THE OXFORD MIDDLETON

Thomas Middleton (1580–1627)—'our other Shakespeare'—is the only other Renaissance playwright who created acknowledged masterpieces of comedy, tragedy, and history; his revolutionary English history play, *A Game at Chess*, was also the greatest box-office hit of early modern London. His achievements extend beyond these traditional genres to tragicomedies, masques, pageants, pamphlets, epigrams, and Biblical and political commentaries, written alone or in collaboration with Thomas Dekker, John Ford, Thomas Heywood, William Rowley, William Shakespeare, John Webster, and others. Compared by critics to Aristophanes and Ibsen, Racine and Joe Orton, he has influenced writers as diverse as Aphra Behn, Anthony Trollope, and T. S. Eliot. Though repeatedly censored in his own time, Middleton has since come to be particularly admired for his representations of the intertwined pursuits of sex, money, power, and God.

The Oxford Middleton, prepared by seventy-five scholars from a dozen countries, follows the precedent of The Oxford Shakespeare in being published in two volumes, an innovative but accessible *Collected Works* and a comprehensive scholarly *Companion*. Though closely connected, each volume can be used independently of the other.

Thomas Middleton and Early Modern Textual Culture: A Companion to The Collected Works. Because Middleton is more representative than any of his contemporaries of the full range of textual practices in early modern England, his works provide an ideal focus for understanding the history of the book, and its relation to the larger history of culture, in this pivotal period. The *Companion* begins, accordingly, with eleven original essays placing Middleton's career in the context of larger cultural patterns governing the creation, reproduction, regulation, circulation, and reception of texts. These essays are followed by a textual introduction and full editorial apparatus for each work, including an account of evidence for its authorship and date of composition. This combination of detail and context provides a foundation for future studies both of Middleton and of early modern culture. The volume's unusual features are described and explained in 'How to Use This Book' (p. 19).

The Collected Works brings together for the first time in a single volume all the works currently attributed to Middleton. The texts are printed in modern spelling and punctuation, with critical introductions and foot-of-the-page commentaries; they are arranged in chronological order, with a special section of Juvenilia. The volume is introduced by essays on Middleton's life and reputation, on early modern London, and on the varied theatres of the English Renaissance. Extensively illustrated, it incorporates much new information on Middleton's life, canon, texts, and contexts; twenty per cent of the works included have never before been annotated. A self-consciously 'federal edition', *The Collected Works* applies contemporary theories about the nature of literature and the history of the book to editorial practice.

http://thomasmiddleton.org

A portrait of the artist as a she-owl: owner of shelved books, the author is imagined as a right-handed scribe with a quill pen, writing (or correcting) symbols in an open codex on a tilted writing desk. The anonymous woodcut, a parody of traditional images of a scholar in his study, first appears on the title-page of Thomas Middleton's *The Owles Almanacke* (1618), printed by Edward Griffin and sold by Lawrence Lisle in his shop at the sign of the Tiger's Head in St Paul's churchyard; it was recycled in satirical broadsides and a pamphlet in the 1650s.

THOMAS MIDDLETON AND EARLY MODERN TEXTUAL CULTURE

A COMPANION TO THE COLLECTED WORKS

General Editors
GARY TAYLOR AND JOHN LAVAGNINO

Associate General Editors
JOHN JOWETT, MACDONALD P. JACKSON,
VALERIE WAYNE, AND ADRIAN WEISS

CLARENDON PRESS · OXFORD

OXFORD
UNIVERSITY PRESS

Great Clarendon Street, Oxford OX2 6DP

Oxford University Press is a department of the University of Oxford.
It furthers the University's objective of excellence in research, scholarship,
and education by publishing worldwide in

Oxford New York

Auckland Cape Town Dar es Salaam Hong Kong Karachi
Kuala Lumpur Madrid Melbourne Mexico City Nairobi
New Delhi Shanghai Taipei Toronto

With offices in

Argentina Austria Brazil Chile Czech Republic France Greece
Guatemala Hungary Italy Japan Poland Portugal Singapore
South Korea Switzerland Thailand Turkey Ukraine Vietnam

Oxford is a registered trade mark of Oxford University Press
in the UK and in certain other countries

Published in the United States by Oxford University Press Inc., New York

British Library Cataloguing in Publication Data

Data available

Library of Congress Cataloging in Publication Data

Data available

Typeset by John Lavagnino
Printed in Italy
on acid-free paper by
Rotolito Lombarda SpA

ISBN 978-0-19-818570-3
ISBN 978-0-19-922588-0 (Works and Companion set)

3 5 7 9 10 8 6 4 2

CONTRIBUTORS

Gary Taylor (General Editor), Florida State University

John Lavagnino (General Editor), King's College London

MacDonald P. Jackson (University of Auckland)

John Jowett (Shakespeare Institute, University of Birmingham)

Valerie Wayne (University of Hawai'i at Mānoa)

Adrian Weiss (independent scholar)

Ilaria Andreoli (Florida State University)

John H. Astington (University of Toronto)

Maureen Bell (University of Birmingham)

Alexandra G. Bennett (Northern Illinois University)

David M. Bergeron (University of Kansas)

†Julia Briggs (De Montfort University)

Douglas Bruster (University of Texas at Austin)

Richard Burt (University of Florida)

Swapan Chakravorty (Jadavpur University)

Cyndia Susan Clegg (Pepperdine University)

Thomas Cogswell (University of California, Riverside)

Ralph Alan Cohen (Mary Baldwin College)

Celia R. Daileader (Florida State University)

Lawrence Danson (Princeton University)

Michael Dobson (Birkbeck, University of London)

Julia Gasper (Open University)

Edward Gieskes (University of South Carolina)

Suzanne Gossett (Loyola University Chicago)

Donna B. Hamilton (University of Maryland, College Park)

Molly Hand (Florida State University)

Trish Thomas Henley (Florida State University)

R. V. Holdsworth (University of Manchester)

Grace Ioppolo (University of Reading)

Coppélia Kahn (Brown University)

Ivo Kamps (University of Mississippi)

Lizz Ketterer (Shakespeare Institute, University of Birmingham)

Theodore B. Leinwand (University of Maryland, College Park)

Kate D. Levin (City College of New York)

Jerzy Limon (Uniwersytet Gdański)

†Harold Love (Monash University)

Jeffrey Masten (Northwestern University)

C. E. McGee (St Jerome's University)

Paul Mulholland (University of Guelph)

Marion O'Connor (University of Kent at Canterbury)

Anthony Parr (University of the Western Cape)

Neil Rhodes (University of St Andrews)

Andrew J. Sabol (Brown University)

Peter Saccio (Dartmouth College)

G. B. Shand (Glendon College, York University)

R. Malcolm Smuts (University of Massachusetts, Boston)

Leslie Thomson (University of Toronto)

Daniel J. Vitkus (Florida State University)

Wendy Wall (Northwestern University)

Stanley Wells (Shakespeare Birthplace Trust)

Linda Woodbridge (Pennsylvania State University)

Paul Yachnin (McGill University)

TABLE OF CONTENTS

CONTENTS

CONTENTS

8

ALPHABETICAL CONTENTS

Full titles, common abbreviations, and alternative titles are all given. Page numbers refer to the Textual Introduction to each work in Part III or, in the case of lost works, to the relevant note in 'Works Included in *The Collected Works*'.

INDEX OF TITLES BY GENRE

LIST OF ILLUSTRATIONS

HOW TO USE THIS BOOK

Gary Taylor

MOST modern readers of Middleton will already have encountered editions of Shakespeare, and readers of this Middleton *Companion* may well have encountered *William Shakespeare: A Textual Companion*, also published by Oxford University Press. But editorial paradigms based upon the unusual conditions of the Shakespeare canon are of limited relevance to Middleton (and many other writers). Rather than simply applying to Middleton modes of editorial practice and critical theory developed to represent another author, we have sought to present Middleton's works in the manner most appropriate to their production and (re)production in early modern culture. In finding their way around a relatively unfamiliar author in a relatively unfamiliar editorial format, readers may be helped by the following description of this book's special features.

Authorship. *The Collected Works* contains texts of all Middleton's known surviving works, and brief descriptions of what we know about his various lost ones. It includes works written by Middleton alone, works written by Middleton in collaboration with other writers, and works by other writers which Middleton later adapted. An overview of the history and the issues surrounding definition of the authorial canon is provided by MacDonald P. Jackson's essay (p. 80). But since such issues have been so central to the history of Middleton's reputation and of Middleton scholarship, Part II of this *Companion* is entirely devoted to determining the canon. 'Works Included in *The Collected Works*' (p. 335) supplies the specific evidence for the authorship of individual works. 'Works Excluded from *The Collected Works*' (p. 444) provides brief explanations for the rejection of works which have sometimes in the past been attributed to Middleton, including some works—*Blurt Master Constable*, *The Family of Love*, and *The Honest Whore, Part II*—which were included in the nineteenth-century collected editions by Alexander Dyce and A. H. Bullen.

Character Names. In the original texts, many characters are not given personal names, but identified by generic social labels (Tyrant, Queen, Lady, Clown, White Queen's Pawn). At other times, a proper name is given somewhere in the text, but speech prefixes and stage directions use the generic label. In the eighteenth century, editors of Shakespeare and other English dramatists began systematically supplying personal names for dramatic characters, whenever they could be found. We have retained the original generic labels in STAGE DIRECTIONS and SPEECH PREFIXES, believing they reflect an emphasis upon social and theatrical roles rather than unique individuals. However,

the texts in *The Collected Works* also provide a single consistent label for each character, which is used in all speech prefixes and stage directions (though in stage directions it may also be supplemented by alternative designations). When there is inconsistency in the labelling of a character in the early witness or witnesses, that variation is described in the Textual Introduction and/or the Textual Notes. We also note and discuss the few cases—most notably, in *A Trick to Catch the Old One* and *A Game at Chess: A Later Form*—where we depart from generic character labels to provide more specific proper names. (See CONSISTENCY.)

Chronology. The textual apparatus in Part III of this *Companion* is arranged in the chronological order of the earliest extant text of each work, from *The Wisdom of Solomon* in 1597 to *Annals* and *Farrago* in 1735. This order situates the material documents in relation to the historical evolution of textual culture. By contrast, *The Collected Works* displays the works in the chronological sequence of their creation. An overview of issues surrounding that authorial chronology is provided by MacDonald P. Jackson's essay (p. 80). 'Works Included in *The Collected Works*' (p. 335) supplies the specific evidence for the dating of individual works.

Compositors. Printed texts were set into type by individual compositors. (See Adrian Weiss's essay, p. 195.) Twentieth-century critical editions of early modern plays devoted much time to the identification and analysis of the their stints of work. But even in the case of the Shakespeare first folio, where the compositors have been studied for eighty years, scholars still dispute some of those identifications. Middleton has not been the beneficiary or the victim of such sustained compositorial analysis, and all such identifications are particularly fragile when dealing with short octavo or quarto texts. Consequently, although the Textual Introductions record and sometimes discuss previous scholarship on compositors, the editors have not engaged in further work of this kind, and—except in the case of the three Middleton collaborations printed in the 1623 Shakespeare folio, the two printed in the 1647 Fletcher folio, and the quarto of *The Revenger's Tragedy*, which have all been extensively studied—we attach little confidence to such identifications.

Consistency. This edition does not attempt to provide or impose a unified view of Middleton or his works. Different EDITORIAL PRACTICES are adopted for different works, and the introductory essays adopt different critical and theoretical perspectives. This diversity is deliberate. It derives from a belief that authors and their readers are better served by a 'federal' than a 'unified' edition. By calling attention to the variety of ways in which the works of an author may be interpreted and edited, a 'federal' edition celebrates the play of difference and acknowledges the foreclosure of possibilities entailed in every act of choice.

Cross-reference. The textual apparatus in Part III of this *Companion* supplies cross-references to each text in *The Collected Works*. The relevant page numbers are given at the end of each textual introduction in the *Companion*, which also supplies page references for the relevant section of 'Works Included in This Edition' and, where necessary, to the music texts in 'Middleton, Music, and Dance'.

Dates. Unless otherwise specified, dates are new style (with the year beginning on January 1).

Editorial practices and principles. The *Companion* includes full bibliographical descriptions of the early documents, critical analysis of their transmission and relationships, and a detailed textual apparatus for each work. *A Game at Chess* survives in more early independent documents than any play of the English Renaissance. By contrast, most of Middleton's works have come down to us in only a single authoritative early manuscript or printed edition, from which all later texts derive. For such single-text works, the editor's primary task is to reproduce, accurately, the substance of that earliest document, and at the same time to make it accessible to modern readers. (See INCIDENTALS and STAGE DIRECTIONS.) However, all forms of early modern textual transmission introduced errors; accordingly, texts have been emended where the editors believe that such an error has occurred. How many emendations have been made in any given work depends in large part upon the quality of the early document, but also in part upon the attitude of the individual editor: some editors are more interested in detecting error, and more adventurous in correcting it, than others. All such emendations, and all variants in authoritative early texts, are recorded in the TEXTUAL NOTES; emendations and variants are not marked in the text of *The Collected Works* (except in the commentary to *Old Law*).

Genres. *The Collected Works* provides readers with an index of titles by literary genre. By contrast, readers interested in early modern textual culture might be more concerned with material and historical categories. The *Companion*'s 'Index of Titles by Genre' (p. 11) groups texts by kinds of manuscript (autograph, scribal, etc.) and print (engravings, folios, quartos, etc.).

Hyphens. Throughout this volume, a hyphen at the end of a line that is really part of the text, and not just introduced because of the line break, is repeated at the start of the following line. This practice reduces ambiguity.

Illustrations. Middleton was unique among playwrights of his time in the number of his works that originally appeared with illustrations. (See John Astington's essay, p. 226.) Both volumes are therefore heavily illustrated. We do not, however, preserve the exact size of the original images, and most images are cropped; we have seldom retained unprinted margins in their full extent. Modern reproductions of early book pages often remove show-through and offset and enhance the contrast between dark ink and white paper, so that they resemble the page of present-day books more closely. In some cases we have left the signs of earlier printing processes in place. The background in the plates from *The Arches of Triumph* (*Works*, p. 225) is not processed to make it uniform, for example; the crooked imposition and poor present condition of three versions of the title-page for *Two Gates* are not corrected (this volume, pp. 600, 601, and 603).

Incidentals. For the Occasional Poems, each edited text in *The Collected Works* (p. 1886) is accompanied by a photograph of the relevant early document; we also reproduce some pages of a manuscript in Middleton's own handwriting in *A Game at Chesse: An Early Form* (*Works*, pp. 1780, 1791). For most works, the text in *The Collected Works* has been modernized to make it more intelligible for contemporary readers; consequently, variants and emendations of punctuation and spelling are not normally recorded in the textual apparatus in Part III of the *Companion*. However, PRESS VARIANTS are recorded, even when the variants only affect incidentals. Moreover, in some cases in the Textual Notes editors discuss the reasons to modernize or not modernize the spelling of particular words. Likewise, in some cases the Textual Notes address issues of punctuation, either because the punctuation is felt to make a substantive difference in the interpretation of the passage, or because the punctuation is relevant to issues of emendation. Finally, *An Early Form* of *A Game at Chess* is printed, in *The Collected Works*, in old spelling and punctuation, which are particularly important in that work, because we possess autograph manuscripts; we therefore provide a full list and discussion of 'Emendations of Incidentals' (p. 884). Whenever punctuation is at issue in the Textual Notes, a caret ∧ indicates the absence of punctuation at that point in *The Collected Works* or one of the textual witnesses being cited in the apparatus.

Indexes. Because the bibliography, canon, and CHRONOLOGY of Middleton's texts will be unfamiliar to most readers, for finding a particular text the main Table of Contents may be less useful than the Alphabetical Contents (p. 9), or the Index of Titles by Genre (p. 11). The alphabetical 'Index to Notes on Modernization' (p. 1167) lists words where the difference between old and modern spelling is significant enough to be recorded in the textual notes. 'A Selective Topical Index' (p. 1175) aims to provide guidance to the more important primary topics treated in Parts I and II and in the TEXTUAL INTRODUCTIONS of Part III, but not to the textual notes. Cyndia Clegg's essay contains a table of all printers, publishers, and licensers of Middleton texts printed between 1597 and 1627 (p. 258). Maureen Bell's essay contains two tables, one of editions of Middleton works printed between 1627 and 1685, the other of printers/publishers and advertisers involved with those publications (pp. 261, 262). John Jowett's essay includes an alphabetical list of known early readers of Middleton's work (p. 322).

Ligatures and 'long s'. Although the texts in *The Collected Works* represent structural features of the TYPOGRAPHY of the original printed editions—the use of black letter type, marginal notes, and multiple columns, for instance—they do not attempt to reproduce local typographical details like ligatures. Nevertheless, in evaluating textual variants and emendations such features may provide important evidence. Therefore, the Textual Notes reproduce, in the citation of witnesses, any original use of ligatures like 'ft', 'fl', and 'ffi'. For the same reason, the Textual Notes preserve the distinction between 'ſ' (the so-called 'long s', usually preferred at the beginning and in the middle of words) and 's' (the normal modern form, usually reserved for the last letter of a word).

Lineation. Early witnesses sometimes misrepresent what seems to be the formal structure of the verse, or the distinction between verse and prose. Such arrangements do not change the meaning of the text, but editors have traditionally emended them to restore what seems to have been the author's formal intentions. Such changes—or variants between early witnesses—are normally recorded in a separate list, following the Textual Notes for the work in question. However, in *A Game at Chess: A Later Form* lineation variants and emendations are incorporated in the Textual Notes.

Metrical Markers. The modernized texts in *The Collected Works* indicate obsolete pronunciations when they seem necessary to the metre of verse lines. A diaeresis indicates that the 'i' in words like 'conversation' should be pronounced as a separate unstressed syllable, so that 'conversation' has five syllables instead of the modern four. Every such diaeresis is editorial, and consequently they have not been recorded among the TEXTUAL NOTES. An accent over the 'e' in words like 'injurèd' indicates that the past participle should be pronounced as a separate syllable, so that 'injurèd' has three syllables instead of the modern two. Middleton's early texts usually indicate the obsolete pronunciation by spelling the past participle 'ed'; by contrast, the elided form is usually spelled 'de' or 't', or with an apostrophe instead of an 'e' before the consonant. Thus, the 'ed' spelling in the early texts is normally represented as 'èd' in *The Collected Works*. When an editor judges that the spelling of the past participle in the early texts misrepresents the author's metrical intentions (by mistakenly eliding the obsolete form, or mistakenly expanding an elided form), then the difference is recorded in the TEXTUAL NOTES.

Press Variants. Where the record of press variants in an early edition is full and complicated—as for example in *The Whole Royal and Magnificent Entertainment*, *The Patient Man and the Honest Whore*, *The Two Gates of Salvation*, and *The Peacemaker*—we provide, immediately following the Textual Notes, a separate list of the variants by forme and page (also giving line numbers to the text in *The*

Collected Works). However, where the number of such variants is small, the list has been incorporated in the Textual Introduction (*The Widow*) or the Textual Notes (*A Game at Chess: A Later Form*).

Scene Divisions. In most cases, the scene divisions and scene numbers in *The Collected Works* were not supplied in the earliest texts. In *A Game at Chesse: An Early Form*, we follow Middleton's own practice in marking act divisions, but not scene divisions. Whenever scene divisions are editorial, they are identified as such in the Textual Introduction or Textual Notes.

Sigla. In the Textual Notes one needs some abbreviated form of reference for textual witnesses; it does not make sense to give their full titles every time we refer to them. It has become normal to identify early texts by formulaic sigla; because the Shakespeare canon is significantly divided into folios and quartos, we are used to sigla like Q1, Q2, F1, F2, etc. Such formulae are unhelpful in the canon of Middleton (and most other writers): no work which appears in quarto also appears in folio, and the difference of format is not textually significant. Moreover, such algebraic notation reifies textual sources, eliminating any reference to history and agency, creating the illusion of mathematical purity and untroubled succession; and it asserts a fundamental distinction between early editions ('Q1') and late ones ('Dyce'). Of course, there are important distinctions between late and early editions, but both are representations of a text, both are mediated, both are fallible. The *Companion* solves this problem of reference to textual sources by systematically referring to agents. All textual sources are identified by a siglum consisting of a proper name. In the case of later editions, this proper name is, as is conventional, that of the editor, where known (DODSLEY, COLLIER, DYCE, BULLEN, etc.). In the case of early editions, that proper name is the name of the printer, who is the agent most directly responsible for producing the material textual product to which we refer. Thus, the siglum for what is traditionally called 'Q1' of *The Revenger's Tragedy* is 'ELD', the siglum for what is traditionally called 'F1' of *The Nice Valour* is 'ISLIP'. This system emphasizes that our textual sources are produced by persons, who differ among themselves; not all printers are alike. It also enables us to refer more precisely to those textual sources. What is traditionally called 'Q3' of *A Game at Chess* is bound as a single book, but it is a product of shared printing; the material object comes from two different printing houses, two different agents. A siglum like 'Q3' not only reifies, but unifies the object to which it refers. The Textual Notes refer to 'MATHEWES' or 'ALLDE', depending on which printing house printed the word or line in question; the Textual Introduction refers to the volume as a whole, which they co-produced, as 'MATHEWES-ALLDE', thus emphasizing its composite nature. This method of reference also makes possible more precise reference to other kinds of texts, which made use of standing type. For instance, 'PURFOOT1' describes not only the first edition of *The Peacemaker*, printed by Thomas Purfoot from manuscript; it also describes sheets A, B, and the inner forme of sheet E of the 'second' edition, which were printed from the same setting of type. Only sheets C, D, and the outer forme of sheet E are a 'new' product, the result of a second representation of the text, which needs to be called 'PURFOOT2'. Likewise, the siglum for a manuscript is normally the name of the scribe. Thus, the copy of *A Game at Chess* now housed at Trinity College, Cambridge, in Middleton's own handwriting, is 'MIDDLETON^T', the superscript 'T' serving to distinguish it from the autograph portions of the manuscript owned in the seventeenth century by the Earl of Bridgewater (which is identified as 'MIDDLETON^B'). Likewise, each of the three manuscripts of the play produced by Ralph Crane is 'CRANE', with a superscript numeral distinguishing them from each other. This arrangement, like the rule for printers, lets us recognize and record different agents operating on the same material object; for instance, the censor George BUC is one of the hands at work on the manuscript of *The Lady's Tragedy*. This system also emphasizes the human links between texts: Ralph CRANE and Nicholas OKES, for instance, mediated more than one work by Middleton. When we do not know the identity of the printer, texts are identified by the name of the publisher, and unidentified scribes are identified by the earliest known owner of the manuscript.

Speech Prefixes. In seventeenth-century texts, speech prefixes are usually abbreviated. The TEXTUAL NOTES do not record expansions of those abbreviations, unless the intention is ambiguous.

Split Verse Lines. Middleton, like other verse dramatists, often divided a verse line between two or more speakers. Early modern texts seldom represent this formal feature visually, and we retain the typical early modern typographical arrangement in *A Game at Chesse: An Early Form*. But elsewhere for the convenience of modern readers we have editorially indented the concluding part(s) of such a divided verse line in order to show the metrical integrity of the line. For instance, in the manuscript of *The Lady's Tragedy* the end of one character's speech and the beginning of the next speech (1.1.208) were written as follows:

> see it effected.
>
> ————————
>
> *Mem.* wth best care, my lord

This is clearly intended as a single iambic pentameter line, which we print as follows:

> See it effected.
> MEMPHONIUS   With best care, my lord.

These editorial manipulations of white space are not recorded in the Textual Notes.

Stage Directions. With Middleton as with other playwrights of his time, the early texts are often deficient in describing stage action, even at so basic a level as the entrance and exit of actors. The stage directions of *The Collected Works* are designed to provide the minimum assistance necessary to make the text theatrically intelligible. Emendations of apparent errors or misreadings are recorded in the TEXTUAL NOTES, but—like similar emendations of the dialogue itself—they are not marked in the text of *The Collected Works*. By contrast, all editorial additions of debatable directions (including, for instance, most asides, indications of the person addressed by a particular speech, and gestures) are printed in *The Collected Works* within square brackets, but they are not recorded in the TEXTUAL NOTES. Instead, the textual apparatus for each play includes (following the PRESS VARIANTS or, if there are none, the TEXTUAL NOTES) a list of every original stage direction, in its original spelling and punctuation, keyed to its position in this edition and (where different) to its exact original location. The apparatus for *A Game at Chesse: An Early Form* gives two lists of stage directions, one of autograph directions, the other of scribal directions. By contrast, in *A Game at Chess: A Later Form* all variants and emendations of stage directions are incorporated in the TEXTUAL NOTES, so that they can be seen as part of the full record of variation and error in the eight extant textual witnesses.

Textual Introductions. The introductions to individual works in Part III summarize previous work on the text (if any), and signal any important innovations or discoveries made by *The Collected Works*.. These introductions vary in length, depending upon the complexity of the textual circumstances: that for *Plato's Cap*, for example, is very brief, while that for *A Game at Chess* is the length of a separate monograph. Every introduction provides for the work in question a bibliographical citation that identifies its early edition(s). 'STC' refers to the revised *Short-Title Catalogue...1475–1640*, ed. Katherine Pantzer *et al.* (1976–85); 'Wing' refers to the revised *Short-Title Catalogue...1641–1700*, ed. Donald Wing *et al.* (1982–98); 'BEPD' refers to W. W. Greg's *Bibliography of English Printed Drama to the Restoration* (1939–59). When dealing with manuscripts, the standard bibliographical reference number is that assigned in Peter Beal's *Index of English Literary Manuscripts* (1980–93). These citations key the discussion to standard reference works, and normally make it unnecessary to provide the kinds of detailed bibliographical information routinely supplied by those authorities. The Textual Introductions also discuss any editorial problem that extends over many scenes—for instance, the 'languages' of cant, Dutch, and dialect in *A Fair Quarrel*, or the fact that the only substantive edition of *Anything for a Quiet Life* is printed almost entirely as prose. Generally, each Introduction states and defends an hypothesis about the nature of the manuscript used by the printer(s), and the relationship of the extant textual witnesses, where there is more than one.

Textual Notes. The notes to individual works in Part III immediately follow the Textual Introduction to that work. They record all editorial emendations of the early witnesses, all substantive variants between authoritative early texts, and all modernizations of spelling that might be disputed. We distinguish between emendations (where the editor believes that the early document contains a mistake, which needs to be corrected) and modernizations (where the editor believes that the early document is correct, but the modern form of the intended word differs significantly from the original form). The difference is illustrated by two adjacent textual notes in *The Wisdom of Solomon Paraphrased*:

3.83 right] DYCE; rghit SIMMES

3.100 Whe'er] SIMMES (Where)

In 3.83, the compositor in the first edition, printed by Valentine Simmes, apparently transposed the types, setting the nonsensical 'rghit' instead of 'right', an error first corrected by Alexander Dyce. In 3.100, 'Where' occurs in the first edition, but 'Where' is an obsolete spelling for 'Whe'er', the elided monosyllabic form of 'Whether'; the textual note records an interpretation, not an emendation. Thus, the emendation 'right' is attributed to DYCE, but the modernization 'Whe'er' is not attributed to an editor, because the reading of SIMMES is correct, by the standards of the time, and has merely been modernized by this edition. Emendations of LINEATION, PRESS VARIANTS and STAGE DIRECTIONS are normally recorded in separate lists, immediately following the Textual Notes. See also INCIDENTALS and SIGLA.

Titles. A number of Middleton's works are given—in separate early documents, or even within the same document—more than one title. In such cases, the running titles in *The Collected Works* vary from page to page, thereby preserving the titular instability of the work throughout the experience of reading it. Thus, on any given opening of *The Collected Works*, the reader may see '*The Nice Valour*' above the left-hand page, and the alternative title '*The Paffionate Mad-man*' above the right-hand page, of the same play. However, in the *Companion* the running titles to the TEXTUAL INTRODUCTIONS and TEXTUAL NOTES remain stable for each work; variant titles in original documents, including variants in the running titles of those documents, are recorded in the initial Textual Note on the title.

Typography. All written and printed texts are embodied forms of language: the size, layout, calligraphy or typography of a text all signal its relationships to other texts, and encode the relationships of its parts to one another. No single book can incorporate the great and deliberate variety of embodiments of Middleton's early texts, and in any case those early embodiments would be unfamiliar and unintelligible to most modern readers. However, *The Collected Works* does call attention to the range and significance of those early embodiments, in part by photographic illustrations, in part by preserving in a modern form the typographical distinctions of the original texts. Thus, the 'black letter' type for certain sections of *The Black Book* is indicated by use of a bolder font (which preserves the emblematic visual 'blackening' of the text, but does so in a form more intelligible to modern readers); the original gothic font is reproduced in the running TITLES, where readers can be reminded of its function without being disturbed by its (to them) illegibility. However, 'black letter' font, or variations in type size, are not systematically recorded in the Textual Notes, unless in a particular case they are relevant to variation or emendation, or to press variants.

Verbal parallels. Previous editing of Middleton has been seriously hampered by the absence of a concordance. In evaluating variants, emendations, and attributions, we have drawn on three new sources: (1) a single copy of a ten-volume draft modern-spelling concordance of Middleton's works, prepared by John Lavagnino in 1994, based upon most but not all initial draft texts of the *Collected Works*, later supplemented by (2) the evolving old-spelling digital database of English drama, poetry, and prose in Literature Online ('LION'), and (3) the even more recent evolving old-spelling digital database of literary and non-literary texts in Early English Books Online— Text Coding Partnership ('EEBO-TCP'). As a result, the *Collected Works* is the first edition to be based on something approaching a comprehensive view of the verbal practice of Middleton and his collaborators, and this *Companion* radically differs from previous Middleton scholarship in its documentation of that practice. Nevertheless, each of our three sources is incomplete, and each overlaps haphazardly with the other two. Consequently, although all cited verbal parallels have been verified and certainly exist, they may on occasion under-represent the range of Middleton's vocabulary or the frequency of some idioms.

Website. At http://thomasmiddleton.org we publish further information relevant to Middleton and his texts, including additional indexes, illustrations, and links to other sites. It is hoped that this expanding site will eventually contain fully searchable texts of *The Collected Works*.

Works Cited. Throughout this *Companion* references are given in an abbreviated form within parentheses. In Part I and Part II, full citations for those authors and works are given at the end of each essay. In Part III, the list of Works Cited at the end of each TEXTUAL INTRODUCTION gives details for works referenced there, in the following TEXTUAL NOTES, and also in the relevant critical introduction and commentary in *The Collected Works*; those lists also provide SIGLA for previous editions of that particular work. *The Collected Works* begins with three introductory essays, on Middleton's life and reputation, Middleton's London, and Middleton's theatres; Part III of this *Companion* begins with bibliographical information on the sources for those three essays.

PREFACE: TEXTUAL PROXIMITIES

Gary Taylor

THE title *The Collected Works of Thomas Middleton* asserts a relationship between a person and a list of texts. The title implicitly claims that any single text written by that person can be fully understood only in the context created by all the texts 'of' that person.

The title of this companion volume, *Thomas Middleton and Early Modern Textual Culture*, links that person and his texts to a vastly larger list of texts, a list whose limits are not defined biographically but temporally and conceptually. However, while the word *and* asserts some relationship between the singular person and the plural list, *and* does not define the nature of the relationship between that proper name and the very vague and less familiar phrase 'Textual Culture'.

The relationship between these two Middleton volumes is modelled on that between two Shakespeare volumes, also published by Oxford University Press: *The Complete Works* (Wells and Taylor 1986), and *William Shakespeare: A Textual Companion* (Wells and Taylor 1987). These two projects are biographically, causally, and visually linked: the design of the Middleton volumes consciously mimics that of our Shakespearean paradigm. Both volumes begin with extensive introductory matter relevant to the whole canon, followed by detailed consideration of the textual and editorial matter of individual works.

Nevertheless, the scholarly apparatus that surrounds the Middleton texts differs from the Shakespeare apparatus, because the Middleton project confronted from the outset a radically different editorial problem. Although the Oxford Shakespeare was based on original research and edited from primary documents, it necessarily set itself the task of synthesizing and re-evaluating a dauntingly capacious body of editorial and textual scholarship. The Oxford Middleton, by contrast, faced a different obstacle: a canon never systematically edited, many works never critically edited according to the standards of post-Victorian bibliography, others never previously annotated or edited at all. Consequently, whereas the Shakespeare *Companion* set out to synthesize and impose order upon a colossal scholarly tradition, this Middleton *Companion* sets out, instead, to lay a foundation for future intellectual enquiry.

Consequently, in place of the Shakespeare *Companion*'s single long 'General Introduction', this *Companion* begins instead with eleven separate essays situating Middleton's extant texts within a larger body of early modern textual practices (Part I). Then follows an account and analysis of evidence for the authorship and date of composition of each of the individual 'Works Included in' and 'Works Excluded from' the Middleton canon (Part II); this process of authorial individuation and chronological positioning necessarily relates the detail of each text to larger patterns created by many other texts. Finally, Part III provides a detailed textual apparatus for each work in *The Collected Works*. But whereas the chronological ordering of Part II, and of *The Collected Works*, reflects the temporal proximities of authorial composition, Part III sequences the works by the date of their earliest surviving documentary witness. It seems appropriate to organize *The Collected Works of Thomas Middleton* along the time-line of the author's own life, especially because the moment of a work's composition was almost immediately followed by the moment of its exposure to a larger public. But the Middleton *Companion* is necessarily more concerned with the chronology of surviving textual witnesses, which need to be situated within the culture and history of textual witnessing.

As I have argued elsewhere (Taylor 1993), Middleton is much more representative than Shakespeare of the full diversity of early modern textual culture. But any attempt to trace Middleton's relationship to textual culture must first define the object of enquiry.

Textual culture is that fraction of a society involved in the production, reproduction, regulation, circulation, and reception of texts. The size and character of that fraction depends upon how we define 'texts', 'society', and 'involved'.[1]

Texts is a more comprehensive category than 'literature', 'books', or 'writing'. Even if we could agree what literature was, it would be impossible to separate its production, reproduction, regulation, circulation, and reception from that of other texts. As material objects, 'books' are much easier to define than 'literature', and the study of textual cultures is now widely characterized as 'The History of the Book'. But that definition of the field is misleading. The material form of the codex—which makes it easier to define a 'book'—itself represents only one of a set of possibilities within a textual culture. Any society that has books also has other kinds of writing, which are 'not-books'. A scrivener like Ralph Crane, who prepared manuscript codices of Middleton plays, had also

---

[1] Since I formulated this definition and advertised the title of this book in the early 1990s, Irvine has described the centrality of grammatica in early medieval 'textual culture', and the journal of the Society of Textual Scholarship, formerly known as *TEXT*, has been re-christened *Textual Cultures* (inaugural issue 2006). See also the 2005 conference on 'Textual Culture' hosted by the Department of English Studies at the University of Stirling; according to the Stirling website, 'textual culture refers to the material processes and ideological formations surrounding the production, transmission, reception, and regulation of texts'.

transcribed innumerable legal documents while working as an underclerk for the Signet Office, the Privy Seal, and the Privy Council (Wilson); a shop like William Jaggard's, which printed three plays partly by Middleton in a famous 1623 folio, also produced countless single-sheet playbills (Greg 22–4). 'Writing' incorporates all of the preceding categories of manuscript and printed texts, but it in turn depends upon an implied opposition to 'speech', an opposition problematic both philosophically and historically. Orality and literacy 'mutually interact and affect each other' (Finnegan, 175), and their interrelations are particularly fascinating in early modern England (Thomas; McKenzie 1990; Fox 2000). Written texts (of plays or ballads or songs, for instance) may be orally composed and/or orally performed; an oral statement (in legal proceedings, for instance) may be graphically recorded; an oral performance of a written text may be transmitted through the memory of a listener, who later writes it down (as, apparently, Edward Pudsey wrote down in his commonplace book passages he remembered from a performance of *The Patient Man and the Honest Whore*).[2]

The complex relationships between literacy and orality, print and manuscript, books and non-books, literature and non-literature, help to define the character of a particular textual culture. But, despite the apparent breadth of the foregoing definition, *texts* is a much more limited category than 'signs'. Clothing and etiquette, for instance, belong to sign systems that may be reproduced, circulated, and semiotically analysed; for many modern cultural critics, a codpiece and a curtsy are both 'texts'. But, sadly, I can't read all signs simultaneously. Even the linguistic culture of a single early modern society is so large and complex that it is difficult to map or conceptualize. It would be impossible, within a single human lifetime, to read all the extant written texts produced in London alone within the lifetime of Thomas Middleton—and the written texts still extant represent only a small fraction of those produced, and the texts written represent only a small fraction of the texts spoken. Textual culture is, as my definition admits, always only a fraction, a subset.

That subset may, of course, overlap with other subsets. A verbal text may be attached, appended, or sewn to a piece of clothing (as probably happened when sinners like Juliet in *Measure for Measure* were sentenced to public penitence in a white sheet); but clothing need not carry a verbal text. Etiquette may include prescribed rituals of address, either oral or written; but it may also prescribe bodily practices which are not linguistic at all. Mathematical and musical notations might be considered distinct languages or sign systems, but in early modern Europe they almost never existed independent of verbal texts. Whenever other semiotic systems incorporate texts, or are incorporated by texts, they become a part of textual culture.

But *texts* is not simply synonymous with 'language'. A text is a technologically reproduced representation of language. For instance, a proverb or a cliché—a verbal formula like 'a mad world' (Dent W880), repeated innumerable times by innumerable users of the language—is a reproduced verbal combination, which we might call a minimal text, one which presumably circulated in both the oral and written culture of early modern England. But we can identify it as a text only because it passed, at some point in its many perambulations and reproductions, through a manual encoding. Only when a piece of a language is taken in hand—written down, printed, engraved, woodcut, sewn, painted, carved in stone—does it become available for distant scrutiny. At our distance, however interested we may be in early modern oral culture, we can hear it only if we can see it, and we can see it only if and where it passed through a manual filter. A text is, for us, handed language.

Hands can produce a language without speech and without any other technological aid. Indeed, Stokoe plausibly argues that signing came before speech. John Bulwer in 1644 published a treatise on 'manuall rhetoricke', describing 'the Naturall Language of the Hand', its 'speaking motions, and discoursing gestures'. His book includes an illustrated 'alphabet of naturall gestures' of the hands and fingers (152–6). But although primate hands can produce meaningful signs, it took machines to produce Bulwer's book (and Stokoe's). Textual culture is fundamentally technological. When Middleton's hand, probably in the spring of 1625, copied out *A Game at Chesse* in the manuscript now preserved in the library of Trinity College, Cambridge, that living hand was holding a modified quill pen, periodically sharpened with a special knife; that quill was designed for transferring a liquid chemical composition called ink (stored in an inkwell, a specially manufactured container) onto a manufactured (once liquid, now solid) recycled compound material called paper, invented by the Chinese and introduced into medieval Europe through Islamic intermediaries. All Middleton's texts began in this way, though most of the Middleton texts still extant were reproduced using additional technologies. But the technological nature of textuality extends beyond Middleton and early modern Europe. The human hand produces a text by using chisels, chemical pigments, brushes, acids, pens, pencils, papyrus, parchment, paper, wood, copper, printing presses. All these text technologies are designed to supplement the fragile human mind and hand by producing a prosthetic, artificial memory system; that prosthesis has been central to the development of complex, geographically dispersed human societies (Taylor 1996, 143–70).

Society is a singular noun, but the reality to which it refers is always plural, compounded, hyphenated (Boon). Societies are never homogeneous or self-contained, geographically, racially, linguistically, or temporally. London

---

[2] Here and throughout these essays, statements about the text, titles, canon, chronology, and transmission of Middleton's works will take for granted conclusions reached by the editors of *The Collected Works*; evidence for those conclusions is provided in the relevant sections of this volume. For Pudsey see Jowett's essay on Middleton's early readers.

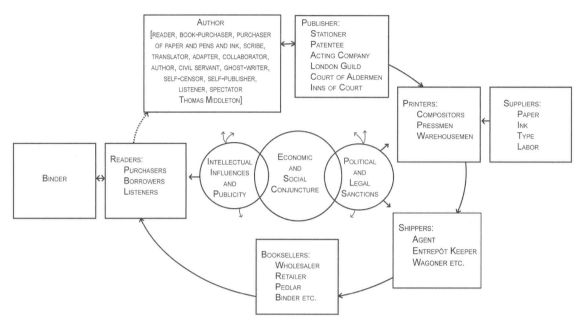

1. Robert Darnton's influential 'Circuit of Communication' (183), based on late eighteenth-century continental textual culture, is here modified to represent early seventeenth-century English textual culture, as exemplified particularly by the career of Thomas Middleton.

is not self-contained; neither is Britain. (No island is an island.) Geographically, Thomas Middleton may never have ventured outside a radius of sixty miles from his birthplace, but his stepfather had sailed to North America, his merchant patrons had contacts as far away as Indonesia, he read imported books and wore imported clothes and ingested imported perishables. Demographically, his texts include representations of Africans, aboriginal Americans, and Asians; native to a great mercantile port, a nexus of the global trade network, he could have encountered live specimens of all these peoples. Linguistically, he wrote texts in English, Latin, French, Spanish, and phonetic Welsh and Dutch; he read texts in English, Latin, Greek, French, Italian, and probably Spanish; within his own lifetime, his own texts were commented upon in texts written in English, French, Italian, Russian, and Spanish. Temporally, he read Aristotle, borrowed Plato's name for the title of a pamphlet, and paraphrased a book of the Old Testament. He internalized texts of a Mediterranean culture more than two millennia old at the time of his birth; he wrote texts about events occurring only weeks before his death; centuries after his death, his own texts continue to reverberate in other texts, like this one.

So defined, the society to which Middleton belonged is itself a complex fraction of a much larger civilization, itself a complex fraction of the global and multi-millennial human community. But it is nevertheless possible to analyse that fraction of a fraction, so long as we define it, not as a natural homogeneous whole, but as an artificial set of co-ordinates in space–time. The internal dynamics of

Middleton's society may be complicated by ghostly multitudes, but those multitudes only concern us to the extent that they affect a volume bounded geographically by the island of Great Britain and temporally by a 'Middleton century', stretching from Middleton's birth (1580) to the publication of *Fifty Comedies and Tragedies* (1679). Here, the limits of a 'society' are being arbitrarily defined in relation to the life and surviving texts of a single individual. Of course, these co-ordinates might be chosen for other reasons: Keith Wrightson, for instance, has written about *English Society 1580–1680*. This century straddles the arbitrary disciplinary divide between 'Renaissance' and 'Restoration', and the change of epistemes which Foucault, just as arbitrarily, locates 'roughly half-way through the seventeenth century' or more precisely in 1657 (Foucault 1971, xxii, 128). But any choice of co-ordinates will be contingent upon the agenda of an investigator, for whom one fraction happens to be more interesting than another.

What interests us here is that fraction of English society in the century between 1580 and 1679 'involved in the production, reproduction, regulation, circulation, and reception of texts'. **Involved** mediates between the specificity of 'texts' and the multiplicities of 'society'. The verb covers many different kinds of engagement, including all of those schematized by Robert Darnton in his image of the circulation of a book (Figure 1). But Darnton's 'Communications Circuit' is, as he acknowledges, obviously too simple to encompass textual culture: it leaves out, most conspicuously, the theatres and churches and law courts, which

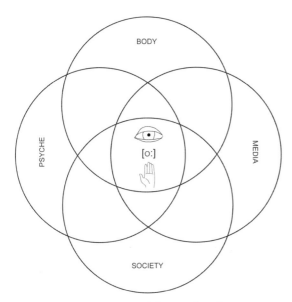

2. Bruce Smith's image of the centrality of acoustic experience—represented by the symbol [o:]—is here modified to include the hand and eye, which also belong at the centre of the nexus of body, society, psyche, and media. Reading a playbill, or an illustrated title-page posted on a wall as an advertisement, might engage only the eyes, while listening to music played by offstage instruments might engage only the ears. Holding a book and reading the words out loud would involve tactile, optical, and aural perception, as would the audience experience of stage dances.

human being can devote all their time and energy to texts. Texts must be fitted into a biological reality dominated by sleeping, eating, excreting, mating, and parenting. And even when creating texts, a person need not engage their entire physical self. When Middleton wrote 'To the King', asking to be released from prison, he urged, 'Use but your royal hand': he does not imagine James speaking a pardon, but signing it. The 'royal hand' is the King's handwriting, but it is also a physical hand, which moves a pen or 'removes' a chessman; and although its movements are, for Middleton, a matter of life and death, for the King they employ only ('but') a fraction of his self, one hand alone (Figure 2). Whether a king or a poet, every individual's relationship to textual culture is necessarily fractional. Likewise, every text's relationship to individuals is necessarily fractional. More than one person is always involved with a text. Every text is what Middleton called a 'farrago' (Taylor 1994).

Textual culture is intrinsically fractional. The study of textual culture is therefore a study of the relationships between dynamic fractions. Moreover, the study of textual culture is itself always fractional, because any such study will be able to focus upon only a fraction of the whole.

Fractions—or 'broken numbers', as they were called in a mathematical treatise published in England in 1608 (Stevin, 7)—were of some interest to early modern textual culture: the modern system of decimalization was developed in Middleton's lifetime. In the sixteenth and much of the seventeenth century, arithmetic tended to justify itself by reference to the more authoritative, visual, concrete procedures of Euclidean geometry. This is particularly easy to do with fractions, because every fraction can be translated into a graph, a set of linear co-ordinates:

A fraction is a way to identify where something sits on a continuum between zero and one, nothing and everything. High literary theory has been obsessed with the impossible absolutes of absence and presence, the incommensurable and the epistemic, 0 and 1. It is perhaps more fruitful to examine the space between 0 and 1 by means of a 'graduated multidimensional' model of intertextual space (Taylor 1993). What matters, then, is not metaphysical presence or its absence, but relative **proximity**, a measurable approach to something which is never reached.

All societies can be, and indeed have been, analysed in terms of proximity. Kinship structures formalize familial distance; class structures formalize economic or social distance; liminal rituals formalize and negotiate the transition between distinct biological or social states within a 'structure that defines status and establishes social distance' (Turner, 100). Xenophobia, ostracism, racism and incorporation magnify or diminish physical and social distance.

If proximity is fundamental to the analysis of societies, it is equally fundamental to the analysis of texts. *All texts are attempts to overcome distance.* The distance to be

in early modern England generated enormous numbers of texts. Moreover, Darnton's circle does not discriminate between different degrees of involvement. Thomas Middleton was 'involved'; but so was an anonymous seventeenth-century provincial rag-picker who sold rags to the owner of a small French paper mill who sold paper to a wholesale export merchant who shipped paper to England where it was bought from the warehouseman by a stationer who printed a posthumous anonymous reprint of Middleton's abridgement of someone else's parody of the whole genre of almanacs (the 1639 edition of *The Penniless Parliament of Threadbare Poets*, which survives in a single unbound copy, now in the Houghton Library of Harvard University). And what about the rag-picker's own suppliers? What about the farmers—in England in Middleton's time, eighty per cent of the population was engaged in agriculture (Clay, I, 68-9, 82, 118, 121)—whose surpluses made possible a division of labour, enabling a small fraction of early modern society to devote itself to the production not of food but of texts made from rags?

The entire structure and economy of a society impinge upon the production and consumption of texts within it. *Everyone* is involved; that is part of the value of a study of textual culture. But *no one* is totally involved. No single overcome may be spatial or temporal. Philippa in *The Widow* has a letter delivered to Francisco in order to overcome the spatial distance between them, and thereby achieve the intimate proximities of sexual intercourse; Middleton paraphrases *The Wisdom of Solomon* in order to make the distant past intelligible to his present, and he writes *Annals* in order to render his present intelligible to a distant future. The manual encoding which produces texts is necessary only when one person is not present to another (in space or time), and must therefore make use of a textual instrument to achieve some degree of proximity.

That is why this book about 'early modern textual culture' is also a book about 'Thomas Middleton'—a single idiosyncratic fractional person. We have chosen Middleton in part because he represents, more than any of his contemporaries, the full range of textual practices in early modern England. His works include an exceptional variety of genres in an exceptional variety of textual forms—in different typefaces and formats of print; in playbooks, miscellanies, and private transcripts for sale or gift; in autograph manuscripts and posthumous editions printed from scribal copies; in texts printed by royal patent, sponsored by corporate authority, or suppressed by ecclesiastical fiat. But we have also chosen to focus upon Middleton as a way of insisting upon the inescapably *personal* dynamics of textual culture. Texts mediate fractional social relationships between involved persons, across space and time. *Thomas Middleton and Early Modern Textual Culture* memorializes the working relationships of many individuals, and creates new relationships between us, its authors, and you, the reader reading this sentence at this moment, who we hope will be part of a community of readers across space and time. Join us, as we put back together the scattered fractions of Thomas Middleton and his textual culture.

WORKS CITED

Boon, James A., *Affinities and Extremes: Crisscrossing the Bittersweet Ethnology of East Indies History, Hindu-Balinese Culture, and Indo-European Allure* (1990)

Bulwer, John, *Chirologia, or, The naturall language of the hand* (1644)

Clay, Christopher, *Economic Expansion and Social Change: England 1500–1700*, 2 vols (1984)

Darnton, Robert, 'What is the History of Books?' (1982) in *The Kiss of Lamourette: Reflections in Cultural History* (1990), 107–35

Dent, R. W., *Proverbial Language in English Drama exclusive of Shakespeare, 1495–1616: An Index* (1984)

Finnegan, Ruth, *Literacy and Orality* (1988)

Foucault, Michel, *The Order of Things* (1971)

Fox, Adam, *Oral and Literate Culture in England 1500–1700* (2000)

Greg, W. W., *The Shakespeare First Folio: its bibliographical and textual history* (1955)

Irvine, Martin, *The Making of Textual Culture* (2002)

McKenzie, D. F., 'Speech—Manuscript—Print', in *New Directions in Textual Studies*, ed. Dave Oliphant and Robin Bradford (1990), 87–109

Smith, Bruce, *The Acoustic World of Early Modern England: Attending to the O-Factor* (1999)

Stevin, Simon, *The Dime*, trans. Richard Norton (1608), in *A Source Book in Mathematics, 1200–1800*, ed. D. J. Struik (1969)

Stokoe, William C., *Language in Hand: Why Sign Came Before Speech* (2001)

Taylor, Gary, 'The Renaissance and the End of Editing', in *Palimpsest: Editorial Theory in the Humanities*, ed. George Bornstein and Ralph G. Williams (1993), 121–49

—— *Cultural Selection* (1996)

—— 'Farrago', *Textual Practice* 8 (1994), 33–42

Thomas, Keith, 'The Meaning of Literacy in Early Modern England', in *The Written Word: Literacy in Transition*, ed. Gerd Baumann (1986), 97–131

Turner, Victor, *The Forest of Symbols* (1967)

Wells, Stanley, and Gary Taylor, with John Jowett and William Montgomery, ed., *William Shakespeare: The Complete Works* (1986)

—— *William Shakespeare: A Textual Companion* (1987)

Wilson, F. P., 'Ralph Crane, Scrivener to the King's Players', *The Library*, IV, 7 (1926), 194–215

PART I: THE CULTURE

THE ORDER OF PERSONS

Gary Taylor

assisted by Celia R. Daileader and Alexandra G. Bennett

'Today we have naming of parts'

Henry Reed

SINCE textual culture depends upon relations between persons, it should be possible to analyse a textual culture by looking at how it represents relations between persons. As it happens, the terminal texts which define our 'Middleton century' are both lists of persons: the parish register which records Middleton's baptism in 1580 (Illus. 1) and the list of 'The Persons represented in the Play' on the first page of *Nice Valour* in the 1679 folio (Illus. 2). The register is the earliest document which identifies Thomas Middleton by name; the 1679 list is the latest substantive text to which a modern editor of Middleton's plays must attend.[1]

These two lists belong to textual genres which have generally been allocated to different disciplines. The 1580 list has become the raw material of biography and demographic history. But historians of individuals and populations have tended to be interested only in the information content of such lists, not their form, or their relation to other kinds of textual production. The 1679 list, attached to a play, is of a kind which students of 'literature' regularly read; it creates an interesting locus of editorial difficulty and an unexplored intersection between social fictions and social facts. It touches on issues—of representation, gender, class, national and racial identity—that have interested many recent literary and cultural critics. But an individual list like that which prefaces *Nice Valour* can only be understood as a fraction of the intertextual field of hundreds of such lists in texts of early modern plays—a field which includes both manuscript and printed texts throughout most of the sixteenth and seventeenth centuries. Thus, the list printed in 1679 leads us from local reading to what D. F. McKenzie called 'the sociology of texts', acknowledging individual agency but positioning it within a quantitative analysis of the playing field within which individual acts occur (McKenzie 1986, 13–16). Moreover, those hundreds of lists, specifically dramatic, can only be understood as a fraction of the vastly larger intertextual field of the innumerable lists of persons in early modern culture. Any satisfactory understanding of an individual list-text, like these exemplary specimens from 1580 and 1679, has to transcend the anecdotalism that has dominated Renaissance studies for the last quarter century; what we need, in place of the anthropological paradigm of 'thick description', is what Douglas Bruster calls 'thin description', or 'deep focus' (2003).

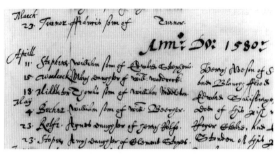

1. Baptisms listed in the parish register of St Lawrence Jewry, London, April 1580

2. Top of the first page of *The Nice Valour* in Beaumont and Fletcher's *Fifty Comedies and Tragedies* (1679)

---

[1] The 1679 collection of *Fifty Comedies and Tragedies* attributed to Francis Beaumont and John Fletcher is, for many of the plays it reprints, an important substantive witness, containing apparently authoritative material not present in earlier extant texts; within that volume, *Nice Valour* is the last text with any connection to the Middleton canon. Recent editors of *Nice Valour* reproduce, with minor changes, the list of 'The Persons represented': see for example Bowers, VII, 438.

Lists of persons provide useful materials for the kind of 'case study', or 'object study', which Roger Chartier has advocated in relation to print culture (1989). But because lists of persons illuminate interrelations between different aspects of early modern textual culture, they enable us to extend the case study approach beyond the confines of print. Moreover, lists of persons—along with lists of words and lists of things—are among the earliest products of literate civilizations (Goody); list-making in itself is not unique to early modern England. Although Foucault naïvely distinguished 'between the age of the theatre and that of the catalogue' (Foucault 1971, 131), catalogues are actually as old as writing, and the 1679 text of *Nice Valour* fuses theatre and catalogue in a combination at least as old as the Athenian and Alexandrian lists of winners at the ancient annual tragic festivals. Because lists of persons occur in all text-making societies, the peculiarities, continuities, and changes in early modern lists should illuminate the peculiarities, continuities, and changes in early modern textual culture. In doing so, they should help us escape the static view of self-contained 'epistemes'—theorized by Foucault, endlessly reiterated by New Historicism, and enforced by the hiring routines of academic institutions—in pursuit of an understanding of the multiple tracks and multiple causes of historical change.

Part I of this essay looks at many different kinds of lists of persons, winnowing the infinitude of potential examples by selecting documents related in some way to the life of Thomas Middleton (Illus. 1–23). From them, I deduce that personal—and authorial—identities in early modern London were categorized by proximities of geography, credit, occupation, genealogy, and value. But these overlapping fractional categories were all in motion, individually and in relation to one another. Early modern textual culture was initially predominantly eclectic (as in Montaigne), but it was moving toward routines of uniformity (as in Locke). Against this background, Part II looks specifically at lists of persons attached to dramatic texts from *c.*1512 to 1679 (Illus. 24–35). From them, I deduce that such 'identification tables' constitute a textual genre that has its own history, driven by particularities of textual production and consumption and by evolving relationships between authors, readers, and booksellers. Part III then relates the two kinds of list, historical and literary, to one another (Illus. 36–52). Can the changing representation of relationships in lists of fictional persons be connected to larger social changes in the perception of geography, gender, labour, and race? Can it be connected to a changing aesthetic of representation? To what extent do such larger changes interact with the particularities of self-differentiating authorial practices?

One thing is immediately clear: the lists of persons in Middleton texts represent human relationships differently than the canonical lists in Shakespeare's, Jonson's, or Dryden's texts. Lists of persons in texts by and about Middleton challenge editors—and readers—to think differently about social and literary identity. They call our attention to critical and editorial problems about human identities and human relationships, which *The Collected Works of Thomas Middleton* has tried to address, or at least acknowledge.

I. Lists of Biological Persons

Lists construct categories of persons. For instance, parish registers—which record baptisms, marriages, and burials—are lists of persons belonging to the category 'participants in certain religious rites in this parish'. The events recorded are textual, not biological: not birth,

3. Taxpayers—including Middleton—from Newington in 1622

intercourse, or death, but the recitation of certain texts prescribed by the Book of Common Prayer. The lists, usually kept by a parish clerk, are organized by place (each parish has its own register), event (each textual rite has its own column, or sequence of pages), and chronology (the names are listed in the chronological order of their participation in the rite). Such a list records the baptism of Thomas, son of William Middleton, in St Lawrence Jewry (Illus. 1); another records that 'Mr. Thomas Middleton' was buried in the churchyard of St Mary's Newington in 1627. Both documents include Middleton in a list of thousands of persons, but they are related to him only by having been, before or after him, the occasion for the performance of the same textual ritual in the same parish. These geographical lists are diachronic; others are synchronic. The lay subsidy roll of 8 March 1622 (Illus. 3) is a list of persons belonging to the category 'non-aristocratic and non-clerical taxpayers in Surrey early in 1622'. This list establishes Middleton's residence in Newington five years before his death, and his wealth relative to other persons in the same place and time. 'Thomas Midleton in goods' differentiates him from others who owned 'land', and the list equates him with the majority of taxpayers, since 'iij^{li}' (three pounds) was the most common assessment of personal wealth, at the low end of a scale which went as high as fifteen pounds. But this still put Middleton in the category of persons wealthy enough to be taxed (Jerkowski *et al.*).

Geography. In all these lists, persons are defined, in part, geographically. At the time of Middleton's birth, English society was still predominantly local and immobile, in terms of personal relations, economies, and government; the size of these local population groups, by our standards, was very small (Braudel, 51–4).[2] Certainly, textual culture in early modern England was a local phenomenon. Individual counties had, to a greater or lesser degree, their own scribal communities (Laslett; Love, 177–84); but textual production, reproduction, and consumption were heavily concentrated in the small triangle bounded by Cambridge, Oxford, and London. The two university towns specialized in the production and circulation of learned texts, especially in Latin, like those which Middleton studied in grammar school and at university; Cambridge and Oxford were also important centres for the production of manuscript miscellanies, like those in which Middleton's epigrams and some of his songs found a place.

Nevertheless, the textual triangle of early modern England was indisputably and overwhelmingly dominated by London. In the Inns of Court it boasted what contemporaries called England's 'third university', like Cambridge and Oxford a centre for the circulation of learned texts and coterie miscellanies. But London had much more than lawyers. Its population was the most literate in England (Cressy). The greater London area (including Westminster) was home to the Stationers' Company, the Scriveners' Company, the theatres, the royal court, and more than one hundred churches. Given this concentration of textual power, it is hardly surprising that all Middleton's works were originally performed or published in London and its suburbs.

Moreover, in almost all these sectors, London's local textual culture was rapidly expanding. In the metropolitan area, population and literacy rose sharply: a larger fraction of London could read, while London itself became a larger fraction of the island's population. Despite efforts at control, the number of printing presses and of journeymen printers grew, as did the number of titles printed (McKenzie 2002); so did the number of theatres and of theatrical performances (Gurr 1989, 1996). The Reformation had stressed the need for a preaching ministry and a literate laity; both these goals, and the theological polemics between Catholics and Protestants, and between different Protestant varieties, textualized religion to an unprecedented extent. Lambeth Palace—the administrative centre of the Church of England—generated and circulated record amounts of ecclesiastical paperwork on the Surrey side of the Thames, just opposite Westminster, while Londoners consumed a quite disproportionate share of the country's new lectures and sermons (Seaver). The legal profession, concentrated in the same small geographical area, was not only growing fast, but also increasingly dependent on printed texts (Baker). The law reports of Chief Justice Edward Coke and the administrative reforms of Chancellor Thomas Egerton—two men in other respects very different—shared an influential commitment to the routine manual inscription of judicial practice.[3] At the same time the conspicuously literary James I greatly intensified and accelerated the textualization of British government. After 1603, he ruled Scotland entirely 'by epistle', and his government tried to impose an unprecedented degree of 'reform in the provinces' (Fletcher; Sharpe 1986); his fondness for hunting led him to spend much of each year on progresses, necessitating a continuous exchange of dispatches with his ministers in London;[4] in the absence of adequate Parliamentary support, royal finances were increasingly dependent upon the sale of monopolies, offices, patents, and titles (Peck). Partly by means of such *ad hoc* textual instruments, secured through connections at court, London livery companies and overseas merchants increasingly dominated English trade (Ashton; Brenner).

English textual culture is, of course, no longer so local. The contributors to the Oxford Middleton come from twelve countries scattered around the globe; only a minority are British subjects. Post-modern textual culture is an increasingly virtual community. This transformation began in the early modern period. By the end of the seventeenth century, a loose collection of localities had become a recognizably national culture (Wrightson)—just as Middleton moved from predominantly local London comedies to the state politics of *A Game at Chess*. This

<hr>

[2] Some of the most influential historical scholarship on early modern England has focused on localities; London, in particular, has been the object of intensive study (Archer, Boulton, Brigden, Finlay, Orlin, Rappaport, etc.).
[3] For more on legal textuality see Gieskes, p. 110 below.
[4] For James's passions for hunting and its effect on bureaucratic routines, see Raumer, II, 201; Lodge, III, 245, 252, 262; Brown, 510, 513; Willson, 179.

emergent national culture was the product, in part, of population mobility and economic interdependence, but it also owed a good deal to that fraction of English society involved in the production, reproduction, circulation, and reception of texts.

The geographical definition of persons, so common in early modern textual culture, depended upon a sense of local identity which early modern textual culture was itself helping to dissolve. Texts produced in London were circulated and read throughout the kingdom. The most important nationalizing texts were the Bibles, catechisms, prayer books, homilies, textbooks, and assize orders by which the Tudor and Stuart regimes successfully imposed some uniformity on the institutions of religion, education, and law; subsidized cartography and history, in the same period, refined and disseminated an image of the nation (Helgerson). But the same pattern was operating, independently of royal encouragement or even desire, at less prestigious levels of textual culture. Middleton in 1604 wished for 'a true-spelling printer' (*Father Hubburd's Tales* 18), and throughout the sixteenth and seventeenth centuries a small community of London printers did create increasingly precise norms of grammar, spelling and punctuation; those norms shaped a new standard for written English, which in time became prescriptive (Price). The increasing power and ubiquity of print helped cause a decline in the prestige of chirographic skill, and by about 1680 the great variety of italic, secretary, and mixed hands had given way virtually everywhere to the more utilitarian mercantile 'round hand' (Petti, 20). In Act 5 of *A Mad World, My Masters* a group of Londoners perform a play at a country house, and in *Hengist, King of Kent* 'a certain company of players' (5.1.68) on tour in the countryside recites a repertory of recognizably London plays. Plays written for and initially performed in London theatres reached the provinces when metropolitan companies toured, or when provincial companies mounted productions of plays written, performed, and printed in London (Murphy 1984).[5] The London theatres also attracted spectators from other parts of the realm (Gurr 1987, 191–204). In 1658 a Newcastle-upon-Tyne bookseller's advertisement included (London) editions of ten plays by Middleton, and his texts were no doubt for sale by other provincial booksellers earlier in the century.[6] The circulation of illicit texts of and about *A Game at Chess* depended on networks of communication by which news and gossip, collected in London, was disseminated up and down the highways of the kingdom (Cogswell, 20–35; Cust; Frearson; Levy 1982, 2002; Watt, 76–7, 295–6). By such means, 'print capitalism' would substitute, for a community confined by locality, one defined instead by a shared written language, a community of 'commodity information' (Anderson). But this change was gradual, and locality remained, throughout Middleton's lifetime, a dominant signifier of personal identity.

Credit. Nevertheless, the geographical categorizing of persons coexisted with an alternative method, which can be seen in many of the same documents. For instance, the tax assessment of 1622 (Illus. 3) is, in effect, a list of persons who owe money to the King, and it belongs to a much larger category of texts. In early modern culture, personal relationships were often categorized in terms of debt. An 'economy of obligation', a culture of personal credit, preceded the development of the institutionalized banking relationships of modern capitalism (Muldrew). In 1612, 'Thomas Middleton a Poett' was included in a list of eighteen debtors of the late Ewen Hebson of Westminster. This list, prepared by a clerk in the Court of Requests, establishes that Middleton must at least occasionally have frequented Hebson's 'verie great haunted Inne' in the Strand, and that he had an economic relationship to Hebson—as did Edward Kirkham, former investor in and manager of the Blackfriars company of child actors. The list also constructs a hierarchy of debt and payment: Middleton was one of only two men from whom some of the debt had been posthumously recovered, and he repaid more than the other. But the list does not establish whether Middleton had any direct relationship with John Halle, esquire, cupbearer to King James, or Richard Ferris, messenger of the chamber, or any of the other fifteen men indebted to Hebson (Eccles, 534–5). Hebson is at the centre of this list; the debtors radiate outward from him, like spokes on a wheel; but the list does not identify any other possible relationships between the spokes. Like much other litigation in this notoriously litigious period, this list illustrates the turmoil created by a gradual transformation in credit relationships, as an occasional reciprocal arrangement between neighbours in a stable local community became a systemic textualized business relationship which linked strangers in an increasingly atomistic and mobile urban environment.

Much of early modern textual culture depended upon credit. Manuscript miscellanies and separates were often prepared by individuals for their personal use and then exchanged among friends without any financial motive or reimbursement; but by the middle of the seventeenth century even such miscellanies were being transformed into printed anthologies, produced for profit. All Middleton's plays and printed texts belonged to a money economy. In 1609 Thomas Dekker called the theatres 'your poets' Royal Exchange', where 'muses' become 'merchants' (98). Certainly, a theatre was an exchange—a market, a retail outlet—for a textual commodity (Bruster 1992, 1–28; Ingram). And production of those textual commodities was normally dependent on credit. In a 1609 lawsuit, what is disputed is whether 'Thomas Middleton de Newington Butts in Com[itatu] Surr[ey] generosum' had paid off his debt to a theatre manager by delivering the text of *The Viper and Her Brood*.[7] An account list of

---

[5] A full record of provincial playing is being accumulated by the volumes of the *Records of Early English Drama* project.

[6] For provincial readers of Middleton's texts, see Jowett, p. 286 below.

[7] For this and other legal documents characterizing texts as property or behaviour, see Gieskes, p. 110 below.

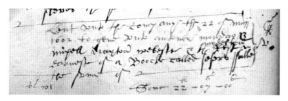

4. First documentary evidence of Middleton as a playwright,
from the records of theatrical entrepreneur Philip Henslowe

1602 (Illus. 4) records payment to a list of playwrights (including Middleton) of an advance toward completion of a new play. The many names listed in what is usually called 'Henslowe's Diary' are almost all records of this kind of economic relationship between persons involved in the production of play texts (Foakes; Carson, 101–41).

Any economy dependent on credit is dependent, also, upon names. You do not need to know someone's name or identity in order to exchange goods of commensurate value, or to exchange money for goods; but if you are giving someone money or goods in exchange for a promise of future delivery of money or goods, then you must be able to identify that person precisely and securely. Plays were always products to which names were attached. Admittedly, English playbills may not have advertised the author of a play until the end of the seventeenth century, and many early printings of plays do not identify their authors. But this namelessness affects the *reproduction* of play texts, not their *production*. Henslowe had to identify authors like Middleton because he had loaned them money and they owed him scripts; that is, Henslowe recognized that scripts are work, that the workers who produce them must be paid, and that he must identify the persons to whom he has loaned money or from whom he has received texts. Entrepreneurs expect loans to be repaid, and authors expect to be rewarded for their labour.

The centrality of rewards is not confined to capitalist, or bourgeois, cultures. The authors of plays in the dramatic festivals of fifth-century Athens were, like Olympic athletes, rewarded with prizes for their success in the competition; the records of those prizes enabled Alexandrian editors to establish the authorship of Athenian plays. In a cultural economy founded upon feudalism, artists—like the bards of Gaelic Ireland—are rewarded by the patronage of an élite, whom they celebrate or condemn by naming them in their songs. Different artistic economies provide different kinds of reward—money, prizes, patronage, applause, esteem—and those differences help shape the structure and development of textual cultures; but there is always a reward, and the distribution of rewards depends upon the identification of workers, of those who produce the work.

But although every textual culture depends upon rewards, not every textual culture depends upon financial debt. Early modern plays differ, historically, from other textual commodities in that their sale required a large ini-

tial investment in purpose-built theatres (which sometimes failed) and a continuing investment in new plays (which sometimes failed). This economic dynamic did not begin to transform drama until the last third of the sixteenth century, but it hit the book trade a century earlier. One consequence of the development of print technology was a radical increase in the capital costs of textual reproduction. The acquisition not only of printing presses, but of stocks of paper and (increasingly varied) founts of type, required a very heavy initial investment, which could only gradually be recouped by the sale of finished texts. In addition to such overheads, stationers had to buy manuscripts from authors; indeed, sometimes they even commissioned texts, particularly translations, thus putting them in the same position as a theatrical entrepreneur, commissioning plays.[8]

Entrepreneurs in both industries responded to this problem in three ways: by creating corporate monopolies to limit competition, by concentrating their resources in areas of high population density, and by specializing their operations. The charter of the Stationers' Company (1557) created a monopoly that controlled the number of authorized printing presses and printers; the *Acte for the Punishemente of Vacabondes* (1572) criminalized all acting troupes that lacked a royal or aristocratic patron. By 1557 the printers, by 1576 the actors, had concentrated their operations in London and its suburbs. Within these metropolitan monopolies, different entrepreneurs began catering to different audiences. The 'War of the Theatres', at the beginning of the seventeenth century, was precipitated by the efforts of the children's companies to identify and dominate an 'élite' sector in what had hitherto been treated, by the adult companies, as an undifferentiated market. The children's companies did not survive, in part because the adult companies co-opted their strategy; in 1608 the King's Men acquired the Blackfriars playhouse, and thereafter offered both indoor and outdoor performances; by the 1630s, plays at the Red Bull and the Fortune were clearly aimed at one clientele, plays at the Blackfriars and Salisbury Court at quite another. In the parallel realm of print, a wave of bankruptcies among the first generation of printers was followed by a progressive division of labour (Greetham, 88, 245–7): between 1580 and 1680 printers permanently separated off from retail booksellers. Even within the retail trade, there was increasing specialization, formalized in the consortium of 'the ballad printers' in the 1620s, leading by the 1650s to the hegemony within a particular market of individual publishers like Playford (music) and Moseley (literature).[9]

In both these sectors of textual culture, an economy based upon debt encouraged a new specialization of identities. The division of labour is, as Durkheim demonstrated, not specific to capitalism, but 'a fact of a very general nature' (41). What capitalism introduced into the textual

---

[8] For more on the economics of printing, see Barnard, McKenzie, and Bell, 568–82, and the essay by Weiss in this volume (p. 195 below).
[9] For Moseley, see Bell, p. 260 below.

economy was an intensified emphasis upon predictability (Knight). In order to reduce the risk of a large capital investment, entrepreneurs sought—and of course still seek—ways to make sales of the eventual mass-produced commodity more predictable. Such predictability was secured through specialized marketing.

Marketing. Specialized marketing is, like reward, a matter of naming. Textual games are played for a reward, and naming ensures that the player who has earned the reward receives it. It is, of course, not necessary to this paradigm that everyone should be able to make a correct attribution; only those in the game who are responsible for distributing a reward need to be able to name who has earned it. Thus, in the late sixteenth century, the general public did not need to know who wrote a play, because the playwright did not receive a reward from the general public; the playwright was rewarded directly by the acting company, or its financial agent. The acting company was in its turn rewarded, for the totality of its performance, by the playgoing public; the playgoing public needed to know whom to reward; consequently, in advertising the performance of a play, early modern playbills identified, not the playwright, or the book-holder, or any of the other invisible persons who contribute to the visible success of a performance, but simply the name of a company of actors and/or its theatre, so that the potential customer would know where to buy the advertised product.

These are all cases of what we might call primary attribution; that is, attribution to the agent to whom a reward would be directed. But players in these economic games sooner or later discover the advantages of secondary attribution. In publishing Middleton's plays, which were most likely to be bought by playgoing readers, stationers regularly featured on the title-page the name of the playing company and/or its theatre; they did so, not because they wished to be fair to the company, but in hopes of increasing their own reward, by providing information which would make their products more attractive to potential consumers. The names of authors would eventually be advertised, by playbills or publishers, for the same reason. Such changes reflect the rise, in early modern England, of a 'consumer culture' (Thirsk), in which texts in particular are evaluated by the same criteria as consumer goods (Hutson, 15–99). Producers seek to reduce their own risk by reducing consumer risk.

In game theory, 'the most important questions of life' are 'for the most part only problems of probability', and 'hope' is a calculation of probabilities which supplies the incentive to experience a loss. The loss is immediate, but one calculates that it is temporary, and will eventually produce a much greater gain.[10] Playgoers and bookbuyers experience a loss—pay money—in advance of any satisfaction; such consumers do not pay *after* watching the performance, or reading the book, which they decide retrospectively was worth a particular sum; instead, they pay *before*, in the 'hope' that they will be satisfied by the product. Secondary attributions are incentives to hope. If

EPILOGUE.

Alſ. ALL *we can doe, to Comfort one another,*
        To ſtay a Brothers ſorrow, for a Brother;
To Dry a Child, from the kinde Fathers eyes
Is to no purpoſe, it rather multiplies :
Your only ſmiles have power to cauſe re-live
The Dead agen, or in their Rooms to give
Brother a new Brother, Father a Child;
If theſe appear, All griefs are reconcil'd.

                                    Exeunt omnes.

        FINIS.

PLAYES newly Printed.

THe *Wild-gooſe-Chaſe,* a Comedy ; written by *Francis Beamont* and *John Fletcher,* Gent'.
    The *Widdow,* a Comedy ; written by *Ben: Johnſon, John Fletcher,* and *Thomas Midleton,* Gent'.

PLAYES in the Preſs.

FIve Playes written by Mr *James Shirley,* being All of his that were Acted at the *Black-Fryers :* Together with the *Court-Secret,* written by the ſame Author, but never yet Acted.

Alſo, The *Spaniſh Gypſies.*

5. Last printed page of *The Changeling* (sig. I3ᵛ), published by Humphrey Moseley in January 1653

consumers have been satisfied by other plays performed by this company, or written by this author, they will be more inclined to pay money to see or read a new play, by the same author or company. For that very reason, in mid-century, booksellers will begin to publish, in one text, advertisements for another (Illus. 5); if consumers liked this play, which this bookseller decided was worth publishing, the same consumers may also like these others, which the same bookseller also decided was worth publishing. A play by James Shirley, published in 1639–40, appended a list of other published plays by Shirley (*BEPD*, pp. 1304–5). Such advertising was aimed at a specific group of consumers, a group already identified by their purchase of a particular book. This marketing strategy would soon be expanded to include published catalogues of plays available from particular booksellers. Such advertisements attempted to establish that a particu-

---

[10] See Laplace, I, 20–25. For my understanding of the potential significance of Laplace's concept I am much indebted to conversations with Brandie Siegfried.

VVit in a Constable	C	Hen. Glapthorn	
VVomans prize	C		
VVoman pleased	C		
VVit at several weapons	C	F. B. Jo. Fletcher	
VVidow	C	Thomas Middleton.	
VVild-goose chase	C	F. B. Jo Flet.	
VVine, Beer, Ale, Tobacco	C	Thomas Middleton	
VVorld tost at tennis	C		
VVoman have her will	C		
VVit in a woman	C		
VVylie beguiled	C		
VViars historie	H	Tho. Decker	
VVestward ho	C	John Webster	
VVeakest goeth to the wall	C		
VVealth and health	C		
VVarning for fair women	C		
VVoman in the moon	C	John Lilly	
VVise for a month	C	F. B. Jo. Fletcher	

Y

Young Admiral	C	James Shirley
Yorkshire Tragedie	T	Will. Shakespeare
Your fine gallants.	C	Thomas Middleton

6. Part of a list of plays included in
the first edition of *Old Law* (1656)

9

R. VV.	Three Ladies of London.	C	Tho. Lodge and Robert Green	Leir and his three Daughters.	H
John Tatham	Love crowns the end.	TC		Looking-glass for London.	H
John Day	Law tricks, or who would have thought it.	C		Liberality & Pro-digality.	C
VV. Chamberlain	Loves Victory.	C		Lady Almony.	C
Tho. Meriton	Love and War.	T		Luminalia.	M
John Lilly	Loves Metamor-phosis.	C		Laws of Nature.	C
	London Chanti-clers.	C	T. B.	Love will find out the way.	C
	Look about you, or, run Red Caps.	C	T. Ford.	Love Alamode.	
			T. Ford.	Loves Labyrinth.	TC
			Geo. Etherege	Levellers Levell'd	I
			Rich. Flecknoe	Love in a Tub.	C
				Loves Kingdom.	TC

M

Will. Shakespear	Merry wives of Windfor.	C	Ben. Johnson	Masque of Owls.	M
Will. Shakespear	Measure for measure.	C	Ben. Johnson	Mortimer's fall.	T
Will. Shakespear	Much adoe about Nothing.	C	Ben. Johnson	Masque of Queens.	M
Will. Shakespear	Midsomer nights Dream.	C	Ben. Johnson	Mercury Vindicated.	M
VVill. Shakespear	Merchant of Venice.	C	James Shirley	Maids Revenge.	T
			Hen. Shirley	Martyr'd Souldier	T
			Tho. Heywood	Maiden head well lost.	C
VVill. Shakespear	Mackbeth.	T	Tho. Midleton	Mad World my Masters.	C
VVill. Shakespear	Merry Devil of Edmonton.	C	Tho. Midleton	Mayor of Quinborough.	C
VVill. Shakespear	Mucedorus.	C	Tho. Midleton	Michaelmas term	C
John Fletcher	Mad Lover.	C	Tho. Midleton	More dissemblers than Women.	C
John Fletcher	Maid in the Mill.	C	VVill. Rowley	Match at Midnight.	T
John Fletcher	Masque of Grays Inne Gent.	M			
John Fletcher	Monsieur Thomas	C	Phil. Massenger	Maid of Honour.	C
John Fletcher	Maids Tragedy.	T	Geo. Chapman	May Day.	C
Ben. Johnson	Magnetick Lady.	C	George Chapman	Monsieur D'Oliv	C
Ben. Johnson	Masque at my Lord Hayes House.	M	George Chapman	Masque of the middle Temple, & Lincolns In	M
Ben. Johnson	Metamorphosed Gypsies.	M	Rich. Brome	Mad Couple well matcht.	C
Ben. Johnson	Masque of Augurs	M	Lord Brooks	Mustapha.	T

B   Barten

7. From Francis Kirkman's 'Exact Catalogue of all the
English Stage-Plays printed, till the present Year 1671'

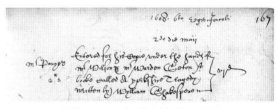

8. First entry of *A Yorkshire Tragedy* in
the register of the Stationers' Company

lar bookseller was a predictable, reliable source for certain kinds of text which certain consumers were especially interested in buying. The same logic led, eventually, to the publication of playlists that identified the author of the play (Illus. 6), and then of playlists that grouped plays by author (Illus. 7). If a consumer liked one work by Middleton, she might expect to like others, which she could find (predictably) in a particular shop. In all these cases, secondary attributions are designed to stimulate market interest in a commodity, and thereby to reduce the risk to entrepreneurs who have already invested considerable sums of money in manufacturing that commodity.

An analysis of textual culture must therefore discriminate between at least two different uses of what Foucault christened 'the author-function' (1977). Anonymity is not, as Foucault claimed, the historical norm; the naming of authors is not simply a mechanism of censorship, enabling governments to punish transgressive authors, or of capitalism, enabling the transfer of property rights between publishers (Foucault, 124).[11] The capitalist publisher, who invests in production of a printed book, does not need an author's name in order to secure his monopoly on a particular textual property. Most of the entries in the Stationers' Register of texts included in *The Collected Works of Thomas Middleton* do not name Middleton as author. Some of them specifically name a different author. For example, an entry on 2 May 1608 (Illus. 8) records Thomas Pavier's right to publish *A Yorkshire Tragedy* 'written by Wylliam Shakespere'. Shakespeare cannot have written the whole play, and most scholars now agree that Middleton wrote it all. But neither Shakespeare

nor Middleton was present when this memorandum was written. The manuscript records a transaction between Pavier and two officials of the Stationers' Company, and it was designed to regulate relationships between Pavier and all other members of the company by granting him the exclusive right to publish this particular text. Its legal

[11] Of the many studies which have adopted and adapted Foucault's theory of the eighteenth-century origins of authorship, see particularly de Grazia, Loewenstein, Masten, and Rose.

force did not depend upon the accuracy of its authorial attribution, but upon the validity of the monopoly that Pavier was claiming from his fellow stationers (Blayney). Why then did Pavier mention Shakespeare? This is only the third time Shakespeare's name had appeared in the Register, and Pavier could have attributed the play to Shakespeare on its printed title-page without naming him in the manuscript register. Perhaps the name was used because Pavier wanted to distinguish this text about a famous Yorkshire crime from *Two Unnatural Murders*, a prose pamphlet about the same crime, which belonged to another stationer (Nathaniel Butter). Middleton's name would have served this purpose as well as Shakespeare's, and one can only guess why Pavier got the name wrong: perhaps Shakespeare (as a representative of the acting company that owned the script) had sold him the manuscript, perhaps Shakespeare was the author of one of the other three parts of *Four Plays in One*, perhaps Pavier believed that Shakespeare's name had greater market appeal than Middleton's. We can only guess at these possibilities because the chief function of the manuscript was to establish Pavier's publishing monopoly. It performed that task efficiently. Attribution of the text to an author, on the other hand, was only tangentially relevant to the transaction being recorded, and here—as often elsewhere—the attribution was botched.

Cases like this have given rise to the belief that the modern concept of authorial agency did not exist in early modern textual culture. But we should not seek for evidence of authorship in documents recording other kinds of claim. The fact that authors' names show up in the Stationers' Register, even though they were not legally necessary there, demonstrates that Londoners habitually attributed texts to authors. So does the equally unnecessary action of a seventeenth-century reader of *The Widow*, who altered the title-page of the 1652 edition to remove the names of Fletcher and Jonson, and attribute the play to Middleton 'alone'. The 'Author' constructed by this handwritten annotation is not, as Foucault would have it, 'a censorship-effect', nor (as Loewenstein would have it) 'a book-effect, a press-effect, a market-effect' (Loewenstein 2002a, 12). *The Widow* contains nothing that would interest a censor, anxious to identify who should be punished: all three of the authors named on the title-page were dead by the time it was printed. The reader's alteration of the title-page did not intervene in the processes that governed the printing or marketing of the text; rather, it resisted the authority of print and marketing. Nor did the alteration increase the value of the owner's book; indeed, given the relative reputations of Middleton, Jonson, and Fletcher in the second half of the seventeenth century, the alteration *decreased* the value of the material object. The reader can only have been motivated by a desire to attribute the work correctly to the individual who had actually done the work.

That desire was not new. Classical Mediterranean and medieval European civilization recognized and celebrated

HVIVS Prologi ratio eò tendit, ut nouo Poetæ ueniam paret quòd non ut reliqui Poetæ, argumentum suo loco narret: tũ deinde, ut ueterem in odium ducat. Postremo, ut Terentium modestissimum, minimeq; errantem comprobet.

9. The playwright Terence addressing the audience on the first page of a 1570 edition of his play *Andria*

individual authorial agency (Vickers, 506–41); classical and medieval scholars took pains to identify authors correctly (Reynolds and Wilson, 1–137). Such habits survived into the age of print. Renaissance editions of Terence pictured 'the poet' himself directly addressing the audience at the start of his plays (Illus. 9). Before the Stationers' Company received its charter, and long before the eighteenth-century Parliamentary and legal battles over authorial copyright, Caxton had published 'The book of fame made by Gefferey Chaucer' (as the 1483 title-page described it). More substantively, living authors could occasionally acquire a patent giving them a monopoly on printed editions of their own work: late in 1610, for instance, John Speed acquired a ten-year royal patent for the printing of his *Genealogies of the Holy Scriptures* (and a map of Canaan), to be inserted in every copy of the new authorized version of the Bible (Hunt). William Alley held his patent 'at the nomination of Thomas Middleton, to print Middleton's *The Peacemaker*'; we do not know what arrangement Middleton had with Alley, but the patent recognizes both Middleton's authorship and his right to nominate the patentee.

Demonstrably, the social category of the author precedes and exceeds censorship, the printing press, and capitalism. But this does not mean that censorship, print, and capitalism had no effect on textual culture or the place of individual authorial agency within it. Rather than creating authors, such forces could in certain circumstances render them invisible. The fear of punishment might make authors or stationers conceal their identity (as happened with the printed editions of *A Game at Chess*). Printing technology has no intrinsic bias against authors, but the names that matter most to the printing industry are the names of owners of printing presses and/or of the wholesale distributors who sell the mass-produced commodities those machines produce. That is still true today: both *The Collected Works of Thomas Middleton* and *Thomas Middleton and Early Modern Textual Culture* name the publisher on the title-page, but neither names all the authors who have contributed to the volume. Unlike most texts, every printed book is the work of more than one labourer. The author, the compositor, the pressman, the bookseller, and potentially many others, divide the work between them. Capitalism—a 'productive mechanism whose parts are human beings'—produces a regimen of 'fractional work'; it 'rivets each labourer to a single fractional detail', making the individual 'the automatic motor of a fractional operation' (Marx, I, 339, 345, 360). Much more than earlier textual regimes, the economy of print has to confront a quantitative problem in attribution: *how many* of the people who worked to produce this text should be acknowledged on the title-page?

This problem was compounded when the heavily capitalized print industry intersected with the heavily capitalized theatre business, because in such circumstances the number of persons doing 'fractional work' inevitably multiplied. But this chronology and causality have been obscured by the overwhelming focus of literary historians on Shakespeare and, to a lesser degree, the commercial theatre system to which he belonged. To scholars with that kind of focus, it may appear that 'in the mid-1590s, playwrights' names begin to appear on title pages' (Loewenstein 2002a, 86). But this statement is false. Playwrights' names did not begin to *appear* in the mid-1590s; they began to *re-appear*. The title-page of the first play printed in England, *Fulgens and Lucrece* (BEPD 1, *c*.1512), declares that it was 'cōmpyled by mayster Henry medwall, late chapelayne to ye ryght reuerent fader in god Iohan Morton cardynall Archebysshop of Caūterbury'. A few decades later (Illus. 10), a play by

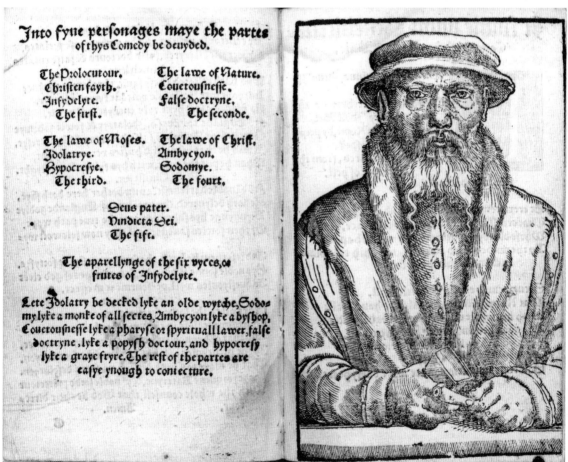

10. An opening of John Bale's *A Comedye concernynge thre lawes* (*c*.1548), with a table of 'personages' and 'partes' facing a woodcut portrait of the author

John Bale included a portrait of the author. Altogether, authors' names appeared on 27 title-pages of dramatic texts from 1512 to 1581, including 18 vernacular plays and entertainments.[12] Attributions then completely disappear from title-pages of commercial plays printed between 1584 and 1594. Historically, the period from 1584 to 1594 is anomalous, not foundational. It could only ever have seemed foundational to Shakespeareans.

What replaced attribution to playwrights, in that anomalous decade, was attribution to one of the new commercial acting companies. Attributions to companies remained a frequent feature of title-pages throughout the early modern period, but gradually after 1594 they were supplemented by attributions to the playwrights who did piece-work for the acting companies: Robert Greene, Thomas Lodge, Robert Wilson, Christopher Marlowe, and Thomas Nashe (all named on 1594 title-pages of commercial plays), John Lyly (first named in 1597), George Chapman and William Shakespeare (first named in 1598). The disappearance of authorial attribution for a decade, combined with its relative infrequency for another decade, demonstrates that the alliance of the theatre with the printing press could effectively render authors invisible. The reappearance of authors on title-pages does not mean that authorship was being invented from scratch; it means that their names were serving some function that was increasingly important to the book trade.

The naming of authors serves different functions in different fractions of a textual culture. At the level of text-production, the identification of authors is central to any of the many systems of reward for textual labour. At the level of text-reproduction, the identification of authors may be a mechanism for reducing the risk, for both sellers and buyers, of investing in a textual commodity. The importance of risk-reducing mechanisms is in part a function of the number of texts available. Historically, most societies with writing systems have been characterized by the circulation of a relatively small number of relatively well-known written texts (Engelsing; Hall; Darnton, 165–67): in such societies, a small number of canonical texts (Scripture, Virgil) could represent a relatively large fraction of textual culture. As the number of texts increases, each individual text becomes a smaller, less easily identifiable fraction of the reading universe. Printing, the commercial theatre, and the Protestant sermon created for the first time in Britain a textual economy characterized by the circulation of large numbers of new and unfamiliar texts. Naming authors helped categorize those texts for the convenience of consumers—for the convenience (in turn) of businessmen who had invested in the reproduction and dissemination of texts.

Such categorizing has, of course, become even more important in our own time, as the information explosion has exponentially increased the number of available texts. *The Collected Works* brings together many texts by Thomas Middleton, in the hopes that readers familiar with some of his texts will be willing to acquire others. The name

> **Our moderne, and present excellent Poets which worthely florish in their owne workes, and all of them in my owne knowledge liued togeather in this Queenes raigne, according to their priorities as neere as I could, I haue orderly set downe (viz) George Gascoigne Esquire, Thomas Church-yard Esquire, sir Edward Dyer Knight, Edmond Spencer Esquire, sir Philip Sidney Knight, Sir Iohn Harrington Knight, Sir Thomas Challoner Knight, Sir Frauncis Bacon Knight, & Sir Iohn Dauie Knight, Master Iohn Lillie gentleman, Maister George Chapman gentleman, M. W. Warner gentleman, M. Willi. Shake-speare gentleman, Samuell Daniell Esquire, Michaell Draiton Esquire, of the bath, M. Christopher Marlo gen. M. Beniamine Iohnsō geleman, Iohn Marston Esquier, M. Abraham Frauncis gen. master Frauncis Meers gentle. master Iosua Siluester gentle. master Thomas Deckers gentleman; M. Iohn Flecher gentle. M. Iohn Webster gentleman, M. Thomas Heywood geutlemen, M. Thomas Middleton gentleman, M. George Withers.**

11. In Edmund Howes's continuation of Stow's *Annals* (1615), Middleton and Wither are the youngest living writers singled out as representatives of modern achievement

of the author is here supplemented by the name of the publisher, Oxford University Press, which carries cultural credentials of its own, which in turn help to reassure potential consumers about the predictable accuracy and importance of this textual commodity. Finally, the list of the names of contributors and their institutions functions as yet another layer of reassurance and predictability. Now as then, names serve a marketing function.[13]

Companies. But that is not their only function. The 1612 lawsuit identified 'one Thomas Middleton a Poett' as one of Hebson's debtors. In 1615 many of the same names that would later appear in publishers' catalogues (Illus. 6–7) had already been listed together in a very different context (Illus. 11). Edmund Howes's approximately chronological list of 'modern ... excellent Poets' was a brief part of his survey of recent English history. John

---

12 For a complete list of authorial names on title-pages through 1581, see Farmer and Lesser, 118; however, they do not call attention to the significance of these figures, being primarily interested in plays from the commercial period after 1576. Saeger and Fassler explicitly exclude pre-1576 drama from their analysis.

13 On this function in relation to post-modern marketing of Shakespeare, see Taylor 1989.

12. The parish register of St Dunstan often identifies the occupation of deceased parishioners

Taylor, in 1620, noted that hemp was among other things used to make paper, upon which many writers 'liuing at this day' displayed their 'worth' (sig. E4):

> ... *Dauis*, *Drayton*, and the learned *Dun*,
> *Ionson*, and *Chapman*, *Marston*, *Middleton*,
> With *Rowley*, *Fletcher*, *Withers*, *Messenger*,
> *Heywood*, and all the rest where e're they are,
> Must say their lines but for the paper sheete
> Had scarcely ground, whereon to set their feete.

Thomas Heywood, in 1635, mentioned 'Tom' Middleton in a list of the nicknames of 'Our moderne Poets' (S1ᵛ). None of these lists was designed to sell a commodity; rather, they were intended to define a community. As such, they resemble the lists, in Middleton's pageants, of famous members of a particular London livery company.

In such lists, personal relationships are defined by membership in an occupational community. Clearly, these groups differ from local communities like the parish of St Mary's, Newington, Surrey, mentioned in other documents. The 'poets' identified by Taylor and Heywood all lived in London or its suburbs, but they were not neighbours, and what connected them was not place-of-residence but kind-of-business. Thus, some parish registers (which establish geographical identities) also record, when naming particular parishioners, their occupation or livery company, thus cross-referencing one kind of community within the context of another (Illus. 12).

Early modern London's textual culture was organized by livery companies, or by occupational communities which aspired to the status of livery companies. Livery companies were hierarchical organizations of people engaged (theoretically or actually) in the same or related work; they combined the richest owners and the poorest workers within a single syndicate; they had internal regulations (designed to control the activities of members) and external privileges, protected by patent or statute (designed to control the activities of non-members). London printing and publishing was almost entirely controlled by one such livery company, the Stationers' Company.[14] Another, the Leathersellers' Company, fought to protect its control of bookbinding, while the Scriveners' Company specialized in the production and reproduction of certain kinds of manuscript. Actors, playwrights, and theatrical entrepreneurs did not have their own livery company, but many of them were free of the Drapers, Goldsmiths, Grocers, or other companies; such membership gave them certain privileges as citizens of London, including the right to bind apprentices (Kathman). Using livery companies as a model, actors like the King's Men organized themselves into joint-stock companies, protected by royal patents, and hierarchically divided into masters (sharers), journeymen (hired men), and apprentices (boys).

'Poets' had no joint-stock companies and no livery of their own. But some belonged to London companies: Ben Jonson was a Bricklayer, Anthony Munday a Draper, John Webster a Merchant Taylor. Others—like George Peele, Thomas Kyd, Thomas Lodge, and Thomas Middleton— were the sons of freemen, though they seem never to have taken advantage of their patrimony. Others still—like Thomas Heywood, William Rowley, and William Shakespeare—belonged to joint-stock companies of actors. As a pervasive feature of social life in early modern London, livery companies provided a model of personal relationships within a trade—a model explicitly invoked in the division, in *News from Gravesend* (1604), of 'all the Rymesters, Play-patchers, Iig-makers, Ballad-mongers, & Pamphlet-stitchers (being the yeomanry of the Company)' from 'all those whom *Theocrytus* calls the *Muses* Byrds (being the Maisters and head-Wardens)' (154–8). Dekker's and Middleton's collaborations with each other and with other poets testify to a livery ethic of occupational sociability and shared labour, equally evident in their pageants (which also involved collaborations with named carpenters). In an entirely different vein, Ben Jonson's insistence upon distinguishing between poets and 'poetasters' (or poets and 'carpenters'), his contractual definition of the proper relationship between authors and those who bought their 'ware' (*Bartholomew Fair* Ind. 59–165), and his pursuit of the reversion to the Mastership of the Revels, can all be seen as attempts to structure and police the profession of literature, along lines suggested by the London livery companies. Jonson envisaged himself as Master of a hierarchical Company, with privileges secured by royal patent—including the right to discipline unqualified interlopers who brought the trade into disrepute.

Nothing came of Jonson's institutional ambitions, or of later seventeenth-century suggestions for a literary

---

14 For livery companies generally, see Seaver, 'Middleton's London' in *Works*, p. 59; for the Stationers' Company in particular, see Clegg, p. 247 below; for the distinction between livery companies and guilds, see Hope.

academy, along the lines of the *Académie française* (founded by Cardinal Richelieu in 1634). Although Jonson became unofficial poet laureate, and Middleton official Chronologer of London, the legitimacy and status conferred by such recognition was purely personal; it did not create a professional structure. Indeed, the livery system—the model for Jonson's policing of privileges and Middleton's collaborative enterprise, alike—was itself beginning to decline, precisely because it restricted the free movement of labour and capital. From the 1590s, Parliament became increasingly hostile to monopolies and exclusionary trading privileges; at the same time, the occupational homogeneity of the livery companies was being undermined from within, as freemen of one company took increasing advantage of the 'freedom of the city' in order to pursue unrelated trades. With the slow disintegration of the livery companies, artisans and labourers became, not collaborators within a secure structure, but isolates competing to sell themselves in an unpredictably changing market-place. The unliveried poets, not the liveried Stationers, heralded the future of textual culture. The first legal recognition of authorial privilege, the Copyright Act of Queen Anne (1709), was secured not by the concerted action of authors demanding a new professional status, but by rivalries between booksellers, occasioned by the collapse of the Stationers' Company monopoly.

Genealogy. In the absence of a real structure of professional relationships, authors invented analogical ones, particularly in the form of feigned (and fained) filiations. The 'sons of Ben'—Richard Brome, Thomas Carew, Lucius Cary (Viscount Falkland), William Cartwright, Sir Kenelm Digby, Robert Herrick, Thomas Nabbes, Thomas Randolph, and Sir John Suckling—belonged to a 'tribe' united by the influence of Jonson; Sir William Davenant, in claiming to be Shakespeare's bastard 'son', literalized the genealogical analogy.

In early modern England, personal identity was predominantly defined by genealogical relationships. In 1623, Samuel Thompson (Windsor Herald) and Augustin Vincent (Rouge Croix Pursuivant) recorded in Latin, in the course of a systematic visitation of gentry families in Surrey, a list of the members of Thomas Middleton's family (Illus. 13). This text registers Middleton's relationship to his biological father William, but does not even mention his stepfather Thomas Harvey; although Harvey was legally and practically his father from the age of six, he is irrelevant to the genealogical line. This Visitation document was often translated and transcribed, and survives in more manuscript copies than any other early text which names Middleton. Indeed, this whole category of manuscripts—lists of genealogical lists—is extraordinarily common (Sims). Wills are even more common, though individual wills were not copied so often. In the lists of beneficiaries in wills, members of the immediate family overwhelmingly predominate: William Middleton, as he lay dying, named only his mother, stepfather, and wife

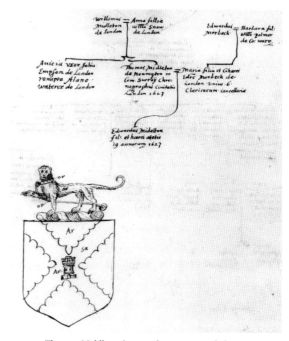

13. Thomas Middleton's genealogy, as recorded in 1623

14. William Middleton's last will and testament

(Illus. 14). Finally, a good deal of litigation—including much of the legal wrangling between Thomas Middleton's mother and his stepfather—originates in disputes over inheritance. Since inheritance legitimized power, property, and status, from the monarch all the way down to the owner of a few 'movables', this pervasive textual emphasis upon genealogy is hardly surprising.

In early modern textual culture, privilege was often transmitted genealogically. Many such transmissions are recorded, for instance, in the lists of members and copyrights kept by the Stationers' Company. George Eld acquired the business which would be involved in the printing of nine Middleton texts by marrying the previous owner's widow. Isaac Jaggard inherited his father William's business, completing the printing of the 1623 folio of Shakespeare's *Comedies, Histories, and Tragedies*. John Okes likewise inherited the printing business of his father Nicholas Okes; Nicholas was involved in the printing of thirteen works by Middleton, John in the printing of two. Like printing presses and company membership, the rights to particular texts could be inherited. Once a stationer had registered a work and acquired the licence to print it, that work became his property; if not sold in the interim, it would, at his death, be bequeathed to another stationer (often through, and with, his widow). Thus, Isaac Jaggard's widow transferred his rights to plays in the 1623 Shakespeare folio to Thomas and Richard Cotes on 19 June 1627; Richard's right to publish *Measure for Measure*, *Timon of Athens*, *Macbeth*, *A Yorkshire Tragedy* and sixteen other 'Shakespeare' plays was, on 6 August 1674, transferred by his widow to Henry Herringman and John Martin; on 21 August 1683, Martin's widow transferred his share to Robert Scott (Schoenbaum, 221–35; Murphy 2003, 51–55).

Genealogical transmission, which often established the *right* to reproduce a text, just as often characterized the *method* by which texts were reproduced. In biological transmission, A begets B who begets C who begets D; in textual reproduction, the first edition of *Timon of Athens* (1623) was copied in the second (1632), which was copied in the third (1663), which was copied in the fourth (1685), which was copied by Rowe (1709), who in turn fathered a succession of eighteenth-century editions. In a genealogy, the ramifying intermediaries of a lineage matter as much as, or more than, the single distant point of origin. After all, for Christians every genealogy had exactly the same starting point: Adam and Eve. In early modern society, it was the number and nature of the *intermediaries* between that shared origin and the divided present that conferred power on some but not others. 'Genealogy,' as Foucault wrote, 'opposes itself to the search for "origins"' (1984, 77). By contrast, philology is anti-genealogical. Philology, unlike genealogy, seeks the origin, and devalues intermediaries. Philology's metaphysical commitment to the origin 'arises from the belief that things are most precious and essential at the moment of birth' (Nietzsche, no. 3). Unlike all editions in the seventeenth century and most in the eighteenth, the text of *Timon of Athens* in *The Collected Works of Thomas Middleton* skips over the successive textual generations between 1623 and 2004, so that the oldest text begets the newest.

The genealogy of anti-genealogical philology, which has come to dominate our own textual culture, can itself be traced to the Renaissance, the Reformation, and the Copernican revolution. These are, of course, complex movements, complexly related, but they are all centrally preoccupied with the problems of textual transmission.

Technical philology developed in the late fifteenth and early sixteenth centuries (Grafton 1991). Modern editing is the child of Renaissance humanism, and modern humanism is the child of Renaissance editing: the recovery of classical culture could only follow from the identification-authentication-interpretation-reproduction-correction of ancient texts. Nor could such practices, once formulated and validated, be confined to secular works (Bentley 1983). The Reformation was, among other things, a textual revolution, in which a small dedicated cadre of editors wielded an influence wholly disproportionate to their numbers or the accuracy of their analysis.[15] One immediate effect of these two interrelated movements—the rise of humanism and Protestantism—was the institutionalization of philology as a university discipline (Grafton 1983, 10; Grafton and Jardine). Once entrenched, the intellectual routines developed in the Renaissance were perpetuated until the eighteenth century, when they began to be applied systematically to vernacular 'classics', creating a new literary canon composed primarily of works produced by early modern textual culture (Taylor 1993).

Both humanism and Protestantism owed the scale and permanence of their extraordinary success in the sixteenth century to the printing press, which could produce thousands of copies of the Aldine editions of Greek classics, of the New Testament edited by Erasmus, of the New Testament translated by Luther or Tyndale. Erasmus himself lived and worked in printers' houses, and much of his international influence was a direct result of his 'consummate mastery of his chosen medium, print' (Jardine, 9). That medium was equally important to the interrelated scientific revolutions of the sixteenth and seventeenth centuries (Eisenstein; Johns). The congruence between humanism and science may seem paradoxical, since new scientific observations had the effect of invalidating the authority of old humanist classics like Pliny and Aristotle. But in all these sixteenth-century intellectual movements, intermediate texts and generations were dismissed as degenerate, as misrepresentations of an originary truth, which could only be recovered by a return to the earliest texts: the Greek and Latin classics (humanism), the Bible (Protestantism), the 'book of nature' (science). All three movements were fundamentally anti-genealogical: they sought to overturn a cultural privilege which had been genealogically transmitted to textual descendants now identified as corrupt.

Early modern textual culture, though still predominantly genealogical in Middleton's lifetime, contained an emergent philological undercurrent. Many of the polemical battles of the sixteenth and seventeenth centuries—which are still being fought in our own century—resulted from clashes between these two viewpoints (Taylor 1994c). In counter-attacks against the new movements, the distinction between distant origin and genealogical

---

15 On the inaccuracy of early modern editing, see Kenney, esp. pp. 1–20.

tradition was simply elided, on the assumption that the origin was perfectly reflected by the tradition; any attack on the intermediaries was thus interpreted as an attack on the source. Lorenzo Valla's *Collatio novi testamenti*, the first humanist work to apply the new techniques of textual and philological criticism to the Vulgate text of the Bible, on occasion criticized both St Augustine and St Thomas Aquinas, and inevitably it often criticized the textually derivative late medieval texts of the Vulgate. Valla's work was immediately attacked by Poggio Bracciolini, who accused Valla of 'scorning the scriptures and slinging darts at Christ', and of deprecating the authority of St Jerome (Bentley 1983, 40–50). The same criticisms were later levelled at Erasmus. Thus, anyone who produced a new edition or translation of a canonical text could be accused of having displaced the original author and substituted themselves: what purported to be a return to the 'oldest' text was interpreted as the creation of a completely 'new' text. Thomas More's *Confutation of Tyndale* complained that Tyndale's English translation of the Gospels was 'not worthy to be called Crystes testament'; it was instead 'Tyndales owne testament' (358). 'Who', Calvin asked, 'will venture to place the authority of Copernicus above that of the Holy Spirit?' (Stimson, 46–7). Philological in his rejection of any intermediaries between him and the original Christianity of the early Scriptures, Calvin was genealogical when it came to the book of nature, preferring an intermediary text to direct observation of the original phenomena.

Calvin was not alone in combining these two attitudes without any sense of their logical incompatibility. The development of all three intellectual revolutions (theological, philological, scientific) depended upon the widespread availability of standard printed texts, which could serve as shared points of scholarly reference, subject to checking, correction, and subsequent reprinting—thereby creating a new point of reference, which could be subjected to the same evolutionary process (Eisenstein, 88–113). As a result, movements whose textual *goals* were anti-genealogical depended upon genealogical *methods* of textual transmission. In the case of the Bible, for instance, the dominant text of the period, the Erasmian anti-genealogical return to Greek manuscripts of the New Testament led to centuries of genealogical retransmission of that hastily constructed 'textus receptus' (Metzger, 95–106). Likewise, in the early modern succession of English translations of the Bible, from Tyndale (1525) to the Authorized Version (1611), each new edition was based upon and incorporated much of the wording of its immediate predecessor—yet each was modified by a scholarly return to editions of the 'original' non-English texts. Genealogical and anti-genealogical methods were combined in the production of a single text. Similar combinations can be seen in the 1604 editions of Middleton's *The Ant and the Nightingale* and Dekker and Middleton's *The Patient Man and the Honest Whore*, where ('corrupting', genealogical) reprints of the first edition incorporate ('improving', anti-genealogical) additions of new material and a new title.

The emergent philological alternative to genealogical transmission transformed the texts Middleton and his contemporaries read, and occasionally affected the way their own texts were transmitted; but it also offered an alternative way for early modern textual culture to represent the relations between persons. Erasmus draped himself in the iconography of St Jerome, and other humanists actually modelled paintings of Jerome, in both cases asserting an identity between a classical and an early modern author (Jardine, 55–82); again, intermediate generations were elided, and the new text/author was imagined as a kind of clone, directly reproduced from ancient seed. By the late sixteenth century, such bracketing of English and classical authors had become a systematic principle of relationship:

> As the Greeke tongue is made famous and eloquent by *Homer, Heſiod, Euripedes, Aeſchylus, Sophocles, Pindarus, Phocylides,* and *Ariſtophanes*; and the Latine tongue by *Virgill, Ouid, Horace, Silius Italicus, Lucanus, Lucretius, Auſonius,* and *Claudianus*: ſo the Engliſh tongue is mightily enriched and gorgeouſly inueſted in rare ornaments and reſplendent abiliments by ſir *Philip Sidney, Spencer, Daniel, Drayton, Warner, Shakeſpeare, Marlow,* and *Chapman.*

This 1598 catalogue of equivalencies (Meres, fol. 280) is original but not eccentric. Jonson saw himself as the English Horace; James I, as the British Solomon. Middleton never represented himself in this way, but that did not prevent others from doing so. In 1652, the actor Alexander Gough commended *The Widow* for its '*neer resemblance to the portracture we have in* Terence'; in 1657, an engraved portrait of Middleton showed him wearing a robe which could easily be interpreted as Roman, and a crown of laurel which could only be interpreted as classical. Such twinning was not confined to the representation of authors. England itself was conceptualized, in Foxe's *Book of Martyrs*, as another Israel, a new elect nation (Haller). London was, in Dekker's 1612 pageant as elsewhere, *Troia-noua*, 'new Troy'. Middleton never used the old genealogies that attributed the settlement of England to a colony of Trojans; instead, he called the Lord Mayor a 'praetor', thereby equating contemporary London and ancient Rome.

Value. All these analogies assert, and thereby construct, hierarchies of value. Early modern English society was, of course, pervasively hierarchical. The designation 'Mr.' in the parish record of Middleton's burial—like the 'Gent.' on the title-pages of many of his works (Illus. 15)—is a marker of social status, justified by the heralds' genealogy (Illus. 13). The subsidy roll (Illus. 3) registers an economic hierarchy within the county. The Oxford matriculation register—in which Middleton's status is corrected downward, from 'generosi fis' to 'plebei' (Eccles 1957, 524)—is one of many indications of the uncertain relationship between social and economic hierarchies: Middleton was the son of a gentleman, but he did not

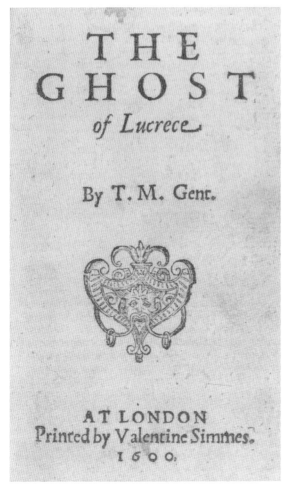

THE
GHOST
of Lucrece

By T. M. Gent.

AT LONDON
Printed by Valentine Simmes.
1600.

15. The first title-page in the Middleton
canon to identify its author as a gentleman

in turn reported directly to the King.[16] The hierarchies which permeated society permeated the institutions of textual culture, and the texts produced by those institutions often reflect that extra-textual social hierarchy. Many of Middleton's title-pages advertise his gentility, a practice very common in the period; occasionally authors go even further, and incorporate a coat of arms in their books. Prefaces and dedications—like those in *The Wisdom of Solomon Paraphrased*, *The World Tossed at Tennis*, and all Middleton's pageant texts—register the subservience of authors to their social superiors. The dedication to *Honourable Entertainments* is typical: the Lord Mayor is listed first (in largest type), then the other aldermen in order of seniority; the smallest type on the page is reserved for the author's initials; he and his texts are only '*Poore Suiters... seruing you*'. Patron-client relations, which structured so much of early modern social life, also structured textual culture.

Such texts merely reflect a hierarchy which is not primarily textual. But textual culture also had hierarchies of its own. The lists of poets compiled by Meres, Howes, Taylor, and Heywood, already quoted, are all selective; they are based upon decisions about which authors were important enough to merit inclusion. In 1615, Chapman described Middleton as '*a poore Chronicler of a Lord Maior's naked Truth*'; Chapman was not just disparaging Middleton, but the whole genre of civic pageantry, which in the hierarchy of textual value seemed to him far inferior to his own translation of Homer. For Chapman, the very popularity of pageantry demonstrated its *textual* vulgarity. Many of the early modern hierarchies of genre are based upon hierarchies of readership: the more common the real or presumed readers of a text, the more despicable the text itself. Ballads, accordingly, were the most contemptible texts of all (Würzbach, 242–84); plays were, for a long time, equally suspect (Bentley 1971, 38–61). In 1617, the satirist Henry Fitzgeffrey complained of

> Bookes, *made of* Ballades: Workes: *of* Playes,
> Sightes, *to be* Read: *of my* Lo: Maiors *day's*:

—thus lumping together Jonson's impressive folio edition of his plays, printed in 1616, with pageant texts like those of Munday and Middleton. Fitzgeffrey's long list of despicables continues with a jibe at pamphlets like Dekker's '*Lanthorn and Candle-light*' and '*A* Quest of Inquirie: (lacke a Douer's)' (recently reprinted with Middleton's *Penniless Parliament of Threadbare Poets* as its 'second part'). Unlike his own poems, such texts were, Fitzgeffrey believed, appropriate only for a '*Pesant*', '*Mecanick* Asse', '*Rusticke*', or '*illiterate Gull*' (A7ᵛ–A8ᵛ, G4ᵛ). The hierarchy of genres of text reflected the social hierarchy of readers of those genres.

But other textual hierarchies were constructed differently. In 1618 or 1619, Ben Jonson claimed that Gervase

have a gentleman's income. As a result, though he was a 'gentleman born', undergraduate Middleton might have faced the prospect of supporting himself through menial manual labour: poor students often worked as servants to wealthier ones (Hargreaves-Mawdsley, 40–1).

Like the larger society to which it belonged, early modern textual culture was pervasively hierarchical. The Stationers' Company and the acting companies were hierarchically organized; so were the political, ecclesiastical and legal institutions which generated so many texts. Middleton's father-in-law, Edward Marbeck, was a Six Clerk; numerous underclerks reported to him, and he reported to the Masters and the Chancellor. Middleton submitted his plays to acting companies, who had to submit them to be licensed by the Master of the Revels, who in turn was subject to the Lord Chamberlain, who

---

[16] The licensing of plays belonged to a complex system of textual regulation, for which see Burt, p. 182 below.

Markham 'was not of the number of the Faithfull'—that is, 'Poets'; Markham was instead 'but a base fellow', and so 'were Day and Middleton' (I, 137). Jonson's list, unlike Fitzgeffrey's, is a list of persons, not genres. Day, Markham, and Middleton had written in most of the same genres as Jonson himself; Jonson distinguishes instead between a class of writers who deserve to be called 'Poets', and another class which deserves no such honorific; the distinction says less about *what* they write, than *how* they write, which is in turn a function of an intrinsic feature of *who* they are. A 'poet', so defined, is, like a king, intrinsically superior to others. This quality has nothing to do with hierarchies in the social world. Middleton and Markham were, technically, gentlemen born; Middleton and Day certainly, and Markham probably, had attended university. Jonson belonged to neither of those elevated social categories. Nevertheless, Middleton was 'base' by the standards of Jonson's 'Faithfull'. Jonson, like Chapman and Fitzgeffrey, used the language of social class: 'base', 'fellow', and 'poore' all locate Middleton among the lower classes. But Jonson was constructing a textual hierarchy independent of, and in competition with, the prevailing social hierarchy. As his reference to 'the Faithfull' makes clear, Jonson divided writers into aesthetic categories modelled on theological ones. Throughout the period, the theological category of the elect—whether achieved by merit or grace—offered an alternative to a merely social hierarchy of value.

In all these examples, the construction of textual hierarchies is obviously related both to the marketing value of proper names and to Jonson's efforts to regularize the profession of authorship. But the impulse to construct a 'canon' did not originate in the early modern period. Deliberate selection is fundamental to memory and the transmission of culture, and that process of selection always depends upon a hierarchy that identifies some texts as more important than others (Taylor 1996). What was new to early modern textual culture was not the *need* to construct textual hierarchies, but the *grounds* on which they were constructed.

Jonson separated the textual hierarchy from the social hierarchy by denying that textual value bore any relation to the writer's social genealogy: Middleton could therefore be, simultaneously, both a gentleman and a 'base' writer. How then was textual value to be determined? Jonson's own status was built, in large part, upon the social prestige of aristocratic patrons who supported and thereby endorsed his work. Jonson's patrons were individuals with widely recognized names; the titles of the epigrams and masques in his *Works* supplied a list of distinguished persons who were known consumers of his work. That list contrasts markedly with the generic categories of reader found in Fitzgeffrey, or in Henry Parrot's 1615 satirical list of visitors to a '*Printers* Stall' who all pick up and comment upon a single book: 'a Statesman', 'my gallant Dycer', 'The mending Poet', 'my *Innes-of-Court-Man*', 'my *Familiar*', 'your Countrey-Farmer', 'A *Puritane*', 'my Seruing-man', 'my

Scholaris' (H4-11). The namelessness of these readers, their reduction to a type, in itself serves to disqualify their judgement of a text. In practice, Jonson explicitly denied the relevance of a writer's genealogy, but—like Fitzgeffrey and Parrot—implicitly accepted the relevance of the genealogies of named readers as an index of value.

Fitzgeffrey, Jonson, and Parrot (and others) were thus resisting the claims of the market as an arbiter of textual value. In the early modern period, the print trade and the commercial theatres created a new market for texts. Success in that new market was determined not by the genealogy of consumers, but by their quantity; indeed, since aristocrats and gentlemen were, by definition, only a small fraction of the population, the new textual market-place depended, increasingly, upon less elevated consumers. In that new market-place, Jonson was not particularly successful: his texts were seldom reprinted in his lifetime, and most of his plays failed in the theatres.

Nonetheless, critics have credited Jonson with inventing the modern conception of literary authorship (Murray; Loewenstein; Bristol, 103-109). If this were true, it would be hard to explain why Jonson's own reputation sank as the modern conception of authorship rose. In fact, Jonson's claim to textual pre-eminence was built, not upon the emergent institutions of financial exchange within an anonymous market, but upon the residual institutions of reciprocal gift-giving within an aristocratic patronage system. Middleton, by contrast, declared that the 'Golden Age' in which kings 'Hung jewels at the ear of every rhyme' was already dead (*Hubburd* 1277). He was not wrong: the number and generosity of literary patrons sharply declined in the last decade of Elizabeth I's reign (Fox). By the 1630s royal and aristocratic patronage had evaporated as a significant or effective life-support system for literary production (Parry). The emergent exchange between writer and receiver was not a personal relationship, one to one, but a commercial relationship, one to many (Taylor 1993).[17] Within the new textual market-places, Shakespeare, Fletcher, and Middleton were all more successful than Jonson.

These competing claims to textual value could be characterized as a conflict between names and numbers. But this was not a simple opposition, because numbers could in turn create names: the theatrical popularity of Shakespeare, Fletcher, or Middleton soon encouraged publishers to use their names to market printed books, so that numbers of consumers helped create recognizable names of authors which in turn assisted the accumulation of further numbers of consumers, which made the names even more recognizable, and so on. Conversely, the rejection of numbers led eventually also to the rejection of names. After all, some of Jonson's court masques also failed, and

---

[17] Middleton had patrons, but they were corporate patrons: his proposals for pageants were vetted by committees of businessmen, representing a livery company or the city. See McMillin, 'Middleton's Theatres', in *The Collected Works*.

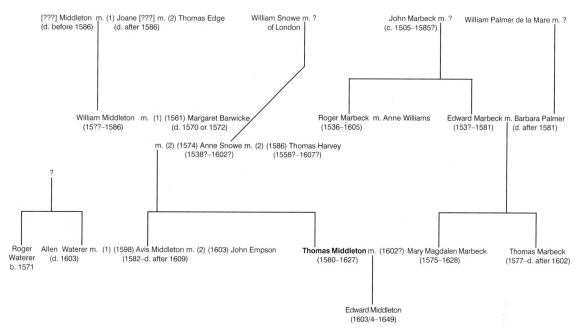

16. Thomas Middleton's genealogy, as constructed by modern scholarship

in the hierarchy of court patronage he was eventually displaced by his collaborator Inigo Jones. Jonson's position, finally, could only be defended by a rejection of all names except his own—a claim to innate value, which others might recognize but could not change, challenge, or imitate. This position rejects any textual hierarchy based on social status or economic power—of producers or consumers—in favour of a hierarchy based upon a mystified self-assessment of individual merit, an aesthetic form of the Calvinist doctrine of election.

Thus, in the end, Jonson's experience of early modern textual culture compelled him to reject genealogical hierarchies just as radically as those hierarchies were rejected by the market-place and the Puritans he despised. As the market-place emphasized the economic independence of each consumer, so Protestantism emphasized the spiritual independence of each Christian. Thomas Middleton felt qualified to write *The Two Gates of Salvation*, and Nicholas Okes published it, even though Middleton was a layman; Middleton paraphrased *The Wisdom of Solomon* without consulting the commentaries deposited by centuries of theologians. His authority in creating such texts was that of any individual reading the Bible—just as his authority for writing *A Game at Chess* was that of any individual reading the news.

As such examples demonstrate, the rejection of genealogy as a source of *textual* authority led, easily enough, to a rejection of genealogy as a source of *political* authority. The connection between these two philological moves could be explicit and direct: the return to the textual origins of English law by antiquarians like Robert Cotton legitimated Parliamentary challenges to royal and ministerial authority in the 1620s (Sharpe 1979)—the subject of many of the entries in Middleton's *Annals* and *Farrago*. The origins of the English Civil War were essentially *textual*: the King, once perceived as the heir of a genealogically transmitted authority, came to be viewed instead as a genealogical interloper, blocking a philological return to a more authoritative constitutional or theological origin. And although the Restoration undid the political revolution of the 1640s, belief in access to an authoritative origin—whether in the self, in the natural world, or in the distant human past—precipitated the philosophical texts of Descartes, Hobbes, and Locke, whose corrosive anti-genealogical effects were more fundamental and permanent.

Mixture. What does the foregoing list of lists tell us about early modern textual culture? It was local, but becoming national. It was often anonymous and multi-purpose, but its dependence upon credit generated an expanding reliance on proper names to appeal to specialist markets. It was organized by restrictive occupational communities, but those were succumbing to the less and less restricted movement of labour and capital. It transmitted privilege genealogically, but a philological (anti-genealogical) ideology and practice were growing more powerful and general. It was pervasively hierarchical, but increasingly divided by disputes over the correct criteria for the construction of such hierarchies of value. Such tendencies create continua, along which individual texts and textual agents can be located, in terms of their proximity to certain residual or emergent, dominant or

17. Gunpowder Plot conspirators

18. This 1662 title-page displays characters from six dramatic texts written by seven authors between 1597 and 1653

dominated positions. But proximity to an emergent position on one such continuum does not guarantee proximity to the emergent position on another continuum; each continuum, each fraction, has its own scale of proximities.[18]

What does the foregoing list of lists of persons tell us about early modern personhood? Again, the lists create continua which enable us to measure the distances between persons: they graph relative proximities of geography, wealth, debt, occupation, fame, status. Again, the separate proximities bear no certain relationship to one another. Even when the same name appears in many lists, the lists tell us different things about that person. Middleton's relationship to these lists is fractional. Each institution within his textual culture is interested in him only in so far as his residence or activities relate to the functions of that institution. Moreover, each list makes arbitrary choices about what is important. For instance, even if we are interested in genealogies, the 1623 list (Illus. 13) omits a good deal of material information, which we can supply from other sources (Illus. 16). As was common, Thomas Middleton's mother's name was omitted from the baptismal record (Illus. 1); as was also common, his own name was omitted from the first state of the title-page of the 1608 edition of *A Trick to Catch the Old One*. In both cases, an early modern list of names neglects the agent of labour; in both cases, the omission tells us something about early modern *ideology*, but it also fails to tell us something about early modern material *reality*. Thomas Middleton did have a mother and *A Trick to Catch the Old One* did have an author, and both facts were acknowledged in many contexts, but they did not seem important to the particular observers who compiled these particular lists.

Though each list strives or claims to be complete, each list gives us only a fraction of a whole—whether that whole is a particular early modern person, or early modern textual culture. Moreover, we cannot describe the whole simply by adding up all the fractions, because the fractions are not subsets of the same set. The sets these lists describe overlap, and at the same time they leave gaps not covered by any set. Society is not the 'founding totality of its partial processes' or 'an ensemble united by necessary laws', but is instead 'unsutured' (Laclau and Mouffe, 95–6, 126, 143, 192), a moving collectivity of overlapping fractions, of 'frontier effects' created by competing articulations of the relationship between fractions.

[18] On proximities see the Introduction, above; Taylor 1993; Taylor forthcoming.

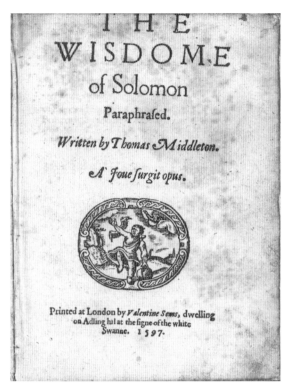

19. The title-page of Middleton's first published work

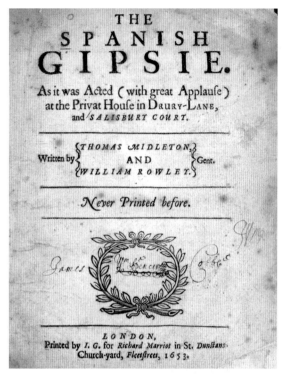

20. This 1653 title-page names two authors, two theatres, and two stationers; the copy now owned by Harvard University adds signatures by different readers

This awareness that a list is fractional, that it does not say enough, creates a desire, in the makers of lists, to supplement the information they supply. I have described the foregoing lists—of inhabitants, credit transactions, authors, genealogies, members of occupational groups, and so on—as though each was a pure list, systematically devoted to a single function. But they often supplement the information they were designed to supply. The burial register, designed to record a person's participation in a rite in one place at one time, adds information about social class; the genealogy, designed to record kinship relations, adds information about location and occupation; the Stationers' Register, designed to record monopoly rights to publish a text, adds the name of an author. All these lists exceed the strict definitions of the set they are meant to describe.

Such 'mixed' lists are characteristic of early modern textual culture. 'Pure' lists of persons can be found—as for instance in an engraving of the Gunpowder Plot conspirators (Illus. 17), an illustrated list of names which creates a strongly unified visual impression, based upon a strictly limited set of identifications. The conspirators, tightly packed together, are unified by political purpose and visual style; the homogeneity of impression is clearly meant to be ominous, to suggest an unnatural and

dangerous cohesion. But the illustrated list of names on the title-page of *The Wits* is much more characteristic of the period (Illus. 18). The characters on the stage represented on that title-page (who come from different plays, authors, genres, theatres, and decades) do not relate to each other at all, and are united only by their apparent inclusion in a miscellany of adaptations—and in fact 'The Changeling', present on this title-page, is not present in the miscellany. The very miscellaneousness of this list was clearly expected to be appealing. Moreover, the apparent difference between these two lists of persons can be subsumed under a larger similarity: both lists mix visual and verbal representations in a manner common in early modern Northern European art (Alpers, 169–221).[19] Finally, the mixedness of the *Wits* page typifies title-pages generally. Thomas Middleton's first title-page (Illus. 19) mixes the names of author and printer, a London address, the name of a Hebrew King, a Latin epigraph quoted from Ovid (*Fasti* 5.111), and a printer's woodblock ornament of Ganymede. Ganymede was the catamite of the Jove mentioned in the epigraph; his story was told in Ovid's

[19] For a fuller analysis of the relations between visual images and texts, see Astington, p. 226 below.

LES CHAPITRES DV
PREMIER LIVRE.

21. Table of contents from Michel,
Sieur de Montaigne's *Les Essais* (1580)

THE CONTENTS.
BOOK I.

22. Table of contents from John Locke's *An
Essay Concerning Human Understanding* (1690)

Fasti, which served sixteenth-century grammar schools as a textbook of Roman mythology.[20] Since Middleton must have delivered *Solomon* to the printer before his seventeenth birthday, he might easily be imagined as a Ganymede figure. This mixture of clashing names and allusions is particular to the title-page of *Wisdom*, but other combinations seem generic. The title-pages of plays often consist of the names of the play, its one or more authors, one or more theatrical companies or venues, one or more printers, one or more booksellers.[21] The names listed on such a title-page are unified, not by any necessary relationship to one another, or to some shared social category, but by their fractional relationships to a text. And such a mixed list could always be mixed even further by the manuscript addition, on the printed title-page, of the names of readers (Illus. 20).

As these mixed lists demonstrate, early modern textual culture was predominantly eclectic. But this eclecticism was itself being challenged by practices which emphas-

ized order, regularity, and strict definitions systematically applied. The difference can be seen in the contrast between two lists at opposite ends of our Middleton century. Montaigne's *Essais* were first published in 1580, the year of Middleton's birth; Locke received from his bookseller copies of the first edition of his own *Essay*—a work he had begun almost twenty years before—in December 1689. Each book contains a list of its contents. The Montaigne list (Illus. 21) is unpredictable, fractional, and eclectic; like the individual essays, the list of essay titles makes

---

[20] I am grateful to Richard Hardin and Anthony Corbeill for tracing this quotation; on *Fasti* in the Tudor curriculum, see Baldwin, 1:84, 124, 291, 339, 341, 387, 2:384, 418, 422, 424, 427–8, 473.
[21] See for example the third state of the title-page of *Trick*, reproduced in Wayne's textual introduction, p. 563 below.

no claims to wholeness or purity of function. As in early modern manuscript miscellanies, a sense of personal identity is created by the interplay of fractions of texts (your own and other people's); new texts are 'composed' by placing together, in new combinations, elements of old texts, creating what Erasmus in 1519 and Middleton in the 1620s called a 'farrago' (Taylor 1994b). Locke's list (Illus. 22) contains, like Montaigne's, a series of titles of short considerations 'Of' certain topics, but Locke's is as conspicuously ordered and systematic as Montaigne's is miscellaneous. Both lists divide a long text into fractions ('books' and 'chapters'), but Locke subdivides the fractions themselves, providing a second list (ten times longer than the first) which breaks down chapters into 'sections', subcategories into sub-subcategories. The 'mixed' is, for Locke, almost inevitably a category of confusion and error.

Of course, these are lists of contents, not lists of persons. But that very distinction may be clearer to us than to early modern readers. The list on the title-page of *Microcynicon* (Illus. 23) belongs to a common category of paratexts attached to literary works, paratexts which combine the functions of lists of persons with the functions of tables of contents. The resulting catalogues are, inevitably, mixed, and their mixedness creates simultaneously their difficulty for editors (the allies of Locke) and their interest for critics (the allies of Montaigne).

II. Lists of Virtual Persons

The mixedness of such lists makes it difficult to know what to call them. Since—as we will see—contemporaries labelled these lists in significantly different ways, we cannot simply adopt an early modern label: by doing so, we would make one of the many early options in some way normative, or anoint it with historical inevitability, and make all the alternatives somehow deviant. I have therefore invented the label 'identification tables'. All these 'tables' (then the most common term for what we would now most commonly call 'lists') identify something; what it is that they identify remains to be seen.

Identification tables are mixed not only in their contents and functions but in their origin and distribution. Middleton's dramatic works epitomize this scatter. By contrast with Shakespeare (where all such tables are posthumous, and none authorial) or Jonson (where tables are systematically authorially supplied), the Middleton canon mixes presence and absence, authors and others, across decades of texts and many different kinds of list. As a result, the treatment of such tables in the Middleton canon illustrates the habits and development, not of a single person, but of a significant fraction of early modern textual culture.[22] Against that larger pattern, we can locate individual texts in terms of their proximity to certain agents, and certain agents in terms of their proximity to certain practices.

Middleton. At the simplest level, some texts have such tables, and some do not. None of Middleton's—or anyone else's—civic pageants contains such a table. Of his plays, nine do not contain a table in any seventeenth-century

23. Middleton's *Microcynicon* (1599)

text. Others, like *Nice Valour* itself, were originally published without a table, but supplied with one later. In trying to determine why some Middleton texts have tables and others do not, we may begin by considering the proximity of tables to Middleton himself. The simplest measure of proximity is chronology: a text published (in printed or scribal form) after the author's death may be copied from an authorial manuscript, but its publication cannot have been directly overseen by the author himself. Posthumous texts are therefore always at least one step removed from the author, whereas texts published in the author's

---

[22] The following account of lists of fictional persons is based upon a database of all such lists in dramatic texts in England during the period 1500–1679, based upon Greg 1939–59 (for English and Latin texts to 1660), supplemented by Harbage (for plays written and published 1660–79), by Greg 1931 (for manuscripts), and by various Malone Society Reprints (for manuscripts discovered or edited since 1931). Most of the work of constructing this database was done by two younger scholars who were, long ago, graduate students working as my research assistants in 1992 (Alexandra Bennett) and 1993 (Celia R. Daileader); without them this essay could not have been written. Their own subsequent publications demonstrate the quality of their work, from which I have greatly benefitted.

lifetime may or may not be. Of dramatic texts published in Middleton's lifetime, six have tables: *The Roaring Girl* (printed in 1611), *Masque of Heroes* (1619), *The World Tossed at Tennis* (1620), *Measure for Measure* (1623), *Timon of Athens* (1623), and *The Witch* (transcribed in 1625?).

On the grounds of chronology, Middleton could have been directly responsible for the presence of a table in any of these six texts. But his proximity to the tables can also be measured by other evidence of his involvement in the publication. He provided a signed epistle to readers for *The Roaring Girl*, a signed Epistle Dedicatory for *The World Tossed at Tennis*, and a post-performance initialled prefatory poem for *Masque of Heroes*; in each case, he was clearly directly involved in the preparation of the text for the press. By contrast, there is no evidence that he had any hand in the preparation of the 1623 Shakespeare folio, where his work as an adapter or junior collaborator in three plays is nowhere acknowledged. The table at the end of *Measure for Measure* apparently derives from the printer's copy, a transcript prepared by Ralph Crane; the (defective) table at the end of *Timon of Athens* seems to be an *ad hoc* printing-house expedient to fill the gap caused by a last-minute decision to substitute the short text of *Timon* in the place originally cast off for the longer text of *Troilus and Cressida* (Wells and Taylor, 468, 501). *The Witch* is harder to place in either of these categories. Middleton wrote a signed dedication, which testifies to his involvement; but the dedication and signature are both in Ralph Crane's hand, which makes it impossible to know whether Middleton ever saw this particular manuscript, or prepared or requested its table.

Tables thus appear in at least three (and possibly four) texts published in Middleton's lifetime under his direct supervision. Two of those texts are collaborative, and the tables might have been provided by Middleton's collaborator. However, Middleton had no collaborator in writing *Masque of Heroes*; the printer's copy was not a manuscript prepared by Ralph Crane; collaborators or scribes cannot explain away the table in that text, which almost certainly was written by Middleton himself. By even the most sceptical account, Middleton seems to have been responsible for at least one table, and may well have been wholly or partially responsible for three others. Why then do tables appear in some of the texts published in his lifetime, but not others?

The most obvious explanation is chronological. Nine Middleton plays were published before 1609; not one contains a table. Moreover, not one contains any evidence of Middleton's involvement in its publication. Two are misattributed (*The Puritan*, *A Yorkshire Tragedy*); one names Middleton's collaborator but not Middleton (*The Patient Man and the Honest Whore*); three others were published anonymously (*The Phoenix*, *Michaelmas Term*, *The Revenger's Tragedy*), and a fourth (*A Trick to Catch the Old One*) was anonymous on its first title-page. Carelessness of attribution accompanies other kinds of carelessness: by the standards of Middleton's early poems or his dramatic works published between 1611 and 1626, the plays printed between 1604 and 1608 are error-prone and poorly proofread. This prevailing carelessness attends a consistent poverty of paratext: no dedications, no epistles, no prefatory epigrams, nothing to indicate that the printer's manuscript had been in any way altered or supplemented to make it more attractive and accessible to readers.

Middleton wrote epistles or dedications to seven different books of his poetry and prose between 1597 and 1609, so the absence of such material from the plays published between 1604 and 1608 cannot be due to any general unwillingness on his part to provide supplementary material for printers. The plays may simply have been printed without his awareness or involvement. It has been plausibly conjectured that most of these texts owe their publication to the financial difficulties of two companies of child actors, who in order to raise cash quickly may have sold their manuscripts of plays by Middleton and several other dramatists (Chambers, II, 22). The companies, having bought the texts from Middleton, were free to sell them to anyone else.

Certainly, the absence of tables in those editions would not be surprising in texts belonging to theatres, particularly the 'playbooks' that contained the signature of the Master of the Revels, authorizing performance.[23] Greg (1931) identified fifteen complete theatrical manuscripts, dating from the 1590s to 1635; only three include a table. All three are late (1622?–33), and none added or altered its list as part of the process of adapting the text for performance.[24] Middleton's *The Lady's Tragedy* (1611), which contains no list, is thus typical of early playbooks. Since *The Lady's Tragedy* belongs to the same year as *The Roaring Girl*, the difference between *Girl* and *Lady* is hard to attribute to any change in Middleton himself, and probably reflects a difference in the function of the two texts. Why does the printed edition have what the theatrical manuscript of the same year does not? Because lists are designed for readers, not actors. But why readers in 1611, and not earlier?

Authorship. The 1611 edition of *The Roaring Girl* marks a shift in several hierarchies. First, the relationship between the two collaborators had changed. In 1604, only Dekker, the senior collaborator, was named on the title-pages of *The Magnificent Entertainment* and *The Patient Man and the Honest Whore*.[25] In 1611, by contrast, *The*

---

[23] For the term 'playbook' (rather than 'promptbook'), and the importance of the distinction, see Gurr 1999.

[24] Greg 1931 lists fifteen in his Category A ('promptbooks'), but admits that *John of Bordeaux* (which he places in Category C) was used as one; from this total of sixteen, I have omitted *The Parliament of Love*, because its initial pages are missing. The lists for *The Two Noble Ladies* (1622–23?) and *The Launching of the Mary* (1633) both occur on title-pages which describe the play's successful performances; Greg notes that each page is a later addition to the manuscript (274, 300), and specifically conjectures that one appears 'to have been added with a view to publication' (275), an explanation equally applicable to the other. The list in *The Welsh Ambassador* (1623?) was written by the same scribe who copied the rest of the text; it was not annotated by any other hand.

[25] Dekker was also apparently foregrounded in at least one early manuscript of *The Bloody Banquet* (composed *c.*1609?), since only his initials appear on the title-page of the 1639 edition.

Roaring Girl not only lists both names, but puts Middleton first, in defiance of alphabetical order. This shift apparently reflects a larger shift in the reputations of the two writers. Before 1611, when Dekker and a collaborator shared title-page credit, Dekker's name was always first; after 1611, Dekker's name was never first, though alphabetically it should always have been.[26] By contrast, Middleton in future would always be named before Rowley, who in turn almost always took second billing among his contemporaries, regardless of alphabetical order.[27] By 1611, Middleton had risen within the hierarchy of his occupational group.

That occupational group was also rising within the hierarchy of textual culture. Despite the fact that they did not possess anything resembling copyright, playwrights increasingly took an independent initiative in selling their texts to printers. Before 1611, Middleton was either uninvolved or invisible in editions of his dramatic works; from 1611 to 1626, none of his dramatic work was published without conspicuous authorial involvement. Moreover, during this later period editions appeared soon after production, in a pattern which owes nothing to the fortunes of theatrical companies, but which would reflect reader and stationer interest in recently performed work. This shift, though unusually clear in Middleton's case, was not confined to Middleton. The 'double sale' of playwrights' labours, about which Thomas Heywood had complained in 1607, was becoming normative, so much so that in the 1620s and 1630s theatres would try to limit the practice by contractual agreements with their leading writers.[28] Playwrights, having in the past surrendered to actors all rights in their texts, were increasingly able not only to resell them to stationers, but also to reclaim those texts from their oral performance. Jonson published an edition of *Every Man in his Humour* which restored material cut by the actors (1600); John Fletcher published, with numerous commendatory verses, *The Faithful Shepherdess*, despite its rejection by audiences (1609); John Webster complained about the treatment on stage of *The White Devil* (1612). Middleton's editions do not grumble anti-theatrically; indeed, the title-page illustrations which characterize Middleton editions from 1611 to 1626 emphasize the visual dimension of performance. But Middleton's editions do, from 1611 on, provide an explicitly authorial written text for readers as a substitute for the oral performance delivered to audiences. As such, they demonstrate that the rise in the status of playwrights involved, not only an increased freedom of economic manœuvre, but a related increase in cultural value.

Canonicity. This shift in the status of playwrights as an occupational group corresponds to a shift in the status of the genre of text they were producing. Although certain religious viewpoints remained hostile to the theatre, and cultural conservatives would continue to lump plays with ballads as the basest of texts, a higher estimate of the status of dramatic entertainments was gradually emerging. That upward shift shows in the proliferation of

more expensive and exclusive indoor theatres, the royal patronage to all the London companies, the acquisition of gentility (William Shakespeare) or great wealth (Edward Alleyn), the increasing employment of professional dramatists by the City and the Court, the dedications to aristocrats, the publication of expensive folio collections. Within the hierarchy of texts, dramatic entertainments were coming to occupy a more dignified place. That new dignity is both reflected and asserted by a burgeoning paratextual apparatus of epigrams, epistles, dedications, commendatory poems, and tables. Identification tables, then, do not appear in isolation. Literally, tables usually appear alongside other paratextual material surrounding a dramatic text—as can be seen in this list, which records percentages of printed plays with identification tables which also contain other supplements:[29]

1581–1600	59%
1601–20	70%
1621–42	81%
1643–60	82%

Not only do such tables prefer company; they become more gregarious over time. They also become more popular over time—as can be seen in this list, which records percentages of printed plays which contain identification tables:[30]

1581–1600	18%
1601–20	41%
1621–42	70%
1643–60	83%
1661–79	96%

The final percentage would be even higher if we excluded plays written earlier but not published until after the Restoration, like the anonymous *Guy of Warwick* (1661) and Middleton and Webster's *Anything for a Quiet Life* (1662), which provide two of only eight exceptions to the rule. By 1668, tables were so mandatory that Margaret

---

26 Dekker was listed before Webster in *Sir Thomas Wyatt*, *Westward Ho*, and *Northward Ho* (all printed 1607), but after Massinger in *The Virgin Martyr* (1622), after Rowley in *The Witch of Edmonton* (1658), and after Ford in *The Sun's Darling* (1656); he received no credit for *The Noble Soldier* (1634, misattributed to S. Rowley), *The Spanish Gypsy* (1653, attributed to Middleton and Rowley alone), or *Lust's Dominion* (1657, attributed to Marlowe alone).

27 In *A Fair Quarrel* (1617), *The World Tossed at Tennis* (1620), *The Changeling* (1653), *The Spanish Gypsy* (1653), and *Old Law* (1657). Rowley is also listed after Heywood in *Fortune by Land and Sea* (1655), after Webster in *A Cure for a Cuckold* and *The Thracian Wonder* (both 1661), after Shakespeare in *The Birth of Merlin* (1662). The only exception is *The Witch of Edmonton* (1657), where he precedes Dekker and Ford.

28 For contracted dramatists, see Bentley 1971, 111–44, and Dutton. However, Bentley and Dutton assume that these later contracts reflect norms which existed from the late sixteenth century. Where they see continuity, I am inclined to see development. For related criticisms of Bentley's assumptions, see Erne, 117–27, Taylor 1989b, 109–11, and Taylor and Jowett, 187–9.

29 This list is based only upon first editions which contain tables. It departs from a mechanical division into twenty-year periods, because the closure of the theatres in 1642 seems a more significant watershed than 1640.

30 I have counted the Beaumont and Fletcher folio of 1647—which does not include tables for any of its plays—as a single text, since it clearly reflects a single publishing decision. Counting each play in that volume separately would reduce the percentage for 1643–60 to 71 per cent.

24–25. Title-page recto and verso of *Everyman* (c.1535)

Cavendish provided one for an unfinished 'Piece of a Play'! In the century after Middleton's birth, the frequency of identification tables more than quadrupled.

This radical change in the frequency in identification tables belongs to a larger complex of shifts in relationships within textual culture: shifts in hierarchies among writers, between writers and actors, between dramatic entertainments and other genres, shifts in the practices and expectations of authors, stationers, and readers. Middleton's 1611 epistle in *The Roaring Girl*—headed 'To the Comic Play-readers, Venery and Laughter' (or, 'To the Comic Play-readers' venery and laughter')—is the first text to recognize, or specifically address, a category of persons called 'play-readers'; indeed, this is the first known use of the compound noun.[31] In *The Roaring Girl* as elsewhere, identification tables are designed to appeal to a new specialist submarket of readers—readers who read plays. Moreover, unlike other paratextual materials, these tables immediately impinge upon the reading of the play text. Epistles or dedications direct attention away from

the play, toward the author or a patron or the play's fate in the theatre; but identification tables inevitably summarize or characterize the play, affecting our assumptions about its fictional persons, and unlike other paratext they are often consulted or cross-referenced during reading, potentially interposing themselves at any point in the text. Consequently, the evolution of such tables provides a unique index to the evolution of a new class of textual consumers, and of their relationship to persons involved in textual production and reproduction.

Title-page characters. The evolution of such tables in printed plays had begun early in the sixteenth century— and it began conspicuously. Since plays, like other books, were normally sold unbound, title-pages served, effectively, as the initial *cover* of the book. As separate sheets that could be posted and displayed, they also served

---

[31] See *OED* 'Play' *sb.* 17, where the first recorded occurrence is exactly a century later (in Shaftesbury's *Characters*). It also occurs in William Prynne's *Histrio-Mastix* (1633), 931.

as the chief mechanism for advertising books (Plant, 248; Farmer and Lesser; Stern).[32] Moreover, since printed books, unlike manuscripts, were normally sold with their pages still uncut, it would have been difficult for readers to browse through the book before buying it; a table on an inside page would be effectively closed to most potential customers. In combination, these physical realities made title-pages much more important, in the relations between booksellers and their customers, than they are now. In the first four vernacular English plays to reach print (*BEPD* 1–5), the title-page displays woodblock images of the characters (Illus. 24–25). Clearly, those illustrations serve as a complete or partial visual list of the play's characters.

Between 1512 and 1562, character woodblocks appeared on the title-pages of eleven vernacular plays (41 per cent).[33] Then the convention abruptly stopped. Between 1562 and 1605, only two new plays—Richard Edwards's *Damon and Pithias* (1571), and Robert Wilson's old-fashioned *The Three Lords and Three Ladies of London* (1590)—were printed with a title-page woodcut showing one or more of its characters.[34] It was also printed in black-letter type, as were most earlier plays but few subsequent ones. When *Damon and Pithias* was reprinted in 1582, the woodcuts disappeared. Although sporadic examples occur in Stuart England, title-page woodcuts were never again so common as in the first half-century of play printing. Middleton, however, was an exception. Between 1611 and 1625, only five dramatic texts written in whole or part by Middleton and performed in commercial theatres were separately printed: *The Roaring Girl*, *A Fair Quarrel*, *The World Tossed at Tennis*, and the two independent editions of *A Game at Chess*. All five have title-pages representing one or more of the play's characters. During the same period when 100 per cent of Middleton's play title-pages were illustrated, forty-two commercial plays by other authors were published for the first time in quarto editions, but only eight had illustrated title-pages (19 per cent).[35] The Middleton play quartos were unusually consistent.

Middleton might have seen, among the secondhand books sold by some London stationers, copies of sixteenth-century printed plays, or his wife might have inherited the book collection of her grandfather, the author John Marbeck, or her father, the lawyer Edward Marbeck. But Middleton's title-pages do not use illustrations in the same way as those earlier books. The Tudor woodcut characters are generic figures, not individuals; for that reason the same woodcuts could be (and were) used with different plays. The title-pages of *Quarrel* and *Tennis* are similarly generic. But unlike the sixteenth-century convention, *Tennis* shows all the play's main characters interacting on the title-page, not isolated in separate woodblocks and not separated between recto and verso. Moreover, the characters displayed by the title-pages of *The Roaring Girl* and *A Game at Chess* (Illus. 26) are startlingly particular individuals. In both cases, those individuals would have been known to many potential readers, but in neither play are they actually named in the text. *The Roaring*

26. Like many early Tudor plays, *A Game at Chess* illustrates and labels many of its characters on the title-page of the first edition

Girl incorporates—as does *Tennis*—a subsequent list of the play's characters; the visual and the textual table complement one another. In contrast, none of the nine early editions or manuscripts of *A Game at Chess* contains a list of characters, although the two agents responsible for most of those texts—the author Middleton and the scribe Ralph Crane—often supplied such lists elsewhere. Any written identification of the characters of *A Game at Chess* would have been far too dangerous. The absence of a list of persons for *Game* is as significant as the presence of such a list elsewhere. Certain names could not be listed in a dramatic text.

---

[32] Manuscripts of some medieval plays also contain identification tables, sometimes elaborately illustrated, and those manuscript precedents may well have influenced early printed editions of plays, in England and elsewhere. I have not attempted a survey of identification tables in medieval manuscripts, because it is unlikely that such practices influenced Middleton or the other producers of such tables between 1580 and 1679.

[33] These figures exclude (a) plays which survive only in fragments which do not include the title-pages, and (b) translations of classical drama.

[34] Undated reprintings of some of the 1512–62 plays continued to use old or new woodcuts: see for instance *Jack Juggler* (*BEPD* 35(a–c)). However, even these reprints are probably no later than 1568. On the old-fashioned dramatic characteristics of Wilson's play, see McMillin and MacLean, 121–56.

[35] Two of the most popular plays of the period, *The Spanish Tragedy* and *Doctor Faustus*, were given new title-pages with woodcut illustrations in 1615 and 1616.

Just as the illustrated title-page of *A Game at Chess* substitutes for a written list of characters, so written lists may have evolved as a cheap alternative to woodcuts. The first extant unillustrated dramatic title-page, *The Nature of the Four Elements* (*BEPD* 6, *c.*1525), instead gives 'the names of the players'. Before 1562, six unillustrated vernacular plays had title-page lists of 'the players names'.[36] Altogether, then, seventeen of the twenty-seven surviving vernacular plays printed between 1512 and 1562 list the play's characters on the title-page, visually or textually or both (63 per cent). Stationers would only have placed this information on so many title-pages if they believed that characters helped sell plays. Clearly, verbal or visual identification tables served as a précis of the play, advertising its interesting characters and suggesting the plot likely to arise from their interactions.

Amateur performances. In itself, the use of printed lists of characters did not drive woodcuts from title-pages, since the two conventions co-existed for four decades. But in 1560 the title-page of *An new enterlude of Impacient pouerte* (*BEPD* 30) showed how 'Foure men may well and easily playe it'. This was not the first play to provide such information, which had already appeared in John Bale's *Three Laws* (*BEPD* 24(*a*), *c.*1548). But Bale's list had been printed late in the book (sig. G1ᵛ), on the same opening as a woodcut portrait of the author (Illus. 10).[37] *Impacient pouerte*'s innovation was providing such information on the title-page. The pattern of doubling is relatively simple, and can coexist on the page with three woodcut figures (recycled from earlier plays).[38] But in 1565 the title-pages of *Darius* and *Lusty Juventus* went further: each gave a list of characters, and specified the number of actors required for a performance, but dispensed with woodcuts. Between 1565 and 1581 at least fourteen title-pages gave such doubling information; none provided woodcuts of the characters. Those fourteen plays represented 56 per cent of the twenty-five original vernacular plays printed in those years. Doubling information is printed on the verso of another title-page; it also appears in two play manuscripts of the same period.[39]

Obviously, such information does not help a potential customer to know whether a text will be an enjoyable or instructive read; it is useful only for someone who contemplates performing the text. The form of these tables, combined with their prominence on title-pages, suggests that, before 1580, booksellers expected a significant proportion of the purchasers of printed plays to be interested, not simply in reading, but actually in performing the plays they bought.

These early editions, complete with casting lists, have been described as texts 'offered for acting', and David Bevington has analysed the lists as evidence for the size and organization of sixteenth-century acting troupes. But itinerant actors can hardly have provided a sufficient market for London booksellers.[40] Nor, in the sixteenth century, had playing yet been confined to professional actors. The title-pages of sixteenth-century plays, with their careful instructions on casting, assured readers that 'you and a few friends can perform this play together'. The title-page of *Damon and Pithias* (1571) recommended the text for 'the proper use of them that hereafter shall haue occasion to plaie it, either in Priuate, or open Audience'. The kind of occasion envisaged is not necessarily a professional performance aimed outward at a paying audience, but a form of playing in which amateurs entertain themselves. Such performances might take place in 'priuate houses, or otherwise'—as suggested on the title-page of *The Conflict of Conscience* (1581). In a period when texts were still often read out loud by one person to a small group of listeners (Chartier 1989b, 147–57), half a dozen friends or relatives reading a play to each other may not have seemed categorically different from other kinds of reading. In a world where most reading was an oral performance, any reader was qualified to perform in a 'play reading'.

The closest parallel to these sixteenth-century title-pages comes, not from the subsequent history of dramatic texts, but from the texts of sixteenth-century music. The connection between music and theatre—two different forms of 'playing'—was much stronger in early modern England than it has since become. In the fifteenth century, 'minstrels' combined both kinds of performance, and songs remained an almost inevitable feature of dramatic texts; one of the first examples of music printing in England was a song printed in John Rastell's play *The Nature of the Four Elements* (*c.*1525), and Middleton's *Triumphs of Truth* (1613) likewise incorporates a musical text. Until 1672, the only public concerts which Londoners might pay to hear were those performed in theatres before, during, and after the play. Moreover, like the drama, the most popular sixteenth-century English music was polyphonic—or, more strictly, polyvocal. Most of this music remained in manuscript, but when it did find its way into print early music title-pages offered readers music 'of foure, fiue, and six parts' (Fraenkel, 55–66). John Day published such 'part books' for the English metrical psalms, beginning in 1563; most books of printed music were imported from the continent, which produced many part-books in the first half of the sixteenth century. Usually, each player had a separate book or 'part', which contained only the music for his or her part (just as an actor's 'part' contained only his own lines); but

[36] Title-page lists without woodcuts: John Heywood's *Play of the Wether* (1533) and *Play of Love* (1534), *Impatient Poverty* (1560), *Nice Wanton* (1560), *Godly Queen Hester* (1561), *Thersites* (1561–3). Title-page lists combined with woodcuts: Heywood's *Four PP* (1544?), *Robin Hood* (1560), *Jack Juggler* (1562). Henry Medwall's unadorned *1 and 2 Nature* (*c.*1530–34) gives 'The names of the players' not at the beginning but the end of the play (sig. i4).

[37] When Bale's play was reprinted in 1562 (*BEPD* 24(*b*)), the original identification table and portrait were removed, and a list supplied on the title-page instead, in place of the elaborate title-page woodcut of the first edition.

[38] The three figures occur in *BEPD* 30(*b*), but not in *BEPD* 30(*a*), which instead has an elaborate architectural frame. One edition of the interlude therefore anticipated *Darius* and *Lusty Juventus* in providing doubling information but no illustrations.

[39] The manuscripts are *Misogonus* (1560–77) and of Merbury's *Marriage of Wit and Wisdom* (1570–79). For transcripts of all such doubling lists, see Bevington, 265–73.

[40] On the economics of print-runs, and the minimum number of copies in an edition, see Weiss, p. 195 below.

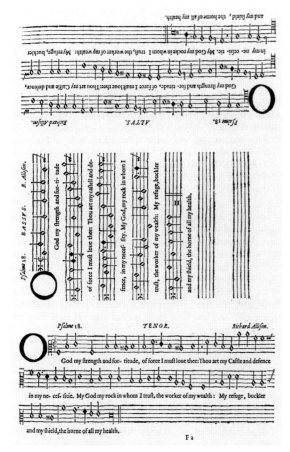

27. Music designed to be read simultaneously by three different people, positioned below, to the right of, and above the page

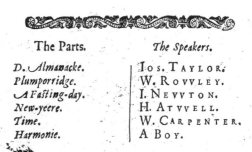

The Parts. *The Speakers.*

D. *Almanacke.*   I os. T AYLOR.
Plumporridge.   W. R ovvley.
A Fasting-day.   I. N evvton.
New-yeere.   H. A tvvell.
Time.   W. C arpenter.
Harmonie.   A B oy.

Two A ntemasqves.

In the firſt, ſixe Dancers.

1. *Candlemas Day.*
2. *Shrouetueſday.*
3. *Lent.*
4. *Ill-May-day.*
5. *Midſommer Eue.*
6. *The firſt Dog-day.*

The ſecond A ntemasqve, preſented by eight B oyes.

Good dayes ———3.
Bad dayes ———3.
Indifferent dayes —2.

The M asqve it ſelfe, receiuing it's Illuſtration from nine of the Gentlemen of the Houſe.

28. Identification table in Middleton's *Masque of Heroes* (1619)

sometimes, all the parts were printed in a single book (Illus. 27), designed so that the players could stand or sit around a table, each reading his own part (Krummel, 34–112). These books presupposed a domestic musical culture, where singing together featured among the rituals of conviviality. The episode recounted by Thomas Morley in 1597 is as typical as it claims to be: 'Supper being ended and music books (according to the custom) being brought to the table, the mistress of the house presented me with a part earnestly requesting me to sing'.

In musical part-books and in plays 'offered for acting', the title-page presumed an active readership: readers were expected to play the text. The list of parts in Middleton's *Masque of Heroes* (1619) presumes very different readers (Illus. 28). That list, which is not printed on the title-page, is not expected to help sell the book. 'The Parts' do not instruct readers on how to perform the play themselves; instead, the list identifies the fictional roles played by particular actors. No doubling of roles is recorded.

Sixteenth-century tables typically had identified a set of parts (which usually included more than one fictional character); they divided a work into a list of separate jobs, to be done by several collaborators. By contrast, the table in *Masque of Heroes* identifies a set of separate fictional characters. The earlier tables had described the relationship *of* readers *to* the text; the later table describes *for* readers relationships *within* the text. The earlier tables had envisaged a group reading communally out-loud; the later table anticipates an individual reading alone silently. The transition from one table to the other marks a stage in what has been called 'the privatization of reading' (Chartier 1989b, 124–47).

Changes in information content attend this change in reading practices. The appended list of professional actors does not look forward to possible future performances, but backward toward an authoritative past performance (Holland, 102–5). It resembles the statement that the 'personage' of Zeal, created by Middleton for the *Magnificent Entertainment*, was 'put on by' the professional actor William Bourne, one of the Admiral's Men (sig. H4). *Magnificent Entertainment* was the first printed dramatic text to identify the actor of a specific role. The list in *Heroes*—which supplies the same kind of information, but does so systematically—says: 'Reader, if you did not see the performance at the Inner Temple, but you do know these actors, then you can imagine how those specific performers would enact these roles.' The names, personalities, and styles of the professional actors provide additional information about the fictional persons of the play. In some cases, the important information is the name of a particular actor; in others, only the type of actor matters (a 'boy' for Harmony, 'gentlemen of the House' for the Nine Worthies). In both cases, the identities of the actors supplement and inform the identities within the text.

Masque of Heroes is, in fact, the first English dramatic text printed with such a cast list, which would become increasingly common as the seventeenth century proceeded.[41] The last English dramatic text with a title-page table of 'parts'—the second issue of *The Conflict of Conscience*, by Nathaniel Woodes—had been printed thirty--eight years before, in 1581. In the four decades between these two texts, between 'you can act' and 'he acted', we can trace a radical transformation in identification tables. This change does not reflect, in any simple way, changes in acting practices. The doubling of parts remained normal after 1580, and cast-size continued to affect the structure of plays (Bradley). In *Michaelmas Term*, for instance, the Country Wench's Father, the Boy, and Sim are all surprisingly absent from the final scene, almost certainly because that is the play's most crowded scene, and the actors who played those roles were doubling other roles already present on stage. But although doubling remained relevant to the structure and performance of plays, it ceased to be relevant to the buyers of published texts. This change apparently represents a transformation in the relationship between dramatic texts and their readers, who went from being an active second person to a passive third.

Acting Companies. What had displaced identification tables and doubling charts from title-pages was the rise of commercial acting companies with fixed London venues. The first play to name a company on its title-page was Richard Edwards's *Damon and Pithias* (1571, reprinted 1582). That title-page offers the text 'as the same was shewed before the Queenes Maiestie, by the Children of her Graces Chappell, except (only) the prologue which is somewhat altered for the proper use of them that hereafter shal have occasion to plaie it, either in Private, or open Audience'. This 1571 title-page, like many from that decade, acknowledges the possibility that buyers may want to perform the play themselves. But it does not provide a doubling chart; 'The Speakers names' are on an inside page (sig. A2^v), without any indication of the number of actors needed for performance. *Damon* is thus a transitional document, advertising its performance by a commercial company, but also encouraging amateur

performance, and naming an author (who was also master of the company in question).

The next eleven title-pages to name playing companies went further. They did not name an author at all (thus insisting on company ownership); they did not envisage or encourage amateur performance, and they lacked identification tables altogether. Moreover, the first example—John Lyly's *Sappho and Phao* (printed twice in 1584, and again in 1591)—began with 'The Prologue at the Black fryers' (sig. A2), identifying a specific theatrical location to supplement the company information on the title-page. The Blackfriars monastery had first been converted for commercial theatrical use in 1576, the same year that the Theatre and the Curtain had been built for outdoor performances. Lyly's *Campaspe* (printed three times in 1584, and again in 1591) repeated this formula: company information on the title-page, no doubling chart or identification table anywhere, a 'Prologue at the blackfriers' (sig. A3). George Peele's *Arraignment of Paris* (also printed in 1584) differed from this formula only in lacking a prologue set in a particular theatre, but 'the Children of her chappell' identified on its title-page played at the Blackfriars. Lyly's *Endymion* (1591) was played, according to the title-page, 'by the Chyldren of Paules', whose name was the same as the name of their theatre, and the epistle from 'The Printer to the *Reader*' confirms this identification of company and venue, referring to performances 'in Paules' and '*by* the children of Paules' (sig. A2; my italics). *Midas* (1592) specifies the same company on the title-page, and opens with 'PROLOGUE IN PAULES' (sig. A2). Only Lyly's *Galathea* (1592) contains nothing that explicitly confirms performance in Paul's, but the title-page attribution to the Paul's boys implies as much.

The companies of boy actors, confined to indoor theatres in London or at court, differed radically from the touring companies of the earlier sixteenth century, or even the professional adult companies with London homes. The adults continued to tour extensively until the second decade of the seventeenth century (Greenfield). Touring usually required smaller casts with more doubling, and consequently plays written for the adult companies at first retained many of the features of earlier sixteenth--century plays (Bevington). The children did not tour, and their writers did not think about doubling patterns in the same way. Moreover, the children's companies apparently had a higher reputation among book-buyers—or at least booksellers—than the adult companies, which were not named on title-pages until 1594. What changed publishing conventions after 1581 was the success of the children's companies and their plays: the three editions

---

41 Webster's *The White Devil* (1612) specifically acknowledges 'Master Perkins', but does not specify his role, or identify any of the other actors. Jonson's *Works* (1616) lists the 'Principle Comedians' at the end of each play, but they are not assigned particular roles; in fact, the play's roles are listed separately, at the beginning of each play. Jonson's list of actors in each play—like the list of 'The Names of the Principall Actors in all these Playes' which prefaces Shakespeare's *Comedies, Histories, and Tragedies* (1623)—serves some of the functions of a set of commendatory verses, or a dedication: the names endorse the text.

6

HERCVLIS FV-
RENTIS.

ARGVMENTVM.

Continet hæc prior Tragœdia querelas Iunonis, & indignationem contra pellices Iouis mariti sui, simúlque contra Herculem ex pellice natum. Continet & Megaræ fletum ob coniugis Herculis absentiam, & ob tædia, minásque Lyci: quippe qui Creonte rege, & filiis occisis, Thebanum imperium occupauerit, eíque vim pariter inferre tentauerit. Mox ab inferis rediens Hercules, cognitis quæ secreta Licus, incedentem illum ad sacrificandum ob partum regnum, interficit. Sed sui in Herculem odij Iuno minimè etiam adhuc oblita, iussit vt is furore corriperetur. Quo actus miserè Hercules coniugi & liberis vitam eripuit. Postremò mente resumpta, illarumque cædium cognito auctore, sibi pariter & manum intulisset vltrò, ni genitoris sui piæ preces intercessissent.

INTERLOCVTORES.

IVNO.	LYCVS.
CHORVS.	HERCVLES.
MEGARA.	THESEVS.
AMPHITRYON.	
	L. AN.

29. The identification table in this 1589 London edition of Seneca (in Latin) exactly duplicates those in earlier continental editions, and was exactly repeated in English translations

ΤΑ ΤΟΥ ΔΡΑΜΑΤΟΣ ΠΡΟΣΩΠΑ.

Δημοσθένης.	Νικίας
Αγοράκριτος ὁ καὶ ἀλλαντοπώλης.	Χορὸς ἱππέων.
Κλέων.	Δῆμο.

30. Jonson cited Aristophanes as a model for his kind of comedy in both *Every Man Out of His Humour* and *Poetaster*, and so he might have been influenced by identification tables in editions of Aristophanes like this one from a 1593 Oxford edition of Ἱππεῖς ('Knights')

a tradition of amateur theatricals, which audiences must have recognized; whenever a practice is professionalized, the new experts must differentiate themselves from the old amateurs.

In the decade from 1581 to 1590, only eight dramatic texts were printed with identification tables—including, in 1581, *The Conflict of Conscience*, the last gasp of a residual popular tradition. Of the remainder, four were translations of Latin plays, one an Inns of Court play, one a royal progress. From 1591 to 1600, of the nine plays printed with tables, five were closet dramas (*BEPD* 97, 108, 116, 132, 147), and two others looked backward to earlier sixteenth-century practice: Marlowe and Nashe's *Dido* (published in 1594, after Marlowe's death), the last play printed with a table on its title-page (but not divided into parts), and *Mucedorus* (1598), which contains a doubling chart (but not on the title-page). During these two decades, identification tables were either confined to learned dramas, or repeated elements of an old convention which had clearly lost most of its authority. But the clearest evidence of uncertainty about the function of such tables is the fact that, from 1591 to 1600, less than 12 per cent of printed dramatic texts provided any sort of table—not only the lowest percentage for any decade of the sixteenth or seventeenth century, but less than a third of the percentage in any other decade.

Between 1581 and 1600, only three dramatic texts (out of ninety-eight) anticipated the norms of the next century. Robert Wilson's *The Three Lords of London* (1590), Henry Porter's *Two Angry Women of Abingdon* (1599), and Ben Jonson's *Every Man in his Humour* (1600) were all performed in the commercial theatre, and each included a table—but not on the title-page and not divided into parts. The two isolated examples at the end of the century were followed by fifteen more in commercial plays published in 1601–6. This spurt of new tables was primarily the work of three men, who in 1605 collaborated on the best-selling *Eastward Ho*: Jonson was responsible for five, Marston for five, Chapman for three. By the end of the decade, the pattern they established had become more general, with examples from Barry, Day, Dekker, Heywood, Mason, and Sharpham. For the decade as a whole, 39 per cent of texts

in one year achieved by *Campaspe* seems to have been a new record for a play, and it was not equalled until 1605 by *Eastward Ho*, another play performed by a children's company, and then not matched again until 1625 (by *A Game at Chess*). Lyly, the best-selling dramatist of the 1580s, did not provide any kind of identification table.

The example of Lyly and the children's companies was followed by the adult companies and their most successful playwrights of the 1580s and early 1590s (Kyd, Marlowe, Greene, Munday, and Shakespeare). Although the adult companies may have toured, they did not encourage amateur performances. Indeed, early commercial plays like *Love's Labour's Lost* and *A Midsummer Night's Dream* (first performed in 1594–6?) seem designed to discredit

59

had tables; in the next decade, the figure rose to 43 per cent, with many more writers represented.

Chapman, Jonson, and Marston, who between them put the new convention into place, were all deliberately 'hard' writers, proud of their own learning, who wrote at least occasionally for the children's theatres, and who more than occasionally despised many of their contemporaries. Their provision of tables belonged to a more general effort to classicize the vernacular theatre. Tables were standard equipment in humanist editions of classical plays, and every Latin play printed in England in the sixteenth and seventeenth centuries had a table. The plays of Chapman, Jonson, and Marston printed in 1600–6 thus combined two traditions which had until then almost always been clearly separated: élite drama (translations, closet plays, learned humanist interludes) and popular theatre (vernacular moralities and commercial plays). The same combination was being effected at the same time by the revived children's companies (1599–1608), which popularized the provision of musical intervals between the five acts of a play—a convention which, like tables, was strongly associated with classical and humanist drama, and which, like tables, would gradually become universal (Taylor and Jowett, 3–50). Both practices connected English drama to a convention simultaneously classical and continental. The commercial theatre's place in textual culture was legitimized by a realignment both temporal and geographical, which associated vernacular plays with texts written and printed across the Channel.

Nevertheless, the new tables in English plays functioned very differently than the seemingly similar tables in classical texts (Illus. 29–30). The mythological characters of classical tragedies had well-known histories and identities, so that a list of Senecan 'interlocutores' served, effectively, as a table of contents (especially since it was usually accompanied by an 'Argumentum', or summary of the action). Moreover, classical plays had very few characters. Indeed, the classical lists had originally served in lieu of individual speech prefixes: early Greek and Latin dramatic manuscripts did not identify the speaker of each speech, but instead simply indicated when speakers changed, and from the list of characters at the beginning of the play the reader was supposed to deduce who spoke which speeches. Renaissance editions of course supplied speech prefixes throughout the text, robbing the lists which preceded the plays of their original function. The new tables of many characters in the English plays (Illus. 31) mimicked the now-vestigial classical convention, but could serve neither of the original functions of the classical lists. Jonson's table supplies almost no information which could be useful to a reader of *Cynthia's Revels*: it tells us nothing about the characters except their names, most of which would have been meaningless to most English readers.[42] It is less interested in categorizing the fictional persons of the play than in categorizing the author's text. It identifies Jonson's play as a member of the category 'canonical literary text', which in turn legitimates Jonson's claim to high status

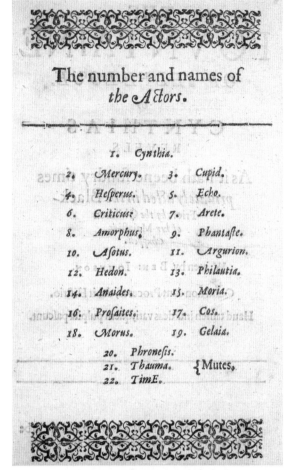

31. Identification table in Jonson's *The Fountaine of Selfe-Love; or, Cynthia's Revels* (1601)

within the hierarchy of his profession. Like other tables, this one gives readers help in reading the text, in this case by telling them to read it with the same attention and reverence they would use in reading Seneca, Terence, or Aristophanes.

Publishers. The rise of the new identity tables in English plays was thus, initially, author-generated. Moreover, to the extent that readers accepted the new authorial identity promulgated by the classical form of these tables, that form was fated to be duplicated by other authors, wishing to categorize themselves in the same flattering way. But as the new tables became conventional, the mere presence of a table lost much of its usefulness in differentiating

The Speakers Names.

The Prologue.	of Miftreffe *Merri-*
Then a Cittizen.	*thought.*
The Cittizens wife, and	Old Mr. *Merry-thought.*
Raph her man, fitting be-	A Squire.
low amidft the Specta-	A Dwarfe.
tors.	A Tapfter.
A rich Marchant.	A Boy that danceth
Iafper his Apprentife.	and fingeth.
Mafter *Humphrey,* a friend	An Hoft.
to the Marchant.	A Barber.
Luce Marchants daughter.	Two Knights.
Miftreffe *Merry-thought,*	A Captaine.
Iafpers mother.	A Sergeant.
Michael, a fecond fonne	Souldiers.

32. Identification table added to the 1635 reprint (printed by Okes for Spencer) of Francis Beaumont and John Fletcher's *The Knight of the Burning Pestle*

The Actors in the Comedy.

SIr *Bounteous Progreffe* an old rich Knight.
Richard Folly-wit, Nephew to
 Sir *Bounteous Progreffe.*
Mafter *Penitent Brothell,* a Country gentleman.
Maw-worme a Lieutenant,
Hobby an Ancient, } Comrades to *Folly-wit.*
Mafter *Ineffe,*
Mafter *Poffibility,* } Two Brothers.
Mafter *Harebraine,* a Citizen.
Gun-water Sir *Bounteous* man.
Iafper mafter *Penitents* man.
Ralph mafter *Harebraines* man.
Two Knights.
One Conftable.
A *Succubus.*
Watch-men.
A Foot-man.

An old Gentlewoman, and mother to the
 Curtizan.
Miftris *Harebraine,* the Citizens wife.
Francke Gulman, the *Curtizan.*
Attendants.

33. Identification table added to the 1640 reprint (printed by Okes for Spencer) of Middleton's *A Mad World, My Masters*

one playwright from another, serving instead to raise the status of plays generally. Eventually, the tables became so strongly associated with the literary merit of a play, so expected a feature of printed plays, that publishers began adding them on their own. A feature which had been author-generated began, within a quarter of a century, to be interpolated by stationers (Illus. 32–33). This shift can be seen clearly in Table I.

In almost every case, the reprints were published posthumously, and in none of the nineteen is there any evidence of authorial involvement in the new edition which added a table. The very first example, the 1623 text of Shakespeare's *2 Henry IV*, is not a strict reprint: it was clearly set from a different manuscript than the earlier quartos, a manuscript that seems to have been a scribal transcript which might already have contained an identification table.[43] But all the other reprints seem to have been set from a copy of an earlier printed edition which did not contain an identification table. Some stationers— Augustine Mathewes, Richard Hawkins,[44] John Spencer, the Moseleys, and the Crookes—show up more than once, but the sheer number of stationers involved is the most striking feature of the record. Never the hobby-horse of a particular stationer, tables were a supplement whose usefulness was widely recognized within the print trade after

the mid-1620s. The practice reached its peak in 1679, in the second 'Beaumont and Fletcher' folio, which added tables to thirty-four plays (including *Nice Valour* and *Wit at Several Weapons*) which had in the past only been printed without them. Notably, five of the six examples between 1625 and 1635 had been plays from the Beaumont and Fletcher canon, clearly regarded as 'literary' by the reign of Charles I.

If stationers could add tables to printed plays, scribes could add them to plays published in manuscript form (Illus. 34–35). The scribal publication of plays itself testifies to their rise in the hierarchy of genres.[45] The earliest evidence of the existence of 'private transcripts'—that is, manuscript copies of a play, specifically made for a reader—comes from 1619 (Greg 1955, 153–4); the earliest extant private transcripts of a commercial play are those of *A Game at Chess* (1624–5), *The Witch* (1625?), and Fletcher's *Demetrius and Enanthe* (1625).

[43] For evidence that the printer's copy might have been a transcript by Ralph Crane, see Honigmann, 165–8.
[44] The interventionist tendencies of Hawkins as a publisher of plays are evident in his expurgated reprints, between 1628 and 1630, of *The Maid's Tragedy, A King and No King,* and *Philaster* (Greg 1955, 151–2); he also published, in 1630, an expurgated reprint of *Othello,* editorially combining features of the 1622 quarto and the 1623 folio texts (Berger).
[45] For scribal publication, see Love (1993) and Love, p. 98 below.

The rise of private transcripts illustrates the complexity of the interactions between different elements of textual culture, providing further proof that 'there was no absolute separation of the handwritten and the printed' (Woudhuysen, 25). Authorial manuscript texts helped create an expanding genre of oral performance, the English commercial play; the success of those oral texts in turn created an expanding demand for printed texts of plays (and printed playbills, which advertised oral performances); the success of printed editions of plays created a practice of reading plays, which in turn created the demand for scribal manuscripts of plays—like *A Game at Chess*—which were not yet available in print. Print, the dominant medium, stimulated a supplement to itself in the residual element of manuscript. 'Private' transcripts were valuable precisely because (like 'private' theatres, but to an even greater degree) they provided to a few what was not available to many. As in Saussurean linguistics, the sign 'manuscript' has meaning only in an opposed relation to some other sign; by the early seventeenth century, 'manuscript' meant 'not-print', and scribal publication created a distinction among readers which was directly related to their social status as persons.[46]

But those social and textual distinctions tend to be blurred by the continual interactions of manuscript and print. Just as the success of supplemental tables as a marker of textual prestige gradually eroded their value as a distinction between authors, so the success of supplemental transcripts was gradually eroded by printed appropriation. The earliest evidence of the existence of private transcripts comes from the epistle to a 1619 edition of *A King and No King*, which indicates that it was printed from such a transcript. Six of the eight earliest extant transcripts were made by Ralph Crane in the mid-1620s, but Crane also apparently prepared manuscripts from which various plays were printed: Webster's *The Duchess of Malfi* (1623), Middleton's *A Game at Chess* (1625), and six plays in the 1623 Shakespeare folio (Wells and Taylor, 20-23).

For the history of identification tables, these interactions are important because they made it easy for tables which originated in private transcripts to find their way into printed texts. Again, such transfers happened almost from the beginning. Shakespeare himself, on the evidence of all the plays published in his lifetime and the great majority published posthumously, did not incorporate a table in his own manuscripts; consequently, the tables appended to the folio plays set from Crane transcripts were almost

[46] Such textual distinctions belong to the more general category of 'distinction'—the foundation of the cultural capital which legitimates class distinction—analysed by Bourdieu.

TABLE I. TABLES ADDED IN REPRINTS 1515-1664

Date	BEPD	Printer	Bookseller	Title
1623	167(b)	William Jaggard	Isaac Jaggard & Edward Blount	2 Henry IV
1625	334(b)	Augustine Mathewes	Miles Partrich	The Scornful Lady
1626	336(b)		John Norton	Englishmen for My Money
1628	363(c)	Augustine Mathewes	Richard Hawkins	Philaster
1630	328(b)		Thomas Jones	Cupid's Revenge
1631	360(c)	Augustine Mathewes	Richard Hawkins	A King and No King
1635	316(b)	Nicholas Okes	John Spencer	The Knight of the Burning Pestle
1637	172(e)	Marmaduke Parsons	Lawrence Hayes	The Merchant of Venice
1640	276(b)	John Okes	John Spencer	A Mad World My Masters
1648	628(b)		Humphrey Moseley	The Goblins
1649	368(b)		Humphrey Moseley	Thierry and Theodoret
1653	537(b)	John Norton	Andrew Crooke	The Conspiracy
1661	574(b)		Andrew Crooke	The Night Walker
1661	643(b)		Humphrey Robinson & Ann Moseley	Beggars' Bush
1662	769(b)		Henry Marsh	Simpleton the Smith
1663	205(j)		W. Gilbertson	Doctor Faustus
1664	166(c)	Roger Daniel, John Hayes, Alice Warren	Philip Chetwin	1 Sir John Oldcastle
1664	222(b)	Roger Daniel, John Hayes, Alice Warren	Philip Chetwin	The London Prodigal
1664	251(b)	Roger Daniel, John Hayes, Alice Warren	Philip Chetwin	The Puritan Widow
1665	306(c)	G. Miller	John Playfere, William Crooke?	The White Devil

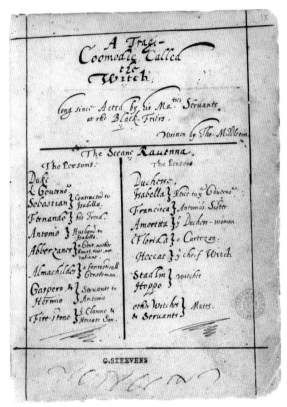

34. Title-page (with identification table) of Middleton's
The Witch, as transcribed by Ralph Crane c.1625

The Scene Vienna.		Thomas. ⎱ 2. Friers.
The names of all the Actors.		Peter. ⎰
		Elbow, a simple Constable.
		Froth, a foolish Gentleman.
Vincentio : the Duke.		Clowne.
Angelo, the Deputie.		Abhorson, an Executioner.
Escalus, an ancient Lord.		Barnardine, a dissolute prisoner.
Claudio, a yong Gentleman.		Isabella, sister to Claudio.
Lucio, a fantastique.		Mariana, betrothed to Angelo.
2.Other like Gentlemen.		Iuliet, beloued of Claudio.
Prouost.		Francisca, a Nun.
		Mistris Ouer-don, a Bawd.

35. Identification table printed in 1623 at
the end of *Measure for Measure*, which was
apparently set from a transcript by Ralph Crane

spective, a table's proximity to the author is related to its date of composition. If a table first published in 1679 was prepared by Middleton himself, then it certainly dates from 1627 or earlier, and may well date from the same year as the play itself; if it was interpolated by the publisher, it probably dates from the year of publication. Thus, the table appended to *Wit at Several Weapons* may date from 1613 or 1679, depending on who prepared it—a difference of two-thirds of a century. Reliable attributions are critical for any historical understanding of the evolution of tables, and what tables may have to tell us about the evolution of textual culture or early modern society.

III. Histories in Fictions

The cultural evolution of identification tables across the seventeenth century can be illustrated by the contrast between *The Roaring Girl* (Illus. 36) and *Wit at Several Weapons* (Illus. 37). These two city comedies were first performed in 1611 and 1613 respectively; their tables were first published in 1611 and 1679 respectively. The 1611 table comes from an edition with multiple evidence of authorial involvement; the 1679 table was added in a reprint, published more than half a century after the death of both authors, in a text which shows no evidence of even indirect authorial involvement, as part of a policy of supplying tables for every play in the collection.[48] Hence, *The Roaring Girl*'s table is authorial and early, the *Wit at Several Weapons* table non-authorial and late. Since the plays have so much in common (date of composition, authorship, social content), the differences between the two tables reflect, not so much a difference in the two plays, but a difference in the conventions by which plays are described. These differences can be categorized in terms of labels, locations, hierarchies, and genders.

Labels. How such tables are labelled reflects a sense of what it is they are. Because different authors may think

certainly created by Crane himself.[47] The same mechanism—printer use of a scribal transcript—could account for the tables in many plays printed after 1623, particularly when those plays were published posthumously.

I began this analysis of tables in Middleton's dramatic texts by distinguishing proximate from posthumous texts. Fortuitously, the end of Middleton's play-publishing career, in 1625, coincides with the rise of scribal and stationer interpolation of tables. Every single one of Middleton's plays first published posthumously was printed, at some point in the seventeenth century, with a table. This uniformity of table-making contrasts, not only with Middleton's overall career, but even with the period 1611-25, when his published texts sometimes (but not invariably) included a table. Some of the tables in posthumous texts may be authorial, but many are demonstrably interpolated.

Editorially, the distinction between authorial and non-authorial tables will affect an editor's willingness to emend or abandon a seventeenth-century table. From the larger perspective of an analyst of textual culture, all these tables are early modern texts, whether prepared by an author, a scribe, or a stationer. But even from that per-

[47] The folio prints lists for *The Tempest*, *The Two Gentlemen of Verona*, *Measure for Measure*, and *The Winter's Tale*, all set from Crane transcripts. It does not print lists for two other plays apparently set from Crane transcripts, *The Merry Wives of Windsor* and *Cymbeline*, apparently in each case due to lack of space on the final printed page of the play.

[48] The 1679 edition published, for the first time, lists of the original casts for many plays, but this evidence was available only for plays in the repertory of the King's Men, and must have derived from oral or written sources connected to that company. The texts of *Wit at Several Weapons* and *Nice Valour* clearly came from some other source.

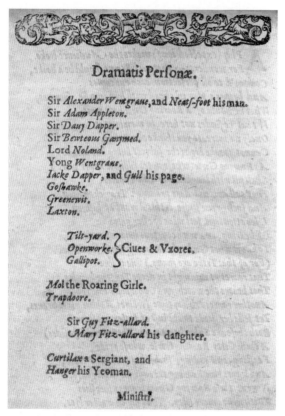

Dramatis Personæ.

Sir *Alexander Wengrane*, and *Neatf-foot* his man.
Sir *Adam Appleton*.
Sir *Dauy Dapper*.
Sir *Bewteous Ganymed*.
Lord *Noland*.
Yong *Wengrane*.
Iacke Dapper, and *Gull* his page.
Goshawke.
Greenewit.
Laxton.

Tilt-yard.
Openworke. } Ciues & Vxores.
Gallipot.

Mol the Roaring Girle.
Trapdoore.

Sir *Guy Fitz-allard*.
Mary Fitz-allard his daughter.

Curtilax a Sergiant, and
Hanger his Yeoman.

Miniftrs.

36. Identification table in Middleton and Dekker's *The Roaring Girl* (1611), with characters not listed hierarchically

358

Wit at several weapons.

A COMEDY.

The Perfons reprefented in the Play.

Sir Perfidious Oldcraft, *an old Knight, a great admirer of Wit.*	Sir Ruinous Gentry, *a decaid Knight,* } Two fharking companions.
Witty-pate Oldcraft, *his Fathers own Son.*	Prifcian, *a poor Scholar,*
Sir Gregory Fopp, *a witlefs Lord of Land.*	Pompey Doodle, *a clown,* Sir Gregories *man, a piece of puff-pafte, like his Mafter.*
Cunningham, *a difcreet Gen.* Sir Gregories *comrade and fupplanter.*	Mr. Credulous, *Nephew to* Sir Perfidious, *a fhallow-brain'd Scholar.*

Women.

Neece *to* Sir Perfidious, *a rich and witty Heir,*	Guardianefs, *to* Sir Perfidious *his Neece, an old doting Croane.*
Lady Ruinous, *Wife to* Sir Ruinous.	Mirabell, *the Guardianeffes Neece.*

The Scene, London.

37. Identification table in Middleton and Rowley's *Wit at Several Weapons*, added in the 1679 reprint of the Beaumont and Fletcher canon (*Fifty Comedies and Tragedies*)

influenced by his elder collaborator's preference.

The history of the labels used for identification tables has been traced by Beckerman, whose conclusions can now be placed in the larger evolution of the genre. Early tables regularly identify 'the players names' or 'names of the players' or specify how many persons are required to 'play' a text; but by the end of the sixteenth century, 'the designation of characters as players...disappears from lists' (63). Obviously, this shift reflects the larger shift, already described, away from the sixteenth-century view of printed plays as 'texts to be performed'. By contrast, 'actors' is a more ambiguous word, referring either to 'performers' or 'doers', to the theatrical performer or the fictive character; it could also be used to distinguish classical 'actors' from modern 'players'. The term 'actors' first appeared in an English table in 1573, in Gascoigne's *Supposes*, translated

differently about what such tables represent, such labels may sometimes distinguish between authors. Studies in attribution have often been able to identify the fractions of a text written by separate collaborators, and internal evidence might in some cases enable us to attribute a table to one author or the other.[49] Thus, the title 'Dramatis Personæ' in *The Roaring Girl* is probably Dekker's phrase, not Middleton's. None of the other Middleton tables published in his lifetime uses that label, and it is infrequent even among posthumous editions.[50] By contrast, the phrase is used to label character lists printed in Dekker's *Satiromastix* (1602), *The Whore of Babylon* (1607), *Match me in London* (1631), *The Noble Spanish Soldier* (1634), *Wonder of a Kingdom* (1634), and *The Bloody Banquet* (1639, attributed on the title-page to 'T.D.' only); the first three of these examples were, like *The Roaring Girl*, all printed in Dekker's lifetime and contain other prefatory material clearly provided by the author.[51] Since *Satiromastix* also represents the very first appearance of 'Dramatis Personæ' in a printed English play, Dekker evidently preferred it, and one way or another Dekker is probably responsible for its appearance in *The Roaring Girl*—either because he wrote it there himself, or because Middleton was initially

[49] The title and form of the list in *The Family of Love* (1608) contribute to the evidence that Lording Barry, not Middleton, wrote that play (Taylor, Mulholland, Jackson). The list there is headed 'Actorum Nomina', a rare form present in only two other English plays: Barry's only other surviving text, *Ram Alley* (1611), and the anonymous *Swetnam the Woman-Hater* (1620). All three texts also list 'Women' characters under a separate subheading.

[50] Of thirteen lists which originate in posthumously published Middleton texts, only three—*The Changeling* (1653), *Hengist, King of Kent* (1661), and *Anything for a Quiet Life* (1662)—adopt the phrase; all are very late, two are collaborative, and the third (*Hengist*) survives in two earlier manuscripts which contain no lists.

[51] By contrast, the four examples in the Dekker canon of alternative labels for such lists all occur in collaborative plays, only one of which was printed in Dekker's lifetime: 'The Actors Names' (Dekker and Ford, *The Virgin Martyr*, 1622; Dekker and Marlowe?, *Lust's Dominion*, 1657), 'Actors Names' (Ford, Dekker, Rowley, etc., *The Witch of Edmonton*, 1658), 'The Names of the Persons' (Ford and Dekker, *The Sun's Darling*, 1656). For Dekker's responsibility for the dramatis personae list and first scenes of *The Bloody Banquet*, see Taylor 2000.

from the Italian, and for the rest of the sixteenth century was limited almost entirely to closet drama; after 1600, 'actors' became common, 'finally appearing in the texts of about 100 plays' (65). Again, this shift coincides with the rise of a new kind of table, which applied features of learned drama to popular plays, in 1600–6: during those years Jonson consistently used the new term. But later he switched to 'Persons', a label which originally appeared in translations of Italian plays (rendering 'Le Persone'). 'Persons' is an English version of 'Personae', which appears in neo-Latin plays printed in England as early as 1581.[52] 'Persons of the Play' and its Latin equivalent, 'Dramatis Personae', by turning toward 'persons', turn away from playing, acting, and roles altogether; but these persons still clearly belong to the play. Thus, in 1620, the table in Middleton and Rowley's *The World Tossed at Tennis* describes 'The Figures and Persons properly raised for employment through the whole masque': 'raised for employment' could refer to persons or performers. By contrast, 'The Persons represented in the Play'—the formula used repeatedly for texts in the 1679 folio, including Middleton and Rowley's *Wit at Several Weapons*—seems to give those persons an independent life in a real world outside the text; these persons are not wholly 'of' the play, but simply appear 'in' it; not 'employed' for it, but 'represented' within it.

Locations. If a play represents persons who exist outside it, where do they exist? In a place, which tables may identify. *The Roaring Girl* table is typical of its time in not giving any indication of where the play's action takes place. The first indications of locale in tables had come in translations of classical and Italian plays (*BEPD* 60, 51, 183), in closet plays by Daniel, Brandon, and Alexander (*BEPD* 132, 147, 260, 261), and in academic drama (*BEPD* 239), from 1573 to 1607; locations did not make the transfer to commercial plays until 1616, when Jonson systematically added them to the tables in his folio. Jonson's move continued his appropriation of élite forms for commercial plays. But the rise of the new tables in the first years of the seventeenth century had been driven by three writers, not one, and the fact that it was so quickly taken up by many other authors indicates that it satisfied a need already shared. Jonson's innovation in providing scene locations was more idiosyncratic, and less quickly adopted. His lead in 1616 was not followed until seven years later, and then only in another folio of plays with which he was conspicuously associated: in the 1623 Shakespeare folio, *The Tempest* was located in 'an vn-inhabited Island' and *Measure for Measure* was re-located in 'Vienna' (Illus. 35).[53] Both texts were printed from manuscripts prepared by Crane, who had worked for Jonson as early as 1618; Crane also prepared the manuscript of *The Witch*, set in 'Rauenna' (Illus. 34). In the 1620s, scene locations were given in a handful of texts prepared for the press by their authors: in 1623 Webster's *The Devil's Law Case*, in 1629 both John Ford's *The Lover's Melancholy* and William Davenant's *Albovine*. In

the next decade, almost 30 per cent of the plays which had tables also had locations, and their frequency continued to rise thereafter. Seven of the eight Middleton tables printed between 1611 and 1652 lack locations (the one exception being *Measure for Measure*, reflecting Crane's practice rather than Middleton's); in stark contrast, five of the six Middleton tables printed between 1653 and 1662 contain locations.[54] This pattern can have nothing to do with Middleton himself; it must reflect a change in reader expectations and stationer practices in the 1650s. By 1679, it was almost inevitable that the table added to *Wit at Several Weapons* should specify 'The Scene London'.

This increase in tables with locations may seem to oppose the larger movement in early modern textual culture, described in the first part of this essay, from local to national self-definition. But greater mobility could, and did, make people more sensitive to the differences between one place and another. The expansion of English overseas exploration and trade introduced the world to Englishmen, and the attendant expansion of news reports from distant parts of the kingdom and the globe made those very different places familiar to an increasing fraction of the population. The temporal and mental *distance* between places decreased, while awareness of the *difference* between places increased. Thus, Middleton's Lord Mayor's pageant of 1613, *The Triumphs of Truth* (1613), belongs to an explicitly local genre, celebrating a particular Londoner and the London livery company to which he belonged; but it also celebrates the East India Company, foregrounds an idealized Black King who addresses the London crowd, and is the earliest extant English dramatic text—indeed, the first popular English text in any genre—to use the word *white* in its modern racial sense (Taylor 2005).

The setting for *The Triumphs of Truth* was London itself: the site of performance was also the site being represented. But by 1613 Inigo Jones had already imported, for English court performances, the conventions of perspective scenery developed in sixteenth-century Italy. Those conventions made it possible for the first time for the persons in a dramatic performance to be 'placed' in a specific visual locale other than the playing space itself. The anachronistic and anatopic world of England's sixteenth-century popular plays, where actors moved across an unspecified *platea*, gave way to an increasing insistence upon a particular fictional *locus*.[55] Titles began to advertise plays situated, not simply in 'London', but in particular contemporary neighbourhoods: after Middleton's *The Puritan, or the Widow of Watling Street* (1606) came Barry's

[52] Thomas Watson's *Antigone* (1581) and William Gage's *Meleager, Hippolytus*, and *Ulysses Redux*, all printed in 1592 (*BEPD* L1–L4).

[53] For Middleton's change of the location from Italy to Vienna, see Taylor 2004.

[54] Present in *The Changeling, Old Law, No Wit/Help like a Woman's, More Dissemblers Besides Women, Women, Beware Women, Anything for a Quiet Life*; not present in *The Mayor of Queenborough*.

[55] I take this terminology from Weimann, esp. pp. 73–85. However, Weimann, like Bentley, presents a static picture of 'Renaissance' drama, anchored upon the 'universal vision' of Shakespeare (251); he does not trace the shifting balance of power between *platea* and *locus*, or explain the developing critical and then practical rejection of *platea*.

Ram Alley (1608). *A Chaste Maid in Cheapside*—performed in 1613, the same year as *The Triumphs of Truth*, but not printed until 1630—was followed by Shirley's *Hyde Park* (1632) and Nabbes's *Covent Garden* (1633) and *Tottenham Court* (1634). The greater use and influence of perspective scenery in the 1630s corresponds with the sudden increase in tables which give locations, and in the 1660s scenery would become a standard feature of the reopened public theatres.

The increasing specificity of place in the performance and publication of dramatic texts may have something to do with the increasing neoclassical emphasis on the three unities. But neoclassical unities of space, time, and action may have been so appealing to seventeenth-century authors and audiences precisely because they reflected a growing sensitivity to the particularities of space and time. During Middleton's lifetime geography became an important subject in English universities (Cormack). Although imported texts initially dominated the discipline, by the time Middleton died England had already begun generating its own contributions to the textualization of space. After the Restoration John Ogilby was named 'King's Geographer and Geographic Printer', producing lavishly illustrated folio descriptions of *Africa* (1669), *America* (1670) and *Asia* (1673), followed by the more domestic *Britannia* (1675) and the cheap *Pocket book of roads* (1679). Living in a world of labelled and measured spaces, readers of the 1678 edition of Thomas Shadwell's adaptation of Shakespeare and Middleton's *Timon of Athens* would presumably have found useful not only the 'Scene Athens' at the bottom of the list of 'Persons', but the later information linking those persons to more specific locations: 'Scene is the Porch or Cloister of the Stoicks. Apemantus speaking to the people and several Senators' (37) and 'Scene the Senate House, all the Senate sitting—Alcibiades' (55). Such localization had not seemed necessary to Shakespeare, Middleton, their first audiences, or their first readers.

Hierarchy. Lists inevitably hierarchize their items, because they must give one item literal priority over another. Hierarchies, indeed, are almost invariably conceptualized as lists, in which the diversity of experience is reduced to an ordered sequence from highest to lowest: the 'great chain of being', as epitomized for instance in Higden's *Polychronicon*—a book Middleton read when writing *Hengist, King of Kent*—was a 'ladder of ascent'. 'In the universal order of things', as in a list, 'the top of an inferior class touches the bottom of a superior' (Tillyard, 26).

But although lists invariably hierarchize, and hierarchies invariably list, the order of lists/hierarchies varies, because that order will be determined by which values are given priority, and the choice of values is arbitrary. Sometimes—as in parish registers (Illus. 1, 12), financial accounts (Illus. 4), annals (Illus. 11), or genealogies (Illus. 13)—the cataloguer's hierarchy is chronological: one name comes before another on the list simply because it came before the other in time. Chronological order may seem neutral, but it may also reflect a value system

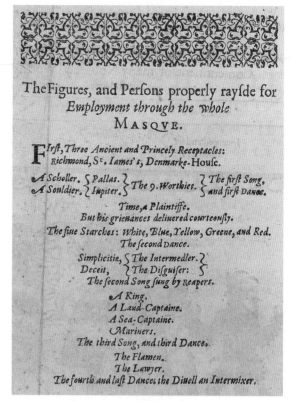

38. Identification table in Middleton and Rowley's *The World Tossed at Tennis* (1620), with characters listed in order of apperaance

in which earliest is most valuable. Humanist philology and Protestant scholarship constructed chronological lists in which the earliest texts were the most valuable; the emergent protocols of seventeenth-century science valued first-hand observation over second-hand reports.

With or without such values, chronological principles can be applied to the construction of identification tables in dramatic texts. Classical plays usually listed names by the order in which they appeared on stage (Illus. 29–30); that sequence had no doubt been useful when texts were written without speech prefixes, but it is also the easiest way for a copyist to compile a list of the roles which appear in a play. *Heroes* (Illus. 28) and *Tennis* (Illus. 38) follow the same procedure. Such lists give priority to the sequence in which, as readers or spectators, we experience the text. So does 'The True Order of his Majesty's Proceeding through London' (*Magnificent* 96–199); such a list would have been needed to marshall the many participants in the correct sequence. In that list the most important name is not at the very beginning or the very end, but in the middle (*Magnificent* 186–87). Such lists reflect a hierarchy which privileges the order of time, of the unfolding event, above all else. Like 'The True Order', a theatrical plat was

39. Part of the theatrical 'plat' of the *Second Part of Seven Deadly sins* (acted by the Chamberlain's Men c. 1597)

40. Identification table in Middleton and Webster's *Anything for a Quiet Life* (1662), with characters listed hierarchically

used, backstage, to marshall actors and their properties in the correct sequence of entrances (Illus. 39). When it is used as the ordering principle for a list of persons, the event hierarchy becomes a textual hierarchy, like any other table of contents, which lists topics in order of appearance.

Alternatively, the ordering of a list may reflect hierarchies which exist outside the theatre. In *Nice Valour* (Illus. 2), the list places all men above all women, and within each gender the list begins with the character of highest social status and descends to the character of lowest social status. This sequence does not reflect the order of appearance in the play: Shamont, for instance, enters at the very beginning of the play, but is placed after the Duke's kinsman, who does not enter until 1.1.184. Such hierarchies are particularly easy to trace in plays which include peers and courtiers, who can be ranked by precise degrees of relationship to the ruler. Likewise, in *Anything for a Quiet Life* (Illus. 40) we move smoothly, predictably down from 'Lord' to 'Sir' to 'Countery Gentleman' to 'Citizen' to 'Lawyer'—a descent from peer to knight to country landed gentleman to city mercantile gentleman to ungentle unliveried professional, and so on down to servants, apprentices, barbers, sergeants, young children—and finally women, who descend in the same order as the men with whom they are paired.

By contrast, in *The Roaring Girl* (Illus. 36), printed fifty years before *Anything for a Quiet Life*, social hierarchy is grossly violated by the very first line of the table,

which not only yokes 'Sir *Alexander Wentgraue*' to 'his man', but also places Wentgrave—and then three other mere knights—above 'Lord *Noland*'. In the 1611 table, the personal servant of a knight precedes a lord. That social impropriety does not result from theatrical propriety, because the 1611 table does not follow the temporal sequence of appearances on stage, either: Mary Fitzallard, the second character to speak, is twenty-second on the list. It places Moll, illustrated by a special woodcut on the title-page, nineteenth. The list therefore does not reflect theatrical sequence, theatrical significance, or social hierarchy.

A revealing example of a mixed list, *The Roaring Girl* uses several different hierarchies in combination. The first five lines include most of the play's highest-ranking characters; then follow the sons of two of the knights, followed by three young gentleman companions. The young are subordinated to the old, and citizens are placed in a second block, below the gentry. But the presence of two personal servants in the first block makes it clear that characters are being grouped, not strictly by rank, but by household. The first block describes the household of Sir Alexander Wentgrave: a community of men which includes his son, his friends, his servant, and various guests, including knights, a lord, and various gentlemen (with their servants). The second block brackets three adjoining households of citizen tradesmen and their wives;

The Names of the principall Perſons.

Mr YELLOWHAMMER, *A Gold-Smith.*
MAVDLINE, *His Wife.*
TIM, *Their Sonne.*
MOLL, *Their Daughter.*
TVTOR *to* TIM.
Sr WALTER WHOREHOVND, *A Suter to* MOLL.
Sr OLIVER KIXE, *and his Wife, Kin to* Sr WALT.
Mr ALLWIT, *and his Wife, Whom* Sr WALT. *keepes.*
WELCH GENTLEWOMAN, Sr WALT. *Whore.*
WAT *and* NICKE, *His Baſtards.*
DAVY DAHVMMA, *His Man.*
TVCHWOOD SENIOR, *and his Wife, A decayed Gentleman.*
TVCHWOOD IVNIOR, *Another Suter to* MOLL.
2 PROMOTERS.
SERVANTS.
WATERMEN.

41. Identification table in Middleton's *A Chaste Maid in Cheapside* (1630), with characters not listed hierarchically

The Men.

1. *Sir Edward Fortune.*
2. *Brabant Signior, and his Page.*
3. *Brabant Iunior, and his Page.*
4. *Planet.*
5. *Puffe, and his Page.*
6. *Iohn Ellis.*
7. *Mamon.*
8. *Flawne his Page.*
9. *Timothy Twedle.*
10. *Iacke Drum.*
11. *Paſquil.*
12. *Mounſieur.*

The Women.

1. *Katherine.*
2. *Camelia.*
3. *Winifride.*
4. *Market Woman.*

42. The identification table in Marston's *Jack Drum's Entertainment* (1601) is the first to divide characters by gender

the anomalous household of Moll, with her single servant, is next, followed by the family household of Sir Guy Fitzallard and his daughter; last comes the occupational pairing of Curtilax and his yeoman. *A Chaste Maid in Cheapside* (written in 1613, printed in 1630) organizes itself in a similar manner (Illus. 41): beginning with the citizen Yellowhammer household, it proceeds to their daughter's suitor Sir Walter Whorehound, then descends through Whorehound's gentry kinsmen and urban dependents to the Touchwood gentry, trailing off with various unattached 'ministri'. In both tables, the sequence of groups reflects the sequence in which the group is introduced on stage, and sequence within each group is influenced—but not consistently determined—by social status.

Mixed lists like those in *The Roaring Girl* and *A Chaste Maid in Cheapside* belong to a position somewhere between purely theatrical lists like *The World Tossed at Tennis* and purely social lists like those in *Nice Valour*. They reflect the complexity of perspective created by the transition from one dominant paradigm to another. Moreover, uncertainties about sequence are themselves interesting evidence of social perceptions. In determining the relative proximity of characters, does social status matter more than genealogy? Should a knight be followed by another knight (as in *The Roaring Girl*), or by his son (as in *Wit at Several Weapons*)? Does economic power matter more than inherited status? Should a wealthy knight precede a lord with 'No Land' (as in *The Roaring Girl*)? Mixed lists answered such questions in various ways.

But although the relative value of wealth or blood might create uncertainties of status, relationships between persons were almost invariably defined, in these tables, in terms of relative status (rich, poor, decayed, knight, lord, citizen) or genealogy (son, daughter, wife, brother, suitor to marry). Although the plots were often driven by credit relationships—Ricardo in *The Widow*, for instance, owes the Second Suitor money—such purely economic connections were almost never recognized as a significant element in the definition of persons. In defining identity, the economic relationships increasingly emphasized by a capitalist economy were ignored; dramatic tables treated family or status or household as foundational. But the most foundational category of all was gender.

Genders. The tables from *The Roaring Girl* and *Wit at Several Weapons* differ most strikingly in their treatment of gender. In *The Roaring Girl*, genders mix, and within household blocks women may be on top of men (Moll over Trapdoor), beside them (*Cives & Vxores*), or below them (Sir Guy over Mary Fitzallard); in the last instance, the gender subordination of female to male may be less significant than the genealogical subordination of child to parent, which similarly structures the table's representation of the relationship between Sir Alexander Wentgrave and his son. By contrast, in *Wit at Several Weapons* women are systematically segregated and subordinated.

The treatment of women in the later table—and in the other tables of the 1679 folio—originated in 1601, with Marston's *Jack Drum's Entertainment* (Illus. 42). A few months later, in a play that mercilessly mocked Marston, Jonson followed Marston's lead (Illus. 43). In the next few years, women were segregated in identification tables in Marston's *Malcontent* (1604) and *Sophonisba* (1606), in Jonson's *Sejanus* (1605) and *Volpone* (1607), in Chapman's *All Fools* (1605), *Sir Giles Goosecap* (1606), and *Monsieur D'Olive* (1606). The three men who established a new convention for identification tables organized most of their own along gender lines.

The divisions in these tables reflect a perceived difference in the outside world, not a difference experienced inside the theatre. The first play with a table to segregate roles by gender, *Jack Drum's Entertainment*, was written for the Children of Paul's, where both male and female roles were played by boy actors; Marston's division between 'The Men' and 'The Women' imposes a biological binary on the characters that does not correspond to a biological binary in the performers. The second example, *Poetaster*, was acted by the Children of the Chapel, where the same conditions applied. The same divisions, by gender, organize tables for the children's companies and the adult companies. Moreover, in the adult companies the boys who played female roles also played young male roles (boys, pages, etc.); the table for Middleton's *Masque of Heroes* (Illus. 28) distinguishes between roles played by adults and roles played by boys, a division with no necessary connection to gender. But gendered tables do not group young male roles with the female roles played by the same boy actors.

This division by gender could not invoke the precedent or authority of classical practice, and it could easily conflict with the representation of theatrical and social hierarchies. Theatrically, it could elevate very minor roles, who speak few if any lines, above protagonists.[56] Socially, it could lead to inversions like that in *More Dissemblers Besides Women* (1657), where the Duchess, the ruler of Milan and the play's highest-ranking character, was placed below a singing master, a dancing master, an usher, and the foolish servant Dondolo.

Perhaps partly because of such difficulties, division by gender was slower to catch on than the tables themselves. *The Roaring Girl* was not alone in rejecting the classification. From 1601 to 1622, gender organized only nine tables in plays not written by Marston, Jonson, or Chapman. But the Shakespeare folio of 1623 contained five, most of them apparently prepared by Ralph Crane (who had earlier worked for Jonson); five more appeared in separate quarto publications by four different authors in 1629. In the next decade they accounted for a third of all tables, and with each succeeding decade they became more common, culminating in their complete dominance

43. Jonson's *Poetaster* (1602) listed female roles, numbered 20 to 24, in a separate column, after and below male roles 1 to 19

of the 1679 folio. The Middleton canon strikingly illustrates this shift. Of the four tables for which Middleton himself seems most clearly responsible—*The Roaring Girl* (1611), *Masque of Heroes* (1619), *The World Tossed at Tennis* (1620), and *A Chaste Maid in Cheapside* (1630), published posthumously but similar to the other three—not one divides the sexes; of the twelve published between 1640 and 1679, all but one is gendered.

Gender triumphed, becoming the most significant of all possible distinctions between persons, an absolute of difference and distance which overcame proximity in every other dimension, genealogical, social, or economic. Why? The change cannot be attributed to the appearance of actresses on the English stage after the Restoration. Theatrical practice had not governed the organization of tables before 1660; why should it govern their organization after 1660? In any case, by the Restoration gendered tables had already become ubiquitous. Rather than the convention of tables changing to reflect a new theatrical convention, it would seem more accurate to say that theatrical convention changed in a way which brought it into line with the already established convention of tables. After all, the play-readers of the 1640s and 1650s (who could not attend performances, because the theatres

---

[56] In recognition of this problem, some tables—like those in *Old Law* (1657) and *The Mayor of Queenborough* (1661)—put such extras in a separate group below the women.

were closed) became the play-makers and playgoers of the 1660s; they brought to the new theatres a set of expectations formed primarily by the reading of plays. To the extent that tables in printed plays made the distinction between men and women foundational and natural, the theatrical blurring of that distinction, when boys played women, began to seem unnatural. Conventions of writing altered performance conventions.

What altered the conventions of writing? Gender, which triumphed in tables in plays, did not feature so conspicuously in the legal and historical lists described in Part I of this essay. But the absence of gender as an organizing principle in those lists results, primarily, from the almost complete absence of women. Early modern textual culture was gendered by exclusion. Just as mothers were omitted from baptismal records which identified fathers, women were systematically excluded from most of the institutions of textual culture: universities, theatres, the legal professions, the church, Parliament. Women usually became agents in textual culture only by some curiosity of inheritance: the textual agency of Elizabeth I descended from her father, of Mary Sidney from her brother Philip, of the printer Alice Warren from her dead husband (whose membership of the Stationers' Company she inherited). The philological imperative—the early modern return to origins, which undermined so much of the old religious, political, and scientific order—did not so obviously challenge the power of gender. By the criteria of the Greek and Roman classics, the Bible or the 'book of nature', gender could claim to be foundational.

But although gender was the most secure and pervasive of all forms of authority in textual culture, even its dominance was fractional and shifting. The exclusion of women was being undermined by both Protestantism and capitalism. Women, like men, could gain direct access to the Bible only if they could read. Women, like men, could attend plays, and if they could read they could buy books: they constituted a growing fraction of consumers in the textual market-place. As early as 1619, Middleton recommended *Masque of Heroes* to readers as a work which was 'counted good' because, being 'meant for ladies', 'ladies understood' it (7–8); by 1693, the *Ladies' Mercury* offered women readers a periodical of their own. What was true of textual consumption was eventually true of textual production. Because commercial playwrights were never organized into a livery company, authors could not control the free movement of labour within their profession, and Aphra Behn was inevitable. As Ralph Waldo Emerson would remark in 1837, 'A man in the view of political economy is a pair of hands' (II, 230). Emerson was complaining about the capitalist division of labour, but if, for the purposes of capitalism, a worker is simply 'a pair of hands', then those hands might just as easily belong to a woman, not 'a man'—as Marx and Engels realized. A decade after Emerson's complaint, they pointed out that 'Differences of age and sex have no longer any distinctive social validity for the working class. All are instruments of labour' (Marx and Engels, 62). In

the view of political economy—or of textual culture—either a man or a woman is just a hand, and gender is fundamentally irrelevant. Consequently, authorship was the first profession in which English women became a significant fraction.

However, these facts only deepen the paradox: if Protestantism and capitalism were breaking down old distinctions between men and women, why did identification tables in plays start insisting on gender distinctions? More must be involved than the personal sexual politics of Marston, Jonson, and Chapman; all three were aggressively misogynist, but the convention would not have been adopted by so many others unless it served a larger social purpose. Wai-Chee Dimock has argued, in another context, that 'gender does its symbolic work primarily by restoring a natural order to a newly denaturalized political order. Against the shakiness of political institutions, gender works with the solidity of a natural fact' (209). As other certainties blink and waver, men cling all the more tenaciously to the authority of sex. Gender began to organize identification tables in 1601, at the tired end of Elizabeth I's reign, just after the failed revolt of the macho Earl of Essex. In 1603 James I restored male rule for the first time in half a century. But any sense of a return to patriarchal normalcy was soon dispelled by the king's relationship with his male favourites, and by the Frances Howard scandals—in which a Catholic wife divorced her Protestant husband, accusing him of impotence and conspiring to poison another man (Lindley; Bellany; McRae). During the controversy over the proposed marriage of Prince Charles to the Spanish Infanta (1620–24), the Protestant nation widely feared that the Prince would be dominated by his Catholic bride; after his accession to the throne in 1625, the influence of his French Catholic wife Henrietta Maria again superimposed gender on fundamental political oppositions. The Stuarts were associated with sodomy or with husbands dominated by Catholic women; their opponents aligned themselves with the former Queen Elizabeth, nostalgically re-invented as the champion of Protestantism and enemy of absolutism (Dobson and Watson, 45–76). It may not be accidental that 1629, the beginning of Personal Rule, was also the first year when gendered tables began appearing in significant numbers in texts by a variety of playwrights, or that they became dominant in the politically tumultuous years between 1640 and 1660.

The political turmoil of those years was itself gendered. The fissures in the old order created 'new opportunities for women—in public speaking, religious and political activism, estate management, and warfare—which in turn generated new texts *pro* and *contra*' (Turner, 77). As has happened in other historical periods, the visible critique or diminution of male power generated a strong backlash. One of the forms that backlash took, in the 1640s and 1650s, was the satirical trope of a Parliament of women (Achinstein 1994a, 131–63; Achinstein 1995; Patton). In 1647 at least five such 'Parliament' texts appeared; two of them include, among their characters,

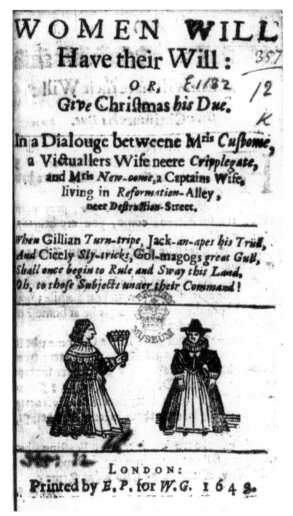

WOMEN WILL

Have their Will: *357*

O, R, *£1/82* 12

Give Chriſtmas his Due. K

In a Dialouge betweene Mᵗⁱˢ *Cuſtome*,

a Victuallers Wife neere *Cripplegate*,

and Mᵗⁱˢ *New-come*, a Captains Wife,

living in *Reformation-Alley*,

neer *Deſtruction-*Street.

When Gillian *Turn-tripe*, Jack-an-apes *his Truſt,*

And Cicely *Sly-tricks*, Gol-magogs *great Gull,*

Shall once begin to Rule and Sway this Land,

Oh, to thoſe Subjects under their Command!

L O N D O N :

Printed by *E. P.* for *W. G.* 1 6 4 9.

44. The freedom of the press that briefly flourished while theatres were closed produced irreverent political pamphlets that mimicked and gendered the title-pages of early morality plays

Middleton and Dekker's Moll Cutpurse.[57] But although these texts name many women, they do not take the form of plays. However, in the following year this satyrical trope combined with one of the new conventions of polemical pamphleteering: beginning with *Canterbury his Change of Diet* (1641), political satire sometimes took the form of a 'play', intended for reading rather than performance. Although they were very short—typically only eight to sixteen pages long—in 1647 and 1648 six such pamphlet playlets included full-page identification tables, like those in full-length printed plays.[58] Then, between April 29 and May 22, 1648, three playlets featuring 'Mistris Parliament' were published, each with a list of names on its title-page; these included Mistris

London (her midwife), Mrs. Synod (her nurse), Mrs. Schisme, Mrs. Priviledge, Mrs. Ordinance, Mrs. Universall Toleration, and Mrs. Leveller (her gossips).[59] All three combined anti-Parliamentary politics, misogynist satire, and a list of female characters featured on the title-page as an inducement to buy the text.

That new convention continued after the execution of Charles I. On December 12, 1649 *Women will have their Will* combined, for the first time since 1562, a title--page list of roles with generic character woodcuts (Illus. 44). Then, on January 30, 1650, the author of previous satires on a 'Parliament' of ladies published a satire on the new 'Commonwealth' of ladies. 'There was a time in *England*,' it begins, 'when men *wore the Breeches*, and debar'd women of their *Liberty*,' but now, rejecting 'the tyranny of men, The *Ladies Rampant* of the times, in their last *Parliament*, knowing themselves to be a part of the *free people* of this Nation, unanimously resolved to assert their own *freedoms*; and casting off the intolerable yoke of their *Lords* and *Husbands*, have voted themselves the *Supreme Authority* both at home and abroad, and setled themselves in the posture of a *Free-State*'. It ends with a long list of the names of real Ladies who can allegedly be found 'upon the *New Exchange* about 6. a clock at night', identifying them all as prostitutes: 'These, and many more you may buy' (Neville, 1–2, 20–21).

Anyone who bought Neville's text also bought a list of women who could be bought. The equation of the com-modified text with commodified women was even more evident when the females for sale are named or displayed on the title-page. The combination of royalist satire, miso-gyny, and prominent lists of female names is intertwined with the development of a 'porno-political rhetoric' that troped resistance to monarchy as a female sexual rebellion against moral, male, matrimonial restraint (Wiseman; Achinstein 1994b; Hughes; Turner, 74–117; Mowry). The Restoration could thus be equated with a return to heteronormativity, the rule of a hyper-heterosexual king over a submissive wife and kingdom, a patriarchal pattern England had not seen in more than a century.

But what was restored had been altered in the interim. Between 1640 and 1660 the textual culture of the public sphere had been, for the first time, pornographized, and the pornography remained after the Restoration, floating free of the political context that had originally legitimated it. The political absolutism of personal rule under Charles I

[57] *The Parliament of Ladies: with their lawes newly enacted* (dated by Thomason April 16, 1647); *An Exact Diurnall of the Parliament of Ladyes* (May 6); *The Parliament of Ladies... The second Edition* (May 18); *The Ladies Parliament* (July 15); *The Ladies, a second time, assembled in Parliament* (September 13). Most or all of these were written by Henry Neville. Those of May 6 and May 18 both include Moll; in the second, 'The Forces of the City under the command of *Moll Cutpurse*, and *Moll Sebran*, two very able Members, were appointed to guard the House, who being there placed with pipes in both their mouthes...' (14–15).
[58] *The Committee-Man Curried* (BEPD 630), A1ᵛ; *The Second Part* (BEPD 631), A2ᵛ; *The Levellers Levelled* (BEPD 635), A1ᵛ; *The Scottish Polytic Presbyter* (BEPD 636), A1ᵛ; *Crafty Cromwell* (BEPD 672), A1ᵛ; *2 Crafty Cromwell* (BEPD 673), A1ᵛ.
[59] *Mistris Parliament Brought to Bed* (April 29, 1648), *Mistris Parliament presented in her Bed* (May 10), and *Mistris Parliament her Gossipping* (May 22).

Perſons Names.

Timon *of Athens*	Mr. *Betterton.*
Alcibiades, *an Athenian Captain.*	Mr. *Smith.*
Apemantus, *a Rigid Philoſopher.*	Mr. *Harris.*
Nicias.	Mr. *Sandford.*
Phæax.	Mr. *Vnderhill.*
Ælius.	Mr. *Leigh.*
Cleon. ⎫	Mr. *Norris.*
Iſander. ⎬ Senators of Athens.	Mr. *Percival.*
Iſidore. ⎪	Mr. *Gillo.*
Thraſillus. ⎭	
Demetrius, Timons *Steward.*	Mr. *Medburne.*
Diphilus, *Servant to* Timon.	Mr. *Bowman.*
Old man.	Mr. *Richards.*
Poet.	Mr. *Jevon.*
Painter.	
Jeweller.	
Muſician.	
Merchant.	
Evandra.	Mrs. *Betterton.*
Meliſſa.	Mrs. *Shadwell.*
Chloe.	Mrs. *Gibbs.*
Thais. ⎫ *Miſtreſſes to* Alcibiades.	{Mrs. *Seymor.*
Phrinias. ⎭	{Mrs *Le-Grand.*
Servants.	
Meſſengers.	
Several Maſqueraders.	
Souldiers.	

Scene *Athens.*

45. Identification table in Shadwell's *Timon of Athens* (1678)

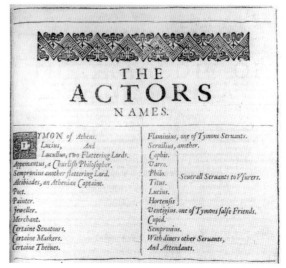

46. Identification table in Shakespeare and Middleton's *Timon of Athens* (1623)

gave way to the sexual absolutism of personal misrule under Charles II. The misogynist polemical playlets of the Interregnum mutated into pamphlets like *Strange Newes from Bartholomew-Fair, or, the wandring-whore discovered, her cabinet unlockt, her secrets laid open, vnvailed, and spread abroad* (1661). Although this title uses key phrases from the political discourse of the previous decades ('Strange Newes', 'cabinet unlocked'), the words have been transformed by a prurient interest in the display of female 'secrets' (genitals). Inside, the reader discovers the playlet format familiar from two decades of polemical pamphleteering: 'A Conference Betwixt the Wandring Whore, Bonny Besse of Whore and Bacon Lane, merry Moll of Duck street, and Pretty Peg of Py-corner' (sig. A2). But these women are not thinly-disguised allegories like 'Mrs. Leveller'. They are simply prostitutes, attached to lewd locations. The title-page of the fifth installment of this pornographic periodical 'dialogue' displays their names and generic attributes ('*Magdalena* a Crafty Bawd, | *Julietta* an Exquisite Whore'); it promises, inside, a longer '*Additional List of the names of the Crafty Bawds, Common Whores*', etc.[60]

By the 1660s the nature of women's inequality in textual culture had decisively changed: it was no longer based upon simple exclusion, upon invisibility, but upon the way their visible presence could be characterized. Women who entered textual culture—whether as actresses or playwrights—became public women; the commercial circulation of their texts among many consumers was figured as sexual promiscuity (King). This trope had been operating since at least the sixteenth century (Wall); but it became less and less effective in preventing women from active participation in textual culture. Like other characterizations, it could be contested, by men or women. Moreover, like other characterizations, it could be re-appropriated. At the very end of our Middleton century, Dryden's adaptation of Shakespeare's *Troilus and Cressida* (1679) is prefaced by a list of 'Persons Represented' which divides the social world of the play into three categories: Trojans, Greeks, and women (B4ᵛ).[61] Both women are Trojans, but they are separated from the male Trojans by nine Greek men, the enmity between the two nations being apparently less foundational than the distinction between male and female. This identification table, which prefaces the play, is itself prefaced by Dryden's essay on 'The Grounds of Criticism in Tragedy', which contrasts Shakespeare's '*more Masculine*' genius with Fletcher's, which was '*more soft and Womanish*'; accordingly, '*the more manly*' Shakespeare '*had an Universal mind, which*

---

60 *The Fifth and last Part of the Wandring whore: A Dialogue* (1661), Wing F888.
61 This division is not original or unique to Dryden: it occurs in the list of 'Actors Names' in Elkanah Settle's *The Conquest of China* (1676), which in descending order lists first 'Tartars', then 'Chineses', then 'Women', with the Chinese women divided from their men by the intervening Tartars. The same tripartite format is also used in Aphra Behn's *The Feign'd Curtizans* (1679): 'Italians', 'English', 'Women'.

The Perſons of the Play.

BRANDINO, *an old Juſtice.*
MARTINO, *his Clerk.*

FRANCISCO⎱
ATTILIO. ⎰ *2 Gentlemen.*

2 Old men Suters to the Widdow.
RICARDO, *A decayed young Gent. and Suter to the*
Widdow.

ANSALDO, MARTIA *diſguis'd.*

LATROCINIO⎫
OCCULTO, ⎪
SILVIO, ⎬ *Thieves.*
STRATIO, ⎪
FIDUCIO. ⎭

VALERIA, *The Widow.*
MARTIA, *Daughter to one of the old*
Suters and ſuppoſed a man.
PHILIPPA, *Juſtice* BRANDINO's *Wife.*
VIOLETTA, *her waiting Maid.*
Officers.
Servants.

47. Identification table in Middleton's *The Widow* (1652)

comprehended all Characters and Passions; Fletcher *a more confined, and limited*' (A3, B3ᵛ). The hierarchy among writers, which Jonson had characterized in terms of a fundamental opposition between the damned and 'the Faithfull', Dryden instead characterizes in terms of gender. Religious opinions, political alliances, forms of government might shift with the accidents of history; gender was essential.

That insistence upon the essentiality of gender could co-exist with more egalitarian views of the relationship between the categories 'men' and 'women'. Indeed, the second half of the seventeenth century, which inscribed gender division into identification tables, also produced a progressive and significant weakening of real male authority, in both theory and practice (Amussen, Staves). Thomas Shadwell's response to this shift was different from Dryden's. In the cast list of Shadwell's adaptation of Shakespeare and Middleton's *Timon of Athens* (1678), women are—by now predictably—divided from men (Illus. 45). But the printer or scribe who added a table at the end of the 1623 text had simply excluded women altogether (Illus. 46). Shadwell not only acknowledges the female prostitutes and masquers who appeared in the original play; he also adds two major women characters— Evadne and Melissa—whose presence radically transforms the narrative. Timon 'the man-hater' becomes a woman--lover; he is rejected not only by a whole group of men (as in the original play), but also by Melissa, the woman he loves; the ingratitude of others to him is matched by his own ingratitude to Evadne; Evadne takes over the role, and some of the speeches, of the male steward who remains faithful to Timon in the original play. Evadne is clearly the play's most admirable character, more admirable than Timon himself. Moreover, the relationship between men and women is represented, like all the play's other relationships, as a human contract between equals, not a divinely sanctioned subordination. Timon and Evadne (unlike Mr and Mrs Betterton) are not married; Timon fails to honour his contractual obligation to Evadne, just as he fails to pay his debts; but Evadne, unlike his male 'friends', does not desert him.

In the 1678 adaptation, women have become more visible, more active, and more generous than in the 1605 original. Of course, women are still not being treated as equals. In Evadne, true love is figured as a free offering, remarkable precisely to the extent that it exceeds a contractual obligation. Of such love, a good woman is capable; romantic generosity is a specifically gendered virtue. At the historical moment when marriage becomes, legally, a merely contractual relationship, women are still encouraged to give men far more than the contract calls for. Female virtue consists in the willing surrender of more than men can demand, legally—and more than men are willing to give in fulfillment of their own contractual obligation. Part of Evadne's appeal as a male image of an ideal female is that, not being his wife, she can make no legal demands of Timon, but she nevertheless gives him everything he could demand of a wife. Evadne is, as Melissa complains, a 'Whore' (Shadwell, 71); but as Alcibiades explains when he rejects Melissa, 'is not one | Kind, faithful, loving Whore, better than | A thousand base, ill-natur'd honest Women?' (83). Honest women are common ('a thousand'); a good whore is rare ('one'). Evadne is the perfect whore: a public woman in a contractual textual economy. Like the ubiquitously gendered identification tables of the second half of the seventeenth century, Shadwell's restructuring of *Timon* assumes and insists that the most important categories in the social world are heterosexual. For Shadwell and the audiences his adaptation pleased for more than a century, it seemed essential that Timon's philosophy— any philosophy—should be gendered.

Nevertheless, gender remained, within identification tables, only one category among many. In early modern textual culture it underwent, with the other categories I have described—labels, locations, and hierarchies—a fundamental shift in reference. Just as the very introduction of the new identification tables, at the beginning of the seventeenth century, implied that the reader should receive rather than re-create the text, so the form of these tables encouraged an increasingly passive relationship to the text. Lists of persons which, in the sixteenth century, had described the unlocalized gender-crossing sequential world

LONDON.	Bur.	Pla.
Margarets new Fishstreet--	123	82
Margarets Pattons ———	77	50
Mary Ab-church ———	98	58
Mary Aldermanbury ——	126	79
Mary Aldermary ———	92	54
Mary le Bow ———	35	19
Mary Bothaw ———	22	14
Mary Coal-church ——	36	11
Mary at the Hill——	152	84
Mary Mounthaw ——	76	58
Mary Sommerset ———	170	192
Mary Stainings ———	70	44
Mary Woolchurch ———	58	35
Mary Woolnoth ———	81	50
Martins Ironmonger-lane	25	18
Martins at Ludgate———	254	164
Martins Orgars ———	83	47
Martins Outwich ———	60	30
Martins in the Vintry———	339	208
Matthew Friday-street--	24	11
Maudlins in Milk-street-	401	23
Maudlins Old-fish-street-	225	142
Michael Bassishaw ——	199	139
Michael Corn-Hill ——	159	79

LONDON.	Bur.	Pla.
Michael Crooked-lane —	144	91
Michael Queen-hith ——	215	157
Michael in the Quern —	53	30
Michael in the Royal—	111	61
Michael in Wood-street--	189	68
Mildreds Bread-street —	60	44
Mildreds Poultrey ———	94	45
Nicholas Acons———	33	13
Nicholas Coal-Abby —	87	67
Nicholas Olaves ———	70	43
Olaves in Hart-street —	266	195
Olaves in the Jewry——	43	25
Olaves in Silver-street —	174	103
Pancras by Soper-lane—	17	8
Peters in Cheap——	68	44
Peters in Corn-hill ——	318	78
Peters at Pauls Wharf-—	97	68
Peters poor in Broadstreet-	52	27
Stevens in Coalmanstreet-	506	350
Stevens in Walbrook—	25	13
Swithins at London-stone-	99	60
Thomas Apostles ———	141	107
Trinity Parish———	148	87

Buried within the 97 Parishes within the Walls, of all Diseases, — 14340.
Where of, of the Plague,—— 9197.

	Bur.	Pla.		Bur.	Pla.
Andrews in Holborn —	2190	1636	Georges Southwark —	1608	912
Bartholmew the Great—	516	360	Giles Cripplegate———	3988	2338
Bartholmew the less —	111	65	Olaves in Southwark --	3689	2609
Brides Parish ———	1481	1031	Saviours in Southwark-	2746	1671
Botolph Algate ———	2573	1653	Sepulchres Parish ———	3425	2420
Bridewel Precinct———	213	152	Thomas in Southwark—	335	277
Botolph Bishopsgate ——	2334	714	Trinity in the Minories-	131	87
Botolphs Aldersgate—	578	307	At the Pest-house———	194	189
Dunstanes the West—	860	642			

Buried in the 16 Parishes without the Walls, standing part within the Liberties, and part without: in Middlesex, and Surrey, and at the Pest-house. ——— } 26972 2
Whereof, of the Plague,——— 17153

48. This demographic table from Graunt's *Natural and Political Observations* (1662) is based on information from parish registers, like those in Illus. 1

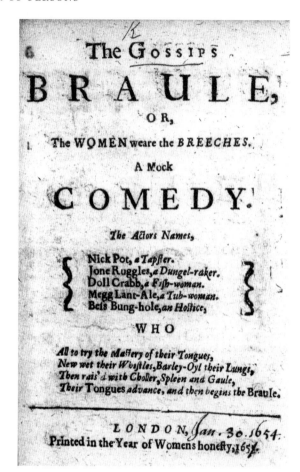

49. *The Gossips Braule* (1655) features characters of both sexes, so the title-page can gender its list of characters (with the man on top) and also identify each by occupational category

of the theatre had, by the end of the seventeenth century, come to refer, more and more systematically, to the grounded, gendered, hierarchical world outside the theatre, the world 'represented in the plays'. The new lists which prefaced plays represented fictional identities and an ordered social world which pre-existed the speeches and actions of the dramatic text, and therefore also pre-existed our own reading of it. Indeed, after the Restoration such tables often pre-existed a spectator's experience of a performed play, as texts were published to coincide with productions, and playgoers like Pepys took an edition with them to the theatre (Holland, 107-110). An audience's epistemological and emotional experience of a play is often shaped by the postponed revelation of personal names (Barton, 23-4); but such revelations are routinely pre-empted by the ubiquitous new tables. Plays often depend upon a concealed relationship or gender, but the new tables— *The Widow* being only one of many examples (Illus. 47)— anxiously rush to identify who these persons really are, and to specify that they are only 'supposed' to be men, or

women, or whatever. The philological return to the origin imagines, and writes, an originary world, which precedes the text which represents it.

Demography. Names, places, relationships and genders are facts in the lived world, and the new tables attempt to describe that world. As such, they belong to a much larger intellectual enterprise, an enterprise evident in the ambitious world-descriptions of Hooke and Newton and Locke, but also evident, most particularly perhaps, in the more mundane work of Sir William Petty and John Graunt, 'Citizen of London'. Graunt's *Natural and Political Observations ... made upon the Bills of Mortality*, published in 1662, initiated the statistical study of populations; in the same year, Petty published *A Treatise of Taxes & Contributions*, to be followed in 1676 by *Political Arithmetick*. In these first classics of demography, based to a large extent upon the lists of persons compiled by parish clerks or tax collectors, individuals were concep-

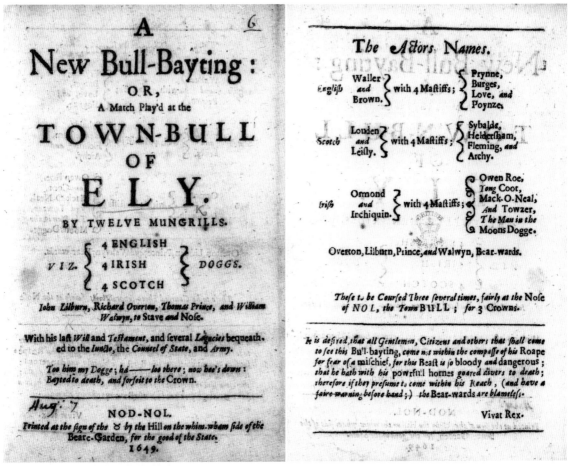

50-51. Both sides of the title-page of this 1649 pamphlet (only sixteen pages long) are dedicated
to displaying and explaining the division of its characters into distinct national groupings

tualized as so many fractions of a political and economic
whole whose behaviour was best understood—and manip-
ulated—mathematically (Illus. 48). As Graunt concluded,
it is 'necessary to know how many People there be of each
Sex, State, Age, Religion, Trade, Rank, or Degree, &c. by
the knowledge whereof, Trade and Government may be
made more certain and Regular' (II, 396).

These preoccupations are evident much earlier in identification tables. We have already examined their treatment
of 'Sex' and 'Rank, or Degree'. But 'Trade' was also
important. Occupations were identified as early as the
1540s, when the title-page of John Heywood's *Four PP*
promised 'A palmer. A pardoner. A potycary. A pedler.'
Beginning in 1605, with Marston's *Dutch Courtesan* and
Chapman's *All Fools* (1605), occupational labels were attached to names, but only for a few of the characters. The
1611 table for *The Roaring Girl* (Illus. 36) named twenty-
-four characters, but specified occupations for only four

(apothecary, sempster, feather-seller, sergeant). But such
labelling became more systematic in subsequent decades
(Illus. 49).

'State'—by which Graunt meant what we would call
nationality—had also been noted in much earlier lists of
persons. Tax-rolls, for instance, systematically identified
resident aliens (also called 'foreigners' or 'strangers');
so, sporadically, did some parish registers. The presence
of aliens in London was dramatized in the 1590s in
plays like *Sir Thomas More* and Dekker's *Shoemaker's
Holiday*, but neither contained an identification table;
but the title character of Marston's *Dutch Courtesan* is
a Dutch woman in London, and distinguished by her
nationality from all the other characters in the play's
printed identification table. Again, such labelling became
more systematic in subsequent decades. By 1649, every
character in a polemical playlet could be broken down
into competing national teams (Illus. 50-51).

Nationalities slide easily into ethnicities. In 1662 Graunt did not include race among his demographic categories, but even before his text was printed a committee of Britain's imperial bureaucracy had started dividing populations into numbers of 'Blacks' and 'Whites'.[62] That happened in London in January 1661. In May, in response to enquiries from that London committee, the President and Council of Barbados directed the compilation of a 'list in every Parish of all the white men and blacks therein'.[63] Middleton had anticipated this binary logic in 1624 when *A Game at Chess* divided the world into a Black House and a White House, but although the White House is clearly England its Black counterpart is Spanish and Italian, not African. The demographic category that bureaucrats in 1661 called 'Blacks' had appeared in English dramatic texts as early as the 1580s, but they were usually called 'Moors' (a religious category) or 'Blackamoors' (a mixed religious and colour category). The noun *black*, on its own, did not appear in a fictional identification table until 1675, when John Crowne's court masque *Calisto* specified 'Two African Women, or Blacks' (b4[v]). The racial sense of the word *white* had been used by Middleton as early as 1613 (*Triumphs of Truth* 408), but it did not show up in an identification table until 1767, when G. A. Steven's farce *The French Flogged* included an Indian King, an English Captain, an Irish Volunteer, two sailors named Ben and Ned, Three Frenchmen, a 'White Lady' and a 'Black Woman'. White is to 'Lady' as black is to lower-class 'woman'—and both are segregated below the men, of whatever nationality or ethnicity. The English had acquired a sense of their own racial whiteness between 1613 and 1661, but whereas such distinctions had to be made explicit in calculating colonial populations, they did not usually need to be spelled out in lists of fictional persons. Different lists obeyed different protocols and served different functions.

Nevertheless, the desire for something 'more certain and regular', articulated by Graunt in 1662, was not confined to demographers. It also shaped the fictional identification tables of the second half of the seventeenth century. The new convention—which would be uniformly imposed in editions of early modern plays until the late twentieth century, and is still dominant today—distributes a temporal flurry of disparate phenomena into ordered atemporal demographic categories. That cannot be said of the four early tables which seem closest to Middleton himself: *The Roaring Girl, Masque of Heroes, The World Tossed at Tennis,* and *A Chaste Maid in Cheapside.* Though they share certain features, each is unique, and it is im-

52. Identification table later added by hand to final page of *Macbeth* in a copy of the 1623 *Comedies, Histories, and Tragedies*

possible to construct from one a formula which would allow us to reconstruct all, or any, of the others. This makes editors of Middleton and his contemporaries uncomfortable. After all, anyone can divide a play into male and female characters, and then sequence those groups by hierarchical proximity; given these principles, any two people would come up with essentially the same table for any play. The new methods for table-making, like the new methods for science-making and chair-making, produce interchangeable reproducible results, results easy for any pair of hands, any scribe or stationer, editor or reader, to supply (Illus. 52).

That is what editors want: to make their results predictable and invisible, to remove the evidence of their own inevitable mediation between author and reader, to give readers the feeling that they are making direct contact with the moment of creation (Taylor 1996, 121–42). But that feeling is an illusion that encourages all kinds of baneful fundamentalisms. All texts are mediated. If editors want to provide tables that represent the relationships between persons in the way that Middleton represented them, then editors cannot provide—or accept—the kinds of uniform identity tables routinely added to plays after Middleton's death. To do so not only misrepresents the nature of editing and the nature of Middleton's representations of persons: it misrepresents the history of individual identities and social relationships. The identification tables in *The Collected Works of Thomas Middleton* are therefore as irregular and unpredictable as Middleton himself, or his characters, or his readers.

---

[62] British Library MS Egerton 2395, fol. 290 (minutes of a committee meeting of the Council of Foreign Plantations, 10 January 1661). The page is reproduced in Taylor 2005, p. 263.
[63] Public Record Office C.O. 31/1, fol. 50a (para. 5). For fuller discussion of the rise of racial demography, see Taylor 2005, 261–71.

WORKS CITED

BEPD: W. W. Greg, *A Bibliography of the English Printed Drama to the Restoration*, 4 vols (1939–59)

OED: *The Oxford English Dictionary Online* (March 2004)

Achinstein, Sharon, *Milton and the Revolutionary Reader* (1994a)

—— 'Women on Top in the Pamphlet Literature of the English Revolution', *Women's Studies* 24 (1994b), 131–63

—— ed., *Gender, Literature and the English Revolution* (1995)

Alpers, Svetlana, *The Art of Describing: Dutch Art in the Seventeenth Century* (1983)

Amussen, Susan Dwyer, *An Ordered Society: Gender and Class in Early Modern England* (1988)

Anderson, Benedict, *Imagined Communities: Reflections on the Origin and Spread of Nationalism* (1983)

Archer, Ian, *The Pursuit of Stability: Social Relations in Elizabethan London* (1991)

Ashton, Robert, *The City and the Court 1603–1643* (1979)

Baker, J. H., 'English law books and legal publishing', in Barnard, 474–503

Baldwin, T. W., *William Shakspere's Small Latine & Lesse Greeke*, 2 vols (1944)

Barnard, John, and D. F. McKenzie with Maureen Bell, eds., *The Cambridge History of the Book in Britain, Volume IV: 1557–1695* (2002)

Barton, Anne, *The Names of Comedy* (1990)

Beckerman, Bernard, 'The Persons Personated: Character Lists in English Renaissance Play Texts', in *Poetry and Drama in the English Renaissance: In Honour of Professor Jiro Ozu*, ed. Koshi Nakanori and Yasuo Tamaizumi (1980), 61–9

Bellany, Alastair, *The Politics of Court Scandal in Early Modern England: News Culture and the Overbury Affair, 1603–1660* (2001)

Bentley, G. E., *The Profession of Dramatist in Shakespeare's Time, 1590–1642* (1971)

Bentley, Jerry H., *Humanism and Holy Writ: New Testament Scholarship in the Renaissance* (1983)

Berger, Thomas, 'The Second Quarto of *Othello* and the Issue of Textual "Authority"', in *Critical Essays on Shakespeare's "Othello"*, ed. A. G. Barthelemy (1994), 144–61

Bevington, David M., *From 'Mankind' to Marlowe: Growth of Structure in the Popular Drama of Tudor England* (1962)

Binns, J. W., *Intellectual Culture in Elizabethan and Jacobean England: The Latin Writings of the Age* (1990)

Blayney, Peter W. M., 'The Publication of Playbooks', in Cox and Kastan, 383–422

Boulton, Jeremy, *Neighbourhood and Society: A London Suburb in the Seventeenth Century* (1987)

Bourdieu, Pierre, *Distinction: A Social Critique of the Judgement of Taste*, trans. Richard Nice (1984)

Bowers, Fredson, gen. ed., *The Dramatic Works in the Beaumont and Fletcher Canon*, 10 vols (1966–1996)

Bradley, David, *From text to performance in the Elizabethan theatre: Preparing the play for the stage* (1992)

Braudel, Fernand, *Civilization and Capitalism: 15th–18th Century*, trans. Siân Reynolds, Vol. I: *The Structures of Everyday Life: The Limits of the Possible* (1981)

Brenner, Robert, *Merchants and Revolution: Commercial Change, Political Conflict, and London's Overseas Traders, 1550–1653* (1993)

Brigden, Susan, *London and the Reformation* (1989)

Bristol, Michael, *Shakespeare's America, America's Shakespeare* (1990)

Brown, Horatio F., ed., *Calendar of State Papers and Manuscripts, Relating to English Affairs, existing in the archives and collections of Venice... Vol. X. 1603–1607* (1900)

Bruster, Douglas, *Drama and the Market in the Age of Shakespeare* (1992)

—— *Shakespeare and the Question of Culture: Early Modern Literature and the Cultural Turn* (2003)

Carson, Neil, *A Companion to Henslowe's Diary* (1988)

Chambers, E. K., *The Elizabethan Stage*, 4 vols (1923)

Chartier, Roger, ed., *The Culture of Print: Power and the Uses of Print in Early Modern Europe*, trans. Lydia G. Cochrane (1989)

—— 'The Practical Impact of Writing', in *A History of Private Life*, Vol. III: *Passions of the Renaissance*, ed. Roger Chartier, trans. Arthur Goldhammer (1989), 111–59

Cogswell, Thomas, *The Blessed Revolution: English politics and the coming of war, 1621–1624* (1989)

Cormack, Lesley B., *Charting an Empire: Geography at the English Universities, 1580–1620* (1997)

Cox, John D., and David Scott Kastan, eds., *A New History of Early English Drama* (1997)

Cressy, David, *Literacy and the Social Order: Reading and Writing in Tudor and Stuart England* (1980)

Cust, Richard, 'News and Politics in Early Seventeenth Century England', *Past and Present* 111 (1986), 60–90

Darnton, Robert, 'First Steps Toward a History of Reading' (1986), in *The Kiss of Lamourette: Reflections in Cultural History* (1990), 154–87

Dekker, Thomas, *The Gull's Horn Book* (1609), in *Thomas Dekker*, ed. E. D. Pendry (1967)

Dimock, Wai-Chee, 'Criminal Law, Female Virtue, and the Rise of Liberalism', *Yale Journal of Law and the Humanities* 4 (1992), 209–47

Dobson, Michael, and Nicola J. Watson, *England's Elizabeth: An Afterlife in Fame and Fantasy* (2003)

Durkheim, Emile, *The Division of Labor in Society*, trans. George Simpson (1964)

Dutton, Richard, 'The Birth of the Author', in *Elizabethan Theater: Essays in Honor of S. Schoenbaum*, ed. R. B. Parker and S. P. Zitner (1996), 71–92

Eccles, Mark, '"Thomas Middleton a Poett"', *Studies in Philology* 54 (1957), 516–36

Eisenstein, Elizabeth L., *The Printing Press as an Agent of Cultural Change: Communications and Cultural Transformations in Early Modern Europe* (1979)

Emerson, Ralph Waldo, 'Doctrine of the Hands', in *The Early Lectures of Ralph Waldo Emerson*, ed. Stephen E. Whicher, Robert E. Spiller, Wallace E. Williams, 3 vols (1959–72), II, 230–45

Engelsing, Rolf, *Der Bürger als Leser: Lesergeschichte in Deutschland 1500–1800* (1974)

Erne, Lukas, *Shakespeare as Literary Dramatist* (2003)

Farmer, Alan B., and Zachary Lesser, 'Vile Arts: The Marketing of English Printed Drama, 1512–1660', *Research Opportunities in Renaissance Drama* 39 (2000), 77–166

Fitzgeffrey, Henry, *Satyres: and Satyricall Epigrams* (1617)

Fletcher, Anthony, *Reform in the Provinces: The Government of Stuart England* (1986)

Foakes, R. A., ed., *Henslowe's Diary*, second edn. (2002)

Foucault, Michel, *The Order of Things* (1971)

—— 'What is an Author?', in *Language, Counter-Memory, Practice*, trans. Donald F. Bouchard and Sherry Simon (1977), 113–38

—— 'Nietzsche, Genealogy, History', in *The Foucault Reader*, ed. Paul Rabinow (1984), 76–100

Fox, Alistair, 'The Complaint of Poetry for the Death of Liberality: The Decline of Literary Patronage in the 1590s', in *The Reign* of Elizabeth I: Court and Culture in the Last Decade, ed. John Guy (1995), 229-57

Fraenkel, Gottfried S., Decorative Music Title Pages: 201 Examples from 1500 to 1800 (1968)

Frearson, Michael, 'The Distribution and Readership of London Corantos in the 1620s', in Robin Myers and Michael Harris, eds., Serials and their Readers (1993), 1-25

Goody, Jack, 'What's in a list?', in The Domestication of the Savage Mind (1977), 74-111

Grafton, Anthony, Joseph Scaliger: A Study in the History of Classical Scholarship, I: Textual Criticism and Exegesis (1983)

—— Defenders of the Text: The Traditions of Scholarship in an Age of Science, 1450-1800 (1991)

Grafton, Anthony, and Lisa Jardine, From Humanism to the Humanities: Education and the Liberal Arts in Fifteenth- and Sixteenth-Century Europe (1986)

Graunt, John, Natural and Political Observations (1662), in The Economic Writings of Sir William Petty, ed. Charles Henry Hull, 2 vols (1899)

Greenfield, Peter H., 'Touring', in Cox and Kastan, 251-68

Greetham, D. C., Textual Scholarship: An Introduction (1992)

Greg, W. W., Dramatic Documents from the Elizabethan Playhouses: Commentary (1931)

—— The Shakespeare First Folio: its bibliographical and textual history (1955)

Gurr, Andrew, Playgoing in Shakespeare's London (1987)

—— The Shakespearian Playing Companies (1996)

—— 'Maximal and Minimal Texts: Shakespeare v. The Globe', Shakespeare Survey 5 (1999)

Hall, David D., 'The Uses of Literacy in New England, 1600-1850', in Printing and Society in Early America, ed. William L. Joyce, David D. Hall, Richard D. Brown, and John B. Hench (1983), 1-47

Haller, William, The Elect Nation: The Meaning and Relevance of Foxe's Book of Martyrs (1963)

Harbage, Alfred, Annals of English Drama, 975-1700, rev. S. Schoenbaum (1964)

Hargreaves-Mawdsley, W. N., Oxford in the Age of John Locke (1973)

Helgerson, Richard, Forms of Nationhood: The Elizabethan Writing of England (1992)

Heywood, Thomas, The Hierarchie of the Blessed Angels. Their Names, Orders and Offices (1635)

Holland, Peter, The Ornament of Action: Text and Performance in Restoration Comedy (1979)

Honigmann, E. A. J., The Texts of 'Othello' and Shakespearian Revision (1996)

Hope, Valerie, Clive Birch, and Gilbert Torry, The Freedom: The Past and Present of the Livery, Guilds and City of London (1982)

Howes, Edmund, The Annales, or Generall Chronicle of England, Begun First by Maister Iohn Stow, and After Him Continued and Augmented with Matters Forreyne, and Domestique, Anncient and Moderne, vnto the Ende of This Present Yeere, 1614 (1615)

Hughes, Ann, 'Gender and Politics in Leveller Literature', Political Culture and Cultural Politics in Early Modern England: Essays Presented to David Underdown, ed. Susan Amussen and Mark Kishlansky (1995), 162-88

Hunt, Arnold, 'Book trade patents, 1603-1640', in The Book Trade and its Customers, 1450-1900, ed. Arnold Hunt, Giles Mandelbrote and Alison Shell (1997), 27-54

Hutson, Lorna, Thomas Nashe in Context (1989)

Ingram, William, The Business of Playing: The Beginnings of the Adult Professional Theater in Elizabethan London (1992)

Jardine, Lisa, Erasmus, Man of Letters (1993)

Johns, Adrian, The Nature of the Book: Print and Knowledge in the Making (1998)

Jonson, Ben, Ben Jonson, ed. C. H. Herford, Percy and Evelyn Simpson, 11 vols (1925-52)

Jurkowski, M., C. L. Smith, and D. Crook, Lay Taxes in England and Wales 1188-1688 (1998)

Kathman, David, 'Grocers, Goldsmiths, and Drapers: Freemen and Apprentices in the Elizabethan Theater', Shakespeare Quarterly 55 (2004), 1-49

Kenney, E. J., The Classical Text: Aspects of Editing in the Age of the Printed Book (1974)

King, Thomas A., '"As if [she] were made on purpose to put the whole world into good Humour": Reconstructing the First English Actresses', Drama Review T135 (1992), 78-102

Knight, Frank H., Risk, Uncertainty and Profit (1965)

Krummel, D. W., English Music Printing 1553-1700 (1975)

Laclau, Ernesto, and Chantal Mouffe, Hegemony and Socialist Strategy: Towards a Radical Democratic Politics, tr. Winston Moore and Paul Cammack (1985)

Laslett, Peter, 'The gentry of Kent in 1640', Cambridge Historical Journal 9 (1947-9), 148-64

Laplace, Pierre Simon, Marquis de, A Philosophical Essay on Probabilities (1812), tr. F. W. Truscott and F. L. Emory (1952)

Levy, F. J., 'How Information Spread among the Gentry, 1550-1640', Journal of British Studies 21 (1982), 11-34

—— 'The Decorum of News', in Joad Raymond, ed., News, Newspapers, and Society in Early Modern Britain (2002), 12-38

Lindley, David, The Trials of Frances Howard: Fact and Fiction at the Court of King James (1993)

Lodge, Edmund, Illustrations of British History, 3 vols (1791)

Loewenstein, Joseph, The Author's Due: Printing and the Prehistory of Copyright (2002a)

—— Jonson and Possessive Authorship (2002b)

Love, Harold, Scribal Publication in Seventeenth-Century England (1993)

Manley, Lawrence, Literature and Culture in Early Modern London (1995)

Marx, Karl, Capital, trans. Samuel Moore and Edward Aveling, 2 vols (1967)

—— and Friedrich Engels, The Communist Manifesto (1848), ed. Frederic L. Bender (1988)

Masten, Jeffrey A., 'Beaumont and/or Fletcher: collaboration and the interpretation of Renaissance drama,' ELH 59 (1992), 337-56

McKenzie, D. F., 'The London Book Trade in the Later Seventeenth Century', unpublished typescript of the Sandars Lectures for 1975-76 (distributed privately, 1976; copies deposited in British Library, the English Faculty Library at Oxford University, and the University Library, Cambridge)

—— Bibliography and the Sociology of Texts (1986; reprinted 1999)

—— 'Printing and publishing 1557-1700: constraints on the London book trades', in Barnard (2002), 555-67

McMillin, Scott, and Sally-Beth MacLean, The Queen's Men and their Plays (1998)

McRae, Andrew, Literature, Satire and the Early Stuart State (2004)

Meres, Francis, Palladis Tamia. Wits Treasury (1598)

Metzger, Bruce, The Text of the New Testament: Its Transmission, Corruption, and Restoration, second edn. (1968)

More, Thomas, The confutacyon of Tyndales answere (1532), ed. Louis A. Schuster, Richard C. Marius, James P. Lusardi, and Richard J. Schoeck, in The Yale Edition of the Complete Works of St. Thomas More, Vol. 8 (1973)

Morley, Thomas, Plaine and Easie Introduction to Practicall Musicke (1597)

Mowry, Melissa M., *The Bawdy Politic in Stuart England, 1660–1714: Political Pornography and Prostitution* (2004)

Muldrew, Craig, *The Economy of Obligation: The Culture of Credit and Social Relations in Early Modern England* (1998)

Murphy, Andrew, *Shakespeare in Print: A History and Chronology of Shakespeare Publishing* (2003)

Murphy, John L., *Darkness and Devils: Exorcism and 'King Lear'* (1984)

Murray, Timothy, *Theatrical Legitimation: Allegories of Genius in Seventeenth-Century England and France* (1987)

Neville, Henry, *Newes from the New Exchange, or The Commonwealth of ladies* (1650)

Nietzsche, F. W., *The Wanderer* (1880), in *Complete Works* (1974)

Orlin, Lena Cowen, ed., *Material London, ca. 1600* (2000)

Parrot, Henry, *The Mastive, Or Young-Whelpe of the Old-Dogge. Epigrams and Satyrs* (1615)

Parry, Graham, 'Patronage and the printing of learned works for the author', in Barnard, 174–88

Patton, Brian, 'The Women Are Revolting? Women's Activism and Popular Satire in the English Revolution', *Journal of Medieval and Renaissance Studies* 23 (1993), 69–87

Peck, Linda Levy, *Court Patronage and Corruption in Early Stuart England* (1990)

Petti, Anthony G., *English Literary Hands from Chaucer to Dryden* (1977)

Plant, Marjorie, *The English Book Trade* (1965)

Price, Hereward T., 'Grammar and the Compositor in the Sixteenth and Seventeenth Centuries', *Journal of English and Germanic Philology* 38 (1939), 540–8

Rappaport, Steve, *Worlds Within Worlds: Structures of Life in Sixteenth Century London* (1989)

Raumer, Frederick von, *History of the Sixteenth and Seventeenth Centuries, Illustrated by Original Documents*, 2 vols (1835)

Reed, Henry, 'Naming of Parts', in *Collected Poems*, ed. Jon Stallworthy (1991)

Reynolds, L. D., and N. G. Wilson, *Scribes and Scholars: A Guide to the Transmission of Greek and Latin Literature*, second edn. (1974)

Saeger, James P., and Christopher J. Fassler, 'The London Professional Theater, 1576–1642: A Catalogue and Analysis of the Extant Printed Plays', *Research Opportunities in Renaissance Drama* 34 (1995), 63–109

Schoenbaum, S., *William Shakespeare: Records and Images* (1981)

Seaver, Paul S., *The Puritan Lectureships: The Politics of Religious Dissent 1560–1662* (1970)

Shadwell, Thomas, *The History of Timon of Athens, The Man-Hater* (1678)

Sharpe, Kevin, *Sir Robert Cotton 1586–1631: history and politics in early modern England* (1979)

—— 'Crown, Parliament and Locality: Government and Communication in Early Stuart England', *English Historical Review* 101 (1986), 321–50

Staves, Susan, *Players' Scepters: Fictions of Authority in the Restoration* (1979)

Stern, Tiffany, '"On each Wall and Corner Poast": Playbills, Title-pages, and Advertising in Early Modern London', *English Literary Renaissance* 36 (2006), 57–89

Stimson, Dorothy, *The Gradual Acceptance of the Copernican Theory of the Universe* (1917)

Stone, Lawrence, *An open elite?: England, 1540–1880* (1984)

Taylor, Gary, *Reinventing Shakespeare: A Cultural History from the Restoration to the Present* (1989)

—— 'The date and auspices of the additions to *Sir Thomas More*', in *Shakespeare and "Sir Thomas More": Essays on the play and its Shakespearian interest*, ed. T. H. Howard-Hill (1989), 101–30

—— 'The Renaissance and the End of Editing', *Palimpsest: Editorial Theory in the Humanities*, ed. George Bornstein and Ralph G. Williams (1993), 121–49

—— 'Bardicide', *Shakespeare and Cultural Traditions*, ed. Roger Pringle *et al.* (1994a), 333–49

—— 'Farrago', *Textual Practice* 8 (1994b), 33–42

—— 'The Rhetorics of Reaction', in *Crisis in Editing: Texts of the English Renaissance*, ed. Randall McLeod (1994c), 19–41

—— *Cultural Selection* (1996)

—— 'Thomas Middleton, Thomas Dekker, and *The Bloody Banquet*', *Papers of the Bibliographical Society of America* 94 (2000), 197–233

—— 'Divine [ ]sences', *Shakespeare Survey* 54 (2001), 13–30

—— 'Shakespeare's Mediterranean *Measure for Measure*', in *Shakespeare and the Mediterranean: The Selected Proceedings of the International Shakespeare Association World Congress, Valencia, 2001*, ed. Tom Clayton, Susan Brock, and Vicente Forés (2004), 243–69

—— *Buying Whiteness: Race, Skin, Slavery from the European Renaissance to African-American Literature* (2005)

—— *Time, Space, Race: A Short Geography and History of Atlantic Racism* (forthcoming)

Taylor, Gary, and John Jowett, *Shakespeare Reshaped 1606–1623* (1993)

Taylor, Gary, Paul Mulholland, and MacDonald P. Jackson, 'Thomas Middleton, Lording Barry, and *The Family of Love*', *Papers of the Bibliographical Society of America* 93 (1999), 213–41

Taylor, John, *The Praise of Hemp-Seed* (1620)

Thirsk, Joan, *Economic Policy and Projects: The Development of a Consumer Society in Early Modern England* (1978)

Tillyard, E. M. W., *The Elizabethan World Picture* (1945)

Turner, James Grantham, *Libertines and Radicals in Early Modern London: Sexuality, Politics, and Literary Culture, 1630–1685* (2002)

Vickers, Brian, *Shakespeare, Co-Author: A Historical Study of Five Collaborative Plays* (2002)

Wall, Wendy, *The Imprint of Gender* (1993)

Watt, Tessa, *Cheap Print and Popular Piety, 1550–1640* (1991)

Weimann, Robert, *Shakespeare and the Popular Tradition in the Theater*, ed. Robert Schwartz (1978)

Wells, Stanley, and Gary Taylor, with John Jowett and William Montgomery, *William Shakespeare: A Textual Companion* (1987)

Williams, Raymond, *Marxism and Form* (1977)

Willson, D. Harris, *King James VI and I* (1956)

Wilson, F. P., 'Ralph Crane, Scrivener to the King's Players', *The Library*, IV, 7 (1926), 194–215

Wiseman, Sue, '"Adam, the Father of All Flesh": Porno-Political Rhetoric and Political Theory in and after the English Civil War', in *Pamphlet Wars: Prose in the English Revolution*, ed. James Holstun (1992), 134–57

Woudhuysen, H. R., *Sir Philip Sidney and the Circulation of Manuscripts, 1558–1640* (1996)

Wrightson, Keith, *English Society 1580–1680* (1982)

Würzbach, Natascha, *The Rise of the English Street Ballad, 1550–1650*, trans. Gayna Walls (1990)

EARLY MODERN AUTHORSHIP:
CANONS AND CHRONOLOGIES

MacDonald P. Jackson

I

'Those who study plays want to know who wrote them.' The statement with which in 1966 S. Schoenbaum began his survey of investigations of the authorship of Elizabethan, Jacobean, and Caroline drama (xv) remains true long after literary theorists first announced the 'death of the author'. Indeed, reports of this demise, as of Mark Twain's, were 'an exaggeration'.[1] There is a sense, obviously, in which a play is the expression of a *Zeitgeist*, a recipient of the current ideologies, a fabrication of the available language, a product of intertextual transactions. Postmodernist theory has increased our awareness of those elements that, entering a text beyond the author's conscious control, become symptomatic of its time and place. But as well as a 'tradition' that encompasses everything from theatre practice to the prevailing cosmology there is the 'individual talent'. Middleton's plays result from the workings of his own creative imagination within a social, literary, and philosophical milieu. They bear the stamp of his distinctive genius.

Writing about *The Revenger's Tragedy* in the *Cambridge Companion to English Renaissance Drama*, Robert N. Watson claims that both traditional literary historians and 'their theoretical antagonists' may legitimately agree that the play 'cannot be safely attributed to any single author'. Traditionalists, he argues, find insufficient evidence to ascribe it either to Tourneur or to Middleton (or to Marston). 'Theoreticians increasingly advocate a new model in which the attribution of any play to any person is misleading, either because plays were not proprietary to their authors in the Renaissance, or because the entire concept of authorship is a sentimental modern fiction disguising the fact that authors (like other individuals) are not really autonomous agents, but products of their cultures' (329–30). *The Revenger's Tragedy*, he points out, is indebted to the literary and dramatic traditions, and expresses the obsessions, of its age.

Watson's remarks themselves betray their specific cultural origins. They could not have been written in the palmy days of attribution studies, when scholars such as H. Dugdale Sykes and E. H. C. Oliphant were busily finding parental homes for the waifs and strays of Elizabethan and Jacobean drama. But Watson's lively chapter, though of its time, is also his. He deserves the credit for it. It belongs to his CV. Qualms about his not being an 'autonomous agent' would be misplaced. Had it been written by somebody else, it would be different, in style

and substance. Renaissance writers were real people too. Middleton earned his living by his writing. It is true that when he handed over his script of *The Chester Tragedy*, let us say, to theatre entrepreneur Philip Henslowe, he retained no authorial copyright, but on 21 October 1602 he received four pounds in exchange and on 9 November a further two pounds (Foakes and Rickert, 205–6). Middleton, whatever he owed to his culture, was the person paid. Henslowe, confronted with the insistent demands of his ever-needy team of playwrights, may often have wished that 'the concept of authorship' could be dismissed as 'a sentimental fiction', but the writers had mouths to feed and came to him with saleable property. And however much *The Revenger's Tragedy* is a product of its period, it either was or was not conceived in Middleton's brain, first penned by him, and sold by him to some theatrical company. Somebody mixed the culturally derived ingredients into the play's new and individual blend.

But does it matter who was, in this sense, its author? I think that it does—that, while the facts of literary history are not always fully ascertainable, we have an obligation to get them as right as we can; that the reasons for assigning *The Revenger's Tragedy* to Middleton are overwhelmingly strong; that the traditional ascription to Tourneur has led critics to misrepresent the play's nature; that it gains in interest from being placed within the Middleton canon; and that Middleton's own insouciance about his reputation with posterity ought not to prevent us, as historians of drama and literature, from examining the evolution of his art, evaluating his achievement, and recognizing his greatness. Commenting on Shakespeare, T. S. Eliot held 'that the full meaning of any one of his plays is not in itself alone, but in that play in the order in which it was written, in its relation to all of Shakespeare's other plays, earlier and later' (136). We may not want to go so far as that—with regard either to Middleton or to Shakespeare—but the sense we receive of 'one significant, consistent, and developing personality' (150) behind the diverse works associated with a major, or even minor, author's name remains an important part of our experience of literature and drama. Which is why there is still a demand for writers' 'collected works'. And, as Schoenbaum went on to remark apropos of wanting

---

[1] Recent discussions of the concept of 'authorship' are too numerous to specify. Sane guidance is provided by Seán Burke, *The Death and Return of the Author* and *Authorship: From Plato to the Postmodern: A Reader*. See also Brian Vickers, *Appropriating Shakespeare*, 101–15.

to know who wrote things, 'The editor needs to decide which works to include in his edition' (xv).

II

During the last few decades the body of literature in English that is deemed worthy of academic study has undergone considerable modification. The security of Shakespeare's place within this changing canon is in part due to there being such a clearly defined 'Shakespeare canon'—a substantial and coherent body of work that we know to be his. Had not his fellow actor–shareholders in the King's Company, John Heminges and Henry Condell, gathered his plays for publication in the First Folio of 1623, seven years after his death, the situation would have been very different. Eighteen of his plays—about half the total—would be unknown to us, including such masterpieces as *Julius Caesar*, *As You Like It*, *Twelfth Night*, *Measure for Measure*, *Macbeth*, *Anthony and Cleopatra*, *Coriolanus*, *The Winter's Tale*, and *The Tempest*. *Henry V* and *The Merry Wives of Windsor* would exist only in corrupt, abbreviated texts, barely recognizable as Shakespearean. Moreover, since the 1600 'bad quarto' of *Henry V* fails to attribute it to Shakespeare, the only item of 'external evidence' for his authorship would be the Epilogue's promise of a sequel to *2 Henry IV*. The manner in which the anonymous *The First Part of the Contention* (1594) and *Richard Duke of York* (1595)—now commonly held to be memorially reconstructed texts of the Folio's *2* and *3 Henry VI*—are connected with Shakespeare would be altogether mysterious. The Folio is crucial to our sense of Shakespeare's achievement. Modern editors accept its definition of his dramatic canon with only minor additions (Taylor 1987). Also, it is widely acknowledged that at least one or two of the plays in the Folio (and in subsequent editions of *The Complete Works*) are collaborative, containing material by dramatists other than Shakespeare. But these adjustments to the Folio's canon have little effect on our sense of 'Shakespeare'.

Heminges and Condell collected Shakespeare's plays in order 'to keep the memory of so worthy a friend and fellow alive', and succeeded beyond all expectation. They may never have undertaken the venture had it not been for the precedent set by Ben Jonson, who fashioned his own memorial with his famous *Works* of 1616. The Jonson Folio was an altogether more self-consciously ambitious volume than the Shakespeare, and there were jibes at the author's pretensions. With meticulous attention to the details of typography and layout and to the selection and ordering of texts, Jonson presented his plays, poems, and masques, to a reading rather than theatre-going public, as the authorized *opera* of an instant classic. In his treatment of speech prefixes and stage directions he imitated classical Latin literature, associating his texts with venerable conventions while perpetuating them through the technology of print. Omitting all his apprentice work and collaborations (including several for Henslowe in the period 1597–1602), suppressing from *Sejanus* all trace of his original

co-author, and thoroughly revising such plays as *Every Man in His Humour*, he projected the image of himself as writer by which he wished to be remembered—independent and in control. He supervised the volume's progress through the printing-house. Jonson constructed a cultural icon. His *Works* bore witness to his individual genius. The volume was designed as the physical monument of a solid authorial persona (Brady and Herendeen; Butler; Dutton 61–9).

The third great Folio collection of Renaissance drama provides a striking contrast. This, published in 1647 by Humphrey Moseley, purported to contain the comedies and tragedies of Francis Beaumont and John Fletcher. There were thirty-five dramatic pieces, including one masque. A Second Folio of 1679 added another eighteen plays. Moseley's Folio, unlike the Shakespeare and Jonson folios, was a purely commercial venture; moreover, the plays were mustered under the aegis not of a single author but of 'Beaumont and Fletcher'. In fact—if for the sake of argument we accept the findings of the latest and most careful investigator—Fletcher wrote on his own fifteen of the Second Folio's fifty-two plays and he had a share in all but three of the remainder, but only nine result from his straightforward dual partnership with Beaumont, who wrote or participated in no more than five others (Hoy). The masque was also Beaumont's. This Folio is essentially a witness to the copious industry of Fletcher, alone and as co-author, not just with Beaumont but, slightly more often, with Massinger, and also (sometimes unwittingly, as provider of a text later revised) with Field, Shirley, Rowley, Webster, Shakespeare, and Ford. Several plays are by three or four hands.

In the second half of the seventeenth century, after the Restoration, Shakespeare, Jonson, and Fletcher (to whom Beaumont's name was sometimes conjoined) were the English Renaissance dramatists to be admired and discussed. For Dryden, in his 'Of Dramatic Poesy: An Essay' (1668) and elsewhere, these are 'the big three' (or 'four') among his predecessors, the most worthy of his critical attention. Dryden weighs the comparative strengths and weaknesses of Shakespeare and Fletcher or of Shakespeare and Jonson. About Middleton he has nothing to say. Middleton's corpus of plays, poems, entertainments, and pamphlets was dispersed over sundry quartos, octavos, and manuscripts of widely varying dates. Uncollected, Middleton disappeared from view, 'untalked of and unseen'.

It was not till 1840 that Alexander Dyce conferred some kind of corporate identity on Middleton's writings with the publication of *The Works*. A. H. Bullen's reprint of 1885–6 made Dyce's canon more readily available, but added almost nothing in the way of new scholarship; its most significant alteration was to omit both parts of *The Honest Whore*, whereas Dyce had included both. Bullen omitted them, simply on the grounds that both had recently been included in his edition of Dekker. Bullen's edition—the form in which most readers encountered Middleton's *œuvre* for more than a century—was a defective reprint of Dyce. But even the canon defined by Dyce was seriously misleading, excluding some of Middleton's finest plays, besides other writings of considerable interest, and including items for which Middleton was not responsible. Dyce omitted some works—*The Two Gates of Salvation*, for instance, and *Honourable Entertainments*—simply because he did not know of their existence. Otherwise, he basically collected anything that had ever been attributed to Middleton in the early modern period. He paid no attention to internal evidence. He did not recognize, in practice, the prevalence in Middleton's time of anonymous publication. The principles adopted by Dyce, and followed by Bullen, would, if applied to Shakespeare, admit to the canon the various apocrypha printed in the Third Folio of 1664, while excluding 'Hand D's' contribution to *Sir Thomas More*. The inadequacies of Dyce's intellectual procedures, and of Bullen's careless reprint, distorted the Middleton canon. Readers, historians, and theatre practitioners interested in Middleton need a better definition of his corpus.

III

How, then, are decisions about what rightly belongs in a *Collected Works of Thomas Middleton* to be made? The evidence for particular inclusions and exclusions in the Oxford edition is described in detail, elsewhere in this volume, in 'Works Included in this Edition: Canon and Chronology' (p. 335). My aim here is not to repeat that information, but to provide an overview of the issues raised, and of the different categories of evidence deployed, in any attempt to establish the canon of an early modern author.

Renaissance autograph manuscripts are rare; printed texts were often published anonymously; when title-pages do make ascriptions they cannot always be trusted; other sources of information—such as the Stationers' Register, Henslowe's Diary, official documents, booksellers' catalogues, and the recorded statements of a playwright's contemporaries—may have nothing pertinent to offer on a given case and are of variable worth; the collaborative preparation of new playscripts and the refurbishing of old ones were features of the Jacobean entertainment industry that complicate any attempt to identify authorial provenance.

Works that have been associated with Middleton differ enormously in the quality of the external evidence for regarding them as his. At one extreme, the authorship of *A Game at Chess* is better attested than that of any other English play of the period. It is preserved in a manuscript wholly in Middleton's own handwriting (including his 'by T.M' on the title-page), in two manuscripts with autograph title-pages displaying the formula 'by Tho: Middleton', and in a manuscript containing dedicatory verses written out and signed 'T.M.' by Middleton himself, as well as in other early manuscripts and quartos. *A Game at Chess* was licensed by Sir Henry Herbert on 12 June 1624 as 'written by Middleton'. Moreover, Middleton's responsibility for this bold anti-Catholic and anti-Spanish

allegory apparently earned him a term in jail: on 18 August 1624 a warrant directed him to appear before the Privy Council, and Middleton, having failed to do so, is mentioned as the 'poet' of the offending theatrical piece in several further State Papers (Howard-Hill, 1–33, 192–213). At the other extreme, for some of the works admitted to the new Oxford *Collected Works* there is no external evidence whatsoever that links them to Middleton. When such evidence does exist, it can seldom be taken on trust, but requires careful assessment.

In such circumstances, resort to the 'internal evidence' of stylistic and sub-stylistic features of the texts themselves is absolutely necessary. But of course this kind of investigation would be impossible did not external evidence establish a core of undoubtedly, or almost undoubtedly, Middletonian writings to serve as basis for the detection of the writer's distinguishing peculiarities. Fortunately, there has been general agreement that at least a dozen plays are of Middleton's unaided authorship, and these span almost the full chronological range of his playwriting career. Admittedly, some of the attributions, on printed title-pages or in catalogues, are quite late, made after Middleton's death in 1627, but scholars have accepted their accuracy because of the clear internal connections among all twelve plays.

I have already mentioned *A Game at Chess*. The first quarto of *Your Five Gallants* (undated, but perhaps 1608) and the second edition of *A Trick to Catch the Old One* (1616) each carry title-page ascriptions to 'T. Middleton'; in the latter case the name expands on the 'T.M.' of the second issue of the first quarto (1608), and these same initials also appear on the title-page of *A Mad World, My Masters* (1608). The precise formula 'Composed by T.M.' (to modernize the spelling) links *A Trick to Catch the Old One* and *A Mad World, My Masters* to the autograph title-page of the Rosenbach Manuscript of *A Game at Chess*, where it recurs. Ralph Crane's scribal transcript of *The Witch* names 'Tho. Middleton' on the title-page and below the author's dedicatory epistle. After Middleton's death, the quarto of *A Chaste Maid in Cheapside* (1630) assigns the comedy to 'Thomas Midelton Gent.' Then on 9 September 1653 Humphrey Moseley entered in the Stationers' Register *More Dissemblers Besides Women, Women, Beware Women*, and *No Wit/Help like a Woman's* as by 'Mr. Tho. Midleton', before eventually publishing all three under the same authorial name in octavos of 1657. Finally, *Hengist, King of Kent; or The Mayor of Quinborough* was entered on the Stationers' Register for 13 February 1661 as 'By Tho: Middleton', and published as his later that year.

Claims made in booksellers' catalogues are intrinsically far less dependable (Greg, 1938–45). *Michaelmas Term* was first attributed to Middleton by Edward Archer in a playlist appended to *Old Law* in 1656; despite Archer's notorious unreliability, that attribution has passed unquestioned, because the anonymous 1607 edition associates the play with the Children of Paul's, for whom several of Middleton's early city comedies were written, and because it is so like them in every detail of its matter and manner. Francis Kirkman's ascription to Middleton of *The Phoenix* in a playlist of 1661 has been accepted for the same reason: this satirical comedy had also been published in 1607 as acted by the Children of Paul's, and it too hits at familiar Middleton targets.

Although the quality of the external evidence for Middleton's authorship even of these twelve plays is variable, the complete consistency of the internal features linking them to one another and differentiating them from other dramatists' plays has ensured their all-but-universal acceptance as wholly his. More doubtful attributions must be assessed in their light. The same rule applies to attempts to apportion shares in collaborations in which Middleton is known or suspected to have taken part.

IV

Schoenbaum's comprehensive and amusing history of attribution studies in English Renaissance drama has served as a cautionary tale to later practitioners. But his mocking scepticism undervalues the achievements of nineteenth- and early twentieth-century scholars such as Fleay, Boyle, Sykes and, above all, Oliphant. Their methods were faulty, their arguments often little more than rationalizations of personal impressions, but the metrical data that they amassed is still of value and their reading in Elizabethan and Jacobean drama was wide and deep; Oliphant in particular read with rare sensitivity to the finer details of verse movement and verbal texture. From 1890 to 1930 Oliphant was unmatched in his appreciation of Middleton's stature as a dramatist, and his ability to detect his hero's hand was almost infallible. It was he who first proposed Middleton as likely author of *The Revenger's Tragedy*, *The Lady's Tragedy*, and *A Yorkshire Tragedy*, and as part-author of *The Bloody Banquet*, and who realized that *Blurt, Master Constable* was not Middleton's but Dekker's; Oliphant's pronouncements on other disputed and collaborative plays associated with Middleton have largely been vindicated by later studies. It was to Sykes's intuition that we owe the recognition that Webster shared with Middleton the writing of *Anything for a Quiet Life* and that *The Spanish Gypsy* is largely the work of John Ford (an ascription supplemented by Oliphant's subsequent realization that Ford had been partnered by Dekker). Sykes's support of the theory that Middleton contributed to *Timon of Athens* also turns out to have been well judged. Oliphant, Sykes, their contemporaries, and their predecessors identified the main canonical problems to be solved in Renaissance drama, and their books and articles are fertile sources of hypotheses to be tested by more objective criteria.

A huge advance in attribution studies in Renaissance drama was made by Cyrus Hoy in his uncovering of diverse 'linguistic patterns' among participants in the 'Beaumont and Fletcher' plays (1956–1962). The techniques had been used by a scattering of earlier scholars, but Hoy applied them with innovative thoroughness. Through meticulous counting of predetermined minutiae

in the earliest printed texts, Hoy demonstrated that the Jacobean playwrights differed from one another in their habits with respect to certain word forms and colloquial contractions. For instance, in his unassisted plays Fletcher strongly preferred *ye*, *'em*, and *has*, to *you*, *them*, and *hath*, and regularly employed such contractions as *i'th'*, *o'th'*, *'has*, and *'s* for *his*. Massinger avoided *ye*, used *'em* less frequently than Fletcher, made liberal use of *hath*, and employed *i'th'* and *'s* seldom, *'has* only once, and *o'th'* never. Fletcher's fourteen plays contain no fewer than 4,507 examples of *ye*, whereas Massinger's fifteen contain only two. So in plays in which the two men collaborated their shares can readily be distinguished. The number of such alternatives possible in the Jacobean period—*does* or *doth*, *I'm* or *I am*, *e'en* or *even*, *ha'* or *have*, *'a* or *he*, *on't* or *of it*, and so on—is very large, so that while any two dramatists will have some preferences in common, most display a distinctive overall pattern.

For the purposes of identification such trivial details are more useful than elements of greater literary import, for they are too inconsequential to encourage imitation and they are relatively unaffected by shifts in genre and stylistic register. Naturally they are subject to alteration by compositors and, more damagingly, scribes. The scribe Ralph Crane demonstrably overrode some of Middleton's habitual preferences, in his transcripts of *The Witch* and *A Game at Chess*, just as he overrode some of Shakespeare's preferences in *The Tempest* and other First Folio plays. Likewise, the 1639 quarto of *The Bloody Banquet* seems to have been set from a manuscript prepared by the same scribe who prepared copy for the 1639 quarto of Robert Davenport's *A New Trick to Cheat the Devil*, and who in both cases imposed some of his own habits (Taylor 2000).

But more often, a detailed investigation of the scribes and compositors who transmitted a play only demonstrates the reliability of the internal evidence. Thus, a knowledge of the stints and habits of First Folio compositors confirms that they cannot be held responsible for the evidence that Shakespeare collaborated with other authors in writing *Henry the Sixth, Part One* (Taylor 1995); likewise, the evidence for posthumous adaptation of *Measure for Measure* cannot be attributed to Ralph Crane (Taylor and Jowett). More generally, the regularity with which the plays of a particular dramatist such as Fletcher or Massinger or Ford are marked by much the same pattern, despite their diverse textual histories, is sufficient guarantee that authorial peculiarities were seldom drastically obscured by agents of transmission. A writer's habits may change over time, but in intelligible ways and without rendering his work unrecognizable.

Hoy's methods have been elaborated in connection with Middleton by Peter B. Murray in a study of *The Revenger's Tragedy*, by David J. Lake and MacDonald P. Jackson in independent surveys of the whole Middleton dramatic canon, and by R. V. Holdsworth in an examination of *Timon of Athens*. Basing their research on seventeenth-century printings or manuscripts (or photocopies of them), both Lake and Jackson checked dozens of items in Middleton's unassisted and undisputed plays and in a control corpus of over a hundred plays by all the prominent dramatists of the time and many of the lesser ones, and then applied the resultant information about Middleton's peculiarities to the doubtful and collaborative works. In forming their control groups both scholars biased the selection in favour of plays roughly contemporary with Middleton's, bearing the closest similarities to his, and written by dramatists who collaborated with him or had been nominated as alternative candidates for the authorship of disputed plays; each read every extant play written for the public stage within the period 1600–1627 (from Middleton's beginnings as playwright to his death); Jackson perused all but a handful of unobtainable plays recorded in the Schoenbaum–Harbage *Annals of English Drama* as written between 1590 and 1630, besides many others outside those dates. Since the two control groups differed and Hoy presented data for certain plays that were in neither of them, while Holdsworth has since compiled tables for all Shakespeare's plays, actual tallies of most pertinent features are available for over two hundred plays altogether. Moreover, Holdsworth, aware of Lake's and Jackson's findings, and seeking further indicators of Middleton's hand, checked stage directions in every available play, in print or manuscript, written between 1580 and 1642, a total of nearly 700 texts; in the course of these checks he kept an eye out for any signs of Middletonian linguistic practices. As well as the contractions, colloquialisms, word forms, and orthographical preferences investigated by Hoy, Lake or Jackson provided tallies for oaths and exclamations, synonymous connectives such as *betwixt* or *between*, *among* or *amongst*, *while*, *whilst*, or *whiles*, the affirmative particles *ay*, *yes*, and *yea*, group speech prefixes such as *All* or *Omnes*, certain rare spellings, unusual words favoured by Middleton, and collocations such as *son and heir*. The data leave no doubt whatsoever that the 'core' Middleton plays share a highly idiosyncratic linguistic and orthographical profile that is almost as reliable a guide to identification as actual physiognomy—or as fingerprinting. Every one of Middleton's twelve undoubted and unaided plays is more like every one of his others than is any play known to be by somebody else. And the fact that one of these Middleton plays, *A Game at Chess*, is preserved in his holograph offers extra reassurance that we are dealing with authorial characteristics.

A brief inventory of the salient discriminators will give some idea of the scope of recent work on the Middleton canon. Middleton employs the following contracted and colloquial forms (to standardize their spellings) at above-average rates: *a'th'*, *e'en*, *'em*, *ex'lent*, *gi'n't* (for 'given it'), *'had*, *'has*, *I'd*, *I'm*, *I've*, *ne'er*, *on't*, *sh'as*, *'tad*, *'tas*, *they're*, *thou'rt*, *upo'th'*, *y'* (as in *y'are* and *y'ave*). Some of these, such as *gi'n't*, *'tad*, and *upo'th'*, are very rare, others more common. He is unusually fond of *a* as a weakened form of *of*, as in *alate* and *a purpose*. Like many playwrights, he makes considerable use of *ha'* and *i'th'* and some of *'s* for *his*, and he is exceptionally partial to enclitic *'t*, particularly after pronouns (as in *for't*). He prefers the modern, 'regulated' uses of the auxiliary verb *do*, rather than the 'unregulated' auxiliary found more often in older, more old-fashioned writers like Shakespeare (Hope). Middleton strongly prefers *does* and *has* to the formal and old-fashioned *hath* and *doth*, and tends to avoid such favourites of other dramatists as *'a* as a colloquial form of *he*, *d'ee* (for *do ye*), *of't*, *shannot*, *t'ee* (for *to ye*), *wonnot*, *ye*, and the variants *'hem*, *o'the*, and *'um*. His most distinctive expletives—all rare and occurring at least ten times more often in his undoubted plays than in Jackson's control corpus—include *a my troth*, *beshrew . . . heart*, *cuds*, *cuds me*, *la you/why la*, *life*, *my life for yours*, *(a) pox*, *puh*, *push*, and *'slife*. Holdsworth, who cites nine examples of *tak't of my word* (or variations, such as *a my/on my/upon my life/soul/truth*) in plays associated with Middleton, was unable to find parallels elsewhere (180). Jackson listed twenty-eight comparatively common oaths, exclamations, and colloquialisms that Middleton employs more liberally than his contemporaries. At the same time, Middleton eschews a wide range of expletives, especially those with a hint of the blasphemous, that pepper the plays of his contemporaries both before and after the passing of the Act to Restrain Abuses of Players in May 1606. During the first decade of the seventeenth century Middleton persisted in preferring *ay* to *yes*, which was replacing it in most quarters, and in later years he remained partial to the old affirmative particle. In group prefixes he favoured *All* over *Omnes*. Among the idiosyncratic spellings sprinkled through his texts are *-cst* in such preterites and past participles as *placst*, *do's* for *does*, *e'm* (instead of *'em* for *them*), *ha's* and *h'as* for *has*, and *theire* for *they're*. Middleton's practices with regard to connectives vary, though his preference for *toward* over *towards* is consistent and, like many dramatists, he avoids *whiles*. He several times employs some very rare words, such as the verb *lin*, and is unusually fond of certain collocations, such as *give him his due* (and the like). Holdsworth discovered that Middleton's and Heywood's texts are the only ones within the period 1602–1624 to furnish several entrance directions in the exact form 'Enter A (or A etc.) meeting B (or B etc.)'. He also compiled statistics on a stylistic trait that he calls 'interrogative repetition', showing that the rate of occurrence in Middleton plays is exceptionally high. The device, a means of maintaining momentum in dialogue, is illustrated at its most straightforward in an exchange between Allwit and Yellowhammer in *A Chaste Maid in Cheapside*, where Allwit says (my italics) 'I am *the sorrier* for't' and Yellowhammer responds, '*The sorrier?* Why, cousin?' In many instances the tone of the repetition is exclamatory, but there is always a clear interrogative element as well. Holdsworth defined the device very carefully, spelling out rules for dealing with ambiguous cases.[2]

---

[2] Jackson attempted a preliminary analysis of the rates of some high-frequency 'function words'—*and*, *it*, *of*, *that*, *to*, and the like—which form the framework upon which any piece of verse or prose is constructed. The findings supported

Such is the identikit of features from which a picture of 'Middleton' may be built up. When doubtful texts are matched against it, the likeness is sometimes so perfect that we can confidently associate them with our man. *The Widow* may instantly be added to the core of twelve 'undisputed and unaided' Middleton plays so as to enlarge their number to thirteen. Though published in 1652 as 'drawn by the art of Johnson, Fletcher, and Middleton', it was excluded from the Jonson and Fletcher Folios, and the catalogues of Rogers and Ley (1656) and Archer (1656) name Middleton alone; so did a seventeenth--century owner of the quarto, who crossed out Jonson's and Fletcher's names on the title-page. Since neither Jonson nor Fletcher specialists have been able to find traces of those authors, there has long been a consensus that the play is wholly, or almost wholly, Middleton's, and the thoroughly Middletonian linguistic profile confirms this orthodox view. In fact Hoy, Lake, Jackson, and Holdsworth draw upon *The Widow* as a source of data concerning Middleton's usages.

A few figures will suggest how compelling the indications of provenance may be. Middleton's liking for contractions with *I* (*I'd*, *I'm*, *I've*) and for *e'en*, *ne'er*, and *on't* is so pronounced that the totals for these six forms alone suffice to differentiate plays of the core canon from those in the control groups. According to Jackson's computations, the lowest total for an unaided Middleton play is 43 for *A Trick to Catch the Old One*. The range for Middleton's twelve remaining unaided plays is 63–144 and the average, to which most of the individual figures approximate, is 90; whereas the range for his one hundred control plays by thirty other dramatists is 0–55 and the average 16.[3] Only Jonson's *Bartholomew Fair* (55) and Rowley's *A Woman Never Vexed* (53) afford raw totals higher than Middleton's lowest, but *Bartholomew Fair* is exceptionally long and *A Woman Never Vexed* considerably longer than *A Trick to Catch the Old One*. Once frequencies have been standardized (as rates per 20,000 words), separation between Middleton and non-Middleton texts is complete. Disputed full-length plays accepted into the Oxford canon as wholly Middleton's afford the following totals: *The Puritan* 94, *The Revenger's Tragedy* 104, *The Lady's Tragedy* 112, *The Nice Valour* 104. Such figures unequivocally categorize these four texts with the Middleton ones rather than with the non-Middleton controls. The eleven rare Middletonian expletives render the same decisive verdict in respect of *The Puritan*, *The Revenger's Tragedy*, and *The Lady's Tragedy*. The eight most distinctive of Middleton's unquestioned plays have the following numbers of instances: *The Phoenix* 13, *A Trick to Catch the Old One* 20, *Your Five Gallants* 30, *Michaelmas Term* 16, *A Mad World, My Masters* 27, *A Chaste Maid in Cheapside* 16, *No Wit/Help like a Woman's* 26, and *The Widow* 16. Sixty-seven of Jackson's one hundred control plays yield no examples at all, and only one has as many as five, one other four, and two others three. The total for *The Puritan*

is 19, for *The Revenger's Tragedy* 14, and for *The Lady's Tragedy* 17.[4]

Since Lake, Jackson, and Holdsworth reached their conclusions, the Chadwyck-Healey electronic database 'Literature Online: English Drama' has made it possible to search some 4,000 plays by 700 dramatists from the late thirteenth century to the early twentieth. Use of this resource confirms that alleged Middleton markers are extremely rare outside his work (Jackson 1998). Take, for example, three unusual expletives: only six plays in the whole of 'English Drama' contain *puh*, *my life for yours*, and *la you/why la*, namely *A Trick to Catch the Old One*, *Your Five Gallants*, *The Widow*, *Wit at Several Weapons*, *The Revenger's Tragedy*, and *The Puritan*. The first three are undoubtedly Middleton's, and the other three have long been associated with him, *Wit at Several Weapons* having been identified by Lake, Jackson, and their predecessors as a collaboration between Middleton and Rowley. The checking in 'Literature Online' of other items that Lake and Jackson claim to be significant affords overwhelming support for the attribution to Middleton of *The Revenger's Tragedy*, *The Puritan*, and *The Lady's Tragedy*, in particular; it also strongly supports other evidence of his part-authorship of *The Bloody Banquet*.

In other cases the 'identikit' resemblance is not to Middleton but to somebody else. An appeal to internal evidence is no mere ploy for aggrandizing the canon. Testing for the Middletonian identifying marks leads to subtractions from the Dyce-Bullen corpus, as well as to additions. It supports the external evidence for Middleton's part-authorship of *The Patient Man and the Honest Whore*; on the other hand, it gives Dekker sole credit for the sequel, *The Honest Whore, Part II*. This example is in many ways emblematic: both Dyce (who included both parts) and Bullen (who excluded both) treated two distinct works as though they were one, and as a result one overestimated and one underestimated Middleton's work. In *The Art of Thomas Middleton*, David M. Holmes was anxious to demonstrate the place of *Blurt, Master Constable* 'in the nexus of Middleton's works' (17), but the play's linguistic profile is utterly unlike Middleton's and remarkably like Dekker's. This comedy, which was in print by 1602 and in which we might expect to find some twenty instances of Middleton's eleven most distinctive expletives, has none at

the ascription to Middleton of *The Revenger's Tragedy*, *A Yorkshire Tragedy*, *The Puritan*, and *The Lady's Tragedy* and the rejection from the Middleton canon of *Blurt, Master Constable* and, less emphatically, *The Family of Love*. Smith has since developed sound statistical techniques for processing and evaluating such data, applying them to *The Revenger's Tragedy* and *Timon of Athens*: Smith's results support Middleton's claim to *Revenger*, but, while consistent with dual authorship of *Timon*, raise doubts over the nature and extent of Middleton's participation in that play. However, it should be said that Smith's work, although mathematically more sophisticated, is based upon smaller databases than the work of Jackson, Lake, and Holdsworth.

[3] This is the arithmetic mean; the median is 15, and the mode (the most frequently occurring total) is as low as 7.

[4] *The Nice Valour*'s two examples are matched or surpassed by only ten per cent of the non-Middleton plays and are similar to totals for plays of Middleton's later period.

all, but teems with Dekker's favourites; *i'faith*, which Middleton used very frequently in all his early plays but which Dekker almost completely avoided, is entirely absent from *Blurt, Master Constable*; and the contractions, connectives, speech prefixes for 'Omnes', and so on, exhibit a pattern that is uniquely Dekker's among dramatists writing for the private theatres around 1602. Likewise, *The Family of Love*, which several critics have considered not only a lively example of 'Jacobean city comedy' but also typically Middletonian in outlook and method, is so deficient in Middleton's distinguishing features that it cannot be accepted as his: a careful evaluation of the evidence strongly suggests that the play is wholly the work of Lording Barry (Taylor, Mulholland, and Jackson).

These negative findings with respect to *Blurt, Master Constable* and *The Family of Love*, far from contradicting the external evidence, help reinforce distinctions between good external evidence and bad. *Blurt, Master Constable* was first assigned to Middleton in Francis Kirkman's catalogue of 1661, and *The Family of Love* remained anonymous until Edward Archer assigned it to Middleton in his catalogue of 1656. These are very late attributions, made by booksellers whose claims are hopelessly unreliable, as W. W. Greg's careful analysis of Archer's and Kirkman's playlists, together with the 1656 list compiled by Rogers and Ley, amply demonstrated. The failure of the linguistic profiles of *Blurt, Master Constable* and *The Family of Love* to match Middleton's simply confirms Archer's and Kirkman's proven unreliability. And this confirmation lends further support, in turn, to the unequivocal verdict of the internal evidence that Middleton wrote *The Revenger's Tragedy*: the traditional ascription to Cyril Tourneur rests on the testimony of Archer, uncritically repeated by Kirkman. The 'Middleton identikit' thus gives warrant for an addition to the Dyce–Bullen canon that further undermines the late-seventeenth-century booksellers' authority and for two subtractions from the Dyce–Bullen canon that work to the same effect.

The same minutiae enable us to return an emphatic answer to W. D. Dunkel's question 'Did Not Rowley Merely Revise Middleton?' One telling detail will illustrate the point. In plays that he wrote alone Rowley never uses *I've*, to which Middleton was so partial. In the four plays and one masque that the Oxford Middleton includes as Middleton–Rowley collaborations—*A Fair Quarrel, The Changeling, The World Tossed at Tennis, Wit at Several Weapons*, and *Old Law*—*I've* occurs twenty-eight times, always within scenes traditionally considered Middleton's handiwork, though his contribution to the actual writing of the five plays is, again according to the orthodox view, somewhat smaller than his partner's. Such a distribution of instances of the contraction must indicate actual collaboration between the two dramatists, not Rowley's mere revision of Middleton's scripts. Holmes's attempt to revive Dunkel's theory that these plays were conceived and composed entirely by Middleton alone, and that Rowley tampered with them later—a theory designed to magnify

'Middleton' at the expense of 'Rowley'—is plainly misguided. The division of labour in plays that Middleton wrote jointly with Dekker or Webster or Shakespeare can usually be deduced by the same means.

But the traditional scholarly concern to apportion shares in co-authored Renaissance plays has come under recent attack, and the whole question of the status of collaborations requires special consideration.

V

Drama is a collaborative art. The pristine script undergoes a complex process of modification as a company of actors and their various functionaries prepare it for its destined realization upon the stage. Without performers, a theatrical space, and an audience a playscript is mere 'words, words, words'. Even in the Jacobean theatre, costumers, carpenters, designers of props, bookkeepers, and musicians, as well as actors, were essential to the co-operative enterprise of turning handwritten signs into live entertainment. And the revival of an old play almost inevitably entailed some alteration of the promptbook that had guided earlier stagings. Scripts evolved to meet changes in public taste and the requirements of different venues. Songs might be interpolated, speeches and whole scenes cut or added or reordered. An originating author is but one of several agents in the creation of the theatrical event for which spectators pay their admission fees.

Moreover, the generation of those initial playscripts themselves was often enough a cooperative venture during the decades in which Middleton was active (Vickers 2002, 18–43). The diary of theatre manager Philip Henslowe records the transactions of a playwriting industry analogous to modern television scriptwriters' joint efforts to meet market demands. Bentley calculates that there are 1,100 or so plays of the period 1590–1642 about which we have evidence of authorship, and that close to 20 per cent 'contained the work of more than one man as either collaborator, reviser, or provider of additional matter'. Since amateur plays were seldom written in collaboration and title-page statements may simplify the true circumstances of composition, he guesses that 'as many as half of the plays by professional dramatists in the period incorporated the writing at some date of more than one man' (199). Nearly two-thirds of the 282 plays mentioned by Henslowe have more than one author. It is not unusual for Henslowe to pay five playwrights for a particular script.

In the frequency with which he collaborated, Middleton is more representative of his age than Marlowe, Jonson, or Shakespeare. Middleton appears to have been the sole author of nineteen extant dramatic texts: the twelve-play 'core' described in Section III above, plus *A Yorkshire Tragedy, The Puritan, The Revenger's Tragedy, The Lady's Tragedy, The Nice Valour, The Widow*, and *Masque of Heroes*. His joint dramatic works include *Wit at Several Weapons, A Fair Quarrel, The World Tossed at Tennis* and *The Changeling* with Rowley; *Old Law* with Rowley and Heywood; *The Patient Man and the Honest Whore, The Bloody Banquet* and *The Roaring Girl* with Dekker; *The Spanish Gypsy* with Dekker, Ford, and Rowley; *Anything for a Quiet Life* with Webster; and *Timon of Athens* with Shakespeare. Further, he seems to have adapted Shakespeare's *Macbeth* and *Measure for Measure*. In addition to these twelve extant collaborative works, Middleton combined with Dekker, Drayton, Munday, and Webster to write the lost *Caesar's Fall, or Two Shapes*, and Dekker explicitly credited him with a speech in *The Magnificent Entertainment*.

The prevalence of collaborative writing for the London stage during the early decades of the seventeenth century has lent extra force to modern critical campaigns for a shifting of emphasis away from 'post-Enlightenment' author-based approaches to the text onto 'the discourses, figures, locations, and cultural practices participating in its emergence', to quote Jeffrey A. Masten (1992, 352). According to the new paradigm, jointly scripted plays epitomize 'the social production of texts'. The apportioning of authorial shares in such works is problematic and ultimately futile. After all, 'the collaborative project in the theater was predicated on *erasing* the perception of any differences that might have existed, for whatever reason, between collaborated parts' (Masten 1992, 342). 'What does it matter who is speaking', asks Masten (337), quoting Foucault quoting Beckett. Even Nicholas Brooke, a critic of an older generation, asserts, in regard to *The Changeling*, that 'the labours of scholarship which have gone into trying to distinguish individual contributions are largely wasted'. Most of the castle plot has been assigned to Middleton, the madhouse plot to Rowley, but (Brooke objects) 'the stylistic tests adduced can only really demonstrate the difference of language between tragedy and comedy, which any single author, especially one brought up on Elizabethan theories, would make' (70).

However, Brooke is wrong and Masten exaggerates. Understanding of 'the social production' of dramatic texts in Renaissance England is surely increased by any information we can glean about the ways in which collaborating playwrights divided their labours. The obstacles to such gleanings are by no means as insurmountable as theorists imply. The fact that in some composite plays the shares of the contributing playwrights cannot be disentangled is itself of interest, since in others the divisions are sharp and clean. Obviously there are various routines by which two or more authors might have contributed to the play texts that survive. The more we can discover about these routines the better. It is true that co-authors, no less than single authors, strive for coherence and unity, but contrast is among the chief principles of Jacobean dramatic construction, so that two playwrights might fully indulge their talents for different kinds of dialogue and nevertheless create a unified aesthetic object. And the linguistic markers that enable us to differentiate Middleton's writing from Rowley's in *The Changeling* are largely impervious to generic shifts between tragedy and comedy: Middleton employs *I've* regardless of stylistic register, whereas Rowley employs it neither in his tragedy *All's Lost by*

Lust, nor in his comedies *A Shoemaker, a Gentleman* and *A Woman Never Vexed*, nor in any of the material, comic or otherwise, in the other plays in which he had a share. Middleton favours the exclamations *puh, push*, and *pish*, whereas Rowley favours *tush*, regardless of context.

In the introduction to her New Mermaid edition of *The Roaring Girl*, Elizabeth Cook claims that 'Attempts to allocate lines or scenes of the play to either Middleton or Dekker beg as many questions as they answer and have tended to be based on pre-existing valuations of each author' (xxxvi). But she too is wrong. Critical 'valuations' of Dekker and Middleton are irrelevant to the techniques used by Lake and Jackson—whose books Cook completely ignores—to determine the probable shares of the two dramatists in the writing of *The Roaring Girl*. Among colloquial contractions and exclamations that Middleton, in his undoubted plays, favours much more than Dekker are *for't, heart, hum, I've, life, on't, pist, puh, push, 'tad*, and *'tas*, and among forms much more commonly found in Dekker's plays are *doth, Gods so, hath, humh, 'sdeath, 'sheart, tush, uds, umh*, and *zounds*. Scenes 3, 4, 5, 8, and 11 (2.1, 2.2, 3.1, 4.1, and 5.2) contain forty-eight examples of the Middleton favourites and only three of the Dekker forms, whereas scenes 1, 2, 6, 7, 9, and 10 (1.1, 1.2, 3.2, 3.3, 4.2, and 5.1) contain thirty-two examples of the Dekker markers and only two of the Middleton ones (Jackson 1979, 95-101). Since neither playwright's avoidance of the other's preferred linguistic forms is absolute, the contrast in *The Roaring Girl* (48:3; 2:32) strongly supports Richard Hindry Barker's sense that in this play 'the shares of the two authors can be determined with some approach to exactness' (270). The same division of scenes leaves seventy-five parentheses in the 1611 quarto's printing of Dekker's share of the comedy, but only four in Middleton's (Jackson 1979, 97). This difference, which cuts across the compositorial stints, is also in line with the two men's contrasting practices, as these may be inferred from the plays they wrote alone. Metrical data and figures for the proportion of polysyllabic words yield similar allocations (Jackson 1979, 100-1, 208-9).

That Middleton's and Dekker's shares of *The Roaring Girl* can so readily be distinguished lends extra significance to the heterogeneous mix of markers in *The Patient Man and The Honest Whore*. In that play the absence of any definite clustering of Middleton's or Dekker's favoured forms—which both, however, occur—indicates a different mode of collaboration from that employed in the later comedy. It would be foolish to ignore such contrasts.

W. H. Auden once reported that in his dramatic collaborations with Christopher Isherwood the accommodation of each man's individual style to the other's allowed a third authorial personality to materialize, distinct from either writer's alone (260). Something akin to this phenomenon can be discerned in several Jacobean plays. The Middleton-and-Rowley pairing is not simply the sum of the two participants. 'Middleton, working alone, did nothing so tragically true as the finest scenes in "The Changeling" or so full of the expression of an extremely poetic sensitiveness as certain passages of "The Fair Quarrel"', declared Oliphant. Whether or not we agree with this judgement, Rowley—a strangely uneven writer, more celebrated in his own day as comic actor—certainly 'seems to have had the ability to draw out Middleton's best' (Oliphant 1929, II, 13). T. S. Eliot considered Middleton's greatest achievement in comedy to be his creation, with Dekker, of the 'perpetually real . . . and human figure of Moll the Roaring Girl' (99). Nevertheless, although Middleton-and-Rowley cannot be straightforwardly equated with Middleton and Rowley or Middleton-and-Dekker with Middleton and Dekker, authors with their personal creative gifts remain crucial agents in the generation of collaborative texts. Middleton and Rowley combined to write plays unlike those of Beaumont and Fletcher or even of Middleton and Dekker. Beaumont and Fletcher could never have created The Changeling. When partnered by Rowley, rather than Dekker, Middleton wrote nothing akin to The Roaring Girl.

Thus, the compound of two authors may produce an effect different than the work of either author in isolation. Failure to recognize this fact not only leads to critical simplifications, reducing dialogic complexity to monologic banality; it can also hamper attempts to determine the authorship of a play in the first place. For much of this century, The Bloody Banquet was excluded from the Dekker canon because Dekker scholars felt that many of its features were unDekkerian, and was excluded from the Middleton canon because Middleton scholars felt that many of its features were unMiddletonian. This conundrum could only be solved by examining the play not as a whole, but scene by scene, in the process demonstrating that unDekkerian features concentrate in scenes which show strong signs of Middleton's authorship, and that unMiddletonian features concentrate in other scenes which show strong signs of Dekker's authorship (Taylor 2000). The resulting play does not belong to either author, but to both.

Twentieth-century writers, collaborating on a film or television script, often sit in one room developing plot and dialogue, scene by scene and speech by speech, through mutual give and take. Presumably English Renaissance dramatists sometimes operated in this way, or reworked, pruned, and expanded each other's drafts in a complicated layering of individual contributions; this may have happened in The Patient Man and the Honest Whore, and again in 2.1 of The Bloody Banquet, where features of both Dekker and Middleton seem inextricably mixed. But the method of collaboration best attested in the early modern theatre involved the allocation to the participating authors of responsibility for structural units—whole acts or scenes. This kind of clear-cut division would have facilitated the meeting of Henslowe's deadlines. Other procedures are theoretically possible, and appear to have been not uncommon in practice—division by 'main plot' and 'sub-plot', by serious and farcical episodes, or by some other categorization of subject matter. An author such as Anthony Munday, whom Francis Meres commended as 'our best plotter', might have sketched an outline for others to fill in (Chambers, 1930, II, 195). And once a script had been completed, one or other of the original collaborators might have given it a last polishing, or somebody else entirely might have revised it long afterwards.

Middleton and Rowley's success as a team was founded on a modus operandi that allowed each to follow his true bent—Middleton's for a skilled probing of the motives and behaviour of psychologically complex characters and for satirical comedy marked by pungent wit and multiple ironies, and Rowley's for a vigorous melodrama of moral blacks and whites and for boisterous clowning. The nature of Middleton's involvement in his collaborations with other playwrights doubtless varied, but, without aspiring to know 'who is speaking' each and every word of these plays, we may legitimately search for clues to the modes of authorial interaction that created them. Attempts to apportion 'shares' in the writing of collaborative plays lack the urgency of attempts to identify the participating authors, since the inclusion or exclusion of a play within The Collected Works of Thomas Middleton depends on Middleton's presence, rather than on the precise extent of that presence. But to take no interest in 'who wrote what' within plays of dual or multiple authorship would be to lack historical curiosity and to hamstring exploration of the art of Middleton, his collaborators, and the Renaissance theatre in general.

VI

But Middleton did not limit himself to the theatre. Unlike Shakespeare, Jonson, and Fletcher, Middleton wrote many civic pageants and a number of topical and popular prose pamphlets. Unfortunately, we cannot assume that such works share the same authorial characteristics as the plays; it is always possible that genre may have affected style. The diversity of Middleton's output adds to the difficulty of determining a canon. And although investigators of canonical problems in the dramatic canon can draw upon more than a century of scholarship devoted to such issues in the plays of Middleton and his contemporaries, much less attention has been paid to authorship problems in non-dramatic genres.

Middleton's civic pageants and entertainments were the most collaborative of all his works. Like a director of Hollywood epics, he organized extravagant spectacles requiring many helpers. Fortunately, few uncertainties of authorship surround Middleton's narrative descriptions of these shows, to which his name is unequivocally attached.[5] His long poems likewise have remained unquestioned since

---

[5] There are minor questions associated with Civitatis Amor and The Sun in Aries. In Civitatis, Middleton's signature occurs at the end of 'The Entertainment at Whitehall', and the following section on 'Prince Charles His Creation' is probably not his. Munday has often been claimed as co-author of Aries.

the discovery of his true date of birth revealed *The Wisdom of Solomon Paraphrased*, *Microcynicon* and *The Ghost of Lucrece* to be juvenilia.

The true extent of his prose writing, by contrast, is much more difficult to determine, in part because such pamphlets were routinely published with little or no indication of authorship. Only three extant non-dramatic works have Middleton's full name on the title-page (*The Wisdom of Solomon Paraphrased*) or appended to a preface (*The Ghost of Lucrece*, *Sir Robert Sherley*). Though *The Peacemaker* was published anonymously, or rather implicitly pseudonymously attributed to King James, an extant manuscript licence specifically attributes it to Thomas Middleton. Three other pamphlets (*Microcynicon*, *The Black Book*, *Father Hubburd's Tales*) attach the ambiguous initials 'T.M.' to some prefatory material; in *The Two Gates of Salvation*, a second issue adds an initialled dedication, linking it to Middleton's post as Chronologer of London. Thus, although there is varying external evidence for Middleton's authorship of eight non-dramatic pamphlets, only one of those—the very first, published when he was seventeen—names him on the title-page. Clearly, no one expected Middleton's name to help sell a pamphlet, and after his trumpeted adolescent entrance into print Middleton himself abandoned the self-importance which would have insisted on conspicuous advertisement of his authorship. It would therefore hardly be surprising if some of his pamphlets, like some of his plays, were published anonymously.

But we can identify such anonymous pamphlets only if we first have a database of undisputed pamphlets. That database has been slow to form. Middleton's non-dramatic canon has only gradually become apparent to modern scholars. Dyce was ignorant of the manuscript evidence for Middleton's authorship of *The Peacemaker*; likewise, *The Ghost of Lucrece* does not appear in the nineteenth-century *Works* because its sole surviving copy did not resurface until the twentieth century; Dyce and Bullen did not include *Two Gates* because they were unaware of the attribution to Middleton in the second issue.

This gradually expanded core canon of non-dramatic works, once established, makes it possible to investigate the relationship between the style of Middleton's plays and the style of his pamphlets. Moreover, although Middleton created characters and wrote speeches in verse for the Lord Mayor's shows, the published pamphlets issued in conjunction with those shows chiefly consist of narrative and descriptive prose; they therefore expand the reliable database of Middleton's non-dramatic prose.

Much of the internal evidence available for plays is not available, or seldom available, for pamphlets. Expletives and colloquial contractions, for example, are far less prevalent in expository or narrative prose than in dialogue for the stage; verse style is easier to describe and quantify than prose style. Moreover, there are a few significant differences between Middleton's habits in plays and his habits elsewhere: in writing dialogue he strongly preferred

the colloquial 'has' and 'does', but in non-dramatic works he normally uses the older 'hath' and 'doth'. Nevertheless, even after all these difficulties have been taken into account, Lake showed that internal evidence could distinguish between pamphlets by Middleton and pamphlets not by him (270–3). The choice of connectives may have confirmatory value, and in some cases a sprinkling of rare Middletonian spellings affords further corroboration. Middleton's hand shows itself most clearly in the sporadic appearance of words and collocations to which he was peculiarly partial and in a heavy accumulation of parallels in thought and expression to his acknowledged works.

The citing of 'parallels' in attempts to identify the authors of Renaissance texts has fallen into disfavour, in reaction to the abuse of such evidence by some earlier investigators, who were too apt to bolster a weak case with mention of a smattering of trivial verbal similarities of a kind that might link almost any two contemporary works, whoever had written them. Both the quality and the quantity of the parallels are crucial in the interpretation of what they imply. Middleton is demonstrably self-repetitive. He echoes other writers infrequently, but often recycles his own ideas, images, and phrases, so that plays, masques, poems, and prose writings are interconnected in an intricate network of striking reminiscences and anticipations. Holdsworth's methodical and persistent exploration of these interconnections has gone far towards re-establishing parallels in the investigator's armoury of usable evidence. The absence from *Blurt, Master Constable*, *2 Honest Whore*, and *The Family of Love*, of significant Middleton parallels strongly confirms the linguistic indications that he had nothing to do with those disputed plays, and the paucity of such parallels in *The Spanish Gypsy* proves that others must be responsible for the bulk of that play. In *The Revenger's Tragedy*, *The Puritan*, *A Yorkshire Tragedy*, *The Lady's Tragedy*, *The Nice Valour*, and certain scenes of *The Bloody Banquet*, by contrast, passages that can be closely paralleled in indubitably canonical plays are reassuringly plentiful. In the collaborative plays Middleton parallels show a marked tendency to cluster within the scenes and sections attributable to him on other grounds. Holdsworth's exhaustive analysis of *Timon of Athens* shows that the shares of Middleton and Shakespeare are, in each case, distinguished by the abundance of parallels with the appropriate collaborating author's corpus and the scarceness of parallels with his partner's.

'Literature Online' allows even greater systematization of such searches for rare phrases and collocations that are shared between an anonymous, collaborative, or disputed, work and rival candidates for its authorship. Comprehensive lists of links with writers belonging to some chronological or other pertinent group can be compiled, and the results analysed. The method, which can identify, from a lineup of writers, the true author of a passage of known provenance, has been fully described by Jackson (1998; 2003, 190–217). Taylor (2002) has employed it to help show that Thomas Heywood contributed 345 lines to *Old Law*.

Early in the twentieth century, parallels were used by Sykes (1925) and Adams to establish that the author responsible for *The Wisdom of Solomon Paraphrased* and *The Ghost of Lucrece* (by 'Thomas Middleton') also wrote *Microcynicon*, *The Black Book*, and *Father Hubburd's Tales* (by 'T.M.'). Using similar evidence, the Oxford Middleton has included five pamphlets published anonymously. Three of these—*The Penniless Parliament of Threadbare Poets*, *Plato's Cap*, and *The Owl's Almanac*—are mock almanacs, clearly linked to one another, generically and textually, and also clearly linked to Middleton's lifelong interest in almanacs. Two other pamphlets—*News from Gravesend* and *The Meeting of Gallants*—seem to be collaborations with Thomas Dekker, with whom Middleton also collaborated in the theatre; both were written in 1603–4, when both men were writing pamphlets in order to earn a living while the theatres were closed by plague.

In all five anonymous pamphlets where Middleton's hand has been detected, the attribution is strengthened by circumstantial evidence. Such circumstantial plausibility also reinforces his claim to the handful of individual poems attributed to him in the seventeenth century: a manuscript epitaph on Richard Burbage, a commendatory poem printed in the first edition of *The Duchess of Malfi*, and a poem about his imprisonment for *A Game at Chess*. Statistical tests are helpless in analysing texts of such brevity, but there is no reason to doubt these attributions: unlike Donne, Middleton was not famous enough to attract casual attributions in manuscript miscellanies. Indeed, his name is much more likely to have been omitted from poems he wrote, than to have been added to poems he did not. The Oxford edition attributes to him three anonymous poems: a verse description of the engraving on the title-page of the first edition of *A Game at Chess*, an epitaph on Sir George Bolles, and a poem celebrating the dedication of the new parish church of St James. Each of these texts is circumstantially linked to Middleton, and each strongly resembles the verbal texture of his acknowledged work.

It is of course entirely possible that Middleton wrote other anonymous poems or anonymous pamphlets. Indeed, if *The Two Gates of Salvation* (mostly an anthology of Biblical passages) and *Sir Robert Sherley* (mostly a translation of a Latin description of a pageant) were not explicitly attributed to him in what appear to be reliable documents, it is unlikely that any literary critic would have suspected or accepted his authorship of either. If he translated other continental works, or composed other religious pamphlets, they would probably escape our detection. Barring the unpredictable rediscovery of lost plays, Middleton's dramatic canon seems relatively fixed; his non-dramatic canon may not be.

VII

Fingerprints, though invaluable for identifying people, tell us nothing about their qualities as human beings. Sim-

ilarly, the linguistic details that help us decide whether a play or pamphlet is by Middleton are of little literary importance, though an orthography that marks colloquial elisions and weakened pronunciations does tend to accompany a poetic style heavily indebted to everyday speech. But to the ear attuned to its rhythms and tones, Middleton's verse is highly distinctive, especially in plays written from 1611 onwards. An attempt at a brief description of Middleton's style, both before and after 1611, inevitably raises the subject of chronology.

In thinking about chronology we need to distinguish between the date at which a work was first exposed to the public, whether in performance or in print, and the date at which it was composed. Performance or publication would usually have followed closely upon completion of the writing of a playscript or pamphlet, but composition is sometimes a protracted business: works may be started and laid aside, to receive intermittent attention over periods of many years. We cannot hope to chart all the details of the evolution of Middleton's writings before their release to the public. Our main ambition must be to determine, if only approximately, the date at which a play was first ready for the stage or a pamphlet or poem for the printing-house. To try to establish dates of this kind is not to privilege study of the author's 'mind and art'. The new historicist or cultural materialist must inevitably share the traditional scholar's concern with chronology. The more precisely a work can be located in time, the more confidently it may be referred to its specific cultural and political context. Critics interested in 'intertextualities' also need to know the order in which texts appeared.

For the dating of Middleton's writings we are reliant mainly on documentation from outside them, on topical allusions within them, and on the ways in which they have influenced, or been influenced by, works whose dates can be fixed with some certainty. The notoriety of *A Game at Chess* ensures that we know precisely when this box-office success was the nine days' wonder of the London stage. The mayoral pageants were designed for specific occasions. *Plato's Cap*, 'Cast at this year 1604, being *Leape-yeere*', and *The Owl's Almanac* in 1618, were, like modern calendars and appointment diaries, obviously written to be marketed by the New Year. Henslowe's record of payment to Dekker and Middleton, some time before 14 March 1604, of five pounds 'in earnest' of *Patient Man and Honest Whore*, and the entry of Part 1 in the Stationers' Register on 9 November 1604 set clear limits between which it must have been completed. For several works there is similarly conclusive evidence. For others the indications are few and ambiguous, so that the range of dates for which different commentators have argued span more than a decade. Nineteenth-century scholars regarded *Hengist, King of Kent; or, The Mayor of Queenborough* as one of Middleton's very first plays; it is now generally assigned to the period 1616–20, and this edition presents new evidence for 1620. Such major readjustments to a chronological ordering of Middleton's works obviously affect our sense of their interconnections, and although in this case we can be reasonably confident that modern scholarship has corrected an earlier mistake, scholars continue to disagree about the dating of some plays. Nevertheless, an account of Middleton's dramatic verse and the changes it underwent may be attempted, if only as a stimulus to further research. The necessary work has barely been begun. Understanding of Middleton's development has yet to profit from the kinds of analysis that have been devoted to the Shakespeare canon.

An immense amount of scholarly activity has gradually built up a clear picture of Shakespeare's stylistic development. During the nineteenth century Fleay, his New Shakspere Society associates, and several German scholars subjected his prosody to minute analysis, calculating the percentages of double endings, run-on lines, trochaic substitutions, anapaestic feet, light and weak endings, and so on, in the blank verse of each play. Twentieth-century scholars have extended and refined this research. When metrical figures are related to chronology, in so far as it can be determined by other means, Shakespeare's verse style can be seen to evolve in intelligible ways. Broadly speaking, the trend is away from a succession of strictly iambic, decasyllabic, end-stopped lines towards greater freedom, variety, and flow. Where external evidence for a Shakespeare play's date of composition is lacking, the metrical figures allow an approximate placing within the overall evolution. Similarly, the formal similes of the early plays give way to a densely metaphoric language in which images blend into one another in kaleidoscopic profusion. Statistical studies of Shakespeare's vocabulary reveal a tendency for plays written at about the same time to share more of their rare-word vocabulary than plays written further apart. An index of 'colloquialism in verse'—in which various contracted and colloquial forms are totalled and related to the number of words within each play's verse—reveals a marked increase in the plays written after 1600. With the help of such data, the approximate order in which Shakespeare's plays were composed has by now been determined to the satisfaction of most scholars (Taylor 1987).

Leeds Barroll and others (Bristol, de Grazia) have decried the use of internal evidence in attempts to establish a Shakespearean chronology. Some of these complaints are specific to the particulars of Shakespeare, and do not apply to Middleton or other authors. For instance, Shakespeare's plays are characteristically set in some other place and/or some other time; so-called 'topical allusions' to current events in contemporary London would therefore be dramatically out of place, and they are correspondingly rare, and sometimes disputed. Middleton, by contrast, characteristically works in a temporal and spatial present, and his texts teem with references to current events, most of them quite indisputable. Intrinsically, as indications of the date of composition, such allusions are much more reliable in Middleton's canon than in Shakespeare's.

But some of the objections raised by sceptics are not specific to Shakespeare, but claim instead to be more generally applicable theoretical strictures. Barroll, for instance, stigmatizes the very term 'internal evidence' as 'most often an oxymoron' (238). But his criticisms rest on a misconception. He takes percentages for a selection of metrical features that rise or fall over Shakespeare's career, shows that they all order the plays differently, and concludes that they are therefore unsatisfactory, because 'If one uses tests whose results are expressed in numbers, quantitative measures must be rigidly adhered to within the scientific universe created' (238-9).

No professional statistician would agree with him. Barroll misrepresents the principle that underlies application of internal tests to matters of dating—the familiar and pertinent statistical concept of *correlation*. The blank verse of Shakespeare's late plays contains more double endings than the blank verse of his early ones, but nobody supposes that each successive play employed a higher proportion of double endings than the one before in a consistent and uniform development, nor that a play for which the percentage is 25 was necessarily composed later than a play for which it is 21. Artistic change is not so steady and predictable. Rather, there is a *relation* between chronological sequence, in so far as it may be established by external evidence, and an inverse rank order based on the magnitude of the percentage of double endings in the plays' blank verse. Mathematical measures of correlation can gauge the degree and significance of this relation. There need not be perfect coincidence between the two orderings for a statistically significant relationship to obtain. Several metrical features correlate with chronology in this way, and when the most reliable are combined into a single index the correlation becomes especially strong.

Indices based on colloquial contractions, on vocabulary links, or on rates of occurrence of function words yield similar correlations with a skeleton chronology based on references to the plays in historical documents, their allusions to contemporary events, and their intertextual connections with datable non-Shakespearean works. Since the different kinds of internal evidence—metrical, orthographical and linguistic, lexical—are independent of one another, when they agree in indicating a particular period for a play's likely date of composition, they come close to settling the matter, even though 'external' confirmation may be lacking. Such considerations cannot tell us whether *Coriolanus* preceded or followed *Antony and Cleopatra*, but they leave us in no reasonable doubt that both plays were written later than, for example, *Othello*. Cautiously interpreted, the evidence of quantifiable stylistic variables is an invaluable aid towards dating a writer's works.

By comparison with Shakespeare's, Middleton's stylistic development has been only roughly charted.[6] Few metrical

---

[6] The fullest analyses of Middleton's style in dramatic poetry are those by Stenger (124-87) and Mincoff. Oliphant offers excellent thumbnail sketches in *Shakespeare and his Fellow Dramatists*, I, 10-12, 21, and *The Plays of Beaumont and Fletcher*, 83-5.

data have been accumulated, and no concordance has existed to serve as basis for statistical analysis of his vocabulary. With the possible exception of Ants Oras's analysis of 'pause patterns', to be described shortly, nothing remotely comparable to the intensive and wide-ranging work of Hoy, Lake, Jackson, and Holdsworth on questions of authorship relating to Middleton has been devoted to uncovering metrical and other stylistic indicators for a Middleton chronology.

As a dramatic poet Middleton has in the past usually been considered 'workmanlike', but less gifted than Webster, for example. The poetic vitality of *The Revenger's Tragedy* has been amply acknowledged, but the credit has gone to Tourneur, formerly thought to have been the play's author. The lukewarm judgement on Middleton as poet owes much to late-Romantic notions of poetry that predate Modernism, let alone more recent movements. In fact, Middleton is a truly remarkable dramatic poet. His achievement as a dramatist is inseparable from his achievement as a poet, for the poetic medium he devised is a subtle vehicle for conveying his characters' anxieties, pretences, and compulsions. His verse is seldom showy. It is less rhetorical than Shakespeare's, mimicking more closely the rhythms and syntax of colloquial speech. But it moves with a peculiar nervous intensity, partly due to the lively interplay between units of sense and line divisions. Middleton's imagery appeals to the intellect, rather than to the eye: it is not flamboyant, but relies on personifications that remain unelaborated and crowd one upon another. At its best Middleton's verse is quick with metaphorical activity. And, as Oliphant noted, he is the one Renaissance dramatist who vies with Shakespeare for 'sovereign mastery of words' (1927, 75). He has an acute awareness of multiple meanings, so that he is not only addicted to the pun and quibble but uses a word less as a single note than as a chord (Ricks 1960, 1961).

As a metrist Middleton was strikingly original, but mainly in his post-1611 plays. His earlier style owed more to rhyme, tolerated more inversions of normal word order, and was somewhat less apt to depart from the decasyllabic norm; but it also mixed prose and verse easily and readily, sometimes moving from one to the other and back again within the same speech. The verse of *The Revenger's Tragedy*, in which the earlier style culminates, is a medium that can accommodate an extraordinary range of tones. The court characters in *The Revenger's Tragedy* may be caricatures of lust and ambition, but their dialogue is eminently speakable. It sounds idiomatic, registers nuances, and invites changes of pace. It conveys a sense of real life that offsets the elements of morality-play abstraction.

Seventeenth-century dramatists rung more and more changes on the basic, end-stopped iambic pentameter line first brought to vigorous life in Marlowe's *Tamburlaine*, but freedom from the tyranny of the norm was accomplished in two main ways, involving two different treatments of line ends. The first was the addition of a final unstressed syllable to create a so-called 'double' or 'feminine' ending.

An occasional variation in the verse of Shakespeare and his early contemporaries, in Fletcher's it became normative: a majority of Fletcher's blank verse lines have feminine endings, and many of these are monosyllables that carry considerable weight. The second was the use of enjambment, or the running-on of the sense from the end of one line into the beginning of the next, with a consequent increase in mid-line pauses and a tendency for these to fall at later points in the pentameter. This feature, too, was at first employed sparingly, but became almost ubiquitous in the verse of such Caroline playwrights as Shirley and Davenant. Extreme forms of enjambment, whereby lines end on prepositions, conjunctions, auxiliary verbs, and the like, can so predominate in a passage of Davenant's verse as to make it seem like chopped-up prose. Shakespeare was among those who adopted a judicious mix of variations, while never allowing the essential structure to collapse. Throughout his career Middleton favoured end-stopping, eschewing the 'weak' and 'light' endings created by extreme enjambment, preferring to gain flexibility through an almost Fletcherian use of feminine endings. Yet Middleton's verse, with its colloquial contractions and natural syntax, has no trace of the lullaby of sentiment that can mark Fletcher's cadences; it has a tense and vibrant music of its own.

Besides double endings, including those in which the extra syllable is emphatic, Middleton had an unusual fondness for 'triple' and even 'quadruple' endings, in which the stressed first syllable of a word such as 'gentlemen' or 'gentlewomen' completes the pentameter line and two or three relatively unstressed syllables follow. Like Fletcher, he often creates double or triple endings by adding vocatives, such as 'sir' or (more idiosyncratically) the trochaic 'madam', to an otherwise complete line. By means of anapaests and other trisyllabic feet he tends to crowd his lines with extra syllables, which in pronunciation may be slurred or elided to fit the measure. Particularly characteristic is his habit of making double endings out of 'on't', 'for't', or some similar contraction, or out of 'else', as in 'You must keep counsel, mother, I am undone else' (*Women Beware*, 1.1.46).

Certain turns of syntax facilitate Middleton's metrical licences and add variety to the strength and position of pausation within lines. Oliphant noted the most conspicuous of these. Endemic is his fondness for making subordinate what in other writers would be a sentence's principal clause, as in 'Will make the rest show nothing, 'tis so glorious' (*No Wit*, 8.195), where the more common construction would be '"Tis so glorious that it will make the rest show nothing'. 'I thank' is frequently used in this manner, as in 'He came in a good time, I thank him for't' (*No Wit*, 6.172). Also characteristic are the employment of emphasizing or confirmatory phrases beginning with 'That' or 'There', as in 'And know it to be mine—there lies the blessing' (*Women Beware*, 1.1.15); conditional approval expressed by 'I'll say that for'; the use of the superlative followed by 'that ever', as in 'Now say if't be not the best piece of theft | That ever was committed'

Play	Double	Rhymed	Slurred
The Phoenix	30	27	29
Michaelmas Term	20	33	32
A Mad World, My Masters	31	29	23
A Trick to Catch the Old One	27	24	14
Your Five Gallants	21	19	23
No Wit/Help like a Woman's	33	15	25
A Chaste Maid in Cheapside	31	9	19
The Witch	32	10	18
More Dissemblers Besides Women	33	11	20
Hengist, King of Kent	24	9	21
A Game at Chess	42	12	—

Table 1. Percentages of verse lines with double
endings, rhyme, and slurred syllables in eleven
Middleton plays, according to Matthew Baird, 1928.

Play	Lines tested	Feminine (per cent)
The Phoenix	250	27
Michaelmas Term	150	24
The Revenger's Tragedy	400	28
The Lady's Tragedy	500	42
No Wit/Help like a Woman's	500	45
A Chaste Maid in Cheapside	400	46

Table 2. Percentages of sampled verse lines with
feminine endings according to Barker, 1945.

(*Women Beware*, 1.1.43–4); and the habit of attaching ability to inanimate things, as in 'Now for a welcome | Able to draw men's envies upon man' (*Women Beware*, 3.1.102–3).

These idiosyncrasies become much more prominent after 1610, although the stylistic shift may seem more sudden and radical than it was, simply because we apparently possess only a single collaborative play written between early 1607 and early 1611 (*The Bloody Banquet*). If more of his dramatic work from that period were extant, the shift might appear more gradual. In any case, the changes in his dramatic verse are potentially quantifiable, but full and accurate figures have not yet been computed. In a thesis of 1928 Matthew Baird presented his calculations of percentages of double endings, rhymed lines, and lines with slurred syllables in eleven Middleton plays. His results are given in Table 1.

The data show a diminution in rhyme after the city comedies, with the last of those having the least rhyme. The figures for 'slurred syllables' fall into no definite pattern, and there appears to be no appreciable increase in double endings until *A Game at Chess*. However, the complete accuracy of Baird's counts may be doubted, and the precise basis of his calculations was not made clear. Figures compiled by Barker (1945), for a small selection of plays and from samples only, agree quite well with Baird's, but show a significant increase in feminine endings in plays written after 1606/7 (Table 2). The probable reason for Barker's percentages being higher than Baird's is that Barker's samples were exclusively of blank verse, in which feminine endings are normally more common than in rhymed lines, and that his 'feminine' endings included 'triple' endings, whereas Baird's perhaps did not.

Data for some collaborative plays that have been tested show Middleton's shares fitting well with his unaided plays of about the same date and differentiate these shares from Dekker's in *The Roaring Girl* and from Rowley's in *A Fair Quarrel*, *The Changeling*, and *Wit at Several Weapons*. According to Baird, in Middleton's scenes of *The Roaring Girl* 34 per cent of the verse lines have

double endings, 14 per cent have rhyme, and 21 per cent have 'slurred syllables', whereas the figures for Dekker's contribution are 14 per cent double endings, 41 per cent rhyme, and 14 per cent 'slurred syllables', in accord with his practices elsewhere. Barker's counts of feminine endings in verse scenes of *The Changeling* show an overall figure of about 54 per cent for Middleton, and 31 per cent for Rowley (Schoenbaum 1955, 211). These figures confirm Pauline G. Wiggin's account of the differences between Middleton and Rowley as metrists. She also noted the relative frequency of triple endings in Middleton's share of *The Changeling*, the prevalence of end--stopped lines, and the orthodox disposition of stresses; in Rowley's share she found almost no triple endings, about twice Middleton's proportion of run-on lines (including those producing weak endings), and frequent inversions of stress in the second and last foot. Wiggin also gives tallies (30–1) that enable us to reckon the percentages of feminine endings in the two dramatists' shares of *A Fair Quarrel*: for Middleton the figure is 46, and for Rowley 26. Over a century ago, Robert Boyle's metrical data for the 'Beaumont and Fletcher' plays included some figures for *Wit at Several Weapons*; when these are converted to percentages and related to the probable division of labour between Middleton and Rowley, the total for Middleton is 42 per cent feminine endings and 9 per cent run-on lines, and for Rowley 24 per cent feminine endings and 19 per cent run-on lines (Jackson 1979, 210). In order to be strictly comparable, counts must be made by one person at one time. The fifty lines that Barker tested in 5.3 of *The Changeling* have inflated his overall percentage for Rowley in that play: Rowley's other scenes are much lower, and 5.3 is probably of mixed authorship. However, it does seem that Middleton used feminine endings more liberally after 1611.

The fullest investigation of any aspect of Middleton's prosody (and the only chronological study which competes in thoroughness with the authorship studies by Hoy, Lake, and Jackson) was undertaken by Ants Oras in the course of his research on pause patterns in the verse of English Renaissance drama. Basing his computations on the earliest printed texts, Oras counted the numbers of pauses falling in the various possible positions—after the first, second, third, fourth, fifth, sixth, seventh, eighth, or ninth syllable within the line. Study of

Play	Percentage of pauses in first half of line
The Phoenix	33.0
Michaelmas Term	30.4
A Mad World, My Masters	22.5
A Trick to Catch the Old One	30.4
The Revenger's Tragedy	33.8
Your Five Gallants	40.0
No Wit/Help like a Woman's	23.4
The Lady's Tragedy	27.7
A Chaste Maid in Cheapside	19.0
The Witch	17.4
More Dissemblers Besides Women	20.9
The Widow	22.7
Hengist, King of Kent	26.5
Women, Beware Women	22.5
The Changeling (Middleton's share)	19.8
A Game at Chess	18.4

Table 3. Ants Oras's figures for percentage of pauses in first half of the pentameter line in Middleton's plays.

Play	Early/late forms
The Phoenix	38/1
Michaelmas Term	31/1
A Mad World, My Masters	63/2
A Trick to Catch the Old One	37/1
The Puritan	51/1
The Revenger's Tragedy	26/0
Your Five Gallants	64/0
No Wit/Help like a Woman's	16/25
The Lady's Tragedy	5/4
A Chaste Maid in Cheapside	7/12
The Witch	0/6
The Nice Valour	4/13
More Dissemblers Besides Women	1/9
The Widow	4/20
Hengist, King of Kent	0/14
Women, Beware Women	3/15
A Game at Chess	2/0

Table 4. Totals for early and late forms in unaided, full-length Middleton plays. Early forms consist of the expletives *a/by my troth*, *by the mass*, *foh*, *la you/why la*, *pist*, *puh*, *'sfoot*, *'slid/'slud*, and *tut*; late forms are *hold my life*, *hoyda*, *pish*, and *o'th'*. Some counts include slight variations, as defined by Jackson 1979, 70-1 and 79, n. 10. Data are drawn from Jackson and Lake.

a wide range of dramatists revealed a changing rhythmic climate, to which individuals responded in different ways. Oras presented his findings in a series of graphs, all drawn to the same scale and showing for each play the percentages of pauses that fall in the nine positions within the blank verse or rhymed pentameter lines. His least vulnerable data—unaffected by scribes or compositors—are for pauses corresponding to divisions of a line between two or more speakers. The graphs for Middleton illustrate the evolution of his pause patterns, each graph tending to be most like that for other plays written at about the same time. Graphs for most early plays show a peak at the sixth syllable, preceded by a lesser but still significant peak at the fourth. In graphs for plays from 1611 onwards the secondary peak recedes or disappears and the main peak at the sixth syllable rises even higher; pauses after the seventh syllable also tend to increase, until in Middleton's share of *The Changeling* and in *A Game at Chess* they outnumber even those after the sixth. As listed in Table 3, Oras's raw figures show pauses in the first half of the pentameter line (after syllables 1–4) decreasing, when these are calculated as a percentage of all pauses except those after the fifth syllable.

Although Oras's data reveal a far from steady chronological development, they are decisive in associating *The Revenger's Tragedy* with the early Middleton, rather than with Tourneur. A mathematical measure of the degree to which Oras's various graphs match one another—the Pearson product moment correlation, using the raw figures—reveals that each of the thirteen core Middleton plays (adding *The Widow* to the unquestioned dozen) affords a closer fit to *The Revenger's Tragedy* than does *The Atheist's Tragedy*, and that closest of all is *A Trick to Catch the Old One*, the very play that was coupled with *The Revenger's Tragedy* in a Stationers' Register entry of 1607.

Oras furnished line-split data for two hundred and fifteen plays beside *The Revenger's Tragedy*: when each of these is in turn matched against it, four of the best dozen matchings prove to be with Middleton plays, namely *A Trick to Catch the Old One*, *The Phoenix*, *Hengist, King of Kent*, and *No Wit/Help like a Woman's*. James Shirley is the sole other dramatist with more than a single play among the top dozen matchings, and he has only two, *The Traitor* and *Hyde Park*, both of which belong to the 1630s—a quarter of a century after *The Revenger's Tragedy* was composed—and share none of its other metrical characteristics. Even if we had no other evidence of Middleton's authorship of *The Revenger's Tragedy*, Oras's counts of pause patterns would establish him as the best candidate (Jackson 1983, 28-9). They also buttress the case for adding *The Lady's Tragedy* to the canon: Oras remarks on 'the extraordinary likeness of its line-split design to the mature patterns of Middleton, quite particularly in those plays closest to it in time, above all that of *The Witch*' (Oras, 32).

Another chronological indicator deserves consideration. Some expletives are more prevalent in Middleton's early plays: *a my troth*, *by my troth*, *by the mass*, *foh*, *la you/why la*, *pist*, *puh*, *'sfoot*, *'slid/'slud*, and *tut*. Three expletives and one contraction appear more frequently in later plays: *hold my life*, *hoyda*, *pish* and *o'th'*. The totals of instances of early and late forms in full-length plays wholly or almost wholly by Middleton are recorded in Table 4.

The most notable feature of Table 4 is the clear division between the first seven plays, composed up to 1607, and the others, datable from 1611 onwards. While the Act to Restrain Abuses of May 1606 might have inhibited Middleton's partiality for *by the mass*, *'sfoot*, *'slid*, and *'slud*, it is unlikely to have influenced the other shifts in usage. *The Bloody Banquet*, for which the count of early/late forms is 10/1, sits comfortably on the early side of the chronological divide.

VIII

Towards the beginning of this essay I maintained the value of reading plays, poems, entertainments, and prose works within their 'authorial' context. The new Middleton canon and chronology results in interesting conjunctions, as one small illustration will show. Working independently on separate plays and separate canons, modern scholars have generally agreed that six plays attributed to Middleton and Shakespeare were written during the period July 1605–July 1606 (probably in this order): Middleton's *A Yorkshire Tragedy*, Shakespeare's *King Lear*, Shakespeare and Middleton's *Timon of Athens*, Middleton's *The Revenger's Tragedy*, Middleton's *The Puritan*, Shakespeare's *Macbeth* (later adapted by Middleton). *The Revenger's Tragedy* was published anonymously in 1607/8, *A Yorkshire Tragedy* was published as Shakespeare's in a quarto of 1608, and *The Puritan* was published in 1608 with the claim that, though acted by the Children of Paul's, it had been written by 'W.S.' These three plays are now included for the first time in an edition of Middleton's collected works. Recognition that Middleton collaborated with Shakespeare on *Timon of Athens* is also recent. We cannot be absolutely sure of the order of composition of the six works, but there is no doubt that they belong to a single period of little more than a year, at the outside.

The strong association between Middleton and the King's Men at this time is in itself an item of theatrical history that has for decades been denied by a long succession of commentators on *The Revenger's Tragedy*. But even more significant are the qualities connecting the plays now gathered together as Middleton's, and as his at a particular time. Consider *A Yorkshire Tragedy* and *The Revenger's Tragedy*. Both have repeatedly been described, by critics from Swinburne onwards, in terms of intensity, fieriness, rapidity, ferocity, vividness, and force.[7] The action of each has been seen as driven by the manic energy of its chief character. The persons in each play have been said to lack rounded humanity but to belong to a dramatic world stripped to essentials and with its own dynamics. The scholar Oliphant (1929) thought *A Yorkshire Tragedy* 'written at white heat'; the director Shelton (1965) thought *The Revenger's Tragedy* 'written in a ferment of excitement' (Scott, 40). It is doubtful whether any other play in the whole of English Renaissance drama could be linked to these two so closely as they have been linked to each other through critical commentary that employs the same adjectives and images. It seems likely that Vindice's savagery in *The Revenger's Tragedy* owes much to the Husband's paranoid violence in *A Yorkshire Tragedy*, with its basis in fact. In any case, the qualities shared by the two plays clearly have their origins in a single, and singular, authorial imagination.

Timon of Athens also has its points of contact with *The Revenger's Tragedy*. As long ago as 1876 F. G. Fleay, who had analysed the metrical features of over two hundred Renaissance plays, reported that results for the 'non-Shakespearean' portions of *Timon of Athens* most closely agreed with those for *The Revenger's Tragedy* (195). In 1909 E. H. C. Oliphant, who also considered *Timon of Athens* to be 'beyond reasonable doubt only partly [Shakespeare's]', proclaimed that 'The tone of III, 1 is that of the *Revenger's Tragedy*' (195–6). In 1968 two critics independently made similar connections. Philip Edwards remarked that if *Timon of Athens* had missed publication in the First Folio, 'We should not have known of Shakespeare's power to write satirical merchant comedy in a style which only Middleton can equal'; he remarked that the dunning scenes in Act 3 of *Timon of Athens* 'have no parallel elsewhere in Shakespeare' (134). Brian Gibbons, finding in Middleton's city comedies a 'tension between the satiric-comic form and the tragic themes of savagery, disease and evil', judged that 'the dramatic manner of Tourneur in *The Revenger's Tragedy* and of Shakespeare in Act III of *Timon of Athens* may be indebted to Middleton's art of comedy' (205). It is now clear that most of those parts of *Timon of Athens* which Fleay regarded as non-Shakespearean, including Act 3, were in fact written by Middleton, who was also the sole author of *The Revenger's Tragedy*. Even in his collaboration with Shakespeare, Middleton's authorial personality has manifested itself to four commentators whose dates of writing span close on a century, whose critical concerns are diverse in the extreme, and who were unaware that they were dealing with a single playwright. Unwittingly, they have conducted an experiment for us—a kind of blind matching. There could scarcely be a neater demonstration that authors, however circumscribed their autonomy, are agents to be reckoned with.

WORKS CITED

Adams, Joseph Quincy, ed., *The Ghost of Lucrece* (1937)
Auden, W. H., interviewed by Michael Newman, in *Writers at Work: The 'Paris Review' Interviews: Fourth Series*, ed. George Plimpton (1976), 243–69

---

[7] Holdsworth, *Three Jacobean Revenge Tragedies*, reprints a range of reactions to *The Revenger's Tragedy*. John Churton Collins called it a 'bleared, rapid and uneven work…fierce and vivid…brilliant and powerful', and wrote of the 'appalling and unrelieved intensity' of Vindice's character, his 'savage and devilish energy' (Holdsworth, *Revenge Tragedies*, 29). Swinburne, *The Age of Shakespeare*, had alluded to the 'fiery jet' of the play's 'molten verse' and to its sustained intensity (1929, II, 94). Eliot applied the adjectives 'fierce' and 'intense', alluded to 'explosiveness', 'rapidity', and 'top speed', and judged that *The Atheist's Tragedy* showed a few 'flashes of the old fire' that had ignited the earlier play, which, like Collins, he also attributed to Tourneur (121–30). Schoenbaum, *Middleton's Tragedies*, also employed the 'flame' figure. Charles Knight described *A Yorkshire Tragedy* in terms of 'ferocity…intensity' (254). John Addington Symonds, *Shakespeare's Predecessors*, likened its effect to a 'flash of lightning' by which we are 'seared and blinded' (435). Swinburne strung together 'fierce… hot…breathless heat…raging rate of speed…fire' (1918, 142). Oliphant (1929) called it 'tense', 'gripping', 'forceful', 'vivid', 'breathless', and 'fiercely naturalistic', thought it 'written at white heat', and remarked on the 'insane fury' of the chief character (II, 25–9).

Baird, Matthew, 'Collaboration of Thomas Dekker and Thomas Middleton'. B.Litt. thesis, University of Oxford, 1928

Barker, Richard Hindry, 'The Authorship of *The Second Maiden's Tragedy* and *The Revenger's Tragedy*', *Shakespeare Association Bulletin* 20 (1945), 51–62

—— *Thomas Middleton* (1958)

Barroll, Leeds, *Politics, Plague, and Shakespeare's Theater: The Stuart Years* (1991)

Bentley, Gerald Eades, *The Profession of Dramatist in Shakespeare's Time 1590–1642* (1971)

Boyle, Robert, 'Beaumont, Fletcher and Massinger', *Englische Studien* 5 (1882), 74–96

Brady, Jennifer, and W. H. Herendeen, eds., *Ben Jonson's 1616 Folio* (1991)

Bristol, Michael, *Shakespeare's America, America's Shakespeare* (1990)

Brooke, Nicholas, *Horrid Laughter in Jacobean Tragedy* (1979)

Burke, Seán, *Authorship: From Plato to the Postmodern: A Reader* (1992)

—— *The Death and Return of the Author* (1992)

Butler, Martin, 'Jonson's Folio and the Politics of Patronage', *Criticism* 35 (1993), 377–90

Chambers, E. K., *William Shakespeare: A Study of Facts and Problems*, 2 vols (1930)

Cook, Elizabeth, ed., *The Roaring Girl*, New Mermaid (1997)

De Grazia, Margreta, *Shakespeare Verbatim: The Reproduction of Authenticity and the 1790 Apparatus* (1991)

Dryden, John, *John Dryden*, ed. Keith Walker (1987)

Dunkel, W. D., 'Did Not Rowley Merely Revise Middleton?', *PMLA* 58 (1933), 799–805

Dutton, Richard, *Ben Jonson: Authority: Criticism* (1996)

Edwards, Philip, *Shakespeare and the Confines of Art* (1968)

Eliot, T. S., *Elizabethan Essays* (1934)

Fleay, Frederick Gard, *Shakspeare Manual* (1876)

Foakes, R. A., and R. T. Rickert, eds., *Henslowe's Diary* (1961)

Gibbons, Brian, *Jacobean City Comedy* (1968)

Greg, W. W., 'Authorship Attributions in the Early Play-lists, 1656–1671', *Edinburgh Bibliographical Society Transactions* 2 (1946), 305–29

Harbage, Alfred, *Annals of English Drama 975–1700*, revised S. Schoenbaum, revised Sylvia Wagonheim (1989)

Holdsworth, R. V., 'Middleton and Shakespeare: The Case for Middleton's Hand in *Timon of Athens*', PhD thesis, University of Manchester, 1982

—— ed., *Three Jacobean Revenge Tragedies* (1990)

Holmes, David M., *The Art of Thomas Middleton* (1970)

Hope, Jonathan, *The Authorship of Shakespeare's Plays* (1994)

Howard-Hill, T. H., ed., *A Game at Chess*, Revels (1993)

Hoy, Cyrus, 'The Shares of Fletcher and his Collaborators in the Beaumont and Fletcher Canon', *Studies in Bibliography* 8 (1956), 129–46; 9 (1957), 143–62; 11 (1958), 85–106; 12 (1959), 91–116; 13 (1960), 77–108; 14 (1961), 45–67; 15 (1962), 71–90

Jackson, MacDonald P., *Studies in Attribution: Middleton and Shakespeare* (1979)

—— ed., *The Revenger's Tragedy, Attributed to Thomas Middleton: A Facsimile of the 1607/8 Quarto* (1983)

—— 'Editing, Attribution Studies, and *Literature Online*: A New Resource for Research in Renaissance Drama', *Research Opportunities in Renaissance Drama* 37 (1998), 1–15

—— *Defining Shakespeare: 'Pericles' as Test Case* (2003)

Knight, Charles, ed., *The Pictorial Edition of the Works of Shakspere*. Second edn. revised, *Doubtful Plays*. New York: Routledge, n.d.

Lake, David J., *The Canon of Thomas Middleton's Plays* (1975)

Masten, Jeffrey A., 'Beaumont and/or Fletcher: Collaboration and the Interpretation of Renaissance Drama', *ELH* 59 (1992), 337–56

—— *Textual Intercourse: Collaboration, Authorship, and Sexualities in Renaissance Drama* (1997)

Mincoff, Marco, 'The Authorship of *The Revenger's Tragedy*', *Studia Historico-Philologica Serdicensia* 2 (1940), 1–87

Murray, Peter B., *A Study of Cyril Tourneur* (1964)

Oliphant, E. H. C., 'Shakspere's Plays: An Examination', *Modern Language Review* 3 (1908), 337–55; 4 (1909), 190–9, 342–51

—— 'Problems of Authorship in Elizabethan Dramatic Literature', *Modern Philology* 8 (1911), 411–59

—— 'A Dekker-Middleton Play, *The Bloodie Banquet*', *Times Literary Supplement*, 17 December 1925, 882

—— 'The Authorship of *The Revenger's Tragedy*', *Studies in Philology* 23 (1926), 157–68

—— *The Plays of Beaumont and Fletcher: An Attempt to Determine Their Respective Shares and the Shares of Others* (1927)

—— ed., *Shakespeare and His Fellow Dramatists* (1929)

Oras, Ants, *Pause Patterns in Elizabethan and Jacobean Drama: An experiment in Prosody* (1960)

Ricks, Christopher, 'The Moral and Poetic Structure of *The Changeling*', *Essays in Criticism* 10 (1960), 290–306

—— 'Word-Play in *Women Beware Women*', *Review of English Studies* NS 12 (1961), 238–50

Schoenbaum, S., *Middleton's Tragedies: A Critical Study* (1955)

—— *Internal Evidence and Elizabethan Dramatic Authorship* (1966)

Scott, Michael, *Renaissance Drama and a Modern Audience* (1982)

Smith, M. W. A., 'The Authorship of *The Revenger's Tragedy*', *Notes and Queries* 236 (1991), 508–13

—— 'The Authorship of *Timon of Athens*', *TEXT* 5 (1991), 195–240

Stenger, Harold L., 'The Second Maiden's Tragedy: A Modernized Edition with an Introduction'. PhD dissertation. University of Pennsylvania, 1954

Swinburne, A. C., *The Age of Shakespeare* (1908)

—— *A Study of Shakespeare*. London: Heinemann, 1918; Golden Pine Edition; first printed Chatto & Windus, 1879

Sykes, H. Dugdale, *Sidelights on Shakespeare* (1919)

—— *Sidelights on Elizabethan Drama* (1924)

—— 'Thomas Middleton's Early Non-Dramatic Works', *Notes and Queries* 148 (20 June 1925), 435–8

Taylor, Gary, 'The Canon and Chronology of Shakespeare's Plays', in Stanley Wells and Gary Taylor (with John Jowett and William Montgomery), *William Shakespeare: A Textual Companion* (1987), 69–144

—— 'Shakespeare and Others: The Authorship of *Henry the Sixth, Part One*', *Medieval and Renaissance Drama in England* 7 (1995), 145–205

—— 'Thomas Middleton, Thomas Dekker, and *The Bloody Banquet*', *Papers of the Bibliographical Society of America* 94 (2000), 197–233

—— 'Middleton and Rowley—and Heywood: *The Old Law* and New Attribution Technologies', *Papers of the Bibliographical Society of America* 96 (2002), 165–217

—— 'Thomas Middleton, *The Spanish Gypsy*, and Collaborative Authorship', in *Words That Count*, ed. Brian Boyd (2004), 241–73

Taylor, Gary, and John Jowett, *Shakespeare Reshaped, 1606–1623* (1993)

Taylor, Gary, Paul Mulholland, and MacDonald P. Jackson, 'Thomas Middleton, Lording Barry, and *The Family of Love*', *Papers of the Bibliographical Society of America* 93 (1999), 213–41

Vickers, Brian, *Appropriating Shakespeare: Contemporary Critical Quarrels* (1993)

—— *Shakespeare, Co-Author: A Historical Study of Five Collaborative Plays* (2002)

Watson, Robert N., 'Tragedy', in *The Cambridge Companion to English Renaissance Drama*, ed. A. R. Braunmuller and Michael Hattaway (1990), 301–51

Wiggin, Pauline G., *An Inquiry into the Authorship of the Middleton–Rowley Plays* (1897)

THOMAS MIDDLETON: ORAL CULTURE
AND THE MANUSCRIPT ECONOMY

Harold Love

The present age inevitably sees the drama of the Renaissance through the spectacles provided by its most substantial material relics—the early printed editions of play texts. It requires a difficult but necessary act of imagination to appreciate the total irrelevance of these relics to the actual business of creating and putting on plays. To the performers, the printed play was at best a distraction and at worst a menace. For a start, copies could be acquired by competitors who might plagiarize them or mount rival performances. Then, the reading of a printed play—mere dialogue, shorn of action and the graces of performance—might create an unfair impression that could prevent a potential theatregoer attending the original; or the rereading of a favourite play, informed by memories of those actions and graces, might satisfy a stimulus that would otherwise have led to a return visit. Brome's contract with Queen Henrietta's company specified that he 'should not suffer any playe made or to bee made or Composed by him for yor subjects or theire successors in the said Companye in Salsbury Courte to bee printed by his Consent or knowledge priuitye or dirreccoñ without the Licence from the said Companie or the Maio^r p[ar]te of them' (Haaker 1968, 298). The publication patterns of the King's Men's house writers point to a similar restriction (Bentley 1971, 264–85).

For most dramatists the printed play too was of little significance. Their main income came from the purchase price offered by the company and, for some, the proceeds of a benefit after the deduction of charges—a confirmed practice after 1660 (but as a third not a second day) which is also specified in Brome's contract of 1638 and other sources of the same decade (Bentley 1971, 128–35). Where the dramatist was responsible for the publication of a play, it seems often to have been as a means of raising money in hard times. Yet publishing booksellers would be unwilling to invade their narrow margins on such cheap products, and some were against offering any payment at all (Love 1993, 57–8). Alternatively, the writer might have to accept his fee in the form of a 'commodity' of copies of the edition, which he then had to dispose of as well as he could. Miller (1959, 160–3) and Bentley (1971, 89–91) cite the case of Richard Robinson who published (non-dramatically) between 1576 and 1600; but the practice was widespread (Love 1978). Such copies might be sold to individual purchasers, with the author acting as distributor, or disposed of to other booksellers, who would naturally offer much less. Or they might be used

for presentations, in the hope of a gift in return, though a printed playbook, even if finely bound and inscribed, was probably much less effective than a manuscript in this role. Thomas Heywood, in presenting a copy of the 1633 printed text of *The Jew of Malta* to Thomas Hammon of Gray's Inn, felt obliged to apologize for the meanness of the offering (Bowers 1973, ii, 259). When a play was paid for by a bookseller, it would presumably be at the two pounds which was the standard fee for a pamphlet (Bentley 1971, 91–3; Taylor 1987, 14 and n.).

Otherwise, the printed play might be used as a means to a dedicatee's donative, which in money terms was traditionally between two and five guineas but could also be a pathway to hospitality and other forms of patronage. Richard Robinson received gifts of 5s., 10s., £2 and £3 (twice) (Bentley 1971, 90), while Roger North, writing of the Restoration period, mentions 'the 3 4 and 5 ginnys' as the usual return for a presentation (Wilson 1959, 344). The two figures suggest a consensual understanding which rose slowly over the intervening century. Yet the dedicating dramatist required skill and good connections if he was to achieve his purpose, since the recipient of an unwanted dedication would feel under no obligation whatsoever to respond. Webster was clearly on shaky ground in dedicating *The Duchess of Malfi* to a nobleman to whom he was a complete stranger—and knew it! Dedications appear with a number of Middleton's entertainments and non-dramatic works, but with none of the plays—though this might mean no more than that he was not personally responsible for their publication. (Only in the case of *The Roaring Girl* with its signed preface, and less certainly in that of *A Trick to Catch the Old One* with its unsigned 'To the Reader', can we speculate that he had deliberately passed over an opportunity to dedicate.) It is also possible that, during much of his career, printed plays may not have been regarded as suitable vehicles for dedication. There is certainly a disparity between pre-1641 practice and that after 1660, when the vast majority of plays carried a dedication, and there was no hesitation about offering even comedies and farces to members of the aristocracy and the royal family. Franklin B. Williams, the scholar best placed to judge, considered that while before 1600 'apart from closet--drama and translations of the classics, plays were not regarded as literature ... by the death of James the custom [of dedication] was general if a play was actually published by its author' (1962, x). Yet, even while respecting this opinion, we need to remember that the number of new playscripts coming into print annually with or without dedications was still only a proportion of those actually performed. And how are we to tell with certainty that a publication was authorial, except by the evidence of a preface or dedication?

Of the few dramatists whose prefaces indicate that they valued the print medium more highly than has been proposed, several must be regarded as seeking justification for work that had failed in performance: *The White Devil* is one famous example. The high esteem felt by Jonson for the printed folio of his 'works' was viewed as eccentric by many of his contemporaries, and he was in a minority in regarding the reading of his plays as being an acceptable substitute, or preferred alternative, to seeing and hearing them in the flesh. It is not until the time of Dryden that we get a clear assertion, uninfluenced by the fate of a particular production, that even adequate performance might in certain respects be intrinsically inferior to attentive, solitary reading:

> In a Play-house every thing contributes to impose upon the Judgment; the Lights, the Scenes, the Habits, and, above all, the Grace of Action, which is commonly the best where there is the most need of it, surprize the Audience, and cast a mist upon their Understandings; not unlike the cunning of a Juggler, who is always staring us in the face, and overwhelming us with gibberish, onely that he may gain the opportunity of making the cleaner conveyance of his Trick. But these false Beauties of the Stage are no more lasting than a Rainbow; when the Actor ceases to shine upon them, when he guilds them no longer with his reflection, they vanish in a twinkling. (*The Spanish Fryar*, in Hooker and Swedenberg, xiv.100)

Of course, materials for a play were often drawn from printed books, and a certain amount of the dramatist's education would have been gained from this source; but even here it is easy to overestimate the influence of the typographical word. Education at the universities in Middleton's time was still conducted to a considerable extent through oral instruction and the study of manuscripts prepared by the tutor, while their libraries were usually barred to undergraduates (Love 1993, 217–24). Intellectual training was not yet irrevocably centred in the assimilation of materials provided by print culture but structured itself instead around the activity of oral disputation (devastatingly guyed in *A Chaste Maid in Cheapside* 4.1), or, for law students, that of mooting.

The theatre's overriding concern, then, was always with the memorial text. David Bradley (1992, 23), in his study of surviving plats, sides, and promptbooks, has stressed the extent to which the stage action of Elizabethan plays was organized through the aural not the written medium:

What the actors were to do when they got on stage and how they were to make their exits appear to be matters of less concern to the Plotter, at any rate as far as making a record went. These matters appear to have been governed largely by the spoken text. Some Plots do not mark exits at all, and, even in promptbooks, exits are frequently overlooked, just as they often are in printed texts. Stage action is almost never described, although in many cases it must have been elaborate: the Plotter merely records the entrances and the properties that are to be carried on.

There was no need to write down what the performer would have divined from the dialogue. Alleyn's side for Orlando contains 'none of the positional markings and scribbled annotations that are typical of a modern player's script': instead, again, he relied on his ears and the fact that what was spoken on stage would have been clearly audible in the tiring-room. There is no cue at all

> for Orlando's disguised, silent entry into the final scene about thirty-seven lines after it begins. Alleyn need have been able to carry in his head no more than a modern actor, but, in order to make a correct entrance here, he must clearly have been able to hear the dialogue and to follow its drift, for the direction for his entrance in the text is placed merely for convenience between speeches, and Orlando's first lines reply to words uttered before that point. (Bradley, 25)

The actors' sides contained their own lines and cues only: they probably never saw a complete text of the play. Once conceived in terms of voice and gesture, the work was recorded in manuscripts but might, even then, require to be retransmitted to the actors as voice. Henslowe records enough occasions on which new work was read aloud by the dramatist to the sharers, usually over wine, to establish that this, rather than the inspection of the script, was the general custom. Censorship might also be conducted through the aural rather than a written text. While George Buc and Henry Herbert, successive Masters of the Revels, worked on and annotated scripts, the patent of a predecessor, Edmund Tilney, who held office from 1579 to 1609, enjoined attendance at a recitation or performance (Bentley 1971, 148–9). (A late survival of this practice was the reading aloud by Thomas Southerne in 1719 of his long-banned *The Spartan Dame* to Congreve, acting as the Lord Chamberlain's agent.) Examining the text in performance or quasi-performance was a sensible discipline given that theatrical words take so much of their meaning from context, gesture, and inflection.

The ideal of composition for voice might extend to a dramatist inventing aloud (like a musician composing at the piano) rather than mentally. Once again our only attested example is from after our period, in some advice to aspiring dramatists by Charles Gildon, drawing in this instance on Aristotle:

When the general Plan is form'd, the Poet should endeavour, before he sets to write, at any time during his penning of the whole Piece, to imitate with his own Body the Gestures and Actions of those Dramatic Persons, to whom he is about to give Words and Sentiments proper to the Passions they are possess'd with; to which I must add, that he should likewise imitate the Voice, and the Utterance; all which join'd together will fix in his Soul the Passion and Characters he is writing, and by that means he can never miss drawing them according to Nature. This was the Method that Otway follow'd, as I have been assur'd by an intimate Acquaintance of his; and to this Method I must in great measure attribute his admirable touching of the Passions. (Gildon 1718, i, 258)

Horace (representing Ben Jonson) is shown composing a poem aloud in *Satiromastix* 1.2, but, seeing he is a character in a play, that is only to be expected: what we need to know is whether his creator Dekker also composed aloud. That some dramatists may have written in this way would be consonant with other information we have about the persistence of orally influenced reading and writing practices into the early modern era. Renaissance pedagogical custom encouraged the use of voice, and even gesture, in private reading as a means both of internalizing what was read and practising the skills of rhetorical delivery. Roger North (1742, 16) in recommending the practice to aspiring lawyers maintained that 'in speaking, a Man is his own Auditor (if he had no others at Hand) to correct himself'. Training in composition within a university system geared to the needs of embryo preachers and advocates was always primarily concerned with the oral text.

Remote from the period of our concern, but illuminating with regard to oral/scribal culture, is the medieval practice by which a letter would be taken to a recipient in order to be read aloud by the bearer and then returned by that bearer to the writer—its function being that of the script for an aural message, not a message in its own right. The practice would be understandable enough for a period when many recipients would have been illiterate; but is also found in the case of letters written in Latin from one learned ecclesiastic to another (Constable 1967, ii, 27–8). If Middleton had written from Oxford to his mother, who signed with a mark and may well have been illiterate, it would have been with the same procedure in view. This exemplifies what Ong (1982, 119) has referred to as the 'residual orality' of the chirographic text. However, the stage, for its own purposes, did preserve another attested medieval practice by which letters would be read aloud by recipients to themselves—possibly still the custom of some readers in Middleton's time. Totally silent reading was certainly known by the sixteenth century but was far from universal.

A practice curious to us but apparently universal in Renaissance England was that by which spelling was taught aurally before the commencement of instruction in writing (Cressy 1980, 20–1). Middleton almost certainly learned to spell in this way. But what is odd viewed from the perspective of a highly literate culture makes perfect sense for one in which the memorized text, available at all times for mental inspection, was more valued than that which lay passively on the page, and the mind permanently stocked with such texts was seen as representing the summit of human learning. Such a mind would also be ready at any time, without preparation, to perform the functions of the advocate in law, the counsellor in government, the controversialist in religion, and, of course, the actor. Today where such skills exist it is largely through the possession of a freak visual memory which retains the image of a scanned page, whereas the older ideal rested firmly on the possession of the word as voice. Ideas as such might be memorized as allegorical pictures, and complex arrangements of particulars disposed around the walls of mentally visualized memory theatres (Yates 1966); but there can be no doubt that verbal memory, at this period, was still strongly aural (Chaytor 1945, 5–21).

The voices, however, are gone. What remains to us from the aural universe of the Renaissance stage are the printed texts and a small but precious body of manuscripts connected with the playhouse and its patrons. In the remainder of this essay I wish to look firstly at the use of manuscripts within the operations of the playhouse; then at the playhouse's relationship to the immense scribal culture beyond its walls; then at Middleton's involvement in both these spheres of scribal work and transmission.

The use of manuscripts within the playhouse

The use of manuscripts within the playhouse has been considered by several scholars, and will be summarized here in its general outlines without taking account of a number of individual departures which are covered in more specialized studies (Bradley 1992, Bentley 1971, Bowers 1966, Greg 1931, Greg 1953, Honigmann 1965, Taylor 1987). The principal documents concerned are the playscript in its various authorial forms, the playhouse master copy and promptbook (when these were not identical), the actors' sides (or 'parts'), the plot or 'plat' (charting entrances and doublings), and a variety of manuscripts connected with the running of the theatre, including playbills, business records, legal documents and correspondence. The agents who might have been involved in their preparation were authors and their amanuenses, if used; the prompter, bookkeeper, stage reviser and plotter (who may—as Bradley points out (1992, 2)—have been one or a number of individuals depending on circumstances); professional scribes such as Ralph Crane; and the playhouse secretary, if this duty was not performed by one or more of the sharers.

In discussing the manuscripts generated by the author we are limited by the paucity of surviving examples and the fact that knowledge about those lost manuscripts which served as the basis for printed editions is invariably speculative. Scholars are accustomed to distinguish two significant stages in the process as that of the 'foul papers' and that of the fair copy, the first being imagined as a rough draft, possibly with sporadic palimpsestic features, and the second the finished version eventually sold to the company. The hypothesizing of these two stages has been helpful in suggesting solutions to textual problems in printed playbooks; however, there can be no certainty either that these were the only manuscripts produced in the course of composition, or that all plays passed through both. On one hand, there is no reason why a dramatist skilled in memorial composition may not have gone straight to fair-copy stage (as, much later, Dr Johnson and Keats did, likewise Mozart in writing out music); while, on the other, it is possible that some dramatists lacked the scribal skills to produce an acceptable fair copy (e.g. Thomas Heywood whose hand puzzles even his modern editors). Certainly, the sometimes mooted notion of a much-interlined set of foul papers seems to belong more to a modern conception of authorial revision than to the rhetorical methods described earlier. It is true that heavily overwritten examples can be found among non-dramatic manuscripts of the time; however, these largely result from the phenomenon of serial composition (Love 1993, 52–4) rather than being primary drafts. The text composed for the ear rather than the eye must often have been in its finished form before commitment to paper. In any case, paper was so expensive that even wealthy writers used it with great economy.

Whatever the nature of the drafting process (and however ingenious the author in extracting advances on work in progress), final payment could only be secured by the presentation of a legible copy to the company. This would then be sent to the Master of the Revels for approval. In one comment, Herbert acknowledges that preliminary editorial work had been done by the King's Men's bookholder, Edward Knight, on what was apparently an authorial fair copy: approval, naturally, was sought not for the author's text but for the form in which it was to be performed by the company (Bentley 1971, 156). It was only when the Master's endorsement was obtained that the prompter could proceed confidently with the preparation of the plat, the sides, and the promptbook. Examples of all of these kinds of document survive and are reproduced and classified in Greg (1931). Further evidence as to the nature of promptbooks can be obtained from printed texts which were set from them and preserve their annotations. It is likely, of course, in some (or many?) cases that an annotated authorial copy *was* the promptbook. Again, fair and foul papers may well have been used together to expedite the rapid copying of sides or additional copies by two scribes working simultaneously. If any conceptual advances are to be made in the understanding of such matters, it will probably be by analogy with the wider field of scribal practice which will be discussed in the next section.

Fredson Bowers, refining Greg's distinctions, has hypothesized thirteen different kinds of copy which may, if they all ever existed, have given rise to printed play texts, indicating that the bibliographical study of printed plays is, in one sense at least, a study of manuscripts at one remove.

(1) author's foul papers; (2) authorial or scribal fair copies not intended for direct theatrical use; (3) foul papers or fair copies partially marked by the prompter as a preliminary for transcription into prompt; (4) scribal transcripts made for private individuals and not for theatrical purposes, the source being foul papers, fair copy, or theatrical prompt book; (5) a manuscript prompt book itself; (6) a scribal transcript of a prompt book; (7) an unrevised copy of an earlier printed edition; (8) an unauthoritatively revised copy of an earlier printed edition, the revisions presumably originating with the publisher or his agent; (9) an authoritatively revised copy of an earlier edition marked by the author; (10) a copy of an earlier printed edition annotated by comparison with some manuscript, usually assumed to be authorial or prompt, preserved in the theatre's archives; (11) a subdivision of the above, consisting of an earlier printed edition marked and used by the theatre company as a prompt book, or another copy of an edition marked for the printer to conform to such a printed prompt book; (12) another possible subdivision of the above, a new and as yet untested theory, which conjectures a scribal transcript made for the printer of such a marked printed prompt book, or else a manuscript made up for the printer by an independent act of conflating a printed edition with a manuscript preserved in the theatre; (13) the 'foul papers', fair copy, prompt book, or transcript of a prompt book of a memorial reconstruction of the text without direct transcriptional link with any manuscript derived from author's autograph, in other words, the copy for a so-called 'bad quarto'. Many of these classes may be mixed by introducing additional manuscript material, as a new scene, of different textual history from that of the main copy; or, in reverse, of introducing leaves from a printed edition to fill out gaps in a manuscript or to obviate transcription in part; or the patching of printed copy by leaves from a different edition. (Bowers 1966, 11–12)

The thirteen is somewhat arbitrary, the total number of permutations being much larger. Our concern at the moment is simply with what the list suggests about the range of scribal activity attending the performance and publication of plays. Obviously no single play could ever have existed in as many forms as Bowers hypothesizes, since there would always have been strong pressure for economy in the consumption and storage of paper quite apart from the cost of copying. In some cases a single book may well have satisfied the needs of the company, albeit one whose text would record several layers of professional intervention. But in an institution in which the handwritten play text served not only as a memory bank for lines, but as an indispensable ancillary to performance, a token of ownership and legal obligation, and an object of commerce in its own right, there must often have been good reason for duplication. One should also remember that the sides, which remained in the possession of the performer not the bookholder, were particularly liable to loss as well as vulnerable to destruction through wear, being the hardest used of all theatrical manuscripts.

The daily work of theatre also gave rise to other documents: accounts, correspondence, legal contracts, and summaries of business dealings, such as the Henslowe diary (Foakes and Rickert 1961). Copy for printed playbills had to be prepared daily and handwritten ones may well have been required in the event of late programme changes. Music, both as notes and tablature, would need to be copied in substantial quantities, with that for the lute, bandora and cittern being of exceptional complexity. All three are found in the popular 'Morley Consort' instrumentation, which seems to have been used in at least some theatres: a glance at Morley's own pieces for the ensemble will indicate the difficulties (Beck 1959). The bookkeeper would have had an archival responsibility for keeping a large library of playbooks, business records and music partbooks repaired and in good order, bearing in mind that, in the calculation of the price of shares in a company, a high monetary value was placed on these materials. We should also remember that the act of inscription required much more preparation then than now: a bookkeeper under any pressure to economize would have needed to prepare his own ink and cut his own quills—and may in any case have preferred for reasons of craftsmanship to do this rather than rely on the inferior bought product (Finlay 1990). Through the activities mentioned, the playhouses' volume of scribal work appears substantial enough for us to speak of them as constituting scriptoria, and to speculate what space within them may have been devoted to writing and the storage of records, and what proportion of their budgets needed to be reserved for that purpose. If keeping play texts secure from rivals was an important consideration, binding too may have been performed within the playhouse rather than scripts being sent out to a bindery. Certainly, it is hard to see how the regular writing required by a busy, metropolitan company could have been handled by a single scribe, if he was also required to serve as prompter.

Bentley (1971, 87) hypothesizes that the copying of sides might have been farmed out to professional scribes such as Ralph Crane, who by his own boast had worked for the King's company (Crane 1620, A6^r); however, it seems to me that a scribe of Crane's calibre (and the fee he would have demanded for his refined skills) would have been wasted on workaday documents. It would have been cheaper to get one of the hired men to assist with such copying on a piece-work basis. Crane, rather, belongs with the external professionals who would have been retained by the major companies: speculatively an

attorney to deal with litigation, a scrivener to prepare business agreements and the simpler writs, a goldsmith to have custody of surplus funds, and perhaps an astrologer to advise on policy decisions. The attorney, the goldsmith and particularly the scrivener would have maintained staffs of trained penmen who would have been available when fine as opposed to workaday writing was required and when scripts were required for sale or presentation.

A final form of activity which demands consideration is the adapting or revision of plays (for the distinction see Kerrigan 1983) for new circumstances of production. Far from being a rare event, it is likely that this happened as often as an old play was brought back into the repertory after a period of neglect. By the 1630s, when a significant proportion of the performances of the established companies was of established repertoire favourites (including perennials like *The Changeling*), work of this kind may well have been at least as important to the salaried playwrights as the writing of new scripts (Bentley 1971, 235–63). But even during Middleton's working lifetime it is clear that there was a constant need to update old scripts to meet the demands of new performers and audiences. He himself adapted *Macbeth* and *Measure for Measure* and had the compliment returned by Shirley for *No Wit/Help like a Woman's*. Restoration practice is again indicative here, since many of the causes that led to the wholesale rewriting of earlier plays (including Middleton's) after 1660 were already operating much earlier. Once again, our evidence for the nature of these revised manuscript versions has for the most part to be gained from anomalies in printed texts; but in one famous case, that of *The Play of Sir Thomas More*, the surviving manuscript is an aggregation of materials in a number of hands (exhaustively discussed in Howard-Hill 1989). The relevance of this to our present enquiry lies in the extent to which it underlines the responsibility of the 'Stage-reviser' (again with Bradley's warning that this function may have been shared around or exercised communally within given companies). Extensive adaptation of plays would exercise a multiplier effect on scribal activity within the company, since it might destroy the capacity of the base manuscript to serve as a promptbook or make an existing promptbook obsolete, as well as requiring the writing of new sides and plats, and possibly a prologue/epilogue (like Middleton's pair in 1602 for *Friar Bacon and Friar Bungay*) or an induction and new music. Often, no doubt, existing documents were reconstructed rather than rewritten, but it should not be assumed that this was always less demanding in terms of time and care. In any case it must sometimes have been more practical to rewrite a much-worn side or plat for which heavy future use was anticipated than to glue in new material.

Use of play manuscripts outside the theatres

With this we move to the knottier question of manuscript as a medium for the transmission of plays beyond the confines of the theatre (Bowers's category 4). This will need to be considered not simply with regard to the fates of individual manuscripts but also as it concerns the relationship of dramatists, actors, and playgoers to a culture of transcription that was still a strong competitor to the press. The broader features of this culture have been considered in Love (1993), to which the reader is referred.

Scribal publication as such is to be distinguished both from print and oral publication (the latter being the primary form with plays, as with sermons) and from the wider phenomenon of scribal transmission, which was basic to every aspect of commercial and administrative activity in early modern England. Some sense of the ubiquity of the handwritten word is given by the range of documents from which we derive our knowledge of Middleton's life and dealings: church registers recording baptisms, marriages and funerals, legal documents (multiple lawsuits involving his mother and stepfather, actions for debt, Privy Council records relating to *A Game at Chess*, records of parish rates paid by his father and himself, his signature in a matriculation book, guild records naming himself and various members of his family, wills of his father and son, and genealogical records relating to his father's coat of arms and his own status as a gentleman. But it is even more sobering to imagine what must have been lost from a lifetime's professional inscription, business and legal transactions, parish and municipal activity, dealings with the secular and ecclesiastical arms of government, and correspondence. Much of both the lost and the surviving heritage would have been recorded in the script of professional clerks and scriveners, a well-rewarded and meticulously trained industrial cadre whose annual consumption of the three staple materials of quills, ink and the high quality paper and parchment surfaces needed for writing was the basis of a significant import trade (Finlay 1990). Seconding the professionals was the large body of non-professionals who had mastered the technology of manual inscription at a more than trivial level and who used it both to circulate texts through communities of the like-minded and to build up personal databases in the form of commonplace books, miscellanies, volumes of 'collections' and assemblages of muniments. Linking the two groups, and responsible for the training of many members of each of them, were the professional writing masters, who were also in many cases virtuosos of an art which, at its highest level, was treasured as one of the noblest accomplishments of civilization. Throughout our period and for much of the century following, the scribe, whether professional or amateur, remained an active competitor of the printer in the duplication of culturally and ideologically important texts. Although unable to compete with the press in quantity, the older medium could still outdo it in rapidity of response, in the capacity to clothe words in appropriate visual dress, and, through the 'reserved' nature of the medium, which protected its products, even when consciously directed at a public, from too promiscuous an availability.

Whereas in print publication a text is made available in a substantial number of copies which can be purchased from booksellers, scribal publication worked through the more subtle method of directing texts into networks of transmission, where they would be replicated according to the degree of interest they aroused. (The present-day practice of distributing texts by e-mail is a helpful analogy.) The contrast is between a form of production that was centralized in the printing shop and one that was to a large extent dispersed among consumers who were also producers. These networks of transmission (or 'scribal communities') were sometimes the creation of private individuals, and sometimes grew from the cultural and political life of institutions. They might establish themselves among alumni of a college, Inn or university, among gentry of a particular county, among clients of a patron, among members of a profession, or among enthusiasts for a discipline or cause. At court their function was usually factional. Although they were in theory bearers of private information, in practice networks would inevitably intersect through having members in common, with the result that shorter texts of more than specialized interest would move rapidly from network to network, until they had achieved nationwide distribution. Transmitted initially, for the most part, as 'separates' of one or two sheets, scribally published texts have survived chiefly as later transcripts in professionally assembled compilations or personal manuscript miscellanies (referred to loosely as 'commonplace books'). Middleton's verse petition to James I (Beal MiT 1–5; addenda 5A) and the song, 'Hence, all you vain delights' from *The Nice Valour* (Beal B&F 112–53) circulated in exactly this way, the latter the most widely transcribed theatre lyric of the whole period.

The other important difference between scribal and print publication was that, instead of production occurring in a single explosive provision of copies, it proceeded continuously, either as a series of editions of one initiated by the intending reader (user publication) or through successive duplications of a master copy. The agents involved in this second, more organized form of copying would either be authors or professional copyists working on an author's or their own account or under contract to booksellers (Love 1993, 35–89). Separates of topical or political significance were offered to the clients of the London newsletter writers, scribal journalists who in some cases maintained scriptoria (Love 1993, 124–6). The newsletter distribution systems acted as national networks feeding material into the local ones.

As early as the reign of James I the audience for scribally transmitted texts and the mechanisms for their circulation were sufficiently developed for many authors to be able to reject the print alternative and circulate their output largely, or in some cases entirely, through the scribal medium. The reasons for this varied: in some cases it arose from what J. W. Saunders, in a remembered phrase, has called 'the stigma of print'—a resistance among the gentry and aristocracy to their work becoming an article of commerce (Saunders 1951). This was also a period at which, for various reasons, a demand arose for materials which were forbidden to the press but which could be provided efficiently, if somewhat expensively, through the scribal medium. The publication of parliamentary proceedings through commercial scriptoria is one profusely documented example; that of satires, lampoons and other kinds of libertine and oppositional writing was obviously another. There is much scattered evidence for contemporary French, Spanish, and Italian writing, and translations from it, being available to Middleton in manuscript (Mulryne 1975), reflecting a wider accessibility to which newsletter writers are known to have contributed (Powell 1977, 56). But, in many cases, the medium was chosen because it was simply more rewarding, both financially and in terms of the search for patronage and influence, than publication through the press. Musicians and music copyists, in particular, could make much more out of compositions sold in manuscript to performers and pupils than they could from print publication. The vast majority of instrumental and sacred vocal music written in England during the seventeenth century was published scribally, and as late as 1669 John Playford found himself obliged to contest the belief that 'no Choice Ayres or Songs are permitted by Authors to come in print' (Playford 1669, A1^r; Love 1993, 63–5). It was presumably for this reason that the Byrd-East monopoly of printed music proved such a failure. The playhouses, being a major source of new songs, may well have been involved in the marketing of manuscript copies. In the Restoration period John Carr made a living 'wrighting the theatricall tunes, to accommodate learners and country fidlers' (Wilson 1959, 29n). Authors, at least in certain specialized genres, might choose to operate in exactly the same way.

The professionalization of scribal authorship appears at its most interesting at a point where the new, streamlined methods of networked distribution blend with established traditions of the presentation of a text by a client to a patron or a series of patrons. While the dedication of a printed text, being a public act, was normally only made once (with Middleton's twice-dedicated *Sir Robert Sherley* a pointed exception), a scribally published work could be presented to several patrons in succession with little danger of detection and for returns that might each time be equivalent to that of the printed dedication. The scribal text could also be a way of establishing factional or professional alliances, as the careers of Donne and Henry King reveal. Writers operating at this social level might not sell copies directly but present them in expectation of a gift or favour in return, often using Middleton's pretext with the Hammond manuscript of *A Game at Chess* of their being a new-year's gift. In both Donne's and King's cases the writer worked from a base within a particular scribal community, Donne's being composed of Inns of Court contemporaries and King's of Oxford colleagues.

While initially writings were meant to remain within these communities, the mechanism of intersection and the employment of professional copyists meant that they soon became a much broader possession, both in the form of collections of works by the writers concerned and, more characteristically, items absorbed into personal or commercially written miscellanies. It can never have taken a writer long to become aware that once the genie of scribal publication was out of the bottle there was no way of returning it. The reputed exclusivity of the medium acted as a spur to obtain texts from networks and to insert new ones into them. Some texts must have existed in hundreds of copies, with many items continuing to be recopied for decades and still surviving today in fifty or more manuscripts. In terms of its ability to promulgate texts, scribal publication was a formidable rival to the press, which in turn looked to it avidly as a source of novelties, but was rarely able to obtain them in accurate copies. Dozens of instances could be cited where the piratical printing of a text from a casually encountered manuscript (or the threat of it) led to the reluctant printing of an authorial text. But even here the surviving manuscripts may still preserve a more authentic form of the work, since print publication demanded a new set of decorums, greater formality, and the suppression of the indecent and heterodox.

The relationship of the theatre to this transmissional practice has never been properly considered; but Middleton is incontestably a crucial figure. The circulation of *A Game at Chess* in 1624–5 is our clearest example from the English Renaissance stage of a 'scribal edition' (its significance will be discussed shortly). However, while at a later period unprinted plays by Fletcher and Massinger are known to have been obtainable in manuscript, there is little evidence for the scribal publication of play texts prior to Middleton's initiative, which may, in any case, have been directed at collectors of anti-Spanish political material rather than admirers of the drama. (Thomas Cogswell has argued for its having been performed and circulated as a follow-up to Buckingham's slanted account of his Spanish voyage with Prince Charles, manuscripts of which enjoy 'a near ubiquity...in surviving gentry collections' (Cogswell 1984, 283).) The possibility of significantly earlier precedents has been considered both by Greg (1954, 45), who regarded it as unproven, and John Jowett (1991, 255) who saw it as unlikely on the grounds that 'the drama simply did not belong to an élite culture in the sense that metaphysical poetry did'. And yet, the fact that there are no earlier *surviving* examples of scribally published play texts would be of little account were we able to accept the assumption of numerous editors (including Bowers in the passage already quoted and Howard-Hill in his work on Ralph Crane) that manuscripts written for reading, rather than the practical work of the theatre, underlie some surviving printed texts. The 1609 *Troilus and Cressida*, nominated by Ernst Honigmann as a possible early consequence of this practice, is currently too controversial an example to be cited with confidence but indicates the *kind* of play which, despite Jowett's insistence, might plausibly have appealed as early as 1603 to an élite readership (Honigmann 1985; Wells and Taylor 1987, 425–6). Certainly, there would be nothing strange in an author, whether or not forbidden the press, seeking patrons' guineas through the scribal medium. The significant query as far as Middleton is concerned is, rather, one that arises from the opening paragraphs of this essay: under what circumstances and at what period can we envisage a reader wishing to possess the manuscript text of a play for the purpose of reading it, rather than attending the theatre?

Jowett is right in assuming that such a reader would need to be wealthy. Humphrey Moseley, in referring to the trade in manuscripts of plays by Fletcher, noted, 'Heretofore when Gentlemen desired but a Copy of any of these *Playes*, the meanest piece here (if any may be called Meane where every one is Best) cost them more then foure times the price you pay for the whole *Volume*' (Beaumont and Fletcher 1647, A4ᵛ). Moseley does exaggerate somewhat: such a manuscript could be produced for well under a pound and handsomely bound for presentation for a few shillings more. The price he has in mind is that of the customary patron's gift rather than a realistic commercial rate. But even a pound was a considerable sum to have tied up in a single manuscript, and one which the playwright could have saved (as many *literati* did) by the simpler, but not necessarily less effective, method of addressing the patron in a manuscript epigram, elegy, verse epistle or sonnet sequence. Jonson's output contains dozens of short poems of compliment of this kind, which we can confidently assume to have performed their function as presented manuscripts prior to their appearance in print. (His awareness of the power of scribal networking is vividly expressed in 'To my Muse, the lady Digby, on her Husband, Sir Kenelme Digby'.) So, as well as needing reasons why a patron would have wanted a scribal copy of a play, we also need reasons why the author would have been prepared to accede to this demanding request, rather than going about his task of begging in some less expensive fashion.

One, partial answer to this may lie in the practice of presenting a patron with an annual new-year's gift. This was a major event of the patron's year, being observed in our period with great formality. Such donations were, needless to say, self-interested, in that the client expected either a gift in return or services and assistance in the year to come: the more substantial the gift the greater the expectation of a return. Patrons measured their own status by the range and value of the gifts they received. While food, clothing, jewels, and plate seem to have been the most common gifts, authors would naturally offer printed books or manuscripts (Miller 1962), the manuscript being the gift of higher status. Ralph Crane made an annual presentation of one to John, Earl of Bridgwater; while, on the other hand, Thomas Heywood, in a passage referred to earlier, found it necessary to apologize for only having a printed play to present (Wilson 1926, 200). Thomas Churchyard, in an illuminating passage, speaks with great frankness about the motives behind such presentations:

Then thought I to beginne the yere:
On Newe yeres daie with some deuice,
And though that many men be nice,

And blushe to make an honest shifte,
I sent eche Lorde a Newe yeres gifte:
Such treasure as I had that tyme,
A laughyng verse, a merrie ryme...
Some thinke this is a crauyng guise,
Tushe holde your peace, world waxeth wise
A dulled horse that will not sturre,
Must be remembred with a spurre:
And where there serues ne spurre nor wand,
A man must needs lead horse in hande.
So I was forste on causes greate,
To see in fire where laye the heate:
And warme their witts that cold did waxe,
But thrust the fire into the Flax...
(Churchyard 1580, C2ʳ–C3ʳ; Miller 1962, 234)

In the opening lines of Dryden's 'To My Lord Chancellor Presented on New-years-day' (Hooker and Swedenberg, i, 38) 'flattering crouds' appear on the day

To give themselves, not you, an happy year;
And by the greatness of their Presents prove
How much they hope, but not how well they love...

The copy of *A Game at Chess* presented by Middleton to William Hammond is by its own statement a new-year's gift. Such gifts belong to the culture of presentation rather than that of commercial sale, but provide a strong reason why playwrights may have been prepared to undertake the preparation of lengthy manuscripts for reading. A company with control over unpublished plays may well have chosen the same means to ingratiate itself with a powerful patron. The King's Men are known to have made new-year's gifts to the Master of the Revels, though their form is not specified (Bentley 1984, 153).

Given the *possibility* of scribal publication of play manuscripts prior to 1624, either by authors or by theatre companies (more will be said about this matter shortly), and the abundant evidence for it after that date, our next problem is how to detect such manuscripts from their outcomes. In the case of the surviving manuscripts it would be through the quality of the script and the absence of any signs of playhouse use: all but one of those in Ralph Crane's hand meet this criterion. The exception is *Sir John Van Olden Barnavelt*, BL MS Add. 18653, which has been marked up by a second scribe to serve as a promptbook; but this probably resulted from the great speed with which this topical play was brought to the stage. In manuscripts the presence of a dedication confirms that they (or an ancestor) were written to be presented. In the case of printed editions the signs are those which betray the piratical capture of scribally published originals in other domains, of which the most important is the *lack* of a dedication or preface. Other kinds of evidence might be a decayed but not hopelessly decayed text (in that it would be unlikely for a play to experience the weight of recopying which produces the more spectacularly corrupt versions of poems and political pieces), the presence of stage directions of an authorial rather than of a prompterial kind, and the absence of the kinds of errors that betray a careless, hard-to-decipher script—manuscripts offered for sale or presentation always being carefully written. Derivation from scribal reading texts might also be suspected when, as in Crane's case, we could identify traces of the orthographical or punctuational practice of a scribe known to have been involved in the preparation of such copies in other contexts and genres; however, our knowledge of such matters is still at a very elementary level, Crane being the only scribe whose habits have been properly studied.

The case of Middleton

Having indicated some of the salient features of the culture and the commerce of scribal transmission, it remains to consider the significance to it of the surviving manuscripts of plays by Middleton, supplementing our knowledge of these with what can be plausibly hypothesized about the lost manuscripts that underlie the printed editions. *A Game at Chess*, being the most straightforward case, will be dealt with first. In the interval between the play's suppression in August 1624 and the appearance of a printed edition at an unknown date in the following year, six surviving manuscripts were produced of which one is wholly in Middleton's hand and three in that of Ralph Crane (Beal MiT 14–19). The two manuscripts written by other scribes each have a title-page (and in one case sections of text) in Middleton's hand. T. H. Howard-Hill (1987, 307; see also Howard-Hill *et al.* 1990, viii–x) has calculated on the basis of a stemmatological analysis of textual variation that 'at least seven more copies of the text must have been made . . . in order to produce the six terminal copies which survive', making thirteen in all. But the total number produced is likely to have been higher still, being limited only by what Middleton, Crane and their assistants could produce over the four months or more during which manuscripts of the play remained a hot property.

The nature of the operation is suggested by the dedication to 'the Worthlie-Accomplish'd, Mr: William Hammond' added by Middleton to one of the manuscripts in Crane's hand:

This, which nor Stage nor Stationers Stall can Showe,
(The Common Eye maye wish for, but ne're knowe)
Comes in it's best Loue, wth the New-yeare forth,
As a fit Present to the Hand of Worth.

In this case we are dealing with a manuscript produced by Crane under Middleton's supervision; in other cases Crane may either have been working for Middleton or going into production on his own behalf, as he did when he added a dedication in his own name to a manuscript of Fletcher's *The Humorous Lieutenant* as *Demetrius and Enanthe* (Beal B&F 59). The production of the 1624–5 manuscripts seems to have been a hurried operation with even the playwright, a far from expert scribe, deleting text for speed and economy. Several exemplars were used in order to streamline copying, including one of the play in a pre-performance state. It should also have been a very profitable process. The dedication to Hammond, despite its

maintaining the fiction of a gift from friend to friend, is likely to have been paid for in one form or another. The copies without dedications may have been commissioned by a bookseller who would know how to make good use of them. The printed edition that brought this happy situation to an end could have been piratical: if not, it was probably pre-emptive in its intention, since the likelihood of a piratical printing rose with every new manuscript that went into circulation. Middleton, Crane and their assistants were engaged in a race against time in the production of copies, knowing that a printed text would be a very desirable addition to any stationer's stall.

The manuscript of *The Witch* (Beal MiT 28) is another case of a presentation manuscript written by Ralph Crane but with a dedication from Middleton, this time to 'the truly worthy and generously affected Thomas Holmes Esquire', a Gray's Inn lawyer (Phelps 1980, 152–4). The opening paragraph would suggest that Middleton seized on some casual words of approval by Holmes in order to pursue him with a copy:

As a true testimony of my ready inclination to your service, I have, merely upon a taste of your desire, recovered into my hands, though not without much difficulty, this ignorantly ill-fated labour of mine.

Bullen (v, 355) thought the manuscript was recovered from the King's company; but there is no assurance that this was the case—indeed the claim of recovery may have been added simply to enhance the value of the gift. What is more significant is Middleton's assurance in the second paragraph that 'For your sake alone she hath thus far conjured herself abroad', suggesting (if we choose to believe him) that the manuscript was a one-off occurrence, not part of a scribal edition.

In the case of *Hengist, King of Kent*, at least three manuscripts must have been in circulation—those that survive as the Folger and Portland copies (Beal MiT 22–3), and that which provided copy for the 1661 printed edition (probably identical with that owned in 1646 by Humphrey Moseley (*Stationers' Register* 4 Sept. 1646)). The first two show signs of promptbook origin and are therefore more likely to have been put into circulation by actors than the dramatist. John Cotgrave may have drawn on a fourth for quotations in his *English Treasury of Wit and Language* (Bentley 1943). Bentley argues on textual and circumstantial grounds that Cotgrave's copy was the same as Moseley's; however, it is just as possible that it was a transcript purchased *from* Moseley, who seems to have acted as a scribal as well as a print publisher. We are unlikely to err in assuming a much larger scribal circulation, since the play's anti-Puritan satire would have kept it topical long after Middleton's death.

Certainly, there seems to have been quite a number of Middleton manuscripts in circulation during the mid-century. Moseley, for one, must have had a sizeable collection, noting in 'To the Reader' of *Women, Beware Women* that the play had been acquired 'amongst others of Mr. Thomas Middleton's Excellent Poems'—no doubt including the group that he registered in 1653 (Middleton 1657, A3ʳ; SR 9 Sept. 1653). Moseley's manuscripts may, of course, have come from the dramatist's family (in which case it would be incorrect to multiply up for the possibility of loss). But, even if this were so (which has not been suggested), neither the manuscripts we do possess nor those that gave rise to the other posthumous editions (to be discussed below) appear to have had any link with Moseley's collection. Abraham Hill's list of plays in manuscript includes two Middleton items, *Your Five Gallants* and the lost *The Conquerors Custom or the Fair Prisoner* (Adams 1939). While it would be going too far on the basis of our present knowledge to suggest that Middleton was a consistent and committed scribal publisher, it is clear that he thoroughly understood the ways by which money or gifts could be obtained through the presentation of play manuscripts.

The final surviving dramatic manuscript, that of the entertainment, *An Invention Performed for the Service of the Right Honourable Edward Barkham, Lord Mayor of the City of London*, is to be viewed together with those of no less than ten of Jonson's masques (two of them in several copies) as evidence of a desire on the part of participants in the celebrations concerned to acquire manuscripts of texts which were not available in print. A study by James Knowles (1992) of the scribal circulation of Marston's *The Entertainment at Ashby* throws considerable light on this practice. Here a second set of copies for distribution had to be prepared after the first was apparently stolen. Henry Lawes's circulation of manuscripts of Milton's *Comus* is a well-known later example (Sprott 1973).

The evidence of the printed editions

Printed editions are relevant to this enquiry firstly in so far as they may be derived from manuscripts prepared for sale or presentation to readers, and secondly in so far as the deliberate withholding of a title from the press—whether by a company or by the author—would have been an incentive to scribal publication. If the insistence came from the company, the scribal medium would have offered the dramatist his only means of further income; however, it is also conceivable that an author in a position to print might, for reasons already given, decide that withholding plays from the press would in the long term lead to better returns.

Taking the Middleton canon as now established we will note a peak of print publication during the years 1607-8 during which no less than ten plays appeared. Some of these were a few years old at the time of publication but a number seem to have reached the press not long after their performance by the Children of Paul's or the Children of the Revels, who, rather than the dramatist, may have been responsible for their publication. (As mentioned, only *The Roaring Girl* offers clear evidence of Middleton's participation and approval.) After 1611 there was a pointed falling off. Apart from *A Game at Chess*, *The World Tossed at Tennis* and the collaborations *A Fair Quarrel* (1617), with a dedication

signed by Rowley, and *Timon of Athens* (a last-minute addition to the Shakespeare folio of 1623) no further plays reached the press prior to Middleton's death in July 1627. This does not indicate any disillusionment with the print medium as such, since from 1613 his city entertainments appeared with great regularity, but surely requires explanation, especially as there was a body of older and new plays which would have been attractive to a print-publisher. These, with their dates of publication given in chronological order, were *A Chaste Maid in Cheapside* (1630), *Wit at Several Weapons* and *The Nice Valour* (1647), *The Widow* (1652), *The Changeling* (1653), *More Dissemblers Besides Women* and *Women, Beware Women* (1657), *No Wit/Help like a Woman's* (1657), *The Mayor of Queenborough* (1661), *Anything for a Quiet Life* (1662), and *The Witch* (1778)—two of which, as we saw, also survive in manuscript. Moreover, unless we are to assume a decline in creativity, there must have been other plays, apart from *The Conqueror's Custom* and *The Puritan Maid*, preserved in manuscript, which have disappeared entirely or survive unrecognized after the kind of metamorphosis described in Alfred Harbage's study (1940) of the unacknowledged reuse of earlier scripts by Restoration revisers. It is true that the mature companies of the 1620s with their repertoires of established favourites had less need for new scripts; but this was not true of the newer companies, and Middleton was nothing if not versatile.

One possible reason for this abstention from the press was that the companies that had purchased the plays refused to permit their publication. Bentley's detailed examination of the evidence for such exclusions (1971, 264-92) considers them as applying primarily to contracted house dramatists, not to freelances such as Middleton; but a company may still have felt possessive about a popular play which remained in repertoire, while the King's Men, at least, could call on the Master of the Revels to suppress undesired printings. *The Changeling*, long-enduring and half Rowley's, could have been vulnerable to this kind of pressure. The other, and in my view more plausible, possibility is that Middleton deliberately withheld work from the press so that he could profit from the sale or presentation of manuscripts. The important thing about this explanation is that it is fully compatible with the first, since a ban on printing would enlarge and sustain the market for the scribally published version. We have no evidence of companies forbidding authors to sell or present manuscripts, but, on the contrary, Moseley's clear statement that this was done even by actors under suitable circumstances (Beaumont and Fletcher 1647, A4ʳ).

In the absence of any hard evidence it would be rash to speculate; but my own strong suspicion is that Middleton would not have been disturbed by any external sanctions that may have kept the plays mentioned from the press, and, even if there had been no such sanctions, would have been in no hurry to print them. After all, even *The Witch* seems to have secured him at least one patron's donative. Returning to the pre-1612 play-publications, we should at least be prepared to admit the *possibility* (though probably in this case a remote one) of a similar practice. Since only one of these editions (*The Roaring Girl*) can confidently be accepted as authorial, the remaining eight must (1) have been initiated by representatives of companies that had purchased the piece, or (2) have been sold by Middleton, but deliberately left unacknowledged and undedicated, or (3) derive from manuscripts written for reading which had fortuitously come into the hands of the bookseller.

The relative probabilities are not easy to estimate. Certainly the children's companies, and their entrepreneurs, were in dire trouble at the period of most intensive publication and the printing of scripts would have been an expected if probably not very profitable form of asset-stripping. On the other hand it would hardly have been engaged in while there was still some chance of their continued use as repertoire. The companies' predicament would, of course, have been understood by Middleton, who may well have felt entitled to cash in pre-emptively by getting to a printer first. As a writer of pamphlets (not all of them acknowledged) he was certainly in close touch with the book trade over the crucial years. Had he chosen such a course, it may well have been politic to disguise his involvement by withholding his name from the printed text. Given these two hypotheses, perfectly capable between them of accounting for the phenomena, it might seem a perverse defiance of Occam's razor to admit a third; yet this becomes a duty as long as the textual evidence has not so far been considered from this particular perspective. The hypothesis would be that Middleton, even at this early stage was selling, or more likely presenting, plays in manuscript and that one or more of these may have fallen into the hands of pirates; for should a bookseller, as George Wither succinctly explained, 'gett any written Coppy into his powre, likely to be vendible; whether the Author be willing or no, he will publish it. And it shallbe contrived and named alsoe, according to his owne pleasure: which is the reason, so many books come forth imperfect, and with foolish titles' (Wither 1624). Future students of the pre-1612 printings should at least take care not to exclude this possibility from consideration.

WORKS CITED

Adams, Joseph Quincy, 'Hill's List of Early Plays in Manuscript', *The Library*, IV, 20 (1939), 71–99

Beal, Peter, *Index of English Literary Manuscripts. Volume 1: 1450–1625 and Volume 2: 1625–1700* (1980–93)

Beaumont, Francis, and John Fletcher, *Comedies and Tragedies Written by Francis Beaumont and John Fletcher gentlemen* (London, 1647)

Beck, Sydney, ed., *The First Book of Consort Lessons Collected by Thomas Morley 1599 & 1611* (1959)

Bentley, Gerald Eades, 'John Cotgrave's *English Treasury of Wit and Language* and the Elizabethan Drama', *Studies in Philology* 40 (1943), 186–203

—— *The Profession of Dramatist in Shakespeare's Time, 1590–1642* (1971)

—— *The Profession of Player in Shakespeare's Time, 1590–1642* (1984)

Boklund, Gunnar, *The Sources of 'The White Devil'* (1957)

Bowers, Fredson, *On Editing Shakespeare* (1966)

—— ed., *The Complete Works of Christopher Marlowe* (1973)

Bradley, David, *From Text to Performance in the Elizabethan Theatre: Preparing the Play for the Stage* (1992)

Bullen, A. H., ed., *The Works of Thomas Middleton* (1885–6)

Chaytor, H. J., *From Script to Print: An Introduction to Medieval Dramatic Literature* (1945)

Churchyard, Thomas, *A Light Bondell of Liuly Discourses Called Churchyardes Charge, presented as a Newe yeres gifte to the ... Erle of Surrie* (London, 1580)

Cogswell, Thomas, 'Thomas Middleton and the Court, 1624: *A Game at Chess* in Context', *Huntington Library Quarterly* 47 (1984), 273–88

Constable, Giles, ed., *The Letters of Peter the Venerable*, 2 vols (1967)

Crane, Ralph, *The Works of Mercy both Corporal and Spiritual* (London, 1620)

Cressy, David, *Literacy and the Social Order: Reading and Writing in Tudor and Stuart England* (1980)

Eccles, Mark, '"Thomas Middleton a Poett"', *Studies in Philology* 54 (1957), 516–36

Finlay, Michael, *Western Writing Implements in the Age of the Quill Pen* (1990)

Foakes, R. A., and R. T. Rickert, eds., *Henslowe's Diary* (1961)

Gildon, Charles, *The Complete Art of Poetry* (London, 1718)

Greg, Sir Walter, *Dramatic Documents from the Elizabethan Playhouses* (1931, repr. 1969)

—— *The Shakespeare First Folio* (1953)

—— *The Editorial Problem in Shakespeare*, 3rd edn. (1954)

Haaker, Ann, 'The Plague, the Theater and the Poet', *Renaissance Drama* NS 1 (1968), 283–306

Harbage, Alfred, 'Elizabethan–Restoration palimpsest', *Modern Language Review* 35 (1940), 287–319

Honigmann, E. A. J., *The Stability of Shakespeare's Text* (1965)

—— 'The Date and Revision of *Troilus and Cressida*', in *Textual Criticism and Literary Interpretation*, ed. Jerome J. McGann (1985), 38–54

Hooker, E. N. and H. T. Swedenberg, Jr., gen. eds., *The Works of John Dryden* (1956–2002)

Howard-Hill, T. H., 'The Author as Scribe or Reviser? Middleton's Intentions in *A Game at Chess*', *TEXT* 3 (1987), 305–18

—— ed., *Shakespeare and 'Sir Thomas More': Essays on the Play and its Shakespearian Interest* (1989)

—— ed., *A Game at Chess*, Malone Society (1990)

Jowett, John, 'Jonson's Authorization of Type in *Sejanus* and Other Early Quartos', *Studies in Bibliography* 44 (1991), 254–65

Kerrigan, John, 'Revision, Adaptation and the Fool in *King Lear*', in Taylor and Warren (1983), 195–245

Knowles, James, 'Marston, Skipwith and *The Entertainment at Ashby*', *English Manuscript Studies 1100–1700* 3 (1992), 137–92

Love, Harold, 'Preacher and Publisher: Oliver Heywood and Thomas Parkhurst', *Studies in Bibliography* 31 (1978), 227–35

—— *Scribal Publication in Seventeenth-Century England* (1993)

Middleton, Thomas, *Two New Playes* (London, 1657)

Miller, Edwin Haviland, *The Professional Writer in Elizabethan England* (1959)

—— 'New Year's Day Gift Books in the Sixteenth Century', *Studies in Bibliography* 15 (1962), 233–41

Mulryne, J. R., 'Manuscript Source-material for the Main Plot of Thomas Middleton's *Women Beware Women*', *Yearbook of English Studies* 5 (1975), 70–4

North, Roger, *The Life of the Right Honourable Francis North* (London, 1742)

Ong, Walter J., *Orality and Literacy* (1982)

Phelps, Wayne H., 'Thomas Holmes, Esquire: the Dedicatee of Middleton's *The Witch*', *Notes and Queries* 225 (April 1980), 152–4

Playford, John, *The Treasury of Musick: Containing Ayres and Dialogues* (London, 1669)

Powell, William S., *John Pory 1572–1636. The Life and Letters of a Man of Many Parts* (1977)

Saunders, J. W., 'The Stigma of Print: A Note on the Social Bases of Tudor Poetry', *Essays in Criticism* 1 (1951), 139–64

Sprott, S. E., ed., John Milton, *A Masque. The earlier versions* (1973)

Taylor, Gary, 'General Introduction' in Wells and Taylor (1987)

—— and Michael Warren, eds., *The Division of the Kingdoms: Shakespeare's Two Versions of King Lear* (1983)

Wells, Stanley, and Gary Taylor, with John Jowett and William Montgomery, *William Shakespeare: A Textual Companion* (1987)

Williams, Franklin B., Jr., *Index of Dedications and Commendatory Verses in English Books before 1641* (1962)

Wilson, F. P., 'Ralph Crane, Scrivener to the King's Players', *The Library*, IV, 7 (1926), 194–215

Wilson, John, ed., *Roger North on Music* (1959)

Wither, George, *The Schollers Purgatory, discovered in the Stationers Common-wealth* (London, 1624)

Yates, Frances, *The Art of Memory* (1966)

'FROM WRONGER AND WRONGED HAVE I FEE': THOMAS MIDDLETON AND EARLY MODERN LEGAL CULTURE

Edward Gieskes

Still in law? I had not breathed else now; 'tis very marrow, very manna to me to be in law: I'd been dead ere this else. I have found such sweet pleasure in the vexation of others, that I could wish my years over and over again, to see that fellow a beggar, that bawling knave a gentleman—a matter brought e'en to a judgement today, as far as e'er 'twas to begin again tomorrow. O, raptures! Here a writ of demur, there a *procedendo*, here a *sursurrara*, there a *capiendo*, tricks, delays, money-laws. (*The Phoenix* 4.115-124)

Tangle, the pseudo-attorney in Middleton's 1603 play *The Phoenix*, rapturously describes his 'sweet pleasure' in the law—in its endless productivity, its ability to transform knave to gentleman, its constant self-renewal, its texts. Like the titular phoenix, Tangle's law rises from the ashes of judgement to begin its argument again. His rapture here (and elsewhere in the play) centres on the vocabulary and documents of the early modern legal profession— the writs of demur, the procedendos, the sursurraras, the capiendos—and much of his speech consists of law-Latin and the names of writs.[1] In Tangle's forty-five years as a 'term-trotter', he has, phoenix-like, 'been at least sixteen times beggared, and got up again, and in the mire again, that [he has] stunk again, and yet got up again' (*Phoenix* 4.126-130). Tangle's fascinated entanglement with legal proceedings resembles that of many contemporary Londoners, not least Middleton himself.

Tangle's ability to dispense advice depends on legal knowledge derived from personal experience of litigation and, by inference, from his absorption of legal terminology and techniques from one of the many legal handbooks published throughout the sixteenth and seventeenth centuries. When Tangle goes mad at the end of the play, his speech is even more laden with names of writs and forms of judgements drawn from such sources than it is early on. The cure for Tangle's law-madness, which revises Jonson's purge of the poetasters in *Poetaster*, is for him to expel the language that has driven him mad.[2] Quieto (the miraculously 'unlawyered' and therefore quiet man) bleeds Tangle:

QUIETO [*opening Tangle's vein over a basin*]
   Now burst out,
   Thou filthy stream of trouble, spite, and doubt.
TANGLE O, an extent, a proclamation, a summons, a
   recognizance, a tachment, an injunction, a writ,

a seizure, a writ of praisment, an absolution, a *quietus est*.
QUIETO
   You're quieter, I hope, by so much dregs.
   Behold, my lord.
   [*Holds up basin to Phoenix*]
PHOENIX   This, why it outfrowns ink.
QUIETO
   'Tis the disease's nature, the fiend's drink.
                    (*Phoenix* 15.308-16)

The blood that flows out of Tangle's arm at the same time this stream of names for written legal instruments flows from his mouth is blacker than the ink in which the writs and law books that afflict him are written, and the couplet associates legal ink with the devil's work: legal ink is the 'fiend's drink'. Tangle's cure is completed when Quieto baptizes him with the 'oil of quietness', saying: 'Thou shalt give up the devil and pray, | Forsake his works, they're foul and black, | And keep thee bare in purse and back. | No more shall you in paper quarrel, | To dress up apes in good apparel' (*Phoenix* 15.324-8). With Tangle's abandonment of 'paper quarrels' and the 'foul and black' written works of the devil, he finds a conscience and is transformed into an 'honest quiet man'. In Tangle's case, the effects of the law—here as 'law-madness'—are intimately linked to its mode of circulation, to writing. Tangle's cure, *The Phoenix*'s final example of chastised corruption, offers a cautionary representation of the powers of the inky material of the law and its texts.

Despite such cautions, an increasing number of Londoners were focusing on the attractions of the law. Lawyers were members of a rising profession and legal training was seen by many as a means of ascending the social ladder.[3]

---

[1] A writ of demur—otherwise known as a demurrer—moved the court to delay action because of a disputed point of law. A procedendo was a writ from a higher court ordering a lower to proceed to judgement. A sursurrara (certiorari) called proceedings in a lower court into a higher (as from a local jurisdiction into a Westminster court). The capiendo was a writ of arrest—for debt, trespass, or other offence. English law operated by means of such writs and much of an attorney's training involved mastering the various forms and purposes of writs.

[2] Jonson's *Poetaster* (1601) closes with Horace (Jonson) administering a purgative to the bad poets Crispinus (Marston) and Demetrius (Dekker) that forces them to vomit up the fustian vocabulary that has contaminated their minds and work. Jonson's purge itself revises his classical source. Here, Quieto's bloodletting purges Tangle of both the vocabulary and the material—ink—which has poisoned him.

[3] See for example, the draper Quomodo's hopes for his son Sim in *Michaelmas Term*—by sending Sim to the Inns of Court, Quomodo hopes to secure a place for his family in the gentry.

Wilfrid Prest writes that 'by the beginning of Elizabeth's reign the law had virtually replaced the church as the career open to talents, the ladder on which young men could climb to power and riches' (Prest *Inns* 21–2). At the same time, the London courts came to dominate England's legal world, drawing more and more business to the courts at Westminster, and with that business came more and more lawyers and their clients. Dekker and Middleton's 1604 plague pamphlet *News from Gravesend* records the wish of London's innkeepers, players, booksellers, drawers, tapsters, butchers, and 'all the rest of the hungry commonalty of Westminster' that Dekker and Middleton's patron Nobody had left for Winchester in the 1603 plague instead of 'all the judges, serjeants, barristers and attorneys' who did flee the city (*News from Gravesend* 295–6). Winchester, Dekker and Middleton write, was much enriched by both lawyers and their clients during the courts' residence, and, by implication, London was impoverished. The London courts brought more than legal business to the city and its suburbs.

Legal jurisdictions abounded in London—and all occupied different courts. London was home to the three ancient common law courts at Westminster (King's Bench, Common Pleas, and Exchequer) as well as the Court of Requests, Star Chamber, Chancery, the Admiralty Court, various guild courts, the Lord Mayor's Court at Guildhall, and the suburban justices (as in Middlesex, before whom Middleton was called on a suit for debt).[4] In addition, both houses of Parliament were courts of law as well as legislative bodies.[5] With all these courtrooms and their associated officials, it is no surprise that to contemporary eyes London appeared to be over-crowded with lawyers, plaintiffs and defendants of various degrees, and tricksters whose livelihood depended on the credulity of those going to law. For example, pettifogging attorneys, corrupt lawyers, and other legal functionaries appear throughout the drama of the period.[6]

However, Middleton's depiction of the law and lawyers in *The Phoenix* does not simply castigate legal practitioners. Responding to Tangle's appearance, Phoenix describes 'sober Law' as an angel deformed by human abuse. Those, he says, who are 'near' to the angel Law do not desire 'to have law worse than war, | Where still the poor'st die first; | To send a man without a sheet to his grave, | Or bury him in his papers' (*Phoenix* 4.222–5). Phoenix draws a careful, and common, distinction between the law as abstract justice (the law praised by common lawyers in published treatises throughout the period) and its practice (the viperous behaviour of the pettifogger). The development of a division between abstract law and its particular, and often corrupt, incarnations enhances the authority of 'the law' as a social institution. The kinds of encomia for the law represented by Phoenix's speech are, paradoxically, rooted in the increasing presence of the paper it complains of. For example, in the course of praising 'sober Law' and its distance from 'paper', Phoenix underscores Tangle's addiction to the law's textuality.

While Tangle is fascinated and finally poisoned by the papers of the law, Phoenix holds that true justice would not want its suitors buried in paper. Nevertheless, as the sixteenth and seventeenth centuries progressed, the law became increasingly bound in paper and that paper becomes an ever-more prominent feature of early modern London.[7]

Early modern common lawyers tended to describe their learning as rooted in memory, and the central formal educational exercises of the Inns of Court were oral—whether they were the formalized readings, case-puttings, and moots or the less formal educational requirements of attending the courts and being resident in the Inns. Despite this self-described oral and memorial legal learning, the actual learning and practice of the law depended crucially on texts—manuscript commonplace books, handbooks, training manuals, reports, digests, etc.—that circulated throughout Middleton's London.[8] Early modern stage representations of the law and lawyers depend as much on the new availability of printed legal texts (which become more and more common over the sixteenth and seventeenth centuries) as they do on conventions about the representation of lawyers.[9] These new forms of legal textuality owe their initial appearance to the convenience printed works offered to practising lawyers and law students in mastering, managing, and using the increasingly unwieldy and massive apparatus of the early modern common law. Law printing begins with the 1481 publication of Littleton's *Tenures*, a text which organizes and categorizes the often bewildering complexities of English land law. Subsequently, lawyers and printers produced endless volumes of law reports, legal manuals, precedent books, treatises, and massive commentaries such as Lord Chief Justice Coke's on Littleton. In addition to specifically professional texts such as these, a variety of less forbidding

---

[4] This is not an exhaustive list, and it excludes some of the civil jurisdictions and other smaller courts. Courts were, however, thick on the ground in early modern London.

[5] Parliament tried, for example, cases of treason and handled the impeachment of public officials. As London's Chronologer, Middleton recorded Parliament's impeachment of Sir Francis Bacon in 1621.

[6] Pettifogger is a term first recorded in the *OED* in 1576 and refers to 'a legal practitioner of inferior status, who gets up or conducts petty cases; esp. in an opprobrious sense, one who employs mean, sharp, cavilling practices; a "rascally attorney".' It is never applied to barristers—those lawyers trained at the four Inns of Court and entitled to appear before the superior courts—and only refers to attorneys. Berger, Bradford and Sondergard list 13 attorneys and pettifoggers, 120 judges and justices, and 65 other lawyers in their *Index of Characters in Early Modern English Drama*. Clerks, bailiffs, constables, scriveners, bailiffs, solicitors and other legal functionaries raise this total considerably.

[7] Printing houses produced large numbers of law-related texts; scriveners producing deeds, bonds, indentures, and some writs abounded; and copies of proclamations, statutes, and ordinances circulated like playbills announcing the law to its audiences. Legal books far outnumbered printed plays throughout the period. For example, in 1580, the year of Middleton's birth, the *Short Title Catalog* records 14 legal texts and Greg records no plays. In 1627, the year of his death, 30 law books were printed and Greg cites only four plays.

[8] Moreover, the statutes produced by Parliament circulated in manuscript and later came to be printed. Statutes *were* law, and their force depended crucially on their written transmission.

[9] See E. F. J. Tucker's *Intruder Into Eden: Representations of the Common Lawyer in English Literature, 1350–1750* for a discussion of the image of the common lawyer.

texts emerged, texts intended to be useful to a broader cross-section of society than the relatively limited group of professional lawyers. The presence and circulation of these texts exerts an important influence on legal education, the image of the professional lawyer, and the dramatic field of early modern London.

I

Legal texts proliferated all though the later sixteenth and seventeenth centuries and mark a transformation in early modern legal culture. Because of print, legal learning became more and more readily available to both aspiring lawyers and interested lay people. For example, as early as 1543, *A Newe Boke of Presidentes in Maner of a Register* (STC 1134) billed itself on the title-page as comprehending 'the very trade of makyng all maner euydence and instrumentes of Practyce, ryght commodyous and necessary for euery man to knowe'. The later *Attourneys Academy* (1623, STC 20163) describes itself as being 'intended for the publique benefit' (title-page) of all Englishmen. This idea of the general usefulness of such texts becomes a common feature of title-pages, and as Prest suggests in his essay 'Lay Legal Knowledge in Early Modern England', a market later in the seventeenth and eighteenth centuries. Yearbooks, reports, and ancient treatises were all printed in the course of the century and new forms of legal writing reached print as well. Manuscript yearbooks, reports, and treatises had been the primary written resources for aspiring lawyers, and many barristers kept extensive notebooks that compiled useful precedents, models for pleading, notes from readings or arguments in court, as well as individual digests of the law that supplemented the aural exercises that formed the core of a lawyer's education. The advent of printed legal literature changed the traditional pattern:

> Within ten years of the introduction of printing into England in the 1470s, the London printers had found a market in the legal profession. The first printed English law book was Littleton's *Tenures* (1481), and by the end of Henry VII's reign a number of year-books were printed ... The effect of printing the year-books was that in time the manuscripts were ousted from the practitioners' libraries. The printed version, with all its many defects, had the apparent advantage of providing the profession with a complete set of reports of accepted authenticity and having a standard method of citation (Baker 207–8).

Printed records of precedent had obvious usefulness for practising lawyers, and students were not slow to see advantages in such texts for their preparations for practice. Venerable manuscript treatises on the common law began to be printed in the sixteenth century: Britton was first printed in 1530, Glanvill in 1554, Bracton in 1569, and Fleta in 1647. These were supplemented by the Year Books (1481 and following and especially Tottell's editions following 1553) and Reports (1571 and following) which became the core of the standard reference library of the common law.[10] In addition to printed volumes of reports, the new printed literature of the law included handbooks, precedent books, recent treatises, and manuals designed to simplify or rationalize the formidable task of learning the law.

The image of the common lawyer who practised in the three ancient common law courts at Westminster or in the provincial circuit courts and assizes dominates stage representations of lawyers in Elizabethan and Jacobean England.[11] Before the sixteenth century, England's courts and laws were as diverse in structure, jurisdiction, and form as the various shires. The common law was merely one of many legal codes available in medieval England. In the fourteenth and fifteenth centuries, provincial courts heard almost as many cases as the London courts, but by the later sixteenth century the courts at Westminster saw the majority of business and wielded greater authority than local jurisdictions.[12] Under the pressure of this vast increase in business, all the Westminster courts underwent reforms intended to improve efficiency. Legal training responded to these reforms by regularizing models of training and practice with the intention of producing a group of well-trained attorneys, clerks, and lesser court functionaries in addition to the barristers and judges.[13] Printers too responded to these changes by producing, among other things, texts which presented forms of pleading, catalogues of writs, and schedules of fees for the reference of both lawyers and their clients.[14]

Despite the fact the lawyers were trained in the Inns and that educational exercises were a normal part of their daily life, the four Inns were less colleges or academies of the law than large professional associations and residences. The Inns' educational role was a kind of side effect of their function as the London offices of practising barristers and attorneys. The early history of the Inns, in so far as it can be reconstructed, demonstrates that aspiring lawyers learned their law in a more or less informal way by attending court at Westminster Hall and living among practising lawyers who, interestingly, were called

---

[10] Walter Cecil Richardson's *History of the Inns of Court* provides a useful survey of these texts.

[11] Other law codes and kinds of lawyers did exist, but their presence and jurisdiction was shrinking in sixteenth- and seventeenth-century England. For example, much of the business of the church courts, staffed by civil lawyers trained in the universities, was being transferred to common law courts.

[12] This process went on in tandem with the progressive centralization of political authority in London under the Tudors. Provincial jurisdictions were not only courts of law but also administrative centres. Provincial courts' legal authority waned as they lost their status as semi-autonomous sites of government. The great provincial councils were increasingly subordinated to the central government.

[13] Prest's *Inns of Court and Rise of the Barristers*, Brooks's *Pettifoggers and Vipers*, and Brian Levack's *Civil Lawyers In England 1603–1642: A Political Study* describe the growth of the legal profession as well as changes in legal training. Legal historians describe a two-tiered legal system with attorneys and solicitors (those who dealt directly with clients and did much of the paperwork related to conveyancing) at a level below that of the barristers (those who were allowed to plead before the judges of the central courts). Attorneys were always far more common that barristers, and their services were more widely available, affordable, and, often, necessary than those of the barristers.

[14] As one example, Thomas Powell's 1623 *Attourneys Academy* presents a listing and description of the procedure of the various courts together with a list of the usual fees charged for actions in those courts. The book closes with an extensive and well-organized index.

'apprentices of the Bench' or 'men of court'. Solid documentation of just what kind of 'learning process' these fourteenth and fifteenth-century law students underwent is scant, but it is clear that it was informal and more concerned with practical matters of procedure than with theoretical jurisprudence.[15] The informality of the early learning exercises kept the details of the law mysterious and relatively unknown to lay people who lacked immediate access to practising lawyers. Budding lawyers learned by immersing themselves in fourteenth-century legal culture, assimilating the practices and knowledge of those whom that culture recognized as legitimate practitioners. The fifteenth century title of 'apprentice of the Bench', held by those admitted to practice, points both to this method of training and to the practical, craft-like, nature of legal practice in the fourteenth and fifteenth centuries.

Aspects of the guild-like legal culture of the middle ages persisted through the sixteenth and into the seventeenth century but, as the profession grew and the common law became more complicated, both students and teachers came to see the need for a more systematic and theoretical method of learning and teaching the law.[16] As David Seipp argues, common lawyers in the sixteenth century 'had carried on for more than three centuries without a comprehensive, systematic treatise describing the whole of their law' (Seipp 61). By the end of the century, he suggests, the need for such a treatise was apparent to many of them. Such a theoretical approach to legal learning had been made necessary by massive change in the nature, scale, and scope of legal business over the course of the second half of the century.[17]

As the law became more complex, the traditional oral exercises and manuscript commonplace books became increasingly inadequate by themselves as a means of providing law students with all the knowledge they needed. In contrast to the fourteenth and fifteenth centuries, where the readings and exercises followed a set pattern and could cover the whole of the law, sixteenth and seventeenth century readings tended to become showpieces of erudition on a narrow topic and made little pretence to covering broad areas of knowledge. The exercises remained tied to the old course of readings, a course that derived from a much earlier state of the field, and were less and less relevant to contemporary concerns.[18] Thus, the exercises were supplemented (and sometimes replaced) by printed texts. In the sixteenth century, legal publishing boomed.

Books such as Littleton's *Tenures* (1481), St German's *Doctor and Student* (1528–30), Plowden's commentaries and reports (1578), Fulbecke's *Direction* (1600), Cowell's *Institutiones* (1605) and *Interpreter* (1607), Finch's *Nomotechnia* (Law French 1613, English 1627), Coke's *Institutes* (1628), Bacon's *Elements of the Common Laws of England* (1630, composed 1590s?), and Dodderidge's *Lawyer's Light* (1629) and *English Lawyer* (1631), to name only a few, all point to a field in the process of rationalization. As legal activity became a more important part of daily life, royal administrators, in concert with the judges

and benchers, saw a need for standardizing requirements for admission to practice for both the upper and lower branches of the profession and focused primarily on ensuring the knowledge and competence of practitioners.[19] Learning the law became an ever more arduous undertaking as the litigation boom continued. Not only did the student have to master the social and rhetorical skills of the legal community (as in the medieval model); he also had to master copious volumes of disorganized legal knowledge. The rapid development of legal publishing was, at least in part, prompted by the desire to organize that knowledge and thus make it easier to absorb.

Littleton's *Tenures* revised an earlier manuscript treatise on the forms of land-ownership under the common law.[20] His book was, as many historians have noted, revolutionary in that it attempted to systematize knowledge that had only existed as disorganized lists and compendia of precedents. Littleton's textbook was divided into two parts: the first dealt with the 'estates' (the kinds of holding from freeholds to non-freeholds) and the second with 'tenures' (the means by which such estates are held). This organization simplified the confusing complexities of English land law into a comprehensible system. By the middle of the sixteenth century, publishers of Littleton included large fold-out charts that laid out the estates on one axis and the tenures on another in order to illustrate points about land law. Baker writes, 'from the date of its first publication in print in 1481 [Littleton] was seized upon by the whole profession as a faithful introduction to the common law of real property' (Baker 216–7). That the profession was in dire need of such introductions is further demonstrated by

---

[15] This is in contrast to the universities whose civil law curriculum concentrated on theoretical texts to the exclusion of practical issues. Newly graduated civilians had to spend several years in Doctor's Commons (which was, interestingly, structured very much like the Inns of Court) learning procedure before they could practise in any of the civil jurisdictions. See Levack's *Civil Lawyers* for a detailed discussion.

[16] The traditional course of learning exercises came under increasing strain in the later sixteenth century, as their inadequacy to the changing times became clearer to practising lawyers. Coke's massive commentaries on Littleton respond, despite their complexity and bulk, to a perceived need for clarification and expansion of this classic text on property law. The guild structure of the old profession was forced to adapt to radically altered conditions in ways that brought it closer to a modern one by adopting new text-based training methods, by formalizing qualifications for practice, and paying more attention to the ethics of practitioners.

[17] If theoretical approaches were made necessary by changes in the legal system, they were made possible by the advancing technology of print which made the texts of the law more easily accessible and, thus, synthesizable.

[18] The *content* lagged behind, but the habits of mind inculcated by the kinds of practices the exercises demanded remained relevant and essential. Later attempts to revive the exercises (which had lapsed entirely during the Civil War) focused on their role in the intellectual formation of aspiring lawyers. See Prest *Inns* chapter 6. That these attempts to revive the exercises failed speaks more to the ineffectiveness of the efforts than the pedagogical usefulness of the old exercises. The failure of the exercises made printed law books still more important.

[19] This is only one example of a concern with training. Even as early as the 1530s, Henry VIII commissioned a report on the status of learning at the Inns of Court. The Denton–Cary–Bacon report (so named for its compilers) provides important early evidence of the nature and quality of legal education in the early part of the century. The report was first printed in *Fortescutus Illustratus* (1663). No period manuscript survives.

[20] Middleton makes a passing reference to Littleton in *Owl* 1671–3: '...inaulated punies must have a silver hair for their capes or else Littleton will not know them.' Littleton was a book so closely associated with the common law that it could serve as a synecdoche for it.

the publication history of Christopher St German's *Doctor and Student*, which was constantly in print throughout the sixteenth and seventeenth centuries.

Doctor and Student and other later manuals filled what came to be perceived as the gaps left by traditional legal training. St German's treatment of equity served not only as an introductory text to the subject, but as a work of legal theory that provided a framework within which to understand the disparate rulings of the common law. For example, St German writes that:

> Equytye is a [ryghtwysenes] that consideryth all the pertyculer cyrcumstances of the dede the which also is temperyed with the sweetnes of mercye. And [such an equytye] must alway be obseruyed in euery lawe of man and in euery generall rewle thereof & that knewe he wel that sayd thus. Lawes couet to be rewlyd by equytye (St German 95).

St German states that 'laws covet to be ruled by equity' and this passage offers a reason why this should be true and asserts that every 'law of man' and every 'general rule' must be submitted to equity, defined as a 'rightwiseness' that considers 'all the particular circumstances of the deed' in question. St German's definition of equity offers a means to understand both the extent and authority of chancery jurisdiction and a way to understand structuring principles of the common law.[21]

William Fulbecke, writing after St German, proposes methods of learning the law that are simpler and more 'convenient' than the usual course of more or less disorganized solitary study punctuated by case-puttings, moots, and readings. Fulbecke addresses the increasing difficulty of learning the law by offering a plan of study. He focuses on issues of conditioning, habitual practices, and the development of reflexes relevant to the practice of the law and pays particularly close attention to the importance of the student's linguistic dispositions and, more importantly, his linguistic habitus. Fulbecke's *Direction* (1600) aims to lead student lawyers to internalize and reproduce the rhetorical and social norms that underwrite the linguistic and social authority of lawyers. The *Direction* makes the mastery of linguistic and social forms a central theme of its educational programme and Fulbecke's deep awareness of the critical role of language in legal practice pervades his work. The legal content of his *Direction* derives mostly from other sources, demonstrating his concern with the *form* of learning rather than its *content*.[22] This emphasis is common to other legal handbooks, most of which promote various logical methods of approaching the learning of the law.[23]

Seventeenth century legal texts continue to combine theoretical jurisprudence designed for the dedicated law student with pragmatic programmes of study, lists of writs, briefs and pleadings to memorize, and continue to make legal learning more accessible to an ever larger number of readers. According to the title-page of Thomas Powell's 1623 *Attourneys Academy*, the volume is a comprehensive treatment of 'the manner and forme of proceeding practically, vpon any Suite, Plaint, or Action whatsoeuer, in any Court of Record whatsoeuer, within this KINGDOME.' Powell's book is one of those most commonly associated with attorneys and its popularity indicates both its usefulness and its ready availability. Moreover, Powell's 'academy', unlike those of the Inns of Court and Chancery, is open to the entire literate population. The book begins with a treatment of the 'manner of proceeding in the CHANCERIE' (B1^r) and proceeds through all the London courts (Requests, Common Pleas, Exchequer, King's Bench, Star Chamber, Parliament, the Lord Mayor's and the Sheriff's Courts) in a systematic fashion. The book presents the rules of each court in great detail. To take an example Middleton would have been familiar with, regarding actions of debt in the Court of Common Pleas, Powell writes:

> First you are to understand of what nature the Action which you would sue must be. If it be for Debt vpon a Bond, you must take a special care that your Originall doe agree with the Bond; For otherwise your proceeding will be erroneous ... If the Sheriffe do returne the Defendant sufficient: Then soon after the said Returne, when the Originall is fyled: The Plaintifs Attourney must goe to the Office of the *Phillozer* of the said County; and there search and be satisfied whether any Attourney haue appeared for the Defendant or no (N3^{r–v}).

Powell continues step by step through the stages of an action for debt and, at each stage, states what both the plaintiff's and the defendant's attorneys need to do. Of Powell's work, Christopher Brooks writes that '*The Attourneys Academy* could not have been an original work by its reputed author ... A number of quite similar works, which date from as early as the 1580s, have been found amongst the papers of attorneys' (Brooks 174). Brooks goes on to suggest that works of this kind were a typical means of acquiring legal knowledge for attorneys. Manuals such as this are common throughout the period—ranging from this kind of handbook for attorneys to collections of models of pleadings for barristers.

The proliferation of legal handbooks of whatever description and derivation is a major feature of early modern legal culture. Where legal knowledge was once acquired and reproduced orally or in manuscripts, the sixteenth and seventeenth centuries saw legal training become increasingly dependent on printed sources. Because the law as practised had much to do with precedent, law books

---

[21] Or what ought to have been the structuring principles. St German's work is filled with similar definitions that explain specific issues while offering insights into general principles. St German alternates between a descriptive and prescriptive mode throughout *Doctor and Student*, often within the same sentence.

[22] The content of legal education would have been readily accessible to a student in printed reports, abridgements, yearbooks, and, of course, through the oral exercises that remained the core of legal training in the Inns.

[23] Abraham Fraunce's successful *Lawiers Logike* (1588) was one of many legal textbooks produced under the systematizing influence of Ramist logic.

tended to base themselves on preceding texts, creating a series of textually-based models for presenting, learning, and deploying the law. Practices once structured primarily by speech come to be structured more and more by writing, and, specifically, by print.[24] These printed sources become ever more common and develop into a significant part of early modern textual culture more generally—law books are available to a broad population and legal language becomes an increasingly common feature of ordinary discourse, at least as that discourse is represented in the drama of Middleton and his contemporaries. At the same time this movement from manuscript to print in legal training was taking place, England saw an incredible increase in litigation. Between 1490 and 1640, cases in late stages in the two most important common law courts (King's Bench and Common Pleas) increased thirteen-fold from about 2,100 to almost 29,000.[25] This increase made litigation an unavoidable fact of London life. Middleton's own experience is instructive on both the frequency of litigation and the way it permeates London's intellectual and social life.

II

Middleton's personal relation to the law and thereby to the culture of the Inns of Court begins early in his life. Mark Eccles, P. G. Phialas, and Mildred Christian discovered and discussed an impressive array of evidence about what Phialas termed Middleton's 'early contact with the law'. Rather than learning his law as a member of Gray's Inn as some early biographers believed, Middleton developed his legal knowledge from the extensive and contentious litigation his family engaged in from the time of his father's death in 1586. In other words, Middleton's legal knowledge was that of an interested layperson—and was likely much the same as that of many of his contemporaries in a highly litigious period. Middleton's early and continuing contact with the law also profoundly influenced his representations of law and lawyers.

Middleton's father was a well-established London bricklayer and tiler with property holdings near the Curtain, in Limehouse, and a house in Catteton Street. His estate was assessed at £335 6s. 2d. upon his death—a considerable sum. The noncupative (oral) will left a third of the estate to be divided between his children Thomas and Avis. The total of this portion was increased by Anne Middleton, Middleton's mother, to 100 marks (£66 13s. 4d.) and was held by the Chamber of London. The money went to the support of the children during their minority.[26] A remainder of £25 was to be paid to Thomas and Avis upon their coming of age. Anne also conveyed the remaining portion of the family's real property 'to three members of the Inner Temple to be held by them in trust, received it back by means of a reversion for ten years, and on the same day conveyed the deeds of the property to her two children, Thomas and Avice [sic] Middleton' (Phialas 188). Her actions took place after William Middleton's death, but before her remarriage to Thomas Harvey. This

set of conveyances was in accordance with William Middleton's wishes and was designed to protect the property from predatory suitors like Harvey. Anne's action, which was clearly in the interests of her children, prompted the litigation that was a dominant feature of Thomas Middleton's youth. Thomas Harvey spent many years attempting to gain control of the Middleton inheritance and these attempts brought the Harveys and Middleton into at least five of London's courts on a regular basis.

London was full of courts of all descriptions. Each of the twelve livery companies operated a court with jurisdiction over its members and their trade, the Lord Mayor had a court at Guildhall, to which Anne Middleton paid her children's portions and before which she appeared when she had herself arrested for debt to secure those portions. Ecclesiastical courts, though increasingly impotent, still operated in London. International law was argued in the Court of Arches and of Admiralty—preserving a small space for the practice of civil lawyers educated in the universities. The great common law courts of King's Bench, Common Pleas, and Exchequer occupied an increasingly overcrowded Westminster Hall. Chancery's equity and common law jurisdictions grew throughout the period. Middleton and his family were involved in one way or another with several of these courts throughout his life. Anne Middleton entrusted Thomas and Avis's inheritance to the Lord Mayor's Court at Guildhall; she and Middleton (and many others) were sued in that court and the Court of Requests. Arrests for debt brought Harvey and Anne before the Equity bench, sureties to keep the peace were taken out in King's Bench, Harvey sued to gain control of the Middleton property in the Court of Requests, and the Middlesex justices arrested Harvey on suspicion of a plot to poison Anne. As a young man, Middleton would have seen a great deal of legal London. That London was polyglot: the Westminster courts used Law French (a kind of Anglo-Norman French which was part of the common law's medieval inheritance), while the so-called English Bill courts (Chancery and Requests) used English, and all used Latin. It was also fundamentally rooted in writing. Most of the mechanisms of the law were written—the bills and writs described in texts discussed above—and, necessarily, most of what we know of Middleton's contact with the law is through written records. The language and writing of the law, which Middleton knew intimately from years of litigation, are a recurring theme of his work.[27]

---

[24] As one example, the structure of a handbook like the *Boke of Presidents* is mirrored by later texts like the *Attorney's Academy*. Part of this has to do with the list-making influence of Ramist logic, but a large part has to do with the imitation of models. Coke's commentary on Littleton, rather than being a systematic treatment of the content of Littleton, proceeds as a line by line glossing of the older texts with the result that Coke's massive work's organization depends on Littleton.

[25] See Brooks *Vipers* 48 ff. Cases in late stages are cases which are past the point where they might settle out of court; the number of suits filed was, naturally, much larger.

[26] Corporation of London Records Office, Common Serjeant's Book I, f. 1ᵛ. See Eccles 1957 for a detailed discussion of the financial arrangements.

[27] The Law Latin tags that Tangle spouts are only one small example of this.

Thomas Harvey, the fundamental cause of much of the litigation that dominates Middleton's youth, was a citizen and grocer involved in trade with the Virginia colony. In 1586, he had recently returned to London after living for a year in Virginia as the cape or head merchant of the Roanoke colony. He appears to have approached Anne sometime in the months after his return from Virginia, and, after she 'had settled her lykinge towards hym, as a fitt manne for her to make choise of', Anne and her trustees decided that he should be made aware of the conveyance. According to a series of depositions from a 1600 Court of Requests suit Harvey filed against Anne, his son-in-law Allen Waterer, and the two surviving trustees, Harvey did not seem discontented with the arrangement at the time (PRO REQ 2/117/15 cited in Phialas). However, 'shortly after the marriage Harvey began to "fynd himsealfe greived for the conveyance that was thus made,"' and after attempting unsuccessfully to collect the leases of the property from the trustees, he applied to the Lord Mayor and Recorder. But his suit was rejected and he was advised to stop his "inuirious dealinges" toward the trustees' (Phialas 189). As Eccles has shown, Harvey and Anne had a far from placid marriage and many of the records relating to them have to do with arrests, actions for debt, and other kinds of litigation. For example, in his 1600 Requests suit, Harvey tells how eight days after the marriage Anne 'had herself arrested in Lord Mayor's Court for the orphans' portions, forcing Harvey to pay them into Guildhall'; how she refused to send him any money while in the Low Countries and how she threatened him with arrest when he returned in 1590. Anne herself accused Harvey of trying to poison her in 1595 and Harvey was committed to Newgate for a month.[28] These quarrels brought the family to court often and certainly exposed the young Middleton to a variety of legal instruments, courts, writs, and types of lawyers. Most of the lawyers who would have been involved in such disputes would have been attorneys—members of what Christopher Brooks terms the 'lower branch' of the legal profession—or, in the case of the poisoning accusation, the Middlesex justices.[29]

According to depositions related to the Requests suit mentioned above, Harvey began making further efforts to secure control of the property around the turn of the century. Middleton, aged about twenty at the time, appears to have been involved in this litigation from its earliest moments and returned from Oxford (where he had matriculated in 1598) to assist his mother with her legal difficulties.[30] The Requests suit Harvey filed in 1600 alleged that 'the defendants had combined to defraud him of the income from certain premises which he allegedly had purchased five or six years before; that his wife made the conveyance [of the Middleton property] after, not before their marriage; that during his second absence from England the defendants had given out that he was "deade beyonde the seas;" and that they had evicted his tenants and kept his income to themselves' (Phialas 188).

One of the depositions in this suit contains the often-cited phrase about Middleton's remaining in London 'daylie accompaninge the players'. It appears that this final effort of Harvey's coincided with Middleton's abandonment of his Oxford studies and the beginning of his association with the London theatres. Not only does legal language and culture influence his plays; litigation is also closely associated with his becoming a professional playwright.

Middleton's personal association with the law continued throughout his life. For example, his wife's father was one of the Six Clerks in Chancery—an important post in an increasingly important court. He was also involved in a series of actions over debt—maintaining his contact with the law and its officers.[31] Early modern debt law, the law exploited by tricksters like Ephestian Quomodo, allowed creditors to arrest both the debtor and his sureties and to extract additional penalties. Actions for debt occupied a great deal of the attention of attorneys, scriveners, barristers, and the courts. In 1609, Robert Keysar—goldsmith and manager of the Children of the Revels—sued Middleton for debt in King's Bench over a £16 bond.[32] Keysar alleged that Middleton failed to repay a loan of £8 10s. made in May of 1606 which was to be paid back in June of the same year. Middleton's answer avers that the delivery of a lost tragedy called *The Viper and Her Brood* satisfied the terms of the bond.[33] Hillebrand was unable to discover the final disposition of the suit, but the incident is indicative of several things. First, Middleton, despite (or perhaps because of) his early contact with the law, remained engaged with litigation all his life, offering a contentious answer to the suit. Second, Middleton's professional life was imbricated with the law—here, his debt was to be satisfied by the production of a playscript—and his relations to Keysar were financial and professional. Finally, the incident also demonstrates that the willingness and ability of theatre professionals to go to law was broad-based and far from restricted to the Burbages, Alleyns, and Henslowes who dominate our picture of early modern theatre.[34] Middleton's literary production displays

---

[28] See Eccles 1957.

[29] Unsurprisingly these are the kinds of legal functionaries who come in for the most criticism in Middleton's plays.

[30] Middleton had already made one such trip in 1599 to assist his mother in a dispute over leases with his brother-in-law Allen Waterer.

[31] He was brought before the justices of King's Bench, Chancery, Requests, and of Middlesex in lawsuits related to debt and the Middleton estate.

[32] KB 27/1416, m. 1056[d]. See Hillebrand.

[33] A lawyer named Michael Moseley represented Middleton in this suit and in another in 1610. Moseley appears to have been an attorney. A Michael Moseley was admitted to Lincoln's Inn in 1559 and another was admitted to the Inner Temple in 1631—the 1559 date seems too early while the 1631 date is too late. In any case, Middleton would not have required a barrister's assistance until much later in the suit. Moseley would have been engaged in drafting Middleton's written answers to the suits, taking out writs, and handling the paperwork associated with the lawsuits. The passage from Powell's *Attorney's Academy* cited above describes the course of action an attorney would take in such a case. Attorneys routinely handled much of the work related to debts.

[34] The list of litigious theatre people is quite large. Lawsuits centred on the disposition of shares in acting companies were common, and some of the best evidence of the terms under which playwrights worked for acting companies derives from a lawsuit alleging that Richard Brome broke the terms of his contract with the Salisbury Court Theatre. See Bentley III.52-4.

his consuming interest with the law and its language, an interest shaped not only by his personal experience with various kinds of litigation, but also by the pervasiveness of early modern legal culture in Middleton's London.[35]

III

> Unlike literary or philosophical hermeneutics, the practice of interpretation of legal texts is theoretically not an end in itself. It is instead directly aimed at a practical object and is designed to determine practical effects...Reading is one way of appropriating the symbolic power which is contained within the text. Thus, as with religious, philosophical, or literary texts, control of the legal text is the prize to be won in interpretive struggles.
>
> Pierre Bourdieu, 'The Force of the Law'

Middleton's work participates in these interpretive struggles over the control of legal texts by insistently foregrounding their role in his literary world. Control of the symbolic power of the law, made apparent by the authority wielded by deeds, warrants, conveyances, etc., is consistently a stake in characters' struggles in Middleton's plays. Martino's pocket full of warrants in *The Widow* is only one example of the way characters attempt to exercise some kind of power through the possession and use of legal papers. The law exercises a world-altering force in many of Middleton's plays and pamphlets and that force resides in the texts in which the law is codified. This is also true of the world Middleton's plays refract—legal texts structure much of early modern London, both literally and metaphorically. Without those texts, for example, the interpretive acts that define legal practice lack authority. Many of the early printed authorities on the common law were commentaries on court cases and Coke's immense work on Littleton took the form of a commentary, a massive act of reading and interpreting. The reading of the law—whether it be the common law or the civil law— is always both a symbolic act making abstract claims about justice and a practical one directed at specific and well-defined ends.[36] Legal reading and writing achieve practical effects and those effects are necessarily bound up in the texts being read and written.

Middleton's work presents tangled relations of legal writing, reading, and practice in that legal texts operate as both objects and agents in many of his plays. The texts of the law circulate throughout the body of Middleton's work like the legal ink that replaces Tangle's blood. Plays like *The Phoenix, Michaelmas Term,* and *The Widow* thematize the law, making it an essential part of the plot and one of the primary movers of the action. Middleton's prose work, from *The Black Book* to *The Penniless Parliament of Threadbare Poets* to *Father Hubburd's Tales,* makes constant and sophisticated reference to the law. Middleton's work, like that of many of his contemporaries, was indelibly marked by the law—by its structures, by its language, and by its textuality.

In *Father Hubburd's Tales,* Middleton depicts the force of the writing of the law in direct terms. The Ant, transformed into a ploughman, describes the death of his landlord and the transfer of the property from the landlord's son to a mercer and merchant through the agency of a scrivener's pen:

> Now was our young master with one penful of ink doing a far greater exploit than all his forefathers, for what they were a-purchasing all their lifetime, he was now passing away in the fourth part of a minute; and that which many thousand drops of his grandfather's brows did painfully strive for, one drop now of a scrivener's inkhorn did easily pass over. A dash of a pen stood for a thousand acres—how quickly they were dashed in the mouth by our young landlord's prodigal fist! (*Hubburd* 480–7)

Like Tangle and Falso's fencing match in *The Phoenix* which blurs the distinction between verbal and physical combat, the scrivener's writing becomes the land the young landlord is signing away. 'One drop' of ink from the scrivener's inkhorn takes the place of 'many thousand drops of his grandfather's brows' and in doing so that one drop of ink does the work of many thousands of drops of sweat.[37] As the Ant notes, when the lawyer and his partners take their 'leaves' of the young landlord, they depart 'heavier by a thousand acres at their parting than they were before at their meeting' (*Hubburd* 541–3). The 'leaves' punningly refer to both the farewells offered by the departing parties and the pieces of paper that carry the land away. The pamphlet thus stages the substitution of legal labour—the writing of a deed—for the physical labour of the heir's ancestors.

The lawyer's substitution of his labour for that of the sweating ancestor—a substitution that destroys what the Ant represents as an idyllic pastoral way of life—refracts an ongoing struggle over principles of social authority into a scene of legal writing. The scrivener's pen, here acting as the hand of the lawyer, replaces a traditional model of landholding in which customary tenants paid customary rents without need for formal writing with one that is legalistic and formal. In the next scene, this new model blasts the Ant and his fellow tenants back to Kent with the

---

[35] As one example of this combination of biographical and textual reference, *The Widow,* printed in 1652 and likely written around 1616, contains numerous references and plot devices deriving from the law. In a parallel to Middleton's own life, the titular widow Valeria conveys her possessions to her brother, the justice Martino, in order to protect them from what she fears are unscrupulous suitors. Additionally, the justice's clerk Martino carries a collection of blank warrants with him at all times in order to be ready to collect fees from anyone who might need one. The writs and warrants of the law circulate throughout the play and drive much of the action.

[36] Legal study in the English tradition is often called 'reading law', a phrase that places texts at the centre of learning the law. In addition, the most formalized of the early modern learning exercises was the reading which was usually based on the reading and interpreting of a particular statute. Becoming a Reader was a necessary precondition for joining the governing oligarchy of the Inns.

[37] Note also how the drops of Tangle's blood, the purging of which cures his 'law-madness', are black as ink. Ink drops, paper, and writing itself exercise an inordinate degree of power in these treatments of the action and effects of the law.

word 'fine' (the fee paid on entry into a new leasehold). Middleton represents the force of the law as explosive, blasting these tenants out of London, and in doing so he testifies to the power of legal writing and engages in a debate over that power and its consequences. Fifteen seconds erases generations of difficult accumulation in this scene, both recognizing the overwhelming power of legal instruments and problematizing that power by suggesting its arbitrariness and isolation from the traditional bonds that, for example, secured the Ant's former way of life. The debate over the power and use of the law, symbolized by the conflict between Phoenix' sober angel of the law and Tangle's paper-drowned practice of it, signals a transformation of the relation between the legal field and its audiences. That transformation—discussed here in terms of Middleton's drama, prose, and verse—depends on the production, transmission, and circulation of legal texts.

WORKS CITED

Anonymous. *Boke of Presidents*. London, 1543.

Baker, J. H. *Introduction to English Legal History*. London: Butterworths, 1990.

Bentley, Gerald Eades. *The Jacobean and Caroline Stage*. Oxford: Clarendon, 1941–1968.

Berger, Thomas L., William C. Bradford and Sidney L. Sondergard. *An Index of Characters in Early Modern English Drama: Printed Plays 1500–1660*. Cambridge: Cambridge University Press, 1998.

Bourdieu, Pierre. 'The Force of the Law: Towards a Sociology of the Juridical Field'. *Hastings Law Journal* 38 (1986–7): 813–857.

Brooks, Christopher. *Pettifoggers and Vipers of the Commonwealth*. Cambridge: Cambridge University Press, 1986.

Christian, Mildred G. 'A Sidelight on the Family History of Thomas Middleton'. *Studies in Philology* 44 (1947): 490–6.

Eccles, Mark. 'Middleton's Birth and Education'. *Review of English Studies* 7 (1931): 431–441.

—— '"Thomas Middleton a Poett"'. *Studies in Philology* 54 (1957): 516–536.

Greg, Walter Wilson. *A Bibliography of the English Printed Drama to the Restoration*. London: Bibliographical Society, 1939–1955.

Hillebrand, Harold. 'Thomas Middleton's *The Viper's Brood*'. *Modern Language Notes* 42 (1927): 35–38.

Jonson, Ben. *Poetaster*. Ed. Thomas Cain. New York: Manchester University Press, 1995.

Levack, Brian. *Civil Lawyers In England 1603–1642: A Political Study*. Oxford: Clarendon Press, 1973.

Phialas, P. G. 'Middleton's Early Contact with the Law'. *Studies in Philology* 52 (1955): 186–95.

Powell, Thomas. *The Attourneys Academy*. London, 1623.

Prest, Wilfrid. *The Inns of Court in Elizabethan England*. Totowa, NJ: Rowman and Littlefield, 1972.

—— 'Lay Legal Knowledge in Early Modern England', in Bush, Jonathan and Alain Wijffels, eds. *Learning the Law: Teaching and the Transmission of English Law 1150–1900*. London: Hambledon, 1999.

—— *Rise of the Barristers*. Oxford: Clarendon, 1986.

Richardson, Walter Cecil. *History of the Inns of Court*. Baton Rouge: Claitor's, 1975.

St German, Christopher. *Doctor and Student*. T. F. T. Plucknett and J. L. Barton eds. London: Selden Society, 1974.

Seipp, David J. 'The Structure of the English Common Law in the Seventeenth Century', in Gordon, W. M. and T. D. Fergus, eds. *Legal History in the Making*. London: Hambledon, 1991.

Tucker, E. F. J. *Intruder Into Eden: Representations of the Common Lawyer in English Literature, 1350–1750*. Columbia, SC: Camden House, 1984.

Waterhouse, Edward. *Fortescutus Illustratus*. London, 1663.

MIDDLETON, MUSIC, AND DANCE

Gary Taylor and Andrew J. Sabol

assisted by John Jowett and Lizz Ketterer

Music! thou modest servant to this place,
Raise chaste delight to do this season grace.
Honourable Entertainments 7.71–2

IN 1597 Thomas Middleton's name appeared for the first time on London bookstalls, fronting a verse paraphrase that interpolated canzons, choristers, dirges, madrigals, roundelays, and interlined song into the biblical *Wisdom of Solomon*.[1] In the same year, John Dowland published *The First Booke of Songes or Ayres* (STC 7091) and Thomas Morley published *A Plaine and Easie Introduction to Practicall Musicke* (STC 18133). By contrast with Middleton's unremarkable quarto, Dowland's and Morley's books were expensive, typographically complex folios with engraved title-pages. Morley's was printed in black and red ink; Dowland's was a physically innovative table-book, one of the first ever published, designed to be read and played simultaneously by four musicians, standing around a table, with the type on each opening of the book facing in three different directions.[2] Beyond their technical sophistication as printed texts, the two folios signaled the increasing importance of music in English society. Dowland had travelled to France, Italy, and Germany; Morley 'was the first English composer to have assimilated thoroughly the Italian idioms of his day' (Caldwell 404). Dowland's folio, despite its size and expense, was his most popular book, reprinted in 1600, 1603, 1606, and 1613; it is still being reinterpreted and recorded today. Morley's folio was also reprinted, and it provides a particularly impressive gauge for the varied part music could play in the life of the average Englishman in the closing years of Elizabeth I's reign. By the turn of the century Morley had composed a rich array of works, including madrigals, balletts, canzonets, lute songs, and keyboard pieces, as well as a remarkable collection of items arranged for a small mixed consort of instrumentalists. This, *The First Booke of Consort Lessons* (1599; STC 18131), in its own time and since, has been treated as an exceptional landmark. Both Dowland and Morley inspired, and were influenced by, a distinguished and exceptional company of contemporary composers that included William Byrd, Thomas Campion, and Orlando Gibbons.

But Byrd and Morley differed from Dowland, Campion, and Gibbons in one important respect: unlike the others, Byrd and his pupil Morley were both monopolists. They made a profit not only from their own music, but from the music of other people. For instance, in 1600 Morley was paid four pounds and fifteen shillings for granting permission for the printing of John Dowland's *Second Book of Ayres* (item 1)—and also received two free copies of the book. This may not seem an extortionate sum, by modern standards, but Morley was one of two patentees, so the total cost of the monopoly was nine pounds, ten shillings; by contrast, the printer of Dowland's volume received only ten pounds for all the work of manufacturing it. Morley must have received a similar payment for the 1600 reprinting of Dowland's *First Booke*.

Morley received this cut because he had been granted, in 1598, a twenty-one-year monopoly on printed music. Morley's was not the first such patent. In 1559 the printer John Day had been given a monopoly on the single most widely used English musical text of the sixteenth and seventeenth centuries, the authorized Book of Psalms by Sternhold and Hopkins, printed 'with apt notes to sing them withal'. Day's patent was renewed in 1567 and 1577, and his son sold it for £9000 to the Stationers' Company, which in 1603 received the new patent, the single most valuable asset in the collective portfolio called 'the English Stock'. Secular song had also been monopolized before Middleton's birth. In 1575 Thomas Tallis and William Byrd were given a monopoly for twenty-one years to 'imprint any and so many as they will of set songe or songes in partes, either in English, Latine, French, Italian, or any other tongues that may serve for musicke either in Church or chamber,' and others were forbidden to import 'any songe or songes made and printed in any forren countrie'. That patent extended to 'the printing of all ruled paper, for the pricking of any song to the lute, virginals or other instrumente'; this was, for some time, the most profitable part of the monopoly, and many examples of printed music paper survive from the sixteenth century. Their patent expired in January 1596, and Morley's *Plaine and Easie Introduction* was printed in the interim between its expiration and Morley's new patent. In fact, the unregulated year 1597 was the high-water mark of English

Andrew Sabol completed a short preliminary draft of this material in 1994. His subsequent illness prevented him from developing it, or correcting proofs. Taylor is responsible for the final form of the essay, for all references to scholarship published after 1994, and for any remaining errors. Items 2, 4, 5, 8, 21, 24, and 25 were not in Sabol's draft survey; transcriptions of the music for these items have been provided by Lizz Ketterer (5) and John Jowett.

[1] 17.104, 164–7, 19.176, 181.
[2] For an example see 'Order of Persons' in this volume, p. 57.
[3] On the music patents see Steele, Krummel, and Smith. For printed music paper see Fenlon and Milsom. Milsom (1999) and Chan (2002) provide useful introductions to the sixteenth and seventeenth century music trade in England more generally.

music publishing in the sixteenth century.[3]

Music could be more easily monopolized than other genres of print because it required special fonts of type, complicated routines of setting, and specialist proofreading. Beginning in about 1473, printers used woodcuts to represent music, and Wynkyn de Worde produced the first known English example in 1495. But this method required a new woodcut for every piece of music. The first music book printed using movable type was produced in Venice in 1501, and Venice dominated music publishing for most of the sixteenth century. Although in the mid-1520s an Englishman, John Rastell, was apparently the first European printer to use the single-impression method that revolutionized continental music printing in the 1530s, Rastell's innovative song sheets, play texts with scores, and musical collections did not inspire other English stationers to follow his lead. During the middle of the sixteenth century, great music publishing firms, sustained by monopoly patents, were established in Venice (Gardano and Scotto) and Paris (Attaingnant), but English music printing languished until Day began publishing the psalms. English secular music had a much smaller, less secure market than psalms, and secular music publishing did not take off until 1588, when the monopolist and composer William Byrd teamed up with the printer Thomas East to issue a historic series of music books, beginning with Italian madrigals set to English texts. That flourishing of native music was the fruit of decades of royal and aristocratic patronage, and of the increasing concentration of English musical resources, performances, and audiences in London. Although it could not compare with Venice, Florence, or Paris, London in 1597 offered Middleton a more varied, cosmopolitan and sophisticated musical culture than England had hosted in any earlier period of its history.[4] Indeed, Middleton's lifetime (1580–1627) almost exactly coincides with the 'golden age' of English lute music (1580–1625), when English composers enjoyed an international reputation.[5]

Whether or not Middleton played the lute, as a gentleman born he should have received some introduction to 'practicall musicke'. More than one London grammar school included music in its curriculum.[6] In 1600 he identified himself as 'Thomas Medius & Gravis Tonus' (*Ghost* 20–21), a masquerade name of a kind found in many Renaissance authors.[7] 'Medius . . . Tonus' puns on the surname 'Middleton,' and the phrase has many meanings; it can be taken to articulate commitment to a poetics of neutrality, ambivalence, the middle, the middle class, the centre, the ordinary, the common good. But since the whole phrase governs the verb *vociferat* ('cries out, speaks with strong emotion'), at its most basic Middleton's self-description refers to the sound of his voice. In the classical Latin of authors that Middleton certainly would have studied in grammar school and university, all three words have musical meanings: *tonus* is tune, note, accent, pitch or timbre, *medius* is neither high nor low, *gravis* is low-pitched, deep.[8] *Medius tonus* might also have been

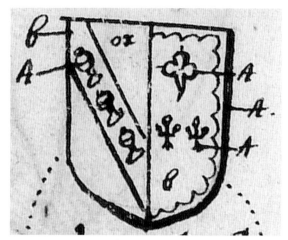

1. Mary (Magdalen) Middleton inherited the arms both of her father's (Morbecke) and mother's (Palmer) families. This gave her the same social status as the two 'gentlewomen' to whom George Kirbye dedicated, in 1597, *The first set of English madrigalls to 4. 5. & 6. voices.*

punning on another early musical meaning, 'semitone'.[9] The phrase might be telling us that Middleton had a typical male voice, probably what we would now call baritone (the mean pitch-range for males), here speaking sadly (because the story of Lucrece is tragic), or that he had an 'ordinary, commonplace' (*medius*) 'bass' (*gravis*) voice. Whatever the exact interpretation, the phrase defines Middleton's art in terms of a musical voice rather than a written text.

Middleton's wife probably shared his interest in music. Mary (Magdalen) Marbeck was descended from two established gentry families (the Marbecks and the Palmers), and her father was much wealthier than Middleton's (Illus. 1). Moreover, her paternal grandfather John Marbeck was a royal musician and composer, still alive when she was

[4] For music printing to 1600 see Agee, Bernstein (1998, 2001), Carter, Cusick, Fenlon, Krummel and Sadie, Pogue; for Rastell, see Milsom (1997) and King; for Elizabethan patronage, see Price.
[5] For 'golden age' see Newton (the first to use the phrase) and Spring, 96–289.
[6] Merchant Taylor's School (whose headmaster, Richard Mulcaster, also composed music), Westminster School, and Christ's Hospital (a charity school, possibly relevant because Middleton was an orphan). See Price, 37–8.
[7] Williams includes it, in the form 'Medius . . . Tonus', in a list of facetious names (p. 318), but he omits 'et Gravis' and gives no definitions, musical or otherwise.
[8] For classical Latin see the definitions and citations in Glare: *medius* (a. 8), '(of musical notes) neither high nor low' (1091), *grauis* (a. 9) '(of a sound) Low in pitch, deep' (775), and *tonus* (n. 2) 'the pitch of a sound . . . a tone' (1949). Elizabethan Latin dictionaries defined *tonus* as 'tune, note, accent' (Lancashire). As this range of definitions suggests, Latin *tonus* would be better translated, in contemporary musical vocabulary, as 'timbre,' a more complex attribute than pitch, representing a synthesis of several factors (Campbell).
[9] See 'Semitonus est medius tonus' and similar phrases in Mathiessen. The fact that Dowland and others defined a 'semitone' as an 'imperfect' tone would also be relevant to Middleton's conviction that 'nothing is perfect born': see Dowland's translation of *Andreas Ornithoparcus his Micrologus, or Introduction: containing the art of singing* (1609), pp. 17–18.

born.[10] In *Women, Beware Women* Fabritio brags that his daughter 'has the full qualities of a gentlewoman. | I have brought her up to music, dancing, what not | That may commend her sex and stir her husband,' and then talks about the money he has spent on training her 'voice' and having her taught to read 'pricksong' precociously (3.2.110-25). Within a year or so of his own marriage, Middleton described 'some unthrifty gentleman's daughter' who, as evidence of 'her bringing up,' could 'run upon the lute very well,' and 'had likewise the gift of singing very deliciously, able to charm the hearer, which so bewitched away our young master's money that he might have kept seven noise of musicians for less charges' (*Father Hubburd's Tales* 602-12). This passage epitomizes the clash between the ideals articulated in conduct-books like Castiglione's European bestseller *Il Libro del Cortegiano*, which particularly commended an ability to play and 'sing to the lute' (M4), and the western tradition that imagined singing women as sirens luring men to their destruction (Austern 1989).[11] We can be sure that the Middleton home did not boast the 'double-gilt' organs or 'the consort of mine own household' of which Sir Bounteous is so proud in *A Mad World, My Masters* (2.1.119, 2.2.160), or all the instruments—'lute, bandora, gittern, | Viol, virginals, and cithern'—that entertain Katherine in *Your Five Gallants* (5.2.9-10). But music and dancing were the chief pleasures of leisure in Middleton's England, and if Thomas and Mary were like other people of their time, place and class they would have wanted to make music. Certainly, as a playwright Middleton was constantly collaborating with musicians.

Texts

Most of the fruit of those collaborations has perished. We often have texts without scores, and sometimes scores without texts, or scores that we cannot confidently connect to their texts. Of course, even when the music is lost, we can sometimes sense its importance. In the *Roaring Girl*, when Moll sits with a viol between her legs, plays the instrument and sings an autoerotic song, the scene (4.1) 'maximizes the viol's sexual connotations, without demeaning the player' (Seligmann 2005, 207). Readers who cannot hear the instrumental accompaniment or see the dance can nevertheless appreciate that 'the masque gone awry' in *Women, Beware Women* 'satirizes the self--mythologizing practices of the elite', and that 'the dancing lesson that fails' in *More Dissemblers Besides Women* 'targets the urban aspirants who supported court power by aping its cultural practices' (Howard, 137). Though we no longer know what music Harmony and her choir sang to the words 'Move on, move on, be still the same' (*Masque of Heroes* 307-22), we can recognize that, like other songs that follow the first dance of a masque, it serves 'the practical function of allowing the dancers a few minutes' rest' (Walls, 107).

Though they are only a small fraction of the music that once accompanied Middleton's texts, the scores that do remain represent almost all the textual varieties of early modern secular music. They include the first song printed in the text of a civic pageant (item 7) and the most popular song written for the commercial theatres before 1642 (item 23).[12] But they also include much music that originated outside dramatic scripts: sung (item 2) and hummed (item 8) snatches of traditional ballads, one traditional dance tune (item 5) and dance tunes by John Dowland (item 21) and William Byrd (item 24), a lute song by Dowland, sampled and sung by a character in a play (item 1), and another lute tune for which Middleton wrote new words (item 6). They include songs that originated in one play, and were later transferred to another (items 12 and 22), music for a masque later transferred to a play (items 9, 10, 13, 14), and a new tune set to Middleton's words for a theatrical revival twenty years after the original performances (item 11). They include music written for a company of adolescent singing actors by one of those choristers (item 3). They include music for twelve dances (items 4, 13-21, 24, 25), though theatrical instrumental music was seldom preserved or identified. They even include—something extraordinarily rare in the period—both music and choreography for two theatre dances, both extraordinarily popular (items 4 and 25).[13] They include songs printed in collections of work by a single composer (items 1, 3, 6, 20) and songs printed in musical anthologies (items 4, 13, 16, 17, 23, 25). They include songs printed using music type fonts designed and manufactured in France and Germany, songs printed from engravings on special rolling presses, and songs circulating in many different kinds of manuscript (a composer's official collection, a musician's working repertory manuscript, a pedagogical manuscript, a woman's private miscellany of favourite songs, a knight's anthology of masque music, etc.). They include manuscript songs written on music paper printed in England, songs printed on special music paper mass-produced and exported from Angoulême for the English market, and one song preserved in a manuscript that used a rare luxury paper imported from Troyes.[14]

The textual reproduction of music 'has long been neglected by historians of the book' (Chartier 325). The textual reproduction of the moving body, what Jacques

---

[10] For John Marbeck see Leaver. His surname is variously spelled by different scholars (Morbeck, Merbecke). Lepet says his wife is entitled to gentry status because she was 'a harper's grand-child' (*Valour* 4.1.294).

[11] Chan (1980) notes that Hoby consistently translates Castiglione's 'uiola' as 'lute' (130).

[12] The popularity of 'Hence, all you vain delights' is measured by the uniquely high number of separate textual sources, especially manuscripts, and especially sources from the first half of the seventeenth century. The two popular dance tunes (items 3 and 25), which appear in every edition of Playford, were printed and distributed in many more copies, but Playford is the only source for both, and those copies all postdate 1650.

[13] Both 'The Slip' and 'The Spanish Gypsy' are among the thirty dances included in all editions of Playford's *Dancing Master*; among those thirty, the only others clearly related to the theatre are 'Kemp's Jig' (from the 1580s) and 'An Old Man's Bones' (sung in Shirley's *Constant Maid*).

[14] For printed music paper (items 4, 20) see Fenlon and Milsom. On the Angoulême trade and Playford's Restoration music books (items 2, 4, 23, 25) see Thompson 1988 and 1995. On the Troyes watermark in Bodleian Mus Sch F.575 (item 23) see Thompson 1998, 146-7.

THE man is bleft that hath

not bent to wicked rede his eare : nor ledde

his life as finners doe, nor fate in fcorners

chaire, 2. But in the law of God the

Lord, doth fet his whole delight : And

in that law doth exercife himfelfe both

day and night.

2. Church music, and particularly psalm singing, would have been the most universal and regular experience of music during Middleton's lifetime. The Sternhold and Hopkins psalm book was the most frequently reprinted text of poetry or music in the sixteenth and seventeenth centuries. 'As a result British printers probably used more music type faces than all of the Protestant printers of the Continent together' (Krummel 1975, 64). Like all editions after 1603, this folio edition (1612) was printed for 'the Company of Stationers'.

twenty-five song and dance texts printed here—the first collection of music associated with the Middleton canon—represent less than an hour of playing time, distributed across seventeen different scripts and more than twenty years of dramatic writing. Nevertheless, these scattered fragments do emphasize an element of Middleton's work that has been obscured by the critical tradition. They illustrate the historical interactions, in his work and in the early modern period generally, of three forms of potentially textualized performance art: theatre, music, and dance.[15] Middleton, after all, described his own activity as a writer with the same word musicians used: he 'composed' his plays.[16] In its analysis of Middleton's 'realism', of his psychological acuity, theological depth, and political daring, of the thematic architecture of his plotting and the layered ironies of his language, twentieth-century criticism resurrected his reputation. But it also described his work in terms that were almost entirely cognitive and mimetic. That academic Aristotelian bias—what Lyotard calls 'textual thinking'—flattens and empties Middleton's art by reducing it to conceptual propositions. Music and dance, in different ways, resist that flattening. Even philosophy now acknowledges that 'the mind is inherently embodied' (Lakoff and Johnson, 3), and dance has always foregrounded that corporeal experience of space, time, and relationships. Music may be invisible but it is never immaterial. Its union of 'feeling and form' links embodied emotional experience to mathematical distributions of frequencies and decibels through time.[17] Thus, music and dance both force us to imagine Middleton through the medium of 'feeling bodies' (Taylor 1998).

Every textual embodiment of music in Middleton's lifetime, and for centuries before and after, depended on notation.[18] Early in the seventh century, Archbishop Isidore of Seville wrote that 'unless sounds are remembered by man, they perish, for they cannot be written down' (*Etymologiarum*, chapter iii, 15). We now know more than Isidore about the history of music notation: late in the twentieth century the musical text of a Hurrian love-song dating from *c.*1800 BCE was transcribed and performed (Wulstan). The ancient Greeks, too, had a notational system. But the musical texts of early modern England belonged to a post-classical western European system that originated in the ninth century, with plainchant. England did not play an important part in the creation of European notation, or its medieval and Renaissance development; like its music fonts, its notation systems were imported.

LeCoq called *le corps poétique*, and the belated evolution of dance notation, has been paid even less attention. 'For thirty thousand years, the memory of culture has been distorted by the uneven development of technologies for making artificial representations of the past' (Taylor 1996, 164). Music and dance notation operate, in part, as boundary markers, calling attention to the limits and anomalies of text technologies, reminding us that they reproduce a mere fraction of the larger culture. Indeed, texts reproduce a mere fraction even of the object of aesthetic desire. Although they are a representative sample of the increasing importance and variety of written music and choreographed dance in early modern textual culture, the

[15] John Rastell was not only an innovator in music printing, but published plays (and probably wrote them), and constructed London's earliest commercial stage (Plomer).
[16] See Taylor 1994, and the title-pages of *Mad World* (1608), *Honourable Entertainments* (1621), and *A Game at Chess* (Rosenbach manuscript, autograph).
[17] 'Feeling and form' is Langer's phrase, but all philosophical accounts of music, beginning with Plato, wrestle with similar conceptualizations: see Bowman and Budd.
[18] Rastell defines notation as 'The written symbols (which may include verbal instructions) by which musical ideas are represented and preserved for future performance or study' (2).

The centuries-long evolution of competing and overlapping systems was driven by many factors.[19] In general, notation evolved to show an increasing number of musical parameters more and more precisely. Nevertheless, early modern musical texts provide much less information than modern staff notation (Illus. 2). Consequently, even when we possess a score, it does not permit us to reconstruct exactly a particular musical performance or musical intention. Much of the detail of the music depended then, and depends now, upon each performer's interpretation, improvisation, and virtuosity, and upon the harmonious collaborative interaction of more than one performer. (This is also true, of course, of early modern dramatic scripts, including Middleton's.)

Dance notation developed even later than music notation. A French manuscript containing seven *basse danses*, conjecturally dated 1445, is probably the earliest known document to record choreographies (Crane). About a decade later, the first treatise on music that included dance descriptions and dance music was written in Ferrara, and in the next few decades Italy produced another eight such treatises, plus fragments (Sparti). The earliest surviving English choreographies—full of Italian and French terminology—occur in a small pocket book miscellany, among the papers of a Derbyshire family, produced c.1500 (Fallows, Nevile). From then until Middleton's death in 1627, only half a dozen English choreographies have been identified, and only one of those was printed (a translated three-column appendix in a teach-yourself-French book, published in 1521).[20] Not surprisingly, scholarship on sixteenth and seventeenth century dance has been slow to develop, and it has intersected with literary studies chiefly in discussion of dances in Shakespeare's plays or Jonson's masques.[21] However, we do not possess original scores or choreographies for any Shakespearean dance, or choreographies for any of Jonson's. For Middleton, by contrast, we possess at least two choreographies (items 4 and 25), and at least twelve dance scores.

The paucity of written choreographies does not indicate a dearth of dance; dance generously punctuated early modern culture and the Middleton canon. We cannot statistically measure its ubiquity in the everyday world, but within the canon variants of the word *dance* appear 142 times (not counting stage directions); one mayoral pageant, two masques, and sixteen plays explicitly require one or more dances. The variety of these dances is suggested by Middleton's technical vocabulary, which includes *canaries, caper, change, cinquepace, coranto, double, galliard, hey, honour, hop, hornpipe, jig, kick, lavolta, leg, measures, morris, pace, round, sides, single, stand, sword-dance,* and *trick.* Even these statistics underestimate the extent to which dance saturated drama. Until 1612, some or all of Middleton's plays would have ended with a 'jig', a short song-and-dance drama unrelated to the fiction of the play itself (Baskervill). Where there was no concluding jig, closure was probably signaled by a formal dance, like that witnessed by a Swiss tourist in 1599. Thomas

Platter visited a theatre on the south bank, saw a tragedy about Julius Caesar, and remembered that, 'zu endt der Comedien dantzeten sie ihrem gebauch nach gar überausz zierlich, ye zwen in mannes vndt 2 in weiber kleideren angethan, wunderbahrlich mitt einanderen' ('at the end of the play they danced according to their custom with extreme elegance, two in men's clothes and two in women's, in wonderful combination with each other').[22] Moreover, all but six of Middleton's extant plays would have been performed, originally, with four intervals between the five acts, and one or more of those intervals routinely included some form of dancing—like the 'Country dance, by the Actors in their Vizards to a new footing' inserted between the end of Act 2 and the beginning of Act 3 in the 1640 edition of *A Mad World, My Masters*.[23] Since all six exceptions predate the legal prohibition on jigs, extra-dramatic dances probably accompanied the original performances of every single Middleton play. Likewise, although the young East Asian 'Indians' who 'dance about the trees' in *The Triumphs of Honour and Industry* are the only dancers specified in any of his Lord Mayor shows, the Jacobean budgets for such shows routinely called for 'greenemen wᵗʰ fireworkę', 'Divells', 'one that went on stiltę', drummers, fifers, trumpeters, ensign-bearers, and 'yᵉ fencer...and his 25 men'.[24] All parades are, in one sense, ritualized street dances.

The concluding jigs are never, and the entr'acte performances rarely, acknowledged in stage directions. Which is to say, most dances remained *totally* outside textual culture. Even when texts indicate that a dance took place, they seldom tell us anything specific about it.[25] In such cases, dance has only *minimally* crossed the boundary into textual culture; text gestures deictically toward

<hr>

[19] About 1420, the solid black notes of medieval music gave way to hollow notes, not because of any change in musical theory or practice, but because paper was replacing parchment as Europe's dominant writing surface, and the concentration of ink in a black note tended to eat through the paper too quickly (Pryer, 1257).
[20] For English sources before 1700 see Ravenhofer, 36–49. I do not count the French manuscript choreographies on the flyleaf of a Latin book printed in Venice in 1497, bequeathed to Salisbury Cathedral eight decades later (shelfmark Y.2.12). I do count 'Here foloweth the maner of dauncynge of bace daũces after the use of fraunce & other places translated out of frenche in englyshe by Robert coplande', appended to Alexander Barclay's *Here begynneth the introductory to wryte, and to pronounce frenche*, printed by Coplande (1521; STC 1386), sig. C4–C4ᵛ. I also include Cambridge University Library MS Ll.1.11 (early 16th century), and four of the seven so-called 'Inns of Court' manuscripts edited by Payne: those associated with Edward Gunther (1563–6), John Willoughby (1594), John Ramsey (1609), and John Stow (1611–21?). Three seventeenth-century manuscripts, all in the British Library—Lansdowne 1115 (fols. 35–8), Sloane 3858 (fols. 15–18), and Add. 41996 (fol. 18)—are not securely dated, but are probably mid-century.
[21] For Shakespeare see Brissenden (academic) and Hoskins (practical). For Jonson see especially Daye and Ravelhofer.
[22] For the original German see Chambers 2:364–5; my translation combines elements from Chambers and Schanzer.
[23] For entr'acte dancing see Austern 1992, 83–92. The six exceptions are *Patient Man and Honest Whore, Yorkshire Tragedy, Timon of Athens, Revenger's Tragedy, Roaring Girl,* and *No Wit/Help like a Woman's,* all first performed in theatres that had not yet adopted the convention of entr'acte music; however, subsequent revivals of those plays probably incorporated act intervals.
[24] Robertson and Gordon, 64, 65, 88, 102.
[25] Dessen and Thomson note that, of the 'almost 350' examples of the direction 'dance' in English professional plays from 1580–1642, the 'most common' occurrence is the single word without elaboration (64).

a domain outside itself. Like the bare word 'song' (which tells us that non-song is the normative form of verbal utterance in plays, but doesn't indicate which song or what music), 'dance' tells us that non-dance is the normative form of stage movement, but the word tells us nothing about which steps are danced, in what pattern, to which music, for how long, at what tempo, or even by how many or whom. Moreover, although many early modern text-directions for 'Song' include lyrics and/or music, early modern directions for dramatic dance never—with one exception, discussed below—include choreographies.

In Middleton's lifetime, almost all dancing remained textless. Specific dances were learned—as, for the most part, dancing continues to be learned—atextually, mimetically, by observing and then attempting to duplicate the bodily movements of someone else. Dancing was 'practiced', and it required 'room to practice in': although a text might usefully be read once, and only once, by a reader confined to a chair or a bed, dancing demanded physical repetition and physical space. The dancing lesson in *More Dissemblers Besides Women* dramatizes this form of teaching. The scene acknowledges that pupils must learn to read written music—'prick-song' (5.1.95)—but it does not consider the possibility of written choreographies. Indeed, Ben Jonson ridicules the very idea of textualizing dance through the character of a Fencer in the antimasque of *Pan's Anniversary* (1620). Like the fencers who performed routinely in Lord Mayor's shows, Jonson's Braggart 'Sonne of the sword' performs the role of usher, whiffler, and presenter, describing himself as a specialist in 'Fencing, Wrestling, Leaping, Dauncing'. He announces that 'a great Clerke, who (they say) can write, and it is shrewdly suspected but he can read too,' will 'make a memoriall' or 'map' of all the dances 'by Brachygraphie' (51-6, 141-5). That last word—a Greek compound for 'short writing'—had first been used in English in the title of Peter Bales' shorthand manual *The arte of brachygraphie* (1590, 1597; STC 1311, 1312), which promised to teach its users 'to write as fast as a man speaketh'. But Jonson might have noticed it in another book, published in the same year that *Pans Anniversarie* was performed, and written by a surveyor named Folkington. His *Art of Brachygraphy* promised 'a speedy dispatch in taking of speeches' (1620, 1622; STC 11122, 11122.5). Whether or not the shorthand systems of Bales and Folkington worked as advertised, their authors presupposed a desire to turn spontaneous speech into text. Jonson's Fencer transforms 'Brachygraphie' into an instrument for turning dance into text. Jonson probably was mocking the ambitious ignorance of the Fencer, but choreography does resemble shorthand, and both are attempts to expand the empire of text. They capture and freeze-frame moving sound-waves and moving feet.

The empire of text was more immediately successful in appropriating two other forms of moving art: the folk tale and the ballad. The early Tudor printer Robert Copland (*fl.* 1505-47) advertised for performers of stories and songs to come to his shop, so that he could write down their words and print them (87). 'At the founding moment of English print culture,' Linda Woodbridge argues, 'the swashbuckling privateers of print colonized the realm of popular storytelling.' Stories that had once circulated orally and anonymously were collected, reshaped, signed, and printed: 'a privatization of what had been collective, a middle-class appropriation of a plebeian art form, a city appropriation of a rural art form, literacy's colonization of the oral . . . a male appropriation of a female art form' (13-14). It is hard to quantify the extent of this expropriation of storytelling because folk tales were not labelled as such, and were usually woven into the texture of legitimated literary genres. But ballads are easier to identify. Although only about 260 specimens survive, it has been estimated that about 4000 single-sheet broadside ballads were printed in the sixteenth century (Livingston 32; Rollins 1919, 281-2). In the registers of the Stationers' Company from its founding in 1557 to the Parliamentary ban of 1642, ballads outnumber books and plays (Rollins 1924, 1). To this massive project of data-capture we owe most of our current knowledge of popular oral culture. Nevertheless, the text technology that made this data-capture possible also created a new regime of intellectual property. 'The Commons of England made this Song', Thomas Deloney recorded; but when he wrote out that ballad and sold it to a printer, the song became the private property of the London stationer Humphrey Lownes, who published the first edition of Deloney's *Jack of Newbury* (1597; STC 6559), and who still owned it when the tenth edition was published in 1626. Like English landowners who enclosed commons land, 'the London book industry took into its private ownership much of the traditional common culture of England, and then charged a rent for using it' (St Clair 50). Indeed, ballads were such a profitable and specialized trade that a broadside cartel was created in the 1620s (Watt 257-95).

The broadside ballads were so profitable because they did not attempt to textualize the music. Instead, they relied upon popular familiarity with existing tunes, or upon balladmongers who sang the ballads they retailed, simultaneously attracting customers and teaching them the melody (Wutzbach 21-3). Thus the printed ballad trade piggybacked on the oral circulation of tunes. We can reconstruct the music for popular songs only if, at some point, someone wrote it down. But anyone capable of transforming a singing voice into written notation was also capable of writing variations on the original tune. Thus, for the sixteenth-century ballad 'Loath to depart' (item 8) we possess musical transcriptions of arrangements by three composers: John Dowland, Giles Farnaby, and Thomas Ravenscroft. Each composer is almost certainly appropriating a tune made by the Commons of England, and modifying it in ways that demonstrate his own musical talent: listeners familiar with the original will appreciate how each composer riffs on his material. For anyone trying to recover an authentic folk tune, or to reconstruct the tune used in Middleton and Rowley's play, this combination of filtering and variation is frustrating.

But the initial fluidity is itself characteristic of folk tale and folk music, with their proliferation of types and versions (Atkinson 1–38), and the foundational 'untextuality' of an oral tradition (Foley 27) will inevitably be altered whenever a text technology captures it. In relation to the original oral performances, it makes little difference whether the music is written down in a private manuscript anthology (Farnaby), printed in a composer's book of songs (Ravenscroft), or both (Dowland).

But this example also demonstrates that the Stationers' Company did not have a monopoly on the commodification of song. The chief early modern institution for the commercial appropriation, transformation, and reproduction, for private profit, of other people's music was not the print trade, but the theatre. Indeed, as Bruce Smith has convincingly argued, a theatre like the Globe was 'the largest, airiest, loudest, subtlest sound-making device fabricated by the culture of early modern England' (1999, 207–8).

Theatres

In the anonymous interlude called *The Triall of Treasure* (1567; STC 24271), for every didactic song sung by the estimable trio of Just, Trust, and Contentation praising those who 'walk upright and just', dozens of additional songs provided the popular Vice figure with a ready means to celebrate the carefree way of life which he espoused. He appeared in various roles—as pedlar, ballad-hawker, thief, or fool—and his repertory, consisting chiefly of verses sung to ballad tunes, three-man's songs, and catches, was richly varied. Wager's interlude *called the longer thou liuest the more foole thou art* (c.1569; STC 24935) includes a character named 'Moros' (from the Greek word meaning 'foolish'), who enters the play '*synging the foot* [= refrain] *of many Songes, as fooles were wont*'; his first speech consists of fragments of eight separate songs (sig. A3). Similar characters show up in Robert Wilson's *Three Lords and Three Ladies of London* (Simplicity), Beaumont's *The Knight of the Burning Pestle* (Merrythought), and Shakespeare's *The Winter's Tale* (Autolycus). In *The Patient Man and the Honest Whore*, Dekker and Middleton assume that the character, or role, is so familiar to actors and audiences that it requires only a single stage direction at the beginning of Scene 6:

> Enter Roger with a stool, cushion, looking-glass, and chafing-dish; those being set down, he pulls out of his pocket a vial with white colour in it, and two boxes, one with white, another red, painting. He places all things in order and a candle by them, singing with the ends of old ballads as he does it.

The playwrights here simply invite the actor to improvise, to sample and mix old ballads however he pleases, as long as he pleases the audience. We could, on the basis of this stage direction, include in the following anthology of music associated with the Middleton canon the tunes of a dozen popular old ballads, like those that Duffin uses to flesh out 'Shakespeare's Songbook'. The verbal content

of the songs Roger sings matters less, dramatically, than their genre (ballads), their age (old), their reduction to the simplest and most familiar verbal units (ends), which can then be creatively re-mixed. The playwrights characterize Roger through the old-fashioned, plebeian songs he sings, and by contrasting him with his employer, the upmarket courtesan Bellafront. Bellafront also, later in the scene, sings snatches of songs, but the verbal content of those songs *does* matter, and is specified in the script.[26] One of the songs she samples in this scene is a fashionable new lute song by John Dowland (item 1). The contrast between the musical tastes of Bellafront and her servant resembles the contrast in *Father Hubburd's Tales*, written the same year, between the regal Nightingale, singing her 'canzonet' (756), and the rustic male Ant, who remembers 'dancing of Sellinger's Round in moonshine nights about Maypoles' (639).

This allusive sampling of popular songs depends on three things. First, the familiarity of the song gives audiences (or readers) the pleasure of instant, shared recognition, and lets the playwright convey a lot of information in a few moments of stage time. Second, the lack of musical copyright allows playwrights and acting companies to appropriate, without fee, the compositional talents both of famous individual composers like Dowland and of the ballad-making Commons of England. Third, the only musical instrument required is the human voice. The scene from *Honest Whore* is typical of the musical structure of most plays written for adult companies performing in outdoor amphitheatres: it contrasts the bass adult male voice (Roger) with the treble adolescent male voice impersonating a woman (Bellafront).[27] Until the 1590s, those companies and theatres seem to have counted on actors to double as musicians (Chan 1980, 32–3).

But if we conceptualize the theatre building itself as 'an instrument to be played upon', then London offered Middleton more than one kind of instrument, and more than one kind of player. The Globe, like other outdoor amphitheatres, 'fostered a broad sound produced by sound waves moving primarily from side to side', by contrast with rectilinear indoor spaces like the Blackfriars theatre and the Middle Temple hall, which 'produced a more rounded sound that was especially suited to ensemble acting, the treble voices of boy actors, and music' (Smith 2004, 137). The mid-sixteenth century formation of acting companies composed largely of 'boy' (adolescent) actors, whose main activity was to serve as choristers for divine service, capitalized on their extraordinary vocal talents. Known variously as the Children of the Chapel Royal, the Boys of St Paul's, or the Children of Windsor, these companies were the most prominent of several shorter-lived additional groups, and the sophisticated song

---

[26] Four stanzas of 'Pretty wantons warble' are given in the anonymous *The Fayre Mayde of the Exchange*, probably written c.1602, printed in 1607 (STC 13317), sig. E1. This song source is not noted by Hoy (2:28).
[27] For early modern plays as musical compositions scored for these different voices see Smith 1999, 222–45.

which they performed implies at once composers writing for the stage, trained voices to sing their compositions, and a cultivated audience capable of understanding and appreciating their work. It was for these groups that dramatists such as Richard Edwards, John Lyly, and George Peele wrote plays richly studded with stage songs of a demanding variety, usually to be sung to the accompaniment of a quartet of viols. Peele's *The araygnement of Paris* (1584), for instance, contains fourteen music numbers, among which are bird-calls mimicked by the high-pitched voices of boys to produce the 'artificial charm of birds'; an antiphonal chorus of gods and muses, the first singing 'within' and the second 'without'; singers taking part in a circular dance; a piper providing accompaniment to his singing companions; a forsaken heroine singing a dramatic lament; a group of knights in armour 'treading a warlike almain, by drum and fife'; a popular catch followed soon after by a sophisticated song in Italian about the goddess Diana; and a concluding chorus in Latin.

At about 1600, the chief choirboy groups were revived, after an intermission of a decade. Ben Jonson, John Marston, and Thomas Middleton made full use of the musical resources of the new companies. Many of their musical offerings featured comic items performed by small groups singing in ensemble. Although their dramatic music repertory was composed largely of solo songs set for small instrumental consorts, usually of viols, it also included dialogue songs for duos and trios to be sung in alternation as well as choral numbers in three or four parts whose variety added special prominence to company scenes. Choirboy plays also offered music before the play began, and during the four intervals between the five acts. A German visitor to the Blackfriars in 1602 reported that 'For a whole hour before, a delightful performance of *musicam instrumentalem* is given on organs, lutes, pandores, mandolins, violins, and flutes' (Gerschow, 29). In the choirboy theatres, music came first—and not just literally. Moreover, the music before, during, and after the play might change from one performance to the next. There was no fixed relationship between the verbal script and the music concert taking place in the same building before the same audience. Music was portable—as we have already seen, in the case of old ballads and Dowland lute songs imported into plays. But this portability also applied to the music specifically composed for particular plays, which would always have been written (if it was written down at all) on separate, loose sheets of paper. Those loose sheets could easily migrate from one playscript to another. Thus, a song first associated with John Lyly's *Campaspe*—'Oh, for a bowl of fat canary'—also shows up in the 1640 edition of *A Mad World, My Masters*; it may have migrated from performance by Lyly's company of boys to the boy company that first performed Middleton's play, at Paul's, or to later revivals at Salisbury Court, but in either case it moved from one play to another. The 'play', as a textual entity, was always a collection of papers, more or less loosely connected, which might

at any point break down into its constituent elements, or absorb new elements to replace the old ones (Stern). Middleton began play-patching early in his career, with the commission to write a new Prologue and Epilogue for *Friar Bacon and Friar Bungay*, and he was still doing so two decades later, when he imported 'Take oh take those lips away' into *Measure for Measure* (item 22).

Most of the incidental stage songs that have been identified from the repertory of the professional acting troupes in early Stuart London—companies like the King's Men, the Children of Paul's, Prince Henry's, and the Lady Elizabeth's—were supplied by a small number of composers whose main activities were carried on in other areas of music, sometimes tangential and sometimes not. Three, in particular, stand out, because they form a natural succession: they were the three chief composers of songs for the King's Men from the accession of James I to the closing of the theatres.

Robert Johnson (*c.*1588–1633) was a well-known contributor to many surviving theatre songs, including, probably, the famous dialogue song in *The Witch* (item 12). Johnson's first patron had been Sir George Carey, who was also the patron of the King's Men. Perhaps that connection inspired his attention to theatrical music. He entered the royal service as lutenist to the King in 1604, and throughout the early years of the century he was much in demand as a performer as well as a composer. His contributions to masque productions were extensive, and about two dozen masque and antimasque dances as well as songs for various masques have been preserved. After his death many of his stage songs were rescued from oblivion by his fellow composer John Wilson, who printed several of them in his *Cheerful Ayres and Ballads* of 1660, the first book of music printed at Oxford.

Wilson, born in 1595, was apprenticed on 11 February 1611 to the actor John Heminges, one of the leaders of the King's Men, for eight years (Kathman). He might have played in the first performances of *The Lady's Tragedy*, later that year; he certainly performed in a late Jacobean revival of Shakespeare's *Much Ado*. His first known musical composition was for *The Masque of Flowers*, in January 1614, and over the next fifteen years he wrote songs for plays by Fletcher, Ford, Brome, and Middleton (items 10 and 22). On 21 October 1622 he was appointed to the London Waits. As Morley had recorded, in dedicating his *Consort Lessons* to the Lord Mayor and Alderman, the City retained and maintained 'excellent and expert musicians to adorn' their 'favours, feasts, and solemn meetings.' In that capacity, Wilson might have composed material for Middleton's mayoral pageants of 1622, 1623, and 1626, or for the abortive London pageant celebrating the accession of Charles I.[28] In 1635, Wilson was appointed as a musician 'for the lutes, viols and voices' to Charles I;

---

[28] Payments to the City Waits were specified in the itemized budgets for Middleton's pageants of 1613, 1617, 1623, and 1626 (Robertson and Gordon). On mayoral pageants and the City Waits more generally, see Burden and Palmer; the latter came to my attention too late to be consulted for item 7.

he accompanied the King to Oxford in 1642, staying on to become Doctor of Music and then Professor of Music. His first work to appear after the conferring of his degree was the *Devotions of His Sacred Majesty in his Solitudes and Sufferings, rendered in verse* (four part-books, 1657).[29]

No less significant is the dramatic music of William Lawes, born in 1582, whose music was not published in print during his lifetime, and whose reputation was overshadowed until very recently by that of his illustrious brother Henry. It is only within the past few decades that William's score for James Shirley's *Triumph of Peace* (1634) as well as those for William Davenant's *The Triumphs of the Prince d'Amour* (1636) and *Britannia Triumphans* (1638) have been made available to establish him as a gifted and far more innovative composer than most of his contemporaries. His fame rests chiefly on his sustained vocal and instrumental scores for these masques, which consist of extended sequences of alternating dialogue passages, arias, and choruses, as well as dances, climactically arranged. But William was also an accomplished composer of music for the commercial theatres, writing twenty-five known settings for twenty-one different plays between 1634 and 1641. In the early 1630s he took over from Wilson as chief composer for the King's Men at the Blackfriars, but he also wrote music for Beeston's Boys at the Phoenix (Wood). Just as playwrights like Middleton wrote new material for old plays, so composers wrote fashionable new music for revivals, and William's setting of a song from *The Widow* is an example (item 11).[30] In 1645, at the siege of Chester, a random shot resulted in William's premature death in mid-career, publicly mourned by the King and many royalists, including his friends and fellow composers John Wilson and John Hinton (item 23) and the music publisher John Playford (1623–87).

Although Playford was not a composer, he is the last important figure in this succession of Stuart musicians associated with Middleton (items 2, 4, 23, 25). 'The first great capitalist of music history' (Krummel 112), Playford probably got his musical education at the cathedral choir school in Norfolk, before taking up an apprenticeship in the London print trade in 1640. After seven years he became a freeman of the Stationers' Company, and from 1647 to 1651 he published twenty-six books, none of them having anything to do with music; twenty-five were political, and 'by 1650 Playford had established himself as a figure of Royalist credentials and sympathies.' Then, from 1651 to 1659, twenty-four of his twenty-seven publications were music books. This seemingly abrupt shift in his business conceals an underlying continuity: the musicians Playford published, and the poets whose lyrics they set to music, were almost all associated with the Stuart court in the years before the outbreak of the Civil War. Like Humphrey Moseley, who catered to the consumer demand for dramatic texts no longer performable, Playford nostalgically sustained a royalist musical tradition, publishing the work of unemployed musicians for 'a now disempowered and disenfranchised audience and clientele' (Lindenbaum).

Movements

The Civil War, which put an end to the music-making of William Lawes, re-directed the career of John Wilson, and laid the foundations for the music publishing of John Playford, reflected divisions in English culture which go back to the Elizabethan period, and which affected attitudes toward music throughout Middleton's lifetime. As early as 1586, John Case—a Fellow of St John's College at Oxford, and author of Latin philosophical treatises—felt obliged to publish *The Praise of Musicke* (STC 20184) in answer to truculent attacks, made principally by Puritans. The very titles of some of his individual chapters—'The Dignity of Music proved both by the rewards and practice of many and most excellent men', 'The Effects and Operation of Music', and 'The Necessity of Music'—resonate with a strong commitment to the art for its use in the general course of life—not only in civil activities, in war-like matters, in the church, but even on the stage. Case responds systematically—and effectively—to Puritan objections that complicated music makes it impossible for all men to sing together, that too much repetition in music makes understanding difficult, and that 'cunning music pleaseth more with the note than the matter' (Boyd, App. C).

This division of opinion about the merits of music can also be traced in Middleton's work. On the negative side, in *Your Five Gallants*, a music school is a front for a brothel, where (punning lewdly) 'musica est ars'; in *Wit at Several Weapons*, a band of musicians is actually a band of thieves; in *The Witch*, 'there is no villainy but is a tune'. On the positive side, in *The Triumphs of Truth* the Lord Mayor will hear 'Truth's celestial harmony' at St Paul's (485);

---

[29] On Wilson's life and musical career see Ashbee and Lasocki, 1157–9, Henderson, and Spink 1974.

[30] Lefkowitz claimed that Lawes also wrote instrumental music for a revival of *The Phoenix* (203), but he did not give a source for the music or the attribution. Wood identifies 'The Phenix' in British Library Add. MS 31429, fol. 40ᵛ; it is not attributed, but she notes that 'the attributions that do appear in this set of partbooks' may 'also apply to the following pieces; Lawes is mentioned on f. 33ᵛ and the next attribution does not appear until f. 42' (59). There is also a keyboard version, not noticed by Wood: 'The ffinex' appears in 'Elizabeth Rogers hir virginall booke', BL Add. MS 10337, fol. 34–33ᵛ (inverted), transcribed by Cofone, p. 68. The Rogers manuscript does not attribute its contents, but it does contain other items by William Lawes and does contain a good deal of theatrical music. These two tunes are quite distinct, but both use the same title and come from approximately the same period. Wood, aware of only the one tune, doubts its association with the play, primarily because 'No records of a revival of Middleton's play during the period when Lawes was writing have been located' (59). But the play was reprinted in 1630, and is quoted repeatedly in Cotgrave's 1655 anthology of passages from plays (see 'Lives and Afterlives', this volume, p. 452); both documents suggest that *The Phoenix* remained popular in the Caroline period, and it would have made sense for a play with such a title to be revived in the theatre with that name. The text explicitly calls for music between scenes 9 and 10: '*Toward the close of the music, the Justice's three men prepare for a robbery*'. This suggests that Middleton was imagining entr'acte music, though none is marked elsewhere in the printed text. Certainly, any 1630s revival would have required entr'acte music. Middleton also probably intended the play to end with music (Austern 1992, 94): the music is not specified in a stage direction, but it would make sense for it to accompany or conclude the climactic cure of Tangle, who finds 'peace's music', which also seems to be acknowledged in the play's last lines, spoken by Phoenix: 'Thus, when all hearts are tuned to honour's strings, There is no music to the choir of kings' (15.344, 349–60). But the fact that 'Phoenix' could refer to the theatre makes attribution of these two pieces to the play very uncertain.

one of the *Honourable Entertainments* celebrates 'Music and archery', the gifts of Apollo; and in *The Triumphs of Love and Antiquity*, 'the musical Orpheus, great master both in poesy and harmony, who by his excellent music drew after him wild beasts, woods, and mountains' epitomizes 'Harmonious government' which can charm and tame the wildness of human and animal nature.

The musical form most strongly associated with the representation of 'Harmonious government' was the masque, a genre of dance drama developed from the mummers' plays of the medieval period and the disguisings so commonly presented at the early Tudor court. Middleton is known to have written three masques. The libretto of *Masque of Cupids*, the first, has been lost, but Jowett (1994) has convincingly identified two songs from the masque (items 9 and 10). By contrast, the libretto of the third masque, *The World Tossed at Tennis*, was printed in 1620, but all the music is apparently lost (or unidentified). Only for the *Masque of Heroes* do we possess both the printed libretto (1619) and a manuscript containing much of the dance music (items 15–20). This difference in the sources—print for the dramatic text, manuscript for the associated music—reflects a more general pattern of textual segregation. Both scripts and scores were used to create dramatic performances, and both might be owned by the same theatre company; Prince Charles's Men performed both the *Masque of Heroes* and *The World Tossed at Tennis*, and in order to do so they would have needed both words and music. But the two types of text were generally produced by different agents (writers *v.* composers), used by different performers (actors *v.* musicians), and reproduced by and for different readers. The potential post-performance market for scripts was large enough to warrant the capital investment necessary to produce printed editions of hundreds of copies; the number of people who could read musical notation—and therefore the maximum potential market—was much smaller, and the appetite of that boutique market was more efficiently served by manuscript copying. Actually, the market for musical texts of even a single masque was further divided between those interested in vocal song and those interested in instrumental consorts. Thus, we possess scores for two vocal songs from *Masque of Cupids*, but no known instrumental music; we possess scores for six pieces of instrumental music for *Masque of Heroes*, but nothing for the vocal songs. This segregation of music from libretto, and of instrumental from vocal music, often makes it impossible to identify which music belongs with which dramatic text. Almost certainly, the items that we identify and reproduce here are only a fraction of the extant music from the period that was once associated with the Middleton canon.

Although Sabol has identified six pieces of instrumental dance music from *The Masque of Heroes*, even for that masque we lack choreographies. That gap is not peculiar to Middleton; we lack choreographies for all English masques before 1650. Given the fact that 'at heart the masque is an entertainment of dancing' (Daye 5), their systematic non-survival is not only unfortunate but remarkable. It demonstrates that anyone interested in reproducing a dance would have done so by imitating a dancer who already knew the steps, rather than by copying or reading a choreography. But it also suggests that the dances may never have been written down, even by the dancing masters who designed them.

James Knowles, in his critical introduction, rightly emphasizes that *The Masque of Heroes* 'challenges Jonsonian models' of court masque. Nevertheless, Middleton retained the classic sequence of dances that the participants in the masque would have expected. 'The masque is a dance drama whose meaning is conveyed primarily through patterned movements and gestures rather than the vocal expression of ideas and ideals' (Sabol 7). The standard dance sequence, outlined by Sabol, can be illustrated by *Heroes*.

1. Dances and songs of the antimasquers: *Heroes* 141.1 (item 15), 231.1–2 (item 16), 266.1 (item 17)
2. Loud music and the discovery of the scene of the masque: 278.1–3
3. Song 1: 279–306
4. Entry dance of the masquers: 306.1–2 (item 18)
5. Song 2: 307–22
6. Main dance of the masquers: 322.1 (item 19)
7. Song 3: 323–31
8. The measures and the revels: 331.1–2
9. Song 4: 332–7
10. Exit dance of the masquers: 337.1 (item 20)

The odd-numbered phases (1, 3, 5, 7, 9) were performed by professional actors, in this case Prince Henry's Men. The word normally used to describe the first phase, 'antimasque', possessed several meanings. As an 'anti-masque' (Jonson's preferred term), it illustrated the obverse of the chief virtues represented by the masquers themselves. As an 'ante-masque' (Middleton's preferred term), it consisted of an episode vividly performed before the masquers appeared, a sequence that might have many different meanings. As an 'antic' masque the term defined the comic or satiric content of its actors' display; as an 'antique' masque it underscored on occasion old-fashioned manners and abandoned customs. The music entitled 'The New Year's Gift' (item 15) was apparently associated with the entry of the presenter figure named New Year. Doctor Almanac chides New Year for goading a sextet of holidays to sin by wilfully causing them to misunderstand their charges rather than by urging them to proceed in a manner to mend their ways. The music for the first antic dance which they perform (item 16) consists of four sections of varying tempo and metre, each of which may be repeated; and each of these four sections varies the measure for a particular individualized display, which (like antic presentations in other Jacobean masques) would more likely be used to support various pantomimic rather than actual formalized dance routines. In each of these sections, one or two of the sextet could successively provide a very short episode distinguishing the nature of his inability to face, let alone comprehend, his charge. The presence of fermatas, or holds, over various notes in the treble parts indicates a musical means of emphasizing a 'stand', in which an actor/dance could assume and accentuate a telling pose.

The principal masquers (appearing in the even-numbered phases 2, 4, 6, 8, and 10) were 'masked', or disguised, typically as historical or allegorical figures; this disguising contributed to the game-like nature of the occasion. In *Masque of Heroes*, the masquers represent the Nine Worthies, and were probably the older and more eminent leaders of the legal profession in the Inner Temple (although sometimes masquers were chosen for their exceptional dancing skills, rather than their social pre-eminence). Their formal dances (items 18, 19, 20) would have been specially choreographed by dancing masters. In this masque Middleton celebrates the legal profession by fashioning masquing roles for the benchers and barristers of the legal societies as heroes who are 'deified for their virtues' (in stark contrast to the sly absurdities advanced by legal professionals in *Old Law*, written at about the same time).

The eighth phase in the structural sequence outlined above, the measures and the revels, is—typically—only minimally represented by the printed text, but in performance it was the most extended and important part of the occasion. 'The measures, formal and grave, and the revels, spirited and energetic, were the popular social dances of the day' (Sabol 15). This part of the masque is, effectively, a formal ball, and it always began with a sequence of 'old measures', invariable in Middleton's lifetime (Payne 8). Middleton did not specify these dances in the printed edition of *Masque of Heroes*, but informed readers of the text would all have known that, when the stage direction calls for the masquers of the Inner Temple to '*make choice of their ladies, and dance*' (331.1–2), they would have begun with these familiar dances in this familiar order. (The parenthetical numbers, below, refer to Ian Payne's transcriptions of the music for these dances, which for six of the eight can be confidently identified from early modern sources.)

1. The Quadran Pavan (139–40)
2. Turkeyloney (144–5)
3. The Earl of Essex's Measures (146)
4. Tinternel (153–4)
5. The Old Almain
6. The Queen's Almain (188)
7. Cecilia Almain
8. Black Almain (201)

It could be argued that these dances, which were certainly performed, should be included in our transcriptions of music for *Masque of Heroes*; doing so would double the number of extant musical texts associated with Middleton's 1619 script, and add eight choreographies. In addition to these guaranteed favourites, manuscript accounts of the 'measures' danced at the Inns of Court also include a less predictable selection of several newer

dances: New Almain, Lorayne Almain, New Cecilia Almain, Brunswick's Almain (182–3), and the Long Pavan. Although these dances appear more haphazardly in the manuscripts, it is likely that one or more of them was danced at this point in Middleton's masque.

As every modern DJ knows, it helps to begin with music and dances that the participants already recognize. This pragmatic logic was formalized in the social dancing of the masque, best described by dance historian Anne Daye. 'Simple dances, well-known to participants, with terre-a-terre steps are the ideal repertoire to start a ball. Participants are comfortable intellectually because they either know the dances or can make a decent showing in them if partnered well. They are also comfortable physically with movements that ease the legs and body gently into action' (17). These were followed by galliards, corantoes, lavoltas, canaries, passamezzi and spagnolette, 'the proving ground of the serious dancers', requiring a great deal of improvisation and 'either a constant rebounding motion or marked elevation in jumps and lifts. These dances are for one couple at a time to show their mastery, while others watched' (18).

None of these ballroom dances—the measures or the revels—are danced in the extant text of *The World Tossed at Tennis*, which represents a text of the masque transformed for performance in a public theatre. The Prologue and Epilogue were certainly added for the new venue; the Prologue's admission that 'we break the stage's laws today | Of acts and scenes' recognizes, among other things, that the continuous action of the masque does not permit a division into five acts, or the performance of four regularly spaced entr'actes. But the printed text also significantly departs from the normal structure of the masque. It is difficult to tell how much of that difference results from adaptation for the public stage, and how much reflects experimentation with the court form. The masque does contain three songs (267–80, 484–95, and 673–81) and at least four dances (297.1, 374.1/406.1, 681.1–3, 811.1–2); it does distinguish between mute, 'discovered' noble dancers (the Nine Worthies) and non-noble dancers who also speak or sing (the Five Starches, the Mariners, the world-tossers). It includes speaking deities that descend on machines, and mute roles for the pages who, at indoor nocturnal masques, functioned as torchbearers (the Nine Muses). All these elements must have originated in the masque libretto. And when the Nine Worthies 'dance' (297.1), they almost certainly recycle one of the three choreographies performed, only a few months before, by the Nine Worthies in the Middleton/Prince's Men *Masque of Heroes* (items 18, 19, 20). But the printed text entirely lacks the crucial eighth element of the sequence: the ballroom dancing of the measures and the revels—which could not be performed in the public theatre, but would certainly have been expected at Denmark House.

We cannot determine whether, or how, the structure of the original court masque was transformed for staging in the public theatres, but the indubitable historical fact of that transfer is more significant than the conjectural detail. Plays had been poaching details of masques for a decade: the dance of satyrs in Shakespeare's *The Winter's Tale* may have been transferred from Jonson's *Oberon* (1611), the morris dance in Shakespeare and Fletcher's *The Two Noble Kinsmen* from Beaumont's *Masque of the Inner Temple and Gray's Inn* (1613); one or more of the witches' dances in Middleton's adaptation of *Macbeth* (1616) may have been recycled from Jonson's *Masque of Queen's* (items 13 and 14). The one constant in these transfers is not the playwright but the acting company: here, the King's Men, who had probably danced all those antimasque roles, and wanted to recycle the dances they had been paid to learn for a single court performance into a theatrical spectacle that could attract paying customers. Neither Jonson nor Beaumont had created, or owned, either the music or the choreography for those dances. If anybody 'owned' the dances, it was the dancers who had danced them, corporealizing them as a series of muscle memories. Like Sellenger's Round, an antimasque dance belonged to anyone who could dance it, as a song belonged to anyone who could sing it, a tune to anyone who could play (or hum) it.

Middleton wrote more masques *within* plays than any of his contemporaries.[31] As early as *Timon of Athens* (1605-6), Middleton had introduced a masque into a play for the public theatres. His Masque of Amazons in Sc. 2, which begins with their entrance 'with lutes in their hands, dancing and playing,' ends with a representation of the measures/revels, as 'The Lords...each single out an Amazon, and all dance, men with women'. Partly through the deliberate 'rupture of court masquing conventions,' Middleton positions himself 'in a consciously extramural and critical fashion,' so that 'the masque offers the audience a satirical commentary on Timon himself—and, by way of the allusion to court masque, on the vices of extravagant consumption and gift-giving embodied in King James' (Jowett 2006). A similarly critical stance seems evident in the double masque of *The Revenger's Tragedy*, probably written a few months later (1606), which begins soon after 'a reveling night, | When torch-light made an artificial noon About the court', when 'some courtiers in the masque, Putting on better faces than their own...Singled out' Antonio's wife. That final verb suggests the normal action of the revels, when noblemen in the masque invited individual women in the audience to dance with them; but in this case 'in the height of all the revels, When music was heard loudest', she was raped, 'amidst a throng', seemingly on the dance floor itself (1.4.26-42). This masque takes place offstage, but Act Five stages two court masques that combine banqueting, music and murder. The wooing masque in *Your Five Gallants* (1607), the wedding masque of the four elements in *No Wit/Help like a Woman's* (1611), the masque of old women in *Old Law* (1619), the rehearsed masque-dance of fools and madmen in *The Changeling* (1622) are all equally ironic. No texts survive which identify themselves as the scores and choreographies for these masques-within-the-play, but any of them might

have appropriated music or dance routines from actual masques, and/or the familiar 'old measures' of the revels repertory. Indeed, why should new music have been specially created for these texts, when the recycling of existing masque music would have added allusively to both the realism and the irony of the play?

But *The World Tossed at Tennis* represents something different: not the usual free circulation of independent units of music and dance, but the wholesale appropriation of an elite form for common consumption. It marks a key transition in the musicalization of the public stage, which will culminate in the eighteenth-century 'whole show', *The Beggar's Opera*, and the rise of melodrama. Before 1600 the adult acting companies made little use of instrumental music, and probably did not have a permanent band of musicians; when they needed extra musical resources, they probably hired some or all of the City Waits (Chan 1980, 32-3). In 1608 the King's Men acquired the Blackfriars theatre and its music consort; 'the new music consort brought the largest single alteration to the King's Men's practices,' leading them among other things to modify the Globe to provide it with a music room (Gurr 368). Between 1608 and 1616 all the adult companies adopted the practice of entr'acte music and dance, which had originated in the small, high-priced venues of the chorister companies (Taylor 1993). In October 1612 'Jigges att the ende of Playes' were banned by the Middlesex authorities (Baskervill 116), inspiring playwrights to begin embedding jigs *within* plays (Mooney).[32] Coincidentally, a year after jigs were suppressed Middleton wrote his first Lord Mayor's show, *The Triumphs of Truth*, and two months later wrote his first masque, the lost *Masque of Cupids*.

In the remaining decade of his career, from 1614 to 1624, Middleton increasingly transformed plays into a de-privatized, 'commons' equivalent of court masques. He did so, in part, by reviving the dumb show. The presence of this seemingly old-fashioned device in such sophisticated late Jacobean plays as *Hengist, King of Kent* (1620), *The Changeling* (1622), and *A Game at Chess* (1624) has seemed odd to many critics. But 'dumb show' is simply a generic label for a carefully choreographed sequence of speechless, stylized movement accompanied by music (Austern 1992, 91-4). In other words, the dumb show is an inset dance drama. We do not think of the Jacobean masque as a form of 'dumb show', but by convention the main masquers did not speak or sing; they participated in a carefully choreographed sequence of speechless, stylized movement accompanied by music,

---

[31] Sutherland 89-90; her tabulation is based on the Bullen canon, and does not include *Timon, Revenger, Weapons,* or *Valour.*

[32] Mooney cites *Fair Quarrel* as the earliest example, not recognizing *Wit at Several Weapons* as a Middleton/Rowley play written within a year of the ban. He attributes this technique to Rowley alone (307), but that assumption is based on earlier attribution studies, which tidily divided the vulgarity of Rowley from the sophistication of Middleton: see the singing, dancing comic material in *Dissemblers, Widow, Heroes,* and *Valour,* and the clown roles in *Hengist* and *Game at Chess;* Rowley does not seem to have contributed any of the 'Gypsy jigs' to *Spanish Gypsy.*

described in elaborate stage directions like those in *Hengist, King of Kent*:

> *Oboes. Dumb Show: enter two villains, enter to them Vortiger, seeming to solicit them; gives them gold, then swears them; exit Vortiger. Enter to them Constantius in private meditation, they rudely come to him, strike down his book and draw their swords upon him. He fairly spreads his arms, and yields to their furies; at which they seem to be overcome with pity, but looking on the gold, kill him as he turns his back, and hurry away his body. Enter Vortiger, Devonshire, Stafford in private conference. To them enter the murderers presenting the head to Vortiger; he seems to express much sorrow, and before the astonished lords makes officers lay hold on 'em, who, offering to come towards Vortiger, are commanded to be hurried away as to execution. Then the lords, all seeming respect, crown Vortiger, then bring in Castiza, who seems to be brought in unwillingly, [by] Devonshire and Stafford, who crown her and then give her to Vortiger, she going forth with him with a kind of a constrained consent. Then enter Aurelius and Uther, the two brothers, who, much astonished, seem to fly for their safety*

This long choreographic stage direction, at the beginning of 2.2, precedes (in the texts) or perhaps accompanies (in performance) a rhyming speech by the presenter Raynulph—in the same metre as the rhyming song that accompanies the long stage direction introducing the Nine Worthies in *The World Tossed at Tennis* (267–80). Raynulph, moreover, is a medieval monk, and it would be entirely appropriate for him to *chant* his lines, here and elsewhere. The distribution of the dumb shows in *Hengist* does not articulate the play's five-act structure, as do the choruses in Shakespeare's *Henry V* and *Pericles*; in *Hengist*, that structure is already established by four intervals of entr'acte music. Each dumb show occurs, instead, in the middle of an act (1.2, 2.2, and 4.3). Moreover, although only three long stage directions are labelled dumb shows, several other directions call for music and action without speech:

> *Music. Enter certain monks...singing as at procession.* (1.1.28.1–3)
> *Alarums and Skirmish* (2.4.0.1)
> *Oboes. [Enter] the King and his train, met by Hengist and Hersus; they salute and exeunt, while the banquet is brought forth. Music plays. Enter Vortiger...* (4.2.0.1–5)

No music has been identified for any of these passages. But the last example is immediately preceded by Simon's lines 'And when that pie is new cut up by some rare cunning pieman, | They shall all lamentably sing, "Put up thy dagger, Simon"' (4.1.24–5). Modern scholars do

not note the fact, but the original audiences would have recognized the last five words as a parody of the words of a popular jig, 'Put up thy dagger, Jimmy,' for which an early tune by Giles Farnaby survives.[33] It certainly would have been ironically and comically appropriate if the instrumental music that plays during the preparation of the banquet—presumably by the commoners in Simon's train—were 'Put up thy dagger'. Indeed, the dramaturgy here resembles the use of 'Wigmore's Galliard' in *Your Five Gallants* (item 5), where the words that cue the stage direction for music are themselves the name of a well-known tune. But in *Hengist* the musical echo serves a more complex, structural function, linking the comic plebeian plot (which serves many of the functions of an antimasque) to the tragic royal plot (which contains all six of these episodes of mime accompanied by music).

Hengist dramatizes not the march but the dance of history. But none of these dumb shows or dance shows occurs in Act 5. The play does, however, end with carefully staged movements that uncannily echo the climactic sequence of many court masques: the initial spectacular appearance of a group of royal and aristocratic masquers above, followed by their gracious descent to the main stage. In the last scene, King Vortiger, Queen Roxana, and the King's favourite (Hersus) all appear 'above', on the battlements of a burning castle—and then in succession each 'falls' into the flames. Like the danced climax of the Jonsonian masque, this spectacularly choreographed ending creates collective 'wonder' (5.2.125), 'astonishment' (127) and 'joy' (208, 219, 221, 222) in the audience, offering the final prospect of 'a fair peaceful kingdom' (225). The final stage direction is for 'music' (Epilogue.10.1).

The long, complex concluding masque in *Women, Beware Women* is even more spectacular, even more carefully choreographed, and even more comprehensively destructive than the final scene of *Hengist*; recent critics have recognized that it represents 'a radical reinterpretation of the symbolic court ceremonies that Middleton relentlessly deconstructs' (Tricomi 127). But this final masque with its mythological and pastoral characters is preceded by another scene of dancing, also performed before the Duke and Duchess. 'By means of the discourses of dancing,' Skiles Howard notes, 3.2 'deconstructs inherited assumptions of all sorts about women, value, and dancing...As no subject-position in the play is untainted, neither are any discourses of dancing' (141). But Howard's critical analysis of dance discourse pays little attention to the actual dancing. Structurally, the earlier 3.2 should be the antemasque or antimasque to the masque presented in 5.1, and indeed the earlier scene contains no mythological figures; instead, it mixes dialogue with song, and includes dancing by the grotesque comic figure of the Ward, a stereotypical antimasquer. Moreover, 3.2 reproduces a structure common in folk dance and jigs,

[33] Baskervill 56 (not citing *Hengist*); Maitland and Squire, CXXVII. Baskervill cites a 1641 pamphlet in which this is one of two 'Scotch jigges', which 'The Fidler he flings out his heels and Dances and Sings'.

the dance-contest between rival suitors (Baskervill 247–88). Middleton had already staged an explicit dance-duel in *Old Law* (item 21); here, both the urbane gentleman Hippolito and the foolish Ward dance with Isabella, in succession. This recognizable jig convention would also have encouraged perception of 3.2 as an antimasque.

But Middleton complicates the expected binary structure. First, the final masque contains no social dancing; it never reaches the final phases of the entertainment, in which male masquers single out female members of the audience and lead them into the revels. By contrast, the 'antimasque' of 3.2 consists entirely of social dancing by guests at the ducal banquet: Hippolito—described as 'a fine-timbered reveler' (3.2.183)—leads out Isabella (a typical move), who changes partners in the second dance (another typical move). Thus, although the play preserves the grounded-clown-antimasque/flying-deities-masque binary, it reverses the normal sequence of dancing: it begins with revels, and ends with a systematically anti-social (indeed, sociopathic) main masque, a climax of discord rather than harmony. Secondly, 3.2 itself reverses the normal order of the masque: it begins with elegant courtly dancing, and is immediately followed by grotesque clown dancing. Thirdly, the Fool normally defeats the Gentleman in dancing-contest jigs, but here the Gentleman has beaten his rival before the dancing even begins; Hippolito is already Isabella's lover, though the Ward is her fiancé. The Ward's clowning probably endears him to at least a significant portion of the audience, which can also be expected to disapprove, morally, of the incestuous extramarital relationship between Isabella and Hippolito. Nevertheless, these allegiances must compete with our actual experience of the dancing.

> *Music. [Hippolito and Isabella] dance, making honours to the Duke and curtsey to themselves both before and after* (3.2.201.1–3)

The perfect symmetrical formality of the etiquette here points to what must be the most noticeable effect of the dance: Hippolito and Isabella dance beautifully together. They embody what Sir Thomas Elyot famously praised as the 'associating of man and woman in dancing, they both observing one number and time in their movings' (77). We know this, despite the absence of a choreography or report of their dance, because the surrounding dramatic script tells us a great deal about these two dancers. Both characters are young and beautiful; both are trained dancers who have been praised, before they begin, for their ability; their long friendship, followed by their more recent experience as lovers, makes them sensitive and responsive to each other's movements, united in what Ravelhofer describes as the 'muscular and acoustic bonding' of social dancing (64). They communicate silently and interactively through what the Renaissance dancing master Fabritio Caroso in 1600 called a 'pedalogue', or 'foot conversation' between a gentleman and lady (164). No one speaks during their dance; they have the undivided attention of the audience, on stage and off, and their performance is immediately followed by the Duke's praise. The aesthetic and emotional effect of this dance—the most perfect romantic couples dance in Middleton, or indeed anywhere in the drama of his time—is at least as powerful as the ironic discourse that surrounds it.

Ironic critical readings of this dance (and others) presuppose an audience's emotional distance from the dance. They ignore what the influential twentieth-century dancer and dance theorist John Martin called 'kinetic empathy' ('the inherent contagion of bodily movement which makes the onlooker feel sympathetically in his own musculature the exertions he sees in somebody else's musculature'). Martin also wrote of 'metakinesis' ('muscular and kinesthetic sympathy linking the dancer's intention to the viewer's perception of it') and 'motor responsiveness'. Roger Copeland called it 'kinetic responsiveness' ('the brand of empathy that most directly unites the dancer and his or her audience'); Adolphe Appia used the phrase 'rhythmic discipline' ('the experience of rhythm in the body by the audience as well as the performer').[34] This process of mimetic contagion is also obviously relevant to the history and sociology of 'dance frenzy' (the tarantella, St Vitus' dance, the Ghost Dance), and to Peggy Phelan's analysis of the relationship between dance and hysteria. Whatever we call it, anyone who regularly attends dance performances will recognize the phenomenon. Indeed, the same 'resonance effect' has been described by film theorists and musicologists.[35]

But this audience echo of the proprioception of the performer takes different historical and social forms, depending on the form of the performance itself. As dance anthropologist Cynthia Jean Cohen Bull argued, spectators are less likely to 'identify physically and kinaesthetically with the dancers' in proscenium arch theatres with very large auditoriums, but more likely to do so if spectators are 'in close proximity to the performance space,' able to 'hear the sound of the dancers' footsteps and breathing.' The effect will also be enhanced by 'the mutual experience of touch', and it will propagate more easily in cultures where dance is a regular part of everyday life. Although Bull did not relate these remarks to the ethnography of early modern London or the architecture of its playhouses, anyone familiar with those field conditions will immediately realize that the early modern theatres were perfect echo chambers for generating kinetic empathy, and that early modern spectators were perfect receptors and transmitters of metakinesis. The wooden platform stage, with an empty space beneath it, was effectively an enormous drum, which dancers could use as a percussion instrument, played with the feet. Moreover, unlike classical dance, the early modern commercial theatre

---

[34] For all these terms, and others, see Monthland, 553–6.
[35] For film, see Kracauer, 158 ('Movement is the alpha and omega of the medium...it seems to have a "resonance" effect, provoking in the spectator such kinesthetic responses as muscular reflexes, motor impulses and the like. Objective movement acts as a physiological stimulus...representations of movement do cause a stir in deep bodily layers'). For music, see Cone's notion of 'vicarious performance' (21).

did not attract passive, well-behaved, physically inhibited ('tight-assed') spectators: it was notorious for the kind of 'participating audience' that Robert Harrold wanted for modern dance, 'taking part in the dance event as a spectator by clapping, singing, shouting encouragement' (Monthland 555). These architectural and social condition help to explain why the jig was so prominent in the history of the early commercial theatre. Middleton himself provides evidence of the importance of kinetic empathy in what are probably his earliest memories of the theatre: in two of his early pamphlets he wrote of the 'lamentable action of one arm' in *Titus Andronicus* (*Father Hubburd's Tales* 936–7) and compared the 'stalking' of Tamburlaine to 'spindle-shank spiders' (*Black Book* 415–18). What stood out in his recollection of those two enormously popular, high-impact plays, first performed when he was between the ages of eight and fourteen, was not ideas, or even sound, but the movement of arms and legs.

These theatrical conditions also affect an audience's experience of the second dance in this scene from *Women, Beware Women*.

> Music. Ward and Isabella dance; he ridiculously imitates Hippolito (3.2.228.1–2)

The Duke and Bianca speak during this dance, and apparently interrupt it before its conclusion; it lacks both the intensity of focus and the formal symmetry of the first dance. Nevertheless, although the Ward as a *character* is clearly no match for Hippolito, the *actor* playing the Ward may be the company's best dancer: it takes extraordinary skill and precision to convincingly perform a specimen of bad dancing, in a way that signals to the audience that the ineptitude is the character's rather than the performer's. Indeed, that is why professional actor/dancers performed the antimasques at court. The Ward's ridiculous dance was almost certainly more athletic than Hippolito's. Like other aspects of such clown roles, it stands half-in and half-out of the fiction: the dance simultaneously displays the ineptitude of the Ward and the tour-de-force charisma of the actor.

Within this context, 'ridiculously imitates' has multiple meanings. First, it demonstrates the potential of what Ravelhofer calls 'dramatic characterization by movement: mimesis by kinesis' (64). This is how all dancing was taught: one dancer imitating the movements of another, more accomplished dancer. This reverses the dynamic of the court masque, because in this normal pedagogical situation the better dancer always dances first. In this sense, the imitation is ridiculous because the act of mimesis so obviously *fails*. It stages the failure of our impulse to kinetic empathy, an impulse that we as spectators share with the Ward. But in so far as the professional performer perfectly imitates the ridiculous dancing of an untaught amateur, the imitation will be ridiculous, will make the audience laugh, because it *succeeds* in its characterization of a fool like the Ward. Finally, the performer who 'ridiculously imitates' might mimic, or mis-mimic, Hippolito's dancing

so astutely that he makes the audience laugh at *Hippolito*, rather than—or in addition to—the Ward.

The Ward's dance must have been specific to *Women, Beware Women*; it could not have been imported from elsewhere, because its function and meaning entirely depend on imitation of Hippolito's dance. *Nice Valour* (1622) also requires a dance that must have been choreographed specifically for that play. But whereas the Ward's dance was probably created by the actor who played the character, and could easily have varied in each performance, the dance specific to *Valour* was apparently choreographed by Middleton (5.1.79.1–5.1.86):

> *Enter Lepet and Clown, and four other like fools, dancing, the Cupid leading, and bearing his Table, and holding it up to Lepet at every strain, and acting the postures*
> [*First strain*]
> LEPET Twinge all, now; twinge, I say.
> *Second strain*
> Souse upon souse.
> *Third strain*
> Douses single.
> *Fourth strain*
> Jostle sides.
> *Fifth strain*
> Knee belly.
> *Sixth strain*
> Kicksy buttock.
> *Seventh strain*
> Down derry.

This passage reminds us that choreographies are simply stage directions. This sequence of stage directions provides the most specific set of dance moves in any early modern English play, and it duplicates the form and some of the vocabulary of the surviving manuscript choreographies. It links specific moves to successive strains of music. 'Douses single' transfers to the douse one of the most common dance moves of the period, the 'single' (usually two steps forward or two steps back, closing the feet). 'Jostle sides' parodies the normal abbreviation 'sides' (indicating that dancers stand side by side). 'Twinge', indicating a sharp pain, often in the abdomen, might suggest a contorted doubling over, in place of the elegant bow normal at the beginning of dances. Knees were used when lifting a partner (Brissenden plate 6a)—though, of course, the joke here depends on the fact that a knee to the belly is not a normal dance move. Kicks are common enough in dances, but 'Kicksy buttock' seems to allude more specifically to *kicksey-winsey*, a word of uncertain meaning and etymology, variously spelled, that the *Oxford English Dictionary* records between 1599 and 1650, associated with galliards, Italian tricks, with something that 'starts up…and goes out again', or something 'here, and there, and here again, and all at once', or something 'overthrown'. Likewise, the phrase 'hey down' occurs in many traditional ballads, and may be related to a specific dance step; alternatively, 'down' is used in choreographies to indicate the opposite of 'up' (closer to the presence); here, 'down' may indicate that the dancers all fall to the floor.

That we cannot recover the exact moves indicated by these instructions is not surprising; the same can be said of most early choreographies. The exceptional feature of this dance is the mere fact of its textualization: the dancers respond to formulaic verbal commands ('Twinge all'), but they also mimic the steps/postures described in Lepet's 'table'. That table is a stage property, a material text that governs everyone's performance. Indeed, Lepet's table epitomizes what Susan Leigh Foster calls 'choreographies of gender': the instructions governing a dance resemble the set of social codes that individuals internalize and interpret in order to construct their own idiosyncratic performance of sexual identity. Specifically, Lepet choreographs masculinity as farcically heroic masochism. A body is male, as James Casey would say, only in so far as it offers itself up for destruction. Moreover, because Lepet is a courtier, whose dance has been specially commissioned, *Nice Valour* mimics, here, the rehearsals for court masques, with a dancing master training courtiers in an original, specially-choreographed series of predetermined moves. Within the fiction, these dancers are not actors, but courtiers; therefore, within the fiction Lepet's dance (near the end of the play) belongs to the masquers. But it clearly belongs to the *genre* of antimasque dances—just as the earlier dance, led by Cupid in 2.1, apparently belonged to the genre of main masques. Middleton again inverts, in a politically significant way, the normal sequence of the Jonsonian masque. But it also seems clear that the earlier dance was not particularly remarkable, formally or musically; it does not need to be, and indeed if it were too interesting it would disrupt the scene. Middleton saves the most dramatic and memorable masquing for the end.

Unfortunately, the music for Lepet's choreography either does not survive or has not been identified—though the music does survive for the extraordinarily popular song 'Hence, all you vain delights' (item 23). By contrast, for *Spanish Gypsy* (1623) we do possess what seems to be an original choreography combined with its original music (item 25). That does not mean that all the play's music was original; indeed, its first dance seems to be sung to an earlier tune by William Byrd (item 24). And others might have appropriated music and moves from Jonson's 1621 masque, *Gypsies Metamorphosed*. Only one piece of music from that masque has survived, and its tune does not fit any of the lyrics in *Gypsy*. However, it—or any of the other dance tunes used in the masque—could have been played to accompany the wordless dance(s) that the Gypsies dance at 3.2.218.1 and 3.2.232.1. Certainly, the middle of 3.2 creatively appropriates the main action of Jonson's masque, in which each Gypsy tells the fortune of one of the noble spectators in a variety of lyric metres. More generally, the play duplicates the structure of the court masque, with a series of exoticized Gypsy dances in Acts 3 and 4 followed, in the final moments of Act

5, by a heterosexual social dance that duplicates many of the features of the revels. But this structure does not simply mirror the masque in order to ape or appropriate élite culture. As Suzanne Gossett emphasizes in her critical introduction, the Gypsy performances mediate and enable the play's emotional trajectory from rape to rejoicing.

The Spanish Gypsy contains more songs and dances than any other play in the Middleton canon. By contrast, *A Game at Chess* is usually read as a political text, not a musical or dance drama. But our initial introduction to the chess game is a dance. 'Music' accompanies the mute, symmetrical entrance of both the White and Black Houses 'in order' (Induction.52.1–2); they do not speak or sing or do anything until 'as in a dance, they glide away' (76). Middleton's image of chess ballet was almost certainly inspired by the dancing chessmen of Rabelais or Colonna (Yachnin); it may have extended beyond the introductory dance to affect the movement of all the characters, which could have been systematically stylized. Certainly, this initial dumb show was followed, in early performances, by four entr'actes, which might also have featured dancing, and by another musical dumb show of symmetrically moving chess pieces (4.3). But Middleton reserved the play's most spectacular choreography for Act 5. The climax of the arrival of the White Knight and Duke in the Black House—mimicking the arrival of Prince Charles and Buckingham in Madrid, eighteen months before—is 'Music' played by invisible musicians (5.1.30.1), followed by the discovery of 'an altar...richly adorned, with tapers on it, and divers statues standing on each side' (33.1–2), followed by a song beginning with the word 'Wonder' (37). During the song, the 'tapers set themselves on fire' (42), then the 'brazen statues move' (44) and finally 'dance' (46.1). These spectacular effects clearly characterize the Catholicism of the Black House as idolatrous (Taylor 2001). But they also unmistakably recall two other court masques associated with a Stuart royal marriage. Francis Beaumont's *The Masque of the Inner Temple and Gray's Inn* (1613), which celebrated the wedding of Elizabeth Stuart to the Elector Palatine, included 'Jupiters *Altar gilt, with three great Tapers vpon golden Candlesticks* burning vpon it: and the foure *Statuaes*, two of gold, and two of siluer, as supporters' (my italics). A song promises us that the statues 'Shall daunce for ioy of these great Nuptialls,' and they do so:

These *Statuaes* were attired in cases of gold and siluer close to their bodie, faces, hands and feete, nothing seene but gold and siluer, as if they had been solid Images of mettall, Tresses of haire as they had been of mettall imbossed, girdles and small aprons of oaken leaues, as if they likewise had been carued or molded out of the mettall: at their comming the Musicke changed from Violins to Hoboyes, Cornets, &c. And the ayre of the Musicke was vtterly turned into a soft time, with drawing notes, excellently expressing their natures, and the Measure likewise was fitted vnto the same, and the *Statuaes* placed in such seuerall postures, sometimes all together in the Center of the daunce, and sometimes in the foure vtmost Angles, as was very gracefull besides the noueltie: and so concluded the first Anti-masque.

This dance was so effective that, after the masque had finished, King James asked for it to be danced again. The dance in *Game* cannot have been identical, because Middleton's statues are 'brazen' rather than gold or silver. But everything else could have been transferred from the masque. Indeed, the music (Sabol 402) might also have been used in *Game*. This recycling of material from the masque would not only have been characteristic of the King's Men's appropriation of music, spectacle, and dance from court entertainments. It would also, for anyone who recognized the allusion, have contrasted the proposed (brazen) marriage of Prince Charles to a Spanish Catholic with the earlier (gold and silver) marriage of Princess Elizabeth to a German Protestant. Indeed, this scene from *A Game at Chess* might have borrowed from two different masques which celebrated the 1613 wedding: *The Lords' Masque*, written by Thomas Campion and designed by Inigo Jones, also contains '*foure Noble women-statues of siluer*' who are 'transformed' into living women during a 'full song' written in the same tetrameters as Middleton's song.[36]

But the spectacular metamorphosis and dance in 5.1 were themselves trumped by the carefully choreographed ending of the play, in which the captured Black pieces are thrown into the bag. That is not a dance. But its formal symmetry mimics the beginning of the revels, as each White aristocrat selects a corresponding Black aristocrat and leads him or her across the stage: the White King the Black King, the White Queen the Black Queen, the White Knight the Black Knight, the White Duke the Black Duke (5.3.200–213). Though it lacks music, this ending duplicates the dance at the end of *Spanish Gypsy* (item 25), a 'longways' dance of four couples.

According to one contemporary witness, the White Knight 'kicked' the Black Knight into the bag (5.3.206.1). Kicks are, of course, potential dance steps, and Lepet's masochistic dance apparently involves being kicked: in another scene Lepet is 'beaten to a tune' (3.4.52), rhythmically pounded to the beat of the music. We normally do not equate dancing with fighting. But if we take an ethnographic approach to dance, if we conceptualize dance studies as performance studies, then we should immediately recognize the overlap between the two forms of early modern movement. The twentieth century defined fencing as a sport and dancing as an art, but 'dancesport' versions of ballroom dancing now aspire to the same Olympic status as fencing, ice-skating and gymnastics (Picart). We have already noted the easy slippage, in masques and Lord Mayor's shows, between dancers and fencers. In Middleton's London, Italians taught fencing as well as dancing. Hippolito, the 'fine-timbered reveler' who out-dances and cuckolds the amateur Ward in 3.2 of *Women, Beware Women*, is also the expert swordsman

who out-duels and murders the amateur Leantio in 4.2. The Nine Worthies of *Masque of Heroes* and *World Tossed at Tennis* are all soldiers; sword-dances and warlike dances are a regular part of the early modern repertoire, popular and courtly. Pre-modern wars were fought to instrumental accompaniment: in such a military regime, soldiers are 'musical', and 'strike . . . to a consort of drum, trumps, and fife' (*Quarrel* 1.1.97–9). Then as now, staged fights are as carefully choreographed as staged dances; indeed, sometimes more carefully choreographed, because unrehearsed swordplay can be more dangerous (Edelman). Moreover, the modern Anglo-American gendering of dance distorts our perception of its relationship to dueling. The stereotype of the 'effeminate' male dancer does not develop until decades after Middleton's death (Jordan). The precision and athleticism of dance aligns it, instead, with early modern martial arts. So does the fact that most dancing, from the morris to the Inns of Court, was all-male. All the dancers in Middleton's plays and masques were males. Whereas postmodern dance studies naturally emphasize the 'male gaze' focused upon the dancing female body, Middleton's spectators (male and female alike) were gazing at, and kinetically empathizing with, male bodies.

Schoenbaum argued that *The Revenger's Tragedy* is a dance of death. Certainly, the first scene, with a skull-wielding presenter and a dumb-show procession of courtiers, supports that reading. Certainly also, Middleton knew the medieval ballad of 'the shaking of the sheets'.[37] But the dance of death was a gender-neutral equal-opportunity dance 'for as many as may be'. Middleton transform the dance of death into something less traditional, less processional, more sudden, violent, elegant, and exclusively male.

> *The revengers dance; at the end, steal out their swords, and these four kill the four at the table in their chairs.*

Jacobean masquers, at the beginning of the revels, stepped out of the frame to select individuals from the audience, inviting them to join the dance. These revengers, likewise, step out of the frame, each choosing a single individual from the audience, and, in a single synchronized movement, each pushes a blade into the startled body of his chosen partner.

The dissolution of the distinction between dancing and fencing can still be seen in southern Italy, especially Puglia, in the traditional *danza scherma* (Monaco). This is an all-male version of a popular folk dance called the *pizzica*, in which a man dances around a woman, trying to seduce her without ever touching her; in the *danza scherma*, two men dance around each other, trying to kill

---

[36] Sabol identifies two pieces of music associated with the Lords' entrance dance (items 73, 191), which immediately follows the transformation of the statues; it is not clear from the text whether the statues/women join in this dance.

[37] In *The Meeting of Gallants at an Ordinary*, 'this youngster daunced the shaking of one sheete within a few daies after' (397) refers to the text of the traditional ballad 'The Dance of Death', which begins 'Can you dance the shaking of the sheets?' Schoenbaum was unaware of this Middleton parallel.

each other. It was originally a knife-dance. Antonio Gramsci acknowledged that, when the two men really hated each other—as Sicilians and Calabrians normally do—'even a practice session turns into something serious and cruel.' In the prison competition Gramsci witnessed, 'the weapons were simple ones: spoons rubbed against a wall in order to leave whitewash marks on clothing'. Unlike the *pizzica* (which has become a major tourist attraction), the *danza scherma* is not often publicly performed, or taught, and the only example I have seen was not advertised, and took place away from the main piazza. But the dance is, as Gramsci claimed, a 'grandiose, unforgettable scene for everyone, actors and spectators alike' (11 April 1927). I found it more intimate than any heterosexual dance I have ever watched, or performed. Though the men were not using knives, each watched and responded to the other as though his life depended on anticipating the next split-second move, flicker, feint, orbiting each other like binary stars with a shared centre of gravity, orbits sometimes circular, sometimes elliptical, closer, farther, the tension relaxing and tightening, the feet constantly moving as though of their own volition, neither man daring to monitor his own footwork because neither could afford to take his eyes off his partner/rival, and the witnesses (witnesses to a performance, which might one felt at any moment become a crime), the witnesses too could not afford to take their eyes off the dancers, aware as we were, aware as they were, that it could all be over in a heartbeat, the heartbeat that stopped a heart from beating, beating to the relentless rhythm of that tamburella, the round tamburella governing the round dance, the men beating the tamburella so violently, repetitively, remorselessly that it left blood on the stretched skin of the instrument. The dancer who won, who ended the dance by a lightning lunge through the other man's defences, the man who if they had been dancing with knives would have cut the other man's throat, never stopped smiling. I had never realized how aggressive, how unnerving, a smile could be. I now imagine Hippolito smiling, in just that way, as he dances with, and deftly skewers, Leantio.

In his adaptation of *Macbeth*, Middleton apparently added the stage direction that requires Macduff to duel and kill Macbeth on stage (5.10.34.2). He scripted the duel between Captain Ager and the Colonel in *Fair Quarrel* (3.1), and the final scene of *Hengist*, where Vortiger and Hersus rhythmically and repeatedly stab each other over the course of fifty lines of dialogue (5.2.86-136). None of these choreographed duets is set to music. But neither is the Old Knight's dance in *Wit at Several Weapons*; as he insists, 'I can dance without music' (5.2.147-8). Dance requires only a body or bodies in rhythmical motion. Academic representations of early modern theatre and culture tend to privilege stillness over motion, the fixed over the ephemeral, the stable text over the moving body (Skantze). The text, after all, is still with us; the moving body has moved on. But we must nevertheless remember, and attempt to describe, 'the phenomenological experience of movement in early modern theatre' (Smith 2004). After all, it was the moving body, not the dead text, which moved early modern spectators. Middleton wrote texts to move bodies.

Editorial Note on the Music

The following transcripts have been modified to the extent that standard modern notation is used: the C clef has been replaced by the G and F clefs, bar lines have been added or rearranged when necessary, and the original key signatures have been replaced by their modern 'equivalents' when the modal colour of a piece is not obscured by that treatment. The original notations of emended passages are given in the individual notes to the music. Editorial accidentals have been used sparingly. Accidentals obviously required by the context are silently added before the notes they affect. Superscript trills are all editorial. Ornaments have been included very rarely, chiefly because the use of appoggiaturas as well as trills was determined largely by the individual performer rather than the composer, as variants between early texts indicate. Fermatas occurring in the middle of an item are retained, but those placed routinely at the end of a piece have been omitted. No indications of tempo or dynamics have been supplied since the dramatic context for each song and the character of the music will be found to be the surest guides to interpretation. Lute tablatures have been transcribed for keyboard. The words that appear with stage songs are taken from the text of *The Collected Works*, unless otherwise noted; full collations of verbal variants are given in the Textual Notes to each passage, elsewhere in this *Companion*.

1. Sorrow, Sorrow, Stay

with the words ``down, down, down I fall''

John Dowland

Middleton text. Sung by Bellafront, the female protagonist and leading boy actor for the Prince's Men, in *The Patient Man and the Honest Whore* (1604), 6.32–3 (*Works*, p. 297).

    Musical copy-text. *The Second Book of Songs and Ayres of*

2, 4, and 5 with Tablature for the Lute and Orpharion, with the Violl da Gamba (1600; STC 7095), C1ᵛ–C2, No. 3, entitled 'Sorrow, sorrow, stay'. The present edition of this dramatic lament includes only the refrain as it appears in both the Canto and viol da gamba parts, the former with text underlay, omitting the first 34 measures. A modern edition of the complete text with specified accompaniment may be found in Fellowes (1922), vol. 5, Part I.

Its use in *The Patient Man and The Honest Whore* is limited to the Canto part, and only to its refrain, beginning in the latter part of the piece with the words 'down, down, down I fall'. We have printed the whole refrain here on the assumption that at least some members of the audience would be familiar with the larger musical and textual context of one of Dowland's most famous melancholy songs, which clearly establishes that Bellafront is contemplating damnation and repentance. See Jorgens, vol. 12, p. 500, for notes on mid-century arrangements of 'Sorrow, sorrow, stay' for solo voice and viols appearing in British Library Add. 17780, ff. 4^v–5^v and in Add. 37402, ff. 58^v–59; these attest to its continuing appeal in the ensuing decades. It may be of interest to note that Middleton mentions Dowland's *Lachrimae* in *No Wit/Help like a Woman's*, 1.229.

This song first appeared in a book that provoked a series of lawsuits (summarized by Dowling), which reveal a great deal about the routines of music printing and publishing in this period. Dowland had been appointed lutenist to Christian IV of Denmark in 1599, and his dedication was written from Elsinore and dated 1 June 1600. On July 15, the book was registered at Stationers' Hall under the name of the music printer Thomas East; by August 2, printing was finished and the books were ready for sale. In the two months between manuscript dedication and printed books, the manuscript had been transported from Denmark to London, and had then been the subject of a series of complicated transactions and transformations. Dowland's wife was paid for his manuscript, which passed from her to George Eastland (who was promised half of any money that the dedication might elicit). Eastland was a gentleman, not a publisher or printer, but he effectively acted the part of a publisher: he acquired and owned the manuscript, paid for the printing, announced on the title-page that copies were to be sold at his house, and supplied members of the Stationers' Company with copies they sold retail. Nevertheless, because he was not a Stationer, Eastland could not register his copyright in the book; East therefore had to act as his proxy. But East himself was acting as a proxy for the holders of the music patent, the composer Thomas Morley and the otherwise unknown Christopher Heybourn. Eastland contacted East, in the first place, because he 'had the name for the true imprintinge of musicke'. They initially drafted a written contract, but East changed his mind about the terms, and the final contract was an oral agreement.

The publisher Eastland paid £20 to Mrs. Dowland for the manuscript; £10 to the printer East, nine pounds and fifteen shillings to the holders of the patent, and two shillings to East's servants in the print shop. Eastland paid 7 pounds 6 shillings 6 pence for the paper, and

another shilling for waste paper. Finally, to East and his servants Eastland paid 2 shillings and sixpence for 'almost A whole weeke worke', according to East: 'for gatheringe collacōninge and mendinge foure falt*e* in the copie booke & not knowne of till the booke was fully finished for the mendinge of wch falt*e* this defendt' and his servant*e* did puse over foure Thowsand sheet*e* or thereaboute'.

East agreed to print a thousand copies of Dowland's book, and in addition one quire of paper to every heap of two reams used therein. The book was a folio and contained twelve and a half sheets; therefore twenty-five reams would be required to print a thousand copies, and from those extra reams could be printed an additional twenty-five copies. The extra copies were to be used 'for proofes & sutch Copie booke as were accustomably to be allowed to one Mr Morly and Mr Heyborne and sutch as did worke in printing of the same'. Unfortunately for Eastland, two of East's apprentices surreptitiously printed thirty-three extra copies, presumably because the success of Dowland's *First Booke* led them to expect a lot of demand for the sequel. Since they legitimately acquired three copies from East and Eastland (their part of the extra twenty-five, explicitly contracted), the two apprentices had thirty-six illicit copies, which they could and did sell for their own profit. Normally, the publisher would not have noticed these black market copies; after all, they represented less than four per cent of the copies he had for sale. But Eastland did not plan to sell any copies until Michaelmas Term: he wanted to distribute presentation copies to music patrons in advance of general publication, hoping to be rewarded for such 'gifts' with more than the retail price. The circulation of the illicit copies therefore spoiled his efforts to maximize his profit by controlling the timing of publication. Moreover, the illicit copies undercut his intended price.

East complained that, although the books cost Eastland only about twelve pence a piece, he 'doth sell the sayd booke for foure shilling*e* six pence a peece in quires, the booke contayninge but twelue sheet*e* and a halfe, to the Companie of Statōners, Albeit other musicke of as great skill or knowledge is sould for two pence the sheete or vnder'. East was not complaining about the retail price, but about the wholesale price at which Eastland sold copies to stationers; those retailers would normally expect to increase the retail price by one-third of the wholesale price, making their own profit from that difference.

The book sold at that price contained only twenty-two short songs. The two folio pages dedicated to 'Sorrow, sorrow, stay' included only sixty words of verse. That is part of the reason music publishers were working for a very specialized market. Like Dowland's *First Booke*, the second was printed in tablature, with different parts facing in different directions on any given opening: the format was designed for performers. For that reason, 'one cannot say that there was a *reading* public for musical printing, but only a *using* public' (Boorman, 227).

2. O brave Arthur of Bradley!

Traditional

O, brave Arthur of Brad·ley, then_____ shall he!

O, brave Arthur of Brad·ley, then_____ shall he!   O, brave Arthur of Brad·ley, then_____ shall he!

Middleton text. *Patient Man and Honest Whore*, 15.448 (*Works*, p. 326). Bellafront, who is pretending to be mad, says 'O, brave Arthur of Bradley then, shall he!' Her first five words are a quotation from the refrain of a ballad, which is repeated several times at the end of each of its eleven stanzas. Though the ballad dates from the sixteenth century, its words were first printed in *Sportive Wit: The Muses Merriment* (1656; Wing P2113), pp. 81–7, and *An Antidote against Melancholy* (1661; Wing D66A), pp. 16–19. The ballad is all about Arthur's wedding, so it is clearly relevant to the context. Singing scraps of old songs is a standard way of indicating madness (most famously exemplified by Ophelia).

Musical copy-text. Chappell points out (2:539–40) that the ballad seems to have been sung to the traditional tune of 'Roger de Coverley', which has been used for many different sets of lyrics. The earliest extant notation for the 'Roger de Coverley' tune was included as one of the additional items (p. 167) in the ninth edition of John Playford's *The Dancing Master* (1695; Wing P2499), printed in oblong duodecimo format. Barlow provides a critically edited modern transcription (item 341, p. 82); the ballad-tune websites of Foxley and Robinson also provide modern versions.

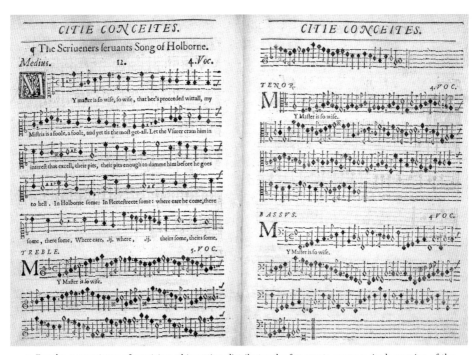

3. For the convenience of musicians this setting distributes the four parts across a single opening of the book. (Compare *Triumphs of Truth*.) The rectangular notes and the absence of bar lines are typical.

3. My master is so wise

Thomas Ravenscroft

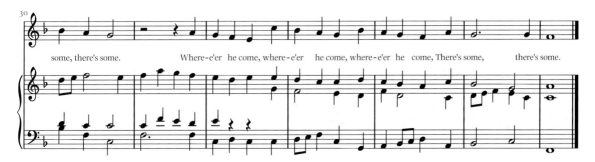

some, there's some.   Where-e'er he come, where-e'er   he come, where-e'er he come, There's some,   there's some.

Middleton text. Sung by Audrey, a younger boy performing for the Children of Paul's, in *A Trick to Catch the Old One* (1605), 4.5.1–4 (*Works*, p. 406).

Musical copy-text. Thomas Ravenscroft's *Melismata Musicall phansies. Fitting the court, citie, and countrey humours. To 3, 4, and 5. voices*, printed by William Stansby for Thomas Adams (1611; STC 20758), item '12.', sig. C3ᵛ–D1, entitled 'The Scriueners seruants Song of Holborne'. (See Illus. 3.) In this title the word 'seruants' is ambiguous, and could be modernized as a singular possessive (servant's) or a plural possessive (servants'). The title of Ravenscroft's book insists on multiple voices, and the music to this song specifies '4.Voc.', identified as Medius, Treble, Tenor, and Bassus. In Middleton's play it is sung by one character, and it is here transcribed as a solo setting to be accompanied by an instrumental consort presumably of viols, for treble, medius, tenor and bassus, the vocal part doubling the instrumental medius part. It is unlikely that the song was sung by four voices in 4.5 of *Trick*, but a four-voice version might have been performed during one of the entr'actes, or Ravenscroft might simply

have treated the instrumental material as vocal in order to accommodate the song to the others in *Melismata*.

Original readings. The setting includes two lines of the lyric which do not appear in the quarto of *A Trick to Catch the Old One*, licensed for printing in 1607 and published in 1608. That quarto was apparently set from an authorial manuscript, not fully prepared for performance or publication. (See the Textual Introduction in this volume, p. 562.) Middleton, or Middleton and Ravenscroft together, might have expanded the song, in the course of rehearsing and preparing the play for performance.

Ravenscroft was a composer as well as an active musician performing in several plays of the Children of Paul's in the early years of the seventeenth century. In his dedicatory epistles he often signs himself T. R. B. M., proud of his bachelor of music degree. A full transcript of this setting appears in Sabol (1959), 3–9, and its opening measures also in Austern (1992), 253. Several items sung in choirboy plays appear not only in *Melismata*, but also in *A Brief Discourse* (1614). His earlier collections—*Pammelia* (1609) and *Deuteromelia* (1609)—consist largely of rounds, catches, and three-men's songs of the day.

4. The Slip

Choreography from Playford.

Longways for as many as will

| Woman | Woman | Woman | Woman |
| Man | Man | Man | Man |

A. Honour to the presence all. A strain played once. Honour to your own. A strain played twice.

B. The two first men take hands, and the two first women take hands, and fall back from each other, men and women open, close again and changes places each with his own. A strain played once. Fall back again, open, close, and change places as before. A strain played twice.

A. First man lead his woman down half way and honour to her. A strain played once. Lead her to the bottom, and honour to her. A strain played twice.

B. Then take hands with the last man, his woman taking hands with the last woman, fall back from each other, open, close, and changes places as before, the four uppermost doing the like at the same time. A strain played once. That again as at first. The strain played twice.

A. The second man lead down his woman as before. A strain played twice.

B. This as before, the rest following in order.

Middleton text. *A Mad World, My Masters* (1605), 5.2.316.1 (*Works*, p. 450). The first edition (1608) does not indicate a final exeunt; the second edition (1640) advertises that the play 'hath been often acted' at the Salisbury Court theatre, and adds a stage direction after the final line, 'The end of the fifth and last Act: marching over the Stage hand in hand'. Both Whitlocke and Kiek identify this final march/dance as 'The Slip'. The title phrase appears seven times in the last scene of Middleton's play; elsewhere in the period it never appears more than twice in any scene, play, or masque, and never elsewhere as a title. The first production would normally have concluded with a dance, and this might have been it: see item 3 for another example of original musical material not present in Middleton's manuscript of a play for Paul's Boys. Alternatively, this particular dance might have been added in Caroline revivals. (Compare item 11.) In either case, 'The Slip' transforms the conventional final jig/dance into something relevant to the fiction. (Compare item 25.)

Musical copy-text. John Playford's *The English Dancing Master* (1651), item 104 (sig. O4ᵛ). The second edition (1652) altered the music, principally by transposing it down a tone from D major to C major. This score was then retained in all subsequent editions. Barlow gives a modernized critical edition of both scores (item 93, p. 35). For a more detailed discussion of Playford, see item 25 below.

Choreography. 'This dance, with its ceremonial tune,' Dean-Smith observes, 'is not so much a "dance" in the social sense as a formal departure...No man dances with a woman other than his own—and as in each repetition the diminished company "honours the Presence", the last couple in the set withdraws from the scene' (88). This is the last dance in Playford's book, and is, as she says, 'a proper conclusion'—but it would also for that reason make a proper conclusion to Middleton's play. Playford imposes heterosexual pairings on all his choreographies, reflecting the norms of mid-century social dancing; but in theatrical dances men often formed couples, so Playford's 'as many as will' could include the entire on-stage cast.

5. Wigmore's Galliard

Traditional

Middleton text. *Your Five Gallants* (1607), from the last speech of Interim 1 to the opening stage direction of Interim 2 (*Works*, p. 615):

> This will make my maister leape out of the bed for ioy, and dance Wigmors galliard in his shirt about the chamber?

> *The Musicke plaies on a while, then enter; Taylbie his man after trussing him.*

For the interpretation of these two short scenes as interim scenes, see Jowett (1999) and the Textual Introduction to *Gallants* in this *Companion* (p. 575). The instrumental music demanded by the stage direction was not played by any character on stage, but by the Blackfriars consort in the music room. The direction does not specify which music plays on, but the preceding speech certainly seems to cue that particular tune. Chappell noted (1:72) that it was common enough to sing old songs, or to play old tunes, at the beginning or end of an Act: in *Summer's Last Will and Testament* (written for indoor 'private' performance at the Archbishop of Canterbury's residence in Croydon, 1592), the Prologue directs the actors to begin the play with 'an old song first', and Barry's *Ram Alley* (1611; STC 1502a), acted by the Children of the Kings' Revels perhaps as early as 1607, ends with 'Strike vp Musick, lets haue an old song' (sig. I4). Chappell also cites Peele's *Ar*a*ygnement of Paris* (1584), where Venus *'singeth an old songe called the woing of Colman'* (3.5), and Marston's *Antonio and Mellida* (1600), where Feliche sings the old ballad, *'And was not good king Solomon'* near end of act 3; but neither of these examples occur exactly at the end of an act, or a marked interval. The more significant point is that all plays of the period made use of what they called 'old songs' or 'old ballads' (phrases that occur at least twenty-one times in plays written between 1580 and 1642). Austern identified more than twenty ballad lyrics with extant broadside tunes in the extant repertoire of the early seventeenth-century children's companies (1992, 231). The anthologies published by Ravenscroft (item 3) also suggest that the children mixed folk and ballad tunes with new compositions (212–19).

Musical copy-text. Trinity College Dublin MS 408/2, p. 112. (See Illus. 4.) The music dates from before 1584, when a 'joyful' broadside ballad called for its tune (STC

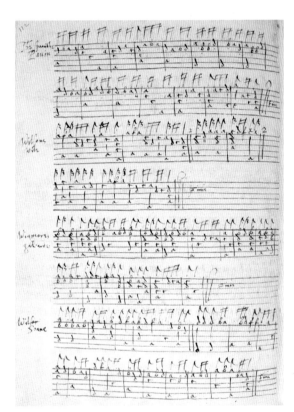

4. Wigmore's Galliard (the third item on this manuscript page) is notated in the style of lute tablature most commonly used in England after 1500. There is a six line 'staff' which represents the six courses of the lute, with the top line corresponding to the highest pitched course on the instrument. The frets of the lute are not numbered, but rather lettered, using a specially designed alphabet which helps the player differentiate between similarly shaped letters. The rhythm of the piece is notated above the 'staff' to which it refers.

12798). This portion of the manuscript, in upright folio format, includes music paper apparently printed by Thomas East (Fenlon and Milsom, 155). Craig-McFeely (408) dates the manuscript *c*.1605, but notes that most of the pieces it contains are at least a decade earlier than that; she classifies it as a pedagogical manuscript. Ward (1967, 85) identified several other early transcriptions: the 'Dallis' lute book, an oblong quarto pedagogical manuscript, compiled by a Cambridge pupil of Thomas Dallis (c.1583–5), Trinity College Dublin MS 410/1 (formerly 'D.3.30'), p. 20 ('Wigorns gayliarde'), p. 36 ('a gailliard'), p. 47 (first strain only, titled 'Le Bride Ale'), and Cambridge University Library MS Dd.v.20 (one of a set of part-books copied by Matthew Holmes), fol. 6 ('Wigmoors Galliarde', a bass viol part). In her discussion of Dallis, Craig-McFeely distinguishes the first example from the latter two, which she instead links to the 'Marsh' lute book in the Dublin Library of Archbishop Narcissus Marsh, Ms Z3.2.13 (c.1595), pp. 420–22. For a facsimile of Marsh see Spencer 1981. Simpson (521), Livingston (210), and various ballad websites reproduce only a portion of the melody from 408/2.

6. Weep eyes, break heart

Michael Cavendish

Weep, eyes, weep, eyes, Break heart, break, break, break heart, My love and I must part, and I must part. Cru-el fates true love do soon-est sever, O, I shall see thee nev-er, nev-er, never, O, hap-py is the maid whose life takes end Ere it knows par-ents' frown or loss of friend.

Middleton text. Moll—played by a boy actor with Lady Elizabeth's Men in 1613—'sings herself to death' with this song in *A Chaste Maid in Cheapside*, 5.2.38–45 (*Works*, p. 952).

Musical copy-text. Michael Cavendish's *14.Ayres in tabletorie to the lute expressed with two voyces and the base*

145

violl or the voice & lute only. 6.more to 4.voyces and in tabletorie. And 8.madrigalles to 5.voices (1598, STC 4878), printed by Peter Short. Cavendish—whose original was transcribed by Fellowes—includes two versions of the song 'Fair are those eyes whose shine must give me life', whose closing burden is 'Weep eyes, weep eyes, break heart, break, break, break heart, and end this restless pain, this restless pain'. The settings are:

> Item x: Cantus with lute tablature and Bassus for bass viol or voice.
> Item xvi: Cantus with lute tablature and with Altus, Tenor, and Bassus parts.

Middleton, presumably attracted by this verbal outburst, retains only this segment of Cavendish's lyric text, supplanting the rest with his own words, which form an alternative to the end of the burden and the opening section of Cavendish's setting. The editorial *Dal Segno* allows for the repeat of the refrain that is stipulated in the text of the play. Cutts (1969) was the first scholar to provide a transcript containing Middleton's version of the lyric text. Middleton's impressive realignment of various segments of Cavendish's music text to suit the lyric that he has composed is ingenious, revealing him to be a subtle adapter and rearranger of a music text to suit his lyric creation.

5. Okes printed fifteen mayoral pageants, but the only other festival book he printed with music was John Squire's *Triumphs of Peace*, for the Haberdashers (1620), where a song is embedded in the middle of the pageant (B1ᵛ–B2). He is not known to have printed any music books. The words of the song appear to be set in the same roman text font as the rest of the book, though with such a small sample of types it's impossible to be certain. 'The eleven staves and their notes could have been set in another shop, tied around, and carried to Okes's shop; then Okes would simply have set the text lines, done the appropriate vertical spacing, and printed the music' (Weiss, private communication).

7. Mother of many honourable sons

Mo - ther of man-y honour-a-ble sons,— Think not thy glass too slow - ly runs, That in Time's hand is set, be - cause

What greater comfort to a mother's heart,— Than to be-hold her son's de-sert, Go hand in hand with love, re - spect,

—Thy worthy son ap - pears not yet. La-dy, be pleas'd the hour grows on; Thy joys will be com-plete anon. Thou shalt be -

—And honour (bless-ings from a-bove). It is of power all griefs to kill, and with a flood of joy to fill. Thy a - ged

hold The man en - roll'd In hon - our's book whom vir - tue rais - es, Love cir - cl'd

eyes, To see him rise With glo - ry deck'd, where ex - pec - ta - tion, Grace, truth, and

round, His tri - umphs crown'd, With all good wish - es, prayers___ and prais - es.

fame, Met in his name, At-tends his Hon - our's con - fir - ma - tion.

Middleton text. Sung by an unidentified 'sweet voice' at Sop Lane End in *Triumphs of Truth* (1613), 90–113 (*Works*, p. 969). The Grocers paid six shillings eight pence for 'the boy who sang in the ship' (Robertson and Gordon 86), part of the water show not described in Middleton's text; a separate payment is recorded for 'the singing boye and alsoe to mr Godfrey whoe did sing at sop lane end' (88).

Musical copy-text. *Triumphs of Truth*, a quarto printed by Nicholas Okes for the Company of Grocers (1613; STC 17904), sig. D3v–D4. This is the first pageant ever printed with a score (see Illus. 5).

The 'musicians' who 'sit playing' for this song were presumably the City Waits, to whom the Grocers paid two pounds, ten shillings (Robertson and Gordon, 86); one of them may also have composed the tune and supplied Middleton or Okes with its score. The City Waits were routinely paid similar sums, whenever detailed accounts for the Jacobean pageants survive. Other musical expenses for the pageant include twenty-five pounds for trumpeters, and more than sixteen pounds for drummers, fifes, ensigns, and flourishers; non-verbal parade music was clearly much more extensive than the song.

It is very likely that its cantus was intended as a solo song, the bassus serving as an unfigured basso continuo upon which various kinds of instrumental accompaniments could be devised.

8. Loath to depart

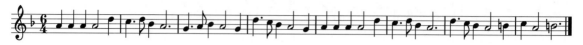

Middleton text. The Clown Pompey Doodle, probably played by William Rowley, in *Wit at Several Weapons* 2.2.248.1 (*Works*, p. 997), exits humming 'Loath to depart'.

Musical copy-text. The ballad existed by 1571; beyond the phrase 'loath to depart', none of its original words have survived, but Middleton and Rowley assume that the tune itself would be so familiar to audiences that they would recognize its title (and the relevance of that title) simply from hearing the tune hummed. John Dowland's setting for lute survives in five manuscripts: Cambridge University MS Dd.ii.11 (professional book in large upright folio, transcribed by Matthew Holmes *c.*1585-95), fol. 9; Dd.ix.33 (professional book in upright folio, transcribed by Matthew Holmes *c.*1600-1605), fol. 68ᵛ-69ᵛ; Glasgow University Library, MS Euing 25 (a personal anthology in oblong folio format, *c.*1610), fol. 28 and fol. 31; British Library Egerton 2046 (Jane Pickeringe's pedagogical lute book in upright folio format, signed 1616, bound in the reign of James I), fol. 33; and Royal Academy of Music MS603 (Margaret Board's pedagogical lute book in upright folio format, more recently in the collection of Robert Spencer), fol. 7ᵛ (*c.*1620-25). Craig-McFeely gives detailed descriptions of all five manuscripts. For facsimiles of Board (which contains some manuscript alterations by Dowland, presumably Margaret's teacher) and Pickeringe, see Spencer (1976, 1985). Giles Farnaby's keyboard variations are contained in the Fitzwilliam Virginal Book (Cambridge Fitzwilliam Museum, MS 168); for modern transcriptions see Maitland and Squire, 2:317-19 and Marlow, item 41. Thomas Ravenscroft's *Deuteromelia*, printed by Thomas Snodham (1609; STC 20757), contains a round or catch for four voices (item 28, sig. F2), incorporating the words 'loath to depart'. Duffin (256) gives a modern transcription of Ravenscroft's tune, apparently because Ravenscroft provides words. However, Ravenscroft's version can hardly be the original: 'sing loath to depart... sing once again' presumes that 'loath to depart' already exists and is familiar.

Since humming provides limited opportunities for harmony (which in any case is not characteristic of sixteenth-century ballad tunes), we have, like Simpson (B288), transcribed only the melody, based on the earliest Dowland source, Dd.ii.11.

9. Cupid is Venus' only joy

Cantus and Bassus with Lute Tablature Transcribed for Keyboard

[1] Cu - pid is Ven - us' on - ly joy,___ But he is a wanton boy, A ver-y, ver - y wan-ton boy. He

[2] Why should not Ven - us chide her son,___ For the tricks that he hath done, The wanton tricks that he hath done? He

shoots at la - dies' na - ked breasts. He is the cause of most men's crests, I mean up - on the___ fore-head, In -

shoots his fier - y darts so thick They wound poor la - dies to the quick, Ay me, with cru - el___ wounding, His

vis - i-ble, but hor-id. 'Twas he first thought up - on the way To keep a la - dy's lips___ in play.

darts are so con - founding That life and strength would soon de - cay. But that it keeps their lips___ in play.

Middleton texts. Probably originally written for *Masque of Cupids* (January 1614), First Song (*Works*, p. 1033), then sung by the male actor Dondolo in *More Dissemblers Besides Women* (1614?), 1.4.89-99 (*Works*, p. 1045), then substituted for the original Welsh song and performed by a boy actor playing the Welsh Gentlewoman in a revival of *A Chaste Maid in Cheapside* (originally 1613, date and venue of revival unknown), 4.1.167-93 (*Works*, p. 943). For this history of the song see Jowett 1994.

Musical copy-text. (A) New York Public Library, MS Drexel 4175, no. xxiv, contains an anonymous vocal setting, the cantus with verse 1 appearing in underlay with verse 2 placed in stanzaic form beneath the cantus, together with an unfigured basso continuo. This version is transcribed in the present edition, and to it is added a transcript of the lute tablature described below.

Cognate versions. (B) New York Public Library, MS Drexel 4175, no. lvi, contains an anonymous cantus with lute tablature. The hand of both cantus and underlay of this version differs from the hand of the preceding version, and a marginal note at its close directs one to 'See no. 24.' An identical and also anonymous version of the cantus, it appears with an unfigured basso continuo, and here verse 1 only is presented in the underlay.

(C) British Library Add. MS 29481, f. 6ᵛ, anonymous: cantus only with underlay of verse 1, and with verse 2 placed beneath in stanzaic form. There are no substantive verbal variants in the lyric text.

Original readings. In m. 15 of the cantus of (A) and (C) the first two quavers read E and C; in (B) they are E and D. In m. 22, in each of the three versions of the cantus the placement of the underlay shows clearly that the word 'lips' is to be sung to three successive quavers and 'in' to only one.

A repeat sign appearing only in (B) for the final couplet of verse 1 at beat 3 of m. 16 provides an ad hoc solution for setting the additional couplet of that verse appearing in the lyric text of *More Dissemblers Besides Women* to virtually the same music as that provided for the final couplet.

Beal in MiT 9-11 lists (A), (B), and (C) as manuscript settings of the mid-seventeenth century, and provides notes on the owners of the manuscripts. He suggests the composer Adrian Batten as one possible owner of (B). Batten is not known to have composed any secular music, and was living in Winchester when *Masque of Cupids* was performed, but he supplemented his church income with work as a music copyist, so he was probably not the setting's composer but might have been its copyist. Jorgens provides photofacsimiles of these three settings in vol. 11 for (A) and (B) and vol. 1 for (C). Cutts (1971) presents diplomatic transcripts of (A) and (B), pp. 46-48. In his transcripts in the vocal part of both (A) and (B) in m. 6, the insertion of a natural before the second quaver on the second syllable of 'very' is editorial and not so noted in his annotations.

10. In a maiden time professed

John Wilson

In a maid-en time pro-fessed / Then we say that life is best. / Tast-ing once the mar-riage life
Cu-pid is an i-dle toy; / Nev-er was there such a boy. / If there are let an-y show
Whilst the world con-tin-ued good / Peo-ple loved for flesh and blood. / Men a-bout them bore the dart

Then we on-ly praise the wife. / There's but one state more to try / Which makes wom-en laugh or
Or his quiv-er or his bow, / Or a wound by him they got, / Or a bro-ken ar-row
That would catch a wom-an's heart. / Wom-en like-wise great and small / With a pret-ty thing they

cry. Widow, wid-ow, of these three / The mid-dle's best, and that give me.
shot. Mon ey, mon-ey, makes us bow. / There is no o- ther Cu-pid now.
call Cun ny, cun-ny, won the men, / And this was all the Cu-pid then.

Middleton text. The second and third stanzas were probably originally written for *Masque of Cupids* (January 1614), Second Song (*Works*, p. 1033); the first stanza is sung, to the same music, by Isabella, a boy actor performing with the King's Men, in *The Witch* (1616), 2.1.131–8 (*Works*, p. 1141). For the song's history see Jowett 1994.

Musical copy-text. (A) Bodleian MS mus. b. 1., f. 21, contains a three-strophe setting for cantus and bassus attributed to John Wilson. Verse 1 only in underlay; verses 2 and 3 in stanzaic form beneath the setting. This item appears in Wilson's autograph (?) song-book, *c.*1656. Facsimile in Jorgens, vol. 7.

Cognate versions. (B) New York Public Library, MS Drexel 4257 (composer John Gamble's manuscript songbook of the mid-seventeenth century), No. 32, is a three--strophe anonymous setting for cantus and bassus. Verse 1 only in underlay; verses 2 and 3 in stanzaic form beneath the setting. Facsimile in Jorgens, vol. 10. This cognate provides the following alternate readings in the underlay to those in the copy text (A) cited above:

1. a maidentime possessed
6. which makes women laugh or cry
13. Or a wound by him begot.,
20. That will win a woman's heart.
24. He was the only Cupid then.

(In the text reproduced in this edition of the setting, the 'women' of l. 6 replaces the copy text's 'woman'.)

See Beal, MiT 29–31; Jorgens, vol. 12, p. 447, and Cutts, No. 5 on p. 7. Spink includes an edition of this item on p. 45, and on pp. 189–90 he briefly characterizes the two manuscripts as noted above.

The lyrics admirably display Middleton's resourceful use of homonyms to achieve unexpected and subtle ambiguities.

11. I keep my horse, I keep my whore

William Lawes

Middleton text. Sung by Latrocinio, an adult male actor in the King's Men, in *The Widow* (1615?), 3.1.22–37 (*Works*, p. 1098). I have preserved the wording of the music manuscript (which differs in a few respects from the text printed in *Collected Works*), because it may represent the text sung in the revival. For variants in all extant texts see Textual Notes.

Musical copy-text. British Library Add. MS 29396, ff. 77[v]–78 for cantus and unfigured basso continuo, where it is attributed to William Lawes. Spink (1971, 190) describes the manuscript as containing songs in the hand of Edward Lowe, *c*.1661–1680. This score must have been written for a revival, because Lawes is not known to have

written theatre music before 1634; the song's appearance in Bodleian Ashmolean MS 38, p. 127, and its attribution there to the play, suggests that it had been revived between 1636 and 1638 (Wood, 16). According to Chan (1979), Add. 29396 is strongly linked to theatrical drolls performed during the Civil Wars and Restoration, which suggests that this song and its scene formed part of such a playlet.

Cognate versions. See Beal, MiT 24–7, for other verse copies; Jorgens, vol. 5, for photofacsimile of the Add. 29396 setting, and vol. 12, p. 435, for notes; Day and Murrie, no. 1536, for its appearance in printed song-books from 1686 (which attribute it to Shakespeare's *1 Henry IV*); and Cutts (1971), p. 57, for a diplomatic transcript.

12a. Come Away, Hecate, Come Away

Setting 1

Robert Johnson (?)

Middleton text. Sung by Hecate, Cat, and witch voices, originally in *The Witch*, performed by the King's Men (1616), 3.3.39–72 (*Works*, p. 1152), then in Middleton's adaptation of *Macbeth*, performed by the King's Men at the Blackfriars (1616), 3.5.34–73 (*Works*, p. 1185). The position of the other voices is ambiguous; therefore in *The Collected Works*, they are editorially imagined offstage or above in *Witch* and onstage in *Macbeth*. Here, in addition to Hecate and the Cat we identify the other party to the song simply as 'Voice', not specifying the number of voices singing, whether they are visible to the audience, or whether they are above. The division of voices is not indicated in the extant music texts. For a detailed discussion of verbal variants in all early texts see this volume, pp. 695, 1002.

Musical copy-text. New York Public Library, MS Drexel 4175, No. liiii, fol. 11; Beal describes this manuscript as once owned by a certain Anne Twice, c.1620, and Spink (1971, p. 190) notes that it contains songs, some with lute accompaniment, possibly before 1620. Because of the Shakespeare connection, the music for this Middleton song has been widely discussed and reproduced: see Long 193–5, Jorgens XI, Brooke 225–33, and Gooch 2:705–83. Austern (1990) situates it within a larger convention of male magicians and female witches as 'impresarios of music and spectacle'; Seligmann (1997) and Henze analyse, from a feminist and musicological perspective, how the triumphant, celebratory, hymn-like music contributes to the characterization of Middleton's witches. No seventeenth-century source attributes the music to Johnson, but Spink (1961) regards the editorial attribution as 'fairly certain' (74), and Henze points out that 'the final portion of the song, representing bells, is highly similar to the final ringing section of Johnson's "Full Fathom Five"' (86). Song type: Dialogue with basso continuo.

Original music readings in fol. 11:

Cantus: m. 27: the natural on B on word 'of' is omitted

Cantus, m. 27: the first minim is a D

6. Unlike the mass-produced anonymity of printed texts, this manuscript represents the personal taste of an individual (Anne Twice), who presumably wrote it with her own hand and also on occasion performed it. The multiple voices of the dramatic score are here transcribed for a single voice, singing to itself (or its selves). It is hard to resist the assumption that the female owner/creator/user of this manuscript identified in some way with the song's 'I' and its triumphant evocation of female power, pleasure, and flight.

12b. Come Away, Hecate, Come Away

Setting 2

Robert Johnson (?)

Lyrics under the music:

Malkin, my sweet spirit, and I O,—what a dain-ty pleasure's this,— To ride in the air when the moon shines fair, And feast and sing and

toy and kiss.— O - ver woods, high rocks, and mountains, O - ver seas and mis - ty fountains, O - ver steeples, towers, and turrets,

[Voice]

We fly by night 'mongst troops of spirits. No ring of bells to our ears sounds, No noise of wolves or

yelps of hounds, No nor the noise of_____ wa - ter's breach, Nor can-nons' throat our height can reach.

Middleton text. See 12a.

Musical copy-text. Cambridge, Fitzwilliam Museum, Mus. 52.D.25, f. 107ᵛ–8. Anonymous dialogue song with basso continuo. Beal describes this manuscript as one owned (in 1659) and partly compiled by John Gamble, c.1630s–50s. The assignment of voice parts is editorial.

Original music readings in ff. 107ᵛ–8:

Cantus, m. 16: last note is an F (a quaver)
Cantus, m. 35: note for '-light' is a crotchet, followed by a crotchet rest.

Bassus, m. 53: last note in the measure is B, a minim
Bassus, m. 7: a flat is omitted before the first note, an E which is a breve

The musical differences in the two versions are very slight. The variants occur principally in the rests separating the change of singers in this dialogue, and they are not haphazard. The cognate strikes one as an edited version arranged by a prompter, if not by singers themselves, to ensure precise entries, and on occasion rests between sections to permit stage movement of vocalists.

13. The First Witches' Dance

Robert Johnson (?)

Middleton Texts. This or the following item was probably danced in *The Witch*, performed by the King's Men at the Blackfriars (1616), 5.2.88.1 (*Works*, p. 1162); then probably incorporated in Middleton's adaptation of *Macbeth*, performed by the King's Men at the Blackfriars (1616). It could be used at 1.3.30 or 4.1.44–60 or 4.1.150.1–2 (*Works*, pp. 1172, 1188, 1189).

Musical copy-text. Robert Dowland, *Varietie of Lute-lessons...Selected out of the best approued Authors, as well beyond the Seas as of our owne Country* (1610; STC 7100), P2ᵛ, the first of several harmonized versions entitled 'The Witches daunce in the Queenes Maske'. This is a setting for solo lute, here transcribed for keyboard. The elegant folio was printed by Thomas Snodham, who had inherited the business (and the musical type-fonts) of Thomas East. (See item 1.) Cutts (1954, 1956) supports the traditional attribution of this music to Robert Johnson, but acknowledges that it is curiously lacking in unusual rhythmic movement.

Cognate versions. British Library Add. 10444, treble, f. 21, 'The first witches dance', bassus, f. 74ᵛ, 'The first of the witches dance'; British Library Add. 17786–91, item 5 'The wyche': consort in five parts for superius, medius, contratenor, tenor, and bassus; British Library Add. 38539, f. 4, 'the wiches Daunce', for lute; Trinity College, Dub. D.1.21, p. 65, for lute. Wilhelm Brade, *Newe Ausserlesene liebliche Branden*, item 49, 'Der Hexen Tantz', consort in five parts. *Board Lute Book*, f. 26. 'The witches Daunce', for lute. Of these, the Add. 10444 and the Add. 17786–91 versions are transcribed in Sabol (1982), items 76 and 247, as well as in Cutts (1971), pp. 14–16, Notes, pp. 125–26. Both the First and Second Witches' Dances appear in Add. 10444 as two of 138 Jacobean masque dances for treble and bassus alone, gathered together (presumably in the 1620s) by Sir Nicholas LeStrange, a music buff with some Inns of Court connections. All of these 138, together with many cognate versions, are included in Sabol 1982.

This music was originally written, by Robert Johnson or some other court musician, for Ben Jonson's fantastically expensive *Masque of Queens*, danced at Whitehall on 2 February 1609; the text of the masque was entered in the Stationers' Register on 22 February, and published soon after in a quarto dated 1609, printed by Nicholas Okes. (See item 7.). The text also survives in a manuscript in Jonson's own handwriting. Dowland's folio includes the music among 'Almaines' (modern 'allemandes'). Allegedly typical of Germans, the allemande was one of the most popular instrumental dance forms in Baroque music, and the basis of much social dancing at the Inns of Court and elsewhere (Payne). Jonson does not name the choreographer for this first, interrupted entry dance, but it was probably Jerome Herne (credited by Jonson with the second antemasque dance, item 14 below) or Thomas Giles (credited with the final dance). The surviving beautiful drawings of masquers, costumes and scenery (by the masque's designer, Inigo Jones) do not include any that represent the witches. In his masque libretto Jonson describes their activities thus:

These Witches, wth a kind of hollow and infernall musique, came forth from thence [Hell]. First one, then two, and three, and more, till they^r number encreased to Eleuen; all differently attir'd; some, wth ratts on they^r heads; some, on they^r shoulders; others wth oyntment-potts at they^r girdles; All wth spindells, timbrells, rattles, or other *veneficall* instruments, making a confused noyse, wth strange gestures . . . These eleuen Witches begiñing to daunce (wch is an vsuall *ceremony* at they^r Convents, or meetings, Where, sometimes, also they are vizarded, and masqu'd) on the sodayne one of them miss'd they^r *Cheife* [Atè], and interrupted the rest. (Herford and Simpson, *Jonson*, 7:283)

Middleton in *The Witch* and *Macbeth* does not give any such detailed directions (or annotate the text, as Jonson does, explaining his learned sources for witch-lore). Although Middleton could have read the printed text of Jonson's masque, he would not have seen the single, private court performance. By contrast, the witches in Jonson's antimasque had probably been performed by members of the King's Men. Therefore, if the King's Men recycled the masque music and the dance in later performances of *The Witch* or *Macbeth*, the channel of appropriation was probably the acting company, rather than Middleton. On the other hand, it is also possible that the dancing of Middleton's witches deliberately differed from Jonson's, in a way that underlined the differences in their dramatic conception and characterization—in which case, the later plays were adapting and responding to the collaborative *Masque of Queens*, rather than merely copying it.

14. The Second Witches' Dance

Robert Johnson (?)

Middleton texts. See First Witches' Dance.

Musical copy-text. Christ Church MS 92r, f. 15, 'The Wiches'. This keyboard version resettles the dance in a slightly different metrical scheme from British Library Add. 10444, which is presumably a version whose bald treble and bassus parts may be somewhat closer to the setting used in Jonson's *Queens* (1609).

Cognate version. British Library Add. 10444, treble f. 21ᵛ, 'The second witches Dance'; bassus, f. 75, 'The second witches Dance'. This version, for treble and bassus alone, appears together with the setting for the first witches' dance described above.

In the libretto of *Queens*, the ninth charm urges that music sound for their dance thus:

At wᶜh, wᵗh a strange and sodayne Musique, they fell into a *magicall Daunce*, full of praeposterous change, and gesticulation, but most applying to theyʳ property: who, at theyʳ meetings, do all thinges contrary to the custome of Men, dauncing, back to back, hip to hip, theyʳ handes ioyn'd, and making theyʳ *circles* backward, to the left hand, wᵗh strange phantastique motions of theyʳ heads, and bodyes. All wᶜh were excellently imitated by the Maker of the *Daunce*, Mʳ. *Hierome Herne* ... In the heate of theyʳ *Daunce*, on the sodayne, was heard a sound of loud Musique, as if many Instruments had giuen one blast. Wᵗh wᶜh, not only the *Hagges* themselues, but theyʳ *Hell*, into wᶜh they ranne, quite vanishd; and the whole face of the *Scene* alterd; scarce suffring the memory of any such thing. (Herford and Simpson, *Jonson*, 7:301)

15. The New Year's Gift

Middleton text. *Masque of Heroes*, performed by the Prince's Men at the Inner Temple (1619), 141.1 (*Works*, p. 1326).

Musical copy-text. British Library Add. 10444, treble, f. 48, 'The new yeares gift'; bassus, ff. 97ᵛ-98, 'The New yeares gift'. This dance is transcribed in Sabol (1982) as item 166 on pp. 256-7.

Original readings. In m. 14 of the treble, notes 4-7 read C D D F, all quavers.

Used as an entry or exit (or both) in *Masque of Heroes* when Doctor Almanac, the presenter, announces the arrival of New Year, of whom the antic bystander Plumporridge says, 'I have ne'er a gift to give him.' The music could therefore cover the dancing entrance of New Year (played by Hugh Atwell, a notoriously skinny actor) and/ or the dancing exit of Plumporridge (played by William Rowley, a notoriously chubby actor). Most of the Jacobean court masques included two antimasque dances and three masque dances (the entry, the main, and the withdrawing dances). The men of the Middle and Inner temples performed masques—and sometimes in their own precincts—in 1613 (by Chapman), 1615 (by Browne), 1619 (by Middleton), and 1621. Since virtually all the other dances for the antics and the masquers of the 1613 and 1615 Inns of Court masques have been identified, the masque dances appearing in Add. 10444—Nos. 175-79 (as numbered in Sabol) comprise a group of two antic and three masque dances for an additional Temple masque, and Nos. 57 and 58 and Nos. 140-42 together comprise a similar group for a different Temple masque. Either of these two groups of five dances may well be considered possible dance tunes for the antimasquers and the masquers of *Masque of Heroes*, although a stronger case may be made for the former not only since the five numbered 175-79 appear in sequence in Add. 10444, but also because the first two appear in cognate versions in John Adson's 1621 *Courtly Masquing Ayres* just two years after the performance of *Masque of Heroes*. See also McGee and Meagher, pp. 70-71.

The source of the 138 dances in Add. 10444 may, as John Ward suggests, have been the dancing masters themselves, who doubtless composed them in the process of teaching their dancing charges their special choreographies, each master with his fiddle in hand. In most cases their simple treble and bassus presentations—perhaps preserved in various notebooks—were later provided with full consort arrangements, usually for four- and five-part strings, by professional composers. While Sir Nicholas also may have derived his two-part versions from manuscript part-books used by consort members in performance, what emerges clearly is that he is not copying from published collections of masque tunes like those of Wilhelm Brade, John Adson, or Thomas Simpson.

16. The First of the Temple Antic

Middleton text. *Masque of Heroes*, performed by the Prince's Men at the Inner Temple (1619), 231.1-2 (*Works*, p. 1328).

Musical copy-text. British Library Add. 10444, treble, f. 50ᵛ, 'The first of the Temple anticke'; bassus, f. 100, 'The first of the Temple Anticke'. This dance is transcribed in Sabol (1982) as item 175 on pp. 263-4.

Original readings. The key signature presented for the first strain, which clearly is in D major, is one sharp in the treble and no sharp in the bassus. Such imprecision is quite commonplace in the amateurish transcripts of Sir Nicholas LeStrange. Fortunately the cognate version noted below clarifies and corrects the score.

Treble

Key signature of one sharp for the first strain.

In m. 7 the fifth note is not preceded by a sharp.

In m. 9 the key signature of one flat replaces naturals at F and at C.

In m. 16, the fifth note is not preceded by a sharp.

In m. 17, the first note is not preceded by a sharp nor is the fourth notes preceded by a natural.

In m. 18, the key signature changes to one sharp.

Bassus

In m. 9, there is no key signature provided.

In m. 12 the second note is a crotchet—a D—augmented editorially by a crotchet D (tied) in m. 13.

In m. 18 no key signature is provided.

Cognate version. John Adson, *Courtly Masquing Ayres* (1621; STC 153), item 9, untitled; consort in five parts for cantus, medius, altus, tenor, and bassus. Adson's book, dedicated to George Villiers, Marquis of Buckingham (who was famous for his dancing) consists of six separate partbooks, printed in quarto by Thomas Snodham (who also printed item 13).

17. The Second of the Temple Antic

Middleton text. *Masque of Heroes*, performed by the Prince's Men at the Inner Temple (1619), 266.1 (*Works*, p. 1328).

Musical copy-text. British Library Add. 10444, treble, f. 51, 'The Second'; bassus, f. 100, 'The second'. This dance is transcribed in Sabol (1982) as item 176 on pp. 264–5.

Original readings.

Treble

No accidentals.

In m. 25, the second note is a crotchet G not tied to the following G.

In m. 26, beats 1–3 consist of the following four notes: a crotchet G and four quavers, A, B, C, D

Bassus

In m. 14, the second note is preceded by a sharp.

In m. 25, the first note is preceded by a sharp.

Cognate version. John Adson, *Courtly Masquing Ayres*, item 8, untitled; consort in five parts for cantus, medius, altus, tenor, and bassus.

18. The First of the Temple Masques

19. The Second of the Temple Masques

20. The Third of the Temple Masques

Middleton text. *Masque of Heroes*, performed by gentlemen at the Inner Temple (1619), 306.1–2, 322.1–2, 331.1–2 (*Works*, pp. 1329, 1329, 1330).

Musical copy-text (First). British Library Add. 10444, f. 51, 'The first of the Temple Masques'; bassus, f. 100ᵛ, 'The first of the Temple Masques'. This dance is transcribed in Sabol (1982) as item 177 on p. 265.

Original readings.

Treble

In m. 14, the second note, a minim F, has been omitted.

In m. 17, the fourth note, a semiquaver, is a B.

Bassus

In m. 16, the first two notes are a minim B and a crotchet C. Here the time values of the notes are reversed.

Musical copy-text (Second). British Library Add. 10444, f. 51ᵛ, 'The Second'; bassus, f 100ᵛ, 'The second'. This dance is transcribed in Sabol 1982 as item 178 on p. 266. **Original readings.**

Treble

In m. 4, the third note is preceded by a flat.
In m. 6, the fourth note is preceded by a sharp.

Musical copy-text (Third). British Library Add. 10444, f. 51ᵛ, 'The third'; bassus f. 100ᵛ, 'The third'. This dance is transcribed in Sabol (1982) as item 179 on pp. 266-7. **Original readings.**

Bassus

In m. 4, the fourth, fifth, and sixth notes are a crotchet G, a quaver F, and a quaver E.

7. The bassus part for all three of the main masque dances. The diminishing vertical lines eventually joining up and fading to an upstroke, at the end of each tune, are elaborate versions of repeat marks; the number of lines of dots may indicate the number of times the section is repeated. The layout of the manuscript in this way (separating parts of the same tune in different sections) suggests that it was copied from separate manuscript parts for the different instruments. Thus, not only were the manuscripts containing dramatic music normally separated from the manuscripts containing dramatic text, but the music for a single song might itself be contained in several separate manuscripts.

21. La Mignard

John Dowland

Middleton text. *Old Law* 3.2.130.1 (*Works*, p. 1367) calls for '*A galliard La miniard*', to which both the young First Courtier and old Lisander dance.

    Musical copy-text. The dance is present in four extant manuscripts: as 'Migniarde' in Cambridge University Library Dd.ii.11.77, fol. 2 (*c*.1585–95); as 'J.D.' in Dd. iii.78.3, fol. 31ᵛ (*c*.1595–1600); as 'Mignarda Jo Dowlande' in Dd xi.33, fol. 29 (*c*.1595–1601), written on music paper printed by Thomas East (Fenlon and Milsom, 151); as 'la miniard' in Cambridge, Trinity College, O.16.2 (*c*.1620–30). The tune is now usually called 'Mignarda', but that title occurs in only one of the manuscripts; the

other two are closer to the form in *Old Law*. The tune is also known as 'M. Henry Noel his Galiard', its title in Dowland's *Lachrimae* (1604; STC 7097), item 14, sig. I1ᵛ–I2 (a table-book format for lute and four instruments such as viols). Since Dowland's music is a galliard, and since Middleton refers elsewhere to *Lachrimae*, the identification seems clear (though it has not been noticed by Middleton's editors). Like other works by Dowland, this one has been very widely transcribed and recorded in modern times. In the play, the tune is evidently played on the viol by the 'Dancer' alone, and so the present score is confined to the cantus of the highly elaborate setting in *Lachrimae*.

22. Take O take those lips away

John Wilson

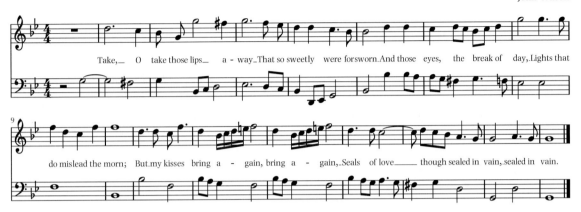

Take,— O take those lips— a - way—That so sweetly were forsworn.And those eyes, the break of day,.Lights that
do mislead the morn; But.my kisses bring a - gain, bring a - gain,.Seals of love——— though sealed in vain,.sealed in vain.

Middleton text. Sung by a Boy in Middleton's adaptation of *Measure for Measure*, performed by the King's Men (1621), 4.1.1–6 (*Works*, p. 1570).

For evidence of Middleton's adaptation of the play, including addition of this song to Shakespeare's original, see Taylor and Jowett, 107–236, *Works*, p. 1542, and this volume, p. 417.

Musical copy-text. Bodleian, Mus. b. 1, f. 19ᵛ, the composer John Wilson's songbook, compiled *c*.1656 ('MS 6' in Jowett's stemma, below).

Original readings. The MS adds a second stanza, as follows:

Hide o hide those hills of snow
that thy froazen bosom beares
on whose topps the Pinkes yᵗ grow
are yet of those yᵗ Aprill weares
But first sett my poore heart free
bound in those Icye chaines by thee

This second stanza belongs to the version of the song in 5.2 of *The Tragedy of Rollo, Duke of Normandy; or, The Bloody Brother*, a play written for the King's Men by Fletcher and Massinger, probably with the assistance of Nathan Field and perhaps another dramatist, between mid-1617 and 1620. Wilson's music indicates a repeat for the last two metrical lines ('But my kisses . . . sealed in vain'), rather than repeating the final three syllables only of the penultimate line ('bring again') and the final line ('sealed in vain'). The verbal repetitions printed here come from the 1623 text of *Measure for Measure*. The musical text given here for those repetitions is editorial, since no early music text is keyed to the version of the song in *Measure*.

Cognate versions. Other music MSS are British Library, Add. MS 11,608, f. 56 (*c*.1656–9); Christ Church, Oxford, MS 434, f. 1 (before *c*.1650); New York Public Library,

MS Drexel 4041, no. 44 (*c*.1640); New York Public Library, MS Drexel 4257, no. 16 (*c*.1659); the song was printed in a series of songbooks issued by John Playford between 1652 and 1669. The first two Playford printings (*Select Musicall Ayres, and Dialogues*, 1652 and 1653) were printed using movable type; but the third (*Select Ayres and Dialogues*, 1659) and fourth (*Treasury of Musick*, 1669) used the same engraved plate. The song is thus reproduced in all three significant seventeenth-century technologies for the textual reproduction of music (manuscript, single-impression movable type, and engraving). Few of the variants in the music texts result from error; almost all represent deliberate alteration to the music. No two manuscripts share even the same positioning of barlines. John Hilton's manuscript (Add. 11,608) freely adds ornamentation, clearly as an after-thought to the original transcription; this is characteristic of the entire manuscript, which seems to have been linked to a group of performers with which Hilton was associated in the 1640s and 1650s (Chan 1979). All manuscripts have incidental variation such as dotted and half notes instead of equal notes, or crotchets split into quavers. In some versions the bass is simplified; in others a phrase in the bass is raised or lowered by an octave. These changes may be dictated by practical circumstance—the capacities of instrument or player. The two manuscripts now in New York transpose the entire song a tone lower, presumably to bring it more comfortably within a singer's range. It seems that anyone who undertook to transcribe the music was competent and perhaps even expected to embellish, simplify, rearrange, or transpose it.

Verbal variants, by contrast, are less frequent and less flamboyant. In the first stanza, the Christ Church MS reads 'that breake the' for 'the break of'; the Playford books have 'that breake of' for the same phrase, 'days, light' for 'day, lights', and 'seals' for 'sealed'. These are the only substantive verbal variants in the music texts of this stanza. Nearly all MS songbooks and verse miscellanies, and early printed texts of both *Rollo* and the song, differ from the Shakespeare Folios in reading 'though' rather than 'but' in the final line; the exception is a MS copied from F4. Numerous other verbal variants occur in stanza 1, as found in texts of the words without the music, and in stanza 2 generally.

General comments. The composer John Wilson (1595–1674) appears to have supplied music for the King's Men, and probably wrote this setting of 'Take, O take' for the company. The song would originally have been performed in *Rollo, Duke of Normandy*, and would later have been lifted from this context to *Measure for Measure* as part of the Middletonian revision. Here it helps break up the continuity of action in the Shakespearean script, providing a theatrically effective opening to the new fourth Act.

The second stanza is entirely inappropriate to the new dramatic setting, as the song's implied addressee is no longer a woman (Edith in *Rollo*) but a man (Angelo in *Measure*). Hence the song as it stands in *Measure* has only one stanza, and the new repetitions in the fifth and sixth lines were no doubt thought to offset the abruption by giving the stanza a stronger close.

The Act probably begins with a discovery; a curtain is drawn back to reveal the jilted Mariana listening to her boy-servant singing a plaintive song in which an abandoned woman addresses her former lover. Both singer and Mariana would therefore be boy-actors. The boy probably accompanied himself on the lute or a similar instrument; the simple bassus of the music gives no more than the key notes for what must have been a fuller accompaniment.

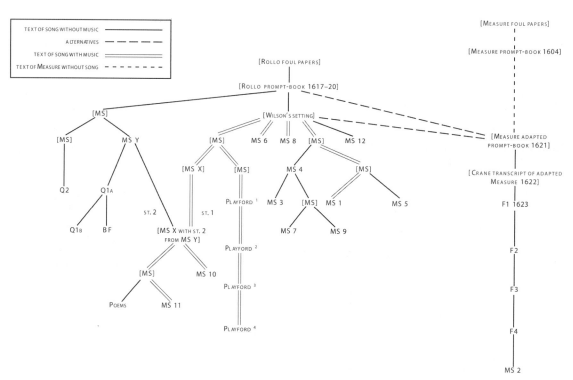

8. John Jowett's summary of the stemma of transmission of twenty-three extant versions of 'Take, O take those lips away', based on his meticulous analysis of text and music variants in Appendix IV of Taylor and Jowett, 272–95.) (This stemma slightly modifies and corrects Figure 10 on p. 295.) Notice that the music was not physically contained in any of the manuscript or print versions of either play; this is typical of early modern theatrical practice, which separated musical scores from the acting company's licensed playbook. All the music texts, and all but one very late manuscript, reproduce the form of the song found in *Rollo, Duke of Normandy*, rather than the adaptation of it in *Measure for Measure*.

23a. Hence, all ye vain delights

Setting 1

John Hilton (?)

Hence, hence,— all ye vain de - lights,———— as short as are the nights where-in you spend your fol-ly. There's

nought in this life sweet, if men were wise to see't, but on-ly Mel - anchol-y. O sweet-est Mel - ancholy!

O sweet-est Mel - ancholy! Welcome fold-ed arms and fix - ed eyes, a sigh that pierc-ing mor - ti - fies, A

look that's fas-ten'd to the ground, A tongue chain'd up, without a sound, Foun - tain heads and path less groves,

Pla - ces which pale pas - sion loves, Moon - light walks, where all the fowls Are warmly hous'd save bats and owls, A

mid - night bell, a part-ing groan: These are the sounds we feed up - on! Then stretch our bones, then stretch our

169

bones in a still gloom-y val-ley. There's noth-ing dain-ty sweet, there's noth-ing dain-ty sweet, but Mel-an-choly.

Middleton text. Sung by the Passionate Madman, an adult actor, in *The Nice Valour*, performed by an unknown company (1622), 3.3.36–54 (*Works*, p. 1698). On Middleton's authorship of the song see this volume, p. 423.

For the many extant texts of the song, see Beal, B&F 125–53 and John Jowett's discussion of Middleton's early readers in this volume, p. 296. For a collation of all verbal variants, see this volume, pp. 1071, 1076.

Musical copy-text. British Library Egerton MS 2013, f. 3ᵛ–4ᵛ; setting for full lyric text for cantus and bassus attributed to John Hilton. The cognate version in Christ Church MS 350 includes a setting of the treble only.

The attribution to Hilton (1599–1657) is dubious. He graduated from Trinity College on 1 July 1626, having spent a decade in Cambridge; he could not have composed the score for the first performance, and is not known to have written original music for any London theatres. Chan notes the songs in Egerton 2013 'appear to have been very carelessly entered and therefore to be unreliable sources' (1990, p. 237). Moreover, the composers' names 'have been added in a different, later hand, and some of the ascriptions are open to question' (Jorgens, 2:vi).

Perhaps this setting or the next may have been sung in different productions of *The Nice Valour*, which was revived at some time between its first performances and the closing of the theatres. Photofacsimiles of each music manuscript are reproduced in Jorgens, vol. 2 and vol. 6; for diplomatic transcripts of each of these two settings see Cutts (1971), pp. 106–9. See also Spink (1971), who on p. 189 describes Bodleian Music School F. 575 as containing 'Mostly lyra-viol music, but also including songs for lute and voice: *c*.1630 or later'. That an incomplete setting of the song survives in Christ Church MS 350 is noted in J. P. Cutts.

9. Note the copyist scribbling out notes and replacing them. This suggests he may be transcribing the music from a memory of its performance.

23b. Hence, all ye vain delights

Setting 2

Cantus

Hence, all ye vain delights, As short, as short as__ are the nights, Where - in__ you__

spend__ your fol - ly. There's nought in this life sweet,__ If men were wise__ to see't, But on -

- ly mel - an - chol - y. Welcome fold - ed arms and fix - ed eyes, A sigh that pierc - ing

mor - ti - fies, A look that's fasten'd to the ground, a tongue__ chain'd up__ with - out a sound.

Middleton text. See preceding item 23a.
Musical copy-text. Bodleian Music School F. 575, f. 7ᵛ,

is a different anonymous setting omitting the concluding
lines of the lyric for cantus and lute tablature.

171

24. The Gypsies' Round

William Byrd

Middleton text. Sung and danced by a group of male and female Gypsies in *The Spanish Gypsy* (1623), 3.1.107-38 (*Works*, p. 1742). Chappell (2:772) conjectured 'Perhaps the words of this round are in Middleton's play...They fit the tune.' It would be more accurate to say that the song seems to have been composed to fit the existing Byrd music. (This is a very widespread practice in the period: witness all the ballads 'to the tune of' X.) This first song and dance is clearly meant to establish an exotic musical and choreographic identity, which would be more easily done if they adapted a familiar tune already long associated with Gypsies.

Musical copy-text. The only known source is the Fitzwilliam Virginal Book (Cambridge, Fitzwilliam Museum, Music MS 32.G.29), p. 321 [item 216], where the tune is attributed to Byrd. The attribution is accepted by modern scholars, and in the standard numeration is 'BK 80'. The manuscript was compiled by the younger Francis Tregian during his imprisonment in the Fleet, 1609-19. It contains over seventy pieces by Byrd, and is thus the largest single source of Byrd's keyboard music. 'On the whole, Tregian's texts are inferior to those of the primary source' (Brown, 2:192), but Tregian is the only source for thirteen pieces, including this one. There are several modern transcriptions: Maitland and Squire, 2:292-6, and Brown, 2:116 (the only edition with a full textual apparatus). Modern recordings are also available.

Byrd's Round is a series of six variations, an elaborate musical art-work that is unlikely to have been played in full in the theatre. We assume instead that the opening section would have been repeated for the four stanzas. The rhythm and tune accord well with the song as printed in *Gypsy*. The words take up most but not all of the first section; the remaining bars could have been played while the Gypsies exeunt dancing.

The present text follows Maitland and Squire's bar divisions, which are based on the MS except that M5-6 are 'divided unequally into three' in the MS. Maitland and Squire add the initial time signature; this edition adds the time signature at M8 and the repeat sign. Maitland and Squire make one notational emendation: in M4 the second bass note, a crotchet, is altered from E to G.

In this edition notes for the following words have been divided from single notes in the MS where two or three syllables are required: M1 'Trip it', M2 'capers! At', M3 'treading', M4 'toys! We', M5 'purses'.

173

25. The Spanish Gypsy

Choreography from Playford.

Longways for eight

Woman	Woman	Woman	Woman
Man	Man	Man	Man

[Honour.] Lead up forwards and back. A strain played once. That again. A strain played twice. Turn all back-to-back; faces again; go all about your women, not turning your faces. That again the t'other way. A strain played once. First and last couple meet, a Double back again; turn all back-to-back; faces again; go about each other, not turning your faces; the other way as much. A strain played twice. The other four as much. A strain played thrice.

Sides all. A strain played once. That again. A strain played twice. Turn back-to-back. Faces again; go about your own [woman] as before. A strain played once. First and last couple meet and go back; turn back-to-back; faces again; take hands and go round; back again. A strain played twice. Then the other four [do] as much. A strain played thrice.

Arms all. A strain played once. That again. A strain played twice. Turn back to back; faces again; go about your own [woman] as before. A strain played once. First and last couple meet; back again; turn back-to-back; faces again; right hands across and go round; then left [hands across and go] round. A strain played twice. The other four [do] as much. A strain played thrice. [Honour.]

Middleton text. *The Spanish Gypsy* (1623). Chappell (1:272–3) proposed that this dance was performed in conjunction with the song 'Come, follow your leader, follow' (3.2.82–113; *Works*, p. 1744). However, the dance

seems more appropriate at 5.3.110.1 (*Works*, p. 1765). See 'Interpretation' below.

Musical copy-text. *The English Dancing Master: or, Plaine and easie Rules for the Dancing of Country Dances, with the Tune to each Dance … printed by Thomas Harper, and are to be sold by John Playford, at his Shop in the Inner Temple neere the Church doore* (1651; Wing P2477), sig. D4 (item 23). Playford entered the book in the Stationers' Register on 7 November 1650; the British Library copy is annotated by Thomason, indicating that he purchased it on March 19, 1651 ('1650' old style). No instruments are specified, but in Playford's *A Musicall Banquet* (1651) he advertised *The English Dancing Master* as 'to be played on the Treble Violl or Violin'; the 1652 title-page also specifies 'to be playd on the Treble Violin'.

The original composer of 'The Spanish Gypsy' is unknown. The compilation and editing of *The English Dancing Master* is normally attributed to its publisher Playford, who signed the preface 'To the Ingenious Reader', which states that 'The Art of Dancing … is a quality that has been formerly honoured in the Courts of Princes, when performed by the most Noble *Heroes* of the Times! The Gentlemen of the Innes of Court, whose sweet and ayry Activity has crowned their Grand Solemnities with Admiration to all Spectators.' This punctuation is confusing: either it distinguishes two venues ('Courts of Princes' and 'Innes of Court') or, more probably, 'the most noble Heroes' are glossed as 'The Gentlemen of the Innes of Court'. Dean-Smith (1957) provides a bibliography of all eighteen early editions, through *c.*1728 (xxi–xxxi); Barlow updates her list of known copies of each edition (13), describes differences in their presentation of the music (5–8), collates the music in all editions and provides a critical modernized text of the music for all the items that he considers 'country dances', which fortunately includes 'The Spanish

Gypsy' (35). Barlow's edition of the music is much more scholarly than the earlier work of Mellor and Bridgewater.

The music was altered in the second edition: *The Dancing Master...The second Edition Enlarged and Corrected from many grosse Errors which were in the former Edition* (1652; Wing P2468A), sig. I3 (item 89). The revised title of the book (omitting 'English') was repeated in all subsequent editions; so was the altered music. It was also printed in Playford's *Musick's Delight on the Cithren* (1666; Wing P2491), sig. C7ᵛ (item 35). The random order of dances in 1651 was changed to alphabetical (by first letter of title) in 1652, and then items were grouped by dance type in 1670 and all subsequent editions.

Choreography. The dance steps are printed, in all Playford's editions, on the same page as, and immediately below, the music. Playford's system for describing dances—the only widely disseminated European dance notation in the seventeenth century—keys formulaic language to a musical score and a brief bird's-eye view of the initial position of the dancers. (See Illus. 10.) His sources for the choreographies are not known, but in form they closely resemble eight English manuscript choreographies from *c.*1563 to 1675, the majority associated with the Inns of Court. 'Country dances' were social dances, incorporated in the 'revels' part of masques at court and elsewhere, where dance partners from the audience joined the per-formers; unlike the specially designed and choreographed dances of the antimasque and main masque (which often required a week of rehearsal), country dances were 'short and easy'. Playford's dance manual reached a very wide audience: even today, 'students with average dancing talents and no previous experience in early repertoire can easily learn one in less than one hour' (Ravelhofer, 44). The best way to make sense of Playford's instructions is not to read them but to act them out, physically.

Though Cecil Sharp published many influential verbal and diagrammatic elucidations of Playford's dance directions (Keller and Shimer), he did not include 'The Spanish Gypsy', presumably because he accepted Chappell's attribution of it to the play, and therefore did not regard it as a genuine folk dance. No modern scholar or dancer has attempted an interpretation of the choreography. Our edited transcription modernizes the spelling and punctuation of Playford, and interpolates a few words in square brackets to clarify the intended sense. The only substantive interpolation is the word 'Honour' at the beginning and end of the dance; most choreographies from the period do not specify this, because it was taken for granted that each dance began and ended with this standard gesture of courtesy, described by Payne: 'The man removes his hat with his hand and carries it gracefully to the side with the inside of the hat towards the thigh. At the same time he

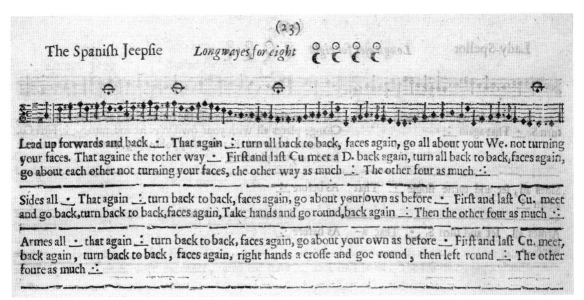

10. The oblong quarto format of Playford's *English Dancing Master* was popular for music printing. The earliest editions devoted entirely to musical notation, printed by Ottaviano dei Petrucci between 1501 and 1520, are oblong quartos. Krummel (1971) estimates that 'about two thousand oblong quarto part-book editions were printed in sixteenth-century Europe' (312). But this format was old-fashioned by 1651, and was changed in all Playford's subsequent editions. The music typeface used by the printer, Thomas Harper, had been inherited from Thomas East (item 1). Playford used special symbols, explained in his introductory Table, to indicate male and female (upper right); but he reversed the usual meaning of the symbols, so that men rather than women were represented by the changeable (quarter) moon, and women by the perfect circle. The four symbols directly above the musical score indicate pauses. Symbols within the choreography are explained in the introductory Table, and translated in our transcript.

draws back either the Left or Right foot, bending the knees of the withdrawn leg as it takes the weight. At the same time he inclines the body forwards (i.e. bow)…trying to maintain eye contact with her throughout. This should be one continuous movement and last for two minim pulses.' He then returns to his opening position 'by repeating these movements in reverse.' The woman, for her part, 'keeps her feet together, bends both knees equally keeping them well turned out, and rises smoothly, in accordance with her partner' (125–6). In English social dancing the honour often also included an embrace.

Only a few items in Playford's choreography require a technical gloss. He assumes, throughout, that the Directions are addressed to a male dancer: hence the verb 'Lead' means that each male dancer leads his female partner. The adverbs 'forward' and 'back' refer to the line of the dance, not the orientation of each dancer to his partner. Although the verb 'go' may seem like an unspecific direction for locomotion, its primary early modern sense was 'walk'—which may be relevant to the vexed question of whether steps should be executed on the flat of the foot or on the toe, or whether they should include hopping or kicking movements. Playford's introductory Table explains that a 'Double' (a very common step in social dances of the period) is 'four steps forward or back, closing both feet'. The phrase 'Arms all', a contemporary explains, 'is to take hands, or by the Arms, and so to turn about and change places; or else go in a single, etc.' (Holme III, 169).

Interpretation. Chappell connected the tune and dance to 'Come, follow your leader, follow' because the metre of that lyric was 'suitable to the air'. There is also a black-letter ballad (STC 10412; Roxburghe 1:544) entitled *The brave English Jipsie*, directed to be sung 'to the tune of *The Spanish Jipsie*', which begins 'Come, follow, follow all, | The English Jipsies call'. The broadside is undated, but it was published by John Trundle (1603–26). The ballad publisher John Wright had entered 'the Spanish Jepsiy' in the Stationers' Register on 28 June 1624; no copy of any text by him with that title is extant, but an exceptionally large proportion of early broadside ballads is lost. It would make sense to assume that the demonstrable success of the play, beginning in the summer of 1623 and extending through court performance in November (and probably beyond), led to composition and publication of a ballad (1624), which in turn led to publication of a response-ballad before Trundle's burial on 12 December 1626 (Johnson 180). Chappell also quotes another ballad, *The Three Merry Cobblers*, written by Martin Parker (Roxburghe 1:408), which begins 'Come, follow, follow me, | To the alehouse we'll march all three'; Chappel seems unaware of the fact that this song is sung entirely by men, whereas Playford's dance calls for mixed couples. Chappell also quotes the first two lines of what he calls 'the most popular song to this tune,' beginning 'Come follow, follow me, Ye fairy elves that be'. This lyric was first printed in *A Description of the King and Queene of Fayries* (1635; STC 21513), which specifies that it should be 'Sung like to the Spanish Gipsie'

(unpaginated, immediately preceding a text of Middleton's 'Hence all you vaine delights', from *Nice Valour*). However, Chappell does not quote the third and fifth lines of the first stanza ('And circle round this greene…Hand in hand lets dance a round'), which demand a round dance, rather than the 'longways' dance specified by Playford.

Chappell also cites songs in *The Boys' Opera* (1730) and *The Fashionable Lady* (1730), which both begin 'Come follow, follow me'. In all these five texts, the sung begins with an iambic trimeter: 'Come, follow, follow me' (or 'all'). That line does not occur in the extant texts of the play. Moreover, the metre of that first line does not match the lilting metre of the first line of 'Come, follow your leader, follow!' (3.2.82), a rhythm exactly repeated in the next line. Other texts 'To the Tune of the *Spanish Gypsie*' also begin with iambic trimetre: Gilchrist (280) cites Robert Coster's 'The Digger's Christmass-Caroll' in *The Diggers Mirth* (1650; Wing C6366A): 'You people which be wise, | Will freedom highly prize' (sig. A2). Wells (200) cites one additional ballad, *Cuckold's Haven* (1638; STC 6101, Roxburghe 1.148), which begins 'Come neighbours follow me | That cuckoldizèd be'. All these citations establish the popularity of the tune; but they do not clearly link the ballad tune to 'Come, follow your leader, follow!'

Beginning with Chappell, all these investigations pay attention to the tune, but ignore the dance. The nature of the song in 3.2 does not fit the nature of the dance Playford describes. Armies are normally all male (like the three merry cobblers), and all-male dancing was common at the Inns of Court and elsewhere; although Eugenia and Preciosa enter in 3.2, nothing in the lyric suggests that the women dance. (If they did dance, they would not dance in couples, but as part of the 'Gypsy army'.) By contrast, nothing in the dance corresponds in any way to the military metaphors or language of the lyric. Playford's dance is not a leader dance, nor an entrance dance, nor an introductory dance, nor an explicitly ethnic dance; it is above all a dance of heterosexual couples—which is not the subject of the song or dance in 3.2.

Nevertheless, the dance must, as Chappell realized, be in some way related to the play. Broadside ballads do not spontaneously generate dances; the play, by contrast, is very explicitly full of dances. Moreover, there was nothing to prompt a song, ballad or dance about one or more Spanish Gypsies until the success of the play. The play took that subject from texts by Cervantes that had not been translated into English; outside the play, the collocation 'Spanish Gypsy' does not appear in Literature Online until 1659, or in EEBO-TCP until 1685. Those databases are not complete, of course, but they do suggest the rarity of the combination, outside this play and a tune that first shows up in an extant ballad text at about the same time.

If we do not assume that the dance described by Playford was danced to accompany 'Come, follow your leader, follow!', then where else in the play might it belong? The Gypsies dance and exit to 'Trip it, Gypsies, trip it fine' (3.1.107–38), but that song does not fit the ballad metre either. (See preceding item.) Nor does 'Dance, sing, and in a well-mixed border' (4.1.42–55), or 'Brave Don, cast your eyes | On our Gypsy fashions' (4.1.86–116), or 'Hence merrily fine to get money' (4.1.138–48). Thus, the Playford tune and dance do not seem to fit the metre or the circumstances of any of the song lyrics in the printed play. But the play's Gypsies also sometimes dance without words. They sing at 3.2.197–217, but only *after* the song does Preciosa tell her father and the others to 'fall to your dancing' (3.2.218)—a speech immediately followed by the stage direction '*Dance*'. Later, the Gypsies exit 'dancing', wordlessly, at 3.2.232.1. Finally, at the end of the play they bid farewell to their life as Gypsies in another 'Dance' without words (5.3.110.1). Thus, in two scenes the Gypsies dance to instrumental music but no vocal accompaniment. Moreover, the same thing happens in John Leanerd's *The Counterfeits* (1679), where at the end of 5.2 'the Spanish Gypsies' are brought on stage for no reason except to perform 'A DANCE' and exit. The tune and dance in Leanerd's play were almost certainly those already familiar to audiences—and they were *not* accompanied by lyrics.

Of the two scenes in *The Spanish Gypsy*, only 5.3 would fit Playford's instructions for the dance. Four heterosexual couples are on stage: Alvarez and Eugenia (leaders of the Gypsies), the Gypsy Pretiosa and Don Juan (who briefly became a Gypsy), Clara and Roderigo (who briefly became a Gypsy), Cardochia and Diego (who both spent time among the Gypsies). The play's final couplet, spoken immediately after the dance, begins, 'On, brides and bridegrooms!', and indeed three of the four couples are bridal pairs; the fourth (the Father and Mother of the Gypsies) are already married. Thus, at 5.3.110.1—and nowhere else—the play provides an arrangement of characters that fits Playford's description of a longways dance for four cross-gender couples.

Moreover, the most remarkable feature of the dance is the direction 'turn back-to-back', which is repeated six times. That is, the couples keep turning their backs to each other. This back-to-back move is compounded with another recurrent move, 'go about each other not turning your faces', which each couple does four times in the first of the dance's three sections: that is, the individual men and women are directed to dance around their partners, without looking at them. The dance thus re-enacts the central action of the play's romantic plots: Roderigo rapes Clara without letting her see him, Don Juan repeatedly 'offers to kiss' Pretiosa but she turns away or otherwise prevents the kiss, Cardochia holds Diego at arm's length while she pursues another man (Don Juan, who turns his back on her). This turning away or turning aside also would have enacted, for the play's first audiences, their political ambivalence about the Spanish Match (Taylor 2008). But although the couples keep turning their backs on each other, this rhythmic rejection oscillates with rhythmic attraction: 'faces again'. The dance embodies a ritual of resisted courtship: the first section begins with the men leading, the second with the couples side by side, the third with them arm-in-arm. In the middle of the second section the couples hold hands; in the final section their hands intertwine, twice.

This final dance would also differ significantly from all the play's previous dances. The first dance introduces and emphasizes the acrobatic agility of the dancers: 'Trip it, Gypsies, trip it fine! Show tricks and lofty capers!…we trip it on the toe…our dances waste our backs…' The lyrics call for the high kicks ('lofty capers') and intricate moves associated with Italian and Spanish dance fashions. It explicitly scorns old-fashioned folk dances ('threading needles…leaping over rapiers'). The only words repeated in the chorus of the second dance (three times) are 'our knackers', foregrounding their exotic castanets; the rest of the lyric ('Follow your leader') implies a specially choreographed mime-dance, imitating a battle, and thereby associating the Spanish Gypsies with Spanish armies. In 4.1 Gypsy dancing is explicitly described as 'antic' (88), and compared to rope-dancing (93–5); it is twice praised as an opportunity 'To show a pretty foot' (146, 148). All these characterizations of the early dances emphasize their exceptional character; they resemble the antic dancing of an antimasque, and/or the specially choreographed displays of the main masque. Theatrically, in order to succeed those dances must impress an audience as spectacular. Notably, these early Gypsy scenes require three characters—Antonio, Carlo, and Christiana—who between them speak only 24 lines, but who cannot be doubled with any other characters; one suspects that these roles were designed to be played by spectacularly fine dancers who were not necessarily fine actors. Notably, these three characters do not appear in the final scene, though the performers were available offstage; apparently, their particular dance talents were not needed here, and the playwrights did not want to raise audience expectations by bringing them back on stage. By contrast with these earlier dances, the choreography Playford labels 'Spanish Gypsy' is, like his 'country dances', not beyond the powers of anyone in the audience. Like the 'revels' or 'measures', it is a social dance, which establishes community. After the dance, the final couplet commands the dancers to 'bend' to the audience, thus explicitly acknowledging their participation. The dance thus ends the play—and the flirtation with Gypsy life temporarily indulged by the characters and the audience. What is apparently the first extant reference to the play in performance refers to 'Gypsy jigs' (see Critical Introduction); this final dance serves many of the functions of the old jigs, but integrates those functions into the play's fictional narrative. It gives the actors a kind of choreographed curtain call; at the same time, like the final number in a modern musical, it is designed to send spectators out of the theatre humming, or whistling, with a rhythm in their steps. It invites imitation—and, to judge by the enduring popularity of Playford's instructions, the invitation was accepted.

How then did this dance, originally wordless, become associated with a broadside ballad? The popularity of the tune and the dance, which like a detachable jig ended the play, invited a ballad-maker to take advantage of both, by providing a simple verbal text that satisfied the conventions of the ballad genre. That text is lost, but we can discern its verbal structure from subsequent ballads that invoked its tune, and especially from the first reply it provoked. That evidence suggests that the original ballad almost certainly began 'Come, follow, follow all'. Clearly, this opening paraphrases the opening of the song in 3.2. The ballad-maker thus seems to have combined the country-dance tune of *The Spanish Gypsy*'s final dance with a paraphrase of elements from the danced song that the Spanish Gypsies use to introduce themselves to a paying audience in 3.2.

WORKS CITED

Agee, Richard, *The Gardano Music Printing Firms* (1998)

Ashbee, Andrew, ed., *William Lawes (1602-1645): essays on his life, times and work* (1998)

—— and David Lasocki, eds., *A Biographical Dictionary of English Court Musicians, 1485-1714*, vol. 2 (1998)

Atkinson, David, *The English Traditional Ballad: Theory, method, and practice* (2002)

Austern, Linda P., '"Sing Again Siren": The Female Musician and Sexual Enchantment in Elizabethan Life and Literature', *Renaissance Quarterly* 42 (1989), 420-48

—— '"Art to Enchant": Musical Magic and its Practitioners in English Renaissance Drama', *Journal of the Royal Musical Association* 115 (1990), 191-206

—— *Music in English Children's Drama of the Later Renaissance* (1992)

Barlow, Jeremy, ed., *The Complete Country Dance Tunes from Playford's Dancing Master (1651-ca. 1728)* (1985)

Baskervill, C. R., *The Elizabethan Jig and Related Song Drama* (1929)

Beal, Peter, comp., *Index of English Literary Manuscripts, 1450-1625* vol. I, parts 1-2 (1980)

Bernstein, Jane A., *Music Printing in Renaissance Venice: The Scotto Press (1539-1572)* (1998)

—— *Print Culture and Music in Sixteenth-Century Venice* (2001)

Borman, Stanley, 'Early Music Printing: Working for a Specialized Market', in *Print and Culture in the Renaissance: Essays on the Advent of Printing in Europe*, ed. Gerald P. Tyson and Sylvia S. Wagonheim (1986), 222-45

Bowman, Wayne D., *Philosophical Perspectives on Music* (1998)

Boyd, Morrison Comegys, *Elizabethan Music and Musical Criticism* rev. edn. (1962)

Brissenden, Alan, *Shakespeare and the Dance* (1981)

Brooke, Nicholas, ed., *Macbeth* (1990)

Brown, Alan, ed., *William Byrd: Keyboard Music*, Musica Britannica, vol. 27-28 (1969-71)

Budd, Malcolm, *Music and the Emotions: The Philosophical Theories* (1992)

Bull, Cynthia Jean Cohen, 'Sense, Meaning, and Perception in Three Dance Cultures', in *Meaning in Motion: New Cultural Studies of Dance*, ed. Jane C. Desmond (1997), 269-88

Burden, Michael, '"For the Lustre of the Subject": music for the Lord Mayor's Day in the Restoration', *Early Music* 23 (1995), 585-602

Caldwell, John, *The Oxford History of English Music*, Vol. I: *From the Beginnings to c.1715* (1991)

Campbell, Murray, 'Timbre (i)', *Grove Music Online*, ed. L. Macy (accessed 22 June 2007), www.grovemusic.com

Caroso, Fabritio, *Courtly Dance of the Renaissance: A New Translation and Edition of the 'Nobiltà di Dame' (1600)*, tr. Julia Sutton and F. Marian Walker (1995)

Carter, Tim, *Music, Patronage and Printing in Late Renaissance Florence* (2000)

Case, John, *The Praise of Music* (1586)

Casey, James, 'Shakespeare and the Destruction of the Male Body', unpublished Ph.D. dissertation (University of Alabama, 2006)

Castiglione, Baldassarre, *The Courtyer*, tr. Thomas Hoby (1561)

Chambers, E. K., *The Elizabethan Stage*, 4 vols (1923)

Chan, Mary, 'John Hilton's Manuscript, British Library Add. MS 11608', *Music and Letters* 60 (1979a), 440-49

—— 'Drolls, Drolleries and Mid-Seventeenth Century Dramatic Music in England', *Royal Musical Association Research Chronicle* 15 (1979b), 117-73

—— *Music in the Theatre of Ben Jonson* (1980)

—— 'A Mid-Seventeenth-Century Music Meeting and Playford's Publishing', in *The Well Enchanting Skill: Music, Poetry, and Drama in The Culture of the Renaissance*, ed. John Caldwell, Edward Olleson and Susan Wollenberg (1990), 231-44

—— 'Music Books', in *The Cambridge History of the Book in Britain, Volume IV: 1557-1695*, ed. John Barnard and D. F. McKenzie (2002), 127-37

Chappell, William, *Popular Music of the Olden Time*, 2 vols (1855-59)

Chartier, Roger, 'Afterword: Music in Print', in Kate van Orden, ed., *Music and the Cultures of Print* (2000), 325-41

Child, Francis James, ed., *The English and Scottish Popular Ballad*, 5 vols (1882-94); reprint edn. (1965)

Cofone, Charles J. F., ed., *Elizabeth Rogers Hir Virginall Booke* (1975)

Cone, Edward, *Musical Form and Musical Performance* (1968)

Copland, Robert, *Complete Poems*, ed. Mary Carpenter Erler (1993)

Craig-McFeely, Julia, 'English Lute Manuscripts and Scribes 1530-1630', Ph.D. dissertation, University of Oxford (1993); published online (2000) at www.ramesescats.co.uk/thesis/

Crane, Frederick, *Materials for the Study of the Fifteenth Century Basse Danse* (1968)

Crewdson, Richard, *Apollo's Swan and Lyre: Five Hundred Years of the Musicians' Company* (2000)

Cusick, Suzanne, *Valerio Dorico, Music Printer in Sixteenth-Century Rome* (1980)

Cutts, John P., 'Jacobean Masque and Stage Music', *Music and Letters* 35 (1954), 185-200

—— 'Robert Johnson: King's Musician in His Majesty's Public Entertainment', *Music and Letters* 36 (1955), 110-25

—— 'The Original Music to Middleton's *The Witch*', *Shakespeare Quarterly* 7 (1956), 203-209

—— 'The Music for *A Chaste Maid in Cheapside*', Appendix II in R. B. Parker, ed., *A Chaste Maid in Cheapside* (1969), 128-37

—— *La Musique de scène de la troupe de Shakespeare: The King's Men sous le règne de Jacques Ier*, second edn. rev. (1971)

Day, Cyrus Lawrence, and Eleanore Boswell Murrie, *English Song-Books, 1651-1702: A Bibliography with a First-Line Index of Songs* (1940)

Daye, Anne, 'Skill and Invention in the Renaissance Ballroom', *Historical Dance* 2 (1991), 12-15

—— '"Youthful Revels, Masks, and Courtly Sights": an introductory study of the revels within the Stuart masque', *Historical Dance* 3 (1996), 5-22

Dean-Smith, Margaret, ed., *Playford's 'English Dancing-Master' 1651: A Facsimile Reprint with an Introduction, Bibliography and Notes* (1957)

Dessen, Alan C., and Leslie Thomson, *A Dictionary of Stage Directions in English Drama, 1580-1642* (1999)

Dowling, Margaret, 'The Printing of John Dowland's *Second Booke of Songs or Ayres*', *The Library*, IV, 12 (1932), 365-80

Duffin, Ross W., *Shakespeare's Songbook* (2004)

Edelman, Charles, *Brawl Ridiculous: Sword-Fighting in Shakespeare's Plays* (1992)

Fallows, David, 'The Gresley Dance Collection, c.1500', *Royal Musical Association Research Chronicle* 29 (1996), 1–20

Fellowes, Edmund H., *The English School of Lutenist Song Writers* (1922)

—— ed., *The Collected Works of William Byrd*, 20 vols (1937–50)

—— ed., *English Madrigal Verse, 1588–1632* (1920), 3rd edn. rev. by F. W. Sternfeld with David Greer (1968)

Fenlon, Iain, and John Milsom, '"Ruled Paper Imprinted": Music Paper and Patents in Sixteenth-Century England', *Journal of the American Musicological Society* 17 (1984), 139–163

Foley, John Miles, *The Singer of Tales in Performance* (1995)

Foster, Susan Leigh, 'Choreographies of Gender', *Signs* 24 (1998), 1–34

Foxley, Eric, 'Music Database', published online (2001) at www.cs.nott.ac.uk/~ef/music/index.htm

Gerschow, Frederic, 'Diary of the Journey of Philip Julius, Duke of Stettin-Pomerania, through England in the Year 1602', ed. Gottfried von Bulow, *Transactions of the Royal Historical Society* NS 6 (1892), 1–67

Gilchrist, Anne G., 'Some Additional Notes on the Traditional History of Certain Ballad-Tunes in the *Dancing Master* (1650)', *Journal of the English Folk Dance and Song Society* 3:4 (1939), 274–80

Glare, P. G. W., ed., *Oxford Latin Dictionary* (1996)

Gooch, Bryan N. S., *et al.*, *A Shakespeare Music Catalogue*, 5 vols (1991)

Gramsci, Antonio, *Letters from Prison*, tr. Lynne Lawner (1973)

Gurr, Andrew, *The Shakespearian Playing Companies* (1996)

Heartz, Daniel, *Pierre Attaingnant, Royal Printer of Music* (1969)

Henderson, H. P., 'The vocal music of John Wilson', Ph.D. dissertation, University of North Carolina (1962)

Henze, Catherine A., 'Invisible Collaboration: The Impact of Johnson's Original Music', *Text & Presentation: The Journal of the Comparative Drama Conference* 22 (2001), 75–87

Herford, C. H., and Percy and Evelyn Simpson, eds., *Ben Jonson*, 11 vols (1925–52)

Holman, Peter, *Four and Twenty Fiddlers: The Violin at the English Court 1540–1690* (1993)

Holme, Randall, *Academy of Armoury* (1688)

Hoskins, Jim, *The Dances of Shakespeare* (2005)

Howard, Skiles, *The Politics of Courtly Dancing in Early Modern England* (1998)

Hoy, Cyrus, *Introductions, Notes, and Commentaries to Texts in 'The Dramatic Works of Thomas Dekker'*, 4 vols (1980)

Johnson, Gerald D., 'John Trundle and the Book Trade 1603–1626', *Studies in Bibliography* 39 (1986), 177–99

Jonson, Ben, *Pans Anniversarie* (1620), in *Ben Jonson*, ed. Herford and Simpson, 7:529–38

Jordan, John Bryce, '"Is He No Man?": The Emergence of the Effeminate Male Dancer in English Restoration Comedy', in *Proceedings of the Society of Dance History Scholars*, ed. J. Willis (1999), 207–16

Jorgens, Elise B., *English Songs 1600–1675, Facsimiles of Twenty-six Manuscripts and an Edition of the Texts*, 12 vols (1986–89)

Jowett, John, 'Middleton's Song of Cupid', *Notes and Queries* 239 (1994), 66–70

—— 'Pre-editorial Criticism and the Space for Editing: Examples from *Richard III* and *Your Five Gallants*', in *Problems of Editing* (special issue of *Editio*), ed. Christa Jansohn and Ursula Schaefer (1999), 127–49

—— 'From Print to Performance: Looking at the Masque in *Timon of Athens*', in *From Performance to Print in Shakespeare's England*, ed. Peter Holland and Stephen Orgel (2006), 73–91

Kathman, David, 'Grocers, Goldsmiths, and Drapers: Freemen and Apprentices in the Elizabethan Theater', *Shakespeare Quarterly* 55 (2004), 1–49

Keller, Kate Van Winkle, and Genevieve Shimer, ed., *The Playford Ball: 103 early country dances 1651–1820: as interpreted by Cecil Sharp and his followers* (1990)

Kiek, Jennifer, '"We'll Have a Crash Here in the Yard": English Country Dance in early modern stage plays: an introduction' (conference paper, *On Common Ground 5: Dance in Drama, Drama in Dance* (2005), available online at www.dhds.org.uk/conference/DHDS-Kiek2005.pdf)

King, A. Hyatt, 'The Significance of John Rastell in Early Music Printing', *The Library*, V, 26 (1971), 197–214

Kracauer, Siegfried, *Theory of Film* (1960)

Krummel, D. W., 'Oblong format in early music books', *The Library*, V, 26 (1971), 312–24

—— *English Music Printing 1553–1700* (1975)

—— 'Musical Functions and Bibliographical Forms', *The Library*, V, 31 (1976), 327–50

—— and Stanley Sadie, ed., *Music Printing and Publishing* (1990)

Lakoff, George, and Mark Johnson, *Philosophy in the Flesh: The Embodied Mind and Its Challenge to Western Thought* (1999)

Lancashire, Ian, ed., *Lexicons of Early Modern English*, leme.library.utoronto.ca/

Langer, Susanne, *Feeling and Form: A Theory of Art Developed from Philosophy in a New Key* (1953)

Leaver, Robin A., 'John Marbecke', *Grove Music Online*, ed. L. Macy (accessed 22 June 2007), www.grovemusic.com

Lecoq, Jacques, *Le Corps poétique* (1997), translated by Simon McBurney as *The Moving Body: Teaching Creative Theatre* (2000)

Lefkowitz, Murray, *William Lawes* (1960)

—— *Trois Masques à la cour de Charles Ier d'Angleterre* (1970)

Lewis, Mary S., *Antonio Gardano, Venetian Music Printer, 1538–1569*, 2 vols (1988–1997)

Lindenbaum, Peter, 'John Playford: Music and Politics in the Interregnum', *Huntington Library Quarterly* 64 (2001), 124–38

Livingston, Carole Rose, *British Broadside Ballads of the Sixteenth Century: A Catalogue of the Extant Sheets and an Essay* (1991)

Long, John H., *Shakespeare's Use of Music: The Histories and Tragedies* (1971)

Love, Harold, *Scribal Publication in Seventeenth-Century England* (1993)

Lyotard, Jean-François, 'How Can the Mind Participate in Communication?', in *Materialities of Communication*, ed. Hans Ulrich Gumbrecht and K. Ludwig Pfeiffer, tr. William Wobrey (1991), 286–302

Marlow, Richard, ed., *Giles & Richard Farnaby: Keyboard Music*, Musica Britannica, vol. 24 (1974)

Mathiesen, Thomas J., ed., *Thesaurus Musicarum Latinarum*, accessed 22 June 2007, www.chmtl.indiana.edu/tml

McGee, C. E., and Meagher, John C., 'Preliminary Checklist of Tudor and Stuart Entertainments 1514–1625', *Research Opportunities in Renaissance Drama* 30 (1988), 1–128

Maynard, Winifred, *Elizabethan Lyric Poetry and its Music* (1986)

Mellers, Wilfrid, *Harmonious Meeting: A Study of the Relationship between English Music, Poetry, and Theatre, 1600–1900* (1965)

Middleton, Thomas, *The Inner-Temple Masque: The Masque of Heroes*, ed. R. C. Bald, in *A Book of Masques, in Honour of Allardyce Nicoll* (1967), ed. T. J. B. Spencer and Stanley Wells, 251–274

Milsom, John, 'Songs and Society in Early Tudor London', *Early Music History* 16 (1997), 235–93

—— 'Music', in *The Cambridge History of the Book in Britain, Volume III: 1400–1557*, ed. Lotte Hellinga and J. B. Trapp (1999), 541–54

Monaco, Davide, *La scherma salentina…a memoria d'uomo: dalla pazziata alla danza scherma* (2006)

Monthland, Valerie, *Dance Words* (1995)

Mooney, Michael E., '"The Common Sight" and Dramatic Form: Rowley's Embedded Jig in *A Faire Quarrel*', *Studies in English Literature* 20 (1980), 305–23

Morley, Thomas, *A Plaine and Easie Introduction to Practicall Musicke*, facs. reprint., ed. R. A. Harman (1937)

—— *The First Book of Consort Lessons*, ed. Sydney Beck (1959)

Nevile, Jennifer, 'Dance in Early Tudor England: An Italian Connection?', *Early Music* 26 (1998), 230–44

Newton, Richard, 'English Lute Music of the Golden Age', *Proceedings of the Royal Musical Association* 45 (1938–9), 63–90

Palmer, Jane, 'Music at the Lord Mayor of London's triumphs, 1604–1708', Ph.D. dissertation, University of London (1994)

Payne, Ian, *The Almain in Britain, c.1549–c.1675: A Dance Manual from Manuscript Sources* (2003)

Phelan, Peggy, 'Dance and the History of Hysteria', in *Corporealities: Dancing, Knowledge, Culture, and Power*, ed. Susan Leigh Foster (1996), 90–105

Picart, Caroline Joan S., *From Ballroom to DanceSport: Aesthetics, Athletics, and Body Culture* (2006)

Plomer, H. R., 'Pleadings in a Theatrical Lawsuit. From the Records of the Court of Requests. John Rastell *v.* Henry Walton', in A. W. Pollard, ed., *Fifteenth Century Poetry and Prose*, 2 vols (1903), 1:307–21

Pogue, Samuel, *Jaques Moderne: Lyons Music Printer of the Sixteenth Century* (1969)

Price, David C., *Patrons and Musicians of the English Renaissance* (1981)

Pryer, Anthony, 'Notation', in Denis Arnold, ed., *The New Oxford Companion to Music*, 2 vols (1983), 1247–68

Pulver, Jeffrey, *A Biographical Dictionary of Old English Music* (1927)

Rastell, Richard, *The Notation of Western Music: An Introduction* (1983)

Ravelhofer, Barbara, *The Early Stuart Masque: Dance, Costume, and Music* (2006)

Ravenscroft, Thomas, *Pammelia, Deuteromelia,* and *Melismata*, facsimile edn. of the American Folklore Society, Inc., vol. XII, ed. by MacEdward Leach and with an Introduction by Matthias A. Shaaber (1961)

Robertson, Jean, and D. J. Gordon, *A Calendar of Dramatic Records in the Books of the Livery Companies of London 1485–1640*, Malone Society *Collections* III (1954)

Robinson, Richard, 'Tunebook', published online (2007) at www.leeds.ac.uk/music/Info/RRTuneBk/tunebook.html

Rollins, Hyder E., 'The Black-Letter Broadside Ballad', *PMLA* 34 (1919), 258–339

Sabol, Andrew J., 'Ravenscroft's *Melismata* and the Children of Paul's', *Renaissance News* 12 (1959), 3–9

—— *Four Hundred Songs and Dances from the Stuart Masque* (1978); reprinted with 'A Supplement of Sixteen Pieces' (1982)

—— *A Score for Thomas Campion's 'The Lords' Masque'* (1993)

Schanzer, Ernest, 'Thomas Platter's Observations on the Elizabethan Stage', *Notes and Queries* 201 (1956), 465–7

Schoenbaum, Samuel, '*The Revenger's Tragedy*: Jacobean Dance of Death', *Modern Language Quarterly* 15 (1954), 201–7

Seligmann, Raphael, 'The Functions of Song in the Plays of Thomas Middleton', Ph.D. dissertation, Brandeis University (1997)

—— 'With a Sword by Her Side and a Lute in Her Lap: Moll Cutpurse at the Fortune', in *Musical Voices of Early Modern Women: Many-Headed Melodies*, ed. Thomasin LaMay (2005), 187–211

Simpson, Claude M., *The British Broadside Ballad and Its Music* (1966)

Skantze, P. A., *Stillness in Motion in the Seventeenth-Century Theatre* (2003)

Smith, Bruce, *The Acoustic World of Early Modern England: Attending to the O-Factor* (1999)

—— 'E/loco/com/motion', in *From Script to Stage in Early Modern England*, ed. Peter Holland and Stephen Orgel (2004), 131–50

Smith, Jeremy L., *Thomas East and Music Publishing in Renaissance England* (2003)

Sparti, Barbara, ed. and tr., *De Pratica Seu Arte Tripudii | On the Practice or Art of Dancing* by Guglielmo Ebreo of Pesaro (1993)

Spencer, Robert, ed., *The Board Lute Book*, with an introductory study and guide to concordances (1976)

—— ed., *The Marsh Lute Book, c.1595*, with an introductory study and guide to concordances (1981)

—— ed., *Jane Pickeringe's Lute Book*, with an introductory study and guide to concordances (1985)

Spink, Ian, ed., *English Songs, 1625–1660*, Musica Britannica, vol. 33 (1971)

—— *English Song, Dowland to Purcell* (1974)

Spring, Matthew, *The Lute in Britain: A History of the Instrument and its Music* (2001)

St Clair, William, *The Reading Nation in the Romantic Period* (2004)

Steele, Robert, *The Earliest English Music Printing: A Description and Bibliography of English Printed Music to the Close of the Sixteenth Century* (1903)

Stern, Tiffany, 'Re-patching the Play', in *From Script to Stage in Early Modern England*, ed. Peter Holland and Stephen Orgel (2004), 151–77

Sutherland, Sarah P., *Masques in Jacobean Tragedy* (1983)

Taylor, Gary, 'The Structure of Performance: Act-Intervals in the London Theatres, 1576–1642', in Taylor and Jowett (1993), 3–50

—— 'Farrago', *Textual Practice* 8 (1994), 33–42

—— *Cultural Selection* (1996)

—— 'Feeling Bodies', in *Shakespeare in the Twentieth Century: Proceedings of the Sixth World Shakespeare Congress*, ed. Jonathan Bate *et al.* (1998), 258–79

—— 'Divine [ ]sences', *Shakespeare Survey* 54 (2001), 13–30

—— 'Middleton, Habsburg, and Stuart: *The Spanish Gypsy* and *A Game at Chess*', *SEDERI* 18 (2008), forthcoming

—— and John Jowett, *Shakespeare Reshaped 1606–1623* (1993)

Thompson, Robert P., 'English music manuscripts and the fine paper trade, 1648–1688', Ph.D. dissertation, University of London (1988)

—— 'Manuscript Music in Purcell's London', *Early Music* 23 (1995), 615–18

—— 'Paper in English Music Manuscripts: 1620–1645', in Ashbee (1998), 143–54

Tricomi, Albert H., *Anticourt Drama in England 1603–1642* (1989)

Walls, Peter, *Music in the English Courtly Masque 1604–1640* (1996)

Ward, John M., 'Apropos "The British Broadside Ballad and its Music"', *Journal of the American Musicological Society* 20 (1967), 28–86

—— 'Newly Devis'd Measures for Jacobean Masques', *Acta Musicologica* 60 (1988), 135-42

Watt, Tessa, *Cheap Print and Popular Piety, 1550-1640* (1991)

Wells, Evelyn Kendrick, 'Playford Tunes and Broadside Ballads', *Journal of the English Folk Dance and Song Society* 3:3 (1938), 195-202

Whitlocke, Keith, 'John Playford's *The English Dancing Master* 1650/51 as Cultural Politics', *Folk Music Journal* 7 (1999), 548-78

Williams, Franklin B., Jr., 'Renaissance Names in Masquerade', *PMLA* 69.1 (1954), 314-23

Wilson, John, *Cheerfull Ayres or Ballads first composed for one single Voice and since set for three Voyces* (1660)

Wood, Julia K., 'William Lawes's Music for Plays', in Ashbee (1998), 11-67

Woodbridge, Linda, 'Patchwork: Piecing the Early Modern Mind in England's First Century of Print Culture', *English Literary Renaissance* 23 (1993), 5-45

Woodfill, Walter L., *Musicians in English Society* (1953)

Wulstan, David, 'The Earliest Musical Notation', *Music & Letters* 52 (1971), 365-82

Würzbach, Natascha, *The Rise of the English Street Ballad, 1550-1650*, trans. Gayna Walls (1990)

Yachnin, Paul, '*A Game at Chess* and Chess Allegory', *Studies in English Literature, 1500-1900* 22 (1982), 317-30

THOMAS MIDDLETON, UNCUT: CASTRATION, CENSORSHIP, AND THE REGULATION OF DRAMATIC DISCOURSE IN EARLY MODERN ENGLAND

Richard Burt

THOMAS MIDDLETON's canon and career present us with quantitatively significant and highly detailed evidence of censorship. Perhaps the best known case of censorship, *A Game at Chess*, continues to receive the most sustained attention of any play censored in the Renaissance. Middleton's *Lady's Tragedy* was also censored. And two other plays, *Hengist, King of Kent* and *The Witch*, may have been censored as well.[1] More crucial than these instances is that the cases themselves are often extremely detailed. There are six manuscripts and three printed quartos of *A Game at Chess*, the total number of manuscripts being significantly larger than that of any other Renaissance play. And the single manuscript of *The Lady's Tragedy* contains evidence of censorship in the censor's own hand. Moreover, there is an unusually full record of contemporary responses to *A Game at Chess*, including a lengthy eyewitness account.[2]

Through Middleton, I want to suggest, we may gain a fuller understanding of how censorship operated and thereby reshape the present debate about it: some critics have argued that censorship was a systematic and fully conscious contractual arrangement; others have argued that it was capricious and arbitrary. Similarly, some have seen the theatre as a prime site of censorship, while others have seen it as exceptional in relation to the censorship of other media. And some have concluded that theatre censorship was severely repressive, while others have argued that it was enlightened, tolerant, and virtually non-existent (Heinemann, 1980; Patterson, 1984; Finkelpearl, 1986; Sharpe, 1987; Worden, 1988; Clare, 1990; Dutton, 1991).

Middleton's contribution to the present debate over whether stage censorship was repressive or lenient lies in the way he forces us to pose a fundamental question that critics have not asked: namely, 'What is censorship?' When debating the relative repressiveness or leniency, efficiency or inefficiency of theatre censorship, critics have largely ignored the way that the similarity between censorship and noncensorship puts the definition of censorship into question, instead assuming that it operates in terms of *removal* and *replacement*; that is, the censor demands cuts from the text and the author or an editor seeks to circumvent the censor by replacing the cut material. Censorship is implicitly defined as a

strictly repressive activity centred in the court and implicitly opposed to the antithetical practice of uncensoring. Within the terms of this model, Middleton is thought to document either cases of radical censorship or, conversely, instances of what Annabel Patterson calls 'those famous puzzling cases of *noncensorship*' (1984, 17).[3] By contrast, I suggest that Middleton's contradictory cases of censorship and noncensorship present us with a more complex and nuanced model of censorship involving *dispersal* and *displacement*. In this model, the difference between censoring and uncensoring is never self-evident.

A quick review of the production and reception of *A Game at Chess* makes this paradox clear. The play was first licensed by the court censor (the Master of the Revels), ran nine days continuously, and was then shut down. Middleton was 'on the run' for some (unknown) time in a failed effort to escape the authorities and was imprisoned for some (unknown) time. The company that acted *A Game at Chess* was briefly prevented from performing. Middleton obtained his release from prison through a witty epigram to King James.[4] He may or may not have been forbidden to write for the stage again. And, remarkably, the company went on to perform *The Spanish Viceroy*, a play on the same subject, without a licence the following year (for which they received no punishment at

---

[1] On *Hengist*, see Bald (1938), and Grace Ioppolo's introduction elsewhere in this edition: *Works*, 1448. On *The Witch*, see Anne Lancashire (1983).

[2] For documentation of these cases, see Bentley, 1941–68, 4:870–7, Gary Taylor's edition of *A Game at Chess* (*Works*, 1825), and Julia Briggs's edition of *The Lady's Tragedy* (*Works*, 833). For the audience response to *A Game at Chess*, see Appendix A of Howard-Hill (1993).

[3] For the case that the play was censored, see Heinemann, 1980. For the opposite case, Patterson (1984, 17) and Howard-Hill (1993, 22). Patterson cites *A Game at Chess* as one of her examples of noncensorship cases. Janet Clare (1990, 198) and Richard Dutton (1991, 237) have confirmed her point. Even Heinemann wonders along similar lines: 'The question remains: given the censorship, how was it possible for the play to be put on at all?' (1980, 165). For further details, see Howard-Hill, who maintains that 'the official reaction to *A Game at Chess* was not harsh' (1993, 22). For an opposing account of the play and of Middleton's career, one that stresses Middleton's progressive politics, see Gary Taylor (1993a).

[4] Those who believe that theatre censorship was repressive might point out that Middleton did not write for the stage after *A Game at Chess*; that his entertainment for Charles I (paid for by the City of London) was cancelled might be taken as further proof of Middleton's lack of favour with the court. But Trevor Howard-Hill quotes (without endorsing) the rumour that 'James, Charles and Buckingham "were all loth to haue it forbidden, and by report laught hartely at it"...and [John Woolley] later passed on the rumour "(how true it is I know not) that the Players are gone to the Courte to Act the game at Chesse before the Kinge, which doth much truble the spanish Amb*ass*ador"....' (22).

all). Middleton continued to receive patronage from the City of London. Moreover, *A Game at Chess* was printed (albeit illegally) in 1625, nine months after the banned performance. The asymmetry between the play's major political transgression and the leniency, the near absence, of repressive consequences suffered by the written text and actors, and the uncertain extent of the penalties suffered by the author, makes the case one that can as easily be called censorship as it can noncensorship.[5]

This ambiguity is a symptom, I believe, of the way early modern stage censorship was dispersed among a variety of regulatory agents and practices and of the fact that it was productive as well as prohibitive, involved cultural legitimation as well as delegitimation.[6] Censorship was more than one thing, occurred at more than one place, and at more than one time. Moreover, Middleton's case allows us to see that texts were displaced from one channel or medium to another (say from print to manuscript or performance to print) not obliterated wholesale. Even an apparently destructive act like a book-burning could be understood as a symbolic rite of purification rather than an attempt to block access to forbidden books completely.[7] Middleton offers, then, less a way of deciding whether particular cases can be classified as either censorship or noncensorship than a call for a more deconstructive definition of censorship, one in which the spatial and temporal location and limits of censorship come into question, in which censorship and editorial revision and literary criticism, censorship and noncensorship, cannot be rigorously distinguished.

Defining censorship in terms of displacement and dispersal displaces and absorbs, so to speak, a definition of censorship as removal and replacement. It is both an alternative categorization and a more inclusive one, both an opposition and an expansion. On the one hand, a dispersal and displacement model of censorship keeps in place a sense of the graduated differences between forms of punishment and repression (between having a hand removed and having a word removed), with 'soft' forms of censorship (like critical censure) at one end of a continuum and 'hard' forms of censorship (like imprisonment) at the other. Yet on the other hand, a dispersal and displacement model unsettles a traditional hierarchy of more or less repressive punishments in so far as it shows that no one form of legitimation or delegitimation necessarily has priority over others. Cultural capital may in some cases count more than economic capital; perhaps even more provocatively, one could say that 'soft' forms of censure may sometimes wound more deeply than 'hard' forms of censorship. More crucially, displacement yokes, often paradoxically, precisely those terms that the more traditional model wishes to oppose: repression and diversity; production and consumption; censoring and uncensoring; public and private, among others.

In discussing the details of Middleton's cases of censorship, fetishism becomes a key term in my analysis of the way censorship permits or blocks entry and access to the literary field. I suggest that censoring is a version of the fetishizing critical practice Naomi Schor (1987) has termed 'reading in detail'. Middleton presents us with what might be called a *fetishized* model of textual culture. In calling censorship fetishistic, I mean that it involves the negotiation and construction of small differences which make the text desirable (either because it is the uncensored version or because it is the censored version).[8] Fetishism involves a mainstreaming practice that increases possibilities for entry and access to the literary field yet, at the same time, allows texts entry not as uncensored wholes (or forbids them entry as censored wholes) but as partial, always already censored versions whose value is constituted by (and which accrues from) their small differences from other versions. In the second part, I explore the possibility of alternative defetishized models of textual culture, ones that would oppose a phallic, patriarchal model of textual production, transmission, and consumption to a feminized, clitoral model or to a sodomitical model. I turn specifically to Middleton's *Game at Chess* in this regard because it thematizes censorship as castration. Understanding censorship through the metaphor of castration, we will see, means that a desire for an uncensored radical politics will inevitably be disappointed.

I

Since it may seem counter-intuitive to think of censorship in terms of dispersal and displacement, let me begin by calling attention to the limitations of the removal and replacement model. This approach assumes a model of textual transmission in which censorship is clearly located in the court censor, or Master of the Revels, as he was known. In this model the process of submitting a theatre manuscript (playbook) to the court censor for licensing would be fairly straightforward. One could trace a line from the text's beginnings to its endings, from plot to foul papers to authorial or scribal promptbook to a licensed promptbook (private transcripts may have been made from the foul papers or from promptbooks) to performance to acquisition by a publisher or printer, then to a compositor (who sets the type and makes corrections), to the printing of the first edition and on possibly to later editions and/or to a theatrical revival and resubmission of the promptbook

[5] For fuller accounts of this case, see Howard-Hill (1993), Clare (1990), Dutton (1991), and Dutton (2001).

[6] For a fuller account of this definition of censorship, see Burt (1993), ix–xv; 1–25; 150–68, Burt (1994b), and Bourdieu (1991). See Francis Barker (1984) for a Foucauldian account of censorship, and see Patterson (1984, 1990) and Norbrook (1994) for an opposing humanist account. See also Post (1998), Hadfield (2001), Clegg (2001), and Müller (2003).

[7] See, for example, a print in John Foxe's *Actes and monuments...* (1563) illustrating the burning of heretical books written by Martin Bucer. At the centre of the illustration is a pile of books being burned. In front of this pile is a procession of priests reading religious books accompanied by torch bearers. As in executions, the burning is a public performance: fire takes on metaphoric significance, not only as a purifying agent (destroying the corrupting influences of heretical books) but as a source of religious illumination—the tapers 'light the way', as it were, toward the true Church and its authorized books.

[8] For a psychoanalytic account of fetishism, see Sigmund Freud (1963). On fetishism and displacement, see Freud (1969) and Mark Wigley (1992). For sympathetic and hostile feminist revisions of Freud's account of fetishism, see Apter (1991); Apter and Pietz (1993); Freedman (1991); Groz (1991); Garber (1991); and McClintock (1993).

for licensing.[9] In this view, censorship is a specific form of intervention and interference in an otherwise clearly transmitted set of signals from the theatre company to the audience: the censor is granted a central kind of interference or imposition, significantly different from the kind of interference introduced, for example, by a printer, whose mistakes could be corrected at will. The underlying assumption here is that the court censor is at the apex and centre of transmission: he would read a manuscript and then assess it positively or negatively, either burning it or licensing it as submitted (or on condition that it be revised). Censorship is understood, then, as a clearly defined (in the sense of limited) activity, located in time and space.

This understanding of censorship is not entirely wrong, of course. The Master of the Revels licensed a text by signing his name and giving his authorization at the end of the text. He had punitive powers and exercised them. In at least one case, he burned a manuscript he was unwilling to license; he demanded that some texts be revised; and one Master, Sir Henry Herbert, threatened authors, theatre managers, and actors with 'publique punishment' (Bawcutt, 1996, 52). The censor's powers were increasingly centralized after 1606. Whereas early in Middleton's career there were a number of censors, including the Bishops of London and dramatists like John Lyly, by the time of his last play, *A Game at Chess*, there was a single court official and his deputies. The (apparent) intervention of the Bishop of London in *Sir John Van Olden Barnavelt* in 1619 is the exception that proves the rule. The Master also put into practice the *Acte to Restraine Abuses of Players*, passed by Parliament in 1606, making it illegal 'jestingly or prophanely [to] speak or use the Holy name of God or Jesus Christ, or of the Holy Ghoste or of the Trinity, which are not to be spoken but with fear and reverence' (Chambers, 1923, Vol. 4, 339).

A closer look at the evidence begins to complicate the assumption that censorship has a precisely defined location and definition. Consider the manuscript of *The Lady's Tragedy*. One sees a number of different markings and a number of different handwritings. Not all of the cuts are in the Master's hand. Some are by the bookkeeper, some by the scribe. Sir George Buc, the Master of the Revels, has, for example, 'struck out a number of oaths in the manuscript, but the specifically Catholic oath "By th' mass" (4.3.94) uttered by the Tyrant, has been deleted by a different hand' (Clare, 1990, 158). Similarly, a wavy line alongside the passage signifies its removal, although again the colour of the ink does not link the instruction directly with Buc. Janet Clare concludes that the cuts and marks imply 'a degree of collaboration between the censor and the playhouse bookkeeper' (1991, 159). She maintains that the manuscript provides 'clear evidence that plays were censored in the playhouse, either in anticipation of the [court] censor's objections or in response to his verbal instructions' (1990, 157). This play is not by any means an exceptional case. *Hengist* evinces a similar dispersal. As R. C. Bald comments, it is unclear whether the play has been censored at all: the cuts may have been made by the actors rather than by the censor (1938, xxx–xxxiii). More recently, Grace Ioppolo in the present edition doubts whether the cuts can be attributed to censorship.

To buttress Clare's point about collaboration, we could add that dramatists might function as censors in the repressive sense. In a discussion of the *Acte to Restraine Abuses of Players*, Gary Taylor (1993b, 51–106) points out that when a text has been expurgated, the source of that expurgation is almost always the theatre. One might infer from the low number of oaths in the Middleton canon, much lower than Shakespeare, that Middleton acted as a self-censor (Lake, 1975, 79). The existence of collaboration is further confirmed by the fact that the Master of the Revels did not double-check to make sure that the acting company had made the revisions he requested. He could rely on the company to obey him, and they generally did (Dutton, 1991, 203).

Thus, censorship was dispersed, not centred in the court, despite the increasing centralization of the Master of the Revels' powers. However much power the Master amassed, that power remained partly decentred by its dispersal even at court and within the Office itself. There were always ecclesiastical censors, and the Revels office had deputies (Clare, 1990; Dutton, 1991; Martin Butler, 1992). In addition to the playhouse exchanges with the Master of the Revels, we could locate the Master himself in patronage faction struggles, as Richard Dutton has pointed out (1991, 247–8). Furthermore, the *Acte to Restraine Abuses of Players* dispersed censorship across all areas of theatrical production and reception in which actors as well as members of the audience could serve as spies and informers (anyone convicted would pay a fine of ten pounds).[10] (The use of spies and informers formed part of a larger pattern of administrative dispersal in early Stuart culture.[11]) And individuals sometimes successfully sued for libel, managing to shut down performances (Clare, 1990, 74; 92–3).

My point that censorship is dispersed confirms a current consensus among critics working on early modern theatre censorship that it operated in terms of complicity and collaboration between censors, authors, and critics rather than in terms of radical oppositions between dumb censors and intelligent literary writers.[12] Richard Dutton has observed that court censorship of the theatre was neither authoritarian nor totalitarian (1991, 205; 217). If the dispersal of censorship meant collaboration and complicity, the question remains: does it alter our understanding of censorship? The fact that censorship was dispersed, some might argue, does not (and should not) significantly alter our sense of it as a repressive practice. Instead, we have

---

[9] A version of this model is described by Gary Taylor (1987).
[10] On spying and the theatre, see Archer (1993).
[11] On this pattern, see Linda Levy Peck (1982).
[12] Patterson's (1984) contribution is perhaps strongest in this regard. She has been seconded directly by Richard Dutton (1991, 9) and indirectly by Natalie Zemon Davis (1990) and Robert Darnton (1991).

only a more rigorous, more nuanced conception of it: censorship remains externally imposed by the court censor and internally self-imposed (as self-censorship) when undertaken by anyone else. Furthermore, censorship would still be located temporally, occurring either before or after performance or publication. That is to say, we would still have a stable model of censorship, one that places it on one side of an axis moving between the opposite poles of repression and freedom, one that opposes agencies and clearly demarcated discursive spaces, one that believes dramatists could choose to collaborate or to resist.

I want to suggest that Middleton presents us with a much deeper sense of collaboration and complicity, one that extends to all points of the agencies and practices of literary consumption and production and thereby calls into question a strict definition of censorship as repression, one that enables censorship to be clearly opposed to noncensorship. Censorship penetrates and is penetrated by literary consumption and production. In defining censorship to encompass state censorship, market censorship, and criticism, I mean that instances of obtrusive suppression belong to a continuum which also includes active support or patronage, as in the support Middleton received from the city for his civic entertainments, or his masques.[13] Criticism, for example, may be regarded not as the antithesis of censorship but as an alternate form of censorship. Criticism is a form of censorship in so far as it involves legitimating certain dramatic discourses and delegitimating others. Criticism operates productively in terms of establishing exclusive hierarchies and repressively as censure (the aim being a kind of post-publication censorship) in order to secure these hierarchies. In the productive sense, criticism, as a form of patronage, establishes capital through élitist forms of censorship: the exclusiveness of a given performance is part of its appeal. The non-alienability of a court masque, say, helps create a sense of the court as the charismatic centre of power.[14]

Consider again the manuscript of *The Lady's Tragedy*. It might appear to provide incontrovertible evidence of censorship in the repressive sense of removal. Crosses and wavy lines, that is, mark passages that the court censor demands be deleted. But things are not all that simple. Take the much discussed change from 'most ladies' to 'many ladies' (Lancashire, 1978, 47; Clare, 1990, 161; Dutton, 1991, 198). What the censor wants removed—'most'—is replaced by the scribe/author/bookkeeper with an alternative—'many'—that is nearly synonymous.[15] Similarly, the tyrant's line 'Your king's poisoned' is changed to the virtually synonymous 'I am poisoned' (A5.2.168/B5.2.143):

And how either of these examples of censorship differ from revision is hard to tell. The marking of a change in the last line of the play from 'Might all be borne so honest to their tombs' to 'Might all be borne so virtuous to their tombs'

looks just like the marking used to change 'Your king's poisoned' to 'I am poisoned' (A5.2.213/B5.2.164):[16]

These examples return us to the ambiguous way a case looks like censorship to some critics and like noncensorship to others. Critics have recently tried to explain the difference between 'most ladies' and 'many ladies' in terms of a specific topical allusion to the Jacobean court that focused on Lady Frances Howard, who divorced her first husband on grounds of non-consummation and who along with her second husband murdered Sir Thomas Overbury (Lancashire, 1978, 47, 276–7; Clare, 1991, 161; Dutton, 1991, 198).

While I would not want to rule out that possibility (though this particular topical allusion has been used to explain the censorship of a surprisingly large number of plays, including Middleton's *Witch*) I think the manuscript shows that the censor's revision cannot be decisively differentiated from theatrical revision in terms of its verbal outcomes.[17] As one editor notes, not all of the marks necessarily suggest censorship, some marking theatrical revision (Lancashire, 1978, 280–1). My point is that this lack of difference suggests that the censor operated productively as a kind of editor. The change from 'most ladies' to the less pointed 'many' softens but, I would argue, hardly neutralizes the topical allusion since in both cases 'ladies' remains as a figure for court corruption. The censor has asked for an editorial revision that involves a fine degree of tact.[18] Editing and censorship thus overlap. And from the fact that the same marks were used by the censor and by actors/authors/bookkeepers in the playhouse we may surmise that censorship and theatrical revision were understood as parallel, complementary activities, not as opposed or different in kind.

Understanding that the censor functioned as an editor allows us, then, to begin to understand the ways in which censorship is structurally complicit with what is

---

[13] Middleton's court patronage can be reviewed in Kawachi (1986).

[14] On the breakdown of a distinction between the masque as inalienable and public theatrical performances of dramatic texts as alienable under the early Stuarts, see Burt (1993, 115–49).

[15] Gary Taylor (1993a) finds similar synonyms in expurgated and non-expurgated oaths in Shakespeare editions.

[16] One could contrast these examples as soft and hard versions of censorship, the revision of 'Your king's poisoned' to 'I am poisoned' regarded as more serious than the revision of 'most' to 'many' because it is more directly political. I would observe, however, that in both cases the displacement of one phrase by another complicates the degree to which soft and hard instances may function smoothly as acceptable replacements. Consider again the substitution of women for court politics. Anne Lancashire notes 'the odd substitution of "woman" for "courtier"' at A2.1.69/B2.1.75, which she points out 'removes one kind of criticism only to add the other' (1978, 277).

[17] Lancashire (1978) uses it to explain censorship of *The Lady's Tragedy* and (1984) to explain censorship of *The Witch*. The same allusion has been used to interpret *The Changeling* as well. See Cristina Malcolmson (1990, 333). As will become clear in the second section of this essay, I think the underlying premises of this kind of topical identification bear scrutiny.

[18] 'Woman' also figures as an object of censorship in *Hengist*: the passage at 4.2.225–32 appears in the two manuscripts but was omitted from the printed edition. See Heinemann (1980, 144).

often taken to be its opposite, namely, criticism.[19] The Master chose plays for performance, and was therefore an extraordinarily important critic as well as a censor: what he liked and thought highly of would get performed at court. As an editor, the censor reads critically in detail. We can adduce further evidence of the censor's critical abilities and interests. It is worth pointing out that George Buc, himself an author and owner of an impressive library, gave *The Lady's Tragedy* the title *The Second Maiden's Tragedy* to differentiate it from Beaumont and Fletcher's (also censored) *The Maid's Tragedy* (Clare, 1990, 165). John Lyly and Ben Jonson both sought to become Master of the Revels (Jonson obtained a reversion to it in 1624). And Sir Henry Herbert (Master of the Revels after George Buc) wrote the following in 1624 in regard to a court performance of Middleton's *More Dissemblers Besides Women*: 'The worst play that ere I saw' (Bawcutt, 1996, 148). Censorship and criticism are complicit, then, in the sense that they are overlapping activities.

Just as literary criticism turns out to be a form of censorship, so too does the market. It is often assumed that court censorship is radically different from market forces. The market is thought to allow into circulation that which censorship seeks to block. And if one allows for market censorship, it is often differentiated from state censorship on the grounds that the former blocks production while the other blocks consumption. In this view, market censorship is better than state censorship. But even this distinction breaks down because it is not always easy to tell the two kinds of censorship apart. Middleton's tragicomedy *The Witch* illustrates the ambiguity by showing that it is difficult to differentiate a censorious reception on the stage from a censorship practised by the court. *The Witch* exists only in a single manuscript and the evidence of its production on stage is a note by Middleton on it. Middleton explains to Thomas Holmes, the person for whom the manuscript was made, that he has '(meerly uppon a tast of yor. desire) recouverd into my hands (though not without much difficultie) This (ignorantly-ill-fated) Labour of mine. Witches are (ipso facto) by ye Law condemned, & yt onely (I thinck) hath made her lie so long in an imprisoned obscuritie' (Steen, 1993, 36). Anne Lancashire has suggested that the phrase 'ignorantly ill-fated' refers not to the play's failure on the stage, as is frequently assumed, but to its political censorship by the Master of the Revels (1983, 162-3). By contrast, I would argue that the phrase is ambiguous: it may be taken literally or metaphorically, the play's lack of stage productions being due to censorship by the court or to what was termed 'censureship' on the public stage.[20]

We can understand further the way that censorship extends to the regulation of consumption by looking at Middleton's reception by competing dramatists. Criticism operated repressively as delegitimating censure. Ben Jonson and George Chapman, who sought to establish literary hierarchies as a way of reforming what they took to be the unacceptable diversity of the popular theatres, regarded

Middleton negatively. In his epistle to his translation of Homer, Chapman used Middleton as an example of Londoners' bad taste. They preferred Middleton's Lord Mayor's pageant, *The Triumphs of Truth*, to Homer: 'why should a poor Chroonicler of a Lord Maior's naked *Truth*, (that peradduenture will last his yeare) include more worth with our moderne wizards, then *Homer* for his naked *Vlysses*, clad in eternall Fiction?' (Steen, 1993, 30-1). Ben Jonson was even more censorious. In *Conversations with Drummond* (1619), he remarks 'that Markham (who added his English Arcadia) was not of the number of the Faithful Poets and but a base fellow that such were Day and Middleton' (cited by Steen, 1993, 35). And Jonson excoriated *A Game at Chess* in *The Staple of News* (1626):

> Lic. What newes of *Gundomar?* Tho. A second *Fistula*,
> Or an *excoriation* (at the least)
> For putting the poore *English-play*, was writ of him,
> To such a sordid vse, as (is said) he did,
> Of cleansing his *posterior's*. Lic. Iustice! Iustice!
> > Tho. Since when, he liues condemn'd to his [chair], at *Bruxels*.
> And there sits filing certaine politique hinges,
> To hang the *States* on, h'has heau'd off the hookes.

> (Howard-Hill, 1993, 212)

The use of a text for toilet paper is as effective a means of taking it out of circulation as burning it. It is worth noting that Middleton too engaged in critical practices. He wrote a commendatory poem to accompany the first publication of *The Duchess of Malfi* and an epitaph on the actor Richard Burbage. Furthermore, references to plays are scattered throughout his dramatic and non-dramatic works. He offered an appreciation of Joseph Hall in the prefatory matter to *The Two Gates of Salvation* (1609) and praised *Utopia* in *The Owl's Almanac* (1618).

Just as the opposition between censoring and uncensoring is troubled by the dispersal of censorship across all aspects of literary consumption, so too is it troubled by its dispersal across all areas of literary production. A number of critics have recently called into question the notion of an original unrevised authentic draft.[21] Texts are revised versions originating out of impure, heteroglossic conversations. Though some manuscripts may rightly be identified as 'authorial' for editorial purposes, there is no unrevised *Urtext* originating out of a single author sitting in his private study.

Middleton allows us to extend this insight into authorial revision to censorship: if texts cannot be unrevised, they cannot be uncensored either. The differences among some of the manuscripts of *A Game at Chess* make it clear that just as there is no point at which one can locate an

---

[19] For a fuller account of the relation between criticism and censorship, see Burt (1993, 27-77) and Burt (1994b).
[20] For instances of *censureship* and for an account of the way its meaning overlapped with *censorship* and *criticism*, see Burt (1993), 30-1, 53, 65.
[21] See Stephen Orgel (1988); Leah Marcus (1988, 1992); Gary Taylor (1993a).

CASTRATION, CENSORSHIP, AND THE REGULATION OF DRAMATIC DISCOURSE

unrevised text, so there is no point at which one can locate an uncensored text. In discussing the lengths of various manuscripts, critics have differentiated between more or less complete versions of the play in terms of whether passages in one version not in another were added after the play was licensed and, if so, whether the censor knew of them or not (Clare, 1990, 193-4; Dutton, 1991; Howard-Hill, 1993, 29-33). The censorship of the play, that is, only makes sense for these critics if at some point in the production of the play, the author/actors circumvented the censor's wishes. They assume that authorial/theatrical revision can be separated from censorship, that Middleton, at the actor's instigation, revised in order to add passages that he feared the censor might not approve (similarly, the actors might have made clear an equation between the hated Spanish Ambassador Gondomar and the Black Knight by using Gondomar's actual litter—required to relieve discomfort from an anal fistula—and one of his actual suits, thereby changing the text's meaning in a way that the court censor presumably could not have anticipated). One critic has used textual evidence to explain the censorship of the play in precisely these terms: 'it is almost certain that the play book which Henry Herbert licensed was somewhat less provocative than the play seen on the stage of the Globe' (Clare, 1990, 193).

But given the complicity between the playhouse and the Master of the Revels, there is no reason to assume that the additions amounted to an evasion of what are presumed to be the censor's politically more conservative desires. As Trevor Howard-Hill points out, 'It is unlikely that the actors would commission a substantial revision unless they were already convinced they could go ahead with performances' (1993, 18). He maintains that the additions make no serious difference: 'That the Black Knight represents Gondomar is transparent in the early version; the additions make the satire no more offensive than it was in the manuscript Herbert approved' (1993, 19). He adds that 'It is possible that Herbert himself might have encouraged enlargement of the satirical depiction of Gondomar' (1993, 32). Indeed, the revisions may have been corrections by the Master of the Revels (1993, 19). In any case, the actors maintained that they had not performed more than had been licensed. When the Privy Council demanded 'whether there were noe other parts or passages represented on the Stage then those expressly contayned in the Booke, they confidently said they added or varied from the same, nothing at all' (Dutton, 1991, 244).

Whereas critics have tended to assume that these manuscripts can be clearly positioned along a line beginning with an uncensored early draft and ending with a licensed final draft in the form of a promptbook or a first edition, I would argue that the manuscripts suggest the reverse. Rather than moving toward a final full draft either in manuscript form or printed form, Middleton and the scribes he used put different versions into different kinds of circulation, some shorter and some longer. As Howard-Hill points out, 'textual analysis reveals that Middleton had decided to make transcripts for sale even before the play had been revised for performance' (1993, 4). This meant that, in one case, a presentation copy was shorter than the performance copy. Whether a particular manuscript is an incomplete transcript or an early draft, whether the additions or omissions were made by the author or by the scribe acting as an editor, whether the additions involve an evasion of the censor or were suggested by the censor, may sometimes all be, in my view, undecidable questions. If there is no moment at which we can definitively establish the author's unrevised text, that is because there is no uncensored original any more than there is an unrevised original. Any search for the origin of censorship will be frustrated by an infinite regression: court censorship (defined in its repressive and productive senses) generates self-censorship in the actors and the author that may be regarded with equal validity as being either an anticipation of court censorship or as following after the suggestions/demands of the censor. The various versions of A Game at Chess suggest that censorship was a negotiation over what will or will not play in a number of different venues, not the establishment of a monumental, authorized, final version.

The details of Middleton's censored plays alert us to a structural complicity much deeper than critics have thus far allowed, a complicity not between opposed agents and spaces but between regulatory agencies at all points of literary production and consumption. This structural complicity, I hope it is now clear, significantly changes our understanding of censorship from a practice that operates in terms of removal and replacement to one that operates in terms of dispersal and displacement. The dispersal of censorship decentres the court censor, who occupies one of many competing sites of authorization and licence that legitimate particular revisions. He is not at the apex of power but is caught up in a contestation over who is going to censor, on the basis of what criteria, and to what extent. The difference between censoring and uncensoring is difficult consistently to determine not only because censorship is dispersed across all points of literary production, transmission, and consumption but because it is a fetishistic practice that involves, as Freud saw, displacement rather than outright removal. Censorship is as much about displacing one version with another, displacing texts from one channel to another, as it is about blocking access or destroying transgressive material. As Thomas Cogswell notes in a discussion of censorship in the 1620s:

> political tracts, sermons and verse, which had no hope of receiving a license, could find a wide circulation in the unofficial market for news. Lack of access to a printing press was not a crippling blow.... Few authors slipped...direct criticism into print in 1623. Yet the government's particularly tight control

of the press in this period did not forestall sim- ilar efforts; it simply forced them into channels that newsletters-writers had developed for circulating their manuscripts. (1989, 21, 45)

Similarly, the *Acte to Restraine Abuses of Players* was directed only at profanity in performance, not in print. The crosses in the manuscript of *The Lady's Tragedy*, for example, may mark passages for removal only during the text's performance.

Displacement is not just about more or less narrow kinds of readership and access, but involves a differential system in which texts circulate and become exchangeable by becoming cultural and economic capital. It involves the commodification of small differences meant to increase the text's value, either by limiting its circulation, say to manu- script (that is, the fact that it can not be shown elsewhere gives the manuscript reader an elevated status as critic, insider, and so on) or by exceeding the limits placed on a given text's earlier circulation—the full uncensored text, as opposed to its performance. As Gary Taylor remarks in a discussion of expurgated texts, 'Although profanities could not be played, they could be printed, or circulated in manuscript.... Once authors and publishers recognize a distinction between the play as performance and the play as literary commodity, the door is opened to various literary embellishments of the theatrical text, including particularly the restoration of material cut in performance' (1993a, 147). Middleton's plays were subject to a series of regulations over literary production and consumption. I take these networks of regulation to be part of the form- ation of what Pierre Bourdieu (1993) terms the *literary field*.[22] According to Bourdieu the literary field emerges as a form of cultural legitimation: texts circulate as negotiable currency, as both symbolic and economic capital, in so far as they are differentiated from other versions in the same or in different media: a text in manuscript form, for example, may be valued over printed versions because a select, élite readership alone has access to it, while a performance may be valued over a printed version because the former is thought to be fuller than the censored printed text; conversely, the printed text may be valued over a performance because the former is regarded as fuller than a censored performance.

Commodities are fetishized not, as Marxists have ar- gued, because they are reified, alienable products of labour (Marx, 1867; Lukács, 1968) but because their value as economic and cultural capital is created within an in- tensely differentiated literary field.[23] As I am defining it, however, commodity fetishism is not just economic or even primarily economic. Cultural critics (Marxists fore- most among them) assume that the market precedes the literary, that fetishism depends on the market. A com- modity aesthetic, so the argument goes, is an effect of capitalism (Haug, 1986). Marxists assume that a specific- ally literary market-place follows upon the emergence of a broader market-place. I am suggesting that the reverse is the case: the commodity is an after-effect of the literary,

modelled upon the literary form: indeed, the market is made possible precisely though fetishism, not the reverse. The proliferation of manuscripts of *A Game at Chess* is due, as we have seen, to the perceived markets for them, some being sold and others presented as gifts, markets here understood to include economic and cultural capital (though patrons sometimes made cash payments, the cash could be less important than the prestige attached to their patronage). I am suggesting, moreover, that all number of texts, ranging from privately circulated manuscripts to publicly circulated printed texts and performances to court performances could be commodities only because they had already been fetishized. What looks like histor- ical specificity from a Marxist perspective—the emergence of a market-place in the sixteenth century—is rather a misrecognized instance of a critical fetishism: 'History' is fetishized as that which stands outside of fetishism.

Now some critics might want to object to my account of censorship as a fetishistic practice on several grounds. Even if texts are not wholly blocked but displaced from one medium or channel to another, they might argue, it would still be crucial to differentiate between more or less narrow channels, 'softer' or 'harder' forms of censorship, greater or lesser access and availability of a text to readers and/or performances to spectators. Indeed, some critics might want to argue, the most diverse range of texts/ performances ought to be able to circulate as broadly and as freely in as big and heterogeneous a market as is possible. If discourses and their circulation were truly diverse, truly free of censorship (in its repressive sense) displacements from official to unofficial channels wouldn't be necessary.

While I am sympathetic to what I would call the diversity position, I also think that many of its funda- mental assumptions about censorship as a strictly repress- ive agency are untenable. To begin with, the circulation of discourses depends on their being commodities. This para- doxically both makes entry and access possible and limits what, where, and how texts can circulate; commodity fet- ishism is not an antidote to regulation but is itself another (paradoxical) form of regulation. A related problem with the diversity position is the correlative assumption that there is a strong opposition between direct and indirect criticism, between official and unofficial discourses; that is, an uncensored criticism would be direct, immediately readable, in short, non-literary (unambiguous, without irony or equivocation). Yet non-literary texts were prosec- uted on the basis of their perceived literary strategies, not because of their naked, unveiled attacks on the Crown. For example, William Prynne's index entry to *Histriomastix*, 'women actors, notorious whores' was taken (mistaken, Prynne maintained) as an attempt to parallel classical

[22] See also Bourdieu (1984) and Bourdieu and Darbel (1990). For a New Historicist use of Bourdieu, see Greenblatt (1989).
[23] For an explicit critique of Marxist notions of commodity fetishism, see Jean Baudrillard, 'Fetishism and Ideology' (1981, 88–101). See also the essays in Apter and Pietz (1993).

Roman and contemporary Caroline courts, to the massive discredit of both. Moreover, the diversity position assumes that there were uncensored versions of a text, however difficult they might be to read critically. The uncensored version might be an unperformed manuscript, a printed text containing material censored which had been for performance, or a performance of a text.

By contrast, I have been suggesting that if censoring is always a matter of censoring in detail, then two points follow: on the one hand, there is no whole uncensored original version but a proliferation of always already revised, always already partial, always already censored versions; on the other, censorship never occurs (one can always locate an 'uncensored' version). Fetishism allows us to see both that uncensoring is an impossibility and to see why the desire for an uncensored text persists, even in countries with no official state censorship apparatus. For if understanding censorship as fetishism shows it always already occurs, the same understanding also shows that the phantasm of an uncensored text appears everywhere. All media can potentially trump the others as the source of the uncensored version. Print can be regarded as fuller than manuscript because it allows for greater access; conversely, a manuscript can also be regarded as fuller precisely because it was not subject to state censorship (*Hengist, King of Kent*, for example, exists in two manuscripts which are fuller than the 1661 printed version). Similarly, theatre may be regarded as harder to police than print because performance is more fluid, allowing the actors to inflect the text's meanings through gestures and props, while, conversely, print may be regarded as fuller than performance because it includes material censored on stage.

But in none of these cases, I would argue, is one getting a completely uncensored version. (In psychoanalytic terms, the fetish 'replaces' what was never there to be removed in the first place, the mother's phallus: the fetishist misreads sexual difference, substituting an originary fullness for an originary lack. In these terms, a censored text would be a castrated text.) To paraphrase Octave Mannoni's (1968) account of the logic of fetishism as a knowledge and disavowal of sexual difference ('Je sais bien, mais quand même...'), we might say that the logic of censorship is as follows: 'I know very well texts are always already censored. Nevertheless, I want the uncensored version of this text.' Fetishizing censorship means affirming and disavowing a difference between censored and uncensored texts. This fetishistic affirmation and disavowal of textual difference is projected in different ways along multiple axes. Texts enter circulation at a variety of points, becoming commodities in terms of various kinds of small differences not only between more or less accessible texts but between more or less well-bound, more or less expensive, more or less well-printed editions. More significantly, censorship is both a means of access and a means of blocking access to the literary field. Commodification both permits entry to this field and excludes it on the basis

of whether or not it can be market-driven. In my view, fetishism can neither be redeemed as a mainstreaming practice nor dismissed as a denial or distortion of difference; rather, it draws our attention to the fact that censorship is not reducible to repression: mainstreaming (bringing something from the margin to the centre, from invisibility to visibility) is not always easy to tell apart from its apparent opposite, namely, censorship in the repressive sense of exclusion and marginalization since a text has to accommodate the constraints of the commodity form in order to circulate in the first place.

II

In addition to enabling us to see that specific cases cannot be definitively classified as instances of censorship or noncensorship, an understanding of censorship as fetishistic throws into relief the way sexuality figures this paradox in early modern culture in general and in Middleton in particular.[24] In Middleton's canon as in those of other dramatists, a sexual metaphorics is the vehicle of a topical politics. For many modern critics, sexuality is a transparent figure for court politics. As we have seen, when discussing 'ladies' in modern accounts of *The Lady's Tragedy* or women in *The Witch*, critics regard the court as the real object of criticism. Similarly, critics of *A Game at Chess* tend to read through or past the play's sexualized figuration of court politics, reading images of gelding, rape, and prostitution as metaphors for religious, moral, or political conflicts (Lancashire, 1978, 234-7; Howard-Hill, 1993, 40-8). But it is precisely the details of this sexual figuration that complicate any easy assignment of a given politics to the play: rather than create stable equivalences that might reinforce a model of censorship as castration (in which castration is precisely a radical removal) the play's sexual metaphorics call into question the self--identity of censorship. Hence, they call into question the difference between censoring and uncensoring. Reading in detail means reading in parts, in terms of a deconstructive account of allegory, a part-to-part relation, rather than hermeneutics, a part-to-whole relation.[25]

If the fetishistic status of censorship means that texts are always already censored, if it attempts to secure, that is, an censored, uncastrated phallic politics of textual potency and plenitude, some critics might wonder whether one might be be able to construct a defetishized model of textual production, transmission and consumption. I want to turn now to *A Game at Chess* to show why this is impossible. Modern critics have made the politics of *A Game at Chess* intelligible by moving away from the literal and the detail (which remain opaque) in the direction of the metaphorical and the abstract (which allows the

[24] For an account of the connections between sexuality and political censorship, see Burt (1993, 132-43) and Boose (1994).
[25] On allegory, see De Man (1979), 188-245. Political critics often assume a more coherent notion of allegory as a decoding of one-to-one correspondences between the text and history. Hence the notable tendency in many so-called New Historicist topical readings to reinscribe Old Historicist critical practices.

play's meaning to become clear). Richard Dutton phrases the usual move in a manner apt for our purposes:

> There is room for debate about the details of the allegory, but the broad outlines could hardly be clearer.... De Domini and Gondomar are, Middleton implies, different faces of the same threat, a relatively sophisticated notion if anyone were looking for a lit-eralistic 'shadowing' of persons and recent events.... The audience was apparently expected to make sense of composite or multi-faceted allusions which may have no literal or one-to-one relation to persons or events. (Dutton, 1991, 239; 241; 241)

The move toward metaphor and a general sense of the play's allegory apparently stems from a desire to save the play from a crude topicality, one that would make it only of antiquarian and non-literary interest. It also assumes a hermeneutic model of censorship—the whole play can be read even if some of the parts can not (they're capable of being dismissed as incidentals that would not change the play's meaning).

But the local allegories and details cannot be so easily dispensed with. For the details turn out not to be incidental but in fact call into question the possibility of allegorizing the whole play. Despite the clarity of particular parallels, the satirical force of *A Game at Chess* remains unclear in modern criticism.[26] Indeed, discussions of this play enact a frequent impasse in censorship studies: the more detailed the case, the more impenetrable it becomes.[27] In searching for an explanation for the censorship of *A Game at Chess*, critics ignore the fact that there is an inconsistency in contemporary accounts, that we get multiple reasons for its performance being shut down: initially the King being personated, and then the satire of Gondomar.[28] Audience response to the play is similarly indefinite. Though we have an extremely full record of responses to this play it too clarifies only parts of the play. An eyewitness account by John Holles is telling in this regard. Calling Holles's report 'the most detailed, intelligent, and (in a reviewer's sense) the most sympathetic of the known descriptions' (1990, 356), A. R. Braunmuller notes that Holles mis-read the White Bishop's Pawn as a 'Spanish euneuch' rather than an English character and that he didn't note parallels obvious to us (1990, 351; 349). Braunmuller concludes that the play leaves us with major questions unanswered ('Was the play an attack on James? on Prince Charles? on the Duke of Buckingham?' [1990, 355]) and with a sense of how undefined the play's reception was: 'Holles' letter...urges us to interpret Middleton's allegor-ical meanings cautiously, to respect the variety and the indefinition that performances and audiences' responses necessarily (every day, every performance) lend to any dramatic "text"' (1990, 356).

Rather than ride over the play's details in order to abstract a general message, then, I want to examine a particular detail through which the play inscribes the overlooking of details as what I would call the impossibility

of a definitively uncensored reading. Middleton figures this impossibility through a specific metaphor for censorship, namely, gelding.[29] Gelding is figured in the White Bishop Pawn's plot (the centrality of which has long been recog-nized by modern critics).[30] It is generally read as a story of the harm done by the Jesuits to the Church of England. As Gary Taylor (2000) has observed, Middleton specifically uses gelding as a metaphor for this harm. Given that cas-tration and censorship became exchangeable terms (Ben Jonson referred to a Jesuit edition of Martial's epigrams as 'Jesuitaru castratus') and given the censorship (in the repressive sense) of the anti-Jesuitical tracts by Thomas Scott and others whom Middleton used as sources, and given that tolerated Jesuitical texts play a central role in the White Queen's Pawn's seduction and prostitution, it is possible, as Taylor (2000) maintains, to see gelding as a metaphor for censorship.[31] While Middleton's gelding metaphor obviously assumes that censorship is painfully repressive, the point of the metaphor, I want to argue, is not to criticize censorship in general but to criticize illegitimate forms of it. The play can be read as a critique of Jacobean censorship—not that it was repressive, but that it was repressive in the wrong way, censoring texts that have been tolerated and tolerating texts that should have been censored. In the 1620s, an almost unlimited number of Jesuit texts were allowed to be circulated while Protestant ones were not (Cogswell, 1989, 20–35). Mid-dleton moralizes censorship not in terms of its presence or absences (as we tend to do) but in terms of who uses it for what ends. The bad censor is a castrator. In a typically Middletonian moral economy, censorship in *A Game at Chess* leads to its own undoing. No forgiveness is available to the Black Bishop's Pawn for having gelded the White Bishop's Pawn. The castrator is castrated, the biter bit.

The play's moral opposition between good and bad cen-sorship self-deconstructs, however, because the figure of castration unsettles rather than underwrites an equation of censorship with repression. Critics have noted that the White Knight's staged confession of his sins in an effort to entrap the Black Knight compromises the moral difference between them (Harper, 88; Braunmuller 1991, 348–9). The White Knight's references to sodomy pertain not only to Olivares (the Black Knight), the favourite of Philip IV, but to Buckingham (the White Knight), the favourite of James I, as well. But, more crucially, the play's moral distinctions self-deconstruct because, as I will make clear

---

[26] See, for example, discussions in Heinemann (1980), Braunmuller (1990), Clare (1990), and Dutton (1991).
[27] See, for example, Dutton's (1991, 10–16) discussion of Ben Jonson's *Sejanus*. Dutton takes it to be an example of the 'sheer impenetrability of so much of the material we have to work with' (10).
[28] These different reasons are rehearsed by Dutton (1991, 237–48). Rather than take into account the multiplicities, critics have often tried to single out one of them as the real explanation.
[29] The following discussion is deeply indebted to Gary Taylor (2000). I thank him for sending me a draft of his stimulating work and for helping to clarify my own account of the way Middleton relates castration and censorship.
[30] See Howard-Hill (1993, 38), for example.
[31] On Jonson, see Burt (1993); on the tracts, see Cogswell (1989).

momentarily, castration is not self-identical. The sexual metaphorics of *A Game at Chess* do not form a chain of binary oppositions with equivalent terms on each side, each moralized, valued in terms of its place above or below another, as if one could say that uncensored is to censored as uncastrated is to castrated, as whole is to part, as plenitude is to lack, as good is to bad.

The coherence of Middleton's moral economy depends on there being a clear difference between castration as a symbolic practice and castration as a literal practice. This distinction allows for a kind of poetic justice: the castrator is castrated in symbolic terms; that is, the Black Knight is not literally castrated as was the White Bishop's Pawn. The Black Knight's crime and his punishment are symmetrical but not identical. The two meanings of castration thus make it possible to differentiate the Black and White sides in moral terms (one side literally castrates, the other side only metaphorically castrates). This difference secures others. There is no good gelder as opposed to a bad gelder. (None of the admirable characters speaks of gelding positively.) And the play does not advocate the gelding of Jesuits (other texts did).[32] But the very doubleness of the meaning of castration (as real and as symbolic) that makes it possible to distinguish in moral terms between those who literally castrate (as bad) and those who do so metaphorically (as good) also calls that distinction into question.

To begin with, *A Game at Chess* never provides us with a literal castration: the play presents us with a gelded chess piece, not a gelded person. To be sure, Renaissance chess pieces were constructed not as abstract shapes but as images of persons. Yet precisely because the White Bishop's Pawn is a chess piece and not a person, he can only be an image of castration, not castration itself. Whether theatrically imaged or not, then, the play gives us only a representation of castration, not *real* castration.[33] (It is perhaps worth adding that for Middleton 'real' castration always appears, as it does for Freud, as figured and displaced. Consider *The Changeling*, in which we are invited to read De Flores's cutting off Alonzo's ring finger as a castration: it recalls both De Flores's earlier image 'I should thrust my fingers | Into her sockets', where 'sockets' means both the fingers of Beatrice-Joanna's glove and her vagina, and an earlier pun on Isabella's ring, both jewel and vagina, into which suitors may 'thrust' their fingers.)[34]

Moreover, Middleton does not limit castration to a single meaning. Castration not only has two negative meanings but a positive one as well. Castration actually empowers the White Bishop's Pawn, makes him lighter and hence faster; it does not make him 'impotent', but instead displaces and disperses his power. In making the Jesuits gelders, Middleton follows a tradition of anti-Catholic literature in which figurative meanings of castration were precisely at stake. Protestants attacked Catholicism as sexually deviant, castration being a sign of that deviancy. Reginald Scot in *Discovery of Witchcraft*, for example,

mocks Catholics who wish to become saints by asking angels to castrate them. Similarly, Barnabe Barnes in *The Devil's Charter* denounces Pope Alexander VI as a sexually deviant monarch by staging a scene in which he castrates a young boy. The point of this tradition was to deprive (one is tempted to say 'castrate') Catholics from assigning castration a positive meaning (say, as celibacy).[35] These symbolic meanings testify to the productivity of castration, a productivity that undermines its self-identity.

Understanding censorship through the metaphor of castration, then, alters our understanding of censorship by revealing its self-deconstructive non-identity. As a multiple and paradoxically repressive practice with positive effects and meanings, castration cannot be reduced to a unified, morally reprehensible practice. The metaphor of castration foregrounds not the literal status of censorship but its (dis)figurative status; that is, castration figures an originary (and paradoxically productive) lack rather than the loss of an originary plenitude; as such, castration is a figure for the way that texts have always already been censored (see Derrida, 1987, 439–42).[36] Castration is a metaphor for the endlessly displaced origin and end of censorship. If censorship has always already occurred, it follows that uncensoring is always reading in detail and hence will never deliver an uncensored 'pay-off', the equivalent of what in the porn industry is termed the 'money shot' (Williams, 1989, 8). Uncensoring is not the opposite of lack, that which replaces castration, the achievement of phallic plenitude. Uncensoring does not lead to an orgasmic moment of pure presence since there is no uncensored text to recover.

If it is clear that censorship of *A Game at Chess* and Middleton's other plays demands that we rethink cen-

---

[32] I thank Gary Taylor for this point and for these references.

[33] The problem the figuration of castration poses to those who want to decode an 'uncensored' politics in the play is crystallized in the questions of whether gelding was theatrically represented, and if so, how? If it was represented, by what details would the White Bishop's Pawn's lack have been signified? More to the point, could it have been represented given that what is being represented is a literal impossibility? In contemporary terms, one might ask 'can a mannequin be castrated?' Perhaps. The nearest analogue I know of is Cindy Sherman's series of 'pornographic' photos of nude, fragmented female mannequins exhibited at Metro Pictures, New York, in 1992. Even here, however, female sexuality is clearly figured. It is not surprising, then, that two reviewers found the images difficult to read (see Hartney, 1992 and Weinstein, 1992), and one notes that 'Sherman's new work has already been enthusiastically misinterpreted as exclusively concerning the link between sex and violence. What has been ignored is that these are mannequins' (Weinstein 1992, 95).

[34] At stake in images of castration is not the difference between real and symbolic, but the economy of substitutions structuring male and female desire whereby something can or cannot be exchanged for something else. On the related problem of glossing and expurgating bawdy puns, see Hedrick (1994).

[35] John Rogers has alerted me to a perhaps even more bizarre Protestant tradition involving foreskin mutilation which tied 'improvement' of the genitalia to the approach of the millennium.

[36] Following Derrida's account of castration as necessarily figured because necessarily misread (i.e. the female body has not been castrated), we could say that censorship too is always metaphorical, available only through a figure which supplements it. I argue (1994a) that censorship's performative, productive status means that its identity is never given, available only through a metaphorical supplement, a supplement which critics often use in an effort to literalize censorship (as with various metaphors of the bodily mutilation, castration among them). For more on this point, see Burt (1993, 150–68) and Bourdieu (1991, 138).

sorship in terms of dispersal and displacement, we are now in a position to make clear that a desire for an uncensored radical politics will always be disappointed. The uncensored, whole, original text is precisely the phantasmatic promise that fetishism offers and always disappoints. A salient contribution of Middleton's case is the way that it puts into question rather than embraces a desire for an original, uncensored, whole text. Uncensoring *A Game at Chess* produces not a single coherent allegory (political, religious, or moral) but dispersed, fragmented allegories which do not come together. Indeed, they do not 'come' at all. While they tellingly link dramatic characters and historical personages, they don't tell the meaning of the parallel. Middleton's play enacts a paradoxical economy of both putting topical parallels into circulation and withholding their whole meaning (both inviting uncensoring and making it impossible). Thus, one arrives at an uncensored general allegory only at the expense of reading in detail, only as it were by not reading. To put the point in its most paradoxical form, uncensoring the play as a whole entails censoring some of its parts.

On the basis of this account of censorship as fetishistic, we can begin to see why there can be no defetishized model of textual culture that might be harnessed to the politics of feminist criticism and/or queer theory. To imagine that uncensoring is an antidote to censoring in the repressive sense is to cling to a fetishistic narrative of textual transmission in which a complete integral text is more or less repressed as it is put into circulation. The uncensored text is implicitly regarded as masculine, an imaginary whole prior to its castration, while the censored text is constructed as feminine, as lacking integrity.[37] This narrative is fetishistic, moreover, in that it constructs a model of textual production and consumption with clear beginnings and endings that either reasserts patriarchal authority over its meaning or reads its textual productivity in phallic terms (the text is productive precisely because it has not been censored/castrated). Critics often tell this story (and perhaps most intensely) in the name of an uncensored politics (either oppositional in the neo-Whig version or consensus in the revisionist version).[38]

In so far as political critics (and here I include all political critics) have (often unconsciously) sought a defetishized, uncensored politics, a whole and original text, they have made a fetish out of oppositional, radical politics. Politics, that is, functions like a commodity rather than as the antidote to commodity fetishism. Just as the commodity constructs a desire which it never satisfies fully (impelling the consumer to purchase another commodity promising to do what the other did not), so each instance of an apparently uncensored radical politics disappoints. Cases of repressive censorship cannot always be decisively distinguished from cases of noncensorship. Local disappointments at not finding clear-cut cases of repressive theatre censorship do not necessarily affect the intensity of the desire for a non-commodified, defetishized, uncensored politics; indeed, one could argue that that desire is hysterically intensified the more it is disappointed.

To imagine that it could be satisfied would be to imagine (mistakenly) that castration ever secured binary oppositions between disavowal and avowal, between distortion and clarity, between visibility and invisibility, between censorship and uncensorship that some anti-fetishism feminist critics think it has (Silverman 1992; Penley 1993).[39] What looks like defetishism (multiple, small differences constituting a clitoral criticism opposed to the single, big difference of a phallic criticism) from another perspective looks like fetishism masquerading as its opposite (small differences being that which enables the construction of a big difference between feminist and patriarchal criticism).[40]

The details of Middleton's cases of dramatic censorship paradoxically place him by showing how hard it is to place him (or any other dramatist) politically.[41] Middleton contributes to contemporary political criticism, indirectly to be sure, in helping to characterize the present in terms of a detumescence of the political, thereby opening up the possibility of an ambivalent, amped up, 'freaked out' critical practice (iconoclastic, scandalous, tabloid), rather than in enabling a History of fetishism that would somehow counter the repressive effects of both commodity fetishism and psychoanalytic models of fetishism.[42] Perhaps Middleton's value lies in the way he might make us face our disappointment at not finding a well-heeled politics, or, to put it another way, at finding that politics are always high-heeled.[43] If we have escaped 'CENSORSHIP' of the sort Middleton faced, we can never escape the fetishistic regulations of discourse that implicitly or explicitly construct a hierarchy of legitimations, enable and limit access to a given reading field.[44]

[37] For an account of fetishism as securing a whole male body at the expense of the female body (which is regarded as lacking), see Silverman (1992).

[38] For a similar formulation, see Haber (1993).

[39] I develop this point more fully in Burt (1994a).

[40] It is perhaps already clear I would argue that any Lacanian informed account of a 'lesbian phallus', of 'displaceability' (see Judith Butler 1992) or of a more polemically, Deleuzian informed anti-psychoanalytic account of masochism (see Shaviro 1993) would not serve as antidotes to Freud's account of castration and fetishism but would instead recapitulate the problems with regard to censorship articulated here.

[41] I say this notwithstanding the reasonably held view of Middleton as unequivocally anti-Spanish, anti-Catholic, and anti-Spanish match. Though there were two sides to the issues dramatized in a play like *A Game at Chess*, Middleton is less concerned with aligning himself on one side or the other than with the way displacement breaks down oppositions. This interest may account for the sometimes surprising reception of Middleton's works. Consider a concrete example. Middleton might be put at one end of an axis, Ben Jonson at the other, with Middleton representing a progressive anti-censorship politics and Ben Jonson representing a reactionary, censorious politics. Yet Jonson was mistaken for Middleton's collaborator on *The Widow* (1615–16).

[42] See Burt 1995. For more on castration and scandal, see Hollier (1984), Saper (1993) and Taylor (2000).

[43] I say this partly to acknowledge that a detumescent or even fully 'castrated' politics can be an instance of phallic politics, as in the Hydra, where cutting of a head only leads to the growth of two more. And it would be a mistake to imagine that a 'new' historicizing practice could lead to a new way of valuing topicality over allegory, or a topicality of fragments over a topicality of the whole reading. These very oppositions would simply secure the same kind of fetishistic desire and disappointment. See Marcus (1990; 1992); Liu (1990); and Fumerton (1990) for accounts of the importance of topicality and the detail in New Historicism. On the self-deconstruction of hermeneutics, see Fineman (1991). For a different account of displacement, one that stresses the reinscription of a stable binary opposition rather than the breakdown of such oppositions, see Dollimore (1991).

[44] I would like to thank Stuart Culver, Barbara Freedman, Judith Haber, Amy Kaplan, Mary Russo, Rebecca Schneider, and Gary Taylor for their conversations

WORKS CITED

Apter, Emily. 1991. *Feminizing the Fetish: Psychoanalysis and Narrative Obsession in Turn-of-the-Century France*. Ithaca: Cornell University Press.

—— and William Pietz, eds. 1993. *Fetishism as Cultural Discourse: Gender, Commodity, and Vision*. Ithaca: Cornell University Press.

Archer, John Michael. 1993. *Sovereignty and Intelligence: Spying and Court Culture in English Renaissance Writing*. Stanford: Stanford University Press.

Bald, R. C., ed. 1938. *Hengist, King of Kent; or The Mayor of Queenborough*. New York and London: Charles Scribner's Sons.

Barker, Francis. 1984. *The Tremulous Private Body: Essays on Subjection*. New York: Methuen.

Baudrillard, Jean. 1981. 'Fetishism and Ideology: the Semiological Reduction'. In *For a Critique of the Political Economy of the Sign*. Trans. Charles Levin. St Louis: Telos Press, 88–101.

Bawcutt, N. W., ed. 1996. *The Control and Censorship of Caroline Drama: The Records of Sir Henry Herbert, Master of the Revels 1623–73*. Oxford: Clarendon Press.

Bentley, G. E. 1941–68. *The Jacobean and Caroline Stage*. 7 vols. Oxford: Clarendon Press.

Boose, Lynda. 1994. 'The 1599 Bishops' Ban, Elizabethan Pornography, and the Sexualization of the Jacobean Stage'. In *Enclosure Acts: Sexuality, Property, and Culture in Early Modern England*, ed. Richard Burt and John Michael Archer. Ithaca: Cornell University Press, 185–200.

Bourdieu, Pierre. 1984. *Distinction: A Social Critique of the Judgement of Taste*. Trans. Richard Nice. Cambridge: Harvard University Press.

—— 1991. 'Censorship and the Imposition of Form'. In *Language and Symbolic Power*, ed. John B. Thompson, trans. Gino Raymond and Matthew Adamson. Cambridge: Harvard University Press, 137–159.

—— 1993. *The Field of Cultural Production: Essays on Art and Literature*. ed. Randall Johnson. New York: Columbia University Press.

—— and Alain Darbel with Dominique Schnapper. 1990. *The Love of Art: European Art Museums and Their Public*. Trans. Caroline Beattie and Nick Merriman. Stanford: Stanford University Press.

Braunmuller, A. R. 1990. '"To the Globe I rowed": John Holles sees *A Game at Chess*'. *English Literary Renaissance* 20: 2, 340–56.

Burt, Richard. 1993. *Licensed by Authority: Ben Jonson and the Discourses of Censorship*. Ithaca: Cornell University Press.

—— 1994a. 'Baroque Down: The Trauma of Censorship in Psychoanalysis and Queer Film Re-visions of Shakespeare and Marlowe'. In *Shakespeare in the New Europe*, ed. Michael Hattaway *et al.* Sheffield: University of Sheffield Press, 328–50.

—— 1994b. 'Introduction: the "New" Censorship'. In *The Administration of Aesthetics: Censorship, Political Criticism, and the Public Sphere*, ed. Richard Burt. Minneapolis: University of Minnesota Press, xi–xxix.

—— 1995. 'Getting Off the Subject: Iconoclasm, Queer Sexuality, and the Celebrity Intellectual'. *Performing Arts Journal* 50/51, 137–50.

Butler, Judith. 1992. 'The Lesbian Phallus and the Morphological Imaginary', *Differences* 4: 4, 133–71.

Butler, Martin. 1992. 'Ecclesiastical Censorship of Early Stuart Drama: The Case of Jonson's *The Magnetic Lady*', *Modern Philology* 89 (May): 469–81.

Chambers, E. K. 1923. *The Elizabethan Stage*. 4 vols. Oxford: Clarendon Press.

Clare, Janet. 1990. *Art Made Tongue-Tied by Authority: Elizabethan and Jacobean Dramatic Censorship*. Manchester and New York: Manchester University Press.

Clegg, Cyndia Susan. 2001. *Press Censorship in Jacobean England*. Cambridge: Cambridge University Press.

Cogswell, Thomas. 1989. *The Blessed Revolution: English Politics and the Coming of War*. Cambridge: Cambridge University Press.

Darnton, Robert. May 16, 1991. 'The Good Old Days'. *New York Review of Books* 38: 9, 44–8.

Davis, Natalie Zemon. 1990. 'Rabelais Among the Censors (1940s, 1540s)', *Representations* 32: 1–26.

De Man, Paul. 1979. *Allegories of Reading: Figural Language in Rousseau, Nietzsche, Rilke, and Proust*. New Haven: Yale University Press.

Derrida, Jacques. 1987. 'Le facteur de la vérité'. In *The Post Card: From Socrates to Freud and Beyond*. Trans. Alan Bass. Chicago: University of Chicago Press, 411–96.

Dollimore, Jonathan. 1991. *Sexual Dissidence: Augustine to Wilde, Freud to Foucault*. Oxford: Oxford University Press.

Dutton, Richard. 1991. *Mastering the Revels: The Regulation and Censorship of English Renaissance Drama*. Iowa City: University of Iowa Press.

—— 2001. *Licensing, Censorship and Authorship in Early Modern England: Buggeswords*. London: Palgrave Macmillan.

Finkelpearl, Philip J. 1986. '"The Comedian's Liberty": Jacobean Censorship Reconsidered', *English Literary Renaissance* 16: 1, 123–38.

Fineman, Joel. 1991. 'The Structure of Allegorical Desire'. In *The Subjectivity Effect in Western Literary Tradition: Essays Toward the Release of Shakespeare's Will*. Cambridge, MA: MIT Press, 3–31.

Foucault, Michel. 1978. *The History of Sexuality, Volume One: An Introduction*. Trans. Robert Hurley. New York: Pantheon Books.

Freedman, Barbara. 1991. *Staging the Gaze: Postmodernism, Psychoanalysis, and Shakespearean Comedy*. Ithaca: Cornell University Press.

Freud, Sigmund. 1963. 'Fetishism'. In *Sexuality and the Psychology of Love*, ed. Philip Rieff. New York: Collier, 214–19.

—— 1969. *An Outline of Psychoanalysis*. Trans. James Strachey. New York: Norton.

Fumerton, Patricia. 1991. *Cultural Aesthetics: Renaissance Literature and the Practice of Ornament*. Berkeley: University of California Press.

Garber, Marjorie. 1991. 'Fetish Envy'. In *Vested Interests: Cross-Dressing and Cultural Anxiety*. New York: Routledge, 118–27.

Greenblatt, Stephen. 1989. *Shakespearean Negotiations: The Circulation of Social Energy*. Berkeley: University of California Press.

Groz, Elizabeth A. 1991. 'Lesbian Fetishism?', *Differences* 3: 2 (1991): 39–54.

about this essay and for their comments on earlier drafts. I am grateful to Gary Taylor for letting me read a copy of his own (then unpublished) work on castration and *A Game at Chess*, to Manfred Pfister for inviting me to present a version of this essay to the Department of English Philology at the Free University, Berlin, to Julie Sanders for inviting me to present a version of it at 'Refashioning Ben Jonson', a conference held at the University of Warwick, and to Cyndia Clegg for inviting me to present a version of it as the keynote paper at 'Liberty, License, and Authority' at the Huntington Library, one of a series of eight conferences in a programme entitled 'Censorship and Silencing: Practices of Cultural Regulation', sponsored by the University of California Institute for Academic Research, the American Academy of Arts and Sciences, and the Getty Center for the Arts. I am also grateful to Julia Briggs for obtaining photographs of the manuscript of *The Lady's Tragedy* from the British Library.

Haber, Judith. 1993. '"True-loves blood": Narrative and Desire in *Hero and Leander*'. Unpublished paper presented at the Third International Marlowe Conference, Cambridge, England.

Hadfield, Andrew. 2001. *Literature and Censorship in Renaissance England*. London: Palgrave Macmillan.

Harper, J. W., ed. 1966. *A Game at Chess*. London: Ernest Benn, Ltd.

Hartney, Eleanor. 1992. 'Cindy Sherman at Metro Pictures', *Art in America* 80: 9, 127–8.

Haug, Wolfgang Fritz. 1986. *Critique of Commodity Aesthetics: Appearance, Sexuality, and Advertising in Capitalist Society*. Trans. Robert Bock. Introduction by Stuart Hall. Minneapolis: University of Minnesota Press.

Hedrick, Don. 1994. 'Flower Power: Shakespearean Deep Bawdy and the Botanical Perverse'. In *The Administration of Aesthetics: Censorship, Political Criticism, and the Public Sphere*, ed. Richard Burt. Minneapolis: University of Minnesota Press, 83–105.

Heinemann, Margot. 1980. *Puritanism and Theatre: Thomas Middleton and Opposition Drama Under the Early Stuarts*. Cambridge: Cambridge University Press.

Hill, Christopher. 1985. 'Censorship and English Literature'. In *The Collected Works of Christopher Hill*. Vol. 1. Amherst: University of Massachusetts Press, 32–72.

Hollier, Denis. 1984. 'Mimesis and Castration, 1937'. *October* 31 (Winter), 3–15.

Howard-Hill, T. H. 1993. 'Introduction'. In *A Game at Chess*, ed. T. H. Howard-Hill. Manchester: Manchester University Press.

Kawachi, Yoshiko. 1986. *Calendar of English Renaissance Drama, 1558–1642*. New York and London: Garland.

Lake, David. J. 1975. *The Canon of Thomas Middleton's Plays: Internal Evidence for the Major Problems of Authorship*. Cambridge: Cambridge University Press.

Lancashire, Anne, ed. 1978. *The Second Maiden's Tragedy*. Baltimore: Johns Hopkins University Press.

—— 1983. 'The Witch: Stage Flop or Political Mistake?' In '*Accompanige the players': Essays Celebrating Thomas Middleton, 1580–1980*, ed. Kenneth Friedenreich. New York: AMS Press, 161–82.

Liu, Alan. 1990. 'Local Transcendence: Cultural Criticism, Postmodernism, and the Romanticism of Detail', *Representations* 32: 75–113.

Lukács, Georg. 1968. 'Reification and Class Consciousness'. In *History and Class Consciousness: Studies in Marxist Dialectics*. Trans. Rodney Livingstone. Cambridge, MA: MIT Press, 83–222.

Malcolmson, Cristina. 1990. '"As Tame as the Ladies": Politics and Gender in *The Changeling*', *English Literary Renaissance* 20: 2, 320–39.

Mannoni, Octave. 1968. 'Je sais bien, mais quand même...' In *Clefs pour l'imaginaire*. Paris: Seuil, 9–33.

Marcus, Leah S. 1988. *Puzzling Shakespeare: Local Reading and its Discontents*. Berkeley and Los Angeles: University of California Press.

—— 1992. 'The Shakespearean Editor as Shrew-Tamer', *English Literary Renaissance* 22: 2, 177–200.

Marx, Karl. 1867. 'The Fetishism of Commodities and the Secret Thereof'. In *Capital: A Critique of Political Economy, Volume I*, ed. Frederick Engels, trans. Samuel Moore and Edward Aveling. New York: International Publishers, 71–83.

McClintock, Anne. 1993. 'The Return of Female Fetishism and the Fiction of the Phallus', *New Formations* 19 (Spring), 1–22.

Müller, Beate, ed. 2003. *Censorship and Cultural Regulation in the Modern Age*. Rodopi.

Newman, Karen. 1991. *Fashioning Femininity and English Renaissance Drama*. Chicago: University of Chicago Press.

Norbrook, David. 1994. '*Areopagitica*, Censorship, and the Early Modern Public Sphere'. In *The Administration of Aesthetics: Censorship, Political Criticism, and the Public Sphere*, ed. Richard Burt. Minneapolis: University of Minnesota Press, 3–33.

Orgel, Stephen. 1988. 'The Authentic Shakespeare'. *Representations* 21: 1–26.

Patterson, Annabel. 1984. *Censorship and Interpretation: The Conditions of Reading and Writing in Early Modern England*. Madison: University of Wisconsin Press.

—— 1990. 'Censorship'. In *Encyclopedia of Literature and Criticism*, ed. Martin Coyle *et al.* London: Routledge, 901–14.

Peck, Linda Levy. 1982. *Northampton: Patronage and Policy at the Court of James I*. London: Allen and Unwin.

Penley, Constance and Sharon Willis. 1993. 'Introduction'. In *Male Trouble*, ed. Penley and Willis. Minneapolis: University of Minnesota Press, vii–xix.

Post, Robert C., ed. 1998. *Censorship and Silencing: Practices of Cultural Regulation*. Oxford: Oxford University Press.

Rose, Jacqueline. 1989. *Sexuality and the Field of Vision*. London: Verso.

Saper, Craig. 1993. 'Scandalography: From Fatty's Demise to Lacan's Rise'. *Lusitania* 1: 4, 87–103.

Schor, Naomi. 1987. *Reading in Detail: Aesthetics and the Feminine*. New York and London: Methuen.

Sharpe, Kevin. 1987. *Criticism and Compliment: The Politics of Literature in the England of Charles I*. Cambridge: Cambridge University Press.

Shaviro, Stephen. 1993. *The Cinematic Body*. Minneapolis, Minnesota: University of Minnesota Press.

Silverman, Kaja. 1992. *Male Subjectivity at the Margins*. New York: Routledge.

Steen, Sara J. 1993. *Ambrosia in an Earthern Vessel: Three Centuries of Reader Response to the Works of Thomas Middleton*. New York: AMS Press.

Taylor, Gary. 1987. 'General Introduction'. In *William Shakespeare: A Textual Companion*. Oxford: Oxford University Press, 1–68.

—— 1993a. 'The Renaissance and the End of Editing'. In *Palimpsest: Editorial Theory in the Humanities*, ed. George Bornstein and Ralph G. Williams. Ann Arbor: University of Michigan Press, 121–49.

—— 1993b. '"Zounds" Revisited: Theatrical, Editorial, and Literary Expurgation'. In Gary Taylor and John Jowett, *Shakespeare Reshaped: 1606–1623*. Oxford: Oxford University Press.

—— 1994. 'Bardicide'. In *Shakespeare and Cultural Traditions: Proceedings of the Fifth World Shakespeare Congress*, ed. Roger Pringle *et al.* Newark, Delaware: University of Delaware Press, 333–49.

—— 2000. *Castration: An Abbreviated History of Western Manhood*. New York: Routledge.

Weinstein, Martin. 1992. 'Cindy Sherman, Metro Pictures, Vivian Horan Fine Art', *Art Forum* 31: 1, 95.

Wigley, Mark. 1992. 'Theoretical Slippage'. In *Fetish*, ed. Sarah Whiting *et al.* Princeton: Princeton Journal and Princeton Architectural Journal, 88–129.

Williams, Linda. 1989. *Hard Core: Power, Pleasure, and the 'Frenzy' of the Visible*. Berkeley: University of California Press.

Worden, A. B. 1988. 'Literature and Political Censorship in Early Modern England'. In *Too Mighty to Be Free: Censorship and the Press in Britain and the Netherlands*, ed. A. C. Duke and C. A. Tamse. Zutphen: De Walburg Press, 45–62.

194

CASTING COMPOSITORS, FOUL CASES, AND SKELETONS: PRINTING IN MIDDLETON'S AGE

Adrian Weiss

By the time Middleton appeared in print in 1597, the various functional aspects of the process of producing printed books had been long established. The centre of the book trade as a whole was the Stationers' Hall at the west end of St Paul's Churchyard, where the large concentration of booksellers 'uttered' their wares from stalls built against the cathedral itself or from multi-storeyed tenements within the cathedral precinct (Blayney, 1990). We know from various sources that 'Paul's' was the Elizabethan equivalent of a modern shopping mall, albeit with an emphasis upon books rather than shoes. Along with other tradesmen, stationers and bookbinders operated from within the side chapels of the cathedral itself (Gair, 21–3). According to Thomas Nashe, a certain ambience was added to the book-perusing environment in the summer of 1596 when 'mr. Harrington of late hath sett up sutch a filthy stinking jakes in poules chuchyard, that the [booksellers] wold give any mony for a cover for it. What shold move him to it, I know not...' (Greg, 1932). Whether Harrington's jakes remained a permanent feature of this hub of the book trade is not known. Visitation reports a few years later list heaps of excrement as an abominable health hazard but Harrington's jakes could not have been the only source (Gair, 22). A sense of Paul's as the hub of the book trade is evoked by Fulke Greville's letter to Walsingham seeking Star Chamber action to stop the unauthorized printing of Sidney's *Arcadia*: 'Sir this day one ponsonby a booke bynder in poles church yard, came to me, and told me that ther was one in hand to print, Sir Philip Sidneys old arcadia asking me yf it were done, with your honors consent or any other of his friends. I told him to my knowledge no, then he advised me to give warning of it, ether to the archebishope or doctor Cosen, who have as he says a copy of it to peruse to that end' (Robertson, xl). The incident reminds us that the stationers operated in a micro-environment where shop talk among apprentices, journeymen, printers, publishers, and booksellers at pubs and coffee houses probably kept the brotherhood fairly well informed about everyone else's business. Long-held notions of secretly-printed bad quartos being used to 'flush out' good texts overlook the realities of the trade. Collaborative business practices involving printing on unhidden presses was the norm.

Harrington's jakes is an appropriate 'signifier' for contemporary opinion of the book trade. The 'vendibility' of a text was generally viewed as the stationers' primary and perhaps only consideration in undertaking its printing and publication. The royal *Injunctions* of 1561 (STC 10095) called for the correction of the 'great abuse in the printers of books, which, for covetousness chiefly, regard not what they print, so they may have gain, whereby ariseth great disorder by publication of unfruitful, vain, and infamous books and papers' (Arber, I.xxxviii–xxxix). Government and ecclesiastical officials, academics, and authors echo this attitude throughout the following century. In fact, it is difficult to find a positive statement about the trade. The stationers never managed to strike a balance in the public's view between the printing of 'worthy' texts and the economic necessity of printing vendible but ephemeral and vain trifles such as Middleton's works. Without a constant flow of the latter through the presses of London, survival in the trade was impossible.

In reality, contemporaries and historians have dealt unfairly with the trade in this respect. A relatively enormous capital investment was required to establish a printing house fully stocked with the range of typefaces needed for a respectable graphic presentation of texts. Based upon figures cited in Arber (III.700–1), Peter Blayney estimates that the ownership of an 'average' functioning single-press printing house (allowed to operate one press and own a second) outfitted with used equipment and type transferred hands at the cost of £140 (1982, 25). Placed in the balance sheet against the wholesale receipts on an edition of, say, 1000 copies of an eight-sheet quarto, a jobbing printer had to turn out a steady and fairly long list of such books for several years to pay off his initial investment. The cost of a new press (about £16) was negligible in relation to the very expensive typefonts that wore out and had to be replaced. Although some exaggeration may underlie his deposition, John Legate claimed in 1588 that he had to spend £200 on new type merely to bring the Cambridge shop of Thomas Thomas up to working standards (McKenzie, 1959, 97). Thomas had used his type for only five years in a shop whose output was relatively low in comparison to similar London establishments. Furthermore, ownership of a printing house did not automatically guarantee success: business acumen clearly was essential for thriving in the trade.

An illuminating example is provided by the changing production level of the shop which passed from Gabriel Simson to Richard Read to Middleton's printer George Eld via the same twice-widowed woman. Read took over the shop in January 1601 and for approximately two years his output was limited to about twenty relatively short jobs. The largest projects were Part 2 of William Cornwallis's *Essays* (STC 5775), a small octavo set in pica roman type, Robert Yarrington's *Two Lamentable Tragedies* (STC 26076), Ben Jonson's *Cynthia's Revels* (STC 14773), and a portion of Jonson's *Every Man in His Humour* (STC 14766) which Read, for some inexplicable reason, shared with Simon Stafford. The five publishers for whom Read printed in 1601–2 never returned for further work.

During 1603, in marked contrast, output surged to at least twenty editions including the Latin drama *Nero* (STC 12551), printed for Edward Blount. A large portion of the shop's output in 1603 is hidden in Eld's section (sheets ²S–³C6) of another of Blount's projects, Florio's translation of Montaigne's *Essayes* (STC 18041), a massive folio in sixes set in pica roman type. (Valentine Simmes, responsible for *The Wisdome of Solomon*, printed the rest.) In 1603 alone, twelve new publishers without prior involvement brought jobs to Eld, including William Aspley, Edward Blount [4], Cuthbert Burby [2], Francis Burton, Jeffrey Chorlton (publisher of *The Blacke Booke*), John Harrison II [2], John Harrison IV, Felix Norton, John Norton 1, Thomas Pavier [2] (publisher of *A Yorkshire Tragedy*), George Potter, and Thomas Thorpe. Of these, Aspley, Blount, Burton, and Thorpe remained frequent customers. During 1604–8, Eld printed six or more editions for Burton [6], Blount [14], Thorpe [7], and Aspley [14: 4 with Thorpe, 1 with Blount; and sections of 4 others as sharing printer]. Eld also began printing for Thomas Adams [9] and John Wright 1, who brought 15 books by 1608 (a total of 56 by 1624). The business from the new clients totalled 64 jobs in the four-year period.

Overall, it is difficult to reject the conclusion that Eld actually took over the shop early in 1603 and was responsible for the dramatic increase in production that endured for the next two decades. As a result of his apparently aggressive quest for work, Eld also succeeded in becoming the 'assign' (the exclusive legal printer) of the two non-stationers who owned the royal patent for the printing of the *Book of Rates for the Custome* (STC 7690.5). Neither Gabriel Simson nor Richard Read ever had the business savvy needed to keep the shop's two presses operating at anything approaching a fraction of the possible production rate. In contrast, Eld did. Consequently, he was able to function as a printer–publisher and capitalize some quite massive publication projects as well as Middleton's *The Puritaine*, *A Tricke to Catch the Old One*, and *The Revengers Tragædie*.

Contemporary criticism of the stationers' trade must be placed in the broader perspective of the availability of the kind of texts that would have generated a more positive view. England simply did not produce the learned and 'worthy' texts that had to be imported from the continent (Clair). However, the conventional opinion that continental printing was universally superior to London printing in appearance and accuracy is based entirely on the output of a few famous printing houses which have received the bulk of scholarly attention. Hundreds of local presses scattered across the continent were turning out work as shoddy as anything printed in London.

Two aspects of the English book trade underscore the disadvantage in which English printers and publishers found themselves regarding the paucity of locally produced 'worthy' texts. The overwhelming majority of learned and scholarly texts were imported from the continent. On the other hand, London publishers and printers certainly did attempt to compete with the continental output of learned Latin texts, the staple of the import book trade, by publishing locally authored Latin works. James Binns has identified about 550 such texts (1550–1640) which can be described as 'serious and solid works...on grammar, rhetoric, logic, and literary theory; on theology, history, politics and law; and on alchemy, medicine, physics, and kindred topics' (1977, 1). Although these texts constitute an insignificant portion of London book production, a surprisingly large number of the active printers and publishers were involved in their publication.

Given the ongoing religious struggles during the period, it is not surprising that the bulk of locally authored serious texts were religious in nature. In one sense, theological treatises, moral tracts, biblical texts such as Middleton's *Two Gates of Salvation* and *Wisdome of Solomon Paraphrased*, sermons, and to a lesser extent, devotional literature, provided the economic underpinning of London printing. The output of most printing houses included a significant portion of such work. For example, Eld's total output of 428 editions from 1603–24 includes 157 religious texts. A sense of the market proportions is available in *A Catalogue of such English Bookes, as lately have bene, and now are in Printing for Publication* (1618), an advertising brochure in which some twenty booksellers and publishers listed their new texts. The 'Divinity' section comprises about eight of the eleven quarto pages; the rest is a potpourri of history, prose narrative, and poetry. Nicholas Okes, Middleton's 'favourite' printer, listed six books in the former section, and five in the latter: five of the eleven were entered in his own name.

The market demand for religious material never abated and it exceeded the output of local authors. Religious works constitute the largest body of translated texts printed during the period. Aside from religious texts and the usually brief continental 'news pamphlet' category, which constituted the second largest group of translations, London publishers (and to a lesser extent, publishing-printers) attempted to make available significant continental works and thus to profit from this market. The Final Report of the Commission appointed by the Privy Council in 1583 to investigate complaints by John Wolfe, Richard Jones, and other printers against the negative impact of royal patents on the printing trade is quite specific about one approach. In principle, a stationer 'hath...to him self any boke [i.e., copyright] that he can procure any learned man to make or translate for him'. The report perhaps exaggerates the extent of the practice which, nonetheless, was sufficiently extensive to bear the weight of the argument: 'a great number of Stationers that kepe no presses or printing [equipment] but put their worke to other[s] [to print] do set learned men on worke to make and translate good bokes, and so have the previlege [copyright] of them... such bokes which are the greatest number of copies [texts] that be printed and much greater number than be in previlege [royal patent], and commonly the most profitable' (Greg, 1967, 127-8). Thus the report indicates that printers and publishers actively sought out and hired 'learned men' either to author or to translate vendible texts. Such recruitment was clearly successful since translations represent a significant portion (ranging between 12% and 24%) of total book-production 1560-1603 (Ebel, 126-7). Entries into the Stationers' Register such as the following indicate it was a healthy business practice. Simon Waterson, Peter Short, and Thomas Adams entered (26 June 1598) four titles comprising the workes of Flaveus Josephus 'To be translated out of French into Englishe. and to be their Copie to printe, bringing better and sufficient authoryty for yt first, and before they print yt.' Three other titles were entered on the same day respectively to Waterson, William Ponsonby, and Master John Cawood, all 'to be printed in English' after translation and upon condition of 'sufficient authoryty'. It is impossible to even speculate about the extent to which locally authored English books were subsidized.

While publishers usually capitalized the printing of large translations and were responsible for the majority of the entries of such texts in the Stationers' Register, a few printers were able and willing to attempt to profit from this market. George Eld undertook several such ventures in collaboration with the indefatigable translator Edward Grimeston, including Jean de Serres's *A General Inventory of the History of France* (STC 22244; 1607) and Jean le Petit's *The Low-country Commonwealth* (STC 15485; 1609), both massive folios equalling the most capital-intensive kind of publishing projects encountered in London printing, and Simon Goulart's *Admirable and Memorable Histories* (STC 12135; 1607), a long quarto in eights (conditional 'sufficient authoryty' entry as noted above). Eld joined in a partnership with Adam Islip for the publication of two of Grimeston's translations: *A General History of the Netherlands* (STC 12374; 1608), a folio in sixes which runs through five alphabets; and *The Generall Historie of Spaine* (STC 17747; 1612), another large folio. One wonders how two printers published such projects.[1]

The Latin texts and the large translation projects show that publishers did not shy away from the risk involved in publishing serious texts. But when a printer undertook such a venture which could tie up his press(es) for the better part of a year, he risked the loss not only of his capital investment but also the cash flow generated by the staple printing of ephemeral texts like Middleton's. As the 1583 Privy Council Commission noted: journeymen and apprentices were 'in better care than the owners [of printing houses], for they are sure to be paied whether the bokes be uttered (i.e., sold) or no, where the owner abideth adventure of many [of the books] to come to [be sold as]

waste paper' (Greg, 1967, 127-8). Furthermore, a printer could not begin to realize a return on his investment until the entire edition was printed.

Given the economic necessity of survival and the inability to compete with continental publishers, it is not surprising that printers, booksellers, and publishers constantly sought out marketable texts regardless of their quality. Students of the drama are familiar with the notion that a new 'hit' was rushed *through* the press in order to take advantage of current interest, provided that a copy of the play could be acquired. In some instances, the sharing of a dramatic quarto among two or more printers certainly suggests that haste was a primary objective (e.g., *Michaelmas Terme*, *A Faire Quarrell*, *A Game at Chesse*; see later discussion). Court masques and civic pageants received similar treatment (e.g., the four different accounts of *The Magnificent Entertainment* published in 1604). However, most of these dramatic quartos were printed by a single printer and required at least two weeks for printing, collation, and delivery to the publisher. Nonetheless, it seems that they were rushed *to* the press. The probability that vendible books were accorded priority by the Masters and Wardens of the Company finds some confirmation in Philip Stubbes's 'sour grapes' complaint that vain trifles were quickly licensed while important theological works commonly experienced delay (Greg, 1956, 47). Thomas Nashe captures the essence of the stationers' behaviour regarding a 'hot' text: '& for the printers there is such gaping amongst them for the coppy of my L. of essex voyage, & t. ballet of the threscore & four knights...' (Greg, 1932). Nashe implies that stationers saw no difference between a text about a major military action led by the popular hero of the day and a silly ballad. Both would sell well. The individual stationer's problem was to acquire the 'coppy' so as to profit from current market interest, and only the printer or publisher who was successful in this pursuit would reap the profits. The sense of intense fraternal competition seen in Nashe's remark certainly is verified in the proceedings of the Stationers' Court regarding violations of copyright.

The fact that printers like Eld and Okes successfully competed with publishers in the quest for vendible texts sometimes obscures the distinction between publishers and booksellers, and publishing-printers.[2] The competitive nature of the trade is clear from two entries on 6 August 1607 when three Paul's Boys plays became available. Eld purchased *The Puritaine* and *Northward Hoe!* and entered both while Thomas Thorpe entered *What You*

---

[1] See also Bracken for data about Stansby, 1611-16; and Gants, 2002, for London data about self-publishing for 1614-18.

[2] The distinction between printer, publisher, and bookseller is sometimes confusing since the terms were used interchangeably during the period. The term **printer** applies only to those individuals who were allowed to own and operate the number of presses specified in the census lists of 1583, 1586, 1615, 1623, and 1636. To add to the confusion, one individual could function in all three capacities. The estate of John Day, for example, included a printing shop and three bookshops, and he published many books as well. 'Index 1. Printers and Publishers' in Volume 3 of the STC (1992) is the authoritative reference for distinguishing publishers and booksellers from printers; this essay uses the forms of names found there.

Will. Title-page imprints, in combination with entries in the Stationers' Register, usually are helpful in determining whether a publisher or the printer himself was responsible for capitalizing the publication of a book. The simple format for imprints—'Imprinted at London by G. Eld.'—along with the entry establish that Eld published as well as printed his two books. At the same time, Thorpe had Eld print his book ('Imprinted at London by G. Eld, for Thomas Thorppe.'). Nicholas Okes, the printer of Middleton's civic pageants, also frequently used this simple format in his copyright books. The record of the payment of £4 to Okes for a presumed 500 copies of *The Tryumphs of Honor and Industry* (1617) by the Grocers' Company reveals the 'silent publisher' type of arrangement that probably lay behind Okes's printing of the pageants: the Grocers' Company could not enter books, but the printer Okes could and did so, but only for *The Triumphs of Truth* (1613), the first in the series. The Grocers' Company took delivery of the edition. While no records exist, publishing-printers such as Okes and Eld and publishers like Thorpe, who had no bookshops, probably made arrangements in advance for distributing books in wholesale lots to various booksellers for marketing.

Publishers sometimes cited only themselves in the short format (e.g., *Histrio-mastix*: 'Printed for TH: Thorpe.') but could include the printer and/or the bookseller (or his address) in the long format. The relations are clear in the full imprint of *The Conspiracy of Byron* (STC 4968) (entered by Thorpe on 5 June 1608): 'Printed by G. Eld for Thomas Thorpe, and are to be sold at the Tigers head in Paules Church-yard', the location of the bookshop of Laurence Lisle, the publisher of *The Owles Almanacke*. Marketing the book through Lisle's bookshop obviously was pre-arranged. However, the printer is frequently omitted, as in the imprint of *A Faire Quarrell*: 'Printed at London for I[ohn]. T[rundle]. and are to be sold at Christ Church Gate. 1617.' Similarly, the imprint of *Your Five Gallants* omits Eld's name but specifies 'Imprinted at London for Richard Bonian, dwelling at the signe of the Spred-Eagle, right over-against the great North dore of Saint Paules Church.' Eld's gillyflower ornament on the title-page exemplifies a common method of a printer claiming his work. The purpose of the detailed addresses is obvious. The absence of a reference to the printer in short-format imprints is a common problem. The identity of the printer is important because it places the handling of a text in the context of his compositors' setting habits as well as the shop's methods of production. Traditionally, printer identification has relied upon the recognition of a printer's ornamental stock and typefonts.[3]

In other instances such as *A Tricke to Catch the Old One* and *The Revengers Tragædie* (both entered by Eld on 7 October 1607), publication by the printer is unambiguous in the rare imprints: 'Printed by G. Eld, and are to be sold at his house in Fleete-lane at the signe of the Printer's Press.' (In a few earlier books from this shop, the phrase 'over against Seacoal Lane' precisely fixed

Eld's location at the corner of Seacoal Lane and Fleete Lane, just west of Paul's.) When the original title of *A Tricke* was printed, Eld had apparently not yet arranged for the sale of the edition: he listed his printing shop as the marketing location although it was not a bookshop and he was not a bookseller. The two resettings of the cancelled title-page indicate that Eld solved the problem of retrieving his investment before pressing the collated books, the final stage of production (see below). Eld sold the entire edition to Henry Rocket during the original printing operation and Rocket thus had the option of cancelling the original title. It is likely that Eld let it be known at Stationers' Hall that he was printing a new drama and needed a buyer for the edition. The new imprint indicates that the book was 'Printed by G: E. and are to be sold by Henry Rockytt, at the long shop in the Poultrie under the Dyall. 1608.' (Additional title-pages were printed in a third setting of the text, probably for use as advertising posters, a practice noted by Middleton in *Owles Almanacke*: 'to paste up your name on every post in the title of a Booke').

Such a transaction involving the sale of an entire impression, or edition, was not altogether extraordinary. It was, in fact, one method of settling copyright or trade disputes in the Court of the Stationers: see, for example, the dispute between Eliot's Court and Joseph Barnes (Arber, II.793–4). Furthermore, the purchase of an entire edition was one method of cornering the market (at least for the moment) for booksellers who did not own copyrights to particularly vendible books. The Final Report of the Privy Council Commission of 1583 in fact recommended that the practice be made illegal, suggesting that 'the companie make an ordinance among them that no boke sellers take up whole empressions or so great quantities to lye by them in stoare till a scarcitie [lead] to the encrease of price or to the hindrance of poor men that thereby cannot have them' (Greg, 1967, 133). Otherwise, the Court settled disputes in various practical manners to protect the interests of the involved parties. In one instance, Humphrey Lownes 1 was given a half year to sell the remaining copies of an edition of the frequently-reprinted *The Pensive Mans Practise* that he had purchased from Richard Bradock on condition that the latter not reprint it until Lownes had sold all copies of his edition. Bradock was ordered to cease printing the new edition and store the already-printed sheets at Stationers' Hall (Greg & Boswell, 64). The tangled web of relations between authors and publishers seems to underlie the settlement ordered by the Court on 14 May 1604. Edward Blount had duly entered *Ben Jonson, his Part of King James his Royall and Magnificent Entertainment* on 15 March 1603 and Simmes printed it before Thomas Man 2 entered *The Magnificent Entertainment* on 2 April 1604, probably

---

[3] For instance, Eld's 'Trumpet-T' ornamented initial and the headpiece on A2 of *Quarrell* suggests his involvement but only the identification of his typefont(s) can prove it (see later discussion). The typefonts show, in fact, that Eld printed sheets A–C and G–K, while Bernard Alsop printed sheets D–F in a shared printing operation. In contrast, only Eld's typefont appears in *Five Gallants*.

a post-printing entry transcribed from a printed copy (Bowers). The Court ordered Blount to sell his remaining four hundred copies to Man at the rate of 6 shillings per ream, the combined cost of the paper and printing (see later discussion). Given the fact that two entirely different texts about the same events were involved, it is difficult to interpret the order as a copyright settlement. More than likely, Man wished to eliminate the competition from Blount's book for market share. The deal eliminated any financial loss on Blount's part since he automatically realized a profit on all the books that he had already sold.

In general, the acquisition of texts is one of the most fascinating issues of printed publication during Middleton's day, but the historical record is nearly blank. Middleton's *Tryumphs of Honor and Industry* is a rare exception since the guild responsible for sponsoring this civic pageant left an expense account (as is the case with several other pageants). Similarly, Henslowe recorded payments to authors for play texts. Otherwise, we are left with the question: how did a given text traverse the gap between the author's personal manuscript copy and the printer's copy from which were printed the 292, 300, 486, 500, 632, 1000, 1200, 1250, or 1500 books that were hawked in Paul's Churchyard or 'uttered' in bookshops scattered across the city? In any event, once a publisher had acquired a manuscript by means fair or foul, the actual production process commenced with the selection of a printer. Joseph Moxon's highly detailed account in *Mechanick Exercises on the Whole Art of Printing* (1683–4) provides a precise knowledge of the actual tools and techniques that were employed in producing books. Given the physical evidence in extant books, it is possible to determine with a fair degree of certainty how Middleton's texts were affected during the hand-printing process.

Prior to the actual production of a book, three stages of preparation were necessary: the transcription of a fair copy; allowance and licensing; and contracting with a printer.

Fair Copy

A fair copy of the text had to be prepared for use by the compositor(s) in setting the type and subsequently by the shop's corrector (and possibly by the author or his agent) in checking printed **proof-pulls** against copy. Significant variations occurred in each of these stages in actual practice. Binns (1977, 1) found that, more often than not, the fair copy was transcribed from the authorial manuscript by a scribe hired by the printer (see also Blayney, 1982, 263–6). Common sense suggests that printers undertook this additional expense for a practical reason. Although a compositor could set type from virtually any rough draft, the quality of printer's copy directly affected the accuracy of typesetting, or **composition**. A manuscript prepared specifically for use by a compositor probably differed from an authorial manuscript in some respects, obviously including legibility. More importantly, a printer would require a transcript that was consistent throughout in terms of the size and spacing of the script, a factor that

is not significant in manuscripts intended for a reader, but critical to a compositor in the process of **casting off** copy (see later discussion).

External Allowance and Internal Licensing

The long series of injunctions, edicts, orders, ordinances, and decrees related to the printing trade required that the manuscript be submitted to the proper authorities *outside* the Stationers' Company whose responsibility was to examine it for heretical, seditious, or treasonable content. As Henry Chettle remarked in regard to his fair copying of *Greene's Groatsworth of Wit* (1592): 'it was ill written, as sometime Greene's hand was none of the best; licensed it must be ere it could be printed, which could never be if it might not be read'. The approval by such an outside authority was termed **allowance** or **authorization** and literally meant that publication of the text was permitted without respect to *who* could publish it. The 10-shilling fee for the perusal process was paid by the publisher. Greg (1956) has noted the probability that the authorizer's review of a manuscript could include cross-examination of the author. Otherwise, it seems that the publisher delivered and retrieved the manuscript which was inscribed with the official 'imprimatur' (see the facsimile, Fig. 35, Blayney, 1982, 260). In cases involving the submission of a manuscript without authorial consent (Brennan, 91), the publisher doubtlessly was responsible.

Following outside allowance, the manuscript or transcription bearing the 'imprimatur' was presented to the Masters, Wardens, or Assistants at Stationers' Hall for the actual licensing for printing. After their approval, the **entry** of the book by the Clerk into the Stationers' Register established ownership of the **copyright** or licence and conferred the exclusive legal right of a printer or publisher to print a text.[4]

By 1582, the entry fee had been normalized to six-pence.[5] The presentation of the authorized copy to Company officials aimed at insuring that no one already owned the copyright to the text. An entry to Okes on 5 February 1606, for example, specifies 'provided that yt be not alreadie entred to any other'. The Clerk had not yet searched the Register's titles. Similarly, the fact that Henry Olney was able to obtain a licence on 12 April 1595 to print a text, which had been previously entered on 29 November 1594 to William Ponsonby with the title 'the

---

[4] The right to enter titles in the Stationers' Register and obtain copyrights was exclusive to members of the Stationers' Company—no one else could. Ignorance of this simple fact as well as the census lists of 1583, 1586, and/or 1615, terms such as 'privilege' and other matters has led to an absurd theory which pits the 'licensed printers' against 'fourteen of the *unprivileged* printers...[who] were obviously not members of the company' in a scenario of government control of printing, censorship and other matters (Boose, 186). Actually, everyone mentioned in the 1599 Bishops' Ban was a member and a licensed printer. Likewise, many of the suppressed titles had been duly entered and licensed. Furthermore, the facsimiles purportedly showing the edicts of June 1, 1599 and June 4, 1599 (Boose, 188, 189) actually reproduce (without any differentiation) the edicts as *printed* in Arber's 1875 transcript, not the actual documents as *written* into the Stationers' Register in 1599.

[5] See Jackson, 1957, about variant fees; Kirschbaum; and Blayney, 1997, about two types of entries.

defence of posey', under the new title *An Apology for Poetrie* indicates that nothing more than a search through the titles in the Register actually preceded licensing. Given the piecework wages economy, the Clerk probably was paid a fee both for his writing the entry and searching the Register although no records exist to support such an inference.

Manuscript in hand, a publisher set about seeing it into print. We can only assume that astute publishers 'shopped around' for the best deal. Negotiations between publisher and printer regarding a printing job doubtlessly occurred at the printer's place of business which was located in his residence, where various rooms served as the 'printing house', the 'warehouse', the 'press room' etc.[6] Overall, it seems reasonable to infer that a printer's wife had a function in the operation of the plant, albeit a menial one. However, in a few instances such as Jacqueline Vautrollier, the ability to function as the master of print in the absence of her husband is absolutely clear in decisions by the Stationers' Court ordering her to cease printing books. It seems quite significant that Lord Burghley entrusted Jacqueline with the printing of one of his more famous propaganda forgeries, *The copie of a letter sent out of England to Don Benardin de Mendoza* (1588). In addition to Jacqueline, the widows of a few printers (Peter Short and Thomas Orwin) printed for a year or two before remarrying. Elizabeth Allde continued printing from 1628–36 under her own name. Henry Bynneman's widow married outside the Company and had to forfeit her possession of his copyrights. Otherwise, copyrights passed with the widows to the new husbands.[7]

The Printing House

Prior to the Great Fire of 1666, London printing shops were set up in a printer's residence rather than in specially designed structures. As Moxon explained, the term 'Printing House' applied, in printer's parlance, specifically to the rooms within his dwelling house in which the printing equipment was installed. Several rooms of a typical three- or four-storey house thus were devoted to the operation of the printing plant. Two structural qualities were desirable, according to Moxon. First, a firm foundation and superstructure were required for the press, so that the force vectors generated by the pressman's 'pull' were focused on the platen by the overhead braces (connected to the ceiling beams) working in opposition to the floor. Lighting was the second consideration in the choice of the room. Ideally, the incoming sunlight was not impeded by contiguous buildings or trees and reached all corners of the room (17). This seems a difficult condition given the London row-houses of the time, not to mention the weather factor (candles were a standard supplemental light source). Further, the press should be located on the north side of the room away from the direct sunlight so that (1) the hard-working pressmen 'may be the less uncommoded' by the heat, and (2) the diffused light best supported the kind of visual recognition required

by work at the press. With the press at the north or west wall, the **heap** of wetted paper would not be exposed to direct sunlight and perhaps dry prematurely before the press-run was completed. Additional space was required for the **horse**, a long knee-height bench upon which the heap and wrought-off sheets were placed, and for the movements of the two pressmen (when operating at **full press**).

Layout and Design

Several matters had to be settled between printer and publisher before production began. Overall, the format of the book (e.g. folio, quarto, octavo), the size of the type used for the text, the size of the edition, and the size and quality of the paper determined the basic cost of the printing job. The hiring of a 'learned corrector' and special requirements for the incorporation of graphic illustrations and tabular material would add to the total cost.

Evolution of Typefaces and Graphics

The publisher's selection of a format for a book established its relative size and the variety of options available for the visual presentation of a text. Middleton's works benefited from the evolution in London printing that occurred during the preceding four decades. By the 1590s, the trade had developed fairly standard typographical and graphical conventions that had begun evolving in the 1550s for different kinds of texts. Prior to the 1550s, English books exhibited, with relatively few exceptions, a numbingly monotonous approach to layout, typography, and ornamentation. In fact, a large number of the pre-1550 books have no separate title-page, but headed the first page of the text with a 'title' such as 'Here begynneth the boke of…' which was more often than not in the same typefont as was used in the text itself. The major limitation on graphic design was an almost total reliance on the black letter **family** of typefaces that was forced on London printers by circumstance. The very few roman and italic typefaces that were available were atrociously awkward in design and poorly cut. The ornamental stock including decorated initials was hardly better.

---

[6] John Twyn read proof in his kitchen and was hung, drawn, and quartered as a result (Blayney, 1982, 197–200). It seems clear that printing house activity spilled over into woman's domain. Printer John Day's son Richard had a personality conflict with Day's second wife Alice. On one occasion Richard came in from the printing house to dinner 'and complained that his stepmother's refusal to provide the workmen with a towel was leading to the spoiling of a lot of good white paper' [during regular sorting in the warehouse]—whereat (Chambers tells us) Alice Day 'wold curse and bay' (Oastler, 66). While such anecdotes add little to our understanding of the printing trade, they remind us that printers were by and large coarse, uneducated tradesmen who laboured hard and long for their keep. Perhaps the world has done them wrong to also expect the refined taste necessary to distinguish between vendible and truly worthy texts that would eventually find their way into the *Norton Anthology*.

[7] For broader studies of women in the book trade, see Bell, 1983 and 1996; she concludes: 'Despite their exclusion from office in the Stationers' Company, women (usually as widows) could operate in the same way as their male counterparts in owning, acquiring, selling, and transferring rights in books, and in the way in which they ran shops and used distribution networks, participating in partnerships and, later in the period, in congers of stationers' (1996, 31).

London printers had to turn to the continent for the printing materials that could produce visually stimulating books. The effect of the increasing availability of continental roman and italic typefaces in the 1550s doubtlessly was reinforced by the influence of humanistic continental printing, particularly from France and Italy. London's use of the new typefaces lagged behind Italian printing by half a century and French printing by three decades (A. F. Johnson, 38–42; Updike, 72–7; Vervliet, 56–61). The use of different typefaces to set off languages and 'marginalize' paratexts in thick humanistic editions of the classics, buttressed with passages of commentaries and notes, was a long-established continental tradition by the time the new romans and italics began appearing in England. Although black letter was still almost totally dominant in 1572, even John Stroud—the 'preacher turned surreptitious printer' who had no training whatever in the trade but nonetheless was responsible for printing Thomas Cartwright's *A Replie to An Answer* (STC 4711; 1573) (often working entirely alone!)—could complain and apologize: 'It falleth out (gentle Reader) that I neyther having wealth to furnishe the Print wyth sufficient varieties of letters [i.e., typefaces], have bene compelled (as a poore man doth one instrument to divers purposes) so to use one letter for three or four tongues.'

The attractive new roman and italic typefaces were first adopted in a minor capacity as emphasis fonts, and gradually they displaced the staple black letter, but never entirely, as the use of the latter became a traditional bibliographical signifier in certain kinds of texts (see below). As a result, the appearance of London books changed dramatically. Overall, the use of ornamented initials and the creation of a typographical hierarchy by the use of a variety of typeface styles and sizes 'coded' the lexical text. The reader understood the relationships of subdivisions to the whole text by 'reading' the bibliographical encoding as well as the lexical text (Weiss, 1992, 91–4).

London printers proceeded through a transitional period lasting through the 1570s that defined the typographical conventions employed thereafter. The remarkable transformation that occurred is apparent from a comparison of the output of Henry Bynneman's shop during 1569–74 and Eld's shop 1603–8. After he outfitted his shop in 1566–9 with a wide range of italics and romans—including three(!) pica roman fonts by Francois Guyot, Pierre Haultin, and the unknown genius who designed the Jean Tournes pica roman—Bynneman continued to rely upon black letter in vernacular English texts 1571–4 but the romans and italics appeared with increasing frequency in settings of paratextual materials such as prefatory epistles, chapter divisions and sub-headings, running titles, tables, and indices. Overall, black letter was used in the large majority of the approximately 70 books (or sections of books) produced by Bynneman in the 1571–4 period. The proportions would change dramatically by the end of the decade. In what appears to be his first exclusively roman and italic book, *A Dictionarie French and English*,

M.D. LXXI (STC 6832; [1569–70] 1571), Bynneman set the French in roman but the English gloss in italic instead of the conventional black letter. The twelve Latin texts produced during the period were set exclusively in romans and italics.[8]

The first extensive appearance of roman and italic in vernacular black-letter texts began in his section (3A–3T7ᵛ, 4E–4K4) of John Calvin's *Commentaries* (STC 4395) which Henry Middleton and Thomas East shared with Bynneman in 1571. The pica romans were used liberally for sizable quotations throughout the book.[9]

The displacement of black letter by roman as the text font in vernacular texts began in 1573, primarily in books in the theological category which were translations of continental works originally printed in roman. Bynneman shifted to the Guyot pica roman as text font midway in his black letter section ('The Tenth Book', 3A–F3ᵛ) of Jean de Serres's *The Three Partes of Commentaries* (STC 22242) for printing 'The King's Letters' (3F4–K2). More significantly, 'The Tenth Book' was a reprint of Bynneman's edition of *A true and plaine report of the Furious outrages of Fraunce* (STC 13847; 1573) in which the vernacular text was printed exclusively in the Guyot roman and italic pica fonts, perhaps the first vernacular prose book containing no black letter whatever. The shift continued in 1574 in some very significant texts. Of the seventeen books produced that year, three major vernacular texts were set in roman type with italic in the emphasis function: two sequential folio editions of John Calvin's *Sermon* [. . .] *vpon the booke of Job* (STC 4444, 4445), followed by Calvins's *Sermons* [. . .] *vpon the epistle to the Galatians* (STC 4449). The formidable 'folio in sixes' format of *Sermons* (STC 4444, STC 4445) must have been priced to a limited market. Purchasers got a bargain nonetheless since each page contained a massive number of types in two columns of 61 lines set in the diminutive Guyot pica (80mm) roman. Economic considerations were probably responsible for this format. Nonetheless, the indispensable annotations in contemporary folio and quarto editions of the Geneva Bible were in even smaller long primer(66mm) and brevier (54mm) roman type.

---

[8] STC 2036, STC 4896, STC 5295, STC 10451, STC 13846, STC 19139, STC 20309, STC 20906, STC 23000, STC 24287, STC 24788a, STC 25004. His later publication history makes it clear that Bynneman invested so heavily in the new roman and italic fonts in order to publish classical as well as 'learned' foreign language texts.

[9] The size of a Renaissance **typefont** is given according to a standard unit of measurement termed the **twenty-line height**. This is the vertical distance between the top of the ascenders in the first line of a setting to the top of the ascenders in the twenty-first line. The **ascender** is that portion of a tall letter which reaches the highest point of a line; it extended to the very end of the body on which the letter was cast. The **descender** extended to the other end of the body. A second measurement termed the **bare-height** is used as the unit for stating the size of a given **typeface**. It consists of the vertical distance from the top of an ascender to the bottom of a descender (e.g. 'l', 'h' and 'g' in 'slight'). The two measurements are necessary because a given typeface was often cast in two (or more) different sets of moulds producing two typefonts with different twenty-line heights but exactly the same bare-height. In other words, the same typeface could be and was cast on different body-sizes. In short, the bare-height confirms the identity of the typeface while the twenty-line height distinguishes between typefonts in that typeface design (Weiss, 1990, 151, note 7).

The typographical medium contributed a non-lexical statement in such applications. Biblical glosses, notes, and commentary, typically set in these small sizes of type, signified 'read carefully—your salvation depends upon it'. However, the difficulty of reading did not increase proportionately. The legibility of small sizes of the **white letter** (as printers referred to roman) was decidedly superior to black letter in such applications. The thin strokes forming the roman and italic letters take much less ink, are less susceptible to blotting, cannot be confused with each other, and hence are more legible. As Viglius Zuichemus noted of Froben's printing types in 1534, 'letters that are too pointed [e.g., black letter] offend the eye, but on the contrary those that are round (e.g., roman, italic) and have been well designed, even when quite small, win the reader's approval' (Gerritsen, 147). That is why roman and italic displaced black letter, whose heavy vertical strokes are ideal for proclamations, ballads, and other such texts which were intended for public reading at a distance. But pica roman type presented no legibility problem in large folios such as Calvin's *Sermons*, Thomas North's translation of Plutarch's *The Lives of the Noble Grecians and Romans* (1579), Geoffrey Fenton's translation of *The History of [Francesco] Guicciardini* (1579), and the Geneva bibles printed by Christopher Barker (see below).

Following the general shift to roman type in theological works, black letter remained as the typographical medium of nonconforming, heretical texts. The effect can be striking. In Eld's printing of *An Apology of Three Testimonies* (STC 19295; 1607), for example, the refuted passages at the head of each section of rebuttal are quoted in black letter type crowded into an excessively indented rectangular area. These blocks of type are engulfed in the contextual roman and italic typefaces, a stranded regiment in tight defensive formation, its back against the wall of the right margin, about to be overwhelmed by the forces of Truth.

By the time Middleton was born (1580), London printers were using a wide range of romans and italics regularly, and an increasing majority of books contained little or no black letter type at all. The typographical conventions that were established during the 1570s resulted in the continued use of black letter in certain kinds of texts which shared one common denominator: they were usually in prose. But a few exceptions occurred even to this most general of categorizations. Each of Middleton's printers produced at least a few items in black letter, but they relied almost exclusively on romans and italics. The output of Eld's shop 1603-8 is roughly typical. Of approximately 130 books and sections of books which Eld printed in that period, Eld used black letter as the text face in about a half-dozen including: *A Fruitefull Meditation* (STC 14377; 1603) [religious reprint]; *The Birth of Mankinde* (STC 21161; 1604) [medical reprint]; *The Shepheards Kalender* (STC 22420; 1604) [quasi-almanac reprint in folio; not Spenser's]; *Riche his Farewell to Military Profession* (STC 20997; 1606), *A Petite Pallace of Pettie his Pleasure* (STC 19822) [prose narrative reprints]; *Belman Pt. 2* (STC 6485) [prose pamphlet]; and *Feareful Newes of Thunders and Lightening* (STC 21511; 1606) ['news' pamphlet]. He also violated the black letter convention of the 'foreign news' category in *A True Report of the Overthrow Given to the Spaniards* (STC 1900; 1605) and in *A True History of the Memorable Siege of Ostend* (STC 18895; 1604) which could be categorized either as 'news' or 'history', both of which could conventionally appear in black letter. Other examples such as *Newes Sent to the Ladie Princesse of Orange* (STC 18834; 1589; printed by John Wolfe in english 94mm roman type) illustrate the variability within the black letter convention. In general, such non-theological prose texts in quarto usually used black letter as the text face, and Middleton's works (*Platoes Cap*, *Meeting of Gallants at an Ordinarie*, *Sir Robert Sherley*, *Penniless Parliament*, and *Father Hubburds Tales*) exhibit the normal mixture of typefaces.

Black Letter: The Commoner's Typeface?

During the past two decades, the study of literacy and publishing in early modern England has produced a curious misunderstanding about the sociological significance of the use of the black letter typeface in the printing of the Elizabethan-Jacobean period. Keith Thomas gives the most detailed expression to the notion that black letter was the typographical medium of the mass of less learned readers, sort of a 'more legible' commoner's typeface. He argues that a child learning to read in the petty schools of Tudor England began with the alphabet in the horn book, proceeded to the Lord's Prayer, *The A. B. C. with the Catechism*, the Primer, and the Psalter: 'what all these learning aids had in common was that they were printed in...black letter' type. Thomas's conclusion that 'black letter was the type for the common people...black letter literacy, in short, was a more basic skill than roman-type literacy' (99) seems reasonable enough when these facts are considered without reference to the relative role of black letter type in the printing of the period as a whole. Actually, this supposed relation is undercut by too many strong contradictions to be taken seriously. The ballads are often cited as primary evidence for the notion that commoners felt more comfortable with black letter and read roman and italic only with difficulty if at all, the converse of the modern reader and black letter (Thomas, 99). The fact is that the romans and italics functioned in ballads as elsewhere: main titles, sub-titles, emphasis, quotations, and verse. In short, ballads forced commoners to become familiar with roman and italic typography from the 1560s onward.

The significance of *The A. B. C. with the Catechism* with respect to typographic literacy is unquestionable: the expanded title describes it as 'an Instruction to be taught and learned of every Childe, before he be brought to be confirmed by the Bishop'. The dialogue (question–answer) format and the doctrinal content (Lord's Prayer, Creede,

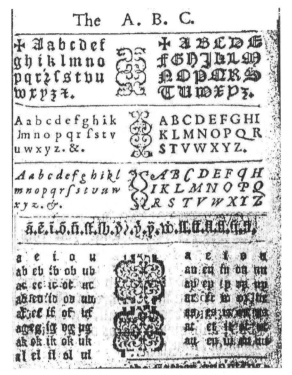

1. The black letter, roman, and italic alphabets on sig. Aiii of *The A. B. C. with the Catechism* (STC 20.8).

syllables, and the text of the sign of the cross (see facsimile in Baldwin, 122). A fragment of another Day edition (STC 20.6; *c*.1584) exhibits the final development of the ABC page which is divided horizontally by rules and vertically by rows of flowers.[12] The layout, but not the typesetting itself, is nearly identical to Thomas Purfoot Sr.'s printings in 1601 and 1605 (see below), as is the mixing of black letter, roman, and italic in the rest of the book.

Incredible as it might seem, the first complete extant copy of the sanctioned little catechism is the edition printed by Thomas Purfoot Sr. in 1605 (STC 20.8). The 1605 ABC page is the same setting of type found in Purfoot Sr.'s 1601 edition (STC 20.7) of Alexander Nowell's version of the catechism (Fig. 1). It includes the black letter, roman, and italic alphabets, and the syllables and ligatures in black letter. Typically, the title-page alternates among the three typefaces (Fig. 2). The title itself, 'The A.B.C.', was set in François Guyot's 40-pt roman, followed by six lines of black letter, Thomas Purfoot Sr.'s printer's mark containing his initials 'T.P.' in roman, the imprint in three sizes of roman, and the royal patent 'Cum Piuilegio' in italic. Hundreds of thousands of Elizabethan children, then, were introduced to the first three letters of the roman alphabet in the titles of the book and the ABC page from as early as 1553. Within the text, both sides of the dialogue are in black letter, but running titles, subtitles, speech prefixes (i.e., 'Maister', 'Scholler'), and the ejaculation 'Lord haue mercy vpon us, and incline our harts to keepe this Law.' repeated by the child after each of the ten commandments, are all in roman type.

In addition to the stand-alone sanctioned catechism, numerous 'alternate' versions lacking the patented ABC page were published which exhibit considerable typographical variation.[13] For example, John Awdely's 1572 edition of Edward Dering's *A briefe and necessary Instruction, Very needefull to bee known of all Householders* (STC 6679) set the text in two sizes of black letter while using roman for running titles, names, quotes, speech prefixes, and marginal scriptural references. John Charlewood's 1577 editions (STC 6679.7, STC 6679.9) switched the marginal references to black letter but set the Lord's Prayer, Creed, and Decalogue in roman type. Charlewood's 1583 edition (STC 6712.3) changed the texts of

Decalogue, 'graces' etc.) of this sanctioned 'small' or 'little' catechism[10] was finalized sometime in the 1560s preceding its appearance in John Cawood's 1569 edition of the *Book of Common Prayer* (STC 2102, sigs. S2–S5[v]) where Archbishop Grindel of York's directives for its universal doctrinal use are appended (see sigs. S5[v]–6; and later editions).

In practice, a pedagogical as well as a doctrinal purpose was served by the 'stand-alone' editions of *The A. B. C. with the Catechism* that were continuously printed in the tens of thousands and sold at a penny or less. In these, the catechism text was preceded by an ABC page which contained alphabets and syllables for teaching children to read.[11] Edward Whitchurch's 1551 edition (STC 20.2; 20.3 is a fragment) seems the first known instance of the official expanded title. The ABC page probably reflects Whitchurch's limited typographic resources: it includes lower and uppercase black letter, rotunda capitals, and roman capitals. The book is exclusively in black letter except for six large roman capitals and one ornamented roman capital. John Day 1 acquired the royal patent for the ABC page and the sanctioned little catechism in 1553. The ABC page of the fragmentary copy of his 1553(?) edition (STC 20.4; lacks the catechism section) set the title 'A,B,C,' in large roman capitals, and includes the black letter and roman alphabets (no italic yet), the table of

---

10 Barker used the descriptive term 'The small Catechisme' (Arber, I.116) while patent holder Richard Day used the title 'the ABC with the little catechism' (Greg, 1967, item 115, 37) in official documents. During the 1560s and after, longer advanced catechisms were published both by the church and individuals. The ABC page was never included in the *Book of Common Prayer* and extremely rarely in other catechisms and primers.

11 Note that the pedagogical function of the catechism overlapped with the hornbook which was just an ABC page either with the text of the Lord's Prayer, or just the sign of the cross ('In the name of the Father etc.'). A child's introduction to reading could begin with either or both.

12 See facsimiles in H. Anders, 34–5.

13 Ian Green has identified over 280 such alternate brief catechisms in the question-answer format intended to improve upon and/or supplement the doctrinal components of sanctioned version during the 1570–1649 period (400). Presumably using the standard edition size of 1250 copies, Green estimated 'that over three-quarters of a million copies of these works were in circulation by the early seventeenth century, in addition to perhaps half a million copies of the official forms' (425).

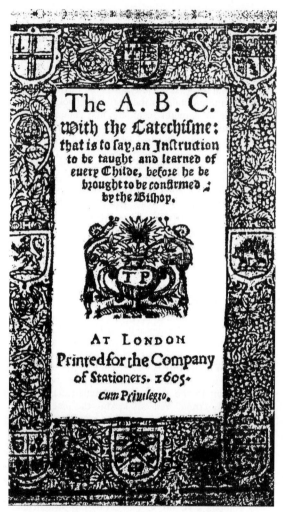

2. Title-page of Thomas Purfoot Sr.'s 1605 edition
of *The A. B. C. with the Catechism* (STC 20.8).

typefaces for the preliminaries (epistle dedicatory, the verse
'Ad Parentes atq; Liberos', and epistle 'To all Children
of a Christian towardnesse'), headings and subheadings,
running titles, and marginal notes. He set the father's explanations in black letter, while the son's humbly framed
questions and answers were set in roman.

In short, Elizabethan children were exposed to roman and italic as well as black letter typefaces from
the beginning of their reading education. The resulting
widespread familiarity with all three typefaces, especially
among commoners, is probably reflected in the typography of the bibles printed from 1575 onward by royal
patent holder Christopher Barker and then his son Robert
Barker (1585). The encroachment on Barker's patent in
1590 by John Legate, printer to Cambridge University,
created a legal conflict that provides insight into market
and typeface literacy issues. Legate had printed in roman
type both the Geneva *New Testament* in the tiny 32mo
format in 1590 (STC 2889), and the whole Geneva *Bible*
in octavo in 1591 (STC 2155). Barker protested vigorously to the Privy Council. The letter of June 1591 from
the Vice-Chancellor and Heads of Cambridge University to
Lord Burghley pleading Legate's case provides an entirely
unique, precise reference to an Elizabethan printer's intended market: 'The suit...is so prejudicial to the poor
man...it could not but tend to his utter undoing; especially Sturbridge-fair now drawing near; being the chiefest
time wherein he hopeth to reap greatest fruit of this his
travail' (Arber, II.819; Greg, 1967, 148-51). Legate's
octavo and 32mo Geneva versions in roman type undeniably were printed for the mass of commoners who visited
this largest of all English fairs (three weeks in September).
Puritan commoners read their Bibles at home and followed
scripture readings in church, even correcting the minister
(Spufford, 33-4), but it is highly unlikely that they lugged
large black letter Bishops bibles in folio to church; rather,
Barker's own production of octavo editions of the Geneva
version was aimed at this Puritan market. The octavo size
was very portable (pocket size) and more importantly, the
most affordable complete *Bible* at about 10-15% of the
cost of a folio and at about 40% of a quarto.[14] Overall,
Barker published 25 octavo editions 1577-1610, all in
roman type (italic emphasis), for a total of approximately
62,500 copies, the largest number in any of the book
sizes. In other words, the cheapest whole bibles on the
market were printed exclusively in roman and italic type.
It seems that only a very large market which included a
mass of roman-reading commoners can account for this
coincidence.[15]

the questions asked by the master to italic type. James
Roberts's 1597 edition (STC 6681) contains only roman
and italic type, but his 1605 edition (STC 6682) reverted
to black letter internally as the text font. In contrast,
Edward Fenton's *So Shorte a Catechism* (STC 10787.2)
went through at least eight editions c.1582-1626 from
at least four different type settings. Only one line changed
(from roman to italic) in the whole 1591-1626 sequence,
demonstrating a basic principle of the period in regard
to reprints: a slavish adherence to the text, layout, and
typographic presentation of earlier editions. Finally, the
typography of John Carpenter's alternate catechism *Con-
templations for the institution of children in the Christian
religion* (STC 4662; 1601) is worth noting. Robert Read
(George Eld's predecessor) employed roman and italic

[14] The allowable price for a book was set by the Stationers' Company according
to the size of the type. These octavo editions used in the range of 53-65 sheets
resulting in a price range of three shillings to three shillings sixpence, unbound.
[15] Barker had obtained a significant exception to the 1250 copy limit in the
Stationers' Company 1587 settlement which permitted 2500 copies per setting of
type in the tiny 'nonpareil' (44mm) size in which Barker's and Legate's octavos
were set (Arber, II.883; 11 December, 1587). So, while he published 45 quarto
editions 1578-1611 (32 black letter, 13 roman), the total number of copies was
approximately 56,250 because of the official limit of 1250 copies per setting of
type. In the folio size, he published thirteen Geneva versions (seven roman, six

Furthermore, the notion that texts aimed at commoners were intentionally printed in black letter to reach the broadest market is fraught with other contradictions. This market theory collapses under the weight of many publications such as Holinshed's massive three-volume *Chronicles* which sold for 20 shillings (new, unbound) in 1577 (F. R. Johnson, 92) and was still evaluated in 1597 at 20 shillings (used and bound) (Hotson, 51). Eld's *Birth of Mankinde* and *The Shepheards Kalender* (noted above) are similar examples. The publishers of such expensive folios in black letter had no illusions about their potential market, but they did not print in the supposed typefaces of the educated and élite. Conversely, a text about kingship by a new King certainly would have appealed to the broadest possible market, a veritable 'text of the century' in the eyes of those 'gaping amongst themselves' for vendible texts in Paul's Churchyard. Nonetheless the syndicate consisting of publishers John Norton 1, George Bishop, Thomas Man, Simon Waterson, and Cuthburt Burby printed editions amounting to an estimated 7500 copies of James I's *Basilikon Doron* (STC 14354; 1603) in english (94mm) roman type. Edward Allde, printer of *The Phoenix* and *Michaelmas Terme*, pirated another 3000 copies of this highly vendible text in english roman type as well.[16]

In some non-theological texts, the intended market niche is precisely specified. *The Surveiors Dialogue* (STC 18640; 1610), for example, is 'Very profitable for all men to peruse, but especially for all Gentlemen, or any other Farmar, or Husbandman.' Clearly the publisher John Busby expected farmers and husbandmen as well as the gentry to read the surveyor's explanations in english (94mm) roman type. Finally, the legalistic wording of the Stationers' price guidelines of 1598 provides mute testimony to the ascendence of the romans and italics: both are specifically stated twice in reference to 'all books being new copies which hereafter shall be printed', but the ordinance makes no reference whatever to black letter (Greg & Boswell, 58–9).

Similarly, attempts to link the hypothesis of the commoner's typeface to class-distinctions in readership overlook conflicting evidence provided by at least a few inventories of libraries owned by the gentry and upper classes. Among the approximately 440 books owned in 1597 by Richard Stonely esquire, Teller of the Queen's Exchequer of Receipt, are black letter editions of prose works by George Whetstone, George Gascoigne (2), Stephen Guazzo, Antony de Guervera, John Lyly, Geoffrey Fenton, Matteo Bandello, Geoffrey Painter and several others (Hotson). The inventory of the 'Lamport Find' (Jackson, 1967) includes 125 books whose titles and authors are still the meat of Elizabethan anthologies: Christopher Marlowe, Shakespeare, Michael Drayton, George Chapman, Sir John Davies, Ben Jonson, Abraham Fraunce, Gervase Markham, Edmund Spenser, and William Warner, all in roman type. Among these, black letter prose texts are represented by William Averill, Nicholas Breton (4), George

Gascoigne, Robert Greene (2), Thomas Lodge, Thomas Nashe, and Thomas Deloney who, like Middleton, wrote for and about the so-called 'middle class'. Two black letter prose pamphlets stick out in this otherwise distinguished list: *The Blacke Booke* and *Platoes Cap*. However, the strongest contradiction of the sociology of genre and black letter occurs at the top end of the class structure. In 1627 the library of Francis, Countess of Bridgewater, amounting to 184 books (excluding 17 French items), included one bound collection of 'Divers Playes by Shakespeare', 'Diverse Playes in 5 thicke Volumes', and 'A Booke of Diverse Playes in Leather', all vain ephemera in the midst of about 160 biblical and religious texts. More significantly, the Countess owned black letter editions of Robert Greene's *A Quip for an Upstart Courtier* and *Greene's Ghost*, *Don Quixote*, *The Pleasant History of Lazarillo de Tormes*, and *The First and Best Part of Scoggins [Merry] Jests*, the very kinds of texts that educated aristocrats supposedly despised (Hackel). In the final analysis, individual taste rather than class-oriented values established a publisher's market, and his choice of typeface had little, if any, effect upon the breadth of that market and potential sales.

Nonetheless, the reprinting of old works in black letter continued into the 1630s long after its general use lapsed. Tradition obviously ruled: the typographical medium became a signifier, created an ambience much in the manner of Spenser's archaic diction, so that the typography of later reprints of famous old works by the likes of Barnaby Rich, George Turberville, George Pettie, and Robert Greene remained exactly as in the first editions. By the 1620s, black letter had been displaced by romans and italics so that its use as a text face (except in reprints) could serve as a bibliographical signifier. It is difficult to reject the hypothesis that when the quarto *A Proclamation Declaring his Majesties Pleasure Concerning the Dissolving of the Present Convention of Parliament* (STC 8677; 1621) was printed in massive double pica (20-pt) black letter in 1621, the choice of typeface was a deliberate effort to somehow borrow something from that antique tradition, perhaps a sense of 'ancient authority' associated with black letter proclamations. But *A Proclamation* was not a proclamation in two senses: (1) it was the King's acquainting of 'Our good Subjects . . . with the reasons' for the dissolution of Parliament; and (2) it was published in the quarto pamphlet format. The only(?) precedent for this form of royal publication occurred in the epistle 'From The King' prefacing William Wilkes's *Obedience or Ecclesiastical Union* (STC 25633) in 1605. In that instance, Eld marginalized

black letter) and seven black letter editions of the official Bishops' version of 1568, the only version that could be used and displayed in churches. Incidentally, the so-called 'black letter' bibles were never exclusively in black letter type after 1575, as roman and italic were used in the emphasis function.

[16] At the same time, Eld's reprinting of another of the new king's texts, *A Fruitfull Meditation* (STC 14377; 1603), illustrates one major factor underlying the use of black letter. Eld simply duplicated the black letter typography of the earlier editions rather than shifting to roman type. But he was aiming at the same market as the printers of *Basilikon Doron*. It is clear that black letter vs. roman literacy was simply not a factor in 1603.

The Induction.

Prologue.

Distroying through Heauens power, what would diftroy.
Welcome our White Knight with lowd peales of Ioy.

Epilogue.

MY Miftris (the White Queene) hathfent me forth
And bad me bow thus lowe to all of worth,
That are true Friends of the White Houfe and Caufe,
Which She hopes moft of this affembly drawes.
For any elfe, by Enuies marke deuoted,
To thofe Night Glow-wormes in the Bagge denoted
Where ere they fit, ftand, or in priuate lurke
They'l be foone knowne by their deprauing worke,
But She's affur'd, what they'le commit to Bayne
Her White Friendfhi is willbuild vp faire againe.

3. The black letter setting of the titles in the Mathewes/Allde
Game at Chesse. The stylistic differences between **typefaces** in the
same **family** can be appreciated by very closely comparing the 'e
g l o' in Mathewes's font ('The Induction', 'Prologue')
and Allde's font ('Epilogue'). Note, for example, the more
acute angle at which the loop joins the bowl of the 'g', the
shorter 'l', narrower 'o' etc. To avoid the expense of another
half-sheet of paper, Allde crammed the 'Epilogue' into the
remaining space at the foot of this page, but to squeeze the
text into that space, he had to switch from his Haultin
pica (82mm) roman to his long primer (66mm) roman.

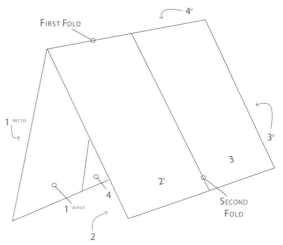

4. The manner of folding the quarto sheet which contained four
type-pages on each side. As in the folio, the sheet is first folded
in half, left to right, then folded again along the new short axis,
left to right, to produce four leaves and eight type-pages. The
source of the terms **inner forme** and **outer forme** is apparent:
the first fold placed the four pages of the inner forme *inside* the
folded sheet. The second fold (left to right) brought pages
2-verso and 3 together and placed page 1-recto at the front of
the folded sheet. The crease at the centre is termed the **gutter**.
The binder stitched and glued the gutters of all the collated
folded sheets of a book together and added the binding
materials. A cut along the crease of the first folds of the sheets
opened the book to produce four free-swinging leaves.

royal authority by setting the epistle in Guyot's double-
-pica (20-pt) roman type. In both instances, the medium
was integral to the message.

When Augustine Mathewes set the titles 'Prologue' and
'The Induction', and Edward Allde the title 'Epilogue', in
A Game at Chesse (STC 17884) in double pica black letter
in 1625 (Fig. 3), the tradition was used in a different
way: to create the impression that the book was printed
on the continent. Mathewes assumed that the reading
public now saw black letter not as a standard English
typeface for notorious new texts but as characteristic of
Northern European countries which continued to use it
as their primary text face. He succeeded well enough so
that, centuries later, the STC still confidently lists, without
query or brackets, the place and printer as 'Lydden, J.
Masse', when in fact Mathewes shared the printing of the
book with Edward Allde in London.

The Formats of Middleton's Works

In bibliographical parlance, **format** simply refers to the
number of type-pages printed on one side of a sheet,
which is then folded one or more times. One side of
a **folio** (2°) contains two type-pages and the other side
also contains two type-pages. When the sheet is folded in
half, left to right, on the short axis, two **leaves** and four
type-pages result. Numbering the type-pages in sequence

reveals that pages one and four are visible on the outside
of the folded sheet, while two and three are 'hidden'
inside, corresponding respectively to the **outer** and **inner
formes**. The smaller formats include additional type-pages
and foldings of the printed sheet. For example, a **quarto**
(4°) sheet contains four type-pages on each side (total of
eight per sheet; Fig. 4). Similarly, an **octavo** (8°) includes
eight type-pages on each side (total of sixteen per sheet), a
duodecimo (12mo) twelve (a total of 24 per sheet), and on
down to the rare 24 (24mo) and 36 (36mo) type-pages.

Folio Format

By Middleton's time, a typographical tradition had been
fairly well established which linked a folio setting with
a larger type size, principally english (94mm), so that in
many instances the actual amount of type per page in
such a folio setting is roughly equivalent to that which
fills a quarto page in pica type (82mm). However, the
Shakespeare Folio (1623: Isaac Jaggard; 1632: Thomas
Cotes, printer of *A Chast Mayd*), in which Middleton's
collaborative work (*Macbeth*, *Timon*, and *Measure for Measure*) appears, was set in two columns of pica roman type,
probably an economizing measure.[17]

[17] See Taylor, 1987, 40-1, for discussion and illustration of the folio format.

Play-Quarto Format

The standard play-quarto format with a black-letter text setting had given way to pica roman type in the 1580s. The format was a speciality niche in the market. A large number of printers never printed play-quartos; many were printed by a group which included Middleton's printers Edward Allde, Thomas Cotes, Thomas Creede, George Eld, Augustine Mathewes, Nicholas Okes, Thomas Purfoot, and Valentine Simmes. The title-page, preliminaries, the first page of the text, and pages on which new acts began, constituted the only areas of variation within the play-quarto format. Options included the choice of typefaces and sizes for the title text, the insertion of horizontal rules in imitation of manuscript practice in dividing sections of the text, the insertion of a printer's or publisher's ornament, and the use of a woodcut or engraving. Ornamented and/or titling-font initials could be inserted at the head of preliminary texts and the main text itself, which, in some cases, is headed by the title in a large face, either italic or roman or both. The preliminaries were printed in a variety of roman and italic typefaces, but pica roman was almost invariably the text face. Richard Bradock (printer of *Yorkshire Tragedy*) printed one of the Paul's Boys' plays (John Marston's *Antonio's Revenge*) in english (96mm) roman, and the two Robin Hood plays in pica black letter (*The Downefall of Robert* [STC 18269] and *The Death of Robert* [STC 18271]). Middleton's play-quartos are conventional in all respects.

Octavo Poetry Format

The use of the octavo format for books of poems began with the watershed book *Songes and Sonetts* published and printed by Richard Tottell first in 1557 (nine editions by 1587; see Carlson regarding the trend to smaller formats). The preliminaries and verse texts were set in black letter (82mm pica and 62mm long primer respectively) but romans and italics provided running titles and poem titles, a minimal typographical variety. Barnabe Googe's *Eglogs, Epytaphes, and Sonettes* (1563) duplicated Tottell's approach except that the title-page reverted to two sizes of black letter. Printer Henry Denham took a big step forward in the 1567 edition of George Turberville's *Epitaphs, Epigrams, Songs and Sonnets* in the title-page and preliminaries. The title-page exhibits a stunningly innovative typographical variety, alternately setting the sequence of the sixteen lines in seven different typefaces and sizes. The compositor obviously enjoyed playing 'musical cases'. Denham's final stroke of innovation consisted of enclosing the title text in a rectangular frame consisting of a double row of printer's 'flowers' (see below). The end result is a new kind of title-page, one in which the text occurs as if it were a prized picture in an highly ornate picture frame. Variation continued within the book itself but the verse texts remained in black letter.

By the 1590s, the texts as well had shifted to roman and italic type. The attention given to ornamentation in the title-pages of early poetry octavos moved into the book itself. Three of Middleton's texts illustrate the conventional

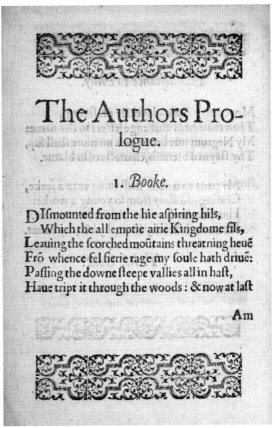

5. Creede's setting of **printer's flowers** in *Micro-cynicon*. Three faint vertical white spaces (top rows) indicate the inner borders of the four pieces that form each row. The horizontal division between rows is not as distinct. Note that the two rows consist of mirror-image castings.

approaches to graphic presentation. Paratextual materials in *Micro-cynicon*, *The Blacke Booke* (a quarto), and *The Ant, and the Nightingale* appeared in large romans and/or italics that were typically used in epistles, prefaces, prologues and the like. Within the text proper, horizontal rows of flowers (as opposed to the rectangular frames of title-pages) appeared either at the head or foot (or both) of the page and created a frame for verse passages or stanzas. Thomas Creede framed the first few pages of *Micro-cynicon* with single rows of flowers above and below, double rows above and below for the 'Prologue' (Fig. 5), and with a single row above beginning on B1. In *The Ant, and the Nightingale*, Creede set Philomel's opening section (B1–4^v) in a balanced four stanzas per page with rows of flowers above and below; the same layout appeared in Philomel's later sections (E2–3 and F4–4^v). Philomel's verse was set off in pica roman type while the prose text of the 'Ant's Tale as Ploughman' (C1–E2) was set in black letter.[18] Similarly, the opening verse text of *The Blacke Booke*, 'A Morall' (B1–2ᵛ), was set in pica roman with rows of flowers above and below; the same roman type was used for emphasis within Lucifer's black letter text.

It is not difficult to believe that the combination of the small octavo format, the use of a variety of sizes of roman and/or italic type, and the framing of the poetry by flowers was deliberately designed to create a specific kind of reader engagement with the text. It aims at a personal intimacy that is impossible in a folio setting which is weighty and cumbersome and relegated to the study or a place with a table for supporting the book. Further, a reader tends to get lost in the page-space of a folio. The 'little Booke in Octavo' format, as Middleton referred to it (*Meeting of Gallants* 201), was inherently portable and could be purposely carried in a small pocket to a reader's favourite haunts, or simply carried against whatever opportunity or need presented itself for a moment of quiet resuscitation from the turmoil of the world. The book itself had to be handled with delicacy and pages turned with fairly precise finger manipulations. The horizontal focus of the eyes need hardly shift in following the lines. Above all, the frames of flowers, delicately engraved and intricately artistic, walled off the annoying world and created a small intimate refuge into which the reader's imagination could flow and be nourished. This extraordinary bibliographical text superbly complimented the lexical text whether the venom of a satirist or the woe of the love poet flowed in it: it was intimate art.[19]

However, *small* did *not* mean *cheap* (the 'short' one-sheet 'cheap print' chapbooks did not yet exist). The pricing guidelines of 1598 tied price to the **size of the type**: an octavo sheet in pica type could be sold for the same halfpenny as a quarto sheet. However, due to the loss of space in the folds, the octavo sheet contained fewer words. The standard practice of setting 25–7 lines per page (vs. 35–8 in a quarto page) at a line-width less than half that of a quarto brought the word-count down even further. Thus a given text of sufficient length could be stretched out to an extra sheet, further raising the relative price of the octavo setting. The purchaser got fewer words per pence in the octavo format as a matter of course. However, when William Ponsonby contracted with Edward Allde to depart from the play-quarto convention in printing Samuel Brandon's *The Tragicomoedi of the Vertuous Octavia* (STC 3544; 1598) in the 'pretty' octavo format replete with frames of flowers and set in long primer (66mm) roman type, he could charge 0.66 pence per sheet instead of 0.5 pence. With roughly seven fewer lines of type per page than in a typical 35–8 line play-quarto and sixteen pages per sheet rather than eight (56 fewer lines per eight type-pages or 112 fewer per sheet), Ponsonby's profit margin expanded accordingly. This closet drama obviously was aimed at a more exclusive market than the typical Middleton play-quarto.

Paper

The choice of edition size and format directly influenced the cost of the paper, a major expenditure in the production balance sheet. As a rule, a **job-lot** of paper was ordered from a paper merchant specifically for a given book. Printers simply could not sink capital into maintaining a warehouse full of paper against future jobs even if they had the storage space. The few settlements recorded in the Stationers' Court Books reveal a consistent practice that probably represents normal procedures regarding 'who supplied the paper'. The printer of a book was invariably paid by the publisher for the paper at a specified amount per ream, or he was paid for both paper and printing at a rate which, when divided into its two parts, roughly agrees with the price per ream plus printing costs.

Sorting according to size and quality was performed on the continent before exportation. Paper was shipped to England in **reams** consisting of 20 **quires** of 24 or 25 sheets each (depending on the source of the shipment). Rejected or damaged sheets formed the **chording quires** at either end of the ream and provided some protection for the 18 inner quires of good paper. A ream thus contained a total of either 480 or 500 sheets, of which either 432 or 450 were good sheets. Both printer and publisher discovered the quality of paper that they had purchased as the warehouse keeper daily opened the reams and built the heap for the next day's printing. Moxon required him to keep an eye trimmed for stained and damaged sheets as much as possible and to pull them (320–1). Moxon's operating assumption is obvious: the printer used whatever paper the merchant delivered. Otherwise, he had the option of buying more expensive paper.

Specific lots of papers are identified by the **watermark** left in each sheet by a decorative wire design woven into the paper **mould**, a rectangular wooden frame (like a picture frame) with thin **wires** (spaced about 1mm) stretched along the short axis. **Chainlines** were woven through the wires along the long axis to stabilize the whole structure.[20] The watermark design as well as the configuration of chainlines permits the accurate identification of paper from a given mould.[21] Research has revealed the rather astounding fact that identifiable moulds continued to produce paper for over a half-century and more (Gravell, 224). Two classes of job-lots of paper are encountered in practice which usually correspond to the different sources and distribution systems (Weiss, 1992, 79–80). Technically, **job-lot** denotes the batch of reams which the London paper merchant assembled at

---

[18] It is worth noting that Eld printed *The Ploughman's Tale* (STC 20035; 1606) in english (96mm) roman type because this particular ploughman speaks in verse. Genre rather than class identity was the determining factor.

[19] Gary Taylor has alluded to the fascinating possibility that Middleton's choice of the title *Micro-cynicon* (i.e., 'little cynic') for his juvenile satire was a deliberate play on the size of the format as well as his age (19 years) (1993, 137).

[20] See illustration, Gaskell, 1972, Fig. 26, 58.

[21] See Stevenson, 1948, 1951–2, 1955; Vander Meulen.

his warehouse and loaded onto his cart for delivery to the printer. A job-lot could be assembled from either one class or a combination of the two classes of continental shipments: (1) homogeneous watermarks from one mill; and (2) a group of heterogeneous, unrelated watermarks without any necessary quantitative proportions.[22] Several circumstances could conceivably combine to produce a sequence of heterogeneous watermarks within a longer book. However, the job-lot itself is, as a rule, responsible for such a sequence in shorter texts such as play quartos, collections of sermons, and pamphlets (for examples see Riddell; Gants, 1998; Weiss, 1999). Failure to recognize this fact has led many editors to idle speculations about 'old remnants gotten at a bargain' or to silly inferences about 'protracted printing'. Another trap consists of confusing two job-lots of paper because of the similarity or presumed identity of the watermarks in two books. Such a similarity underlies the claim that *A Tricke to Catch the Old One* and *The Revengers Tragædie* (both entered on 7 October 1607 by Eld and printed by him) were printed from the same job-lot of paper even though the papers exhibit significant differences, including the appearance of the initials 'BD' in the latter book. In reality, this **family of watermarks**, a single-wire oval joined at both ends by single-wire extensions to a variety of hearts and clovers, and sometimes enclosing initials or other designs, was extremely common. Representatives of the family appear in at least 14 books by Eld in the 1604-8 period as well as in books by Simmes and other printers. It is clear that a stable distribution route furnished London with a regular supply of these papers. In short, there is no guarantee that the two job-lots of papers constitute a single order from one merchant at one time, or even that they came from the same London paper merchant.

The publisher's decision about the size of an edition was the key factor that determined the overall cost of production. The 1586 Star Chamber Decree established a maximum edition size of '1250 or 1500 copies' from a single setting of type. A unique reference demonstrates that London printers required a *minimum* edition size of 100 copies (Woodfield 2). It simply was not worth the financial return to set up to print such a small edition since typesetting required an absolute minimum amount of time regardless of the size of an edition; the same is true of the various preparations and adjustments performed by the pressman. Otherwise, the extant numbers of known edition sizes spread across a wide range from 292 to 3000. The reference to '1250 or 1500 copies' has led to rather silly inferences about the edition sizes of some of Middleton's dramatic quartos (e.g., 'normally large' etc.) among a host of other books. The number of extant copies of a book is usually worked into the equation, an equally silly proposition given the random process of preservation across four centuries.

The amount of paper ordered depended upon the total number of copies to be printed (**edition size**) and the number of sheets in a single copy (the **collation**, expressed in the sequence of **signatures**).[23] Determining the collation figure required that the printer **cast off** the manuscript copy, a tedious process which, in barest terms, involved counting the total number of letters and spaces in the copy, and then transforming that figure into the number of sheets required by the format of the edition and the sizes of type to be used (e.g., four type-pages per sheet in a folio, eight in a quarto, sixteen in an octavo etc.). Moxon provided a detailed description of the process of casting off (239-44). Irregularly written copy presented the greatest challenge in casting off. The three methods described by Moxon produce a gross estimate which could then be further refined by close attention to several kinds of details. The compositor had to work through the manuscript, adding and subtracting spaces and lines to compensate for: variations in the relative width of the writing, abbreviations (fairly numerous in the writing of the time), blank lines above and below chapter or section headings or stage directions, the different size of type used in the former, the insertion of ornamented or titling initials, the narrower body-width of words set in italic, and so on. Moxon's confidence in explaining one detailed example reassures us that compositors were able to perform this complicated process with sufficient accuracy to estimate that 127 pages of manuscript copy containing 191,135 letters would transfer into 123 quarto pages set in english (94mm) type which, when divided by eight (the number of type-pages in a quarto sheet), yielded the final figure of fifteen sheets with a remainder of three pages of text left for the sixteenth sheet.

Although Moxon does not make the point, the number of pages remaining for the final, partially filled sheet is of considerable importance in terms of production costs. A compositor could estimate the overall total number of sheets (e.g., sixteen) without performing the more refined and time-consuming measurements and calculations and thus save time. The refined page-total was necessary in instances of belated delivery of copy to be inserted into a planned position in the text (Weiss, 1992, 100-2). The refined page-total also could establish whether a half-sheet could be saved. If the remainder was less than four full pages of type in a quarto setting, these pages could be printed by the **half-sheet imposition** method. The four type-pages 1, 1^v, 2, and 2^v were imposed in an arrangement which, after cutting the sheet in half and folding, yielded two copies of the half-sheet. Alternately, half-sheet imposition was commonly employed in play-quartos to print the last four pages of the text and

---

[22] See the beta-radiographs of the heterogeneous watermarks in the Okes *Lear* [1608], Blayney, 1982, Fig. 7, 98; see also heterogeneous marks and paper sizes in the Jonson *Workes*, Gants, 1995.

[23] Each sheet was assigned a letter, its 'signature', in alphabetical order so that, for example, *Game* with its ten sheets collated sigs. A–K (the letter 'J' was not yet in use). In turn, each leaf of a folded sheet was given a number, or A1 through A4 in a quarto, and finally, the term 'recto' was applied to the side of the leaf with its outer edge at the right side, and the term 'verso' to the opposite side. In an open book, the 'verso' side is on the left, the 'recto' on the right. In general, a signature without a superscript is assumed to mean recto, while the verso is always given with the superscript 'v', i.e., B2^v.

the four pages of the half-sheet containing the title and preliminaries. The presence of a conjugate watermark in one of the half-sheets A and K of the Huntington Library copy of *Quarrell* (RB 62593) demonstrates that Eld used the method to save a half-sheet in this Middleton quarto (Fig. 6).[24]

Paper and Printing Costs

The historical record for the period is almost totally blank in regard to actual costs of printing and paper vs. retail prices. The settlement between Peter Short and the syndicate of twelve publishers for the former's printing of the fifth edition of John Foxe's *Book of Martyrs* (STC 11226; 1596) is the only extant balance sheet which permits a cost analysis.[25] Overall, Short was paid 17 shillings and 6 pence per finished book for both paper and printing, resulting in a profit margin of 6 shillings and 6 pence per book. The payment to Short included the cost of the paper at 7 shillings per ream: each book used 1.11 reams of paper (501 sheets). The printing cost thus amounted to slightly less than 10 shillings per book. The publishers as a group had to sell about 876 books to break even on their investment for the stated edition size of 1200 copies. However, this quite high break-even point is due primarily to the very high price of the paper: the few other recorded settlements cite the paper cost at 3 to 4 shillings per ream, representing the average grades like 'pott' paper. A few records cite totals of 6 to 8 shillings per ream for the combined costs of paper and printing. Nicholas Okes's receipt of £4 for printing Middleton's *The Tryumphs of Honor and Industry* is all the more interesting as a result. Again, we must make a reasonable assumption that the edition size was 500 copies (the edition size of other pageants), but even if it was 1500, Okes took the Grocers to the cleaners:

Edition size	500
Collation: actual numbers of sheets	1250
sig. A = 500; B = 500; C = 250	
(half-press imposition)	

	pence	*shillings*
Paper cost for 1250 sheets of 'Pott' (2.78 reams @ 48d. (4s.) per ream)	134d.	
Payment from Grocers' Guild	960d.	(80s.)
Production cost (= payment less paper cost)	826d.	(68.8s.)
Cost per ream for paper and printing (= payment/2.78 reams)	345d.	(28.75s.)
Presswork & composition per day (1.5 days maximum required time)	550d.	(45.8s.)

The final two lines tell the tale. Okes in effect charged the Grocers 28.75 shillings per ream instead of the normal 6 to 8 shillings! Any attempt to explain the grossly inflated production costs would be pure speculation. However, F. R. Johnson noted that such commemorative editions

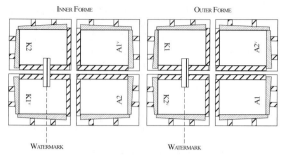

6. The arrangement of the eight type-pages of half-sheets A and K in Middleton's *Faire Quarrell* (1617). The watermark will appear conjugate in one half-sheet when the half-sheet imposition method is used.

sold at a premium (93), and that Middleton's *Inner-Temple Masque* (1619) fetched 1.33 pence per sheet (107). Regardless, the Grocers obviously had no desire to recoup their investment through sales. But the reason for Okes's continued interest in printing pageants is fairly obvious.

Building the Heap

It was the warehouse keeper's task to divide the quires of paper shipped as reams of 432 or 450 good sheets (the eighteen middle quires) into **tokens** of 250 sheets (Moxon, 320-2), the hourly unit of presswork for printing one side of the sheets. We are compelled to believe this hourly unit because extant references agree exactly on the rate (McKenzie, 1959, 101-2; Moxon, 292, 485). Moxon required that the warehouse keeper sort through the chording quires for sheets that could be salvaged. In some instances, he worked in remnants of leftover papers from a recent job that was just being finished or had been a few days previous (Blayney, 1982, 79-81; Weiss, 1992, 79, note 13). Once the warehouse man built a heap sufficient for the next day's job, he carried it to the printing house after the pressman had finished the current day's printing. The pressman then wet the paper by drawing it through a specially designed trough containing clean water (Moxon, plate 29, 280). The paper had to be damp so that the thick varnishy ink could be absorbed into the fibers of the paper: the platen of the press did not exert sufficient force to complete the transfer of ink from the

---

[24] Watermark evidence provides conclusive proof of certain aspects of presswork, as in this case. However, its usefulness is sometimes severely restricted by the minuscule number of copies of a book that are extant or available. For example, Holdsworth (197-8) correctly reasoned that sigs. A and K were printed by the half-sheet method, but none of the four copies that he examined provided the necessary evidence of **conjugacy**, i.e., watermarks in the correct position for that particular method of imposition. However, had he examined just the Huntington Library copy, he would have found the evidence. Similarly, I had examined twenty copies of John Marston's *Malcontent* Q3 (STC 17481; 1605), printed by Simmes (A–G) and Eld (H–I), before finding a watermark in the twenty-first that permitted fixing the date of the book in the 1605 production schedule of Eld's shop. See also Mulryne on half-sheet imposition in *More Dissemblers Besides Women* and *Women Beware Women*.

[25] The settlement is printed in Greg & Boswell, 51. The analysis here is based upon the reasonable assumption that this book was sold for the same 24 shillings that was charged for the third edition; see Oastler, 28, and 76, note 24; and F. R. Johnson on the stability of retail prices.

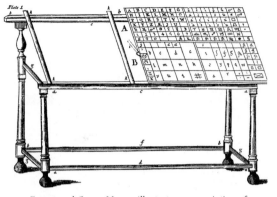

7. Frame and Cases. Moxon illustrates one variation of the lay of the upper and lower cases. The arrangement of the alphabets and punctuation was standard, but the compositor loaded special symbols, accented letters, or block capitals to suit the job. The second pair of cases containing the typefont for emphasis and quotation was placed in the open space to the left of the text-font cases.

8. The ligatures commonly used during Middleton's age. The 'tall s' (like the 'f' but without a crossbar) usually was used in the medial position of words, the short modern 's' for the terminal position. At times compositors combined the two in the medial position because of a shortage of the ff ligature. Note the stylistic differences between the pica roman ligatures cut by Claude Garamond (l. 1) and the Tournes pica. The Tournes ligatures are 0.2–0.3mm taller in addition to differences in weighting (boldness) and design. Garamond's english (96) roman ligatures (l. 3) are very similar to his pica, but since each typeface had to be cut separately (no 'scalable fonts' in those days!), a master punchcutter's letter-designs varied among his different sized typefaces. Note particularly the pica vs. the english 'ct'. The second line includes the Tournes 'g' and the Haultin 'g' (see below, Fig. 19).

type to dry paper. The wetted heap was left in place on the horse awaiting the next morning's printing.

Composition

While the warehouse keeper was building the heap, the compositor was at work setting the next day's type-pages. Normally, a compositor was expected to set two formes per day. This was the most critical of his duties, which also included assembling the type-pages for the press, making corrections in the metal as called for by proofing, rinsing and drying the type after printing, and distributing the type back into the cases. The compositor usually shared space with the press in the 'printing house' room. The compositor's 'printing stuffe' included three major items: the **type-cases**, the **frame**, and the **composing stick**.

The printing types were placed in a pair of **type-cases**, each a shallow rectangular box divided into a large number of separate compartments (**sort-boxes**) of varying sizes which were determined by the relative frequency of appearance of the letters in an English text (Fig. 7). The pattern in which the sort-boxes were arranged was termed the **lay of the case** (Moxon, 193–5; Gaskell, 1969). During the actual setting of types, two pairs of cases (e.g., a pair containing roman type and a second pair containing italic, or whatever combination of text- and emphasis-type was being used) from which a text was being set were placed upon a specially designed frame. Moxon's dimensions and discussion indicate that English compositors stood, so that the front of the frame was positioned at approximately waist-height. The 1588 inventory of Thomas's shop includes two 'great stools', probably similar to the modern 'bar stool', upon which his compositors must have sat while setting type (Morris).

The variety of typefonts in different faces and sizes kept by a printer determined the number of cases and frames that were needed. The inventory of Thomas's single press shop lists seventeen pairs of cases and six frames (Morris).

The lay of the case can sometimes provide cogent typographical evidence in determining whether a suspected error in a text must be attributed to manuscript copy or to compositorial error. Each letter comprising the words of a text represents a single piece of type which was picked from its **sort-box** by one reach of the compositor's hand. Hence, the proximity of sort-boxes is a key criterion for resolving spelling cruxes. The emendation of Creede's setting 'iugling' in *Micro-cynicon* (5.96) to 'juggling' by Alexander Dyce, for example, overlooks the fact that the 'u' and 'n' sort-boxes are contiguous: the letter in question (a 'u', not an inverted, or **turned**, 'n') could easily represent either a mis-reach into the 'u' sort-box, or the retrieval of a 'u' that was mistakenly **distributed** previously into the 'n' sort-box. Furthermore, the use of 'ingling' in the title of Satire 5 and the list of characters on the title-page (e.g., 'Ingling *Pyander.*') weighs heavily against the emendation.

The **ligatures** can provide especially valuable typographical evidence since they consist of two or three joined ('ligata') letters cast as the face of a single piece of type (Fig. 8). Except for the 'fi' and 'fl' ligatures, the rest have been eliminated from most modern typography. In a modern setting, 'first stewes' (*Game* 5.3.18) appears to contain eleven letters separated by one space, requiring twelve reaches into the case. Actually, only nine reaches occurred to set the original. The phrase 'side a dish of fish' (*Five Gallants* 1.1.300) is even more illuminating (Fig. 9). Thus the number of reaches involved in the setting of a word as well as the proximity of sort-boxes can resolve various kinds of textual cruxes (McLeod, 1984). The Harvard copy of *The Phoenix* (Price, 1962), for example, contains the uncorrected state of the setting 'any way to bee rid of her ſhould rid my torment'; the corrected state in the remaining copies changes 'ſhould rid' to 'would rid'. The question is: which word did Middleton actually write?

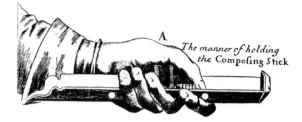

first stewes
side a dish of fish

9. Ligatures in use.

A
The manner of holding
the Composing Stick

B

The manner of Emtying
a Stick of Letter.

10. Composing Stick. (A) The compositor held the composing
stick in the left hand, picked a type out of the case with the
fingers of his right hand, added it to the growing line, then
compressed and held the types in place with the thumb.
He began setting a line at the left cheek; the types were
upside-down and mirror-image. (B) Once the stick had filled
with five or six lines, he placed a **reglet** (a thin stick) against the
top line (bottom line in illustration B), compressed the lines
of type against the reglet, and deftly flipped the lines of
type away from the stick and placed them on the alley.

Since both settings make clear sense and represent a single
reach into the case (e.g., one reach for an 'fh' ligature,
not two reaches for an 's' and an 'h'), the location of
the 'fh' sort-box directly above the 'w' sort-box provides
the solution. The only possible reason for the change is
that the alert corrector noticed the error and restored the
'would' reading from manuscript copy. It is clear that the
compositor mistakenly pulled an 'fh' ligature rather than
a 'w', and that the correction is attributable to proofreading against manuscript copy. Middleton's intention is thus
clarified: divorce 'definitely will relieve' instead of 'might
relieve' 'my torment'.

In addition, the mixture of ligatures in different typefaces in a typefont can provide a fairly reliable clue to
the identity of an unknown printer. Peter Short's pica
roman font, inherited from Henry Denham, contained the
rare 'ꝏ' ligature, found also in the mixed pica roman
font of William White (printer of *Penniless Parliament*).
White's font also contains the entirely unique 'th' and 'ch'
ligatures, 'markers' which identify White as the printer of
a book.

The **composing stick** was the compositor's basic tool in
which he set the lines of type (i.e. **composition** or **composing**) in the most crucial stage of the textual transmission
process (Fig. 10). Lighting was especially important in
regard to the location of the compositor's frames, and
Moxon would have them placed at the side of the room
where 'the Light may come in on his Left hand; for else
his Right hand plying between the Window-light and his
Eye might shadow the *Letter* [i.e., the type in the cases]
he would pick up' (17). Thus the compositor relied upon
visual recognition as well as motor-control in picking
types from the case and setting them in the stick. The
'Visual Ray' of his eyes 'very quickly' darted back and
forth between copy and case. For the sake of efficiency, the
compositor memorized a unit of text such as five words or
even a whole sentence, then proceeded to set each letter,
separating words with a space, until the line was filled,
or nearly so. If the final word did not quite reach to the
right cheek, it was necessary to insert additional spacing
material between letters in words and between words in
order to **justify** the line and achieve the tight fit that kept
the types from falling out of the type-page during the
various transfers it would experience before ending up on
the bed of the press. The compositor had spacing materials
in a variety of widths for use in justification. The reference
standard for type-body width was based upon the letter
'm', the widest letter.[26] Blanks in this width were termed

em-quadrats, em-quads, or simply **ems**. The **en-quad** was
half the width of the **em-quad**.[27]

Compositors employed a variety of justification techniques. Readers usually are unaware of the fact that, to
a compositor's eye, the white space between the end of a
shorter verse line and the right margin is not simply empty
white space, but is an area tightly packed with faceless
pieces of lead. Every line of types had to be justified (Fig.
11). The most rudimentary justification involved adjusting
the spaces between words to justify a line and is most
obvious in l. 14 where wide spaces and en-quads were
used before and after the punctuation and between the
words, and l. 15 where en-quads were inserted between all
words except for the em-quads between 'vp' and 'all' and

[26] This width was unique to each individually designed typeface, so no universal
value for a given size category of typefaces was possible. For example, different
pica roman typefaces differed in the width of the 'm', so it was not possible to
state a width such as '22mm' that would apply to all the different designs in the
pica size.

[27] In addition, larger quads were cast in multiples of the em-quad, e.g., 1-em ×
2-ems, 1-em × 4-ems, and multiples of line heights, e.g., 2-ems × 2-ems, 3-ems
× 4-ems etc. The term **space** technically refers to blanks which were a fraction
of the em-quad: two widths were generally used measuring respectively four and
seven spaces to the em-quad.

11. Justification: *The Puritaine*, B3, lines 12–31.

12. Indenting the stick produces a right margin defined by an imaginary vertical line at the end of the longest lines in a group. Setting to narrow measure, Bernard Alsop's compositor for *A Faire Quarrell* **turned-over** '(you.' (from l. 5) onto the line above although it could have fit in the full measure, moved the speech prefix left by the width of an en-quad, and eliminated the space after the comma, as he did in l. 6, where the speech prefix exhibits normal indentation. The en-quad spacing between 'Indeed' and 'I' forced compression in the rest of the line.

'at' and 'your' (see also ll. 19 and 21). In contrast, l. 12 is spaced normally except for the comma at 'Marke,quatha'.

Spelling was still in a fluid state so that a compositor could adjust line-length by choosing between the short and long forms of many words, such as high frequency pronouns ('he/hee', 'she/shee', and 'we/wee'), auxiliary verbs ('do/doe', 'be/bee'), terminal 'y/ie', words with doubled medial and terminal vowels and consonants, contractions, and elisions. In addition, ligatures and discrete letters could be juggled to achieve a better justification fit. In general, compositors seem to have developed personal habitual preferences for patterns of alternate spellings that can in some cases distinguish the alternating stints of two compositors in setting a text (Hinman, 1941).[28] Literal rhymes in which orthography matches sound ('eye-rhyme') have been found to influence compositorial spelling preferences (Reid). In some cases, the use of variant spellings as a justification technique has been found to change a compositor's otherwise consistent preferences (Kable). For example, the use of long/short forms for justification is evident in l. 17, where Eld's compositor began with his (and Middleton's) preferred long spelling 'Wee' (see l. 27), spaced normally until the end of the line, then reverted to the short form 'we' to justify the line. Even though he omitted spaces before and after the comma in l. 12, he retained his preferred long form 'doe' but had to resort to the short forms of 'he' (vs. l. 20 'hee') and 'shew' (see also 'know' l. 17). Similarly, the long form 'blowe' began l. 20 (see also l. 15) but use of 'hee' forced reversion to the short forms 'blow' and 'me'. Interestingly, he preserved the doubled terminal consonants of 'Corporall' despite justification needs (ll. 14, 18, and 26). The choice of alternate terminations for 'drye' (l. 15) and 'lie' (l. 19) are probably justification-related. The short form 'spirit' (l. 14) is retained although the doubling of the medial consonant ('spirrit') could have helped justify the spaced-out line (as is the case with 'here's' in l. 19). The

short form 'Lether' (l. 29) permitted normal justification spacing. Note that Eld's compositor maintained a consistent indentation of speech prefixes despite justification needs; other compositors adjusted this indentation as a justification technique.[29]

In play-texts dominated by short verse lines, justification sometimes placed a severe strain on the supply of spacing materials and compositors sometimes resorted to techniques such as inserting several em or longer dashes (9mm, 12mm, 18mm) even when this punctuation was not in printer's copy. For example, throughout most of *Puritaine*, Eld's compositor used 3–5 regular dashes, depending upon the justification needs. At B3:25, he resorted to an 8mm long-dash, and began line 30 with a regular dash, but then set an 18mm long-dash. Neither long-dash is a justification solution. The pressure on the supply of spaces and quads is somewhat less obvious in play-texts such as Middleton's which frequently mix prose and verse passages on many pages.

The most significant saving of spaces and quads in verse/prose play texts could be realized by employing the technique known as **indenting the stick** (McKenzie, 1973). A stack of large quads of one size could be set against the right cheek of the stick in advance of setting lines of verse and in effect create a narrower **measure**, or line-width of the body of a text.[30] However, indenting still required the use of normal justification techniques (Fig. 12). In some instances, indenting caused errors that required extraordinary solutions (Fig. 13).

Once the stick was filled with four or five lines of packed type firmly justified, the compositor carefully transferred the collection of types and spaces to the **galley**, a rectangular wooden frame with a sliding tray called the **slice** (Fig. 14). A compositor was usually equipped with several

---

[28] Current compositorial analysis as a method is quite primitive and unreliable in the context of a scientific statistical analysis of populations of alternate choices, given the extremely limited samples upon which such analyses are based. As a result, the compositorial analyses that have been performed on Middleton's plays (as well as the rest) have produced largely contradictory identifications.

[29] For additional illustrations of justification techniques, see Taylor, 1987, 45.

[30] The general practice was to set the measure of the text to a width that was the equivalent of the height of twenty lines of the typefont in use.

> B. Q. p. We doe not always feeke, the faith wee liue by,
> Nor euer fee our growth, yet both worke vpward.
> W. Q. p. It was well applied, but may I fee him too.
> B Q. p. Surely you may, without all doubt or feare,

13. Nicholas Okes's compositor for *A Gam^e at Chæss* indented the stick from about l. 3 to l. 27 in sig. G1 of *Game* Q1 and ran into a problem. He spaced the words in the first half of l. 18, then omitted spacing in the second half only to find the line was short, and filled it with the alternate spelling 'wee'. He omitted an em-quad and space from the indention of the speech prefix of l. 20, separated it from the text with a narrow space, and was able to complete the line with normal spacing. However, at some point, either the compositor or the corrector realized that two words had been omitted from ll. 18–19, either in the printer's copy manuscript or during type setting (or both). As a solution, the final two words of l. 18, 'live by', were set separately as marginalia and slipped out of alignment along with the indenting column of quads, a not uncommon result of indenting the stick.

sizes of galley to handle a range of type-page sizes (but not exactly corresponding to any).[31] Each successive group of lines was transferred to the galley until the compositor estimated that he had set a page. He then added a line of blanks into which the signature and catchword were inserted. Final adjustments for the correct alignment and justification of the lines as a whole page were made and then the type-page was tied tightly around several times with string and was placed upon a piece of paper on a flat surface (usually a **letterboard**, a finely planed hardwood plank) to await further processing. A misunderstanding of the galley and the process has led to a naïve reliance upon the number of lines per page as evidence of the stints of different compositors and/or corrections for earlier miscalculations produced by 'hasty casting off'. The end results include fantastical scenarios such as: 'by sheer error he set his galley for 39 lines for the first three pages of the inner forme. At F4^r he corrected to 38 lines'. The simple fact is that the galley had no kind of adjustment whatever. A variety of factors could produce variations in the number of lines per page, chiefly compositorial error or a lack of concern.

After the compositor had set enough pages for at least one side of sheet, the next step was to **impose** the type--pages (Fig. 15). Supposing that the job involved one of Middleton's quarto play texts, the compositor transferred four tied-around type-pages in succession from the storage surface to the **correcting stone**, a slab of marble (or perbeck) mounted on a strong oak frame with four sturdy legs about three feet high and with drawers to store the **furniture**. The four type-pages were arranged carefully on the stone so that the pages would appear in the proper sequence in the printed sheet after it was folded twice as noted earlier. The compositor then began assembling, or **imposing**, the quarto **forme**, that is, the combination of materials needed for printing one side of the sheet, namely, the four type-pages, the **chase**, and the assorted pieces of wood comprising the furniture. A rectangular iron frame measuring roughly 22in × 18in (or about

14. The four to six lines of justified types were transferred from the stick to the galley until a sufficient number of lines for a page had accumulated.
(1) The **galley** (A) itself consisted of a rectangular base about 1/4-inch thick and three low sides which had grooves to allow the **slice** to slide in and out. The slice (d) was a rectangular board about 1/8-inch thick with a handle: it was trimmed to exactly fit the grooves in the sides of the galley (a, b, c).
(2) During imposition, the compositor held the slice (d) with the left hand while sliding the tied-around type-page onto the imposing stone (B) with the right hand.

56cm × 46cm), the chase was divided into halves for the imposition of a folio forme (two type-pages) by the insertion of a **short-cross** bar across its width, or into four quarters for a quarto forme (four type-pages) by the addition of a **long-cross** bar along its length.[32] The chase was lowered onto the stone around the type-pages. The large gaps between the type-pages and sides of the chase had to be filled. Rectangular flat **head-sticks** and **gutter-sticks** were inserted between the type-pages and one long side of the chase as well as between the type--pages themselves. Then long wedge-shaped **foot-sticks** and **side-sticks** were inserted along the other three sides of the chase. Finally, the **quoins**, small wedge-shaped wood blocks, were positioned between the sides of the chase and the foot-sticks and side-sticks.[33] To complete the process, the compositor **locked up** the forme by driving the quoins tightly home with his mallet and the **shooting-stick**, a

---

[31] The Thomas inventory lists four sizes of galley; see McKenzie, 1959.

[32] The cross bars were dovetailed at the ends to fit into notches at the midpoint of each of the chase's side-bars, and at their centres so as to lay flush when both were installed (Moxon, 228–33, 408; Gaskell, 1972, Fig. 43, 79). As a rule, chases came in pairs for an obvious reason: both formes could be assembled independently. With a single chase, the imposition of the second forme of a sheet would have to wait until the first forme was off the press, rinsed, and **stripped**.

[33] Compositors had many sizes of the sticks and quoins to fit various sizes and numbers of imposed type-pages in the various formats.

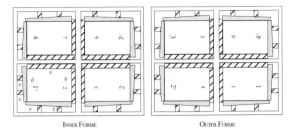

INNER FORME   OUTER FORME

15. The arrangement of the four type-pages of each imposed forme: the page numbers appear at the top where the running titles would appear in a real setting; the signatures are at the bottom. The printed sheet exhibits a mirror-image of the arrangement. The wooden 'sticks' which filled the gaps between the type-page and the chase are: (*a*) the **gutter-stick**, (*b*) the **head-stick**, (*c*) the **side-stick**, and (*d*) the **foot-stick**. Four wedge-shaped **quoins** (*e*) were driven home to compress each type-page of the **locked-up** forme. The quoins were loosened during proof corrections and stop-press corrections to permit the removal of mis-set types and the insertion of correcting types. In **single-skeleton** printing, the set of four running titles stayed in the same position in both formes so that they appear to have been transferred from outer forme to inner forme, e.g., pages 1 to 2, 2^v to 1^v, 3 to 3^v, and 4^v to 4, and vice versa in returning to the outer forme.

16. Mid-eighteenth-century illustration of hand-presses similar to those used in Middleton's time.

wedge-shaped stick about 6 inches long. The quoins were loosened during proofing and stop-press corrections, and then driven home again. This combination of wedge--shaped side-sticks, foot-sticks, and quoins was the key to the success of the locked-up forme and, in effect, compressed the types, furniture, and chase into a solid assembly of lead, wood, and iron which could be moved around without danger of disintegration. Needless to say, the forme was quite heavy, given the total weight of the iron chase and the four slabs of lead type (about one inch thick) of which it was constructed! In discussing the rinsing process, Moxon noted: 'And if the *Form* be not too heavy, in this position he lifts it up to the *Rincing-trough*; but if it be too heavy, as most commonly it is...' (195).

The compositor was rewarded for his labour by having to carry the locked-up forme to the press for the initial **proof-pull**. It appears that most printers kept a spare old press for this purpose so that the current forme on the main press (or presses) need not be displaced (Moxon 312; Blayney, 1982, 41). According to Moxon, the pressman had to interrupt work at the main press whenever the compositor requested a proof-pull (302). The **proof-sheet** was passed to the corrector who read it (sometimes against printer's copy but not always) and marked necessary corrections (Blayney, 1982, 191). Having transferred the forme back to the correcting stone, the compositor unlocked the forme enough to permit him to pick out offending types with the tip of his bodkin (like an ice pick), to insert correcting types, and to re--justify to accommodate the changes in line-length that inevitably resulted from the difference in body-widths of the exchanged types. He was not paid for these corrections

'in the metal', a definite motivation for 'setting it right the first time'! The long-held notion that a single proof-pull was the norm in early printing has more recently been dispelled.[34] It seems clear that at least two proofs were necessary to achieve the printed condition of most texts. (Moxon describes an ideal sequence of four stages, 233–9.) 'Learned correctors' were often employed for biblical and theological texts.[35]

After the final wave of corrections, the compositor delivered the forme to the press, where the pressman proceeded with his immediate preparation for printing. Once on the press, any further corrections were performed without removing the forme from the press, which is what the term **stop-press corrections** means. The claim that all four formes of sheets A and B of *The Phoenix* were imposed at the same time and alternatively bouncing on and off the press(es) in a random sequence for two stages of correction each is absurd. The fact that many of Middleton's play texts exhibit but a few stop-press corrections (none in *Five Gallants*) need not be a source of amazement or taken as evidence of hasty and carefree printing (e.g., 'another indication that the actual printing was done rapidly').

The early printing press was a complicated machine comprised of two sections, the **carriage** and the **press**. The carriage and its associated parts are visible to the left of the press labelled 'Fig. 2' in Fig. 16. The **stone** (marble or limestone) sat on the **plank** which slid in and out of the press on two rails for the processing of each sheet. The **beater** inked the type by rolling two leather **ink balls** with handles attached on the two type--pages of the folio forme that is imposed on the stone. The **pressman** placed a sheet of paper on the **tympam**, a rectangular wood frame connected by iron hinges to

[34] See especially McIlwraith; Blayney, 1982, 188–219; and Hammersmith, 1985, 1988.
[35] Our knowledge of the identities of both in-house and outside 'learned correctors' during the period is extremely limited: only a few have been identified. Elizabeth Story Donno's ground-breaking paper (1989) about Abraham Fleming presents an overview of the subject as well as the most detailed discussion of the career of a professional learned corrector.

The trick will proue an euerlafting Scarecrow,
To fright poore gallants from our rich-mens daughters,
Enter the Lady Ager, with two feruants.
Sifter? lue fuch a ioy to make you a wel-come of,
Better you neuer tafted, *Lady,*Good fir fpare it not,
B
Lady.

17. Pull-back in *A Faire Quarrell*. During imposition, the speech 'Lady, Good fir spare it not,' was pulled back from the first line of B1^v for an unknown reason. It may be a repercussion of an adjustment made on that page or later. The catchword 'Lady.' was an integral part of the original setting of B1 and tied-around with the rest of the type-page. Eld's compositor forgot to change it after the pull-back, so that it does not agree with the first word of B1^v, 'Ruff.'. The entire page was set to the narrow measure (indented stick) with the right margin at the end of 'daugh' and 'not,'. Note that 'ters.' has slipped out of alignment, a common effect of indenting the stick. These types were embedded in a column of quads that was added to the type-page in the galley, the method used for setting marginalia.

What is without you worthie, I negleﬅ,
In you is placﬅ the worth that I refpeﬅ:
Vouchfafe vnequalld Virgin whereon I iuﬅly kept,
Accept this worthleffe fauor from your feruants arme, the hal-
The true and perfeﬅ number of my fighs.   (lowed beades,
Kat. Mine cannot equall yours, yet in exchange , accept and
*Fitfg.*Euen as my ile rate it?   (weare it for my fake,
Golaſt. Heart? *Fitſgraue* in fuch bofome fingle-loues?
Enter fiue Gallants at the farther dore.
B 2
So

18. The excessive cramming at the very bottom of sig. B2 (ll. 29–37) of *Your Five Gallants* leaves little doubt of non-simultaneous setting by formes, with the outer forme of B having been set first and probably imposed already. The cramming occurs at the very end of the B1^v–2 unit of the inner forme and represents the final stick of type set for the page: the rest of the lines were in the galley and the compositor chose to make all adjustments in the stick. Extraordinary portions of ll. 32 and 34 are turned-under. Since Fitzgrace and Katherine have spoken in verse (narrow measure) for most of the page, an editor would have to consider the possibility that the compositor mis-cast four lines of verse as just two lines. Note the foul-case 'ct' ligature in l. 33, which contrasts with the correct Haultin 'ct' ligatures in ll. 29–30.

the plank and covered with parchment backed by cloth or sheets of paper. The density of the packing material controlled the sharpness of the impression made in the printed paper by the type. Connected to the outer end of the tympan with iron hinges, the **frisket** was a metal frame covered with parchment. Two rectangular holes exactly corresponding to the positions of the two type-pages were cut in the parchment to mask off the rest of the sheet. After placing the sheet on the tympan, the pressman closed the frisket onto the tympan, leaving exposed (through the frisket cut-outs) only the portions of the sheet that were to be impressed.[36] The pressman then swung the folded tympan–frisket assembly onto the imposed forme, so that the frisket mask was between the paper and the inked type-pages. The sheet was ready to be impressed (printed). The pressman slid the whole carriage assembly into the press until the first type-page was directly under the platen, pulled on the large bar to print the first page, and repeated the process for the second page (see the right press labelled 'Fig. 3' in Fig. 16). Two pulls were required because the **platen** which pressed the paper down onto the inked type-pages was only half the size of the chase (Moxon, 292–7). The pull exerted large upward and torque forces so that the presses had to be braced with (usually) six diagonal beams to the ceiling. The carriage was then retracted from the press, the tympan and frisket unfolded, the printed sheet removed, and the processing of the next sheet begun. The pressmen worked through the first side of the sheets (the **white paper**) in the **heap** before **turning** the heap, removing the first forme from the press, installing the second forme, and **perfecting** the second side of the sheets.[37] At any time during a press-run for a Middleton play, then, it was necessary that only one quarto forme containing four type-pages had to be imposed and corrected to keep the press in operation.

Setting by Formes

For the sake of discussion, it has been assumed that the compositor set all eight pages of a quarto sheet before proceeding to the imposition stage. However, this was not necessarily true. Given the need for the speed of composition to balance with the printing of the current forme at the press so that a new forme would be ready as soon as the current forme was finished, compositors resorted to a technique of saving time which could create unsolvable problems during imposition and cause deletions from a text. The simplest method, setting the eight pages **seriatim**, that is, from first page to last in sequence, presented no problems. In the quarto format, at least seven type-pages had to be set before the inner forme (1^v, 2, 3^v, 4) could be imposed. The simultaneous setting **by halves** (the first half of a sheet set by one compositor and the second half by the other) presented one additional problem which could be solved easily. The segment of copy given to the first compositor (e.g., the first four type-pages, or signatures 1-recto, 1-verso, 2-recto, and 2-verso, herein simply pages 1, 1^v, 2, 2^v, and so on) could exceed his space so that a few lines still remained after he reached the very bottom of the fourth type-page (2^v). This overflow problem could easily be resolved during imposition simply by adding the lines to the top of the fifth page (3), and shifting an equivalent number of lines forward in the remaining pages. Conversely, a line or partial line could be pulled back to the bottom of the previous page to solve a setting problem (Fig. 17).

[36] The holes that were cut in the frisket corresponded to the number of type-pages in the forme being printed, i.e., four holes for a quarto, eight for an octavo, and so on.

[37] A single pressman performed both functions (inking; preparation of sheet and pulling) at **half-press** at a rate rather less than half that obtained at **full-press** (Blayney, 1982, 42–3). Incidentally, the standard work-rate was 1250 sheets perfected per day at full-press. That amounts to 5000 pulls and 2500 sides printed (Moxon, 292, 484–6).

Setting **by formes**, however, could result in casting-off errors that forced compositors to resort to drastic measures such as omitting words and lines or cramming the excess text into available space at the end of a setting unit (Fig. 18). Theoretically, the method saved considerable time, especially when only one compositor was at work, since he only had to set four instead of seven type-pages before imposing the first forme. However, a significant portion of the time-saving would have been lost to the necessity of precise and accurate casting off. Nonetheless, he could set pages 1, 2^v–3, and 4^v, and then impose the outer forme, returning to set 1^v–2 and 3^v–4 while the outer forme was on the press. And therein lies the catch! If a line or two remained at the bottom of page 2 or 4 and could not be worked in by various techniques of compressing the type in the 1^v–2 or 3^v–4 page units, it was impossible to transfer the extra line(s) to the outer forme because it was already on the press! He therefore had to delete something—a few words, an entire line, or a stage direction—from the text in order to make it fit.

Modern textual editors, armed with a superficial knowledge of the casting off problem in setting by formes, often leap to incorrect conclusions on the basis of two faulty assumptions. First, the appearance of any of the compression or expansion methods is usually taken as conclusive proof of setting by formes.[38] However, many of these methods were also used for routine justification purposes. Second, it is assumed that the compositor cast off the *entire* eight pages of a sheet before setting either forme. Common sense suggests otherwise. A single compositor only needed to cast off the pages that he would *not* be setting at once. For setting the outer forme first, then, he could set page 1, cast off pages 1^v–2, set pages 2^v–3, cast off pages 3^v–4, and set page 4^v. Two advantages emerged. First, the time lost to casting off was at least halved. And second, the potential for error decreased significantly because setting depended upon the casting off of only two pages at any time rather than seven. The need for accurate casting off virtually dissipated if two compositors worked simultaneously on their respective formes. The casting off in this situation did not require precise accuracy since any excess lines could be moved between the two compositors' pages. Thus pages 1 and 1^v could be set simultaneously, then compositor A could 'eyeball' printer's copy for a ballpark estimate of the page-break between pages 2 and 2^v, and then begin setting without interrupting compositor B's setting of page 1^v and 2. Compositor B would do the same to estimate the page-break between 3 and 3^v, and so on.

W. Speed Hill's analysis of the casting-off markings in the Pullen manuscript (225 folios of 'eminently legible copy') which served as printer's copy of Book V of Richard Hooker's *Of the Lawes of Ecclesiasticall Politie* (1597) confirms this logic. Although this was a folio in sixes, which required that pages 3^v–4 of the inner forme be set before imposition could proceed, Hill found that 'compositor [B] typically cast-off the earlier pages in the inner forme (1–3^r) twice as frequently as the

19. Haultin and Tournes 'g'. In the Tournes ('S-face') typeface design (right), the bowl (top oval) is narrower, is positioned to the left of the centre of the loop (bottom oval), and slants to the left. In the Haultin ('Y-face') design (left), both bowl and loop are roughly equal in size, centred vertically, and positioned roughly equal distances above and below the baseline.

remaining pages (3^v–6^v). Compositor A, however, cast off every page of his thirteen gatherings at least once' (Hill 147). Surprisingly, Hill found that the compositors used expedients such as variant spellings 'but sparingly', and that the decrease in the number of lines per page from 47 in sheet B and the first two pages of sheet C to 46 thereafter is inexplicable but absolutely not related to casting off error. Most significant, however, is Hill's finding that, given the bibliographical evidence in the printed book, an analytical bibliographer 'could not even suspect the sort of adjustments that took place to even out pages' (159). The practical application by textual editors of the theory of setting by formes, in short, requires a general overhaul.

Finally, non-simultaneous setting by formes either by one or two compositors can produce exclusive patterns of typographical usage that are isolated to just one forme of a sheet. The most common usage pattern consists of the **substitution** of letters in a second typeface for normal letters because of a **shortage** of the latter. The wrong-face letters are called **foul-case** letters because they contaminate the stylistic purity of the typefont in a particular pair of cases. Two general categories of foul-case letters obtain: (1) letters from a different family, e.g., black letter types or italic types in a roman font, roman types in an italic font etc. (see below, Fig. 21), and (2) letters from the same family of typefaces, but in a different style established by the unique features of design and size created by an individual punchcutter, e.g., the Tournes pica roman 'g k w' letters in a Haultin Y-font. The first category is easily detected, but the second requires a more or less expert familiarity with the variety of typeface designs within a given family and size (Weiss, 1989, 542–3). For example, the subtle stylistic difference between the 'g' in the two faces can be seen in Fig. 19.

Armed with this insight, a close examination of the eleven 'g' types in Fig. 11 reveals that the 'g' in 'right' (l. 21) exhibits the characteristics of the Tournes design, and is obviously different from the letters seen in nearby words 'strong inough' (l. 19), 'Newgate', and 'Ludgate' (l. 22) which represent the Haultin face. Since Eld's pica roman font as a whole exhibits the Haultin typeface design, the Tournes 'g' is a **wrong-face** or **foul-case** letter. That wrong-face 'g' in 'right' is a member of the **foul-case cluster** (i.e., a group of different letters of the

---

38 See for example, Daalder and Moore, 246–8.

wrong design) created during the setting of texts in which Eld's compositors alternated his Tournes and Haultin pica roman fonts, a practice which usually produced such cross-contamination or fouling of both fonts.

Scholars naïvely assume that each instance of fouling represents the deliberate choice of a compositor while setting the text in question. Hence, the setting of the text is viewed as an isolated event in the lifetime of a typefont. Nothing could be farther from the truth. A typefont undergoes a constant sequence of modifications during its life beginning with its very first use, and its state in a given text is the sum total of these modifications (for further discussion see Weiss, 1990, 126–40; Weiss 1991, 207–13; Weiss 1992, 81–5). Consequently, the appearance of foul-case letters in a text can only be defined as 'substitution' in the context of the font's life history. The *a priori* condition for concluding substitution is that the same foul-case letter or foul-case cluster never have appeared previously in a setting which used the typefont in question. In general, deliberate fouling was occasioned by the fact that the supply of a particular letter had been depleted as damaged and worn types were discarded over a period of time; as a result, the quantity of types in that sort-box was inadequate to meet the demands of a text, so that the compositor introduced wrong-face letters to supplement the supply. Two categories of fouling must be distinguished: **resident** and **transient**. In transient fouling, a compositor more or less successfully purged the foul-case letters from the font either immediately during the next distribution or sequence of distributions (Weiss, 1990, 132–4). However, unpurged letters remained resident in the typefont thereafter. In dealing with 'substitutions', then, a compositorial choice to foul the font is not at issue. The issue is *when* that act occurred: during the setting of a given page in this text, or during the setting of a previous text. Genuine 'substitutions' that are isolated to a later page in one forme of a sheet indicate a strong probability that the text was set by formes and can thus alert an editor to the possibility that the sometimes subtle errors of omission associated with setting by formes might be present.

Play texts were especially vulnerable to shortages since the supply of an italic capital letter often came under severe **sort-pressure** because the names of two or more characters begin with that letter. Phoenix, Proditor, Fidelio, Falso, Furtivo, and Fucato appear in a great many scenes in *The Phoenix*. Obviously, the compositor(s) required a large supply of italic 'P' and 'F' for setting the speech prefixes, and if the supply became exhausted during the setting of a forme, the compositor had to substitute roman capitals unless he scavenged italic capitals from a previous forme awaiting distribution. The basic question is: were roman 'P', 'F', and other capitals drawn into the italic font during the setting of *The Phoenix* in 1607? Was this a result of current sort-pressure? A survey of a few books printed by Allde in the proximate period suggests that it was not. As early as 1606, a roman 'P' 'substitutes' for its italic counterpart in a prose text with absolutely

20. 'P': (1) Earlier in *Puritaine* A3:26 'Parson'. (2) *Five Gallants* A4:36: 'Pri.' (3) D1:10: 'Pax'. (4) E2:28: 'Purs.'

no sort-pressure whatever; additionally, 'H' and 'R' were 'substituted' despite the large number of italic capitals in these sorts (*The Examination* [STC 23464]). The play text *Cupid's Whirligig* (STC 22380; 1607) required no 'P' or 'F' 'substitutions', but moderate-to-high 'substitutions' occurred with roman 'E K L M N W'. The same kind of 'substitutions' in the absence of sort-pressure occurs in other of Allde's books in the period. Two conclusions are apparent: (1) the roman letters fouling the italic font are probably attributable in large part to resident fouling; and (2) Allde's compositor(s) habitually reached for roman capitals even when no need existed. A misunderstanding of the history of the font in question can thus lead to an incorrect conclusion that a text was set by formes.

The pattern of appearance, furthermore, should be unequivocal for demonstrating current substitutions: in one forme only, and in a late page of that forme, unless it can be proven by evidence of recurrent identified types that a distribution occurred early in the setting of that forme. The most preposterous instance of tailoring this general axiom to suit the appearance of supposed 'substitutions' occurs in regard to *The Phoenix*: 'Therefore, a majority of roman initial capitals in one of the first formes of an edition leads to the inference that the forme was composed after another which succeeds it textually, but which has a majority of italic capitals' (Price, 1962, 422; also 1967, 214–15); that is, a setting sequence of B(outer), B(inner), A(inner), and A(outer) without an intervening distribution of any of the four formes. The fact that at least two identifiable types recur in both sheets A and B disproves this hypothesis for the simple reason that one physical type cannot be in two formes at the same time. In some instances, it is possible to conclude that a 'substituted' letter is actually a resident foul-case letter. For example, the roman 'P' in the speech prefix at A3:15 reappears in the speech prefix at B3:33 with a new set of lowercase italic letters. Given the habits of Allde's compositor(s), this type most probably was distributed from A3:15 back into the italic case from whence it was retrieved in setting B3:33. In other instances, current substitution can be proven by the movement of an identified type. In *Five Gallants*, for example, the roman 'P' in the prefix 'Pri.' at A4:36 was distributed back into the roman case, retrieved to set 'Pax' in the text at D1:10, and again substituted in 'Purs.' at E2:28 (Fig. 20). Two factors leave little doubt about current substitution at E2:28: (1) the 'P' was definitely retrieved from the roman case, and (2) the pattern of appearance suggests sort-depletion in the context of the

Snr. Marry in plaine tearms I know not what to fay to him, the wound *I* can affure you enclines to *Paralifme*; and I find his body *Cacochimicke*: being then in feare of Feuer and in-flamation, I nourifh him altogeither with *Viands refrigerating* and giue for potion the iuyce of *Sauicola*, diffolu'd with water *Cerefolium*: I could doe noe more Lady, if his beft *Guiguimos* were diffeuered. *Exit.*

21. The mixing of roman 'I' and italic '*I*' in a typical passage in Eld's section of *A Faire Quarrell*, G4ᵛ, ll. 25–31. The ratio of 2:3 approximates that found on other such pages. The commas in ll. 29 and 30 are foul-case as well, mixed in from an english (94mm) roman typefont. Note also the wide justification spacings before and after the commas in contrast to the non-spaced comma in l. 28. An example of an identifiable uniquely damaged type, the 'w' in 'know' in l. 25, is clear even in this reproduction. When examined at high magnification (30×), it can be absolutely identified as the 'w' at sig. C3:20 as well, the last sheet printed by Eld before he moved to sheet G. Since sig. C3 exhibits the same proportion of foul-case italic *I* as does G4ᵛ, it is clear that the two pages were set from the same type-case. However, to the naked eye, the damaged 'w' in Alsop's section at F3ᵛ:34 ('new') appears identical to Eld's 'w' but very significant differences are noticeable at high magnification.

distribution of type from sheet D. Within the E1ᵛ–E2 unit of the inner forme, no substitutions occur in the setting of 10 italic '*P*' on E1ᵛ, and *only* roman 'P' (11) occur on page E2.[39]

In contrast, the history of Eld's Granjon pica italic font as well as the pattern of appearance raises doubt about current substitution at A4:36. Speech prefixes in previous texts including *The Puritaine* exhibit extensive fouling of the Granjon pica italic font in the absence of sort-pressure in various sorts including the '*P*', so that the appearance of five roman 'P' on A3ᵛ along with seven italic '*P*', followed by six italic '*P*' on A4 *before* the two roman 'P' were set, suggests that italic '*P*' were still available for setting A3ᵛ. Resident fouling and compositorial habits thus rule out current substitutions on A4. These two factors were obviously at work in two later appearances of Eld's Granjon pica italic (*Troilus and Cressida* and *Histrio--mastix*) where the first speech prefix in each text was set with a resident roman 'P'.

Similarly, italic capitals can be introduced into the roman text font in response to shortages, and the same principles apply as with speech prefixes. Sort-pressure on the roman capital 'I' (or any other) sort may occur because of the nature of the dialogue with the result that italic capital '*I*' is substituted. In some play texts such as *A Faire Quarrell*, the out-of-place italic '*I*' are grossly apparent in both Eld's (A–C, G–K) and Alsop's (D–F) sections of the text (Fig. 21). Since both use an identical typeface (Pierre Haultin's pica roman Y-face), one effect of these supposed 'substitutions' is to create the impression that a single typefont which was short of roman 'I' was used to set the whole book, and hence that it was printed by a single printer. The reality is that the foul-case italic '*I*' were resident for at least two years

in both Eld's and Alsop's typefonts. Further, both had large fonts, probably distributed into two pairs of cases with unequal contamination levels. The alternation of the pairs of cases in unequal stints produced an erratic pattern of 'substitutions' that could drive an editor to the brink of madness (see Holdsworth's comment, 185). However, a survey of other books in the two fonts reveals exactly the same helter-skelter pattern. In the final analysis, most of the fonts used in Middleton's books exhibit resident fouling of one sort or another.[40] In fact, the foul-case cluster in one of the two pairs of cases containing the pica roman font used by Augustine Mathewes in *Quarrell* (1621) is so distinct as to permit an accurate, unquestionable assignment of the type-pages either to the A cases or B cases, probably reflecting the stints of two compositors. Similarly, fonts owned by different printers can sometimes be distinguished by their different foul-case clusters. However, absolute identification of a typefont requires evidence consisting of uniquely damaged types (Fig. 20).

Finally, a conclusion that a book was set by formes is occasionally based upon a study of the movement of iden-tified damaged types through a book, a method developed by Charlton Hinman (1963) which provides conclusive proof of the relation between the intricately related stages of setting and distribution in presswork. Unfortunately, such analyses are usually based upon the ill-conceived Turner Principle (Blayney, 1982, 92–3) which states that, when types from both formes of the previous sheet appear in only one form of the current sheet, setting could only have been by formes (Watson, Holdsworth). The simple truth is that the alleged absence of recurrent types is negative evidence incapable of supporting any such conclusion: in most instances, it reflects the *failure* of the investigator to *find* recurrent types. A subsequent investigator may find the overlooked types. Conversely, more sophisticated methods of type-identification at high magnification (20×–30×) may reveal that the claimed identifications exhibit an error rate of 40% or higher.[41]

---

[39] The importance of establishing the extent of the distribution of type from previous formes before concluding current substitution should be noted. When both formes of the previous sheet have been distributed, all italic letters are available for setting in the current sheet. However, if only a portion of the previous two formes has been distributed, the italic types remaining in the undistributed forme are not available unless the forme is off the press and scavenging is possible. In this instance, the movements of identified types from sheet D to sheet E demonstrate that all pages of the outer forme of sheet D were distributed before the setting of inner E was completed. The distribution sequence probably was D4ᵛ, D1, D3, D2ᵛ (note that the type-pages can be distributed in any sequence). Of the sixteen types which move from sheet D to sheet E, fourteen are from the outer forme of D, including three italic letters ('S', 'P', and 'M') from speech prefixes. Although the two exceptional types move from D4ᵛ to E4ᵛ, D4ᵛ was distributed before the setting of E1ᵛ, and D1 (containing no italic '*P*') before the setting of E2. Types from inner D bypass sheet E, suggesting that inner D was distributed after the setting of inner E. The fact that the distribution of D1 released no italic '*P*' for setting in E2 although other types from D1 appear in E2 establishes the basic condition for sort-depletion that would require current substitutions in E2.

[40] These include the fonts used by Middleton's printers Edward Allde, Bernard Alsop, Richard Bradock, Thomas Cotes, Thomas Creede, George Eld, Augustine Mathewes, Nicholas Okes, Thomas Purfoot, and Valentine Simmes.

[41] Weiss, 1988, 240–3, and Table 266–8; Watson's type identifications for *Tricke* exhibit such an error rate.

Skeletons, Running Titles, and Presswork

Once the pressman, cranking out four sheets per minute, completed machining the first forme (the white paper heap), he removed the forme from the bed of the press, carried it to the washing trough, thoroughly scrubbed the ink from the letterpress with a strong lye solution, and leaned it against a wall to drain while awaiting rinsing and drying, and the **distribution** of the type back into the cases by the compositor. The press was ready for the second forme to perfect the heap.

As noted earlier, a **pair** of chases was a distinct advantage at this stage in production. The locked-up quarto forme is composed of four independent components: the four type-pages, a set of four running titles, the chase, and the furniture. In bibliographical parlance, the latter components without the type-pages are called the **skeleton forme**, or simply the **skeleton**. The process of **stripping** the forme commenced with its unlocking, followed by the careful removal of the chase and other parts of the skeleton. In **single-skeleton** printing, one set of four running titles is encountered in both formes of a sequence of sheets throughout an entire book. If indeed the entire skeleton was transferred piece by piece from the wrought-off forme to the new forme as Moxon described (229–31), valuable time would inevitably have been lost: the imposition of the new forme had to await the stripping of the previous forme. Only then could proof-pulls be taken and the forme corrected. Meanwhile the press would lay idle.

However, a single set of running titles does not invariably indicate single-skeleton printing. Although Moxon assumed the use of a single chase (perhaps for the sake of simplifying discussion), no physical necessity required that the furniture and/or the chase inevitably be transferred as a unit along with the set of running titles. As Peter Blayney felicitously remarked, 'four bones do not a skeleton make' (1982, 124–5). In fact, the transfer of the four running titles may indicate nothing more than that the group of letters were picked out of the wrought-off forme as soon as it came from the press and then immediately inserted into the running title line of a second skeleton which had been filled with quads during imposition. The process required only that the line be re-justified to accommodate the substitution of letters for quads. Numerous instances of changes in the spacing between the words of running titles, and indeed in the spacing between letters, can all be attributed to such a process; if the running title line as a whole had been transferred, its original justification would preclude any tinkering with the spacing of the words and letters (Fig. 22).

The fact that chases came in pairs made the process feasible, given a second factor that is quite important. Moxon's discussion and illustration (227–31 and plate 28) indicated that the frame which supported the correcting stone included drawers for storing the sticks used for furniture in previous jobs. Thus, Moxon did not, as modern editors assume, discuss 'constructing' a skeleton in the sense of a carpentry project, that is, planing rough

22. Changes in spacing as running title C migrates through Okes's edition of *Game*. The justification adjustments affect the indentation (not shown) from the left margin as well as the spacings between the four units '*A*', '*Game*', '*at*', and '*Cheſſe*'. Had the furniture and running titles been transferred as intact units, no observable variations would have occurred.

pieces of wood into sticks of the right shape and size. Rather, in assembling the very first skeleton for a book, the compositor 'seeks out *Inner Side* and *Head-sticks* of such thickness' as will fit (228). If the available sticks are too thin 'and he cannot find any to his intended thickness, he puts a *Scaboard* (i.e., a shim) or two' to build up the thickness. Given the supply of sticks and the method of 'constructing' a skeleton, then, it was a simple matter to construct a second skeleton by imposing the four type-pages in the exact positions on the stone as used for the first forme, and then to proceed. The skeleton was built around the imposed type-pages, not the other way around. In short, single-skeleton printing, the legendary 'most inefficient method of feeding a single press', probably was two-skeleton printing in many instances.

Eld's common practice of employing the single-skeleton method presents a totally baffling situation when measured against the traditional view. In *Five Gallants*, for example, one skeleton with a set of four running titles is used for *both* formes of sheets A, C, E, and G, while a second skeleton with another set of four titles prints *both* formes of B, D, F, and H. Given accepted wisdom, this has to represent the most inefficient method imaginable. Fortunately, Eld had two presses, so the logical solution has been to claim that each skeleton was constructed to feed a separate press, 'so that the actual printing was done rapidly and without need of waiting for the compositors'. Just how single-skeleton printing could be 'done rapidly' in any situation seems of no concern in that scholar's view. However, the results yielded by the formula 'number of skeletons = number of presses' are entirely illusory. The appearance of a 'new' skeleton for H(o) of *Game* (Fig. 23), for example, led to the inference that 'there were two presses used in the last signatures [e.g., H, I, and K] of [OKES¹]; otherwise, there would have been no need to make up a third skeleton' (Nascimento, 387). However, Okes was permitted only one operating press and the movements of recurrent types through the two editions prove that he used only that one press. Similarly, in *Five Gallants* and other play texts by Eld which were printed with alternating single skeletons, recurrent types invariably move from sheet to sheet, e.g., types from sheet A move to sheet B, from B to C, and so on. Furthermore, in this play types from *both* formes of the previous sheet appear in the next sheet *except* from D(i), and it is possible that D(i) was not distributed until after the setting of both formes of E was completed. The typographical evidence thus shows that only one press was used because only one forme was imposed at any given time. Consequently, the other chase was always available for imposing the next forme either with the alternate set of four running titles for the next sheet, or with quads awaiting the release of the set used in the printing forme of the current sheet. It is impossible to determine why Eld's compositors chose to employ alternating single skeletons, but to feed two presses simultaneously was *not* their objective.

The advantage of using two sets of four running titles in two skeletons, one for the inner forme and the other for the outer forme, should be readily apparent. The method is seen in several of Middleton's play texts, including *Game*, *Tricke*, and in both Eld's (B-C, G-K) and Alsop's (D-F) sections of *Quarrell*. Unlike the alternating single-skeleton

method, it is easy to understand how this method was ideal for feeding a single press efficiently. In *Game*, for example, C(o) could be imposed with the set of titles that was used in B(o) while B(i) was still on the press, and C(o) could be transferred to the press immediately after B(i) was wrought off. The compositor could then strip B(i) and transfer the inner-forme titles to C(i) at his leisure, and so on for subsequent sheets.

However, interpretation of the evidence left by the method is frequently skewed by the long-held notion that the process occurred with perfect regularity throughout a book *à la* Moxon's description, so that any disruption of the regularity must therefore indicate some sort of interruption of presswork and a consequent 'slowing down' or 'delay' in printing. That in turn usually leads to the mandatory inference about the deterioration in printer's copy that is characteristic of foul-papers. But the fact is that in many, if not most, instances, the apparent irregularity is regular in various ways. Thus the sets of running titles remain in their appropriate formes in transferring through sheets A to G of *Game*, but **rotate** (i.e., switch positions within the forme) in moving from sheet to sheet. They simply were not transferred according to Moxon's perfectly regular procedure (Fig. 23). In moving from sheets G to H, however, the two sets break up in random fashion and are joined by new running titles, and then proceed to rotate and switch formes from sheets H through K of OKES¹, H through K of OKES², and sheets G through B of OKES² (printed in reverse order). Rotations and switching of formes begin in F(o) of *Tricke* after a regular movement through sheets B to E. Rotations occur between sheets B and C of *Quarrell*, followed by a switching of formes upon Eld's return in G through I. The running titles both rotate and shift between formes in the three sheets (D–F) printed by Alsop. In general, these movements indicate that the four quadrants of the skeletons were not transferred as single intact units. In some instances, warped gutter sticks do not accompany their respective running titles from sheet to sheet, clear proof that the components of the

	Sheets	B		C		D		E		F		G	
Outer Formes	3 / 4v	C	D	C	D	C	D	C	A	C	A	B	D
	2v / 1	-	-	B	A	A	B	D	B	B	D	A	C
Inner Formes	4 / 3v	g	h	h	f	f	h	f	g	f	g	g	h
	1v / 2	f	e	e	g	g	e	e	h	h	e	e	f

		H		2H		I		2I		K		2K	
Outer Formes	2 / 3	2	3	2	3	g	4	g	4	C	-	C	-
	1 / h	1	h	1	h	A	e	A	e	5	D	5	D
Inner Formes	D / f	D	f	D	f	D	f	2	3	g	4	C	e
	5 / C	5	C	5	C	5	C	1	h	f	h	5	D

23. Running-Title Rotations in *A Gam^e at Chæss*, printed by Okes

skeleton were not transferred as an intact unit. However, these irregularities simply are not evidence of presswork in any sense. The movements of recurrent types show that composition, imposition, and distribution continued in a regular sequence throughout these books. *No interruption or delay whatever occurred*, and therefore, *no* inferences about the quality of printer's copy are possible. In the final analysis, running title movements prove next to nothing about presswork except that, at a particular point in imposing a new forme, a compositor retrieves a running title and 'seeks out' sticks that fit. A quarto skeleton consisted of an absolute minimum of thirty-two pieces of wood in addition to the four running titles. Unlike the bones of a skeleton, no cartilage held the whole lot together.[42]

Shared Printing

The practice of shared printing has been silently assumed in earlier references such as 'Eld's and Alsop's sections of *Quarrell*'. In 'The Prevalance of Shared Printing' (1973), Blayney demonstrated that, in fact, a significant proportion of books of all sizes were printed by two or more printers. The sharing strategy was one of two standard solutions to the problem of maintaining a consistent flow of jobs through a printing shop and thus maintaining good relations with clientele to ensure repeat business. First, a printer could resort to the strategy of producing two or more books concurrently, for example, by scheduling two sheets of book A for Monday–Tuesday, printing a sheet of book B on Wednesday, two sheets of book C on Thursday–Friday, and another sheet of A on Saturday. In this manner, three publishers could be held at bay with encouraging reports of progress. Second, if he found that incoming jobs exceeded the limits of this **concurrent production** method of juggling of books and publishers, a printer could take the printer's copy for a section of one book around the corner to another shop and have it printed there.

Identifying the divisions of labour in a shared book is the preliminary task confronting the bibliographer. While a change in aspects of printing style established earlier in a book can raise the possibility of sharing, sharing can only be confirmed by more substantive typographical evidence of three kinds ranked in order of certainty: ornamental stock, a font composite, and identified types. A failure to understand this principle underlies a recent disastrous 'reappraisal of some of the most important evidence relating to the textual history of *The Honest Whore*' (Daalder and Moore, 243).[43]

The identification of a printer's ornamental stock (i.e., ornamented letters, engravings, woodcuts, etc.) is fairly reliable evidence of his work in a book but must be approached with some suspicion for various reasons such as, for example, the common practice of borrowing ornamental materials (Weiss, 1991, 191–203). Since ornamental stock usually occurs but infrequently in most books, divisions of labour can only be proven beyond doubt by a change in typefonts which creates a boundary

between sections of a sequence of sheets.[44] A printer's typefont can be identified by two kinds of typographical evidence.

First, a comprehensive composite of a typefont's mixture of correct-face and wrong-face types provides conclusive evidence of a printer's identity and section in a shared book.[45] For example, composites alone show conclusively that *Whore* Q1 and Q2 were printed in four sections by Valentine Simmes (Simmes-S, sigs. A–B), Thomas Creede (Creede-4, sigs. C–D), Simon Stafford (Stafford-EF, sigs. E–F), and George Eld (Eld-Y1, sigs. G–K). Each of these typefonts occurs in other books signed and known to be printed by the respective printers. Furthermore, neither John Windet's nor Thomas Purfoot's contemporary pica roman fonts appear anywhere in the two editions.[46]

Second, unique damage to specific types as detected at high magnification (20×–30×) in original copies (*never in reproductions!*) of a printer's book permits the absolute identification of his typefont in other books (Weiss, 1988, 238–41; 1991, 203–27). The fact that *Whore* Q1–Q2 ends with a fourth printer's section consisting of sheets G–K, and the fact that the printer was George Eld, is absolutely demonstrated by a list of identified types linking the font of G–K to other books signed and printed by Eld.[47]

Overall, the typographical evidence demonstrates a shared printing in four shops, hence the identities of the actual compositors who set the text following the actual setting and work methods characteristic of each shop. As a result, Daalder and Moore's convoluted discussion of the

[42] On the additional problem of the unreliability of running title identifications and consequent presswork conclusions, see Weiss, 1988, 242–5; Weiss, 1991, 198.

[43] The erroneous reconstruction of the printing history in the study fails to recognize the difference in evidential certainty between font composites and identified damaged types and, for example, incidental components of the printing process such as running titles (Weiss, 1990, 159, note 40; Weiss, 1991, 189), skeleton formes, methods of signing, compositor's measure, number of lines per page, and compositorial spelling preferences and setting habits, none of which can prove either shared printing or the identity of a printer and his work in a book. The study argues as if all carried equal weight.

[44] The exception to this rule involves printers like George Eld who always had in use two pica roman fonts in different typefaces and sometimes alternated the two fonts in an unshared book.

[45] For discussion of composites and the typefont discriminants found in various fonts, including those seen in *Whore*, see Weiss, 1988, 251–5; 1989, 543; 1990, 97–127, 144–9; 1991, 206–15; 223; 1992, 75–7, 82–5.

[46] Although Daalder and Moore cited my 1990 study, they apparently were unaware of my 1991 study and 1989 review of W. Craig Ferguson's *Pica Roman Type* and its extensive errors of font identification, including the latter's confusion of Windet-4 for Creede-4 in C–D and Purfoot-H2 for Stafford-EF in E–F and Eld-Y1 in G–K (see also 1991, 185, 192–3, 208, 209, 213, 214; 1992, 76). Clearly they did not understand the significance of the analyses of the discriminants of the four typefonts used in *Whore*, relying instead upon earlier arguments based upon incidental components (see note 43) and Ferguson's mistaken identifications (245–6, 251–2). No evidence consisting of composite discriminants or identified types was offered to support their conclusions.

[47] The rhetorical notions of 'convincingly argued' and 'if we assent to Weiss's belief' (251) that inform Daalder and Moore's approach are irrelevant in the context of concrete bibliographical facts consisting of even a very short list of identified types connecting Eld's Y-1 font in other of his books to the target book: type 'a1', *Honest Whore* STC 6501 G2v:25 = STC 17480 B3:18 = STC 17481 I1v:24; type 'b1', STC 6501 H1:14 = STC 4963 B1:9 = STC 17481 H2:2 = STC 25760 D1v:29; type 'ff1', STC 6501 I3:1 = STC 4971 C2v:36 = STC 14429.5 A4:20 = D3v:17 = STC 17479 D4v:3; type 'o1', STC 6501 H1:23 & K4:34 = STC 14429.5 C4:25 = F1:25 = STC 17481 H1v:11. Thus Eld *absolutely* printed G–K. No argument is needed to 'convince' anyone to accept this 'belief'.

textual history of *Whore* simply collapses on its illusory foundation: except for Simmes in A–B, the wrong printers, shops, compositors, sections.

The division of labour usually implies the circumstances which occasioned the sharing strategy. The basic issue is whether work progressed on two or more sections of a book simultaneously or sequentially: in the former situation, printing time would be cut in half (or a quarter, or whatever proportions result from the fractional number of sections which were farmed out). Since casting off was required for dividing copy for simultaneous shared printing, the same batch of potential dangers discussed in regard to setting by formes beset this approach. In general, equal sections *suggest* simultaneous printing, but do *not* *prove* it. *The Whole Magnifycent Entertainment* (STC 6513), for example, was divided into four equal sections for four sharing printers with primary printer Allde picking up the remaining sheet I, but we can never be sure that the book was printed in five days (one day for setting the first sheet of each section, two days for printing two sheets, two days for drying, collation, and pressing). Doubts are raised about such an inference because of the divisions in some books such as *The Honest Whore* in which primary printer Valentine Simmes printed sheets A–B, Thomas Creede did sheets C–D, Simon Stafford did E–F, and Eld did G–K. Until Eld's four-sheet section, it appears that a deliberate plan to give two sheets to each printer for simultaneous printing obtained, but the final four-sheet section destroys the symmetry and thus the inference of a pre-planned sharing strategy to compress production time. Hence, the classic two-section pattern, although it appears to be a deliberate strategy to permit simultaneous printing, may in fact represent sequential printing (Weiss, 1991, 223, and note 44; Weiss, 1992, 74, 77–8). The sharing of *Game* between Augustine Mathewes (A–D) and Edward Allde (E–I) is in two roughly equal sections, but simultaneous printing does not necessarily follow. In contrast, Eld's division of *Quarrell* virtually proves sequential printing. He clearly responded to unforeseen circumstances after printing sheets B and C by passing copy to Bernard Alsop, only to recall the job three sheets later and finish it himself. Eld was involved in several other jobs shared in this kind of asymmetrical pattern.

Another kind of sequential pattern occurs in *Michaelmas Terme*, where primary printer Thomas Purfoot printed sheets A and B, and for whatever reason, passed the rest to sharing printer Edward Allde. George R. Price's incredibly elaborate tissue of interdependent conjectures about the attempts of compositors to compensate for a sequence of inaccurate castings off is based, quite simply, on his mistaken notion that Allde was the primary printer (1966, 327–31). In terms of known sharing practice, the primary printer always did the title-page (e.g., the first sheet), usually including his imprint and/or ornament (for rare exceptions, see Weiss, 1991, 193–4, 200–3). In many instances, he also printed sheet B and passed later sheets to other printers, sometimes reserving the

final section of a book for himself. In regard to Purfoot and Allde, the two were involved in the sharing of at least two dozen books with various printers during 1605–8, and in every instance, this pattern of primary printer and title--page was followed. In short, there was *no* 'Dividing the Copy for *Michaelmas Terme*' through casting off: Purfoot simply printed the first two sheets and then passed the rest to Allde, just as he had done with other texts such as *Monsieur d'Olive* and other printers such as William White. He was using the same method a decade later when he printed sheets A and B of *The Peace-maker* (one of his last jobs) with his imprint on the title-page, and passed C–H to William Stansby, recently identified by Paul Mulholland as the sharing printer on the basis of identified types evidence. For the later partial reprints, he reallocated sheet C to a second (unidentified) sharing printer because the amount of type left standing during this ongoing printing operation exceeded the supply that was available in the two shops.

Collation, Pressing, Packaging

Regardless of whether a book was printed in one, two, three or more shops, the final stage of production took place in the primary printer's warehouse. Prior to collation, the damp perfected sheets were hung along the centre crease for drying in overlapping groups on racks that were designed specifically for the purpose and suspended from the ceiling beams of the warehouse room (Moxon, plate 32, 314; see Dane for relation to press variants). The warehouse keeper then laid out the heaps of dried sheets in a row, and took one sheet from each stack to collate a complete book (if shorter than twenty-five sheets or so). The collated book was folded in half along the short axis. This placed the crease at the top edge of a quarto sheet between the running titles. Finally, a stack of gathered books (probably an entire edition of play-quartos) was placed on the **standing press**, and as Moxon noted, the warehouse keeper cranked the platen down 'with his main Strength to Squeeze and *Press* the *Books* as close and tight as he can together: and so lets them stand in *Press* about a Day and a Night' (318; plate 33, 319). After pressing, each stack of gathered books was then tied into bundles, and either placed in storage or delivered to booksellers who had to wait this extra day even for the most vendible texts. In the hand-printing period, 'rushing a book through the press' took longer than implied by common myths about printing at 'maximum efficiency' and 'with all due haste'. The purpose of pressing the gathered sheets may not be immediately apparent. When the platen forced the damp paper onto the type-pages, the paper literally stretched down and around the letters on the faces of the types. The end result was an incredibly heavy embossing of about 3/32 inch. Even after pressing, most books (including Middleton's) exhibit embossing of sufficient height to permit accurate identification of the last forme through the press (Povey).

No records exist as to a standard unit of books for wholesale transactions. Plantin allowed a discount of about 16% on books exported to London shops. F. R. Johnson inferred that London printers allowed a discount of about 20% (93). The Privy Council Commission's report of 1583 mentioned the **quaterne** (twenty-five books) as a unit, but said nothing of the actual wholesale discount for bulk purchases from printers or publishers by booksellers. The quaterne certainly seems to have been encouraged as a unit since a free book was included as a bonus in an order of this size.

The final transformations of the gathered book began at the bookseller's shop where the sheets had to be disassembled, re-folded as per format, and re-collated for offering to the public unbound as a packet of folded sheets tied crosswise with cord (and sometimes loosely stitched together at the gutter). The title-page functioned as the modern dust jacket in advertising the book because it was well-nigh impossible to examine the contents of the packet of folded sheets (unless it was a folio). The sheets had not been **opened** at the top to produce free--swinging leaves, nor had the rough deckle edges of the sheets been trimmed (**cut**) to permit 'thumbing through' the book. As a result, those horrendously long title-page texts included as much detail as space would permit to entice customers. Without doubt, Middleton's *The Blacke Booke* exhibits the most stunningly innovative title-page advertising gimmick of the entire period. This title-page, in its perfect opaqueness, tells prospective purchasers absolutely nothing about its contents and thus inevitably arouses curiosity. We are left with the question: was Middleton's creative instinct responsible for this stroke of genius in toying with bookshop browsers?

WORKS CITED

Arber, Edward, *A Transcript of the Registers of the Company of Stationers of London 1554–1640 A. D.*, 6 vols (1876)

Baldwin, T. W., *William Shakespeare's Petty School* (1943)

Bell, Maureen, 'A Dictionary of Women in the London Book Trade, 1540–1730', unpublished M.L.S. dissertation, Loughborough University, 1983

—— 'Women in the English Book Trade 1557–1700', *Leipziger Jahrbuch zur Buchgeschichte* 6 (1996), 13–45

Binns, James, 'STC Latin Books: Evidence for Printing-House Practice', *The Library*, V, 32 (1977), 1–27

—— 'STC Latin Books: Further Evidence for Printing-House Practice', *The Library*, VI, 1 (1979), 347–54

Blayney, Peter W. M., *The Bookshops in Paul's Cross Churchyard* (1990)

—— 'The Prevalence of Shared Printing in the Early Seventeenth Century', *Papers of the Bibliographical Society of America* 47 (1973), 437–42

—— 'The Publication of Playbooks', in *A New History of Early English Drama*, ed. John D. Cox and David Scott Kastan (1997), 383–422

—— *The Texts of 'King Lear' and their Origins* (1982)

Boose, Lynda E., 'The 1599 Bishops' Ban, Elizabethan Pornography, and the Sexualization of the Jacobean Stage', in *Enclosure Acts: Sexuality, Property and Culture in Early Modern England* ed. Richard Burt and John Michael Archer (1994), 185–200

Bowers, Fredson T., 'Textual Introduction', in *The Dramatic Works of Thomas Dekker*, 4 vols, ed. Fredson T. Bowers (1953–61)

Bracken, James K., 'Books from William Stansby's Printing House, and Jonson's Folio of 1616', *The Library*, VI, 10 (1988), 18–29

Brennan, Michael, 'William Ponsonby: Elizabethan Stationer', *Analytical & Enumerative Bibliography* 6–7 (1982–3), 91–110

Carlson, David, 'Formats in English Printing to 1557', *Analytical & Enumerative Bibliography* 2–3 (1988–9), 50–57

Clair, Colin, 'Christopher Plantin's Trade-Connexions with England and Scotland', *The Library*, V, 14 (1959), 28–45

Daalder, Joost, and Anthony Telford Moore, 'Breaking the Rules: Editorial Problems in Dekker and Middleton's *The Honest Whore, Part I*', *Bibliographical Society of Australia and New Zealand* 20 (1996), 243–87

Dane, Joseph A., 'Perfect Order and Perfected Order: The Evidence from Press-Variants of Early Seventeenth-Century Quartos', *Papers of the Bibliographical Society of America* 90 (1996), 273–301

Donno, Elizabeth Story, 'Abraham Fleming: A Learned Corrector in 1586–87', *Studies in Bibliography* 42 (1989), 200–211

Ebel, Julia G, 'A Numerical Survey of Elizabethan Translations', *The Library*, V, 22 (1967), 104–27

Gair, Reavley, 'Second Paul's: Its Theater and Personnel: Its Later Repertoire and Audience (1602–6)', in *The Elizabethan Theater VII*, ed. G. Hibbard (1979), 21–45

Gants, David L., *A Digital Catalogue of Watermarks and Type Ornaments Used by William Stansby in the Printing of The Workes of Beniamin Jonson* (London: 1616) (1995), available online at http://www3.iath.virginia.edu/gants/

—— 'A Quantitative Analysis of the London Book Trade 1614–1618', *Studies in Bibliography* 55 (2002), 185–213

—— 'Patterns of Paper Use in the *Workes of Beniamin Jonson* (William Stansby, 1616)', *Studies in Bibliography* 51 (1998), 127–153

Gaskell, Philip, 'The Lay of the Case', *Studies in Bibliography* 22 (1969), 125–42

—— *A New Introduction to Bibliography* (1972)

Gerritsen, Johan, 'Printing at Froben's: An Eye-Witness Account', *Studies in Bibliography* 44 (1991), 144–63

Gravell, Thomas L., 'The Need for Detailed Watermark Research', *Restuator* (Copenhagen), 4 (1980), 221–6

Greaves, Richard L., *Society and Religion in Elizabethan England* (1981)

Greg, W. W., *A Companion to Arber* (1967)

—— 'Decrees and Ordinances', *The Library*, IV, 7 (1927), 395–425

—— *English Literary Autographs 1550–1650* (1932)

—— 'Samuel Harsnett & Hayward's *Henry IV*', *The Library*, V, 11 (1956), 1–10

—— 'Was the First Edition of *Pierce Penniless* a Piracy?', *The Library*, V, 7 (1952), 122–4

—— and E. Boswell, *Records of the Court of the Stationers' Company from 1576 to 1602—from Register B* (1930)

Hackel, Heidi Brayman, "A catalogue of my ladies bookes at London': the Countess of Bridgewater's London library', in *Reading Material in Early Modern England: Print, Gender, Literacy* (2005), Appendix

Hammersmith, James P., 'Frivolous Trifles and Weighty Tomes: Early Proof-Reading at London, Oxford, and Cambridge', *Studies in Bibliography* 38 (1985), 236–51

—— 'The Proof-Reading of the Beaumont and Fletcher Folio of 1647: Introduction', *Papers of the Bibliographical Society of America* 82 (1988), 17–51, and subsequent installments

Hill, W. Speed, 'Casting Off Copy and the Composition of Hooker's Book V', *Studies in Bibliography* 33 (1980), 144–60

Hinman, Charlton, 'Principles Governing the Use of Variant Spellings as Evidence of Alternate Setting by Two Compositors', *The Library*, IV, 21 (1940), 78–94

—— *The Printing and Proof-Reading of the First Folio of Shakespeare*, 2 vols (1963)

Holdsworth, R. V., 'A Critical Edition of Thomas Middleton's *A Fair Quarrel* (1617)' (B. A. Thesis, University of Oxford, 1971)

Hotson, Leslie, 'The Library of Elizabeth's Embezzling Teller', *Studies in Bibliography* 2 (1949–50), 49–61

Jackson, William A., 'The Lamport Hall–Britwell Court Books', in *Records of a Bibliographer: Selected Papers of William Alexander Jackson* (1967), 121–33

—— 'Variant Entry Fees of the Stationers' Company', *Papers of the Bibliographical Society of America* 51 (1957), 103–10

Johnson, A. F., *Type Designs: Their History and Development* (1959)

Johnson, Francis R., 'Notes on English Retail Book-prices, 1550–1640', *The Library*, V, 5 (1950), 83–112

Kable, William S., 'The Influence of Justification on Spelling in Jaggard's Compositor B', *Studies in Bibliography* 20 (1967), 235–9

Kirschbaum, Leo, 'The Elizabethan Licenser of "Copy" and his Fee', *Review of English Studies* 13 (1937), 453–5

McIlwraith, A. K., 'Marginalia on Press-Corrections in Books of the Early Seventeenth Century', *The Library*, V, 4 (1949), 238–48

McKenzie, D. F., '"Indenting the Stick" in the First Quarto of *King Lear*', *Papers of the Bibliographical Society of America* 68 (1973), 125–30

—— 'Notes on Printing at Cambridge *c*.1590', *Transactions of the Cambridge Bibliographical Society* 3 (1959), 96–103

McLeod, Randall, 'Spellbound', in *Play-Texts in Old Spelling*, ed. G. B. Shand and Raymond C. Shady (1984), 81–96

Morris, John, 'Restrictive Trade Practices in the Elizabethan Book Trade: the Stationers' Company vs. Thomas Thomas 1583–8', *Transactions of the Cambridge Bibliographical Society* 4 (1964–8), 276–92

—— 'Thomas Thomas [part 2]', *Transactions of the Cambridge Bibliographical Society* 4 (1964–8), 339–62

Moxon, Joseph, *Mechanick Exercises on the Whole Art of Printing* (1683–4), ed. Herbert Davis and Harry Carter (1962)

Mulholland, Paul, 'Thomas Middleton's *The Two Gates of Salvation* (1609): An Instance of Running-title Rotation', *The Library*, VI, 8 (1986), 18–31

Mulryne, J. R., 'Half-Sheet Imposition and Running-title Transfer in *Two New Playes by Thomas Middleton*, 1657', *The Library*, V, 30 (1975), 222–32

Nascimento (Zimmerman), Susan, 'Thomas Middleton's *A Game at Chesse*; a Textual Study' (Ph.D. diss., University of Maryland, 1975)

Oastler, C. L., *John Day, the Elizabethan Printer* (Oxford Bibliographical Society, Occasional Publication, 1975)

Povey, Kenneth, 'The Optical Identification of First Formes', *Studies in Bibliography* 13 (1960), 189–90

Price, George R., 'The First Edition of *Your Five Gallants* and of *Michaelmas Term*', *The Library*, V, 8 (1953), 23–9

—— 'Setting by Formes in the First Edition of *The Phoenix*', *Papers of the Bibliographical Society of America* 56 (1962), 414–27

—— 'Dividing the Copy for *Michaelmas Term*', *Papers of the Bibliographical Society of America* 60 (1966), 327–36

—— 'The Early Editions of *A Trick to Catch the Old One*', *The Library*, V, 22 (1967), 205–27

Reid, S. W., 'Compositional Spelling and Literal Rhyme', *The Library*, V, 30 (1975), 108–15

Riddell, James, A., 'The Concluding Pages of the Jonson Folio of 1616', *Studies in Bibliography* 47 (1994), 147–154

Robertson, Jean, ed., *The Countesse of Pembroke's Arcadia* (1973)

Spufford, Margaret, *Small Books and Pleasant Histories: Popular Fiction and its Readership in Seventeenth-Century England* (1981)

Stevenson, Allan, 'New Uses of Watermarks as Bibliographical Evidence', *Studies in Bibliography* 1 (1948), 151–82

—— 'Chain Indentations in Paper as Bibliographical Evidence', *Studies in Bibliography* 6 (1955), 181–195

—— *Observations on Paper as Evidence* (1961)

—— 'Watermarks are Twins', *Studies in Bibliography* 4 (1951–2), 57–91

Taylor, Gary, 'General Introduction', in *William Shakespeare: A Textual Companion*, ed. Stanley Wells, Gary Taylor, *et al.* (1987), 1–68

—— 'The Renaissance and the End of Editing', in *Palimpsest: Editorial Theory in the Humanities*, ed. George Bornstein and Ralph G. Williams (1993), 121–49

Thomas, Keith, 'The Meaning of Literacy in Early Modern England', in *The Written Word: Literacy in Transition*, ed. Gerd Baumann (1986), 97–131

Updike, Daniel Berkeley, *Printing Types: Their History, Forms, and Use* (1962)

Vander Meulen, David L., 'The Identification of Paper without Watermarks: The Example of Pope's *Dunciad*', *Studies in Bibliography* 37 (1984), 58–81

Vervliet, H. D. L., *Sixteenth-Century Printing Types of the Low Countries* (1968)

Watson, George J., ed., 'A Critical Edition of Thomas Middleton's *A Tricke to Catch the Old One* (1608)' (B. Litt Thesis, University of Oxford, 1968)

Weiss, Adrian, 'Reproductions of Early Dramatic Texts as a Source of Bibliographical Evidence', *TEXT: Transactions of the Society for Textual Scholarship* 4 (1988), 237–68

—— review of W. Craig Ferguson, *Pica Roman Type in Elizabethan England*, *Papers of the Bibliographical Society of America* 83 (1989), 539–46

—— 'Font Analysis as a Bibliographical Method: the Elizabethan Play-Quarto Printers and Compositors', *Studies in Bibliography* 43 (1990), 95–164

—— 'Bibliographical Methods for Identifying Unknown Printers in Elizabethan/Jacobean Books', *Studies in Bibliography* 44 (1991), 183–228

—— 'Shared Printing, Printer's Copy, and the Text(s) of Gascoigne's *A Hundreth Sundrie Flowres*', *Studies in Bibliography* 45 (1992), 71–104

—— 'Watermark Evidence and Inference: New Style Dates of Edmund Spenser's *Complaints* and *Daphnaida*', *Studies in Bibliography* 52 (1999), 129–54

Woodfield, Denis B., *Surreptitious Printing in England 1550–1640* (1973)

VISUAL TEXTS: THOMAS MIDDLETON AND PRINTS

John H. Astington

IN 1657 Humphrey Moseley brought out three previously unpublished Middleton plays in two editions, both of which were prefaced with an engraved portrait of the author: *No Wit/Help like a Woman's* (Wing M1985) and *Two New Plays* (Wing M1989; see Illustration 1). This is the only likeness—or supposed likeness—of Middleton which survives; since it appeared thirty years after his death and it contains no indication either of who made it or what other picture it may be based on we have some reason to suspect it. It is not a particularly accomplished engraving, and the half-length portrait is rather stiff and formal. The subject is seen at a three-quarter face angle, turned to the left. The body is largely covered with a dark cloak or gown, the right hand emerging from the sleeve at lower centre and holding what is probably a handkerchief, tucked into the palm and with the ends falling over the fingers. The figure wears a plain white falling collar around the rather awkwardly represented neck, with large braided tassels descending over the inner doublet. Curling shoulder-length hair frames a broad face, with large eyes, a long, prominent nose, and a small mouth. The subject wears a small moustache and a carefully trimmed line of beard below the lip to the chin, a rather dandyish touch to an otherwise sober exterior. A conventional crown of laurel is worn around the head. Below the shadowed rectangular space in which the framed portrait is set a decorative cursive script reads '*Vera Effigies Tho: Midletoni Gent:*'.

If this legend is true, and the engraving was made in 1657, the engraver was working from a portrait made during Middleton's life. The general impression the engraving creates is of a younger rather than an older individual: perhaps the sitter is about thirty, but he could be ten years younger, and therefore the picture may show something of Middleton's vision of himself as a university man. The laurel crown signifies accomplishment as a poet, but this detail could simply be the engraver's addition. How good a likeness the source picture may have been is an open question, but although qualities of a good portrait may have suffered at the hands of the evidently mechanical technique of the engraver, the face seems to have had some care given to it. We can probably regard this picture as providing us, through a double filter of representation, with an impression of Middleton at about the middle of his life.

Although we can know nothing about the original portrait, the work of the engraver can be examined comparatively. I would identify the engraving as the unsigned work of Thomas Cross, who worked for Moseley on other

1. Engraved portrait of Middleton, used as a frontispiece for *Two New Playes... Written by Tho. Middleton, Gent.* (1657)

books, who produced a number of other conventional portraits of poets and dramatists, and whose style is consistent with the techniques apparent in the Middleton plate; a number of his catalogued plates are unsigned (Hind, vol. 3, 277–326). The standard reference on his work points out both that 'he was not a very skilled craftsman' and that, despite that fact, it 'seems highly probable' that he 'engraved portraits only for book publishers, in fact that he was employed exclusively by them' (Hind, vol. 3, 277). He worked from 1644 until the 1680s, and produced a considerable number of portraits during the 1650s. There is also some evidence, not mentioned by Hind and his successors, that Cross printed and sold pictures from his own premises, so that he may have printed engravings for Moseley on his own press.[1]

Most immediately the Middleton picture may be compared with two portraits of dramatists Cross made, and signed, for publication by Moseley in 1653 and 1655: those of Richard Brome for *Five New Plays*, and of Philip Massinger for *Three New Plays*. In both the subject is plainly dressed, turned to a three-quarter face angle, and set against an unlocalized background of horizontal shading lines, complicated somewhat in the Massinger picture by cross-hatching to the right of the figure. Both show a laurel halo hanging over the subject's head, rather than the crown of the Middleton composition. The Massinger portrait is particularly similar to the Middleton print in format, visual scheme, and legend, which announces that it too is a 'Vera ac Viva Effigies' of its subject; again it is a posthumous portrait with no known source. The similarity of the visual presentation of the dramatists together with the 'New Plays' formula of the titles of the books rather suggest that Moseley was establishing a recognizable series, for commercial reasons: a sort of 'standard authors' collection. But despite the mechanical similarity of the portraits the features of the faces are quite distinct, within the evident limits of Cross's style, and demonstrate that the engraver was making an effort to represent distinct originals.

If further confirmation of Cross's authorship of the engraving is required, one can observe that 'Vera Effigies' is a recurrent formula of the legends below his portraits, and although he uses a wide variety of scripts, the elaborate and not entirely successful flourishes we see decorating the lettering in the Middleton plate can be matched, for example, in his signed portraits of Sir Robert Cotton, Richard Kilburne, and Richard III (Hind, vol. 3, plates 153b, 155b, 160b). The initial T of Middleton's first name is particularly close in formation to that of Cross's own signature, in an italic style, of the name he shared with the dramatist.

The portrait, then, was made by a man who is unlikely ever to have seen Middleton himself, but the limitations of whose style make it seem likely that he was closely following the picture he had been given to copy. Any such picture probably came into Cross's hands through the publisher; how and from whom he may have acquired it is impossible to tell, but by his own account Moseley took care with such illustrations to his books. The Beaumont and Fletcher Folio of 1647 was prefaced by a portrait of John Fletcher engraved by William Marshall, and in his introductory address to the readers Moseley describes his efforts to acquire a likeness of Fletcher's collaborator: 'I was very ambitious to have got Mr. *Beaumonts* picture; but could not possibly, though I spared no enquirie in those *Noble Families* whence he was descended, as also among those Gentlemen that were his acquaintance when he

was of the *Inner Temple*' (Greg, vol. 3, 1234). Middleton's acquaintances must have included many actors: at least one actor, William Cartwright, kept a collection of pictures which included portraits of his fellows, and perhaps there were other such repositories of theatre memorabilia during the interregnum (Bentley, vol. 2, 404–5). But a painted portrait or miniature is most likely to have remained in Middleton's family, and therefore may have been in the possession of his grandson, Richard, in the 1650s. Lacking more knowledge, we must guess at the guardianship of his picture between the date of his death and its appearance in print, much as we must guess at that of the manuscript plays between the closing of the theatres and publication.

The prefatory portrait was a common type of illustration in printed books from an early date, and upon which more care for authenticity and accuracy was generally expended than it evidently was on other illustrated material. Pictures in printed plays naturally invite speculation about their relationship to the contemporary stage; a valuable collection and discussion of such material is to be found in R. A. Foakes's *Illustrations of the English Stage 1580–1642*. The illustrating of the title-pages of published English plays with pictures of famous scenes or characters began in earnest early in the reign of James I, and forms part of the general increase in illustrated publications throughout the Stuart period (Watt, 140–50). The fashion for decorated printed plays of a hundred years earlier had produced texts embellished with generic woodcut figures (Davidson, 128–41), but Jacobean publishers spent money on illustrations that were specifically designed for given plays. Simply by counting the figurative illustrations reproduced in Greg's *Bibliography* one can observe that decade by decade between 1590 and 1640 there is a steady increase in the number of decorated play texts (with a slight recession in the 1620s), so that between 1630 and 1640 four times as many illustrated plays were published as in the 1590s. In both the earlier Tudor period and in the Stuart years pictorial decoration was used to attract readers and buyers, and its range in the early seventeenth century can be represented by the elaborate full-page engraving created by William Hole for the Ben Jonson folio *Works* in 1616—detailed, erudite, and classical—and in the same year by the perky vernacular woodcut block used to enliven the title-page of William Haughton's play *Englishmen for my Money* (Corbett and Lightbown, 144–50; Foakes, 166; see Illustrations 2 & 3).

Apart from their considerable difference in intention and effect these two pages also demonstrate two quite different techniques of reproduction. The engraving or etching is made by cutting lines and marks into the surface of a sheet of copper, respectively with a steel tool or with acid; when the sheet is inked the dampened paper is pressed tightly

[1] The 1656 broadside 'The Great Sins of Drunkeness and Gluttony' (Wing G1755), illustrated with engravings copied from Dutch sources, was 'to be sold by T. Crosse, in Py-corner, in *Green-dragon*-court'. Judging by the lack of other surviving publications, Cross's enterprise—assuming T. Crosse the printseller to be identical with the engraver—was occasional, unsuccessful, or both.

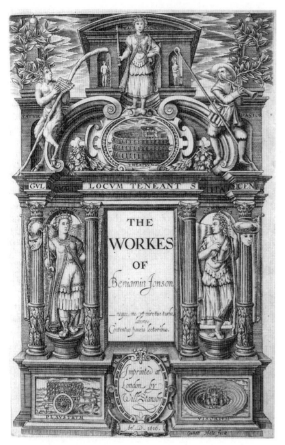

2. Title-page of Ben Jonson, *Workes* (1616)

3. Title-page of William Haughton,
Englishmen for my Money (1616)

against it to take an impression of the marks cut into the plate, which hold the ink. Woodcuts, like type, print an impression of their raised plane surface; the technique of woodcut is to remove or recess those parts of the block which are not to print black in the finished picture. A further consequence of this difference is that woodcuts could be printed concurrently with movable type—both could be set into formes and printed in one process. The engraved plate, however, must be printed in a rolling press—in which plate and paper are squeezed very firmly together—an entirely different machine from the hand press used for printing type. If type and engraving were to appear together in the finished book, the paper had to be printed twice in two distinct processes (Landau and Parshall, 21–30).

As might be imagined, therefore, engraved illustration tended to be reserved for more expensive and ambitious books, at least in the earlier seventeenth century. Woodblocks were generally far more durable than the copper plates used for engravings, which wore quickly in the press, and had to be reworked periodically (Watt, 141–

2). Woodblock illustrations, initial letters, and printers' ornaments could sustain a great deal of printing, and last for a surprisingly long time. Further, as Peter Blayney has pointed out, many smaller printing houses appear to have worked with only one fully operative press, and they were probably incapable of printing engravings (Blayney, 31–43, 463–4). In addition to the technological distinction between woodcuts and engravings, a difference of class, technique, or status is that Jacobean woodcuts are invariably anonymous, whereas etchings or engravings are usually signed with the name or initials of their makers. Engravers appear to have made more money than their largely unknown fellow-craftsmen who created woodblocks. The production of engraved pictures was considered an art, practised by named individuals; the making of woodcut prints a craft, the membership of which we know little about. This is not so much a reflection of any

4. Title-page of *Two Most Unnatural and Bloody Murders* (1605)

5. Title-page of *Sundry Strange and Inhumane Murders* (1591)

inherent artistic superiority of the engraved plate as an expressive medium as of the relative ease and speed of execution, the capacity for fine detail of line and shading, and the control over the pictorial effect which the designer of the picture might achieve himself. Since the technique of engraving is so much nearer to drawing, the creator of an image was far more likely himself to execute the plate used for printing; a complex woodcut design required a high degree of skill in cutting the block, which was frequently carried out by a separate craftsman (Landau and Parshall, 23).

The relative difficulty of creating fine and detailed effects in woodcuts might be taken as one reason why many Jacobean printed illustrations strike us as naïve or awkward, but we should think of their visual style as chosen as much as imposed by limitations of technique or skill. Although we know very little about the identity of the woodcut craftsmen it seems likely that at least some of them produced other kinds of graphic work— in decorative painting of plaster, woodwork, and glass, in portrait and genre painting, in designs for embroidery, tapestry, and ceramics, and indeed in engraving— where their visual style might be different, and their identity as maker might be acknowledged (Davies, 81– 4; Watt, 146). No doubt many craftsmen were capable of the fine and detailed work required for printers' ornaments, borders, and decorated initials. But prints for popular publications in the Jacobean period—illustrations to ballads, almanacs, broadsides, and pamphlets dealing with disasters, prodigies, and crimes—invariably adopt a naïve decorative style which shows little of the representational realism of contemporary 'high' art. Planar composition, deliberate distortion of perspective, of spatial relationships, of anatomical proportion, gesture, and facial expression characterize a style which is consciously formal, somewhat grotesque, and amusing. That is to say that its intent was to entertain, although what we may find amusing about Jacobean woodcuts today may not correspond too closely to the kinds of pleasurable response they aroused in their original viewers. Evidently, however, popular woodcuts conformed roughly to a recognizably exaggerated, non-realistic style which was calculated to stimulate a generic expectation about the kind of printed material it was used to decorate, much as the typography of mass-market newspapers or the visual conventions of drawing and colouring in modern comic books create or confirm the expectations of those who buy them.

Published plays inhabited ambiguous territory in the marketing world of seventeenth-century bookstalls, and such ambiguity is reflected in the ways they were illustrated. They could be serious literature, as was Jonson's *Works*, and as were the two university plays in Latin, *Ignoramus* and *Pedantius*, both published with engraved frontispieces in 1630 and 1631 (Foakes, 128-9, 132-3). In so far as plays belonged to the unserious world of public entertainment, however, they might be sold alongside jest books, news pamphlets, and ballads, and decorated accordingly. Most illustrations to plays published before the Restoration are conceived in the disjunctive, exaggerated conventions of the popular woodcut. Perhaps the most famous images of this kind, at least as they are known through reproduction in modern texts, are the woodcut illustrations to *The Spanish Tragedy* (1615) and *Doctor Faustus* (1616). Both have been used as evidence for the appearance of plays on the contemporary stage, although even a brief survey of woodcuts in non-dramatic texts will reveal that many of their pictorial details are generic rather than specific (Davies, plates). Both woodblocks were also subsequently used to decorate ballads, the first on a versified narrative of the subject of the play (STC 23012 [1620?]), but the second as the decoration to 'The Tragedy of Doctor Lambe' (STC 19272; 1628), where it serves as a general indication of the 'great supposed Coniurer'. Several other woodcuts appeared both in play texts and ballads, and one might say that even if play texts were not genuinely 'popular' literature in the usual sense of that term, they were illustrated, perhaps as an advertising ploy, as if they were. Furthermore, the reuse of pictorial material reveals a frankly decorative attitude towards what it represents. All kinds of woodblocks, some of them a century old, were used to ornament publications during the Jacobean years. Woodcut illustrations were conceived within formal, non-realistic conventions, and although they may have been made to represent a particular event or person connected to a given publication they were also evidently regarded generically: a picture of an execution made for a pamphlet in 1614 will turn up in a ballad on another event in 1615. Illustrations could be generic signs as much as they were particular depictions, and there is no distinct boundary between these two functions. As evidence of things in the Jacobean world, therefore, contemporary woodcut illustrations should be treated very cautiously. The 1605 pamphlet Middleton used as a source for *A Yorkshire Tragedy*, *Two Most Unnaturall and Bloodie Murthers* (STC 18288), is a case in point (see Illustration 4). In the title-page picture Calverley is not armed with a knife, as he is both in the pamphlet account and in the play, but with some kind of cudgel, and his oddly disjointed victims are all the same size: the children are not infants. There is an odd figure with clawed hands and feet emerging from the left frame, and an entirely superfluous dog in the right middle ground—although technically there is no ground: all the figures float in white space. The explanation of this crude and odd arrangement of figures is that the publisher—Nathaniel Butter, who also illustrated plays—has re-used

an old woodblock, first published in 1591 on the title-page of *Sundrye Strange and Inhumaine Murthers* (STC 18286.5; see Illustration 5). This block, made for the book, shows the devilish Ashford father and his hired assassin, armed with an axe, standing over the bodies of three adolescent children. The background shows a dog miraculously discovering a murdered child—a separate incident recounted in the book. For the 1605 pamphlet the old block has been thoroughly but crudely cut down to serve the Calverley story, with which it has no connection at all.

Although he may have been aware of the arbitrary decorative quality of some printed illustrations to books, Middleton seems to have been particularly interested in the visual presentation of his own published work, to a degree unique among contemporary dramatists. During the second half of his career four of Middleton's dramatic works were decorated with original illustrations: *The Roaring Girl* (1611), *A Fair Quarrel* (1617), *The World Tossed at Tennis* (1620), and *A Game at Chess* (1625). The first three of these were published with woodcuts forming part of the title-page, and the last with two distinct engraved title-pages. In addition *The Black Book* (1604) was printed with a xylographic decoration which was specifically cut for that publication, and *The Owl's Almanac* (1618) is decorated with a title-page woodcut in the manner of the plays; in the same year *The Peacemaker* contains a decorative woodcut print of the royal arms and initials on the leaf facing the title-page, while the 1626 edition of *The Triumphs of Health and Prosperity* bears on its title-page a print of the Drapers' Company arms, from a woodcut which is quite likely to have been made for the book.[2] I propose to speak of the four figurative woodcuts as a group, then to pass to the illustrations for *A Game at Chess*, which like so much else to do with the play have a particular and distinct context.

When an illustration was specifically made for a substantial book the author was frequently responsible for its design (Corbett and Lightbown, 45-6). Playbooks were neither substantial publications nor always directly connected with an author, in that the dramatist had sold the play to the acting company, which might subsequently sell a text to a publisher. The decision to decorate the title-page with an illustration—and the great majority of published quarto plays were not so decorated—probably lay usually with the publisher, who, if he consulted anyone at all, would have spoken to the person or persons from whom he had acquired the text. Neither Kyd nor Marlowe, long dead when their plays were first provided with woodcut illustrations, had any say in the matter.

---

[2] *The Two Gates of Salvation* (1609) was printed with a woodcut border (McKerrow and Ferguson 100) first recorded in 1559, but in Nicholas Okes's possession between 1609 and 1612 (Blayney, 459). Two of the six surviving copies of *Civitatis Amor* (1616; Huntington and Yale) have a half-length portrait of Prince Charles, engraved by Francis Delaram, bound as a frontispiece to the text, the work of a later antiquarian collector. The print, which is larger than the page size of *Civitatis Amor*, was made for the folio volume *The Surveyor*, by Aaron Rathborne, published in the same year (STC 20748; Hind, vol. 2, 217).

The Roaring Girle.

OR

Moll Cut-Purse.

As it hath lately beene Acted on the Fortune-stage by
the Prince his Players.

Written by T. Middleton and T. Dekkar.

My case is alter'd, I must worke for my liuing.

Printed at London for Thomas Archer, and are to be sold at his
shop in Popes head-pallace, neere the Royall
Exchange. 1611.

6. Title-page of *The Roaring Girl* (1611)

7. Plate from Jacob de Gheyn, *The Exercise of Arms* (1607)

On the other hand, some Jacobean writers clearly were involved in the publication of their plays: Webster's address 'To the Reader' at the beginning of *The White Devil* (1612) announces that he regards himself as responsible for 'publishing this Tragedy', and it has been assumed that he read the proofs of the published text. Where there is other evidence of authorial involvement in a printed play, then, we might guess, if it is illustrated, that the author(s) may have had some role in creating the pictorial decoration also. As it happens, Middleton signs an address 'To the Comic Play-Readers' which prefaces the text of *The Roaring Girl*, William Rowley a dedication to *A Fair Quarrel*, while both of them appear to be responsible for prefatory matter in the text of *The World Tossed at Tennis*. But to understand why and how a play was illustrated it is probably at least as important to think of the publisher, and possibly the printer, as it is to consider the author or authors. In the present context this involves some consideration of the other contemporary work, specifically the illustrated work, of the publishers of Middleton's plays.

In the Jacobean years nineteen distinct editions of dramatic texts were published with pictorial woodcuts (among them *The Roaring Girl*, *A Fair Quarrel*, and *The World Tossed at Tennis*). These nineteen appeared above the names of twelve publishers or groups of publishers: of these twelve only five published more than one illustrated play, and no one published more than three. Given these figures it would be hard to regard any one stationer as a specialist in illustrated play texts, and if indeed the option of illustrating a play lay with the publisher then no given publisher seems particularly more likely to have chosen to do so. But it is wrong to regard woodcuts in plays as especially distinct from similar illustrations used in other publications; a more significant question may be how frequently publishers issued illustrated texts of any kind.

Thomas Archer and John Trundle, publishers of *The Roaring Girl* and *A Fair Quarrel* respectively, were the first to decorate title-pages with illustrations directly related to the printed play. Even their contemporary Nathaniel Butter, in his illustrated editions of Heywood's *If You Know Not Me, You Know Nobody* (1605, 1623, 1639) and Samuel Rowley's *When You See Me, You Know Me* (1613), conforms more closely to the sixteenth-century practice of decorating plays with generic illustrations which would serve—and did serve—just as well in another context.

Trundle's lively comic woodcuts to the play *Nobody and Somebody* (1606), by contrast, seem to represent actors in costume for the parts (Foakes, 94–5, 62–3), as well as referring to Trundle's own shop-sign in the Barbican, which presumably showed 'No-body' much as he appears in the printed illustration. In both woodcuts, one of which appears on the title-page and the second following the end of the play, a single standing figure is shown in a plain square frame, set on a ruled perspective floor which terminates at an undifferentiated plain background. All of the earlier seventeenth-century theatrical woodcuts follow the convention of showing a single figure connected with the play in characteristic costume and gesture: that to *The Roaring Girl* is typical (see Illustration 6). Within an upright rectangular plain frame Moll, in men's clothes and holding a sword and a pipe, stands facing the observer, slightly turned to the right. Beneath her feet a fairly shallow wooden floor is represented by retreating perspective lines, which once again terminate at a ruled horizon with a blank background above it. Either a stage or an interior location may be loosely suggested by this part of the picture, but it is first and foremost a simple conventional sign of depth, and a basis for a lively and interesting figure to be anchored by the shadowing around her shoes. (If one pays the incidental detail of the floor too much attention, one begins to realize that the figure is not foreshortened to match the high viewpoint from which the sharply angled floor is seen—a distraction, given the non-realistic conventions of representation in popular woodcuts.)

The woodcut is quite detailed in its execution, and its design achieves a satisfying expression of the combined dynamism and insouciance of the title character. One of its most interesting visual details, the pipe with its curling whiff of smoke, is also one of the earliest depictions of a growing cultural practice—the smoker, including the woman smoker, was to become a favourite genre subject in Dutch art later in the seventeenth century. When Moll smokes in the play (Sc. 2) she is dressed '*in a frieze jerkin and a black saveguard*', so that the illustration is not recording a given moment in the action so much as the more sensational manifestations of Moll's career as a roarer. The details of the male costume she wears are related to the text of the play (Foakes, 99; Gomme, 2), as is the raised sword, in pictorial terms both an amusing symbol and a diagonal accent which contrasts with the swirling lines of the cloak and its shadowing. R. A. Foakes notes that the sword is carried in the left hand, and speculates as to whether the actual Mary Frith or the actor of Moll may have been left-handed. But Moll is not ready to fight, and her right hand is occupied in managing her pipe; the sword has been unhooked from the belt, but is still within its scabbard, and the hangers fall over Moll's arm above the hilts of the sword. This may indeed presage a fight—the woodcut to *A Fair Quarrel* shows scabbards and hangers on the ground behind the duelling pair— and the details both of cloak and sword at the ready may reflect the action in Sc. 5, where Moll appears in male

dress for the first time in the play to confront Laxton, and where a stage direction specifies that she '*puts off her cloak and draws*' (61.1). The pipe-smoking is quite unrelated to this passage, however, and the ostentatious sword may simply be another aspect of roaring.

Otherwise the stance has an ironic resemblance to the postures of military drill, in illustrations of which the sword can be shown as being held diagonally across the front of the body, the point appearing above the left shoulder (Kist, 10). Moll's clothing, indeed, is interestingly close to that shown in the first and most influential illustrated book of military drill, Jacob de Gheyn's *The Exercise of Armes* (The Hague, 1607); de Gheyn's second series of Dutch musketeers, all rather differently dressed in each of forty-three plates, wear decorated wide-brimmed hats, high collars, and capacious breeches ('the great Dutch slop' of the play) with lively bows at the knee (see Illustration 7). The woodcut was certainly not directly copied from any one of these plates, but they may have provided some general stylistic influence, a point to which I shall return below.

Moll's female identity is revealed in the woodcut partly by the indication of a visibly protuberant right breast, rather sketchily (and anatomically oddly) shown with a few curved lines. This detail may or may not have been made evident on stage via the male actor's doubly disguised body. Foakes reminds us that the woodcut may equally be making reference to Mary Frith herself; I tend to think that precise representation of either the real person or the actor in the part is not what the illustration is attempting. With the stage in mind, however, one might compare the woodcut illustration of the disguised Aspatia in the 1619 edition of *The Maid's Tragedy* (Foakes, 115), who wears a costume similar to Moll's in a number of respects, but whose breasts are given an even more perfunctory graphic treatment. Both the pictured Moll and Aspatia show signs of the conventions of cross-dressing which probably did part of the stage tradition, however. Moll's hair does not fall below her ears, and may be compared with the longer male hairstyles in the *Fair Quarrel* woodcut, with Amintor's in *The Maid's Tragedy* picture, or with those of de Gheyn's soldiers. Tucking the longer hair of a female wig up into the male hat was one stage convention of cross-dressed disguise: the first quarto of *Philaster* (1620) includes a stage direction which clearly indicates a method of throwing off male disguise, when the unnamed daughter of Leon, who spends most of the play as the page Bellario, '*Kneeles to* LEON, *and discovers her haire*'.

The Roaring Girl was the second play with an illustrated title-page to be published by Thomas Archer and printed by Nicholas Okes, and it forms part of a group of Archer's publications which were decorated with woodcuts between 1603 and 1615. The other illustrated play, *The History of the Two Maids of Moreclack* (1609; Foakes, 96–7), follows the same general conventions of page layout and of visual scheme within the woodcut as does *The Roaring Girl*. The upright rectangle of the woodcut block frames the quirky full-length figure of John of the Hospital, who is anchored only by shadows beneath his feet in an otherwise entirely unlocalized space. To that extent the figure is cruder than the picture of Moll, and the drawing and shading are both stiffer and less unified than in the later picture: there is little stylistic evidence to suggest they were made by the same hand. An earlier woodcut, used to illustrate *Diogines Lanthorne* (1607), has more of the detail and assurance we see in *The Roaring Girl* print, although again there is little sign of common workmanship. A pamphlet published in the year following *The Roaring Girl*, *The Arraignment of John Selman* (1612) is decorated with a fairly rough figure of the criminal, a cutpurse, while in 1615 two distinct editions of Joseph Swetnam's *The Arraignment . . . of Women* bear two different decorative female figures on their title-pages, blocks which are quite generic, although they differ in style, and which were later much used in ballads.

There is little indication, therefore, that Archer consistently employed one craftsman to provide his woodcuts; rather each job is likely to have been commissioned ad hoc. Archer's shop, in Pope's Head Alley, near the Royal Exchange, was in one of the centres of printselling, and possibly therefore of printmaking, in early seventeenth--century London; it was the address of John Sudbury and George Humble, and in 1634 Henry Peacham specifically mentioned it as a place to acquire imported prints (Rostenberg, 1–18). Not only was Archer likely to have found printmakers in his immediate vicinity, but those artists and craftsmen had access to continental models, should they have chosen to consult them, in the local shops of printsellers and print publishers. My suggestion that the figure of Moll may show some influence of the de Gheyn plates is made partly with this local circumstance in mind; *The Exercise of Armes* is likely to have been for sale in Pope's Head Alley.

How Archer may have commissioned the picture—that is to say how he described what he wanted—raises the questions of whether he saw the play on stage or whether he spoke either to the actors or the authors. Middleton's signed preface 'To the Comic Play-readers', in the course of which he makes reference to Moll's costume, suggests that he may have collaborated on other aspects of the production of the book; he rather than Archer may have spoken or given written notes to the designer of the block.

The attractive and lively picture of Moll Cutpurse was never reused, so far as is apparent from surviving publications. Blocks showing single figures were much in demand for ballads and broadsides, and quite inappropriate blocks were frequently used to illustrate a cheap text simply because they were visually attractive. That such an amusing block was never reprinted seems to suggest that it was damaged or lost following the production of the book—woodblocks produced for a specific occasion could have a protracted afterlife in other contexts.[3]

The woodcut illustration to *A Fair Quarrel*, which shows the duel between the Colonel and Captain Ager

8. Title-page of *A Faire Quarrell* (1617)

in 3.1 of the play, is made in a far more exaggerated style than is that to *The Roaring Girl* (see Illustration 8). The rather phantasmagoric effects of distorted proportions and stiff postures were possibly originally meant to be somewhat tongue-in-cheek, while a modern viewer is taxed to find a visual meaning in the print that could be anything other than ridiculous. Either the woodcut is very inept, or it is designed to parody the physical and emotional tension of the duel. The central diagonals of the crossed swords are undermined by the stronger lines of the discarded scabbards, which create a crazy geometrical rhythm with the extended disproportionate legs of the figures, carrying through into the lines of the bodies and arms, and the bloated pyramidal shape of each figure from knees to crown. The diagonal lines on the two doublets and on the breeches of the left--hand figure continue the jazzy disharmonic effect of the

[3] There seems to me to be little likelihood that the woodcut influenced the engravings of women smoking (as 'Gustus' in a series of prints of the Five Senses) produced by Jan Bara and George Glover (early 1630s and late 1640s[?]: Hollstein, vol. 1, 95; Hind, vol. 3, 98–9, 247–8). Thus the article by W. A. Thorpe, which gives an account of wall paintings based on the Bara prints, is mistaken in connecting the 'Gustus' picture with Moll. The later Restoration engraved portrait of Mary Frith may have some connection with the Bara prints of thirty years earlier, but is probably iconographically independent.

233

Three Bloodie Murders:

The first, committed by *Francis Cartwright* vpon *William Storre*, Mr. of Art, Minifter and Preacher at *Market Raifin* in the countie of *Lincolne*.

The Second, committed by *Elizabeth Iames*, on the body of her Mayde, in the Parifh of *Egham* in *Surrie*: who was condemned for the fame fact at Saint Margarets hill in Southwark, the 2. of Iuly 1613. and lieth in the White Lion till her deliuerie: difcouered by a dombe Mayde, and a Dogge.

The Third, committed vpon a ftranger, very lately, neere *High-gate* foure miles from *London*: very ftrangely found out by a Dogge alfo, the 2. of Iuly. 1613.

Imprinted at London for *Iohn Trundle*, dwelling in Barbican 1613.

9. Title-page of *Three Bloody Murders* (1613)

picture. Any tension or danger seems to be of entirely the wrong kind: the duellists are at risk of tripping or lumbering into a hit, or simply of collapsing. As in earlier woodcuts a shallow ground for the figures is established by an undulating, shadowed horizon—indicating an exterior rather than an interior location—behind which there is a completely uncharacterized vacant space. Because of the conventional shallowness of the ground and the strength of emphasis of the woodcut lines the designer has trouble subordinating the background details of the discarded hats and scabbards: their relationship in depth with the foreground figures is not successfully established, and they invade the composition as if they were on the same vertical plane—the fighters contend with objects floating around their knees and feet. In format, the squarish rectangular plain frame of the woodcut is set horizontally in the printed title-page, rather than vertically as in the early single-figure woodcuts: the 'scenic' woodcut, which shows more than one figure in action, beginning with *The Spanish Tragedy* cut in 1615, is invariably laid out in this way.

John Trundle published this play in some kind of collaboration with Edward Wright, whose shop 'at Christ Church Gate' is advertised as where it was to be sold. This arrangement had begun some years before the publication of *A Fair Quarrel*, and it was to continue through the publication of *The World Tossed at Tennis*. Both men produced a good deal of illustrated material, much of it at the lower end of the market, and hence in a fairly rough, vernacular visual style. Although Trundle's earlier play woodcuts—to *Nobody and Somebody* and to *Greene's Tu Quoque* (1614)—are amusing and specific depictions of characters in costume, that to *A Fair Quarrel* seems more loosely generic, and is nearer in style to the illustrations for pamphlets on crimes and disasters, which formed part of Trundle's and Wright's output. R. V. Holdsworth has suggested that the picture was probably 'copied out of one of the many fencing manuals', while simultaneously pointing out that the details of the *Fair Quarrel* scene are rather different from those in fencing books (Holdsworth, 2). I can find no evidence of copying, although the general conventions of fencing pictures undoubtedly had some influence on the woodcut. Most illustrations in such manuals, even those produced in England, attempt and usually achieve a far clearer and more unified style. That which perhaps is closest is Joseph Swetnam's *The Schoole of the Noble and Worthy Science of Defence*, published in the same year as the play with a title-page woodcut showing two men fighting with absurdly large two--handed swords, a print which vies with the duelling scene in vernacular awkwardness. It also demonstrates the same convention of a shallow undulating foreground on which the combatants stand, with vacant space behind them. That visual scheme is carried through the six different woodcuts in the text of the book, although the figures are rendered there with considerably more sophistication and success.

On stylistic grounds I think that the design for *A Fair Quarrel* shows more sign of influence from the popular prints published by Trundle and Wright; the woodcut was probably made by one of the craftsmen they employed for such publications. A good example of such work is the title-page to the 1613 pamphlet *Three Bloodie Murders* (STC 18287a; see Illustration 9), which shows a horrific scene of murder and dismemberment presented with a similarly jolly graphic absurdity to that of the *Fair Quarrel* picture. In this case a hat dislodged from the victim and his severed lower right leg have the same arbitrary decorative quality as trees on the horizon, or a particularly elaborate plant in the right middle ground. Otherwise the print is not of the extreme technical simplicity of the most primitive of such penny-dreadful scenes, but is quite carefully shadowed and modelled; the skill it displays is rather more than that shown in the woodcut to the play.

The relationship between the actual murder of William Storre and its representation in a woodcut is a symbolic one. The scene is an 'artist's impression', as we now say, in which the draughtsman strives to present particular events in a manner understandable to the viewer. The same is true of the illustration of a scene from a play, in which certain given fictional circumstances will dictate what actions or people are shown in a print, but not necessarily how they are shown. If, in this case, the printmaker takes care to follow certain indications dictated by the text—that the Colonel (the left-hand figure) is older than Captain Ager, that the fight has some outdoor location, rather vaguely referred to at several points in the play—other visual signs do not have a particularly close connection with the play text, nor, probably, with its staging. Thus the discarded hats and scabbards may have been concomitant effects of drawing the swords, but both men involved in this fight have seconds, and the duel is prepared for with long preliminaries: it is not a hasty scrap. Similarly the spurs, a suicidal impediment to serious fencing, one might think, are probably a conventional visual sign of social rank or military status. There is no indication in the play that the combatants approach or leave on horseback the vague location where they fight. Hence one could not confidently regard this picture as indicating what the actors may have worn on stage—the figures are simply dressed as generic gentlemen.

I have been suggesting that the publishers may have had rather more to do with this woodcut than with that illustrating *The Roaring Girl*. No great ingenuity need have been spent in conceiving any more than in executing it. A largely generalized duel scene relates directly to the title of the play, and the block could easily have been reused to provide decorative prints elsewhere, although once again nothing survives to show that it was.[4] Nevertheless, one of the authors—in this case William Rowley—prefaces the text with a dedication, so that one or both may have been consulted over the book's appearance. If indeed either made specifications for an illustration they cannot have been very detailed or demanding, or else they were subsequently ignored.

As a publishing venture *The World Tossed at Tennis* was a triple collaboration among John Trundle and George Purslowe, to whom it was entered in the Stationers' Register, and Edward Wright, whose address once more appears on the title-page. Purslowe printed it; he also operated as a bookseller, and in both roles he handled a good deal of illustrated material.

The woodcut illustration to the masque, in the horizontal rectangular format common in the 'scenic' convention of illustrated dramatic texts, shows a good deal more careful attention to representing the events and characters than does the picture to *A Fair Quarrel*; eight of the characters from the masque are shown, six of them surrounding a globe, an important stage property in the action, while an intriguing bunched curtain appears hanging below the top of the frame (see Illustration 10). As Foakes points out, the woodcut apparently represents the point towards the end of the masque where the various claimants to control over the world dance, passing the globe from one to another and fending off the efforts of Deceit and the Devil to seize it (Foakes, 120-1). But there is a good deal about *The World Tossed at Tennis* which is puzzling, from its title to its stage directions, and it is

10. Title-page of *The World Tossed at Tennis* (1620)

not clear whether the printed text represents the masque as finally adapted for the commercial theatre, some literary indication of the original shape of the projected royal entertainment, or a mixture of both. Hence there is some confusion between on the one hand the sequence in which the world is first entrusted by Jupiter to Simplicity, and passed successively to the King, the Land Captain, the Sea Captain, the Flamen, and the Lawyer, and on the other the dance in which this ceremonial relay is repeated, but in which the characters are named as abstractions: *Majesty, Valour, Law, Religion,* and *Sovereignty*. *Majesty* and *Sovereignty* are presumably embodied in one character, the King (although in the projected masque the plan may have been to deliver the globe to James himself). *Law* and *Religion* are clear enough, but which of the two captains becomes *Valour*? Simplicity is not mentioned in the directions for the dance. Once again,

4 The woodblock lasted until at least 1622, when a third edition of the play was published. (There are two distinct editions in 1617, the second with additions.) Trundle had assigned his rights in the play to Thomas Dewe, who published the third quarto with the same print on the title-page, so that part of the agreement evidently involved the transfer of a physical object. The play was not subsequently reprinted before the 1640s, but the ownership of copy was transferred twice more in the 1620s, and the woodblock may have passed its remaining life in storage at a number of locations before cracking, being eaten by woodworm, or simply getting lost (Greg, vol. 2, 494-6).

A QVIP FOR AN VPSTART COVRTIER:

OR,

A quaint diſpute betweene Veluet breeches and Cloth breeches.

Wherein is plainely ſet downe the diſorders in all Eſtates and Trades.

London printed by G. P. 1620.

11. Title-page of *A Quip for an Upstart Courtier* (1620)

then, the woodcut, although it represents the action in some ways, conflates and selects rather than records. The only indication within the text that characters support the globe together involves five characters (or as few as three?) rather than six, when after the dance '*They all deliver the orb up to the King*'. There is little sign in the woodcut that the pictured figures may be dancing, and although a visual opposition is established between the supporters of the world and the forces of evil, it seems more likely that on stage there was a symmetrical arrangement on either side of the globe and the throne: '*the Law confounding Deceit, and the Church the Devil*' (812.10–11).

Hence I disagree somewhat with Foakes's identification of the figures supporting the globe. It is clear that the background pair are the Lawyer (left) and the Flamen, or churchman (right). The foreground figures are the Sea Captain (left) and Simplicity (right), who is dressed as a countryman, and whose appearance may reflect that of

Rowley, who probably played the part. Foakes suggests that the middle figure on the left is the King, since he wears a feathered hat and pointed beard similar to those in many representations of James. But the evident sign of a king (rather than *the* king) whether on stage or in graphic images was the crown, and I think that this figure's feathered hat, gorget, sword, boots, and spurs bespeak the Land Captain. Who then stands opposite him, since such a plainly dressed figure wearing a hat can hardly be the King either? Foakes, rather confusingly, calls him Valour, but I think he must be meant as the Scholar, who begins and ends the masque in the company of the Soldier, and who remains on stage throughout the action, it appears. One would not imagine that it is intended he be included among the '*all*' who deliver the globe to the King, but that is no reason to prevent his being there in a design based on the masque. He stands, appropriately, as a supporter of the world opposite a soldier, if not the Soldier.

The characters are largely dressed as conventional social types, as presumably they would have been on the stage, although one must guard against too easy an assumption that the pictured characters are wearing stage costume. The appearance of Simplicity, as a countryman carrying a staff, is connected by Foakes to the fool's costume, but it is as likely to be related to 'Cloth Breeches' as he is shown in the woodcut to the edition of *A Quip for an Upstart Courtier* printed by Purslowe in 1620 (STC 12303; see Illustration 11: the courtier figure in the cut also resembles the Land Captain), a print which is related in turn to an earlier woodcut of 1592, of which copies were used in ballads from the 1620s to the Restoration. 'Court and country' figures in various guises form a popular graphic theme, and Simplicity shares many features of costume and gesture with other contemporary woodcut prints of rustics. Similarly the spirited depiction of the Devil, who 'has a splendid costume', according to Foakes, is a rather elaborate version of an iconographic commonplace in contemporary popular illustrations: demons and devils are more often than not black, and equipped with horns, tails, claws, and not infrequently a phallus (Davies, 464–71). A lively vernacular example can be seen in the title-page woodcut to Trundle and Wright's 1614 pamphlet *Anthony Painter the Blaspheming Caryar* (STC 19120; see Illustration 12).

It is plain that the woodcut was designed to exhibit the action of the masque, and therefore perhaps to sell a rather unusual product, but its attractive rendering of figures is not matched by a sophisticated sense of pictorial space. The figures are set within a completely neutral blankness; no ground is established beyond that of the shadowing beneath their feet, but a number of other spatial conventions are used—ineptly—to create some depth. Thus Deceit, upstage of the Sea Captain, is shown as smaller, but that vastly exaggerated perspective is not matched in the group to the right, who might be described either as being seen from a high viewpoint, but not foreshortened, or as a short, blunt human pyramid, a problem created

12. Title-page of *Anthony Painter* (1614)

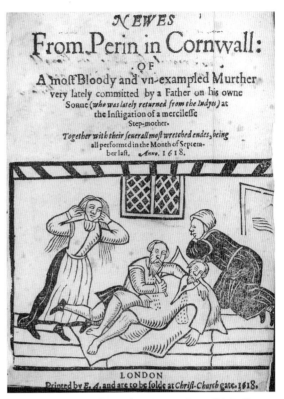

13. Title-page of *News from Perin in Cornwall* (1618)

by the unreadable vertical plane of the globe, on which foreground and background figures lay their hands with equal ease. The curtain has always attracted interest in commentary on this print, and it may indeed have been specified by the designer(s) as a visual reminder that this fiction was made for the royal stage rather than the commercial theatre; it may equally have been a design solution—and again an inadequate one—to the representation of pictorial depth. That is to say that because of the busy, crowded figure group the designer may have chosen not to make a conventional representation of a retreating floor or stage—as we have seen, detail easily becomes distracting in Jacobean woodcuts—but to suggest space with the hint of a ceiling above. This hardly works, since curtaining usually hangs vertically, but the idea may be derived from the perspective ceiling represented in a woodcut of 1618, published by Edward Wright. This is a fairly crudely drawn murder scene used on the title-page and again within the text of *Newes from Perin in Cornwall* (STC 19614; see Illustration 13). Little depth is established by the floorboards on which the murder is taking place, the lines of which run horizontally parallel with the frame of the picture, but the insistent black beams of the strip of

ceiling shown below the top of the frame converge on a vanishing point. Woodcut representations rarely use the space above the figures to create depth, but the 1618 cut gives a clear example of the technique, and the print for *The World Tossed at Tennis* may be following it.

The woodcut was made by one of the anonymous workmen who frequently provided blocks for Purslowe, Trundle, and Wright, but there is every sign that he was given quite explicit and detailed instructions, and hence more reason to think in this case that one or more of the authors may have contributed to them. The print rivals that to *A Game at Chess* in its lively representation of characters and actions, and there is possibly a common thread of authorial input behind the two pictures. Middleton signed a dedicatory epistle to the published book, and 'Simplicity'—presumably Rowley—an address to the reader (Bentley, 4, 909). If Rowley indeed acted in the masque his guidance on the illustration would perhaps be particularly sought.

After 1620 *The World Tossed at Tennis* was not republished until the nineteenth century, but the lively block which was cut for it had a bibliographical career for another sixty-five years. Nearly the whole block was printed as the second illustration to a satirical Royalist ballad, 'A New Game at Cards', which is undated and

14. Title-page of *The Owl's Almanac* (1618)

15. Title-page of *Doctor Faustus* (1620)

bears no colophon, but appears to have been produced between 1646 and 1648. Copies of the ballad survive in the Euing and Roxburghe collections, and appear to be identical with a copy in the Bodleian Library which is recorded in Wing's *Short Title Catalogue* as N642, and dated 1655–1680. A date in the 1640s seems far likelier, given both the political circumstances the ballad addresses and its anonymity. The woodblock seems to have been trimmed so as to leave the figure group only, possibly on the top by cutting across the holes through which the type would originally have been inserted—titles are not printed above the Devil, Deceit, and the World. Fragments of the side frame survive; the bottom rule appears to have been trimmed off. In the context of the ballad the figures read as the various contemporary contestants for the kingdom, cheered on by the devil, so that the absence of an identifiable king among the group becomes particularly significant. At some subsequent time the block was split or broken, to leave two pieces, one of which printed the figures of the Devil and Deceit, with a fragment of the ruled frame to the left and a line corresponding to the left edge of the Sea Captain's breeches to the right. This decorative pair of figures was used with other pieces to illustrate the ballads 'The Good Fellow's Resolution' (1678–

80), 'London's Drollery' (1680), and 'Strange and True News from Westmoreland' (1685), the last being possibly the final appearance of a print from the woodblock (Wing L359, S2697, S5836; *Roxburghe*, vol. 6, 343; 4, 221; *Pepys*, vol. 2, 155). The second piece of the original block, showing the globe and its supporters, illustrates 'A godly song for all penitent Sinners' (*Pepys*, vol. 2, 50; not in Wing?).

In the case of the woodcut to *The Owl's Almanac* we seem to be on firmer ground in detecting satirical intent; it prefaces a mock prognostication, the words '*mirth*' and '*Merrie*' appear above it, and the learned owl inscribing astrological signs in a book is a piece of Aesopian whimsy (see Illustration 14). But the actual composition of the picture is not noticeably different from many other woodcuts which one could not confidently assume to have been parodic: for instance the formally arbitrary rendering of a shooting in *A True Relation of a Most Desperate Murder* (STC 24435; Davies, plate 94), published by Lawrence Lisle in the year before he brought out *The Owl's Almanac*. The tendency of the conventions of woodcut—skewed perspective, lack of depth, lack of focus, distortion of proportion—to produce caricature and bizarre effects is entirely appropriate to the satirical context in this case; the woodcut is simultaneously parodic and entirely typical of popular illustration.

Its designer took a venerable iconographic formula—that of the learned man in his study—and simply changed the man into an owl. As a symbol of folly the owl was common in sixteenth-century satirical literature and the prints which accompanied it, notably in the Eulenspiegel publications (Welsford, 35, 43-7). But long before the printed book the visual conventions of the enclosed study, with writing desk, shelf of books, and window, are apparent in medieval paintings and drawings of the evangelists and church fathers. In the former case the human figures are frequently accompanied by their symbolic beasts, and there may be a further visual joke in the woodcut in this connection: the beast has taken over as writer, but is far from being the eagle of St John. The targets are chiefly secular, however. The iconography of the enclosed room with particular furniture had been assimilated, via portraits of Renaissance humanists and scholars, to signify the learned man, simply, and it was widely used in serious portrait engravings of the first half of the seventeenth century. In woodcuts its conventions famously appear in the 1616 illustration to *Doctor Faustus* (Foakes, 109-11; see Illustration 15, of 1620 edn.), to which *The Owl's Almanac* print, appearing just two years later, may be making some satiric reference. Faustus is not seated in his woodcut, but his room has a steeply angled floor of tiles in perspective, and a diamond-paned window, with books and an astrolabe on a shelf—all elements which appear in *The Owl's Almanac* picture. In addition, the absurd gown and, especially, the ruff which the owl wears may be making some reference to the figure of Faustus, while the symbols in the owl's book are those inscribed in Faustus's magic circle. But as a whole the parody is generic rather than specific, and the visual idea is simple: once again it is suggested by the title of the book. The illustrator neatly guys a visual genre to match the author's mockery of the style and content of the almanac.

Once again the woodcut survived for reuse later. The Thomason Tracts collection contains two satirical broadside ballads and a quarto pamphlet directed against the interregnum astrologer and almanac-maker William Lilly, 'Strange Predictions', 'Lillies Banquet', and *Lillyes Lamentations*: Thomason has dated the first and last November 1652, and the other December 1653 (Wing S5916, L2204, L2206). All feature the squarish woodcut from *The Owl's Almanac*: on the broadsides it is printed centrally towards the top of the sheet, and in the pamphlet it appears as on *The Owl's Almanac* title-page. The block had evidently sustained some damage to the frame, which is broken in a number of places, in the intervening thirty-odd years, and there are a number of worm-holes, but otherwise it has printed cleanly. The picture again appears in the context of satires on astrological prediction, rather indicating that those who used it may have known its history, or have expected their readers to have done

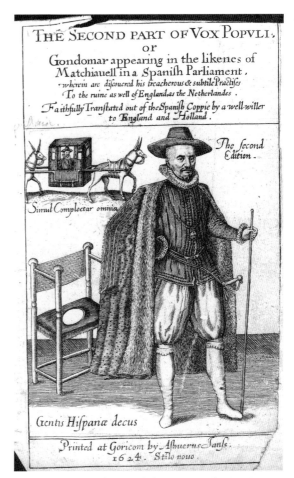

16. Title-page of Thomas Scott, *The Second Part of Vox Populi* (1624)

so. The connection it established between the owl and Lilly, a favourite target of Royalist abuse in the late Commonwealth and early Restoration period, survived in the engraved title-pages to the 'Montelion' mock-almanacs of 1659-61, where another learned owl presides.

The remaining illustrations published during Middleton's lifetime and connected with his works were produced under conditions quite different from those examined so far: they are the famous title-page engravings to *A Game at Chess*. The furore surrounding the play's production in August 1624 had made it famous, and that was perhaps why the published book was chosen to be decorated with the relatively expensive medium of an engraved illustration: it is the first English quarto play text with an engraved title-page. The two plates used to illustrate the three editions of the play are related to the engraved title-page (Illustration 16) of a book Middleton used as a source for *A Game at Chess*, Thomas Scott's *The Second Part*

17. Title-page of *A Game at Chess*, Okes's edition (1625)

of *Vox Populi* (1624). The engraver or engravers of the two plates for the published play used the *Vox* engraving as a visual source for both pictures of the Black Knight, Gondomar (Bald, 14–15), and two other illustrations in Scott's book influenced the engraving made for the two quartos printed by Nicholas Okes (traditionally, but perhaps wrongly, called 'Q1' and 'Q2'). A. M. Hind assigned the anonymous engravings in Scott's book to the Dutch artist Crispijn de Passe the elder (Hind, vol. 2, 43–46), but *The Second Part of Vox Populi*, despite its spurious claim to have been 'Printed at Goricom [Gorinchem, in the Netherlands] by Ashuerus Janss', was actually printed in London by Okes, and it seems likely that the engraved title-plate, which was altered twice during the production of two editions of the book, was produced in London also, and that the engraver—not de Passe, whose workshop was in Utrecht—worked in cooperation with Okes. In addition there is a pirated edition of the book, printed by William Jones (STC 22104), with a title-page copied from the third state of the *Vox* plate, and copies of the other engravings in the text; these were certainly made in London. The context of the illustrations to Scott's books as it is presented by Hind might make one think that the *Game at Chess* plates also were made outside England. Given the bibliography of *The Second Part of Vox Populi* it seems more likely, despite the probably spurious claim of the title-page to the quarto printed by Augustine Mathewes and Edward

Allde (traditionally, but perhaps wrongly, called 'Q3')—'*Ghedruckt in Lydden by Ian Masse*' [Printed in Leiden (?) by Jan Masse]—that they too were engraved in London, possibly under Middleton's close direction; they may have been made by one of the engravers involved in the various states of the *Vox Populi* plates.[5]

The plate to the Okes quartos has drawn more attention from commentators on the play, particularly in the light of its possible demonstration of what was seen on the stage of the Globe 'nine days together' in August 1624 (see Illustration 17). As a physical object it had certain peculiarities which show themselves in the surviving prints which were made from it. First, it was larger than the page size of the printed book, with the result that copies are frequently cropped, or folded to fit within the bound volume. This is not a unique circumstance in seventeenth-century book production—large prints were indeed made to be folded within smaller books—but title-pages, the outside of an unbound book, were not usually designed to be larger than the regular page size; in this case it is probably a sign of distinct and not entirely well coordinated production of the plate and the printed text. It also may suggest a reason why a new plate, smaller than the other, was required.[6]

Confusion over the size of the plate may explain the smaller underlettering at the top; it seems that the lettering of the title was laid out on a smaller scale, then expanded in size and width of line, the partly engraved letters being ineffectively erased. Thus, for example, a smaller A appears above and to the left of the top central letter, and 'Chaess', it seems, may have first been spelled 'Chess'. The rearrangement of the text may explain some evident mistakes: the small super- and subscript terminal e to 'Game' and 'nine', and the final d of 'Acted', which protrudes beyond the rule of the frame. The plate was also scratched in a number of places before printing, and marked with what appears to have been a slip of the engraver's hatching tool, in a diagonal line down the upper left side of the plate. (Most of these marks, being fairly light, do not usually show in photographs, although some of the underlettering can be seen in good reproductions.) Taken together these indications seem to be of haste or uncertainty in production of the plate.

The plate in the Mathewes/Allde quarto is therefore a more satisfactory job of work in a number of respects, although it is, as R. C. Bald says, 'less elaborate' than the first plate. Yet not only does its design reproduce elements also found in the Okes plate, but its lettering is similar in a number of details: I find it quite likely that the same

[5] I am indebted to Peter Blayney for sharing with me his detailed knowledge of the *Vox Populi* imprints. Adrian Weiss identified the printers of the *Game at Chess* quartos: see the General Textual Introduction to *Game* in this *Companion*, p. 712.
[6] In the British Library copy C.34.d.38 the larger title-page is fitted into the bound volume by folding the bottom and right-hand edges of the sheet. The full size of the bound pages is 135 mm. (to spine) by 183 mm.; the entire sheet of the title-page measures 142 mm. by 178 mm., while the ruled frame of the plate measures 134 mm. by 177 mm. Hind gives the dimensions of the Okes plate as 7" by 5 3/4", and those of the Mathewes/Allde plate as 6 3/8" by 4 1/8" (Hind, vol. 2, 386–87).

engraver produced both plates, evidently taking more care with lettering in his work on the Mathewes/Allde one.

The Okes title-page design features three rectangular spaces divided by two horizontal rules across the page. The smallest is at the top, and contains the lettering of the title, with two boxed lateral legends above the rule, referring to the pictured group in the rectangle below: 'The Black-House' and 'The White-House'. This middle rectangle is approximately twice as deep as that above it, and contains a centred group of eight seated figures around a table, on which a chessboard sits; the figures are identified by legends next to or above their heads. The bottom rectangle is largest, showing three standing figures in the foreground, with a background detail of three captured figures shown from the chest upwards, enclosed in a large bag. The space all the figures occupy is defined by a horizon and shadowing (a stage?); the three prominent figures are once again identified by labels over their heads, and each has a speech ribbon containing words quoted or paraphrased from Middleton's play or its sources.

The lowest panel is most closely related to the play on stage, perhaps, while the central one is an artist's interpretation both of the framing situation and the moment in the Induction where 'Enter severally the White House and Black House, as in order of the game' (Induction.52.1–2). As Foakes notes, however, 'there is nothing in the play to show that they sat at a table' (Foakes, 123). The pictured figures sit, I think, not only because the illustration gives a clear visual indication of the competition dramatized in the play, but also because the engraver is copying a visual composition which is used twice in *The Second Part of Vox Populi*, and to which he may be making a quite deliberate reference, as his central lower figure of Gondomar refers to the earlier picture on the title-page of Scott's pamphlet (Hind, vol. 2, plate 18). Two plates are printed within the text of Scott's work, of 'The Spanish Parliament' and of a council of English Jesuits and priests (Illustration 18), both showing seated figures around tables, with evident similarities of grouping and viewpoint to the *Game at Chess* group. The gestures of the two arrangements of *Vox* figures have obvious affinities with all the characters in the later picture, and the dress is reflected in that of the White and Black Dukes and Bishops; the Jesuit council is identified with individual legends in a manner similar to the *Game* group. The lateral background windows in both *Vox Populi* pictures suggest why the engraver in the *Game* picture places his boxed titles identifying the houses where he does, and indicate that if he had had more space to elaborate he would have drawn windows (rather than theatrical doors) in those positions, to suggest an interior.

The engraver seats his group at a table partly because the situation is easily read visually, but also because the table with seated figures has an immediate iconographic context for the literate viewer with Protestant sympathies: it suggests Catholic intrigue, inside and outside England. The addition of the chessboard to the table indicates the battle against Catholic plots, and the removal of the foreground figures opens the table to the viewer's observation

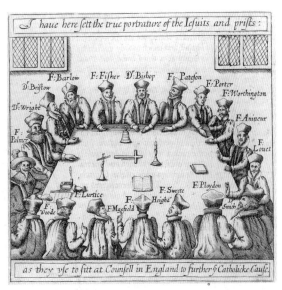

18. Jesuit council, from Thomas Scott,
The Second Part of Vox Populi (1624)

and judgement, as in a theatre. But while playing a variation on the compositions in the *Vox Populi* pictures, the engraver is also invoking other iconographic traditions, and in the first case quite consciously so. Perhaps the most famous icon of the Jacobean Protestant opposition was that 'invented by' the Puritan Samuel Ward, engraved in Amsterdam in 1621, the publication of which led to Ward's examination by the Privy Council and subsequent imprisonment (Hind, vol. 2, 394–5; plate 247). This picture, much copied and alluded to in subsequent visual satire and propaganda, shows the events of 1588 on the left, and those of 1605 on the right. Centrally at the top a glory frames the Holy Letters, and an eye directs a converging beam of light towards the cellars of Parliament on the right, with the legend 'VIDEO RIDEO'. We see, centrally, immediately below heaven, a group of figures seated around a table, sheltered under a tent-like structure which has been opened like a theatrical discovery space; the curtains are held back by two demons, whose faces leer from behind them. The devil, disguised in friar's robes, sits centrally facing us, and around the table are seated the Pope, a Spanish general, and various ecclesiastics and monks. This picture constitutes a central visual touchstone of the Protestant politicians. One of its chief symbols is a hellish conclave, to which the engraving of 'The Spanish Parliament' is making direct reference: in the latter picture the devil emerging from behind the cloth of state and the ecclesiastic with the crossed staff are evident allusions to Ward's engraving. The engraving for Middleton's play is at a further remove, and set within a rather different context, but the sinister implications of figures seated around a table are meant to be read, I believe, as part of the visual information.

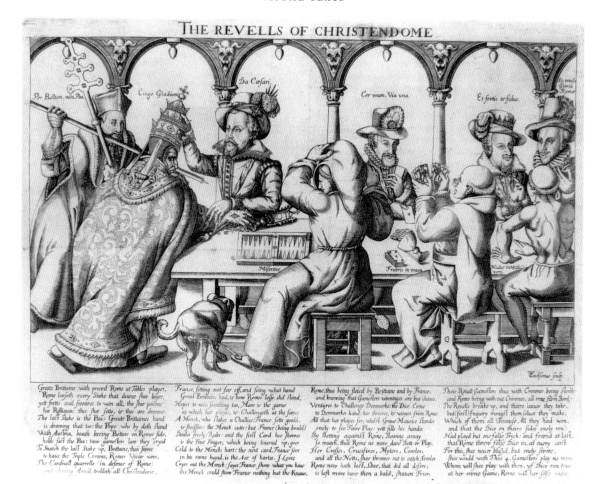

19. Thomas Cockson, *The Revells of Christendome* (1609)

The form the illustrator gives to Middleton's conceit—famous figures seated at a board game—has venerable iconographic roots, and raises the question of whether Middleton may have taken the idea from visual sources in the first place. He may indeed, as John Robert Moore has suggested, have been specifying a particularly Spanish game, but the allegory is an entirely traditional satirical pictorial motif. As a symbol of conflict, the chessboard with competing human figures upon it appears in a printed illustration to the medieval *Pèlerinage de la vie humaine* (1485; Camille, 276–81). The earliest example I have located of a specifically political contest, a woodcut from 1499, shows potentates from the Italian wars seated around a table playing cards, with Lodovico Sforza cheating (Shikes, 9). Thomas Cockson's 'The Revells of Christendom' (1609; see Illustration 19) is particularly interesting in showing James, together with Henry IV of France, Prince Maurice of the Netherlands, and Christian IV of Denmark, seated at a table and engaged in play, at cards and backgammon, with a group of monks. James is resisting the efforts of the Pope and a cardinal to grasp the winnings, and the situation satirizes the peace negotiations between the United Provinces and Spain (Hind, vol. 1, 254–5; plate 134). The picture is directly copied from a Netherlandish print of *c.*1600, 'Hola ghy roouers tspuel is noch ierst beghonnen' ('Look, you robbers, the game has not yet begun'), which originates the visual polemic of Catholic cheaters (and losers) and Protestant opponents: Maurice of Nassau is seated in the position where James sits in Cookson's version (Harms, vol. 2, 120–1). More immediately prior to *A Game at Chess* an anonymous German print of 1621 shows Tilly and Mansfeld seated opposite each other at a backgammon table, with miniature castles and fortified towns for stakes (Harms, vol. 2, 294–5). The engraver places Middleton's play within a European graphic tradition, but Middleton himself is quite likely to have known it. The particular meaning of the game motif in the north-European Protestant graphic tradition was that of resistance to Catholic guile. Middleton's play in performance probably relied on a recognition by its audience—or at least by some members of it—of such an iconography, while the illustration to the published play closes the circle.

Before turning to the lower of the illustrated panels I have two further comments on the group at the table. The engraver evidently used printed portraits as his primary source for depicting the characters. He knew or had been told that the chess-piece personae corresponded to great ones, but used pictures of the great ones themselves to create his own picture. Unless the actors did the same— and they may have done so in the case of Gondomar at the least—the engraving probably bears little relationship in terms of costume and physiognomy to what everyone saw at the Globe. The White King is recognizably James (but a rather younger James than the worn-out man of 1624–5), the Fat Bishop corresponds roughly to the larger figure immediately below him, while the others bear a more approximate resemblance to their known or assumed originals (Moore, 762–3). What is striking, however, is that both kings wear identical crowns, and White King/James is certainly not wearing the crown of England, a fact that any engraver with access to the standard portraits on sale in the print shops would have known. The rival monarchs are wearing players' crowns, so that we are observing either a deliberate avoidance of *lèse-majesté* or an invocation of the stage; were the latter true we would have to consider who may have directed this visual detail. The second point is perhaps simply one of design, an illustrator's visual choice for effect: the game on the exaggeratedly large and thick chessboard is entirely meaningless, consisting of undifferentiated and solely white pieces arranged chequer--like, with one exception, on only the black squares; the board itself, impossibly, is four squares deep by eleven squares wide. Either the engraver did not understand chess very well or the game itself was an incidental detail in the directions he was given to compose the plate.

The lower pictorial panel shows three major characters from the play, identified through their portraits with their originals: Marc Antonio de Dominis, Bishop of Spalato ('*the Fatte Bishop*'), Diego Sarmiento de Acuña, Count Gondomar ('*the Black Knight*'), and Charles Stuart, Prince of Wales ('*the White Knight*'). The iconography of these portraits was first explored by Bald, who reproduces an engraving of de Dominis by Elstrack (1617), and an engraving of Gondomar after Velázquez. Foakes reproduces two painted portraits of Gondomar which may be sources of some of the prints of him (Foakes, 123, 125). The general point is that all three figures were portrayed in numerous prints, accessible in the London print shops. De Dominis was painted by Michiel Mierevelt in 1617, and that portrait is the basis for three prints, two by Renold Elstrack and one by Willem Delff (Hind, vol. 2, 172–4; plates

M. ANT. DE DOMINIS COM. PAL. ARCHIEP. SPALAT. DALM. ET CROAT. PRIMAS.

Scriptura, Patres, Concilia nolunt tegi. | Episcoparum, Ecclesiam, Christum, fidem;
Et ipsa gestit evolare veritas. | Mea penna, lingua, vita, mores, ipsa asserit.
Sum Christianus, Catholicus Presul equi. | Nec plus obire valeo, nec fas est minus.

Joannes Bill excud.

20. Renold Elstrack, engraved portrait of Marc Antonio de Dominis, Bishop of Spalato (1617)

92c, 92d; Hollstein, vol. 5, 160; Illustration 20). The book and the outstretched left hand in the *Game at Chess* composition can be seen as separate details in the two Elstrack prints. Gondomar's likeness was engraved by both Simon and Willem de Passe, both prints appearing in 1622 (Hind, vol. 2, 257, 289; plates 153a, 177a), but the main source is the figure from the *Vox Populi* plate, which was evidently based on a portrait or print related to the Madrid picture reproduced by Foakes. The engraver's adaptation of the *Vox* picture is rather unusual, in that the angle of the head is maintained while the rest of the body is reversed; the right leg (left in original) is moved to a closed position, slightly to the rear; the sword is erased, while the staff in the left hand of the original is replaced by the letter in the right hand of the adapted figure; the left hand and arm (right in original) are moved to form a confidential gesture across the chest towards the figure's right.

There are very many portrait prints of Prince Charles, but the immediate source for the pose and dress of the figure of the White Knight is a small print by either Simon de Passe or John Payne, from about 1622 (Hind, vol. 2,

21. Title-page of *A Game at Chess*, Mathewes-Allde edition

255, 300–1; plate 188a). The engraver adapts the pose so that the head is turned in profile, and he brings Charles up to date by adding the beard he had grown at some time later (Howard-Hill). The fabric of the breeches of the standing figure matches that of the sleeve in the portrait bust (which in the adaptation is covered by the figure's cloak). The riding boots and spurs are hardly required by the dramatic situation at the end of the play (whence the White Knight's line comes), and suggest that the engraver may also have used an equestrian portrait to assemble his figure. Alternatively, the White Knight might have worn the boots and spurs in 5.1, which in other respects visually alludes to Charles and Buckingham's arrival in Madrid.

Given these correspondences it seems quite unlikely that the illustrator is attempting to represent the play in performance, even making allowance for the conflation of 3.1 and 5.3 of Middleton's play to create 'the scene'. Hence the relationship between the 'bag' shown in the centre left background and whatever device the King's Men may have used at the Globe is suspect at the least. The 'dialogue' similarly does not bear a close relationship to the surviving texts, but its very lack of relationship is suggestive about the plate's composition. The White Knight's speech scroll contains the most direct quotation: 'We give thee checkmate by | Discovery, King—the noblest mate of all' (5.3.160–1). The words of the Fat Bishop are an abbreviated paraphrase of 'Pray, keep your side and distance' (3.1.28), while the Black Knight's 'line' does not occur in any surviving text of the play; he refers only obliquely to the proffered letter as 'fair greetings to your reverend virtues | From Cardinal Paulus, your most princely kinsman' (3.1.25–6). Bald's note on Middleton's possible source, the pamphlet *Newes from Rome: Spalato's Doome* (1624), quotes the text from which the playwright created this episode in the play: 'For (saith hee [Gondomar]) I can shew you *a letter* lately come to my hands *from his Holinesse*' (Bald, 147; my emphasis). Either the engraver (or his director) was working from yet another text of the play, or—as seems to me most likely—the directions for the plate came from Middleton himself, who in choosing suitably simplified motifs for illustration came up with words for the Black Knight which he remembered from his reading, possibly at a date after the first performance of the play (Howard-Hill).

Middleton may have wanted to keep his head down—and if he did indeed design the plate, he declares its theatrical production, not its literary authorship—yet he was evidently being deluged with requests for copies of the play. His role in the illustration of the text, given the very specific textual quotations from the three standing characters, from the play and one of its sources, was probably close and direct: I think that he must have described what he wanted fairly fully. He had worked with the printer of the play, Nicholas Okes, on many texts over the course of the preceding fifteen to sixteen years, and Middleton's choice of engraver—if the choice was his—was perhaps influenced by his reading of Thomas Scott's pamphlet, and possibly facilitated by political circles interested in the distribution of other literature sympathetic to Scott's anti-Spanish outlook. The visual allusions of the plate connect the printed play with the Puritan pamphlets of Thomas Scott, and suggest that Middleton's work is waging the same political war by other means.[7]

The Mathewes/Allde plate (Illustration 21) may have been made by the same engraver who made the other. One of the reasons for a new illustration, as we have seen, may have had to do simply with book production; a second may have been that the Mathewes/Allde quarto, containing a variant text of the play and produced by different printers, may not have been authorized by the same stationer; a third reason may have been political. In the new design, which is directly related to the Okes one, all the White House characters—that is the English court—are removed, leaving the two famous villains dominating the foreground, and imprisoned in the bag in the background. The chessboard from the Okes design

---

7 On Scott and his circle see Lake.

lies on the ground as a visual clarification of the title of the play, and the foreground figures plant their feet on it to indicate their participation in the game as pieces rather than players, or, more subtly, their ambiguous status. The chess game itself the engraver has made more convincing in terms of the positions of the pieces, but all the visible pieces are black, so it really makes no more sense than that in the other picture. But the removal of the identifiable figures, principally of Prince Charles and King James, may represent some attempt to cool down the scandalous nature of the play as a book for sale in London after the succession of Charles as King.

That the rearrangement of the design may have been simply the engraver's simplification for a rather smaller plate, however, might be indicated by the retention of the now redundant and rather misleading titles to the two houses. But these have also been reversed from their other position; the engraver knew that Gondomar was black and the Fat Bishop white (in 3.1). The figures and their speech scrolls are based, clearly enough, on the Okes design, but some variations have been made. Gondomar now holds a stick in his left hand, and the figure as a whole is more recognizably a reversed version of the figure on the title-page of *The Second Part of Vox Populi* (see Foakes, 124). The figures no longer join their hands on the proffered letter, but the bishop rather imperiously extends a palm for it; the change is probably dictated by the scale at which the engraver has chosen to show the figures, relative to the available width of the frame. As it is, the bishop looks rather uncomfortably jammed towards the left, and the full sweep of the furred cloak of Gondomar, evidently the figure preferred by the illustrator, falls outside the right frame of the plate.

In short, however, the Mathewes/Allde plate to *A Game at Chess* gives us little that we can connect to the play itself, since it may be visually derivative from the Okes plate. The simplification of its design, as I suggest, may represent an attempt to render the appearance of the book less inflammatory—a choice which the engraver is unlikely to have taken without direction—while retaining a representation of the most famous impersonation which the actors had made in the summer of 1624, that of Gondomar. Although we now know a good deal more about the printing of all three quartos of the play, Middleton's involvement in the production of Mathewes/Allde remains difficult to judge, and we therefore cannot say whether the title-page shows his influence.[8]

Middleton's memorable characters and dramatic situations lend themselves readily to illustration, from Moll Frith to the Black Knight, and the picturing of his characters continued after his death. Shortly after Middleton's portrait appeared in 1657 the publishers Henry Marsh and Francis Kirkman brought out *The Wits* (1662), an anthology of short farces and extracts from pre-Restoration plays. No Middleton text is present among them, but the anthologists may originally have planned to include a piece from the madhouse scenes of *The Changeling*,

22. Frontispiece to *The Wits* (1662)

since the famous engraved frontispiece showing seven performers on a stage features at top left a character identified by the legend 'Changling', who is otherwise unrelated to the contents of the book (see Illustration 22). The figure wears a long buttoned coat, a curious high cap in the form of a mitre, and appears to have a hornbook hanging from his belt (we recall that Lollio undertakes to turn his charges into scholars); he has an inclined head and foolishly hanging hands. If, as seems likely, this figure is meant to represent the disguised Antonio (although there are other comic changeling characters in other Stuart plays), we may have some kind of indication of the appearance of the actor in what evidently was a popular and memorable role.[9] As it happens the engraver of *The Wits* plate, John Chantry, had already made pictures of

[8] For further discussion of the relationship of the Mathewes/Allde quarto to the Okes quartos, see General Textual Introduction to *Game*, at p. 712 in this *Companion*.

[9] The limitations of the evidence of the plate are examined in Astington.

Beatrice-Joanna, Alsemero, Vermandero, De Flores, and the Piracquo brothers, in a plate for the illustrated edition of John Reynolds's *The Triumphs of God's Revenge against... Murder* (1657; Wing R1309), an earlier edition of which book was Middleton's source for the murder and seduction plot. In his work on the Reynolds plate it seems unlikely that Chantry would have been guided by memories of Middleton's play, but in the theatrical context of *The Wits* he has made an attempt to reanimate a vivid stage figure from before the wars. And although the character is probably the creation of his collaborator, Middleton is implicitly included among the pantheon of wits, with Shakespeare, Shirley, and Fletcher: his place there is endorsed pictorially.

WORKS CITED

Astington, John H., 'The Wits Illustration, 1662', *Theatre Notebook* 47 (1993), 122–40

Bald, R. C., ed., *A Game at Chesse* (1929)

Bentley, Gerald Eades, *The Jacobean and Caroline Stage*, 7 vols (1941–68)

Blayney, Peter W. M., *The Texts of King Lear and their Origins. Volume I. Nicholas Okes and the First Quarto* (1982)

Camille, Michael, 'Reading the Printed Image: Illuminations and Woodcuts of the *Pèlerinage de la vie humaine* in the Fifteenth Century', in *Printing the Written Word*, ed. Sandra L. Hindman (1991), 259–91

Corbett, Margery, and Ronald Lightbown, *The Comely Frontispiece* (1979)

Davidson, Clifford, *Illustrations of the Stage and Acting in England to 1580* (1991)

Davies, Marie-Hélène, *La Gravure dans les Brochures Illustrées de la Renaissance Anglaise 1535–1640* (1979)

Euing = Dixon, M., ed., *The Euing Collection of English Broadside Ballads* (1971)

Foakes, R. A., *Illustrations of the English Stage 1580–1642* (1985)

Gomme, Andor, ed., *The Roaring Girl* (1976)

Greg, Walter Wilson, *A Bibliography of the English Printed Drama to the Restoration*, 3 vols (1939–57)

Harms, Wolfgang, *Deutsche Illustrierte Flugblätter des 16. und 17. Jahrhunderts*, 4 vols (1985–7)

Hind, Arthur M., Margery Corbett, and Michael Norton, *Engraving in England in the Sixteenth and Seventeenth Centuries*, 3 vols (1952–64)

Holdsworth, Roger V., ed., *A Fair Quarrel* (1974)

Hollstein, F. W. H., *et al.*, *Dutch and Flemish Etchings, Engravings, and Woodcuts ca. 1450–1700*, 69 vols (1949–2004)

Howard-Hill, T. H., *Middleton's 'Vulgar Pasquin'. Essays on 'A Game at Chess'* (1995)

Kist, J. B., *Jacob de Gheyn, The Exercise of Armes: A Commentary* (1971)

Lake, P. G., 'Constitutional Consensus and Puritan Opposition in the 1620s: Thomas Scott and the Spanish Match', *The Historical Journal* 25 (1982), 805–26

Landau, David, and Peter Parshall, *The Renaissance Print* (1994)

McKerrow, R. B., and F. S. Ferguson, *Title-Page Borders Used in England and Scotland, 1485–1640* (1932)

Moore, John Robert, 'The Contemporary Significance of Middleton's *Game at Chesse*', *PMLA* 50 (1935), 761–8

Pepys = Latham, R., ed., *Catalogue of the Pepys Library at Magdalen College, Cambridge. The Pepys Ballads*, 5 vols (1987)

Rostenberg, Leona, *English Publishers in the Graphic Arts 1599–1700* (1963)

Roxburghe = Ebsworth, J. W., ed., *The Roxburghe Ballads*, 8 vols (1877–95; repr. 1966)

Shikes, Ralph E., *The Indignant Eye* (1969)

Thorpe, W. A., 'Portrait of a Roaring Girl', *Country Life* 100 (1946), 1070–2

Watt, Tessa, *Cheap Print and Popular Piety, 1550–1640* (1991)

Welsford, Enid, *The Fool* (1935)

''TWILL MUCH ENRICH THE COMPANY OF STATIONERS': THOMAS MIDDLETON AND THE LONDON BOOK TRADE, 1580–1627

Cyndia Susan Clegg

'Seen and Allowed' or banned and burned; printed 'cum privilegio', surreptitiously, or legally but without licence; published by performance alone, by manuscript circulation, or 'cast up' to the booksellers 'in Paul's Churchyard, Popeshead Alley, and at Temple Bar' (*Plato's Cap*, 31–3), Thomas Middleton's works epitomize London publishing in the author's lifetime. Between Middleton's birth in 1580 and his death in 1627, the London book trade was largely within the domain of the London Company of Stationers; indeed all the printers, publishers, and booksellers involved in Middleton's works were free of the Company, and many were members of its Livery.[1] Middleton's relation to the book trade, then, can be fully understood only within the context of the Stationers' Company. From the perspective of the Stationers, printing and selling books, pamphlets, plays, civic pageants, masques, broadsheets, ballads, and a host of government business forms and registers was primarily a commercial venture—a venture that *The Nice Valour* shows Middleton understood well. In this play Lapet remarks that his book, *The Uprising of the Kick And the Downfall of the Duello*, 'sells gallantly' and ''Twill much enrich the Company of Stationers' (4.1.327-8, 5.3.7, 11). The Company's regulations and customs, as well as the internal Court of Assistants that enforced them, largely concerned themselves with maintaining orderly trade practices to protect both the Stationers' Company's monopoly on printing and individual Stationers' rights to the titles they owned. The Stationers' interests, however, were not alone in affecting the retail book trade. The regimes of Elizabeth I and James I employed royal prerogative to patronize several printers and publishers, a few non-Stationers, and writers of specialized items; they also sought, though not always successfully, to control political and religious opposition by controlling the printed word. Thomas Middleton's printed works, representing a range of genres, were published over the course of three decades, during the reign of two monarchs. The conditions of their publication reflect the customary practices of the London Stationers on the one hand, and the special interests of two English monarchs on the other.

Two events in the publishing history of Middleton's works result from direct government engagement with the printed word. Tudor and Stuart monarchs recognized the printed word's potential power to enhance their religious, political, and cultural ends—or, less frequently, to

interfere with their ends. From the earliest days of printing English monarchs supported royal printers (who were not necessarily Stationers) to print their proclamations, orders, and injunctions—in short, to give voice to their political power. The Crown also issued patents to ensure that certain kinds of books would be printed—not only catechisms, Bibles, and prayer books to affect belief, but classics to further learning, music to sustain the arts, and maps to facilitate political action. They also issued patents to patronize particular printers and authors. Such was the case with James I's patent for Thomas Middleton's *Peace--maker*. On 19 July 1618 the Domestic State Papers record a patent to William Alley to print and sell Middleton's *The peace-maker, or Great Britain's Blessing*, followed by this notation:

> It may please Your most Excellent Majestie This Bill conteyneth your Majestie's licence and priviledge unto William Alley, during seaven yeares, (at the nomination of Thomas Midleton) for the sole printing, and selling, of a small booke, lately made by the said Midleton, called the Peace-Maker, or Great Brittains blessing . . .

Rhodes Dunlap views King James's signature on the licence as a 'fact of James's personal involvement' (Dunlap, 85) and as evidence that the views Middleton expressed in the pamphlet (praising peace and attacking the vices opposing peace, particularly duelling) conformed with the King's own (Dunlap, 90). Dunlap observes that the licence was drawn up in such a way that it 'might make the publication a profitable one for Middleton' (Dunlap, 85), but it is difficult to ascertain why this would be so beyond whatever remuneration Middleton might have received for selling his text. The privilege is extended not to Middleton but to William Alley, who is not a member of the Stationers' Company. In effect, the royal patent

---

[1] To be 'free' of the Stationers' Company was to have attained full membership in one of four ways: by completing an apprenticeship to an independent master who was himself free of the Company; by being the son of a Stationer (provided he was a 'freeman' at the son's birth); by purchasing membership (redemption); or by transferring (translating) membership as a freeman from another company. The regular membership of the company was known as the yeomanry, with the Company's senior membership constituting the 'Livery', those members who attended the Lord Mayor and voted in parliamentary and mayoral elections. Admission to the Livery was a purchased privilege—but one which was essential for anyone aspiring to Company leadership (Blagden 1960, 35-7).

allows Alley to circumvent the monopoly on printing and bookselling conveyed to the Stationers by their charter and upheld by decrees in the Court of Star Chamber in 1566 and 1586. Alley's privilege, which assures him the sole right to print (or have printed) and sell Middleton's *Peace-maker* for seven years, reserves to Alley the profits of his enterprise and protects him from interference from the Stationers. For non-Stationer Alley, the king's privilege was not only desirable but necessary.

The most visible kind of royal interest in printing—besides those occasions when the government was called upon to intervene in matters regarding trade governance—came in the form of press control. The governments of both Elizabeth I and James I took considerable (though largely intermittent) interest in pre-print censorship or authorization, and while elaborate mechanisms were put in place, official authorization never achieved the kind of hegemony that it has been credited with. It never prevented treasonous or seditious texts, particularly from the continent, from being available in England, nor did it prevent the legal English publication of texts like John Hayward's *The first part of the life and raigne of king Henrie the IIII*, which was ordered burned even though it was published with official approval. While English law designated certain kinds of texts as illegal, and thus actionable in the law courts, on some occasions the only means by which the government could censor a printed book it regarded as offensive was by royal edict or proclamation. Elizabeth issued proclamations to condemn or suppress objectionable texts eleven times during her reign. James issued a similar proclamation only once, though he ordered books he personally disliked burned at Paul's Cross or equally public squares in Oxford and Cambridge at least six times during his reign.

One Middleton work, the anonymously published *Micro-cynicon*, fell prey to an unusual act of official suppression, the so-called 'Bishops' Ban'. On 1 June 1599 the Archbishop of Canterbury, John Whitgift, and the Bishop of London, Richard Bancroft, engaged in an act of censorship that lacked precedent during the reign of Elizabeth because it was unmotivated by concerns about treason or conformity, and because it extended to a group of text legally printed by members of the London Stationers, including Middleton's *Micro-cynicon*. The bishops ordered the Stationers to cease printing satires, epigrams, and any works by Thomas Nashe and Gabriel Harvey. They prohibited printing histories without Privy Council allowance or printing plays 'excepte they bee allowed by suche as have aucthorytie' (Arber, 3: 677–8). Further, their order specified that nine books, mostly epigrams and satires (including *Micro-cynicon*) be seized and brought to the Bishop to be burned. Motivated by concerns about religious conformity and sedition, various Archbishops of Canterbury had acted to suppress religious works, but these were printed abroad or by underground presses and rarely involved members of the London book trade.[2] The books that were burned had been published from London

Stationers' presses (most of them had been printed two or three years before the 1599 order) and were neither religious nor seditious. The motivation for the order was unstated, but it did appear during a climate of heightened political anxiety.[3] 1599, a difficult year for Elizabeth's government, saw the invasion of Ireland under the command of the highly controversial Robert Devereux, the Earl of Essex. Some members of the government, anxious about the mission and its choice of leader, associated the satires with Essex's opponents. Whether or not the satires were intentionally about Essex, they were received as being so, and Archbishop of Canterbury Whitgift, a member of the Privy Council, took the extraordinary action of suppressing any texts that might conceivably be read as oppositional.[4]

While the Stationers conformed to the 1599 Bishops' order to confiscate and burn certain works, it is not at all clear that the ban had any lasting effect. English histories continued to be published without Privy Council authorization, and plays were published without necessarily being 'allowed by those that have authority'.[5] Despite the ban against satires and epigrams, Zachariah Pasfield, a prebendary of St Paul's and an ecclesiastical authorizer, allowed *The letting of Humours Blood*, which was subsequently burned by a Stationers' Court order on 6 October 1600 along with 'other Popishe books & things that were lately taken' (Greg and Boswell, 79). In 1601 two satiric pamphlets, *The Whipping of the Satyre* and *The Whipper of the Satire*, both duly authorized, were published without consequence. And after the deaths of Elizabeth I and Archbishop Whitgift epigrams regularly appeared in the Registers as well as numerous satiric pamphlets,

[2] Besides the well-known censorship campaign against the Martin Marprelate tracts in 1588, works suppressed by the church include: *A Commission sent to the pope and Convenres of freres by Sathen* (suppressed 27 February 1587); John Knox's *The First booke of the history of the reformation of religion within the realm of Scotland* (suppressed 1587); 'one barrell and ii firkers of books of Alexander Humes' Doing' ('by a warrant of his grace and other high commissioners' dated 2 December 1594). Alexander Hume was, according to the *DNB*, a Scottish poet and an 'ardent' Puritan. On 15 August 1595 at the Archbishop of Canterbury's commandment, five books (all apparently foreign) were burnt in Stationers' Hall (Arber, 2: 40). Among these were 'Thesaurus Principium', 'Ministromachia' [Cardinal Stanislaus Rescius, Cologne, 1592], 'Rosseus de re publica' [William Rainolds, *De justa Republicae Chrestianae*, Douay, 1590; Antwerp, 1592], 'Little French bookes in 8 and Surius Chronicle' [Laurentius Surius, probably his hagiographical history, Cologne, 1572]. Religio-political interests probably motivated this censorship since Rosseus's book addressed the English succession, a subject prohibited by statute.

[3] Presented with this uncommon circumstance, scholars have usually followed G. G. Perry and Charles Gillett in accepting the works' 'licentiousness' as grounds for justifiable ecclesiastical suppression. Most of the works specifically named in the order, drawing upon classical models of Ovid, Juvenal, and Martial, indeed contained highly sexualized discourse. Since the Latin writers' works had been widely available in England in the sixteenth century, and most had been printed under royal patents, licentiousness alone seems an unlikely cause for the bishops' order.

[4] For a complete discussion of the evidence relating to the relationship between the bishops' 1599 order and the Earl of Essex, see Clegg 1997, chapter 9.

[5] For instance, on 28 August 1599, the plays *Edward III and the Tanner of Tamworth* and *The history of the life and death of master SHORE and JANE SHORE his Wyfe* were entered in the Stationers' Registers. On 7 September 1599, the ecclesiastical authorizer Charles Sonybanck, rather than a member of the Privy Council, is shown as the official authorizer of the history, *The life and Deathe of THOMAS WOOLSEY Cardinal*, in a Register entry.

including four by Middleton (*Platoes Cap*, *The blacke booke*, *The ant and the nightingale*, and *The meeting of gallants at an ordinarie*). *The blacke booke*, in its prologue, addresses directly the issue of satire and censure and implicitly flouts earlier censorship when it says,

> And I account him as a traitor to virtue who, diving into the deep of this cunning age, and finding there such monsters of nature, such speckled lumps of poison as panders, harlots and ruffians do figure, if he rise up silent again, and neither discover or publish them to the civil rank of sober and continent livers... Wherefore, I freely persuade myself, no virtuous spirit or judicial worthy but will approve my politic moral...And thus far I presume, that none will or can except at this, which I call *The Black Book*... (11–28)

The pamphlet returns to the issue in its concluding lines:

> Now sir, what is your censure now? You have read me, I am sure....Methinks I hear you say nothing, and therefore I know you are pleased and agree to all, for *Qui tacet consentire videtur*. And I allow you wise and truly judicious, because you keep your censure to yourself. (823–31)

The official authorizer agreed and, saying nothing, extended his approval to Middleton's satiric pamphlet, the 1599 furore over satire forgotten or ignored.

While government interests directly affected Middleton's *Peace-maker* and *Micro-cynicon*, the principal forces that influenced the printing and dissemination of Middleton's literary works were economic. By the time Middleton's works were beginning to be printed in the last years of the sixteenth century and the first of the seventeenth, the Stationers' Company, strengthened by the 1586 Star Chamber Decree, had obtained a veritable monopoly in the book trade. The London Company of Stationers had received official recognition as a London guild in 1557 when their royal charter conferred on them the exclusive right to engage in printing along with the privileges and practices common among the older guilds.[6] The charter not only granted the Stationers' Company its corporate right to exist and assigned to the company the power to govern itself and the trade, it also conferred on its members in perpetuity the sole economic benefits of printing. Except for the right reserved to the Crown to issue patents (privileges), the Stationers' Company charter transferred authority over printing from the Crown to the Stationers' Company. The Stationers, however, were not government 'henchmen'. The company charter created in the Stationers' Company an entity that functioned with considerable independence from the Crown and whose principal interest was in securing exclusively for its members the benefits of a growing economic market. To accomplish this, the Company issued licences, or copyrights, giving to printers and publishers the exclusive right to manufacture the titles they registered with the Company. Company licences were distinct from ecclesiastical authorization that

had been instituted in the 1559 Elizabethan religious settlement and was reaffirmed by the 1586 Decrees for Order in Printing issued by the Star Chamber.[7] The Company issued its licences for many texts that did not receive official authorization, though the Company Masters and Wardens apparently required official approval for certain classes of texts—books in foreign languages, translations, and books with religious or political contents. The kind of 'illegal printing' that most concerned Stationers' Company officials was either printing outside the Company or printing by a Company member against the licence of another member. A major challenge to the Stationers' Company's control of the book trade that was mounted in the 1570s and early 1580s by dissatisfied journeymen printers and non-Stationers led to the 1586 Star Chamber Decree, which upheld the Stationers' monopoly and strengthened their power. The Decree ensured that all printing in England, except for presses at Oxford and Cambridge universities, was confined to London and placed in the control of the Stationers and the few non-Stationers who enjoyed royal patents. It upheld the Company's power to enforce its monopoly through its Court and its right to search for and seize illegal presses.[8] By exercising these rights, the Company effectively eliminated competition from members of the Drapers' Company engaged in bookselling, and thereby extended their monopoly from printing to bookselling (Johnson 1988).

By the end of the sixteenth and the early part of the seventeenth centuries when the works of Thomas Middleton and his peers appeared in print, publishing practices and notions of textual property were well established in the London book trade. Once a text was identified through either royal patent or the Stationers' Company's licence as being someone's 'copy', the printer or bookseller who owned the right exercised full control over when, if, and how many times the text would be printed and reprinted, and derived the primary economic benefits from the text's publication.[9]

The journey from author's manuscript to printed text was largely a cooperative venture between a publisher—

---

[6] While the custom of the city allowed men free of one company to engage in the trade of another—a bricklayer, if he chose, could sell fish—the 1557 charter's printing monopoly to the Stationers' Company was an extraordinary benefit to the Company. The other rights the charter conferred were customary: self-regulation, keeping apprentices, and engaging in searches to protect the trade from 'foreigners' (non-members) and poor workmanship as well as the privilege to form a livery which gave the company voting rights in London and parliamentary elections and participation in the city's governance.

[7] The Decree's call for outside authorization by ecclesiastical officials had not really introduced anything new, but Archbishop of Canterbury John Whitgift's establishment of a panel of correctors subsequent to the decree did. By appointing official authorizers, Whitgift effectively established a bureaucracy whose presence, though it may have led to an increase in entries receiving authorization in the Stationers' Registers, often turned official authorization into perfunctory perusal and promotion.

[8] See Clegg 1995. For a complete discussion of the London Stationer's Company, see Clegg 1996.

[9] After 1587, however, if a work was not kept in print, the Stationer might lose his right to the copy. On 4 December 1587 the Court of Assistants issued a Company order which stated that if the owner of a copy allowed it to go out of print, he could be required to reprint it, and if he failed to do so, the copy might be reprinted for the use of the Company.

often a bookseller—and a printer. During the reign of James about eighty per cent of the printed works entered in the Stationers' Registers were published by booksellers,[10] though some printers acted as their own publishers and maintained retail outlets, and some works appeared through the subsidy of publishers who were neither printers nor booksellers. Thirteen of the thirty-nine Middleton works printed during the author's lifetime appeared through the efforts of George Eld and Nicholas Okes, who both published and printed these texts.[11] The publisher provided the capital for the venture and usually procured the manuscript, probably buying it outright. The specialization that emerges when publishers' and printers' names are correlated with the texts they produced suggests that publishers maintained fairly regular relationships with certain writers and particular acting companies. Robert Milbourne, who primarily published Puritan, anti-Arminian, and anti-papal writings, remarked on a Stationer's dependence on personal relationships for his business in a 1629 'Printer's Epilogue' to a work by Daniel Featly. After having experienced near financial ruin from a publishing venture, Milbourne says he had 'been beholding to my good friends for some good Copies' for the subsequent recovery, his friends having found vendible texts for him to publish (*Cygnea Cantio*, 40). Similarly, the printer publisher Nicholas Okes clearly provided a consistent outlet for Middleton's civic pageants, pointing to a fairly regular relationship between publisher and author.

Once a publisher obtained a text, usually in manuscript form, he generally obtained approval for the work from an ecclesiastical or government 'authorizer'. Although existing documents indicate that such authorization was requisite, between 1558 and 1627 never more than half the texts printed in any given year received official authorization. Most important for a publisher was the Company licence. He obtained this by showing his 'copy' to the Stationers' Company master or wardens who conferred the Company's 'licence' to print the text. The Stationers' Company clerk entered the licence and the name of the official authorizer (if there was one) in the Company's Registers as an official record of ownership. In the Registers the word 'licence' refers to the ownership of copy. The Registers clearly distinguish this ownership from ecclesiastical or state approval, which they refer to as 'authorization' or 'allowance'. Alternatively, a printer might have already possessed the 'licence' to print a particular work by virtue of a privilege, or patent, granted by royal prerogative for a particular work or class of works. The word 'licence' appears regularly in Elizabethan printing patents to indicate such a privilege. In this case, the printer did not necessarily need to seek authorization or enter his 'copy' in the Stationers' Registers. According to the terms of John Day's 1567 patent for all metrical psalms, the *ABC with the little catechism*, and Nowell's catechisms, Day was to submit these works for clerical scrutiny 'according to her Majesty's Injunctions', though patents to other printers for non-religious works did not

specify that authorization was requisite (*Calendar of Patent Rolls, Eliz.*, 4: 108; 6: 217). Similarly, though royal patent assured a printer's right to copy, by the early seventeenth century patented works, outside of those printed by the King's printer, were frequently entered in the Stationers' Registers.

Once the right to a copy was established, the publisher placed the manuscript in the hands of a master printer (printing house operator and press owner) who proceeded to print it. It was common for a dedication or epistle to the reader (usually solicited by the printer or publisher) to be added in the shop while the manuscript was being prepared for printing. The epistle 'To the Reader' in *The world tost at tennis* acknowledges the practice of adding introductory materials when its poet-persona says that the work is 'a toy brought to the press rather by the printer than the poet, who requested an epistle for his pass to satisfy his perusers how hitherto he hath behaved himself' (Epistle.7–10).[12]

Whatever liberties a printer might take in adding supplementary materials in the printing house, Company customs and ordinances dictated print shop practices. Company ordinances required that the printed text would carry the printer's name, the city, and the year of publication, as did all Middleton texts with the exception of the three surreptitious editions of *A Game at Chesse*. This information appeared in an imprint on the title-page, final page, or, sometimes, both. In addition, a printer might use the title-page to advertise a royal patent ('*cum privilegio regiae*' or, as in Middleton's work *The peace-maker*, simply '*cum privilegio*'), or for plays and entertainments, the acting company and a distinguished performance ('*A faire quarrell* as it was acted before the King'). Company ordinances, reflecting concern for conditions in the book trade, prescribed practices that sought to ensure adequate employment levels in a trade where skilled labour exceeded product demand. They called for hiring journeymen printers rather than apprentices for certain tasks, restricting the number of apprentices, specifying the maximum number of copies that could be printed from a single setting of type (either 1250 or 1500 copies), and prohibiting printing from standing type. They also made provisions for the Company's poor.[13]

When the printer had completed the printing and collation of the book, copies were then sent to the publisher,

[10] Statistics in this study derive from my computer database containing the records of the Stationers' Company. These records have been collated against the *Short Title Catalogue*, 2nd revised edn., to obtain a more complete record of printers, publishers, and booksellers. Henceforth, references to the *Short Title Catalogue*, 2nd edn., will appear as STC.

[11] Additionally both Eld and Okes printed Middleton texts for other publishers. And Thomas Creede printed an additional seven Middleton texts for other publishers.

[12] That this is not Middleton himself addressing the reader is apparent from his subsequent characterization of the poet ('begot in Brentford, born on the Bankside of Helicon') as being 'fair-spoken, never accused of scurrilous or obscene language' (Epistle.11, 14–15)—hardly the author of *Micro-cynicon*.

[13] Orders to this effect were issued by the Master, Wardens, and Assistants on 4 December 1587.

who sold the book wholesale and/or retail to other book-sellers in the Stationers' Company and to provincial book-sellers. (Of course, if the printer was himself the book's publisher, he sold the edition himself.) Surviving account books and inventories of booksellers' stocks that appear in wills and other legal instruments attest to the fact that booksellers regularly sold not only the works they published but those published by fellow Stationers, though, as we shall see, it is likely that a given bookseller's stock often appealed to a particular clientele. Books were sold both bound and unbound. Retailers, however, often hired a specialist binder to stitch and bind some of their copies. The standard material used for binding books was inexpensive sheep or calf, though a more expensive tooled calf binding could be contracted for by a bookseller's special clients. Texts in quarto, the common format for pamphlets and plays, were stitched at the gutter and tied crosswise with string, but rarely bound (Gaskell, 146–7). The actual prices that booksellers charged varied according to whether a work was unbound or bound, and, if bound, to the kind of binding. The Stationers' Company in 1598 passed an ordinance against excessive book prices, prescribing a maximum unbound wholesale price of a penny for two sheets for books in pica or english sizes of type, or a penny for a sheet and a half for books in the smaller brevier type. According to Francis R. Johnson, retail book prices were remarkably stable between 1550 and 1640, reflecting conformity to the Company's specifications; a publisher, however, did set his prices 'not upon the prosaic basis of cost of production plus a reasonable profit, but upon his estimate of how much the book-buyer would pay' (90). At ten sheets, Middleton's *Michaelmas terme*, then, could have sold for around five pence, but like other play quartos it probably sold for six pence, the price paid for *A mad world, my masters* in 1608 (Blayney 1982, 391). At the Company's prescribed price, the three-sheet *Masque of heroes* would have sold wholesale for one and a half pence, while it retailed for fourpence unbound (Johnson, 106), consistent with the typical price for a longer masque.

Ever since E. K. Chambers observed that in Middleton's time the 'average' play text was 'probably derived from a play-house "book" handed over by the actors to the printer' (3: 193), early modern playwrights have been presumed innocent of any participation in the printing of their works. The associations of Middleton with particular publishers and printers, however, points to significant author involvement in publishing—an involvement which is borne out by the texts themselves. Middleton frequently mentions printing and publishing practices in epistles dedicatory. His play, *The Nice Valour*, offers the theatregoer (and reader) a more sustained look at authors and printing through the character Lapet, who has authored a book. Lapet not only examines proof for his book, *The Uprising of the Kick And the Downfall of the Duello*, he specifies the kinds of type the printer should use ('Bid him put all the thumps in pica roman' and the 'kicks', 'all in *italica*', 4.1.237, 239–40) and laments the printer's choice of

paper ('He prints my blows upon pot-paper too, the rogue, | Which had been proper for some drunken pamphlet', 4.1.245–6). While Middleton's experience with particular printers may have been unusual, it was not unique. His frequent collaborator, Thomas Dekker, worked with most of the same Stationers as Middleton. Similarly, seventy-two per cent of the works of Middleton's contemporary, the 'water poet' John Taylor, appeared in print through the auspices of just two printer-publisher partnerships—Edward Allde printed fifty-five per cent of them for Henry Gosson and George Eld printed seventeen per cent in a publishing partnership with Miles Flesher. Middleton's own associations with and references to printers and printing offer us a special window through which we can view the world of London publishing. What emerges is a picture of commercial activity shaped as much by personal relationships and political and religious loyalties as it is by official authority. Members of the printing trade joined together to assure that certain texts or kinds of texts became available to specialized markets, and some of these publishers formed distinctive associations with the authors or playing companies that could provide them with vendible texts. Middleton appears to have associated with at least three networks of printers and booksellers during his writing career. These associations were shaped both by the genres and the years in which Middleton was writing. With one important exception—*A Game at Chesse*, whose special circumstances of publication will be considered later—Middleton's works appeared in print through the regular efforts of London Stationers.

Middleton's earliest printed work, *The wisdome of Solomon paraphrased* (1597), was published and printed by Valentine Simmes, who also published and printed *The ghost of Lucrece* in 1600. Simmes's printing interests were as varied as his career was chequered. Simmes entered neither of Middleton's early works in the Registers, not because of their contents but because Simmes generally held a low regard for regular practices and official regulations.[14] While in later years Simmes would share printing with Thomas Creede in two Middleton/Dekker collaborations, it appears that in the case of *Micro-cynicon* (1599) Thomas Bushell outdid Simmes for 'some good copy', and gave the printing to Creede.

Thomas Creede appears at the centre of the earliest network of Middleton's printers and publishers, most of whom published his poetry and verse satires. In 1599 Creede printed *Micro-cynicon* for Thomas Bushell. He had also printed Joseph Hall's *Virgidemiarum* (1597), one of its sources (George, 22). Though Bushell published Middleton's satire, and indeed, together with his partner Chorlton, seems to have sustained a relationship with the author, Creede could as well have introduced Middleton to Bushell and Chorlton, since Creede's name reappears frequently in association with Middleton. With the exception

---

[14] Simmes had been arrested during the Marprelate controversy, and he was in trouble in 1595 for printing the *Grammar and Accidence* against patent. William Jackson notes that he printed recusant books (381n).

of John Davies's *Epigrams* all the satires mentioned in the 1599 Bishops' Ban were printed by three men, Thomas Creede, Richard Bradock, and James Roberts.[15] The satires were popular and sold well. Roberts's imprint appeared in the three editions of Marston's *Scourge of Villany*, although he gave Q3 to Bradock for the actual printing (see Weiss, 1991, fn.42, 220-21), and the two parts of Hall's *Virgidemiarum* appeared in four editions before 1599. Here is a clear instance of printers specializing in a particular kind of work and of a relationship between Middleton and a printer being driven by genre. Besides *Micro-cynicon*, Creede printed several other Middleton pamphlets, including both editions of *Father Hubburds tales* (1604), both editions of *The blacke booke* (1604), *The meeting of gallants at an ordinarie* (1604),[16] and *The penniles parliament of threed-bare poets* (1608). The only Middleton satiric pamphlet which Creede did not print, *Platoes Cap* (1604), was published by Bushell and Chorlton and printed by Thomas Purfoot.

The booksellers for whom Creede and Purfoot printed Middleton's pamphlets actively traded in works that appealed to the interests of a popular audience. In Bushell and Chorlton's shop 'at the Great north door of Paul's', Middleton's satiric pamphlets would have been sold alongside works by Nicholas Breton and Barnaby Rich. About half of the shops' holdings were works of popular literature, the other half being political and religious. Among the religious works sold were Samuel Gardiner's *Dialogue of Ireneus and Antimachus*, P. Cotton's *Hellish Councel of Jesuites regarding the Murther of the King*, *The Burial of Alice Wellington, a Recusant* and *The Arraignment of the Priests Drury and Davy*. These works reflect interests strongly Calvinistic and anti-papal but well within the mainstream. While we cannot be certain that Middleton shared the interests of these printers and publishers, he certainly showed them his respect in the epistle to the reader in the first edition of *The ant and the nightingale: or father Hubburds tales*:

> I never wished this book better fortune than to fall into the hands of a true-spelling printer and an honest-stitching bookseller; and if honesty could be sold by the bushel like oysters, I had rather have one Bushel of honesty than three of money. (56-61)

Middleton apparently held the bookseller of the second edition, *Father Hubburds Tales*, in equally high regard. In the first edition he had labelled Chorlton 'an honest-stitching bookseller', and in the second, Cotton is 'an honest-minded' one. Cotton's publishing and bookselling interests, like those of Bushell and Chorlton, included a substantial number of strongly anti-papal and Calvinist religious works, including works by William Perkins, the eminent Calvinist divine, and by Calvin himself. Barley's publishing interests were similar to Bushell and Chorlton's. In Barley's shop Middleton's *The penniles parliament* would have been in the company of works reflecting

Barley's publishing interests in 'entertaining, instructing and improving the members of his own [tradesman] class'—travel tales, cony-catching pamphlets, pamphlets of moral advice, and sermons (Johnson, 36).

Middleton's associations with Creede and Purfoot for the printing of his early non-dramatic works extended to printing and publishing plays and entertainments entirely or in part by Middleton. While Bushell and Chorlton served as a common link between the two printers for the prose, little seems to tie Purfoot, his fellow printers, and their publishers to Creede, his fellow printers, and their publishers, except that both groups worked with Middleton and his collaborators. Thomas Purfoot, who had printed *Platoes Cap* in 1604, joined with Edward Allde to print *Michaelmas terme*. Arthur Johnson, a regular play publisher, published them both. Allde also printed *The phoenix* (1607). Middleton's associations with these two printers can be viewed as the usual happenstance of trade associations—trade printers printing for publishers. Purfoot, however, had the printing of *The peace-maker* for which Middleton procured a royal printing privilege. Furthermore, while Allde and Purfoot shared printing on only a few occasions and were not partners, the kinds of works they printed were remarkably similar. Both actively printed works we regard as traditionally literary, with nearly half of their output being works by the writers John Day, Thomas Dekker, John Marston, Samuel Rowlands, Thomas Middleton, and John Taylor. Both printed works favourable to James I and works interested in international politics. And both printed surprisingly few religious works; those that they did print were predominantly anti-Catholic.

In the same year that Thomas Creede printed two of Middleton's pamphlets (1604), he served as the primary printer for two dramatic works principally by Dekker on which Middleton collaborated. Creede shared the printing of two editions of *The magnificent entertainment* with Edward Allde, Humphrey Lownes, George Eld, and Valentine Simmes, and he shared *The honest whore* with Valentine Simmes (the play's principal printer), George Eld, and Symon Stafford. While only Simmes and Creede had printed Middleton works before 1604, Simmes, Creede, Allde, and Stafford had all printed works by Dekker.[17] Shared printing

---

[15] The 31 March 1597 entry for all six books of Hall's work specified 'to be printed at all tymes by Thomas Creede'. Richard Bradock, apparently Creede's assign in Hall's satire, subsequently entered the last three satires in the Registers, presumably with Creede's consent since no court records indicate that action was taken against Bradock for printing against the entry licence.

[16] *The meeting of gallants at an ordinarie* was printed by Creede and sold by Matthew Law, a former Draper. The 1604 edition was not entered in the Stationers' Registers. On 8 January 1608 John Trundle and Richard Sergier entered *Powles Walke or a gallant Dismasked*, which the STC identifies with Middleton's *The meeting of gallants at an ordinarie*. Trundle and Sergier's entry is an unusual one. Both Creede and Law were alive and still working in London, and nothing exists that would indicate that they assigned their interests to Trundle and Sergier. Nor does the 1608 entry indicate an assignment (such an indication was customary). The 1608 entry must have been for an entirely different work.

[17] Simmes printed *Shoemaker's Holiday* (1600); Stafford *Old Fortunatus* (1600); Allde *Satiro-mastix* (1602) and *Patient Grissill* (1603); and Creede *The Wonderful Year* (1603).

such as this was arranged by the printers or publishers, and while it did not involve Middleton and Dekker, it points to a pattern of associations among printers, many of whom served as principal printers for these writers.

Although Creede ceased to print Middleton texts after 1604, Eld, Allde, and Purfoot continued to be associated with publishing and printing Middleton's works. In 1607-8 seven plays which we now know to be Middleton's appeared in print; George Eld printed three of them: *The puritane widow*, *A tricke to catch the old-one*, and *Your five gallants*. As we shall see, Eld may not have known Middleton to be the author of *The puritane widow* (1607), but two months later Eld's title-page attribution for *A tricke to catch the old-one* (1608) indicates Eld's knowledge of Middleton's authorship. Since Eld served as printer-publisher for *A tricke*, he may have purchased the text directly from Middleton. He continued to print Middleton texts for several years. In 1616 Eld printed sheets A–C of the second edition of *A tricke to catch the old-one*. In 1617 he shared printing of *A faire quarrell* with Bernard Alsop (D–F), and in 1621 he printed the second edition. Eld also printed the *Honourable entertainments* (1621), which, like most other Middleton civic pageants and entertainments, was not entered in the Register.

The seventeen years over which Eld published or printed Middleton's plays suggest a working relationship between the writer and printer. Freed of the Company in 1600, Eld ran his own printing house between 1603 and his death in 1624. He was a printer/publisher who printed for himself as well as other publishers in the trade. Middleton may well have found Eld's shop a useful resource. Eld printed Dekker's *Lanthorne and Candlelight*, a source for *Michaelmas terme*, and *The Charge of Sir Francis Bacon Knight touching Duells*, the principal source for *The peace-maker* (George, 19). Of the 211 works entered in the Stationers' Registers which Eld printed, thirty-one per cent were literary (including seventeen plays), twenty-nine per cent consisted of current news, both local and from the continent, and twenty-six per cent were religious. Eld printed religious works for Robert Milbourne and John Wright, both of whom regularly published Puritan divines. Eld's own religious interests may be reflected in his both publishing and printing several works by Thomas Draxe and Arthur Dent. Dent was a nonconformist preacher who refused to subscribe to the oath supporting the Book of Common Prayer. Draxe was generally more moderate though he translated the writings of the Puritan theologian William Perkins for an edition printed in Geneva. Eld's Puritan interests, as well as his associations with Milbourne and Wright, suggest a network of writers, publishers, printers, and government authorizers linked by religious interests. Eld was associated through this network with the publisher Robert Milbourne, whom Middleton mentions in the preface to the second issue of *Two Gates of Salvation*. This group of associations were particularly important to Middleton when he was writing *A Game at Chesse*. Nearly all the works which Middleton

'quarried...for phrases and information rather than plot materials' were published by Robert Milbourne (George, 22).[18]

While Eld, Allde, and Purfoot dominated the printing of Middleton plays during the author's lifetime, Nicholas Okes printed most of Middleton's pageants and civic entertainments. The association between Okes and Middleton began in 1609 when Okes printed *The two gates of salvation*.[19] Okes was not particularly motivated by religious interests, so another factor must have brought the two together. In 1609 and 1612 Okes shared with Edward Allde the printing of three almanacs for the Stationers' Company, which in 1603 had acquired the royal privilege to print all almanacs. While Allde may have served as a liaison in this instance, the important relationship between Okes and Middleton for pageants more likely was established through Middleton's frequent collaborator, Thomas Dekker. Okes had printed four Dekker works between 1607 and 1609 for various publishers. In 1611 Okes printed Middleton and Dekker's *The roaring girle*, a text whose title-page illustration points to the writers' participation with the printer. In 1612 Okes printed and probably published Dekker's pageant for Lord Mayor Swinnerton, *Troia-nova triumphans*, which he entered in the Registers on 21 October. In 1613 Middleton wrote his first Lord Mayor's show, *The triumphs of truth*, for the installation of Thomas Myddelton from the Company of Grocers. This was the first of seven civic pageants that Okes printed and the first and last Middleton entertainment that Okes entered in the Registers. Okes also printed *Civitatis amor* (1616), *The triumphs of honor and industrie* (1617), *The triumphs of love and antiquity* (1619), *The triumphs of honor and vertue* (1622), *The triumphs of integrity* (1623), and *The triumphs of health and prosperity* (1626). Why Okes entered one pageant in the Registers and not the others is not entirely clear. He may have entered the first work and learned thereafter that custom did not require that this sort of work be entered. Other examples of Lord Mayor's shows that were not entered suggest that this may have been the case, including Anthony Munday's *The triumphs of re-united Britania* (1605) and *Chruso-Thriambos* (1611), both printed by William Jaggard, as well as his *Himatia-Poleos* (1614, printed by Allde) and *Metropolis Coronato* (1615, printed by Purslowe). Another explanation for non-entry may be seen in a 1613 bookkeeping entry in the Grocers' Company records for Middleton's *Triumphs of truth* that suggests that the status of pageants may have been distinctive. Among the charges for the pageant is one for £4 'Paide to Nicholas Oaks, Stacioner for the prynting of [blank] bookes' (*Collections*, 3: 87). While this might be seen as indicating that the pageants were some kind of 'private' publications that did not require entrance,

18 T. G., *The Friers Chronicle* (1622); J. Gee, *Foot out of the Snare* (1624); J. Gee *New Shred of the Old Snare* (1624); P. Gosselin, *The State-Mysteries of the Jesuites* (1623); and T. Robinson, *Anatomie of the English Nunnerie at Lisbon* (1622).
19 Okes had shared the printing with Ballard of *A mad world, my masters* in 1608, but Middleton's knowledge of this is unlikely.

the Grocers Company's payment to Okes rather than the status of pageants is the distinctive feature here. The Stationers' Registers more regularly record the entrance of pageants than company accounts record payments to printers. On only one other occasion does a record exist for a printer being paid directly, and that was again to Okes in 1617 for another Middleton pageant, *The tryumphs of honor and industrie*. Far more typical is the record of payment to Dekker for his 1612 *Troia-Nova Triumphans* which reads: 'paid to Mr Hemyngs and Mr Thomas Dekker, the Poet for the devise of the Land Showes…one Pageant called Neptunes Throne…One pageant called vertues Throne, and for the printing of the bookes of the Speeches…One hundred fourscore, and seaventeene poundes' (*Collections*, 3: 85). Apparently, the usual practice was for a company to make a lump-sum payment to the pageant-maker, who would then arrange the printing. While it appears that the printing was exclusively for the company staging the show—as a kind of show souvenir—this may not always have been the case. The title-page of Dekker's 1612 pageant shows that it was to be sold by Wright. Alternatively, Okes may have availed himself of his licence, but chose not to pay the fee for entering the licence in the Registers, assuming little likelihood of competition for his copy. This also seems to be the case with *Civitatis amor*, again not entered in the Registers, but clearly a commercial publication, since the title-page carries 'Printed by Nicholas Okes for Thomas Archer, and are to be sold at his shop in Popes-head-Pallace'.

During the years that Okes was printing Middleton entertainments, two pageants appeared that Okes did not print: *The sunne in Aries*, printed by Edward Allde, and *Honorable entertainments*, printed by George Eld. Both appeared in 1621, and neither was entered in the Registers. In 1621 twenty-five works came out from Okes's printing house, and it is entirely possible that he was too busy to print pageants whose marketability relied upon their currency. Since Middleton already had relationships with these Stationers, it is not unusual that they should print these works, particularly in regard to Allde who had printed other pageants.

One of the most extraordinary publishing events effected by Middleton's associations in the printing trade was the illegal publication of *A Game at Chesse*. Circumstances surrounding *A Game at Chesse* offer an unusual glimpse into book trade practices in early modern England. The play's unprecedented popularity and subsequent suppression undoubtedly suggested a market whose potential would merit whatever risks a printer might incur. The King's Men's 1624 performances of Middleton's *A Game at Chesse*, an anti-Catholic, anti-Spanish play that T. H. Howard-Hill describes as propagating 'attitudes to Spain fervently maintained by most politically aware Englishmen in the middle of 1624' (Howard-Hill 1995, 108), ran for an unprecedented nine days from 6–17 August, to what contemporary reports described as 'very great enjoyment' and the 'great applause of the people' (Howard-Hill, 1995,

73). While the play provoked no riot among its London audiences, it offended the Spanish Ambassador, Don Carlos de Coloma, who complained to James I, that 'his players' had performed a play in which 'his Majesty the king of Spain, Count Gondomar, and the Archbishop of Spalato' were 'personified' (*CSPD* 12, 325). A 12 August letter from the King's secretary, Sir Edward Conway, to the Privy Council called upon them to cite the author and performers of the play before the council, to examine the comedy, imprison those most at fault, and see that means be taken for the 'severe punishment' of the offenders (*CSPD* 12: 325). The play's performance was suspended, and Middleton and the players were summoned before the Council, and though the 'poet…shifted out of the way', the players submitted their play book with the Master of the Revels's licence, and were prohibited from playing until the King allowed it. The King's reluctance 'to punish the innocent, or utterly to ruin the Company' (*CSPD* 12: 331) led to the Company's timely vindication, though performance of *A Game at Chesse* was prohibited (Dutton, 245–6).

On 20 August when news was abroad that 'Middleton the Poet' was being sought for writing *A Game*, the Venetian Ambassador, Alvise Valaresso, wrote that the Spaniards having been 'touched from their tricks being discovered…the Spanish ambassador has made a remonstrance, and it is thought that they will at least punish the author' (*CSP, Venetian, 1623–1628*, 425). A verse petition to the King for the release of its poet who 'lye[s] nowe vnder hatches in ye ffleete' that appeared in many manuscripts has been widely received as evidence of Middleton's punishment. Shortly after the play's performance was stayed, Middleton engaged in what Howard-Hill describes as 'a premeditated course of preparing texts of the play for sale, for presentation to patrons…and for surreptitious publication' (Howard-Hill, 1987, 306). The six extant manuscripts, the earliest of which is dated 13 August 1624 and the latest New Year's Day 1625, and the other copies (at least thirteen) that must have existed between the extant states, attest to the efforts of Middleton to capitalize on *A Game at Chesse*'s enormous theatrical success (and notoriety). Middleton's handwriting is seen in three of the six surviving manuscripts, one of which is entirely in his hand, and he wrote out the manuscript copy for Okes's edition. Therefore, Middleton was closely involved in the multiplication of texts of his play after performances were stopped. His personal involvement in their production argues that Middleton's time in prison was short.

Middleton's engagement with the manuscript production of *A Game at Chesse* has been misread by Janet Clare as representative of a prohibition upon circulation (Clare, 197). That the play was printed 'surreptitiously', probably after James I's death, would appear to lend credence to Clare's understanding, except that documentary evidence does not suggest that any effort was made to prevent the production and circulation of manuscripts. The matter of printing is a bit more complex. The three quartos of the play, unlicensed by the Stationers' Company, and hence not reviewed by official authorizers (that is, submitted for pre-print censorship) were printed in London without an imprint indicating the play's publisher, printer, place of imprint, date, or author. Although the lack of these attributes defines 'surreptitious' printing, their absence from the texts of *A Game at Chesse* has been misread as evidence of continental printing. Adrian Weiss's recent work on the quartos has established that all three were printed in London by members of the London printing establishment. While the government's reaction to the play's performance would certainly have suggested to *Chesse*'s publishers that the play would not receive official authorization for print, it is important to note that at this time the print authorizer for plays was the Master of Revels! Even though Herbert, whose licence for *A Game at Chesse*'s performance had recently been scrutinized, would surely not have granted permission to print the play, no evidence exists to suggest that the government engaged in increased surveillance of scribes and printers after the August clamour the performance provoked.

The question then remains of what circumstances surrounded the printing of *A Game at Chesse*. From an analysis of typography, Adrian Weiss has established that Nicholas Okes printed two of the editions of the play (conventionally known as Q1 and Q2) in a single continuous job.[20] Standing type from near the end of the first was re-used immediately thereafter in the second. Both Howard-Hill and Gary Taylor agree that Okes's text was printed from a manuscript closely associated with Middleton himself. While it is not at all unreasonable to assume that Middleton's play, like most printed texts in the early seventeenth century, was purchased outright by Okes, neither is Middleton's direct involvement in publication implausible. Okes's printing of several Middleton texts suggests some relationship between the two men. In this instance Middleton's involvement with scribal publication—himself serving as scribe and apparently encouraging the activities of Ralph Crane, the King's Men's scribe—argues an unusual engagement with publication, particularly since he may have introduced variants in the printed text that do not appear in manuscripts attributable to him. Middleton might have approached Okes with his provocative text in part because he understood Okes's character and had a long-term working relationship with him. Okes was an entrepreneurial risk-taker. Blayney characterizes him as possessing 'determination, initiative, and perhaps more than a little chicanery' (Blayney 1982, 28). Okes's own career and casual regard for regulation suggest that he may have felt that the risk involved in printing *A Game at Chesse* was outweighed by the financial reward. Okes had, after all, only three years before surreptitiously printed without consequence *Vox Populi* (Blayney 45), Thomas Scott's anti-Spanish pamphlet which served as one of Middleton's sources for *A Game at Chesse*.[21] Okes's surreptitious printing activities might be seen as exceptional except that an anonymous informant's letter to Secretary of State Sir

George Calvert sometime around or after 1620 suggests a regular trade in 'illegal' books:

> Althoughe such bookes as vox populi, and other suche as daylie tooe audaciouslie are dispersed, are forbidden and ought by noe good subiect be intertained or openly divulged, yet (as I am lykewayes crediblie given to vnderstand) there bee dyuers stationers soe soone as they heare of anie such bookes, as haue noe publicke authoritie they indevo[r] vpon whatsoever condic[on] to gett them in theire hands... (Greg 1967, 177)

The printing of *A Game at Chesse*'s other quarto (conventionally known as Q3) is another matter entirely. According to Weiss it was printed by Edward Allde and Augustine Mathewes, also a London Stationer, who sought to create the impression of continental printing by using black letter for the setting of the two title-words 'Epilogue' and 'Prologue'. Howard-Hill identifies the Allde/Mathewes edition with the line of manuscripts that derived from Ralph Crane's 'Archdale' manuscript (the earliest extant copy). Allde, who had printed two other Middleton texts, *The Sun in Aries* for Gosson and *The Phoenix* for Johnson, had on a few occasions published texts he printed. Augustine Mathewes, though principally a trade printer, engaged in some publication with his partner, John Norton. Allde and Mathewes may either have published *A Game at Chesse* or printed it for another publisher, though it is impossible to say which. In 1624 Mathewes had printed Edward Elton's *Gods Holy Minde* for Richard Milbourne, which, although duly authorized and licensed, was subsequently burned. Milbourne frequently employed Mathewes, whose interest in publishing anti-Catholic, anti-Arminian tracts and sermons coincided with Milbourne's. Milbourne testified to the ruin that the burning of *Gods Holy Minde* caused to his business (*Cygnea Cantio*, 40), and this ruin, in turn, may have affected Mathewes's business. Having lost Milbourne's hire, Mathewes may have become willing to incur some risk in a printing venture that promised considerable return. Furthermore, Mathewes was no stranger to risk. He was one of four Stationers fined by the Court of Assistants in 1621 for printing George Wither's *A Motto*

---

[20] Adrian Weiss, private correspondence, 14 May 1993.
[21] Though published anonymously, *Vox Populi*'s author was discovered to Sir Dudley Carleton on 3 February 1621. Despite the King's displeasure at the pamphlet, the author was protected from official sanctions. On 20 November 1622 Thomas Locke wrote to Carleton:

> I did this day accompanie mr Scotts brother to the B͞p: of Norwich [Samuel Harsnett] who professeth himself readie to do yo[r] l͞p any seruice in this or ought else And hath referred him to the Archb: of Cant [George Abbot] of whom when they have spoken togither he dowbteth not but he shall receiue a satisfactorie answere touching his brother whereof I do not make any great dowbt vnlesse he should be pressed by the higher powers, for hee told me that he hath proceded no further against him then a sum͡ons... (Greg 1967, 176)

A further letter on 15 November confirmed that Harsnett 'promised that there shalbe no further proceeding against mr Scott' and that Harsnett would issue an order so that Scott 'may avoid danger' (Greg 1967, 177).

without authorization or licence (Jackson, 135). (Nine of the twenty-nine texts Mathewes printed in 1625 were not entered in the Stationers' Registers.)

For Mathewes, Allde, and Okes, printing the texts of *A Game at Chesse* represented instances of Company printers employing legal presses to print for profit texts which were technically 'illegal' by Company standards (unlicensed and unentered). Should the printers have been discovered, the risks were twofold: the Company could have imposed fines for unlicensed printing, and the government could have suppressed the work and ordered the destruction of unsold copies and imprisonment of the printers and author. That the government did not suppress the printed texts of *A Game at Chesse* and punish their printers points either to a certain degree of government disinterest or to an ineffectual mechanism for detecting and suppressing literature perceived as transgressive— or both. The Stationers' Company here clearly was not a mechanism for censorship. *A Game at Chesse* was not printed by the kind of 'underground' presses that had printed the Marprelate tracts in the 1580s. Okes, Allde, and Mathewes were Company members, and though *A Game at Chesse* was not printed legally, none of the printers was the subject of Company sanctions. Indeed, some fellow Stationers must have known of the printing and seen it as somewhat routine (if we are to believe Calvert's informer). There may have been a certain unexpressed compact among Stationers to support each other in matters where they supported the expression of certain political views. Such a compact need not have extended throughout the trade, but almost certainly other Stationers must have known of the actions of *A Game*'s printers and chosen not to reveal them. Equally important is the fact that, despite its earlier suppression of performance, the government took no action in the face of the appearance of three editions of the play. In effect, it acquiesced in the circulation of possibly 3000–4000 copies.

If Middleton's occupation with publishing *A Game at Chesse* in some ways resembles Ben Jonson's interest in ensuring the folio publication of his *Works* in 1616, so does his total uninvolvement with the publication of other plays look like his other contemporary, William Shakespeare. Like Shakespeare, Middleton was clearly uninvolved with the publication of some of his works. Considering these publications, while it may offer little insight into Middleton *per se*, reminds us of the kind of widespread publishing practices that existed in early modern England that provide the basis for the more usual conclusions about printing and authorship. These practices create a background against which Middleton's participation with his printers and publishers stands in high relief. Middleton was not likely to have been involved in the printing of his works in three kinds of circumstances—the first in cases of misattribution, the second when acting companies facilitated the printing of a play or plays, and the third when a work was printed along with and under the title of another work or other works. Misattribution is the most distinctive category, and two of Middleton's works belong here. *A*

Yorkshire tragedy (1608), printed by Richard Bradock for Thomas Pavier, carried Shakespeare's name on the title-page, and *The puritane widow* (1607) identifies W.S. as its author. The misattribution of *A Yorkshire tragedy* was probably deliberately dishonest (Wells and Taylor (1987) 140). *The Puritane*'s 'W.S.' may have been a more honest mistake. *The Puritane* had been performed by the Children of Paul's and was part of a 'flood' of plays performed by the company that appeared in print in 1607–8, around the time that the company broke up. This was the first of four Middleton plays performed by the Children of Paul's that Eld printed, and his attribution of 'W.S.' may indicate he was unaware of the author's identity. The Children of Paul's apparently facilitated the printing of some of the plays that had been in their repertoire. The numerous plays from the Children of Paul's repertoire that appeared in print in 1607–8 indicates that the company, perhaps in financial straits, was selling its manuscripts to raise money. One Middleton play performed by the Children of Paul's, *A mad world, my masters*, was printed by Henry Ballard for the frequent dramatic publishers Walter Burre and Eleazar Edgar, so in this case, the more customary arrangement between an acting company and publisher saw this play into print.

In an entirely different situation another acting company, the King's Men, figured prominently in the printing of plays in which Middleton collaborated—the publication of the Shakespeare first folio. In 1623 Shakespeare's *Comedies, Histories, and Tragedies*, published by W. Jaggard, Blount, Smethwick, and Aspley and printed by W. Jaggard, included *Timon of Athens*, *Macbeth*, and *Measure for Measure*, all of which contained extended passages that have been attributed to Middleton. Two circumstances of the folio's publication argue against any Middleton involvement in the volume's production. First, the acting company, which owned the manuscripts, functioned as the 'author', and organized the publication. Second, as a collaborator (co-author or adapter) in works included in an edition published in part to honour the primary author, Middleton was doubly unimportant.

On two occasions Middleton's dramatic talents found another outlet besides plays—masques. His *Masque of heroes* was printed by William Stansby for John Browne in 1619, and his and William Rowley's *World tost at tennis* was printed by George Purslowe for Trundle. Both appeared at a time when the popularity of Middleton's plays apparently kept them out of the printers' shops, and in both cases publishers who regularly traded in popular drama found a way to use Middleton's popularity to their advantage. Printed as they were outside of Middleton's usual associations in the print trade, it seems unlikely that Middleton was involved in their publication. That *World tost at tennis* is touted as 'a toy brought to the press rather by the printer than the poet' supports this.

These circumstances, uninformative as they are about Middleton and his associations, remind us of some important aspects of London publishing. Publishing was a collaborative venture in which printers, booksellers, acting companies, and writers participated in varying degrees. Even in instances where Middleton clearly did not participate in the process of publication, associations were formed and networks existed. Furthermore, that this work could be misattributed, altogether unattributed, or 'owned' by an acting company points to the ambiguous status of an 'author' in early modern England. In the years 1607 and 1608, when four of Middleton's plays were first printed, authorship was unrecorded in the Stationers' Registers nearly one third of the time. This, of course, poses problems for studying a writer's involvement with publishing, especially in the earlier years of Middleton's career. Because crediting authorship was only becoming important to printers at the end of the sixteenth century and the beginning of the seventeenth, we should not assume that an unidentified author was an unknown author. This seems to be particularly true when we consider the networks that emerge among the printers of Middleton's early pamphlets and plays. These patterns suggest that whether or not Middleton was acknowledged by his publishers and printers, he knew them and may well have worked with them directly. In the later years Middleton's associations are somewhat easier to trace. Indeed, this should not be surprising since by the time that Shakespeare's *Comedies, Histories, and Tragedies* was printed in 1623, authorship went unrecorded only one-tenth of the time. Even though between 1597 (when Middleton's first text appeared in print) and Middleton's death in 1627, the changing status of authorship altered attribution, the regular patterns of association between Middleton and his printers and publishers found throughout Middleton's career attest to the author's emerging importance in the early modern period. These authors may not have enjoyed the ownership of their literary properties that from the eighteenth century on copyrights would ensure them; based on Middleton's experiences with the Stationers, however, we can no longer assume that Ben Jonson was the only early modern dramatist interested in publication.

Thomas Middleton emerges from this study of his associations in the London print trade as an author who joined with the sixteenth- and seventeenth-century publishers and printers of his works in an enterprise that sought to reap the benefits—economic and ideological—of the burgeoning print culture. At the centre of this culture the London Stationers exercised considerable power and independence, and even when government regulation infringed in theory on their liberties, the practices of individual printers and booksellers effectively forged a liberty that reaped them rich economic rewards. For the pamphlets, plays, civic entertainments, and masques written by Middleton, this commercial activity can be associated with a full complement of practices. From the official suppression of *Micro-cynicon* to the royal favour he found for printing *The peace-maker*, Middleton experienced the extremes of official engagement with the printed word. Furthermore, financial gain motivated both the promotion and withholding of Middleton texts. Like the works of other popular dramatists, many of Middleton's plays were withheld from printing by the acting companies. Most of his works, though, appeared through the agency—legal and illegal—of entrepreneurial Stationers whose interests were largely financial. While the government undoubtedly acted effectively *ad hoc* to suppress works it considered undesirable—the Bishops' Ban of *Micro-cynicon* or the Privy Council's suppression of the performance of *A Game at Chesse*—the Stationers were equally effective in reviving satire and printing copies of *Game* as long as a market existed for the works. Even when the mechanisms for providing official authority for works to be licensed became more efficient after the 1586 Star Chamber Decree, Stationers and authorizers, sometimes independently and sometimes working together, found ways to bring works with strong popular appeal and particular religious interests to the book-buying public, even though some of those works might displease the government. The works of Thomas Middleton that appeared in print in the author's lifetime did so because they appealed to these interests—interest in religion, in civic and guild pride, in current politics, and in fads and fashions (literary and social)—and not because they conformed to some rigidly inscribed official notion of allowable literature. Middleton's literary heritage shows that he understood and was personally engaged by the greatest influence on early modern print culture—the market.

THE WORKS OF THOMAS MIDDLETON PRINTED BETWEEN 1597 AND 1627

Year	SR Entry	Title	Collaborator	Printer	+ Printers	Publisher	Bookseller	Authorizer
1597	not	The wisdom of Solomon paraphrased		Simmes		no		
1599	not	Micro-cynicon		Creede		Bushell		not
1600	not	The ghost of Lucrece		Simmes		no		
1604	01.08.03	Jacke of Dover, including Penniless Parliament		White		Ferbrand		
1604		The meeting of gallants at an ordinarie		Creede			Law	
1604	04.01.03	The Ant, and the nightingale: or father Hubburds tales		Creede		Bushell	Chorlton	Hartwell
1604		Father Hubburds tales: or the ant and the nightingale, anr. edn.		Creede		Cotton		
1604	04.03.21	Platoes Cap		Purfoot		Bushell, Chorlton		Harsnett
1604	04.03.22	The blacke booke, 2 edns.		Creede		Chorlton		Murgetrod
1604	04.04.02	The magnificent entertainment	Dekker	Creede	Eld, Simmes, Stafford	Man, T.		Pasfield
1604	04.11.09	The honest whore	Dekker	Simmes	Creede, Eld, Stafford	Man, T.	Hodgets	Pasfield
1607	07.05.09	The phoenix		Allde		Johnson		Buc
1607	07.05.15	Michaelmas terme		Purfoot	Allde	Johnson		Buc
1607	07.08.06	The puritane widow	[Init. W. S.]	Eld		Eld		Buc
1607	07.10.07	The revengers tragedy		Eld		Eld		Buc
1608	07.10.07	A trick to catch the old-one		Eld		no		Buc
1608	08.03.22	Your five gallants		Eld		Bonian		Buc
1608	08.05.02	A Yorkshire tragedy	[Title-p. W. Shakespeare]	Bradock		Pavier		Wilson
1608	08.10.04	A mad world, my masters		Ballard	Okes	Burre, Edgar		Segar for Buc
1608		The penniles parliament of three-bare poets		Creede		Barley		
1609	09.05.30	Sir Robtert Sherley, sent ambassador		Windet		Budge		Etkins
1609	not	The two gates of salvation, or the mariage of the old and new testament		Okes		no		
1611	not	The roaring girle	Dekker	Okes		Archer		
1613	13.11.03	The triumphs of truth		Okes		no		
1613	not	Entertainment at the Opening of the New River, with Triumphs of Truth		Okes		no		
1615		The honest whore, 3rd edn.		Okes				
1616		A trick to catch the old-one, anr. edn.		Eld			Langley	
1616	not	Civitatis Amor, The Cities Love		Okes		Archer		
1617	not	A faire quarrell	Rowley	Eld	Alsop	Trundle	Wright	
1617	not	The tryumphs off honor and industrie		Okes		no		
1618	18.01.22	The Owles almanacke, 2 edns.		Griffin		Lisle		Taverner
1618	not	The peace-maker		Purfoot				Cum Privilegio
1619		The peace-maker, 2nd edn.		Purfoot				Cum Privilegio
1619	19.07.10	Masque of heroes		Stansby		Browne		Buc
1619	not	The triumphs of love and antiquity		Okes				
1619	not assn	The Peace-maker, 3rd edn.		Beale				Cum Privilegio
1620	20.07.04	The world tost at tennis	Rowley	Purslowe		Trundle	Wright	Buc
1620	not	The Mariage off the old and new testament, anr. issue of Two Gates of Salvation		Okes				
1620	not	The peace-maker, 4th edn.		Beale				Cum Privilegio
1621		The peace-maker, 5th edn.		Beale				Cum Privilegio
1621	21.09.02	A faire quarrell, 2nd edn.	Rowley	Mathewes		Dewe		
1621	not	Honorable entertainments		Eld				
1621	not	The sunne in Aries		Allde		Gosson		
1622	not	The triumphs of honor and virtue		Okes		no		
1623	23.11.08	Macbeth, in Comedies, Histories & Tragedies	Shakespeare	Jaggard, W		Blount, Smethwick, Aspley, Jaggard		Worrall
1623	23.11.08	Measure for Measure, in Comedies, Histories & Tragedies	Shakespeare	Jaggard, W		Blount, Smethwick, Aspley, Jaggard		Worrall
1623	23.11.08	Timon of Athens in Comedies, Histories & Tragedies	Shakespeare	Jaggard, W		Blount, Smethwick, Aspley, Jaggard		
1623	not	The triumphs of integrity		Okes		no		
1623	not	The Duchess of Malfi, with Middleton's 'Webster'		Okes		Waterson		
1625	not	A game at chess as it was acted		Okes		no		
1625	not	A game at chess as it was acted, partial reprint		Okes		no		
1625	not	A game at chess as it was acted, anr. edn.		Mathewes, Allde		no		
1626	not	The triumphs of health and prosperity		Okes		no		
1627	not	Two gates of salvation, anr. issue w. cancel title 'God's Parliament House'		Okes, J		no		

WORKS CITED

Arber, Edward, *A Transcript of the Registers of the Company of Stationers of London, 1554–1640*, 5 vols (1875)

Blagden, Cyprian, *The Stationers' Company: A History, 1403–1959* (1960)

Blayney, Peter W. M., *The Texts of 'King Lear' and their Origins* (1982)

—— *The Bookshops in Paul's Cross Churchyard* (1990)

Bullough, Geoffrey, '*The Game at Chesse*: How It Struck a Contemporary', *Modern Language Review* 49 (1954), 156–63

'A Calendar of the Dramatic Records in the Books of the Livery Companies of London, 1485–1640', *Collections of the Malone Society*, vol. 3 (1954)

Calendar of the Patent Rolls in the Public Record Office, Elizabeth I, 1558–1603, 9 vols (1939–86)

Calendar of State Papers, Domestic, for the Reign of James I, vol. 12 (1859)

Calendar of State Papers, Venetian, 1623–1625, vol. 18 (1912)

Chambers, E. K., *The Elizabethan Stage*, 4 vols (1923)

Clare, Janet, '*Art made tongue-tied by authority': Elizabethan and Jacobean Dramatic Censorship* (1990)

Clegg, Cyndia Susan, 'The 1586 Decrees for Order in Printing and the Practice of Censorship', *Ben Jonson Journal*, 2 (1995), 9–29

—— 'The Stationers' Company of London', *Dictionary of Literary Biography*, 170 (1996), 275–91

—— *Press Censorship in Elizabethan England* (1997)

Dunlap, Rhodes, 'James I, Bacon, Middleton, and the Making of *The Peace-Maker*', *Studies in the English Renaissance Drama*, ed. Josephine W. Bennett, Oscar Cargill, and Vernon Hall, Jr. (1959), 82–94

Dutton, Richard, *Mastering the Revels: The Regulation and Censorship of English Renaissance Drama* (1991)

Elizabeth I, *The Quenes Majesties Injunctions* (1559)

Featly, Daniel, *Cygnea Cantio* (1620)

George, David, 'Thomas Middleton's Sources: A Survey', *Notes and Queries* 216 (1971), 17–24

Greg, W. W., *A Companion to Arber* (1967)

—— and E. Boswell, *Records of the Court of the Stationers' Company 1576–1602—from Register B* (1930)

Heath, Baron, *Some Account of the Worshipful Company of Grocers of the City of London* (1869)

Howard-Hill, T. H., 'The Author as Scribe or Reviser? Middleton's Intentions in *A Game At Chess*', *TEXT* 3 (1987), 305–18

—— *Middleton's 'Vulgar Pasquin': Essays on 'A Game at Chess'* (1995)

Ioppolo, Grace, *Revising Shakespeare* (1991)

Jackson, William A., ed., *Records of the Court of the Stationers' Company 1602 to 1640* (1957)

Johnson, Francis R., 'Notes on English Retail Book-prices, 1550–1640', *The Library*, V, 5 (1950), 83–112

Johnson, Gerald D., 'The Stationers Versus the Drapers: Control of the Press in the Late Sixteenth Century', *The Library*, VI, 10 (1988), 1–17

Perry, G. G., and Charles Gillett, *Burned Books*, 2 vols (1932)

Stephen, Leslie, and Sidney Lee, *et al.*, *Dictionary of National Biography* (1885–1925)

Weiss, Adrian, 'Bibliographical Methods for Identifying Unknown Printers in Elizabethan/Jacobean Books', *Studies in Bibliography*, 44 (1991) 183–228

—— private correspondence, 14 May 1993

Wells, Stanley, and Gary Taylor, with John Jowett and William Montgomery, *William Shakespeare: A Textual Companion* (1987)

BOOKSELLERS WITHOUT AN AUTHOR, 1627-1685

Maureen Bell

THERE is a gap in seventeenth-century book trade history which coincides with the closure of the theatres during the Interregnum. This is not surprising: the scholars who established historical bibliography—notably Greg and McKerrow—had a particular interest in dramatic literature, and their bibliographical enquiries were focused especially on Renaissance drama. In his Sandars Lectures in 1976, D. F. McKenzie remarked on the consequences, for book trade historians, of this link between historical bibliography and Renaissance drama:

> The English book trade has commanded a scholarship of the highest standard for the period up to 1640; but for the rest of the 17th century, it may not be unfair to say, we have scarcely begun either to formulate the kinds of question that historical enquiry might try to answer, or even to edit, as evidence, the basic documents which must serve it. (*London Book Trade*, 16)

Although substantial work has now been done on discrete aspects of trade practices in the period after 1640—on publications such as newspapers and periodicals, seditious pamphlets, parliamentary printing; issues of legislation, censorship and control; particular groups of stationers involved in opposition publishing in the Restoration period—we still lack editions of some of the documents which would enable us to look at the workings of the trade as a whole. In particular, the period between 1640 and 1660 remains largely uncharted, as far as the day-to-day running of the trade is concerned.[1] In English literature, too, there is a similar problem: courses tend to divide the period into Renaissance drama on the one hand and Restoration drama on the other, and despite new work on the Caroline drama, students and teachers alike continue to conceptualize seventeenth-century drama as disjunctive, broken by the Civil War, apparently 'restored' after 1660 in a radically different cultural context.[2]

In investigating the posthumous publication of Middleton's plays, both of these gaps—in book trade history, and in drama—will have to be negotiated.[3] In following the trail of Middleton's plays, however, we have a path (or, rather, an irregular series of stepping-stones) to lead us through the unmapped territory of the Interregnum; and, in the process of following it, we can usefully confront and interrogate the apparent disjunction. The trail will take us from the author's death to the early years of the Restoration. Between 1627 and 1685 twenty of Middleton's plays appeared in a variety of forms and formats, and were—according to their imprints—handled by a multiplicity of booksellers, some of them publishers, others only retailers.[4]

The distinction between the terms used in the last sentence needs to be made clear at the outset. 'Publishing', in our sense, was not in this period a separate function from printing or bookselling. The person who financed publication by buying rights to a book and by paying for the printing costs, and who organized the book's distribution, is the person whom I shall—anachronistically—describe as the publisher. In the seventeenth century that role was not identified as it is today, and might be carried out by any stationer (the printer or the bookseller) or by an interested party outside the trade (the author, a religious or political group) who provided both financial backing and a distributive network alongside (or instead of) the usual retail outlets. During the earlier part of the century, there had been a shift in power within the book trade: printers, once the driving force in the Stationers' Company, which regulated the trade, had by mid-century lost their pre-eminence to the publisher/booksellers. Increasingly in this period it was booksellers rather than printers who owned the rights in copies, and it was booksellers who held the highest offices within the Company itself.[5] In an age when there was no copyright in the modern sense, the entrance of a book's title in the Stationers' Register constituted a statement of ownership; rights of ownership thus established could be transferred by agreement between owners and became, in effect, perpetual monopolies. The point of this digression into book trade terminology is to insist, at the outset, on the fact of publishing as a *trade*: printers and booksellers took financial risks when they decided to act as publishers, tying up in printed sheets capital which could only realize a profit (and thus enable more publishing) when the books were sold. Publishing a

---

[1] *A Chronology and Calendar of Documents Relating to the London Book Trade, 1641–1700*, ed. D. F. McKenzie and M. Bell, provides a guide to the period, bringing together records from the *Calendar of State Papers Domestic*, the Lords' and Commons' Journals, Reports of the Historical Manuscripts Commission, and extracts from the Court Books of the Stationers' Company. See R. Myers, 'The Records of the Worshipful Company of Stationers and Newspaper Makers', for a list of the principal unpublished records of the Company.
[2] Exceptions to the general neglect of this material are Martin Butler's *Theatre and Crisis 1632–1642*, Lois Potter's *Secret Rites and Secret Writing* and Andrew Gurr's *Playgoing in Shakespeare's London* which, despite its title, covers the period to 1642.
[3] For the posthumous publication of Middleton's non-dramatic work, *The Penniless Parliament*, see the Textual Introduction to the work, p. 469. John Astington deals with the posthumous use of prints originating in earlier Middleton editions (in his essay, p. 226).
[4] For details of the booksellers involved, see Table 2 below.
[5] For accounts of these developments, see Cyprian Blagden, *The Stationers' Company* and John Feather, *A History of British Publishing*.

TABLE I. MIDDLETON'S PLAYS 1627–85: DATES OF PUBLICATION

Dates of earlier editions are added where appropriate. Folios are signalled by 'F' after the date. 1647F and 1679F = the Beaumont and Fletcher folios; 1623F, 1632F, 1663F, 1664F, and 1685F are all Shakespeare folios. Asterisks denote adaptations.

Greg no.	Title	Dates published
204	*Honest Whore*	1604/1605/1615/1616/1635
243	*Phoenix*	1607/1630/[?1656 lost edn?]
244	*Michaelmas Term*	1607/1630
251	*Puritan*	1607/1664F/1685F
272	*Yorkshire Tragedy*	1608/1619/1664F/1685F
276	*Mad World*	1608/1640
402	*Timon of Athens*	1623F/1632F/1663F/1664F/1678*/1685F
404	*Macbeth*	1623F/1632F/1663F/1664F/1673/1674*/1685F
433	*Chaste Maid*	1630
567	*Bloody Banquet*	1639
652	*Nice Valour*	1647F/1679F
666	*Wit at Several Weapons*	1647F/1679F
705	*Widow*	1652
712	*Changeling*	1653/1668
717	*Spanish Gypsy*	1653/1661
766	*Old Law*	1656
778	*No Wit/Help*	1657/1677*
Collection	*Two New Plays [Women Beware & More Dissemblers]*	1657
815	*Mayor of Quinborough*	1661
821	*Anything for a Quiet Life*	1662

book required both investment and a judgement of the likely market for such a book. To put it crudely, and allowing for some exceptions in the publishing of propaganda and vanity items, no stationer would usually be interested in financing the publication of a book for which there was no discernible market. I think it worth labouring this point simply because it is so readily missed, even by those whose interest is primarily in the organization of the book trade. The bookseller Humphrey Moseley, for example, who published several of Middleton's plays and whom we shall meet later in this discussion, has been characterized repeatedly as 'the chief publisher of the finer literature of his age' (Plomer; *DNB*); his 'ideals' as a publisher have been deduced from prefaces addressed to the reader of his books (Reed). What has not been inspected is Moseley's activity as a commercial publisher concerned to make a living in a competitive, capital-intensive business. Inspecting Moseley's practice from this angle would alter the perspective, from a Moseley hailed as precursor of the liberal humanist literary critic to a Moseley whose commercial interests involved identifying and actively developing a new market in what we—retrospectively—call 'literature'.[6]

A Survey of Middleton Publications

To start, then, with Middleton. A tabulation of the edition dates of the plays (Table 1) and of the publishers and booksellers involved (Table 2) enables us to survey the period 1627 to 1685 as a whole. Such a survey will immediately raise questions about the usual time-bands (pre-1640, 1641–60, after 1660) which are conventional in discussing the period. A few of the plays we are considering had already appeared in print during Middleton's lifetime (*Honest Whore*, *Phoenix*, *Michaelmas Term*, *Puritan*, *Yorkshire Tragedy*, *Mad World*, *Timon of Athens*, and *Macbeth*), though not all had been attributed to Middleton. A larger number appeared in print for the first time, most of them in the 1650s when the theatres were closed. By the time that the first edition of *Anything for a Quiet Life* was published, in 1662, Middleton had been dead for thirty-five years. By the time that *The Puritan* was reprinted in 1664 (in the Shakespeare folio), fifty-seven years had passed since its first publication in 1607. Such long gaps, both between first performance and first edition, and between first and second editions, raise a question central to the workings of the book trade and to the reception of Middleton's plays: why would anybody be interested in publishing these old plays? In pursuing that central question we shall need to look at the variety of forms of publication, who the publishers and booksellers were, the circumstances in which they were operating, and the

---

[6] The lack of attention to Moseley's business has, since the time of completing this essay, been remedied by Paulina Kewes, whose '"Give me the sociable pocket-books..."': Humphrey Moseley's serial publication of octavo play collections' demonstrates Moseley's commercial innovations. I very much regret that this publication came too late for me to incorporate some of its many insights into the above: while it does not focus on Middleton, it offers a welcome and detailed account of Moseley's publication of plays.

TABLE 2. EDITIONS 1627–85: THE PUBLISHERS AND BOOKSELLERS INVOLVED

Title	SR entries	Edition date: Publisher/bookseller	Advertised by
Chaste Maid	[Constable] 1648 R. Thrale 1681 B. Thrale	1630 Constable	
Michaelmas Term	1607 Johnson 1630 Meighen 1646 M. Meighen & Bedell	1607 Johnson 1630 Meighen	1656 Bedell & Collins
Phoenix	1607 Johnson 1630 Meighen 1646 M. Meighen & Bedell	1607 Johnson 1630 Meighen	1656 Bedell & Collins
Timon of Athens	1623 Blount & Jaggard 1630 Cotes & Allott 1637 Cotes/Legatt & Crooke 1674 Martin & Herringman 1683 Scott & Herringman	1623 Jaggard/Blount/Smethwick/Aspley 1632 Smethwick/Aspley/Hawkins/Meighen & Allott 1663 Chetwin 1664 Chetwin 1678 [Shadwell alteration] 1685 Herringman/Brewster/Bentley/Chiswell/Knight/ Saunders	1685 Herringman/ Knight/Saunders
Macbeth	1623 Blount & Jaggard 1630 Cotes & Allott 1637 Cotes/Legatt & Crooke 1674 Martin & Herringman 1683 Scott & Herringman	1623 Jaggard/Blount/Smethwick/Aspley 1632 Smethwick/Aspley/Hawkins/Meighen & Allott 1663 Chetwin 1664 Chetwin 1673 Cademan 1674 Chetwin/Clark [Davenant adaptation] 1685 Herringman/Brewster/Bentley/Chiswell/Knight/ Saunders	1685 Herringman/ Knight/Saunders
Honest Whore	1604 Man	1604 Simmes/Hodgets 1615 Okes/Basse 1635 Okes/Collins	
Bloody Banquet		1639 Cotes	
Mad World	1608 Burre/Edgar 1613 Burre/Hodgets 1630 Spencer	1608 Burre 1640 Spencer	1660 Moseley
Valour & Weapons	1660 Robinson & Moseley 1671–3 Martin/Herringman [& Marriot?]	1647 Robinson & Moseley 1679 Martin/Herringman & Marriot	1650–60 Moseley 1679–86 Herringman
Widow	1652 Moseley 1667 Herringman	1652 Moseley	1653–60 Moseley 1668 Herringman
Changeling	1652 Moseley	1653 Moseley 1668 Anne Moseley & Dring	1653–1660 Moseley 1672 Dring
Spanish Gypsy	1624 Wright [Marriot] 1659 Moseley	1653 Marriot 1661 Crofts/Kirkman	1653–60 Moseley 1662 Kirkman, Marsh
Old Law		1656 Archer	1661 Crofts
No Wit/Help	1653 Moseley	1657 Moseley 1677 Curtis [adaptation]	1656 Moseley
Two New Plays	1653 Moseley	1657 Moseley	1656–60 Moseley
Mayor of Quinborough	1646 Robinson & Moseley 1661 Herringman 1673 Martin & Herringman	1661 Herringman	1661–86 Herringman
Quiet Life		1662 Marsh/Kirkman	1662 Marsh
Puritan	1607 Eld	1607 Eld 1664 Chetwin 1685 Herringman/Brewster/Bentley/Chiswell/Knight/ Saunders	1685 Herringman/ Knight/Saunders
Yorkshire Tragedy	1608 Pavier 1626 Brewster/Bird 1630 Cotes 1674 Martin & Herringman 1683 Scott & Herringman	1608 Pavier 1619 Pavier 1664 Chetwin 1685 Herringman/Brewster/Bentley/Chiswell/Knight/ Saunders	1685 Herringman/ Knight/Saunders

market for printed plays. We need to bear in mind, too, that the period between 1627 and 1685, covering the years immediately before Civil War, the Interregnum, and the Restoration years, enmeshes both producers and consumers of texts in political, legislative, and social shifts which touch every aspect of the enquiry, from the performance of plays and the regulation of the book trade to the political and ideological positions out of which the category 'literature' was produced.

a. Before the Civil War

Between Middleton's death and the beginning of the Civil War, eight of his plays were published. Four of these were quarto reprints: *The Phoenix* and *Michaelmas Term* (both printed for Richard Meighen in 1630), *The Honest Whore* (printed by Nicholas Okes and sold by Collins, 1635) and *A Mad World, My Masters* (printed by John Okes for Spencer, and sold by Becket, 1640). Only two first editions of Middleton plays were published: *A Chaste Maid in Cheapside*, published by Constable in 1630 and *Bloody Banquet*, published in 1639 by Cotes. Two more plays, *Timon of Athens* and *Macbeth*, which had been included in the Shakespeare first folio of 1623, were reprinted as part of the 1632 Shakespeare folio. I shall hold over discussion of plays which appeared in collections, including the Shakespeare folios, until later.

The 1630 reprints of *The Phoenix* and *Michaelmas Term* can be said to share a certain 'house style'. Both were printed by Thomas Harper and other plays printed by Harper for Meighen have strong resemblances. Greg notes, for example, that the imprint of *The Phoenix* is from the same setting as that in the 1630 edition of *Cupid's Whirligig*, which Harper also printed for Meighen. Both Middleton plays had originally been published by Johnson in 1607, and the rights were assigned by Johnson to Meighen (along with two more plays, *Cupid's Whirligig* and *The Merry Wives of Windsor*) on 29 January 1630.[7] There is nothing unusual about this transfer of rights from one publisher to another, and it occurs again in relation to the other two reprints of this period, *The Honest Whore* and *A Mad World*.[8] The deals behind such transfers, and the size of payments made by the bookseller buying rights from another, remain in most cases obscure; but the practice was commonplace, and the recording of such transfers in the pages of the Stationers' Register ensured both that the process was documented and legalized in the eyes of the Company, and that the new owner's rights were established and protected for the future against infringement. As physical objects, the texts of the three reprints from the 1630s (*The Phoenix*, *Michaelmas Term*, and *The Honest Whore*) are unremarkable: they are plain, unpaginated, unadorned (no extra information, such as character lists or prefaces, is added). In all respects they look like 'ordinary' quarto plays of the period. All three refer to the companies which acted the plays. The Meighen plays both state that they were 'sundry times acted by the Children of Paules', and *The Honest Whore* was 'Acted by her Maiesties Servants with great Applause'.

The title-pages of both the Meighen plays thus simply reprint those of the 1607 editions, reproducing verbatim the information supplied in 1607 about the 'Children of Paules'. Since it was in or around 1607 that the company closed, the title-page information would be more than twenty years out of date by 1630. The only deviation from the 1607 title-pages is the addition, on the title-page of *Michaelmas Term*, of the false, but common, claim that the play is 'Newly corrected'. The title-page of *The Honest Whore* (1635), however, adds information not present in earlier editions of the play and which relates to a current acting company. 'Her Maiesties Servants' were Queen Henrietta's Company, by 1635 established at the Phoenix/ Cockpit in Drury Lane as the chief rivals of the King's Men. This company retained in its repertory a number of older plays which had been performed by earlier companies, including (in addition to *The Honest Whore*) *A Mad World, My Masters*, *The Changeling*, and *The Spanish Gypsy*.

Of the twelve Middleton plays which were published for the first time after his death, only two, *A Chaste Maid in Cheapside* and *The Bloody Banquet*, appeared in the pre-Civil War period. *A Chaste Maid* was published as 'neuer before printed' in 1630 by Francis Constable. Constable published relatively few plays: most of his output up to 1640 was religious, with some medical/ anatomical works, some works on 'gentlemanly' arts and a little poetry. *A Chaste Maid* was only the third play he had published in fifteen years as a publisher-bookseller. Like *The Phoenix* and *Michaelmas Term* published in the same year, the *Chaste Maid* title-page harks back to earlier performances: 'As it hath beene often acted at the Swan on the Banke-side, by the Lady Elizabeth her Servants'. That company's connection with the Swan probably ended around 1613 (Edwards *et al.*, p. 89), so the title-page information is hardly topical. On the evidence of this 1630 first edition, taken together with the two reprints of 1630 (*Phoenix* and *Michaelmas Term*), the publishers' pitch seems to have been largely nostalgic, providing plain texts with no elaboration (*Chaste Maid* is the only one to provide even a list of dramatis personae) and reproducing performance information which was no longer current. If this is the result of a deliberate decision, then we might deduce an appeal to the 'good old days' of the theatre as perceived nostalgically by the play-buyer of the early 1630s. Equally, though, there may have been no such decision: the printers, instructed to reprint the play using earlier editions as copy-text, may simply have done their job efficiently and literally, so that the

---

[7] For all entries of copies in the Stationers' Register (hereafter SR), the reader is referred to Edward Arber's *A Transcript of the Registers of the Company of Stationers of London, 1554–1640*, and the continuation for 1640–1708 by G. E. Briscoe Eyre.

[8] In the case of *A Mad World* the transfers are fully documented: on 4 October 1608 it was entered by Burre and Edgar; on 19 April 1613 Edgar transferred his half-share to Hodgets, and on 2 July 1630 Burre's widow transferred her rights to Spencer. There is no record of Man's transfer of *The Honest Whore*, but the absence (presumably implying a private negotiation) is not in itself unusual.

apparent nostalgia may be no more than the result of faithful reprinting.

Slight deviations from this pattern have already been noted (the current acting information of *The Honest Whore*, the dramatis personae of *Chaste Maid* and the 'Newly corrected' claim of *Michaelmas Term*) as small but possibly significant indications of updating. That these features are representative of a growing trend towards presenting the plays as current rather than nostalgic becomes apparent when we turn to the plays at the decade's end: *The Bloody Banquet* of 1639 and *A Mad World* of 1640. The former, published by Thomas Cotes as by 'T.D.', offers no information about performance or company, but it does present the reader with more than the plain play text. The title-page uses rows of ornament for display and presents a Latin tag ('Hector adest secumque Deos in proelia ducit. | Nos haec novimus esse nihil'). As well as a list of dramatis personae, scene divisions are supplied. The publishing history of the play is obscure: Cotes did not enter the play in the Stationers' Register, and there is no indication of his source. What is clear is that either the scribe who prepared the manuscript or the publisher who supplied copy to the printer was attentive to its formal presentation as a marketable object. The last of the pre-war reprints, *A Mad World* (1640), shows substantial signs that the publisher is conscious of contemporary performance, and of the age of the play. *A Mad World* is in several respects the 'odd one out' among the four reprinted plays of the decade. It is the only one of the four which offers more than the text of the play: an address of 'The Printer and Stationer to the Gentle Reader' (signed 'I.S.', i.e. John Spencer, the publisher); a list of 'Actors in the comedy'; and, after the text of the play, a 'Catch' whose relationship to the play probably points to a recent performance. That the play appears in its second edition so long (thirty-two years) after the first is not explained directly, but clearly has something to do with contemporary performances. Instead of repeating the 1608 title-page (which refers, like the Meighen reprints, to the 'Children of Paules') the 1640 edition claims that the play 'hath bin often Acted at the Private House in Salisbury Court, by her Majesties Servants'. Queen Henrietta Maria's Men, broken up and evicted from the Phoenix Theatre during 1636–7, played at Salisbury Court until the closure of the theatres in 1642 (Bentley, *Jacobean and Caroline Stage*, vol. I, p. 237). Rather than simply reprinting the first quarto edition of 1608, as is the case with the 1630s reprints, the 1640 edition of *A Mad World* both corrects the text and adds stage directions which suggest some alteration of the play for the Salisbury Court performances. Despite (or because of?) its being a recently-performed play, the address of 'The Printer and Stationer to the Gentle Reader' is rather defensive in its presentation of an author 'whose knowne Abilities will survive to all Posterities, though hee be long since dead'; he refers to 'the liking of the Spectators, and commendations of the Actors', suggesting that the plot's lack of surprises ('In the reading of one *Act* you ghesse the consequence') is its virtue ('for here is no bumbasted or fustian stuffe; but every line weighed as with ballance; & every sentence placed with judgement and deliberation'). He wants to 'prevent a censure that may arise in the reading of this Comedy' by explaining that:

> here & there you shall find some lines that doe answer in meetre, which I hope will not prove so disdainefull, whereby the booke may be so much slighted, as not to be read; or the *Authors* judgement undervalued as of no worth. Consider (gentle Reader) it is full twenty yeares since it was written, at which time meetre was most in use, and shewed well upon the conclusion of every Act & Scene. My prevalent hope desires thy charitable censure...

The mixed messages of the publisher's address are interesting: the play is old, even old-fashioned, yet it has been recently performed and applauded; it has qualities which the 'Gentle Reader' may be expected to approve ('ballance', 'judgement', 'deliberation' rather than 'bumbasted or fustian stuffe') yet its use of 'meetre' is unfashionable. The author is known to be 'long since dead' but the publisher's grasp of the play's real age is shaky: 'it is full twenty yeares since it was written' is an underestimate of at least twelve years. If the three reprints of the 1630s are largely repetitive, reprinting the plays uncritically from the first editions of more than twenty years before, then Spencer's 1640 edition of *A Mad World* seems to point in a very different direction.

The publisher Spencer, who had been apprenticed to the bookseller Walter Burre, may never have operated independently as a bookseller. His first three publications were published in partnership with the bookseller Bartlet, whose shop seems to have provided the retail outlet for Spencer during 1624; between 1625 and 1630, during which time Spencer published only one book, Spencer may well have been doing something else for a living. In 1630 he acquired the rights in *A Mad World*, *The Alchemist* and *Epicoene*, along with six other titles, from Burre's widow (SR, 3 July 1630); at around the same time he had taken up the post of Librarian at Sion College. Occasionally thereafter (in 1630, 1635, 1638, 1639) a publication appeared in his name. The imprint of *A Mad World* stating that the book is to be sold by James Becket, at the latter's shop in the Inner Temple gate, suggests as do other Spencer imprints that Spencer had no shop of his own. James Becket's shop would have been an appropriate outlet for the book, since Becket acted as bookseller for other printers and publishers (in particular the Okes family of printers) and his stock included works by Heywood, Dekker, and Shirley. In 1640 Spencer presumably saw some possibility of capitalizing on the rights which, as a freeman of the Stationers' Company, he still owned, despite his having ceased to practise as a stationer. Performance of the play at Salisbury Court perhaps gave him an opportunity for a new edition. The hesitations of the prefatory address, however, suggest that he was unsure of his market, perhaps because as practising librarian rather than bookseller he was not confident of being in tune with his likely readership. Perhaps, too, as a tradesman turned 'professional' gentlemanly reader, he was aware that he was trying to interest a more 'polite', private-playhouse readership in a play which they (and he himself?) might regard as old and unsophisticated: hence his alteration and elaboration of the bare play text.

Compared with the other reprinted Middleton plays of this decade, the 1640 *Mad World* looks, at first, distinctly odd. Like *The Honest Whore* it is precisely linked to recent performance by both company and theatre, but it is the only one dressed up with preface, dramatis personae, additional stage directions, corrections and 'Catch'. Yet despite its difference from the reprints of ten years earlier, it is clearly part of a trend which had been developing during the 1630s. Individual features of several plays (*Honest Whore*, *Chaste Maid*, *Michaelmas Term*, and *Bloody Banquet*) have suggested a move towards addressing a discriminating readership, elaborating the bare play text into a literary product, and in this context the 1640 *Mad World* can be seen to be part of a process already under way. To follow the process further, we must go beyond 1640; but after the appearance of *Mad World* in 1640, no more Middleton plays in single editions would appear for twelve years.

b. The 1650s and early 1660s

If it is possible to speak of a boom in the posthumous publication of Middleton's plays, it happened principally in the years between 1652 and 1657, and carried over into the early years of the Restoration. *The Widow*, *The Changeling*, and *Old Law*, as well as *The Spanish Gypsy*, attributed wrongly to Middleton, were all published for the first time. As well as these quarto plays, there was an attempt at a small-scale Middleton collection: in 1657 *Two New Plays*, containing *More Dissemblers Besides Women* and *Women, Beware Women*, was published in octavo by Moseley, who also published a single octavo edition of *No Wit/Help like a Woman's*, which was clearly intended to be sold either separately or together with the *Two New Plays*, to suit the customer. 1661 and 1662 saw two more Middleton plays in print for the first time (*The Mayor of Quinborough* in 1661, *Anything for a Quiet Life* in 1662) and a reprint of *The Spanish Gypsy* in 1661.

Compared with the plain quartos of the pre-war period, the plays of the 1650s and early 1660s are elaborately tricked out, designed to appeal both to a nostalgia for performance and to an interest in the plays as literary artefacts. The pull of the 'good old days'—that is, the days of the Caroline theatre, not those of the plays' original performances—is immediately apparent from the title--pages, which refer consistently to the acting companies and playhouses of the 1630s. The playhouses mentioned are the Blackfriars (*The Widow*, *The Mayor of Quinborough*, and *Anything for a Quiet Life*); the 'Privat house in Drury-Lane'—that is, the Cockpit (*The Changeling*, *The Spanish Gypsy*); and Salisbury Court (*The Changeling*,

The Spanish Gypsy, and—possibly—*Old Law*). The title--page formula foregrounds the old days of performance ('As it was Acted...'), the play's favourable reception ('with great Applause'), the playhouses themselves and the courtly associations of actors or performance ('by His late Majesties servants'). That the first edition is the first is frequently stressed: phrases emphasizing that the play is 'Printed by the Originall Copy' (*The Changeling*) or that it was 'Never Printed before' (*The Changeling*, *The Spanish Gypsy*, *Anything for a Quiet Life*) appear on the title-pages.

No longer is the play text presented bare and un-adorned. Lists of dramatis personae consistently preface the plays. *The Widow* goes further by offering an address 'To the Reader' by the actor Alexander Gough and *The Mayor of Quinborough* has an address by the stationer. The octavo plays of 1657 go even further, with an engraved portrait of the author which appears consistently in copies of *Two New Plays* and is occasionally prefixed to the companion volume, *No Wit/Help like a Woman's*. *Two New Plays* is prefaced by the publisher's address to the reader, and a poem by Nathaniel Richards, 'Upon the Tragedy of my familiar Acquaintance. Tho. Middleton'. The plays' status as literature, and as part of a specific literary culture, is thus insisted upon, not only by the title-page formulae, but by the accretion of extra-textual apparatus.

The other remarkable feature of these plays as printed objects is the way in which they have become the carriers of information about *other* plays. Play lists and advertisements for other plays available from the bookseller appear at the end of these plays with a new regularity. *The Changeling*, *The Spanish Gypsy*, *Old Law*, *Two New Plays*, *No Wit/Help* all carry such lists, varying in length from a handful of plays (three, in the 1661 *Spanish Gypsy*; four in the 1653 *Changeling*) to much longer lists such as those in Moseley's elaborate catalogue found in copies of *No Wit/Help* and *Two New Plays*. Some of the plays carry general advertisements, rather than lists of titles, stating that 'most sort of Playes' are available from the shop of the bookseller.[9] In one extraordinary case, a catalogue of plays becomes an integral part of the volume: in Archer's edition of *Old Law* the title-page offers the play itself '...Together with an exact and perfect Catalogue of all the Playes, with the Authors Names, and what are Comedies, Tragedies, Histories, Pastoralls, Masks, Interludes, more exactly printed than ever before'. In this case, the catalogue is offered partly as an elaborate advertisement of books obtainable from Archer and from another bookseller, Robert Pollard: 'And all these plaies you may either have at the Signe of the Adam and Eve, in Little Britain [Archer's shop]; or at the Ben Johnson's Head in Thredneedle-street, over against the Exchange [Pollard's shop]'. That this catalogue was, in itself, a

---

[9] Variants of the 1661 edition of *The Spanish Gypsy* advertise the shops of the different booksellers who appear in the imprints: the Crown (Robert Crofts) and the Jo: Fletcher's Head (Francis Kirkman).

commodity worth advertising on the title-page is surely suggestive: by categorizing the plays and by supplying author names (however inaccurately), Archer was perhaps offering to *cognoscenti* collectors a check-list of printed plays which would be of intrinsic interest beyond its advertising function, against which they could compare their own collections, identify plays in a specific genre, or by a particular author, and of course suggesting whose shops could best satisfy the list of desiderata generated by using the catalogue in this way. In Archer's *Old Law*, the apparatus of collecting printed plays seems to have reached a status equivalent to the play itself. In passing, we may also note that the naming of booksellers' shops has taken on a new twist: that bookshops are now called the 'Ben Johnson's Head' or, in another instance, the 'Jo: Fletcher's Head', suggests a degree of specialization in plays by the time of the Restoration which uses the author's reputation as marketing ploy. No 'Shakespears Head' appeared until Jacob Tonson's move to the Strand in 1710, and the choice of Jonson and of Beaumont and Fletcher by early Restoration sellers of plays indicates those authors' greater appeal for Restoration readers and playgoers.[10] We may notice, too, that the playwrights chosen by booksellers as signs of excellence had been the first to be canonized by the publication of collected folio editions.

So what had happened in the 1640s?

This brief survey of Middleton's posthumously-published plays alerts us to a number of questions which the rest of this essay will attempt to explore. Some are questions which relate specifically to Middleton: why does the publication of *first* editions of his plays apparently 'take off' in the 1650s? Does Middleton's work appeal to a specific readership? Has its status as literature changed by the time of the Restoration? Who were the stationers involved in these publications, and why did they publish Middleton? There are questions, too, which relate more broadly to the status of printed plays in general, and to the status of Elizabethan and Jacobean playwrights in the Restoration period. Was there really, as seems likely from the comparison of pre-war and post-1650 editions of Middleton's plays, a shift in the way plays were presented to the reading public? If so, what developments in the market for printed plays, and perhaps in their profitability for stationers, were at work? All of these questions—about Middleton, about plays as 'literature', about booksellers, readers and markets—are interconnected, and in what follows I shall make no attempt to deal with them as if they can be separated. The first difficulty in tracking the developments signalled by the evidence of Middleton's plays would seem to be the yawning twelve-year gap in the publications discussed above. Some changes during the 1630s in the presentation of printed plays have already been identified, culminating in the 1640 edition of *A Mad World*, which has much in common with the editions of the 1650s. The 1640s, so far ignored in this discussion, clearly need to be inspected. As far as Middleton is concerned, the decade seems barren. The two

Middleton plays which were published were not attributed to Middleton: *Nice Valour* and *Wit at Several Weapons* both appeared in the Beaumont and Fletcher folio of 1647, published by Robinson and Moseley. Yet although no single quarto editions appeared, the rights to Middleton's plays were changing hands between booksellers, with their transactions recorded in the Stationers' Register. It is by following up these events that we can bring into focus the 1640s as an important period in the development of play-publishing. In doing so, we shall pay particular attention to Humphrey Moseley, the publisher of the Beaumont and Fletcher folio of 1647, and the bookseller who had an interest in ten of the Middleton plays published between 1640 and 1661.

Moseley's first appearance as the publisher of Middleton was his inclusion of *Nice Valour* and *Wit at Several Weapons* in the Beaumont and Fletcher folio collection, *Comedies and Tragedies*, of 1647. The publication of plays in folio, begun by Jonson, was—even by 1647—a rare phenomenon. In Jonson's folio *Works* the inclusion of the plays served to raise the status of drama to that of poetry. Subsequently, other collected works began to include plays (e.g. two plays in the 1633 edition of Fulke Greville's *Certaine Learned and Elegant Workes*) but no other collection consisting principally of plays moved into folio during the 1630s to join those of Jonson and Shakespeare. (The small exception to this statement is the 1637 edition of Alexander's *Recreations with the Muses*, containing his *Monarchicke Tragedies*—which are closet plays.) After the 1647 Beaumont and Fletcher collection, no other author's plays were issued collected in folio until Killigrew's were published by Herringman in 1664. Folio was, then, an unusual format for plays throughout this period, and nearly all published plays were printed in less prestigious (and less expensive) quartos. The standard selling price for quarto plays was, at least until about 1640, sixpence: not expensive, but slightly higher than the average for books of that size and length. The sixpenny retail price seems to have been conventional for quarto plays regardless of the length (and therefore the manufacturing costs) of the individual play. Evidence of booksellers' lists and inventories is patchy for the whole of the seventeenth century, but in surviving inventories from the years up to 1640 printed plays seem not to have been held in great esteem by the booksellers who handled them. For example, in a 1616 York bookseller's inventory, which lists about 750 titles in more than 3,000 copies, only Ben Jonson's folio *Works* are treated in the same way as the majority of non-dramatic books, in being given a separate entry in the bookseller's stock list: all other plays are entered simply as 'Twenty-seven Playe bookes, of sortes'—the kind of 'job lot' treatment also accorded to sermons and almanacs (Barnard and Bell, *York Book Trade*).

---

[10] See Gary Taylor, *Reinventing Shakespeare*, especially pp. 26–8, for discussion of the relative status of these playwrights at the Restoration.

While the folio format remained the exception, rather than the rule, for the publication of plays throughout the century, the idea of issuing an author's 'collected works' clearly became more usual: as a publishing format, the 'collected works' or 'collected poems' volume caught on. Using Greg's information on collections (*BEPD*, vol. III) to identify those containing plays we can see that, after a slow start, the 'collected works' as a marketable commodity really takes off at the end of the 1630s (see Appendix).[11] In some ways this may have been an *ad hoc* development: clearly, booksellers were aware that one way to sell more plays was to issue as a collection the separate editions of plays left unsold. In 1639 someone (probably Walkley) published two tragedies by May which could be sold separately or together as a collection; in the same year another publisher (probably Fussell, with whom Humphrey Moseley started out as a bookseller) had a single leaf printed to provide a title-page for the plays of Nabbes, presumably with the intention of converting his stock of old, separately printed plays into a form saleable as a 'new' collected edition. This kind of reissue of old stock with a new title-page was a common enough way for booksellers to breathe new life into stock that was not moving; they needed, after all, to try to get *some* return on unsold books in order to reinvest in new ones. Customers, however, may have resented the practice (as I do when—stupidly—I buy a copy of a book which I already have, simply because I didn't recognize it in its new cover). In his preface to the Beaumont and Fletcher volume, Moseley's opening words allude to this practice:

> Before you engage farther, be pleased to take notice of these Particulars. You have here a *Newe Booke*; I can speak it clearly; for of all this large Volume of *Comedies* and *Tragedies*, not one, till now, was ever printed before. A *Collection of Playes* is commonly but a *new Impression*, the scattered pieces which were printed single, being then onely Republished together: 'Tis otherwise here.

Though some of Moseley's other claims (e.g. for the continuous printing of the volume) are false, he is here telling the truth: the Beaumont and Fletcher folio is, in itself, an extraordinary publishing event. To understand what Moseley and his partner in the venture, Humphrey Robinson, were doing, and to discover the relationship between Moseley—principal publisher of Middleton in the 1640s and 1650s—and his authors, we have to set this publication in the context of Moseley's career as a bookseller, pausing for a moment to establish his involvement in play-publishing up to this point, before returning to consider the inclusion of Middleton's plays in the works of Beaumont and Fletcher.

Humphrey Moseley's bookselling career began in 1627 (the year of Middleton's death) when he was made free of the Stationers' Company and began to work in partnership with another bookseller called Nicholas Fussell. As well as publishing a few books together, mostly devotional and religious works, they were buying large numbers of books from other publishers for retail in their shop.[12] Stationers' Company records show that in 1636 they were in dispute with Bourne over £76 6s. 7d. owed by them to Bourne for books received from him in 1633. Moseley and Fussell claimed that Bourne had not supplied them with all the books agreed, and refused to pay up until Bourne fulfilled his obligation. The dispute was settled after arbitration, and the fact that Fussell and Moseley agreed to pay the revised sum of £68 16s. 7d. in the space of the following week suggests that they were not short of ready cash (Jackson, 281-3).

Moseley had begun to enter copies in the Stationers' Register in his own right in 1634; by 1637 he had moved into his own shop, the Prince's Arms in St Paul's Churchyard, where he stayed for the rest of his life. Moseley's publishing in the years up to 1640 continued in much the same vein as his ventures with Fussell: a staple of devotional and religious works, with—from around 1638—a growing proportion of history, verse and polite literature such as Bacon, More, *The Academy of Compliments*, and Paolo Sarpi. As a publisher, Moseley was hardly a specialist in plays. Indeed, between 1627 and 1640 he published only one play, Zouch's *The Sophister. A Comedie...* in 1639. Fussell seems to have become interested in plays at the same time: in 1639 he took over another stationer's stock of plays by Nabbes. He had new title-pages printed for the individual plays, as well as a title-page which he used to reissue the separate plays as a set, 'Collected into one Volume'.[13]

As a bookseller, however, if not as a publisher, Moseley clearly had some strength in the area of play texts. A surviving bill for books bought from Moseley's shop, dated March 1641, lists sixty-seven plays by title, plus nine more books ('New poems & historyes') and gives prices. The plays in quarto and octavo are sixpence each; folio plays either one shilling or one shilling and sixpence. Two Middleton plays appear in the bill: the 1635 edition of *Honest Whore* and the 1640 *Mad World*.[14] Unfortunately, the identity of the customer is not known. While plays were certainly not the only books sold by Moseley, and were as yet of no specific interest to him as a publisher, and although the chance evidence of one surviving bill is hardly conclusive, this list of plays with their dates does show that Moseley either had in stock, or was able to obtain, a large number of plays published by a variety of stationers. The list gives dates for almost all the plays, and all of them are recent editions: mostly from the previous three or four years, and none earlier than 1634. It seems likely, therefore, that the list draws on Moseley's own stock, built up over the previous six years, when he began as an independent publisher. Interestingly, the

---

[11] Early examples are the collections of plays by Lyly (1632, duodecimo) and Marston (1633, octavo).

[12] This is suggested by their reissues with cancel title-pages, such as STC 15713, 13991, 14832.

[13] See Greg, *BEPD*, vol. III, p. 1098; STC, note to 18337, Nabbes's *Playes, maskes, epigrams, elegies, and epithalamiums*, 1639.

[14] The list (PRO SP16/478) is printed by Reed as Appendix I, pp. 132-3.

prices given in Moseley's list demonstrate the stability in retail prices of quarto plays: sixpence had been the usual price since Elizabethan times.[15] By 1641, then, Moseley had established himself as a fairly prosperous bookseller with some publishing experience and was now looking to buy up more copies for publication. As yet, though he clearly had an extensive stock of printed plays, he had not in any sense become a specialist in drama. That he did so, on an unprecedented scale, is clear from his entries in the Stationers' Register in the 1640s and 1650s.

The rights to publish plays were not necessarily the author's, to dispose of as he liked. In the case of plays by dramatists who worked as professionals, contracted to or otherwise 'attached' to an acting company, the play became the property of that company. To obtain plays for legal (rather than pirated) publication, the publisher needed to buy the right to publish either from the author or from the company, and to register the copy with the Stationers' Company which could be required (though not necessarily relied on) to protect the interests of the legal owner of any published work. It is not particularly surprising, then, to find that on 7 August 1641, the Lord Chamberlain wrote to the Master and Wardens of the Stationers' Company asking them to forbid the printing of any play belonging to the King's Men without consent, and enclosing a list of sixty plays whose printing was to be forbidden.[16] What is more surprising is that five years later, in 1646, Moseley and Humphrey Robinson entered in the Stationers' Register, as their copies, thirty-eight of the plays in the Lord Chamberlain's list. Many of the plays protected by the Lord Chamberlain in 1641 appear in the Stationers' Register in the same order as in the 1641 list. In 1653, in another large Stationers' Register entry, Moseley (alone, this time, which suggests financial independence) included another thirteen from the 1641 list. It seems that he had managed to buy up, perhaps in two lots, the very plays whose printing the King's Men had earlier tried to prevent.[17] The major publication of Beaumont and Fletcher's plays in 1647 was clearly done with the consent of the actors, ten of whom signed the dedication. Why, in 1646, was Moseley able to do what had been specifically forbidden in 1641?

The 1641 protection list was issued at around the time of the playhouse closure of 1641 occasioned by plague. Political events of that year presumably added to the King's Men's feeling of insecurity. *The Stage-Players Complaint*, dated by Bentley as contemporary with the Lord Chamberlain's list, expresses the players' apprehension:

But I'le assure you 'tis to be feared: For Monopolers are downe, Projectors are downe, the High Commission Court is downe, the Starre Chamber is down, & (some think) Bishops will downe, and why should we then that are farre inferior to any of those not justly feare, least we should be downe too? (Bentley, *JCS*, vol. I, p. 65n.)

By 1646 some of the playhouses were reopening surreptitiously; the date of the brief revival of performance suggests perhaps that Moseley's wholesale buying up of plays that year might be connected with an obvious— if suppressed—public desire for performances. There is no evidence, however, that the Blackfriars theatre ever tried to reopen after 1642: indeed, Bentley remarks on the oddity that despite the King's Men being the most successful company in the pre-war period, there is no evidence of surreptitious playing at the Blackfriars during the whole of the Interregnum (*JCS*, vol. VI, p. 40). The playhouse was eventually pulled down in 1655. By 1646, the players must have decided to earn money as best they could, and selling the publication rights to their plays was an obvious option. There is, of course, no evidence for the negotiations which lie behind the Moseley/Robinson entry of 1646, and we can only guess how much the booksellers paid for the copies they entered. The cost to Moseley and Robinson must have been considerable, since publication of a single play (*The Wild-Goose Chase*, first in the 1641 list but lost until 1652, when it was published) could be hailed as a considerable benefit to the actors:

> In this late dearth of wit, when *Jose* and *Jack*
> Were hunger-bit for want of fowl and Sack
> His nobleness found out this happy meanes
> To mend their dyet with these WILD-GOOSE scenes,
> By which he hath revived in a day
> Two Poets, and two Actors, with one Play.[18]

The purchase of the rights, plus the financing of the folio, must have been a huge investment. The costs of paper and printing for large works often proved financially ruinous to English publishers who relied on imported paper.[19] Moseley's emphasis on the cost in his 'The Stationer to the Readers' is unlikely to be exaggeration for effect:

> 'Twere vain to mention the *Chargeablenesse* of this Work; for those who own'd the *Manuscripts*, too well knew their value to make a cheap estimate of any of these *Pieces*, and though another joyn'd with me in the *Purchase* and *Printing*, yet the *Care & Pains* was

[15] F. R. Johnson, 'Notes on English Retail Book-prices, 1550–1640' has, for example, Marlowe's *Edward II* priced at sixpence in 1595 (the year after its publication), in a Cambridge physician's library list. Johnson's assertion that 'about 1635 a sudden rise in the prices of books occurs, amounting to at least 40 per cent' is not substantiated by the 1641 Moseley list, however.

[16] The list is printed by Bentley, *Jacobean and Caroline Stage* (hereafter *JCS*), vol. I, pp. 65–6.

[17] SR, 4 Sept. 1646 (49 plays entered to Moseley and Robinson) and SR, 9 Sept. 1653 (42 or 58 plays entered to Moseley alone; the total is doubtful, because of confusion over subtitles).

[18] Quoted by Bentley, *JCS*, vol. II, p. 505. Jose and Jack were the King's Men actors Joseph Taylor and John Lowin. Moseley appealed for the lost play in his preface to the Beaumont and Fletcher folio, saying that the manuscript had been borrowed and not returned.

[19] In the 1580s the printer Henry Bynneman was apparently ruined financially by his attempt to publish a large dictionary, and the publication of Foxe's '*Book of Martyrs*' involved John Day in borrowing large sums (Barnard and Bell, 'The Inventory of Henry Bynneman'). By 1632 it was beyond the scope of any individual to finance the Foxe work, with the price set at 46s. 8d. per volume, and needing sixteen partners to handle its reprinting (Jackson, *Records*, 434).

wholly mine, which I found to be more then you'l easily imagine, unless you knew into how many hands the Originalls were dispersed. They are all now happily met in this Book, having escaped these *Publike Troubles*, free and unmangled.

No details of the edition size are known, so we can only guess as to the size of Moseley and Robinson's investment. An edition size of 1,000 copies, perhaps even more, seems likely, since there was no second edition until 1679. Peter Blayney suggests that the Shakespeare folio of 1623 was probably printed in an edition of no more than 750 copies, since after nine years a new edition was needed. If the gap between first and second editions is a good guide, then the absence of a second edition of Beaumont and Fletcher until 1679 argues a large edition size. The pre-eminence of Beaumont and Fletcher amongst playgoers and play--readers throughout the century would indicate a market at least equal in size to that for the Shakespeare folio, so Moseley and Robinson must have printed enough copies not only to satisfy immediate demand but also to keep the market supplied for the next three decades. Precise estimates are difficult, but using Blayney's calculations for the Shakespeare folio and what we know of the pricing of Jonson's folio as guides, we can point to an initial investment in paper and printing costs of between £245 and £330 for an edition of 1,000; a larger print run of 1,500 could bring the costs to as much as £480. To the costs of paper and printing should be added the initial cost of buying the rights to the plays, such incidental expenses as fees for Stationers' Register entries, and perhaps some additional payments made to individuals to persuade them to release manuscript copies in their possession.[20]

Robinson, it seems, was a backer rather than an active mover in the enterprise. Buying the rights, presumably from the ten actors who signed the dedication (of whom John Lowin was the first signatory), did not necessarily mean that copies of the manuscripts simply changed hands. Rather, what the transaction involved was the transfer of the right to publish. The fact that in Moseley's Stationers' Register entries the titles of plays were sometimes garbled suggests that the clerk was working from a list, rather than from actual manuscript copies of the plays.[21] Moseley still needed to track down at least some of the copies whose rights he had bought, but which the King's Men had lost, mislaid or lent out. His failure to find *The Wild-Goose Chase* indicates that this was not always an easy task, and the statement about the missing play suggests that Moseley was holding out some hope until the last moment that it would turn up.

The question which obviously arises is why Moseley and his 'silent partner' Robinson should go to such trouble and expense to bring out what would be an expensive book in a format which, for plays, was unusual. Jonson's folio (volume one) sold for nine or ten shillings unbound; the Shakespeare first folio cost fifteen shillings unbound and prices of sixteen shillings, eighteen shillings and sixpence, and twenty-two shillings are recorded for

the 1632 edition. Binding made the volumes still more expensive: Jonson's folio in a plain calf binding cost thirteen or fourteen shillings, and more elaborate bindings would add significantly to the purchaser's bill. What little evidence we have of book prices suggests that there was some inflation in this period. Why produce, at a time of political and financial uncertainty, an expensive book of this kind; a book, moreover, of old plays?

Martin Butler's discussion of the folio as an extravagant statement of royalist propaganda goes some way to explaining the motivation of the volume. Its dedication to Philip, Earl of Pembroke and Montgomery, reminding him of his patronage to the 'sweet Swan of Avon' and referring to the stage as 'now withered, and condemn'd, as we feare, to a long Winter and sterilitie' reads as a plea that Pembroke should support the now out-of-work actors. Shirley, the company's associated dramatist before the closure, supplied a preface 'To the Reader' which laments 'the Authentick witt that made Blackfriars an Academy' and offers reading as a substitute for seeing:

> And now Reader in this Tragicall Age where the Theater hath been so much out-acted, congratulate thy owne happinesse, that in this silence of the Stage, thou hast a liberty to reade these inimitable Playes.

The past is still within reach:

> It is not so remote in Time, but very many Gentlemen may remember these Authors & some familiar in their conversation deliver them upon every pleasant occasion so fluent, to talke a Comedy...

The commendatory verses pledge the allegiance, as it were, of a host of prominent writers and royalist public figures. But the publication of the volume was not simply an act of loyalist fervour on the part of Moseley and Robinson: to invest so heavily they must have made some serious calculation of the likely market. Recent discussions of the 1630s have emphasized the differentiation in playhouse repertories and in their audiences in this period. The Blackfriars, in the years preceding the war, had a prestige which the open-air public theatres did not, and in Butler's words 'it is clear that a flourishing literary world was gradually being established' (Butler, 105). The circulation of plays as literary texts was part of that process, and there is evidence that gentleman-connoisseurs were borrowing, lending, copying out, and collecting playbooks. Moseley's own remarks in the Beaumont and Fletcher folio suggest as much: a person of quality's borrowing of the manuscript of *The Wild-Goose Chase*, and its subsequent loss 'by the negligence of a Servant' points to the lending and circulation of plays in this form. Moseley's sales pitch

---

[20] An edition size of 1,500 is not out of the question. In 1639 a Davenant play was to be printed in an edition of 1,500 (Jackson, *Records*, 325).

[21] The SR entry of 4 Sept. 1646, while not identical to the Lord Chamberlain's list of 1641, contains several groups of plays which are given in exactly the same order as in the 1641 list. Perhaps the common source is a list held by the King's Men, now lost.

includes a comparison of the relative costs of his printed volume with the going rate for manuscript copies of single plays:

> Heretofore when Gentlemen desired but a Copy of any of these Playes, the meanest piece here…cost them more then foure times the price you pay for the whole Volume.

Moseley may be exaggerating for effect ('four times' would mean that manuscript copies cost £3 or £4 each); but it indicates the existence of a flourishing market for manuscript plays. His knowledge that gentlemen *cognoscenti* were prepared to pay extravagant prices for manuscript copies must have encouraged Moseley in his assessment of the financial risks—and potential profits—involved in this unusual venture. The rapid growth of Moseley's publishing activities in the following years suggest that his investment paid off, and that he himself was instrumental in developing a market for printed plays which capitalized on the already established interest in the collection of manuscripts.[22] In the following years (see Appendix) he continued to put together collections of plays and poems, though his excursion into folio format was perhaps not entirely successful. In his preface to the Cartwright collection of 1651, which was an even more elaborate (and elaborately royalist) endeavour than the Beaumont and Fletcher folio, he explains that octavo has been preferred to folio because 'it is such weather that the most ingenious have least money'. Moseley may have created a selling point out of his own need to keep down paper and printing costs. Equally, though, he may have recognized the declining spending-power of his customers. By 1651, many of the royalists remaining in England found their disposable income severely limited. In 1643 Parliament had ordered the sequestration of the estates of those giving assistance to the King; in 1645, another order provided for royalists to regain their estates by 'compounding' (Ashton, *English Civil War*, 191, 269). After Charles's execution, with the restoration of monarchy an unlikely prospect, royalists at home and those exiled abroad negotiated to pay large fines and forfeits in order to hold on to a portion of their property, and many were reduced to living on credit while these negotiations went on.

The question remains, what are plays by Middleton (and others) doing in the folio? The two Middleton plays, *Nice Valour* and *Wit at Several Weapons*, are not the only plays written by authors other than Beaumont and Fletcher inserted into the volume. Moseley claims them all, of course, as genuine:

> as it is all New, so here is not any thing Spurious or impos'd; I had the Originalls from such as received them from the Authors themselves; by Those, and none other, I publish this Edition.
>
> And as here's nothing but what is genuine and Theirs, so you will finde here are no Omissions: you have not onely All I could get, but All that you must euer expect. For (besides those which were

formerly printed) there is not any Piece written by these Authours, either Joyntly or Severally, but what are now publish'd to the World in this Volume.[23]

This is, of course, what connoisseur buyers would want to hear. If Moseley had been seriously concerned to establish authenticity, help was at hand: Sir Aston Cokayne, who wrote one of the commendatory verses, knew that some of the attributions were spurious, and protested on behalf of Massinger in particular:

To Mr. Humphrey Mosley and Mr. Humphrey Robinson

> In the large book of Playes you late did print
> (In Beaumonts and in Fletchers name) why in't
> Did you not justice? give to each his due?
> For Beaumont (of those many) writ in few:
> And Massinger in other few; the Main
> Being sole Issues of sweet Fletchers brain.
> Fletchers chief bosom-friend inform'd me so.
> Ith' next impression therefore justice do,
> And print their old ones in one volume too:
> For Beaumonts works, & Fletchers should come forth
> With all the right belonging to their worth.[24]

No one, however, protested on behalf of Middleton. What is interesting here is that the myth of Beaumont and Fletcher's lifelong collaboration is already in place, and that other playwrights are sucked in to the newly created canon. The heyday of Beaumont and Fletcher is already part of a golden past, and the gentility of these two playwrights is in keeping with the emerging status of plays as a gentlemanly interest. As well as praising their intelligence and 'Wit' ('being furnished with Arts and Sciences by that liberall education they had at the University'), Moseley is careful to mention 'those Noble Families, whence [Beaumont] was descended' and 'those Gentlemen that were his acquaintance when he was of the Inner Temple'. These playwrights are thus claimed as 'one of us' for the gentleman-connoisseur of royalist sympathies. Middleton could hardly be as appealing. The two Middleton plays which were published in the folio were clearly late arrivals. Having bought the rights and acquired copies of twenty-five of the twenty-six plays he intended to use (*The Wild-Goose Chase* failed to turn up until some years later), Moseley then acquired copies of four more plays, which were added to the Stationers' Register entry of 1646.[25] He split up the copy into eight sections and distributed them among several printers but, presumably while printing was going on, he obtained five more manuscript plays, which included *Nice Valour*

---

[22] Harold Love, *Scribal Publication in Seventeenth-Century England*, p. 67, quotes Roger North as mentioning '3 or 4' guineas as the usual price for a manuscript presented by the author. See Love, p. 64, for similar prices for music, and pp. 65–70 for the authorial publication of play manuscripts.

[23] 'The Stationer to the Readers', Beaumont and Fletcher *Comedies and Tragedies*, 1647, sig. A4.

[24] Cockayne, *Chain of Golden Poems*, 1658; the poem is printed by Reed, p. 67.

[25] The plays must have arrived after the SR entry of 1646, possibly from a different source, and they were not entered until 1660.

and *Wit at Several Weapons*.[26] Thus Middleton was a last-minute entrant in the folio, but once included, the two plays stayed in the canon, being reprinted in the enlarged edition of 1679 and being transferred between stationers as part of that collection of plays. Thomas Berger has observed in relation to Shakespeare that, once 'folio'd', plays are never again set free.[27] They become part of a particular collection, associated with a particular author, and as property the rights move *en bloc* between stationers. Once they have appeared in folio, the plays hardly ever again appear in quarto editions until the adapted quartos of the later seventeenth century. This phenomenon is observable in the case of Middleton not only here, with the two plays which became part of the Beaumont and Fletcher folio, but also with *Timon of Athens* and *Macbeth*, which were sucked into the 1623 Shakespeare folio, and with *The Puritan* and *A Yorkshire Tragedy*, which became 'Shakespeare's' in the 1664 folio. The latter two, unlike the others, had been published in separate quarto editions before they appeared in the Shakespeare folio. Once published in folio, however, neither appeared separately in quarto again during the seventeenth century.

The market for printed plays

We know that collections of printed plays were being accumulated as early as 1610. Sir John Harington's papers contain what appears to be a catalogue of 135 plays in his possession. That he was a serious collector seems certain: a third of his collection were plays published before 1600 (a quarter of all plays known to have been in print in that period); he had half of the plays known to have been published between 1590 and 1599; and he had copies of six out of every seven plays printed between 1600 and 1609–10, when he apparently stopped collecting. Henry Oxinden's list of between 1663 and 1665 is assumed by Greg (on the evidence of the dates of the plays) to refer to a collection made many years earlier—the bulk of it by 1615. But Oxinden's activity as a collector need not necessarily be contemporary with the publication dates of the plays: Oxinden's list, although of plays which were old in 1663, might nonetheless be evidence of a collection made more recently—even as late as the 1640s or 1650s.[28] It is the possibility of a new market in 'old' plays (in manuscript, in original early sixteenth-century printed editions, and in newly printed form) that I would like to explore further.

Several developments in the trade in the middle years of the century suggest that publishers and booksellers were growing more conscious of their potential markets and were moving towards offering their customers—that is, both retail booksellers and individual customers—more information about the books they could supply. One development was the compilation of book catalogues. The earliest known catalogue of English publications was compiled and published by Andrew Maunsell in 1595. In it, books are divided into broad subject areas: divinity, mathematics, and so on. As Greg observes 'Maunsell, like Sir

Thomas Bodley, regarded plays as beneath notice' (*BEPD*, vol. III, p. 1294). Maunsell's catalogue, like Jaggard's of 1618, and like the Frankfurt Mess-Katalog, was probably aimed at booksellers, rather than individual buyers, as a trade publication to inform booksellers of what books were available and from which printers and booksellers they could be obtained. The long series of Frankfurt Book Fair Catalogues, which informed Europe's booksellers of the new books traded at the fair, included no works in English, though John Bill's English edition of the catalogue (1617–27) included from 1622 some English books as a supplement. In 1631 a catalogue of recent English and Latin books appeared, with the stated intention of being the first in an annual series (a kind of early *Books in Print*) but no subsequent editions appeared. Up to this point, plays were very rarely included in catalogues, and were never listed in any quantity. Plays, it seems, were of little significance in the context of the trade as a whole.

The earliest known catalogues specifically of plays appeared in the mid-1650s. Rogers and Ley issued 'An Exact and perfect Catalogue of all *Playes* that are Printed' as part of their edition of *The Careless Shepherdess* (1656), and in the same year Edward Archer's edition of *Old Law* included his lengthy catalogue of plays for sale, which is clearly based on the recent Rogers and Ley catalogue, but elaborated to give more names of authors and to categorize plays by type. That these two catalogues were printed in editions of single plays suggests that the booksellers of 1656 were assuming a specific play-buying market. The size of that market is difficult to judge, and estimates of the size of the playgoing public before the closures are of little help since the proportion of the audiences capable of reading, rather than hearing and seeing, a play would be only a part of the whole. Gurr (76) points to the Blackfriars as the playhouse most frequently named on the title-pages of plays published during Charles I's reign, and it seems likely that it was especially amongst the audiences of the 'private' hall playhouses that purchasers and readers of printed play texts would have been found. A sixpenny quarto play would have been too expensive for an apprentice or servant who could afford to watch a play at an outdoor theatre for a penny. But for those who could afford to pay sixpence for a Lord's room, or the much higher prices at the indoor theatres, sixpence for a copy of a play would not be difficult to find. The hall playhouses, of which the Blackfriars was, by the 1630s, the most socially select, had a minimum admission price of sixpence; a place on a bench in the pit cost one shilling and sixpence and a box alongside the stage would cost two

---

[26] For details of the make-up of the volume and a reconstruction of events, see *BEPD*, vol. III, pp. 1013–17.
[27] Thomas Berger, 'Shakespeare in Caroline England: Problems and Possibilities', unpublished paper given at the Society for Textual Scholarship Conference, April 1993.
[28] *BEPD*, vol. III, pp. 1306 ff. and 1313 ff. prints both lists. Both collections contained plays by Middleton. Harington had copies of *Mad World*, *Your Five Gallants*, *Puritan Widow*, *Yorkshire Tragedy*, *Phoenix*, *Michaelmas Term*. Oxinden's list includes *Yorkshire Tragedy*, *Game at Chess*, *Michaelmas Term*; the play listed as *The Converted Courtesan* was the second edition of *Honest Whore*.

shillings and sixpence. For literate playgoers used to these prices, the sixpenny price of a quarto would be a manageable sum. Gurr cites the accounts of Edward Heath, who between 1629 and 1631 made forty-nine visits to playhouses, regularly paying one and sixpence or two shillings for his seat. During the same period, he bought ten play books. For some enthusiasts, playgoing and play-reading were complementary, and there is in particular evidence that students of the Inns of Court 'confined themselves to the hall playhouses and their repertoire of playbooks' (Gurr, 26-7, 76). A market for printed plays thus pre-existed the closure of the theatres, but it consisted of a specific sector of the total playgoing public; once playgoing became impossible, this same segment—defined by social status and wealth as well as literacy—became the target for enterprising publishers like Moseley, who enticed them to redirect towards booksellers the disposable cash no longer spent on performances. Since the theatre had been a lucrative commercial enterprise in the 1630s, money which had then been spent on theatre-going must now have become available for redistribution to other parts of the economy.

Moseley's activity as a retailer of plays (the 1641 bill) and his large-scale venture into play publishing (the Stationers' Register entry of 1646 followed by the Beaumont and Fletcher folio in 1647) are significant moments, both in his career and in the development of the market for plays. But his activity between 1647 and 1656, the year of Rogers and Ley's and Archer's play catalogues, is also important to the direction of play-publishing in particular and 'literary' publishing more widely. Like other bookseller-publishers, Moseley might add, sometimes to fill out the last leaf of a book, a list which acted as an advertisement of other books available from his shop. This was becoming a usual practice, and is in itself unremarkable. What is remarkable, however, is the extent to which this small advertisement became more and more elaborated, until it took on the character of an extensive book catalogue, in which plays became a substantial category. While short advertising lists integral to the text continued to appear in his books (for example, his 1653 edition of *The Changeling* advertises as 'newly printed' a handful of plays: *The Wild-Goose Chase*, *The Widow*, Shirley's *Five Plays* and *The Spanish Gypsy*), Moseley began to have printed more extensive lists which could be issued either separately or bound in with publications of the same size. It seems that his printer kept the type standing, and updated it regularly to take into account not only Moseley's most recent publications but also his plans for those not yet printed. Greg has distinguished seven different versions of these separate lists between 1650 and 1660, each more elaborate than its predecessor. Among Moseley's innovations as the lists progressed were more elaborate subject categories, specific information about the latest publications, and information about books to be published shortly. The first of these lists, dated 1650, is printed on four octavo leaves and simply divides the books into three sections: histories, poems, and sermons and divinity. The following year he

introduces new categories to signal his most recent publications: 'Bookes newly Printed this present yeare...', 'More Bookes newly printed...' and 'These Bookes I have now in the Presse'. By 1653 the stress on newness has grown; this year's books are now further subdivided, to distinguish 'Books printed this Tearm', and after the list of books in the press are more, headed 'These Bookes I doe purpose to Print very Speedily'. In the 1654 list, each subject-category in the list (including plays) has a 'lately printed' subsection, and the 'Choice Poems' list is followed by a new section, 'Incomparable Comedies and Tragedies written by several Ingenious Authors'. By 1656, what had started out as a four-leaf list has more than doubled to ten leaves; his last list, issued in 1660 when Moseley was ill (he died in January 1661), has sixteen leaves and the last section perhaps acknowledges his precarious state of health in substituting for 'very Speedily' (in the usual 'These Bookes I doe purpose to Print very Speedily') the words 'Deo Volente'.[29]

Moseley's innovations in advertising were a response to his growing involvement in publishing. Before the venture of the 1647 folio, he had issued a few of what Greg calls 'Collections'—collections of several works by single authors: Milton's poems in 1645, Shirley and Suckling in 1646. After 1647 he became the most prolific publisher in this line of book: of seven such works published between 1645 and 1649, he was the publisher of six. In all, between 1645 and 1659, he published seventeen such collections, far more than any other publisher: of Milton (1645), Shirley (1646, 1653, 1655), Suckling (1646, 1648, 1658, 1659), Beaumont and Fletcher (1647), Cavendish (1649), Carew (1651), Brome (1653), May (1654), Massinger (1655), Carlell (1657), and Middleton (1657) (see Appendix).

Apart from the evidence of the surviving books themselves, we can turn to the Stationers' Register for information about Moseley's development as a publisher. The striking thing about Moseley's entrance of copies is the way in which he frequently entered not just one or two books, but long lists of titles.[30] In 1646, as well as the large block entry of King's Men's plays, he is found buying up copies from other booksellers (sometimes, half-shares in titles, held by different stationers, which are then reunited, as it were, to give Moseley the sole rights). Apart from the 1646 and 1660 entries, made with Robinson and thus dividing the rights between them, Moseley usually entered copies alone, as sole publisher: in 1653 he entered forty-two plays in one lot, as well as acquiring rights in fourteen titles from Marriot. More transfers from other stationers were recorded in 1659, as well eleven books entered to Moseley alone.[31] Moseley was buying up copies

---

[29] The portions of Moseley's lists which contain plays are given by *BEPD*, vol. III, pp. 1173-81, as 'Separate Lists I-VIB'.

[30] While block entries are by no means unusual, and occur earlier than this (for example, in the entries of the ballad partners earlier in the century), Moseley's long entries are unusual in that they contain so many plays.

[31] SR, 4 Oct. 1646; 31 Oct. 1646; 22 Feb. 1648; 12 Apr. 1648; 9 Sept. 1653; 12 Dec. 1653; 20 Dec. 1653; 11 Jun. 1659; 29 Jun. 1660.

at an impressive rate from 1646 onwards; indeed, he was buying up copies at a much faster rate than he could publish them. More than eighty of the plays he entered are now lost, and although a few may have been printed and have subsequently disappeared, it is likely that the majority of them were never printed at all. Moseley's entries in the Stationers' Register remain for nearly all of them the sole record of their existence.[32] The sources of his plays are not recorded, and while a large number can be traced to the King's Men and rather fewer to his buying out of other bookseller-publishers, there remains a number whose provenance is obscure. It is possible that, once he became established as a publisher with a particular interest in plays, private individuals may have offered him their own manuscript copies for use as printer's copy. Dead authors, disbanded acting companies and a now defunct Revels Office could raise no objections. That individual owners felt they were at liberty to offer play manuscripts for publication is clear from Cockayne's preface to the 1658 edition of his poems and plays, where he says that he had intended to print Fletcher's *Mad Lover* with his own verses, having had the manuscript for several years: 'when I found the Players were prohibited to act, I writ these poor Verses with an intention to have had the *Mad Lover* printed single, and them [i.e. his verses] to have waited on it'.[33]

Plays were not, of course, the only kinds of publications issued by Moseley. His interest in contemporary poets (many of royalist tendencies) is clear from the list of collections given above. He also specialized in translations, many of them from French, and many of them romances (such as those by de Scudery) which represented French-exiled royalist taste and presumably, by fashionable extension, therefore appealed to closet royalists at home. If, as Lois Potter has convincingly argued in *Secret Rites and Secret Writing*, romance provided a safe mode of literary discourse for readers of royalist sympathies, then Moseley was clearly out to tap precisely that market. In his prefaces Moseley laments the loss of the King ('the Sun-set of that Majesty from whose auspicious beams he [Suckling] derived his lustre') and the state of the times; in dedicating to Lady Anne Lucas the translation of *Artamenes*, and its continuation (1653, 1654) he offers romance as veiled speech:

> our Author in this hath so laid his Sceans, as to touch upon the greatest Affairs of our Times: for, Designs of War and Peace are better hinted and cut open by a Romance, than by downright Histories; which, being barefac'd, are forc'd to be often too modest and sparing; when these disguiz'd Discourses, freely personating every man and no man, have liberty to speak out.

and

> The former Volume left Cyrus at the Block; This shews what means were us'd to preserve him, a Felicity which all good Princes have not enjoy'd.

Many more examples from Moseley's prefaces could be offered.[34] What is important to note is that he extended and elaborated the idea of the stationer's address to the reader, so that it becomes an important framing device for the texts he offers, and elevates his own taste, as discriminating publisher, as well as focusing the elements of 'wit', nostalgia, latent royalism, and gentlemanly connoisseurship which he sees as appropriate to his readers.

Why publish Middleton?

If this is the characteristic mode of Moseley's publications in the 1650s, what place has Middleton in his publishing programme? During the 1650s Moseley (see Table 2) published first editions of *The Widow* (1652) and *The Changeling* (1653) as quarto single plays, and in 1657 brought out a collection of Middleton plays: *Two New Plays* and *No Wit/Help like a Woman's*. In the context of Moseley's prolific production the Middleton collection is both small-scale and late in Moseley's publishing programme. Earlier publications by Moseley either failed to recognize Middleton's authorship at all (the plays in the Beaumont and Fletcher folio) or represented Middleton as one of a collaborative team: Moseley's edition of *The Widow* is attributed to Jonson, Fletcher, and Middleton, and his *Changeling* names Rowley as joint author. For the first time, the 1657 collection offers Middleton as a single author. As well as these plays, Moseley was accumulating the rights to others by Middleton which remained unpublished until after his death. *Nice Valour* and *Wit at Several Weapons* had already been acquired in 1646 and published in the Beaumont and Fletcher folio of 1647; in the same batch of plays, Moseley entered as his *The Mayor of Quinborough* (formerly known as *Hengist*); and in 1659 the ownership of *The Spanish Gypsy* (by 'Middleton and Rowley') was transferred to him from Richard Marriot, who had published an edition in 1653. It is likely, too, that he was buying up old stocks of plays from other booksellers: in his list of 1660 he was advertising *A Mad World, My Masters*, presumably Spencer's edition of 1640, amongst his own publications.

The question of Middleton's publication by Moseley is—at least in part—answered very simply by the evidence already offered that throughout the period 1646 to 1660 Moseley was buying up every 'old' play that came his way. Middleton's plays came to him as part of job lots bought from acting companies, from individuals who possessed manuscripts, and from other booksellers who transferred their rights to Moseley either as one-off sales to raise cash

---

[32] *BEPD*, vol. II: Lost plays nos 33, 45, 53–7, 58–102, 122–5, 159–84. Of the plays in the SR entry of 9 Sept. 1653 (58 plays), 45 are listed by Greg as lost. Another 27 are lost from the SR entry of 1660 (37 plays).

[33] 'The Authors Apology to the Reader' in Cockayne's *Small Poems* (i.e. *Chain of Golden Poems*), 1658, sig. A3. Reprinted in *BEPD*, vol. III, pp. 1240–1.

[34] Quotations are from 'The Stationer to the Reader', *Artamenes* (1653) and 'To The Right Honourable And Most Perfectly Noble, The Lady Anne Lucas', *The Continuation of Artamenes* (1654). The meaning of the name of the hero, Cyrus, is given in the former as being 'a bright Sun'. Reed, pp. 73–103, usefully brings together a number of Moseley's prefaces and epistles dedicatory.

or, perhaps, to discharge debts to Moseley for books supplied by him wholesale. In a sense, Moseley's buying up of copies was indiscriminate: in concentrating on expanding the market for plays he must have assumed that the copies he acquired would eventually pay off as investments even if he never published them himself. Even without published new editions, Moseley's ownership of rights and of manuscript copies could prove useful. In 1655 Moseley published an anthology of extracts from English plays, compiled by John Cotgrave, with the title *English Treasury of Wit and Language*. The collection is remarkable in that it selects its verse extracts, 1,686 in all, exclusively from plays, whereas previous anthologies had favoured poetry. The plays used as sources are not identified in the text, but Bentley's analysis of the volume indicates an overwhelming concentration on plays published post-1600, and a strong representation of Caroline dramatists. Middleton is represented in the volume by more than a hundred quotations. Notably, *The Mayor of Quinborough* is quoted twelve times, second in frequency among the Middleton plays only to *Fair Quarrel*.[35] Comparison with the 1661 quarto of *The Mayor of Quinborough* and with the two surviving manuscript copies of the play suggests that Cotgrave was using as his source the same manuscript used as the copy-text in 1661. This raises the possibility that as publisher, and perhaps even as instigator of the project, Moseley gave Cotgrave access to his own stock of plays, including those that he had bought but not yet published.[36] The publication of an anthology of this kind in 1655 is entirely consistent with Moseley's development as a play-publisher. *English Treasury* presents drama as the repository of didactic gems; Cotgrave's hierarchy of sources, as expressed by frequency of quotation, mingles the folio 'greats' with contemporary playwrights such as Shirley, Davenant, and Nabbes.[37] The prominence of Greville in the collection is attributed by Bentley to Cotgrave's predilection for moralistic tragedy, to the author's 'exalted rank', and to the relative ease with which passages can be extracted from aphoristic rhymed verse. Cotgrave's own statement 'To the Courteous Reader' claims for drama the virtue of 'Wit' and draws the reader into the circle of 'such as know best use of them':

> indeed the Drammatick Poem seems to me (and many of my friends, better able to judge then I) to have been lately too much slighted, not onely by such, whose Talent falls short in understanding, but by many that have had a tolerable portion of Wit, who through a stiffe and obstinate prejudice, have (in neglecting things of this nature) lost the benefit of many rich and usefull observations, not duly considering, or believing, that the Framers of them, were the most fluent and redundant Wits that this age (or I thinke any other) ever knew...

This is recognizably the language of Moseley's own prefaces, presenting the fruits of Cotgrave's 'Recreation in these much distracted times' to a discerning readership.[38]

In his design and marketing of those Middleton plays which he published in full, Moseley was concerned to 'package' them in line with his own (and his customers') interests. The collection of 1657 is not only a collection of Middleton plays: it is a collection of 'woman' plays. The thematic packaging is unusual and perhaps fortuitous. In looking at his remaining Middleton plays, Moseley must have seen this grouping as a striking possibility; the absence of the other as yet unpublished plays which Moseley could have included, since he owned the rights, suggests a deliberate selection of these three. The 'woman' topic may have had a particular marketing value in 1657. The 1640s and 1650s had seen the emergence into public, and published, debate of women on both sides of the political and religious divide, and the mass petitions of women addressed to Parliament and in support of sectarian and republican ideals had become a joke amongst royalists, who lampooned them in mock-petitions.[39] Vocal and active women, as preachers, writers, sectarian activists, participants in sieges and battles, had exemplified the upturning of the political and social order. At the same time, as petitioners to the parliamentary committees on sequestration and compounding, and as managers of houses, estates and the complicated finances of shattered fortunes, royalist women themselves had taken on public roles as representatives of exiled or disgraced husbands, travelling to London to attend sometimes lengthy hearings. Such wives gained both financial control and an income (allocated by committee) specifically for themselves and their children, and in the process of obtaining their income they experienced an independent life in the city (Fraser, chap. 11). Women had a public presence as never before, and in this context, the collection of three 'women' plays may have had a topical resonance.

Title-pages in Moseley's editions of Middleton plays stress the performances at private playhouses: Blackfriars (*The Widow*) or Drury Lane and Salisbury Court (*The*

[35] Bentley (1943), with a narrower view of the Middleton canon, counts only 78 quotations. See p. 452 for figures based on the canon as defined by this edition.
[36] *English Treasury* deserves full analysis in its own right (Bentley's is a sampling of an annotated copy). The relationship between the plays used by Cotgrave as sources and the known stock of Moseley could thereby be clarified; moreover, the politics of the volume—which may be consistent with Moseley's mode of publishing—need investigation.
[37] Neither Greville nor Nabbes fits easily into a programme of sentimental royalism; neither do some of the writers who figure in Moseley's list of 'collected' poets (such as Milton). I am indebted to Simon Shepherd (private correspondence) for indicating the inadequacy of the category 'royalist' in this context, and the need for a term which would open up a space where royalist and anti-royalist criticism of court might meet (along the lines of Butler's designation 'town').
[38] The politics of the volume might also be illuminated by a comparison with other collections, such as Cox's *Actaeon and Diana* (1655, 1656) and the later *Wits* volumes which, in their presentation of drolls, belong perhaps more to the world of the Red Bull audience than to that of the Blackfriars. For the cultural meaning of 'wit' and a reading of the politics of theatrical place and space, see Shepherd and Womack (1995).
[39] Spoofs on the idea of female parliaments were written by Henry Neville: *The Ladies Parliament* (1647), *The Ladies, a Second Time, Assembled* (1647), and *The Commonwealth of Ladies* (1650). Royalist parodies of women's petitions were *A Remonstrance of the Shee-Citizens of London* (1640) and *The Ladies Remonstrance* (1659). See entry for 'Petitions' (pp. 263-70) in Bell, Parfitt, and Shepherd, *A Biographical Dictionary of English Women Writers*.

Changeling). The preface to *The Widow*, written by Alexander Gough, who had acted with the King's Men at Blackfriars, links Jonson, Fletcher, and Middleton with the achievements of Scipio and Laelius in 'subduing their Countries enemies' and providing their countrymen with 'recreation and delight' in order 'to banish...folly and sadness'. A variant of the 1653 *Changeling*, printed without an imprint, was possibly intended for presentation or private circulation rather than for sale (*BEPD*, no. 712). The collection issued in 1657 claims Middleton as an important author: an engraved portrait appears in both parts, *Women, Beware Women* has a commendatory poem by Nathaniel Richards, an address 'To the Reader' emphasizes Middleton's 'Excellent Poems' and 'Reputation', and lists of dramatis personae are given. Moseley's extensive booklist of 246 items is also part of the package. In 1640 John Spencer had been hesitant about the old-fashioned style of *A Mad World*; by 1657 Moseley was offering Middleton as a high-status commodity. Moseley's 'To the Reader' is, perhaps, revealing:

> I was not a little confident but that his name would prove as great an Inducement for thee to Read, as me to Print them: Since those Issues of His Brain that have already seen the Sun, have by their worth gained themselves a free entertainment amongst all that are ingenious: And I am most certain, that these will in no way lessen his Reputation, nor hinder his Admission to any Noble and Recreative Spirits.

The idea of 'seeing the light of day' is conventional enough, but Moseley's version of it ('that have already seen the Sun') has, perhaps, more point. Signalled by the familiar use of 'for thee' (rather than 'for you'), the 'Sun', a loaded term politically, may suggest to a 'connoisseur' reader a courtly context for Middleton's plays. If 'the Sun' is indeed a coded claim to royal associations for Middleton's plays, performed by the King's Men and even for the King as audience, then 'all that are ingenious'—the connoisseur-readers/collectors of plays—are positioned very firmly as royalists. And it is to these 'Noble...Spirits', whose leisure and income allows them their 'Recreative' pursuits, that Moseley's Middleton is offered as representative of a culture which Moseley's product helps to sustain. As the Beaumont and Fletcher folio demonstrates, the elevation of playwright-as-noble-genius and the myth-making of a golden past was already happening in 1647. Ten years later, the process has co-opted Middleton into the myth of cavalier sensibility. The original context of Middleton's career, his politics, his relationship to the stage and to the authorities are all irrelevant, forgotten or suppressed. The author is dead. There are no friends to speak up for him as Cockayne did for Massinger. Middleton's work is a commercial property to be exploited to best advantage (i.e. profit) by its owner. The free market economy has apparently triumphed.

Competition

The limited extent of that triumph can be seen in what happened to Middleton's plays in the early years of the Restoration. The logic of the operation of the free market (we are told) is competition. So far, throughout the 1650s, Moseley had dominated the trade in play-publishing, though he did not have a monopoly. Some publishers made an occasional venture into the field: both the Rogers and Ley play catalogue and Archer's edition of *Old Law* with his catalogue are apparently isolated examples, possibly opportunist ventures into a market which Moseley's prodigious advertising and series of regularly updated publications lists had helped to shape. The Meighen/Bedell/Collins partnership presented potentially more serious competition. Richard Meighen, older than Moseley and the publisher of Jonson's folio of 1616, during the 1630s established a strong line in play-publishing, with editions of *Michaelmas Term*, *The Phoenix*, quarto plays by Fletcher, Shakespeare, Goffe, Shakerley and Davenant, and a share in the 1632 Shakespeare folio and the second and third Jonson folios. Meighen died around 1642, just as Moseley was developing his business; Meighen's widow, Mercy, joined forces with Gabriel Bedell to keep the business going, and in 1650 Thomas Collins joined the partnership. But while the partners continued to publish plays previously owned by Richard Meighen, and issued advertising lists of their plays in 1653 and 1656, their plays are nearly all plays from the 1630s; few new plays were acquired and as the business prospered and diversified Bedell moved into law books, Collins issued proclamations on behalf of the Council of State, and Mercy, having married Collins, was involved in importing Bibles.[40] Their plays, while remaining part of their trade, were not the focus of the business after Richard's death.

The Restoration, however, brought less orthodox competition, which found an opening during the first three or four years of the 1660s when some confusion (as the changes consequent on the restoration of monarchy were worked through) encouraged entrepreneurial initiative. The resulting struggle for pre-eminence in the new order affected both the book trade and the theatre. Stamping out the republican press was a particular priority for the authorities, and new legislation on printing centred on the repression of sedition. The revival of the theatre gave rise to disputes and even legal challenges, as rival theatres and acting companies claimed rights which had lapsed or been overruled during the Interregnum. New plays were urgently needed; meanwhile, the rights to the old repertoires were fiercely contested. The survival of a letter

---

[40] The Meighens' publishing activity can be traced through STC; see also Plomer, and *BEPD*, vol. III for advertising lists. A Mercy Collins was prosecuted in 1653 for importing English Bibles printed abroad (see *CSPD* entries for 7 Jun. and 16 Jun. 1653 [Council of State, vol. I 69, 236-40, 335]). This may be Richard's widow, remarried to her new business partner, or possibly a daughter of the same name. A remarriage and change of surname would explain Plomer's assumption that Mercy Meighen died or retired at around this time. A son of Thomas Collins, named Gabriel (after Gabriel Bedell?) was freed in 1685 (McKenzie, *Apprentices*, no. 919).

from Moseley to Sir Henry Herbert, who was trying to assert the traditional prerogative of the Revels Office against the grants made by Charles II to new theatre companies, suggests that Moseley had a direct link, through his ownership of publishing rights, to the revival in performance. The letter was endorsed, in Herbert's hand, 'From m^r Mosely Concerninge the Players &c. Aug. 30-60.':

Sr

I haue bene very much solicited by the Gentlemen Actors of the Red Bull for a Note under my hand to certifie unto your Wor^p. what Agreement I had made with M^r. Rhodes of the Cock-Pitt Playhouse; Truly (S^r) I am so farr from any Agreement with him, that I neuer so much as treated with him, nor wth. Any from him; neither did I euer consent Directly or Indirectly, y^t hee, or any others should Act any Playes that doe belong to mee without my Knowledge, and Consent had & Procured. And the same allsoe I doe Certifie concerning The Whitefryers Playhouse, & Players. S^r. This is all I haue to trouble you withall att Present, & Therefore I shall take the Boldnesse to,

Remaine,
Your Wor^p. most Humble Seruant
Humphrey Moseley[41]

John Rhodes's company of players at the Cockpit were being harassed on two fronts: by Davenant and Killigrew, the recipients of Charles's favour, who complained of Rhodes's exorbitant admission fees, and by Herbert, who persisted in acting as if he retained his pre-war power. Charged by Herbert with justifying his erection of a playhouse 'at yor p⟨er⟩ill', Rhodes ignored Herbert's warrant and sent the terse reply 'That the Kinge did authorise Him'. Herbert insisted that Rhodes reduce his rates in line with Blackfriars prices, and sent to the players a further instruction:

And you are Hereby further required to bringe or sende to me All such old Plaies As you doe Intende to Acte at ye saide playhouse, that they may be reformed of Prophanes & Ribaldry, at yor perill

A petition from the Cockpit players complained both of Killigrew's attempts to suppress them, and of Herbert's powerlessness to intervene, despite their weekly payment to him of protection money. The company eventually made terms with Davenant—terms entirely favourable to him—in November 1660, and the list of players bound by the contract includes a John Moseley.[42] It is conceivable that this John Moseley was related to the bookseller; perhaps the suspicion of a deal between Humphrey Moseley and Rhodes was aroused by a personal connection with the actor in Rhodes's company. Whatever the reason, and despite Moseley's denial of any such deal, the implication of the exchange between him and Herbert raises the question of how far, at the Restoration, Moseley's rights to plays might extend. In particular, having bought up the

plays of a whole company, as he did with the King's Men, did he now assume that the plays were 'his': not only his to publish, but his to license, in effect, for performance by an approved company? The episode remains a mystery, but as well as illustrating the confusion over rights, grants and monopolies at the Restoration, and the apparent muddle of old and new claims, it gives a hint that Moseley's practical and financial interest in plays as commodities may have stretched beyond publication to performance itself. John Rhodes, according to Downes's *Roscius Anglicanus*, had himself been a bookseller; the only record of such activity is that a man of that name was selling second-hand books in 1628, and it is not clear whether the bookseller and the former wardrobe-keeper at the Blackfriars were the same person.[43] That Moseley, despite his denials to Herbert, might have come to some agreement with Rhodes is suggested both by the repertoire of the company, which as listed by Downes consisted almost entirely of plays bought up by Moseley, and by the appearance of John Moseley as actor. Little is known of the actor, except that he played women's parts until the replacement of boys by women in 1661 and (again, according to Downes) died around 1673.[44] John Moseley was presumably a young man in 1660, and it is tempting to connect negotiations between Humphrey Moseley and John Rhodes with an apprenticeship for John Moseley. Until evidence of the relationship between the two Moseleys is found, however, that remains conjecture.

Something of the new circumstances arising at the Restoration can be deduced from an examination of the Middleton plays which appeared in 1661 and 1662. Two plays, *The Mayor of Quinborough* (1661) and *Anything for a Quiet Life* (1662), appeared in print for the first time in these years as well as a second edition of *The Spanish Gypsy*, attributed in its first edition of 1653 to Rowley and Middleton, and reprinted in 1661. This second edition of *The Spanish Gypsy*, a play owned by Moseley though never published by him, appeared in 1661 in two variants: one published for Robert Crofts which advertised his shop, the Crown, as the source of 'most sort of playes', and the other for Francis Kirkman, advertising his shop, the John Fletcher's Head, as able to satisfy the demands of 'any Gentlemen' who there 'may be furnished with all the Playes that were ever yet Printed'. Crofts's version lists as 'Printed for Robert Crofts' three plays, two of which are *Old Law* and *The Careless Shepherdess*—that is, the two 1656 plays containing Archer's and Rogers and Ley's play catalogues. Presumably Crofts had acquired copies of the 1656 editions and was passing them off as his own publications; it is interesting that he chooses to publicize

---

41 Moseley's letter is now in the Harvard Theatre Collection; see Thaler for a facsimile (facing p. 122) and Herbert's endorsement (p. xiii), and Bawcutt (p. 229) for a transcription of Moseley's text.
42 Bawcutt documents the long battle for control (pp. 88–93), and prints the surviving documents (pp. 229–40).
43 For Downes's claim, see the Milhous and Hume edition of *Roscius Anglicanus*, p. 43 (p. 17 in the original text); Plomer.
44 *Roscius Anglicanus*, ed. Milhous and Hume, 44, 46, 74, 115.

himself as a play-seller by advertising those particular plays, which because of their catalogues must have had a particular attraction for play collectors. Kirkman was not a stationer at all: it is clear from his prefaces to later publications that he had been a scrivener, that he had collected plays himself, had amassed a considerable collection, and that—his business as a scrivener having done badly—he decided to set up shop with his own collection as the nucleus of his stock.[45] He had already attempted bookselling in 1656, but had done badly, and returned to his trade as a scrivener. Clearly the Restoration gave him confidence to try again, and in association with the stationers Nathaniel Brooke, Thomas Johnson, and Henry Marsh he began to publish plays. The first edition of Middleton's *Anything for a Quiet Life* was printed by Johnson for Kirkman and Marsh in 1662. The source for their edition may have been a manuscript in Kirkman's collection; prior to this edition, there is no mention of the play in the Stationers' Register, and the publishers of this edition did not themselves enter it as theirs. The title-page, as is usual, connects the play with a specific playhouse and company. Although in this case there is nothing to suggest that Kirkman and Marsh did not have the right to publish the play—the Stationers' Register has no record of a prior claim—it remains the case that many of the plays published by Johnson, Kirkman, and Marsh were, strictly speaking, pirate editions: that is, they reprinted plays owned by other stationers who had registered their ownership in the usual way with the Stationers' Company. Johan Gerritsen has identified ten pirated plays published in 1661 which can be attributed to this group, with Kirkman as the central figure. For a time they got away with it, though clearly they caused a great deal of annoyance to the rightful owners of the plays they pirated. Moseley's rights in *The Spanish Gypsy*, for example, were contravened by their edition, and although Moseley himself had not got around to printing the play, a pirate edition would sabotage any future edition, since it is unlikely that the market—even though swollen by the influx of the courtly and fashionable to London—would be able to sustain two editions of the same play. In effect, such piracies scuppered the investment in rights which Moseley had bought up over the previous decade.

Kirkman was not only selling plays, but was stepping into exactly the area of specialization which Moseley had defined for himself. In *The Thracian Wonder* Kirkman says: 'If any Gentlemen please to repair to my House afore--said, they may be furnished with all manner of English, or French Histories, Romances, or Poetry; which are to be sold, or read for reasonable Considerations.' Perhaps in emulation of Moseley, Kirkman habitually supplied prefaces to his publications, and it is worth quoting at length from one of them (from *A Cure for a Cuckold*, 1661), to demonstrate the difference of approach. Here Kirkman outlines his own career, and presents himself as a reader/collector turned publisher:

Gentlemen,

It was not long since I was onely a Book-Reader, and not a Bookseller, which Quality (my former Employment somewhat failing, and I being unwilling to be idle) I have now lately taken on me. It hath been my fancy and delight (ere since I knew any thing) to converse with Books; and the pleasure I have taken in those of this nature (viz. *Plays*) hath bin so extraordinary, that it hath bin much to my cost; for I have been (as we term it) a Gatherer of *Plays* for some years, and I am confident I have more of several sorts than any man in *England*, Book-seller, or other: I can at any time shew 700 in number, which is within a small matter all that were ever printed. Many of these I have several times over, and intend as I sell, to purchase more; All, or any of which, I shall be ready either to sell or lend to you upon reasonable Considerations...

The Expedient of Curing a Cuckold (after the maner set down in this *Play*) hath bin tried to my knowledge, and therefore I may say *Probatum est*. I should, I doubt, be too tedious, or else I would say somewhat in defence of this, and in Commendation of *Plays* in general, but I question not but you have read what abler Pens than mine have writ in their Vindication. Gentlemen, I hope you will so incourage me in my beginnings, that I may be induced to proceed to do you service, and that I may frequently have occasion in this nature, to subscribe myself

Your Servant
Francis Kirkman.

His tone, compared with Moseley's, is confidential, chatty and enthusiastic. In his later prefaces, he reminisces about clandestine performances of drolls at the Red Bull and elsewhere, grows sentimental about actors, and speaks of the manuscripts he has which he would like to see in print. He offers plays for sale and on loan, and is concerned to collect more. A dig at Moseley is perhaps intended by Kirkman's remark in *The Thracian Wonder* that in promising to publish more plays 'I shall not (as some others of my profession have done) promise more then I will perform in a year or two, or it may be never...'. Moseley's elaborate advertising of plays 'in the press' and to be printed 'speedily' did not always bear fruit, and he certainly bought up copies beyond the rate at which he could publish them, holding on to many (like *The Spanish Gypsy*, *The Mayor of Quinborough*, and the lost Middleton play entered in the Stationers' Register in 1653 as 'The Puritan Maid, Modest wife & wanton widdow') which he never published. In another Marsh/Kirkman publication, *The Wits, or, Sport upon Sport* (1662), a collection of drolls and extracts from plays which includes an image of *The Changeling* in its title--page woodcut, Marsh's preface deliberately refuses the pretensions which Moseley's style of preface, projecting

---

[45] A number of his prefaces are given by *BEPD*, vol. III.

the publisher as literary critic, had consistently promoted. Here Marsh pokes fun at the 'literary' publisher's usual style of address to the reader, by asserting

> Now I must tell you, my *Plot* with my *Humours* is clearly for sale; for I intend to raise no other reputation to my self then that of Ready Money...

Clearly there were those in the trade, Marsh among them, who saw Moseley's public image (at its most hyperbolic in the Beaumont and Fletcher folio and in the Cartwright collection of 1651) as one which conveniently effaced the connections between literature and profit. In bursting Moseley's literary bubble, Marsh reminds us, and his readers, that publishing is a capitalist enterprise. In the same volume, Marsh prints a long list of books for sale which, in its elaborate layout, looks as if it is modelled on Moseley's series of lists. Kirkman and Marsh were moving in on Moseley's territory shamelessly.

By 1662 the competition between the Moseley and the Kirkman/Johnson/Marsh faction had become intense. Moseley himself had died at the beginning of 1661, but his wife and daughter carried on the business with the help of Moseley's two apprentices. The last Middleton play owned by Moseley to come out in a first edition was *The Mayor of Quinborough*. It seems likely that the printing was already in progress, or at least planned, when Moseley died. It was entered in the Stationers' Register by Henry Herringman thirteen days after Moseley's death, and the confusion of its form of entrance perhaps indicates the hurry of Herringman stepping in to relieve the Moseley women at a time of bereavement.[46] Though no Restoration performance of the play is known, parts of it had remained current via Cotgrave's *English Treasury* of 1655 and *Wit Restored* of 1658 and the 'Oliver' sub-plot clearly afforded royalist wits material for topical expansion. The Stationer's address celebrates both the joke and the restoration of 'wit':

> You have the first flight of him I assure you; this *Mayor* of *Quinborough* whom you have all heard of, and some of you beheld upon the Stage, now begins to walk abroad in Print; he has been known sufficiently by the reputation of his Wit, which is enough (by the way) to distinguish him from ordinary mayors; but Wit you know, has skulk'd in Corners for many years past, and he was thought to have most of it that could best hide himself...I know you will agree with me, upon your better acquaintance with him, that there is some difference in point of Wit, betwixt the *Mayor* of *Quinborough*, and the *Mayor* of *Huntingdon*.

The 1661–2 editions of Middleton plays neatly demonstrate the fracture in the market: Moseley's rights in *The Spanish Gypsy* were overridden by Kirkman and Marsh; Moseley's rights held in the case of *The Mayor of Quinborough*, though he did not live to see it published, and in the case of *Anything for a Quiet Life* Kirkman seems

to have located a manuscript which had evaded Moseley completely. The competition between the Moseley and the Kirkman/Marsh factions soon became public. In 1661, in their edition of Beaumont and Fletcher's *Beggar's Bush*, Anne Moseley and Humphrey Robinson attacked Kirkman in a note printed on the title-page of some copies:

> You may speedily expect those other Playes, which *Kirkman*, and his Hawkers have deceived the buyers withall, selling them at treble the value, that this and the rest will be sold for, which are the onely Originall and corrected copies, as they were first purchased by us at no mean rate, and since printed by us.

Kirkman countered with an 'Advertisement' in his edition of *The English Lovers* (1662):

> *Courteous Reader,*
> Those books and plays specified in the preceding Catalogue, I acknowledge to be my own Copies, and printed by my direction and order, but whereas in the title page of a Play called *Beggars Bush*, I am charged with printing and publishing that play and others, and to have exhausted the Prices of them, I desire notice may be taken that I printed none of them, but whosoever did, though he have printed them in a fairer Character and better Paper, yet can and will afford them as cheap as any whose Covetousness makes them print them in a character, and Paper not fit for any Gentleman to look on.

Kirkman, then, stands accused of selling (interestingly, through hawkers who perhaps hung around outside the newly-opened theatres) pirated plays at extortionately high prices; Kirkman counters by protesting his innocence ('I printed none of them' is—technically—true, since he was not a printer) and accusing Anne Moseley and her partner of using shoddy materials unworthy of their 'Gentleman' customers. Even if Kirkman's prices *were* high, he was clearly attracting enough customers for Anne Moseley and Humphrey Robinson to fear for their own rights, and the latter's resort to placing a 'genuine product—accept no substitute' message on the title-page of *Beggar's Bush* indicates their frustration. It may be that a price war was in progress in 1661 and 1662. I can find no evidence of the prices charged by Moseley for his publications of the 1650s, but factors such as likely inflation in the cost of imported paper, the higher production costs of elaborate collections as against simpler quartos, and a general inflation in book prices, would probably have resulted in higher prices than had obtained in the 1640s and earlier.

The threat posed by Kirkman, Johnson and Marsh did not last long, however, because the market was not really,

---

[46] SR, 13 February 1661. This appears as a simple entry by Herringman of the whole play, when in fact—since Moseley and Robinson shared ownership—Herringman's entry should have transferred only Moseley's half to himself. In 1673 Robinson's executor sold his remaining half-share to Martin and Herringman.

of course, a free one at all. The Stationers' Company, concerned above all to ensure the 'orderly' running of the trade by protecting its members' rights, eventually asserted itself. Marsh, a member of the Company who—perhaps unlike the naïve Kirkman—must have known the risks he was taking, apparently baled out, leaving Kirkman holding the stock which, after a raid on his shop, was confiscated. That the searchers seized 1,400 playbooks suggests that Kirkman had accumulated (legally or not) a considerable stock. Kirkman went out of business, to re-emerge in 1665 when Marsh's death gave Kirkman an opportunity to secure Marsh's estate as reparation for debts owed him, thereby taking over Marsh's shop and stock and starting out again as a bookseller (Plomer).

How long the Moseley women continued to run the business is not clear. Anne was buying copies in 1661 and as late as 1668 was still publishing: an issue of *The Changeling*, published with Thomas Dring, came out that year. Gradually, some of Moseley's rights were transferred to other stationers, principally Herringman who, by acquiring Robinson's shares in works he had jointly owned with Moseley, became the leading literary bookseller--publisher of the Restoration period. Many of the transfers must have been agreed privately between the Moseley women, Robinson and Herringman, since far from all of Moseley's copies can be traced through the Stationers' Register. Private contracts must have been regarded as sufficient protection in many cases.

Rethinking the Restoration: authors, markets, booksellers

Investigating the posthumous publication of Middleton's plays has forced us to inspect the book trade of the Interregnum period, and in particular the role of Moseley as publisher. As a consequence, the reopening of the theatres at the Restoration can be seen not as a 'new' phenomenon, dislocated from the supposedly anti-theatrical Interregnum period, but as an event produced within a cultural context which was being fashioned in print in the 1640s and 1650s. On the evidence presented here, it is arguable that the Restoration theatre can only be understood in relation to a shift in the cultural valuation of drama and of playwrights which is *continuous* with the emerging literary scene of the Caroline period.

a. Authors

The emergence of a 'canon' of dramatists is clear. Folio editions conferring status on a small minority of dramatists had a material effect: in elevating those specific playwrights as authors; in making the rights in their works capital assets to be accumulated, exchanged and transmitted from publisher to publisher; and in inhibiting the publication of those plays in other formats. Folio works unsupervised by their authors (Jonson of course was the only one to have exerted any control), constructed by players and publishers, were high-cost investments; the desire to satisfy the buyer/collectors made 'completeness' a selling point. Along with the need to offer new editions as 'improved' (and still more 'complete') versions, this

meant that folio editions attracted, almost magnetically, the works of others—single authors, or multiple collaborators—to swell them. The final evidence of this, as it touches Middleton, is the addition of *The Puritan* and *A Yorkshire Tragedy* to the Shakespeare folio of 1664. Its publisher, Chetwin, had been in dispute with the Stationers' Company over his right to publish the Shakespeare plays. That he added to the existing plays, offering in his 1664 edition not only the already accepted Shakespeare works but also 'seven Playes, never before Printed in Folio' (of which *The Puritan* and *A Yorkshire Tragedy* are two), suggests an attempt to go one better than the previous editions. Similarly, whereas the 1647 Beaumont and Fletcher folio offered thirty-five plays, the second edition published by Martin, Herringman, and Marriot in 1679 contained fifty, and was advertised as having 'all that were formerly Quarto and Folio put together into one Volume'. Just as soap powders can only wash ever whiter, folio collections could only get bigger in order to demonstrate that they were new and improved versions of the old product, superseding the older editions and forcing the serious collector/reader to buy anew. In the process, authors less easily identifiable, or perhaps less easily marketable, were absorbed; and those difficult products, plays of multiple authorship, were reduced to the most easily marketable name.

By 1661, when the cataloguing and classifying of plays was becoming increasingly refined, Kirkman the collector--turned-bookseller produced an 'exact catalogue' of plays in which the authors are beginning to be shuffled into some kind of rank order. The plays are listed under letters of the alphabet, though within each letter they are not in strict alphabetical order. First, under each letter, he consistently places the plays of three authors: Shakespeare, Jonson, and Fletcher. It is not surprising, perhaps, that he sees as most important those authors who alone have been published in folio collections; more interesting, as Greg notes, is the fact that although Shakespeare is given precedence, 'as a rule it is only the plays of the folio that come at the beginning, other attributions appear later' (*BEPD*, vol. III, pp. 1338–53). Neither *The Puritan* nor *A Yorkshire Tragedy*, despite being attributed by Kirkman to Shakespeare, heads its respective group of plays. The connection between folio publication and the valuation of 'important' plays could hardly be more clearly demonstrated. By 1671, when he issued a revised catalogue, Kirkman had gone further in developing a rank order of important playwrights: this time, the ten authors whom he considers notable take precedence in each alphabetical section, rather than the three of 1661. His 'method' for ordering the authors is, at least in part, quantitative:

First, I begin with *Shakespear*, who hath in all written forty eight. Then *Beaumont and Fletcher* fifty two. *Johnson* fifty, *Shirley* thirty eight, *Heywood* twenty five, *Middleton* and *Rowley* twenty seven, *Massenger* sixteen, *Chapman* seventeen, *Brome* seventeen, and

D'Avenant fourteen; so that these ten have written in all, 304. The rest have written under ten in number, and therefore I pass them as they were in the old Catalogue, and I place all the new ones last.[47]

In fact, his calculation is slightly wrong: he attributes seventeen plays to Middleton, four to Rowley, and five to them jointly, making twenty-six in all. Dekker is a notable absentee: his total (of ten plays in the 1661 catalogue) includes several plays of which he is joint author; their allocation to the other author reduces his status, in Kirkman's system, to the point of invisibility. Kirkman is careful to distinguish between the rank order produced in this way and any critical evaluation of the playwrights' relative merits: 'I shall not be so presumptuous, as to give my Opinion, much less, to determine or judge of every, or any mans Writing, and who writ best ...'. Yet the apparently quantitative ranking order is not free of judgement: 'I begin with Shakespear' despite the fact that more plays are attributed both to Beaumont and Fletcher and to Jonson. Heywood is placed before Middleton and Rowley, perhaps because Kirkman is concerned to point to the fact that counting printed plays can misrepresent an author's output: Heywood, as Kirkman reports, 'hath had an entire hand, or, at least, a main finger in the writing of 220 ...'.

The catalogue-making tendency, which we have observed as, in part, a development of booksellers' advertising practices and, in part, a specific and increasingly elaborate books-in-print service for the play-collector, had in itself an effect on how authors were perceived. Above all, catalogues (like folio collections) privilege the single author. Joint authorship and multiple authorship are subsumed to a 'main author' heading, and (as happens elsewhere, in relation to collectively written texts by women and by Quaker groups) the need for a single name—at most, a pair of names—works to obscure the collective nature of writing in this period.[48] Kirkman's awareness of the partiality and the misrepresentations occasioned by attention to printed texts is clear: he knows that many plays were written collaboratively, that there are many more in manuscript as yet not available to the play-collector, and that Heywood's 'main finger' cannot be represented in a list such as this. Formulations such as 'Waler and others' necessarily obscure the 'others'.[49] Thus the very act of catalogue-making works with the emerging formulations of the 'man of wit' and poet-as-gentleman-genius to reinforce ideas of unitary, individual authorship.[50] Play as printed product helps to produce author-as-marketable-commodity; the drama as a specifically *literary* form, as well as its author, becomes detached from the original circumstances of production. In a situation where the printing of plays was free of any supervision, intervention or correction on the part of their authors, printed drama was owned, produced and marketed by the booksellers. It would seem likely, then, that the relationship of living playwright and publisher after the Restoration rested on ideas of authorship and cultural valuations of printed

drama which had been developed in the pre-Restoration years by bookseller-publishers like Moseley. Gary Taylor has pointed to the position of new playwrights, particularly Dryden, overshadowed by the established 'greatness' of Shakespeare, Jonson, and Beaumont and Fletcher. Writing new plays involved a peculiarly difficult negotiation with the past (*Reinventing Shakespeare*, chap. 1). D. F. McKenzie has demonstrated that in the case of Congreve and Tonson the relationship of author to publisher, and to the printed text itself, was radically different from what had existed in the Elizabethan–Jacobean period (McKenzie, *London Book Trade*).

The consequences for Middleton are interesting. By 1671, on the evidence of Kirkman's catalogue, Middleton is a 'ranking' playwright. As single author, though, he is compromised by the bracketing with Rowley. Unlike the Beaumont and Fletcher pairing, enshrined (however misleadingly) in folio early on, the pairing of Middleton and Rowley is not strong enough, with only five plays according to Kirkman, to attain legendary status, yet it weakens Middleton's output as a single author. Work of Middleton's has been by now dispersed and effaced: sucked into the folios of Beaumont and Fletcher and Shakespeare. The rules for 'great authors' have already been set, and fixed, by the gobbling folios to which some of Middleton's work has already fallen prey. The seventeen plays left to his name are not enough, in Kirkman's terms—which are those of the collector as much as the bookseller—to lift Middleton to the front rank of playwrights whose plays number forty-eight, fifty or even fifty-two.

A glance forward, to the fate of Middleton's plays in the last decades of the century, is instructive. No more first editions were published, and the few single reprints issued were not what they seem. In 1668 Anne Moseley had republished *The Changeling*, for sale by Thomas Dring; in fact her 'edition' was simply a reissue of remaining stocks from Moseley's 1653 edition with a new title-page linking the play to its performance by the Duke's company at the Theatre in Lincoln's Inn Fields, and advertising Dring's shop as furnishing 'most sorts of Plays'. Current performance provided Anne Moseley and Thomas Dring with a way of reinvigorating copies printed fifteen years earlier. In 1673 *Macbeth* was being performed in a version altered by Davenant. William Cademan's edition of *Macbeth* of the same year was an attempt to cash in on the popularity of Davenant's adaptation, ahead of Davenant's publishers, but is in fact a cheat: despite its claim to be the current version, Cademan's text is the old one, and Davenant's adaptation was published the following year. The only other new editions are similarly linked to performance and, again, are adaptations: in 1677 Langley Curtis published, as *The Counterfeit Bridegroom: or the Defeated Widow*,

[47] 'An Advertisement to the Reader', printed in full by *BEPD*, vol. III, p. 1358.
[48] For the argument as it affects women writers, and in particular Quakers, see Bell, Parfitt, and Shepherd, *A Biographical Dictionary*, p. xvii.
[49] Entry for *Pompey* in his list of 1661.
[50] For a discussion of the development of the unitary subject in drama itself, see Catherine Belsey, *The Subject of Tragedy*.

an adaptation of *No Wit/Help* performed at the Duke's Theatre, and the following year saw the publication of Shadwell's alteration of *Timon*, as *The History of Timon*. In each case, publication was entirely due to performance; in three cases the play had been adapted or altered, and in a fourth the claim to adaptation was (misleadingly) implicit. Middleton as author has disappeared.

b. The market

In the early seventeenth century the sixpenny play had been, like the penny almanac, a generic rather than specific item of a bookseller's stock. That some people collected quarto plays is clear from the evidence of Harington. By 1641, if the surviving list from Moseley's shop is in any way indicative, a customer might be buying plays in bulk, and a bookseller like Moseley was in a position to supply the latest plays from a variety of publishers. A developing *cognoscenti* market, centred in particular on the 'private' playhouses, was already in place by 1640, and the 1640 edition of *A Mad World, My Masters* would seem to be symptomatic of that shift. Quarto plays of the Interregnum signalled, on their title-pages, their connections with particular playhouses, companies, and royal performances; folios and the 'collected works' format enhanced their cultural and material status. Accretions to texts (prefaces, lists of dramatis personae, dedicatory poems and addresses, engraved portraits) worked to the same end. The meaning of, for example, Middleton's *Two New Plays* of 1657 was constructed within this set of literary, cultural, and political valuations; their original context and meanings were thus overwritten, and Middleton too has become a brand-name commodity. *The Mayor of Quinborough* is marketable in 1661 as a royalist joke: the 'Oliver' plot capable of elaboration at Cromwell's expense.

It is tempting—but possibly misleading—to generalize about readers on the evidence of the printed texts alone. It is easy to forget the constraining factors which narrowed the market: the geographical proximity of the booksellers and their shops, the relatively small proportion of the population they served (the readership of printed plays is necessarily narrower than the audience for public— or even private—performance), and there is nothing to tell us to what extent the interest in printed plays was an urban phenomenon, or whether there was a wider provincial market. Parliamentary, radical and sectarian literature travelled fast throughout the country, and elaborate distribution networks for 'seditious' literature kept the country well-supplied. If, as I have suggested, there is a strong element of royalist consolation in the literary publishing of the Interregnum, then the lists and catalogues developed in particular by Moseley may have been a way to generate sales outside London. In part the catalogues may have supported a kind of mail-order service as far afield as there were interested customers, even as far as royalists exiled on the Continent and anxious to obtain English books.

The second-hand market in older printed editions of plays—as with second-hand books more generally—is hard to pin down. Booksellers' inventories in this period make no distinction between new and second-hand books, which seem to have been treated the same as new books and shelved amongst them. (Similarly, in the early years of printing, book-owners do not distinguish between manuscript and printed books.) The circulation of second-hand plays was probably widespread, but largely unidentifiable. Booksellers continued, throughout the period, buying up unsold copies and selling them on, sometimes with new title-pages claiming them as their own publications. One piece of evidence is the survival of a label printed for Thomas Dring, advertising his shop as supplying 'most Sorts of Plays' (*BEPD*, vol. III, p. 1155). Dring, Anne Moseley's partner in the 1668 *Changeling*, was principally a law stationer from 1649 to 1668, yet his label is found in a number of plays printed in the first half of the century, one of them dating from as early as 1598. His sideline in plays was perhaps aimed at the Inns of Court men who must have constituted a large part of his clientele, and it seems that he would buy and sell plays both new and old. In 1669, the resilient Kirkman was still advertising himself as a buyer of libraries and parcels of old books, and from the beginning of the Restoration he had been offering 'all the Playes that were ever yet Printed' both for sale and to be 'read for reasonable Considerations'. The retail trade involved both publication and pseudo-publication, the sale of old and new stock, the buying and selling of second-hand and manuscript copies, and even facilities for lending. A customer could find combined in one shop the functions which, today, we differentiate as specialist areas.

Manuscript circulation was part of the trade, and remained so for some time as Moseley's remarks in the preface to the Beaumont and Fletcher folio of 1647 suggest. But the late Caroline playhouse-related culture (with all its nostalgia, literary pretension and court connections, as well as its articulation—via writers such as Nabbes—of an oppositional politics) could only be sustained, once the theatres had been closed, by printing— in its mass production, a substitute for performance, a replacement of the collective experience of the audience by the shared readership/ownership of the texts. New editions and new collections of old plays stressed their authenticity, their completeness and their faithfulness to the originals: a conservation and re-presentation of the cultural values and social activities of a particular Caroline milieu. While play manuscripts would continue to circulate, and copies would be sought by collectors, printed texts could reach and consolidate a bigger market than could manuscript. For the wealthy collector, however, manuscript plays were still of interest. The notebooks of Abraham Hill (1635–1721) provide some evidence of a Restoration book-collector's interests. Hill, who inherited a fortune in 1660, noted books he bought at auction ('Shakespeares Playes—0-16-0'; 'Collection of Playes— 0-3-6') and among his papers is a handwritten list of plays, perhaps made from the stock of a bookseller, or from a collection which was on the market privately. He lists fifty-one manuscript plays, plus twenty-six printed plays. The first in the manuscript list is 'The Conquerors custome or the fair prisoner Tho Middleton'; beside 'Your 5 gallants' he notes '(is in print)' and the same play occurs in the list of printed plays as 'Your five Gallants = T:Midleton'. The annotation of several of the manuscript play titles as 'is in print' perhaps suggests that manuscripts were only of interest when of plays previously unknown, or otherwise obtainable; Hill's 'is in print' may indicate that for the play-collector, manuscript was supplementary rather than of interest in itself. The sales of private libraries attended by Hill between 1678 and 1685 suggest not only a growing specialist interest in collecting, but also a development in the second-hand and antiquarian market for printed books which raised prices (Adams).[51]

c. The booksellers

Tracking Middleton's plays through the mid-century offers a new dimension to the history of the book trade in the Interregnum. Book trade history has concentrated on the period as one of turmoil and disruption, and with good reason. The significant moment for the stationers was the abolition of Star Chamber and the High Commission in 1641. The controls on the trade, tightened most recently by the 1637 Star Chamber Decree, were now removed, and the effectiveness of the Company as a controlling agency waned as it was subjected to a series of internal challenges to power: printers argued for a company of their own, separate from booksellers, and there were arguments over the monopolies claimed by the Company. Civil war affected other aspects of the trade: booksellers who relied on imports found their businesses disrupted, and there was a boom in news and propaganda publishing which may have dented the market for the ordinary bookseller's less sensational stock in trade. Printers, who had long complained of the lack of enough work to occupy their ever-increasing numbers, were now in demand for the quick printing of broadsides, news-sheets and topical polemic, and need no longer take account of the old restrictions on numbers of presses and master printers allowed to operate within London. This explosion of print, its topicality, its propaganda uses, have attracted most attention.[52] Attending to Middleton, however, necessitates a shift in focus: away from the fast-moving, rapid-response world of political and religious controversy and news and towards the less exciting world of the non-radical and conservative bookseller.

What is clear from the brief reconstruction of Moseley's activities as a publisher, however, is not only that he was far from neutral in the political conflict, but that he could fashion a publishing programme instrumental in sustaining (even, in part, creating) the cavalier ethos. From his translations of French romances to his presentation of 'old' plays, his prefaces and the texts themselves are shaped to speak to a dominant literary culture fashioned from the gentlemanly-connoisseur cultural values already observable in the immediate pre-war years. His catalogues and lists of books, with their rapid updating, the news of

books 'in the press' and those 'to be speedily printed', have an urgency which perhaps is part of the wider emphasis on offering 'the latest' in news and debate. The speed of his activities—buying up copies, putting together collections, keeping the customer informed—mirrors the news values of his society, though in very different form. In its elaborate, high-status packaging of literature, Moseley's publishing countered (and relegated to vulgarity?) the cheap and hastily produced news-propaganda of the parliamentary side. Equally, though, his apparent urgency may have been a contrivance, a sales ploy, to arouse and to consolidate consumer interest. At the moment of triumph, the Restoration, Moseley died; but the 'literary' booksellers of the Restoration—Herringman, Tonson— were clearly building on a conception of bookselling which Moseley had developed through the 1640s and 1650s. Herringman, who stepped in on Moseley's death to publish *The Mayor of Quinborough*, was Moseley's de facto successor. Having begun his business in 1652, by the time of Moseley's death Herringman was in a position to buy up many of Moseley's rights, as well as those of other publishers. In the following years, Herringman became the leading publisher of collections, of plays and of poetry; he was involved in both the Beaumont and Fletcher second folio of 1679 and the fourth Shakespeare folio of 1685. From 1668 he dominated the publication of collections in the way that Moseley had done previously, publishing collections by Denham, Carew, Suckling, Davenant, Jonson, and Cowley (see Appendix). More than ever, the ownership of literary works was being concentrated in the hands of a small group of publishers, amongst whom Herringman was pre-eminent. The sheer scale of investment involved in accumulating rights and in publishing more and bigger folio collections was beyond the means of any single entrepreneur. Even the earliest folio collections, of Jonson and Shakespeare, had required partnerships of publishers to finance them, and after the Restoration the trend to syndicates (now called 'congers' in the trade) accelerated as expenses rose. The ownership of the Beaumont and Fletcher plays is a good example of the process. In 1646 Moseley and Robinson had bought the rights to the King's Men's plays, in the following year they had published the folio in joint names, and as partners had presumably shared both costs and profits. Robinson's half-share was sold in 1671 to Martin and Herringman (who thereby became quarter-sharers). What became of Moseley's share is not clear, though it apparently ended up with Marriot, and was later split between Bentley and Magnes. This process of fragmentation of shares indicates the increasing capital value of the rights to 'old' works, and the increasing investment needed for new editions. In order to achieve the publication of the 1679 folio, the

---

[51] Love (p. 67) suggests that Hill's list may represent Kirkman's collection of plays.

[52] For the details of legislative changes and attempts at regulation throughout this period, see F. S. Siebert, *Freedom of the Press in England 1476–1776*. Blagden, *The Stationers' Company*, chronicles the internal wrangles within the Company.

syndicate needed not only the rights to the original folio plays, but also to the additional plays which expanded the collection to fifty. The financial need for partnerships and syndicates is made visible in the Appendix's details of collections published between 1680 and 1700.[53] Against such concentrations of capital investment, individual competitors made little headway. Early attempts to muscle in (Marsh) were seen off quickly; maverick enthusiasts (Kirkman) had no long-term effect on the transfer of rights (which is to say capital) and proved if anything conducive to maintaining consumer interest. Competition like Kirkman's was really only at the retail end; he was never a substantial publisher. Such limited, and ultimately powerless, competition was no problem. In such a context, the power of the copy-owning publishers was paramount. The relationship between the bookseller--publisher and the author necessarily underwent a process of renegotiation. Moseley's image, developed through his prefaces and through his publications programme, had elevated the bookseller from tradesman to literary expert. This image was as much a part of his legacy as his accumulation of copies. It was inherited and developed both by Herringman, whose shop—at a more fashionable address than Moseley's—became a lounging place for literary gentleman, and by Tonson, whose literary and social pretensions reached apotheosis in the circle called the Kit-Kat Club. The publishers' need for *new* works, however, gave authors some power too; they too could begin to assert their interests within this new social and economic formation. The increasingly professionalized relationships of Restoration playwrights and their publishers—Dryden and Herringman, or Dryden and Tonson, or Congreve and Tonson—must be seen in this context. Our understanding of their position as *living* authors writing a commodity called 'literature' is enlarged by knowing what had happened earlier in the century; and in particular, by knowing what had happened to a dead author called Middleton at the hands of a publisher called Moseley.

Appendix. Collections, 1630-1700

This list of collected works is based on *BEPD*, vol. III, and therefore is limited to collections which include dramatic works by pre-Restoration authors. Thus, collections of poems (such as Donne's) are excluded, unless they include any dramatic material, nor will Restoration playwrights be found here.

* = separate issues—probably designed to be sold either together or separately
** = 'made up' collections—really reissue of separate editions with a new title-page added to present the separate works as a 'collection'. Some of these may have been one-off title-pages printed for individual collectors, and therefore may not be relevant to booksellers' practice at all (e.g. 1652 Chapman and Marston; possibly 1639 Nabbes). Some, however, were deliberate reissues of old or bought-up stock, offered as a 'new' collection.

1630
1631 Jonson v. II [Meighen]
1632 Lyly [Stansby/Blount]; Shakespeare [Cotes/ Smethwick/Aspley/Hawkins/Meighen/Allott]
1633 Greville [Seile]; Marston [Sheares]
1634
1635
1636
1637 Alexander [Harper]; Heywood [Hearne]
1638 Randolph [Bowman]
1639 May* [Walkley]; Nabbes** [Fussell]
1640 Carew [Walkely]; Jonson v. I [Bishop]; Jonson v. II reissue [Meighen]; Randolph [Bowman]; Tatham [Best]
1641 Jonson v. II reissue [Meighen]; Killigrew [Crooke]
1642 Carew [Walkley]
1643 Randolph [pirated]
1644
1645 Milton [Moseley]
1646 Randolph reissue [?]; Shirley [Moseley]; Suckling* [Moseley]
1647 Beaumont and Fletcher [Robinson and Moseley]
1648 Suckling [*?] [Moseley]
1649 Cavendish [Robinson and Moseley]
1650
1651 Carew [Moseley]; Cartwright [Moseley]
1652 Chapman [**?]; Marston [**?]; Randolph reissue [Bowman]
1653 Beaumont [Blaiklock]; Brome [Moseley, Marriot & Dring]; Shirley [*?] [Robinson and Moseley]
1654 May* [Moseley]
1655 *Actaeon and Diana* etc [Cox]; Massinger [Moseley]; Shirley suppl* [?Moseley]
1656 *Actaeon and Diana* etc reissue [Archer]; Goffe [Bedell and Collins]
1657 Carlell [Moseley]; Middleton [Moseley]; Shirley** [Kirton]; Tatham reissue [Burden]
1658 Cokayne [Godbid]; Mayne** [Davis]; Suckling* [Moseley]
1659 Brome [*?] [Crooke and H. Brome]; Mayne reissue** [Davis]; Suckling* [Moseley]
1660 Beaumont reissue [Hope]
1661 Lower** [Kirkman]; Webster & Rowley* [Kirkman]
1662 Cokayne [*?] reissue [Stephens/Kirkman]; Cox Wits [Marsh]; *Gratiae Theatrales* [Daniel/?]; Lower** reissue [Kirkman]
1663 Shakespeare [Chetwin]
1664 Killigrew [Herringman]; Shakespeare reissue [Chetwin]; Randolph [Bowman]
1665 Davenant [Bedell and Collins]
1666
1667
1668 Denham [Herringman]; Randolph [Bowman, Crosley]

53 Publication by subscription was another response to the increasing expense of publishing large-scale works in this period.

1669 Cockayne reissue [Kirkman]
1670 Carew [Herringman]
1671 Carew reissue [Herringman]; Denham
[Herringman]
1672 Cox *Wits* [Kirkman]; Suckling ?piracy [?]
1673 Cox *Wits* [Kirkman]; Milton [Dring]
1674
1675
1676 Suckling reissue [Herringman]
1677
1678
1679 Beaumont & Fletcher [Martin, Herringman,
Marriot]
1680
1681 Cowley Pt II [Harper, Tonson]
1682 Cowley Pt II [Harper, Tonson]
1683 Davenant [Herringman]
1684 Cowley Pt II [Harper, Swalle]; Denham
[Herringman, Knight, Saunders]
1685 Shakespeare [Herringman, Brewster, Chiswell,
Bentley, Knight, Saunders]
1686
1687
1688
1689 Cowley Pt II [Harper]; Cowley Pts II/III [Harper]
1690
1691
1692 Jonson [Herringman, Brewster, Basset, Chiswell,
Wotton, Conyers]
1693 Cowley Pt I [Herringman, Bentley, Tonson,
Saunders, Bennet]
1694
1695 Milton [Tonson]
1696 Suckling [Herringman, Bentley, Tonson, Bennet,
Saunders]
1697
1698
1699
1700 Cowley Pt I [Herringman, Tonson, Bennet];
Cowley Pt II [Harper]; Cowley Pts II/III [Harper]

WORKS CITED

Adams, J. Q. 1939. 'Hill's List of Early Plays in Manuscript'. *The Library*, IV, 20: 71–99.
Arber, Edward. 1875–7. *A Transcript of the Registers of the Company of Stationers of London, 1554–1640 A.D.*. 5 vols. London.
Ashton, R. 1978. *The English Civil War*. London: Weidenfeld & Nicolson.
Barnard, John, and Maureen Bell. 1991. 'The Inventory of Henry Bynneman (1583): a Preliminary Survey'. *Publishing History*. 29: 5–46.
Barnard, John, and Maureen Bell. 1994. *The Early Seventeenth-century York Book Trade and John Foster's Inventory of 1616*. Leeds: Leeds Philosophical and Literary Society.
Bawcutt, N. W. (ed.). 1996. *The Control and Censorship of Caroline Drama: The Records of Sir Henry Herbert, Master of the Revels 1623–73*. Oxford: Clarendon Press.

Bell, Maureen, George Parfitt, and Simon Shepherd. 1990. *A Biographical Dictionary of English Women Writers 1580–1720*. Hemel Hempstead: Harvester; Boston: G. K. Hall.
Belsey, Catherine. 1985. *The Subject of Tragedy: Identity and Difference in Renaissance Drama*. London and New York: Methuen.
Bentley, G. E. 1941–68. *The Jacobean and Caroline Stage*. 7 vols. Oxford: Oxford University Press.
—— 1943. 'John Cotgrave's *English Treasury of Wit and Language* and the Elizabethan Drama'. *Studies in Philology*. 40: 186–203.
Berger, Thomas L. 1993. 'Shakespeare in Caroline England: Problems and Possibilities'. Unpublished paper, Society for Textual Scholarship Conference, April 1993.
Blagden, Cyprian. 1960. *The Stationers' Company: a History, 1403–1959*. London: George Allen and Unwin.
Blayney, Peter. 1991. *The First Folio of Shakespeare*. Washington: Folger Shakespeare Library.
Briscoe Eyre, G. E., and C. R. Rivington. 1913–14. *A Transcript of the Registers of the Worshipful Company of Stationers from 1640–1708 A.D.* 3 vols. London: Roxburghe Club.
Butler, Martin. 1984. *Theatre and Crisis 1632–1642*. Cambridge: Cambridge University Press.
Calendar of State Papers: Domestic Series, 1547–1704 (CSPD). 1856–1972. London: Public Record Office.
Dictionary of National Biography (DNB). Ed. L. Stephen and S. Lee. 1921–2. 22 vols and suppl. London.
Downes, John. 1708. *Roscius Anglicanus*. Ed. J. Milhous and R. D. Hume, 1987. London: Society for Theatre Research.
Edwards, P., *et al.* 1981. *Revels History of Drama in English, vol. IV, 1613–1660*. London: Methuen.
Feather, John. 1988. *A History of British Publishing*. London and New York: Routledge.
Fraser, Antonia. 1984. *The Weaker Vessel: Woman's Lot in Seventeenth-century England*. London: Weidenfeld & Nicolson.
Gerritsen, Johan. 1958. 'The Dramatic Piracies of 1661'. *Studies in Bibliography*. 11: 117–31.
Greg, W. W. 1939–59. *A Bibliography of the English Printed Drama to the Restoration*. 4 vols. London: Bibliographical Society.
Gurr, Andrew. 1987. *Playgoing in Shakespeare's London*. Cambridge: Cambridge University Press.
Jackson, William A. (ed.). 1957. *Records of the Court of the Stationers' Company 1602 to 1640*. London: Bibliographical Society.
Johnson, F. R. 1950. 'Notes on English Retail Book-prices, 1550–1640'. *The Library*, V, 5: 83–112.
Kewes, Paulina. 1995. '"Give me the sociable pocket-books...": Humphrey Moseley's serial publication of octavo play collections'. *Publishing History*, 38: 5–21.
Love, Harold. 1993. *Scribal Publication in Seventeenth-Century England*. Oxford: Clarendon Press.
McKenzie, D. F. 1976. *The London Book Trade in the Later Seventeenth Century*. Sandars Lectures.
—— 1961. *Stationers' Company Apprentices 1605–1640*. Charlottesville: Bibliographical Society of the University of Virginia.
—— 1974. 'Stationers' Company Apprentices 1641–1700'. Oxford Bibliographical Society Publications: NS 17.
—— and Maureen Bell (eds.). 2005. *A Chronology and Calendar of Documents Relating to the London Book Trade, 1641–1700*. 2 vols. Oxford: Oxford University Press.
Myers, R. 1983. 'The Records of the Worshipful Company of Stationers and Newspaper Makers'. *Publishing History*, 13: 89–104.
Plomer, H. R. *et al.* 1977. *Dictionaries of the Printers and Booksellers who were at work in England, Scotland and Ireland, 1557–1775*.

London: Bibliographical Society. (Reprint in one volume of the original volumes, 1907–32.)

Potter, Lois. 1989. *Secret Rites and Secret Writing: Royalist Literature, 1641–1660*. Cambridge: Cambridge University Press.

Reed, J. C. 1929. 'Humphrey Moseley, Publisher'. *Oxford Bibliographical Society Proceedings and Papers*. II: 57–142.

Shepherd, S., and P. Womack. 1995. *English Drama: a cultural history*. Oxford: Blackwell.

Siebert, F. S. 1965. *Freedom of the Press in England 1476–1776: the Rise and Decline of Government Control*. Urbana: University of Illinois Press.

Taylor, Gary. 1989. *Reinventing Shakespeare: a Cultural History, from the Restoration to the Present*. New York and Oxford: Oxford University Press.

Thaler, Alwin. 1922. *Shakspere to Sheridan: A Book about the Theatre of Yesterday and To-Day*. Cambridge: Harvard University Press.

FOR MANY OF YOUR COMPANIES:
MIDDLETON'S EARLY READERS

John Jowett

THIS study identifies readers of Middleton's works by name; it notes, where possible, details of their social and intellectual environment, and it explores the nature of their interaction with the text. The aim is to provide a map, albeit merely a sketch-map, of the circulation of these works in the seventeenth century. Any such study is premised on the significance of readers' contributions to what D. F. McKenzie and others have called the 'sociology of the text'. It is desirable to investigate the meanings that readers constructed and the responses they made. Yet in the case of Middleton those reactions are all too rarely observable. Moreover, they cannot usually be measured in relation to the meanings the author intended, a difficult proposition at best that is here exacerbated by Middleton's characteristically weak or entirely absent control of the texts' circulation. This essay is, of necessity, a study of some kinds of dispersal that can follow when the author's presence is, from the outset, fragmented.

Though the role of readers is well recognized in literary studies, it has often been noted of the reception theories of Wolfgang Iser, Roland Barthes, and others that these seminal theorists of the reader neglect or ignore the position of actual readers in history.[1] This is especially true of Iser's non-empirical reader whom Iser himself describes as a 'transcendental construct' of the text. In contrast, criticism influenced by Mikhail Bakhtin historicizes the reader, emphasizing the dialogic aspects of a text seen as 'inseparably enmeshed in the communication event', an event in which the reader plays an active part.[2] The significance of the historically-situated reader is recognized as well in various studies of the history and historicity of the book, including D. F. McKenzie's attempts to broaden the scope of bibliography, Roger Chartier's examinations of the cultural uses of print, Margaret Spufford's study of seventeenth-century popular fiction, and Tessa Watt's work on the production and reading of ballads, broadsides, and chapbooks. It is nonetheless striking that, although Andrew Gurr (1987) has studied the social composition and attitudes of theatre audiences and assembled a list of all known London playgoers, there are no comparable accounts of the readers of early modern English writers.

The present study attempts to provide such an account for Middleton. It reaches towards a description of Middleton as a cluster of disparate texts that claim or discover or have thrust upon them certain social and cultural positions by virtue of the way they addressed readers and were read. Any such attempt is bound to remain provisional. Reading is an unspectacular activity that leaves few traces—especially in a period that boasted virtually no professional criticism and little literary journalism. A description obtained by aggregating particles of specialized evidence that come into view only when the reader ceases to be silent and untraced is bound to be fractional.

The actively responding reader who does gain notice communicates the text onwards in a way that is comparable with those various agents in the reproduction of the text that I will refer to as textual transmitters. Indeed there are circumstances—the highly characteristic seventeenth-century circumstance of the miscellany-compiler for example—in which the distinction between reader and transmitter becomes hard to sustain. Lisa Jardine and Anthony Grafton have drawn attention to the central role of collation and parallel citation in allowing the text to be embedded in context in early modern academic reading. In non-academic situations too the manifested evidence of reading can be manipulation of the text rather than commentary on it. Because the period finds meagre space for formalized records of readers' responses, it may actually be ahistorical to expect that a reader-response approach as it is known can survive historicization. Exceptionally, as Jardine and Grafton demonstrate, one may find a careful, regular annotator such as Gabriel Harvey, and in his case deduce the quality and purpose of his intellectual response as a humanist scholar from his comments. But even with Harvey, where one can be relatively precise about his reaction to a classical historian such as Livy, there is less evidence for his response to texts as aesthetic objects, and little commentary on a popular contemporary dramatist even when, as in the case of William Shakespeare, there is at least some written response. It is a feature of the early modern cultural milieu that readers did not give drama from the professional theatre the serious intellectual consideration that it was afforded from the eighteenth century onwards. And the same is true of other semi-popular genres in which Middleton participated. The nearest approximation to an articulate close reader until the later years of the seventeenth century was often a

---

[1] See, for example, Eagleton 1983, 83-4, and compare Holub, 96-101 and 128-9.

[2] Medvedev and Bakhtin, p. 120. Bakhtin is a particular influence on Jerome McGann, who, writing as a textual scholar, emphasizes 'the entirety of the poetic event' including the history of reception (McGann, 18-23).

textual transmitter. It is not only inevitable but appropriate that these transmitters will figure large in the present account, both as readers in their own right and as those who provide for yet new readers.

Yet one can scarcely begin to understand the circulation of Middleton books without some notion of the currency of reading in early modern England. Literacy was increasing through the seventeenth century. At mid-century, male literacy, judged by the ability to write one's name, stood at about 30% amongst the adult male population and considerably lower amongst women, though the proportion of women readers to women writers was probably higher than with men. School libraries could be quite substantial, but there were few parish and civic libraries before 1640, and a substantial personal collection of books was relatively rare. Sears Jayne's list of libraries totalling fifteen or more volumes between 1500 and 1640 identifies 848 such collections for the entire period. Even this apparently low figure inevitably understates the sparsity of book-gathering, for Jayne's research concentrates on Oxford and Cambridge inventories: the universities would have produced a heavy concentration of wealthy and academic readers. Nevertheless, Peter Clark has pointed out that a number of richer members of the non-academic laity owned extensive libraries (96–7). Sir Edward Dering bought 41 books in a single day, and in 1623 purchased nearly 200 volumes including plays by Ben Jonson and Shakespeare (see below).

Clark's main findings derive from his study of 2,771 inventories of the townspeople of Canterbury, Faversham, and Maidstone. This represents perhaps a 30% sample of adult citizens dying in these towns, but perhaps as high as 75% of the people dying with any significant amount of property at all. Within this sample, by the early seventeenth century books were owned by about 40% of men and 25% of women. Yet the sample is itself heavily weighted towards men because they were the usual property-holders, and the inventoried women might actually over-represent women readers. Jayne's research, based on more substantial book-ownership, identified only three woman readers. Given the academic environment he reviews, the imbalance is perhaps not surprising, but Paul Morgan has noted that only 1% of the book ownership labels listed in STC names women. As regards social class, Clark indicates that even amongst those labourers and servants who were sufficiently propertied to leave inventories, book-ownership was practically non-existent. Higher up the social hierarchy and the hierarchy of literacy, up to 85% of yeomen were sufficiently literate to sign their names, and over a third owned books. It was the exception not to do so in the professional and gentry classes.

There is less information as to the numbers of these volumes, though in most cases it would have been small. As for their titles, it is clear that the Bible and religious literature dominated overwhelmingly, and that secular works other than books on law and history figured little. Cheaper books, including much secular literature, often escaped listing by title in inventories. Some of the people whose estates were inventoried could have owned Middleton books and we would be none the wiser.

The towns that Clark surveys were relatively prosperous and in relatively close contact with London as the centre of book production. Book ownership was still sparser in poorer and more remote counties. In London it would have been more common. The literacy rate of London artisans and merchants was two or three times higher than that of their rural counterparts (Chartier 1989, 116). Even though the bookselling industry had developed an efficient provincial distribution system by the middle of the seventeenth century (Morgan, 208), the circulation of Middleton's works must have been heavily concentrated in London, where books were more available and readers more numerous.

One cannot speak of Middleton's works without considering the meaning of such an entity, and this raises questions relating to the validity of an edition such as the Oxford Middleton as a *post hoc* aggregation of separate texts. There are questions also as to the categorical value of Middleton's name from the point of view of the seventeenth-century readers of these texts. Middleton was often a collaborator, often an anonymous writer, and his published editions displayed misattributions. His name would have meant relatively little to most of his early readers, most of whom would have been able to associate him with only a relatively small number of plays, pageants, and non-dramatic works published at various times and for various readerships. Most purchasers of Middleton would have been buying texts whose authorial underpinning was weak, absent, or misleading. The texts are dispersed as a result of the absence of a comprehensive authorial enclosure, and further as a result of the variety of genres, publishers, dates of publication, book-formats, and modes of textual presentation. And to a much greater extent, the readers too are scattered.

Envisaged Readers, Fictional and Real

There are several possible starting points for a study of Middleton's readers. One of them is the texts themselves, at the point where they target and address their envisaged readers. An epistle 'To the Comicke, Play-readers, Venery, *and* Laughter' is prefixed to *The Roaring Girl*; in it Middleton claimed that 'The book I make no question, but is fit for many of your companies, as well as the person it selfe, and may bee allowed both Gallery roome at the play-house, and chamber-roome at your lodging'. Whereas the play presents Moll as a crusader against the commodification of sex, Middleton's blurb for the book as a saleable object wryly makes an analogy that at face value assumes that she was a prostitute. The book, and so inferably Moll, 'may bee allowed...chamber roome at your lodging'. That face-value reading of the epistle's construction of Moll might be accepted by the fictional Simplicity S.P.D., the '*well-vnderstanding*' reader invoked in the mock-epistle to *The World Tossed at Tennis*. A more discriminating reader would note Moll's actual virtue in the play, and discover a less directly jocular but more complimentary sense of the utterance. Moll, and the book, will be fit companions because their bold familiarity will be a stalking-horse for moral edification. They share in their capacity to be taken into the chamber-room for purposes that would most obviously be erotic, but may prove otherwise. By either interpretation, Middleton's vocative address produces both the figure of the authorial speaker and a community, or communities, of addressees. Moll is she of whom I know you know, and could be invoked as such because the real-life Mary Frith was notorious. But the familiarity is a guise. Middleton could not claim to know the readers even of the first edition. The invoked readers, being non-specific, know Moll by reputation only, and the sense in which she is said to be known remains enigmatically unclear. How is one supposed to read this epistle in order to feel addressed inclusively? When Middleton writes 'the person it selfe', does 'it selfe' where one would expect 'herself' denote a text, a dramatic role, a boy actor, a transvestite? Is the community textual, theatrical, social? Or is the book invoked, as Genevieve Love has suggested, as an anti-communal commodity that provokes an autoerotic response in the chamber-room? If the book happens to be in the hands of a woman, is the text then read against itself, or does the ungendered phrase 'Comicke, Play-readers' permit some kind of reading of the subsequent epistle in which there is no trace of masculine nudge? Must we assume that the readers of comedies are wished venery and laughter, or is it possible that Venery and Laughter are the personificatory names of comic-spirited play-readers, or, as Mulholland suggests in his edition, that the epistle 'in an alternative reading may be dedicated to the play-reader's venery and laughter' (p. 68)?

As these questions show, the notion of Middleton's readers is problematic, even if we focus on a single play that is prefaced with an address to its recipients, and even if we ignore the fact that it was written in collaboration with Thomas Dekker. The epistle's equivocation between the private familiarity of the bedchamber and the public anonymity of the market-place is paradigmatic of the relation between author and reader in the circumstances of print culture.[3] As is often the case with such epistles, the text tells us nothing concrete of actual readers, only of fictional readers wishfully predicated by the text itself. The collective readers, whether assumed to be comic playreaders, gentlemen, wits, or citizens, are constituted as a homogeneous group that is an idealized simplification of any actual readership. The outsider accepts the fiction of familiarity as a compliment, or accepts her or his exclusion.

The Roaring Girl is one example where the position of the reader is posed explicitly. Another is *The Black Book*, with its epistle 'To all those that are truly Vertuous, and can touch Pitch and yet neuer defile themselues'. Here a space begins to open up not only between actual and

supposed reader, but also between actual and supposed writer. At face value the epistolary document belongs to the community of the Puritan virtuous, yet it is more likely to be taken as an ironic dedication that supposes the actual reader to be a cynical wit—as is signalled by the references to Thomas Nashe's satiric *Pierce Penniless* in the poem printed after the epistle and titled 'A Moral'.

In such cases Middleton plays on the fictive possibilities of dedications and epistles, drawing on the example of Gabriel Harvey, Thomas Nashe, and Robert Greene, whose diatribes, satires and repentances were so often cast in epistolary form. A more extremely fictional example is *Father Hubburd's Tales*, which is introduced with a mock-dedication 'TO THE TRVE Generall Patron of all *Muses, Musitians, Poets, & Picture Drawers*, Syr *Christopher Clutch-Fist*' and signed by the fictional persona Oliver Hubburd. Hubburd can be taken to stand for Middleton—to the extent that some scholars have cited Hubburd's autobiography in order to flesh out Middleton's early life, identifying Clutchfist with an ungrateful Baron William Compton, the dedicatee of *The Ghost of Lucrece* (Adams, ed., 1937, xxiii–xxx). Such an identification is plausible enough, but it means neither that Compton was sent a copy of the pamphlet, nor that we can assume that he read it, nor that readers would usually have recognized the allusion.

Clutchfist is an invention, and only in addition to that may he be a caricature of an actual miserly patron. In the epistle prefixed to *The World Tossed at Tennis*, the speaker Simplicity and the addressee his kinsman Simplicity are pure fictions. Indeed the speaker is a figure in the masque itself, and so makes a more spectacular leap from his textual confines than Rosalind at the end of Shakespeare's *As You Like It* or Weatherwise at the end of *No Wit/Help like a Woman's*, escaping drama as the mode of representation as well as the fictivity of the dramatic action, so as to become an author in his own right.[4] This mock epistle in which writer and reader belong to the same family parodies more typical epistles and dedications to the reader, including Middleton's own, in which the reader is characterized and defined in relation to the writer's subject-matter and disposition. It might specifically recall the apparent absurdity of Middleton's dedication of *The Triumphs of Truth* to his namesake the Lord Mayor Sir Thomas Myddelton, where the text actually prints the form 'Middleton' indifferently to indicate both the author and the dedicatee. The epistle to *The World Tossed at Tennis* uses this mirroring of author in reader to mock the hermeneutic circle that inevitably flows between the textualized epistle-author and the presupposed addressee and reader. Simplicity greets Simplicity, but the construction and validation of meaning is far from simple.

---

[3] On the early modern market-place and the public sphere, see Halasz.
[4] Simplicity has been thought to represent Middleton's collaborator in the masque Rowley on the assumption that Rowley as actor in the Prince's Men would have played the role. But by 'socially allusive' I mean a vehicle for satire.

In the examples discussed so far, the textual speaker is located at various points between the poles of author and fictional invention. One text breaks this convention, following instead the conventions of scripted speech and other formal addresses. In the epistle 'To our Loving Subjects' in *The Peacemaker*, Middleton speaks through the mouth of the King himself. By this act of impersonation, King James is seen to be introducing an apology in praise of himself. In fact the author is alternating his speaking voice from that of the King to that of the praiser of the King.

Epistles actually or supposedly aimed at particular readers stand in enigmatic relation to the anonymous medium of print, for after all the letter is a personal and private form of writing usually confined to a single manuscript copy. If the addressing voice can become ambiguous, so too can the identity of the addressee. A work of Calvinist piety, *The Two Gates of Salvation* (1609) is printed anonymously; it is only by referring to the 1620 reissue with its new preliminaries that we can identify Middleton as the author. It has an open-ended and anonymous dedication, headed 'TO THE VERY WORthy deseruer of all true honours, and constant louer of Religion and Learning', after which there is a white space deep enough to accommodate a name. The dedication closes 'Deuotedly most affectionately to your' after which no more words are printed. A word such as 'servant' seems to have been omitted as well as the writer's name, leaving the very relationship between signatory and addressee open. The blank spaces below the dedicatory heading and the end of the dedication seem to have been left for completion in the writer's own hand (in complete contrast with the dedication in Ralph Crane's transcript of *The Witch*, where even the author's name has been transcribed). The implication might be that Middleton proposed to dedicate the book to various different individuals. We have moved from the letter as a singular means of address, and even from the printed letter as a replication of the singular in near-identical form, to the reindividuated printed letter. It produces a scattering of the addressee as each and every copy of the book is left to be completed and personalized by hand. The notion of dispersed dedication mapping out a community of the virtuous is something alien to our presuppositions that a compliment will be specific and preferably unique. The position of inscriber is as unregulated as that of dedicatee. Theoretically at least, any purchaser might trespass on the authorial prerogative to dedicate, making a present of the book by treating the dedication as his or her own godly gift-card. Whether such an act should be regarded as an acceptable practice or as a subversion of the text is hard to say, but it certainly lies well within the range of logical possibilities that the text presents.

When his texts are published with authorial intent, Middleton shows himself to be unusually aware of the reader, which is to say unusually active in constructing the textual reader. The diversity of his texts reflects itself in the diversity of assumed book-buyers. *The Two Gates of Salvation* invokes godly readers, whereas the self-consciously literary *Ghost of Lucrece* follows its dedication with an Invocation in Latin, which implies an academic readership. Middleton identified *Microcynicon* generically and in terms of anticipated readers by alluding to Joseph Hall, who had introduced Juvenalian satire to English readers; *Microcynicon* opens with '*His defiance to Envy*', thereby imitating Hall's introduction to his Satires with *A Defiance to Envy*. Middleton does not usually define his readership purely in terms of social class. Other writers commonly addressed 'gentlemen readers', a phrase that makes assumptions about both class and gender. Middleton does so only in the epistle attached to *The Wisdom of Solomon Paraphrased*, an early work that the seventeen-year-old Middleton aimed at an otherwise unexampled height by dedicating it to the Earl of Essex. In contrast, the verses attached to *Masque of Heroes* refer to the ladies in the masque's audience, and so might elicit a female readership.

Addresses to readers are fictional but allusive means to real ends. The ends are to promote and consolidate actual readerships. In this, Middleton was far more active than, for example, Shakespeare, though his activity primarily reflects the diversity of his writing practices and his regular publication of printed civic pageants. Otherwise the contrast would be less apparent: Middleton provided an authorial address to only one play from the public stage; Shakespeare wrote carefully meditated dedications of the two narrative poems he brought to the press. Though inevitably respectful to his patrons, Middleton is familiar with his general readers. He does not, like Jonson, stand aloof, hector, educate; he does not offer himself as the only authoritative reader of his own text. More modestly, he draws his audience into a circle whose admission price is a few pence.

Numbering Readers: Edition Sizes and Reprinted Texts

The various non-specific epistles and dedications attached to Middleton's works show the author's real or assumed sense of his readers. But a description of Middleton's readers does not lie at the mercy of authorial intention. In the case of printed books a consideration of edition sizes and edition numbers can yield some information about the numbers of Middleton's readers. In a very small minority of cases these readers can be identified as dedicatees, patrons, known owners of copies. Similar information is available for manuscripts, where circulation is far more restricted and the chances of pinpointing the recipient are much higher.

STC and Wing recognize eighty-one editions of Middleton works in the period up to 1670.[5] Amongst these may be found both true reprints and variant states of the original edition. There is a surprisingly large number of the latter in the Middleton canon. Standing type was reprinted in *The Patient Man and the Honest Whore*, *Magnificent Entertainment*, and *A Game at Chess*. The two issues of *Father Hubburd's Tales*, *The Revenger's Tragedy*, *A Trick to Catch the Old One*, *Sir Robert Sherley*, *The Changeling*,

---

[5] See Appendix A for a listing of all editions.

and *Hengist* are all practically identical apart from the variant imprints. W. W. Greg suggested that the variant issue of *The Changeling* that lacks the stationer's name may have been intended for private circulation (Greg 1939–59, ii, 828), though it is perhaps more likely that the publisher Moseley was responding to intensified opposition to the publication of plays in early 1653 (Lawrence, 37–8). In other cases, a variant title-page might accompany a cancel, as is the case with *The Triumphs of Truth* (reissued in 1613, the year of original publication, with a text of *His Lordship's Entertainment* appended to the original printing), and the 1617 second impression of *A Fair Quarrel* (which introduces 'new additions').

The Stationers' Company imposed a maximum print-run of 1,500 from a single setting of type. In many of the cases just reviewed the intention was probably to exceed this maximum by giving the impression of bringing out a genuine new edition. It is generally considered that by the sixteenth century an edition quantity of less than 500 would have been regarded as uneconomical (Gaskell, p. 161), but, although a run of 1,000 to 1,500 was common, there were circumstances, as Adrian Weiss shows elsewhere in this volume, in which a print-run might be as low as 100. Blayney finds the economics of publishing less favourable than Gaskell, suggesting that there would be only a modest return, depending on the rate of sales, on a fully sold print-run of 800. As most play quartos could not be expected to sustain a maximum print-run and go to a second edition, Blayney suggests that a typical print-run might be based on the expectation of 800 copies being sold (Blayney 1997, 396). The likelihood of a non-dramatic text being reprinted in a stationer's working lifetime does not differ much from that of a play quarto, so Blayney's figure can cautiously be accepted for Middleton's works as a whole. But there are circumstances in which a single edition was printed in different issues, and in these cases the issues can for present purposes be counted as editions. The implications for the total number of copies sold of reset imprints, expanded editions, and reprints from standing type will vary, but most instances suggest a long print-run in the first instance, and open up some possibility of anything up to 1,500 further sales. Given a working figure of 800 for a print-run, it is erring on the side of caution to treat them as separate and, on average, typical editions. But the figure of 800 itself needs revising downwards to produce an estimate of actual purchasers. Blayney's stationer calculates, of course, that he will print as many copies as he can expect to sell, but some of the editions that were not reprinted would certainly have failed to sell completely. I therefore hazard an estimate of 750 purchasers per edition. This would suggest that Middleton had over 60,000 purchasers.

Any such estimate must be set against the relatively low population of early modern England (between four and five million in the early-to-mid-seventeenth century), low literacy levels, and the concentration of the book-trade in one corner of the land. On the other hand, the total is spread over the best part of a century of book production. In contrast with this slow but steady individualized consumption, it has been calculated that as many as 22,000 spectators saw *A Game at Chess* during its nine-day run, over 100,000 people may have witnessed *The Magnificent Entertainment*, and tens of thousands would have seen each of Middleton's mayoral pageants. Moreover, the estimated number of purchasers has only the most broadly indicative value, and says even less about actual readers. By no means all purchasers would be readers, though, as both the range of leisure activities and the proportion of income available to spend on them were by modern standards restricted, there is less scope for a book lying unread after it had been bought. It would be more usual for a single copy to circulate within a group of family or friends, or pass on to a second owner; and indeed the names inscribed in copies of various works show examples of such circulation. The names of both Maria and Thomas Detton appear on their copy of *Sir Robert Sherley*; the title-page of *More Dissemblers Besides Women* in a copy of the 1657 *Two New Plays* is inscribed 'For my boy'. The same book has the names Arthur Ryland [1] and a 'Japlud Secundus' [2]. The unique extant edition of *Ghost of Lucrece* has some manuscript doggerel by two kinsmen, George [3] and Richard Fallowes [4], but the book was probably purchased by the 'G.O.' [5] who appears on the covers, and it subsequently came into the hands of Giles Paulet [6].[6] No less than four names appear in the National Library of Scotland copy of *Fair Quarrel*. The inscribed names are just the tip of an iceberg of shared reading.

There are therefore various uncertainties at play if one conjectures a readership by multiplying the number of known editions. Nevertheless, a reprint can be taken as a reaction to readers' responses, and usually a positive one. It most often indicates that the original edition has sold out, and the timing of reprints gives at least an approximate insight into a work's popularity. These true reprints can be divided between more or less immediate reissues that reflect a continuous and high level of demand for the text and later reprints that suggest a renewed or renewable interest in it.

Some early reprints no doubt sold well in the first edition because the work was intensely topical. *The Peacemaker* (1618), *The World Tossed at Tennis* (two editions in 1620), and *A Game at Chess* (1625), all works written to mark or respond to a public occasion, stimulated for a variety of reasons a greater interest amongst readers than, for example, the topical but unreprinted mayoral pageants. The explosive *A Game at Chess* was issued in two substantive quartos (STC 17882 and 17884), the first of which was reprinted (17883); the reprint was itself reissued with a new preliminary half-sheet (17885). All these editions

---

[6] The numbers given in brackets after the mention of a reader provide a reference system that allows the alphabetical listing in Appendix E to be used as an index.

seem to have appeared within a single year, and as all were illegal there would have been no effective limit on the print-run. *The Peacemaker* was even more in demand, though a less momentary phenomenon. Between 1618 and 1621 there were no less than five editions. Apart from *Penniless Parliament* (which, like *The Peacemaker* and *A Game at Chess* appeared without Middleton's name on it), Middleton thus gained his widest popularity as a published writer when he pretended to be King James and when he represented him in a play.

Every indication is that *A Fair Quarrel* was a popular stage-work. Prior to its first publication in 1617 it had already been revised, probably for a stage revival; it enjoyed Court performance before 1620 (Holdsworth, ed., xiv–xv), and a new edition appeared in 1622. *The Phoenix* (1630), *Michaelmas Term* (1630), *The Patient Man and the Honest Whore* (1615–16, 1635), and *A Mad World, My Masters* (1640) were issued by new publishers in search of new readers after a much longer delay, indeed several decades after their original publication. The Shakespeare Folio was reprinted in 1632, in 1663–4 (the edition in which *The Puritan* and *A Yorkshire Tragedy* were included for the first time as Apocryphal works), and in 1685. The Beaumont and Fletcher Folio, which included two plays, *The Nice Valour* and *Wit at Several Weapons*, now thought to be largely by Middleton, was reissued in 1679. Particular circumstances or events were able to renew the demand for a book. Whereas the reprints of *Phoenix* and *Michaelmas Term* reiterated the information on the first title-page, the 1640 edition of *A Mad World, My Masters* was reissued after a theatrical revival at the Salisbury Court theatre, and its title drew attention to the fact. The attribution of *A Yorkshire Tragedy* to William Shakespeare acquired new significance when Thomas Pavier [7] brought together a series of 'Shakespeare' plays for publication in quarto; Pavier's project thus gave new life to an old play and ultimately precipitated its appearance in the third Shakespeare Folio. Anne Moseley's [8] 1668 reissue of *The Changeling*, which was largely made up of leftover sheets of her husband's edition of 1653, advertised on the title-page the success of a recent revival by the Duke of York's players. The repackaging of the 1609 printing of *The Two Gates of Salvation* first as *The Marriage of the Old and New Testaments* in 1620 and then as *God's Parliament House* in 1627 testifies to very slow sales indeed; clearly a significant stock remained eighteen years after the original print-run, and the illusion of an entirely new book was created to stimulate new interest.

Book format, quality, and price determined who might actually buy. The Shakespeare Folio, and later the Beaumont and Fletcher Folio, were large and expensive books that brought texts Middleton had adapted or co-authored to a restricted group of affluent readers. It is estimated that the Shakespeare Folio sold at fifteen shillings for the unbound book and one pound for the bound volume in plain calf (Blayney 1991, 25–6). But cost was not the only distinguishing mark of a folio. As Roger Chartier has noted, 'It was during the last centuries of the hand-copied book that a lasting hierarchy was established between the great folio volume, the "shelf-book" of the universities and of serious study, which had to be propped up to be read, the humanist book, more manageable in its mid-sized format, which served for classical texts and new works of literature, and the portable book, the pocket book or the bedside book of many uses, religious and secular, and of a wider and less selective readership' (Chartier 1989, p. 2). The play folios of Jonson, Shakespeare, and Beaumont and Fletcher were encroaching upon a format traditionally reserved for scholarly study.

At the other extreme, the quartos and even cheaper octavos would often have had no intellectual pretension and would have sold for a few pence. One halfpenny per sheet was the legal maximum price for books (Plant 1965, 221), and we know of purchases of *A Mad World* for sixpence, and *Masque of Heroes* for fourpence. A play such as *The Patient Man and the Honest Whore*, emanating from the large public auditorium of the Fortune Theatre to be printed in large quantities in quarto format, must have reached out to a popular readership of apprentices and journeymen. Like printed ballads, printed plays were literary artefacts based on an oral performance text. None-theless, a play quarto was considerably more demanding on the semi-literate reader than a short broadside ballad illustrated with woodcuts, and it was several times more expensive. Middleton's prose pamphlets and pamphlet de-scriptions of Lord Mayor's shows were usually shorter than plays, and correspondingly cheaper. *The Penniless Parliament of Threadbare Poets* might have found thread-bare purchasers; editions of this black letter pamphlet were made up of just three sheets.

Short popular quartos and octavos might have been sold alongside broadsheets by chapmen. Tessa Watt has described how one Middleton reader, Frances Wolfreston, purchased 'penny godlinesses' and merry books, staple fare of the chapmen, but also quartos distributed by ballad publishers; 'It seems likely that she relied upon chapmen travelling the midlands for reading material between visits to more substantial shops' (Watt, 316). Wolfreston may have acquired her more substantial quarto volumes on visits to Birmingham and Coventry, as well as London. Certainly Middleton's books would most dependably have been bought in London, very often in Paul's Cross Church-yard, and so neighbouring the St Paul's theatre that produced many of his early plays. *Mad World*, *Michaelmas Term*, and *The Phoenix* are examples of Paul's Boys' plays issued from across the road in the Churchyard (Blayney, 1990). Only one Middleton edition was manufactured outside London, Thomas Finlason's [9] Edinburgh 1604 reprint of *The Magnificent Entertainment*, which was clearly brought out to satisfy Scottish public curiosity about the Scottish king's reception in the south. We know of one English provincial bookseller who, half a century later, publicized a number of Middleton titles to his customers in Newcastle-upon-Tyne. William London's [10] printed catalogue of 1658 listing 'the most vendible Books in England' testifies to a trade that must have continued in other, less remote, centres of population, and indicates one route whereby readers dispersed over England might have acquired their books. Included amongst just over a hundred plays are *Michaelmas Term* (1630), *The Phoenix* (1630), the Beaumont and Fletcher Folio (1647), the Shakespeare Folio (1632), *Old Law* (1656), *The Patient Man and the Honest Whore* (1635), *The Widow* (1652), and *The Changeling* (1653) (Greg 1939–59, 1299–1301). Middleton is not named, but in a supplement of 1660 he is the only dramatist to be mentioned; the supplement introduces *No Wit*, *More Dissemblers* and *Women, Beware Women*, all attributed to their author. The catalogues testify both to the popularity of plays as texts to be read, and to the reading of Middleton as an identified author, far from both the time and place of theatre performance.

Copies purchased in London directly by individual readers did not necessarily remain in the city. Courtiers and students of the Inns of Court are two specific and literate groups of people who were not permanently resident in London but had cause to be there for limited or extended periods. Though King James attempted, with little success, to send the gentry back to the counties, those that could afford to see and be seen in London usually did so. By their visits to London and voluntary or constrained returns home, the rural gentry spread books through the land; and indeed we know of Middleton book-owners in Kent, Salop, Staffordshire, and elsewhere.

Collaboration

The first readers of a text would be its writers. Despite the well-known anecdote that Robert Browning claimed not to understand his own poem, the author must always be an advantaged reader. Authorial revisions, such as are found in *A Fair Quarrel* and, more extensively, *A Game at Chess*, can be taken as an author's response as reader of his own text, just as Middleton's revisions of *Macbeth* and *Measure for Measure* can be taken as a reflection of his response to Shakespeare's plays. To Thomas Middleton [11] himself should be added the names of his collaborators:[7] Anthony Munday [12], Thomas Dekker [13], Michael Drayton [14], William Rowley [15],[8] William Shakespeare [16],[9] John Webster [17], John Ford [18], and Thomas Heywood [19]. These men certainly read at the very least the Middleton portions of the dramatic works to which they contributed, and the complete text will embody some mutual reader-response. Middleton's collaborators are amongst his most important readers.

Middleton actively collaborated with the scenic designers of his civic pageants as well as the dramatists (see Bergeron, 252–5). Garret Christmas [20], who is named at the end of *Antiquity*, *Aries*, *Virtue*, *Integrity*, and *Prosperity*, was the chief designer of the later pageants.[10] For *Industry*, Middleton was assisted by Rowland Bucket [21], whom he accounts 'chiefe master of the work', and 'my well approoued friend *Henry Wilde* [22] and *Iacob Challoner* [23], partners in the businesse'. He names Robert Norman [24] as Christmas's partner in *Antiquity*.

Reading and Reproducing the Text

Scarcely less notable than the first makers of the text as a semantic system are those who subsequently reproduced it, whether through theatrical performance or the production of new physical documents. In contrast with the conception of the reader as a recipient that is evoked, for example, by the term 'reception theory', these figures may be described as textual transmitters. Of course, neither receivers nor transmitters are inert, and indeed the distinction between them begins to founder when a particular act of reading leads on to a response such as annotation that takes the form of text. As McKenzie puts it, 'New readers make new texts and their new meanings are a function of their new forms' (20). The transmitters are indeed intrinsically caught up in a process of physical reinscription that does not apply to reading as it is usually understood. But the process involves reading, and that reading can be intimate and responsive.

Middleton's texts were processed by actors and other theatrical personnel, by scribes, miscellanists, and composers, by stationers and their employees. In some cases they were adapted by other writers. If they were plays they were subject to censorship by the Masters of the Revels; if they were to appear in print they required licensing by the ecclesiastical authorities or their agents. Most or all of these people would read at least some of the text. The nature of the reading activity is in every case specialized, and accordingly would vary considerably from one to another. And they are usually involved in repositioning the text: moving it away from the author, directing it towards further readers, redefining and diversifying the relation between text and reader.

Theatre

The various processes of bringing the authorial script towards performance on the stage can be seen most vividly in the manuscript of *The Lady's Tragedy*. Shortly after he copied the play, the scribe went over it, not only correcting his own mistakes but also adding what are evidently authorial revisions on separate slips of paper. Other interventions came from a playhouse reviser, who introduced sixteen marginal stage directions. He also seems to have been responsible for pasting the revision slips in the margin of the main manuscript, and identified the actor who would speak otherwise unassigned lines written in one of the slips (Lancashire, ed., 8–9). Sir George Buc, as Master of the Revels, supplied the play's licence to be performed subject to reformations. Changes in accordance with his demands and other minor revisions were effected by a third playhouse annotator. As Lancashire notes of dramatic manuscripts more generally, 'individual correctors did not necessarily make only one kind of change in a

---

[7] For full discussion of the contributions of collaborators, see the 'Canon and Chronology' section of the present volume.
[8] See below for Rowley as actor in Middleton's dramatic works.
[9] Shakespeare may have acted in *Timon of Athens*, *The Revenger's Tragedy*, and *A Yorkshire Tragedy*.
[10] Heinemann, 122, n. 3, indicates that Christmas may have been a Puritan.

MS' (Lancashire, ed., 11). A large number of other minor corrections cannot be assigned with confidence to any of the agents identified; further hands may have introduced some of them, and one of these hands might have been Middleton's.

The playhouse reviser of *The Lady's Tragedy* identified points in the text where the King's Men actors 'm^r Goughe' (Robert Gough) [25] and 'Rich Robinson' [26] were to appear. Gough played a noble, probably Memphonius. The note for the boy Robinson, later one of the company's most prominent actors, specifies that he takes the leading female role of the Lady. These two annotations provide a reminder that the most vital group of textual transmitters, and the most conspicuous of all to the original audiences, would have been the actors who performed Middleton's plays. They would have read and memorized their roles in the manuscripts of actors' parts, and would have been familiar with the rest of the play. A full listing of the actors who inferably must have or are likely to have performed in Middleton's dramatic works would include most if not all of the regular professional actors active between 1601 and 1624. For present purposes attention may be confined to specific theatrical figures who are more certainly known to have read plays or played parts in them.[11] Here may be included not only the actors themselves but also the sharers' committees and managers who selected plays for performance and, comparable to the professional theatre's sharers and managers, the guild committees that read and approved proposals for pageants.

Early in Middleton's dramatic career, the theatrical manager Philip Henslowe [27] issued payments to Middleton for several works. Henslowe probably had at least some say in the choice of scripts (Carson, 32–3), but this was the main responsibility of the leading sharers. Henslowe's *Diary* often indicates the sharer at whose managerial appointment the payments were made, and who therefore had most immediate responsibility for the play in question. Thomas Downes [28] of the Admiral's Men authorized payments for *The Two Shapes* (*Caesar's Fall*) on 29 May 1602, and for the new prologue and epilogue to *Friar Bacon and Friar Bungay* on 14 December of the same year. Payments for *The Chester Tragedy* were made at the appointment of Edward Juby [29], of the same company, on 21 October and 9 November. A few weeks previously, on 3 October, John Duke [30], of Worcester's Men, authorized Middleton to be paid for the unnamed play.

The 1604 text of *The Magnificent Entertainment* gives detailed information about those involved in a dramatic production of a very different kind. On sig. H4 'W. *Bourne*, one of the seruants to the young Prince' is named as the player of Zeal, whose speech Middleton wrote; '*Bourne*' is a textual error, for the actor in question must be William Birde [31] of the Prince's Men. A note on I3^v-4 notes 'those who gave the maine direction, and undertooke for the whole busines': William Friselfield [32], George Mosse [33], John Knight [34], Paul Isacson [35], Samuell Goodrick [36], Richard Wood [37], and George Heron [38], 'Over whom, Stephen Harrison Joyner [39] was appointed chiefe; who was sole Inventer of the Architecture'. These directors were evidently City personnel and have no known association with the professional theatre.

At about the time when *The Magnificent Entertainment* was produced Middleton turned to the boys' companies for employment. Whereas the affairs of the adult companies were run by principal actors, the boys were usually under adult supervision and entrepreneurial management. Paul's Boys, the most regular performers of Middleton's plays in the early years, was run by Edward Pierce [40], who was joined, apparently in late 1605, by Edward Kirkham [41] (Chambers, ii, 21–2). Their rivals the Children of the Blackfriars, who performed *Your Five Gallants* and the lost *The Viper and her Brood*, were managed after the *Isle of Dogs* scandal of February 1606 on a sharing system like that of the adult companies, but with Robert Keysar [42] as overseer (Chambers, ii, 52; Gurr 1992, 53–4). The managers of both companies would have been responsible for reading Middleton's manuscripts and accepted them for performance.

Masque of Heroes was performed, according to the title-page, by gentlemen of the Inner Temple, but the named actors who gave the production professional strength are more immediately associated with Prince Charles's Men. Joseph Taylor [43] (Doctor Almanac) was on the brink of a successful career as Burbage's replacement with the King's Men. Middleton's collaborator William Rowley played Plumporridge, a characteristic fat clown's part; he probably later appeared as the Fat Bishop in *A Game at Chess*.[12] The gaunt part of a Fasting Day was taken by John Newton [44]; Hugh Atwell [45] performed New Year, fittingly, if, as Rowley's elegy of 1621 indicates, he was a little man. William Carpenter [46] played Time.

In 1623 John Heminges [47] and Henry Condell [48] introduced a collection of Shakespeare plays that included a Middleton collaboration and probably two Middleton adaptations. Heminges was no longer acting by the time of Shakespeare's death, and Condell may have retired from acting around 1619; thus Condell could have played in the adapted version of *Macbeth*, and either actor could have appeared in *Timon of Athens* and Middleton's other early to middle work for the King's Men. Middleton wrote an elegy on the death of Richard Burbage [49]; this gives strong reason to suppose that Burbage acted in Middleton plays, though the elegy does not single out plays or roles for special mention.

Thomas Heywood (1635) mentions Middleton amongst other dramatists. Heywood was an actor as well as a dramatist, but he performed with a company, the Worcester's-Queen Anne's men, with which Middleton

---

[11] I note all identifiable actors up to 1642, and subsequently major theatrical figures only.
[12] As mentioned above, it is also sometimes conjectured that he also played Simplicity in *The World Tossed at Tennis*.

had no known association. Three otherwise unknown actors—Robert Briggs [50], Blackson [51], and Robert Str[atford?] [52]—can be more firmly connected with Middleton, for they are named in the prompt stage directions of *Hengist* (Bald, ed., 1938, xx–xxi and xxviii). Two actors with Queen Henrietta's Men can similarly be associated with the role of Antonio in Caroline revivals of *The Changeling*; contemporary references indicate that the part was evidently taken by William Robbins [53] and later Timothy Reade [54] (Bawcutt, ed., xxvii–xxviii). In John Rhodes's [55] late-Interregnum production of the play, Thomas Betterton [56] is recorded to have played De Flores, and Thomas Sheppey [57] played Antonio (Bentley, *Jacobean and Caroline Stage*, vol. 4, p. 862). Shortly before the Restoration, *The Widow* was one of the plays put on by pre-1642 actors at the Red Bull.

The Widow subsequently passed into the repertory of the new King's Men at the Theatre Royal under the management of Thomas Killigrew [58]; so too did *More Dissemblers*, *Hengist*, and plays in the Fletcher canon. *The Nice Valour*, *More Dissemblers*, *Hengist* ('The Mayor of Quinborough') and *The Widow* are all named in the 1669 catalogue of plays allotted to Killigrew (Nicoll, 353–4). Sir William Davenant [59] had acquired rights to a number of plays by Shakespeare and others as early as 1660; amongst them are *Measure for Measure* and *Macbeth*, both of which were subsequently staged in adapted form by his company, the Duke of York's Men. A number of other plays from the Shakespeare and Fletcher folios, including *Timon of Athens* and *Wit at Several Weapons*, were assigned to Davenant a few months before the allocation to Killigrew. A decade later Shadwell's adaptation of *Timon* played at Davenant's Dorset Garden theatre. Thomas and Mary Betterton [60] were well known for their performances in the leading roles of *A Trick to Catch the Old One* and *The Changeling*, which had also came into the hands of the Duke of York's Men, as did *No Wit/Help like a Woman's*, adapted as *The Counterfeit Bridegroom*. In the latter, Sir Oliver was played by Anthony Leigh [61], and his follower Sam by John Richards [62] (Gewirtz, 58).

As part of the regular processing of manuscripts in the course of becoming official playbooks, the various Masters of the Revels would have read and allowed all of Middleton's plays that reached performance. Plays written for the Children of the Blackfriars (which certainly included the lost *Viper and Her Brood*) would have been submitted for licensing to Samuel Daniel [63], who had been allocated the duties of the Master of the Revels for this one company.[13] Sir George Buc [64] licensed *The Lady's Tragedy* subject to reformations; he may have censored *Hengist* (Bald, ed., 1938, xxxii–xxxiii), but probably also selected it for Court performance. It is amongst the plays listed on Revels Office slips; the note 'Maior of Quinborough' is in another hand, but Buc added the now more familiar title 'or Hengist K. of Kent'.

Sir Henry Herbert [65] was confirmed as Master of the Revels in 1623. *More Dissemblers* was relicensed for revival in the same year, and *The Changeling* received its approval early in 1624 (Bawcutt 1996, 146 and 148). Herbert would have been responsible for selecting *More Dissemblers* for Court performance, yet described that Court performance in a marginal note to his record of the event as 'The worst play that e'er I saw' (Bawcutt 1996, 148). Despite its controversial subject-matter, *A Game at Chess* too was licensed by him (Bawcutt, 152, 153, 154; Bentley 1941–68, iv, 871 and 874).

Though he never saw a printed text, Herbert 'read' *More Dissemblers* in at least three ways: he engaged in the physical and mental operations of interpreting the ink-marks on the manuscript as signs; he scanned the manuscript professionally with a view to detecting inadmissible material and new alterations; and he came up with a judgement based on a 'reading' or interpretation of the play on the stage. Similar overdeterminations of the reading process are involved when a play is adapted for theatrical revival. An adapter must necessarily read very actively in both literal and interpretative senses of the word—with the added complication that the outcome is a new performance text which is not only a response to the old play but also becomes itself the basis for further acts of reading.

Adaptation was a process with which Middleton, as adapter of *Macbeth* and *Measure for Measure*, was himself familiar. Curiously, Middleton's own re-vision of Shakespeare became the starting point for some of the earliest Restoration adaptations by Davenant, whose first attempts at rewriting Shakespeare were directed towards the very plays Middleton had reshaped. He worked *Measure for Measure* together with material from *Much Ado About Nothing* to result in *The Law against Lovers* of 1662, and produced his version of *Macbeth* in the following year. If Middleton thus anticipated the Restoration practices of adapting Shakespeare, then, as Davenant had connections with the pre-Interregnum theatre, he may conjecturally have been aware of the example Middleton had set. Davenant extended Middleton's introduction of songs into *Macbeth* by preserving the Hecate scenes and developing the play further towards an operatic piece. In contrast, he opposed the tendency of Middleton's reworked *Measure*. Bawdry was jettisoned. The role of Mariana was deleted, and hence the adaptation's one song was lost. The 'bed-trick', highlighted in the adaptation, was abandoned. In a conclusion scarcely imaginable from the hand of Middleton, Davenant allowed Isabella and Angelo to be reconciled in marriage. The Restoration taste for adapted versions of plays from the earlier age was later gratified with Thomas Shadwell's [66] version of Shakespeare and Middleton's *Timon of Athens*, produced in 1678, and revived in 1694 with music by Henry Purcell [67]. Thus

---

[13] It is not clear whether his responsibilities continued after 1606. See Gurr 1992, 54.

Timon, like *Macbeth*, became operatic. Shadwell's text facilitated this transmutation by allowing Timon a loyal and rich fianceé who joins him in his cave in the woods. Many of the lines Middleton wrote for the Steward Flavius are transferred to her: a conspicuous reversal of Shakespeare and Middleton's insistence that all Timon's relationships are defined primarily in terms of economic dependence, and that women are peripheral.

Restoration reworkings of Middleton did not generally acknowledge their origins. Attitudes to literary borrowing were strung out between the free and easy practices of the less innovatory theatrical adapters and the censorial comments of Gerald Langbaine, whose critics accused him of an obsessive interest in plagiarism. Reflecting this interest, Langbaine annotates Restoration borrowings, and so provides a convenient chart of the fortunes of Middleton plays. As he notes, two of the characters in Davenant's *The Wits* might be modelled on counterparts in *Wit at Several Weapons* (Langbaine 1691, 216), and parts of *A Chaste Maid in Cheapside* were 'stollen *verbatim*' (504) in *The Life of Mother Shipston*, a play now attributed to Thomas Thompson [68]. John Leanerd [69], whom Langbaine calls a 'confident Plagiary', lifted the Gypsy scenes from *More Dissemblers* for his 1678 comedy *The Rambling Justice* (319–20).

A year earlier, a dramatist usually identified as Aphra Behn [70] (but possibly Thomas Betterton) brought *The Counterfeit Bridegroom* to the stage. This farcical comedy closely follows and retains much of the language of *No Wit*, especially the Low-water/Goldenfleece plot. The adapter extended an emphasis on the female characters that is already pronounced in Middleton's play; Marston Stevens Balch considers that this might offer some confirmation that Behn was the dramatist responsible. No Restoration adaptation follows a Middleton original more closely (Balch, 1–58). 'Only an Old Play of *Middleton's*', Langbaine noted dismissively (Langbaine 1691, 529), but as the play was perhaps with a due caution published as anonymous, he could not blame the adapter. *The Counterfeit Bridegroom*, and perhaps *No Wit* as well, were raided by the Drury Lane actor and hack dramatist George Powell [71] in his compilation of borrowings *A Very Good Wife*, but there is little by way of a reader's response detectable here (Balch, 59–73).[14] Behn herself seems to have been particularly drawn to Middleton, perhaps on account of a wit that with a little modification suited Restoration taste well as much as for his focus on female characters, though the latter quality made his plays relatively congenial to the restored stage with its female actors. According to Langbaine, Behn took the character of Follywit in *A Mad World, My Masters* and transcribed 'Part of the Language' of the play for *The City Heiress*, which also drew on the plot of *Trick to Catch the Old One* (Langbaine 1611, 19); she 'so well esteem'd' *Masque of Heroes* (the same that was, in Middleton's words, 'made for Ladies') that she borrowed from that too for the same play (p. 372). The device in *The Lucky Chance* (1686) of the female seducer who surrounds herself with a Circean atmosphere of sorcery and insists

on blindfolding her lover to protect her reputation seems to hark back to *The Bloody Banquet*, and has analogues in *The Witch* as well.

There are earlier precedents for what, even in the seventeenth century, was beginning to be seen as the opportunism that helped shape the Restoration stage. Lord David ('Lordling') Barrey [72], in *Ram Alley*, and Philip Massinger [73], in the Welborne plot of *A New Way to Pay Old Debts*, had both taken freely from Middleton's *A Trick to Catch the Old One*. In contrast, James Shirley [74], in reviving *No Wit* at the St Werburgh Street theatre in Dublin, was probably content to add a new prologue and act divisions, and to make perhaps no more than one minor revision by way of updating the play—though the act divisions and revision could be the work of someone else involved in the revival, such as John Ogilby [75], who as manager of the theatre is likely at least to have read the play. Shirley's Prologue was printed in his *Poems, Etc.* of 1646. It may be read in the *Collected Works*, where it is appended to *No Wit*. A new prologue and epilogue were supplied for the Restoration revival of *The Widow*, but their author is unknown; they were printed in William Hickes's [76] *London Drollery, or The Wits' Academy* (1673) (Bentley 1941–68, iv, 901).

Manuscript

Amongst Middleton's closest readers must have been the professional scribes who prepared manuscripts for the theatre and for private readers. These manuscripts are mostly lost, and their makers unknown. But Ralph Crane [77] transcribed *The Witch* into an attractive little quarto-sized manuscript. In its layout it draws eclectically on the conventions appropriate to manuscript and printed book; it is clearly tailored as a gift for presentation. Crane also copied three extant manuscripts of *A Game at Chess*, one of them, the Malone manuscript, from the same stock of paper as *The Witch* (Greg and Wilson, ed., 1950, viii). It is strongly inferred that he supplied a lost manuscript that served as copy for the printed text designated Q3 and for the later scenes of Q1.[15] He is the scribe of the extant manuscript of 'A Song in Several Parts' (Howard-Hill 1972, 11); he also probably prepared the copy for Webster's *Duchess of Malfi*, which was prefaced by Middleton's commendatory verse 'Upon this Masterpiece of Tragedy'.[16] In modern terms, Crane can be regarded as editor as well as scribe. He extensively modified the punctuation and the forms of contractions he found in his copy, and in plays he might alter the wording of stage directions, correct speech-prefixes, regularize act or scene divisions, and modify some of the profanity (Howard-Hill

---

14 When Behn's own novel *Oroonoko* was dramatized by Thomas Southerne he added scenes modelled most probably on *The Counterfeit Bridegroom*. Balch, 74–113, details this and other borrowings from the adaptation, but only *The Counterfeit Bridegroom* itself draws directly and demonstrably on Middleton's play.
15 Howard-Hill, ed., 1990, viii-x, and 1993, 6–8 and 49–51, draws on Bald, ed., 1938, and Nascimento.
16 It has been proposed as well that the printer's copy for *Women, Beware Women* was in Crane's hand (Mulryne in Middleton 1975, xxvi-xxvii; Howard-Hill 1992, 126), but in my view this seems unlikely.

1972 and 1992). In most respects his changes were concerned with presentation rather than substance, even if he took a broad view as to what might fall within the scope of presentation.

In many other respects Crane was a careful and dutiful transcriber. In other situations, such as where a scribe happened to be compiling a verse miscellany, he might see much less obligations to the copy, and there are considerable possibilities for substantive textual variation, and indeed creative alteration or addition. One Middleton song, 'Hence, all you Vain Delights' (*The Nice Valour*, 3.3.36–54), makes a spectacular entry into the culture of manuscript transmission and publication. As well as being copied into an exceptionally large number of miscellanies, it was set to music, adapted, and imitated. This wide and various proliferation is not at all by virtue of the song's appearance in the Beaumont and Fletcher Folio of 1647, for many of the manuscripts date from the 1630s, long before that volume became available. Peter Beal lists forty-one extant manuscripts containing the lyric, which is a higher figure than for any other play-song. Many of these miscellanies and songbooks can be ascribed to a compiler or early owner. The multiple manuscripts are intriguing not only because they contain a substantial number of named owners and readers, but also because they show the text thriving in extreme dislocation from its original author and theatrical environment. Its success depends on that dislocation, or rather on the new set of associations generated by the environment of manuscript culture.

'Hence, all you Vain Delights' was subject to the usual and in this case extensive adaptations by way of verbal alterations and cutting. In addition it was provided variously with a new stanza, a parody, and an 'answer'.[17] A verse miscellany, Bodleian MS Rawl. poet. 84, contains two copies of 'Hence, all you Vain Delights' onto which a six-line stanza from 'The Farewell' by Henry King (1592–1668) has been grafted.[18] The result, on ff. 66–65^v, is:

A Song

Hence all you Vaine delights
As short as are the nights
Wherein you spend your folly
Thre's nothing truly sweet
If men were wise to see't
But onely melancholy
Welcome, folded armes, and fixed eyes
A sight that peircing mortifies
A looke that's fastned to the ground
A Tongue chaind up without a sound
Fountaine heades, and pathlesse groues
Places which Pale Passion loues
Moon light walkes when all the Fowles
Are warmely hous'd saue bats, and Owls
A midnights bell, a parting groane
These are the sounds we feed upon
Then stretch our bones in a still gloomy Vally

Theres nothing truly sweet
My woful monument shall be a Cell
The murmur of the purling brooke may [*sic*] knell
And for my epitaph the rocks shall groane
Eternally, If any aske the stone
What wretched thing doth in that compasse lye
The Hollow Eccho answer will Tis I: I:

The presence of lines by King—a lyric poet associated with John Donne, Jonson, Robert Burton, King James, and King Charles—confirms the 'cavalier' spirit of the culture into which the song was migrating. This process of transformation is taken a stage further in British Library Add. MS 47111, f. 11, where the addition of the King stanza at the end is counterbalanced by omission of the six lines that usually open the song. It is beginning to metamorphose beyond recognition.

These adaptations are unlikely to represent Henry King's own responses to the song, but rather would have been put together by compilers who married two poems to bring forth a small brood of new ones. William Strode [78], on the other hand, certainly knew the poem, which in manuscript circulation was often given the title 'On Melancholy'. There are numerous manuscript copies of Strode's reply, sometimes headed 'Opposite to Melancholy'; both poems were published in *Wit Restored* (1658), compiled by Sir John Mennes [79] (1599–1671) and published by Robert Pollard [80], Nathaniel Brooks [81], and Thomas Dring [82]. They are headed '*The lover's Melancholy.*' and '*The answer, by Dr. Stroad.*' Strode's answer-poem may be cited from one of his autograph manuscripts (Corpus Christi, MS 325):[19]

---

[17] I am grateful to Anne Forde, who transcribed all British manuscripts of the song in an unpublished MA dissertation (University of Birmingham, 1994), for pointing out the augmented and truncated British Library Add. MS 47111 and the Ashmole imitation.

[18] The last lines are considerably variant on the stanza as printed in King's *Poems, Elegies, Paradoxes, and Sonnets* (1657):

My woful Monument shall be a Cell,
The murmur of the purling brook my knell;
My lasting Epitaph the Rock shall grone:
Thus when sad Lovers ask the weeping stone,
What wretched thing does in that Center lie?
The hollow Eccho will reply, 'twas I.

A manuscript in King's hand (Bodleian MS Mal. 22, f. 13^v) gives a text closer to the conflation:

My wofull Monument shall be a Cell,
The murmur of the purling brook my Knell.
And for an Epitaph, the Rock shall groane
Eternally: if any ask the Stone
What wretched thing does in that compasse ly,
The hollow Eccho will reply, 'Twas I.

A substantively invariant text of this version of the stanza appears in Bodleian MS Eng. poet. e. 30, also in King's hand.

[19] See also Dobell, in Strode 1907, 15. For the song's textual development and a facsimile of another autograph manuscript, see Croft, i, 42–3. On the authorship of 'Hence, all you Vain Delights', which Dobell includes as a Strode poem, see 'Canon and Chronology', under *Nice Valour*. The misattribution to Strode probably arises because it appears in several manuscripts immediately before 'An Opposite to Melancholy'. This is a common cause of misattribution; for another Strode example see Hobbs, 185.

An Opposite to Melancholy.

Returne my Joyes and hither bring
A tong not made to speake but sing;
A Jolly spleene, an Inward Feast,
A Causeless Laugh without a Jeast;
A Face which Gladnes doth annoynt,
An Arme for Joy flung out of Joynt;
A sprightfull Gate that leaues no print,
And makes a Feather of a Flint;
A Heart that's lighter then the Aire,
An Eye still dancing in its sphere,
Strong Mirth which nothing shall controwle,
A Body nimbler than [a] some Soule;
Free wandring thoughts on all things not tied to
    Muse,
Which think on all things, nothing chuse,
Which er'e we see them come are gon;
These Life itself doth liue upon.
Then take no Care but only to be Jolly;
To be more wretched then we must is Folly.

Middleton's lyric and Strode's reply were probably known to Milton [83]. As J. B. Leishman argues (120–59), they probably supplied a model for his own paired poems 'L'Allegro' ('Hence, loathed Melancholy') and 'Il Penseroso' ('Hence, vain deluding joyes').[20] Middleton's text, unlike the separated lyric, was written 'impersonally' for the dramatic score; Milton's later epic poetry owes much to the antagonistic traditions of drama. It is interesting to note how the intellectual exercise of adapting a lyric into a new dialogue gives rise to a bridge between the two dialogic writers.

'Hence, all you Vain Delights' stimulated, as well as Strode's reply and Milton's elaboration, another response that comes close to parody. In his folio-sized and ostentatiously royalist miscellany book (Bodleian, MS Ashmole, 36.37), Elias Ashmole [84] inscribed line-for-line, alongside his transcription of the song itself, the following ingenious Cavalier rebuttal:[21]

Come all my deare delights,
As pleasing as the Nights,
Consum'd in Bachus drenches;
Ther's nought in this world sweete,
If Men had Eyes to see't;
Save only Wine, & Wenches.

Welcome circling Armes, & rowling Eyes,
A Laugh that peirceth through ye skies,
A Wench that's prostrate on ye ground;
A Tongue yt yeilds a pleasing sound;
Maiden heads, & deedes of Love,
Things wch freer *Accons*[22] move,
And smiles of pleased weights;
Sporting walkes, when all ye Fowles
Doe sleepe secure saue Batts & Owles;
Theis are our free Delights.

Midnight healths, & parting Bowles,
Theis are ye things yt glad or Soules;
Then strech yor Bones on Taverne benches,
There's nothing sweete, save Wine, & Wenches.[23]

In addition to these examples of elaboration and response, the same song circulated widely in manuscript, both songbook and verse miscellany.[24] In one instance it is inscribed at the back of a richly-decorated fifteenth-century astrological manual (Bodleian, MS Lyell 37).[25] It appears as the last of a number of later insertions on spare leaves and other blank spaces, and as such finds company with 'Esops Fables in Meter', an English quotation from Du Bartas, and the dramatic fragment headed 'Cambridg Speakers Bande. Cuffe Ruffe.'.[26] A setting of the song ascribed to John Hilton [85] (1599–1657) is preserved in a mid-seventeenth-century songbook, and an alternative, anonymous, and probably earlier setting is found in two other manuscripts. It is the anonymous setting that might be from the theatre. But the widespread reproduction of the song and engagement with it in manuscript contexts shows that it had truly shifted from the theatrical milieu to the arena of manuscript circulation. No other lines by Middleton, and few by any writer, can have engaged individual seventeenth-century minds so actively and variously.

As has been seen, readership and transmission become two aspects of a single activity when a text or a portion of a text is included in a personal miscellany. Selection assumes prior reading, and indeed requires that the passage concerned has been read with special attention and approval. The manuscript's owner will more often than not be the scribe who copies the passage from its source document. In the following instances the scribe or the manuscript's owner can be identified.

A decade before Ben Jonson's [86] host Drummond of Hawthornden [87] heard Jonson describe Middleton as a base fellow, Drummond became the earliest known compiler of passages from Middleton plays. His manuscript verse miscellany *Ephemeris* of 1606–14 (National Library of Scotland, MS 2059) includes extracts from both *Mad World* and *Your Five Gallants*. Drummond owned a copy of the latter play. Middleton's short poem addressed to King James, 'To the King', survives in a number of manuscripts,

[20] Milton's pair of poems was first published in Humphrey Moseley's edition of Milton's *Poems* in 1645, two years before Humphrey Robinson and Moseley brought out *Nice Valour* in the Beaumont and Fletcher Folio. See below for Moseley as a publisher of Middleton.

[21] The royalist emphasis is established in the opening poem, 'Vpon the meeting of the King and Queene vpon Edge-hill'. Before f. 21 a copy of the pamphlet 'Sol in Ascendente: Or, The glorious Appearance of Charles the Second' (1660) has been sewn in. 'Come all my deare delights' appears a few leaves later, on f. 26.

[22] Or possibly 'Aecons'. I suspect a mistranscription of 'Amors' or 'Actions', which might be taken as evidence that Ashmole did not compose the lines.

[23] There is a longer but less salacious version of the parody with a musical setting in British Library, Egerton MS 2013.

[24] All known manuscripts are listed and described in Beal, *Index*, vol. I, part 1, pp. 93–5. For details of ascribable manuscripts, see Appendix C below.

[25] Later owned by R. Twopeny of Ipsden, Wallingford.

[26] A text of the latter, under the title *Ruff, Band, and Cuff*, edited from Folger MS J.a.2, can be found in *Jacobean Academic Plays*, 133–8.

one of which is a miscellany compiled within a few years of the *Game at Chess* uproar, in 1624–8 (British Library Add. MS 29492). The compiler was Sir Thomas Dawes [88]. Another copy is found in a miscellany apparently compiled by Sir Thomas Hulse [89], and later included in a composite volume put together by Peter Le Neve [90] (1661–1729). Middleton's short epitaph 'On the Death of Burbage' appears in Robert Bishop's [91] verse miscellany of *c*.1630 (Rosenbach MS 1083/16). By 1691 it was owned by Joseph Harrison [92]. John Evans's [93] *Hesperides, or the Muses' Garden*, prepared *c*.1655, is better known for its Shakespearean passages, amongst which there were twenty-seven from *Measure for Measure* and nineteen from *Timon*, but we learn from Evans's index (preserved in the Folger Library, MSS V. a. 75, V. a 79, and V. a. 80) that he also included extracts from *The Phoenix* and *A Mad World*.

Middleton's songs circulated widely in both verse miscellany and song-book, and attributable manuscripts of Middleton songs are listed below in Appendix C. Music--makers, like the compilers of verse miscellanies, frag-mented songs from plays and gathered various pieces together in new configurations. In addition to the set-tings of 'Hence, all you Vain Delights', several music manuscripts include settings of Middleton songs (Beal, Cutts). A full study of these books, the collocations they produce, the textual adaptations they originate, and the responses to the text implied by the musical setting, is far beyond the scope of this essay. But here, at the least, a highly idiosyncratic group of Middleton 'readers' can be identified. The songbook compiled by the composer and musician John Gamble [94] (d. 1687) contains Robert Johnson's [95] setting of 'In a Maiden Time Professed' from *The Witch*. Johnson's setting is also found in John Wilson's [96] volume of mostly his own song settings prepared *c*.1656, which may be in the hand of the com-poser, cathedral organist, and music copyist Edward Lowe [97] (*c*.1610–1682), or someone else associated with the Oxford music circle of the 1650s. The early seventeenth--century manuscript compiled by the musician John Bull [98] (*c*.1562–1628) preserves Johnson's arrangement of 'Come away, come away' from the same play. In a song-book of about 1620 once owned by Anne Twice [99] there is the Johnson setting of 'Come away, come away' and two anonymous settings of 'Cupid is Venus' Only Joy', the song performed in *More Dissemblers Besides Women* and *A Chaste Maid in Cheapside*. The latter lyric has the same arrangement in a manuscript songbook prepared *c*.1630, once owned by Richard Elliotts [100], and inscribed (in another hand) with the date 1668. Beal conjectures that the composer is Adrian Batten [101], though this attri-bution is insecure: Batten worked on Anglican church music and is not known to have composed secular or instrumental music, let alone settings for smutty lyrics.[27] Edward Lowe (1610–82), composer, musical copyist, and organist at Christ Church, Oxford, was, like Batten, a native of Salisbury, and Batten was for some time his

scholar. As well as probably acting as copyist in John Wilson's songbook, he assembled two large anthologies of music; the song 'I keep my horse' from *The Widow* is given what is probably a late musical setting by William Lawes [102] in one of them. To these various scribal examples may be added a music manuscript that found its way into print. Thomas Ravenscroft's [103] collection of songs, canons and catches *Melismata* (1611) includes the song 'My Master is so Wise' from *A Trick to Catch the Old One*. Ravenscroft, who had been a chorister at St Paul's before taking his music degree in 1605, may possibly have composed the music. All these settings may be examined in the collection of the music from Middleton's texts at p. 119.

As Robert Johnson was evidently employed to write songs for the King's Men, his settings of songs from *The Witch* may well have been composed for the theatre. It is characteristic of music circulation in the early and middle parts of the seventeenth century that composers such as Bull and Wilson should have been active in the copying and gathering of song settings. To some extent, then, the Middleton words become fortuitously drawn into a specialized field of manuscript circulation. In a late--Renaissance musical culture that sought to give equal weight to words and music, the lyrics can scarcely have been ignored. Furthermore, the efflorescence of Middleton songs in music does not depend on a theatrical origin for the song. Edward Lowe and John Hilton, at least, had no known connection with the London theatre.[28]

'Now this Book is every Reader's': Print[29]

In this section I will focus on those involved in the pro-duction and reproduction of Middleton's texts as printed books who had a sufficiently active interest for them to be, of choice or necessity, readers. The stationers who were engaged in book-production solely as a master printers can be passed by quickly, for they would have had no particular reason to give the copy or the printed book more than a cursory glance. In contrast, the compositors necessarily paid scrupulously close attention to the words on the page, but they set their copy in a mechanical fashion with limited attention to the words' semantic sig-nificance, and their response as readers was minimal. A less mechanical but still only minimally 'literary' reading would be given by the printer's correctors. In the case of the 1590s stationer John Danter we know that Thomas Nashe acted as corrector and that Henry Chettle worked on the acquisition, editorial preparation, composition, and perhaps correcting of some of Danter's books, but there are no comparably nameable figures involved in the printing of Middleton texts.

Even before a book could be printed it required licensing for print. This form of official control was separate from

---

[27] See the entry on Batten in Sadie.
[28] Neither is named in the index in Bentley 1941–68, vii.
[29] Quotation from Humphrey Moseley's epistle 'To the Reader' in Cartwright 1651.

the court-based system for regulating the performance of plays, falling under the jurisdiction of the ecclesiastical courts. London publishing was therefore under the authority of the Bishop of London. Yet we know of more Middleton books approved for publication by the office of the Master of the Revels than by any other licensor. The early seventeenth century saw a new practice of delegating approval to specialized authorities, 'doctors, lawyers, scholars, and the like' (Greg 1955, 109). The Master of the Revels came to act in this capacity as an expert in dramatic literature. Hence Buc's name appears as the licensing authority for the publication of eight Middleton plays in the Stationers' Register.[30] His deputy, Sir William Segar [104], gave authority for *A Mad World, My Masters*, and his successor Herbert did the same for *Chaste Maid*.

The Stationers' Register records several other licensors of Middleton works published during his lifetime, none of whom seems to have been connected with the office of the Revels. Authority for publication of *The Magnificent Entertainment* and *The Patient Man and the Honest Whore* came from Zachariah Pasfield [105], prebendary of St Paul's, deputizing for the Bishop of London. One John Wilson [106]—not the composer—licensed *A Yorkshire Tragedy*. *Sir Robert Sherley* was authorized by Richard Etkins [107], who was consulted primarily over works connected with European affairs in much the same way as the Masters of the Revels were sought out for plays. The previously unpublished plays in the Shakespeare First Folio, however, were licensed by Dr Worrall [108], probably the divine Thomas Worrall. During the Interregnum another ecclesiastical figure, Henry Langley [109], rector of St Mary's, Newington (earlier Middleton's parish church), gave authority for *Hengist*.[31] Sir Nathaniel Brent [110] licensed the 1650s editions of *The Widow* and *The Changeling*. After the theatres reopened, Sir Robert L'Estrange [111] was licensor for the Restoration adaptations of *Timon of Athens*, *More Dissemblers*, and *No Wit* when they appeared in print.[32]

The actual publishers and booksellers who dealt with Middleton books are considered more fully elsewhere in this volume, but something needs to be said here of their potential as readers and their role in constructing a readership. A publisher contemplating investing money in production of a book from a manuscript would usually read the manuscript in order to assess its suitability. Middleton's publishers up to 1670 are therefore included in the list of readers below. Even amongst publications in Middleton's lifetime, the plays at least would often have been sold without contact between publisher and author. *The Peacemaker* provides a documented case of such contact in a non-dramatic work, for King James gave William Alley [112] a special licence for the sole printing and selling of the book 'at the nomination of Thomᵃˢ Middleton'.[33]

Whereas Middleton's own addresses and dedications sometimes sought to conceive of readers in terms of their particularity, Middleton's later publishers and other preface-writers tended to speak to the readers as less specifiable figures, whilst particularizing the dead author. The effect is to set up an intertextual reading community organized around the idea of the author. Previously this had been possible in a patchy and informal way around 1606-8, when a number of Middleton plays from the boys' companies appeared in print within a short period of time, some of them naming Middleton or T.M. as the author, and again in the years when Middleton was writing civic pageants, when his name came to denote a specific and specialized authorial activity.

When he addressed the reader in his 1640 reissue of *A Mad World, My Masters*, the publisher John Spencer [113] was able to observe the original edition's advice that the play was 'Composed by T.M.'; he reprinted it and added the dignification 'Gent.'. Whether this refinement suggests that Spencer knew T.M.'s identity is unclear, but if he did he declined to pass this information on to his readers. Yet Spencer showed himself to be an acute and critical reader in his own right. As well as stationer, he was librarian at Sion College. In his epistle, the first sustained reader's response to a Middleton work, Spencer eschews the language of conventional compliment and recommends the play to the discerning reader who is able to make an historical adjustment in evaluating what had already become an old play. He speaks as a man of learning as much as a bookseller, and his attitude is at moments surprisingly apologetic:

> here & there you shall find some lines that doe answer in meetre, which I hope will not prove so disdainefull, whereby the booke may be so much slighted, as not to be read; or the *Authors* judgement undervalued as of no worth. Consider (gentle Reader) it is full twenty yeares since it was written, at which time meetre was most in use, and shewed well upon the conclusion of every Act & Scene.

Spencer fears that the faults he identifies may affect sales.[34] In his more positive comments, Spencer presents a Middleton who can be read for his modernity, a writer who rejects bombast for balanced and well-judged sentences:

> In the action, which is the life of a Comedy, and the glory of the Author, it hath bin sufficiently expressed, to the liking of the Spectators, and commendations of the Actors; who have set it forth in such lively colours, and to the meaning of the Gentleman that

---

30 *The Phoenix, Michaelmas Term, The Puritan, The Revenger's Tragedy, A Trick To Catch the Old One, Your Five Gallants, Masque of Heroes*, and *The World Tossed at Tennis*

31 And also twenty nine plays in the Beaumont and Fletcher Folio, but these do not include the Middleton pair.

32 For licensors of selected books of all kinds up to 1640, see Greg 1962. For licensors of plays and entertainments listed in Greg 1939-59, see iii, 1480-7.

33 Licence dated 19 July 1618, excerpted in Greg, ed., 1967, 163, and printed in facsimile and full transcription in the present volume, 660.

34 What he rejects is not verse (most Caroline comedies have more verse than *Mad World* itself), but rhyme (*OED*'s sense 19 of *answer* is 'to make a responsive sound, as an echo').

true penn d [*sic*] it, that I dare say few can excell them, though some may equall them. In the reading of one *Act* you guesse the consequence, for here is no bumbasted or fustian stuffe; but every line weighed as with ballance; & every sentence placed with judgement and deliberation.

Spencer's Middleton anticipates the sharp and witty writer who would be adapted for the Restoration stage.[35]

Humphrey Moseley's [114] Middleton of the 1650s was one of a number of pre-Interregnum dramatists whom the publisher issued in a uniform series of octavo volumes combining cheap format with relatively high cultural aspiration (Bell, 'Booksellers'; Kewes). In his epistle 'To the Readers' in his edition of Cartwright (1651), Moseley justifies the octavo format in these terms: 'If you ask, why its crowded in so scant a Volume? 'tis for your own sakes; we see it is such weather that the most ingenious have least money; else the Lines are as long as in Folio, and would equall those of trebble its price'.[36] The reference is to the fines and confiscations that had been exacted against the defeated Royalists. Moseley thus slanted his decision as a publisher so as to present it as an act of cultural alignment. The plays can no longer be performed and their admirers are impoverished; the two predicaments have the same cause, and cheap reading editions are the solution. Moseley compensated for the economy by supplying dignifications such as epistles and authorial portraits.

Two of Moseley's editions of works in the Middleton canon were prefixed with commendatory material. Alexander Gough [115], an actor with the King's Men in the Caroline period who became engaged in surreptitious theatrical performances during the Interregnum, has been described as the publisher of *The Widow* (1652). This is not technically true, for the publisher is Moseley, but Gough's address to the reader of *The Widow* makes it clear that he has sought out the publisher in order to 'present' the play to the readers. His role is the same as in the 1653 edition of *The Queen, Or, The Excellency of Her Sex* (published as anonymous but attributed to Ford). Though this play is described on the title-page as 'Found out by a Person of Honour, and given to the Publisher, Alexander Goughe', and one of the complimentary verse writers calls him 'Midwife Goughe', the play was actually published by Thomas Heath. In his epistle in *The Widow* Gough offers only vague comment on the play itself, but his address is crucial for retrieving Middleton as a named and canonical author, setting unfolioed Middleton alongside his supposed co-authors, folioed Jonson and Fletcher. Gough repeats the title-page attribution, describing the play as a '*lively piece, drawn by the art of* Johnson, Fletcher, *and* Middleton', and makes a virtue of their supposed collaboration by saying that it 'is thought to have a neer resemblance to the portraiture we have in *Terence* of those worthy minds, where the great *Scipio* and *Lælius* strove to twist the Poets Ivy with the victors Bayes'. Apart from the reprinted attribution of *Mad World* to 'T.M.' in 1640, this is the

first book to mention Middleton as its author since 1630 (*Chaste Maid*), and Moseley's first publication to name him. It is probably no coincidence that at this the beginning of Moseley's 1650s Middleton revival the dramatist's name is ushered in after prestigious collaborators whose hand in the play was an invention.

Moseley had already acted as co-publisher of the Beaumont and Fletcher Folio of 1647, and went on to issue *The Changeling, No Wit*, and *Two New Plays* (these being *More Dissemblers Besides Women* and *Women, Beware Women*); his widow Anne was to issue another edition of *The Changeling*. Some copies of *Two New Plays* and *No Wit/Help like a Woman's* were bound with an engraving of Middleton. The portrait presents a dignified authorial figure who implicitly upholds the excellence of the dramatic works. In an epistle attached to *Two New Plays* Moseley makes a statement as Middleton's publisher. Though he had probably read the manuscripts as a matter of course before deciding to issue them, he does not offer critical responses, but rather he carries forward the canonical project to the readers, invoking 'His name', 'his Reputation', and 'the Author in his deserved Esteem'. Moseley, in promoting that which he describes as a given authorial entity, is actually bundling up an entirely new vendible package.

Nathaniel Richards's [116] commendatory verse to *Women, Beware Women* in *Two New Plays* is much less apologetic about the theatrical past than Gough's epistle, and more explicit than Moseley's in terms of critical response. Richards emphatically insists on the play's success on stage:

Women beware Women; 'tis a true Text
Never to be forgot: Drabs of State vext,
Have Plots, Poysons, Mischeifs that seldom miss,
To murther Vertue with a venom kiss.
Witness this worthy *Tragedy*, exprest
By him that well deserv'd among the best
Of *Poets* in his time: He knew the rage,
Madness of Women crost; and for the Stage
Fitted their humors, Hell-bred Malice, Strife
Acted in State, presented to the life.
I that have seen't, can say, having just cause,
Never came *Tragedy* off with more applause.

Richards was author of *The Celestial Publican*, a work that combines Puritan religious sentiment with misogynist, anti-Court and anti-Jesuit satire, as well as the anti-tyrant play *Messalina* and *Poems Sacred and Satirical*. He dedicated works to the Parliamentary leader Alderman Thomas Sterne and to Viscount Rochford, the former associate of the parliamentarian Sir John Eliot (Heinemann, 171, n. 34). His response to Middleton's play is informed by his earlier writing against the Caroline court in *The Celestial*

---

[35] For further comment on Spencer's epistle, see Bell, 'Booksellers', in this volume.
[36] For a reprinting of Moseley's various epistles and dedications, see Reed, 73–103.

Publican, where he had already used the phrase *drab of state*:

> Neuer was any great Arch-mischiefe done,
> But by a Whore, or a Priest, first begun . . .
> A glorious shee *Smocke-statist* can amaze,
> Fire famous Troy, and set the world at gaze.
> A *Drab of State*, is a consuming Flame,
> Oft, fiers the Hearts of Princes, past reclaime,
> Turnes Ioy, to deepe and Melancholy sadnesse,
> Poysons the Bloud, and fils the braine with madnesse,
> *Why should she else, with painting seeme more
> faire?
> *Suffer her naked *Breasts* lie open bare? (sig. H1ᵛ–2)

As these lines already suggest, drama that was forbidden from representing the Stuart Court and moral satire whose only referent could be that Court shared the same discursive materials. Richards's commendatory poem is therefore neither a pure response to the text nor an oblivious reworking of his own earlier writings; those writings are already caught up in a response to the drama that enables the mixture of satire and melodrama found in passages such as these. *Women, Beware Women* itself was probably known to Richards long before it appeared in print, for there are echoes of it in all his published work. Mulryne, in his editions of the play (1962, i, pp. ii–iv; 1975, xxii), has pointed out reminiscences of it in *Messalina* and *Poems Sacred and Satirical*, but as *The Celestial Publican* (1630) is Richards's earliest published work, and as the phrase *drab of state* occurs in it, it would do well to establish reminiscences here too. For instance:

> When my soule-erring Eyes, staring behold
> A dang'rous Strumpet, flame in glit'ring gold,
> (And murd'ring Beauty; sparkling from her Eye
> Burning Temptation) (sig. F6)

This passage recalls Leantio's lines in *Women Beware*:

> When I behold a glorious dangerous strumpet
> Sparkling in beauty, and destruction too (3.1.95–6)

The all-important difference is that Middleton's lines are heavily laden with dramatic irony: Leantio is smugly celebrating the joys of marriage immediately after the scene in which his wife, unknown to him, has become the Duke's mistress. In his commendatory poem Richards seems similarly oblivious to the ironic possibilities of the play's title. Ignoring such complexities, he apprehends Middleton as a Pauline and misogynist anti-Court moralist, transporting the poet 'in his time' into an era when the Court was abolished, but to a moment within that era when the return of monarchy was becoming possible. Such transportation might have been quite literal if, as Mulryne persuasively suggests, Richards owned the manuscript of *Women, Beware Women* that in 1657 became the printer's copy. Richards is important as a careful and appreciative, if highly partial, reader of a play that was otherwise strangely neglected in its own century.

The various forms of textual transmission—theatrical and literary, manuscript and print—converge in John Cotgrave's [117] *English Treasury of Wit and Language* (1655), published also by Humphrey Moseley. Cotgrave is a miscellanist whose compilation appears in print, and whose interest was exclusively in the more or less defunct theatre. Rather ineffectively perhaps, he recognizes the commercial imperatives of the print industry. His book is in part designed to 'make my able and ingenious friend, the Stationer, a gainer by it', but though Moseley was engaged in the publication and sale of many of the plays quoted, his potential to benefit from Cotgrave's promotion of the 'best of our English DRAMMATICK POEMS' was actually limited. Cotgrave could not have stimulated interest in specific Moseley books, for he does not identify play-titles and dramatists. Instead he compiles an extensive collection of play quotations gathered under various thematic headings, selecting what he calls 'rich and usefull Observations' on a given subject that are expressed with 'almost a prodigious accrewment of their [the dramatists'] luxuriant fancies' (epistle 'To the Courteous Reader', in Cotgrave 1655). Despite embracing these 'luxuriant fancies', he is, therefore, a moral utilitarian. He can be seen as an Interregnum play-reader actively constructing a new view of the drama, and indeed his acts of selection and implied criticism constitute a kind of authorship in their own right. He seems aware of the difficulties that lie in squaring the spirit of his own times—at worst (as he recognizes in his address to the reader) a 'stiffe and obstinate prejudice'—with the drama's reputation for moral frivolity. The examples he chooses therefore seek to illustrate intellectual poise and even stylistic exuberance in the service of just observation and moral wisdom.

Attributions for Cotgrave's anonymous passages can be derived from the annotations in William Oldys's signed copy dated 1730, now in the Bodleian Library. John Munro's examination of the handwriting detected two or possibly three hands, none of them that of Oldys; he noted that the ascriptions 'are remarkably accurate and show a very extensive knowledge of the drama' (Ingleby, ed., ii, 52). Gerald Eades Bentley has likewise commended the 'thorough and careful searches' of the annotators (Bentley 1943, 194). These late seventeenth-century and early eighteenth-century textual investigators placed a high value on the identification of works and authors that contrasts vividly with Cotgrave's indifference. Their commitment to authorial canonicity meant that they read widely in the drama and retained much of their reading. Like Langbaine, they knew Middleton well.

As for Cotgrave, if one judges by the number of quotations devoted to each dramatist, if one reverses Cotgrave's active hostility to identifiable texts and authors,[37] and sets aside the very unknowability of the Middleton canon as an

---

[37] As Bentley notes, Cotgrave depersonalized quotations by suppressing personal names of dramatic characters, in keeping with the practices of commonplace-book compilers (Bentley 1943, 191). The extracts are contrived to stand as specimens of poetry rather than dramatic dialogue—but anonymous poetry.

entity, Middleton was equal with Shakespeare as his most favoured dramatic writer. In his analysis of the ascriptions in the Oldys copy, Bentley records 78 quotations from Middleton, to which may be added one for *Nice Valour*, one for *Wit at Several Weapons*, eight for *Bloody Banquet*, sixteen for *The Patient Man and the Honest Whore*,[38] seven for *The Puritan*, eleven for *Timon*, and twenty-five for *Revenger's Tragedy* (Bentley, 'English Treasury', pp. 195–9).[39] This amounts to 147 quotations from Middleton works: a figure exactly equal with Shakespeare,[40] and distinctly ahead of the other leading contenders, Beaumont and Fletcher at 112 (which includes the Middleton plays), Chapman at 111, Jonson at 111, Fulke Greville at 110, and Webster at 104.

Cotgrave's English drama is distinctly didactic. He is attracted especially to sententious plays.[41] Cotgrave draws extensively on Middleton plays printed between 1604 and 1639, with the exceptions of *Your Five Gallants*, *A Trick to Catch the Old One*, and *A Yorkshire Tragedy*. The only new Middleton plays to be printed in the 1640s were the two appearing in the Beaumont and Fletcher Folio. Cotgrave offers no quotations from the plays of the early '50s, *The Widow* (1652) and *The Changeling* (1653), which were presumably published too late to find a place in his collection. Of the included Middleton plays, Cotgrave quotes most extensively from *The Revenger's Tragedy* (twenty-five quotations).[42] Other titles, in descending order of popularity, are: *A Fair Quarrel* (fourteen), *Hengist* (twelve, probably culled from Moseley's unpublished manuscript of the play),[43] *The Phoenix* (twelve), *Timon of Athens* (eleven; of the Shakespeare plays, only *Hamlet* exceeds this total), *A Mad World, My Masters* (nine), *The Roaring Girl* (nine), *The Bloody Banquet* (eight), *Michaelmas Term* (eight), *The Puritan* (seven), *Chaste Maid* (four), *A Game at Chess* (three), *The Nice Valour* (one), and *Wit at Several Weapons* (one).

Cotgrave favours Middleton, and values a number of plays that are now often regarded as marginal to Middleton's reputation, or that could not have been known to the compiler himself as Middleton plays. Ironically, and in marked contrast to the dramatists gathered in folio, the confusion as to what Middleton actually wrote make it impossible for him to have articulated or even conceived of such a preference. Even if he had wished to know it, Cotgrave simply could not have realized that Middleton was his favourite dramatist. It is symptomatic of Middleton's lack of prestige as a canonical dramatist that he is so conspicuously favoured by a process of selection whose criteria ignore authorial attributions.

In startling contrast with Richards's view of Middleton as an outraged exposer of corruption and Cotgrave's sententious Middleton, the publisher Henry Herringman's [118] address to the readers in his 1661 edition of *Hengist* appropriates Middleton to the post-Interregnum order. Herringman commends the play's wit and drollery, presenting it as a corrective to the sour excesses of humourlessness attributed to the Cromwellian period. There is some rather strained jesting about Mayor Oliver, and nothing is said about the play's potential anti-Court

sentiments. Middleton, only four years previously the castigator of Court decadence perceived by Richards, now enters the Restoration gratuitously dressed as an anti-Puritan wit.

Middleton in Early Book Collections

Book catalogues tend to come from scholarly readers whose shelves found limited space for vernacular literature. Latin remained the language of scholarship; works of theology, philosophy, and history usually predominated. Even when, later in the century, collections included works by Milton, Shakespeare, Jonson, Sidney, or Spenser, they neglected dramatists who had not been gathered in folio. There are no mentions of Middleton works in the personal libraries recorded in the Cambridge University inventories, nor in those catalogued in the two published volumes of *Private Libraries in Renaissance England*, nor in the unpublished database of the *PLRE* project.[44] These negative findings are, however, much less conclusive than they appear, for cheap quarto and octavo editions of vernacular literary texts were commonly not listed separately in inventories, but neglected entirely or subsumed under an entry for various other, unnoteworthy, books (Chartier 1989, p. 128). Yet even the recorded holdings of the literary figures Gabriel Harvey, John Donne, Ben Jonson, John Milton, and William Congreve omit any reference to Middleton, as do those of Lancelot Andrewes, John Locke, and John Evelyn. Sir Edward Dering [119] is known to have been interested in drama and a regular playgoer in the 1620s, but only by virtue of owning, apparently, two copies of the 1623 Shakespeare Folio would he have found a place for any Middleton on his shelves.

Early to mid-seventeenth-century records of Middleton works in private collections are largely confined to readers with a special interest in accumulating printed plays. The pioneer was Sir John Harington [120], translator of *Orlando Furioso*. Greg estimates that Harington drew up lists of plays in his possession (British Library MS Add. 27632) in the winter of 1609–10 (Greg 1939–59, iv, 1307). He appears to have owned about six out of seven of the plays printed between 1600 and that date, and he catalogues seven Middleton titles.[45] In 1641

---

[38] The Oldys copy identifies twenty-six quotations as from *The Honest Whore*, but does not distinguish between the play Middleton contributed to and *2 Honest Whore*, a play with which Middleton was not involved.

[39] I discount Middleton's Shakespeare adaptations, *Macbeth* (four) and *Measure for Measure* (ten).

[40] The Shakespeare total includes the Middleton collaboration and adaptations but excludes *The Puritan*, which Cotgrave refers to as a Shakespeare play.

[41] Such as Chapman's *Conspiracy of Biron* (twenty-seven quotations), and *Revenge of Bussy D'Ambois* (twenty seven), Greville's *Alaham* (sixty-three) and *Mustapha* (forty-seven), Jonson's *Cataline* (thirty-three) and *Sejanus* (twenty-eight), and Webster's *Duchess of Malfi* (forty), and *White Devil* (thirty-six).

[42] There is in addition at least one unidentified passage from this play.

[43] Bentley 1943, p. 193. As Bentley points out, the quotations agree with the later printed text against the Lambarde and Portland manuscripts. Moseley entered the play in the Stationers' Register in 1646. *The Widow* and *The Changeling*, which Cotgrave does not quote, were not entered until 1652.

[44] Leedham-Green; Fehrenbach and Leedham-Green, eds. Elisabeth Leedham-Green kindly checked the full database for Middleton titles.

[45] His omissions of plays printed by 1610 are *The Patient Man and the Honest Whore* and *A Trick to Catch the Old One*.

Humphrey Moseley drew up a selection of plays and a few other books available in print for a private customer. It represents potential elements in a private collection. Of Middleton's plays, Moseley includes only *The Patient Man and the Honest Whore* (reprinted 1635) and *A Mad World, My Masters* (reprinted 1640). The actor and bookseller William Cartwright [121] wrote a commendatory verse for the 1647 Beaumont and Fletcher Folio and was himself published by Moseley; Cartwright's collection of up to five hundred plays can scarcely have failed to encompass a number by Middleton. The collection passed on to Dulwich College in 1687, but there is no extant catalogue, and so the titles of Cartwright's books are not known. Parts, perhaps large parts, of the Dulwich College collection were probably acquired by David Garrick to form part of his collection now in the British Library (Kahrl and Anderson, 3 and 18). Middleton works in the collection include most of his printed plays (Kahrl and Anderson, 194–5). Henry Oxinden's [122] list of printed plays, though compiled in 1663 or later, describes a collection compiled for the most part by 1615, with a few additions after that date. Of Middleton plays in print by 1615, Oxinden lists seven, omitting only *The Puritan, A Mad World*, and *The Roaring Girl*. The intermittent later plays in his collection include *A Game at Chess*, but no other Middleton play.

Amongst the seventeenth-century bibliophiles who built up collections that were to form the core of Renaissance dramatic literature in secular libraries, Langbaine is again of special prominence. In 1688, in the Preface to *Momus Triumphans*, Langbaine [123] claimed to be '*Master of above* Nine Hundred *and* Fourscore *English* Plays *and* Masques, *besides* Drolls *and* Interludes'. These included most of Middleton's drama that had been printed. His *Momus Triumphans* is centrally an annotated list based on the title-pages of his collection. It is divided into two parts, the first of which is itself divided into '*Declared* Authours', authors identified by initials, and anonymous plays, and the second an index printing titles by alphabetical order. Unlike the booksellers who compiled lists of titles available from their shops, Langbaine read and studied the plays in his possession. He claimed as much in the Preface to *Momus Triumphans*, and the information he gives in this pamphlet and in the more substantial *Account of the English Dramatic Poets* (1691) bears witness to a close knowledge of many plays. Langbaine's reading is organized around his project to convert bare play--lists into an account of dramatists as authors who contributed a defined body of work. To this end, as well as identifying plagiarism, he investigates authorship, sources, and publication details, and he makes an estimate of the worth of some of the plays. As already noted, he detects later thefts from *Chaste Maid, More Dissemblers, No Wit, Mad World, Trick to Catch the Old One, Masque of Heroes*, and *Wit at Several Weapons*. In the Middleton section of the *Account* (Langbaine 1691, 370–75) he also identifies sources for *The Changeling, A Fair Quarrel, Hengist*, and *Women, Beware Women*, and gives brief

descriptions of *Hengist* and *The Triumphs of Love and Antiquity*. He describes *A Trick to Catch the Old One* as 'an Excellent Old Play', and accounts the language and plot of *Mad World* as 'very diverting'.[46]

Though he admits to having never seen *The Roaring Girl*, all this is more than enough to suggest that Langbaine was probably Middleton's fullest and closest reader before the nineteenth century. Yet his sense of Middleton as a dramatist is constrained by the limits of the information available to him (it was he who first attributed *The Revenger's Tragedy* to Tourneur) and a prejudice in favour of the dramatists issued in folio. Recollecting Gough's account of the authorship of *The Widow*, he wrote of Middleton in relation to Jonson and Fletcher that, 'like the Ivy by the Assistance of the Oak, (being joyn'd with them in several Plays) he clim'd to some considerable height of Reputation'. The past tense of 'clim'd' can look back no further than the 1650s: it would have been impossible for any reader to think of Middleton in these terms in his lifetime. To Langbaine, Middleton's worth very much depends on his being 'fit to be receiv'd into a *Triumvirate*, by two such Great Men', for the plays he wrote alone 'speak him a Dramatick Poet of the Second Rank' (Langbaine 1691, 370–1). As we now see it, Middleton actually collaborated very little with these dramatists, the excellence of *The Widow* is all his own, and many of his other plays are much higher esteemed. Nevertheless, at a time when Middleton's plays were falling out of print and being ransacked like stone ruins for new building material, Langbaine actively attempted to reverse the dispersal of the Middleton canon, such as it recognizably was, by those he zealously called the plagiaries.[47]

Many of Langbaine's books came to Worcester College, Oxford. The collector William Gower [124] purchased all or a large part of his collection. Langbaine's copies of *The Widow* and *Anything for a Quiet Life* are preserved in the College library, and its copies of *A Chaste Maid in Cheapside* and *The Phoenix* appear to have been Gower's copies. In 1691 Langbaine described *More Dissemblers Besides Women, Women, Beware Women*, and *No Wit/Help like a Woman's* as 'all in one Volume'; extant early bindings of the three plays in one are rare, so it is likely that the example in Worcester College is another of Langbaine's books sold to Gower. Confirmation comes from the annotation 'Nº 635', which is in Langbaine's manner. A note on the title-page of Thompson's *Life of Mother Shipton* in a hand C. H. Wilkinson, in 'The Library of Worcester College', identifies as Gower's reads: 'Part of

---

[46] Much of the information is already briefly noted in *Momus Triumphans*. The pamphlet also gives, opposite the heading 'Tho. Middleton', a cryptic note reading 'v. Fletcher'. The Fletcher entry does not elaborate, but as *The Widow* is listed under Jonson, the note may indicate that Langbaine was aware of Middleton's presence in the 1647 Folio.

[47] The subtitle of *Momus Triumphans* is 'The Plagiaries of the English Stage Exposed in a Catalogue'. It should be remembered that title and subtitle were foisted on the book by an unidentified opponent of Langbaine, and were satirical towards him, but in *plagiary* the interpolator picked up a term Langbaine repeatedly favoured. (The term had also been used, perhaps for the first time with reference to plays, in Moseley's epistle to Cartwright.)

this Play stolen from yᵉ Citty M⟨ | & pᵗ from Chast Maid in Cheapside p Middleton': evidence of attentive reading on a premise of authorial property akin to Langbaine's.

As Wilkinson points out, the Worcester College collection can also be associated with the names of John Playford and Sir William and Dr George Clarke. Playford [125] published the scores of several songs from Middleton's plays. Sir William Clarke [126] was Assistant Secretary to the Army Council in England 1645–50, Secretary to Oliver Cromwell in Scotland 1650–51, and Secretary to General George Monck 1651–60, before becoming Secretary of War under the restored monarchy in 1661–6. In what looks almost like a symbolic act of cultural realignment, he bought fourteen plays from John Playford in the early days of the new regime in 1661. Clarke was, or became, an avid collector of playbooks. Worcester College Library holds a copy of Francis Kirkman's playlist (which includes twenty-seven plays under the authorial label 'Middleton and Rowley') annotated in Sir William's hand.[48] He marked over 300 titles with a cross and added notes of other titles; the plays so recorded are inferably those in his possession. Of Middleton's works, crosses appear opposite A Fair Quarrel, The Patient Man and the Honest Whore, A Mad World, My Masters, Michaelmas Term, Hengist, Old Law, and The Widow. A manuscript annotation records 'Middleton. Any thinge for a quiet life'. William's son George [127], Secretary of War, Joint Secretary to the Admiralty, then Lord of the Admiralty, augmented the collection. He is known also to have owned copies of the 1647 Beaumont and Fletcher Folio and the third and fourth Folios of Shakespeare.

Much more precise and straightforward than the evolutionary development of the Worcester College collection is the founding of the Pepys Library at Magdalene College, Cambridge. Apart from a few posthumous additions, these are simply the books of Samuel Pepys [128] himself. As well as Restoration folios of Beaumont and Fletcher (1679) and Shakespeare (1685), his library contains two single-text volumes of Middleton plays: The Phoenix (1607) and Hengist (1661) (Smith et al. 1978). He noted that he had been reading Hengist, 'a simple plays', whilst travelling home to dinner then to Woolwich and Deptford on 16 June 1666 (Pepys, vii, 168–9). Emmanuel College Library, Cambridge, acquired many of its seventeenth-century printed books from Archbishop William Sancroft [129] (Master 1662–5) or John Breton [130] (Master 1665–75). In these circumstances it is difficult to attribute an individual book to a specific early owner, but either Sancroft or Breton might be the source for its copies of A Game at Chess and Mad World (1640) (Wood). Likewise, some of the Middleton items in the British Library could derive from Sir Robert Cotton's [131] library, which formed the nucleus of the original collection, whilst others probably came from the collection of Edward Harley [132], second Earl of Oxford. The divine Thomas Plume [133] (1630–1704) built up a collection of books that included the 1647 Beaumont and Fletcher Folio; his books

passed to the Plume Library in Maldon (Deed and Francis). According to the List of Books in Guildhall Library, this library includes in its collections A Chaste Maid in Cheapside, Civitatis Amor, His Lordship's Entertainment, The Phoenix, Health and Prosperity, Honour and Industry, The Triumphs of Truth, The Changeling (1653) and the Shakespeare First Folio. The selection of titles in this strong representation of Middleton reflects his association with the City, and the books could well have been acquired in the seventeenth century.

Middleton's works were haphazardly acquired by individuals and institutions who were less systematically concerned with the drama as an entity in its own right. Pre-eminent here is Robert Burton [134], author of The Anatomy of Melancholy. He gathered an extensive collection of books largely on topics of immediacy, if not novelty, to the curious seventeenth-century mind; it is supposed to have amounted to about 2,000 volumes. Most are Latin works of intellectual enquiry, but there are also what Sir Thomas Bodley described, with reference to his own criteria for collection, as 'baggage books', including plays. 'I can see no good reason to alter my opinion, for excluding suche bookes, as almanckes, plaies,' Bodley wrote to his librarian Thomas James in 1612, 'Happely, some plaies may be worthy the keeping: but hardly one in fortie' (Bodley 1926, 121–2). Burton was happy to acquire what he called 'new books every day, pamphlets, currantoes, stories, whole catalogues of volumes of all sorts'.[49] In this library Beaumont, Dekker, Greene, Thomas Heywood, Middleton, and Shirley were represented, but amongst recorded works Shakespeare was not. Many of these books went to the Bodleian Library after Burton's death, and so redressed Bodley's conscious omissions.[50] Others went to Christ Church, Oxford. The Middleton works known to have been in Burton's library are the plays Michaelmas Term (1607), The Phoenix (1607), and A Fair Quarrel (1622), the entertainments The Magnificent Entertainment (1604), Civitatis Amor (1616), and Masque of Heroes (1619), and the prose work Sir Robert Sherley (Osler, Bensley, et al; Kiessling).[51] Only one of these is annotated. The recto of the front flyleaf in Burton's copy of Sherley, now in the Bodleian Library (4° L81 (6) Art.), is inscribed with three items making up seven lines. The writing is cropped and illegible.

There are other identifiable people known to have possessed Middleton texts. The library of the seventeenth-century book collectors in the Isham family of Lamport, Northamptonshire, includes copies of Black Book

---

[48] I am grateful to Frances McDonald for privately identifying the hand.
[49] Cited by Raymond Irwin, in his 'General Introduction' to Wormald and Wright, 9.
[50] In fact the Shakespeare First Folio notably was not treated as a baggage book, but as one of the one in forty: it was purchased and sent to William Wildgoose for binding shortly after publication (Madan, Turbutt, and Gibson).
[51] Yet the mentioned books are not entered in the Bodleian catalogue of 1674, which instead records The Changeling, No Wit/Help like a Woman's, and Two New Plays under Middleton and The Widow under Jonson (cross referenced); it also includes the Beaumont and Fletcher Folio of 1647 and the Shakespeare Folio of 1664.

and *Plato's Cap* (Jackson 1967). Both were published by Jeffrey Chorlton in 1604, so John Isham [135] (1582–1651; first Baronet of Isham 1627) may have directly or indirectly purchased them both from Chorlton's shop soon afterwards. The eclectic book collection of the Oxford antiquarian Brian Twyne [136] (1579?–1644) found space for works on 'angling, chess, dogs, gardening, horses, geomancy, necromancy, serpents, stenography, witches, and much else beside' (Ovenell, 17). About a score of these 350 volumes contained various and mostly minor literary works.[52] There is a single Middleton–Dekker title, *The Roaring Girl*. The subject matter probably appealed to Twyne's curiosity. Drummond of Hawthornden (1585–1649) owned a number of playbooks; amongst them was *A Game at Chess* (STC 17884) as well as *Your Five Gallants* (MacDonald, ed.). Another copy of *Game at Chess* (STC 17882; Bodleian Vet A2.e.177) is inscribed with the owner's name 'Leonard Diggs' [137]. Digges was author of a commendatory verse in the Shakespeare First Folio. The founder of the Merton College librarianship, Dr Griffin Higgs [138], built up his own private library of books, ranging widely in subject. The drama is represented barely; but one exception, probably acquired for its historical rather than dramatic interest, is *The Magnificent Entertainment* (Morrish). In contrast, William Percy [139], son of the eighth Earl of Northumberland, was himself an amateur playwright, and is the probable source for the collection of Jacobean play quartos in the Petworth library. These books include *Michaelmas Term*, *The Phoenix*, and *The Revenger's Tragedy*. The first two of these were boys' company plays written for the Children of Paul's, a company for whom Percy wrote, or pretended he wrote, a number of pieces.[53] George Thomason (d. 1666) [140], London publisher, friend of Prynne and Milton, owned copies of *Hengist* and *Old Law*.[54] In a manuscript probably compiled between 1677 and 1703, the affluent collector Abraham Hill [141] lists plays of which, it may be inferred, he owned manuscript copies. These include an otherwise unknown 'The Conquerors custome or the fair prisoner' by 'Tho Middleton' and 'Your 5 gallants' (Bentley 1941–68, iv, 865–6). In addition to these English and Scottish book owners was the Spanish ambassador Gondomar. The catalogue of Gondomar's collections in the Royal Library in Madrid lists, among Gondomar's English books still in the collection, a copy of the 1613 edition of *Triumphs of Truth*. Gondomar began his first period as ambassador in London in 1613, the year the entertainment was performed and first published. He was later to be satirized in *A Game at Chess*.

One collectable Middleton book must have been valued not for its actual author but for its association with James I. *The Peacemaker* was acquired by both Silvester Petyt [142] for the provincial church and grammar school libraries he consolidated at Skipton, Yorkshire (*Catalogue of the Petyt Library*), and by John Bagford [143], the ballad-collector, small-scale printer, and would-be historian of

printing, whose extensive gathering of English printed books later came into the possession of the British Library (1964) (Wolf). Both collectors were active *c.*1700.

Bagford is anticipated in a small way by Frances Wolfreston [144] (1607–77), who is well-recognized as a collector of chapbooks and popular literature (Morgan; Watt, 314–17; MacLean; Roberts, 300–302). Wolfreston was the eldest of twenty-two children of George Middlemore and Frances Stanford. After her marriage in 1631 she lived at Statfold, near Tamworth, in Staffordshire. There she built up a collection of chapbooks and quartos; amongst the latter are a number of plays by Shakespeare and other dramatists. Wolfreston probably acquired a book issued as early as *The Penniless Parliament* (1608) by inheritance or second-hand purchase. Some years later she obtained *A Description of the King and Queene of Fayries* compiled by 'R. S.' [145] (1634), which contains a printed text of the Middleton song 'Hence, all you Vain Delights' printed with the heading '*The Melancholly Lovers Song*' facing an engraving of a naked man and woman in a rock cell. It was published three years after her marriage. The unique copy of the first edition is inscribed with her name.[55]

The extensive holdings of the Anglican cathedral libraries include a number of Middleton books, or books that contain Middleton texts (McLeod). Canterbury, Norwich, and Exeter all held copies of the 1632 Shakespeare Folio; Southwell held the 1647 Beaumont and Fletcher Folio. York obtained two items of royalist interest, *The Magnificent Entertainment* and *The Peacemaker* (two copies, both of sheets C to E only), and one of local interest, *A Yorkshire Tragedy*. St Paul's library includes four Middleton plays, all of which were probably first performed by St Paul's Boys: *A Mad World, My Masters*, *Michaelmas Term*, *The Phoenix* (two copies), and *A Trick to Catch the Old One*. Here the local relevance of the book to the library is even more immediate than with York's *Yorkshire Tragedy*. Yet although the St Paul's theatre was probably inoperative after 1606 (Bentley 1941–68, vi, 86), and plays from the Paul's repertoire, including most of Middleton's early city comedies, appeared in print in 1607–8, none of the cathedral library's Middleton holdings dates from this period. Its five copies are of the reprinted editions brought out in 1616 (*Trick*), 1630 (*Michaelmas Term* and *Phoenix*), and 1640 (*Mad World*). Might a former chorister, adolescent in the early 1600s, have acquired these books for the cathedral during the Civil Wars?[56]

---

[52] Ovenell notes works by Nicholas Breton, Henry Constable, Greene, Fulke Greville, Gabriel Harvey, Jonson, John Lyly, Thomas Nashe and John Partridge.

[53] Miller, 62–3; I am grateful to Christine Buckley for pointing this article out to me, and for a number of helpful suggestions.

[54] The British Library copy of *Hengist* is annotated in Thomason's hand, and the title is entered in his MS Index and the flyleaf of Thomason E1085 (Kahrl, 194–5).

[55] See below for comment on Wolfreston as a woman reader.

[56] The only other Paul's plays I have noted as held in the Cathedral library are John Lyly's *Six Court Comedies* (1632): another 1630s edition.

Dedicatees and Patrons: Printed Books

A full listing of the dedications in Middleton texts and collections containing Middleton texts is given below in Appendix B. The following remarks are concerned, more narrowly, with specific readers who are addressed or invoked by Middleton.

Middleton's first book known to have appeared in print is *The Wisdom of Solomon Paraphrased* (1597), which, with no little presumption, Middleton dedicated to Robert Devereux [146], Earl of Essex. As Essex had the honorific role of chief literary patron on Queen Elizabeth's behalf, dedication of a work to him was almost tantamount to offering it to the Queen herself. He was also probably regarded as the successor to Leicester as champion of the Puritan cause. In both respects the dedication accords with the poem's Calvinist-tinged Protestant Elizabethanism (Shand). Middleton went on to present his juvenile *Ghost of Lucrece* (1600) to Baron Compton [147]. Compton succeeded to his father's titles and estates in 1589, and in 1599 married Elizabeth, heir to 'the rich John Spencer', Lord Mayor of London in 1594–5; Elizabeth was reputed to bring a dowry of £28,000.[57] A would-be adventurer, Compton was recalled by the Queen from the proposed Cadiz expedition in 1596 and refused permission to sail with Essex to the Azores in 1597. Despite his wealth, he is not otherwise known as a literary patron, but as *The Wisdom of Solomon Paraphrased* had been dedicated to the Earl of Essex, his connection with Essex may be significant (Adams, ed., 1937, xxiii–xxv).

Masque of Heroes was written for performance at the Inner Temple. This specific theatre audience would presumably influence the readership of the printed text, which may have been of similar composition to that of *Microcynicon*. But the preliminaries raise a question of gender. The masque was performed by the gentlemen of the Inner Temple to an audience of ladies, as is made clear both on the title-page and in the poem headed 'The Masque'. As might be expected on economic grounds, there is no open appeal to or for a female readership, but there may nonetheless be an implication that a dramatic text '*made for Ladies*' is in some sense suitable for ladies to read. Three later texts are, like *Masque of Heroes*, presented in ways that draw attention to their occasion. *Sir Robert Sherley* celebrates the ambassadorial achievements of Sir Robert Sherley [148], and is dedicated, in different issues, to his father Thomas [149] and his brother Thomas [150]. Sherley was a noted venturer as well as a diplomat. *The World Tossed at Tennis* is described on the title-page as 'Prince Charles his Creation', indicating that it was commissioned by Prince Charles for Court performance by the company he patronized, the Prince's Men.[58] Finally, the editions of *A Game at Chess* make specific and varied reference to the scandalous nine-day run on the stage. Heinemann (pp. 166–9) conjectures that the play and its producers would probably have been protected by a powerful magnate, whom she identifies as William Herbert, Earl of Pembroke. Howard-Hill similarly conjectures that Sir Henry Herbert

as Master of the Revels might have consulted Pembroke in his capacities as both his kinsman and the Lord Chamberlain (Howard-Hill, ed., 1993, 21–2), citing John Woolley's letter of 20 August to William Trumbull: 'Middleton the Poet is sought after, and it is [thought] supposed shall be clapt in prison, if he does not cleere him selfe by the Mr. of the Reuells, who alowed of it; and it is thought not wthout leaue, from the high powers I meane the P[rince]. and D[uke]. if not from the K[ing].' (Howard-Hill, ed., 1993, 203). It might be questioned whether the *Duke* in question could possibly be the *Earl* of Pembroke, and indeed Gary Taylor's account of the play in the present edition is sceptical towards the suggestions of Howard-Hill and Heinemann alike.

Some of the more firmly documented examples considered in the previous paragraph complicate any monologic account of Middleton as a Puritan or anti-Court dramatist. King James's special licence for Middleton's nominee to print and publish *The Peacemaker* suggests that the King was himself an approving reader who saw that tract as a favourable expression of royal policy. But Middleton's links with the City were strong, especially in the second half of his life as a writer. He made a junior contribution to the pageant marking the entry of King James into the City of London (1604), and he later wrote a series of annual shows and other entertainments for the Lord Mayors of London. It would, however, have been leaders of the guild company responsible for the year's performance who would have chosen the pageant-writer in the first place. A 1619 Skinners' Guild record notes that the 'poettes' Munday, Middleton, and Richard Grimston 'all shewed to the table their severall plottes for devices for the shewes and pagente against Symon and Judes tide and each desired to searve the Companie'.[59] Middleton's *Triumphs of Love and Antiquity* was selected for performance.

Middleton's involvement with the city authorities began in 1613 with work for Sir Thomas Myddelton [151]. For Sir Thomas Myddelton's Lord Mayor's show Middleton wrote *The Triumphs of Truth*, a spectacular and dramatic pageant that evidently cemented an alliance with the City. Middleton supplied an entertainment for performance on the day of Sir Thomas's election as Lord Mayor at the New River, a work of civic engineering that had been designed, executed, and partly financed by Sir Thomas's brother Hugh [152].[60] He composed the lost *Masque of*

---

[57] G. R. Hibbard, in his edition of *Merry Wives of Windsor*, suggests that 'the Fenton–Anne Page story reflects the affair between Lord Compton and Elizabeth Spencer' (Hibbard, ed., 1973, 48), making it strangely possible that Shakespeare's Fenton and Middleton's Clutchfist (see above) are responses to the same person.

[58] The word *creation* is not here used in the modern sense 'production of imaginative art', which was not available at the time, but is a conceit playing on the title's *The World*. The example may notwithstanding be added to those cited by Stephen Orgel of a text's authority deriving from the patron rather than the author.

[59] Bergeron, 188–9. Beverill's pasteboard in *No Wit* is probably a similar plot for the device of the wedding masque.

[60] The title-page also names Sir John Swinarton, Lord Mayor before Sir Thomas, and Sir Henry Montagu, City Recorder.

Cupids when the King instructed Sir Thomas, still Lord Mayor, to entertain the newly-married Robert Carr, Earl of Somerset [153] and Frances Howard [154] early in 1614. The 1616 pageant *Civitatis Amor*, the City's celebration of the investiture of Prince Charles [155] as Prince of Wales, was followed by an intermittent series of 'Triumphs' for the annual Lord Mayor's shows: in 1617 for George Bolles [156]; in 1619 for William Cokayne [157]; in 1621 for Edward Barkham [158]; in 1622 for Peter Proby [159]; in 1623 for Martin Lumley [160], and in 1626 for Cuthbert Hacket [161]. There are other pieces whose occasion suggests likely recipients for the printed souvenir: *The World Tossed at Tennis*, though commissioned by Prince Charles, was published in honour of the wedding of Cokayne's daughter Mary [162] to Charles, Lord Howard, Baron of Effingham [163], and one of the *Honourable Entertainments* was performed at the wedding celebrations.

Middleton's activities as City Chronologer must have extended beyond writing lost annals and extant entertainments. He probably wrote the epitaph on the death of the Lord Mayor George Bolles (see *Works*, p. 1890), which was commissioned by his widow Joan [164]. This and the poem on the consecration of the church of St James (*Works*, p. 1891) were included in Munday's 1633 expanded edition of John Stow's *Survey of London*. Munday had included a text of *His Lordship's Entertainment* in his earlier 1618 revision.

In 1620 Middleton reissued *The Two Gates of Salvation* as *The Marriage of Old and New Testaments* with a new dedication 'To the two noble examples of friendship and brotherhood', Richard Fishbourne [165], a Mercer, and John Browne [166], a Merchant Taylor. Both were of Puritan sympathies (Heinemann, 126). John Chamberlain, in a letter of 26 October 1616, indicates that they were known for importing corantoes printed in Holland (Heinemann, 157). Fishbourne, early in his career a privateer and participant in Sir Francis Drake's 1587 Cadiz expedition, traded with the Low Countries, dealing in silks and clothing. Most of these activities suggest an anti--Spanish stance (Heinemann, 259–60). It is curious that William Strode, whom we have already met, should have written an elegy for him after his death in 1625. *Honourable Entertainments* (1621) correlates the book itself as an assemblage of entertainment texts with an assemblage of the city dignitaries before whom the original performances took place. It was dedicated to the twenty-six aldermen of London, and the title-page names them all. The roll includes the present Lord Mayor, nine former mayors, ten future mayors, and the London Recorder. The average age of these men must have been over fifty, and their accumulated wealth would have been formidable.

The city dignitaries who employed Middleton most often, Myddelton and Cokayne, were both from families of minor country gentry. Myddelton in particular grew spectacularly wealthy. In his early business career he worked as export merchant and factor to Ferdinando Poynz. He was a founding member of the East India Company and

an adventurer in the Virginia Company, but made most of his money through usury. Some of it he spent in promoting Puritan lecturers and backing publication of the first 'popular' Welsh Bible, but he signalled his upward mobility by purchasing Chirk Castle and its estate. The Myddelton brothers financed both Raleigh and Drake, and their kinsman William was himself a privateer. Cokayne was a leading member of the Merchant Adventurers Company. He helped finance William Baffin's north-west voyages, but is best known for originating the disastrous Cokayne Project, backed by the Earl of Somerset and other members of the Howard faction. It aimed to add value to exported wool by dying and dressing it in England, but collapsed in 1616. Cokayne bought large estates in several counties. As Strode commemorated Fishbourne, Donne preached Cokayne's funeral sermon.

The city patrons who fostered Middleton in his capacities as Chronologer and pageant-writer, though they represented a broad artisan constituency, in themselves belonged to a distinctive and wealthy élite. The Lord Mayors were rich and successful entrepreneurs who invested in trade and land far removed from the city itself. A number of them had been associated with privateering in the 1590s, and a number, sometimes the same individuals, participated in the developing New World trade of the Jacobean period (Heinemann, 170). Both activities were consistent with the anti-Spanish politics of Puritan sympathizers. The point here is not to suggest the political complexion of Middleton as a writer but to describe the environments in which he was read. Middleton was a poet for the city élite, and no doubt for many trade guild members of lesser substance as well. Middleton's city-oriented publications constitute a relatively large, homogeneous, systematically published group of texts which are issued with dedications and given manifest authorial direction towards a specific readership. But this visible, coherent, indeed one might say official, author–reader relationship misrepresents the author. Though numerically they represent a significant proportion of Middleton's titles, the texts are short, and therefore make up only a small proportion of his overall output as a writer. Moreover, books without dedications are not books without readers. Most of Middleton's writing enters less controlled reading environments in which readers reveal themselves possessing his works in situations that the texts themselves do not predict. Middleton the City Chronologer and pageant-writer is only one facet of Middleton.

Manuscript Owners

This section is not concerned with manuscript miscellanies in which fragments of Middleton's writing are collocated with selected passages from other writers. The textual relocations and alterations associated with such manuscripts have been discussed above as processes of active transmission, and the identifiable miscellany owners are recorded below in Appendix C. It remains here to consider a small group of play manuscripts which can be assigned to particular owners. The group subdivides into manuscripts prepared by Ralph Crane and the scribal manuscripts of *Hengist*.

Of the two extant manuscripts of *Hengist*, one can be ascribed to the collections of the Dukes of Portland, of Welbeck Abbey, Nottinghamshire (University of Nottingham, Portland MS Pw V 20). The family also owned a manuscript (Portland MS Pw V 37) containing the song 'Hence, all you Vain Delights'. Sir Richard Weston [167] (1577–1635), created first Earl of Portland, was Middleton's contemporary; his political sympathies lay with Spain, he adhered to Catholicism, and was admired by the Spanish ambassador Gondomar. King James sent Weston and Sir Edward Conway to the Rhine states (1620) and Brussels (1622) to negotiate a peace settlement over the Palatinate dispute (Gardiner, iii, 361–87; iv, 301–71). In 1624 they presented the Commons with Buckingham's anti-Spanish report on the Spanish Match negotiations. It is of course by no means certain that Sir Richard was responsible for acquiring the manuscript for the Portland collection, and one might wish on account of its more obvious relevance to the Palatinate wars that the play were *A Game at Chess* rather than *Hengist*. Weston's partner Conway [168] is also thought to have owned a Middleton dramatic manuscript. The *Invention for the Lord Mayor* was transcribed *c*.1622 in a manuscript (Public Record Office, SP. 14/129/53) that probably came into Conway's possession. He had been knighted by Essex in 1596 at the sacking of Cadiz, and after his travels on diplomacy became one of the principal secretaries of state in 1623.

Middleton, Crane, and others engaged in some intense scribal publication of *A Game at Chess*, presumably concentrating their activity in the period immediately after the play's banishment from the stage. The Malone manuscript of *A Game at Chess* has a dedication 'To the Worthilie Accomplish'd Mr: William Hammond.' [169]:

This which nor Stage nor Stationers Stall can showe,
The Common Eye may wish for, but ne're Knowe,
Comes in it's best Loue wth the New-yeare forth,
As a fit Present to the Hand of Worth.

A Seruant to youre
Vertues,
T.M.

The script's presentation to Hammond as a New Year gift can be assigned to January 1625 (Howard-Hill, ed., 1990, ix). Hammond was, according to Heinemann, 'a rich Puritan member of the Haberdashers'' (Heinemann, 169–70). Bald suggests that he 'belonged to a coterie of Middleton's civic patrons', for he, along with John Browne, was left £5 in Fishbourne's will (Bald, ed., 1929, 137).[61] It is at least possible that Hammond was the cousin of Nathaniel Richards or that man's son. Nathaniel's brother Gabriel left most of his estate to William Hammond, 'eldest son of my cousin William Hammond of St. Albans, Esq.'.[62] The same manuscript, according to Bald, seems at some later point to have belonged to 'J Pepys' [170], probably John Pepys (1576–1652) of Salisbury Court, London (Bald, ed., 1929, 28).[63] The rather untidy Bridgewater–Huntington manuscript of the same play, in part in Middleton's own hand, presumably came into the possession of Sir John Egerton, first Earl of Bridgwater [171]. Egerton was son of a strongly Protestant and anti-Spanish father; Milton was later to write *Comus* in celebration of his initiation as President of Wales. Ralph Crane, the scribe employed to prepare other transcripts of the play, had close connections with Egerton, for his poem *The Works of Mercy* was dedicated to him in 1621, and his transcript of *The Faulty Favourite* was presented as a New Year's gift in 1632 with a dedication describing the manuscript as '*my yeerely Destinate* to some Corner... of yo[r] learned and well-stord *Library*'. It was probably therefore Crane who brought the play manuscript to Egerton's library (Howard-Hill 1984, 156).[64] Another transcript of *A Game at Chess* was owned by Sir Thomas Browne [172], author of *Religio Medici*. The sale catalogue of his library includes 'A Game at Chesse, a Comedy, written by Tho. Middleton, an. 1620'.[65] And Howard-Hill makes the plausible conjecture that the Trinity manuscript derives from the collection of Patrick Young [173] (1584–1652), Librarian to King James I and King Charles I (Howard-Hill, ed., 1990, x).[66]

Alongside the textual dispersal of *A Game at Chess* came its writer's confinement. The short poem 'To the King' is Middleton's petition to King James [174] for enfranchisement after his imprisonment for his authorship of the play. Though there is no evidence for any extant manuscript having been in the King's possession, he presumably must have been sent a copy.

Middleton dedicated Crane's transcript of *The Witch*, which the Malone Society editors date at *c*.1624–5 (Greg and Wilson, ed., vii–viii), 'To the truely-worthie *and generously-affected* Thomas Holmes *Esquier*' [175]. Middleton claims to have recovered the text from its 'im=prisond-Obscurity' 'meerely upon a tast of yo[r] desire'. Wayne H. Phelps considers Holmes is likely to be the son of a citizen and Haberdasher of London who went to Emmanuel College, Cambridge, and Gray's Inn; but Elizabeth Schafer has argued instead for the Winchester organist and composer of the same name. Though it is not clear that this Holmes was entitled to the designation 'esquire', Schafer's proposal is otherwise attractive. In particular, Thomas's father John trained Edward Lowe in Salisbury before the latter took up duties at Christ Church, Oxford, and Lowe, as we have seen, probably transcribed

[61] For a critique of Bald's and Heinemann's inference of a Puritan coterie, see Bawcutt 1999.
[62] Bentley, *Jacobean and Caroline Stage*, vol. 5, p. 1001. St Albans might be the school where Nathaniel taught rather than the town.
[63] Another John Pepys (1601–80) was father of the diarist Samuel.
[64] Christine Buckley has privately pointed out a connection between this reader of Middleton and his City patron Sir Thomas Myddelton. Anne Myddelton, Sir Thomas's daughter, was daughter-in-law of Mary Egerton, Sir John's daughter.
[65] Bodleian MS Rawl. 390, no. 11; cited in Wilkin, ed., iv, 470.
[66] Young's collection eventually came to Roger Gale (1672–1744), whose library was given to Trinity College in 1738.

a setting of a song from the very play in question. This may not be a coincidence even though the play transcript must have preceded the song transcript by many years, and the possible connection is intriguing at least.

One senses with the *Hengist* manuscripts that the connection between author and reader is tenuous at least. The manuscripts of *A Game at Chess* and *The Witch* emanate, if not from Middleton himself, then from his immediate textual environment. Crane was a colleague, a co-transcriber. Middleton gifted the Malone *Game at Chess* to its recipient, who is associated with other dedicatees, and Crane is likely to have brought the Bridgewater–Huntington manuscript to its new owner. A taste of Thomas Holmes's desire brought him a copy of *The Witch*. Scribal publication enables a relatively immediate author–reader relationship.

Readers' Responses: Marginalia, etc.

Like other books, Middleton's printed texts were subject to inscription with marginal notes and other forms of inscription. Middleton has no scholastic annotator of the ilk of Gabriel Harvey; the inference to be drawn is not that Middleton had no intellectual readers but rather that his texts were not perceived as works of intellectual authority demanding urgent mediation. In other respects the forms of annotation vary considerably. Many inscriptions, far from playing a role of mediation, are completely disregardful of the text, but even these can tell us something of the reader.

A note written in Latin, in a copy of *Sir Robert Sherley*, records what appears to be a relic of feudal obligation. The note is tidily appended to the text, which is itself a translation from Latin; there may be an obscure sense of decorum at work here. The mind-set of this book-owner may be contrasted with that of the person who scribbled a memo across the top of a page of *The Revenger's Tragedy* noting that a member of the household ate a twopenny loaf at a single meal. Dyce's copy of *The Widow* has financial accounts written in pencil on p. 64. It may be the 'boy' to whom a copy of *Two New Plays* was presented who responded to the text by doodling columns of loops down the margins of successive pages. Books inhabit households as well as libraries; they come into the hands of the unconcerned. In an economy where paper was a relatively expensive commodity, spare white spaces in books that had outlived their value as texts readily served as notepaper.

It was reasonably common for a book to be inscribed with its owner's signature, and where the name can be identified we are given a valuable insight into the circulation of the book. In his edition of *Women, Beware Women*, Mulryne was able to posit the identities of two early eighteenth-century owners of copies, John Cowcher and Edward Bearcroft. Further research might reveal more about the likes of Edward Palmer, owner of *Father Hubburd's Tales*, or John Jenkins, owner of *Mad World*. Unfortunately it is the élite reader who is most readily identified. Sometimes the link between a signed

name and a historical person can only be conjectured. For example a copy of *God's Parliament House* is inscribed with the names of John Robinson [176] and H. Burton [177]. Burton might be Henry Burton, the Puritan martyr, associate of William Prynne, and harsh critic of royalist drama. The Calvinist piety of the work and implicit Parliamentarianism of its title might be especially appropriate to such a figure, but although he is a plausible candidate the identification must remain insecure. Robinson is unlikely to be either the pastor of the Pilgrim Fathers who sailed to America in 1620 or the notable royalist (1617–81). The man in question is more probably the actor with the King's Revels, one of the writers of commendatory verse for Nathaniel Richards's *Messalina*. As we have seen, Richards was himself a Calvinistic reader of Middleton, and may have been related to William Hammond, dedicatee of the Malone manuscript of *A Game at Chess*. Herein lies a possible embryonic network of Middleton readers.

Several early readers of the Shakespeare Folio can be identified, whether by virtue of a signature or an established ancestry of ownership. Most interesting potentially from the Middleton point of view is Gondomar [178]. A Folio copy, now lost, is reported to have been acquired by Gondomar in 1623, and to have contained manuscript interpolations in English, many of them in verse (Lee, 13). The nineteenth-century evidence is, however, anecdotal and unreliable, and the copy may not have existed (Pujante). The Durham Cathedral copy of the Folio was bequeathed by the Laudian bishop John Cosin [179]. Other owners mentioned by Lee are the herald Augustine Vincent [180] (who was presented with a copy by William Jaggard); the first Lord Arundel of Wardour [181]; John Hackett, Bishop of Lichfield [182]; Colonel John Lane [183] (who protected Charles II after the Battle of Worcester); Ralph Sheldon [184] (Warwickshire antiquary and landowner); Charles Killigrew [185] (Restoration theatrical manager), whose copy passed on to William Congreve [186]; Dr Daniel Williams [187] (dissenting divine and benefactor of London); and Cotton Mather [188] (Puritan minister of Boston, Massachusetts, and activist in the persecution of the Salem witches). Mather is the earliest American reader of Shakespeare and Middleton who can be conjectured with any confidence.[67] Lee established further owners and annotators in his 'Notes and Additions to the Census of Copies': the Oxford bookseller Richard Davies [189], who bought the Bodley copy after the library acquired the 1664 Third Folio; the County Durham gentleman and antiquary Gilbert Spearman [190], who inscribed his copy 'Liber G. Spearman Dunelm. 1695'; a certain 'Tho: Bourne' [191]; the inscribers of 'the Lady Sarah Hearst' [192], 'the Ladie Ann Grey' [193], and 'The Lady Mary Bucckinham' [194]; the addressee and writer of a note to Viscount Cholmondeley [195] (whom Lee specifies as Robert Cholondeley, created Viscount of

[67] The origin of the Mather family copy is unfortunately an inference; there is no Cotton Mather signature.

Cholmondeley in 1628, and Earl of Leinster in 1645) and his wife (Catherine) [196], signed 'Robert Shakerley' [197].

The commonest response to reading was a marginal cross or line highlighting a passage. This widespread form of annotation often cannot be tied to a particular owner, or even a particular century. In the case of the British Library copy of *Two New Plays* that has over sixty phrases and passages underlined, it is possible to conjecture that the marks were introduced in the late seventeenth century, as p. 17 has a marginal note probably in the same ink reading 'says the wi[t] in the pla[in] Dealer', alluding to William Wycherley's play of *c.*1676. If in other instances the date of marginal markings is unascertainable, it is likely that most such interventions belong to the seventeenth century, and not only because the book might be most actively read when relatively new. Selection of memorable phrases and passages is consonant with the compilation of commonplace books. With some readers the process of selection in the printed book may have been followed by transcription; with others the selection may have been an analogous but alternative activity pursued as an end in itself.

Particular lines are usually selected as a mark of approval, but selection can also lead to expurgation. The New York Public Library copy of Pavier's 1619 edition of *A Yorkshire Tragedy* contains a series of vigorous deletions, mostly of profanity. Victims are not only strong oaths such as 'Masse' and 'Slid' and the name of God, but also the mild 'Faith', references to damnation, and the unpleasant but theologically uncontroversial 'plague founder thee' (perhaps taken as an impious call on God's powers). Exception is also taken to a joke at the expense of hypocritical Puritans, 'Neyther of eyther, as the Puritan Bawde sayes', which is changed to 'Neyther of eyther, as thay say'. This last alteration points away from the otherwise intriguing possibility that the annotator was bringing the text into line with the requirements for theatrical performance after the 1606 Act outlawing profanity; instead one might posit a Puritan reader who liked the play as a moral fable but was repeatedly disturbed by the language of its telling.

Words such as the reference to *The Plain Dealer* in *Two New Plays* are clearer indications than crosses and deletions as to who marked the book and when; they might also tell something of the reader's reaction to the text. One reader of *More Dissemblers Besides Women* (perhaps the named Arthur Ryland or 'Japlud Secundus') intervened in a variety of ways in the copy inscribed 'For my boy'. On the title-page a note classifies the play as one that concerns 'women V. men'. The title's words 'comedy' and 'by' are Latinized, in schoolboy fashion, as 'comedia' and 'par', and the thistle of the printer's ornament is elaborately copied. Less passively, the final blank leaf of the book has been inscribed with various quotations and paraphrases of passages from both *More Dissemblers* and *Women, Beware Women*. They show a taste for striking or even quirky similes, metaphors and turns of phrase. This reader's Middleton is a clever, extravagant, and memorable stylist. An

annotator of *The Puritan* thought otherwise: in the Latin motto at the end of the play 'Deus dedit his quoq[ue] finem', 'Deus' is crossed out and 'Diabolus' written above. Here is a wry-faced negative response.

None of the types of annotation mentioned so far is of much use to the modern student of Middleton and his texts, but in other cases a reader might supplement the title-page information, correct printers' errors, make annotations of a 'theatrical' nature, or provide information relating to the purchase of the book. We know that *Mad World* sold for sixpence because a buyer inscribed: 'Iohn Ienkines November 24th: 1608 pre. 6d/'. In a copy of *The Phoenix* in the British Library, the title-page adds the information otherwise missing, 'Written by Tho Middleton. Gent.' The Folger's *Trick to Catch the Old One* expands the title-page identification of the author from 'T.M.' to 'T.Middleton'. In *The Widow*, Dyce copy, the title-page attributions to 'Ben Johnson' and 'John Fletcher' are crossed out, and the word 'alone' is written after 'Tho: Middleton', and the Wellesley copy corrects the authorship to 'Tho: Middleton'; both early annotators anticipate the findings of more recent scholarship. Contextual information is added in two copies of *A Game at Chess*. A British Library copy explains that the Fat Bishop is 'bish. of Spalatto', and that the Black Knight is 'Gundomar'. One of the Dyce copies adds a short account of Middleton's 'To the King', and provides the text of the poem.

Some inscribers supply early readings that might emend the text or usefully amplify it. Handwritten notes in the Bodleian copy of *Microcynicon* make three corrections to the text, two of them necessary and the third plausible. In a Folger copy of *Trick* there is a whole series of such alterations. Plays, of course, invite interventions that modify or add to the account of the dramatic action. A Folger copy of *The Patient Man and the Honest Whore* (1604; Folger 1, K2v) introduces a missing speech-prefix, 'Ans' (with long 's') inked in where a speech prefix is missing; the same library's edition of *Trick to Catch the Old One* (1608) includes amongst its annotations some additions and corrections to the stage directions; the British Library copy of the 1616 reprint of *Trick* interpolates a series of entrances and an exit; *The Changeling* (1653) in the New York Public Library supplies the critical directions for De Flores to stab Alsemero and for Alsemero to die. In none of these instances does it seem necessary to posit that the printed text was being prepared for use as a promptbook; it seems instead that even though most of the directions that have been cited can be inferred from the printed dialogue, some readers were more active in constituting the play as imaginary theatre than the text immediately allowed. The resulting annotation affords the earliest textual stipulation of action that modern editors often need to specify in their scripts. If in these and other cases there is no need to assume that the annotator had access to a manuscript or knew the play on the stage, amplifications are occasionally not so readily explained as independent editorial inference on the part of the annotator. The Yale copy of the 1657 *Two New Plays* provides a number of detailed stage directions for Act 5 of *Women, Beware Women* that are so specific that Mulryne has plausibly argued that they might reflect the annotator's experience of the play on the stage (Mulryne 1975).

Ungeneralizable though it may be, a record of such annotations is an illumination of reading practices. Appendix D is a list of the marginalia and other inscriptions that I have found or that have been reported to me. It is far from exhaustive, and should be read as a large and representative sampling of such material. The handwriting is rarely that of a professional scribe, and indeed is often casual scrawl; the boundary between formed letters and non-literal doodle is sometimes indistinct. For these reasons transcription can sometimes be hazardous, and another eye will sometimes find readings at variance with my own. Annotations that are fairly certainly post-seventeenth-century have not been recorded.[68]

Readers' Responses: Comment on Middleton

Some of the early commentary on Middleton usefully compiled by Sara Jayne Steen responds to his works on stage—for example George Chapman's sneer at *The Triumphs of Truth*, Orazio Busino's description of *The Triumphs of Honour and Industry*, the Spanish Ambassador's indignant account of *A Game at Chess*, or Samuel Pepys's comments on *The Widow* or *The Changeling*, seen as part of an evening's entertainment. Comment reflecting a knowledge of Middleton's work is sometimes discouraging. The chronicler Edmund Howes's [198] catalogue of 'present excellent Poets' lists them 'according to their priorities as neere as I could', placing Middleton next to the last, before only George Wither (*Annales*, 1615; see Taylor, 'The Order of Persons', p. 40). But the 'priorities' in question are those of age rather than literary quality. In contrast, Jonson's dismissal of Middleton as a 'base fellow' (Jonson, 1525–52, i, 137) is almost certainly a judgement on the quality of his writing rather than his social origins. In *Praise of Hemp-Seed* (1620) the Water Poet, John Taylor [199], is more positive, listing Middleton amongst twelve living poets 'Which do in paper their true worth display'; the name '*Middleton*' is clunkily rhymed with 'learned *Dun*' (i.e. John Donne). Joseph Mead's [200] uncomprehending 1625 response to *Game at Chess* (not in Steen; see Critical Introduction to *Later Form*, *Works*, p. 1826) was not based on the quality of the work but on his lack of knowledge of chess. Toward mid-century an even more enthusiastic anonymous reader sung Middleton's praises:

Facetious *Middleton* thy witty Muse,
Hath pleased all, that books or men peruse
If any thee dispise, he doth but show,
Antipathy to wit, in daring so:
The fam's above his malice and 'twilbe,
Dispraise enough for him, to censure thee.
(*Wits Recreation* (1640), in Steen, 58)

This description of a 'facetious' Middleton appeared in the same year as the publisher John Spencer's praise of Middleton's stylistic poise, in his reissue of *A Mad World, My Masters*.

Mentions of Middleton in Restoration literary biographies by Edward Phillips and William Winstanley are little more than lists of information from title-pages, and even Winstanley's comment that *Michaelmas Term* 'is highly applauded for both the plot and the neatnes of style' (Steen, 65). Langbaine's closer engagement with Middleton has already been discussed.

Middleton's Early Readers, Anonymous and Nameable

One kind of conclusion for this study is Appendix E, which provides a list of all the readers recorded in this essay. No hard cut-off can be sustained between textual production and consumption. A text can be produced upon the impulse of a patron and recipient such as a Lord Mayor of London, to the extent that such a figure might, as Stephen Orgel has argued, share in the text's authorship. In the varied ways that have been described, during transmission the text is simultaneously produced and reproduced. Annotation enlarges the text, and an annotator's corrections can become an accepted part of the text in its edited received form; this is the case with some of the annotations in the Yale *Two New Plays*, which are accepted into Mulryne's and most subsequent editions of *Women, Beware Women*. What is visible to us in all these situations is the most active end of the reading process. The professionals engaged in transmitting Middleton's works figure disproportionally amongst his visible readers, because they are more readily identified. They are all men apart from Anne Moseley, publisher of the 1668 edition of *The Changeling*, and they are all known in other capacities.

The paucity of evidence for a female readership does not mean that women avoided Middleton's works. Indeed *Masque of Heroes* is unusual in being directed at a female auditory, and Aphra Behn found Middleton's plays especially congenial to adaptation. Furthermore, 'paucity' is a relative term. As noted above, the STC listing of ownership labels indicates a female participation of 1%, whereas the present study, despite its inclusion of professional groups that largely or wholly exclude women, identifies seventeen woman readers, between 5% and 6% of the total. One of them is Frances Wolfreston. It is impossible to know how representative or otherwise were Wolfreston's tastes amongst gentlewomen in country houses. Undoubtedly her collection would have been unusually large, but she can be singled out as an identifiable woman collector on account of the very particular attitude she took towards the books she owned. In her will they were bequeathed to her youngest surviving son Stanford [201], vicar of Wooten Wawen in Warwickshire, on two conditions: that he made them available for loan by his brothers and sisters, and that he kept them together as a collection

---

[68] I am grateful to the following colleagues in the *Collected Works* for passing on information on marginalia: Suzanne Gossett, Paul Mulholland, G. B. Shand, Gary Taylor, Leslie Thompson, and Wendy Wall. Laetitia Kennedy has dated the handwriting and checked the transcription in a number of books in the Folger Shakespeare Library.

(Morgan, 204). It is probably in order to identify this collection and distinguish it from her husband's property that she is so careful to inscribe her name in her books. The formation of this group of texts gathered together under the woman's name is motivated by neither economic nor antiquarian value, but rather it has in view the informal education of her children and, perhaps, a desire to maintain the cohesion of her family after her death. What is marked out from the husband is reserved for something approaching collective ownership amongst the children. It is perhaps no coincidence that the son who assumes guardianship bears her mother's maiden name.

In much the same way as with women readers, the weighting towards affluent patrons and culturally sophisticated transmitters offers no testimony against a more popular readership, and indeed the non-élite humdrum reader is certainly to be found in the marginalia of the printed texts. In other respects it would be hard to mistake the diversity of the cultural milieux that have been surveyed. Some of Middleton's texts enter the arenas of cheap print and the popular piety documented by Tessa Watt; others were read by royalty and great lords. Readers vary in religion from Calvinist to Catholic.[69] In physical distribution they are spread from Spain to Edinburgh (and even to the New World if one includes Cotton Mather, as a reader of Shakespeare, amongst readers of Middleton). Middleton circulated at court, in the city, in ecclesiastical environments, at the universities, in country houses of the gentry, amongst merchants, politicians, lawyers, wits, theatregoers, musicians, and Puritans.

In his youth Middleton sought authorial emergence in non-dramatic works through ambitious acts of patron-seeking. A few years later, Middleton was a published city-comedian. This happened not only or even primarily because he excelled in the genre, but also because the collapse of some of the boys' companies offered a window of opportunity for authorial emergence in print. In the years between Middleton's appointment as City Chronologer and the *Game at Chess* affair, the only play to appear in print with Middleton's name on it was *A Fair Quarrel*, and that was a collaboration ostensibly at least brought to the press by Rowley. Any momentum later achieved by Moseley towards establishing Middleton as a prestigious dramatic author in his octavo-format series of dramatic publications foundered after the Restoration when Middleton texts rapidly fell out of print and, despite Langbaine's protestations, became a quarry for adapters. Middleton's supposed association with Fletcher and Jonson as advertised on the title-page of *The Widow* and his partnership with Rowley in the still-popular *The Changeling* ensured that he was remembered chiefly as a collaborator and so in the second rank of dramatists. The poem 'Hence, all you Vain Delights'—now thought to be by Middleton himself, but attributed first to Beaumont and Fletcher and subsequently to Strode—was freely copied, altered, adapted, expanded, conflated, and set to music. In this case the loss of original authorial tag facilitated a peculiarly rich recycling of the text. And this is symptomatic: viewed as a whole, the Middleton canon had a weak authorial underpinning. On the one hand his texts were vulnerable to loss and misappropriation; but they could perhaps also enjoy greater scope for diversification and cultural mobility. Middleton's texts often reached their readers through systems invented by intermediaries, even when, as in the case of Moseley's project, the system was itself author-based. The transmitting reader was vital in repositioning the individual text for subsequent readers. Most of them had left the author behind and were thinking forward to their own audience. In this version of transmission and reception, the author's readers are utterly without loyalty to him.

In some respects Middleton initiated the process. It could be possible for a freelance dramatist, as opposed to a contracted 'ordinary poet', to be given permission to print his plays (Dutton, Brooks), but Middleton showed only occasional desire to take advantage of any such opportunity, or little success in doing so; major plays became hostages of fortune. If Middleton the pageant writer had his works published and duly credited as a matter of course, Middleton the pamphleteer was notably anonymous. There may be a significant connection between his dignified but limiting official identity as City Chronologer later in his career and his anonymity as author of such unconformable and unattributed or fictitiously attributed works as *The Owl's Almanac* or *The Peacemaker*: invisibility in such texts may have held advantages for the Chronologer. But the reticence runs deeper, and is probably related to Middleton's polymorphism as a writer. This variable and often invisible author as read in the seventeenth century differs profoundly from the author as studied in the modern university curriculum. A 'Collected' Middleton such as is presented in the present volumes depends on an editorial act of willed centripetalism against the dispersive energies of production, circulation, and reading. Those energies might well remain recognized in our own readings of Middleton.

Appendices

A. Publishers

The following list gives STC/Wing number, title (standard form of reference as used in the *Collected Works* except in the case of collections), date of publication, publisher.

STC Titles

6181 *Bloody Banquet* 1639: Thomas Cotes [202]
6501 *Patient Man* 1604: John Hodgets [203]
6501.5 *Patient Man* 1604: Valentine Simmes [204]
6502 *Patient Man* 1605: Valentine Simmes
6503 *Patient Man* 1615: Robert Basse [205]
6504 *Patient Man* 1616: Robert Basse

[69] If indeed the owner of *God's Parliament House* was the Puritan martyr Henry Burton, it is noteworthy that his co-martyr William Prynne was cruelly parodied by another Middleton reader, William Strode, in his Laudian play *The Floating Island*.

6505 *Patient Man* 1635: Nicholas Okes [206]
6510 *Magnificent Entertainment* 1604: Thomas Man jr. [207]
6512 *Magnificent Entertainment* 1604: Thomas Finlason
6513 *Magnificent Entertainment* 1604: Thomas Man jr.
6515 *Owl's Almanac* 1618: Laurence Lisle [208]
6515.5 *Owl's Almanac* 1618: Laurence Lisle
12199 *News from Gravesend* 1604: Thomas Archer [209]
14387 *Peacemaker* 1618: Thomas Purfoot [210]
14388 *Peacemaker* 1619: Thomas Purfoot
14388.3 *Peacemaker* 1619: John Beale [211]
14388.5 *Peacemaker* 1620: John Beale
14388.7 *Peacemaker* 1621: John Beale
17154 *Microcynicon* 1599: Thomas Bushell [212]
17781 *Meeting of Gallants* 1608: Thomas Creede [213]
17874.3 *Father Hubburd's Tales* 1604: Thomas Bushell
17874.7 *Father Hubburd's Tales* 1604: William Cotton [214]
17875 *Black Book* 1604: Jeffrey Chorlton [215]
17877 *Chaste Maid* 1630: Francis Constable [216]
17878 *Civitatis Amor* 1616: Thomas Archer
17882 *Game at Chess* [1625]: Nicholas Okes (printer)
17883 *Game at Chess* [1625?]: Nicholas Okes (printer)
17884 *Game at Chess* [1625?]: Edward Allde [217] and Augustine Mathewes [218] (printers)
17885 *Game at Chess* 1625: Nicholas Okes (printer)
17885.5 *Ghost of Lucrece* 1600: Valentine Simmes
17886 *Honourable Entertainments* 1621: George Eld [219]
17887 *Masque of Heroes* (*Inner Temple Masque*) 1619: John Browne [220]
17888 *Mad World* 1608: Walter Burre [221][70]
17889 *Mad World* 1640: John Spencer
17890 *Michaelmas Term* 1607: Arthur Johnson [222]
17891 *Michaelmas Term* 1630: Richard Meighen
17892 *Phoenix* 1607: Arthur Johnson
17893 *Phoenix* 1630: Richard Meighen
17894 *Sir Robert Sherley* 1609: John Budge [223]
17894.5 *Sir Robert Sherley* 1609: John Budge
17895 *Sun in Aries* 1621: Henry Gosson [224]
17896, 17896a *Trick to Catch the Old One* 1608: George Eld
17897 *Trick to Catch the Old One* 1616: Thomas Langley [225]
17898 *Triumphs of Health and Prosperity* 1626: Nicholas Okes
17899 *Triumphs of Honour and Industry* 1617: Nicholas Okes
17900 *Triumphs of Honour and Virtue* 1622: Nicholas Okes
17901 *Triumphs of Integrity* 1623: Nicholas Okes
17902 *Triumphs of Love and Antiquity* 1619: Nicholas Okes
17903 *Triumphs of Truth* 1613: Nicholas Okes
17904 *Triumphs of Truth* and *His Lordship's Entertainment* 1613: Nicholas Okes
17904.3 *Two Gates of Salvation* 1609: Nicholas Okes

17904.5 *Two Gates of Salvation* 1620: Nicholas Okes
17904.7 *Two Gates of Salvation* 1627: Nicholas Okes
17906 *Wisdom of Solomon Paraphrased* 1597: Valentine Simmes
17907 *Your Five Gallants* 1608: Richard Bonian [226]
17908 *Roaring Girl* 1611: Thomas Archer
17909 *World Tossed at Tennis* 1620: George Purslowe [227][71]
17910 *World Tossed at Tennis* 1620: George Purslowe
17911, 17911a *Fair Quarrel* 1617: John Trundle [228]
17912 *Fair Quarrel* 1622: Thomas Dewe [229]
19307 *Penniless Parliament* 1614: William Barley [230]
19307.5 *Penniless Parliament* 1637: John Beale
21512.5 *A Description of the King and Queen of Fairies* 1634: Richard Harper [231]
21513 *A Description of the King and Queen of Fairies* 1635: Richard Harper
21531 *Puritan* 1607: George Eld
22273 Shakespeare Folio 1623: William Jaggard [232], Edward Blount [233], John Smethwick [234], William Aspley [235]
22274–22274e.5 Shakespeare Folio 1632: John Smethwick, William Aspley, Richard Hawkins [236], Richard Meighen [237], Robert Allott [238]
22340 *Yorkshire Tragedy* 1608: Thomas Pavier
22341 *Yorkshire Tragedy* 1619: Thomas Pavier
24149 *Revenger's Tragedy* 1607: George Eld
24150 *Revenger's Tragedy* 1608: George Eld

Wing Titles

B1581 Beaumont and Fletcher Folio 1647: Humphrey Robinson [239], Humphrey Moseley
J1015 *Widow* 1652: Humphrey Moseley
M1048 *Old Law* 1656: Edward Archer [240]
M1714 *Wit Restored* 1658: Robert Pollard, Nathaniel Brooks, Thomas Dring
M1979 *Anything for a Quiet Life* 1662: Francis Kirkman [241], Henry Marsh [242]
M1980 *Changeling* 1653: Humphrey Moseley
M1981 *Changeling* 1653: Humphrey Moseley
M1982 *Changeling* 1668: Anne Moseley
M1984, M1984A *Hengist* 1661: Henry Herringman
M1985 *No Wit* 1657: Humphrey Moseley
M1989 *Two New Plays* 1657: Humphrey Moseley
S2913 Shakespeare Folio 1663: Philip Chetwin [243]
S2914 Shakespeare Folio 1664: Philip Chetwin

B. Dedications and Prefaces in Printed Books

Wisdom of Solomon Paraphrased (1597): Dedicated to Robert Devereux, Earl of Essex, and with an epistle to the gentlemen readers, both addresses signed 'Thomas Middleton'
Microcynicon 1599: Verse epistle '*His defiance to Envy*', signed 'T.M. Gent.'

---

[70] Entered in the Stationers' Register jointly by Burre and Eleazar Edgar; the latter's share was transferred to John Hodgets in 1613.
[71] Entered in the Stationers' Register jointly to Purslowe and John Trundle.

Ghost of Lucrece (1600): Dedicated 'To the Right Honorable, and my very bountiful good Lord, my Lord Compton', signed '*T.M.*'

Father Hubburd's Tales (1604): Mock dedication 'To the True Generall Patron of all *Muses, Musitians, Poets, & Picture Drawers, Syr Christopher Clutch-Fist*', signed 'Oliver Hubburd'; and epistle 'To the Reader', signed 'T.M.'

Black Book (1604): Epistle to the reader, signed 'T.M.'

News from Gravesend (1604): 'Tee [*sic*] Epistle Dedicatory. *To Him, that (in the despite and never-dying--dishonour of all empty-fisted Mecen-Asses) is the Gratious, munificent, and golden Rewarder of Rimers: singular pay-maister of Songes and Sonnets: Unsquint-eyde Surveyor of Heroicall Poems: Chiefe Rent-gatherer of Poets and Musitians: And the most valiant Confounder of their desperate debts: And to the comfort of all honest Christians. The now-onely-onely-Supper-maker to Enghles & Plaiers-Boyes, Syr Nicholas Nemo, alias Nobody*', signed 'Devoted to none but thy selfe, *Some--body*'

Mad World (1640 edition): 'The Printer and Stationer to the Gentle Reader'

Sir Robert Sherley (1609): Some copies with a dedication to Sir Thomas, Sir Robert's brother, signed 'Thomas Midleton'; others with another unsigned dedication to Sir Thomas, Sir Robert's father

Two Gates of Salvation (1609): dedication headed, 'To the very worthy deserver of all true honours, and constant lover of religion and learning' and unsigned

Roaring Girl (1611): Epistle 'To the Comic Play-readers', signed 'Thomas Middleton'

Truth (1613): Epistle to Sir Thomas Myddelton, signed 'Thomas Middleton'

Fair Quarrel (1617): Dedication to 'Robert Grey Esquire [244], one of the Grooms of his Highnesse Bed--Chamber', signed 'William Rowley'

Honour and Industry (1617): Dedicated to George Bolles, Lord Mayor, Puritan, and Sabbatarian; signed 'T.M.'

Owl's Almanac (1618): Dedication to Sir Timothy Thornhill [245] signed 'L.L.' (Laurence Lisle, the publisher)

Peacemaker (1618): Fourteen-page Epistle 'To all Our true-loving, and Peace-embracing Subjects', unsigned

Masque of Heroes (1619): Short poem to the reader, headed 'The Masque', signed 'T.M.'

Love and Antiquity (1619): Dedicatory verses to Sir William Cokayne, Lord Mayor, signed 'Tho. Middleton'

Marriage of Old and New Testaments (1620): Dedicated to Richard Fishbourne and John Browne, signed 'Tho: Middleton, Chronologer for the Honourable City of London'

Tennis (1620): Epistle Dedicatory to the marrying couple: 'To the Truly-Noble, Charles, Lord Howard, Baron of Effingham, and to his Vertuous and Worthy Lady, the Right Honourable, Mary, Lady Effingham, Eldest Daughter of the truly Generous and Judicious, Sʳ William Cokayne, Knight, L. Maior of this City, and L. Generall of the Militarie Forces'. Also, epistle 'To the well-wishing, -well reading *Understander, well--understanding Reader; Simplicitie S.P.D.*', signed '*Your kinde and loving Kinsman, Simplicitie.*'

Honourable Entertainments (1621): Dedicated to:

Sir Francis Jones [246] (1560?-1622?, Haberdasher, Lord Mayor 1620-21)

Sir John Garrard [247] (1546?-1625, Lord Mayor 1601-2)

Sir Thomas Bennet [248] (1550?-1627, Mercer, Lord Mayor 1603-4)

Sir Thomas Lowe [249] (1550-1623, Haberdasher, Lord Mayor 1604-5)

Sir Thomas Myddelton (1551?-1631, Grocer, Lord Mayor 1613-14, and see above)

Sir John Jolles [250] (d. 1621, Draper, Lord Mayor 1615-16, pageant by Munday)

Sir John Leman [251] (1544-1632, Alderman, Lord Mayor 1616-17; member and warden of Fishmongers' Company; inauguration with pageant by Munday (*Chrysanaleia: The Golden Fishing*); knighted 1617; John Vicars dedicated his translation of Francis Herring's poem of the Gunpowder Plot, *Mischief's Mystery*, to him)

Sir George Bolles (1538-1621, Grocer, Lord Mayor 1617-18)

Sir William Cokayne (1561?-1626, Skinner, Lord Mayor 1619-20, and see above)

Heneage Finch [252] (d. 1631, Recorder, later MP for London 1623-6)

Edward Barkham (d. 1634, Draper, Sheriff 1611-12, Lord Mayor 1621-2)

Alexander Prescot [253] (d. 1622, Goldsmith, Lord Mayor 1611-12)

Peter Proby (1565?-1625, Grocer, Sheriff 1614-15, Lord Mayor 1622-3)

Martin Lumley (1580?-1631, Draper, Sheriff 1614-15, Lord Mayor 1623-4)

William Gore [254] (d. 1624, Merchant Taylor, Sheriff 1615-16)

John Gore [255] (1570?-1636, Merchant Taylor, Sheriff 1615-16, Lord Mayor 1624-5)

Allan Cotton [256] (Draper, Sheriff 1616-17, Lord Mayor 1625-6)

Cuthbert Hacket (Draper, Sheriff 1616-17, Lord Mayor 1626-7)

William Halliday [257] (d. 1623, Mercer, Sheriff 1617-18)

Robert Johnson [258] (1565?-1626, Grocer, Sheriff 1617-18)

Richard Herne [259] (d. 1625, Sheriff 1618-19)

Hugh Hamersley [260] (Haberdasher, Sheriff 1618-19, Lord Mayor 1627-8)

Richard Deane [261] (Skinner, Lord Mayor 1628-9; Puritan)

MIDDLETON'S EARLY READERS

James Campbell [262] (Ironmonger, Sheriff 1619–20, Lord Mayor 1629)

Edward Allen [263] (1563?–1626, Fishmonger, Sheriff)

R. Ducie [264] (Merchant Taylor, Sheriff, Lord Mayor 1630–31).

Sun in Aries (1621): Dedicatory verses to Edward Barkham, Lord Mayor, signed 'Tho. Middleton'

Honour and Virtue (1622): Dedicatory verses to Peter Proby, Lord Mayor

Integrity (1623): Dedicatory verses to Martin Lumley, Lord Mayor (who was upwardly mobile; the pageant praises greatness derived from merit), signed 'Tho. Middleton'

Shakespeare First Folio (1623): Epistle 'To the Reader' signed 'B.J.'; dedication to William Herbert, Earl of Pembroke [265] and his brother Philip, Earl of Montgomery [266], and epistle *To the great Variety of Readers*', both signed by Heminges and Condell; commendatory verses by Jonson, Hugh Holland, Leonard Digges, and 'J.M.' (James Mabbe)[72]

Health and Prosperity (1626): Dedicatory verses to Cuthbert Hacket, Lord Mayor, signed 'Thomas Middleton'. Heinemann suggests the almost obsequious stance adopted to Charles in some speeches could be an attempt to appease him after the refusal of a group of wealthy London citizens to grant him a loan of £1,000,000, but notes also that Hacket anticipated Lord Mayors of the following decade in having no discernable anti-Court affiliations.

Shakespeare Second Folio (1632): Adds new commendatory verses, including an epitaph to Shakespeare by John Milton and a poem signed 'J.M.S.'

Beaumont and Fletcher Folio (1647): Dedication to Philip Herbert Earl of Pembroke signed John Lowin, Joseph Taylor, Richard Robinson, Robert Benfield, Eylard Swanston, Thomas Pollard, Hugh Clark, William Allen, Stephen Hammerton, and Theophilus Bird; Epistles 'To the Reader' signed James Shirley, 'The Stationer to the Readers' signed Humphrey Moseley, and 'To the Stationer' signed 'Grandison'; commendatory verses by: H. Howard, Henry Moody, Thomas Peyton, Aston Cokayne, John Pettus, Robert Stapylton, George Lisle, J. Denham, 'Edw. Waller', Richard Lovelace, William Habington, James Howell, Thomas Stanley, Roger L'Estrange, Robert Gardiner, John Webb, George Buc, John Earle, 'J. M.', Jasper Maine, William Cartwright, Richard Corbet, Ben Jonson, Robert Herrick, John Berkenhead, Edward Powell, G. Hills, Joseph Howe, T. Palmer, Alexander Brome, John Harris, Henry Harrington, Richard Brome, James Shirley, and Humphrey Moseley

Widow (1652): Epistle to the reader, signed Alexander Gough

Two New Plays (1657): Epistle to the reader, unsigned; commendatory verses by Nathaniel Richards

Hengist (1661): Publisher's epistle to the reader (Henry Herringman)

C. Songs in Ascribable Miscellanies

1. Nicholas Burghe's [267] miscellany of *c*.1638 (Bodleian MS Ashmole 38) includes Latrocinio's song, described as 'Thee Highe Lawyers Song in the playe called the Widdowe'. Burghe was himself a poet; around 1632–5 he was probably imprisoned for debt with the King's Men sharer John Heminges's son William. The manuscript was later owned by Ashmole. The only known copy of William Heminges's *Elegy on Randolph's Finger* (which contains lines on immigrant Amsterdam Puritans' admiration for *A Game at Chess*) appears in this manuscript in Burghe's hand, and for this reason it has been conjectured that the manuscript was prepared in prison (Smith, ed., 1923, pp. 8–9; Bentley 1941–68, iv, 541–2).

2. A copy of the same song headed 'On a purse Taker' appears in another miscellany of *c*.1630 (British Library Add. MS 10309) once owned by Margaret Bellasys [268]. Beal identifies her as the Margaret Bellasys who was the daughter of Thomas, Lord Fauconberg (1577–1653).[73] She was granddaughter of Sir Henry Cholmley of Roxby and Whitby, Yorkshire, who was perhaps related to the younger man of same name who owned Harvard MS Eng 703, which contains 'Hence, all you Vain Delights'. Margaret married in 1619, and died, still a young woman, in 1624.

3. The song from *The Witch* beginning 'In a maiden time professed' is included in Daniel Leare's [269] miscellany probably written while he was at Christ Church, Oxford, before he entered the Middle Temple in 1633 (British Library Add. MS 30982). The flyleaf is inscribed 'Daniell Leare, his Booke witnesse William Strode', in a hand that may be Leare's own conscious imitation of Strode (Hobbs, 189). The words should be read as a gesture of affiliation rather than testimony that Strode might have known the contents including Middleton's song (Hobbs, 190, points out that Leare was second cousin of Strode, and may have been tutored by him at Christ Church). Leare's manuscript contains a transcription of a large grouping of Strode's poems, probably taken directly from his autograph manuscript, including two copies of 'An Opposite to Melancholy' and the elegy for Fishbourne. Other names are inscribed, as Beal notes: 'John Leare' [270], probably Daniel's younger brother; 'John Scott' [271], who matriculated at Christ Church in 1632; 'Anthony Eyans his booke Amen', *i.e.* the Anthony Eyans [272] who married Daniel

---

[72] I have not included dedication writers of the Shakespeare and Beaumont and Fletcher folios amongst Middleton's readers. But it would be implausible to suppose that Jonson and Milton at least had not read the Shakespeare plays in which Middleton had a hand.

[73] Gary Taylor (1985) has drawn attention to another person of the same name, the wife of Sir William Bellasis (d. 1640) of Morton House, Co. Durham, the eldest daughter of Sir George Selby, of Whitehouse, in the same county; she died in 1671. But, as Taylor recognizes, Beal's candidate is more plausible.

Leare's niece Dorothy Leare [273] in 1663 (Beal, II, ii, 355).

4. 'Hence, all you Vain Delights' is preserved in the manuscripts listed in the Textual Introduction to *Nice Valour*.[74] The following give indications of owners or readers:

B&F 112: Aberdeen University Library MS 29, compiled *c.*1630s, inscribed on a flyleaf 'Elizabeth Lane hir booke' [274] and on another 'Johannes Finch' [275]: possibly either the parliamentarian, Speaker of the 1629 Parliament, impeached in 1640 (1584–1660), or the son of Heneage Finch, physician and member of the Royal Society (1626–82);

B&F 113: Bodleian MS Ashmole 36.37, in the hand of Elias Ashmole (1617–92), in a composite volume of verse collected by him, mid-seventeenth century;

B&F 114: Bodleian MS Eng. poet. c. 50, compiled *c.*1630s–40s, owned by Peter Daniell [276] of Oxford and later inscribed with the names 'Thomas Gardner' [277], 'James Leigh' [278], and 'Petrus Romell' [279], song headed 'on Melencholie', with Strode's reply;

B&F 115: Bodleian MS Eng. poet. e. 14, compiled in Oxford *c.*1630s, owned by Henry Lawson [280], song headed 'The Image of Melancholly';

B&F 116: Bodleian, MS Firth e. 4, dedicated to Lady Afra Harflete [281], p. 72 (*c.*1640);

B&F 119: Bodleian MS Mus. Sch. F. 575, mid-seventeenth century music book owned by William Iles [282] (perhaps related to Thomas Iles, canon of Christ Church), who in 1673 sent it to Dr John Fell [283], Dean of Christ Church, for use in the Music School;[75]

B&F 121–2: Bodleian MS Rawl. poet. 84, compiled mid-seventeenth century, belonged to the Paulet family [284] (see Giles Paulet above; as Kewes notes, Moseley's edition of Shirley's *The Sisters*, in *Six New Plays* (1652) was addressed to William Paulet); owned in 1659 by Egigius Frampton [285]; two copies of the song, with an added stanza by the poet Henry King (1592–1669);

B&F 126: British Library Add. MS 26844, otherwise mostly autograph poems by Charles Montagu, Earl of Halifax [286] (1661–1715; member of the Whig Junto), compiled end of seventeenth century;

B&F 127: British Library Add. MS 47111, compiled by Sir John Perceval [287] (1629–65), probably while at Magdalene College, Cambridge, *c.*1646–9, song omitting first stanza;

B&F 129: British Library Sloane MS 542, compiled *c.*1630s, owned by Nathaniel Highmore [288] (1613–85), who wrote the scientific tract *History of Generation* (1651), dedicated to Robert Boyle, and was first to describe the antrum of the upper jaw;

B&F 130: British Library Sloane MS 1792, compiled early 1630s, probably by 'I. A.' [289] of Christ Church, Oxford, later owned by Robert Killigrew

[290] (perhaps Thomas Killigrew's son); Strode's reply is found two leaves previously in the same manuscript;

B&F 131: Cambridge University Library MS Dd. 6. 43, compiled late seventeenth century, owned by William Godolphin [291] (probably Sir William, the ambassador and Catholic convert, 1634?–96) and Henry Savile [292] (the diplomat, 1642–87);

B&F 132: Cambridge University Library MS Gg. 1. 4, compiled *c.*1658 probably by J. Hinson [293], who owned the miscellany, song headed 'Melancholly', dedicated to Thomas Martin [294], Bishop of Durham 1632–59, lacks first stanza;

B&F 135: Folger MS V. a. 124, compiled *c.*1650–57 by Richard Archard [295], song headed 'On Melancholy'; followed by Strode's answer poem;

B&F 136: Folger MS V. a. 125, Part I, compiled by Richard Boyle, Viscount Dungarvan [296] (1612–98) (royalist, elder brother of the scientist Robert Boyle), *c.*1630s, song headed 'Verses made of Melancholy';

B&F 137: Folger MS V. a. 160, p. 2 (2nd series), compiled by Matthew Day [297], Mayor of Windsor, *c.*1633–4, song headed 'A Melancholy meditation', second stanza placed first;

B&F 144: Harvard MS Eng. 703, compiled by or for Sir Henry Cholmley [298], brother of Sir Hugh Cholmley (1600–57), *c.*1624–41;

B&F 145: Huntington HM 46323, compiled by one or two members of the Calverley family [299], *c.*1623–30s (Sir Richard Calverley was active in the early 1620s as a Court official responsible for making ready venues for Court entertainments and plays);

B&F 149: St John's College, Cambridge MS S. 32 (James 423), owned and possibly compiled by John Pike [300] of Cambridge, *c.*1636–40s.

D. Marginalia, etc.

Books are listed by order of publication.

Wisdom of Solomon Paraphrased (1597), *British Library,* C. 39. e. 49

E2, line 7: 'x' opposite 'The longer that the wicked lives on earth'.

Microcynicon (1599), *Bodleian*

Prologue.25: 'the the' altered to 'the' by striking out the repetition.

6.3: 'Why' corrected to 'way'.

Epilogue.6: 'must have' changed to 'have'.

---

[74] This list is based on Beal, *Index*, pp. 93–5.
[75] A note on a verso at the beginning of the songbook reads:

M[r] William Iles: Sent thes ten Bookes to D[r] Fell Deane of ch: ch: in oxford [wherof] for ye use of the publick musick scoole whereof 5 of them are of one sort & the other 5 of a nother, they are mark[t] with ye 10 first figures at the topp of this page that soe it may bee discouered which is wantinge

And on the opposite recto, in the same hand: 'William Iles. 1673'.

Microcynicon (1599), Huntington

Title-page has ink signature 'Iohes Playdell'[?]. [301] Epilogue.6: 'must have' changed to 'have'.

Ghost of Lucrece (1600), Folger

'G.O.' is written on the covers of the unique copy. This is evidently the original owner. On the inside of the front cover is 'Giles' and below this ultraviolet photography reveals the full name 'Giles Paulet' (perhaps of the family that owned a manuscript miscellany containing the Middleton song 'Hence, all you Vain Delights'; see above). B2ᵛ–3 identifies other seventeenth-century owners as George and Richard Fallowes: 'George ffallowes is the trwe oner of this booke and he that stealeth this booke he shall be hanged on a houcke and If the hocke do faille he shale be hãged on anile and If the naile do cracke he shall be ha:'; then, 'George ffallowes is the trewe oner of this boke and he that stealeth this booke he shall be'; then, 'Richard ffallowes is my nam and If with my pen I rot the same and If my pen ⟨pen⟩ hit had bin Better I woould amend eueri letter' (Adams, ed., 1937; confirmed by G. B. Shand).

Father Hubburd's Tales (1604), Folger

Title-page: 'Edw: Palmer' [302], in a hand c.1625 or mid-seventeenth century (Laetitia Kennedy).

Black Book (1604), British Library, C. 27. b. 2

Crosses in margin at B4ᵛ, 12; C3, 17; C4, 2; D1ᵛ, 9; D2ᵛ, 7 (of main text); D3, 2 up; D4ᵛ, 10; F2ᵛ, 11 up.

Black Book (1604), Folger

C1 has partially cropped and only partly legible note running down outer margin in secretary hand.

Patient Man and the Honest Whore (1604), Folger 1

K2ᵛ, 5 lines up: 'Ans' (with long 's') inked in where speech prefix is missing.

The Puritan (1607), British Library, C. 34. l. 4

H4, Latin motto: 'Deus' crossed out and 'Diabolus' written above.

Revenger's Tragedy (1607), British Library, C.34. e. 11

Copy for an edition of Tourneur's plays, extensively marked up in two or more hands with alterations to punctuation, modernizations of spelling, emendations, and casting off. Also, in earlier hands: B2ᵛ: 'P Gu…' smudged and running off cropped page. Then 'John' [303]. Then doodle in left margin. E3: Deletion of 'Meete' after 'Amb.' and, five lines below, deletion of 'O this' after 'For this,'. H1: Note in secretary hand, top of page, first word and top of letters of second and third words cropped: ')a no⟨t⟩e that at one mele pan eat [corrected from "et"] a tow peny lofe'.

The Phoenix (1607), British Library, 161. a. 68

Title-page, below 'THE PHOENIX': 'Written by Tho Middleton. Gent.'

Mad World (1608), E2 copy

Title-page: 'Iohn Ienkines [304] November 24ᵗʰ: 1608 pre. 6ᵈ/'.

Penniless Parliament (1608), Folger (unbound)

A3 (above start of text): 'frances wolfreston] hor bouk' in a mid-seventeenth century hand.

Trick (1608), British Library, C.34. d. 42

E1, lines 5–6: 'but were it to marry a chin not worth a haire now' underlined.
E4, line 5 (near end of Act 3): 'cunnycatching' underlined.

Trick (1608), Kemble–Devonshire, Folger

Title-page: 'Gewer' [305] (evidently an owner's name; see also Kemble–Devonshire Tennis, 1620) and 'pleasant', both in the same hand, probably second half of the seventeenth century.

Trick (1608), Folger

Contains marginalia in an early hand:
Title-page: 'idleton' after 'T. M.'; 'Edw. worseley' [306] below and right of ornament. Worseley could conceivably be the Jesuit (1605–76), but if so he is unlikely to have been the first owner.
B2, 3 lines up: 'my' marked marginally for insertion before 'Nephew'.
B3, line 4: 'mouth' underlined and marginally corrected 'moneth'.
C1ᵛ, line 22: 'thike' underlined and corrected 'thinke'.
C4, line 20: 'Enter Lucr' opposite 'Wit. Vncle?'
E1ᵛ, 1 line up: 'in' underlined and corrected 'it'; foot of page: 'Enter George'.
E2ᵛ, 14 lines up: 'I bee' underlined and marginally corrected to 'I'le'. 6 lines up: 'he' underlined and marginally corrected to 'the'.
E3ᵛ, line 11: 'Enter Audry' opposite 'remember'.
E4ᵛ, line 8, opposite 'Hoord?': 'Enter Luker' written to right and deleted; 'As within' to left; line 22: s.p. 'Luc.' crossed out and marginally corrected 'Curt.'
F2, line 9: 'Enter witgood' added opposite 'see where he comes' and below 'Exit.'
F3ᵛ, line 6: 'wee' smudged and 'wee' noted in margin.
F4ᵛ, 6 lines up: 'Enter Hoste' added opposite 'newes!'
G1ᵛ, line 2: 'Exit' added opposite 'reuenge yet'; line 15: 'Enter Witgood' opposite 'here he comes'.
G4ᵛ, 9 lines up: 'Breake' underlined and marginally corrected 'breed'.
H1, line 22: 'the' interlined before 'theefe' and added marginally; line 23: 'Is this' underlined and corrected 'This is'.
H1ᵛ, bottom: 'has better skill' underlined and written out to right.

H2, line 20: 'Enter La⟨⟩' (cropped) added right of 'Madame you are welcome to'; 5 lines up: 'Enter brot⟨h⟩ | and 2 ot⟨h⟩ | ' opposite 'brother'.

Final leaf: written out in Roman script, old spelling, round 's' except for first of 'ss', with imitation running title and 'FINIS.'

Your Five Gallants (1608), British Library, C. 34. d. 44

A4, line 10: 'x' opposite '*Frip*. Nay I let twelue alone'.

B1, line 8: 'x' opposite 'friends—are you a maide. *Nou*. Yes, in the last quarter sir'.

B1ᵛ, line 16: 'x' opposite 'obseruer of a saltseller, priuy to nothing but a close-stoole, or'.

B2, line 3: line under 'prickt so'.

B4, line 22: 'x' opposite 'myle hence, beleeue that: his friends are of the olde fashi-'.

E2, line 19: 'x' opposite '*Puss*. You must pardon me sir, I must a little play the Vintner'; line 21: 'x' opposite '*Tayl*. Alasse ther's no conscience in that sir, shall I enter into'; line 26: line looped round end of '*Purs*. Masse that's the diuill, I thanke you heartily, for hee's [cal'd the prince ath' world]'.

F1, line 12: vertical mark opposite '*Tayl*. I would had staide him,'.

G2, l, 15: 'x' opposite 'my company so long, 'tis now about the nauill of the day, vpon [the belly of noone]'.

H3, line 15: 'x' opposite '*Go*. Last man we spoke on, Maistr Bowser.'

Your Five Gallants (1608), Glasgow University

Title-page: Title copied immediately below, and 'for' written below 'friers'. Sig. 1ᵛ, alphabet from a to k (cropped) and 'for'.

C4ᵛ: 'F' followed by two crosses with loop underlinking arms. F4ᵛ: Various faint orange marks, amongst them 'Gold' opposite the erroneous speech prefix 'Bung'.

Sherley (1609), British Library, C. 1119. dd. 21

A1 (unprinted leaf): 'maria Detton' [307] running upwards in large, rounded letters. Also, other way round, 'W. Warde' [308] and 'Willm A Warde'.

Title-page: Lettering in a distinct hand from those of A1. Either side of 'ENGLAND': 'F' and 'T'. Further right: scrolled lettering perhaps representing 'Tho' followed by 'Detton' [309].

B2ᵛ, upwards in left margin: 'Thomas Detton of Detton | in the Countie of Salop | gentleman.'

B4ᵛ, left margin: large letters, cropped and illegible, probably in the same hand as Maria Detton's name on A1.

C1: Top, 'The'. right margin: 'T[?] R', cropped, and 'The | thow'.

C4ᵛ, left margin: 'De Hugford ⟨pro⟩ qu⟨e⟩ W.ᵐᵘˢ tenet de Hono⟨rᵉ⟩ ⟨inve . . .⟩ pro servic' inveniend vnum ho.ᵐ cum arcu et tribus [sat] sigittis in temp. querᵉ in exercitu [⟨yf⟩] Wallie Rs ⟨Dent⟩ coram me J'.[76]

Patient Man and the Honest Whore (1615), British Library, 644. b. 19

Title-page: Subtitle and first part of author's name copied by hand.

In the text, marginal 'X' with a bar joining the upper limbs used for emphasis.

K4ᵛ, bottom right: '880' (recorded in Kahrl and Anderson, 124).

Trick (1616), British Library, 644. b. 78

Title-page, above title, 'Cit Warinse' [310].

A4ᵛ: line 3: 'exiunt:/' opposite 'of our Country'; lines 4–5: 'Enter 2 gentlemen' opp '1. Whose that?' and '2. Oh, the common . . .'.

B1, line 17, 'wille nille': 'against the' interlined for insertion before 'wille', and 'nille' deleted.

B3ᵛ (towards the end of Act 1) 'Enter Gulfe | & Dampit' left of 'the Roague has spied . . . a poxe search you . . .'.

B4 'Enter Ser:' at foot of page after 'Translation now sir' (end of Lucre's speech opening Act 2).

C2, 6 lines up: 'Enter George./' after Lucre calls 'George—'.

C2ᵛ, line 17: 'Enter George' left of end of Lucre's speech beginning 'Ah Sirrah, that rich widdow'.

D3, right of line 20: illegible scrawl.

Fair Quarrel (1617a), Huntington

Inserts scene divisions of the type 'Scena 3' at D3ᵛ, line 13, F4ᵛ. Line 15, H2, line 6.

Marks brackets around a number of passages, and quotation marks at the opening of 2 lines. Corrects 'frialeto' by inscribing 'y' over 'o'.

D3ᵛ: where the Physician says 'Nay Master', 'Master' is corrected to 'Mistriss'.

G3: probably miscorrects at 4.1.128–31: 'hee throw . . . vpon him' becomes 'I throw . . . vpon me'.

Fair Quarrel (1617a), National Library of Scotland

In left margin of B1ᵛ, alongside the Captain's Friend's speech about Captain Ager's youthful nobility (beginning 1.1.39), 'Although unruelly'.

E3: under the Act notation, the name 'Mr. Peter Bar'. [311]

E4ᵛ: in the margin, 'My lou'.

H3ᵛ: 'John Gowlin' [312] (or 'Dowlin').

I2ᵛ: fragments: 'John', 'Joh'.

I3ᵛ: 'Rep' (?), '⟩ller', 'Barrett'. [313][77]

I4ᵛ, 'Elizabeth W. Haynes [314], John Noynes [315]'.

Fair Quarrel (1617a), Harvard

F1ᵛ: marginal direction at 3.1.160, 'Col Fall' (or possibly 'Falls').

[76] I am grateful to Richard Proudfoot for providing a transcript of this item.

[77] A John Barrett performed in Richards's *Messalina* with the King's Revels, c.1634; but might this Barrett be the same as 'Mr. Peter Bar'?

Masque of Heroes (1619), *Folger*

B1ᵛ: cropped and irrecoverable marginal note, keyed with a caret to 'my Ladies *Hole*ᴧ'.

Yorkshire Tragedy (1619), *in Pavier bound collection, Folger*

Title-page: 'Edward Gwynne' [316] (book-collector, resident of Furnival's Inn, former owner of several books now in the Folger; see Jackson 1934–5).

Yorkshire Tragedy (1619), *New York Public Library*

Title-page, below and right of title: 'ABC'. Right of ornament: copy of oval medalion with part of the motto inscribed between the lines.

Heavy deletions, with occasional substitutions in an early seventeenth-century hand, as follows (deletions marked in square brackets, manuscript substitutions in bold, interlineations between slashes):

A1: '*Oliuer* [Masse]'; 'Neyther of eyther, as [the Puritan Bawde] / **thay** / say[es]. **but stay** [Slidd] I heare *Sam*, *Sam's* come, heere tarry, come [ifaith], now'.

A1ᵛ: '*Am.* Honest fellow *Sam*, welcome [ifaith],'. '*Oliuer* [Ile sweare] / **truly** / thou art, thou maist set vp'. '*Amb.* [Faith] ye ieast'.

A2: '*Sam.* But speake in your conscience [ifaith]'. '*Amb.* [Faith] lets heare it'.

A2ᵛ: '*Amb.* [Faith] that's excellent'.

A3: '*Enter Husband.* | *Hus.* [Pox] / **Fie** /'. '**ime undon** [Ime damnd, Ime damnd]'. 'Nay tis certainly true: [for he that has no coyne,] | [Is damnd in this world]'. '*Hus.* [A vengeance] strip thee naked'. '*Wife.* Bad, turnd to worse? **o! beggery!** | [Both beggery of the soule, as of the body.] | [And] so much vnlike'.

B2: '*Enter Wife in a riding suite, with a seruingman.* | *Ser.* [Faith] mistris'.

B3: 'What [the diuell]? how now?'.

B4: '*Hus.* Oh [God, oh.] **mee oh:**'.

B4ᵛ: 'vndone thee, [thy damnation has beggerd thee], that'.

C1: 'I haue don't [ifaith]: terrible'.

C2ᵛ: '*Hus.* Dost thou preuent me still? | *Wife.* Oh [God!]'. '*Ser.* [Sbloud], you haue vndone vs all sir'.

C3ᵛ: 'Oh, I am sorely bruisde, [plague founder thee],'.

C4: '[Sfoot], a man may dice vpon it'.

Tennis (1620), *British Library, C. 34. g. 5*

Marginal pencil marks correspond to notes at end in rebinding paper.

Tennis (1620), *Kemble–Devonshire, Folger*

Title-page: 'Gewer' (evidently an owner's name; see also Kemble–Devonshire *Trick*) and 'sorry', both in the same hand, probably second half of the seventeenth century.

Tennis (1620), *Folger*

At least 2 hands are present. Annotations on: B2 (illegible); B3 'Emphasis Capitals' (which must be from a more recent hand); E1, undeciphered name.

Seventeenth-century annotation to *Measure for Measure*.

Tennis (1620), *Worcester College*

'The Figures': Part of the page missing and replaced with blank insert. Missing names written in: (a) opposite '*A King*': 'A Land Captain. Deceit as a souldʳ'; (b) below insert: 'A Sea Captain Deceit as a Purser. The Mariners Song.'

God's Parliament House (1621), *British Library, C. 19. 3127*

Title-page: 'John | Robinson.' left of 'LONDON'. 'Burton' at top.

¶1: 'Gods parl | house' and 'H Burton' right of ornament. Burton's name is in the same hand as appears on the title-page. 'Parl' cropped. 'New Testament' in same hand down right edge, top of lettering cropped.

Fair Quarrel (1622), *British Library, 644. b. 80*

Title-page: initialed 'W: C' (with traces of cropped lettering below).

H2ᵛ: pencil cross enclosed in circle opposite 2 lines in the Captain's speech beginning 'May then that glorious reward': 7–8 (The crowne...Let 'em) and 10 (I feele it).

Fair Quarrel (1622), *Worcester College*

Final leaf missing and made good with handwritten transcription.

Shakespeare Folio (1623), *Folger Copy 54*

F1 (first page of *Measure*): 'Scene—Vienna.', in a 'later seventeenth century' hand (Laetitia Kennedy): see illustration.

Shakespeare Folio (1623), *Folger Copy 63*

'x' marked, in a similar ink to the other marginalia, opposite various lines in *Timon*, all spoken by Apemantus:[78]

---

[78] Copy 63 is a composite volume, and there appear to be no 'x's or annotations elsewhere in it.

gg2ᵛ: *Ape.* Thy Mothers of my generation . . .
Ape. Should'st haue kept one . . .
Ape. No I will do nothing . . .
gg3: Heere's that which is too weake to be a
sinner,
gg4: *Ape.* Dost Dialogue with thy shadow?
gg4ᵛ: *Ape.* Would I had a Rod in my mouth . . .
Ape. There will litle Learning dye . . .

hh4, (a) opposite '*Phrinica*': 'phrinia', and opposite
'*Timandylo*': 'Tymandra', in a hand of the first half of
the seventeenth century (Laetitia Kennedy); opposite
'man': 'men'.
hh6: several lines of Latin below 'The Actors Names',
in a hand of the first half of the seventeenth century
(Laetitia Kennedy).

Game at Chess (1625?), Okes 1, *British Library, C. 34. l. 23*

Title-page: Under 'the Fatte Byshop' is written 'bish.'
[then head of figure] 'of Spalatto'; under 'B Knight'
is written, to the right of his hat, 'Gundomar:'; both
in thick black ink.

Game at Chess (1625?), Okes 2, *British Library, C. 34. d. 38*

B1, Induction title: initials 'E. C.' [317]

Game at Chess (1625?), Okes 2, *National Art Library, Victoria and Albert Museum, Dyce Collection, no. 6561, 25. D. 42*

After nyne dayse wherein I have heard some of the
acters say they tooke fiveteene hundred Pounde the
spanish faction being prevalent gott it supprest the
chiefe actors and the Poett Mr. Thomas Middleton
that writt it committed to prisson where hee lay
some Tyme and at last gott oute upon this petition
presented to King James
A harmles game: coyned only for delight
was playd betwixt the black house and the white
the white house wan: yet stille the blacke doth
bragge
they had the power to put mee in the bagge
use but your royall hand. Twill set me free
Tis but removing of a man thats mee.

Game at Chess (1625?), Okes 2, *Folger 2*

Title-page[?]: 'let mee [know?] whether you [haue?]
yet fetched [???] your owne[e' in a hand of c.1625
(Laetitia Kennedy) and perhaps a bookseller's note
(Gary Taylor).

Game at Chess (1625?), Allde/Mathewes, *British Library, C. 34. d. 37*

B1ᵛ: Several annotations. B2, right margin, written top
to bottom opposite first 3 speeches: 'James [?] ?omes'.
F1ᵛ, top: 'Spencer Dag' (or perhaps 'Day') [318]. Lettering might extend indistinctly over page number

'38'. Running upward in right margin: 'paun'. Lower
down margin, letters 'Y' and 'B'.
F2, down right margin, apparently 'Domes' [319].

Game at Chess (1625?), Allde/Mathewes, *Worcester College, LRB. 54*

A2: Written in ink under Prologue is 'Campden' [320]
(presumably one of the Viscounts: Baptist Hicks,
1551–1629, son of a rich citizen of Cheapside;
Edward Noel, 1582–1643, royalist; Baptist Noel,
1611–82, royalist colonel).

Chaste Maid (1630), *British Library, C. 34. f. 9*

On the title-page, written upwards along right edge,
scrawl that appears to, but surely cannot, read
'39 Jaco.', and further down, in a smaller hand,
'abols', 'wbols', 'aboles', or 'wboles' (or could it be
'whores'?).

Patient Man and Honest Whore (1635), *Folger*

76 oaths crossed out, following a strict definition
of what constitutes profanity, including 'pox' and
'faith'.
'X' marked beside 19 passages.
C4: 'trouble' and I2ᵛ: 'ay', both c.1700 (Laetitia
Kennedy).

Widow (1652), *British Library, 644. e. 55*

Title-page, around ornament: 'Wᵐ Jolwood [321] his
book | Juno 25ᵗʰ. 1679'. Above this, various scribbles
including secretary and italic 'S's, 'Widdow', and
'Gent' (opposite printed 'Gent').
I3, line 9: Square bracket to left of 'Had Law unfortunately put you upon me', and, boxed, to right, 'D
prim' (cropped).

Widow (1652), *National Art Library, Victoria and Albert Museum, Dyce Collection, 25. 50.6*

Pencil scribbles (accounts) on bottom of p. 64.

Widow (1652), *National Art Library, Victoria and Albert Museum, Dyce Collection, 25. A.99*

On the title-page, '*Ben Johnson*' and '*John Fletcher*' are
crossed out, and the word 'alone' is written after '*Tho: Middleton*', followed by 'dr H H' [?].

Widow (1652), *National Art Library, Victoria and Albert Museum, Dyce Collection, 26. 24.a*

Above right of head title, first page (sig.?): 'Elizabeth
[?]' [322] (surname smeared).

Widow (1652), *Wellesley*

'Tho: Middleton' added to title-page.

Widow (1652), *Worcester College*

K1ᵛ, below printed text: 'Paid 0—1—6'.

Changeling (1653), *New York Public Library, Berg Collection*

D4, right, opposite 'secresie? I must silence you.': 'Stabs
him'. Right, opposite '*Def.* I must silence you.': 'Dies'.

Old Law (1656), *British Library, 644. e. 86*

'Thomason's copy' noted opposite title-page in leaf added for new binding.

Title-page, imprint: L of 'LONDON': 'Aut 6.'. Right of 'LONDON': 'August 6'; second '6' of '1656' crossed out and corrected to '5'.

No Wit (1657), *British Library, 162. d. 33*

H2ᵛ: 'C' as marker opposite 'methinks... joy'.

H3ᵛ, between 'ears' and 'FINIS', to right: 'plegs ph: p⟨⟩' (cropped).

No Wit (1657), *British Library, 643. b. 38*

Title-page: 'E. Cooper' (18–19th c.?).

Underlining in same manner as *Two New Plays*, 643. b. 37.

Two New Plays (1657), *British Library, 162. d. 28*

More Dissemblers title-page has various notes: 'Arthur Ryland | his book' (top left); 'Ryland' (below this); 'women V. men' (below title); 'comedia/' (below 'COMEDY'), 'par' (right of 'BY'); also 'Liber Arthuri', 'For my boy', 'J | Japlu⟨⟩' (for 'Japlud'); and a copy of the thistle in the ornamental device.

A3, below 'To the Reader': 'Japlud Secundus'.

C4–E5: scribbles in right margin of all rectos but D2, with heavy seepage to versos. Begin as doodles based on 'D' and other caps; soon degenerate to scribble.

Blank O4 inscribed with mixed hand that seems distinct from other hands in the book:[79]

blush—a star shot from butys cheek.

Lk ye sun my I sheiniy lks on Earths corrupt.

yet shin⟨e

clear itself. Peece of Tuchwood—get wʰ child⟨.

We're ful of wants & cannot welcome worth.

Eting Egs, turne into a Cock in 24 howers.

ill me⟨

Idolatry to honʳ a Fool—for he's but ye Image of am⟨

Tis but begging 3 or 4 yrs further & haɤe her.

Weeping. Cannt Ere be as wel exprest in a gd look, but in⟨

stil se her face in a fountaine, it shows lk a Cuntry Mayd dressing her head by adish of water.

Chide sometimes—wʰ best friends invited to a [banket] feast,

nt al swᵗ meates—but sower & salt.

Pefermᵗ from sin & lust shoots up quickly as Gardiners crops

in rottenest grownds.

As tall as she sold in a fayr for 2ᵈ.

Sin wthout Conscience—a Monster whal forhd & no Eye⟨

Glistring whore shines lk serpents—wʰ Crtsun's on h⟨

Drunkrds to a ⟨m⟩yst Heven wrath—offer?] vomit in sacrif⟨

Friendship dang. as Curtiz. yt wil kiss into pouerty emin⟨e

—shame lk a Prisnʳ set al wᵗʰ Halbards.

Wk folks unto yt pr Po⟨ldi⟩ar. stuff' yᵘ may weigh yᵘ by oz.

Two New Plays (1657), *British Library, 643. b. 37*

Over 60 phrases and passages underlined. Makes the correction of speech prefixes on N1. Probably late seventeenth-century as p. 17 has margin note probably in the same ink reading 'says the wi[t] in the pla[in] Dealer'. See *No Wit*, British Library, 643. b. 38, marked similarly.

Two New Plays (1657), *Bodleian, Malone copy*[80]

Title-page: signed 'I Cowcher 17⟨'.

O3ᵛ: 'In. Cowcher of Balliol College in [Ox]ford March 16th 1727–8 in Determining Batchelour'. Mulryne (1975) notes that John Crowcher was son of Richard Crowcher of Malvern Parva, Worcestershire.

Two New Plays (1657), *National Art Library, Victoria and Albert Museum, Dyce Collection*

B1: 'Ed. Bearcroft' (or 'Barcroft') [323]. Mulryne suggests Edward Bearcroft who matriculated at Queen's College, Oxford on 6 March 1709, BA 1712, MA (Merton) 1715.

Two New Plays (1657), *Library of Congress*

Title-page: 'TWO' inked out by hand and '3' written to the left of it; the bracket left of the two printed titles extended downwards, and '3 [extended bracket] No Wit like a Woman's' carefully handwritten in black ink.

Two New Plays (1657), *Texas*

G8ᵛ, stage direction for the entry of Hippolito and Isabella: 'Hippolito' crossed out and 'maie' (or 'maid') written above.

H1, opposite '*Enter the Ward...*': almost undecipherable note, perhaps 'yᵉ 2 Prenn'.

N1: opposite 'And the Devil after you...': 'Stabs him'; opposite 'Breaks both together': 'Dies'.

O1ᵛ, opposite 'My own ambition...': 'Dies'.

O2, opposite 'And cut off time and pain': 'Dies'.

O3, opposite 'Tasting the same death...': 'Dies'.

Two New Plays (1657), *bound with No Wit, Worcester College*

Blank leaf, two leaves before title-page: 'Ri⟨' and tabular subtraction of 1677 from 1689 to give 12.

On following blank leaf: 'Nᵒ 635'.

Title-page, below title: 'Also another called noe Witt or Helpe Like a womans./' (with 'Witt' above 'or' and 'Helpe' below).

---

[79] I am again grateful to Richard Proudfoot for providing a transcript. I have rechecked the readings and made some minor changes. Mulryne's transcript, in his 'Annotations', is less complete, and varies.

[80] Details of the annotations in this book and the Dyce, Texas, and Yale copies are from Mulryne 1975.

Two New Plays (1657), *Yale*

L8^v, above 'fear' in 'Of this corruption, fear': 'before'.

N1: prefix '*Lean.*' before 'I'll hurry...' deleted, and 'Le' written in left-hand margin opposite previous line; opposite 'And the Devil after you...': 'strikes'; opposite '*Within.* Help...': 'Lean: falls'; opposite 'Breaks both together': 'Dies'.

N3, opposite ''Tis time we parted...': 'To Hip:'.

N8, opposite '*Hebe* give that...': 'To the Duke | the wrong cup | by mistake'.

N8^v, opposite 'I offer to thy powerful Deity': 'whilst the incense | sends up a poisond | smoke'.

O1: opposite 'Never denies us...': 'Throw's flameing | gold upon Isabella | who falls: dead'; opposite 'Then with a stamp': 'guardian sinkes'.

O1^v, opposite last word of 'For which I am punish'd dreadfully and unlook'd for': 'which'.

O2: opposite 'Run and meet death...': 'runs on a habbart'; opposite '*Bran.* Not yet, no change...': 'looke[i]ng on the | Cardinal'; opposite '*Bran.* Nor yet': 'lookeing still at the | Cardinal'; opposite 'strength': 'Duke falls'.

O2^v, opposite 'Her ignorant...': 'stabs her self' (in another hand?).

O3, opposite 'Tasting the same death...': 'she dies'.

Hengist (1661), *British Library, 644. f. 10*

Title-page, 'March 28' in George Thomason's hand (Bald, ed., 1938).

Quiet Life (1662), *Worcester College*

Title-page, below '*Never before Printed*': '2^d conc. [?] the Adventure of George & the Barber.'

E. Index of Names

To enable reference from the following alphabetical listing to the essay and earlier Appendixes, the readers' names are numbered sequentially at the person's first significant mention, and these numbers are reproduced below.

WORKS CITED

Adams, Joseph Quincy, ed., Thomas Middleton, *The Ghost of Lucrece* (1937)

Balch, Marston Stevens, *Thomas Middleton's 'No Wit, No Help Like a Woman's' and 'The Counterfeit Bridegroom' (1677) and Further Adaptations* (1980)

Bald, R. C., ed., Thomas Middleton, *A Game at Chesse* (1929)

—— ed., Thomas Middleton, *Hengist King of Kent: Or, The Mayor of Queenborough* (1938)

Barrey, David ('Lording'), *Ram Alley: Or, Merry Tricks* (1611)

Barthes, Roland, *Image, Music, Text*, trans. Stephen Heath (1977)

Bawcutt, N. W., ed., *The Control and Censorship of Caroline Drama: The Records of Sir Henry Herbert, Master of the Revels 1623–73* (1996)

—— 'Was Thomas Middleton a Puritan Dramatist?', *Modern Language Review* 94 (1999), 925–39

—— ed., Thomas Middleton and William Rowley, *The Changeling* (1958)

Beal, Peter, *Index of English Literary Manuscripts*, vol. I, 1450–1625, 2 parts (1980), and vol. II, 1625–1700, 2 parts (1987, 1993)

Behn, Aphra, *The City Heiress* (1682)

—— *The Lucky Chance* (1687)

Behn, Aphra (?), *The Counterfeit Bridegroom* (1677)

Bentley, Gerald Eades, *The Jacobean and Caroline Stage*, 7 vols (1941–68)

—— 'John Cotgrave's *English Treasury of Wit and Language* and the Elizabethan Drama', *Studies in Philology* 40 (1943), 186–203

Bergeron, David M., *English Civic Pageantry 1558–1642* (1971)

Blayney, Peter W. M., *The Bookshops in Paul's Cross Churchyard*, Occasional Papers of the Bibliographical Society 5 (1990)

—— *The First Folio of Shakespeare* (1991)

—— 'The Publication of Playbooks', in *A New History of Early English Drama*, ed. John D. Cox and David Scott Kastan (1997), 383–422

Bodley, Sir Thomas, *Letters to Thomas James*, ed. G. W. Wheeler (1926)

Brooks, Douglas A., *From Playhouse to Printing House: Drama and Authorship in Early Modern England* (2000)

Catalogue of the Petyt Library at Skipton, Yorkshire (1964)

Carson, Neil, *A Companion to Henslowe's Diary* (1988)

Cartwright, William, *Comedies, Tragicomedies, with Other Poems* (1651)

Chambers, E. K., *The Elizabethan Stage*, 4 vols (1923)

Chartier, Roger, 'General Introduction: Print Culture', in Chartier, ed., *The Culture of Print: Power and the Uses of Print in Early Modern Europe*, trans. Lydia G. Cochrane (1989), 1–10

—— *The Cultural Uses of Print in Early Modern France*, trans. Lydia G. Cochrane (1987)

—— *The Order of Books: Readers, Authors, and Libraries in Europe between the Fifteenth and Eighteenth Centuries*, trans. Lydia G. Cochrane (1994)

—— 'The Practical Impact of Writing', in Chartier, ed., *A History of Private Life*, vol. 3, *Passions of the Renaissance*, trans. Arthur Goldhammer (1989), 111–59

Clark, Peter, 'The Ownership of Books in England, 1560–1640: The Example of Some Kentish Townsfolk', in *Schooling and Society: Studies in the History of Education*, ed. Lawrence Stone (1976), 95–111

Cotgrave, John, *The English Treasury of Wit and Language* (1655)

Croft, P. J., *Autograph Poetry in the English Language: Facsimiles of Original Manuscripts from the Fourteenth to the Twentieth Century*, 2 vols (1973)

Cutts, John P., *La Musique de scène de la troupe de Shakespeare: The King's Men sous le règne de Jacques Ier*, second edn. rev. (1971)

Davenant, William, *The Law against Lovers*, in *Works*, 2 vols (1673), vol. 2, pp. 272–329

Deed, S. G., with Jane Francis, *Catalogue of the Plume Library at Maldon, Essex* (1959)

Dutton, Richard, 'The Birth of the Author', in *Text and Cultural Change in Early Modern England*, ed. Cedric C. Brown and Arthur F. Marotti (1997), 153–78

Eagleton, Terry, *Literary Theory: An Introduction* (1983)

Fehrenbach, R. J., and E. S. Leedham-Green, eds., *Private Libraries in Renaissance England: A Collection and Catalogue of Tudor and Early Stuart Book-Lists*, 2 vols (1992–3)

Forde, Anne, 'The Transmission and Circulation of a Theatre Song: "Hence all you Vain Delights"', MA dissertation (University of Birmingham, 1994)

Gaskell, Philip, *A New Introduction to Bibliography* (1972)

Gewirtz, Arthur, *Restoration Adaptations of Early 17th Century Comedies* (1982)

Greg, W. W., *A Bibliography of the English Printed Drama to the Restoration*, 4 vols (1939–59)

—— *Licensers for the Press, &c. to 1640: A Biographical Index, Based Mainly on Arber's 'Transcript of the Registers of the Company of Stationers'* (1962)

—— *Some Aspects and Problems of London Publishing between 1550 and 1650* (1955)

—— ed., *A Companion to Arber* (1967)

—— and F. P. Wilson, ed., Thomas Middleton, *The Witch*, Malone Society Reprints (1950 for 1948)

Guildhall Library, *A List of Books Printed in the British Isles and of English Books Printed Abroad Before 1701 in Guildhall Library*, 2 vols (1966–7)

Gurr, Andrew, *The Shakespearean Stage 1574–1642*, 3rd edn. (1992)

—— *Playgoing in Shakespeare's London* (1987)

Halasz, Alexandra, *The Marketplace of Print: Pamphlets and the Public Sphere in Early Modern England* (1997)

Heinemann, Margot, *Puritanism and Theatre: Thomas Middleton and Opposition Drama under the Early Stuarts* (1980)

Henslowe, Philip, *Diary*, ed. R. A. Foakes and R. T. Rickert (1961)

Heywood, Thomas, *The Hierarchy of the Blessed Angels* (1635)

Hibbard, G. R., ed., William Shakespeare, *The Merry Wives of Windsor* (1973)

Hickes, William, *London Drollery: Or, The Wits' Academy* (1673)

Hobbs, Mary, 'Early Seventeenth-Century Verse Miscellanies and Their Value for Textual Editors', *English Manuscript Studies 1100–1700* I (1989), 182–210

Holdsworth, R. V., ed., Thomas Middleton and William Rowley, *A Fair Quarrel* (1974)

Holub, Robert C., *Reception Theory: A Critical Introduction* (1984)

Howard-Hill, T. H., 'The Bridgewater–Huntington MS of Middleton's *Game at Chess*', *Manuscripta* 28 (1984), 145–56

—— *Ralph Crane and Some Shakespeare First Folio Comedies* (1972)

—— 'Shakespeare's Earliest Editor, Ralph Crane', *Shakespeare Survey* 44 (1992), 113–29

—— ed., Thomas Middleton, *A Game at Chess, 1624*, Malone Society Reprints (1990)

—— ed., Thomas Middleton, *A Game at Chess* (1993)

Ingleby, C. M., ed., *The Shakspere Allusion-Book: A Collection of Allusions to Shakspere from 1591 to 1700*, 2 vols (1909)

Iser, Wolfgang, *The Act of Reading: A Theory of Aesthetic Response* (1978)

Jackson, William A., 'Edward Gwynne', *The Library*, IV, 15 (1934–5), 92–6

—— 'The Lamport Hall–Britwell Court Books', in *Records of a Bibliographer: Selected Papers of William Alexander Jackson* (1967), 121–33

Jacobean Academic Plays, ed. Suzanne Gossett and Thomas L. Berger, Malone Society Reprints, *Collections*, vol. 14 (1988)

Jardine, Lisa, and Anthony Grafton, '"Studied for Action": How Gabriel Harvey Read His Livy', *Past and Present* 129 (1990), 30–78

Jayne, Sears, *Library Catalogues of the English Renaissance* (1956)

Jonson, Ben, *Works*, ed. C. H. Herford and Percy and Evelyn Simpson, 11 vols (1925–52)

Kahrl, George M., with Dorothy Anderson, *The Garrick Collection of Old English Plays* (1982)

Kewes, Paulina, '"Give me the Sociable Pocket-books…": Humphrey Moseley's Serial Publication of Octavo Play Collections', *Publishing History* 38 (1995), 5–21

Kiessling, Nicholas K., *The Library of Robert Burton*, Oxford Bibliographical Society *Publications* NS 22 (1988)

King, Henry, *Poems, Elegies, Paradoxes, and Sonnets* (1657)

Lancashire, Anne, ed., *The Second Maiden's Tragedy* (1978)

Langbaine, Gerard, *Momus Triumphans: Or, The Plagiaries of the English Stage Exposed in a Catalogue* (1688)

—— *An Account of the English Dramatic Poets* (1691)

Lawrence, Robert G., 'A Bibliographical Study of Middleton and Rowley's *The Changeling*', *The Library*, V, 16 (1961), 37–43

[Leanerd, John,] *The Rambling Justice* (1678)

Lee, Sidney, 'Notes and Additions to the Census of Copies of the Shakespeare First Folio', revised edn. (1906)

—— *Shakespeares Comedies, Histories, & Tragedies… Containing a Census of Extant Copies* (1902)

Leedham-Green, E. S., *Books in Cambridge Inventories: Book-lists from Vice-Chancellor's Court Probate Inventories in the Tudor and Stuart Periods*, 2 vols (1986)

Leishman, J. B., *Milton's Minor Poems*, ed. Geoffrey Tillotson (1969)

Love, Genevieve, '"This Child was Sent to me": Addressing print and performance frames in Marston, Heywood, Middleton &

Dekker' (unpublished seminar paper presented at the Shakespeare Association of America Annual Meeting, 2000)

Love, Harold, *Scribal Publication in Seventeenth-Century England* (1993)

Madan, F., G. M. R. Turbutt, and S. Gibson, *The Original Bodleian Copy of Shakespeare (The Turbutt Shakespeare)* (1905)

MacDonald, Robert H., ed., *The Library of Drummond of Hawthornden* (1971)

McGann, Jerome J., *The Beauty of Inflections: Literary Investigations in Historical Method and Theory* (1985)

McKenzie, D. F., *Bibliography and the Sociology of Texts* (1986)

McLeod, Margaret S. G., *The Cathedral Libraries Catalogue: Books Printed before 1701 in the Libraries of the Anglican Cathedrals of England and Wales*, vol. 1, *Books Printed in the British Isles and British America and English Books Printed Elsewhere* (1984)

MacLean, Gerald, 'Literacy, Class, and Gender in Restoration England', *TEXT* 7 (1994), 307–35

Massinger, Philip, *A New Way to Pay Old Debts* (1632)

Medvedev, P. N., and M. M. Bakhtin, *The Formal Method in Literary Scholarship: A Critical Introduction to Sociological Poetics*, trans. Albert J. Wehrle (1978)

Miller, Edward, 'A Collection of Elizabethan and Jacobean Plays at Petworth', *The National Trust Year Book* (1975–76), 62–4

Milton, John, *Poems* (1645)

Morgan, Paul, 'Frances Wolfreston and "Hor Bouks": A Seventeenth-Century Woman Book-Collector', *The Library*, VI, 11 (1989), 197–219

Morrish, P. S., *Bibliotheca Higgsiana: Catalogue of the Books of Dr. Griffin Higgs (1589–1659)*, Oxford Bibliographical Society, Occasional Publications, 22 (1990)

Mulholland, Paul, ed., Thomas Middleton and Thomas Dekker, *The Roaring Girl* (1987)

Mulryne, J. R., 'Annotations in Some Copies of *Two New Plays* by Thomas Middleton, 1657', *The Library*, V, 30 (1975), 217–21

—— *A Critical Edition of Thomas Middleton's 'Women Beware Women'*, unpublished dissertation (Cambridge University, 1962)

—— ed., Thomas Middleton, *Women Beware Women*, (1975)

Nascimento, Susan, 'The Folger Manuscripts of Middleton's *A Game at Chesse*: A Study in the Genealogy of Texts', *Publications of the Bibliographical Society of America* 76 (1982), 159–95

Nicoll, Allardyce, *A History of English Drama 1660–1900*, vol. 1, *Restoration Drama 1660–1700* (1952)

Orgel, Stephen, 'What is a Text?', *Research Opportunities in Renaissance Drama* 24 (1981), 3–6

Osler, William, Edward Bensley, *et al.*, 'Robert Burton and the Anatomy of Melancholy', *Proceedings and Papers of the Oxford Bibliographical Society* I (1927), 159–246

Ovenell, R. F., 'Brian Twyne's Library', in Oxford Bibliographical Society *Publications*, NS 4 (1952, for 1950), 1–42

Phelps, Wayne H., 'Thomas Holmes, Esquire: The Dedicatee of Middleton's *The Witch*', *Notes and Queries* 225 (1980), 152–4

Pepys, Samuel, *Diary*, ed. Robert Latham and William Matthews, 11 vols (1970–83)

Plant, Marjorie, *The English Book Trade: An Economic History of the Making and Sale of Books*, 2nd. edn. (1965)

Pujante, A. Luis, 'But Was There Ever a "Spanish" First Folio?', in *Shakespeare and Spain*, ed. José Manuel González and Holger Klein, *Shakespeare Yearbook* 13 (2002), 17–29

Ravenscroft, Thomas, *Melismata* (1611)

Reed, John Curtis, 'Humphrey Moseley, Publisher', *Oxford Bibliographical Society Proceedings and Papers*, vol. 2, part 2 (1929, for 1928), 57–142

Richards, Nathaniel, *The Celestial Publican: A Sacred Poem* (1630)

Roberts, Sasha, 'Reading the Shakespearean Text in Early Modern England', *Critical Survey* 7 (1995), 299–306

S., R., compiler, *A Description of the King and Queene of Fayries* (1634)

Sadie, Stanley, ed., *The New Grove Dictionary of Music and Musicians*, 20 vols (1980)

Schafer, Elizabeth, 'Thomas Holmes of Winchester and Salisbury: The Dedicatee of Thomas Middleton's *The Witch?*', *Notes and Queries* 241 (1996), 188–90

—— ed., Thomas Middleton, *The Witch* (1994)

Shadwell, Thomas, *The History of Timon of Athens* (1678)

Shand, G. B., 'The Elizabethan Aim of *The Wisdom of Solomon Paraphrased*', in *'Accompaninge the players': Essays Celebrating Thomas Middleton, 1580–1980*, ed. Kenneth Friedenreich (1983), 67–77

Shirley, James, *Poems, Etc.* (1646)

Smith, G. C. Moore, ed., *William Hemminge's Elegy on Randolph's Finger Containing the Well-Known Lines 'On the Time-Poets'* (1923)

Smith, N. A., with H. M. Adams, D. Pepys Whiteley, and J. C. T. Oates, *Catalogue of the Pepys Library of Magdalene College, Cambridge*, Vol. 1: *Printed Books* (1978)

Spencer, Christopher, *Davenant's 'Macbeth' from the Yale Manuscript: An Edition, with a Discussion of the Relation of Davenant's Text to Shakespeare's* (1961)

Spufford, Margaret, *Small Books and Pleasant Histories: Popular Fiction and its Readership in Seventeenth-Century England* (1981)

Steen, Sara Jayne, *Ambrosia in an Earthern Vessel: Three Centuries of Audience and Reader Response to the Works of Thomas Middleton* (1993)

Strode, William, *Poetical Works*, ed. Bertram Dobell (1907)

Taylor, Gary, 'Some Manuscripts of Shakespeare's Sonnets', *Bulletin of the John Rylands Library* 68 (1985), 210–46

Watt, Tessa, *Cheap Print and Popular Piety, 1550–1640* (1991)

Wilkin, Simon, ed., Sir Thomas Browne, *Works*, 4 vols (1835–6)

Wilkinson, C. H., 'The Library of Worcester College', *Proceedings and Papers of the Oxford Bibliographical Society* 1 (1927), 263–320

Wolf, Melvin H., *Catalogue and Indexes to the Title-Pages of English Printed Books Preserved in the British Library's Bagford Collection* (1974)

Wood, P. Worsley, *A Hand-List of English Books in the Library of Emmanuel College, Cambridge, Printed before MDCXLI* (1915).

Wormald, Francis, and C. E. Wright, eds., *The English Library before 1700* (1958)

PART II: THE AUTHOR

INTRODUCTION: THE MIDDLETON CANON

Gary Taylor

ONE major goal of *The Collected Works of Thomas Middleton* has been to define the Middleton canon; a second goal has been to establish a provisional, but nevertheless reasonably reliable, chronology for that canon. We began the project, in the mid-1980s, assuming that we would simply reproduce the canon defined by Jackson and Lake. Over twenty years we have, in fact, been able to resolve some problems left by those earlier investigations, and to pay more attention than they did to Middleton's non--dramatic canon. Some of that new work on Middleton's canon and chronology has already been published; some of it is published here for the first time. The cumulative results of the century-long investigation of the canon are evident in the differences between *The Collected Works* and the nineteenth-century editions of Dyce and Bullen. They were simply unaware of the existence of *The Ghost of Lucrece*, *The Two Gates of Salvation*, and *Honourable Entertainments*. We have confirmed the complete rejection of three plays they both considered Middleton's: *Blurt Master Constable*, *The Honest Whore, Part Two*, and *The Family of Love*. We have confirmed too the presence of a collaborator in *Anything for a Quiet Life* and of two additional collaborators in *The Spanish Gypsy*. We have confirmed Middleton's whole or part authorship of *A Yorkshire Tragedy*, *Timon of Athens*, *The Revenger's Tragedy*, *The Puritan Widow*, *The Bloody Banquet*, *The Lady's Tragedy*, *Wit at Several Weapons*, *Macbeth*, *The Nice Valour*, and *Measure for Measure*. We have identified two new Middleton poems, and provided evidence for his adaptation of *The Penniless Parliament of Threadbare Poets*, his authorship of *Plato's Cap* and *The Owl's Almanac*, and his part-authorship of *News from Gravesend* and *Meeting of Gallants*. Since Dyce and Bullen made no attempt at establishing a Middleton chronology, *The Collected Works* is the first edition to give readers a chance to experience the historical sequence of his work.

I was the sole author of the essay on 'Canon and Chronology' in the *Textual Companion* to Shakespeare (Wells and Taylor, 69–144). By contrast, this section of the Middleton *Companion* is a pervasively collaborative enterprise. MacDonald P. Jackson's essay in Part I (p. 80) introduces the parameters of the problem, a history of scholarly efforts to solve it, and a survey of the most important kinds of evidence. Jackson and I have worked together on the list of 'Works Excluded', just as we have worked together, over two decades, in evaluating the evidence that establishes the borders of the canon. Almost all the individual entries in 'Works Included' were written by the editor(s) of that text in *The Collected Works*; each

entry presents and analyses the evidence for both the authorship and the date of a single work; each entry is signed by the contributor responsible for it. One scholar has not signed any of those entries, but R. V. Holdsworth has been so generous, so knowledgeable, and so astute so often in these and other matters that we have listed him among the Contributors to this *Companion*.

Nevertheless, in the end someone had to decide which works should be printed in *The Collected Works*. I have made the final decisions, but always after consulting with Jackson, and sometimes with one or more of other associate general editors. We have included works only if we are confident of Middleton's authorship of part of them. There may well be other works still to find. Although his fondness for certain interjections and contractions clearly distinguishes his early work, in the 1620s the linguistic markers that once distinguished him start to become more common. At the same time, with the appointment of a new and stricter Master of the Revels in 1622 some of Middleton's favourite oaths and interjections apparently began to be censored (or self-censored). Over the length of a whole play, enough strong evidence remains to distinguish him clearly from other playwrights. But collaborations might be harder to detect—especially if the evidence were disturbed by scribal preferences, or if Middleton was only one of three or four collaborators, as in *The Spanish Gypsy*. Notably, several of the plays 'Excluded from *The Collected Works*' cluster in the period 1621–4, and are probably collaborative. If such ambiguities remain at the edges of the intensely studied dramatic canon, we must suspect that there are many more in the poems and pamphlets. It is difficult to establish the authorship of unattributed short poems. Without external evidence, few people would have suspected Middleton's authorship of *Sir Robert Sherley*, where translation muddies the waters. Middleton might have translated other works, especially in the theatrically lean years of 1608–9 and 1624–7. Translations, like short poems, are often difficult to attribute.

In matters of chronology individual editors usually confine themselves to the evidence for dating that particular work, without necessarily adjudicating whether it was written just before or just after another work by Middleton. But the printed edition of *The Collected Works* must put one before the other. Again, someone must decide, and in this edition I have been that someone. Some of those decisions are arbitrary, because the available evidence does not securely establish the sequence of two adjacent works. For example, I have placed *The Widow* before *The*

Witch only because *The Widow's* minimal references to the Overbury trials might reasonably precede the full-blown dramatization/allegorization of those same trials in *The Witch*. Likewise, I have put *A Fair Quarrel* later than either because that puts the play closer to *The Peacemaker*.

Finally, some documents and the issues they raise extend beyond the purview of any single editor in *The Collected Works*. Several Middleton plays are named on fragments of waste-paper inserted into a manuscript of Sir George Buc's *History of Richard III* (British Library, Cotton MS Tib.E.X). Marcham reproduced and transcribed all the scraps, but did not discuss their significance; Chambers (1925), in a review of Marcham, first analysed the material, and in particular the four scraps which contain lists of plays. These lists include the titles of one Middleton play (*Hengist*), three Middleton–Rowley collaborations (*Wit at Several Weapons*, *Old Law*, *Fair Quarrel*), and one Rowley play (*All's Lost by Lust*). Authors are not given for any of the plays; the interest of the material is confined to its significance for dating them. Chambers tentatively dated the material 1619–20, and his conclusion has been repeated, usually without analysis or qualification, in all subsequent discussions.

The scraps can be dated by a conjunction of three kinds of evidence. First, all the scraps concern, and apparently originate in, the Revels Office during Buc's official tenure there; there is no reason to believe, and every reason to doubt, that he would have had access to Revels Office papers after he was removed as Master of the Revels. Marcham does therefore seem to be right in asserting 'an absolute limit of writing between 1610 and 1622' for these waste-paper fragments (7). As Chambers observes, scraps other than the play-lists are or can be confidently dated (1) no earlier than 1617 (2) 1615 or after (3) from 1611 to 1617 or later (4) 16 May 1619. Most of the scraps are not dated or datable, but the earliest secure date in 1615, and the latest May 1619.

Second, the dedication to the manuscript in which the scraps are inserted is dated '1619' (f. 4); typically, dedications and other such front matter are the last things to be written. The scraps seem to have been used for later additions/revisions to the manuscript. Their insertion in the manuscript therefore would seem most likely to have occurred in 1619 or later. Buc died on 22 October 1622; he was known to be mad, and deprived of his office, on 29 March 1622; the last evidence of his performing any official duties is his licensing for publication of *Herod and Antipater* on 22 February 1622; he may have been relieved of some of his duties in the Revels Office itself by 21 December 1621 (Eccles, 481–84).

Third, a number of the plays in the play-lists themselves can be confidently dated by other means. Most of Chambers's analysis is devoted to such evidence. However, Chambers himself cautions that 'it must not be taken for granted that all the lists belong to the same year'; subsequent scholars ignore this caveat, perhaps because Chambers himself reduces it to a subordinate clause in

Revels Office scrap paper with 'An ould Lawe [ ] a['

a sentence which ends 'consistent with the production or revival of quite a substantial proportion of the plays concerned about 1619 or 1620' (404). But the caveat is crucial: the other, datable scraps might belong to different years between 1611 and 1619, and each play-list needs to be analysed separately.

The list most convincingly datable in 1619–20 is also the shortest (f. 211ᵛ), containing only '[Kni]ght of Malta' and '[Seco]nd part of Falstaff | [not p]laid yᵉⁱˢ 7. yeres.' Chambers dates the first of these two items '1615–19', but Bentley shows, more precisely, that it must have been written between autumn 1616 and very early 1619 (3:352–3); Burbage, who leads the cast list published in the 1679 Fletcher folio, was buried on 16 March 1619, and in order for him to have performed in it the play must have been completed by February 1619 at the very latest. It seems likely that the second play is Shakespeare's *2 Henry IV*; since *Sir John Falstaffe* and *The Hotspur* were acted at court during the Christmas season of 1612–13, in the Christmas season of 1619–20 it might have been seven years since *2 Henry IV* had been played at court. This interpretation accords with the brief range of dates for the first performances of *Malta*. However, we do not know which plays were performed at court in the years from 1612–13 through 1622, and it is possible that *2 Henry IV* was performed in 1613–14 or 1614–15, so that seven years would have to be counted from those dates. Nevertheless, this scrap can hardly be earlier than late 1619.

Unfortunately, the other play-lists are even less securely datable. The first (f. 70ᵛ) contains Beaumont and Fletcher's *The Captain* (1612), Shakespeare's *Winter's Tale* (1609–10?), Shakespeare and Fletcher's *Two Noble Kinsmen* (1613), and Jonson's *Volpone* (1606). It cannot be earlier than late 1613, but could belong to any other date until 1622. Of the eight plays in the second list (f. 197ᵛ), only four are securely datable: *Hamlet* (1600–1601), *Philaster* (1609), *Maid's Tragedy* (1611), *Albumazar and Trinculo* (March 1615). *The Tradgedy of Jeronimo* is probably Kyd's perenially popular *Spanish Tragedy* (1589?), but might be *1 Jeronimo* (Eccles, 479). Chambers identifies 'The Falce Frend' with Fletcher's *The False One* (datable by an actor list to 1619–23), but Bentley rejects this conjecture (5:1331). Without that identification, the most we can say is that the second play-list was written between 1615 and 1622.

The final list, in which *ould Lawe* appears, is the longest. Of its fifteen plays, only seven are datable: *Witt at [Several Weapons]* (1613-14?), *A Fair Quarrel* (1614-17), *All's Lost by Lust* (1618?), *Titus and Vespatian* (1592?), *Epicoene* (1609), *The Dutch Courtesan* (1604), *D'Ambois* (1606?), and *A Woman's a Weathercock* (1612). The latest play here—as Chambers did not know—is Rowley's *All's Lost*, which must be later than June 1618 (Bentley, 5:220). Chambers tries to link *Bussy D'Ambois* to its probable revival by the King's Men in 1615-19, but only one of the plays on this list belonged to them; most belonged to other companies, so there are no grounds for taking Chapman's play as evidence of a late date.

Each list therefore could have been written at a different time: list one in late 1613 or after, list two in 1615 or after, list three in 1619-20 or after, list 4 in June 1618 or after. Moreover, the writing of the list only establishes that a play existed by the time that list was written. Thus, the third list cannot have been written earlier than March 1615; *Hengist*—which is included on that list—could have existed as early as 1615, and must have existed before April 1622. Similarly, the fourth list seems to be later than June 1618; *Old Law* therefore could have existed as early as June 1618, and must have existed before April 1622. In both cases—as is demonstrated by the inclusion, in the three long lists, of plays perhaps as early as *The Spanish Tragedy* and *Hamlet*—the play might have been written much earlier than the list was written.

Whether we can go beyond this range of dates in dating *Old Law* or *Hengist* depends upon the plausibility of Chambers's conjectures. His conclusion that 'the lists represent plays which the Revels Office had at some time or times under consideration for performance at court' seems sound. They cannot be lists of plays by the same author, or licensed for publication at the same time, or licensed for performance at the same time. The chief function of the Revels Office, in relation to such plays, was the selection and preparation of those to be performed at court, normally in the extended Christmas season. Most of the plays were, at one time or another, performed at court, or written by admired and popular authors whose plays were often enough performed at court. We know from lists of plays performed in other Jacobean court seasons that they included both new plays and revivals of older plays. Three of the plays in these lists—Jonson's *Volpone*, Marston's *Dutch Courtesan*, Field's *Weathercock*—are individually crossed out; this fact supports Chambers's conjecture that the lists are, not of plays actually performed at court in a certain season, but of plays being considered for the court season; the absence of dates and companies also supports this conjecture, for that information would be necessary once actual performances were fixed or paid for.

But the (apparently correct) conjecture that the lists served the same function must be separated from the (much more dubious) conjecture that they all belong to the same date, 1619-20. The four scraps listing plays cannot ever have been part of a single sheet of paper; moreover, all but the first is followed by sufficient blank space to make it clear that we have the end of a list. The second list alone has the remains of marginal numbers (2, 3, 4) opposite some plays but not others; it also contains the only alterations demonstrably in Buc's hand, rather than the scribe's (the addition of 'or Hengist K. of Kent' after the alternative title 'Maior of Quinborough', and the addition of 'or Love Lies a bleeding' after the alternative title 'The History of Philaster').

Another way of looking at this evidence would be to ask: how many of the plays on any given list might be new? We would expect a list of plays being considered for court performance to include some new material, and it would be odd if the subsequent accidental curtailing of the lists eliminated only the new plays. The first list consists of four identifiable plays, all datable, the last being Fletcher and Shakespeare's *Two Noble Kinsmen* (1613). Of the eight plays in the second list, two—'The Scholler turnd to schoole againe' and 'The Falce Frend'—are otherwise unknown, and might therefore have been new whenever the list was compiled; of the others, the latest securely identifiable is 'The Cambridge Playe of Albumazar and Trinculo' (March 1615), and the only other play which might be later is *Hengist*. The third list contains one play that was certainly old and another that could have been new. Of the fifteen in the fourth list, five—'Henrye the vna...', 'the Cittye', 'the House is Haunte...', 'Looke to the Ladye', 'A Turkes too good for hi...'—are otherwise unknown, and therefore might have been new whenever the list was compiled; of the ten others, eight would clearly have been revivals; the latest securely identifiable is *All's Lost*, which could have been new as early as the winter season of 1618-19. The only other play which could be later, or also new in 1618-19, is *Old Law*. One might therefore suspect that both Rowley plays were new. But although the external evidence would support such a dating, it by no means enforces it.

On the strictest interpretation of the evidence, this scrap of paper establishes that *Old Law* existed in some form by March 1622 at the very latest. However, if—as seems highly probable—the lists do indeed represent plays being considered for the court's winter season, this date can be pushed a bit further back: the last court season Buc could have overseen was that of late December to early February 1621-22. In order to be considered for that season, before it began, and therefore to be included on a list of candidates for court performance, a play would have needed to be finished—and presumably performed publicly—by December 1621.

The scrap of paper that mentions *Old Law* must have been written later than June 1618, and therefore it might have been used in preparation for the Christmas court seasons of 1618-19, 1619-20, 1620-21, or 1621-22. And *Old Law* must have been completed and performed, in some form, before the end of 1621.

WORKS CITED

Bentley, G. E., *The Jacobean and Caroline Stage*, 7 vols (1941–68)

Bullen, A. H., *The Works of Thomas Middleton*, 8 vols (1885–6)

Chambers, E. K., review of Marcham, *Review of English Studies* 1 (1925), 481–4

Dyce, Alexander, ed., *The Works of Thomas Middleton*, 5 vols (1840)

Eccles, Mark, 'Sir George Buc, Master of the Revels', in *Thomas Lodge and Other Elizabethans*, ed. C. J. Sisson (1933)

Jackson, MacDonald P., *Studies in Attribution: Middleton and Shakespeare* (1979)

Lake, David J., *The Canon of Thomas Middleton's Plays: Internal Evidence for the Major Problems of Authorship* (1975)

Marcham, Frank, *The King's Office of the Revels 1610–1622: Fragments of Documents in the Department of Manuscripts, British Museum* (1925)

Wells, Stanley, and Gary Taylor, with John Jowett and William Montgomery, *William Shakespeare: A Textual Companion* (1987)

WORKS INCLUDED IN THIS EDITION:
CANON AND CHRONOLOGY

The Wisdom of Solomon Paraphrased   1597

Middleton's authorship is clear from external evidence: his name appears on the title-page, and under both dedicatory epistles.

The poem's dedication to Essex, and thus probably its printing, may be dated quite precisely: it must have occurred after 18 March 1597, on which date Essex became Master of the Ordnance (which title he is given by Middleton), and before 28 December of the same year, when he became Earl Marshal (a title not included in the dedication). Absence of any mention of the Azores expedition (late June-late October 1597) suggests that the dedication may date from between 18 March and Essex's departure in late June, an inference perhaps supported by the dedication's (admittedly figurative) mention of 'sowing time'.

G. B. Shand

SEE ALSO

Text: *Works*, 1919
Textual introduction and apparatus: this volume, 461

Microcynicon 1599

While it is now accepted that Middleton is the author of *Microcynicon*, critics in the nineteenth century were hesitant to attribute this satire to him. The title-page does not bear any author's name, although the book's opening 'Defiance to Envy' is signed by 'T. M. Gent'. In the *Poetical Decameron* (1820), John Payne Collier argued against Middleton's authorship on aesthetic and stylistic grounds, noting in particular that the attribution is ambiguous. Because 'T. M.' seems to refer to the author in the third person in the *Defiance*, naming himself simply as 'the author's mouth', Collier speculated that Middleton authored only the preliminary poem. Allusions to the author's dispersed and segmented persona, however, were common in satire; and mouth imagery resurfaces in *Microcynicon*'s references to vomiting, gorging, and spitting. In light of satiric convention and the *Defiance*'s linkages to the rest of the text, we can read T.M.'s self-identification as corroborating his authorship of the entire book. Dyce and Bullen were persuaded enough by the attribution to include *Microcynicon* reluctantly in their editions, and subsequent critics have followed their assessment of the text's authorship.

In general, scholars' scepticism about Middleton's authorship is premised on two lines of thought: it was mistakenly believed that Middleton was born in 1570 rather than 1580; and *Microcynicon* was judged to be inferior to the later plays. Swinburne, for instance, thought it impossible that a writer of such talent could produce verse that 'modulates the whine of an average pig'. It is ironic that critics denied Middleton's authorship on aesthetic grounds, given that Renaissance writers believed a rough speaking voice and a harsh metrical style to be appropriate to satire. When critics devalue *Microcynicon*, they appear, in fact, to express their discomfort with its genre, which is self-consciously messy, fragmentary, and filled with metrical irregularities.

In the early twentieth century, critics presented internal and external evidence to argue for Middleton's authorship. The erroneous birthdate, which had led scholars to declare it impossible that a mature 28-year-old could have written such juvenilia, was corrected by Mark Eccles in 1931. H. Dugdale Sykes (1925) offered substantial evidence for stylistic links between *Microcynicon* and other early works attributed to Middleton. Sykes argued, for instance, that *Microcynicon* shares with *Solomon* Middleton's characteristic fondness for compound adjectives ('hard-soft'); for

imagery involving tools of the trade (ink and paper); for particular rare words and images ('nigrum', tennis imagery); and for certain rhetorical features (antithesis, especially compounded with other figures). Norman Brittin (1946) furthered this analysis by supplying significant rhetorical links between *Solomon*, *Ghost* and *Microcynicon*. Further evidence is found in the fact that *Microcynicon* bears the same attribution as *A Mad World, My Masters* and *A Trick to Catch the Old One*; and five of Middleton's first six satiric works—*Microcynicon*, *Black Book*, *Meeting*, *Gravesend* and *Hubburd*—were all printed by Thomas Creede. In noting that Creede published roughly half of the satires that Middleton wrote during his life, we discover a working relationship between Renaissance printer and author, one that revolved around a specific genre of writing. Composite evidence thus places *Microcynicon* firmly within Middleton's canon. Both Adams and Irwin offered detailed summaries of the debate about *Microcynicon*'s authorship. Once the more fundamental evidence establishes the work as Middleton's, it is possible to see links between the city life satirized in these verses and his later satiric comedies—for instance, in his interest in rogue literature, the theme of the spendthrift heir, and transvestism.

The 1599 date of publication, imprinted on Creede's text and narrowed to the earlier part of that year by the Bishop's Ban on 1 June 1599, has never been disputed. Because *Microcynicon* imitates Hall's *Virgidemiarum*, the second portion of which was entered into the Stationers' Register on 30 March 1598, we can assume that Middleton, an eighteen-year-old student at Oxford, wrote this book between April 1598 and May 1599. The possible allusion to Marston's *Pygmalion* (1598) in the fifth satire also verifies the time of writing as fairly close to the publication date; *Pygmalion* was entered in the Stationers' Register on 27 May 1598. Adams suggested that the poem is indebted to Guilpin's *Skialetheia*, which was published in September 1598; this would push the time of writing until the period between autumn 1598 and May 1599.

Wendy Wall

SEE ALSO

Text: *Works*, 1974
Textual introduction and apparatus: this volume, 465

WORKS CITED

Adams, Joseph Quincy, 'Introduction' to his edition of Thomas Middleton, *The Ghost of Lucrece* (1937)
Brittin, Norman Aylsworth, *The Early Career of Thomas Middleton (1597–1604)* (unpublished Ph.D. diss., University of Washington, 1946)
Collier, John Payne, *The Poetical Decameron or Ten Conversations on English Poets*, 2 vols (1820), 1, 281–402
Eccles, Mark, 'Middleton's Birth and Education', *Review of English Studies* 7 (1931), 431–41
Irwin, Larry Wayne, *A Critical Edition of Thomas Middleton's 'Micro-cynicon', 'Father Hubburds Tales', and 'The Blacke Booke'* (unpublished Ph.D. diss., Univ. of Wisconsin, 1969)
Swinburne, Algernon Charles, 'Thomas Middleton', *The Nineteenth Century* 19 (1886), 138–53
Sykes, H. Dugdale, 'Thomas Middleton's Early Non-Dramatic Works', *Notes and Queries* 148 (1925), 435–8

The Ghost of Lucrece   1600

Middleton's authorship of *Ghost* is indicated by the initials T.M. which appear on the title-page and three more times in the dedicatory sonnet and invocation; in addition, the author calls himself '*Thomas Medius & Gravis Tonus*' (20-1), in an obvious play on his name. The poem is clearly Middletonian in the nature and intensity of its disillusioned and angry focus on the violation of idealized female chastity. Finally, *Ghost* shares some rare lexical features with *Solomon*, such as 'incolants' (evidently a Middleton coinage) and 'steven' (uniquely understood as crown, probably deriving from Greek *stephanos*, and anticipating the much later coinage, 'stephane').

J. Q. Adams suggests that Middleton actually wrote the poem somewhere between 1596 and 1598, although it was only published in 1600. Adams's theory stems from his evolutionary assumptions about style and intentionality: he sees *Ghost* as more skilled than *Solomon* (1597), but less so than *Microcynicon* (1599). This leads him to propose and then bolster an argument for deliberately delayed publication; but although the idea of early composition (possibly while Middleton was still at Oxford) might be attractive, nothing in Adams's argument is inevitable.

G. B. Shand

SEE ALSO

Text: *Works*, 1989
Textual introduction and apparatus: this volume, 467

WORK CITED

Adams, Joseph Quincy, ed., *The Ghost of Lucrece* (1937)

The Penniless Parliament of Threadbare Poets   1601

The earliest known edition of *The Penniless Parliament of Threadbare Poets* appeared in 1604 (STC 14291; see Textual Introduction). Its publisher, William Ferbrand entered *The Second Part of Jack of Dover* in the Stationers' Register on 3 August 1601. This second part was presumably *Penniless*, the first part or *Jack of Dover*, the original jestbook, having already been printed. *Penniless* itself is a revised version of *The Feareful and Lamentable Effects of Two Dangerous Comets*, a mock-prognostication by 'Simon Smellknave' published in 1591. This would mean that *Penniless* must have been composed at a date between the 1591 source and 1601, the date of the SR entry and most probably of the lost first edition.

Jack of Dover was apparently an earlier work, originally published without *Penniless*. The opening of *Jack of Dover* betrays the original plan when it mentions Jack's search 'in most of the principal places of England' for the 'fool of all fools' (A2). The one-man quest is changed into a conference in which Jack joins a group of starving scholar-poets in St Paul's Cathedral, each of whom relates a jest about a fool from one part of the country. Six stories (Fools of Berkshire, Devonshire, Cornwall, Hampshire, Essex, and London) retain Jack's older first-person narrative, which

elsewhere has been revised into a dialogue with insertions such as '(quoth another of the jury)' and 'quoth Jack of Dover'. These were clearly the last six jests, although that of the Fool of Berkshire was imposed out of sequence. The tales are printed in the right order in the quarto edition entitled *Jack of Dover's Merry Tales* printed by John Beale in 1615 (see Textual Introduction). The latter provides further evidence for the discrete nature of the jestbook. The second tale in it is titled 'How the Fool of Hereford was chosen Foreman of the Jury, and of the speech he uttered to the rest of his fellows' (A4). The caption seems a survival from the unrevised jestbook since it is followed by no such election or speech. There are other differences (see Textual Introduction), the most significant being that the jests in the 1615 edition trail off with Jack announcing that he has found the fool of all fools, while the 1604 text moves on to *Penniless* without Jack having reached the end of his quest.

Penniless, however, pre-dates the changes made to *Jack of Dover*, since there were clearly two stages in the revision. Whoever revised *Comets* into a mock-parliament had planned a discrete work. The opening sentence addresses 'all such as buys this book' (ll. 1-3), showing that the work was meant for independent publication, and the closing words, 'till my next return' (l. 388), use the authorial first-person without looking back at *Jack of Dover*. Even in the 1604 quarto, the two sections carry distinct running heads. Publishing *Penniless* as a separate work was hence a logical step, one that William Barley took in 1608 (STC 19307).

The internal evidence for dating *Penniless* is inconclusive, since any or all of the new markers could have been inserted at the second stage of the revision, when *Penniless* was attached to *Jack of Dover*. In ll. 233-4 the reference to the conquest of Granada in *Comets*, B4ᵛ, is replaced with a mention of the siege of Boulogne, an event which dates back to 1544. More helpful is the change from 'they will destroy the King of Spain' in *Comets*, B3ᵛ (an allusion to Philip II who died in 1598) to 'they will destroy Tyrone' (ll. 176-8). The Irish revolt led by Hugh O'Neill, the Earl of Tyrone, began in 1595. Although defeated by Lord Mountjoy, Tyrone did not surrender formally until April 1603. In *The Wonderful Year* published in 1603, Dekker speaks of 'wild Ireland' becoming 'tame' (Wilson 1925, p. 20, l. 6). Given the context in *Penniless*, the substitution would have been pointless if Tyrone were still not considered a threat. The change thus favours a date before April 1603, and it would certainly have been relevant in 1601. The rebellion and the trial of the Earl of Essex, to whom Middleton had dedicated *Solomon*, took place that year, and Middleton was present in London on the day of the uprising. The mention of Tyrone would recall the failed Irish expedition under Essex, which initiated the course of events leading to his revolt. The same could be said of the revision in ll. 283-4 decreeing that those who 'go to the wars and get nothing may come home poor by authority', where only the words 'come home poor' are from *Comets*. The change to 'these dangerous times' in ll.

258-9 from the source-phrase 'these times' (*Comets*, C1) would suit 1601, and one may suspect an allusion to the trial in ll. 318-20, where the revised text mentions those who 'boldly forswear themselves'.

Another updating changes 'prank it on the stage' in *Comets*, C1, to 'prank about the new playhouse' (ll. 247-8). This seems a reference to the first Fortune built in 1600. The Globe, built in 1598, was not as new when Ferbrand entered the book in August 1601. Performances at the Fortune, which drew big crowds along with the low-life crew hinted at in the passage, began in late 1600 or 1601 (Chambers, II, 173; Wickham, II, pt. 1, 281), and the change would, once again, be relevant in 1601. Finally, the phrase 'every fool in his humour' (l. 1) in the opening sentence added by the reviser may be alluding to Jonson's *Every Man in His Humour*, acted in late 1598 and printed in 1601, the corresponding dates for *Every Man Out* being 1599 and 1600. Once more, the allusion fits a date of 1601, the year in which *Poetaster* and *Satiromastix* were published. In the latter Dekker taunted Jonson for bringing on the stage '*Every Gentleman in's humour* and *Every Gentleman out on's humour*' (4.2.56-7). Middleton, who was to work with Dekker and others on *Caesar's Fall* for Henslowe the following year, would be tempted to make an arch reference to Jonson's plays in late 1601, when the war of the theatres was at its most intense.

It seems then that when Ferbrand entered the second part of *Jack of Dover* in August 1601, the revision of *Comets* into *Penniless* was already complete. The internal evidence suggests that the changes to *Comets*, as we have them, were made not long before.

The unrevised setting of six *Jack of Dover* jests and the traces of the original integrity of *Penniless* make it unlikely that the same author wrote the two tracts. There is further evidence to suggest that the two were written by different authors working independently. *Jack of Dover* includes the story of a man whose wife, after shouting at him, empties a chamber pot on his head, an event he likens to rain after thunder (B4-4ᵛ). A version of the story appears in the 49th jest in *Merry Tales, Witty Questions and Quick Answers* (1567; Hazlitt, I, 2, 65), where the henpecked husband (as in the Wife of Bath's Prologue) is Socrates. This version was obviously known to Smellknave, since he mentions Socrates in the allusion to the story retained in *Penniless*, ll. 152-4. In *Jack of Dover*, Socrates becomes 'a certain poor labouring man in Lincoln' (B4), just as the wit of Demosthenes in Jest 69 of *Merry Tales* (Hazlitt, I, 2, 88-9) is given to 'a widow woman dwelling in Westchester' (C1). It seems improbable that the author of *Penniless* would leave the Socrates story unaltered if he were also the author of *Jack of Dover*, or even if he were a different person who had planned *Penniless* as a sequel.

One can dismiss, therefore, the possibility of Middleton's authorship of *Jack of Dover*, a book which shows none of his verbal traits. Nevertheless, it appears that the reviser who retouched *Jack of Dover* to clear the ground for *Penniless* was also using Smellknave's text. In the opening paragraph of *Jack of Dover*, clearly added or altered to change Jack's first-person tale into his encounter with the poets, the latter are said to be 'as necessary in a commonwealth as a candle in a straw-bed' (A2), a line which is lifted from *Comets*, B2.

The Authorship of *Comets*: Foulweather, Smellknave, and Nashe

Smellknave's 'Epistle to the Reader' (A2) acknowledges his debt to Adam Foulweather, whose comic prophecy *A Wonderful Strange and Miraculous Astrological Prognostication*, also published in 1591, was attributed to Nashe in a sale-list appearing in Samuel Egerton Brydges's *Censura Literaria*, VII (1808), 10 (McKerrow, V, 138). McKerrow considered the attribution apocryphal, adding that any claim on Nashe's behalf must explain the work's relationship to Smellknave's *Comets* and the lost *A Book Entitled Francis Fair Weather*, entered in the Stationers' Register on 25 February 1591 (McKerrow, IV, 476-7, and V, 138-9).

According to McKerrow, the reason for attributing Foulweather's mock-prophecy to Nashe was that it was thought to be a parody of the *Astrological Discourse upon the Conjunction of Saturn and Jupiter* written by Richard Harvey, brother of Gabriel, in 1583. There is a dubious clue to Foulweather's identity in Gabriel Harvey's description in *Pierce's Supererogation* (1593) of Andrew Perne, who became Vice Chancellor of Cambridge and who, according to Nashe, opposed Gabriel's candidature for Public Oratorship there (III, 94, ll. 19-20), as 'a fair prognostication of a foul weather' (*Works*, II, 300). Gabriel's allusion strengthens the impression that the pseudonymous Foulweather was involved in the Harvey-Nashe quarrel.

There might be stronger grounds for saying the same of Smellknave. The pseudonym itself recalls that used by Nashe—'Cutbert Curry-knave'—in *An Almond for a Parrot* the previous year. A remarkable concentration of themes from Nashe may be sampled in the following passage:

> But oh you ale-knights, you that devour the marrow
> of the malt, and drive whole aletubs into consump-
> tions, that sing *In Crete when Dedalus*, over a cup, and
> tell Spanish news over an alepot, how unfortunate
> are you, who shall piss out that which you have
> swallowed down so sweetly,... the rot shall infect
> your purses, and eat out the bottom .... (B1ᵛ-B2)

In *Have with You to Saffron Walden*, Nashe named 'In Crete when Dedalus' as the song which to Gabriel Harvey was '*food from heaven*' (III, 67, ll. 26-7); in *Strange News* he claimed that the bibulous Greene 'pissed as much against the walls' in a year as the Harvey brothers did in three (I, 287, ll. 19-20; note that 'Spanish news' is altered to 'strange news' in *Penniless*, l. 114); in the same work Nashe refuted Gabriel's charge that he had lifted the proverb 'The devil's dancing school is in the bottom of a man's purse that is empty' out of Tarleton (I, 305, ll. 28-32).

There are other parallels, and a full treatment of the evidence would need to consider the whole of *Comets*. Nevertheless, it might be useful to note a few which occur in passages included in *Penniless* and which are not derived from Foulweather.

24 grace] A similar use of 'grace' to mean both 'lustre' and 'blush' links it to 'gold' in *The Unfortunate Traveller*: 'that not the professors have the greatest portion in grace; that all is not gold that glisters' (II, 34, ll. 14–16).

36 new steeple] 'though not this age, yet another age three years after the building up the top of Paul's steeple' (*Have with You to Saffron Walden*, III, 31, ll. 19–21).

38–9 whether false dice or true be of the most antiquity] See *Unfortunate Traveller*, II, 217, ll. 27–9.

68 tympany] 'Hero, for that she was pagled and tympanized' (*Lenten Stuff*, III, 199, ll. 30–1).

88–9 poulters shall kill more innocent poultry] Compare the criticism of the English for 'the murder of innocent mutton' and 'the unpluming of pullery' in *Pierce Penniless* (I, 201, ll. 20–1).

102 stare] (= boast, threaten): 'swears and stares' (*Pierce Penniless*, I, 170, l. 32). The phrase 'swear and stare' also occurs in *Comets*, A3ᵛ.

111–12 *fiery facias*] 'with the very reflex of his *fieri facias*' (*Unfortunate Traveller*, II, 230, l. 30).

130–2 worms in the churches in London shall keep their Christmas at midsummer in their bellies] Nashe uses the same comparison between the belly and a church-vault in *Pierce Penniless* (I, 200, l. 1) and *Summer's Last Will and Testament* (l. 1031).

165 simples] 'their [physicians'] simples in this case wax simple fellows' (*Unfortunate Traveller*, II, 230, l. 1).

169 one shirt to shift them] 'A man in his case hath no other shift, or apparel…but he must thus shift otherwhile for his living' (*Have with You to Saffron Walden*, III, 75, ll. 4–6).

232 Turk] 'now they set up their faces (like Turks) of grey paper, to be spit at for silver games in Finsbury Fields' (*Pierce Penniless*, I, 240, ll. 7–9).

234–5 dangerous weapon against a mud wall] 'piss out all their wit and thrift against the walls' (*Pierce Penniless*, I, 206, ll. 15–16).

270 whole quart for a penny] 'a penny a quart' (*Have with You to Saffron Walden*, III, 84, l. 16; *Summer's Last Will and Testament*, l. 1134).

270–1 St Thomas onions shall be sold by the rope] 'a twopenny rope of onions' (*Have with You to Saffron Walden*, III, 58, ll. 34–5).

291–2 louse in an old doublet] 'not a louse in his doublet was let pass' (*Unfortunate Traveller*, II, 223, ll. 11–12).

292–3 fool and his bauble] 'What's a fool but his bauble?' (*Summer's Last Will and Testament*, ll. 63–4).

305 halfpenny loaves] 'than desire (with the baker) there might be three ounces of bread sold for a halfpenny' (*Pierce Penniless*, I, 202, ll. 16–18); 'not like the baker's loaf, that should weigh but six ounces' (*Summer's Last Will and Testament*, ll. 885–6).

308 sudden or rather sodden] 'and to die suddenly, as Fol Long, the fencer, did, drinking *aqua vitae*' (*Pierce Penniless*, I, 208, ll. 22–3).

324 more gold than iron] 'another that had twilted all his truss full of counters, thinking, if the enemy should take him, he would mistake them for gold, and so save his life for his money' (*Unfortunate Traveller*, II, 233, ll. 6–9).

365 beef] 'beef-witted gull' (*Terrors of the Night*, I, 370, l. 18); 'bury not your spirits in beef-pots' (*Christ's Tears over Jerusalem*, II, 122, l. 23).

366–7 simper it] 'simpering of thy mouth' (*Almond for a Parrot*, III, 349, l. 10).

383–4 ten precepts…in the art of scolding] 'tempted beyond her [the shrew's] ten commandments' (*Strange News*, I, 321, l. 20).

385 Chapel of Ill Counsel] 'Convocation Chapel of sound counsel' (*Have with You to Saffron Walden*, III, 22, l. 9).

It appears that Smellknave, if he was not Nashe, had an insider's knowledge of Nashe's fight with the Harveys a year after Richard Harvey's *Lamb of God* fired the first shot and, what is more surprising, a year before Nashe's known replies began to come out. The publisher of *Comets*, John Busby (the elder), would have been an interested party in the quarrel in 1591, since he was to market three editions of *Pierce Penniless* in the next two years. Smellknave's printer was John Charlewood, who had also prepared the first edition of *Pierce Penniless* in 1592, and, before that, *The Anatomy of Absurdity* in 1589.

The case for Middleton's authorship of *Penniless* does not depend upon a conjectural attribution of *Comets*. However, the Nashe-connection may not be altogether irrelevant. Although Middleton in *Hubburd* accused others of plagiarizing Nashe, he himself, in the year *Hubburd* was published, lifted passages verbatim from Smellknave for *Plato's Cap*. *Plato* takes care to remind readers of its generic lineage, using the pseudonym 'Adam Evesdropper', modelling Mihill Mercurie's prefatory poem, even in its rhyme-scheme, on Martin Merry-mate's in *Comets*, and recalling Nashe's gibes in *Pierce Penniless* (I, 196–7) against Richard Harvey's prognostication on the 'conjunction of Saturn and Jupiter' (*Plato*, 214). Nashe's works were called in by the bishops in 1599 at the time Middleton's own *Microcynicon* was burnt, and although the ban did not stop publication of Nashe's works (McKerrow, V, 34), he seems to have ended his days in dismal poverty. This at least is what Middleton leads us to believe in *Black Book*, written as a sequel to *Pierce Penniless*. Nashe's death presumably encouraged publishers to exploit his notoriety, and Ferbrand himself brought out another sequel to *Pierce Penniless* in 1606, Dekker's *News from Hell*. Between 1601 and 1605, Middleton adopted a propagandist stance on Nashe's behalf, pleading his cause against the Harveys in *Hubburd* (252–7), and quoting a couplet from *Pierce Penniless* in *Yorkshire Tragedy* (4.87–8). The title of *Penniless* seems designed to recall Pierce Penniless ('exceeding poor scholar', Middleton calls him in *Black Book*, 796), Nashe's self-portrayal in *Have with You to Saffron Walden* as a poet 'in a threadbare cloak' (III, 26, l. 16), and his description of a poor scholar in *Strange News* as a 'threadbare cloak' (I, 306, l. 17). Even the idea of the mock-parliament could have come from the mock-legalese in the Introduction to *The Unfortunate Traveller*, where the porch is called the 'parliament house' of court-pages (II, 208, l. 15). The reviser replaces the porch with a variant of the 'penniless bench' of insolvent loungers in Oxford, mentioned in *Foulweather* (III, 383, l. 35) and in *The Black Book* (462–3).

The Authorship of *Penniless*

Doctor Merryman

An octavo edition of *Penniless* only was brought out by John Beale in 1637 (STC 19307.5), attributing the work to 'Doctor Merry-man'. The pseudonym was used by Samuel Rowlands in *Democritus, or Doctor Merry-man his Medicines* (1607) and *Doctor Merry-man: or Nothing but Mirth* (1616). Ferbrand published many of Rowlands's works between 1600 and 1609, including *The Letting of Humour's Blood in the Head-Vein* (1600, printed by White), *Ave Caesar* (1603, printed by White and co-published by George Loftus), *Look to It, for I'll Stab Ye* (1604, sold by Loftus; 1604, another edition printed by White), *Humour's Looking Glass* (1608), *The Famous History of Guy, Earl of Warwick* (1609), and *The Knave of Clubs* (1609).

Beale had acquired the rights to *Penniless* on 12 November 1614; he acquired from Loftus the rights of Rowlands's *The Melancholy Knight* (1615) on 2 December 1614, and in 1631 he printed an edition of Rowlands's *Democritus, or Doctor Merry-man his Medicines* for R. Bird. Beale may have attributed *Penniless* to 'Merryman' because he took Rowlands to be the author of all the tracts he had acquired from Ferbrand and Loftus, or because he wished to link the 1637 *Penniless* with the 1631 *Democritus*. In any case, 'Doctor Merryman' was among the stock pseudonyms for writers of parodic almanacs. The prefatory verse in Smellknave's *Comets* was signed by 'Martin Merry-mate', the publisher of *Owl* called himself 'Jocundary Merry-brains' on the title-page, and in *Have with You to Saffron Walden* (1596), published before any of Rowlands's 'Merryman' tracts were out, Nashe taunted Gabriel Harvey after accusing him of ghosting Gabriel Frende's almanacs: 'What, a grave Doctor a base *John Doleta*, the almanac-maker, Doctor *Deus-ace* and Doctor *Merry-man*?' (III, 72, ll. 8–9). The title-page of Beale's edition calls Merryman 'the merry fortune-teller' in spite of *Penniless* being a mock-parliament rather than a mock-prophecy. The pseudonymic credit is late and vague, the Ferbrand–Rowlands link bears weakly on the attri-

bution of the primary revision, and if Rowlands was at all involved, he probably came in at the second stage.

Rowlands's works provide a few verbal parallels, of which three may be worth recording. But none of these is significantly close, and only one (l. 208) is located in the material added to *Comets*.

205 locked in their own bosoms] 'The Knave of Clubs he any time can burn, | And find him in his bosom, for his turn' (*Letting of Humours' Blood*, D5^v)

208 Footman's Inn] 'That he at last in footman's inn must host' (*The Knave of Hearts*, C3^v)

241 mince pie] 'He lives not like Diogines, on roots: | But proves a mince-pie guest unto his host' (*Letting of Humours' Blood*, A7^v)

Rowlands's name figures in a cryptic note by Malone to the title of *Letting of Humour's Blood* in a copy of Joseph Ritson's *Bibliographia Poetica* (1802), p. 317: 'Stolen from Nash's papers after his death in 1600. So says T. Middleton' (Bullen, VIII, 63n). Rowlands, however, may have published his book before Nashe's death, which took place in or before 1601. Malone apparently took the phrase 'humorous theft' in *Hubburd*, where Middleton is complaining of 'Drones' who steal Nashe's honey (269), for a reference to *Letting of Humour's Blood*. McKerrow (V, 151n) dismissed Malone's note, observing that Rowlands was drawing on Lodge's *Wit's Misery* (1596), which in turn quarried Nashe's *Pierce Penniless* (1592). In any case, Middleton implies that there was more than one writer plagiarizing Nashe after his death, and there is no clue that the passage in *Hubburd* was specifically accusing Rowlands.

Anthony Nixon

Comets was adapted by Anthony Nixon in *The Black Year* in 1606. It is easy to dismiss the possibility of Nixon's authorship of *Penniless*. *Black Year* copies *Comets* directly and, barring the use of 'prove' in the joke about long-bearded men (B1^v; *Penniless*, l. 6) and the change from 'beneath' to 'below' (B2^v; *Penniless*, l. 43), there is no trace in the text of Nixon's awareness of *Penniless*.

The Case for Middleton

While there is nothing in the external situation to make Middleton's involvement in *Penniless* implausible, the case for his authorship rests entirely on verbal and thematic parallels. It is not possible to trace his preferred oaths, contractions, connectives, and verbs in a work to which his contribution was verbally minimal. *While* appears once as a connective, although there is also a single use of the more Middletonian *whilst*. *Amongst* (× 5), however, outnumbers *among* (× 1), and twice the latter form in *Comets* (B4^v, C1^v) is altered to the more Middletonian *amongst* (ll. 236, 289). *Betwixt* and *between* are each used once.

But the 'Middletonian' way with such variants deduced from the plays are not always reliable for the non-dramatic works and juvenilia. For instance, *hath* (× 7) is consistently used instead of the more usual *has*. Lake's list on p. 273 (Table III.2) shows that there is not a single use of has in 6 of the 7 non-dramatic works studied, *Peacemaker* being the only tract to use the form (× 5). On the other hand, there are nearly 80 uses of *hath* against a single *has* in *Solomon*. This pattern is consistent for other non-dramatic texts, and with other 'unMiddletonian' forms such as *doth*. Middleton's preferences in these matters were demonstrably different for dramatic and non-dramatic texts, and for colloquial and formal styles. Moreover, the verbal conventions of *Penniless* are twice removed from Middleton's known habits, being both borrowed and parodic.

That Middleton used a phrase repeatedly elsewhere is no clinching argument for his authorship of an anonymous work which uses it once or twice, especially when the controls required are the texts of not just a few known playwrights, but any number of obscure pamphleteers. But the evidence begins to look compelling when so many parallels are found concentrated in the quantitatively small additions and changes. There are only 1532 'new' words that are not present in the source, and these constitute a fraction over 36 per cent of the text of *Penniless*. Again, around 37 per cent of the 'new' words are the formulaic phrases of Parliamentary statutes, which leaves us with a sample-pool slightly short of 1000 words. While many of the instances below may be paralleled from other possible claimants, there is no other writer who will offer an echo for what is nearly every bit of the new material added to *Comets*. Moreover, one would need to account for the fact that such additions appear in a work which Middleton definitely plundered in *Plato* and which he drew on till very late in his career.

There is one parallel which is especially close. The clause 'for them that want shoes to wear boots all the year' in ll. 29–31 is an addition for which the source is Foulweather's line 'such as have no shoes to go barefoot' (ed. McKerrow, III, 381, l. 22). Foulweather is speaking of poor men who fast even on Sundays, while the line in *Penniless* can also imply cheats and abraham men who cannot afford stockings and wear riding boots to hide their loot as much as their bare legs (see l. 5: 'and a pair of boots, but no stockings', also an addition). The joke is repeated almost verbatim in *Owl*, 2320–1: 'Our sirs that want shoes must trash out their boots'. The words I emphasize are different from Foulweather's and the same as in *Penniless*, while 'trash out' furthers the oddness of wearing riding boots for walking. Middleton frequently mocks the new fashion of wearing wide, turned-down boots, and associates them with rakes and cheats. See 'ripping up the bowels of wide boots' (*Black Book* 657–8); 'booted Michaelmas term', 'a curious pair of boots of King Philip's leather', and 'upon those fantastical boots' (*Hubburd*, 363, 407–8, 413); 'Signior Stramazoon and Signior Kickshaw... with their dirty boots' (*Meeting*, 173–4); 'Cheaters booted' (*Roaring Girl*, 11.221); 'they're [termers] well booted for all seasons' *Witch*, 1.1.75, etc. One might argue that Middleton was borrowing from the unMiddletonian *Penniless*, especially since there are other echoes of *Penniless* such as those of ll. 110–12, 117–18 (the *fiery faces* joke and 'infect your purses and eat out the bottoms ere you be aware') in *Owl* (see 297, 327). The question that would then have to be answered is why Middleton should *also* need to lift the minor additions in *Penniless* for *Owl* when he had used *Comets* as a direct source for *Plato* more than a decade earlier, and had drawn on Foulweather and Smellknave for many other lines elsewhere. The likelihood of the same writer being responsible for *Penniless* and *Owl* is strengthened by a few of the other parallels listed below.

20   a pint of muscadine with eggs] 'a pint of malmsey and oil' (*Comets*, B3). Compare 'riotous eggs and muscadine' (*Black Book*, 645–6); 'brothel at noonday and muscadine and eggs at midnight' (*Trick*, 3.1.76–7); 'buttered his lecherous guts, with eggs and muscadine' (*Owl*, 799–800).

21–2   those that clip that they should not shall have a horse-nightcap for their labour] 'such as clip that they should not' (*Comets*, A4, brought across from another context to add the rest). The idea of the halter ('horse-nightcap') was there in the sentence in *Comets* ('assured... of a cord'). The change introduces the 'horse/whores' pun, as habitual in Middleton as the use of horse-riding in a bawdy context. Compare 'you've a horse to ride upon' (*Phoenix*, 13.47); 'instead of a French horse, practise upon their mistresses' (*Black Book*, 331–2); 'how many horses hast thou killed in the country with the hunting of harlotries' (*Meeting*, 305–6); 'The horse and he lies in litter together', 'to my [the courtesan's] Cousin Horseman', 'To lie with their horsekeeper' (*Mad World*, 2.4.92–3, 3.2.247, 3.3.101); 'My [Tailby's] horse waits for me' (*Five Gallants* 3.1.19); 'Maybe his groom O'th' stable begot me...He could ride a horse well' (*Revenger*, 1.2.135–6); 'they are the same jades...that have drawn all your famous whores to Ware' (*Roaring Girl*, 5.18–19); 'To marry a whore in London...Brentford horse-races' (*Chaste Maid*, 5.4.87–92); 'lay with her horsekeeper' (*Weapons*, 3.1.281); 'with one light horse' (*Witch*, 5.1.77); I keep my horse, I keep my whore (*Widow*, 3.1.22); 'Mars will take horse at the armourer's shop and never leave riding till he fall in the amorous lap' (margin-note: 'Soldiers are whoremasters'), 'whurry of their coach-horses' (*Owl*, 1211–12, 1257–8); 'He that loves a horse well, | Must needs love a widow well' (*Old Law*, 2.2.57–8), etc. The word 'clip' attracts an association with whores elsewhere in Middleton; compare 'when he clips his whore' (*Mad World* 4.5.53); 'Here sometimes ladies practise...Court, clip, and exercise our wits upon' (*Five Gallants*, 2.1.69–72). In *Comets*, 'clip' seems to imply stealing by cutting or shearing, whereas in *Penniless*, the substitution of 'horse-nightcap' for 'cord' and the consequent 'horse/whores' pun, extends the meaning of 'clip' to include 'embrace', as in the examples from *Mad World* and *Five Gallants*.

37-8 cony-catchers to fall together by the ears about the four knaves at cards] 'there shall be war between the four knaves at cards' (*Comets*, A4ᵛ). The phrase 'fall together by the ears' is recurrent in Middleton in contexts which involve cheating. Compare 'he [Dampit] set the dogs together by th'ears' (*Trick*, 1.4.19-20); 'they [law books] were almost together by the ears' (*Hubburd*, 731); 'an they fall together by the ears', 'and the sun near ent'ring into th'Dog sets 'em all together by th'ears' (*No Wit*, 4.301-2, 9.478-9); 'They [lawyers] fall to th'ears about it', 'I have a device will bring you together by th'ears again' (*Quiet Life*, 1.1.215, 3.2.227-8). There are occasional uses of the same idiom in Rowlands; see *Letting of Humour's Blood*, E4ᵛ.

143 which shall assail them about midnight] To the source in *Comets*, B2ᵛ, is added the phrase 'about midnight'. The title-page of *Comets* has an astrological motif with 'Twelve a'clock at midnight' inscribed on it, because the comets were expected to strike 'after twelve of the clock at midnight...to all sorts of married folk especially' (B2ᵛ), (see *Phoenix*, 15.11-12: 'stuck not a comet...| Upon the dreadful blow of twelve last night?') The reviser's addition, suggested by Smellknave's mention of married couples, is consistent with Middleton's chronic linking of dissipation with midnight. 'Midnight' is again added in a lewd context in ll. 372-4, 'spirits with aprons shall much disturb your sleeps about midnight', from *Comets*, D2: 'as all the *crinite* comets in Christendom cannot disturb us of our sleeps, (I mean such comets as wear aprons...)'. Compare 'To make midnoon midnight...Midnight with sin' (*Solomon*, 17.184-5); 'adulterously train out young ladies to midnight banquets' (*Phoenix*, 15.98-9); 'voluptuous meetings, midnight revels', 'Midnight, still I love you' (*Yorkshire*, 2.7, 2.81); 'muscadine and eggs at midnight' (*Trick*, 3.1.77); 'For, after twelve has struck, maids look for one' (*Five Gallants*, 1.1.165); 'O, hour of incest!... twelve o'clock at night', 'twelve o'clock at night upon the rushes' (*Revenger*, 1.3.63-9, 2.2.80-81); 'vent his private bottle-ale at midnight', 'roars at midnight in deep tavern bowls' (*Roaring Girl*, Epistle.28, Prologue.17); 'About the peace of midnight...When all the world's a gamester' (*Lady*, 1.2.197-200); 'I feel thy wrongs at midnight', 'an ill conscience at the fall of midnight' (*No Wit*, 1.28, 9.255); 'a sin stamped last midnight' (*Widow*, 5.1.128); 'come by water to the backdoor at midnight', 'midnight surfeiter' (*Witch*, 2.1.49, 2.1.80); 'visit your taverns at midnight' (*Owl*, 1848-9); 'contract myself at midnight to the larder-woman', (*Women Beware*, 1.2.116), etc.

159 Bow Bell in Cheapside] 'bells of Barking'. (*Comets*, B3). In *Quiet Life*, 1.1.137-8, a scene sometimes assigned to Webster, there is mention of the harshness of Bow Bell: 'And in | These fits Bow Bell is a still organ to her'. The comparison of harsh voices to bells

is familiar in Middleton; compare *Meeting*, 280, *Lady*, 2.3.23, and *Roaring Girl*, 3.314-15.

168 French *morbus*] 'French pox' (*Comets*, B3). Compare *Quiet Life*, 2.4.20-21: 'O fie, youth, pox is no word of art. *Morbus gallicus*, or *neopolitanus* had been well.' The joke appears in a scene which shows no Webster-markers (see Jackson, pp. 142-4). The coy evasion of the word 'pox' is mocked also in *Five Gallants*, 3.1.11 ('my French adversary'), and *Owl*, 2022 ('The French something').

189-90 in these our latter days] 'this latter time' (*Comets*, B3ᵛ). Compare 'of our latter days' (*Micro-cynicon*, 1.9); 'of these latter days' (*Phoenix*, 9.87); 'in these latter days' (*Michaelmas*, 1.3.9). A similar change, needed to erase a trace of the yearly forecast, is made in ll. 305-8: 'Chaucer's books...shall in these days' from 'Chaucer's books shall this year' (*Comets*, C2). The phrase 'in these days' is present elsewhere in *Comets* (C1ᵛ). Although formulaic, the phrase is recurrent in Middleton: *Trick*, 1.1.99; *Revenger*, 1.3.65, 2.2.25; *Lady*, 1.2.118; *Owl*, 294; *Hengist*, 4.2.39; etc.

248-9 to seek out their old master Captain Cropear] This addition contains an alliterated name (like John Findfault in ll. 387-8), created by a verb-noun compound, familiar in Middleton (Christopher Clutchfist in *Hubburd*, Sim Suckspiggots, Susan Scoldout, and Tib Tittlebasket in *Owl*). However, 'Simon Smellknave' itself is a name of this kind. But 'cropear' reappears in *Owl*, 2203-4: 'or a crop-eared courser to his mill-bruised beans' (the context involves shirkers and cowards, and 'beans' suggests punishment). There is a pun, involving the 'ear' of the corn, a 'crop'. A similar pun on 'ear' occurs in *Phoenix*, 2.63-4: 'before the corn comes to earing, 'tis up to the ears in high collars'. The punishment for felony is linked to a pun on ears again in *Quiet Life*, 2.2.136-7: 'Not a word more, goodman Snipsnapper, for your ears'. See also 'Justice Cropshin' (*Five Gallants*, 1.1.9).

284-8 And those that play fast and loose with women's apron-strings may chance make a journey for a Winchester pigeon...physician's purgatory] An addition. 'Apron-strings', with a quibble on 'fast', reappears in *Owl*, 925-6: 'she that followed Virgo (as fast as her apron-strings would give her leave)'. For jokes on Winchester pigeons/geese, see *Meeting*, 580; and *Owl*, 301. On 'physician's purgatory', see 'A physician...I have put you to your purgation' (*Mad World*, 3.2.17-19); 'In purgatory?...There's physicians enough there to cast his water' (*Puritan*, 4.1.14-16).

320-1 for almanac-makers to tell more lies than true tales] The liars in the source passage were 'Such as have skill in physiognomy' (*Comets*, C2ᵛ). Jokes against the bogus prophecies of almanacs are more frequent in Middleton than any other playwright of his time. In addition to the mock-almanacs, the extended satire in *No Wit*, and Doctor Almanac in

Heroes, compare 'an almanac in my pocket, and three ballads in my codpiece' (*Yorkshire*, 1.27–8); 'Happen but true tomorrow, almanac' (*Puritan*, 3.5.254); 'if all almanacs lie not' (*Roaring Girl*, 7.26); ''Light, that's six hundred more than any almanac has' (*Weapons*, 3.1.67); 'Like *The Wise Masters* and the almanacs' (*Valour*, 5.3.13), etc.

329–30 And he that hath once married a shrew... beware how he come into the stocks again] An added joke, with a pun on 'stocks', meaning the instrument of punishment and the frame in which a horse is confined for shoeing. *Owl*, 2310–11, has a similar pun on 'stocks', where shoemakers are told 'you can cast the best gentleman in the land into your stocks'.

367–8 dare manfully set upon a shoulder of veal] 'dare make incision in a shoulder of veal' (*Comets*, D2). The point of the change seems to be to link the treatment of the veal to the setting upon a 'veal', i.e. a gull, by the sergeant or robber (sheriff's officers and criminals are equated in such phrases as 'the sheriffs of Salisbury Plain' and 'Sergeant of Salisbury Plain' in *Black Book*, 312–13, 680). A similar pun on 'a target of veal' occurs in *Owl*, 2209. 'Clapping' or setting upon a shoulder is frequently associated with the sergeant or bailiff in Middleton. Compare 'sergeants... with one clap on your shoulder' (*Hubburd*, 24–6); '*claps him on the shoulder*' (*Mad World*, 4.1.29.1–2); 'They [sergeants] have struck a fever into my shoulder' (*Puritan*, 3.3.85); 'a sergeant cares but for the shoulder of a man' (*Roaring Girl*, 7.146–7); 'Now for a shoulder of mutton' (*Chaste Maid*, 2.2.162); 'set upon his right shoulder—thy sergeant Counterbuff' (*Quiet Life*, 3.2.1–2), etc. Moreover, the comic collocation of 'manfully' with eating recurs in *Weapons*, 2.1.26: 'earn my supper manfully'.

381–2 may eat mutton on fasting days] An addition, adapting two verse lines: 'May instead of red herrings, | Eat mutton in Lent' (*Comets*, D1ᵛ). There are many mentions of 'fasting days' in Middleton, and of the dodging of the statutory ban on flesh. Compare 'never came home drunk but upon fasting nights' (*Mad World*, 1.1.15–16); 'puritanical scrape-shoes, flesh o' good Fridays' (*Puritan*, 1.3.10–11); 'we eat no flesh on Fridays' (*Owl*, 425–6, see also 1323, 1585); 'Nobody minds Fasting Day; | I have scarce been thought upon o' Friday nights' (*Heroes*, 45–6); 'like your fasting days before red letters in the almanac' (*Quiet Life*, 5.1.74–5); 'as many fasting days | A great desire to see flesh stirring again' (*Women Beware*, 4.1.32–3), etc.

There are a number of other parallels which, although minor, serve to corroborate the positive evidence for Middleton's hand.

Title Compare 'the parliament of inward smart' (*Solomon*, 17.108). A singer in *Microcynicon* has a 'threadbare coat' (4.50), and Truth is 'threadbare' in *Truth* (294).

1 for the increase of every fool in his humour] This phrase in the added opening paragraph, while alluding to Jonson's plays, uses 'humour' in a way which is as instinctive with Middleton as with the second suitor in *Widow*. Among closer parallels, see 'a very kind-natured soul... in her humour... in all her humours' (*Five Gallants*, 4.5.39–42).

16 red petticoats] 'Venus' (*Comets*, A4). 'Petticoat' means a prostitute in *Weapons*, 4.1.288: 'Some petticoat begot him'. For the same association, see also 'this petticoat has been turned' (*Five Gallants*, 1.1.77); 'stript for a petticoat', 'Not the petticoat? that were holiday upon working day' (*Quiet Life*, 2.2.206, 239–40). For '[adjective] petticoat', compare 'embroidered petticoat' (*Phoenix*, 12.130); 'taffeta petticoat' (*Five Gallants*, 1.1.7, 1.1.75–6); 'velvet petticoats' (*Weapons*, 1.1.52). Similar changes are made in ll. 221–3 (see below), and ll. 264–6: 'they shall go into Petticoat Lane', from 'they shall go into Brothel houses' (*Comets*, C1).

30–2 he that hath never a cloak... witness old Prime, the keeper of Bedlam dicing house] In this added clause, there is a quibble on 'Priam' and 'Prime'. The second could be a real person, but the context of the dicing house suggests an allusion to the game of primero (compare the name Primero in *Five Gallants*, and 'to my youngest sons Gleek and Primavista' in *Heroes*, 105–6). Compare the wordplay in *Weapons*, 4.1.56–7: 'the prime villain... A wicked prime.'

42–3 while the husband stands painting below] *Comets*, A4ᵛ, had 'beneath' in place of 'below'. This minor change is consistent with Middleton's habit in referring to interiors. Compare 'whilst her husband sat below by the counter' (*Hubburd*, 879); 'below i'th' hall' (*Weapons*, 4.1.25); 'Sat like a drone below' (*Women Beware*, 1.3.87).

55–6 by the help of women's hands] An addition. Compare 'with a woman's hand' (*Mad World*, 3.2.269); 'in women's hands' (*Hengist*, 3.2.8)

221–2 shall sell their freehold for tobacco pipes and red petticoats] 'shall sell their freehold for peas pottage' (*Comets*, B4ᵛ). Attacks on tobacco are frequent in the period's literature, including in texts by Rowlands (*Letting of Humour's Blood*, Epig. 18). Middleton links tobacco specifically with bankruptcy in *Hubburd* 447–8: 'and he might very fitly take tobacco there, for the lawyer and the rest made him smoke already'. Smoking is blamed for the decline of the gentry and of hospitality in *Peacemaker*, 506–7. See also *Phoenix*, 2.59–61.

243 Dagger in Cheap] 'Woolsack' (*Comets*, C1). Compare 'the Dagger pies can testify' (*Quiet Life*, 5.1.73–4).

268–70 if the brewers of London buy store of good malt, poor bargemen at Queenhithe shall have a whole quart for a penny] 'if the brewer of Putney buy store of good malt, they about Richmond and Mortlake shall have a whole quart for a penny' (*Comets*, C1).

Middleton's sympathy for 'poor bargemen' is evident in *Chaste Maid*, 4.3. Queenhithe is spelled 'Queen-hive', which agrees with the preferred form in *Chaste Maid*, 2.2.186, and *Quiet Life*, 5.2.33; see also 'Queen Hive' in *Weapons*, 5.1.69. (The form 'Queene-hith' appears in Crane's transcript of *Witch*, 1.1.86.)

297 salmon shall be better sold in Fish Street] 'cod shall be better sold than the bean' (*Comets*, C2). 'Salmon' is used to mean a prostitute, with a quibble on 'cod's-head' immediately following in a scene given to Dekker in *Roaring Girl*, 9.92–3. For unsavoury allusions to Fish Street and New Fish Street, see *Black Book*, 239–40; *No Wit*, 4.305; *Owl*, 496, 1284; and *Heroes*, 53.

344–5 they go a-fishing on Salisbury Plain] An addition to the passage on poor soldiers in *Comets*, C4ᵛ. Salisbury Plain, a haunt of robbers and crooks who posed as poor soldiers, appears in *Black Book*, 313, 680.

378–80 he that is plagued with a cursed wife to have his pate broke quarterly, as he pays his rent] In *Comets*, the date on which the comets appear is 25 March, the legal quarter-day. The pun on 'quarterly' (divided into quarters, quarterly payment of rents) in the addition, however, may be compared to puns on 'quarters' elsewhere in Middleton: 'those lousy quarters' (*Valour*, 3.4.39); 'Last quarter, with thieves at Newgate' (*Owl*, 1166).

387–8 assaults of Sir John Findfault] Besides being a verb–noun alliterated compound, this name for the carping critic in the paragraph added at the end has an echo in the player's address to the critics in the audience in *Hengist*, 5.1.138: 'And for your finding fault our hope is greater'.

The phrases inserted to mimic parliamentary legislation are formulaic, and there are instances elsewhere in Middleton (see *Michaelmas*, 2.3.440, for 'have commission', and *Phoenix*, 10.70, for 'by authority').

There is one change which might appear to be not quite typical of Middleton, the one from 'that are born under this kind goddess' (*Comets*, C4ᵛ) to 'which are sworn true servitors to women's pantables' (ll. 347–8). *Comets* has the form 'pantofle' on D3, and this form appears in *Quiet Life*, 4.2.50. The quarto of *Quiet Life* was published in 1662, and the fidelity of the extant text to authorial preferences is doubtful. Besides, the forms could be treated as indifferent variants. Massinger's *The City Madam*, printed in 1654 from a holograph promptbook, uses the form 'pantables' (3.1.95), whereas *A New Way to Pay Old Debts*, printed in 1633 from what is also thought to have been his autograph manuscript, has 'pantofle' (1.1.137).

Middleton's works echo other passages in *Penniless* that are derived directly from *Comets*. Such parallels demonstrate when Middleton borrowed material from Smellknave elsewhere, the point of the joke or quibble was almost invariably the same as in *Penniless*.

65 heap up riches for another] Middleton echoes the idea elsewhere. See *Five Gallants*, 1.1.131–2; *No*

Wit, 4.35–7; *Dissemblers*, 2.3.107–8; *Women Beware*, 3.3.91–2, 3.4.38–9.

102 sound trebles] For quibbles on 'sound base' and 'sound treble', see *Black Book*, 177; *Five Gallants*, 1.1.99.

147 sheep's head] *Owl*, 677–8 ('this cornuted husband of the sheep's heads').

156 Essex calves] *Owl*, 274–5 ('the two Essex calves have sucked each other dry').

158 sheep's skin] *No Wit*, 9.11; *Owl*, 2223–4 ('Furriers and glovers...for your sheepskins').

172 upland grounds] For a similar quibble on 'uplands', see *Trick*, 1.1.3.

270–1 St Thomas onions shall be sold by the rope] See *Changeling*, 1.2.207–8, for a similar link between a rope of onions and the hangman's rope.

273 falling band] For the same quibble on 'falling', see *Patient Man*, 7.51; *Five Gallants*, 1.1.81–5; *Roaring Girl*, 1.16–17.

318–19 neither write nor read] A recurrent phrase and idea in Middleton; see *Michaelmas*, 1.2.300; *Black Book*, 75 ('yet can neither read nor write'); and *Women Beware*, 1.2.128.

The lists above exclude the verbatim parallels in *Plato*, of which there are many instances (the major ones involve ll. 6–7, 16 18, 35–9, 40–1, 47–50, 56–8, 71–4, 76–8, 83–6, 89–93, 99–104, 203–6, 213–19, 263–6, 292–5, 369–70 in *Penniless*). There is a dilemma in arguing that *Penniless* and *Plato* are by the same author. If *Plato* is too close to the fresh material in *Penniless*, one could say that Middleton is borrowing from the non-Middleton *Penniless* rather than from *Comets*; if not, the two could be said to be by different authors plagiarizing *Comets*.

There is no doubt that *Plato* uses *Comets* directly. *Plato*'s prefatory epistle and poem are modelled on the ones in *Comets*, and it includes passages omitted in *Penniless* (e.g. 'shameless drabs shall be still gadding about the streets for figs, almonds and confects' in *Plato*, 358–9 is taken from *Comets*, B4, and omitted in *Penniless*). Even when the two pamphlets quote the same lines from *Comets*, *Plato* goes back to the unmediated form ('dreadful war' in *Comets*, A4ᵛ and *Plato*, 270, 'fall at square' in *Penniless*, l. 41; 'bailiffs' in *Comets*, A4ᵛ and *Plato*, 319, 'sergeants' in *Penniless* l. 49; 'nostrils' in *Comets*, B1 and *Plato*, 339, 'noses' in *Penniless* l. 77; 'flesh' in *Comets*, B1ᵛ and *Plato*, 285, 'meat' in *Penniless*, l. 93; 'brothel-houses' in *Comets*, C1 and *Plato*, 366, 'Petticoat Lane' in *Penniless*, l. 265, etc.).

But there are also elements common to *Penniless* and *Plato* that do not derive from *Comets*. *Plato* starts with an address to 'all those that are laxative of laughter' (compare 'I am of such a laxative laughter' *Puritan*, 3.5.87–8), and mentions 'brows too full of Saturn, that sullen planet that never laughs' (13–14), recalling 'such as...laugh not...shall be condemned to melancholy' in the opening paragraph of *Penniless* (ll. 1–4; compare 'to make them laugh a little' *Owl*, 1458). *Plato* has 'foisting John' and 'plain-dealing John' in the closing paragraph, and concludes with 'And farewell John' (380); *Penniless* mentions 'Sir John Findfault' in its closing paragraph (ll. 387-8). *Plato* couples 'salt salmon and fresh cod' (85), and quibbles on 'quarter' (cut into quarters, a quarter of the year): 'Red herring may go hang himself then for a twelvemonth...until the hungry ploughboys cut him down and quarter him' (88-90). 'Midnight' appears with the same connotation in a different context (101), as does 'shoulder-clappers' (128). The almanac-joke reappears in an altered form (113, 296), although *Plato*, like *Comets*, pretends to be an almanac itself. Old Fish Street, Smithfield, and Cheapside are all mentioned in *Plato* (201, 266-7). A phrase in another alteration, 'may as boldly forswear themselves' (ll. 318-20) from 'may boldly quit themselves of forgery' (C2ᵛ), appears in a different place in *Plato*, 233-4: 'makes the gallants forswear themselves'. These parallels strike the right balance of distance and proximity between the two pamphlets so as to allow the possibility of common authorship. As with *Owl*, the alternative is to admit the odd conclusion that Middleton needed to steal minor additions from *Penniless* at a maturer phase in his career, even when he continued to refer to the original *Comets* in his mock-almanacs and other texts.

In two places, the revisions may have biographical import. The source for ll. 320-2 read, 'they that will sail without compass, may have shipwreck without remedy' (*Comets*, C2ᵛ). The change to 'they that go to sea without victuals may suffer penury' may be recalling the plight of Middleton's stepfather, who was among Ralegh's marooned and starving crew Drake brought back from Roanoke Island in 1586.

The second alteration suggests that the reviser was involved with the theatre. By changing 'prank it on the stage' (*Comets*, C1) to 'prank about the new playhouse' (ll. 247-8) the brunt of the joke is shifted from players to the sharpers in the audience. *Penniless* also rejects a censure of players: 'as famous in idleness, as dissolute in living' (*Comets*, B2). Among contemporary playwrights, Dekker is the only one whose work contains several echoes of *Penniless*, and the major ones are listed below.

32 old Prime, the keeper of Bedlam dicing house] For an instance of the link between 'midsummer' madness and 'old Priam', compare: 'Whilst Troy was swilling sack and sugar, and mousing fat venison, the mad Greeks made bonfires of their houses: old *Priam* was drinking a health to the wooden horse, and before it could be pledged had his throat cut' (*Wonderful Year*, p. 25, ll. 1-5).

176 great noise of wars in taverns] 'those terrible noises...that live by red lattices and ivy-bushes' (*The Bellman of London*, p. 307).

183 building in steeples] 'do jackdaws dung the top of Paul's steeple still' (*Westward Ho*, 2.1.31-2); 'Some (seeing me so patient to endure crows and daws) pecking at my ribs, have driven tame partridges over my bosom' (*The Dead Term*, D4).

218-19 (if candles could tell tales)] 'to throttle him [candlelight] from telling tales' (*The Seven Deadly Sins*, D3).

232 Turk] 'turned to a Turk, and set in Finsbury for boys to shoot at' (*The Shoemaker's Holiday*, 2.3.55-6).

270-1 St Thomas onions shall be sold by the rope] 'two hundred pounds in St Thomas's onions...they could get wenches enough to cry and sell them by the rope' (*Lantern and Candlelight*, p. 331).

351 bestow a new suit of satin] 'I will bestow on you a suit of satin, | And all things else to fit a gentleman' (*2 Honest Whore*, 3.2.139-40).

The parallels hardly amount to evidence for the authorship of *Penniless*, since none except the first concerns the changes and additions to Smellknave's text.

Swapan Chakravorty

SEE ALSO

Text: *Works*, 2003
Textual introduction and apparatus: this volume, 469

WORKS CITED

Bullen, A. H., ed., *Works* (1885-6)
Chambers, E. K., *The Elizabethan Stage*, 4 vols (1923)
Edwards, Philip and Gibson, Colin, eds., *The Plays and Poems of Philip Massinger*, 5 vols (1976)
Grosart, A. B., ed., *The Works of Gabriel Harvey*, 3 vols (1884-5)
Hazlitt, W. C., ed., *Shakespeare Jest-Books*, 3 vols (1864)
Wickham, Glynne, *Early English Stages: 1300 to 1600*, 3 vols (1959-81)
Wilson, F. P., ed., *The Plague Pamphlets of Thomas Dekker* (1925)
Wilson, F. P., *Shakespearian and Other Studies*, ed. Helen Gardner (1969)

Caesar's Fall; or, Two Shapes   May 1602

For this work, see Feldmann and Tetzeli von Rosador, 'Lost Plays', in *Works*, 328.

The Chester Tragedy   October–November 1602

For this work, see Feldmann and Tetzeli von Rosador, 'Lost Plays', in *Works*, 328.

Friar Bacon and Friar Bungay   December 1602

For this work, see Feldmann and Tetzeli von Rosador, 'Lost Plays', in *Works*, 330.

The Phoenix   1603-4

Few critics have doubted that Thomas Middleton is the author of *The Phoenix*, although his name does not appear on the editions of 1607 or 1630, nor in the Stationers' Register entries of the same years. Middleton's name was first associated with the play in 1661, when Francis Kirkman ascribed the play to 'Tho. Middleton' in his catalogue of English plays (*BEPD* 1138-52). The only critic to cast serious doubt on Middleton's sole authorship was Daniel B. Dobson who in 1954 offered internal evidence that small portions of the play were written by Dekker. Dobson, however, found his arguments refuted convincingly by Brooks in 1965 (Brooks, 27–40), and by David Lake in 1975 (Lake, 31). Brooks's efforts to determine Middleton's sole authorship on the basis of mostly linguistic and thematic evidence are, by Brooks's own admission, inconclusive (41–60). But Lake argues with justifiable confidence that 'The Phoenix is certainly Middleton's, as it exhibits nearly the full range of features' which characterize A Game at Chess, a work of which Middleton's authorship is beyond question (Lake, 31).

The Phoenix was entered in the Stationers' Register on 9 May 1607; but it was written earlier, probably between the spring of 1603 and early 1604. The title-page of the 1607 quarto tells us that the play was performed before James I by the 'Children of Paules'. A possible date of the performance, 20 February 1604, can be established with some certainty. E. K. Chambers quotes from a letter by Philip Gawdy stating that 'Ther hath bene ij playes this shroftyde before the king and ther shall be an other to morrow' (Gawdy, 141; Chambers, IV, 118 n. 4). One of these 'ij playes' may well have been The Phoenix. Separate entries in the Chamber Accounts record two payments of £10 each made on 20 February 1604 to Prince Henry's company and to 'Edward Pearce m^r of the children of Powles' (Chambers, IV, 169). Since there is no indication that the Paul's Boys performed before the King at court at any other time, it is reasonable to conclude that one of the plays referred to by Gawdy is the same for which the Paul's Boys were paid on 20 February 1604; and, if the title-page of the 1607 quarto speaks true, that play was The Phoenix. This, then, also establishes the latest possible date of composition. Internal evidence, based on style and on two topical allusions, can be used to establish an earliest possible date. The style, which indicates early Middleton, is detailed in Brooks. The topical allusions are to 'Irish money' (10.144) and James's carpet knights. As Maxwell points out, Irish money refers to debased coins which the crown of England imposed on the Irish between 1601 and 1603. The twice-repeated joke at the expense of knights (he's no gentleman, sir, he is only a knight [6.148, 9.3–4]), Maxwell argues, refers to James's 'promiscuous creation of knights' in the spring of 1603 as he made his way from Edinburgh to London.

Lawrence Danson and Ivo Kamps

SEE ALSO

Text: *Works*, 94
Textual introduction and apparatus: this volume, 529

WORKS CITED

Brooks, John Bradbury, ed., *The Phoenix* (1980)
Chambers, E. K., *The Elizabethan Stage*, 4 vols (1923)
Dobson, Daniel B., 'Thomas Middleton's City Comedies' (dissertation, Columbia, 1954)
Gawdy, Philip, *Letters of Philip Gawdy of West Harling*, ed. Isaac Herbert Jeayes (1906)
Maxwell, Baldwin, 'Middleton's *The Phoenix*', *Joseph Quincy Adams Memorial Studies*, James G. McManaway, Giles E. Dawson, Edwin E. Willoughby, eds. (1948)

News from Gravesend   Late 1603

The pamphlet describes the severe outbreak of plague which began in May 1603. The only surviving early edition is dated 1604. The prose epistle was written 'in the tail of the plague' (25–7) and 'now at Christmas' (39–41), which must refer to the Christmas season of 1603–4. The poem which follows was, as Wilson noted (p. 232), apparently written earlier: 'Come back again' (959) makes it clear that the runaways have not yet returned, and implies a date in the autumn of 1603.

The separate dates of composition may be relevant to problems of attribution. The work was originally published anonymously. The prose epistle, which appears to have been written later than the poem, is consistently written in the first person singular, which occurs 80 times. By contrast, the first person plural occurs only seven times. Six of those plurals, moreover, are general references to Englishmen, and only one refers to the author(s): 'Accept... these curtal rhymes of ours' (694–5). Significantly, this sole instance of the plural refers to the plural authorship of the poetry, not the epistle itself. In the verse, these pronoun proportions are completely reversed: the first person singular occurs only seven times, and the plural 57 times. Moreover, only one of those singulars is authorial ('my verse', 912). By contrast, most of the plural pronouns in the poem are authorial, from the first verse lines to the last. The poem begins as 'We drink a health in wholesome rhyme' (443), then addresses Apollo ('we invoke thy aid', 444), and proceeds with appeals to 'Arm us', 'Teach us', and 'Inspire us'; it ends with another appeal to 'Make us' and a reference to 'our prophesying pen'. Throughout, the poetry is described as a joint product: 'our verse', 'our tragic song', 'our strong verse', 'our ink', 'our lines', 'our panting muse', 'our verse', 'our muse'. And the action which produces this verse is also plural: 'we will write', 'we'll mix', 'how can we choose | But have a sad and drooping muse', 'we write', 'We must not lose you... Whose acts we one day may rehearse | In marble numbers', 'We mean not', 'We would conclude'. On the basis of this consistent pattern of pronoun use, it seems reasonable to conclude that the verse was originally written by two or more authors, one of whom later single-handedly wrote the prose epistle.

The prose epistle appears to have been written entirely by Dekker; as Wilson noted and as our own investigations have confirmed, it is full of parallels to Dekker's acknowledged works, and no one has noticed any significant parallels with the Middleton canon. Dekker was also undoubtedly responsible for parts of the verse: Wilson observed in particular that the apostrophe to London (beginning at 744) also occurs, virtually verbatim, in Dekker's share of *Magnificent Entertainment*, written at about the same time. But Wilson himself noted four consecutive significant parallels (between 1026–7 and 1055) to *The Black Book* and *The Puritan*. He also recorded a number of striking parallels between *Gravesend* and *Meeting*. (See the discussion of the authorship of *Meeting*, below.) Wilson's own evidence thus suggests that the two authors of the verse were Dekker and Middleton, who were clearly collaborating on other projects in 1602–4. Moreover, *Gravesend* was printed by Thomas Creede, who also in 1604 printed *Black Book* and *Hubburd* (by Middleton) and *Meeting* and *Magnificent Entertainment* (by Middleton and Dekker).

This conclusion has been reinforced by two investigations of verbal parallels: Roger Holdsworth (looking for Middleton parallels) and Robert Maslen (looking for Dekker parallels). Holdsworth (private communication, February 1992) proposed that Middleton wrote the last seven pages of the pamphlet, citing parallels from 980 to 1159. (I have added to his list further parallels at 989 and 1052–3.)

980–7 the usurer...flesh...gold Turns into tokens... chest...infectious breast...When all his coin... golden] 'usurers...amongst their golden hills: when I have changed Their gold into dead tokens, with the touch Of my pale-spotted and infectious rod, When with a sudden start and ghastly look, They have left counting coin, to count their flesh, And sum up their last usury on their breasts, All their whole wealth locked in their bony chests' (*Meeting* 74–84)

989 heaven, earth, and seas] 'earth, the sea, or heaven' (*No Wit* 1.67)

990–3 covetous rooting mole (That heaves his dross above his soul...To die...stamped full of] 'covetous rooting moles That heave their gold thrice higher than their souls...to die stamped full of' (*Meeting* 86–7, 97)

995 (being boiled in wine)] '(gone to bed in wine)' (*Revenger* 1.3.60)

998 his saint] For the figurative use of 'his saint', compare *Valour* 5.3.184, *Quarrel* 1.1.21, 4.3.6, *Changeling* 1.1.158, 5.3.53.

1003–19 drunken men...More than tavern-tokens new Stamped upon his breast and arms...he'll scarce have Time to go sober to his grave. And then to die...none can reel to heaven] 'What is't to die stamped full of drunken wounds, Which makes a man reel quickly to his grave' (*Meeting* 97–8)

1006 Stamped] For afflictions 'stamped' upon their victims see *Weapons* 2.1.28, *Widow* 5.1.128, *Hengist* 5.2.89, *Women Beware* 4.2.37

1019 none can reel to heaven] 'reel to hell' (*Ghost* 508, *Revenger* 5.1.51), 'a drunkard now to reel to the devil' (*Witch* 1.2.233–4)

1026–7 The adulterous and luxurious spirit Pawned to hell and sin's hot merit] 'spirit Pawned to luxurious and adulterous merit' (*Black Book* 51). Middleton rhymes 'spirit' and 'merit' at *Solomon* 3.113–4 and

3.119–20, *Ghost* 423–5, *Quarrel* 5.1.427–8, *Antiquity* 224–5.

1028 his leprous soul] *Women Beware* 5.1.246

1030–7 blood...infernal flood...The heat of all his damned desires...fires, His riots...His marrow wasted] 'O that marowless age Would stuff the hollow bones with damned desires, And stead of heat kindle infernal fires' (*Revenger* 1.1.5–7, followed by 'blood' and 'riot', ll. 10–11)

1043 Lazy lieutenants without bands] 'villainous lieutenant without a band' (*Black Book* 153–4)

1044 muffled half-faced] 'half-faced, muffled' (*Puritan* 3.5.4)

1049–50 Two gnawing poisons cannot lie In one corrupted flesh together] 'Two kings on one throne cannot sit together' (*Women Beware* 5.1.264), 'gnawn With poison' (*Revenger* 5.1.100–101)

1052–5 not a strumpet...Dreads this contagion or his threats, Being guarded with French amulets] 'harlots...armed (as they term it) against all weathers of plague and pestilence, carrying always a French supersedeas about them for the sickness' (*Meeting* 372–4)

1052–3 a strumpet...That lives and rises by her fall] 'Rise, strumpet, by my fall' (*Women Beware* 4.2.43); for the paradox see also *Phoenix* 13.41, *Hubburd* 1069, *Michaelmas* 1.3.44, *Yorkshire* 2.179, *Revenger* 1.2.183–4, 4.2.189, *Lady* A2.1.166–7.

1073–4 this stroke of force That turns the world into a corse] 'If a bastard's wish might stand in force, Would all the court were turned into a corse' (*Revenger* 1.2.35–6)

1076 Emptying whole houses to fill graves] 'whole households emptied to fill up graves' (*Meeting* 607–8)

These parallels, concentrated in less than one hundred lines of text, seem to me absolutely convincing: they involve complex concatenations of language and image. I am not convinced by Holdsworth's parallels for the conclusion of the pamphlet: the use of the adjective 'speckled' (1077), an allusion to Aesculapius (1110), a proverbial reference to mushrooms (1113), and an identification of 'carbuncles' and 'blains' as symptoms of the plague (1159). All can be matched by Dekker.

Maslen's examination of verbal links between *Gravesend* and the Dekker canon (private communication, January 1994) usefully supplements the work of Wilson and Holdsworth. In 503–917, Maslen identifies additional striking parallels with Dekker's *Wonderful Year*, *English Villainies*, and *Rod for Runaways*. In the lines which contain a sudden concentration of Middleton links, he has not found a single parallel of comparable intensity. The end of the pamphlet yields three parallels, between 1080–141, all to *Wonderful Year*. The parallels between *Gravesend* and *Wonderful Year* are widely scattered through the latter, and (despite the suspicions of Holdsworth) there seems to me at present no reason to suspect Middleton's hand anywhere in that pamphlet. Therefore the parallels at the end of the pamphlet suggest Dekker's authorship, rather than Middleton's.

MacDonald P. Jackson (private communication, February 1994) adds some further indications that Middleton may be responsible for 972–1076. The aphetic form ''mongst' (common in Middleton) occurs three times in these lines, and nowhere else in the pamphlet. More important, the percentage of feminine endings in this passage is 20.8 (22 out of 106 lines), whereas that for the rest of the poem is 8.2 (50 in 612 lines). 'A chi-square test (with Yates's correction) yields...a probability of considerably less than 1 in 1000 that the difference is due to chance.' These figures would be even more striking if the Middleton section were assumed to begin at 980 (where the strong Middleton parallels actually start), because lines 972–9 contain no feminine endings.

It is possible that Middleton was responsible for short passages elsewhere in the poem, and also possible that some passages result from mixed writing; further investigation may be able to trace his presence elsewhere. But we have here attributed to him, conservatively, only one passage, which contains sustained evidence of his work. The exact borders of this passage are open to dispute. Middleton may have continued writing after 1076, but there is no clear evidence that he did so, and the awkward mid-sentence shift from a repeatedly singular infestation ('season...stroke...it') to a plural one ('plagues...are... they're') could be the result of a change of authors. There is another minor inconsistency near the beginning of the Middleton parallels. At 962–71, the poem warns the magistrates who have abandoned London that if they do not return now, they may face, later, 'A deadlier siege'. This is characterized as a 'bold thought', which calls for 'pardon'; the implication would seem to be that the citizens who have been abandoned by their leaders will, when those leaders finally return, rebel against them. What follows, at 972, is something rather different: not a prediction of rebellion, but a sustained fantasy about the plague attacking the city's wealthiest inhabitants (those who have fled). Moreover, the claim ''Tis now the beggars' plague' (972) might seem to contradict the portraits, earlier in the poem, of rich Londoners struck down by the disease. These are minor inconsistencies, which would almost certainly not be noticed by any reader, but they could result from a shift of author. And the sarcastic phrase 'most tragical' (979) also occurs in Black Book 273 and Plato's Cap 308. Certainly, if Dekker had ended 'The horror of the plague' at 971 (or 979), and begun 'The cure of the plague' at 1077, the join would have been more seamless than it is now.

Wilson concluded that Gravesend was probably composed before Meeting. His evidence is hardly conclusive, but Middleton's share of Gravesend belongs to the poem, which does seem to have been written in the autumn, and therefore to be earlier than Meeting.

Gary Taylor

SEE ALSO

Text: *Works*, 132
Textual introduction and apparatus: this volume, 474

WORK CITED

Wilson, F. P., ed., *The Plague Pamphlets of Thomas Dekker* (1925)

Father Hubburd's Tales Early January 1604

Middleton's text was entered in the Stationers' Register on 3 January 1604 with the variant title *The Nyghtingale and the Ante. A Jove surgit opus*, evidence that a manuscript that had not yet been modified for the printing project was presented at Stationers' Hall for licensing. The printed editions bear the variant titles *The Ant and the Nightingale, or Father Hubburd's Tales* (CREEDE 1) and *Father Hubburd's Tales, or the Ant and the Nightingale* (CREEDE 2). Middleton's *The Black Book* was entered ten weeks later on 22 March 1604. These three editions were printed by Thomas Creede using his large sixteen-point roman fount for setting a preliminary text in each. There is no reason to doubt that the sequence of entry dates reflects the dates (including the usual lead time for preparations) of the printing of CREEDE 1 and *The Black Book*. However, the printing of CREEDE 2 did not immediately follow CREEDE 1. The sixteen-point roman type used in 'To the Reader' in CREEDE 1 was distributed for another intervening printing job, requiring a resetting of that text for the printing of CREEDE 2. Similarly, all of the pica roman and pica black letter used in the main text was distributed between printings. Thus the printing date of CREEDE 2 cannot be determined precisely, but it definitely was separated from the printing of CREEDE 1 by at least one other printing job.

The attribution of the work to Middleton is based upon the fact that the epistle 'To the Reader' is signed 'T.M.' (in combination with ubiquitous parallels with Middleton's other works).

The date of composition coincides with Middleton's pamphlet writing activity during the closing of the theatres in 1603–4. However, the composition of the work appears to have been an ongoing process. It seems likely that Middleton first completed and sold the manuscript containing *The Nyghtingale and the Ante* to Thomas Bushell and then wrote the preliminaries ('To the Reader' and 'The Epistle Dedicatory') in preparation for the printing of CREEDE 1. But Middleton did not completely execute his concept of the expanded work in time for the first edition. Those two preliminary texts require the second edition's addition of the third tale (The Scholar's Tale) and its associated verse links for completeness. The gist of the reference to Queen Elizabeth's death 'They that forget a queen, soothe with a king' (200) suggests composition later (perhaps considerably later) than April 1603, as do the references to James I's selling of knighthoods ('hundred-pound feat of arms', 6) and to his early reign (222–5). In addition, Gary Taylor has noted that the rather specific reference 'our gentleman slept not there all the Christmastime, but had been at court and at least in five masques' (650–3) probably refers to masques and entertainments at court during the Christmas 1603 holiday (although the number might be exaggerated). Four other references also indicate that Middleton was attempting during composition to evoke a very current setting relative to the printing date. The description of the ploughmen's ruined Christmas (637–44) certainly has that effect. More importantly, the ploughmen return to London 'three days before the term' (648–9), a reference to Hilary term which usually commenced on January 13. Given the amount of time required for the preparation and printing of CREEDE 1, the earliest readers of CREEDE 1 could have assumed that the ploughmen's disaster had just happened. Similarly, the plot to arrest Clutch-Fist described in the Epistle Dedicatory (16–27) is planned for Candlemas term which commenced on February 2, a week or two after the book would have appeared in book shops. Finally, The Soldier's Tale concludes in the very frosty weather of winter. As a whole, these temporal references merely evoke a current holiday setting as opposed to a sequence of events—the ant's three experiences as a human could not have concluded almost simultaneously, nor could he have told the tales to Philomel during the previous summer/autumn. Nonetheless, the references suggest that the printed text of CREEDE 1 most likely represents what Middleton had completed by early January 1604, while the additions in CREEDE 2 were written between the printing of CREEDE 1 and CREEDE 2.

Adrian Weiss

SEE ALSO

Text: *Works*, 164
Textual introduction and apparatus: this volume, 476

The Meeting of Gallants at an Ordinary
January–February 1604

For the purposes of establishing Middleton's authorship, there is little new data to add to Lake's analysis of spelling and lexical evidence. This evidence includes Middletonian features such as '-cst' endings, preterite or past participle forms ending in '-de', favoured Middleton interjections such as 'marry', 'puh', and ''sfoot', and echoes of phrases in *The Black Book*, *Father Hubburd's Tales*, and early Middleton plays. Several of these parallels have been adduced by Wilson; others are recorded below.

To this evidence, however, must be added Gary Taylor's case for Thomas Dekker's part-authorship. As it happens, the parallels with Middleton's works are found in the verse 'Dialogue' and the first seven and one half pages of the prose section. With the exception of the final twenty lines of the pamphlet, the concluding two and one half pages supply no Middleton parallels, but seven parallels with Dekker's works (Wilson). The conclusion seems to be by Middleton since it contains one parallel and an example of his characteristic '-cst' ending (Lake). Definitive

statements about the precise division of authorship are clearly out of the question here, but on the basis of internal evidence it is reasonable to attribute the pamphlet principally to Middleton with an addition by Dekker very near the text's conclusion.

As Wilson pointed out, *The Meeting of Gallants* was probably written in late January or early February 1604. Shuttlecock and Jinglespur have not seen each other since 'the decease of July', and Jinglespur remarks later that 'the moon hath had above six great bellies since we walked here last together'. Also, James's 15 March entry into London is not mentioned. To this evidence can be added Shuttlecock's remark that 'the bells ringing all about London as if the Coronation day had been half a year long'. James's Coronation took place 25 July.

Middleton Parallels

6   Hole-stopping prisoners] *Hubburd*, 1043–4 'stop some prison hole with me'

70   double-damnèd] *Game*, 2.2.62, 'that would double-damn him'; *Black Book*, 28, 'it doubly damns the Devil'

124   Shuttlecock] *Hubburd*, 376–8, 'His head was dressed up in white feathers like a shuttlecock, which agreed...well with his brain (being nothing but cork)'

124   Jinglespur] *Hubburd*, 417–18, 'he walked the chamber with such a pestilent jingle that his spurs over-squeaked the lawyer'

153   satin] *Black Book*, 229–30, 'that smooth glittering devil satin'

156   hell] *Black Book*, 48, 'hell the very shop-board of the earth'

188   black gentleman the Term] The leading figure in the Induction to *Michaelmas Term* is the term itself, attired in 'civil black'.

357   worthy Stow's *Chronicle*] *Puritan*, 4.2.305–6, 'This were wonderful and worthy Stow's *Chronicle*.'

Paul Yachnin

SEE ALSO

Text: *Works*, 186
Textual introduction and apparatus: this volume, 491

WORK CITED

Wilson, F. P., ed., *The Plague Pamphlets of Thomas Dekker* (1925)

Plato's Cap
March 1604

Wilson was the first to suggest the possibility of Middleton's authorship. He found that *Plato's Cap* had 'the same racy and spirited style' as Dekker and Middleton's prose-works of the period, and continued: 'I am not rash enough to attribute *Plato's Cap* to Middleton, still less to Dekker, but the perusal of it is to be recommended to any editor of Middleton. I observe...that *Plato's Cap* was published jointly by Geoffrey Chorlton...and Thomas Bushell, that *Father Hubbard's Tales* was published by Bushell and sold by Chorlton, that Chorlton also published *The Black*

Book, and that Anthony Wood's copy of *Plato's Cap* in the Bodleian is bound up with *The Wonderfull Year*, *The Meeting of Gallants*, and *The Black Book*'.

In addition to the circumstantial evidence and the general sense of recognition the text arouses in scholars familiar with Middleton, there is also persuasive internal evidence. Jackson (1982) pointed out the use of the unusual verb 'lin' ('whose tongues will never lin jangling' [76-7]) in the pamphlet. In his census of 132 early modern English plays, Lake found no examples of the combinaton of 'lin' + present participle in non-Middleton plays, but six in plays by Middleton and one other instance in *The Black Book*. Roger Holdsworth (private communication) adduced both 'give them their due' and 'son and heir' as Middletonisms in *Plato's Cap*, and indeed, as Lake has shown, they are as commonplace in Middleton as they are rare in other writers of the period. Finally, *Plato's Cap*'s 'Satin is the chiefest devil' and 'Velvet that old reveller' (306-7) echoes *The Black Book*'s 'glittering devil satin, and that old reveller velvet' (229-30). To this evidence can be added numerous verbal parallels with Middleton's other works (see below), an allusion to a play by Marlowe (a common feature of Middleton's prose works), and a fondness for satirizing almanacs.

Plato's Cap was entered in the Stationers' Register 21 March 1604. There is no external way, however, of setting a *terminus ad quo*, although the material of the pamphlet was, of course, current in 1604 ('The revolution of this present year 1604'), and Middleton was at that juncture perhaps compelled by the closing of the theatres to write for the popular press. It seems likely that *Plato's Cap* would have been written just after *The Meeting of Gallants*. Since the latter was written in late January or early February, a probable time of composition for *Plato's Cap* is February or March 1604. It is important to note in this regard that the Almanac year began in March, so that *Plato's Cap* would have been a new-year publication, timed more or less to issue alongside the crop of regular almanacs.

Middleton Parallels

1 laxative of laughter] *Puritan*, 3.5.87-8, 'I am of such a laxative laughter that, if the devil himself stood by, I should laugh in his face'

77 never lin jangling] *Widow*, 5.1.205-6, 'never lin wagging'; *Black Book*, 348: 'never lin galloping'

127 prisoners...holes] *Hubburd*, 1043-4 'stop some prison hole with me'

256 white feather] The landlord's son in *Hubburd*, 376-7, trades his father's estate for fashionable frivolities, one of which is a hat of 'white feathers'.

268 six to one] *Puritan*, 3.3.30-3, 'I have been one of the six myself that has dragged as tall men of their hands, when their weapons have been gone, as ever bastinadoed a sergeant'

302-3 sew...out] *Meeting of Gallants*, 250-1, 'sewing of false seeds, which peep out'

304-5 hell...linings] *Black Book*, 48-50: 'hell the very shop-board of the earth, | Where, when I [i.e., the Devil] cut out souls, I throw the shreds | And the white linings of a new-soiled spirit'

306-7 Satin...reveller] cf. *Black Book*, 229-30: 'devil satin, and that old reveller velvet'

312 false bodice] *Black Book*, 142-3, 'false bodice'

337 reel-pots] *Black Book*, 487, 'reel-pots' (*OED* cites *Black Book* as only instance)

Paul Yachnin

SEE ALSO

Text: *Works*, 198
Textual introduction and apparatus: this volume, 492

WORKS CITED

Jackson, MacDonald P., 'An Allusion to Marlowe's *The Jew of Malta* in an Early Seventeenth-Century Pamphlet Possibly by Thomas Middleton', *Notes and Queries*, NS 29 (1982), 132-3

Wilson, F. P., 'Some English Mock-Prognostications', *The Library*, IV, 19 (1938), 6-43

The Black Book   March 1604

There is little reason to doubt *The Black Book*'s long--accepted place in the Middleton canon. *The Epistle to the Reader* is signed by a T.M. who has intimate knowledge of Oxford, London, and the theatre, and the pamphlet, as David Lake points out, bears a number of Middleton's stylistic trademarks: the use of 'lin', 'luxur', 'puh', 'faith', 'marry', 'they're', and the preference for 'amongst' and 'beside.' Lake also points to the Italian backside joke (474-6) as a Middleton marker. To this one might add instances of Middleton's early propensity for bilingual puns or playful etymological refinements of meaning in such items as 'shoe-penny' (706), where he plays on *chopine* (pronounced *cioppini*), and 'geometrical' (309-10), where he savours the Greek roots. H. Dugdale Sykes argued the integral place of the pamphlet in Middleton's early works in 1925, and R. V. Holdsworth has recently pointed out (and made persuasive critical use of) parallels between *The Black Book*'s disguised anatomizing observer and that same device in almost all Middleton's early plays. All such evidence is circumstantial, of course, but its cumulative weight places the onus surely (and perhaps impossibly) on the disintegrator to prove a case for any other authorship candidate.

The xylograph title-page, used in both editions of *The Black Book*, is dated 1604. Middleton evidently composed the pamphlet between autumn of 1603 and early spring of 1604, well after the funeral of Queen Elizabeth (28 April 1603, mentioned at 427-8) and 'the last plaguy summer' (211-12) which followed. *The Black Book* was licensed on 22 March [1604], and summer might seem to be just around the corner once again as the pamphlet appears: there is a shadowed suggestion (771-3) that Lucifer's visit coincides with Easter, and Lieutenant Frig-beard is already lamenting the unfortunate origins of his new summer suit (372–4).

G. B. Shand

SEE ALSO

Text: *Works*, 207

Textual introduction and apparatus: this volume, 493

WORKS CITED

Holdsworth, R. V., ed, *Three Jacobean Tragedies* (1990)

Sykes, H. Dugdale, 'Thomas Middleton's Early Non-Dramatic Works', *Notes and Queries* 148 (20 June 1925), 435–8

The Magnificent Entertainment   1603–4

The planning and preparation of the pageants accompanying the royal entry of 15 March 1604 is relatively well documented in references scattered through the State Papers Domestic of the Public Record Office (London), the Cecil papers at Hatfield House and records of the London Corporation. Initial planning began very shortly after Elizabeth's death in March of 1603 and must have proceeded rapidly, since the entry was originally intended to take place in July, on the day of James's coronation. A major outbreak of plague resulted in a decision, apparently reached toward the end of June, to postpone the entry indefinitely. By January it had been rescheduled to take place during Lent, although the exact date remained unsettled until mid-February.

The pageant speeches and arches that have come down to us therefore could have been written and designed at any time between early spring of 1603 and late winter of the next year. Probably most of the pageants were well along by the time the decision to postpone was reached, but it seems likely that revisions and additions continued until a date shortly before the entry itself. Evidence that has so far come to light does not permit more definite conclusions.

Ben Jonson his Part of King James his Royal and Magnificent Entertainment was registered with the Stationers' Company on 19 March, and Thomas Dekker's *Magnificent Entertainment* on 2 April. Harrison's *Arches of Triumph* apparently was never entered in the Stationers' Register, although the title-page bears the date 1604. It would have been produced as quickly as possible, before interest in the event it commemorated had had time to cool, probably soon after 16 June, the date of its dedicatory epistle.

Middleton's speech for Zeal at the fifth arch is recorded in Dekker's text, which also provides the authority for its attribution.

R. Malcolm Smuts

SEE ALSO

Text: *Works*, 224

Textual introduction and apparatus: this volume, 498

The Patient Man and the Honest Whore
March–September 1604

Although Middleton is not named on the title-page of the early editions, Henslowe's payment of £5 some time in 1604 prior to 14 March to 'Thomas Dekker and Middleton in earnest of their play called the patient man and the honest whore' lends firm external support to him as a collaborator on the play. The title-page ascription to Thomas Dekker alone, as David J. Lake suggested, may have arisen from the publisher supplying the name. Recent studies of Middleton's involvement allot him a substantial share of the writing as well as a probable hand in its shaping, though a distinctly smaller portion than Dekker.

Henslowe's record of the play points to early 1604 as the date of composition. But Hippolito's servant's jocular remark, 'Indeed, that's harder to come by than ever was Ostend' (10.31–2), is a topical allusion to the siege of Ostend by Spanish forces from 5 July 1601 to 11 September 1604. The reference seems to imply that the siege had ended, which would situate it after 11 September 1604. If so, the allusion presumably represents an addition made in the course of the play's theatrical run, which suggests further that *The Patient Man and the Honest Whore* was still on the stage in the latter part of 1604.

In his review of linguistic evidence bearing on the authorship and collaborative shares of *The Patient Man and the Honest Whore* MacDonald P. Jackson notes the play's metrical homogeneity and correspondence of its metrical characteristics to Dekker's work. He also draws attention to the appearance of a range of oaths and exclamations favoured by Dekker and shunned by Middleton that occur throughout the play (e.g. 'in God's name', 'alack', 'sblood', 'O God', 'God so', 'God's my life', 'sheart', 'Godamercy', 'zounds', 'by God', 'God's my pittikins', 'tush', 'snails', 'marry gup', 'plague found you', 'God bless him', and other oaths that invoke the deity). Against these he observes a number of characteristic Middleton forms (e.g. 'for't' × 8, 'on't' × 4, 'puh' × 4, and 'heart' × 1). In addition twelve examples of what Jackson cites as 'the eleven most distinctively Middletonian expletives' occur (besides the four instances of 'puh': 'la you'/'why la' × 6, 'beshrew…heart' × 1, and 'cuds' in the form 'cods life'); and 'e'en', encountered only twice in six Dekker plays, turns up on nine occasions in *The Patient Man and the Honest Whore*. A peculiarity of the disposition of linguistic forms, however, is that they tend not to be concentrated in specific scenes, which defeats the task of identifying with any certainty the extent of Middleton's contribution. The linguistic data nevertheless lead Jackson to conclude that 'Middleton must have had a hand not merely in the planning of the play but in the actual writing of it too.' He further notes in support of the first two of Scenes 5, 7, and 9, which reveal clear signs of Middleton's presence, that they are almost entirely free of parentheses—a Dekker trait—containing only one parenthesis each as against 59

351

parentheses in the rest of the play. Although he records G. R. Price's contention that Middleton's responsibility mainly concerned the scenes in which Candido is tested, in an effort to explain the inconsistencies in linguistic evidence more or less throughout Jackson proposes that 'Middleton wrote the first draft of some scenes and perhaps even of a large portion of the play, but that Dekker was largely responsible for its final form.' Such an explanation would in his view square with various signs of Dekker's presence, including the mixture of Middleton and Dekker forms in many scenes, the relatively low proportion of three-syllable Latin words, and the likelihood that the manuscript from which the play was set was in Dekker's hand.

David J. Lake's examination of linguistic and other evidence relating to collaboration and authorship makes reference to many of the same features noted by Jackson but supplements them with citations of word/phrase collocations found in other plays of Middleton's undoubted authorship. Lake additionally considers *The Patient Man and the Honest Whore* scene by scene (in two instances, part-scenes) drawing attention to discriminators that signal each author. Like Jackson, he finds the strongest evidence of Middleton in Scenes 5 and 7 in which various Middleton expressions bolster the oaths and other features; he divides Sc. 5 into two parts, in the first of which to 5.140 he cites the Middleton forms 'puh' and 'pah' (in contrast to Jackson, he distinguishes these exclamations), 'on't' × 2, the phrase 'sons and heirs' (5.33), the spelling 'Ha's'—for 'he has'—(5.57), and the contraction 'exlent' (5.93). In addition, Lake notes that an 'ay'/'yes' ratio of 5:1 is consistent with Middleton. But Dekker does not appear to be entirely absent from this part of the scene: Lake notes the oath ''sblood' × 2, which suggests Dekker, as well as George's use of 'affable' in his sales pitch at 5.24–5, which occurs in a similar circumstance elsewhere in Dekker. In the second part of the scene, beginning with Candido's Wife's speech at 5.142, Lake finds in the oath 'God's my life' evidence of Dekker's presence, which he feels is confirmed by the oath ''sheart' at 5.216. He further observes that the spelling 'they're' at 5.191 may point to Middleton. This spelling conforms to that encountered in *Hubburd*, which, like the section of *The Patient Man and the Honest Whore* in which it occurs, was printed by Creede.

Lake similarly splits Sc. 7 into two parts: 7.1–60 and 7.61–283. Citing a collection of particularly distinctive features, he claims the first part of the scene to accord closely with an 'early Middletonian manner' ('Spoke like', 7.12; 'faith' × 3; 'troth' × 3; 'mass', 'puh', 'sh'as', and 'ay' but no 'yes'). This section is not entirely free of Dekkerisms, however ('Lacedemonian', 'mallicolly' (melancholy), 'beside'). Lake sees more sustained evidence of Dekker in the second part of the scene ('Sneales' (God's nails); 'as God judge me'; 'O Lord', 'tush', 'it's', 'Omn[es]' × 3). The scene appears to contain signs of Middleton also, however ('ay'/'yes' ratio of 5:2; 'save... harmless', 7.279; 'covert-baron', 7.280), especially in the final speech of George.

Through much of the play's other scenes Lake discerns evidence of both dramatists, but preponderantly of Dekker. In Sc. 1 he notes Dekker's presence in the oaths 'in God's name' (1.5) and ''Sblood' (1.62) and the spelling 'woud' (1.81); but Middleton is signalled by two instances of the speech heading '*All*', the oath 'birlady' (1.106), and an 'ay'/'yes' ratio of 3:1. In Sc. 2 practically all evidence points to Dekker; the only features Lake identifies that may indicate Middleton are the oath 'puh' and a single instance of ''has'. Three instances of the phrase 'la you now', not found in Dekker, and an 'ay'/'yes' ratio of 2:0 in Sc. 3 support Middleton's presence; but Lake finds Infelice's exclamation on waking, 'O God, what fearful dreams?' (3.36) and the verse up to this point (without further comment) more likely to be Dekker's. Although the indicators of Sc. 4 are relatively weak, they point in both directions: 'ay' × 3 (no 'yes') and 'on't' × 2 for Middleton; and ''sblood' for Dekker. Scene 6 contains abundant evidence that supports Dekker ('God's my pittikins', 'God's my pity', 'God's so', 'by th'', 'Lord' × 2, 'God-a-mercy', 'umh' × 4, 'wut' (woot), 'wou'd' × 4, 'it's' × 4, 'Omni' × 3 [sic], 'marry-muff' × 2, 'ay'/'yes' 4:10). Against the clear signs of Dekker, however, a number of particularly distinctive Middleton spellings crop up ('e'm': 6.19, 'facst': 6.130, 'fac'st': 6.157) together with the contraction 'T'has' (6.317) and the exclamation 'Pah' (6.259). Lake assigns Sc. 8 to Dekker alone on the basis of the oaths 'God's my life' (8.17), 'God damn me... if' (8.61), and 'marry gup' (8.73) and no significant signs of Middleton. In Sc. 9 he finds evidence of both dramatists: 'Omn[es]', ''Sblood', and the spellings 'th'art' × 3 and 'th'are' suggest Dekker; 'ay'/'yes' 3:0, 'subaudi' (9.20), and 'son and heir' (9.62) point to Middleton. In Sc. 10 Lake discerns relatively little support for Middleton. Evidence is restricted to the phrase 'by their copy' (10.4) and the spelling 'they're' × 2 (in a section printed by Eld, who gives this spelling also in *Five Gallants* and *Trick*). Against these traits he cites the ten pairs of parentheses, some enclosing single words, as signs of Dekker. The brief Sc. 11 contains little clear evidence of either dramatist, but 'God sa' me' (11.42) signals Dekker. Although the oaths ('God's my life', 12.28; ''sblood', 12.74; 'O' God's name', 12.179) and two instances of 'umh' (12.70), indicate Dekker's presence, the 'ay'/'yes' ratio of 10:1 from 12.61 to the end of the scene in conjunction with an instance of 'Troth' (12.34) point to the involvement of Middleton. In the remaining scenes Lake finds relatively few signs of Middleton and a number of features associated with Dekker. Linguistic markers are relatively few in Sc. 13, but against the possible Middleton forms 'w'are' (13.26) and 'Thei'r' (13.33), an instance of 'umh' (13.75) points to Dekker. Sc. 14 contains two Dekker traits: 'It's' (14.75) and 'Omn[es]' and no significant sign of Middleton. The strongest evidence favouring Middleton's presence in the play's final three scenes Lake locates in the Sweeper's speech at 15.126–7, which contains the phrases 'sons and heirs' and 'by... copy'; in addition, two instances of 'mass' and one each of 'on't' and 'comfort' occur. Various traits associated with Dekker are sprinkled through this scene: 'O God' × 2, 'God so' × 2, 'by th' Lord' × 2, 'God's santy', 'tush', 'Omn[es]' × 13, 'wut' × 2, 'it's' × 3, an 'ay'/'yes' ratio of 8:10, and an ''em'/'them' ratio of 14:8.

The overlapping and widely distributed evidence of both Dekker and Middleton leads Lake to conclude that the collaboration between the two dramatists on this play was very close. He further proposes that Middleton may have composed the first drafts of a number of scenes subsequently revised by Dekker. Jackson and Lake thus independently reach much the same conclusion in their attempt to account for the apparent presence of both writers in many scenes though they may differ over certain local allocations.

In addition to linguistic and other traits characteristic of Middleton, situational elements, plotting motifs and strategies, and aspects of characterization found in *The Patient Man and the Honest Whore* emerge in other of his plays. Whether these betray Middleton's involvement here or his subsequent reworking of material or ideas picked up from Dekker is generally impossible to determine. But as several commentators have remarked, Candido has a strong affinity to two other Middleton creations: Quieto in *Phoenix*, which very likely immediately preceded *The Patient Man and the Honest Whore* in sequence of composition and accordingly argues against Middleton's reworking of Dekker, and Water Chamlet, who likewise has a shrewish wife and a servant named George in *Quiet Life* (1621), written considerably later. Further, the distinct change in the character of Candido in *The Honest Whore, Part 2*, which Peter Ure persuasively argues constitutes a fundamental misunderstanding of his nature, prompted this critic to surmise that the Candido of the original play is chiefly a product of Middleton's imagination. A host of elements present in *The Patient Man and the Honest Whore* arises in later Middleton works. As Roger Holdsworth has pointed out, Hippolito's contemplation of his supposed dead beloved over a skull and portrait anticipates the opening of *Revenger*. Another prefiguring of this play occurs at 13.40–5, as Doctor Benedict sketches in a situation close to that faced by Vindice and Hippolito in their final moments. Beyond these correspondences, Cyrus Hoy has drawn attention to a highly characteristic Middleton image that occurs at 9.99–100 in *The Patient Man and the Honest Whore* and 1.3.117–19 and 4.4.79–81 in *Revenger* among other instances in his work. The sham funeral procession interrupted by Hippolito is a motif Middleton would make use of in a string of plays: *Puritan Widow, Michaelmas*, and *Chaste Maid*. And the plot device involving two lovers thought to be dead in *Chaste Maid* is conceivably a development of the situation involving Infelice and Hippolito in *The Patient Man and the Honest Whore*. In addition, Bellafront's circumstance in many respects corresponds to that of the Courtesan in *A Trick to Catch the Old One*. The present play contains the earliest instance in Middleton or Dekker's work of a female disguised as

page—a favourite Middleton device—which together with an imaginary Milan setting occurs in *More Dissemblers*. Further, numerous striking correspondences between *The Patient Man and the Honest Whore* and *Changeling*, two plays that essentially frame the Middleton canon, have been noted by Hoy and others. Chief among these is the unfolding of a serious plot with a parodic parallel action, each of which has at its heart a transformed woman, and a madhouse setting. Middleton returned to and worked over aspects of this early collaboration at various points throughout his subsequent career.

Paul Mulholland

SEE ALSO

Text: *Works*, 285
Textual introduction and apparatus: this volume, 507

WORKS CITED

Holdsworth, Roger, ed., *Three Jacobean Revenge Tragedies* (1990)
Hoy, Cyrus, *Introductions, Notes, and Commentaries to texts in 'The Dramatic Works of Thomas Dekker'*, 4 vols (1980), vol. 2
Price, George R., *Thomas Dekker* (1969)

Michaelmas Term   November–December 1604

Michaelmas Term was entered in the Stationers' Register without notice of its author. The title-pages of neither the 1607 nor the 1630 edition includes a playwright's name. In 1656, due to a typographical error in Rogers and Ley's catalogue appended to *The Careless Shepherdess* (*BEPD*), Chapman is listed as the author of *Michaelmas Term* (Greg sensibly assumes that Chapman's name was meant to follow the masque listed in the following line). The play is first attributed to Thomas Middleton in 1656, in Edward Archer's generally unreliable list published with a quarto edition of *The Old Law* (*BEPD*). The play is then ascribed to Middleton in Francis Kirkman's catalogues of 1661 and 1671 (*BEPD*). The play looks very much like the work of the author of *A Trick to Catch the Old One* and *A Mad World, My Masters*, and Middleton's sole authorship has not been questioned. Linguistically, it fits the pattern of other plays assigned solely to Middleton (Lake, Jackson).

Michaelmas Term was almost certainly written between 1603, following the accession of James I, and early 1606, prior to the last performance of the Children of Paul's (Bald; Maxwell; Levin; Price). The anti-Scots satire centred on Andrew Lethe indicates a post-accession date of composition. Maxwell argues that the 'sixpence British' (1.2.309) that Andrew Lethe gives his mother refers to the new coinage, ordered 11 November 1604, wherein James is styled *Mag. Brit.*. Thomasine's lines at 2.3.226–31 and 378–80 have been taken by some to refer either to the hanging and quartering of Francis Clarke, in Winchester, on 29 November, 1603, or to the execution of Sir Everard Digby, at the west end of St Paul's, on 30 January 1606. However, Maxwell sensibly points out that while this and comparable, contemporary dramatic allusions probably refer to the execution of those involved in the Gunpowder Plot, Middleton may well have had some other, less notorious, public execution in mind. Dekker's *Whore of Babylon* (c.1606–7) includes a passage about 'women at an Execution, that can endure to see men quartred alive' (2.1.112–3).

Falselight's line about the 'passage to Middleburgh' being stopped 2.3.400 represents an uncertain allusion. No particular Spanish blockade, English edict, Dutch attack, or piracy can be adduced with any confidence.

Taken together, the foregoing evidence points to composition at some point between very late 1604 and early 1606. If we account for theatre-closing in time of plague (Barroll), *Michaelmas Term* could have been first performed in November or December 1604, during much of 1605 before October, or in early 1606.

Theodore B. Leinwand

SEE ALSO

Text: *Works*, 337
Textual introduction and apparatus: this volume, 535

WORKS CITED

Bald, R. C., 'The Chronology of Middleton's Plays', *Modern Language Review* 32 (1937), 33–43

Barroll, Leeds, *Politics, Plague, and Shakespeare's Theater: The Stuart Years* (1991)

Levin, Richard, ed., *Michaelmas Term*, Regents Renaissance Drama Series (1966)

Maxwell, Baldwin, 'Middleton's *Michaelmas Term*', *Philological Quarterly* 22 (1943) 29–35

Price, George R., ed., *Michaelmas Term* and *A Trick to Catch the Old One* (1976)

A Trick to Catch the Old One　　Spring 1605

The authorship of *Trick* has never been disputed. The revised title-pages of the first edition of 1608 identify the play as 'Compoſde by T.M.'; the second edition of 1616 spells out the attribution, 'By T. Midleton.' The only ascription to an author other than Middleton was Edward Archer's 1656 identification of 'Will. Shakespeare.' as its author in the 'Catalogue of all the plays that ever were printed' accompanying his edition of *The Old Law* (*BEPD* 766), but W. W. Greg has observed that two out of three of Archer's new attributions were 'careless blunders or irresponsible guesses'. *Trick* was correctly ascribed to 'Tho. Midleton' in Kirkham's Catalogues of 1661 (*BEPD* 820) and 1671.

The play was performed by the Children of Paul's at a time when Middleton was writing other scripts for that company. 1604 is the earliest date accorded it, which is supported by the mention at 4.4.214 of Master Mulligrub, a character from John Marston's *The Dutch Courtesan*. That play was performed sometime from 1603 to 1605 and printed in 1605. The song sung by Audrey at the beginning of 4.5 in *Trick* was written by Thomas Ravenscroft, whose *Melismata* of 1611 prints the music for it as no. 12. Reavley Gair proposes that this song was perhaps Ravenscroft's last contribution to Paul's Boys before he left the company to read music at Cambridge in 1604, adding that Ravenscroft may even

have performed the role of Audrey. George J. Watson and W. J. Lawrence caution, however, that little or no residence at Cambridge would have been required for the B.A. that Ravenscroft received in 1605, so he may have had subsequent associations with the company (1968b).

Sampson tentatively glosses Dampit's reference at 3.4.4 to 'Powis' new buildings', printed in Eld as 'Poouyes', as an allusion to a wooden building in Paul's Churchyard erected by a leathermaker named Povey contrary to orders from James I in 1605 and 1607 prohibiting the use of timber in building construction. Sampson says the building was therefore destroyed, and he cites Stow's *Annals* as his source for this information. Yet I can find no reference to such a building in the relevant editions of the *Annals* continued by Howes and published in 1615 and 1631, which do, however, identify the first proclamation as having a date of 1 March 1605 and remark that it 'took small effect', so that a second was made on 12 October 1607. The passage adds that 'some were censured in the Star Chamber for building contrary to the tenor of the first proclamation' on 16 October 1607 but says nothing about demolition. This information might be read as implying that there was no attempt to enforce the first proclamation before 16 October 1607, in which case the situation would be irrelevant to *Trick* since the play was licensed on 7 October 1607. Without further evidence to support Sampson's gloss, it appears insignificant to attempts to date the play. If, however, a reference to the demolition of Povey's buildings due to the proclamation were found, it would suggest that the play could not have been written before 1 March 1605.

George Watson (1968a) dates the play with reference to two other dramatic texts, Ben Jonson's *Volpone* and Dekker and Webster's *Northward Ho*. He settles on a date of 'some time after late 1605 or early 1606' due to *Trick*'s imitation of the latter. This case is altered in Watson's B.Litt. thesis completed later in the same year (1968b), where no mention is made of *Volpone*, and *Northward Ho* is taken to have been influenced by *Trick*, which leads to a revised date 'in 1604 or possibly early 1605.' Watson adduces the same parallels in each instance between the two plays—the disguise of a whore as a rich gentlewoman, 'the deception of suitors in order to gain money from them, a young man who deceives an older relative about the true identity of the whore, the whore's marriage to somebody more interested in her money than in herself, and the final revelation of the true state of affairs', as well as verbal parallels between *Trick* at 5.2.169–70 and 5.2.177 in this edition and *Northward Ho* at 2.2.11–14 and 3.1.129–32 respectively in Fredson Bowers's edition. I would concur with Watson's second thoughts, although his change of mind offers evidence that the parallels can be read either way.

E. K. Chambers dates *Northward Ho* at the end of 1605, with May, 1605 and February, 1606 as its outer limits. This information would argue for early to mid-1605 as a likely date for the composition of *Trick*, and it has the advantage of correlating with other evidence that from

August 1605 to July 1606, Middleton's calendar was full. It would also suggest that the parallels originally observed by Watson between *Trick* and *Volpone* can now be read as Middleton's having influenced Jonson's comedy. R. B. Parker's 1983 edition of the latter concludes that 'it seems likely...that the play first occurred to [Jonson] in late January or early February 1606; was written in late February and early March; and was first produced before 25 March 1606'. These dates correlate well with a 1605 composition of *Trick*. In support of this possibility, Roger Holdsworth has observed in a note to me that *Volpone*'s opening address to his gold, 'O thou son of Sol,...let me kiss, | With adoration, thee' (1.1.10–12) is similar to Witgood's enthusiastic address to his newly-recovered mortgage, 'Thou soul of my estate, I kiss thee' (4.2.85). Other parallels between the two plays observed by Watson include their subject matter ('the legacy hunting of the one and the rich widow hunting of the other') and the single stratagem of 'a clever schemer's manipulation of the other characters' greed' articulating the intrigue. 'More specifically, the three creditors of *A Trick* resemble the three birds of prey in *Volpone* in their unctuous flattery of their deceiver, in their competitive suspiciousness about one another, and in the uncharacteristic liberality to which they drive themselves in hope of fat rewards' (1968a). These lines of influence traced by Watson and also observed by Brian Gibbons might now be reversed to make Jonson the debtor. His having termed Middleton 'a base fellow' in 1618–19 does not preclude his having reworked Middleton's material.

A terminal date of 1606 has been generally observed for *Trick* on the grounds that the Children of Paul's performed at court for the last time on 30 July 1606. Hence the play might have been written anytime from 1604 to October, 1607, but its likeliest date of composition is in early to mid-1605.

Valerie Wayne

SEE ALSO

Text: *Works*, 377
Textual introduction and apparatus: this volume, 562

WORKS CITED

Chambers, E. K., *The Elizabethan Stage*, 4 vols (1923)
Dekker, Thomas and John Webster, *Northward Ho*, in Thomas Dekker, *Dramatic Works*, ed. Fredson Bowers (1964)
Gair, Reavley, *The Children of Paul's: the story of a theatre company*, 1553–1608 (1982)
Gibbons, Brian, *Jacobean City Comedy*, 2nd edn. (1980)
Holdsworth, R. V., private correspondence, 27 August 1993
Jonson, Ben, *Volpone or, The Fox*, ed. R. B. Parker (1983)
Lawrence, W. J., 'Thomas Ravenscroft's Theatrical Associations', *Modern Language Review* 19 (1924), 418–23
Sampson, Martin W., ed., *Thomas Middleton* (1915)
Stow, John, *The Annals of England*, continued by E. Howes (1615 and 1631)
Watson, George J., ed., *A Trick to Catch the Old One* (1968a)
—— ed., 'A Critical Edition of Thomas Middleton's *A Trick to Catch the Old One* (1608)' (B.Litt. thesis, Oxford, 1968b)

A Mad World, My Masters   Summer 1605

The title-page of the first edition (1608) of *A Mad World, My Masters* asserts that the play '*hath bin lately in Action by the Children of Paules*. Composed by T. M.' The second edition (1640) varies the attribution slightly: 'Composed by *T. M. Gent.*' The author's name is first spelled out as 'Thomas Middleton' in the Catalogue of Edward Archer (1656) (*BEPD*, Archer 364) and as 'Tho. Middleton' in the catalogues of Francis Kirkman (1661, 1671) (*BEPD*, Kirkman 407). Middleton's unaided authorship has never been questioned.

Since Follywit alludes at 1.1.64–5 to James I's widespread bestowal of knighthoods (which began in 1603) and since the theatres were closed by plague until spring 1604, the date of first performance cannot be earlier than the latter year. Henning moreover has pointed out that the reference to 'some hundred pounds in fair spur-royals' (2.6.112–13) indicates a later *terminus a quo*, July 1605. In that month, according to Brooke, minting of these gold coins was renewed for the first time since 1592. Although characters eagerly pursuing money may be allowed some fantasy about the object of their desire, the wear and clipping to which coins were subjected make it unlikely that gold coins in circulation for at least thirteen years would still be considered 'fair'. The last recorded performance of the Paul's boys was in July 1606, and their plays began to reach the Stationers' Register in May 1607. Gair maintains that the company continued performing at least intermittently until 1608, but the documents he quotes are general attacks on the theatre that do not positively assert performance by Paul's boys. We are fairly safe in holding that the play first appeared between midyear 1605 and late 1606.

Peter Saccio

SEE ALSO

Text: *Works*, 417
Textual introduction and apparatus: this volume, 586

WORKS CITED

Brooke, George C., *English Coins from the Seventh Century to the Present Day* 3rd edn. (1950)
Gair, Reavley, *The Children of Paul's: The Story of a Theatre Company, 1553–1608* (1982)
Henning, Standish, ed., *A Mad World, My Masters*, Regents Renaissance (1965)

A Yorkshire Tragedy   1605

The play can have been written no later than 2 May 1608, when it was entered on the Stationers' Register, and no earlier than the publication of the source pamphlet (STC 18288) which was entered on 12 June 1605. Calverley was executed on 5 August 1605. Absence of reference to his fate may simply reflect Middleton's use of a single source. Maxwell however argued that the play was probably finished before Calverley had been sentenced, which would mean that it was written within the weeks immediately following publication of the source. The use of oaths suggests composition before the Act to Restrain Abuses of May 1606.

Attribution to Shakespeare both on the title-page and in the Register is probably a deliberate fraud, and has met with little belief. It may be relevant that another Middleton play, *The Puritan Widow*, had been ascribed to 'W.S.' when it was published not long before *A Yorkshire Tragedy*. Evidence for Middleton as author has grown since Lake published his study, in which he allowed for Shakespeare's possible authorship of the first scene. Jackson's view that Middleton wrote the whole play is strongly supported by Holdsworth. Conceivably, as Taylor suggests, Shakespeare wrote one of the other parts of the four plays in one, but we have no evidence of this composite work other than that provided by *A Yorkshire Tragedy*.

Stanley Wells

SEE ALSO

Text: *Works*, 455
Textual introduction and apparatus: this volume, 592

WORKS CITED

Holdsworth, R. V., '*A Yorkshire Tragedy* and the Date of *Timon of Athens*' (privately circulated, 1993)
—— 'Middleton's Authorship of *A Yorkshire Tragedy*', *Review of English Studies* NS 45 (1994), 1–25
Taylor, Gary, '*A Yorkshire Tragedy*', in Stanley Wells, Gary Taylor, *et al.*, *William Shakespeare: A Textual Companion* (1987), 140–1

Timon of Athens 1605–1606

There are no mentions of *Timon of Athens* before it was entered in the Stationers' Register in 1623 in anticipation of the First Folio of William Shakespeare's *Comedies, Histories, and Tragedies*. An anonymous academic play *Timon* of *c*.1602 (Victoria and Albert Museum, Dyce MS 52) may have some relation to the present work (for the dating, see Bulman), but the nature and direction of any influence are by no means clear. Indeed, the only definite and datable source is Sir Thomas North's translation of Plutarch's 'Life of Marcus Antonius' and 'Life of Alcibiades' in *Lives of the Noble Grecians and Romans* (1579). The terminal dates are thus 44 years apart.

A reference to the Gunpowder Plot of late 1605 is possible at 7.32. Although *Timon* may plausibly have been written at about this period on other grounds, the allusion is too uncertain to give this dating much added credibility or exactitude, and the Plot was remembered by Middleton and others many years after the event. The plausibility of the year 1605 depends on the play's position in the canons of its authors, Shakespeare and Middleton (see below). A Shakespeare–Middleton collaboration printed in the Shakespeare First Folio would almost certainly have been written for the King's Men. Seen in this context, the absence of act divisions in the Folio text gives an immediate clue as to the play's date, for it might suggest that it was written before the company began performing with act intervals in response to their occupancy of the Blackfriars Theatre in August 1608.

Shakespeare drew on the 'Life of Marcus Antonius' for *Julius Caesar* (1599) and for *Antony and Cleopatra* (1606?). When writing *Coriolanus* (1608?), he would have found the 'Life of Alcibiades' paired with that of Coriolanus. Timon is mentioned in both 'Alcibiades' and 'Marcus Antonius', and so it is possible to imagine him coming to Shakespeare's attention as he revisited Plutarch when writing the late Roman plays. On this basis Chambers (1930) is often followed in assigning the play to 'between *Coriolanus* and *Pericles* in 1608' (I.483). However, this inference is insecure, as Shakespeare had studied Plutarch's 'Marcus Antonius' for *Julius Caesar* before 1600, and it takes no account of the absence of act-breaks. Shakespeare probably owned a copy of North's translation, and the bare details of the Timon story had wide currency.

Much more importance must be attached to the evidence arising from internal stylistic tests of the sections of the play attributed to Shakespeare, which also challenges Sandra Billington's case, on the basis of a reference to Timon of Athens in John Marston's *Jack Drum's Entertainment* (1600), for an earlier date. Taylor's colloquialism--in-verse test (Wells and Taylor, 1987) places this portion between *All's Well that Ends Well* (*c*.1604–5) and *Macbeth* (1606) (Wells, Taylor, *et al.*, 1987, p. 128), and Jackson (1979, p. 155), similarly analysing Shakespeare's share for the distribution of rare vocabulary, placed it at 1604–5. These investigations strikingly converge in suggesting that *Timon* was written *c*.1605. It probably precedes *The History of King Lear* (1605–6), the Shakespeare play with which it has the strongest affinities of plot, style, and philosophical disillusionment.

Holdsworth, looking at the Middleton material from the point of view of Middleton's dramatic writing, similarly concluded that the play most convincingly fitted the period 1604–6. During these years Middleton is particularly associated with city comedies performed by the boys' companies, but he also wrote *Yorkshire Tragedy* (1605) and *Revenger's Tragedy* (1606), both, it seems, for Shakespeare's company. There is no period of Middleton's career when a collaboration with Shakespeare on a tragedy would be more likely.

The presence of Shakespeare's hand in the play is uncontested. No work in the 1623 Folio has been discredited as a play written exclusively or at least partly by Shakespeare. The case for Shakespeare is reinforced by the stylistic tests mentioned above: they would not be expected to yield coherent results if the portions tested were not very substantially in his hand. Though Charles Knight suggested that *Timon* might be of joint authorship as early as 1838, it is the presence of the collaborator's hand that needs more strenuous justification.

Certainly the play's inclusion in the Folio does not exclude the possibility of collaboration. *Henry VI Part One* and *All is True* (*Henry VIII*) are other examples of Folio plays that can similarly be ascribed to Shakespeare and others; *Titus Andronicus* may be another. What is unique to the case of *Timon* is that there is bibliographical evidence indicating that the play was not originally planned to have its present place in the collection. A surviving cancel shows that work began on setting *Troilus and Cressida* in the pages finally occupied by *Timon*. Irregularities of format further confirm that the space originally allotted to *Troilus* was reduced so that *Timon* could substitute for it (see Textual Introduction). Either *Timon* was planned to appear later in the volume or it was not planned to appear at all. The first possibility cannot logically be ruled out, but most critics find in these circumstances some support for the view that *Timon* was not originally intended to form part of the collection. If so, the Folio editors chose to exclude it as their first choice and later to include it as an expedient; the play's status within the canon as they saw it is marginal. Cases of dual authorship were clearly troublesome to the editors, who opted in favour of the collaborations mentioned above but, on what criteria we do not know, rejected *Pericles*, *The Two Noble Kinsmen*, *Cardenio*, and perhaps other authorially variegated plays.

The bibliographical circumstances are therefore suggestive that *Timon* is not of single authorship, but the case for Middleton's hand, first mooted by Wells (1920) and Sykes (1924, pp. 1–48), depends on internal evidence. Such evidence eventually emerged in convincing detail and form in the published work of Lake (1975) and Jackson (1979), and, much more comprehensively, in Holdsworth's dissertation (1982) and forthcoming book devoted specifically to the question of the play's authorship. These critics between them end the mid-century anti-disintegrationist consensus that accepts the Folio attribution to Shakespeare at face value. Lake argues persuasively that the rough-draft theory of the text is incapable of explaining the play's stylistic irregularities— irregularities, that is, by Shakespearean standards. He describes the high incidence of rhyme and the combination of prose, blank verse, and rhyme in a single speech as non-Shakespearean but consistent with Middleton, and he identifies linguistic forms and verbal preferences that point further to Middleton. Lake remains tentative in his conclusions; not so Jackson, who surveys inconsistencies in the spelling and abbreviation of certain names, contractions, linguistic forms, verbal parallels, interjections, function words, rare words, and the spelling of 'o(h)', and is confident in concluding from this diverse array of indicators that Middleton must have written parts of *Timon*. Holdsworth draws on a remarkably detailed knowledge of Middleton's works in order to conduct a systematic and discriminating study of significant verbal parallels between those works and the Middletonian parts of *Timon*.

Between them, these studies make up an impressive case for Middleton's presence in the play, and in such a way as to suggest a joint venture rather than the revision of one writer's work by the other. However, a statistically sophisticated study of function words by Smith (1991) has cast doubt on whether the 'Middletonian' sections can in fact have been written by Middleton. Indeed, Smith comes to the paradoxical conclusion that, despite his confirmation of a division between authors, Shakespeare is actually more likely to have written the 'Middletonian' sections

than the 'Shakespearean' sections. In a private communication, Jackson has pointed out that some of Smith's evidence may have been subject to chance fluctuation because of the relatively small size of the non-Shakespearean sample. He adds that 'it may be significant that the type--token tests, which deal with samples of 3,000 and 5,000 words—so that the "Middleton" sections of *Timon* don't suffer from the disadvantage of being smaller than the comparative material—place *Timon-M* within the Middleton range and outside the Shakespeare range for 5,000 word samples, and within the Middleton range and on the fringe of the Shakespeare range for 3,000 word samples'. Smith is unable from his evidence to posit an alternative collaborator or collaborators, and he underestimates the extent and value of the evidence that has been assembled in Middleton's favour. It remains possible that the 'Middleton' section contains some material by a third dramatist, or that Shakespeare's own hand contaminates the authorial profile of the 'Middleton' scenes, but the case for Middleton as Shakespeare's sole or main collaborator remains convincing.

According to Holdsworth the following passages can be attributed to Middleton:

1.276–86 (?)
Sc. 2
4.0.1–4.44.1 (??)
4.116–4.228.1, parts (?)
Scs. 5–10
11.0.1–11.35 (?)
11.104.1–11.114.1
13.0.1–13.29.1 (?)
13.30–51
14.459.2–14.538.1

Jowett (1993) suggests the following minor modifications to Holdsworth's account. Middleton may have introduced other minor additions to Shakespeare scenes: he probably added the silent figure of the Mercer at the beginning of Sc. 1 and the passage over the stage of senators at 1.38.1–1.41.1; as Holdsworth suggested, a short passage at 14.66–9 is also Middletonian in idiom. Sc. 4 is thoroughly collaborative, with 4.4–115 showing intermixed signs of both authors. In the remainder of the scene the most distinctively Shakespearean sections are ll. 160–70 ('Heavens...given') and 199–226 ('They answer... sink'), with Middleton perhaps partly responsible for the passage before l. 160, and perhaps wholly responsible for the passage between the Shakespearean sections and the scene's final couplet. Though if taken alone the evidence of Sc. 4 is indecisive, it appears from the text as a whole that Middleton wrote his contributions after Shakespeare had stopped working on his, sometimes, as most clearly in Scs. 1, 11, and 14, adding material to Shakespeare scenes.

By proportion, Middleton assumed responsibility for about one-third of the play. By sequence, the beginning of the play is thoroughly collaborative, the early--middle scenes are mostly Middleton, and the remainder is mostly Shakespeare. By subject matter, Middleton took the banquet scene (Sc. 2), the central scenes with Timon's creditors and Alcibiades's confrontation with the Senate, and most of the episodes figuring the Steward; Shakespeare was left to concentrate on the opening, the scenes dealing most fully with Timon himself, and the conclusion. Shakespeare gave the play its schematic structure, and gave Timon his inspired, misanthropic, universalizing rage. Middleton added comic social nihilism, but also introduced some brief moments that question Timon's later cynicism about human worth. Complementarity, contest, and contradiction are intrinsic to *Timon*. As a play jointly authored by Shakespeare and Middleton it is vibrantly unique.

John Jowett

SEE ALSO

Text: *Works*, 471
Textual introduction and apparatus: this volume, 704

WORKS CITED

Billington, Sandra, 'Was *Timon of Athens* Performed before 1604?', *Notes and Queries* 243 (1998), 351–3
Bulman, J. C., 'The Date and Production of *Timon* Reconsidered', *Shakespeare Survey* 27 (1974), 111–27
Chambers, E. K., *William Shakespeare: A Study of Facts and Problems*, 2 vols (1930)
Holdsworth, R. V., *Middleton and Shakespeare: The Case for Middleton's Hand in 'Timon of Athens'*, unpublished Ph.D. diss. (University of Manchester, 1982, and forthcoming as book)
—— '*A Yorkshire Tragedy* and the Date of *Timon of Athens*' (privately circulated, 1993)
Jowett, John, ed., *Timon of Athens* (1993)
Knight, Charles, ed., William Shakespeare, *Comedies, Histories, Tragedies, & Poems*, 55 parts [1838–43]
Smith, M. W. A., 'The Authorship of *Timon of Athens*', TEXT 5 (1991), 195–240
Sykes, H. Dugdale, *Sidelights on Elizabethan Drama* (1924)
Wells, Stanley, and Gary Taylor, with John Jowett and William Montgomery, *William Shakespeare: A Textual Companion* (1987)
Wells, William, '*Timon of Athens*', *Notes and Queries* 112 (1920), 226–9

The Viper and Her Brood   Spring 1606

For this work, see Feldmann and Tetzeli von Rosador, 'Lost Plays', in *Works*, 332.

The Puritan Widow   Mid-1606

Entered in the Stationers' Register by George Eld on 6 August 1607, *The Puritan Widow* was subsequently published in a quarto edition. The title-page bears the date 1607, attributes the printing to Eld, the acting to the Children of Paul's, and the authorship to 'W. S.'

In 1656, Archer's play list expanded 'W. S.' to 'Will. Shakespeare.' Subsequently, the play was included in the Third Folio (1664) of the works of William Shakespeare, an edition which also included for the first time *Pericles*, *Locrine*, *Sir John Oldcastle*, *Thomas Lord Cromwell*, *The London Prodigal*, and *A Yorkshire Tragedy*. Of this group, the title-pages of the first editions of *Locrine* and *Cromwell* also give the author as 'W. S.' These seven plays were also included in the Fourth Folio (1685), in Rowe's Shakespeare editions (1709, 1714), and in the supplement to Pope's Shakespeare (1728). (The inclusion of these plays in these Folios is discussed in Taylor 1986.) In 1780, Edmond Malone declared the play not by Shakespeare. Virtually all critics have concurred on the basis of style alone; the fact that Shakespeare did not write for Paul's Boys provides confirming external evidence.

With concurrence on the play's not being by Shakespeare, the authorship issue has, in the past, focused in part on searching for other writers with the initials 'W. S.' who were connected to the theatre. While various possibilities have been pursued (Wentworth Smith, W. Smith, William Sly, William Stanley, Earl of Derby), no convincing case for attributing the play to any of these people has been made, although such study has fostered continuing speculation that the desire to sell a larger number of books was the motivation for using initials that might suggest that the play was by Shakespeare. It is just as possible, however, that other material conditions made these initials attractive, especially given that the play treats ecclesiastical matters in a controversial manner; if those initials could raise market value, they also had a legitimizing effect. Eld would have been sensitive to such issues; in 1605, the controversial *Eastward Ho*, printed by Eld, had been censored, and Ben Jonson and George Chapman had been imprisoned.

Whatever the case and with few exceptions, most scholars since Malone (including, in chronological order, Bullen, Fleay, Hopkinson, Ward, Tzeutschler, Chambers, Dunkel, Eccles, Christian, Maxwell, Heaven, Williamson, Barber, Kaiser, Lake and Jackson) have identified Middleton as the sole or primary author of *The Puritan Widow*; the ground-breaking and confirming 1931 essay by Eccles virtually removed the issue from further dispute. Exceptions include Brooke's speculation (1908) that the play was Marston's, and Barker's (1958) that the play sounded more like Rowley or a disciple of Middleton's. Swinburne, Symons, and Heinemann have also dissented.

An earlier obstacle to claiming authorship for Middleton, and the obstacle that influenced Brooke's attribution, is the cluster of allusions to Oxford University ('quadrangle', 'battelled', 'Jesus College', 'Welshman' [1.2.32–9]); Brooke, for example, attributed the play to Marston, partly on the grounds that Marston had attended Oxford. In 1931, such reservation dissipated with Eccles's evidence that Middleton had matriculated at Queen's College, Oxford, his date of subscription being 7 April 1598.

Since 1931, most scholars have spoken of Middleton's authorship with the same confidence as Eccles, who found the play to be in every respect like other writing of Middleton's. Eccles noted the presence of many contractions associated with Middleton, including 'h'as', 'sh'as', 't'as', 't'ad', and 'uppo'th'', as well as such characteristically Middletonian turns of phrase as 'give him his due' and 'troth you say true', use of 'trashing' and 'comfort', and of interjections 'Push', 'puh', 'why', ''sfoot', and 'mass'. There remains scattered speculation that Middleton may have had a collaborator. Following Eccles's lead, Lake and Jackson did extensive stylistic analysis, which for them confirmed Eccles's conclusions. The important dissenter on the matter of authorship is Heinemann, who, dismissing the validity of stylistic analysis, argued against Middleton's authorship on the grounds that the view of puritans represented in the play is inconsistent with Middleton's moderate puritanism, a view which my critical introduction in this edition disputes.

The date of the play is almost certainly 1606. The reference in 3.5.134-5 to the 'Act passed in Parliament against conjurors and witches', an act passed in 1604 during James's first session of Parliament, sets the date of the play no earlier than 1604. As Maxwell has indicated, a related detail is the reference, in 'Britain gold | Of the last coining' (3.4.162), to the indenture on 11 November 1604, providing for a coinage that would carry the king's new title, King of Great Britain. The Stationers' Register entry for the play, 6 August 1607, sets the later limits for the date.

The only source identified for *The Puritan Widow*, George Peele's *Merry Conceited Jests of George Peele*, at once further clarifies and further problematizes the matter of dating. In *The Puritan Widow*, two of George Pieboard's schemes to outwit the sergeants who have arrested him and to rediscover the gold chain that has been lost (in 3.3 and 3.4, and in 3.5 and 4.2, respectively) have analogues in Peele's *Jests* 2 and 11. Peele is also recognized as the namesake of Pieboard ('peel' being a board for removing pies and other baking from an oven). But how and when Middleton had access to these jests is uncertain; the possibility of a close connection between Middleton and Peele merits serious consideration and further study. Entered in the Stationers' Register on 14 December 1605, the first surviving edition printed in 1607, *Jests* may have been available to Middleton in manuscript; analogues to the jests that Middleton uses can also be found in other sources. As David Horne has noted, an analogue to the jest by which the chain is found (3.4, 4.2) occurs in Reginald Scot's *The Discovery of Witchcraft* (1584), which represented the conventional protestant view that conjuring was a device of popery to deceive the people. As interesting as this analogue is for this play, the pun on Peele's name argues for a definite link between *The Puritan Widow* and specifically Peele, and the December 1605 date of entry in the Stationers' Register once again calls attention to 1606 as the year when the material may have been available for Middleton's use.

Most other details suggest a date of 1606. Fleay uncovered the fact that the play's reference to the fifteenth of July falling on a Tuesday corresponded with the 1606 calendar, information that may suggest that the play's date is in or close to July. Basing his conclusion partially on Fleay, Holdsworth suggests a date prior to mid-July and perhaps also prior to Shakespeare's writing *Macbeth*. Sir Godfrey's remark, as he invites everyone to a banquet,

that 'the ghost i'th' white sheet sit at upper end o'th' table' (4.2.355-6) is not, according to Holdsworth, a reference to Banquo's ghost in *Macbeth*, dated between November 1605 and August 1606, but a repetition of language that Middleton had used in *The Black Book* and in *The Meeting of Gallants at an Ordinary*. Also considering the possibilities of a date in 1606, Maxwell considers the reference to 'George Stone the bear' being baited by 'three dogs at once' (3.5.15-16). While acknowledging that such a reference to one of the most well-known bears at Bear Garden may have been common practice, Maxwell nevertheless speculates that further evidence may be adduced for the 1606 date from a petition to the king by Philip Henslowe, then Keeper of the King's Bears, which indicates that the bear died during late July or early August, 1606, at a baiting before the king of Denmark.

Attention to corporal oaths in 1606 is consistent as well for dating a play with a character named 'Corporal Oath'. Beginning in February, the 1606 session of Parliament turned its attention to developing policies in reaction to the 5 November 1605 discovery of the Gunpowder Plot. As McIlwain and Milward have outlined, those policies included instituting an oath of allegiance which was aimed at extracting from Catholics allegiance to the king as their temporal ruler. Given the other details for dating, it is significant that this oath was published on 25 June 1606. Of course, as Leonard Levy and Patrick Collinson have emphasized, corporal oaths, especially the oath *ex officio mero*, were of regular concern to all religious dissidents, including protestant nonconformists. During the 1606 session of Parliament, the oath *ex officio* was discussed in the Commons, with the puritan Nicholas Fuller (on 13 March) leading the debate against it. In 1607, Fuller would defend Richard Mansel and Thomas Ladd for refusing to take the oath *ex officio* and would publish his arguments against this oath in *The Argument of Master Nicholas Fuller, in the Case of Thomas Ladd and Richard Mansel, his Clients*, also in 1607.

According to Chambers, there is no record of performances by Paul's Boys after 30 July 1606, when they played the lost play *Abuses* for James and the King of Denmark (presumably during the same visit that witnessed the death of George Stone). Chambers supported his speculation that Paul's Boys shut down after that date by noting the plays associated with Paul's Boys that were printed in 1607 and 1608. The Middleton plays in this group include *The Puritan Widow*, *Michaelmas Term*, *The Phoenix*, *A Mad World, My Masters*, *A Trick to Catch the Old One*, *Your Five Gallants*. Of those printed in 1607, the title-pages of *The Puritan Widow*, *The Phoenix*, and *Michaelmas Term* all indicate the connection to Paul's Boys. Title-pages also announce a Paul's Boys connection for *A Mad World, My Masters* and *A Trick to Catch the Old One*, printed in 1608. The title-page of *Your Five Gallants*, also printed in 1608, identifies a connection with the Children of the Chapel. Bald has contended that, with the demise of Paul's Boys, *Mad World* and *Trick* passed out of Paul's Boys to new owners.

Contrary to Chambers, Gair has speculated that Paul's Boys was still playing in 1608. As evidence, he refers to William Crashaw's Paul's Cross sermon, 14 February 1608, which denounces the stage representation of Puritans as hypocrites in characters who take their names from the parishes of St Antholin's and St Mary Overie—obvious references to *The Puritan Widow*'s Nicholas St Antlings and Simon St Mary Overies. Gair speculates that this reference to *The Puritan Widow* means that Paul's Boys were still playing. But it is also possible that the play's fresh currency for Crashaw derived specifically from the printed version, as opposed to a recent playing, of the play. As Crashaw writes, the 'church and state [are] dishonoured . . . not on the stage only, but even in print'.

Donna B. Hamilton

SEE ALSO

Text: *Works*, 513
Textual introduction and apparatus: this volume, 540

WORKS CITED

Bald, R. C., 'The Chronology of Middleton's Plays', *Modern Language Review* 32 (1937), 33–43

Barber, Charles, 'A Rare Use of the Word "Honour" as a Criterion of Middleton's Authorship', *English Studies* 38 (1957), 161–8

Barker, Richard Hindry, *Thomas Middleton* (1958)

Brooke, C. F. Tucker, ed., *The Shakespeare Apocrypha* (1908)

Bullen, A. H., ed., *Works of Thomas Middleton* (1885, rpt. 1964), vol. 1

Chambers, E. K., *The Elizabethan Stage* (1923), vols 2, 4

Christian, Mildred G., 'Middleton's Acquaintance with the Merrie Conceited Jests of George Peele', *PMLA* 50 (1935), 753–60

—— 'A Sidelight on the Family History of Thomas Middleton', *Studies in Philology* 44 (1947), 490–6

Collinson, Patrick, *The Elizabethan Puritan Movement* (1967)

—— 'The Downfall of Archbishop Grindal and its Place in Elizabethan Political and Ecclesiastical History', in *Godly People: Essays on English Protestantism and Puritanism* (1983), pp. 371–97

—— 'Lectures by Combination: Structures and Characteristics of Church Life in 17th-Century England' in *Godly People: Essays on English Protestantism and Puritanism* (1983), pp. 467–98

Crashaw, William, *The sermon preached at the Cross, Feb. 14, 1607* (1608)

Dobson, Daniel B., 'Allusions to the Gunpowder Plot in Dekker's *Whore of Babylon*', *Notes and Queries* 6 (1959), 257

Dunkel, Wilbur, 'The Authorship of *The Puritan*', *PMLA* (1930), 804–8

Eccles, Mark, 'Middleton's Birth and Education', *Review of English Studies* 7 (1931), 431–41

—— '"Thomas Middleton a Poett"', *Studies in Philology* 54 (1957), 516–36

Fleay, Frederick G., *A Biographical Chronicle of the English Drama, 1559–1642* (1891), vol. 2

Fuller, Nicholas, *The argument of Master Nicholas Fuller, in the case of T. Ladd, and R. Mansel, his clients* (1607)

Gair, W. Reavley, *The Children of Paul's* (1982)

Heaven, Sidney, ed., *The Puritaine or The Widow of Watling Street* ([1955])

Heinemann, Margot, *Puritanism and Theatre: Thomas Middleton and Opposition Drama under the Early Stuarts* (1980)

Hopkinson, A. F., ed., *The Puritan, or the Widow of Watling Street* (1894)

Horne, David H., *The Life and Minor Works of George Peele* (1952)

James I, *The Political Works of James I*, ed. C. H. McIlwain (1918; rpt. 1965)

Kaiser, Donald Frederick, ed., *A Critical Edition of 'The Puritan; or, the Widow of Watling Street'*, University of Wisconsin diss., 1966

Levy, Leonard W., *Origins of the Fifth Amendment: The Right Against Self-Incrimination* 2nd edn. (1986)

Malone, Edmond, ed., *Supplement to the Edition of Shakespeare's Plays Published in 1778 by Samuel Johnson and George Steevens* (1780), vol. 2

Maxwell, Baldwin, *Studies in the Shakespeare Apocrypha* (1956)

Milward, Peter, *Religious Controversies of the Jacobean Age: A Survey of Printed Sources* (1978)

Pope, Alexander, ed., *The Works of Mr. William Shakespear* (1728), vol. 9

Rowe, Nicholas, ed., *The Works of Mr. William Shakespear* (1714), vol. 8

Scot, Reginald, *The discovery of witchcraft* (1584)

Swinburne, Algernon C., *Thomas Middleton*, ed. Havelock Ellis (1887) vol. 1

Symons, Arthur, 'Middleton and Rowley', *The Cambridge History of English Literature*, ed. A. W. Ward and A. R. Waller (1910), vol. 6

Taylor, Gary, 'Canon and Chronology: Works Excluded from this Edition', in Wells, Stanley, and Gary Taylor, with John Jowett and William Montgomery, *William Shakespeare: A Textual Companion* (1987), 134–141

Tzeutschler, Artur, *Das Drama 'The Puritan': Eine literarhistorische Untersuchung* (1909)

Ward, Adolphus W., *A History of English Dramatic Literature to the Death of Queen Anne*, 2nd edn. (1899), vol. 2.

Williamson, Marilyn L., 'Middleton's Workmanship and the Authorship of *The Puritan*', *Notes and Queries* 202 (1957), 50–1

The Revenger's Tragedy   Late 1606

External evidence for the authorship of *Revenger* is contradictory and inadequate, but, rightly assessed, it favours Middleton. Although Eld's quarto of 1607/8 was anonymous, the play had been registered, on 7 October 1607, in a joint entry with *Trick*, and the practice of coupling plays on the Stationers' Register was, throughout the entire Elizabethan and Jacobean periods, confined to those with a single author (Lake, pp. 140–2). *Sejanus* and *Volpone*, for example, were linked in this way, without mention of Jonson's name, and there are co-entries (the first also anonymous) for plays by Lyly, Shakespeare, and Chapman.

Apparently confirming the inference to be drawn from the double entry is a phrase in Nathaniel Richards's commendatory verse to *Women Beware* (1657). Richards, avowedly a 'familiar acquaintance' of Middleton, refers to 'drabs of state', evidently as a deliberate quotation from *Revenger*, 4.4.72, since he employs the whole line, 'A drab of state, a cloth o' silver slut', in his own tragedy *Messalina*. It seems natural to conclude that while praising *Women Beware* Richards intended a glancing allusion to an earlier masterpiece that he knew to have been written by his friend (Lake, 1975, pp. 141–2; Holdsworth, 1990, pp. 123–4).

However, in his catalogue appended to an edition of *The Old Law* in 1656 Edward Archer attributed 'Revenger' to 'Tournour', and in 1661 and 1671, in two further playlists, Francis Kirkman expanded title and author to 'Revengers Tragedy' and 'Cyrill Tourneur' (*BEPD*, 3, 1319-55). Kirkman's repetition of Archer's ascription has no independent authority: his lists were based on those of his predecessors and repeat obvious mistakes. Greg, who undertook a careful evaluation of the seventeenth-century playlists, calculated that Archer blundered in at least two out of every three of his new attributions (Greg, 1938-45, pp. 316-17). Archer's testimony is clearly worth very little. Judging from his overall performance, he is much more likely to have got the author of *Revenger* wrong than right.

Foakes (1966, p. xlviii), Ross (p. xiv), Schoenbaum (1966, p. 201), Parfitt (p. xiii), Schuman (p. 61), and others have considered it unlikely that Archer would have assigned the play to a dramatist so obscure as Tourneur, if he was not really its author. But this belief cannot survive an inspection of the catalogue itself. What he ought not to have done in theory, Archer did in fact. His errors included the assignment of *Love's Labour's Lost* to William Sampson, and he made new and incorrect ascriptions to other equally obscure writers—for example, Lewis Machin, Thomas Goffe, Thomas Newman, and Ludovic Lloyd. As Greg observed, his crediting of *Revenger* to the author of *The Atheist's Tragedy* 'may rest on no more than similarity of title' (p. 318), the obvious cause of his misattribution of *Every Woman in her Humour* to Jonson.

Eld's title-page claims that *Revenger* had been 'sundry times acted by the King's Majesty's Servants', and editors supporting Archer's ascription to Tourneur have urged that during the period 1603-1607 Middleton was writing not tragedy for the King's company of adults but city comedy for boy actors to perform at private theatres (Foakes, 1966, p. xlviii; Ross, pp. xiv-xv; also Schoenbaum, 1966, p. 209). But neither the argument from genre nor the argument from company attachments withstands scrutiny. Middleton had written tragedies for Henslowe as early as 1602 and claimed to have completed *The Viper and her Brood*, a tragedy, in May 1606 (see 'Lost Plays', *Works*, p. 332). *Revenger* often reads like an adaptation of Middleton's comic and satiric art to material that is 'tragic' mainly in its lethal violence, and among the most conspicuous features of Middletonian drama is the ease with which it moves between the genres. Nor was Middleton's connection with the boy actors at all binding. Middleton was one of several 'prolific professionals' who appear 'never to have had any long sustained company attachment, but to have sold [their] plays here and there' (Bentley, 1971, p. 35); and a great deal of evidence has now accumulated for an association, however non-committal, between Middleton and the King's Men dating from precisely the period at which *Revenger* appears to have been written (see *Yorkshire* and *Timon*, and, in a later period, *Lady* and *Macbeth*—all tragedies). In contrast, there is 'no evidence to connect Tourneur with the King's Men before (or after) 23 February 1612, when his lost play, *The Nobleman*, was performed by them. In fact, there is nothing to suggest that he wrote for the stage at all before composing *The Atheist's Tragedy*, now usually dated about 1610' (Jackson, 1983, p. 17). What company performed *The Atheist's Tragedy* is not known. The clues under this head point to Middleton, not Tourneur.

A just evaluation of the meagre external evidence is decisively confirmed by the internal evidence. This, broadly speaking, is of two kinds: (*a*) subjective, literary-critical, and concerned with theme, structure, atmosphere, mind-set, and moral purpose; and (*b*) objective, bibliographical, and concerned with statistical analysis of linguistic, stylistic, orthographical, and lexical features. The more subjective types of enquiry have reached opposite conclusions. Some critics find the play akin to *The Atheist's Tragedy* in 'the more intangible qualities which evade strict analysis, in mood, general temper and moral fervour' (Foakes, 1953, p. 138) and see a philosophical development from the earlier to the later tragedy (Nicoll, Jenkins, Adams, Ornstein, Peter, Ribner); others stress the vast disparity between *Revenger* and Tourneur's undoubted play in their dramatic and poetic quality, and detect Middleton's plot structure, modes of expression, ironic viewpoint, or Calvinist sense of human depravity in the anonymously published work (Oliphant, Dunkel, Mincoff, Barker, Schoenbaum 1955, Frost, Stachniewski). Disagreement of this nature is not surprising. Inconclusive critical debates surround almost every major English Renaissance play. In contrast, the more objective tests applied to *Revenger* all point unequivocally to Middleton's authorship, and this convergence is explicable only if he did indeed write the play.

The evidence, much of it accumulated fairly recently by Murray, Lake, Jackson, and Holdsworth, is summarized in the introduction to Jackson's facsimile edition (1983) of Eld's quarto. Lake (1971) has also proved that the scraps of objective evidence adduced by Nicoll and Foakes (1966) in favour of Tourneur's authorship are worthless. In its linguistic preferences—the pattern of choices among contractions, colloquial forms, connectives, particles, and the like—and in its favoured spellings of some of these *Revenger* is Middletonian to a degree that distinguishes it from all extant non-Middleton plays of the period 1590-1630, and from Tourneur's *The Atheist's Tragedy* more markedly than most. Scribal or compositorial interference cannot explain this finding. Middleton's characteristic pattern is not simply a matter of orthography but involves a liking for turns of phrase and metrical variations that can incorporate such favourites as 'e'en' and 'on't'. More significantly, any adjustments to the text by compositors or scribes should have been random in their effect, making *Revenger* less Middletonian as often as more so. The consistency with which Middleton's favoured forms, recurring from play to play, are matched by *Revenger* is obviously not due to accidents of transmission.

Moreover, much of the other evidence is of a kind that only the severest forms of textual corruption could substantially have affected. For example, Middleton favours some highly unusual oaths and exclamations. *Revenger* contains fourteen instances of the most distinctive, linking it with the eight Middleton plays that have at least thirteen instances and sharply differentiating it from a control corpus of one hundred non-Middleton plays, sixty-seven of which (including *The Atheist's Tragedy*) have no instances at all, with only one play affording as many as five; and unlike that play, Chapman's *May-Day*, *Revenger* is remarkably free from expletives avoided by Middleton but commonly employed by his fellow dramatists. Also, statistical testing of high-frequency words shows that rates of use for *Revenger* associate it with Middleton's plays and dissociate it from *The Atheist's Tragedy*: Jackson's work in this area has been refined by Smith (1991), who has exposed the statistical flaws in Morton's 'stylometric' methods (Smith, 1989). Metrical features, especially the distribution of pauses within the pentameter line, closely match *Revenger* to Middleton's plays of about the same period and point to Middleton as a likely author (Oras, pp. 28–31; Lake, 1975, pp. 257–69; Jackson, 1983, pp. 27–29). Holdsworth's (1982) count of cases of 'interrogative repetition' in over a hundred contemporary plays reveals that *Revenger* uses this stylistic device with a distinctively Middletonian liberality. Negative checks, using a large control sample of plays by other dramatists, have confirmed the genuine significance of the presence in *Revenger* of certain unusual Middleton words, phrases, and collocations; and striking verbal parallels abound. The remarkably exact and extensive parallel, between *Revenger* 4.2, and *Mad World* 3.3, which was pointed out by Barker (1958, pp. 70–1), goes far beyond the normal bounds of borrowing between authors and implies either gross plagiarism or common authorship.

Commenting on Jackson's much fuller (and comprehensively documented) summary in his facsimile edition (1983), Wheeler agreed that the various kinds of evidence 'point decisively away from Tourneur and more compellingly toward Middleton than to any of his contemporaries'. He found this predominantly sub-stylistic evidence 'persuasive in itself', but judged that it would 'continue to have trouble overcoming the inertia of tradition' until supplemented by studies demonstrating the play's 'integral thematic connections' to Middleton's whole canon (p. 405). This challenge has since been met by Holdsworth in his close-packed account of 'The Revenger's Tragedy as a Middleton Play'. Holdsworth shows how *Revenger* combines elements from all Middleton's earlier works and how these are in turn redeployed in his subsequent tragedies. He amply substantiates his claim that in its modes of thought and expression *Revenger* fits perfectly into the 'constantly unfolding pattern of continuities' within the Middleton canon (1990, p. 80).

A complete review of the extensive literature on the authorship of *Revenger* is beyond the scope of this summary. Schuman offers a full history, which, however, fails to evaluate the various contributions correctly and stops short of the decisive contributions of Lake, Jackson, and Holdsworth; Steen's bibliography lists most relevant books, articles, and dissertations that appeared before its cut-off point (1978, with some coverage of 1979–81); Jackson (1979, pp. 159–78) outlined the case for Middleton as it then stood and rebutted the arguments of sceptics; and a brief assessment of the evidence has since been provided by Loughrey and Taylor. Cavils about Lake's methods, in reviews of his book by Foakes (1977) and Shand, have been shown by Holdsworth (1982, pp. 73–5) to be misconceived. Jackson (1979, pp. 36–9) exposed the flaws in Proudfoot's strictures on Murray's case. The resources of the Chadwyck-Healey electronic database, *English Drama*, reveal that some of the Middleton markers used by Lake and Jackson to identify him as author of *Revenger* are even rarer outside his work than they claimed (Jackson, 1998). And Corrigan, seeking to tie *Revenger* more securely to the Middleton canon, has argued that the play exhibits a characteristic 'tendency to react to changes in popular or personal literary taste by exploring and exploding earlier modes of writing' (p. 292).

While it is possible to be definite about the authorship of *Revenger*, an exact date of composition cannot be determined. Clues to an approximate one are furnished by its debts to other plays. The influence of *Hamlet* is obvious, and other connections, established or suspected, are mainly within the first few years of the seventeenth century (1600–04), such as Chettle's *Hoffman* and Marston's *Malcontent*, *Antonio's Revenge*, and *The Fawn* (Foakes, 1966, pp. lxvii–lxviii). Vindice's remarks at 4.4.43–5 recall one of the most memorable lines of *Othello* (1.2.60). However, links with two other plays add a year or two to the likely *terminus a quo*. *Revenger* shares with *Volpone* a cast of grotesque humours with apt Italian names (with the besieged Castiza a less insipid counterpart to the virtuous Celia), a central intriguer unaware of the applicability of his satirical quips and maxims to himself, and elements of savage farce, and there is a close relationship between the two plays' 'wooing' scenes (*Revenger* 2.1 and *Volpone* 3.7). The Revels editor firmly assigns *Volpone* to the early months of 1606 (Parker, pp. 8–10). Holdsworth (1980) argued that Jonson, rather than Middleton, may have been the debtor, but whatever the direction of the influence, it was probably exerted shortly after the earlier of the two plays was first produced. Probable echoes of *King Lear* as encountered in the theatre reinforce the evidence from *Volpone*. Spurio, though a far less complex character than Shakespeare's Edmund, is, like him, a lustful illegitimate son whose schemes against his father and stepbrother are motivated by desire to avenge his bastardy; and *Revenger* contains several verbal reminiscences of *King Lear*, detailed by Holdsworth (1985, p. 63). Taken together these seem unlikely to be due to chance, and, in view of Taylor's strong argument that *King Lear* 'was not completed before the autumn of 1605' (1982, p. 407), make it a plausible guess that *Revenger* was written in 1606. A possible reference at 2.2.168 to the Gunpowder Plot of 5 November 1605 would fit such a date. The relationships of the play to *Yorkshire*, *Puritan*, and Middleton's share of *Timon* also suggest that *Revenger* was written in early spring 1606 (see 'Early Modern Authorship: Canons and Chronologies').

MacDonald P. Jackson

SEE ALSO

Text: *Works*, 547
Textual introduction and apparatus: this volume, 548

WORKS CITED

Adams, Henry H., 'Cyril Tourneur on Revenge', *Journal of English and Germanic Philology* 48 (1949), 72–87
Barker, Richard H., 'The Authorship of the *Second Maiden's Tragedy* and *The Revenger's Tragedy*', *The Shakespeare Association Bulletin* 20 (1945), 51–62, 121–33
—— *Thomas Middleton* (1958)
Bentley, G. E., *The Profession of Dramatist in Shakespeare's Time* (1971)
Corrigan, Brian Jay, 'Middleton, *The Revenger's Tragedy*, and Crisis Literature', *Studies in English Literature, 1500–1900* 38 (1998), 281–95
Dunkel, W. D., 'The Authorship of *The Revenger's Tragedy*', *PMLA* 46 (1931), 781–5
Foakes, R. A., 'On the Authorship of *The Revenger's Tragedy*', *Modern Language Review* 48 (1953), 129–38
—— Review of David J. Lake, *The Canon of Thomas Middleton's Plays*, *Modern Language Review* 72 (1977), 895–7
—— ed., *The Revenger's Tragedy*, Revels (1966)
Frost, David L., *The School of Shakespeare* (1968)
Greg, W. W., 'Authorship Attributions in the Early Play-Lists, 1656–1671', *Edinburgh Bibliographical Society Transactions* 2 (1938–45), 305–29
Holdsworth, R. V., 'Middleton and Shakespeare: The Case for Middleton's Hand in *Timon of Athens*' (Ph.D. diss., University of Manchester, 1982)
—— 'Middleton and William Perkins: A Biblical Echo in *The Revenger's Tragedy*', *Notes and Queries* 230 (1985), 61–3
—— '*The Revenger's Tragedy*, Ben Jonson, and *The Devil's Law Case*', *Review of English Studies* NS 31 (1980), 305–10
—— ed., *Three Jacobean Revenge Tragedies* (1990)
—— '*A Yorkshire Tragedy* and the Date of *Timon of Athens*' (privately circulated, 1993)
Jackson, MacDonald P., 'Editing, Attribution Studies, and Literature Online: A New Resource for Research in Renaissance Drama', *Research Opportunities in Renaissance Drama* 37 (1998), 1–15
—— ed., *The Revenger's Tragedy, Attributed to Thomas Middleton: A Facsimile of the 1607/8 Quarto* (1983)
Jenkins, Harold, 'Cyril Tourneur', *Review of English Studies* 17 (1941), 21–36
Lake, David J., '*The Revenger's Tragedy*: Internal Evidence for Tourneur's Authorship Negated', *Notes and Queries* 216 (1971), 455–6
Loughrey, Brian, and Neil Taylor, eds., *Thomas Middleton, Five Plays* (1988)
Mincoff, Marco, 'The Authorship of *The Revenger's Tragedy*', *Studia Historico-Philologica Serdicensia* 2 (1940), 1–87
Morton, A. Q., 'Authorship: the nature of the habit', *Times Literary Supplement*, 17–23 February 1989, 164, 174
Murray, Peter B., *A Study of Cyril Tourneur* (1964)
Nicoll, Allardyce, ed., *The Works of Cyril Tourneur* (1929)
Oliphant, E. H. C., 'The Authorship of *The Revenger's Tragedy*', *Studies in Philology* 23 (1926), 157–68
Oras, Ants, *Pause Patterns in Elizabethan and Jacobean Drama* (1960)
Ornstein, Robert, *The Moral Vision of Jacobean Tragedy* (1960)
Parker, R. B., ed., Ben Jonson, *Volpone or, The Fox*, Revels (1983)
Peter, John, *Complaint and Satire in Early English Literature* (1956)
Proudfoot, G. R., Review of Peter B. Murray, *A Study of Cyril Tourneur*, *Notes and Queries* 212 (1967), 233–37
Ribner, Irving, *Jacobean Tragedy* (1962)
Ross, Lawrence J., ed., *The Revenger's Tragedy* (1966)
Schoenbaum, S., *Internal Evidence and Elizabethan Dramatic Authorship* (1966)
—— *Middleton's Tragedies: A Critical Study* (1955)
Schuman, Samuel, *Cyril Tourneur* (1977)
Shand, G. B., Review of David J. Lake, *The Canon of Thomas Middleton's Plays*, *Shakespeare Studies* 11 (1978), 311–14
Smith, M. W. A., 'Statistics and Authorship', *Times Literary Supplement*, 17–23 March 1989, 278
—— 'The Authorship of *The Revenger's Tragedy*', *Notes and Queries* 236 (1991), 508–13
Stachniewski, John, 'Calvinist Psychology in Middleton's Tragedies', in R. V. Holdsworth (ed.), *Three Jacobean Revenge Tragedies* (1990), pp. 226–47
Steen, Sara Jayne, *Thomas Middleton: A Reference Guide* (1984)
Taylor, Gary, 'A New Source and an Old Date for *King Lear*', *Review of English Studies* NS 33 (1982), 396–413
Wheeler, Richard, 'Recent Studies in Elizabethan and Jacobean Drama', *Studies in English Literature, 1500–1900* 24 (1984), 373–410

Your Five Gallants   1607

The title-page of the quarto states the play's authorship unequivocally: 'Written by T. Middleton.' The ascription has not been contested, and in its linguistic texture and characteristics of style and dramatic construction the play is entirely at one with Middleton's practices.

As to when he wrote it, according to the Stationers' Register, the play had 'been acted by the Children of the Chappell' before its entry on 22 March 1608. Bald argues that the play was written at least 15 months before its entry in the Register. He bases that conclusion on his belief that Middleton had originally composed the play for the Children of Paul's, who had already performed several of Middleton's works and who had disbanded by the middle of 1606. His earliest suggested date is 1604, but a date before November 1605 seems most unlikely in view of what seems to be a reference to the Gunpowder Plot when the servant Hieronimo Bedlam refers to 'the Fifth of November, a dismal day' (2.2.13–14). To get around the evidence of this reference, Bald suggests that the play that the title-page testifies was performed by the Blackfriars' Children might have been a revision of an earlier work (p. 35). Maxwell sees the allusion to the Gunpowder Plot as a reason to date the play from November 1606, since 'it suggests that Middleton had experienced one anniversary of the lamentable day' (p. 38). Fleay suggests an even later date because of the play's numerous references to the plague which he believes more appropriate after the terrible plague summer of 1607, and, using what he sees as a specific chronology in the play, he concludes that the play was written in November of 1607 for a December performance (II, pp. 94–5).

Colegrove, remarking on the general 'looseness' of the play's plot, disputes the possibility of such exact dating, but nonetheless joins Chambers (III, p. 440) and Maxwell (p. 39) in accepting 1607 as the probable year of the play's composition; this later dating is accepted in the 1989 edition of Harbage (p. 96). Colegrove points out that the scene in the Mitre tavern resembles one of the jests in *The Merry Conceited Jests of George Peele*, a pamphlet published in 1607 (20–21). Taken together, the topical evidence for a date in 1607 weighs more than Bald's suggestion of an earlier date based largely on his unsubstantiated contention that Middleton wrote an earlier version of the play for the Children of Paul's.

Ralph Alan Cohen with John Jowett

SEE ALSO

Text: *Works*, 597
Textual introduction and apparatus: this volume, 575

WORKS CITED

Bald, R. C., 'The Chronology of Middleton's Plays', *Modern Language Review* 32 (1937), 33–43
Chambers, E. K., *The Elizabethan Stage*, 4 vols (1923)
Colegrove, Clare Lee., ed., *A Critical Edition of Thomas Middleton's 'Your Five Gallants'*, Ph.D. diss. (University of Michigan, 1961); issued in book form 1979
Fleay, F. G., *A Biographical Chronical of the English Drama*, 2 vols (1891)
Harbage, Alfred, *Annal of English Drama, 975–1700*, 3rd edn., rev. Sylvia Stoler Wagonheim (1989)
Maxwell, Baldwin, 'Thomas Middleton's *Your Five Gallants*', *Philological Quarterly* 30 (1951), 30–9

The Bloody Banquet   1608–9

The only substantive edition, the COTES quarto of 1639, attributes the play to 'T.D.'. Archer's play-list (*BEPD* 567) attributes it to 'Thomas Barker', an apparent misreading elsewhere attached to plays by Thomas Dekker; Anthony a Wood, a much more reliable and also demonstrably independent source, explicitly attributes the play to Thomas Dekker (Baugh 409). Dekker's work is sometimes elsewhere identified by initials; Dekker also often placed Latin mottoes below his titles. Lake and Jackson show that the linguistic evidence rules out Thomas Drue, the only other dramatist with the same initials. Taylor (2000) has pointed to a variety of internal evidence for Dekker's authorship of 1.1, 1.2, 1.3, 2.2, 2.4, and 5.1.110.2–5.1.248.1; that evidence is supplemented below. Dekker apparently wrote all the scenes of the Lapyrus narrative, as well as the opening and closing scenes which connect the two plots.

Middleton's part-authorship was first suggested by Oliphant, who pointed out that the title-page of the Middleton–Dekker play *Patient Man and Honest Whore* attributes it to Dekker alone. Lake and Jackson hesitated to confirm Oliphant's suggestion, because of some discrepancies in the linguistic evidence; but Lake suggested, and we

have been able to confirm, that COTES was printed from a scribal transcript. (See Textual Introduction.) The scribe's habits, which can be documented elsewhere, interfered with half a dozen linguistic features; the anomalies noticed by Lake and Jackson therefore must be discounted, as scribal rather than authorial. Jackson's statistical evidence (1998) has shown that the play's expletives would in themselves be sufficient to warrant attribution to Middleton; Taylor (2000) marshals additional evidence from expletives, verbal parallels, and linguistic forms to establish Middleton's authorship of 1.4, 2.3, 3.1, 3.3, all of Act Four, and 5.1.1–5.1.110.1. Evidence of collaboration is provided by the distribution of distinctive authorial features in different scenes of the play; by differences in the naming of characters (Tyrant, Lodovico, Sextorio); and by the false scene division in COTES at 5.1.110.2, where a change of authors was misinterpreted as a change of scenes. (See Textual Notes.) The evidence of mislineation also supports Middleton's authorship, and the proposed division of scenes between the collaborators. (See Textual Introduction.)

The play's brevity has led to suggestions that COTES prints an abridged text; Schoenbaum provided some specific evidence of adaptation, developed by Taylor (2000). Acts Two, Three, and Five are anomalously short, and the second Chorus (2.5) seems particularly likely to be the work of an unknown adapter, replacing two or more scenes of the Lapyrus plot, originally written by Dekker. The same anonymous writer was also probably responsible for the Induction, and may have made minor alterations elsewhere. The adaptation seems to have affected disproportionately Dekker's share of the original play, because the adapter found the Lapyrus plot less interesting than the Tymethes plot.

The original play must have been written after publication of the second edition of William Warner's *Pan his Syrinx* (1597), its chief source. Lake suggested that it belonged to the very beginning of Middleton's career, but Taylor (2001) shows that a series of topical allusions in 2.1 refer to events in 1606+ (drunkenness at court), 1608–9 (dearth), and 1608–9 (piracy). Versification and verbal parallels, in the shares of both authors, also point toward the end of the first decade of the seventeenth century.

A manuscript in the Lord Chamberlain's office establishes that in 1639 the play belonged to the repertory of Beeston's boys, playing at the Cockpit (Chambers 337); the history of this company suggests that they must have acquired the play from the first Prince Charles's Men (1608–25), the Queen Anne's Men (1603–19), or the Children of the Revels playing at the Blackfriars (1600–13). Dekker is not known to have written for the Blackfriars boys. Queen Anne's Men make similar use of dismembered limbs in Heywood's *Golden Age* (1610?). The date and authorship of the adaptation have not been established. Dekker did not die until 1632, but the play might have been adapted by someone else while he was still alive.

Some evidence of the date of the adaptation may be given by 3.2. If the adapter was responsible for the Induction and 2.5, and if (as Taylor suggested) part of 2.5 replaced a Lapyrus scene which originally stood between 3.1 and 3.3, then it is worth considering whether the same adapter might have been responsible for the extant 3.2. The adapter could normally get rid of material from the uninteresting Lapyrus plot by simple omission, but if he had removed an original Lapyrus scene between 3.1 and 3.3 he would have had to replace it with something, in order not to violate the law of re-entry: Roxano and Tymethes exit at the very end of 3.1, and enter at the very beginning of 3.3. The extant 3.2, which fills this gap, is the only scene of the Tymethes plot which, according to Taylor, was not written by Middleton; if by Dekker, it would be his only contribution to that plot (besides the opening and concluding episodes, which connect the two narratives). Taylor's only reason for attributing 3.2 to Dekker was that it contains absolutely no evidence of Middleton, but does use 'hath' twice; if we are sure that Middleton and Dekker are the only two hands in a text, then 'hath' becomes evidence for Dekker, but of course many other writers used it, and we already have evidence of a third, adapting hand in Banquet. (Neither the Induction nor 2.5 uses 'hath' or 'has', so we have no other evidence of the adapter's preference.) On the other hand, the scribe also seems to favour 'hath', so the form cannot in itself be considered compelling evidence for Dekker, or compelling evidence against Middleton. The complete absence of Middleton's oaths or linguistic forms might be attributed to the relative brevity of the scene (35 lines, shorter than any of the scenes confidently attributable to Middleton here); but the fact that not one of the twenty rhymed lines contains a feminine rhyme is hard to explain away, as is the speech prefix 'Omnes', very rare in Middleton, common in Dekker, and not characteristic of the scribe's other work. Moreover, there is no Middleton parallel for the scene's only contraction, t'all (3.2.5).

The scene is dramatically useful: it gives the Young Queen a speaking appearance in Act Three, and makes explicit her role as stage manager of the love-banquet; it also establishes an ironic contrast between the loyal servants who pledge their faiths to her in 3.2, and Roxano, who in 3.1 decides to betray her. If it formed part of the original play, it might have been the first scene of Act Three, where its position would encourage a contrast between the Young Queen and the Old Queen (in the conjectured original scene at the end of Act Two). The alternating plots often create such contrasts, the Old Queen and Young Queen are juxtaposed in 1.3/1.4, and 'I pour my life into your breasts' (3.2.12) could have pointedly recalled the life-giving breasts of the Old Queen as wet-nurse to her own child. The adapter, wishing to abridge the Lapyrus plot, might have decided simply to move this scene from its original location, to fill the gap between 3.1 and 3.3. This might also explain the

apparently erroneous 'Exeunt' in COTES at 3.2.34; if the scene were placed before 3.1, then the servants need not exit before the Young Queen, in order to prepare the banquet which opens 3.3.

If in everything but its position the scene belongs to the original unadapted script, then we would expect Middleton to have written it. But if the scene were an addition to the first draft, an afterthought designed to highlight the contrast between the two Queens, it might have been written by the dominant partner, Dekker. The Young Queen's praise of 'Honest Roxano' (3.2.31-2) may echo Othello's praise of 'Honest Iago'; Dekker was more prone than Middleton to imitate Shakespeare. But the phrase also suggests the equally ironic 'Honest De Flores' (Changeling 4.2.38, 4.2.58, 5.2.9); Roxano's relation to the Young Queen at several points resembles De Flores's relation to Beatrice-Joanna. In particular, the Young Queen's 'he's no needful' (3.2.29) recalls Beatrice-Joanna's 'A wondrous necessary man' (Changeling 5.1.92), and her praise of him as 'so officious' (3.2.32) recalls Beatrice-Joanna's rebuke of De Flores for being 'officious' (Changeling 1.1.231). The concatenation of links to Changeling is certainly remarkable, and presumably accounts for Oliphant's attribution of the scene to Middleton. But is Changeling being anticipated here (by Middleton, the author of both sets of passages), or is a scene in Banquet written by one of the collaborators being remembered by the other collaborator in Changeling?—or is Changeling being remembered by a Caroline adapter? Changeling was in the repertory of Beeston's Boys, and it is impossible to rule out the possibility that an adapter working in or for that company might have been influenced by that popular play, in writing a short scene for Banquet. Although the larger pattern of verbal parallels between Banquet and the Middleton and Dekker canons cannot be easily dismissed, it seems impossible to arbitrate between the various competing explanations for the links to one popular later play in this one passage of 3.2.

Certainly, if 3.2 was not part of the original play, then the adaptation would seem to postdate Changeling (1622). But we do not feel confident in attributing the scene to Middleton, Dekker, or the adapter.

The following notes on the authorship of particular scenes, collected by both editors, supplement the evidence published in Taylor (2000).

Title-page The Bloody Banquet] In Dekker's prose work A Strange Horse-Race (1613) one of the sections is headed 'The Bankrout's Banquet' (Grosart III). The Bachelor's Banquet, which Grosart also includes, is not now considered to be by Dekker.

Persons Drammatis Personae] Dekker's favoured form. Middleton preferred the heading 'Persons'.

1.1.2 The speech prefix 'Omn.' is rare in Middleton: in plays of his sole authorship, it occurs three times (once each in Hengist, Women Beware, and Nice Valour); all three examples occur in late texts, and in plays where other prefixes for group speeches are more common.

By contrast, 'Omnes' is very common in plays written by Dekker after 1599: *Blurt* (17), *Satiromastix* (10), *Honest Whore* (43), *Whore of Babylon* (36), *If This Be Not a Good Play* (84), etc. It occurs again in 3.2 (also apparently not by Middleton, and possibly by Dekker).

1.1.26–7 For a similar example of the work-ethic (and its familiar metaphor from bees) being used in a highly ironic fashion by a character undoubtedly evil, see the speech of Shackle-soule, a devil disguised as a Friar, in Dekker's *If This Be Not A Good Play the Devil Is In It*: 'PRIOR How? Sin to feed religious Votaries! SHAC Rather to nourish idle vagabonds: The Cleargy of other lands, haue with much pietie And thrift destroyde those drones, that lazily Liue eating up the labours of the bee' (1.3.162–168). It is not the idea that is unusual, but its ironic twist, which can be found again in 1.3.8–9 below, a scene which is definitely by Dekker.

1.1.64 The fleecing of young heirs is a frequent concern of Dekker's early pamphlets. In *If This Be Not A Good Play* Dekker shows Bartervile, a London usurer, fleecing a young gentleman, and a more detailed account occurs in *Lantern and Candlelight* chapters iii–iv, particularly in the sections 'The gull-groper', 'The Gull' and 'City-hunting': 'And thus are young heirs cozened out of their Acres before they well know where they lie' (Grosart III, 224). See also note to 2.1.63–4 below.

1.3.8–9 Ironic. See note to 1.1.26–7 above. Dekker, whose works, especially *The Shoemakers' Holiday*, can be seen as exemplifying the Protestant work-ethic, was also aware of how such moralism could be misapplied.

1.3.13–14 Two attempted rapes occur in another Dekker work, *The Virgin Martyr*. The play is a collaboration with Massinger, but the rape-attempts are found in a Dekker scene, 4.1. Sapritius comments on Antoninus's hesitation, 'A souldier, and stand fumbling so' (4.1.98).

1.3.19–23 In *Four Birds of Noah's Ark*, Dekker wrote 'A Prayer for a Souldier going to a battell', and 'A Prayer, or Thanksgiving for a Souldier after victorie' (Grosart V, 28, 29).

1.4.29 Italian padlocks] 'There is a gem I would not loose, kept by the Italian under lock and key' (*Mad World* 1.2.22–23); 'How would you have women locked?—With padlocks, father; the Venetian uses it' (*Chaste Maid* 4.4.4–5).

1.4.60 Compare to Middleton's *Mad World* 5.2.308 'you pledge none but me' where there is a bawdy meaning in the toast; also *Changeling* 5.3.168–71, *Ghost* 128–131, *Lady* 2.3.67.

2.1 Oliphant attributed this scene to Dekker; Taylor (2000) does not attribute it to either author. Both the linguistic evidence ('has') and—more strongly—two oaths (mass, I warrant) point to Middleton; there are occasional examples of 'I warrant' in most of Dekker's plays, but Lake records no examples of 'mass'

in Dekker after *Satiromastix*. In 2.2, by contrast, both the linguistic evidence and the oath 'snails' identify Dekker; 'snails' points as strongly to Dekker as 'mass' points to Middleton. Moreover, the scene division between 2.1 and 2.2 is suspect (see textual notes), and may reflect a change of authors. Perhaps a scene of mixed writing.

2.1.2 usurer's conscience] Dekker attacked usurers habitually: in *If This Be Not A Good Play* the usurer Bartervile teaches the devil a few tricks, and when in the last scene he is welcomed to Hell, it is said of him: 'Golde to get | Hee would hang a Citie, starue a Countrey' (5.4.257–8). But Middleton attacked usurers at least as often as Dekker. For the specific collocation of usurer and conscience, see *Widow* 3.1.46–7, 'no more conscience in us than in usurers?' For the transition from conscience to wolf, see *Trick* 1.3.38 ('the wolf of thy conscience').

2.1.5 devour a widow and three orphans at a breakfast] In Dekker's *The Rauens Almanacke*, a dishonest usurer is made to drink a potion made of 'the teares of poore men, distilled from their eies through the anguish of thy extortion…tempered with the cursses of Widdowes and Orphanes, whome thou hast brought to beggery' (Grosart IV, 239).

2.1.26 A murrain on them] Holdsworth (1994) finds several parallel usages in Middleton: 'A murrain meet 'em', *Revenger* 3.6.84; 'A murrain meet 'em', *Mad World* 2.6.77; 'A murrain on you', *Hengist* 5.1.263. But Dekker has 'how a murrain' (*Shoemaker* 4.2.48) and 'what a murrain' (*Westward Ho* 5.4.108). What seems particular to Middleton is the oath 'a murrain meet'; the form here is less certain.

2.1.28–9 as for example] Often used by Middleton, but rare elsewhere: *Meeting* 586, *No Wit* 3.190–1, *Weapons* 4.1.223, *Tennis* 481, *Women Beware* 1.1.81, *Measure* 1.2.25. See Taylor and Jowett, 204, 223. Small does not record any instances of 'example' in the undisputed Dekker dramatic canon.

2.1.33–4 Holdsworth (correspondence) notes that the image 'just as many sorts as there be knaves in the cards…that's four' echoes two early Middleton pamphlets: 'a battle between the four knaves at the cards for superiority' (*Plato* 275–6) and 'the four knaves at the cards shall suddenly leap from out the bunch' (*Penniless Parliament* 246–7).

2.1.48 Dekker mentions Long Lane in several other works including *The Wonderful Year 1603*, 'Vsurers and Brokers (that are the Diuels Ingles, and dwell in the long lane of hell' (Grosart, I, 87). In *Westward Ho!* (a collaboration between Dekker and Webster) Birdlime reports that he 'prest three knaues my Lord, hirde three Liueries in Long-Lane, to man her', (2.2.45–46). In *Northward Ho!* (Dekker and Webster again) Doll says 'Why I tel thee Iack Hornet, if the Diuel and all the Brokers in long lane had rifled their wardrob, they wud ha been dambd before they had fitted thee thus' (2.1.13–15). In *The Rauens Almanacke* (1609),

Dekker's Epistle, which is addressed to the young gallants of London, prognosticates 'you shall be...so full of health, that you will scorne to keep your beds, but for more securitie, put the brokers of Long Lane in trust to keepe them for you' (Grosart IV, 175). And in Dekker's *A Strange Horse-Race* (1613), one item in the Devil's last will and testament is 'that all the Brokers in Long-lane be sent to me with all speed possible, because I haue much of them laid to pawn to me, which will, I know, neuer be redeemed...' The lack of capital letters in two of these examples resembles COTES here. But 'Long Lane' also appears in Middleton's *Owl* 2496.

2.1.63 in wax] Holdsworth (1994) calls attention to Middleton's use of this rare image of a man in wax, parallel to *Yorkshire* 1.51–2 ('pawned his lands, and made his university brother stand in wax') and *Michaelmas* 4.1.45–6 ('trust his land in wax'). The association of wax with gulling young men of their land also crops up in Dekker's *Lantern and Candlelight* (1608): 'a young Novice...they lay upon the Anvill of their wits, till they have wrought him like wax, for him-selve aswell as for them: to doe any thing in wax...' (Ch. IV, 'How the Warren is Made', Grosart III, 232). But this parallel does not contain the actual phrase 'in wax', or the metaphorical transfer of the wax from the legal document to the land or the person it binds. Moreover, the Middleton parallels clearly antedate *Banquet* and the Dekker parallel in *Lantern*.

2.1.68 In Dekker's *If This be Not a Good Play* the notorious pirates Ward and Dantziger are welcomed into Hell by Pluto and his devils, together with one Schellum who 'scourd the Seas so well, | Charon will make him ferriman of hell' (5.4.87–88). Schellum is mentioned again in passing in *A Strange Horse-Race* (Grosart III, 349). But Middleton refers to pirates in all three of his plays of 1611: *Roaring Girl* 10.136, *No Wit* 9.150, *Lady* 3.1.72.

2.1.74–6 Compare to Dekker's *Match Me In London*, where Cordolente says, 'But as the weake | And smaller flyes i'th Spiders web are tane | When greater ones teare the web, and free remaine, | So may that morall tale of you be told, | Which once the Wolfe related: in the Fold | The Shepheards kill'd a sheepe and eate him there; | The Wolfe lookt in, and seeing them at such cheere, | Alas (quoth he) should I touch the least part | Of what you teare, you would plucke out my hart' (4.1.58–66). Compare also to a passage in *Sir Thomas Wyatt*, a Dekker-Webster collaboration: 'Great men like great Flies, through lawes Cobwebs breake, | But the thin'st frame, the prison of the weake' (5.1.99–100). Bacon's *Apothegms* 181 attributes this latter saying to Queen Elizabeth; it seems to have been proverbial.

2.2.9–10 In *Patient Grissil* (1599), a Dekker collaboration with Chettle and Haughton, Dekker writes a very emotive scene in which the peasant-born Grissil is prevented by her cruel husband, the Marquis,

from breast-feeding her two new-born infants: 'see heer's a fountaine, Which heauen into this Alablaster bowles [sic], | Instil'd to nourish them', (4.1.123–4). In *Banquet* this image is particularly powerful juxtaposed to that of the famished Queen and her two infants. We may also compare Dekker's 'A Prayer in time of Famine', from *Four Birds of Noah's Ark*: '...but open the entrals of the earth, that shee may give to man and beast their wonted sustenance. As thou hast made mouthes, so make meate to fill those mouthes; lest otherwise Christians feed upon the blood of Christians...' (Wilson, 148).

3.3.125 drinking drunk...horrible] Compare 'drink drunk' (*Michaelmas* 1.2.129, *Mad World* 1.1.18) and 'horribly drunk' (*Puritan* 1.4.183).

4.2.57–8 Go: | Report we are forty leagues off] Resembles Antonio's feigned absence for the same reason—suspicion of his wife—in *Witch* 3.2.168–169, and the excuses given by both the Duke in *Revenger* ('rid forth', 5.1.121–4) and Anselmus in *Lady* ('walked forth', 1.2.79).

4.3.51 O miserable youth, none saves thee now] Resembles the Duchess's decision to kill Almachildes after he has told her he has killed the Duke in *Witch* 4.1.46.

4.3.124–5 Hapless boy, | That never knew how dear 'twas to enjoy] Resembles Almachildes in *Witch* 3.1.34–5 'I had hard chance | To light upon this pleasure, that's so costly', i.e. it may cost him his life to sleep with the Duchess.

4.3.210 O hadst thou not confessed! Hadst thou no sleight?] Resembles *Witch* 4.3.54 where Antonio, thinking his wife has betrayed him, says, 'Had it been hid, and done, 't had been done happy...' despite the fact that he has been to great lengths to discover it.

4.3.218 AMBO] A Latin speech prefix that I have never found in Dekker (J.G.).

4.3.240–1 treachery...treacherous; 257 treacher] Spelled 'trechery...trecherous...Trecher', paralleling Middleton's spellings in *Game*: 'Trecher' at 4.2.8 and 'Trecherie' at 4.4.14 (Holdsworth, correspondence).

4.3.282 The bottom drink's the worst in pleasure's cup] See note to 1.4.60 above. In *Mad World* we find 'you pledge none but me. | And since I drink the top, take her...I spice the bottom' (5.2.308–10). Also *Ghost* 127–8 and *Lady* 2.3.122–3 (Holdsworth, correspondence).

5.1.27 T'abuse] Five times elsewhere in Middleton: *Witch* 4.2.101, 5.1.66, *Valour* 5.3.126, *Widow* 1.1.192, *Hengist* 4.2.27; never in Dekker's concorded dramatic canon.

5.1.110.2 *blazing star*] Several times in Middleton, but also in Dekker at *2 Honest Whore* 4.2.52.

5.1.229 What are you] The Old King does not recognize his wife at first: compare 4.3.128–30. The dangers the Young Queen went on to relate were feigned; those of the Old Queen are real. This symmetry of construction, whereby the true and the false are presented in antithesis, is typical of Dekker's best plays, and ultimately relates back to the militant Protestant vision of the world as an apocalyptic confrontation. This strongly suggests Dekker's hand in the design of the play.

Gary Taylor and Julia Gasper

SEE ALSO

Text: *Works*, 641
Textual introduction and apparatus: this volume, 1020

WORKS CITED

Baugh, A. C., 'A Seventeenth Century Play List', *Modern Language Review* 13 (1918), 401–11

Chambers, E. K., ed., 'Dramatic Records: The Lord Chamberlain's Office', in Collections: Vol. II. Part III, gen. ed. W. W. Greg (1931), 389–90 (reproducing Public Record Office xii:5/134)

Grosart, A. B., ed., *The Non-Dramatic Works of Thomas Dekker*, 5 vols (1884–1885)

Holdsworth, R. V., 'Middleton's Authorship of *A Yorkshire Tragedy*', *Review of English Studies* NS 45 (1994), 1–25

Jackson, MacDonald P., 'Editing, Attribution Studies, and *Literature Online*: A New Resource for Research in Renaissance Drama', *Research Opportunities in Renaissance Drama* 37 (1998), 1–15

Oliphant, E. H. C., '*The Bloodie Banquet*: A Dekker-Middleton Play', *Times Literary Supplement* (17 December 1925), 882

Schoenbaum, Samuel, ed., *The Bloody Banquet* (1961)

Small, V. A., R. P. Corballis, and J. M. Harding, *A Concordance to the Dramatic Works of Thomas Dekker*, 5 vols (1984)

Taylor, Gary, 'Gender, Hunger, Horror: The History and Significance of *The Bloody Banquet*', *Journal for Early Modern Cultural Studies* 1 (2001), 1–45

—— 'Thomas Middleton, Thomas Dekker, and *The Bloody Banquet*', *Papers of the Bibliographical Society of America* 94 (2000), 197–233

—— and Jowett, John, '"With New Additions": Theatrical Interpolation in *Measure for Measure*', in *Shakespeare Reshaped 1606–1623* (1993), 107–236

Wilson, F. P., ed., *The Plague Pamphlets of Thomas Dekker* (1925)

Sir Robert Sherley   Spring 1609

This pamphlet was entered in the Stationers' Register on 30 May 1609. On the same day its publisher, John Budge, was fined for having printed the pamphlet before it was authorized (Jackson, 443). To allow time for printing, it must have been completed at some point earlier in May, at the latest. It cannot have been written before Sherley's arrival in Cracow, in autumn 1608, and almost certainly was not written before publication of its Latin source, *Encomia Nominis & Negocij D. Roberti Sherlaeii*, printed in Cracow with a title-page dated '1609' (Shand).

The authorship of this pamphlet is established by the single surviving copy (British Library G.6673) of a separate issue (STC 17894.5) containing a dedication to Sir Thomas Sherley (Additional Passage A), signed 'THOMAS MIDLETON.' (sig. [A3]). The playwright is the only person with that name otherwise known to have been writing and publishing in the period (or recorded in STC).

Moreover, the fact that the playwright can be unequivocally linked to another pamphlet completed and printed at about the same time, *Two Gates*, demonstrates that he was engaged in writing texts for publication rather than performance in 1609.

Without the single surviving dedication page, no one could have assigned this pamphlet to Middleton on the basis of its stylistic features. Translation of another author's work presumably diminished the free play of Middleton's own verbal preferences. However, Lake demonstrated that *Sherley*'s preference for 'amongst', 'toward', and 'whilst' fit the pattern of Middleton's other pamphlets and pageants (273). The original dedication signed by Middleton has a number of phrases that might suggest his authorship. R. V. Holdsworth noted that 'so neere kinne to one another in Actions of Fame and Honour' is 'certainly a favourite Middleton formula' (private communication, 18 September 1990). Middleton uses 'near' before 'kin' (both words variously spelled) at least seven times elsewhere, including 'so neere kinne to' in *Revenger* 1.3.25, the only example of the identical phrase identically spelled in LION or EEBO. Likewise, 'Actions of Fame and Honour' contains the same key words as 'Fame and honour | Of righteous actions' (*Tennis* 801–2); LION offers nothing else comparably close. The collocation 'happy father' occurs also in *Women Beware* 3.2.202; LION records only nine other occurrences printed between 1597 and 1662. The exact phrase 'the selfe same office' occurs also in *Revenger* 1.3.178; in the same period LION records only one other example, and EEBO only four. The closest online parallel for 'your long desired ariuall in' (possessive pronoun, adverb, past participle, the unusual spelling 'ariuall', the preposition 'in') is 'his most wished ariuall in' (*Triumphs of Integrity* 43). The phrase 'to performe the like' occurs in *Chaste Maid* 3.2.77, and only once elsewhere in LION. Although 'eternizing' shows up eleven times in LION in this period, only one example—in *Dissemblers* 1.2.20—is preceded by 'to' or 'unto'. Finally, the salutation, 'Your Worships, in his most selected studies', closely resembles the salutation at the end of the Dedication to *Honourable Entertainments*: 'Euer obedient in his Studies'. Again, LION offers nothing comparable. Given the brevity of the sample, this verbal evidence confirms that the playwright is the Thomas Middleton who wrote this dedication, and hence (presumably) the rest of the text.

We know that *Sherley* must have been finished by mid-May 1609; we know that *Two Gates* cannot have been completed before April 14 (see below), and perhaps not until after April 24 (when Hall's sermon was entered in the Stationers' Register). It is possible that the reference to Hall's sermon in the preliminaries to *Two Gates* was written just after the sermon was given or printed, and that Middleton completed his translation of the much shorter and less complicated text of *Sherley* immediately afterwards. It is impossible to be sure which pamphlet was written or printed first. I have placed *Sherley* earlier because it must have been completed in the spring of 1609, whereas *Two Gates* could have been completed later.

Gary Taylor

SEE ALSO

Text: *Works*, 673
Textual introduction and apparatus: this volume, 598

WORKS CITED

Jackson, William A., ed., *Records of the Court of the Stationers' Company 1602 to 1640* (1957)
Shand, G. B., 'Source and Intent in Middleton's *Sir Robert Sherley*', *Renaissance and Reformation* 19 (1983), 257–64

The Two Gates of Salvation 1609

The initials 'T. M.' appear at the end of the preface to *The Two Gates of Salvation* (B4; l. 190), and Middleton's authorship is confirmed by the dedication in the cancel prelims of the 1620 issue, which gives both his name ('Tho: Middleton') and newly acquired title ('Chronologer to the Honourable Citie of London'). The pamphlet's multiple titles together with the erroneous binding into the BL 1 copy of the 1627 issue of a dedicatory epistle from *Epphata to F. T.* by Samuel Collins gave rise to confusion about its date and authorship not resolved until the appearance of the revised *Short-Title Catalogue*. Among the likely results of this confusion are that the work was not included in the editions of Dyce or Bullen, has never been edited, and is still miscatalogued in various reference works and libraries. My bibliographical examination of *Two Gates* has revealed that the main body of the text in all copies, which runs from B1 to H4, was impressed in 1609. Further, on the strength of his dedication to the 1620 issue the initials of the preface must be Middleton's.

The work cannot have been completed earlier than 14 April 1609, the date on which Joseph Hall's *Passion Sermon* was delivered at Paul's Cross; Middleton refers to this sermon in his preface at l. 130.n. There is no Stationers' Register entry; the title-page of the Emmanuel College copy—the only surviving copy that possesses the original title-page and preliminaries—is dated 1609. Leeds Barroll has established that the theatres were closed from July 1608 to January 1610 because of an extended outbreak of the plague (Barroll 179–84). Plague conditions over this period inevitably took their toll on dramatists' livelihoods. Litigation from these years reveals that Middleton found himself unable to repay a number of debts (Hillebrand, Eccles, Schoenbaum). His strained financial circumstances very likely connect with resort to non-dramatic writing as it had in 1603–4. *The Two Gates of Salvation* would appear then to have come into existence as a measure designed to relieve Middleton's pecuniary woes. The work's unusual collection of different titles and running titles may in this light represent a strategy aimed at eliciting more money from a number of prospective patrons. Whether or not such an explanation for this curious feature of *Two Gates* is accurate, the period immediately following Hall's

sermon as the date of composition fits the circumstances intimately.

Paul Mulholland

SEE ALSO

Text: *Works*, 683
Textual introduction and apparatus: this volume, 600

WORKS CITED

Barroll, Leeds, *Politics, Plague, and Shakespeare's Theater: The Stuart Years* (1991)
Eccles, Mark, '"Thomas Middleton a Poett"', *Studies in Philology* 54 (1957), 516–36
Hillebrand, H. N., 'Thomas Middleton's "The Viper's Brood"', *Modern Language Notes* 42 (1927), 35–8
Mulholland, Paul, 'Thomas Middleton's *The Two Gates of Salvation* (1609): An Instance of Running-title Rotation', *The Library*, VI, 8 (1986), 18–31
Schoenbaum, Samuel, 'A New Middleton Record', *Modern Language Review* 55 (1960), 82–4

The Roaring Girl Spring 1611

The title-page ascription of *The Roaring Girl* to 'T. Middleton and T. Dekkar' and the preface to readers signed 'Thomas Middleton' have provided sufficient assurance of Middleton's part in the play, strengthened by agreement that it is characteristic of his work in many ways. Debate has centred on determining his part in the collaboration with Dekker. Dating, on the other hand, has proven more controversial.

Date. The title-page provides a *terminus ad quem* of 1611 for the play. Until Paul Mulholland's 1977 article, however, dates before 1611 had been accepted. In 1923 E. K. Chambers, following Bullen, proposed 1610. On the basis of an entry concerning Mary Frith in *The Consistory of London Correction Book* dated 1605, discovered and published by Francis W. X. Fincham in 1921, in 1925 Chambers revised his date to 1604–5, supporting Fleay's 1884 proposal. In 1937, R. C. Bald proposed a date of 1607–8, based on similarities between the canting scene (scene 10) and Dekker's *The Belman of London* and on allusions in the text.

With Mulholland's discovery that the *Correction Book* entry had been wrongly dated 1605, its correct date being 1612, the earlier dates proposed were cast in doubt. Mulholland's arguments that the play was written early in 1611, performed in late April or early May and printed by the end of the same year, rest mainly on its connections to the *Correction Book* entry, and have not been challenged. That entry of 27 January 1612 recounts Mary Frith's confession that 'three quarters of a year since' she sat upon the stage of the Fortune Theatre 'in the public view of all the people there present in man's apparel and played upon her lute and sang a song'. Strikingly similar to scene 8 of the play, in which Moll Cutpurse, dressed as a man, plays a viol and sings, the events described in this account also invite a parallel with the Epilogue, which promises 'The Roaring Girl herself, some few days hence, | Shall on this stage give larger recompense' (34–

5). If, as Mulholland suggests (and Cyrus Hoy agrees), there is 'a reasonable chance that Mary Frith may have stood in for the actor impersonating her' in this scene or a part thereof, then the play's first performance would be dated nine months before her court confession, in late April or early May of 1611. The title-page notes that the play 'hath lately been acted on the Fortune-stage' and the play contains several allusions to the Fortune, further strengthening connections with Mary Frith's confession.

Finally, Mary Frith's confession refers to her punishment in Bridewell 'for the misdemeanors aforementioned' at the Fortune, a period of imprisonment that occurred before similar more recent infractions in St Paul's 'since upon Christmas Day at night.' Mulholland notes that this imprisonment might explain the quotation printed on the left side of the title-page portrait of Moll, 'My case is alter'd, I must work for a living.' Hoy finds support for this suggestion in a passage from Dekker's *If This Be Not a Good Play, the Devil Is In It*, which was written after mid-January 1611, referring to Moll Cutpurse as 'late a sore-tormented soul' who has been 'beating hemp in Bridewell' (5.4.105 ff.).

Mary Frith's confession on 27 January was followed by her penance at St Paul's Cross on 9 February, so dated and described in a letter by John Chamberlain. Nine days later, 'a book concerning Mall Cutpurse' was entered by Ambrose Garbrand in the Stationers' Register, and on the same day a fine, also paid by Garbrand, was recorded in *Records of the Court of the Stationers' Company 1602–1640* 'for printing the book of Moll Cutpurse without entering it'. Thus it is clear that the book, dated 1611 on its title-page, was already in print by February 1612.

Mulholland makes two inferences from the conjunction of the two entries with Mary Frith's penance. First, he suggests that it explains Garbrand's connection with the book, because Garbrand 'had a stall conveniently located near the site of the penance' and was 'very likely a friend of' Thomas Archer, who is listed as publisher on the title-page. In stating that 'The legal proceedings involving Mary Frith ... apparently resulted from the play's performance (to which Middleton very likely alludes)', Mulholland suggests that Garbrand was trying to capitalize on the recent spectacle of the penance by selling the book before entering it in the Stationers' Register. Second, Mulholland regards the fine entry as confirming that the Register's entry of 'a book concerning Mall Cutpurse' refers in fact to *The Roaring Girl*, the subtitle of which is 'Moll Cut-purse.'

Mulholland also finds, in several topical allusions, internal evidence to support a date of March or April 1611 for the play's composition. First, in 10.314–16 Moll mentions a knight 'who lost his purse at the last new play i'the Swan'. Records indicate that from about 1599 to 1611 the Swan was primarily a sporting arena, and plays were not performed there. Second, in 7.213–16, Gull mentions a butcher who 'dry beat' a sword-bearing man, a reference that accords with an incident, entered in *Middlesex County Records* on 26 February 1611, in

which two butchers were accused of abusing gentlemen at the Fortune. Third, in defending her reputation in scene 10, Moll makes reference to 'an Italian pander' who knows 'all the close tricks of courtesans' (10.347–9). Her argument is strongly reminiscent of Thomas Coryate's problematic description of the courtesans of Venice in *Coryat's Crudities* (1611), and the link is strengthened by the fact that Prince Henry both financed the publication of *Crudities* and served as patron of the company at the Fortune Theatre. Finally, Greenwit delivers a citation asking Gallipot to appear in Bow Church 'upon *Crastino Sancti Dunstani*—this Easter Term' (9.254), which accords with the calendar of 1612 if the Easter Term of that year is meant, or if the allusion is more casual, with the time of year of the play's composition suggested by other topical evidence.

Authorship. Dekker and Middleton previously collaborated on *I Honest Whore*, for which Lake believes Middleton mainly supplied first drafts which Dekker revised, and *The Magnificent Entertainment*, to which Middleton contributed a single speech. Both works are dated 1604. Apparently, *The Roaring Girl* was their last joint venture. Dyce (1840) thought Middleton's 'by far the greater part', but Bullen (1885) proposed a much more exact scene by scene division, with both dramatists at work in several scenes. Next, Price (1944) attempted a thorough scene by scene analysis, based partly on linguistic features, and reached conclusions markedly different from Bullen's. Barker (1958), differing only slightly from Price, proposed a division on the basis of stylistic traits and parallels of style, plot, and characters with the dramatists' other works. His division runs as follows: Dekker, scenes 1, 2, 7, 9, 10; Middleton, scenes 8 and 11; Middleton and Dekker, scenes 3, 4, 5, and 6, with each dramatist's share varying greatly from scene to scene. Barker does not assign the Prologue or Epilogue.

In two separate studies based on similar methodologies unlike those of Price and Barker, Lake (1975) and Jackson (1979) proposed divisions of authorship substantially in agreement with each other. Identifying and tabulating 'stylistic and sub-stylistic minutiae' such as expletives and contractions that occur often in each author's work and never or seldom in the works of other dramatists, features that can be quantified and assessed numerically, Lake and Jackson proposed the following division: Dekker, scenes 1, 2, 6, 7, 9, 10; Middleton, scenes 3, 4, 5, 8, 11. While Lake assigns the Prologue and Epilogue to Middleton, Jackson believes they were written by Dekker.

Mulholland's reassessment in his 1987 edition of *The Roaring Girl* importantly qualifies the conclusions of Lake and Jackson, however. He cautions against any scene by scene division, arguing that most scenes show evidences of both authors' hands and, citing stylistic features not subject to quantification as well as those tabulated by Lake and Jackson, believes that statistics mislead where evidence of authorship is meager or contradictory. To summarize his most significant modifications of Lake and Jackson: he finds traces of Middleton in scenes 1 and

2, thinks that 'traits of both are mingled throughout' scene 6, concurs with the attribution of scene 10 to Dekker but points to 'a number of Middleton traits... [that] hint at Middleton's involvement in the scene if only as reviser or transcriber'. Largely concurring with Jackson, he considers the Epilogue 'very likely Dekker's' as well as the Prologue. In conclusion, he states that 'Few scenes point conclusively to either dramatist as the main writer'. Citing Cyrus Hoy's belief that 'the designation "Middleton and Dekker" is the only one appropriate for much of the play', Mulholland proposes that the authors revised each other's work so that their writing overlapped, but notes that where plot motifs have antecedents they derive mostly from Middleton.

Coppélia Kahn

SEE ALSO

Text: *Works*, 726
Textual introduction and apparatus: this volume, 610

WORKS CITED

Bald, R. C., 'The Chronology of Middleton's Plays', *Modern Language Review* 32 (1937), 37–9

Barker, Richard Hindry, *Thomas Middleton* (1958)

Bullen, A. H., ed. *The Works of Thomas Middleton* (1885), vol. I, xxxvi–xxxvii

Chamberlain, John, *Letters*, ed. Norman McClure (1939), vol. I, 334

Chambers, E. K., *The Elizabethan Stage* (1923), vol. III, 296

—— 'Elizabethan Stage Gleanings', *Review of English Studies* I (1925), 75–8, 182–6

Coryat, Thomas, *Coryats Crudities* (1611), STC 5808

Dekker, Thomas, *If This Be Not a Good Play, the Devil Is In It, The Dramatic Works of Thomas Dekker* ed. Fredson Bowers (1958), vol. III

Dyce, Alexander, ed., *The Works of Thomas Middleton* (1840), vol. II

Fincham, Francis W. X., 'Notes from the Ecclesiastical Court Records at Somerset House', *Transactions of the Royal Historical Society*, 4th series, 4 (1921), 103–39

Fleay, F. G., 'Thomas Middleton: Annals of His Career', *Shakespeariana* I (October 1884), 297–300

Hoy, Cyrus, *Introduction, Notes, and Commentaries to texts in 'The Dramatic Works of Thomas Dekker'*, edited by Fredson Bowers (1980), vol. III, 3–9

Mulholland, Paul, 'The Date of *The Roaring Girl*', *Review of English Studies* NS 28 (1977), 18–31

—— 'Introduction', *The Roaring Girl*, Revels Plays (1987)

Price, George R., 'The Shares of Middleton and Dekker in a Collaborated Play', *Papers of the Michigan Academy of Sciences, Arts, and Letters* 30 (1944), 601–615

No Wit/Help like a Woman's — Summer 1611

The play is attributed to Middleton in the Stationers' Register entry of 9 September 1653, in Humphrey Moseley's advertising catalogues, and on the title-page of the 1657 edition ('BY | Tho. Middleton, Gent.'). These are late witnesses and derive from a single source, but that source is probably the copy manuscript. Middleton's stylistic traits are pervasive. There are no serious grounds to doubt that Middleton wrote the entire play unaided.

George discusses the implications of Weatherwise's use of maxims from Thomas Bretnor's almanac of 1611. He shows that the play almost certainly belongs to that year, which may be defined as running from January to December in the new style, as in almanacs. The play's action can be dated to 12 June; see 7.105. This and other references to summer, June in particular, and the high incidence of almanac maxims from this time of year, suggest that the play was written or performed around June. George postulates that borrowings from later in the almanac's year indicate later stages of composition; this postulate should perhaps be treated with some scepticism.

James Shirley revived the play for the Werburgh Street theatre in Dublin in 1638. The year can be stipulated because of a specific reference to the current year as 1638 at 7.293. The text's linguistic characteristics rule out any pervasive revision by Shirley, and if he altered the text elsewhere, his hand has not been traced. See Textual Introduction.

John Jowett

SEE ALSO

Text: *Works*, 783
Textual introduction and apparatus: this volume, 1149

WORK CITED

George, David, 'Weather-wise's Almanac and the Date of Middleton's *No Wit No Help like a Woman's*', *Notes and Queries* 211 (1966), 297–301

The Lady's Tragedy — Autumn 1611

The strange and strangely beautiful tragic poem which could not have come down to us under a stupider or less appropriate title than that apparently conferred on it by the licensor of *The Second Maiden's Tragedy*, must by all evidence of internal and external probability be almost unquestionably assigned to the hand of Middleton. The masterly daring of the stage effect, which cannot or should not be mistaken for the merely theatrical audacity of a headlong impressionist at any price, is not more characteristic of the author than the tender and passionate fluency of the flawless verse.

Thus Swinburne on Middleton in *The Age of Shakespeare* (1908), attributing the play largely on the basis of his own excellent ear for verse: it takes a poet to recognize a poet. Swinburne had first considered the play's authorship more than thirty years earlier, in his introductory essay in the second volume of Shepherd's *Works of George Chapman* (1875), which reprinted 'The Second Maiden's Tragedy' in a section of 'Doubtful Plays and Fragments'. Here he begins by dismissing the name of Thomas Goffe (which at some stage had been written beside those of 'Will Shakspear' and George Chapman, on the final page of the single surviving manuscript), and takes up the suggestions of an earlier poet, Thomas Lovell Beddoes, who had observed in 1830, 'Tieck has translated *The 2nd Maiden's Trag[edy]* and attributes it to Massinger, I must ask him, Why? the poisoning and painting is somewhat like him but also like Cyril Tourneur—& it is too imaginative for old Philip' (650). Swinburne acknowledged that *The Lady's Tragedy* shared its gruesome climax with *The Revenger's Tragedy* (then attributed to Tourneur) and Massinger's *The Duke of Milan*, and yet, '[t]he style is certainly and equally unlike that of Chapman, Massinger, or Tourneur; but it is very like the style of Middleton.... Was there but one grain of external evidence,... I should not hesitate in assigning to [Middleton's hand] the workmanship of this poem also'.

Swinburne found in *The Lady's Tragedy* more resemblances to Middleton's later plays (such as *The Witch*, *The Changeling*, and *Women, Beware Women*) than to the earlier *Revenger's Tragedy*. There are, nevertheless, many thematic and linguistic echoes of *The Revenger's Tragedy* in it, but as long as *The Revenger's Tragedy* was attributed to Tourneur, they served only to confuse the question of their common authorship still further. The solution, that both plays were in fact by Middleton, was tentatively proposed by E. H. C. Oliphant, the major reconstructor of the canon, in 1911, and more confidently in his seminal essay of 1926.

The case for Middleton's authorship was argued by Barker in an article of 1945, while Schoenbaum's *Middleton's Tragedies* (1955) refuted the view that the playwright had begun his career by writing comedies and ended with tragedies, demonstrating instead that Middleton had written tragedies at every stage of his career. He traced a clear line of development from *The Revenger's Tragedy* through *The Lady's Tragedy* and *Hengist, King of Kent*, culminating in *The Changeling* and *Women, Beware Women*—to this list we can now add the collaborative *Bloody Banquet*, whose Tyrant anticipates the Tyrant of *The Lady's Tragedy*. In a later book, *Internal Evidence and Elizabethan Dramatic Authorship*, Schoenbaum wrote less confidently: the fact that the manuscript corrections in *The Second Maiden's Tragedy* were not in Middleton's hand constituted a stumbling block for him, though, as Anne Lancashire would point out, there was no reason why they should have been—indeed, there was no evidence of Middleton's hand anywhere in the manuscript. In the 1970s, working independently, Lake and Jackson both published studies that employed linguistic tests to establish a new Middleton canon. For both scholars, *The Revenger's Tragedy* and *The Lady's Tragedy* represented Middleton at his most characteristic, and Jackson used the latter to introduce the kinds of test to which he submitted the rest of the canon.

In addition to typical linguistic preferences and individual usages, *The Lady's Tragedy* displays numerous situations, themes, figures and turns of speech that are highly characteristic of Middleton's dramaturgy, not only in earlier plays (which might be explained away in terms of their influence), but also in a variety of authenticated works composed after 1611. The most immediately striking parallels are, however, with *The Revenger's Tragedy* (1606), with its anti-court satire, a parent attempting to lure a beautiful daughter to a life of sin, the death

of a chaste woman threatened by a lustful ruler, and the subsequent use of her poisoned skull/body as the murder weapon to destroy him. There are many more minor echoes: for example, Govianus's satirical account of a fashionable education (A1.1.84-96) is reminiscent of Vindice's speech at 2.1.209-223, and before that, of passages in *The Black Book* (220-32) and *Father Hubburd's Tales*, where the ant/ploughman similarly complains of 'fines' (525-644).

Though Lancashire did not finally set Middleton's name on the title-page of her edition, she effectively accepted his authorship and gave a valuable account of the play's relationship to the rest of the canon, pointing out a series of figurative parallels between Votarius's soliloquy repenting of his adultery at 2.2.1-21 and that of Sir Penitent Brothel which opens Act 4 of *A Mad World, My Masters*: both include favourite images of sexual temptation, damnation, and gaming. In 5.1, the Wife's 'play', intended to persuade her husband of her innocence, also parallels scenes of play-acting that backfire when overtaken by real events in the last act of *A Mad World, My Masters*, in the Mayor plot of *Hengist, King of Kent* and, with comparably tragic consequences, in the masque at the end of *Women, Beware Women*. Sophonirus's soliloquy as a complacent cuckold (1.1.35-54) anticipates the creation of Allwit in *A Chaste Maid in Cheapside* (especially 1.2.12-56), while the language and imagery of the play often resemble those of *No Wit/Help like a Woman's* (also dating from 1611), despite major differences in mood and subject matter. There, too, Middleton seems to have invented one of the plots, linking it closely with another plot adapted from an identifiable source. The earliest possible date for the composition of *The Lady's Tragedy* is May 1610, when the fanatical François Ravaillac murdered Henry IV of France and was spectacularly tortured to death (see A5.2.141). Buc licensed it on 31 October 1611 and it would have gone into rehearsal and performance during the following weeks.

'Presumably the scribe...made a very faithful copy of the author's papers' observed Lake (188), noting that the manuscript closely followed Middleton's writing practice, even in matters of spelling and punctuation: not only do many of Middleton's preferred contractions and elisions appear, but so do some of his idiosyncratic spellings, for example, the '-cst' endings of the manuscript, as in 'forcst' at 1.2.91, 'forc'st' at 3.1.97, 'plac'st' and 'grac'st' at 4.4.14, 4.4.16. Also characteristic is his use of the speech heading 'All', instead of 'Omnes' (at A3.1.231/B3.1.228, 4.3.56, 4.3.69 and A5.2.179/B5.2.149), and his use of numbers in speech headings, for example when referring to the 'fellows' in Act 3 or the soldiers in Act 4. Several distinctive forms, identified by Howard-Hill in his edition of Middleton's holograph of *A Game at Chess*, are also observable here, for example the oddly placed apostrophe in 'wa'st' at 1.1.13 (compare *Game*, 3.1.102). Middleton made regular use not only of exclamation and question marks, but also of the *punctus percontativus*, a reversed question-mark used to indicate a rhetorical, as opposed to an actual question (described and illustrated by Parkes).

Examples occur at 1.1.13, after 'bould', and at 1.1.71–2 (not all of them are registered as such in Greg's transcript). More eccentrically, he sometimes combined punctuation marks, for example placing question marks over commas, e.g. at A2.1.115, A2.3.51, A53/B45 (see Howard-Hill, *Chess*, xix; Bawcutt, 7). Jackson (1983) argued for Middleton's authorship of *The Revenger's Tragedy* on the grounds that it appeared to have been set from a manuscript in Middleton's own hand; the manuscript of *The Lady's Tragedy* yields comparable evidence that the scribe closely followed Middleton's working draft.

With the exception of Sir George Buc's, none of the hands that appear on the manuscript has been positively identified, so that they have continued to provoke speculation: in 1989, Eric Rasmussen claimed that nine words written in the margin at B5.2.35—'where is he', followed by 'Sol. he is come my lord', deleted—were in Shakespeare's hand. He went on to argue that the addition slips, in the hand of the scribe who had copied out the rest of the manuscript, were also by Shakespeare, instancing verbal similarities. Yet even if his initial conjecture could be established beyond doubt and those nine words were indeed in Shakespeare's handwriting, this would do no more than add to the long list of non-authorial interventions in the text. It certainly does not substantiate any larger claims concerning the authorship of the addition slips, since there is no further evidence to connect them with the marginal insertion at B5.2.35, as MacDonald Jackson pointed out in his reply to Rasmussen (1990). Instead, Jackson demonstrated that the addition slips also reflect Middleton's preferred forms, such as ''em' over 'them' (at B1.1.198), 'e'en' (twice, at B2.1.5 and B5.1.166), and the idiosyncratic form 'alate' (at B4.2a.1), which also occurs twice in the main text (at 2.2.73 and 4.1.70).

An altogether more extravagant claim was advanced in 1994, when Charles Hamilton, a lifelong student of Shakespeare's handwriting, published an edition of the play entitled *The Lost Play of Cardenio, or The Second Maiden's Tragedy*. He claimed not only that this was the lost work by Shakespeare and Fletcher, known to have been acted at court in 1612, but also that the whole manuscript was in Shakespeare's handwriting. Hamilton had been struck by the fact that Cervantes's story of 'The Curious Impertinent', which provides the source for the Wife plot of *The Lady's Tragedy*, is actually inset within the long and diffuse tale of Cardenio and Dorothea that occupies so much of part one of *Don Quixote*, though their juxtaposition does not, of course, make them identical. The story of Cardenio has nothing to do with the action of Middleton's play, and in any case Shakespeare's lost play can be roughly reconstructed from Lewis Theobald's 1728 rewrite, *Double Falshood: or, The Distrest Lovers* (and it bears no relation to the plot of *The Lady's Tragedy*). Long before that, the printer Humphrey Moseley had made two quite separate entries for *Cardenio* and *The Second Maiden's Tragedy* in the Stationers' Register for 9 September 1653.

Julia Briggs

SEE ALSO

Text: *Works*, 839
Textual introduction and apparatus: this volume, 619

WORKS CITED

Barker, Richard Hindry, 'The Authorship of *The Second Maiden's Tragedy* and *The Revenger's Tragedy*', *Shakespeare Association Bulletin* 20 (1945), 51–62, 121–33

Bawcutt, N. W., ed., 'Ralph Crane's Transcript of *A Game at Chess*' by Thomas Middleton, *Collections XV*, Malone Society (1993)

Beddoes, Thomas Lovell, *Works*, ed. H. W. Donner (1935)

Hamilton, Charles, ed., *The Lost Play of Cardenio, or The Second Maiden's Tragedy* (1994)

Howard-Hill, T. H., ed., *A Game at Chess* by Thomas Middleton, Malone Society (1990)

Jackson, MacDonald P., ed., *The Revenger's Tragedy: A Facsimile of the 1607/8 Quarto* by Thomas Middleton (1983)

—— 'The Additions to *The Second Maiden's Tragedy*: Shakespeare or Middleton?' *Shakespeare Quarterly* 41 (1990), 402–7

Johnson, Lowell E., ed., *No Wit, No Help Like a Woman's* by Thomas Middleton, Regents Renaissance Drama (1976)

Lancashire, Anne, ed., *The Second Maiden's Tragedy*, Revels Plays (1978)

Oliphant, Ernest H. C., 'Problems of Authorship in Elizabethan Dramatic Literature', *Modern Philology* 8 (1911), 411–59

—— 'The Authorship of *The Revenger's Tragedy*', *Studies in Philology* 23 (1926), 157–168

Parkes, Malcolm, *Pause and Effect: Punctuation in the West* (1992)

Rasmussen, Eric, 'Shakespeare's Hand in *The Second Maiden's Tragedy*', *Shakespeare Quarterly* 40 (1989), 1–26

Schoenbaum, Samuel, *Middleton's Tragedies: A Critical Study* (1955)

—— *Internal Evidence and Elizabethan Dramatic Authorship* (1966)

Swinburne, Algernon Charles, 'Essay', *The Works of George Chapman*, ed. R. H. Shepherd, vol. 2 (1875)

—— 'Thomas Middleton', *The Age of Shakespeare* (1908)

A Chaste Maid in Cheapside   Spring 1613

Middleton's name is given in full on the title-page of the first printed edition of *Chaste Maid*, and, although his name does not appear in the Stationers' Register entry for the play, the play is thoroughly Middletonian and its authorship has not been questioned. According to Lake, it is one of the twelve plays long agreed by scholars to have been written unassisted by Middleton.

As Parker has demonstrated, much evidence points to the play's first having been acted in 1613. The title-page of the first edition (1630) says the play has been 'often acted at the Swan on the Banke-side, by the Lady Elizabeth her Seruants'. This company, Lady Elizabeth's Men, came into existence and was licensed in April 1611, and moved into the Swan after signing an agreement with Philip Henslowe on 29 August 1611. By autumn 1614, they had moved to Henslowe's new theatre, and never returned to the Swan, which they had vacated by December 1613, to judge from a letter to Henslowe from Robert Daborne (9 December 1613) indicating the company's readiness to move into the new theatre (*Henslowe Papers*, ed. W. W. Greg, 79), and from John Taylor's report of January, 1614, indicating their absence from the Bankside at that time (in 'The True Cause of the Watermen's Suit concerning Players'). The reference in the play to Moll's swan song (5.2.48) may be an allusion to the imminent closing of the Swan. Title-page evidence plus what we know about the acting company and the theatre, then, produce a *terminus ad quem* of April, 1611 and a *terminus a quo* of December, 1613 or perhaps a little later.

Internal evidence for date comprises a rich crop of topical allusions, the most important being references to extraordinarily strict dietary regulations during Lent. As Parker shows, London regulations were extra strict in 1613 because 'a bad harvest in 1612 had left the cattle without winter feed, and consequently there were fears of a dearth' (xxx). During this year, even the usual blanket exemptions for the ill and for pregnant women were suspended, a state of affairs mentioned in the play: the promoters tell Allwit that his excuse 'my wife lies in' will 'not serve [his] turn' (2.2.100-1) when it comes to buying meat, and the Wench runs off (she claims) to fetch a document, a 'true authority from the higher powers' (2.2.151), comprising a special licence to buy meat, even though her mistress is ill—a condition that would have obtained only in 1613, since ordinarily an ill person would come under the blanket exemption and not need a special licence. Of course, conditions obtaining in 1613 *might* have been made the subject of a play in 1614 or even 1620 (or 1920, for that matter). One should always be wary of making simple, one-to-one equations between literature and life. However, given the narrow range of dates established by references to acting company and theatre (above), it makes sense to suspect that the satire on Lenten regulations was a bid for the immediate response and appreciation of an audience suffering at that very moment from the harsh regulations, or at least recalling them clearly from a few months before. (The time-scheme within the play stretches from before Lent to about Easter—see Parker, xxxi.) Such topical allusion loses its immediate force with the passage of time, and although the connection between marketed meat and other kinds of marketed flesh operates at a deeper symbolic level in the play, one not so diminished by the passage of time, the irksomeness of specific regulations and surveillance practices would still have greater public appeal in the time in which it was experienced.

Several smaller details also point to 1613 or slightly earlier. Tim's alarm at the prospect of being whipped may allude to the suicide, in 1612, of the son of the Bishop of Bristol, to avoid the disgrace of being whipped (see Chamberlain I: 335, entry for 12 February 1612). Rider's Dictionary, mentioned at 4.1.97, was the subject of a copyright suit which was brewing in 1613 but which did not come to a head until late 1615 (see Sisson). Mistress Allwit's extravagant lying-in may reflect contemporary amazement at the spectacular expense of the lying-in of the Countess of Salisbury in 1613 (see Chamberlain I: 415, entry for 4 February 1613), a possibility supported by several references to countesses in the text; however,

extravagant lyings-in were a very common literary topic in Renaissance literature. More convincing as dating reference, the water-house mentioned at 1.2.29 is probably the reservoir completed by goldsmith Hugh Myddelton; Thomas Middleton wrote *His Lordship's Entertainment* for its opening on 29 September 1613. Windmills are referred to at 1.2.29: there were windmills for waterpumping in two parts of the city at this time, and on 21 September 1612, patents were taken out for a new type of water-house with windmill, which was supposed to be the subject of a public demonstration (see Parker, 21). The emphasis on (and idealization of) the watermen (4.3, 4.4) may bear some relation to the watermen's petition to the Privy Council in January 1614, which grew out of 'the watermen's resentment at the decrease in their vital theatre business' (Parker, xxxii; see John Taylor's contemporary account). A symbiotic relationship existed between the watermen and the Bankside theatres like the Swan, which owed their viability to water taxis; the praise lavished on watermen in *Chaste Maid* would make little sense outside the context of the Swan Theatre at which the play was acted no later than December of 1613, shortly before the watermen's complaint.

Parker's suggestion that the brief jostling between the comfit-maker's wife and the apothecary's wife at 2.4 reflects a trade quarrel brewing in 1613-14 between the grocers and the apothecaries seems rather strained. More persuasive is his linking of the Kix plot with the Essex divorce case: the full story of this scandal did not become public until 1614, but it was the subject of much gossip in 1613. Parker writes, 'It seems inconceivable that the Kix situation, with its public quarrelling about impotency, talk of drugs and divorce, implication of the lady's scandalous past at court (3.3.50-3), and good offices of a third person who is really the lady's lover, could have failed to recall the current scandal. The very name "Kix" resembles "Essex"' (xxxiv). Parker's seeing in the mention of 'the foreman of a drug-shop' (1.2.37) a veiled allusion to Simon Forman, 'the most notorious dealer in love philtres in London', later implicated in the Essex scandal (xxxiii-xxxiv) is less convincing.

Though (as I suggest in the Critical Introduction) *Chaste Maid* stands in an almost antimasque relation to *The Triumphs of Truth* (1613), the one cynically satirizing the city while the other high-mindedly idealizes it, a number of echoes make it entirely believable that the two were composed in the same year. Most striking, the phrase 'religious wholesome laws', which Touchwood Senior applies to the Lenten meat laws in *Chaste Maid* (2.1.113)—critics have taken this uncharacteristic pronouncement as either irony or a sop to James I, who promoted the laws—recurs as 'wholesome and religious laws' in *Truth* (142), in a transparently non-ironic context, in reference to London's good governance. 'Zeal', an allegorical character in *Truth* (where he is the champion of Truth) is a recurrent word in *Chaste Maid*: Touchwood Junior and a Puritan gossip both apply it to sexual ardour (1.1.153,

3.2.34), while the disguised Allwit uses it to describe his alleged family-spiritedness in revealing the scandalous behaviour of Sir Walter Whorehound (4.1.207). The leading allegorical figure of evil in the antimasque portion of *Truth* is named Error, recalling the fuss Yellowhammer makes over Maudline's use of the word 'errors' in *Chaste Maid* (1.1.25–34). The climax of *Truth* takes place in Cheapside, to which the masquers travel (literally) by boat and floating island across the Thames, recalling the boat chase in *Chaste Maid* which is the culmination of Moll's second elopement attempt. The allegorical doings at the Mount Triumphant in *Truth*'s Cheapside wryly recalls Tim's censored but clearly obscene closing lines at the end of *Chaste Maid*: 'and for my mountains, I'll mount upon——' (5.4.115–16). One of the characters at the Mount Triumphant, appropriately for the year *Chaste Maid* was onstage, is Chastity. Considering the 'base marriage' theme in *Chaste Maid*, it is unsurprising to find, in *Truth*, Truth's ringing declaration, 'What is greatness if not joined with grace? | Like one of high-blood that has married base.' *Chaste Maid*'s talk of 'no woman made without a flaw…But 'tis a husband solders up all cracks' (1.1.36–8) finds an echo in *Truth*'s mention of civic authority being 'so pure a crystal' that any corruption will 'appear soon in some crack or flaw'. Bergeron also discusses these two works together, noting, for example, the Seven Deadly Sins in *Truth*, and the appearance of the same sins in the behaviour of *Chaste Maid*'s characters (one could also adduce the centrality of the number seven in *Chaste Maid* as does Van den Broek—though seven is too common a number to clinch dating by). But while interesting, Bergeron's remarks seem too general to cast much light on the *date* of the play.

Though some individual pieces of evidence for the date 1613 are debatable, the accumulation of evidence from topical reference and from resemblances to *The Triumphs of Truth* is impressive, and combined with the narrow range of possibility as established by the title-page's evidence on theatre and company, this evidence renders fairly firm a date of 1613 for the first acting of the play.

Linda Woodbridge

SEE ALSO

Text: *Works*, 912
Textual introduction and apparatus: this volume, 1011

WORKS CITED

Bergeron, David, 'Middleton's Moral Landscape: *A Chaste Maid in Cheapside* and *The Triumphs of Truth*', in *Accompaninge the Players: Essays Celebrating Thomas Middleton*, ed. Kenneth Friedenreich (1983), 133–46
Chamberlain, John, *The Letters of John Chamberlain*, ed. Norman Egbert McClure, 2 vols (1939)
Greg, W. W., ed., *The Henslowe Papers, being Documents Supplementary to Henslowe's Diary* (1907)
Parker, R. B., ed., *A Chaste Maid in Cheapside* (1969)
Sisson, C. J., 'The Laws of Elizabethan Copyright: the Stationers' View', *The Library*, V, 15 (1960), 8–20
Taylor, John, 'The True Cause of the Watermen's Suit concerning Players', in *All The Works of John Taylor, the Water Poet* (1630)
Van den Broek, A. G., 'Take the Number Seven in Cheapside', *Studies in English Literature, 1500–1900*, 28 (1988), 319–30

The Manner of his Lordship's Entertainment
September 1613

The title-page of this entertainment, which is included at the end of *The Triumphs of Truth*, indicates that Middleton is the author: 'By T. M.' This page also notes the performance on 'Michaelmas Day last'; that is, on 29 September 1613.

David M. Bergeron

SEE ALSO

Text: *Works*, 961
Textual introduction and apparatus: this volume, 629

The Triumphs of Truth   October 1613

The title-page indicates Middleton's authorship ('By Thomas Middleton') and the date of performance ('on the morrow next after Simon and Jude's day, October 29, 1613').

Preparations, according to the records of the Grocers company, began in February 1613, at which point Anthony Munday had offered a 'Device or project in writing'. Middleton's name appears in guild records for April 1614: 'Paid to Thomas Middleton Gent for the ordering overseeing and writing of the whole Device and also for the apparelling the personage in the Pageant the sum of £40.' Munday received £149, which included costs for apparel and for the transportation of the pageant devices. John Grinkin, the artificer, received £310 for all the other expenses incurred for the production, that is, the construction of the devices.

David M. Bergeron

SEE ALSO

Text: *Works*, 968
Textual introduction and apparatus: this volume, 627

Wit at Several Weapons   Late 1613

Although *Weapons* was first printed in the Beaumont and Fletcher folio of 1647, complete with an epilogue apparently crediting at least two acts to Fletcher, and is listed as a Fletcher play by Robert Gardiner's commendatory poem elsewhere in the same volume (c2), most scholars who have studied the play since the late nineteenth century have taken it to be the work of Middleton in collaboration with William Rowley. The external evidence for Fletcher's authorship provided by the 1647 folio is in fact by no means overwhelming: the volume appeared, after all, twenty years after the deaths of Fletcher, Middleton, and Rowley, and its contents certainly include much material written by neither Beaumont nor Fletcher, as contemporary readers recognized. The folio's original Stationers' Register entry of September 1646, moreover, omits to mention both *Weapons* and another play now attributed to Middleton, *Valour* (along with four works by Fletcher), suggesting that at that late stage in the volume's preparation its publisher Humphrey Moseley did not have manuscripts of these two Middletonian plays in his possession: both may have been only belated and uncertain additions to the Fletcher canon, mentioned in Gardiner's poem solely on Moseley's authority. Furthermore, the 'Epilogue at the Reviving of this Play' printed after *Weapons* proves on inspection not to be an epilogue at all but a prologue, and to have no conclusive connection with this particular play. (See Textual Introduction, p. 1062.)

The question of the play's authorship was first reconsidered in the light of internal evidence in the 1880s, when a number of literary scholars were beginning to experiment with statistical tests for authorship based on metre and style, and the more sophisticated and reliable such methods have become, the more firmly *Weapons* has been attributed not to Fletcher but to Middleton and Rowley. F. G. Fleay first made the attribution in 1886 (apparently on no other grounds than intelligent guesswork), and it was reaffirmed by E. H. C. Oliphant in 1891 on considerations of metre, rhyme, and vocabulary. Fleay nonetheless placed sufficient faith in the 1647 folio to believe Fletcher had a minor share in the play, and Oliphant thought it to be a revision of an earlier play by both Beaumont and Fletcher. The view that Fletcher collaborated in the play as it stands, however, has lost favour over the course of the twentieth century, with commentators from G. C. Macaulay (1932) through Robb (1950) to Barker (1958) attributing it entirely to Middleton and Rowley, the latter pointing out a number of parallels with other Middleton plays: the Old Knight–Wittypate plot with the Witgood–Lucre plot of *Trick* and the Follywit–Sir Bounteous plot of *Mad World*, and the situation of Lady Ruinous Gentry in 2.1 with that of Mistress Low-water in Sc. 2 of *No Wit*.

The attribution to Middleton and Rowley has been decisively confirmed by the work of Cyrus Hoy (1960), David Lake (1975) and MacDonald Jackson (1979), whose analyses of the play, looking in particular at the distinctive incidence of different inflections, oaths and contractions compared to the usage of a number of Renaissance playwrights in plays of undisputed sole authorship, all agree in assigning *Weapons* to Middleton and Rowley. Hoy recognizes Middleton's hand in parts of the text by the frequency with which he uses 'ha'', 'h'ad', 'sh'as', 'sh'ad', 'a'th' and the exclamation 'Puh' or 'Push', and points out that the unusual adjective 'frampold' (3.1.300) is also found in *Heroes* (63) and one of the Middletonian sections of *Roaring Girl* (5.11): Rowley's authorship of the remaining scenes is betrayed by his predilection for the contraction ''um' (them) and the interjection 'Tush'. Lake further adduces Middleton's fondness for the contractions 'I've', 'I'm', 'I'd', 'we're', 'they're', 'gin't', 'y'ave', 'i'' and 'on't' and the oaths 'light', 'cuds', ''snigs' and ''slid', and elsewhere in the play traces Rowley's habitual use of 'Lord', ''snails' and 'Ud'so'. Jackson points

to some more distinctively Middletonian expletives and idioms, 'cuds me', 'my life for yours', 'a my troth', 'la you', 'shrew my heart' and 'a purpose', and establishes that the frequency with which 'e'en', 'I'm', 'I'd', 'I've', 'ne'er' 'on't', and ''t' appear in certain parts of the play tallies closely with Middleton's practice in other works, while the comparative infrequency of parentheses elsewhere helps mark these Middletonian sections from those of the more bracket-prone Rowley. Not surprisingly, the play's only two editors since these studies appeared, Sharp and Turner, have no hesitation in publishing the play as the work of Middleton and Rowley (Sharp, indeed, offers further evidence along similar lines in support of the attribution), although both are at pains to record Hoy and Lake's lingering belief that Middleton and Rowley might have merely been revising a lost part-Fletcherian ur-*Weapons*. The case for this view, however, depends heavily on a single word, 'slubber', at 5.1.329, which Hoy notes occurs frequently in Fletcher, and is surely decisively weakened by the fact that the same verb is used by Middleton in *Five Gallants* (2.4.56).

Speculations about missing source-plays aside, the dating of *Weapons* as it stands is a comparatively simple matter. Apart from the first edition itself, there is only one piece of external evidence involved, a scrap of Revels Office waste paper (preserved with the manuscript of Sir George Buc's *History of Richard III*) which lists a number of plays thought to have been under consideration for court performance in 1619 or 1620 (helpfully reproduced by Marcham; see also the discussion above, p. 332). Along with two other Middleton and Rowley collaborations, *Quarrel* and *Old Law*, the list includes the title *Witt at*: although the remaining words have been destroyed by a tear, this is almost certain to refer to *Weapons*, since no other known play has a title beginning with these two words. On this testimony, the latest possible date for *Weapons* would be 1620, and internal evidence allows us to fix an earliest possible date too: at 5.1.220-1 Sir Gregory refers to the New Exchange in the Strand, which did not open until 1609, and at 4.1.359-62 and 5.1.43-8 the Clown talks about visiting the New River at Islington, construction of which began in the same year. The waterway was completed in 1613, an event celebrated by Middleton in *His Lordship's Entertainment* and *Truth*, and the nature of the Clown's allusions (which prophesy sceptically about the river's future, suggesting it is still new and of topical interest, but make it clear that it is already full of water) make it almost certain that *Weapons* too belongs to 1613. (Attempts to fix an earlier date on isolated parts of the play, usually by taking the chronology of Sir Ruinous's fraudulent military history at 1.2.164-82 at face value, have been uniformly unconvincing).

The date of 1613 gives *Weapons* a special place in the canon as the earliest of Middleton's extant collaborations with William Rowley (*Weapons*, *Quarrel*, *Old Law*, *Tennis*, *Changeling*, and *Gypsy*), and the method by which the two playwrights divided their work on this first joint project is thus of particular interest. Hoy, Lake, and Jackson

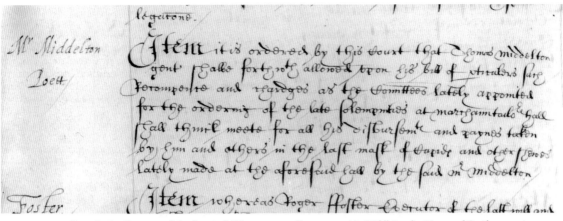

Entry in the *Repertory* of the Court of Aldermen regarding payment to Middleton for *Masque of Cupids*.

all agree in their assignation of scenes between the two collaborators, giving 1.1, 2.1, 3.1, and all of Act 4 to Middleton and the remainder to Rowley, and this division of the play is supported by a striking feature of the 1647 first edition, the inconsistency with which its speech prefixes and stage directions refer to Lady Ruinous Gentry. She is '*Lady Gentry*' and '*Lady*' in 2.1 and 4.1, but '*Lady Ruinous*' and '*L.Ruin*' in Act 5, and this discrepancy almost certainly reflects Middleton's and Rowley's respective practice in their foul papers. (The same probably applies to variations in the Old Knight's surname, given in hyphenated form as '*Old-craft*' and '*Old-Craft*' in Middleton's 1.1 and 3.1 but simply as '*Oldcraft*' in Rowley's 2.4).

It is clear from this that the two writers worked very closely together, presumably from a plot devised in collaboration, since their shares of the play do not divide according to story-line (with Middleton and Rowley contributing roughly equivalent portions of the Wittypate–Old Knight and Cunningame–Niece intrigues), and Hoy, Lake, and Jackson agree that at times Middleton contributed brief passages to Rowley's scenes and vice versa, with a particularly high percentage of such composite writing in Act 5. The fraudulent Greek and Syriac of 1.2.201–28, for example, are highly characteristic of Middleton, although the remainder of the scene is certainly by Rowley, and the last, prose section of the Clown's conversation with Cunningame in Middleton's 4.1 (ll. 343–62) is likely to be by Rowley, who wrote all the Clown's other dialogue (probably for performance by himself) and always has him speak in prose. Despite the closeness of the collaboration and the overall cohesion of the play, this predilection for prose on Rowley's part (with Middleton, as in most of his comedies from *Chaste Maid* onwards, writing predominantly in verse) is only one of a number of distinctions between the playwrights' respective scenes, the most pervasive (though least easily evidenced) being the difference in tone between Middleton's satirical irony and Rowley's more whimsical vein of farce.

It may be that both playwrights' recognition of the discrepancies between, for example, the bitter, malcontented Cunningame of Middleton's scenes and the comparatively undistinguished intriguer of Rowley's helped to motivate the much neater division of labour between serious and comic plots that characterizes the later work of this extraordinarily successful partnership.

Michael Dobson

SEE ALSO

Text: *Works*, 983
Textual introduction and apparatus: this volume, 1062

WORKS CITED

Barker, Richard Hindry, *Thomas Middleton* (1958), 177–80
Fleay, F. G., 'The Chronology of the Plays of Beaumont and Fletcher and Massinger', *Englische Studien* 9 (1886), 25
Hoy, Cyrus, 'The Shares of Fletcher and his Collaborators in the Beaumont and Fletcher Canon (V)', *Studies in Bibliography* 13 (1960), 77–108
Macaulay, G. C., *The Cambridge History of English Literature* (1932), VI, 38
Marcham, Frank, *The King's Office of the Revels* (1925), 14–15
Robb, Dewar M., 'The Canon of William Rowley's Plays', *Modern Language Review* 45 (1950), 129–41
Sharp, Iain, ed., *Wit at Several Weapons*, unpublished dissertation, University of Auckland (1982), 4–42
Turner, Robert Kean, ed., *Wit at Several Weapons*, in Bowers, Fredson, general ed., *Dramatic Works in the Beaumont and Fletcher Canon* (1966–1996), vol. 7 (1989), 301–3

Masque of Cupids January 1614

Evidence for Middleton's involvement is provided by the proceedings of the Court of Aldermen in *Repertory* 31 (pt. 2), which is also the only source for the title of the masque. On Tuesday, 18 January 1614, the entry runs:

M[r]. Middleton Poett. Item it is ordered by this Court that Thomas Middleton gent. shalbe forthw[i]th allowed upon his bill of p[ar]ticulers such Recompence and chardges as the Co[mm]ittees lately appointed for the ordering of the late solempnities at Marchauntailors hall shall thinck meete for all his disbursem[en]t[es] and paynes taken by him and others in the last mask of Cupids and other shewes lately made at the aforesaid hall by the said M^r. Middelton (fol. 239^v).

The entertainment is often called the *Masque of Cupid*, but James R. Sewell, City Archivist of the Corporation of London Records Office, confirms the plural reading:

The word 'Cupids' is, I am sure, intended to be a plural although I can see why confusion has arisen. There is definitely a character after the 'd', although it is arguable as to whether it is an unusual letter 's' or a more than usually abbreviated 'es' mark. The same mark appears in words in the following entry and on the opposite page (written in the same hand) in contexts where it is clearly a plural indicator, particularly after final tall letters such as 'l' and 'd'. There are also examples of final 'd's in singular words with no such mark following, so it cannot be merely a common scribal flourish.

M. T. Jones-Davies and Ton Hoenselaars

SEE ALSO

Text: *Works*, 1033
Textual introduction and apparatus: this volume, 630

More Dissemblers Besides Women   1614

More Dissemblers was entered in the Stationers' Register on 9 September 1653 as a play by Middleton. The 1657 *Two New Plays* of which it is one are described as 'WRITTEN | By *Tho. Middleton*, Gent.'. The attribution is considered secure.

The earliest known mention of the play is the relicensing entry in Sir Henry Herbert's lost office-book of 17 October 1623, George Chalmers's 1799 transcript of which reads:

For the King's Company. An Old Play, called, *More Dissemblers besides Women*: allowed by Sir George Bucke; and being free from alterations was allowed by me, for a new play, called, *The Devil of Dowgate*, or *Usury put to use*: Written by Fletcher.

Bentley (IV, p. 888) explains how in transcription two separate entries became confused. There is no record associating the King's Men with the play before 1623, but the inference that the company owned the play since its first performance may be allowed to stand.

Dissemblers evidently precedes *The Widow* because it gives in full the song 'Come, my dainty doxies' that is quoted more briefly in that play; *The Widow* is no earlier than later 1615, but as it could have been written several years later it does not put an upward limit on the date for *Dissemblers*. Lake (1967), revising Bald's (1936) approximate guess of *c*.1615, suggests that the play was

written in 1619. His arguments may be summarized as follows:

1. The reference to 'This dear time of black velvet' seems to indicate that the play was written during a period of mourning. There were two royal deaths in the second decade of the seventeenth century: Prince Henry (6 November 1612) and Queen Anne (2 March 1619). Lake argues for the latter being more plausible as a source of allusion.

2. The incidence of feminine endings approximates to that in Middleton's later plays.

3. The oaths favoured in the pre-1617 comedies are relatively scarce in *Dissemblers* as they are in other later plays.

4. The play's title picks up on the feminist controversy of the mid-decade, especially Joseph Swetnam's *Arraignment*.

Some of these arguments need qualifying. The reference to black velvet could be no more than a reference to an expensive and fashionable cloth, but is likely to be explained internally with reference to the Duchess's protracted seven years' mourning. It is clear that the Duchess and presumably her court wear mourning garments at the beginning of the play, and the Duchess's rejection of mourning garments in 2.1 would be all the more striking if it were not followed by the court. The evidence of feminine endings is inconclusive, as it places *Dissemblers* in a period spanning from 1612 to 1627. Lake's test on the frequency of oaths is suggestive, and cannot plausibly be dismissed as minor revision of a transcript for the 1623 court performance as Herbert implies that the manuscript was the original one with Buc's licence in it. Nevertheless, this evidence looks as though it is fallible. If it were applied to *Women Beware*, it would place that play earlier than *Dissemblers* itself, a sequence hard to entertain (see discussion of *Women Beware* below). Moreover, the low occurrence of oaths seems to put *Dissemblers* markedly later than *The Widow*, which, as already noted, is unlikely. Perhaps oaths are disfavoured because in many scenes they would be inappropriate. Finally, the link with the feminist controversy is less convincing than in the case of *Women Beware* and need not urge a late date. For example, Francis Beaumont's *The Woman Hater* is dated *c*.1606, so its title cannot refer to Misogynus in the play *Swetnam the Woman Hater* (1617-18); Field's *A Woman is a Weathercock* probably dates from 1609; most importantly, Middleton's own *No Wit/Help like a Woman's* was written in 1611.

Bromham (1980) claims further support for the 1619 dating by identifying the play's Lord Cardinal with de Dominis, Archbishop of Spalatro, the temporary convert to Protestantism whom Middleton satirized as the Fat Bishop in *Game at Chess*. Yet even if *Dissemblers* was written in 1619 there is some doubt as to whether the Archbishop would have already been an object of English Protestant contempt, for rumours of his conversion back to Catholicism began to circulate only towards the end of 1620, by which time the mourning for Queen Anne would have been a thing of the past (Lake suggests that the demand for black velvet slackened in June 1619). Even if he had been available as a suitable object of satire, it would remain unlikely that the play's supposed allusions to him would have been effective. The Cardinal's addiction to ritual and his tendency to sanctify the Duchess make satiric capital out of his Catholic affiliations, but not in terms specific to de Dominis. Bromham parallels his boast of having written entire books of the Duchess's chastity with de Dominis's own industrious book-production, but books are common theatrical emblems of real or false piety (Lactantio carries a book when he enters sanctimoniously at 1.2.95.1), and the Cardinal's works in praise of the Duchess are important within the play for the way they literally inscribe her within a set pattern of behaviour. Middleton may further have been echoing the commentary in the Rheims bible, which says of widowhood that St Ambrose and St Augustine have written 'books intitled thereof, and made it next to virginitie' (Fulke, 1589, Rheims annotation to 1 Timothy 5:3). The supposed allusion is too dubious to be taken as evidence for the play's date.

It seems clear that *Dissemblers* picks up on John Webster's *Duchess of Malfi*, which was probably first performed about October 1613, as a play about a widowed duchess facing the prospect of remarriage, and this might alert us to the possibility of an earlier date—and, unless the direction of influence runs the other way, which is highly unlikely, it rules out a date of completion before late 1613. That date can be pushed further on to early 1614. Jowett (1994) argues that the song 'Venus is Cupid's Only Joy' was taken from Middleton's lost *Masque of Cupids*, performed on 4 January 1614, as perhaps also was the idea behind the play's own 'masque of Cupid' scene, 1.3. Strictly speaking the sequence between the one-stanza song in the play and the two-stanza version in music manuscripts derived (most probably) from the masque is indeterminable. But if the song travelled from *Dissemblers* to the masque, it subsequently went on from there to *Chaste Maid*, where a three-stanza version was probably introduced for a revival; in this case the song must have switched genres twice. Furthermore, the appearance of Cupid in 1.3 of *Dissemblers* intrudes elements of masque, suggesting again that the play was influenced by *Masque of Cupids* rather than vice versa. Middleton had already, in 1611, borrowed from a pageant to supply the framework for the masque scene in another play: the wedding masque in *No Wit* is influenced by the 1604 Entertainment to welcome King James to London, to which Middleton contributed the speech of Zeal. The odds on the direction of influence between *Masque of Cupids* and *Dissemblers* are heavily stacked. The play is unlikely to predate January 1614.

In transposing the song from masque to play, and adapting it accordingly, Middleton might have been prompted by the topicality of the masque as part of the celebration of the most notorious Court marriage in the reign of James I. Is it mere coincidence that two major theatrical precursors for *Dissemblers*, the *Masque of Cupids* and *Duchess of Malfi*, were written within a few months of

each other? That the play also seems to pick up on events of 1612–13 can be discounted as evidence for earlier composition, but might further strengthen the case for early 1614 as against 1619. At 1.2.120 Lactantio expresses a fear of meeting 'a witch far north'. This certain allusion would point most precisely to the Lancashire witch trials. The alleged witches were executed at Lancaster in August 1612, and were made famous in 1613 by Thomas Potts's *The Wonderful Discovery of Witches in the County of Lancaster* (entered in the Stationers' Register on 7 November 1612). At 5.1.8–9 (in the same scene as the reference to black velvet) the Page expresses 'a great longing in me | To bite a piece of the musician's nose off'. This odd desire has, of course, a sexual imputation, and makes reference to strange food-longings during pregnancy, but it also looks like an allusion to an event related by John Chamberlain in a letter of 25 February 1613 to Sir Dudley Carleton:

> Here was an odde fray fell out the last weeke twixt one Huchinson of Greyes Ynne and Sir German Poole, who assaulting the other upon advantage, hurt him in three or foure places, and cut of three of his fingers before he could draw his weapon, whereupon inraged he flew upon him and getting him downe bit of a goode part of his nose and caried yt away in his pocket.

As against these possible allusions, there may have been a general association between the north of England and witches, the Page's odd longing is self-explanatory within the text, and Middleton may have responded to his own *Masque of Cupids* and Webster's *Duchess of Malfi* at any time after 1613 notwithstanding their proximity. Neverthless, the evidence for the earlier dating preponderates, and on this basis we place *Dissemblers* in early 1614.

John Jowett

SEE ALSO

Text: *Works*, 1037
Textual introduction and apparatus: this volume, 1131

WORKS CITED

Bald, R. C., 'The Chronology of Thomas Middleton's Plays', *Modern Language Review* 32 (1937), 33–43

Bentley, G. E., *The Jacobean and Caroline Stage*, 7 vols (1941–68)

Bromham, A. A., 'Middleton's Cardinal of Milan', *Notes and Queries* 225 (1980), 155–7

Chamberlain, John, *Letters*, ed. Norman Egbert McClure, 2 vols (1939)

Fulke, William, *Text of the New Testament of Jesus Christ tr. by Papists at Rheims* (1589)

Jowett, John, 'Middleton's Song of Cupid', *Notes and Queries* 239 (1994), 66–70

Lake, David J., 'The Date of *More Dissemblers Besides Women*', *Notes and Queries* 221 (1976), 219–21

The Widow   Winter 1615–6

The Widow was said, upon its first publication in 1652, to have been 'Written by { Ben: Johnson | John Fletcher |

Tho: Middleton. } Gent.' However, in one copy of that edition (Victoria and Albert, D25A99), a seventeenth-century owner crossed out the first two names, and after Middleton's name appended 'alone'; in another copy (Wellesley) an early hand has written 'Tho: Middleton'. No seventeenth-century collection of the works of either Jonson or Fletcher included *The Widow*. The play-lists by Rogers and Ley and by Archer (both 1656) attribute the play to Middleton alone; Kirkman's lists (1661, 1671) include it under Middleton and Rowley. Clearly, some early readers, for whatever reason, doubted that Jonson and Fletcher had anything to do with this play.

These early doubts have been confirmed by subsequent scholarship. Herford and Simpson find no stylistic trace of Jonson in the play (X, 339). Hoy's linguistic study dismisses the play from the canons of either Fletcher or Jonson; Lake and Jackson provide extensive evidence of Middleton's sole authorship, as does Levine in his edition of the play (vii–xx).

Whoever was responsible for the false identification of Jonson and Fletcher as collaborators, its motives are not difficult to discern. No new play attributed to Middleton had been published since 1630; in the intervening 22 years, only a single play quarto—the 1640 reprint of *Mad World*—had carried his name. By contrast, Jonson's works had been published in a prestigious folio as recently as 1640, Fletcher's in 1647. The attributions to Jonson and Fletcher are, in the circumstances, as suspect as the attribution to Middleton is unexpected and therefore credible.

The fraud might have been deliberately perpetrated by the publisher Humphrey Moseley, or by the actor Alexander Gough, who contributed an epistle 'To the Reader', and probably sold the manuscript to Moseley. (See Textual Introduction.) From 1626 into the 1630s Gough played women's parts for the King's Men at the Blackfriars (Bentley II, 446–7); born in 1614, he could only have known the play through revivals. That such a revival took place is confirmed by the survival of a musical setting for Latrocinio's song at 3.1.22–37; this setting, in British Library Add. MS 29396, ff. 77^v–78, is attributed to 'Mr Will: Lawes'. Cutts claims that this setting was composed for the play's original performances, when Lawes was in his middle teens (*Musique*, 154); but, if we discount *The Widow*, Lawes has no known links to the theatre until 1634 (Lefkowitz 6–12). That song itself is so inextricably a part of the scene, and so Middletonian in its manner and vocabulary, that it must have formed part of the original play; but Lawes seems to have composed a new setting. It would be most economical to assume that the new setting was composed for the same revival(s) through which Gough became familiar with the play.

Gough could well be responsible for the title-page claim that the play had been 'Acted at the private House in *Black-Fryers*, with great Applause, by His late MAJESTIES Servants.' These claims—of successful performance at the most prestigious theatre by the most prestigious company—could have been invented by the publisher Moseley, in order to encourage sales of the book; or they could have been invented by Gough, in order to encourage Moseley to buy the manuscript from him. But the venue and company are plausible enough, given what else we know about Gough's career. Moreover, *The Widow* was included in the list of sixty plays which the Lord Chamberlain, on 7 August 1641, forbade the Stationers from publishing 'without [the King's Men's] knowledge and consent' (Greg 1911, 367–8). This letter independently confirms that the play belonged to the King's Men, and that it was current enough in their repertoire to be worth protecting. However, the title-page almost certainly refers, not to the original company, theatre, and performances, but to a posthumous revival. This probability may, in itself, account for the misattribution: Gough, who knew the play only through a late revival, may not have been entirely certain of its authorship.

This interlocking evidence for a revival (not fully recognized by previous scholars) is potentially significant in relation to both authorship and date. The extant play might include some non-Middletonian material added or altered on the occasion of the revival. Fletcher died in 1625, and there is no evidence for Jonson engaging in theatrical hack-work in the last decade of his life; the evidence for a revival thus does nothing to support either's title-page claims to a part of this text. However, another hand or hands might be present, and the Prologue and Epilogue—printed separately at the end of the text—are particularly likely candidates for interpolation. (See Textual Notes.) Moreover, Middleton did not often provide his plays with prologues and epilogues. (See discussion of *Nice Valour*, below.) Since previous studies of the play's authorship have not isolated these lines for scrutiny, I have paid them particular attention.

Prologue

Prologue.1   Christmas] also the subject of extensive discussion in *Owl* (1618), *Heroes* (1619), and *Honourable Entertainments* 7 (1621), which date from approximately the same period of Middleton's career.

Prologue.2   This hour presents t' you] this hour presents me with *Mad World* 4.5.78 (in both cases, what is presented precedes this clause); this hour presents thee to my heart *Women Beware* 1.1.6–7; the play which we present *Mad World* 5.2.22

Prologue.2   t' you] (a contraction not common in Middleton, but compare 't' him ... t' me' at *No Wit* 4.281–2)

Prologue.3   all th'ambition] All my ambition Is but *Tennis* 587–8; their ambition Does reach no higher *Valour* 2.1.19–20

Prologue.3   't has] (a common enough Middleton contraction)

Prologue.3   fullest aim] whole aim *Revenger* 1.1.74, all my aim *Quarrel* 1.1.9, *Widow* 5.1.297, great aim *Witch* 4.1.48

Prologue.3–4 and . . . aim . . . to win] and my aim | Has
   been to win your love *Game* 4.4.43–4
Prologue.4 Bent at] *Michaelmas* 2.1.112, *Widow*
   4.1.119; Bend at *Dissemblers* 4.1.29
Prologue.5 not quite] *Witch* 4.1.8, *Hengist* 3.3.284, *Women Beware* 1.3.85
Prologue.6 Wearied with sports] We wearièd ourselves
   with our delight *Solomon* 5.63

Epilogue

5.1.457 likings] *Michaelmas* 3.1.52, *Life* 2.1.95
5.1.459 that's not handsome] 'tis not handsome *Women
   Beware* 2.1.43
5.1.459 trust me, no] 'Trust me' is very frequent in
   Middleton, and is preceded by 'no' three times (*Mad
   World* 4.5.11, *Roaring Girl* 10.313, *Women Beware*
   3.2.61).
5.1.460 your loves understood] understood my love
   Michaelmas 4.4.78, our loves the better understood
   Civitatis 54, your grace and love by pleased signs
   understood *Hengist* Epilogue.9, all love's worth . . . understood *Integrity* 302. The rhyme understood/good
   occurs in the prologue poem to *Heroes* (8–9) and the
   epilogue poem to *Hengist* (9–10).
5.1.462 I ha' no money] I have no money *Michaelmas*
   2.3.143, *Widow* 2.1.91

Most of these parallels only confirm that Middleton *could*
have written the Prologue and Epilogue; but the parallels
for Prologue.2, Prologue.3–4, and 5.1.460 are, I believe,
difficult to dismiss. It is also notable that the parallels tend
to cluster in works apparently written about the same time
as *The Widow*. Moreover, as *A Game at Chess* demonstrates,
Middleton himself might decide to add a prologue and
epilogue at some point between completion of a full draft
of the play and its first performances. Such additions
might also be made on the occasion of court performance;
these paratexts would be particularly appropriate for the
Christmas play-season at court.

There is no documentary evidence for the date at which
The Widow was composed and first performed. The song
quoted at 3.1.18 ('Come, my dainty doxies') is given in
full in *Dissemblers* 4.2.56–81. Since *The Widow* does not
use the entire text of the song, but instead only quotes
its refrain, and claims that the song itself is already well-
-known, it seems reasonable to infer that the song was
first performed in *Dissemblers* (where it is given in full, and
not treated as an already-familiar piece). If this reasoning
is correct, then *Dissemblers* presumably antedates *The
Widow*. However, the date of *Dissemblers* is also disputed;
it could be placed anywhere between 1614 and 1619.
(See above.)

More internal evidence for *The Widow*'s date of composition is provided by Martino's reference to 'yellow bands'
being 'hateful' and connected to hanging (5.1.51–4). As
scholars have long recognized, this must refer to the
hanging of Mrs. Anne Turner, on 15 November 1615.
The Widow therefore presumably postdates the hanging.
The difficulty is in knowing how long after that execution

this allusion could have been written. Levine gives an extensive account of references to yellow bands in the period
(xxi–xxvi). They demonstrate only that the fashion remained subject to strong opinions long after the execution;
indeed, Jones and Stallybrass demonstrate that the hostility to yellow bands, and their association with the hanging
of Turner, continued into the 1650s. Although Levine
argues that bands were no longer generally 'hateful' after
about May 1617, Jones and Stallybrass doubt that they
went out of fashion at court, even in the immediate af-
termath of the execution, showing that they remained a
staple of court clothing until c.1625. Moreover, when or
if they went out of fashion is only relevant if we take
the ridiculous old-fashioned Martino as a reliable index
of contemporary fashion. The joke here might result from
Martino's failure to recognize that yellow bands were back
(or still) in fashion. Or the hatefulness of the fashion might
again have become sharply topical when, on 30 January
1621, King James, riding through the streets of London
on his way to the first opening of Parliament in seven
years, saw a window full of ladies 'all in yellow bands',
and 'cried out aloud, "A pox take ye!"' (D'Ewes, I:170).
In itself, this passage is desperately uncertain evidence of
the play's date of composition.

Another allusion to the Overbury trials may occur in the
dialogue following the apparently accidental discovery of
the letter; Martino dismisses it as 'nothing', Phillipa retorts
that 'A letter' has 'been many a man's undoing', and
Martino replies 'So has a warrant' (1.1.138–40). A letter
from Frances Essex to Simon Forman was dramatically
produced at the trial of Mistress Turner on 9 November
1615, when it was stated to have been found accidentally
some time after Forman's death in one of his pockets
(D'Ewes, II:345–6).

Francisco's claim that he is 'used to' playing women's
parts (1.2.111) may also point to a similar date. Both
Barton (p. 228) and Happé (p. 128) conjecture that Dick
Robinson (formerly a boy actor playing women's parts)
played the 'young gallant' Wittipol in Jonson's *The Devil
is an Ass*, and that Jonson's play explicitly calls attention
to Robinson's transition from playing young women to
playing young men. *The Devil is an Ass* was probably
first performed by the King's Men, at the Blackfriars,
in November or December of 1616. This is the same
company which later owned *The Widow*, and performed it
in that same theatre. If they originally owned *The Widow*,
Middleton's play could be exploiting the same transition
exploited by Jonson, at what must have been about the
same time. (The shift would only have been news when
it was new.) This series of suppositions is attractive, but
hardly definitive; every boy actor grows up, and many of
them transitioned into adult playing, and Middleton need
not have been referring to the same actor/transition as
Jonson.

Finally, 4.2.3–16 closely resembles a passage (sig. F2)
in *The Honest Lawyer*, by 'S.S.', entered in the Stationers'
Register on 14 August 1615 and published with a title-
-page dated '1616'.

GRIPE The stone, the stone: I am pitifully grip'd with
the stone. I ha' lost my pissing.

VALENTINE

...Let's see. Me thinks—a little Gun-powder
Should have some strange relation to this fit.
I have seene Gun-powder oft drive out stones
From Forts and Castle-walls, huger then he
Has any in his reynes or bladder, sure.

If either passage is indebted to the other, Middleton must
be the debtor, since his play cannot have been written
until after *The Honest Lawyer* was entered. However,
Middleton might have been struck by this passage during
a performance; the influence, if any, need not have waited
until *The Honest Lawyer* reached print. On the other hand,
he need not have read the play immediately after it was
printed. The parallel therefore tends to confirm only that
The Widow is associated with events which took place late
in 1615 or in 1616.

In conclusion, *The Widow*, written by Middleton alone,
cannot have been completed before December 1615,
and may have been completed in the subsequent twelve
months; if the Prologue belonged to the original script, the
play would seem to have been written late in the year, but
the year in question could be 1615 or 1616. Any more
precise or reliable dating depends upon a more precise or
reliable dating of *Dissemblers*.

Gary Taylor

SEE ALSO

Text: *Works*, 1078
Textual introduction and apparatus: this volume, 1084

WORKS CITED

Barton, Anne, *Ben Jonson, Dramatist* (1984)

Bentley, G. E., *The Jacobean and Caroline Stage*, 7 vols (1941–68)

Cutts, John P., *La Musique de scène de la troupe de Shakespeare: The King's Men sous le règne de Jacques Iᵉʳ*, second edn. rev. (1971)

D'Ewes, Sir Simonds, *The Autobiography and Correspondence*, ed. J. O. Halliwell, 2 vols (1845)

Greg, W. W., ed., *Collections*, Parts IV and V, Malone Society Reprints (1911)

Happé, Peter, ed., *The Devil is an Ass* (1994)

Herford, C. H., and Percy and Evelyn Simpson, ed., *Ben Jonson*, 11 vols (1925–52)

Hoy, Cyrus, 'The Shares of Fletcher and his Collaborators in the Beaumont and Fletcher Canon (V)', *Studies in Bibliography* 13 (1960), 77.–108

Jones, Ann Rosalind, and Peter Stallybrass, *Renaissance Clothing and the Materials of Memory* (2000), 63–85

Lefkowitz, Murray, *William Lawes* (1960)

Levine, R. T., ed., *A Critical Edition of Thomas Middleton's 'The Widow'* (1975)

The Witch   Mid-1616

Proclaimed on the title-page of the manuscript in which
the play survives, Middleton's authorship of *The Witch*
has never been in doubt. The date of its composition
has, however, been the focal point of the best of such
critical discussion as *The Witch* has received. The drift

of consensus has been to date the play ever later in
Middleton's career: where its first editor took it to have
been written 'long before' 1603 (Steevens, 1778, 1793),
its most recent editors agree upon 1616 (Esche, 1993;
Schafer, 1994; this edition). The evidence adduced for
dating *The Witch* can be divided into four categories:
intertextuality; theatre history; stylistic teleology; and
topicality.

Intertextuality: Under discussion here are variously constructed relations between *The Witch* and several other
Jacobean plays. Its early editors addressed its relationship
to *Macbeth*, with which *The Witch* shares some subject
matter, the name of one *dramatis persona* (Hecate), and
the titles of two songs ('Come away, Hecate' and 'Black
spirits'). The qualitative superiority of Shakespeare's play
being unanimously, and more or less eloquently, asserted
by all early critics of *The Witch*, what preoccupied them
was a question of temporal priority. Given the uncertainties around the date of Shakespeare's play and about the
status of the earliest text in which it survives, the most
such discussion can establish about the date of Middleton's was that its composition antedated the publication,
in the Shakespearean First Folio, of the earliest extant
text of *Macbeth*. With 1623 as a *terminus ad quem*, the
relationship of *The Witch* to Ben Jonson's *Masque of Queens*
provides a *terminus a quo*. Jonson's play can be indisputably dated by its performance on 2 February 1609; and
while the extent of the overlap between the two texts is
not great, Jonson's does appear to have been the earlier
and therefore establishes a *terminus a quo* early in 1609
(Lawrence, 32–3; Wickham, 175). Less helpful for dating
of *The Witch* is the possible relationship between it and
The Atheist's Tragedy (George, 209–10). The latter play,
ascribed to Cyril Tourneur, can be confidently dated to
1611; but here neither the direction, nor even the fact, of
indebtedness is sufficiently safe to secure a dating of the
former.

Theatre History: The theatrical provenance of *The Witch*
is proclaimed on the title-page of the manuscript: 'acted
by His Majesties Servants at the Blackfriars'—thus, after
the King's Men took over the playhouse in 1609 (Bentley,
904). For two of the songs in *The Witch* there exist settings
which are convincingly ascribed to composers associated
with the King's Men: Robert Johnson, who is credited with
the setting for 'Come Away, Hecate', worked for the King's
Men principally from 1610 to 1616 or 1617 (Spink, 6);
and John Wilson, who claimed the setting of 'In a Maiden
Time Professed' as his own, from about 1615 (Brooke,
225). If it be assumed both that it was for performance by
the King's Men that each composer wrote his respective
setting of a song for *The Witch*, and also that each was
writing at about the same time as the other, then the
probable date is restricted to the years 1615–1617.

Stylistic Teleology: Within Middleton's career, *The Witch*
is one of the plays which mark his transition from comedy
to tragedy (Schoenbaum, 7–8; McElroy, 155–215; Asp,
211–57; Ewbank, 156). Other plays in this tragicomic
group can be assigned to more or less secure and precise

dates around the middle of the second decade of the seventeenth century: *Dissemblers* to 1614; *Old Law* to 1618-19; and *Quarrel*, in which affinities with *The Witch* are particularly strong, to 1616. *The Witch* can also be situated in another Middletonian transition—from the mimetic mode of the city comedies which he wrote until 1613 to the allegorical mode of the civic entertainments which he wrote from 1613 on. Its resolution and its spectacular sequences of song and dance are analogous with the conventions of a court masque (Lancashire, 171). Moreover, its visual and its verbal languages indicate an above-average acquaintance with iconographical handbooks and an interest in inventing theatrical terms for the images and descriptions circulated in such texts.

Topicality: A scattering of topical references—to the law against witchcraft (Epistle), to the popularity of tobacco (2.1.80-9), to the proliferation of knighthoods (2.1.84), and to an East Indian voyage (2.1.63-4)—are of little use for a firm assignment of *The Witch* to any particular year within the reign of King James I. More helpful are the play's many analogies with, and apparent allusions to, the court scandals surrounding the divorce of Frances Howard from Robert Devereux in 1613, her marriage to Robert Carr at the end of that year, and the Overbury murder trials in 1615 and 1616 (Bald, 41; Lancashire, 163-9; Bromham, 1980; Bromham and Bruzzi, 1990; 24-7). In so far as these correspondences are accepted as evidence that *The Witch* addressed these scandals, they are also negative evidence against dating the play before the middle of 1614 and positive evidence in favour of a date some time in 1616, probably June or later. *Masque of Cupids*, which Middleton is thought to have written for the celebrations surrounding the Howard/Carr wedding, was performed—on four days' notice—at Merchant Taylors' Hall on 4 January 1614. (John Wilson wrote the music for another masque marking the occasion.) It is quite unthinkable that Middleton would have written *The Witch* before the death of the Countess's omnipotent great--uncle, Northampton, in the summer of 1614; it is highly improbable that he would have done so before the ascendancy of George Villiers over Carr from the spring of 1615; and it is unlikely that the play was written before the trials, throughout the autumn of 1615, of the agents in the Overbury murder case. Those trials gave wide publicity to enough of the criminal 'facts' for Middleton to have set about recasting them as dramatic fiction by the beginning of 1616. The mirroring of the printed image of Lady Pride in the broadsheet *Mistress Turner's Farewell to all Women* (reproduced in *Works*, 45) by the stage image of Francisca at 2.3.31-7 establishes 14 November 1615, the date of Anne Turner's execution, as the earliest possible *terminus a quo*. However, the probable *terminus a quo* is six months later. The correspondence between the outcomes of Middleton's play and of the Countess's trial suggests that the composition of the former followed the conclusion of the latter. Additionally, there is the correspondence between the play and the anti-Somerset riddle which, concatenating 'a maid, a wife, a widow, and a whore',

must postdate her husband's trial and condemnation. The couple were tried on successive days, 24 and 25 May 1616. Public interest in the scandals, and particularly in the Countess, continued to be intense in the summer of 1616. Pleas for equal justice, and for the convicted aristocrats to suffer the same penalty as had their agents, did not end with her pardon on 15th July but continued even into the autumn (Lindley, 186). Overall, the middle of 1616 looks likeliest as a date of composition, for performance the following autumn/winter in the course of the King's Men's 1616-17 season at the Blackfriars.

Marion O'Connor

SEE ALSO

Text: *Works*, 1129
Textual introduction and apparatus: this volume, 995

WORKS CITED

Asp, Carolyn, *A Study of Thomas Middleton's Tragicomedies*, Salzburg Studies in English Literature: Jacobean Drama Studies, Vol. 28 (1974)

Bald, R. C., 'The Chronology of Middleton's Plays', *Modern Language Review*, 32 (1937), 33-43

Bentley, G. E. *The Jacobean and Caroline Stage*, vol. 4: *Plays & Playwrights* (1956)

Bromham, Antony A., 'The Date of *The Witch* and the Essex Divorce Case', *Notes and Queries* 225 (1980), 149-57

—— and Zara Bruzzi, *'The Changeling' and the Years of Crisis, 1619-1624: A Hieroglyph of Britain* (1990)

Brooke, Nicholas, ed., *Macbeth* (1990)

Esche, Edward J., ed., *The Witch* (1993)

Ewbank, Inga-Stina, 'The Middle of Middleton', in Murray Biggs, Philip Edwards, Inga-Stina Ewbank, and Eugene M. Waith, eds., *The Arts of Performance in Elizabethan and Early Stuart Drama: Essays for G. K. Hunter* (1991), 156-72

George, David, 'The Problem of Middleton's *The Witch* and its Sources', *Notes and Queries* 212 (1967), 209-11

Johnson, Samuel, and George Steevens, eds., *The Plays of William Shakespeare* (1778), revised edn. Isaac Reed, vol. 7 (1793)

Lancashire, Anne, '*The Witch*: Stage Flop or Political Mistake?', in Kenneth Friedenreich, ed., *'Accompaninge the Players': Essays Celebrating Thomas Middleton, 1580-1980* (1983), 161-81

Lawrence, W. J., 'The Mystery of *Macbeth*: A Solution', in *Shakespeare's Workshop* (1928), 24-38

Lindley, David, *The Trials of Frances Howard: Fact & Fiction at the Court of King James* (1993)

McElroy, John F., *Parody and Burlesque in the Tragicomedies of Thomas Middleton*, Salzburg Studies in English Literature: Jacobean Drama Studies, Vol. 19 (1972)

Schafer, Elizabeth, ed., *The Witch* (1994)

Schoenbaum, Samuel, 'Middleton's Tragicomedies', *Modern Philology*, 54 (1956), 7-19

Spink, Ian, 'Robert Johnson and Seventeenth-Century Theatre Music', in *Shakespeare's Lutenist* (1993), 5-6

[Steevens, George, ed.,] *A Tragi-Coomedie Called The Witch* (1778)

Wickham, Glynne, 'To Fly or Not to Fly? The Problem of Hecate in Shakespeare's *Macbeth*', in *Essays on Drama and Theatre: Liber Amicorum Benjamin Hunningher* (1973), 171-82

Macbeth (adaptation)   Autumn 1616

Macbeth was first printed in 1623 in William Shakespeare's *Comedies, Histories, and Tragedies*. The astrologer

Simon Forman saw a performance at the Globe on 20 April 1611 (Bodleian MS Ashmole 208, X, fols. 207-207^v). Most scholars believe that the play was originally written several years before Forman saw it. That conclusion is based partly on topical allusions, partly upon stylistic evidence.

An allusion to Banquo's ghost has been plausibly detected in Beaumont's *Knight of the Burning Pestle* (*BEPD* 316; composed 1607?), 5.1.22-30. The choice of a Scottish and demonic subject suggests that the play was written after James I's succession. James was touching for 'the king's evil' (4.3.144) as early as November 1604. The reference to equivocation coupled with treason at 2.3.8-11 very probably alludes to the trial of the Gunpowder Plot conspirators (January-March 1606). The reference to 'the Tiger' (1.3.6-24) may allude to the terrible voyage experienced by a ship of that name which arrived back at Milford Haven on 27 June 1606 and at Portsmouth Road on 9 July, after an absence which lasted almost exactly 'weary se'ennights nine times nine' (Loomis). The allusion to Antony at 3.1.57 suggests that *Macbeth* was written at about the same time as Shakespeare's *Antony and Cleopatra* (1606-7?).

Various internal evidence specific to the Shakespeare canon tends to confirm these topical allusions. A test of rare vocabulary links *Macbeth* most clearly to three tragedies—*Hamlet*, *Troilus and Cressida*, and *King Lear*—written between 1600 and 1605 (Slater); a composite metrical test and a colloquialism-in-verse test both place it after *Lear* (1605?) and Shakespeare's share of *Timon of Athens* (1605?) but before *Antony* (1606-7?) (Taylor, 128-9). A test of pauses within verse lines also places it after *Lear* but before *Antony* (Oras). All of this evidence would be compatible with composition in 1606, and most scholars agree that the play was originally written by Shakespeare alone in that year.

The foregoing internal evidence deliberately excludes certain sections of the play, widely believed to be later interpolations. It has been known since 1788 (Reed) that the two songs identified in stage directions in 3.5 and 4.1 appear in Middleton's *The Witch*. The date of *The Witch* has been the subject of much dispute, but no one believes it was written before 1608, and most recent scholarship inclines to 1616 (see above), a decade after the original composition of Shakespeare's play. Full texts of both songs appear in Davenant's 1672 adaptation of *Macbeth* (Spencer); Davenant is unlikely to have had access to *The Witch*, and therefore probably acquired the songs from the pre-Restoration promptbook of the King's Men (Greg and Wilson). As early as 1869, Clark and Wright proposed that the songs had been interpolated into Shakespeare's play on the occasion of a theatrical revival. This conjecture has been widely accepted. The songs draw upon Scot, an important source for Middleton's play, but not otherwise used in *Macbeth*, or in Shakespeare's other Jacobean plays. The Hecate song in 3.5 clearly requires efficient and quiet flying machinery. Such machinery was clearly available at the Blackfriars

theatre (Smith, 414-18); its availability at the Globe is, at best, uncertain, and no one doubts that the Blackfriars had better facilities for this kind of spectacle. The King's Men did not begin using the Blackfriars until two or more years after Shakespeare first composed *Macbeth*. Moreover, Holdsworth's comprehensive survey of English plays written before 1642 demonstrates that the form of the entrance direction for Hecate at 3.5.0.1-2—'*Enter the three Witches, meeting Hecat*'; Enter A, meeting B—is rare in early modern drama, outside Middleton. Middleton uses it ten times in his undisputed works (including two examples in the autograph *Game at Chess*); in the other 623 plays, masques, and shows from the period 1580-1642, it occurs only 27 times. Of those, many come from Thomas Heywood's plays, and ten assume that 'B' is already on stage (which is not true of any of the Middleton examples). No one suspects Heywood here. Elsewhere in the Shakespeare canon, it appears only in a Middleton scene in *Timon of Athens* (1.2.0.2). Shakespeare instead prefers 'Enter severally' or 'Enter A at one door, B at another'. Holdsworth also notes a cluster of verbal parallels between the songs, the lines introducing them, and the Middleton canon. Finally, the two songs are associated with Hecate, a figure who appears in only two English dramatic texts from the period 1500-1660: *Macbeth* and *The Witch* (Berger 53). She appears only in the two affected scenes of *Macbeth*, but is prominent throughout *The Witch*. The Hecate material—spectacular, dispensable, written in a different style and introducing a new character—is typical of 'new additions' (Kerrigan). And Forman does not mention the Hecate passages, though they might be expected to interest him.

Cumulatively, as almost all scholars have recognized, this is compelling evidence for the presence in the 1623 text of late interpolations written by Middleton. It must be emphasized that this conclusion has been reached by *Shakespeare* scholars. (Of the authorities cited above, only Holdsworth had a strong interest in Middleton.) This fact is important for two reasons. First, the attribution of parts of *Macbeth* to Middleton cannot be dismissed as part of a campaign to aggrandize the Middleton canon; most scholars who have given the Hecate material to Middleton have, in the same breath, excoriated it. Second, previous scholarship on this issue has been conducted by people who know a great deal about Shakespeare, and relatively little about Middleton. A more balanced assessment of the authorship problem demands equal attention to possible corroborative evidence in the Middleton canon.

If the original play, written c.1606, was adapted, then the date of the adaptation depends first on the nature of the relationship between *Macbeth* and *The Witch*, and then upon the date of Middleton's play. There is no evidence that the play was altered more than once. Nosworthy argued for an adaptation c.1611, but this was part of an attempt to claim that Shakespeare himself was responsible for adding the Hecate material; few scholars have been persuaded by this scenario, and none should be. Brooke, who accepts Middleton's presence in the extant text, nevertheless suggests that the adaptation of *Macbeth* preceded composition of *The Witch*, and may have occurred as early as 1609-10 (65-6). However, he provides no evidence for this conclusion, beyond the assertion that it is 'the more probable sequence'. If *Macbeth* were altered in 1609-10, it would seem likely that Shakespeare himself would do the altering (as he did with *King Lear*)—and the passages most clearly identifiable as alterations are by Middleton, not Shakespeare. From the perspective of the Middleton canon, too, it makes more sense for *The Witch* and the adapted *Macbeth* to belong to approximately the same period, rather than being separated by (as Brooke proposes) five to seven years; certainly, the verbal parallels between adapted passages and the rest of the Middleton canon do not encourage so early a dating as Brooke proposes.

It therefore seems to us, as to most other scholars, that the adaptation of *Macbeth* followed composition of *The Witch*, which we date in 1616. According to this hypothesis, the adaptation could have been done at any time between spring 1616 and spring 1623. However, if *The Witch* was suppressed for political reasons, then the King's Men would have had an incentive—if they were going to make use of the songs from that play at all— to use them soon; the author would already have been paid for the script, a composer may have been paid for the music, the boy actors may already have learned the songs. Moreover, in November 1616 Middleton's *Civitatis* claims that the 'many thousand faces' of a crowd 'Look like a moving wood' (139); this image is not suggested by anything in the context, and looks like Middleton's reminiscence of a part of *Macbeth* which no one believes that he wrote. *Macbeth* seems to have been fresh in Middleton's mind in autumn 1616. The most likely date for the adaptation would thus seem to be the summer or autumn of 1616 (shortly after Shakespeare's death).

If Middleton contributed the Hecate passages, then it is obvious that he may also be present elsewhere: once the *existence* of a collaborator has been established, external evidence becomes irrelevant, and the claims of the two authors (in this case, Shakespeare and Middleton) and two dates (in this case, 1606 and 1616) must be weighed as objectively as possible, purely on the basis of internal evidence. Clark and Wright, in fact, suspected Middleton's hand, not only in the Hecate scenes, but in 1.2, 1.3, 2.3, and in more than a dozen miscellaneous short passages elsewhere; Fleay found him even more often (1876, 1886). But much of this commentary was casual, and almost entirely based upon a conviction that any perceived contradiction, awkwardness, or bombast should be attributed to a demonized interpolator. It provoked a conservative reaction from scholars like Chambers and Muir, who demolished a good deal of weak speculation. For instance, Shakespeare's authorship of the speeches of the Porter in 2.3 (denied by Clark and Wright) has been demonstrated by Fleay, Muir, and others. The attribution problem is not a matter of assigning blame, but of

determining what kinds of changes were normally made in Jacobean revivals, and which areas of the text resemble the writing of Middleton more than Shakespeare.

Most of the play is demonstrably Shakespeare's. The linguistic markers which Hoy, Lake, and Jackson identified in Middleton's work are sparse; in particular, the striking contrast between the linguistic profile of *Timon* and that of *Macbeth* makes it clear that we are dealing, in *Macbeth*, not with collaborative composition by the same two authors who created *Timon* but with late adaptation, where the adapter's presence is more fugitive. This linguistic evidence is confirmed by studies of syntax (Burton, Houston) and imagery (Spurgeon, Clemens); the verbal texture of the play is overwhelmingly Shakespearean.

Abridgement

Nevertheless, if Shakespeare wrote the great majority of the extant text, that does not mean that the extant text includes everything he wrote. Middleton almost certainly abridged the original. The play's anomalous brevity is easily statistically demonstrated by comparison with non--collaborative texts in Wells and Taylor's original-spelling edition (which gives consecutive line numbers for each play). If all that Middleton did was add the Hecate material, then the original play would have been only 2049 lines long—shorter than any play in the Shakespeare canon except *Comedy of Errors* (1778). Unlike *Errors*, *Macbeth* is not a comedy, not an early work, and not confined by the unities of time and place. Shakespeare's comedies (average 2566) are consistently briefer than his histories (average 3032) and tragedies (average 3046). Of 16 comedies, only three contain *more* than 2800 lines (*All's Well*, *Winter's Tale*, and *Cymbeline*); of the other 21 histories and tragedies, only six contain *less* than 2800 lines (collaborative *Titus*, collaborative *1 Henry VI*, *Richard II*, *King John*, *Caesar*, and collaborative *Timon*). Noticeably, all three long comedies were written between 1603 and 1610; discounting *Timon* (which combines Middleton's compression with Shakespeare's expansiveness), all the shorter historical-tragical plays date from before 1600. There are two clear patterns in the length of Shakespeare's plays: comedies are shorter than histories and tragedies, and early plays are shorter than late ones. In fact, Shakespeare was at his most consistently expansive between 1602 and 1610. Discounting the collaborative *Timon* and the collaborative and corrupt *Pericles*, the nine plays Shakespeare wrote in the four years before and the four years after *Macbeth* average 3106 lines. The shortest of those nine plays is in fact *Measure for Measure*, another text apparently adapted by Middleton; without it, the average would be 3156. By either of these measurements, *Macbeth* is massively anomalous: less than two-thirds the average length of the other Shakespeare plays in the period of its original composition, less than two-thirds the average length of Shakespeare's other tragedies.

These figures would be even more anomalous if we took account of the nature of the copy behind other Shakespeare histories and tragedies, as defined by Wells and Taylor's *Companion*. Discounting the Shakespeare-Middleton *Timon*, the shortest tragedies are *Titus* (early, collaborative) and *Julius Caesar* (deriving from a late promptbook). The shortest histories are *1 Henry VI* (collaborative) and *King John* (set from the promptbook of a late revival). Among histories and tragedies entirely by Shakespeare which survive in an apparently uncut untheatrical text, the shortest text is *Richard II* (at least 2746 in its original state, and shorter in performance, since the quarto and folio texts have both apparently been cut). *Macbeth*, written in a more expansive period of Shakespeare's career, is only 75 per cent as long as this shortest parallel. On the basis of such comparisons, it seems likely that anywhere from 700 to 1200 lines have been cut.

There is also another piece of evidence that the play has been cut. As I noted in 1987, without the Hecate material the play fits the normal Shakespeare profile for the distribution of function words, with one exception: the frequency of 'by' is far too low (86). This discrepancy cannot be due to Middleton's authorship of any large proportion of the text, but it could be due to an abridgement which abbreviated existing scenes and speeches, partly—as in *A Game at Chess*—by eliminating subsidiary clauses (like those which begin with 'by').

The play's brevity has been defended by critics who believe it is somehow thematically relevant, but Brooke has forcefully refuted such claims (55–6). As can be seen by examination of the abridgement of Middleton's own *A Game at Chess* (Bawcutt), astute cutting leaves a play's essential narrative intact, without leaving any sense of incoherence or yawning gaps; it gives us the same story, but in a compressed and accelerated form. To the extent that critics have admired the speed and intensity of *Macbeth*, they have been admiring artistic virtues much more characteristic of Middleton than of Shakespeare. As the preceding figures demonstrate, and as many more impressionistic critical evaluations have testified, Shakespeare was a 'generous' writer; as the comparable statistics for Middleton's plays demonstrate, and as many more impressionistic critical evaluations (like those quoted above by Jackson, 'Early Modern Authorship') have testified, Middleton specialized in a leaner, brisk abruptness.

Middleton's contributions to *Macbeth* were thus apparently of two kinds: cuts and additions. The cuts will be, by definition, very difficult to identify. Coghill made a strong case that the original play included an appearance of King Edward the Confessor, probably in what is now 4.3. Fleay (1876), noting that Angus speaks only seventeen lines in the extant text and 'is not of the slightest use in the play', plausibly conjectured that 'Middleton has cut down Angus's part in the original play by omitting scenes in which he appeared'. Two stage directions—at 1.2.44.2 (Angus) and 2.3.87.1 (Ross)—suggest that the scenes in which they appear once contained a part for characters who are, in the abridgement, eliminated from them. (See text notes.)

In 1.2, moreover, there is other evidence of abridgement. Most of the scene's extant dialogue is clearly Shakespeare's. Linguistically, the use of the -eth inflection (2) and the two occurrences of 'hath' (68) are characteristic of Shakespeare, not late Middleton. The vocabulary and imagery are also predominantly Shakespeare's. He used 'multiplying' (11) as an adjective three times, all *c*.1603–8 (*All's Well*, *Coriolanus*, *Timon* 4.1), and also collocated 'natures' and 'villainy' (*Timon* 14.19–20); 'brandished steel' (17) echoes 'brandish...steel' (*Richard II* 4.1.50); Shakespeare often, and Middleton never, associates blood with the verb 'smoke' (18); 'valour's minion' (19) is likely to be Shakespeare's, who used 'minion' much more often than Middleton (22, vs. 4), and specifically in possessive constructions ('Mars's hot minion' *Tempest* 4.1.98, 'Fortune's minion' *1 Henry IV* 1.1.83); 'carved out his passage' (20) resembles 'Be his own carver and cut out his way' (*Richard II* 2.3.144); the aphetic verb form 'gins' (25), never used by Middleton, occurs seven times in Shakespeare, once of the sun (*Cymbeline*), five times between 1600 and 1610; 'surveying vantage' (31) echoes 'survey the vantage' (*Richard III* 5.3.15); Shakespeare, but not Middleton, associates 'supply' with 'fresh' and 'men'; Shakespeare contrasts 'hare' and 'lion' (35, *1 Henry IV* 1.3.196); 'cannons overcharged' (37) recalls the 'overchargèd gun' of *Contention* 3.2.331; Shakespeare uses the verb 'reek' of blood and bodies in battle, and often has characters 'bathe' in blood (35); 'say sooth' (36), 'doubly redoubled' (38), 'memorize' and 'Golgotha' (40) are all Shakespearean, as are 'craves composition' (60) and 'deign' (61). Moreover, a number of words and phrases—'sergeant' (3), 'the western isles...of kerns and gallowglasses' (12–13), 'cousin' and 'valiant...gentleman' (24), 'Sweno' (60), 'Saint Colme's Inch' (63) and 'thane of Cawdor' (65)—all come from Holinshed, and hence presumably from the original text. Holinshed here also includes a storm which wrecks ships (25); while the content comes from Holinshed, the language comes from Shakespeare, for although Middleton uses 'direful' once, in Shakespeare it occurs eight other times, including 'direful...wreck' [of a ship in a storm] (*Tempest* 1.2.26).

But although most of what remains in the scene is Shakespeare's, the extant scene almost certainly differs from his text. Chambers, Wilson, and Brooke plausibly argue that the dialogue of the original scene has been abridged, resulting in various kinds of metrical, syntactical, and narrative strain. Although Middleton cannot have written all of those lines himself, he may well have combined some of his own writing with material culled from a longer original (as he does, for instance, in *Penniless Parliament*). Cutting or transposing material might have entailed writing new bridging phrases or passages.

Holdsworth, surveying all the extant dramatic texts from 1580 to 1642, demonstrates that the opening stage direction ('*Enter.... meeting a bleeding Captain*') is, here as in 3.5, strong evidence for Middleton's presence. Although the word 'meeting' does occur in stage directions by other playwrights, the formula 'Enter X meeting Y' (where both

X and Y are entering) is rare outside Middleton's work, and never occurs in Shakespeare except in the Middletonian sections of *Timon* and here in *Macbeth* (Holdsworth, 169–218). There are also several verbal parallels linking Middleton to the speeches of the bleeding captain. His first words—'Doubtful it stood' (7)—combine 'it stood' with a qualifying adjective, a phrase-pattern found nowhere else in Shakespeare but duplicated at *Dissemblers* 1.2.182 ('it stood blest'). There is no parallel in Shakespeare for the image of 'two spent swimmers that do cling together | And choke their art' (8–9), but Middleton has 'much like the *art* of swimming ... *swimmer* ... *swims* ... *swim* ... *choked*' at *Weapons* 1.1.16–29; Shakespeare never uses the verb 'cling' in this sense (OED 1), but Middleton does three times (*Revenger* 1.3.61, 4.4.64, *Women Beware* 3.1.107). The transitional phrase 'but all's too weak' (15) uses the collocation 'all's too', unparalleled in Shakespeare, but found in Middleton at *Mad World* 5.1.119 and *Lady* 4.3.126; 'all too weak' (*Dissemblers* 3.1.257) is the closest parallel for the whole phrase in either canon. A summarizing phrase like this could easily cover a cut. For 'unseamed him from the nave to th' chops' (22)—which has no parallel in Holinshed, where MacDowald commits suicide—the closest parallel is 'rip thee down from neck to navel' (*Witch* 5.1.14); neither author uses 'unseamed' elsewhere, but Shakespeare never elsewhere uses the word 'seam' at all, which appears at least six times in Middleton, including the verb 'seamed' (*Meeting of Gallants* 201). Another set of overlapping parallels suggests that Middleton wrote 'So from that spring, whence comfort seemed to come, | Discomfort swells' (27–8). There is no Shakespeare parallel for 'seemed to come'; Middleton has '*seemed* she strove *to come*' (*Women Beware* 1.2.23) and 'seem to come' (*Widow* 5.1.246). Although both authors juxtapose 'comfort' and 'come', Middleton does so much more often, and only Middleton also juxtaposes 'come' and 'discomfort' (*Mad World* 3.2.213–4), or associates 'comfort' with liquids (*Mad World* 3.2.78, *Puritan* 3.1.48, *Five Gallants* 4.6.16, *Solomon* 19.104), or with the verb 'spring' ('sprung forth fruits of comfort', *Roaring Girl* 11.95). Middleton also, unlike Shakespeare, collocates the noun spring and the verb 'swells' (*Entertainments* 10.47). The phrase 'that spring' occurs twice in Middleton (*Solomon* 4.125, 7.253), and 'that [adjective] spring' three times (*Hengist* 4.3.4, *Game* 1.1.197, 4.1.140); Shakespeare never uses 'that' before 'spring'. Moreover, a textual crux at the end of the preceding line suggests that this whole clause may displace something which has been cut (see text note at 1.2.26). After this Middletonian clause comes 'Mark, King of Scotland, mark' (28), for which both canons provide parallels ('Mark, Marcus, mark', *Titus Andronicus* 3.1.143, beginning of verse line; 'Mark, autumn, mark', *Entertainments* 8.14, end of verse line). The following line—'No sooner Justice had, with Valour armed'—is more Middletonian; although both authors use the phrase 'no sooner', it is more common in Middleton (27, eight at the beginning of a sentence) than in Shakespeare's

much larger canon (19, only twice at the beginning of a sentence); moreover, Shakespeare never links 'justice' and 'valour', as Middleton does at *Invention* 38 ('Justice and valour')—in a speech spoken by an 'armed' figure (22).

The likeliest reason for Middleton having written the opening stage direction, and some phrases within the scene, is that the original text has here been abridged or compressed. Noticeably, the Middleton parallels all concentrate in a few lines (8–9, 15, 22, 27–9), none of which is dependent upon Holinshed. This pattern itself suggests adaptation; otherwise, the non-Shakespearean parallels should have been distributed randomly throughout the text. Moreover, all the Middletonian lines deal with the defeat of McDonwald, and the transition from those events to the Norwegian attack; I see no evidence of Middleton after the first mention of 'the Norwegian lord' (31). Shakespeare, who began writing onstage battle scenes at the beginning of his career, in the three Henry VI plays, was still staging battles as late as *Antony and Cleopatra* (1606–7?) and *Coriolanus* (1608?), but even then a younger generation of playwrights and playgoers were beginning to think it rather old-fashioned and ridiculous to represent a battle with 'three rusty swords, And help of some few foot-and-half-foot words' (Ben Jonson, revised *Every Man in His Humour*, Prologue.9–10); indeed, Jonson's satire here was clearly aimed at Shakespeare. The Blackfriars playhouse, which the King's Men acquired in 1608, was much less suitable for such scenes than the Globe (Gurr, 131–2). By 1616, a playwright like Middleton, asked to adapt Shakespeare's *Macbeth*, might have begun by abridging the battle sequence with which it had begun. Just as *Coriolanus* has a sustained battle sequence in Act One, so *Macbeth* as written by Shakespeare might have staged some of the material which 1.2 narrates. Or that scene itself might have begun with a conversation between Duncan and other lords before the entry of the bleeding sergeant; if Middleton deleted that opening conversation, he would have needed to compress two entrance directions into one—which is exactly what his characteristic formula (Enter X meeting Y) does. Either scenario would explain why 1.2 combines material dealing with *two* separate sets of battles, the first against MacDonwald (7–30), the second against Norway and Cawdor (31–68); either scenario would explain why Middleton is most clearly visible, verbally, in the first sequence. Although we cannot be certain of which explanation is correct, it does seem certain that the first twenty-nine lines of 1.2, at least, represent abridged, adapted, and mixed writing.

Forman and Act One, scene three

Additions are much easier to identify than deletions. For possible Middleton additions to the original play, we have both external and internal evidence. If *Macbeth* was adapted in 1616, Forman in 1611 must have attended a performance of the unadapted text. Forman's account—here reproduced from Chambers, II.337–8—is therefore valuable evidence of Shakespeare's play before Middleton adapted it. (To facilitate analysis, I have inserted, in square brackets, scene-references to the extant text.)

In Mackbeth at the Glob, 161[1], the 20 of Aprill Saturday, ther was to be obserued, firste, howe [1.3] Mackbeth and Bancko, 2 noble men of Scotland, Ridinge thorowe a wod, ther stode before them 3 women feiries or Nimphes, And saluted Mackbeth, sayine, 3 tymes vnto him, haille Mackbeth, king of Codon; for thou shalt be a kinge, but shalt beget No kinges, &c. Then said Bancko, What all to Mackbeth And nothing to me. Yes, said the nimphes, haille to thee Bancko, thou shalt beget kinges, yet be no kinge. And so they departed & [1.4] cam to the Courte of Scotland to Dunkin king of Scotes, and yt was in the dais of Edward the Confessor. And Dunkin bad them both kindly wellcome, And made Mackbeth forth with Prince of Northumberland, and sent him hom to his own castell, and appointed Mackbeth to prouid for him, for he would sup with him the next dai at night, & [1.6-1.7] did soe. And Mackebeth contriued to kill Dunkin, & thorowe the persuasion of his wife [2.1-2.2] did that night Murder the kinge in his own Castell, beinge his guest. And ther were many prodigies seen that night & the dai before [2.3, 2.4]. And when Mack Beth had murdred the kinge, the blod on his handes could not be washed of by Any meanes, nor from his wiues handes, which handled the bloddi daggers in hiding them, By which means they became both moch amazed & Affronted. The murder being knowen, Dunkins 2 sonns fled, the on to England, the [other to] Walles, to saue them selues, they being fled, they were supposed guilty of the murder of their father, which was nothinge so. [3.1] Then was Mackbeth crownded kinge, and then he for feare of Banko, his old companion, that he should beget kinges but be no kinge him selfe, he contriued the death of Banko, and caused him [3.3] to be Murdred on the way as he Rode. [3.4] The next night, being at supper with his noble men whom he had bid to a feast to the which also Banco should haue com, he began to speake of Noble Banco, and to wish that he wer ther. And as he thus did, standing vp to drincke a Carouse to him, the ghoste of Banco came and sate down in his cheier behind him. And he turninge About to sit down Again sawe the goste of Banco, which fronted him so, that he fell into a great passion of fear and fury, Vtterynge many wordes about his murder, by which, [3.6] when they hard that Banco was Murdred they Suspected Mackbet.

[3.6, 4.3] Then MackDoue fled to England to the kinges sonn, And soe they Raised an Army, [5.2–5.9] And cam into Scotland, and at Dunston Anyse overthrue Mackbet. [4.2] In the meantyme whille Macdouee was in England, Mackbet slewe Macdoues wife & children, and [5.10] after in the battelle Mackdoue slewe Mackbet.

[5.1] Obserue Also howe Mackbetes quen did Rise in the night in her slepe, & walke and talked and confessed all, & the doctor noted her wordes.

Forman kept these notes for his own satisfaction, not ours, and it is clear that some parts of the story interested him more than others. Consequently, as his corresponding account of *Cymbeline* demonstrates, he could fail to mention whole scenes if they did not strike him, or only mention the brief part of a scene which seemed relevant to his summary. Forman's summary demonstrates that the extant text does not eliminate anything which Forman thought most significant to the story. Again, this fits the profile of the abridgement of *A Game at Chess*, which preserves those features of the full play remarked upon by the many contemporary references to its performance.

Forman records one spectacular effect that does not appear in the extant text: in what corresponds to 1.3, he has Macbeth and Banquo 'riding'. Scragg considered it unlikely that Macbeth appears on horseback, but her argument underestimated the evidence for adaptation and abridgement of the original text. Two of the three unequivocal examples of a (property, or live) horse cited by Dessen and Thomson occur in plays performed at the Globe, before (*Alarum for London*) and after (*The Late Lancashire Witches*) the original performances of *Macbeth*. The effect may seem crude, but Shakespeare throughout his career demonstrated his ability to transform crude conventions into mechanisms of great theatrical and symbolic impact. Such a staging would have been impossible in an indoor playhouse like the Blackfriars. Since *Witch* was designed for performance at the Blackfriars, it is reasonable to assume that *Macbeth* was adapted for the same playhouse, and the change of theatrical venue would account for this change in the text. The removal of the horse(s) almost certainly resulted in some abridgement of the text of 1.3.

Anything *not* mentioned by Forman could be an addition, but need not be. As already noted, there is already a consensus that the Hecate scene (3.5) and her speeches in 4.1 are interpolations. This suggests that Middleton supplemented the supernatural and spectacular aspects of the play, and he is therefore likeliest to have affected 1.1, 1.3, and 4.1. But the addition of the Hecate material, in itself, would have compelled other changes to the play, because of its major consequences for casting requirements.

If all the play's witches were, like other female roles, played by boy actors, then the added scene 3.5 would have required eight boy actors (3 witches, 3 spirits, Hecate, a spirit like a cat small enough to join Hecate on a flying machine), and the expanded scene 4.1 would also have required eight boy actors (6 witches, Hecate, one boy doubling as two speaking child-apparitions). Bradley has concluded that 'after about 1600, boys rarely doubled' (44); if he is right, the 1623 text of *Macbeth* would have required thirteen boy actors (if the witches were played by boys). But even with doubling, the 1623 text makes extraordinary demands on the company. These figures in themselves corroborate the conclusion that Hecate is an addition to the original script, because no King's Men play of the first decade of the seventeenth century requires so many boy actors. In fact, such demands would have been impractical at any period of the company's history. The play therefore was almost certainly altered in at least two respects to accommodate the impossible demand for boys created by the Hecate additions.

First, the gender of the three original witches was changed. Throughout Shakespeare's dialogue they are referred to as 'sisters', and therefore female. Likewise, in Forman's account the three figures Macbeth and Banquo meet in 1.3 are '3 women feiries or Nimphes'. But that gender designation contradicts the explicit reference to 'beards' in Banquo's first speech to the sisters (ll. 42–4). Although Forman's account sometimes (understandably) confuses unfamiliar proper names which he only *heard*, this is the only case where the extant text explicitly contradicts what Forman says he heard *and saw*, and since these characters presumably appeared in at least three scenes it is hard to explain how Forman could have taken them for women if they were bearded. To explain this discrepancy, Shakespeare scholars have been forced to conjecture that Forman's account of the play has, here alone, been contaminated by Holinshed, Shakespeare's source, who calls these figures 'nymphs or fairies'. But why should Forman draw upon Holinshed here, and nowhere else? Traister 'found no references to Holinshed among Forman's' very extensive surviving papers (171). Brooke, in defence of his thesis that Forman has been contaminated by Holinshed, objects that the words 'nymphs' and 'fairies' are 'not in the play, not likely ever to have been, and not likely to have occurred to anyone as a description of the Weïrd Sisters as played by male actors in 1611' (234–5). But whether they were played 'by male actors in 1611' is the very point at issue here, and Brooke has no basis for the claim that the words are 'not likely ever' to have been in the play; of course, anyone who needed to change the gender of the witches would have to eliminate any such reference from the text, and Brooke himself acknowledges that Middleton has significantly abridged the original text. Shakespeare, in this very speech as elsewhere in *Macbeth* and other plays, often took over phrases and images from Holinshed, and Shakespeare is certainly more likely than Forman to have echoed 'nymphs' and 'fairies' from Holinshed. In Shakespeare's sources, in his dialogue, in an early account of a performance of his play, the three witches are consistently female.

I suggested in 1987 (129) that Banquo's whole speech might have been added, or substituted for something else, when the play was adapted. But there is compelling evidence of Shakespeare's presence in parts of Banquo's speech. First, the collocation 'wild . . . attire' comes from Holinshed's account of this episode, and therefore is more likely to come from Shakespeare (who read Holinshed when writing the play) than from Middleton (who shows no signs of having read Holinshed when adapting the

play). With 'look not like' (39) compare 'looks not like' (*Ado* 4.1.68); with 'choppy finger laying upon her skinny lips' (42–3), compare *Troilus* 1.3.240 ('Peace! . . . lay thy finger on thy lips') and *Othello* 2.1.221 ('Lay thy finger thus', with the same meaning). On the other hand, Shakespeare only used 'inhabitants' (39) once elsewhere; it is common in Middleton, occuring eleven times, including three instances of 'the inhabitants', an exact parallel for the elision 'th'inhabitants' (*Quiet Life* 5.2.91), and—most important—'the earth's inhabitants' (*Owl* 544). The contraction 'on't' (40) is also more frequent in Middleton than Shakespeare. Finally, and most significantly, for Banquo's crucial statement about beards ('you should be women, But that your beards'), the closest parallel in either canon is at *Patient Man* 10.193–5: 'fear he *should be* a *woman*, for some *women* have *beards*; marry, they are half witches'. The point here is not that Middleton was the only writer of the period to gender witches equivocally; there would have been nothing remarkably original about a decision to give the witches beards. But they were not bearded in Shakespeare's source, or in the play Forman saw in 1611, and the language in which their beards are described in the adapted text is Middletonian.

Thus, the only speech in which the gender of the three witches is confused contains evidence of mixed writing, and the most Middletonian part of that speech is the very part which explicitly gives the witches male characteristics. Moreover, there is a very practical reason for that alteration: if the three witches have beards, they can be played by bearded adult actors. At least in its abridged and adapted form, the play does not make heavy demands on the adult side of the company; its most crowded scene (1.6) contains only eight speaking adults. Thus, switching the gender of the witches allowed them to be recast, transferring the acting burden to the men, and thus freeing the company's boys to handle the interpolated material in 3.5 and 4.1. The Hecate interpolations virtually forced the company to recast the witches. Moreover, since the witches would originally have been played by boy actors, in 1606 and 1611, those boys would either have become adult actors (in which case they could keep the parts they already knew), or stopped acting altogether (in which case someone else would have to learn the lines, and it might as well be a man as a boy).

Act Four, scene one

The expanded demand for boy actors also seems to have affected 4.1 itself. The lines immediately following the witches' exit 149–50 seem to be Shakespeare's: Shakespeare elsewhere has 'this pernicious' (*Errors* 5.1.242, *Richard II* 4.1.325), 'stand accursed' (*Kinsmen* 5.3.23), 'aye' (17 times), and 'in the calendar' (*John* 3.1.86, *Caesar* 2.1.42, *All's Well* 1.3.4), and Middleton provides parallels for none, or for any other distinctive feature of the sentence. By contrast, (152–60) may well be by Middleton. Macbeth has already seen the witches vanish once (in 1.3); why should he need to ask Lennox if he saw them leave, and why should he be surprised by Lennox's denials? But the dialogue between Macbeth and Lennox almost exactly duplicates a passage in *Mad World* 4.1. In both scenes, a character (Macbeth, Penitent Brothel) has an encounter with supernatural evil in female form (witches, a succubus) characterized by singing, dancing, and chanted couplets; immediately after the supernatural exit, in a short speech the character first exclaims, and then calls in a servant (Lennox, Jasper), who despite repeated questioning insists that no one has exited—thus confirming that the supernatural character(s) did not simply leave, but somehow vanished; the protagonist (Penitent, Macbeth) then reflects on this information, re-solves on a new course of action, and exits. Shakespeare never wrote anything comparable to this elsewhere. (The emblematic tournament in Sc. 6 of *Pericles* belongs to the part of the text written by George Wilkins.) Since *Mad World* (1605) was acted before the original *Macbeth* (1606), Shakespeare might have been influenced by see-ing Middleton's play performed. But the 'Middletonian' character of this short passage extends to its language. Macbeth must always have spoken some lines in response to the witches, and two sentences—'Let this pernicious hour Stand aye accursèd in the calendar' (150–1) and 'Infected be the air whereon they ride And damned all those that trust them' (155–6)—seem Shakespearean, and could have belonged to Macbeth's original scene-closing soliloquy here. But the actual exchanges with Lennox about the witches' exit and Macduff's flight con-tain nothing notably Shakespearean. Macbeth claims that he 'did hear The galloping of horse' (156–7); but it is difficult to fit such a sound effect into the preceding se-quence, without distracting and confusing the audience. Shakespeare never elsewhere uses the word 'galloping'; Middleton does (*Black Book* 348). In the parallel scene in *Mad World*, the exchanges about the succubus's vanishing lead to an exchange about hearing: 'I not hear her? 'Sfoot, one may hear the rustling of their bums...' (4.1.86–7). Middleton's 'one may *hear the* rustl*ing of*' matches, syntactically and rhythmically, *Macbeth*'s 'I did *hear the* gallop*ing of*'. Macbeth then asks 'Who was't came by?' Shakespeare never elsewhere uses the collocation 'who was't'; Middleton does (*Women Beware* 3.2.102). Lennox answers ''Tis two of three...' (158). The collocation 'two or three' appears five times elsewhere in Shakespeare; but it appears 23 times in Middleton's (significantly smaller) canon (not counting appearances in scenes attributed to collaborators, or in stage directions). Lennox then reports that 'Macduff is fled to England' and Macbeth replies 'Fled to England?' (159). This exchange is an example of what Holdsworth defines, very precisely, as 'interrogative re-petition'; Middleton uses it three times more often than Shakespeare (236–67). These exchanges with Lennox are followed by Macbeth's long speech (161–73), which closes the scene. Holdsworth has expressed doubts about Shake-speare's authorship of that speech; I believe it contains writing by both Middleton and Shakespeare. (See below.)

Brooke, responding to Holdsworth's suspicions about the final speech, notes that earlier editors did not sus-pect this part of the scene as an interpolation—Macbeth's closing speech does not add to the supernatural and spectacular elements of the play, and there is no other evidence that Middleton wrote speeches for the protag-onist. Holdsworth himself offers no explanation for this anomalous interpolation. But both the closing speech and the earlier exchange with Lennox serve a simple practical function: they expand the amount of playing time which passes between the preceding mass exit and the beginning of the next scene. That next scene, 4.2, opens with the entrance of two characters (Macduff's wife and son) who would have been played by boy actors. Without the pro-longed ending of 4.1, the boy actor playing Hecate would have had very little time to transform into one of the other characters needed in the following scene.

Of course, as originally written the three weïrd sisters would have been played by boy actors, and one or more of them would probably have had to double as the Wife or Son in 4.2. However, in the original scene they could have left the stage after the word 'depart', at the very beginning of the stately and elaborate dumbshow of eight kings (128). The addition of Hecate's speech (143–50) and another dance (1–2) postponed the exit of the scene's 'Hecate and the other three witches'; Hecate certainly would have been a boy actor (and so might her three companions have been). This change created a need for more dialogue to cover the backstage transformation. Without the added material in ll. 152–73, only four lines would have been available for the change of role and gender. The verbal evidence for Middleton's authorship of lines at the end of the scene thus corroborates the casting evidence for practical changes consequent upon the addition of the Hecate passages.

The Hecate additions, their effect upon the play's cast-ing, and the adaptation's general emphasis upon expand-ing and transforming the supernatural and spectacular element of the play all suggest that we must pay particular attention to 4.1. Middleton has already been generally ac-knowledged as the author of 39–60 and 143–4.1.150.2; the evidence of casting and of verbal parallels, described above, adds much of 153–73 to Middleton's share of the play. On the other hand, Shakespeare seems just as clearly responsible for 1–38, 61–3, 81–3 (on the basis of the witch's trochaic metre, vocabulary, and style), and for most of Macbeth's speeches, which means that—despite Forman's silence—Shakespeare wrote a scene in which Macbeth revisited the three witches. Therefore, the extant scene appears to be of mixed authorship, and Middleton may well be responsible for more than the material already identified.

There is textual evidence of theatrical dislocation in the stage direction at 4.1.128.1–2, which suggests that Banquo is an addition to the show of kings (see text note); if so, then the lines referring to him (140–2) may also be interpolated. These lines, notably, immediately precede the acknowledged addition at 143–4.1.150.2. However effective dramatically, Banquo's presence gives the witches power over the dead, something which is nowhere else implied, and which indeed would seem to suggest that Banquo's spirit is in hell (an implication not likely to please a Stuart monarch descended from Banquo); the earlier appearance of his ghost has no such implications, and neither does the appearance of the 'eight kings', since they are merely images of the future. Moreover, Middleton uses the phrase 'points at' (or 'points to') to interpret a mute theatrical gesture four times elsewhere: 'See, see, he points to heaven, as who should say...' (*Hengist* 1.3.111), '*Vermandero points to him*' (*Changeling* 4.1.0.6), '*Points to the physician*' (*Quarrel* 5.1.271.1), and '*she points to her breasts, as meaning she should nurse it*' (*Banquet* 2.5.0.13–14). In *Changeling* this phrase is followed, in the same dumbshow direction, by someone '*smiling*' and the appearance of the ghost of a man he has murdered; in *Banquet* the 'it' is her child, and in *Quarrel* it identifies the father of an onstage child (as Banquo is here pointing to his descendants). There are no such verbal parallels, in dialogue or stage directions, in the Shakespeare canon.

The three apparitions also seem suspect. Like Hecate, the cat, the three spirits and the three additional witches, they are supernatural and spectacular and appear nowhere else in the play. Davenant's adaptation does not include them, though Davenant elsewhere further expanded the play's supernatural elements; Davenant could, of course, have cut them on his own initiative, but he may have been encouraged to do so by a manuscript which made it clear that they were added to the original text. The apparitions are superfluous: the three prophecies—which seem Shakespearean, occur in Holinshed, and are linked to the rest of the play—could just as easily be delivered by the three weïrd sisters, who deliver the prophecies in 1.3, and are described by Holinshed as 'endued with knowledge of prophecy' (Bullough, 495); in Holinshed, these final quibbling prophecies come from 'a certain witch' (Bullough, 500). That this was Shakespeare's intention is suggested by 3.4.135, where Macbeth, having announced that he will visit the weïrd sisters, says 'More shall they speak'; likewise, in 4.1.77–8 Macbeth proposes to ask something, and the witches tell him to speak and promise to answer. This plan, implied in the source and in two different passages written by Shakespeare, is abandoned and contradicted by 78a–80, which sets up the appearance of the apparitions; these two lines (in a different metre than the preceding and following speeches by the witches) contain two instances of Middleton's favoured contraction ''em' (out of only five in the whole play); Shakespeare never elsewhere uses the collocation 'call 'em', which appears in Middleton seven times elsewhere (four of them imperatives, as here). These same two lines also introduce the idea that these supernatural figures have 'masters'; within these lines, and the Hecate additions, the weïrd sisters seem to be free-floating agents. In other words, these lines, like the Hecate additions, reduce the apparent independence of the original witches.

Although Macbeth's visit to the witches is anticipated in 3.4, and their prophecies echo through the remainder of the play, the apparitions themselves are elsewhere mentioned only at 3.5.26–9 (in the middle of a Middleton scene). Although both Shakespeare and Middleton occasionally use the word 'apparition' in dialogue, according to Dessen and Thomson it occurs in stage directions in only three plays written for the commercial theatres between 1580 and 1642: here in *Macbeth*, in Middleton's *Game at Chess* 3.1.395.2, and in *Cymbeline* 5.5.123.1; however, in *Cymbeline* the phrase '*as in an Apparition*' probably derives from Ralph Crane, because it duplicates—even in its punctuation—the exact phrase '(as in an Apparition)' found in two of Crane's transcripts of *Game at Chess* (CRANE[2-3]). (For Crane as the scribe who prepared the printer's copy for *Cymbeline*, see Wells and Taylor, 604.) Moreover, the three apparitions resemble the emblematic staging of Middleton's civic shows, entertainments and masques; there is nothing like them elsewhere in Shakespeare. Compare, for instance, the 'cuckoo sitting on a tree' in the masque at *Five Gallants* 5.1.108, or the equally emblematic trees in *Banquet* Act 2, and in the pageants of *Truth*, *Industry* and *Virtue*; or 'the emblem' at *Owl* 616 of 'a child playing with a dog'; or the allegorical 'personage of armour representing Honour', or 'Honour with two armed hands' which dominates 'Invention' (1–74).

Finally, since Hecate's speech at 4.1.143–50 is given the speech prefix 'I', it seems probable that she is also meant to speak the other speeches in the apparition sequence—as she does in Davenant's adaptation. (See text notes.) In the rest of the play, the witches speak in a rotation which emphasizes their eery corporateness; in the apparition sequence, four speeches in a row are assigned to 'I', who also speaks the first speech after the sequence (4.1.124), when the characteristic rotation resumes. Whether or not we interpret 'I' as Hecate, the apparition sequence is, in this as in other respects, anomalous. Moreover, the apparition sequence, like the Hecate additions, makes extra demands on the company's child resources: two of the three apparitions are children, and although they might be played by the same actor, even a single child actor would increase the number required by the original play, without the apparitions.

If the prophecies are original and the apparitions interpolated, then 4.1.81–111 must—like 1.2.7–29—contain mixed writing, which it is no doubt impossible to disentangle to everyone's satisfaction, since Middleton would have been mixing a few phrases of his own with material from Shakespeare, some of which may have been moved from its original position. Thus, 'but one word more' (89) may be Middleton's, since the phrase never elsewhere appears in Shakespeare, but is duplicated at *Five Gallants* 1.1.102; the phrase belongs to the mechanics of the apparitions, not the content of the prophecies. On the other hand, 4.1.81–6 must be Shakespearean; not only are they written in the trochaic metre characteristic of

Shakespeare's other witch incantations, but they include Shakespeare's favoured 'hath', and apparently draw upon material in Holinshed and Apuleius, with which Shakespeare was certainly familiar, and Middleton probably not. (See commentary notes in Furness.) Likewise, 4.1.102–6 seem Shakespearean, particularly the phrase 'the round and top of sovereignty': for Shakespeare and hendiadys, see Granville-Barker (I, 169) and Wright. The phrase 'the issue of' appears 16 times elsewhere in Shakespeare, including 'the issue of King Polixenes' (*Winter's Tale*); Middleton does not have any parallels. Middleton has 'of a king' three times, but all are in the early *Solomon*; Shakespeare has the phrase 29 times elsewhere. Shakespeare has 'upon his...brow' twice (*Romeo*, *Twelfth Night*); I have found no Middleton parallels.

I have conjectured that Middleton borrowed these lines from their Shakespearean locations later in the scene. What is now 4.1.81–6 could have originally conjured the show of kings; the demand that the figures reveal their 'office' is more relevant to Macbeth's request about Banquo's issue, and to the show itself, than it is to the apparitions, and 'show' would then be echoed by the witches' 'show show show'. Likewise, what is now 4.1.102–6 could have originally belonged to Macbeth's speech reacting to the show of kings. Holinshed remarks that only two of the Stuart monarchs 'were of full age, when the title of the kingdome descended unto them' (390/b/9–11); the fourth was six years old, the fifth seven years old, the seventh 'one yeere, five moneths and ten daies old'; Mary, 'the eight of the name of Stewards, being but seven daies old, was crowned queene of Scots'; James I himself, the ninth, was only 'about a yeere old' (390/b/25–48). As Brooke observes, this passage was probably Shakespeare's source for the number of Stuart kings (74); but in the show as it stands in the 1623 text, nothing is made of this record of premature crowning, so important to James I himself, and to the play's own interest in childhood. What is now 4.1.102–6 would easily fit the metre, if inserted after 'seventh' at what is now 4.1.134; indeed, since Shakespeare elsewhere treats 'sovereignty' as trisyllabic, this transposition actually produces a sequence more metrically regular than the 1623 text.

This hypothesis also—with the word 'rises' and the fact that an infant would have difficulty walking across the stage—implies that the 'show of eight kings' ascends from the trapdoor. Davenant has them '*pass by*', and Shakespeare editors since Theobald have also assumed that 'Eight kings appear in order and pass over the stage'; even when editors do not adopt Theobald's direction, they imagine that the kings 'exeunt' (Globe), or move around 'backstage' and 're-enter' (Brooke 176). But that the eight kings ascend, rather than simply enter, is implied by the first line of Macbeth's reaction to them: 'Thou art too like the Spirit of *Banquo*: Down:' (128, omitted by Davenant). The last word 'Down', always understood as an imperative, indicates that Macbeth wants the figure to go back where he has come from, to go down instead of coming up. If 4.1 includes the three apparitions, who

rise from the trapdoor and descend back into it, then to have the eight kings do the same thing would be anticlimactic, the mere repetition of a stage effect already used only minutes before; therefore, in the adapted text it makes good theatrical sense for the eight kings to pass over the stage. But in a version of 4.1 without the apparitions, there would be every reason to have the kings ascend from the trapdoor. Indeed, why else insist that the cauldron sinks before the kings appear? In Jonson's *Masque of Queens*, after their dance the witches 'vanish' at the same time as their 'cave'; it would surely have been more dramatic to have *Macbeth*'s witches and cauldron 'vanish' simultaneously. But the cauldron would have to 'sink' before the kings appear, if the kings were themselves rising from the same trapdoor into which the cauldron has to sink. Thus, at least two elements of the extant text—the timing of the cauldron's disappearance, and the word 'down'—suggest that the eight kings originally ascended through the trapdoor; if this effect was transferred to the (interpolated) apparitions, then it would be natural for Middleton to transfer some lines from the original theatrical effect to the new effect, using the same technique.

If the adaptation transfers to the interpolated apparitions sequence some material which originally belonged elsewhere in the scene, then it may also have transposed other material in the scene. In particular, a few lines of Macbeth's closing soliloquy (161–73) might well have been Macbeth's response to the first prophecy. After he is told to 'beware Macduff beware the Thane of Fife', Macbeth's only response is 'Whate'er thou art, for thy good caution thanks. Thou hast harped my fear aright' (85–8). Later, after hearing the second prophecy, he immediately responds 'Then live Macduff' (96)—although he did not, after the preceding prophecy, threaten to kill Macduff, or anyone else. Part of such a threat, which we might have expected after the first prophecy, instead comes at the very end of the scene:

> the castle of Macduff I will surprise
> seize upon Fife give to th'edge o'th' sword
> his wife his babes and all unfortunate souls
> that trace him in his line

These lines surely belong to the original play. Without them, Lady Macduff and her son are not mentioned or introduced before their appearance at the beginning of 4.2. Middleton never uses the plural 'babes' after *Solomon*, and never uses the noun after *Chaste Maid*; Shakespeare, by contrast, uses the plural 25 times elsewhere, and the noun 71 times in total, from the beginning to the end of his career. Here, 'his wife his babes' is echoed in 4.3 ('to leave his wife, to leave his babes...your wife and babes savagely slaughtered'), and 'babe' appears three times elsewhere in the play in passages undoubtedly Shakespearean; there are no such collocations of 'wife' and 'babes' in Middleton. Shakespeare, unlike Middleton, also offers parallels for 'th'edge' (*Hamlet* 1.3.77), 'edge o'th'' (*Antony* 2.2.116, *Pericles* 3.3.35), 'edge...

sword' (*Cymbeline* 3.4.34), 'give . . . edge . . . sword' (*Henry V* 1.2.27, 'gives edge unto the swords'), and 'trace him' (*Hamlet* 5.2.119); Shakespeare also uses the double contraction *o'th'* much more often than Middleton (289 to 101).

Part of Macbeth's final speech in the scene is therefore unquestionably Shakespearean. So, too, is the first line of that speech: 'Time thou anticipat'st my dread exploits'. Compare *Troilus* 4.5.2 ('anticipating time'), *Othello* 2.1.76 ('anticipat'st our thoughts'), and *History of Lear* 7.118 ('dread exploit'). Middleton, again, offers nothing comparable; the Shakespeare parallels, in this line and the others, predictably cluster in the years around 1606. And this line, like the others, could originally have been written as a reply to the first prophecy. Indeed, in its current position it requires the verb 'anticipate' to take a meaning ('forestall') which *OED* first records in this passage, and does not record again until Goldsmith's *Vicar of Wakefield* (which quite possibly takes it from *Macbeth*). Shakespeare often gave words new meanings, but here the new meaning ('prevents me from accomplishing') is virtually the opposite of the old one ('accelerates the accomplishment of'). The usual meaning would be perfectly intelligible as a response to the first prophecy—which, by warning him to beware Macduff, anticipates the attack on Macduff he has already been considering, and thus at the outset of the prophecies seems to confirm their accuracy.

It is possible that almost all of Macbeth's final speech (161–71) was originally part of his response to the first prophecy; only its last two lines clearly demand their present context. But the rest of Macbeth's final speech lacks the tightly interwoven texture of Shakespearean parallels found in these lines, and instead echoes with Middletonian phrases. Holdsworth had noticed some Middleton parallels in Macbeth's last speech here; I have therefore conducted an independent examination of the verbal texture of the entire speech. As in 1.2, lines containing strong clusters of Shakespearean parallels can be distinguished from lines containing Middleton clusters. There is nothing distinctly Shakespearean from 'The flighty purpose' to 'thought and done' (162–6), or from 'No boasting' to 'where they are' (170–3). Both Shakespeare and Middleton contrast 'thoughts' with 'acts'. Most readers might think 'firstlings' Shakespearean, but Middleton also uses it, and in fact has the more precise parallel 'firstlings . . . shall be' (*Michaelmas* 2.1.166). The closest parallel for 'the deed go' is 'the deed goes' (*Widow* 1.2.224). Both Shakespeare and Middleton describe 'thoughts' as 'royal', but for 'crown my thoughts with acts' Middleton offers a better parallel than Shakespeare: 'till the deed crown the will' (*Phoenix* 15.25)—a passage which, as Holdsworth notes, also contains, within four lines, 'now', 'think', and 'act'. Middleton, unlike Shakespeare, has the collocation 'No boasting' (*Entertainments* 3.28). Notably, the lines which cannot certainly be attributed to Shakespeare are those which insist upon the immediacy of his action—something entirely appropriate

here, at the end of the scene, but less obviously appropriate as a response to the first prophecy, in the middle of the scene. Middleton might well have transposed lines from Macbeth's response to the first prophecy, and then added lines of his own to Shakespeare's, in order to provide time for the costume change by extending the ending of the scene.

My conjecture here that certain lines originally associated with the show of kings have been moved to the apparitions sequence, and that lines originally associated with the first prophecy were moved to the end of the scene, is (necessarily) speculative. However, the exact attribution of words or lines matters less than the conclusion that the device of the three apparitions, and the current form of the ending of the scene, both probably belong to Middleton's adaptation. Middleton thus contributed more to this scene than has been suspected—which would account for the fact that, in Hope's analysis, not only 3.5 but also 4.1 departs from Shakespeare's sociolinguistic preferences in the direction of Middleton's. As originally written, 4.1 probably contained the dialogue transferred from 1.3, the opening cauldron-charm by the weïrd sisters, followed by their prophecies and a show of eight ascending kings; as adapted, it has become a longer, more spectacular, much more important scene, with its additional song, Hecate, apparitions, reappearance of Banquo, reappearance of Lennox with news about Macduff, and concluding soliloquy by Macbeth. It has also been given more prominence by the addition of 3.5, which prepares for it, and by its position immediately after an act interval. Middleton's changes have made this scene the centre of the play.

Act Three, scene six

The original performances would not have included act intervals (Taylor 1993). These may have been added before Middleton adapted the play, but even if that were the case, he might have altered their position, as he reshaped the play by addition and subtraction; their current position therefore belongs, passively or actively, to the adaptation. Shakespeare's original would have been played without interruption; the adaptation would have been played with four act intervals. Not recognizing this distinction has created some confusion in discussions of the play. For instance, editors have sometimes argued that 3.6 has been moved from its original position (after 4.1), in order to divide 3.5 and 4.1; in a performance without act intervals, the exeunt of the weïrd sisters at the end of 3.5 could not have been immediately followed by their entrance at the beginning of 4.1—but that sequence would cause no difficulty in the adaptation, where an act break intervenes. Davenant's adaptation, which retains the act interval and the position of 4.1, omits 3.6 altogether, so that the witches exit at the end of Act Three and enter again at the beginning of Act Four. Moreover, if 3.6 had originally been placed after 4.1, then by moving it to its current position Middleton would have gained nothing, and have *created* a doubling problem for boy actors between the end of 4.1 and the beginning of

4.2 (discussed above). We can, I think, be fairly confident that the scene never belonged after 4.1. On the other hand, Brooke is equally misguided when he claims that 3.6 'would always have been needed to separate 3.4 from 4.1' (52). Even without the Hecate material Macbeth does not enter until forty-one lines after the beginning of 4.1; no intervening scene (or act break) would be required to separate his exit at the end of 3.4 from his entrance in 4.1.

The current position of 3.6 therefore can owe nothing to the purely mechanical demands of scene-sequencing, in either the original text or the adaptation. Nevertheless, the extant text of 3.6 does cause a knot of interrelated problems, ably articulated by Brooke (51–3). In 3.6, 'Macbeth knows of Macduff's flight', but at the end of 4.1 'he is told of it and reacts with violent shock.' However, this contradiction is created by the very lines (4.1.152–73) which we have reason to believe might have been added or relocated by Middleton (see above). Without the (added) lines in 4.1, there is no contradiction created by 3.6. Since the verse of 3.6 is unmistakably Shakespearean, and its presence in the play is attested by Forman, the obvious explanation for the contradiction is that Macbeth's knowledge of Macduff's flight in 3.6 represents Shakespeare's original intention, and that Macbeth's onstage discovery of Macduff's flight in 4.1 represents Middleton's adaptation. The Smock Alley promptbook in the 1670s omitted 3.6 entirely, and so have a great many later productions of the play (Halstead, 800c); this might have been Middleton's intention, or the actual practice of the King's Men after 1616. But the duplication only affects twenty lines, which could have been cut without damage to the rest of the dialogue; indeed, there is some evidence that the text has been adjusted to make it possible to cut those lines, while retaining the rest. (See text notes.) The added lines at 4.1.152–73 seem intended to displace 3.6.23–23j, 30a–31, which were inadvertently printed. The printing of lines which should have been cancelled is not surprising: deletion marks were often ignored by printers and other copyists, deliberately or accidentally. The other adapted text in the 1623 folio, *Measure for Measure*, also prints a passage which should have been deleted to make way for its replacement.

One effect of this cut in 3.6 would have been to remove the play's first reference to King Edward the Confessor; as noted, Coghill has plausibly argued that Edward originally appeared in what is now 4.3. (See text note at 4.3.242a.) Coghill attributed the cut to a censor; but it is perhaps more likely to be the work of the adapter. The Calvinist Middleton would almost certainly have objected to Shakespeare's celebration of a Catholic saint and an onstage Catholic miracle. (See Taylor 2001.)

It may be helpful to trace the interrelationship of the conjectured adaptions in 3.5, 3.6, 4.1, and 4.3. By the addition of 3.5, Middleton expanded the play's supernatural spectacularity. Further enlarging the play's theatrical spectacle and its demonic supernatural elements, in 4.1

Middleton added Hecate, three more witches, a witches' dance, an exchange emphasizing the strangeness of the witches' disappearance, three apparitions, and a reappearance by the ghost of Banquo; by these changes, combined with the anticipatory addition of 3.5, he transformed 4.1 into the dramatic centre of the play. But the changes at the end of 4.1 duplicated, dramatically, some material that had merely been reported in 3.6; therefore, some lines in 3.6 were marked for omission. Those cancelled lines involved not only Macduff, but King Edward, constituting in fact the play's first identification of the sainted English monarch; in 4.3, Middleton further reduced the English king's role, by turning an actual stage appearance (and miracle) into a briefly reported offstage action. In 4.3, therefore, Middleton reduced theatrical spectacle, which may seem to contradict the logic of his adaptation; but the spectacle he apparently eliminated would have represented a holiness specifically Catholic, whereas the supernatural spectacles he added were unmistakably unholy.

Act Four, scene two

Braunmuller (259–60) suggests that 2.3.116–22 may be a later addition, because of the 'repetition bracket' there. The term 'repetition brackets' was coined by Wilson (1918, 173–4), and the phenomenon was fully documented by Turner: it refers to a repetition, by the same character, of the same words, which often indicates revision in a dramatic manuscript, designed not to disrupt the existing actor's part except through a tidy and self-contained addition or deletion. The lines seem to be Shakespeare's, though: compare 'an auger's bore' (*Coriolanus*) 'upon the foot of fear' (*1 Henry IV*). Moreover, the point of a repetition bracket is for the same words to be spoken by the same actor, and here 'look to the lady' is spoken by two different characters.

Braunmuller does not discuss an even clearer example of repetition brackets, with the repeated phrase 'how wilt thou do for a father' spoken by the same actor, at 4.2.38–58. In fact, the passage in question does not seem to have been doubted by anyone. Strindberg and others have criticized the entire scene (Rosenberg, 541–2); in 1878 Leighton (recorded in Furness) dismissed the entire 'conversation between Lady Macduff and her pretty infant … unworthy of Shakespeare', but his personal distaste for what he called 'a flat and wrong conversation between mother and child under the circumstances' did not pinpoint the lines bracketed by the repetition, or examine any stylistic evidence. The scene as a whole, and most of the conversation between mother and child, is undoubtedly Shakespeare's, so these complaints about the whole simply discredit themselves as serious contributions to the objective study of authorship.

Up to this point, the scene has been written entirely in verse, and afterwards it returns to verse; here, between the repetition brackets, even the most determined eighteenth-century editors were unable to produce uninterrupted verse. Linguistically, this passage contains the only example in *Macbeth* of *i'faith*, and one of only four examples of *'em* (two of the others in passages already assigned to Middleton). Middleton frequently, and Shakespeare rarely, uses the oath *i'faith* or the contraction *'em* (with or without apostrophes, and with various spellings); the combination of the two, so close together (13 intervening words) is even more Middletonian. In Shakespeare the two words only appear in the same Act once elsewhere (in *Merry Wives*, where they are separated by 165 intervening words). In English drama before 1642, they appear within 20 words of each other on only 37 other occasions: 25 times (69 per cent) in the Middleton canon—*Patient Man* (3), *Mad World*, *Michaelmas*, *Five Gallants* (3), *Puritan* (2), *No Wit*, *Weapons* (8), *Widow* (4), *Old Law* (2)—three times in Chapman's *May Day*, once each in Dekker and Webster's *Westward Ho*, Tourneur's *Atheist's Tragedy*, Fletcher and Massinger's *Knight of Malta*, Brewer's *Lovesick King*, Jonson's *Gypsies Metamorphosed*, Dekker and Ford's *Sun's Darling*, the anonymous *Fatal Marriage*, *Knave in Grain*, and *Thracian Wonder*, and twice in Kirk's *Seven Champions* (1638?). Notably, the only examples before 1606 come from Middleton and Chapman, and Middleton is responsible for 25 (81 per cent) of the 31 examples before 1623. The two plays with the most examples are *Wit at Several Weapons* and *The Widow*, written in 1613-16, near the conjectured date of the adaptation of *Macbeth*. If we limit the search to 13 intervening words or less, all the examples from *Patient Man*, *Michealmas* and *Mad World* are eliminated, as are *Fatal Marriage* and *Sun's Darling*; Middleton's canon contains 20 of the remaining 35 examples. More significantly, perhaps, this leaves only three plays with examples before the original composition of *Macbeth*, none in print in 1605-6, and none performed by Shakespeare's company; the first to be published were *Puritan* (1607), *Five Gallants* (1608), and Chapman's *May Day* (1611). Middleton is much more likely to have produced this combination than Shakespeare (or any other writer); the combination in such proximity is much more likely to have been written after the original composition of *Macbeth* than in early 1606.

Other collocations and verbal parallels in the passage reinforce this statistical evidence. (1) The phrase 'any market' appears in *Widow* (three words away from *'em*), and nowhere else in English plays of 1580-1642 except this passage (where it is four words away from *'em*). (2) In one of the scenes of *Patient Man* most clearly attributed to Middleton, 'buy em' occurs 18 words before 'ifaith'; 'buy *'em*' occurs once in Shakespeare—in *Tempest*, which does not contain the oath at all; indeed, the collocation appears nowhere else in plays of the period. (3) Middleton, but not Shakespeare, has the idiom 'sell...again' (*Michaelmas*, specifically 'sell 'em agen', thus linking the phrase to *'em*, as in *Macbeth*); 'sell...again' appears only three times elsewhere in plays of the period, and is never elsewhere near *'em*. (4) 'I can buy' occurs in *Puritan*, but never in Shakespeare, and only five times elsewhere in plays of the period. (5) Middleton has 'yet i'faith' (*Widow*), which appears ten times elsewhere, and never in Shakespeare.

(6) Both Shakespeare and Middleton have 'Why one that' once elsewhere, but only in *Chaste Maid* is it an answer to a question—specifically, a mother's answer to her son's question ('what's a Foole Mother?'). The phrase appears only three times elsewhere, and none is as close to *Macbeth* as *Chaste Maid*. (7) 'I, that he was' resembles 'I, that he raz'd' in *Measure* 1.2 (a Middleton scene); 'I that he can...yfaith' (*Patient Man*, spoken by 'Wife', in a Middleton scene), and *Puritan*'s 'I that he did, ifaith' (which gets 'i'faith' as well). The phrase 'I that he' appears 16 times elsewhere, never in Shakespeare, and only once elsewhere in the vicinity of 'I'faith' (in the anonymous *Look about You*). (8) The idea that 'all' should be 'hangd' (these words in this order and this sense) occurs in *Lady* 4.2, and no other period play; in fact, in that passage a tyrant-king proposes to 'have 'em all hangd vp'—not only juxtaposing 'all...hangd' but also 'hangd vp' and *'em*, all present in this passage. (9) MacD. P. Jackson (private communication) also observes that 'swear and lie' occurs at *Weapons* 1.1.262 (a Middleton scene), and in only six other plays of 1576-1642, none of them by Shakespeare. These strong Middleton parallels come from eight plays written between 1604 (*Patient Man*) and 1621 (the adaptation of *Measure*).

As always happens, a complete search of phrases and juxtapositions in the passage turns up many idioms common to both writers, and several that are unique to Shakespeare. This is not surprising, since the same thing happens in texts of undoubted authorship (Taylor 2002). (1) *Nay how* occurs in *Taming* (Nay how now), and in a Wilkins scene of *Pericles* (Nay how absolute); neither is a question. It occurs eleven times in other plays of 1580-1642—more often than any of the phrases or collocations, listed above, which point to Middleton. This is very dubious evidence of authorship, not only because of the relative frequency of the idiom, but because 'how' picks up and responds to a question that was undoubtedly part of the original text ('how wilt thou do...nay, how will you do'). So 'how' was already required by the context, and the format resembles Middleton's fondness for interrogative repetition (described by Holdsworth), with an interjection being followed by a repetition of the words of the immediately preceding speaker. (2) *Timon* 2.1 has 'buy...twenty', an apparently unique collocation; this is a scene attributed to Shakespeare. Again, though, this is not strong evidence. As Schoenbaum and many others have insisted, collaborative works featuring the two authors under debate are intrinsically uncertain data. Moreover, the idea of twenty lovers/spouses, or of a choice of twenty, does occur in Middleton: 'choice of twenty' (*Witch*) refers to love-charms used to attract a mate; in *Valour* a character asks Cupid for 'twenty more' women (as Lady Macduff is here contemplating talking about twenty *more* potential husbands), *Five Gallants* compares a woman to a pie in which 'twenty may dip their sippits'. (3) Shakespeare has 'buy...a husband' in *Measure* 5.1; again, since *Measure* contains writing by Middleton, it is not the most reliable evidence of Shakespeare's practices.

Middleton has the same idea in *Women Beware* ('Men buy their slaves, but women buy their masters'), though the word 'husband' does not appear in the phrase itself; Middleton also has, twice elsewhere, 'husband...buy' (the actual order of the words in *Macbeth*). For four other sets of Shakespeare parallels there are no such doubts. (4) The phrase 'Was my father' appears three times in Shakespeare (never as a question), and nineteen times in other plays. (5) The juxtaposition 'father' *near* 'traitor' also appears three times in Shakespeare (never as a question), and nine times elsewhere. (6) Shakespeare has 'all traitors' in *As You Like It* (sixteen times elsewhere); (7) 'must be hang'd' appears in *Merchant* (and ten times elsewhere, including a Peele scene of *Titus Andronicus* and a Fletcher scene of *Two Noble Kinsmen*). But all these parallels (4–7) are specific to the context of the existing original scene, which throughout concerns her husband, his father, and the accusation of treason (which is punished by execution). Parallels specific to a narrative context—especially if that narrative context was inherited rather than chosen—are not good evidence of authorship Moreover, two of these last four parallels ('was my father' and 'all traitors') appear more often in the drama of the period than any of the cited Middleton parallels; the other two occur ten and ten times in other playwrights, more than any of the Middleton parallels except 'yet i'faith'. The more common an idiom, obviously, the less reliably it identifies an individual writer. Finally, the surviving Shakespeare canon is larger than Middleton's (and better concorded). Nevertheless, despite the mathematical advantage Shakespeare has in such comparisons, there is not a single convincing verbal parallel that points to Shakespeare rather than Middleton.

The subject matter of this exchange would have been particularly relevant after the Overbury trials, and hangings, of 1615–16. Wilson (1950) tried to connect this scene to the trials of the Gunpowder plots conspirators early in 1606, but the only possible connection is the accusation of treason, which is raised in the earlier, original part of the scene; it thus belongs to the context into which the suspected addition had to be fitted. In any case, the prosecution in the Overbury conspiracy had originally planned to accuse the Earl of Somerset of treason, and treason was repeatedly invoked in the trials of other conspirators, so even that detail is not unique to 1606. The Porter's reference to 'equivocation' was obviously pertinent after the Jesuit defence following the Gunpowder plot; by contrast, the issue in the Overbury trials was perjury ('swear and lie')—and a woman's remarriage (to a Scot). Moreover, the question 'must they *all* be hanged' was also especially relevant in the wake of the Overbury trials, where the two highest-ranking plotters, the Earl and Countess of Somerset, were conspicuously *not* hanged (though others were). This, again, differs from the situation in 1606, and is not particularly relevant to the situation of the Macduff family. The very first sentence of the putative additional material, 'how will you do for a husband?', could have reminded spectators in the autumn of 1616 of Frances Howard, who had been pardoned by King James in July, but whose husband, the Earl of Somerset, was under a death sentence until 1624, so that he was, in law, already 'dead'. (See Marion O'Connor's introduction to *Witch*.) Frances Howard had given birth to a daughter in 1615, so she was a mother. Hence, all the elements of this passage—perjury, remarriage, a mother whose husband is legally but not yet actually 'dead', a husband/father/Scot suspected of treason, the question of whether 'all' would 'be hanged'—are relevant to the autumn of 1616. In considering the date of the adaptation (above), I have not listed this passage as evidence that Middleton adapted *Macbeth* in the summer or autumn of 1616, partly because I came to that earlier conclusion a decade before I suspected this passage, and partly because this passage has not been previously identified as Middleton's work. To cite it as evidence for the date of the adaptation would therefore make the argument circular. Instead, on the basis of other evidence for the date of the adaptation, I consider these topical connections to the Overbury plot primarily useful as an *explanation* for the interpolation.

The passage thus combines (a) a clear repetition bracket, suggesting the presence of additional material; (b) an unexplained switch from verse to prose, remarked upon by critics since the eighteenth century; (c) mathematically strong linguistic evidence for Middleton; (d) unique verbal parallels that point much more strongly to Middleton than to Shakespeare; (e) material that would have been topical in 1616 but not 1606; and (f) additions to the parts played by boy actors, typical of other aspects of the adaptation.

Only one sentence in the passage between the repetition brackets seems clearly to have been written by Shakespeare: compare 'Now God help thee': to 'God help thee' in *As You Like It* and 'Now God help thee' in *1 Henry IV*. More generally, the use of 'God' is typical of Shakespeare, not Middleton, and typical of plays written in 1606 or earlier, not 1616. The passage as originally written must therefore have included it.

> Yes he is dead. Now God help thee poor monkey,
> but how wilt thou do for a father?

The first line is an iambic pentameter verse line with an extra unstressed syllable at the end (a 'feminine' ending); the second is a nine-syllable verse line which lacks a final stressed syllable. Middleton's insert would have been marked to occur after 'yes he is dead'—that is, in the middle of what would originally have been a verse line. Notably, JAGGARD has a line break here, exactly at the point where the interpolation seems to have begun; the break was emended away by ROWE to produce verse. JAGGARD also has a line break, twenty lines below, after 'Now God help thee poor monkey'; that line break was emended away by POPE to produce prose. Subsequent editors, not suspecting an interpolation, have tended to follow ROWE and POPE. Thus, the repetition bracket is here combined with a disruption of the lineation of the text at both ends of the bracketed passage. The copyist might not have realized that the added passage should have displaced 'Now God help thee poor monkey'—or the copyist might have thought that it had been cut only in deference to the 1606 Act to Restrain Abuse of Players, and decided to retain it, as he retained many other examples of 'God' that should have been censored. In any case, some textual confusion around the edges of an addition, with or without repetition brackets, is not unusual.

Beginning and Ending Details

Finally, Middleton's presence may also be responsible for two small but significant changes at the beginning and end of the play. Though some scholars have doubted 1.1, it must be primarily Shakespeare's. In the first line, 'shall we three meet again' echoes 'we three . . . shall meet again' (*Richard II* 2.2.143). Shakespeare uses 'meet again' eleven times, Middleton only once (in the early *Microcynicon*). Middleton never uses the word 'hurlyburly'; Shakespeare does (*1 Henry IV* 5.1.78) and also has 'lost and won' (of a battle) at *Antony* 3.11.70, written almost contemporaneously with *Macbeth*. The phrase 'ere set of sun' is almost identical with 'ere the sun set' (*Two Noble Kinsmen* 3.6.184); more generally, Shakespeare collocates 'ere . . . sun' five times (never in Middleton), and collocates 'sun' and 'set' much more often than Middleton.

However, one line of the scene is probably Middleton's. There is no parallel in Shakespeare for 'greymalkin' or 'malkin'; 'Malkin' is a witch's familiar at *Witch* 3.3.60, and the word appears again in *Owl* 1645; a character gives 'paddock-brood' to a witch in *Witch* 1.2.219, and in the same play 'I come' is repeated by Hecate four times in response to a summons from a spirit, a statement quickly followed by the names of four spirits in three short lines. The six words in which all this vocabulary evidence occurs are also anomalous metrically. Of the scene's other nine (Shakespearean) lines, at least seven and probably eight are trochaic, all rhyme, and all are between six and nine syllables long; these six words, by contrast, form a regular unrhyming iambic pentameter line. They are also associated with a textual dislocation, recognized by all editors since Pope: JAGGARD (wrongly) attributes everything after 'Greymalkin' to ALL. (See Textual Notes.) This textual irregularity could easily have resulted from the marginal interpolation of the six new words. They have the effect of changing the character of the three weird sisters, explicitly associating them with contemporary beliefs about witchcraft, and preparing for the kinds of material added in the Hecate scenes. Moreover, the added line implies added stage business, for 'I come' and 'Paddock calls' are—as Davenant's stage direction makes clear—responses to a summons or noises from offstage (as in 3.5).

There may also be another explanation for Middleton's intervention at this point. As noted above, Middleton apparently wrote the opening stage direction for 1.2, which comes only one short speech after this line. This line might have been changed, not only for what it adds, but in order to replace something else which, because of the abridgement of the play, was no longer appropriate.

At the end of the play, Middleton may be responsible for a change of staging: at the end of 5.10, Macbeth and Macduff

> *Exeunt fighting. Alarums*
> *Enter Fighting, and Macbeth slaine*

Many editors, beginning with Pope, omitted the second direction. As Brooke notes, the 'unusual effect' created by these two directions resembles that in *Changeling* 3.1.10.2 ('*Exeunt at one door and enter at the other*'); there, De Flores is leading Alonso to his death, and in both cases the empty stage intensifies the suspense before a death. It may also have been needed to permit some sort of special effect for Macbeth's death (which many later productions have also sought). Alternatively, the stage direction might be a solitary fossil of a cancelled scene, inadvertently retained. In either case, some adaptation seems to have occurred in connection with this direction.

Summary

Middleton seems to have been responsible for 1.1.8, 1.3.43–5, 3.5.0.1–3.5.74, 4.1.39–60, 140–4.1.150.2, 152–73, 4.2.38–56, and 5.10.34.1–2 (151 lines); Middletonian and Shakespearean writing seem to be combined in 1.1.10, 1.2.0.2–1.2.29, 1.3.38–42, and 4.1.78a–111 (72 lines); Middleton apparently made several major transpositions: transferring lines from 4.1 to 1.3, and transferring lines within 4.1 and within 4.3. Other short passages of Middletonian or mixed writing may be impossible to detect, but what can be detected includes about eleven per cent of the extant play. Middleton may also be responsible for cutting one quarter or more of the original text.

Gary Taylor

SEE ALSO

Text: *Works*, 1170
Textual introduction and apparatus: this volume, 690

WORKS CITED

Bawcutt, Nigel, ed., 'Ralph Crane's Transcript of *A Game at Chess*, Bodleian Manuscript Malone 25', in *Collections XV*, Malone Society (1993), 1–110

Beaumont, Francis, (and John Fletcher?), *The Knight of the Burning Pestle*, in *The Dramatic Works in the Beaumont and Fletcher Canon*, gen. ed. Fredson Bowers, I (1966)

Berger, Thomas L., William C. Bradford and Sidney L. Sondergard, *An Index of Characters in Early Modern English Drama: Printed Plays 1500–1660* (1998)

Bradley, David, *From text to performance in the Elizabethan theatre: Preparing the play for the stage* (1992)

Braunmuller, A. R., ed., *Macbeth*, New Cambridge Shakespeare (1997)

Brooke, Nicholas, ed., *Macbeth*, Oxford (1990)

Bullough, Geoffrey, ed., *Narrative and Dramatic Sources of Shakespeare*, vii (1973)

Burton, Dolores M., *Shakespeare's Grammatical Style* (1973)

Chambers, E. K., ed., *Macbeth* (1915)

—— *The Elizabethan Stage*, 4 vols (1923)

Clark, W. G., and W. A. Wright, eds., *Macbeth* (1869)

Clemen, Wolfgang H., *The Development of Shakespeare's Imagery* (1951)

Coghill, Nevill, 'Macbeth at the Globe, 1606–1616 (?): Three Questions', in *The Triple Bond: Plays, Mainly Shakespearean, in Performance*, ed. Joseph G. Price (1975), 223–239

Dessen, Alan C., and Leslie Thomson, *A Dictionary of Stage Directions in English Drama, 1580–1642* (1999)

Fleay, F. G., *Chronicle History of the Life and Work of William Shakespeare* (1886)

—— *Shakespearean Manual* (1876)

Furness, Henry Howard, ed., *Macbeth*, New Variorum, rev. edn. (1903)

Granville-Barker, Harley, *Prefaces to Shakespeare*, 2 vols (1958)

Greg, W. W., and F. P. Wilson, ed., *The Witch* (1950)

Gurr, Andrew, *The Shakespearian Playing Companies* (1996)

Halstead, William P., *Shakespeare as Spoken: A Collation of 5000 Acting Editions and Promptbooks of Shakespeare*, vol. 10 (1979)

Holdsworth, R. V., 'Middleton and Shakespeare: The Case for Middleton's Hand in *Timon of Athens*', unpublished Ph. D. thesis, University of Manchester (1982)

Hope, Jonathan, *The authorship of Shakespeare's plays: A socio--linguistic study* (1994)

Houston, John Porter, *Shakespearean Sentences: A Study in Style and Syntax* (1988)

Hoy, Cyrus, 'The Shares of Fletcher and his Collaborators in the Beaumont and Fletcher Canon', *Studies in Bibliography* 8 (1956), 129–46; 9 (1957), 143–62; 11 (1958), 85–106; 12 (1959), 91–116; 13 (1960), 77–108; 14 (1961), 45–67; 15 (1962), 71–90

Kerrigan, John, 'Revision, Adaptation, and the Fool in *King Lear*', in *The Division of the Kingdoms: Shakespeare's Two Versions of 'King Lear'*, ed. Gary Taylor and Michael Warren (1983), 195–245

Loomis, F. A., 'Master of the Tiger', *Shakespeare Quarterly* 7 (1956), 457

Muir, Kenneth, ed., *Macbeth* (1951)

Nosworthy, J. M., *Shakespeare's Occasional Plays* (1965)

Oras, Ants, *Pause Patterns in Elizabethan and Jacobean Drama: An Experiment in Prosody* (1960)

Pope, Alexander, ed., *Works*, 6 vols (1723–5)

Reed, Isaac, ed., *The Witch* (1778)

Rosenberg, Marvin, *The Masks of Macbeth* (1978)

Schoenbaum, Samuel, *Internal Evidence and Elizabethan Dramatic Authorship* (1966)

Scot, Reginald, *The Discovery of Witchcraft* (1584)

Scragg, Leah, 'Macbeth on horseback', *Shakespeare Survey* 26 (1973), 81–8

Slater, Eliot, 'Word Links from *Troilus* to *Othello* and *Macbeth*', *The Bard* 2 (1978), 147–9

Smith, Irwin, *Shakespeare's Blackfriars Playhouse* (1964)

Spencer, Christopher, ed., *Davenant's 'Macbeth' from the Yale Manuscript* (1961)

Spevack, Marvin, *Complete and Systematic Concordance to the Works of Shakespeare*, 9 vols (1968–80)

Spurgeon, Caroline, *Shakespeare's Imagery and What It Tells Us* (1935)

Taylor, Gary, 'The Canon and Chronology of Shakespeare's Plays', in Stanley Wells, Gary Taylor, *et al.*, *William Shakespeare: A Textual Companion* (1987), 69–144

—— 'The Structure of Performance: Act-Intervals in the London Theatres, 1576–1642', in Gary Taylor and John Jowett, *Shakespeare Reshaped 1606–1623* (1993), 3–50

—— 'Divine [ ]sences', *Shakespeare Survey* 54 (2001), 13–30

—— 'Middleton and Rowley—and Heywood: *The Old Law* and New Attribution Technologies', *Papers of the Bibliographical Society of America* 96 (2002), 165–217

Traister, Barbara Howard, *The Notorious Astrological Physician of London: Works and Days of Simon Forman* (2001)

Turner, Robert Kean, 'Revisions and repetition brackets in Fletcher's *A Wife for a Month*', *Studies in Bibliography* 36 (1983), 178–90

Wells, Stanley, and Gary Taylor, gen. eds., *William Shakespeare: The Complete Works: Original Spelling Edition* (1986)

—— Gary Taylor, *et al.*, *William Shakespeare: A Textual Companion* (1987)

Wilson, John Dover, 'The copy for *Hamlet*', *The Library*, III, 9 (1918), 153–85

—— ed., *Macbeth*, New Shakespeare (1947)

—— ed., *Macbeth*, New Shakespeare, rev. edn. (1950)

Wright, George T., 'Hendiadys and *Hamlet*', *PMLA* 96 (1981), 168–93

Civitatis Amor   October 1616

The title-page does not indicate an author. Middleton's name appears on sig. B2, 147 of this edition: 'Tho. Middleton'. Clearly Middleton wrote the scenes at Chelsea and Whitehall, but his authorship of the rest of the quarto has been disputed since the nineteenth century. The report of the actual investiture ceremonies and the Order of the Bath ceremonies follows very closely—often verbatim—the text of *The Order and Solemnity of the Creation of the High and Mighty Prince Henry... Prince of Wales* (London: W. Stansby for John Budge, 1610; STC 13161; BEPD 291). In all likelihood Middleton or the publisher adapted this earlier text for the purpose of reporting Prince Charles's festivities, but changing the names.

From records of the Corporation of London and of the Fishmongers guild we learn that the guild lent some of its properties from the Lord Mayor's Show of that year, Munday's *Chrysanaleia* (Tuesday, 29 October), to Middleton's pageant on the river. The Corporation's records give the date of Thursday, 31 October for the pageant. The running at the ring was on Saturday, 2 November, according to the text of *Civitatis Amor*, and its title-page gives the date of the actual creation of Charles as Prince of Wales: Monday, 4 November 1616.

David M. Bergeron

SEE ALSO

Text: *Works*, 1204

Textual introduction and apparatus: this volume, 632

A Fair Quarrel   Late 1616

The title-page of the 1617 quarto of *A Fair Quarrel* states that the play was 'Written By *Thomas Midleton* and *William Rowley*. Gentl'. There has never been any doubt that both men participated in its composition, though in Rowley's dedication to Robert Grey he makes no mention of a second author. Since the pioneering work of Pauline Wiggin in 1897 editors have disagreed only about the ascriptions for sections of the first and last acts, in particular 1.1.1-93, 1.1.394-425, and 5.1.393-448. That Middleton wrote 2.1, 3.1, 3.3, 4.2, and 4.3, and Rowley 2.2, 3.2, 4.1, 4.4, and the uncontested lines of 1.1 and 5.1, all critics agree.

Wiggin, and Price after her, give the whole of Act 1 to Rowley; Hoy, Lake, Jackson, and Holdsworth (1974) believe that Middleton wrote the opening of the first scene, up to Russell's speech beginning 'How now, gallants?' Recently Holdsworth has concluded that Middleton was also responsible for the end of Act 1, lines 394-425. He bases his claim on a 'dense concentration' of Middleton parallels in the passage, comparing 1.1.405-6, 'Wise men begets fools, and fools are the fathers | To many wise children', to *Women, Beware Women* 2.1.162, 'Fools will serve to father wise men's children', and pointing out that 'He shall so stir thee up!' (1.1.422) is an example of Middleton's frequent use of *stir* with a sexual innuendo (Holdsworth, 1984, 245).

Wiggin, Price, and Lake would give the end of the last act, from the entrance of Captain Ager and his party, 5.1.393-448, to Middleton; Hoy, Jackson, and Holdsworth (1974) agree that the entire last act is Rowley's. However, Holdsworth has now changed his mind and added the contested lines to his previous attributions to Middleton.

According to Holdsworth, the divisions of the first and last acts of *A Fair Quarrel* 'are in line with Middleton and Rowley's standard working arrangement of beginning or ending their stints at the moment of entry of a principal character or characters, often coinciding with a significant moment of development in the plot'. He does acknowledge two possible objections to the division proposed here: the first is that there is no significant development to explain the change of authors at 1.1.93; the other is the presence of two examples of '*um*, a normally reliable Rowley indicator, in 1.1.394-425.

There is not, finally, enough material in the contested sections to allow for a full statistical analysis of linguistic differences. The greatest uncertainty exists about 1.1.394-425, which Holdsworth is alone in ascribing to Middleton, and which contains linguistic material suggesting Rowley. Nevertheless, Middleton's participation in the first and last acts fits the general impression of close collaboration throughout, with the involvement of both authors in both major plots. Middleton introduces Russell, Lady Ager, Captain Ager, and the Colonel; writes the powerful scenes between Ager, his mother, and the Colonel; and tidies up the end of the duelling plot. Rowley is responsible for the remainder of Jane's history; the confrontation between the Colonel and Captain Ager that builds to the provocative phrase, 'Son of a whore!'; and both of the roaring scenes.

This edition accepts Holdsworth's modified division of the authorship, while acknowledging that doubt remains about 1.1.394-425. In summary, the ascriptions are as follows:

Middleton: 1.1.1-93, 1.1.394-425, 2.1, 3.1, 3.3, 4.2, 4.3, 5.1.393-448.
Rowley: 1.1.93-393, 2.2, 3.2, 4.1, 4.4, 5.1.1-392.

The limitations of date on *A Fair Quarrel* are set by its publication in 1617 and its echoes of Peter Lowe's *A Discourse of the Whole Art of Chirurgery* (1612), where Middleton found the professional jargon of the Surgeon (4.2 and 5.1). The play was probably composed in 1615-1616, in which years the invasion of private property to search for saltpetre (1.1.240-4), roaring boys, and duels were all much in the public eye. Although searches for saltpetre had long been a source of annoyance, there is a possibility that patents granted to the Earl of Worcester in 1613 and again in 1617 had reawakened concern (Holdsworth, 1971, citing *Analytical Index . . . to Archives*, 218-220). More importantly, in 1616 the saltpetre men encountered so much resistance that they complained of difficulty in renting carts, with a resulting scarcity of gunpowder; Price suggests that the Privy Council order of 22 May 1617 enforcing public cooperation responded to a crisis that 'had probably arisen about a year earlier' (xviii, citing *CSPD*, 356, and *Acts of the Privy Council*, 47-8, 132-3).

Roaring boys or street ruffians were a notable sight in London throughout this period. In *The Alchemist* (1610), Kastril, like Chough, has come up to London to learn to quarrel and take tobacco from the 'angry boys'. By 1614, in *Bartholomew Fair*, Jonson refers to the brawlers as roaring boys. The conjunction of roaring boys and 'vapours' in *Bartholomew Fair* is sometimes taken to suggest that Middleton and Rowley were influenced by that play, in which Rowley as one of the Prince's Men may have acted the part of Zeal-of-the-Land Busy (Holdsworth, 1974, xiii). Yet Jonson, Middleton, and Rowley could also have been responding separately to a topical problem. Apparently the boys were especially troublesome in 1615; Holdsworth (1971, 31) cites a letter from the end of that year in which Sir Simonds D'Ewes complains that 'divers sects of vicious persons, under particular titles, pass unpunished or regarded, as the sect of Roaring Boys, Bravadoes, and such like' (Halliwell, II, 324-5). In the same year, 1615, Webster added 'A Roaring Boy' to the sixth edition of Overbury's *Characters* (Holdsworth, 1974, xiv n. 7).

King James issued his first proclamation against duelling in 1613 (Stone, 120) and his second in 1614. This was the beginning of 'a vigorous government campaign against duelling in which James, Bacon, and Henry Howard, Earl of Northampton, the Lord Privy Seal, all had a hand, and which ultimately involved Thomas Middleton' in writing *The Peacemaker* (Parker, 60). In 1616 Gervase Markham was heavily fined for a challenge, and in 1617 James himself went to the Star Chamber to pass sentence on two Inns of Court men who had arranged a duel (Holdsworth, 1971, 118, citing Maclean). Thus in 1616-17 a play entitled *A Fair Quarrel* would be especially timely.

The additional scene, expanding on interest in the roaring boys and probably on the theatrical success of Chough and Trimtram, was most likely added early in 1617. This would allow time after the performance for it to be printed and inserted in the remaining copies of the first issue, and for the second issue still to be dated 1617.

Suzanne Gossett

SEE ALSO

Text: *Works*, 1212
Textual introduction and apparatus: this volume, 633

WORKS CITED

Acts of the Privy Council, 1616–1617 (1890)
Analytical Index to . . . Records . . . Preserved Among the Archives of the City of London 1579–1664 (1878)
Calendar of State Papers Domestic . . . 1603–1610 (1857)
Halliwell[-Phillipps], J. O., ed., *The Autobiography and Correspondence of Sir Simonds D'Ewes*, 2 vols (1845)
Holdsworth, R. V., ed., *A Critical Edition of A Fair Quarrel*, Thesis, Linacre College, Oxford (1971)
—— ed., *A Fair Quarrel* (1974)
—— 'Sexual Puns in Middleton, Chapman, and Dekker', *Notes and Queries* NS 31 (1984), 242–247
Hoy, Cyrus, 'The Shares of Fletcher and his Collaborators in the Beaumont and Fletcher Canon (V)', *Studies in Bibliography* 13 (1960), 77–108
Lowe, Peter, *A Discourse of the Whole Art of Chirurgery* (1612)
Maclean, J., ed., *Letters from George Lord Carew to Sir Thomas Roe* (1860)
Parker, Brian, '*A Fair Quarrel* (1617), the Duelling Code, and Jacobean Law', *Rough Justice: Essays on Crime in Literature*, ed. Martin L. Friedland (1991), 52–75
Price, George R., ed., *A Fair Quarrel* (1976)
Stone, Lawrence, *The Crisis of the Aristocracy, 1558–1641*, abridged edn. (1967)
Wiggin, Pauline, *An Inquiry into the Authorship of the Middleton-Rowley Plays* (1897)

The Triumphs of Honour and Industry

October 1617

The title-page includes the usual information about the performance occurring on the day after Simon and Jude's day, 29 October 1617. Middleton's name does not appear on the title-page; but instead it occurs at the end of the dedication: 'At your honour's service, T. M.'

The Grocers paid Middleton £282, which included payment for the 'ordering overseeing and writing of the whole device', as well as construction costs, transportation expenses, and costumes. Munday received £5 'for his pains in drawing a project', and Thomas Dekker £4 'for the like'.

David M. Bergeron

SEE ALSO

Text: *Works*, 1253
Textual introduction and apparatus: this volume, 643

The Owl's Almanac   January 1618

The Owl's Almanac was published in 1618 under the pseudonym 'Mr. *Iocundary Merrie-braines*', a name which gives no clue as to the real author of the pamphlet. The notoriously unreliable John Payne Collier attributed the work to Thomas Dekker and claimed that he had seen a copy so ascribed in an early hand. Although there is no record of this copy, Collier's attribution was the basis for listing *Owl* in the Dekker canon and it appears under Dekker in the revised *Short Title Catalogue*, albeit with a note stating that it is not by him. F. P. Wilson was sceptical about the attribution, commenting that the author was 'no imitator of Dekker's sentiment or style', and in the introduction to his diplomatic reprint of *Owl*, Don Cameron Allen gave cogent reasons why the work could not be by Dekker. He argued that Dekker was not accustomed to publishing his work anonymously or under a pseudonym; that the period between 1613 and 1625, which he spent mainly in prison, was quite unproductive of prose work; that he would be unlikely to write a dedicatory epistle to himself; and that the style of the pamphlet is unlike Dekker's. He suggested instead that the author may have been Samuel Rowlands on the grounds of a similarity in prose style.

The claims of Rowlands can quickly be dismissed. The author of *Owl* was an extremely clever parodist with a prose style which is quick, supple, and verbally inventive; the pamphlet is undoubtedly one of the liveliest examples of comic prose writing in the Jacobean period. Rowlands, however, wrote very little prose (his only work entirely in prose is *Greene's Ghost Haunting Cony-catchers*, c.1602), and this is uniformly mediocre. He is a completely unoriginal writer. Furthermore, Rowlands was consistently hostile to the theatre, while the theatrical allusions in *Owl* (434–5, 1124–6, 1234, 1428.n, 1456–8, 2419–20, and 2514–16) show that the author was pro-theatre and probably himself a playwright. Rowlands, according to Edmund Gosse, was 'in all probability . . . not a man of any classic learning', yet there is a significant amount of classical quotation and allusion in *Owl*. Finally, Rowlands was quite systematic about putting his name or initials on his work, and his popularity with pamphlet readers from 1598 onwards would have given him and his publisher every reason to advertise his identity.

Allen does, however, note that 'Middleton has been mentioned' as the author of *Owl*, though unfortunately he does not identify his source, and we have not been able to trace it. Gary Taylor independently identified Middleton as the probable author in 1992, in the course of a systematic examination of anonymous non-dramatic works published during Middleton's working lifetime; my own investigation has confirmed his conclusion and expanded its evidentiary basis. In the first place, the comic prose style of *Owl*, which is so distinctive, links it to *Black Book* (1604) and through *Black Book* to Nashe. Middleton seems quite consciously to have figured himself as Nashe's successor or inheritor, and *The Owl's Almanac* is, like *Black Book*, a work which Nashe referred to, but never wrote. Nashe's talent is praised in *The Ant and the Nightingale*

(1604), where other writers (probably including Rowlands) are accused of plagiarizing him after his death; he is quoted verbatim in two lines of *A Yorkshire Tragedy* (1605-6), and is the source for a passage in *Hengist, King of Kent* (between 1616 and 1619). Middleton is also the only Jacobean pamphlet writer really to capture the manner of Nashe, and considerable evidence of this early influence survives in *Owl*. This stylistic aspect of the text is discussed more fully in the Critical Introduction. In the second place, Middleton's interest in almanac parody is particularly well attested. He had worked on two mock-almanacs early in his career, *Penniless Parliament* (1601) and *Plato's Cap* (1604), and almanac parody appears frequently in his dramatic work through to *Heroes* (1619). Instances of this are recorded in the Critical Introduction, but it is worth emphasizing here the particular significance of two works. In *No Wit/Help like a Woman's; or The Almanac* (1611), almanac parody is a major theme of the play as a result of Weatherwise's obsessive reliance on his almanac as an oracle. Particular points of comparison are his banquet in 2.1, which is laid out to resemble the astrological anatomy mocked so extensively in *Owl*, and his story of the 'daughter which was called Virgo' in the same scene, which is similar to the Owl's story of 'the young wench (called Virgo)' who loses her [maiden]head in Cheapside (157-62). *Masque of Heroes*, which Middleton wrote for the Inner Temple within a year of *Owl*, is based entirely upon almanacs: the principal character is a Doctor Almanac; the second antemasque presents Good Days and Bad Days; there is close parody of Bretnor (the catchphrase 'the gear cottons' [252, 260.6] echoes 'this gear will cotton' in *Owl*, 2122-3), and there are references to Madam Leak and the sacking of the Cockpit by the apprentices (204-5; *Owl*, 434-5).

Other factors which link Middleton to *Owl* are its illustrated title-page, characteristic of his publications from 1611 to 1626, and the extensive satire on the City livery companies. The latter, which Allen identifies as the most original feature of *Owl*, had appeared earlier in a less developed form in the satirical references to trades and occupations in *Plato's Cap*. The author of *Owl* was also interested in civic pageants: 'you know what the citizens will give for one to welcome his majesty to London' (1627-9); 'some of them [buildings] that bow to my Lord Mayor when he rides by their front' (2281-2)—this immediately after an allusion to Orpheus, a speaker in the Lord Mayor's pageant that Middleton wrote in 1619; and 'My Lord Mayor's posts must needs be trimmed against he takes his oath' (2362-3). In view of Middleton's employment on civic pageants, the satire on the City companies would have given him a reason to conceal his authorship with a pseudonym. Almamac parody is, in general, an anonymous or pseudonymous genre, as is demonstrated by Middleton's two other forays into the genre, and in the same year as *Owl* he is known to have published an anonymous pamphlet, *The Peacemaker*. Middleton's attitude to his name is, therefore, quite different from that of Rowlands. Finally, the author of *Owl* had read Sir

Thomas More's *Utopia* (621-3), the acknowledged source for an episode in *Women, Beware Women*, c.1621, and he was familiar with, and complimentary of, Dekker's works (604-5).

The above evidence makes a strong circumstantial case for Middleton's authorship by itself, but it needs to be supported by the more detailed evidence supplied by verbal parallels with Middleton's other works, and the following examples of significant words, phrases, and allusions suggest that the verbal texture of *Owl* is indeed Middletonian:

3-4   Calculated as well for the meridian mirth of London] 'like the front of a new almanac, as thus: calculated for the meridian of cooks' wives', *Roaring Girl*, 3.46-7; 'Thus am I fain to calculate all my words | For the meridian of a foolish old man', *Women Beware*, 1.2.11-12

158-62   young wench (called Virgo)...maid was afraid to have lost her head] 'Virgo...maidenheads... young wanton wenches', *Plato*, 134

175   good doings] 'good doings', *Plato*, 170

180   cap-case] 'capcase', *Yorkshire Tragedy*, 1.26; *Changeling*, 3.4.46

318-19   Tailors have been troubled with stitches] 'Tailors shall be mightily troubled with the stitch', *Plato*, 302

319   yards] (pun on penis): 'yard', *Plato*, 229 (same pun)

330   phlegethontical] 'phlegetontic', *Ghost*, l. 118

347-8   Since the dancing horse stood on the top of Paul's] 'as well as the horse go a-top of Paul's', *Black Book*, 563-4; 'easier now for his horse to get up atop of Paul's', *Meeting*, 419-20

355-6   Since the German fencer cudgelled most of our English fencers] also 'go into the field with a fencing German', 1859-60: 'I have struck up the heels of the high German's size', *Roaring Girl*, 3.382-3; 'the high German's throat', *Roaring Girl*, 5.90 (Bullen cites *Owl*)

357-8   Since yellow bands...came up] also 'a gallant's pocket with yellow band', 2467-8: 'hateful | As yellow bands', *Widow*, 5.1.53-4; 'the love she bears him starches yellow', *Dissemblers*, 5.1.104-5

429-30   The dominical letter 'L'...signifies either a lord or a pound] 'the dominical letter being "G", I stood for a goose', *No Wit*, 7.293-4

476-7   Cancer...a crab well buttered is excellent meat] 'Cancer, buttered crabs will be good meat', *Plato*, 120

496-7   Pisces...in Fish Street] 'Pisces...in Old Fish Street', *Plato*, 201

575   Monsieur into England] 'in the days of Monsieur', *Black Book*, 230; 'in Monsieur's days', *Mad World*, 4.2.21

581   Charles's Wain] (also 'Charles's Wains', 1240; for Ursa Major): 'Charles's Wain', *No Wit*, 9.666-7

670   golden fleeces] (under *Aries*): Lady Goldenfleece sits at the sign of Aries in *No Wit*, 4.105

674   uberous] 'uberous', *Hengist*, 2.4.140 (predates first citation in *OED*)

764   lug] (as in bear-baiting): 'lugged', *Changeling*, 2.1.82

813 Don Fire-Drake] 'fire-drakes', *Five Gallants*, 3.1.114; *Weapons*, 2.1.23; *Witch*, 1.1.94

1054-5 Oceanus the senior sea god] 'Ocèanus the sea, that's chief of waters', *No Wit*, 7.296

1096 ambitiosoes] 'Ambitioso', character in *Revenger* (not in *OED*)

1186-7 apple-squire] 'apple-squire', *Quarrel*, 4.4.121

1237-8 the morrow after Simon and Jude's day] 'the morrow after Simon and Jude', *Quiet Life*, 1.1.69-70 (i.e. 29th October, Lord Mayor's Day)

1285-6 The Sun in New Fish Street draws excellent French wines] 'Ho, Sol in Pisces! The sun's in New Fish Street', *No Wit*, 4.305-6

1339-40 a cracked crown...at the goldsmith's] 'cracked crowns...by goldsmith stalls', *Plato*, 265-6

1450.n *Stultorum plena sunt omnia*] '*plena stultorum omnia*', *Hubburd*, 65

1463 desperate as a piece of rash] 'desperate-rash', *Plato*, 309

1514 jerk] ('yerke' in GRIFFIN): 'yerked', *Black Book*, 516 ('yerkt' in CREEDE); 'yerking', *Hubburd*, 368 ('yerking' in CREEDE)

1619 hot-shots] 'hot-shots', *Hubburd*, 821 (first example in *OED*)

1637-9 a little fall will make a salt look like Grantham steeple with his cap to the alehouse] 'wresting them quite awry like Grantham Steeple', *Black Book*, 329

1654-5 gentlemen's spurs...shall jingle] 'Signor Jingle-spur', *Meeting*, 124

1664 gripple] 'gripple-minded', *Quiet Life*, 1.1.72-3

1672 punies] (i.e. novices): 'puny', *Revenger*, 1.3.154

1682 marry-muffs] 'marry-muff', *Hubburd*, 1005; *Meeting*, 199 (first citations in *OED* as sb.)

1739 block] (under *Haberdashers*): 'haberdashers... block', *Plato*, 372-8 (same pun)

1921 black jacks] 'black jack', *Witch*, 1.1.44

1933 bene-bouse] 'ben bouse', *Roaring Girl*, 10.170

2048 muchatoes] 'muchatoes', *Black Book*, 167

2113 loose-livers] 'loose liver', *Mad World*, 3.2.18

2205-6 Woolner (that cannon of gluttony)] 'those two cormorants and Woolners', *Black Book*, 19

2244 penny-fathers] 'penny-father', *Black Book*, 493; *Hubburd*, 1233; 'penny-fathers', *Meeting*, 440

2251 voider] 'voider', *No Wit*, 6.210; *Game*, 5.3.97

2261 lobcocks] 'lobcocks', *Plato*, 202

2268 the Lenten-faced usurer] 'a Lenten-faced fellow, the usurer's man', *Black Book*, 247 (only example in *OED*)

2362-3 My Lord Mayor's posts must needs be trimmed] 'We will attend his worship...for so much the posts at his door should signify', *Puritan*, 3.4.11-13

2409 ill-faced] 'ill-faced' *Hengist*, 3.1.47; *Changeling*, 2.1.53

2462 geometrical dimensions] (under *highways*): 'geo-metrical thieves...measure the highways', *Black Book*, 309-10

2513 doorkeepers] (i.e. pimps): 'door-keeper', *Black Book*, 385-6

In conclusion, then, we have as the principal evidence of Middleton's authorship, first, techniques of comic prose style which identify the Owl as a successor to Nashe; second, an extensive interest in almanac parody; third, connections with the City livery companies and an interest in civic pageants, and finally a remarkable degree of verbal parallel between *Owl* and other works in the Middleton canon.

Neil Rhodes

SEE ALSO

Text: *Works*, 1274
Textual introduction and apparatus: this volume, 641

WORKS CITED

Allen, Don Cameron, ed. *The Owles Almanacke* (1943)

Collier, John Payne, *A Bibliographical and Critical Account of the Rarest Books in the English Language*, 2 vols (1865)

Gosse, Edmund W., 'Memoir on Samuel Rowlands' in *The Complete Works of Samuel Rowlands*, eds. E. W. Gosse and S. J. H. Herrtage, 3 vols (1880)

Wilson, F. P., 'Some English Mock-Prognostications', *The Library*, IV, 19 (1938), 6-43

The Peacemaker   July 1618

Although *The Peacemaker* was published anonymously in its succession of editions, the pamphlet strives to give the impression that it was the work of the king. This circumstance was very likely responsible for its assignment to James I in the *Short-Title Catalogue*, one of the consequences of which is the miscataloguing of the work in many reference works and libraries. The licence granted by James I to William Alley 'at ye nomination of Thom^as Midleton' for 'ye sole printing, and selling of a small booke, lately made by the said Midleton, called the *Peace maker* or *Great Brittains blessing*', first noticed by A. H. Bullen, establishes the pamphlet's authorship with some certainty. W. W. Greg was indisposed to accept the Thomas Middleton named in the licence as the dramatist, however, and proposed instead that it had been 'written by some unidentified Thomas Middleton'.

In defence of the dramatist's authorship a number of correspondences between the pamphlet and other Middle-ton works, especially the Middleton–Rowley collaboration, *A Fair Quarrel*, have caught the attention of a number of commentators, who have found suggestive resonances of various kinds linking *The Peacemaker* with the Mid-dleton canon. David M. Holmes, for example, remarks upon the pamphlet's reworking of a passage borrowed from *The Charge of Sir Francis Bacon Knight, His Majesty's Attorney General, touching duels, upon an information in the Star Chamber against Priest and Wright* in an attempt to demonstrate that Middleton's adapted version coordin-ates intimately with the characterization and dramatic situations of *A Fair Quarrel*. In this he argues that *The Peacemaker* stands in significantly closer relation to *A Fair Quarrel* than does the source passage. And Brian Parker, in addition to examining correlations between the play and the fourth section of the pamphlet dealing principally with the duelling question, notes the equation between tobacco smoking and 'roaring' in the Captain Albo addition to the Chough plot and in *The Peacemaker* ll. 504–21.

The paucity of linguistic evidence pointing to the dramatist Middleton's presence is in no small measure attributable to the fact that the relatively formal prose of the work banishes elisions, oaths, exclamations, and a range of other features that investigators such as David J. Lake and MacDonald P. Jackson have established as distinctive markers of his style. In his Appendix III dealing with Middleton's works other than plays Lake includes *The Peacemaker* in Table III(2), noting the distribution of 'between'/'betwixt' as 1:5, 'toward'/'towards' as 3:0, and 'while'/'whilst'/'whiles' as 1:1:0; in addition he lists no instances of 'ha's' out of five occurrences of 'has', and no instances of 'do(')s' out of nine of 'does'. Apart from the table Lake does not discuss the question of the authorship of the work, apparently assuming it to be by the dramatist. With the exception of the data concerning 'ha's' and 'do's', the frequencies of the other words are entirely consistent with the ranges Lake sets out in relation to Middleton plays written after 1610. Distributions of the words cited above in *Women, Beware Women* are 1:10, 2:1, and 2:0:0 and in *A Game at Chess* 1:4, 1:0, and 0:4:0. Important overlooked evidence however concerns an instance of the Middleton spelling 'Do's' (B2; l. 126) and, no doubt because it occurs only in the Lambeth Palace Library copy of the work (containing the earliest state of the forme in question), a '-cst' preterite, a feature treated elsewhere as a particularly significant and distinctive Middleton fingerprint: 'embracſt' (A3ᵛ; l. 21). The absence of 'ha's' is possibly attributable to the involvement of a scribe, as noted below. Two occurrences of 'comfort', two of 'why' (as an interjection), and two instances of 'tast' (for 'taste'; A4ᵛ, B2ᵛ; ll. 45, 161) perhaps also deserve mention.

Bullen, the first editor to include *The Peacemaker* in the Middleton canon, wondered if the prefatory epistle may have been written by James I. But the highly unusual and idiosyncratic '-cst' preterite is clearly not a spelling favoured by the king: it does not occur in any of a range of his works examined (e.g. 'traduced' is found in *Basilikon Doron* and 'inforced' in James's *Speech to Parliament* of 19 March 1604). Further, forms associated with James's Scottish style common in the king's works (e.g. 'trew') are absent.

Also of significance in the matter of discerning linguistic features distinctive of Middleton is *The Peacemaker*'s derivative nature in setting out passages taken verbatim chiefly from *The Charge of Sir Francis Bacon Knight* (published in early 1614), first noted by Dunlap, and the incorporation of extensive citations from Seneca's works, on occasion apparently in the author's own rendering, but mostly taken from the translation by Thomas Lodge; in addition, a few lines are drawn from Henry Howard, Earl of Northampton's *A Publication of His Majesty's Edict and Severe Censure against Private Combats and Combatants*, the latter two noted for the first time by this edition. Like Middleton's prose in the work, that of Bacon, Lodge, and the Earl of Northampton is practically devoid of those features that have proved useful as authorship determinants in the investigation of dramatic works. As with his citations from Bacon, in adapting Lodge's Seneca for use in *The Peacemaker*, Middleton generally modernizes verb forms such as 'careth' and 'looketh' to 'cares' (l. 384) and 'looks' (l. 419) and adds or alters the style of the original, usually in modest ways. For the most part such changes do not, however, introduce linguistic forms or spellings that point in his direction. The probability that apart from the preface the manuscript of *The Peacemaker* used by the printers was in the hand of a scribe adds a further layer shrouding traits typical of Middleton.

In his discussion of *The Peacemaker* Dunlap comments on the frequency of praises of peace in Middleton and their similarity to sentiments expressed in the pamphlet, citing the civic pageants, *The Triumphs of Honour and Industry* (1617) and *The Triumphs of Integrity* (1623), and the masque, *The World Tossed at Tennis*, ll. 878–84 (1620). He additionally makes reference to Middleton's 'entertainment by water', *Civitatis Amor*, which commemorated Prince Charles's creation as Prince of Wales in 1616. The allegorical figure of Peace in this civic entertainment sang a song at the landing of Charles at Whitehall. Middleton's link to the prince on this occasion spurs consideration of a potential connection between the Lambeth Palace Library copy of *The Peacemaker*, which is clearly associated with Prince Charles, and the writing of the pamphlet. The lack of further evidence consigns any judgement on the matter to speculation, however. As Norman A. Brittin points out, a further significant relationship between *The Peacemaker* and Middleton's civic writing concerns the manner in which each section of the pamphlet is framed in the opening couplet in terms reminiscent of the 'triumphs' of a pageant.

Dunlap also draws attention to a correspondence between the rhetoric of the opening of *The Peacemaker*'s preface ('The glory of all virtues is action; the crown of all acts, perfection; the perfection of all things, peace and union', ll. 12–13) and that of a civic pageant of 1613 written to celebrate the opening of a new waterworks ('Perfection, which is the crown of all inventions, swelling now high with happy welcomes to all the glad well-wishers of her admired maturity...', *His Lordship's Entertainment* ll. 12–14). Beyond Dunlap's citations, the phrase, 'angle of the World' at l. 615 in *The Peacemaker* exactly matches that in the opening line of Ignatius's first speech in the Induction to *A Game at Chess*. The possibility that the same author is responsible for the duplicated words is strengthened by the context, which in both instances concerns restriction imposed on the spread of malicious interests. In contrast to works of a dramatic nature imitation would seem an unlikely explanation for such correspondences.

In conjunction with the external evidence of state documents that nominate Thomas Middleton as the author of *The Peacemaker*, internal evidence of various kinds persuasively argues that the Middleton in question was the dramatist. Although the individual components of the internal evidence are of varying degrees of strength, the cumulative effect is the provision of substantial support for the proposition that the Middleton who composed *The Peacemaker* was the same as the Middleton who was responsible for a wide range of works in other literary forms and genres.

The date of the licence, 19 July 1618, provides a *terminus ad quem* for the composition of *The Peacemaker* since the manuscript must have been in final or near-final form for examination prior to the licence's granting. The pamphlet contains two loose references to the age of James I (ll. 67–8), but as neither is strictly accurate (the second probably dependent on the first), they are of no value as dating evidence. Allusions in the early part of the pamphlet to diplomatic missions involving foreign powers relate chiefly to negotiations completed in 1613 or 1614. The pamphlet's publication either on the eve of the outbreak of the Thirty Years War or soon after the inception of hostilities lends to citation of foreign peace initiatives and successes a presumably unwitting ironic cdge.

According to its title-page, Middleton and Rowley's *A Fair Quarrel*, published in 1617, was performed before James I as well as publicly. As Bentley notes, since the title of this play is listed along with others on undated waste-paper of the Revels Office from about 1619-20, there is a possibility that it was under consideration for another court performance at this time. Performance at court—perhaps on more than one occasion—attests to the play's popularity with the king. Brian Parker has suggested that the anti-duelling stance of *A Fair Quarrel* together with the proximity in dates between it and *The Peacemaker* prompts speculation that James or Bacon may have called upon Middleton to write a pamphlet aimed at denouncing lawless private combats together with other threats to peace within the kingdom. If the proposition has any validity, Middleton would presumably have been at work on *The Peacemaker* between some time in 1617 and July 1618. Such a time scheme is consistent with all evidence that has yet come to light, but does not rule out the possibility of an earlier starting date.

Paul Mulholland

SEE ALSO

Text: *Works*, 1306
Textual introduction and apparatus: this volume, 648

WORKS CITED

Bacon, Francis, *The Charge of Sir Francis Bacon Knight, His Majesty's Attorney General, touching duels, upon an information in the Star Chamber against Priest and Wright* (1614)
Bentley, Gerald Eades, *The Jacobean and Caroline Stage*, 7 vols (1941–68), vol. 4
Brittin, Norman A., *Thomas Middleton* (1972)
Dunlap, Rhodes, 'James I, Bacon, Middleton, and the Making of *The Peace-Maker*', *Studies in the English Renaissance Drama*, ed. Josephine W. Bennett, Oscar Cargill, and Vernon Hall, Jr. (1959), 82–94
Greg, W. W., *A Companion to Arber* (1967), pp. 56–7 and 163–4
Holmes, David M., *The Art of Thomas Middleton* (1970)
Howard, Henry, Earl of Northampton, *A Publication of His Majesty's Edict and Severe Censure against Private Combats and Combatants* (1613/1614)
Lodge, Thomas, tr., *The Workes of Lucius Annæus Seneca* (1614)
Parker, Brian, '*A Fair Quarrel* (1617), the Duelling Code, and Jacobean Law', in *Rough Justice: Essays on Crime in Literature*, ed. Martin L. Friedland (1991), 52–75

Masque of Heroes   January 1619

The title-page of the first edition identifies the author as 'Tho. Middleton'; the prefatory poem is signed 'T. M.' It was entered in the Stationers' Register on 10 July 1619 as '*The Temple Maske. Anno. 1618.*' This places its performance in the Christmas season which that year ran from 6 January (Twelfth Night) to 2 February (Candlemas); '1618' refers to the legal year, which did not change until March 21. It is not identified in the Inn's records (Inderswick 2:116), but Bald notes that 'The costs of such an entertainment as this were probably defrayed from a special fund collected by the officers for Christmas and were not included in the accounts of the Inn itself' (253). Bald also notes that 'Twelfth Night' is referred to in the past tense (l. 92) and 'Candlemas' in the future tense (l. 139).

Gary Taylor

SEE ALSO

Text: *Works*, 1324
Textual introduction and apparatus: this volume, 646

WORKS CITED

Bald, R. C., ed., *The Inner Temple Masque, or Masque of Heroes*, in *A Book of Masques: In Honour of Allardyce Nicoll*, gen. eds. T. J. B. Spencer and Stanley Wells (1967), 251–74
Inderswick, Frederick, ed., *Calendar of Inner Temple Records*, 2 vols (1898)

'Burbage'   March 1619

'Burbage' is attributed to 'Tho. Middleton' in the only known copy of the poem (Rosenbach MS 1083/16), a miscellany compiled by Robert Bishop c.1630, and edited by Redding. The rarity of attributions to Middleton in manuscript makes this particular attribution more credible: his was not a name routinely attached to other men's work. For 'visible eclipse' see *Phoenix* 4.213: 'the clouds That get between thy glory and their praise, That make the visible and foul eclipse'. LION finds no other parallel before 1784. For 'interposing' near 'eclipse' see *Tennis* 794 ('eclipse that, interposing'); LION finds no other instance of the collocation before Smollett. The use of Bretnor's Almanac is also characteristic of Middleton. (See commentary.) The Freemans suggested that the poem was a forgery by John Payne Collier, who first printed it; they did not know of the surviving manuscript.

Gary Taylor

SEE ALSO

Text: *Works*, 1889
Textual introduction and apparatus: this volume, 992

WORKS CITED

Freeman, Arthur, and Janet Ing Freeman, *John Payne Collier: Scholarship and Forgery in the 19th Century* (2004)
Redding, David Coleman, *Robert Bishop's Commonplace-Book: An Edition of a Seventeenth Century Miscellany*, unpub. Ph.D. thesis, University of Pennsylvania (1960)

An/The Old Law   1618–19

There is, for *Old Law*, no record of licensing, no reference to an acting company for which the play was written or by which it was first performed, and no early record of attribution—none of the desirable documentary evidence by which one might confidently fix the identity of the playwrights or a date of composition and first performance. There is, nevertheless, an abundance of evidence for date and authorship; but it has not always been recognized, and in particular the relationships between the various kinds of evidence have not been logically articulated.

The title-page of the first edition (1656) states that the play was written 'By *Phil. Massinger. Tho. Middleton. William Rowley.*' The attribution to Middleton and Rowley is confirmed by a great range and variety of internal evidence. Price, Barker, Lake and Jackson agree, on the basis of linguistic and stylistic analyses, that Middleton wrote scenes 2.2, 3.2, and 4.2 and that Rowley wrote at least parts of 4.1 and 5.1—to which all but the earliest and least sophisticated of these investigators (Price) would add 3.1. Barker had concluded that Rowley was 'certainly concerned in [1.1] and may have written it all' (186); Jackson and Lake—working later, independently, and with more reliable and extensive data—assign it to Rowley. (Although printed in 1982, Shaw's edition takes no account of Lake or Jackson, and is demonstrably unreliable.)

The distinction between Middleton and Rowley may at some points be less secure than this consensus would suggest. Jackson notes, following Cyrus Hoy, that a few very unusual spellings characteristic of Rowley 'are almost entirely absent from plays partly Rowley's which were first printed, as *Old Law* was, after about 1650' (130). Rowley's contribution may therefore be underestimated by recent studies. Moreover, as Masten observes (private communication), linguistic and stylistic analyses sometimes seem influenced by—or at moments of methodological difficulty default to—earlier, more transparently ideological views of the dissimilarities of Middleton and Rowley, differences that collaboration may have diminished, effaced, or altered over time. Gossett has cogently generalized that many attempts to separate Middleton from Rowley eventuate in a related set of binary oppositions (verse/prose,

serious/comic, high/low, noble/common). Morris, for example, wrote of one *Old Law* passage in 1902 (before the advent of systematic linguistic analysis): 'If, now, the line and a half containing the feminine pronouns and the coarse Rowleyesque figure be removed, the improved verse and the finer taste are like Middleton's' (42). Criticism of the play much more recent than Morris continues to set Rowley's 'crassness' in opposition Middleton's 'moral dignity' (Shaw xxi), and Barker writes that 'what now looks like Rowley may sometimes be corrupt Middleton or even corrupt Massinger' (186). Such assumptions of profound authorial difference can influence (and undermine) ostensibly systematic analysis of collaborative texts. Jackson, for example, views the linguistic evidence in 4.1 of *Old Law* as inconclusive, and specifically finds 'no linguistic evidence of Rowley's presence'; nevertheless, and despite a list of characteristic Middletonisms he cites, he assigns the scene to Rowley because it 'is one of the Gnotho scenes, which in their farcical clowning seem characteristic of Rowley's work' (129).

Masten's specific critique of these earlier studies (which I have quoted in the preceding paragraph) is certainly justified. But in addition to these general problems with the distinction between Middleton and Rowley, there is a problem more particular to *Old Law*. The biases to which Masten takes exception affect all the Middleton–Rowley collaborations; chronologically, *Old Law* belongs to the middle period of their partnership, not at either extreme, and it should be no more or less affected by such considerations than any other Middleton–Rowley play. Nevertheless, it is—by general consent—'undoubtedly the most difficult one of the Middleton–Rowley group' from the perspective of attribution (Barker, 186). The real problem posed by this play is not the exact distribution of scenes or passages to Middleton or Rowley, but the third name on the 1656 title-page.

Massinger was cited alone as the play's author in the catalogue of plays sometimes bound with the 1656 edition (see Textual Introduction). But that is probably a consequence of the fact that his name is listed first on the title-page; the 1656 play list normally gives only a single author for collaborative plays, and that author is usually the first in the sequence of collaborators named on the title-page of an edition already available. The 1656 edition and the play list were both published by Edward Archer. Masten has shown that authorship was secondary to Archer's purposes in compiling the play list. Certainly, where we can check Archer's authorship attributions against reliable early sources, Archer was wrong twice as often as he was right (Greg 1946).

Most scholars have doubted Massinger's involvement. The surviving Massinger canon is large, and includes an autograph manuscript play, so there is plenty of reliable evidence of Massinger's stylistic norms. Studies of Massinger's overall linguistic profile by McIlwraith and Hoy—without any bias in favour of Middleton or Rowley, with whom they were little concerned—demonstrate the consistency of his preferences. Those preferences are not present in *Old Law*. His most recent editors note that '*The Old Law* is no longer accepted as Massinger's' (Edwards and Gibson, 1:li); 'it is now generally agreed that Massinger can have had little or nothing to do with the writing of the play. It has been argued that Massinger revised it, but the evidence is not strong' (1:xix). Lake and Jackson found no evidence of Massinger. Price had 'argued that Massinger revised it', but no one else has attempted to make a case for Massinger, and Price's claims have been refuted in detail by Taylor (2002).

Lake's analysis found one scene ('5.1a': 5.1.1–5.1.347.1) that could not be attributed to Middleton, Rowley, or to Massinger at any period of his career for which we have stylistic evidence. Jackson provided other evidence that ruled out Middleton or Massinger. Lake suggested that 5.1a might have been written by Daborne, Day or Heywood (207–8). But a comprehensive survey of the internal evidence does not support Day or Daborne (Taylor 2002). Heywood is the only early modern playwright surveyed by Lake whose linguistic profile perfectly matches that found in 5.1.1–347. Taylor provides extensive lexical evidence (based on computer databases) that clearly assigns 5.1a to Heywood, whether the raw data is analysed in terms of gross totals, totals adjusted for canon size, totals from collaborative works, or totals adjusted for canon size and collaboration and date. 'No other attribution based on internal evidence has ever been subjected to such thorough negative checks' (Taylor 2002, 207).

Rowley's earliest known work was written for the Queen's Men in 1607–8; Heywood was a sharer in that company, as both actor and leading writer. Heywood and Rowley collaborated on *Fortune by Land and Sea*, probably written in the same period. They collaborated again in 1625, teaming with Webster on *A Cure for a Cuckold*. Rowley's collaborations with Heywood thus stretched from the beginning to the end of Rowley's career. Heywood's presence thus does not help to date the play. Middleton and Rowley's first known collaboration occurred in 1613, but they might have collaborated earlier.

The play was named in a list of plays on a fragment of waste-paper inserted into a manuscript of Sir George Buc's *History of Richard III* (British Library, Cotton MS Tib.E.X, fol. 247), which contains the words (in a scribal hand, not Buc's) 'An ould Lawe [ ] a['; damage to the paper has created a lacuna before and after the final 'a'. The evidence for dating all these scraps is discussed in the introduction to this Chronology (p. 332). Taylor there concludes that the scrap that mentions *Old Law* must have been written later than June 1618, and might have been used in preparation for the Christmas court seasons of 1618–19, 1619–20, 1620–1, or 1621–2. *Old Law* must have been completed and performed, in some form, before the end of 1621.

The following internal evidence has been adduced for the date of the play (given in the order in which the passages appear in the play):

—'He that has been a soldier all his days | And stood in personal opposition | 'Gainst darts and arrows, the extremes of heat, | And pinching cold, has treacherously at home | In his securèd quiet by a villain's hand—' (1.1.237–41). This may allude to the execution of Sir Walter Ralegh on 29 October 1618 (Taylor, 2002).

—the 'dark eclipse' and 'sad events' (1.1.104–5) may allude to the eclipses of 1619, which an epitaph by Middleton ('Burbage') connected to the deaths of Queen Anne on 2 March 1619 and Richard Burbage on 13 March 1619 (Taylor, 2002).

—the mention of a footman's race (2.1.256–8), taken to be an allusion to a race described at some length in a letter written 10 April 1618 (Maxwell, 143–5).

—the allusion to Dr William Butler (2.1.274–5), who died on 29 January 1618, but whose reputation was considerable from 1612 (when he treated Prince Henry during his final illness) until well after his own death (*DNB* 3:542).

—Masten's commentary notes a possible allusion to John Bullokar's *Expositor* (3.1.30), published in 1616, 1621; or to his father William Bullokar's *Orthographie*, published 1580, with a related text in 1586. Since *Old Law* cannot have been written in the 1580s, the later texts are the more obviously relevant; but the ambiguity of this evidence makes it of uncertain value in dating the play.

—the clerk's mentioning of the year 1599 (3.1.34). The most precise date in the play, this is of dubious value in determining its date of composition, since it may simply function to make subtraction easier for the audience to follow. It is impossibly early for any of the collaborators associated with the play in 1656 (Eccles; Maxwell, 140).

—the dramatic display and discussion of 'corruption' and 'figure-casting' (3.1.98–107). This may allude to the Navy scandal of summer and autumn 1618, and the even greater corruption scandal involving Thomas Howard, Earl of Suffolk, Lord Treasurer, the highest official in the King's government. Chamberlain's letters are full of news about that scandal for more than a year, as the trial was anticipated in January 1619 and delayed and delayed until October (Taylor, 2002).

—the possible allusion to *Hiren: or The faire Greeke* (4.1.53), published in 1611 and written by William Barksted, a player certainly associated with Prince Charles's Men in March 1616 (Bentley 1:211). When he left the company is not known.

—the controversy over the Common Law (5.1.232), highlighted by Edward Coke's dismissal from the King's Bench in November 1616 (Bromham). In fact, disputes between defenders of the Common Law and defenders of royal prerogative continued until the Civil War.

—the publication of *GOD and the King*, with its patriarchalist rhetoric and emphasis on the fifth commandment, in 1615 (Bromham).

With the one explicable exception of '1599', the allusions above all fall within the range 1615–19. Six occur within the period from 29 January 1618 to 13 March 1619. It thus seems unlikely that the play was originally completed before the second half of 1618. A date in late March or April 1619 would account for all the evidence. The London theatres were forbidden to play during Lent, which in 1619 began on 16 February. All the London theatres were closed from Queen Anne's death on 2 March until her burial on 13 May (Bentley 1:5–7). Thus, *Old Law* must have had its first performances before 16 February or after 13 May 1619.

If *Old Law* was written at any time between 1615 and 1619, it must have been written for Rowley's company, Prince Charles's Men; he is not known to have worked with any other company between 1609 and 1622. It is possible, but relatively unlikely, that Heywood would have collaborated on a play for Prince Charles's Men before the death of Queen Anne (Taylor 2002). The reference to eclipses and sad events, combined with Heywood's presence, favour completion after 2 March 1619 and a first performance after 13 May 1619. The Revels Office scrap paper is best explained on the assumption that *Old Law* was being considered for a performance at court in the 1619–20 winter season.

After the death of Queen Anne there was a major reorganization of the London companies, with Prince Charles's Men moving from the Red Bull to the Cockpit—formerly the home of Queen Anne's company, now owned by the impresario Christopher Beeston, himself a former member of that company. The Cockpit in 1619 thus brought together Prince Charles's Men with properties and people formerly associated with the Queen's Men (Gurr 402–5). A collaboration between Rowley and Heywood at that moment would have made sense. It is theoretically possible that Heywood adapted the play after the deaths of Middleton and Rowley, but the hypothesis of posthumous adaptation was originally raised only in order to explain the otherwise inexplicable title-page attribution of part of the play to Massinger. Nothing in Heywood's contribution, or any other element of the play, suggests or requires a theory of late revision.

The quarto title-page states that the play was 'Acted before the King and Queene at *Salisbury House*, and at severall other places, with great Applause'. This statement almost certainly refers to performances during the reign of Charles I. The 'Queen' who witnessed a performance must have been either Queen Henrietta Maria (who could have done so between 1625 and 1642) or Queen Anne (before March 1619). The more likely reference, for any reader in 1656, was Henrietta Maria.

Bentley conjectured that the title-page might refer to the actual residence ('Salisbury House') of the Earl of Dorset (6:87). But there is no record of such a performance, or of other performances at that venue. 'House' could mean 'playhouse', and it seems altogether more likely that the 1656 title-page refers to The Salisbury Court theatre. It opened c.November 1630 (Bentley 6:87). Again, this suggests that the play was successfully revived in the reign of Charles I. During the closing of the theatres between March and November 1625, Prince Charles's Men disappeared, as part of a general reorganization of all the London theatres, which (with the exception of the King's Men) were controlled by impresarios rather than actors in the next reign. The Salisbury Court theatre at various times hosted Queen Henrietta's Men, the King's Revels Men, and the second Prince Charles's Men; these companies at other times played at the Cockpit, the Fortune, and the Red Bull, and any one of them could therefore account for the 'and severall other places' of the title-page. All three companies owned some old plays which had belonged to pre-1625 companies; Queen Henrietta's Men, in particular, owned a number of old Rowley titles (*All's Lost by Lust, Fortune by Land and Sea, Hymen's Holiday, The Witch of Edmonton*). They seem likelier than any other company to have owned *Old Law* in the 1630s. This assumption would align *Old Law* with *Changeling* and *Spanish Gypsy*, which, according to their title-pages, were acted at both the Cockpit and Salisbury Court. Butler argues that the Beeston's Boys' 1639 repertory protection list prevented the relocated Queen's from acting any of their old Cockpit repertory (116); Bill Lloyd (private communication, 31 May 2007) suggests that they did begin to act some (*Gypsy, Old Law, Changeling*, perhaps *Wit Without Money*), which led William Beeston to have the protection list issued.

Gary Taylor

SEE ALSO

Text: *Works*, 1335
Textual introduction and apparatus: this volume, 1123

WORKS CITED

Barker, R. H., *Thomas Middleton* (1958)
Barksted, William, *Hiren: or The faire Greeke* (1611)
Bentley, G. E., *The Jacobean and Caroline Stage*, 7 vols (1941–68)
—— *The Profession of Dramatist in Shakespeare's Time, 1590–1642* (1971)
Bromham, A. A., 'The Contemporary Significance of *The Old Law*', *Studies in English Literature, 1500–1900* 24 (1984), 326–39
Bullokar, John, *An English Expositor: Teaching the Interpretation of the hardest words vsed in our Language* (1616)
Bullokar, William, *Bullokars Booke at large, for the Amendment of Orthographie for English speech* (1580)
Butler, Martin, 'Exeunt Fighting: Poets, Players, and Impresarios at the Caroline Hall Theaters', in *Localizing Caroline Drama: Politics and Economics of the Early Modern English Stage, 1625–1642*, ed. Adam Zucker and Alan B. Farmer (2006), 97–128
Eccles, Mark, 'Middleton's Birth and Education', *Review of English Studies* 7 (1931), 431–41
Edwards, Philip, and Colin Gibson, eds., *The Plays and Poems of Philip Massinger*, 5 vols (1976)

God and the King (1615)

Gossett, Suzanne, 'Major/Minor, Main Plot/Subplot, Middleton/?', *Elizabethan Theatre XV*, ed. Ted McGee and Lynne Magnusson (2002)

Greg, W. W., 'Authorship Attributions in the Early Play-lists, 1656–1671', *Edinburgh Bibliographical Society Transactions* 2 (1946), 305–29

Gurr, Andrew, *The Shakespearian Playing Companies* (1996)

Hoy, Cyrus, 'The Shares of Fletcher and his Collaborators in the Beaumont and Fletcher Canon (V)', *Studies in Bibliography* 13 (1960), 77–108

Masten, Jeffrey A., 'Ben Jonson's Head', *Shakespeare Studies* 28 (2000), 160–168

Maxwell, Baldwin, *Studies in Beaumont, Fletcher, and Massinger* (1939)

McIlwraith, A. K., 'The Life and Works of Philip Massinger' (unpublished doctoral thesis, Oxford University, 1931)

Morris, Edgar Coit, 'On the Date and Composition of *The Old Law*', *PMLA* NS 10 (1902), 1–70

Price, George R., 'The Authorship and the Manuscript of *The Old Law*', *Huntington Library Quarterly* 16 (1953), 117–139

Shaw, Catherine M., ed., *The Old Law* (1982)

Taylor, Gary, 'Middleton and Rowley—and Heywood: *The Old Law* and New Attribution Technologies', *Papers of the Bibliographical Society of America* 96 (2002), 165–217

The Triumphs of Love and Antiquity

October 1619

The title-page indicates the performance on 29 October 1619, and that Middleton was the author: 'By Tho. Middleton Gent.' Records of the Skinners company show planning as early as May 1619. An entry for 1 July reads: 'Lastly Anthony Munday, Thomas Middleton and Richard Grimston poets, all showed to the table their several plots for devices for the shows and pageants...and each desired to serve the Company.' The guild appointed additional committees on 13 July. Obviously the company eventually chose Middleton's plan for the pageant.

David M. Bergeron

SEE ALSO

Text: *Works*, 1399
Textual introduction and apparatus: this volume, 672

The World Tossed at Tennis

February–April 1620

The title-page of George Purslowe's edition of *Tennis* indicates that the work was 'Invented and set down by Thomas Middleton and William Rowley, Gentlemen.' While Middleton's authorship has never been in doubt, the question of precisely which parts of the masque are his and which Rowley's has caused some debate. Since the time of Fleay, critics have agreed unanimously that the material in the main masque prior to the entrance of the Starches (374.1) is Rowley's, that which follows Middleton's. This distribution of shares of the work has been based on a sense of general stylistic similarities between this work and other

works by the two authors. Sketchy (but still more convincing) studies of close verbal parallels (Barker, Holdsworth, Robb), of hard words (Barker), of specific features of style (Robb), and of distinctive usages (Wiggin, Lake, Hoy, Jackson) confirm the assignment of the first part of the text to Rowley and the second part to Middleton. The same studies produce disagreements about particular passages: Hoy, for example, argues persuasively that Rowley wrote the speech of the Lawyer (772–83) because it includes two instances of 'vm', a form that he and other scholars treat as a Rowley signature. Stork and Robb give Middleton the Dedication and the Prologue while attributing to Rowley the prose speeches of Simplicity; Barker and Lake disagree, the former simply dismissing Rowley's claim to the authorship of these speeches as unsubstantiated by Stork, the latter setting forth the Middletonisms ('they're', 'i'their', 'I'm') that appear in Simplicity's prose.

The debate concerning the authorship of Simplicity's speeches is in part a conflict between critics who situate the masque in theatre history and critics who analyse it as a configuration of words. Given Rowley's prominence in the Prince's Men and Simplicity's Epistle on behalf of the poet, it has become a commonplace of commentary on *Tennis* to suggest—tentatively of course—that Rowley played Simplicity. Although the casting remains uncertain, this association has encouraged critics to accept the possibility that Rowley the actor also wrote the speeches of Simplicity.

This edition accepts the general division of the masque proper of *Tennis* into two parts demarcated at the entrance of the Starches, what precedes their entrance being Rowley's work, what follows largely Middleton's. However, this general division of shares does not include all parts of the entertainment or of the book. Signed by Middleton, the Dedication is clearly his. The Epistle seems to be Rowley's for it is self-consciously artificial in style—in Robb's words, 'balanced, stiff, affected, steering from pun to pun, from quibble to quibble, from forced witticism to forced witticism' (138–9). There is insufficient evidence to determine the authorship of the Prologue, or of the Epilogue for that matter. Both have been assigned to Rowley but only because of his direct involvement in the performance of the masque in the public theatre, for which performance the two speeches were written. Finally, this edition gives the Induction to Middleton on the strength of Roger Holdsworth's analysis of literary and verbal similarities between it and other works by Middleton. In an early draft of a note on the authorship of the Induction (generously provided by Dr Holdsworth), he sums up the linguistic features that favour Middleton:

> Rowley pointers such as *tush* and *'um* do not appear, and *hath*, which Middleton generally avoids, does not either, while *has* (10, 50) occurs twice (once as *ha's* [50], a common Middleton spelling). There are two instances of *doth* (32, 91), which Middleton firmly avoids in his plays, but in his entertainments it is in fact quite frequent.... The spelling evidence

suggests that the copy for the Induction may well have been in Middleton's autograph. Particularly significant is *do's* on B2ᵛ (33). This form links the Induction to Middleton's share of the masque proper, where it occurs twice (475, 856), it is consistently the spelling of *does* which Middleton uses in the Trinity MS of *Game*, and it is frequent in his pageants (*Aries* has five examples of it). A large majority of the Induction's other spellings follow Middleton's preferences: for example, 'doe' (8), 'ayre' (8, 49), 'Rivall' (20), 'Oh' (44), 'yeere' (46), 'layd' (51), 'agen' (54), 'lowd' (63), 'yfaith' (70), 'e're' (74, 94), 'dayly' (84), 'stayres' (87), 'ioynt' (88), 'Solsticie' (61), 'eternitie' (90), 'bee' (92), 'lyes' (94), 'Royall' (30, 38, 72, 81), 'maiesticall' (28), 'shee's' (27). Two of Middleton's favourite oaths appear—*yfaith* (twice) (35, 70) which Jackson (69) finds that Middleton uses eight times more often than other dramatists, and *by my troth* (69) about four times more often.

Holdsworth goes on to note literary parallels between *Tennis* and other entertainments by Middleton: a sisterhood of three buildings reappears in *Entertainments*; *Aries* also uses the rare word *re-edified* (195); and the first lines of the Induction echo those of *Heroes*, 'Fasting Day, | Why art so heavy?' (41-2). The Induction is also a kind of drama—an occasional entertainment, an urban manor house show—at which Middleton was adept, especially by this point in his career; he had already been engaged by the Inns of Court to write a masque, by the city of London to collaborate on a pageant for the royal entry of James I, by the Skinners and the Grocers to produce Lord Mayor's shows, and by the Lord Mayor and aldermen to write a series of shows for their entertainment.

The masque was written and performed sometime between 28 September 1619, when King James granted Denmark House to Prince Charles, and 4 July 1620, when the book was entered in the Stationers' Register. A few topical references justify narrowing these limits to late February and mid-April 1620. The Soldier mentions by name *Hic Mulier* and *Haec Vir* (32-3), two pamphlets which were, like *Tennis*, printed for John Trundle; the former was entered in the Stationers' Register on 9 February, the latter on 16 February. The 'frenzy of apparel' (368), satirized in the masque, was particularly intense at this time. James I rekindled the debate and sharpened its focus when he enjoined the clergy late in January to castigate women for their sartorial extravagance. By 12 February, John Chamberlain (289) could report to Dudley Carleton that the players and the ballad-makers had joined the ranks of the preachers in castigating women. The appearance of the Starches also seems appropriate for the spring of 1620. Jupiter identifies these characters as 'the youngest daughters of Deceit' (407), an epithet justified by the relicensing of the starchmakers in 1619 and by new fashions requiring dyed, starched fabrics. However, the Starches did not represent the same threat after 5 May 1620 when James I issued a proclamation against the making of starch (STC 8633). The outside limit for the writing of *Tennis* can be pushed back another few weeks, to mid-April, given the description of Prince Charles as 'Minerva's valiant'st, hopefull'st son', who 'early in his spring puts armour on' (865-6). The lines allude to his first tilt, preparations for which were made throughout February and March. The tilt, cancelled in 1619 because of the Queen's death, took place on 24 March and again on 18 April 1620. *Tennis* was probably composed between the publication of *Hic Mulier* and the second running of Prince Charles's first tilt.

Two attempts have been made to specify precisely the first performance of the masque. Noticing the only other record from 1620 of an entertainment at Denmark House sponsored by Charles, Fleay inferred that *Tennis* was performed on 4 March 1620. The proposal is attractive because Chamberlain's account of the festivities on that occasion connects it to tennis and notes that a banquet rather than a feast (see *Tennis*, Induction.73) was provided: 'The King came to London before Shrovetide; much feasting and jollity. The Prince gave a ball and banquet at Denmark House, the cost of which he lost in a wager at tennis with Buckingham; many mistresses and valentines were there, a custom grown into request lately; abundance of sweetmeats provided, but no supper' (292). What is missing from this description is any reference to a dramatic production, let alone a masque. Wiggin claimed on the strength of Middleton's dedication that *Tennis* celebrated the marriage of Charles Howard and Mary Cokayne on 22 April 1620, but in so doing confused the presentation of the book of the masque as a wedding gift with a presentation of the show. As Bentley argues (908), both Fleay and Wiggin assume that what was intended and prepared must have been performed as such. However, if the masque were performed at court, poets, printer, and publisher would surely have turned that fact to account. Instead of acknowledging that *Tennis* was 'intended for a royal night' (Prologue.12) or that it was 'prepared for his Majesty's entertainment at Denmark House' (Induction.0.1-2), they would have advertised the fact that it was performed under those privileged conditions, just as the title-page does try to capitalize on the Swan audience by noting performances 'to the Contentment of many Noble and Worthy Spectators'.

C. E. McGee

SEE ALSO

Text: *Works*, 1408
Textual introduction and apparatus: this volume, 667

WORKS CITED

Arber, Edward, ed. *A Transcript of the Register of the Company of Stationers of London; 1554-1640 A.D.* (1876), 3: 315
Barker, Richard Hindry, *Thomas Middleton* (1958), 190-1
Bentley, Gerald Eades, *The Jacobean and Caroline Stage*, 7 vols, vol. 4 (1956)
Chamberlain, John, *The Letters of John Chamberlain*, ed. Norman Egbert McClure, 2 vols (1939)
Fleay, F. G., *A Biographical Chronicle of the English Drama* (1891), 2:100

Hoy, Cyrus, 'The Shares of Fletcher and his Collaborators in the Beaumont and Fletcher Canon (V)', *Studies in Bibliography* 13 (1960), 77-108

Robb, Dewar M., 'The Canon of William Rowley's Plays', *Modern Language Review* 45 (1950), 129-41

Stork, C. W., ed., *'All's Lost by Lust' and 'A Shoemaker a Gentleman'* (1910), 41

Wiggin, Pauline G., *An Inquiry into the Authorship of the Middleton-Rowley Plays* (1897), 40

Honourable Entertainments
April 1620–April 1621

'Honorable Entertainments, composed for the service of this Noble Citie' are described on the title-page of the 1621 edition as 'Invented by Thomas Middleton'.

Anthony Parr

SEE ALSO

Text: *Works*, 1434
Textual introduction and apparatus: this volume, 673

Hengist, King of Kent June–December 1620

The first attribution of the play to Middleton appears in Henry Herringman's Stationers' Register entry (13 February 1661), and on the title-page of the edition published by Herringman (1661). There is no reason to doubt this attribution of the play entirely to Middleton. Swinburne and Stork suggested that Rowley might have written the comic scenes, but that conjecture has been refuted by Bald, Lake, and Jackson. The linguistic texture, style, structure, characterization, and design of the play clearly resemble those found in other plays written by Middleton from 1615 to 1620.

The play's date of composition is not so simply or confidently determinable. Because it contains dumb shows, Dyce considered it one of Middleton's earliest plays (1:122); Bullen rightly rejected such 'evidence', but believed that *Hengist* 'was originally an early play, but that it underwent considerable revision at a late date' (1:xviii). Between 28 November 1596 and 2 April 1597 Henslowe recorded payments for the purchase of properties and receipts from twelve performances of a 'ne[w]' play called 'valteger', performed by the Admiral's Men; on 20 November 1601 the company bought from Edward Alleyn 'a Boocke called vortiger', probably a different spelling of the same name. On 22 June 1597 Henslowe recorded receipts from a performance, by the same company, of a play not marked as 'ne', called 'henges'; scholars have generally assumed that this was 'amost certainly' or 'very probably' the same play as 'valteger'/'vortiger' (Greg, 2:181, 185), but it might be a second play. These records caused much confusion in early scholarship on the play. Fleay cited them as evidence that *Hengist* was Middleton's first play (2:104). Eccles (1931), having proven that Middleton was born in 1580—and thus only sixteen when 'valteger' was 'ne[w]'—pointed out that 'so famous and

dramatic a story as Hengist's…would naturally attract more than one author; most of the important reigns in British history were dramatised twice at least' (436-7). As Eccles also noted, the play's verse—feminine endings, run-on lines, and the rarity of rhyme—can hardly be earlier than '1606-1607'. *Hengist* also seems linked, by literary allusions, to plays of 1615-21, not those of the mid-1590s (Holdsworth). It is of course theoretically possible that Middleton was revising an old play by someone else, but if so the revision has left no traces. Moreover, since he clearly consulted various historical sources directly, he need not have been influenced by the earlier play(s) at all. Finally, it is hard to explain how a play originally owned and performed by the Admiral's Men could have become—as Middleton's *Hengist* was—the property of the King's Men.

The composition of *Hengist* has been more fruitfully connected with another play, which is extant: William Rowley's *The Birth of Merlin; or, The Child Hath Found his Father*, published in 1662. Bald argued persuasively, from the two plays' treatment of their historical materials, that *Merlin* 'is clearly later than Middleton's play' (xxii). Bald's analysis of the two plays' relationship to their sources was subsequently confirmed by Udall's more detailed and sophisticated discussion (80-84). When Bald and Udall analysed the relationship of the two plays, the date of *Merlin* was not known. But Bawcutt has since published a transcript of parts of the lost record book of the Revels Office, recording the licensing of Rowley's play: 'The *Childe hath found his Father*, for perusing and allowing of a New Play, acted by the Princes Servants at the Curtayne, 1622' (Bawcutt, 136). As Bawcutt notes, this is the alternative title of the play published in 1662, and clearly establishes that it was new in 1622. Since Middleton's play cannot be later than December 1621 (see below), this record confirms Bald's and Udall's arguments that *Merlin* is later.

It also confirms Bald's belief that *Merlin* and *Hengist* originally belonged to different companies (although it reverses the direction of movement he had proposed). On 7 August 1641 'The Maior of Quinborow &' was included in a list of plays belonging to the King's Men, which the Lord Chamberlain forbade the printers to publish without the company's consent (Chambers 1931, 398-99); it belonged by then to the King's Men, and there is no evidence that it ever belonged to anyone else. Bawcutt's evidence now proves that *Merlin* was first performed by Prince Charles's Men, the company to which Rowley belonged in 1622; it thus supports the 1662 attribution of the play to Rowley, and disproves the 1662 identification of Shakespeare as Rowley's collaborator.

External evidence establishes that *Hengist* was written and performed before the licensing of *Merlin* in 1622. The title of Middleton's play appears as the first in a list of play titles written by a scribe on a sheet inserted into George Buc's *History of King Richard III* (British Library, Cotton MS Tib.E.X, fol. 197[v]):

e Maior of Quinborough

Below this title, Buc himself (whose hand is clearly identifiable, and distinguishable from that of the scribe) wrote:

or Hengist K. of Kent

Buc's hand here was identified by Eccles (1933, 478–9). The play list must have been written on one side of this sheet of paper before the other side was used for Buc's *Richard III*. Bald notes that 'the corrections on the inserted scraps' in Buc's manuscript were 'probably still later in date' than the manuscript itself, which is dated '1619' (xiii). We do not know when in 1619 the manuscript was originally completed, or exactly when the scraps were subsequently inserted; the latest datable scrap is from 16 May 1619, but of course different scraps may have been used at different times. The insertions could have been made at any time between early 1619 and Buc's madness and death in 1622.

This is one of several scraps of paper that apparently originated in the Office of the Revels; the nature and dating of these scraps as a whole is discussed at length above. (See the Introduction to this Chronology, p. 332.) These lists must have been written before Buc's madness led to his expulsion from the Revels Office (March 1622); they were probably lists of plays being considered for performance in the long winter season at court; the last such season that Buc supervised was that of 1621–2, and therefore such lists could be no later than November 1621.

However, we know of six plays performed by the King's Men at court in the winter season of 1621–2: Massinger's (lost) *The Woman's Plot* (5 November 1621), the lost *The Woman is Too Hard for Him* (26 November), Fletcher's *Island Princess* (26 December), *Pilgrim* (1 January 1622), *Wild Goose Chase* (24 January), and *Coxcomb* (5 March). The payment for all six, made on 27 March 1622 to John Heminges, is recorded in Inner Temple MS 515, No. 7 (first transcribed by Murray, 2:193). Since this payment covers performances over a four month period, it presumably includes all the plays given by the company during that period. The play-list which contains *Hengist* includes at least three other plays which belonged to the King's Men: Beaumont and Fletcher's 'The Maides Tragedy', Shakespeare's 'The tradgedy of Ham⟨...', and Beaumont and Fletcher's 'The History of Phil⟨...⟩ or Love lies a bleed⟨...⟩'. None of the other plays on the list is known to have belonged to any other company, and therefore this scrap might contain only a list of candidates from the King's Men. In any case, it does contain four plays belonging to the King's Men, but does not contain any of the six King's Men plays actually performed at court in the winter season of 1621–2. Whatever may be true of the other play-lists on the other scraps, this one at least does not seem to belong to preparations for the 1621–2 court season. If Chambers (1925) was right about the original function of the scraps—and that remains the most probable explanation—then the scrap that contains *Hengist* must have been written for some earlier season.

It could therefore date from no later than November or December 1620.

This conclusion is supported by an element of the play, apparently not noted by previous investigators: the fact that the titular 'Mayor of Queenborough' is a 'tanner' (3.3.99, 109, 188, 253, 2.4.116). His profession follows naturally from his function in the story (cutting the hide into strips), but it was Middleton who made him a Mayor and a comic politician. Middleton began working for the city government in 1613, and increasingly often after autumn 1616, and he could have acquired his familiarity with the antics of local politicians at any time during those years. But in 1621, the Lord Mayor Edward Barkham (for whom Middleton wrote *The Sun in Aries* and 'An Invention') transferred from the Leathersellers to the Drapers; he therefore had belonged for virtually his entire life to the same company as men like Simon. It seems most unlikely that Middleton, in the first year of his appointment as City Chronologer, would have wanted to write a play which goes out of its way to ridicule a Mayor who had been a leatherseller. This internal evidence tends to confirm my interpretation of the Revels Office scrap, in ruling out 1621. *Hengist* therefore seems to have existed by December 1620, but the external evidence does not enable us to fix an earlier date.

There is no reason to suppose that all the scraps in Buc's manuscript date from the same period; on this particular scrap, the latest play securely datable is 'The Cambridge Playe of Albumazar and Trinculo', written by Tomkis, and performed for King James at Cambridge in March 1615 (Chambers 1923, 3:498). All the other datable plays on the list are earlier, some much earlier: 'The Tradgedy of Ham' and 'The Tradgedy of Jeronimo'. The otherwise undated plays contained on the list—including *Hengist*—could therefore theoretically have been written as early as *Hamlet*, or as late as the writing of the list. The list itself *must* have been written after March 1615, but that does not prove that any play named on it was completed after March 1615.

Chambers (1925) equated another play on this list—'The Falce Frend'—with Fletcher's *The False One* (datable by an actor list to 1619–23); but Bentley rejects this conjecture (5:1331). Without that identification, we have no evidence that the list was written after April 1615. It is perhaps more likely that scrap paper would come from more recent years, but it is not inevitable: as anyone knows who recycles paper, older scraps can get mixed with much younger ones. But it is worth emphasizing that even if we accept Chambers's conjecture, it would not establish that *Hengist* itself was written in or after 1619. The scrap provides a latest-possible date for *Hengist*, but in itself does nothing more.

The names of the actors 'Robrt St' (Stratford?), 'Robb Briggs', and 'Blackson' appear in both manuscripts (see textual notes to 2.1.31–2, 2.4.2, and 4.2.233–5); Ioppolo (2003, xvii) suggests that these may be actors living in London in the 1610s or 1620s (one John Blackston died in 1617, another in 1621), but unfortunately we cannot identify the actors securely, and the names cannot be used to date the play.

For any dating more specific we are dependent on internal evidence. As Bald realized, the reference to 'a great enormity in wool' (1.3.98) apparently alludes to 'a glut of wool on the market and a general disorganisation of the wool trade', caused by Sir William Cokayne's attempt to monopolize the dyeing of domestic wool before it was exported; this prompted a boycott of English wool by other countries, with disastrous economic consequences for England's major export trade. A full account of the economic consequences is given by Friis; Ioppolo shows that this background is relevant not only to the specific line cited by Bald, but to the whole scene of the petitioners' complaints and the subsequent treatment of Oliver (91–2). These allusions 'would be appropriate in 1616 and 1617 and again, say from 1619 onwards' (Bald xiv).

Ioppolo also argues that two other issues that permeate the play—proving a woman's chastity and protecting the country from foreign invasion—point to political scandals during these same years: the notorious annulment of the marriage of Lady Frances Howard and her subsequent trial for the murder of Thomas Overbury (1613–16), and the political power struggle among James's appointed deputies in Jersey beginning in 1616. (See Critical Introduction.) The Howard scandal remained notorious for decades, and although it confirms that the play can be no earlier than c.1616 it does not otherwise narrow the range of possible dates. For Jersey I have independently examined the *Calendar of State Papers Domestic*. Although rumblings of the dispute in Jersey are recorded in April 1614 (*CSPD* 12:540-41), it escalated dramatically in 1616, with charges by Herault in April leading to counter-charges by Peyton in July, and thereafter it was almost continuous until February 1621 (*CSPD* 12:550-631); it persisted, indeed, for some years after, but these later events are of no relevance to the dating of *Hengist*. As Bird said in a letter to his fellow commissioner Conway, 'I have been very much tried with our Jersey business' (27 March 1620, 12:621), and he was not alone. The events primarily disturbed the inhabitants of Jersey itself, but news of them did circulate in London, once the Privy Council became involved. According to a letter of 15 March 1617, John Herault of St Sauveur in Jersey had 'ben here these fowre or five moneths attending at the counsaile table about some contentions and complaints made of him by Sir John Payton governor of the yle of Gersey' (Chamberlain 2:63). On 13 March 1617 Sir Edward Conway was appointed to deal with the problem (*CSPD* 9:445); on 19 July 1617 Chamberlain reported Conway and his companions had 'returned out of Gersey, whether they were employed to compound the differences twixt the Governor and the inhabitants' (2:88). Together these allusions suggest that the play cannot be earlier than mid-1616 or early 1617.

The Jersey troubles were eventually overshadowed by the troubles in Bohemia (beginning in May 1618); these intensified King James's efforts to arrange a dynastic marriage as part of an international peace settlement. The growing influence of the Spanish ambassador (Gondomar), the anxieties over the prospect of the projected royal marriage to a foreign woman of another religion, the invasion of Protestant territories by Catholic troops in eastern Europe, the increasing toleration of English Catholics—all these would have provided a topical backdrop to *Hengist* in 1619 or 1620. There were real fears of foreign invasion in Kent routinely, for hundreds of years. On 27 March 1619 Chamberlain reported that 'We had a great alarme the last weeke by the fiering of almost all the beacons in Sussex and Kent, upon a mistaking by reason of the burning of certain furzes or ferne neere a beacon in Sussex: but it fell out not altogether amisse for the people shewed themselves forward enough to arme and make head' (2:226). The play's 'several references to the British throne as elective...would have had a particular resonance after September 1619, when James's son-in-law Frederick was elected to the Bohemian throne, an event which precipitated war in Europe and threatened to draw England in against the German emperor' (Briggs, 492). The topicality of this historical material in 1619–20 is indicated by an apparently unrelated manuscript play in Latin entitled *Fatum Vortigerni* (British Library, MS Lansdowne 723), written by Thomas Carleton and performed at Douai in August 1619 (McCabe).

The internal evidence so far surveyed makes it very unlikely that *Hengist* could have been written before the summer of 1616, and probably not before early 1617, when the dispute in Jersey attracted more public attention. The year least likely to fit the foregoing allusions would be 1618, when the wool crisis seemed (briefly) to be abating, and the implications of events in central Europe were not yet so clearly linked to English interests, or to the events of Middleton's play. Early 1619 can be ruled out for other reasons. The usual injunction on playing during the forty days of Lent (Gurr, 86–7) was in that year extended in both directions by particular misfortunes. On 21 January 1619 the London Common Council ordered the King's Men to stop performing in the Blackfriars; the order was not revoked until 27 March. But all the London theatres were closed from Queen Anne's death on 2 March 1619 until her burial on 13 May (Bentley 1:5-7). Although the King's Men may have shifted their operations to the Globe from 21 January until the beginning of Lent (February 16), the Globe was not an attractive venue in winter, and for ten years they and their customers had grown accustomed to it as a summer venue only (Gurr). At the very least, the King's Men lost eleven weeks in spring 1619, and unless they ignored the ban on playing during Lent they lost three months; before Lent, they lost another three weeks of the use of their normal winter house (where *Hengist* was performed, according to the 1661 title-page). Even if Middleton wrote *Hengist* in early 1619, it could not have had its first performances until the second half of May. That brings us close to early September, when Chamberlain—and presumably other Londoners—heard about Frederick's election in Bohemia. The disputes in Europe after May 1618 almost certainly interested and affected many more Londoners than the dispute in Jersey; Chamberlain's letters, for instance, devote many pages to the crisis in Europe and the fears it precipitated at home, but only two sentences to Jersey.

There are thus two distinct periods into which *Hengist* might be most plausibly fitted, with a gap between them: late 1616 to early 1618, or September 1619 to December 1620. Although the internal evidence so far surveyed is not decisive, it does tend to favour the later period (when the Jersey dispute and the dispute in central Europe overlapped, providing the fullest topical background to the text). So does the external evidence: the closer we get to 1619, the closer we get to the date of the Buc manuscript in which the scraps appear.

Stylistic evidence also favours the later date. As noted below, *Hengist* is closely aligned with Middleton's plays of 1621-4 both metrically and in its treatment of unusual oaths. (See *Nice Valour*.) Its structure also represents an innovation not seen in his earlier tragedies and tragi-comedies. Like the ambiguously titled *Changeling* (1622), it combines a tragic plot ('Hengist, King of Kent') with a comic plot ('The Mayor of Queenborough'); one ends happily, the other unhappily. This represents a major departure from the dominant conventions of tragicomedy, which Middleton had accepted in *The Witch* (1616), *Fair Quarrel* (1616), and *Old Law* (late 1618-19). Neither genre is subordinated to the other; instead, the two are juxtaposed in a way that compels a composite emotional response to the whole. It seems relatively improbable to suppose that five or six years separated Middleton's two known examples of this generic experiment.

None of this evidence allows us to arbitrate between autumn 1619 and 1620. Heinemann (147) suggested that the contested election for Mayor in Middleton's play echoed a dispute over the Parliamentary election for Queenborough, in early November 1620; one of the parties in this dispute was Philip Herbert, Constable of the Castle at Queenborough (brother of the Earl of Pembroke, Lord Chamberlain and patron of the King's Men). Middleton would certainly have been sympathetic to the Protestant alliances of the Herberts at this point. But Heinemann's argument depends upon Middleton's knowledge of two letters sent to Queenborough in November 1620, and concerns its Member of Parliament, not its Mayor; it would allow very little time for the play to be licensed, performed publicly, and considered for the court winter season of 1620.

A better explanation for the play's emphasis upon Queenborough (and in particular its Mayor) is provided by an event and a text that were notoriously public, not private, and particularly likely to have interested Middleton. Briggs pointed out that Middleton's historical sources placed Hengist's 'Tong' castle elsewhere in Kent, thus distinguishing it from Queenborough Castle (493). But in July 1619 Queenborough castle was the objective of John Taylor ('the water poet') and his Bankside companion

Robert Bird. Bird had wagered that he could row down the Thames to Queenborough in a paper boat. They left London on the evening ebb tide of 25 July, their progress observed by 'thousands of people' on the banks of the Thames, 'And thousands more' in boats and barges; after two miserable and dangerous nights on the water, at dawn on Monday

> The sight of *Quinborough* castle did appear.
> That was the famous monumentall marke,
> To which we striu'd to bring our rotten barke:
> The onely ayme of our intents and scope...
> But being come to *Quinborough* and aland...
> The Maior of *Quinborough* in loue affords
> To entertaine vs, as we had been Lords;
> It is a yearely feast kept by the Maior...
> We to the Maior gaue our aduenturous boat...
> He to his house inuited vs to dine,
> Where we had cheare on cheare, and wine on wine,
> And drinke, and fill, and drinke, and drinke and fill,
> With welcome vpon welcome, welcome still...
> Which when the Maior did know, he presently
> Tooke patient what he could not remedie.

In the play, immediately after Simon is elected Mayor Hengist gives him money for 'your feast'; the Barber promises to 'drink [his] health with trumpets', but Simon corrects that to 'sack-butts': 'That's the more solemn drinking for my state; No malt this year shall fume into my pate' (3.3.249-52). When we next see Simon, 'the Mayor of Queenborough...with all [his] brethren' ceremonially welcomes visitors to the town and castle (4.1.1-2); this scene is immediately followed by 'the banquet' for the guests (4.2.0.3). In Simon's next scene, the Mayor elaborately welcomes a mere footman, who tells him that Hengist 'Intends this night to make merry with you'; Simon replies, 'Why was I chosen Mayor, but that great men Should make merry with me? There's a jest indeed' (5.1.26-30). Simon then gives elaborate instructions for preparation of the feast. Players arrive, and Simon, rather than allow them to perform in the town hall, insists 'my house will...serve' (5.1.66-7). Simon is then cheated, and can do nothing about it. None of this material—the repeated emphasis on welcoming visitors, drinking and feasting at his own house, exaggerating the importance of an ordinary visitor, being disappointed of his expectations—is in Middleton's known sources, and it all corresponds with the role of the actual Mayor of Queenborough in Taylor's publicity stunt.

Middleton might have heard of all this in July 1619, when Taylor made the little town of Queenborough a temporary sensation. But the bizarre voyage to Queenborough is more likely to have attracted attention and gossip than the behaviour of the Mayor when they arrived. Taylor's account of the trip—including the lines I have quoted describing his arrival and treatment by the Mayor—was entered in the Stationers' Register on 22 May 1620, and presumably published soon after, in a quarto dated '1620' entitled 'The Praise of Hemp-seed with The Voyage of Mr. *Roger Bird* and the Writer hereof, in a Boat of browne-Paper, from *London* to *Quinborough* in *Kent*.' Middleton is likely to have taken an interest in this pamphlet, because its long first part—'The Praise of Hemp-seed'—includes a catalogue of 'Poets ancient and moderne, the best sort mentioned' (to which the prefatory table of 'The Contents of This Booke' calls attention). Middleton himself is one of the twelve living poets identified as 'the best sort'. His sometime collaborators Rowley and Heywood are also included; both—like another Middleton collaborator, Dekker—were friends of Taylor, who as a waterman was particularly well known among London's theatrical community (Capp, 41-4). In the Preface to the same pamphlet Taylor refers specifically to Middleton's *Ant and the Nightingale*: 'One wrote the Nightingale and lab'ring Ant'. In *Chaste Maid* Middleton had gone out of his way to praise watermen.

Middleton is thus much likelier to have known Taylor's pamphlet than to have had access to private letters from noblemen to officials in the town of Queenborough. And there seems little doubt that any connection between the pamphlet and the play resulted from Taylor's influence on Middleton, and not vice versa. Taylor's pamphlet is autobiographical, describing actual events of 1619; Middleton's play departs from all historical sources in those places where it resembles Taylor's pamphlet. If the play had already existed, Taylor would surely have mentioned it; his works generally are full of such citations, and the Mayor of Queenborough became one of Middleton's most famous characters. It thus seems likely that Taylor's pamphlet was a significant influence on Middleton's play—in which case, *Hengist* cannot have been completed before mid-1620.

Gary Taylor

SEE ALSO

Text: *Works*, 1451
Textual introduction and apparatus: this volume, 1029

WORKS CITED

Bald, R. C., ed., *Hengist, King of Kent or The Mayor of Queenborough* (1938)

Bawcutt, N. W., ed., *The Control and Censorship of Caroline Drama: The Records of Sir Henry Herbert, Master of the Revels 1623-73* (1996)

Bentley, G. E., *The Jacobean and Caroline Stage*, 7 vols (1941-68)

Briggs, Julia, 'Middleton's Forgotten Tragedy *Hengist, King of Kent*', *Review of English Studies* NS 41 (1990), 479-95

Capp, Bernard, *The World of John Taylor the Water-Poet* (1994)

Chamberlain, John, *The Letters of John Chamberlain*, ed. N. E. McClure, 2 vols (1939)

Chambers, E. K., *The Elizabethan Stage*, 4 vols (1923)

—— Review of Marcham, *The King's Office of the Revels 1610-1622*, *Review of English Studies* 1 (1925), 481-4

—— ed., 'Dramatic Records: The Lord Chamberlain's Office', in *Collections II.3*, Malone Society (1931), 321-416

Eccles, Mark, 'Middleton's Birth and Education', *Review of English Studies* 7 (1931), 431-41

—— 'Sir George Buc, Master of the Revels', in *Thomas Lodge and Other Elizabethans*, ed. C. J. Sisson (1933), 409-506

Fleay, F. G., *A Biographical Chronicle of the English Drama, 1559-1642*, 2 vols (1891)

Friis, Astrid, *Alderman Cockayne's Project and the Cloth Trade* (1927)

Greg, W. W., ed., *Henslowe's Diary*, 2 vols (1904-8)

Gurr, Andrew, *The Shakespearian Playing Companies* (1996)

Heinemann, Margot, *Puritanism and Theatre: Thomas Middleton and Opposition Drama under the Early Stuarts* (1980)

Holdsworth, R. V., 'The Date of *Hengist, King of Kent*', *Notes and Queries* 236 (1991), 516-19

Ioppolo, Grace, 'Sexual Treason, Treasonous Sexuality, and the Eventful Politics of James I in Middleton's *Hengist, King of Kent*', *Ben Jonson Journal* 3 (1996), 87-107

—— ed., *Hengist, King of Kent, or The Mayor of Queenborough by Thomas Middleton*, Malone Society (2003)

McCabe, W. H., 'Fatum Vortigerni', *Times Literary Supplement* (15 August 1935), 513

Murray, J. T., *English Dramatic Companies 1558-1642*, 2 vols (1910)

Stork, C. W., ed., *William Rowley: All's Lost by Lust and A Shoemaker a Gentleman* (1910)

Swinburne, A. C., 'Introduction', *Thomas Middleton*, Mermaid series (n.d.), I, xxii

Udall, Joanna, ed., *A Critical, Old-Spelling Edition of The Birth of Merlin (Q 1662)* (1991)

Women, Beware Women   Summer 1621

No identifiable allusion to *Women Beware* would survive if the play had not been brought to print. It is first mentioned in the Stationers' Register entry of 9 September 1653, and is there ascribed to 'Mr. Tho: Midleton'. The ascription is repeated on the title-page of the 1657 *Two New Playes* ('WRITTEN By Tho. Middleton, Gent.') and the separate title-page for *Women Beware* itself ('By Tho. Middleton, Gent.'). In the preliminary matter to *Two New Playes*, Nathaniel Richards concurs, claiming special knowledge: *Women Beware* is 'The Tragedy of | My Familiar Acquaintance, | THO. MIDDLETON'. The play is in every respect highly characteristic of Middleton, and his sole authorship has not been questioned.

In the absence of any external evidence the play's date is difficult to ascertain. Fleay (1891), Schelling (1908), and Cope (1961) accepted relatively early datings of 1612-14. Their dependence on parallels with *The Triumphs of Truth* (1613) is suspect, not least because Middleton could be self-imitative at distant points in time. To cite one example they give, comparable imagery of infectious mists can be found as early as *Wisdom of Solomon*. The earlier dating is not widely accepted, though there are two points that can be taken in its favour. First, the incidence of oaths favoured in the city comedies is relatively high in the play and would be consistent with pre-1617 (see Lake, 1976). Second, the play makes exceptional demands on the number of actors, and in particular boy actors, in much the same way as *A Chaste Maid in Cheapside*, and Dutton (1999) has conjectured that performance could have been by the same combined company of Lady Elizabeth's Men supplemented with players from the Queen's Revels Boys that has been hypothesized for the first performances of that play in 1613.

Metrical evidence lends some support to critics' general impression of the play's maturity (Mulryne, 1962). Middleton's play-title has been thought to pick up lines from *Swetnam the Woman-hater Arraigned by Women* (performed 1617-18, published 1620), but more closely echoes an undated broadside on Anne Turner (see Critical Introduction, *Works*, p. 1489), who was tried for murder in 1616 (for an account, see Lindley, 1993). This area of interest indicates at least that the play is post-1616. Most recent discussion focuses on where the play should be placed within the period defined by Bald's proposal (1937) of *c*.1621 and Oliphant's proposal (1929) of 1627 (the year of Middleton's death), though the claims of 1617-20 should not be discounted.

Several points that have been adduced in favour of one date or another can be discounted. The reference to wearing wigs as a result of venereal disease (3.3.68) has been seen as another allusion to Swetnam or to the misogynist pamphlet *Haec Vir* (1620) (Mulryne, 1975), but similar references are found in plays of various dates, including Middleton's own. Maxwell (1943) took the reference to hasty marriage 'As if they went to stock a new-found land' (1.2.61) to be an allusion to the sixty women who went to the Virginia colony between July and November 1621 to become wives of male colonists. But Jacobs (1941) and Mulryne noted earlier such projects in 1618 and 1619, and pointed out that Middleton is echoing himself at *Roaring Girl* 4.72-3. Two other discountable details relate to a late dating. Sir Thomas More's *Utopia*, a passage from which evidently lies behind Sordido's proposal that Isabella should be viewed naked (2.2.118-19), was reprinted for the first time since 1597 in 1624, but Middleton refers to *Utopia* by name before this date, in 1618 (*Owl* 620.n). An emphatically discountable point is that composition after 1621 would be indicated if Middleton's interest in chess had been stimulated exclusively by studying the game of the Italian player Greco, who was resident in London 1622-4 (see J. R. Moore, 1935). Bawcutt (1987) has pointed out that Middleton was conversant with chess from Arthur Saul's *The Famous Game of Chess-Play*, published in 1614 and subsequently reissued in an edition revised by John Barbier in 1618. Middleton closely echoes this work at 2.2.301; his wording is slightly but significantly closer to Barbier's 1618 edition. Here at least is further evidence for composition after 1617, but not necessarily after 1621.

Indeed, first performance after 1621 is unlikely on two other accounts. Sir John Astley's and Sir Henry Herbert's records as Masters of the Revels begin in 1622. Edmond Malone, in James Boswell's Variorum Shakespeare, vol. 3, p. 153, published selective transcriptions of these documents. *Women Beware* does not appear in them. Although the transcriptions are incomplete, Malone owned a copy of this particular play, and he would have had an interest in recording its licence. Bawcutt has located a previously unpublished transcription by Jacob Henry Burn that considerably supplements Malone's records for 1622-5, but *Women Beware* does not feature in these items either. Hence the likelihood of *Women Beware* having been first performed in these years correspondingly narrows again.

Moreover, Hoy (1980) conclusively demonstrates that the play influences in its plot and therefore antedates Dekker's *Match Me in London*. *Match Me* was relicensed by Henry Herbert on 21 August 1623 (Bawcutt, 1996). Herbert testifies that the original licence was issued by George Buc, who on account of his madness was removed from office in March 1622. As Martin Wiggins has privately pointed out, *Women Beware* therefore simply must have been performed or otherwise made available to Dekker before March 1622, and indeed, if one allows time for Dekker to write *Match Me*, it is improbable that Middleton's play is later than 1621.

One argument that has been adduced in favour of 1621 carries limited significance if taken in isolation, but adds circumstantial weight once a date after 1621 is ruled out. Mulryne, in his commentary, connects Bianca's mention of pirates at 3.1.153 with Sir Robert Mansell's expedition against Mediterranean pirates; reports of a major battle were reaching London in July 1621, and Mansell's ships returned to Plymouth on 22 September. They had not achieved their object, for on 20 October Chamberlain recorded the capture of fifty-seven merchant ships by pirates. However, Chamberlain records Dutch pirates and Dunkirkers as in the London news again in 1623, 1624, and 1625. Of particularly urgent concern were Turkish pirates active on the seas west of England and taking slaves from Cornwall in 1625. The matter was raised in the House of Commons, as a result of which an attack was launched against them. The reference to pirates is therefore of little value if taken in isolation for a 1621 dating. But that year is the only one that is compatible with both Herbert's testimony and the topical issue of pirates (and it is also consistent with the reference to women migrants to Virginia, and, for that matter, allusions to Swetnam or *Haec Vir*).

First performance in 1621 would accord with one other possible allusion. Mulryne (1975) upheld Maxwell's suggestion (1943) that the comment on the Duke's age of fifty-five at 1.3.89-93 may be a piece of flattery aimed at King James, who was fifty-five on 19 June 1621. Holdsworth (1993) questions this, arguing that it may be no more than an indication of mature manhood, as similar ages are twice elsewhere in Middleton. He also objects that James would not relish comparison with a rapist, though the Duke has not been identified as such at the relevant moment in the play, and a compliment could work independently of a more general analogy between the living person and the role. Middleton is not elsewhere arbitrarily precise about the age fifty-five, except in the case of Antigona in *Old Law*; her exact age is crucial to the plot, and she is not a man lauded for his sexual maturity. The detail is at least suggestive.

Notwithstanding Dutton's intriguing suggestion in favour of 1613, the combined evidence of metre, references to the Swetnam controversy and/or Anne Turner, and the probable dependence on a 1614 book for knowledge of chess, probably in its 1618 reprinting, all suggest a later date. Correspondingly, in the absence of more concrete indications, Malone's and Burn's joint failure to transcribe any reference to the play in the years beginning 1622, and Herbert's testimony to Buc's original licence of *Match Me*, must be taken as suggesting composition in or before 1621. The more credible of the alleged topical allusions tend to converge on 1621 itself. Given a date of 1621, these allusions further help to narrow the date within that year. All would have been topical between July (the month following the King's birthday) and October–November. But the time lapse between composition and performance of *Women Beware*, composition of *Match Me*, and licence of the latter play before March 1622, perhaps encourages a dating closer to July.

John Jowett

SEE ALSO

Text: *Works*, 1493
Textual introduction and apparatus: this volume, 1140

WORKS CITED

Bald, R. C., 'The Chronology of Middleton's Plays', *Modern Language Review* 32 (1937), 33–43

Bawcutt, N. W., 'New Light on Middleton's Knowledge of Chess', *Notes and Queries* 232 (1987), 301–2

—— ed., *The Control and Censorship of Caroline Drama: The Records of Sir Henry Herbert, Master of the Revels 1623–73* (1996)

Boswell, James, ed., *Plays and Poems of William Shakespeare*, 21 vols (1821)

Chamberlain, John, *Letters*, ed. Norman Egbert McClure, 2 vols (1939)

Cope, Jackson I., 'The Date of Middleton's *Women Beware Women*', *Modern Language Notes* 76 (1961), 295–300

Dutton, Richard, ed., *'Women Beware Women' and Other Plays*, by Thomas Middleton (1999)

Fleay, F. G., *A Biographical Chronicle of the English Drama, 1559–1642*, 2 vols (1891)

Holdsworth, R. V., 'Notes on *Women Beware Women*', *Notes and Queries* 238 (1993), 215–22

Hoy, Cyrus, *Introductions, Notes, and Commentaries to texts in 'The Dramatic Works of Thomas Dekker'*, 4 vols (1980), vol. 3

Jacobs, Elizabeth R., ed., 'A Critical Edition of Thomas Middleton's *Women Beware Women*', unpublished Ph.D. dissertation (Wisconsin, 1941)

Lake, David J., 'The Date of *More Dissemblers Besides Women*', *Notes and Queries* 221 (1976), 219–21

Lindley, David, *The Trials of Frances Howard: Fact and Fiction at the Court of King James* (1993)

Maxwell, Baldwin, 'The Date of Thomas Middleton's *Women Beware Women*', *Philological Quarterly* 22 (1943), 338–42

Moore, J. R., 'The Contemporary Significance of Middleton's *Game at Chesse*', *Publications of the Modern Language Association of America* 50 (1935), 761–8

Mulryne, J. R., 'A Critical Edition of Thomas Middleton's *Women Beware Women*', Ph.D. dissertation, 2 vols (Cambridge University, 1962)

—— ed., *Women Beware Women* (1975)

Oliphant, E. H. C., ed., *Shakespeare and His Fellow Dramatists*, 2 vols (1929)

Parker, R. Brian, 'A Critical Edition of Thomas Middleton's *Women Beware Women*', unpublished Ph.D. dissertation (University of Liverpool, 1955)

Schelling, Felix E., *Elizabethan Drama 1558–1642*, 2 vols (1908)

'Bolles'   September 1621

One of Middleton's official duties as City Chronologer might have been the writing of epitaphs for former Lord Mayors. This is the only epitaph in English written for a Lord Mayor who died during Middleton's term as Chronologer (Cokayne). Bolles died on 1 September 1621 and was buried in St Swithin's parish church, London; Middleton had written *The Triumphs of Honour and Industry* to celebrate his election as Lord Mayor in 1617.

In conjunction with the date and official status of the poem, two features of its vocabulary and form most strongly suggest Middleton's authorship. *OED*'s earliest example of the noun *praetorship* in reference to mayoralty is from Middleton's *Virtue* 225 (1622); Middleton used it even earlier in the same sense in the headnote at *Entertainments* 5.3 (1621). The 1621 passage is followed by an 'epitaph', the only text so labelled anywhere in the Middleton canon; the word 'epitaph' appears three times in fifty lines of that entertainment. The only other occurrences of *praetorship* in this specialized sense in the Literature Online database, or the Early English Books Online digitized database (as of June 2006), occur in Dekker's *London's Tempe* (1629) and in Heywood's *Londini Sinus Salutis* (1635), *Londinii Speculum* (1637) and *Porta Pietatis* (1638). Neither Dekker nor Heywood had any known association with Bolles, or did any known writing for the City of London in the early 1620s. Although Heywood used the word more frequently than Middleton, all his examples postdate the Bolles epitaph and Middleton parallels by more than a decade. By contrast with the Heywood and Dekker parallels, both Middleton parallels date from within a year of the Bolles epitaph, which uses the same word in the same rare sense. Moreover, in the parallel in *Virtue*—'this high place, which praetorship is termed'—Middleton explained its meaning to the London public, making it clear that at the time the word was newly coined and unfamiliar. By the time Dekker and Heywood adopted it, no such explanations were needed. This evidence suggests that Middleton invented this sense of the word *praetorship* in 1621. He was certainly capable of such compounds. He apparently invented five other words by appending the -ship suffix to an existing noun: *rivalship* (*Five Gallants* 1.1.271, antedating *OED*'s first example), *hagship* (*Witch* 2.2.9), *ravenship* (*Owl* 168, not in *OED*), *coxcombship* (*Gypsy* 4.2.76, not in *OED*), and the specific sense of *mothership* at *Game* 4.2.45.

The disyllabic *-ion* suffix at the end of a verse line is—as Oliphant noted (84)—characteristic of Middleton, who combines this obsolescent accentuation with a style which is in other respects consistently modern and colloquial. In his civic verse, for instance, Middleton rhymes affection/one, conversation/won, dissolution/on, expectation/on, progression/on, suggestions/ones. The Bolles epitaph combines this obsolescent syllabification with an unusual rhyme, compassion/man; a comparable -an/-on rhyme occurs at *Antiquity* 428–9 (upon/man). Both the unusual features of the rhyme in the first couplet of the Bolles epitaph are paralleled at *Antiquity* 455–6, where Middleton rhymes pampilïon/swan.

This odd syllabification and rhyme are combined with a diction—like Middleton's, especially in his civic work—otherwise distinctly plain and modern, as can be seen by contrast with the epitaph for Sir Thomas Smith, a former sheriff of London (d. 4 September 1625, buried in Sutton at Hone). The Smith epitaph (Cokayne, 5) uses the auxiliary verb 'doth' in its first line, and syllabic -ed twice; the Bolles epitaph uses neither of these obsolescent forms (which are relatively rare in Middleton, particularly by the 1620s). Like the 'Epitaph' at *Entertainments* 5.31–50, the Bolles epitaph is written in a succession of couplets that contain no feminine endings.

Other aspects of the vocabulary and imagery of the poem are also consistent with Middleton's authorship in 1621. The rhythm and grammar of the first two lines strongly resemble the first two lines of the dedication to *Antiquity* (1619), which begins with a similar triumvirate of abstract nouns ('Love, triumph, honour . . .'). I searched Literature Online for examples—in the canons of Dekker, Heywood, Middleton and Munday—of the three first words of the epitaph in comparable lists without *and* (the rhetorical figure polyptoton). Dekker yielded 'beauty, honour, store' (*Troia-Nova*, 1612); Heywood, 'power, honour, glory' (*Hierarchy of the Blessed Angels*, 1635); Munday, 'truth, virtue, honour' (1616). None of these examples combines *honour* with a Latinate noun of three syllables or more, as does the Bolles epitaph. By contrast, both Middleton parallels for polyptoton with one of these three words combines it with latinate and polysyllabic nouns: 'Honour, Religion, Piety, Commiseration' (*Industry* 222–3) and 'Integrity, Watchfulness, Equality, Providence, Impartiality' (*Virtue* 245–6). Because Vickers (2002) has demonstrated that authors may be differentiated by the frequency with which they begin verse lines with the preposition *of*, I checked the same four canons for the phrase 'Of honour' as the beginning of a line: there were no Munday parallels, the sole Dekker example came from 1604, the examples in Heywood came from 1613, 1636, and 1637. By contrast, one Middleton parallel (*Aries* 64) dates—like the Bolles epitaph—from 1621; another was written in 1624 (*Game at Chess* 4.4.47).

Of the poem's three first words, *integrity* is the rarest. It does not appear in Munday's canon at all, and only five times in the works of Dekker (1607–31) and five times in those of Heywood (1607–38). By contrast, Middleton uses it fifteen times: once in *Fair Quarrel*, all the remainder in texts written between 1619 and 1626, including

a mayoral pageant entitled and prominently featuring *Integrity* (1623).

The phrase 'those three' occurs six times in Middleton *Revenger*, *Gallants*, *Widow*, *Aries*, *Integrity*, *Entertainments*; 'of this man' occurs at *Valour* 3.1.66 (We may commend the carriage of this man in't). 'Filled up' occurs at *Revenger* 1.4.32 and *Game* 5.2.93; here, three virtues fill up a lifetime, and in *Integrity* 'virtuous government' 'Filled all those years' (161). *Man* and *lifetime* are collocated at *Valour* 2.1.157; *conscience* and *discharged* at *Valour* 5.2.46; *know* and *feel* at *Valour* 2.1.149, 3.2.136. *Grave* is Middleton's favourite adjective for a lord mayor or alderman (eleven times); the collocation 'honourable, grave' occurs at *Entertainments* 8.103. 'One man's fame' combines two phrases which elsewhere appear separately often in Middleton: 'one man's' (seven times), 'man's fame' (three times). 'Living name' occurs at *Chaste Maid* 5.4.12 and in 'Malfi'; 'to oppress' at *Quarrel* 5.1.424, *Game* 1.1.321. 'Crown a soul' echoes 'my soul crowned' (*Old Law* 4.2.47–8). Middleton collocates *praise* and *just* (or *justly*) at *Timon* 2.217 and *Integrity* 313; in the same line, Middleton combines 'praise . . . her life . . . read', as at *Dissemblers* 1.1.5 ('read her life and praise'). Middleton collocates *worthy* and *wife* (*Lady* 1.2.22), *true* and *worth* (*Weapons* 1.1.173, *Aries* 144, 289), *true* and *bed* (*Dissemblers* 5.2.167). The phrase 'of his worth' occurs in *Game* 3.1.162 (of his worth comprized in). It also appears once in Dekker, once in Heywood, but not at all in Munday. The collocation 'of his bed' occurs at *Phoenix* 8.180. I have found nothing in the poem which contradicts Middleton's verbal preferences, and the overwhelming majority of the vocabulary parallels come from works Middleton wrote between 1613 and 1626.

Gary Taylor

SEE ALSO

Text: *Works*, 1890
Textual introduction and apparatus: this volume, 992

WORKS CITED

Cokayne, G. E., *Some Account of the Lord Nayors and Sheriffs of the City of London: During the First Quarter of the Seventeenth Century, 1601-1625* (1897)
Oliphant, E. H. C., *The Plays of Beaumont and Fletcher* (1927)
Vickers, Brian, *'Counterfeiting' Shakespeare: Evidence, Authorship, and John Ford's 'Funerall Elegye'* (2002)

Measure for Measure (adaptation)

October 1621

Jowett and Taylor (171–7) reconsider the date of *Measure* in the light of discussions by Lever, Eccles, and others, and conclude that it was probably written no earlier than September 1603 and no later than late 1604. Shakespeare's authorship is undoubted, on account of the play's inclusion in the 1623 Folio (JAGGARD) and its attribution to 'Shaxberd' in a record of performance on 26 December 1604 in the Revels accounts.

Jowett and Taylor's hypothesis of adaptation was originally developed while Marcus was preparing a fresh examination of the play's topical allusions. One of the passages Marcus places within the context of 1604 is the opening of 1.2, which Jowett and Taylor firmly identify as part of the later adaptation. It remains for the present account to respond to Marcus's reading of the passage, and to argue for the relative strength of placing it within the context of the later adaptation.

The broader picture of allusion drawn in by Marcus involves the play as a whole. The Duke is not, she suggests, a historical Duke of Vienna, but the historical Duke of Vienna's brother, namely Archduke Albert, ruler of the Spanish Netherlands. This interpretative manœuvre need not be challenged here, for it is almost entirely separate from the considerations that apply to the 'King of Hungary' passage in 1.2. Indeed, by taking the Duke away from Vienna, Marcus widens the separation. The opening of 1.2 can be considered on its own terms.

As Marcus notes (following Keeton, 374-6), in 1604 the title 'King of Hungary' could not pertain to an independent national monarch; it could refer only to the Holy Roman Emperor, Rudolf II (187). This seems correct. Bennett (8-11) indicates that István Bocskai, the leader of the Protestant revolt against the Empire, was offered the title King of Hungary by the Turkish Porte in 1604. But the chronology of events is more drawn-out than such a statement suggests, and the events before the recorded Court performance of *Measure* are such that the putative allusion would probably have been puzzling even in Hungary itself. Bocskai's important victory at Adorján was on 14 October 1604. On 20 November Bethlen Gábor, accompanied by a Turkish chiaus, brought to Bocskai, from the Turkish Porte, the ensignia of the princes of Transylvania. It was not until 21 February 1605 that the Transylvanian parliament at Marosszerda elected Bocskai as Prince; his inauguration was on 14 September of that year. It would have been both presumptive and inaccurate to style Bocskai King of Hungary in 1604, and it seems highly unlikely that an English audience would have understood any such reference. A further difficulty in assuming a reference to Bocskai is that to do so pushes the date of the composition of *Measure* to the latest possible limit. Unless one is committed to sustaining an allusion to Bocskai's revolt, the play may actually have been written as early as September 1603, and there are no specific reasons for dating it later than March 1604 (Jowett and Taylor, 171-7).

Lever had noted (xxxi) that there was in fact no peace treaty involving the Hungarians in 1603-4. Marcus accommodates this apparent difficulty. She notes that in the passage in *Measure* the 'composition' has not yet been agreed: 'If the Duke with the other dukes come not to composition with the King of Hungary, why then, all the dukes fall upon the King'. The conflict between the King of Hungary, and 'the Duke and the other Dukes' refers, she suggests, to the Austrian archdukes' deprivation of Rudolf, as King of Hungary, of direct political control of areas under his administration. 'All the dukes fall upon the King' therefore refers not to an attack against the Hungarians, but to a quarrel within the Imperial dynasty. This interpretation is hard to sustain, partly because Lucio does, after all, sound as though he is speaking of negotiations to end a military dispute between the Hungarians and the Viennese, but also and not least because the crisis to which she refers did not come to a head until a few years after 1604. Crown Prince Matthias obliged Ferdinand to make peace with the Hungarians in 1605, which led to the Peace of Vienna and the Peace of Zsitvatorok in 1606, events probably already too late to be in the air of anticipation in London in 1604. It was only the events of 1608 that by Marcus's reading most fully fulfil Lucio's prediction. On 28 March, Matthias declared a mobilization of the nobility in Western Hungary and Austria, seemingly to protect the peace achieved at Vienna and Zsitvatorok, but implicitly to oppose Emperor Rudolf. Rudolf surrendered his power over Hungary, Croatia, and the Austrian perennial provinces in favour of Matthias on 25 June. By Marcus's interpretation, Rudolph is called King of Hungary rather than Emperor because this is the title, or at least one of the titles, of which he might be deprived. Clearly this assumes foreknowledge: a London audience of 1604 is most unlikely to have been aware that Matthias would 'fall upon' Rudolf in this way some four years later.

Conceding that the revolt of the Hungarian estates is after all an issue of immediate allusion, Marcus accepts its relevance to the First Gentleman's immediate riposte, 'Heaven grant us its peace, but not the King of Hungary's'. By her reading, the referent switches from the dynastic quarrel of 'the Dukes fall upon the King' to the Emperor's intended 'pacification' of Hungarian Protestants. There is no consistency of allusion between the 'composition' with the King of Hungary and the King of Hungary's 'peace', and no immediate antithesis between the possibility that the dukes might 'fall upon the King' and the King of Hungary's 'peace'. The need to assume such bewildering shifts of focus reflects the strain in making the passage fit the 1604 date. And here again the play's composition would have to be pushed towards the very end of 1604 to make a reference to the Hungarian revolt at all possible.

It might be suspected too, on the negative evidence that there are few if any books known to have been published on political affairs relating to Hungary in 1603-4, that English interest in them and knowledge about them was limited at this time. The Duke of Holstein's visit to London to procure, according to John Chamberlain, 'a levie of men to carie into Hungarie' in support of Bocskai (Chamberlain, I, 198) failed, and so is scarcely a token of popular enthusiasm for the Hungarian cause. Marcus's claim that 'Left-wing Protestant circles received the slightest news from the Continent with almost incredible speed and watched the Habsburg suppression extremely closely' (188) is unsubstantiated with reference to Hungary in 1604. Her evidence of 'lively cultural exchange between English and Hungarian Protestants' is one-way in the wrong direction: books by English Puritan divines that found their way into Hungarian Protestant libraries.

In view of the wider arguments for later adaptation, the question here is whether Marcus succeeds in locking the date of the passage in question to 1604 sufficiently firmly to make a case for later interpolation unsustainable. It seems that she does not. There is no reason to suppose that the interpretation of events she offers would have been even intelligible, let alone of immediate interest, to an English play audience of 1603-4. As will be seen below, and in the Critical Introduction and commentary to the present edition, even with regard solely to the allusion to Hungary, a later date when English interest in the King of Hungary was running at an unprecedented height fits considerably better than 1604. It can still follow, then, and indeed it does follow far more plausibly than not, that Middleton wrote a passage to replace the original opening of the scene.

The adaptation must have occurred after John Fletcher wrote 'Take, O take those lips away' for *Rollo, Duke of Normandy*, as the hypothesis of adaptation is based on the argument that the song was transferred from *Rollo* to *Measure*. *Rollo* appears to have been written mid-1617 or 1619-20 (Taylor and Jowett, Appendix 3); the earliest date for the adaptation of *Measure* is therefore mid-1617. It can be surmised from Charlton Hinman's analysis of the chronology of printing that sheets F and G, on which *Measure* is printed, would have been machined in about April 1622 (Hinman, I, 342-7), and if we allow a week or so for Crane to prepare his transcript, this can be taken as the latest possible time for any alterations in the theatrical manuscript as Crane copied it.

Jowett and Taylor (177-86) find a number of allusions in the adapted part of 1.2 that point strongly to 1621 as the year this passage was written: the economic depression of 1619-24, England's unofficial engagement in the Thirty Years War as of April 1621, Hungarian raids just outside Vienna that began in August 1621 (and were being reported in news-sheets published between 18 September and 6 October), the negotiations for a peace between the King of Hungary and the Empire proceeding in late 1621, the English expedition against pirates that departed on 20 September 1620 and returned on 22 September 1621 (for details of the expedition and its significance as the major campaign against pirates in the reign of James I, see Hebb), the reported loss of fifty-seven merchant ships to pirates on 20 October 1621 (Chamberlain, II, 365). As is explained in the Critical Introduction, and developed at greater length in Jowett, 'Audacity', a news-sheet published on 6 October (STC 18507.32), as well as recording the incursions of the Budianer Hungarians, makes particularly detailed reference to a number of dukes meeting with the King of Hungary. Thus the allusions to pirates and the Thirty Years War converge on late October 1621. A slightly later date is, however, possible. Sir John Digby gave his speech to Parliament on 26 November reporting on his

negotiations in Vienna for peace. Public interest in the possibilities of 'composition' or war would have been at their height during the Parliamentary debate that followed. But the passage was presumably written before news reached England in early 1622 of the Treaty of Nikolsburg, by which 'composition' between Vienna and the King of Hungary was confirmed.

The evidence for Middleton's authorship of parts of the adapted text is given in full in Jowett and Taylor; it is summarized and in many details extended in the Critical Introduction and commentary of this edition. In 1993, Jowett and Taylor suggested that the lines after the song in 4.1 were written by John Webster or an unidentified theatre functionary or minor dramatist. They gave three reasons for doubting Middleton's authorship of the interpolated lines after the song; none of them, however, is compelling.

a) There are three occurrences of 'hath'. This is uncharacteristic of Middleton, but it is wholly characteristic of Crane. In any Crane text, the presence of 'hath' is normal, whoever the author. Thus, the presence of 'has' in 1.2, because it contradicts Crane's preference, is good evidence of the underlying copy; by contrast, the presence of 'hath' here is simply evidence for Crane. In *Game*, where we can check Middleton's autograph, Crane texts repeatedly change authorial 'has' to 'hath'. This particular linguistic evidence is therefore intrinsically unreliable. Moreover, 'hath' is not, as Jowett and Taylor claimed, good linguistic evidence for Webster. Webster's fondness for 'hath' dates from his earlier plays (and may have been augmented in *Duchess of Malfi* by Crane, who is thought to have prepared the copy for this play as for *Measure*). By *Devil's Law Case* and *Anything for a Quiet Life* Webster preferred 'has' as strongly as Middleton. Of the candidates Jowett and Taylor considered plausible, only Massinger still preferred 'hath'—and he is ruled out by the presence of prose.

b) Jowett and Taylor also urged 'the metrical regularity of the verse'. That claim was based on a restricted understanding of the variety of verse in Middleton's plays. There are patches of perfect regularity, even in his latest plays. He is particularly likely to write regular iambic pentameter when he is writing couplets (four of the nine lines here), though numerous examples can be found in unrhymed lines too.

c) Jowett and Taylor's third reason for dismissing Middleton was the 'general blandness' of these lines. This is poor evidence for an attribution, especially in a passage where a simple transition for plot purposes was what was needed and supplied.

Is Webster nonetheless a likelier author of these lines than Middleton? Most of the words and phrases in the passage are commonplace and could be found in many writers. Jowett and Taylor pointed out that the vocabulary is compatible with Webster, but, quite apart from the expressly Middletonian diction discussed below, it is at least equally compatible with Middleton throughout. The following is a brief record of expressions well exampled in Middleton's works, with the nearest Middleton phrasing noted in brackets where it is not identical:

Here comes a man (here comes the man, here comes a fellow, here comes a scholar); Hath often [past participle]; discontent; I cry you mercy; I…well could wish (I could well wish); I…wish You had not found me here so (I thought you had not come so, you shall always find me so); musical; excuse me; and believe me; believe me so (prove me so; disparage me so; deceive me so; believe me, so do I); my mirth is much (my mirth is such, much mirth); mirth…woe (woe…mirth); displeased; pleased; 'Tis good; hath such a (has such a); charm; good…harm (harm…good); provoke; anybody; enquired; enquired for (enquire for); today; much upon; much upon this time (much about this time); upon this time I have (by this time I have); I have promised here to meet (I have promised her to do't); here to meet (to meet here); enquired after (enquire after); I have sat; sat…day (sat upon this day); constantly (especially 'I…will constantly embrace it'); I do…believe you (I do believe you, I well believe you); the time is come (the time of their offence is come, the time is yet to come, the time that is to come, etc); even now; I shall crave your forbearance (I'd crave your present kindness, I must crave a discharge from you); forbearance (forbear); Maybe; call upon you (call upon thee, call upon me); anon; for some advantage to yourself (for your advantage, no advantage, strong advantage, better means and opportunity to yourself).

This list plays little part in advancing a positive case for Middleton's hand, but it does show that the writing is at least compatible with Middleton. More positively, every one of the verbal features that are absent in Webster's work can be paralleled in Middleton: 'break off' (Puritan 3.1.22, Antiquity l. 121, Women Beware 4.3.0.4); 'haste…away' (Mad World 5.1.155; Widow 4.2.54); 'away, make haste' (Game 2.1.190); 'quick' (adverbial) (at least 17 examples in Middleton); 'still' (verb) (Valour 3.2.114: 'stills'); 'brawling' (brawl not found in Webster as a noun or verb or adjective; Middleton has it four times, including the adjectival participle: 'some brawling lawyer', Hubburd l. 1200).

Against this, there is Webster's 'I am ever bound to you' as a parallel for Mariana's 'I am always bound to you'. But whereas Webster does not have a parallel for the key collocation, 'always bound', Middleton does: 'always bound to', Michaelmas 4.2.24; he also has the exact same sentence, minus 'always', at Widow 2.2.141, 'I am bound to you'. The idea of the line also appears in 'I am bound eternally to' (Hengist 1.3.183), 'I'm bound in soul | Eternally to' (Women Beware 2.2.426–7), 'I had been bound | Perpetually unto' (Changeling 3.4.130–31). In addition, Middleton has 'I am bound to' seven more times. So a key piece of evidence urged in favour of Webster is actually better paralleled in Middleton. Another key parallel for

Webster was 'Here's a man of comfort' for Measure's 'Here comes a man of comfort'. Middleton does not have 'man of comfort'—although he has '[noun] of comfort' many times, and 'man of [abstract noun]' twice. We can now add that Middleton collocates 'man' and 'comfort' twice ('man's comfort', Lady 1.2.189; 'man's cold comfort', Owl l. 527). What is missing from the Webster parallel is the word 'comes'. This is precisely the aspect of the sentence that is most distinctively Middletonian. Middleton repeatedly collocates 'comfort' and 'come': No Wit 1.149.1–151, 'Enter Grace Twilight | O, are you come? | Are any comforts coming?'; Weapons 3.1.238, 'Come I to thee for comfort'; Heroes l. 185, 'This is my comfort, I shall come'; Chaste Maid 5.1.60, 'Of comforts coming toward me'; Changeling 2.1.96–7, 'comes | To bear down all my comforts'; Women Beware 1.1.2–3, 'Welcome with all the affection of a mother | That comfort can express'. Most remarkable is Quarrel 4.2.37–8, 'man most ridiculous. | I come to him for comfort, and he tires', where the collocation of 'man', 'come', and 'comfort' combines with 'come' and 'comfort' occupying exactly the same metrical positions as they do in the line from Measure. A related double collocation with 'man' also occurs in the passage from Owl ll. 526–7 already cited: 'commiserated man's cold comfort'. The come | comfort collocation is good evidence for Middleton.

So too is the couplet rhyme-sequence 'so … woe … charm … harm', which compares with the quatrain rhyme-sequence 'show … harm … woe … charm' in Solomon 13.97–100. Here, 'Striving to heal himself, did himself harm' has a similar thought and chiastic structure to 'To make bad good, and good revert to harm'. Webster never uses 'charm' at the end of a line, let alone as a rhyme-word. Another, if less distinct, pointer towards Middleton is 'My mirth it much displeased, but pleased my woe', which is echoed in 'My mirth was but dissembled, and seeming joys but counterfeit' (No Wit 9.308–9). Though 'my mirth' occurs once in Webster's works, there is no similar construction. Further evidence of the Middletonian temper of these lines comes in the collocation of 'stilled my brawling discontent', 'mirth', the sequence '[abstract noun] is the nurse of [abstract noun]', and the suggestion that music has the power 'to good provoke to harm'.

Hence, quite apart from the consideration that Middleton was involved in the adaptation elsewhere, he is more likely to have contributed these lines than any other dramatist. He is also the most probable author of the short dialogue between the Justice and Escalus at the end of 2.1. The Calvinist temper, the mixture of verse and prose, and the appearance of a rhyme already noted in 4.1, 'so' with 'woe', all suggest Middleton's hand.

Another modification of the conclusions reached in Jowett and Taylor (1993) concerns Pompey's speech at the beginning of 4.3. Jowett and Taylor noted that it is entirely separable from the rest of the scene and contains a number of Middleton idioms, but they allowed the balance to fall in Shakespeare's favour. It is now apparent that the case for Middleton writing this allusive and satirical speech is stronger than was then allowed. The reference to the old women being dead has been connected with the plague outbreak of 1603–4, but high mortality amongst the old could equally well be an effect of the depression that was at its worst in 1621, and this connects well with other themes in the speech of opportunistic trading in commodities and beggary as a result of debt. The topicality of duelling with 'rapier and dagger', was not, as Jowett and Taylor previously accepted, specific to the period around 1603–4; it was a court preoccupation reflected in Middleton's writing from *A Fair Quarrel* to *The Peacemaker* to *The Nice Valour*, works ranging between 1614 and 1622. Jowett and Taylor noted a number of parallels from Middleton's work, but made the caveat that most of them date from Middleton's early writing rather than the period around 1621. We can now add further examples from Middleton's maturity, but in any case the speech is a set-piece of city comedy writing; many of the Middleton parallels are from city comedies, and Middleton wrote most of his city comedies in the early years of the century. Jowett and Taylor's final point in Shakespeare's favour is the analogy between this speech and beginning of the Porter scene in *Macbeth*, but there are significant differences too. The Porter's speech has a formal structure based on the offstage knocking, whereas the Clown's speech is a Middletonian catalogue based on Middletonian names. Of course Middleton would have been particularly familiar with *Macbeth* as a result of adapting that play, so the Porter scene is an example that could easily have influenced his adaptation of *Measure*. The arguments in favour of Shakespeare are all vulnerable, and the strength of the parallels with Middleton's work, as detailed in the commentary and modified only by the presence in Shakespeare but not Middleton of the details mentioned in the textual note to this passage, speaks for itself.

Other more localized indications of Middleton's hand are discussed in the Critical Introduction and commentary. Nowhere is a passage identified as an addition of 1621 more plausibly assigned to another dramatist. This is not to say that Middleton necessarily worked unaided, but that any contribution from other hands was presumably more in the nature of theatrical annotation than dramatic composition. A specific example of a series of changes that could have been introduced either by Middleton or by another person is the suppression of profanity. Indeed, this could logically belong to an earlier revival of about 1606–8, though, as there is no evidence of such a revival, the presumption can be allowed that these changes too were made in 1621.

Measure has the same claim to be represented in this edition as does *Macbeth*, or Sir William Davenant's adaptation of *Measure* in an edition of Davenant. The work undertaken for the present edition both extends the scope of the adaptation and affirms the presence of Middleton's hand in passages that previously seemed to be more plausibly the work of someone else. This recent research benefits from the availability of electronic databases such as *Literature Online*, which have made it possible not only to confirm and modify previous suggestions but also to develop new ones. The use of such resources has enabled us not only to confirm the strength of the case for Middleton's claim for authorship of these passages as compared with Shakespeare's, but also to confirm the particularly Middletonian quality of the language as against the habits and preferences of other writers.

John Jowett

SEE ALSO

Text: *Works*, 1547
Textual introduction and apparatus: this volume, 681

WORKS CITED

Barroll, Leeds, *Politics, Plague, and Shakespeare's Theater: The Stuart Years* (1991)
Bennett, Josephine Waters, '*Measure for Measure' as a Royal Entertainment* (1966)
Chamberlain, John, *Letters*, ed. N. E. McClure, 2 vols (1939)
Eccles, Mark, ed., *A New Variorum Edition of Shakespeare: 'Measure for Measure'* (1980)
Hebb, David Delison, *Piracy and the English Government, 1616–1642* (1994)
Hinman, Charlton, *The Printing and Proof-Reading of the First Folio of Shakespeare*, 2 vols (1963)
Jowett, John, 'The Audacity of *Measure for Measure* in 1621', *Ben Jonson Journal* 8 (2001), 1–19
—— and Gary Taylor, '"With New Additions": Theatrical Interpolation in *Measure for Measure*', in Taylor and Jowett, 107–236
Keeton, George W., *Shakespeare's Legal and Political Background* (1967)
Lever, J. W., ed., *Measure for Measure*, by William Shakespeare (1965)
Marcus, Leah, *Puzzling Shakespeare: Local Reading and Its Discontents* (1988)
Taylor, Gary, and John Jowett, *Shakespeare Reshaped 1606–1623* (1993)

The Sun in Aries   October 1621

The title-page attributes the pageant to Middleton ('By Tho. Middleton, Gent.') and indicates the date of performance as 29 October 1621. G. E. Bentley, *Jacobean and Caroline Stage* (4:895), and others have suggested that Munday collaborated on the show with Middleton. Obviously, as the guild records make clear, the two poets worked together on the show; but apparently only Middleton wrote the pageant, as the title-page indicates. Middleton, Munday, and Garret Christmas, the artificer, received a payment of £140 for all the major expenses, according to the records of the Drapers. Since 1613, Munday had occasionally assisted with Middleton's pageants.

David M. Bergeron

SEE ALSO

Text: *Works*, 1589
Textual introduction and apparatus: this volume, 674

Anything for a Quiet Life Late 1621

The generally accepted date of composition, 1621, is based only on several internal details, summarized by F. L. Lucas. The Guiana voyage referred to at 1.1.167–8 is almost certainly the last one made by Ralegh in 1617–18. The allusion to the litigation between Chief Justice Coke and his wife (5.1.247–8) indicates a date between 1617 and 1621. The mention of soldiers going to the Palatinate (5.1.112) probably refers to Sir Horace Vere's expedition of July 1620. Finally, the reference to the Standard in Cheapside as 'new' (1.1.52) suggests a date quite late in 1621. The long-delayed rebuilding was apparently not finished until early October (Stow, *Annales*, p. 1034). With no contradictory evidence, 1621 seems a likely date of composition.

Although the title-page says the play was 'Written by *Tho. Middleton*, Gent.', A. H. Bullen thought he detected James Shirley's hand but did not say why, and in 1921 Dugdale Sykes offered evidence of verbal parallels and borrowings in concluding that 'most of it is Webster's', a view supported by E. H. C. Oliphant. In response, W. D. Dunkel presented similarly detailed verbal evidence to defend his opinion that the play is Middleton's, with Webster as either collaborator or reviser. Sykes's attribution of much of the play to Webster is generally supported and furthered by Lucas in his edition. G. E. Bentley completely rejects this evidence and the attribution to Webster, but this conclusion reflects his generally dismissive attitude to internal evidence rather than his own analysis. For his part, William Power rejects Bentley's conclusion and offers evidence that *Anything for a Quiet Life* is the product of collaboration, although he does not say with whom. In a nice if misplaced piece of circularity, Nancy Ruth Katz follows the title-page assertion that Middleton is the sole author. But subsequent, independent attribution studies by David J. Lake and MacDonald P. Jackson provide statistical support for a division of the play between Middleton and Webster. Both studies give Webster all of Act 1; Act 2, Scene 1; and 4.1. Middleton is credited with the larger share: 2.2–2.4; all of Act 3; and 4.2. For Act 5, Jackson argues that 'the linguistic evidence...would encourage a theory of mixed authorship', whereas Lake attributes 5.1 to Webster and 5.2 substantially to Middleton. Lake gave Webster 4.2.1–44, but Jackson (2006) provides convincing evidence of Middleton's authorship. As these disagreements suggest, it is often difficult to divide the play rigidly between the two authors. Certainly, it is unlikely that they wrote in isolation of each other; rather, they probably not only worked together but edited and altered each other's work as they went along.

Leslie Thomson

SEE ALSO

Text: *Works*, 1596
Textual introduction and apparatus: this volume, 1160

WORKS CITED

Bentley, G. E., *The Jacobean and Caroline Stage*, vol. 4 (1956), 859–61

Bullen, A. H., ed., *Thomas Middleton, Works* (1885), vols 1, 5
Dunkel, W. D., 'The Authorship of *Anything for a Quiet Life*', *PMLA* 43 (1928), 793–9
Jackson, MacDonald P., '*Anything for a Quiet Life*, IV.ii.1–44: The Hazards of Collaboration', *Notes and Queries* 53 (2006), 87–90
Katz, Nancy Ruth, ed., *Anything for a Quiet Life*, unpublished dissertation, University of California, Berkeley (1975)
Lucas, F. L., ed., *The Complete Works of John Webster* (1927), vol. 4
Oliphant, E. H. C., '*Anything for a Quiet Life* by Thomas Middleton and John Webster', *Notes and Queries*, XII, 10 (1922), 11
Power, William, 'Double, Double', *Notes and Queries* 204 (1959), 4–8
Stow, John, *Annales*, rev. Edmund Howes (1631: STC 23340)
Sykes, H. Dugdale, 'A Webster-Middleton Play: *Anything for a Quiet Life*', *Notes and Queries*, XII, 9 (1921), 181–3, 202–4, 225–6, 300

An Invention April 1622

The title is given in full at the front of the manuscript, and specifies Middleton's authorship: 'Written by Tho. Middleton'. The performance took place during the Easter holidays of 1622.

Anthony Parr

SEE ALSO

Text: *Works*, 1446
Textual introduction and apparatus: this volume, 675

The Changeling May 1622

Date

Malone is the source of our date for *The Changeling*, through a note in his copy of the 1653 quarto (Bodleian Mal. 246 (9)):

> Licensed to be acted by the Lady Elizabeth's servants at the Phoenix, May 7, 1622. by Sir Henry Herbert Master of the Revels.

Malone's information came from the lost record book of the Revels Office. N. W. Bawcutt has shown that the licence was actually issued by Sir John Astley; Herbert did not become Master of the Revels until July 1623.

Thirty and one-half years later, on 19 October 1652, the London bookseller Humphrey Moseley would enter the play in the Stationers' Register:

> Entred...under the hands of Sr Nath: Brent and Master Thrale warden, a comedie called, The changeling, written by Rowley (*Transcript*, 1.403)

All indications suggest that *Changeling* was printed the following January, 1653 (see 'Textual Introduction').

Authorship

The 1653 title-page declares that the play was 'Written by { *THOMAS MIDLETON*, and *WILLIAM ROWLEY.* } Gent." (with the authors' names enclosed in brackets and centred, Middleton above Rowley). Traditionally, scholars have followed Pauline Wiggin's division of authorship; her study, published in 1897, bases its claims on unrecorded metrical tests performed on Dyce's edition of Middleton. Wiggin assigned Rowley the first and last scenes of the play and the hospital scenes, giving Middleton the rest (i.e. the bulk of the castle plot). The work of Lake and Jackson has tended to confirm this division. Increasingly, however, readers have moved toward a model of collaboration *within* scenes. Following Oliphant, Hoy saw 4.2 to the entrance of Tomazo as Rowley's work (theretofore the scene given to Middleton alone), and Holdsworth has suggested Middleton's hand throughout 5.3, attributing most or all of the first 121 lines to him. Both suggestions are convincing. To them I would add that Middleton appears to have had a hand in 1.1, especially Alsemero's opening soliloquy.

Douglas Bruster

SEE ALSO

Text: *Works*, 1637
Textual introduction and apparatus: this volume, 1094

WORKS CITED

Bawcutt, N. W., ed., *The Control and Censorship of Caroline Drama: The Records of Sir Henry Herbert, Master of the Revels 1623-73* (1996)

Holdsworth, R. V., 'Notes on *The Changeling*', *Notes and Queries* 234 (1989), 344-46

Hoy, Cyrus, 'The Shares of Fletcher and his Collaborators in the Beaumont and Fletcher Canon (V)', *Studies in Bibliography* 13 (1960), 77-108

Oliphant, E. H., ed., *Shakespeare and His Fellow Dramatists: A Selection of Plays Illustrating the Glories of the Golden Age of English Drama* (1929)

Transcript of the Registers of the Worshipful Company of Stationers from 1640-1708 A.D., ed. Eyre, Rivington, and Plomer, 3 vols (1913-14)

Wiggin, Pauline G., *An Inquiry into the Authorship of the Middleton-Rowley Plays* (1897)

The Nice Valour   September 1622

The Nice Valour; or, the Passionate Madman first appeared in the 'Comedies and Tragedies, Written by Francis Beaumont and John Fletcher' (1647); the Stationers' Register entry of 29 June 1660 (supplementing the original Humphrey Moseley entry, by adding the six texts not registered in 1647) also attributes it to Beaumont and Fletcher (*BEPD*, p. 68). However, it has been known since 1647 that inclusion in the 1647 folio was dubious evidence for authorship by 'Beaumont and Fletcher'. Even Bentley, perhaps the most rigidly conservative of modern scholars on issues of attribution, acknowledged that 'the possibility that [*Valour*] is not a Beaumont and Fletcher play should not be ignored' (3:384).

Given the uncertainty of the external evidence, scholars have no choice but to evaluate the internal evidence for authorship. Noting that his nineteenth-century predecessors Dyce (10, 295), Fleay (I, 196-7), Boyle (7:74,

8:40, 53-4), and Bullen (309) had all been dubious about Fletcher as sole author, Oliphant (1927) suggested possible shares in the play by Beaumont, Fletcher, and Middleton, with Middleton probably as reviser rather than collaborator (439-51). Hoy, in the most influential modern survey of authorship problems in the Beaumont and Fletcher canon (1960), found 'traces' of Fletcher in *The Nice Valour*, but attributed the 'major share' of the play to Middleton. Hoy established Middleton as sole author of Act 3 and 5.1, and suggested that Acts 1, 2, and 4, 5.2, and 5.3 were by Middleton with Fletcher; in other words, he found Middleton throughout the play, and no signs of unassisted Fletcher. Lake (1975), from the perspective of the Middleton canon, seconded Hoy's conclusions; Lake attributed a large share of the play to Middleton on the grounds of the internal evidence offered by contractions, exclamations, oaths, affirmatives, colloquialisms, and collocations. On the basis of evidence in some cases overlapping but in others supplementing Lake's, Jackson (1979) identified Middleton as 'almost' the sole author, finding no evidence of Fletcher; in 1998 he added further evidence in the rare spelling 'froath'. The still-unpublished but extensive research of R. V. Holdsworth on authorship problems in the Middleton canon has led him to conclude that Middleton is the 'sole author' of the play. One aspect of Holdsworth's evidence, available in his 1982 dissertation, is Middleton's demonstrable fondness for 'interrogative repetition' (236-67); *Valour*, with a rate of 24 for every thousand speeches, is well within Middleton's range (close to *Game at Chess*'s rate of 26, for instance); by contrast, Fletcher very seldom used the device, averaging only 11 per thousand speeches in the five plays surveyed by Holdsworth. The play's most recent editor, George Walton Williams (1989), endorsed Holdsworth's conclusion (communicated to him privately), adding that the use of rhyming couplets at the ends of scenes also indicates Middleton rather than Fletcher. The history of twentieth-century scholarship on the play's attribution is a history of increasing confidence in Middleton's authorship.

Although all modern investigators attribute at least a significant part of the play to Middleton, there has been no such unanimity about whether the play was revised. Dyce (*Fletcher*, 10, 295) raised the issue of revision, a recurrent problem in the Fletcher canon, and all subsequent investigators have therefore felt compelled to address it. Lake, for instance, suggests that there may be 'traces of Fletcherian syntax...perhaps a substratum nearly buried by thoroughgoing Middletonian revision'; Jackson, faced with the spectre of such revision, is unwilling to rule it out entirely; Williams reports the view of his general editor, Fredson Bowers, that the play was probably revised; Hoy is unsure whether the indications of abridgement also indicate revision. Amid all this wavering a reader might be led to think that there must be some evidence which is complicating the picture, and preventing scholars from arriving at the otherwise-indicated conclusion that Middleton was the first and only author of the text.

However, there is in fact no real evidence, external or internal, that the play was ever revised. The text is unusually short when viewed from the perspective of the long-winded Fletcher's canon, but not from the perspective of the tight-lipped Middleton's; its alleged inconsistencies are no more numerous or significant than might be found in virtually every play of the period. Although such details often bother scholars, they are never noticed by audiences, and such inconsistencies are sometimes almost certainly deliberate, the playwright wishing to create one effect at one point in the play, and another elsewhere (Taylor, 1985). Why, in any case, should revision result in greater narrative incoherence? One might just as easily postulate that revision would identify and correct minor inconsistencies, rather than adding to them. The fact that prologue and epilogue refer to the 'poet', singular, indicates that one person was considered to be responsible for the play as it was produced; this evidence does not support theories of revision or collaboration. Moreover, the prologue's claim that the author did not like to write prologues is consistent with Middleton's authorship. Middleton wrote few prologues or epilogues (Taylor, Mulholland, Jackson, 233–4). The original version of *A Game at Chess*, for instance, does not contain a prologue or epilogue; both were added in the eventual theatrical script. If only one person was responsible, the evidence overwhelmingly points to that one person being Middleton. Nor would Fletcher's complete absence be unparalleled in the 1647 folio: most scholars now attribute *The Laws of Candy* entirely to Ford (Hoy 1996, 661–3), and *Wit at Several Weapons* entirely to Middleton and Rowley (see above).

The Prologue does refer to 'the reviving of this play'— but that simply proves that the play was performed again, at some time between its original composition/ performance and the publication of the prologue in 1647 (or, more plausibly, before the closing of the theatres in 1642). This prologue, incidentally, speaks of the author in the past tense, suggesting that he was dead at the time of the revival; that would locate the revival after Middleton's death (1627). But it tells us nothing about the original date of composition.

There is no known literary source for the play, or any early document which fixes its date of composition; any dating must therefore depend upon internal evidence. Dyce (*Fletcher*, 10, 363) had interpreted 'Your Herring prov'd the like, able to buy Another *Fishers* Folly' (5.3.25–6) as an allusion to George Walker's 1624 pamphlet, *Fisher's Folly Unfolded* (STC 24959). But Baldwin Maxwell proved that 'Fisher's Folly' was a London landmark, and showed that the play refers to the hypothetical purchase of a notoriously extravagant and expensive house, not to the hypothetical purchase of a cheap quarto pamphlet never reprinted; he cites references to the house dating from 1603 to 1660. Maxwell then goes on to build a circumstantial case for composition in 1615, which has been accepted without discussion by subsequent investigators (Hoy, Lake, Jackson).

But Maxwell's destruction of Dyce's case for 1624–5 is much more convincing than the construction of his own case for 1615: as he says himself, 'most of this evidence is slight and much of it subject to more than one interpretation' (128); Bentley dismisses 'all of it' as 'highly uncertain' (3:383). Fleay had suggested a date of composition soon after 1613 (I, 196–7); although his conjecture was wholly unsubstantiated, it seems to have influenced both Lawrence and Maxwell, leading them to search for links between the play and events of the middle of the second decade of the seventeenth century.

There are six components to Maxwell's case. One is an admittedly dubious interpretation of 'and your *Pasquil* Went not below the mad-caps of that time' (5.3.26–7) to mean that '*Pasquils nightcap* (1612) sold as well as did the Mad-cap pamphlets (1600) of the time of the *Herring* (1598–1600)' (128); this complicated scenario ignores the multiplicity of titles that 'Pasquil' and 'mad-caps' might cover, and in any case would only date *Valour* in 1612 or later. Secondly, Maxwell takes references to the apparently best-selling texts of 'the *Wise Masters*, and...The hundred *Novels*' (5.3.15–16) as allusions to *The Seven Wise Masters of Rome* and *A C. Merry Tales*, two texts transferred in separate transactions in the Stationers' Registers on October 29 and November 6, 1615 (125); but both transactions involved many texts, transferred as a result of the death of previous owners, and there is no evidence that such business transactions were public knowledge, or that new editions of either text appeared in 1615—and indeed 'The hundred *Novels*' might refer to collections of Boccaccio or Painter, rather than to a jestbook. Clearly, these two pieces of 'evidence' are not evidence at all.

Third, Maxwell adopts a conjecture by W. J. Lawrence, first recorded (and rejected) by Oliphant (1927, 444–5). At 4.1.361–3, Lepet, talking about his pamphlet, says 'I hope To save my hundred gentlemen a month by it, Which will be very good for the private house.' Weber had first suggested that 'the private house' referred to an indoor or hall playhouse; profits at such a playhouse would indeed be increased by the survival of more of their gentry clients. Weber's interpretation seems correct, and indeed it is difficult to imagine what else the sentence might mean. But Lawrence insisted on 'the significance of the use of the word "house" in the singular', asking 'at what time after 1610 was the Blackfriars the sole private theatre?', and answering 'the spring of 1615'. Lawrence's reconstruction—which Maxwell adopts as one of his six pieces of evidence for a 1615 date—depends upon a whole series of dubious suppositions. First, 'the private house' may mean not 'the only private house' but merely 'this private house.' Secondly, there was also a period 'in 1616–17 between the closing of Porter's Hall...and the opening of the Cockpit' (c.March 1617). Both these objections were raised by Oliphant; the second point extends the chronological range of Lawrence's interpretation to

1617, and the first entirely eliminates the chronological significance of the passage. Moreover, Maxwell wants not to treat Porter's Hall (patented on 3 June 1615, and in use for an indeterminate period afterwards) as a 'private' theatre, although it was clearly a hall playhouse. Either (probably) this passage is not a precise chronological allusion at all, or (less probably) it is more precise than Maxwell wants to acknowledge, limiting composition to the first five months of 1615 or to the twelve months preceding March 1617.

Maxwell's other evidence for 1615 is reconsidered in Taylor (2001). First, the play's attitude toward duelling postdates official proclamations of late 1613 and early 1614, but might belong to any subsequent year. Second, 'Your Herring prov'd the like, able to buy Another *Fishers Folly*' (5.3.25–6) seems to allude to the only Jacobean purchase of Fisher's Folly, in July 1616, by Lady Harrington (upon whose name the sentence puns). Third, an anecdote about King James kicking a Gentleman of his Chamber, which seems to be an important source for the play's plot, cannot date from earlier than the end of 1617, when Endymion Porter became secretary to Buckingham.

Taylor then suggests other links between the play and events at court in the period 1617–22: the wholesale dismissal of the sovereign's entourage, their replacement by men of lesser rank, and the golden handshakes promised to those dismissed (1617–24); the superfluous episode in which the Duke dismisses his Huntsman (2.1.308–10), contrasted with the King's response to news of the invasion of the Palatinate (September 1620); the extraneous reference to City bankruptcies (5.1.84), rampant in 1621–2, and spectacularly including the bankruptcy of the outgoing Lord Mayor in 1621, on the day of Middleton's pageant; the claim that 'your commons seldom fight at sharp, But buffet in a warehouse' (5.3.39–40), which may refer to physical fights between members of the Parliament of 1621; the Clown's extraneous description of the Passionate Lord/kinsman's breaking of casements, paid for by the Privy Purse (3.1.52–5), which seemingly echoes the scandalous breaking of windows by John Villiers, Buckingham's mad brother, in June 1622, and the maintenance the King immediately ordered; the Passionate Lord's relationship to the Cupid, which resembles the marriage, that same summer, of Buckingham's other brother, Christopher Villiers. He also argues that Robert Burton's *Anatomy of Melancholy* (completed December 1620, published 1621) was a major source for the play, and that the play's ambivalence about violence is best explained by the political circumstances of the early 1620s.

Cumulatively, these associations, if accepted, establish that the play cannot have been written before the summer of 1622. The references, in the opening scene, to the equinox on September 13 (1.1.41–2) and to 'the country's coming up' (1.1.230), presumably at the beginning of Michaelmas Term, suggest that it opened in the autumn of that year; this inference is reinforced by the play's only other specific reference to a time of year, Lepet's claim that

he has only been a gentleman 'since Lammas'—1 August (4.1.329). Middleton's calendar was very full in the eighteen months between January 1621 and May 1622: by contrast, it is unusually empty in the eighteen months from June 1622 to December 1623. Given Middleton's own fascination with almanacs, the passage at 1.1.41–2 almost certainly reflects the actual date of the equinox in the year of composition. In 1622, it fell on September 13, according to English almanacs; but in 1616, 1620, and 1624, it fell on September 12. *Valour* is accordingly unlikely to date from those years, but it could certainly belong to autumn 1622.

Stylistic evidence supports this re-dating of the play. In an exemplary statistical analysis of verse structure, Ants Oras showed that the pattern of mid-line pauses, within iambic pentameter lines, could clearly differentiate various early modern authors, and also in some cases reflected the chronological evolution of a single author's style. The most reliable of all indicators of such caesurae is the splitting of a verse line between two different speakers; unlike patterns of punctuation, which may be affected by compositors, scribes, or modern editors, the division of a verse line between speakers clearly represents an authorial intention. Oras did not provide statistics for *Valour*, but because the splitting of verse lines is so unambiguous and easy to count, it is possible to provide statistics for the play which are compatible with the methods used by Oras. (In compiling this data I have, in order to prevent circularity, used the text of the play edited by Williams, so that decisions about which part-lines to indent and treat as single verse lines are not being influenced by my own assumptions about the play's authorship or date.) I list below the number of such splits after each of the first nine syllables of verse in *Valour*, first in raw numbers, then in percentages:

	1	2	3	4	5	6	7	8	9	TOTAL
	3	7	6	26	35	77	90	22	9	275
%	1.0	2.5	2.2	9.4	12.7	28.0	32.7	8.0	3.3	

What is remarkable here is the relationship between pauses after the sixth and the seventh syllables. Of the 21 plays written in whole or part by Middleton surveyed by Oras, in only three do the totals and percentages for the seventh syllable exceed those for the sixth: in *Anything for a Quiet Life* (21.9, 31.7), in Middleton's share of *The Changeling* (31.0, 36.5), and in *A Game at Chess* (30.3, 37.0). The figures for *Quiet Life* may be disturbed by the presence of Webster, who in the 1620s apparently began to prefer the seventh position; nevertheless, it is remarkable that *Quiet Life*, *Changeling*, and *Game* date from late 1621, May 1622, and summer 1624 respectively. Oras also gives statistics for total percentage of pauses in the first half of the line (after 1, 2, 3, 4, 5), and of pauses after even syllables (2, 4, 6, 8); in the first category, *Valour* (28.4) is closest to *Hengist, King of Kent* (26.5), while in the second category (42.9) it is closest to *Quiet Life* (42.7) and Middleton's share of *Changeling* (44.0). This feature thus links *Valour* to plays dated 1620, 1621, and 1622.

Other features of *Valour* also point to a later date than Baldwin's. First, there is the relatively small number of Middleton's most characteristic oaths: only two of the eleven most distinctively Middleton oaths, and only a dozen of the less distinctive twenty-eight (Jackson, 141). The parallels for such low totals are all late plays: *Hengist* (1) and *Women Beware* (2) are the only plays with two or fewer of the most distinctive oaths, and the only play with a lower total for the less distinctive oaths is *A Game at Chess* (7). Jackson, not aware of this chronological pattern, had concluded that the oaths 'point less certainly to Middleton's authorship'; but in fact they agree perfectly with the pattern we should expect in a Middleton play written in 1622. Likewise, the sole piece of evidence that Lake cited as evidence that Fletcher had a hand in the play was the preference of 'yes' (15) over 'ay' (9), which reverses Middleton's usual preference for the obsolescent form (194). But in fact Middleton's preference eventually changed. The only plays in which 'yes' strongly predominates are all late: *Women Beware* (21/17), the collaborative *Quiet Life* (35/6) and *Game* (14/10). Even if we restrict ourselves to the scenes in *Quiet Life* which Lake attributes to Middleton, the preference remains intact (13/6). Thus, in three Middleton plays clearly attributable to 1621-4, 'yes' predominates 48/33. *Valour* fits this pattern perfectly. It also fits—as Lake noted (195)—Middleton's late preference for 'betwixt' (8) over 'between' (0): Lake compared *Women Beware* (10/1), but he could also have cited *Game* (4/1). Lake also noticed some rare oaths in *Valour* for which there are Middleton parallels only in his late plays (194). In all these features, there is a chronological pattern to Middleton's preferences, and *Valour* fits the 1620s end of that spectrum, not the middle period. Thus, the stylistic evidence reinforces the evidence of topical allusions.

Oliphant argued that the play seemed unlikely to have been acted by the King's Men; it was not in the list of plays given by the King's Men to Moseley for publication in 1641 (Chambers, 398-99), and the 1679 folio does not provide a list of the original cast, as it does for most plays which belonged to the King's Men. The other plays in the 1660 entry—all late additions to the plan for the folio—are *Wit at Several Weapons* (now attributed to Middleton and Rowley: see above), *The Fair Maid of the Inn* (licensed after Fletcher's death, and containing perhaps only a single scene of his writing), *The Masque of Gray's Inn and the Inner Temple* (entirely by Beaumont), *Four Plays in One* (by Field and Fletcher) and *The False One* (by Massinger and Fletcher). Three of these five added texts clearly did not belong to that company; neither, apparently, did *Valour*. In the short final speech of the play's chief comic character, Lepet describes himself as 'The heaviest gentleman that e'er lost place' (5.3.88); although *heaviest* clearly means 'saddest', it might also plausibly allude to the size of the comic actor William Rowley, who was

indeed a gentleman. Without some such twist, the speech provides an uncharacteristically lame conclusion to an otherwise hilarious dramatic role. Certainly, the physical farce, the jokes on farting, and the contrast between a fat Lepet and his starved servant Galoshio, would fit Rowley's career profile. Rowley did not begin acting for the King's Men until August 1623 (Bentley 5:1016). If I am right in thinking Lepet was written for Rowley, in 1622, then this would provide further evidence that it was written either for Lady Elizabeth's Men at the Phoenix (like *Changeling* and *Gypsy*), or for the Prince's Men. However, if the play were acted by Lady Elizabeth's Men it might have been included—like *All's Lost by Lust*, *Changeling*, and *Gypsy*—in the 1639 list of plays owned by Beeston (Chambers 389-90). Since we know from the Prologue that the play was revised between its first performances (1622?) and the closing of the theatres (1642), its absence from the Beeston list cannot be explained by its having permanently fallen from the repertoire. By a process of elimination this suggests that *Valour* may have been written for the Prince's Men.

Since the internal evidence for composition of the whole play, and the stylistic evidence for its place in Middleton's chronology, both date from a period when Fletcher was still alive, the Prologue cannot be used as evidence that Middleton's presence results from late revision of an original work by Fletcher. In any case, the kind of revision imagined by scholars from Oliphant to Bowers—so extensive that it has left almost no traces of Fletcher himself—is unparalleled in the Fletcher canon, and intrinsically implausible. As Kerrigan demonstrated, theatrical texts were very unlikely to be revised in that systematic fashion.

It is of course possible that some 'new additions' were made to the play on the occasion of its revival; one might attribute the whole of the original to Middleton, and yet acknowledge that one detachable element or two was written by another author after his death. Prologues and epilogues were frequently added, and the Prologue in particular is very unlikely to be Middleton's work: it refers to the original author in the past tense (suggesting it is a posthumous addition to the text). The epilogue, by contrast, speaks of the author in the present tense, and is stylistically compatible with Middleton; moreover, in explicit contrast to the Prologue, its title does not link it to a revival.

It might be argued that the song 'Hence, all you vain delights' was a posthumous interpolation, by another author, on the occasion of that revival. Songs were sometimes added to plays. However, that seems unlikely in this case. The song belongs to a sequence of songs, each representing a different mood of the character's madness, and this musical structure seems intrinsic to the whole dramatic narrative; moreover, the rest of the scene in which the song appears is clearly Middletonian. And the earliest surviving text of the song dates from Middleton's lifetime: *Nice Valour* was apparently first performed late in

1622, and the earliest manuscript of the song (INNS[1]) is part of a miscellany that contains no material later than 1625. (For manuscript sigla, see Textual Introduction.)

Some manuscripts (LANE, OXFORD[2], OXFORD[3], OXFORD[7]) attribute the song to William Strode (1602–45), and Edmond Malone accepted this attribution (in manuscript notes first published by Rimbault). But this attribution clearly derives from the fact that Strode wrote a reply, 'An Opposite to Melancholy', which immediately follows the song in some manuscripts; even when the two poems are not juxtaposed, they often occur in the same miscellanies. In the circumstances, the unattributed poem could easily be contaminated by its well-attributed companion. The more relevant fact is that MENNES explicitly attributes to Strode only the reply (which it printed for the first time). In the only critical edition of Strode's poetry, Forey rejects the attribution, as does Beal. Although there are two Strode autograph texts of 'An Opposite', the song from Nice Valour does not appear in any of Strode's surviving autograph collections. And although Strode's was the most popular reply to the original poem, it was not the only one; Henry King wrote another, and a third is anonymous. If Strode had written both the original and the reply, as companion pieces, it is hard to imagine why another author would write an alternative reply. Finally, the song appears more often as an independent poem (thirty-one seventeenth-century texts) than as part of a diptych with Strode's 'An Opposite' (seven seventeenth-century texts). The earliest printed version (HARPER, 1634) entitles the poem 'The melancholly Lovers Song', suggesting an awareness of its place in the play; 'Song in y[e] praise of Melancholly' (OXFORD[2]) and 'The Lovers Melancholy' (OXFORD[7], MENNES) also connect the thriving manuscript circulation to the specific dramatic context of Nice Valour. It is common, indeed normal, for manuscript texts of lyrics from plays not to be attributed to the dramatist. Thus, the manuscript tradition of the song does nothing to cast doubt upon Middleton's authorship of this song, as part of the original text of the play.

Gary Taylor

SEE ALSO

Text: Works, 1683
Textual introduction and apparatus: this volume, 1070

WORKS CITED

Bald, R. C., *Bibliographical Studies in the Beaumont and Fletcher Folio of 1647* (1937)

Beal, Peter, *Index of English Literary Manuscripts: Volume I: 1450–1625* (1980); *Volume II: 1626–1700* (1987–93)

Bentley, G. E., *The Jacobean and Caroline Stage* (1956)

Boyle, Robert, 'Beaumont, Fletcher and Massinger', *Englische Studien* 7 (1884), 66–87; 8 (1885), 39–61

Bullen, A. H., 'John Fletcher' (1889), in *Dictionary of National Biography*, ed. Leslie Stephen and Sidney Lee (1921–2), 7:303–11

Chambers, E. K., ed., 'Dramatic Records: The Lord Chamberlain's Office', in *Collections: Vol. II. Part III*, gen. ed. W. W. Greg, Malone Society (1913), 321–416

Dyce, Alexander, ed., *The Works of Beaumont and Fletcher*, volume 10 (1843–6)

Fleay, F. G., *A Biographical Chronicle of the English Drama*, 2 vols (1891)

Forey, Margaret A., *A Critical Edition of the Poetical Works of William Strode, excluding The Floating Island*, unpublished B. Litt. thesis (Oxford University, 1966)

Hoy, Cyrus, 'The Shares of Fletcher and his Collaborators in the Beaumont and Fletcher Canon (V)', *Studies in Bibliography* 13 (1960), 77–108

—— ed., *The Laws of Candy*, in *The Dramatic Works in the Beaumont and Fletcher Canon*, gen. ed. Fredson Bowers, vol. 10 (1996)

Jackson, MacDonald P., 'Editing, Attribution Studies, and *Literature Online*: A New Resource for Research in Renaissance Drama', *Research Opportunities in Renaissance Drama* 37 (1998), 1–15

Kerrigan, John, 'Revision, Adaptation, and the Fool in *King Lear*', in *The Division of the Kingdoms: Shakespeare's Two Versions of King Lear*, ed. Gary Taylor and Michael Warren (1983), 195–246

Maxwell, Baldwin, *Studies in Beaumont, Fletcher, and Massinger* (1939), 116–35

Oliphant, E. H. C., *The Plays of Beaumont and Fletcher* (1927)

Oras, Ants, *Pause Patterns in Elizabethan and Jacobean Drama: An experiment in Prosody* (1960)

Rimbault, Edward F. R., 'Song in Fletcher's play of *The Nice Valour*', *Notes and Queries*, I, 1 (5 January 1850), 146–7

Taylor, Gary, *Moment by Moment by Shakespeare* (1985)

—— Paul Mulholland, and MacDonald P. Jackson, 'Thomas Middleton, Lording Barry, and *The Family of Love*', *Papers of the Bibliographical Society of America* 93 (1999), 213–41

—— 'Thomas Middleton, *The Nice Valour*, and the Court of James I', *The Court Historian* 6 (2001), 1–36

Williams, George Walton, ed., *The Nice Valour*, in *The Dramatic Works in the Beaumont and Fletcher Canon*, gen. ed. Fredson Bowers, vol. 7 (1989)

The Triumphs of Honour and Virtue

October 1622

The title-page assigns the pageant to Middleton: 'By Tho. Middleton, Gent.' It also provides the usual date of performance, 29 October. The Grocers records for 1622 indicate a payment of £220 to Middleton and Christmas for all the expenses of the pageant, including the 'ordering overseeing and writing of the whole device'.

David M. Bergeron

SEE ALSO

Text: Works, 1719
Textual introduction and apparatus: this volume, 676

'St James'

January 1623

These verses were written for an official City of London ceremony, the consecration of the church of St James, restored by the City; the Lord Mayor, both sheriffs, and sixteen Aldermen were present, and even more clearly than the epitaph for Sir George Bolles the poem written for this event would seem a natural commission for the City's paid chronologer-poet. Barkham, the Lord Mayor emphatically praised in the poem, had been celebrated in Middleton's *Aries*. Since the consecration occurred on New

Year's Day 1623, the verses would have been written too late for inclusion in *Honourable Entertainments* (1621).

The source for these verses, the 1633 expansion of Stow's *Survey of London*, does not attribute them. It also prints three separate sets of verses in connection with the ceremony, separating them with prose passages; there is no guarantee that all three sets of verses were written by the same author.

I. Middleton's authorship of the first, and longest poem, is suggested not only by the occasion, but by the plainness of the diction, and by a series of verbal parallels with his work (particularly works written in 1613 or after). The most plausible alternative candidate, in terms of that occasion, would be Anthony Munday, himself a Draper— although Barkham had translated to the Drapers only months before his inauguration, to the Company's dismay, which makes any personal connection with Munday less likely. In fact, Munday seems ruled out by the note at the end of the description of the consecration of Saint James in the 1633 edition, which concludes: 'Nor could I have said so much of this new Church, but only by the friendly help and assistance of my honest well-willer, *George Cooper*, Clerke there, who under his own hand delivered the same to mee' (149). Munday would not have needed Cooper's assistance if he had written the verses himself.

I have nevertheless checked the Munday, Dekker, and Heywood canons (since all three wrote extensively for the City, and provide at the very least a sense of the language common to such work) and the Wither canon (for reasons explained below); if the canons of those authors do not afford parallels I have searched more extensively in the databases for the period. I list the resulting parallels below, with an asterisk to identify particularly striking collocations (that is, those which occur in only one or two of the five canons examined). I have also listed some other parallels, with explanations of why they are not asterisked, and some additional parallels, which seem to me interesting, but are not in themselves reliable evidence, and not counted in the final totals.

1 As Dauid] Once each in Dekker and Wither. A dubious parallel, because the connection to David is clearly related to the occasion (the building and consecration of a temple).
*1 rest afford] The only comparable collocation in any of the five candidate canons is 'affords' and 'rest' at end of adjacent lines in *Entertainments* 6.15-16.
2 he had found] Not in Wither.
*2 found a...out] Heywood, *English Traveler*
*3 so this man] Munday, *Zelauto* (1580)
*3 this man of worth] 'that man of worth' *Truth* 717. LION identifies no parallels for 'man of worth' in Dekker, Heywood, or Munday. LION drama 1576-42 has nineteen other examples, and Wither one, but none of [demonstrative pronoun] 'man of worth' (which shows up only once elsewhere in the period, in a poem by John Ashmore published in 1621).

4 mirror of these later days] 'Mirror of times' *Magnificent* 2144
4 later days] *Virtue* 122. Not in Dekker or Munday, but Wither has 'these later days' (*The Protector*, 1655).
5 the worthy] immediately juxtaposed with name: *Lady* 5.1.81, *River* (3), *Prosperity* 124.
*5 immortal name] 'name immortal' *Owl* 535-6, *Hengist* 1.3.185. Dekker mocks the phrase in *Satiromastix*; the collocation does not appear in Heywood, Munday, or Wither; LION drama 1576-1642 has no other parallels. In poetry published before 1660 it appears about twenty times.
6 Marble's too weak] for the idea, compare 'outlasting brass or marble' *Valour* 4.1.101
7 industry and care] 'care and industry' (*Microcynicon* 3.119, *Civitatis* 29, *Industry* 290, *Changeling* 1.2.5); 'industry and carefulness' *Truth* 73-4. Collocation once in Heywood (1641), once in Dekker (1614), not in Munday or Wither.
*10 altars still to raise] Heywood, *Troia Britanica*, 'Altars raise'; *Solomon* 'Erect an altar' (9.8.70).
*11 receive a blessing] 'receive a blessing' *Weapons* 4.1.4, 'receive your blessing' *Phoenix* 9.16. Not in Dekker, Heywood, or Munday. The only drama parallels are one in Lodwick Carlell and two in Fletcher; Wither has 'a blessing may receive' (*Britain's Remembrancer*, 1628).
*12 honour's seat] For the collocation compare 'seat of honour' *Industry* 190, 'honourable seat' *Industry* 25-6, 'honoured seat' *Aries* 286 (always of a Lord Mayor's office, which is seven times described as a 'seat'). Dekker later uses 'Honor'd Seate' once (*Brittannia's Honor*, 1628) in the same sense, and the same phrase also appears in the anonymous *Look about You* (1600), which may be Dekker's; no similar collocation appears in Heywood, Munday, or Wither. Among other playwrights, Brome, Brandon, Chapman, Davenant, and Mary Sidney have 'seat of honour' (once each); the only exact parallel for 'honour's seat' comes from Robert Wilson (d. 1600).
*12 honour's seat] Middleton five times uses the construction '[possessive abstract noun] seat' (judgement's, virtue's, affection's); LION has no parallels in Dekker, Heywood, Munday, or Wither.
12 scarce warm] Once each in Dekker and Heywood; Wither, *Faire-virtue* (1621), 'scarce warmeth' (not an exact parallel).
*13 pious work] 'pious works' *Entertainments* 8.4, *Invention* 85. Not in Dekker, Heywood, or Munday; eleven times elsewhere in period plays, only Massinger matching Middleton's two examples. But Wither has six examples, including one singular.
*15 charge the...city bears] 'charge, the City of London, bearing' *Prosperity* 23-4; 'the city bears' *Prosperity* 66. Dekker has 'the City beares' (*Troia-Nova*), but Heywood, Munday, and Wither have neither element of the phrase. In period plays, Fletcher has 'charge

the city' once (in a different sense), but there are no other parallels for 'city bears'.

15 the honourable city] *Truth* 22, 'this honourable city' *Industry* 183, *Virtue* 177, 261–2. Not in Wither.

*16 whose bounty in full nobleness] 'whose bounty and nobleness' *Integrity* 248, *Prosperity* 187. Not in Dekker, Heywood, or Munday; 'whose bounty' appears eight other times in period drama, and once in Wither, but never elsewhere followed by 'nobleness' (for which there are no parallels in LION poetry or prose published before 1660, either).

17 best condition] 'best condition' *Women Beware* 1.2.170, 'best conditions' *Quarrel* 2.1.53. Heywood has the singular once (1639), and Wither twice; of other playwrights living in 1621, Chapman, Fletcher, and Shirley each have one example.

*17 in such wise] seven times in Wither, twice at the end of a rhyming line, once rhyming with 'rise' (*Vaticinium causuale*, 1654). Not in Middleton, Dekker, Heywood, or Munday (but in King James Bible 1 Macchabees.xiv).

*18 bettering] *Industry, Hengist, Weapons*; not in Dekker, Heywood, Munday, Wither. In LION plays of 1576 to 1642, the only other parallels are one in Shakespeare (d. 1616), and three in Ford.

*18 by their ruin rise] Compare the collocation of 'ruin' and 'raised' in *Tennis* Induction.80, *Hengist* 5.2.97; 'raises...ruinous' *Witch* 1.2.133. No comparable collocation in other candidates.

*19 noble faithful] *Valour* 1.1.73–4: 'faithfully effected. And how does noble'. No comparable collocation in Dekker, Heywood, Munday, Wither.

20 Amongst] Munday strongly prefers 'among'.

20 religious men] Once each in Munday, Wither; five times in Heywood.

23 masterpiece] Middleton uses 'masterpiece' nineteen times (18 of them in *Quarrel* or after); rare in other candidates.

23 zeal and care] *Aries* 133 ('Zeale, Care'), 212 ('Zealous Care'); *Antiquity* 432–3 ('Care, Zeale'); *Women Beware* 1.3.23 ('When his care's most, that shows his zeal'). The collocation also occurs once each in Munday (*Watch-woord*, 'care, zeale, and loue') and Wither (*Britain's Remembrancer*, 'zealous care').

*25 Now...I arrive] now I arrive *Mad World* 1.1.61, I arrive now *Industry* 156. No parallels in Dekker, Heywood, Munday, or LION drama 1576–1642, or LION poetry and prose published before 1660.

25 blessed foundress] 'bless the founders' *Entertainments* 8.72, 'prays for the Founder, bless' *Chaste Maid* 1.2.14–15

*27 held the fame] 'held by fame' *Integrity* 283. No parallel collocation in Dekker, Heywood, Munday, or LION drama 1576–1642, or LION poetry and prose published before 1660.

*29 since I touch...so near] 'since I am touched so near' *Witch* 5.3.113. No parallels in Dekker, Heywood, Munday, Wither, or LION drama 1576–1642, or pre-1660 LION poetry and prose.

*30 observe what] 'observe what' *Lady* 1.1.162–3, *Truth* 607, *Revenger* 3.5.18. Not in Heywood, Munday, or Wither.

30 observe...notes] 'observe...note' *Michaelmas* 1.2.122. No parallels in Dekker, Heywood, Munday; among period prose writers and poets, Leighton, Mulcaster, and Peacham each have one example of 'observe and note'.

30 notes remarkable] 'notes' are 'strange' (*Women Beware* 4.2.72) or 'not usual' (*Virtue* 140). The word 'remarkable' (*Owl* 291, *Integrity* 120) is not recorded in Munday.

32 Prime prior] elsewhere in Middleton 'prime' villain, gallant, commander, incendiary, president zealot (1613–24)

*32 falling to worst] *Solomon* 10.16.147–8 'fall, Turne best to worst'. No comparable collocations in Dekker, Heywood, Munday, Wither.

*34 which is rare] *Old Law* 2.2.178; 'which is a rare' *Dissemblers* 1.2.83. No parallels in Dekker, Heywood, Munday, Wither. In other plays of the period, 'which is rare' occurs only twice (anonymous *Nobody and Somebody* 1606; Shirley's *lady of Pleasure* 1637); 'which is' followed by one word then 'rare' once each in Brome, Chapman, Daniel, and Davenant. Middleton is the only author with two parallels. Ten examples of 'which is rare' in poetry and prose before 1660.

*35 worth observing] 'worth th'observing' *Witch* 4.1.87, 'worth observation' *Old Law* 2.1.116. Not in Dekker, Munday, or Wither; 'worth observation' in Heywood (1635); the only comparable parallel in drama of the period is Massinger's 'worth your obseruing'.

38 Fitz-Alwin of the Drapers' Company] a marginal note in 1633 says that 'This is mistaken by Mr. Stow'; Middleton always—in *Aries, Integrity*, and *Prosperity*—treats Fitz-Alwin as a member of the Drapers.

*39 fame now shines so clear] 'in fame shines clearer' *Hengist* 1.1.33; 'virtues...shine clear now' *Entertainments* 4.16–17; 'now shines bright' *Michaelmas* 1.2.68; 'shines more cleere' *Aries* 274. Middleton frequently uses 'shine' of abstract nouns. See also 'clear fame' *Game* 3.1.165, 'clear-eyed fames' *Hengist* 5.2.163. Dekker, Heywood, Munday, and Wither provide no parallels for 'fame...shines', or for the juxtaposition of 'fame(s)' and 'clear*'; the drama of the period has no examples of 'fame...shines', which shows up in the poetry and prose of the period only three times (once by National Richards, twice by John Taylor—two authors who both wrote in praise of Middleton). In drama the juxtaposition with 'clear*' shows up once in Fletcher, twice in Shirley, and once in the anonymous *Guy of Warwick*. Dekker has one parallel for the collocation 'now' and 'shine*'

(*Old Fortunatus*, 1599), and two for 'shines cleere' (*Satiromastix*, 1602); Wither has 'shine clearer' once (*Schollers Purgatory* 1624). Middleton uses 'so clear' (variously spelled) eight times, more than any other candidate.

40   of the same Society] *Industry* 163. Four times in Munday; not in Dekker, Heywood, or Munday.

Of asterisked phrases or collocations, Middleton has parallels for 23, Dekker 5, Heywood 3, Wither 3, Munday 2. That is, Middleton's total almost doubles the sum of all four others, and is more than four times the number of the nearest rival (Dekker). [These totals are types, not tokens; that is, they count the existence of a parallel, without attending to the number of such parallels in an author's work.] If one paid attention to the quality or density of the parallels, Middleton's dominance would be even greater.

II. The second set of verses does not directly concern the role of the City, but focuses instead upon explication of a religious emblem. Middleton often provided such glosses for elements of his civic pageants, but very little verbal detail here suggests Middleton. The one phrase that initially seemed to be strong evidence for Middleton ('free donation') was actually common in only one other writer, George Wither. Since Wither began publishing religious verse in 1619, and had connections with important clergy and with King James by 1622, he seemed a plausible alternative candidate. I therefore checked these verses for parallels, in LION, in the canons of Middleton or Wither. The results strikingly contrast with the pattern of parallels in the first forty verses. Again, I've checked for parallels in all five canons, and eliminated those that show up in three or more. Because the passage is so short, I have also checked all parallels that pass this first screening (against five canons) against the LION database of authors alive in 1622-3, and against the database of EEBO-TCP (June 2006).

1   The rising...Sunne] Middleton has 'the rising' twice; however, the collocation with 'sun' appears nowhere else in Middleton, but eleven times in Wither. (Once in Munday, twice in Heywood, three times in Dekker.) Since it appears in four canons, it has not been counted.

*1   the cleere Gospels] Wither, *Schollers Purgatory* (1624): 'the light of the gospell begann to shine clearer' (81). The collocation does not appear in Middleton, Dekker, Heywood, or Munday.; LION finds only one other (earlier) parallel. However, in EEBO the collocation (which has to be checked manually) appears 44 times just in authors whose names begin with the letter A.

*1   Gospels Sunne] *Integrity* ('the sun-beames of the Gospell'). The collocation does not appear in Wither, Dekker, Heywood, Munday; LION finds only one other (later) parallel. EEBO has 19 examples from authors whose names begin with the letter A; this idiom therefore seems to be less common than the preceding one.

1-2   Sunne...donation] For Middleton rhyming disyllabic -ion (as here) see notes on the Bolles epitaph. Wither's parallels for 'free donation' (see below) rhyme it with 'expectation' and 'augmentation', in both cases treating 'ion' as one syllable, not two. Wither's *Motto* (1621) and *Hymnes and Songs of the Church* (1623) do not contain a single example of disyllabic -ion; but it does occur in his earlier *Abuses Stript* (1613): 'search't on/confusion' ('Of Man'); 'groweth on/proportion' ('Satyr.I'), 'opinion/resolued on' ('Satyr.2'), 'goe on/presumption' (twice), and 'Alcharon/Religion' ('Satyr.4').

2   Is through the] Wither, *Collection of Emblems* (1635), XXVIII (beginning a verse line); *Hymnes and Songs of the Church* (1623). Twice in Heywood's *Troia Britanica* (1609), neither example at the beginning of a verse line; Middleton twice has ''tis through the' (*Phoenix, Mad World*). No parallels in Dekker, Munday.

2   Senates] Wither, *Prosopopoeia Britannica* (1648). The possessive does not appear in Middleton, Dekker, or Munday. However, inflections of a noun are not strong evidence.

*2   free donation] *Game* 5.1.31. Not in Dekker, Heywood, Munday; no other parallel in LION plays 1576-1642; the only other LION parallels are three from Wither: *Vox Pacifica* (1645), *A Suddain Flash* (1657), and *A Triple Paradox* (1661). This phrase suggests that Middleton or Wither is likelier than any other poet of the period to have written these verses, but it does not arbitrate between them: Wither has more parallels, but they are later, and the syllabification is different. EEBO-TCP lists 70 other examples of the phrase before 1700, so it clearly belongs to the shared religious vocabulary of the period.

3   bright Sunne] Middleton, *Truth, Antiquity*; Wither, *Exercises* (1620), *Faire-virtue* (1621). More common in Dekker and Heywood. Not counted because present in four canons.

*3   God of might] Wither, *Hymnes and Songs* (1623). Not in Middleton, Dekker, Heywood, Munday; 23 LION examples, 91 EEBO examples.

4   and the light] Wither, *Exercises* (1620). Twice in Dekker, once in Munday.

*5   the blessed Spirit] Wither, *Britain's Remembrancer* (1628); *Peacemaker* 717. Not in Dekker, Heywood, Munday. The exact sequence and spelling occurs in LION three times, and in 215 EEBO works.

*5   of truth and right] *Prosperity* 141 (specifically, 'stars of truth and right,' thus sharing this passage's celestial imagery, and rhyming 'right' with 'light'). Dekker has 'Truth, and Right' (*Troia-Nova*), but LION has no examples of the four-word phrase from living authors; EEBO has only 28 other examples, and only two before 1623.

*6   as these three] *Women Beware* 5.1.103; Dekker, *Wonderful Year*. These are the only LION parallels for authors alive in 1622-3; EEBO has 79 examples.

7 are all one] *Puritan* 2.1.86. Three times in Dekker, twice in Heywood.

*7 one sun…three one God] For 'one sun', 'one God', and the conceit of these lines, compare Wither's *Hymnes and Songs* (1623): 'And sure we are, those *persons Three* | Make but one *GOD*, and thou art Hee. | The *Sunne* a *Motion* hath we know | Which *Motion* doth beget vs Light; | The *Heat* proceedeth from those *two* | …Yet, though this *Motion*, *Light* and *Heate*, | Distinctly by themselues we take; | Each in the other hath his seat, | And but one *Sunne* we see they make | …So, in the *God-head* there is knit | A wondrous threefold *True-loue-knot*' (SONG LIX., *Trinity Sunday*). Wither also used 'one Sun' in *Prince Henries obsequies* (1612); Dekker has two examples, Heywood one, of this two-word phrase, which is therefore not in itself reliable evidence. (LION has 17 entries among living authors, EEBO 209). It is harder to search, mechanically, for parallels in the period for the thought and imagery of the whole passage. The philosophical coupling of 'one God' to 'one sun' is an ancient idea; it can be found in a compendium of medieval thought, *Batman vppon Bartholome his booke De proprietatibus rerum* (1582): 'there is one God, one world of one God, one Sunne of one world' (Bii^v); LION and EEBO identify another ten examples in the period. But there is nothing in them about the Trinity. However, in a passage of popular and admired Sylvester's translation of *Du Bartas his deuine weekes and workes* (1611) the two phrases are linked to the Trinity: 'The greater World hath but one Sun to shine, The lesser but one Soule, both but one God, In Essence One, in Person *Trinely*-odde' ('The Magnificence', in Snyder, 1328–30). Sylvester does not break the 'one sun' down into its constituent parts, to parallel the three parts of the Trinity. Of the five primary candidates, only Wither combines (1) 'one God' and 'one sun', (2) and links them to the trinity, breaking the sun down into three parts. I have counted this as a single parallel, and the next phrase as a second.

*7 one God] This phrase appears in *Old Law* 3.1 (a Rowley scene) and nowhere else in the Middleton canon, but twice in Wither: *Britain's Remembrancer* (1628), and the passage quoted in the previous note. LION hass another fifteen examples among living authors; EEBO identifies 7175 occurrences. Although the terms of my search require this to be listed as a strong parallel, it is far and away the commonest idiom so identified here.

8 *Allelujah* speakes] Compare '*Halelujah* sing' in Wither's *Prince Henries Obsequies* (1612) and *Britain's Remembrancer* (1628). All the more than 300 examples of the word I have found in Wither's canon use the initial 'h'; so do the dozen Heywood examples. By contrast, Dekker has 'Alleluia' (*Noahs arke*, 1609) and 'Alleluiah' (*Rod for Runaways*, 1625). The presence of the word in three canons makes it weak evidence,

and the lack of known parallels in Middleton and Munday means that the unusual spelling here might be their preference (as it was clearly not the presence of Wither, and apparently not the preference of Heywood or Dekker). In any case, a single word is always weak evidence.

8 the rayes] Compare 'the rayes' in Wither, *Britain's Remembrancer* (1628), and 'the ray' in *Faire-virtue* (1622), both at the end of a rhyming line. No such parallels in the other candidates, but Middleton has 'near the principal rays' (*Aries* 200), and 'the… rayes' also appears in Wither and Heywood, so this is not a strong parallel.

9 Three in One] *Solomon* 3.114 ('All three in one make one thrice-happy spirit'). The phrase appears three times in Wither's *Hymnes and Songs* (1623), once each in Dekker and Heywood. In itself it thus occurs in four of the candidates, and cannot be considered good evidence; I cite it only for the contextual parallel in Middleton.

*9 may only haue] *Lady* B1.1.210. No exact parallel in any of the other candidates, or (according to LION) in any other writer alive in 1622–23. EEBO identifies only thirteen examples, one of them the notes to the 1561 Geneva Bible Daniel 4:34 ('that God may onely haue the glorie'), which seems to be echoed here.

The totals here are much more problematic than for the first group of verses: Middleton 6, Wither 6, Dekker 1, Heywood 0, Munday 0. Although this pattern confirms that Dekker, Heywood, and Munday had nothing to do with this event, the contrast with the earlier verses (Middleton 23, Wither 3 vs. Middleton 6, Wither 6) is remarkable. Two of these rare phrases are shared by both writers ('free donation', 'the blessed spirit'), and the two different collocations with 'Gospel' (sun/clear) effectively cancel each other out (though the Wither parallel is more than twice as common in the period than the Middleton one). This leaves, on Middleton's side, 'of truth and right', 'of these three', and 'may only haue': these three parallels have no necessary connection to the emblem they describe, but seem to be independent authorial mannerisms, and given the huge size of the Wither canon it seems significant that he never uses them. Together these three parallels have one LION parallel among living writers, and 120 EEBO parallels. By contrast, the three remaining Wither parallels occur 39 times in LION, and 7277 times in EEBO. Simply in terms of relative frequencies elsewhere, the Middleton parallels are much stronger. One of the Wither parallels ('God of might') was familiar from church services, and the other two— 'one God' with the threefold sun—might be explained by specific circumstances of the occasion not chosen by the poet: the verses describe a 'fair monument' in the church, and the design of that monument refers to that church's long historical association with the Trinity. Generally, Wither's canon contains much more explicitly religious writing than Middleton's, so he has a larger sample size for commonplace religious phrases. On balance, then, the evidence is probably best explained by Middleton's authorship of the lines—especially given the much more asymmetrical evidence for his authorship of the preceding and following verses, and the unifying description of the Court of Aldermen as a 'Senate' in all three sets of verses.

III. The final set of verses is a single couplet, and by definition such a small data sample provides less reliable evidence of authorship. However, in Stow it is preceded by a list of the names of Lord Mayor and Aldermen, which associates it with the Middleton verses more strongly than with the verses that might be Wither's. I transcribe the prose below.

This Temple received Consecration the morrow after New-yeeres day, in the yeere 1622.

The Right Honourable, Sir *Peter Proby* being then Lord Maior; and the Right Worshipfull, Mr. *Iohn Hodges*, and Sir *Humfrey Hanford*, Knight, Sheriffes, and Aldermen.

The names of all the rest of the Honourable Senators, all worthy Patrons of this pious worke, and then present at the consecration:

Sir *Iohn Garrard.*
Sir *Thomas Bennet.*
Sir *Thomas Lowe.*
Sir *Thomas Middleton.*
Sir *Iohn Leman.*
Sir *William Cokayne.*
Mr. *Martin Lumley.*
Mr. *William Goare.*
Mr. *Iohn Goare.*
Mr. *Allen Cotton.*
Mr. *Cuthbert Hacket.*
Mr. *William Holliday.*
Mr. *Robert Iohnson.*
Mr. *Richard Hearne.*
Mr. *Richard Deane.*
Mr. *Robert Ducie.*
Aldermen.

The italicized couplet that immediately follows this list of aldermen refers to 'this Senate', apparently an allusion to the list. Elsewhere the St James verses refer to 'a Senate' and 'the Senate', but 'this' must refer to some antecedent, and the list of 'Senators' seems to be that antecedent. Moreover, for the first two sets of verses the 1633 edition indicates a specific place in the church where they are written; no such locale is given for the third set of verses, which would therefore seem to be part of the monument mentioned in connection with the second set of verses. The implication of these arguments is that the names of the Mayor, Sheriffs, and Aldermen were placed on the monument, with these verses above or below them. There is no guarantee that the author of the final couplet wrote the preceding prose, which chiefly consists of a list of names; but the author of the verses was clearly aware that they would be situated in relation to the list of names, and the identification of the Court of Aldermen as 'Senators'

fits the three references to a Senate, one in each of the three sets of verses.

In the couplet itself, there are two phrases with strong Middleton parallels, and nothing comparable for any other candidate. For all three sets of verses, the totals are Middleton 31, Wither 9, Dekker 6, Heywood 3, Munday 2.

1 This sacred] *Civitatis* 244. Not in the other four canons. But LION has 196 parallels among living writers, and EEBO 1387.

1 structure which] Wither, *Britain's Remembrancer* (1628). Also in Heywood. Middleton elsewhere has 'this fair structure', Wither 'this crippled structure'. Only two other LION examples, and 93 in EEBO. These first two phrases cancel each other out, as weak indicators of Middleton or Wither.

1 this Senate] *Old Law* 1.1.138 (probably by Rowley). Not in other candidates at all.

1 fames] For the verb compare 'whom Tradition fames' (at the end of a rhyming verse line) in Wither's *Verses Intended* (1662). But this is poor evidence, because all the candidates use *fame* as a verb, and particular forms of a verb are not good authorship markers.

2 hath] Middleton strongly preferred 'has' in his dramatic works (especially by the 1620s), but did use 'hath' on formal occasions, in his other poems of 1619–25, and in his other religious works; Wither overwhelmingly preferred 'hath' (2730 to 8 in his poetry in LION). This single linguistic form is therefore unreliable evidence.

*2 stil'd] With the sense 'styled' at *Prosperity* 151 ('stil'd the Fountayne of') and *Integrity* 172 ('stilde by the name of the Temple of Integrity'). The parallels involve not only the unusual verb (which also occurs in *Truth*) but its inflection in combination with the other elements of the phrase: (1) 'styled the *noun* of', (2) 'styled...the Temple of'. Heywood has parallels for the first, but I have found no other parallels in the other candidates, and no uses of the verb in Munday or Wither. (It is not possible to do a simple LION or EEBO count, since every example of all possible inflections and spellings of the verb would have to be checked for the correct meaning.)

*2 the Temple of Saint] See preceding note and *Truth* 425 ('the Temple of Saint Paul'). Nothing comparable in Wither, Dekker, Heywood, Munday; this is the only LION parallel for living authors. EEBO has another 24 examples, but only five before 1623, and all but one refer to Catholic or Muslim houses of worship; in the one exception, Thomas Flatman's *John Juan Lamberto* (1661), 'the Temple of Saint Maryovers' is clearly satirical. Middleton thus provides the only known parallel for serious use of the phrase in reference to an English Protestant church.

Gary Taylor

SEE ALSO

Text: *Works*, 1891
Textual introduction and apparatus: this volume, 992

WORK CITED

Snyder, Susan, ed., *The Divine Weeks and Works of Guillaume de Saluste Sieur Du Bartas*, 2 vols (1979)

The Spanish Gypsy   July 1623

The title-page of the first edition (1653) claims that the play was 'Written by *THOMAS MIDLETON, AND WILLIAM ROWLEY*. Gent.' This claim is repeated in subsequent editions and Stationers' Register entries throughout the seventeenth century (Padhi, xii–xix, lxix–lxxiv). Although someone with access to an authoritative manuscript annotated one copy of the first edition, s/he did not challenge the title-page attribution; *Gypsy* thus differs significantly from *The Widow*, where the title-page attribution was challenged by at least two early readers. It is possible the attribution was made on the original licence for the play. Malone transcribed the licensing of the play onto his own copy of the 1653 edition; he did not identify the play's authors—which means either that the licence did not specify authorship, or that it specified the same two authors as the first edition. More positively, in a list of manuscript plays belonging to Beeston's Boys in 1639, *Gypsy* is grouped with other Middleton–Rowley plays: 'Alls Lost by Lust: The Changeling: A fayre quarrell: The spanish gipsie: The World' (Chambers, 390, reproducing Public Record Office xii:5/134, p. 337). The only known play which fits the fifth item in this sequence is Middleton and Rowley's *The World Tossed at Tennis*. The list begins with five plays by Fletcher, then five by Massinger, then thirteen by Shirley, then these five, then three by Ford; it is hard to deny that the plays are being grouped, here, by author. So someone associated with Beeston believed that the play belonged in the Middleton and/or Rowley canon in 1639, fourteen years before the first edition (Taylor). The compiler of the Beeston list, in 1639, had no commercial reason, indeed no conceivable reason, to deliberately misattribute the play. Moreover, because the play was originally licensed, on 9 July 1623, to one of Beeston's companies (Bawcutt, 141), the Beeston document originates in the institution responsible for the play's first productions, and for subsequent revivals in the 1620s and 1630s. The suggestion (made by Sykes and seconded by Lake) that the publisher of the 1653 quarto deliberately misattributed the play to Middleton and Rowley must therefore be dismissed. Both Dekker and Ford (Lake's alternative candidates) were much more popular in print than Middleton or Rowley in the two decades before *Gypsy* was published. The external evidence that *Gypsy* belongs in the Middleton canon is thus 'exceptionally strong' (Taylor).

Nevertheless, Middleton and Rowley's authorship has been disputed for most of the twentieth century. In 1924 Sykes argued that the play 'came substantially, if not wholly, from the pen of John Ford' (183). Ford's presence in at least some scenes has since been demonstrated, using a variety of linguistic evidence, by both Lake and Jackson; even Padhi, determined to reclaim the play for Middleton and Rowley, had to concede that Ford probably also contributed.

No one, however, has been convinced that Ford was the sole author. In 1935 Sargeaunt, in a book on Ford which accepted his authorship of much of the play, specifically denied that he could have written 4.1 (41–52). In 1929 Oliphant concluded that *Gypsy* 'certainly seems in the main to be from the workshop of Ford and Dekker' (II, 18); in 1975 Lake attributed it wholly to Ford and Dekker. But Jackson refused to commit himself on the identity of Ford's collaborator(s), and Padhi denied Dekker's presence altogether; more importantly—because he is a more objective observer, and a champion of the very method Lake deployed—Cyrus Hoy concluded that 'the case for Ford's presence in the play is a good deal stronger than the one that Lake is able to make for Dekker' (III, 234).

Linguistically, late Dekker is difficult to distinguish from late Middleton and Rowley. Moreover, the evidence for scribal interference and theatrical expurgation (detailed in the Textual Introduction) renders unreliable some of the usual discriminants between them. Lake's case for Dekker therefore depended, in large part, on a handful of verbal parallels. Holdsworth, in his work on *Timon of Athens* and *A Yorkshire Tragedy*, had demonstrated the value of verbal parallels, but only if one systematically surveyed the entire text; more recently Jackson, using newly available electronic resources, has shown that it is now possible to evaluate such parallels by comprehensive negative checks against the whole corpus of early modern drama. Lake's citation of Dekker parallels did not satisfy the rigorous criteria demanded by Holdsworth or Jackson. Nevertheless, Oliphant's and Lake's intuitions were right. Taylor and Jackson are able to demonstrate—using a computer-assisted comprehensive survey of verbal parallels in certain areas of the text, coupled with comprehensive negative checks—that Dekker certainly seems to have written most of 2.1, 2.2.119–75, and parts of 3.2.

But the presence of Dekker and Ford does not demonstrate the absence of Middleton and Rowley; if we are to abandon the evidence of the 1653 title-page, we have no reason to assume that the play was written by two authors (rather than three or four). Taylor demonstrates that, although the linguistic pattern for *Gypsy* is demonstrably anomalous for a Middleton–Rowley collaboration, it is equally anomalous for a Dekker–Ford collaboration. Moreover, the distribution of the linguistic evidence falls into alternating patterns that suggests the collaboration of all four writers. The strongest linguistic evidence for Ford clusters in three scenes (3.3, the middle of 5.1, and the beginning of 5.3); there is a comparable clustering of linguistic evidence for Middleton in two scenes (the end of 1.5 and the middle of 3.2). Moreover, the very techniques for evaluating verbal parallels which support Dekker's claim to authorship of some of the Gypsy material also support Middleton's claim to authorship of the end of 1.5 and the middle of 3.2.

Four-party collaborations make it intrinsically difficult to identify the authors of particular passages, because there is no guarantee that one author wrote an entire scene (especially a long one with multiple subsections, like 2.1 or 3.2). The linguistic tests used successfully by Hoy, Jackson, and Lake to solve so many attribution problems in early modern drama depend on statistically significant repetitions, and are therefore most successful with plays by a single author, or divided between two; with smaller samples they lose most of their effectiveness. Any survey of the evidence must therefore consider the text in terms of distinct sub-scenes or detachable elements. But even such structural divisions may underestimate the complexity of such a collaboration. For instance, either Rowley or Middleton might have contributed jokes, speeches, or passages to the prose of Sancho and Soto, even in scenes primarily written by Dekker.

The overlapping linguistic evidence (Taylor) and phrasal evidence (Jackson and Taylor) is complemented by metrical statistics. Metrical evidence has, for decades, been generally discredited, because some earlier scholars used it indiscriminately and over-enthusiastically; moreover, the critical attack on formalism has made it unfashionable to take seriously the formal features of Renaissance texts. But two simple, easily-duplicated metrical tests distinguish these four candidates most of the time: Middleton and Rowley used 'feminine endings' (an extra unstressed syllable at the end of a line) more often than Ford and Dekker; Ford and Dekker made much more use of iambic pentameter lines with exactly ten syllables. The following verse statistics do not count part-lines (six syllables or less), songs or couplets (formally distinct from the iambic pentameter dialogue norm). That is, these statistics describe metrical practice in the play's 'blank verse'.

1.1.47-55 (9 blank verse lines): 5 feminine (55%), 0 regular. This is a small sample at the very end of the scene—most of the scene is in prose—and may not be statistically significant. Ford is ruled out of the prose beginning of the scene by linguistic evidence; the metrical statistics fall wildly outside the ranges of Dekker or Ford.

1.2 (12 lines): 3 fem (25%), 5 reg (42%). A short scene entirely in verse, producing another small sample, but one in striking contrast with the preceding scene. Metrically it fits Ford or Dekker; it contains an unusually high concentration of linguistic evidence (*I'm*, *'em*, *has*, *does*) that tells against Ford. It is possible that this verse scene and the verse segment at the end of the preceding scene should be considered as a single stretch of writing—no scene division is marked in the quarto, and the first scene does not end with a couplet—rather than two separate sections. It would then consist of 21 blank verse lines (a sample more likely to be significant), eight with feminine endings (38%) and five regular (28%). These figures would not be characteristic of Ford

or Dekker. The metrical irregularity of 1.2.1 (ten syllables, but not iambic) would be characteristic of Rowley: see 4.3.

1.3 (102 lines): 37 fem (36%), 53 reg (52%). Almost everyone assigns this scene to Ford, on the basis of strong verbal parallels; linguistic evidence—including three instances of *hath*—is compatible with his authorship.

1.4 (14 lines): 8 fem (57%), 3 reg (21%). The first percentage is far higher than any Ford or Dekker scene; the second is far lower than any Ford or Dekker scene. This short scene introduces the Don Juan plot, and metrically resembles Middleton or Rowley more than Ford or Dekker.

1.5.1-73 (71 lines): 30 fem (42%), 29 reg (41%). Assigned Ford on the basis of verbal parallels; linguistic evidence compatible with Ford's authorship. Metrically at the edge of Ford's range.

1.5.73-end (46 lines): 23 fem (50%), 13 reg (28%). As with linguistic evidence, the metrical evidence is in striking contrast with the first part of the scene. Linguistic evidence (Taylor) and verbal parallels (Taylor and Jackson) assign this passage to Middleton.

2.1 (37 lines): 13 fem (35%), 14 reg (38%). The bulk of this scene's prose is by Dekker, on the basis of verbal parallels and other evidence canvassed by Lake; it also uses Guzman as a major source. The ratio of feminine endings is significantly higher, and the ratio of regular lines significantly lower, than any other Dekker scene. One area of verse that might not be Dekker's is at 2.1.104-13, the 'changeling' passage, which could easily be a late insert: of its ten lines, six (60%) have feminine endings, while only four (40%) are regular iambic pentameter. Since Middleton or Rowley would have the most reason to add this passage, it would make sense if one of them wrote it; the proportion of regular lines, the absence of arhythmia, and the interrogative repetition, all favour Middleton. If this detachable passage were subtracted, the rest of the scene's twenty-seven verse lines would include only seven feminine endings (27%) and twelve regular iambic pentameters (44%). These modified figures better fit Dekker.

2.2.1-118 (119 lines): 36 fem (30%), 56 reg (47%). Clara plot, usually assigned to Ford.

2.2.119-75 (11 lines): 1 fem (9%), 6 reg (55%). A small metrical sample; most of the passage is prose. Clearly distinct linguistically and stylistically from the Clara part of the scene. The bulk of the vocabulary evidence assigns this scenelet to Dekker (Taylor and Jackson). As noted in the Textual Introduction, the final four lines of the scene (2.2.176-9) are probably a later addition, and therefore might have a different author than the rest of the material. The only other known example of the verb *Gypsify* occurs at *Dissemblers*

4.2.183; the only examples of turning the adjective *typsy* into a comic polysyllable are *typsify* here and *tipsitaptrapolonian* at *Owl* 1683–4; *Dissemblers* 4.2.77–78 contains the only known example, before the 1670s, of the rhyme Gypsy/tipsy; Dekker does not use any form of the words *typsy* or *camel* elsewhere. There are three examples of the word *gambols* in Middleton, only one each in Dekker and Ford. Thus, strong verbal evidence for Middleton is concentrated in the final lines of the scene, which seem on other grounds to represent a distinct layer of the text's evolution.

3.1.1–29 (23 lines): 5 fem (22%), 12 reg (52%). Metrically not Rowley or Middleton.

3.1.30–106 (27 lines): 8 fem (29%), 14 reg (52%). Metrically either Ford or Dekker. The contraction *it's* (85) tells against Ford; the form *wut* (61) appears in Dekker but none of the others. Lake cited numerous Dekker parallels, and a more systematic study of vocabulary confirms Dekker for this passage, and for the song at 107–38 (Jackson and Taylor).

3.2.1–50 (42 lines): 17 fem (40%), 18 reg (43%). Metrically more like Ford than Dekker; unlike Rowley. This conversation among nobles and gentry differs in subject matter and style from the rest of the scene, after the entrance of the Gypsies. Lake recognized that 3.2 is 'of mixed authorship' and that 'Ford may be present at the beginning of the scene' (224): Sykes noted a Ford parallel in the first two lines.

(51–2). Juan's aside, which is not integrated into the metrical structure of the surrounding lines, could have been interpolated by another hand, after the surrounding dialogue had been written. Among the four authors, the only parallel for the collocation 'shoot...wide' is at *Roaring Girl* 4.196 (a Middleton scene); *holds not* occurs only at *Old Law* 2.2.42 (a Middleton scene) and *The Maid in the Mill* 4.1 (a Rowley scene in a play licensed by the Master of the Revels on 29 August 1623, and thus written within weeks of the completion of *Gypsy*). Middleton also used the contraction *'mongst* at least 34 times, much more frequently than all the other candidates combined; this is its only occurrence in the play. Middleton was elsewhere responsible for much of the Don Juan/Preciosa plot.

3.2.54–5, 58–77. Soto's Prologue could have been separately written, as prologues often were; the tumbling metre, followed by prose, is characteristic of Rowley, who seems to have been responsible for the other play-with-the-play (4.3). However, because they contain no blank verse, they are not counted in these statistics.

3.2.56–7. Juan's aside, and the line that cues it, could have been interpolated by another hand, after the surrounding dialogue had been written. Metrically,

as aligned in this edition, this includes a feminine ending; but the lineation is uncertain, and therefore unreliable evidence. 'How, how' occurs in Dekker, Ford, and Middleton, but the interrogative repetition is most characteristic of Middleton. The collocation of the full form *I am* followed by the contraction *I'm* occurs in Dekker once ('I am no Frier, see I'm poore') and Ford once ('I am the sorrier, sir; I'me loath'). But there are three examples in Middleton, and—unlike either of the preceding parallels—two of the Middleton examples are rhythmically identical to 'I am a-fire, I'm sure': 'I am no fool, I'm sure' (*Old Law* 2.1.109), 'Though I am old, I'm free' (*Widow* 2.2.176). There is also a parallel in *Dissemblers* 4.2.18 and at *Weapons* 5.1.254–5 ('I'm o'er shoes, I'm sure, upon the dry bank'), but that final example might be by Rowley. Nevertheless, the preponderance of evidence would favour Middleton, who was responsible for much of the Don Juan/Preciosa plot.

3.2.78–81 (4 lines): 2 fem (50%), 2 reg (50%). A small sample, but metrically not like Ford or Dekker. Don Juan's speech, in particular, is entirely composed of Middletonian phrases: 'I should be sorry else' appears in *Hengist* 5.1.27 and *Widow* 5.1.147 (where it immediately follows 'troa'). The other three authors provide parallels for neither the sentence as a whole nor the conjunction 'sorry else'. There are also multiple Middleton parallels for the verbal conjunctions 'yes sure', 'sure 'tis,' and ''tis she'; though the Dekker canon also contains parallels for all three, only at *Witch* 2.1.199 is *'tis she* followed by *sorry*, as here. See Textual Notes (3.2.81) for the speech prefix error, which may indicate that the passage, or at least Don Juan's speech, has been added by a second hand.

(3.2.82–113, 197–217): Probably both songs are by Dekker (Taylor and Jackson), but they could have been written separately, and in any case are not counted in these statistics.

3.2.114–94 (24 lines): 10 fem (42%), 6 reg (25%). Vocabulary and linguistic evidence point to Middleton (Taylor and Jackson). Metrically, not Ford or Dekker. This passage most closely resembles, metrically, the ending of 1.5 (also assigned to Middleton by linguistic and vocabulary evidence).

3.2.218–30 (13 lines): 7 fem (54%), 4 reg (31%). This passage, to the exit of the Gypsies, is uncharacteristic of Dekker or Ford, metrically.

3.2.233–42 (9 lines): 7 fem (78%), 2 reg (22%). A small sample, but clearly uncharacteristic of Dekker and Ford. Rowley? Middleton? Mixed? Combining these two transitional passages to produce a more significant sample, 3.2.218–42 has 22 lines, 14 with feminine endings (64%), and only 6 regular (27%), outside the range of Dekker or Ford.

3.2.242-98 (55 lines): 20 fem (36%), 26 reg (47%). 'There are no very good authorship indicators here' (Lake). Metrically more like Ford than anyone else; same plot material as other Ford scenes. If combined with the preceding uncertain transitional material, the ending of the scene would have 77 lines, with 34 feminine (44%) and 32 regular (42%). This would be just within Ford's range; Clara is mentioned at 219 and 237-40. But it is not self-evident that all those sections belong together.

3.3 (102 lines): 43 fem (43%), 42 reg (41%). Clearly by Ford, linguistically (*whiles, d'ee, hath*).

4.1.1-148 (15 lines): 5 fem (33%), 7 reg (47%). Metrically not Middleton or Rowley (though most of the scene is rhymed, and therefore outside these statistics). Sargeaunt argued convincingly against Ford's authorship. Lake assigned to Dekker on the basis of phrasal evidence and linguistic compatibility.

4.1.149-210 (51 lines): 20 fem (39%), 19 reg (37%). Feminine ending ratio higher than any Dekker section; regularity ratio lower than any Dekker section. Metrically this is more like Middleton than Dekker. Middleton is elsewhere most clearly associated with the Don Juan plot, and a number of verbal parallels support attribution of this segment to him. Holdsworth points out (private communication, 22 June 2003) that the phrase 'obsceane language' occurs, in the Literature Online database, only here (l. 205) and at *Tennis* Epistle.15.

4.2 (66 lines): 27 fem (41%), 25 reg (38%). Both ratios (and the relation between them) rule out Dekker, and the verse seems too regular for Rowley. Lake could find no evidence for Dekker (225); *it's* (4.2.36), *has* (74) and *does* (100, 101) rule out Ford. The contraction *to th'* before a consonant (20, 99) is characteristic of Middleton. The name Lollio (83, 86) is one of the play's three connections to *Changeling*. Lake considers the asseveration in 'Protest, my Lord' (58) a Middletonism. As noted by Padhi (cvii), 'The plot being full' (55) is closely paralleled by 'The plot's full then' (*Women Beware* 4.2.214). 'This young she-Gypsy' (52) echoes the Spanish title of Cervantes's tale *La Gitanilla*; Middleton read and wrote Spanish. The scene contains five examples of Middleton's characteristic interrogative repetition (18, 31, 39, 60, 93) in only 52 speeches (and related forms of iterative repetitions occur at lines 44, 104, and 105).

4.3 (123 lines): 68 fem (55%), 29 reg (24%). Metrically, this is not Dekker or Ford. The high ratio of feminine endings could be Middleton's, but Rowley seems more likely. Rowley rather than Middleton is suggested by lines like 'Of your love measure us forth but one span. We do (though not the best) the best we can' (12-13). The first line, like the

second, has ten syllables, but is very uneasy as iambic pentameter. (Because they form a couplet, these lines were not counted in the statistics.) 'Art thou one of his curs to bite me too?' (47) is spoken by Alvarez, who elsewhere in the inset play always speaks verse, and obviously does so in the very next line. Again, though the line has ten syllables, the iambic rhythm is very uncertain. There are other examples I do not quote here because one may dispute whether they are prose or verse. But that is always precisely the problem with Rowley's 'verse'. The scene's metrical peculiarity cannot be attributed to an effort to differentiate the 'play within the play' formally, because there is no metrical difference between those areas of the scene and the rest. This scene is also distinct from the Gypsy scenes clearly attributable to Dekker in that it makes no use of Guzman as a source. The formula 'My Lord De Carcamo' (4.3.118) appears nowhere else in the play; elsewhere he is identified as 'Francisco de' (1.5.91, 2.1.243, 3.2.0.1) or 'my lord of' (3.2.233, 5.3.88), 'the earl of' (2.2.66), or 'the count of' (5.3.1) Carcamo. There is an extempore inset play based on Italian models in *The Three English Brothers* (1607) by Day, Rowley, and Wilkins. Padhi cites good Rowley parallels for the pun on gravel (17), 'I drop at nose' (18), 'Bucaphalus' (49), 'Trim, tram' (78), and 'Lapland' (133-4).

5.1 (195 lines): 66 fem (34%), 93 reg (48%). Linguistically Ford.

5.2 (55 lines): 15 fem (27%), 34 reg (62%). 'There is no good evidence here' (Lake, 225). The metrical pattern suggests Dekker or Ford.

5.3.1-95 (95 lines): 38 fem (40%), 40 reg (42%). Linguistically Ford.

5.3.96-112 (5 lines): 1 fem (20%), 3 reg (60%). The verse sample here is too small to be significant. The Sancho/Soto material at the end of the play does not contain any of the pro-Ford linguistic markers; Lake notes that Ford does use 'ha'' occasionally (5.3.105), but there are only four examples in his seven whole plays; it is much more frequent in both Dekker and Middleton, either of whom are more likely to have written this material than Ford. Lake's whole hypothesis started from the recognition that Ford is unlikely to be responsible for the 'Gypsy' material.

The division of authorship proposed here metrically distinguishes the different authors identified in the play on other grounds. If we add the scenes certainly by Ford (3.3, 5.1, 5.3.1-95) or almost always assigned to him on the basis of phrasal parallels and compatible linguistic evidence (1.3, 1.5.1-73, 2.2.1-118), the 688 full blank verse lines most clearly attributed to Ford contain 250 feminine endings (36%) and 317 regular lines (46%), with a range of 34-42% for feminine endings, and a range of 41-52% for regular lines. By contrast, the two passages most clearly assigned to Middleton on linguistic grounds (1.5.74–end, 3.2.114–94) have 70 full blank verse lines, with 33 feminine endings (47%) and 19 regular iambic pentameters (27%). If we added the other distinct scenes and scenelets specified above (1.4, 2.1.104–13, 4.1.149–210, 4.2), the 218 blank verse lines most plausibly assigned to Middleton have 97 feminine endings (44%) and only 73 regular lines (33%), with a range of 39–60% (feminine endings) and 21–41% (regular lines). Middleton's lowest range for feminine endings barely overlaps with Ford's highest range (between 39 and 42%), while Middleton's highest regularity barely overlaps with Ford's lowest (41%). But in no Middleton scene do regular lines outnumber feminine endings; in only one Ford scene (1.5.1–74) do feminine endings outnumber regular lines, and then just barely (30/29). The 123 blank verse lines in the one scene most plausibly assigned to Rowley (4.3) have the highest ratio of feminine endings for an extended pasage (54%) and one of the lowest ratios of regular lines (24%); neither figure is within the range of either Dekker or Ford. By contrast, the four passages most confidently assignable to Dekker, on the basis of phrasal parallels and linguistic compatibility—2.1 (except 104–13), 2.2.119–75, 3.1.30–106, 4.1.1–148—contain only 81 blank verse lines, 21 with feminine endings (26%) and 38 regular (47%), with ranges of 9–33% (feminine) and 35–55% (regular). Dekker's scenes always contain more regular lines than feminine endings; the percentage gap is never less than 10%. The oldest of the four playwrights, Dekker's metrical practice is the most regular, reflecting Elizabethan rather than Jacobean norms. Rowley, apparently the youngest of the four, and certainly the one whose writing career began latest, is the least regular.

Blank verse statistics omit much of the play, and it is therefore significant that the pattern of interrogative repetition produced by the divisions of authorship proposed here is also characteristic of the different authors. As Holdsworth discovered, Middleton used this device more often than any of his contemporaries. In the corpus of 112 plays checked by Holdsworth, only Middleton plays exceed 40 such repetitions per 1000 speeches. The passages here assigned to Ford contain nine such repetitions (as strictly defined by Holdsworth) in 344 speeches, a rate of 26 per 1000 speeches, close to the average for Ford calculated by Holdsworth (23). Rowley has the lowest average of any of the four dramatists (21 per 1000), and the material assigned to him here, 4.3, with only two interrogative repetitions in 117 speeches, has the lowest rate in the play (17 per 1000). By contrast, the passages assigned to Middleton in the preceding analysis contain 12 examples in only 186 speeches, a rate of 65 per 1000. In Holdsworth's tables, only Middleton's *Puritan*, with 72 per 1000, has a higher rate. The scenes given to Dekker by Lake contain 25 such repetitions in 555 speeches, a rate of 45 per 1000—higher than any Dekker play, and much higher than his average (29

per 1000). The four passages here most confidently assigned to Dekker—2.1 (minus the 'changeling' passage), 2.2.119–75, 3.1.30–106, 4.1.1–148—contain 10 repetitions in 240 speeches, producing a rate of 42 per 1000. That is more plausible, but still too high, and suggests that those scenes may contain some Middleton writing. Eight of the ten given to Dekker occur in 2.1, and since Middleton has already been identified as the author of one insertion in that scene (2.1.104–13), he might also be responsible for others. The last strong phrasal evidence for Dekker occurs before the entrance of Don Juan, which also corresponds with the exit of all the Gypsies except Preciosa and her mother (at line 2.1.229). If Middleton were responsible for the ending of the scene, Dekker's overall total would be a much more plausible 8 repetitions in 223 speeches (36 per 1000). Alternatively, Middleton might be responsible for some of the scene's prose.

If the plot/scenario for the play was written primarily by one author, Middleton is the likeliest candidate. Rowley can be confidently identified in only one long scene, and Dekker—alone of the four collaborators—was apparently responsible only for parts of scenes, contributing mostly lyric verse and prose. None of Middleton's three partners ever produced a work of such polyphonic complexity, orchestrating so many plots and tones. Middleton is also the only one of the four who had used Cervantes before (for *Lady's Tragedy*), and the only one who definitely could read Spanish (because *Honour and Industry* contains a speech written in Spanish). The play seems based on the Spanish original 'Novela de la Gitanilla' (1613) rather than the French translation 'La Belle Egyptienne' (1620). The diminutive, employed by the Spanish title and by frequent repetition in its text, is echoed in the 'little' applied to Preciosa fourteen times in the play, including specifically 'little Gypsy' (2.1.222) and 'young she-Gypsy' (4.2.52). Moreover, although Middleton does not seem to have written much if anything in Act Five, the stage direction at 5.1.0.2 resembles the dumbshow bridal processions at *Women Beware* 4.3.0.1 and *Changeling* 4.1.0.1, and the direction for the very unusual scene-break between 5.1 and 5.2 ('Ex. at one dore; Enter presently at the other') has parallels in *Five Gallants*, *Lady*, and *Changeling*. This suggests that Ford (who wrote 5.1) and Ford or Dekker (who wrote 5.2) may have been working from a plot outline with entrances and exits written by Middleton.

The play must have been completed by 9 July 1623, when it was licensed by Herbert. One passage (3.2.246–52) could not have been written before mid-May, when news reached England of a similar incident involving Archy Armstrong. (See commentary note.) This is a turning point in the plot; the text *might* have been retrospectively altered to incorporate a topical reference, but four authors could easily have written the entire play in six weeks or less.

Gary Taylor

SEE ALSO

Text: *Works*, 1727
Textual introduction and apparatus: this volume, 1105

WORKS CITED

Bawcutt, N. W., ed., *The Control and Censorship of Caroline Drama: The Records of Sir Henry Herbert, Master of the Revels 1623-73* (1996)

Chambers, E. K., ed., 'Dramatic Records: The Lord Chamberlain's Office', in *Collections: Vol. II. Part III*, gen. ed. W. W. Greg (1931), 389-90 (reproducing Public Record Office xii:5/134, p. 337)

Hoy, Cyrus, *Introductions, Notes, and Commentaries to texts in 'The Dramatic Works of Thomas Dekker'*, 4 vols (1980)

Oliphant, E. H. C., *Shakespeare and His Fellow Dramatists*, 2 vols (1929)

Padhi, Shanti, 'A Critical Old-spelling Edition of *The Spanish Gipsie* by Middleton, Rowley (and possibly Ford)', unpub. D.Phil. thesis (Oxford University, 1984)

Sargeaunt, M. Joan, *John Ford* (1935)

Sykes, H. Dugdale, *Sidelights on Elizabethan Drama* (1924)

Taylor, Gary, 'Thomas Middleton, *The Spanish Gypsy*, and Collaborative Authorship', in *Words That Count*, ed. Brian Boyd (2004), 241-73

—— and MacDonald P. Jackson, 'Middleton, Dekker, and *The Spanish Gypsy*: Protocols for Attribution in Cases of Multiple Collaborators' (forthcoming)

The Triumphs of Integrity   October 1623

The title-page attributes the pageant to Middleton ('By Tho. Middleton, Gent.') and records the date of performance as 29 October 1623. The Drapers' records again indicate a payment to Middleton and Christmas, this time £150 for the pageants. Middleton also received £3 for 'making of a breakfast and fire for the children of the pageants'. Anthony Munday, who wrote the water entertainment, called *The Triumphs of the Golden Fleece*, received a payment of £35 for 'an Argoe'.

David M. Bergeron

SEE ALSO

Text: *Works*, 1768
Textual introduction and apparatus: this volume, 679

'Malfi'   November 1623

The only known text of this poem, in the 1623 edition of *Malfi*, attributes it to 'Thomas Middletonus | Poëta et Chron. Londinensis'. No one has doubted the attribution. Akrigg plausibly argued that Middleton's poem (which like other prelims might have been supplied just before publication of the quarto of Webster's play) refers to the Shakespeare first folio, which was published shortly after 8 November 1623.

Gary Taylor

SEE ALSO

Text: *Works*, 1894
Textual introduction and apparatus: this volume, 992

WORK CITED

Akrigg, G. P. V., 'Middleton: An Allusion to the Shakspere First Folio?', *Shakespeare Association Bulletin* 21 (1946), 25-6

Annales   1620-3?

The existence of this work was noted by the antiquary and editor William Oldys (1696-1761), in an undated manuscript note in a copy of Gerald Langbaine's *An Account of the English Dramatick Poets* (1691), now in the British Library (C.28.g.1); the note is interlined on pp. 370-1, at the beginning of Langbaine's entry for Middleton.

> There are two MSS of this Author's in being which have never been taken Notice of in any Acct of him. They were Sold in an Auction of Books at the Apollo Coffee House in Fleet Street abt the year 1735 by Edw Lewis but puffd up to a great price, bought back, & coud not afterwds be recoverd. They are entitled, I. Annales: or a Continuation of Chronologie; conteyninge Passages and Occurrences proper to the Honnoble City of London: Beginninge in the Yeare of our Lorde 1620. By Thomas Midleton then received by there Honnoble. Senate as Chronologer for the Cittye. There are in it, these Articles under the Year 1621—On Good Fryday in the Morn died John (King) Lord Bp of London—28 May. Fra. Ld Verulam comitted to the Tower. (Seal taken from him the last day of April)—27 Decr. Sr. Edwd Coke committed to the Tower.—Decr. The Fortune Play-House, situate between White Crofs Street and Golding Lane, burnt, &c II. Middleton's Farrago: In which there [there repeated and cancelled] is—The Earl of Efsix his Charge agt Visct. Wimbleton, & the Viscts. Answr.
> —The Treaty & Articles of Marriage between Pr. Cha: & Hen. Maria.
> —Parliamentary Matters, 1625-26.
> —Habeas Corpus 1627 &c

Middleton presumably began writing the *Annales* after his appointment as City Chronologer. This appointment was recorded in the City of London *Repertories*, Volume XXXIV, fol. 540v, transcribed (and modernized) in a note in *Analytical Index to the Series of Records known as the Remembrancia* (1878), 305, and from there quoted for the first time by Bullen (I, l–li):

> [1620, 6th September, 18th James I.—] Tho: Middleton [in the margin] Item this daie was reade in Courte [of Aldermen] a peticon of Thomas Middleton gent and vpon Consideracon thereof taken and vpon the sufficient testimonie this Courte hath receyued of his seruices pformed to this Cittie. This Courte is well pleased to entertaine and admitt the said Thomas Middleton to collect and sett downe all Memorable actes of this Citty and occurrents thereof and for such other imployments as this Courte shall have occasion to vse him in. But the said Thomas Middleton is not to

putt any of the same actes soe by him to be collected into print wthout the allowance and approbacon of this Courte. And for the readynes of his service to the Cittie in the same imployments This Courte doth order that he shall receiue from henceforth out of the Chamber of London a Yearelie fee of vi^{li} xiii^s iiij^d. and the first payment to begin at Michaelllmas Next.

Since even Dyce missed this record, it is unlikely that Oldys knew of it; it provides independent confirmation of the Oldys report that the *Annales* began in 1620. Presumably the seller noted some samples from 1621 because it was the first full year, and/or a more dramatic year, containing as it did a politically divisive Parliament. The first item listed for 1621, John King's death, occurred on 31 March 1621; according to the official calendar, the new year began on 25 March, so King's death could have been the first entry for 1621. The 'Fortune Play House' burned down on 9 December 1621 (Bentley, VI, 133), so the latest entry recorded by Oldys for the *Annales* is 27 December 1621. The '&c' presumably indicates that *Annales* continued for at least some time after December. We can therefore be reasonably certain that Middleton kept the annals from September 1620 until at least early 1622. In fact, Middleton was actively writing for the City through at least August 1623. See *Honourable Entertainments*, 'Bolles', 'St James', *An Invention*, and the following records of payments:

[20 November 1620]: 'Item, this day vppon consideracon taken by this Court of the peticon of Thomas Middleton gent. this Court is well pleased to order that his yearely fee of six poundes thirteene shillings and foure pence payable out of the Chamber of London shall from henceforth be encreased to Tenn poundes p Anum duringe the pleasure of this Court And the first quarters payment to be made at our Ladye daye next:' (Rep. 35, fol. 76, with marginal note 'Peticon Middleton').

17 April 1621: 'Item, this day vppon the humble peticon of Thomas Middleton Chronologer and Inventor of ho:^{ble}: entertainem^{ts}: for this Citty, this Court is pleased for and towards his expences in the pformaunces thereof to graunt vnto him the no^{i}racon and benefitt of one psone to be madde free of this cittye by redempcon (the same psone beinge first p^{r}sented and allowed of by this Court and to be one of the number of ten to be new made free at this Easter and payinge to M^r: Chamblen to the Citties vse the some of six shillings and eight pence./' (Rep. 35, fol. 148^v, with marginal note 'M^r: Middletons graunt:'). This record indicates that Middleton could have had himself made 'free' of the City, and therefore a citizen, but there is no evidence that he ever did so, and he probably preferred to sell this grant to the highest bidder. It was presumably paid in conjunction with the publication of *Honourable Entertainments*.

7 May 1622: 'Item, this day vppon the humble peticon of Thomas Middleton the Citties Chronolger: This Court is pleased for his better encouragement in his laboures and services to the Citty to graunt' etc., as above (Rep. 36, fol. 129^v, with marginal note 'Petic$\bar{o}$ Middleton:'). This payment might have been made for *An Invention*.

17 September 1622: 'Item this Day vppon the humble peticon of Thomas Middleton the Cittyes Chronologer This Courte is pleased for his better incouragem^t. to order that M^r. Chamblen shall pay vnto him the some of fifteene pounds as of the guifte of this Courte./' (Rep. 36, fol. 249, with marginal note 'Tho: Middleton xv^l.').

6 February 1622/23: 'Item, this day vppon the humble peticon of Thomas Middleton the Cities Chronolger this Court is pleased to take into their consideracon the services of the saide peticoner expressed in his peticon and thereupon to order that M^r. Chamblen shall pay vnto him the some of Twenty pound as of the guifte of this Court./' (Rep. 37, fol. 95, with marginal note 'Middleton xx^{li}'). This payment might have been made for 'St James', consecrated on 2 January.

24 April 1623: 'Item this daye vpon the humble peticon of Thomas Middleton the Cities [blank space left in original, filled in pencil at a later date with the word 'Chronologer'] and for his better incoragm^t to doe his best service to this Cittye, this Court of theire especiall favour doth graunt vnto him' etc, one freedom of the city (Rep. 37, fol. 151^v; there are no marginal notes on this page at all).

2 September 1623: 'Item this daie vpon the humble peticon of Thomas Middleton gent. the Cities Chronologer, this Court vouchsaved, to order that M^r. Chamblen shall paie vnto him the some of Twentie markes of the guifte of this Court for and towardes the charges of the service, latelie pformed by him att the shuting att Bunhill before the Lord Maior and Aldren[?], and for his service to bee pformed att the Conduitt heades;/' (Rep. 37, fol. 240, with marginal note 'Middleton: 20^{tie}: markes./').

Middleton might have continued work on the *Annales* until his death. But this is the last record of payment I have found, and on 1 February 1626 the Common Council resolved to end Middleton's annual salary (then recorded as ten pounds) 'unless he give this Court satisfaction according as was intended he should do when the said pension was first granted him' (Rep. 41, fols. 216–9).

Gary Taylor

SEE ALSO

Account: *Works*, 1907

A Game at Chess   May–August 1624

Middleton's authorship is attested by Sir Henry Herbert's licence of 'A new play called *A Game at Chesse*, written by

Middleton' on 'June 12. 1624' (Bawcutt 1996, 152), by a letter from John Woolley on 20 August 1624 (Bawcutt 1996, 153), by a Privy Council order of 30 August 1624 (Howard-Hill 1993, 207), by an autograph manuscript (now in Trinity College, Cambridge), by the autograph title-pages of two other manuscripts (one now in the Folger Library, the other in the Huntington Library), and by an autograph dedication to another manuscript (now in the Bodleian Library). The relevant autograph pages have all been collected and reproduced (Howard-Hill 1990, Plates 1–11). Further attributions to Middleton occur in an anonymous note on the title-page of a copy of the second quarto (once owned by Alexander Dyce, and now in the Victoria and Albert Museum), and by various copies of Middleton's verses 'To the King' (for all which, see the separate discussion of the authenticity of those verses at p. 441). In 1631–2 the playwright William Heminges attributed to 'Middleton' a 'learned Excercise gaynst Gundomore' (presumably *Game*) in his 'Elegy on Randolph's Finger' (Steen, 55).

The play was performed from August 5 to August 14, 1624 (Howard-Hill 1991). Three significantly different versions of the work survive: an *Early* form, preserved in a manuscript now at the Folger Library (CRANE¹), an abridged reading text preserved in a manuscript now at the Bodleian Library (CRANE³, reproduced by Bawcutt 1993), and a lost playbook owned by the King's Men and signed and licensed by Herbert. (For details of these texts and their relationships, see the General Textual Introduction.) All these versions date from the year 1624. The only surviving witness to the abridged reading text contains a dedication by Middleton, describing it as a gift for 'the New-yeare' (i.e. 1 January 1625); there is no reason to believe that the abridgement predates the August performances. The title-page of the sole surviving copy of the *Early* form is dated 'August 13° Anno Dm 1624'. This is clearly the date of the transcription, not of the *Early* form itself; by August 13, the revised version of the play had been in performance for more than a week. The final version of the King's Men's playbook must have existed by August 4, at the latest; the *Early* form must have existed by June 12, at the latest.

Middleton cannot have completed the *Early* form before mid-May. One of his sources—the enlarged fourth edition of John Gee's *The Foot out of the Snare* (STC 11704)—was entered in the Stationers' Register on May 1. Another important source, Thomas Scott's *The Second Part of Vox Populi* (STC 22103) (1624), was not registered, but 'contains a letter dated May 3 which, even if it were a fiction, would have lacked plausibility if publication took place before that date. So the pamphlet was probably published *after* May 3' (Howard-Hill 1993, 18).

Beginning with Bald in 1943 (175), some scholars have conjectured that the text that Sir Henry Herbert licensed was the *Early* form, and did not include the major revisions performed in August. This conjecture directly contradicts the documentary evidence that the King's Men submitted the licensed book to the Privy Council. If so

conspicuous a part of the performed play as the Fat Bishop had not been licensed by Herbert, it is hard to understand why the actors thought they could get away with such an outrageous lie, or why their claims were accepted by the Privy Council. Against this documentary evidence there are allegedly 'weighty objections' (Howard-Hill 1995, 98). For convenience it will be best to number Howard-Hill's objections, and consider each separately.

1. '[T]here seems very little chance that Middleton could have completed the shorter version of the play, submitted it to the King's Men, and revised it with substantially new...material within the five-week period' between early May and June 12. There are two distinct issues here. One concerns the time-gap between completion of a play and its licensing. 'Middleton had to prepare a fair copy, the players must have read and discussed it, and time was required for Herbert's approval' (Howard-Hill 1993, 56). But Herbert probably read it the day he licensed it—which could have been the day he received it; Middleton (or someone else) could easily have made a fair copy in one day; actors typically read a new script over dinner. Theoretically, the fair copy could have been prepared on June 11, read and approved by the actors that evening, submitted to the Master of the Revels early on the morning of June 12, and approved by Herbert late that afternoon. Of course, this process may not have been completed that quickly; but it could have been, and we have no proof that it did not. The second issue is Middleton's own rate of composition. Howard-Hill himself concludes that Middleton wrote the entire play, in its first version, within 'about five weeks' (Howard-Hill 1995, 93). This is not implausible; Jonson publicly asserted that 'five weeks fully penned' *Volpone* (Prologue.16)—which is more than half again as long as the *Early* form of *A Game at Chess*. Five weeks for *Early* would require a rate of composition of 375 lines per week, or 53 lines a day. At that rate Middleton could easily have composed all the additions within six days. If Middleton wrote at Jonson's rate in composing *Volpone* (about 85 lines per day), Middleton could have completed *Early* in 22 days, and the revisions in another four. Hence, Howard-Hill's first objection cannot be accepted, because it depends upon unverifiable assumptions about Middleton's rate of composition and about the time required for licensing.

2. 'To make provision for [writing the additions before June 12] would push the beginning of composition back into March and raise the question of why Middleton did not use the first edition of Gee's *Foot out of the Snare*'. This objection depends upon the first; it has no merit in itself. Moreover, it assumes that Middleton could have done no work at all on the play before the publication of the enlarged edition of Gee. We know nothing about Middleton's writing process. The central political conceit of the play—that Charles and Buckingham went to Madrid in order to 'discover' or expose Spain's dissembling about the Spanish Match—reproduces Buckingham's February 'Account' to Parliament (Cogswell); the account was very

widely circulated in manuscript, and undoubtedly even more widely circulated orally by the 'St Paul's walkers' and others.

3. Assuming that the additions were written before June 12 'would leave the gaping gulf of June to August, when, it seemed, nothing much was happening.' But Howard-Hill himself notes that the gap between licensing and first performance was unpredictable. Moreover, MacIntyre demonstrates that 'white clothing was not much used either in the theater or in practical life', and that 'when the King's Men needed white costumes for Middleton's play, they probably had to have most of them made', specially tailored and usable for this play only (316–17). Costumes were always the most expensive capital outlay for a new play, and the King's Men would not have wanted to invest large sums of money in creating so many new and expensive costumes especially for this play until after the text had successfully passed through the censor's office (Taylor 2005, 133, 413).

4. 'And, more conclusively, it would make it quite difficult to explain why Crane was preparing a transcript...of the version that lacked one of the play's principal box-office attractions even during the run of the play.' But the revisions had undoubtedly been written before the first performance, on August 5; hence, the problem of explaining CRANE[1] remains, regardless of exactly when the revisions were composed.

5. 'Finally, it would make the curious relationships among [the printed quarto editions of 1625] and other Crane transcripts prepared before 1625 even less explicable than they now are.' In other words, completion of the revisions before June 12 creates problems for Howard-Hill's own stemmatic analysis of the relationships between the various surviving texts of the play. But it is not immediately apparent, or self-evident, that the exact date of the revisions—at some point between late May and late July—should affect the relationships between copies of the revised version of the play, all produced between August 1624 and May 1625. Again, this objection depends upon Howard-Hill's own conjectures; there is no documentary evidence to support it, and no logical necessity for such assumptions. (For objections, on quite other grounds, to Howard-Hill's stemma see the General Textual Introduction.)

In conclusion, these objections seem conjectural and unwarranted. If we accept the unchallenged testimony of the King's Men to the Privy Council, the version licensed by Herbert on 12 June was the version they performed. Middleton must have completed that version, including the added material concerning the Fat Bishop, by June 10 at the very latest. Even if the added material were written quickly, it probably took four to six days to complete. This would put completion of *Early* between June 4 and June 6, at the very latest. It thus seems likely that Middleton had finished *Early* by 31 May 1624, give or take a few days, and that the revisions were written within a week.

Gary Taylor

SEE ALSO

Text: *Works*, 1779 and 1830
General textual introduction: this volume, 712

WORKS CITED

Bawcutt, N. W., ed., *Ralph Crane's Transcript of 'A Game at Chess'*, Bodleian Manuscript Malone 25, in *Collections XV*, Malone Society (1993)
—— ed., *The Control and Censorship of Caroline Drama: The Records of Sir Henry Herbert, Master of the Revels 1623–73* (1996)
Cogswell, Thomas, 'Thomas Middleton and the Court, 1624: *A Game at Chess* in Context', *Huntington Library Quarterly* 47 (1984), 273–88
Howard-Hill, T. H., ed., *A Game at Chess by Thomas Middleton 1624*, Malone Society (1990)
—— 'The Unique Eye-Witness Report of Middleton's *A Game at Chess*', *Review of English Studies* 42 (1991), 168–78
—— ed., *A Game at Chess*, Revels Plays (1993)
—— *Middleton's 'Vulgar Pasquin': Essays on 'A Game at Chess'* (1995)
MacIntyre, Jean, *Costumes and Scripts in the Elizabethan Theaters* (1992)
Steen, Sara Jayne, *Ambrosia in an Earthern Vessel: Three Centuries of Audience and Reader Response to the Works of Thomas Middleton* (1993)
Taylor, Gary, *Buying Whiteness: Race, Culture, and Identity from Columbus to Hip Hop* (2005)

'To The King'   Autumn 1624

The poem is attributed to Middleton in Bodleian MS Rawlinson Poet. 152, f. 3 ('The petition of poet Midleton'), in an Inns of Court manuscript now at Meisei University, p. 62 ('Middletons Verses'), in a handwritten note on the title-page of a copy of the printed text of *A Game at Chess* now in the Dyce collection ('and the Poett Mr. Thomas Middleton...committed to prison where hee lay some Tyme and at last gott out upon this petition'), in a miscellany compiled by Sir Thomas Dawes, now British Library Add. MS 29492, f. 43 ('T.M.', below the last line). Tannenbaum, reproducing the Dyce copy, claimed it was a forgery, but he was unaware of the other copies; two of them were later transcribed by Wagner.

Gary Taylor

SEE ALSO

Text: *Works*, 1895
Textual introduction and apparatus: this volume, 992

WORKS CITED

Tannenbaum, Samuel A., 'A Middleton Forgery', *Philological Quarterly* 12 (1933), 33–6
Wagner, B. M., 'A Middleton Forgery', *Philological Quarterly* 14 (1935), 287–8

'Hammond'   December 1624

The only known copy of this poem is Middleton's autograph, and signed. No one has doubted the attribution.

Gary Taylor

SEE ALSO

Text: *Works*, 1896
Textual introduction and apparatus: this volume, 992

'Picture'   Spring 1625

The poem appears opposite the title-page of the first edition of *A Game at Chesse*, printed by Nicholas Okes in May 1625. Harper claimed that 'This poem is probably not by Middleton, for it appears to have been written by someone who was ignorant of chess and who was misled by the scene on the title page of Q1 and Q2 into misinterpreting the ending of the play' (96). The claim that the author 'was ignorant of chess' is presumably based on lines 5 (where 'check' is given to the White Knight) and 13 (where 'checkmate' is given to the Black Knight). This is dubious evidence of authorship. First of all, 'Knight' and 'King' are substituted for one another often in texts of *Game*, because Middleton regularly abbreviated the designations of chess pieces in a way scribes and compositors found confusing or ambiguous; he sometimes used 'K.' for 'Knight', and even when he wrote 'Kt.' it might easily be misread as 'K.' or 'Ki.' So the alleged authorial error might be only a compositorial error, encouraged by the prominence of 'the White Knight' and 'the Black Knight' on the engraved title-page. However, even this explanation is probably not necessary. In the play itself, Middleton imagines the characters not only as chess pieces, but as players, playing a game of chess against characters from the other side; this is especially true of his portrayal of the Black and White Knight. Moreover, as I argue in the Critical Introduction to 'A Later Form', the primary field of reference in the play was historical; chess was a secondary metaphor. Historically, as readers in 1625 knew, by going to Madrid Charles I had 'checkmated' the plans of Gondomar: by May 1625, that 'White Knight' had become a King. The alleged chess error, which Harper took as evidence that Middleton did not write the poem, is as deliberate as any of the play's violations of chess logic. It is relatively unlikely that anyone else wrote the frontispiece poem, especially because the quarto was printed, from what seems to have been an authorial manuscript, by Okes, with whom Middleton had often worked. (Harper was unaware of the identity of the printer.) Middleton is unique among playwrights of the period in his frequent use of illustrated title-pages (see 'The Order of Persons'). All these factors make it likely that Middleton supplied Okes not only with a manuscript of the play, but with ideas for an illustration, and a poem to accompany the engraving.

   Middleton's authorship is also suggested by the style of the poem—including its use of octosyllabic iambic couplets, as in *Macbeth*, *Gravesend*, etc. I note some verbal parallels below.

1–2   A game at chess...Between the Black and White House] 'A harmless game...by the Black House and White' ('To the King', 1–2; variants include 'Betwixt the Black House and the White'). The closest parallel in *Game* itself is 'A game at chess Betwixt our side and the White House' (Induction.42–3). This suggests that the author was more influenced by Middleton's poem 'To the King' than by the printed text of *Game*.

3   crown-thirsting policy] 'honest-profitable policy' *Plato* 142 (a compound adjective before the same noun)

5   check often gives] 'I give you check and mate to your white king' (*Women Beware* 2.2.304). Middleton does not use the idiom 'give check' in *Game*.

8   give the blow] 'give the fearful'st blow' *Game* 3.1.68; compare also 'blow you gave' *Changeling* 5.3.103, 'give your blow' *Valour* 1.1.116.

9   all their craft] all the craft *Game* 5.2.57

11   circumspective] Middleton uses 'circumspect' three times; also 'circumspection' (*Valour* 2.1.27) and 'circumspectly' (*Lady* 5.2.60)

11–12   prudency Gives checkmate] 'the prudent'st part to check' *Chaste Maid* 2.1.13

12   Gives checkmate by discovery] 'We give thee checkmate by discovery' *Game* 5.3.159; 'I gave him checkmate by discovery' *Game* 5.3.173.

17   Plain-dealing] *Plato* 354

18   Defeats the cheats] 'Cheated and defeated!' (*Mad World* 5.2.171)

18   cheats] Middleton uses the plural noun at *Roar* 10.264, *Weapons* 1.1.84, 2.1.34, and *Hengist* 5.1.238.

18   and pride] Middleton elsewhere uses this kind of doubling of abstract nouns, with pride as the second item, at *Truth* 328 'insolence and pride', *Quarrel* 2.1.116 'joy and pride', *Valour* 4.1.191 'scorn and pride', *Quiet Life* 5.1.263 'Envy and pride'; with pride as the first of such a pair, five times (including 'pride and falsehood' *Game* 5.3.218).

Gary Taylor

SEE ALSO

Text: *Works*, 1897
Textual introduction and apparatus: this volume, 992

WORK CITED

Harper, J. W., ed., *A Game at Chess* (1966)

Lost Pageant for Charles I
December 1625–April 1626

The 'Brief Account' in *Works* quotes all the relevant documents known to me. For attribution purposes the key document is the memorandum of 6 June 1626: 'Mr. Christmas and Mr. Middleton referring themselves to this Court, noe further moneys shalbe paid unto either of them, but that Mr. Christmas shall forthwith cause the said Pageants to bee taken downe, and to have the same for his full satisfaccon' (*Repertories of the Court of Aldermen* 40, f. 256).

Gary Taylor

SEE ALSO

Account: *Works*, 1898

WORKS CITED

Beaven, Alfred B., *The Aldermen of the City of London* (1908)

Bentley, G. E., *The Jacobean and Caroline Stage*, 7 vols (1941–68), 7:60 (masque)

Brenner, Robert, *Merchants and Revolution: Commercial Change, Political Conflict, and London's Overseas Traders, 1550–1653* (2003)

Calendar of State Papers Venetian, Volume 19: *1625–1626*, ed. Allen B. Hinds (1913), 31, 51, 89–90, 271, 294, 464

Chamberlain, John, *Letters*, ed. Norman McClure, 2 vols (1939)

Corporation of London, *Journal*, vol. 33, fol. 182; 34, fol. 159b, 163

Corporation of London, *Repertories of the Court of Aldermen*, vol. 37, fol. 240; vol. 39, fol. 172, 183b

Jackson, William A., 'Racan's *L'Artenice*, An Addition to the English Canon', *Harvard Library Bulletin* 14 (1970), 183–90

Mead, Joseph, British Library MSS Harleian MSS 389, 390 (letters to Sir Martin Stuteville)

Pearl, Valerie, *London and the Outbreak of the Puritan Revolution: City Government and National Politics, 1625–1643* (1961)

Weldon, Anthony, *The Court and Character of King James Whereunto is now added the Court of King Charles* (1651), 177

Williams, Sheila, 'The Lord Mayor's Show in Tudor and Stuart Times', *Guildhall Miscellany* 10 (1959), 1–18, citing (p. 11) 'Upon my Lord Majors day, being put off by reason of the Plague' from *Wit and Drollery* (1656), pp. 37–39

Withington, Robert, *English Pageantry: An Historical Outline*, vol. 1 (1918), 236

The Triumphs of Health and Prosperity
October 1626

The title-page indicates Middleton's authorship—'By Tho. Middleton, Gentleman'—but uncharacteristically does not provide the date of performance. It would have been the traditional day after Simon and Jude's day, 29 October. Although Middleton and Christmas eventually received a payment of £125 from the Drapers, the payment had been postponed 'in regard of the ill performance thereof'.

David M. Bergeron

SEE ALSO

Text: *Works*, 1903
Textual introduction and apparatus: this volume, 1010

Farrago
1626–7

The existence of this lost manuscript work was noted by the antiquary and editor William Oldys (1696–1761), in an undated manuscript note in a copy of Gerald Langbaine's *An Account of the English Dramatick Poets* (1691), now in the British Library (C.28.g.1). For a transcription and discussion of the authenticity of this document, see *Annales*, p. 438 above. The items listed by Oldys cover political events of 1625–7. The final item is 'Habeas Corpus 1627': the opening rounds of the historic Five Knights Case began in late June 1627, not long before Middleton's burial on 4 July 1627. Since Dyce in 1840 was the first scholar to identify the date of Middleton's death, this further confirms the authenticity of the Oldys note. Moreover, the earliest item ('Parliamentary Matters, 1625–26') would put the beginning of the manuscript in the period following *A Game at Chess* and Middleton's imprisonment, and during the same time as his work on the pageant for Charles I; the manuscript's interest in national politics certainly fits this period of Middleton's career.

Gary Taylor

SEE ALSO

Account: *Works*, 1909

The Conqueror's Custom; or, The Fair Prisoner
undated

For this work, see Feldmann and Tetzeli von Rosador, 'Lost Plays', in *Works*, 331.

The Puritan Maid, the Modest Wife, and the Wanton Widow
undated

For this work, see Feldmann and Tetzeli von Rosador, 'Lost Plays', in *Works*, 330.

A Right Woman
undated

For this work, see Feldmann and Tetzeli von Rosador, 'Lost Plays', in *Works*, 328.

WORKS EXCLUDED FROM THIS EDITION

MacDonald P. Jackson and Gary Taylor

Blurt Master Constable

Entered in the Stationers' Register on 7 June 1602 and published in a quarto of 1602 (*BEPD* 188), which left the play anonymous but claimed that it had been 'priuately acted by the Children of Paules'. It was ascribed to Middleton by Kirkman in his unreliable catalogue of 1661 (*BEPD* 761; see iii. 1341, item 74). Oliphant (1926), the first scholar to question this attribution, proposed Dekker as alternative candidate, and compelling evidence has since accumulated against Middleton's authorship and in favour of Dekker's. This is summarized by Lake (1975), Berger (1979), and Jackson (1979).

The Birth of Merlin

First published by Francis Kirkman and Henry Marsh in 1662 as 'Written by *William Shakespear* and *William Rowley*' (*BEPD* 822). Kirkman had already made this attribution in his play list of 1661 (*BEPD* 761; see iii. 1341, item 8). Dominik's thoroughly unsatisfactory case for accepting it is undermined by the recent realization that, under its alternative title *The Child Hath Found His Father*, *The Birth of Merlin* was licensed in 1622 as 'A New Play' to be acted by Prince Charles's Servants at the Curtain (Gunby). Although collaboration between Rowley and Shakespeare, who died in 1616, is thus ruled out, Rowley's revision of a script to which Shakespeare had contributed remains theoretically possible. But whereas Rowley's style is evident in the play, Shakespeare's is not. Rowley appears, however, to have had a collaborator who could write scenes and speeches of considerable power (Robb). Middleton is among playwrights who have been proposed. In her scholarly edition of the play, Udall summarizes the various theories. None has proved persuasive, and Jackson (1979) found the text notably lacking in Middleton markers.

The Captain

The play (*BEPD* 642) was first printed in the 1647 Beaumont and Fletcher folio. In his survey of authorship problems in that canon, Oliphant remarks 'that the first fifteen speeches of III.2 I would certainly give to Middleton were there positive signs of his presence elsewhere; but the only other scenes showing signs of him (and these not convincing) are the latter part of I.3 and IV.5. In each scene Fletcher is present and there is nothing in this Middleton-like work that may not be his' (165–6). Other scholars have not pursued this suggestion, but given Oliphant's extraordinary ability to identify Middleton's style it is worth recording.

The Copie of a Letter...concerning the proceeding at Winchester

The title-page of a 1603 quarto (STC 17151) claims that the letter was 'written from Master T. M. neere Salisbury, to Master H. A. at London'. Bald suggested that Middleton was the said T.M. (36). Eccles (1957) showed that the author was Thomas Moffatt, who lived near Salisbury (523–4).

The Family of Love

The famelie of loue Acted by the children of his Maiesties Reuells was published anonymously in 1608, in a quarto printed by Richard Bradock for John Helmes (STC 17879, *BEPD* 263); it had been entered in the Stationer's Register on 12 October 1607, 'as yt hath bene Lately acted by the Children of his Maiesties Reuelles' (Arber 3:360). It was first attributed to Middleton in Edward Archer's play-list (1656), which is notoriously unreliable (Greg). Nevertheless, Archer's attribution led Dyce to include it in his edition; Dyce was copied by Bullen, with the result that the play seemed securely attached to the Middleton canon, and was regarded as Middleton's by literary critics and reference works throughout the nineteenth and twentieth centuries. However, Oras demonstrated that the pattern of breaks in verse lines in *Family* did not fit any period of Middleton's career; both Lake and Jackson independently demonstrated that the linguistic pattern in the play differed radically and systematically from the pattern in Middleton's genuine work. Lake was unaware of the work of Oras and Jackson; to explain the anomalies in his own linguistic data, Lake conjectured that a very early Middleton play had subsequently been heavily revised by Lording Barry. But Taylor, Mulholland, and Jackson showed that the play could not have been written earlier than the second half of May, 1605; they also provided further evidence (in the pattern of contractions, oaths, and verbal parallels) for Barry's authorship of the entire play, and against Middleton's authorship of any part of it. Barry's only other known play, *Ram Alley* (1611)—STC 1502, BEPD 292—was written for the same minor theatre company, the Children of the King's Revels, with which Barry was financially associated (Gurr, 361–5; Bly; Kathman; Munro); Middleton had no known association with that company. The Prologue specifies that the play was written by a single author ('his' repeated three times);

this contradicts Eberle's conjecture that it was written collaboratively.

The Historie of Scotland...Done into English by T.M.

In some catalogues a 'Thomas Middleton' is credited with this translation, published in 1646, of a history 'during the minority of King James written in Latine by Robert Johnston' (Wing J880). The Preface, signed by 'T.M.' (sig. A4), quotes a text of '1639' (sig. A4) and between that date and the signature refers to 'my infant quil'. The initials might stand for a 'Thomas Middleton', but he cannot have been the playwright.

The Life of a Satyrical Puppy, Called Nim

This pamphlet, first published in 1657 by Humphrey Moseley (Wing M82A), is attributed on the title-page to 'T.M.', and the same initials sign the dedication to 'George Duke of Buckingham' (sig. A2ᵛ). An advertisement for 'Books Printed for Humphrey Moseley' lists, among 'Books I do purpose to Print very speedily', this very title (no. 226), attributing it to 'W.D'. However, mistakes much more often occur in advertisements than in prefaces, and the advertisement by its own testimony precedes the printing of the pamphlet; hence, if anything Moseley corrected what he regarded as his mistaken attribution to 'W.D.' It is hard to see why 'T.M.' would sell more copies than 'W.D.' The pamphlet is occasionally attributed to Thomas May, but Gibson demonstrated that it cannot have been written by May, that its topical references situate it clearly in the mid-1620s, and that the dedication must therefore address the first Duke of Buckingham, George Villiers, raised to the dukedom in 1623 and assassinated in 1628; finally, she suggests that 'T.M.' might have been Middleton (298–306). Her suggestion has been repeated by McRae (29–30). Certainly, the pamphlet's lively and precise satire of London life might suggest Middleton, and if he was forbidden to write plays after A Game at Chess he might have tried his hand at satire and sought patronage from Buckingham, on the grounds that the Duke would have approved of the politics of the banned play. Moreover, Buckingham remained popular through 1624 and most of 1625. It is difficult to be sure what a picaresque proto-novel written by Middleton at the end of his life would sound like, but the narrative better fits the experience of William Davenant than Middleton. Like the narrator, Davenant moved as a young man from the provinces to London, arriving in 1622, and he was immediately connected to court circles, first in the household of Frances Howard, then that of Fulke Greville. The unusual spelling 'scituation' (78) occurs five times in Davenant, who is also much more likely than Middleton to have written (p. 45) 'Patience: that Rose-lip'd Cherubim' (with its obvious echo of Othello's 'Patience, that young and rose-lipped Cherubim'), immediately followed by 'infant morn' (with its echo of Richard III). Searching LION for rare phrases that link the Life to anybody living within the period 1550–1650, we have found a conspicuous absence of

verbal links to Middleton. The strongest unique parallel we have noticed is 'she seems an intire Scabbe; a great proportionable Boyle' (p. 85), which remarkably resembles 'thou appear'st Like an intire proportionable Boyle' (again of a woman) in Davenant's The Cruel Brother (printed 1630, written 1627). Life's use of connectives is absolutely consistent: they are always 'whilst' (29 times), 'between' (11, plus 1 ''tween'), 'amongst' (5), 'towards' (7), and 'besides' (20). By contrast, Middleton uses the alternatives 'whilst' and 'while' and 'between' and 'betwixt' in about equal numbers (Lake, Table I.1, Band 2(d), Band 2 Segment 2 for plays, p. 273 for non-dramatic texts), and his non-dramatic works show a preference for 'betwixt'. He prefers 'amongst' and 'beside', and has a very strong preference for 'toward'. The many parentheses are also atypical of Middleton. Although scribal or compositorial interference cannot be ruled out, we have found no positive internal evidence for Middleton, in linguistic preferences or spellings or phrasing, to counteract this negative stylistic evidence. Davenant seems a likelier candidate.

A Match at Midnight

Entered in the Stationers' Register on 15 January 1633 and published in that year as 'Acted by the Children of the Revells. Written by W. R.' (BEPD 476). In his play list of 1656, the unreliable Archer expanded the initials to 'William Rowley', to whom the play has usually been credited (BEPD 766; see iii. 1335, item 401). However, several scholars, beginning with Fleay, have supposed that Rowley collaborated with Middleton or revised a script originally by him (Chambers). The matter has since become complicated by doubts whether Rowley had anything to do with the play. Robb regarded it as entirely Rowley's, but Hoy's linguistic evidence challenged this ascription. Hoy noted in particular that the rate of usage of ye is much higher than in any writing that can more confidently be assigned to Rowley. Young, who surveys and evaluates evidence for the play's authorship in his edition of A Match at Midnight, concludes that probably neither Rowley nor Middleton had a hand in it. The pattern of contracted and colloquial forms and the choice of expletives are difficult to reconcile with an ascription to Rowley, Middleton, or the two playwrights in collaboration.

Pimlico; or Run, Red-Cap

Entered in the Stationers' Register on 15 April 1609 and published anonymously in the same year (STC 19936). The poem is a lively celebration of the London place of resort, Pimlico, and the ale of that name. Pimlico Gardens were not in the present Pimlico but in Hogsdon, now Hoxton. The writer is thoroughly familiar with London, knowledgeable about his English literary predecessors, is interested in the theatre of his time, and has a sharp satirical wit. In this pamphlet he interpolates John Skelton's The Tunning of Eleanor Rumming within his own poem. He alludes to the popularity of Shakespeare and Wilkins's Pericles. Some phrases call Middleton to mind, but there are more striking links to other city playwrights and poets, such as Ben Jonson and Thomas Dekker. The large number of parentheses and the absence of Middletonian contractions tell against Middleton's authorship.

The Second Part of the Honest Whore

Entered in the Stationers' Register on 29 April 1608 and again on 29 June 1630, the second time with an ascription to Thomas Dekker, which was repeated on the title-page of 1630 quarto, when the play first reached print (*BEPD* 435). There is no external evidence connecting Middleton to this Second Part, as opposed to the First Part, of *The Honest Whore*, and while Lake (1975) and Jackson (1979) found ample evidence of Dekker's hand throughout, they detected no signs of Middleton's.

The True Narration of the Entertainment of His Royal Majesty

Printed by Thomas Creede for Thomas Millington in a quarto of 1603, having been entered in the Stationers' Register on 9 May of that year (STC 17153). The dedication 'To the Reader' is signed 'T. M.' Eccles suggested that the initials were Middleton's. Lake, examining the connectives, showed that the strong preferences for *besides* and *towards* over *beside* and *toward* were unparalleled in Middleton's non-dramatic works or early plays and added: 'nor are there any spellings in *Narration* which point to Middleton'. In view of the absence of features that distinguish other pamphlets as Middleton's, it seems likely that 'T. M.' is the publisher Thomas Millington.

The Witch of Edmonton

The play was written between 21 April and 29 December 1621 (Hoy 3: 233). The title-page of the 1658 first edition (Wing R2097) claims that the play was 'composed into a tragi-comedy by divers well-esteemed poets, *William Rowley, Thomas Dekker, John Ford*, &c.' Scholars interested in attribution problems have generally ignored the '&c', and focused their attention on assigning scenes to Rowley, Dekker, or Ford. Hoy, for instance, repeatedly refers to the play's 'trio of authors', as though the 'etcetera' did not exist. But the external evidence clearly establishes the presence of at least one, possibly two, other collaborators. The three named authors collaborated with Webster on *Keep the Window Waking* in 1624, and the same three apparently collaborated with Middleton on *The Spanish Gypsy* in 1623. Middleton, Ford, and Rowley all wrote commendatory poems for Webster's *Duchess of Malfi* in 1623; Middleton and Webster collaborated on *Anything for a Quiet Life* in 1621, and of course Rowley often collaborated with Middleton between 1613 and 1623. Thus, the title-page '&c.' might well refer to Middleton, or Webster, or both. Although Middleton would never be mistaken for Ford, in individual scenes or speeches—especially in prose—he can sometimes be difficult to distinguish from Dekker, Rowley, or Webster. In general, the smaller the

sample size, and the longer the chronological gap between original composition and first edition, the more difficult it is to prove the presence of Middleton, or any other collaborator, on the basis of internal evidence alone. It might be possible to resolve this problem through a systematic analysis of verbal parallels, using comprehensive online databases, but we have not attempted this. Nevertheless, *Edmonton* is one of the more plausible candidates for further investigation.

WORKS CITED

Arber, Edward, ed., *A Transcript of the Registers of the Worshipful Company of Stationers, 1554-1640* (1857)

Bald, R. C., 'The Chronology of Middleton's Plays', *Modern Language Review* 32 (1937), 33-43

Berger, Thomas Leland, ed., *A Critical Old-Spelling Edition of Thomas Dekker's 'Blurt, Master Constable' (1602)* (1979)

Bly, Mary, *Queer Virgins and Virgin Queens on the Early Modern Stage* (2000)

Chambers, E. K., *The Elizabethan Stage*, 4 vols (1923)

Dominik, Mark, *William Shakespeare and 'The Birth of Merlin'* (1985)

Eberle, Gerald J., 'Dekker's Part in *The Family of Love*', in *Joseph Quincy Adams Memorial Studies*, ed. James G. McManaway *et al.* (1948), 723-38

Eccles, Mark, '"Thomas Middleton a Poett"', *Studies in Philology* 54 (1957), 516-36

Gibson, Leonie J., 'Formal Satire in the First Half of the Seventeenth Century, 1600-1650', unpublished DPhil, Oxford (1952)

Greg, W. W., 'Authorship Attributions in the Early Play-lists', *Edinburgh Bibliographical Society Transactions* 2 (1946), 305-26

Gunby, David, 'Rowley, William (1585?-1626)', *Oxford Dictionary of National Biography*, ed. H. C. G. Matthew and Brian Harrison, 60 vols (2004), 48.25-27

Gurr, Andrew, *The Shakespearian Playing Companies* (1996)

Hoy, Cyrus, *Introductions, Notes, and Commentaries to texts in 'The Dramatic Works of Thomas Dekker'*, 4 vols (1980)

—— 'The Shares of Fletcher and his Collaborators in the Beaumont and Fletcher Canon (V)', *Studies in Bibliography* 13 (1960), 77-108

Kathman, David, 'Lording Barry', *Oxford Dictionary of National Biography* (2004)

McRae, Andrew, *Literature, Satire and the Early Stuart State* (2004)

Munro, Lucy, *The Children of the Queen's Revels: A Jacobean Theatre Repertory* (2005)

Oliphant, E. H. C., 'The Authorship of *The Revenger's Tragedy*', *Studies in Philology* 23 (1926), 157-68

—— *The Plays of Beaumont and Fletcher: an attempt to determine their respective shares and the shares of others* (1927)

Oras, Ants, *Pause Patterns in Elizabethan and Jacobean Drama* (1960)

Robb, Dewar M., 'The Canon of William Rowley's Plays', *Modern Language Review* 45 (1950), 129-41

Taylor, Gary, Paul Mulholland and MacD. P. Jackson, 'Thomas Middleton, Lording Barry, and *The Family of Love*', *Papers of the Bibliographical Society of America* 93 (1999), 213-41

Udall, Joanna, ed., *A Critical, Old-Spelling Edition of 'The Birth of Merlin' Q 1662* (1991)

Young, Stephen Blase, ed., *A Critical Old-Spelling Edition of 'A Match at Midnight'* (1980)

PART III: THE TEXTS

THOMAS MIDDLETON: LIVES AND AFTERLIVES

Gary Taylor

I. Survey of Sources

'Thomas Middleton: Lives and Afterlives' draws upon a tradition of scholarship that was a century and a half old when I began my own research. The first scholarly biography was that in Alexander Dyce's 'Some account of Middleton and his works', in his edition of *The Works of Thomas Middleton*, 5 vols (1840), I, ix–lvii. Almost a century elapsed before the next significant compilation of new material. Mark Eccles—in 'Middleton's Birth and Education', *Review of English Studies*, 7 (1931), 431–41—established the date of Middleton's birth and his immediate family connections. Further details of the life were published in: J. Q. Adams, ed., *The Ghost of Lucrece* (1937); Mildred G. Christian, 'A sidelight on the family history of Thomas Middleton', *Studies in Philology* 44 (1947), 490–6; David George, 'Thomas Middleton at Oxford', *Modern Language Review* 65 (1970), 734–6; P. G. Phialas, 'Middleton's Early Contact with the Law', *Studies in Philology* 52 (1955), 186–94; S. Schoenbaum, 'A New Middleton Record', *Modern Language Review* 55 (1960), 82–4. The most important twentieth-century synthesis of known and new material was produced by Mark Eccles: '"Thomas Middleton a Poett"', *Studies in Philology* 54 (1957), 516–36. My own Middleton entry in *The Oxford Dictionary of National Biography* (2004) takes account of these sources, and others described below, but it does so within the necessarily restricted space and generic restrictions of a dictionary entry. Most of the biographical facts in 'Lives and Afterlives', and most of the primary manuscript sources listed below, were first identified in these earlier sources. However, I have been able to add a few details to the record. (See also Seaver, below.)

Like Eccles in 1931 and 1960, in 2004 I overlooked W. M. Myddleton's edition of *Chirk Castle accounts, AD 1605–1666* (1908); the records there of Sir Thomas Myddleton (b. 1586) include the note 'Given Mr. Myddleton the Poet o 10 o' [=10 shillings]. This note (p. 12) is not dated, but it occurs between 'At London Novem. 1613' (p.11) and 'To Mr. Tymothie for Mich. quarter ... 5 o o' (p. 12, i.e. 5 pounds). Hence the gift to the poet seems to belong to November 1613, soon after performance and publication of *Triumphs of Truth*.

Eccles (1931) first identified Middleton's baptismal record, and his parents, in the parish records of St Lawrence Jewry, now in the Guildhall. These records have since been published in an edition by Clarke (1940), which facilitates a systematic examination of the parish population, and a clearer reconstitution of the Middleton family. The parish recorded the marriage of a 'William Midleton' to 'Margrett

Barwicke' on 21 November 1563; one 'Margarett Middleton' died on 17 August 1570, and another on 11 February 1572. There was apparently more than one Margaret Middleton; one might have been the child of Robert or George Middleton, and the other was probably the Margaret who had married William Middleton in 1563. But there is no evidence of any other William Middleton in the parish between 1552 (when a mercer of that name died) and 1676; the William married in 1563 was widowed by 1572, and Thomas's father William was married in 1574 (to a woman in her mid-thirties). Since Thomas's father William acquired a coat of arms in 1568, he was certainly twenty-one by 1568, and probably older. So his marriage to Margaret in 1563 is plausible chronologically, and if he was first married in 1563 his second marriage was to a woman not conspicuously (if at all) older than himself. It therefore seems likely that the same William Middleton married Margaret Barwicke in 1563 and Anne Snowe in 1574.

There were in 1563 two women in the parish named Margaret Barwicke. One was married (on 3 November 1554) to William Barwicke; one was William's eldest daughter (baptized six days after the marriage, on 9 November 1554). In the plague of 1563, William Barwick died (24 September), followed by Mary (25 September), Margaret and Cicely (11 October), and Susan (18 October), thus wiping out the entire family, except for one surviving Margaret, the widow (and heir), who married William Middleton two months later.

Thomas and Avis were the only children of William Middleton alive in January 1586, when he died; but he might have fathered other children who predeceased him. Eccles (1931) regarded Bridgett Middleton (baptized 3 April 1575, buried 27 May 1576) as a daughter of Anne and William; but he did not note that Elizabeth Middleton (baptized 11 April 1577, buried 12 January 1581) might also have belonged to the same family.

I have discovered a new document about William Middleton, recording a dispute between him and the Bricklayers, which resulted in his immediate elevation to the livery of the company and subsequent election as Warden. The dispute was adjudicated by the Court of Aldermen, and their judgement is recorded in Repertory 19, fol. 169–169^v, 5 February Elizabeth 19: 'item yt was orderyd and decreyd by this Co^{r}te, that the M^r and Wardens of the Company of the Brycklayers shall forthwth receyue Wyllm̄ Myddleton Brycklayer into the liuery of their sayd company, and that the sayd Myddleton shall haue and enioye as many appntyzes as any other pson of the sayd lyuery, not hauinge byne Wardyne of the sayd company nowe hathe and enioyethe. And the sayd M^r and Wardens of the Company of the Brycklayers psente here in this Co^rte, dyd faythfully promyse to the same, that they wth thassente of their sayd lyuery wolde at the next ellecon of newe Wardens of their sayd companye nomynate ellecte and chuse the sayd Willm Middleton to be one of their sayd Wardens, and that then the sayd Mydleton shall haue and take as many apptizes as any other pson wch hathe byne Warden of the same company, W^ch promise the sayd M^r. and Wardens were by this Co^rte, strongly charged and commandyd to obserue'. Unfortunately this record gives no indication of the basis for the dispute or for the ruling in Middleton's favour.

The Bricklayers were one of the poorest London companies—or, at the very least, were perceived to be so. Although Eccles had noted the 1582 assessment of William Middleton's wealth, the publication of a transcription of the entire subsidy roll has made it possible to contextualize Middleton's standing among members of his own parish (Lang, 190, 211), and the status of the Bricklayers among London companies (Lang, Table II, p. lxxi). In 1582 the Goldsmiths were ranked by the assessors at the top of all the London guilds (assessed for 10 pounds); seventeen other companies were assessed between 6 pounds 8 shillings (Fishmongers) and one pound (Cordwainers). The Tylers & Bricklayers are thirty-fifth in the list (5 shillings 4 pence). Notably for historians of textual culture, the Scriveners are twenty-fifth in the list (13 shillings 4 pence), assessed at more than twice the wealth of the Stationers, who are thirty-first (6 shillings 8 pence). 'There is no time at which London valuations for the subsidy can be taken as representing actual worth in goods or income, or even as an index of actual wealth. They can probably be taken as an indication of wealth rank order as that was widely perceived' (Lang, li).

I have not been able to identify the gentry family to which William Middleton allegedly belonged, despite an examination of all the pedigrees and coats of arms listed in Sims; some arms are similar, but none identical, and no pedigree includes an appropriate William. Nor have I been able to identify which of the Palmer families of Warwickshire Barbara Palmer (Edward Marbecke's wife, and Middleton's mother-in-law) belonged to. However, the 1623 Middleton genealogy (College of Arms C.2, 328^v) does contain the coat of arms of 'Morbeck and Palmer' (reproduced on p. 120 of this Companion); that coat of arms also appears, separated from the Middleton genealogy, in Harleian MS 1433 (fol. 196^v).

I have, however, learned more about Edward Marbecke, Middleton's father-in-law. There is no evidence of his attendance at Oxford, Cambridge, or the Inns of Court; he probably rose to Six Clerk by being promoted from within, a career pattern common enough in the Tudor Chancery (Prest 1981). He is not listed in Hardy, who identifies known Six Clerks from 1545 to 1842 (pp. 106–9); however, records of such officers are spotty for the

sixteenth century. He appears five times in the parish registers of St Dunstan's in the West from 1571 to 1577; but neither he nor any other Marbecke appears there from 1580 to 1623. It is clear that many Chancery officials lived in this parish: the register records the burials of 'Thomas Pole one of the six clerks of the chancery' (27 July 1601), 'Raph Buckley a clerke of the Chancery' (27 October 1601), 'Richard Melson gent and a clerk in the Chancery' (1 February 1603), 'Anne Andrews ... out of the house of the Six Clarkes' (3 October 1603), 'William Yerley gent. clarke of the Chancery' (21 June 1604), 'Roger Gill clerk of the Chancery' (6 July 1604), 'Thomas Madox gent and clerke in the Chancery' (28 February 1607), 'Edward Bishopp a Clerke in the Chancerie' (18 December 1609), 'John Torr gent. a Clerke of the Chancery' (4 December 1611). No record of Marbecke's burial is recorded there, but Marbecke was dead by 1581 (Fitch, 276). 'Barbara Marbeck' is identified as the 'relic' of 'Edwardus Marbecke' of St Dunstan in the West on 16 December 1581 in the testamentary records of the Commissary Court of London (Guildhall MS 9168.13, 248^v). This means that Edward Marbeck died when his daughter Mary/Magdalen was about six, long before Middleton met and married her. I have discovered nothing further about Barbara Palmer.

I have found one tantalizing suggestion, which may be a ghost, of the date of Middleton's marriage. In the online genealogical database of the Church of Latter Day Saints, a query about the marriage of Thomas Middleton, in England at any time between 1601 and 1605, produced the record '1602, London, married Mary Madelen Morbecke, b. 1582'. The name 'Morbecke' is an acceptable alternative spelling of 'Marbecke'. Before Eccles (1960), scholars had assumed that Middleton was married twice, first to Mary, then later to Magdalen; Eccles proposed that he married only once, to a woman named 'Magdalen', and that 'Maria' was a scribal mistake for 'Magdalena' (536). I had proposed 'Mary Magdalen' as his wife's name in drafts of 'Lives and Afterlives' as early as 1994, but had not published that conjecture. I have, unfortunately, been unable to trace the source of the information in the genealogical database, which I discovered only shortly before The Collected Works went to press. If verified, it would mean that Mary Magdalen was born a few months after the death of her father, and that she must have been baptized somewhere other than the parish of St Dunstan in the West. The record would also confirm my own suggestion that her full name was 'Mary Magdalen'. The record gives no indication of Middleton's own date of birth, which suggests that whoever was responsible for entering this information in the database was unaware of scholarship on the poet.

Another record which may or may not refer to the poet is recorded in Surrey Wills (Archdeaconry Court, Herringman Register), Surrey Record Society, Vol. IV (1920), p. 203 (fol. 467, item 880): among the 'Debtors' listed in the will of 'Ralphe Mower of Wiphurt, in the par. of Cranly, yeoman' (proved 5 April 1604) was 'Mʳ Midleton'.

It may help future investigators to know that the few surviving records of the Surrey Quarter Sessions—now located in the Surrey Record Office (Kingston upon Thames) and in the More–Molyneaux Collection of the Guildford Muniment Room—do not contain any material relevant to Middleton.

Heinemann claimed that Middleton was a 'Puritan', a biographical assertion based in part on claims about his personal associations and patrons; the details have been more thoroughly investigated by Bawcutt, who challenges much of her evidence. My own view is that Middleton was a life-long Calvinist, but not a 'Puritan'; like many other mainstream Calvinists—including George Abbot—he found himself increasingly opposed to the foreign and ecclesiastical policies of the Stuarts in the 1620s (Taylor 1994, 2001). In at least one other detail Heinemann is demonstrably wrong: she states that Middleton 'was admitted to membership of the Drapers' Company by redemption' in 1626 (169). The Archivist of the Drapers' Company, Penelope Fussell, confirms (letter of 7 December 1993) that a 'Thomas Middleton' was admitted on 10 January 1626, but the Thomas in question was the son of Richard Middleton (d. 1624) of the parish of St Michael Cornhill; he was baptized in that parish on 9 July 1597, and married 'Clare Avere' there on 1 February 1626. Clearly, he was not the playwright.

Less clearly, guild records cast doubt on the identification of Allen Waterer as a clothworker. Various records cited by Eccles (1931) identified him as such, and a check of the documents confirms his transcriptions: 'Item Allyn Waterer Cloth Worker and Avice his wife daughter and Orphan of William Middleton Brickleyer' (CLRO Repertory 24, fol. 267ᵛ, 3 August 1598) 'Allanes Waterer Civis et Clothworker London' (Journal 24, fol. 322ʳ). Nevertheless, the Archivist of the Clothworkers' Company, Dr E. Wickham, conducted three searches of the records from 1575–1605, and for family connections searched 'the lists of Freeman from 1528, when the Clothworkers' records begin, to 1605; no-one surnamed Waterer appears, nor anything remotely phonetically similar, appears … My argument has to be that the Clothworker records imply that he was not a Freeman…. We believe that the Clothworker records *are* absolutely complete for the period but I cannot insist that this is so' (4 February 1994).

For Newington in Middleton's lifetime I have drawn upon Aubrey (5:132–54), Johnson (114–18), and Darlington (65, 81–94, 127–8). Earlier scholars had cited Middleton's tax payments in the 1620s, but I have re--examined the rolls for information about his exact location (Blackman Street) and wealth relative to his neighbours. The Newington parish records have been examined by previous Middleton scholars; they contain no additional information about Thomas Middleton or his descendants, but I have applied the statistical methods of Wrigley and Schofield to the birth and death rates in order to calculate the probable population of the parish. Other evidence

suggests that his son Edward did continue to live in Newington after the death of both his parents. The published index of Surrey probate records includes 'Edward Middleton of Newington, gent. [PRO: PCC 1649]' (Webb 345). I have not found this record, but PCC 1647 Fines, fol. 135b, does contain what appears to be his will [proved 25 November 1647 by Edmond Browne]:

> I Edward Middleton of Newington Butts in ye County of Surry gent being sound of minde and of body doe nominate and appoint this my last will and testament that is to say: First I bequeath vnto my loving frend Elizabeth Browne wyfe of Edmond Browne five poundₑ to buy her mourning after my decease Item I giue and bequeath to Edward Browne youngest sonne of ye sayd Edmond ten poundₑ … Item I giue to the poore of Newington aforesaid one pound Item I giue and bequeath to the poore of the parish of Lambeth ten shillings All the rest of my goodₑ & chattels both real & psonall I giue & bequeath to my trusty & welbeloved frend Edmond Browne of the pish of Thorpe in the County of Surrey whome I ordayne my sole executor of this my will … In witnes wherof I haue hereunto sett my hand & seale the vijth day of Aprill, 1645. Ed. Middleton

Middleton's son was a gentleman named Edward, living in Newington in the 1620s, and I have found no one else of the name who fits these facts. Unfortunately, the will, if his, identifies no members of his own family. Theoretically, 'Elizabeth Brown' might be his daughter, and 'frend' might be used of a near relation (*OED n.* 3), but in the circumstances one would expect—and a biographer would certainly prefer—the more specific 'daughter' or 'sister'. This record suggests that Edward died unmarried and childless. I once believed that Edward had a son, because a gentleman named Richard Middleton with the same coat of arms was living in the adjoining parish of St Saviour's in 1662 (Add. MS 5533, fol. 151ᵛ). That manuscript, a copy of the 1662 Visitation of Surrey, attaches 'Richard Middleton' to the same coat of arms as William, Thomas, and Edward, but it does not give him a crest or a genealogy. But the original of the 1662 Visitation, now in the College of Arms (D.15, fol. 93), does give his genealogy, and demonstrates conclusively that he is not a descendant of either Edward or Thomas. He might be a distant cousin, because the genealogy goes back to a 'William Middleton of Sussex' in the fourth generation (which would be the same generation as the father of Thomas). The 1568 grant to William claimed that he had 'ben of longe time one of the bearers of these Armes', but the herald could 'finde no Creaste therevnto belonging or appertayninge', and hence assigned the 'Ape passant' (Vincent 162, fol. 215, transcribed in its entirety by Dyce, 1:ix–xii). It may therefore be significant that the genealogy of Richard Middleton in 1662 has the coat of arms, but not the crest; perhaps 'William Middleton of Sussex' was the father of William Middleton the bricklayer. The exact nature of the connection must remain speculative. What is now certain is that the Richard Middleton of 1662 was not Edward's son or heir. Thomas Middleton's last direct (legitimate) descendant seems to have died between 1645 and 1647.

Various manuscripts of 'To the King' claim that Middleton was imprisoned 'in the Fleet', i.e. the Fleet Prison. Unfortunately, commitment lists for the Fleet Prison, held in the Public Record Office (ref PRIS1) do not begin until 1685. One miscellaneous series (PRIS10) contains material dating from 1628. Therefore, the claim cannot be independently verified. However, critics of James I were regularly imprisoned in the Fleet in the 1620s (Howard-Hill 79–80).

The little existing scholarship on Middleton's reputation has been limited to accounts of single works (usually in editions) or confused by uncertainties over the canon. For an overlooked early allusion to *Hengist*, which links Middleton and Shakespeare, see Munro. For the importance of the first generation after the death of an artist to the subsequent history of his or her reputation, see Lang and Lang, and Taylor 1996. Steen (1993)—the first comprehensive survey, and very useful—is unfortunately based on the Dyce canon.

Likewise, Bentley's account (1943) of the 1,686 quotations in Cotgrave (1655) defines the Middleton canon by Bullen's edition. Bentley, on that basis, identifies 78 quotations from Middleton. I have subtracted from his total seven quotations from *The Family of Love*, but added *Nice Valour* (1), *Wit at Several Weapons* (1), *The Bloody Banquet* (8), '*1 Honest Whore*' (1), *The Puritan Widow* (7), *Timon of Athens* (11), and *The Revenger's Tragedy* (25), giving Middleton a total of 116. This figure is surpassed only by Shakespeare (for whom I count 149, subtracting seven from *The Puritan* but adding two from *The Two Noble Kinsmen*); the nearest rival is 'Beaumont and Fletcher', with 112. However, Bentley counts quotations from collaborative works under the names of both collaborators. If, according to Bentley's rule, we count the eleven quotations from *Timon of Athens*, four from *Macbeth*, and ten from *Measure for Measure* in both canons, Middleton's total would be raised to 141. Moreover, Bentley's figures, and the preceding calculations, are based entirely on quotations whose authors or play titles are named by the manuscript annotator of Cotgrave. Those annotations do not distinguish between the two parts of *Honest Whore*; I have checked them all, and identified eleven in *Part One*, which should therefore be added to Middleton's total, raising it to 152. I have also checked all unattributed quotations by looking for their key words in Literature Online. I hope to publish the full record in future, but here will limit myself to the most frequently quoted playwrights, Middleton and Shakespeare. This electronic search has identified seventeen additional Middleton quotations, from *Bloody Banquet* (pp. 144, 225, 257, 291), *Mad World* (309), *Phoenix* (23), *Puritan* (233), *Revenger* (57, 122, 281, 304), *Roaring Girl* (64, 79, 82, 120, 176),

and *Valour* (216), but only eight additional Shakespeare quotations, from *All's Well* (278), *Cymbeline* (74), *Hamlet* (199), *Pericles* (285), *Tempest* (224), *Troilus* (103, 226), *Twelfth Night* (94). The annotators were better at attributing Shakespeare quotations, which is not surprising, given the fact that almost all of them came from a single book, the *Comedies, Histories, and Tragedies*, probably in its 1663–4 edition. The full record of Cotgrave's selections would thus, according to Bentley's rules, put Middleton in first place, based on 169 entries (10 per cent of all citations), with Shakespeare a close second, with 157. If we assigned Middleton's adaptations of Shakespeare entirely to the original dramatist, Shakespeare would take first place (157), with Middleton an even closer second (155). However, it should also be noted that all thirty-eight Shakespeare plays were in print in the 1630s, and Cotgrave quoted twenty-seven of them, including twenty-five from the folio; by contrast, Middleton's plays were scattered in individual quartos, and Cotgrave does not quote *Trick*, *Yorkshire*, or *Your Five Gallants*, probably because they had long been out of print. Bentley notes that Cotgrave cited only one play printed between 1650 and 1655; if we take 1650 as the effective cut-off date, then *Changeling*, *Spanish Gypsy*, and *Widow* were unavailable. Certainly, Cotgrave's anthology was published before the printing of *Women, Beware Women, More Dissemblers, No Wit, Old Law, Quiet Life, Witch*, and *Lady*. Cotgrave nevertheless quotes seventeen plays from the Middleton canon (including the three that overlap with the Shakespeare canon). If we assign Middleton's two Shakespeare adaptations entirely to the original writer, then about twice as many Shakespeare plays were available to Cotgrave.

II. PRIMARY SOURCES: MANUSCRIPT

Published Transcriptions

Bannerman, W. Bruce, ed., *The Visitations of the County of Surrey, Made and taken in the years…1623* (1899)

Clark, Andrew, ed., *Register of the University of Oxford*, vol. II, *1571–1622* (1888)

Clarke, A. W. Hughes, ed., *The Register of St Lawrence Jewry. London, 1583–1676*, Part I, Harleian Soc. Publ., 70 (1940)

Gordon, D. J., and J. Robertson, *A Calendar of Dramatic Records in the Books of the Livery Companies of London 1485–1640*, Malone Society Collections III (1954)

Henslowe's Diary, ed. R. A. Foakes and R. T. Rickert (1961)

Historical Manuscripts Commission, *The Manuscripts and Correspondence of James, First Earl of Charlemont*, 12th Report, Appendix, Pt. X, 2 vols (1891)

Lang, R. G., ed., *Two Tudor subsidy assessment rolls for the City of London: 1541 and 1582*, London Record Society no 29 (1993)

Leishman, J. B., ed., *The Three Parnassus Plays (1598–1601)* (1949)

Overall, W. H. and H. C., eds., *Remembrancia: Analytical Index to the Series of Records Known as the Remembrancia 1579–1664* (1878)

Bodleian Library

Wood E.5
Gough Oxon. 16

British Library

Additional MS 4963, fol. 171 (1623 genealogy, copy)
Additional MS 5533, fol. 151^v (Richard Middleton arms, 1662)
Harleian 1046, fol. 203 (1623 genealogy, copy)
Harleian 1397, fol. 174 (1623 genealogy, copy)
Harleian 1433, fol. 126 (1623 genealogy, copy) and fol. 196^v
   (Morbecke and Palmer arms)
Harleian 1441, fol. 88 (William Middleton grant, English copy)
Harleian 1561, fol. 213^v (1623 genealogy, copy)

Clothworkers' Hall

CM: Court Orders I–III 1536–1605
RF: Register of Freemen I 1545–1661
WA: Renter and Quarter Wardens' Accounts I–IV 1528–1613

College of Arms

Vincent 162, fol. 215 (William Middleton grant, 23 April 1568)
C.2, Visitation of Surrey, 1623, fol. 328^v (genealogy, Latin
   original)
D.15, Visitation of Surrey, 1662, fol. 93 (Richard Middleton
   genealogy and arms)

Guildhall

Commissary Court of London

MS 9168.13, fol. 248^v (Edward Marbecke)
MS 9171.17, fol. 4, 10 February 1586 (William Middleton's will)

Cutlers

MS 7147 I Wardens Account Books (1586–1621)
MS 7159 I–II Register of Apprentice Bindings (1575–1627)

Grocers

MS 11,571 I–X Wardens' Accounts (1454–1622)
MS 11,588 I–II Court Minute Books (1556–1616)

Tylers and Bricklayers

MS 3043 I Court Minutes (1580–1667)
MS 3054 I Masters and Wardens' Accounts (1606–31)

Parish Registers

MS 6974 St Lawrence Jewry
MS 10342 St Dunstan's in the West
MS 17602 St Dioniss

Local History Library, London Borough of Southwark

Southwark Archives 1032, 1033 (vestry minutes, St Mary's
   Newington)

London Metropolitan Archives

Archdeaconry of London

Act Book 3, fol. 187 (Allen Waterer estate)

Corporation of London, Aldermen's Court Repertories

Rep. 19, fol. 169–169^v, 5 February 1577 (William Middleton v.
   Bricklayers)
Rep. 21, ff. 291, 332v, 367 (inheritance of Avis and Thomas),
   fol. 437, 18 May 1587 (auction of Harvey's goods)
Rep. 24, fol. 207 (Avis's portion, 1598)
Rep. 25, fol. 221 (Thomas's portion, 1601)
Rep. 42, fol. 89 (widow Magdalen Middleton petition)

Corporation of London, Common Serjeant's Book I

fol. Iv (inventory of William Middleton's estate)

Corporation of London, Journals

22, f. 103v
25, f. 260

Corporation of London, Letter Books

BB, fol. 93
'&c' (1584–90), fol. 147v

Middlesex Sessions Files

January 1608/9 (Roger Waterer)

Middlesex Sessions Rolls

330/28, 331/15 (Anne Harvey accusation; Thomas Harvey
   reply, 30 September 1595)
399/45. Allen Waterer arrest (396/15), who is juror in several
   lists in 1601 (393/23, 91; 413/10)
402/30 (Thomas Harvey as surety 1 June 1602)

Parish Registers

X92/30 St George the Martyr Southwark
X92/60 St Mary's Newington
X9/1–2 St Saviour's Southwark

Public Record Office

Chancery

C.2.Eliz. S.[S.] 16/48, Chancery bill date 4 February 1591 (Anne
   Harvey's letters of administration)
C.2.Eliz. S.S. 16/48 Answer by Thomas Harvey 10 February 1591
C.24/170 (petition of William Middleton to Lord Chancellor,
   1584)
C 24/283/44 *ex parte* Dawson vs. Harvey *et al.*
C 24/291/55 Deposition of Paul Whitmore
C 54/1693 (deed TM signed 29 June 1600)

Exchequer

E/178/3288 (arrest of Harvey)
E 179/186/406 and 420 (Thomas Middleton subsidy assessment
   8 March 1622, 25 October 1624)
E 179/251/16, membrane 103 (William Middleton subsidy assessment, 1582)

King's Bench

KB 27/1416/1056d (Keysar sue TM for Viper & Brood, 1609)
KB 27/1424/828 Harper vs. Middleton
KB 29/222/32d (William Middleton 1585 surety)
KB 29/233, membranes at end (1595/6)
KB 29/236/137 Waterer vs Harveys, etc.
KB 29/238/137d, Pardon for Waterer 4 June 1601

Prerogative Court of Canterbury

5 Windsor (William Middleton's will)
62 Hayes (Roger Marbecke's will)

Requests

Req. 1/24, Decrees and orders, p. 526, 29 November 1608; other
   references pp. 296, 386, 417
Req. 2/26/90, Depositions for Harvey to prove contempt by
   Waterer
Req. 2/53/18, *ex parte* Richardson v. Anne Harvey
Req. 2/63/4, Bill dated 10 June 1600 (Thomas Harvey)
Req. 2/63/37, Replication by Harvey November 1600
Req. 2/79/58, Bill dated 23 October 1588; Answer 31 October;
   Demurrer 31 October; Answer 12 November; Replication 25
   January 1589
Req. 2/87/44, Anne Harvey's answer dated 20 October 1600
Req. 2/87/58, Bill by Thomas Harvey dated 6 December 1600;
   also includes (by mistake) answer by John Jackson, 4 May 1601

Req. 2/117/15, Answer of Thomas Drury dated 12 May 1601

Req. 2/224/15, Deposition of Thomas Harberte dated 2 February 1602

Req. 2/224/19, Depositions (Philip Bond, John Kyrby, Thomas Dawson, Anthony Snode) dated 8 February 1601

Req. 2/430, pt 2, Thomas Middleton debt

Req. 2/436, Answer of Anthony Richardson, 11 May 1606

Req. 2/468, Dawson

Req. 2/473, Empson v. Hayes and Waterer

Req. Witness Book, witnesses to be called for Dawson

III. PRIMARY SOURCES: PRINT

Aubrey, John, *The Natural History and Antiquities of Surrey*, 5 vols (1719)

Beaumont, Francis, (and John Fletcher?), *The Knight of the Burning Pestle* (1613)

The Book of Common Prayer, 1559: The Elizabethan Prayer Book, ed. John E. Booty (1976)

Brinsley, John, *Ludus Literarius* (1612)

Brown, William Wells, *The Travels of William Wells Brown*, ed. Paul Jefferson (1991)

Calvin, John, *Institutes*, trans. Ford Lewis Battles, Library of Christian Classics (1961)

Clark, Andrew, ed., *The Shirburn Ballads 1585–1616* (1907)

Donne, John, *The Sermons of John Donne*, ed. Evelyn M. Simpson and George R. Potter, 10 vols (1953–62)

Drayton, Michael, *Works*, ed. J. William Hebel, 5 vols (1932)

Eliot, T. S., 'London Letter: May, 1921', *Dial*, 70 (June 1921), 687

—— 'Thomas Middleton' (1927), *Selected Essays*, third edn. (1951), 161–70

Harman, Thomas, *A Caveat for commen Cursetors* (1567)

Harriot, Thomas, *A Briefe and True Report of the New Found Land of Virginia* (1588)

Jonson, Ben, *Ben Jonson*, ed. C. H. Herford, Percy and Evelyn Simpson, 11 vols (1925–52)

Knights, L. C., *Drama and Society in the Age of Jonson* (1937)

Lowell, James Russell, *Early Prose Writings* (1902)

Massinger, Philip, *Plays and Poems*, ed. Philip Edwards and Colin Gibson, 5 vols (Oxford, 1976), I, xxii–xxviii

Meres, Francis, *Palladis Tamia*, ed. Arthur Freeman (1973)

Mulcaster, Richard, *Positions* (1581)

Perkins, William, *A Commentary on Galatians*, ed. Gerald T. Sheppard, Pilgrim Classic Commentaries (1989)

Rollins, Hyder E., ed., *A Pepysian Garland: Black-letter Broadside Ballads of the years 1595–1639* (1922)

Stow, John, *A Survey of London*, ed. Charles L. Kingsford, 2 vols (1908)

Tilney, Edmund, *The Flower of Friendship*, ed. Valerie Wayne (1992)

Trollope, Anthony, *Notes on the Old Drama*, ed. Elizabeth R. Epperly (1988)

Tudor Royal Proclamations, ed. Paul L. Hughes and James F. Larkin, 3 vols (1964–9)

Tynan, Kenneth, review of *Women, Beware Women*, in *The Observer*, 8 July 1963

Virginia Voyages from Hakluyt, ed. David B. Quinn and Alisson M. Quinn (1973)

Wilson, Thomas, *Arte of Rhetorique* (1560), ed. G. H. Mair (1909)

Woolf, Virginia, *Letters*, ed. Nigel Nicholson and Joanne Trautmann, 6 vols (1975–80)

IV. SECONDARY SOURCES

Akrigg, G. P. V., 'Middleton: An Allusion to the Shakspere First Folio?', *Shakespeare Association Bulletin* 21 (1946), 25–6

Balch, Marston Stevens, 'Contemporary Imitations of Thomas Middleton', *Jacobean Miscellany*, Vol. I (1981), 47–79

—— 'The Dramatic Legacy of Thomas Middleton: A Study of the Uses of His Plays from 1627 to 1800', unpublished Ph.D. dissertation, Harvard University (1931)

Bald, R. C., 'The Chronology of Middleton's Plays', *Modern Language Review* 32 (1937), 33–43

Baldwin, T. W., *William Shakspere's Petty School* (1943)

—— *William Shakspere's Small Latine and Less Greeke*, 2 vols (1944)

Barroll, Leeds, *Politics, Plague, and Shakespeare's Theater: The Stuart Years* (1991)

Baskervill, C. R., *The Elizabethan Jig and Related Song Drama* (1929)

Bawcutt, N. W., 'Was Thomas Middleton a Puritan Dramatist?', *Modern Language Review* 94 (1999), 925–39

Bentley, Gerald Eades, 'John Cotgrave's *English Treasury of Wit and Language* and the Elizabethan Drama', *Studies in Philology* 40 (1943), 186–203

—— *The Profession of Dramatist in Shakespeare's Time, 1590–1642* (1971)

Bergeron, David, *English Civic Pageantry 1558–1642* (1971)

Blayney, Peter, *The Texts of King Lear and their Origins*, Vol. I, *Nicholas Okes and the First Quarto* (1982)

Boulton, Jeremy, *Neighbourhood and Society: A London Suburb in the Seventeenth Century* (1987)

Bouwsma, William J., *John Calvin: A Sixteenth Century Portrait* (1988)

Bowlby, John, *Attachment and Loss*, 3 vols (1969–80)

Bray, Alan, *Homosexuality in Renaissance England* (1982)

Brodsky, Vivien, 'Widows in Late Elizabethan London: Remarriage, Economic Opportunity and Family Orientations', in *The World We Have Gained: Histories of Population and Social Structure*, ed. Lloyd Bonfield, Richard M. Smith and Keith Wrightson (Oxford, 1986), 122–54

Butler, Martin, *Theatre and Crisis 1632–1642* (1984)

Cave, Terence, *The Cornucopian Text: Problems of writing in the French Renaissance* (1979)

Clare, Janet, '*Art made tongue-tied by authority': Elizabethan and Jacobean dramatic censorship* (1990)

Clark, Sandra, *The Elizabethan Pamphleteers: Popular Moralistic Pamphlets 1580–1640* (1983)

Clarkson, Paul S., and Clyde T. Warren, *The Law of Property in Shakespeare and the Elizabethan Drama* (1942)

Collinson, Patrick, *The Religion of Protestants: The Church in English Society 1559–1625* (1982)

Cohen, Charles Lloyd, *God's Caress: The Psychology of Puritan Religious Experience* (1986)

Cressy, David, *Education in Tudor England* (1975)

—— *Literacy and the Social Order: Reading and Writing in Tudor and Stuart England* (1980)

Croll, Morris W., *Style, Rhetoric, and Rhythm* (1966)

Daileader, Celia R., *Eroticism on the Renaissance Stage: Transcendence, Desire, and the Limits of the Visible* (1998)

—— 'Back-door Sex: Renaissance Gynosodomy, Aretino, and the Exotic', *English Literary History* 69 (2002), 303–34

—— 'The Courtesan Revisited: Thomas Middleton, Pietro Aretino, and Sex-Phobic Criticism', in *Italian Culture in the Drama of Shakespeare and his Contemporaries*, ed. Michele Marrapodi (forthcoming, 2007)

Darlington, Ida, *Survey of London*, vol. XXV, *St George's Fields: The Parishes of St George the Martyr, Southwark and St Mary, Newington* (1955)

Dutton, Richard, *Mastering the Revels: The Regulation and Censorship of English Renaissance Drama* (1991)

Elliott, Vivien Brodsky, 'Single Women in the London Marriage Market: Age, Status and Mobility, 1598–1619', in R. B. Outhwaite, ed., *Marriage and Society* (1981), 81–100

Finkelpearl, Philip, *John Marston of the Middle Temple* (1969)

Finlay, Roger, *Population and Metropolis: The Demography of London 1580–1650* (1981)

Fitch, Mark, ed., *Index to Testamentary Records in the Commissary Court of London (London Division), Vol. III 1571–1625* (1985)

Foakes, R. A., *Illustrations of the English Stage 1580–1642* (1985)

Frost, David L., *The School of Shakespeare: The Influence of Shakespeare on English Drama, 1600–42* (1968)

Goldberg, Jonathan, *Writing Matter: From the Hands of the English Renaissance* (1990)

Grafton, Anthony, and Lisa Jardine, *From Humanism to the Humanities: Education and the Liberal Arts in Fifteenth- and Sixteenth-Century Europe* (1986)

Greene, Thomas M., *The Light in Troy: Imitation and Discovery in Renaissance Poetry* (1982)

Griswold, Wendy, *Renaissance Revivals: City Comedy and Revenge Tragedy in the London Theatre, 1576–1980* (1986)

Gurr, Andrew, *Playgoing in Shakespeare's London* (1987)

Halpern, Richard, *The Poetics of Primitive Accumulation: English Renaissance Culture and the Genealogy of Capital* (1991)

Hardy, Thomas Duffus, *A Catalogue of Lords Chancellors, Keepers of the Great Seal, Masters of the Rolls, and Principal Officers of the High Court of Chancery* (1843)

Heinemann, Margot, *Puritanism and Theatre: Thomas Middleton and Opposition Drama under the Early Stuarts* (1980)

Hennessy, George, *Novum Repertorium Ecclesiasticum Parochiale Londinense* (1898)

Helgerson, Richard, *Self-Crowned Laureates: Spenser, Jonson, Milton and the Literary System* (1983)

Hind, Arthur M., Margery Corbett, and Michael Norton, *Engraving in England in the Sixteenth and Seventeenth Centuries*, 3 vols (1952–64)

Holdsworth, R. V., 'Middleton and Shakespeare: The Case for Middleton's Hand in *Timon of Athens*', unpublished Ph.D. dissertation, University of Manchester (1982)

Howard-Hill, T. H., *Middleton's 'Vulgar Pasquin': Essays on 'A Game at Chess'* (1995)

Hoy, Cyrus, 'The Shares of Fletcher and his Collaborators in the Beaumont and Fletcher Canon (V)', *Studies in Bibliography* 13 (1960), 77–108

Jackson, MacDonald P., *Studies in Attribution: Middleton and Shakespeare* (1979)

Johannson, Bertil, *Law and Lawyers in Elizabethan England* (1967)

Johnson, David J., *Southwark and the City* (1969)

Jones, W. J., *The Elizabethan Court of Chancery* (1967)

Lake, David, *The Canon of Thomas Middleton's Plays* (1975)

Lang, Gladys Engel, and Kurt Lang, *Etched in Memory: The Building and Survival of Artistic Reputation* (1990)

Leinwand, Theodore B., 'Shakespeare and the Middling Sort', *Shakespeare Quarterly* 44 (1993), 284–303

Lewalski, Barbara Kiefer, *Protestant Poetics and the Seventeenth-Century Religious Lyric* (1979)

Magrath, J. R., *The Queen's College*, 2 vols (1921)

McConica, James, ed., *The History of the University of Oxford*, vol. III: *The Collegiate University* (1986)

Miller, Edwin H., *The Professional Writer in Elizabethan England: A Study of Nondramatic Literature* (1959)

Munro, Lucy, 'A Neglected Allusion to *Perciles* and *Hengist King of Kent* in perforamnce', *Notes and Queries* 51 (2004), 307–10

Oliphant, E. H. C., 'The Authorship of *The Revenger's Tragedy*', *Studies in Philology* 23 (1926), 157–68

—— 'A Dekker–Middleton Play, *The Bloodie Banquet*', *Times Literary Supplement*, 17 December 1925, 882

—— *The Plays of Beaumont and Fletcher* (1927)

—— 'Problems of Authorship in Elizabethan Dramatic Literature', *Modern Philology* 8 (1911), 411–59

—— ed., *Shakespeare and His Fellow Dramatists* (1929)

Peck, Linda Levy, *Court Patronage and Corruption in Early Stuart England* (1990)

Prest, Wilfrid R., *The Inns of Court under Elizabeth I and the Early Stuarts, 1590–1640* (1972)

—— ed., *Lawyers in Early Modern Europe and America* (1981)

Rappaport, Steve, *Worlds Within Worlds: Structures of Life in Sixteenth Century London* (1989)

Revis, Matthew, 'Life at Oxford University, 1598–1601' (unpublished paper, 1993)

Roberts, Marilyn, 'A Preliminary Check-List of Productions of Thomas Middleton's Plays', *Research Opportunities in Renaissance Drama* 28 (1985), 37–61

Rollins, Hyder E., *An Analytical Index to the Ballad-Entries (1557–1709) in the Registers of the Company of Stationers of London* (1924)

Rozett, Martha Tuck, *The Doctrine of Election and the Emergence of Elizabethan Tragedy* (1984)

Saffady, William, 'The Effects of Childhood Bereavement and Parental Remarriage in 16th century England: the Case of Thomas More', *History of Childhood Quarterly* (1973), 311–24

Seaver, Paul S., *The Puritan Lectureships: The Politics of Religious Dissent 1560–1662* (1970)

—— *Wallington's World: A Puritan Artisan in Seventeenth-Century London* (1985)

Simon, Joan, *Education and Society in Tudor England* (1966)

Sims, R., *An Index of Pedigrees and Arms contained in the Heralds' Visitations in the British Museum* (1849)

Slack, Paul, *Impact of Plague in Tudor and Stuart England* (1985)

—— *Poverty and Policy in Tudor and Stuart England* (1988)

Smith, Bruce R., 'Reading Lists of Plays, Early Modern, Modernist, Postmodern', *Shakespeare Quarterly* 42 (1991), 127–44

Smuts, R. Malcolm, 'The Court and Its Neighbourhood: Royal Policy and Urban Growth in the Early Stuart West End', *Journal of British Studies* 30 (1991), 117–49

Spufford, Margaret, 'First Steps in Literacy: The Reading and Writing Experiences of the Humblest Seventeenth-Century Spiritual Autobiographers', in *Literacy and Social Development in the West*, ed. Harvey J. Graff (1981)

Steen, Sara Jayne, *Ambrosia in an Earthern Vessel: Three Centuries of Audience and Reader Response to the Works of Thomas Middleton* (1993)

—— *Thomas Middleton: A Reference Guide* (1984)

Stachniewski, John, 'Calvinist Psychology in Middleton's Tragedies', in *Three Jacobean Revenge Tragedies: A Casebook*, ed. R. V. Holdsworth (1990), 226–46

Sugden, Edward H., *A Topographical Dictionary to the Works of Shakespeare and His Fellow Dramatists* (1925)

Taylor, Gary, 'Bardicide', *Shakespeare and Cultural Traditions*, ed. Roger Pringle *et al.* (1994), 333–49

—— *Buying Whiteness: Race, Culture, and Identity from Columbus to Hip-Hop* (2005)

—— *Castration: An Abbreviated History of Western Manhood* (2000)

—— *Cultural Selection* (1996)

—— 'Farrago', *Textual Practice* 8 (1994c), 33–42

—— 'Feeling Bodies', in *Shakespeare in the Twentieth Century:*

Proceedings of the Sixth World Shakespeare Congress, ed. Jonathan Bate *et al.* (1998), 258–79

—— 'Forms of Opposition: Shakespeare and Middleton', *English Literary Renaissance* 24 (1994), 283–314

—— *Reinventing Shakespeare: A Cultural History from the Restoration to the Present* (1989)

—— 'The Renaissance and the End of Editing', in *Palimpsest: Editorial Theory in the Humanities*, ed. George Bornstein and Ralph G. Williams (1993), 121–49

—— 'Thomas Middleton, *The Nice Valour*, and the Court of James I,' *The Court Historian* 6 (2001), 1–36

Thomas, Keith, 'The Meaning of Literacy in Early Modern England', in *The Written Word: Literacy in Transition*, ed. Gerd Baumann (1986), 97–131

—— *Religion and the Decline of Magic* (1971)

—— *Rule and Misrule in the Schools of Early Modern England* (1976)

Todd, Margo, *Christian Humanism and the Puritan Social Order* (1987)

Tricomi, Albert H., *Anticourt Drama in England 1603–1642* (1989)

Tyacke, Nicholas, *Anti-Calvinists: The Rise of English Arminianism c. 1590–1640* (1987)

Venn, J. and J. A., *Alumni Cantabrigienses*, 4 vols (1922–27)

Watt, Tessa, *Cheap Print and Popular Piety, 1550–1640* (1991)

Webb, Cliff, ed., *Surrey Probate Records to 1650* (1990)

Wendorf, Richard, *The Elements of Life: Biography and Portrait Painting in Stuart and Georgian England* (1990)

Williamson, George, *The Senecan Amble: a study in prose form from Bacon to Collier* (1951)

Wolff, Dorothy, *Thomas Middleton: An Annotated Bibliography* (1985)

Wrightson, Keith, *English Society 1580–1680* (1982)

Wrigley, E. A., 'Family Limitation in Pre-Industrial England', *Economic History Review*, II, 19 (1966), 82–109

—— and R. S. Schofield, *The Population History of England, 1541–1871: A Reconstruction* (1981) (1952–64)

Würzbach, Natascha, *The Rise of the English Street Ballad, 1550–1650*, trans. Gayna Walls (1990)

MIDDLETON'S LONDON

Paul S. Seaver

WORKS CITED

Primary (manuscript)

Corporation of London Records Office

Journal 24, 33, Repertory 23, Remembrancia I.

Guildhall Library

Bridewell Royal Hospital, Court Minutes, vol. I, Microfilm 510.
Cutlers' Company, Court Minutes, 1602–1670, MS 7151/1.
Cutlers' Company, Wardens' Account Book, 1586–1621, MS 7147/1.
Grocers' Company, Charges of Triumphs, 1613–1624, MS 11,590.
—— Court of Assistants, 1556–1591, MS 11,588/1
—— Court of Assistants, 1591–1616, MS 11,588/2.
—— Court of Assistants, 1616–1639, MS 11,588/3.
—— Wardens' Accounts, 1590–1601, MS 11,571/8.
—— Wardens' Accounts, 1601–1611, MS 11,571/9.
Merchant Taylors Company Court Minutes, 1562–1574, Microfilm 325.
St Lawrence Jewry, Vestry Minutes, 1556–1669, MS 2590/1.
Tylers and Bricklayers' Company, Court Minutes, 1580–1667, MS 3034/1.

Primary (printed)

Beard, Thomas, *The Theatre of God's Judgements* (1597)
Birch, Thomas, ed., *The Court and Times of Charles the First*. Vol. I. London, 1848.
—— ed., *The Court and Times of James the First*. Vol. II. London, 1849.
Groos, G. W., ed. and trans., *The Diary of Baron Waldstein*. London, 1981.
Harrison, William, *The Description of England*, ed. Georges Edelen. Ithaca, NY, 1968.
Hinds, A. B., ed., *Calendar of State Papers and Manuscripts, relating to English Affairs, Existing in the Collection of Venice, 1617–1619*. Vol. XV. London, 1909.
Hughes, Paul, and James F. Larkin, eds., *Tudor Royal Proclamations*. Vols. II & III. New Haven, 1969.
Johnson, Richard, *A Song of Richard Whittington* (1612).
Larkin, James F., and Paul Hughes, eds., *Stuart Royal Proclamations*. Vol. I. Oxford, 1973.
Larkin, James F., ed., *Stuart Royal Proclamations*. Vol. II. Oxford, 1983.
Loftis, John, ed., *The Memoirs of Anne, Lady Halkett and Ann, Lady Fanshawe*. Oxford, 1979.
McIlwain, C. H., ed., *The Political Works of James I*. Cambridge, Mass., 1918.
Niccols, Richard, *Londons Artillary* (1616).
Schofield, Bertram, ed., *The Knyvett Letters (1620–1644)*. London, 1949.
Stow, John, *A Survey of London* (1603), ed. C. L. Kingsford. 2 vols. Oxford, 1908.

Secondary

Archer, Ian, *The Pursuit of Stability. Social Relations in Elizabethan London*. Cambridge, 1991.
Barker, Richard Hindry, *Thomas Middleton*. New York, 1958.
Beier, A. L., 'Engine of Manufacture: the Trades of London', in A. L. Beier and Roger Finlay, eds., *London 1500–1700* (London and New York, 1986), 141–67.
Bennett, H. S., *English Books and Readers 1603–1640*. Cambridge, 1970.
Borsay, Peter, *The English Urban Renaissance: Culture and Society in the Provincial Town, 1660–1770*. Oxford, 1989.
Boulton, Jeremy, *Neighbourhood and Society. A London Suburb in the Seventeenth Century*. Cambridge, 1987.
Brenner, Robert, *Merchants and Revolution. Commercial Change, Political Conflict, and London's Overseas Traders, 1550–1653*. Princeton, 1993.
Chartres, J. A., 'Food Consumption and Internal Trade', in A. L. Beier and Roger Finlay, eds., *London 1500–1700* (London and New York, 1986), 168–96.
—— *Internal Trade in England 1500–1700*. London, 1977.
Clark, Peter, and Raymond Gillespie, eds., *Two Capitals: London and Dublin 1500–1840*. Oxford, 2001.
Clay, C. G. A., *Economic Expansion and Social Change: England 1500–1700*. Vol. I. Cambridge, 1984.
Dale, T. C., *The Inhabitants of London in 1638*. 2 vols. London, 1931.
Dietz, Brian, 'Overseas Trade and Metropolitan Growth', in A. L. Beier and Roger Finlay, eds., *London 1500–1700* (London and New York, 1986), 115–40.
Dodd, A. H., 'Mr. Myddelton the Merchant of Tower Street', in S. T. Bindoff, J. Hurstfield, and C. H. Williams, eds., *Elizabethan Government and Society* (London, 1961), 249–81.
Earle, Peter, *A City Full of People. Men and Women of London 1650–1750*. London, 1994.
Eccles, Mark, '"Thomas Middleton a Poett"', *Studies in Philology*, 54 (1957), 516–36.
Finlay, Roger, *Population and Metropolis. The Demography of London 1580–1650*. Cambridge, 1981.
—— and Beatrice Shearer, 'Population Growth and Suburban Expansion', in A. L. Beier and Roger Finaly, eds., *London 1500–1700* (London and New York, 1986), 37–59.
Forbes, Thomas R., 'By what disease or casualty: the changing face of death in London', in Charles Webster, ed., *Health, Medicine, and Mortality in the Sixteenth Century* (Cambridge, 1979), 117–39.
Foster, Frank Freeman, *The Politics of Stability. A Portrait of the Rulers in Elizabethan London*. London, 1977.
Grassby, Richard, *The Business Community in Seventeenth-Century England*. Cambridge, 1995.
Griffiths, Paul and Mark Jenner, eds., *Londinopolis. Essays in the Cultural and Social History of Early Modern London*. Manchester, 2000.
Gurr, Andrew, *Playgoing in Shakespeare's London*. Cambridge, 1987.

Harding, Vanessa, 'The Population of London 1550–1700: a review of the published evidence', *London Journal*, 15 (1990), 111–28.

Jordan, W. K., *The Charities of London 1480–1660*. London, 1960.

Lindley, K. J., 'Riot Prevention and Control in Early Stuart London', *Transactions of the Royal Historical Society*, 5th series, 33 (1983), 109–26.

Maclure, Millar, *The Paul's Cross Sermons 1534–1642*. Toronto, 1958.

Manley, Lawrence, ed., *London in the Age of Shakespeare: An Anthology*. London and Sidney, 1986.

—— 'From Matron to Monster: Tudor-Stuart London and the Languages of Urban Description', in Heather Dubrow and Richard Strier, eds., *The Historical Renaissance* (Chicago, 1988), 347–74.

Manning, Robert B., *Village Revolts. Social Protest and Popular Disturbances in England, 1509–1640*. Oxford, 1988.

Merritt, J. F., ed., *Imagining Early Modern London. Perceptions and Portrayals of the City from Stow to Strupe 1598–1720*. Cambridge, 2001.

Orlin, Lena Cowen, ed., *Material London, ca. 1600*. Philadelphia, 2000.

Palliser, D. M., *The Age of Elizabeth*. London and New York, 1983.

Pelling, Margaret, and Charles Webster, 'Medical Practitioners', in Charles Webster, ed., *Health, Medicine, and Mortality in the Sixteenth Century* (Cambridge, 1979), 165–235.

Pettegree, Andrew, *Foreign Protestant Communities in Sixteenth- -Century London*. Oxford, 1986.

Power, M. J., 'The East and West in Early Modern London', in E. Ives *et al.*, eds., *Wealth and Power in Tudor England* (London, 1978), 167–85.

Prest, Wilfrid, *The Inns of Court under Elizabeth I and the Early Stuarts 1590–1640*. London, 1972.

—— *The Rise of the Barristers*. Oxford, 1986.

Rappaport, Steve, *World within Worlds: Structures of Life in Sixteenth-Century London*. Cambridge, 1989.

Seaver, Paul S., *The Puritan Lectureships*. Stanford, 1970.

—— *Wallington's World*. Stanford, 1985.

—— 'Work, Discipline, and the Apprentice in Early Modern London', in Penelope Gouk, ed., *Wellsprings of Achievement: Cultural and Economic Dynamics in Early Modern England and Japan* (Aldershot, Hampshire, 1995), 159–79.

Shoemaker, Robert B., *Prosecution and Punishment: Petty Crime and the Law in London and Rural Middlesex, c.1660–1725*. Cambridge, 1991.

Slack, Paul, 'Metropolitan Government in Crisis: the response to the plague', in A. L. Beier and Roger Finlay, eds., *London 1500– 1700* (London and New York, 1986), 60–81.

—— *Poverty and Policy in Tudor and Stuart England*. London, 1988.

Smith, David L., Richard Strier and David Bevington, eds., *The Theatrical City: Culture, Theatre and Politics in London 1576– 1649*. Cambridge, 1995.

Spufford, Margaret, *Small Books and Pleasant Histories. Popular Fiction and Its Readership in Seventeenth-Century England*. London, 1981.

Stone, Lawrence, 'The Residential Development in the West End of London in the Seventeenth Century', in Barbara Malamant, ed., *After the Reformation* (Philadelphia, 1980), 167–212.

Ward, Joseph P., *Metropolitan Communities. Trade Guilds, Identity, and Change in Early Modern London*. Stanford, 1997.

Watt, Tessa, *Cheap Print and Popular Piety, 1550–1640*. Cambridge, 1991.

Wrigley, E. A., 'A Simple Model of London's Importance in changing English society and economy 1650–1750', *Past and Present*, 37 (1967), 44–70.

MIDDLETON'S THEATRES

Scott McMillin

WORKS CONSULTED

Armstrong, William A. 'Actors and Theatres'. *Shakespeare Survey* 7 (1964), 191–204

Astington, John H. 'A Drawing of the Great Chamber at Whitehall in 1601'. *REED Newsletter* 16 (1991), 6–11

—— *English Court Theatre 1558–1642*. Cambridge: Cambridge University Press, 1999

—— ed. *The Development of Shakespeare's Theatre*. New York: AMS Press, 1992

Barlow, Graham F. 'Wenceslas Hollar and Christopher Beeston's Phoenix Theatre in Drury Lane'. *Theatre Research International* 13 (1988), 30–43

Barroll, J. Leeds. *Politics, Plague, and Shakespeare's Theater*. Ithaca: Cornell University Press, 1991

—— *et al., The Revels History of Drama in English, Vol III: 1576–1613*. London: Methuen, 1975

Bentley, G. E. *The Jacobean and Caroline Stage*. 7 vols. Oxford: Clarendon Press, 1941–68

—— *The Profession of Dramatist in Shakespeare's Time: 1590–1642*. Princeton: Princeton University Press, 1971

—— *The Profession of Player in Shakespeare's Time: 1590–1642*. Princeton: Princeton University Press, 1984

Bergeron, David M. *English Civic Pageantry 1558–1642*. Columbia, S. C.: University of South Carolina Press, 1971

—— ed. *Pageantry in the Shakespearean Theater*. Athens, Ga.: University of Georgia Press, 1985

Berry, Herbert. 'The Playhouse in the Boar's Head in Whitechapel'. In *The Elizabethan Theatre* 1, ed. David Galloway. London: Macmillan, 1969, pp. 45–73

—— *Shakespeare's Playhouses*. New York: AMS Press, 1987

—— 'The Stage and Boxes at Blackfriars'. *Studies in Philology* 63 (1966)

Bradbrook, Muriel C. 'The Politics of Pageantry'. In *Poetry and Drama, 1570–1700: Essays in Honour of Harold F. Brooks*. Ed. Antony Coleman and Antony Hammond. London: Methuen, 1981, pp. 60–75

Bruster, Douglas. *Drama and the Market in the Age of Shakespeare*. Cambridge: Cambridge University Press, 1992

Cerasano, S. P. 'The Business of Shareholding, the Fortune Playhouse, and Francis Grace's Will'. *Medieval and Renaissance Drama in England* 2 (1985), 231–52

—— 'The Chamberlain's–King's Men'. In Kastan, ed., *A Companion to Shakespeare*, pp. 328–45

Chambers, E. K. *The Elizabethan Stage*. 4 vols. Oxford: Clarendon Press, 1923

Clare, Janet. *Art Made Tongue-Tied by Authority: Elizabethan and Jacobean Dramatic Censorship*. Manchester: Manchester University Press, 1990

Cook, Ann J. *The Privileged Playgoers of Shakespeare's London*. Princeton: Princeton University Press, 1981

Dessen, Alan C. *Elizabethan Stage Conventions and Modern Interpreters*. Cambridge: Cambridge University Press, 1984

—— and Leslie Thomson. *A Dictionary of Stage Directions in English Drama, 1580–1642*. Cambridge: Cambridge University Press, 1999

Dutton, Richard. *Mastering the Revels: the Regulation and Censorship of English Renaissance Drama*. Iowa City: University of Iowa Press, 1991

Edmond, Mary. 'Peter Street, 1553–1609: Builder of Playhouses'. *Shakespeare Survey* 45 (1992), 101–14

Foakes, R. A. *Illustrations of the English Stage, 1580–1642*. Stanford: Stanford University Press, 1985

—— 'Tragedy at the Children's Theatres after 1600: a Challenge to the Adult Stage'. In *The Elizabethan Theatre* 2, ed. David Galloway. Waterloo: Archon, 1970, pp. 37–59

Gair, Reavley. *The Children of Paul's: The Story of a Theatre Company, 1553–1608*. Cambridge: Cambridge University Press, 1982

Gurr, Andrew. 'Money or Audiences: the Impact of Shakespeare's Globe'. *Theatre Notebook* 42 (1988), 3–14

—— *Playgoing in Shakespeare's London*. Cambridge: Cambridge University Press, 1987

—— *The Shakespearian Playing Companies*. Oxford: Clarendon Press, 1996

—— *The Shakespearean Stage: 1574–1642*. 3rd edn. Cambridge: Cambridge University Press, 1992

—— *The Shakespeare Company, 1594–1642*. Cambridge: Cambridge University Press, 2004

—— and John Orrell. *Rebuilding Shakespeare's Globe*. New York: Routledge, 1989

Harris, John, and A. A. Tait. *Catalogue of the Drawings by Inigo Jones, John Webb and Isaac de Caus at Worcester College Oxford*. Oxford: Oxford University Press, 1979

Harris, Jonathan Gill, and Natasha Korda, eds. *Staged Properties in Early Modern Drama*. Cambridge: Cambridge University Press, 2002

Heinemann, Margot. *Puritanism and Theatre: Thomas Middleton and Opposition Drama Under the Early Stuarts*. Cambridge: Cambridge University Press, 1980

Hill, R. F., and F. P. Wilson, eds. *Dramatic Records in the Declared Accounts of the Office of Works: 1560–1640*. Malone Society Collections, Vol. 10 (1977)

Hillebrand, Harold Newcomb. *The Child Actors: a Chapter in Elizabethan Stage History*. Urbana: University of Illinois Press, 1926

Hosley, Richard. 'The Playhouses'. In Barroll *et al., The Revels History of Drama in English, Vol. III*, pp. 121–235

Howard, Jean E. *The Stage and Social Struggle in Early Modern England*. London: Routledge, 1994

Ingram, William. *The Business of Playing: the Beginnings of the Adult Professional Theater in Elizabethan London*. Ithaca: Cornell University Press, 1992

Kastan, David Scott, ed. *A Companion to Shakespeare*. Oxford: Blackwell, 1999

King, T. J. 'Staging of Plays at the Phoenix in Drury Lane, 1617–42'. *Theatre Notebook* 19 (1965), 146–66

Kipling, Gordon. 'Richard II's "Sumptious Pageants" and the Idea of the Civic Triumph'. In Bergeron, ed., *Pageantry in the Shakespearean Theater*, pp. 83-103

—— 'Triumphal Drama: Form in English Civic Pageantry'. *Renaissance Drama*, NS 8 (1977), 37-56

Knutson, Roslyn. *Playing Companies and Commerce in Shakespeare's Time*. Cambridge: Cambridge University Press, 2001

—— *The Repertory of Shakespeare's Company: 1594-1613*. Fayetteville: University of Arkansas Press, 1991

Leggatt, Alexander. *Jacobean Public Theatre*. London: Routledge, 1992

Lopez, Jeremy. *Theatrical Convention and Audience Response in Early Modern Drama*. Cambridge: Cambridge University Press, 2003

Mackintosh, Iain. 'Inigo Jones—Theatre Architect'. *Tabs* 31 (1973), 95-105

Mullaney, Stephen. *The Place of the Stage: License, Play, and Power in Renaissance England*. Chicago: University of Chicago Press, 1988

Nelson, Alan H. 'Hall Screens and Elizabethan Playhouses: Counter-Evidence from Cambridge'. In Astington, ed., *The Development of Shakespeare's Theater*, pp. 57-76

Nungezer, Edwin. *A Dictionary of Actors*. New Haven: Yale University Press, 1929

Orgel, Stephen. *The Illusion of Power: Political Theater in the English Renaissance*. Berkeley: University of California Press, 1975

—— *Impersonations: The Performance of Gender in Shakespeare's England*. Cambridge: Cambridge University Press, 1996

Orrell, John. *The Human Stage: English Theatre Design, 1567-1640*. Cambridge: Cambridge University Press, 1988

—— 'Inigo Jones at the Cockpit'. *Shakespeare Survey* 30 (1977), 157-68

—— 'The Theatre at Christ Church, Oxford, in 1605'. *Shakespeare Survey* 35 (1982)

Paster, Gail Kern. 'The Idea of London in Masque and Pageant'. In Bergeron, ed., *Pageantry in the Shakespearean Theater*, pp. 48-64

Reynolds, G. F. *The Staging of Elizabethan Plays at the Red Bull Theatre*. New York, 1940

Rowan, D. F. 'A Neglected Jones/Webb Theatre Project: "Barber-Surgeons' Hall Writ Large".' *Shakespeare Survey* 23 (1970), 125-9

—— 'A Neglected Jones/Webb Theatre Project, Part II: A Theatrical Missing Link'. *The Elizabethan Theatre* 2, ed. David Galloway. Toronto, 1970, 60-73

Rutter, Carol Chillington, ed. *Documents of the Rose Playhouse*. Rev. edn. Manchester: Manchester University Press, 2001

Shapiro, Michael. 'The Children of Paul's and Their Playhouse'. *Theatre Notebook* 36 (1982), 3-13

—— *Children of the Revels: The Boy Companies of Shakespeare's Time and Their Plays*. New York: Columbia University Press, 1977

Smith, Irwin. *Shakespeare's Blackfriars Playhouse*. New York, 1964

Sturgess, Keith. *Jacobean Private Theatre*. London: Routledge, 1987

Thomson, Peter. *Shakespeare's Theater*. 2nd edn. London: Routledge, 1992

Wickham, Glynne. *Early English Stages*. 3 vols. New York: Columbia University Press, 1963-81

THE WISDOM OF SOLOMON PARAPHRASED

Edited by G. B. Shand

The Wisdom of Solomon Paraphrased (STC 17906) was printed by Valentine Simmes in 1597. There is no record of licensing in the Stationers' Register. The book is a quarto, its prelims irregularly arranged: A1 (blank except for a large signature A printed on recto), [A2, missing], B2 (blank, unsigned, apparently congruent with B1), A3 (title-page), A4, B1. In place of the missing A2, the half sheet containing B1 has been turned back to fill the gap. The remainder of the quarto, divided up four stanzas to the page, is regularly arranged on twenty-three sheets. From B to Bb two skeletons were used in regular alternation, one printing outer and inner B, the other outer and inner C, and so on. There is one break in this pattern, when the first skeleton misses a turn, leaving skeleton two to set P, Q, and R. Skeleton two is turned between outer and inner R.

There was some uncertainty about typographical format at the outset, and outer B sets off with rather too short a measure, but quickly adjusts this. Catchwords end the first five sheets of text (B–F), but not thereafter. Marginal indications of verse number, after Verse 1, use an unaccompanied numeral through B, C, and outer D. Thereafter, the word 'Verse' or an abbreviation of it always appears. The second and third of these variations in format might have resulted from interruptions in the setting.

Although only four copies of the book have survived (Bodleian Library, British Library; Huntington Library, Yale University Library), thirty-two press variants occur, scattered through fourteen formes. On the whole, correction is of nontextual features (turned letters, incorrect verse numbers, and so on), but three substantive corrections and a few emendations of punctuation also occur. No two surviving copies are identical, and no extant copy has corrected or uncorrected sheets throughout. The Bodleian copy has a duplicate of corrected sheet C, bound between D and E. The largely neat and attentive job of printing, and the frequency of correction, conceivably reflect Middleton's personal attention, although 1597 was a relatively slow year in Simmes's shop (Ferguson), and the corrections might simply be evidence of workmen with time on their hands.

SEE ALSO

Text: *Works*, 1919
Authorship and date: this volume, 335

WORKS CITED

Previous Editions

Dyce, Alexander, ed., *Works* (1840), vol. 5
Bullen, A. H., ed., *Works* (1886), vol. 8

Other Works Cited

Biblia Sacra cum glossa ordinaria...et Postilla Nicolai Lirani (1617)
Book of Common Prayer 1559, ed. John E. Booty (1976)
Brittin, Norman, *The Early Career of Thomas Middleton*, dissertation, University of Washington (1946)
Calvin, John, *Institutes of the Christian Religion*, tr. Ford Lewis Battles, ed. John T. McNeill (1961)
Campbell, Lily Bess, *Divine Poetry and Drama in Sixteenth-Century England* (1961)
Critici sacri, ed. John Pearson *et al.* (1698)
Ferguson, W. Craig, *Valentine Simmes* (1968)
Geneva Bible, facsimile, intro. Lloyd E. Berry (1969)
Lapide, Cornelius a, *Commentaria in Scripturam Sacram*, vol. 8 (1881)
Lok, Henry, *Ecclesiastes, Otherwise Called the Preacher* (1597)
Marlowe, Christopher, *Works*, ed. Fredson Bowers, 2 vols (1973)
Midrash Rabbah, ed. H. Freedman and Maurice Simon (1939)
Roston, Murray, *Biblical Drama in England from the Middle Ages to the Present Day* (1968)
Shand, G. B., 'The Elizabethan Aim of *The Wisdom of Solomon Paraphrased*', in *'Accompaninge the players': Essays Celebrating Thomas Middleton, 1580–1980*, ed. Kenneth Friedenreich (1983), 67–77
Tilley, Morris Palmer, *A Dictionary of the Proverbs in England in the Sixteenth and Seventeenth Centuries* (1950)

TEXTUAL NOTES

1.4 sits] SIMMES, BULLEN; sit DYCE. The first of many instances (and the only one recorded in these notes) where Dyce regularizes verb agreements. Bullen returns to Simmes's reading wherever Dyce's notes record such emendation; where Dyce regularizes silently, Bullen follows silently.

1.5 ear] SIMMES (eare); care DYCE

1.19 tempting] SIMMES temting

1.36 friend] DYCE; frinds SIMMES

1.86 inequal] DYCE; ineqall SIMMES

2.17 conjoinèd] DYCE; conoyined SIMMES

2.35 An] DYCE; And SIMMES

2.53 they] DYCE; the SIMMES

2.102 spite] DYCE; fpght SIMMES

2.172 bodies'] SIMMES (bodies); body's DYCE

2.182 cave] THIS EDITION; crue SIMMES; core DYCE. It is more likely that Simmes's compositor made the single error of setting r for a (side by side in Moxon's case), than the double error of first selecting a wrong type u, and then transposing it with the r. Compare 'Frm'd' for 'Fam'd' in John Wilmot's *Poems on Several Occasions* (Antwerpen [London], c.1680), C2.

2.207 bonds] SIMMES (bands)

2.224 avail] DYCE; aualie SIMMES

3.29 load] SIMMES (lade)

3.43 infirmity's] DYCE; infiirmities SIMMES

3.56 O] SIMMES (Oh); Or DYCE

3.78 see] DYCE; see see SIMMES

3.83 right] DYCE; rghit SIMMES

3.100 'Whe'er] SIMMES (Where); Or DYCE

3.113 wisdom's] DYCE; wifedomess SIMMES

3.125 Three] SIMMES (corr. [Yale]), DYCE; Their SIMMES (uncorr.)

4.73 sect] SIMMES (sex)

4.75 connect] SIMMES (connex)

5.10 stand] THIS EDITION; ftands SIMMES

5.91 e'en] SIMMES (eu'ne)

5.94 tine] THIS EDITION; teeme SIMMES; team DYCE

5.160 against] SIMMES (agen)

6.93 before] DYCE; defore SIMMES

6.106 course] SIMMES (corfe)

6.121 coyish she] SIMMES (~ fhee); possible error for *coyish shie* (i.e., shy)?

6.132 Shall] DYCE; Sall SIMMES

6.160 her plea's rejection] THIS EDITION ∧ ∧ rejection SIMMES

6.166 banner] SIMMES (bonner)

7.13 matrix] SIMMES (matrice)

7.94 travail] SIMMES (trauell)

7.118 maintainer] DYCE; maintatiner SIMMES

7.184 have] THIS EDITION; had SIMMES

7.191 show,] fho∧ SIMMES

8.7 *Verse 2*] THIS EDITION; SIMMES, apparently assuming that this stanza completes Middleton's paraphrase of Geneva's *Verse 1*,

leaves it unnumbered, with the result that the paraphrase of Geneva's *Verse 3* is then misnumbered 2. The error persists until *Verse 14*, which SIMMES numbers *Verse 13 14* so that *Verse 15* will be correctly identified. SIMMES's error is repeated by DYCE and BULLEN.

8.8 lodge] SIMMES (Bodleian, Huntington); body (bodie) SIMMES (British Library, Yale)

8.15 heaven] SIMMES (Bodleian, Huntington); haven SIMMES (British Library, Yale)

8.115 unmeets] SIMMES (vnmeetes)

9.67 subject] SIMMES; subjects DYCE; *OED* records *subject* as a collective singular only in Shakespeare after 1600.

9.72 heaven] DYCE; heau'n SIMMES

10.76 fears] DYCE; fears SIMMES

10.137 shall we file] DYCE; fhall file SIMMES

11.2 fears] DYCE; fear SIMMES

11.35 stone] THIS EDITION; ftore SIMMES, DYCE; the reference is to the stone from which Wisdom produced water (21), and which the idolatrous misconstrue as the agent of the miracle (25 and 33).

11.42 prize] DYCE; przie SIMMES

11.82 shows] DYCE; shoes SIMMES

11.168 new] DYCE; nw SIMMES

12.110 mould] SIMMES (moule)

12.157 fire-dust] BULLEN, suggested by DYCE; fire-durft SIMMES

12.167 teen] SIMMES (teene); team DYCE

13.40 rinsed] SIMMES (wrencht); *OED*'s earliest record of this spelling variant is from 1663, although 'rench' is recorded in 1591

14.3 its] SIMMES (it); while 'its' had come into colloquial use by the end of the 16th century, 'it' remained the literary form of the neuter possessive pronoun.

14.10 has] THIS EDITION; haue SIMMES

14.21 providence] DYCE; pouidence SIMMES

14.47 world's] THIS EDITION, proposed by DYCE; world SIMMES

14.179 life's] SIMMES (lifes); lives DYCE

14.223 Corruption's] THIS EDITION; Corruption SIMMES

15.118 hands.] THIS EDITION; hand: SIMMES

16.258 old] DYCE; olds SIMMES

17.50 opposite] DYCE; oppfite SIMMES

17.59 denied] THIS EDITION; dinide SIMMES; divide DYCE, apparently assuming foul case or a turned 'u'. But the sort is clearly an 'n', and the past tense of 'deny' is demanded by the context.

17.72 Connecting] SIMMES (Connexing)

17.102 fear] DYCE; feate SIMMES

18.104 mischief's] DYCE mifcchiefes SIMMES

18.170 thorough] SIMMES (through); emended for metre

18.236 drew] SIMMES (draw'd)

19.76 corpse] DYCE; coarfe SIMMES

19.169 sheep] DYCE; fhheepe SIMMES

19.200 the] DYCE; te SIMMES

PRESS VARIANTS

The four surviving copies of SIMMES are at the Bodleian (B), British Library (BL), Huntington Library (HN), and Yale (Y).

Sheet B (outer forme)

Corrected: B, HN, Y
Uncorrected: BL

Sig. B2ᵛ

1.80   to composition] to compoſition *corr*; tocompoſition *uncorr*

Sig. B3

1.116   joy.] ioy, *corr*; ~ᴧ *uncorr*

Sig. B4ᵛ

1.170   Whose] Whose *corr*; Wᶸoſe *uncorr*

Sheet C (inner forme)

Corrected: B, HN
Uncorrected: BL, Y

Sig. C1ᵛ

2.36   goes] goes. *corr*; ~ᴧ *uncorr*

Sheet D (outer forme)

Corrected: B, HN, Y
Uncorrected: BL

Sig. D1

2.196   true.] true: *corr*; ~, *uncorr*

Sig. D2ᵛ

3.1   Verse 1] Verſe 1 *corr*; ᴧ 1 *uncorr*

Sig. D3

headline   CHAP. 3 *corr*; ~ 1 *uncorr*
3.36   immortality?] immortalitie? *corr*; ~. *uncorr*
3.45   ease,] eaſe, *corr*; ~,) *uncorr*

Sig. D4ᵛ

headline   CHAP. 3 *corr*; ~ 1 *uncorr*

Sheet E (outer forme)

Corrected: Y
Uncorrected: B, BL, HN

Sig. E1

3.125   Three] Three *corr*; Their *uncorr*
3.136   found.] found: *corr*; ~, *uncorr*

Sig. E4ᵛ

4.107   say] ſay, *corr* ~ᴧ *uncorr*;

Sheet E (inner forme)

Corrected: B, BL, Y
Uncorrected: HN

Sig. E1ᵛ

headline   CHAP. 3 *corr*; ~ 4 *uncorr*
3.145   Verse 15] Verſe 15 *corr*; Verſe 1 *uncorr*
3.157   Verse 16] Verſe 16 *corr*; ~ 2 *uncorr*

Sig. E2

3.169   Verse 17] Verſe 17 *corr*; ~ 5 *uncorr*

3.181   Verses 18, 19] Ver.18 19 *corr*; Verſe 6 *uncorr*

Sheet F (outer forme)

Corrected: B, HN, Y
Uncorrected: BL

Sig. F1

4.123   gyre,] gire, *corr*; ~; *uncorr*

Sheet H (outer forme)

Corrected: BL
Uncorrected: B, HN, Y

Sig. H3

headline   CHAP. 6 *corr*; ~ 5 *uncorr*
6.187   earthly] earthly *corr*; eaᴚthly *uncorr*

Sheet K (outer forme)

Corrected: B, HN
Uncorrected: BL, Y

Sig. K2ᵛ

8.8   lodge] lodge *corr*; bodie *uncorr*
8.15   heaven] heauen *corr*; hauen *uncorr*

Sig. K4ᵛ

8.109   tongue,] tongue, *corr*; tongᴧ *uncorr* (both BL and Y appear
        to print left margin of 'u')

Sheet O (outer forme)

Corrected: B, HN, Y
Uncorrected: BL

Sig. O3

signature   O3 *corr*; Oᴧ *uncorr*

Sheet O (inner forme)

Corrected: B, BL, Y
Uncorrected: HN

Sig. O1ᵛ

11.141   flame] flame *corr*; flame *uncorr*

Sig. O2

11.162   eyes?] eyes. *corr*; ~ᴧ *uncorr*

Sheet T (inner forme)

Corrected: B, BL, HN
Uncorrected: Y

Sig. T4

headline   Paraphraſed. *corr*; Chapter XVI. *uncorr*

Sheet X (outer forme)

Corrected: B, HN, Y
Uncorrected: BL

Sig. X2ᵛ

17.98   That] That *corr*; Thet *uncorr*
17.98   should] ſhoulde *corr*; ſhoulda *uncorr*

Sheet Y (outer forme)

   Corrected: B, BL, HN
   Uncorrected: Y

Sig. Y2^v

18.119   vaults] vaults, *corr*; ~; *uncorr*

Sheet Aa (outer forme)

   Corrected: BL
   Uncorrected: B, HN, Y

Sig. Aa1

18.228   harms.] harms. *corr*; ~$_\wedge$ *uncorr*

MICROCYNICON: SIX SNARLING SATIRES

Edited by Wendy Wall

Microcynicon presents few textual problems for an editor. This slim volume of six 'snarling' satires was first published in octavo form in 1599 by the printer Thomas Creede for Thomas Bushell. Copies of the original edition (STC 17154) are found in the Huntington and the Bodleian with no textual variants between them. Creede's text appears to be fairly clean and well-printed, with only a few missing catchwords and problems in numbered headings. Both copies contain minimal ink corrections made by an unknown hand, which emends the incorrectly numbered headings on C5–C6 and C7 as well as altering a verb tense on the last page. These notations are recorded in the textual notes and attributed to ANNOTATOR. Irwin argues that the annotator is a late sixteenth-century hand, but not Middleton's. The cleanness of the text suggests that great care was taken in publishing this work. *Microcynicon* contains the usual bizarre Renaissance punctuation, especially at the end of verse lines; Creede peppers the text with colons. Aside from minor oddities (discontinuities in the large capital lettering that opens each satire and in the ornamental lace borders that decorate the twenty-four leaves of the text), the text is carefully printed. Few emendations are necessary.

Microcynicon was not entered in the Stationers' Register. We are fortunate to have access to any copies of the first edition given that *Microcynicon* was burned shortly after it was published. On 1 June 1599 the Bishop of London and the Archbishop of Canterbury ordered that ten books, mainly satires, be destroyed. The Stationers' Register indicates that *Microcynicon* was indeed burnt at Stationers' Hall three days after the initial decree, and was not reprinted at all in the seventeenth century. The text has been edited only four times since its initial appearance in print. This work thus has its place in a history of censorship, and this vexed history is perhaps ironically responsible for enabling us to have an extremely stable text.

SEE ALSO

Text: *Works*, 1974
Authorship and date: this volume, 336

WORKS CITED

Previous Editions

Bullen, Arthur Henry, ed., *Works* (1886), vol. 8

Dyce, Alexander, ed., *Works* (1840), vol. 5
Irwin, Larry Wayne, *A Critical Edition of Thomas Middleton's 'Micro-cynicon', 'Father Hubburds Tales', and 'The Blacke Booke'* (unpublished Ph.D. diss., Univ. of Wisconsin, 1969)
Utterson, Edward Vernon, ed., *Microcynicon* (1842)

Other Works Cited

Adams, Joseph Quincy, ed., Thomas Middleton, *The Ghost of Lucrece* (1937)
Alden, Raymond MacDonald, *The Rise of Formal Satire in England, Under Classical Influence* (1899; repr. 1962)
Apperson, G. L., *English Proverbs and Proverbial Phrases* (1929)
Boose, Lynda E., 'The 1599 Bishops' Ban, Elizabethan Pornography, and the Sexualization of the Jacobean Stage', in *Enclosure Acts: Sexuality, Property, and Culture in Early Modern England*, eds. Richard Burt and John Michael Archer (1994), 185–200
Bredbeck, Greg, *Sodomy and Interpretation: Marlowe to Milton* (1991)
Collier, John Payne, *The Poetical Decameron or Ten Conversations on English Poets*, 2 vols (1820), I, 281–402
Garber, Marjorie, *Vested Interests: Cross-Dressing and Cultural Anxiety* (1992)
Guilpin, Everard, *Skialetheia, Or A Shadow of Truth*, in *Certain Epigrams and Satires*, ed. D. Allen Carroll (1974)
Hall, Joseph, *Virgidemiarum* (1597–8), in *Satires*, ed. Samuel Weller Singer (1824)
Horace (Quintus Horatius Flaccus), *Satires and Epistles*, trans. and ed. Niall Rudd (1973)
Kernan, Alvin, *The Cankered Muse: Satire of the English Renaissance* (1959)
Langley, Thomas, *An Abridgement of the Notable Works of Polidore Vergil* (1546)
Marlowe, Christopher, *Doctor Faustus*, ed. John D. Jump (1965)
Marston, John, *Pygmalion's Image and Certain Satires* (1598) and *The Scourge of Villainy* (1598), in *Works*, ed. A. H. Bullen, vol. 3 (1887)
Nashe, Thomas *Works*, ed. R. B. McKerrow, revised F. P. Wilson, 5 vols (1958)
Rankins, William, *Seven Satires* (1598)
Rich, Barnaby, *The Excellency of Good Women* (1613)
Shakespeare, William, *The Complete Works*, gen. eds. Stanley Wells and Gary Taylor (1986)
Swinburne, Algernon Charles, 'Thomas Middleton', *The Nineteenth Century* 19 (1886), 138–53
Taylor, Gary, 'The Renaissance and the End of Editing', *Palimpsest: Editorial Theory in the Humanities*, ed. George Bornstein and Ralph G. Williams (1993), 121–149
Tilley, Morris Palmer, *A Dictionary of the Proverbs in England in the Sixteenth and Seventeenth Centuries* (1950)
Wither, George, *Abuses Stript and Whipt* (1617)

TEXTUAL NOTES

Title-page Following the title, cast of characters and motto is one of Thomas Creede's devices—the emblem of a griffin seated on a stone or a book under which is a ball with wings (see McKerrow, 339). This is followed by the printer's identification: Imprinted at London by Thomas Creede, | for Thomas Buſhell, and are to be ſold | at his ſhop at the North doore of | Paules Church. 1599.

The Huntington copy has an ink signature (Iohes Playdell?).

Defiance.2 mask'st] THIS EDITION; mak'ſt CREEDE

Defiance.5 Miscontrarieties] CREEDE (miſſe contrarities)

Defiance.14 satire-days] CREEDE (Satyr-dayes)

Defiance.15 Than] CREEDE (then)

Defiance.16 nigrum] CREEDE (Negrum)

Prologue.2 *Book 1*] CREEDE (1. Booke.)

Prologue.9 veilèd] THIS EDITION; vaild CREEDE

Prologue.11 threat'ning] THIS EDITION; threating CREEDE; threatening DYCE

Prologue.22 before] CREEDE (beforne)

Prologue.25 the] ANNOTATOR; the the CREEDE

Prologue.36 satirist] CREEDE (Satyriſt)

1.2 *Satire 1*] CREEDE places this line after 'Insatiate Cron', but his order does not match the pattern established in subsequent satires.

1.24 Burse] CREEDE (burs)

1.39 immortal I] THIS EDITION (*conj.* DYCE); I mortall I CREEDE

1.41 Avarus] CREEDE (Auarus)

1.44 O'er] CREEDE (Ore)

1.58 complaint] BULLEN (*conj.* DYCE); compt CREEDE

1.60 bankërupts] CREEDE (bankerouts)

2.16 Engirt] DYCE (Ingirt); CREEDE (In girt)

2.19 he] DYCE; yee CREEDE

2.22 he] DYCE; ſhe CREEDE

2.23 chariot] CREEDE (Charrot)

2.58 endur'd] DYCE; endured CREEDE

2.60 lascivious] DYCE; lasciuions CREEDE

2.67 there] CREEDE (their)

2.68 the appointed] THIS EDITION; th'appointed CREEDE

2.68 whos'] CREEDE (whose)

3.7 pride's] THIS EDITION; Pride CREEDE

3.11 Bandied] CREEDE (banded)

3.24 Than] CREEDE (then)

3.29 their] CREEDE (there)

3.72 high-prized] CREEDE (hie prizde); high-pric'd DYCE

3.107 hussy] CREEDE (huswife)

3.116 th'amiss] CREEDE (th'amis)

3.121 unloads] CREEDE (unlades)

4.4 than] CREEDE (then)

4.38 chats] CREEDE (chates)

4.41 truth] CREEDE (troth)

4.55 An] CREEDE (and)

4.59 fiddlers] DYCE; fidler CREEDE

4.61 The other] DYCE; (the tother) CREEDE

5.18 seized] DYCE; CREEDE (ceasd)

5.43 indeed] CREEDE (in deed)

5.96 juggling] CREEDE (iugling). DYCE speculates that this could be a misprint for 'ingling', but given that the two were used interchangeably, 'juggling' is easily correct. Most likely both words would have been suggested by 'iugling'. But see the discussion by Weiss in this volume, p. 211.

6.3 Way] ANNOTATOR; Why CREEDE. The annotator's otherwise unauthoritative emendation makes sense in the context of the dialogue. The Innocent appropriately announces his arrival with a boisterous exclamatory phrase that prompts the Satirist's rebuke.

6.3 pure] poor DYCE

6.6 ha't] DYCE; hate CREEDE

6.21 their] CREEDE (there)

Epilogue.1 Epilogue] DYCE; Epilouge CREEDE

Epilogue.2 oft] DYCE; of CREEDE

Epilogue.6 must have] had ANNOTATOR

THE GHOST OF LUCRECE

Edited by G. B. Shand

The Ghost of Lucrece (STC 17885.5) was printed in London by Valentine Simmes in 1600. It was not entered in the Stationers' Register. Simmes produced an attractive small three-sheet octavo, of which only one copy has survived. An early owner had the poem bound together with four other works probably perceived as companion pieces: Shakespeare's *The Passionate Pilgrim* (1599 second edition, but containing two sheets of the otherwise lost first edition, probably from the same year), Shakespeare's *The Rape of Lucrece* (third edition, 1600—unique), E.C.'s *Emaricdulfe* (1595), and Shakespeare's *Venus and Adonis* (1599—unique). This remarkable assembly of unique materials was discovered in 1920 in a lumber-room of Longner Hall near Shrewsbury, and is now in the Folger Shakespeare Library. *Ghost* is bound in immediately after Shakespeare's *Lucrece*.

Analysis of *Ghost*'s spelling and setting preferences indicates a single compositor. While there is little evidence as to the nature of the printer's copy, the poem appears cleanly printed, presumably from authorial fair copy. (The frequent lack of concord between subject and predicate, as at 42, 120, 123, etc., appears to be a feature of Middleton's text, rather than evidence of textual corruption.) A curious feature is the setting of upper-case I for T twice on B5, perhaps because the compositor sometimes had difficulty recognizing upper-case I during distribution (which would also account for the foul-case error of upper-case I for lower-case l on B1^v).

SEE ALSO

Text: *Works*, 1989
Authorship and date: this volume, 337

WORKS CITED

Previous Edition

Adams, Joseph Quincy, ed., *The Ghost of Lucrece* (1937)

Other Works Cited

Augustine, Saint, *The City of God Against the Pagans*, tr. Marcus Dods (1950)
Bate, Jonathan, *Shakespeare and Ovid* (1993)
Bromley, Laura G., 'The Lost Lucrece: Middleton's *The Ghost of Lucrece*', *Papers in Language and Literature*, 21 (1985), 258–74
Campbell, Lily Bess, ed., *The Mirror for Magistrates* (1960)
Daniel, Samuel, *The Complaint of Rosamond*, in *Poems and A Defense of Rhyme*, ed. Arthur Colby Sprague (1930)
Donaldson, Ian, *The Rapes of Lucretia: A Myth and its Transformations* (1982)
Drayton, Michael, *Matilda* (1594)
Gascoigne, George, *Certain notes of Instruction*, in *The Complete Works*, ed. John W. Cunliffe (1907)
Greene, Robert, *Ciceronis Amor: Tully's Love* (1589)
Heywood, Thomas, *The Rape of Lucrece*, ed. John Pearson (1874)
Jed, Stephanie, *Chaste Thinking: The Rape of Lucretia and the Birth of Humanism* (1989)
Kerrigan, John, *Motives of Woe: Shakespeare and 'Female Complaint'* (1991)
Kyd, Thomas, *The Spanish Tragedy*, ed. Philip Edwards (1959)
Livy, *Historia*, ed. B. O. Foster (1919)
—— *The Roman History*, tr. Philemon Holland (1600)
Marlowe, Christopher, *Works*, ed. Fredson Bowers, 2 vols (1973)
Middleton, Thomas, *Works*, ed. Alexander Dyce (1840)
Ovid, *Fasti*, ed. Sir James George Frazer and G. P. Goold (1931, 1959)
Painter, William, *The Palace of Pleasure*, ed. Joseph Jacobs (1890)
Paster, Gail Kern, 'Leaky Vessels: The Incontinent Women of City Comedy', *Renaissance Drama*, NS 18 (1987), 43–65
Peele, George, *Polyhymnia* (1590)
Shakespeare, William, *The Complete Works*, ed. Stanley Wells and Gary Taylor (1986)

TEXTUAL NOTES

10 twins] SIMMES (twines). While 'twines', meaning 'strings' or 'strands', cannot be ruled out entirely here, SIMMES's spelling is an acceptable sixteenth-century form of 'twins', and the image of two-fingered baptismal blessing thus created is compelling in context.

18 honour's] SIMMES (Ho.)

24 *coeptis*] ADAMS; *cæptis* SIMMES

207 bandied] SIMMES (banded)

214 lids] ADAMS; Iiddes SIMMES

239 tyrant] SIMMES (Tyr-ant)

240 aunt] ADAMS; Ant SIMMES

245 Racks] SIMMES (Wrackes)

248 heart] hearts SIMMES, ADAMS. While SIMMES's reading might refer generally to the sympathetic hearts of the audience, the first-person singular of the rest of this stanza, describing the specific impact of the rape on Lucrece herself, suggests that she speaks here of her own wounded heart.

261 lose] SIMMES (loofe)

322 That] ADAMS; Ihat SIMMES

324 That] ADAMS; Ihat SIMMES

392 slept'st] flepft SIMMES, ADAMS

408 losers] SIMMES (loosers)

426 her] ADAMS; het SIMMES

527 Saint] SIMMES (S.)

528 Saint] SIMMES (S.)

582 Lord] SIMMES (L.)

614 shuttles] THIS EDITION; fhickles SIMMES, ADAMS. ADAMS glosses 'shuttles', apparently assuming that SIMMES's spelling is acceptable, although *OED* records no such form; 'shittle', an acceptable spelling of 'shuttle', is used elsewhere by Middleton, and might easily be misread 'shickle'. If, however, SIMMES's 'shickles' does reproduce what Middleton actually wrote, it is barely conceivable that there is a playful glance at 'shekels'.

616 Combing] SIMMES (Keaming), ADAMS. An obsolete spelling of 'Kembing', itself obsolete except in dialect.

THE PENNILESS PARLIAMENT OF THREADBARE POETS

Edited by Swapan Chakravorty

ON 3 August 1601, the following entry was made in the Stationers' Register:

William ffyrbrand Entred for his copie vnder the hand of master Seton The second parte of Jack of Dover
vj^d

The first known edition of *Penniless* was printed in London by William White and published by William Ferbrand in 1604 as the second part of the anonymous 'IACKE | OF | DOVER, | HIS | Queſt of Inquirie, or | his priuy ſearch for the verieſt | Foole in England' (STC 14291). In this quarto (WHITE), *Penniless* begins on sig. E3^v, under the subtitle 'Heere beginneth the pen-|niles Parliament of threed-bare Poets', and ends on sig. G4. It starts with an ornamental initial letter and has a running head (*The penniles Parliament | of threedbare Poets*) different from that of the preceding material.

There is, however, reason to believe that the two parts were printed together in 1601. F. P. Wilson (pp. 316–17) noted Hayward Townshend's report in *Megalopsychy* (1682) of a complaint brought in the Commons by Henry Doyley on 16 December 1601 against a libel entitled *The Assembly of Fools*. The latter was examined by the Privy Council and found to be an innocent 'Old Book, Entituled, *The Second Part of* Jack *of* Dover'. Its printer reportedly dwelt '*right over* Guild-Hall-Gate', an address which agrees with that given for Ferbrand in the imprint of the 1600 edition of Robert Armin's *Fool upon Fool*. The charge of insulting Parliament and the involvement of Jack of Dover's name in the title make it likely that Ferbrand printed the jests and the mock-parliament together in 1601 (FERBRAND).

The first edition in which *Penniless* is extant as a separate work is the 1608 quarto (STC 19307) printed for William Barley (BARLEY) by an unidentified printer. The new title reads 'THE | PENNILES | PARLIAMENT | OF | Threed-bare Poets: | OR, | All mirth and wittie Conceites.' The quarto, of which two copies survive in the Folger and Huntington Libraries, is set in black letter. It reproduces the ornamental initial letter of WHITE, and retains the subtitle 'Heere beginneth etc.'. The laced border at the end of the text closely resembles the one above the subtitle in WHITE.

Penniless itself is a revision of Simon Smellknave's *Fearfull and lamentable Effects of two dangerous Comets* (*Comets*), a mock-prognostication for 1591 (STC 22645), printed, like BARLEY, in black letter. There is one clue which might seem to indicate that *Comets* was used as printer's copy for WHITE. The phrase 'The belles of Barking'

on sig. B3 of *Comets* is changed to 'Bow Bell in Cheapside' in *Penniless* (l. 159). The words which follow, 'if they breake not', should have been revised to read 'if it break not'. The change to the singular is made in BARLEY, but the plural 'they' remains unaltered in WHITE, sig. F3. In spite of the dependence suggested by the error, it seems improbable that WHITE was set from a marked-up copy of *Comets*. The error could be authorial or compositorial. For all its reliance on *Comets*, the text of *Penniless* involves considerable rearrangement, changes and omissions. The sequences of passages in the two texts are different, phrases are transposed across pages and contexts, and lines which originally belonged to verse are inserted into prose passages. To take a few instances, ll. 7–12 were part of 'The Epiſtle to the Reader' in *Comets* (sig. A2), the words 'those that clip that they should not' in ll. 20–2 are taken from a passage on sig. A4 in *Comets* and inserted into another which may be found on sig. B3, and ll. 375–6 are paraphrased from four verse lines on sig. C3^v.

WHITE may have been set from the lost (FERBRAND) or, less plausibly, from the reviser's manuscript. BARLEY, on the other hand, appears to have been set either from WHITE, or, more probably, a source which WHITE followed. Of the WHITE errors repeated in BARLEY, 'markt' (l. 43), 'gives' (l. 154), and 'woman' (l. 255), for 'mark', 'give' and 'women' respectively could have had their source in a manuscript. But 'ventrouſty' (l. 265) is a foul case error in WHITE which is left uncorrected in BARLEY, although BARLEY rectifies WHITE's use of a wrong ligature in l. 215 ('Miſtreſte' for 'Miſtreſſe'). A link between the two texts is also suggested by the care taken in the setting of sheets A and B of BARLEY to make the line-breaks coincide, despite the use of black letter, with those in WHITE, often by spelling out ampersands and contractions and *vice versa*, or by oscillating between indifferent orthographic variants (*shall/shal, we/wee, manner/maner*, etc.). The reason for this seems to be that the copy used by Barley's printer was cast off at what is now the end of G1^v in WHITE, and the work divided into two segments, the first covering sheets A and B, and the second sheet C. To make the end of sheet B coincide with that of G1^v in WHITE or its equivalent in WHITE's source, it was found necessary to space out the copy on sig. B4, where a paragraph from WHITE is split and the formulaic initial word 'Furthermore' is added to the sundered clause (l. 246). There was no such pressure in setting sheet C, and errors increase as paragraphs and line-breaks coincide with diminishing regularity with those in WHITE. Sheet C shows another revealing difference, the hyphen being dropped from 'threed-bare' on the recto running heads. Of course, if WHITE is a line-by-line reprint of the lost 1601 edition, the pattern in BARLEY may derive from FERBRAND rather than WHITE itself.

BARLEY is the first available edition in which *Penniless* is treated as a discrete work. It contains at least one important passage missing in WHITE (l. 5), and a few substantive variants show that the printer had access to an exemplar more authoritative than WHITE. For instance, 'faft' and 'with a' make better sense than WHITE's 'feaft' and 'without' in ll. 28–9 and 88–90 respectively, although in each case the change inverts the meaning. 'Authorial' preferences in paragraphing, spelling and punctuation have only limited consequence where such things are determined by the exigencies of plagiarism, revision and hasty production. The paragraph-divisions in BARLEY do not seriously affect the text, and may even be authoritative, simulating the layout and black-letter font of printed Parliamentary decrees and royal proclamations. These details may derive from an earlier manuscript or FERBRAND, since the hyphenation and capitalization of BARLEY are on the whole more consistent than those in WHITE.

WHITE thus seems derived from a text which had bibliographical links with BARLEY, but which did not contain errors that occur in the latter. In many such instances, WHITE's readings are supported by *Comets* (see ll. 41, 121, 135, 159, 172, 221, 223, 227, 307, 309, 318, 324, 338–9, 353, 366). WHITE and BARLEY are thus bibliographically similar, but each contains authoritative readings missing in the other. Such evidence indicates (as was pointed out to me by the general editor) that both derive independently from FERBRAND. When books from this period are known to have been printed in multiple editions, and some of these editions survive in single copies (we possess only one copy of WHITE and two of BARLEY), it is more than likely that there were other editions which have not come down at all (Willard).

FERBRAND, therefore, would have been the ideal control-text for *Penniless*. In its absence, this edition is eclectically constructed from both WHITE and BARLEY. In deciding between variants, we have checked the source-reading in *Comets*. Hence, the evidence of *Comets* is indicated in the collation whenever one of the variants agrees with it. (Since *Comets* is not a text of *Penniless* proper, it is italicized, rather than printed in small capitals, like other sigla.) Such a comparison suggests that WHITE was closer to FERBRAND, and this edition prefers WHITE for indifferent variants when there is no corresponding material in *Comets*.

Although *Penniless* itself is a revision of *Comets*, the reviser's opening sentence speaks of 'all such as buys this book' (ll. 1–3), a clear signal that the revision was not planned as a sequel to the *Jack of Dover* jests. To make way for the material from Smellknave, the jests themselves were revised from Jack's first-person narrative to an exchange between him and a group of down-at-heel poets gathered at what was thought to be Duke Humphrey's tomb in St Paul's Cathedral. In the only surviving copy of WHITE (at the Bodleian library), six of the jests (Fools of Berkshire, Devonshire, Cornwall, Hampshire, Essex and London) retain Jack's older first-person story. The evidence points to two stages in the revision: first *Comets* is transformed into *Penniless*; second, *Jack of Dover* is adapted to accommodate what was not originally a sequel. It seems likely that the same reviser who adapted *Comets* also altered the first and last paragraphs of the *Jack of Dover* jests in WHITE to prepare for the transition to *Penniless* (see Canon and Chronology). The relevant extracts are hence included in this edition as Additional Passages.

On 12 November 1614, John Beale acquired the rights in *Penniless* from Barley's widow, and a quarto entitled *Jacke of Dovers merry tales* was published by him in 1615 and sold by Richard Higgenbotham (BEALE[1]; STC 14292). The title says *Whereunto is annexed The Pennileſſe Parliament of Three-bare Poets*, although the sequel is not present in the only known copy (at the Bodleian). The last tale (Fool of London) ends abruptly in BEALE[1], and about 12 lines present in WHITE are dropped. While WHITE repeats the closing parenthesis in which Jack says that he has not found the fool he is looking for, BEALE[1] closes on sig. F4 with Jack announcing that he has now found the fool of all fools. The link passage in WHITE (Additional Passage B) does not follow, the black-letter characters taper off to FINIS and laced borders appear at the foot of the text. *Penniless*, however, figures in *The Table of the Contents* on A2[v].

The same six jests retain the first-person narrative as in WHITE. But the numbered tales with headings summarizing the jests indicate a different printer's copy. These do not seem later additions since the heading for Tale II on sig. A4 points to a layer of the text older than WHITE (see Canon and Chronology). In WHITE, the matter of C2[v] appears on D1[v], that of D1[v] on D4[v], and that of D4[v] on C2[v]. As a result, the jest involving the Fool of Berkshire is placed out of sequence. The jest appears in the right place in BEALE[1]. However, the tale of the Fool of Derby is cut short after a couple of lines in BEALE[1], and the next tale begins on E1, apparently because of faulty casting off.

Beale brought out a discrete octavo edition of *Penniless* in 1637 (BEALE[2]; STC 19307.5). It introduces a substantial number of new paragraph-breaks, and reproduces the shorter paragraphs of quire C in BARLEY. BEALE[2] elsewhere follows the readings in WHITE and BARLEY almost in equal proportion, and introduces errors and variants absent in both. Most of these variants, as also the expanded title, are followed in the octavo edition printed for John Wright (the younger) in 1649 (WRIGHT; Wing P1398). Wright omits around 827 words (not counting minor variants), the exclusions made in units that correspond to the paragraph divisions in BEALE[2]. It seems that WRIGHT is derived from BEALE[2]. The printer may have checked earlier editions as well, since in a number of places the text in WRIGHT follows WHITE or BARLEY or both rather than BEALE[2]; however, some of these corrections might have been made independently of any textual source; moreover, WRIGHT might derive not from Beale's 1637 edition, but from the apparently lost 1615 edition, or from another lost edition printed between 1615 and 1637. With so popular a text, lost intermediate editions are a real possibility.

Penniless was reprinted from BARLEY by William Oldys in the first volume of *The Harleian Miscellany* in 1744 (OLDYS). It was revised by Thomas Park in 1808 for the first volume of the ten-volume reissue of the *Harleian Miscellany* published by John White and John Murray (PARK). It was printed again in the third volume (1809) of the chronological reissue in twelve volumes by Robert Dutton (MALHAM). The editor was supposedly J. Malham, who wrote the Preface to the collection. OLDYS modernizes the spelling and grammar, introduces a few errors, and omits two statutes (ll. 289–93, 312–16). OLDYS also numbers the mock-statutes, ignoring the irregular and exigent nature of paragraph-breaks in BARLEY. PARK and MALHAM reproduce the text in OLDYS. The differences between them are minor, except for one variant recorded in the Textual Notes (l. 206–7). Two more reprints appeared in the nineteenth century: T. Wright's edition in *Early English Poetry, Ballads, and Popular Literature of the Middle Ages*, Percy Society, 7 (1842), and Charles Hindley's for the second volume of his *Old Book Collector's Miscellany* (1872). Both editions are without authority, being straight reprints of OLDYS.

SEE ALSO

Text: *Works*, 2003
Authorship and date: this volume, 337

WORKS CITED

Previous Editions

Jack of Dover, His Quest of Inquiry, or His Privy Search for the Veriest Fool in England (1604)
The Penniless Parliament of Threadbare Poets, or, All Mirth and Witty Conceits (1608)
Jack of Dover's Merry Tales, or His Quest of Inquiry, or Privy Search for the Veriest Fool in England, Whereunto is annexed The Penniless Parliament of Threadbare Poets (1615)
The Penniless Parliament of Threadbare Poets, or The Merry Fortune-Teller (1637)
The Penniless Parliament of Threadbare Poets, or The Merry Fortune-Teller (1649)
MALHAM, J., ed., in *The Harleian Miscellany*, 3 (1809)
OLDYS, W., ed., in *The Harleian Miscellany*, 1 (1744)
PARK, T., ed., in *The Harleian Miscellany*, 1 (1808)

Other Works Cited

Armin, Robert, *Fool upon Fool, or Six Sorts of Sots* (1600)
Bosanquet, E. F., *English Printed Almanacks and Prognostications* (1917)
Butler, Samuel, *Hudibras*, ed. John Wilders (1967)
Chakravorty, Swapan, '"Upon a sudden wit": On the Sources of an Unnoticed Pun in *The Revenger's Tragedy*', Notes and Queries 240 (1995), 344–5
Chartier, Roger, *The Cultural Uses of Print in Early Modern France*, trans. Lydia G. Cochrane (1988)
Clark, Peter, 'A Crisis Contained? The Condition of English Towns in the 1590s', in Peter Clark, ed., *The European Crisis of the 1590s: Essays in Comparative History* (1985), 44–66

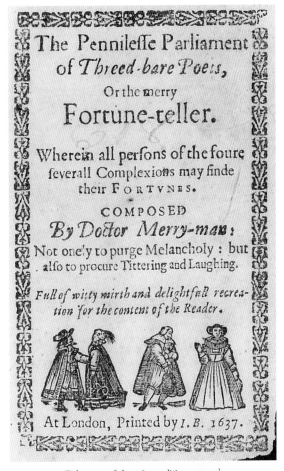

Title-page of the 1637 edition, BEALE[2].

Clark, Sandra, *The Elizabethan Pamphleteers: Popular Moralistic Pamphlets 1580–1640* (1983)
Dean, James, 'Artistic Conclusiveness in Chaucer's *Parliament of Fowls*', *The Chaucer Review* 21 (1986), 16–25
Elton, G. R., ed., *The Tudor Constitution: Documents and Commentary* (1960; 2nd edn., 1982)
Febvre, Lucien, and Martin, Henri-Jean, *The Coming of the Book: The Impact of Printing 1450–1800*, trans. David Gerard, ed. Geoffrey Nowell-Smith and David Wotton (1976; Verso edn., 1978)
Fitzgeffrey, Henry, *Satyres and Satyricall Epigrams* (1617)
Grosart, A. B., ed., *The Non-Dramatic Works of Thomas Dekker*, 5 vols (1884–6)
—— ed., *The Works of Gabriel Harvey*, 3 vols (1884–5)
Harriss, G. L., 'Medieval Doctrines in the Debates on Supply, 1610–1629', in Kevin Sharpe, ed., *Faction and Parliament: Essays on Early Stuart History* (1978), 73–103
Mandrou, Robert, *From Humanism to Science 1480–1700*, trans. Brian Pearce (1978)
McKerrow, Ronald B., ed., *The Works of Thomas Nashe*, 5 vols (1904–10; with corrections and supplementary notes by F. P. Wilson, 1958)

Neuburg, Victor E., *Popular Literature: A History and Guide* (1977)

Orrell, John, 'Building the Fortune', *Shakespeare Quarterly* 44 (1993), 127–44

Rhodes, Neil, *Elizabethan Grotesque* (1980)

Rowlands, Samuel, *Democritus, or Doctor Merry-man His Medicines* (1607)

—— *Doctor Merry-man: or Nothing but Mirth* (1616)

Smellknave, Simon, *Fearful and Lamentable Effects of Two Dangerous Comets* (1591)

Smith, J. C., and de Selincourt, E., eds., *Spenser: Poetical Works* (1912)

Willard, Oliver M., 'The Survival of English Books Printed before 1640: A Theory and Some Illustrations', *The Library*, IV, 23 (1942–3), 171–90

Wilson, F. P., *Shakespearian and Other Studies*, ed. Helen Gardner (1969)

Young, Edward, *Conjectures on Original Composition* (1759), in Edmund D. Jones, ed., *English Critical Essays (Sixteenth, Seventeenth and Eighteenth Centuries)* (1922; rpt. 1947), 270–311

TEXTUAL NOTES

Title   *The ... Poets*] There is no separate title-page for *Penniless* in WHITE. The section is subtitled 'Heere beginneth the pen-|niles Parliament of threed-bare Poets' (see note on l. B.10 and Textual Introduction). THE | PENNILES | PARLIAMENT | OF | Threed-bare Poets: | OR, | All mirth and wittie Conceites. BARLEY; The Pennileſſe Parliament | of *Threed-|-bare Poets*, | Or the merry | Fortune-teller. | Wherein all perſons of the foure | ſeverall Complexions may finde | their FORTUNES. | COMPOSED | *by Doctor Merry-man*: | Not onely to purge Melancholy: but | alſo to procure Tittering and Laughing. | *Full of witty mirth and delightfull recrea-|tion for the content of the Reader.* BEALE², WRIGHT

2   buys] doe buy BEALE², WRIGHT

3   laughs] laugh BEALE², WRIGHT

3   he hath] they haue BEALE², WRIGHT

5   and ... stockings‚] BARLEY; ~ at all on BEALE², WRIGHT; *not in* WHITE

6   is] *not in* WHITE

16   their hair] WHITE, BARLEY, *Comets*; their the ~ BEALE²; the their ~ WRIGHT

20   taste] WHITE+, *Comets*; take WRIGHT

22   not] WHITE, BARLEY, *Comets*; ~ clip BEALE², WRIGHT

22   have] ſhave WRIGHT

25   hath] WHITE+, *Comets*; haue BEALE²

29   fast] BARLEY+, *Comets*; ſeaſt WHITE

33–9   In ... antiquity.] *not in* WRIGHT

39   true be] be true BEALE²

39   the] *not in* BEALE²

41   superiority] WHITE+, *Comets*; ſeperioritie BARLEY

42   chamber] WHITE+, *Comets*; Camber WRIGHT

43   painting] WHITE, BARLEY, *Comets*; panting BEALE², WRIGHT

43   mark] BEALE², WRIGHT; markt WHITE, BARLEY. The error was probably caused by anticipating 'markes', which follows in l. 44.

44   letters] BARLEY+, *Comets*; letter WHITE

45   lawfully be] be lawfully BEALE²

48   masters] WHITE+, *Comets*; Maſter BEALE²

52   through] BARLEY, *Comets*; throughout WHITE+

54   money before] WHITE, BARLEY, *Comets*; their ~ any good BEALE², WRIGHT

57   Those] WHITE+, *Comets*; and thoſe BEALE²

63   as] WHITE, BARLEY, *Comets*; ~ at laſt BEALE², WRIGHT

64   gather] WHITE, BARLEY, *Comets*; and ~ BEALE², WRIGHT

71   a] WHITE, BARLEY, *Comets*; the BEALE², WRIGHT

73, 74   some] WHITE, BARLEY, *Comets*; Some ſhall haue BEALE², WRIGHT

73   migrain] WHITE (Megram)

76   some] WHITE, BARLEY, *Comets*; Some ſort of people ſhall haue BEALE², WRIGHT

77   such a] WHITE, BARLEY, *Comets*; such there be that haue a ſcent or BEALE², WRIGHT

81–3   some ... themselves] WHITE+, *Comets*; *not in* WRIGHT

81   some] WHITE, BARLEY, *Comets*; Otherſome BEALE²

82   keep never] neuer keep BEALE². Source line in *Comets*, sig. B1, has 'find neuer'.

83   themselves] WHITE, BARLEY, *Comets*; ~ withall BEALE²

88   poulters] WHITE+, *Comets*; poulterers WRIGHT

90   with a] BARLEY, BEALE²; without WHITE, WRIGHT. Source line in *Comets*, sig. B1ᵛ, reads 'with'.

91   and] WHITE+, *Comets*; *not in* WRIGHT

100   nimmers] BARLEY+, *Comets*; Nimners WHITE

102   stare] WHITE+, *Comets*; starve WRIGHT

106   get] WHITE, BARLEY, *Comets*; can get BEALE², WRIGHT

106   swords] THIS EDITION (G.T.); Sworde WHITE+. The error seems to been made in adapting the reading in *Comets*, sig. B1ᵛ, 'by the sword'.

107   treasurer] WHITE, BARLEY, *Comets*; ~ or purſer of the ſhip BEALE², WRIGHT

107   anything] WHITE, BARLEY, *Comets*; any money BEALE², WRIGHT

108   build] WHITE+, *Comets*; built BEALE²

108   in] WHITE+, *Comets*; on BEALE²

110   further] furthermore BEALE²

112   *facias*] THIS EDITION (G.T.); *faces* WHITE, BARLEY; *facies* BEALE², WRIGHT, *Comets*

113   into] WHITE+, *Comets*; in WRIGHT

113   that] WHITE, BARLEY, *Comets*; and ſuch that vſe to BEALE², WRIGHT

116   down] WHITE, BARLEY, *Comets*; *not in* BEALE², WRIGHT

121   husbands] WHITE, WRIGHT, *Comets*; Hubſands BARLEY; huſband BEALE²

126–38   Furthermore ... reading.] *not in* WRIGHT

126   Ale] WHITE, BARLEY, *Comets*; ſtrong ~ BEALE²

127   his] WHITE, BARLEY, *Comets*; the BEALE²

128   liquor] WHITE, BARLEY, *Comets*; ~ therewith BEALE²

131   their] WHITE, BARLEY, *Comets*; ~ the BEALE²

133   were] WHITE, BARLEY, *Comets*; *not in* BEALE²

135   fees] WHITE, BEALE², *Comets*; fee BARLEY

138   lines] WHITE, BARLEY, *Comets*; ~ herein BEALE²

138   reading] WHITE, BARLEY, *Comets*; ouermuch reading of the ſame BEALE²

140   exquisite] WHITE+, *Comets*; requiſite WRIGHT

140   judgements] Iudgement BEALE², *Comets*

141   of] WHITE, BARLEY, *Comets*; which are of the BEALE², WRIGHT

145   have] WHITE+, *Comets*; *not in* WRIGHT

146   doth] doe BEALE², WRIGHT

149–55   As ... Parliament.] *not in* WRIGHT

150   of the] of ‚ WHITE. The dropped article, which should have been the first word on sig. F3 in WHITE, remains the

catchword on sig. F2ᵛ.

151 thereof] hereof BEALE²

154 give] OLDYS; giues WHITE+

155 act] this ~ BEALE²

158 juryman] ~ in this cafe BEALE², WRIGHT

159 it] they WHITE. Source line in *Comets*, sig. B3, reads 'they break not', since the pronoun refers to the 'belles of Barking'. See Textual Introduction.

160 patents] pattent BEALE²

162 dinners] dinner BEALE², *Comets*

162 custom] WHITE, BARLEY, *Comets*; ~ is to haue BEALE², WRIGHT

165 christened] WHITE, BARLEY, *Comets*; firft borne BEALE², WRIGHT

166 Beside] WHITE, BARLEY, *Comets*; Besides that BEALE², WRIGHT

167 teacher] WHITE, BARLEY, *Comets*; teachers BEALE², WRIGHT

168-74 The...Tyburn.] *not in* WRIGHT

172 grounds] WHITE, *Comets*; ground BARLEY, BEALE²

175 it] BEALE², WRIGHT; ~ is WHITE, BARLEY

177 power] WHITE+, *Comets*; powder WRIGHT

180 Silk] Alfo ~ BEALE², WRIGHT

187 wits] WHITE+, *Comets*; wit BEALE²

206 careless] WHITE (careles), BEALE², WRIGHT; Carles BARLEY. BARLEY drops the first 'e', leading to a confusion with 'carles', meaning churls or base persons (*OED sb* 2). OLDYS and MALHAM follow the BARLEY reading, while PARK follows WHITE. Source line in *Comets*, sig. B4, reads 'careleffe'.

207 on] WHITE, BARLEY, *Comets*; altogether vpon BEALE², WRIGHT

207 on] WHITE, BARLEY, *Comets*; vpon BEALE², WRIGHT

211 apple] WHITE, BARLEY, *Comets*; ~ and a pint of wine BEALE², WRIGHT

213-16 It...her.] *not in* WRIGHT

213 established] eftablifh BARLEY

214 those‚] WHITE, BARLEY, *Comets*; the‚ BEALE²

215 mistress] miftreff BARLEY, BEALE², *Comets*; Miftrefte WHITE

217 Also] And WRIGHT

219 take] WHITE+, *Comets*; thinke WRIGHT

219 Also] And WRIGHT

221 shall catch] WHITE+, *Comets*; will cach BARLEY

223 for] WHITE+, *Comets*, *not in* BARLEY

227 whither] WHITE+, *Comets*; whether BARLEY

228 unpublished] unpunifhed WRIGHT

229-30 contentions] contention WRIGHT, *Comets*

231 at] WHITE+, *Comets*; at at WRIGHT

232-9 For...eyes.] *not in* WRIGHT

234 won] WHITE (wan)

234 Boulogne] WHITE (Bullen). OLDYS retains the archaic spelling. The word is spelled in this way in *The Bachelor's Banquet*, 1, 193; and Samuel Butler, *Hudibras*, 1.1.308, where it rhymes with 'woollen'.

238 hath lost] WHITE, BARLEY, *Comets*; loft both BEALE²

240 O] WHITE+, *Comets*; But oh WRIGHT

242 a] WHITE+, *Comets*; *not in* BEALE²

244 that] WHITE, BARLEY, *Comets*, *not in* BEALE², WRIGHT

244 is] WHITE, BARLEY, *Comets*; *not in* BEALE², WRIGHT

250 shall] WHITE+, *Comets*; all WRIGHT

251 It] Furthermore it BARLEY. The addition of the word in BARLEY is needed to begin the new paragraph created at this point to space out the copy (see Textual Introduction).

251 shall] all WRIGHT

255 women] THIS EDITION; woman WHITE+. Source line in *Comets*, sig. C1, has 'Women'.

261-4 And...them.] *not in* WRIGHT

265 vent'rously] BEALE², WRIGHT; ventroufty WHITE; Ventroufity BARLEY. OLDYS emends to the uncontracted form 'venturously'. The wrong ligature in both texts suggests the dependence of BARLEY on WHITE, or of both on a lost earlier edition. Source line in *Comets*, sig. C1, uses the correct ligature.

269 Queenhithe] WHITE (Queene-hiue)

276 Porters'] WHITE, BARLEY, *Comets*; Also ~ BEALE², WRIGHT

278 amongst] WHITE, BARLEY, *Comets*; among BEALE², WRIGHT, *Comets*

280-1 The...falchions.] *not in* WRIGHT

282 mind] WHITE, BARLEY, *Comets*; minds BEALE², WRIGHT

283-4 the wars] ‚ ~ BARLEY, BEALE²

284 get] can get BARLEY, BEALE²

285 apron-strings] Aporne-ftringes WHITE

287 *Noli me tangere*] *Nole me tangeri* WHITE

288 the] *not in* BEALE², WRIGHT

293 bauble] WHITE (bable). The archaic spelling stresses the 'bauble/babble' pun.

295 and] and Church men and BEALE², WRIGHT

296 the] a BEALE², WRIGHT

297 be] WHITE, BARLEY, *Comets*; ~ fold BEALE², WRIGHT

299 by the statute] by Statute BARLEY; *not in* WRIGHT. The article is consistently present elsewhere in *Penniless*.

300-2 It...evening.] *not in* WRIGHT

302 inclined] BARLEY+, *Comets*; inclining WHITE

305 halfpenny] WHITE+, *Comets*; halfe-peny BARLEY

306-9 Chaucer's...her.] *not in* WRIGHT

307 were] WHITE, *Comets*; ~ before BARLEY, BEALE². There is a tear in the page at this point in BEALE², but the space indicates two words.

308 abroad] WHITE, BARLEY, *Comets*; broad BEALE²

309 comment] WHITE, BEALE², *Comets*; cemment BARLEY

313-16 Also...labour.] *not in* WRIGHT

314 in] WHITE, BARLEY, *Comets*; *not in* BEALE²

314 day] BARLEY, BEALE², *Comets*; pay WHITE. The error in WHITE seems due to a turned 'd'.

315 where they] WHITE, BEALE², *Comets*; wheye the BARLEY

318 sometime] WHITE, *Comets*; fometimes BARLEY+

321 sea] Seas BARLEY

324 a] WHITE, BEALE², *Comets*; *not in* BARLEY, WRIGHT

328 fever] THIS EDITION; fauour WHITE+; The error seems to have arisen from a misreading of the word in *Comets*, sig. C3ᵛ, 'feuor'.

336 have] WHITE+, *Comets*; have have WRIGHT

338-9 hot ‚ rheums] WHITE+, *Comets*; ~ that ~ BARLEY. An anticipatory error in BARLEY; 'that' follows later in the line.

346-52 Furthermore...charges.] *not in* WRIGHT

348 servitors] Seruitor BEALE²

353 you] WHITE+, *Comets*; your BARLEY

357-9 In...rheum.] *not in* WRIGHT

360 more] WHITE, BARLEY, *Comets*; *not in* BEALE², WRIGHT

361-3 It...barelegged.] WHITE+, *Comets*; *not in* WRIGHT

366 better] WHITE+, *Comets*; other BARLEY. BARLEY anticipates 'other' appearing later in the line.

373-4 But...midnight.] *not in* WRIGHT

373 sprites] WHITE; Spirits BARLEY; Spriits BEALE²

387 safe] *not in* BEALE², WRIGHT

A.1 *Jack...Inquiry*] WHITE; Iacke of Douers | *Queft of inquirie for the verieft* | Foole *in England.* BEALE¹

A.12 there] WHITE; where BEALE¹

A.17 this] WHITE; the BEALE¹

A.20 discovered] WHITE; difcouereth BEALE¹

A.23 digestion] BEALE¹; difieftion WHITE

B.1-9 'Well,'...fools.'] WHITE; *not in* BEALE¹

B.10 Here...*Poets*] WHITE, BARLEY; *not in* BEALE¹, BEALE², WRIGHT

NEWS FROM GRAVESEND: SENT TO NOBODY

Edited by Gary Taylor

THE extant copies of *News from Gravesend* (STC 12199) were 'Printed by T.C. for Thomas Archer, and are to be solde at the long Shop vnder S. Mildreds Church in the Poultry.' The 'T.C.' identified on the title-page was Thomas Creede; in all other instances, the specified address is associated with Henry Rocket, not Thomas Archer. The first edition, a quarto of six sheets dated 1604—hereafter CREEDE—was also apparently the last, until F. P. Wilson included the work in his collection of *The Plague Pamphlets of Thomas Dekker* (1925). This is the first edition since Wilson's, and the first ever in modern spelling.

SEE ALSO

Text: *Works*, 132
Authorship and date: this volume, 346

WORKS CITED

Previous Edition

Wilson, F. P., ed., *The Plague Pamphlets of Thomas Dekker* (1925)

Other Works Cited

Barroll, Leeds, *Politics, Plague, and Shakespeare's Theater: The Stuart Years* (1991)
Boccaccio, Giovanni, *The Decameron*, trans. G. H. McWilliam (1972)
Bowers, Fredson, ed., *The Dramatic Works of Thomas Dekker*, 4 vols (1953–61)
Braudel, Fernand, *Capitalism and Material Life, 1400–1800* (1973)
Bullein, William, *A Dialogue Against the Fever Pestilence*, ed. Mark W. Bullen and A. H. Bullen, Early English Text Society (1888)
Camus, Albert, *La Peste* (1972)
Creighton, Charles, *A History of Epidemics in Britain*, 2 vols (1891–4)
Defoe, Daniel, *A Journal of the Plague Year*, ed. Anthony Burgess and Christopher Bristow (1966)
Hoy, Cyrus, *Introduction, Notes, and Commentaries to texts in 'The Dramatic Works of Thomas Dekker'*, 4 vols (1980)
Lodge, Thomas, *A Treatise of the Plague* (1603), in *The Complete Works of Thomas Lodge*, 4 vols (1883), vol. 4
Nashe, Thomas, *The Works of Thomas Nashe*, ed. R. B. McKerrow (1904)
Palliser, D. M., *The Age of Elizabeth* (1992)
Shelley, Mary, *The Last Man*, introd. Brian Aldiss (1985)
Shrewsbury, J. F. D., *A History of Bubonic Plague in the British Isles* (1970)
Slack, Paul, *The Impact of Plague in Tudor and Stuart England* (1985)
Wilson, F. P., *The Plague in Shakespeare's London* (1963)

TEXTUAL NOTES

1   *The*] WILSON; TEE CREEDE
3   Maecen-asses] CREEDE (Mecæn-affes)
12–13   *Apophthegms*] CREEDE (Apothegmes)
26   caviar] CREEDE (*Caueare*)
35   swam] CREEDE (fwom)
37   Plancius] WILSON; *Plamius* CREEDE
42   Queenhithe] CREEDE (Queene-hyue)
52   Sultan] CREEDE (Soldan)
60   impreses] CREEDE (impræfaes)
62   taffeta] CREEDE (Taffaty)
81   Latin-sellers] CREEDE (lattin-fellers)
87   hate them] WILSON; hate him CREEDE
100   *Dicite*] WILSON; *Dieite* CREEDE
121   them] WILSON; him CREEDE
166   whenas] CREEDE (when as)
173   stilts] WILSON; ftilttes CREEDE
211   off] CREEDE (of)
225, 319   smelled] CREEDE (smelt)
236   broke] CREEDE (brake)
276   commendations] WILSON; commendatious CREEDE
297   saving] fauing CREEDE (B3ᵛ, text); hauing CREEDE (B3, catchword)

303   whinny] THIS EDITION; weihy CREEDE. I cannot find CREEDE, or anything resembling it, in *OED*; perhaps spelled 'wenhy'.
308   sweat] CREEDE (fwet)
335   o'] CREEDE (a)
393   roost] CREEDE (roaft)
401   jostling] CREEDE (iuftling)
421   lain] CREEDE (lyen)
425   swooning] CREEDE (fwounding)
433   will] CREEDE (Britwell); wil CREEDE (Bodleian)
482   accite] CREEDE (Bodleian); atcite CREEDE (Britwell, Huntington)
490   her] WILSON; *not in* CREEDE
514   shrieking] CREEDE (fhriking)
616   give] THIS EDITION; giues CREEDE. The collocation 'leap... and gives' calls awkward attention to the difference in the number of the verbs, and there is no intervening noun to account for the shift.
621   within] WILSON; wirhin CREEDE
667   Rhine] CREEDE (rhein)
710   lot] THIS EDITION; *Lott* CREEDE. The capitals and italics makes it clear that CREEDE interprets this word as an allusion to the Old Testament figure who escaped from Sodom; but such an allusion seems wildly inappropriate here.

716 antic] CREEDE (Antique)

721 Has] WILSON; Had CREEDE

729 care] CREEDE; charge THIS EDITION *conj.*

741 Turned] THIS EDITION; Turned CREEDE (= Turnèd)

742.n *Apostrophe ad civitatem*] THIS EDITION; *A postr | ad Ciui | tem.* CREEDE. The marginal note is cropped in all surviving copies, and begins in the right margin in a space between lines 742 and 743; WILSON begins it after 745.

744 Altar] WILSON; Alrar CREEDE

777 rend] CREEDE (rent)

780 loon] CREEDE (Lowne)

796 ostriches] CREEDE (Eſtridges)

799 wave] WILSON; waues CREEDE

809 Whitsun] CREEDE (Whiſſon)

812 eas'ly] CREEDE (eaſely)

843 fold] WILSON; fold CREEDE

847 desperate] WILSON; deſperare CREEDE

863 the pride] THIS EDITION; ther ~ CREEDE; thy ~ WILSON *conj.*

911 wife's] CREEDE (wiues)

914 lain] CREEDE (lyen)

922 ha'p'ny] CREEDE (halfe-penny)

937 What] WILSON; who CREEDE

952 now] THIS EDITION; *not in* CREEDE. The line is a syllable short, and 'now' provides the contrast which seems to be required between the reproof of the city governors which occurs here in the poem and the praise of them which is promised 'one day' (949): 'We will praise you in the future, but *now* you are making a mistake.' Alternatively, CREEDE's 'methinkes' might be a compositorial substitution for the rarer, old-fashioned 'methinketh'.

983 infectious] WILSON; infeċtions CREEDE

989 breathed] THIS EDITION; breath CREEDE. The change seems necessary for the sense: God 'breathed' heaven, earth, and seas in two senses: they were created by his command (he literally breathed them into existence), and he gave life, breath, to all the creatures in them. For comparable religious uses of the verb *breathe*, see *Solomon* 7.172, 18.67, *Hengist* 4.4.55. The error—omission of the last letter of manuscript 'breathd'—could easily have resulted from contamination by 'death' in the preceding line.

1010 in] WILSON; on CREEDE

1053 her] THIS EDITION; the CREEDE. The strumpet does not live by 'any' fall, but specifically by her own fall (both physical and figurative).

1054 his] THIS EDITION; her CREEDE. The plague is elsewhere male: a king (467) whose snares are 'his' (978). Moreover, 'her' in this context is unfortunately ambiguous, because it seems most obviously to refer to the female strumpet of the previous lines, rather than the (not specifically gendered) 'contagion'. Emendation to 'his' removes the ambiguity, and brings the gendering of the plague into conformity with the rest of the poem. Moreover, 'his threats' could refer either to the plague or backward to the (equally impotent) threats of the plague-stricken former lover. The error could have arisen from a misplaced correction in foul proofs: 'her' should have been substituted for 'the' in the preceding line, but was instead substituted for 'his' in this line.

1113 mushroom] CREEDE (miſhrump)

1118 dearths] THIS EDITION; deaths CREEDE. The emendation is suggested not only by the rhyme, but by rhetoric and sense: 'twenty deaths' (a ridiculously small number, in the circumstances) is not a fit parallel for 'ten plagues.'

THE NIGHTINGALE AND THE ANT
and FATHER HUBBURD'S TALES

Edited by Adrian Weiss

THOMAS MIDDLETON'S *Father Hubburd's Tales, Or The Ant and the Nightingale* was published in two editions dated 1604. The first, CREEDE 1 (STC 17874.3; formerly STC 17881), bears the title-page:

THE ANT, | AND THE | Nightingale: | OR | FATHER | *Hubburds* Tales. | [Thomas Bushell's device, McKerrow no. 313] | LONDON | Printed by T.C. for Tho: Bushell, and | are to be solde by *Ieffrey Chorlton*, at his | Shop at the North doore of | Paules, 1604. |

In the second edition, CREEDE 2 (STC 17874.7; formerly STC 17880), the titles were reset in a reversed order, Creede's device was substituted for Bushell's, and a new publisher and point of sale was indicated in the imprint:

FATHER | Hubburds Tales: | OR | THE ANT, | And the Nightingale. | [Thomas Creede's device, McKerrow no. 299] | LONDON | Printed by T.C. for William Cotton, | and are to be solde at his Shop neare ad-|ioyning to Ludgate. 1604. |

The text was entered in the Stationers' Register on 3 January 1604 to Thomas Bushell with the usual fee of sixpence: 'Entered for his Copie vnder the handes of Master Abraham Hartwell and the wardens A booke called. *The Nyghtingale and the Ante. A Ioue surgit opus*'. The variance of the entry title as well as the incorporation of the motto (or 'posie') 'A Ioue surgit opus.' used by Middleton in *The Wisdom of Solomon Paraphrased* (1597) leaves no doubt that the work was presented for licensing in manuscript form prior to printing. As a general rule, the title in a manuscript already modified for printing before licensing agrees with the printed title-page of the first edition. However, the issue of what Middleton's manuscript contained remains a major problem because the texts of the two editions differ substantially in terms of length: CREEDE 1 lacks about one-fifth of the text found in CREEDE 2. The addition of the third tale in CREEDE 2, however, has a major impact upon the work.

Our understanding of Middleton's text is complicated by several factors. For clarity's sake in the following discussion, the units comprising the complete text should be noted in their order of appearance and respective positions by signature in the two editions with CREEDE 1 cited first, followed by cross-references to the text of this edition (all line references are to *Father Hubburd's Tales*):

(1) *A2* title-page; *A1* CREEDE 2 (main heading THIS EDITION)

(2) *A3* Oliver Hubburd's dedicatory epistle; *A2* CREEDE 2 (1–48 THIS EDITION)

(3) *A4* Middleton's epistle 'To the Reader'; *A3* CREEDE 2 (49–82 THIS EDITION)

(4) *B1* introductory verse frame; *A4* CREEDE 2 (83–275 THIS EDITION)

(5) *C1* transitional prose paragraph to the first tale (*C1ᵛ* blank); *B4* CREEDE 2 (276–90 THIS EDITION) (*B4ᵛ* blank CREEDE 2)

(6) *C2* 'The Ant's Tale when he was a Ploughman'; *C1* CREEDE 2 (291–742 THIS EDITION)

(6b) *E2* Prose transition to 'The Nightingale's Canzonet'; *D3ᵛ* CREEDE 2 (743–5 THIS EDITION)

(7) *E2* 'The Nightingale's Canzonet' and one stanza link to second tale; *D3ᵛ* CREEDE 2 (746–808 THIS EDITION)

(8) *E3ᵛ* 'The Ant's Tale when he was a Soldier'; *E1* CREEDE 2 (809–1047 THIS EDITION)

(9) *F4–F4ᵛ* concluding stanzas for The Soldier's Tale, 'FINIS'; *E4ᵛ–F1* CREEDE 2 includes the portion of CREEDE 1's concluding stanzas up to 1072 THIS EDITION, where the new materials are inserted for CREEDE 2; the remaining concluding stanzas of CREEDE 1 appear on *F4* of CREEDE 2 (1267–83 THIS EDITION)

CREEDE 2 *Additions:*

(10) *F1* new linking verses introducing the third tale (1073–92 THIS EDITION)

(11) *F1* 'The Ant's Tale when he was a Scholar' (1093–257 THIS EDITION)

(12) *F4* new stanza concluding the scholar's tale (1258–66 THIS EDITION)

(13) *F4* final concluding stanza from CREEDE 1 *F4ᵛ*; 'FINIS' (1267–83 THIS EDITION)

The textual problem, and it is a major one indeed, is that a substantial portion of the text, namely, 'The Ant's Tale, when he was a Scholar' and its linking verses (units 10–12), appear only in CREEDE 2; it is entirely absent from CREEDE 1 and no reference to it is made in the first edition. Thus two radically different texts were published in the same year (1604 imprints), the second longer than the first by a complete section. The basic question is: was the scholar's tale deleted for the first edition and then restored in the second, or was it unavailable until the second edition?

Three hypotheses are possible: (1) Middleton's manuscript lacked the scholar's tale in any form, and it was supplied later for the second edition; (2) the manuscript contained the scholar's tale in a form not suitable for publication (i.e., unrevised, incomplete), and Bushell decided to publish the section of the manuscript that was ready; and (3) the manuscript was complete but Bushell caused the deletion of the scholar's tale and linking verses.

Deletion, Restoration Hypothesis

George R. Price is the chief proponent of the third option. Since his elaborate hypothesis has never been refuted in detail, and has even been described in terms such as 'a good case for suppression [i.e., deletion]' and 'argued his case so persuasively', it must be considered at length. In summary, Price theorizes:

> It is best to discuss the omissions first, and by means of a theory of the history of the text.... Possibly Bushell (rather recently launched in business) was striving for economy, and having found, when the printing was well along, that the pamphlet would run into sheet G, requested Creede to keep it within six gatherings... to assume that Middleton was given or sought no opportunity to read proof may be extreme, but seems the likeliest explanation of what happened... it is likely that Middleton went to Bushell and asked for a corrected edition of his pamphlet, and that, Bushell having yielded, Creede persuaded Middleton to allow the new edition to be printed in his shop... In sum, the author's protest against the mishandling of his tract probably caused the publication of the corrected version very soon after the first. (182–4)

It should be noted that no circumstances such as censorship or political repercussions, the usual problems with satiric texts, can be identified by Price to supplement this 'economizing' theory. J. Q. Adams suggested the possibility that Bushell's desire to avoid 'giving offense' to 'the niggardly Lord Compton, dedicatee of *The Ghost of Lucrece* (1600)' because of the personal satire in the scholar's tale was a possible motive for its deletion (xxvi), but Price correctly dismisses this theory because Middleton let the dedication stand (182): both the dedication and the concluding paragraph of the scholar's tale repeat essentially identical details. Otherwise, several stretches of credibility are obvious at first glance in Price's 'deletion, restoration' hypothesis. The major weakness in this and most other 'deletion, restoration' hypotheses is that no textual evidence is available to prove them. The absence of a unit of text in a shorter first edition is apparent only by virtue of its presence in a longer second edition. In contrast, when a longer text is reprinted in a shortened version, no hypothesis is necessary: the omission of a portion of a text undeniably produces an 'absence'. Likewise, when an author adds or deletes materials through revision in a sequence of two editions, the textual evidence is undeniable.

Although Price is on fairly solid ground in interpreting five passages to mean 'more than two metamorphoses of the Ant' (182–3), as he admits, the words 'three' or 'thrice' are not specified: the self-reflexive textual references are open-ended, and not limited to three or any other number of tales. In fact, 'others' and 'all the rest' are certainly less limiting than the 'one more' that Price settles on. Price ignores other variations such as 'durst once again | Venture amongst perfidious men?' (795–6). The narrative structure of *Father Hubburd's Tales* allows for an unlimited addition of further tales. One could argue that Middleton's lack of specificity in these self-reflexive comments is designedly open-ended. After all, not every author of a collection of prose tales started out with a tritameron's, an heptameron's, or a decameron's worth in mind. History shows that if the initial book proved successful, an author could continue with, for example, a second part, a third part, and perhaps a fourth part on some popular subject such as cony-catching or a belman's experiences. That was inherent in the nature of Elizabethan prose pamphlets. Price's other arguments simply will not stand close scrutiny either.

First, the notion that a publisher would unilaterally decide to amputate a text finds no support in the extant evidence of author–publisher relations as seen in authors' prefaces to second, longer editions (Binns, 1977, 1979; Yamada, 143–56). Nonetheless, Price believes that 'A publisher's decision to sacrifice the academic and autobiographical portions of a tract aimed at the populace is more likely than the author's attempt to amplify a popular work by this sort of material' (183). He fails to address three issues: (1) would Middleton's readers have known that this material was autobiographical, and would they therefore have found it somehow objectionable; (2) would Bushell have deleted the material for that reason; and (3) was Middleton too shy to add such material? As a whole, Price's hypothesis about the deletion of the scholar's tale requires a sequence of such ungrounded and indeed unprovable 'likelihoods' which defy common sense and 'crunch' the text to fit the hypothesis.

As Price admits, the assumption that Middleton did not read proof is 'extreme', both in general terms of printing-house practices, and in terms of the relatively stable state of the text which is common to both editions. Moreover, the substantive revisions of the text found in CREEDE 2 leave no doubt of Middleton's direct involvement with that edition (see discussion below in 'Quality of Proofing: Hatfield Inner-F'). To argue that he had no involvement in CREEDE 1 is absurd. But Middleton's resulting 'irritation' at belatedly discovering the unsuspected amputation of his text is utterly essential to Price's scenario because that is the necessary condition for Middleton's 'dissatisfaction' with Bushell's unilateral action and the occasion for the angry young author confronting the 'untrustworthy' publisher with the demand 'for a corrected edition'. Joel H. Kaplan surely is correct in arguing that Price's 'deletion, restoration' view 'overestimates the importance of a fledgling author with few connections of any importance when [Price] pictures an incensed Middleton demanding a second edition to repair the damage Bushell had done to the first' (173–4). Where Price got the notion that, however 'incensed', an author either in 1604 or 1949 could 'demand' the capitalization of a new edition is puzzling. It was utterly improbable in 1604, when the publisher, *not* the author, owned the copyright and the text: he was legally free and justified to do whatever he wished with his property. Only one instance is known from the period in which a publisher was *forced* to reprint a text—in that case, Thomas Newman's illegal first edition of Sidney's *Astrophel and Stella* was called in, apparently by Lord Burghley, and Newman was forced to print a new edition (Brennan 95). Middleton simply did not have the Sidney family's influence, especially at this early stage in his career.

Further, the text itself contradicts the image of publisher–author relations imagined by Price. The fact that the punning compliment to Bushell in the first edition was transferred into the second edition with a significant positive revision presents no difficulty to Price. That is, in his epistle 'To The Reader', Middleton remarks: 'I never wished this book better fortune than to fall into the hands of a true spelling printer, and an honest-stitching bookseller; and if honesty be sold by the bushell like oysters, I had rather have one *Bushell of honesty* than three of money' (56–61). The 'honest-stitching' reference is quite significant in regard to the 'deletion, restoration' hypothesis. Usually, most books were sold unbound as a stack of folded, unopened, and uncut gatherings tied around with string. Either the publisher, bookseller, or purchaser could send the packet to a bookbinder, who then proceeded to open, cut, and stitch the gatherings into a bound book. In this context, 'honest-stitching' means specifically that no gatherings or leaves were left out during the process so that the bound book was 'perfect' or complete. Contemporary records indicate that defective books were at times sold with leaves or whole gatherings missing (see Francis R. Johnson). Middleton's choice of phrase thus verifies that the text of CREEDE 1 is complete and unabridged. Nonetheless, for the second edition, Middleton revised 'honest-stitching' to 'honest-minded', raising the compliment a notch: exactly what Price means when claiming that '"honest-minded" is ambiguous' (185) is totally unfathomable. If anything, a trade skill is replaced by a reference to a quality of character, signifying a businessman who lives up to his word. This would definitely not apply to a publisher who double-crossed an author by deleting one-fifth of his text, as Price claims about Bushell.

Price's author–publisher scenario and his relegation of the revision 'honest-minded' to 'ambiguous' seems to arise from his tangled view of printer's copy and the role of the printer Creede. He notes: 'The reappearance of any compliment to Bushell in the second edition appears contradictory of the history [see above] described, but a plausible explanation can, I think, be found' (185).

Price then suggests that Creede, not Middleton, was responsible for the revision to 'honest-minded': 'possibly Creede himself used a little irony here'. In other words, Price believes that the printer Creede revised to 'honest-minded'—perhaps as some sort of inside joke? This suggestion raises an obvious question: how did Middleton miss this meddling with his text, especially given Price's supposition that he was so recently incensed at Bushell for being double-crossed by him?

Price skirts the difficulty by adjusting his hypothesis about the proofing of the text to fit his scenario, claiming that other variants in 'To the Reader' point to the conclusion that this text in CREEDE 2 was set 'from an uncorrected copy of [CREEDE 1], and probably not proof-read at all'. Thus, not only did Middleton not read proof of this part of CREEDE 1, Price apparently would have us believe that he left the job of revision to the printer. However, 'To the Reader' was an exception. Similar substantive revisions in the rest of the text render 'doubtless' that the compositor 'worked, somewhat carelessly, from a copy of [CREEDE 1] corrected by the author' (187). But it could not have been a 'thoroughly corrected copy' because of several errors that passed into CREEDE 2 (188). In fact, that he worked from a corrected copy is not certain at all: 'I think he used a manuscript...while setting the text proper of [CREEDE 2]' (186). Given this thoroughly muddled explanation of printer's copy and the proofing process in which most conceivable binaries are operative (i.e., manuscript/CREEDE 1, proofed/not proofed, corrected/uncorrected, by Middleton/by Creede, carelessly/carefully etc.), each and every textual variant can be privileged or marginalized at will, the appropriate agent responsible for the variant selected, and the version of copy-text chosen to suit the theory. In short, the dismissal of the 'honest-minded' revision as non-authorial simply has no foundation in the bibliographical evidence.

Despite the obvious evidence of Middleton's attitude toward Bushell, who supposedly massacred Middleton's text, Price sweeps away the admitted contradiction to his scenario thus: 'a plausible explanation can, I think, be found. I know of no evidence that Middleton's disposition was vindictive (his vein of irony suggests the contrary); very likely, having asked for and obtained a resetting of the tract, he did not take the trouble to rewrite the foreword' (185). Given this insight, Price's hypothetical attribution of the revision 'honest-minded' to Creede is not actually necessary, for, if it is meant ironically, Middleton's 'vein of irony' certainly would have been adequate for the job. On the other hand, Middleton actually could have rewritten 'To the Reader' without being vindictive in the least. Authors' prefaces to second editions almost always *apologize* to readers for the publisher's haste in printing an incomplete or unrevised work, which then becomes the occasion for a new expanded edition. Vindictive attacks on the first publisher are extremely rare. For example, during the transfer of copy for Thomas Nashe's *Pierce Penilesse* from Richard Jones (the copyright owner and publisher of the first edition) to John Busby, Jones passed along

Nashe's 'A private Epistle of the Author to the Printer' which Busby then printed at the head of his new edition as if it were a standard author's epistle 'To the Reader'. Actually, it was a private letter in which Nashe, having heard that a second edition is underway, complains that Jones published too hastily: 'you know very well that it [the first edition] was abroad a fortnight ere I knew of it, and uncorrected and unfinished it hath offered itself to the open scorn of the world. Had you not been so forward in the republishing of it, you should have had certain Epistles to Orators, to insert to the later end....These were prepared for *Pierce Pennilesse* first setting forth, had not the fear of infection detained me with my Lord in the country' (Harrison, 1). Despite the injustice, Nashe offers the new material for inclusion in a third edition if it comes to that. In other words, he attempts to sell that material to Jones in his letter. The reality of author–publisher relations is clear: an author would be unwise to totally antagonize a publisher who had purchased a manuscript from him because that would cancel any potential future purchases by the publisher.

Now, had Bushell actually deleted the scholar's tale, it is difficult to imagine that Middleton would not have informed the reader of that fact, especially since CREEDE 2 was being put forth by a new publisher, William Cotton. Middleton, in effect, no longer needed Bushell since he had found a new publisher. And his tone need not have been vindictive. But Middleton did not revise the epistle to explain why the new edition had an additional tale. He simply heightened the compliment to Bushell. An author would normally, it seems, *want* to explain such a situation. Indeed, it is difficult to imagine Middleton *not* doing so if Bushell actually had published an incomplete text—even if Price's assessment of Middleton's 'disposition' is correct. In effect, the bibliographical evidence of revision and its implications regarding the publishing history of the text are rejected by Price in favour of pseudo-evidence consisting of his vague assessment of Middleton's 'disposition' and Creede's bent for ironic practical jokes. In terms of the collaborative publishing practices of the period, exemplified by the transfer of *Pierce Penniless* from Jones to Busby for a second edition, common sense suggests that the publisher of a first edition might have had no desire to risk a furthur investment in a second edition even though the first might have sold well. A successful first edition produces a degree of market saturation that increases the possibility of loss on unsold copies of a second edition. In this context, Gerald D. Johnson has observed that the original publisher's financial risk in a second edition was reduced by passing ownership of the copyright to the new publisher either for a price or for a share of the profits (3). Whatever the actual arrangement here, Cotton clearly was willing to take the risk in publishing the expanded text in a second edition.

Next, Price ignores the natural progression in 'deletion, restoration' cases consisting of a shorter text undergoing an expansion. The addition of new material is usually noted on the title-page, an obvious ploy aimed at enticing buyers of the earlier edition, or in some manner in a prefatory text. For example, the title-page of the third edition of John Marston's *The Malcontent* (STC 17481, 1604) calls attention to two new textual units: the 'augmentations' 'by Marston' and 'the Additions' 'Written by John Webster'. When feasible in the context of the structure of a work, the narrator could comment editorially about new material. For example, in *The Third and Last Part of Cony-Catching* (STC 12283, 1592), Robert Greene retells a tale from *The Second and Last Part* (STC 12282, 1592) in expanded form and editorially notes: 'This tale, because it was somewhat misreported before, upon talk had with the poor cutler himself, is set down now in true form and manner how it was done; therefore is there no offence offered, when by a better consideration, a thing may be enlarged or amended....' Conversely, the narrator in the first edition could note that a text is incomplete or unfinished, as does G. T. in introducing 'The reporter's conclusion unfinished' in Gascoigne's *A Hundreth Sundrie Flowres* (STC 11635, 1573) where, in addition to the subtitle, G. T. notes that he had 'not recovered a full ende of this discourse'. In some instances, a combination of bibliographical evidence and self-reflexive references in the text itself establish the probability that expansion, not 'deletion, restoration', is responsible for new material in a second edition (see Weiss, 1992, 98–102). In the present instance, the sequence of titles is reversed: 'Father Hubburd's Tales' is the main title, with 'The Ant and the Nightingale' as the subtitle. In terms of bibliographic encoding, the first edition has become a subset of a work bearing a new title: to the perceptive reader, this would indicate a new version of the work which contains the earlier version.

Finally, the theory that Bushell discovered, 'when the printing was well along', that the text 'would run into a seventh gathering', ignores the basic realities of the printing business. Paper had to be purchased before printing began, and even the most crude and inaccurate casting off of Middleton's manuscript, assuming that it contained the full text, would have revealed the need for a seventh gathering. Given the type-page size of the first edition, it would have been blatantly apparent to Creede (or to his compositor—even when drunk) that the scholar's tale (units 10–12) would not merely 'run into a seventh gathering', but indeed would fill almost an entire seventh gathering. For Price's economizing theory to work, we would have to assume that Creede and/or Bushell approached the job with an unbusinesslike attitude such as: 'well, let's pick up a couple reams of paper to start with, use this pica black letter type and set the measure to about 78mm or so, and then see how things move along'. Joseph Moxon is clear about the preparations for a job: the manuscript must be cast off to determine 'how much *Written Copy* will make an intended number of *Sheets* of any assigned *Body* [i.e, size of type] and *Measure* [i.e., the length of the widest line of type on a page]' (239). If indeed the manuscript contained the scholar's tale, Creede would have informed Bushell of the simple fact that, by widening the measure to about 86mm, setting the type close-spaced, 36 lines to the page rather than 34, the entire text would fit into six sheets, as indeed it does in CREEDE 2. Significantly, Price overlooks an obvious bibliographical fact that destroys his theory that Bushell deleted the third tale to avoid paying for an extra sheet. The wide measure of roughly 83–86mm is maintained up to page D1^{v} in CREEDE 1. On D2 and thereafter, the measure is narrowed to roughly 76–79mm. This adjustment demonstrates the printer's decision to stretch out the text to fill six gatherings rather than to avoid overflow into a seventh gathering. Otherwise, about three pages of sheet F would have been left blank. Creede's strategy, in short, was aimed at wasting, *not* saving paper. In a word, Price's economizing argument is pure poppycock.

Finally, the fact that the second edition was published by William Cotton rather than Bushell without a record of the transfer of copyright in the Stationers' Register is not as puzzling as M. A. Shaaber (15–16) and Price (183) would have it seem. As long as the gentlemen's agreement between the two publishers was honoured, no copyright action would ensue in the Court of the Stationers. For example, the transfer of *Pierce* from Jones to Busby noted earlier was neither entered nor did subsequent court action occur. The collaborative publishing practices of the period often led to such arrangements (Gerald D. Johnson, 2–3).

Expansion Hypothesis

The addition of a self-contained text (units 10–12) such as the scholar's tale in the second edition requires that two possibilities must be examined: (1) the scholar's tale was not in the manuscript that was used for printer's copy for CREEDE 1 at all; or (2) it was present in the manuscript in an incomplete or unrevised state and, as a result, not printed in the first edition. Both hypotheses assume that Middleton's text evolved in stages.

Price senses the possibility that stages of textual evolution are hinted at by the difference in the three titles affixed to Middleton's text: 'It is also noteworthy that the entry [title] evidently represents Middleton's first intention, and it has a natural order, for the nightingale is the first speaker' (180). Aside from the issue of Middleton's original intention, the most important fact is that the clerk at Stationers' Hall in all likelihood faithfully reproduced the title of the text as written in the manuscript licensed by the Wardens for entry into the Stationers' Register. This is the standard criterion for differentiating between post-printing entries of printed books, which duplicate the printed title, and manuscripts, whose titles often enough are not yet modified for the printed title-page. Price's observation, therefore, is valid, but he fails to pursue the implications with respect to possible stages of textual evolution. (The second change in title for CREEDE 2 will be considered below in that context.)

A second aspect of the entry title is significant: it indicates that Middleton's 'posie', a Latin motto used in courtly circles in earlier decades as an identification device, appeared on the manuscript title-page. For example, at the time when George Gascoigne wrote his version of the Philomel myth (1575), he was in his 'Tam Marti, quam Mercurio' phase in his sequence of posies. Middleton used the posie 'A Jove surgit opus' earlier in *Solomon Paraphrased* (1597) as well as in this manuscript. It seems plausible that Middleton was associating himself with courtly poets as he had done in his *Ghost of Lucrece*, which, interestingly enough, was dedicated to Lord Compton, whose wife Lady Compton was the dedicatee of Edmund Spenser's *Mother Hubburd's Tales*. (No such 'posie' appears in either CREEDE 1 or CREEDE 2 and, in fact, Middleton is not identified as the author on their title-pages.) But these details do not precisely define the contents of Middleton's manuscript beyond the obvious fact that two interlocutors are involved (as in the medieval verse *debate* 'The Owl and the Nightingale' and others). It should be apparent that the body of the text as printed in CREEDE 1 (units 4, 6–9) functions perfectly well as a self-contained literary work: an unidentified narrator creates a framing device, beginning with an Ovidian description of sunset and concluding with a description of sunrise, for the interaction between the ant and the nightingale. Such descriptions commonly served as the setting for the Philomel myth, a natural consequence of the fact that the nightingale sings at night. Middleton need not have known any particular treatment of the myth such as Gascoigne's *Complaint of Philomene* in this respect. Any of a number of narrative frames could have served as a model. Although, as Price argues, five passages suggest that more than one tale is incorporated in the body of the work, the references lack specificity as to number and are fundamentally ambiguous when taken as self-reflexive comments on the text. Nowhere is it even implied that the ant will *tell* whatever number of tales is suggested by 'all the rest' (803). Literally, these passages refer to the ant's sequence of human transformations, *not* to the number of tales that he will tell. In contrast, for example, Oliver's reference to 'my first Epistle' (1249) in CREEDE 2 at the end of the scholar's tale is precise: it points specifically to the dedicatory epistle which appears as the first text in this book. This is textual evidence of the nature of the structure of the bibliographical artifact CREEDE 2 (see Weiss, 1992, 98–9). But Price's five passages simply do not constitute self-reflexive textual evidence of the structure of the book. In short, it is almost certain that a manuscript containing only the body (units 4, 6–9) of the printed text of CREEDE 1 was presented for licensing at Stationers' Hall.

Furthermore, it is clear that Middleton's 'To the Reader' and Oliver's Epistle Dedicatory (units 2–3) are additions to Middleton's manuscript and, indeed, to his original conception of his work. Normally, it is logical to assume that the body of a text was composed first, and once the manuscript was purchased by a publisher, an author provided preliminary texts in preparation for printing. But this norm is not 'evidence', especially in a situation like this, where a preliminary text such as Oliver's dedication is directly self-referenced within the body of the text. Now, a reader who has nodded in agreement with this obvious insight must then accept its implications with regard to the evolution of Middleton's text. For the body of the text as found in CREEDE 1 makes no such reference, and in fact, the ant does not acquire the identity of Oliver Hubburd within the body of the text until CREEDE 2. In CREEDE 1, we know that the Oliver Hubburd of the dedication is the narrator of the prose tales *only* because Middleton tells us so in 'To the Reader': 'Father Hubburd tells them [i.e., tales] in the small size of an ant' (75–6). Otherwise CREEDE 1, apart from 'To the Reader', establishes no more specific a connection than that someone named Oliver Hubburd dedicates a book (which he presumably authored) to Sir Christopher Clutch-Fist. In that book, an ant, who remains nameless, talks to Philomel and tells her two stories.

The absence of the identification of the ant in CREEDE 1 seems quite significant in terms of the role of revision in textual evolution. The ant is confronted in CREEDE 1 with a perfect situation for revealing his name, if indeed Middleton had already decided that he would have one. That Middleton made no effort in the body of the text as found in printer's copy to name him Oliver is apparent in the bond-signing scene of the ploughman's tale. The ant signs with an emblematic mark, not with a name. To provide the ant with a name for CREEDE 1 through revision of the manuscript would have been a quite simple matter. This is a natural situation for the ant to make a typical comment such as: 'But I, not so simple as they laughed me for, *not being able to write Oliver Hubburd*, drew the picture of a knavish emblem....' (498–500). Such a parenthetical revision could have been inserted interlinearly or in the margin. It was not, and hence the ant in the body of the text of CREEDE 1 is nothing more than a specific ant from an undefined ant nest.

Furthermore, the identification of the ant as Oliver Hubburd in Middleton's 'To the Reader' of CREEDE 1 creates several structural problems which transform the self-contained, internally consistent manuscript portion of the text (units 4, 6–9) into the incomplete and confusing expansion seen in CREEDE 1. In the manuscript version, a single omniscient narrative voice is sustained throughout: it sets the scenes, makes transitions, and referees the dialogue between the nightingale and the ant in verse, with two exceptional passages in prose (see below). Middleton is assumed to be the framing narrator in this version. The manuscript version thus is like all other such framed narratives, whether in prose or verse. In contrast, the dedication and 'To the Reader' of CREEDE 1 identify Oliver as the fictitious persona who writes this particular book and dedicates it to Clutch-Fist, his nemesis. This creates an ambiguity in the narrative structure, especially when the dedication is considered in context with 'To the Reader'. The dedication implies that Oliver wrote the whole book and hence that he functions as the omniscient narrator who creates the framing device, as the ant as interlocutor, and finally, as the ant as the sub-narrator who tells the prose tales. However, in 'To the Reader', Middleton credits Oliver only as the sub-narrator of the tales and claims the book as his own in thirteen references such as 'Why I call these *Father Hubburd's Tales* is not to have them called in again' (62–3).

More significant, however, are the problems created in regard to the textual relationship of the dedication to the body of the text in CREEDE 1. On the one hand, as J. Q. Adams perceptively notes:

> ...it is further significant that the name 'Hubburd' does not appear in the text of the first edition, and was introduced into the text of the second edition (not as 'Father Hubburd' but 'Oliver Hubburd') only once, and that parenthetically (and unnecessarily) in the last twelve lines of the last tale, as the name of the poor young scholar himself—rather inconsistently since neither of the preceding speakers is given a name. (xxvi)

A second inconsistency emerges. Nothing within the text itself contributes to our understanding of the tone and content of the dedication. On the one hand, Philomel cautions the ant against railing (252), and the ant complies, maintaining a controlled, moderate tone except in his outburst against dicing, which he does not repeat verbatim for the nightingale: 'Here I began to rail like Thomas Nashe against Gabriel Harvey, if you call that railing' (655–6). At another low point, he remarks that he fell into 'these passionate, but not railing speeches' (1028–9). At worst, then, the ant's outer limit of invective is: 'At dice? At the devil...for that is a dicer's last throw!' (654–5). Otherwise, the ant passively endures the injustices done to him in his two transformations without striking back. In short, the venomous, railing attack on Clutch-Fist in the dedication, with its references to his habit of scavenging usable components from the books presented to him as dedicatee, has no connection whatever to the body of the text—the dedication is an 'orphan' text in CREEDE 1. A reader's normal response after reading CREEDE 1 with the dedication in mind would be: 'why is he so angry about Clutch-Fist's scavenging habit?' The concluding paragraph of the scholar's tale, added in CREEDE 2, provides the missing parentage. There we learn that, after writing and having printed a 'quaint volume, fairly bound up in principal vellum, double-filleted with leaf-gold, strung most gentleman-like with carnation silk ribbon; which book, industriously heaped with weighty conceits, precious phrases, and wealthy numbers, I, Oliver Hubburd...presented [it] to Sir Christopher Clutch-Fist, whose bountiful virtue I blaze in my first Epistle' (1243–9). The sarcasm here resonates with the anger of the dedication: Clutch-Fist has scavenged the carnation silk ribbon, the 'principal vellum' of the book's covers, and presumably the gold-leaf gilding of Oliver's book. Thus, Middleton clearly conceived of the dedication and Oliver's concluding paragraph as interlocking, self-relexive textual units. These two units (2, 11), written by Oliver, frame the body of the work in the second edition. The latter unit is necessary to illuminate the dedication's thinly veiled threat that 'certain line-sharkers' (16–17) (presumably including Oliver himself) have plotted with 'the best common play-plotter in England' (22) to ambush Clutch-Fist during Candlemas term (February 2).

In summary, the differences between CREEDE 1 and CREEDE 2 suggest three stages of textual evolution. The manuscript which was presented to the Wardens for entry contained the body of the text (units 4, 6–9) as found in CREEDE 1, a straight-forward, self-contained work consisting of two prose tales enclosed in a standard framing device in verse. Then Middleton expanded his original concept to include an identity for the ant, composed 'To the Reader' and Oliver's dedication in time for the printing of CREEDE 1, but made no effort at revising the body of the text to include any reference to the ant's new identity. Finally, he completed the third tale for CREEDE 2 in which the relationship of the ant to the writer of the dedication is finally clarified. Only at this stage was the identity of the ant as Oliver Hubburd revealed in the third tale.

Next, the two exceptional prose passages within the text of CREEDE 1 must be addressed in regard to whether they were present in the manuscript version. Both constitute technical flaws in the verse framing device. Middleton knew that decorum required consistency in this respect, and his possible models would have all confirmed the necessity of sustained verse, or conversely, sustained prose, in a framing device. The fact that the transitional paragraph (unit 5, 276–90) is in prose is obviously a failure to sustain the framing verse narrative which has obtained to this point, and which will be sustained to the end of the work, except for the second, brief, prose passage (unit 6b) which introduces Philomel's canzonet at the end of the first tale. Two aspects of the first prose passage are evidence of a later stage of composition.

First, although the prose transition adds a delightful depiction of the setting and the 'stalking' diminutive ant who fears no audience, the paragraph is structurally redundant. The final stanza of the verse frame actually introduces the first tale, and in the same fashion as the verse introduction to the second tale: 'And now to you, Sir Ant: | On with your prose . . . | And, as I like the matter, I will sing | A canzonet to close up everything' (270–5). The tale begins, after the prose transition, with the ant's continuation of the dialogue: 'I was sometimes, most chaste Lady Nightingale . . . ' (292). In effect, the setting of scene in the prose transition interrupts the smooth flow of the dialogue. To this point, the narrator has successfully handled the description of setting and action in verse. The obvious question is: why did Middleton violate decorum at this point? Complicating the issue is Middleton's habitual shifting between prose and verse in his dramatic works, a disregard of decorum that drives editors to the brink of insanity. But a critical difference obtains. Although Middleton writes those shifts, characters speak them, and no principle of decorum requires that a character sustain either prose or verse throughout a speech. In fact, the opposite is true: shifts between prose and verse were a

recognized technique for conveying shifts of mood, levels of importance, and so on. But here, the genre demands consistency. To accept the prose transition as part of the manuscript version, we have to believe that Middleton, having undertaken to frame his prose tales in verse, arrives at the point where the first tale is to be told, turns the floor over to the ant at the end of the final stanza of the verse frame, but then decides to dash off a prose paragraph as an extension of the verse frame before the ant has a chance to begin his prose narrative.

Second, verbal echos between the prose transition and 'To the Reader' strongly suggest contemporaneous composition. In the latter, Middleton arrogantly challenges the reader: 'Then, to condemn these tales following because Father Hubburd tells them in the small size of an ant is even as much as if these two words *God* and *Devil* were printed in one line, to skip it over and say that line were naught because the devil were in it' (74–9). In the prose transition, the narrator describes the ant as 'not afraid to tell tales out of the villainous school of the world, where the devil is the schoolmaster . . . But for fear I interrupt this small actor in less than *decimo sexto*, I leave, and give the ant leave to tell his tale' (282–90). He has indeed interrupted the ant, and very likely, the original structure of the narrative. Aside from that, another technical problem is apparent. Since the two passages contain nearly identical terms, share satiric subject matter and satiric tone, and are both self-reflexive intrusions by a narrator, who is the narrator of the prose transition who states 'I leave, and give the ant leave to tell his tale . . . .'? Is it Middleton, Oliver the writer of the dedication, or Oliver as the ant? An editor is sorely pressed to attribute the passage to one or the other. Thus the similarities suggest contemporaneous composition with the phrases and attitude of the first passage fresh in mind while writing the second. The prose transition (unit 5), in short, most probably was an interpolation made for the printing of CREEDE 1.

In contrast, the brief prose transition (unit 6b) to Philomel's canzonet, presents no such technical difficulties because it belongs there: 'The remorseful nightingale, delighted with the ant's quaint discourse, began to tune the instrument of her voice, breathing forth these lines in sweet and delicious airs' (743–5). The elegiac tone is entirely consistent with that which is maintained throughout the framing verses. Since the passage lacks rhyme and metre when rearranged in stanzaic form, it cannot be an instance of mislineation by a compositor. It seems possible that Middleton jotted it down in haste, intending to return later and revise the passage into verse. Regardless, a reader glides through the passage without noticing that it is prose simply because it sounds exactly like the rest of the framing verse, but unlike anything in the prose tales.

Finally, the major question about the scholar's tale and its linking verses must be confronted: was this material composed at the same time as the body of CREEDE 1? Several factors suggest a later date of composition. First, the new verse transition (unit 10) to the scholar's tale in CREEDE 2 contrasts sharply with the contextual elegiac tone and moral perspective that is maintained throughout CREEDE I. Philomel, previously a sober moralizing figure, abruptly steps out of character momentarily. Up to this point, Philomel has consoled the ant regarding the impact of the world's greed upon his two human transformations. But upon learning that the ant selected 'a scholar's gown' as his third transformation, Philomel exclaims:

A needy scholar? Worse than worst,
...
I thought, thoud'st leaped into a law-gown, then
There had been hope to have swept up all again.
But a lank scholar? Study how you can,
No academe makes a rich alderman. (1085-92)

This perspective is antithetical to the Philomel of CREEDE I. Indeed, the greed embodied by rich lawyers, mercers, scriveners, cony-catching gallants, cavaliers, whores, and aristocratic ladies in the first two tales now becomes the value which underlies her surprised response. The ant cannot 'become rich' as a scholar! Given the fact that this contradictory depiction of her character occurs as a result of an interpolated text in a second edition, it is reasonable to infer two separate compositional efforts. The same is true of the ant. In the new third tale, he rails venomously against rich usurers and then, lost in his own rage at the injustice of his poverty, against gold—because he envies and greedily covets what others have. This breaks from his Horatian moderation in the original two tales where he consistently complies with Philomel's incomplete threat 'Or if in bitterness thou rail like Nashe' (252) by detachedly describing vice but not viciously attacking it.

After the identity of the ant is firmly established with the addition of the scholar's tale, the title can be reversed to reflect the privileged function of Oliver Hubburd. The title of CREEDE 2 is a logical step: Middleton's 'To the Reader' in CREEDE I explains 'Why I call these *Father Hubburd's Tales*' (62), explicitly identifying that as the main title. However, it serves merely as the subtitle in CREEDE I. Middleton doubtlessly had conceived of the final stage of the evolution of his text when writing his epistle and Oliver's dedication for CREEDE I, but he had not yet fully implemented it. The title-page of CREEDE I thus represents an intermediate stage of revision in which the subtitle 'Father Hubburd's Tales' has been added to the main title 'The Ant and the Nightingale'. In CREEDE 2, finally, 'Father Hubburd's Tales' becomes the main title and 'The Ant and the Nightingale' the subtitle. In regard to the issue of printer's copy, the preservation of the running title of CREEDE I, i.e., '*The Ante, and the Nightingale.*', in CREEDE 2 despite the change of priority in the title-page is undeniable bibliographical evidence that a corrected copy of CREEDE I functioned as printer's copy for CREEDE 2.

Moreover, Middleton left one revealing unrevised loose end in the structure of the final version. The scholar's tale concludes: 'at which ruthful prospect I fell down and swooned, and when I came to myself again, I was

an ant, and so ever since I have kept me' (1255-7). This is perfect stuff for a deconstructionist: the text self--annihilates because this final line denies its basic fiction— if the ant had no further human transformations, then the ant as Oliver Hubburd of the dedication is an impossibility. Oliver writes the dedication to attack Clutch-Fist *after* discovering the latter's scavenging of his book and *after* falling down and swooning.

In summary, it is impossible to believe that the new material in CREEDE 2 is contemporaneous with the concept of the work and the creative effort that produced the body of the text as found in the manuscript version. The textual evidence as a whole points in the opposite direction, that is, the new material was not present in the original manuscript version. That text is seamless and internally consistent; the printed versions exhibit such serious structural flaws as to suggest that Middleton made no revisionary attempt to more smoothly incorporate the new material into the conjecturally reconstructed manuscript version (units 4, 6-9). Hence, the present edition presents both the manuscript and the final versions as discrete texts (see discussion below, 'Copy-text').

Printing History

Thomas Creede printed both editions as evidenced by the ornamental stock as well as the typefounts, particulary the 40-point roman titling fount used exclusively by Creede. Furthermore, the same setting of type was used in both editions to print the dedication. Progressive damage to a significant portion of the standing types in the dedication conclusively identifies *Father Hubburd's Tales* (STC 17874.7) as the second to be printed (CREEDE 2). Both editions fill six gatherings despite the addition of the scholar's tale to CREEDE 2, a unit consisting of about six pages of prose and 26 lines of verse. The space-saving compression in CREEDE 2 was achieved primarily through an increase in type-page size and through an erratic effort at crowding lines.

CREEDE I exhibits a type-page (Huntington copy) measuring approximately 145mm × 83-86mm from A2-D1^v with 33 lines of text per page (excluding the signature/ catchword line); at D2, the measure was narrowed to about 76-79mm for the remainder of the book (D2-F4^v). The reason for this modification is obscure, as it does not coincide with any bibliographical unit of processing (e.g., between gatherings, between formes). Rather, that it occurs on the second type-page of the inner forme shows that setting was seriatim rather than by formes. The modification has the effect of stretching out the text to fill most of signature F, but whether this was the objective is moot. Sheet F would have been needed in any event. However, it is clear that the wide measure of 83-86mm was dictated by the necessity of setting the long verse lines of the introductory section (unit 4), and accommodating the width of the frames consisting of rows of flowers above and below on these pages (B1-B4^v). For some obscure reason (possibly a new setting of the flowers at the bottom of the page) the compositor set a space between the two right-most flowers of the top frame on B4^v, thus widening its earlier width (as found on B3^v) to 87mm. The fact that the preliminaries are set to the narrow measure suggests that they were set last using the measure of signatures D2–F4^v, and that work began with the wide measure of signature B. This sequence would conform to the 'normal' practice of printing the preliminaries last.

In terms of size, the setting of CREEDE 2 approaches a normal quarto. The type-page size was expanded to approximately 149mm × 86mm with 36 lines of text per page. As the first page of The Ploughman's Tale illustrates (CREEDE 1, sig. C2; CREEDE 2, sig. C1), the gain amounts to about 4.5 lines per page through D1^v; from D2 on, the measure of CREEDE 2 is about 8–10mm wider than in CREEDE 1, producing an even greater gain per page. An extra page was gained by shifting the title-page from sig. A2 to sig. A1; however, the blank versos of the title and the prose transition (unit 5) were preserved. The compositor of CREEDE 2 followed the layout of CREEDE 1 until the first tale, where the compression began. He faithfully reset Middleton's epistle 'To the Reader' line-for-line with minor variants in the incidentals and two significant textual emendations, and duplicated the CREEDE 1 setting of the first section of introductory verses (unit 4) and the prose transition (unit 5), again with variants in incidentals. However, he ignored CREEDE 1's shift to black letter in the prose transition, continuing to set from the cases containing Creede's Tournes pica roman in which the verse section is set.

The claim that CREEDE 2 almost immediately followed CREEDE 1 because the type of the Epistle Dedicatory was left standing (Shaaber, Price, Kaplan) ignores the printing context in Creede's shop. The key fact is that only the 94mm roman section of CREEDE 1 was left standing. Creede had a quite ample supply of this 94mm roman fount (a standard text-fount) and could afford to leave fifty narrow lines standing, since he most frequently used the Tournes pica in quarto roman settings. In contrast, the 16-pt roman used in 'To the Reader' was not a text-fount and Creede probably had a quite limited supply that was only adequate for setting brief preliminary texts such as this. Unless an immediate reprint was scheduled, his compositor most probably would have distributed the 16-pt roman since Creede liked using it for preliminaries, as he did for 'The Epistle to the Reader' (A3–4) in The Black Book, which was entered on 22 March 1604, about ten weeks after CREEDE 1. In the mean time, two other entered books (25 January, 22 February) were printed by Creede. It is tempting to conjecture that the epistle of CREEDE 2 had to be reset because the 16-pt roman fount was distributed for Black Book. However, ten of the twenty books printed by Creede in 1604 were not entered, and it is impossible to say which of these (if any) were printed between CREEDE 1 and Black Book. In any event, the distribution of the 16-pt roman certainly indicates that CREEDE 2 was not printed on the heels of CREEDE 1, but only after one or more intervening books requiring the 16-pt roman had

been printed in the mean time (see Weiss, 1999, 62–4, about contextual type usage).

Running-Title Movements and Printing Method

Price based his conclusion that CREEDE 1 was printed in quarto-form using cut sheets of large paper upon his analysis of running titles. Although his running-title identifications are largely erroneous, a re-examination of the running titles strongly suggests that his conclusion was correct (188–9). Running-title movements can, in fact, demonstrate whether a book was printed as a quarto or as an octavo in fours using either the normal or the half-sheet methods of imposition. However, the running titles of CREEDE 1 present a serious problem because of the compositors' method of transferring them from forme to forme.

The difficulty of identifying recurrences of specific titles arises from the fact that the titles were not moved, for the most part, as intact units. Only two titles exhibit exactly identical types and spacings which were transferred without modification: #2 appears at B1^v, B3^v, and C3^v, and #7 appears at B3^v, C4^v, and probably E1^v. Otherwise, other apparent recurrences exhibit changes in spacings and types. In some cases, the recurrence can be confirmed by other characteristics. (The complete running title divides into two typographical units based upon the compositor's manipulations: unit A consists of 'The Ant, and the', while 'Nightingale' is unit B). For example, title #8 contains the misspelled 'Ning tingale' on C1 which is corrected to 'Ningtingale' on D3^v and moves to E3^v. However, while this second typographical unit ('#8B') moves to F2^v, either some types were reset in unit A, thereby producing a narrower measure, or a new setting of unit A appears in F2^v. In short, the compositor scavenged unit #8A 'The Ant, and the' from the wrought-off inner forme of E. Next, the swash-N used in unit B appears in eight formes. Four of these exhibit identical damage to the swash-N descender (#6B) and the settings of unit B are identical in B4, D1, E1, and F2. However, the initial 'T' of unit #6A is either damaged (right arm-serif sheared away) or replaced in going from B4 to D1. The move to E1 eliminates an en-space or so between units A and B, and a further compression of the inter-word space as well as replacement with a roman 'T' accompanies the move of #6A to F2. Overall, the title is the same, but only unit #6B remains unmodified. However, the same is not true of the four other appearances of a swash-N setting. While the swash-N of B3 possibly moves to C3, the word is entirely reset, as is the unit A portion of the title of B3. Then unit B of C3 moves to D3, and probably to E3. However, the A unit is reset in each later appearance (D3, E3). Two new settings appear in inner-D and retain their position in the forme in moving to inner-E (#10: D4 to E4; #11: D2 to E2). The new titles in D2 and D4 are accompanied by a narrowing of the measure from about 86mm to 76mm as noted above. These changes coincide with evidence that a second compositor began setting at D2. Finally, neither unit can be identified in the titles of E2^v and E4^v, or in five of the titles from sheet F (F1, 3, 3^v, 4, and 4^v); nor does #5 appear after B2.

Despite the limited nature of the evidence, the movements are sufficient to strongly suggest that the book was printed as a quarto on large sheets cut in half before machining. First, in normal 'octavo in fours' printing, the corresponding formes (i.e, outer or inner) of two successive signatures are imposed in the chase; for example, pages 1, 2^v, 3, and 4^v of both signatures A and B for printing the outer forme of the first sheet of paper, of signatures C and D for the second sheet, and so on. The other side of the sheet is backed by the inner formes of the corresponding signatures. Eight running titles are required since no title can appear in corresponding formes of successive sheets. Several sequences of recurrences (#2, #3B, #6–6B, #8, #10, and #11) violate the basic criterion that no title can recur in the corresponding forme of successive signatures. Second, the same criterion applies to printing two half-sheets of octavo worked together and then cut in half before folding. In the third method of printing an octavo in fours, that is, half-sheet imposition for work and turn, both formes of a signature are imposed in the chase and are printed on both sides of the octavo sheet so that two quarto sheets result after cutting the octavo sheet in half. Since eight separate titles are required, no title can reappear in both formes of a signature. This criterion is violated only in signature B, where #2 appears at B2^v and B1^v. Otherwise, signatures C–F could have been printed by the half-sheet work and turn method. However, given the fact that signature B uses no regular running titles, the evidence does not eliminate the possibility that signatures A and B were printed by the other octavo methods. Overall, the evidence points to quarto printing on half-sheets.

The watermark evidence is ambiguous with respect to method of printing because of the size of paper used in the book. The papers in CREEDE 1 (Folger copy) exhibit extraordinarily wide-spaced chainlines of about 38–40mm which are vertically oriented, the normal orientation for octavo printing; the same orientation would obtain if the large sheets had been cut in half for quarto printing. Similarly, the positions of the marks in the top gutter would be the same. The watermarks seen in A1, B2, and E3–4 have disintegrated to the point where it is impossible to state with any certainty what the original design was (e.g., pot, vase, grapes, etc.). No evidence of watermarks is found in signatures C, D, and F.

Printer's Copy and Creede's Compositors

Price based his view that CREEDE 2 was set from manuscript copy rather than a corrected copy of CREEDE 1 on an analysis of substantive variants. He found that, of a group of 39 variants, CREEDE 1 was superior in 17 instances and CREEDE 2 in 22 instances, and argued that the proportion of superior readings should be significantly higher if CREEDE 2 had been set from a corrected copy of CREEDE 1 (186–8). However, if the list of variants is analysed with

respect to the nature of the differences, it is clear that the 17 readings of CREEDE 1 are 'superior' simply because a word or a letter was omitted by the compositor of CREEDE 2. In one instance (not noted by Price), the incorrect change (1279) of *flew* in CREEDE 1 to *flew* in CREEDE 2 is obviously a result of foul-case due to mis-distribution of visually similar types. In other instances, compositorial eyeskip is the readily apparent cause of the difficulty, as in the omission of -the- from *Never-|lesse* (946) and the misspelling of *Prit-|ter* (58) at line-breaks, or the omission of *it* from the phrase *vyed it* (965–6) at a page-break. If the compositor of CREEDE 2 had worked directly from manuscript copy, the print-copy conditions for these kinds of omission simply would not have been present. In other words, he could only have been setting from a printed copy of CREEDE 1.

In some instances, it seems that faulty memorization, misreading, or auditory memorial confusion produced the error in CREEDE 1, since a single letter is involved. For instance, a fatigued compositor could easily set the correct-sounding *once complain* after having memorized several lines containing *ones complain* (190) and *as wings* for *his wings* (383). Similarly, two instances each of *men* for *me* (177, 1018) and *on* for *one* (696, 901), *set* for *sent* (867), *the* for *thy* (1064), and *the* for *they* (586) point to habitual kinds of errors committed by Creede's two compositors, and are what we would expect from Akihiro Yamada's study of them during the 1603–10 period. Both were prone to omit letters and single words; the latter most frequently are pronouns, auxiliary verbs, connectives, articles, and adjectives. Each of the omissions in CREEDE 2 has numerous correspondences in Yamada's table of errors (196–8) and lists (164–82, 184, 216–37). Similarly, in his study of Creede's printing of *The Black Book*, G. B. Shand found that the second edition introduces 37 errors, of which twelve are substantive (326) and correspond in kind to those noted above.

In contrast, the 22 superior readings of CREEDE 2 are substantive corrections, emendations, or additions. It is clear that a very careful proofing of a copy of CREEDE 1 might have produced some of the corrections noted above. The work of a corrector is obvious in one instance. Price points to the failure to completely correct the mispunctuation with parentheses of the clause 'at (passage I | meane: (for...' (CREEDE 1, D4^v; 666–8) as evidence that 'a thoroughly corrected copy of' CREEDE 1 could not have been used for setting CREEDE 2. But the fact is that a correction was attempted which closed the parentheses but left the leading parenthesis in the wrong position: 'at (passage I meane:) for...' (CREEDE 2, D2^v). The partial correction points to a corrector reading for obvious typesetting errors without an eye to sense (see below for similar corrections in inner-F of CREEDE 2).

Similarly, the subtlety of many of those variants involving a single letter or a change of pronoun or tense suggests a degree of attention to sense not usually to be expected of a corrector. Certainly the revision of *honest--stitching* to *honest-minded* in 'To the Reader' has no plausible explanation either in terms of compositorial or proofing error and points to an authorial proofing and revision of the copy of CREEDE 1 used as printer's copy for CREEDE 2. On the other hand, the omission of the entire clause (a full line in CREEDE 2) 'which agreed so well with his brain (being nothing but cork)' (377–8) from CREEDE 1 is a different situation (Yamada found a 'disturbing tendency' of Creede's compositors to commit such errors [187]). Since the omission of this non-essential clause has no effect upon the completeness of the sentence, the case is equally strong for restoration by a corrector reading against manuscript copy, by Middleton proofing CREEDE 1 and catching the omission, or by Middleton adding the clause for CREEDE 2. In any event, since the text was set seriatim, a stop-press correction in CREEDE 1 would have required a major, time-consuming adjustment involving the insertion of this clause on C3^v and an extremely complicated forward movement of type involving the shifting of excess words to each line below, and the re-justification of all the lines on the remaining pages of sheet C (see Moxon, 235–6). Middleton probably would have been convinced by Creede to allow the omission in this circumstance; in fact, Creede would have, in all probability, simply refused to do the insertion.

In addition to the line-for-line resetting of 'To the Reader', one additional bit of evidence conclusively points to the use of a corrected copy of CREEDE 1 as copy for setting CREEDE 2. As Kaplan argued, CREEDE 2's erroneous setting of *fltnt* for the *flipt* of CREEDE 1 can only result from setting from CREEDE 1. The descender of the *p* in *flip* has been sheared away, giving 'the author's *slipt* the appearance of *slint*, the word the compositor was presumably trying to set', which was a variant of *slent* (meaning *slipt*) (175). The mis-setting of the *t* for the *i* evidences compositorial confusion in trying to decipher his printed copy. Illegibility in manuscript copy simply does not work as an explanation, since the confusion depends entirely upon damage to a printing type.

The line-for-line resetting of 'To the Reader' conclusively demonstrates that it was set from a corrected copy of CREEDE 1. Price's judgement regarding the final line of A4, *for I entreat here neither of Rug-*, continued overleaf *ged Beares, or Apes* (65–6), is certainly in error. (The catchword in both editions is *-ged*.) He inexplicably chooses the setting *Rug-|ged* as the corrected form of the adjective modifying *Beares*, even though *Rag-|ged* is the form in two of three copies of CREEDE 1 and both copies of CREEDE 2. He cites the later use of *rugged* in the phrase 'rugged Souldier' (805) but there is no textual relation whatever between the two instances. One could more plausibly argue that the London scene and the later reference to bear-baiting would most probably evoke the image of a 'ragged bear' whose coat has been repeatedly torn by the bear-trap jaws of mastiffs. Unfortunately, nothing is known of the content of this specific 'Tale of Mother Hubburd' (63) which is the actual context of the reference to bears and apes. The subtitle of Edmund Spenser's *Prosopopoia* is 'Or Mother Hubberds Tale', but no record of it being called in exists. Moreover, a fox and an ape are the main characters.

In short, the evidence demonstrates that the CREEDE 1 portion of CREEDE 2 was set from a corrected copy of CREEDE 1 worked over by both Middleton and a corrector, while the additions for CREEDE 2 obviously were set from manuscript.

Quality of Proofing: Hatfield Inner-F

Price's general contention that CREEDE 1 was, at best, 'carelessly corrected' is dispelled by the evidence of stop-press corrections in inner-F of the Hatfield copy of CREEDE 2 (unknown to Price). The fact that CREEDE 1 contains only two stop-press corrections is clearly the result of a rather rigorous final stage of proofing. Kaplan found 17 stop-press corrections in inner-F of the Hatfield copy. This high rate of error far exceeds that which Yamada found in Creede's books for the period (see discussion, 183–90), and provides some insight into the quality of the final stage of stop-press correction in CREEDE 2 (and by implication, CREEDE 1).

Several errors fall into the categories noted above (see the Press Variants section below for a list). Four corrections involve a restoration of an omitted pronoun *I* in *but think* to *but I think* (1249), the addition of a letter in *bakfide* to *backfide* (1250-1), and a comma in *fhowde in learning*, to *fhowde, in learning* (1110) which is essential for the sense, and a space inserted correcting *Icould* to *I could* (1125). Five other corrections of incidentals include the closing of a parentheses in *Madame; to Madame)* (1252), one corrected misspelling (*plentuous* to *plenteous*, 1145), a replacement of an ampersand with *and* (1105), and additions of a terminal *-e* (*old* to *olde*, 1109) and a terminal *-l* (*ful* to *full*, 1129) in lines shortened by other corrections.

Six others are substantive. One omission seems clearly attributable to the compositor's habitual faulty memorization: the setting of *Bookes* for *Booke* (1266) is an obvious instance. However, a second omission illustrates the principle that corrections often produced new errors. Hatfield-F set the incorrect *reward* (1103), but in the process of correction, the compositor set *rereward* instead of the correct *rearward*, perhaps misinterpreting the corrector's mark. A misreading of manuscript copy or auditory confusion could have led to the setting of *Batchelors gowne* instead of the correct *Batlors gowne* (1109), but the compositor may have mistaken the latter, worn by the lowest level of academics, for the former, or just not known the difference. Two involve the change of a word: *courfe* for *growth* (1129), and *Linnens* for *Limbes* (1134). These two are clearly attributable to authorial revision, since a misreading of manuscript copy, however illegible, is virtually impossible.

And finally, one variant provides unquestionable evidence either of correction by the author or a precise proofing against a manuscript copy which preserved Middleton's unique spelling forms. The form *forft* (F2:2) is corrected to Middleton's characteristic *forcft* (1134). Interestingly enough, the other compositor changed the

Middleton form *forcſt* at C4^v:1 (CREEDE 1) to *forced* at C3:19 in CREEDE 2 (430). Overall, the corrected state of inner-F is on par with the rest of the two editions, with no obvious need for further corrections except in the case of *rereward* as noted above. As a whole, then, CREEDE 2 was proofed rather closely.

Creede's Compositors

The work of Creede's two compositors (designated 'A' and 'B'), as Yamada determined, is difficult to distinguish because of the many spelling preferences shared by the two (see Hinman). Yamada plausibly inferred this to be an effect of the master/apprentice relationship. Price's view that both editions were set from manuscript copy is puzzling, since it seems to ignore his own evidence that CREEDE 1 preserved 71 spellings 'closer to Middleton's form' while CREEDE 2 only preserved 27 (187). In any event, he overlooks the fact that many of A's and B's preferences overlap Middleton's, in effect nullifying the evidence that seems to demonstrate setting from a holograph manuscript. It seems that only two of Middleton's preferences survive the overlap. The compositors generally preserved Middleton's *agen* vs. *again* in verse settings. As noted above, of the two instances of Middleton's *forcſt* vs. *forced* undeniably set from manuscript (CREEDE 1, C4^v:1; CREEDE 2, F2:2), one was changed in resetting CREEDE 2 (430). The Middleton spelling *ballac'ſt* (CREEDE 1, E4:32) was preserved in CREEDE 2 (E1^v:19) (857), probably because of the compositor's unfamiliarity with the word. On the other hand, several Middleton spellings are never followed, such as medial *-ei-* (*beleive*), but with one notable exception. In CREEDE 1 at F3^v:10 (1027), the compositor encountered the Middleton spelling *feild*, set a ligature by habit for this word, and then finished with what he saw in the manuscript, producing the oddity *fiel̄ds*. Creede's men never set *-d-* preceding soft *-g-* after *-n-* (*plundge*); Middleton's *yfayth* is never set with the medial *-ay-*; and *onely* is never set with terminal *-lie* (*onelie*). (It is worth noting that the medial *-ei-* is preserved in six instances in Creede's setting of *The Black Book* [Shand, 326].) Several Middleton preferences are levelled by compositorial preferences such as: doubled medial and terminal consonants *-nn-* (*donne*), *-pp-* (*uppon*) and *-tt-* (*gett*); medial *-ay-* (*agaynst*); the single medial *-t-* consonant in *litle*; and the doubled vowel in *bee* and the pronoun group (*hee*, *shee*, *wee*). In short, these and an array of other spellings render CREEDE 1 and CREEDE 2 indistinguishable from other texts set by A and B. In other words, the majority of presumed Middleton preferences in CREEDE 1 and CREEDE 2 can be as probably attributed to compositors A and B as to Middleton.

The difficulty of distinguishing compositorial stints in the two editions is compounded by two factors: (1) the shared preferences of Creede's two compositors as described by Yamada; (2) the influence of justification upon compositorial spelling preferences in prose, which constitutes a majority of the text. Nonetheless, two hands can be distinguished on the basis of several high-frequency preference groups. Overall, approximately 320 variants

distinguish the two editions; of these approximately 280 involve changes in spelling (not including substitutions of an ampersand for *and* or a tilde for various letter combinations). The statistically significant changes include the following, where the numbers of occurrences include only changed spellings, not the entire number of instances of a given spelling.

(1) In setting pronouns, the compositor of CREEDE 2 changed the long form (*hee*, *shee*, *mee*) to the short form (*he*, *she*, *me*) in 17 of 18 instances. However, the long forms do not occur before D2 in CREEDE 1.

(2) Similarly, Middleton's exclusive preference for medial *-y-* in dipthongs (*-oy-*, *-ay-*, *-ey-*) dominates the setting of CREEDE 1 (32/12), but the ratio is reversed in favour of medial *-i-* (12/32) in CREEDE 2.

(3) Terminal *-y*, *-yes*, and *-s* are the preferred forms of CREEDE 1; the ratio of 29/12 is reversed in CREEDE 2.

(4) Finally, the ratio for doubled medial consonants *-pp-* and *-tt-* is also reversed in CREEDE 2 (10/2).

It should be noted that verbal spellings show no consistent pattern either in regard to distinguishable preferences or to changes for CREEDE 2. Among other spelling variants, changes are made in specific forms but these occur at such a low frequency as to be statistically insignificant. Again, justification problems in prose settings probably influenced these changes as much as compositorial preferences. However, the overall tendency is for resetting in the short form.

The evidence for two compositors in CREEDE 1 is less certain. However, a shift occurs at D2 to the long pronominal forms (*hee* etc.) that continues until E4, and then at F2 and after at a statistically significant level. Similarly, a greater preponderance of medial *-y-* as well as terminal *-ie* obtains. The problem is as Yamada noted, namely, that neither of Creede's compositors had exclusive preferences, but rather shared most preferences, with A distinguished from B primarily on the basis of magnitude of inclination to use one form over the other. Nonetheless, the fact that the shift in magnitudes occurs at D2 where the measure is shortened from 80–83mm to 76–79mm can hardly be coincidental, and strongly suggests that a second compositor took over at that point.

Copy-text

The selection of copy-text, editorial approach, and presentation in this edition depends first upon sorting out the relationship between the two printed texts of CREEDE 1 and CREEDE 2 in regard to Middleton's 'final intention' for his work.

At the outset, it must be recognized that this relationship does not primarily consist of what might be termed 'micro-revisions' which produce a series of variant readings of words, phrases, or even paragraphs in the two texts. In such a case, as G. Thomas Tanselle notes, an editor is faced with 'determining which stage of intention is to take precedence over the others and be incorporated into the main text' (18). The editor's task thus consists of making critical choices between earlier vs. later readings. As is clear from the Textual Notes, revisions and corrections did occur at this level, but almost all of the substantive variants consist of an omitted letter or word (in one instance an omitted clause) in one or the other edition, and are, for the most part, attributable to compositorial error, but not to authorial revision. As a whole, the portions of the text that appear in CREEDE 1 are stable and exhibit no internal revisions in going to CREEDE 2 except for the two clearly authorial revisions in the preliminaries (and possibly the added or restored clause at 377–8). Thus the text of CREEDE 1 reached its final state before printing. In other words, Middleton considered the text of CREEDE 1 fully revised and completed when he committed it to print even though CREEDE 1 did not include the third tale (units 10–12). Furthermore, the addition of these units did not require any modification to the text of CREEDE 1. If revisions were done to the text of units 10–12, they were done independently of the text of CREEDE 1. In short, on the 'micro-revisions' level, Middleton's intentions for the texts of both CREEDE 1 and CREEDE 2 were finalized when each was printed.

Next, the difference between the two texts must be considered on what might be termed the 'macro--revisions' level, or in this case, more appropriately 'macro-additions'. The view, espoused by Price, that the completed final text found in CREEDE 2 was present in printer's copy for CREEDE 1 and amputated by the publisher can be rejected for the reasons cited in earlier discussion. There is simply no factual basis for rejecting the inference that CREEDE 1 represents a deliberate and consensual printing of the text in an uncompleted state.

Hence, the magnitude of difference between the two states of the text requires a critical assessment in the context of the textual situation described by Tanselle: 'revisions are sometimes so radical that they alter the nature or conception of a work and in effect produce a new work; in such cases it is probable that the earlier version and the later one are best treated as two separate works, each worthy of a critical edition' (18). The fundamental question, then, is whether CREEDE 1 and CREEDE 2 differ in such a manner as to represent two different works.

In fact, they do not. Although the insertion of the third tale and its introductory verses 16 lines from the end of CREEDE 1 substantially enlarges the text, CREEDE 2 simply represents a further evolution of the conception of the work already evident in CREEDE 1. CREEDE 1's naming and characterization of Oliver Hubburd in 'To the Reader' and 'The Epistle Dedicatory' shows that, at the time of printing, Middleton's conception of his work included the scholar's tale. As CREEDE 2 demonstrates, his final intention was a work in which the information supplied in The Scholar's Tale would elucidate the issues of the identity of the writer of the Epistle and the source of his anger.

Thus CREEDE 2 cannot be considered a new version of CREEDE 1 because it does not fundamentally differ from CREEDE 1 in terms of Middleton's conception. In order to say that it does, we would have to accept the irrational proposition that Middleton decided to preface CREEDE 1 with a vituperative Epistle Dedicatory signed by one Oliver Hubburd, and then, only after CREEDE 1 was printed, did he conceive the idea of adding the third tale in order to explain the unanswered issues raised in the Epistle. In short, the additions of CREEDE 2 are not, in any sense, 'revisions' or 'changes' of the conception of the work exhibited in CREEDE 1, but rather, function as actualizations of potentials implicit in CREEDE 1. Thus, taken together, CREEDE 1 and CREEDE 2 represent two stages in the evolution of a single conception of Middleton's work. It is impossible to determine why Middleton allowed the printing of the partially-realized concept. However, the shift in publishers between the two editions is undeniable. Perhaps he applied the strategy of Nashe's 'A Private Epistle of the Author' noted above and approached Cotton with the offer of the new material. His decision could have been, in some undefinable way, related to the shift in publishers, but in the final analysis, to suggest such specific scenarios is purely ungrounded speculation. Shaaber's notion that a sell-out occasioned an immediate reprinting and led to the publisher requesting the new material is a case in point (15).

Finally, the fact that the preliminaries of CREEDE 1 do not cohere with the body of the text (units 4, 6–9) underscores the presence of two different concepts of the work in CREEDE 1 (and by extension, CREEDE 2). The body of the text in no way implies the presence of the preliminaries. In fact, when the body of the text is read apart from the preliminaries, nothing suggests their absence. In other words, the body of the text of CREEDE 1 functions as a self-contained work with no outward-looking conceptual threads. In Tanselle's terms, the preliminaries of CREEDE 1 and the additions of CREEDE 2 so fundamentally alter the conception represented in the body of the text, in which the major character was an unnamed ant, as to produce a new work. Thus CREEDE 1 must be viewed as an uncompleted expression of that new work, which is found in CREEDE 2 in its completed form. Furthermore, it is clear that the 'original' work that was substantially changed to produce the 'new' work (in Tanselle's terms) is the body of the text (units 4, 6–9) of CREEDE 1.

In short, both the bibliographical evidence and critical considerations lead to the selection of CREEDE 2, collated with CREEDE 1, as copy-text for this edition of *Father Hubburd's Tales*, the final version of the work.

The evidence that the manuscript presented for entry in the Stationers' Register contained only the body of the text suggests the approach taken in this edition. Two options are available for differentiating the two versions of the work in an edition. A single clean reading text of the final version can be presented with textual notes indicating the location and sequence of additions, allowing the reader to construct (with great difficulty) a mental concept of the 'original' (manuscript), 'transitional' (CREEDE 1), and 'final' (CREEDE 2) versions. However, the necessity of flipping between reading text and textual notes would largely obscure the dramatic impact of the additions. In contrast, presenting the 'original' version in a separate text and encouraging the reader to read it first will lead to a clearer appreciation of the evolution of Middleton's work from manuscript to final printed version. Hence, this edition presents the 'original' version, *The Nightingale and the Ant*, as a separate text which is conjecturally reconstructed by extracting the body of the text (units 4, 6–9) verbatim from the final printed version. The Textual Notes and Commentary are keyed to *Father Hubburd's Tales*.

SEE ALSO

WORKS CITED

Editions

CREEDE, Thomas, printer, *The Ant, and the Nightingale* (1604)
CREEDE, Thomas, printer, *Father Hubburds Tales* (1604)
DYCE, Alexander, ed., *Works*, 5 vols (1840), vol. 5
BULLEN, A. H., ed., *Works*, 8 vols (1885–6), vol. 8
IRWIN, Larry Wayne, ed., *A Critical Edition of Thomas Middleton's Micro-Cynicon, Father Hubburd's Tales, and The Blacke Booke*, unpublished Ph.D. diss. (University of Wisconsin, 1969)

Other Works Cited

Adams, J. Q., 'Introduction', in *The Ghost of Lucrece*, ed. J. Q. Adams (1937), i–xviii
Arber, Edward, *A Transcript of the Registers of the Company of Stationers of London, 1554–1640*, 5 vols (1875)
Binns, James, 'STC Latin Books: Evidence for Printing-House Practice', *The Library*, V, 32 (1977), 1–27
—— 'STC Latin Books: Further Evidence for Printing-House Practice', *The Library*, VI, 1 (1979), 347–54
Brennan, Michael, 'William Ponsonby: Elizabethan Stationer', *Analytical & Enumerative Bibliography* 6–7 (1982–3), 91–110
Harrison, G. B., ed., *Thomas Nash: Pierce Penilesse, his Supplication to the Divell (1592)* (1924)
Hibbard, G. R., 'Introduction', in *Three Elizabethan Pamphlets* (1951), 11–34
Hinman, Charlton, 'Principles Governing the Use of Variant Spellings as Evidence of Alternate Setting by Two Compositors', *The Library*, IV, 21 (1940), 78–94
Johnson, Francis R., 'Printers' "Copie Books" and the Black Market in the Elizabethan Book Trade', *The Library*, V, 1 (1946), 97–105
Johnson, Gerald D., 'John Busby and the Stationers' Trade, 1590–1612', *The Library*, VI, 7 (1985), 1–15
Kaplan, Joel H., 'Printer's Copy for Thomas Middleton's *The Ant and the Nightingale*', *Papers of the Bibliographical Society of America* 81 (1987), 173–5
Moxon, Joseph, *Mechanick Exercises on the Whole Art of Printing* (1683–4), Herbert Davis and Harry Carter, eds. (1962)
Nashe, Thomas, *Pierce Penilesse his Supplication to the Divell* (1592)
Price, George R., 'The Early Editions of Thomas Middleton's *The Ant and the Nightingale*', *Papers of the Bibliographical Society of America* 43 (1949), 179–90
Read, Conyers, *Lord Burghley and Queen Elizabeth* (1960)
Shaaber, M. A., '*The Ant and the Nightingale* and *Father Hubburd's Tales*', *Library Chronicle of the University of Pennsylvania*, 14 (1947), 13–16
Shand, G. B., 'The Two Editions of Thomas Middleton's *The Blacke Booke*', *Papers of the Bibliographical Society of America* 71 (1977), 325–8
Tanselle, G. Thomas, 'Texts of Documents and Texts of Works', in *Textual Criticism and Scholarly Editing* (1990), 3–23
Weiss, Adrian, 'A "Fill-in" Job: The Textual Crux and Interrupted Printing in Thomas Middleton's *The Triumphs of Honour and Virtue*', *Papers of the Bibliographical Society of America*, 93 (1999), 53–73
—— 'Rhetoric and Satire: New Light on John Marston's Pigmalion and the Satires', *Journal of English and Germanic Philology*, 71 (1972), 22–35
—— 'Shared Printing, Printer's Copy, and the Text(s) of Gascoigne's *A Hundreth Sundrie Flowres*', *Studies in Bibliography* 45 (1992), 71–104
Yamada, Akihiro, *Thomas Creede: Printer to Shakespeare and his Contemporaries* (1994)

TEXTUAL NOTES

Title   The Nyghtingale and the Ante. A Jove surgit opus *Stationers' Register*; THE ANT, | AND THE | Nightingale: | OR | FATHER | *Hubburds* Tales. CREEDE 1; FATHER | Hubburds Tales: | OR | THE ANT, | And the Nightingale. CREEDE 2.

1   *The Epistle Dedicatory*] THIS EDITION; supplied from running title (A2ᵛ CREEDE 1; A3ᵛ CREEDE 2)

40   a pair] THIS EDITION; a a ~ CREEDE

50   I should] CREEDE 1; ₄ ~ CREEDE 2

58   printer] CREEDE 1 (Printer); Prit-|ter CREEDE 2

58   honest-minded] CREEDE 2; honeſt-ſtitching CREEDE 1

66   ragged] Rag-|ged CREEDE 1 (Folger, Malone), CREEDE 2 (British Library, Hatfield); Rug-|ged CREEDE 1 (Huntington). The word is split at the catchword position of sig. A3 in all copies. Folger and Malone represent the corrected state of the forme in CREEDE 1 which passed to CREEDE 2.

80   Companies] CREEDE 1; Companie CREEDE 2

140   judgement's] CREEDE 1 (Iudgements); Iudgement CREEDE 2

154   this sentence] CREEDE 2; their ~ CREEDE 1

177   poor me] CREEDE 2; ~ men CREEDE 1

190   ones complain] CREEDE 2; once ~ CREEDE 1

203   morning's sun.] CREEDE 1 (mornings Sun!); morning Sunne. CREEDE 2

276–90   With this, ... his tale.] *blackletter in* CREEDE 1; *roman in* CREEDE 2

349   and if] CREEDE 1; ~ if if CREEDE 2

353   I have heard] CREEDE 1; ~ ₄ ~ CREEDE 2

359   we had] CREEDE 1; we we ~ CREEDE 2

362   offered] CREEDE 2; offering CREEDE 1

364   the bowing] CREEDE 1; ₄ ~ CREEDE 2

368   jerking] CREEDE (yerking)

377–8   which agreed so well ... nothing but cork)] CREEDE 2 (Cork); *not in* CREEDE 1

383 His wings] CREEDE 2 (his); as ~ CREEDE 1
418 jingle] CREEDE (Gingle)
425 approach] CREEDE 2; approacht CREEDE 1
522 for 'tis easier] CREEDE 1 (~ ti's ~); ∧ ~ ~ CREEDE 2
525 that] CREEDE 1; ȳ CREEDE 2
554 scent] BULLEN; cent CREEDE
577 one] CREEDE 2, CREEDE 1 (Malone, Folger); and CREEDE 1 (Huntington)
585 gentlewomen] CREEDE 1 (Gentlewomen); Gentlewoman CREEDE 2
586 they,] CREEDE 1 (they ∧); the ∧ CREEDE 2
590 go still] CREEDE 1; ~ ∧ CREEDE 2
594 vaulting] CREEDE (vauting)
609 besides] CREEDE 2; beside CREEDE 1
660 volley] CREEDE 2; valley CREEDE 1
677 the host] BULLEN; *not in* CREEDE
683 we not] CREEDE 1; ∧ ~ CREEDE 2
694 then] CREEDE 1; *not in* CREEDE 2
696 one side] CREEDE 2; on ~ CREEDE 1
712 grown as] CREEDE 1; *not in* CREEDE 2
732 *habeas*] THIS EDITION; *Habes* CREEDE
753 carriage] THIS EDITION (Taylor); marriage CREEDE. Gary Taylor conjectures that 'marriage' is a compositorial misreading of the minims 'c' and 'm' which are easily confused in the secretary hand. I would add that a compositor, unaware of the musical sense of 'carriage' as 'meaning conveyed by words' (i.e., the idea 'Small bodies can have little wrong' in this instance), might have easily chosen to set 'marriage' although it makes no sense in this context.
780 men's] CREEDE 2 (mens); mans CREEDE 1
785 And] CREEDE 2; *not in* CREEDE 1
797 *Ant.*] CREEDE 2; *not in* CREEDE 1
828 other] CREEDE 1; *not in* CREEDE 2
851 washed shape] CREEDE 2 (waſht-ſhape); waſh-ſhape CREEDE 1

860 and a] CREEDE 1; ~ ∧ CREEDE 2
867 sent] CREEDE 2 (ſent); ſet CREEDE 1
872 eelskins] CREEDE 1 (Eel-|ſkins), CREEDE 2 (Ele-|ſkins)
901 on] CREEDE 2; one CREEDE 1
929 the first] CREEDE 2; ~ CREEDE 1
946 Nevertheless] CREEDE 1; Never-|leſſe CREEDE 2
965-6 vied it] CREEDE 1; ~ ∧ CREEDE 2
980 my bleeding] CREEDE 1; ∧ ~ CREEDE 2
982 towards] CREEDE 2; toward CREEDE 1
1011 warm lapped] CREEDE 1 (warm lapt); ∧ ~ CREEDE 2
1018 me leaden] CREEDE 2; men ~ CREEDE 1
1027 Moorfields] CREEDE 2 (Moore fields); Moore fieilds CREEDE 1
1035 turns] CREEDE 2 (turnes); for-|tunes CREEDE 1. 'Turns' seems to agree best as referent of the question 'doth reeling Fortune...?', which is raised two sentences earlier and evokes this answer.
1042 of brown] CREEDE 2; of of ~ CREEDE 1
1047 slipped into an ant] sli[p]t into an Ant CREEDE 1; ſltnt CREEDE 2. The descender of the damaged 'p' in CREEDE 1 has been sheared away, producing the appearance of an 'n'. Dyce's reading of CREEDE 2 as 'stint' overlooks the use of the ſl, not the ſt ligature. Kaplan is probably correct: 'Here [CREEDE 2's] erroneous "sltnt" results not from the problems of reading manuscript, but from a badly damaged "p" in [CREEDE 1] which gives the author's "slipt" the appearance of "slint", the word Creede's compositor was presumably trying to set.... *OED* records "slint" as a variant of "slent" (meaning slipt).'
1064 thy body] CREEDE 2; the ~ CREEDE 1
1073-266 So here...or plough] CREEDE 2; *not in* CREEDE 1
1103 rearward] CREEDE 2 (rereward)
1255 swooned] DYCE; CREEDE (ſounded)
1279 flew] CREEDE 1; flew CREEDE 2. Ligature mis-setting error due to the extremely similar visual appearance of the ſl and fl ligatures, or alternately, to a previous foulcase mis--distribution of ligature types.

PRESS VARIANTS

CREEDE 1

Copies collated: FOL Folger; MAL Malone; HN Huntington

Sheet A (inner forme)

Sig. A4

66 ragged] Rag-|ged FOL, MAL; Rug-|ged HN

Sheet D (outer forme)

Sig. D3

577 one of] FOL, MAL; and of HN

CREEDE 2

Copies collated: BL British Library; H Hatfield House, Hatfield, Herts.

Sheet F (inner forme)

Sig. F1ᵛ

1103 rearward] rereward BL; reward H
1105 and] BL; & H

1109 old] olde BL; old H
1109 batteler's] Batlors BL; Batchelers H
1110 showed, in learning] ſhowde, in learning BL; ſhowde in learning, H
1125 I could] BL; Icould H
1129 full] BL; ful H
1129 course] courſe BL; growth H

Sig. F2

1134 linens] Linnens BL; Limbes H
1134 forced] forcſt BL; forſt H
1145 plenteous] BL; plentuous H

Sig. F3ᵛ

1249 but, I think,] but I thinke BL; but thinke H
1250-1 backside] backſide BL; bakſide H
1252 madam]] Madame) BL; Madame; H
1252 book] booke BL; Booke H
1261 more] BL; where H
1266 book,] Booke, BL; Bookes H

THE MEETING OF GALLANTS AT AN ORDINARY

Edited by Paul Yachnin

No early edition is extant other than a quarto published in 1604. The title-page of that edition informs us that it was 'printed by T[homas] C[reede] and ... sold by Mat[t]hew Lawe, dwelling in Paules Churchyard'. The text comprises four gatherings: A1 is the title-page, A1^v is blank, D3^v and D4 are blank. Except for the title-page, section and speech headings, running titles, and a few individual words and lines, the pamphlet is printed in black letter. Four copies of CREEDE (STC 17781) survive. Two are in the Bodleian, a third is in the British Library, and a fourth in the Pierpont Morgan Library. The present edition, like Wilson's, is based on Wood 616 in the Bodleian.

On 8 January 1608 John Trundle and Richard Sergier entered a work entitled *Powles Walke or a gallant Dismasked*, in the Stationers' Register. Although the STC cites this entry as referring to *The Meeting of Gallants at an Ordinary*, it does not have the usual characteristics of an assignment to other stationers (see Cyndia Susan Clegg's discussion in this volume, p. 252), and no corresponding reprint is known. It probably refers to a different work.

SEE ALSO

Text: *Works*, 186
Authorship and date: this volume, 349

WORKS CITED

Previous Editions

Halliwell, James Orchard, ed., *The Meeting of Gallants* (1841)
Wilson, F. P., ed., *The Plague Pamphlets of Thomas Dekker* (1925)

Other Works Cited

Barroll, Leeds, *Politics, Plague, and Shakespeare's Theater: The Stuart Years* (1991)
Chamberlain, John, *Letters*, ed. Norman Egbert McClure, 2 vols (1939)
Creighton, Charles, *A History of Epidemics in Britain*, 2 vols (1891–4)
Dekker, Thomas, *The Wonderful Year* (1603), in *Plague Pamphlets*, ed. F. P. Wilson
Gerard, John, *The Herbal* (1597)
Hoy, Cyrus, *Introductions, Notes, and Commentaries to Texts in 'The Dramatic Works of Thomas Dekker'*, 4 vols (1980)
Lodge, Thomas, *A Treatise of the Plague* (1603)
Slack, Paul, *The Impact of Plague in Tudor and Stuart England* (1985)
Wilson, F. P., *The Plague in Shakespeare's London* (1927)

TEXTUAL NOTES

13   farthest] WILSON (fardest); farideſt CREEDE, HALLIWELL
22   know'st] CREEDE (knoweſt). Metrical emendaton.
25   mak'st] CREEDE (makeſt). Metrical emendation.
29   speak'st] CREEDE (speakeſt). Metrical emendation.
43   maim'd] CREEDE (maimed). In collocation with trisyllabic 'soldiers', 'maim'd' preserves metre and balance of line.
116   want'st] CREEDE (wanteſt). Metrical emendement.
124   Signor] CREEDE (Signior). The spelling of 'signior' is modernized throughout.
149   ensign] CREEDE (Antient). 'Ancient' was a corrupt form of 'ensign' in use from sixteenth to eighteenth century.
154   Besides] CREEDE (befide)
193   besides] CREEDE (befide)
236   Cornhill] CREEDE (Cornewell)
276   tattered] CREEDE (tottered)
314   anchovies] CREEDE (Anchouifes)
402   [SIGNOR JINGLESPUR]] THIS EDITION. CREEDE, HALLIWELL, and WILSON give (by default) the following sentence to the Host, although clearly it is spoken to rather than by him. It could be assigned to any of the gallants, so the present edition's choice of Jinglespur is arbitrary.

404   HOST] THIS EDITION
467   words] CREEDE (worde)
541   SIGNOR JINGLESPUR] CREEDE (Gingle-fpur)
614–22 Sit ... them] THIS EDITION (Taylor). CREEDE prints this section earlier, just before the Host's tale of the 'merry accident ... about Shoreditch' (506–8). Although the Host's phrasing, 'now I return' (503–5), suggests that his 'capering' was taken somewhat into account in the manuscript-copy provided to the printer, the detailed conclusion here can hardly be reconciled with the continuation of the 'meeting'. Perhaps the section beginning with the 'Shoreditch' tale was added at the last moment, but the original conclusion was neither moved nor revised as it should have been.
619–22 With ... them] THIS EDITION (Taylor). In CREEDE, the concluding paragraph is assigned (by default) to the Host. Since it cannot logically be spoken by him, and since it does not resemble a stage direction, the present edition indents it and sets it off in italics in order to highlight its strongly interruptive character. In this paragraph, as at the end of *Black Book* (822–31), we suddenly hear the previously unheard voice of an omniscient narrator.

PLATO'S CAP

Edited by Paul Yachnin

Plato's Cap was entered in the Stationers' Register 21 March 1604: 'to Thomas Bushell & Jeffrey Charlton—Entered for their copy under the hands of Master Harsnett and the wardens a book called *Plato's Cap Cast at this Year 1604 being Leap Year*'. The only edition before the present one was published in a well set-up quarto printed in 1604 'for Jeffrey Chorlton' by Thomas Purfoot. It comprises four gatherings; A1 is blank, A2 is the title-page (the verso of which is blank), D4 is blank. The main body of the work (B1–D3) is printed in black letter. Three copies of PURFOOT (STC 19975) survive—in the British Library (imperfect), Bodleian, and Huntington. STC records a fourth copy in the Milton S. Eisenhower Library of Johns Hopkins University, but that is only a positive photostat. This edition is based on the Huntington Library copy.

SEE ALSO

Text: *Works*, 198
Authorship and date: this volume, 349

WORKS CITED

Chettle, Henry, *Kind-Harts Dream* (1593)
Dekker, Thomas, *The Gull's Hornbook* (1609), in *Thomas Dekker*, ed. E. D. Pendry (1967)
—— *The Wonderfull Yeare* (1603), in *The Plague Pamphlets of Thomas Dekker*, ed. F. P. Wilson (1925)
The Fearful and Lamentable Effects of Two Dangerous Comets, 'By Simon Smell-knave' (1591)
Jack of Dover, His Quest of Inquiry (1604)
Jackson, MacDonald P., 'An Allusion to Marlowe's *The Jew of Malta* in an Early Seventeenth-Century Pamphlet Possibly by Thomas Middleton', *Notes and Queries*, NS 29 (1982), 132–3
Nashe, Thomas, *Pierce Pennyless his Supplication to the Devil* (1591), in *The Works of Thomas Nashe*, ed. Ronald B. McKerrow, rpt. with corrections, ed. F. P. Wilson, 5 vols (1958)
Nixon, Anthony, *The Black Year* (1606)
Stow, John, *A Survey of London* (1603), ed. Charles Lethbridge Kingsford, 2 vols (rpt. 1971)
Wilson, F. P., 'Some English Mock-Prognostications', *The Library*, IV, 19 (1938), 6–43
A Wonderful, Strange and Miraculous Prognostication 'By Adam Fouleweather' (1591), in *The Works of Thomas Nashe*, ed. Ronald B. McKerrow, rpt. with corrections, ed. F. P. Wilson, 5 vols (1958)

TEXTUAL NOTES

36 *Mihell*] PURFOOT (Mihill)
66 not indented in PURFOOT
91 Gizzard] PURFOOT (Gizzern)
110 Barbaries] PURFOOT (Barberies). If the primary witticism has to do with 'pothecaries and 'barberies' (barber-shops), then the original spelling is to be preferred; however, 'Barbaries' (pagans) as primary with a glance at 'barberies' makes better grammatical sense and provides the more normal reading.

170 Brentford] PURFOOT (Brandford)
239 taffeta] PURFOOT (taffatie)
312 bodice] PURFOOT (bodies)
314 bodice] PURFOOT (Bodies)
381 an etc] PURFOOT (a &C)

THE BLACK BOOK

Edited by G. B. Shand

THOMAS CREEDE, whose 1604 output included the two editions of *Hubburd*, also printed *The Black Book* (STC 17875 and 17875.5) twice that year, both times for the bookseller Jeffrey Chorlton, whose licence to publish it, dated 22 March 1604, appears as follows in the Stationers' Register: 'Entred for his copy under the handes of the wardens and master | Murgetrod A Book Called *the black book*...vj d.' Both editions consist of six sheets (A1 and F4, both blanks, usually lacking). The first edition is a reasonably well-set quarto (CREEDE 1) of which three copies survive (Bodleian/Wood 616; Folger and Yale). CREEDE 2, a mixed second edition, is mainly an inattentive and evidently hasty line-by-line resetting of CREEDE 1, surviving in six copies (Bodleian/Malone 640, British Library, and St John's College, Oxford; Harvard, Huntington, and New York Public Library). Sheet A of this second edition, and eight pages scattered through E and F have been reimposed from CREEDE 1's standing type. Apparently, *The Black Book* was more popular than Chorlton had anticipated, and when it sold quickly he had Creede rush a second edition into print to capitalize on the demand.

While it had previously been assumed that CREEDE 2 and CREEDE 1 were simply uncorrected and corrected states of a single edition, CREEDE 2 being the earlier, a fuller analysis of the evidence in 1977 was able to distinguish the two editions, each of which is internally homogeneous in both typesetting and paper quality. Their order is confirmed by progressive deterioration of the title-page (A2) as it passed from the first edition to the reprint. 'Breakage in the woodcut border immediately above the place of publication is identical in all copies of CREEDE 1, but considerably worse in several copies of CREEDE 2. The exception here is the Huntington copy of CREEDE 2, which however has picked up the half-sheet A2-3 from CREEDE 1—its title-page shows the least damage of all nine survivors of both editions' (Shand). Thus CREEDE 2's numerous errors, extending even to the running title on F2 ('The Blake Bocke'), are attributable to a rushed resetting, rather than to an uncorrected early state. One reason for the haste may have been to ensure that the two editions, bearing the same title-page and lineation, would appear to be one, thus avoiding any further licensing fee.

CREEDE 2 makes twenty-two substantive changes in the text, which are recorded in the Textual Notes. The majority of these substantive variants result from compositor error. In addition, there are almost two hundred incidental variants between the two texts, including, on CREEDE 2's E1 and E4^v, textbook examples of error due to spillage in the process of reimposing standing type: in the first instance, consecutive line endings 'Polt-' 'which' and 'rotten' now appear as 'Poh', 'whiclt' and 'rotten-'; and in the second, 'fhoulder' in the bottom line has been spilled and picked up as 'oulfhder'. CREEDE 2 does correct six spelling errors found in CREEDE 1, but it shows no sign of reference to any other authority, and cannot be said to have any authority of its own.

Sheet A, Lucifer's prologue in sheet B, and the personified Black Book's first-person Epilogue on F3^v are set predominantly in roman, with names and foreign terms in italic, but the main body of the pamphlet (Lucifer's narrative, and the text of his bequest) is in black letter, with names and phrases sometimes in roman, sometimes italic. Sandra Clark has argued that while the gothic black-letter typeface, common in contemporary popular pamphlets, 'probably implied cheapness, haste, and all the other qualities of catchpenny journalism', it was also falling out of more general use, and was thus 'associated with a certain kind of old-fashioned and familiar writing'. In the case of *The Black Book*, however, it seems to have another signifying function, as Gary Taylor has noted, combining with the solid black panel of its woodcut title-page to create a pamphlet which is materially what its name promises, a literally black book.

SEE ALSO

Text: *Works*, 207
Authorship and date: this volume, 350

WORKS CITED

Previous Editions

Bullen, A. H., ed., *Works* (1886), vol. 8
Dyce, Alexander, ed., *Works* (1840), vol. 5
Irwin, Larry Wayne, *A Critical Edition of Thomas Middleton's 'Micro-cynicon', 'Father Hubburds Tales', and 'The Blacke Booke'* (unpublished Ph.D. diss., University of Wisconsin, 1969)
Judges, A. V., ed., 'The Testament of Laurence Lucifer', i.e., *The Black Book* (590-821), in *The Elizabethan Underworld* (1930)

Other Works Cited

Clark, Sandra, *The Elizabethan Pamphleteers: Popular Moralistic Pamphlets 1580-1640* (1983)
Collier, John Payne, 'The Black Book By T. M[iddleton]' (manuscript notes in the Folger Shakespeare Library)
Dessen, Alan, *Shakespeare and the Late Moral Plays* (1986)
Greene, Robert, *The Black Book's Messenger* (1592)
—— *Disputation Between a He Cony-catcher and a She Cony-catcher* (1592)
Hall, Joseph, *Virgidemiarum* (1597)
Hibbard, G. R., *Three Elizabethan Pamphlets* (1951)

Hutton, Luke, *The Blacke Dogge of Newgate* (1596)

Marlowe, Christopher, *Works*, ed. Fredson Bowers, 2 vols (1973)

Middleton, Thomas, *The Ghost of Lucrece*, ed. J. Q. Adams (1937)

Nashe, Thomas, *Works*, ed. R. B. McKerrow, vols 1, 3, 5 (1958)

Paster, Gail Kern, *The Idea of the City in the Age of Shakespeare* (1985)

Rhodes, Neil, *Elizabethan Grotesque* (1980)

St Augustine, *The City of God Against the Pagans*, vol. 4 (1966)

Shakespeare, William, *The Complete Works*, ed. Stanley Wells and Gary Taylor (1986)

Shand, G. B., 'The Two Editions of Thomas Middleton's *The Blacke Booke*', *Papers of the Bibliographical Society of America* 71 (1977), 325-8

Spenser, Edmund, *Mother Hubberds Tale* (1591)

Stowe, John, *A Survey of London. Reprinted from the Text of 1603* (1971)

Taylor, Gary, 'The Renaissance and the End of Editing', *Palimpsest: Editorial Theory in the Humanities*, ed. George Bornstein and Ralph G. Williams (1993), 121-149

Tilley, Morris Palmer, *A Dictionary of the Proverbs in England in the Sixteenth and Seventeenth Centuries* (1950)

Walker, Gilbert, *A manifest detection of the most vyle and detestable use of Diceplay* (1552)

Webster, John, *The White Devil*, ed. John Russell Brown (1960)

Whitney, Geffrey, *A Choice of Emblems* (1586)

Wilson, F. P., ed., *The Plague Pamphlets of Thomas Dekker* (1925)

The Wyll of the Devill, With his x. detestable Commaundementes (1825)

TEXTUAL NOTES

These notes include substantive variants between CREEDE 1 and CREEDE 2.

66 sow] CREEDE; throw DYCE, apparently suspecting compositor error in the repeated rhyme-word. G.T. conjectures 'row' in 67, implying 'poke' in both agricultural and sexual senses. But CREEDE's sense is clear, and there is occasional precedent for repeated rhyme-words, for instance in *Revenger*, where we also find such repetition in a triplet at 1.1.114-6.

72 hands] hand CREEDE, DYCE. Rhyme in the *Moral* is irregular, and *OED* records no instance of 'between' taking a singular object.

77 they're as] they're ∧ CREEDE; they are DYCE

86 their heavy] CREEDE 1 (their heauie); heir theauie CREEDE 2

89 breathe] CREEDE 1; breath CREEDE 2

102 base-metalled] CREEDE (base mettald). While *OED* records only *base-mettled*, the obvious collocation here with 'Gilded' and 'copper' suggests a deliberately playful spelling on Middleton's part, a recognition of a reading (in addition to a hearing) audience.

130 risse] CREEDE (rizze). CREEDE employs both spellings, twice each.

136 | 'How?] CREEDE prints one paragraph ending before 'Why, for shame!'(220). DYCE suppresses even that division, continuing the first paragraph all the way to 286.

142 others] other CREEDE

143 truth] CREEDE (troath)

155 fitly] CREEDE 1; filthy CREEDE 2

163 damned] CREEDE; dammed DYCE. See Commentary.

167 mustachios] CREEDE (Muchatoes)

181 Cold Harbour] CREEDE (Cole-harbour)

206 eleventh] 11. CREEDE; second DYCE (evidently misreading CREEDE's 11 as roman numeral II). 'The number eleven... stands for trespassing against the law and consequently for sin', according to St Augustine, *The City of God* 15.20.

213 inductions] DYCE; inductious CREEDE 1; inudction CREEDE 2

233 Pooh] CREEDE (puh). This typical Middleton item occurs also at 564.

271 began to spit] CREEDE 1; began spit CREEDE 2

321 clause] DYCE; clawe CREEDE

342-3 for't, where'er] CREEDE 1 (for't, where 'ere); for it, where euer CREEDE 2

364 excusest] CREEDE 1; excuse CREEDE 2

372 be a cross] CREEDE 2; be crosse CREEDE 1

377 Frig-beard] CREEDE; Prigbeard DYCE. DYCE is followed by BULLEN and JUDGES, the latter of whom adds a note: 'Orig. *Frig--beard*, apparently a misprint'! DYCE's reading is apparently a rare self-referential bowdlerism. *OED* records no instance of *Frig-beard* before 1708 (and none whatsoever of *Prigbeard*).

416 show] CREEDE 1 (fhowe); showd CREEDE 2

427 snatched] CREEDE 1; scattered CREEDE 2

429 foul] CREEDE 1 (foule); soule CREEDE 2

439 Bridge] DYCE; Bride CREEDE

440 is a mad] CREEDE 2; is mad CREEDE 1

455 my intents in particulars] CREEDE; my intents; in particular DYCE

462-3 like the Mayor's Bench at Oxford] inked out in the Folger copy of CREEDE 1

464 pawed] CREEDE 1 (pawde); pawnde CREEDE 2

473 swoon] CREEDE (sowne)

481 those things] CREEDE 2; that things CREEDE 1. While one might as readily emend to 'that thing', CREEDE 2's plural is preferred for its concurrence with 'faiths and troths', 'curds and whey.'

485 villains] DYCE; villainies CREEDE

494 my] CREEDE 1; thy CREEDE 2

516 jerked] CREEDE (yerkt)

525 how] CREEDE 1; haw CREEDE 2

531 hear] CREEDE 1 (heare); here CREEDE 2

573 worldlings] DYCE; worldings CREEDE

576 Well, into my tiring-house] In the right-hand margin beside this paragraph on E1, the Folger copy of CREEDE 1 contains a cropped fragment of contemporary secretary verse: 'This geare to pas to bring, and all such fooles ar[] | nothing fete to understand this thenge.'

587 stops] CREEDE 1 (ftoppes); stoopes CREEDE 2

598 *Imprimis*] CREEDE *Inprimis*

620 with] DYCE; with with CREEDE

622 wriggle-eyed] CREEDE (rigle-eyde). Collier ingeniously proposed 'rigol-eyed', the sense being 'round-eyed'; but given Middleton's use, in *Chaste Maid* 3.2.65, of 'riggle-tail', DYCE's interpretation (adopted here) is equally acceptable.

660-1 wine-pipes] CREEDE 2 (winepipes); wine-pippes CREEDE 1

672 towns] possibly CREEDE's error for 'gowns' (conj. G.T., who notes Latrocinio's description of a closely analogous practice in *Widow*, 4.2.35-8); but to shift towns in the sense of fleeing from place to place is a reasonable understanding of CREEDE.

713 Cornhill] CREEDE (Cornewell). DYCE, reading 'Cornwall', ventures the guess that the reference is to a Cornish wrestler,

but F. P. Wilson (*Plague Pamphlets*, 240) argues convincingly that by CREEDE's 'Cornewell' is intended 'Cornhill'.

730 running] CREEDE; cunning DYCE. The collocation with 'reins', as in the common Elizabethan description of urinary discharge, 'running of the reins', renders emendation superfluous.

731 offices. Beside,] ~: ~ₐ CREEDE; ~ₐ~. DYCE

735 black] DYCE; balcke CREEDE
773 endeavour] DYCE; enduour CREEDE 1; endoure CREEDE 2
792 thee] DYCE; thy CREEDE
801 or pierced] CREEDE; o'erpierced (G.T. *conj.*)
822 Epilogue... *Book*:] THIS EDITION
829 *tacet*] DYCE; *tacit* CREEDE
831 CREEDE repeats FINIS after the Epilogue.

PRESS VARIANTS

This is a complete list of differences between CREEDE 1 (the Folger copy) and the resetting, CREEDE 2 (the Harvard copy). For clarity, the readings are all printed using modern typefaces; the modern-spelling lemma is in roman when the original passage was in roman or italics, and in sans serif when it was black letter.

Sheet B (outer forme)

B1 (roman)

41 theatre] *Theator* CREEDE 1; *Theater* CREEDE 2
42 numbered] numbred CREEDE 1; numbeed CREEDE 2
43 devils] Diuels CREEDE 1; Diuells CREEDE 2
48 shop-board] ſhop-boord CREEDE 1; ſhop-borrd CREEDE 2
50 white linings] white-lynings CREEDE 1; white linings CREEDE 2
53 like] like CREEDE 1; llke CREEDE 2

B2ᵛ (roman)

109 Pierce] *Peirce* CREEDE 1; *Pierce* CREEDE 2

B3 (black letter)

113 nightgown] Night-gowne CREEDE 1; night-gowne CREEDE 2
114 taverns] Tauernes CREEDE 1; Tauerns CREEDE 2
119 Devil] diuill CREEDE 1; diuell CREEDE 2
124 been] bœn CREEDE 1; bene CREEDE 2
127 dreadful] dreadfull CREEDE 1; dreadful CREEDE 2
128 watchmen] watchmen CREEDE 1; watch men CREEDE 2

B4ᵛ (black letter)

185 Is] is CREEDE 1; Is CREEDE 2
193 said] sayd CREEDE 1; sayde CREEDE 2
194 twinkling] twinckling CREEDE 1; ~, CREEDE 2
203 and] and CREEDE 1; aed CREEDE 2
203 blackness] blackeneſſe CREEDE 1; blackneſſe CREEDE 2
206 eleventh] 11 CREEDE 1; ~ CREEDE 2 (second 1 in roman)
207 show] ſhew CREEDE 1; ſhow CREEDE 2

Sheet B (inner forme)

B1ᵛ (roman)

59 fire.] fire. CREEDE 1; ~: CREEDE 2
61 Globe,] Globe: CREEDE 1; ~, CREEDE 2
62 companies] Companyes CREEDE 1; Companies CREEDE 2
63 villainies] Villanyes CREEDE 1; villanies CREEDE 2
65 affection] Affection CREEDE 1; affection CREEDE 2
67 betwixt] berwixt CREEDE 1; betwixt CREEDE 2
68 field's] Feilds CREEDE 1; Fields CREEDE 2
68 womb] wombe CREEDE 1; wome CREEDE 2
71 do] doe CREEDE 1; do CREEDE 2
73 fat] fatte CREEDE 1; fat CREEDE 2
73 swains] Swaynes CREEDE 1; Swaines CREEDE 2
74 Do] Doe CREEDE 1; Do CREEDE 2
77 judgement] Iudgement CREEDE 1; iudgement CREEDE 2
78 Newgate] *New-gate* CREEDE 1; *Newgate* CREEDE 2
79 spirit.] spirit. CREEDE 1; ~, CREEDE 2
80 black] blacke CREEDE 1; black CREEDE 2
80 music,] Muſicke, CREEDE 1; ~. CREEDE 2

B2 (roman)

85 Fleet Street] *Fleet-ſtreet* CREEDE 1; *Fleet-ſtreete* CREEDE 2
86 their heavy] their heauie CREEDE 1; heir theauie CREEDE 2
89 breathe] breathe CREEDE 1; breath CREEDE 2
93 Pierce] *Peirce* CREEDE 1; *Pierce* CREEDE 2
98 returns] returnes CREEDE 1; returnes CREEDE 2
101 Strumpets] Strumpets CREEDE 1; Strumpets CREEDE 2
101 theatres] *Theators* CREEDE 1; Theators CREEDE 2
103 To] To CREEDE 1; To CREEDE 2

B3ᵛ (black letter)

130 first] furſt CREEDE 1; firſt CREEDE 2
137 she] ſhœ CREEDE 1; ſhe CREEDE 2
138 house] house CREEDE 1; heuse CREEDE 2
140 watchword] watch-word CREEDE 1; watch word CREEDE 2
141 stones] ſtones CREEDE 1; ſtœnes CREEDE 2
147 feather beds] Featherbeddes CREEDE 1; Feather-beddes CREEDE 2
151 nearer] nœrer CREEDE 1; nearer CREEDE 2
153 he] he CREEDE 1; hœ CREEDE 2
154 been] bene CREEDE 1; bœne CREEDE 2

B4 (black letter)

155 fitly] fitly CREEDE 1; filthy CREEDE 2
156 He] he CREEDE 1; hœ CREEDE 2
157 old] old CREEDE 1; olde CREEDE 2
158 been] bene CREEDE 1; bœne CREEDE 2
160 been] bene CREEDE 1; bœne CREEDE 2
163 be] be CREEDE 1; bœ CREEDE 2
174 dangling] dangling CREEDE 1; dengling CREEDE 2
176 champion] Champion CREEDE 1; Campion CREEDE 2

Sheet C (outer forme)

C1 (black letter)

213 inductions] inductious CREEDE 1; inudctions CREEDE 2
214 upon] vpon CREEDE 1; vppon CREEDE 2
216 villain] villaine CREEDE 1; villain CREEDE 2
217 practised] practizd CREEDE 1; practized CREEDE 2
218 Devil] Diuel CREEDE 1; Diuell CREEDE 2
224 widow's] Widdowes CREEDE 1; Widowes CREEDE 2
224 shillings!] ſhillings! CREEDE 1 (black-letter text, italic exclamation point); ~: CREEDE 2 (all black letter)
225 land] Land, CREEDE 1; ~, CREEDE 2
229 devil] Diuel CREEDE 1; Diuell CREEDE 2
230 reveller] Reveller CREEDE 1; Reueller CREEDE 2
232 money] mony CREEDE 1; money CREEDE 2

C2ᵛ (black letter)

277 charcoal] Charcole CREEDE 1; charcole CREEDE 2
283 possible] poſſible CREEDE 1; prſſible CREEDE 2
289 conscience.] conscience, CREEDE 1; ~? CREEDE 2
290 clientess] clyenteſſe CREEDE 1; clyĕteſſe CREEDE 2
291 quarter] quarter, CREEDE 1; ~, CREEDE 2
294 mercer] Mercer CREEDE 1; mercer CREEDE 2

C3 (black letter)

306 villainy] villanie CREEDE I; Villanie CREEDE 2
307 know] know CREEDE I; knowe CREEDE 2
309 thieves] Thieues CREEDE I; Thæues CREEDE 2
312 clerks] Clerkes CREEDE I; Clarkes CREEDE 2
312 sheriffs] Shiriffes CREEDE I; Sheriffes CREEDE 2
321 common law] Common-Lawe CREEDE I; Common Lawe CREEDE 2

C4ᵛ (black letter)

371 world] worlde CREEDE I; world CREEDE 2
372 know] know CREEDE I; knowe CREEDE 2
372 be a cross] be Croffe CREEDE I; be a Croffe CREEDE 2
373 Phlegethon] Phlegeton CREEDE I; Phlegeton CREEDE 2
376 Pierce] Pierce CREEDE I; Pierce CREEDE 2
378 words] words CREEDE I; werds CREEDE 2
378 me] me CREEDE I; mæ CREEDE 2
379 changed] chaungde CREEDE I; changed CREEDE 2
379 Pierce Penniless] Pierce-Pennileffe CREEDE I; Pierce-Pennileffe CREEDE 2
383 Pierce] Pierce CREEDE I; Pierce CREEDE 2
383 Penniless] Pennileffe CREEDE I; Pennileffe CREEDE 2
383-4 mad-cap's] Mad-caps CREEDE I; Mad-cappes CREEDE 2
388 devil] diuell CREEDE I; Diuell CREEDE 2
389 aqua vitae] Aqua vitæ CREEDE I; Aqua-vitæ CREEDE 2
390 villainy] Villanie CREEDE I; villanie CREEDE 2
392 Pandarus] Pandarus CREEDE I; Pandarus CREEDE 2
catchword   indæde, CREEDE I; indæd, CREEDE 2

Sheet C (inner forme)

C1ᵛ (black letter)

234 usurer] Usurer: CREEDE I; ~ₐ CREEDE 2
234-5 impossible] impos-|sible CREEDE I; impos-|siible CREEDE 2
237 will] wil CREEDE I; will CREEDE 2
238 smell] smel CREEDE I; smell CREEDE 2
242 will] wil CREEDE I; will CREEDE 2
245 unmerciful] vnmerciful CREEDE I; vnmercifull CREEDE 2
247 Lenten-faced] Lenten-faced CREEDE I; Lenten faced CREEDE 2
249 together] together CREEDE I; together CREEDE 2
249 pitiful] pittiful CREEDE I; pittifull CREEDE 2
252 await] awayt CREEDE I; awaite CREEDE 2
254 Candlemas] Kandelmas CREEDE I; Kandle-mas CREEDE 2

C2 (black letter)

264 upon] vp-|on CREEDE I; ap-|on CREEDE 2
267 again,] againe, CREEDE I; ~ₐ CREEDE 2
271 began to spit] began to spit CREEDE I; began spit CREEDE 2
272 money] mony CREEDE I; money CREEDE 2

C3ᵛ (black letter)

325 me] me CREEDE I; mæ CREEDE 2
332 practise] practize CREEDE I; practise CREEDE 2
332 vaulting] vaulting CREEDE I; Vaulting CREEDE 2
333 worthy] worthie CREEDE I; worthy CREEDE 2
333 be] bæ CREEDE I; be CREEDE 2
333 Somerset] So-|merset CREEDE I; Somer-|set CREEDE 2
335 maintained] maintaynde CREEDE I; maintainde CREEDE 2
339 city-horse] Cittie-horfe CREEDE I; Citie-horfe CREEDE 2
341 city] Cittie CREEDE I; Citie CREEDE 2
342 for't] for't CREEDE I; for it CREEDE 2
343 where'er] where | 'ere CREEDE I; where | euer CREEDE 2
343 London] London-| CREEDE I; ~ₐ| CREEDE 2
346 another tide] another Tide CREEDE I; another tyde CREEDE 2

C4 (black letter)

353 need] næd CREEDE I; næde CREEDE 2

357 angels] Angells CREEDE I; Angelles CREEDE 2
357 A bawd] a Bawde CREEDE I; A Bawde CREEDE 2
358 packthread] Pack thread CREEDE I; Pack-thread CREEDE 2
363 Italian] Italian CREEDE I; Iitalian CREEDE 2
364 fashion?] fafhion? CREEDE I; ~: CREEDE 2
364 excusest] excufeft CREEDE I; excuse CREEDE 2
364 negligence] negligence CREEDE I; negligance CREEDE 2
365 summer's] Summers CREEDE I; Sommers CREEDE 2
366 For] For CREEDE I; for CREEDE 2
catchword   worlde CREEDE I; world CREEDE 2

Sheet D (outer forme)

D1 (black letter)

403 she] fhe CREEDE I; fhæ CREEDE 2
404 apparel] apparel CREEDE I; apparell CREEDE 2
408 narrow] narrow CREEDE I; rarrow CREEDE 2
411 tattered] tottred CREEDE I; tottreb CREEDE 2
416 show] fhowe CREEDE I; fhowd CREEDE 2
416 little] litle CREEDE I; little CREEDE 2

D2ᵛ (black letter)

453 Penniless] Pennileffe CREEDE I (final e in black letter); ~ CREEDE 2 (entirely in roman)
458 wapper-eyed] wapper-eyd CREEDE I; wapper-eid CREEDE 2
462 Penniless] Pennileffe CREEDE I; Pennileffe CREEDE 2
463 Pierce] Peirce- CREEDE I; Pierce- CREEDE 2
464 pawed] pawde CREEDE I; pawnde CREEDE 2

D3 (black letter)

472 jacket,] Iacket; CREEDE I; ~, CREEDE 2
473 swoon] sowne CREEDE I; sownde CREEDE 2
478 Well] Well CREEDE I; Whell CREEDE 2
478 scudded] scuddded CREEDE I; scudded CREEDE 2
479 Exchange-time] Exchange-time CREEDE I; Exchange time CREEDE 2
481 those] that CREEDE I; those CREEDE 2
485 how] howe CREEDE I; how CREEDE 2
486 how] howe CREEDE I; how CREEDE 2
494 my] my CREEDE I; thy CREEDE 2

D4ᵛ (black letter)

540 bets] Betts CREEDE I; Bettes CREEDE 2
550 me,] mæ, CREEDE I; ~) CREEDE 2
551 being] bæing CREEDE I; being CREEDE 2
560 may] may CREEDE I; moy CREEDE 2
562 murderer] Murde-|rer CREEDE I; Murthe|rer CREEDE 2

Sheet D (inner forme)

D1ᵛ (black letter)

421 field] Field CREEDE I; Fielde CREEDE 2
421 trampled] trampled CREEDE I; trambled CREEDE 2
422 upon] vpon CREEDE I; vppon CREEDE 2
426 pieces] peices CREEDE I; pieces CREEDE 2
427 snatched] snatcht CREEDE I; scatterd CREEDE 2
427 King's Street] Kings Streete CREEDE I; Kings-Streete CREEDE 2
429 foul] foule CREEDE I; soule CREEDE 2
437 bowling alley] Bowling-Alley CREEDE I; Bowling Alley CREEDE 2
439 London] London CREEDE I; ~ CREEDE 2 (first o in blackletter)
440 is a mad] is mad CREEDE I; is a mad CREEDE 2
441 Pierce] Peirce CREEDE I; Pierce CREEDE 2

D3ᵛ (black letter)

496 replied:] replyed. CREEDE I; ~: CREEDE 2
497 Diabla] Deiabla CREEDE I; Deiable CREEDE 2
498 tabla.] Tabla. CREEDE I; Table, CREEDE 2

504 buff doublet] Buff-Doublet CREEDE 1; Buffe,Doublet CREEDE 2
506 lace] Lace CREEDE 1; Lgce CREEDE 2
508 same] same CREEDE 1; sams CREEDE 2
510 poor] pᴏore CREEDE 1; pᴏoze CREEDE 2
516 away] away CREEDE 1; ~, CREEDE 2

D4 (black letter)

524 lurching] lurching CREEDE 1; lurchtng CREEDE 2
524 cast] Cast CREEDE 1; cast CREEDE 2
525 how] how CREEDE 1; haw CREEDE 2
526 upon] vpon CREEDE 1; vppon CREEDE 2
527 Captain,] Captaine, CREEDE 1; ~ₐ CREEDE 2
530 me] me CREEDE 1; mæ CREEDE 2
531 hear] heare CREEDE 1; here CREEDE 2
532 Darkness.] Darkneſſe, CREEDE 1; Darkeneſſe. CREEDE 2
533 companies] Companies CREEDE 1; Crmpanies CREEDE 2
536 dexterity] dexterity CREEDE 1; dexteritie CREEDE 2

Sheet E (outer forme)

E1 (black letter)

572 polt-foot] Polt-|fœte CREEDE 1; Poh, | fœte CREEDE 2
573 which] which CREEDE 1; whiclt CREEDE 2
574 rotten,] rotten, CREEDE 1; ~- CREEDE 2

E2ᵛ (black letter)

606 Beside] beside CREEDE 1; dbeside CREEDE 2

E3 (black letter)

640 Devil] Diuell CREEDE 1; Diuel CREEDE 2
645 eggs] Egges CREEDE 1; Egs CREEDE 2

E4ᵛ (black letter)

712-13 cog-shoulder] Cog-ſhoulder CREEDE 1; Cog-oulſhder CREEDE 2
catchword   a CREEDE 1; a both CREEDE 2

Sheet E (inner forme)

E1ᵛ (black letter)

587 whey countenance] whay-countenance CREEDE 1; whay countenance CREEDE 2

587 stops] ſtoppes CREEDE 1; ſtooppes CREEDE 2

E2 (roman/italic titles, black-letter text)

591 old wealthy bachelor] olde wealthy Bachiler CREEDE 1; old Batchiler CREEDE 2

E3ᵛ (black letter)

654 deliver] Deliuer CREEDE 1; deliuer CREEDE 2
655 very] ve-|ry CREEDE 1; very CREEDE 2
660-1 wine-pipes] wine-pippes CREEDE 1; wine-pipes CREEDE 2
663 behind] behinde CREEDE 1; behind CREEDE 2

E4 (black letter)

673 henceforward] henceforward CREEDE 1; hence forward CREEDE 2
684 Item,] Item, CREEDE 1; ₐ CREEDE 2

Sheet F (outer forme)

F1 (black letter)

719 pimple your] pimple your CREEDE 1; pimpleyour CREEDE 2

Sheet F (inner forme)

F2 (black letter)

762 upon] vpon CREEDE 1; vppon CREEDE 2
764 Bias] Bias CREEDE 1; Bias CREEDE 2
766 and so] & so CREEDE 1; and so CREEDE 2
766 ketlers] Ketlers CREEDE 1; ketlers CREEDE 2
772 eleven] Leuen- CREEDE 1; Leauen- CREEDE 2
773 know] know CREEDE 1; knowe CREEDE 2
773 endeavour] enduour CREEDE 1; endoure CREEDE 2
775 upon] vpon CREEDE 1; vppon CREEDE 2
778 upon] vpon CREEDE 1; vppon CREEDE 2

F3ᵛ (roman)

824 think] think CREEDE 1; thinke CREEDE 2
828 know] know CREEDE 1; knowe CREEDE 2
830 wise] Wise CREEDE 1; wise CREEDE 2
830 judicious] Iudicious CREEDE 1; Iudicious CREEDE 2

THE WHOLE ROYAL AND MAGNIFICENT ENTERTAINMENT

Edited by R. Malcolm Smuts

FOUR separate published accounts of James I's triumphant entry into London on 15 March 1604 appeared within about three months of the event: Thomas Dekker's *Magnificent Entertainment*, Ben Jonson his *Part of King James his Royal and Magnificent Entertainment*, Stephen Harrison's *Arches of Triumph* and Gilbert Dugdale's *Triumph of Time*. While it was common in early modern Europe to commemorate great public ceremonies like James's coronation entry with a printed volume, the appearance of four different tracts about one event was distinctly unusual. The explanation for the proliferation of texts appears to lie partly in a professional rivalry between Dekker and Jonson and partly in the ambitions of Harrison and Dugdale. Of all the authors, Dekker came closest to furnishing a complete account, including a narrative framework and transcripts not only of the speeches he himself composed, but also one by Middleton at the sixth arch, and four Latin orations delivered by the Recorder of London, a student of the Merchant Taylors' School and representatives of the communities of Dutch and Italian merchants. His volume also briefly describes Jonson's pageants, leaving out the speeches, which could easily have been incorporated, however.

Unfortunately, Dekker and Jonson had satirized each other during the so-called war of the theatres and remained on bad terms. They also differed philosophically in their approach to the entry, in ways that affected both the narrative style and the typographical layout of the text. Although we do not know the exact circumstances, it is therefore easy to understand why collaborative publication proved impossible. Instead of supplying Dekker with copies of his speeches Jonson rushed into print with a volume containing his three pageants for the 15 March entry, along with a *Panegyre* delivered at the opening of James's first Parliament four days later and an earlier *Entertainment of the Queen and Prince at Althorp*. This volume was entered in the Stationers' Register on 19 March by Edward Blount, as 'A part of the king's majesties right royal and magnificent entertainment through his honorable city of London the 15 of March 1603; so much as was presented in the first and last of their triumphal arches. With a speech made for the presentation in the Strand erected at the charges of the lords knights gentlemen and other the inhabitants of the City of Westminster with the liberties of the Duchy of Lancaster, both done by Benjamin Jonson.' The printers recorded on the title-page were V. Simmes and G. Eld. Jonson's decision to publish his speeches for the coronation entry together with the 'Pangeyre' and 'Althorp Entertainment' looks like a further attempt to emphasize his association with the new King and royal court, thus upstaging his rival.

Dekker's volume was entered in the Stationers' Register about a fortnight later on 2 April, by Thomas Man the younger, as 'A book called *The Magnificent Entertainment given to King James, Queen Anne his wife and Henry Frederick the Prince Upon the Day of his Majesty's Triumphant Passage from the Tower through his Honorable City and Chamber of London the 15 of March 1603.*' On May 14 the Stationer's Company ordered Blount to sell the 400 copies of *Ben Jonson his Part* remaining in his possession to Man, at the rate of six shillings a ream, the combined cost of paper and printing. This decision most likely represents a settlement between the two publishers, allowing Man to eliminate the competition from Blount's book, while covering Blount's costs and allowing him to realize a profit on any copies already sold. In any case, Man thereafter had sole rights over both publications.

Dugdale's tract was registered with the Stationers' Company on 27 March, by Ralph Blore or Blower 'under the hands of Master Hartwell and the Wardens'. The title was listed as '*The Time Triumphant or the True Model As Well of the King's Majesty's First Coming into England as Also his Royal Progress from the Tower through the City the 15 of March 1603 to his Highness' Manor of Whitehall.*' The publisher was J. Windet (STC 12863). It looks very much like a freelance effort to capitalize on public demand for works relating to the new King and the ceremonial events marking the opening of his reign. Dugdale wrote from the perspective of a spectator following the royal procession on foot and seeking to grasp the meaning of pageants often seen from a distance. He had no access to the speeches recorded by Dekker and Jonson, and generally gives a very sketchy account of the main pageants. He does record a few details mentioned in no other accounts, however, such as an appearance by saints George and Andrew near the Fenchurch Street arch. He provides a less stylized account than Dekker of both the crowd's response to the royal family and James's sometimes brusque reaction to the crowd; and he gives complete transcripts of two speeches ignored by the other volumes that do not seem to have been part of the official pageantry at all but probably originated in efforts by individuals or small groups to welcome the King in their own way.

Harrison's beautiful folio, which was never registered with the Stationers, must have been considerably more expensive than any of the other volumes. Its elaborate title-page and seven additional engravings by William Kip (and others?) also took longer to prepare, delaying publication probably until June. Harrison incorporated text verbatim from both Dekker and Jonson, including the major pageant speeches, to which he added his own prefatory material and a few passages explaining architectural features of the arches. His relations with Dekker—who supplied one of two commendatory poems at the start of the volume—seem to have been excellent. His decision to publish separately almost certainly derived from a desire to preserve a permanent visual record of the arches he had designed, something that an unillustrated quarto could not achieve. The title-page states that *Arches of Triumph* was sold directly from Harrison's house in Lime Street, indicating that he had underwritten the costs of publication.

The text presented here, *The Whole Royal and Magnificent Entertainment, with the Arches of Triumph*, derives primarily from Dekker. We have, however, substituted Jonson's descriptions of his pageants at Fenchurch Street, Temple Bar and the Strand, while adding three textual passages and the engraved illustrations from Harrison, and a list of the order of the royal procession from a manuscript among the State Papers Domestic in the Public Record Office, London (SP14/6, item 97). This source material has been rearranged to produce a sequential narrative, with Dekker's summaries of Jonson's pageants and portions of Dugdale's tract incorporated in the commentary or as additional passages. The commentary also draws upon a manuscript Wardrobe account for the entry (Public Record Office LC2/4(5)). The arrangement of the source materials within the text is as follows:

1–95: Harrison, *preliminary materials*.

96–199: Manuscript, '*True Order of His Majesty's Proceeding*'.

200–451: Dekker, *initial description of the entry and account of the cancelled pageant beyond Bishopsgate*.

451–98: Harrison, *description of the first arch at Fenchurch, called* Londinium.

499–865: Jonson, *account of the Fenchurch arch and pageant*.

866–2218: Dekker, *accounts of the second through sixth arches and oration at St Paul's school*.

2218–43: Harrison, *account of the seventh arch,* The Templum Jani, *at Temple Bar*.

2244–643: Jonson, *account of the arch and pageant at Temple Bar and the pageant in the Strand*.

2644–725: Dekker, *concluding materials*.

2726–92: Harrison, '*Lectori Candido*' postscript.

A: Dugdale, *account of the events at the Tower*.

B: Dekker, *account of the Fenchurch arch and pageant*.

C: Dugdale, *incident during the Italians' Pageant*.

D: Dugdale, *speech at the Conduit*.

E: Dekker, *account of the arch and pageant at Temple Bar*.

F: Dekker, *account of the pageant in the Strand*.

All the volumes incorporated in our text have a relatively uncomplicated history, except for Dekker's *Magnificent Entertainment*. *Ben Jonson his Part* was not reissued until the appearance of the Folio *Works* published by STANSBY in 1616 (STC 14751). As Herford and Simpson point out, a number of careless mistakes in the Latin of the Folio text show that Jonson did not bother to read it before the printing. We have therefore used the original SIMMES-ELD quarto (STC 14756; *BEPD* 200) as our control-text, while making a few emendations on the basis of the STANSBY Folio and the second Folio of 1640 published by R. BISHOP (STC 14753). Herford and Simpson collated eleven copies of the original quarto, recording a number of variants reproduced below, virtually all involving no more than minor differences in spelling and punctuation or the correction of obvious mistakes. As part of the process of modernization we have expanded many of the abbreviations in Jonson's marginal notes to make them more intelligible. We have also altered a handful of citations where Jonson's reference does not correspond to modern editions of the text he was citing, noting the changes in the textual notes. We have not, however, corrected other apparent discrepancies, such as rearrangements in the word order of Latin titles, since these may provide clues to the edition Jonson used or evidence that he was citing texts from memory. Throughout our text, Latin ligatures and accents have been eliminated, in conformity with modern usage, except where they appear to reproduce typographical features of inscriptions on the arches.

The engravings in *Arches of Triumph* were reissued without the text by J. Sudbury and G. Humble in 1613 but thereafter the work was not reprinted until 1829, when John Nichols included it in volume I of *Progresses of James I*. We have used the 1604 edition as our control-text. Dugdale's volume also was not reprinted until Nichols's *Progresses of James I*. Edward Arber included a modern-spelling edition in *The English Garner* (1871), subsequently re-edited by C. H. Firth in *Stuart Tracts 1603-1693*, the volume we have consulted. Both Nichols and Firth occasionally took liberties with the text, whose convoluted syntax and printing errors admittedly present numerous problems. We have used the 1604 BLOWER quarto (STC 7292) as our control-text. The most valuable modern discussion of Dugdale's importance as a source for James's first London entry is David Bergeron's.

The publishing history of Dekker's *Magnificent Entertainment* (*BEPD* 202) presents considerably more difficulties. Two further editions appeared in 1604. One published in Edinburgh (STC 6512) derived from the original London edition (STC 6510), differing from it only in a few, mostly insignificant details. A second London edition, however, entitled *The Whole Magnificent Entertainment* (STC 6513) includes new English translations of three Latin speeches and some altered readings from the original text. In 1955 Fredson Bowers, building on earlier work by Sir W. W. Greg, produced an extensive analysis of the two London editions. He argued that the first was printed in five different houses, probably to speed production. Sheets A–B were produced by Thomas CREEDE, the printer listed on the title-page; F–H by Humphrey LOWNES; I by Edward ALLDE and C–D and E by two other, unidentified printers.

The first of these was identified as Simon STAFFORD by Adrian Weiss (1991). The second edition (*Whole Magnificent Entertainment*) lists Allde as the printer, but the work was actually divided again, this time among four houses. Whenever possible standing type from the first edition was reused, although the insertion of new material required considerable resetting and other adjustments. In *Whole Magnificent Entertainment* ALLDE was responsible for sheets A–B and I, LOWNES for G–H and STAFFORD for C–D, while the unknown printer of E in the first edition did both E and F. The following table, adapted from Bowers, summarizes the division of responsibilities for both editions and identifies lines reset in the second edition by the designation ''. The remaining lines were printed from standing type. We have followed the convention used throughout *Collected Works* of differentiating two different editions by the same printer with a number placed after his name.

	First Quarto	Second Quarto
200–451^r A–B	CREEDE	ALLDE
866–98 C1^v–2	STAFFORD	STAFFORD
899–950^r C2^v–3	STAFFORD1	STAFFORD2
950–1004 C3^v–4	STAFFORD	STAFFORD
1005–24^r C4^v	STAFFORD1	STAFFORD2
1025–37 D1 top	STAFFORD	STAFFORD
1038–55^r	not set	STAFFORD2
1056–65^r D1 foot	STAFFORD1	STAFFORD2
1066–113 [...hands] D1^v–2 (1083–4 reset)	STAFFORD	STAFFORD
1113–61^r [upon...] D2^v–3	STAFFORD1	STAFFORD2
1160–209 D3^v–4 (lines 1189–93 reset)	STAFFORD	STAFFORD
1210–27^r D4^v	STAFFORD1	STAFFORD2
1228–50^r E1–1^v (top)	UNKNOWN1	UNKNOWN2
1251–464 E1^v (line 7)–4^v	UNKNOWN1	UNKNOWN2
1465–691^r [...side in] F1–4^v	LOWNES	UNKNOWN
1689–719^r [that...of an] G1	LOWNES1	LOWNES2
1719–68 [Arbor...] G1^v–2	LOWNES1	LOWNES2
1768–804^r G2^v–3 (line 6)	LOWNES1	LOWNES2
1805–29^r [...which] G3 (remainder)	LOWNES1	LOWNES2
1827–88 [colour...] G3^v–4	LOWNES1	LOWNES2
1888–913^r G4	LOWNES1	LOWNES2
1914–29 H1	LOWNES1	LOWNES2
1929–77^r	omitted	LOWNES2
1978–2044^r (English for Latin)	LOWNES1	LOWNES2
2045–157 H3–4^v	LOWNES1	LOWNES2
2158–217; 2644–725 I1–4	LOWNES1	LOWNES2

Bowers found that in the second London edition significant emendations occurred only in Latin passages and in LOWNES's sheets G–H, corresponding to lines 1689–2157 of our text. On the basis of internal evidence Bowers concluded that changes in the Latin, which Dekker had not written, were probably due to the unknown translator, but that G–H were most likely corrected by Dekker himself. We have accepted the implications of this conclusion, using *Magnificent Entertainment* as the control-text but following Bowers in making some alterations based on *Whole Magnificent Entertainment* for lines 1689–2157.

In addition to comparing the three editions, Bowers collated sixteen copies of the first London edition. We have recorded the variants he identified, along with about thirty substantive differences between Dekker's original text and parallel sections of *Arches of Triumph*. These last present a final editorial difficulty, particularly in the case of the translations of Latin orations which are not found in *Magnificent Entertainment*. In this instance we cannot be certain that Harrison derived his text from Dekker. It is not certain that *Whole Magnificent Entertainment* was published before *Arches of Triumph*; and even if it was, Harrison might have obtained manuscript text from the translator of the Latin or some other source.

Several of the variants appear to represent small but deliberate changes, rather than casual slips. In the translation of the Italian merchants' speech, for example, Dekker's text several times employs 'you' and 'your' where Harrison's substitutes 'thou' and 'thine'. In these instances it is difficult to know which construction to prefer, although Harrison's seems more consistent with usage throughout the rest of text. In another case, however, *Whole Magnificent Entertainment* supplies a plainly superior reading. For the couplet, '*Aspice ridentem per gaudia Plebis Olympum, | Reddentem et plausus ad sua verba suos*' (1259–60) it translates: 'Behold, Heaven itself laughs to see how thy subjects smile, and thunders out loud plaudits to hear their *aves*' (1298–9). In Harrison this becomes: 'Behold, Heaven itself laughs to see thy subjects smile and thunder out loud plaudits, to hear their *aves*.' Although Harrison's sentence makes more sense, since there is no record of a thunderstorm on 15 March 1604, it misconstrues the grammatical structure of the Latin. It is therefore either a careless mistake or an incompetent revision. In the absence of more conclusive evidence, this seems sufficient reason to mistrust variant readings from *Arches*, even when they appear superficially more plausible than the text supplied by Dekker's volume.

The manuscript 'True Order of his Majesty's Proceeding through London' is preserved as volume 6, item 97 of the State Papers Domestic for the reign of James I in the Public Record Office, London. Although drawn up for the Earl Marshal's Commission, a committee responsible for overseeing the procession, it is certainly a rough draft rather than a fair copy of the final, authoritative list. Nichols printed a very similar Order based on two other manuscripts, one then privately owned and the other among the Cotton Manuscripts of the British Museum. Nichol's Order, while very similar to that in the Public Record Office, does include a few additional marchers and some other supplementary information. These changes probably reflect late emendations by the Commission itself or the scribes working under its supervision. We have therefore incorporated them into our Order, while noting the discrepancies in the textual notes.

Throughout the commentary translations of passages from Latin texts have been taken, wherever possible, from Loeb Classical Library editions.

SEE ALSO

Text: *Works*, 224
Authorship and date: this volume, 351

WORKS CITED

Previous Editions

Bowers, Fredson, ed., *The Dramatic Works of Thomas Dekker* (1955), vol. 2
Bullen, A. H., ed., *Works of Thomas Middleton* (1886), vol. 7
Dyce, Alexander, ed., *Works of Thomas Middleton* (1840), vol. 5
Herford, C. H., and Simpson, Percy and Evelyn, eds., *Ben Jonson* (1925–52), vol. 7
Nichols, John, *Progresses of James I*, vol. 1 (1828)

Other Works Cited

Bergeron, David, 'Gilbert Dugdale and the Royal Entry of James I (1604)', *Journal of Medieval and Renaissance Studies* 13 (1983), 111–25
Bowers, Fredson, 'Notes on Standing Type in Elizabethan Printing', *Papers of the Bibliographical Society of America* 40 (1946), 205–24
Hoy, Cyrus, *Introductions, Notes, and Commentaries to Texts in 'The Dramatic Works of Thomas Dekker'*, 4 vols (1980)
Stow, John, *Chronicles* (1631 edition)
Weiss, Adrian, 'Bibliographic Methods for Identifying Unknown Printers in Elizabethan/Jacobean Books', *Studies in Bibliography* 94 (1991), 183–228

TEXTUAL NOTES

Title *The ... Triumph*] A composite of the titles of the three works from which this edition is drawn: Dekker's *Magnificent Entertainment*, Ben Jonson his Part of King James his Royal and Magnificent Entertainment and Harrison's *Arches of Triumph*.

74 *laurel*] THIS EDITION; *laurer* WINDET

97 1604] PRO MSS. (1603). In this period the English customarily began the new year on March 25 (Lady's Day) rather than January 1; our text and notes use the modern convention throughout.

101 Harbingers] NICHOLS (Harbengers); Harbengenger PRO MSS.
101 Porters] NICHOLS; Porter PRO MSS.
115 Aldermen ... London] NICHOLS; *not in* PRO MSS.
117 The Prince's Serjeant] NICHOLS; *not in* PRO MSS.
118 Advocate] PRO MSS.; Advocate and Remembrancer NICHOLS
119 Queen's Attorney] PRO MSS.; NICHOLS has 'The Queen's Counsell at Lawe' preceding the King's Advocate; it is difficult to know whether these officials marched side by side or if the Queen's Attorney preceded the King's Advocate by a step.
120 Attorney and Solicitor] PRO MSS.; Attorney {The King's Solicitor} Sir Francis Bacon, The King's Counsell at Lawe NICHOLS. Since Bacon was the King's Solicitor NICHOLS effectively duplicates his place in the procession.
121 of the] PRO MSS.; at NICHOLS
122 Serjeants] PRO MSS.; Serjeant at Law NICHOLS. There were several King's Serjeants.
124 Secretaries for the French and Latin Tongues] NICHOLS reverses the order of the secretaries and Knights Bachelors.
128–9 Queen's Council at Law] NICHOLS; *not in* PRO MSS.
127 Pursuivants] NICHOLS; *not in* PRO MSS.
142 The ... England] NICHOLS; *not in* PRO MSS.
145 Knights and] NICHOLS; *not in* PRO MSS.
151 Governor] NICHOLS adds his name, Sir Thomas Challoner
178 together] PRO MSS.; *not in* NICHOLS
175–8 Serjeants ... swords] NICHOLS; *in left margin only* PRO MSS.
175–8 but ... swords] PRO MSS.; *not in* NICHOLS

179–81 Lord ... Usher] NICHOLS; PRO MSS. places the Lord Mayor on the right.
180–1 Garter ... Arms] NICHOLS; Garter Prince PRO MSS.
186 Gentlemen] PRO MSS.; *not in* NICHOLS
186 Footmen] NICHOLS *adds* and Esquires
186–7 of ... Stable] NICHOLS; *not in* PRO MSS.
189 Vice ... King] PRO MSS.; King's Vice Chamberlain NICHOLS
191 Queen's ... Chamberlain] PRO MSS.; *not in* NICHOLS
194 Master ... Horse] The repetition of this entry (see l. 188) probably refers to separate Masters of the Horse of the King and Queen. The Wardrobe accounts indicate that a spare horse did accompany Queen Anne (see commentary).
199 with ... follow] NICHOLS; *not in* PRO MSS.
204 1604] CREEDE (1603). See note to l. 97–8 above.
209 Martial] Throughout we have followed the modern procedure of placing the name of the author of a quotation, in full, *after* and *below* the inset quotation; the original texts give an abbreviated form of the name just before the first word of the quotation (as though it were a speech prefix).
252 a long] BOWERS; along CREEDE
351 those] NICHOLS; these CREEDE
388 mechanicians] CREEDE (mychanitiens)
451 gates.] We have omitted the phrase 'of which the first was erected at Fenchurch' from CREEDE in order to create a smoother transition into the full descriptions by Jonson and Harrison.
491 architrave] architive CREEDE
503 perspective] THIS EDITION; prospective SIMMES–ELD, STANSBY, HERFORD–SIMPSON
546.n *Manlio*] HERFORD–SIMPSON; Mallii SIMMES–ELD, STANSBY
561.n Proverbs 8:15] Jonson or his printer incorrectly placed this note beside the previous scriptural quotation. We have restored it to its correct position.
567.n *tam*] HERFORD–SIMPSON; *not in* SIMMES–ELD
599 TAMESIS] Both Harrison and Dekker spell the name 'Thamesis', whereas Jonson leaves out the h. We have

613.n *clausula 6*] THIS EDITION; *cl. 5.* SIMMES–ELD, STANSBY, HERFORD–SIMPSON

628 cruse] SIMMES–ELD (cruze)

636.n Eucharisticon] THIS EDITION; Epu. SIMMES–ELD, STANSBY, HERFORD–SIMPSON

641 Veneration] BISHOP; *Veneratio* SIMMES–ELD, STANSBY

652 ribboned] SIMMES–ELD (ribanded)

653 trifolium] THIS EDITION; trifoly SIMMES–ELD, STANSBY, HERFORD–SIMPSON

688 pila] BISHOP, HERFORD–SIMPSON; peila SIMMES–ELD, STANSBY

717–28 *Maximus . . . suum.*] Italics in SIMMES–ELD; Roman capitals in STANSBY and HERFORD–SIMPSON. Harrison's illustration shows the inscription in italics; we have regarded this as decisive.

727 *heres*] THIS EDITION; haeres SIMMES–ELD, HERFORD–SIMPSON

740 complimental] THIS EDITION; complementall SIMMES–ELD, STANSBY, HERFORD–SIMPSON

747 their] THIS EDITION; the SIMMES–ELD, STANSBY, HERFORD–SIMPSON

770 Briton] THIS EDITION; Brittane SIMMES–ELD; Britaine HERFORD–SIMPSON

782.n *urbo*] STANSBY, HERFORD–SIMPSON; urbe in SIMMES–ELD

798 Zeal.'] THIS EDITION. Jonson did not close the quotation.

803 tide.'] THIS EDITION. Jonson did not close the quotation.

815 weak.'] THIS EDITION. Jonson did not close the quotation.

817 lose] SIMMES–ELD (loose)

853.n Frederick II] SIMMES–ELD (*Frederick* fecōd); *Frederick* ⟨the⟩ fecōd HERFORD–SIMPSON

853.n Christian] THIS EDITION; Christierne SIMMES–ELD

853.n IV] SIMMES–ELD (the fourth)

858.n Charles . . . Elizabeth] SIMMES–ELD (*corr*); *not in* SIMMES–ELD (*unc*); supplied by HERFORD–SIMPSON from STANSBY

950 roof] BOWERS; roote STAFFORD, FINLASON

950 erected] ALLDE; directed STAFFORD

1058 *Belgians*] STAFFORD. Italics retained to indicate a Latinate term for the modern counterparts to the north Gallic tribe of the *Belgae*, here corresponding to inhabitants of both the northern and southern Netherlands. Thus a synonym for Dutchmen in l. 1066.

1144 *nobili*] THIS EDITION; *Nobile* UNKNOWN1 and 2

1233 *celebre*] BOWERS; *Celeb:* UNKNOWN1 and 2

1250 *et*] UNKNOWN2; *at* UNKNOWN1

1262 *onus*] UNKNOWN2; *vnus* UNKNOWN1

1264 *Ardua res*] 2 UNKNOWN2; *Arduares* UNKNOWN1

1266 *hominis*] BOWERS; *homines* UNKNOWN1 and 2, FINLASON

1267 *temperat*] FINLASON; *temperet* UNKNOWN1 and 2

1270 *ille*] BOWERS; *illa* UNKNOWN1 and 2, FINLASON

1278 *At*] BOWERS; *Aut* UNKNOWN1, FINLASON

1279 *Assidet*] BOWERS; *Assidat* UNKNOWN1 and 2, FINLASON

1288 *Quos fovit*] *Quos fouit* BOWERS; *Quosfouit* UNKNOWN1 and 2

1291 *diu Panthaici*] BOWERS *Deum Panthaeci* UNKNOWN1; *Diù Panthaici* UNKNOWN2; *Deus Panthaeci* FINLASON

1292 *innumeros*] BOWERS (*Innumeros*); *Iunumeros* UNKNOWN1, FINLASON

1293 *tui*] BOWERS; *tua* UNKNOWN1 and 2

1299 plaudits] UNKNOWN1 (plaudities)

1308 holds] BOWERS; hold UNKNOWN2

1313 Religion] We have preserved initial upper case letters for key nouns in this passage, since allegorical personification seems to be implied.

1321 lavishly] UNKNOWN2, BOWERS; *not in* WINDET

1333 you] UNKNOWN2, BOWERS; thee WINDET

1334 your] UNKNOWN2, BOWERS; thy WINDET

1334–5 then under hers] UNKNOWN2, BOWERS; under hers WINDET

1336 grandfathers . . . many] UNKNOWN2, BOWERS; *not in* WINDET

1366 jutted] THIS EDITION; jetted UNKNOWN1 and 2, BOWERS

1415 *Arete*] UNKNOWN2; *Arate* UNKNOWN1, FINLASON

1470 Dries] WINDET (engraving); Drie LOWNES, FINLASON

1516 drunk] LOWNES, UNKNOWN, FINLASON; drunk up WINDET, BOWERS

1538 Fairyland] THIS EDITION; Fairie land LOWNES; cf. Dekker's *Whore of Babylon* (1608), where 'Fairie land' is the allegorical name of England.

1570–1 clear, straight] LOWNES (errata); cleare strength LOWNES (text), FINLASON; during UNKNOWN

1576 that during] CREEDE (errata), ALLDE; aluring LOWNES (text), FINLASON

1693 Sylvans] *Syluans* LOWNES2; *Syluanus* LOWNES1

1700 choristers] LOWNES1 (queristers)

1709–10 eighteen . . . twelve] 18 . . . 12. LOWNES1; 16 . . . 10 LOWNES2, FINLASON

1717 terms] LOWNES2; frames LOWNES1, FINLASON

1726 forty-four] 44. BOWERS; 4. LOWNES1 and 2, FINLASON

1741 *caducaeus*] *Caducæus* BOWERS; *Caducæns* LOWNES1, FINLASON

1746 on] BOWERS; of LOWNES1, FINLASON

1806 *Chorus*] LOWNES1, FINLASON; *A Chorus* LOWNES2

1862 ONE] THIS EDITION; *not in* LOWNES1 and 2, BOWERS

1882 he] CREEDE errata, BOWERS; had LOWNES1

1895 Had . . . stayed] CREEDE errata; Here ſtayed had ſtill LOWNES1 (text); Here staide hee still! LOWNES2

1924 choristers] LOWNES1 (Quiristers)

1941 *primariae*] LOWNES2; *primaria* LOWNES1 (*corr*); *prima via* LOWNES1 (*unc*)

1957 *emittantur*] LOWNES2; *emittuntur* LOWNES1

1971 *eum*] THIS EDITION; *cum* LOWNES1 and 2

1978–2044 THE ORATION . . . Almighty etc.] LOWNES2; *not in* LOWNES1, FINLASON

2016 *didicit*] *dedicit* LOWNES2; *not in* LOWNES1

2055 risse] LOWNES1 (riz). This unusual past tense of *rise* is characteristic of Middleton, and suggests he may have been responsible not only for the speech but the description of the arch.

2061–2 body. | As] THIS EDITION (*conj.* Taylor). All previous editions insert a period and break the paragraph after 'mounts', l. 2064.

2072 *Arete*] DYCE; *Arate* LOWNES1

2107 engine] LOWNES2; Eronie LOWNES1, FINLASON

2114 *et*] LOWNES2 *at*; LOWNES1

2117 praters] LOWNES2; parts LOWNES1

2127 the same] THIS EDITION (*conj.* Taylor); these men LOWNES1

2137 move] THIS EDITION; moved LOWNES1

2143 human] LOWNES1 (humaine). Human, humane and humaine were variant spellings of the same word in this period; 'human' rather than 'humane' seems appropriate to the context.

2192 [FIRST SINGER]] THIS EDITION; *not in* LOWNES1

2202 [RUMOUR]] THIS EDITION; *not in* LOWNES1

2207 Which] THIS EDITION; With LOWNES1

2210 [FIRST SINGER]] THIS EDITION; *not in* LOWNES1

2210 lose] LOWNES1 (loose)

2261 adscribe] THIS EDITION (*conj.* HERFORD–SIMPSON); abſcribe SIMMES–ELD; aſcribe STANSBY. Jonson uses the same Latinate form in *Sejanus*: see *OED*.

2266 *nominantur*] HERFORD–SIMPSON; *nominatur* SIMMES–ELD

2287–92 QVI...BRITANNOS] STANSBY, HERFORD–SIMPSON; *Qui...Britannos* SIMMES–ELD

2295–6 IVRANDASQVE...*FATENTES*] HERFORD–SIMPSON; *Iur andasǫ...fatentes* SIMMES–ELD

2307.n Cephisodotus] HERFORD–SIMPSON; *Cephif-|odotus* SIMMES–ELD

2346 bore] SIMMES–ELD (bare)

2401 Poscimvs] HERFORD–SIMPSON; POSSIMVS SIMMES–ELD

2447 fantasy] THIS EDITION; Phantasy SIMMES–ELD

2449.n the page 272.] SIMMES–ELD (the Page. D.3.)

2461 blessed] SIMMES–ELD; b[l]est HERFORD–SIMPSON. Since 'blessed' and 'best' both make sense in context there seems insufficient reason to emend the original text.

2492 lose] SIMMES–ELD (leefe)

2496.n rata fit] HERFORD–SIMPSON; ratafit SIMMES–ELD

2511 dis-ease] THIS EDITION; (disease SIMMES–ELD)

2524 PVLCHERRIMÆ] THIS EDITION; PUVCHERIMAE SIMMES–ELD; PVLCHER(R)IMÆ BISHOP, HERFORD–SIMPSON

2531 FVNESSIMAM] SIMMES–ELD; FUNESTISSIMAM STANSBY, HERFORD–SIMPSON

2546–54 Thus...days] SIMMES–ELD; 'In the Strand.' STANSBY

2641.n detestatam,] HERFORD–SIMPSON; ~∧ SIMMES–ELD

2642.n caput 23] THIS EDITION; *cap.* 25 SIMMES–ELD

2687 summa.] fumma. | fumma. LOWNES1

A.3 emptied] THIS EDITION; emptye BLOWER

A.4 and] THIS EDITION; *not in* BLOWER

A.19 seeming] THIS EDITION; feeing BLOWER

A.20 of] THIS EDITION; in of BLOWER

B.9 on] THIS EDITION; one CREEDE

C.3 [the arch]] THIS EDITION; it BLOWER. This alteration has been made for clarification.

C.9 few] THIS EDITION; five BLOWER

C.16 downy] THIS EDITION; dawny BLOWER

D.10 third] THIS EDITION; 3 BLOWER

E.7 *Quadrifronti*] THIS EDITION; QUADRIFRONTI BLOUNT; Quadri fronti ALLDE

PRESS VARIANTS

Press Variants in Dekker (Creede et al.), adapted from BOWERS

Copies collated by BOWERS:
BM1 (British Library C.34.c.23)
BM2 (British Library Ashley 612)
Bodl (Bodleian Mal. 602[1])
Dyce (Dyce Collection, National Art Library, Victoria and Albert Museum)
CLUC (W. A. Clark Library)
CSmH (Huntington Library)
CtY (Yale University)
DFo (Folger Shakespeare Library)
DLC (Library of Congress)
ICN (Newberry Library)
IU (University of Illinois)
MB (Boston Public Library)
MH (Harvard University)
NN (New York Public Library)
NNP (Morgan Library)
TxU (University of Texas)

Sheet B (inner forme)

Corrected: BM1, Bodl, CSmH, DLC, MH, NN, TxU
Uncorrected: BM2, Dyce, CLUC, CtY, DFo, ICN, IU, MB, NNP

Sig. B1ᵛ

336 frighted] *frighted corr*; *fraighted unc*

Sig. B2

354 joys,] *Ioyes, corr*; ~ ∧ *unc*
355 world,] *world, corr*; ~ ∧ *unc*
360 Dilexere] *Dilexere corr*; *Delexere unc*

Sig. B3ᵛ

437 whose] *corr*; *whom, unc*

Sig. B4

B.9 greces] *Grices corr*; *Gate unc*

Sheet C (outer forme)

Corrected: IU, NNP
Uncorrected: BM1, BM2, Bodl, Dyce, CLUC, CSmH, CtY, DFo, DLC, ICN, MB, MH, NN, TxU

Sig. C3

949 pilasters] *Pilafters corr*; *Pelafters unc*

950 pedestal] *Pedeftall corr*; *Padeftall unc*

Sheet H (outer forme)

First stage corrected: BM1, Dyce, CLUC, DFo, ICN, MB, MH, NN, TxU
Uncorrected: BM2, NNP

Sig. H1

1927 one of] *corr*; one *unc*

Sig. H2ᵛ

1967 scholae] *fcholæ corr*; *fchola unc*
1972–3 *Annam,*] *corr*; ~ ∧ *unc*
1974 stirpis] *ftirpis corr*; *ftripis unc*

Sig. H3

2047 being] *corr*; *beeing unc*
2057 building] *corr*; *bnilding unc*
2066 being] being *corr*; *beeing unc*

Second stage corrected: CtY

Sig. H2ᵛ

1965–6 adscribere.] *adfcribere, corr*; ~. *unc*

Sig. H3

2055 posterns risse up] pofternes riz vp *corr*; pofternes. *Viz.* Vp *unc*
2063 need] neede *corr*; minde *unc*

Third stage corrected: Bodl, CSmH, DLC, IU

Sig. H2ᵛ

1973 reliquamque] *corr*; *relinquamque unc*
1974 summa] *fumma corr*; *fummam unc*

Sheet H (inner forme)

First stage corrected: DFo, NN
Uncorrected: BM1, BM2, Dyce, ICN, MB, MH, NNP

Sig. H1ᵛ

1941 primariae] primaria *corr*; *prima via unc*

1943 *demortui*] *corr; de mortui unc*
1943 *spei*] *ſpei corr; ſpe unc*

Sig. H2

1949 *summae*] *ſummæ corr; ſumma unc*

Second stage corrected: Bodl, CLUC, CSmH, CtY, DLC, IU, TxU

Sig. H4

2113.n *Astraea*] Aſtræa *in right margin corr; ~ in left margin unc*
2114 *virgo*] *virgo *corr;* ‸~ *unc*
2114 *Saturnia*] *corr; Satarnia unc*

Historical Collation of Early Editions of Dekker, *Magnificent Entertainment*, **adapted from** BOWERS

253 countenances] countenance ALLDE
257 breasts] Breste: FINLASON
269 *inter fictos*] Inter fictos BOWERS; *Interfictos* FINLASON
288 for] *not in* ALLDE
291 would] will FINLASON
311 is] in ALLDE
360 *Dilexere*] Delexere CREEDE (unc), ALLDE
399 plotted] blotted FINLASON
412 wakened] weakened FINLASON
430 above] about ALLDE
432 bannerets] Banners ALLDE
437 whose] whom, CREEDE (unc), ALLDE
441 speak] speake BOWERS; spake ALLDE
893.n Gracious Street] *not in* FINLASON
911 out] *not in* ALLDE
930 *otia fecit*] otiafecit FINLASON
936 his] her ALLDE
950 erected] directed ALLDE, FINLASON
1025 Speech] speach in Latine. ALLDE
1037-55 The Italians'...even all.] *not in* CREEDE, FINLASON
1114 in her] ‸ her FINLASON
1120 *Utroque*] Viroque FINLASON
1127 pursued] sude FINLASON
1213-15 QVOD...APERIT] ALLDE *sets inscription in small italic lower case to save space*
1270 *ille*] illa
1308 holds] hold ALLDE
1361.n Soper Lane] *not in* FINLASON
1477 *Fame*] Fama FINLASON
1536 Is't] it's FINLASON
1543 is't] it's FINLASON
1579 'tis] it is FINLASON
1582 here] there ALLDE
1612 conqueror] Conquerors ALLDE
1618 BOWERS following ALLDE adds in the margin 3. *Cuppes of Golde given by the Cittie*
1631-2 BOWERS following ALLDE adds in the margin *The Pageant at the litle Conduit*
1691 in] *not in* ALLDE
1696 cornetts] *Cornets* BOWERS; *Comets* ALLDE
1701 the ditty] *not in* FINLASON
1718 twenty] 25. BOWERS; 20. CREEDE, ALLDE
1886 *Chorus*] *not in* CREEDE, FINLASON
1895 Had still he stayed] from CREEDE errata; Here staide had still CREEDE (text), FINLASON; Heere staide he still ALLDE
1897, 1898 he] from CREEDE errata; had CREEDE (text), FINLASON
1901 equally] equall CREEDE, FINLASON
1929-77 *Oratio...Dixi*] *not in* ALLDE
1941 *dotatum*] dodatum FINLASON
1941 *primariae*] prima via CREEDE (unc); priamria CREEDE (corr), FINLASON

1954 *Regiam*] Regiæ FINLASON
2110 nobleman...ploughman] Noblemen...Ploughmen FINLASON
2144 thy] by FINLASON
2152 property] properties FINLASON
2183 *Thomas*] Tho. CREEDE, ALLDE; T. FINLASON
2189 of] of the FINLASON
2214 and princely] *not in* FINLASON
2659 closed] close FINLASON
2668 *In freta*] Infreta ALLDE
2668 *umbrae*] unbræ ALLDE
2669 *pascit*] pascet FINLASON
2719-24 To...were.] *not in* ALLDE, FINLASON

Substantive Variants Between Parallel Texts of Dekker, *Magnificent Entertainment* **and Harrison,** *Arches of Triumph*

1033-4 *rex nobilissime, salve*] *not in* WINDET
1039 your] thy
1040-1 your...your] thy...thy
1042 your] thy
1048 you did] thou didst
1049 your] thine
1049 you said that] thou saidst
1055 thus we cry, all] *not in* WINDET
1298 see how thy] see thy
1299 thunders] thunder
1310 teaches] teacheth
1321 lavishly] *not in* WINDET
1327 of them] then
1333 you] thee
1334 your] thy
1334 then] *not in* WINDET
1336 grandfathers...so many] *not in* WINDET
1468 in] is
1470 Dries] Dry
1516 drunk] LOWNES, UNKNOWN, FINLASON; drunk up WINDET, BOWERS
1519 dost] doest BOWERS; doth WINDET
1642 here not] heere, not BOWERS; not heere WINDET
1645-60 to deliver...whilst all] *not in* WINDET
1660 here] heere BOWERS; *not in* WINDET
1662-3 for...infinite] *not in* WINDET
1675 so now] now so
1691 in] *not in* WINDET
2137 move] WINDET; moude BOWERS
2144 virtue] Vertues
2155 figured all in] which here figure

Press Variants in *Ben Jonson his Part*, **Adapted from** HERFORD-SIMPSON

Copies collated by HERFORD-SIMPSON:
A1 (British Library C.34.b.20)
A2 (British Library C.39.d.1)
B (Gough copy, Bodleian Library, Oxford)
C1 and C2 (The Huth copy and another copy in the Guildhall Library, London)
D (All Souls College Library, Oxford)
E (Trinity College Library, Cambridge)
F (Rylands Library, Manchester)
G (Dyce Collection, National Art Library, Victoria and Albert Museum)
H (copy of the late T. J. Wise)

Sig. A2

506 *mira constantia*] A1, A2, C1, C2, D, E, F, G; *mirâ constantiâ* B, H

508 *copia*] A1, A2, C1, C2, D, E, F, G; *copiâ* B, H
519 *hyperbole*] Hyporbole A1, A2, C1, C2, D, E, F, G; Hyperbole B, H

Sig. A2ᵛ

525 above mentioned...of] above-mentioned Title | of C1, C2, D; above mentioned | Title A1, A2, B, E, F, G, H
526 the King's chamber] the Kings Chamber C1, C2, D; *the Kings Chamber* A1, A2, B, E, F, G, H
527 empire: for] Empire | for C1, C2, D; Em-|pire: for A1, A2, B, E, F, G, H
528 kingdom, Master] Kingdome | Maister C1, C2, D; King-|dome M. A1, A2, B, E, F, G, H
534 shields through them,] ~: C1, C2, D; shieldes thorow them; A1, A2, B, E, F, G, H
537 Ireland.] ~; C1, C2, D; *Ireland.* A1, A2, B, E, F, G, H
547-8 Virgil...*penitus*] *Virg.—Et penitus* C1, C2, D; And *Virg.* | *—Et penitus* (centred) A1, A2, B, E, F, G, H
550-1 the...set] The Shields their | precedency and distinc-tions At her feete was set | C1, C2, D; The Shieldes the | precedency of the Countries and their distincti-|ons. At her feete was set | A1, A2, B, E, F, G, H
552-4 THEOSOPHIA...garments] THEOSOPHIA, or *Divine wise-dom, al in white, a blew mantle seeded* | *with Stars, a crowne of Stars upon hir head; he gar* | C1, C2, D (with catchword 'ments'); THEOSOPHIA, A1, A2, B, E, F, G, H (with catchword 'or', and two lines taken over to A3ʳ). To adjust the page, the printer took out the 'white' lines above and below 'GENIVS VRBIS', l. 567.

Sig. A3

554 head...garments] head; hir gar | ments C1, C2, D; head. Hir gar-|ments A1, A2, B, E, F, G, H
555 clearness.] ~: C1, C2, D; Cleerenesse. A1, A2, B, E, F, G, H
556-7 dove,...serpent:] Dove;...Serpent; C1, C2, D; ~,...~: A1, A2, B, E, F, G, H
559.n Matthew 10:16] *ranged with 'Dove', l. 556* A1, A2, F; *ranged with 'Estote', l. 557-8* B, C1, C2, D, E, G, H
561.n Proverbs 8:15] *ranged with 'word', l. 558-9* A1, A2, F; *ranged with 'PER ME', l. 561* B, C1, C2, D, E, G, H
567.n *Antiqui...14*] *ranged with the white line below* GENIVS VRBIS C1, C2, D; *ranged above* 'GENIVS VRBIS' *between ll. 565 and 567* A1, A2, B, E, F, G, H
567.n rerum...quam] rerum existi-|marūt Deum: | et vrbib. quam | A1, A2, C1, C2, D, E, F, G; rerū exxistima-|runt Deum: & | tam vrbib. quā | B, H

Sig. A3ᵛ

600 the river] The River *indented* A1, A2, C1, C2, D, E; *No paragraph* B, H
600 the city in] the Ci-|ty; in A1, A2, C1, C2, D, E, F, G; the City; | B, H

Sig. A4

632 And...place] *centred* A1, A2, C1, C2, D, E, F, G; *begins the line* B, H

Sig. A4ᵛ

658.n *Aeneid* I] *Æne. 1 above* QVA...PORTA C1, C2, D; *ranged with* QVA PORTA A1, A2, B, E, F, G, H
660 wind] winde, C1, C2, D; ~; A1, A2, B, E, F, G, H
662.n *Aeneid* I] *Æne. 1 ranged with* Taken, l. 659 C1, C2, D; *between ll. 659, 659* A1, A2, B, E, F, G, H
662 *porta*] porta, C1, C2, D; ~ₐ A1, A2, B, E, F, G, H

Sig. B3

782.n *ab urbo*] ab urbe A1, A2, C1, C2, D, E, F; ~ urbo B, H

785.n *Cressa...nota*] A1, A2, C1, C2, D, E, F; *Creſſâ...notâ* B, H

Sig. B4

821.n chief serjeant] chief Serieant A1, A2, C1, C2, D, E, F; chiefe ~ B, H
823.n some...the] some particu-|lar allusion to | his name, | which is *Be-|net*, and hath | (no doubt) in | time bin the | A1, A2, C1, C2, D, E, F; some particular | allusion to his | Name, which | is *Benet*, and | hath (no doubt) | in time bin the | B, H
835.n persons] A1, A2, C1, C2, D, E, F; Persons B, H
835.n humanity...Greek] Humanity, & | in frequent | use with al the | Greek A1, A2, C1, C2, D, E, F; Humanitie, and | in frequent vse | with all the | Greeke B, H
On this page the notes have been reset, probably owing to a derangement in type. The original setting is neater and has the lines more evenly balanced.

Sig. B4ᵛ

843.n *Lactantatius*] *Lactant.* A1, A2, C1, C2, D, F; *Luctatius* [a miscorrection for *Lactantius*] B, E, G, H
848 And] A1, A2, C1, C2, D, F; *~ B, E, G, H
848.n To the] A1, A2, C1, C2, D, F; *~ B, E, G, H
858 With...*those*ᵉ] With those (e) A2, C2; With (e) those A1, B, C1, D, E, F, G, H
858.n Charles...Elizabeth] A1, B, C1, D, E, F, G, H; *not in* A2, C2

Sig. C1

2255 *vocabant*;] A1, A2, C1, C2, D, E, F; ~ₐ B, H

Sig. C1ᵛ

2258.n *Albricus...imagine*] Abb. in | deorum | imag. A1, A2, C1, C2, D, E, F; Alb. in | deorum B, H
2260-1 winter—and adscribe] *Winter,)...adscribe* A1, A2, C1, C2, D, E, F; *Winter,...adscribe* B, H

Sig. C2

2292 SANGVINEA] *sanguineâ,* A1, A2, C1, C2, D, E, F, G; ~ₐ B, H
2295 IVRANDASQVE] *Iur andsaʒ* A1, A2, C1, C2, D, E, F, G; *Iur andasǯ* B, H
HERFORD–SIMPSON also noted a number of fine adjustments of type on this page, especially involving the long italic '*ſ*'.

Sig. C2ᵛ

2307.n him.] ~ₐ A1, A2, C1, C2, D, E, F, G; ~. B, H
2315 IN NVMERIS] IN NVMERIS A1, A2, C1, C2, D, E, F, G; INNVMERIS B, H
2318.n Silius Italicus] *placed one line above in* A1, A2, C1, C2, D, E, F, G;
2320 triumphs] Tryumphes A1, A2, C1, C2, D, E, F, G; Triumphes B, H
2324 first handmaid] *type disordered* A1, A2, C1, C2, D, E, F, G; *type adjusted* B, H

Sig. C3

2329 rest.] Rest; A1, A2, C1, C2, D, E, F, G; ~: B, H
2337 *mandataque*] *mandataʒ* A1, A2, C1, C2, D, E, F, G; *mandataǯ* B, H
2338 *Imperiosa*] A1, A2, C, C2, D, E, F, G; *Imperioso* B, H

Sig. C3ᵛ

2360 was] ~. A1, A2, C1, C2, D, E, F, G; ~ₐ B, H
2365 medicine;] Medicine: A1, A2, C1, C2, D, E, F, G; ~: B, H. The wrong-fount colon was reproduced in STANSBY.

Sig. C4

2383 cornucopia] *Coruncopia* A1, A2, C1, C2, D, E, F, G; *Cornu-copia* B, H

Sig. C4ᵛ

2401 Poscimvs] POSSIMVS A1, A2, C1, C2, D, E, F, G; *POSCIMVS* B, H

Sig. D1

2416.n *Flamines dicti*] *Flamines diciti* A1, A2, C1, C2, D, E, F, G; *Filamines dicti* B, H

2418.n Which in] Whichin A1, A2, C1, C2, D, E, F, G; Which in B, H

2420.n *Pone*] *pone* A1, A2, C1, C2, D, E, F, G; *ponè* B, H

Sig. D1ᵛ

2435 calendar] *Calender* F; *Kalender* A1, A2, B, C1, C2, D, E, G, H

2437 feast] *feast*; F; ~ₐ A1, A2, B, C1, C2, D, E, F, G, H

2438 Perenna] PERENVA F; PERENNA A1, A2, B, C1, C2, D, E, G, H

2438 guest;] *guest*; A1, A2, C1, C2, D, E, G; ~ₐ B, H

2458 Who] *c.w.: Whose* F; Who A1, A2, B, C1, C2, D, E, G, H

Sig. D2

2461 His and] *His and* F; *His, and* A1, A2, B, C1, C2, D, E, G, H

2480 cense] *sence* F; *cense* A1, A2, B, C1, C2, D, E, G, H

2484–2484.n thy…masculine] *the Masculine* F; *thy Masculine* A1, A2, B, C1, C2, D, E, G, H

2484.n *pependit*] *pependi* F; *pependit* A1, A2, B, C1, C2, D, E, G, H

2485 My] *c.w.: That* F; My A1, A2, B, C1, C2, D, E, G, H

Sig. E1ᵛ

2638 sing] *sing*ₐ C2; sing, A1, A2, B, C1, D, E, F, G, H

THE PATIENT MAN AND THE HONEST WHORE

Edited by Paul Mulholland

HENSLOWE'S payment of £5 to 'Thomas deckers & Midleton in earneste of ther playe Called the pasyent man & the onest hore' at some point in 1604 prior to 14 March, the date of the subsequent entry, marks the first recorded reference to the play and supplies a dating limit for its composition. *The Patient Man and the Honest Whore* was entered in the Stationers' Register on 9 November 1604 by Thomas Man the younger: 'Entred for his copye vnder the hand of mʳ Pasfeild A Booke called. The humours of the patient man. The longing wyfe and the honest whore.' The play was released in what may for convenience be described as three editions in quarto form in a relatively brief span of time (STC 6501, 6501.5, and 6502; *BEPD* 204). In the second edition use of a combination of standing type from the impression of the first together with reset type renders the relationship between the two considerably more intimate and complex than is usual in separate editions. The third 'edition' is made up entirely of sheets imposed from type set for the first edition and, with minor adjustments, the second. The title of the play in the first edition, 'The Honeſt Whore', was altered to 'The Converted Curtezan' in the second, and, apparently in deference to the running titles of leftover first-edition sheets, reverted to 'The Honeſt Whore' in the third edition. The subtitle, 'With, The Humours of the Patient Man, and the Longing Wife.', is essentially invariant in the three editions.

W. W. Greg surmised that John Hodgets, whose name appears in the first-edition imprint as publisher, 'Printed by V. S. for Iohn Hodgets, and are to be folde at his ſhop in Paules church-yard', probably acted merely as bookseller, in light of the entry to Man and the altered form of the imprint on the third-edition title-page: 'Printed by V. S. and are to be fold by Iohn Hodgets at his ſhoppe in Paules church-yard'. The latter form of the imprint appears also in the only copy of the second edition that preserves the title-page, the Bute copy of the National Library of Scotland, which was unknown to Greg. Although the initials, 'V. S.', in all three imprints point to Valentine Simmes as the printer, Simmes was responsible only for the initial two sheets; the remaining eight sheets were shared among three other printers, each of whom retained his first-edition allocation in printing the second edition. SIMMES–CREEDE–STAFFORD–ELD1 (the first edition) was probably published in November 1604, and SIMMES–CREEDE–STAFFORD–ELD2 (the second edition), since it too bears the date 1604, soon after; SIMMES–CREEDE–STAFFORD–ELD3 (the third edition), with its change in imprint date to 1605, very likely appeared early in the

new year. Simmes's xylographic 'THE', which appears on all of the title-pages, sustained some damage to the 'T' prior to or during the printing of SIMMES–CREEDE–STAFFORD–ELD3; this damage is not apparent in the same xylographic used in *The Malcontent* Q3 printed by Simmes in early (Weiss 1990, 136, queries January) 1605. The fourth edition (1615 or 1616), which Greg established used SIMMES–CREEDE–STAFFORD–ELD1 as copy text, and the fifth (1635), which Fredson Bowers established used the fourth as copy text, were both printed by Nicholas Okes. Neither has authority.

In his review of the evidence bearing on the nature of the printer's copy Bowers concludes that the manuscript was probably foul papers or a non-theatrical transcript of them, noting: permissive stage directions; the discrepancy in speech prefixes and in certain stage directions for Candido's Wife ('*Viola*' in Sc. 2, A4ᵛ–B2 in SIMMES1, A4ᵛ–B1 in SIMMES2; '*Wife*' in Sc. 4, B4 and thereafter); the partial sequence of scene numbering running from Scenes 7 to 13 but omitting the heading for Sc. 12; and the absence of clear signs of playhouse origin in the form of unambiguously imperative stage directions and the like. The appearance of the character-name discrepancy within the section of the play set by Simmes's compositor establishes that it originated in the manuscript. In Sc. 15, however, the specification in a stage direction and in speech headings of the actor, Towne, a member of Prince Henry's Men who performed the play at the Fortune, is a most unusual detail for a non-theatrical text (I3–I3ᵛ; 15.102.1). This feature may signify that the role was written expressly for this actor, a circumstance which gave rise to citation of his name in the manuscript; or perhaps it represents a late addition or revision like the reference to the siege at Ostend (10.31–2).

Through fount analysis Adrian Weiss has shown that the first and subsequent editions were set in four sections: A–B, C–D, E–F, and G–K. Valentine Simmes printed only sheets A and B (Simmes-S1 fount), which contain a characteristic seen in other texts printed by him: use of medial 'v' and 'j'. In addition, the running titles in this section are lower-case roman with initial capitals. Two skeletons were probably used, and the printer's measure was 90 mm. For sheets C and D an S-fount and 'a resident cluster of foul-case italic capitals' identify the printer as Thomas Creede (Creede-4 fount); a smaller printer's measure (87 mm.) and running titles given in italic capitals were used in these sheets. Two complete sets of running titles point to the likely use of two skeletons in this section. Further type changes and the presence of tell-tale damaged type signal the printer of sheets E and F to be Simon Stafford (Stafford-EFb fount). Though Greg, and subsequently Bowers, concluded that E–K was the work of a single printer, members of a foul-case cluster and identified types in sheets G to K point to George Eld as responsible for this section (Eld-Y1 fount; Weiss 1990, 125, 132, 135, 138; 1991, 223). Identification of Stafford and Eld as the printers of the final portions of the text dismisses a range of associated puzzling elements and problems involving, for example, the supposed use of two presses for the section E–K, and the transference of type from one printer to another occasioned by an imagined switch from three printers in SIMMES–CREEDE–STAFFORD–ELD1 to four printers in SIMMES–CREEDE–STAFFORD–ELD2. One press apparently printed Stafford's sheets E–F, and one press Eld's G–K. Stafford's sheets were imposed and printed using the same single skeleton (both formes).

In Eld's section a single skeleton printed H; but another skeleton equipped with different settings of running titles was apparently used for both formes of G, and that skeleton also printed inner I and both formes of K. The skeleton used for H, with different settings of some running titles, was used for outer I. Except for some variations in thickness, the paper is fairly uniform throughout surviving copies; a different watermark appears in sheet H of the FOLGER1 copy, but this is not inconsistent with job-lots of this quality of paper. Scene numbers running from Sc. 7 to Sc. 13 but omitting Sc. 12 are exclusive to the E–F and G–K sections; the numbering abruptly ceases after Sc. 13, which is the last scene-break in G–K (H2ᵛ). Failure to assign scene numbers in the early part of the play may be due to a simple printing error. As Bowers pointed out, the fact that the numbers begin at Sc. 7 on E2 demonstrates that they came from the manuscript, since the printer of E–F would be unlikely to know otherwise how many scenes preceded those marked in his section. The scene markings are internally consistent in each section: Stafford employs the form 'SCENA 7.' etc.; Eld '11.SCE.' and '13.SCE.'

Division of printing among four printers almost certainly signifies hasty production as in the case of Dekker's *Magnificent Entertainment*, in which Thomas Man the younger was also involved as publisher. Other similarities connecting these two works lie in the use of standing type and the introduction of apparently authoritative corrections in the second edition. A rate of roughly four edition-sheets per week for a single-press establishment (Blayney, 43) suggests that SIMMES–CREEDE–STAFFORD–ELD1 was probably printed in the space of a week or so. Eld's four sheets establish this minimum overall production time. The presence of standing type for SIMMES–CREEDE–STAFFORD–ELD2 would inevitably mean that the second edition could be completed within a significantly shorter time-span.

The SIMMES–CREEDE–STAFFORD–ELD1 title, 'The Honeſt Whore', head-title, and corresponding running titles were altered in SIMMES–CREEDE–STAFFORD–ELD2 to 'The Converted Curtezan'. As noted above, the imprint was also changed

to reflect John Hodgets's capacity as bookseller (Man was obviously the publisher). No clear evidence has come to light to explain what may have prompted the title change or who may have been responsible for it; but circumstances that have escaped the notice of previous commentators in this regard perhaps deserve attention. While T. M. Parrott and others have seen Marston's *The Dutch Courtesan* as an 'intentional retort' to the Dekker–Middleton play, discussion has not extended to include the latter's alternate title. The main obstacle to establishment of a clear link between the two plays relating to the title change from *The Honest Whore* to *The Converted Courtesan* is the problem of pinning down the date of *The Dutch Courtesan*. The printing of *The Patient Man and the Honest Whore* SIMMES–CREEDE–STAFFORD–ELD1 in November 1604 and SIMMES–CREEDE–STAFFORD–ELD2, which also bears the date 1604, not long afterward, narrowly defines dating limits for such a connection.

Although *The Dutch Courtesan* has not been dated more precisely than between 1603 and early 1605, late 1604 is consistent with and does not unduly attenuate such evidence as has so far been adduced. This date is particularly well aligned with *The Dutch Courtesan*'s title-page, which specifies that the play was performed by the Children of Her Majesty's Revels, a company granted this title 4 February 1604. It is not known whether Marston's play originated with this company or was revived by them. But in either case, whether intended or not, Marston's representation of the title courtesan, Franceschina, may well have been perceived by Dekker as a challenge to the comparatively sentimental portrait of the reformed prostitute, Bellafront. The title, *The Converted Courtesan*, may accordingly have been designed as a riposte to Marston and/or an attempt to exploit any topical interest generated by *The Dutch Courtesan* and suggestions of rivalry between the dramatists, and possibly companies, if *The Patient Man and the Honest Whore* was still in the repertory. In view of both the so-called 'war of the theatres', in which Dekker, Marston, and Jonson participated, and subsequent developments of contention between Dekker and Jonson—and probably Marston—and their respective companies over Dekker and Webster's *Westward Ho* at Paul's and Chapman, Jonson, and Marston's *Eastward Ho* at Blackfriars, the possibility of Dekker's instigation of the change in title seems highly plausible, though in the absence of further evidence incapable of proof.

Two of the three extant copies of SIMMES–CREEDE–STAFFORD–ELD2 lack the title-page and final leaves of text. The only perfect copy known (National Library of Scotland—NLS) interestingly differs from the others in some particulars. As Bowers notes, the missing leaves in two of the three surviving copies are probably the result of accidental rough handling rather than a sign that the second edition may have been suppressed. Although the Stationers' Company forbade resort to standing type to print more than the legally allowed size of edition-sheet (e.g., 1250 or 1500), a similar second-edition venture involving a combination of standing and reset type in roughly equal proportions may be seen in Dekker's *Magnificent Entertainment*. On such occasions in which the cost of producing copies beyond the permitted limit was diminished by partially circumventing the need for duplicate typesetting, the publisher presumably arranged with his printers to negotiate terms acceptable to their compositors over a mutually agreed amount of resetting. Shared printing makes standing type a more realistic proposition, as it ties up much less of any one printer's type-supply. In the cases that have come to light, suspicion that such an arrangement was in place is increased by the availability of the authors for correction and revision in connection with the second printing. If not planned from the outset, the decision to print SIMMES–CREEDE–STAFFORD–ELD2 was very likely taken soon after the printing of SIMMES–CREEDE–STAFFORD–ELD1 was embarked upon since the type would otherwise have been distributed in the usual way. Although the survival of only a single copy does not encourage speculation, SIMMES–CREEDE–STAFFORD–ELD3 may also have figured in the plan, as it would seem too much of a coincidence for there to be a good supply of spare sheets, from different sources, of all the book. It is tempting to speculate that the change of title, although possibly prompted by Marston's *The Dutch Courtesan*, may have served also to mask an apparent attempt to exceed the permitted size of edition sheet.

The SIMMES–CREEDE–STAFFORD–ELD2 typography and running titles indicate that the second edition adhered to the four-fold division of SIMMES–CREEDE–STAFFORD–ELD1: Simmes A–B 'The converted Curtezan.', Creede C–D 'THE CONVERTED | CVRTIZAN.', Stafford E–F '*The conuerted Courtizan.*', and Eld G–K '*THE CONVERTED | CVRTIZAN.*'. The proportion of standing to reset type in the play's 78 pages is equivalent to roughly 42 pages to 36. Where resetting is restricted to one forme, only the outer forme is involved. This circumstance possibly constitutes a stratagem of deliberate deception aimed at shrouding an overuse of standing type since the inner forme would be less conspicuous in uncut copies. The standing/reset type proportion varies by section as printed in the different shops. Unless the publisher or some other interested party oversaw production of the second edition as a whole, identification of the printer of each of the four sections of SIMMES–CREEDE–STAFFORD–ELD1 and 2 would appear to oppose the possibility of an intention to balance the overall proportion of standing to reset type advanced as a means to account for otherwise puzzling unequal amounts of resetting in some formes and in different sections. Local conditions specific to the individual sections perhaps offer the most plausible explanation. In some instances the quantity of resetting may reflect the timing of receipt of instructions to hold imposed type for a second edition; in a few cases it appears to be related at least in part to accidentally pied type; but, as Adrian Weiss has communicated to me privately, type-supply offers the likeliest explanation for most instances of different quantities of standing type

in each section. In Simmes's part, both formes of A (6 pages) are standing type; and both formes of B (8 pages) are reset. Creede's portion contains three pages of inner C and both formes of D in standing type (11 pages); outer C and C1ᵛ of inner C are reset (5 pages). The inner formes of E and F and three pages of outer F are standing in Stafford's section (10 1/2 pages); outer E, F1, and parts of F2ᵛ (possibly only disturbance) and F3 of outer F are reset (essentially 5 1/2 pages). Eld's section contains the smallest proportion of standing to reset type: inner H, inner I, inner K and K1 and K4ᵛ of outer K are standing (14 pages); both formes of G, outer H, outer I, K2ᵛ and K3 of outer K are reset (18 pages).

Resetting of C1ᵛ only of inner C was possibly brought about because the printer had already begun to break up CREEDE1 type before word arrived to hold it for a second edition. The resetting of F1 and the bottom seventeen and a half lines of F3 in outer F was probably occasioned by pied type; disturbance to the initial seven lines of F2ᵛ is very likely related. In his Textual Introduction Bowers curiously notes that the top sixteen lines were reset, but in his collation lists an altered stage direction near the top of the page as occurring in standing type, and a change six lines from the bottom in reset type. Examination of the letterpress of STAFFORD2 establishes unequivocally that the type of the lower half of the page differs from that of STAFFORD1 and that the type of the upper half, though registering disturbance, is the same. Resetting in K is confined to the adjacent inner pages of the outer forme (K2ᵛ–3). Since Eld had already accumulated several formes of standing type by the time the formes of the play's final sheet came to be set, resetting in outer K is unlikely to have any connection with late instructions to retain it for reprinting. In Eld's section, which calls for the largest stock of type, fourteen pages of standing type coupled with resetting for each sheet in turn very likely stretched his supply to its limit. Distribution of both formes of G, outer H, outer I, and two pages of outer K was probably dictated by a need to replenish a dwindling reserve as setting progressed. In other sections the proportion of standing to reset type in the main very likely reflects similar shortages at the respective establishments. Where distribution of single pages or parts of a forme was involved, the number of pages distributed was most likely governed by the quantity of type required to complete the setting of a new forme or the resetting of a forme previously broken up. In such cases the order of pages selected for distribution is random. Partial distribution additionally stood to save time over distribution of a whole forme and may have been resorted to on this account. Normal distribution practices coordinated with type-supply, then, are the likeliest primary determinants of the proportion and pattern of standing type in each section.

Standing-type formes in SIMMES–CREEDE–STAFFORD–ELD2 include A (both formes), most of inner C, D (both formes), inner E, most of F (both formes), inner H, inner I, inner K, and two pages of outer K. In most of these corrections and revisions affect both accidentals and substantives. Some, like those in both formes of sheet A, are in themselves of indeterminate origin. Others, extending much farther than the competence of a proof-corrector, appear in all other formes of SIMMES–CREEDE–STAFFORD–ELD2 standing type except for both formes of sheet F, inner I, and possibly inner H. Too few copies of SIMMES–CREEDE–STAFFORD–ELD1 survive to establish whether when only minor variants occur in a standing-type forme of SIMMES–CREEDE–STAFFORD–ELD2 such variants were introduced in SIMMES–CREEDE–STAFFORD–ELD1 in the course of proof-correction or in the course of SIMMES–CREEDE–STAFFORD–ELD2 impression, since the extant SIMMES–CREEDE–STAFFORD–ELD1 copies preserve what may amount only to the uncorrected SIMMES–CREEDE–STAFFORD–ELD1 state. Bowers proposes as a 'working hypothesis' that 'the invariant formes in known copies of Q1 [SIMMES–CREEDE–STAFFORD–ELD1] (supplemented by some sheets of Q3 [SIMMES–CREEDE–STAFFORD–ELD3 F and I]) represent the corrected state of the type if variance ever existed; and hence we are bound to assume that the observed Q2 [SIMMES–CREEDE–STAFFORD–ELD2] variants in standing type were in fact made subsequent to Q1 impression.'

Although a number of corrections may have originated from an editor or proof-corrector, others appear to call for the authority of an author. Those that reveal sophistication beyond what would reasonably be expected of a proof-corrector include CREEDE1 'Malauella' to 'Malauolta' at 6.114 (D1), the rewriting of 6.352-4, 496, 501, and 506 (D4, E2), and the alteration of Bellafront's CREEDE1 'What' to 'Whaat' (6.45; C4), and possibly 'doſt' at 5.237, to 'doeſt' (C3^v), which, although a preferred Dekker spelling, is, as Bowers notes, 'scarcely unique with him'. In addition, the introduction of new readings that can scarcely have stood in the manuscript copy for SIMMES–CREEDE–STAFFORD–ELD1 and instances of relining prose as verse suggest the scrupulousness of an author. The likelihood of authorial presence behind these and other alterations in SIMMES–CREEDE–STAFFORD–ELD1 standing type enforces acceptance of them, unless at specific points contamination of some other description is strongly suspected.

Less clear is the authority of variants in reset formes of SIMMES–CREEDE–STAFFORD–ELD2. With a few exceptions, in the formes of only inner and outer B and pages K2^v and K3 of outer K are there clear signs that variants in reset type betray authorial presence. Most other reset-type variants can be accounted for by printing-house proofing probably without reference to any copy. In sheet B numerous alterations point to an author. These involve relineation of verse (B2: 3.19-20), scrupulous attention to points of detail (e.g. 'alterd' to 'alter' B2^v: 3.44; 'the' to 'thy' B2^v: 3.56), and instances of possible revision (e.g. 'olde dames' to 'mad-caps' B1^v: 2.135, 'God knowes' to 'good knaues' B2^v: 3.52, 'haunts' to 'hnrts'—a misprint for 'hurts'—B3: 3.71). In its reset state sheet B additionally incorporates dozens of spelling and punctuation changes. In Eld's section, G–K, a cluster of authoritative variants appears in the reset K3 of outer K that comprises fairly extensive revisions chiefly of several of Bellafront's speeches. Apart from these Bowers isolates six instances with any claim to authority in the reset type elsewhere in the section; but his observations call for some revision in light of apparently overlooked evidence. He inadvertently reverses the first variant cited: ELD1's 'Benedeƈt' on G3 (10.192) is corrected to 'Benediƈt', not the other way round as reported. He also notes the addition of 'up' (G3: 11.4) and correction of 'Poli' to 'Poh' in the stage directions at 11.0.2 (G3), 12.56.1 and the speech prefix at 12.72 (G4^v), but remarks that all of these may be credited to printing-house initiative and do not require authorial intervention. The sense of the passage calls for the introduction of 'up'; and reference to the inner forme of G, where on G3^v of ELD1 'Poh' is five times spelled correctly and in a sixth instance was press-corrected from 'Poli' to 'Poh', could have given rise to discovery and correction of the erroneous form in ELD2.

Possibly worthy of addition to Bowers's list is the change from ELD1 'deept' on H3 to 'dipt' (13.43), which may signify authorial sophistication of the order noticed in D1. While it might be argued that this and 'Benediƈt' involve normalization of an odd 'e' spelling, in the case of 'deept'/'dipt', the two words derive from different roots and have somewhat different meanings. Such distinctions seem more likely to arouse an author's rather than a compositor's sensibilities. Further, this alteration lends additional force to the possibility of authorial involvement in the change from 'for' to 'far' (13.35) on the same signature (H3) in providing evidence of more than a single instance in this forme. Relineation of prose as verse on I2^v (15.46-9 and 15.59-61) provides for Bowers the clearest evidence of an author's editorial involvement.

Bowers unaccountably asserts that reset K2^v contains no variants. ELD2 introduces at 15.399 the speech heading, 'Anſel:', which, despite placement a line early (possibly attributable to the compositor's misunderstanding of the correction), clearly corrects a fault in the ELD1 setting and identifies the speaker of the last speech on the page. Since the speech prefix is missing in all surviving copies of ELD1, and since this printed text rather than the original manuscript was presumably used as the copy text for the reset parts of ELD2, detection of the error by the authority responsible for other, farther-reaching changes elsewhere seems plausible. In order to explain the variants at the foot of K3, Bowers cites revision in the initial line of standing K3^v ('and had not you it leerer' to 'and that naughty man had it, had you not leerer' 15.444-5), which he presumes to be 'of a piece with', or a continuation of, corrections called for at the bottom of the preceding page and the likely source of those corrections. But the addition of 'Anſel:' on K2^v possibly renders such an explanation unnecessary. A mark directing the compositor to supply a missing speech prefix on K2^v, which in turn drew his attention to corrections on the adjacent page, obviates the need for reference to a correction that spans the two formes of K.

As Bowers points out, an editor of *The Patient Man and the Honest Whore* must confront the unusual circumstance whereby authorial correction/revision is found in standing type but in relatively few reset pages. Accordingly, the present edition essentially adopts the policy set out by Bowers in respect to the authority of reset pages (extended to include the overlooked pages noted above), but rejects his account of how this circumstance may have come about. Although the possibility that minor changes are authoritative cannot be ruled out, authorial correction can only be accepted in formes where it can be demonstrated; further, the pattern of demonstrable authority can be explained without assuming wider authorial correction.

Bowers proposes that a marked bound copy of SIMMES-CREEDE-STAFFORD-ELD1 was passed from printer to printer in reverse order beginning with Eld, which would allow each in turn to incorporate correction/revision into his standing-type formes and Simmes to do so in sheet B in the process of resetting that sheet. The additional time required for binding a copy of SIMMES-CREEDE-STAFFORD-ELD1, which would tie up a substantial portion of each printer's pica roman fount from production while awaiting arrival of corrected copy, the unlikely notion that the respective sheets travelled around London intact in place of division and distribution to the respective printers, and one or two other problematic matters render Bowers's explanation untenable, however. A particular oddity in the suggested sequence would be the doubling back to Addling Hill, south-west of St Paul's, the location of the shops of both Stafford and Simmes (Eld's printing house was located west of St Paul's in Fleet Lane, and Creede's was east or south-east of St Paul's in the Old Exchange). Also difficult to reconcile with his explanation is Bowers's apparent disregard of substantial revision in reset pages in Eld's section. Changes introduced in two pages of reset outer K and arguably elsewhere (see above) establish that, in this section at least, authorial correction/revision is found in both standing and reset type. In place of an intact marked copy passed from printer to printer, sheets printed by each of the other shops were probably sent to Simmes's establishment by twos and fours so that each printer received his two or four corrected/revised sheets soon after corrections or revisions had been made. Whether changes to standing type in the sections printed by Creede and Stafford constitute the full complement of authoritative correction/revision called for in their respective sheets or, if not, some other as yet unknown factor was responsible for restriction of such correction/revision to their standing type is impossible to determine on the basis of evidence that has so far come to light. Intriguing and exasperating as the question may be, however, its resolution seems unlikely to affect editorial policy regarding the relative authority of variant readings.

In two recent studies Joost Daalder and Antony Telford Moore adopt a much more permissive approach to variants and thereby extend the limits of authority considerably beyond those proposed by Bowers and significantly further than the present analysis. The authors essentially argue that variant readings found in the second edition, whether in standing or reset type, improve (frequently in a manner that exceeds compositorial judgement) those of the first, and accordingly should be accepted as authoritative (and possibly authorial). Among other matters examined is a rejection of Adrian Weiss's positive identification of Creede, Stafford, and Eld as printers of sheets C to K in favour of John Windet (C–D) and Thomas Purfoot (E–K) in the first edition, with the addition of another printer, possibly Simon Stafford, who took over sheets E and F from Purfoot for the second (Daalder and Moore 1996, 245, 251–2). Daalder and Moore regrettably do not elaborate on analysis of type identification in support of their printer allocations; and in the absence of such evidence the case for Windet and Purfoot appears unpersuasive and far from compelling. Unfortunately, the 1996 study setting out these investigators' rationale for a more liberal approach to the question of authority in the early editions of *The Patient Man and the Honest Whore* appeared too late for a fuller and more detailed response here.

Bowers's discussion of NLS sheet E, which alone among the sheets of this copy of SIMMES-CREEDE-STAFFORD-ELD2 contains the running title, '*THE HONEST WHORE.*', can be revised and supplemented in light of unconsidered evidence. The stages of press correction in sheet E demonstrate that while both formes of NLS sheet E are re-imposed (the inner from standing and the outer from reset type), they represent earlier states than those in other copies of STAFFORD2 sheet E (including the STAFFORD2 sheet in SIMMES-CREEDE-STAFFORD-ELD3). In the standing inner forme, the NLS copy contains two readings shared with STAFFORD1: on E2 occurs the uncorrected reading, 'A', found in all copies of STAFFORD1 and corrected in the BODLEIAN and FOLGER2 copies of STAFFORD2 to 'I' (7.23); and on E3^v at 7.116 STAFFORD1 and NLS read 'thrumb' where other copies of STAFFORD2 have 'thrum'. The NLS copy's alterations to the STAFFORD1 state include not only the probably authorial revision of Bellafront's line near the top of E2 (6.496) but a number of other changes that help to establish its position in the printing sequence. On E1^v NLS and other copies of STAFFORD2 read 'I see' at 6.476, corrected from STAFFORD1's 'See'. Several other significant variants appear on E3^v and E4: at 7.121 STAFFORD1's 'here' is corrected in STAFFORD2 (including NLS) to 'heres'; and at 7.141 STAFFORD1 reads 'thrum', whereas NLS and other STAFFORD2 copies give 'thump'. On E4 at 7.169 STAFFORD1's 'min-|gle' is altered in STAFFORD2 (including NLS) to 'Nin-|gle'. Incorporation of the revised form of Bellafront's speech and several other corrections common to the BODLEIAN and FOLGER2 copies of STAFFORD2 together with the uncorrected state of 'A' and 'thrumb' establishes that NLS sheet E represents an intermediate state between that of STAFFORD1 and that found in other copies of STAFFORD2 including inner E of STAFFORD3. This evidence is consistent with the anomalous NLS running title, '*THE HONEST WHORE.*', which may be seen to derive from that phase of printing that preceded alteration of the running title to '*The converted Courtizan.*' Duplication of the running-title positions of NLS sheet E in STAFFORD1 sheet F prompts investigation of the relationship between these sheets. The key question in this relationship centres on the direction of the running-title transfer: i.e. whether they were moved from E to F or the reverse. Transfer from E to F would presume that the reset state of E was ready for impression before either forme of F in its STAFFORD1 state had been set and carries a number of implausible attendant implications: the cancel of an entire forme for no apparent reason; corrections to the other forme of a kind unexampled in SIMMES–CREEDE–STAFFORD–ELD1 (both of which foreshadow what happens regularly in SIMMES–CREEDE–STAFFORD–ELD2, but before the STAFFORD1 sheet F was printed); and the chance inactivity of the compositor when the first version of the E formes were printed (that neither forme of F had been imposed by the time both formes of E had been printed seems improbable). Accordingly, the likelihood is that the transfer was from F at the completion of its print run in an unreset state to the STAFFORD2 state of E, the outer forme of which had in the mean time been reset, and the inner forme subjected to authorial correction. Since sheets G–K of both ELD1 and 2 were printed in a different shop, no correspondence such as Bowers speculates on is possible between the running titles of E–F and G–K.

In reset outer E the presence of the 'HONEST WHORE' running titles in the same settings as seen in STAFFORD1 similarly argues that the state of this forme is earlier than that of outer E in the STAFFORD2 copies with the 'Courtizan' titles. Apart from the running titles the reset type contains no variants in outer E. To account for the unusual circumstance of NLS sheet E Bowers offers two possibilities: a number of copies of sheet E may have been impressed before the headline error was detected, or additional sheets may have been machined 'to make up a short count in Q1'. The fact that the irregular sheet E appears in a copy of SIMMES–CREEDE–STAFFORD–ELD2 rather than 1 would seem to oppose the latter possibility, however. As noted below, NLS sheet E is oddly balanced by sheet E in the Dyce copy of SIMMES–CREEDE–STAFFORD–ELD3, which similarly has running titles mismatched with those in other sheets. Bowers's claim that NLS contains only one reading variant from the other SIMMES–CREEDE–STAFFORD–ELD2 copies ('let' corrected from 'le' G4: 12.17) overlooks a second correction in the inner forme of this sheet: on G3ᵛ NLS prints 'beard' (11.19) in place of 'beasd' in the BODLEIAN and FOLGER2 copies.

The third edition, SIMMES–CREEDE–STAFFORD–ELD3, which survives in a single copy (Victoria and Albert Museum—V&A) with an imprint date of 1605, is in fact little more than a composite of previously imposed sheets from SIMMES–CREEDE–STAFFORD–ELD1 (C–D, F–G, I–K), a sheet of the same impression as SIMMES–CREEDE–STAFFORD–ELD2 (E), and sheets re-impressed from SIMMES–CREEDE–STAFFORD–ELD2 type (A–B, H), with a variant title-page, which reverts to 'The Honeſt Whore' in the title and head-title on A1 and A2 respectively, and in sheets A, B, and H from SIMMES–CREEDE–STAFFORD–ELD2

gives corresponding reset running titles. The 'HONEST WHORE' running titles of the SIMMES–CREEDE–STAFFORD–ELD1 sheets are no doubt responsible for the return to this title in SIMMES–CREEDE–STAFFORD–ELD3. In preserving the running title, 'The conuerted Courtizan.', sheet E in the SIMMES–CREEDE–STAFFORD–ELD3 copy demonstrates that it is of the same impression as that in SIMMES–CREEDE–STAFFORD–ELD2, a fact confirmed by collation with sheet E in the BODLEIAN and FOLGER2 copies. Whether any significance attaches to the instances of sheet E bearing mismatched headlines in both this and the NLS copy is difficult to determine. But the coincidence of anomalous headlines involving the same sheet in two copies prompts consideration of a relationship between them. To the possibilities advanced by Bowers to account for the faulty running titles of the NLS copy (erroneous impression of STAFFORD2 sheet E with STAFFORD1 running titles and a special make-up print run) may be added a third, which has implications for the circumstances of both the NLS and the V&A copies. Assuming that the count of E sheets bearing the respective running titles was closely coordinated with that of other sheets, if sheet E had been taken from the wrong end of the pile when the NLS copy was made up, a sheet (or sheets, if, as would seem likely, more than one copy was involved) with the wrong running title would in consequence be left over when the sheets for SIMMES–CREEDE–STAFFORD–ELD3 were assembled.

Sheet E is unique among STAFFORD2 sheets in not surviving in a state that reflects reversion to the original running title, a circumstance that may indicate that an extended run of sheets, or simply an 'over run' of the usual kind, bearing the 'HONEST WHORE' running titles was made in anticipation of SIMMES–CREEDE–STAFFORD–ELD3. In this respect the order of exemplars in this heap of sheets would differ from that of the heaps of other sheets in which a substitution of running titles was made late in the run for alignment with the SIMMES–CREEDE–STAFFORD–ELD1 titles. As Bowers notes, if additional copies of SIMMES–CREEDE–STAFFORD–ELD3 were to come to light some variation in the assortment of sheets from SIMMES–CREEDE–STAFFORD–ELD1 and SIMMES–CREEDE–STAFFORD–ELD2 would be likely. Formes in two of the sheets from SIMMES–CREEDE–STAFFORD–ELD1 which compose SIMMES–CREEDE–STAFFORD–ELD3 are represented in the uncorrected state: outer C, the variants of which are found only in the SIMMES–CREEDE–STAFFORD–ELD3 copy, and inner G; outer K is from the first stage of correction. Although Bowers's proposal that the early states of these formes possibly indicate that they were held back as slightly defective and later used as 'remainders' has some appeal, the uncorrected state of outer K (i.e. an earlier state than that in SIMMES–CREEDE–STAFFORD–ELD3) in the Huntington copy of SIMMES–CREEDE–STAFFORD–ELD1 argues against it. Perhaps the sheets bearing the formes' early states were simply at or near the bottom of the respective heaps of sheets left over when the decision to retitle the play and to print a second edition was taken. Apart from alterations contingent upon the change of the play's title affecting re-impressed SIMMES–CREEDE–STAFFORD–ELD2 sheets A–B and H used in SIMMES–CREEDE–STAFFORD–ELD3, they are invariant on SIMMES–CREEDE–STAFFORD–ELD2. No changes were made in the type of STAFFORD3 sheet E between STAFFORD2 and STAFFORD3 impressions. The textual authority of SIMMES–CREEDE–STAFFORD–ELD3 accordingly extends no farther than the authority of the respective sheets of SIMMES–CREEDE–STAFFORD–ELD1 or SIMMES–CREEDE–STAFFORD–ELD2 in other copies.

The following table summarizes the relationship between SIMMES–CREEDE–STAFFORD–ELD1 and SIMMES–CREEDE–STAFFORD–ELD2 in terms of the present edition:

1.0.1–2.68 (*Enter at one*...hee haz|) A2–4^v standing; slight disturbance affecting A3.

2.68–5.43 (not all...cleaner.|) B1–4^v reset

5.44–120 (*Geo.* You may...vext or moou'd?|) C1–1^v reset

5.121–2 (He has...angry : no,|) C2 reset: these lines were transferred from the top of C2 in CREEDE1 to the foot of C1^v in CREEDE2 to allow for the relineation of prose as verse in Fluello's aside on C2, 5.149–54 (*A filuer*...impatience.).

5.123–59 (The beft...100. Duccats.|) C2 standing; rearrangement of 5.149–54 and disturbance of 5.137 (man,patient boue wrong or woe,) and 5.140–140.1 (—*George*...*Exit George*.)

5.160–226 (*Pior.* Ile pledge...mifplace it.|) C2^v–3 reset

5.227–6.12 (Out of...looke|) C3^v mainly standing: some disturbance affects the type and a few words appear to have been reset.

6.13–55 (worfe now...to day.|) C4 standing; some disturbance to several lines.

6.55–99 (*I lay*...a manchet-*Ex.*|) C4^v reset

6.100–314 (*Caft.* Her's...fweepe vp all.|) D1–3 standing; some slight disturbances affecting spacing on D2^v.

6.315–47 (I fhould be...a fourth,|) D3^v mainly standing: beginning at 6.335 (Indeed ?) parts of the left side of the page pied and were reset as required.

6.348–419 (Should haue...your graues.|) D4–4^v standing

6.420–57 (From fooles...vertuous thoughts,|) E1 reset

6.458–7.24 (And on...y'are welcome.|) E1^v–2 standing

7.25–113 (*Fuft.* The Deuils...cambrick fir?|) E2^v–3 reset

7.114–97 (*Fuft.*Sfoot...your miftris.|) E3^v–4 standing

7.198–235 (*Wife.* Come...Carpet. *Enter George.*|) E4^v reset

7.236–78 (*Cand.*O well...patience.|) F1 reset

7.278–10.39 (*Wi.* Prythee...fweet skill,|) F1^v–4^v standing (except for some disturbance in the top seven lines of F2^v, 8.75–84 (*Rog.* Scuruy...

Pandar), and resetting of the last seventeen and a half lines of F3, 9.41–59 (I am not as...difeafes,|))

10.40–12.72 (Hath from...walking in there.|) G1–4^v reset

12.73–110 (*Cram.* No matter...me warme,|) H1 reset

12.111–85 (I thanke...nothing can,|) H1^v–2 standing

12.186–13.64 (Ile fweare...noble friend|) H2^v–3 reset

13.64–14.7 (*Hip.* Few...lies.|) H3^v–4 standing

14.8–48 (*Geo.* O yes...*firke mony*,|) H4^v reset

14.49–84 (As Parfley...mad men|) I1 reset

14.85–15.37 (*Caft.* I haue...none|) I1^v–2 standing

15.37–112 (goes to be...where he is|) I2^v–3 reset

15.113–95 (*Caft.* And...fee ime|) I3^v–4 standing

15.195–244 (ouer head...vnruly thus.|) I4^v reset

15.245–371 (1 *Mad.* Whip...good lucke.|) K1–2 standing

15.372–444 (*Bel.* You...calde|) K2^v–3 reset

15.444–554.2 (a Maidenhead...*Finis*) K3^v–4^v standing

The present edition uses SIMMES–CREEDE–STAFFORD–ELD1 as control text based on fresh collation of the four surviving copies together with those sheets of SIMMES–CREEDE–STAFFORD–ELD1 preserved in SIMMES–CREEDE–STAFFORD–ELD3. The analysis set out above calls for acceptance as authoritive those alterations to standing type in SIMMES–CREEDE–STAFFORD–ELD2 (with a small number of exceptions) and, among changes in reset type, only those encountered in sheet B and the reset pages of outer K. Otherwise, except in those instances in which variant readings preserved in unauthoritative reset type have been thought necessary or fitting, such variants have been rejected.

The present edition departs from the traditional practice initiated by Dyce of dividing the play into five acts in favour of preservation of the scenic structure partially set out in the early printed texts. Since *The Patient Man and the Honest Whore* contains no clear indications of a five-act structure, a return to fifteen scenes seems appropriate.

Although the play has by editorial convention since 1840 been entitled *The Honest Whore, Part 1*, in adopting *The Patient Man and the Honest Whore* this edition aims to restore the title that appears in Henslowe's diary, the earliest reference to the work. Henslowe's citation, in addition to occurring within a theatrical as opposed to a print context, balances the play's two main centres of interest by its provision of a unified double paradox. By contrast, the editorially conventional title, in featuring only a single paradox, misrepresents the play in important ways and additionally gives a sense of incompleteness. The second-edition print title, *The Converted Courtesan*, is deficient for similar reasons; and, in any case, this title appears to have been prompted by the specifically topical interest generated by Marston's *The Dutch Courtesan*. The first edition printed title and subtitle, *The Honest Whore*, with the Humours of the Patient Man and the Longing Wife, may have been provided by the publisher rather than either of the authors. Although *The Honest Whore, Part 1* usefully distinguishes this play from Dekker's sequel, the original play is no more likely to have been referred to as *Part 1* than other works that have spawned sequels when first produced, performed, or published. The Stationers' Register entry cited above significantly preserves Henslowe's order while adding as a third term reference to 'the longing wife', thereby lending support to *The Patient Man and the Honest Whore*.

Bowers minimizes the likelihood that Middleton may have been involved in the process of correction and revision, claiming his part in the play to be 'relatively minor'. But recent studies by David J. Lake, MacDonald P. Jackson, and Cyrus Hoy of the respective shares of the two authors disagree with him on this point. Although Dekker may have been responsible for revision of the play prior to and possibly in the course of printing, practically none of the changes introduced affects scenes or parts of scenes which betray Middleton's presence, or alters traits associated with Middleton.

SEE ALSO

Text: *Works*, 285
Music: this volume, 137
Authorship and date: this volume, 351

WORKS CITED

Previous Editions

Dodsley, R., ed., *A Select Collection of Old Plays*, 12 vols (1744), vol. 3

Reed, Isaac, ed., *A Select Collection of Old Plays*, 12 vols (1780), vol. 3

Scott, Walter, ed., *The Ancient British Drama*, 3 vols (1810), vol. 1

Collier, J. P., ed., *A Select Collection of Old Plays*, 12 vols (1825–27), vol. 3

Dyce, Alexander, ed., *Works*, 5 vols (1840), vol. 3

Shepherd, R. H., ed., Thomas Dekker, *Dramatic Works*, 4 vols (1873), vol. 2

Rhys, Ernest, ed., *The Best Plays of the Old Dramatists: Thomas Dekker* (1894)

Neilson, William Allan, ed., *The Chief Elizabethan Dramatists* (1911)

Walley, Harold Reinoehl, and John Harold Wilson, eds., *Early Seventeenth-Century Plays 1600–1642* (1930)

Spencer, Hazelton, ed., *Elizabethan Plays* (1933)

Bowers, Fredson, ed., Thomas Dekker, *Dramatic Works*, 4 vols (1955, rev. edn. 1964), vol. 2

Other Works Cited

Anon., *The Batchelars Banquet*, ed. F. P. Wilson (1929)

Berlin, Normand, 'Thomas Dekker: A Partial Reappraisal', *Studies in English Literature, 1500–1900* 6 (1966), 263–77

Blayney, Peter W. M., *The Texts of 'King Lear' and their Origins: Nicholas Okes and the First Quarto* (1982)

Bowers, Fredson T., *Bibliography and Textual Criticism* (1964)

—— 'Thomas Dekker: Two Textual Notes', *The Library*, IV, 18 (1937), 338–41

Daalder, Joost, and Antony Telford Moore, 'Breaking the Rules: Editorial Problems in Middleton and Dekker's *The Honest Whore, Part 1*', *Bibliographical Society of Australia and New Zealand Bulletin* 20 (1996), 243–87

—— '*Mandrakes* and *Whiblins* in *The Honest Whore*', *Studies in Philology* 94 (1997), 494–507

—— 'New Variants in the First Part of Dekker's *The Honest Whore*', *Notes and Queries*, NS 42 (1995), 342–4

Erasmus, Desiderius, 'Of the young man and the evil disposed woman', in *A Modest Mean to Marriage*, tr. Nicholas Leigh (1568)

Gies, Frances and Joseph, *Women in the Middle Ages* (1978)

Greene, Robert, 'The Conversion of an English Courtesan', in *A Disputation between a He Cony-Catcher and a She Cony-Catcher* (1592)

Greg, W. W., 'The Early Editions of Thomas Dekker's *The Converted Courtezan* or *The Honest Whore, Part I*', *The Library*, IV, 10 (1929), 52–60

—— '"The Honest Whore" or "The Converted Courtezan"', *The Library*, IV, 15 (1935), 54–60

Hoy, Cyrus, *Introductions, Notes, and Commentaries to texts in 'The Dramatic Works of Thomas Dekker'*, 4 vols (1980), vol. 2

Jackson, MacDonald P., *Studies in Attribution: Middleton and Shakespeare* (1979)

Kahn, Coppélia, *Man's Estate: Masculine Identity in Shakespeare* (1981)

Kistner, A. L., and M. K., '*1 Honest Whore*: A Comedy of Blood', *Humanities Association Bulletin* 23 (1972), 23–7

—— *Middleton's Tragic Themes* (1984)

Lake, David J., *The Canon of Thomas Middleton's Plays* (1975)

Leggatt, Alexander, *Jacobean Public Theatre* (1992)

Marcham, Frank, 'Correspondence: The Early Editions of Thomas Dekker's *The Converted Courtezan* or *The Honest Whore, Part I*', *The Library*, IV, 10 (1929), 339

Parrott, T. M., ed., George Chapman, *The Plays and Poems* (1914)

Pudsey, Edward, Commonplace Book: Bodleian Library MS. Eng. poet. d. 3. fol. 80

Reynolds, George F., 'Another Principle of Elizabethan Staging', *The Manly Anniversary Studies in Language and Literature* (1923), 70–7

Schoenbaum, S., 'Middleton's Share in "The Honest Whore", Parts I and II', *Notes and Queries* 197 (1952), 3–4

Spencer, Hazelton, 'Correspondence: The Undated Quarto of *1 Honest Whore*', *The Library*, IV, 16 (1935), 241–2

Ure, Peter, 'Patient Madman and Honest Whore: The Middleton–Dekker Oxymoron', *Essays and Studies* 19 (1966), 18–40

Weiss, Adrian, 'Bibliographical Methods for Identifying Unknown Printers in Elizabethan/Jacobean Books', *Studies in Bibliography* 44 (1991), 183–228

—— 'Font Analysis as a Bibliographical Method: The Elizabethan Play-Quarto Printers and Compositors', *Studies in Bibliography* 43 (1990), 95–164

Woodbridge, Linda, *Women and the English Renaissance* (1984)

TEXTUAL NOTES

In the following notes 'SIMMES1' and 'SIMMES2', 'CREEDE1' and 'CREEDE2', etc., depending on which printer set the relevant section, are used to designate the first and second 'editions' (SIMMES–CREEDE–STAFFORD–ELD1 and SIMMES–CREEDE–STAFFORD–ELD2) of *The Patient Man and the Honest Whore*. Similarly, SIMMES–CREEDE–STAFFORD–ELD3 and OKES4 represent the third and fourth 'editions'. The textual notes include a brief account of the relationship of standing to reset type at the start of each section. Where variant readings occur in standing and reset type, these are designated (S) and (R) respectively. Uncorrected and corrected readings are signified by (A) and (B) respectively.

Title The Patient Man and the Honest Whore] THIS EDITION; THE [xylographic] | Honeſt Whore, | With, | The Humours of the Patient Man, | and the Longing Wife. SIMMES1; THE [xylographic] | Converted Curtezan | With, | The Humours of the Patient Man, | and the Longing Wife. SIMMES2. The title adopted by the present edition attempts to recover what may well have been the play's original *theatrical*, as opposed to printed, title. Henslowe refers to *The Patient Man and the Honest Whore* in the earliest record of the play. See Textual Introduction.

Persons THIS EDITION; *not in* SIMMES1 & 2.

Sc. 1 THIS EDITION; ACTUS PRIMUS. SCÆNA PRIMA. SIMMES1 & 2; ACT I. SCENE I. DYCE. This edition has adopted the fifteen-scene structure partially preserved in SIMMES1 & 2's demarcation of Scenes 7 to 13 (omitting Scene 12) in preference to the act/scene division traditional since Dyce.

1.0.1–5.43 *Enter . . . cleaner.*] SIMMES1 & 2. This section of the play was printed by Valentine Simmes. Authoritative changes introduced into sheet B of reset SIMMES2 point to authorial presence. Reset sheet B runs from 2.68–5.43 (*not all . . . cleaner.*).

1.0.2 *scutcheons*] SIMMES1 & 2 (Scut-|chins)

1.0.3 *Trebazzi*] SIMMES1 & 2 (Trebatzi). This and other names have been modernized to their conventional modern Italian forms.

1.0.4 *Castruccio*] SIMMES1 & 2 (Caſtruchio). See note to 1.0.3 above.

1.0.5 *others. At . . . door*] NEILSON; *others at . . . doore.* SIMMES1 & 2. The punctuation in SIMMES1 & 2 indicates entrances associated with the funeral from two separate stage doors and no specification of the entrance point of Hippolito and Matteo. Since a re-arrangement of punctuation clears up the problem, compositorial error is the likely source. Apart from other considerations, two trains of mourners converging on the stage produce an unusual and unlikely pattern. Repositioning the full stop after '*others*' generates stage action at once clear, plausible, and effectively keyed to the play's primary opposed interests (at this stage of the narrative): a single funeral procession emanating from '*one door*' flanked on the other side of the stage by the entrance of Hippolito restrained by Matteo '*at another door*'.

1.0.6 *Matteo*] SIMMES1 & 2 (Matheo). See note to 1.0.3 above.

1.5 ALL THE MOURNERS] SIMMES1 & 2 (*All*)

1.9 you're] SIMMES1 & 2 (y'are)

1.17 ALL THE MOURNERS] SIMMES1 & 2 (*All*)

1.23 withered] DODSLEY 1 (wither'd); withered SIMMES1 & 2. The blank verse is regular in the passage in which *withered* appears and calls for metrical emendation to an unvoiced 'ed' preterite ending.

1.45 torment] SIMMES1 & 2; torrent *conj.* DYCE. Although not adopted by any editor, as Bowers remarks, Dyce's suggestion of 'torrent' is appealing especially in view of the flood image of 1.49–51, and water images in the Duke's speeches in Sc. 3. The SIMMES1 & 2 reading, 'torment', makes good sense, however, and, in contrast to 'torrent', additionally betrays that the Duke is nettled by Hippolito.

1.53 Nay, nay] SIMMES1 & 2 (Na, na)

1.54 Forwhy] SIMMES1 & 2 (For why); For why, DODSLEY 1. In accordance with Dyce and subsequent editors, *forwhy* is treated as a conjunction meaning 'because'. The absence of punctuation following SIMMES1 & 2's 'For why' supports such a reading. Although Bowers regards SIMMES1 & 2's colon at the end of the preceding line as rather heavy, and possibly cause for seeing *forwhy* adverbially, meaning 'for what reason', followed as in DODSLEY 1–3 by a comma, Hoy notes several parallel instances of a colon before the conjunction *forwhy*.

1.55 corpse] SIMMES1 & 2 (coarſe)

1.72 scarecrow] SIMMES1 & 2 (ſcarre-crowe)

1.73 Wrestle] SIMMES1 & 2 (wraſtle)

1.82 powder] SIMMES1 & 2 (powlder)

1.84 alicant] SIMMES1 & 2 (Aligant)

1.97–8 An . . . morning—] SIMMES1 & 2 (and . . . morning.)

1.97 ate] eat SIMMES1 & 2 (eat), SPENCER. SIMMES1 & 2's 'eat', though a common preterite form (it occurs also at 13.8), has been normalized to *ate*.

1.104 dead—drunk] NEILSON; dead drunke SIMMES1 & 2. The dash before *drunk* employed by Neilson underscores and clarifies Matteo's joke.

1.130 Infelice's] SIMMES1 & 2 (Infælices)

Sc. 2 DODSLEY 1; *not in* SIMMES1 & 2; ACT I. SCENE II. DYCE

2.6 *clarissimo*] SIMMES1 & 2 (Clariſſimo); clarissimo's DYCE. As Bowers notes, Dyce's emendation 'reflects the sense intended but is not required by the construction'.

2.29.1 *Viola, Candido's Wife*] THIS EDITION; *Viola* SIMMES1 & 2. Although SIMMES1 & 2 print *Viola* in this stage direction and in stints of different length as a speech heading in this scene (the whole scene in SIMMES1, the first part of the scene to 2.105 in SIMMES2). In the latter part of this scene beginning on B1ᵛ (2.106) in SIMMES2 and in subsequent scenes through the remainder of the play in SIMMES–CREEDE–STAFFORD–ELD1 & 2 the character is cited as *Wife* in speech headings and *Candido's Wife* in stage directions. This generic style carries implications for the dramatists' conception of the character. '*Viola*' is, however, both textually authorized and helpful to the reader, and has been preserved on this account.

2.33 WIFE] BOWERS; *Viola* SIMMES1 (*to end of scene*), SIMMES2 (*to bottom of B1*, 2.105). See note to 2.29.1 above.

2.44 two hundred] SIMMES1 & 2 (200.)

2.60 powder] SIMMES1 & 2 (powlder)

2.97 *Emblems*] SIMMES1 & 2. Editors from Dodsley 1 to Rhys masked Fustigo's ignorance by emending to *Problems*, a medical book published in London in 1595. The reading of SIMMES1 & 2 was restored by Neilson.

2.98 o'th'] SIMMES1 & 2 (ath)

2.102 mustachio] DODSLEY 1; muſtacho SIMMES1 & 2. SIMMES1 & 2's 'muſtacho' is a common variant of *mustachio*.

2.129 four hundred] SIMMES1 & 2 (400.)

2.130 lieutenant] SIMMES1 & 2 (Lievetenant)

2.135 madcaps] SIMMES2(R) (mad-caps); olde dames SIMMES1. A possible instance of authorial revision, but compositorial misreading cannot be ruled out.

2.136 o'my naunts] SIMMES2(R) (a my naunts); a mine aunts SIMMES1. A possible instance of authorial revision.

2.138 He's] SIMMES1 (Haz), SIMMES2(R) (H'az)

2.144 roars‸] SIMMES2(R); roares? SIMMES1. The reset SIMMES2 reading has been adopted in the belief that it reflects authorial revision. As discussed in the Textual Introduction, both formes of sheet B were completely reset, but in their reset states incorporate authoritative alterations. The change in punctuation is presumed to be among these. Bowers prefers SIMMES1's roares?, conjecturing that the query may be intended 'to represent a sample of Fustigo's swaggering'.

Sc. 3 DODSLEY 1; not in SIMMES1 & 2; ACT I. SCENE III. DYCE

3.0.1 Enter] DYCE; not in SIMMES1 & 2

3.0.1 Benedict] SIMMES2(R); Benedicke SIMMES1. As with a number of other variant readings between SIMMES1 and 2 in sheet B, the reset 'Benedict' is presumed to be authorial.

3.5 near] DODSLEY 1; meere SIMMES1 & 2. SIMMES1 & 2's meere is apparently the result of a misreading of minims; as the passage makes clear (especially 3.18), the glass is not 'mere [i.e. completely] spent', but 'near [i.e. almost] spent'.

3.6 Benedict] SIMMES2(R) (Benedict); Benedicke SIMMES1. See note to 3.0.1 above.

3.11 See] SIMMES2(R) (see); fweete SIMMES1. SIMMES1's 'sweete' makes little sense in the context and is possibly derived from compositorial misreading or misconstruction of the MS.

3.14 crust] DYCE; ruft SIMMES1 & 2. As Bowers observes, the imagery of a stream in winter (picked up again at 3.56–7) supports Dyce's emendation, although 'rust' escaped correction in reset SIMMES2.

3.32 Benedict] SIMMES2(R) (Benedict); Benedick SIMMES1. See note to 3.0.1 above.

3.35 Bergamo] SIMMES2(R); Bergaine SIMMES1. The SIMMES1 reading is clearly faulty—apparently the result of minim error combined with a final 'o' misread as an 'e'.

3.37 Infelice] SIMMES1 (Infælifha); Infælica SIMMES2(R). In accord with practice observed elsewhere, modern Italian forms of character names have been adopted. In the case of Infelice, the spellings 'Infelice' and 'Infælice' occur in subsequent scenes.

3.40 midst] SIMMES2(R); deadft SIMMES1. The SIMMES1 reading defies sense and is undoubtedly mistaken—most likely the result of compositorial misreading.

3.41 cup] SIMMES2(R); cap SIMMES1. As elsewhere, the SIMMES1 reading is faulty—presumably the result of a/u confusion.

3.44 alter] SIMMES2(R); alterd SIMMES1. Since a central element of the Duke's account concerns the suddenness of his daughter's transformation, SIMMES2's present tense seems more appropriate, and as in other instances in sheet B may reflect authorial revision.

3.52 BOTH SERVANTS] SIMMES1 (2 Servants); 2 Ser. SIMMES2(R). The Duke's praise to his good knaves, 3.52, supports the clear plural of the SIMMES1 reading. The abbreviated SIMMES2 form may have been intended to represent both servants, but it is undistinguished from the form used elsewhere as a speech heading for the second servant.

3.52 good knaves] SIMMES2(R); God knowes SIMMES1. The SIMMES1 error is likely to have arisen from a simple compositorial misreading of the MS.

3.54 Infelice] SIMMES1 (Infælifhæ); Infelica SIMMES2(R). See note to 3.37 above.

3.56 thy] SIMMES2(R); the SIMMES1. SIMMES1's 'the' is presumably a simple compositorial error.

3.66 I'd] SIMMES2(R) (Ide); Ile SIMMES1. The Duke's statement is clearly conditional and accordingly supports reset SIMMES2's abbreviation of 'I would'. The SIMMES1 reading may have come about through compositorial misreading.

3.71 hurts] SIMMES2(R) (hnrts); haunts SIMMES1. Although a case can be mounted in support of the SIMMES1 reading, in line with other apparently authoritative alterations encountered in the reset state of this sheet, the SIMMES2 reading makes clear sense and has been adopted as a probable authorial revision or correction.

3.76 deer] SIMMES1 & 2 (diere)

3.78 goddess] SIMMES2(R); gods SIMMES1

3.78 Cyprian] SIMMES2(R) (Ciprian); Coprian SIMMES1. The SIMMES1 reading, which is clearly at fault, may have arisen from compositorial misreading.

3.83 her] SIMMES2(R); it SIMMES1. The SIMMES2 reading may be the result of authorial revision.

3.89 Benedict] SIMMES2(R) (Benedict); Benedick SIMMES1. See note to 3.0.1 above.

3.92 may] SIMMES1; way SIMMES2. The clearly faulty SIMMES2 reading presumably springs from simple compositorial error.

Sc. 4 DODSLEY 1; not in SIMMES1 & 2; ACT I. SCENE IV. DYCE

4.20 will't] SIMMES1 & 2 (wilt)

4.52 tempted] SIMMES2(R); tempred SIMMES1. This change from SIMMES1's 'tempred', introduced in reset SIMMES2, makes a distinct improvement in sense, and so argues that it is the authoritative reading notwithstanding Bowers's caveat that confusion of 'r' and 't' is so frequent that the error may rest with either word. No simple explanation of 'tempred' corresponding to its sense at 4.31, for example, satisfactorily supports it here; even an ironic twist would need to turn itself inside out to do so, and then be uncertain of success.

Sc. 5 DODSLEY 1; not in SIMMES1 & 2; ACT I. SCENE V. DYCE

5.0.1–2 Enter…shop] SIMMES1 & 2; George and two Prentices discovered: enter Viola. DYCE

5.12 ALL THREE IN THE SHOP] SIMMES1 & 2 (All three)

5.44–6.419 GEORGE You may…to your graves:] CREEDE1 & 2. This section of the play was printed by Thomas Creede. Eleven pages of standing type are found in sheets C and D of CREEDE2 comprising all but C1ᵛ (5.82–120 'Sblood… moved?) of inner C (5.121–59 He has…ducats. and 5.227–6.55 Out of…today,) and practically all of both formes of sheet D (6.100–419 Here's…graves:). The remainder of this section, embracing outer C, C1ᵛ, and various pied lines on D3ᵛ including the bottom six (6.343–7 Shall I…a fourth), is reset in CREEDE2.

5.55 you're] CREEDE1 & 2 passim (y'are)

5.61 e'en] CREEDE1; euen CREEDE2(R). The expansion of e'en in CREEDE2 produces a hypermetrical line—probably a compositorial error.

5.63 conscionably] CREEDE1; confcionable CREEDE2(R)

5.63 eighteen shillings] CREEDE1 (18.s.); 18. CREEDE2(R)

5.66 seventeen] CREEDE1 & 2 (17.)

5.87 WIFE] DYCE (Vio.); Mist. CREEDE1 & 2

5.88 gentleman] CREEDE1 (Gentle-man); gentleemen CREEDE2(R). As Candido speaks only to Castruccio here, the reset CREEDE2 reading is in error. The same mistake in reset type occurs at 5.107.

5.107 gentleman] CREEDE1; Gentlemen CREEDE2(R)

5.108 Pray] CREEDE1; not in CREEDE2(R)

5.126 'twould] CREEDE2(s); would CREEDE1. Parallelism with the preceding line in addition to sense argues forcefully in favour of the standing-type CREEDE2 reading.

5.129 We are] CREEDE2(s); Were CREEDE1. The CREEDE2 reading restores the line's metre.

5.131 leese] CREEDE1 & 2. Although 'leese' and 'lose' carry the same meaning, the former is a morphologically distinct form rather than a mere spelling variant and has been retained on this account.

5.133 penn'orth] CREEDE1 & 2 passim (penworth)

5.137 patient 'bove] CREEDE2(s) (patient, boue); patient boue CREEDE1. Insertion of a comma before 'boue' in disturbed (possibly reset) type of CREEDE2 very likely records the compositor's misreading—or misplacement—of an apostrophe.

5.153 hundred] CREEDE 1 & 2 (100.)

5.156 to you] CREEDE2(s); you CREEDE1

5.159 hundred] CREEDE 1 & 2 (100.)

5.161 off;] CREEDE1 & 2 (off:); off, DYCE. The colon following 'off' in CREEDE1 & 2 connects the expression 'play't off' with the contemporary idiom found also in Hal's speech to Sir John in 1 Henry IV, 2.5.16–17. In telling Pioratto to play't off Fluello urges him to finish his drink; to me— is either a request to Pioratto to toast him or a call for the silver and gilt beaker, which he intends to make off with to vex Candido (and thereby to save Castruccio's wager, as set out in their asides 5.149–56), to be passed to him. Dyce's removal of punctuation following off presumably infers, as Bowers suggests, a transposition of pointing.

5.182 our] CREEDE1; your CREEDE2(R). The CREEDE1 reading allows Castruccio, who had been the instigator of the pretty sportive conceit (4.4) to move Candido's patience and of the wager of a hundred ducats, to conceal his debt in their general failure.

5.188 lie] CREEDE1 (lye); be CREEDE2(R). As elsewhere in this section, the authority of CREEDE1 is generally superior to reset CREEDE2 in apparently standing in closer relation to the MS, and has been followed on this account.

5.190 calm] CREEDE1; all calme CREEDE2(R). The addition of 'all' in CREEDE2 is difficult to account for: it would seem to be too distant from 'all' at 5.188 to have been contaminated by it. But since the reset type of this section is generally considered to be farther from the MS than the original setting, the latter has been followed.

5.196 Exit George] CREEDE1 & 2 (to the right of 'now?', 5.198). A shortage of space would appear to have been responsible for postponement of George's exit direction. The lineation of the final verse lines of Candido's speech (5.195–6) is abandoned and the line is turned over, and the first line of Viola's begins on the immediately following line ending a line below with 'now?'; the exit direction is right justified on this line. Viola's prose speech continues on the next line. The progress of the scene seems best served by repositioning the exit direction immediately after Candido's order.

5.211 sir] CREEDE1 & 2 passim (fyr)

5.219 wife's] CREEDE1 & 2 passim (wiues)

5.230 shame;] DODSLEY 1; fhame, CREEDE1 & 2. Bowers comments at length on the intricacies of this passage and difficulties associated with different punctuation found in the sequence running from 5.230–6 in CREEDE1 and CREEDE2(s). The pointing adopted reflects in the main his conclusions. Stronger punctuation than that provided by CREEDE1 & 2 is called for after shame to set off the following statement, which concludes with which is most cruel (5.234) and draws a contrast between the provocation given Candido and the feebler grounds which drive worldlings to exact cruel retribution, even loss of life. Alternative pointings fail to make clear

the contrast Candido describes or to establish that those who lose their lives are the victims of many worldlings. Punctuation changes introduced by the CREEDE2 corrector, as Bowers observes, indicate that he was apparently mistaken in his attempt to recover the passage's sense.

5.237 dost] CREEDE1 (doft); doeft CREEDE2(s). The CREEDE1 reading produces a decasyllabic line; the apparent extra syllable in the following line would probably be absorbed by the pronunciation of spirit as 'sprite'.

5.241 courtier] CREEDE2(s); carter CREEDE1. The CREEDE1 reading is manifestly faulty—presumably a result of compositorial error.

Sc. 6 THIS EDITION; not in CREEDE1 & 2; ACT II. SCENE I. DYCE

6.0.3 vial] CREEDE1 & 2 (violl)

6.9 here's] CREEDE1 & 2 (her's)

6.9 two] CREEDE1 & 2; twe CREEDE1

6.17 and] CREEDE2(s); not in CREEDE1

6.32–3 Down, down, down, down, I fall | Down, and arise I never shall] CREEDE2(s) (Downe, downe, downe, downe, I fall downe and arife, I neuer | fhall); Downe, downe, downe, down, I fall downe and arife, downe, I neuer fhall arife. CREEDE1. The appearance of the song from which this excerpt is taken, 'Sorrow, sorrow stay, lend true repentant tears', in John Dowland's Second Book of Songs or Airs (1600) provides an additional, independent authority for the song's correct wording. The phrasing of the conclusion of the song in the upper two voices in Dowland's collection closely matches the lyrics sung by Bellafront in standing CREEDE2 and accordingly provides collateral support for the authority of CREEDE2 over CREEDE1. The correspondence between CREEDE2 and Dowland is not exact, however. The initial sequence of descending notes through four statements of 'down' begins with 'but', and a repetition of 'and arise' immediately follows its first statement prior to the concluding 'I never shall'. But perhaps the snippet sung by Bellafront is not intended to give a faithfully detailed rendering of Dowland. The CREEDE1 wording interestingly conforms at one point with the bass voice of Dowland: 'I fall, downe & arise, downe', but it then departs from the song's 'and arise, arise I never shall'; if the base line were followed for this passage in its CREEDE1 version, possibly inadvertent transposition accounts for the rearrangement of the final phrase, 'I never shall arise'. Against this, however, is the opening fourfold sequence of 'downs', which in the bass line consists of six statements of the word. Alternatively, the CREEDE1 arrangement may merely represent a bungled attempt to repeat the 'down and arise' in the text of the song printed between the staves of music in the edition published in 1600.

6.34 mistress] CREEDE1 & 2 (M.)

6.37 of] CREEDE2(s); if CREEDE1. The CREEDE2 alteration in standing type corrects an apparently simple compositorial error.

6.42 no] CREEDE2(s); in CREEDE1. Although the readings in CREEDE1 and CREEDE2 may appear indifferent, the alteration introduced in CREEDE2 is clearly deliberate and seems designed to register Roger's repudiation of Bellafront's remark on his appearance solicited initially at 6.40.

6.45 Wha-at] CREEDE2(s) (Whaat); What CREEDE1. The standing type of CREEDE2 adds an 'a' to CREEDE1's 'What' apparently to record an extended syllable—possibly a feature of performance; Bellafront's sha-all at 6.269 suggests that this kind of utterance is characteristic of her.

6.52 BELLAFRONT] CREEDE2(s); Hell. CREEDE1

6.52 Roger] CREEDE1 & 2 (Ro.)

6.54 Sing, pretty] CREEDE1 & 2 (*Sing pretty*); (Sing) s.d. COLLIER. Numerous contemporary songs and madrigals incorporate this injunction into the text of their lyrics (apparently repeated in *warble*), so there seems no need to suppose that it is a stage direction as do several modern editors. The two preceding directions (6.24.1 and 6.45.1), both of which appear on the same page as this line, are indicative and accordingly do not encourage treatment of *Sing* as an imperative direction despite possible indications of space shortage. The line in which *Sing, pretty* occurs is the final line on the page and is preceded by doubled-up speeches. Since it does not occupy the full printer's measure, however, an alternative arrangement that clarified *Sing* as a direction, if that is what it is, would presumably have been possible.

6.67.1 *Roger fetches*] CREEDE2(R); *Roger Fetch* CREEDE1. Although the indicative occurs only in reset type, the grammar of CREEDE1 is clearly at fault. 'Roger' was possibly inscribed in the margin—an indication perhaps that the name was added at some stage subsequent to the original writing out of the MS.

6.76 *Exit for a candle*] CREEDE1 & 2 (*Exit. for a candle.*)

6.78.1 *Enter Roger*] CREEDE1 & 2(R) ((*Enter Roger.*)

6.85 angels] CREEDE1 (Angels); Anhels CREEDE2(R)

6.98 three shillings and sixpence] CREEDE1 & 2(R) (iij.s.vi.d.)

6.100 Herculean] CREEDE2(s); *herculaniā* Creede1. Possibly an instance of authorial revision or correction.

6.102 Faugh] CREEDE1 & 2 passim (Fah)

6.108–9 I there...scorn't] CREEDE1 & 2. Bowers remarks that although CREEDE1 & 2's 'I' may be read as a pronoun or exclamation (ay), he favours the former. He also notes that other editors have inserted a pronominal 'I' before *scorn't*, but regards the CREEDE1 & 2 usage as possibly a representation of current 'fashionable speech' which omitted the pronoun, as in numerous instances in *The Honest Whore, Part 2*.

6.114 Malavolta] CREEDE2(s); *Malauella* CREEDE1. In this and other changes involving names introduced in standing CREEDE2 the alterations appear to signal the intervention of an author.

6.117 Lollio] CREEDE2(s); *Lollilo* CREEDE1. See note to 6.114 above.

6.137 Sordello] CREEDE2(s); *Lord Ello* CREEDE1. See note to 6.114 above.

6.143 to] CREEDE2(s); of CREEDE1. Since the standing-type CREEDE2 reading is clearly correct, CREEDE1's 'of' presumably derives from compositorial error of some kind.

6.157 a-tilt] THIS EDITION (Dyce); a litle CREEDE1 & 2. Dyce's conjecture has considerable appeal. It is at once more idiomatic (the term occurs also at 15.305) and sounds rather more convincing in Roger's pretence than CREEDE1 & 2's 'a litle'. A simple misreading of the MS could have given rise to the error.

6.187 heed] CREEDE2(s); heard CREEDE1. As in other instances involving corrections introduced in standing type for the CREEDE2 impression, the alteration marks a clear improvement and may be attributable to authorial intervention.

6.194 —[*To Bellafront*] Beseech you, sweet.—] BOWERS; -beseech you sweete, CREEDE1 & 2. The punctuation in this passage follows Bowers and assumes that *Beseech you, sweet* is a parenthetical remark addressed to Bellafront, accompanied presumably by stage business of some kind either aimed at enlisting her aid to draw Hippolito into their company, or requesting permission or approval from her to *bestow a banquet* upon him. This arrangement is designed to reflect the notion that Fluello urges Hippolito not to shun their fellowship be-

cause of Infelice's death (*for all that*) and accordingly invites him to join Bellafront's circle. As Bowers notes, Dyce and subsequent editors place a dash after *for all that* presuming this phrase to mark the conclusion of a 'parenthetic apology to Bellafront for Fluello's praise of Infelice and the assertion that this praise does not affect their admiration of Bellafront.' *Come, let us serve under the colours of your acquaintance still* is more likely addressed to Hippolito, however; and *Beseech you, sweet* seems more plausible and natural in reference to Bellafront than Hippolito, especially since the speaker has just made Hippolito's acquaintance but is clearly on familiar terms with Bellafront.

6.197 the] CREEDE2(s); my CREEDE1. Creede1's 'my' is apparently the result of compositor error.

6.207 Never; trust me,] BOWERS (Neuer, trust me); Neuer truft me CREEDE1 & 2. Stronger punctuation after *me*, as Bowers points out, runs counter to the idiom, restated by Hippolito at 6.229, which is favoured here over the alternative arrangement (e.g. 2.33) for character consistency.

6.215 have it] CREEDE2(s); ha CREEDE1

6.222 your] CREEDE2(s); you CREEDE1

6.228 ALL THE GALLANTS] CREEDE1 & 2 (*Omni.*)

6.239 O] CREEDE1 & 2 (Oh)

6.240 Hippolito] DYCE; *Hipolitos* CREEDE1 & 2

6.242 an] CREEDE1 & 2 (&)

6.244 Bellafront] CREEDE2(s) (*Bellafronte*); *Bellafronta* CREEDE1

6.244 An] CREEDE1 & 2 (&)

6.264 for] CREEDE2(s); I, for CREEDE1. Possibly an instance of authorial revision.

6.266 It's...Antelope] CREEDE1 & 2 (*Its done at Th'antilop*). Italicization in CREEDE1 & 2 sets off the statement in an unusual manner—possibly an indication that the line mimicked a phrase of a song or well-known catchphrase now lost.

6.274 —your scurvy mistress here—] CREEDE2(s) (your scurny miftris heere,); *not in* CREEDE1. The CREEDE2 addition may be a revision or correction, either of which may derive from authorial intervention.

6.285–6 six shillings] CREEDE1 & 2 (vi.s.)

6.295 please stay] CREEDE1; pleafey CREEDE2(s) [*type dropped out*]

6.297 If I may] CREEDE2(s); *Hipo. If* may CREEDE1

6.319 O] CREEDE1 & 2 (ô)

6.340 would] CREEDE2(s); could CREEDE1

6.352–4 if you'll...my eyes...and led] CREEDE2(s); beleeue it, I | No fooner had laid vpon your prefence, | But ftraight mine eye conueid CREEDE1. Although he adopts the CREEDE2(s) reading for this passage, Bowers preserves CREEDE1's 'mine' over CREEDE2(s)'s 'my', presumably because he sees no call for emphasis. CREEDE2(s)'s more emphatic 'my' may be intentional, however, and is presumably a component of the authorial revision evident elsewhere; it has been preferred on this basis.

6.356 fashion] CREEDE2(s); paffion CREEDE1. The CREEDE1 reading is probably the result of compositorial misreading; its correction in standing-type CREEDE2, however, may derive from authorial involvement.

6.377 It's] CREEDE2(s) (Its); Is CREEDE1. Bowers discusses at some length the thorny matter of the two corrections in this speech and links them to problems of mislineation in CREEDE1 & 2: CREEDE1 'Is' to CREEDE2(s) 'Its', and CREEDE1 'Is' to CREEDE2(s) 'Tis' (6.379), only the first of which has been accepted. He argues that 'Its' at 6.377 is the correct reading. 'Tis', two lines later, on the other hand, could have been brought about by the same or another compositor's failure to observe that the correction had already been made.

If a marginal indication were not precisely placed, moreover, as is frequently the case, a glance at the corrected page could give the impression that it had not yet been corrected, thus giving rise to the second, erroneous alteration. Bowers remarks also on the scheme of the speech and its progress from considering first Bellafront's soul and then her body. He accordingly reads *For* at 6.376 as 'as for' rather than 'because'. Misconstruction as 'because' may have led the CREEDE I compositor to set '*Is*' for '*Its*'. As a misplaced correction at 6.379, '*Tis*' offers an alternative reading for the correction at 6.377. Against this Bowers points out that the compositor's use of a lower case 't' in his correction of '*Is*' at 6.377 is incompatible with a corrector's marginal marking of '*Tis*'. Further, if, as seems likely, only a 't' had been marked for insertion, '*Its*' is very likely the correct reading. Although '*tis*' is without question the favoured form in the play (69 usages), '*it's*' occurs ten times excluding the present instance. But '*it's*' is also a form specifically associated with Dekker and appears on three other occasions along with a range of other evidence of Dekker's presence in this scene. Accordingly, *It's* is the form adopted.

6.377 shore] CREEDE I & 2 (fhoare)

6.379 Is] CREEDE I; Tis CREEDE2(s). See note to 6.377 above.

6.407 Back-doored] DODSLEY I; Blacke-doord CREEDE I & 2. Several scholars have in recent decades established the authority of this emendation first adopted by Dodsley. R. K. Turner connected the sense of *back-doored* with 'anal intercourse' (*Notes and Queries* 205 (1960), 25–6) citing a passage from Marston's *Insatiate Countess*, Act II (ed. Wood, III, 29). Additional support has been provided by Richard Levin (*Notes and Queries* 208 (1963), 338–40), MacDonald P. Jackson (*Notes and Queries* 209 (1964), 37), and Hoy.

6.420–10.39 From fools...sweet skill] STAFFORD I & 2. This section of the play was printed by Simon Stafford. Sheets E and F in STAFFORD2 contain eleven pages of standing type: the inner formes of E (6.458–7.24 *And on...welcome.* and 7.114–97 '*Sfoot...mistress.*) and F (7.278–8.74 *Prithee, George...a pox?*) and three pages of outer F: F2ᵛ–F3 (8.75–9.59 *Scurvy...diseases,*), and F4ᵛ (10.0.1–10.39 *Enter... skill*); outer E, F1, and part of F3 of outer F are reset (essentially 5 pages).

6.461 Lust] STAFFORD I & 2 (*Luft*)

6.465 mete] STAFFORD I & 2 (meat)

6.476 I see] STAFFORD2(s); See STAFFORD I

6.491 O] STAFFORD I & 2 (Oh)

6.496 His weapon left here?] STAFFORD2(s); What! has he left his weapon heere behind him, | And gone forgetfull? STAFFORD I. An instance of authorial revision.

6.498 master] STAFFORD I & 2 (M.)

6.501 cleave my bosom on] STAFFORD2(s); split my heart vpon STAFFORD I. An instance of authorial revision.

6.506 Not look! Not bid farewell!] STAFFORD2(s); not bid farewell! a fcorne! STAFFORD I. An instance of authorial revision.

6.505.1 Exit] DODSLEY I; *Exeunt* STAFFORD I & 2

Sc. 7 STAFFORD I & 2 (SCENA 7.); ACT III. SCENE I. DYCE

7.1 gentleman] THIS EDITION; Gentlemen STAFFORD I & 2. Since Fustigo is the only potential customer present, the singular seems more appropriate. Similar confusion over 'gentleman' and 'gentlemen' at 5.88 and 5.107, although in a section printed in a different establishment, suggests that the error was not uncommon—possibly attributable to the orthography.

7.23 I] STAFFORD2(s)(B); A STAFFORD I, STAFFORD2(s)(A)

7.31 melancholy] STAFFORD I & 2 (mallicolly). Although the STAFFORD I & 2 spelling could perhaps be defended as an alternate form or as a malapropism, *OED* records it as a spelling common in the 16th C. for the noun at least (it is curiously not listed for the adjective). In light of its currency in this connection, modernization seems the most sensible treatment.

7.47 lip] STAFFORD I; lips STAFFORD2(R). The plural form, *lips*, like other variants which occur on this sheet in reset STAFFORD2, is without authority—presumably the result of compositorial error. Moreover, the singular here echoes the singular at 7.45.

7.53 sh'has] STAFFORD I & 2 (fha's)

7.66 thee] STAFFORD I & 2 (the)

7.73 Zounds] STAFFORD I & 2 (Zwounds)

7.79 thorough] STAFFORD I (thorow); through STAFFORD2(R)

7.85 do't.] STAFFORD I & 2; do't. [*Exit Second Prentice.* DYCE. See note to 7.91 below.

7.91 *Exit Second Prentice*] BOWERS; *Exit* I. *prentice* STAFFORD I & 2. Acceptance of STAFFORD I & 2's direction, '*Exit* I. *prentice*', calls for emendations involving an earlier exit for Second Prentice and alteration of the speech heading from '2. *pr.*' to 'I. *pr.*' at 7.88. Assignment of the exit to First Prentice is more likely mistaken. Emendation to '*Exit Second Prentice*' makes better stage sense and more neatly resolves attendant difficulties since it follows up the opportunity this character has created to leave the stage in search of material stored in the warehouse (which need not be acted upon), and enables him to return a few moments later with the pretence of Signor Pandulfo to remove Candido from the on-stage action. As Bowers argues, no call for apprentices beyond George and the first or second is required at 7.108–9 and 7.140, a consideration that takes some account of the personnel resources of the theatre; Fustigo is most likely beaten only by these three at 7.152.1 (the signal for other prentices to enter, 7.80–1, is never sounded). Further, reassignment of this exit direction to Second Prentice removes the need for speeches delivered within at 7.108–9 and 7.140.

7.107 FUSTIGO...Ay, when...pieces?] STAFFORD I; *not in* STAFFORD2(R)

7.108 ALL THE PRENTICES] STAFFORD I & 2 (*Omn*[*es*].)

7.112 you're] STAFFORD I & 2 *passim* (yare)

7.116 thrum] STAFFORD2(s)(B); thrumb STAFFORD I & 2(s)(A)

7.121 Here's] STAFFORD2(s); here STAFFORD I

7.134 thread] STAFFORD I & 2 (thrid)

7.136 twenty] STAFFORD I & 2 (20.)

7.140 ALL THE PRENTICES] STAFFORD I & 2 (*Omn*[*es*].); Prentices [*within*]. DYCE. See note to 7.91 above. Dyce's arrangement calling for a statement from offstage prentices is related to the exit of First Prentice prescribed by STAFFORD I & 2 at 7.91 and a presumption that the sequence outlined by Second Prentice, 7.79–84, is followed precisely.

7.141 thump] STAFFORD2(s); thrum STAFFORD I

7.151 ALL THE PRENTICES] STAFFORD I & 2 (*Om*[*nes*].); Geo., First and Sec. P., and other Prentices rushing in. DYCE. See note to 7.140 above.

7.158 does 't] STAFFORD I & 2 (dooft)

7.169 ningle] STAFFORD2(s) (Ningle); mingle STAFFORD I. Presumably the result of misreading due to minim error.

7.170 folly] STAFFORD I(B) & 2(s); ᴌy STAFFORD I(A)

7.202 on edge] STAFFORD I & 2 (an edge)

7.213 fashioned] STAFFORD I & 2 (fafhioned). The preterite ending in STAFFORD I & 2 calls for metrical emendation to preserve the iambic pentameter.

7.214 O] STAFFORD1 & 2 (oh)

7.216 Troth] STAFFORD1; Truth STAFFORD2(R)

7.218 thief's] STAFFORD1 & 2 (Theeues/theeues)

7.247.1 *Exit*] STAFFORD1 & 2 (*Exit Ge.*)

7.258 master] STAFFORD1 & 2 (M.)

7.280 covert-baron] STAFFORD1 & 2 (couert barne)

Sc. 8 STAFFORD1 & 2 (SCENA 8.); ACT III. SCENE II. DYCE

8.19 twelve] STAFFORD1 & 2 (12.)

8.20 BAWD] OKES4; *not in* STAFFORD1–3. Although no heading precedes the Bawd's speech, the speech begins on a new line and is indented.

8.33 ambergris] STAFFORD1 & 2 (Amber greece)

8.35 O] STAFFORD1 & 2 (oh)

8.54 that slave] STAFFORD1 & 2 (that flaue). Understood to be in apposition to *Thou* (presumably directed to Roger), the reading of STAFFORD1 & 2 makes adequate sense. Bowers surmises that *that* may have been misread for a repeated *thou* (yᵘ), or a manuscript 'yᵉ' misread as 'yᵗ', but dismisses these alternatives as no more attractive than the STAFFORD1 & 2 reading.

8.61 God damn…within!] STAFFORD1 & 2 (*God dam me, Gentlemen, if fhe be within,*). Recourse to italics in STAFFORD1 & 2 may simply signify emphasis or quotation, or may be designed to register a more sophisticated effect such as Bellafront's mimickry of the bawd or Roger.

8.63–4 every man…vocation] STAFFORD1 & 2. The sense, 'let every man abide in his vocation', could plausibly be conveyed in performance; so, although the phrase is elliptical, there seems no warrant for emendation.

8.66 gentlemen.] DODSLEY 1; gentlemen? STAFFORD1 & 2

8.93 Milan] STAFFORD1 & 2 (Millain)

Sc. 9 STAFFORD1 & 2 (SCENA 9.); ACT III. SCENE III. DYCE

9.1 BELLAFRONT] DYCE; *not in* STAFFORD1 & 2. Although STAFFORD1 & 2 omit the speech heading, there can be no doubt of the speaker.

9.6 gallant's] DODSLEY 1; *gallant* STAFFORD1 & 2. The possessives of each representative type specified earlier in the song argues strongly for emendation to *gallant's*.

9.10 O] STAFFORD1 & 2 (Oh)

9.19.1 *Fluello, and*] STAFFORD2(S); *Fluello,* STAFFORD1

9.29 forgot] STAFFORD1 & 2 (forgat)

9.54 being slaves] STAFFORD1; being flaue STAFFORD2(R). The reset STAFFORD2 reading is presumably the result of compositorial error.

9.55 blossoms] STAFFORD1; bloffom STAFFORD2(R). The lower right part of F3 appears to have pied and was reset; the resetting presumably gave rise to the error.

9.60–9 And all…alone] STAFFORD1 & 2(S). A narrow printer's measure was used for these lines. In this section four lines, 9.61, 62, 67, and 68 (com-|pany), were justified.

9.62 gallants] DYCE; gallät STAFFORD1 & 2(S). The line in which 'gallant' occurs occupies the full width of a narrow measure used for Bellafront's verse speech and resorts to 'gallät' apparently to conserve space. A lack of room may have been responsible for the failure to set the final 's'. Dyce's emendation is aptly keyed to the context and connects with the plural at 9.60.

9.72 fist] STAFFORD1 & 2 (fyfte)

9.78 ALL THE REST] STAFFORD1 & 2 (*Omn[es].*)

9.113 O] STAFFORD1 & 2 (Oh)

9.120 Marry, faugh] STAFFORD1 & 2 (mary foh)

Sc. 10 STAFFORD1 & 2 (SCENA 10.); ACT IV. SCENE I. DYCE

10.5 master] STAFFORD1 & 2 (M.)

10.40–15.554.2 Hath…*Finis*] ELD1 & 2. Sheets G to K were printed by George Eld. Sections of ELD2 printed from standing type consist of inner H (12.111–85 *I thank…nothing can*; and 13.64–14.7 *Few…lies?*), inner I (14.85–15.37 *I have…none* and 15.113–95 *And where…I'm*), inner K (15.286–371 *lessons…good luck.* and 15.444–521 *a maidenhead…Loathe it?*) and K1 (15.245–86 *Whip me? Out… bawdy*) and K4ᵛ (15.522–554.2 *For he…Finis*) of outer K. The remaining parts, both formes of G, outer H, outer I, K2ᵛ and K3 of outer K are reset.

10.63 plots] ELD2(R); plot ELD1. Although it appears in the reset ELD2 state, the plural appears to be the appropriate reading. ELD1's singular may be attributable to compositorial error.

10.74 gayness] ELD1 & 2 (*Gay-nes*)

10.88 wicked faces] ELD1 & 2. Bowers notes the analogous collocation of painters and wrinkled faces in Dekker's *Whore of Babylon*, 2.1.125, together with an occurrence of *wicked* in *The Shoemakers' Holiday*, 3.2.45, and questions whether the reading 'wrinkld faces' might have been intended, though the error which generated *wicked* would need to have been duplicated independently. In an attempt to make sense of *wicked* he postulates that Dekker may have indulged in a forced private pun involving 'wicks' = lips, the allusion being to ugly faces featuring prominent lips or large mouths.

10.94 person] ELD1 & 2 (parfon)

10.100 for] ELD1 & 2; from DYCE. The Servant's statement appears to play on the special appeal of a cross-dressed female. His citation of foods considered to be aphrodisiac are accordingly keyed to an imagined exciting encounter with a woman dressed as a man (a similar reference occurs in *Roaring Girl*, 8.45–56). Dyce's emendation improbably sets the effect of stimulating foods against a woman appealingly dressed in breeches. Even in the unlikely circumstance that the cross-dressed Bellafront was deemed unattractive, it would be difficult to reconcile the Servant's reference to aphrodisiac dishes with fortified resistance to her.

10.131 *buon coraggio*] ELD1 & 2 (*Boon couragio*). The spelling of ELD1 & 2 corresponds most closely to the Italian *buon coraggio*, which connects with the nominal setting in Milan.

10.147.1 *Exit*] ELD1 (*to right of* 10.145); *not in* ELD2(R)

10.153 beat'st] ELD2(R) (beatft); beats ELD1

10.168 might'st] ELD1; mighteft ELD2(R). The line in which 'might'st' occurs is already hypermetrical, so the additional syllable called for by 'mightest' is most likely without authority—probably a simple compositorial error.

10.182 He'll] ELD1 & 2 (Hele)

10.183 O] ELD1 & 2 (oh)

10.184 Though] OKES4 (Tho); The ELD1–3

10.200 Go.—Woman] ELD1 (go: woman); goe woman ELD2(R). The punctuation of ELD1 coordinates with Hippolito's *Go* addressed to his servant (rather than Bellafront as other editors, presumably guided by ELD2, have supposed), followed by *Woman, fare thee well* directed to Bellafront. Possibly the ELD2 compositor misread the colon as a lightly printed 'e'.

Sc. 11 ELD1 & 2 (11. SCE.); ACT IV. SCENE II. DYCE

11.0.2 *Poh*] ELD2(R); *Poli.* ELD1. The compositor of ELD1 apparently misread the MS in setting *Poli* for *Poh* here and elsewhere.

11.4 up] ELD2(R); *not in* ELD1

11.7 nine] ELD1 & 2 (9.)

11.19 beard] ELD1, ELD2(R)(B); beasd ELD2(R)(A)

11.27 I'll] ELD1 & 2 (ile); ide BOWERS. Bowers's emendation, although attractive, is not essential; the ELD1 & 2 reading makes sense as it stands. In addition, the simple future conveys an element of immediacy lost in 'I'd'.

11.34 tavern] ELD1 (taueren); tauern ELD2(R). ELD1's spelling probably resulted from a misplaced final 'e'; the ELD1 spelling at 11.40 is 'tauerne'.

11.48 *Exit*] NEILSON; *Exeunt* ELD1 & 2. Various arrangements of exit directions are possible, but that adopted deviates only marginally from ELD1 & 2, involving emendation of *Exeunt* to *Exit*. Poh apparently leaves the stage earlier than the others, who talk of him briefly after he departs.

11.49 *Poh is*] ELD2(R) (*Poh is*); *Poli*. Is ELD1. The compositor of ELD1 apparently misconstrued the erroneously spelled *Poli*. as a speech heading and set the speech beginning 'Is as tall . . .' as the joint declaration of Crambo and Poh (Poli).

Sc. 12 THIS EDITION; ACT IV. SCENE III. DYCE

12.18 court'sy] ELD1 & 2 (curtzy)
12.56.1 Poh] ELD2(R); Poli ELD1
12.72 POH] ELD2(R); *Poli*. ELD1
12.82.1 [*Exit Candido . . . cloth*]] THIS EDITION; *not in* ELD1 & 2. ELD1 & 2 offer no assistance in clarifying whether Candido or Second Prentice is sent to fetch the *striped canvas* (12.79). Dyce designated Second Prentice to fetch the cloth in his stage direction but wondered in a footnote if Candido should perform this duty. Candido's eagerness to serve as an apprentice in this scene provides the primary rationale for his exit to retrieve the canvas. The adopted arrangement carries the additional benefits of giving George an opportunity to act with a measure of authority not previously seen, and of providing sharper definition to the comic inversion.

12.88 O] ELD1 & 2(R) (ô)
12.97 Zounds] ELD1 & 2(R) (Zownes)
12.108 CRAMBO *and* POH] ELD1 & 2 (*Both*)
12.117 phrase] ELD2(s); praife ELD1.
12.118.1 Candido's] ELD2(s); his ELD1
12.120 OFFICER] ELD1 & 2 (*Off*.). Although more than one officer enter at 12.118.1, ELD1 & 2 do not distinguish them in the distribution of speeches. Any reassignment to one or division between the two would be arbitrary since no pattern of speech, attitude, position or other traits sets them apart.

12.125, 128, 136, 167 O] ELD1 & 2 (oh)
12.172 sewster's] THIS EDITION; Sifters ELD2(s); Cifters ELD1. The emendation adopted is closely related to ELD1 & 2's variants of 'sisters' in both spelling and sound. It additionally conveys the sense of the passage more effectively.

12.179 O' God's] ELD1 & 2(s) (A Gods)
Sc. 13 ELD1 & 2 (13. SCE.); ACT IV. SCENE IV. DYCE
13.14 pour't] ELD1 & 2 (power't)
13.35 far] ELD2(R); for ELD1. A possible instance of authorial revision.
13.43 dipped] ELD2(R) (dipt); deept ELD1. Reset ELD2's 'dipt' possibly records the kind of sophistication associated with an author witnessed elsewhere (cf. *far* at 13.35). Alternatively, 'dipt' may stand as a modernization of ELD1's 'deept', a word that, if not obsolete, probably verged on obsolescence by 1604. If ELD2's alteration amounts to no more than this, the reading may be accepted as an unauthoritative but correct emendation of ELD1. The sense of *dipped* seems more closely coordinated than the sense of *deeped* with the passage in which it occurs: the doctor wishes to allay any fears the Duke may have concerning his readiness to undertake other murderous acts—possibly against the Duke himself—now that the Duke believes him to be tainted with the blood of one man. The degree of immersion suggested by *dipped* appears

better suited to the doctor's argument than the hyperbole of 'deeply plunged' ('deept').

13.54 digs] ELD1; dig ELD2(R)
13.58 he's] ELD1 & 2(R) (has)
13.60 January] ELD1 & 2(R) (Ianiuere)
13.63 I'th' lurch] ELD2(R) (Ith lurch); Itch lnrch ELD1
13.66 send] ELD1 & 2(R); sent DODSLEY I. The ELD1 & 2 reading is satisfactory in denoting an action continuing into the present; emendation to the preterite is unnecessary.
13.96 her own interment] ELD1 & 2(s). The reference is to the supposed burial of Infelice following the funeral of Sc. 1, of which she has been kept in ignorance. Doctor Benedict has by *letters* (13.95) informed Infelice of events that have transpired without her knowledge; no emendation is called for.
13.109 bands] ELD2(s); bonds ELD1
Sc. 14 THIS EDITION; *not in* ELD1 & 2(s); ACT V. SCENE I. DYCE
14.7 George] ELD1 & 2(s) (Geroge)
14.52 stormiest] DODSLEY I (stormyest); ftormeft ELD1 & 2(R). The omission of 'i' in ELD1 & 2 would be a very easy error in a row of minims, especially with the influence of *calmest*. Elision would presumably resolve the metre problem.
14.53 True] DYCE; Tame ELD1 & 2(R). ELD1 & 2's 'Tame' could have come about as a result of a simple misreading. As Bowers notes, it is more likely that a misreading gave rise to 'Tame' than that the Wife contests the argument of the final line of George's cheese-trencher posy, pointing out that 'tame' rather than 'calm' husbands make their wives stormy; and that her storming days are over.
14.59.1 Sinezi] OKES4; Sinere ELD1–2(R)–3. The opening stage direction to Sc. 1 and references at 15.63, 15.90, and the stage direction at 15.86.2 establish that *Sinezi* is the correct form.
14.60 O] ELD1 & 2 (Oh)
14.83 DUKE] OKES4; Caft[ruchio]. ELD1–2(R)–3. Since Castruccio has not yet entered when this order is given, and Castruccio seeks to know where the Duke is in his initial line, the speech heading is clearly at fault. The problem is most readily resolved by reassigning the line to the Duke.
Sc. 15 THIS EDITION; *not in* ELD1 & 2; ACT V. SCENE II. DYCE
15.28 amongst] ELD1 & 2(s) (amonft)
15.35 so] OKES4; o ELD1–2(s)–3
15.46 ALL THE REST] ELD1 (Omn[es].), ELD2(R) passim (Omn[es].)
15.52 CASTRUCCIO] ELD2(R); Chaftruchio ELD1
15.59 O . . . O] ELD1 & 2 (Oh . . . oh)
15.59-61 Son, . . . hence?] ELD2(R); Sonne . . . your | enemy . . . hêce. ELD1. The rearrangement of Anselmo's speech as verse in reset ELD2 may well signify authorial presence behind this and one or two other changes on this page (K2ᵛ).
15.68-9 You . . . disguise, | O happy man!] THIS EDITION; You . . . Friers. | Hip[olito]. O bleft . . . man. ELD1 & 2. The ELD1 & 2 arrangement obscures both versification and rhyme. The arrangement adopted completes the pentameter (with allowance for elision) and establishes the rhyme with *eyes*.
15.68 disguise] ELD2(R); difguifde ELD1
15.72 not] ELD2(R); nor ELD1. The reset ELD2 reading has been preferred on the basis of possible authorial intervention on this page (I2ᵛ) collateral with the relineation of Anselmo's speech as verse (15.59-61).
15.79 frighted] ELD2(R); fraighted ELD1. ELD1's 'fraighted' is not listed by OED as a variant spelling of *frighted*; it may be an idiosyncratic spelling springing either from the MS or the compositor.

15.83   O] ELD1 & 2 (Oh)

15.102.1   *Enter...Sweeper*] THIS EDITION; *Enter Towne like a ſweeper.* ELD1 & 2. ELD1 & 2 preserve the name of Thomas Towne, an actor with the Admiral's (subsequently Prince Henry's) Men at this point. The citation of the actor's name in the stage direction and in speech headings (see note to 15.106 below) is an unusual feature for a non-theatrical text.

15.103   O] ELD1 & 2 (Oh)

15.106   SWEEPER] DYCE; *Tow.* ELD1 & 2 *passim*

15.116   A'mighty] ELD1 & 2 (a mighty)

15.124, 132, 135   O] ELD1 & 2 (Oh)

15.148   countryman] ELD2(s) (Country man); Country men ELD1

15.153   Anselm] ELD2(s); *Anſelmo* ELD1. ELD2's '*Anselm*' is presumed to be authorial.

15.175   He's] ELD1 & 2 (Has)

15.177   himself] ELD2(s); his wits ELD1. A possible instance of authorial revision.

15.194   further] ELD1 & 2 (furder)

15.207   ALL THE VISITORS] ELD1 & 2(R) *passim* (*Omn[es]*.)

15.214   verjuice] ELD1 & 2 (vergis)

15.235   goes] ELD1; goe ELD2(R)

15.235   O, O, O] ELD1 & 2(R) (oooh)

15.254   O, O] ELD1 & 2(s) (oh, oh)

15.263   save] ELD1(B) and ELD2(s); haue ELD1(A)

15.271   SECOND MADMAN] ELD1 & 2(s); Third Mad. DYCE. Presumably on the strength of the manner in which Anselmo introduces them, Dyce reversed the speech headings of the Second and Third Madmen. But ELD1 & 2's arrangement can stand; Second Madman is probably so named because he is the next madman to speak, not because he entered before his fellow.

15.278   O] ELD1 & 2(s) (ô)

15.292   THIRD MADMAN] ELD1 & 2(s); Sec. Mad. DYCE. See note to 15.271 above.

15.303, 305   thou't] ELD1 & 2(s) (thow't)

15.304, 307   Woo't] ELD1 & 2(s) (Wut)

15.305   a-tilt] ELD1 & 2(s) (a tilt)

15.309   O! O!] ELD1 & 2(s) (Ooh!)

15.329   curtsy] DODSLEY 1 (curt'sy); curſie ELD1 & 2(s)

15.342   Three] ELD2(s); The're ELD1

15.353   Marry, faugh] ELD1 & 2(s) (mary ſo)

15.361   one, two, three, and four] ELD1 & 2(s) (1. 2. 3. and 4.)

15.364-5   you ha' good...spun] ELD2(s); heres your fortune ELD1. An instance of authorial revision.

15.367.1-15.368   [*Infelice*] *bows a little* | The] THIS EDITION; Bow a little, the ELD1 & 2(s) (*prefixed as text to* 15.368). ELD1 & 2's setting of *bow a little* in roman, undistinguished from Bellafront's speech, seems most likely to derive from a stage direction. Bellafront has no clear reason to bow; but Infelice has been advised by Hippolito to *steal hence* when she *spies time* (15.351). In the arrangement adopted here she attempts to steal away as Bellafront appears to reach the end of her speech, bowing to her as a prelude to parting; but Bellafront continues and forestalls her escape.

15.375   wit] ELD1(B) & ELD2(R); wet ELD1(A)

15.375-7   Troth...here] THIS EDITION; Troth ſo does your noſe, nay lets ſhake hands with you too: | Pray open, heres a fine hand, | Ho Fryer ho, God be here ELD1; Troth ſo does your nofe: nay lets ſhake hands with you too | Pray open, hers a fine hand, | Ho Frier ho, God be here ELD2(R). Irregular versification in combination with miscued rhymes reveal the lineation of ELD1 & 2 to be faulty. The rhyme of *nose* in the first line of Bellafront's speech with *goes* (15.374) establishes that this part line completes that begun by Matteo (*O, your*

wit drops.). A full blank verse line ending with *pray open* follows; and a pattern emerges when the parallelism of *Here's a fine hand...* and *Here's a free table...* is recognized. Each is part of an iambic pentameter line and each rhymes with a tetrameter.

15.387   ALL THE GALLANTS] ELD1 (*Omn[es]*.) and ELD2(R) *passim* (*Omn[es]*,)

15.399   She's mine by marriage] ELD1; *Anſel[mo]*: Shees mine by marriage ELD2(R). See note to 15.400 below.

15.400   ANSELMO] ELD2(R) ('*Ansel:*' prefixed to 15.399); not in ELD1. ELD1 is clearly at fault in failing to provide a speech heading for Anselmo at this point; and reset ELD2 introduces the heading a line early—possibly derived from the compositor's misunderstanding of the correction. If, as seems likely, ELD1 were used as copy-text for ELD2, the addition of the speech heading may be a result of authorial attention.

15.419   conquered] ELD2(R) (conquerd); conquered ELD1. The reset ELD2 reading registers a metrical correction—possibly a sign of authorial revision.

15.423-4   content; | I throw...consent.] DODSLEY 1; confent, | I throw...confent. ELD1-2(R)-3; confent, | I throw... content. OKES4. As Bowers notes, reset ELD2 provides no guidance on the matter of which *consent* is correct. Bowers favours retention of *consent* at 15.423 and emendation to *content* at 15.424, arguing that the first instance is more likely to have contaminated the second, as is usual in such cases, and cites the independent support of OKES4. Despite Bowers's claim that 'No serious change in meaning is involved whichever *consent* is emended to *content*', however, the traditional emendation of the first *consent* to *content* produces what appears to be a reading that coordinates more naturally with the sense of the passage: *Yours now is my content* accordingly means 'what contents you now contents me'; and the Duke's *consent* in the following line confers his blessing on the marriage.

15.425   fine fortune-teller? God's me] ELD2(R); good girle, for finding the Frier in the wel? gods ſo ELD1. An instance of authorial revision.

15.427   for telling how...not?] ELD2(R); because I am ſo good a fortune teller. ELD1. An instance of authorial revision.

15.431   soul?] ELD2(R); foule? I know you: Is not your name Mathæo. ELD1. An instance of authorial revision.

15.432-41   MATTEO No...very fine jewel] ELD2(R); [*Bell[afront]*.] I know you: Is not your name *Mathæo*. | *Mat[hæo]*. Yes lamb. | *Bell[afront]*. Baa, lamb! there you lie for I am mutton; looke fine man, he was mad for me once, and I was mad for him once, and he was madde for her once, and were you neuer mad? yes I warrant, I had a fine iewell once, a very fine iewell and that naughty man ſtoale it away from me, a very fine iewell ELD1. An instance of authorial revision. Neither ELD1 nor ELD2(R) gives Matheo the answer *No* at 15.432, but Bellafront's *nay*, 15.433, and a possible pun on *noses*, 15.434, call for a negative reply to her question at 15.431. Bowers conflates ELD1's *for* with the reset ELD2 phrase *I am mutton*, 15.438-9, but the passage makes clear sense without resort to the ELD1 reading.

15.432   No] BOWERS; You ELD2(R). See previous note.

15.443-4   golden jewel, hark, 'twas] ELD2(R); very rich iewell, ELD1. An instance of authorial revision.

15.444-5   that naughty...not] ELD2(s); had not you it ELD1. An instance of authorial revision.

15.448   *Singing*] THIS EDITION (Taylor); not in ELD1

15.448   O] ELD1 & 2(s) (ô)

15.449   then, shall he!] ELD2(s); then? ELD1. An instance of authorial revision.

15.458 Father] ELD2(s); Nay then, father ELD1. An instance of authorial revision.

15.470-2 first mad'st me…brow] ELD2(s); didſt firſt turne my foule black, | Now make it white agen, I doe proteſt, | Ime pure as fire now, chaſte as *Cynthias* breſt ELD1. An instance of authorial revision.

15.496-7 husband, that…Orlando] ELD2(s); husband mad ELD1. An instance of authorial revision.

15.507 DUKE Why, signor, came you hither? | CANDIDO O my good lord!] ELD2(s); *not in* ELD1. An instance of authorial revision.

15.510 was my] ELD2(s); was yet my ELD1. An instance of authorial revision.

15.514 O] ELD1 & 2(s) (ô)

15.532 patience] ELD1 & 2(s) (*Patience*)

PRESS VARIANTS

1. Press Variants in SIMMES–CREEDE–STAFFORD–ELD1

Copies collated:

(i) BL (British Library C.34.c.24)
FOLGER1 (Folger Shakespeare Library—copy 1)
HUNT (Henry E. Huntington Library)
NYPL (New York Public Library)

(ii) V&A (the CREEDE–STAFFORD–ELD1 sheets, C-D, F-G, I-K, found in the unique copy of SIMMES–CREEDE–STAFFORD–ELD3 in the Dyce Collection, National Art Library, Victoria and Albert Museum, London)

Sheet C (outer forme)

Corrected: BL, FOLGER1, HUNT, NYPL
Uncorrected: V&A (CREEDE3)

Sig. C2ᵛ

5.183 cheaters] CREEDE1(B); chraters CREEDE1(A)

Sig. C4ᵛ

6.65 damned] dambde CREEDE1(B); dambe CREEDE1(A)
6.77 Fluello?] *Fluello?* CREEDE1(B); ~. CREEDE1(A)

Sheet E (inner forme)

Corrected: BL, FOLGER1
Uncorrected: HUNT, NYPL

Sig. E4

7.170 folly] STAFFORD1(B); ₐl₍ₐ₎y STAFFORD1(A)

Sheet G (inner forme)

Corrected: FOLGER1
Uncorrected: BL, HUNT, NYPL, V&A (ELD3)

Sig. G2

10.118 woo] wooe' ELD1(B); ~. ELD1(A)

Sig. G3ᵛ

11.49 CRAMBO Poh is] *Cram.Poh. is* ELD1(B); *Cram.Poli. Is* ELD1(A)

Sheet K (outer forme)

First stage corrected: V&A (ELD3)
Uncorrected: FOLGER1, HUNT

Sig. K2ᵛ

15.375 wit] ELD1(B); wet ELD1(A)

Second stage corrected: NYPL

Sig. K1

15.263 save] faue ELD1(B); haue ELD1(A)

Third stage corrected: BL

Sig. K4ᵛ

15.541 sings,] ſings, ELD1(B); ~⌐ ELD1(A)

2. Press Variants between SIMMES–CREEDE–STAFFORD–ELD1 and Standing Type in SIMMES–CREEDE–STAFFORD–ELD2

The following list attempts to set out changes introduced in standing type originally set for SIMMES–CREEDE–STAFFORD–ELD1 prior to (and in the case of one forme, in the course of) impression of SIMMES–CREEDE–STAFFORD–ELD2.

Copies collated:
(i) FOLGER2 (Folger Shakespeare Library—copy 2)
BODLEIAN (Bodleian Library, Oxford)
NLS (National Library of Scotland, Edinburgh)

(ii) V&A (Dyce Collection, National Art Library, Victoria and Albert Museum, London: sheets E and H)

Sheet A (outer forme)

First stage corrected: BODLEIAN, NLS, FOLGER2
Original: SIMMES1

Sig. A1

BODLEIAN and FOLGER2 lack A1.
title-page line 2 Converted Curtezan] SIMMES2; Honeſt Whore, SIMMES1
title-page lines 8-9 and are to be folde by Iohn | Hodgets at his ſhoppe] SIMMES2; for Iohn Hodgets, and are to | be folde at his ſhop SIMMES1

Sig. A3

1.58 MATTEO] *Matheo* SIMMES2; *Mathew* SIMMES1

Sigs. A2ᵛ, A3, A4ᵛ

running title The converted Curtezan.] SIMMES2; The Honeſt Whore. SIMMES1

Second stage corrected: V&A

Sig. A1

title-page line 2 Honeſt Whore] SIMMES3; Converted Curtezan SIMMES2
title-page line 10 1605] SIMMES3; 1604 SIMMES2

Sigs. A2ᵛ, A3, A4ᵛ

running title The Honeſt Whore.] SIMMES3; The converted Curtezan. SIMMES2

Sheet A (inner forme)

First stage corrected: BODLEIAN, NLS, FOLGER2
Original: SIMMES1

Sig. A2

head-title *Converted Curtezan*] SIMMES2; *Honeſt Whore* SIMMES1

Sigs. A3ᵛ, A4

running title   The converted Curtezan.] SIMMES2; The Honeſt Whore. SIMMES1

Sig. A4

1.141   lived so long] livde, ſo long SIMMES2; livde ſo long, SIMMES1

Second stage corrected: V&A

Sig. A2

head-title   *Honeſt Whore*] SIMMES3; *Converted Curtezan* SIMMES2

Sigs. A3ᵛ, A4

running title   The Honeſt Whore.] SIMMES3; The converted Curtezan. SIMMES2

Sheet C (inner forme)

Corrected: BODLEIAN, NLS, FOLGER2
Uncorrected: CREEDE1

Sig. C2

Two lines from the top of C2 (5.120–1) in CREEDE1 were transferred to the foot of C1ᵛ in CREEDE2.

running title   *CVRTIZAN.*] CREEDE2; *THE HONEST WHORE.* CREEDE1
5.126   'twould] CREEDE2; would CREEDE1
5.129   We are] CREEDE2; Were CREEDE1
5.129   here] CREEDE2; heere CREEDE1
5.137   patient] patient, CREEDE2; ~ₐ CREEDE1
5.137   woe] wo CREEDE2; woe CREEDE1
5.150–4   beaker...impatience.] beaker, ſure twil fret him, | It cannot chooſe but vexe him, *Seig. Caſtruchio,* | In pittie to thee, *I* haue a cõceit, | Wil faue thy 100. Duckets yet,twil doot, | And worke him to impatience. CREEDE2; beaker: I haue a tricke to worke vp-|on that beaker, ſure twil fret him, it cannot chooſe but vexe | him, *Seig. Caſtruchio,* in pittie to thee, *I* haue a cõceit, wil faue | thy 100. Duckets yet, twil doot, & work him to impatience. CREEDE1
5.159   Here to you,] heere to you CREEDE2; -heere you CREEDE1

Sig. C3ᵛ

running title   *THE CONVERTED*] CREEDE2; *THE HONEST WHORE.* CREEDE1
5.227   sufferance] ſufferance CREEDE2; ſufferaence CREEDE1
5.231   grounds—] grounds; CREEDE2; groundes, CREEDE1
5.233   palm,] palme, CREEDE2; ~: CREEDE1
5.235   lives.] liues: CREEDE2; ~, CREEDE1
5.237   dost] doeſt CREEDE2; doſt CREEDE1
5.241   courtier] CREEDE2; carter CREEDE1
6.4   I'm] *I'me* CREEDE2; *Ime*
6.9   two] CREEDE2; twe CREEDE1

Sig. C4

running title   *CVRTIZAN.*] CREEDE2; *THE HONEST WHORE.* CREEDE1
6.17   and your poker] CREEDE2; your pocker CREEDE1
6.17–18   together upon] together | vpon CREEDE2; together vp-|on CREEDE1
6.19   hams] hammes CREEDE2; hames CREEDE1
6.32–3   down...shall] *downe, I fall downe and ariſe, I neuer* | *ſhall.* CREEDE2; *down, I fall downe and ariſe, downe, I ne-|uer ſhall ariſe.* CREEDE1
6.37   of] CREEDE2; if CREEDE1
6.42   no, faith] no faith, CREEDE2; infaithₐ CREEDE1
6.45   Wha-at] Whaat CREEDE2; What CREEDE1

6.52   BELLAFRONT] *Bell.* CREEDE2; *Hell.* CREEDE1

Sheet D (outer forme)

Corrected: BODLEIAN, NLS, FOLGER2
Uncorrected: CREEDE1

Sig. D1

running title   *CVRTIZAN.*] CREEDE2; *THE HONEST WHORE.* CREEDE1
6.100   Herculean] Herculian CREEDE2; herculaniã CREEDE1
6.114   Malavolta] *Malauolta* CREEDE2; *Malauella* CREEDE1
6.117   Lollio] *Lollio* CREEDE2; *Lollilo* CREEDE1
6.135   salt] falt CREEDE2; fault CREEDE1
6.137   Sordello] *Sordello* CREEDE2; *Lord Ello* CREEDE1
6.139   citizen] itizen CREEDE2; Citizen CREEDE1
6.143   to a] CREEDE2; of a CREEDE1

Sig. D2ᵛ

running title   *THE CONVERTED*] CREEDE2; *THE HONEST WHORE.* CREEDE1
6.232   can;] can, CREEDE2; ~ₐ CREEDE1
6.244   Bellafront] *Bellafronte* CREEDE2; *Bellafronta* CREEDE1
6.251   melancholy] me-|(lancholy CREEDE2; ma-|(lancholy CREEDE1
6.264   for] CREEDE2; I for CREEDE1
6.273–4   mistress...here] miſtris in | minde, your ſcurny miſtris heere, CREEDE2; miſ-|treſſe in mind CREEDE1
6.277   hackney] hackny CREEDE2; hackney CREEDE1

Sig. D3

running title   *CVRTIZAN.*] CREEDE2; *THE HONEST WHORE.* CREEDE1
6.295   please stay,] pleaſeyₐ CREEDE2; pleaſe ſtay, CREEDE1
6.296   much.] much.' CREEDE2 (with lowered comma from the line above); much. CREEDE1
6.297   If] *If I* CREEDE2; *Hipo. If* CREEDE1

Sig. D4ᵛ

running title   *THE CONVERTED*] CREEDE2; *THE HONEST WHORE.* CREEDE1

Sheet D (inner forme)

Corrected: BODLEIAN, NLS, FOLGER2
Uncorrected: CREEDE1

Sig. D1ᵛ

running title   *THE CONVERTED*] CREEDE2; *THE HONEST WHORE.* CREEDE1
6.159   accursed] accurs'd CREEDE2; a curſt CREEDE1
6.170   presently,] CREEDE2; ~ₐ CREEDE1
6.180   servant—] ſeruantₐ CREEDE2; ~? CREEDE1
6.187   heed] CREEDE2; heard CREEDE1

Sig. D2

running title   *CVRTIZAN.*] CREEDE2; *THE HONEST VVHORE.* CREEDE1
6.197   the] CREEDE2; my CREEDE1
6.214   wench.] CREEDE2; ~: CREEDE1
6.215   have it] haue it CREEDE2; ha CREEDE1
catchword   *Hipe.*] CREEDE2; *Hipo.* CREEDE1

Sig. D3ᵛ

Six lines at the foot of the page appear to have been reset in CREEDE2.

running title   *THE CONVERTED*] CREEDE2; *THE HONEST WHORE.* CREEDE1
6.334   red] read CREEDE2; red CREEDE1

6.340　would] CREEDE2; could CREEDE1
6.341　drown] CREEDE2; drowne CREEDE1
6.341　spheres] ſpheres CREEDE2; ſphers CREEDE1

Sig. D4

running title　*CVRTIZAN.*] CREEDE2; *THE HONEST WHORE.* CREEDE1
6.352　if you'll believe] if youle beleeue CREEDE2; beleeue it, I CREEDE1
6.353　My honest tongue, my eyes no sooner met you] My honeſt tongue, my eyes no ſooner met you, CREEDE2; No ſooner had laid hold vpon your preſence, CREEDE1
6.354　But they conveyed and led] But they conueid and lead CREEDE2; But ſtraight mine eye conueid CREEDE1
6.356　fashion] faſhion CREEDE2; paſſion CREEDE1
6.377　It's] Its CREEDE2; Is CREEDE1
6.379　Is] Tis CREEDE2; Is CREEDE1

Sheet E (inner forme)

First stage corrected: NLS
Original: STAFFORD1

Sig. E1ᵛ

6.476　I see] I ſee STAFFORD2; See STAFFORD1

Sig. E2

6.496　His weapon left here?] his weapon left heere? STAFFORD2; What! has he left his weapon heere behind him, | And gone forgetfull? STAFFORD1
6.501　cleave my bosom on] cleaue my boſome on STAFFORD2; ſplit my heart vpon STAFFORD1
6.506　Not look! Not bid farewell!] not looke! not bid farewell! STAFFORD2; not bid farewell! a ſcorne! STAFFORD1

Sig. E3ᵛ

7.121　Here's] heres STAFFORD2; here STAFFORD1
7.141　thump] STAFFORD2; thrum STAFFORD1

Sig. E4

7.169　ningle] Nin-|gle STAFFORD2; min-|gle STAFFORD1

Second stage corrected: BODLEIAN, V&A, FOLGER2

Sig. E1ᵛ

running title　*The converted Courtizan.*] STAFFORD2(B); *THE HONEST WHORE.* STAFFORD2(A), STAFFORD1

Sig. E2

running title　*The converted Courtizan.*] STAFFORD2(B); *THE HONEST WHORE.* STAFFORD2(A), STAFFORD1
7.23　I] STAFFORD2(B); A STAFFORD2(A), STAFFORD1

Sig. E3ᵛ

running title　*The converted Courtizan.*] STAFFORD2(B); *THE HONEST WHORE.* STAFFORD2(A), STAFFORD1
7.112　thrum] STAFFORD2(B); thumb STAFFORD2(A), STAFFORD1

Sig. E4

running title　*The converted Courtizan.*] STAFFORD2(B); *THE HONEST WHORE.* STAFFORD2(A), STAFFORD1

Sheet F (outer forme)

Sig. F1

This signature was reset.
　　Corrected: BODLEIAN, NLS, FOLGER2
　　Uncorrected: STAFFORD1

Sig. F2ᵛ

running title　*The conuerted Courtizan.*] STAFFORD2; *THE HONEST WHORE.* STAFFORD1
8.83　walk] walke STAFFORD2; walk STAFFORD1

Sig. F3

running title　*The conuerted Courtizan.*] STAFFORD2; *THE HONEST WHORE.* STAFFORD1
9.41　I…I] I…I STAFFORD2; I…I STAFFORD1
9.42　I was…I'll] I was…Ile STAFFORD2; I was…Ile STAFFORD1
9.45　thou'rt] thart STAFFORD2; th'art STAFFORD1
9.52　than] then STAFFORD2; thē STAFFORD1
9.52　poisons] poiſons STAFFORD2; poyſons STAFFORD1
9.54　being slaves] being ſlaue STAFFORD2; being ſlaues STAFFORD1
9.55　seldom…ere…blossoms] ſeldom…e're…bloſſom STAFFORD2; ſeldome…ere…bloſſoms STAFFORD1

Sig. F4ᵛ

running title　*The conuerted Courtizan.*] STAFFORD2; *THE HONEST WHORE.* STAFFORD1

Sheet F (inner forme)

　　Corrected: BODLEIAN, NLS, FOLGER2
　　Uncorrected: STAFFORD1

Sig. F1ᵛ

running title　*The conuerted Courtizan.*] STAFFORD2; *THE HONEST WHORE.* STAFFORD1
8.34　silk] ſilke STAFFORD2; ſilk STAFFORD1
8.35　a body] a | body STAFFORD2; a bo-|dy STAFFORD1

Sigs. F2, F3ᵛ, F4

running title　*The conuerted Courtizan.*] STAFFORD2; *THE HONEST WHORE.* STAFFORD1

Sheet H (inner forme)

　　First stage corrected: BODLEIAN, NLS, FOLGER2
　　Original: ELD1

Sig. H1ᵛ

running title　*THE CONVERTED*] ELD2; *THE HONEST WHORE.* ELD1
12.117　phrase] phraſe ELD2; praiſe ELD1
12.118　Help] help ELD2; helpe ELD1
12.118.1　*Candido's*] ELD2; *his* ELD1
12.123　Officers?] officers? ELD2; ~‸ ELD1

Sig. H2

running title　*CVRTIZAN.*] ELD2; *THE HONEST WHORE.* ELD1
12.171　cord!] corde! ELD2; ~, ELD1
12.172　sewster's] Siſters ELD2; Ciſters ELD1

Sig. H3ᵛ

running title　*THE CONVERTED*] ELD2; *THE HONEST WHORE.* ELD1
13.81　mourning] ELD2; morning ELD1
13.87　wooed] woode ELD2; wode ELD1
13.90　thither—] thither——— ELD2; ~? ELD1

Sig. H4

running title   *CVRTIZAN.*] ELD2; *THE HONEST WHORE.* ELD1
13.106   away this night] away (this night) ELD2; ~, ~ ~ₐ ELD1
13.109   bands] ELD2; bonds ELD1
13.120   spread] ſpred ELD2; ſprede ELD1

Second stage corrected: V&A

Sigs. H1ᵛ, H3ᵛ

running title   *THE HONEST WHORE.*] ELD3; *THE CONVERTED* ELD2

Sigs. H2, H4

running title   *THE HONEST WHORE.*] ELD3; *CVRTIZAN.* ELD2

Sheet I (inner forme)

Corrected: BODLEIAN, NLS, FOLGER2
Uncorrected: ELD1

Sig. I1ᵛ

running title   *THE CONEVRTED*] ELD2; *THE HONEST WHORE.* ELD1
14.97   Monastery] *Monaſterie* ELD2; *Monaſtarie* ELD1

Sig. I2

running title   *CVRTIZAN.*] ELD2; *THE HONEST WHORE.* ELD1

Sig. I3ᵛ

running title   *THE CONVERTED*] ELD2; *THE HONEST WHORE.* ELD1
15.148   countryman] Country man ELD2; Country men ELD1
15.153   Anselm;] *Anſelm,* ELD2; *Anſelmo.* ELD1

Sig. I4

FOLGER2 lacks I4.
running title   *CVRTIZAN.*] ELD2; *THE HONEST WHORE.* ELD1

Sheet K (outer forme)

Corrected: BODLEIAN, NLS (FOLGER2 lacks sheet K)
Uncorrected: ELD1

Sig. K1

running title   *CVRTIZAN.*] ELD2; *THE HONEST WHORE.* ELD1

Sig. K4ᵛ

BODLEIAN lacks K3–4.
running title   *THE CONVERTED*] ELD2; *THE HONEST WHORE.* ELD1

Sheet K (inner forme)

Corrected: BODLEIAN, NLS (FOLGER2 lacks sheet K)
Uncorrected: ELD1

Sig. K1ᵛ

running title   *THE CONVERTED*] ELD2; *THE HONEST WHORE.* ELD1

Sig. K2

running title   *CVRTIZAN.*] ELD2; *THE HONEST WHORE.* ELD1
15.342   Three] ELD2; The're ELD1
15.342   gudgeons?] gudgeons! ELD2; ~, ELD1
15.346   here;] here, ELD2; ~ₐ ELD1
15.364–5   you ha'...spun;] you ha good fortune (now [turned under] | O fee, fee what a thred heres ſpun, ELD2; heres your fortune, ELD1

Sig. K3ᵛ

BODLEIAN lacks K3.
running title   *THE CONVERTED*] ELD2; *THE HONEST WHORE.* ELD1
15.444–5   that naughty man had it, had you not] ELD2; had not you it ELD1
15.449   then, shall he!] then ſhall he! ELD2; then? ELD1
15.458   Father] ELD2; Nay then, father ELD1
15.470   first mad'st me] firſt madſt me ELD2; didſt firſt turne my foule ELD1
15.470–1   me | White...now] mee white as before, I vow to thee Ime now ELD2; it white agen, I doe proteſt ELD1
15.472   As chaste...brow] As chaſte as infancy, pure as *Cynthias* brow ELD2; Ime pure as fire now, chaſte as *Cynthias* breſt ELD1

Sig. K4

BODLEIAN lacks K4.
running title   *CVRTIZAN.*] ELD2; *THE HONEST WHORE.* ELD1
15.496–7   husband,...Orlando] husband, that was as patient as *Iob*, to be more mad then euer was *Orlando* ELD2; husband mad ELD1
15.498   placed] ELD2; placde ELD1
15.499   Yonder] yonder ELD2; youder ELD1
15.507   DUKE Why...hither?] Duke. why Signior came you hether? | Cand. O my good Lord! ELD2; *not in* ELD1
15.510   was my] ELD2; was yet my ELD1

STAGE DIRECTIONS

Except at 10.147.1, and occasional minor discrepancies in spelling, fount, and punctuation, the stage directions between SIM-MES–CREEDE–STAFFORD–ELD1 and SIMMES–CREEDE–STAFFORD–ELD2 are in general agreement. The following list records the directions found in SIMMES–CREEDE–STAFFORD–ELD1 except where SIMMES–CREEDE–STAFFORD–ELD2 is significantly variant; in such instances readings from both are given.

1.0.1–7   *Enter at one doore a Funerall, a Coronet lying on the Hearſe, Scut-|chins and Garlands hanging on the ſides, attended by* Gaſparo | Trebatzi, Duke *of* Millan, Caſtruchio, Sinezi. Pioratto | Fluello, *and others at an other doore. Enter* Hipolito *in diſcon-|tented apparance:* Matheo *a Gentleman his friend, labouring | to hold him backe.*
1.46.1–2   *Exeunt with funerall.*
1.71.1   *Mathæo holds him ins armes*

1.148   *Exeunt.*
2.0.1–2   *Enter* Fuſtigo *in some fantaſtike Sea-suite at one | doore, a Porter meets him at another.*
2.29   *Exit. (to right of 2.28)*
2.29   *Enter* Viola. *(after 2.28)*
2.151   *Exit. (after 2.150)*
2.152   *Exit.*
3.0.1–2   Gaſparo *the Duke,* Doćtor Benedicke, *two ſervants.* SIM-MES1; Gaſparo *the Duke,* Doćtor Benedićt, *two ſervants.* SIM-MES2(R)
3.83   *Exit.*
3.89   *(Exeunt. (after 3.87)*
3.100   *Exeunt*
4.0.1   *Enter* Caſtruchio, Pioratto, *and* Fluello.
4.63   *Exeunt.*

5.0.1–2   *Enter Candidoes wife, George, and two prentices | in the* | *fhoppe.*
5.11.1   *Enter Caftruchio, Fluello, and* Pioratto.
5.45.1   *Enter Candido.* (*to right of* 5.45)
5.140.1   *Exit George.* (*to right of* 5.140)
5.144.1   *Enter Georg.*
5.147.1   *Exit George.*
5.156.1   *Enter George.* (*to right of* 5.156)
5.182.1   (*Exeunt.* (*to right of* 5.182)
5.196   (*Exit George.* (*to right of* 5.198, 'now')
5.209.1   (*Exit.* (*to right of* 5.208)
5.209.2   *Enter Caftruchio, Fluello, Pioratto, and George.*
5.247.1–2   (*Exeunt.*
6.0.1–8   *Enter Roger with a ftoole, cufhin, looking-glaffe, and* | *chafing-difh,* | *Thofe being fet downe, he pulls out of his pocket,* | *a violl with* | *white cullor in it. And* 2. *boxes, one with white,* | *another red* | *painting, he places all things in order & a candle* | *by thē, finging* | *with the ends of old Ballads as he does it. At* | *laft Bella-|front (as he rubs his cheeke with the cullors, whiftles* | *with-|in.*
6.15.1–3   *Enter Bellafronte not full ready, without a gowne, fhee* | *fits* | *downe, with her bodkin curles her haire, cullers her lips.*
6.22.1   *Exit.*
6.24.1   *She fings.* (*to right of* 6.25 *set on one line*)
6.45.1   *She fings.* (*to right of* 6.45)
6.61   *One knocks.* (*to right of* 6.59)
6.67.1   *Roger Fetch in Fluello, Caftruchio, and* Pioratto. CREEDE1; | *Roger fetches in Fluello, Caftruchio, and* Pioratto. CREEDE2
6.76   *Exit. for a candle.* (*to right of* 6.76)
6.78   (*Enter Roger.* (*to right of* 6.78.1)
6.99   *Ex.*
6.143.1–4   *Enter Matheo and Hypolito, who faluting the Com-|* | *pany, as a ftranger walkes off. Roger comes in fadly behind them,* | *with a potle-pot, and ftands aloofe off.*
6.179   *Exit.* (*to right of* 6.178)
6.190.1   *Tabacco.* (*to right of* 6.190)
6.234.1   *Exit.* (*to right of* 6.234)
6.272.1   *Enter Roger.* (*to right of* 6.272)
6.282   *Exeunt.* (*to right of* 6.281)
6.290.1   *Enter Hipolito.* (*after* 6.291)
6.291   *Exit.* (*to right of* 6.291)
6.477.1   *Exit.* (*to right of* 6.477)
6.499.2   *Enter* | *Hipo.* (*opposite* 'doing' *and* 'me,' 6.500)
6.505.1   *Exit* | *Hipol.* (*opposite* 6.505 *and* 6.506)
6.508   *Exeunt.*
7.0.1–2   *Enter Candido, his wife, George, and two Prentices in the* | *fhop: Fuftigo enters, walking by.*
7.91   *Exit* 1. *prentice.* (*to right of* 7.90)
7.101.1   *Enter the* 2. *Prentice.* (*to right of* 7.101)
7.105   *Exit.* (*to right of* 7.105)
7.153.1   *Enter Can.* (*to right of* 7.153)
7.186   *Exit.* (*to right of* 7.186)
7.186.1   *Enter an Officer.* (*to right of* 7.185–6)
7.190.1   *Exit* | *Off.* (*opposite* 7.190 *and* 7.191)
7.210.1   *Exit.* (*to right of* 7.210)
7.228   *Exit George.*
7.234.1   *Enter George.* (*to right of* 7.235)
7.247.1   *Exit Ge.* (*to right of* 7.247)
7.251.1   *Enter Geo.* (*to right of* 7.251)
7.257   *Exit.*
7.259.1   *Enter Can-|didoes wife.* (*opposite* 'two.', 7.259, *and* | 'gone?', 7.260)
7.283.1   *Exeunt.* (*to right of* 7.283)
8.0.1   *Enter a Bawd and Roger.*
8.29.1   *Enter Bellafronte.* (*to right of* 8.29)

8.72   *Exit.*
8.93   *Exeunt.*
9.0.1–2   *Enter Bellafronte with a Lute, pen, inke and paper* | *being* | *placde before her.*
9.0.3   *Song.*
9.9.1   *Shee* | *writes.* (*opposite* 9.8 *and* 9.9)
9.19.1   *Enter Matheo, Caftruchio, Fluello, Pioratto.* STAFFORD1; | *Enter Matheo, Caftruchio, Fluello, and* Pioratto. STAFFORD2(S)
9.89.1   *Exeunt.* (*to right of* 9.89)
9.125   *Exit.*
10.0.1–2   *Enter a feruant fetting out a Table, on which he places* | *a fcull, a picture, a booke and a Taper.*
10.13.1   *Enter Hipolito.* (*to right of* 10.13)
10.37   *Exit.*
10.91.1   *Enter his feruant.*
10.109.1   *Reades.* (*to right of* 10.109)
10.115.1   *Enter Bellafronte like a Page.*
10.126.1   *Enter his Seruant.*
10.147.1   *Exit.* (*to right of* 10.145; ELD1; *not in* ELD2(R))
10.189.1   *Enter his feruant.* (*to right of* 10.190)
10.200.1   *Exeunt.* (*to right of* 10.200)
10.209   *Exit.*
11.0.1–2   *Enter Fuftigo, Crambo and Poli.* ELD1; *Enter…Poh.* ELD2(R)
11.48   *Exeunt.*
11.51.1–2   *Exeunt.* (*to right of* 11.51)
12.0.1–2   *Enter Condidoes wife, in her fhop, and the* | *two Prentises.* ELD1; *…Candidoes…* ELD2(R)
12.18.1   *Enter George.* (*after* 12.16)
12.27.1–2   *Enter Candido, and Exit prefently.* (*after* 12.26)
12.54.1   *Enter Candido like a Prentife.*
12.56.1   *Enter Crambo and Poli.* ELD1; *Enter…Poh.* ELD2(R)
12.67   *Exit.*
12.97   *He ftrikes him.*
12.108   *Exeunt,*
12.118.1   *Enter his wife, with Officers.* ELD1; *Enter Candido's…* ELD2(S)
12.179.1   *Exe.* (*to right of* 12.179)
12.183   *Exeunt.*
12.186   *Exit.*
13.0.1   *Enter Duke: Doctor: Fluello, Caftruchio, Pioratto.* ELD1; | *Enter Duke: Doctor, Fluello, Caftruchio, Pioratto.* ELD2(R)
13.51   *Exit.*
13.54.1   *Enter the Doctors man.*
13.61.1   *Enter Hipolito.* (*to right of* 13.62)
13.63   *Exit.*
13.121.1   *Exeunt.*
14.0.1–3   *Candido's wife, and George: Pioratto* | *meetes them.*
14.6   *Exit.* (*to right of* 14.5)
14.59.1   *Enter Duke, Fluello, Pioratto, Sinere.*
14.83.1   *Enter Caftruchio.* (*to right of* 14.83)
14.91.1   *Exeunt.* (*to right of* 14.91)
14.121.1   *Exeunt.* (*to right of* 14.121)
14.125   *Exit.*
15.0.1   *Enter Frier Anfelmo, Hipolito, Mathæo, Infæliche.*
15.37.1   *Enter Fluello.* (*to right of* 15.38)
15.81.1   *Exeunt.* (*to right of* 15.81)
15.86.1–2   *Enter to Fluello, the Duke, Caftruchio, Pioratto and* | *Sinezi from feuerall dores muffled.*
15.102.1   *Enter Towne like a fweeper.* (*to right of* 'Mas content.', | 15.102)
15.152.1   *Enter Anfelmo.* (*to right of* 15.155)
15.154   *Exit.*
15.180.1–2   *Difcouers an old man,* | *wrapt in a Net.* (*opposite* | 'vext.', 15.180 *and* 'soule.', 15.181)

15.326.1 *Exeunt.* (*to right of* 15.326)
15.326.2 *Enter Bellafronte mad.*
15.342.1–2 *Enter Hipolito, Mathæo, and Infæliche difguifde* | *in the Habets of Friers.* (*after* 15.344)
15.367.1 *Bow a little* (*prefixed to* 15.368)

15.381.1 *difcouers* | (*them.* (*opposite* 'Frier', 15.382, *and* 'Haha haha.', 15.383)
15.487.1 *Enter Candidoes wife and George.*
15.499.1 *Enter Candido with Anselmo.*
15.554.1 *Exeunt.*
15.554.2 *FINIS.* (*in large type*)

LINEATION NOTES

1.90 O, Thursday.] DODSLEY 1. In SIMMES 1 & 2 Hippolito's speech is set on the same line as '—let me see—Thursday' concluding Matteo's preceding speech, possibly implying a part verse-line (as, for example, at 3.36). The surrounding prose in this passage gives no support for verse here, however.

3.4–5 The glass, | The hour-glass.] BOWERS; the glasse, the houre-glasse. SIMMES 1 & 2

3.19–20 weigh | Mine own] SIMMES 2(R); wey mine | Owne SIMMES 1

5.88–90 No, . . . not] THIS EDITION; *prose* CREEDE 1 & 2

5.95–7 Ay, . . . husband] THIS EDITION; *prose* CREEDE 1 & 2

5.107–9 Look . . . custom] DYCE; *prose* CREEDE 1 & 2

5.149–54 A silver . . . impatience] CREEDE 2(S); *prose* CREEDE 1

5.154–5 Sweet . . . conceit.] DYCE; *1 line* CREEDE 1 & 2. The page in CREEDE 1 & 2 on which this line occurs (C2) contains evidence of space shortage of various kinds. Condensation of a part and full verse line into a single line of type is presumably related to the other strategies to conserve space.

5.158–9 I . . . ducats] DYCE; *prose* CREEDE 1 & 2

5.168–9 Blurt . . . all] DYCE; *prose* CREEDE 1 & 2

5.174–5 You . . . sin] DYCE; *1 line* CREEDE 1 & 2

5.178–9 Nay, . . . Candido] DODSLEY 1; *verse* CREEDE 1 & 2: good one: | Candido ('one:' turned under)

5.195–6 The constable's . . . again.] DYCE; *1 line* CREEDE 1 & 2

5.222–3 Then . . . angry] DYCE; *1 line* CREEDE 1 & 2

6.25–8 Cupid . . . fail] BOWERS; *2 verse lines* CREEDE 1 & 2: naile, | faile

6.32–3 Down . . . shall] THIS EDITION; *2 lines* CREEDE 2(S): neuer | fhall; *2 lines in a different wording* CREEDE 1: ne- | uer . . . arife. See textual note to 6.32–3.

6.39–40 If you do . . . now?] THIS EDITION; *2 lines set as verse* CREEDE 1 & 2: fort: | now?

6.54–5 Sing . . . today] THIS EDITION; *1 verse line* CREEDE 1 & 2. See textual note to 6.54.

6.223–4 I must . . . well] DYCE; *1 line set as verse* CREEDE 1 & 2

6.371–2 Then . . . do't] DODSLEY 2; *2 verse lines* CREEDE 1 & 2: wafted, | doo't

6.373–4 Lend . . . soul] BOWERS; *1 line* CREEDE 1 & 2. Various alternative lineations, each of which involves more than one short line, are possible; but that adopted has been preferred because it produces a single short line of considerable force.

7.166–7 A surgeon . . . cousin] BOWERS; *prose* STAFFORD 1 & 2

7.252–3 So, so . . . sight] DODSLEY 2; *prose* STAFFORD 1 & 2. Turned lines, doubled-up speeches, and entrance directions set to the right of speeches indicate that space was short on this page (F1). The setting of these two lines of verse as prose may have come about as another space-saving strategy.

10.31 Indeed . . . was] DODSLEY 1; *1 line* ELD 1 & 2. The line in ELD 1 & 2 occupies less than the full printer's measure and may accordingly signify a verse line; but the Servant on only one occasion unequivocally speaks verse (10.22–3), and the passage surrounding this speech is prose.

10.112–13 temperem . . . vela] DYCE; *1 line* ELD 1 & 2

12.33 What . . . thee?] SCOTT; *set as a separate line* ELD 1; *set as prose* ELD 2(R). In ELD 1 only 'faw.' occupies the preceding line and 'What' is capitalized; whereas in reset ELD 2 the lineation has been rearranged so that Candido's Wife's speech occupies the full printer's measure and is set in the conventional form of prose, but with altered punctuation after 'faw:' and a lower-case 'w' for 'what'.

12.177–8 And . . . whither?] DYCE; *1 line* ELD 1 & 2

14.108–9 Is't . . . say] DODSLEY 2; *1 line* ELD 1 & 2

15.10–11 O . . . fear] DYCE; *1 line* ELD 1 & 2

15.22–3 Can . . . safe] DYCE; *1 line* ELD 1 & 2

15.46–9 Then . . . here] ELD 2(R); *prose* ELD 1. The page containing this passage (I2v) bears evidence of a shortage of space; the arrangement of verse as prose is presumably related to other instances of conservation.

15.59 O God, O God!] NEILSON; *set on same line as* he would neuer open his lips. ELD 1 & 2

15.59–61 Son . . . hence?] ELD 2(R); *prose* ELD 1: your | hēce. See note to 15.46–9 above.

15.68–9 O . . . man] THIS EDITION; *1 line* ELD 1 & 2

15.87 Who's . . . away,] THIS EDITION; *2 lines* ELD 1 & 2: Lord. | away,

15.89–90 What's . . . legs] ELD 1; *1 line* ELD 2(R)

15.95 You . . . Not yet.] ELD 2(R); *2 lines* ELD 1: yet. | yet.

15.369–70 For . . . Tuck] THIS EDITION; *2 lines* ELD 1 & 2: ioy. | Tucke

15.375–7 Troth . . . here] THIS EDITION; *3 lines* ELD 1 & 2: (too: | hand, | here. See textual note to 15.375–7.

15.446–7 Had . . . thee] DYCE; *prose* ELD 1 & 2

15.470 now make me] BOWERS; *prefixed to* 15.471 ELD 2(S). See textual note to 15.470–2.

THE PHOENIX

Edited by Lawrence Danson and Ivo Kamps

OUR copytext for *The Phoenix* is the first edition of the play, a quarto text consisting of 38 leaves, printed by Edward Allde in 1607 (STC 17892; *BEPD* 243(*a*)). The entry in the Stationers' Register on 9 May of that year reads: 'Ent. A. Johnson: lic. G. Bucke: a booke called The Phenix'. A later entry in the Stationers' Register reveals that on 29 January 1630 the copyright of *The Phoenix* was transferred from Arthur Johnson to Richard Meighen, for whom a second edition of the play was printed in the same year by Thomas Harper (STC 17893; *BEPD* 243(*b*)). Harper's printing, except for some minor changes in spelling, a few corrections and new mistakes, merely aims to reproduce Allde's quarto text. HARPER post-dates Middleton's death and its printing shows no evidence of the author's involvement. It is of little value in the editorial process.

ALLDE does not mark act or scene divisions. But the stage direction at the start of Sc. 10, with its reference to 'the music', clearly indicates that Middleton was thinking of a performance in which the acts would be separated by musical intervals (as was universal in the children's companies after 1599, and probably before: see Taylor and Jowett, 8). The absence of act divisions in ALLDE is evidence that the edition was not set from a theatrical manuscript or a literary transcript, either of which would have been likely to indicate such divisions. The present edition indicates scene divisions whenever the stage is cleared, but not, unlike DYCE, BULLEN, and BROOKS, act divisions, since the editorial insertion of the latter would, except between Sc. 9 and Sc. 10, be arbitrary.

Brooks argues that Middleton's 'foul papers' lie behind ALLDE. His argument is based on (1) the spelling and punctuation, which are consistent with Middleton's practice elsewhere, (2) the stage directions, and (3) two possible inconsistencies in nomenclature. Relying on W. W. Greg's principles of text identification as set out in *The Shakespeare First Folio*, Brooks proposes that the stage directions in ALLDE are 'either too full and "literary" (10.71.1-2, 12.208-12.209.1) or too vague (10.0.1, 9.1-2).' Furthermore, Proditor refers to the Prince as 'Phoenix' (2.138) (which, the speech prefixes throughout the text indicate, is his name) even though 'Phoenix' is also the name by which he goes while in disguise (rendering the disguise useless). A similar inconsistency occurs when the Captain refers to Prince Phoenix as 'duke' (8.286). These apparent contradictions, Brooks reasonably suggests, are of the kind we encounter in an author's draft, and they would probably have been cleared up by a scribe transcribing the promptbook.

The Huntington Library copy of ALLDE includes an extra leaf in the back containing the prologue and epilogue to John Mason's *The Turk*.

The present edition has benefited from Brooks's scholarship, and records Brooks's collation of press variants *in totem*.

SEE ALSO

Text: *Works*, 94
Authorship and date: this volume, 345

WORKS CITED

Previous Editions

Brooks, John Bradbury, ed., *The Phoenix* (1980)
Bullen, A. H., ed., *Works* (1885), vol. 1
Dyce, Alexander, ed., *Works* (1840), vol. 1

Other Works Cited

Blount, Thomas, *A Law-Dictionary and Glossay* (1717)
Bouvier, John, *Bouvier's Law Dictionary*, ed. William Edward Baldwin (1934)
Chambers, E. K., *The Elizabethan Stage* (1923), vol. 4
Kamps, Ivo, 'Ruling Fantasies and the Fantasies of Rule: *The Phoenix* and *Measure for Measure*', *Studies in Philology* 42 (1995), 248-73
Kantorowicz, Ernst, *The King's Two Bodies: A Study in Medieval Political Theory* (1957; repr. 1981)
Kirkman, Francis, *A True, perfect, and exact Catalogue of all the Comedies, Tragedies, Tragi-Comedies, Pastorals, Masques and Interludes, that were ever yet printed and published, till this present year 1661...*, ed. John S. Farmer (1913)
Shakespeare, William, and John Fletcher, *All is True (Henry VIII)*, William Montgomery, ed., *The Complete Works*, gen. eds. Stanley Wells and Gary Taylor (1986)
Taylor, Gary, and John Jowett, *Shakespeare Reshaped 1606-1623* (1993)

529

TEXTUAL NOTES

1.43   yields] DYCE; yeeld ALLDE
1.59   chosen] chose ALLDE
1.92   not] DYCE; no ALLDE
1.135.1   *Exit Phoenix*] DYCE; *Exit Phoen* at end of preceding line in ALLDE
1.166.1   *Exit Niece*] DYCE; *Exit* at end of preceding line in ALLDE
2.64   earing] HARPER; earning ALLDE
2.70   consumed] HARPER; cansumde ALLDE
2.72.1–2.73   *Enter…LADY*] In ALLDE the Lady is referred to by her name, Castiza, and also as the Captain's wife, but most frequently by the generic term, Lady. DYCE, BULLEN, and BROOKS all opt for Castiza, but this edition identifies characters in speech headings by the designation most frequently used in the stage directions and speech headings of the control text.
2.79   LADY] BROOKS (*subs.*); *cap.* ALLDE
4.6   guests] BROOKS; Gueſſe ALLDE
4.11   under] HARPER; vdder ALLDE
4.12   sir] HARPER; ſit ALLDE
4.23   towed] DYCE; toward ALLDE
4.33   a] HARPER; *not in* ALLDE
4.36   Iwis] I wus ALLDE
4.46   FIRST SUITOR] DYCE; ALLDE (1). We have expanded the speech headings for all the suitor characters throughout this edition.
4.201   Maid] THIS EDITION; Made ALLDE. All editions before this one accept ALLDE. That reading does make sense. However, the first five lines of Phoenix's speech are an apostrophe to a figure named law gendered as a female angel, a modest and virginal *maid*. We have amended *made* to *maid* because *made* unnecessarily disrupts the sequence and distracts from the image of a personified female law.
4.233   lord] ALLDE (L.)
4.266   gentlemen] HARPER; Gentleman ALLDE
6.134   waists] ALLDE (waſtes)
6.155   have] DYCE; has ALLDE
6.164   handkerchiefs] ALLDE (handkirchers)
6.167   KNIGHT] DYCE; *Fal.* ALLDE
8.107, 8.110   lord] ALLDE (L.)
8.126   fault] ALLDE (faul)
8.156   faces] DYCE; face ALLDE
8.196   posy] DYCE; poesye ALLDE
8.235   is] DYCE; *not in* ALLDE
8.284   know] DYCE; knowes ALLDE

8.321   harm] DYCE; haime ALLDE
9.104   SUITOR] *Whin.* ALLDE
9.109   SUITOR] *Whi.* ALLDE
9.109   good] HARPER; god ALLDE
9.175–6   A writ…dagger] DYCE; ALLDE gives this part of speech to Falso
9.185   i'] BROOKS; ALLDE a
9.231   TANGLE] HARPER; F*alſ.* ALLDE
9.237   demurs] *Demurres* ALLDE
9.237   pluries] *Plures* ALLDE
9.237   sursurraras] DYCE; *Surſurarers* ALLDE
10.9   to] HARPER; *not in* ALLDE
10.41   LATRONELLO] HARPER; *Enter* ALLDE
10.81   scarce] HARPER; ſcare ALLDE
10.91   Fucato] BROOKS; Fuca ALLDE
10.144   master] ALLDE (Ma.)
10.185   I'll] DYCE; *Fals.* Ile ALLDE
10.203   knees] HARPER; kees ALLDE
12.13–14   bliss. | Then] DYCE; bliſſe: | *Prod.* Then ALLDE
12.31   tenure] DYCE; tenor ALLDE
12.67   BOTH SUITORS] DYCE; *Both.* ALLDE
12.85   possibly] THIS EDITION; poſſible ALLDE
13.34–5   [*Giving money*]] DYCE
13.56   Metrezza Aureola] Mettreza Auriola ALLDE
14.76   *Exit…Officer*] THIS EDITION; *Exeunt* ALLDE. BROOKS has *Exeunt* [*severally*], but it is likely that the Officer would try to arrest the Gentleman for helping the Knight escape.
15.45   ALL] DYCE; *Prod. All* ALLDE
15.58   Soul-quicking] ALLDE (soule qucking)
15.67   here?] DYCE; What's here my Lord? ALLDE. 'my lord' is deleted as mistaken repetition of Proditor's exclamation 'My Lord?' in the next line: otherwise line is extra-metrical
15.169   stings] ALLDE *corr.*, DYCE; ſtrings ALLDE *uncorr.*
15.207   LUSSURIOSO…NOBLES] THIS EDITION; *All.* ALLDE. As BROOKS notes, ALLDE is incorrect because, 'presumably, some of the courtiers present were loyal to the duke' and because 'Falso is not included in the general amnesty.' The general point is valid, except that it is Proditor, not Falso, who does not receive clemency.
15.275   He's] BROOKS; Has ALLDE
15.293.1   [*Quieto…Tangle*]] THIS EDITION. In light of what Quieto is about to do to Tangle, it seems reasonable to assume that the latter will have to be constrained.
15.311   an] ALLDE (and)

PRESS VARIANTS

This list of press variants is adopted from BROOKS.
   The 1607 quarto was printed by Edward Allde; there are eleven copies:

HUNT = Huntington Library
WIDE = Widener Library, Harvard University
FOLG = Folger Shakespeare Library
BOD = Bodleian Library, Oxford University
BL 1 = British Library, copy 1
BL 2 = British Library, copy 2
PEPYS = Pepys Library, Cambridge University

PFORZ = Pforzheimer Collection, University of Texas at Austin
YALE = Yale University Library
V&A = Dyce Collection, National Art Library, Victoria and Albert Museum, London
NYPL = New York Public Library

Sheet A (inner forme)

Corrected: HUNT, WIDE, BL 1, BL 2, PEPYS, PFORZ, YALE, V&A, NYPL
Uncorrected: FOLG, BOD

Sig. A3ᵛ

1.83 kingdoms] Kingdomes *corr.*; Countreys *uncorr.*

Sheet B (outer forme)

> *First stage corrected:* FOLG, PFORZ, NYPL
> *Uncorrected:* WIDE

Sig. B1

headline *The Phœnix]* *corr.*; *The Pœnix. uncorr.*
2.11 ha't] *corr.*; ha'e *uncorr.*
2.13 married] *corr.*; ɯarried *uncorr.*
2.14 'Sfoot] S'foot *corr.*; Sfoo't *uncorr.*
2.15 over] ouer *corr.*; ~? *uncorr.*
2.19 trick] Tricke *corr.*; Trike *uncorr.*
2.20 abominable, I] abhominable ∧ I *corr.*; ~ ? ~ *uncorr.*
2.20 you, now] you ∧ now *corr.*; ~ , ~ *uncorr.*
2.20 see't.] see't: *corr.*; ~ ∧ *uncorr.*
2.21 women—] Women—*corr.*; ~?—*uncorr.*
2.24 't'ad] t'ad *corr.*; ta'd *uncorr.*
2.26 pretty] pretty ∧ *corr.*; ~, *uncorr.*
2.30 together] *corr.*; togethers *uncorr.*
2.35 honest?] *corr.*; ~: *uncorr.*
2.40 hear] heare *corr.*; heere *uncorr.*
2.42 aboard] aboord *corr.*; abroad *uncorr.*

Sig. B2ᵛ

2.99 Count] *corr.*; count *uncorr.*
2.108 count] Count *corr.*; count *uncorr.*
2.108 you.] you: *corr.*; ~ ∧ *uncorr.*
2.112 rumoured?] rumord? *corr.*; rumorde. *uncorr.*
2.118 great.] great: *corr.*; ~ ∧ *uncorr.*
2.119 him] him∧ *corr.*; ~, *uncorr.*
2.119 virtues,] Vertues, *corr.*; ~∧ *uncorr.*
2.126 believed?] beleeu'd? *corr.*; ~, *uncorr.*
2.127 him. I] him: I *corr.*; ~,~ *uncorr.*
2.129 matter. H'as] matter: ha's *corr.*; ~,~ *uncorr.*
2.134 society] soscietie *corr.*; solicitie *uncorr.*

Sig. B3

headline *The Phœnix.]* *corr*; *The Phœnix. uncorr.*
2.141 vile;] vilde: *corr.*; ~, *uncorr.*
2.142 honour.] honour, *corr.*; ~∧ *uncorr.*
2.147 married?] *corr.*; ~: *uncorr.*
2.148 relieve] relieue *corr.*; reliue *uncorr.*
2.148 be] *corr.*; bee *uncorr.*
2.152 hold] *corr.*; holde *uncorr.*
2.152 that,] that: *corr.*; ~∧ *uncorr.*
3.2–5 LADY...entreat it—] *Lad.* I...this, | Tis...my | honour...welcome, | if...it—*corr.*; ∧I...this. | *Ladie:* Tis... friend | vnto...euer | welcome,...it. *uncorr.*
3.3 granted.] grāted: *corr.*; granted, *uncorr.*
3.4 honour] honour∧ *corr.*; ~, *uncorr.*
3.5 it—] *corr.*; ~. *uncorr.*
3.8 LADY 'Tis] *Lad.* Tis *corr.*; *Ladie.* Tis *uncorr.*
3.8 lord; such] Lord, such *corr.*; L. such *uncorr.*
3.9 too] *corr.*; to *uncorr.*
3.10 see me] *corr.*; se mee *uncorr.*
3.10 forth.] forth: *corr.*; ~∧ *uncorr.*
3.10–3.10.1 LADY And honourably welcome. *Exeunt]* *Lady.* And honourably welcome. | *Exuent. corr.*; ∧and honourably welcome. | *Lady. Exuent. uncorr.*

Sig. B4ᵛ

headline *The Phœnix.]* *corr.*; *The Phœnix. uncorr.*
4.78 *testes] corr.*; *testis uncorr.*

4.87 and] *corr.*; aud *uncorr.*
4.90 your worship] *corr.*; ∧worship *uncorr.*
4.94 the cause] *corr.*; ∧ cause *uncorr.*
4.100 nunc] Nunc *corr.*; Nuuc *uncorr.*
4.101 venire] Venire *corr.*; Venere *uncorr.*
4.109 thee?] *corr.*; ~, *uncorr.*
4.112 PHOENIX] *Phœ, corr.*; *Phœ. uncorr.*

> *Second stage corrected:* HUNT, BOD, BL 1, BL 2, PEPYS, YALE, V&A

Sig. B1

2.10 am I] Am I *corr.*; I am *uncorr.*
2.28 marry:] marrie: *corr.*; ~, *uncorr.*

Sig. B2ᵛ

2.119 him] him, *corr.*; ~∧ *uncorr.*
2.119 virtues,] Vertues: *corr.*; ~, *uncorr.*
2.119–21 Put...foe.] Put...Vertues: | Or...know | This...foe. *corr.*; prose in WIDE, FOLG, PFORZ, NYPL
2.120 him] him, *corr.*; ~∧ *uncorr.*
2.120 wisdom] wisdome: *corr.*; ~, *uncorr.*
2.124 singly] singlie *corr.*; simplie *uncorr.*
2.124 my best gladness—] (my best gladnes) *corr.*; ,~~~, *uncorr.*

Sig. B3

2.148 would] *corr.*; should *uncorr.*
2.149 kill or] kil, or *corr.*; kill∧ or *uncorr.*
2.150 gentle] ∧ gentle *corr.*; a gētle *uncorr.*
2.151 a divorce] a Diuorce *corr.*; ∧ Diuorce *uncorr.*
2.151 shall] shal *corr.*; shall *uncorr.*

Sig. B4ᵛ

4.83 o' th' pillory] ath Pillorie *corr.*; oth Pillorie *uncorr.*
4.99 costs] *corr.*; cost *uncorr.*

Sheet B (inner forme)

> *First stage corrected:* BOD, BL 2
> *Uncorrected:* WIDE, FOLG, PFORZ, NYPL

Sig. B1ᵛ

2.63 i'th' city] i'the Cittie *corr.*; 'the Cittie *uncorr.*

Sig. B4

4.54 to you] *corr.*; to yet *uncorr.*

> *Second stage corrected:* HUNT, BL 1, PEPYS, YALE, V&A

Sig. B4

4.44 law-worm] Law-worme *corr.*; Laɯw-worme *uncorr.*

Sheet C (inner forme)

> *Corrected:* HUNT, WIDE, FOLG, BL 1, BL 2, PEPYS, PFORZ, YALE, V&A, NYPL
> *Uncorrected:* BOD

Sig. C1ᵛ

4.180 suits.] suits: *corr.*; ~, *uncorr.*

Sig. C2

4.197 company.] companie. *Exit. corr.*; companie. ∧ *uncorr.*
4.202 virgin,] *corr.*; ~. *uncorr.*
4.203 sale,] *corr.*; ~. *uncorr.*
4.210 incorruptible;] incorruptible, *corr.*; ~: *uncorr.*
4.210 wise.] wise, *corr.*; ~∧ *uncorr.*

Sig. C3ᵛ

5.4 away.] *corr.*; ~? *uncorr.*
5.12 Revenue!] Reuenewe! *corr.*; Reuennewe? *uncorr.*

5.34   They're] th'are *corr.*; their *uncorr.*

Sig. C4

6.7   therein?] *corr.*; ~. *uncorr.*
6.12   will?] *corr.*; ~, *uncorr.*
6.14   welcome,] *corr.*; ~ₐ *uncorr.*
6.25   sir,] *corr.*; ~: *uncorr.*

Sheet D (outer forme)

Corrected: HUNT, WIDE, FOLG, BOD, BL 1, BL 2, PEPYS, PFORZ, V&A, NYPL
Uncorrected: YALE

Sig. D4ᵛ

8.145   furthermore, I the said, of] furdermore (I the said) of *corr.*; furdermore, I the saide of, *uncorr.*
8.149   in or] *corr.*; ₐor *uncorr.*
8.149   said] *corr.*; saide *uncorr.*

Sheet E (outer forme)

First stage corrected: BL 2
Uncorrected: FOLG

Sig. E1

8.207–8   A, B, C?...Ah] A.B.C? ah *corr.*; A.B.C. A *uncorr.*

Sig. E2ᵛ

8.291   captain,] Captaineₐ *corr.*; ~, *uncorr.* This may be an inking rather than a press variant.

Sig. E3

8.339   gone.] gone: *corr.*; gon: *uncorr.*
8.343   brightness] brightnes *corr.*; bightnes *uncorr.*

Sig E4ᵛ

9.76   wise and love] wise, and loue *corr.*; wise, ₐ loue *uncorr.*
9.97–8   late...The] late—The *corr.*; late.—the *uncorr.*

Second stage corrected: HUNT, WIDE, BOD, BL 1, PEPYS, PFORZ, YALE, V&A, NYPL

Sig. E4ᵛ

9.96   enough] ynough *corr.*; ynought *uncorr.*

Sheet F (outer forme)

Corrected: HUNT, WIDE, BOD, BL 1, BL 2, PEPYS, PFORZ, YALE, NYPL
Uncorrected: V&A

Sig. F1

9.109   good] god *corr.*; gour *uncorr.*
9.109   coming] comming *corr.*; cōming *uncorr.*
9.112   Tangle!] *corr.*; ~. *uncorr.*
9.114   fence:] Fence: *corr.*; ~, *uncorr.*
9.119   When] when *corr.*; wheu *uncorr.*
9.121   instantly.] instantly: *corr.*; ~, *uncorr.*
9.131   What, what!] *corr.*; ~, ~, *uncorr.*
9.132   labour.] labour: *corr.*; ~, *uncorr.*
9.135   quarter.] quarter: *corr.*; ~, *uncorr.*

Sig. F2ᵛ

9.232   by'r Lady. I] birlady—I: *corr.*; ~—~ₐ *uncorr.*
9.233   remove, do] Remoue, doe *corr.*; Remooue, doe *uncorr.*
9.237   pluries] Plures *corr.*; Plurs *uncorr.*
9.237   sursurraras] Surfurarers *corr.*; Surfurarer *uncorr.*
9.238   longswords—] Longswords: *corr.*; Longswordₐ *uncorr.*

9.238   delays—all] Delaies: al *corr.*; Delaies, all *uncorr.*
9.240   good] *corr.*; Good *uncorr.*

Sig. F3

9.245   see at length law. I shall have law. Now] see at length law, I shal haue law: now *corr.*; ₐ at length lawe, I shall haue lawe, now *uncorr.*
9.256–7   an overthrow] an o-|uerthrowe *corr.*; ano-|uerthrowe *uncorr.*
9.268   by th'] by'th *corr.*; by'th the *uncorr.*
9.270   certo] Certo *corr.*; Corto *uncorr.*
9.274   he shall] hee shall *corr.*; heele shall *uncorr.*
10.0.2   prepare] *corr.*; drepare *uncorr.*

Sig. F4ᵛ

10.75   Ha?] ha? *corr.*; ~. *uncorr.*
10.76   knows,] knowes, *corr.*; ~ₐ *uncorr.*
10.79   uprightness] vp right-|nes *corr.*; vpright-|nes *uncorr.*
10.104   you] *corr.*; ye *uncorr.*
10.106   By] *corr.*; by *uncorr.*

Sheet I (inner forme)

Corrected: FOLG, BL 1, PEPYS, YALE
Uncorrected: HUNT, WIDE, BOD, BL 2, PFORZ, NYPL

Sig. I1ᵛ

15.11   Ah, stuck] Ah! Stucke *corr.*; ~, ~ *uncorr.*
15.27   act] Act. *corr.*; Actc, *uncorr.*

Sig. I2

15.41   both!] both, *corr.*; ~. *uncorr.*
15.51   possession] *corr.*; posession *uncorr.*

Sig. I3ᵛ

15.144   thieves] theeues *corr.*; threeues *uncorr.*
15.147   liberty] liber-|tie *corr.*; liber= | tie *uncorr.*

Sig. I4

15.169   stings] *corr.*; strings *uncorr.*

Half-sheet K (outer forme)

Corrected: HUNT, WIDE, FOLG, BOD, BL 1, BL 2, PEPYS, PFORZ, YALE, NYPL
Uncorrected: V&A

Sig. K1

15.223   mistress] Mistris *corr.*; Master *uncorr.*
15.229   favours?] Fauours? *corr.*; ~. *uncorr.*
15.232   common—] common: *corr.*; ~, *uncorr.*
15.232   subtle] subtill *corr.*; suptill *uncorr.*
15.233   three] Three *corr.*; three *uncorr.*
15.237   curse] cursse *corr.*; curse *uncorr.*
15.237   ill-got] il-got *corr.*; ill-got *uncorr.*
15.239   freedom] Freedome *corr.*; freedome *uncorr.*
15.239   be] *corr.*; bee *uncorr.*
15.243   those] *corr.*; these *uncorr.*

Sig. K2ᵛ

15.335   war's] *corr.*; war, *uncorr.*
15.341   patience.] patience, *corr.*; ~ₐ *uncorr.*
15.341   feel] feeleₐ *corr.*; ~, *uncorr.*
15.342   conscience] Conscience *corr.*; conscience *uncorr.*
15.343   all,] al, *corr.*; all, *uncorr.*
15.347   Now] 'Now *corr.*; ₐNow *uncorr.*
15.347   least] *corr.*; left *uncorr.*
15.349   honour's] Honors *corr.*; honors *uncorr.*

Half-sheet K (inner forme)

Corrected: HUNT, WIDE, FOLG, BOD, BL 1, BL 2, PEPYS, PFORZ, YALE, V&A
Uncorrected: NYPL

Sig. K1ᵛ

15.266   wealth] wealth, *corr.*; ~, *uncorr.*
15.267   perjured's] Periur'ds *corr.*; periur'd *uncorr.*
15.271   guard!] *corr.*; ~. *uncorr.*
15.272   father] Father *corr.*; father *uncorr.*
15.274   on't.] on't, *corr.*; ~. *uncorr.*
15.275   law-mad] Law-mad *corr.*; law-mad *uncorr.*
15.276   yea!] *corr.*; ~. *uncorr.*
15.278   solicitor] Solister *corr.*; Solisiter *uncorr.*
15.283   Away, I'll] Awa,yile *corr.*; Away ile *uncorr.*
15.286   disease.] disease, *corr.*; ~. *uncorr.*
15.288   ink,] Inke, *corr.*; ~. *uncorr.*

Sig. K2

15.291   ha] hah *corr.*; hah, *uncorr.*

15.291   rejoice] reioice *corr.*; reioyce *uncorr.*
15.291   too] *corr.*; to *uncorr.*
15.294   She never] She neuer *corr.*; She, she neuer *uncorr.*
15.294   fight—] fight, *corr.*; ~. *uncorr.*
15.295   grace.] grace, *corr.*; grace *uncorr.*
15.298   I'm] I'me, *corr.*; ~. *uncorr.*
15.298   counsel.] counsel, *corr.*; ~. *uncorr.*
15.301   patience] *corr.*; pacience *uncorr.*
15.303   Yea!] *corr.*; ~, *uncorr.*
15.310   O,] Oh, *corr.*; Oh— *uncorr.*
15.312   seizure, a writ] Seyfure, | a Writ *corr.*; Seyfuse, a | Writ *uncorr.*
15.314   QUIETO You're] *Qui.* You'r *corr.*; *Quie.* Your *uncorr.*
15.314   dregs] Dreggs *corr.*; Druggs *uncorr.*
15.315   lord.] Lord: *corr.*; ~. *uncorr.*
15.315   ink.] Inke: *corr.*; ~. *uncorr.*
15.317   Ply-fee, sick] Ply-fee, sicke *corr.*; Phyfee, flie, sicke *uncorr.*
15.318   O!] oh! *corr.*; ~ ¡ *uncorr.*
15.322   cheap that] cheape, that *corr.*; ~, ~ *uncorr.*

STAGE DIRECTIONS

1.0.1–2   *Enter the old Duke of Ferrara, Nobles, Proditor, | Lussurioso, and Infesto, with Attendants.*
1.30.1   *Enter Prince attended by Fidelio.*
1.73.1   *Exeūt (right)*
1.73.2   *Manet Phoenix and Fidelio*
1.135.1   *Exit Phoen. (right, opposite the first half of the split verse line 1.135)*
1.141.1   *Enter Neece. (right)*
1.166.1   *Exit (right, opposite 1.165)*
1.168   *Exit. Fidelio. (flush right)*
2.0.1   *Enter the Captaine with Souldiering fellowes.*
2.41.1   *Exeunt (right)*
2.72.1   *Enter his Lady.*
2.99.1   *Enter Seruus.*
2.103.1   *Enter Proditor.*
2.138.1   *Exit. (right)*
2.160   *Exit. (right)*
3.0.1   *Enter Proditor with the Captaines wife.*
3.10.1   *Exeunt.*
4.0.1–2   *Enter a Groome before Phoenix, and Fidelio, | alighting into an Inne.*
4.45.1   *Enter Tangle with two futers.*
4.189.1   *Enter Groome.*
4.198   *Exit (right, opposite 4.197)*
4.232.1   *Enter Tangle, with Captaine.*
4.269   *Exit (right)*
4.284   *Exeunt. (right)*
5.0.1   *Enter Iewellers wife with a Boy.*
5.9.1   *Enter Knight.*
5.37   *Exeunt. (right)*
6.0.1   *Enter two suters with the Iustice Falso.*
6.48.1   *Exeunt, (right)*
6.122.1   *Enter Knight with Iewellers wife.*
6.165.1   *Exeūt. (right, opposite 6.165)*
6.172   *Exeunt. (right, opposite 6.172)*
7.0.1–2   *Enter Phoenix and Fidelio.*
7.24.1   *Exeunt*
8.0.1   *Enter Captaine his Ladie following him.*
8.35.1   *Enter Proditor.*
8.36   *Exit. (right)*

8.58.1   *Enter Phoenix and Fidelio both disguized.*
8.259   *Exit. (right)*
8.298.1   *Enter his Lady.*
8.342.1   *Exit. (right)*
8.347   *Exeunt. (right)*
9.0.1   *Enter Iustice, Knight, Iewel.*
9.92   *Exit. (right)*
9.101.2   *Enter Tangle.*
9.277   *Exeunt. (right)*
10.0.1–2   *Toward the close of the musick, the Iustices three men | prepare for a robberie.*
10.0.3   *Enter Iustice Falso, vntrust.*
10.9.1   *Enter two of his men tumbling in, in False beards.*
10.71.1–2   *Enter Phoenix, Fidelio being robd, Constable, Officers | and the Theefe Furtiuo.*
10.208.1   *Exeunt. (right)*
10.213.1   *Enter Neece.*
10.257   *Exeunt. (right)*
11.0.1   *Enter Knight, and Iewella.*
11.22   *Exeunt. (right)*
12.0.1   *Enter Proditor, and Phoenix.*
12.26.1   *Exit. (right)*
12.30.1   *Voices within. (right)*
12.42.1   *Enter Tangle with two after him.*
12.67.1   *Exeunt: (right)*
12.80.1   *Enter Iustice Falso.*
12.97.1   *Enter 1. (right, opposite 12.98)*
12.101.1   *Enter 2. (right, opposite 12.102)*
12.132   *Exeunt. (right)*
12.143.1   *Enter Fidelio.*
12.160.1   *Enter Quieto. (right, opposite 12.159)*
12.178.1   *Enter his Boy.*
12.203.1   *Enter two Officers.*
12.205.1–2   *Iars the Ring of the Doore, the Maide enters | catches him.*
12.209.1   *Takes in Phoenix, amazde.*
12.215.1   *Exeunt. (right)*
12.220   *Exeunt (right)*
13.0.1   *Enter Phoenix with the Maide.*
13.4   *Exit. (right)*

13.10.1   *Enter Iewell.*
13.105   *Exeunt.* (right)
14.0.1   *Enter Knight, two Officers after him.*
14.36.1   *knockes.* (right, opposite 14.36)
14.51.1   *a Boxe* (right)
14.61.1   *Enter a Gentleman with a Drawer.*
14.66.1   *Blinds the officer.* (right, opposite 14.67)
14.76   *Exeunt.* (right)
15.0.1   *Enter Proditor and Phoenix.*

15.41.1   *Enter Lussurioso, and Infesto two Lords.* (after the end of 15.41)
15.53.1   *Horn winded.* (right)
15.53.2   *Enter Fidelio.*
15.107.1   *Enter Iustice Falso.*
15.204   *Exit.* (right, opposite 15.203)
15.210.1   *Enter Iewell: with Fidelio.* (after 15.212)
15.268.1   *Enter Tangle madde.*
15.279.1   *Enter Quieto.* (right)
15.350.2   *FINIS.*

LINEATION NOTES

1.22   He...lord] DYCE; *1 line* ALLDE
1.23–4   Had...again] DYCE; *prose* ALLDE
1.59–60   They're...mine] DYCE; *prose* ALLDE
1.61   What...more] DYCE; *1 line* ALLDE
1.123–4   And...brother] DYCE; *prose (but 2 lines)* ALLDE
1.126   You...lord] DYCE; it is ambiguous whether the line is *prose or verse* in ALLDE
1.129–31   When...assister] DYCE; *prose* ALLDE
1.158–9   Write...mother] DYCE; ALLDE: *2 lines* father-in-law, the |
1.162–5   Nothing...will] DYCE; *prose* ALLDE
2.89–94   What...man] DYCE; *prose* ALLDE
2.96–7   Then...do't] DYCE; *1 line* ALLDE
2.98–9   What...into] DYCE; *1 line* ALLDE
2.99–103   How...him] DYCE; *prose* ALLDE
2.104–5   I'll...captain] DYCE; *1 line* ALLDE
2.105–6   O...pricksong] DYCE; *prose* ALLDE
2.107–8   My...you] DYCE; *1 line* ALLDE
2.110–16   My...lord] DYCE; *prose* ALLDE
2.122–5   That's...Fidelio] DYCE; *prose* ALLDE
2.159   Him...tread] DYCE; occupies 2 lines in ALLDE, and its intention is ambiguous
3.8–10   'Tis...forth] DYCE; *prose* ALLDE
4.56–7   O...sir] DYCE; *1 line* ALLDE
4.58–9   But...sir] DYCE; *1 line* ALLDE
4.190–1   Sir...sir] DYCE; *1 line* ALLDE
4.281–4   I...enterèd] DYCE; *prose* ALLDE
6.3   Please...word] DYCE; *2 lines* ALLDE: yourself |
6.161–5   Keys...wise] THIS EDITION; *prose* ALLDE
6.166–7   I...sweetly] DYCE; *1 line* ALLDE
8.3–12   Hence...oak] DYCE; *prose* ALLDE
8.17–19   O...credit] DYCE; *prose* ALLDE
8.34–5   No...chapman] DYCE; *prose* ALLDE

8.41–4   O...sight] BROOKS; *4 lines, intention ambiguous* ALLDE lord she | yet | appear |
8.185–6   That...minute] DYCE; *prose* ALLDE
8.253   I...bosom] DYCE; *prose* ALLDE
8.260–1   O...you] BROOKS; *1 line* ALLDE
8.261–3   Stranger...quickly] DYCE; *prose* ALLDE
8.313   But...it] DYCE; *unassimilated part line* ALLDE that | his
9.39   Pray...niece] DYCE; *prose* ALLDE
9.57–8   As...you] DYCE; *verse* ALLDE
10.227–8   O...loss] BROOKS; *prose* ALLDE
10.233–4   But...examination] DYCE; *prose* ALLDE
10.235–9   Henceforth...leave 'em] DYCE; *prose* ALLDE
10.242–3   That...nature] DYCE; *prose* ALLDE
10.250–1   I...furnished] DYCE; *prose* ALLDE
12.6   Be...lord] DYCE; *1 line* ALLDE
12.17   O...brain] DYCE; *1 line* ALLDE
12.23   You...mischief] DYCE; *1 line* ALLDE
12.26   Look...fashion] THIS EDITION; *2 lines* and | fashion ALLDE
12.159–60   I...temper] DYCE; *2 lines sir* | ALLDE
12.173–4   He's...variance] DYCE; *prose* ALLDE
15.3–4   Ay...us] DYCE; *1 line* ALLDE
15.13–14   About...duke] DYCE; *1 line* ALLDE
15.85–6   He...lord] DYCE; *1 line* ALLDE
15.86   Most...guard] DYCE; *1 line* ALLDE
15.124–5   Falso...name] DYCE; *prose* ALLDE
15.187–8   Without...Fidelio] DYCE; *1 line* ALLDE
15.191   Madam...lord] DYCE; *1 line* ALLDE
15.193–4   My...again] DYCE; *1 line* ALLDE
15.204   Away...idle] DYCE; *prose* ALLDE
15.217–18   Now...now] BROOKS; *prose* ALLDE
15.230–1   Stand...city] DYCE; *prose* ALLDE
15.263–4   Her...her] DYCE; *prose* ALLDE
15.271–2   Under...himself] DYCE; *2 lines* Father | ALLDE
15.292–3   Ah...patience] DYCE; *1 line* ALLDE
15.342–4   I...music] DYCE; *prose* ALLDE

MICHAELMAS TERM

Edited by Theodore B. Leinwand

Michaelmas Term (STC 17890) was entered in the Stationers' Register on 15 May 1607. The publisher, Arthur Johnson, 'Entered for his Copie vnder the hands of Sir Georg Buc knight & the wardens A Comedy called Mychaelmas terme'. The play itself was printed in quarto in the same year (Greg, #244), with the following title-page: 'MICHAELMAS | Terme. | AS | IT HATH BEEN SVN-| dry times acted by the Children | *of Paules.* | [ornament] | AT LONDON, | *Printed for A.I. and are to be* | sould at the signe of the white horse in | Paules Churchyard. | An. 1607.' (*BEPD* 244).

Printed by Thomas Purfoot and Edwarde Allde, the quarto includes numerous, detailed stage directions (mostly entrances—see, for example, 3.1.0.2–6), but does not mention properties or anticipate entries. Price (1966) counts twenty-four entrances and thirty exits omitted. Levin notes 'the vague or inconsistent designations of some of the characters'. The printers' copy may well have been Middleton's own manuscript, rather than a theatre prompt book or a scribal transcription. Purfoot and Allde frequently print the playwright's verse as prose.

Greg was the first to note that Purfoot printed sheets A and B (through 2.1.27–8), and Allde, sheets C through I. In the only published study of the printing of the play, Price (1953, 1966) argues that Allde, as the primary printer, cast off copy so that Purfoot could print A–B, then cast off copy again when he received the sheets from Purfoot and went on to print C–I. However, Adrian Weiss (1993) demonstrates that Price misunderstood shared printing and got things backward. Weiss argues that Purfoot, whose device appears on the title-page, was the primary printer. Purfoot would have printed the first two sheets and then passed his copy to Allde. Allde, whose device appears at the end of the text, then printed C–I. As Weiss notes, 'Purfoot and Allde were involved in the shared printing of about twenty-four books with other printers in the proximate period (1605–1608) and in all cases, the primary printer did the title page.' When Purfoot shared *Dutch Courtesan* with Jaggard, he printed A–E with his imprint on the title-page. There would have been no need to cast off type.

Certainly there is no need to imagine (with Price) an error in casting off copy in Allde's shop to account for the difference between the number of lines per page in A–B and then C–I. As Weiss notes, 'variation in the number of lines per page is quite common in the period, especially in dramatic texts, and in many instances, the texts can be shown to have been set seriatim with no casting-off of copy'.

Weiss effectively refutes Price's contention that the large ornament at the end of *Michaelmas Term* (McKerrow: Allde Nr. 17) indicates the printer. Such ornaments often fill the empty portion of a final page because they assure 'a level surface at type-height' during printing. Price's specification of the number of compositors who set *Michaelmas Term* (as well as the number of presses employed) is equally fanciful.

Stop-press corrections were made in each shop. Purfoot's man may have returned to the manuscript at 1.2.26, and the same might apply to Allde's corrector at 3.4.233. The variant at 2.3.381 cannot with certainty be said to entail a correction. Press variants listed in this volume derive from Levin's and Price's (1976) collations.

On 29 January, 1630, Arthur Johnson (with the 'Consent of Mr Purfoote Warden') transferred his copyright of 'Cupids Whirlegig', 'The merry Wives of Winsor', 'Michalmas terme', and 'The Phenix' to Richard Meighen (Greg). Meighen engaged the printer Thomas Harper, and in 1630, a second, quarto edition (STC 17891) appeared with the following title-page: 'MICHAELMAS | TERME. | AS | IT HATH BEENE | SVNDRY TIMES ACTED | BY THE CHILDREN | of PAVLES. | *Newly corrected.* | [ornament] | *LONDON:* | Printed by *T.H.* for *R. Meighen,* and are to be sold | at his Shop. next to the Middle-Temple Gate, and in | *S. Dunstans* Church-yard in *Fleet-street,* | 1630.'

Harper's edition is a page-for-page and line-for-line reprint of the Purfoot–Allde quarto. Middleton was no longer alive when Harper's shop inconsistently modernized the spelling of the first quarto, made a number of new corrections, failed to make others, and even made new errors. The copyright was transferred, on 7 November 1646, to Meighen's widow, 'Mrs: Mercie Meighen. & Gabriell Beadell'. The play next appears in a list of books available at the Fleet Street shop of Meighen, Bedell, and T. Collins in the 1653 edition of *Cabala, Mysteries of State* (*BEPD* 2A2) and later, among books printed for Bedell and Collins listed in the 1656 edition of Thomas Goffe's *Three Excellent Tragedies* (*BEPD* R6). William London's catalogue of 'the most vendible Books in England' (1658) includes *Michaelmas Term* (*BEPD* 2F1), as does Richard Rogers and William Ley's catalogue of plays included in their edition of Goffe's *The Careless Shepherdess* (1656). In this last instance, the play is attributed to 'Chapman', but Greg sensibly assumes that Chapman's name was meant to follow the masque listed in the following line.

Both the 1607 and 1630 quartos denote act divisions beginning with Act Two. Neither quarto marks scene divisions. In keeping with the principles of this edition,

Michaelmas Term's 'Inductio' appears as Act 1, Scene 1; consequently this edition of the play has three scenes in the first act.

SEE ALSO

Text: *Works*, 337
Authorship and date: this volume, 353

WORKS CITED

Previous Editions

Bullen, A. H., ed., *Works* (1885), vol. 1

Dyce, Alexander, ed., *Works* (1840), vol. 1

Levin, Richard, ed., *Michaelmas Term*, Regents Renaissance Drama Series (1966)

Price, George R., ed., *Michaelmas Term*, dissertation, University of Wisconsin (1941)

—— ed., *Michaelmas Term* and *A Trick to Catch the Old One* (1976)

Sampson, Martin W., ed., *Thomas Middleton* (1915)

Schelling, Felix E. and Matthew Black, eds., *Typical Elizabethan Plays* (1949)

Taylor, Michael, ed., *Thomas Middleton: A Mad World, My Masters and Other Plays* (1995)

Other Works Cited

Booth, Stephen, *'King Lear', 'Macbeth', Indefinition, and Tragedy* (1983)

Chambers, E. K., *The Elizabethan Stage*, 4 vols (1923)

Eliot, T. S., *Selected Essays* (1934)

Greg, W. W., *A Bibliography of the English Printed Drama to the Restoration*, vols 1 and 3 (1939 and 1957)

Grosart, Alexander B., ed., *The Non-Dramatic Works of Thomas Dekker*, 5 vols (1884)

Guilpin, Everard, *Skialetheia. or A shadowe of Truth* (1598)

Herford, C. H., and Percy & Evelyn Simpson, eds., *Ben Jonson*, 11 vols (1925–52)

Leinwand, Theodore B., *The City Staged: Jacobean Comedy, 1603–13* (1986)

—— 'Redeeming Beggary/Buggery in *Michaelmas Term*', ELH 61 (1994), 53–70

L[enton], F[rancis], *The Young Gallants Whirligigg* (1629)

Marotti, Arthur F., *John Donne, Coterie Poet* (1986)

Nashe, Thomas, *Pierce Penilesse* (1592)

Paster, Gail Kern, *The Idea of the City in the Age of Shakespeare* (1985)

Price, George R., 'The First Edition of *Your Five Gallants* and of *Michaelmas Term*', *The Library*, V, 8 (1953), 23–9

—— 'Dividing the Copy for *Michaelmas Term*', *Papers of the Bibliographical Society of America* 60 (1966), 327–36

Prynne, William, *Histrio-mastix* (1633)

Smith, Bruce R., *Homosexual Desire in Shakespeare's England* (1991)

Stubbes, Philip, *The anatomie of abuses* (1583)

Swinburne, A. C., *The Age of Shakespeare* (1908)

Weiss, Adrian, personal correspondence, 4 August 1993

TEXTUAL NOTES

1.1.0.1 Incipit Actus Primus] THIS EDITION; *not in* PURFOOT; all subsequent act divisions appear in PURFOOT–ALLDE

1.1.34 hither] PURFOOT (hether); also at 3.1.301

1.1.67 do] LEVIN (*conj.*); *not in* PURFOOT. Levin transposes 'we call' to make sense of the interrogative form, but he conjectures that the compositor may have dropped 'do' after 'Why'.

1.2.26 newly] PURFOOT (cor.); *not in* PURFOOT (uncor.)

1.2.83 itch] HARPER; icth PURFOOT

1.2.86 look sleek] HARPER; looke, seeke PURFOOT

1.2.94 in] SAMPSON; *not in* PURFOOT

1.2.102 Ne'er] PURFOOT (Ne) possibly a compositor's misprint

1.2.109 some] HARPER; some some PURFOOT

1.2.147 Who? 'Tis!] PRICE; Whose tis? PURFOOT; Who's this? HARPER

1.2.248 of] PURFOOT (off)

1.2.256 Prithee] PURFOOT (Prethe)

1.2.270 on't] PRICE (*conj.*); out PURFOOT. Levin notes that going from Scotland to London would be a journey 'up' (cf. 1.1.0.4, 1.1.13, 1.2.117, etc.), not a journey 'out'. He conjectures that the compositor reversed the 'n' in his type (cf. 2.2.33, etc.).

1.2.277 knight] HARPER; Knight PURFOOT

1.2.281 christened] PURFOOT (kersen'd)

1.2.282 disguise] DYCE; disquire PURFOOT. PURFOOT's 'disquire' may be Middleton's nonce word for 'rob me of my squiredom', but the passage would then require 'does [not] disquire me'.

1.2.291 an't] PURFOOT (and); see discussion in note to 4.7.156 in Gary Taylor's edition of *Henry V*

1.3.1 HELLGILL] DYCE; Pand[er] PURFOOT–ALLDE throughout scene and in some stage directions and speech prefixes

1.3.16 thou shalt] PRICE; thou that shalt PURFOOT

1.3.40 dissemble] SAMPSON (*conj.*); dissembler PURFOOT

1.3.61 till] PURFOOT (tell)

2.1.7 gentleman] HARPER; genrleman PURFOOT

2.1.22 impressure] PURFOOT (impressier)

2.1.95 knew] DYCE; know ALLDE

2.1.104–5 o' their...o' their] DYCE (*subst.*); a'th their...a'th their ALLDE

2.1.194 sleight] ALLDE (slight)

2.2.0.2 *enticed*] HARPER (entic'd); entt(?)ic'd ALLDE

2.2.3 thatched] ALLDE (thatcht)

2.2.33 fond] HARPER; foud ALLDE

2.3.24 errand] BULLEN; errant ALLDE

2.3.63 fool] HARPER; foote ALLDE

2.3.104 *into the shop*] LEVIN; *not in* ALLDE. That he may appear in the middle of business, Quomodo feigns conversation with a customer within.

2.3.107.1 *Enter Thomasine above*] DYCE; 'Tomazin above' ALLDE (after line 2.3.224)

2.3.152, 158, 183 Gum] DYCE; Goome ALLDE

2.3.185 Brentford] ALLDE (Brainford)

2.3.210, 400 Middleburgh] ALLDE (Middleborrow)

2.3.275 gentleman] ALLDE (catchword); genleman ALLDE (text)

2.3.322 Drop, damn] DYCE; Drop Dam ALLDE

2.3.348 piece] BULLEN; price ALLDE

2.3.358 You've] ALLDE (Ye'ave)

2.3.381 he] ALLDE (corr.); *not in* ALLDE (uncorr.)

2.3.385 R's] SAMPSON; R. ALLDE

2.3.385 E's] SCHELLING; E. ALLDE

2.3.445 proper springall] DYCE; proper, springfull ALLDE

2.3.450 *spemque*] HARPER (spemꝗ); sprinꝗ ALLDE

2.3.462 to] ALLDE (too)

2.3.484 and...my] ALLDE (and my). The text is corrupt here; perhaps 'now have I' or 'have got' has dropped out.

2.3.486.1 *Finis*] ALLDE (uncorr.); *Finit* ALLDE (corr.)

3.1.0.5 *Mistress Comings*] *not in* ALLDE

3.1.0.5 tirewoman] HARPER; Tyrewomen ALLDE

3.1.12 COURTESAN] Curt[ezan] ALLDE (*throughout scene*). At this point in the play, speech-prefixes in ALLDE cease referring to the 'Country Wench'.

3.1.41.1 *a Servant*] SAMPSON; *one* ALLDE

3.1.42 SERVANT] DYCE; 1 ALLDE (also at l. 45)

3.1.50 too] ALLDE (to)

3.1.70 MISTRESS COMINGS] HARPER (Com); Coin ALLDE

3.1.83, 85 punk] ALLDE (pung)

3.1.85 to] HARPER; ro ALLDE

3.1.94 'em] ALLDE (am)

3.1.117 FATHER] DYCE; Sho ALLDE

3.1.215 beshrew] ALLDE (beshrow)

3.1.242 off] ALLDE (of)

3.1.243 doted] ALLDE (dooted)

3.1.263 MOTHER GRUEL] HARPER (Gruil.); Guil. ALLDE

3.1.281 REARAGE *and* SALEWOOD] DYCE; All ALLDE

3.1.290 banns] ALLDE (banes)

3.1.295 'fraid] ALLDE (fraide)

3.3.37 know 'tis] HARPER; knew tis ALLDE

3.3.39 knew] DYCE; knowe ALLDE

3.3.55 enough] ALLDE (enow)

3.4.10 lecher] DYCE; leather ALLDE

3.4.10 a] HARPER; *not in* ALLDE

3.4.71 angrily] ALLDE (angerly)

3.4.90 bach'lors] HARPER; batchler ALLDE

3.4.136 dreamt] HARPER (dream't); dream ALLDE, probably due to a letter having dropped out or failed to print

3.4.138 bring] HARPER; ring ALLDE, probably due to a letter having dropped out or failed to print

3.4.153 therefore] HARPER; therfeore ALLDE

3.4.166 debts] ALLDE (depts)

3.4.174 bands] ALLDE (Bonds)

3.4.225 seven] HARPER; seanen ALLDE

3.4.226 shrewd] ALLDE (shroud)

3.4.233 to't] DYCE; too't ALLDE

3.4.265-6 'he] LEVIN; quotation marks begin next line in ALLDE

3.5.3 in] HARPER; jn ALLDE

3.5.39 Gentlemen] HARPER; Gntlemen ALLDE

3.5.58 Master] HARPER; maistet ALLDE

3.5.67 venture] ALLDE (venter)

4.1.45 Quomodo] HARPER; Qmomodo ALLDE

4.1.55 free man] ALLDE (freeman)

4.1.56 whither] ALLDE (whether)

4.1.70 sleight] ALLDE (slight)

4.2.2 COURTESAN] Curt[ezan] ALLDE (*throughout scene*)

4.2.17 punishment] HARPER; punishent ALLDE

4.2.28 generation's] HARPER (Generations); Generatious ALLDE

4.3.30 i'th'] LEVIN; 'ith the ALLDE

4.4.2 wringing] ALLDE ringing

4.4.3 tears] ALLDE (catchword); *not in* ALLDE (text)

4.4.23 One] HARPER; Ont ALLDE

4.4.31 QUOMODO] LEVIN; ALLDE assigns this speech, and the succeeding response to Sim, to Bead[le].

4.4.34 lest] ALLDE (least)

4.4.41 hear] HARPER; feare ALLDE

5.1.48 Easy] SAMPSON; Blastfield ALLDE. The compositor may have picked up the 'Master Blastfield' six lines above; if we retain the quarto's 'Blastfield', then with Levin, we could give the sarcastic phrase—'Sweet Master Blastfield'—to Easy at the start of the next line.

5.1.67 months] DYCE; *not in* ALLDE

5.1.101 thither] ALLDE (the ther?)

5.1.102 Quomodo] HARPER; Qnomodo ALLDE

5.1.109 Who? 'Tis] LEVIN; Whose? tis ALLDE; Who's? this HARPER

5.2.5 COURTESAN] Curt[ezan] ALLDE

5.2.7 enough] ALLDE (ynow)

5.3.15 They're] ALLDE (their)

5.3.75 I] HARPER; I, ALLDE. ALLDE's comma suggests 'Ay', but HARPER is consistent with 'I warrant' throughout the play.

5.3.96 SALEWOOD] DYCE; Gent[.] ALLDE

5.3.103 COURTESAN] Curt[.] ALLDE (also at 5.3.107)

5.3.111 lashes] HARPER; lastes ALLDE

5.3.115 SALEWOOD] DYCE; Gent[.] ALLDE

5.3.140 Mistress] HARPER; Maister ALLDE

5.3.141 against] ALLDE (agen)

5.3.159 hither] ALLDE (heather)

5.3.159 then were] PRICE; *not in* ALLDE

PRESS VARIANTS

This list of substantive variants in PURFOOT–ALLDE derives from Levin's collation of copies in the Folger Library (Clawson-Bridgewater copy), the Houghton Library at Harvard, the Henry E. Huntington Library, the Yale Elizabethan Club, and the British Museum (Ashley 1154, and C34.d.40). For particular variants, Levin also consulted the Folger's Cole Orton Hall copy, and copies in the Chapin Library at Williams College, the Boston Public Library, and the Pforzheimer Collection, University of Texas at Austin.

Sheet A (inner forme)

1.2.26 is newly fallen] *corr* (falne); is falne *uncorr*

Sheet B (inner forme)

1.2.196 Horn we'll—] *uncorr* (horne weele); horne—weele *corr*

1.2.206 this is kindness] *corr* (kindnes); this kindnes *uncorr*

1.2.294-5 him now, I can tell you] *corr* (now,ₐ); him I can you now *uncorr*

1.2.297 behaviour] *corr*; haviour *uncorr*

1.2.298 His] *corr*; Hee *uncorr*

1.3.19 decking] *corr*; deckning *uncorr*

1.3.39 thing] *corr*; things *uncorr*

Sheet C (outer forme)

2.1.155 great] *corr*; good *uncorr*

Sheet D (outer forme)

2.3.255 discharged] *uncorr*; discharg'd *corr*

2.3.276-7 a...neither] *corr*; a stranger to me, I meere neither *uncorr*

2.3.393.1 *Falselight*] *corr* (Falslight); *Flaslight uncorr*

Sheet D (inner forme)

2.3.158 Master...Master] *corr*; Mister...Mister *uncorr*

2.3.185 Brentford] Brainford *corr*; Braniford *uncorr*

2.3.381 cut, he will] *corr*; cut, will *uncorr*

Sheet E (outer forme)

2.3.433 will] *corr* (wil); we wil *uncorr*

3.1.60   of] *corr*; of of *uncorr*

Sheet E (inner forme)

2.3.486   of] *corr*; for *uncorr*
2.3.486.1   *Finis*] *uncorr*; *Finit corr*

Sheet F (outer forme)

3.4.136   dreamt] in ALLDE, either dream' or dream

Sheet G (outer forme)

3.4.170   too...too] *corr*; to...to *uncorr*
3.4.200   faces] *corr*; face *uncorr*
3.5.79.1   *Finis*] *corr*; *Finit uncorr*

Sheet G (inner forme)

3.4.233   to't] *corr* (too't); to eate *uncorr*
3.4.233-4   in us more pity] *corr* (~ pittie); more pittie in us *uncorr*
3.4.248   and] *corr*; aud *uncorr*
3.4.266   rape] *corr*; reape *uncorr*
4.1.13   face, iwis!] *corr* (ywis![?]); ~‸ ywis, *uncorr*
4.1.51   upon't] *corr* (uppon't); uppon,t *uncorr*

Sheet I (inner forme)

5.3.30   counterfeit] *corr* (counterfet); connterfet *uncorr*
5.3.157   suit] *corr* (sute); suite *uncorr*

STAGE DIRECTIONS

1.1.0.2–5   Inductio. | *Enter Michaelmas Terme in a whitish* | *Cloake, new come up out of the countrey, a Boye* | *bringing his Gowne after* | *him!*
1.1.29.1   Musicke | *playing.* (at left margin, to the left of a brace enclosing 1.1.29.1–3)
1.1.29.1–4   *Enter the other 3. Termes, the first bringing in a* | *fellowe poore, which the other 2. aduanceth, gi-*|*uing him rich Apparell, a page, and a pandar.*
1.1.29.5   Exit.
1.1.53   Exeunt.
1.1.75   Exit.
1.2.0.1–2   *Enter at one dore Maister Rerrage, meeting* | *Maister Salewood.*
1.2.42.1–2   *Enter master Cockstone, a Gentleman meeting master* | *Easye of Essex.*
1.2.78.1–2   *Quomodo with his two spirits, Shortyard* | *and False-light.*
1.2.89   Exit Fals. (right, opposite 1.2.89)
1.2.133   (*Exit.*
1.2.135   (*Exit.*
1.2.209   Exeunt.
1.2.317   (*Exit.*
1.2.322   Exit.
1.3.0.1–2   *Enter Lethes Pandar with a Country wench.*
1.3.62   Exeunt.
2.1.0.1–3   Actus Secundus. | *Enter Rerrage, Salewood, Lethe,* | *Easye, with Shortyard* | *alias Blastfield, at dice.*
2.1.184.1   *Enter a Drawer.*
2.1.196   Exeunt.
2.2.0.1–2   *Enter the Countrie-Wenches Father, that was enttic'd for* | *Leth:*
2.2.38   Exit
2.3.0.1–2   *Lethes Mother enters with Quomodoes wife with the* | *Letter.*
2.3.34.1   *Enter Quomodo and his Daughter Su.*
2.3.76.1   *Enter Falslight.*
2.3.88   Exit.
2.3.90   Exit.
2.3.100.1   *Enter Maister Easie, with Short-yard, alias Blastfield.*
2.3.181.1   *Enter Boy.*
2.3.225   *Tomazin aboue.* (moved to 2.3.107.1 in edited text)
2.3.327.1   *Enter Dustbox the Scriuener.*
2.3.347.1   *Enter Falslight like a Porter, sweating.*
2.3.380   Exit.
2.3.393.1–2   *Enter Falslight with the cloath.*
2.3.443.1   *Enter Sim.*
2.3.466.1   *Enter Falslight for Maister Idem.*
2.3.481   Exeunt.

2.3.486   Exit.
2.3.486.1   *Finit Actus secundus.*
3.1.0.1–6   Incipit Actus Tertius. | *Enter Lethes pander, Helgill, the* | *Coũtrie wench comming in with* | *a new fashion Gowne drest Gentlewoman like, the Taylor* | *pointes it, and a Tyrewomen busie about her* | *head.*
3.1.41.1–2   *Enter one bringing in her Father in disguise to* | *serue her.*
3.1.72   Exeunt
3.1.75.1   *Enter Lethe with Rerage and Salewood.*
3.1.134.1   *Enter Shortyard with Easie.*
3.1.205.1   *Enter Mother Gruill.*
3.1.279   Exit.
3.1.281   Exeunt
3.1.287   Exeunt.
3.1.291   Exit.
3.1.304   Exit.
3.2.0.1   *Enter Easie with Shortyards Boy.*
3.2.19   Exit.
3.2.24   Exit.
3.3.0.1–2   *Enter Shortyard and Falslight like a Sarieant and a* | *Yeoman to arrest Easie.*
3.3.21.1   *Enter Easie with the Boy.*
3.3.63   Exeunt.
3.4.0.1   *Enter Quomodo with the Boy.*
3.4.135   Exeunt.
3.4.192.1–2   *Enter Shortyard and Falslight, like wealthy Cittizens* | *in Sattin sutes.*
3.4.260   Exeunt.
3.5.25.1   *Enter Easie with Shortyard like a Cittizen.*
3.5.62   Exit.
3.5.65   Exeunt after Lethe.
3.5.79   Exeunt.
3.5.79.1   *Musicke. Finis Actus tertius.*
4.1.0.1–4   Incipit quartus. | *Enter Quomodo, his disguised spirits,* | *after whom Easie* | *followes hard.*
4.1.65   Exit.
4.1.121   Exit.
4.2.0.1   *Enter Curtezan with her disguised father.*
4.2.29   Exeunt.
4.3.0.1   *A Bell Toales, a Confused crie within.*
4.3.3.1   *Enter Shortyard and the Boy.*
4.3.23   Exit.
4.3.23.1   *Enter Tomazin with Winefride her maide* | *in hast.*
4.3.39   Exit.
4.3.44.1   *Enter Rerage, Curtezans Father following.*
4.3.81   Exeunt.
4.4.0.1   *Enter Quomodo like a Beadle.*

4.4.16.1   *Enter the Liuerie.*

4.4.52.1–3   *A counterfet Coarse brought in, Tomazin, and al the |*
    mourners equally counterfeit.

4.4.54.1   *Enter Easie.*

4.4.56   *Falls downe in a fayned swound.*

4.4.70   *Pointing after the Coffin.*

4.4.74   *Exeunt.*

4.4.82.1   *Finis Actus Quartus.*

5.1.0.1–3   *Incipit Quintus et Ultimus. | Enter Shortyard with*
    writings, hauing cousned Sim | Quomodo.

5.1.13.1–2   *Enter Quomodoes Wife marryed to Easie.*

5.1.48   *Exit.*

5.1.60.1   *Enter Quomodo.*

5.1.133   *Exit.*

5.1.135   *Exeunt.*

5.2.0.1   *Enter Lethe with officers, taken with his Harlot.*

5.3.0.1–2   *Enter Iudge, Easie, and Tomazin in talke with him.*

5.3.92.1   *Enter Officers with Lethe and the Harlot.*

5.3.167.1   *FINIS*

LINEATION NOTES

1.1.1–2   Lay...gown] DYCE; *1 line* PURFOOT

1.2.61–2   Is't...yourself] DYCE; *prose* PURFOOT

1.2.65–71   One...weakest] DYCE; *prose* PURFOOT

1.2.86–8   Go...cunning Falselight.] DYCE; *prose* PURFOOT

1.2.104–12   Puh...lands] DYCE; *prose* PURFOOT

1.2.116–17   Ah...me] DYCE; *prose* PURFOOT

1.2.119–21   I...Happily] LEVIN; *prose* PURFOOT

1.2.157–69   That...dew] DYCE; *prose* PURFOOT

1.2.177–8   Do...memory] DYCE; *1 line* PURFOOT

1.2.196–7   At...that] DYCE *1 line* PURFOOT

1.2.261   That's...then] DYCE; *separate line* PURFOOT

2.3.344   I...sir] DYCE; *separate line* ALLDE

3.1.42   I've...whose] DYCE; *separate line* ALLDE

3.1.54   Be...hope] PRICE; *separate line* ALLDE

3.1.118–19   But...busy] LEVIN; *prose* ALLDE

3.1.147   I...sir] PRICE; *separate line* ALLDE

3.3.1   So...that] DYCE; *separate line* ALLDE

4.1.75–6   I...wood] DYCE; *one line* ALLDE

4.2.6–7   That...men] DYCE; *prose* ALLDE

4.2.19–20   To...distant] DYCE; *prose* ALLDE

4.4.15–16   I'll...low] DYCE; *prose* ALLDE

4.4.77–9   Delay...us] PRICE; *prose* ALLDE

5.1.2   heir] DYCE; *first word of next line in* ALLDE

5.1.28–30   Why...you] DYCE; *prose* ALLDE

5.1.33–6   You...'em] DYCE; *prose* ALLDE

5.2.1–2   Heart...disgraced] DYCE; *one line* ALLDE

5.3.8   No] DYCE; *ends previous line* ALLDE

5.3.14–15   O...Thomasine] DYCE; *prose* ALLDE

5.3.27–8   Stay...lord] DYCE; *one line* ALLDE

5.3.32–3   Why...am] DYCE; *prose* ALLDE

5.3.49–50   All...see't] DYCE; *prose* ALLDE

5.3.59–60   My...wife] DYCE; *one line* ALLDE

5.3.64–8   He...me] DYCE; *prose* ALLDE

5.3.78–80   Is...'em] DYCE; *prose* ALLDE

5.3.80–1   My...me] DYCE; *one line* ALLDE

5.3.104   I'll...too] DYCE; *separate line* ALLDE

5.3.109   O, intolerable] DYCE; *separate line* ALLDE

5.3.129–30   I...punishment] DYCE; *prose* ALLDE

5.3.133–4   Whom...pardon] DYCE; *one line* ALLDE

5.3.137–8   Knave...quiet] LEVIN; *prose ?* ALLDE

5.3.144–50   I'll...lordship] LEVIN; *prose* ALLDE

5.3.158–62   This...thee] LEVIN; *prose* ALLDE

THE PURITAN WIDOW *or* THE PURITAN *or*
THE WIDOW OF WATLING STREET

Edited by Donna B. Hamilton

The Puritan Widow was entered in the Register of the Stationers' Company on 6 August 1607, by George Eld, who entered *Northward Ho* on the same day:

> Geo. Elde Entred for his copie vnder thande of Sr. Geo. Bucke Knight and the wardens a booke called the comedie of the Puritan Wydowe

The only known quarto (ELD) was printed in 1607 (STC 21531; *BEPD* 251); its title-page specifies that the play was performed by the Children of Paul's and that George Eld was the printer:

> THE PURITAINE Or THE WIDDOW of Watling-ſtreete. *Acted by the Children of Paules.* Written by W. S. Imprinted at London by G. ELD. [device 320] 1607.

In addition to *Northward Ho* (*BEPD* 250) and *The Puritan Widow*, other plays printed by Eld in 1607 include *Lingua: or, the Combat of the Tongue and the Five Senses* (*BEPD* 239), *What You Will* (*BEPD* 252), and *The Revenger's Tragedy* (*BEPD* 253).

ELD consists of 31 leaves, the title-page and 59 printed pages (A3 through H4). At the end of H4, after 'Exeunt', appear the words '*Deus dedit his quoq finem*', and below them 'FINIM.' The text is printed in roman type, with speech headings in italic and stage directions in predominantly italic type, but frequently in combination with words (often character names) in roman type. The verso signatures and the last recto of each gathering are unsigned. Catchwords occur regularly, but with some inconsistencies and errors. On B1, the catchword is 'Peece', and on the following page 'Peace'. When a speech heading is used as the catchword, there is inconsistency in whether the catchword gives the name in abbreviated form, and also inconsistency in the spelling of abbreviated forms; for example, on B2ᵛ, the catchword is '*Frailtie*', while the speech heading on B3 is '*Frail*', while on B4ᵛ the catchword is '*Nich.*' and the speechheading on the following page is '*Nic.*'. On E3, the catchword is '*Gent.*' but Pieboard has the first speech on E3ᵛ. Kaiser has suggested appropriately that a short speech from the Gentleman may have been dropped, a possibility that this edition records in the text. The running title is 'THE PURITAINE WIDDOW'. Adopted in THIS EDITION for the title of the play, these words differ from ELD's title-page but correspond to the Stationers' Register entry, as well as to the running title in DANIEL. Different spellings of the speech headings for

Pieboard led Kaiser to conclude that the play was set by two compositors, one of whom used 'Pye.' or 'Pie.', the other 'Pyb.' or 'Pib.'

Kaiser and Lake use the inadequacy of several stage directions for exits or entrances to argue that the quarto is based on the author's manuscript copy (or, according to Kaiser, a scribal copy of the author's manuscript), but not on a promptbook. For example, at 1.1.117, the direction 'Exeunt mother and daughters' is followed by a soliloquy by Moll, one of the daughters. Similarly at the end of 4.3, after Sir Godfrey has invited everyone to a banquet, there occurs the stage direction 'Exit', but the daughter Frank remains on stage for a soliloquy. At the beginning of 3.2, the stage direction signals an entrance for Puttock and Ravenshaw but omits Dogson, who has a prominent role in the scene. For other discrepancies, see the Textual Notes. Further, the presence of many contractions especially associated with Middleton, and identified in Eccles's seminal article of 1931 (including 'h'as', 'sh'as', 't'as', ''t'ad', and 'uppo'th''), together with Lake's evidence that Eld's compositors reproduced contractions as they found them in copy, further corroborates both Middleton's authorship of the play and Eld's use of the author's manuscript copy.

One character name requires comment. In keeping with the usage that predominates in ELD, this edition uses 'Frank' (a nickname for 'Frances') to refer to the older daughter of the Widow. In speech headings and stage directions, ELD usually uses this nickname, variously spelled as 'Franck', 'Franke', or 'Frank'; only in conversation on G1ᵛ and H1ᵛ, and in a stage direction on H3, does ELD use the name 'Frances'. In contrast to ELD, the 1664 Shakespeare folio edition—the first edition of *The Puritan Widow* to list *dramatis personae*—and all subsequent editions list this character in the *dramatis personae* as 'Frances' and refer to her in speech headings as either 'Frances' or 'Fran.' This modern spelling edition restores ELD's predominant use of the nickname 'Frank' (by using it in the persons list, speech headings, and stage directions), while also retaining 'Frances' in the two instances where this form of her name occurs in character speeches.

This edition reproduces the act divisions in ELD (which includes divisions labelled *Actus Primus*, *Actus 3*, *Actus 4, and Actus 5. Scen. 1*), and follows all later editions by inserting Act 2 at the point where ELD gives the stage direction 'Enter Moll, youngest daughter to the Widow, alone'. ELD contains no other scene divisions.

After ELD, the next printing of the play was by DANIEL, for inclusion with six other plays (now not regarded as William Shakespeare's) in the 1664 folio edition of the plays of Shakespeare; these seven plays were also included in 1685, which was published by a consortium and printed by multiple printers who have not been identified.

This edition is indebted to the work of Richard Proudfoot, who gave me access to his unpublished collations of ELD. I have independently collated the copies of Eld (except as noted in Press Variant collations) and of later editions as listed below, and am wholly responsible for any errors in this edition. Theodore Leinwand and John Duffy assisted me with the notes to the text.

SEE ALSO

Text: *Works*, 513
Authorship and date: this volume, 358

WORKS CITED

Previous Editions

The puritaine or the widdow of Watling-street (1607)
Mr. William Shakespear's Comedies, Histories, and Tragedies (1664)
Mr. William Shakespear's Comedies, Histories, and Tragedies (1685)
Rowe, Nicholas, ed., *The Works of Mr. William Shakespear* (1714), vol. 8
Pope, Alexander, ed., *The Works of Mr. William Shakespear* (1728), vol. 9
Shakespeare, William, *The Puritan: or, the Widow of Watling-street*, printed by R. Walker, 1734
Shakespeare, William, *The Puritan: or, the Widow of Watling-street*, printed by J. Tonson, 1734
Malone, Edmond, ed., *Supplement to the Edition of Shakespeare's Plays Published in 1778 by Samuel Johnson and George Steevens* (1780), vol. 2
Simms, William Gilmore, ed., *A Supplement to the Plays of William Shakespeare* (1848)
Tyrrell, Henry, ed., *The Doubtful Plays of Shakespeare* ([1851])
Hazlitt, William, ed., *The Supplementary Works of William Shakespeare* (1852)
Hopkinson, A. F., ed., *The Puritan, or the Widow of Watling Street* (1894)
Brooke, C. F. Tucker, ed., *The Shakespeare Apocrypha* (1908)
Heaven, Sidney, ed., *The Puritaine or The Widow of Watling Street* ([1955])
Kaiser, Donald Frederick, ed., *A Critical Edition of 'The Puritan; or, the Widow of Watling Street'*, University of Wisconsin diss., 1966

Other Works Cited

Bawcutt, N. W., 'Was Thomas Middleton a Puritan Dramatist?', *Modern Language Review* 94 (1999), 925-39

Bullard, J. V., ed., *Constitutions and Canons Ecclesiastical 1604* (1934)
Burrage, Champlin, *The Early English Dissenters, 1550-1641* (1912; rpt. 1967), vols 1, 2
Chambers, E. K., *The Elizabethan Stage* (1923), vols 2, 4
Christian, Mildred G., 'Middleton's Acquaintance with the Merrie Conceited Jests of George Peele', *PMLA* 50 (1935), 753-60
Collinson, Patrick, *The Elizabethan Puritan Movement* (1967)
—— 'The Downfall of Archbishop Grindal and its Place in Elizabethan Political and Ecclesiastical History', in *Godly People: Essays on English Protestantism and Puritanism* (1983), pp. 371-97
—— 'Lectures by Combination: Structures and Characteristics of Church Life in 17th-Century England' in *Godly People: Essays on English Protestantism and Puritanism* (1983), pp. 467-98
Crashaw, William, *The sermon preached at the Cross, Feb. 14, 1607* (1608)
Dobson, Daniel B., 'Allusions to the Gunpowder Plot in Dekker's *Whore of Babylon*', *Notes and Queries* 6 (1959), 257
Eccles, Mark, 'Middleton's Birth and Education', *Review of English Studies* 7 (1931), 431-41
—— '"Thomas Middleton a Poett"', *Studies in Philology* 54 (1957), 516-36
Gair, W. Reavley, *The Children of Paul's* (1982)
Gasper, Julia, *The Dragon and the Dove: The Plays of Thomas Dekker* (1990)
Haigh, Christopher, 'From Monopoly to Minority: Catholicism in Early Modern England', *Transactions of the Royal Historical Society*, 5th series, 31 (1981), 129-47
Heinemann, Margot, *Puritanism and Theatre: Thomas Middleton and Opposition Drama under the Early Stuarts* (1980)
Hill, Christopher, *Society and Puritanism* (1964)
Lake, David J., *The Canon of Thomas Middleton's Plays* (1975)
Lake, Peter, *Anglicans and Puritans* (1988)
Maxwell, Baldwin, *Studies in the Shakespeare Apocrypha* (1956)
Milward, Peter, *Religious Controversies of the Jacobean Age: A Survey of Printed Sources* (1978)
Perkins, William, *A golden chaine, or the description of theologie, containing the order of the causes of salvation and damnation* (1591)
Power, William, 'Middleton's Way with Names', *Notes and Queries* 205 (1960), 56-60
Rogers, Thomas, *A golden chaine, taken out of the psalmes of King David* (1579)
Scot, Reginald, *The discovery of witchcraft* (1584)
Seaver, Paul S., *The Puritan Lectureships: The Politics of Religious Dissent, 1560-1662* (1970)
Stow, John, *A survay of London* (1598)
Strype, John, *The Life and Acts of John Whitgift* (1824), vol. 3
Stubbes, Philip, *The rosarie of christian praiers and meditations* (1583)
Williams, Dorothy Ann, 'Puritanism in the City Government, 1610-40', *The Guildhall Miscellany* vol. 1, no. 4 (1955), 3-14

TEXTUAL NOTES

Title The Puritan Widow] THE PVRITAINE Or THE WIDDOW
of Watling-ſtreete *with THE PVRITAINE WIDDOW for
running title* ELD; THE PURITAN: OR, THE Widow of Wat-
lingſtreet *with same words repeated for running title* 1685; The
Puritan: or, The Widow of Watling Street *with* The Puritan
for running title MALONE. *The Puritan Widow as title in* THIS
EDITION *corresponds to the Stationers' Register entry*, the
comedie of 'the Puritan Widowe', *and the running title in* ELD.

1.1.0.3 Frank] ELD (Frank, Franck, *or* Franke), *but usually*
Franck *in speech headings, except for* Frank *at* 4.2.28 *and*
4.2.301. Franke *occurs in the s.d. at* 4.2.300.1. *At* 4.2.48,
5.1.26, *and* 5.4.0.3, *she is called* Frances ELD (Francis).

1.1.45 cards] ELD; charts MALONE

1.1.54 corpse] THIS EDITION; coarſe ELD. *This edition uses the
spelling* 'cor'se' *for all versions in* ELD *of the word* 'corpse',
including 'coarse' *and* 'corps'.

1.1.81 choir] ELD (Quire); o' the choir MALONE

1.1.87 too hot] MALONE; ſo hot ELD; too good SIMMS

1.1.108 vow...his] DANIEL; now...her ELD

1.1.113 this...This] MALONE; their...their ELD

1.1.115 this] MALONE; their ELD

1.1.117.1 Exeunt [Widow] and Frank] ROWE; Exeunt mother and
daughters ELD

1.1.120 widows'] STEEVENS; widows POPE; Widdowers ELD; wid-
owers' HOPKINSON. *Hopkinson, like Malone, suggests that*
'widdower' *was applied to both sexes.*

1.1.123 to] ELD; too DANIEL. *If spittle is taken to mean spit or
saliva, then* 'to nigh' (*i.e. almost as far as*); *if taken to mean*
'spital' *or* 'hospital', *then* 'too nigh'. *The context suggests
that the former is the primary meaning.*

1.1.135 between] ELD; betwixt DANIEL

1.1.148 roost] ELD (roast)

1.2.7 your] *corrected copies of* ELD; yours *uncorrected copies of*
ELD

1.2.23 ensign] ELD (Antient)

1.2.50 nothing to lose but] ELD; nothing in the world but DANIEL

1.2.56 and thereby] ELD; that thereby ROWE

1.2.60 affliction] Affliction ELD; affection DANIEL (*and all subsequent editions*). *The context does not, however, support
that emendation. Pieboard is explaining that all that his
education has resulted in is the ability to tell the horrible
truth about his life, that he is a beggar, a condition made
worse by peacetime. Though he knows this point may offend
some people, he insists on making it; he will not* 'cog with
[flatter] peace', *not be* 'afraid to say' *what is true. Hence,
his satiric words will be an* 'affliction' *to many (as indeed
Middleton's satire in the play was to Crashawe).*

1.2.80 our only] ELD; the onely DANIEL

1.2.85 a fortune-teller, a fortune-teller] ELD; a fortuneteller
MALONE

1.2.86 Very proper] ELD; A Fortune-teller? Very proper. MALONE.
Malone regarded the repetition of 'a Fortune-teller' *in* 1.2.85
as a printer's error.

1.2.87 of] ELD; *not in* DANIEL

1.2.93 those] ELD; these DANIEL

1.2.103 sh'as] ELD; she's DANIEL; she has MALONE

1.2.103 on't] ELD; of it MALONE. THIS EDITION *retains throughout
Middleton's characteristic* 'on't' *and does not substitute* 'of't'.

1.2.110 derive] ELD; drive DANIEL

1.3.12 SIMON, FRAILTY, *and* NICHOLAS] THIS EDITION; All ELD; *not
in* HEAVEN, *who adds s.d.*, They recoil, and in their horrified
embarrassment exclaim mildly.

1.3.22 dry] ELD; three MALONE

1.3.36 swoon] 1685; sowne ELD

1.3.44 feet] ELD; Fleet 1685

1.3.64 we must] DANIEL; me must ELD

1.3.75 up] ELD; *not in* 1685

1.3.76 fall] DANIEL; falls ELD

1.4.0.1–3 The prison Marshalsea. Enter Captain Idle at one door,
George Pieboard and old soldier Skirmish speaking within at
another door] THIS EDITION; The Prison, Marshalsea. Enter
Captaine Ydle at one dore, and old souldier at the other. George
Py-board, speaking within. ELD; A room in the Marshalsea prison.
Enter Idle; to him afterwards Pyeboard and Skirmish MALONE

1.4.5 Is't] ift ELD; has it MALONE

1.4.52 Does] ELD (Do's); doth DANIEL

1.4.87 that. Ne'er] DANIEL; that but ne'er ELD

1.4.89 'im] DANIEL; him TONSON; 'em ELD

1.4.121 quoth a] ELD (quo'the)

1.4.132 second] ELD (2.)

1.4.133 quoth a] ELD (qua tha)

1.4.135 knew] ELD; know DANIEL

1.4.136 makes so little] ELD; makes it so little ROWE

1.4.142 done't] ELD (don't)

1.4.148 shall] ELD; will DANIEL

1.4.163 but it shall be] MALONE; but be ELD

1.4.169 at] ELD; at a DANIEL

1.4.175 hands] ELD; sides HOPKINSON

1.4.181 against] ELD (again); against DANIEL. 'Again' *for*
'against' *is a colloquial form.*

1.4.189 raged] ELD (ragde)

1.4.200 three-times-thrice-honey] ELD (hunny)

1.4.210 harmless] MALONE; harmless. Exit Nicholas ELD. ELD
placed an 'exit' *for Nicholas at both* 1.4.210 *and* 1.4.212.
Beginning with DANIEL, *printers retained the first* 'exit' *but
deleted the second, until* MALONE, *who deleted the first and
restored the second.* THIS EDITION *follows* MALONE.

1.4.212 Exit Nicholas] ELD, MALONE; *not in* DANIEL

1.4.239 Know] ELD; I know DANIEL

1.4.254 ensign] ELD (Anci-|ent)

1.4.256–7 in heaven] ELD; in the even STEEVENS

1.4.259 if] ELD; *not in* MALONE

2.1.0.1 Incipit Actus Secundus] ROWE; *not in* ELD

2.1.10 do't] ELD; dote MALONE

2.1.28.1 Enter Sir John Pennydub] HEAVEN *places S.D. here; at*
27 ELD; *after* 'time' MALONE

2.1.32 e'en now] ELD (enow); e'now 1685; even now MALONE

2.1.55 Pennydub] DANIEL; Penny-Dab ELD

2.1.97 sure to another] ELD; sure to have MALONE

2.1.117 your] DANIEL; yours ELD

2.1.119 quoth a] ELD (qua tha)

2.1.176 and] DANIEL; and and ELD

2.1.209 guests] 1685; ELD (guesse)

2.1.234–5 the elder two of you] THIS EDITION; two of you the
elder shall run mad ELD; of you two the elder DANIEL; of you
two the eldest ROWE; the two elder of you shall run mad
HOPKINSON; two of you—the elder—shall run mad KAISER.
*Malone speculated that the words had been transposed at
the press.*

2.1.250   possible] possible ELD; possibly MALONE

2.1.283.1   *Exeunt Widow and Frank*] Exit Wid. and Fran. ROWE; Exit ELD

2.1.310   among] ELD; amongst 1685

3.1.13   Suds, a] ELD; Sud's a DANIEL; Suds is a TONSON

3.1.14.1   *Enter...soldier*] follows 15 ELD

3.1.14.1   *soldier*] 1685; soulders ELD

3.1.15, 17, 21   what's o'clock] ELD (what's a clock); what is't o'clock MALONE

3.1.16   Jack o'th'] ELD (Jacke at'h); Jack at th' DANIEL; Jack at the ROWE

3.1.21.1   *Enter Corporal*] THIS EDITION; after 23 ELD; after 'corporal', 3.1.22 HOPKINSON. In THIS EDITION, characters enter before their entrance is announced by another character.

3.1.27   balk] ELD (bawk)

3.1.40   knew] *corrected* copies of ELD; know *uncorrected* copies of ELD

3.1.44, 46, 54   Corporal] POPE; Captain ELD

3.1.53.1   *Pieboard stands aloof*] THIS EDITION; Exit MALONE; *goes out* HEAVEN

3.1.58   him] ELD (hem)

3.1.58   [*stepping forward*]] THIS EDITION; *Re-enter Pyeboard* MALONE; *Scene 2 Re-enter Pyeboard* HOPKINSON

3.2.0.2   *and Frailty*] THIS EDITION; *not in* ELD. The Widow indicates his presence 5.

3.2.8   superior] ELD; surgeon STEEVENS. See Commentary note.

3.2.30   lief] ELD (liue)

3.2.37   gaskins] ELD (Gascoines)

3.2.48   are] ELD; is MALONE

3.2.86   Besides] DANIEL; Beside ELD

3.3.0.1–2   *with Yeoman Dogson*] DANIEL; *not in* ELD

3.3.1   hostess] DANIEL; Hostesses ELD

3.3.10   Besides] ELD; because MALONE

3.3.15   doublets] DANIEL; doublers ELD

3.3.24   Have an eye, ay] THIS EDITION; Have an eye, eye ELD; Have an eye, have an eye DANIEL

3.3.52   You] ELD; you'll MALONE

3.3.61   to] ELD; *not in* DANIEL

3.3.70–1   Mistress] DANIEL; Misters ELD

3.3.76   swear] ELD; fear MALONE

3.3.91   is] ELD; are HOPKINSON

3.3.92   Has my wit] ELD; have MALONE; has my wits ROWE

3.3.95   from] DANIEL; ELD (fro)

3.3.97   is touchstone] ELD; the touchstone MALONE

3.3.103   we] DANIEL; me ELD

3.3.119   ha't] ELD (hate), DANIEL; have it MALONE

3.3.130   He's] ELD; hast HOPKINSON

3.3.131.3   withinside] DANIEL; *with inside* ELD; *at the door of a gentleman's house at the inside of the stage* MALONE. 'This stage direction is a good illustration of the simplicity of Elizabethan stage requirements. The author did not intend a change of scene' (BROOKE).

3.4.4   your] DANIEL; you ELD

3.4.17   yeoman] ELD; yeomen HOPKINSON

3.4.21–2   you...your] him...his MALONE. ELD wording emphasizes the proverbial.

3.4.42–4   PIEBOARD...GENTLEMAN] In ELD, Pieboard's 'I have the thing here for you, sir' is the last line of speech on E3. The catchword at the bottom of E3 is 'Gent.' But the first speech heading at the top of E3ᵛ is 'Pyb.' Most likely, ELD omitted a short speech by the Gentleman. DANIEL assigns 3.4.42–4, 'I...sir', to 'Gent.'

3.4.50   fangs] ELD; hands DANIEL

3.4.63   make happy] ELD; make a happy DANIEL

3.4.75   at] ELD; at a DANIEL; of a WALKER

3.4.94   sergeants] ELD; sergeant HOPKINSON

3.4.99   gentleman] DANIEL; Centlemen ELD

3.4.119   then] ELD; *not in* DANIEL

3.4.123   his] *corrected* copies of ELD; her *uncorrected* copies of ELD

3.4.128   fifty shillings] DANIEL; fift-ſhillings ELD

3.4.140.1   *Gentleman*] Gentlemen ELD

3.4.143   God] ELD; Give SIMMS

3.4.143   good e'en] ELD (god den)

3.5.24   set] ELD; *not in* DANIEL; shalt sure be free SIMMS

3.5.44–5   let's to conjuring, let's to conjuring] ELD; let's to conjuring DANIEL

3.5.64   tell] ELD (till), DANIEL

3.5.95   else] ELD; 1685 omits 'else' from 95, and adds it after 'lin' in 94; ROWE follows 1685; *not in* MALONE; *not in* HOPKINSON, who later wrote it in by hand in a copy now in the Folger.

3.5.106   if] 1685; *not in* ELD

3.5.113   Cry Prisoners] ELD; *Prisoners cry within* MALONE

3.5.134   passed in] ELD (past in); of DANIEL

3.5.137   therein] ELD; there DANIEL

3.5.143   sir] ELD; *not in* DANIEL

3.5.161   above] ELD (aboue); about DANIEL

3.5.193   Wilt] ELD (Woult), ROWE; Wilt thou HOPKINSON

3.5.199   fees] DANIEL; fee's ELD

3.5.208   fine] ELD; five DANIEL

3.5.238.1–2   *Pieboard [opens] an almanac, and [takes aside] the Captain*] THIS EDITION; *Pyeboord with an Almanack and the Captaine* ELD; *Opens an almanack, and takes Captain Idle aside* MALONE

3.5.242   fifteen] ELD; fifteenth ROWE

3.5.248   sixteen] ELD; sixteenth ROWE

3.5.291   PIEBOARD *and* CAPTAIN] THIS EDITION; Pye. Idle. MALONE; Tip. Cap. ELD; Capt. POPE

3.5.295   truly] ELD; heartily DANIEL

4.1.6   have as big a heart] ELD; have a heart DANIEL

4.1.26   two] ELD (too), DANIEL

4.1.36   o'the] ELD (a'the); DANIEL oth'; i'the MALONE

4.2.12   man o' cunning] ELD (man a cunning); a man cunning DANIEL; a cunning man MALONE

4.2.26   now] ELD; *not in* DANIEL

4.2.35   quit] THIS EDITION; quite ELD

4.2.37–8   bears you] ELD; bears to you DANIEL

4.2.45   MUCKHILL Yet...fairer.] ELD; *not in* DANIEL

4.2.57   Go] ELD; to DANIEL

4.2.58   TIPSTAFF *and* MUCKHILL] ELD (Both)

4.2.59.1–2   *Exeunt Tipstaff and Muckhill; [Widow, Frank and Frailty go into an adjoining room]*] Exeunt Sir Andrew, Sir Oliver, and Frailty. The Widow and Frances go into the adjoining room HOPKINSON; *Exit* ELD. ELD's sparse direction 'Exit' may indicate that the exit direction was first omitted in typesetting and later added to the end of 4.2.59.

4.2.60.1   *Enter Nicholas*] THIS EDITION; *not in* ELD. Godfrey has told Nicholas, 'Step in,' and then asked him to 'Look, is the coast clear.' Nicholas' affirmative response (4.2.62) suggests that he has entered and has looked over the situation before responding.

4.2.62   cat's] ELD (Cattes); Carter's DANIEL

4.2.63.1   *Enter Sir Godfrey, Captain, Pieboard, and Edmond*] THIS EDITION; *Enter Sir Godf. Capt.Pyb.Edm.Nick* ELD. THIS EDITION has Nicholas enter at 4.2.60.1.

4.2.64   your] ELD; our DANIEL

4.2.70   here] ELD; in't DANIEL

4.2.87   o'er] ELD (ore); of MALONE

4.2.88   tell] ELD; tell you DANIEL
4.2.94   care] *Idle and Pieboard retire to the upper end of the room* MALONE
4.2.100   leaves] ELD; pieces DANIEL
4.2.101.1–2   *Sir Godfrey … room*] HOPKINSON; runs in ELD (printed as part of Edmond's speech); DANIEL recognized 'runs in' as a s.d. and set it opposite and next to 'Thunders'. THIS EDITION provides an exit for Nicholas here so that he can re-enter after he is called at 4.2.168.
4.2.110–39   *Sir Godfrey … within*] ELD. This s.d. initiates a series (4.2.110–41) of off-stage comments by Godfrey and the Widow. MALONE eliminated s.d. at 4.2.110–11, and marked this point and all of the rest of the off-stage speeches by Godfrey and Widow in this section as 'at the door.' THIS EDITION preserves the s.d. from ELD at 4.2.110–11, but uses 'within' for the speeches of the Widow and for other speeches of Godfrey, thereby allowing maximum flexibility in staging.
4.2.126–7   *Hounslow, Hockley te Combe Park*] ELD (hounslow, hockley te comme parke)
4.2.141.1   *Sir Godfrey goes in*] ELD. Although MALONE eliminates this s.d., its significance lies in that it verifies that Godfrey has been visible to the audience during his speeches of the preceding lines.
4.2.159   dancer] ELD; dancer's DANIEL
4.2.169.1   *Enter Sir Godfrey, Widow, and Nicholas*] THIS EDITION; Enter Sir Godfrey, Widow, Frances, and Nicholas after 172 MALONE. Captain has called for Sir Godfrey and Nicholas in 4.2.168.
4.2.182.1   *[Exeunt Sir Godfrey, Widow, and Nicholas]*] THIS EDITION; *supposed to goe* ELD; *Exeunt Widow, Sir Godfrey, Frances and Nicholas* MALONE. Nicholas must exit because ELD has him re-enter with Sir Godfrey and Widow at 4.2.236.1.
4.2.183   EDMOND (*at keyhole*)] ELD (*Edm.at keyhoole*); at the door MALONE
4.2.188.1   *Enter Edmond*] after 187–8 MALONE
4.2.219   thus, and again] ELD; thus again DANIEL
4.2.229.1   *pulls … nose*] MALONE; ELD after 230
4.2.255   hug you] ELD; *not in* DANIEL
4.2.274   full] ELD; *not in* DANIEL
4.2.275   waking] DANIEL; walking ELD
4.2.277.1   *Enter the coffin of the Corporal*] ELD; 4.3 MALONE; 'No change of scene intended by author' BROOKE. The action indicates a discontinuity in place, but continuity in action; no change of scene is required.
4.2.306   were] ELD; is DANIEL

4.2.320   who] ELD; where DANIEL
4.2.323   ever] ELD; *not in* DANIEL
4.2.323   his] ELD; *not in* DANIEL
4.2.331   quoth a] ELD (qua tha)
4.2.342   SKIRMISH] ELD (Skir.); Sher DANIEL
4.2.352   Mum] ELD (mun)
4.2.356   at upper] ELD; at the upper MALONE
4.2.357–8   *[Exeunt … Frank]]* MALONE; Exit ELD
5.1.18   help'] help ELD; helpt DANIEL
5.1.33   Britons] ELD (Brittaines)
5.3.29   ye'll] BROOKE; ſheelle ELD; ſhe'll DANIEL; you'll HAZLITT
5.3.34   seven] ELD (seauen); heaven DANIEL. In DANIEL, 'You ſee he loves me well; up before heaven.'
5.3.35   at eleven] DANIEL; at a eleuen ELD
5.3.36   I'll] DANIEL; Iee ELD
5.4.0.4   *two knights*] ELD. Because these two knights are in addition to the knights Pennydub, Muckhill, and Tipstaff, THIS EDITION adds 'two knights' to the Persons List
5.4.8   handful] ELD (hand full); handfull DANIEL; handful 1685 (not 'bandful' as Brooke records)
5.4.18   your] DANIEL; you ELD
5.4.30   heard] ELD; heare SIMMS
5.4.34   not] DANIEL; nor ELD
5.4.36   wonder] ELD; wonder'd MALONE
5.4.62   need] ELD; needed DANIEL
5.4.62   others] ELD; other MALONE
5.4.64   villainies] ELD; villains DANIEL
5.4.79   nearer] ELD; near DANIEL
5.4.88   hath] ELD; have DANIEL
5.4.103   Pennydub] Sir Joh. ELD; Sir Godf. DANIEL
5.4.107   into] ELD; in DANIEL
5.4.109   give ye] ROWE; giue ELD; give me DANIEL
5.4.109.1   *Exeunt*] DANIEL; *Exeunt* followed on the next line by *Deus dedit his quoque finem* ELD. The Latin means, 'God has given an end to these things also', and is a modified version of *Aeneid* 1.199: 'God will give an end to these things also.' According to Steevens, the Latin sentence at the end of ELD appears also at the end of *Leicester's Commonwealth* and many other books, and was introduced by the printers not the authors. I concur with Steevens, primarily because DANIEL has omitted the sentence. Incidentally, the sentence does not occur in the 1584 editions of *Leicester's Commonwealth*; it does occur in the 1641 editions, as *Iamque opus exegi, Deus dedit his quoque finem*, where it is attached not to *Leicester's Commonwealth*, but to the end of Thomas Rogers's poem *Leicester's Ghost*, which is printed at the back of the volume.

PRESS VARIANTS

The sixteen known copies of Eld are listed below. Of the copies of Eld listed below, I have collated (at first hand or by photocopy) all but N, B, and BB. This edition reproduces the press variants identified by Richard Proudfoot, and turned over to me for the purposes of this edition. The Proudfoot notes which were given to me include no press variant collations for HN1, HN2, and BB; additionally, they include no notes for D2ᵛ in FOLGER1, N, Y; D3ᵛ in FOLGER1, N, Y, B, BL1, BL2, TCC; D4 in FOLGER1, N, Y, B, BL1, BL2, TCC; E1 in FOLGER1, N, Y, B, H; E2ᵛ in FOLGER1, FOLGER2, N, Y, B, H, BL1, BL2, BOD, TCC; E4ᵛ in FOLGER1, N, Y, B, H, BOD; G1ᵛ (4.2.19, FRANK) in N, Y, B, H, BL1, BL2, BOD, TCC, NLS.

> FOLGER1: Folger Library, unbound, imperfect
> FOLGER2: Folger Library, Howe
> N: Lenox Library, New York Public Library
> Y: Yale, Elizabethan Club
> H: Harvard, White Collection
> B: Barton Collection, Boston Public Library
> BL1: British Library: C.12.g.15
> BL2: British Library: C.34.1.4
> BOD: Bodleian Library: Mal.218
> TCC: Trinity College, Cambridge: Capell R234
> HN1: Huntington 1: 69198
> HN2: Huntington 2: 69199
> STRAT1: Stratford-upon-Avon, Shakespeare Centre: S.R.51.09, /1607, imperfect
> STRAT2: Stratford-upon-Avon, Shakespeare Centre: 51.09 R, imperfect
> NLS: National Library of Scotland: Bute 533
> BB: Bibliotheca Bodmeriana

FOLGER1 contains title-page through G3, and H, which is loose and (according to the Folger card catalogue) 'from another copy'; missing sections have been supplied in manuscript (with variants in spelling and punctuation) in a seventeenth-century hand. STRAT1 contains only the title-page through C4ᵛ. STRAT2 lacks H4, which has been supplied in a substitute typed facsimile leaf, possibly based on an eighteenth- or nineteenth-century edited text. Running titles are complete in Y, H, HN1, HN2, and NLS.

Sheet B (outer forme)

> *Corrected*: FOLGER1, FOLGER2, Y, H, B, BL1, BOD, TCC, HN1, HN2, NLS, STRAT1, STRAT2
> *Uncorrected*: N, BL2

Sig. B1

1.2.7 your] your *corr.*; yours *uncorr.*

Sheet D (outer forme)

> *Corrected*: B, BL1, TCC, HN2
> *Uncorrected*: FOLGER1, FOLGER2, Y, H, BL2, NLS, BOD, HN1, STRAT2

Sig. D2ᵛ

2.1.276 leave 'em] leaue 'em *corr.*; leaue m . *uncorr.*

Sheet D (inner forme)

> *Corrected*: FOLGER1, FOLGER2, Y, H, BL1, BL2, BOD, TCC, HN1, HN2
> *Uncorrected*: NLS, STRAT2

Sig. D3ᵛ

3.1.40 knew] knew *corr.*; know *uncorr.*

3.1.50 upon] vpon *corr.*; vpon [MARK] *uncorr.*

Sig. D4

3.2.21 villains] Villains *corr.*; Villians *uncorr.*

Sheet E (outer forme)

Sig. E1

> *Corrected*: FOLGER1, FOLGER2, Y, H, BL1, BL2, BOD, HN1, HN2, NLS, STRAT2
> *Uncorrected*: TCC

3.2.76 choose] choofe *corr.*; choufe *uncorr.*
3.3.1 hostess] Hofteffes *corr.*; Hoftffes *uncorr.*
3.3.2 arrest] areft *corr.*; rreft *uncorr.*
3.3.7 RAVENSHAW] Rauen *corr.*; Raaen *uncorr.*
3.3.9 sergeant] Seriant *corr.*; Sariant *uncorr.*
3.3.11 conveyances] Conuayances *corr.*; Conuaaynces *uncorr.*

Sig. E2ᵛ

> *Corrected*: FOLGER1, FOLGER2, Y, H, BL1, BL2, BOD, TCC, HN1, HN2, STRAT2
> *Uncorrected*: NLS

3.3.131 Come,] come, *corr.*; come; *uncorr.*

Sig. E4ᵛ

> *Corrected*: FOLGER1, FOLGER2, Y, H, BL1, BL2, BOD, HN1, HN2, NLS, STRAT2
> *Uncorrected*: TCC

3.4.123 his] his *corr.*; her *uncorr.*
3.4.124 to] to *corr.*; ro *uncorr.*

Sheet E (inner forme)

> *Corrected*: FOLGER2, HN1, NLS, STRAT2
> *Uncorrected*: FOLGER1, N, Y, H, B, BL1, BL2, BOD, TCC, HN2

Sig. E3

3.4.38 welcome, sir] welcome fir *corr.*; welcomefi r *uncorr.*

Sheet G (inner forme)

Sig. G1ᵛ

> *Corrected*: FOLGER2, Y, H, BL1, BL2, BOD, TCC, HN1, HN2, NLS
> *Uncorrected*: FOLGER1, STRAT2

4.2.19 FRANK] Frank. *corr.*; [MARK] Frank *uncorr.*

> *Corrected*: FOLGER1, N, Y, H, B, BL2, BOD, TCC, HN1, HN2, STRAT2, NLS
> *Uncorrected*: FOLGER2, BL1

4.2.29 TIPSTAFF] Tip. *corr.*; Ti p *uncorr.*

Sheet H (outer forme)

Sig. H1

> *Corrected*: FOLGER2, N, Y, H, B, BL1, BL2, BOD, TCC, HN1, HN2, NLS, STRAT2
> *Uncorrected*: FOLGER1

4.2.316 starts,] ftarts, *corr.*; ftarts; *uncorr.*

THE PURITAN WIDOW

STAGE DIRECTIONS

1.1.0.1 *ACTVS PRIMVS.*
1.1.0.2–7 *Enter the Lady* Widdow-Plus, *her two Daughters* Franke
    and | Moll, *her husbands Brother an old Knight* Sir Godfrey,
    with | *her Sonne and heyre Maister* Edmond, *all in moorning
    appar-*|*ell,* Edmond *in a Cypresse Hatte. The Widdow wringing
    her | hands, and bursting out into a passion, as newly come from
    the Bu-*|*riall of her husband.*
1.1.112 *Drawing out* | *her husbands* | *Picture.* (right, opposite
    1.1.113–15)
1.1.117.1 *Exeunt mother and daughters.*
1.1.127 *Exit Moll.*
1.1.135 *Exit Sir Godfrey.*
1.1.152 *Exit.*
1.2.0.1–2 *Enter* George Py-bord *a scholler and a Cittizen and unto
    him an* | *old souldier,* Peter Skirmish.
1.2.115.1–2 *Enter Captaine* Idle, *pi-*|*nioned, & with a guarde* | *of
    Officers passeth ouer* | *the Stage.* (right, opposite 1.2.114–17)
1.2.132 *Exeunt.*
1.3.0.1–6 *Enter at one doore Corporall* Oth, *a Vaine-glorious fellow,*
    | *and at the other, three of the Widdow Puritaines Ser-*|*uingmen,*
    Nicholas Saint-Tantlings, Simon Saint-|Mary-Oueries, *and*
    Frailtie *in black scuruie mourning* | *coates, and Bookes at their
    Girdles, as comming from* | *Church. They meete.*
1.3.25.1 *Corporall breaths vpon Frailtie.* (right)
1.3.74.1 *Exit Corporal, Nicholas.*
1.3.76 *Exit Simon and Fraylty.*
1.4.0.1 *The Prison, Marshalsea.*
1.4.0.1–3 *Enter Captaine* Ydle *at one dore, and old souldier* | *at
    the other.*
1.4.0.2–3 George Py-boord, *speaking within.* (below s.d. at
    1.4.0.1–3 and right)
1.4.3.1 *Entring.* (right, opposite 'friends' at 1.4.4)
1.4.34.1 *Cap. blowes a pipe.* (right)
1.4.37.1 *Corporall and Nicholas* | *within.* (right, opposite 1.4.38–
    40)
1.4.210 *Exit Nicholas.* (right, opposite 1.4.210; deleted in this
    edition because same s.d. occurs opposite 1.4.212)
1.4.212 *Exit Nich.*
1.4.257 *Exeunt.*
2.1.0.2–3 *Enter* Moll *yongest Daughter to the Widdow:* | *alone.*
2.1.16.1 *Enter Frailtie.*
2.1.28.1 *Enter Sir Iohn Penny-Dub.* (after 2.1.27)
2.1.37–8, 40.1 *Kissing: Ent. Wid-*|*dow &* Sir Godfr. (grouped
    together and far right, opposite 2.1.41–2)
2.1.42 *Exeunt.* (near right, after 'gallery' at 2.1.42)
2.1.63.1 *Enter Simon.* (right)
2.1.75.1 *Enter Frailtie.*
2.1.83.1–2 *Enter the suters Sir* Andrew Tipstaffe, *Sir* Oliuer |
    Muck-hill, *and* Penny-dub.
2.1.121.1 *Going out, Muckhill and sir Godfrey.* (right)
2.1.125 *Exit Muckhill.* (right, opposite 2.1.123)
2.1.125.1 *Enter George Py-boord, the scholler.* (right)
2.1.139 *Exit Frailtie.*
2.1.140.1 *Enter Daughters.* (after 2.1.139)
2.1.283.1 *Exit.*
2.1.285 *Exit*
2.1.311 *Exit Py-Boord.*
2.2.0.1 *Enter* Nicholas Saint Tantlings *with the chaine.*
2.2.8 *Exit Nich.*
3.1.0.1 *Actus 3.*

3.1.0.2 *Enter* Simon Saint Mary-Oueries *and* Frailty.
3.1.14.1 *Enter old Skirmish the soulders.* (after 3.1.15)
3.1.21 *Enter Corporall.* (after 3.1.23)
3.1.37.1 *Draw.* (right)
3.1.39 Simon *runs in.* (right)
3.1.41.1 *Enter Py-boord.* (after 3.1.43)
3.1.47.1 *Enter Officers.* (right)
3.1.58.1 *Exeunt with Skir.*
3.1.67 *Exit Pyboord.*
3.2.0.1 *Enter the Widdow with her two Daughters.*
3.2.10 *Exit Frailtie.*
3.2.19.1 *Enter Sir Godfrey in a rage.*
3.2.45.1 *Enter Fraylty.*
3.2.64.1 *Enter Nicholas.*
3.2.90 *Exeunt,*
3.3.0.1–3 *Enter two seriants to arrest the Scholer* | George
    Pyeboord.
3.3.40.1 *Entet Pyeboord.*
3.3.65 *Exet Dogson.* (right, opposite 3.3.66)
3.3.80.1 *Making to tie his garter.* (right, opposite 3.3.82)
3.3.131.1–3 *Exeunt with him, passing in they knock at the doore
    | with a Knocker with inside.*
3.4.34.1 *Enter Gentleman.* (after 3.4.32)
3.4.101 *Exit George.*
3.4.140.1 *Enter the Gentlemen.*
3.4.173 *Exeunt.*
3.4.181 *Exit.*
3.5.0.1–2 *Enter in the Prison, meeting George and Captaine,* |
    George *comming in muffled.*
3.5.112.1 *The Crie at Marshalsea.*
3.5.118.1–2 *They salute: and* Py-board *salutes* | *Maister* Edmond.
    (right, opposite 3.5.118–19)
3.5.128.1 *Whispering.* (right)
3.5.196.1 *Enter Keeper.* (right)
3.5.201 *Exet Keeper.*
3.5.238.1–2 Pyeboord *with an Almanack* | *and the Captaine.*
    (right, opposite 3.5.238–9)
3.5.295 *Exeunt.*
4.1.0.1 *Actus. 4.*
4.1.0.2 *Enter* Moll, *and Sir* Iohn Penny-dub.
4.1.36 *Exeunt.*
4.2.0.1 *Enter Widdow, with her eldest Daughter* | Franck *and*
    Frailtie.
4.2.20.1 *Enter Sir* Oliver Muck-hill, *and Sir* | Andrew Tip-staffe.
4.2.22 *Exit Frailtie.*
4.2.45.1 *Enter Frailtie.* (right)
4.2.47.1 *In her eare.* (right)
4.2.59.1 *Exit.*
4.2.60 *within Sir* Go. (right, opposite 4.2.61)
4.2.63.1 *Enter Sir* Godf. Capt. Pyb. Edm. Nick. (right, opposite
    4.2.64)
4.2.100 *Thunders.* (right, opposite 'runs in—'. See s.d. 'runs in,'
    4.2.101.1–2.)
4.2.101.1–2 —runs in— (printed as though it is part of the
    speech that ends 'deuill already' at 4.2.101; all editions
    beginning with DANIEL recognize it as a s.d.)
4.2.110–11 *Sir* Godfrey *through* | *the keyhole? within.* (right,
    opposite 4.2.110–11)
4.2.141.1 *goes in.* (right)
4.2.182 *supposed to goe.* (right)

4.2.183   *Edm. at keyhoole.* (right, opposite 4.2.183)
4.2.225.1   *Iustles him.* (right, opposite 4.2.225)
4.2.229   *Puls him by the Nose.* (near right, after 4.2.230)
4.2.236.1–2   *Enter Sir* Godfrey, Widdow, Franck, Nicholas | *with the Chaine.*
4.2.238.1   Edm. *strikes him.* (right, opposite)
4.2.265.1   *Enter Frailtie.*
4.2.277.1   *Enter the Coffin of the Corporall, the souldier bound, and | lead by Officers, the Sheriffe there.*
4.2.300.1   *Franke comes to him.* (right)
4.2.341.1   *Exeunt, pushing in the corpes.*
4.2.357   *Exit.*
5.1.0.1   *Actus* 5. *Scen.* I.
5.1.0.2   *Enter in hast Maister* Edmund *and* Fraylite.
5.1.20   *Exit* Frailty:
5.1.29.1   *Enter Captaine and Pie-boord.*

5.1.44.1   *Enter musitians.*
5.1.48   *Exeunt omnes.*
5.2.0.1   *Eneter Sir* Iohn Penidub, *and* Moll *above lacing | of her clothes.*
5.2.18   *Exeunt.*
5.3.0.1   *Enter Sir* Oliuer Muck-hill, *Sir* Andrew Tip-staffe, | *and old* Skirmish *talking*
5.3.29.1   *Enter a seruant.*
5.3.36.1   *Exeunt.*
5.4.0.1–6   *Enter the two Bridegromes* Captaine *and* Scholler *after them, Sir | Godfrey and Edmond, Widdow chandge in apparell, mistris | Francis led betweene two Knights, Sir Iohn Penny-dub and | Moll: there meetes them a Noble man, Sir Oliuer Muckil, | and Sir Andrew Tip-staffe.*
5.4.109.1   *Exeunt omnes.*
5.4.109.2   *FINIS.*

LINEATION NOTES

1.2.115–18   Puh...Idle] MALONE; *4 lines* ELD, with s.d. set to their right: Peter| he| me|; DANIEL sets s.d. above these lines and reproduces the line breaks in ELD
2.1.82–3   now?| Villain] villain| MALONE: now| ELD
2.1.148–50   Ay...attention] THIS EDITION; *2 verse lines* ELD: uneffected|; *prose* MALONE. 'Ay' replies to and balances 'Fear' in line preceding it.
2.1.219   Nor...flatter] ROWE; *2 lines* ELD: widow|
2.1.283   'Tis...higher] ROWE; *2 lines* ELD: Lady|
3.1.50–1   Down...villain] *2 lines, prose* DANIEL; *1 line* (turned under) ELD
3.1.56–7   Go...prison] *2 lines* ELD: then|. But in ELD, no s.d. between the two lines, and their intention is ambiguous. *prose* HOPKINSON, with s.d. after 3.1.57.
3.4.6–7   Ay...me] *prose* MALONE; *2 lines, verse* ELD: me|
3.3.66–7   Pray...me] MALONE; *verse* ELD: go|; and its intention is ambiguous. *Exit Dogson* set to right of 'go'.
3.4.23–4   A pretty...now] MALONE; *verse* ELD: methinks|; in ELD, shift from setting as prose to setting as verse corresponds with the end of an 'aside'.
3.4.88   [*Exit Gentleman*]] MALONE; *not in* ELD
3.4.89–90   I'll...now] *prose* MALONE; *2 lines* ELD: worship|; in

ELD, line division corresponds with a change in the person Pieboard is addressing.
3.4.119–21   Ay...that] MALONE; *verse* ELD: myself| tonight| that|
3.4.160–2   Why...coining] MALONE; *verse* ELD: much| protest| gold
3.5.18–19   The...suffice] MALONE: wits|; *1 line* ELD
3.5.113–14   Good...Godfrey] ELD; lines scan as hexameters; *prose* MALONE
4.2.28–9   Yes...favour] DANIEL; *1 line* ELD
4.2.60–1   Step...clear] THIS EDITION; *1 line* ELD
4.2.101.1–2   *Sir Godfrey...room*] HOPKINSON; runs in (printed as part of Edmond's speech) ELD; DANIEL recognized 'runs in' as a s.d. and set it opposite and next to 'Thunders'.
4.2.174–5   Laid...garden] MALONE; *verse* ELD: dropped|
4.2.243–4   A...sir] MALONE; *1 line* ELD
4.2.299–300   How...all] MALONE; *2 lines* ELD; man|; s.d. set to right of 'all'
5.2.2–3   Who's...I] ROWE; *1 line* ELD
5.4.26–7   'Sfoot...Nicholas] *2 lines, prose* DANIEL; *1 line* ELD
5.4.73–4   DANIEL; *prose* ELD
5.4.99–100   MALONE; *verse* ELD; lady|

THE REVENGER'S TRAGEDY

Edited by MacDonald P. Jackson

THE earliest record of *The Revenger's Tragedy* is in a double entry in the Stationers' Register on 7 October 1607:

> Geo. Elde Entred for his copies vnder thandes of S^r
> Geo. Buck & thwardens. Twoo plaies thone called the
> revengers tragedie thother. A trick to catche
> the old one xij^d

Eld printed the two play quartos on the same stock of paper and in the same font of type (Price, 1960, 1967). Both exhibit variant title-pages. *Trick*, which bears the date 1608, was originally anonymous but was ascribed to 'T.M.' in its second state, and *Revenger*, anonymous in all copies, is dated 1607 in some and 1608 in others. The 1607/8 quarto of *Revenger*, consisting of nine full sheets, is the sole seventeenth-century edition of the play (STC 24149–50; *BEPD* 253). Presumably printing took place late in 1607 and early in 1608. Edgerton fully substantiated Greg's assertion that books were normally dated according to modern calendar years.

The title-page of *The Revenger's Tragedy* provides just one of thirty-three stop-press corrections that were revealed by Price's and Ross's collation of nine copies of Eld's quarto held in libraries in the United States, Jackson's collation of the two Bodleian Library copies, his checking of the states of ten further copies, Nicoll's inspection of the Gollancz copy, and Foakes's examination of London copies that have since been checked by Jackson. At least two dozen copies are known to survive. The variant formes are A(o), D(i), E(i), E(o), F(o), G(o), H(i), and H(o), the last of these existing in three states. Most of the corrections are trivial and 'cosmetic', but many of the twenty in sheet H are substantive and appear to have been made with reference to the manuscript.

For the quarto of *Revenger* Eld employed a two-skeleton method of printing, the same two skeletons being used for sheets A, B, D, F, H, and I, and a second pair being created for the machining of sheets C, E, and G. This suggests that two presses were used for the central section of the play, sheets C–G. The stints of two compositors can be distinguished and related to this pattern, as Jackson's bibliographical analysis sought to demonstrate (1981). A wide range of typographical and spelling evidence indicates that one workman ('Y') set A2, B1–B2^v, D1–D2^v, E1–E2, E4^v, F3–G2^v, H3–H3^v, H4^v, I1^v, and I2^v, and that a different man ('X') set the rest of the text. (The title-page, A1, cannot be assigned, and A1^v is blank). Apparently, over the middle section of the quarto, when two presses were in operation, the compositors shared the typesetting equally, but over the first two and last

two sheets one man did the bulk of the typesetting for a single press. In terms of the line numbering of the present edition, the division of labour was as follows:

> X: 1.1.34–1.2.67, 1.3.3–2.1.156, 2.2.43–2.3.12, 2.3.113–3.4.50, 3.5.10–159, 4.2.40–4.4.72, 4.4.147–5.1.34, 5.1.73–113, 5.1.150–84, 5.3.1–5.3.128.2 (minus 5.3.13.1)
> Y: 1.1.0.1–1.1.33, 1.2.68–1.3.2, 2.1.157–2.2.42, 2.3.13–112, 3.4.51–3.5.9, 3.5.160–4.2.39, 4.4.73–146, 5.1.36–72, 5.1.114–49, 5.1.185–5.3.0.4 (plus 5.3.13.1)

Although the bibliographical evidence is copious, the distinguishing of compositorial stints is inevitably a matter of uncertain inference. It is likely that the two compositors worked on other quartos printed by Eld in the years surrounding publication of *Revenger*, since several of these yield similar contrasting patterns of spelling and typographical preferences (Jackson, 1981, 166–7).

The quarto of *The Revenger's Tragedy* contains a sprinkling of minor corruptions, which closely resemble the substantive mistakes corrected by the press-reader. Twenty-seven of the press variants occur on Compositor X's forty-four pages and five on Compositor Y's twenty-six, and the quarto errors that remain fall into a similar pattern, X's stints yielding about twice as many as Y's in proportion to their lengths. The apparent difference in the accuracy of the two typesetters has been taken into account in this edition's treatment of readings that are suspect but defensible. Since, as editors agree, the two men were almost certainly setting from authorial papers, some unsatisfactory quarto readings may have faithfully preserved Middleton's own accidental omissions and slips of the pen. In addition, the successful printing-house attempt to fit the text exactly to nine quarto sheets doubtless influenced the layout and may well have had an occasional effect on the wording.

Moreover, the pattern of substitution of anomalous types in speech prefixes suggests that the quarto may have been set by formes, rather than seriatim. In sheet D, for example, all four pages of the inner forme (D1^v, D2, D3^v, and D4) use the standard italic '*V*' in prefixes for Vindice; whereas in pages of the outer forme, apart from the first (D1), the substitute roman 'V' greatly predominates (D2^v, D3, D4^v). There is not, however, any clear evidence that miscalculations in 'casting off' of copy have caused the compositors severely to cramp the text or to waste space, though turnovers and abbreviations save a line here and there.

The evidence for authorial copy is substantial. A serviceable promptbook would have required an altogether less erratic series of stage directions, and many of those that the quarto does provide carry descriptive details of an authorial kind, as when Antonio enters at 1.4.0.1-2 as '*the discontented Lord* Antonio, *whose wife the Duchesses youngest Sonne rauisht*' or when, as the Duchess and Spurio enter arm in arm at 4.3.0.1-2, '*he seemeth lasciuiously to her*'. This edition adds some eighteen entry directions that are completely absent from the quarto, though implied by the dialogue, and supplements a few others. There is some confusion over the numbers of nobles, gentlemen, officers, and attendants who participate in certain scenes. Editorial attempts to resolve these ambiguities concerning minor characters are discussed in the textual notes. From Act 4 onwards such characters are usually designated by mere numerals in speech prefixes, which is a potential source of confusion in 5.1, especially, where '1' and '2' are made to stand for two different pairs of persons. Spurio is so named in speech prefixes but is '*the Bastard*' in several stage directions. There is no evidence that the manuscript had been annotated by a bookkeeper concerned with properties or sound effects necessary to theatrical performance. However, somebody does appear to have expurgated a reference to God at 4.4.14, presumably some time after the passing of the Act to Restrain Abuses of Players on 27 May 1606.

As the studies by Price, Murray, Lake, and Jackson show, in its use of colloquial contractions and other such linguistic forms, in its spelling of these, and in its numerous orthographical links with the Trinity holograph of *A Game at Chess*, Eld's quarto shows every sign of having been set directly from a manuscript in Middleton's hand. To cite one small, but tell-tale detail, in *Revenger* four stage directions are punctuated with quite meaningless question marks, as in '*Enter the other Maske of entended murderers?*' on I3ᵛ. Middleton's question marks and exclamation marks, like those of other writers of his time, are not always readily distinguishable from each other and seventeenth-century compositors sometimes use question marks where we would use exclamation marks. In the Trinity MS of *Game* Middleton three times ended an otherwise perfectly normal stage direction with an exclamation mark, and four exclamation marks and four question marks can be found ending stage directions in the printed texts of other Middleton works—*Five Gallants*, *Michaelmas*, *Trick*, *Entertainments*, and *Puritan*. Werstine, Long, and others have challenged the New Bibliographers' attempts to distinguish between Renaissance plays printed from 'foul papers' and those printed from 'prompt book' copy; they have shown that acting companies tolerated considerable muddle and variety in their theatrical playscripts. Even so, it seems unlikely that the manuscript that served as copy for *The Revenger's Tragedy* could have been used to regulate performances, and highly probable that it had been penned by the author.

Perhaps an editor's main difficulty is in deciding on lineation. The longer verse speeches present few problems, but series of brief exchanges may offer scope for various editorial arrangements. Middleton's abrupt transitions from verse to prose and back again, even within a single speech, his tendency at times to nudge either medium towards the other, and his liking for hypermetrical exclamations and short phrases that interrupt the basic iambic pentameter appear to have perplexed the compositors on several occasions and can make it hard to determine the most appropriate setting-out. The matter has been fully discussed by Foakes (1953; 1966, lvii-lxii), though not in relation to Middleton's metrical practices: some of his proposals for the dovetailing of speeches produce uncharacteristic enjambements and have been rejected in later editions, including this one. The extent to which the quarto mislines the dialogue should not be exaggerated. It often seems surprisingly sensitive to Middleton's probable intentions, and most of its sudden switches to prose come at precisely those points where the reader loses any sense of an iambic beat.

One short passage will illustrate some of the points at issue. At the bottom of H2ᵛ and top of H3 (4.4.70-6 in the present edition), where Vindice and Hippolito have been rebuking their mother for her willingness to prostitute Castiza to Lussurioso, Eld's quarto reads:

> *Vind.* There had beene boyling lead agen,
> The dukes sonnes great Concubine:
> A drab of State, a cloath a siluer slut,
> To haue her traine borne vp, and her soule traile i'th
>   durt; great.
> *Hip.* To be miserably great, rich to be eternally
>   wretched.
> *Vind.* O common madnesse:
> Aske but the thriuingst harlot in cold bloud, . . .

Foakes prints:

> *Vind.* There had been boiling lead again.
> The duke's son's great concubine, a drab of state,
> A cloth o' silver slut, to have her train
> Borne up, and her soul trail i'th' dirt—great!
> *Hipp.* To be miserably great; rich to be
> Eternally wretched.
>   *Vind.* O common madness!
> Ask but the thriving'st harlot in cold blood, . . .

This creates (after the short opening line) a succession of lines of ten or eleven syllables. But it breaks up Eld's one regular (and effective) iambic pentameter, 'A drab of state, a cloth o' silver slut', and it renders Eld's immediately preceding line less forceful: if this is scanned as beginning and ending with iambs that enclose three strongly stressed one-syllable feet ('The dúke's són's gréat cóncubíne'), it becomes expressively emphatic. Nor does the last line of Vindice's speech, as printed by Eld, seem impossible for Middleton: if we ignore the last word ('great') for the moment, it seems a nicely balanced six-stress line, with the antitheses pointed up by the alliteration of 'train' and 'trail'.

But here questions of lineation are bound up with questions of actual wording. Foakes's 'to have her train | Borne up, and her soul trail i'th' dirt—great!' is attractive, but the modern ironic colloquialism that we hear in the last word, though nicely suited to Vindice's characteristic tone, was not available to Middleton. Dodsley expunged 'great' and punctuated Hippolito's speech, 'To be great, miserable; to be rich, eternally wretched', which is lame. Collier transferred 'great' to Hippolito, so that he begins, 'Great, to be miserably great'. This balances 'rich, to be eternally wretched'. Yet the exact repetition of 'great' in the first half of the line is less pointed than the consonance of 'rich...wretched' in the second. Recalling the 'graced pallace' in Folio *King Lear* (1.4.224) that is a 'great pallace' in the 1608 Quarto (4.240), and noting the ease with which the Middletonian spelling 'gract' could be misread as 'great', we may propose 'Graced, to be miserably great; rich, to be eternally wretched'. Such a line is overloaded with no fewer than seventeen syllables, but it has only six beats, echoing the previous one and sharing its antithetical quality, and little is to be gained by splitting it. The present edition emends 'great' to 'graced' and transfers the word to Hippolito.

> VINDICE To have her train borne up and her soul trail
> i'th' dirt!
> HIPPOLITO Graced, to be miserably great; rich, to be
> eternally wretched.
> VINDICE O common madness!

I have, in this instance, reverted to Eld's lineation, except for the transfer of one word.

One further feature of the quarto's lineation should be mentioned. On 128 occasions a new speech begins within the line on which the previous speech ends. In the vast majority of instances the new speech is very short, consisting of five or fewer words, and so does not go beyond the shared line. From this aspect of the quarto layout nothing can be inferred about Middleton's sense of the structure of his verse. Eld's compositors were simply anxious to conserve space when such opportunities presented themselves, becoming more so over the later part of the play. This is clear from the fact that speches sharing lines become progressively more common: there are 18 in sheets A–C, 48 in sheets D–F, and 62 in sheets G–I. It is only from F3 onwards that any speeches of more than one line begin on the same line as the previous speech ends: there are nine examples altogether, and in five of these the *previous* speech occupies only the single part-line.

The quarto divides the play into four acts. The fourth is much the longest, and editors have begun a fifth act at a suitable place for such a break, on the assumption that the heading has been accidentally omitted. Act-divisions in a quarto published as early as 1607/8 would normally imply association with one of the boys' companies playing at a private theatre, as Taylor (1993a) shows, but the

title-page states that the play had been acted by the King's Men. Evidently the provision of act intervals had become habitual to Middleton while he was writing for the Children of Paul's. It is possible that when he began *The Revenger's Tragedy* he still had performance by one of the boys' companies in mind, but the casting pattern, which fits an adult company, suggests otherwise (Taylor, 1993, 139–40).

By far the greatest contribution to the editing of Eld's text was made by Dodsley, whose alterations are nearly all genuine corrections. Hazlitt's many emendations, in contrast, are mostly misconceived. Later editors have initiated few substantive changes to the dialogue but have profitably paid attention to the arrangement of the verse and to the provision of necessary stage directions. The commentary of this edition is especially indebted to Foakes (1966), whose thorough work of annotation has helped all his successors, and to Ross, Parfitt, and Loughrey and Taylor.

This edition is based on Jackson's facsimile of the Huntington Library copy of the quarto that is dated 1608, a copy with all formes in the corrected state. The text has been methodically checked against the Bodleian Library's two copies of the quarto, while other copies named in the inventory of press variants have been examined over typographical details. In the Textual Notes references to Foakes and Gibbons are to their original editions, unless the revised editions are specified by date.

SEE ALSO

Text: *Works*, 547
Authorship and date: this volume, 360

WORKS CITED

Previous Editions

Busi, Anna, *The Revenger's Tragedy* (Bari: Adriatica Editrice, 1985)
Collier, John Payne, Dodsley's *A Select Collection of Old Plays* (1825–7), vol. 4; source of proposed emendations by Gilchrist
Collins, John Churton, *The Plays and Poems of Cyril Tourneur* (1878), vol. 2
Corrigan, R. W., *The Revenger's Tragedy*, Chandler Editions (1962)
Dodsley, Robert, *A Select Collection of Old Plays* (1744), vol. 4
Fluchère, Henri, *La Tragédie du Vengeur*, Collection Bilingue des Classiques Étrangers (1958)
Foakes, R. A., *The Revenger's Tragedy*, Revels (1966)
—— *The Revenger's Tragedy*, Revels Student Editions (1996)
Fraser, Russell A., and Norman Rabkin, *Drama of the English Renaissance* (1976), vol. 2
Gibbons, Brian, *The Revenger's Tragedy*, New Mermaid (1967, revised 1991)
Gibson, Colin, *Six Renaissance Tragedies* (1997)
Gomme, A. H., *Jacobean Tragedies* (1969)
Harrison, G. B., *The Revenger's Tragedy*, The Temple Dramatists (1934)
Hazlitt, W. Carew, Dodsley's *A Select Collection of Old English Plays* (1874–76), vol. 10
Huston, John Dennis, and Alvin Kernan, *Classics of the Renaissance Theatre: Seven English Plays* (1969)
Jackson, MacDonald P., *The Revenger's Tragedy, Attributed to Thomas Middleton: A Facsimile of the 1607/8 Quarto* (1983)

Loughrey, Brian, and Neil Taylor, Thomas Middleton, *Five Plays* (1988)

Maus, Katharine Eisaman, *Four Revenge Tragedies* (1995)

Nethercot, Arthur H., *Stuart Plays* (1971); a revision of C. R. Baskervill, V. B. Heltzel, and Arthur H. Nethercot, eds., *Elizabethan and Stuart Plays* (1934)

Nicoll, Allardyce, *The Works of Cyril Tourneur* (n.d. [1930])

Oliphant, E. H. C., *Shakespeare and his Fellow Dramatists* (1929), vol. 1

Parfitt, George, *The Plays of Cyril Tourneur*, Renaissance and Restoration Dramatists (1978)

Reed, Isaac, Dodsley's *A Select Collection of Old Plays* (1780), vol. 4; source of proposed emendations by Steevens

Ross, Lawrence J., *The Revenger's Tragedy*, Regents (1966)

Rylands, G. H. W., *Elizabethan Tragedy: Six Representative Plays* (1933); follows old Mermaid text

Salgādo, Gāmini, *Three Jacobean Tragedies* (1965)

Scott, Sir Walter, *The Ancient British Drama* (1810), vol. 2

Symonds, John Addington, *The Best Plays of Webster and Tourneur*, Mermaid (1888)

Thorndike, Ashley H., *Webster and Tourneur*, Masterpieces of the English Drama (1912)

Trussler, Simon (introduced by), *The Revenger's Tragedy*, Swan Theatre Plays (1987); text based on Foakes, but with alterations for Royal Shakespeare Company production of 1987 indicated

Other Works Cited

Bowers, Fredson, *Elizabethan Revenge Tragedy, 1587–1642* (1940)

Dollimore, Jonathan, *Radical Tragedy* (1984)

Edgerton, William L., 'The Calendar Year in Sixteenth-Century Printing', *Journal of English and Germanic Philology* 59 (1960), 439–49

Ekeblad (Ewbank), Inga-Stina, 'On the Authorship of *The Revenger's Tragedy*', *English Studies* 41 (1960), 227–33; reprinted and reorganized as 'The Structure of *The Revenger's Tragedy*' in *Three Jacobean Revenge Tragedies* (1990), ed. R. V. Holdsworth, pp. 58–65; quotations are from this reprint

Eliot, T. S., *Elizabethan Essays* (1934)

Foakes, R. A., 'On the Authorship of *The Revenger's Tragedy*', *Modern Language Review* 48 (1953), 129–38

Holdsworth, R. V., '*A Fair Quarrel*: Additions and Corrections to the New Mermaid Edition' (forthcoming, 1993)

—— ed., *Three Jacobean Revenge Tragedies* (1990); includes his '*The Revenger's Tragedy* as a Middleton Play', pp. 79–105, and '*The Revenger's Tragedy* on the Stage', pp. 105–20

Howarth, R. G., 'Who's Who in *The Revenger's Tragedy*', in *A Pot of Gilliflowers: Studies and Notes* (Cape Town, 1964), pp. 70–1

Jackson, MacDonald P., 'Compositorial Practices in *The Revenger's Tragedy*, 1607–08', *Papers of the Bibliographical Society of America* 75 (1981), 157–70

—— *Studies in Attribution: Middleton and Shakespeare* (1979)

Lake, David J., *The Canon of Thomas Middleton's Plays* (1975)

Leavis, F. R., 'Imagery and Movement', *Scrutiny* 13 (1945), 119–34 (120–2); reprinted in *The Living Principle* (1975)

Leech, Clifford, 'A Speech-Heading in *The Reuengers Tragedie*', *Review of English Studies* 18 (1941), 335–6

Long, William B., 'Stage-Directions: A Misinterpreted Factor in Determining Textual Provenance', *TEXT* 2 (1985), 121–37

Maxwell, J. C., 'Two Notes on *The Revenger's Tragedy*', *Modern Language Review* 44 (1949), 545

Mulryne, Ronnie, and Margaret Shewring, *This Golden Round: The Royal Shakespeare Company at the Swan* (1989)

Murray, Peter B., 'The Authorship of *The Revenger's Tragedy*', *Papers of the Bibliographical Society of America* 56 (1962), 195–218; incorporated in his book, *A Study of Cyril Tourneur* (1964)

Napier, C. S., '*The Revenger's Tragedy*', *Times Literary Supplement*, 13 March 1937, 188

Nashe, Thomas, *The Unfortunate Traveller* (1594)

Price, George R., 'The Authorship and the Bibliography of *The Revenger's Tragedy*', *The Library*, V, 15 (1960), 262–77

—— 'The Early Editions of *A trick to catch the old one*', *The Library*, V, 22 (1967), 205–27

Salingar, L. G., '*The Revenger's Tragedy* and the Morality Tradition', *Scrutiny* 6 (1937–38), 402–22; reprinted and abbreviated in *Three Jacobean Revenge Tragedies*, ed. R. V. Holdsworth (1990), pp. 37–51; quotations are from this reprint

Sheldon, Brian, Remarks on producing *The Revenger's Tragedy*, quoted in Michael Scott, *Renaissance Drama and a Modern Audience* (1982)

Sher, Antony, Remarks on playing Vindice, in *This Golden Round*; see under Mulryne

Swinburne, Algernon Charles, *The Age of Shakespeare* (1887, 1908)

Taylor, Gary, 'The Renaissance and the End of Editing', in *Palimpsest: Editorial Theory in the Humanities*, ed. George Bornstein and Ralph G. Williams (1993), 121–49

—— 'The Structure of Performance: Act-Intervals in the London Theatres, 1576–1642', in Gary Taylor and John Jowett, *Shakespeare Reshaped 1606–1623* (1993a), pp. 3–50

Trevis, Di, Remarks on producing *The Revenger's Tragedy*, in *This Golden Round*; see under Mulryne

Waith, Eugene M., 'The Ascription of Speeches in *The Revenger's Tragedy*', *Modern Language Notes* 57 (1942), 119–21

Wells, Stanley, '*The Revenger's Tragedy* Revived', in G. R. Hibbard, ed., *Elizabethan Theatre: VI* (1978), 105–33

Werstine, Paul, 'McKerrow's "Suggestion" and Twentieth-Century Shakespeare Textual Criticism', *Renaissance Drama* 19 (1988), 149–73

—— 'Narratives about Printed Shakespeare Texts: "Foul Papers" and "Bad" Quartos', *Shakespeare Quarterly* 41 (1990), 65–86

THE REVENGER'S TRAGEDY

TEXTUAL NOTES

Persons THIS EDITION; *not in* ELD. A list (incomplete) was first
provided by Collins.

1.1.0.1 *Incipit…Primus*] THIS EDITION; *not in* ELD. Eld heads
'*ACT.I. SCÆI.*', and similarly divides at Acts 2 and 4,
specifying Act only at Act 3; no division is indicated at Act 5,
its placing in the present edition being that first adopted by
Collins; Reed began Act 5 with the scene here numbered 4.3.
Eld does not mark scene divisions. The formulas introduced
into this edition to open and end the acts ('*Finis Actus Primi*',
and so on) are those which Middleton himself most favours.
Eld includes the final '*FINIS.*' (in that form).

1.1.0.2 *Vindice*] ELD (Vendici). Hereafter he is Vindice on Compositor X's pages, and either Vindice or Vindici on Compositor
Y's; Y also has Hippolito as '*Vindicies brother*' on D2. Speech
headings, after the first ('*Vindi.*') are for '*Vind.*' or '*Vin.*'

1.1.0.3 *his*] REED; *her* ELD

1.1.0.3 *Spurio the Bastard*] ELD (Spurio *the bastard*). In Eld's
quarto Spurio is so called in speech prefixes and in one
other stage direction (2.3.36.1–2). In four directions he is '*the
Bastard*' (1.2.0.2, 3.5.203.1, 4.3.0.1, 5.3.48.2); this edition
adds Spurio's Italian name to the English designation.

1.1.5, 1.3.29, 1.3.135 exc'llent] ELD (exlent). Middleton's disyllabic spelling.

1.1.6 Should] DODSLEY; Would ELD. Vindice's words are an
exclamation ('O, [to think] that…'), like Hamlet's 'That it
should come to this!' (1.2.137), though Nicoll (like most
editors), retaining Eld's reading, implausibly suggests that 'it
may be construed as a curse'.

1.1.36 Outbid,] THIS EDITION; Out-bid like ELD. The emendation,
which improves the sense and regularizes the metre, is based
on the assumption that 'like' has been accidentally repeated
from the immediately preceding line, where it is in the same
position.

1.1.40 show'st] ELD (fhouſt)

1.1.46 off] ELD (of). This Middleton spelling recurs at 1.2.30 and
2.1.17; the two forms were interchangeable, and 'off' is used
for modern 'of' at 3.5.94, 4.1.49, 4.2.109, and 5.1.75.

1.1.49.1 his] DODSLEY; her ELD

1.1.50 death's] ELD *corr* (deaths); death ELD *uncorr*

1.1.53 Puh] ELD. This Middletonian exclamation of dismissal
or contempt is often modernized to 'Pooh', but it is closely
related to Middleton's 'Push', phonetically, as well as func-
tionally, and the more modern double vowel makes too much
of what is a mere bilabial explosion.

1.1.62 I have] ELD; I've SYMONDS. Symonds's contraction may
represent the intended pronunciation, but stress on 'have'
gives Hippolito the more meaningful intonation, and 'Faith'
can be considered extrametrical.

1.1.62 shoved] ELD (fhooud)

1.1.70 time] ELD; fame HAZLITT. Hazlitt's emendation would create a 'Shakespearean' doublet ('fame and common rumour')
of a kind favoured by Middleton in this play, as in line 74:
'the whole aim and scope of his intent'.

1.1.97 to] ELD (too). The spellings were interchangeable; Eld
again uses 'too' for modern 'to' at 1.3.54, and 'to' appears
for modern 'too' at 1.1.124, 1.4.36, and 5.1.114.

1.1.101 mole] ELD (*Moale*). Eld also italicizes '*French*'.

1.1.103 coin] ELD (quoyne)

1.1.108 court] DODSLEY; Cour ELD

1.1.108 MOTHER] ELD. This generic title, always used by Eld in
speech prefixes and stage directions, is retained throughout
this edition. At 1.3.127 Lussurioso identifies her to the
disguised Vindice as 'Madam Gratiana, the late widow', but
she is never addressed by that name.

1.1.120 unnatural] DODSLEY; vnnaturally ELD

1.1.125 through] ELD; tho' DODSLEY

1.2.0.2 *Spurio the Bastard*] ELD (ₐthe Baſt-| ard)

1.2.0.4 *youngest, Junior*] ELD (yongeſt,ₐ)

1.2.11 FIRST JUDGE] ELD (*Iud.*). In the scene's later speech prefixes
Eld differentiates the two judges.

1.2.15 cered] ELD (feard)

1.2.16 cerecloths] REED (serecloths); fearce clothes ELD

1.2.30 their] DODSLEY; therr ELD

1.2.39 metal] ELD (mettall)

1.2.42 fast] DODSLEY; firſt ELD

1.2.47 JUNIOR] ELD. The character is so designated in speech
prefixes. Eld's stage direction at 3.4.0.1 reads '*Enter in prison*
Iunior *Brother*', thus distinguishing typographically between
the last two words. So this edition calls him Junior, the
suggestion of the modern Americanism being appropriate
enough.

1.2.52 made] ELD (mad)

1.2.59 condemned] DODSLEY (condemn'd); condemned ELD (=
condemnèd)

1.2.65 methinks] DODSLEY; my thinks ELD

1.2.65 'sessed] ELD (ceaft). The modernization was made by
Dodsley; 'cessed', which *OED* gives as a separate headword
(with 'cease' as a variant spelling) and 'ceased' are also
possible.

1.2.81 Pox] ELD (Pax)

1.2.88.1 *Exit Junior with a Guard*] ELD (*Exit with a garde*)

1.2.99 double-loathèd] THORNDIKE (double-loathed); double
loathd ELD. Sounding the 'ed' ending gives a regular iambic
pentameter.

1.2.99 or] DODSLEY; and ELD. Eld's text might be punctuated
with a comma after 'meat' and taken to mean 'kill her lord
as he is eating and sleep quietly after' (Nicoll), but it is more
probable that 'and' has been caught from the previous line;
while eating or while sleeping are both times at which the
Duke would be especially vulnerable.

1.2.116 He's] ELD (Ha's)

1.2.120, 127, 167 SPURIO] DODSLEY (*Spu.*); Spi. ELD

1.2.129 't as] ELD ('tus); 'tis DODSLEY

1.2.144 thou'rt] ELD (thou'art)

1.2.145 in thy] DODSLEY; in ELD

1.2.145 mine] THIS EDITION (Holdsworth); minde ELD. The word
both emphasizes a distinction between the items that are
coupled, and yet 'thought and minde' is lamely pleonastic,
whereas 'thy…and mine' (a construction much favoured by
Middleton) follows appropriately from 'our' in the previous
line. The compositor might easily have misread 'mine' as
'mind' and spelled the latter word according to his own
preference. Compare 'Thy wrongs and mine' at 1.1.57.
(Holdsworth's conjecture was communicated in a private
letter to the editor.)

1.2.160 commandèment] ELD (commandement). ELD's spelling
of the word indicates the four-syllable pronunciation required
by the metre.

552

1.2.183 risse] ELD (rise); rose DODSLEY. Editors follow Dodsley, but 'risse' (in various spellings, but with 'i' as the vowel) is a favourite Middletonian form of the past tense of the verb 'to rise'.

1.2.187 met] ELD; meet DODSLEY. Dodsley's emendation puts line 187 in apposition to the exclamation 'O, damnation meet!' (= fitting), and may be right, but Eld's clandestine meeting between damnation and adultery seems not inappropriate. Reed, followed by Ross among more recent editors, took an intermediate course by placing a comma after 'met'.

1.2.196 beholden] ELD (beholding)

1.3.0.1-2 *in disguise as Piato*] ELD (*in difguife*)

1.3.6 mistress] ELD (Mistrs)

1.3.6 mistresses] DODSLEY; Mistesses ELD

1.3.40 cònstrue] ELD (conster)

1.3.48 Fool to] ELD (Foole, to); S'foote, to COLLINS

1.3.59 procreation] DODSLEY; procrearion ELD

1.3.74 loud] ELD; wide DODSLEY

1.3.84 woman] ELD; women SYMONDS. Eld's usage is analogous to that in 'Some father' at 1.3.60.

1.3.90 depth] ELD (depht); possibly a Middleton spelling analogous to his 'strenght' for 'strength'.

1.3.106 is] ELD; as REED (Steevens). Eld's version of Lussurioso's construction is vindicated by *OED, Defend*, II.5.b.

1.3.139 my] DODSLEY; me ELD

1.3.157 th'age] THIS EDITION (Collins); age ELD. Foakes and others interpret Eld's 'age' as referring to the middle or old age of the mother. Ross, in contrast, glosses 'age' (which he retains unaltered) as 'the age', and Salgādo, also following Eld, explains 'in league with age' as 'in tune with the times', which gives more point to 'nowadays' and its position in the sentence. The play is very conscious of the depravity of 'this age' (1.3.23, 1.4.55, 2.1.115), and this alternative interpretation seems to me the more plausible; but idiom prohibits it without Collins's emendation, proposed in his commentary but not printed in his text; 'th'' might easily have been accidentally omitted after 'with'.

1.3.159 Does't] ELD (Doft)

1.3.185 blood] DODSLEY; good ELD. The end-of-line repetition of 'good' is accepted by Nicoll and defended by Holdsworth (1993) as playing on different shades of meaning of the word. It makes sense, but sounds intolerably lame. The rhyme 'blood'/'good' is the most common in the play, occurring in four other places; here 'blood' means 'disposition' or '(strength of) character'.

1.4.15 Placed] ELD (Plastc'd)

1.4.21 wrong] THIS EDITION; wrongs ELD. A rhyme with 'tongue' ('Tong' in ELD) is almost certainly intended, and Antonio has suffered an overwhelming wrong.

1.4.36 step-duchess' monster] ELD (ftep Duches—Monfter)

1.4.38, 5.3.94 heard] ELD (hard)

1.4.49 She's] ELD (Sh'as)

1.4.55 near] ELD (nere)

1.4.68 Should] DODSLEY; Sould ELD

1.4.76 miracle] DODSLEY; miralce ELD

2.1.0.2 *the . . . Hippolito*] ELD (*the fifter*)

2.1.24 own] ELD (one)

2.1.27.1-2 *and bearing a treasure chest*] THIS EDITION; *not in* ELD. The need for such a direction is argued by Holdsworth (1990), p. 111.

2.1.33 myself] ELD (my felfe); my sex HAZLITT (Gilchrist)

2.1.66 in't, mark] DODSLEY; it ~ ELD

2.1.86 Men] ELD; If men HAZLITT. Hazlitt's insertion spells out the logic of Vindice's sentence; 'an' (= if) might have been accidentally dropped between 'can' at the end of line 85 and 'Men' at the beginning of this one.

2.1.89 still fools] HAZLITT; ~ foole ELD

2.1.102 may well] ELD; well may FOAKES. Since Foakes does not record an emendation, he may have made the alteration (in which he is silently followed by Loughrey and Taylor) inadvertently; it creates a slightly more naturally and meaningfully stressed line, but the less regular original is not uncharacteristic of Middleton's verse.

2.1.130 madam] DODSLEY; Mad-man ELD

2.1.147 should] DODSLEY; fhouldft ELD

2.1.149 wouldst] THIS EDITION; would ELD. I assume that a miscorrection has attached the 'ft' ending to 'fhould' in line 147 instead of to 'would' in this line. The normal inflection here is 'thou wouldst', just as the normal inflection in line 147 is 'should we'.

2.1.151 others] DODSLEY; other ELD

2.1.157 she] HAZLITT; you ELD. The third person pronoun sharpens Castiza's irony; Eld's 'you' has presumably been caught from the end of the previous line. Hazlitt's reading was suggested by a manuscript note in 'one of the former edits.'

2.1.192 That] ELD; Ay, that OLIPHANT. The emendation would regularize the metre, and several speeches hereabouts begin with 'I' (= 'Ay').

2.1.197 musics] ELD (Musicks); music DODSLEY. The plural is used by Cloten in *Cymbeline*, 2.3.37, and the page in Eld on which the word occurs was set by the more reliable Compositor Y.

2.1.199 wear] ELD (were)

2.1.216 mete] ELD (meat)

2.1.225 low] FOAKES; loue ELD. Eld spells 'show'st' as 'fhouft' at 1.1.40; so 'loue' may conceivably be an eccentric spelling of 'lowe', but a contemporary reader would inevitably have understood 'loue' as 'love', to which Dodsley modernized. Though Parfitt defends 'love', it makes little sense.

2.1.244 *Exit Mother*] ELD (*Exit.*), after Mother's speech

2.1.247 turn] DODSLEY; tnrne ELD

2.2.55 cheeks] DODSLEY; checkes ELD

2.2.60 i'faith] DODSLEY; ifath ELD

2.2.66 an] DODSLEY; a ELD.

2.2.88.1 *Exit Lussurioso*] ELD (*Exit.*), after Lussurioso's speech

2.2.121 word] ELD *uncorr*; world ELD *corr*. Eld appears to have miscorrected this word while making a genuine correction to the next.

2.2.121 sweeter] ELD *corr*; sweete ELD *uncorr*. The comparative sharpens Spurio's exclamation. To Spurio the news ('word') is sweet because of the sweeter opportunity it presents him with. Editors have failed to note this correction.

2.2.126.1 *Exeunt Spurio and Servants*] ELD (*Exeunt.*)

2.2.130 fees] ELD. Collins claimed that the word stands 'for phease or pheese, which means tatters or hangings' (the black funeral trappings) and most editors have repeated this gloss, but the word is unknown to *OED*, in these or any other spellings, and no example has ever been cited. Collins describes 'phease' as 'a substantive derived from the verb' and refers the reader to the section on 'fease' in Hensleigh Wedgwood's *A Dictionary of English Etymology* (London, 1859-65); this is *OED*'s verb 'feaze', meaning to unravel a rope or fray the end of a stick, but neither Wedgwood nor *OED* gives evidence of a closely related noun that could be used of funeral hangings. 'Frees' is a possible Jacobean spelling of 'frieze', in the sense either of (a) 'a coarse wollen cloth with a nap' or (b) of 'that part of an entablature between the architrave and the cornice'; but neither meaning is quite apt enough to encourage emendation. If Collins's 'phease or pheese' could have been authenticated, I should have printed it as a modernization. As it is, we must assume a 'telescoping of sense' (Foakes) whereby the exorbitant fees are equated with the display, unless the 'fees' are perquisites, as when a hangman obtains his victim's clothes.

2.2.135   sunset] ELD *corr* (Sun fet); Snn fet ELD *uncorr*

2.2.148   The] ELD (catchword on D4); *Vind.* The ELD. Vindice's speech beginning 'Who's this comes?' in line 147 has a normal speech prefix in Eld's quarto; it is the last line of dialogue on D4 and at the top of D4^v (line 148) the prefix is repeated. The fact that the catchword on D4 is 'The' suggests that no redistribution of the dialogue between Vindice and Hippolito is needed, though Dodsley gave Hippolito 148–9 and Collier gave him all of 147.

2.2.167.1   *Exeunt Lussurioso and Vindice*] ELD (*Exeunt*), turned down below line-end

2.3.4   they're] ELD (their)

2.3.5   spleen] DODSLEY; pleene ELD

2.3.17   lawyers. Guard!] ELD (Lawyers gard). Collins was the first editor to see that the Duke must be calling for guards.

2.3.17.2–3   *sons ... Supervacuo*] ELD (*sonnes*)

2.3.18   grace] DODSLEY; Gtace ELD

2.3.32   words] DODSLEY; word ELD. The emendation seems more idiomatic and improves the rhyme with 'swords'.

2.3.33.1   *dissemble a flight*] ELD. The three words are in the right-hand margin, the first two beside line 34 and the last beside line 35, and it is unclear whether they refer to Vindice and Hippolito or to the Duchess. But in line 28 Vindice has proposed to make a politic retreat, and although the phrase is odd, it is probably intended to mark the brothers' covert escape. Foakes, who interprets the direction in this way, is nevertheless probably right to add an exit for the Duchess as well (see note on 2.3.34.1).

2.3.34.1   *Exit Duchess*] FOAKES; *not in* ELD. The Duchess has nothing further to say in the scene and there is no other point in it at which she can conveniently make her exit; in fact modern editors apart from Foakes provide none for her. Eld's *Exeunt* directions at 2.3.56.1, 2.3.102.1, and 2.3.121.1 seem specific to particular sets of other characters, whom editors name, and the Duke's speeches at 102–10 and 122–30 are clearly soliloquies. 'It seems appropriate that she should go off with the duke's words of comfort in her ears', as Foakes remarks.

2.3.36.1   *two ... villains*] ELD (₍his villaines.)

2.3.42   to] DODSLEY ro ELD

2.3.56.1   *Lussurioso ... Guards*] THIS EDITION; *not in* ELD. Other editors do not specify the Nobles (two of whom speak after their entry at 2.3.17.2), but Eld's *Exeunt* presumably includes them, since they are given an entry at 2.3.110.1 (and again two speak).

2.3.74   That] ELD; That's THIS EDITION *conj.*

2.3.75   father] ELD; fathers DODSLEY

2.3.102.1   *Exeunt ... Supervacuo*] ELD (*Exeunt*)

2.3.103   o'er't] ELD (or't); on't DODSLEY

2.3.119   Why, rise] THIS EDITION; Which, rise ELD; Arise DODSLEY; Which—[*To them*] rise FOAKES; Rise HARRIER. The sudden breaking off of sense assumed by Foakes seems pointless. Ross and Parfitt try to impart meaning by introducing a parenthesis. Parfitt reads: 'Which (rise my lords) your knees sign: his release.', and assumes the antecedent of 'Which' to be 'liberty'. Ross, who punctuates similarly, avoids interpreting the Duke's previous two lines as an aside,

and concludes line 118 with a comma, so that it becomes the antecedent. Neither version would readily be intelligible on stage, and it is improbable that the key command to rise would be uttered parenthetically. 'Which', repeated from the previous line, appears to have corrupted some monosyllabic exclamation (metrically desirable), such as 'Why' or 'Nay': the former is more readily explicable as a misreading or missetting.

2.3.121.1   *Exeunt Nobles*] ELD (*Exeunt.*), turned down below line end

3.1.15   Blessed] DODSLEY (Blest); Blaft ELD

3.1.25.1   *Exit Supervacuo*] ELD (*Exit.*), after Supervacuo's speech

3.3.3   We] ELD *corr*; Were ELD *uncorr*

3.3.13   Already, i'faith] DODSLEY; Alrearly ifath ELD

3.3.14   he that] THIS EDITION (FOAKES); that ELD. Insertion of the pronoun improves the sense. Eld's line is metrically regular if 'impudent' is stressed on the second syllable, but the adjective is normally stressed on the first syllable (as at 1.2.190, 1.4.41, 3.5.17, and 4.2.194; at 5.1.128 it could be stressed on either the first or second syllable). Inclusion of the pronoun renders line 14—'And he that is least impudent soonest dies'—metrically acceptable whether 'impudent' is stressed on the first syllable (and 'that is' is pronounced as printed) or on the second (and 'that is' is elided in pronunciation).

3.3.14   impudent] ELD (Impudent); imprudent HAZLITT. As Foakes remarks, 'the emphasis in the play on impudence ... supports the reading of Q as an ironic comment on Junior Brother.'

3.3.27.1   *Exeunt Officers*] ELD (*Exeunt.*)

3.4.7.1   *He ... letter*] ELD (*Letter.*)

3.4.15   I'll be mad!] Ross, followed by several other editors, inserts after this direction for Junior to tear up the letter, and another after line 57 ('Would I'd been torn in pieces when I tore it') for him to try to piece it together again. This would provide some amusing stage business, but at line 57 'tore it' probably means simply 'opened it'. Junior's desperate punning in line 57 is weakened by taking 'tore it' to mean 'tore it in pieces'.

3.4.62   dunce] ELD (Duns)

3.5.63   he] ELD; she FOAKES. Foakes's emendation makes the absurdity that of women who stake their fortunes on their made-up faces; it requires a comma after 'set' in line 64. It creates a pun on 'set' = placed as cosmetics (they spend a fortune on them). But although Foakes finds the jump from singular 'she' to plural 'their' (64) in accord with 'the author's habit of generalizing', one would expect 'are not they', rather than 'is not she'. On the whole, 'he' gives at least as strong a meaning: 'Is not he absurd who stakes his fortunes on the painted faces of godless women?'

3.5.63   absurd] ELD (absur'd)

3.5.103   poisoned] DODSLEY (poison'd); poyfoned ELD (= poisonèd)

3.5.112   sign] ELD (fine); sin REED; fine COLLINS. *OED* records 'sine' as a good seventeenth-century spelling of 'sign', and inspection of several copies of the quarto makes the difference between the 'fi' and 'fi' ligatures quite clear; so Parfitt is wrong to suppose that Eld reads 'fine' (which he calls 'perfectly acceptable' in the sense 'a fine lady') and to describe Gibbons's 'sign' as an emendation. Ross also seems to have misread Eld. Of course an editor might legitimately decide to emend to 'fine'.

3.5.114   need] ELD; needs THIS EDITION *conj.* The plural is much more common in this kind of locution; in the analogous 'must needs' it is almost invariable.

3.5.129   FIRST GENTLEMAN] ELD (*Gentle.*)

3.5.164 slobbering] HAZLITT; Flobbering ELD

3.5.175 not] ELD corr; nor ELD uncorr

3.5.184 Villain!] ELD (Villaine?). Eld's question mark presumably represents an exclamation, as Vindice replies in kind to the Duke's reference to Vindice and Hippolito as 'villains'. Vindice has identified himself, his brother, and the 'bony lady' as 'Villains all three' at line 153, so is unlikely to be questioning the Duke's appellation; a question would seem to require an exact echo of the Duke's plural.

3.5.185 hires] ELD; hire DODSLEY. The singular may seem more idiomatic, but 'hires' was set by the more accurate of Eld's two compositors, and OED cites Wyclif's late fourteenth-century 'the hires of sin, death' (modernized); a touch of biblical archaism ('hires' for 'wages') would suit Vindice's sententious saying.

3.5.203.1 the Bastard Spurio] ELD (the Baſtard₍)

3.5.218 banquet's] REED; Banqueſts ELD. All editors have followed Reed. This makes pleasure guest of banquet, and so personifies 'banquet' as well as 'pleasure'; and Eld's capital suggests personification, since the word is not capitalized on the three other occasions on which it appears within a line (1.1.47, 3.5.188, 5.3.0.4). It is only reluctance to credit Eld's compositor with responsibility for that subtle capital 'B' that prevents me from placing the apostrophe after the 's' and so having pleasure as guest of banquets (that is, a guest at banquets).

3.6.12 SUPERVACUO] REED; Spu. ELD

3.6.15 Led] ELD (Lead)

3.6.25 our] DODSLEY; out ELD

3.6.44 woo] ELD (woe)

3.6.46 stead] ELD (ſteed)

3.6.54 AMBITIOSO and SUPERVACUO] ELD (Both.)

4.1.1.1 Enter Hippolito] THIS EDITION; Enter Luſſurioſo with Hippolito ELD, at 4.1.0.2. Since Hippolito remarks at 4.1.3 on the oddity of Lussurioso's summoning him only to dismiss him, Hippolito's entry should presumably be placed after Lussurioso's initial call.

4.1.9 You're] ELD (Ye'are)

4.1.13 He'd] ELD (Had)

4.1.23 desperate] DODSLEY; deſperare ELD

4.1.31 lordship] DODSLEY; Lorship ELD

4.1.38 next] ELD; vexed OLIPHANT conj.

4.1.38 come] DODSLEY; comes ELD

4.1.39.1 Exit] ELD (Exit Vin.)

4.1.40 He's] ELD (Has)

4.1.68 thee,] ELD (thee); the DODSLEY. Eld's quarto does not elsewhere spell the definite article 'thee', so Dodsley's reading should probably be considered an emendation, rather than a modernization. It would make the line metrically a little more regular, and there is something to be said for the impersonality of 'the brother'.

4.1.72.1 The Nobles enter] DODSLEY; ELD prints in roman as part of line 72, where (coincidentally, we must assume), it completes the pentameter (while providing a feminine ending).

4.1.81 FIRST GENTLEMAN] 3 ELD. Two of the nobles who enter at 4.1.72.1 are designated '1' and '2' in speech prefixes. One of the new group entering at 4.1.79.1 speaks lines 81 and 89, but Middleton thinks of him simply as a third voice.

4.2.13 the] ELD; thee the THIS EDITION conj.

4.2.32 turn] ELD (turne); tune THIS EDITION conj. The conjectural emendation would more obviously fit Vindice's musical image in 4.2.27–30, but see Commentary.

4.2.36 I've] ELD (I'ave)

4.2.38 he's] ELD (h'as)

4.2.40 Duke's] DODSLEY; Duke ELD

4.2.41.1 Vindice snatches] ELD (Snatches)

4.2.46 on] HAZLITT; on't ELD

4.2.46 —heaven!] ELD (—heauen!); omit THIS EDITION conj. Lussurio's extrametrical exclamation may have arisen through misunderstanding of a manuscript annotation designed to expurgate 'God' from the same sentence; compare 4.4.14. But his reflex use of 'heaven!' as a mere expression of surprise may be read as comically, and unwittingly, reinforcing the point he has just made.

4.2.64 LUSSURIOSO] SYMONDS (Gilchrist); Hip. ELD

4.2.75 rattles] ELD (rotles)

4.2.76 threatening] ELD (threatning)

4.2.80–1 You...for it] Vindice may intend play on the contradiction between 'not chose but like' and 'give nothing for' = not care for at all; but this would require omission of Eld's 'me' on the assumption that it had been caught from the line below.

4.2.80 choose] ELD (chose)

4.2.88 He's] ELD (Has)

4.2.98 pockets] ELD (pock₍), 'ets' having dropped to the end of the next line

4.2.102 heartily] ELD (heartly)

4.2.110, 5.1.111 clothes] ELD (cloths)

4.2.118 your asking] DODSLEY; you rasking ELD

4.2.126 covetous] ELD (couetuous)

4.2.128 threatened] DODSLEY (threaten'd); threatened ELD (= threatenèd)

4.2.142 fine] COLLINS; fiue ELD; few HAZLITT

4.2.151 their] ELD; this DODSLEY. Several editors have followed Dodsley, but 'their' is presumably proleptic, referring to 'these news' in the next line.

4.2.171 Exit] ELD (Exit Hippo.)

4.2.174 Thou] DODSLEY; thon ELD

4.2.192.1 Exit] ELD (Exi. Luſſ.)

4.2.198 There it goes] Editors, assuming that the words indicate a prompt heavenly response to Vindice's rhetorical question, have added a direction for thunder here, but the expression is a catchphrase marking sudden inspiration. See Commentary.

4.2.215 We,] DODSLEY; Me₍ ELD

4.2.216 Shall] ELD corr; Shalt ELD uncorr

4.2.222 grain] ELD corr (graine); graihe ELD uncorr

4.3.0.1–2 the Bastard Spurio] ELD (the Baſtard)

4.3.0.3–4 his brother Ambitioso] ELD (his Brother)

4.3.5 Exeunt Duchess and Spurio] ELD (Exeunt.)

4.3.6 Woult] ELD. Recent editors emend (or modernize) to 'Would', 'Wouldst', or 'Would't', but Eld's is a separate colloquial form (more commonly 'wolt', 'wou't' or 'woltow') for 'wilt thou', used by Middleton in Puritan (four times) and Yorkshire, as noted by Lake (p. 148), who found one instance in Marston's What You Will; 'wolt' occurs in the Shakespearean part of Pericles, 15.112. See OED, Will, v.¹.A.3.a and 6.a.

4.3.15 waist] ELD (waſte); waists DODSLEY. Errors involving 's' endings are common in Compositor X's stints, and Dodsley may be right, but the singular is possible here (on the reasoning that a woman has only one waist).

4.3.16, 4.4.0.1 their] ELD (there).

4.3.16–18 about...Exeunt] DODSLEY; about. Exeunt. | Sup. Come...preuent, | Or...repent. ELD corr; about, | Or...repent. Exeunt. | Sup. Come...preuent, ELD uncorr. ELD originally reversed the order of 17 and 18, giving 18 to Ambitioso. When the sequence was corrected, the stage direction was incorrectly moved from after 'repent.' to after 'about.'

4.4.3   parent] DODSLEY; Parents ELD
4.4.12   knew'st] ELD *corr* (knewſt); knowſt ELD *uncorr*
4.4.14   thou only God] ROSS (Swinburne); *Thou onely,* you powers
ELD. Dodsley omitted 'Thou only' and Symonds omitted
'you'. Nicoll altered Eld's four words to 'you [heavenly]
powers'. Foakes, following Thorndike, punctuates the speech
as follows: 'Ah, is't possible? Thou only? You powers on
high, | That women should dissemble when they die!'
Swinburne's conjecture, supported by Price, is preferable.
Presumably 'Thou onely God' was censored and underlined
or scored through for deletion, and 'you powers' substituted;
the printer eliminated 'God' but mistakenly retained and
italicized 'Thou onely'.
4.4.41   'tis] ELD *corr*; to't ELD *uncorr*
4.4.43   tears] ELD *corr* (teares); tares ELD *uncorr*
4.4.44   Wet will make iron] ELD *corr*; Wee will make you ELD
uncorr (state 1); Wet will make you ELD *partially corr* (state 2)
4.4.53   rinse] ELD (rence)
4.4.60   seld] ELD (ſild)
4.4.64   clinged] ELD *corr* (cling'd); cling ELD *uncorr*
4.4.71   The Duke's] ELD *corr* (The dukes); Dukes ELD *uncorr*
4.4.73-4   dirt! | HIPPOLITO Graced, to] THIS EDITION; durt; great.
| Hip. To ELD. Dodsley omitted 'great', while Collier trans-
ferred it to the beginning of the next speech, by Hippolito.
The present editor accepts Collier's transfer and emends the
adjective, so that Hippolito's line—'Graced, to be miserably
great, rich to be eternally wretched'—is neatly balanced,
with consonance linking the first and last words of each
half ('Graced...great; rich...wretched'). We may guess that
Middleton first wrote the line without 'Graced', and added it
marginally, in order to secure this phonetic and syntactical
pattern, but that the word was misread (under the influence
of 'great' in 71 and 73-4) and misplaced. The press variants
at 71 and 73-4, involving the omission and restoration of
single words, suggest that the manuscript copy was confusing
for the compositor at this point. The emendation is further
discussed in the Textual Introduction. 'Graced' is a word
favoured by Middleton, who used it over a dozen times.
Most editors end Vindice's speech with an anachronistic
exclamation: 'Great!'
4.4.74   to be miserably] ELD *corr* (To ~); Too miserably ELD *uncorr*
4.4.93.1   *Exeunt Vindice and Hippolito*] ELD (*Exeunt.*)
4.4.141   their] ELD; her SYMONDS
4.4.149   not] ELD; but SYMONDS
4.4.157   Be] REED (Steevens); Buy ELD
5.1.10   enough] ELD (enow)
5.1.12   faith's] ELD *corr*; faith ELD *uncorr*
5.1.17   show] ELD; shown FOAKES
5.1.18-19   he died] ELD *corr*; hee did ELD *uncorr*
5.1.35   loathsome] ELD *corr* (loathſome); leathſome ELD *uncorr*
5.1.44   stifle] DODSLEY; ſtifle ELD
5.1.54   mad-breast] ELD *corr* (mad breſt); mad beaſt ELD *uncorr*.
Gibbons is the only other recent editor to accept 'breast' as a
genuine correction. Maxwell plausibly defended it as creating
a compound ('Thou art a mad-breast') on the analogy of
'mad-brain'. Lussurioso is commenting appreciatively on
Vindice's extravagant fancy and bizarre wit, as when he
called him 'a mad apprehensive knave' at 2.2.82.
5.1.58   nake] ELD *corr*; make ELD *uncorr*
5.1.80   Duchess, all,] ELD (Ducheſſe,all?); Duchess; tell, DODSLEY
5.1.86   SORDIDO] 1 ELD. From lines 85 and 91 it can be inferred
that Eld's (and presumably Middleton's) '1' and '2' are

Sordido and Nencio. Since they have been named in the
dialogue they cannot be allowed to remain anonymous in
the speech prefixes—or in the stage directions at 5.1.85.1
and 5.1.92.1.
5.1.87   NENCIO] 2 ELD.
5.1.95   furthest] ELD (fordeſt)
5.1.102   LUSSURIOSO] ELD (*Lus.*); *not in* DODSLEY. Ross follows
Dodsley in giving the line to Vindice.
5.1.104   FIRST NOBLE [*within*]] ELD (1)
5.1.105   SECOND NOBLE [*within*]] ELD (2). The questions they ask
suggest that the extras (clearly not those of lines 86, 87, and
91) are heard as voices before they materialize as Nobles at
5.1.105.1. Eld's '2' and '1' at 110 and 111 are interpreted as
prefixes for these two Nobles, who have first spoken offstage
as they are about to enter (5.1.105.1).
5.1.122   FIRST GENTLEMAN] ELD (1). The numeral here and at
line 130 appears to denote a different character from that
discussed in the previous note. This edition calls him 'First
Gentleman', in order to identify him with the character who
in 4.1.81-2 spoke of the Duke as having 'privately rid forth'.
Hence also the need to include Gentlemen along with the
Nobles entering at 5.1.105.1.
5.1.140   [FIRST] NOBLE] ELD (*Nob.*). Here and at lines 151, 153,
155, 157, 160, and 165, Eld abandons the use of numerals
as speech prefixes and uses '*Nob.*' or '*Nobl.*' instead. Clearly
one Nobleman takes the lead. This edition (like Gibbons's)
gives him all the speeches except those at line 151 and
155; at least two speaking Noblemen are present (lines
110-12), and the seven speeches might be distributed in
various ways. Perhaps the First Noble should be identified as
Sordido, but the Noble seems too much a spokesman on state
concerns to be Lussurioso's contemptible henchman (whose
name, according to Florio, means 'absurd, filthy, corrupt,
unclean, beastly'), though his words may be hypocritical in
the manner of Buckingham ensuring Richard Gloucester's
acceptance of the crown.
5.1.148   sov'reign] THIS EDITION; forraine ELD. There has been no
completely convincing gloss on Eld's adjective. The postulated
misreading would have been very easy ('fov' being seen as
'for'), and 'sov'reign markets' has the advantage of punning
on markets in 'rulers' and in 'coins'. *Old Law* has similar
wordplay—'As he is my sovereign, I do give him two crowns
for it' (5.1.357-8)—though in a scene probably written by
Rowley. *Owl* 1188-9 juxtaposes 'reign' and 'markets'.
5.1.151, 5.1.155   [SECOND] NOBLE] ELD (*Nob.*)
5.1.164   Spread] ELD; Speed HAZLITT. Whereas in this edition
'Calling...son' (163-4) is parenthetical, Hazlitt places a
comma after 'happiness' and a colon after 'son'. This is one of
Hazlitt's few attractive emendations, but seems unnecessary
even so. See Commentary.
5.1.171.1   *Exeunt...Hippolito*] ELD (*Exeu.* Bro.)
5.1.172   have at] DODSLEY; haue ELD
5.1.176   SUPERVACUO] ELD (*Sup.*). See note on 5.3.53 for a discussion of this and the next three speech prefixes.
5.1.177   AMBITIOSO] COLLINS (*Amb.*); And. ELD
5.1.184   *Exit*] ELD (*Exit* Super.)
5.1.185   'Tis] ELD ('tis)
5.1.187   *Exit*] ELD (*Exit* Ambi.)
5.2.8   FIRST LORD] ELD (1)
5.2.8   SECOND LORD] SYMONDS; 3 ELD
5.2.13   tale] ELD (taile)
5.2.24   THIRD LORD] ELD (3)

5.3.0.1–2   *young . . . Lussurioso*] ELD (*young Duke*)

5.3.0.4   *banquet*] THIS EDITION; *banquet. A blaſing-ſtar appeareth.* ELD. Foakes remarks that Eld's 'could be an anticipatory direction' (of a kind that is quite compatible with foul papers, rather than promptbook, copy). This edition transfers the appearance of the comet to line 5.3.13.1, where Lussurioso is first startled by it. It is, on the whole, unlikely that such a spectacular effect could remain unremarked during the preceding thirteen lines of dialogue (see Holdsworth (1990), pp. 110–11).

5.3.1   FIRST NOBLE] ELD (*Noble.*)

5.3.5   SECOND NOBLE] ELD (*Nob.*). Since the scene's third speech for a Noble is prefixed '3.*Nob.*' and the Nobles' speeches are numbered from that point onwards, the first two speeches must be for the First and Second Nobles.

5.3.13.1   *A blazing star appeareth*] ELD (~ blaſing-ſtar ~ at 5.3.0.4); see note on 4

5.3.14   *thee . . . start?*] ELD (thee, what art thou? madſt me start?). Depending on how this elliptical, nine-syllable line is punctuated, two substantive emendations are possible. Hazlitt, assuming haplography, read 'thou? [thou] mad'st'. Alternatively, punctuating as in this edition, one might supply the elided relative pronoun: 'thou that mad'st'. But the slight metrical irregularity seems acceptable within Lussurioso's staccato outcry.

5.3.23   wear] ELD (were)

5.3.27   most] ELD; most near DODSLEY

5.3.40.1–2   *two . . . Hippolito*] ELD (*two Brothers*)

5.3.46.1   *Exeunt . . . Lords*] ELD (*Exeunt.*, after 'ling'ring' in line 46)

5.3.48   *Exit*] ELD (*Exit Vin.*)

5.3.48.2   *stepsons . . . Supervacuo*] ELD (*Step- ſons*)

5.3.48.2–3   *Bastard Spurio*] ELD (*Baſtard*)

5.3.48.4   *The Duke Lussurioso*] ELD (*the Duke*)

5.3.49   LUSSURIOSO O, O!] ELD, before line 48.1

5.3.51   FOURTH NOBLE] ELD (4). The Fourth Man of Eld's (and presumably Middleton's) direction at 5.3.48.3 is always '4' in Eld's speech prefixes.

5.3.53   SUPERVACUO] FLUCHÈRE (Napier); *Spur.* ELD. This is the minimal emendation, implying Eld's misreading, or accidental setting, of '*Super*' as '*Spur*'. At 3.6.12 Eld's '*Spu*' is certainly a mistake for '*Sup*'. More extensive alterations were proposed by Nicoll, Waith, and Howarth. At 3.1.13 and 3.6.18 Ambitioso claimed to be heir; so Nicoll exchanged Ambitioso's two speech prefixes for Supervacuo's two at 5.1.176–87 to give Supervacuo the words 'And do you think to be duke then, kind brother?' This entailed also exchanging

the names (included by Eld) in the brothers' separate exits at 5.1.184 and 5.1.187. Waith and Howarth would reassign the speeches here in 5.3 so as to have Ambitioso speak all of 51–3, and Supervacuo the first half of 54 ('Thou Duke? Brother thou liest'), before Spurio adds 'Slave, so dost thou', and the Fourth Noble caps that in turn. Such reorganization is tempting, but Foakes gives grounds for thinking that it would be 'pressing the idea of consistency too far', since Ambitioso and Supervacuo are both eager to be Duke and 'what matters to the audience' is 'their rivalry in villainy'. The theory behind Waith's changes would have to be that Middleton himself left his foul papers inconsistent and that the speech prefixes would have been revised for the performance script.

5.3.57.1   *Enter . . . Guards*] THIS EDITION, *not in* ELD. Editors bring on Antonio and the requisite guards, but unless further attendants enter here, nobody will be both present and alive to hear Antonio's final speech (126–8) and take part in the last *Exeunt.*

5.3.57   traitor] COLLINS; Traytors ELD. Dodsley retained the plural and took Eld's immediately preceding 'this' to be a spelling of 'these'.

5.3.60   make‸] REED; wake, ELD. Some editors retain 'wake', but the implication that the eyes become bloodshot during a nightmare muddles the point; the emphasis should be on the bloody spectacle affecting Antonio now.

5.3.64   unhallowed] ELD (vnhollowed)

5.3.70   'Sblood] DODSLEY; Sloud ELD, which Collins interpreted as ''Slud'. 'Sbloud' is the Eld spelling of ''Sblood', but 'Sloud' would be abnormal for Middleton as a spelling of ''Slud', to which Collins modernized.

5.3.89   may] DODSLEY; nay ELD

5.3.94   I ne'er] THIS EDITION; I not ELD; I've not DODSLEY. As a parallel to Eld's construction Foakes cites 'It not concernèd me' in *Antony and Cleopatra*, 2.2.39, but while this placing of 'not' in front of the verb is quite common in Shakespeare and other dramatists (though more so in the present tense, as Foakes notes), I know of no exact parallel to Eld's 'I not hard of the like', where the meaning would be not 'I did not hear' but 'I have not heard'. 'I ne'er heard' is idiomatic and Middletonian; compare 'the like ne'er heard of' at 4.2.122. The spelling 'ne'r' could easily have been misread, or 'not' might be the compositor's 'memorial' error. The passage occurs on a page set by the less reliable of Eld's two workmen.

5.3.94   of the] ELD; the OLIPHANT

5.3.101   to] DODSLEY; two ELD

5.3.110   murd'rers] DODSLEY (murderers); murders ELD

5.3.128.1   *Exeunt*] OLIPHANT; *Exit.* ELD. See note on line 5.3.57.1 above.

PRESS VARIANTS

The following extant copies of Eld's quarto have been recorded:

*B(1) Bodleian, Oxford, 1607, Malone 856
*B(2) Bodleian, Oxford, 1608, Malone 202 (lacking sheet B)
*BPL Boston Public Library, 1607
*BL(1) British Library, London, 1607, C.34.e.11
*BL(2) British Library, London, 1608, C.12.f.8
*BL(3) British Library, London, 1608, 644.c.80
*Ch Chapin Library, Williams College, Williamstown, Mass., 1607
*Cla William Andrews Clark Library, Los Angeles, Calif., 1607
*D(1) Dulwich College, London, 1607, O.a.2
*D(2) Dulwich College, London, O.a.5 (lacking title-page)
*F(1) Folger Shakespeare Library, Washington, DC, 1607
*F(2) Folger Shakespeare Library, Washington, DC, 1608
*Har Harvard University, Cambridge, Mass., 1607
*Hun(1) Huntington Library, San Marino, Calif., 1607
*Hun(2) Huntington Library, San Marino, Calif., 1608
IG Sir Israel Gollancz, 1608
K King's College, Cambridge, 1608
*M(1) Magdalene College, Oxford, 1607, Arch.D.4.9
*M(2) Magdalene College, Oxford, 1608, Arch.D.4.10
NLS National Library of Scotland, Edinburgh, 1607
P Princeton University, Princeton, N.J., 1608
TCU Texas Christian University, Fort Worth, Texas, 1607
*VA(1) Victoria and Albert Museum, London, 1607, Forster
*VA(2) Victoria and Albert Museum, London, 1608, Dyce
*W Worcester College, Oxford, 1608
*Y(1) Yale University, New Haven, Conn., 1607, Childs
Y(2) Yale University, New Haven, Conn., 1608

Price and Ross collated nine copies located in the United States, and Jackson has collated or checked twelve British copies. Foakes examined the British Library and Dulwich Library copies without giving complete information about the states of their formes, and Nicoll was also aware of several variants and had looked at the Gollancz copy (which may no longer be in private hands). To the total of thirty-one variants discovered by Price and Ross subsequent investigations have added only two. Neither Price in his article (1960) nor Ross in his edition recorded all variants, but for Jackson's facsimile (1983) Price provided an almost complete list, to which two variants noted by Ross and two recently detected by Jackson may be added; Price also privately communicated full details of the states of formes in the nine American copies. The table below presents these details, together with those for copies scrutinized by Jackson. The twenty-one copies checked are marked with an asterisk in the inventory above.

Twenty of the variants are in sheet H, in which the pattern of correction is most complicated. The Boston and Chapin copies have one variant on H2ᵛ in an intermediate state, and two copies, one in the Bodleian and one in the British Library, are corrected on the first page, H1ᵛ, of the inner forme, but not on H2 or H3ᵛ– 4. Several copies bearing the 1607 date nevertheless exhibit the corrections to A2ᵛ and A4ᵛ. According to Nicoll the Gollancz copy has both formes of sheet H in the corrected state and the variant on G3 in the uncorrected state. The variant on E3 was noticed only during a final checking of the text, so that information about the states of most copies is not available.

Besides true variants, there are a few readings where loosening of type has affected the printing of some copies: 'about' on D3, catchword; 'Without' on E1ᵛ, catchword; 'Mock off thy head.' on G1, 3.6.82; and 'pockets' on G3ᵛ, 4.2.98. Damage to type and variations in inking may also create readings that look like press variants but are not. Nicoll was several times misled by reliance on a photostat of BL(2) as his foundation text. In some copies two letters of the headline on D4 and F4 have been accidentally transposed to read 'ERVENGERS'.

Sheet A (Outer Forme)

Corrected: B(1), B(2), BPL, BL(1), BL(2), BL(3), Ch, Cla, D(1), F(1), F(2), Har, Hun(1), Hun(2), M(2), VA(2), W; but B(1), BPL, BL(1), Ch, Cla, D(1), F(1), Har, Hun(1) have 1607 imprint
Uncorrected: D(2), M(1), VA(1), Y(1)

A1

imprint   1608] corr; 1607 uncorr

A2ᵛ

1.1.47   laughter] laughter, corr; laughter_ uncorr
1.1.50   death's] deaths corr; death uncorr

A4ᵛ

1.2.38   woman! Are] woman; are corr; woman are uncorr
1.2.60   well] well, corr; well. uncorr

Sheet D (Inner Forme)

Corrected: Ch, F(1), Hun(2), VA(2)
Uncorrected: B(1), B(2), BPL, BL(1), BL(2), BL(3), Cla, D(1), D(2), F(2), Har, Hun(1), M(1), M(2), VA(1), W, Y(1)

D4

2.2.121   word, sweeter occasion] world,fweeter occafiõ corr; word, fweete occafion uncorr
2.2.135   sunset] Sun fet corr; Snn fet uncorr

Sheet E (Outer Forme)

States of copies unknown except B(1) uncorr., Hun(2) corr.

E3

3.3.3   We] corr; Were uncorr

Sheet E (Inner Forme)

Corrected: B(1), B(2), BPL, BL(1), BL(2), BL(3), Ch, Cla, D(1), D(2), F(1), F(2), Hun(1), Hun(2), M(1), M(2), VA(1), VA(2), W, Y(1)
Uncorrected: Har

E3ᵛ

3.3.20   people] corr; poeple uncorr

Sheet F (Outer Forme)

Corrected: B(1), B(2), BPL, BL(1), BL(2), BL(3), Ch, Cla, D(1), D(2), F(1), F(2), Har, Hun(1), Hun(2), M(1), M(2), VA(2), W
Uncorrected: VA(1), Y(1)

F1

3.5.21   appointed] appoynted, corr; appoynted: uncorr

F3

3.5.168   father] Father, corr; Father, uncorr

3.5.175 not] *corr*; nor *uncorr*

Sheet G (Outer Forme)

Corrected: BL(1), D(1), F(1), F(2), Har, Hun(1), Hun(2), VA(2), Y(1)

Uncorrected: B(1), B(2), BPL, BL(2), BL(3), Ch, Cla, D(2), M(1), M(2), VA(1), W

G3

4.2.57 To...lord.] To...Lord. | *corr*; To...much. | *Vin.*Tis... at the | *uncorr*

Sheet H (Outer Forme)

Corrected: B(2), BL(1), Cla, F(1), Hun(2), M(2), VA(2)

Partially corrected (4.4.43–4 in intermediate state): BPL, Ch

Uncorrected: B(1), BL(2), BL(3), D(1), D(2), F(2), Har, Hun(1), M(1), VA(1), W, Y(1)

H2ᵛ

4.4.41 beyond...'tis] be yond...'tis *corr*; beyond...to't *uncorr*

4.4.43 tears] teares *corr*; *state 2 only*; tares *uncorr*

4.4.44 Wet will make iron] Wet will make yron *corr*; Wee will make you *uncorr state 1*; Wet will make you *uncorr state 2*

4.4.64 clinged] cling'd *corr*; cling *uncorr*

4.4.71 The Duke's] The dukes *corr*; Dukes *uncorr*

H3

4.4.74 to be miserably] To be miserably *corr*; Too miserably *uncorr*

H4ᵛ

5.1.54 mad-breast] mad breſt *corr*; mad beaſt *uncorr*

5.1.58 nake] *corr*; make *uncorr*

Sheet H (Inner Forme)

Corrected: B(2), BL(1), BL(3), Cla, D(2), F(1), F(2), Hun(2), M(1), M(2), VA(1), VA(2), W, Y(1)

Corrected on H1ᵛ only: B(1), BL(2)

Uncorrected: BPL, Ch, D(1), Har, Hun(1)

H1ᵛ

4.2.216 Shall] *corr*; Shalt *uncorr*

4.2.222 grain] graine *corr*; graihe *uncorr*

4.3.16 about.] about.*Exeunt. corr*; about, *uncorr*

4.3.17–18 SUPERVACUO Come...prevent, | Or...repent.] *Sup.*Come...preuent, | Or...repent. *corr*; Or...repent.*Exeunt.* | *Sup.*Come...preuent, *uncorr*

H2

4.4.12 knew'st] knewſt *corr*; knowſt *uncorr*

4.4.19 thee] *corr*; the *uncorr*

4.4.31 disguise] diſguize, *corr*; diſguize, *uncorr*

H4

5.1.12 faith's] *corr*; faith *uncorr*

5.1.18–19 he died] *corr*; hee did *uncorr*

5.1.32 me! You] me; you *corr*; me you *uncorr*

5.1.35 loathsome] loathſome *corr*; leathſome *uncorr*

STAGE DIRECTIONS

1.1.0.1 *ACT* 1 *SCÆ.* 1.

1.1.0.2–3 *Enter* Vendici, *the Duke, Dutchesse,* Lusurioso *her sonne,* | Spurio *the bastard, with a traine, passe ouer the* | *Stage with Torch-light.*

1.1.49.1 *Enter her brother* Hippolito.

1.1.134 *Exeunt.*

1.2.0.1–4 *Enter the old Duke,* Lussurioso, *his sonne, the Duchesse: the Bast-*|*ard, the Duchesse two sonnes* Ambitioso, *and* Super-uacuo, *the* | *third her yongest brought out with Officers for the Rape two* | *Iudges.*

1.2.88.1 *Exit with a garde.*

1.2.92.1 *Exe. manet Du.*

1.2.175 *Exit.*

1.2.202 *Exit.*

1.3.0.1–2 *Enter* Vindici *and* Hippolito, Vindici *in disguise to* | *attend L.* Lussurioso *the Dukes sonne.*

1.3.185 *Exit.*

1.4.0.1–4 *Enter the discontented Lord* Antonio, *whose wife the Duchesses* | *youngest Sonne rauisht; he Discouering the body of her dead* | *to certaine Lords: and* Hippolito.

1.4.77.2 *Exeunt.*

2.1.0.1 *ACTVS.* 2. *SCÆ.* 1.

2.1.0.2 *Enter* Castiza *the sister.*

2.1.27.1 *Enter* Vindice *her brother disguised.*

2.1.31.1 *A boxe ath eare to her Brother.*

2.1.40 *Exit.*

2.1.237.1 *Exit.*

2.1.243 *Exit.*

2.1.253 *Exit.*

2.2.0.1 *Enter* Lussurioso, *with* Hippolito, | Vindicies *brother.*

2.2.15.1 *Exit.*

2.2.88 *Exit.*

2.2.103.1 *Enter* Hippol.

2.2.126.1 *Exeunt.*

2.2.167.1 (*Exeunt* (turned down below line-end)

2.2.171 *Exit.*

2.3.0.1 *Enter againe.* (right of 2.3.1)

2.3.17.1 *Enter Nobles and sonnes.*

2.3.33.1 *dissemble a* | *flight.* (right, opposite 2.3.34–5)

2.3.36.1–2 *Enter* Spurio *with his villaines.*

2.3.56.1 *Exeunt.*

2.3.59.1 *Exit.*

2.3.102.1 *Exeunt.*

2.3.110.1 *Enter Nobles.*

2.3.121.1 (*Exeunt.* (turned down below line-end)

3.1.0.1 *ACT.* 3.

3.1.0.2 *Enter* Ambitioso, *and* Superuacuo?

3.1.25 *Exit.* (right of Superuacuo's speech)

3.1.28 *Exit.*

3.2.0.1 *Enter with the Nobles,* Lussurioso *from pryson.*

3.2.6 *Exeunt.*

3.3.0.1 *Enter* Ambitioso, *and* Superuacuo? *with Officers.*

3.3.27.1 *Exeunt.*

3.3.30 *Exeunt.*

3.4.0.1 *Enter in prison* Iunior *Brother,*

3.4.7.1 *Letter.* (on same line as, and immediately preceding, first words of letter)

3.4.79 *Exeunt.*

3.5.0.1 *Enter* Vindici *with* Hippolito *his brother.*

3.5.34 *Exit.*

3.5.43.1 *Enter* Vindice, *with the skull of his loue drest vp in Tires.*

3.5.156.1 *stamping* | *on him* (right, opposite 3.5.156–7)

3.5.203.1 *Enter the Bastard meeting the Dutchesse.*

3.5.218.1 *Exeunt.*

3.5.223   *Exeunt.*
3.6.0.1–2   *Enter the Dutchesse two sonnes, Ambitioso & Super-*
vacuo.
3.6.53.1   *Enter Lussurioso.*
3.6.64   *Exit Luss.*
3.6.90.1   *Exeunt.*
4.1.0.1   ACT. 4. SCEN. 1.
4.1.0.2, 4.1.1.1   *Enter Lussurioso with Hippolito.* (one entry in
ELD, at beginning of scene)
4.1.27.1   *Enter Vind.* (right, opposite Vindice's speech at 4.1.29)
4.1.39.1   *Exit Vin.*
4.1.61   *Exit.*
4.1.72.1   The Nobles enter. (printed as part of 4.1.72, but
preceded by a dash)
4.1.89   *Exeunt.*
4.2.0.1–2   *Enter Vindice and Hippolito, Vind. out of his disguise.*
4.2.41.1–2   *Snatches of | his hat and | makes legs | to him.* (right,
opposite 4.2.40–2)
4.2.171   *Exit Hippo.*
4.2.177.1   *Enter.Hip.*
4.2.192.1   *Exi. Luss.*
4.2.225.1   *Exeunt.*
4.3.0.1–4   *Enter the Dutches arme in arme with the Bastard: he
seemeth lasci-|uiously to her, after them, Enter Superuacuo,
running with a ra-|pier, his Brother stops him.*
4.3.5   *Exeunt.*
4.3.18   *Exeunt.* (right of 4.3.16 in ELD corr)
4.4.0.1–3   *Enter Vindice and Hippolito, bringing out there Mother
| one by one shoulder, and the other by the other, with | daggers
in their hands.*
4.4.93.1   *Exeunt.*

4.4.157   *Exeunt.*
5.1.0.2–3   *Enter Vindice and Hippolito.*
5.1.30.1   *Ent. Luss.*
5.1.85.1   *Enter all.* (right of 5.1.85)
5.1.169.1–3   *Exeunt Duke | Nobles and Duchesse.* (right, opposite
5.1.169 and first word of 5.1.170)
5.1.171.1   *Exeu. Bro.*
5.1.184   *Exit Super.*
5.1.187   *Exit Ambi.*
5.2.0.1–2   *Enter Vindice & Hippolito, with Piero and other Lords.*
5.2.31.1   *Exeunt.*
5.3.0.1–4, 5.3.13.1   *In a dum shew, the possessing of the young
Duke. | with all his Nobles: Then sounding Musick. | A furnisht
Table is brought forth: then enters the Duke | & his Nobles to
the banquet. A blasing-star appeareth.* (all at beginning of 5.3)
5.3.40.1–2   *Enter the Maske of | Reuengers the two Brothers, and
| two Lords more.* (right, opposite 5.3.40–1)
5.3.41.1–2   *The Reuengers daunce? | At the end, steale out their
swords, and these foure kill the foure at | the Table, in their
Chaires It thunders.*
5.3.46.1   *Exeunt.* (right, after Vindice's speech at 5.3.46)
5.3.48   *Exit Vin.*
5.3.48.1–7   *Enter the other Maske of entended murderers? Step-
-sons; Bastard; | and a fourth man, comming in dauncing, the
Duke recouers a | little in voyce, and groanes,—calls a guard,
treason. | At which they all start out of their measure, and
turning towards | the Table, they finde them all to be murdered.*
(after Lussurioso's 'O, O!' at 5.3.49)
5.3.55.2   *Enter the first men.*
5.3.125.1   *Exeunt.*
5.3.128.1   *Exit.*
5.3.128.2   FINIS.

LINEATION NOTES

1.2.30–1   Good...uglier] THORNDIKE; *1 line* ELD
1.2.87–8   Brother...rest] REED; *prose* ELD
1.2.129–30   I...now] THIS EDITION; name| ELD
1.2.134–8   Of...windows] HAZLITT; *prose* ELD
1.2.141–2   And...basins] THORNDIKE; *prose* ELD
1.3.17–18   Nay...looks] COLLINS; *prose* ELD
1.3.30–2   So...hand] THIS EDITION; *prose* ELD
1.3.41   What...profession] FOAKES; *2 lines* ELD: been|
1.3.44   A...together] FOAKES; *2 lines* ELD: lord|
1.3.60–1   Some...mother] OLIPHANT; *prose* ELD
1.3.61   and...daughter-in-law] OLIPHANT; *1 line* ELD
1.3.68–70   That...scape] FOAKES; *verse* ELD: damned| twelve|
1.3.102–3   Push...fortunes] FOAKES; *1 line* ELD
1.3.125–7   We...widow] OLIPHANT; *prose* ELD
1.3.151   O...lord] GIBSON; *prose* ELD
1.3.156   Why...name] SYMONDS; *prose* ELD
1.4.8–9   Would...colours] COLLIER; cheeks| ELD
2.1.41   It...nigh] COLLINS; *2 lines* ELD: box|
2.1.75–8   Therefore...already] THIS EDITION; *3 lines* ELD: friend|
poor|
2.1.83–4   O...task] SYMONDS; *prose* ELD
2.1.121–2   These...woman] GOMME; *1 line* ELD
2.1.134–5   O...heart] COLLINS; yonder| ELD
2.1.170–1   It...now] FOAKES; *1 line* ELD
2.1.178–9   'Tis...honesty] REED; *1 line* ELD
2.1.188–9   O...ravished] FOAKES; *1 line* ELD
2.1.190   'Slid...grace] FOAKES; *2 lines* ELD: honour|
2.1.195–6   Ready...eaten] REED; *1 line* ELD

2.1.203–5   Ay...i'faith] ROSS; *prose* ELD
2.2.22–3   Then...now] THORNDIKE; *1 line* ELD
2.2.31–2   But...mother] SYMONDS; *prose* ELD
2.2.103–4   Brother...tell you] THIS EDITION; of you| ELD
2.2.139–40   To...apace] FOAKES; proclamation| ELD
2.2.156–7   I'd...bastard] FOAKES; *1 line* ELD
2.2.157–8   This...now] FOAKES; *1 line* ELD
2.3.9–10   O...days] OLIPHANT; *1 line* ELD
2.3.26–7   I am...good] OLIPHANT; *1 line* ELD
2.3.30–1   You...here] OLIPHANT; *1 line* ELD
2.3.40–1   To...him] OLIPHANT; *1 line* ELD
2.3.41–2   Troth...there] OLIPHANT; *1 line* ELD
2.3.54–5   It...us] OLIPHANT; *1 line* ELD
2.3.56–7   No...better] FOAKES; *1 line* ELD
2.3.61–2   So...death] OLIPHANT; life| ELD
2.3.65–7   Is't...further] THIS EDITION; *prose* ELD
2.3.90–1   I...released] REED; *1 line* ELD
2.3.97–8   'Tis...pass] FOAKES; *1 line* ELD
3.2.2–3   But...you] OLIPHANT; *1 line* ELD
3.4.3–4   My...'em] REED; *1 line* ELD
3.4.8–15   Brother...mad] OLIPHANT; *quotations from letter alternate with comments on it, one line each* ELD
3.4.24–5   Ha...why] FOAKES; *1 line* ELD
3.5.2–3   O...forehead] COLLINS; *1 line* ELD
3.5.10–12   Are...lady] FOAKES; secrets| price| ELD
3.5.37–8   To...men] THIS EDITION; *1 line* ELD
3.5.121–2   So...minute] OLIPHANT; *1 line* ELD
3.5.144–5   Lady...O] COLLINS; *prose* ELD

3.5.146–7   Brother...eyeballs] FOAKES; *1 line* ELD
3.5.166–7   Is...then] OLIPHANT; *1 line* ELD
3.5.176–7   But...Duke] OLIPHANT; *1 line* ELD
3.5.198–9   We...object] COLLIER; Brother | ELD
3.6.2–3   Ay...that] FOAKES; *1 line* ELD
3.6.3–4   Your...what] FOAKES; *1 line* ELD
3.6.31–2   My...allotted] FOAKES; *1 line* ELD
3.6.37–8   I...yourself] OLIPHANT; *1 line* ELD
3.6.43–4   He...it] FOAKES; *1 line* ELD
3.6.45–6   He...due] COLLIER; *1 line* ELD
3.6.46–7   But...oaths] COLLIER; *1 line* ELD
3.6.58–9   Released...it] THIS EDITION; Released | ELD
3.6.70–1   The...came] OLIPHANT; *1 line* ELD
3.6.74–5   Our...furies] THIS EDITION; *1 line* ELD
3.6.87–8   Well...vengeance] SCOTT; *prose* ELD
4.1.1–2   My...in] OLIPHANT; lord | ELD
4.1.4–5   Your...employment] OLIPHANT; *1 line* ELD
4.1.7–8   He...honour] OLIPHANT; *1 line* ELD
4.1.15–16   'Tis...you] REED; *1 line* ELD
4.1.16–17   Neglect...it] OLIPHANT; *1 line* ELD
4.1.29–30   Away...thee] OLIPHANT; *1 line* ELD
4.1.36–7   Mum...dumb] HAZLITT; *1 line* ELD
4.1.54–6   It...dwells] OLIPHANT; *2 lines* ELD: honour |
4.1.56–7   Why...court] COLLINS; *1 line* ELD
4.2.29–30   Like...sadly] OLIPHANT; *1 line* ELD
4.2.32–3   'Sfoot...upon't] OLIPHANT; *1 line* ELD
4.2.45–6   Nimble...heaven] OLIPHANT; name | ELD
4.2.130–1   I'll...me] OLIPHANT; *1 line* ELD
4.2.140–1   Would...done] FOAKES; lord | ELD
4.2.152–3   Brought...for't] COLLINS; *1 line* ELD
4.2.158–9   Has...wasted] OLIPHANT; *1 line* ELD
4.2.159–60   If...cause] OLIPHANT; *1 line* ELD

4.2.178–9   Now...slave-pander] OLIPHANT; *1 line* ELD
4.2.184–5   'Twas...wit] OLIPHANT; *1 line* ELD
4.2.187–8   You...him] OLIPHANT; *1 line* ELD
4.2.219–21   It...pursuit] GIBSON; *prose* ELD
4.2.222–3   Nay...colour] OLIPHANT; *1 line* ELD
4.3.6–7   Hold...now] OLIPHANT; *1 line* ELD
4.3.13–14   A...shame] OLIPHANT; *1 line* ELD
4.4.23–4   But...not] SALGĀDO; *1 line* ELD
4.4.33–4   O...so] THORNDIKE; *1 line* ELD
4.4.37–8   O...true] OLIPHANT; *1 line* ELD
4.4.51–2   O...soul] FOAKES; *1 line* ELD
4.4.73–4   To...Graced] COLLIER; *1 line and reading* great *where this edition has* Graced ELD
4.4.119–20   Of...flame] REED; breath | ELD
4.4.141–3   An...beggars] SYMONDS; *2 lines* ELD: son |
4.4.149–50   Indeed...honest] REED; *1 line* ELD
5.1.43–4   Puh...breaths] OLIPHANT; *1 line* ELD
5.1.59–60   Troth...for't] ROSS; *1 line* ELD
5.1.98–9   Hark...again] FOAKES; *1 line* ELD
5.1.100–1   O...poison] SYMONDS; *1 line* ELD
5.1.107–9   Behold...disguised] OLIPHANT; *prose* ELD
5.1.112–13   That...lie] FOAKES; *1 line* ELD
5.1.129–30   Maintain...execution] THORNDIKE; *1 line* ELD
5.1.135–6   Why...wits] COLLINS; *1 line* ELD
5.1.182   This...mighty] GIBSON; *prose* ELD
5.2.1–2   My...countries] OLIPHANT; *1 line* ELD
5.3.44–5   So...enough] OLIPHANT; *1 line* ELD
5.3.56–7   Pistols...Duke] FOAKES; *1 line* ELD
5.3.79–80   And...departed] FOAKES; *1 line* ELD
5.3.96–8   All...him] GIBBONS; now | it | ELD
5.3.102–3   My...he] OLIPHANT; *1 line* ELD
5.3.115–16   Brought...time] HAZLITT; *1 line* ELD
5.3.123–4   To...true] OLIPHANT; enough | ELD

A TRICK TO CATCH THE OLD ONE

Edited by Valerie Wayne

A Trick to Catch the Old One (BEPD 262, STC 17896–17897) was licensed to George Eld on 7 October 1607 along with *The Revenger's Tragedy* and issued with a 1608 date on all title-pages of the first edition (ELD1). The account in the Stationers' Register reads: 'George Elde Entred for his copies vnder th[e h]andes of Sir George Buck and th[e] wardens. Twoo plaies th[e]one called *the revengers tragedie* th[e]other. *A trick to catche the old one* . . . xijd.' The original title-page of the play, printed on A2, did not identify the author; its title was followed by the information, '*As it hath beene lately Acted, by the Children of Paules.*' This title-page was cancelled and another was printed on A1 with more information about performances and a reference to the author: 'As it hath beene often in Action, both at Paules, and the Black-Fryers. *Prefented before his Maieftie on New-yeares night last.* Compofde by T.M.' George Eld remained the printer of the play on this revised title-page, and Henry Rocket was identified as its bookseller. The revised title-page is also extant in another state that is discussed in detail below. A second edition of the play appeared in 1616 (ELD2): it identified the play further as 'By T. Midleton' and included the same performance information as appeared on the revised title--pages of the first edition. Eld was named as printer and Thomas Langley as bookseller. The text of each of these quarto editions required eight sheets and ended on H4ʳ.

Harold Newcomb Hillebrand is the only historian who asserts that the play was associated first with the Children of the Revels and then taken over to Paul's in the early months of 1606, when Edward Kirkham left as master of the Children at Blackfriars to go to the other company. This assumption leads Hillebrand to support F. G. Fleay and J. T. Murray in identifying *Trick* as one of the two plays that were performed at court by Paul's boys before the last day of March, 1606, and therefore, he infers, on 1 January of that year. The account does not explain why a play not licensed until October 1607 and printed either late in 1607 or early in the following year would refer on its title-page to a performance 'before his Maieftie on New-yeares night last'; nor does it take into account Middleton's and Ravenscroft's associations with the Children of Paul's in the years preceding 1606.

E. K. Chambers, W. W. Greg, William Roy Dawson, and Andrew Gurr propose instead that the play moved from Paul's to the Blackfriars boys around 1607 and was performed by the latter before the King on 1 January 1609. The company is known to have appeared at court during Christmas 1608–9. Greg accounts for the discrepancy of a 1608 date on a title-page referring to a performance on 'New-yeares night last' of 1609 by supposing that it 'indicates the legal not the calendar year', conceding that the earlier date 'may, however, have been retained inadvertently' after the printing of the cancelled title-page. This chronology has the advantage of explaining why the title-page was changed to include the Blackfriars and the performance before the King; it has the disadvantage of supposing, in Greg's formulation, a distance of nearly a year between what he terms the first and second issues, a delay that is implausible from Eld's point of view and unsupported by the play's printing history, including the likelihood that at least one of the revised title-pages was printed before the book was collated, folded, and pressed.

Working from the evidence of the printed book, George R. Price and George J. Watson prefer the possibility of a court performance on New Year's night of either 1607 or 1608. Watson observes that 'there are no grounds for assuming (as Chambers and [Greg] unconsciously seem to do in the case of this play) that the records of performances at court are comprehensive and exhaustive' (1968b), and Gurr does note the court performance of an unnamed play by the Blackfriars boys on 1 January 1607. William Edgerton's finding that early printers customarily used the calendar year rather than the legal year (beginning on March 25) in printing books calls into question Greg's assertion in *BEPD* that the 1608 date refers to the legal year. Books published late in one calendar year could also be dated as of the following year: *The Revenger's Tragedy* has one first-edition title-page dated 1607 and another dated 1608. So it is even more unlikely that a title-page printed early in 1609 by the same press would bear the date of 1608. Price and Watson's position seems the most convincing way of accommodating all the information we have about the printing of the play. What it does not offer is an explanation for the changes in the title-page of the first edition.

The information provided on the two revised title-pages is of three different sorts: the author is identified by his initials, the additional performances by the Blackfriars boys and at court are included, and Henry Rocket replaces George Eld as bookseller though not as printer. Eld gained access to at least three of the nine or more plays that he printed in 1607 because of Paul's closing after July, 1606. *The Puritan Widow* and *Northward Ho*, both Paul's plays, had been licensed to him in August of 1607 and were printed by him before the end of the year. *What You Will*, also from Paul's, was licensed in August to Thomas Thorpe and printed by Eld. *Trick* and *The Revenger's Tragedy* were licensed in October and show the same family of watermarks, so they were printed on paper that Eld may have purchased at the same time. Since Paul's was the source for so many of the plays that Eld had recently printed, it is understandable that he would associate *Trick* with the others, especially if he had acquired some or all of them directly from the company. Yet unlike those other plays, *Trick* continued to be performed after 1606 because it was transferred to the Blackfriars. The connection between *Trick* and the other Paul's plays might explain what is otherwise puzzling, that Eld apparently knew of its earlier performances but overlooked the more recent productions at Blackfriars and before the King.

I would propose, then, that the first title-page of *Trick* reflects its association with some of the other plays that Eld printed in 1607: he or his employees probably assumed that a play from Paul's was only a Paul's play, as three others had been. When Eld was informed or reminded, presumably while *Trick* was still in press, that it was a play by 'T.M.' which had also been performed elsewhere, and when Rocket became its bookseller, Eld set another title-page and, if the outer forme of A had already been printed, passed sheet A through the press a second time, probably at Rocket's request and expense. The added information would clearly enhance the sale of the play, and Rocket stood to gain from the advertisement of a new venue for that sale. It is possible that Middleton himself provided some of this information, particularly since Eld had attributed *The Puritan Widow* to 'W.S.' and printed *The Revenger's Tragedy* without any attribution just months earlier. But Rocket's association with the book is likely to be the single most important reason for the printing of the revised title-pages.

That Eld printed this revision by passing sheet A through the press another time is evident from the two copies of the edition in the Bodleian Library, both of which begin the text on A3. One copy has A1 cut off and shows the original title-page on A2, which is conjugate with A3 (Malone 797); the other copy shows the revised title-page on A1, with A2 cut off and its stub remaining, and A4 conjugate with A1 (Malone 812). Adrian Weiss argues that the business transaction between Eld and Rocket must have occurred during the original printing operation and before sheet A had been collated, folded, and pressed. Had the transaction occurred after these operations, the crease in the top edge of the folded sheet A probably would have been so tight as to render the process of unfolding the sheets and making register extremely difficult, even after re-wetting. Distortion of the sheets would have been unavoidable, and no such distortion is evident in the extant copies.

The revised title-page was also set another time by Eld, because the type on the Huntington Huth copy, an illustration of which appears here, differs from some other extant copies including the Huntington's Kemble–Devonshire. The words, spellings, and spacings in the Huntington Huth state are identical to that in Kemble–Devonshire, but Adrian Weiss has identified at least 42

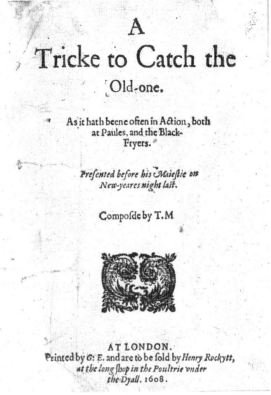

The Huntington Huth title-page of the first edition, which represents a different state of the revised title-page from the Huntington's Kemble–Devonshire copy. The variations that are most visible without enlargement are due to the inked-in portions in the right-hand bottom third of the page, such as the word 'vnder', but there are also discrepancies in type. The page is constructed from three pieces of paper, and the absence of a full stop after 'T.M' is the result of a new piece being joined where the punctuation mark would have been.

types from Eld's shop that occur in one but not in the other. The Huntington Huth title-page is not conjugate with the remaining leaves in the sheet. Why Eld had to set the revised title-page twice is unclear, but title-pages could be used to advertise books as well as sell them, so Rocket may have wanted extra ones to give notice of his new purchase.

The title-page of the Huntington Huth copy was reconstructed from three pieces of possibly contemporary laid paper (David Gants): a portion tipped or glued in that follows the book's gutter until it angles to the right near the bottom of the page; an almost v-shaped piece having the same watermark as the other sheets in the book, on which all of the actual type of this page is printed; and an outer sheet that completes the page. On this third, blank sheet someone working in ink that was made to look like type has most skilfully completed the portions of the title-

-page that were absent from the second, v-shaped, printed piece of paper. The inked-in portions extend through the right-hand bottom third of Eld's scroll ornament to the centre of the imprint beneath it, half of which was torn away. Discrepancies between this title-page and the state represented by the Kemble–Devonshire copy are visible in the lack of a full stop after 'Compofde by T.M', where the third, right-hand sheet begins just before the 'M' and extends through the right-hand side of the ornament; the inked portion of the ornament is also made to look like more of a mirror image of the left side than in the other copies, and the inked words 'sold', 'vnder', and the date '1608' also show variations.

My conjecture is that the Huntington Huth title-page was pieced together and bound in the early nineteenth century. Two of the fly-leaves have watermarked dates of 1800, and the copy is marked as 'Bound by C. Smith' in type or a stamp that Weiss identifies as from the late eighteenth or early nineteenth century. There was a C. Smith in business as a mapseller and publisher on the Strand who flourished from 1803 to 1821, and he would probably have had someone in his shop capable of the skilful inking that completes the title-page's ornament and imprint. This copy was in any case bound before 1877, when John Kershaw, whose bookplate appears on the inside cover, sold it at a Sotheby's sale in July (William Younger Fletcher). It was then or at a later date purchased by Huth and sold at the Huth sale in 1916 to Henry Huntington (*Catalogue of the Huth Collection*).

This evidence suggests that Eld's shop went to even greater lengths to print the revised title-page than we have thought. The scarcity of extant copies of the original title-page—only two exist (Malone 797 and the BL Ashley copy) and the Malone copy is definitely conjugate with the other leaf in the sheet—also suggests that the book was not widely sold in this form. I have not been able to compare the Huntington Huth copy with those at other locations, but it is quite possible that it is not a unique instance of this state of the revised title-page.

The copy-text for all previous critical editions by Charles Barber (1968), George R. Watson (1968b), William Roy Dawson, Jr. (unpublished Ph.D. dissertation, 1969), and George R. Price (1976), as for the present one, is the 1608 edition of the play. While Price's 1967 essay, 'The Early Editions of *A trick to catch the old one*', is perhaps the best known bibliographical analysis of the play, George Watson's B.Litt. thesis for Oxford University, completed less than a year after his own New Mermaids edition of the play, provides the most lucid and extensive account of its printing history, takes issue with many of Price's conjectures, and includes other information unavailable in his published edition.

At the beginning of 4.5, a four-line song appears that was written by Thomas Ravenscroft, who was affiliated with Paul's Boys. A six-line version of the song is printed in Ravenscroft's *Melismata* of 1611, where the music for it is no. 12. The lineation is the same in each text, but *Trick's* version does not include the first two lines. Gary Taylor

and John Jowett point out that the reference in those lines to a 'wittol' (an acquiescent cuckold) would make them inappropriate to the play (*Shakespeare Reshaped*), since Dampit is not clearly married. The remaining lines are, however, not only relevant but include a pun on Dampit's name—'There's pits enough to damn him, before he comes to hell' 4.5.2—and references to Holborn and Fleet Streets, the locations named in association with him at 1.4.60.

The list of forty press variants among the fifteen extant copies of the 1608 edition that appears here was compiled first by recording all variants identified by the four previous editors of critical editions and including in that collation the Folger Shakespeare Library's copy of the play, of which they were unaware. Other variants have been added to this list as necessary. I collated the original quartos at the British Library, Eton College, the Victoria and Albert Museum, the Bodleian and the Huntington libraries. Dr Hector Macdonald and Ms Ashlynn Pai examined and collated the copy in the National Library of Scotland; Mr Paul Quarrie checked three variants in the copy at Eton College; and I collated all remaining copies and variants by xerox or microfilm. The collation shows that correction was made in the following formes: outer A (apart from the revised title-pages), outer and inner B, outer and inner C, inner D, outer and inner E, outer and inner G, and inner H. The outer forme of E was corrected in two separate stops, as Price observes, but in the second instance two changes were made rather than one. The present account adds at least one more corrected forme and twelve or more variants to those noted in any single previous edition.

Both Watson and Price assert that (1) the play was set by formes (certainly for Watson, probably for Price); (2) that it was cast off; and (3) that mistakes or idiosyncrasies in its composition, such as crowding on the page, required economy measures to 'save space' on the affected pages. Watson's conclusion that the play was set by formes was based on negative evidence: e.g., broken type in the outer forme of B does not appear again in his analysis until the inner form of C, which leads him to conclude that the outer form of C 'must have been composed before B(o) was distributed'. However, a more recent analysis of the play's type by Adrian Weiss contradicts these conclusions. Weiss finds three types that appear in B(i) (one in $B3^v$ and two in $B1^v$) and again in C(i) (in C2, $C3^v$ and C4). In later signatures, similar recurrences disprove Watson's hypothesis that type recurred 'from outer forme to inner forme of the subsequent gathering, and from inner forme to outer forme of the next gathering but one (B(o) to C(i), B(i) to D(o))'. Specifically, three types observed by Weiss move from C to D in patterns contradicting this principle, two from D to E, two from E to F, two from F to G, and one from G to H. These patterns of recurrence charted by Weiss are more appropriate for a text set seriatum than one set by formes, because both formes of one sheet would have been distributed before the composition of the next sheet was complete.

Having concluded on a more regular pattern of setting by formes, Watson then finds the pattern disturbed in the setting of sheets F and G. But this irregularity within a more regular pattern might instead offer support for the overall pattern posited by Weiss: that there was no haste in setting the play and that normal breaks in the composition from one sheet to the next would have been highly probable. Weiss also finds on the basis of embossing evidence that all outer formes were printed first except for sheet A, where the evidence is not clear enough to support a definite conclusion.

Seriatum composition is also more appropriate for the play because it would not have required that the text be cast off. Joseph Moxon's 1683-4 account of how he as a printer performed this task indicates how complicated it could be for a text that included as much prose as appears in *Trick*, even allowing for the misconstrual of some verse as prose. It would probably have taken more time to count every letter and space and adjust for the width of small or large pieces of type and ligatures in order to set the play by formes than to set it seriatum. Price posits that after 576 lines of type had been set through part of outer C, a second and 'more exact casting off was made' that adjusted the estimate of the whole text from 2,100 lines to 2,144. The compositors' desire to finish the play on H3^v then led them to increase the number of lines per page to 37, 38, and even 39. But the amount of work involved in doubly casting off much of the play makes this scenario highly unlikely. The account of the printing of the play offered by Price often suggests, as here, that it is possible to reconstruct activities and motives in Eld's shop with a kind of precision that this editor more often associates with historical fiction.

Whether the play would have been set by one compositor using one case, as Watson thinks, two compositors working from two cases and feeding two presses, as Price contends, or three compositors using one press as Dawson believes, has yet to be illustrated convincingly. Watson offers sound reasons for questioning Price's identification of compositors on the basis of spelling, since Price ignores evidence from his own analysis that contradicts his position and Watson's accounts of spelling and type recurrences suggest a different pattern. Weiss's findings also provide other reasons to doubt Price. For example, the latter's account of a shortage of italic capitals no longer obtains if both formes of A were distributed before B1^v and B4^v were set. The long-range recurrences between one or more intervening sheets that appear in Weiss's analysis indicate a likelihood of two compositors working from two pairs of cases in irregular stints. Neither case appears to have been idle during the setting of a single sheet except for A and B. Weiss's examples include the following: 1 type appears in all sheets except H; 3 types recur in CDFGH; 4 types recur in DFGH; 6 types recur in CDFH. These patterns do not disprove the theory that the play was set by formes, but they make it very unlikely.

Both Price and Watson relate the generally crowded character of most pages of *Trick* to the peculiarities of its printing and the need to save space on the page. Watson counts twelve turn-overs and turn-unders, nearly ninety instances of a speech being set on the same line as the end of the previous speech, as many as sixteen stage directions (excluding single-worded 'exits' and 'exeunts') squeezed into the last line of a speech, and 'three important entrances (on E1, E2, and E4)...maladroitly placed at the foot of the page'. The lineation notes to the present edition include the speech prefixes in the lemma in order to indicate some of these instances of over-crowding. If space-saving manœuvres such as these were anomalous in Eld's texts, they might indicate irregularities in the printing of *Trick* or the state of the manuscript from which it was set. However, having examined nine other plays printed by Eld from 1607 to 1609—Barnes's *The Devil's Charter* (1607), Chapman's *Byron's Conspiracy and Byron's Tragedy* (1608), Dekker and Webster's *Northward Ho* (1607), Marston's *What You Will* (1607), Middleton's *The Puritan Widow* (1607), *The Revenger's Tragedy* (1607-8), and *Your Five Gallants* (1608), Shakespeare's *Troilus and Cressida* (1609) and Tomkins's *Lingua* (1607)—I find these features occurring so frequently that I would question their indicative character. The only plays among these texts that do not show signs of crowding are Chapman's *Byron* and Tomkins's *Lingua*. The former is entirely in verse and so would have been much more easily cast off; the latter is a university play that might have been printed with considerably more care than other dramatic texts.

While white space on the page is attractive to us, it was more troublesome to Renaissance compositors because it depleted their supply of quads or blanks. The features observed by Price and Watson might instead be attempts by Eld's compositors to fill up white space with type rather than further reduce their limited resources of quads. Another indication that Eld's shop did not have ample quads to spare is the use of unusually long dashes—of 5, 9, or even 18 millimetres in length—frequently at the end of a line or speech where quads would otherwise have been needed. These long dashes occur in the first edition of *Trick* at sigs. C3, C4^v, D2^v, E4, G and G2^v. They also occur in the seven other texts from Eld's press that show features of crowding. So it is very unlikely that the long dashes are 'Middletonian', as Watson suggests, or that the other characteristics of crowded pages are traceable to anomalies in the printing of the play or the author's manuscript. Corroborative evidence can be seen in the second quarto of *Trick* printed in 1616, which has an even greater number of long dashes that are more clearly attributable to constraints on the compositor rather than to the copy from which the text was set.

George Watson devotes fourteen pages to an analysis of the nature of the copy for the first quarto and concludes that it was 'the author's autograph manuscript not fully prepared either for the theatre or the press' (1968b). I would agree with this conclusion, which is also shared by the other editors. I count twenty-nine entrances missing from the stage directions, as does Watson, who also identifies a total of sixty instances where directions for entrances, exits, and more important stage business need to be supplied. Numbers are often used in place of names for speech prefixes for Onesiphorus Hoard, Limber and Kix at 1.1.110-48, for the three creditors at 2.2.55-75, 3.1.4-69, 4.3.1-62 and 4.4.206-98, and for unnamed gentlemen associated with Lucre and Hoard. This practice introduces two ambiguities: (1) who is meant by '3' when only two unnamed gentlemen are on stage at 3.3.33; and (2) how can one distinguish Lucre's friends on the one hand, who are referred to in the stage directions as gentlemen or first and second gentlemen and in speech headings as '1' and '2', from Hoard's friends on the other hand, who are referred to in the same way. A genuine conflict occurs in 4.1, when the character designated as '1' of that scene opens it by celebrating the marriage of Hoard and Jane (4.1.1-5) and then vouches for Lucre's willingness to sign over the mortgage to Witgood at 4.1.72-4. This conflation of the friends of Lucre and Hoard has been removed in the present edition by the assignment of speeches by Hoard's first and second gentlemen to Lamprey and Spitchcock (see textual note to 3.1.111.1), a change that also reduces the unnamed gentlemen cluttering the quarto texts.

Many other features of the text reflect its lack of preparation for the theatre. Watson observes that the stage direction introduced by Dilke at 2.1.325.1 is necessary for understanding the rebuff that Jane gives to Sam Freedom. I would add that without adequate stage directions at 3.1.192-3.1.201.1, editors and readers have been unable to recognize that action as Jane's being coaxed and coerced into the spousal. Eighteen lines of the scene between Witgood and the three creditors following 3.1.29 are printed in this edition as an additional passage because they appear to be an earlier version of 3.1.1-29, providing still further evidence that the manuscript copy may have been authorial. The quarto's mislineation of verse as prose has been observed by most of the play's editors. Watson counts about thirty instances, affecting over sixty lines, where no space would have been saved by setting the text as prose, which argues against attributing such a practice to the compositors. Mislineations of verse as prose also occur in Middleton's holograph manuscript of *A Game at Chess*, and one finds many habits of spelling and punctuation in *Trick* that correlate with that manuscript. These are analysed persuasively by Watson (1968b) and Barber.

All of this evidence provides a convincing case for concluding that the copy from which the first quarto was set was in Middleton's own handwriting, either his foul papers or a fair copy that he made of them. That copy was not so foul as to produce serious problems of comprehension for the play's compositors; it was sufficiently legible to be adequate for printing the play. But it had discrepancies sometimes seen in authorial copies, even fair ones, such as inconsistent speech headings for minor characters, an absence of stage directions, and the inclusion of a brief, unrevised passage. One can say with greater assurance that the play was not printed from a promptbook, and

Watson seems on reasonable ground when he proposes that the promptbook of *Trick* was sold to the Blackfriars' company after the dissolution of Paul's boys, and the authorial manuscript went to Eld to be printed.

SEE ALSO

Text: *Works*, 377
Music: this volume, 140
Authorship and date: this volume, 354

WORKS CITED

Editions Consulted

Barber, Charles, ed., *A Trick to Catch the Old One* (1968)
Baskervill, Charles R., ed., *Stuart Plays* (1934), rev. edn., Virgil Heltzel (1971)
Bullen, A. H., ed., *Works* (1885), vol. 2
Dawson, William Roy, Jr., 'A Critical Edition of Thomas Middleton's *A Trick to Catch the Old One*', (dissertation, University of Tennessee, 1969)
Dilke, C. W., ed., *Old English Plays* (1815)
Dyce, Alexander, ed., *Works* (1840), vol. 2
Ellis, Havelock, ed., *Thomas Middleton* (1887)
Lawrence, Robert G., ed., *Jacobean and Caroline Comedies* (1973)
Loughrey, Brian, and Neil Taylor, eds., Thomas Middleton, *Five Plays* (1988)
Neilson, William Allan, ed., *The Chief Elizabethan Dramatists* (1911)
Price, George R., ed., Thomas Middleton, *Michaelmas Term and A Trick to Catch the Old One, a critical edition* (1976)
Sampson, Martin W., ed., *Thomas Middleton* (1915)
Spencer, Hazelton, ed., *Elizabethan Plays* (1933)
Taylor, Michael, ed., *A Mad World, My Masters, Michaelmas Term, A Trick to Catch the Old One, No Wit, No Help Like a Woman's* (1995)
Watson, G. J., ed., *A Trick to Catch the Old One* (1968a)
—— ed., 'A Critical Edition of Thomas Middleton's *A Trick to Catch the Old One* (1608)' (B.Litt. Thesis, University of Oxford, 1968b)
White, T., ed., *The Old English Drama* (1830)

Other Works Cited

Balch, Marston Stevens, *Thomas Middleton's 'A Trick to Catch the Old One', 'A Mad World, My Masters', and Aphra Behn's 'City Heiress'* (1981)
Behn, Aphra, *The City Heiress*, in *The Works of Aphra Behn*, ed. Janet Todd, vol. 7 (1996)
Catalogue of the Huth Collection of Printed Books and Illuminated Manuscripts, Fifth Portion [1916?]
Chambers, E. K., *The Elizabethan Stage*, 4 vols (1923)
The Complete Collection of State Trials [Cobbett's State Trials], vol. 3, ed. T. B. Howell (1816), col. 414
Coryate, Thomas, *Coryats Crudities* (1611)
Cronin, Lisa, 'Professional Productions in the British Isles since 1880 of plays by Tudor and Early Stuart Dramatists (excluding Shakespeare), A Checklist', *Renaissance Drama Newsletter*, Supplement 7 (1987)
Dalton, Michael, *The Country Justice, 1619* (1973)
Dawson, Anthony B., 'Giving the Finger: Puns and Transgression in *The Changeling*', *Elizabethan Theatre* 12 (1993), 93-112
Digges, Leonard, *A prognostication everlasting of right good effect* (1576)
Downes, John, *Roscius Anglicanus, or An Historical Review of the Stage*, ed. Judith Milhous and Robert D. Hume (1987)
Dukore, Bernard, private communication, 27 August 1993

E., T., *The Law's Resolutions of Women's Rights* (1632)

Edgerton, William L., 'The Calendar Year in Sixteenth-Century Printing', *Journal of English and Germanic Philology* 59 (1960), 439-49

Eliot, T. S., 'Thomas Middleton', *Times Literary Supplement*, 30 June 1927

Fleay, F. G., *Biographical Chronicle of the English Drama 1559-1642* (1891)

Fletcher, William Younger, *English Book Collectors*, ed. Alfred Pollard (1902)

Gair, Reavley, *The Children of Paul's: the story of a theatre company 1553-1608* (1982)

Gants, David, private communication, July 2000

Gibbons, Brian, *Jacobean City Comedy*, 2nd edn. (1980)

Gowing, Laura, *Domestic Dangers: Women, Words and Sex in Early Modern England* (1996)

Greg, W. W., *A Bibliography of the English Printed Drama to the Restoration*, vol. I (1939)

Gurr, Andrew, *The Shakespearian Playing Companies* (1996)

Heinemann, Margot, *Puritanism and Theatre: Thomas Middleton and Opposition Drama under the Early Stuarts* (1980)

Hillebrand, Harold Newcomb, *The Child Actors* (1926)

Jonson, Ben, *Volpone, or the Fox*, ed. R. B. Parker (1983)

McKerrow, R. B., *Printers' and Publishers' Devices in England and Scotland 1485-1640* (1949)

Moxon, Joseph, *Mechanick Exercises on the whole Art of Printing* (1683-4) (1958)

Murray, J. T., *English Dramatic Companies* (1910)

Neuman, Michael, letter to John Lavagnino, 6 June 1994

Parker, R. B., 'Middleton's Experiments with Comedy and Judgement', *Jacobean Theatre*, Stratford-upon-Avon Studies I (1960), 179-99

Partridge, Eric, *Shakespeare's Bawdy*, rev. edn. (1969)

Paster, Gail Kern, 'The City in Plautus and Middleton', *Renaissance Drama* NS 6 (1973), 29-44

Price, George R., 'The Early Editions of *A trick to catch the old one*', *The Library*, V, 22 (1967), 205-27

Quaife, G. R., *Wanton Wenches and Wayward Wives: Peasants and Illicit Sex in Early Seventeenth Century England* (1979)

Ravenscroft, Thomas, *Melismata, Musical Fancies, 1611* (1971)

Roberts, Marilyn, 'A Preliminary Check-List of Productions of Thomas Middleton's Plays', *Research Opportunities in Renaissance Drama* 28 (1985), 37-61

Rowe, George E., Jr., *Thomas Middleton and the New Comedy Tradition* (1979)

Shapiro, Michael, *Children of the Revels: The Boy Companies of Shakespeare's Time and Their Plays* (1977)

Sharpham, Edward, *A Critical Old Spelling Edition of the Works of Edward Sharpham*, ed. Christopher Gordon Petter (1986)

Steen, Sara Jayne, *Ambrosia in an Earthern Vessel: Three Centuries of Audience and Reader Response to the Works of Thomas Middleton* (1993)

Stonex, A. B., 'The Usurer in Elizabethan Drama', *Publications of the Modern Language Association* 31 (1916), 190-210

Taylor, Gary and John Jowett, *Shakespeare Reshaped, 1606-23*, (1993)

Tilney, Edmund, *The Flower of Friendship*, ed. Valerie Wayne (1992)

Todd, Janet, and Elizabeth Spearing, eds., *Counterfeit Ladies* (1994)

Wayne, Valerie, 'Assuming Gentility: Thomas Middleton, Mary Carleton, and Aphra Behn', *Women and Politics in Early Modern England, 1450-1700*, ed. James Daybell (2004), 243-56

—— 'The Sexual Politics of Textual Transmission', *Textual Formations and Reformations*, ed. Laurie E. Maguire and Thomas L. Berger (1998), 179-210

Weiss, Adrian, private correspondence on the printing history of *A Trick to Catch the Old One*, July-November, 1993

Williams, Gordon, *A Glossary of Shakespeare's Sexual Language* (1997)

Williams, Gwyn, 'The Cuckoo, the Welsh Ambassador', *Modern Language Review* 51 (1956), 223-5

TEXTUAL NOTES

Persons   *not in* ELD

1.1.15-18   He...stranger.] Italics in ELD

1.1.28.1   *Enter Jane*] THIS EDITION; *Enter Curtizan.* ELD. This change is made because Middleton's use of 'courtesan' has been taken to identify a professional prostitute, whereas the character has only been Witgood's mistress; in 3.1 she becomes a wife when she marries Hoard, although ELD's stage directions remain the same (with one exception noted at 4.1.0.2-4 below). See Critical Introduction and Wayne, 'The Sexual Politics of Textual Transmission'. Not subsequently recorded; but see list of Eld's stage directions.

1.1.29   Jane] THIS EDITION; Curt. ELD. See previous note. Not subsequently recorded.

1.1.41   Forgive.] ELD (For giue_∧)

1.1.47   courtesan] ELD (Currizan)

1.1.57   embryo] ELD (Embrion). ELD's is the original form of the word, now obsolete (*OED*). The modernization makes more recognizable the procreative language that Witgood uses in 1.1.57-8 and Jane repeats at 1.1.61-2.

1.1.83   furnished] ELD (furnifht); finish'd DILKE

1.1.108   now] DILKE; no ELD

1.1.110-11   ONESIPHORUS...LIMBER] DYCE; I...2. ELD. Throughout scene.

1.1.110   Who's] ELD (Whofe)

1.1.131   wife's] ELD (wiues)

1.1.148   KIX] DYCE; 3. ELD

1.2.26   sleight] ELD (flight)

1.3.7   balsamum] ELD1(b) (Balfamum); Balsum ELD1(a)

1.3.12   indifferency] THIS EDITION (conj. Jowett); indifferences ELD. ELD's plural form is not justifiable, so Jowett suspects the copy had 'indifferencie'.

1.3.62   off] ELD (of)

1.3.62.1   *Manent*] ELD (*Manet*)

1.3.73.1   *Moneylove strikes Sam*] ELD (*Strikes him.*)

1.3.75   month] ELD2; mouth ELD1

1.4.4.1   *Enter...apart*] BARBER; *not in* ELD; after 'footman' 1.4.31-2 DILKE; after 1.4.28 DYCE. Watson observes that the scene is more comic when Witgood's remarks occur while the two usurers are on stage; and lines 5-6 imply that they are.

1.4.16, 23   mastiff] ELD (masty)

1.4.17   commandments] DYCE; commandement ELD

1.4.18   began first] ELD1; first began ELD2

1.4.47   armadas] ELD (armadoes)

2.1.9   penn'orth] ELD (penworth)

2.1.16   SERVANT] DILKE; Ser.2. ELD

2.1.38   Meddler] ELD (Medler). The name is spelled 'Meddler' in ELD in the next line and 'Medler' in all other occurrences (2.2.63, 4.4.254, 4.4.255, 4.4.259, 5.2.59). At 5.2.162-

3 Witgood remarks that since he is married, 'there's no meddling with mine aunt' (medling ELD), drawing on the word's meanings of sexual congress (*OED* v.5), as well as mingling in general and interference in particular. 'I will neither meddle nor make was proverbial' (Tilley M548), and a much-quoted passage on spousal duties said that 'the office of the husband is, to deale and bargaine with all men, of the wyfe, to make or meddle with no man' (Edmund Tilney, *The Flower of Friendship*, ll. 731–3). Another meaning of the word stems from its association with the medlar tree, the fruit of which was eaten when it was partly rotten. Middleton used this meaning in *Women Beware* 4.2.97–100: 'he that marries a whore looks like a fellow bound all his lifetime to a medlar-tree—and that's good stuff: 'tis no sooner ripe but it looks rotten'. Both meanings relate to this character, and all previous editions have retained the ambiguity by using the spelling 'Medler'. That decision is, however, inconsistent with the modernization of other names in the text. Given the choice between 'Meddler' and 'Medlar', I have selected the form that encompasses more meanings, including sexual activity, and is also appropriate to a character who affects the play's events by blocking others' plans and realizing those in her own interest as much as this one does.

2.1.49   He's] ELD (has)
2.1.65   her?] ELD2; he.? ELDI. The last letter of the word may have broken in printing, since the remaining mark is irregular.
2.1.66   H'as] ELD (has)
2.1.105 have] ELD2 (haue); hane ELDI
2.1.107 Pox] ELD (Pax). Also at 4.4.139, 4.4.210.
2.1.109 unknown] ELD2; vnknowe ELDI
2.1.123 swoon] ELD (Sowne)
2.1.126 you] ELD2; your ELDI
2.1.141 HOST] ELD2; Hoftis. ELDI
2.1.152 Tomorrow's] ELD (to morrowes)
2.1.175 deceives] ELD2 (deceiues); dceaues ELDI(a); decaues ELDI(b). See press variants.
2.1.190–3 When…lands] DILKE, DYCE and some modern editors such as BARBER, WATSON, LAWRENCE, and LOUGHREY–TAYLOR treat this as an aside; BARBER, DAWSON and PRICE do not. Since the passage might be spoken within George's hearing and George is clearly aware of the change in Lucre's treatment of Witgood, marking it as an aside unnecessarily limits the way it might be performed.
2.1.223 to blame] ELD (too blame)
2.1.287, 338, 3.1.58, 229, 4.4.57 beholden] ELD (beholding)
2.1.315 your] ELD2; yours ELDI
2.1.325 fifteenth] ELD (15)
2.1.349 above] ELDI; about ELD2. Spencer and Watson take 'above' to refer to the upstairs rooms.
2.1.356 ye] THIS EDITION tee ELD; t'ye DILKE; t'ee NEILSON. Compare A.7, I warrant yee ELD. 'Tee' is probably a misprint for 'yee'.
2.1.363 Jenny] ELD (Ginnee), also DILKE and all editors through SAMPSON; Jinny SPENCER; 'Ginny BASKERVILL; Ginny LOUGHREY–TAYLOR.
2.1.368 against] ELD (againe)
2.1.372 standing] ELD2; ftranding ELDI. The error in ELDI is corrected in the next line, 'ftanding'.
2.2.51   plague] ELD2 (plague), plauge ELDI. BARBER notes that *plauge* is Middleton's own spelling, as evident in the Trinity manuscript of *Game*.
2.2.53   Lucre] ELD2 (*Lucre*); *Lucer* ELDI

3.1.30   I am to raise] Eighteen lines from ELD have been omitted prior to this line and printed as an additional passage at the end of the text, on the grounds that they are an undramatic repetition of the preceding twenty-nine lines in the scene and may have been an earlier version of it. PRICE initiates this procedure in his edition and offers his reasons in his earlier essay, 'Early Editions', pp. 216–17. The Second Creditor in the scene provides Witgood with the same information twice, at 3.1.7–8 and A.9–10, and on the second occasion Witgood responds as if he has never heard it before (A.11).
3.1.61   They're] ELD2 (They'r); The'ar ELDI
3.1.104 bestowed] ELD2 (beftow'd); deftowp ELDI(a); deftowd ELDI(b)
3.1.109 our] ELD2; out ELDI
3.1.111.1 *Lamprey and Spitchcock*] THIS EDITION; *and Gentlemen* ELD. Some previous editors of the play, DYCE, SPENCER, LAWRENCE, WATSON, and LOUGHREY–TAYLOR, propose that the anonymous two gentlemen who speak against Witgood in 3.1, eventually become advocates of Hoard's marriage to Jane, and compete with each other over their contributions to the spousal at 3.3, are Lamprey and Spitchcock, but none of them regularizes the speech headings or stage directions. MICHAEL TAYLOR does in his 1995 edition, but see note 3.3.94.1. This change is necessary for the following reasons: (1) There is a clear confusion between two speech prefixes for '1.' or 'First Gentleman' who speaks in 4.1. The first (4.1.1–5) is an advocate for Hoard because he begins the scene by celebrating the marriage; the second is an advocate for Lucre because he vouches for the latter's willingness to sign over the mortgage to Witgood (4.1.72–4). Changing the 'First Gentleman' to Lamprey eliminates this duplication and is consistent with the character's role in other scenes. (2) At 3.1.219–21 Hoard specifically says that the two gentlemen who are with him then at the spousal will participate in the feigned abduction at Cole Harbour, and the speech prefixes in ELD at 4.1 identify them in the later scene as Lamprey and Spitchcock. (3) Without designating the gentlemen acting on Hoard's behalf in 3.1 and 3.3 as Lamprey and Spitchcock, it is unclear how the latter move from their apparently unbiased position as 'honest, even-minded gentlemen' in 1.3.11 to becoming straightforward advocates for Hoard's interests in 4.1. With the designation, however, that shift is explained by the remark at 3.1.230 by the First Gentleman that ''Tis for our credits now to see't well ended', referring to the marriage. (4) The change provides continuity between the character who offers Jane a jointure ('join land to land', 3.1.191) and clasps her hands with Hoard's in the handclasp at 3.1.201.1 and the character who celebrates the joining of hearts and hands in their marriage at 4.1.1–5. (5) It eliminates the unnecessary duplication of Hoard's two gentlemen in 3.1 and 3.3 and Lamprey and Spitchcock in 1.3, 4.1, 4.5 and 5.2; and it permits the doubling of one of these characters for Lucre's first or second gentlemen. (6) It includes those who brought about the spousal in the final wedding celebration at 5.2. Their exclusion, which might have been necessary because of the doubling of roles, would otherwise be inappropriate. To make this change, stage directions and speech prefixes in 3.1, 3.3, and the first speech of 4.1 specify the unnamed gentlemen as Lamprey and Spitchcock. Emendations are recorded for stage directions in each of these scenes.
3.1.111.2 *Host as servingman*] ELD (Host,—servingman.)
3.1.132–3 LAMPREY…SPITCHCOCK] M. TAYLOR; 1. … 2. ELD. Throughout scene.

3.1.136.1 *Enter Jane. Witgood watches while concealed*] BARBER; *not in* ELD. Other editors have Witgood enter or look in at 3.1.185, but his remarks at 3.1.235–40 suggest he has watched much of the scene. He even acknowledges his own complicity in the spousal at 5.2.158–9: 'and where could I bestow her better than upon your pitiful worship?' See note to 3.1.185.

3.1.158 HOARD] ELD (text) (*Ho.*); *Ho∫t.* ELD (c.w.)

3.1.185 *aside*] BARBER; *not in* ELD1; (*Peeping out.*) DILKE; [Witgood *enters apart*] LOUGHREY–TAYLOR

3.1.213 very day] ELD2; very uery day ELD1

3.1.222 suddenly] ELD2; ∫nddenly ELD1

3.1.229 engaged] ELD2 (engag'de); engade ELD1

3.1.234 *Exeunt Hoard . . . Spitchcock*] M. TAYLOR, *Exeunt Hoard and Gentlemen* DYCE; *Exeunt* ELD

3.1.263 i'faith] WATSON; faith ELD. As Watson observes, there is some evidence of an initial 'i' in ELD1, but it is badly damaged.

3.2.0.1 *Enter*] *not in* ELD

3.2.12 it] ELD2; in ELD1

3.2.15 hand] DILKE; hard ELD, with space suggesting slippage or damage around the 'r' or 'n'

3.2.16 (*Reading*)] ELD *Reades.*

3.2.16–20 *Dearer . . . Witgood*] ELD also italicizes the note and signature.

3.3.0.1–2 *Lamprey and Spitchcock*] M. TAYLOR; *and two Gentlemen* ELD.

3.3.4 Up . . . gentlemen] Lamprey and Spitchcock may exit here and reenter at 3.3.19 or 3.3.22, since they have been directed to go *up those stairs.* However, Lamprey's remark that 'yon room's fittest' 3.3.36 probably refers to a room downstairs and, as Hoard adds, 'next the door' 3.3.36, so Lamprey and Spitchcock may not exit at all.

3.3.11 WILLIAM (*within*)] BASKERVILL; *Within.* ELD, *functioning as a speech prefix.*

3.3.22–3 LAMPREY . . . SPITCHCOCK] THIS EDITION; 1. . . . 2. ELD. Through scene; but see next note.

3.3.33 LAMPREY] THIS EDITION; 3. ELD; 1 [GENT.] BASKERVILL

3.3.36.1–3 *Exit . . . Drawer*] This exit and entrance may occur at roughly the same time, avoiding a cleared stage. See textual note to 3.3.68.1–2.

3.3.50 prigging] DILKE; Priggin ELD

3.3.55 Alas] THIS EDITION; ˌa∫∫e ELD all copies except for the Huntington Huth copy, which has aˌ∫∫e. Since Spencer's suggestion, it has been evident that type dropped out of the case; but the Huntington Huth copy shows that the word began with an 'a' in this forme and may have been improperly corrected. Jane begins two earlier speeches with 'Alas' at 3.1.171 and 3.1.204.

3.3.66 I'll do] ELD1(b) (Ile do); I bee do ELD1(a); Ay, boy, do DILKE

3.3.68.1–2 *Exeunt . . . Vintner*] This exit and entrance may occur in such close conjunction that they occasion near misses and avoid a cleared stage, as at 3.3.36.1–3. A scene division at either point would disrupt the continuity of the action that is important to these events (Paul Mulholland).

3.3.74 the] DILKE; he ELD

3.3.94.1 *Gentlemen*] ELD. M. TAYLOR identifies these gentlemen as Limber and Kix, but since, together with Onesiphorus Hoard, they discuss Jane as a courtesan at 1.1.110–48 and expose her identity at 5.2.68–106, the gentlemen who enter with Lucre (only one of which speaks) and offer their support for the recovery of 'the widow' at 3.3.102 and 3.3.123–5, are different characters.

3.3.109 thirsts] DILKE; thrifts ELD

3.3.118 traced 'em] ELD (trac'de e'm)

3.3.128.1 *Exeunt*] DYCE; after 3.3.127 ELD

3.3.130 *Exit*] DYCE; *Eixt* ELD1; *not in* ELD2

3.4.2 armada] ELD (Armado)

3.4.2 '99] ELD; '89 DILKE (*conj.*); '98 SAMPSON (*conj.*). As Spencer points out, this is probably not 'an error for '89 (when there was a terrific thunderstorm); the point is the long lapse of time'.

3.4.3 lightning] ELD2; Lighting ELD1

3.4.4 Powis'] ELD (Poouyes). See commentary note.

3.4.12 bed] ELD2; bed Bed ELD1

3.4.29 knew] ELD2; knenw ELD1

3.4.30 penn'orth] ELD (pennort)

3.4.33 this] ELD2; ths ELD1

3.4.50 coxcombry] DILKE; coxcombre ELD

3.4.63 Mistress] ELD2 (Mi∫tris); Mi∫ters ELD1

4.1.0.2–4 Hoard . . . Spitchcock] THIS EDITION; Hoord, *the Widdow and Gentlemen, he married now.* ELD; Hoard *and Courtezan, as just married, with* Gentlemen DILKE; Hoard, *Courtezan, Lamprey, Spichcock, and* Gentlemen. DYCE

4.1.1 LAMPREY] M. TAYLOR; 1. ELD. The presence of Lamprey and Spitchcock in this scene is marked in ELD by speech prefixes at 4.1.12, *Lamp.*, and following, and at 4.1.100, *Spich.*

4.1.20 JANE] THIS EDITION; *Lu.* ELD; *Court.* DILKE

4.1.47 friends] ELD2; friend ELD1

4.2.11 LUCRE] ELD2 (*Luc.*); Ln: ELD1

4.2.13 *Exit*] DYCE; after 'instantly' at 4.2.12 ELD

4.2.15 how now] ELD2; how ELD1

4.2.85–90 Thou . . . in.] Italics in ELD

4.3.12 The rioter is caught!] There is no exit for the boy following this line in ELD or any other edition, although he has no further lines in the scene. His presence may add to those on stage opposing Witgood; on the other hand, he could exit after this line or after Witgood's entrance with the sergeants at 4.3.15.1.

4.3.68 CREDITORS] BARBER; *Cit.* ELD; 1 *Cred.* DILKE. SAMPSON divides the speech between the three creditors, with the lines of the first ending at 'puritans', the second at 'hear 'em', and the third at 'i'faith!'.

4.4.7 wise] ELD2; wife ELD1

4.4.32 caps] ELD (capes). See Francis Bacon's reference to usurers wearing orange-tawny 'bonnets' in commentary note.

4.4.32.1 *Enter*] DILKE; after 'worship' at 4.4.34 ELD

4.4.55 champaign] ELD (Champion-)

4.4.59 your] ELD2, DILKE; you ELD1

4.4.82 Mistress] ELD2, DILKE (Mi∫tris); Mi∫trs ELD1

4.4.90 marquise] ELD (Marquesse)

4.4.92 Yea] ELD (yee)

4.4.99 precontract] ELD (præcon-|tract). Also at 4.4.100 without word division.

4.4.125 examine] ELD (ezamine)

4.4.145 drawn. Within there!] DILKE; drawne-within there ELD1(a); drawn, within there ELD1(b)

4.4.146 SERVANT] ELD; 1. ELD

4.4.147 directions] ELD2; derictions ELD1

4.4.174.1 [*They talk apart*]] DILKE; *not in* ELD; [Draws Courtesan *aside*] BASKERVILL. The phrasing of BASKERVILL's stage direction, which is adapted with modifications by BARBER and WATSON, implies that Witgood is the active agent in initiating the private conversation. However, as the talk between them continues, it is evident that Jane also wishes to object to Witgood's involving her in further deceit in order to cover his debts to the creditors.

4.4.199   I will] THIS EDITION (conj. Jowett); ile ELD; I'll DILKE

4.4.223   trick] ELD (*Trick*). The word is also italicized in two further instances before the end of the play, probably to call attention to the relation between these tricks and the play's title, as *Trick* at 4.4.297 and as *Tricks* at 4.5.95.

4.4.267   immovables] ELD2 (immoueables); immouerables ELD1

4.4.298   *Exeunt Creditors*] ELD (*Exeunt*)

4.4.307   *Exeunt*] DILKE; after 'farewell' at 4.4.306 ELD

4.5.0.1   *A curtained...forth*] THIS EDITION; *Dampit the Vſurer in his bed* ELD. All editors follow ELD, but Dampit is not revealed until 4.5.5–6.

4.5.0.1–2   *Enter Audrey...curtains*] THIS EDITION; *Audry spinning by.* ELD and subsequent editions

4.5.0.2   *and sings*] THIS EDITION; *Song* ELD; DYCE and subsequent editors give the song to Audrey.

4.5.1–4   Let...some] Ravenscroft's *Melismata* includes two lines at the beginning of this song that do not appear in ELD:

Y maſter is ſo wiſe, ſo wiſe, that hee's proceeded wittall,
my Miſtris is a foole, a foole, and yet tis the moſt get-all.

The following variants occur between the lines from the song that appear in ELD and STANSBY's printing of *Melismata*:
4.5.2   There's pits] their pits, their pits STANSBY
4.5.2   comes] goes STANSBY
4.5.4   Where'er] Where ere ELD; Where eare STANSBY
4.5.4   there's some, there's some] there some, there some *in the first instance of this refrain*, theirs some, theirs some *in the second instance* STANSBY

4.5.5.1–2   *Enter Boy...bed*] THIS EDITION; *not in* ELD; DYCE and subsequent editors include Boy at the opening of the scene, but he has nothing to do (unless he sings the song). Dampit's command functions as his cue.

4.5.6.2   *Enter Lamprey and Spitchcock*] DILKE; *Enter Gentlemen.* ELD. DILKE's emendation was occasioned by the speech prefixes *Lamp.* and *Spich.* in the subsequent dialogue.

4.5.12   muckender] ELD (muckinder)

4.5.21   preyed] ELD (pray'd)

4.5.28   girnative] ELD (gernatiue)

4.5.28   mullipode] ELD (mullipood)

4.5.29.1   *Enter Sir Lancelot and another gentleman*] PRICE; *Enter other Gentleman* ELD1; *Enter other Gentlemen.* ELD2; *Enter Sir Lancelot and others* DILKE; *Enter other Gentleman [i.e., Sir Lancelot]* BASKERVILL. WATSON and LOUGHREY-TAYLOR follow BASKERVILL, but Holdsworth is probably correct that Lancelot's 'us' at 4.5.31 refers to at least one person besides himself.

4.5.30   Yea] ELD (Yee)

4.5.128   *firmae*] DYCE; *firme* ELD

4.5.132   Heyday] ELD (Hoyda)

4.5.168   This' exc'lent. Thief] ELD1 (This exlent, theefe); This excellent, theefe ELD2; This [is] excellent! thief DILKE; This exc'llent thief BASKERVILL. I have accepted Holdsworth's contention that these are two Middletonian contractions, 'this' for 'this is' and 'exlent' for 'excellent'.

4.5.181   An't were] ELD2 (Ant were); Ant twere ELD1

4.5.203   GULF] ELD2 (*Gul.*); Lul: ELD1

5.2.21.1   *Enter Lamprey and Spitchcock*] DILKE; *Enter two gentlemen.* ELD. Hoard identifies the two gentlemen by name at 5.2.22.

5.2.55, 56   guests] ELD (gueſſe), the obsolete plural form of 'guest'

5.2.66   smack] DILKE, ſmerck ELD

5.2.67.1   *Both...turn back*] THIS EDITION; *Both turne back.* at 5.2.68 ELD; *Both turn back* at 5.2.67.1 DILKE

5.2.74   feared] THIS EDITION (Jowett); fread ELD; 'fraid DILKE

5.2.97   strumpet] ELD2 (Strumpit); Srumpet ELD1

5.2.106.1   *with the Niece*] DYCE (*and Niece*); *not in* ELD. Six editors through Baskervill follow Dyce by including Joyce in the closing events of the play; Price is the only editor since Baskervill to have done so. It is nonetheless appropriate for Witgood's wife to be on stage when he reveals his marriage to her at 5.2.160–1, and earlier in the scene Joyce proclaims that the feast 'serves fit for my wedding dinner, too' (5.2.20–1). Her presence also makes Witgood's new marriage, which is the more conventional counterpart to Hoard's and Jane's, much more visible in the final moments of the play. Names of characters are omitted elsewhere from Eld's stage directions, so this would not be an unusual instance.

5.2.144–5   before twenty, | Twenty] DYCE (*conj.*); before, twenty ELD. DYCE's emendation, which occurs in prose lines in his text, nonetheless makes the continuation of verse much more possible. At the page break in ELD from H3 to H3ᵛ, corresponding in this edition to the end of 5.2.139, the text moves from poetry to prose. Editors since DILKE have set the next four lines as poetry, ending at 'man's love', 5.2.143; this is the first edition to set the entire speech as verse. Dyce's addition of 'twenty' on the basis of sense allows the next two lines to scan. BULLEN and ELLIS accept Dyce's emendation; other editors do not. LAWRENCE glosses 'before' at 5.2.144 to mean before marriage, but marriage has not been referred to earlier in the speech, so the object of 'before' and 'after' is unclear without the emendation. Since 'young virgins' are mentioned at 5.2.147, Dyce's conjecture is appropriate. It has the further advantage of explaining how a compositor might have dropped the word, since it would have appeared twice in the manuscript with only a comma separating those instances.

5.2.185   reclaimed] SPENCER; reclaim'd DILKE; reclaymed ELD, which incorrectly implies -èd (Jowett)

5.2.196   Ribboned] ELD1 (Riband); ELD2 (Ribband); Reband DILKE; Ribbon M. TAYLOR. Most editors follow Dyce in using 'Riband', which is an obsolete spelling for 'ribboned' (*OED*).

PRESS VARIANTS

For an account of different printings of the title-page of the first edition, see Textual Introduction.

Sigla and copies collated:

BL1 British Library, C.34.d.42
BL2 British Library, Ashley 1158
ED National Library of Scotland, Bute 366
ET Eton College
F Folger Shakespeare Library [H4 missing, supplied in manuscript copied from ELD2]
H Harvard University Library
HN1 Huntington Library, Kemble-Devonshire 292
HN2 Huntington Library, Huth copy, 62577
O1 Bodleian Library, Malone 797
O2 Bodleian Library, Malone 812
TX1 University of Texas at Austin
TX2 University of Texas at Austin, formerly Pforzheimer
VA1 National Art Library, Victoria and Albert Museum, Dyce 33.1
VA2 National Art Library, Victoria and Albert Museum, Dyce 33.2
Y Yale University Library

Sheet A (outer forme)

Corrected: BL1, BL2, ET, F, H, HN1, HN2, O1, O2, TX1, TX2, VA1, VA2, Y
Uncorrected: ED

Sig. A3

1.1.4   sunk] funck *corr*; fnnck *uncorr*

Sheet B (outer forme)

Corrected: BL1, ED, ET, F, H, HN1, HN2, O2, TX1, TX2, VA1, VA2, Y
Uncorrected: BL2, O1

Sig. B3

1.3.72   MONEYLOVE] *Mony. corr*; *Monyt. uncorr*

Sheet B (inner forme)

Corrected: BL1, BL2, ED, F, H, HN1, HN2, O1, O2, TX1, TX2, VA1, VA2, Y
Uncorrected: ET

Sig. B1^v

1.2.43   money. Now] money: now *corr*; money now *uncorr*
1.2.50   purpose?] purpofe? *corr*; purpofe, *uncorr*
1.2.50   year?] yeare? *corr*; yeare, *uncorr*
1.2.54   covey] Couy *corr*; Coue *uncorr*
1.2.57   *hostis*] *hoftis corr*; *Hoftis uncorr*

Sig. B2

1.3.7   balsamum] Balfamum *corr*; Balfum *uncorr*
1.3.26   nephew,] Nephew, *corr*; Nephew‸ *uncorr*
1.3.34   want it] want it *corr*; want ir *uncorr*

Sig. B3^v

1.4.33   once, too] once too; *corr*; once too‸ *uncorr*

Sig. B4

1.4.62   fooliaminy] Fooli-aminy *corr*; Foole-aminy *uncorr*

2.1.2   nephew! Why] Nephew: why *corr*; Nephew, why *uncorr*
2.1.6   me?] mee : *corr*; mee , *uncorr*
2.1.9   penn'orth] penworth: *corr*; pennorth, *uncorr*

Sheet C (outer forme), one correction

Corrected: BL1, BL2, ET, H, HN1, HN2, O1, O2, TX1, TX2, VA2, Y
Uncorrected: ED, F, VA1

Sig. C2^v

2.1.175 deceives] decaues *corr*; dceaues *uncorr*
2.1.204 from] frō *corr*; from *uncorr*
2.1.205 chief] cheife *corr*; chife *uncorr*

Sheet C (outer forme), another correction

Corrected: BL1, O2, VA2
Uncorrected: BL2, ED, ET, F, H, HN1, HN2, O1, TX1, TX2, VA1, Y

Sig. C1

2.1.57   faith.] faith : *corr*; faith, *uncorr*. ['faith' is the last word at the right hand margin, and it concludes a speech. The colon is located considerably beyond the margin of printed words and below the line of type. These differences probably reflect a stop press correction, since other speeches end in this text, even on this signature, with a colon; but given the number of uncorrected copies, this would be an anomalous time in the press run for a correction to occur.]

Sheet C (inner forme)

Corrected: BL1, BL2, ET, H, HN1, O1, O2, TX1, TX2, VA2
Uncorrected: ED, F, HN2, VA1, Y

Sig. C1^v

2.1.116 think] thinke *corr*; thike *uncorr*

Sheet D (inner forme)

Corrected: BL2, ED, ET, F, H, HN1, HN2, O1, O2, TX2, VA1, VA2, Y
Uncorrected: BL1, TX1

Sig. D2

2.2.63   Meddler] Medler *corr*; medler *uncorr*

Sig. D3^v

3.1.104 bestowed] deftowd *corr*; deftowp *uncorr*
3.1.106 First] firft *corr*; firift *uncorr*
3.1.111.1 *Lamprey and Spitchcock*] Gentlemen *corr*; *Gentleman uncorr*
3.1.118 come, thou'rt] com e,thou'rt *corr*; com e,‸hou'rt *uncorr*

Sig. D4

3.1.123 better] better *corr*; bettre *uncorr*
3.1.148 gentlemen] Gentlemen *corr*; Centlemen *uncorr*

Sheet E (outer forme), first correction

Corrected: BL1, BL2, ED, ET, F, H, HN2, O1, O2, TX1, TX2, VA1, VA2, Y
Uncorrected: HN1

Sig. E1

3.1.204 love not] loue not *corr*; loue no *uncorr*

Sig. E2[v]

3.3.55   Alas] ˏaſſe *corr*; aˏſſe *uncorr*

Sheet E (outer forme), second correction

Corrected: BL2, ET, HN2
Uncorrected: BL1, ED, F, H, HN1, O1, O2, TX1, TX2, VA1, VA2, Y

Sig. E2[v]

3.3.66   I'll] Ile *corr*; I bee *uncorr*

Sheet E (inner forme)

Corrected: BL1, BL2, ED, ET, F, H, HN1, HN2, O1, O2, TX1, TX2, VA1, VA2
Uncorrected: Y

Sig. E4

3.4.35   Audrey-prater] *Audrie*-prater *corr* [without ie ligature]; *Audrie*-prater *uncorr* [with ie ligature]

Sheet G (outer forme)

Corrected: BL1, BL2, ED, ET, F, H, HN2, O1, O2, TX1, TX2, VA1, VA2, Y
Uncorrected: HN1

Sig. G3

4.4.302.1   [*Niece*] *is above*] She is aboue. *corr*; *not in uncorrected copy as stage direction, but the word 'aboue' is inserted in the previous line, after 'ſome'*

Sig. G4[v]

4.5.141   Behold] behold *corr*; behole *uncorr*

4.5.142–4.5.142.1   usurer . . . *Gulf*] vſurer . . . Gulf *corr*; vſure . . . Gulfe *uncorr*. [These are the first and last words on the type line.]

Sheet G (inner forme)

Corrected: BL1, BL2, ED, ET, F, H, HN1, O1, O2, TX1, VA2, Y
Uncorrected: HN2, TX2, VA1

Sig. G1[v]

4.4.145   drawn. Within] drawne-within *corr*; drawne, within *uncorr*

Sig. G2

4.4.214   Mulligrub's] Muligrubs *corr*; Mulgraues *uncorr*

Sig. G3[v]

4.5.28   mullipode] mullipood *corr*; mullipoop *uncorr*

4.5.29   concupiscency] concupiſcency *corr*; concupiſcenty *uncorr*

Sheet H (inner forme)

Corrected: BL1, BL2, ED, ET, HN2, O1, TX1, Y
Uncorrected: H, HN1, O2, TX2, VA1, VA2

Sig. H4

5.2.181   tarry,] tarry, *corr*; tarryˏ *uncorr*

STAGE DIRECTIONS

1.1.0.2   *Enter Witt-good a Gentleman, solus.*
1.1.28.1   *Enter Curtizan.*
1.1.148   *Exeunt.*
1.2.0.1   *Enter at one doore*, Witt-good, *at the | other* Host.
1.2.65   *Exeunt.*
1.3.0.1–3   *Enter at seuerall doores, old* Lucre, *and old* Hoord, | *Gentlemen comming betweene them, | to pacifie 'em.*
1.3.62.1   *Exeunt.* | [blank line] *Manet* Sam *and* Monyloue.
1.3.73.1   *Strikes him.*
1.3.73.2   *Exit.*
1.3.81   *Exit.*
1.4.0.1–2   *Enter* Wit-good *and the* Host.
1.4.76   *Musick. Exeunt.*
2.1.0.1   *Incipit ACT. 2.*
2.1.0.2   *Enter* Lucre.
2.1.18.2   *Enter* Host *like a Seruingman.*
2.1.154   *Exit.*
2.1.169   *Exit.*
2.1.199   *Exit.*
2.1.214.1   *Enter* Wit-good.
2.1.373   *Exit.*
2.1.400   *Exeunt.*
2.2.0.1   *Enter* Hoord *and* Monyloue.
2.2.41   *Exit.*
2.2.54.1   *Enter three Creditors.*
2.2.75   *Exeunt.*
2.2.80   *Musick. Exit.*
3.1.0.1   *Incipit ACT. 3.*
3.1.0.2   Wit-good *with his Creditors.*
3.1.70.1   *Exit.*
3.1.77.1   *Enter* Curtezan.
3.1.111   *Exit.*
3.1.111.1–2   *Enter* Hoord *and Gentlemen with | the* Host,— seruingman.
3.1.130   *Exit.*
3.1.234   *Exeunt.*
3.1.234   *Enter* Wit-good.
3.1.241.1   *Enter* Lucre?
3.1.264   *Exit.*
3.2.0.1   Hoord *and his Neece.*
3.2.6   *Exit.*
3.2.16   *Reades.* (centred on separate line)
3.2.22   *Exit.*
3.3.0.1–2   *Enter with a Drawer*, Hoord, *and two Gentlemen.*
3.3.36.1   *Exit.*
3.3.36.2–3   *Enter* Wit-g: Curt: *and* Host.
3.3.65.1   *Enter* Hoord *with Gentlemen.*
3.3.68.1   *Exeunt.*
3.3.68.2   *Enter* Wit-good *and* Vintner.
3.3.87.1   *Enter* Host.
3.3.94.1   *Enter* Lucre *with Gentlemen.*
3.3.113.1   *Enter* Host.
3.3.128.1   *Exeunt.*
3.3.130   *Eixt.*
3.4.0.1   *Enter* Dampit, *the Vsurer drunke.*
3.4.77   *Exit.*
4.1.0.1   *Incipit ACT. 4.*
4.1.0.2–4   *Enter at Cole-harbour*, Hoord, *the* Widdow | *and Gentlemen, he married now.*
4.1.29.1   *Enter* Lucre. (after 'you', 4.1.28)
4.1.91.1   *Exeunt.*
4.1.101   *Exeunt.*
4.2.0.1–2   *Enter* Lucre *with Gentlemen meeting* Sam Free-dome.
4.2.13   *Exit.* (after 4.2.12)

4.2.26.1   *Enter* Lucre.
4.2.67   *Exit.*
4.2.68.1   *Enter Wife:*
4.2.79   *Exeunt:*
4.3.0.1   *Enter three Creditors.*
4.3.9.1   *Enter a Boy.*
4.3.15.1   *Enter* Wit-good *with Seriants.*
4.3.62.1   *Enter Host.*
4.3.72   *Exeunt.*
4.4.0.1   *Enter Hoord.*
4.4.32.1–2   *Enter All.* (after 4.4.34)
4.4.83.1   *Enter Curtizan altred in Apparell.*
4.4.298   *Exeunt.*
4.4.302.1   *She is aboue.*
4.4.307   *Exeunt.* (after 4.4.306)
4.5.0.1   *Dampit* the Vsurer in his bed, *Audry* | spinning by.

4.5.0.1–2   Song. (at left margin, opposite 4.5.2. The verse lines of the song are indented.)
4.5.6.2   *Enter Gentlemen.*
4.5.29.1   *Enter other Gentleman.*
4.5.142.1   *Enter Hoord with Gulf.*
4.5.181.1   *drawes his dagger.*
4.5.203   *Exeunt.*
5.1.0.1   *ACTVS.* 5.
5.1.0.2   *Enter Lucre and* Wit-good.
5.1.19   *Exeunt.*
5.2.0.1–2   *Enter Hoord tasting wine the* Host *following* | *in a Liuery cloake.*
5.2.8   *Exit.*
5.2.21.1   *Enter two gentlemen.*
5.2.40.1   *Exeunt.*
5.2.67.1   *Both turne back.* (after 'know', 5.2.68)
5.2.106.1   *Enter* Wit-good, *and* Lucre.
5.2.204.2   FINIS.

LINEATION NOTES

1.1.34   Hence...tarantula] DILKE; *prose* ELD
1.1.51–2   Fate...thee] DILKE; *new prose paragraph* ELD
1.1.55–8   Spoke...over it] DYCE; *prose* ELD
1.1.112–15   You will...courtesan] DYCE; *prose* ELD
1.1.116–19   You...calmest] THIS EDITION; *prose* ELD; brother| adversaries| fight| calmest| DYCE
2.1.222–4   You might...offence] DYCE; *prose* ELD
2.1.226–7   It was...now] WATSON; *1 line* ELD
2.1.241–2   -match...credit] DILKE; *1 type line* ELD
2.1.299–300   -band's...Aunt] DILKE; *1 type line* ELD
2.2.42–3   Fool...love] DYCE; *prose* ELD
2.2.51–4   Fall...all] DILKE; *prose* ELD
2.2.55–6   FIRST...I...faith] DILKE; *1 type line* ELD
2.2.76–8   Good...will] DYCE; *prose* ELD
3.1.16–17   again...i'faith] DILKE; *1 type line* ELD
3.1.22–3   WITGOOD...all] DYCE; *1 type line with turn under* ELD
3.1.23–4   FIRST...us] DYCE; *1 type line* ELD
3.1.24–8   For...securities] DYCE; *prose* ELD
3.1.39–40   You do...take it] DYCE; *prose* ELD
3.1.44–5   I hope...rites] DYCE; *prose* ELD
3.1.45   -riage...firmly] DILKE; *1 type line* ELD
3.1.59–60   money...it] DILKE; *1 type line* ELD
3.1.79–80   WITGOOD...news] DILKE; *1 type line* ELD
3.1.86–7   Among...gentleman] DYCE; *prose* ELD
3.1.90   Speaks...it] DILKE; *1 type line* ELD
3.1.93   Than...Excellent] DILKE; *1 type line* ELD
3.1.96–7   To...uncle] DILKE; *1 line* ELD
3.1.131–2   Now...worth] DYCE; *prose* ELD
3.1.142–3   Do...confess] DILKE; *prose* ELD
3.1.162   So...suffices] DILKE; *1 type line* ELD
3.1.168–9   Nor...gentleman] DILKE; *prose* ELD
3.1.174–6   A...can] DYCE; miseries| swallow| ELD
3.1.190   You...say] DILKE; *1 type line* ELD
3.1.191–2   He...desire] DILKE; *prose* ELD
3.1.192   you...come] DILKE; *1 type line* ELD
3.1.195–6   But...sir] DILKE; *1 type line* ELD
3.1.205–6   Well...seek] THIS EDITION; *1 type line* ELD; widow| DYCE
3.1.207   Before...best] THIS EDITION; *1 type line* ELD; before| gentlemen| best| DYCE
3.1.229   Still...sir] DILKE; *1 type line* ELD
3.1.235   O...eternally] DILKE; *1 verse line* ELD

3.1.250–1   -lowed...rumoured] DILKE; *1 type line* ELD
3.3.2–3   gentlemen...Hist] DILKE; *1 type line* ELD
3.3.5–6   HOARD...sir] DILKE; *1 type line* ELD
3.3.16–17   DRAWER...How] DILKE; *1 type line* ELD
3.3.30   LAMPREY...i'faith] DILKE; *1 type line* ELD
3.3.34–5   By th'...more] DYCE; *prose* ELD
3.3.35–6   you...fittest] DYCE; *1 type line* ELD
3.3.44–5   WITGOOD...sir] DILKE; *1 type line* ELD
3.3.55–6   Alas...mistress] DILKE; *1 type line* ELD
3.3.60–1   gone...forsooth] DILKE; *1 type line* ELD
3.3.64–5   BOY...him] DILKE; *1 type line* ELD
3.3.69–72   I...making] DYCE; *prose* ELD
3.3.73–4   I'll...her] DILKE; *prose* ELD
3.3.77–8   know...Drawer] DILKE; *1 type line* ELD
3.3.79–80   VINTNER...sir] DILKE; *1 type line* ELD
3.3.82–3   BOY...Out, sir] DILKE; *1 type line* ELD
3.3.90–1   HOST...yet] DILKE; *1 type line* ELD
3.3.102–3   FIRST...it] DILKE; *1 type line* ELD
3.3.105–6   LUCRE...confederates] DILKE; *1 type line* ELD
3.3.109–10   That...malice] DILKE; *prose* ELD
3.3.118   HOST...Well] DILKE; *1 type line* ELD
3.3.118–19   HOST...Harbour] DYCE; *1 line* ELD
3.3.121–2   Kind...breasts] DILKE; *1 line* ELD
3.4.9–10   DAMPIT...gentleman] DILKE; *1 type line* ELD
3.4.63–4   -serpine...Fooh] DILKE; *1 type line* ELD
4.1.1–5   Join...lips] ELD, DILKE, BARBER; hands| bands| part| heart| women| yeoman| slips| DYCE, WATSON
4.1.17–18   Let...his] DYCE; *prose* ELD
4.1.18–19   act...true] DILKE; *1 type line* ELD
4.1.20–1   You...him] DYCE; *prose* ELD
4.1.23   LAMPREY...in] DILKE; *1 type line* ELD
4.1.24–6   Hear...exercise] DILKE; *prose* ELD
4.1.30–1   O...Hoard] DILKE; *prose* ELD
4.1.31–2   excellent...ha!] DILKE; *1 type line* ELD
4.1.32–4   I...thus] DYCE; *prose* ELD
4.1.38–40   To...rascal] DILKE; O| by| ELD
4.1.58–9   Why...it] THIS EDITION; *prose* ELD; mind| DYCE
4.1.59–62   Ay...i'faith] THIS EDITION; *prose* ELD; performed| contained| DYCE
4.1.63–4   That...effect] DYCE; *prose* ELD
4.1.65–6   Why...I would] PRICE; *prose* ELD; than| hopes| DYCE
4.1.72–4   We'll...fullness] DYCE; *prose* ELD

4.1.78-9   When...terms] DILKE; *prose* ELD
4.1.89-91   So...ha] DYCE; *prose* ELD
4.1.98   HOARD...now] DILKE; *1 type line* ELD
4.1.99   HOARD...Hoard] DILKE; *1 type line* ELD
4.2.1   My...nephew] DYCE; *2 verse lines* ELD: law |
4.2.2   SAM...How] DILKE; *1 type line* ELD
4.2.7-8   your...in] DILKE; *1 type line* ELD
4.2.18   FIRST...Gentlemen] DILKE; *1 type line* ELD
4.2.19-20   Sorrow...it] DYCE; *prose* ELD
4.2.24   But...gentlemen] DILKE; *1 type line* ELD
4.2.26-9   Nephew...comes] DYCE; *prose* ELD
4.2.41-2   FIRST...nephew] DILKE; *1 type line* ELD
4.2.43-4   You...this] DYCE; *prose* ELD
4.2.46-7   But...you] DYCE; *prose* ELD
4.2.47   enough...certain] DILKE; *1 type line* ELD
4.2.48-9   Much...nephew] DYCE; *prose* ELD
4.2.51-2   Although...nephew] DYCE; *prose* ELD
4.2.58   You...No] DILKE; *1 type line* ELD
4.2.59   WITGOOD...true] DILKE; *1 type line* ELD
4.2.77-8   With...mocked] DYCE; *prose* ELD
4.2.78-9   LUCRE...ha] WATSON; *1 line* ELD
4.2.79-80   He...another] WATSON; *prose* ELD; them | DILKE
4.2.83-4   I...follies] DILKE; *prose* ELD
4.3.10-11   BOY...boy] DILKE; *1 type line* ELD
4.3.32-4   SECOND...fifty] DILKE; *1 type line* ELD
4.3.63-4   HOST...come] DILKE; *1 type line* ELD
4.4.36-7   liveries...sir] DILKE; *1 type line* ELD
4.4.40-1   You...perfumer] DILKE; *1 type line* ELD
4.4.61-2   want...sir] DILKE; *1 type line* ELD
4.4.65-6   HOARD...sir] DILKE; *1 type line* ELD
4.4.69-70   perfumer...sir] DILKE; *1 type line* ELD
4.4.105-7   -jurious...me] DILKE; *1 type line* ELD
4.4.117-18   And...Wife] DILKE; *1 type line* ELD
4.4.130-1   Let...offered you] DILKE; *prose* ELD
4.4.141-3   Excellent...hither] DYCE; *prose* ELD
4.4.145-6   there...Sir] DILKE; *1 type line* ELD
4.4.153   Away...quickly] DYCE; *prose* ELD
4.4.160   HOARD...spent] BULLEN; *1 type line* ELD
4.4.161-2   WITGOOD...sure] BULLEN; *1 type line* ELD
4.4.165-6   WITGOOD...name] DYCE; *1 line* ELD
4.4.172-3   Shall...first] SPENCER; *prose* ELD
4.4.174   WITGOOD...Shame] SPENCER; *1 type line* ELD
4.4.178-9   which...Excellent] DILKE; *1 type line* ELD
4.4.185-6   No more...you] DYCE; *1 line* ELD

4.4.188-9   Call...time] DYCE; *prose* ELD
4.4.189   Wife...bitter] DYCE; *prose* ELD
4.4.190-200   Master...sir] THIS EDITION; *prose* ELD
4.4.200-1   Would...i'faith] THIS EDITION; *prose* ELD
4.4.228-9   much...sir] DILKE; *1 type line* ELD
4.4.231-2   WITGOOD...said] DILKE; *1 type line* ELD
4.4.272-3   as...come] DILKE; *1 type line* ELD
4.4.303-4   NIECE...life] DILKE; *1 type line* ELD
4.5.20-1   sir...man] DILKE; *1 type line* ELD
4.5.26-7   I ha'...ha!] DILKE, *1 type line* ELD
4.5.45-6   I was...sir] DILKE; *1 type line* ELD
4.5.73-4   LAMPREY...sir] DILKE; *1 type line* ELD
4.5.76-7   DAMPIT...Lancelot] DILKE; *1 type line* ELD
4.5.78-9   DAMPIT...Pythagorical] DILKE; *1 type line* ELD
4.5.96-7   give you...possible] DILKE; *1 type line* ELD
4.5.102-3   learned advice...Enough] DILKE; *1 type line* ELD
4.5.106-7   LAMPREY...spouting] DILKE; *1 type line* ELD
4.5.154-5   the name...widow] DILKE; *1 type line* ELD
4.5.169   Is...usury] DILKE; *1 verse line* ELD
4.5.197-8   house...best] DYCE; *1 type line with long dash after 'house' suggesting a shift from prose to verse* ELD
5.1.9-10   WITGOOD...How] DILKE; *1 type line* ELD
5.1.12-13   i'faith...that] DILKE; *1 type line* ELD
5.2.9-11   HOARD...sir] DILKE; *1 type line* ELD
5.2.19-21   Fear...too] THIS EDITION; *prose* ELD
5.2.35-6   HOARD...bride] DILKE; *1 type line* ELD
5.2.72-3   -ry...man] DILKE; *1 type line* ELD
5.2.75-6   that you...brother] DILKE; *1 type line* ELD
5.2.95-6   LIMBER...Ha] DILKE; *1 type line* ELD
5.2.97-8   KIX...Gentlemen] DILKE; *1 type line* ELD
5.2.99-100   ONESIPHORUS...living] DILKE; *1 type line* ELD
5.2.101-2   ONESIPHORUS...Speak] DILKE; *1 type line* ELD
5.2.108-9   Why...widow] DYCE; *prose* ELD
5.2.110-11   Why...whore] NEILSON; *prose* ELD
5.2.111   she's...knave] DILKE; *1 type line* ELD
5.2.113   *Probo tibi*, nephew] DILKE; *1 line* ELD
5.2.125   LUCRE...strumpet] DYCE; *1 type line* ELD
5.2.125-8   Nay...thought] DYCE; *prose* ELD
5.2.140-9   Thank...forever] THIS EDITION; *prose* ELD. See Textual Note to 5.2.144-5.
A.1-4   I...foes] THIS EDITION; *prose* ELD; now | incitement | such | DYCE
A.7-8   You...ill-willer] DYCE; *1 line* ELD
A.17-18   my...O, O, O] DILKE; *1 type line* ELD

YOUR FIVE GALLANTS

Text edited by Ralph Alan Cohen with John Jowett

Your Five Gallants (BEPD 266) was entered in the Stationers' Register on 22 March 1608. The entry records 'A plaie called The Fyve Wittie Gallantes as it hath ben acted by the Children of the Chappell'. Neither the Stationers' Register nor the title-page of the only seventeenth-century edition mentions a printer, but the device on the title-page of that single edition was George Eld's (McKerrow #320β), and the quarto (STC 17907) is printed in a font (Eld–Y2) used by Eld beginning in 1607. The title-page reads, 'Your fiue Gallants. | As it hath beene often in Action | at the Black-friers. | Written by T. Middleton'. Eld printed the book 'for *Richard Bonian*, dwelling at the signe of the Spred-Eagle, right ouer-against the great North dore of Saint *Paules* Church'. The quarto bears no date, but there is no reason to believe that its publication was delayed beyond 1608, the year when it was entered.

The text is poor, and is a particularly clear example of a play printed from an authorial draft. The repeated squeezing of verse passages into prose perhaps reflects on a lack of clear distinction in the manuscript. Stage directions are seriously inadequate, even though this is a play whose intelligibility depends on small actions, many of them requiring props that go from hand to hand. Even the basic entrances and exits are inconsistent and often missing entirely. Speeches are often misassigned, and occasionally not assigned at all. The speech prefixes for minor characters are particularly unstable. That problem is exacerbated by the fact that characters are frequently designated with a numerical speech prefix—the numbers '1' and '2' at one time or another represent fellows, courtesans, servants, gentlemen, and constables. This feature is so prevalent that it suggests a provisional and unfinalized text.

Scene divisions are unmarked. The text indicates the beginnings of 'ACTVS. 2.' and 'ACT. 5.' in the same position as in this edition, but Eld's one other marked act-break, 'Finis Actus 3 | ACTVS. 4.', appears where this edition follows Dyce and others in ending Act 2.

Worst of all for the prosperity of the play, a major passage of almost four pages (F2–F3ᵛ; Interims 1 and 2) is almost certainly misplaced. Eld immediately follows the end of Act 2 (Eld's 'Finis Actus 3') not with the Interim scenes as in this edition, but with Tailby's entrance in which he is reading a letter from a mistress in Kingston. Eld therefore concurs with this edition in beginning the new act with the letter-reading, but delays the scenes identified in this edition as Interims 1 and 2 until after the last scene in editorial Act 3. Tailby's letter in 3.1 is certainly the one that he receives from Mistress Newblock

in Eld's text much later (after 3.4; sig. F3), and of course, the reading of the letter should follow, not precede, its arrival. Eld has clearly transposed material.

Its proper location can be determined by considering the sequence of events that leads on from Tailby losing his clothes at the dicing table in 2.4. The episode positioned as Interim 1 in the present edition shows the serendipitous arrival of clothes while Tailby is supposedly still abed after his bad night with the dice. It is the action that follows most closely the exit from the Mitre at the end of Act 2. Jack's line that Tailby 'played away half his clothes last night' confirms this supposition. Interim 2 shows Tailby enter as he finishes dressing in his newly-acquired suit, and he goes on to receive a beaver hat that restitutes another loss from the night before. Until Tailby is furnished with new clothes he cannot leave home to meet his next mistress. The Interim sequence is therefore coherent within itself in Eld, but both episodes are mislocated. Colegrove discusses this transposition in her edition (1979, 44–7), where, following the suggestion first made by Fleay (1891) and later echoed by Bald (1945) and Maxwell (1951), she was first to put the material back in order.

Maxwell's explanation for this error was that the 116 lines—apparently 'exactly enough to fill four pages of the manuscript copy'—were 'intended for discard, but instead found their way into a later spot' (32). This edition instead identifies the moved scenes as an entr'acte sequence (see Jowett, 'Pre-editorial Criticism'). Picking up on the Middletonian term 'interim' as used by Tailby in 2.1 in a way that suggests an interval in theatrical time juxtaposed with music (as well as an interval in 'real' time), we apply it to these scenes in preference to more formalized or classicized terms such as 'interlude', 'entr'acte', or the Jonsonian 'intermean'.

As the stage directions make clear, the episodes are performed amidst music: '*In the midst of the musick, enter one . . .*', '*The Musicke plaies on a while, then enter . . .*'. In other words, the action interrupts the music that, as was usual in the hall theatres, plays during the act interval. The first, shorter, Interim episode clearly has music played before and after it. An arrangement that has been considered but rejected for the present edition is that our Interim 2 should be marked as a new beginning to Act 3. The reason why this cannot be countenanced is that Tailby is given an exit at the end of this scene and, in the reconstructed sequence, an immediate re-entry. Keeping him on stage would conflict with the stage directions, one of which was supplied for the expanded text; moreover, the transition from the end-of-scene type of soliloquy to the reading of the letter would be extremely awkward theatrically. If, on the other hand, the music associated with the act interval strikes up once more, there is no objection to the re-entry after it. Eld's quarto does not this time specifically call for music, but this is far from a decisive consideration in a text so generally deficient in supplying stage directions.

The two Interim scenes literally have no place in the original five-act sequence, and so, in an unusual and indeed experimental piece of stagecraft, they are forced into the space between two acts. It is probably no coincidence that Francis Beaumont's *Knight of the Burning Pestle*, performed by the Children of the Queen's Revels in the same period (probably c.1607–8) has short Interlude scenes after each act. Middleton's Interims are nevertheless distinctive, in that they develop the same action as the rest of the play, and they are confined to one act interval. Though Ben Jonson's *Staple of News* would later have 'Intermeans' of up to 88 lines, the length of the combined episodes is striking too. If the second scene is indeed an Interim followed by music, the boundary between act-interval and act is entirley blurred.

The theory that these scenes, far from being discarded material, were added as an afterthought provides a much more satisfactory account of Eld's transposition. Maxwell had to suppose the coincidence that the episodes intended for discard happened conveniently to begin at the top of a fresh sheet and end at the bottom of another sheet; his account depends on the pages being both removed and reinserted. If, however, the scenes were belatedly *added* to the manuscript, they must have been written on separate leaves in the first place, and it would be a simple matter for them to be inserted at the wrong point. If, as we accept, editors have identified the right point at which to begin Act 4, the Interims simply appear at the wrong act interval. (It is tempting, then, to imagine that the transposition contributed to the prematurely numbered act-break, but it is hard to see just how the one might have led to the other.)

Another suspected transposition has been rejected in this edition. Dyce relocated the short scene identified in this edition as 2.3 to the end of 2.1. The text has been considered suspect because it returns to the brothel, the scene of 2.1, so soon after leaving it in 2.2. Maxwell sought to explain Eld's error by suggesting that 'the order of two sheets was accidentally reversed or, if the play was written on both sides of the sheets making up the copy, that the printer erroneously set the later side first' (Maxwell, 31). But there are difficulties with the transposition theory, and with Maxwell's account in particular. First, as with his explanation of the larger transposition of Interims 1 and 2, Maxwell has to assume that the unit of theatrical action coincided with the page--breaks of the manuscript, which is not readily to be expected. Moreover, the two passages that change places, 2.1 and 2.2, are both too short to occupy a full page of a typical theatrical manuscript. And, quite apart from the

mechanics of the assumed error, the text's stage directions are specifically written for the sequence of action in Eld. The text supplies a plural '*Exeunt.*' after 2.1.345 that clears the stage ready for Fitzgrave's entry, a re-entry for Tailby ('*Enter Whore Gal.*') opposite 'Oh the parting of vs twaine,' and a speech-prefix for Tailby before that line; these would all be incorrect or redundant if the text was written for Tailby to remain on stage.

Such circumstances oblige us to consider anew whether the text might here play successfully as Eld prints it. Colegrove (44) objects to Tailby's entry at the Mitre at the beginning of 2.4 straight after leaving Primero's house as a violation of the so-called 'law of re-entry', but, as Taylor has shown in relation to Shakespeare's *Henry V*, re-entry is 'a perfectly acceptable procedure' provided that a character enters in different company (Wells and Taylor, 1979, 95). This is especially the case if the entry involves a large group in which the re-entering character may be preceded by others. Moreover, it seems likely to us that music would be played within at the beginning of this scene too (see textual note to 2.4.0.1–2), and this would separate Tailby's exit from his re-entry in the same way as at the beginning of 3.1.

In other respects Eld's arrangement is as plausible as Dyce's, and in some ways preferable. The Novice and Tailby exeunt together, and the scene with Fitzgrave is a short interlude occupying the time that we will guess they spend in lovemaking. Tailby then enters as from this encounter ('the parting of us twain'), only to be joined together immediately with Mistress Newcut. Perhaps Dyce balked at the display of sexual prowess. But Eld's arrangement gives a comic edge to lines such as Mistress Newcut's 'Ah, sweet gentleman, he keeps it up stately' that is lost in the transposition, and the play's return to the brothel provides a comic equivalent in the recursive movement of the stage action to Tailby's return to a new sexual encounter.

As to the more general sloppiness of the printing, no one has yet offered a convincing scenario. Price (1953) claimed that the printing was done on the cheap in a hurry. As evidence of haste he offers the theory that two presses were used, and to prove that the costs were cut he theorizes that the paper was 'old stock got at a bargain' (24). Weiss, however, on the basis of a careful study of type movement, concludes that 'the recurrence evidence leaves no doubt that the play was printed on a single press'. As for Price's conjecture that the publisher Richard Bonian went bargain shopping for paper remnants, Weiss points out that Price's examination of the paper could not have distinguished old from new, and adds that because paper was extremely expensive 'there were no "old stocks of paper" lying about in London warehouses'.

Given the muddled state of Eld's quarto, Dyce's edition is a notable accomplishment. Dyce sorts through the confusion of speech headings, applies consistent entrances and exits, divides the play into logical acts and scenes, and recasts prose into verse. Bullen follows Dyce closely and does little to improve on his work. The editorial fortunes of Middleton's play took a turn for the better, however, in Colegrove's painstaking edition. This edition benefits throughout from her work.

Two editorial procedures that respond to the character of the text deserve mention. In Eld, speeches just a few words long are often set on the same type-line as the previous speech or the end of it, irrespective of whether the text set in this way makes up a verse line. In this edition, as there is in general no significance for the editorial lineation in part-lines set on a single type-line for the lineation, cases are not recorded in the Lineation Notes. As the Eld quarto is unusually far from self-consistency in its provision of stage directions, we have not sought to distinguish between on the one hand emending its deficiencies to a notional norm and on the other hand supplementing that norm to the requirements of the fully edited text. In this respect we have adopted a procedure at variance with the usual editing of stage directions elsewhere in the *Collected Works*. All added stage directions and parts of stage directions appear in square brackets.

SEE ALSO

Text: *Works*, 597
Music and dance: this volume, 143
Authorship and date: this volume, 363

WORKS CITED

Previous Editions

Dyce, Alexander, ed., *Works* (1840), vol. 2
Bullen, A. H., ed., *Works* (1885), vol. 3
Colegrove, Clare Lee., ed., *A Critical Edition of Thomas Middleton's 'Your Five Gallants'*, Ph.D. diss. (University of Michigan, 1961); issued in book form 1979

Other Works Cited

Bald, R. C., 'The Chronology of Middleton's Plays', *Modern Language Review* 32 (1937), 33-43
—— 'The Foul Papers of a Revision', *The Library*, IV, 26 (1945), 37-50
Barker, Richard Hindry, *Thomas Middleton* (1958)
Chambers, E. K., *The Elizabethan Stage*, 4 vols (1923)
Fleay, F. G., *A Biographical Chronicle of the English Drama*, 2 vols (1891)
Jowett, John, 'Pre-editorial Criticism and the Space for Editing: Examples from *Richard III* and *Your Five Gallants*', in *Problems of Editing* (special issue of *Editio*), ed. Christa Jansohn and Ursula Schaefer (1999), 127-49
Maxwell, Baldwin, 'Thomas Middleton's *Your Five Gallants*', *Philological Quarterly* 30 (1951), 30-9
Price, George R., 'The First Edition of *Your Five Gallants* and of *Michaelmas Term*', *The Library*, V, 8 (1953), 23-9
Sugden, Edward H., *A Topographical Dictionary to the Works of Shakespeare and His Fellow Dramatists* (1925)
Wells, Stanley, and Gary Taylor, *Modernizing Shakespeare's Spelling, with Three Studies in the Text of 'Henry V'* (1979)

TEXTUAL NOTES

Prologue.0.1–Prologue.1 *Presenter or prologue . . .* PRESENTER] THIS EDITION; *Presenter or prologue*, ELD. Eld runs these words straight on with the words printed in this edition as the Presenter's speech, which are likewise in italic. So Prologue.1–8 are printed entirely as a stage direction. At least the second part of the passage includes an address to the audience or the reader, and cannot be a stage direction ('I warrant you'). As the text as a whole shows many signs of not having been given any special preparation for the reader, it seems that at least part of the present passage is dramatic speech. Moreover, Eld's opening words '*Presenter or prologue*' strongly imply a dramatic role, a figure whose function would be to speak a verbal prologue. This edition prints the entire passage as the Presenter's speech for the following reasons:

(*a*) the passage is printed uniformly;

(*b*) although stylistically the passage shifts from theatrical idiom to speech idiom, it does not readily divide into two distinct blocks;

(*c*) theatrically speaking, it would be very useful to give verbal identification to the five gallants;

(*d*) having the Presenter describe the choreography of the opening blocking starts the play off in a way that foreshadows the formal symmetry of the masque of gallants at the end of the play, with the Presenter serving roughly the same function as Katherine does in the masque when she gives each gallant his Latin tag;

(*e*) having the Presenter speak such lines as 'kiss these three wenches and depart in a little whisper and wanton action' while that action takes place on stage is in keeping

with the disarming metatheatrics which operate throughout the play.

That the dramatic technique is Middletonian (and can be used in a less whimsical fashion) can be seen by comparing the opening of *Revenger's Tragedy*, where Vindice comments on the Duke and his family as they pass over the stage in dumb-show. Eld's compositor probably misunderstood a speech that had been written in italic to distinguish it from the main body of the play. There would be a heading '*Presenter or prologue*' doubling as a speech-prefix, as with the heading 'Prologue' in the Trinity manuscript of *Game*.

Prologue.7 *Hactenus*] DYCE; hactcnus ELD

1.1.0.1 *Actus Primus*] DYCE (ACT I.); *heading not in* ELD. What we identify in this edition as the Prologue logically stands outside the five-act structure. Whether there would have been a short musical interlude is impossible to say, but it would be appropriate and effective for a light musical accompaniment to have been played during the Prologue itself; this could have been briefly continued after the Presenter's speech.

1.1.1 ARTHUR] DYCE; 1. ELD. Excepting 1.1.61, where he appears as '2.', Arthur is represented by '1.' in Eld's text.

1.1.2 FIRST FELLOW] COLEGROVE; 2. ELD. As in Eld it is Arthur who assumes the speech-prefix number '1.', the '*fellow*' comes to be numbered '2.' here; but subsequently, through some confusion, it seems to be the same figure who is identified as '3.'. DYCE, however, envisaged two Fellows, following Eld in identifying the speaker of 1.1.2 as the Second, and identifying Eld's '3.' as the First.

1.1.6   FRIP] ELD (*Frip.*). Previous editors expand to 'Frippery' in stage directions, but there is no basis on which to assume that his name is anything more than Frip. *Frippery* in full occurs only once in Eld, and there (1.1.190) with only indirect reference to the character's name. In the few stage directions to name him, '*Enter Frip.*' (4.2.0.1) is not evidence for a contraction, as directions regularly end with full stops; the stage direction at 5.2.23, '*Frip.* Bowes to her,' is indecisive, as, like the other directions in the series, it is set as though it were a speech-prefix followed by a speech; the unstopped '*Frip presents her...*' (5.2.25.5–6) is evidence against a written contraction. Similarly, in dialogue there is no instance of a full stop where it would not be expected irrespective of whether 'Frip' were an abbreviation. As all words in *OED* beginning 'Frip-' relate to frippery, there is no uncertainty as to what the short name signifies.

1.1.31   ARTHUR] DYCE; 3. ELD

1.1.33   FIRST FELLOW] DYCE; 3. ELD. For the rest of his appearance on stage, the First Fellow is represented by '3' in Eld's text.

1.1.42   I'll...presently.] ELD. DYCE reassigns the line to Frip; but the First Fellow may simply be speaking to Arthur, who before exiting indicates his desire to be tipped.

1.1.55   safely] ELD; safety *conj.* JJ

1.1.58.1   *Enter...trunk*] COLEGROVE; *after* 1.1.60 ELD

1.1.61   ARTHUR] DYCE; 2. ELD

1.1.69   SECOND FELLOW] DYCE (*identifying him as the speaker of 1.1.2: see note*); COLEGROVE (*introducing a new speaker as in this edition*); 4. ELD. The Second Fellow is represented throughout by '4.' in Eld's text.

1.1.70   FRIP] *Frip* ELD (c.w.); *Frie.* ELD (*text*)

1.1.85   gentlewomen's] DYCE; gentlewomans ELD

1.1.85   falls] ELD (faules); faults *conj.* JJ

1.1.103   hazard] DYCE; haxard ELD

1.1.178   gallant] DYCE; Gallants ELD

1.1.199   Ye] ELD (yea)

1.1.234   I hope] BULLEN; hope ELD

1.1.247   changed] DYCE; chande ELD

1.1.257.1   *Enter Arthur*] THIS EDITION (RAC); *not in* ELD. Arthur exited earlier with the Second Fellow at 1.1.109 and would logically re-enter when Frip calls. Alternatively, Arthur might have re-entered with the Novice at 1.1.208.1.

1.1.265   PRIMERO] DYCE; *Ar.* ELD. Arthur should have exited with the Novice, so Dyce is probably correct in reassigning the line to Primero. His further emendation of 'mass, sir' for Eld's 'maister', however, seems unnecessary. One running joke throughout the play is the excessive courtesy with which these rogues use one another, and the imputation here could be virtually 'maestro'.

1.1.278   *Exit Primero*] DYCE; *after* 1.1.277 ELD

1.1.278.1   *Frip...clothes*] THIS EDITION (JJ); *not in* ELD. This transformation seems essential to make sense of the soliloquy, at the end of which Frip offers 'to continue change' (1.1.313–14).

1.1.284   appear] appearce ELD

1.1.308   not] DYCE; nor ELD

1.1.317–18   in...dagger] DYCE; & *Andrew Lucifers* Rapier and dagger, in the knights ward ELD. Perhaps a misunderstood interlineation.

1.1.329   than] DYCE; them ELD

1.2.0.1   *Mistress*] ELD (*Misters*). Perhaps not an error: *OED* records the spelling 'Misterss'.

1.2.7   perfection of my joys,] THIS EDITION (JJ); perfections of myioye: ELD; perfection of my joy DYCE. The erratic plural 'perfections' (contrast 1.2.3) is better explained if transferred from 'ioye', and plural *joys* accords with *desires*.

1.2.20–2   to...kept] DYCE; whereon I iustly kept, | Accept this worthlesse favor from your seruants arme, the hallowed beades, ELD (*with* 'lowed beades,' *as turn-over*). In Eld, 'whereon I iustly kept' appears at the position of the editorial 'to', which is not in Eld. The layout in Eld strongly suggests that 'the hallowed beades whereon I iustly kept' was added after the rest, with 'whereon I iustly kept' placed as a turn-up. Either the turn-up obscured the preposition 'to', or the compositor omitted it in an attempt to produce some sort of sense. The line is necessary to the sense of the passage: either the extant words replace a first draft of the line, or Middleton's mind was running ahead of his hand, causing an initial omission.

1.2.26   soul] THIS EDITION (JJ); *not in* ELD; life DYCE. *Soul* fits the religious language better than *life*, and a compositor sensing a touch of blasphemy could have consciously or unconsciously omitted the word. Compare 2.2.3–4.

1.2.26.1   *Enter five gallants*] DYCE; *after* 1.2.27 ELD.

1.2.39   ne'er] ELD (neare)

1.2.64, 66   GALLANTS] *All.* ELD

1.2.66.2   they...them] COLEGROVE; *after* 'Exit.', 1.2.65.1, ELD; *after* 'Ugh', 1.2.67, DYCE

1.2.67   Ugh!] ELD (Ough.)

1.2.68.1–2   *The...pocket-gallant*] COLEGROVE; *right, opposite ll. 67–8* ELD

1.2.97.2   *Finis Actus Primus*] THIS EDITION; *not in* ELD

2.1.36   FIRST COURTESAN] *Curt.* ELD. She is subsequently identified by number.

2.1.49.1   *Primero's Boy*] Without evidence to the contrary, it is safe to assume that Primero's boy is not the same as Pursenet's. For one thing, it is improbable, though not impossible, that a single boy played music and picked pockets simultaneously. For another, having two different boys means that Middleton has given each of his five gallants a servant.

2.1.53.1   *Enter all*] DYCE; *after* 2.1.55–6 ELD

2.1.55–7   this...Whence] DYCE; this, | [*indent*] *Purfn.* Gentleman his parts deserue it, *Enter, All* | Whence ELD. ELD clearly prints the speech-prefix for Pursenet on the wrong type-line.

2.1.100   ALL THE COURTESANS] *All.* ELD

2.1.135–7   PRIMERO...A] BULLEN; *Pri.* My wits must not stand idle, Slife hee's in a ficke trance? | [*indent*] *Golft.* A ELD. Goldstone is the gallant who is proud of his wits and is about to put them to use, and if Primero is meant to speak here, only the observation about Frip's distraction seems appropriate.

2.1.154   The truest...gentleman] An interesting instance of Middleton's splitting a verse line between two characters not in the same conversation which may suggest the speed and fluidity of the movement in the original production.

2.1.155   and has so] ELD; and so BULLEN

2.1.163   never] DYCE; nere ELD

2.1.168   Goldstone] DYCE; *Boufer* ELD. Colegrove rejects Dyce's emendation and argues, 'It seems equally likely, however, that the courtezan is here calling on a bystander (the disguised Fitsgrave) for help...'. The following arguments might support Dyce's change: (*a*) Goldstone and the Second Courtesan are in a private conversation that neither would want overheard; (*b*) Fitzgrave ('Bowser') has not been involved in the dialogue for forty-five lines and will not speak again for another seventy; (*c*) Fitzgrave ('Bowser')—against character—does not respond at all to the lady in distress. But a misreading of literals is most unlikely, and, as Bowser has not been named previously in Eld either in dialogue or stage directions, eyeskip or memorial error are just as implausible.

2.1.208 FULK] DYCE; I. ELD. Similarly in the following exchange except at 2.1.221, where the speech-prefix is less ambiguously 'I. *Seruing.*'. Fulk is not given an entry.

2.1.223 GOLDSTONE] ELD. Dyce, followed by Bullen and Colegrove, reassigns this speech to Pursenet. The logic is that in his preceding and following speeches, Goldstone is clearly not indifferent. But the speech falls at the top of a page (C2ᵛ) in Eld, and the catchword '*Gold.*' at the foot of the previous page confirms that Goldstone was given the line in the manuscript. Presumably Goldstone unexpectedly changes tack to pre-empt any dispute.

2.1.228–9 then. | PURSENET Boy] DYCE; then: Boye ELD. Eld continues the speech it attributes to '*All*' without a line-break.

2.1.228, 270 ALL THE REST] *All.* ELD

2.1.237 'Twill] DYCE; till ELD

2.1.244–6 PURSENET...thee?] THIS EDITION (JJ); *Goldſt.* What money haft about thee? | *Purſ.* Looke you ſir, ELD; *GOL.* What money hast about thee? Look you DYCE. By Dyce's emendation, it is hard to account for the presence of a regularly set but redundant speech-prefix for Pursenet in Eld. It therefore seems more likely that a speech of three words for Pursenet, perhaps written as a marginal addition or interlineation in the manuscript, was mislocated in Eld in such a way that it ran on with the rest of Goldstone's speech. In the text as emended in this edition, 'Look you, sir' can be taken as Pursenet's address to Bungler, drawing his attention to 'Bowser's' latest ſit, and incidentally allowing Goldstone more privacy in negotiating with Frip. The words happen to complement what previous editors have recognized as an unassimilated part-line, 'When I have lost her favour', to give a regular pentameter.

2.1.309 you're firm] THIS EDITION (RAC); your ſinne ELD; you ſin DYCE

2.1.333 'Tween] DYCE; Turne ELD; Twin JJ *conj.* Eld's *Turn* isn't quite possible even as 'reverse, exchange', for the verb is still not equivalent to eliminating difference.

2.1.339 bodies∧] DYCE; bodie, ELD

2.1.343 wear] ELD (were)

2.2.0.1–2.2.25.1 *Enter...Exit*] ELD. All previous editors since Dyce have transposed the scene so that it continues the action at the end of 2.1. See Textual Introduction.

2.2.11 KATHERINE'S SERVANT] THIS EDITION (RAC); I. ELD; Ser. DYCE. Similarly 2.2.16 and 2.2.19.

2.2.23 that] DYCE; That's ELD

2.3.0.1 *Enter whore-gallant*] THIS EDITION (JJ); *right, opposite* 2.3.1 *not in* DYCE

2.3.30 *Exeunt*] *Exit.* ELD

2.4.0.1 *Music within*] THIS EDITION (JJ); *not in* ELD. The end of the music would mark the end of supper within, would allow a space between the exit and re-entry of Tailby and Primero, and would provide an opportunity to set out the dicing table and chairs.

2.4.0.2 *enter all at once*] *position as in* DYCE; *right, opposite* 2.4.1 ELD

2.4.9 FIRST COURTESAN] I. ELD. The lack of unambiguous referent in Eld is clarified at 2.4.9, 'I *Cur.*', but potential confusion resumes at 2.4.18 and subsequently, when 'I.' is the prefix for Fulk.

2.4.18 VINTNER] THIS EDITION (RAC); *not in* ELD. Eld prints '*Within* Anon, anon ſir' in parentheses.

2.4.21 FULK] DYCE; I. ELD. Similarly throughout the rest of the scene, except at 2.4.318 ('*Ful.*'), 2.4.322 ('*Fulk.*'), and 2.4.340 ('*Fu.*').

2.4.28 quarreler] THIS EDITION (RAC); quarter her ELD; chatterer DYCE; quatre-trois COLEGROVE *conj.*

2.4.72 FITZGRAVE] *Bow.* ELD. Fitzgrave is disguised as 'Bowser' throughout the scene. Eld uses '*Bow.*' as his speech heading here and at 2.4.75–6, and '*Bou.*' at 2.4.342.

2.4.131–2 Mew! | TAILBY Where] THIS EDITION (JJ); Mew, where ELD. DYCE instead emends Eld's speech-prefix, giving both 'Mew' and 'Where...bones' to Tailby. But it is easier to suppose a missing speech-prefix than corruption of '*Tay.*' or '*Tayl.*' to '*Purs.*'. Pursenet's next speech (2.4.146) is also a monosyllable.

2.4.159 wary] THIS EDITION (JJ); weary ELD

2.4.162 thee] THIS EDITION (RAC); tee ELD; 't ye DYCE

2.4.167 FULK] DYCE; 5. ELD. Fulk resumes his usual prefix 'I.' at 2.4.172.

2.4.169 thine] DYCE; mine ELD

2.4.178 ever be] COLEGROVE; be euer be ELD; be ever DYCE

2.4.183 against] ELD (againe)

2.4.192 fogger] ELD (fooker). Eld's spelling echoes the German *fucker* or *focker* as variants on the name *Fogger*. A pun on the English verb *fuck* seems unlikely, though would be almost inevitable in modern performance were pronunciation to be based on Eld's form.

2.4.213 against] ELD (agen)

2.4.203 ALL THE REST] *All.* ELD

2.4.260 TAILBY] DYCE; *not in* ELD. Since Goldstone has just won, he cannot be complaining of not having won a hand. The manuscript probably indicated a new speech, as Eld otherwise unnecessarily begins a new line of type.

2.4.260 o'] DYCE (a'); ath ELD

2.4.314 FULK] COLEGROVE (Dyce); *Purſ,* ELD; *GOL.* DYCE. It may be significant that the three following speech-prefixes for Fulk identify him by name, instead of as 'I.', for the first time. Perhaps an unfamiliar '*Fu.*' was misread '*Pu.*' and expanded towards conformity with the neighbouring prefixes '*Pursn.*'.

2.4.363 near] DYCE; meere ELD

2.4.383 vintner] DYCE; Vintne ELD

2.4.412–13 on. | GOLDSTONE Nay] DYCE; on.Nay ELD. Eld continues the type-line. But Goldstone is the one who wants to linger so that he and Fulk can retrieve the hidden goblet.

2.4.418.2 *Secundus*] THIS EDITION; 3. ELD

Interim 1.0.1–Interim 2.95.1 *In...Exit*] *position of scenes as in* COLEGROVE (Fleay); *after* 3.4. See Textual Introduction.

Interim 1 THIS EDITION (JJ); ACTVS. 4. ELD; ACT III SCENE I DYCE (*following* ELD's *sequence of scenes*)

Interim 1.1 JACK] DYCE; I. ELD. Similarly throughout scene. He is identified as Jack in the speech-prefixes for Interim 2.

Interim 1.2 MISTRESS CLEVELAND'S SERVANT] THIS EDITION (RAC); 2. ELD; SER. DYCE. Similarly throughout scene.

Interim 2 THIS EDITION (JJ); *heading not in* ELD; ACT III SCENE II DYCE

Interim 2.37 MISTRESS NEWBLOCK'S SERVANT] THIS EDITION (RAC); I. ELD; Ser. DYCE; *Second Servant* COLEGROVE. Similarly throughout following dialogue.

Interim 2.79 MISTRESS TIFFANY'S SERVANT] THIS EDITION (RAC); 2. ELD; *Ser.* DYCE; *Third Servant* COLEGROVE

Interim 2.82 All-Hallowtide] ELD (all hollandide)

Interim 2.92 Take] DYCE; Takes ELD

3.1.0.1 *Tertius*] DYCE (III); 4. ELD. See Textual Introduction.

3.1.30 sweet] DYCE; ſweere ELD

3.1.32–3 him....Boy.] him.— | Boy ELD; DYCE *begins a new scene* (3.2) *before* 'Boy'. Such is the magic of theatre that Pursenet can indicate a change of place simply by crossing the stage and masking himself with his scarf. An exit and re-entry is unnecessary and contrary to Jacobean stage convention, though it might effectively underscore the same joke about theatrical illusion. See Critical Introduction.

3.1.118–27 'Master Tailby...want nothing'] ELD puts into italics the words that Pursenet reads from the letter.

3.1.135 a lord] DYCE; A.L. ELD

3.1.144 him] ELD; her DYCE

3.1.147 The] THIS EDITION (JJ); There ELD. Compare 3.3.21.

3.2.22 behind] DYCE; bekinde ELD

3.2.22 high] THIS EDITION (JJ); not in ELD. Dyce first noted that a
word seems to be missing. *Standing high* equivocates between
'held in high esteem', 'standing in a vulnerable position', and
'with an erect penis, sexually preoccupied'. *High* contrasts
with *reels* in the following line. Dyce established the following
four lines as rhyming couplets in a speech Eld sets as prose;
the emendation allows a further six lines to be set as verse.

3.2.25 men] DYCE; me ELD

3.3.0.1 *Fitzgrave...Gentleman-Gallants*] THIS EDITION (JJ); *two
Gentlemen* ELD. Eld identifies two speakers, '1.' and '2.'; the
first is clearly Fitzgrave. Previous editors have concluded with
apparent good sense that Fitzgrave is one of the two Gentlemen. But 3.3.14 sounds as though the speaker is petitioning
Fitzgrave on behalf of himself and another; it is likewise two
gentlemen, not one, of whom Fitzgrave asks 'Stands your
assistance firm?' at 5.1.73; and Fitzgrave's discovery by 3.3
of three 'sophistical' gallants would symmetrically correspond
with the presence of altogether three 'good' gentlemen, in anticipation of the symmetrical groups of five in the final scene.
The designation 'Gentleman-Gallants' establishes continuity
between 3.3, 5.1, and 5.2 (see note to 5.1.73–4).

3.3.1 FITZGRAVE] DYCE; 1. ELD. Similarly throughout the scene.

3.3.5 A GENTLEMAN-GALLANT] THIS EDITION; 2. ELD; GEN DYCE.
Similarly throughout the scene.

3.3.11 *subaudi*] DYCE; *fubands* ELD

3.3.16 faints] ELD; faires ELD

3.3.16.1 *Exeunt*] Exit. ELD

3.4.0.2 FIRST] ELD (1.)

3.4.2 FIRST COURTESAN] *Curt.* ELD. The ordinal is given in the
subsequent speech-prefixes.

3.4.36 St George's Day] Fleay's suggestion, in view of his dating
of November–December 1607, that 'St George's Day (April
23) seems to have been put in for St Andrew's (Nov. 30), to
avoid offending the King' (*Biographical Chronicle* (1891), vol.
2, 94) is not especially convincing. Perhaps the significance
of mentioning an April festival in a play set in November
is its sheer implausibility, unless the inconsistency is merely
authorial oversight.

3.4.40 Not] ELD; No *conj.* JJ. Error is especially plausible in view
of the beginning of Pursenet's previous speech, 'Notable'.

3.4.51 Yea] ELD (Yee)

3.4.58 it] DYCE; ir ELD

3.4.88 truth] DYCE; truh ELD

3.4.90 it] ELD; him *conj.* JJ. There might originally have been a
short rhyming couplet.

3.4.91 Would I had] THIS EDITION (JJ); I would had ELD; I would
[I] had DYCE

3.4.97 look] DYCE; luck ELD. The compositor may have misinter-
peted a spelling such as 'luke'.

3.4.99 limed] THIS EDITION (Dyce); linde ELD

3.4.121 he's] DYCE; his ELD

3.4.141 hundred] ELD (hundreth)

3.4.164 worships] ELD. Should logically be singular 'worship'.
Perhaps an affectation or lisp.

3.4.174 sham'-legged] ELD (fhamlegd). '?Wooden-legged (but
perh. error for *shamble-legged*)' (*OED*). The one quotation in
OED (1688) reads 'One James Caulket,...a Dyer...sham
leg'd, goes somewhat foundered'. In both this and the

present Middleton instance, 'shamble-legged' seems the sense
required. As both texts read 'sham' they might reflect an
idiomatic contraction of an orally awkward phrase rather
than a shared error.

3.4.179.1 *Finis Actus Tertius*] THIS EDITION; *not in* ELD

4.1.0.1 *Actus Quartus*] COLEGROVE (*subst.*); *not in* ELD. DYCE,
following the sequence of scenes in Eld, began Act 4 with
the present Interim scenes before Act 3, making the present
4.1 the third scene of the Act. See Textual Introduction.

4.2.38 lend] ELD; lead DYCE. It seems appropriate that the
pawnbroker should be jocularly 'lent'.

4.3.0.1–2 *Bungler, meeting Marmaduke*] THIS EDITION (RAC, *following* Dyce *for identification of the roles*); *Gall.* ELD.

4.3.40 *Exit Bungler*] DYCE; *after* 4.3.39 ELD

4.3.71 *Exit Goldstone*] DYCE; *right, opposite* 4.3.70 ELD. Eld begins
a new type-line after 'then', suggesting that the exit should
have been printed here, as might the otherwise redundant
'Goldst.'.

4.4.3 thee] ELD (the)

4.4.5.1 *Enter Piamont*] ELD. Colegrove moves this stage direction
a sentence later, so that Piamont enters just as the Boy sees
him. Eld's positioning, however, makes more sense because
the imagined scene is the middle aisle at St Paul's, a place
where gallants promenaded, and having Piamont there while
the Boy takes a moment or two to spot him helps to give the
impression of a large or crowded space.

4.4.26 by troth] ELD. For the idiom, compare *Women Beware*
3.1.28.

4.4.37–8 once. | ...PIAMONT...Do] DYCE; once: do ELD. This
edition follows Dyce, but the assignment of the speech to
Pursenet in Eld can work on a stage. Pursenet, after all,
is trying to think of a 'device' to distract Piamont and
pick his pocket. That device, which is nowhere explained
in this scene, is to faint near Piamont and to pick his pocket
when he stoops to assist. Middleton may have intended that
Bungler be walking with Piamont in unheard conversation
during Pursenet's diatribe against one-handed salutes and
that Pursenet suddenly get the idea for his 'device' after he
says 'at once'. By interrupting the two other men and asking
Bungler, 'Do you walk, sir?', Pursenet gets closer to his prey
without seeming to single him out. Piamont's line beginning
'Farewell then, sir—' would then be a courteous departure in
response to Pursenet's interruption, and Pursenet's fainting
device might follow it immediately. In this way Eld's text
might be played so as to make sense on stage, though it
reads less well than Dyce's alteration.

4.4.37.1–3 *He...and Boy*] THIS EDITION. See 4.6.1–4. Dyce conjectures that 'a portion of this scene has dropt out, and that
the incident of the swoon took place here on the stage, after
Pursenet had tried all other mean of surprising Piamont's
caution' (291). Bald ('Foul Papers', 42) agrees: 'It is unlike
Middleton (or any other playwright, for that matter) to dramatize the unsuccessful attempt to rob Pyamont, and then pass
over so cursorily the trick which secured the prize'. Lines may
be missing, or the script may not have been fully written at
this point. But the action can be silent and need not have required any text. In the James Madison University production,
this stage business simply occurred during the conversation
between Bungler and Goldstone. We here identify it instead
as a piece of self-contained mime. Bungler seems likely to be
involved in assisting Pursenet, as this creates a situation in
which Piamont has occasion to address him afterwards (but
see previous note).

4.4.75 *Exeunt*] Exit. ELD

4.5.16   gentleman] DYCE; gentlemen ELD

4.5.21, 22   guests] ELD (gueſſe)

4.5.37   Yea] ELD (Yee)

4.5.44   have not] DYCE; haue ELD

4.5.45, 55   ye] ELD (yea)

4.5.55   BUNGLER] ELD (Bun.); Gol. BULLEN. Bullen appears to think this line is Goldstone promoting his trick, but it might just as easily be Bungler arguing that his own 'humour'—his ability to keep his countenance—will contribute to the jest. Goldstone's next line, 'Faith, I'll try you for once,' is thus his submission to Bungler's assurance.

4.5.65   your] DYCE; you ELD

4.5.75   stay] DYCE; ſtray ELD

4.5.91   MARMADUKE] Mar. ELD (c.w.); Man. ELD (text)

4.5.92   board] DYCE; boore ELD

4.5.93   cousin?—(Sings) Cousin] DYCE; couzen:—ſings—couzen ELD. Dyce, by putting 'Cousin, cousin, did call, coz?' into italics, suggests that these are the words that Bungler sings. The point seems right, that Bungler is so childlike in his excitement about being part of a prank that he acts suspiciously. In this case he 'sings' his words like one who ruins a surprise party might in a sing-song way tell the honouree that 'someone's having a birthday today'.

4.5.94   cozen] THIS EDITION (JJ); couze ELD. Editors usually take 'couze' as a spelling of coz. But there seems to be play on the expression to call cousins (i.e., familiarly to call each other cousins) and cozen as 'cheat'; coz will not tolerate the latter.

4.7.7   sweet] DYCE; ſeewte ELD

4.7.22.1   whisper] position as in DYCE; follows previous line in ELD

4.7.26   goldsmith] DYCE; goldsmits ELD

4.7.30   is] DYCE; 'tis ELD

4.7.46-7   FIRST CONSTABLE ... SECOND CONSTABLE] Cunſt. ... 1. ELD. Eld's numerically identified First Constable is the second one to speak. The prefix '1.' continues to 4.7.65-6, and returns at 4.7.78; elsewhere the prefix is 'Cunst.' (or 'Cun.'). Dyce, Bullen, and Colegrove identify Eld's 'Cunst.', the first constable to speak, as the Second Constable. To simplify matters, this edition names the first speaker as 'First Constable' and the second speaker as 'Second Constable', and continues accordingly to distinguish between 'Cunst.' and '1.'.

4.7.101   Let't] THIS EDITION (JJ); lets ELD; Let DYCE

4.7.121   a'] ELD (a)

4.7.141   a-swash] THIS EDITION (JJ); aſway ELD. DYCE emended 'lookt asway' to 'look, a' 's way'. OED's quotations catch the contemptuous sense of a-swash: 'Se how she loketh ashosshe, or aswasshe, is she nat a prowde dame' (1530), 'huffingly, swaggeringly, aswash' (1611). The literal sense is 'obliquely, aslant', from which we understand 'suspicious' (compare askance), but in light of these quotations we also gloss 'swaggering'.

4.7.145   out] DYCE. This is the usual editorial reading, though ELD evidently reads 'ont', which, as 'on't', would make a kind of sense.

4.7.185   ALL THE REST] All. ELD. Likewise 4.7.208.

4.7.202   Truth] ELD (troth)

4.7.208   Admiral] ELD (Admirall); Admirable DYCE. OED offer two instances of admiral as an adjective, dated 1611 and ?1650, describing it as a by-form of admirable caused by confusion with sb. admiral.

4.7.228   staged] DYCE; ELD (ſta'gde)

4.7.229   Are...Bowser] DYCE; why what lacks Bowſer, are you too well, too ſafe ELD

4.7.244   ALL THE GALLANTS] ELD (All.)

4.7.272   possibly] THIS EDITION (RAC); poſſible ELD

4.7.274.2   Finis Actus Quartus] THIS EDITION; not in ELD

5.1.37   scratch] DYCE; ſcrath ELD

5.1.38   others] DYCE; vs ELD

5.1.64   NEWCUT] DYCE; not in ELD. Newcut alone has previously mentioned a husband, and indeed the scene seems to be making comic play of her new widow's attire.

5.1.66   THIRD COURTESAN] ELD (3.). DYCE, observing that the Third Courtesan 'had "set her affections" on Tailby', attributes the speech to the First Courtesan. We see no reason, however, why one courtesan might not willingly vouch for another in bringing Goldstone's oaths in question ('in this who would not feign', 5.1.68); or, alternatively, why Goldstone might not have made promises to another courtesan without respect to where her affections had been set.

5.1.71   FITZGRAVE] DYCE; Frip. ELD

5.1.73-4   FIRST GENTLEMAN-GALLANT...SECOND GENTLEMAN-GALLANT] 1. Gal. ... 2. Gal. ELD. These prefixes signal that from here on in the scene speech-prefixes consisting of numbers only (except 5.1.96, '2. Gal.') refer to gallants, not courtesans. This edition (JJ) introduces the more specific designation 'Gentleman-Gallants', (a) to accord with Eld's description of what are almost certainly the same figures as 'Gentlemen' in 3.3 and at 5.2.18.5-8, (b) to distinguish them from the two Ancient Gentlemen in 5.2, and (c) to distinguish them from the five rogue-gallants.

5.1.75   BUNGLER] DYCE; 3. ELD. Similarly 5.1.99. Should these lines be spoken by Piamont, who has already been given appropriate speech-prefixes at 5.1.80 and 5.1.90, or Bungler, who is given appropriate speech-prefixes later in the scene at 5.1.190 and, problematically, at 5.1.196 (see note)? As Bullen remarked, 'Hitherto Bungler has been represented as an arrant ass,—the last person Fitzgrave would have taken into his confidence' (234). But clearly Bungler is indeed one of the trusted gentleman-gallants. The immediate context leads one to favour Bungler over Piamont, because he is the only gentleman-gallant not otherwise identified in the passage. Moreover, Bungler, unlike Piamont, has previously, at 2.1.105-10, had a conversation with Primero, and it is the mention of his name that provokes the interjection at 5.1.99. Oblique confirmation comes from 5.1.83-4. These lines are given no separate speech-prefix in Eld, but as a riposte to the Gentleman-Gallant's apparent failure to understand Latin they need attributing to another figure. That figure is again most likely to be Bungler, and for a similar reason: the discussion of how those who are not university scholars fail to understand Latin tags likewise picks up from the conversation between Bungler and Primero in 2.1. There is therefore a point of reference shared between 5.1.83-4 and 5.1.99, and it is reasonable to suppose that Bungler spoke both.

5.1.83   BUNGLER] THIS EDITION (RAC); not in ELD; Sec. G. DYCE. See previous note.

5.1.101   Occultos] DYCE; occulos ELD

5.1.104   SECOND GENTLEMAN-GALLANT Excellently] ELD (text) (2. Excellently); 1. Exccel. ELD (c.w.)

5.1.117   their] DYCE; their | their ELD

5.1.144-5   Bowser. | FITZGRAVE First] DYCE; Bowcer, firſt ELD. The speech-prefixes in this passage must have been inadequately marked.

5.1.160-1   her.' | TAILBY Right] THIS EDITION (RAC); her, right ELD

5.1.196   FITZGRAVE] DYCE; Bungl. ELD. Bungler is watching the proceedings from above, and it is unlikely that even he would address one of the gallants on whom he is spying. The compositor might have misinterpreted 'Bou.', standing for Fitzgrave's disguised role of Bowser (as at 5.1.204-5 and 5.1.213), influenced by 'Bungl.' a few lines above at 5.1.190.

5.1.198 You] THIS EDITION (JJ); *Purſ.* You ELD; FIT You DYCE. It may be suspected that the correspondence between speech-prefixes and dialogue was thrown out because 'You haue it ſir' was written on a separate line in the manuscript. See also following note.

5.1.199 PURSENET] DYCE; *Boy.* ELD

5.1.204 Master] THIS EDITION (JJ); *Bou.* Maiſter ELD; FIT Master DYCE (*assigning* 'These...father', 5.1.202-5, *to the Boy*). Eld provides two consecutive speech-prefixes for Fitzgrave: 'Ftif.' at 5.1.202-3 and 'Bou.' (his disguised role as Bowser) at 5.1.204-5. As the latter form appears again at 5.1.213, there is nothing uniquely irregular about it. The duplication probably occurs because the speech switches from recitation of the speech to 'Bowser's' interjection to Goldstone. It may appear that the recitation more properly belongs to the Boy. This would apply equally to 5.1.210-11, which Dyce also reassigns—but the double error is implausible, and in Eld the Boy specifically hands over to Fitzgrave at 5.1.202: 'To you Maister, proceede'. Perhaps he is not yet 'perfect' in his speech after all. The difficulty in the passage lies not simply in explaining the distribution of speeches between the Boy and Fitzgrave, but in understanding why the insults do not offend the gallants when there is no alternative official script. It seems likely that the insults are part of the script itself, which we have been told will be in Latin and will 'present their dispositions more liberally' (5.1.117). Evidently the Latin is mostly translated for the sake of the audience, but it is to be imagined that the gallants are hearing the original Latin.

5.1.210 a] DYCE; an ELD

5.1.211 *corporis*] DYCE; *corpus* ELD

5.1.230 that] THIS EDITION (RAC); the ELD

5.1.232 sheriff] DYCE (*shrieve*); Sheerſe ELD

5.1.234 Exeunt] '(Exit.' *bracketed as turn-over on following type-line* ELD

5.2.6 charms] DYCE; ſwarmes ELD

5.2.9 [SINGERS] [*within*]] THIS EDITION (JJ); *not in* ELD

5.2.18.15-5.2.23 *The...her*] In ELD the lines first identified by DYCE as stage directions for the gallants to bow are printed as if they were speeches ('Purſn. Bowes to her.', etc.), and each line that Katherine speaks has its own speech-prefix for her to do so. Eld's direction '*The speech: their action.*' strongly implies a tabular layout in the manuscript. This edition (JJ) is the first to re-establish it.

5.2.24 Are] *Kath.* Are ELD

5.2.37 no sort to be] THIS EDITION (RAC); new forth to ELD. Bullen questions the original, which makes no sense; clearly Fitzgrave's 'Betrayed?' means, as he explains, that he finds betrayal inappropriate for such unworthy creatures.

5.2.48 FIRST ANCIENT GENTLEMAN] I. ELD

5.2.48 SECOND ANCIENT GENTLEMAN] 2. ELD

5.2.90 when they] DYCE; when the ELD

5.2.91 They] DYCE; The ELD

5.2.92 FITZGRAVE] DYCE; *not in* ELD

5.2.98-9 And...down.] *set off with two lines of blank space and printed in italic in* ELD

5.2.99.1 *Exeunt*] DYCE; *not in* ELD. It is possible that the actors stayed on stage for their ovation before making an exit, and it is even possible in an indoor theatre that, following the applause, some or all of the actors may have mingled in the house. But in the present text the absence of a stage direction does not in itself have particular significance.

Parts ELD gives no list of persons. In the final scene there are altogether no less than eighteen people on the stage who in this scene or earlier have speaking parts. This assumes that the five shield-boys are made up of two Courtesans, the Novice, Newcut, and Pursenet's Boy. If, instead, a third Courtesan played a shield-boy and Pursenet's Boy had a separate role, the total would be nineteen. On the two gentlemen or gallants consolidated as 'Gentleman-Gallants' in this edition, see note to 5.1.73-4. A saving of boy actors could have been achieved if two adults involved in producing the play stepped in to play the two 'Ancient Gentlemen', who speak just one line apiece. By redistributing some lines in the final scene, the James Madison University production managed with only twelve actors (see Textual Introduction). The only other time there was a problem was when Frip calls for Arthur in 2.4 and an actor playing that part was onstage doubling as Fulk.

PRESS VARIANTS

Colegrove collated the eleven extant copies of *Your Five Gallants*, which are as follows:

BOD Bodleian Library
BL 1 British Library, C. 34 d. 44
BL 2 British Library, 162 d. 29
DYCE 1 Dyce Collection, National Art Library, Victoria and Albert Museum, 6550 18. K. 28
DYCE 2 Dyce Collection, National Art Library, Victoria and Albert Museum, 6550 26. Box 32. 3
ETON Eton College Library
HARV Harvard University Library
HUNT Huntington Library
LCON Library of Congress
PFOR Pforzheimer Collection, University of Texas at Austin
YALE Yale University, Elizabethan Club

We reproduce in full the press variants noted by Colegrove. A number result from uneven inking or loose type, sometimes producing incompatible groups of copies showing variant readings within a single forme. In the formes affected, the readings that most certainly represent true stop-press corrections are marked with an asterisk below.

Sheet B (outer forme)

Sig. B2ᵛ

*1.2.47 me. If] BL 1, BL 2, DYCE 2, HARV, PFOR, YALE; ~, if *others*

Sig. B3

1.2.84 graced] grac'd *all but* HUNT; grac d HUNT
1.2.85 observed] obſeru'd *all but* BOD; obſeru d BOD

Sheet C (outer forme)

Sig. C1

2.1.113 have] haue BOD, BL 2, DYCE 1, ETON, HARV, YALE; ha e *others*

Sheet C (inner forme)

Sig. C1ᵛ

2.1.122 ladies] Lad ies BL 1, BL 2; Ladi es *others*

Sheet D (outer forme)

Sig. D3^v

2.4.274   sir,] BL 1, DYCE 1, DYCE 2; ~. LCON; ~$_\wedge$ *others*

Sheet D (inner forme)

Sig. D2

2.4.131   dice!] ~. BL 1, DYCE 1, LCON, YALE; ~$_\wedge$ *others*

Sheet F (outer forme)

Sig. F2^v

Interim 2.0.1   plays] *'plaies' all but* LCON; plai s LCON

Interim 2.0.1   Tailby] Taylbee *all but* BOD; Taylb e BOD

Interim 2.18   Jack,] Iacke$_\wedge$ BL 1, HARV; Iacke, *others*

*Interim 2.24   you] BOD, BL 2, DYCE 2, ETON, HARV, HUNT, PFOR, YALE; your BL 1, LCON, DYCE 1

Interim 2.27   playing:] ~$_\wedge$ BOD, BL 2, DYCE 2, YALE

*Interim 2.28–9   now down…rise to] and nowne,…down-rise…if | your yeares riseto BL 1, DYCE 1; and nowne,… downe rise…if | your yeares riseto LCON; now downe,… rise…if your | yeares rise to *others*

*Interim 2.31   that's] whats BL 1, DYCE 1, LCON; thats *others*

Interim 2.31   reason] rea on HARV; reafon *others*

Sig. F3

Interim 2.66   do.] ~$_\wedge$ BL 1, DYCE 1, LCON, YALE; ~. *others*

Interim 2.80   you, your] HUNT, LCON; ~, ~ *others*

Sheet G (outer forme)

Sig. G4^v

4.7.26   goldsmith,] goldsmits, BL 1, BL 2, DYCE 2, LCON, PFOR, YALE; goldsmits$_\wedge$ *others*

Sheet G (inner forme)

Sig. G1^v

4.4.0.1   Enter] Ente HARV, LCON, YALE

Sig. G2

*4.4.32   Where's] where s BOD, HARV, HUNT

Sig. G3^v

4.6.4   much$_\wedge$] *comma printed in* BL 1, BL 2, DYCE 2, HUNT, *badly inked or broken in* ETON, LCON; *not visible in* BOD, DYCE 1, HARV, PFOR, YALE

Sig. G4

*running title   GALLANTS BOD, HARV, HUNT; GALLA NTS *others*

Sheet H (outer forme)

Sig. H1

4.7.52   whilst,] *all but* DYCE 1; ~; DYCE 1

Sheet H (inner forme)

Sig. H2

*4.7.168–70   while?…brothers…i'faith?]   ~?…~?…~?   *all but* LCON; ~,…~,…~. LCON

4.7.170   on's] on s BL 1, DYCE, ETON, HUNT

Sig. H3^v

5.1.1   wary,] ~$_\wedge$ HUNT

*5.1.7–8   twitterlights; | You] ~$_\wedge$ you LCON; ~,y ou *others*

5.1.12   you,] BOD, DYCE 2; ~, *others*

5.1.18–19   rose-leaves] ~, DYCE 1, ETON, HARV, LCON, PFOR; ~$_\wedge$ *others*

*5.1.20   smooth] fmoothe *all but* LCON; Smouthe LCON

Sheet I (outer forme)

Sig. I1

5.1.116   compendious] BL 2, DYCE 1, DYCE 2, HARV; compend ous *others*

Sig. I2^v

5.2.18.12   her [Katherine];] her, BL 2, DYCE 1, DYCE 2, HARV, HUNT, PFOR; ~$_\wedge$ *others*

Sig. I3

5.2.44   contains—] containes. HARV, LCON; ~, *others*

STAGE DIRECTIONS

Prologue.0.1–Prologue.8   *Presenter or prologue, passing ouer the Stage, the Bawde-gallant, | with three wenches gallantly attirde, meetes him, the whore-Gal-|lant, the pocket-Gallant, the cheating-Gallant, kisse these three | wenches, and depart in a little whisper and wanton action: now | for the other the Broker--Gallant, hee sits at home yet I warrant | you, at this time of day, summing vp his pawnes, hactcnus quasi | inductio, a little glimpse giuing.*

Prologue.8.2–1.1.0.3   *Enter a fellow.*

1.1.5.1   *starts back.*

1.1.54.1   *Exit.*

1.1.58.1   *Enter his man bringing a trunke.* (right, opposite 1.1.60)

1.1.111.1   *Enter Bawde-Gallant, Primero?*

1.1.278   *Exit Prime.* (right, opposite 1.1.277)

1.1.330.1   *Exit.*

1.2.0.1   *Enter Misters Katherine with Fitsgraue a Gentleman.*

1.2.26.1–2   *Enter fiue Gallants at the farther dore.* (after 1.2.27)

1.2.65.1   *Exit.*

1.2.66.2   *They looke scuruily vpon* Fitsgraue, *and he vpon them.* (after 'Exit.', 1.2.65.1)

1.2.68.1–2   *The boy in a corner, with his | maister pocket-Gallant.* (right, opposite ll. 66–7)

1.2.81   *Exit.*

1.2.97.1–2   *Exit.*

2.1.0.1–2   ACTVS. 2. | *Enter* Primero, *the Bawde-Gallant, meeting* Mistresse | New-cut *a Marchants wife.*

2.1.53.1–2   *Enter, All* (right, opposite 2.1.55–6)

2.1.120.1–5   *The Song, and hee keepes time, showes | seuerall humors and moods: the boy in | his pocket nims away* Fitsgraues | Iewell here, *and exit.*

2.1.296   *Exeunt.*

2.1.296.1   *Enter whore-Gallant.*

2.1.316.1   *Exit.*

2.1.345.1   *Exeunt.*

2.2.0.1   *Enter Fitsgraue.*

2.2.21   *Exit.*

2.2.25.1   *Exit.*

2.3.0.1   *Enter Whore Gal.* (right, opposite 2.3.1)

2.3.30   *Exit.*

2.4.0.1–2   *Enter all at once.* (right, opposite 2.4.1)

2.4.18   *Within*

2.4.418   *Finis Actus 3.*

3.1.0.2   ACTVS. 4. | *Enter* Taylbee *reading a letter.*

3.1.1   *reads.*

3.1.102   *Exit.*
3.3.0.1   *Enter two Gentlemen.*
3.3.16.1   *Exit.*
3.4.0.1–2   *Enter Pursnet and his 1. Curt.*
3.4.96.1   *he thumps*
3.4.155.1   *Exeunt all but* Gold; *and Curtisan.*
3.4.179   *Exeunt.*
Interim 1.0.1–3   *In the midst of the musick, enter one bringing in a suite of Satin, | knocks at Taylbees doore, enter his man.*
Interim 2.0.1–2   *The Musicke plaies on a while, then en-|ter; Taylbee his man after trussing him.*
Interim 2.75.1   *Enter another.*
Interim 2.95.1   *Exit.*
4.1.0.3   *Enter* Goldstone *calling Maister Bowser.*
4.2.0.1   *Enter Frip.*
4.2.13.1   *Enter Pursnet.*
4.2.19   *Exit.*
4.2.19.1   *Enter Fitsgraue.*
4.3.0.1   *Enter* Goldst: *and Gall.*
4.3.40   *Exit* Bung. (right, opposite 4.3.39)
4.3.40.1–2   *Enter Fitsgraue.*
4.3.70   *Exit.* Goldst. (right, opposite 4.3.69)
4.3.92   *Exit.*
4.4.0.1   *Ente Pursnet and his boy.*
4.4.5.1   *Enter Piamont.*
4.4.46.1   *Enter* Goldst. *and his man disguisde both.*
4.4.75   *Exit.*
4.5.0.1   *Enter Mistresse* New-cut *and Marmaduke.*
4.5.19.1   *Enter Bungler and* Goldst. *disguized.*
4.5.108.1   *Enter Goldstone.*
4.5.119.1   *Exeunt.*
4.6.0.1   *Enter Pyamont.*
4.6.12.1   *Enter Pursnet.*

4.6.49   *Exit.*
4.7.22.1   *whisper.* (right, opposite 4.7.21)
4.7.22.1   *Enter Taylbee.*
4.7.274.1   *Exeunt.*
5.1.0.1–4   ACT. 5. | *Enter Curtizans.*
5.1.29.1   *Enter Fitsgraue.*
5.1.70.1   *Exeunt.*
5.1.79   *Exit.*
5.1.234   (*Exit.* (bracketed as turn-over on following type-line)
5.2.0.1   *Enter the Virgin betweene two antient gentlemen.*
5.2.8.1–5.2.9   *Himne.*
5.2.18.1   *Cornets.*
5.2.18.2–14   *Enter the maske, thus ordered. A torchbearer, a sheeld-|-boy, | then a masker, so throughout, then the sheeld boyes fall at one end, | the torchbearers at the other; the maskers ith middle, the torch-|bearers are the fiue gentlemen: the sheeld-boies the whores in boies | apparel: the maskers the fiue Gallants, they bow to her she rises | and shewes the like, they dance but first deliuer the sheeldes vp; shee | reades.*
5.2.18.14–15   *The speech : their action.*
5.2.19   *Pursn. Bowes to her.*
5.2.20   *Gold. Bowes to her.*
5.2.21   *Tailbe Bowes to her.*
5.2.22   *Prim. Bowes to her.*
5.2.23   *Frip. Bowes to her.*
5.2.25.1–6   *They going to dance, each vnhaspes his weapon from his side, | and giues em to the torch-bearers.* Katherine *seemes dis-|trustfull, but then* Fisgraue *whispers to her and falls backe. | At the end of which all making an honor,* Frip *presents her | with that chaine of Pearle.*
5.2.27.1   *Pursnet stamps.*
5.2.28.1   *All lay hands on him.*
5.2.99.2   FINIS.

LINEATION NOTES

1.1.133–6   Well...hands] DYCE; *prose* ELD
1.1.142   That happens...yours] DYCE; *verse* ELD: well|
1.1.153–4   'Twas...year] DYCE; *1 line* ELD
1.1.156–7   Many...patrimonies] THIS EDITION (RAC); fatted| ELD. These lines probably scan with 'over' and 'With the' monosyllabic, and '-ed me' as an amphibious foot.
1.1.269–71   I...enough] DYCE; *prose* ELD
1.1.274–5   Nothing...face] DYCE; *prose* ELD (but type-line ends 'place')
1.1.278–9   I...brightness] DYCE; *1 line* ELD
1.1.302–12   Nor...worse] DYCE; *prose* ELD
1.1.326   Quick...daughter] THIS EDITION (JJ); Quick...Now *prose*, To...daughter *verse-line* ELD
1.2.20–2   Vouchsafe...kept] DYCE; kept| beads| ELD. Dyce unscrambled the following:

Vouchsafe vnequalld Virgin whereon I iustly kept,
Accept this worthlesse fauor from your seruants arme, the hal-
The true and perfect number of my sighs. (lowed beades,

1.2.24–5   Mine...sake] DYCE; *1 line* ELD
1.2.33–4   See...themselves] DYCE; *prose* ELD
1.2.37–9   I take your wishes...insulted] COLEGROVE; I take... suits *prose*, I ne'er insulted *verse-line* ELD
1.2.73–4   Active...soul] DYCE; *1 line* ELD. The compositor seems to have been saving space in this speech to enable Act 1 to end at the foot of the page (sig. B3), presumably in

accordance with the casting-off mark. See the two following notes.
1.2.77–80   Hope...alone] THIS EDITION (JJ); *3 lines* ELD: rank| cause|; *5 lines* DYCE: purchase| rank| cause| it|
2.1.165–6   'Slight...heart] DYCE; on't| ELD
2.1.177–8   Than...me] DYCE; do| ELD
2.1.218   I'll...gallants] COLEGROVE; *2 lines* ELD: tonight|; *speech in prose* DYCE
2.1.226–7   Why...far] DYCE; *verse* ELD: mind|
2.1.228–30   ALL...away] See textual note to 2.1.228–9.
2.1.233–4   Nothing...fury] DYCE; *1 line* ELD
2.1.236–7   Whoo...noise] DYCE; *1 line* ELD
2.1.243–4   How...favour] DYCE; *1 line* ELD
2.1.292–3   More...sir] DYCE; *1 line* ELD
2.1.295–6   The...them] DYCE; *1 line* ELD
2.1.302–3   Push...garden] THIS EDITION (RAC); *1 line* ELD; walk| DYCE; did| COLEGROVE
2.1.318–20   Pox...longing] DYCE; *prose* ELD
2.1.327–8   By this...dear self] DYCE; *prose* ELD
2.1.329–30   Ha...soul] THIS EDITION (RAC); *1 line* ELD
2.1.330–1   Ay...oaths] DYCE; *1 line* ELD
2.1.342–3   Forgive...ring] DYCE; *1 line* ELD
2.2.7–8   But...he] DYCE; *1 line* ELD
2.2.22–4   Thou'rt...stol'n] DYCE; *verse-line* (yet|) *followed by prose* ELD
2.3.2–3   Hath...married] DYCE; *1 line* ELD
2.3.10–11   Valle...lillo] THIS EDITION (RAC); *1 line* ELD

2.3.12–13 Vallee...lillo] THIS EDITION (RAC); *1 line* ELD

2.4.7–8 Ourselves...ho] DYCE; *1 line* ELD

2.4.11–13 Ay...three] DYCE; *prose* ELD

2.4.107–8 As...others] DYCE; *verse* ELD: i'faith |

2.4.126–30 Has...her] DYCE (*also setting* 'Here's...rose-noble' (2.4.124–5) *as verse:* angel |); *prose* ELD

2.4.155–6 'Tis...men] THIS EDITION (RAC); *verse* ELD: sir |

2.4.352 All's...welcome] DYCE; *verse-line* ELD

Interim 2.86–9 Faith...keeps] DYCE; *prose* ELD

Interim 2.92–3 Well...hair] THIS EDITION (JJ); *3 lines* ELD: i'faith | legs |; *3 lines* DYCE: i'faith | me |. Dyce added the metrical emendation 'still' after 'friends'.

3.1.13 Who...carouse] DYCE; *prose* ELD

3.1.30–3 This...Boy] DYCE; *2 lines* ELD: greet |

3.1.105–13 Let me...heaven] DYCE; *prose* ELD

3.1.118–27 'Master...nothing.'] DYCE. In ELD the material in quotations appears in italics and Pursenet's interjections follow on the next type-line, with the exception of 'A pox... wench:' which follows *royals in't...* after a space on the same line.

3.1.175–6 Deliver...boy] THIS EDITION (JJ); *prose* ELD

3.1.182–3 I have...I go] DYCE; *prose* ELD

3.2.17–22 My...high] THIS EDITION (JJ); *prose* ELD (*omitting* 'high')

3.2.23–6 Or take...then] DYCE; *prose* ELD

3.4.2–3 Welcome...instantly.] DYCE; *prose* ELD

3.4.5–6 O...delight, my] THIS EDITION (JJ); remain | ELD

3.4.14–15 'Twas...you] DYCE; *1 line* ELD

3.4.85–6 Who...it] DYCE; me | ELD

3.4.112–17 Thou graceless...o'er 'em!] DYCE; *prose* ELD

4.3.71 You...then] *verse-line* ELD. In the manuscript the line-break probably anticipated the exit Eld misplaces on the previous line.

4.3.77 The...forehead] DYCE; *prose* ELD

4.4.30–1 O...leisure] THIS EDITION (JJ); *prose* ELD. The mock-Ciceronian lament is fitting as verse, and by Middletonian criteria scans adequately. *Grown* (ELD 'growne') might be disyllabic (growen).

4.4.32–5 Where's...had it] DYCE (*but dividing* 'Or...forgot' *after* 'waist'); *prose* ELD. The line Dyce divides is probably a hexameter with 'Or the' and 'with the' both pronounced as monosyllables.

4.4.74–5 Nay...cousin.] DYCE; *verse* ELD: way, cousin |

4.5.25–6 There...faithfully] DYCE; *verse* ELD: coz |

4.6.41–3 The...sir] DYCE; *verse* ELD: Paul's |

4.7.11–20 He...you] THIS EDITION (JJ); *prose* ELD; lives not | look'st not | ground | pearl | *then as this edition* DYCE; conveyance | *then as this edition to* 'matter', 4.7.19, *then prose* RAC *conj.*

4.7.100–1 Now...i'faith] DYCE; *prose* ELD

4.7.124–9 Another's...mine] DYCE *prose* ELD

4.7.199–204 With...shall choose] DYCE; *prose* ELD

4.7.209–10 For instance...done] DYCE; *1 line* ELD

4.7.228–31 You'll...operation] DYCE; *prose* ELD

4.7.239–41 Pawn...five] THIS EDITION (RAC); *prose* ELD; brothers | DYCE

5.1.8–9 You...suspicion] DYCE; *prose* ELD

5.1.43–5 Why...night] ELD *begins a new type-line after* 'marriage', *but otherwise sets as prose*

5.1.52–5 You...pleasure you] DYCE; *prose* ELD

5.1.61–2 Will...Hark you] THIS EDITION (JJ); *1 line* ELD

5.1.63 And...match] DYCE; *2 lines* ELD: another |

5.1.65 Goldstone...me] DYCE; *2 lines* ELD: marriage |

5.1.95 *Fratremque patremque*] *on a separate type-line* ELD

5.1.101 the...*honores*] *on a separate type-line* ELD

5.2.18 Anon...found.] COLEGROVE; *1 line* ELD

5.2.45–7 You...bawd] DYCE; *prose* ELD. The switch to prose occurs across a forme-break (I3–I3ᵛ), and is probably compositorial.

A MAD WORLD, MY MASTERS

Edited by Peter Saccio

A Mad World, My Masters (*BEPD* 276) was entered in the Stationers' Register on 4 October 1608. Blayney transcribes the entry as follows:

> Wa. Burre. Entred for their copie vnder
> Elea. Edgar. the hand*e* of m^{r} Segar deputy
> of S^{r}. Geo. Bucke / and the
> Wardens Hand*e* also beinge
> to yt. A Booke called. A Mad
> World (my Maysters)
> } vj^{d}

The title-page of the ensuing quarto edition (STC 17888) advertises the play '*As it hath bin lately in Action by the Children of Paules*' and asserts that it was 'Printed by *H.B.* for WALTER BVRRE, and are to be sold in Paules Church--yard, at the signe of the Crane. 1608.' Greg identified H.B. as Henry Ballard, but Henning discovered that the printing was in fact divided between the shops of Henry Ballard (signatures A–E) and Nicholas Okes (signatures F–H and the half-sheet I). In the present text, the break between the two sections falls at 3.3.116–18. BALLARD–OKES divides the text into numbered acts. Scenes are not numbered, and the use of blank space to mark scene--breaks is variable in both sections.

The title-page of the second edition (STC 17889) asserts that the play 'hath bin often Acted at the Private House in *Salisbury Court*, by her Majesties Servants' (i.e. Queen Henrietta's Men). It was 'Printed for *J.S.* and are to be sold by *James Becket*, at his Shop in the inner Temple Gate. 1640.' Greg identified J.S. as John Spencer and the unnamed printer as John Okes, Nicholas's son. (In the textual commentary below, the 1640 edition will be identified as J. OKES to distinguish it from the OKES section of 1608.) J. OKES adds five items to the text, none of which can be attributed to Middleton: a preface to the reader signed with Spencer's initials, a list of dramatis personae, stage directions at the ends of Acts 2 and 5 presumably reflecting production at Salisbury Court, and 'The Catch for the Fifth Act, sung by Sir Bounteous Progress to his guests'. (As Bullen noted, this song, 'Oh for a Bowl of fat Canary', was first printed in 1632 as part of *Campaspe* 1.2 in Edward Blount's edition of John Lyly's *Six Court Comedies*. Although Lyly's plays call for songs, none appear in the original quartos: the authorship of the songs Blount printed is unknown.) Aside from these items J. OKES is a reprint of BALLARD–OKES, amending a few errors and adding more. BALLARD–OKES is our only authority for the text of *Mad World*.

The Ballard section of the 1608 edition is well printed: the surviving ten copies exhibit no variants and relatively few errors. Eberle and Taylor, relying chiefly on the abbreviation of speech headings and the use of apostrophes in contractions, discerned two compositors at work. They assign to one compositor the whole of sheets A, B, and C (1.1.1–2.6.47), as well as D4^{v}–E2^{r} (3.2.42–192) and the final page, E4^{v} (3.3.75–118). They assign to a second compositor D1^{r}–D4^{r} (2.6.48–3.2.41) and E3^{v}–E4^{r} (3.2.266–3.3.74). They differ over other passages in the Ballard section. Eberle admits that the evidence for some of these assignments is slight.

Although unaware that sheets F–I were printed in a different shop, Eberle and Taylor recognized from the introduction of a new set of running titles that printing had been somehow interrupted. All twentieth-century editors have concluded that the N. OKES section of the play was set by an inept compositor, some of whose frequent blunders were corrected in press. Blayney prints the fullest list of variants. Eight pages (six in sheet F and two in sheet H) exhibit no variants in the surviving copies. Two pages in sheet F (3.3.159–4.1.58) and the remainder of the play from 4.5.0.2–4.5.1 (with the exception of the two pages in H, 5.1.105–45 and 5.2.185–227) exist in both uncorrected and corrected states, with seven of these pages manifesting an additional phase of correction.

Eberle, Taylor, and Henning suppose that the printer's copy used was an autograph copy, perhaps 'foul papers'. Eberle develops the argument most fully, considering the patterns of spelling and contraction, and errors supposedly arising from ambiguous handwriting, in relation to the autograph MS of *A Game at Chess* at the Huntington Library. Since some autograph features might well be preserved in a scribal copy, since a compositor may in turn select among such features, and since Eberle also used such features to distinguish among compositors, conclusions about the precise nature of the copy are unwarranted. Whatever the origin of the copy, the stage directions show an interesting mixture of vagueness and precision. It is not clear how many watchmen appear in 1.2 or how many comrades Follywit has (Lieutenant, Ensign, one to play the Footman, and at least one more since four speak serially in 5.2). On the other hand, the ceremonies of arrival and welcome at Sir Bounteous's house in 2.1 and the stage arrangements surrounding the Courtesan in 3.2 are detailed with some elaboration. These directions were written by some one whose imaginative or real eye was keen for theatrical effect.

Despite the variants in the OKES section of 1608, *Mad World* presents relatively few editorial problems. In the first and second editions of *Old Plays*, Dodsley and Reed satisfactorily emended about half of the puzzling readings in BALLARD–OKES that had not been already corrected by J. OKES. This edition departs from earlier ones in only two major respects. At 4.3.54 Follywit, disguised as the Courtesan, leaves a room in Sir Bounteous's house with the latter's jewels. Sir Bounteous then enters for a soliloquy and remains for a scene with Gunwater. Presumably because the fictional location remains the same, previous editions mark this as one continuous scene. Follywit's exit, however, momentarily clears the stage of all actors, and his parting words form an emphatic rhymed couplet directed at the audience. I have therefore marked his exit with a scene break, indicating Sir Bounteous's soliloquy and dialogue with Gunwater as 4.4. The remaining scenes of Act 4 become 4.5 (Penitent's second repentance scene) and 4.6 (Follywit's wooing of the Courtesan).

The second innovation arises from a problem of nomenclature and the presence or absence of proof correction. The oddest feature of the N. OKES section of 1608 (unchanged by J. OKES) is the variation in three character names. Gunwater has become Gumwater, Master Penitent Brothel's last name is twice given as Once-Ill, and Master Harebrain is sometimes Harebrain, sometimes Hargrave, and sometimes Shortrod. Do these changes result from the incompetence of Nicholas Okes's compositor (Henning), from authorial revision (Frost), or haste and indecision on Middleton's part (a possibility considered by Eberle and Henning)?

The three cases differ. The difference between Gunwater and Gumwater is a simple minin error, easily attributable to a compositor. As Henning argued, the overall superiority of Ballard's compositors suggests that they were more likely to reflect copy accurately here. 'Gunwater' is, moreover, on two grounds the more appropriate name. Gun-washings (the liquid resulting from the cleansing of guns) are suitable for a country knight's steward who is introduced receiving orders to supply game birds for a feast. The phallic associations of the name (gun + water, which often means semen in Middleton) are consistent with this character's attempt to seduce his master's mistress and with Middleton's sexual punning throughout the play.

'Once-Ill' occurs only in the stage directions opening Master Penitent's two repentance scenes (4.1 and 4.5). It reflects the character's change of heart and it echoes 'Brothel': it is thus probably authorial. Since Penitent's surname occurs nowhere else in the final acts, however, the variant is trivial and has no effect in stage performance.

In the case of Harebrain, the frequency and grouping of the variants create a more complex problem. Harebrain's wife is referred to as 'Mistress Hargrave' twice in the dialogue between Penitent and Jasper at 4.1.75–6. 'Hargrave' then recurs in 4.5, twice in dialogue, twice in stage directions, and once as an abbreviated speech heading (*Harg.*). On the same page (G2^r) as this speech heading and one of the stage directions, Harebrain's four

other speeches in the scene are prefixed by his full original surname. 'Hargrave' thus appears to be a simple (and quite possible) misreading by an inept compositor, intermeddled with the original surname and uncorrected in proof. At 5.1.10 and 15–16, Sir Bounteous effusively addresses his guest as 'Master Shortrod', once at the start of a page so that 'Short-' also occurs as the catchword. The character's three speeches in this brief passage, however, are prefixed *Harebrain* and *Hareb.* (There is no entry direction naming him.) In 5.2, the character's name occurs only in his eighteen speech headings, as *Short.* (fifteen times) and *Short. R.* (thrice). Speech headings are not heard by an audience, but in this scene they mattered enough in Okes's printing shop to receive five corrections. One amends bad spacing, an operation that may be conducted without reference to copy. Three add the unnecessary *R.* to *Short.*, and the remaining one corrects a mistaken catchword between H4^r (inner forme) and H4^v (outer forme). These changes strongly suggest reference to copy and rule out what in any case is a very unlikely misreading of Jacobean handwriting. 'Shortrod' therefore appeared in the manuscript and is of course a highly appropriate name for a cuckold. It is possible that Middleton revised the character's name but carried out the revision incompletely, in which case the revision may have gone in either direction. This edition acts on a different solution, that the character's full name is Master Shortrod Harebrain, on the same pattern as Master Penitent Brothel, and that he is twice addressed as Master Shortrod in the same way that Penitent is often called Master Penitent. (Both Eberle and Taylor wonder in passing whether 'Shortrod' is a first name, but Taylor nonetheless emends to 'Harebrain'. Eberle retains 'Shortrod' where OKES prints it only because his dissertation seeks to reproduce the 1608 text verbatim.) Accordingly, although speech headings are regularized, I have retained the two dialogue uses of 'Shortrod' and used the character's full name in the list of Persons in the Play and in some stage directions. The full name points both to his own sexual anxiety and (like 'Follywit') to the madness of the whole action. It is also appropriate that he should actually be addressed as Master Shortrod by Sir Bounteous, who frequently savours his guests' names.

SEE ALSO

Text: *Works*, 417
Music and dance: this volume, 142
Authorship and date: this volume, 355

WORKS CITED

Previous Editions

Dodsley, Robert, ed., *A Select Collection of Old Plays*, vol. 5 (1744)
Reed, Isaac, ed., *A Select Collection of Old Plays. The Second Edition*, vol. 5 (1780)
Scott, Walter, ed., *The Ancient British Drama*, vol. 2 (1810)
Collier, J. Payne, ed., *A Select Collection of Old English Plays. A New Edition*, vol. 5 (1825)
Dyce, Alexander, ed., *Works*, vol. 2 (1840)

Bullen, A. H., ed., *Works*, vol. 3 (1885)

Eberle, Gerald J., ed., *A Critical Edition of Thomas Middleton's A Mad World, My Masters* (dissertation, University of Wisconsin, 1945)

Taylor, M. J., ed., *A Critical Old-Spelling Edition of Thomas Middleton's A Mad World, My Masters* (1608) (dissertation, University of Birmingham, 1963)

Henning, Standish, ed., *A Mad World, My Masters* (1965)

Salgādo, Gāmini, ed., *Four Jacobean City Comedies* (1975)

Frost, David L., ed., *The Selected Plays of Thomas Middleton* (1978)

Other Works Cited

Behn, Aphra, *The City Heiress, or, Sir Timothy Treat-all* (1682)

Blayney, Peter W. M., *The Texts of King Lear and their Origins Volume I: Nicholas Okes and the First Quarto* (1982)

Bullock, Christopher, *The Slip* (1715)

Daileader, Celia R., *Eroticism on the Renaissance Stage: Transcendence, Desire, and the Limits of the Visible* (1998)

—— 'The Courtesan Revisited: Thomas Middleton, Pietro Aretino, and Sex-Phobic Criticism', in *Italian Culture in the Drama of Shakespeare and his Contemporaries*, ed. Michele Marrapodi (forthcoming, 2007)

Eberle, Gerald J., 'The Composition and Printing of Middleton's *A Mad World, My Masters*', *Studies in Bibliography* 3 (1950), 246–52

Johnson, Charles, *The Country Lasses, or, The Custom of the Manor* (1715)

Keeffe, Barrie, *A Mad World, My Masters*, rev. edn. (1980)

Kenrick, William, *The Spendthrift, or, A Christmas Gambol* (1778)

Macnally, Leonard, *The April Fool, or, The Follies of a Night*, acted 1786. Larpent MS, Huntington Library

Moore Smith, G. C., 'Notes on Mr. K. Deighton's "The Old Dramatists: Conjectural Readings, 1896"', *Notes and Queries* 117 (1908), 302

Webster, John, *The Duchess of Malfi* (1612)

TEXTUAL NOTES

1.1.0.3 Ensign Oboe] THIS EDITION; *Antient Hoboy* BALLARD

1.1.31 And] J. OKES; dna BALLARD

1.1.71 lord] DODSLEY; L. BALLARD. This abbreviation, which is the usual but not invariable practice of BALLARD–OKES, has been expanded throughout this edition.

1.1.88.1 Master] J. OKES; M. BALLARD Usually abbreviated as *M.* or *Mast.* in BALLARD, expanded throughout this edition.

1.1.91 *Exeunt all but Penitent*] SALGĀDO; *Exit.* BALLARD. All editions from DYCE forward expand this direction to the same effect in varying words.

1.1.126 Shirt] *conj.* COLLIER; Skirt BALLARD

1.1.198 indecent] DODSLEY; un-decent BALLARD

1.1.202 well] REED; *not in* BALLARD

1.2.0.1 *Master Shortrod Harebrain*] THIS EDITION; *Mast. Harebrain* BALLARD On this character's name, see Textual Introduction.

1.2.67 a] COLLIER; *not in* BALLARD

2.1.52 (*laughs*) Puh!] COLLIER; Laughs, puh— BALLARD

2.1.84 lord's] *conj.* REED; love's BALLARD

2.1.99 is] J. OKES; in BALLARD

2.1.101 house] DODSLEY; houses BALLARD, retained by HENNING, SALGĀDO, FROST

2.2.18 champaign] DODSLEY; champion BALLARD

2.2.19 chambers] FROST (*conj.* Deighton in Moore Smith); champers BALLARD, reprinted by all editors before FROST, most expressing uncertainty about the meaning. 'Champers' may be horses, which makes sense after 'champaign grounds'. Sir Bounteous, however, speaks of something 'in my house': he may be hinting at further 'pleasure' of a 'venereal' sort. A b/p error is easy by foul case, or by eyeskip to 'champion' 4 words earlier.

2.2.27 portmanteau] REED; portmantua BALLARD. The word recurs in the robbery scenes, and is here consistently modernized.

2.4.1 A VOICE WITHIN O!] THIS EDITION; BALLARD prints '*Within.* Oh.' on the line immediately below the Courtesan's final words and the exeunt direction of 2.3, before a space marking the scene break.

2.4.13.1 [*Exeunt all but Ensign*]] THIS EDITION. The Ensign's l. 14 appears to cover the empty stage time while Follywit and the other comrades fetch Sir Bounteous.

2.4.54 not] FROST; *not in* BALLARD. Although Sir Bounteous could deliver the BALLARD reading on a note of glad, demented martyrdom, obsequiousness toward Lord Owemuch is his normal tone.

2.5.43 quacksalving] J. OKES; guacksalving BALLARD

2.5.55 Harebrain's] REED; Harebraine BALLARD

2.6.91–2 FOLLYWIT...LIEUTENANT] THIS EDITION. BALLARD assigns ''Slid, here's a house haunted indeed' to Lieutenant (without marking his entrance) and 'A word with you, sir' to Sir Bounteous. All editions follow, with DYCE adding Lieutenant's entrance direction before his line. But 'a word with you, sir' is the natural way for the entering Lieutenant to address Follywit, from whom it draws a suitably abrupt response. Sir Bounteous would not call a servant 'sir'. That leaves Follywit as the only person free to speak of the haunted house, a line appropriate to his play-acting.

2.6.111 ribbon] THIS EDITION; riband BALLARD

3.1.88 think] J. OKES; hinke BALLARD

3.2.8 'im] THIS EDITION; e'm BALLARD

3.2.104 gentlemen] J. OKES; gentleman BALLARD

3.2.115 kinds] FROST; kind BALLARD

3.2.153 gentlemen] DODSLEY; gentleman BALLARD

3.2.170.1–2 [*Penitent supplies a chamber-pot. She feigns farting and excreting*]] THIS EDITION. No previous edition specifies the action prompting the sudden exit of Inesse and Possibility after their repeated resolution to stay except FROST, who directs that the Courtesan be lifted upon a bedpan. Jacobean physicians used both emetics and laxatives ('power upward and downward', 3.2.131), but the latter is supported by the references in this scene to purgation (18–19) and stool (197 and 234). For theatrical effect the feigned action should be noisy, which is not explicit in FROST.

3.2.253 you stand] J. OKES; yous stand BALLARD

3.3.31 shrewd] DODSLEY; shrode BALLARD

3.3.144, 146 Kew] THIS EDITION; Cue N. OKES

3.3.146 Q] THIS EDITION; C N. OKES, followed by all editors, presumably because of the spelling 'Cue' and because P and C are the initial letters of two 'landing places for lechers', prick and cunt. But this reading, as well as overlooking a familiar alphabetical sequence, prefers a written pun to a spoken one: Cue/Kew sounds not like C but like Q, and queue, the tail, is another well-known site of lechery. Follywit has just remarked that "'tis a monkey-tailed age' (138–9).

4.1.0.2–3 *Master Penitent Brothel*] REED; *Master Penitent, Once-Ill* N. OKES. Penitent's new surname occurs only in the entry--directions here and at 4.5.0.1–2. M. TAYLOR suggests that, separated by the comma, 'once-ill' is a descriptive adjective rather than a name, but this does not account for the second occurrence. See Textual Introduction.

4.1.21 clock] J. OKES; clack *and* cloak *in different states of* N. OKES.

4.1.29 bear] DODSLEY; better N. OKES. DODSLEY's emendation makes sense of an otherwise perplexing phrase. Presumably Penitent makes a gesture appropriate to a vow.

4.1.35 Thou'rt] N. OKES (Th'art)

4.1.48 our] DODSLEY; her N. OKES.

4.1.58–9 seized . . . Seize] DODSLEY; seard . . . Ceare N. OKES

4.1.71.1 *Succubus stamps and exit*] DODSLEY; *Succu.* Stamps—[space] *and Exit* N. OKES

4.1.75, 76 Harebrain] DODSLEY; *Hargrave* N. OKES

4.2.0.2 *Gunwater*] HENNING first regularized the name in this form throughout the text. From this point to the end of the play N. OKES prints the name as *Gumwater* or an abbreviation thereof. See Textual Introduction for the superiority of the Gunwater reading,

4.2.26 know] J. OKES; knew N. OKES

4.5.1 RAFE] THIS EDITION; [*Servus*] N. OKES, who uses the Latin generic term for the character's speech headings throughout this scene. THIS EDITION substitutes his personal name, which has been established in the dialogue and speech headings of 3.1.

4.5.4 Harebrain] DODSLEY; N. OKES prints *Hargrave* through this scene in spoken text and stage directions; the speech prefixes at ll. 74, 82, 86, and 89 are *Harebrain*.

4.5.66 his] DYCE; her N. OKES

4.6.23 lady] M. TAYLOR; Ladies N. OKES. Editors from REED to SALGĀDO suggest that the phrase is a throwaway addressed to women in the audience. Since the eager Follywit does not otherwise greet the Mother, whose entry direction occurs on the same line of print, the phrase makes more sense as an ingratiating address to her.

4.6.59–60 restraint upon flesh] J. OKES; restraint ont upon flesh N. OKES, although retained with a comma after 'on't' by HENNING, SALGĀDO, and FROST, looks like an awkward anticipation of 'upon't' in the next line.

4.6.77 maid] DODSLEY; man N. OKES

4.6.109 track] REED; tract N. OKES

4.6.138 geld some charges] THIS EDITION (G.T.); get some charges N. OKES. The reading 'get' seems to give the exact opposite of the required sense: by crashing his uncle's dinner party Follywit will *save* the expenses ('charges') of a wedding banquet of his own. The most economical way of producing the correct sense is to emend the common word 'get' to the unusual word 'geld' (which might easily have been misread

by the compositor as 'gett'). Middleton often elsewhere uses 'geld' metaphorically: see *Puritan* 3.5.55, *Owl* 1622, *Widow* 1.1.116, etc.

4.6.148.2 *Finit Actus Quartus*] HENNING; *Actus Quintus* N. OKES. The closing act-tags are dropped by all subsequent editions except HENNING. and the literal transcripton of EBERLE.

5.1.0.1 *Incipit Actus Quintus et Ultimus*] THIS EDITION; *Actus Quintus : Vlls.* N. OKES

5.1.10, 15–16 Master Shortrod] N. OKES, J. OKES, DODSLEY; emended to 'Master Harebrain' by REED and all subsequent editions except EBERLE's literal transcription. All editions assign the character's speeches in this scene to 'Harebrain'. See Textual Introduction for the argument that the character's full name is Master Shortrod Harebrain.

5.1.27.1 *Enter Servus [clumsily]*] THIS EDITION. All editions until HENNING follow N. OKES's strange reading *Semus* for what was presumably *Servus* here and in the speech directions of ll. 29 and 46. HENNING, SALGĀDO, FROST substitute 'servant'. *Clumsily* is deducible from context.

5.1.46 LIEUTENANT] THIS EDITION; N. OKES is followed by all editors in assigning the speech to *Semus/Servus*. The speaker, however, must be privy to Follywit's plot, whereas the servant behaves and is addressed as one of Sir Bounteous's household.

5.1.62 your] J. OKES; you N. OKES

5.1.105 Soft] M. TAYLOR; post N. OKES, retained by SALGĀDO. All other editors follow DODSLEY in emending to 'pox'. Although 'pox' is an epithet elsewhere used by Sir Bounteous, M. TAYLOR rightly points out that a word is needed to introduce the aside, a function more naturally performed by 'soft' than 'pox'.

5.1.139 FOLLYWIT Excellent well, sir] J. OKES; *not in* N. OKES. Follywit presumably says something here, since Sir Bounteous's subsequent question is printed on the next line with a new speech prefix.

5.1.150 for] THIS EDITION; *not in* N. OKES

5.2.2 HAREBRAIN] REED. In N. OKES the character's name appears throughout the speech prefixes of this scene as *Short.* or *Short. R.* It does not occur in stage directions or dialogue.

5.2.7 yclept] COLLIER; ecclipped N. OKES

5.2.77–8 THIRD COMRADE . . . FOURTH COMRADE] DYCE; 2 . . . 3 N. OKES. Two other comrades, Lieutenant and Ensign, have just spoken.

5.2.152 HAREBRAIN] REED; *Nub.* N. OKES, *Gum* J. OKES. Some editors follow J. OKES in assigning the speech to Gunwater/Gumwater. He is not otherwise indicated as being on stage in 5.2, nor does he ever address Sir Bounteous by name. It is a guest's line.

5.2.258 A piece, a piece] Given the sexual overtones of groping in a man's pocket, there is no need to emend N. OKES's 'peece' to 'prize', as all editors beginning with DYCE have done. THIS EDITION simply modernizes the spelling.

5.2.316.1 *Exeunt*] J. OKES; *not in* N. OKES

STAGE DIRECTIONS

1.1.0.2–3 *Enter Dick Folly-wit, and his confrts, Lieftenant Mawe-|worme, Antient Hoboy, and others his Comrades.*

1.1.88.1 *Enter M. Penitent Brothel.*

1.1.91 *Exit.*

1.1.120.1 *Enter Curtizan.* [after 'aim', l. 118]

1.1.140 *Exit. Penitent.*

1.1.140.1 *Enter mother.*

1.1.186.1 *Enter Ineffe, and Poffibilitie.*

1.1.204 *Exeunt.*

1.2.0.1 *Enter Maft. Harebraine.*

1.2.5.1 *Enter two or three.*

1.2.24.1 *Exeunt.*

1.2.61 *Exit.*

1.2.69.1 *Enter wife & Curt.*

1.2.156   *Exit.*
1.2.165   *Exeunt.*
1.2.165.1   *Finit Actus Primus.*
2.1.0.1   *Incipit Actus Secundus.*
2.1.0.2   *Enter Sir Bounteous with two Knights.*
2.1.6.1   *Exeunt at one doore.*
2.1.6.2–3   *At the other, enter in haſt a footman.*
2.1.52   Laughs, [printed as spoken text]
2.1.89.1–2   *Enter Folly-wit like a Lord with his Comrades in | blew coates.*
2.1.95   *Exit.*
2.1.157.1–3   *A ſtraine plaid by the Conſort, Sir Bounteous makes a Court-|ly honour to that L and ſeemes to foot the tune.*
2.1.166.1–2   *The Organs play, and couerd diſhes march ouer the Stage.*
2.1.170.1   *Exeunt.*
2.1.170.2   *A ſong to the Organs.*
2.2.0.1–3   *Enter ſir Bounteous with Folly-wit, and his conſorts | toward his lodging.*
2.2.24   *Exit.*
2.2.49.1   *Exit.*
2.3.0.1   *Enter Curtizan with her man.*
2.3.7   *Exeunt.*
2.4.1.1–2   *Enter in a masking ſute with a vizard in his hand, | Folly-wit.*
2.4.6.1–2   *Enter the reſt Vizarded.* [after 'lads', l. 7]
2.4.15.1–2   *Enter with Sir Bounteous in his night-gowne.*
2.4.66.1   *Exit.* [after 'feast you', l. 65]
2.4.74.2–2.4.75   *Enter Antient.* [after 'sure', l. 75]
2.4.103.1   *Exeunt.*
2.5.0.1   *Enter Curtizan with M. Penitent Brothel.*
2.5.58   *Exeunt.*
2.6.0.1   *Voyces within.*
2.6.6.1–2   *Enter Sir Bount. with a cord halfe vnbound, Foot. with | him.* [after 'old worshippe', l. 7–8]
2.6.23   *Exit.*
2.6.101.1   *(Curtens drawn* [opening parenthesis only]
2.6.131   *Exit.*
2.6.134   *Exeunt.*
2.6.134.1   *Finit Actus Secundus.*
3.1.0.1   *Incipit Actus Tertius.*
3.1.0.2–4   *Enter Maſter Harebraine with two elder brothers, Maſter | Ineſſe, and Maſter Poſſibilitie.*
3.1.9   *Exit.*
3.1.68   *Exit.*
3.1.132   *Exeunt.*
3.2.0.1–4   *Viols, Gallipots, Plate, and an Houre-glaſſe by her. The | Curtizan on a bed, for her counterfeit fitt. | To her, Maſter Penitent Brothell, like a Doctor of Phiſick.*
3.2.93   *Exit.*
3.2.102.1–2   *Enter M. Ineſſe and Poſſibilitie.*
3.2.176.1   *Enter Miſt. Harebrain.*
3.2.191.1   *Exeunt.*
3.2.191.2   *Enter M. Harebraine liſtening.*

3.2.247.1   *Enter Wife with Maſter Penitent.*
3.2.266.1   *Exeunt.*
3.2.268.1   *Exit.*
3.3.0.1–2   *Enter Folly-wit with Lieftenant Maw-worme, Antient | Hoboy, and the reſt of his conſorts.*
3.3.160   *Exeunt.*
3.3.160.1   *Finit Actus Tertius.*
4.1.0.1   *Incipit Actus Quartus.*
4.1.0.2–3   *Enter in his chamber out of his ſtudie, Master Pænitent, Once-|Ill, a Booke in his hand reading.*
4.1.29.1–2   *Enter the Diuell in her ſhape, claps him on | the ſhoulder.*
4.1.71.1   *Succu. Stamps—and Exit.*
4.1.94   *Exeunt.*
4.2.0.1–2   *Enter at one doore Sir Bounteous, at another Gum-water.*
4.2.30   *Exit.*
4.2.32   *Exit.*
4.3.0.1–2   *Enter Gumwater with Follywet in Curtizans diſguize, | and maskt.*
4.3.30   *kisses her Exit.*
4.3.54.1   *Exit.*
4.4.0.1   *Enter Sir Bounteous.*
4.4.34.1   *Exit.*
4.4.57.1   *Exit.*
4.5.0.1–2   *Maſter Pænitent Once-Ill-knocking within; | enter a Seruus.*
4.5.2.1   *Enter Master Pænitent.* [printed as part of opening s.d.]
4.5.14–4.5.14.1   *Enter mistreſſe Hargraue.*
4.5.67.1   *Enter | Hargraue.* [right of ll. 67 and 68]
4.6.0.1   *Enter Follywit, the Curtizan ſtriuing from him.*
4.6.5   *Exit.*
4.6.22.1   *Enter the Mother.* [after 'Ladies', l. 23]
4.6.56   *Exit.*
4.6.71.1   *Enter Mother bringing in ſtriuingly the Curtezan.*
4.6.143.1   *Exit.*
4.6.148.1   *Exeunt.*
4.6.148.2   *Actus Quintus.*
5.1.0.1   *Actus Quintus:Vlls.*
5.1.0.1   *Enter buſilie Sir Bounteous Progreſſe for the feaſt.*
5.1.27.1   *Enter Semus.* [after 'good Sir Bounteous', l. 26]
5.1.85.1   *Enter Mother and Curtelan.* [after 'dissemble it', l. 88]
5.1.114.1   *Exit,*
5.1.121.1   *Enter Folly-wit.* [after 'ready', l. 122]
5.1.123   *Takes it off.* [after 'on', l. 5.1.124]
5.1.161   *Exit.*
5.2.0.1–2   *Enter Sir Bounteous and all the Gueſts.*
5.2.17.1   *Euter for a Prologue Folly-wit.*
5.2.17.2   *Prologue.*
5.2.27   *Exit.*
5.2.46.1   *Folly-wit returnes in a furie.* [after 'betrayed', l. 47–8]
5.2.71.1   *Enter Conſtable with them.*
5.2.127.1   *Exit.*
5.2.205.1–2   *Enter Follywit in his owne ſhape, and all the reſt.*
5.2.316.2   *FINIS.*

LINEATION NOTES

1.1.2–3   What...society] COLLIER; *verse* BALLARD: thee | bounty |
1.1.130   Did...time] THIS EDITION; *prose* BALLARD. In J. OKES, REED, HENNING, and SALGĀDO the words fit into a single line of type. Since they do not otherwise differentiate between verse and prose, it is unclear whether they saw that this is a line of blank verse in the middle of a prose passage.
1.1.162–4   Fifteen...still] THIS EDITION; *verse* BALLARD: maidenhead | yet | still |
1.1.184   'Twill...own] COLLIER; *prose* BALLARD
1.2.4–5   I'll...i'faith] THIS EDITION; *1 line* BALLARD
1.2.10–12   To rob...numbers] COLLIER; *prose* BALLARD
1.2.20–4   Let...sir] THIS EDITION; *prose* BALLARD
1.2.28   The...Peace!] REED; *prose* BALLARD
1.2.110–11   My...me] COLLIER; *1 line* BALLARD
1.2.119–22   Think...Come] THIS EDITION; *prose* BALLARD
1.2.161–2   Keep...it] DYCE; *prose* BALLARD
2.1.90–1   Footman!...lord] DODSLEY; *1 line* BALLARD
2.1.98–9   You've...welcome] HENNING; *verse* BALLARD: self | welcome |
2.1.100–2   In...presume] DYCE; *verse* BALLARD: houses | presume |
2.2.44–7   In gold...lads] THIS EDITION; *verse* BALLARD: I | forsooth | lads |
2.5.20–4   I only...sickness] DYCE; *verse* BALLARD: hitherto | admittance | please you | conveyed it | sickness |
2.6.44–5   I like...lodging] REED; *1 line of verse* BALLARD
3.1.17–18   True...said?] THIS EDITION; *1 line* BALLARD
3.1.20–1   Is...handled?] THIS EDITION; *prose* BALLARD
3.1.30–3   Did...Harebrain!] REED; *verse* BALLARD: midst | wife | Harebrain |

3.1.46   When...weeping] THIS EDITION; *prose* BALLARD
3.1.55–8   Shake...thing] THIS EDITION; *prose* BALLARD
3.1.86–7   Now...me?] SALGĀDO; *verse* BALLARD: gone | me? |
3.2.32–3   The plague...Good] DODSLEY; *1 line* BALLARD
3.3.25–6   They...already] THIS EDITION; *prose* BALLARD
3.3.157–8   Twelve-penny...scribes] REED; *prose* N. OKES
4.1.30–3   What...grace] DYCE; *prose* N. OKES
4.1.34–6   Leave...bone] HENNING; *prose* N. OKES
4.1.63–4   Fa...la] THIS EDITION; N. OKES *prints the 20 sung syllables so that 2 complete the metre of l. 62, 15 occupy the next line, and 3 an additional line*
4.3.52   Now...below] DYCE; *prose* N. OKES
4.4.11–12   How...Gullman] DYCE; *prose* N. OKES
4.5.18–19   Puh...there] DYCE; *1 line* N. OKES
4.5.75–7   Forever...wife] DYCE; *2 lines* N. OKES: will | wife |
4.6.20–2   Face...on't] THIS EDITION; *prose* N. OKES
4.6.52–3   She will...lives] DYCE; *prose* N. OKES
4.6.82–6   Why...now] THIS EDITION; *prose* N. OKES
4.6.93–6   Men...look] DYCE; *3 lines* N. OKES: sir | passage | look |
4.6.105–6   Why...wench] DYCE; *prose* N. OKES
4.6.122   'Sfoot...dies] DYCE; *prose* N. OKES
4.6.144–5   If...well] DYCE; *prose* N. OKES
5.1.99–100   She...Buz] DODSLEY; *1 line* N. OKES
5.1.103–6   Away...sir] DYCE; *prose* N. OKES
5.1.110–14   You're...me] THIS EDITION; *prose* N. OKES
5.2.67–9   *For...him]* COLLIER; *prose* N. OKES
5.2.70–1   Being...shame] DODSLEY; No | N. OKES
5.2.119–21   *As fast...thieves!]* DODSLEY; *1 line* N. OKES
5.2.212–13   Thanks...friends] THIS EDITION; *prose* N. OKES

A YORKSHIRE TRAGEDY

Edited by Stanley Wells

A Yorkshire Tragedy (STC 22340; *BEPD* 272) was entered to Thomas Pavier in the Stationers' Register on 2 May 1608: 'Mr Pavyer Entered for his Copie vnder the handes of Mr Wilson and master Warden Seton A booke Called A yorkshire Tragedy written by Wylliam Shakespere … vj^d'. The play appeared in a quarto of four sheets with the title-page: 'A | YORKSHIRE | Tragedy. | *Not ſo New as Lamentable* | and true. | *Acted by his Maieſties Players at* | the *Globe.* | VVritten by VV. Shakſpeare. | [device: McKerrow 280] | AT LONDON | Printed by *R.B.* for *Thomas Pauier* and are to bee ſold at his | ſhop on Cornhill, neere to the exchange. | 1608.' The title-page device (McKerrow 280) identifies the printer as Richard Bradock. The title-page is A1; there is no list of characters, and the playtext begins on A2 with the heading 'ALL'S ONE, | *OR,* | One of the foure Plaies in one, called | a *York-ſhire* Tragedy: as it was plaid | by the Kings Maieſties Plaiers.' It is undivided into acts or scenes. Six copies are recorded, two in the British Library, and one each in the Bodleian, Corpus Christi, Oxford, the Folger Shakespeare Library, and the Huntington Library.

Though Bradock was an experienced printer of plays, and *A Yorkshire Tragedy* was printed late in his career, it is a poor piece of work. Two skeleton formes were used; the Malone Society edition records over 100 press variants, occurring in every forme and all but seven pages; they include more than sixty changes in punctuation, corrections of turned letters, and reallocations of speech prefixes; even so, many obvious errors, such as commas at the ends of speeches, wrong fount punctuation, and turned letters, remain. In the absence (noted by G. H. Blayney) of evidence of reference to copy in the process of correction, the present edition is based on the premise that uncorrected readings provide the best guide to what lay in the manuscript.

Everything indicates that the printers worked from authorial foul papers. There are many signs that the text as printed represents the author very much in the process of hasty composition, writing with the source pamphlet in front of him and leaving decisions crucial to the play's staging to be sorted out later. This is most apparent in the episode in which the Husband throws the Maid downstairs (5.11–12), which does not appear to be conceived in fully theatrical terms, in uncertainty about which servants should speak which lines in Sc. 5, and in the survival of the speech prefix 'Kni.' at 6.11.1 which appears to represent an uncancelled remnant of an abandoned intention (see Textual Notes). Less conclusive as evidence is the namelessness of all the characters except those in the opening scene; there may have been good reasons for not using actual names when writing for the theatre, where more vigilant censorship would operate, and Middleton had a penchant for leaving even major characters nameless; it is possible, however, that while removing names in the first draft he would have provided fictitious names for at least some of the characters in a final version, as Wilkins does in *The Miseries of Enforced Marriage*.

Use of personal names is not the only respect in which the first scene is anomalous. Its links with the source pamphlet are far less close than those of the rest of the play, the servants portrayed in it take no further part in the action (at least under their own names), and its relationships in general with the rest of the play, while not so tenuous as to justify the criticism that it is irrelevant, have not been evident to all the play's critics. The scene's function has been ably defended by Jackson, and Holdsworth (1994) provides ample evidence of Middleton's authorship. Nevertheless, if we discount the theory that it was added by a different writer from the rest of the play, the possibility remains—as Baldwin Maxwell and others have suggested—that Middleton himself wrote it after his initial act of composition was completed. Its freedom of invention, along with its use of personal names, suggests that it may have been composed in a more relaxed frame of mind than what follows.

Although the relationship between the opening scene and the rest of the play presents a fascinating puzzle, and although hypotheses about it may influence performance, it has little if any bearing on editorial method.

The play was reprinted by William Jaggard for Thomas Pavier in 1619 (STC 22341; *BEPD* 272(*b*)) from a copy of Bradock's quarto with all the formes corrected. It next appeared in the 1664 issue of the Shakespeare Third Folio (Wing 2914; *BEPD* 272(*c*)) in the section printed by Roger Daniel, and then in the Fourth Folio of 1685 (Wing 2915; *BEPD* 272(*d*)), where its printer has not been identified. As will be seen from the list of Works Cited, the play has often been reprinted since then; many of the editions listed do not, however, constitute fully re-edited texts.

SEE ALSO

Text: *Works*, 455
Authorship and date: this volume, 373

WORKS CITED

Other Editions

Brooke, C. F. Tucker, ed., in *The Shakespeare Apocrypha* (1908)

Cawley, A. C., and B. Gaines, ed., *A Yorkshire Tragedy* (1986)

Collier, J. P., ed., in *The Plays and Poems of William Shakespeare* (1878)

DANIEL, Roger, and others, printers, in William Shakespeare, *Comedies, Histories, and Tragedies* (1663-4)

Dominik, M., ed., in *Shakespeare-Middleton Collaborations* (1988)

Feldman, S., ed., *A Yorkshire Tragedy* (1973)

Hazlitt, W., ed., in *The Doubtful Plays of William Shakespeare* (1897)

HERRINGMAN, Henry, and others, publishers, in William Shakespeare, *Comedies, Histories, and Tragedies* (1685)

Hopkinson, A. F., ed., in *Shakespeare's Doubtful Plays*, 11 parts (1890-5, 1, 1895)

Knight, Charles, ed., in *The Pictorial Edition of the Works of William Shakespeare*, 8 vols (1839-43), 8

Kozenko, W., ed., in *Disputed Plays of William Shakespeare* (1974)

Malone, E., ed., in *Supplement to the Edition of Shakespere's Plays Published in 1778 by Samuel Johnson and George Steevens*, 2 vols (1780)

Moltke, M., ed., *Doubtful Plays of William Shakespeare* (1869)

Oliphant, E. H. C., ed., in *Shakespeare and his Fellow Dramatists*, 2 vols (1929)

Rowe, Nicholas, ed., in *The Works of Mr. William Shakespear . . .*, 6 vols (1709), vol. 6

Rubinstein, H. F., ed., in *Great English Plays* (1928)

Scott, Walter, ed., in *Ancient British Drama*, 3 vols (1810), 1

Simms, W. G., ed., in *A Supplement to the Plays of William Shakespeare* (1848)

Sturgess, K., ed., in *Three Elizabethan Domestic Tragedies* (1969)

Tyrrell, H., ed., in *The Doubtful Plays of Shakespeare Revised* (1851)

A Yorkshire Tragedy (Pavier, 1619)

A Yorkshire Tragedy ([Tonson], 1735)

A Yorkshire Tragedy (R. Walker, 1735)

Other Works Cited

Adams, H. H., *English Domestic or Homiletic Tragedy, 1575 to 1642* (1943)

Blayney, G. H., 'Variants in Q1 of *A Yorkshire Tragedy*', *The Library*, V, 11 (1956), 262-7

Clark, Sandra, *The Elizabethan Pamphleteers: Popular Moralistic Pamphlets 1580-1640* (1985)

Eliot, T. S., *The Letters of T. S. Eliot*, ed. Valerie Eliot, Vol. 1 (1898-1922), (1988)

Holdsworth, R. V., 'Two Emendations in Middleton's *A Yorkshire Tragedy*', *Notes and Queries* NS 39 (1992), 361-3

—— 'Middleton's Authorship of *A Yorkshire Tragedy*', *Review of English Studies* NS 45 (1994), 1-25

—— '*A Yorkshire Tragedy* and the Date of *Timon of Athens*' (privately circulated, 1993)

Jackson, MacDonald P., *Studies in Attribution: Middleton and Shakespeare* (1979)

Lake, David J., *The Canon of Thomas Middleton's Plays* (1975)

Maxwell, B., *Studies in the Shakespeare Apocrypha* (1956)

TEXTUAL NOTES

1.13   here's] STURGESS *after* BRADOCK *corr.* (her's); hers BRADOCK *uncorr.*; here he is MALONE

1.14-15   news. | OLIVER] BRADOCK *corr.* (news‸ [*indent*] Oliue; *as part of text* BRADOCK *uncorr.*

1.16.1   *Enter Sam furnished with things from London*] *after* 1.23, *omitting* '*Enter Sam*' BRADOCK. The quarto direction appears to be an indication for properties rather than an entry direction.

1.22   RALPH *and* OLIVER] BRADOCK (*Amb.*)

1.41   RALPH *and* OLIVER] BRADOCK (*Ambo.*)

1.49   her own] BRADOCK (here owne)

1.74   RALPH *and* OLIVER] BRADOCK (*Am:*)

1.78   RALPH *and* OLIVER] BRADOCK (*Am.*)

1.79   SAM] HERRINGMAN; *not in* BRADOCK

2.47   upo' th' soil] CAWLEY-GAINES; vppot'h foole BRADOCK; but upoth' fool DANIEL. See Barry Gaines, *The Library*, V, 27 (1972), pp. 142-3. Sturgess defends Bradock, glossing 'live a life of riot', which is possible if strained; Holdsworth ('Two Emendations . . .') writes that 'Any emendation should . . . retain' Bradock's 'foole', but is uncertain whether Bradock 'should stand unemended.'

2.65   you're] BRADOCK (y'are)

2.73   mortgaged] BRADOCK (morgadge)

2.87   *spurns her*] *at end of line* BRADOCK

2.105   true trouble] STURGESS, *conj.* G. H. Blayney; true troubled BRADOCK (*uncorr.*); trouble trouble, BRADOCK *corr.* A difficult crux, partly because of the idiosyncratic style of the Husband's utterance. Cawley and Gaines say that 'emendation is not really necessary since corrected [Bradock] gives a satisfactory reading: the doubling of *trouble* is in keeping with the Husband's tendency to repeat words and phrases passionately . . .'. Nevertheless the uncorrected state, though nonsensical, is likely to be closer to the manuscript, and 'troubl[e]d' would be an easy misinterpretation of 'trouble';

Sturgess's reading supposes that the press corrector, faced with nonsense, was 'over-zealous' in altering 'true' to 'trouble' in an attempt to make sense of the passage. See G. H. Blayney, *The Library*, V, 11 (1956), p. 266. John Jowett conjectures (privately) 'a true trouble treble[d]', supposing cursory consultation of copy or unclear mark-up by the corrector.

2.119   *Exeunt Gentlemen*] *as here* THIS EDITION; *after* admonitions BRADOCK. It seems likely that the Husband's words should at least be addressed to the backs of the Gentlemen.

2.128   Or] BRADOCK *corr.* (or); O BRADOCK *uncorr.*

2.128.1   *Exit Servant*] JAGGARD; *not in* BRADOCK

2.134   follies] JAGGARD; follie BRADOCK

2.151   deceived] deceived (= èd) BRADOCK

2.154   proclaimed] proclaimed (= èd) BRADOCK

2.159   'T'as] BRADOCK (Ta's)

2.161   HUSBAND] JAGGARD; *not in* BRADOCK

2.163   Wilt] BRADOCK (Woult)

2.172   you] THIS EDITION; *not in* BRADOCK. Sense and metre support the emendation; misreading would have been easy.

2.173   You're] BRADOCK (Y'are)

2.178   On . . . sore] JAGGARD; On her your posterity, let only sin be sore BRADOCK; On her [and] your posterity, [nor blame | Your overthrow;] let only sin be sore BROOKE; On your posterity; let only sin be sore STURGESS. Brooke's conjecture assumes the need for a rhyme for 'shame', but compare e.g. 5.3. Sturgess appears to assume accidental failure to cancel a first thought.

2.181   left] BRADOCK. Various emendations have been conjectured to avoid repetition from the previous line (e.g. 'cleft', Collier, 'reft', Sturgess), but none is particularly convincing, and the sense is adequate.

2.188   Ay,] BRADOCK (I?)

3.11 withered] withered (= èd) BRADOCK

3.14 on] BRADOCK (one)

3.17 deserts] BRADOCK; defects STURGESS. Sturgess's emendation posits an easy misreading, but *OED*'s definitions of deserts include 'demerits' and 'characteristics deserving punishment'.

3.41 dowry] BRADOCK; poor dowry *conj.* Taylor. Taylor's conjecture is attractive, but the scene is modulating into prose. Cawley and Gaines print the whole of this speech as prose, but it is set out as verse in Bradock.

3.48 *spurns her*] BRADOCK (*at end of line, after* 'overjoyed')

3.51 state] BRADOCK; estate STURGESS. Emendation seems unnecessary, even though the pamphlet has 'estate' in the corresponding passage.

3.71 *To...fear*] BRADOCK (*at end of line, after* 'news', *running on to following line*)

3.79 *Husband...Servants*] not in BRADOCK

3.80 WIFE (*alone*)] BRADOCK ('Wif. alone' *at end of line*)

3.82 offered] offered (= èd) BRADOCK

4.1 You're] BRADOCK (y'are)

4.17 ponderous] BRADOCK (pandorus)

4.19 might] BRADOCK; and might JAGGARD. Sturgess adopts, but does not record, Jaggard's reading.

4.39–40 SERVINGMAN Sir? | HUSBAND Fill] CAWLEY–GAINES; Sir Hu. Fil BRADOCK; Hus. Fill...JAGGARD; Hu. Sir, Fil BROOKE. As Cawley and Gaines remark, omission of a speech prefix (as at 5.16) is likely.

4.40 *Exit...wine*] after 4.41, BRADOCK

4.40 Servingman] BRADOCK (feruant)

4.43.1 *Servingman*] not in BRADOCK

4.44 You've] BRADOCK (y'aue)

4.47.1 *Drink both*] BRADOCK (*at end of* 4.47)

4.54.1 *with Servingman*] not in BRADOCK

4.62 we're] BRADOCK *uncorr.* (were); we are BRADOCK *corr.* Cawley and Gaines follow the corrected reading; Brooke reads 'were', but if, as seems likely, this is closer to the manuscript it is probably an abbreviation.

4.86 for to live] BRADOCK; to relieve SIMMS; to deliver CAWLEY–GAINES. Cawley and Gaines gloss 'to live as I would like to'; perhaps 'to find the means to keep myself' would be more apt. In any case emendation seems unnecessary.

4.97 visors] BRADOCK (vizards)

4.100 *strikes him*] BRADOCK (*at end of line*)

4.105 crouch] THIS EDITION *conj.* Holdsworth; Couch BRADOCK; coach JAGGARD. Most earlier editors followed Jaggard's unauthoritative reading; Sturgess reverted to Bradock, glossing 'low bow', which is essentially the sense of Holdsworth's proposed emendation. See Holdsworth, 'Two Emendations...'.

4.108 *stabs him*] BRADOCK (*at end of line*)

5.0.1 *Wife*] BRADOCK (*mother*)

5.7.1 *Enter...bleeding*] THIS EDITION; *after* O! BRADOCK

5.15.1 *Wife wakes*] BRADOCK (*after* 'children', 5.16)

5.16 *Wife*] JAGGARD; *not in* BRADOCK

5.24 *stabs...arms*] BRADOCK ('stabs...in' *at end of* 5.24, 'her arms' *at end of following line*)

5.25 *gets...her*] BRADOCK (*at end of* 5.24)

5.36 thrown] JAGGARD; thowne BRADOCK

5.51 He's] BRADOCK (H'as)

5.56 MASTER'S SERVANT] THIS EDITION, *after* BRADOCK (*Ser.*); Servants CAWLEY–GAINES. According to Cawley and Gaines this line 'seems to be given to the two servants entering with the Master...'. It could be spoken by one or both. It seems to imply knowledge not immediately available to the Master, so to this extent would come more appropriately from the servant who has been felled, but the Master's description of him as 'all faint and bloodied' is against this. The staging would make best sense if one or both of the servants entered in advance of the Master.

5.67 SERVANT] CAWLEY–GAINES; 1 *Ser.* BRADOCK

5.67.1 *Exeunt...Servants*] BRADOCK (*Exit Mr and feruants.*), *after previous line*

5.78 rent] BRADOCK. An alternative modernization is 'rend', as the spellings were not distinct.

5.83 purposed to] BRADOCK; purpose to MALONE. The emendation, though plausible, is not necessary.

5.84.1 *Enters two Servants*] BRADOCK; *Enter a servant* MALONE. Though only one servant is needed, the author presumably had in mind the two who enter with the Master.

6.11.1 *Cry within*] JAGGARD; *Kni.* BRADOCK. It seems likely that Bradock's '*Kni.*' represents an original intention to bring on the Knight (suggested by the 'Sir John Sauill' of the source) at this point, abandoned in favour of the added episode with the Master of the College.

6.16 ALL BUT HUSBAND] *not in* BRADOCK

6.18 feats] BRADOCK (fates). See Cawley and Gaines, note to VIII. 19.

6.22 prisoned] prisoned (= èd) BRADOCK

6.26 He's] BRADOCK (H'as)

7.1 Endangered] Endangered (= èd) BRADOCK

7.2 KNIGHT'S GENTLEMAN] THIS EDITION; 4 *Gen.* BRADOCK; Gentlemen. CAWLEY–GAINES. It is immaterial which of the Knight's companions speaks these speeches.

7.6.2 *Husband as*] not in BRADOCK

7.33 shame...shame] BRADOCK; sin...shame *conj.* Malone.

8.2 endangered] endangered (= èd) BRADOCK

8.20 ne'er] JAGGARD; near BRADOCK (*probably a spelling variant*)

8.32.1 *Children laid out*] as here THIS EDITION; *after* l. 34, BRADOCK

8.50 have part] CAWLEY–GAINES; leaue part BRADOCK; live apart *conj.* Steevens.

8.50 OFFICER] JAGGARD; *not in* BRADOCK

8.62.1 *Exeunt...halberds*] 'Exeunt' *after* 'distress' *in previous line*

8.62.1 *and Officers*] *not in* BRADOCK

8.63 unmurdered] unmurdered (= èd) BRADOCK

8.69 pardon my] BRADOCK; pardon—my CAWLEY–GAINES; pardon for my JAGGARD

PRESS VARIANTS

This list derives from the Malone Society edition, which collates the six known copies:

BL: British Library C.34. l5
Bod: Bodleian Library Malone 34 (Bod)
CCC: Corpus Christi College Library, Oxford
F: Folger Shakespeare Library
H1: Huntington Library 69371 (Kemble–Devonshire copy)
H2: Huntington Library 69372 (Church copy)

Variants occur in all formes as follows:

A (inner) *corr.* Bod, CCC, F; *uncorr.* BL, H1, H2.

A (outer) *corr.* Bod, CCC, F; *uncorr.* BL, H1, H2.

B (inner) *corr.* BL, Bod, CCC, F; *uncorr.* H1, H2. (B4 in H2 is a pen and ink facsimile.)

B (outer) *second corr. state in* BL, Bod, CCC, F; *first corr. state in* H2 (and see above.); *uncorr.* H1.

C (inner) second corr. state BL, F, H1, H2; *uncorr.* Bod.
C (outer) *corr.* BL, H1, H2; *uncorr.* Bod, CCC, F.
D (inner) *corr.* Bod, CCC, F; *uncorr.* BL, H1, H2.
D (outer) *corr.* Bod, CCC, F; *uncorr.* BL, H1, H2.

Sheet A (inner forme)

Sig. A2

1.13 here's…come,] her's⌃…come, BRADOCK *corr.*; hers,…come BRADOCK *uncorr.*
1.14-15 news. | OLIVER…does mine] news | *Oliue*…doe's mine BRADOCK *corr.*; news…does | mine BRADOCK *uncorr.*

Sheet A (outer forme)

Sig. A2ᵛ

1.26 wires] wyers⌃ BRADOCK *corr.*; wyers, BRADOCK *uncorr.*
1.37 Why] Why? BRADOCK *corr.*; Why⌃ BRADOCK *uncorr.*

Sig. A3

1.59 here] heere, BRADOCK *corr.*; heere⌃ BRADOCK *uncorr.*
1.69 gentlewomen] gentle women BRADOCK *corr.*; gentle weo-men BRADOCK *uncorr.*

Sig. A4ᵛ

2.68 to.] BRADOCK *corr.*; to⌃ BRADOCK *uncorr.*

Sheet B (outer forme)

Sig. B1

2.91 give] giue BRADOCK *corr.*; glue BRADOCK *uncorr.*
2.97 slave] flaue BRADOCK *corr.*; flauc BRADOCK *uncorr.*
2.99 blood!] blood, BRADOCK *corr.*; blood⌃ BRADOCK *uncorr.*
2.102 yield.] yeeld, BRADOCK *corr.*; yeeld? BRADOCK *uncorr.*
2.103 Speedily, speedily] *line not indented* BRADOCK *corr.*; *line indented* BRADOCK *uncorr.*
2.104 hour] howre BRADOCK *corr.*; how BRADOCK *uncorr.*
2.105-6 trouble…evils] trouble trouble,…euils BRADOCK *corr.*; true troubled…euills BRADOCK *uncorr.*
2.107 strumpet and bastards, strumpet] ftrumpet, & baftards, ftrum= | pet BRADOCK *corr.*; ftrumpet, & baftards⌃ ftrum= | pets BRADOCK *uncorr.*

Sig. B *omitted Huntington copy only*

Sheet B (inner forme)

Sig. B1ᵛ

2.114 name.] name: BRADOCK *corr.*; name⌃ BRADOCK *uncorr.*
2.116 you.] BRADOCK *corr.*; you, BRADOCK *uncorr.*
2.121 would] wud BRADOCK *corr.*; wad BRADOCK *uncorr.*
2.126 HUSBAND] Huf. BRADOCK *corr.*; Huf⌃ BRADOCK *uncorr.*
2.127 she…of,] fhe…of: BRADOCK *corr.*; fhee…of⌃ BRADOCK *uncorr.*
2.128 Or…home.] *line not indented* BRADOCK *corr.*; *line indented* BRADOCK *uncorr.*
2.128 Or] or BRADOCK *corr.*; o BRADOCK *uncorr.*
2.129 not.] BRADOCK *corr.*; not, BRADOCK *uncorr.*
2.130 I] I. BRADOCK *corr.*; I⌃ BRADOCK *uncorr.*
2.131 you.] BRADOCK *corr.*; you⌃ BRADOCK *uncorr.*
2.138 Lie] Lie BRADOCK *corr.* (*c.w.*, *text*), BRADOCK *uncorr.* (*text*); Lei BRADOCK *uncorr.* (*c.w.*)

Sig. B2

2.141 HUSBAND] Huf. BRADOCK *corr.*; Hu. BRADOCK *uncorr.*
2.151 devil] deuill BRADOCK *corr.*; deuil BRADOCK *uncorr.*
2.152 HUSBAND] Huf. BRADOCK *corr.*; Hu. BRADOCK *uncorr.*
2.154 HUSBAND] Huf. BRADOCK *corr.*; H. BRADOCK *uncorr.*
2.156 GENTLEMAN] Gent. BRADOCK *corr.*; *omitted* BRADOCK *uncorr.*

2.156 O ignoble thought!] *line indented* BRADOCK *corr.*; *line not indented* BRADOCK *uncorr.*
2.157 *no speech prefix* BRADOCK *corr.*; *Gent.* BRADOCK *uncorr.*
2.157 I am…idle] *line not indented* BRADOCK *corr.*; *line indented* BRADOCK *uncorr.*
2.159 monster] monfter, BRADOCK *corr.*; monfter⌃ BRADOCK *uncorr.*
2.160 love.] loue, BRADOCK *corr.*; loue⌃ BRADOCK *uncorr.*

Sheet B (outer forme)

Sig. B2ᵛ

2.168 ground] BRADOCK *corr.*; grond BRADOCK *uncorr.*
2.179 this] BRADOCK *corr.*; this BRADOCK *uncorr.*

Sig. B3

2.188 I'd] Id'e BRADOCK *corr.*; Ide BRADOCK *uncorr.*
3.0.1 *Servingman*] feruingman BRADOCK *corr.*; f *broken in* BRADOCK *uncorr.*
3.16 as] BRADOCK *corr.*; as if BRADOCK *uncorr.*

Sheet B (inner forme)

Sig. B3ᵛ

3.28 SERVINGMAN] Ser. BRADOCK *corr.*; Şer. BRADOCK *uncorr.*
3.36 where] BRADOCK *corr.*; were BRADOCK *uncorr.*
3.37-8 down with it, down…o'th' ground] down with it, downe…oth ground BRADOCK *corr.*; down with it, down…oth the groūd BRADOCK *uncorr.*
3.41 dowry] Dowrie BRADOCK *corr.*; Dow rie BRADOCK *uncorr.*
3.44 usage] vfage, BRADOCK *corr.*; vfage (*punctuation in* BRADOCK *corr. probably damaged comma*)
3.46 provided] prouided⌃ BRADOCK *corr.*; prouided. BRADOCK *uncorr.*
3.46 court] Court BRADOCK *corr.*; court BRADOCK *uncorr.*
3.48 spurns] , fpurns BRADOCK *corr.*; ʃpurns BRADOCK *uncorr.*

Sig. B4

3.58 your] BRADOCK *corr.*; yonr BRADOCK *uncorr.*
3.62 mine] BRADOCK *corr.*; mink BRADOCK *uncorr.*
3.71-2 devil?…now?…news!] deuel?…now?…news? BRADOCK *corr.*; deuell⌃…now⌃…news, BRADOCK *uncorr.*
3.75 villain] villaine BRADOCK *corr.*; villiane BRADOCK *uncorr.*
3.75 Quick, short] quick, fhort BRADOCK *corr.*; quick fhorte BRADOCK *uncorr.*
3.76 sir] fir BRADOCK *corr.*; fir BRADOCK *uncorr.*

Sheet B (outer forme)

Sig. B4ᵛ

3.80 WIFE] Wi. BRADOCK *corr.*; *omitted, line not indented* BRADOCK *uncorr.*
3.90 become] BRADOCK *corr.*; bccome BRADOCK *uncorr.*
3.91 here…beggars?] here,…beggers, BRADOCK *corr.*; here⌃…beggers⌃ BRADOCK *uncorr.*
4.5 my] BRADOCK *corr.*; me BRADOCK *uncorr.*

Sheet C (outer forme)

Sig. C1

4.11 prisoner, all…amazed,] prifoner, al⌃…amazed, BRADOCK *corr.*; prifoner⌃ all,…amazed BRADOCK *uncorr.*
4.13 these] thefe BRADOCK *corr.*; theis BRADOCK *uncorr.*
4.18 brother,] BRADOCK *corr.*; brother⌃ BRADOCK *uncorr.*
4.19 employments,] Imployments, BRADOCK *corr.*; Imployments⌃ BRADOCK *uncorr.*
4.30 you] BRADOCK *corr.*; yov BRADOCK *uncorr.*
4.33 Sir,] Sir: BRADOCK *corr.*; Sir⌃ BRADOCK *uncorr.*
4.38 wrongs.] BRADOCK *corr.*; wrongs- BRADOCK *uncorr.*
4.38 there!] there? BRADOCK *corr.*; there, BRADOCK *uncorr.*

Sheet C (inner forme)

Sig. C1ᵛ

4.38.1 Servingman] ſeruingman BRADOCK *corr.*; ſermiugman BRADOCK *uncorr.*

4.41 sake!] fake‸ BRADOCK *corr.*; fake, BRADOCK *uncorr.*

4.45 sake.] fake, BRADOCK *corr.*; fake‸ BRADOCK *uncorr.*

4.50 you.] you: BRADOCK *corr.*; you. BRADOCK *uncorr.*

4.51 answer] anſwere BRADOCK *corr.*; auſwere BRADOCK *uncorr.* (*also in first corrected state*)

4.55 man,] man‸ BRADOCK *corr.*; man? BRADOCK *uncorr.*

4.56 beggared thee!] beggerd thee, BRADOCK *corr.*; beggerd thee? BRADOCK *uncorr.*

4.61 forbidden!] forbidden, BRADOCK *corr.*; forbidden‸ BRADOCK *uncorr.*

4.62 we're] we are BRADOCK *corr.*; were BRADOCK *uncorr.*

Sig. C2

4.68–9 posterity,…beggars?…done,…done't i'faith,] poſte-|ritie, …beggars: …done, …don't yfaith: BRADOCK *corr.*; poſte-|ritie‸ …beggars‸ …done …dont yfaith‸ BRADOCK *uncorr.*

4.73 mine, mine] mine: Mine BRADOCK *corr.*; mine. Mine BRADOCK *uncorr.*

4.75 down, it] downe; it BRADOCK *corr.*; downe‸ it BRADOCK *uncorr.*

Sheet C (outer forme)

Sig. C2ᵛ

4.105 brother.] brother: BRADOCK *corr.*; brother‸ BRADOCK *uncorr.*

4.108 Bleed, bleed,…beg, beg.] BRADOCK *corr.*; Bleed‸ bleed‸…beg‸ beg? BRADOCK *uncorr.*

Sig. C3

5.7 desolation—] deſolation: BRADOCK *corr.*; deſolation‸ BRADOCK *uncorr.*

5.13 tongue] tongue. BRADOCK *corr.*; tongue‸ BRADOCK *uncorr.*

5.16 cried?] cride? BRADOCK *corr.*; cride‸ BRADOCK *uncorr.*

5.24 WIFE O] Wi. Oh BRADOCK *corr.* (*c.w.*, *text*), BRADOCK *uncorr.* (*text*); Oh BRADOCK *uncorr.* (*c.w.*)

Sheet C (inner forme)

Sig. C3ᵛ

5.28 There's] Ther's BRADOCK *corr.*; Thers BRADOCK *uncorr.*

5.34 master?] maſter, BRADOCK *corr.*; maſter, BRADOCK *uncorr.*

5.35 me?] BRADOCK *corr.*; me, BRADOCK *uncorr.*

5.37 tug thee,] BRADOCK *corr.*; tug thee‸ BRADOCK *uncorr.*

5.41 beggar.] begger: BRADOCK *corr.*; begger‸ BRADOCK *uncorr.*

5.47 I want] I wan BRADOCK *corr.* (*c.w.*); I want BRADOCK *corr.* (*text*), BRADOCK *uncorr.* (*c.w.*, *text*)

Sig. C4

5.50 to] BRADOCK *corr.*; lo BRADOCK *uncorr.*

5.51 He's] H'as BRADOCK *corr.*; Ha's BRADOCK *uncorr.*

5.73 mangled too?] māgled too? BRADOCK *corr.*; mangled too‸ BRADOCK *uncorr.*

5.75 soon] ſoone BRADOCK *corr.*; ſooue BRADOCK *uncorr.*

Sheet C (outer forme)

Sig. C4ᵛ

5.78 hair,] haire: BRADOCK *corr.*; haire‸ BRADOCK *uncorr.*

5.89 house] houſe BRADOCK *corr.*; honſe BRADOCK *uncorr.*

Sheet D (outer forme)

Sig. D1

6.11 Dispatch] Diſpatch BRADOCK *corr.*; Diſdatch BRADOCK *uncorr.*

Sheet D (inner forme)

Sig. D3ᵛ

8.72 must] muſt BRADOCK *corr.*; mnſt BRADOCK *uncorr.*

STAGE DIRECTIONS

1.0.1 *Enter* Oliuer *and* Ralph, *two seruingmen.*

1.16 Sam calls within, *where are you there?* (after 1.15)

1.16.1 *Furnisht with things from London.* (after 1.23)

1.80 *Exeunt.*

2.0.1 *Enter wife.*

2.24.1 *Enter Husband.*

2.35 *Exit.*

2.39.1 *Enter Husband | againe.* (opposite 2.39–40)

2.87 *spurns | her at end of line* (opposite 2.87–8)

2.99 *holding his hands in | his pockets* (opposite 99–100)

2.103 *Exit.*

2.108.1 *Enter three Gentlemen heering him.*

2.119 *Exeun Gent,* (after 2.120)

2.120.1 *Enter a seruant.*

2.128.2 *Enter a Gentle man.*

2.163.1 *They fight and the | Husbands hurt.* (after 'fruitful', 2.67)

2.165.1 *Fight agen.*

2.167.1 *Husband falls downe.*

2.180 *Exit:*

2.188.1 *Exi*

3.0.1 *Enter wife in a riding suite with a seruingman.*

3.28 *Exit.*

3.33.1 *Enter Husband.*

3.48–9 *spurns her* (after 'overjoyed', 3.48–9)

3.70.1 *Enters a seruant very hastily.*

3.71 *to his man | Seruant in a feare* (after 3.71)

3.79 *Exeunt.*

3.80 *Wif. alone* (at end of line)

4.0.1 *Enter the Husband with the master of the Colledge.*

4.38.1 *Enter a seruingman.* [sermiugman BRADOCK *uncorr.*]

4.40 *Exit seruant | for wine.* (after 4.41)

4.43.1 *Enter with wine.*

4.47.1 *Drink both.* (at end of line)

4.54.1 *Exit.*

4.81.1 *Teares his haire.*

4.93.1 *Enters his little sonne with a top and a scourge,*

4.97.1–2 *Husb,takes vp the childe by the skirts of his long | coate in one hand and drawes his dag-|ger with th'other.*

4.100 *strikes him* (at end of line)

4.108 *stabs him.* (at end of line)

4.112 *Exit with his Sonne.*

5.0.1 *Enter a maide with a child in her armes, the mo-|ther by her a sleepe.*

5.7.1 *Enter husband with the boie bleeding.* (after 5.7)

5.8.1 *Striues with her for the | child.*

5.12.1 *Throws her down.*

5.15.1–5.17.1 *W.wakes. | catches vp the yongest.* (after 'children', 5.16)

5.24 *Stabs at the child in | hir armes.* (after 5.24)

5.25 *gets it from hir.* (after 5.44)

5.27.1   *shee's hurt and sinks downe.*
5.28.1   *Enter a lusty seruant.*
5.37   *ouercomes him.*
5.42.1   *The Master meets him.*
5.49.1   *Exeu.*
5.55.1   *Enter Master, and two seruants.*
5.67.1   *Exit Mr and seruants. (after 5.67)*
5.84.1   *Enters two seruants.*
5.89.1   *Exeunt*
6.0.1   *Enter Husband as being thrown off his horse, And falls:*
6.8.1   *Crie within*

6.15.1   *Euter M. of the Colledge, 3,Gentlemen,and others | with Holberds. | Finde him.*
6.33–7.0.1   *Exeunt | Enters a knight with two or three Gentlemen.*
7.6.1   *Enter the master of the colledge and the rest, | with the prisoner.*
7.27.1   *Exit prisoner.*
7.33.1–8.0.1   *Exit. | Enter Husband with the officers,The Maister and gen-|tlemen as going by his house.*
8.4.1   *Enter his wife brought in a chaire.*
8.32.1   *Children laid out. (after 8.33)*
8.62.1   *Exeunt | Husband with holberds (after 8.61)*
8.75.1   *FINIS.*

LINEATION NOTES

Note: In view of the large number of editions of this work, many of them reprints with only minor changes, a systematic collation of the lineation has not been attempted. Most of the necessary changes originate with Malone; this list notes further changes occurring in Sturgess's and the Revels editions without necessarily implying that they had not been made before.

2.39   As...him] STURGESS; *2 lines* BRADOCK: spirit |
2.45   Fool...beggars] MALONE; *verse* BRADOCK
2.52–3   O beggary...man] STURGESS; *1 line* BRADOCK
2.55–6   He...credit] THIS EDITION; *prose* BRADOCK
2.96–8   Look...hands] MALONE; *prose* BRADOCK
2.98   But...nails] MALONE; BRADOCK *starts a verse line at* 'to'.
2.103   I...speedily] MALONE; BRADOCK *prints* 'I...shall' *as verse and starts prose with* 'Speedily'
2.105–6   A...me] THIS EDITION; *prose* BRADOCK
2.162–3   To...bed] MALONE; fruitful | BRADOCK
2.165–6   Have...me] STURGESS; *1 line* BRADOCK
3.44–9   usage...torments] MALONE; *verse* BRADOCK: pity | pro- vided | credit | me | overjoyed |
3.78–9   From...me] MALONE; *verse* BRADOCK: so, university |

4.41   Bruised...sake] MALONE; *verse* BRADOCK
4.42–3   A...'em] MALONE; mortal | BRADOCK
4.72–3   and...was mine] MALONE; *verse* BRADOCK
4.84–6   In...live] MALONE; *prose* BRADOCK
4.89–91   Who...interest] MALONE; *prose* BRADOCK
4.108–11   Bleed...see] THIS EDITION; *6 lines* BRADOCK: beg, beg | disgrace | base | fates | faces | see |
5.10–11   Are...Downstairs] MALONE; *prose* BRADOCK
5.37–9   O...haste] MALONE; *prose* BRADOCK
5.74–5   I...him] MALONE; *prose* BRADOCK
5.85–6   Please...within] MALONE; *prose* BRADOCK
6.6–8   In...meadows...beast] MALONE; *prose* BRADOCK
7.6–7   The...justice] STURGESS; *prose* BRADOCK
7.9–10   Do...on] STURGESS; *prose* BRADOCK
7.30   It...man] MALONE; so | BRADOCK
8.1–2   I...endangered] MALONE; *prose* BRADOCK
8.6–7   O...laws] MALONE; *prose* BRADOCK
8.9–10   How...dead] STURGESS; *prose* BRADOCK
8.18–19   Seven...nails] MALONE; *prose* BRADOCK
8.62–3   O kind...unmurdered] MALONE; *2 lines* BRADOCK: com- forted

SIR ROBERT SHERLEY

Edited by Jerzy Limon and Daniel J. Vitkus

Sir Robert Sherley first appears in a quarto edition of 1609. It was entered in the Stationers' Register on 30 May of that year:

> John Budge. Entered for his copy in a Courte holden this day a booke called the travells of Sir Robert Sherley he sayth yt is aucthorised by master Etkins ⎱ vj^d

The quarto was printed by J. Windet 'for *Iohn Budge*, and are to bee sold at his Shop at the Great South doore of Pauls.' It survives in six copies, one of which—the British Library's Grenville copy (STC 17894.5)—contains a unique cancel dedication to Sir Robert's brother, Sir Thomas, and is the only one that is signed by Thomas Middleton; it is printed here as Additional Passage A. The other five copies contain an unsigned dedication to Sir Robert's father, also Thomas; this dedication is printed as Additional Passage B. Most of Middleton's text is a free translation of Andreas Loeaechius's (i.e. Andrew Leech's) *Encomia Nominis & Negocij D. Roberti Sherlaeii*, published in Cracow early in 1609. Middleton's other source is Strabo's *De Situ Orbis Libri XVII*. The quarto is collated A–C4, and there are no apparent press variants among the six extant copies. (Apart from the British Library which has both variant copies, copies of STC 17894 are at the Bodleian Library, Chatsworth, the Folger Shakespeare Library, and Yale University Library.) The current text is based on the British Library Grenville copy.

SEE ALSO

Text: *Works*, 673
Authorship and date: this volume, 368

WORKS CITED

Previous Editions

Bullen, A. H., ed., *Works* (1886), vol. 8

Other Works Cited

Baumer, Franklin L., 'England, the Turk and the Common Corps of Christendom', *The American Historical Review* (1945), 26–48
Calendar of State Papers and Manuscripts, Relating to English Affairs, Existing in the Archives and Collections of Venice, and in other Libraries of Northern Italy, ed. Rawdon Brown *et al.*, 40 vols (1864–1947)

Cartwright, John, *The Preacher's Travels. Wherein is set downe a true Journall, to the confines of the East Indies, through the great Countryes of Syria, Mesopotamia, Armenia, Media, Hircania and Parthia. With the Authors retourne by the way of Persia, Susiana, Assiria, Chaldaea, and Arabia, Containing a full survew of the knigdom [sic] of Persia: and in what termes the Persian stands with the Great Turke at this day: also a true relation of Sir Anthonie Sherleys entertainment there* (1611)
Chamberlain, John, *Letters*, ed. Norman Egbert McClure, 2 vols (1939)
[Cottington, Robert?], *A True Historicall Discourse of Muley Hamets Rising...* [including] *The adventures of Sir Anthony Sherley* (1609)
Day, John, William Rowley, and George Wilkins, *The Travailes of the Three English Brothers* (1607)
Leech, Andrew, *Iouis arbitrium: sine hæreditarium, Iacobo... primo...regi, in Angliam, Franciam, & Hyberniam, diuinitus collatum* (1603)
Loeaechius, Andreas [Andrew Leech], *Decas Anagrammatum. Quá suis ipsorum donantur nominibus ... Iosephus Iusoila ... Nicolaus Firleus ... Stanislaus Lanscoronscius ...* (1608)
—— *Elogium sermae heroinae, Mariae Archiducissae Austriae...ex tituli anagrammate...* (Cracow, 1606)
—— *Encomium insigniorum illmae domus Comorouianae. Elogia tribus superstitibus fratribus data. Iusta duobus mortuis soluta... Accessit carmen in xenium...* (Cracow, 1607)
—— *Encomia Nominis & Negocij D. Roberti Sherlaeii* (Cracow, 1609)
—— *Sermis Archiducibus Austriae Maximiliano eiusq[ue] sorori virgini, Mariae Christiernae: alteri votum, vt Magni Patris incitatus exemplo, clarissimis in patriam meritis nominis sectetur consequaturq[ue] immortalitatem: alteri paraenesis, ne ob hominum opiniones. De hoc quod humanitús malis artibus factum est, quicquam de animo optimé sibi conscio remittat. Xenii nomine eb Andrea Loeaechio...dicatum* (Cracow, 1606)
Nixon, Anthony, *The Three English Brothers* (1607)
Parry, William, *A new and large discourse of the travels of Sir Anthony Sherley Knight by sea and over land, to the Persian empire* (1601)
Patterson, W. B., *King James VI and I and the Reunion of Christendom* (1997)
Shand, G. B., 'Source and Intent in Middleton's *Sir Robert Sherley*', *Renaissance and Reformation* 19 (1983), 257–64
Shirley, Evelyn Philip, *The Sherley Brothers* (1848)
Strabo, *The Geography*, ed. H. C. Hamilton and W. Falconer (1906) ['Persis' in vol. III, pp. 129–41]
A True report of Sir Anthony Shierlies iourney overland to Venice, frō thence by sea to Antioch, Aleppo, and Babilon. And soe to Casbine in Persia: his entertainment there by the Great Sophie: his oration: his letters of credence to the Christian princes: and the priviledg obtained of the Great Sophie, for the quiet passage and trafique of all Christian marchants, throughout his whole dominions (1600)

TEXTUAL NOTES

118 *Servus...Liber*] LEECH, WINDET. BULLEN emends this, unnecessarily, to 'Liber, ast hero servus'.

121 Encomiums] WINDET (Encomions)

178 Ast Liber, Servus Hero] LEECH, WINDET. BULLEN emends this, unnecessarily, to 'Liber, ast servus hero'.

208 renowned] THIS EDITION, following BULLEN's note; renowmed WINDET

225 behests] BULLEN *conj.*; heasts WINDET

237 scimitar] WINDET (Semyter); BULLEN (scymitar)

270 goal] WINDET (Gole)

315 also of] THIS EDITION; alfo ∧ WINDET

384 diserta] BULLEN; deferta WINDET

388 Scoti] WINDET; BULLEN thought this was a misprint for a 'Swede' and emended 'Scoti' to 'Sueci'. He did not know that Andreas Loeaechius was neither Polish nor Swedish, but Scottish.

B.12 I thought] THIS EDITION; ∧ ~ WINDET

THE TWO GATES OF SALVATION

Edited by Paul Mulholland

THE quarto pamphlet, *The Two Gates of Salvation Set Wide Open: or, The Mariage of the Old and New Teftament*, was originally printed in 1609 by Nicholas Okes (STC 17904.3). Confusion generated by variant cancel titles, misattribution in the unrevised STC to S. Collins (deriving from a dedicatory epistle from another work misbound into the British Library second copy), and clear identification of the actual author restricted to a single surviving copy have militated against recognition of the pamphlet as the work of Thomas Middleton. It has not previously been edited. The copy at Emmanuel College, Cambridge, is unique in preserving the initial half-sheet bearing the original title-page and preliminaries. A title-page border (McKerrow 182) exclusive to this copy occurs in other Okes books, as does a decorative initial 'G' (Miller G1) found on B1 in all surviving copies. *The Two Gates of Salvation* was reissued in 1620 under the title 'THE | MARIAGE | OF THE OLD | AND NEW | TESTAMENT' with a cancel title-page and preliminaries (a different dedicatory epistle) constituting a half-sheet, which, on the basis of the title-page ornament (McKerrow 311), was apparently printed by George Purslowe (STC 17904.5). Only a single copy of this issue survives—the British Library first copy (BL 1). A third issue dated 1627 contains a cancel title-page and no preliminaries printed by John Okes and titled, 'GODS | Parliament-|HOVSE: | OR, | The Marriage of the Old | and New Teftament' (STC 17904.7). Four copies of the 1627 reissue are known: Bodleian Library, British Library second copy (BL 2), Lambeth Palace Library (formerly at Sion College), and the George Peabody Library of The Johns Hopkins University. In addition to these six complete copies, a fragment constituting approximately the bottom third of the 1609 title-page is preserved in a volume in the British Library: Bagford 5927, no. 212 (Blayney, 413). Although no surviving copy contains the title, 'CELESTIALL PARALELS. | OR | The Prophets and the Euangelifts | *Embracing*', its appearance as a title to the preface in LAMBETH prompts the speculation that it may have served in this capacity. Since the 1627 cancel title-page affixed to this copy appears on three other copies, two of which have different head-titles, the cancel title presumably does not disclose the original intentions. The head-titles of both BL 2 and PEABODY, like BL 1 and EMMANUEL, read 'THE MARIAGE | OF THE OLD AND | *New Teftament*' while BODLEIAN reads 'GODS | PARLIAMENT | *Houfe*'. The Stationers' Register contains no record of the work.

From a bibliographical point of view *Two Gates* has a number of curious features—foremost among them is the provision of three different paired sets of running titles

The title-page of the solitary complete exemplar of the original edition of *The Two Gates of Salvation, Set Wide Open, or The Marriage of the Old and New Testament* (1609), printed by Nicholas Okes.

in three of the six surviving copies; the other three copies have a mixture of running-title sets (consistent within any given sheet) that includes examples of those preserved in the other three copies together with two sets not found elsewhere. The five matched pairs of running titles are as follows:

The Mariage of the old | and new Teftament. (BL 1 throughout; BL 2 sheets B, F, H; BODLEIAN sheets F, H; PEABODY sheets B, G)
The firft Gate. | The fecond Gate. (EMMANUEL throughout; PEABODY sheets E, F, H)
The lower Houfe. | The vpper Houfe. (BODLEIAN sheets B, D, E, G; BL 2 sheets D, E, G; PEABODY sheet D)

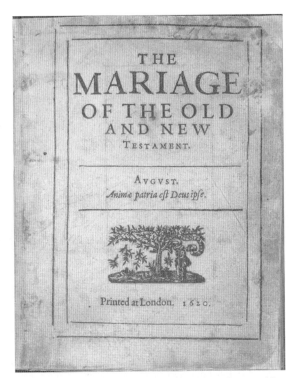

The cancel title-page of the second issue, apparently printed by George Purslowe, bearing one of the pamphlet's variant titles, *The Marriage of the Old and New Testament* (1620), from the only known surviving copy. Variant running titles and preface titles in several copies strongly suggest that the pamphlet when originally printed was equipped with variant titles.

> The Prophets. | The Euangelifts. (LAMBETH throughout)
>
> Law. | Grace. (BL 2 sheet C; BODLEIAN sheet C; PEABODY sheet C)

The sequence set out above slightly revises that presented in my earlier study (1986) in its reversal of the positions of the fourth and fifth set. The first and second sets of running titles coordinate closely with the titles given to the pamphlet in the 1609 and 1620 issues: 'THE TWO GATES OF SALVATION, *Set wide open:* OR The Mariage of the Old *And new Teftament*.' and 'THE MARIAGE OF THE OLD AND NEW TESTAMENT' respectively; the third set appears designed to link up with the title found in the 1627 issue: 'GODS Parliament-HOVSE: OR, The Marriage of the Old and New Teftament'; and the final two sets seem devised for the head-title preserved in LAMBETH: 'CELESTIALL PARALELS. *OR* The Prophets and the Euangelists *Embracing*.' The issue dates, of course, are unlikely to have any bearing on the range of titles that may have appeared on the occasion of the release of any issue, although the title common to all four 1627 copies suggests that this title served the pamphlet without regard

to the disposition of head-titles and running titles. The present edition attempts to convey the variant nature of the work's multiple titles and numerous running titles by making them all available over the body of the text.

Running titles begin on B1^v, where in three copies (EMMANUEL, LAMBETH, BODLEIAN) '*The Preface.*' appears and continues until B3^v (B4 contains no running title). On B4^v in these copies the running titles listed above are set in italic fount: EMMANUEL, '*The firft Gate.*'; LAMBETH, '*The Prophets.*'; BODLEIAN, '*The lower Houfe.*'. An italic setting of '*The fecond Gate.*' running title on C1 in EMMANUEL matches the corresponding italic title on B4^v. The three other copies (BL 1, BL 2, PEABODY) contain italic fount versions of '*The Mariage of the old | and new Teftament.*', that begin on B1^v and, except for B4, continue in their italic form through the remainder of the sheet. BL 1 is unique in preserving the italic rendering of '*The fecond Gate.*' on C1. On this page in BL 2, BODLEIAN, and PEABODY an italicized '*Grace.*' is found.

The transference of two settings of each pair of running titles and four sets of rules (i.e. one set per page) from forme to forme more or less throughout the work establishes that it was not printed from standing type but from a single imposition of each forme and further that a single skeleton forme was employed. I have discussed the multiple sets of running titles together with several related matters at greater length in an earlier study (1986). As the distribution of running titles among the six surviving copies reveals, three of the copies with the 1627 cancel title contain a mixture of running titles. One of the consequences of this is a series of mismatches at points where a running title found in one sheet is juxtaposed with that of another sheet, as, for example, '*The lower Houfe. | Grace.*', in BODLEIAN on B4^v and C1. Such arrangements are unlikely to have been intentional. But the fact that all instances occur in copies bearing the 1627 cancel title-page possibly suggests that copies defective in this way were held back until this date. After her husband's death Middleton's widow, Mary Magdalen, found herself in desperate circumstances and petitioned the city for money (Barker); the release of any remaining imperfect copies of *Two Gates* at this time may be related to her condition of poverty. The assortment of mismatched sheets is difficult to account for unless Okes's workmen were remiss in keeping a careful count of the number of sheets impressed with each title. The appearance of the 'Law. | Grace.' title only in sheet C of three copies and 'The vpper Houfe. | The lower Houfe.' in sheet D of three copies would seem to support such an explanation.

A book of this nature would normally be equipped with only one set of paired running titles which would proceed from one forme to the next in an orderly fashion and, possibly in an abbreviated form, reflect the work's title. The five sets of running titles (no clear evidence survives to establish whether this is the full complement) are accordingly most unusual and, together with variant titles and head-titles preserved in the reissued copies, direct attention to a puzzling element of complexity in what would appear to be a relatively straightforward work. This in turn prompts speculation as to the purpose of the book's extraordinary features. The unique extant copy of the 1609 issue, EMMANUEL, contains a 'factotum dedication', that is, a dedication with the spaces left blank for manuscript completion of the name of the dedicatee and the signature of the author. Might the alternate titles and running titles signal an attempt to give the appearance of different works to prospective patrons, or to create the impression at least of a work catering in part to individual interests or sensibilities? The likely motive underlying such designs would be generating more money—a motive entirely consistent with Middleton's circumstances when the work was originally published. Since the first two issues are known only in single copies, whether the substitute titles and other variants were part of a plan in 1609 and/or calculated from the start for subsequent reissues is impossible to determine.

In contrast to the blank dedication of the 1609 issue is the naming in the 1620 issue of two prominent Puritans as the dedicatees, Mr Richard Fishbourne and Mr John Browne. Further, the 1620 dedication is accompanied by the author's name and recently acquired title, 'Chronologer for the Honourable Citie of London'.

The ornament that appears on the 1620 cancel title--page depicts an olive tree and an old man whose outstretched right hand extends to a pruned limb of the tree. Severed branches are suspended in mid air or lie on the ground. A scroll bearing the text 'NOLI ALTUM SAPERE' loops over the abbreviated limb, runs behind the extended hand, and serpentines above the man. A. A. Bromham correctly identified the source of the caption as Romans 11:20, the latter part of which in the Latin Vulgate Bible reads 'noli altum sapere, sed time': 'be not high-minded [i.e. proud], but fear' (Geneva). In place of this critic's misidentification of the olive tree as the tree of knowledge, however, Patricia Parker has pointed out in correspondence that the contextual passage in Romans 11 (assisted by glosses in the Geneva and/or Geneva-Tomson Bible) clarifies and elaborates the significance of the image and accompanying text: the Jews who are unbelievers are the broken branches, Abraham is the tree's root, and believers are wild olive branches that may be grafted onto the tree. Despite the absence of the symbol of his martyrdom— a sword—the aged figure very likely represents St Paul himself, with the scroll standing in for the apostle's other iconic symbol—a book. His hand's grasp of a pruned limb suggests that he is engaged in an act of branch removal linked to the first part of Romans 11:20: 'Well, through unbelief they are broken off'. Middleton includes Romans 11:9-10 (79.II) in *The Two Gates*, a scriptural passage that makes allusion to the blind or preposterous zeal of Jews who fail to acknowledge the authority of the Gospel (i.e. broken branches). As McKerrow points out, the ornament used by Purslowe is a copy of a much earlier device found in many books printed by the Etienne family; and the version in Purslowe's possession occurs in various publications bearing his imprint. In light of the links

The ornament from the title-page of *The Marriage of the Old and New Testament* (1620).

and resonances between the ornament and particularly 79.II of this pamphlet, not to mention the new dedication and self-identification as City Chronologer, however, it is tempting to speculate that Middleton may have had a hand in selecting it for the 1620 issue.

The printed text of *Two Gates* is free of gross errors or other evidence of corruption. In some formes several stages of correction have survived, not infrequently to effect relatively inconsequential changes—presumably a reflection of care in printing or, since publication of this work was clearly initiated by Middleton, authorial supervision. On a number of occasions the stages of correction helpfully coincide with rotation of the sets of running titles and accordingly provide evidence relating to the order of their impression. In sheet F, for example, two stages of correction in addition to the original state are preserved. In the earliest state of inner F are found the following uncorrected readings: 'becaufe hee' (in the margin of F1ᵛ; 44.I.c), 'and -|ther' (F2; 45.II.1), and 'foone' (F3ᵛ; 54.I.1) in BL 1, BL 2, and BODLEIAN, which carry the running titles 'The Mariage of the old | and new Teftament.' in this sheet. The faulty readings are corrected to 'becaufe hee', 'and o-|ther', and 'fonne' in EMMANUEL and PEABODY, the running titles of which are 'The firft Gate. | The fecond Gate.' LAMBETH, equipped with the running title, 'The Prophets. | The Euangelifts.', contains a subsequent correction from 'confi-|dene' to 'confi-|dence' (in the margin of F4; 56.II.c). Evidence of correction in other formes similarly betrays the sequence of title rotation and suggests that the order (i.e. as set out above) was adhered to systematically at least until sheet H, which is anomalous in several respects (e.g. the order of formes through the press observed elsewhere was reversed in this sheet: outer H, which consists of only three pages, was impressed before inner H). Such corrections as are preserved are fairly routine and fall within the competence of a proof-corrector; none calls for specific reference to the manuscript. On G4ᵛ and H1 an Old and a New Testament passage are mistakenly reversed and a marginal note accompanied by a hand with a pointing index finger on H1 directs the reader to the error (76.I and 76.II). The reversal was probably allowed to stand because sheet G had already been perfected when it was noticed. Given the scheme of the work, which with only a few exceptions is organized according to the sequence of New Testament books, the error's discovery is not dependent upon, but neither is it inconsistent with, authorial intervention.

A particular editorial 'problem' posed by *The Two Gates of Salvation* concerns a number of instances in which the printed text is manifestly at fault. Some of these involve erroneous readings in scriptural citations, others mistaken or imprecise marginal references. The question of which to emend and which to leave alone calls for the articulation of and adherence to a governing policy of some kind. In the present edition only those errors that appear to be compositorial in origin have been emended. This includes, for example, the reading 'gracious', xii.I.4, which conflicts with the sense of the passage and stands at variance with the Bible Middleton used as his source. Since 'grievous' in the manuscript may plausibly have been misread as 'gracious' by the compositor and Middleton is rather less likely to have mistranscribed the word from his printed source, the faulty word has been emended. By contrast, a marginal reference to 'Exod. 24:17' accompanying ll. 60–1 of the Preface appears to be a, presumably inadvertent, authorial error for 'Num. 24:17'. Since the attendant circumstances do not throw suspicion on the compositor as the source of the mistaken reference, it has been allowed to stand. In other cases the scriptural references to cited passages fail to record the full extent of the biblical quotation or are otherwise imprecise. The following is a list of inaccurate references and other erroneous readings that have not been emended but which are discussed in the Commentary and, in some cases, Textual Notes: Preface.60.n; ii.I.s; ii.II.s; iii.II.s; vii.II.s; viii.I.s; ix.II.s; x.II.s; xi.I.s; xii.II.s; xiii.I.s; xiii.II.s; 5.II.s; 11.II.s; 20.II.s; 29.II.s; 32.I.s; 35.I.s; 39.II.s; 40.I.s; 43.II.s; 50.I.s; 51.I.c; 53.II.s; 55.II.s.

Among the interesting features of the early printed text of *The Two Gates of Salvation* is its unusual texture of italic and roman typefaces. In the pamphlet's Preface italic type appears to be used chiefly for emphasis, though resort to it at times verges on the idiosyncratic. In the body of the work proper the italic type used predominantly for scriptural passages is set against roman marginalia and references. In some instances inconsistencies in a generally observed pattern occur, as, for example, in the case of quotation of key words from a biblical passage in the accompanying marginal note. Such words or phrases are for the most part in roman type, but on a few occasions italics are used. This edition attempts to preserve the contrast between italic and roman type as a deliberate feature of design and presentation, but apart from a few exceptional instances does not attempt to iron out inconsistencies.

References to passages in the body of the work are by section number, testament (I for Old, II for New), and line number or marginal column (s for source, c for commentary). Thus 65.II.4 refers to section 65, New

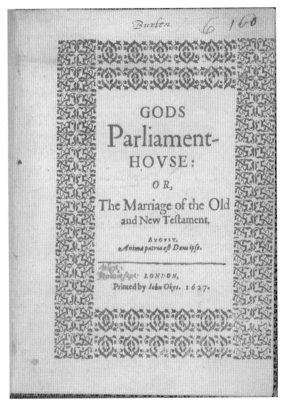

The cancel title-page of the third issue printed by John Okes, bearing another of the variant titles, *God's Parliament House, or The Marriage of the Old and New Testament* (1627), from one of the four surviving copies.

Testament passage, line 4. The early printed text contains two numbered sequences of sections, the first running from 1 to 17 and the second from 1 to 92; in this edition the first sequence is printed with roman numerals to distinguish it from the second. The introductory and concluding sections in these sequences are identified as a, xviia, o, and 92a in references.

SEE ALSO

Text: *Works*, 683
Authorship and date: this volume, 369

WORKS CITED

Barker, R. H., *Thomas Middleton* (1958)

Blayney, Peter W. M., *The Texts of 'King Lear' and their Origins*, vol. i, *Nicholas Okes and the First Quarto* (1982)

Bromham, A. A., and Zara Bruzzi, *The Changeling and the Years of Crisis, 1619–1624: A Hieroglyph of Britain* (1990), 140

Hall, Joseph, *The Passion Sermon* (1609; STC 12693.7)

McKerrow, R. B., *Printers' and Publishers' Devices in England and Scotland 1485–1640* (1913)

Miller, C. William, 'A London Ornament Stock: 1598–1683', *Studies in Bibliography* 7 (1955), 125–51

Mulholland, Paul, '*The Two Gates of Salvation*: Typology, and Thomas Middleton's Bibles', *English Language Notes* 23 (1985), 27–36

—— 'Thomas Middleton's *The Two Gates of Salvation* (1609): An Instance of Running-title Rotation', *The Library*, VI, 8 (1986), 18–31

TEXTUAL NOTES

In the following notes reference is made to corrected (OKES B) and uncorrected (OKES A) states; but readers should refer to the list of Press Variants for a record of relationships in changes to type that span multiple stages. These are frequently coordinated with rotation of the series of five running titles. Omitted from the following notes are corrections involving elements not represented in the modernized text; these include, for example, the series of markers cited in the Preface, 172–83. The latter are, however, recorded among the Press Variants.

Title   The Two Gates...Testament OKES; THE MARIAGE OF THE OLD AND NEW TESTAMENT. PURSLOWE; GODS Parliament--HOVSE: OR, The Marriage of the Old and New Teftament JOHN OKES. As only a single copy of the early printed text survives with the original title-page, the title of the work is taken from this copy. The evidence provided by alternative wordings at the start of the Preface and subsequent issues suggests, however, that the pamphlet may originally have been printed with variant titles.

Preface.24   surgeon] OKES (Chirurgi|on)

Preface.27   sins] THIS EDITION; fonnes OKES. The OKES reading, 'fonnes', shifts attention away from the transgression of Adam to the exoneration of subsequent generations. Although this is not indefensible, the focus seems rather to be concentrated more directly on balancing the treason of the first Adam against the absolution of the second (Christ); besides, Christ's death quitted not only Adam's *sons*, but his daughters, his wife, and himself. Emendation to 'sins' reflects this. A simple misreading of the manuscript could have been responsible for the error.

Preface.31   bore] OKES (bare)

Preface.53   four thousand] OKES (4000.)

Preface.60   sung] OKES (song)

Preface.85   kingdom] OKES (* Kingdome). Asterisks in OKES link the citation from Isaiah to 'Kingdome' in the text. These are the only such instances in the Preface.

Preface.85.n   Isa. 54] OKES (*54). See preceding note.

Preface.102–3   were...was] OKES B; was...were OKES A. Correction of this undoubtedly mistaken reading clearly signals direction, with implications for the sequence of running titles.

Preface.127   *sepulchre*] OKES (Sepulchre). The pattern of italicization in the earlier part of this sentence (*Manger...Manger, Croffe...Croffe*) suggests that the second occurrence of 'Sepulchre' ought also to be italicized. The compositor could easily have failed to observe a mark to this effect in the manuscript.

Preface.141   guide] OKES (guid)

Preface.143   whilst] OKES (whileft)

Preface.157   sprung] OKES (fprong)

a.I.2   revealed] OKES (reueled)

ii.I.2   bore] OKES (bare)

iii.I.1, iii.II.2, 3, vii.II.1   Bethlehem] OKES (Beth-leem)

iv.II.c   *parientis...parientis*] THIS EDITION; *patientis...patientis* OKES. OKES's '*patientis*' in neither instance connects with the context and is most likely mistaken; '*parientis*' answers the apparent need in both citations. The error could easily

have arisen from a simple compositorial misreading of the manuscript.

v.I.s   Judg. 13:5] THIS EDITION; *Iudg*. 13. | 15. OKES. The OKES reading most likely represents a compositorial misreading of the manuscript; but an authorial error cannot be ruled out.

vii.I.3   all the] THIS EDITION; *the all* OKES. OKES's '*the all*' cannot have been intended (the passage reads 'all the' in the Geneva Bible, the source for this citation); the error probably arose from an accidental transposition of the words by the compositor.

vii.II.1   Jewry] OKES (Iury)

viii.II.c   *solvitur*] THIS EDITION; *foluiter* OKES. A simple compositorial misreading.

viii.II.c   *immolatur*] THIS EDITION; *imolatur* OKES. The single '*m*' of the OKES reading may signify nothing more than the vagaries of Jacobean spelling; but the compositor may have neglected to supply a tilde over the '*m*'.

ix.II.3   spoken] OKES (fpaken)

x.II.1   forty...forty] OKES (40. ... 40.)

xii.I.2   land of] THIS EDITION; *land* OKES. Omission of the preposition is most likely a compositorial slip, especially since it appears in the following parallel reference on the same line.

xii.I.2   Zabulon] OKES (Zebulon)

xii.I.4   *grievous*] THIS EDITION; *gracious* OKES. A compositorial misreading of '*gracious*' for '*grievous*' is a plausible explanation for this error, and rather more likely than Middleton's misreading of the printed Geneva Bible.

xii.II.6–7   sat...sat] OKES (fate...fate)

xiv.II.4   prophet] OKES (Prohphet)

xiv.II.4   bore] OKES (bare)

xv.I.c   humility] OKES B (humi-|ity); humi-|lity OKES A. Probable evidence of direction; but a case such as this involving the migration of a loose sort carries less authority than a correction.

xvii.II.1   Zecharias] OKES (Zacarias)

0.I.4   Are...bands] THIS EDITION; are...in | heauenly bands OKES. In OKES only the second line of the couplet is set as a separate verse line; the preceding component of the pair is run on as a continuation of the prose introduction. Relineation as a pentameter line recovers the balanced couplet. Presumably the compositor failed to recognize the pair of rhymed lines.

0.II.4   Are...bands] THIS EDITION; are...mari-|age...bands OKES. As in the parallel Old Testament introduction, only the second line of the couplet is set as verse in OKES. See preceding note.

7.I.4   two] OKES (too)

8.II.4   enemies] THIS EDITION; *enemy* OKES. Since the allusion in the source passage in the Geneva or Geneva-Tomson Bibles is plural, the singular in OKES is presumably due to compositorial error.

10.I.c   expoundeth] OKES (expon-|deth)

14.II.2   son] OKES (Sunne)

16.II.2   spoke] OKES (fpake)

22.I.4   desert] OKES (defart)

28.II.2 *overthrew*] THIS EDITION; *ouerthrow* OKES. OKES's 'ouerthrow' is clearly in the wrong tense—possibly the result of a compositorial misreading of an 'o' for an 'e', or an instance of foul case.

29.I.4 *mightst*] OKES (*mighteſt*)

31.II.s Matt. 21:42] THIS EDITION; *Mat.21.24* OKES. Reversal of the digits of the verse number probably stems from compositorial error.

35.II.1 *through*] OKES (*tho-|rough*)

36.II.c *Josephus*] OKES (*Ioſeph.*). The reference has been expanded in the interests of clarification.

37.I.s Isa. 13:9, 10] THIS EDITION; *Eſ.13.9 | 9.10* OKES. Duplication of the citation of verse 9 from Isaiah 13 in OKES presumably derives from some form of confusion—either in the manuscript or on the part of the compositor, or both.

38.I.c *Father*] OKES B (*Fa-|ther*); *fa-|ther* OKES A. Evidence of direction.

40.I.s Ezek. 18:7] THIS EDITION; *Ezech. | 7.* OKES. OKES omits citation of the chapter from Ezekiel—either a simple compositorial oversight or a reflection of a lapse in the manuscript.

40.II.3 *a-hungered*] OKES (*an hungred*)

43.I.s Ezek. 11:7, 8, 9, 10] THIS EDITION; *Ezec.11* OKES. Omission of the verse reference may be a compositorial oversight; but, unless the whole of the chapter is the intended reference, an authorial lapse is also possible.

44.II.1 *be come*] THIS EDITION; *be-|come* OKES. The hyphen in OKES's 'be-|come' mistakenly gives the impression of one rather than two words; a manuscript line-break after '*be*' may have contributed to the compositor's perception of the two separate words as divided syllables of '*become*'.

44.II.3 *sat*] OKES (*ſate*)

45.II.1 *and other*] OKES B (*and o-|ther*); *and -|ther* OKES A. Evidence of direction.

46.II.3 *there's*] OKES (*theirs*)

53.I.4 *bore*] OKES (*bare*)

54.I.1 *son*] OKES B (*sonne*); *soone* OKES A. A signal of direction.

55.I.2 *Sidon*] OKES (*Zidon*)

55.I.s Kgs.] OKES (*King.*)

56.II.c *confidence*] OKES B (*confi-|dence*); *confi-|dene* OKES A. As in other such instances, correction clearly signals sequence of impression.

57.II.1 *load*] THIS EDITION; *lade* OKES

58.II.2 *bore*] OKES (*bare*)

64.II.2 *Aceldama*] OKES (*Aceldema*)

65.I.1-4 *pour...pour*] OKES B (*powre...powre*); *power...power* OKES A. A number of press corrections on this page provide evidence of direction.

65.I.5 *show*] OKES B (*ſhew*); *ſhow* OKES A. See note to 65.I.1-4.

65.I.c abundance...than] OKES B (a|būdance more | generally thē); a-|dance more ge-|nerally then OKES A. See note to 65.I.1-4.

68.I.c *Adam*] OKES B; *Adam* OKES A. See note to 65.I.1-4.

68.II.c *Abraham*] OKES B; *Abraham* OKES A. See note to 65.I.1-4.

76.I.1-8 *I will sow...sons of the living God.*] THIS EDITION; *I will call...children of the liuing God.* OKES. By some error, presumably compositorial, the passages for 76.I and 76.II were reversed in OKES. The error, of course, could have escaped notice until the setting of outer H, which uniquely preceded the inner forme through the press, was underway. Since the first stage of the mistake occurred on the final page of outer G (G4ᵛ) with a setting of verses from Romans in place of those from Hosea, and since the outer forme of sheet G perfected the inner, correction of the error would have involved the expense of an additional edition-sheet quantity of paper, possibly the resetting of inner G if it had been distributed by the time that the sheet was perfected, and reimpression of both formes. In place of this a more economical course was taken which took the form of a marginal note to the misplaced Hosea passage drawing attention to the error and the proper arrangement of the citations accompanied by a left-pointing hand.

76.II.1-4 *I will call...children of the living God.*] THIS EDITION; *I will ſow...ſonnes of the liuing God.* OKES. See preceding note.

76.II.c *not in* THIS EDITION; This verſe | muſt bee reade | on the Pro-|phets ſide, | Page.48. | ☞ OKES. See preceding note. Since the presumably compositorial error involving the reversal of the passages for 76.I and 76.II has been corrected in this edition, the marginal note alerting the reader to the appropriate placement of the Old and New Testament passages is not required.

77.I.s Nah.] OKES (*Nahum.*)

80.II.2 Zion] OKES (*Sion*)

82.I.3 *my*] THIS EDITION; *his* OKES. The OKES reading, 'his', makes no sense in the context and is unsupported by any versions of the Bible Middleton appears to have consulted in composing *The Two Gates*. The adopted reading is that found in the Geneva Bible, the source of this passage.

84.I.s Hos.] OKES (*Hoſea*)

85.I.c *meaning*] OKES B; *menning* OKES A. Additional evidence relating to direction.

86.I.c *of his*] OKES B (of | his); of | of his OKES A. See preceding note.

87.II.1 *revealed*] OKES (*reueiled*)

89.I.1 *plague*] OKES B; *plauge* OKES A. See note to 85.I.c.

89.I.2 *quit*] OKES (*quite*)

90.II.1 *wings*] OKES B; *wnigs* OKES A. See note to 85.I.c.

PRESS VARIANTS

In some instances sequence is uncertain. Such cases mainly involve the sequence of as many as five sets of rotated running titles; but the order of impression of the pamphlet's three head-titles on B1 is likewise unclear. Doubtful stages have been marked with an asterisk (*).

Copies collated (abbreviations listed to the left):

BODLEIAN Bodleian Library, Oxford (1627)
BL 1 British Library copy 1 (1620)
BL 2 British Library copy 2 (1627)
EMMANUEL Emmanuel College, Cambridge (1609)
PEABODY The George Peabody Library, The Johns Hopkins

University, Baltimore, Maryland (1627)
LAMBETH Lambeth Palace, London; formerly Sion College, London (1627)

Sheet B (outer forme)

First Stage Corrected: EMMANUEL
Uncorrected: BL 1, BL 2, PEABODY

B2ᵛ

running title *The Preface.* corr; *The Mariage of the old* unc

B3

running title *The Preface.* corr; *and new Teſtament.* unc

$B4^v$

running title   *The firſt Gate. corr*; *The Mariage of the old unc*

   Second Stage Corrected: BODLEIAN

$B1$

Preface.1–2   The Marriage of the Old and New Testament] GODS | PARLIAMENT | *Houſe. corr*; THE MARIAGE | OF THE OLD AND | *New Teſtament. unc*

$B2^v$

Preface.102–3   were…was] were…was *corr*; was…were *unc*

$B4^v$

running title   *The lower Houſe. corr*; *The firſt Gate. unc*

   Third Stage Corrected: LAMBETH

$B1$

Preface.1–2   The Marriage of the Old and New Testament] CELESTIALL PARALELS. | OR | The Prophets and the Euangelifts | *Embracing. corr*; GODS | PARLIAMENT | *Houſe. unc*

$B4^v$

running title   *The Prophets. corr*; *The lower Houſe. unc*

Sheet B (inner forme)

   First Stage Corrected: BODLEIAN, EMMANUEL, LAMBETH
   Uncorrected: BL 1, BL 2, PEABODY

$B1^v$

running title   *The Preface. corr*; *The Mariage of the Old unc*

$B2$

running title   *The Preface. corr*; *and new Teſtament. unc*

$B3^v$

running title   *The Preface. corr*; *The Mariage of the Old unc*

Sheet C (outer forme)

   First Stage Corrected: EMMANUEL
   Uncorrected: BL 1

$C1$

running title   *The ſecond Gate. corr*; *and aew Teſtement. unc*

$C2^v$

running title   *The firſt Gate corr*; *The Mariage of the old unc*

$C3$

running title   *The ſecond Gate. corr*; *and new Teſtament. unc*

$C4^v$

running title   *The firſt Gate. corr*; *The Mariage of the old unc*

   Second Stage Corrected: LAMBETH

$C1$

running title   *The Euangelifts. corr*; *The ſecond Gate. unc*

$C2^v$

running title   *The Prophets. corr*; *The firſt Gate unc*

$C3$

running title   *The Euangelifts. corr*; *The ſecond Gate. unc*

$C4^v$

running title   *The Prophets. corr*; *The firſt Gate. unc*

   Third Stage Corrected: BL 2, BODLEIAN, PEABODY

$C1$

running title   *Grace. corr*; *The Euangelifts. unc*

$C2^v$

running title   *Law. corr*; *The Prophets. unc*

$C3$

running title   *Grace. corr*; *The Euangelifts. unc*

$C4^v$

running title   *Law. corr*; *The Prophets. unc*

Sheet C (inner forme)

   First Stage Corrected: EMMANUEL
   Uncorrected: BL 1

$C1^v$

running title   *The firſt Gate. corr*; *The Mariage of the old unc*

$C2$

running title   *The ſecond Gate. corr*; *and new Teſtament. unc*

$C3^v$

running title   *The firſt Gate. corr*; *The Mariage of the old unc*

xv.1.c   humility] humi-|^{l}ity *corr*; humi-|lity *unc*

$C4$

running title   *The ſecond Gate. corr*; *and new Teſtament. unc*

   Second Stage Corrected: LAMBETH

$C1^v$

running title   *The Prophets. corr*; *The firſt Gate. unc*

$C2$

running title   *The Euangelifts. corr*; *The ſecond Gate. unc*

$C3^v$

running title   *The Prophets. corr*; *The firſt Gate. unc*

$C4$

running title   *The Euangelifts. corr*; *The ſecond Gate. unc*

   Third Stage Corrected: BL 2, BODLEIAN, PEABODY

$C1^v$

running title   *Law. corr*; *The Prophets. unc*

$C2$

running title   *Grace. corr*; *The Euangelifts. unc*

$C3^v$

running title   *Law. corr*; *The Prophets. unc*

$C4$

running title   *Grace. corr*; *The Euangelifts. unc*

Sheet D (outer forme)

   First Stage Corrected: EMMANUEL
   Uncorrected: BL 1

$D1$

running title   *The ſecond Gate. corr*; *and new Teſtament. unc*

$D2^v$

running title   *The firſt Gate. corr*; *The Mariage of the old unc*

D3

running title   The fecond Gate. *corr*; and new Teftament. *unc*

D4ᵛ

running title   The firft Gate. *corr*; The Mariage of the old *unc*

　　Second Stage Corrected: BL 2, BODLEIAN, PEABODY

D1

running title   The vpper Houfe. *corr*; The fecond Gate. *unc*

D2ᵛ

running title   The lower Houfe. *corr*; The firft Gate. *unc*

D3

running title   The vpper Houfe. *corr*; The fecond Gate. *unc*

D4ᵛ

running title   The lower Houfe. *corr*; The firft Gate. *unc*

　　Third Stage Corrected: LAMBETH

D1

running title   Tꞅe Euangelifts. *corr*; The vpper Houfe. *unc*

D2ᵛ

running title   The Prophets. *corr*; The lower Houfe. *unc*

D3

running title   The Euangelifts. *corr*; The vpper Houfe. *unc*

D4ᵛ

running title   The Prophets. *corr*; The lower Houfe. *unc*

Sheet D (inner forme)

　　First Stage Corrected: EMMANUEL
　　Uncorrected: BL 1

D1ᵛ

running title   The firft Gate *corr*; The Mariage of the old *unc*

D2

running title   The fecond Gate. *corr*; and new Teftament. *unc*

D3ᵛ

running title   The firft Gate. *corr*; The Mariage of the old *unc*

D4

running title   The fecond Gate. *corr*; and new Teftament. *unc*

　　Second Stage Corrected: BL 2, BODLEIAN, PEABODY

D1ᵛ

running title   The lower Houfe. *corr*; The firft Gate *unc*

D2

running title   The vpper Houfe. *corr*; The fecond Gate. *unc*

D3ᵛ

running title   The lower Houfe. *corr*; The firft Gate. *unc*

D4

running title   The vpper Houfe. *corr*; The fecond Gate. *unc*

　　Third Stage Corrected: LAMBETH

D1ᵛ

running title   The Prophets. *corr*; The lower Houfe. *unc*

D2

running title   The Euangelifts. *corr*; The vpper Houfe. *unc*

D3ᵛ

running title   The Prophets. *corr*; The lower Houfe. *unc*

D4

running title   The Euangelifts. *corr*; The vpper Houfe. *unc*

Sheet E (outer forme)

　　First Stage Corrected: EMMANUEL, PEABODY
　　Uncorrected: BL 1

E1

running title   The fecond Gate. *corr*; and new Teftament. *unc*

E2ᵛ

running title   The firft Gate. *corr*; The Mariage of the old *unc*

E3

running title   The fecond Gate. *corr*; and new Teftament. *unc*

E4ᵛ

running title   The firft Gate. *corr*; The Mariage of the old *unc*
38.I.c   Father] Fa-|ther *corr*; fa-|ther *unc*

　　Second Stage Corrected: BL 2, BODLEIAN

E1

running title   The vpper Houfe. *corr*; The fecond Gate. *unc*

E2ᵛ

running title   The lower Houfe. *corr*; The firft Gate. *unc*

E3

running title   The vpper Houfe. *corr*; The fecond Gate. *unc*

E4ᵛ

running title   The lower Houfe. *corr*; The firft Gate. *unc*

　　Third Stage Corrected: LAMBETH

E1

running title   The Euangelifts. *corr*; The vpper Houfe. *unc*

E2ᵛ

running title   The Prophets. *corr*; The lower Houfe. *unc*

E3

running title   The Euangelifts. *corr*; The vpper Houfe. *unc*

E4ᵛ

running title   The Prophets. *corr*; The lower Houfe. *unc*

Sheet E (inner forme)

　　First Stage Corrected: EMMANUEL, PEABODY
　　Uncorrected: BL 1

E1ᵛ

running title   The firft Gate. *corr*; The Mariage of the old *unc*

E2

running title   The fecond Gate. *corr*; and new Teftament. *unc*

E3ᵛ

running title   The firft Gate. *corr*; The Mariage of the old *unc*

E4

running title   The fecond Gate. *corr*; and new Teftament. *unc*

Second Stage Corrected: BL 2, BODLEIAN

E1ᵛ

running title   The lower Houſe. *corr*; The firſt Gate. *unc*
E2

running title   The vpper Houſe. *corr*; The ſecond Gate. *unc*
E3ᵛ

running title   The lower Houſe. *corr*; The firſt Gate. *unc*
E4

running title   The vpper Houſe. *corr*; The ſecond Gate. *unc*

Third Stage Corrected: LAMBETH

E1ᵛ

running title   The Prophets. *corr*; The lower Houſe. *unc*
E2

running title   The Euangeliſts. *corr*; The vpper Houſe. *unc*
E3ᵛ

running title   The Prophets. *corr*; The lower Houſe. *unc*
E4

running title   The Euangeliſts. *corr*; The vpper Houſe. *unc*

Sheet F (outer forme)

First Stage Corrected: EMMANUEL
Uncorrected: BL 1, BL 2, BODLEIAN

F1

running title   The ſecond Gate. *corr*; and new Teſtament. *unc*
F2ᵛ

running title   The firſt Gate. *corr*; The Mariage of the old *unc*
F3

running title   The ſecond Gate. *corr*; and new Teſtament. *unc*
F4ᵛ

running title   The firſt Gate. *corr*; and new Teſtament. *unc*

Second Stage Corrected: PEABODY

F1

41.II   * *corr*; ¶ *unc* [reference-mark]

Third Stage Corrected: LAMBETH

F1

running title   The Euangeliſts. *corr*; The ſecond Gate. *unc*
F2ᵛ

running title   The Prophets. *corr*; The firſt Gate. *unc*
F3

running title   The Euangeliſts. *corr*; The ſecond Gate. *unc*
F4ᵛ

running title   The Prophets. *corr*; The firſt Gate. *unc*

Sheet F (inner forme)

First Stage Corrected: EMMANUEL, PEABODY
Uncorrected: BL 1, BL 2, BODLEIAN

F1ᵛ

running title   The firſt Gate. *corr*; The Mariage of the old *unc*
44.I.c   because he] becauſe hee *corr*; becauſe hee *unc*

F2

running title   The ſecond Gate. *corr*; and new Teſtament. *unc*
45.II.1   *and other*] *and o-|ther corr*; *and -|ther unc*
F3ᵛ

running title   The firſt Gate. *corr*; The Mariage of the old *unc*
54.I.1   son] ſonne *corr*; ſoone *unc*
F4

running title   The ſecond Gate. *corr*; and new Teſtament. *unc*

Second Stage Corrected: LAMBETH

F1ᵛ

running title   The Prophets. *corr*; The firſt Gate. *unc*
F2

running title   The Euangeliſts. *corr*; The ſecond Gate. *unc*
F3ᵛ

running title   The Prophets. *corr*; The firſt Gate. *unc*
F4

running title   The Euangeliſts. *corr*; The ſecond Gate. *unc*
56.II.c   confidence] confi-|dence *corr*; confi-|dene

Sheet G (outer forme)

First Stage Corrected: EMMANUEL
Uncorrected: BL 1, PEABODY

G1

running title   The ſecond Gate. *corr*; and new Teſtament. *unc*
G2ᵛ

running title   The firſt Gate. *corr*; The Mariage of the old *unc*
68.I.c   *Adam*] *Adam corr*; *Adam unc* [roman to italic A]
G3

running title   The ſecond Gate. *corr*; and new Teſtament. *unc*
68.II.c   *Abraham*] *Abraham corr*; *Abraham unc* [roman to italic A]
G4ᵛ

running title   The firſt Gate. *corr*; The Mariage of the old *unc*

Second Stage Corrected: BL 2, BODLEIAN

G1

running title   The vpper Houſe. *corr*; The ſecond Gate. *unc*
G2ᵛ

running title   The lower Houſe. *corr*; The firſt Gate. *unc*
G3

running title   The vpper Houſe. *corr*; The ſecond Gate. *unc*
G4ᵛ

running title   The lower Houſe. *corr*; The firſt Gate. *unc*
79.I   *not in corr*; * *unc* [reference-mark]

Third Stage Corrected: LAMBETH

G1

running title   The Euangeliſts. *corr*; The vpper Houſe. *unc*
G2ᵛ

running title   The Prophets. *corr*; The lower Houſe. *unc*
G3

running title   The Euangeliſts. *corr*; The vpper Houſe. *unc*

$G4^v$

running title   The Prophets. *corr*; The lower Houſe. *unc*

Sheet G (inner forme)

   First Stage Corrected: PEABODY
   Uncorrected: BL 1

$G1^v$

65.I.1   *pour*] *powre corr*; *power unc*
65.I.c   more generally] more | generally *corr*; more ge-|nerally *unc*
65.I.c   than] thē *corr*; then *unc*
65.I.4   *pour*] *powre corr*; *power unc*
65.I.5   *show*] *ſhew corr*; *ſhow unc*

$G2$

65.II.7   *show*] *ſhew corr*; *ſhow unc*

   Second Stage Corrected: EMMANUEL

$G1^v$

running title   The firſt Gate. *corr*; The Mariage of the old *unc*
$G2$
running title   The ſecond Gate. *corr*; and new Teſtament. *unc*
$G3^v$
running title   The firſt Gate. *corr*; The Mariage of the old *unc*
$G4$
running title   The ſecond Gate. *corr*; and new Teſtament. *unc*

   Third Stage Corrected: BL 2, BODLEIAN

$G1^v$
running title   The lower Houſe. *corr*; The firſt Gate. *unc*
$G2$
running title   The vpper Houſe. *corr*; The ſecond Gate. *unc*
$G3^v$
running title   The lower Houſe. *corr*; The firſt Gate. *unc*
$G4$
running title   The vpper Houſe. *corr*; The ſecond Gate. *unc*

   Fourth Stage Corrected: LAMBETH

$G1^v$
running title   The Prophets. *corr*; The lower Houſe. *unc*
$G2$
running title   The Euangeliſts. *corr*; The vpper Houſe. *unc*
$G3^v$
running title   The Prophets. *corr*; The lower Houſe. *unc*
$G4$
running title   The Euangeliſts. *corr*; The vpper Houſe. *unc*

Sheet H (outer forme)

   First Stage Corrected: EMMANUEL, PEABODY
   Uncorrected: BL 1, BL 2, BODLEIAN

$H1$

running title   The ſecond Gate. *corr*; and new Teſtament. *unc*
$H2^v$
running title   The firſt Gate. *corr*; The Mariage of the old *unc*
85.I.c   meaning] meaning *corr*; menning *unc*
86.I.c   of his] of | his *corr*; of | of his *unc* [BL 2 cropped]
89.I.1   *plague*] *plague corr*; *plauge unc*
$H3$
running title   The ſecond Gate. *corr*; and new Teſtament. *unc*

   Second Stage Corrected: LAMBETH

$H1$
running title   The Euangeliſts. *corr*; The ſecond Gate. *unc*
$H2^v$
running title   The Prophets. *corr*; The firſt Gate. *unc*
$H3$
running title   The Euangeliſts. *corr*; The ſecond Gate. *unc*

Sheet H (inner forme)

   First Stage Corrected: EMMANUEL, PEABODY
   Uncorrected: LAMBETH

$H1^v$
running title   The firſt Gate. *corr*; The Prophets. *unc*
$H2$
running title   The ſecond Gate. *corr*; The Euangeliſts. *unc*
$H3^v$
running title   The firſt Gate. *corr*; The Prophets. *unc*
$H4$
running title   The ſecond Gate. *corr*; The Euangeliſts. *unc*
90.II.1   *wings*] *wings corr*; *wnigs unc*

   Second Stage Corrected: BL 1, BL 2, BODLEIAN

$H1^v$
running title   The Mariage of the old *corr*; The firſt Gate. *unc*
$H2$
running title   and new Teſtament. *corr*; The ſecond Gate. *unc*
$H3^v$
running title   The Mariage of the old *corr*; The firſt Gate. *unc*
$H4$
running title   and new Teſtament. *corr*; The ſecond Gate. *unc*

THE ROARING GIRL

Edited by Coppélia Kahn

The Roaring Girl was first printed in quarto by Nicholas Okes in 1611 (*BEPD* 298, STC 17908). Several headbands and an ornamental initial identify him as the printer. The title-page reads:

> The Roaring Girle. | OR | *Moll Cut-Purſe.* | As it hath lately been Aᵈted on the Fortune-ſtage by | *the Prince his Players.* | Written by *T. Middleton* and *T.Dekkar.* | [woodcut illustration] | Printed at *London* for *Thomas Archer*, and are to be fold at his | ſhop in Popes head-pallace, neere the Royall | Exchange. 1611.

Dramatis Personæ appears on the verso. The play was entered in the Stationers' Register on 18 February 1612:

> Ambr. Garbrand Rd of him for then-
> trance of a booke
> concerninge Mall   } vjd.
> Cutpurse

A fine is recorded on the same date in *Records of the Court of the Stationers' Company 1602 to 1640*, ed. William A. Jackson (1957):

> Ambr: Garbrand *received* of him for
> a fyne for printinge
> the booke of Moll   } vij^d
> Cutpurse wᵗʰout
> entringe it

Mulholland (1987) posits that the entry was made by Garbrand rather than by Archer because Garbrand was a friend of Archer and had a stall located near the site of Mary Frith's penance in St Paul's Churchyard, which she had performed only nine days earlier, on 9 February 1612. Thus, he implies, Garbrand could take advantage from selling the play concerning the same notorious figure. A transfer of copyright from Thomas Archer to Hugh Perry dated February 1631 is also recorded in the Stationers' Register; it was formerly thought to be the original entry.

It is generally agreed that printer's copy was fair. Mulholland (1977) supports Bowers's claim that it was non-theatrical, citing the precisely placed stage directions, with a relatively small number of missing exits (eight). On the basis of inconsistency between imperative and indicative stage directions, Price claimed the copy was theatrical, but Mulholland (1977) argues that its five imperatives are insufficient evidence; that where instructive stage directions might be expected, they are lacking; and that many stage directions have a literary quality. Bowers also proposed that printer's copy was a scribal transcript from authorial fair copy, made before prompt copy was prepared, and that Middleton's preface bears 'the tone of an author introducing an approved publication to the public', suggesting that Middleton might have provided printer's copy. He also noted, however, that though Middleton similarly provides a preface to *The Family of Love*, he also indicates that he didn't provide copy for that play. Price believed that Dekker supplied it; Lake refuted his theory; and the present edition attributes *The Family of Love* to Lording Barry rather than Middleton. Mulholland is sceptical of all attempts to identify the source of printer's copy, on the grounds that evidence of the hand of printer's copy, the playwrights' shares in it, and the compositors' stints is either inadequate or so mutually contingent as to prevent confident conclusions. He does propose, though, that unusually light punctuation terminating speeches and peculiarly Middletonian forms in scenes attributed to Dekker (e.g. 'i' the') suggests that Middleton may have had a hand in the printer's copy.

Price, Bowers, and Mulholland agree that the text was printed from a single skeleton; setting was by formes, and printing was careful. Adrian Weiss, however, doubts that either running title movements or substitutions of roman capitals in speech prefixes (both used as evidence) can prove setting by formes. There has been considerable disagreement about the number of compositors. Price argued for five; Bowers disagreed on the grounds that Okes had a one-press shop, and argued for three; Mulholland (1987) argues for two or three, and rejects Price's attempt to identify compositors on the basis of speech prefix transfers (1984). He identifies them as A and B, alternating irregular stints from sheets B to E inclusive, and D, who took over from A and B to complete the remaining formes, including most of sheet A. Type recurrences suggest that most of the play was set from a single case. Speech prefix transferences, type shortage peculiarities, the use of a single case of type by several compositors, and setting by formes instead of *seriatim* (unusual in single-skeleton printing) all suggest that the text was set and printed concurrently with others.

Mulholland (1987) has determined that proof correction is preserved in nine of the text's twenty-four formes, and that only sheet H shows evidence of correction in both formes. The invariant formes are mainly clear of major errors, which suggests that they may have been proofed for literals at an early stage. Inner I was extensively reset, possibly because, Bowers suggested, an accident caused the type to pie in the course of proof correction. There are two sets of significant variants, in inner I and inner D. Mulholland argues that the reset substantive variants in inner I lack authority, the original setting being closer to manuscript copy (1987), while the reverse is true of variants on inner D (1984), which he discovered in a single copy of Okes in the Robert H. Taylor Collection of the Firestone Library, Princeton University. He maintains, for both textual and literary reasons, that the inner D variants, involving altered speech prefixes and consequent reallocation to different characters of several speeches at the end of scene 3, provide the authoritative reading.

These variants occur in sig. D4^r, and Mulholland (1984) uses two of them to argue that the variants are corrected and authoritative. The first replaces a speech prefix for Mistress Gallipot with one for Mistress Openwork. If spoken by Mistress Gallipot, the line has no particular point; if spoken by Mistress Openwork, it pertains to her earlier tiff with her husband over Moll and to her new involvement with Goshawk. The second variant places a new speech prefix, for Master Gallipot, before the catchword, thus splitting between Tiltyard and Gallipot a speech formerly allocated to Gallipot. Combined with a new line given in the variant to Mistress Tiltyard, it creates a vignette centring on the Tiltyards which helps justify their presence (he makes his first appearance here, and she has previously spoken only seven lines) and which, according to Mulholland, 'does not really square with the Gallipots', who formerly spoke the lines. Mulholland has collated twelve copies of Okes and includes a list of press variants in his edition (1987).

Okes contains several unusual features. Bowers regarded two speech heading discrepancies, S.Dap. and variants in scene 3, Sir Dauy. and variants in scene 7 as inconsequential because he believed both scenes to be Dekker's, but Mulholland (1987) disagrees, believing that Middleton may have had a hand in scene 7 and that the variant form could be his. Other peculiarities occur in the list of characters. Dramatis Personae is Dekker's form, as is Ministri for servants. Two characters who appear only in none are omitted from the list, and the forms 'Wentgrave' for Sir Alexander, 'Young Wentgrave' for Sebastian, and 'Neats-foot' are used there only, all of which according to Mulholland (1977) may reflect an early stage of composition. Only an initial Act I, scene 1 designation is provided in Okes; I have followed the scene divisions of previous editors and in accordance with the policy of this edition, have not interpolated act divisions but rather have numbered scenes successively. I have followed Mulholland's regularization of the canting in scene 10, which accords with OED spellings and those in recent modernized editions of Dekker's underworld pamphlets.

I have relied upon Mulholland's collation of the editions of Reed, Scott, Collier, Dyce, Bullen, Ellis, Bowers, and Gomme; he also consulted the editions of Shepherd (an original-spelling text with the most obvious misprints corrected), Farmer (a photographic facsimile of the British Library 162.d.35 copy of Okes), and Fraser and Rabkin. Reed initiated modernization, corrected obvious errors,

and provided some commentary. Scott and Collier substantially reproduce his edition, with minor changes. Later editors take most of their changes from Dyce's edition; Bullen's is mainly based on it, and Ellis draws from Dyce and Bullen. (The 'edition' of Marble is an exception, as despite its title it does not include a text of the play at all, only an introduction and annotations.) Bowers introduced new readings and relineations; his edition is enhanced by Cyrus Hoy's Introductions, Notes, and Commentaries. Gomme presents some new emendations.

Mulholland's Revels Plays edition (1987) is meticulous and trustworthy. I have followed it, with some departures in lineation, emendation, and stage directions, using as copy-text the copy of Okes in the Robert H. Taylor Collection of Princeton University Library. I am grateful to Prof. Mulholland for supplying me with a photographic copy of it.

SEE ALSO

Text: Works, 726
Authorship and date: this volume, 369

WORKS CITED

Previous Editions

Bowers, Fredson, ed., The Dramatic Works of Thomas Dekker (Cambridge, 1953–61), vol. III (rev. 1966)
Bullen, A. H., ed., Works (1885), IV
Collier, J. P., ed., A Select Collection of Old Plays (1825), vol. VI
Dyce, Alexander, ed., Works (1840), II
Ellis, Havelock, ed., The Best Plays of Thomas Middleton, The Mermaid Series (1890), vol. II
Farmer, J. S., ed., The Roaring Girl, Tudor Facsimile Texts (1914), rpt. AMS (New York, 1973)
Fraser, Russell A., and Norman Rabkin, eds., Drama of the English Renaissance II: The Stuart Period (New York, 1976)
Gomme, Andor, ed., The Roaring Girl, The New Mermaids (1976)
Marble, Paul F., An Edition of 'The Roaring Girl', Brown University M.A. dissertation (1933)
Mulholland, Paul, ed., A Critical Modern-Spelling Edition of 'The Roaring Girl', by Thomas Middleton and Thomas Dekker, University of Birmingham doctoral dissertation (1975)
—— ed., The Roaring Girl, Revels (1987)
Reed, Isaac, ed., A Select Collection of Old Plays (1780), vol. VI
Scott, Walter, ed., The Ancient British Drama (1810), vol. II
Shepherd, Richard Herne, ed., The Dramatic Works of Thomas Dekker (1873), vols I, III (1873)

Other Works Cited

Anon., Hic Mulier: or, The Man Woman (1620) and Haec-Vir: or The Womanish-Man (1620), rpt. The Rota, University of Exeter (1973)
Anon., The Life and Death of Mary Frith, Commonly Called Moll Cutpurse (1662), ed. Randall Nakayama (1993)
Anon., The Life of Long Meg of Westminster (1620), rpt. Short Fiction of the 17th Century, ed. Charles Mish (1968)
Anon., 'On Marriage', Certaine Sermons or Homilies (1623), rpt. ed. Mary Ellen Rickey and Thomas B. Stroup (1968)
Belsey, Catherine, The Subject of Tragedy: Identity and Difference in Renaissance Drama (1985)
Bowers, Fredson T., 'Textual Introduction', The Roaring Girl in The Dramatic Works of Thomas Dekker, vol. 3 (1958), 3–9

Bullen, A. H., ed., 'Preface', *The Roaring Girl* in *Works* (1885), vol. 4

Butler, Judith, *Gender Trouble: Feminism and the Subversion of Identity* (1990)

Case, Sue-Ellen, *The Roaring Girl* (author's manuscript, 1979)

Chamberlain, John, *Letters*, ed. Norman Egbert McClure, 2 vols (1939)

Coates, Richard, 'The First American Placename in England: *Pimlico*', *Names* 43 (1995), 213-27

Comensoli, Viviana, 'Play-making, Domestic Conduct, and the Multiple Plot in *The Roaring Girl*', *Studies in English Literature, 1500-1900* 27 (1987), 249-66

Dawson, Anthony B., 'Mistris *Hic* and *Haec*: Representations of Moll Frith', *Studies in English Literature, 1500-1900* 33 (1993), 385-404

Dekker, Rudolf and Lotte van de Pol, *The Tradition of Female Transvestism in Early Modern Europe* (1989)

Dugaw, Dianne, *Warrior Women and Popular Balladry 1650-1850* (1989)

Eliot, T. S., 'Thomas Middleton', *Times Literary Supplement*, 30 June 1927

Fenton, James, 'Roaring Girls and Passionate Trends', Harvard Theatre Collection (May 1983)

Garber, Marjorie, 'The Logic of the Transvestite: *The Roaring Girl* (*1608*)', *Staging the Renaissance: Reinterpretations of Elizabethan and Jacobean Drama*, ed. David Scott Kastan and Peter Stallybrass (1991), 221-34

—— *Vested Interests: Cross Dressing and Cultural Anxiety* (1992)

Gibbons, Brian, *Jacobean City Comedy* (1968)

Helms, Lorraine, 'Roaring Girls and Silent Women: The Politics of Androgyny on the Jacobean Stage', *Women in Theatre*, ed. James Redmond (1989), 59-73

Hendricks, Margo, 'A Painter's Eye: Gender and Middleton and Dekker's *The Roaring Girl*', *Women's Studies* 18 (1990), 191-203

Howard, Jean E., 'Crossdressing, the Theatre, and Gender Struggle in Early Modern England', *Shakespeare Quarterly* 39 (1988), 418-40

—— 'Sex and Social Conflict: the Erotics of *The Roaring Girl*', *Erotic Politics: Desire on the Renaissance Stage*, ed. Susan Zimmerman (1992), 170-90

Hoy, Cyrus, *Introduction, Notes, and Commentaries to texts in 'The Dramatic Works of Thomas Dekker'*, edited by Fredson Bowers (1980), vol. III

Jardine, Lisa, *Still Harping on Daughters: Women and Drama in the Age of Shakespeare* (1983)

Jones, Ann Rosalind, and Peter Stallybrass, 'Fetishizing Gender: Constructing the Hermaphrodite in Renaissance Europe', *Body Guards: the Cultural Politics of Gender Ambiguity*, ed. Julia Epstein and Kristina Straub (1991), 80-111

Kahn, Coppélia, 'Whores and Wives in Renaissance Drama', *In Another Country: Feminist Perspectives on Renaissance Drama*, ed. Dorothea Kehler and Susan Baker (1991), 246-60

Knights, L. C., *Drama and Society in the Age of Jonson* (1937)

Leggatt, Alexander, *Citizen Comedy in the Age of Shakespeare* (1973)

Mulholland, Paul, 'The Date of *The Roaring Girl*', *Review of English Studies* NS 28 (1977), 18-31

—— 'Some Textual Notes on *The Roaring Girl*', *The Library*, V, 32 (1977), 333-43

—— '*The Roaring Girl*: New Readings and Further Notes', *Studies in Bibliography* 37 (1984), 159-70

—— 'Let Her Roar Again: *The Roaring Girl* Revived', *Research Opportunities in Renaissance Drama* 28 (1985), 15-27

Nakayama, Randall, 'Introduction', *The Life and Death of Mistress Mary Frith* (1993)

Orgel, Stephen, 'The Subtexts of *The Roaring Girl*', *Erotic Politics: Desire on the Renaissance Stage*, ed. Susan Zimmerman (1992), 12-26

Price, George, 'The Manuscript and Quarto of *The Roaring Girl*', *The Library*, V, 11 (1956), 180-6

Repertories of the Court of Aldermen, Corporation of London Records Office, Rep. 30, fol. 184[r] (26 September 1611)

Rose, Mary Beth, 'Women in Men's Clothing: Apparel and Social Stability in *The Roaring Girl*', *English Literary Renaissance* 14 (1984), 367-91

Shepherd, Simon, *Amazons and Warrior Women: Varieties of Feminism in 17th Century Drama* (1981)

Simon, Francesca, 'The Honest Cutpurse at the Play', *The Sunday Times*, 24 April 1983

Stubbes, Philip, *The Anatomie of Abuses* (1583)

Ungerer, Gustav, 'Mary Frith, alias Moll Cutpurse, in Life and Literature', *Shakespeare Studies* 28 (2000), 42-84

Wardle, Irving, 'Distant Echo of Jacobean Mirth: *The Roaring Girl*, Barbican', *The Times*, 27 April 1983

Warman, Christopher, 'Moll Who Took Her Role Seriously', *The Times*, 23 April 1983

Weiss, Adrian, private communication

TEXTUAL NOTES

Persons.0.2   *The Persons of the Play*] Dramatis Perfonæ OKES

Persons.1   Wengrave] REED; Wentgrave OKES

Persons.2   NEATFOOT] REED; *Neatſ-foot* OKES

Persons.3   SIR THOMAS Long] COLLIER; *not in* OKES

Persons.18   TEARCAT] COLLIER; *not in* OKES

Persons.19   Fitzallard] DYCE; Fitz-allard OKES

Persons.21   CURTALAX] MULHOLLAND; Curtilax OKES; Curtleax DYCE

Persons.23   Ministri] DYCE (*subst.*); Ministri OKES

Persons.23-4   FELLOW...CUTPURSES] THIS EDITION

Epistle   The Epistle OKES (as running title to second page of Dedication in OKES)

Epistle.0.1   *Play-readers*,] OKES; Playreaders: MULHOLLAND. I prefer OKES's reading because it suggests a slight ambiguity concerning whether 'venery and laughter' are what 'playreaders' possess or what the playwright is offering them in the form of his play.

Prologue   DYCE; *Prologus* OKES; placed before Dramatis Personae in OKES

Sc. 1   THIS EDITION; Act. I Scœ 1. OKES. This is the only act or scene heading in OKES. BOWERS divided Act 1 into two scenes; the other act and scene divisions were introduced by DYCE and have been accepted by all subsequent editors.

1.22   dined] REED; dyed OKES.

1.35   i'th'] REED; ith the OKES

1.37   quench this,] OKES; quench this fire DYCE

1.85   brows,] DYCE; brow: OKES

2.82   winds] SCOTT; wind OKES

2.91   talked] DYCE; talke OKES

2.94   cards] OKES; cares BOWERS

2.199 h'as] REED; has OKES

3.41.1 *At the tobacco shop*] MULHOLLAND

3.80 *(blowing smoke in their faces)*] THIS EDITION; *he blowes tobacco in their faces*, right, OKES

3.81 *[coughing]*] MULHOLLAND

3.106 Jack Dapper] I.Dap. OKES

3.110 *[Receiving purse from Mistress Gallipot]* MULHOLLAND

3.144 errand] OKES (arrant)

3.168 snail] GOMME, MULHOLLAND; snake OKES

3.174 Heyday] REED; Haida OKES

3.179 arrantest] REED (arrant'st); arrants OKES

3.199 marrowbone] COLLIER; maribone OKES

3.207 an ounce] an an ounce OKES

3.234 i'the] SCOTT; ith the OKES

3.263 *[Strikes him]*] DYCE

3.288 Brentford] OKES (Brainford) *passim*

3.315 St Antholin's] OKES (Saint Antlings)

3.354 *[Whispers]*] MULHOLLAND

3.373 errands] OKES (arrants)

3.406 *[Exit Openwork with Moll]*] DYCE (*subst.*)

4.10 two-leaved] OKES *subst.* (two leaud); two-lewd COLLIER

4.27 They're] MULHOLLAND; the're OKES

4.73 *[Moves away from him]*] MULHOLLAND

4.74 *[Retires]*] MULHOLLAND

4.81 *[Takes measurements]*] MULHOLLAND

4.82 Heyday] MULHOLLAND; Hoyda OKES

4.109 *[comes forward]*] MULHOLLAND

4.115 *[comes forward]*] DYCE (*subst.*)

4.127 bewitched] REED (*subst.*); bewitch OKES

4.160 Many one,] OKES (*subst.*); Mary, one BOWERS

4.161 Forseek] MULHOLLAND; For seeke OKES. I follow Mulholland's reading of OKES's 'For seeke' as meaning either seek out or weary oneself with seeking (*OED*).

5.3 *[gives money]*] MULHOLLAND

5.12 you,] REED; your OKES

5.13 coached] OKES (*subst.*); couched GOMME

5.61.1 *She puts off her cloak and draws*] right, after 62 OKES; *She puts off her cloak and draws [her sword]* BOWERS, MULHOLLAND; *put off her cloak*, right, opposite 62, *Draws her sword*, right, opposite 63, DYCE

5.95 wives,] THIS EDITION; wives— MULHOLLAND; wiues. OKES

5.114 slanderers] COLLIER; slanders OKES

5.127 voyage] DYCE (*subst.*); viage OKES; visage REED

5.131 surgeon's] OKES (Chirurgions)

5.155.1 *She comes towards him*] THIS EDITION; OKES right, opposite 156

5.159 Yea] DYCE; Ye OKES; Yes REED

5.159.1 Turns] *Turne* OKES

6.12 What is't?] THIS EDITION; whats ist OKES; Whats' is't? MULHOLLAND

6.13 Heyday] MULHOLLAND; hoyda OKES

6.31 Fie, fie!] DYCE; fih - - - fih OKES

6.33 sting] REED; sing OKES

6.47-8 *[Produces a letter]*] MULHOLLAND

6.84.1 *[He sneaks behind her]*] MULHOLLAND

6.84.2 *She tears the letter*] THIS EDITION; after 6.85 MULHOLLAND; to the right of 'I'le see't.' OKES

6.178.1 *[Talks apart with Mistress Openwork]*] MULHOLLAND

6.195 *[To Tiltyard]*] MULHOLLAND

6.249 lain] THIS EDITION; OKES (line); MULHOLLAND (lien)

6.254 now] REED; uow OKES

6.267.1 *[Exit Gallipot]*] DYCE; *Exit Maifter Gallipot and his wife.* OKES (after first part-line of 267). As Mulholland argues, OKES s.dd. indicate a premature exit for Gallipot and his wife.

Dyce's exits allow Gallipot to hear his wife's response, and Mistress Gallipot to hear Laxton's misogynistic comment.

7.3.1 *[Sir Alexander talks apart with Trapdoor]*] MULHOLLAND; *Sir D. Dapper and Sir A. Appleton talk apart.* DYCE

7.46-7 *[As in a quarrel]*] MULHOLLAND

7.47 Fox] OKES (Foxe); For REED; Pox DYCE

7.75, 7.78, 7.115 ALEXANDER *and* SIR ADAM] Both OKES

7.103 be placed] DYCE *conj.*; beg plac't OKES; beg place REED (Steevens's note)

7.114 sprites] DYCE, MULHOLLAND; spirits OKES. Cf. 9.133.

7.125 honesty] OKES; honestly GOMME

7.170 Greyhound] OKES (Grayhound)

7.173, 7.176, 7.178 CURTALAX *and* HANGER] Both OKES

7.180 and—and] MULHOLLAND; and and OKES; and REED

7.184 nook] REED; uooke OKES

7.217 MOLL *and* TRAPDOOR] Both OKES

7.217 Honest...Fly] MULHOLLAND; Honest Serieant fly, flie OKES; Honest Gull fly; fly SCOTT; Trap. Honest servant, fly! Moll. Fly, DYCE; Honest sir fly, flie BOWERS. I have followed Mulholland in retaining OKES, in line with his suggestion that Moll first tries to divert the sergeant's attention by calling to him, then urges Jack Dapper to flee.

7.221 *[Moll holding him]*] DYCE

7.224 *[To Trapdoor]*] MULHOLLAND

7.227 *[To Hanger]*] MULHOLLAND

7.229.1 *[Exeunt Curtalax and Hanger]*] MULHOLLAND

8.33 would] OKES; 'twould REED

8.36 glisterings] OKES (gilsterings)

8.37 mysteries] OKES; miseries DYCE *conj.*

8.43.1 *(He kisses Mary)*] *Kisses Mary* MULHOLLAND; *kiss* OKES

8.52 Moll. Troth...seriously:] MULHOLLAND; Moll, troth...seriously, OKES

8.56 of] OKES; or BOWERS

8.75 *[Draws]*] MULHOLLAND

8.77.1 *[Takes down...viol]*] MULHOLLAND

8.90 hang] MULHOLLAND; hung OKES

8.95 Thou'rt] MULHOLLAND; th'art OKES

8.102.1 *The Song*] REED; right, opposite 104 OKES

8.144 ballads:] BOWERS; ballets, OKES

8.147 wardrobes] DYCE; wardrops OKES

8.148 *[to Mary]*] MULHOLLAND

8.149 *[to Sebastian]*] MULHOLLAND

8.153 sigh] DYCE; sight OKES

8.154 *[aside]*] MULHOLLAND

8.154 Will't] ELLIS; wilt OKES

8.156 *[aside to Moll and Mary]*] MULHOLLAND

8.156 *[Aloud to Moll]*] MULHOLLAND

8.159 *[Aside to Moll]*] MULHOLLAND

8.160 *[Aloud]*] MULHOLLAND

8.160 *[Offering money]*] MULHOLLAND

8.165 *[aside]*] MULHOLLAND

8.168.1 *[He comes forward]*] DYCE (*subst.*)

8.172 fingering] MULHOLLAND; fingring. OKES

8.186 an] ELLIS; and OKES

8.216 *[Gives money]*] MULHOLLAND

8.218 on't] OKES (an't)

9.13 flown] THIS EDITION; flin'e OKES; fline MULHOLLAND, who cites fline as the old form for flown

9.94.1 *[They put on masks]*] DYCE (*subst.*)

9.96 *[Talks apart with Mistress Gallipot]*] MULHOLLAND

9.108 Your] OKES; you'r, BOWERS

9.128 Damn] Dambe OKES

9.133 sprites] COLLIER (*subst.*); spirits OKES. I follow Mulholland in emending 'spirits' for rhyme; cf. 7.114.

9.135 them] BOWERS; then OKES
9.142 MISTRESS GALLIPOT] SCOTT; Mist.Open. OKES. I follow Mulholland's adoption of Scott's emendation; reassigning this speech makes sense of Mistress Openwork's remark at l. 143 and of Goshawk's response to it.
9.152 [to Mistress Gallipot]] MULHOLLAND
9.153 [to Mistress Openwork]] MULHOLLAND
9.167 [aside to Mistress Openwork]] MULHOLLAND
9.169 [to Openwork]] MULHOLLAND
9.172 MISTRESS GALLIPOT] OKES; Mistress Openwork GOMME
9.183 OPENWORK] DYCE; Mist. Open. OKES. In reassigning this speech to Openwork, I follow Mulholland, who suggests that a compositor's speech-prefix transfer error assigned this speech to his wife.
9.190.1 Draws out his sword] Draw out his sword OKES
9.198 him—the] him:—the OKES; him; [in] the DYCE
9.219 OPENWORK] SCOTT; Mist. Open. OKES. I follow Mulholland in reassigning this speech to Openwork; its moralizing coheres better with his other speeches in this scene than with his wife's.
9.230 core] REED; chore OKES
9.231 ay] DYCE; I OKES; aye (= even) REED; BOWERS omits
9.245 snuffling] DYCE; snafling OKES
9.283 [Aside to Laxton]] MULHOLLAND
9.284 [Aside to Mistress Gallipot]] MULHOLLAND
9.285 [Aloud]] MULHOLLAND
9.289.1 [Removes hair-piece]] MULHOLLAND
9.292 surgeon] OKES (Chirurgion)
9.302 Gilt] ELLIS; Get OKES, MULHOLLAND; Gelt DYCE; COLLIER omits. I emend because 'gelt' (as Mulholland notes) isn't recorded at this date as an adjective in OED, and the meanings of 'get' applied here are rather strained. 'Gilt' best conveys the sense presumably intended of gilded, golden.
9.308 enough!] THIS EDITION; enough, OKES
10.22 SIR THOMAS] T.Long OKES
10.40 handkerchief] OKES (handkercher)
10.103-7 Ick, mine here...frollick, mine here.] As in SCOTT; black letter in OKES
10.108 [About to give money]] DYCE (subst.; after 109)
10.167 kinchin] REED; kitchin OKES

10.170 booze] BULLEN (subst.); baufe OKES
10.179 queer] DYCE; quire OKES
10.196-7 [Hits and kicks him]] MULHOLLAND
10.224 pannam] BOWERS; pennam OKES
10.224 lap] BULLEN; lay OKES
10.226, 233 MOLL and TEARCAT] BOWERS (subst.); not in OKES
10.229 harmans] MULHOLLAND; Hartmans OKES
10.230 Tearcat] OKES (subst.); Moll SCOTT
10.230 queer] DYCE; Quire OKES
10.237 Romford] OKES (Rumford)
10.267 Than] MULHOLLAND; :hen OKES
10.313 trust] REED; rrust OKES
10.316 Swan] MULHOLLAND; Swanne, OKES
10.320 [Exeunt Cutpurses]] MULHOLLAND
11.5 has] OKES (ha's)
11.6 breaking?] REED; breaking: OKES
11.12 Blackfriars!] COLLIER; Blacke Fryars, OKES
11.15 Heyday] MULHOLLAND; Hoyda OKES
11.16 [Exit]] GOMME
11.22 has] GOMME; had OKES
11.23 gaskin-bride] GOMME; Gaskoyne-bride OKES
11.47 Alexander—] REED; Alexander. OKES. I follow Mulholland's reading of Reed: 'Goshawk speaks first to Sir Guy and is then interrupted when he begins to address Sir Alexander.'
11.66 [to Sir Alexander]] MULHOLLAND
11.92 [aside to Goshawk]] MULHOLLAND
11.92 [aside to Greenwit]] MULHOLLAND
11.105 an] MULHOLLAND; and OKES
11.141 who? This Moll!] who this Mol? OKES; who this? Moll? REED; who's this? Moll! DYCE; who is this Mol? BOWERS; who? this' Moll! MULHOLLAND. Mulholland argues that 'this' can be a contraction of 'this is', citing four instances from Middleton and two from Shakespeare. His reading implies that there is or can be a single Moll, while mine, retaining OKES's words, implies that there might be more than one 'Moll'.
11.164 And] OKES; an MULHOLLAND
11.187.1 [Servant fetches deeds]] MULHOLLAND
11.209 an] MULHOLLAND; and OKES
11.221 Cheaters] DYCE conj.; Cheates OKES
11.259 gentlewomen] DYCE; gentlewoman OKES
Epilogue SCOTT; Epilogus, OKES

PRESS VARIANTS

Press variants were established by Paul Mulholland in his 1987 Revels Plays edition of The Roaring Girl. He collated the following twelve copies at first hand or on microfilm. Abbreviations are given below; the state of the copy and provenance, if known, follow in parentheses.

BL 1: British Library 162.d.35 (cropped: many running titles affected; lacks A1, M4)

BL 2: British Library, Ashley 1159 (slightly cropped; some running titles restored in ink; lacks A1, M4; T. J. Wise's copy)

BODLEIAN: Bodleian Library, Oxford University, Malone 246 (1) (lacks A1, M4)

BOSTON: Boston Public Library, Massachusetts (lacks A1, M4)

CCC: Corpus Christi College, Oxford University, φB.1.3 (5) (some inked-in alterations; Brian Twyne's copy)

FOLGER: Folger Shakespeare Library, Washington, D.C. (badly inked; A4 bound before A3; lacks A1, H2, M4; ? Isaac Reed's copy)

HUNTINGTON: Huntington Library, San Marino, California (lacks A1, M4; leaves disbound and remounted; John Philip Kemble's copy)

NLS: National Library of Scotland, Bute.368 (lacks A1, M4)

PFORZHEIMER: Carl H. Pforzheimer Collection, University of Texas at Austin

PRINCETON: Robert H. Taylor Collection, Princeton University

V&A: Victoria and Albert Museum, National Art Library, D.26, Box 33/4, Dyce Collection (lacks A1, M4)

YALE: Beinecke Library, Yale University, 1977/2724 (lacks sheet A, M4; Norman Holmes Pearson's copy)

Sheet A (outer forme)

State a: BL 1, BOSTON.
State b: BL 2, BODLEIAN, CCC, FOLGER, HUNTINGTON, NLS, PFORZHEIMER, PRINCETON, V&A.

Sig. A3

Epistle.16 statute] Sta-|ute OKES State a; Sta-|tute OKES State b

Epistle.17 codpiece] cod-peice OKES State a; cod-peece OKES State b

Epistle.17 book] booke OKES State a; book OKES State b

Sig. A4^v

Persons Dramatis] Drammatis OKES State a; Dramatis OKES State b

Sheet B (inner forme)

> *State a*: FOLGER.
> *State b*: BL 1, BL 2, BODLEIAN, BOSTON, CCC, HUNTINGTON, NLS, PFORZHEIMER, PRINCETON, V&A, YALE.

Sig. B1^v

1.26 in truth, sir] intruthfir OKES State a; in truth fir OKES State b
1.37 slakes] flackes OKES State a; flakes OKES State b
1.38 sayst] faith OKES State a; faift OKES State b
1.39 viva] viue OKES State a; viua OKES State b
1.41 What] Wthat OKES State a; What OKES State b
1.42-3 brought...Neatfoot] brough_t_...Neatfoo te OKES State a; brought...Neatfoote OKES State b. In State a, the t has slipped down and intrudes into the middle of 'Neatfoote' in the line below.

Sig. B2

1.62 Ha!] Ha: OKES State a; Ha! OKES State b
1.63 shape?] fhape: OKES State a; fhape? OKES State b
1.66 prey] pray OKES State a; prey OKES State b
1.66 eyes] eyes, OKES State a; eyes_ OKES State b
1.69 a loathed] aloathed OKES State a; a loathed OKES State b
1.86 gold] gold, OKES State a; gold_ OKES State b
1.90 heir?] heire, OKES State a; heire? OKES State b

Sig. B4

2.63 met] met, OKES State a; met_ OKES State b
2.85 fray] fray, OKES State a; fray_ OKES State b
2.86 mad,] mad_ OKES State a; mad, OKES State b
2.87 question] question, OKES State a; question_ OKES State b

Sheet C (inner forme)

> *State a*: BL 1, BOSTON.
> *State b*: BL 2, BODLEIAN, CCC, FOLGER, HUNTINGTON, NLS, PFORZHEIMER, PRINCETON, V&A, YALE.

Sig. C2

running title Girel OKES State a; Girle OKES State b
2.187 I'm] Ime OKES State a; I'me OKES State b
2.189 I'm] Ime OKES State a; I'me OKES State b
2.209 Simon] ‾imon OKES State a; Simon OKES State b
2.212 I'll] ile OKES State a; Ile OKES State b
2.214 burnt?] burnt. OKES State a; burnt? OKES State b

Sheet D (inner forme)

> *State a*: BL 2, BODLEIAN, CCC, FOLGER, HUNTINGTON, PFORZHEIMER, V&A, YALE.
> *State b*: BL 1, BOSTON, NLS.
> *State c*: PRINCETON.

Sig. D4

Variants between states a and b–c

3.419-20 Hogsden] Hogf-|dcn OKES State a; Hogf-|den OKES States b, c

Variants between states a–b and c

3.416 OPENWORK] *Gal.* OKES States a–b; *Open.* OKES State c
3.417 GALLIPOT] *Tilt.* OKES States a–b; *Gal.* OKES State c

3.419 TILTYARD] *Gal.* OKES States a–b; *Tilt.* OKES State c
3.423 TILTYARD] *Gal.* OKES States a–b; *Tilt.* OKES State c
3.424 TILTYARD] *Gal.* OKES States a–b; *Tilt.* OKES State c
catchword Come OKES States a–b; *M.Gal.*Come OKES State c

Sheet H (outer forme)

> *State a*: NLS.
> *State b*: BL 1, BL 2, BODLEIAN, BOSTON, CCC, FOLGER, HUNTINGTON, PFORZHEIMER, PRINCETON, V&A, YALE.

Sig. H1

7.196 child] child, OKES State a; child_ OKES State b
7.196 debts] debts_ OKES State a; debts, OKES State b
7.217 sergeant] Seriant OKES State a; Serieant OKES State b
7.217-18 Fly, Master] flie|Maifter OKES State a; flie Maifter OKES State b
7.223 sergeants] Seriants OKES State a; Serieants OKES State b

Sig. H2^v

8.66 Moll] *Moll,* OKES State a; *Moll*_ OKES State b
8.68 nine] mine OKES State a; nine OKES State b
8.72 pity] pitty, OKES State a; pitty_ OKES State b
8.78 viol] viall_ OKES State a; viall, OKES State b
8.85 put us] put vs OKES State a; put|vs OKES State b
8.85 as well as] as well OKES State a; as wel as OKES State b
8.85 can: it] can: it OKES State a; can:it OKES State b

Sig. H3

8.113 again?] againe. OKES State a; againe? OKES State b

Sig. H4^v

8.211 them] them. OKES State a; them_ OKES State b
8.214 house,] houfe OKES State a; houfe, OKES State b
8.214 heart.] heart . OKES (BL 1, BL 2, BOSTON, HUNTINGTON, PFORZHEIMER, V&A, and YALE); heart. OKES (BODLEIAN, CCC, NLS, and PRINCETON); h eart . OKES (FOLGER). This apparent press-variant does not conform to the pattern of press correction seen elsewhere in the sheet.
8.218 three] there OKES State a; three OKES State b

Sheet H (inner forme)

> *State a*: NLS.
> *State b*: BL 1, BL 2, BODLEIAN, BOSTON, CCC, FOLGER, HUNTINGTON, PFORZHEIMER, PRINCETON, V&A, YALE.

Sig. H3^v

8.142 execution] excution OKES State a; execution OKES State b
8.163 quarter] qnarter OKES State a; quarter OKES State b

Sheet I (inner forme)

> *State a*: BL 2, BOSTON, CCC, FOLGER, NLS, PFORZHEIMER, PRINCETON, V&A, YALE.
> *State b*: BL 1, HUNTINGTON. 'State b*' signals a passage that was completely reset and not just corrected.
> *State c*: BODLEIAN. 'State c*' signals a passage that was completely reset and not just corrected.

Sig. I1^v

running title Girle OKES State a; Girle OKES States b*, c*
9.61 the] the OKES State a; *omitted* OKES States b*, c*
9.65 deal they] deale they OKES State a; they deale OKES States b*, c*
9.69 done] done OKES State a; donc OKES States b*, c*
9.72 will] will OKES State a; wil OKES States b*, c*
9.78 Why] why OKES States a, c; wh_ OKES State b
9.80 do] doe OKES State a; do OKES States b, c
9.85 duck me] duckmee OKES State a; duck mee OKES States b, c

9.98 pothecary-ship] Potticariſhip OKES State a; Poticariſhip OKES States b*, c*

Sig. I2

9.100–2 LAXTON I...LAXTON No?] *Lax.* I...*Lax.* No? OKES State a; *Lax.·* I...*Lax* No? OKES States b, c. In OKES, these two speech headings are on consecutive lines, one above the other; in states b and c the stop after the second speech heading has migrated up into the previous line.

9.131 some beldame] ſome beldame OKES State a; ſomebeldame OKES States b, c

Sig. I3ᵛ

9.203 makes] makes OKES State a; m akes OKES States b, c

9.203 petticoat] peticote OKES State a; peticot e OKES States b, c

9.204 Besides] beſides OKES State a; beſide OKES States b, c

9.206 moon] moone OKES State a; moon OKES States b, c

Sig. I4

9.232 try] try, OKES State a; try∧ OKES States b*, c*

9.233 you] you, OKES State a; you∧ OKES States b*, c*

9.234 'twas] t'was OKES State a; 'twas OKES States b*, c*

9.235 beat] beat OKES State a; beate OKES States b*, c*

9.239 MISTRESS OPENWORK] *Mist, Open.* OKES State a; *Mist. Opeu,* OKES States b*, c*

9.239 No.] No:—— OKES State a; No: - - - - OKES States b*, c*

9.240 OPENWORK] *Maiſt.* OKES State a; *Mai.* OKES States b*, c*

9.242.1 and] and OKES State a; *aud* OKES States b*, c*

9.242.2 sumner] *Sommer* OKES State a; *Somner* OKES States b*, c*

9.244 GALLIPOT] *Gal.* OKES State a; *Gall.* OKES States b*, c*

9.245 GREENWIT] *Green.* OKES State a; *Greene.* OKES States b*, c*

9.245 snuffling] ſnaſling OKES State a; ſnaſling OKES States b*, c*

9.247 GALLIPOT] *Gal.* OKES State a; *Gall.* OKES States b*, c*

9.248 I]——I OKES State a; - - - - I OKES States b*, c*

9.248 head, sir] headſir OKES State a; head ſir OKES States b*, c*

9.251 sir.] ſir, OKES State a; ſir. OKES States b*, c*

9.252 GREENWIT] *Green.* OKES State a; *Greene.* OKES States b*, c*

9.253 and you] and you | OKES State a; and | you OKES States b*, c*

9.254 do] do OKES State a; doe OKES States b*, c*

9.254 see—Crastino] ſee, *Craſtina* OKES State a; ſee, *Craſtino* OKES States b*, c*

9.256 GALLIPOT] *Gal.* OKES State a; *Gall.* OKES States b*, c*

9.257 GREENWIT] *Green.* OKES State a; *Greene.* OKES States b*, c*

Sheet K (outer forme)

State a: HUNTINGTON, V&A.

State b: BL 1, BL 2, BODLEIAN, BOSTON, CCC, FOLGER, NLS, PFORZHEIMER, PRINCETON, YALE.

Sig. K1

9.316 being] beng OKES State a; being OKES State b

Sheet M (outer forme)

State a: BL 1, BL 2, BOSTON, HUNTINGTON, NLS, PFORZHEIMER, PRINCETON.

State b: BODLEIAN, CCC, FOLGER, V&A, YALE.

Sig. M1

11.162 charity] charity? OKES State a; charity, OKES State b

11.163 bargain,] bargaine, OKES State a; bargaine? OKES State b

11.166 SIR GUY] *Aitz-All.* OKES State a; *Fitz-All.* OKES State b

STAGE DIRECTIONS

[Printed following the Prologue:]

Dramatis Personæ.

Sir *Alexander Wentgraue,* and *Neats-foot* his man.

Sir *Adam Appleton.*

Sir *Dauy Dapper.*

Sir *Bewteous Ganymed.*

Lord *Noland.*

Yong *Wentgraue.*

Iacke Dapper, and *Gull* his page.

Goshawke.

Greenewit.

Laxton.

Tilt-yard.
Openworke. } Ciues & Vxores.
Gallipot.

Mol the Roaring Girle.

Trapdoore.

Sir *Guy Fitz-allard.*

Mary Fitz-allard his daughter.

Curtilax a Sergiant, and

Hanger his Yeoman.

Ministri.

1.0.1–4 Act. 1. Scœ. 1. | *Enter* Mary Fitz-Allard *disguised like a sempster with a case for* | *bands, and* Neatfoot *a seruingman with her, with a napkin on* | *his shoulder, and a trencher in his hand as from table.*

1.29 *Exit* Neatfoote, (right, opposite 28)

1.37.1 *Enter* Sebastian Wengraue *with* Neatfoote.

1.54 *Exit* Neat-foote.

1.123.1 *Exeunt*

2.0.1–3 *Enter Sir* Alexander Wengraue, Sir Dauy Dapper, Sir Adam | Appleton, Goshake, Laxton, *and Gentlemen.*

2.32.1 *Enter* Sebastian and | *M.* Greene-wit.

2.42.1 *Enter three or foure Seruingmen, and* Neatfoote.

2.57.1 *Exeunt* seruants. (right)

2.144 —aside. (right)

2.179 *Exit* Sebastian.

2.184.1 *Exeunt all but sir* | Alexander.

2.189.1 *Enter* Ralph Trapdore (right)

2.259 *Exeunt.*

3.0.1–6 *The three shops open in a ranke: the first a Poticaries shop, the next* | *a Fether shop: the third a Sempsters shop:* Mistresse Gallipot | *in the first,* Mistresse Tiltyard *in the next,* Maister Openworke | *and his wife in the third, to them enters* Laxton, Goshawke *and* Greenewit.

3.50.1 *Shee puts it to the fire.*

3.80 *he blowes tobacco in their faces.*

3.103.1 *Enter* I. Dapper, *and his man* Gull. (right)

3.136 *Exit* Gul.

3.153.1 *At the Fether shop now.*

3.163.1 *At the Sempsters* | *shop now.*

3.177.1 *At the Tobacco shop now.*

3.180.1 *Enter* Mol *in a freese Ierkin and* | *a blacke sauegard.*

3.219.1 *The Fether shop againe.*

3.228.1 *The Sempster shop.* (right, opposite 229)

3.252.1 *Enter a fellow with* (opposite 251 *with following line of text blank*) | *a long rapier by his side.* (right)

3.270 *Exit fellow.*

3.312.1 *Fall from them to the other.*

3.323.1 *The Fether shop.* (right)

3.339.1 *The Sempsters shop.*

3.357.1 *Enter Ralph Trapdore* (right, opposite 358)

3.380.1 *Mols* trips vp his heels he fals. (opposite 378)

3.392 *aside.* (right, opposite 393)

3.398 *Exit Trapdore*

3.398.1 *Mol meets Laxton* (right, opposite 399)

3.401.1 *then Openworke.* (right, opposite 401)

3.406.1 *The bel rings.*

3.413.1 *Exeunt Gallants.*

3.413.2–3 *Enter Maister Gallipot, Maister Tiltyard, and seruants | with water Spaniels and a ducke.*

3.424 *spits in the dogs mouth.* (right, opposite 423)

4.0.1 *Enter Sebastian Solus.*

4.3 *Enter Sir Alexander | and listens to him.* (right, opposite 3–4)

4.18.1 *Enter Mol and a porter | with a viall on his backe.* (right, opposite 18)

4.27.1 *Exit Porter.*

4.76.1 *Enter a Tailor.*

4.106 *Exit Mol.*

4.108 *Exit Taylor.*

4.194 *Exit Sir Alexander*

4.208 *Exit Sebastian.*

5.0.1–2 *Enter Laxton in Graies-Inne fields with the Coachman.*

5.24.1 *Exit Coachman with his whip.*

5.28 *clocke three* (in left-hand margin)

5.37.1 *Enter Mol like a man.*

5.61.1 *Shee puts of her cloake and drawes.* (right, after 62)

5.115 *They fight.* (right, opposite 116)

5.131 *Exit Laxton.*

5.141.1 *Enter Trapdore.*

5.152.1 *Shee iustles him* (right)

5.155.1 *She comes towards him.* (right, opposite 156)

5.159.1 *Turne his hat.*

5.162.1 *Philips him.*

5.197 *Exeunt omnes*

6.0.1–2 *Enter Mistresse Gallipot as from supper, her husband after her.*

6.45 *Exit Maist.Gallipot.*

6.57.1 *She reads the letter.*

6.79.1 *Enter Maister Gallipot hastily.*

6.84.1 *She teares the letter,* (right, opposite 84)

6.160.1–2 *Enter Maister Tiltyard, and his wife, Maister Goshawke, and Mistresse Openworke.*

6.204.1 *Exeunt all but Gallipot and his wife.*

6.211.1 *Enter Laxton muffled.*

6.267 *Exit Maister Gallipot and his wife.* (right, below first part of 267)

6.271 *Exit Laxton.*

7.0.1–3 *Enter Sir Alexander Wengraue: Sir Dauy Dapper, Sir Adam | Appleton, at one dore, and Trapdore at another doore.*

7.52 *Exit Trapdore*

7.111.1 *Enter Seriant Curtilax and Yeoman Hanger.*

7.115.1 *Exeunt Alex. and Adam,*

7.180 *Exit S.Dauy*

7.184.1 *Enter Mol and Trapdore.*

7.205.1 *Enter Iacke Dapper and Gul.*

7.220.1 *Exit Dapper and Gull.*

7.233.1 *Exeunt.*

8.0.1 *Enter Sir Alexander Wengraue solus.*

8.4.1 *Enter Trapdore* (right, opposite 3)

8.38 *Exeunt.*

8.38.1 *Enter Sebastian, with Mary Fitz-Allard like a page, and Mol.*

8.43–8.43.1 *Kisse*

8.104 *The song.* (right)

8.106.1 *Enter Sir Alexander behind them.*

8.219 *Exit Alexander.*

8.224 *Exeunt omnes.*

9.0.1 *Enter Mistresse Gallipot, and Mistresse Openworke.*

9.73.1 *Enter Goshawke.*

9.95.1 *Enter Laxton muffled.*

9.109 *Exit Laxton.*

9.110.1 *Enter Maister Openworke.*

9.190.1 *Draws out his sword*

9.242.1–2 *Enter Maister Gallipot, and Greenewit like a Sommer, | Laxton muffled a loofe off.*

9.354.1 *Exeunt omnes.*

10.0.1–2 *Enter Iacke Dapper, Moll, Sir Beautious Ganymed, | and Sir Thomas Long.*

10.47.1 *Enter the Lord Noland.*

10.63 *They walke.*

10.64.1 *Enter Trapdore like a poore Souldier with a patch o're one eie, and | Teare-Cat with him, all tatters.*

10.117.1 *Pull off his patch*

10.220.1 *The song.* (right, opposite 226)

10.259.1 *Exeunt they two | manet the rest.* (right, opposite 258–9)

10.276.1–2 *Enter a Cutpurse very gallant, with foure or fiue men after | him, one with a wand.*

10.372 *Exeunt.*

11.0.1–2 *Enter Sir Alexander Wengraue, Goshawke and | Greenewit, and others.*

11.6 *Enter a seruant.* (right, opposite 5)

11.13.1 *Enter Trapdore.*

11.18.1 *Enter sir Fitz-Allard.*

11.91 *Exit Fitz-Allard.*

11.96.1 *Enter Moll.* (right)

11.102 *Exit Moll*

11.124.1 *Enter a seruant.* (right, opposite 125)

11.128.1–2 *Enter Mol maskt, in Sebastians hand, and Fitz-Allard.*

11.140.1 *They unmaske her.* (right)

11.168.1–2 *Enter the Lord Noland, and Sir Bewtious Ganymed, with Ma-|ry Fitz-Allard betweene them, the Cittizens and their | wiues with them.*

11.228 *Enter Trapdore.* (right, opposite 229)

Epilogue.38.1 FINIS.

LINEATION NOTES

Persons.1–2   Sir Alexander...man] *1 line* OKES
Persons.9   Jack Dapper...page] *1 line* OKES
Epistle.0.1–Epistle.32   To the Comic Play-readers...Thomas Middleton] *38 lines* OKES
2.43–4   You...asleep] MULHOLLAND; *1 line* OKES
2.92   Pray...end] BOWERS; *2 lines* OKES
3.54–5   O pardon...smoke] BULLEN; *verse* French | smoke OKES
3.61–2   Push...gallants] *1 line* OKES
3.72–3   O...to 'em] DYCE; *verse* manners | 'em OKES
3.169–71   I...mouse] DYCE; *prose* OKES
3.179–80   I dare...upon't] MULHOLLAND; *verse* Tobacco | upon't OKES
3.216–17   Some...woman] ELLIS; *verse* man | woman OKES
3.308–9   A match...there] *1 line* OKES
3.310–11   The hour...Three] *1 line* OKES
3.358   Mass...is] COLLIER; *1 line* OKES
3.390–1   at a...Ay?] *1 line* OKES
3.397–8   I...kindness] COLLIER; *verse* mistress-ship | kindness OKES
3.407–8   Hark...munch] BULLEN; *verse* gentlemen | munch OKES
3.434   Come...away] MULHOLLAND; *prose* OKES
4.48–54   The most...faithfully] DYCE; *prose* OKES
4.54–5   A pox...now] MULHOLLAND; *1 line* OKES
4.133–4   O...own] REED; *prose* OKES
4.140–1   What sayst...indictment] DYCE; *prose* OKES
5.62–4   Yes...tongue] DYCE; *prose* OKES
5.64–8   There's...'em] COLLIER; pace | 'em OKES (ambiguous as verse or prose)
5.79–80   That...lifetime] DYCE; *verse* sight | lifetime OKES
5.113–14   Would...thine] COLLIER *1 line* OKES
5.164–6   I...sir] MULHOLLAND *verse* often | sir OKES
5.169–70   Your...too] DYCE; *prose* OKES
5.196–7   I'll...do] DYCE; *1 line* OKES
6.53–4   Laxton...praise] COLLIER; *prose* OKES
6.56–7   'Lack...To the point] MULHOLLAND *1 line* OKES
6.84   Steal...steal] BOWERS; *prose* OKES
6.84   What...see't] BOWERS; *1 line* OKES
6.85–7   O would...undone] BOWERS *prose* OKES
6.87–8   What ails...tear'st] DYCE; *1 line* OKES
6.94–7   When...dead] COLLIER; *prose* OKES
6.112–13   Sweet Prue...bosom] COLLIER; *1 line* (turned over) OKES
6.140–1   I'll tell...thee] DYCE; *prose* OKES
6.151–4   Forty...Prue] COLLIER; *prose* OKES
6.174   Has...stomach] DYCE; *verse 1 line* OKES
6.223–4   He...you] REED; *prose* OKES
6.237–9   Um...sending] DYCE; *prose* OKES
6.246–8   I'll...diseased] DYCE; *verse* common | diseased OKES
6.265–6   Yes...part] COLLIER; *1 line* (turned over) OKES
6.267–8   With...wit] MULHOLLAND; *1 line* OKES
7.103–4   When...prisoner] DYCE; *1 line* OKES
7.112–13   I know...you] DYCE; *1 line* OKES

7.116–17   This...sir] DYCE; *verse* he | sir OKES
7.132–3   That's...circle] *1 line* OKES
8.18–19   She...myself] DYCE; *prose* OKES
8.30–4   It's...for] *prose* OKES
8.143   That...England] MULHOLLAND; *prose* OKES
8.149–51   No poison...he be] MULHOLLAND; *prose* OKES
8.156   Life...it] MULHOLLAND; *1 line* OKES
8.173–4   Ay...her] *1 line* OKES
8.178–9   Ay...'em] *1 line* OKES
8.180–2   Forty...on't] *2 lines* OKES us |
9.100–1   I must...No] *1 line* OKES
9.137–8   Ha?...eyes] MULHOLLAND; *1 line* (turned over) OKES
9.144–5   Is't...yet?] MULHOLLAND; *prose* OKES
9.152–3   Do I...Rarely] *1 line* OKES
9.169–71   Why...whore] *prose* OKES
9.173–4   With...morning] MULHOLLAND; *prose* OKES
9.174   Oars...sir] MULHOLLAND; *1 line* OKES
9.175–204   Rack...wife's] MULHOLLAND; *prose* OKES
9.239–40   No...that] MULHOLLAND; *1 line* OKES
9.268–71   Trust...swore] MULHOLLAND; *prose* OKES
9.276–7   What...pound] MULHOLLAND; *prose* OKES
9.283–4   I'll...spitting] MULHOLLAND *prose* OKES
9.288–95   Nay,...company] MULHOLLAND; *prose* OKES
9.299–303   A...On] MULHOLLAND; *prose* OKES
9.308–13   My bed...will] MULHOLLAND; *prose* OKES
9.324–5   Yet...wins] MULHOLLAND; *prose* OKES
9.347   If...life] MULHOLLAND; *2 lines* OKES
9.351   Tarry...jest] MULHOLLAND; *2 lines* OKES
10.103–7   Ick...here] SCOTT; *7 lines* OKES Teare Cat | Dutchlant | beasa | gaeb | cop | halle | here
10.264–74   A...liquor] COLLIER; Divine | bread, | late | die | full | Lorde | opening | OKES
10.304–5   Zounds...Ha] *1 line* OKES
10.344   To raise...it] MULHOLLAND; *1 line* OKES
10.346   Suppose...Well] MULHOLLAND; *2 lines* OKES
10.349   Hearken...here] MULHOLLAND; *3 lines* OKES
10.365–70   Good...constable's] REED; world: | that? | whipped | rather | constable's | OKES
11.9–11   And...soaking] DYCE; *prose* OKES
11.14–15   Your...now at Tower] REED; *2 lines* ramp | Tower OKES
11.16–18   Which...shame] DYCE; *2 lines* care | shame | OKES
11.53–4   How...distractions] DYCE; *1 line* OKES
11.85–6   If...beggar] DYCE; *1 line* OKES
11.110–11   Like...them] DYCE; *1 line* OKES
11.120–1   Age...drunkenness] DYCE; *1 line* (turned under) OKES
11.125–6   Your...hand] DYCE; *1 line* OKES
11.133–4   Before...pardon] DYCE; *1 line* OKES
11.134–5   My...it] DYCE; *1 line* OKES
11.164–6   No...me] DYCE; *2 lines* advantage | me | OKES
11.233–5   Pardon...gentleman] DYCE; *prose* OKES
Epilogue.26–7   REED; *1 line* OKES

THE LADY'S TRAGEDY

Edited by Julia Briggs

THE TEXT of the play here entitled *The Lady's Tragedy* is preserved in a single manuscript, bound with two other playscripts and fragments of a third in a volume owned by the British Library (BL MS Lansdowne 807). This manuscript, carefully transcribed on 23 folio sheets for performance by the King's Men, and submitted by them to the Revels Office for approval, also served as the company's promptbook. From it, one can reconstruct different versions of the play—from the earliest, as the scribe originally copied it out from Middleton's working papers, to the latest, as it was performed at Blackfriars, with the cuts imposed by the censor Sir George Buc, six additional passages supplied by the playwright, and a range of further cuts, alterations and stage directions added during rehearsal—the resulting text having been politically damped down and dramatically speeded up. This edition juxtaposes the earliest and latest versions, so that readers may see for themselves the ways in which a Renaissance play was revised during production.

The manuscript is beautifully and clearly written, but has been extensively corrected and revised by at least two further hands; five slips containing additional speeches, copied out by the original scribe, have been attached at different points. The sequence in which the various deletions, alterations and additions were made is difficult to establish with certainty, and neither the hand of the SCRIBE nor that of the most frequent REVISER has been positively identified—though neither resembles that of Middleton, as it appears in the Trinity manuscript of *Game at Chess*, for example (see discussion in 'Early Modern Authorship: Canons and Chronologies', page 371).

The only hand so far identified is that of Sir George BUC, who wrote out the licence, made corrections at A5.2.168/B5.2.143, 3.1.161 and perhaps 4.3.102, and almost certainly a number of other deletions and marginal markings as well. BUC's task was to remove any words or passages that might be politically dangerous (such as damaging references to royalty or the court, or to recent events), or else might give offence (such as gratuitous oaths—'Heart!' and 'Life!' are regularly deleted, as is 'By the mass!'). A substantial number of such changes have been made to the original text, though it is impossible to tell how many of the words or lines marked for deletion, either by being scored through or indicated by a cross or a vertical line in the margin, were thus marked by BUC himself. Deletions often necessitated the addition of alternative words or phrases and these were probably supplied by the REVISER(s) at the playhouse, while the playhouse itself may also have participated in the censorship process, either before the script was sent to BUC or after it returned from him. Jacobean stage censorship has increasingly come to be seen as a collaborative process in which the companies cooperated with the Revels office (see Patterson's account generally, and on *The Lady's Tragedy* in particular, Clare, 158–9, and Dutton, 194). Howard-Hill has argued that a series of blue-pencil crosses visible in the margins should be associated with BUC, in which case he appears to have made grammatical as well as political corrections (Howard-Hill, 176–7), thus further complicating the attribution of individual interventions.

The main REVISER (who may also have been the BOOK-KEEPER or prompter) has made a series of alterations on the manuscript, filling in a lacuna in the text (at 4.3.38; the other line containing a lacuna, 5.1.168, has been deleted); substituting words where they have been deleted (e.g. at A5.1.186–7/B5.1.192 and A5.2.141/B5.2.116, and almost certainly at 1.2.165, A2.1.81/B2.1.78 and A5.2.212/B5.2.164), and making a series of minor adjustments to the metre (e.g. at 1.1.21, 1.1.37 and A1.1.137/B1.1.118) or the phrasing (e.g. at A2.1.158/B2.1.119, 4.3.28 and 4.3.69). While some of these alterations result in greater metrical regularity, as many or more are either apparently pointless or constitute changes for the worse, as Jackson has pointed out (*Studies in Attribution*, 28).

The most extensive additions to the play are those made on the additional slips: these were written out by the original SCRIBE on a single folio sheet, cut into five pieces and fastened to the manuscript at places marked with a circle in the margin by the BOOKKEEPER. No corrections have been made on the slips themselves, so they were probably added after the manuscript had returned from the Revels office and been 'reformed', in accordance with BUC's instructions, but before the play went into production. Further substantial cuts seem to have been made after their insertion, since in the final scene Helvetius's part has been cut altogether, although the addition at B4.2a.1–11 prepares us for his reappearance.

In general, the purpose of the additional passages seems to have been to tighten up the plot. The first three additions (B1.1.198, B1.1.208–15, B2.1.3–10) address the implausibility of the Tyrant allowing Govianus and the Lady to be imprisoned together (it is, of course, essential to the plot that they should be); the fourth (B4.2.38–41) explains why Govianus is free to visit the Cathedral. The fifth addition (B4.2a.1–11) advances the plot and demarcates a break between the Tyrant's exit at the end of 4.2 and his re-entry elsewhere in the following scene, a break insisted upon by contemporary stage convention.

The sixth addition (B5.1.166–79) allows Anselmus to die only after having learned the truth about his wife's adultery.

Finally, extra stage directions have been written in an italic hand in the left margin. These were added after the paste-in slips, since one of them, 'Enter Mr Gough' (B4.2a.0.1), identifies the speaker of the fifth addition which would otherwise remain unattributed. This is one of two points where entrances are marked with the actors' own names, the other being 'Enter Lady | Rich Robinson' (B4.4.42.7)—both are names of King's Men actors (see Critical Introduction). These entries, in an italic hand, are the work of the BOOKKEEPER, and are likely to have been made during rehearsal. It is quite possible that these and the other stage directions entered on the manuscript were written in the italic hand of the main reviser, in which case that REVISER was also the BOOKKEEPER. The presence in the text of the hands belonging to the SCRIBE and the BOOKKEEPER, and the absence of that of the author recalls the Induction to Jonson's *Bartholomew Fair* (1614) where the bookkeeper, with the 'scrivener' in attendance, draws up a contract with the audience. Playwrights evidently recognized that, at a certain point, their work passed into the control of the scrivener and bookkeeper, before it could reach its audience.

Although it was entered in the Stationers' Register on 9 September 1653 (by Humphrey Moseley, as 'The Maids Tragedie, 2nd Part'), the play was not printed until the nineteenth century, after it had been acquired by the British Museum. In the mid-seventeenth-century it had belonged to the stationer Humphrey Moseley, along with a number of other King's Men play scripts, and in the following century it was owned by the antiquary John Warburton, who had it bound with the other texts that had escaped the general destruction of his collection: 'After I had been many years Collecting these MSS Playes, through my own carlesness and the Ignorace of my Ser, in whose hands I had lodged them they was unluckely burnd or put under Pye bottoms, excepting ye three which followes. J.W.' At his death, it was acquired by the first Marquis of Lansdowne and from him by the British Museum in 1807. As 'The Second Maiden's Tragedy', it was first published in 1824, then twice in 1875 and again in 1892.

Since then, two major editions have appeared: in 1910 W. W. GREG published a diplomatic transcript of the manuscript, recording and attributing the various corrections as far as he was able to, and in 1978 Anne LANCASHIRE produced an excellent modern-spelling edition with a full scholarly apparatus, including a collation of all previous editions. More recently, it has been implausibly edited by Charles Hamilton as *Cardenio, or The Second Maiden's Tragedy* (see note on 'Authorship and Date'), and by Martin Wiggins, under the title *The Maiden's Tragedy*. The latter 'attempts to edit the play "forward" towards a theatrical text' while at the same time restoring Buc's cuts, and criticizing Lancashire for producing 'a version

of the text that never existed'. Wiggins's edition is published in a collection of *Jacobean Sex Tragedies* where it precedes Fletcher's *Tragedy of Valentinian*—although *Valentinian* evidently influenced *The Lady's Tragedy* and is undoubtedly the earlier play. (See commentary notes at A4.2.38 and B5.1.192.)

The textual apparatus to this edition differs from that of any preceding edition, because we have printed two separate versions, with (accordingly) two analytically distinct sets of Textual Notes. The first set records emendations and variants arising from the original version of the text, as represented by the SCRIBE's completed transcript, before it had been altered by BUC, any REVISER, or the BOOKKEEPER. These notes also record cases where the SCRIBE has made what appear to be running corrections to his own work, resulting in substantive variants to the text. Where the SCRIBE's self-corrections do not produce variant words, but only variant spellings or variant punctuation, these are recorded in a separate list of 'Incidental Variants'; where they do not affect the words themselves, but only their arrangement as verse, they are incorporated in the Lineation notes. The second set of Textual Notes records emendations and variants relevant to the Performance Text, incorporating changes made by BUC, the BOOKKEEPER, by any other unidentified REVISER, and on the addition slips transcribed later by the original scribe (identified, when performing that function, as SCRIBE^{2}). It is seldom clear which of these agents was responsible for a particular change; accordingly, the notes record such uncertainties, while making no attempt to discriminate between different REVISERS.

SEE ALSO

Text: *Works*, 839
Authorship and date: this volume, 371

WORKS CITED

Previous Editions

BALDWYN, Charles, (printed for), *The Second Maiden's Tragedy* in *The Old English Drama* (1824), vol. 1

TIECK, Ludwig, trans., *Shakspeare's Vorschule*, 'Der Tyrann, oder die zweite Jungfrauen-Tragoedie' (1829), vol. 2

HAZLITT, W. C., ed., *A Select Collection of Old English Plays* (1875), vol. 10

SHEPHERD, R. H., ed., *The Works of George Chapman* (1875), vol. 2

HOPKINSON, A. F., ed., *The Second Maiden's Tragedy* (1892)

GREG, W. W., ed., *The Second Maiden's Tragedy*, Malone Society (1910, backdated to 1909)

STENGER, Harold L., Jr., ed., *The Second Maiden's Tragedy* (Ph.D. dissertation, University of Pennsylvania, 1954)

LANCASHIRE, Anne, ed., *The Second Maiden's Tragedy*, Revels (1978)

Hamilton, Charles, ed., *The Lost Play of Cardenio, or The Second Maiden's Tragedy* (1994)

Wiggins, Martin, ed., *The Maiden's Tragedy*, in *Four Jacobean Sex Tragedies* (1998)

Other Works Cited

Allman, Eileen, *Jacobean Revenge Tragedy and the Politics of Virtue* (1999)

Bergeron, David M., 'Art within *The Second Maiden's Tragedy*', *Medieval and Renaissance Drama in England* 1 (1984), 173–86

Bushnell, Rebecca W., *Tragedies of Tyrants: Political Thought and Theater in the English Renaissance* (1990)

Clare, Janet, '*Art made tongue-tied by authority*': *Elizabethan and Jacobean Dramatic Censorship* (1990)

Dutton, Richard, *Mastering the Revels: The Regulation and Censorship of English Renaissance Drama* (1991)

Erasmus, Desiderius, *The Education of a Christian Prince* (1516), trans. Lester K. Born (1936), 190

Greenblatt, Stephen, 'Remnants of the Sacred in Early Modern England', *Subject and Object in Renaissance Culture*, ed. Margreta de Grazia, Maureen Quilligan and Peter Stallybrass (1996), 337–45

Holdsworth, R. V., '*The Revenger's Tragedy* as a Middleton Play', *Three Jacobean Revenge Tragedies: a Casebook*, ed. R. V. Holdsworth (1990), 79–105

Howard-Hill, T. H., 'Marginal Markings: the Censor and the Editing of Four English Promptbooks', *Studies in Bibliography* 36 (1983), 168–77

Jackson, MacDonald P., *Studies in Attribution: Middleton and Shakespeare* (1979)

Lake, David J., *The Canon of Thomas Middleton's Plays* (1975)

Levin, Richard, *The Multiple Plot in English Renaissance Drama* (1971)

Moore, A. Telford, '"Shey"' in Jacobean and Caroline Drama', *Notes and Queries* 238 (1993), 228–9

Patterson, Annabel, *Censorship and Interpretation: The Condition of Reading and Writing in Early Modern England* (1984)

Schoenbaum, Samuel, *Middleton's Tragedies: A Critical Study* (1955)

Stachniewski, John, 'Calvinist Psychology in Middleton's Tragedies', in *Three Jacobean Revenge Tragedies: a Casebook*, ed. R. V. Holdsworth (1990), 226–47

TEXTUAL NOTES

As explained in the textual introduction, the two versions set out in the present edition coexist as layers of writing in a single manuscript, copied out by a single scribe who wrote out the whole text, here presented as version A, the Original Version.

The record for version B, the Performance Version, derives from changes made to the scribe's text by a series of revisers. It has thus been editorially reconstructed from the scribal base text, taken in combination with the revisers' changes. The revisers also had a retrospective influence on how version A is read, since they have sometimes corrected errors they came across while working through the scribe's text.

Textual notes to the Original Version (version A) have been provided when and where a doubt arises over what the scribe has written, or when the process of modernizing the text has altered the original reading significantly. The scribe's idiosyncrasies or errors can obscure the text he was copying in one of two ways: (*a*) he corrected himself in mid-flow of his writing (*currente calamo*), rewriting initial mistakes or misreadings or altering his own earlier (mis?)readings (sometimes the editor must decide whether the scribe has corrected himself rightly or wrongly); or, (*b*) the scribe's manuscript gives readings that the editor considers need emending, or correcting (in the second case, it is sometimes a reviser who has suggested a necessary amendment).

Textual notes to the Performance Version (version B) are of a somewhat different nature, since they are seldom directed towards establishing the text in terms of individual readings; instead, they record how the censor (Buc) and the reviser(s) modified the scribe's manuscript text. These notes are mainly concerned to record later alterations and additions, or the precise extent of the cuts marked in the manuscript's margins.

A. Notes on the Original Version

Title The Lady's Tragedy] THIS EDITION (*conj.* Taylor); This second Maydens tragedy BUC. Buc's provisional title has no authority; for a justification of the new title, see the Critical Introduction.

Persons *not in* SCRIBE

A1.1.8 on] SCRIBE, o *altered from* i

A1.1.29 care] SCRIBE, *written over* charge (*erased*)

A1.1.34.1 *Exit*] SCRIBE (*Exit Mempho:*)

A1.1.37 her her] SCRIBE, *second* her *interlined*

A1.1.52 one] REVISER (?), *altered from* ones SCRIBE (*final letter uncertain*)

A1.1.54 *Exit*] SCRIBE (*Exit Sophonirus*)

A1.1.72 too] SCRIBE (to), *second* o *added by* REVISER (?)

A1.1.80 FIRST NOBLE] LANCASHIRE; *3. Noblemā* SCRIBE. Memphonius and Sophonirus are the first two noblemen; '3 *Noble.*' also speaks at ll. 96, 99 and '4 *Nobl.*' at l. 99.

A1.1.86 cònstrue] SCRIBE (conster)

A1.1.87 wife's] SCRIBE (wyues)

A1.1.87 women] SCRIBE, e *altered from* a

A1.1.117 too] SCRIBE (to), *second* o *added by* REVISER

A1.1.127 hither] SCRIBE (hether, th *altered from* re *and* er *added*)

A1.1.138 any] SCRIBE, y *altered from* n

A1.1.146 affection] SCRIBE, *a final* s *erased*

A1.1.179 Has] SCRIBE, s *altered from* v

A1.1.180 Like...way] SCRIBE, *originally omitted, then interlined*. See also textual note on B1.1.161.

A1.1.206 thy] SCRIBE, *altered from* our

A1.2.0.1 Lord] SCRIBE (L). The title is often thus abbreviated (e.g. at 1.2.132, 1.2.155, etc.).

A1.2.34 rest] SCRIBE (Rest), R *altered from* br (*correction in dark ink, possibly made by* REVISER)

A1.2.48 that] SCRIBE, at *altered from* e

A1.2.61 upon] SCRIBE (vpon), v *altered from* o

A1.2.91 to] SCRIBE, *interlined*

A1.2.120 he] SCRIBE, *interlined*

A1.2.161 part] SCRIBE, *preceding word* port (?) *written, then crossed out*

A1.2.212 O, you...heart,] SCRIBE, *first written between* 1.2.209–10, *then crossed out*

A1.2.257.1 *Exit*] SCRIBE (*Exit Votarī*)

A1.2.282 but in] SCRIBE, n *probably altered, perhaps from* s

A1.2.285 ill....I‸ thank] STENGER; ~, I, ~ SCRIBE

A1.2.288 a] SCRIBE, *altered, perhaps from beginning of* h

A1.2.290 *Exit*] SCRIBE (—/*Exit lady.*)

A2.1.31 my] SCRIBE, y *altered from* e

A2.1.39 left'st] SCRIBE (left's)

A2.1.48 through] SCRIBE (thoroughe)

A2.1.56 mind] SCRIBE, m *altered from* k

A2.1.59 beholden] SCRIBE (beholding)

A2.1.75 What] SCRIBE (what), h *altered from* th

A2.1.76 on't] SCRIBE (an't)

A2.1.80 thee] SCRIBE, *second* e *added* (?)

A2.1.82 the] SCRIBE, *interlined*

A2.1.166 ascent] SCRIBE (asscent), c *inserted*

A2.2.18   Delights] BALDWYN; delight SCRIBE

A2.2.31   LEONELLA] SCRIBE (Leo.), *speech heading altered from* Wife (*erased*)

A2.2.55   the] THIS EDITION (*conj.* T. W. Craik); *omitted* SCRIBE

A2.2.83.1   *Exit; manet Votarius*] SCRIBE (*Exit Leonela | manet Votarius*)

A2.2.139   *Exit*] SCRIBE (*Exit Anselm*ˢ.)

A2.2.151   And...pardon.] SCRIBE, *crossing out* Exit *in right margin*

A2.3.19   ha't] SCRIBE (ha'ate)

A2.3.23   saint's] SCRIBE (Sance)

A2.3.28   tempt'st] SCRIBE (temp'st)

A2.3.39   own] SCRIBE, *interlined*

A2.3.62   when] SCRIBE, *possibly* wher

A2.3.80   to me] SCRIBE, to *interlined, in place of* wᵗʰ (*deleted*)

A2.3.81   Thou'lt] SCRIBE (thow't)

A2.3.92   plainness] SCRIBE (playnes)

A3.1.0.2   *and a servant*] SCRIBE, *added later*

A3.1.24   a friend] SCRIBE, *written twice, the second crossed out*

A3.1.45   LADY] SCRIBE, *altered from* Gou (*erased*)

A3.1.53   we're] THIS EDITION (*conj.* T. W. Craik); neer SCRIBE

A3.1.67   Then] REVISER, *inserting* n; the SCRIBE

A3.1.165   Where] SCRIBE, *a final* s *partly erased*

A3.1.200   king] SCRIBE (kinge), *a final 's' smudged out*

A3.1.204   his] SCRIBE, s *altered, possibly from* r (?)

A3.1.206   SECOND FELLOW] SCRIBE (2), *altered from* 1

A4.1.0.2   *Wife*] THIS EDITION; *Lady* SCRIBE. This substitution, made for the sake of clarity, also occurs at 5.1.37.2 and 5.1.120.2.

A4.1.1   Prithee] STENGER (*conj.* GREG); pry SCRIBE

A4.1.13   in] SCRIBE, *interlined*

A4.1.25   We shall] SCRIBE (wee shall), ee *written over* h (*erased*)

A4.1.33   ha't] SCRIBE (haate)

A4.1.63   *Exit*] SCRIBE (—*Exit Votarius*)

A4.1.66, 67   Say ye?] THIS EDITION; sha yee? SCRIBE. See A. Telford Moore, '"Shey"' in Jacobean and Caroline Drama'. Previous editors read 'Pshaw, ye!' or 'Pshaw ye!', wrongly deriving 'sha' from a later interjection.

A4.1.68   now] BALDWYN; noe SCRIBE

A4.1.128   As] BALDWYN; are SCRIBE

A4.1.139   ha't] SCRIBE (ha'te)

A4.2.1   FIRST NOBLE] TIECK; *2 Noble.* SCRIBE (Memphonius being the first).

A4.2.14.1   *Exit*] SCRIBE (—*Exit Memph.*)

A4.2.38   Afranius] THIS EDITION; Atranius SCRIBE. As this is not a possible Roman name, it must be a scribal error for 'Afranius', who appears in Tacitus, and in Fletcher's *Valentian* (see Textual Introduction, and Commentary on this line).

A4.2.46   from] SCRIBE, *altered, probably from* in

A4.3.20   year] SCRIBE, *preceded by* faire (*deleted, probably by* SCRIBE)

A4.3.38   [   ]] *lacuna in* SCRIBE; ffear REVISER

A4.3.40   a] THIS EDITION; *omitted* SCRIBE

A4.3.54   Set to] SCRIBE (setto)

A4.3.100   weep] SCRIBE, *interlined*

A4.3.107   sin] SCRIBE (Syn), *altered from* Sim

A4.3.120   pity] SCRIBE (pittie), p *altered from* d (?)

A4.4.1   eye] BALDWYN; eyes SCRIBE (?), *but the final* s *is uncertain*

A4.4.1   melts] SCRIBE, *final* s *possibly added* (?)

A4.4.39   to] SCRIBE, *altered from* et

A4.4.42   send] SCRIBE (sende), *final* e *altered from* s

A4.4.80   *Exit*] SCRIBE (*Exit Lady.*)

A5.1.2   with] SCRIBE (wᵗʰ), w *altered from* y

A5.1.8   Lock] SCRIBE (locke), c *altered from* o

A5.1.11.1   *He...closet*] SHEPHERD (*subst.*); *Exit* SCRIBE. Anselmus is on stage to speak ll. 30–7, so presumably here goes to the closet, in accordance with instructions given at ll. 8–9.

A5.1.27   thou'lt] SCRIBE (thow't)

A5.1.65   preys] BALDWYN; pray SCRIBE

A5.1.80   I'll] SCRIBE (ile), l *altered from* s *and* e *added*

A5.1.82   she] SHEPHERD; he SCRIBE

A5.1.98   LEONELLA] SCRIBE (Leo.), L *written over beginning of* V *or* W

A5.1.108   LEONELLA] SCRIBE (Leo.), L *written over beginning of* W

A5.1.148   Hear] SCRIBE (here), *first read as* 'hear' *in* THIS EDITION

A5.1.168   a [breath]] THIS EDITION; A [*lacuna*]— SCRIBE, *followed by something smudged out, then a space*; Point, jot *or* whit LANCASHIRE *conj.* Previous editors leave a space or adopt the REVISER's cut that avoids this line altogether.

A5.2.37   ladies'] SCRIBE (ladies)

A5.2.98   but, alas,] SCRIBE (but alas), *with* but a *recopied at the beginning of* 5.2.99 *and crossed out*

A5.2.102   those] BALDWYN; the those SCRIBE

A5.2.118   Our] SCRIBE (our), u *altered from* r

A5.2.128   robber of] SCRIBE, of *interlined*

A5.2.147   weather] SCRIBE, *written over an erasure*

A5.2.152   charged] SCRIBE (chargd), g *altered from* d

A5.2.153.1   *same*] BALDWYN; shame SCRIBE

A5.2.177   Then] SCRIBE, en *altered from* ou *or* on

A5.2.206.1–2   *The Spirit...it*] ALL EDITIONS; five words of the stage directions have lost initial letters where the margin has been torn.

B. Notes on the Performance Version

B1.1.2   Have] REVISER, *altered from* hath SCRIBE, *and rewritten in the right margin*; ink cross, right margin, and large pencil and ink crosses, left margin BUC. For the attribution of these markings to BUC, see Howard-Hill, 'Marginal Markings', 176–7.

B1.1.5–6   Flattered...dignity.] The Second | Maydens Tragedie *written in the right margin in an unidentified seventeenth-century hand*

B1.1.21   'Tis] REVISER (t'is), *altered from:* it is SCRIBE

B1.1.37   own] REVISER (owne), *interlined*; one SCRIBE

B1.1.38   gi'] REVISER, *altered from:* giue SCRIBE. See also B3.1.121.

B1.1.40   On] REVISER; wᵗʰ SCRIBE

B1.1.61   title] REVISER; titles SCRIBE, *final* s *deleted* (?)

B1.1.79   Then...farewell.] THIS EDITION *cuts after this line and resumes at* A1.1.99/B1.1.80 (*conj.* Greg); A1.1.80–98 *in* SCRIBE ('how's that...Fare yoᵘ well Sʳ') *marked to be cut.* A1.1.80 ('how's that Sir') *is unmarked and* REVISER *has added a question mark. The first half of* A1.1.81 ('waightie and serious,—') *has been deleted, and a line in the left margin indicates a cut from* A1.1.82 *to* A1.1.99, *though its limits are not precise. Greg's conjecture seems preferable as it produces the most coherent dialogue. The Tyrant's change of mind* (A1.1.99/B1.1.80) *is necessary for the action that follows.*

B1.1.85   to afflict] REVISER, *altered from:* t'afflict SCRIBE

B1.1.91   he'll] REVISER, *altered from:* he will SCRIBE, *by first deleting* wi, *then inserting* 'll *after* he *and deleting* wi'll.

B1.1.94   Whence] REVISER, *altered from:* Black? whence SCRIBE, *by deleting the first word*

B1.1.115   hast] REVISER, *altered from:* hadst SCRIBE

B1.1.118   Thou'rt] REVISER (th'art), *altered from:* thow art SCRIBE

B1.1.134   pains] REVISER, *altered from:* paine SCRIBE

B1.1.140   in curses] REVISER, *altered from:* in a curse SCRIBE

B1.1.152 this...that] REVISER; that...thy SCRIBE

B1.1.161 Like...way] *this line originally omitted, then interlined by* SCRIBE; *large pencil cross, left margin,* B1.1.160–2 BUC. Howard-Hill ('Marginal Markings', p. 177) suggests that BUC's cross drew attention to an omitted line, subsequently written in by SCRIBE.

B1.1.164 greatness.] A1.1.184–7 *in* SCRIBE ('A woman...husbands,') *deleted with diagonal lines by* REVISER

B1.1.188 Lovers'] REVISER (Louers), r *interlined*; Loue's SCRIBE

B1.1.198 'Tis...you!] SCRIBE[2] *in first addition slip, not in* SCRIBE; *a circle in the left margin at* B1.1.198–9, *indicating the point of insertion for these 2 lines* BOOKKEEPER

B1.1.208–15 TYRANT Nay...me.] SCRIBE[2] *in first addition slip, not in* SCRIBE; *a circle in the left margin at* B1.1.207–16, *indicating the point of insertion for these eight lines* BOOKKEEPER

B1.2.8–9 Dominions...jailer] *smudged pencil cross, left margin* BUC (?) *may indicate a possible cut*

B1.2.15 spirits] *followed by* all honest Courtiers! SCRIBE, *deleted by* REVISER

B1.2.165 brazen] REVISER, *interlined*; Courtiers SCRIBE

B1.2.225 I] *preceded by* heart, SCRIBE, *deleted by* REVISER

B1.2.253 I'm] *preceded by* heart SCRIBE, *deleted by* REVISER

B1.2.254 her!] A1.2.254–5 *in* SCRIBE ('sin's...pieces') *deleted by* REVISER

B1.2.280 has] REVISER (?); his SCRIBE

B1.2.286 Have] *preceded by* life SCRIBE, *deleted by* REVISER

B1.2.313 I'm...news,] 'swer' *or* 'swor', *written in faint ink, right margin*

B2.1.1–11 Who is't...father] SCRIBE[2] *in second addition slip, replacing and enlarging on* A2.1.1–4 SCRIBE; *a circle in the left margin at* B2.1.2, *indicating the point of insertion for these ten and a half lines* BOOKKEEPER

B2.1.20 Think?] A2.1.13–14 *in* SCRIBE ('yoᵘ come...for me') *deleted by* REVISER

B2.1.63–84 Say you...husband,] *pencil line in right margin* BUC. This line was probably intended to indicate problems rather than a definite cut, since there are further crosses, corrections and changes in BUC's hand within it.

B2.1.71 servant] BUC (*in pencil in right margin*); frend SCRIBE (*large pencil cross in left margin, and a small pencil cross at* frend *itself*)

B2.1.72 servant?] THIS EDITION; frend SCRIBE. See preceding note.

B2.1.75 woman] BUC (*interlined; large pencil cross, left margin*); Courtier SCRIBE

B2.1.77 mistresses.] A2.1.72–81 *in* SCRIBE ('that glister...forgotten') *marked for omission and crossed out by* REVISER

B2.1.78 The King] REVISER; he SCRIBE. This change was made to compensate for the preceding cut.

B2.1.104 creature] A2.1.108–38 *in* SCRIBE ('o hadst...the world,') *bracketed for omission by* REVISER. Within that larger cut, there is a further pencil line from A2.1.108–10, apparently made by BUC, and A2.1.121 has also been deleted.

B2.1.115 surgeon!] smarte on sowle SCRIBE, *deleted by* REVISER. A2.1.149–54 *in* SCRIBE ('thow't feele...formes;') *marked for omission by* REVISER

B2.1.119 path] REVISER; waie SCRIBE

B2.2.100 'Tis] *preceded by* life, SCRIBE, *deleted by* REVISER (*or* BUC, *conj.* Greg)

B2.3.39 flesh?] A2.3.40–5 *in* SCRIBE ('youle prefer...haue em!') *marked for omission by* REVISER

B2.3.44 greatness?] A2.3.50–2 *in* SCRIBE ('And must...place?') *marked for omission by* REVISER

B2.3.47 our] REVISER (oʳ.); my SCRIBE

B2.3.48 with him] A2.3.56–8 *in* SCRIBE ('she might...spoilde him,') *deleted by* REVISER

B2.3.49 in't] A2.3.59 *in* SCRIBE ('and marde me a good workeman') *deleted by* REVISER

B2.3.71 I'll] A2.3.81 *in* SCRIBE ('thow't feele thy self light shortlie,') *deleted by* REVISER

B2.3.81 mistress] REVISER; gentlewoman SCRIBE

B2.3.110 seize] REVISER (*deletes* on); ceaze on SCRIBE. See also B2.3.111, B3.1.44.

B2.3.111 seize] REVISER (*deletes* on); ceaze on SCRIBE

B3.1.21 gi'm] REVISER, *altered from:* giue him SCRIBE

B3.1.44 seize] REVISER (*deletes* on); ceaze on SCRIBE

B3.1.67 Then] REVISER; the SCRIBE

B3.1.161 some] BUC *interlined (large pencil cross in left margin)*; great SCRIBE (*deleted by* REVISER, *perhaps after* BUC's *addition*)

B3.1.188 SECOND FELLOW] REVISER (2); 1 SCRIBE. The fellows are referred to only by numbers. See also B3.1.192.

B3.1.188 Farewell] *preceded by* heart, SCRIBE, *deleted by* BUC (*large pencil cross in left margin,* B3.1.187–8)

B3.1.192 FIRST FELLOW] REVISER (1); Goui SCRIBE

B3.1.210 She's] *preceded by* life SCRIBE, *deleted by* REVISER

B3.1.218 died.] A3.1.218–21 *in* SCRIBE ('twas a...for it;') *deleted by* BUC (*pencil cross with ink cross over it in the left margin*)

B3.1.229 without her] A3.1.232–43 *in* SCRIBE ('faith she... after death!') *marked for omission by* REVISER

B4.1.12 You'd] *preceded by* life SCRIBE, *deleted by* REVISER

B4.1.74 man's] THIS EDITION (*conj.* Taylor); mens BUC *interlined (smudged pencil cross, left margin)*; knightes SCRIBE

B4.2.37.1 Enter...soldiers] SCRIBE (Enter 1 Soldier). This stage direction was later concealed beneath the third addition slip (see next note), and 'Enter Soldiers' was written by BOOKKEEPER in the left margin, opposite B4.2.35.

B4.2.37–42 The men...Cathedral] SCRIBE[2] *in third addition slip, replacing and enlarging on* A4.2.38–9 SCRIBE; *a circle in the left margin at* B4.2.37, *indicating the point for the insertion for these five and a half lines* BOOKKEEPER

B4.2.47 Does] *preceded by* life SCRIBE, *deleted by* REVISER

B4.2a.0.1 Enter Mr Gough] BOOKKEEPER *in left margin, opposite* B4.2.60; ~ *as* Memphonius (*conj.* GREG). This stage direction names the actor who spoke the additional lines, rather than the character. He re-enters, marking a new scene, here numbered B4.2a, though the time and place are apparently continuous with the previous action.

B4.2a.1–11 What...free] SCRIBE[2] *in fourth addition slip, not in* SCRIBE; *a circle in the left margin below* B4.2.60, *indicating the point of insertion for these eleven lines* BOOKKEEPER

B4.2a.6 Nobles'] BALDWYN; noble SCRIBE[2]. This emendation is necessary to provide a plausible antecedent for 'they' (B4.2a.7).

B4.3.28 fearful] REVISER; limber SCRIBE

B4.3.36 living] *followed by* thats my humour sir! SCRIBE, *deleted by* REVISER

B4.3.38 fear!] REVISER (ffear!); *lacuna* SCRIBE

B4.3.45 What] *preceded by* life SCRIBE, *deleted by* BUC (?)

B4.3.47 villain] REVISER; Stone Cutter SCRIBE

B4.3.69 Lay to your hands again] REVISER; wher be thease lazie handes agen SCRIBE

B4.3.79 How] *preceded by* life SCRIBE; *deleted by* BUC (*a smudged pencil cross in the left margin*)

B4.3.94 Thou'rt] *preceded by* Bi'th masse SCRIBE; *deleted by* REVISER

B4.3.102 many] BUC (?) *interlined (large pencil and ink crosses in the left margin)*; most SCRIBE

B4.3.131 Must] *preceded by* life, SCRIBE, *deleted by* REVISER

B5.1.72 Shall] *preceded by* life SCRIBE, *deleted by* BUC (?)

B5.1.94   He] *preceded by* life SCRIBE, *deleted by* BUC (?)

B5.1.106   You] *preceded by* heart SCRIBE, *deleted by* BUC (?)

B5.1.126   Must] *preceded by* heart SCRIBE, *deleted by* BUC (?)

B5.1.164   our] REVISER (*interlined*); twoe SCRIBE

B5.1.166–B5.1.179.1   ANSELMUS O thunder…lust!' [*He*] *dies*] SCRIBE[2] *in fifth addition slip, with 'quiet' written in as a cue, above B5.1.165; not in* SCRIBE *and probably added later by* REVISER; *a circle in the left margin at B5.1.165, indicating the point for insertion of these fourteen lines* BOOKKEEPER

B5.1.181   Brother,] REVISER *adds* Goui. *at the start of this line, replacing speech heading deleted at A5.1.166. A5.1.166–74 in* SCRIBE ('*Goui* Is death…more comely;') *marked for omission by* REVISER, *though A5.1.174/B5.1.180 is retained in* THIS EDITION *to get the bodies offstage. Within the larger cut, A5.1.167–9* ('Lass…staie?') *deleted by* REVISER, *perhaps to avoid lacuna at A5.1.168.*

B5.1.192   And I must through] REVISER (thorow); Tyrant…my self. SCRIBE

B5.2.19   any.] A5.2.20–3 *in* SCRIBE ('By this hand,…for't') *marked for omission by* REVISER

B5.2.21   living] A5.2.26 *in* SCRIBE ('and…hence,') *deleted by* REVISER

B5.2.25   colour] A5.2.31–2 *in* SCRIBE ('and thinck…hindraunce,') *deleted by* REVISER. See following note.

B5.2.26   But fate is my hinderer] REVISER (*with 's' at the end of 'fate' apparently deleted*); but *Fates* my hindraunce, SCRIBE (*probably deleted by accident*)

B5.2.31   for a picture drawer] THIS EDITION. *The preceding half-line in* SCRIBE ('for a Court schoolemaster,') *has been deleted by* REVISER, *but* LANCASHIRE *points out that 'for' is necessary for the sense of the remaining line.*

B5.2.34   charged him] A5.2.40–7 *in* SCRIBE ('to fit…wages') *marked for omission by* REVISER

B5.2.35   Where is he] REVISER, *added in the right margin, and preceded by a semicolon. The insertion is followed by 'Sol. he is come my lord' in the right margin, A5.2.41, and then deleted, presumably because it anticipated B5.2.35.*

B5.2.42   for this?] A5.2.56 *in* SCRIBE ('and kept in the worst Corner?') *deleted by* BUC (?)

B5.2.66   but few] BUC (?), *interlined*; at Courte SCRIBE

B5.2.113   Govianus!] A5.2.127–38 *in* SCRIBE ('*Goui* o thow… too?') *marked for omission by* BUC (?). *There are two slanting ink crosses, left margin, against A5.2.130–1, and at A5.2.132, a short vertical line beside A5.2.133–4, and a short horizontal line between A5.2.135–6.*

B5.2.116   th'extremest] THIS EDITION; the extremest REVISER; the Frenchmens SCRIBE. *The elision preserves the metre.*

B5.2.139   further] *followed by* nowe SCRIBE, *deleted by* REVISER

B5.2.143   I am poisoned] BUC (*large pencil and square ink crosses, left margin*); yo[r] kinges poisond SCRIBE

B5.2.147   all] REVISER, *interlined*; both SCRIBE

B5.2.148   obeyed.] A5.2.173.4–A178 *in* SCRIBE ('*Enter Helvetius*…Torments:') *marked for omission by* REVISER. *From here to the end of the play, cuts have been made to avoid the re-entry of Helvetius.*

B5.2.149.1   *A flourish*] BOOKKEEPER. BALDWYN *places the direction after the line, but before it is also possible.*

B5.2.150   GOVIANUS Well] THIS EDITION (*conj.* Greg); A5.2.180–94 *in* SCRIBE ('*Goui* I cannot…express it') *marked for omission by* REVISER. *The beginning and end of this cut are uncertain since the marginal line begins in the middle of a sentence (at A5.2.181, after 'I cannot better') and continues through to A5.2.195, leaving an awkward transition, best resolved by Greg's proposal. Within this larger cut, the speech heading for Helvetius at A5.2.189 has been deleted, and three of his lines, at A5.2.189–91, have been further marked for omission; speech headings for Memphonius at A5.2.192 and Helvetius at A5.2.193 have also been deleted. Probably at an intermediate stage, Helvetius's speech at A5.2.189–91 was intended to be cut and his lines at A5.2.193–4 reattributed to Memphonius: see note to B5.2.148, above.*

B5.2.156   lived.] A5.2.201–6 *in* SCRIBE ('here place…blest *Spirit*') *marked for omission by* REVISER. *Although the line marking the cut extends to B5.2.206, it is likely to have ended with 'Scilence;', thus retaining Govianus's next words, 'o welcome blest Spirit'.*

B5.2.164   virtuous] REVISER; honest SCRIBE

INCIDENTAL VARIANTS

1.2.213   use] SCRIBE (vse), v *altered from* w (?)

A1.2.260/B1.2.259   watched] SCRIBE (watcht), *first* t *altered from* r *or* c (?)

A2.1.22/B2.1.28   renew] SCRIBE, r *altered from* n *or* v (?)

2.2.40   he would] SCRIBE, d *perhaps altered from beginning of* l

A2.3.120.1/B2.3.110.1   *Exeunt*] SCRIBE (Exiunt), i *altered from* e

A2.3.123/B2.3.113   their] SCRIBE, ir *altered from* r (?)

3.1.61   Prithee] SCRIBE (pry thee), t *altered from* f

3.1.83   destruction] SCRIBE, e *altered from* i (?)

A3.1.231.1/B3.1.228.1   *Exeunt*] SCRIBE, e *possibly altered from* i

4.1.127   As] SCRIBE, *possibly altered*

4.2.0.1   *discontentedly*] discontedly SCRIBE

A4.2.40/B4.2.43   holy] SCRIBE, o *altered*

A4.2.57.1/B4.2.60.1   *Exeunt*] SCRIBE (Exunt), 5 *minims, the last altered to a* t (?)

4.3.9   monument] SCRIBE, *first* m *altered from* n

4.3.94   thou'rt] SCRIBE (thow'rt) *altered from* thort

4.3.131   now] SCRIBE, w *apparently altered from* u

4.4.13.1   *wondrous*] wrondrous SCRIBE

5.1.27   missed] SCRIBE (myst), y *altered from* i

5.2.13.2   paleness] SCRIBE (paileness), i *inserted; first* e *altered from beginning of* l

A5.2.170/B5.2.145   with] SCRIBE (w[th], w *altered from* t)

STAGE DIRECTIONS

A. Original Version

All stage directions in this version are scribal.

A1.1.0.1–2 *Actus Prim.ˢ* (left, opposite 1.1.0.4)

A1.1.0.3–5 *Enter the new Vsurping Tirant; The Nobles of | his faction, Memphonius, Sophonirus, Heluetius | with others, The right heire Gouianus depos'de,*

A1.1.34.1 *Exit Mempho:*

A1.1.54 *Exit Sophonirus*

A1.1.111.1 *Enter with the | Lady clad in Black.—* (left, opposite 1.1.110–11)

A1.1.211.1 *Exiunt Lady and | Govianus* (right, opposite 1.1.211–12)

A1.1.235 *Exiunt.*

A1.2.0.1–2 *Enter L Anselmus the deposde kinges brother, wᵗʰ | his Frend Votarius*

A1.2.69.1 *Enter Wyfe.* (left, opposite 1.2.70)

A1.2.111.1 *Exit Wife*

A1.2.153 *Exit Ansel:*

A1.2.165.1 *Enter Wife*

A1.2.257.1 *Exit Votariˢ*

A1.2.262.1 *Enter Leonela.*

A1.2.290 *—/Exit lady.*

A1.2.293.1 *Enter Bellarius | Mufled in his | cloke.* (left, opposite 1.2.292–4)

A1.2.331.1 *—Exiunt*

A2.1.0.1 *Actus: 2:ᵈᵘˢ·* (left, between 2.1.0.2 and 2.1.1)

A2.1.0.2 *Enter the ladye of Gouianus, wᵗʰ a Servaunt.*

A2.1.3.1 *Enter Heluetius*

A2.1.104.1–2 *Enter Gouianus | discharging a | Pistoll.* (left, opposite 2.1.103–4)

A2.1.169 *Exiunt*

A2.2.0.1 *Enter Votarius | sadly.*

A2.2.21.1 *Enter Wife*

A2.2.25.2 *Enter Leonela.* (left, just above 2.2.26, and supplying speech heading)

A2.2.46.1 *Enter Anselmus.*

A2.2.77.1 *—Exunt wife and Anselmˢ.*

A2.2.83.1 *Exit Leonela | manet Votarius* (right, opposite 2.2.83–4)

A2.2.99.1 *Enter Bellarius— | passing ouer the | Stage.* (left, opposite 2.2.99–101)

A2.2.117.1 *Enter Anselmus*

A2.2.139 *Exit Anselmˢ.*

A2.2.151 *—Exit* (deleted S, and written in at 2.2.153–4, below)

A2.2.151.1–2 *Enter Anselmus: a | dagger in his hand | wᵗʰ Leonela.* (left, opposite 2.2.150–1)

A2.2.155 *Exit | Votarius* (right, opposite 2.2.153–4)

A2.2.174 *—Exit./*

A2.2.177 *—Exit.*

A2.3.0.2–3 *Enter the Tyrant with Sophonirus Memphonius | and other Nobles.*

A2.3.8.1 *Enter | Helvetius* (left, bracketed, opposite 2.3.7–8)

A2.3.93.1 *Enter Guard* (left, opposite A2.3.94/B2.3.84 and supplying speech heading)

A2.3.101.1 *—Exit.*

A2.3.120.1–2 *—Exiunt | Manet Sophonirus—* (right, opposite A2.3.120/B2.3.110)

A2.3.126 *—Exit.*

A3.1.0.1 *Actus Tertius* (left)

A3.1.0.2 *Enter Gouianus with his | Ladye. and a servaunt.* (right, opposite 3.1.0.1)

A3.1.7.1 *—Exit*

A3.1.12.1 *Enter Servaunt.*

A3.1.23.1 *Enter | Sophonirus* (left, bracketed, opposite 3.1.23–4)

A3.1.46.1 *Enter Servˢ.* (left, opposite 3.1.47 and supplying speech heading)

A3.1.54.1 *Enter Seruant* (left)

A3.1.62 *—Exit*

A3.1.149.1–2 *Runs at her and | falles by the way | in a Sound.* (right, opposite 3.1.148–9)

A3.1.163.1 *—Kills her self* (right, bracketed)

A3.1.163.2 *A great knocking | agen.* (right, bracketed, opposite 3.1.164–5)

A3.1.187.1 *Enter the Fellows | well weopend.* (right, opposite 3.1.187–8)

A3.1.231.1–2 *Exeunt | Manet Gouianus* (right, opposite 3.1.230–1)

A3.1.255.1 *—Exit.*

A4.1.0.1–2 *Actus Quartus: Enter Votarius wᵗʰ Anselmus Lady.*

A4.1.63 *—Exit Votarius*

A4.1.64.1 *Enter Leonela.* (left, opposite 4.1.65 and supplying speech heading)

A4.1.138.1 *—Exit Wife*

A4.1.139.1 *Enter | Belarius.* (left, bracketed, opposite 4.1.138–9)

A4.1.166.1 *Exiunt.*

A4.2.0.1–2 *Enter Tirant wondrous discontedly:/ | Nobles afarr of.*

A4.2.14.1 *—Exit Memph.*

A4.2.37.1 *Enter 1 Soldier.* (left, opposite 4.2.37 and supplying speech heading)

A4.2.41 *—Exit.*

A4.2.51.1 *Enter. 1 Sould.* (left, opposite 4.1.52 and supplying speech heading)

A4.2.54 *—Exit*

A4.2.57.1 *—Exunt*

A4.3.0.1–4 *Enter the Tirant agen at a farder dore, which opened, brings | hym to the Toombe wher the Lady lies buried; The Toombe | here discouered ritchly set forthe;*

A4.3.130.1–2 *Exiunt | Manet 1 Sol.* (right, opposite 4.3.130–1)

A4.3.136 *—Exit*

A4.4.0.1–2 *Enter Gouianus in black, a booke in his hand, | his page carying a Torche before hym.*

A4.4.13.1–2 *Gouianus kneeles at | the Toomb wrondrous | passionatly, His | Page singes.* (right, opposite 4.4.13)

A4.4.13.3 *The songe.* (centre)

A4.4.42.1–5 *On a sodayne in a kinde of Noyse like a Wynde, | the dores clattering, the Toombstone flies open, | and a great light appeares in the midst of the | Toombe; His Lady as went owt, standing iust | before hym all in white, Stuck with Iewells | and a great crucifex on her brest.*

A4.4.80 *Exit Lady.*

A4.4.90 *—Exit.*

A5.1.0.1–2 *Actus Quintus. Enter Votarius with Anselmus the Husband.*

A5.1.11.1 *—Exit.* (Anselmus is still on stage to speak 5.1.30–7, so presumably here enters the closet, as instructed at 5.1.8–9).

A5.1.16.1–2   —*Exit.*

A5.1.16.2–3   *Leonella aboue in a Gallery | with her loue Bellarius.* (left)

A5.1.29   *Descendet Leonela.*

A5.1.37.1   /*Locks him self in* (right)

A5.1.37.2–3   *Enter Anselmus Lady with Leonella.* (left)

A5.1.82.1   *Enter Votarius | to the doore | w^(th)in* (left, opposite 5.1.82–4)

A5.1.112–A5.1.112.1   *kills | Leonela* (right, bracketed, opposite 5.1.112.1)

A5.1.120.1–3   *They make a daungerous passe at one another | the Lady purposely runs betwene, and is kild | by them both.* (right)

A5.1.142.1   —*Ansel: dies*

A5.1.143.1   *Enter Gouianus with Servauntes*

A5.1.165.1   —*Dyes.*

A5.1.187   *Exit*

A5.2.0.2   *Enter Tyrant with Attendauntes.*

A5.2.13.1–8   *They bringe the Body in a Chaire drest up in black veluet which setts out the | pailenes of the handes and face, And a faire Chayne of pearle crosse her brest | and the Crucyfex aboue it; He standes silent awhile letting the Musique | play, becknyng the soldiers that bringe her in to make obeisaunce to her, and | he hym self makes a lowe honour to the body and kisses the hande*

A5.2.13.9   *A song within in Voyces.* (centre)

A5.2.47.1   *Enter 3 Souldier with Gouianus.* (left)

A5.2.153.1–2   *Enter the Ghost | in the shame form | as the lady is | drest in the | Chayre* (right, opposite A5.2.151–5/B5.2.126–30; a line links it to the end of A5.2.154/B5.2.129)

A5.2.167.1   *Enter | Nobles* (left, bracketed, opposite A5.2.166–7/B5.2.141–2)

A5.2.173.3   *Enter | Helvetius* (left, bracketed and deleted, opposite A5.2.173–4/B5.2.148–9)

A5.2.206.1–2   *The Spirit enters | agen and stayes to | goe out with the | body as it were | attendinge it.* (left, opposite A5.2.205–9/B5.2.157–60)

A5.2.213.3–4   *Recorders or other solempne | Musique plays them owt* (right)

A5.2.213.5   *ffinis* (centre right)

B. Stage Directions Added in Performance Version

All these are in the prompter's hand except B5.1.165, which is in the hand of the scribe.

B1.1.0.6   *A Senate* (left, opposite B1.1.2)

B1.1.221.1–2   *A Florish* (left, under B1.1.221)

B2.3.0.4   *A florish* (left, opposite B2.3.1)

B2.3.116.1–2   *A florish* (left, opposite B2.3.115)

B3.1.139.1   *Knock* (left, opposite B3.1.138)

B3.1.146.1   *Knock* (left, opposite B3.1.145)

B3.1.162.1   *knock* (left, opposite B3.1.162)

B3.1.163.2   *knock* (left, at B3.1.165)

B3.1.184.1   *Knock | w^(th)in* (left, opposite B3.1.183–4)

B4.2.37.1   *Enter Soldiers.* (left, at B4.2.35)

B4.2a.0.1   *Enter M^r | Goughe* (left, opposite B4.2.60)

B4.4.42.7   *Enter Ladye | Rich Robinson* (left, opposite B4.4.42.3–4)

B5.1.116.1–2   *Ente: Bellarius* (left, opposite B5.1.111)

B5.1.165   —/*dyes.*

B5.2.11.1   *Enter soldiers | W^(th) the Ladye* (left, at B5.2.10–11)

B5.2.12.1   *ii. musick* (left; the number is arabic, and refers to the eleventh gathering of the manuscript)

B5.2.149.1   *Florish* (left)

LINEATION NOTES

1.1.73–5   But that…reign] THIS EDITION; *2 lines* SCRIBE: dignity |

A1.1.152/B1.1.133   Like an old man,] SCRIBE, *written at the end of* A1.1.151/B1.1.132, *then crossed out*

A1.2.14–15   Is…courtiers] LANCASHIRE; spirits | SCRIBE

1.2.157–8   He…back] BALDWYN; *1 line* SCRIBE

A1.2.297–9/B1.2.296–8   As you…servants] THIS EDITION; muffler | you | SCRIBE

A2.1.14   If you] SCRIBE, *at end of* A2.1.13, *then crossed out and rewritten on next line*

2.2.101   business?] SCRIBE; *after this, 'my eye catcht so much knowledge' written and then crossed out*

2.3.21–2   Hark…you] SHEPHERD; *1 line* SCRIBE

2.3.22–3   O…bell] SHEPHERD; *2 lines* SCRIBE: tongue |

A2.3.125–6/B2.3.115–16   That…it] LANCASHIRE; *2 lines* SCRIBE: him |

3.1.12–13   Does…now] HOPKINSON; *1 line* SCRIBE

3.1.30   Home] SCRIBE, *at the end of* 3.1.29, *then crossed out and written on the next line*

3.1.100–1   Lady…heart] THIS EDITION; *2 lines* SCRIBE: now |

3.1.139–40   Enough…Hark!] THIS EDITION; *1 line* SCRIBE

4.1.63–4   Go…thee] SHEPHERD; *1 line* SCRIBE

4.1.66–8   Say ye…company] LANCASHIRE *conj.*; *2 lines* SCRIBE: say ye |

4.1.101–3   I…you] STENGER; *6 lines* SCRIBE

4.1.143–4   Did…adventurous] STENGER; *1 line* SCRIBE

4.2.7–8   I…already] SHEPHERD; *1 line* SCRIBE

4.2.12–13   That…thyself] SHEPHERD; *1 line* SCRIBE

4.2.36–7   Of…there] SHEPHERD; *1 line* SCRIBE

B4.2.37–9   The…released] SHEPHERD; *2 lines* SCRIBE: employment |

4.3.5–8   I…her] FIRST SOLDIER *speaks the only prose in the play here, and below, at* 4.3.46–9, 4.3.57–8.

4.3.39–40   I'm…Cathedral] THIS EDITION; *1 line* SCRIBE

4.4.64–5   He…Tyrant] SHEPHERD; *1 line* SCRIBE

4.4.86–7   Before…counsel] SHEPHERD; *1 line* SCRIBE

A5.2.31–2   And…yet] SHEPHERD; yet | SCRIBE

A5.2.42–3/B5.2.41   To…thee] SHEPHERD; youth | SCRIBE

A5.2.100–1/B5.2.98–100   To…again] SHEPHERD; *1 line* SCRIBE

A5.2.104/B5.2.106   Of] SCRIBE, *originally written at the end of* A5.2.103/B5.2.89 *and smudged out*

A5.2.126/B5.2.127   'Twas] SCRIBE, *originally written at the end of* A5.2.125/B5.2.111 *and crossed out*

A5.2.175–7   Helvetius…'em] SHEPHERD; *1 line* SCRIBE

A5.2.211–12/B5.2.162–3   Lead…rooms] SHEPHERD; *1 line* SCRIBE

THE TRIUMPHS OF TRUTH

Edited by David M. Bergeron

THE text of *The Triumphs of Truth* appears in two separate issues (STC 17903 and 17904; *BEPD* 311–2). Printed by Nicholas Okes, the text is a quarto of four sheets. The expanded issue (STC 17904) includes the text of *The Manner of his Lordship's Entertainment* and serves as the control-text for this edition, designated OKES1B. The title-page was entirely reset. In OKES1A (STC 17903) it bears the imprint 'Printed by Nicholas Okes, dwelling at the signe of the | Hand, neere Holbourne-Bridge, 1613.'; OKES1B adds a reference to *The Manner of his Lordship's Entertainment* (see the textual note to l. 15 below) and shortens the imprint to '*LONDON*, | Printed by NICHOLAS OKES, 1613.' On 3 November 1613 the printer entered the book in the Stationers' Register: 'Ent. N. Okes: a booke called The Tryumphes of Truth, of all the showes, pagiantes, Chariotes, &c. on the Lord Maiours day, Octobris 29, 1613.' This is the only time that a printer entered one of Middleton's pageant texts in the Register.

Nicholas Okes the printer received a payment of £4 for printing the book, probably the usual 500 copies, based on guild records for other pageants. The record in the Grocers accounts for 1613 unfortunately leaves a blank when indicating the number of copies. But we cannot know whether this payment covered both issues of the text. In any event, as Greg observes, 'This publication is unusual.' Greg speculates that the printer may have intended two separate editions, one of *Truth* and the other of *The Manner*. When the copy for *The Manner* came to the print shop, the earlier text of *Truth* was still standing; and the printer decided to combine them. Greg erroneously assumed that the second issue was printed from standing type without examining for evidence that suggests a single impression. It seems clear that the formes (except for outer A) were impressed only once.

Adrian Weiss has demonstrated that the type is the same for both issues—therefore, one press run with only the title-page of STC 17904 being reset (private correspondence). Almost all press correction appears on outer formes of sheet B and C. The outer forme of C contains the largest number of changes. The only substantive change appears on C2^v, 524–7—an obvious mis-setting due to compositorial eyeskip which misplaced three words of the speech. Both issues include at the end of *Truth* the musical notation for the song sung at 90–113. This is Middleton's only pageant text that includes a musical score and the first pageant text to contain such.

SEE ALSO

Text: *Works*, 968
Music: this volume, 147
Authorship and date: this volume, 375

WORKS CITED

Previous Editions

The Progresses of King James the First, ed. John Nichols (1828), vol. 2
Thomas Middleton, *Works*, ed. Alexander Dyce (1840), vol. 5
Some Account of the Worshipful Company of Grocers, J. B. Heath (1854)
Thomas Middleton, *Works*, ed. A. H. Bullen (1886), vol. 7

Other Works Cited

Aubrey, John, *Aubrey's Brief Lives*, ed. Oliver Lawson Dick (1950)
Bald, R. C., 'Middleton's Civic Employments', *Modern Philology* 31, (1933), 65–78
Bergeron, David M., *English Civic Pageantry 1558–1642* (1971)
—— 'Middleton's Moral Landscape: *A Chaste Maid in Cheapside* and *The Triumphs of Truth*', in '*Accompaninge the players*': *Essays Celebrating Thomas Middleton, 1580–1980*, ed. Kenneth Friedenreich (1983), 133–46
—— 'Thomas Middleton and Anthony Munday: Artistic Rivalry?', *Studies in English Literature, 1500–1900* 36 (1996), 461–79
—— 'Stuart Civic Pageants and Textual Performance', *Renaissance Quarterly* 51 (1998), 163–83
Bradbrook, M. C., 'The Politics of Pageantry: Social Implications in Jacobean London', in *Poetry and Drama 1570–1700: Essays in Honour of Harold F. Brooks*, ed. Antony Coleman and Antony Hammond (1981), 60–75
Bromham, A. A., 'Thomas Middleton's *The Triumphs of Truth*: City Politics in 1613', *The Seventeenth Century* 10 (1995), 1–25
Chapman, George, *Homer's Odyssey* (1614)
Fuller, Thomas, *The Worthies of England*, ed. John Freeman (1952)
Heath, J. B., *Some Account of the Worshipful Company of Grocers of the City of London* (1854)
James I, *The Political Works of James I*, ed. Charles H. McIlwain (1918)
Leinwand, Theodore B., 'London Triumphing: The Jacobean Lord Mayor's Show', *Clio* 11 (1982), 137–53
Paster, Gail Kern, 'The Idea of London in Masque and Pageant', in *Pageantry in the Shakespearean Theater*, ed. David M. Bergeron (1985), 48–64
Robertson, Jean, and D. J. Gordon, *A Calendar of Dramatic Records in the Books of the Livery Companies of London 1485–1640*, Malone Society, Collections III (1954)
Stow, John, *Survey of London* (1598, 1603, 1618, 1633)
Wickham, Glynne, *Early English Stages 1330 to 1660* (1959–81)
Williams, Sheila, 'Two Seventeenth Century Semi-Dramatic Allegories of Truth the Daughter of Time', *The Guildhall Miscellany* 2 (1963), 207–20

TEXTUAL NOTES

15 Middleton] In OKES1B the following lines appear after Middleton's name: Shewing alfo his Lordfhips Entertainement vpon *Michaelmas* day laft, being the day of his Election, at that moft Famous and Admired Worke of the Running Streame, from *Amwell-Head* into the Cefterne at *Iflington,* being the fole Coft, Induftry and Inuention of the Worthy Mᵣ· Hᴠɢʜ Mɪᴅᴅʟᴇᴛᴏɴ of *London,* Gold-fmith.

16 *The Epistle Dedicatory*] ᴛʜɪꜱ ᴇᴅɪᴛɪᴏɴ; *not in* ᴏᴋᴇꜱ

144 *led*] ᴏᴋᴇꜱ (*lead*)
169 *they've*] ɴɪᴄʜᴏʟꜱ; *they haue* ᴏᴋᴇꜱ
216 *attends*] ᴛʜɪꜱ ᴇᴅɪᴛɪᴏɴ; attend ɴɪᴄʜᴏʟꜱ; *attnds* ᴏᴋᴇꜱ
418 *pass*] ɴɪᴄʜᴏʟꜱ; *not in* ᴏᴋᴇꜱ
569 her] ɴɪᴄʜᴏʟꜱ; her a ᴏᴋᴇꜱ
681 *this*] ɴɪᴄʜᴏʟꜱ; *not in* ᴏᴋᴇꜱ
741 *they'll*] ᴏᴋᴇꜱ (*the'ile*)
780 chariot] ɴɪᴄʜᴏʟꜱ; cariot ᴏᴋᴇꜱ

PRESS VARIANTS

Copies collated: British Library (2), National Library of Scotland, Folger, Guildhall, Pforzheimer Collection (University of Texas at Austin). One of the BL copies is STC 17903, which is designated below as ʙʟ1. All the other copies are of STC 17904, the expanded version of the text; they are invariant. The contrast below is between ʙʟ1 and the other copies.

Sheet B (outer forme)

Sig. B1

176 won] *wonne* ʙʟ1; *wunne*
199 stand] ftands ʙʟ1; stand

Sig. B2ᵛ

282 *herd*] *heard* ʙʟ1; *Heard*

Sig. B3

321 impudence] Im-|pudence ʙʟ1; Im-|pudēce
322 forceth] forces ʙʟ1; forceth
323 Truth] Truth ʙʟ1; *Truth*

Sheet C (outer forme)

Sig. C1

422 *temples*] Temple ʙʟ1; *Temples*
423 *Moor,*] *Moor,e* ʙʟ1; *Moore,*
434 *adore.*] adore: ʙʟ1; *adore*
446 *mistress*] Mihrefse ʙʟ1; Miftreffe
448 *friend*] Frend ʙʟ1; *Friend*

Sig. C2ᵛ

517 *friends*] Frends ʙʟ1; *Freinds*
524–7 *Vanish, give way* . . . *and beams*] At this her powerfull command, the Vanifh, giue | Way, Cloude fuddenly rifes, and changes into a | bright fpredding Canopy, ftucke thicke with Starres, | and beames ʙʟ1; *Vanifh, giue Way.* | At this her powerfull command, the Cloude | fuddenly rifes, and changes into bright fpred-|ding Canopy, ftucke thicke with Starres, and | beames

Sheet D (inner forme)

Sig. D4

794 *FINIS.*] FINIS. ʙʟ1; *not in others*

THE MANNER OF HIS LORDSHIP'S ENTERTAINMENT

Edited by David M. Bergeron

THIS brief quarto pageant of one sheet, printed by Nicholas Okes, appears with the text of *The Triumphs of Truth* (STC 17904, *BEPD* 312) as an independent section at the end of the book. Anthony Munday in his continuation of Stow's *Survey of London* (1618) includes a description of the entertainment and the speeches.

SEE ALSO

Text: *Works*, 961
Authorship and date: this volume, 375

WORKS CITED

Previous Editions

The Progresses of King James the First, ed. John Nichols (1828), vol. 2
Thomas Middleton, *Works*, ed. Alexander Dyce (1840), vol. 5
Thomas Middleton, *Works*, ed. A. H. Bullen (1886), vol. 7

Other Works Cited

Aubrey, John, *Aubrey's Brief Lives*, ed. Oliver Lawson Dick (1950)
Fuller, Thomas, *The Worthies of England* (1662)
Hardin, William, '"Pipe-Pilgrimages and Fruitfull Rivers": Thomas Middleton's Civic Entertainments and the Water Supply of Early Stuart London', *Renaissance Papers* 1993 (1994), 63–73
Stow, John, *Survey of London* (1618, 1633)

TEXTUAL NOTES

3   Swinnerton] OKES (Swinarton). The spelling has been changed to bring it into conformity with the more recent spelling of this proper name.

12   This edition has omitted the beginning lines of the text because they exactly repeat a passage from the title-page ('The manner...London', ll. 1–6).

THE MASQUE is not extant unless the songs presented here are fragments of it.

'Cupid is Venus' Only Joy'

The first song derives from a number of printed and manuscript sources, and is for this reason textually complicated. Different versions or parts of the song are found in:

(*a*) three versions of stanzas 1 and 2, or stanza 1 alone, in music manuscripts:

> British Library Additional MS. 29481, fol. 6ᵛ: stanzas 1 and 2; the vocal part with stanza 1 underlaid and stanza 2 at the foot of the page;
>
> New York Public Library, Drexel MS. 4175, Item 24: stanzas 1 and 2; treble and bass notation with stanza 1 between staves and stanza 2 below the score;
>
> New York Public Library, Drexel MS. 4175, Item 56: stanza 1 only; treble and lute tablature with stanza between staves;

(*b*) Thomas Cotes's 1630 printing of *Chaste Maid*, at 4.1.167–93: stanzas 1 and 2, followed by another stanza as in *Chaste Maid* in this edition;

(*c*) Thomas Newcomb's 1657 printing of *Dissemblers*, at 1.4.89–99: stanza 1 only, with an added couplet after l. 7.

Cutts cogently suggests that the song in *Chaste Maid* is an interpolation replacing the anticipated song in Welsh by the Welsh gentlewoman. The music manuscripts evidently represent the underlying two-stanza version on which the two different printed versions were based. The revisions for both plays were presumably by Middleton, as was the original song: the diction and ideation are characteristic of his style. The manuscripts probably derive from a third dramatic text written before either play. This text is probably the lost masque (Jowett).

Apart from the textual problem in l. 12 discussed below, the text in the manuscripts is stable. None of the variants between these manuscripts and the printed plays demonstrates error in the manuscripts.

'Cupid is an Idle Toy'

This song survives in two versions in music manuscripts: John Wilson's songbook dated 1656, Bodleian MS Mus.b.1, and John Gamble's songbook dated 1659, New York Public Library, Drexel MS 4257.

The stanzas are written after another Middleton song, 'In a Maiden Time Professed', which also appears in *The Witch* at 2.1.131–8 without the present stanzas. In private correspondence, Raphael Seligmann has suggested that the stanzas exclusive to the music manuscripts might

both derive from the *Masque of Cupids*. I am grateful to Seligmann for his information and comments. See also Marion O'Connor's textual introduction to *The Witch*, p. 995, and note to 2.1.138.

Stanza 1 is a reworking of 'Only Joy' stanza 1, and in each song stanza 2 develops different parallels and contrasts with the preceding stanza. The songs are intimately related. It might be argued that the stanzas actually make up a single song. The objections are that (*a*) the two pairs offer contradictory statements, the first that Cupid has a strong influence here and now, the second that he is now no longer effectual, being an 'idle toy' whose period of influence belongs to the past; (*b*) the pairs are of different length and stanzaic form. For these reasons, and in recognition also of their separate textual provenances, the two pairs of stanzas are here presented as separate songs, the second in effect offering a response to the first. It is possible either that the two pairs were sung at different points in the masque, perhaps by a Cupid, or that they were sung in sequence but by different singers.

SEE ALSO

Text: *Works*, 1033
Authorship and date: this volume, 377
Music: this volume, 149 ('Cupid is Venus' only joy'), 151 ('Cupid is an idle toy')

WORKS CITED

Augustine, *The City of God against the Pagans*, trans. E. McCracken, *et al.*, 7 vols (Cambridge and London, 1957–72)

Bacon, Francis, *The Works of Francis Bacon*, ed. J. Spedding, R. L. Ellis and D. D. Heath, 14 vols (London, 1857–74)

Bartlett, Phyllis Brooks, ed., *The Poems of George Chapman* (New York: Russell & Russell, 1962)

Beaumont, Francis, *The Masque of the Inner Temple and Gray's Inn*, ed. Fredson Bowers, in Bowers, gen. ed., *The Dramatic Works in the Beaumont and Fletcher Canon*, vol. 1 (Cambridge, 1966)

Bentley, G. E., *The Jacobean and Caroline Stage*, 7 vols (Oxford: Clarendon Press, 1941–68)

Carew, Thomas, *The Poems*, ed. Rhodes Dunlap (Oxford: Clarendon Press, 1948)

Carey, John, *John Donne: Life, Mind and Art* (London: Faber & Faber, 1981)

Chambers, E. K., *The Elizabethan Stage*, 4 vols (Oxford: Clarendon Press, 1923)

Clode, Charles M., *The Early History of the Guild of Merchant Taylors of the Fraternity of St. John the Baptist, London, with Notices of the Lives of Some of its Eminent Members*, 2 vols (London, 1888)

Cutts, John P., *La Musique de scène de la troupe de Shakespeare: The King's Men sous le règne de Jacques Iᵉʳ*, second edn. rev. (1971)

Davis, Walter R., ed., *The Works of Thomas Campion: Complete Songs, Masques, and Treatises, with a Selection of the Latin Verse* (London: Faber & Faber, 1969)

Dubrow, Heather, *A Happier Eden: The Politics of Marriage in the Stuart Epithalamium* (Ithaca and London: Cornell UP, 1990)

Ebreo, Leone, *Dialoghi d'Amore/The Philosophy of Love*, trans. F. Friedeberg-Seeley and Jean H. Barnes (London: The Soncino Press, 1937)

Grierson, Herbert J. C., ed., *The Poems of John Donne*, 2 vols (Oxford: Clarendon Press, 1912)

Herford, C. H., and P. and E. Simpson, eds., *Ben Jonson*, 11 vols (Oxford: Clarendon Press, 1925–52)

Hesiod, *Theogony*, trans. Hugh G. Evelyn-White, Loeb Classical Library (London, 1968)

Horne, David H., *The Life and Minor Works of George Peele* (New Haven, 1952)

Hyde, Thomas, *The Poetic Theology of Love* (London and Toronto: Associated University Presses, 1986)

Jones-Davies, M.-T., *Inigo Jones, Ben Jonson et le masque* (Paris: Didier, 1967)

Jowett, John, 'Middleton's Song of Cupid', *Notes and Queries* 239 (1994), 66–70

Lancashire, Anne, 'The Witch: Stage Flop or Political Mistake?' in

'*Accompaninge the players': Essays Celebrating Thomas Middleton, 1580–1980*, edited by Kenneth Friedenreich (New York: AMS Press, 1983), 161–81

McClure, Norman Egbert, ed., *The Letters of John Chamberlain*, Memoirs XII, Pts. I and II, The American Philosophical Society (Philadelphia, 1939)

Mercer, Eric, *English Art 1553–1625* (Oxford: Oxford University Press, 1962)

Mulcaster, Richard, *Positions*, ed. Henry Barnard and R. H. Quick (London, 1887)

Nicoll, Allardyce, *Stuart Masques and the Renaissance Stage* (London, 1938)

Nichols, John, *The Progresses, Processions, and Magnificent Festivities of King James the First*, 4 vols (London, 1828)

Puttenham, George, *The Arte of English Poesie*, ed. G. D. Willcock and A. Walker (Cambridge, 1936)

Sidney, Sir Philip, *The Old Arcadia*, ed. Katherine Duncan-Jones (1985; rpt. Oxford: Oxford University Press, 1999)

Spencer, T. J. B., ed., *A Book of Masques in Honour of Allardyce Nicoll* (Cambridge, 1967)

White, Beatrice, *Cast of Ravens: The Strange Case of Sir Thomas Overbury* (London: John Murray, 1965)

TEXTUAL NOTES

1.0.1 [First] Song] THIS EDITION; THE SONG *Chaste Maid*; SONG *Dissemblers*

1.2 he is] MSS, *Chaste Maid*; he's *Dissemblers*

1.8 thought] MSS, *Dissemblers*; taught *Chaste Maid*

1.10–18 Why…play.] BL, DREXEL 24, *Chaste Maid*; not in DREXEL 56, *Dissemblers*

1.11 tricks] MSS; *prankes Chaste Maid*

1.12 The…done?] added in margin, DREXEL 24; not in BL. This line, which partly repeats l. 11, may have been missing in the underlying copy common to the two music MSS. It is required for the musical setting, though this would not be immediately obvious as in both MSS the stanza is written below the musical setting, not alongside the notation. The DREXEL 24 scribe may have reconstructed it. In this case the word 'wanton' would be guesswork, but effective guesswork as *Chaste Maid* testifies to the same reading.

1.14 wound] BL, DREXEL 24; *hurt Chaste Maid*

1.15 Ay] BL, DREXEL 24; *Ah Chaste Maid*. 'Ah' may be an error, as 'Ay me' echoes 'I mean' in the same position in stanza 1.

1.17 strength] BL, DREXEL 24; *sence Chaste Maid*. 'Strength' might have been thought to blur the gender distinction and have been later revised for this reason. Compare following note.

1.18 it] BL, DREXEL 24; *he Chaste Maid*. The text in *Chaste Maid* is again more securely gendered, perhaps in response to the dramatic context.

2.0.1 [Second Song]] THIS EDITION; *not in MSS*

2.5 they got] WILSON; begott GAMBLE

2.7 bow] WILSON (bough). The spelling differentiates the pronunciation from 'Bow' (l. 4).

2.9 world] GAMBLE; wold WILSON

2.12 would catch] WILSON; will winn GAMBLE

2.15 Cunny] WILSON (Cunny), GAMBLE (Cony)

2.16 And this was all the] WILSON; Loe was the only GAMBLE. WILSON seems correct, as it summarizes both 'Cunny' and 'the dart'.

CIVITATIS AMOR

Edited by David M. Bergeron

THE text of *Civitatis Amor*, printed by Nicholas Okes (STC 17878; *BEPD* 338), has few textual problems. This quarto text has three sheets. Some copies now include a frontispiece engraving of Prince Charles, but this is a later addition from a separate publication (see John Astington, 'Visual Texts', this volume, 230).

SEE ALSO

Text: *Works*, 1204
Authorship and date: this volume, 398

WORKS CITED

Previous Editions

The Progresses of King James the First, ed. John Nichols (1828), vol. 3
Thomas Middleton, *Works*, ed. Alexander Dyce (1840), vol. 5
Thomas Middleton, *Works*, ed. A. H. Bullen (1886), vol. 7

Other Works Cited

Chamberlain, John, *The Letters of John Chamberlain*, ed. Norman Egbert McClure, 2 vols (1939)
Munday, Anthony, *Chrysanaleia: The Golden Fishing* (1616)
—— *London's Love to Royal Prince Henry* (1610)
The Order and Solemnity of the Creation of the High and Mighty Prince Henry ... Prince of Wales (1610)
Spenser, Edmund, *The Complete Poetical Works of Spenser*, ed. R. E. Neil Dodge (1936)
Stow, John, *Annales*, rev. Edmund Howes (1631)
—— *Survey of London* (1603)

TEXTUAL NOTES

39–42 a personage ... followeth] This statement reappears in 46–9, only slightly changed. Both appear on the inner forme on sheet A on adjoining pages. Lines 46–9 are set as a kind of heading, which may account for the repetition.
57 NEPTUNE] THIS EDITION; *not in* OKES
85 *climb*] OKES (*clime*)

104 NEPTUNE *Sound on.*] I construe this as an order from the speaker Neptune, but the text creates some confusion at the bottom of sig. B1. In rather large Roman type the text reads: 'Neptune——Sound——On——'. Perhaps this is the printer's way of delineating this prose statement from London's preceding verse speech.
184, 235, 291 Pembroke] OKES (*Penbrooke*)
288 night] nighr OKES
399–400 Earl of Northumberland] OKES (*E. Northumb.*)

PRESS VARIANTS

Copies collated: British Library (BL), Huntington (HN), Guildhall (GH).

Sheet A (outer forme)

Sig. A3

20 this] GH; his BL, HN

Sig. A4ᵛ

65 city] Citie BL, HN; *Citie*, GH

Sheet A (inner forme)

Sig. A3ᵛ

28 marshalled] Marſhall'd GH; Marſh'alld BL, HN

Sheet B (inner forme)

Sig. B2

127 *This,*] HN, GH; This BL

Sheet C (outer forme)

Sig. C4ᵛ

416 *Sir William ... Lord Stourton.*] BL, HN; *not in* GH
421 *Sir William ... Lord Beauchamp.*] *Sir William ... Lord Beauchampe.* BL, HN; *not in* GH
437 *Viscount Villiers*] Vicount *Villiers* BL, HN; Viconnt *Villiers* GH
437–40 the Viscount Wallingford, ... Carew, etc.] the Vicount *Wallingford, ... Carew, &c.* BL, HN; *not in* GH

A FAIR QUARREL

Edited by Suzanne Gossett

THE first edition of *A Fair Quarrel* (BEPD 352) was published in 1617 in two issues (STC 17911, 17911a), neither of which was entered in the Stationers' Register. The title-page of the first issue states that the play was 'Acted before the King | *and diuers times publikely by the* | Prince his Highnes Seruants' and that the quarto was 'Printed at London for *I.T.* . . . to bee sold at | Christ Church Gate. 1617.' Greg identified I.T. as John Trundle and, based on the ornament on A2, recognized the printer as George Eld.

The second issue differs from the first by a cancel title--page, which alerts readers to the expanded text. 'A Faire Quarrell. | With new Additions of Mr. *Chaughs* and | *Trimtrams* Roaring, and the Bauds Song. | *Neuer before Printed.* | *As it was Acted before the King, by the Prince* | his Highnesse Seruants.' The rest of the page follows the text of the original, though it was newly set up. The second issue contains an additional scene, intended as 4.4, printed on three leaves. The first recto of this scene, identified as H4, states at the bottom, 'Place this at the latter end of the fourth Act.' and the scene was inserted between H3 and the original H4. The title-page and the additions were printed on one sheet, and the new title-page was then cut off and pasted in place.

The text of the play is clear, without many simple errors, though there is a certain amount of mislineation. The lack of errors may suggest authorial proofreading, particularly since Rowley was involved enough in the publication to write a dedication. Holdsworth and Price agree that the copy for the first-issue quarto was a fair copy of the authors' foul papers; the descriptive nature of the stage directions, as well as two omitted entrances (4.2.0.1; 5.1.194.1) and five omitted exits (1.1.219; 1.1.252.1; 4.1.253.1; 4.3.96; 5.1.233.1), may indicate that this copy had not undergone full revision in the theatre as a promptbook. A particular source of confusion, which would be intolerable to a book holder, concerns the identification of minor characters. The Captain's Friends and the Colonel's Friends are identified only by numbers, a special problem in 3.1 where each man has two friends with him. Furthermore, no lines are assigned to the Colonel's second friend, but the Colonel's confidante is sometimes named 'Col. 1. Friend' (3.1.169), sometimes 'Colonels Second' (4.1.0.2), and sometimes '1 Liefetenant' (4.2.58). That these are the same individual is an editorial decision. Finally, in 4.1 there is a '2. Roarer' (4.1.75.1) but no 1. Roarer.

On the other hand, the manuscript underlying the added scene appears to have come from the play house; the headings are more regular than in the rest of the text, and the stage directions take the imperative form, 'Sing Baud' (Holdsworth, 1974, xliii). The most difficult question facing an editor of the play is where to place this scene in a modern edition. Holdsworth put it, as instructed, at the end of the fourth act; Price placed it in an appendix. G. E. Bentley praises Trundle for 'one of the most explicit statements made by a Jacobean publisher about the revisions he found in his copy' but he is wrong when he asserts that Trundle 'prints the new material as he has evidently received it, on additional pages bound in at the end and not distributed through the play' (*Profession*, 243–4). The surviving copies of the second issue, at Harvard, Eton College, and the Dyce Collection (National Art Library Victoria and Albert Museum), have 4.4 placed, as instructed, after 4.3.

The additional scene is tightly integrated into the play. It forms a counterpart to 4.1, in which Chough learns at the roaring school the lessons he practises in 4.4; it fills out the tripartite plot structure; it elaborates both the character of Chough and the theme of women's questionable virtue; it slyly satirizes the military pomp of Captain Ager and the Colonel through Captain Albo. Given Priss's metatheatrical reference to the 'new play', the additional material seems to be an afterthought capitalizing on the popularity of the original roaring scene. Rowley may or may not have consulted Middleton about it. Yet, since the play is completed, rather than distorted, by the added material, I have followed Trundle's direction and inserted the scene at the end of the fourth act.

Holdsworth considered it impossible to determine whether the manuscript behind the first issue was in the hand of one or both of the authors, but judged Rowley the more likely scribe (1974, xl–xli); Price more definitively asserted 'that the handwriting of both authors appeared in the manuscript, and that Rowley himself edited it for the press' (1976, xiii). This last is likely: though the characteristic linguistic patterns of each author appear in the scenes commonly assigned to him, Rowley wrote the epistle dedicatory and the greater proportion of the play itself. As Holdsworth pointed out, the act headings, in the form 'Actus primus, Scæna prima', are typical of Rowley. (There are no scene headings within the acts.) Furthermore, although Holdsworth now believes that Middleton wrote 1.1.394–425 (see 'Canon and Chronology'), the passage contains two examples of "um", usually a reliable Rowley indicator. If the ascription to Middleton is correct, the presence of "um" suggests that Rowley was copying his collaborator's work in this section.

In his thesis Holdsworth did a textual analysis of the quarto, and on the basis of regular variations in line length, number of lines per page, catchword setting, and spelling argued that there were two different compositors: A set signatures B1^r through C4^v (1.1.1–2.1.82); B set signatures D, E, and F (2.1.83–3.3.16); A then completed the text through K2^v, with the exception that B set K1^r (5.1.359–92). More recently, Adrian Weiss has demonstrated, on the basis of foul-case clusters and identified types present in other books, that there were not merely two compositors but two printers. Eld shared the book with a second printer, Bernard Alsop, with Eld printing signatures B–C and G–K and Alsop signatures D through F. And despite the return to the spelling 'Chaw' instead of 'Chau' for the speech prefixes on K1^r, Weiss finds that this page, like the rest of K, was set in Eld's shop in his type-font.

Eld and Alsop are difficult to tell apart. Both men used a pica roman type-font. Both fouled the text with mis-placed italic *I*s (Weiss). In both printers' parts there is an occasional substitution of *t* for *r*. This is presumably a foul case error, probably indicating that some of the types, as they deteriorated, had become almost indistinguishable. Examples include 'gitle' for 'girl' (1.1.399); 'gtace' for 'grace' (2.1.190); 'teciprocall' for 'reciprocall' (2.2.60); 'thetes' for 'theres' (3.1.42); and 'bting' for 'bring' (3.1.95). Only one of these, 'teciprocall' on D4^v, receives a stop-press correction. As the example at 1.1.399 is on C3^r (Eld), while other examples are in Sig. D and E (Alsop), these variations are not significant in dividing the printing stints.

There are thirteen extant ELD–ALSOP copies, ten of the first issue and three of the second. All but one were collated by Holdsworth, and I have added a collation of the remaining copy, found in the Library of Congress. Only one of the stop-press variants is potentially significant: at 1.1.42 the New York Public Library Arents Collection copy gives 'wisdom' instead of 'courage' as an attribute surprising in one as young as Captain Ager. I have followed Holdsworth in adopting this reading, as it makes more sense in the passage and anticipates later similar praise of the Captain.

Two of the surviving copies of ELD–ALSOP are incomplete and the missing sections are supplied in manuscript. The University of Chicago copy, damaged or defective, includes a manuscript portion running from 4.2.42 to 5.1.62 and copied from a first issue without the additional scene. The hand is secretary and the changes are largely of spelling, with the occasional omission of a word. The Huntington copy of ELD–ALSOP was a first issue to which has been added the supplementary scene, copied out in a fine italic hand on paper that is mid-18th century or later.

On 2 September 1621, John Trundle transferred his rights in the play to another publisher, as shown by the following entry in the Stationers' Register:

[Thomas Dewe.]
Idem. Assigned ouer vnto him by John Trundle these 2 play bookes followinge at a full court holden this Day.   xij^d
    A faire quarrell.
    Greenes Tu quoque

As a result Dewe published a second edition in 1622; Price and Holdsworth identify the printer as Augustine Mathewes. Holdsworth concludes that the second quarto was set up from a copy of the second issue of ELD–ALSOP, and that, since the authors had nothing to do with the new edition, it is merely an 'unauthoritative reprint' (1971, 130). The Huntington Library has two copies of MATHEWES. Hn 62591 includes B3–4^v totally reset as C1–2^v. B4^v is short a line, '*Iane.* Plant some other?' (1.1.380), which appears as the last line on C2^v. The catchword is appropriately adjusted. In the other copy, Hn 62590, B3–4 are cancelled and the gutter edges glued together before binding. Greg, who lists copies of MATHEWES in different states, suggests that the error was not discovered in the print shop, because existing copies from which leaves have been removed are doctored in different ways.

One of the two Huntington copies of MATHEWES is completed, from 5.1.161 to the end, in manuscript; two contemporary secretary hands, and two inks, are evident. The copyists were working from another copy of MATHEWES, as the variations demonstrate, and at least one did not always understand his text. This is most clearly revealed at 5.1.336–8, where he turned Fitzallen's pretended anger at learning of Jane's sexual history from 'This is a sweet epithalamium | Unto the marriage bed, a musical | Harmonious Io! Sir, you've wronged me' into 'This is a sweet epithalamium unto the marriage bed, a musicall harmonious o Sir, you've wronged me.'

The copyist's failure to understand the Greek exclamation is suggestive. *A Fair Quarrel* contains a number of special 'languages'—Dutch, roaring, the jargon of surgery—any of which may have caused errors in the course of copying and printing. Each of these special forms of discourse poses a slightly different problem to the textual editor. The Nurse's Dutch is at least in part a comic stage convention, found in such other plays as Marston's *The Dutch Courtesan*, Dekker's *The Shoemaker's Holiday* and Middleton's *No Wit/Help like a Woman's*. It is sufficiently unidiomatic to demonstrate that it was written by someone who did not know the language at all well. Under the circumstances I have usually preserved the spelling found in the quarto. The seventeenth-century spelling is provided in the notes from *A Copious English and Netherdutch Dictionary*, by Henry Hexham, enlarged by Daniel Manly (Rotterdam, 1675).

Middleton's source for the surgeon's professional terms in 4.2 and 5.1 was, as Holdsworth discovered, Peter Lowe's *A Discovrse of the Whole Art of Chyrvrgerie*, 2nd edn., 1612. In his edition Holdsworth corrects the language of the text to bring it into agreement with Lowe, assuming that 'the mangling was not deliberate, but largely the combined result of errors or peculiarities already in Lowe and errors by a scribe or compositor'. For example, he emends 'turmafaction' to 'tumefaction' (4.2.17) as in Lowe. In his desire for correctness Holdsworth also changes 'guiguimos' to 'ginglymus' (4.2.35), even though it does not occur in the 1612 edition of Lowe ('Jargon', 452–3). Such a procedure assumes that because Middleton consulted a surgical manual he intended the surgeon's speeches to be correct. However, the tone of the interchange between the sister and the surgeon suggests that the medical man is made unsympathetic specifically by his insistence on using incomprehensible professional jargon when the concerned sister begs for 'plain terms' (4.2.28). Middleton may well have allowed his language to be either intentionally or carelessly incorrect. I have not, therefore, regularly corrected it.

The language of roaring is usually consistent, but several words, particularly 'bronsterops', appear in variant forms. This cant word—which appears only in scenes ascribed to Rowley—is spelled *bronsterops* seven times and *bronstrops* six times in the play. Given the frequency of vowel elision throughout the language of the play, it may have been pronounced the same way regardless of the spelling. The variation presumably indicates compositorial unfamiliarity with the word, except at 5.1.156, where Russell replies to Chough's accusation, 'thy daughter is a bronstrops' by asking 'A bronsterop? What's that, sir?' On this occasion the variation seems to indicate Russell's unfamiliarity with the roaring cant. OED gives *bronstrops*, with a citation from *A Fair Quarrel*. The two-syllable form appears in Rowley and Webster's *A Cure for a Cuckold*, 4.1.123–4, where Compass says a wench is 'A Tweak or *Bronstrops*—I learnt that name in a Play'. As *A Cure for a Cuckold* was not published until 1661, however, it cannot serve as evidence. I have regularized to *bronsterops* throughout because at 5.1.321 this form is required by the rhythm of the song.

SEE ALSO

Text: *Works*, 1212
Authorship and date: this volume, 398

WORKS CITED

Previous Editions

Bullen, A. H., ed., *Works* (1885), vol. 4
Dyce, Alexander, ed., *Works* (1840), vol. 3
Ellis, Havelock, ed., *Thomas Middleton* (1890, repr. 1969)
Holdsworth, R. V., ed., *A Fair Quarrel*, Thesis, Linacre College, Oxford (1971)
—— ed., *A Fair Quarrel* (1974)
Lamb, C., ed., *Specimens of English Dramatic Poets* (1808)

Oliphant, E. H. C., ed., *Shakespeare and His Fellow Dramatists* (1929)
Price, George, ed., *A Fair Quarrel* (1976)
Sampson, Martin, ed., *Thomas Middleton* (1915)

Other Works Cited

Acts of the Privy Council, 1616–1617 (1890)
Analytical Index to … Records … Preserved Among the Archives of the City of London 1579–1664 (1878)
Arber, Edward, *A Transcript of the Registers of the Company of Stationers of London: 1554–1640 A.D.*, Vol. 4 (1877)
Barber, John, 'Doing more than was done by Shakespeare', *Daily Telegraph* (10 February 1979)
Bentley, Gerald Eades, *The Jacobean and Caroline Stage*, 7 vols (1941–68)
—— *The Profession of Dramatist in Shakespeare's Time, 1590–1642* (1971)
Brissenden, Alan, review of *A Fair Quarrel*, ed. R. V. Holdsworth, *Review of English Studies* NS 27 (1976), 211–12
Calendar of State Papers Domestic … 1603–1610 (1857)
Gossett, Suzanne, 'Sibling Power: Middleton and Rowley's *A Fair Quarrel*', *Philological Quarterly* 71 (1992), 437–57
Gurr, Andrew, *The Shakespearean Stage 1574–1642*, 3rd edn. (1992)
Halliwell[-Phillipps], J. O., ed., *The Autobiography and Correspondence of Sir Simonds D'Ewes*, 2 vols (1845)
Hayne, Victoria, 'Performing Social Practice: The Example of *Measure for Measure*', *Shakespeare Quarterly* 44 (1993), 1–29
Hexham, Henry, *A Copious English and Netherdutch Dictionary*, enlarged by Daniel Manly (1675)
Holdsworth, R. V., 'The Medical Jargon in *A Fair Quarrel*', *Review of English Studies* NS 23 (1972), 448–54
—— 'Sexual Puns in Middleton, Chapman, and Dekker', *Notes and Queries* NS 31 (1984), 242–7
Levin, Richard, *The Multiple Plot in English Renaissance Drama* (1971)
Lowe, Peter, *A Discovrse of the Whole Art of Chyrvrgerie*, 2nd edn. (1612)
Maclean, J., ed., *Letters from George Lord Carew to Sir Thomas Roe* (1860)
Parker, Brian, '*A Fair Quarrel* (1617), the Duelling Code, and Jacobean Law', *Rough Justice: Essays on Crime in Literature*, ed. Martin L. Friedland (1991), 52–75
Price, George R., 'The First Edition of *A Faire Quarrell*', *The Library*, V, 4 (1949), 137–41
Richards, Bernard, 'Corrections and Additions to Recent Editions of Middleton and Rowley's *A Fair Quarrel*', *Notes and Queries* NS 27 (1980), 154–55
Stone, Lawrence, *The Crisis of the Aristocracy, 1558–1641*, abridged edn. (1967)
Stow, John, *A Survey of London*, ed. Charles Lethbridge Kingsford (1908)
Webster, John, *A Cure for a Cuckold*, ed. F. L. Lucas (1927)
Weiss, Adrian, Analysis of type-fonts in *A Fair Quarrel*, personal communication (1994)
Wiggin, Pauline, *An Inquiry into the Authorship of the Middleton-Rowley Plays* (1897)

TEXTUAL NOTES

Epistle.5   'em] ELD ('um). The spelling 'um is typical of Rowley; Middleton uses 'em, and the form is regularized to this throughout.

Epistle.7   part-takers] ELD. DYCE, following MATHEWES, changes to partakers, but the pun is part of the metaphor of 'this great world' as a stage.

1.1.0.1   *Incipit Actus Primus*] THIS EDITION; *Actus primus, Scæna prima.* ELD. I have similarly regularized the headings for each act from Rowley's to Middleton's style.

1.1.2   the t'other] ELD (the other)

1.1.7   o'er] ELD (ore). Previous editors have emended to *o'her*, but Alan Brissenden pointed out in a review of Holdsworth that *ore* is an acceptable form of *o'er* and so appears at 1.1.89, *oretaken*. The phrase 'too careful or too tender' is appealing, but the syntax would be even looser. Holdsworth notes that *or* 'nowhere appears in [ELD–ALSOP] with a final *e*'.

1.1.28   know] ELD. Holdsworth (correspondence) now suggests emending to *knew*, but Russell's line makes sense as it stands, with *would* having the force of *would demand to be*.

1.1.42   wisdom] ELD *NY copy only*; courage ELD *all other surviving copies. Wisdom* is the reading of only one surviving copy, but Holdsworth, who first found and accepted the variant, pointed out that it yields a superior sense. Though the Captain is younger than his superior, he excels in the characteristics traditionally associated with advancing age, wisdom and moderation. Russell articulates this at 1.1.126, 'wisdom in men grows up as years increase'. Presumably the error was discovered late and only a few copies were corrected. MATHEWES also reads 'courage'.

1.1.66   not] DYCE; nor ELD

1.1.122   digest] ELD (disgest)

1.1.139   demons] ELD (*Dæmons*)

1.1.150   Nay 'tis] ELD; ~, ~ DYCE (followed by all editions). The comma obscures the ambiguities of Russell's statement, which appears encouraging while actually threatening.

1.1.166   diminuting] PRICE; diminiting ELD. Price notes that *OED* marks the verb rare and does not record *diminiting*, but the word may merely be the result of a minim error.

1.1.171   you are] THIS EDITION; yeare ELD; ye are DYCE

1.1.289   be] HOLDSWORTH; by ELD. Holdsworth points out that the emendation is made marginally in the Harvard copy, but it is impossible to tell when this occurred.

1.1.353   present] DYCE; prsent ELD

1.1.387   master] ELD (M)

1.1.392   to] DYCE; ro ELD. In the typeface of both ELD and ALSOP it is frequently difficult to differentiate between t and r.

1.1.399   girl] DYCE; gitle ELD. See note to 1.1.392.

1.1.404, 425   'em] ELD ('um). Although Holdsworth argues that a cluster of Middleton usages demonstrates his reappearance in the final lines of this act, Rowley's characteristic *'um* at these two points suggests, at the least, that he may have copied the passage out, unconsciously introducing his preferred forms.

1.1.425.1   *Finis Actus Primus*] THIS EDITION; *not in* ELD. I have added similar headings at the end of each act, following Middleton's usual style.

2.1.29   frailty] DYCE; fraileto ELD; frailtie to MATHEWES

2.1.96   off] ALSOP (of)

2.1.104   off] ALSOP (of)

2.1.117   firm] ALSOP; *firm faith* PRICE. An ellipsis of *reputation* or *belief* is likely as an omission, and *firm* as the sign of his sword also makes sense. The line is metrically complete as is.

2.1.212.1   *Enter … Ager's*] THIS EDITION; after 'friends', l. 211 ALSOP

2.2.1   mistress] DYCE; Master ALSOP. Presumably a mistaken expansion of M in the manuscript.

2.2.8   fine] DYCE; fiue ALSOP

2.2.34   What's] MATHEWES; what ALSOP

2.2.129   beholden] ALSOP (beholding)

2.2.129   our] DYCE; out ALSOP

2.2.131   o'erthrown] THIS EDITION; ouerthrowne ALSOP. The emendation is metrical.

2.2.150   RUSSELL] MATHEWES; *Kuff.* ALSOP

2.2.218   afire] PRICE; a fire ALSOP

3.1.42   there's] DYCE; thetes ALSOP

3.1.46   come. Do] DYCE; comed, do ALSOP

3.1.77   rejoiced] ALSOP (reioyc'st)

3.1.82   For] DYCE; Eor ALSOP

3.1.152   deceive's] ALSOP (deceiues)

3.1.170   us] DYCE; v; ALSOP

3.1.176   stings] DYCE; ſtrings ALSOP

3.1.184.1   *Exit, led by his Friends*] THIS EDITION; *Exeunt, | led by them.* ALSOP

3.2.4   forstoore] ALSOP; forstoor HOLDSWORTH. Holdsworth claims the word comes from Md. Dutch *verstoren*, meaning hinder, and changes the spelling, but the word is not in Hexham and *verstoren* used transitively means to upset or frustrate. The nurse takes the Physician's phrase, 'I must not tell', as his reluctance to praise the child in its presence, and reassures him that the baby cannot understand. Therefore, the verb is *verstaen*, understand, as at line 20, and the Physician modifies his phrase to 'I cannot tell' to clarify his meaning, that it is not possible to determine the value of a child.

3.2.6   price] ALSOP (priſe)

3.2.12   one] ALSOP (on)

3.2.13   lieben fader] apparently a mixture of languages: German *lieb* with the characteristic Dutch *n* added, and Dutch *vader*, though it is German (*vater*) where the *v* is pronounced as f.

3.2.48   Is't] ALSOP

3.2.98   In deed] HOLDSWORTH; indeed ALSOP

3.2.110   price] ALSOP (priſe)

3.2.134   above you] DYCE; aboue ALSOP. The addition of 'you' allows the Physician to exit on a rhyming couplet, 'love you/above you', and editors since Dyce have assumed that a word has dropped out. Rhyming couplets are common in Rowley's sections: compare 3.2.169–75.

3.3.8   Whither] ALSOP (whether)

3.3.10   whither] ALSOP (whether)

4.1.0.2   *Colonel's First Friend*] Colonels Second ELD. In ELD–ALSOP this character is variously identified as Col. 1. Friend (3.1), Colonel's Second (4.1) and 1 Liefetenant (4.2). Like Dyce and Holdsworth, I assume that these are different titles for the same character, and that the Colonel's other friend is mute. In this reading the significance of 'second' is the same as that of lieutenant, i.e. the Colonel's assistant officer who seconds him in the duel and in other matters. Price, however, interprets *Colonels Second* as *Colonel's Second Friend* (65n), 'master of the Roaring School and therefore "first roarer" … the other is the Colonel's companion' (5n). There is no evidence, however, to demonstrate which friend is the master of the School. Price's assumption requires arbitrary assignment of speeches to the second friend.

4.1.0.2 *Roarer*] &c. ELD. The speech prefix in 4.1.70 and further is *2. Roar*; Dyce accordingly calls for 'several roarers', and is followed by Holdsworth. Price assumes that the master of the roaring school is the first roarer and therefore this is the second one. It could as easily be the Usher who is understood as the first roarer. However, there is no indication that more than one speaking Roarer is present.

4.1.16 then] ELD *corrected copies*; the ELD *uncorrected copies*. See press variants.

4.1.70 ROARER] See note to 4.1.0.2.

4.1.112 bronsterops] ELD (Bronſtrops). At 5.1.321 the rhythm of Chough's song requires that the word be *bronsterops*, suggesting that this is the full form. The shortened form, and the variation between forms, may reflect compositorial uncertainty. The word only appears in scenes ascribed to Rowley, so collaboration is not responsible for the variation. The word is regularized to bronsterops throughout this edition, with the exception of Russell's confused repetition at 5.1.156.

4.1.129 TRIMTRAM] DYCE; *Chau* ELD. A repetition of the preceding prefix.

4.1.133 demons] ELD (Dæmons)

4.1.135 gentlemen] DYCE; gentleman ELD

4.1.181 Dungcrower] THIS EDITION; dungcoer ELD. Holdsworth proposed emending to dungcart, as *rt* is easily misread as *er* in a secretary hand. Price believed the word was an error for dungcock. Richards, however, is surely right in proposing *dungcrower*, though he explains only that 'the argument concerns roaring speech'. At this point Chough is maintaining the superiority of one species of birds, the choughs, to another, the rooks, and so the term *dungcrower*, denigrating Trimtram as an inferior bird, is apposite.

4.1.194 you] ELD *corrected copies*; *not in* ELD *uncorrected copies*. See press variants.

4.1.239 say] ELD *corrected copies*; sap ELD *uncorrected copies*. See press variants.

4.2.7 oesophag] HOLDSWORTH; *Orſophag* ELD. Probably an e/r misreading by the compositor.

4.2.11 syncope] DYCE; *Syncops* ELD

4.2.17 turmafaction] ELD; tumefaction HOLDSWORTH. This may be a minim error, but it could also be intentional.

4.2.17 quadrangular] DYCE; *Quadragular* ELD. As the word is not exclusively medical, I have corrected it.

4.2.23 sarcotrick] ELD (*Sarcotricke*); sarcotic HOLDSWORTH. Given Middleton's fondness for the word *trick*, this may be an intentional pun.

4.2.34 sanicola] HOLDSWORTH; *Sauicola* ELD. Probably an example of turned case.

4.2.35 guiguimos] ELD; ginglymus HOLDSWORTH. While gin/gui may be minim misreadings, the remainder of the word is different enough that we cannot assume Middleton wrote the term correctly.

4.2.58 *Colonel's First Friend*] *1 Lieſetenant* ELD

4.2.97 comforts] The *s* is poorly printed in several of the surviving copies and could be a blot or comma, but it is confirmed by the Folger copy.

4.3.28 off] ELD (of)

4.3.67 ay] ELD (*I*). Either 'I' or 'ay' makes sense. Holdsworth points out that *ay* is spelled *I* over a dozen times in the play, and that the imperative phrase is frequent in Middleton, appearing, for example, several times in *Old Law*.

4.4 This scene is found in the second issue only, between H3 and H4, with a note at the bottom of the first page: 'Place this at the latter end of the fourth act.' See Textual Introduction for fuller discussion.

4.4.1 VOICE (*within*) Hem!] THIS EDITION; *Hem, within.* ELD

4.4.55 the] DYCE; the the ELD

4.4.91 gentle] DYCE; Gentile ELD

4.4.209 TRIMTRAM] DYCE; *not in* ELD, which gives the entire speech to Chough.

4.4.214 three] DYCE; two ELD

5.1.8 but] DYCE; by ELD

5.1.32 pursue] ELD; escape DYCE. Dyce and Holdsworth argue that the second *pursue* is eyeskip, a repetition of 5.1.31. But Brissenden points out that Rowley was given to such quibbling repetitions, and Holdsworth now believes that the second *pursue* is correct. Jane hopes for the apparently loathsome fate of exposure because it will avert her marriage to Chough.

5.1.71 am] DYCE; an ELD

5.1.91.1 *Physician draws his sword*] THIS EDITION; *drawes his sword* ELD. It must be the Physician who draws, as Chough asserts that he'll 'never draw' and urges the Physician to 'put up and speak freely' (5.1.98-9).

5.1.127 be] DYCE; de ELD

5.1.130 twenty-nine] THIS EDITION; tenty nine ELD. Though editors from Dyce to Holdsworth gloss tenty nine as meaning nineteen, it is not in *OED* and Price proposes that it is a printer's error.

5.1.154 is] DYCE; in ELD

5.1.156 bronsterop] ELD. See note at 4.1.112.

5.1.245 then] THIS EDITION; they ELD

5.1.248 a] MATHEWES; *not in* ELD

5.1.287 mean't so] HOLDSWORTH; meant to ELD; meane to MATHEWES. Holdsworth's emendation makes sense of the passage. Alternatively, it could be that Chough says 'I do not mean to either' in response to Trimtram, in which case a speech prefix is missing.

5.1.335 whole] ELD (hole). The original spelling emphasizes the pun.

5.1.396 gastrolophe] ELD; gastroraphy HOLDSWORTH, following Lowe

5.1.414 Thou'st] ELD (th'ast)

5.1.431 him] DYCE; h'um ELD; 'em HOLDSWORTH. Dyce does not explain his emendation. Holdsworth argues that as the sister is the nominee of the will the gift is to both. But legally, as soon they are married the Captain will have full control of the sister's property. It is he who returns the will to the Colonel, starting the new contest in generosity between the men. The Colonel's intent is to enrich the Captain, who is 'like to have charge', and the gift is to him.

PRESS VARIANTS

The collation is basically that done by Roger Holdsworth in his 1971 thesis for Linacre College, Oxford. I have added a collation of the copy at the Library of Congress, which Holdsworth did not see. In checking his list I have made a few corrections and additions (especially another stop-press alteration to the outer forme of Sheet D), and have excluded Sig. B2ʳ 1.1.61, where Holdsworth lists a comma after 'me' as a correction in the New York copy. This comma is visible, to varying degrees, in all the other corrected copies, and is an inking problem.

Issue 1 (STC 17911)
c University of Chicago Library (lacks H, the contents of which are supplied in contemporary manuscript copied from ELD on eight leaves)
E National Library of Scotland
F Folger Shakespeare Library
HI Harvard University Library
HN Henry E. Huntington Library (additions supplied in contemporary manuscript from MATHEWES on three leaves inserted between H3 and H4)
L British Library
LC Library of Congress
NY New York Public Library Arents Collection
O Bodleian Library
Y Yale University Library

Issue 2 (STC 17911a)
D Dyce Collection, National Art Library, Victoria and Albert Museum
EN Eton College Library
H2 Harvard University Library

Sheet A (inner forme)
Corrected: C, E, F, HI, L, LC, NY, O, Y, H2.
Uncorrected: D.

Sig. A2

catchword   the] *corr.*; th *uncorr.*

Sheet B (outer forme)
Corrected: C, F, HN, LC, O, D, EN, H2.
Uncorrected: E, HI, L, NY, Y.

Sig. B1

head-title   Quarrell. *corr.*; Quarrel. *uncorr.*

Sig. B2ᵛ

1.1.103   meets too hard,] meets to hard, *corr.*; meets to | (hard, *uncorr.*

Sheet B (inner forme)
Corrected: NY.
Uncorrected: C, E, F, HI, HN, L, LC, O, Y, D, EN, H2.

Sig. B1ᵛ

1.1.42   wisdom] wisdome *corr.*; courage *uncorr.*

Sheet D (outer forme)
Corrected: E, F, HN, H2.
Uncorrected: C, HI, L, LC, NY, O, Y, D, EN.

Sig. D1

2.1.84   Such] Such *corr.*; Snch *uncorr.*

Sig. D2ᵛ

2.1.208   wedlock] wedlocke *corr.*; wedlorke *uncorr.*

Sig. D4ᵛ

2.2.60   reciprocal] reciprocall *corr.*; teciprocall *uncorr.*

Sheet D (inner forme)
Corrected: HI, O, NY.
Uncorrected: C, E, F, HN, L, LC, Y, D, H2.

Sig. D4

running title   *A Faire Quarrell. corr. Faire Quarrell. uncorr.*

Sheet E (outer forme)
Corrected: C, E, F, HI, HN, LC, NY, O, Y, D, EN, H2.
Uncorrected: L.

Sig. E1

2.2.103.1   Enter] *corr.*; Euter *uncorr.*
2.2.103.1   Trimtram] Trimtram. *corr.*; Triutram. *uncorr.*
2.2.121   CHOUGH] Chaw. (*c.w., text*) *corr.*; ☐haw. (*c.w.*), Chaw. (*text*) *uncorr.*

Sheet E (inner forme)
Corrected: C, E, F, HI, HN, LC, NY, O, Y, D, EN, H2.
Uncorrected: L.

Sig. E3ᵛ

3.1.50   boasting] boafting, *corr.*; boafti *uncorr.*

Sheet F (outer forme)
Corrected: E, HI, HN, L, LC, NY, Y, H2.
Uncorrected: C, F, O, D, EN.

Sig. F4ᵛ

3.3.8   he?] *corr.*; he *uncorr.*

Sheet F (inner forme)
Corrected: E, HI, HN, L, LC, NY, Y, H2.
Uncorrected: C, F, D, O, EN.

Sig. F1ᵛ

3.1.163   against] againft *corr.*; aga/nft *uncorr.*

Sheet G (inner forme)
Corrected: C, E, HI, HN, L, NY, O, Y, D, EN.
Uncorrected: F, LC, H2.

Sig. G1ᵛ

4.1.16   then] *corr.*; the *uncorr.*
4.1.27   shall] fhal *corr.*; fhall *uncorr.*
4.1.27   lecture] Lecture *corr.*; Lectue *uncorr.*

Sig. G3ᵛ

4.1.179   Choughs] Chaughes *corr.*; Chaughis *uncorr.*
4.1.191   excellent] *corr.*; excelent *uncorr.*
4.1.194   you] *corr.*; ‸ *uncorr.*
4.1.195   CHOUGH] Chaugh *corr.*; Chauogh *uncorr.*

Sig. G4

4.1.222   with] *corr.*; w th *uncorr.*

4.1.238   yesterday] *yeſterday corr.*; *yeſterbay uncorr.*
4.1.239   say] *ſay corr.*; *ſap uncorr.*

Sheet H (outer forme)

Corrected: E, F, H1, HN, L, LC, NY, O, Y, D, EN.
Uncorrected: H2.

Sig. H4ᵛ

5.1.29   then] *corr.*; n *uncorr.* In C, this line is part of the
manuscript insert which substitutes for gathering H, and the
word is omitted entirely.

Sheet I (outer forme)

First stage corrected: C, E, H1, L, LC, NY, O, Y, D, EN, H2.
Uncorrected: F.

Sig. I3

5.1.250   *catchword* If *corr.*; ‸ *uncorr.*

Second stage corrected C, D, EN.
Uncorrected: E, F, H1, HN, L, LC, NY, O, Y, H2.

Sig. I3

signature   I3 *corr.*; Iᴢ *uncorr.*

Holdsworth adds one other stop-press variant, the resetting of the
title-page of the first issue in the outer forme of half-sheet A (A1).

Corrected: C, F, HN, L, LC, O, Y.
Uncorrected: E, H1, NY.

The resetting centred and brought closer together the authors'
names immediately above the illustration. The left hand bracket
and the names were moved to the right, and the right hand
bracket and 'Gentl.' moved to the left, reducing the overall width
of the type.

Variants among the copies of ELD are also due not to stop-press
correction but to accidents in printing, particularly unevenness in
inking. A full collation of the Library of Congress copy increases
Holdsworth's list of such accidents as follows:

1.1.37   *Russ.*] Russ LC
1.1.105   brought home] broughthome *all copies except* C, HN, D
1.1.263   *Russ.*] Russ F
1.1.365   words,] words NY
2.1.155   How?] How. D
2.2.189   shall] sh ll LC
3.1.28   wilfully] wilful y LC
3.1.31   it,] it LC
3.1.125   him] h m C, F, D
3.1.137   beyond] b yond F
3.1.146   lost,] lost C, E, F, H1, O, D, EN
4.1.1   sir,] sir NY
4.1.5   of] oᶠ LC
4.1.21   *Chau.*] Chau LC
4.1.23   *Trim.*] Trim LC
4.1.90   roaring] (*c.w.*); roarin (*c.w.*) C, E, HN; LC is clipped above
the catchword
4.1.231   foule] foul LC

Three pseudo-readings are due to smudges or marks on the paper:
3.2.68   you,] you; L
4.1.24   sir.] sir, D
5.1.376   groome] grooms D

STAGE DIRECTIONS

1.1.0.1   *Actus primus, Scæna prima.*
1.1.0.2   *Enter Master Russell Solus.*
1.1.24.1   *Enter the Lady Ager, with two seruants.*
1.1.28.1   - - - - *she weepes*: (right, with dashes immediately
following 'My Sonne!')
1.1.33.1   *Exeunt Lady and her Seruants.*
1.1.36.1-2 *Enter a friend of the Colonells, and another of | Captaine
Agers.*
1.1.51.1   *Enter the Colonell and Captaine Agar.*
1.1.130.1 *Enter Fitzallen and Iane.*
1.1.145.1 *Kisses her.* (right, opposite 1.1.145)
1.1.187.1 *Exit with weapons.* (right, opposite 1.1.187)
1.1.193   (*aside.*) (after 1.1.194)
1.1.217.1 *Enter Russell and a Seruant.*
1.1.227   *a side.* (right, after 'mist it.')
1.1.232.1 *Enter Seruant.*
1.1.261.1 *Enter two Sergeants in disguise.*
1.1.365.1 *Exit with his friend.* (right, opposite 1.1.365)
1.1.366.1 *Exit Capt. and his friend.* (right, opposite 1.1.366)
1.1.367   *Exit.* (right, opposite 1.1.367)
1.1.393.1 *Exit | Fitz. with Officers* (right, opposite 1.1.392-3)
1.1.393.2 *Enter Russell.*
1.1.425   *Exeunt.* (right, opposite 1.1.425)
2.1.0.1   *Actus Secundus, Scæna prima.*
2.1.0.2   *Enter Captaine Ager.*
2.1.34.1   *Enter the Lady Ager.*
2.1.86.1   *Strikes | him.* (right, opposite 2.1.90-1)
2.1.208.1 *Exit Lady.* (right, opposite 2.1.208)

2.1.211   *Enter two friends of Captaine Agers.*
2.1.250.1 *Exeunt.*
2.2.0.1   *Enter Physitian and Iaue.*
2.2.53   *Exit Physitian.* (right, opposite 2.2.53)
2.2.64.1   *Enter Physitian, and Anne his sister.*
2.2.103.1 *Enter Russell, Chawgh, and Trimtram.*
2.2.204.1 *Exit Russ. Iane, Phys. An.*
2.2.240.1 *Exeunt.* (right, opposite 2.2.240)
3.1.0.1   *Actus Tertius. Scæna Prima.*
3.1.0.2   *Enter Captaine Ager with his two friends.*
3.1.45.1   *Enter Colonell and his two friends.*
3.1.112.1 *Offers to go | away.* (right, opposite 3.1.111-12)
3.1.168.1 *Exeunt Captaine and his friends.*
3.1.184.1 *Exeunt, | led by them.* (right, opposite 3.1.183-4)
3.2.0.1-2 *Enter Physitian, Iane, Anne, Dutch Nurse with the child.*
3.2.15.1   *Giue. | money.* (right, opposite 3.2.15-16)
3.2.18.1   *Giues her | money.* (right, opposite 3.2.17-18)
3.2.21   *Aside.* (right, opposite 3.2.21)
3.2.22.1   *Giues her money.* (right, opposite 3.2.22)
3.2.27   *Exeunt Ann. and Nurse.* (right, opposite 3.2.27)
3.2.69   *Aside.* (right, opposite 3.2.69)
3.2.117.1 *Spits,* (right, opposite 3.2.117)
3.2.134   *Exit Phys.* (right, opposite 3.2.134)
3.2.140.1 *Enter Anne.*
3.2.175   *Exeunt.* (right, opposite 3.2.175)
3.3.0.1   *Enter the Lady Ager, meeting one of her seruants.*
3.3.4.1   *Enter Seruant.*
3.3.37   *Exeunt Seru.* (right, opposite 3.3.37)

3.3.44 *Exit.* (right, opposite 3.3.44)
4.1.0.1 *Actus quartus, Scæna prima.*
4.1.0.2-3 *Enter the Colonels Second.. Vsher &c. with Chaugh and Trim.*
4.1.35 *reads his bill* (right, opposite 4.1.34)
4.1.75.1 *Exit 2. Roarer.* (right, opposite 4.1.73)
4.1.133.1 *Enter 2. Roarer with Wine, and Vapor with Tobacco.*
4.1.194.2 *Enter a Seruant.*
4.1.203 *Exit seruant* (right, opposite 4.1.202)
4.1.255 *Exeunt* (right, opposite 4.1.255)
4.2.0.2 *Enter the Colonels Sister, meeting the Surgeon.*
4.2.35 *Exit.* (right, opposite 4.2.35)
4.2.58 *1 Liefetenant reads.*
4.2.121 *Exeunt* (right, opposite 4.2.121)
4.3.0.1 *Enter Captaine Ager.*
4.3.15.1 *Enter the Lady Ager.*
4.3.72.1 *rises.* (right, opposite 4.3.72)
4.3.90 *Exit Lady.* (right, opposite 4.3.90)
4.3.92.1 *Enter a Seruant.* (after 4.3.93)
4.3.103.1 *Enter the Colonels Sister.*
4.3.107.1 *She kneeles.* (right, opposite 4.3.107)
4.3.124 *Exit.* (right, opposite 4.3.124)
4.4.1.1 *Hem, within.* | *Enter Captaine Albo, a Baud and a Whore.*
4.4.50.1 *Enter Chaugh and Trim.*
4.4.62.1 *Iustle.* (right, opposite 4.4.62)
4.4.117.1 *Sing Baud.*
4.4.233 *Exeunt Chaugh and Trim.* (right, opposite 4.4.233)

4.4.237 *Exeunt.* (right, opposite 4.4.237)
5.1.0.1 *Actus Quintus, Scæna prima.*
5.1.0.2 *Enter Phisition: Iane as a Bride.*
5.1.32 *Exit Iane* (right, opposite 5.1.32)
5.1.36.1 *Enter Trimtram with Rosemarie.* (after 5.1.37)
5.1.57 *within.*
5.1.62 *Exit Trim* (right, opposite 5.1.61)
5.1.63.1 *Enter Chaugh.*
5.1.91.1 *drawes his sword* (right, opposite 5.1.91)
5.1.124.1 *Enter Trimtram*
5.1.129.1 *Lookes in an Almanacke.* (right, opposite 5.1.129)
5.1.142 *Exit Trim.* (right, opposite 5.1.142)
5.1.145 *Exit Phisition.* (right, opposite 5.1.145)
5.1.147.1 *Enter Russell and Trimtram.*
5.1.208.1 *Enter Iane and Anne.*
5.1.253.1 *Enter his Seruant.*
5.1.264 *Exit Ser.* (right, opposite 5.1.264)
5.1.264.1 *Enter Phisitian, Nurse, with the childe.*
5.1.271.1 *Poynts to the* | *Phisitian.* (right, opposite 5.1.271-2)
5.1.297.1 *Enter Seruant with Fitzallen.*
5.1.318 *sings.*
5.1.319 *Sings.*
5.1.392.1-2 *Enter Captaine Ager, Surgeon, Lady Ager Colonells* | *Sister, two friends.*
5.1.405 *giues him money.* (after 5.1.404)
5.1.411.1 *Enter Colonell with his too friends.*
5.1.448.1 *Exeunt Omnes.*

LINEATION NOTES

1.1.39-40 Young...disgrace] OLIPHANT; *prose* ELD
1.1.50-1 Here's...blood] DYCE; *prose* ELD
1.1.60-3 Words...in't] THIS EDITION; pass| opinion| fame| in't| ELD
1.1.87 Have...sir] DYCE; *2 lines* ELD: nobler|
1.1.181 No...sir] DYCE; *2 lines* ELD: quarrel|
1.1.182-3 Why...climate] DYCE; *prose* ELD
1.1.217 He...cue] DYCE; *2 lines* ELD: returned|
1.1.220-1 Sir...sir] OLIPHANT; you| ELD
1.1.231-2 Ha...humh] DYCE; again| ELD
1.1.234 What...you, sir?] HOLDSWORTH; *2 lines* ELD: What say you, sir [first time]|
1.1.248-9 But...varlets] DYCE; *1 line* ELD
1.1.265-6 I...pray] HOLDSWORTH; gentlemen| ELD
1.1.267-8 This...that?] DYCE; name| ELD
1.1.276 A thousand...substance] DYCE; *2 lines* ELD: pounds|
1.1.277-9 Good...men] BULLEN; *prose* ELD
1.1.283-9 Ye...accessory] HOLDSWORTH; proving| better| tribe| him| sir| here| accessory| ELD
1.1.314 Sir...plots] DYCE; *2 lines* ELD: wronged|
1.1.324 I...others] HOLDSWORTH; *2 lines* ELD: debts|
1.1.334 Else...themselves] HOLDSWORTH; *2 lines* ELD: knaves|
1.1.366 Come...now] HOLDSWORTH; *2 lines* ELD: 'twas|
2.1.72 The...touchwood] DYCE; *2 lines* ELD: enraged|
2.1.86-7 Thou...thee] DYCE; *1 line* ALSOP
3.1.15-16 Why...that] PRICE; then| ALSOP
3.1.57-8 Slight...methinks] DYCE; *prose* ALSOP

3.1.97-8 Choose...good] DYCE; *1 line* ALSOP
4.1.102-3 Cyclops...Briarean] DYCE; *1 line* ELD
4.2.21 Pox...fired] HOLDSWORTH; *prose* ELD
4.2.26-8 Sacro-halter...him] THIS EDITION; *prose* ELD
4.2.85-7 Alter...content] DYCE; article| love| ELD
4.3.51 I...on't] DYCE; *2 lines* ELD: deed|
4.3.83 You...not] DYCE; *2 lines* ELD: to't|
4.3.87-90 Deserve...you] DYCE; again| fame| ruin| you| ELD
4.3.97 O...gentlewoman] DYCE; *2 lines* ELD: then|
4.4.72-3 A...roarers] DYCE; *1 line* ELD
4.4.137-8 Or...etc] DYCE; *1 line* ELD
4.4.146-7 And...etc] DYCE; *1 line* ELD
4.4.148-9 Melodious...hippocrene] DYCE; *1 line* ELD
4.4.150-1 Sweet-breasted...tweak] DYCE; *1 line* ELD
4.4.152-3 Delicious...panagron] DYCE; *1 line* ELD
4.4.154-5 Calumnious...sindicus] DYCE; *1 line* ELD
4.4.231-2 Farewell...bronsterops] DYCE; *1 line* ELD
5.1.40-1 Pray...today] THIS EDITION; *prose* ELD
5.1.77-8 Take...you] DYCE; *prose* ELD
5.1.84-5 Your...have] DYCE; *prose* ELD
5.1.144-5 I'll...evidence] DYCE; *prose* ELD
5.1.207-8 Rather...comes] DYCE; *1 line* ELD
5.1.217 And...hope] DYCE; *2 lines* ELD: too|
5.1.230-1 I...malice] DYCE; *3 lines* ELD sister| office|
5.1.255-6 Do...Dick] THIS EDITION; *prose* ELD
5.1.352-6 Your...child] DYCE; *prose* ELD
5.1.405 There's...together] DYCE; *prose* ELD

THE OWL'S ALMANAC

Edited by Neil Rhodes

The Owl's Almanac makes its first appearance in an entry in the Stationers' Register on 22 January 161[8], which reads: 'Entred for his Copie under the hands of master TAVERNOR and master Swinhowe warden, A booke Called *DICKE DIVER-DEEPES, or Owles Almanacke*'. There are two quarto editions of the text, one collating sig. A–I⁴ (STC 6515) and the other sig. A–H⁴ (STC 6515.5), both printed in 1618 by Edward Griffin for Laurence Lisle. It can be established that STC 6515 is the earlier of the two by four months, for at sig. B4 there is a reference to a German fencer who 'cudgelld most of our English Fencers now about a moneth past' (355–6), which has become at sig. B2ᵛ of STC 6515.5 'cudgelld most of our English Fencers now about 5 moneths past'. The textual change is a clear attempt to keep the almanac up to date.

The only subsequent edition of the text is a diplomatic reprint, without commentary or textual notes, prepared by Don Cameron Allen in 1943. Allen collated copies of the first edition in the British Library, Folger Shakespeare Library, and Henry E. Huntington Library, and found no press variants. He was not, however, aware of the second edition, which was identified in the revised STC. In this edition STC 6515 is referred to as GRIFFIN 1 and STC 6515.5 as GRIFFIN 2. GRIFFIN 2 was clearly set up from GRIFFIN 1, as it repeats GRIFFIN 1's typographical errors such as reversed parentheses; the present edition has been prepared from the Huntington Library copy of GRIFFIN 1, which has been collated for significant variants with the Harvard copy of GRIFFIN 2.

SEE ALSO

Text: *Works*, 1274
Authorship and date: this volume, 400

WORKS CITED

Previous Editions

Allen, Don Cameron, ed., *The Owles Almanacke* (1943)

Other Works Cited

Bretnor, Thomas, *A New Almanack and Prognostication* (1617)
Collier, John Payne, *A Bibliographical and Critical Account of the Rarest Books in the English Language*, 2 vols (1865)
Franklin, Benjamin, *Poor Richard Improved* in *The Writings of Benjamin Franklin*, ed. A. H. Smyth, 10 vols (1905–7)
Grosart, A. B., ed., *The Non-Dramatic Works of Thomas Dekker*, 5 vols (1884–6)
Gosse, Edmund W., 'Memoir on Samuel Rowlands' in *The Complete Works of Samuel Rowlands*, eds. E. W. Gosse and S. J. H. Herrtage, 3 vols (1880)
Hutson, Lorna, *Thomas Nashe in Context* (1989)
Paylor, W. J., ed., *The Overburian Characters* (1936)
Pond, Edward, *A President for Prognosticators* (1609)
Rhodes, Neil, *Elizabethan Grotesque* (1980)
Stow, John, *A Survey of London*, ed. C. L. Kingsford (1971)
Wilson, F. P., 'Some English Mock-Prognostications', *The Library*, IV, 19 (1938), 6–43

TEXTUAL NOTES

13 to speak] GRIFFIN 1; ſpeake GRIFFIN 2
154–5 thrown by] GRIFFIN 1 (throne-by)
179 The first return] GRIFFIN 2; GRIFFIN 1 uses digits 1, 2, 3 etc.
220 wain] THIS EDITION; GRIFFIN (Wayne). The spelling draws attention to the pun.
244–5 of those five hundred] GRIFFIN 1 (of thoſe 500); of theſe 500 GRIFFIN 2
249 owns] THIS EDITION; GRIFFIN (owes)
289 heard] GRIFFIN 2; heard there GRIFFIN 1
322 Seville] GRIFFIN (Sivill). The earlier spelling indicates the pronunciation (as in 'civil').
329 Ralph] GRIFFIN, (*Ra:*). Presumably an abbreviation of Ralph or Rafe.
356 a month] GRIFFIN 1; 5 moneths GRIFFIN 2
361 coaches] GRIFFIN (caroches)
473, 496 govern] GRIFFIN 1; governes GRIFFIN 2
549 Pyrodes] THIS EDITION; Pyrotes GRIFFIN
558 *withered, Daphne*] GRIFFIN 1; *withered ₄ Daphne* GRIFFIN 2
575–6 *Poena et Pecunia*] GRIFFIN (*Poena & Pecunia*)

583 Humorism] THIS EDITION; Humoniſme GRIFFIN 1; Humaniſme GRIFFIN 2. GRIFFIN 2 appears to correct GRIFFIN 1, but 'humanism' seems improbable as a vice to be categorized with bribery and malice. Although the first citation of 'humorism' in *OED* is 1831, and has a different meaning from the term here, it fits the present context and seems entirely possible as a coinage. See 'humoralities', 1732.
650 wide-throated] GRIFFIN 1; winde-throated GRIFFIN 2
696 on behalf of] THIS EDITION; in behalfe of GRIFFIN 1, GRIFFIN 2
751 murd'rous] THIS EDITION; Mardrons GRIFFIN. Probably a misreading of 'murdrous'.
753 sakers] GRIFFIN (ſacres)
791 corpse] GRIFFIN (courſe)
795 *testudineo*] THIS EDITION; *teſtudine* GRIFFIN
822 scare] GRIFFIN (ſcarre)
842.n bawl] GRIFFIN 1 (*ball*); GRIFFIN 2 (*baule*)
859 plaudit] GRIFFIN 2; plandit GRIFFIN 1
862 retreat] GRIFFIN (retrait)
866 nurture] THIS EDITION; nuture GRIFFIN

894 pilled] GRIFFIN 1 (pild); GRIFFIN 2 (pilde)

898 youngsters] THIS EDITION; yonſters GRIFFIN 1; (yongſters) GRIFFIN 2

925 *balance*] THIS EDITION; *Ballanced* GRIFFIN

998 such another] GRIFFIN 1; ſuch an other GRIFFIN 2

1003 traitor's] GRIFFIN 1; Trayterous GRIFFIN 2

1007.n *More anger yet*] This appears to be a marginal note which has been misplaced into the text in GRIFFIN.

1065-6 bonfires] GRIFFIN (bone-fires)

1079 fount] GRIFFIN (font)

1127 hoisted] GRIFFIN (hoiſed)

1141 forcible] GRIFFIN 2; GRIFFIN 1 (forceable)

1155 content] GRIFFIN 1; contentment GRIFFIN 2

1161.n ◯] GRIFFIN (⊙)

1167.n ☾] THIS EDITION (Lavagnino); ☽ GRIFFIN

1174.n ☽] THIS EDITION (Lavagnino); ☾ GRIFFIN

1218 compare] GRIFFIN (*Compar*); 'compar' seems a possible spelling but is not recorded in *OED*.

1258 whurry] GRIFFIN (whorry). See 'whurrying', l. 845

1276.n-1293.n *Purging...Hair*] GRIFFIN 1; the marginal glosses from ll. 1276.n-1293.n are omitted in GRIFFIN 2

1347 Catiline] GRIFFIN (Cataline)

1400.n *Billingsgate*] GRIFFIN 1 (*Belingſgate*); GRIFFIN 2 (*Bellingsgate*)

1438 hundred] THIS EDITION; hundreth GRIFFIN

1446.n *your hole*] THIS EDITION; *you hole* GRIFFIN

1468 Euclioes] THIS EDITION; Enclioes GRIFFIN

1499 cinnamonian] GRIFFIN 2; GRIFFIN 1 (Synnamonian)

1514 jerk] GRIFFIN (yerke). The word or spelling 'yerk' is now confined to Scots or dialect usage; the almost synonymous *jerk* would in early texts have the spelling 'ierk', for which 'yerk' is a natural alternative spelling. Compare Troian/Trojan/Troyan.

1514 currants] GRIFFIN (Curranes)

1548 Now you] THIS EDITION; Nor you GRIFFIN

1549 mantles] THIS EDITION; mantle GRIFFIN

1600, 1621, 1984 metamorphose] GRIFFIN (metamorphise)

1604 beholden] GRIFFIN (beholding)

1646 malkin] GRIFFIN (Mawkin)

1655 jingle] GRIFFIN (gingle)

1664 pelleters] GRIFFIN (Pelliteers)

1668 braggadocian's] GRIFFIN (Braggadotians)

1676, 1888, 2341 cony] GRIFFIN (cunny)

1688 visor] GRIFFIN (vizard)

1696 you dapper lances] THIS EDITION; you dapper Lannoes GRIFFIN. Although there are a number of coinages ending -oes in the text, 'Lannoes' seems to make no sense and is probably a misreading of 'launces'; see 'they shall pierce'.

1700 shall be counted] GRIFFIN 1; ſhall ſo be counted GRIFFIN 2

1804 crew] GRIFFIN (crue)

1805 corpse] GRIFFIN (corpes)

1808 shall lie] THIS EDITION; as lie GRIFFIN

1853 old wine excellent] THIS EDITION; old excellent GRIFFIN

1869 Lyaeus his honour] THIS EDITION; Lyens his hoʳ GRIFFIN. This makes no sense and may be a misreading of 'Lyeus' (Lyaeus = Bacchus), which would fit the context.

1872 renew] GRIFFIN (renue)

1882 a-work] GRIFFIN (a worke)

1888 sheep-shear] GRIFFIN 1 (ſheepſhare)

1906 count] THIS EDITION; court GRIFFIN

1906-8 your sable...your ebon...your cerulean] THIS EDITION; their ſable...their Ebon...their Crulean GRIFFIN

1908 cerulean] THIS EDITION; Crulean GRIFFIN

1909 embassady] THIS EDITION; Embaſidie GRIFFIN

1920 user] THIS EDITION; uſuer GRIFFIN

1922-3 rosin cans] GRIFFIN (Rozen canns)

1935 bagpudding] GRIFFIN (bagg-pudden)

1958 life] GRIFFIN (liffe)

1978 metal] GRIFFIN (mettle)

2007 sink at every] THIS EDITION; ſinke euery GRIFFIN

2029 surgeons] GRIFFIN (Chirurgians)

2057 foresaid] THIS EDITION; forefound GRIFFIN. Neither 'forefound' nor 'forefound' is recorded in *OED*, and the context suggests 'aforesaid'; probably a misreading.

2057 surgeon] GRIFFIN (Chirurgian)

2057 crease-fist] THIS EDITION; creſ-fiſt GRIFFIN 1, GRIFFIN 2. GRIFFIN's reading is not recorded in *OED* and 'crease-fist' (i.e. 'clench-fist') seems more likely as a coinage.

2108 precedents] GRIFFIN (presidents)

2112-13 binder, good loose-livers] THIS EDITION; bindergood looſe-livers GRIFFIN 1; binder ˌ good looſe livers GRIFFIN 2

2128 knock at a post] GRIFFIN 2; knocke at poſte GRIFFIN 1

2131 abundance] GRIFFIN 2; abundant GRIFFIN 1

2134 yea verily] THIS EDITION; yet verily GRIFFIN. 'yet' is probably a misreading ('yea verily' mimics the puritan's sermon).

2135 your] THIS EDITION; you GRIFFIN. 'your' makes more grammatical sense.

2165 blessing] THIS EDITION; bleſſe GRIFFIN

2166 Sulla] *Silla* GRIFFIN

2204-5 crop-eared courser] GRIFFIN (croopeard coarſer)

2205.n Woolner] GRIFFIN (*Wolner*)

2237-8 horse-ridge cushioners] GRIFFIN 1, GRIFFIN 2 (horſe-rigde-cuſhioners)

2258 rode] GRIFFIN (rodde)

2275 abundance] GRIFFIN (a bundance)

2285 aproned] THIS EDITION; capround GRIFFIN. A possible misreading. 'Capround' is not recorded in *OED* and the first citation of 'aproned' is 1628.

2291 Baucis] THIS EDITION; *Baneis* GRIFFIN

2326 dumb] GRIFFIN 1 (dombe)

2350 Dardan] THIS EDITION; Pardan GRIFFIN. Misreading or foul-case error: Dardan = Trojan (see commentary).

2351 fere] GRIFFIN (pheare)

2375 *But the smoke...painter*] set as verse in GRIFFIN

2376 clue] GRIFFIN 1; GRIFFIN 2 (*Cleue*)

2389 *Basileu*] THIS EDITION; *Baſilus* GRIFFIN.

2440 week] GRIFFIN 1; weeken GRIFFIN 2

2466 one purse for twenty] THIS EDITION; 20 purſes, for one GRIFFIN

2514 afire] GRIFFIN (a fire)

THE TRIUMPHS OF HONOUR AND INDUSTRY

Edited by David M. Bergeron

The Triumphs of Honour and Industry (STC 17899; *BEPD* 351) was printed by Nicholas Okes, who received a payment of £4 for 500 copies, according to the records of the Grocers guild. This quarto text consists of three sheets.

On sig. B3 Okes radically changes the font to a large italic for the listing of several nationalities (153–5). This change on the outer forme of sheet B may indicate a miscalculation in casting off copy or a deliberate stretching of the text. Once the printer recognized that he did not have enough text to fill up the space on the outer forme, he shifted to a larger font and thereby took up about two-thirds of the page.

No press variants were found among the extant copies: British Library, National Library of Scotland, Guildhall, and Huntington.

J. B. Heath prints an exceptionally detailed list of the expenditures for this pageant based on Grocers records (Guildhall Library MS 11590). Heath should, however, be used with caution. His transcription alters some words, omits others, inconsistently renders spelling and punctuation, reorders a portion of the account, and misreads several numbers. Quotations from the 1617 Grocers records in the commentaries on *Honour and Industry* and the *Busino Account* are taken from the original manuscripts.

SEE ALSO

Text: *Works*, 1253
Authorship and date: this volume, 400

WORKS CITED

Previous Editions

Thomas Middleton, *Works*, ed. Alexander Dyce (1840), vol. 5
Thomas Middleton, *Works*, ed. A. H. Bullen (1886), vol. 7

Other Works Cited

Analytical Index to the Series of Records Known as the Remembrancia, 1579–1664 (1878)
Beavan, Alfred B., *The Aldermen of the City of London*, 2 vols (1913)
Bergeron, David M., ed., *Pageants and Entertainments of Anthony Munday: A Critical Edition* (1985)
Beveridge, Sir William, *Prices and Wages in England*, vol. 1 (1939)
Birdwood, G., ed., *The Register of Letters, etc., of the Governor and Company of the Merchants of London Trading into the East Indies, 1600–1619* (1965)
Brenner, Robert, *Merchants and Revolution* (1993)
Calendar of State Papers, Domestic, 1611–1618, ed. Mary Anne Everett Green (1858)
Calendar of State Papers, East Indies, 1617–1621, ed. W. Noel Sainsbury (1870)
Calendar of State Papers, Venetian, 1617–1619, ed. Allen B. Hinds (1909)
Chaudhuri, K. N., *The English East India Company* (1965)
Clark, G. N. and Jonkheer W. J. M. Van Eysinga, *The Colonial Conferences Between England and the Netherlands in 1613 and 1615* (1951)
Clode, Charles M., *The Early History of the Guild of Merchant Taylors*, 2 vols (1888)
Daly, Peter, *et al.*, eds., *The English Emblem Tradition* (1988)
Dekker, Thomas, *Troia-Nova Triumphans* (1612)
Diehl, Huston, *An Index of Icons in English Emblem Books, 1500–1700* (1986)
Dodd, A. H., 'Mr. Myddelton the Merchant of Tower Street', in S. T. Bindoff, J. Hurstfield, and C. H. Williams, eds., *Elizabethan Government and Society* (1961), 249–81
Fedorowicz, J. K., *England's Baltic Trade in the Early Seventeenth Century* (1980)
Foster, Frank F., 'Merchants and Bureaucrats in Elizabethan London', *The Guildhall Miscellany* vol. 4, no. 3 (1972), 149–60
Franklyn, Julian, *An Encyclopedic Dictionary of Heraldry* (1970)
Grocers Company Charges of Triumphs, Guildhall Library MS 11,590, fos. 10ᵛ–12ᵛ
Gurr, Andrew, *Playgoing in Shakespeare's London* (1987)
Heath, John Benjamin, *Some Account of the Worshipful Company of Grocers* (1854)
Herford, C. H., and Percy and Evelyn Simpson, eds., *Ben Jonson* vol. 10 (1950)
Hinton, R. W. K., *The Eastland Trade and the Common Weal* (1959)
Jonson, Ben, *The Case is Altered*, in *Ben Jonson*, eds. C. H. Herford and Percy Simpson, vol. 3 (1927)
—— *The Masque of Queens*, in *Ben Jonson*, eds. C. H. Herford and Percy and Evelyn Simpson, vol. 7 (1941)
Jordan, W. K., *The Charities of London: 1480–1660* (1960)
Kayll, Robert, *The Trade's Increase* in *Harleian Miscellany*, vol. 4 (1808–11)
Lang, Robert G., 'London's Aldermen in Business: 1600–1625', *The Guildhall Miscellany* vol. 3, no. 4 (1971), 242–64
Malone Society, *Collections* III (1954)
Masters, Betty R., 'The Mayor's Household Before 1600', *Studies in London History* (1969), 95–114
McClure, Norman Egbert, ed., *The Letters of John Chamberlain*, vol. 2 (1939)
Munday, Anthony, *Camp-bell* (1609)
—— *Chrysanaleia* (1616)
—— *Himatia-Poleos* (1614)
—— *Metropolis-coronata* (1615)
Okayama, Yassu, *The Ripa Index* (1992)
Orgel, Stephen and Roy Strong, eds., *Inigo Jones*, vol. 1 (1973)
Prockter, Adrian and Robert Taylor, *The A to Z of Elizabethan London* (1979)
Rabb, Theodore K., *Enterprise and Empire* (1967)
Riggs, David, *Ben Jonson* (1989)
Rogers, James E. Thorold, *A History of Agriculture and Prices in England*, vols 5 and 6 (1887)
Sandys, George, *A Relation of a Journey begun An: Dom: 1610* (1973)

Stone, Lawrence, 'Inigo Jones and the New Exchange', *The Archaeological Journal* 114 (1957), 106–21

Stow, John, *The Survey of London* (1603, reprinted 1971)

—— *The Survey of London*, ed. Anthony Munday (1618)

—— *The Survey of London*, ed. John Strype (1727)

Willan, T. S., *Studies in Elizabethan Foreign Trade* (1959)

—— *The Early History of the Russia Company* (1968)

Williams, Sheila, 'The Lord Mayor's Show in Tudor and Stuart Times', *The Guildhall Miscellany* 10 (1959), 3–18

TEXTUAL NOTES

3, 12   Bolles] OKES (BOVVLES)

9   The Epistle Dedicatory] OKES (running title, A3^v)

61   peace] peaee OKES

67   *has*] OKES (*ha's*); A recurring spelling of this word, probably Middleton's own.

77–8   *Behold…hands*] OKES creates a space between 76–7, apparently trying to lengthen the text.

81   *and*] DYCE; *ana* OKES

132   *ahora*] OKES (*agora*)

134   *a*] OKES (*Al*)

136   *deseos*] OKES (*deſſi eos*)

138   *dignidad*] DYCE; *digmday* OKES

138   *su*] DYCE; *lu* OKES

153–5   An Englishman…Muscovian] By use of large font and generous spacing, Okes makes this list occupy nearly two-thirds of sig. B3.

160   Justice] THIS EDITION (*conj*. Levin); *Induſtry* OKES

165   divers] OKES (diuerſe)

231   On] THIS EDITION. OKES begins a new paragraph here, probably in another effort to stretch the text.

233   her] DYCE; het OKES

235   And] THIS EDITION. OKES begins a new paragraph here. See 231.

243   guests] OKES (Gueſſe)

258   HONOUR] THIS EDITION; The ſpeech…OKES. The omitted material simply duplicates the preceding paragraph and looks like more space-wasting. See 231.

261   *hope's*] OKES (*hopes*)

ORAZIO BUSINO'S EYEWITNESS ACCOUNT OF 'THE TRIUMPHS OF HONOUR AND INDUSTRY'

Translated and annotated by Kate D. Levin

THE *Busino Account* (Biblioteca Marciana MSS. Italiani--Classe VII, 1122 [7451], cc. 98–100) was written by Orazio Busino in a relatively clear early-seventeenth--century humanist hand, although the ink is extremely faded in places. The manuscript, consisting of three leaves, is currently bound into a volume with Busino's other letters to the Contarini family; a few words are obscured by the binding. A small sketch, also by Busino, appears in the top right-hand corner on the reverse of the second leaf. The text has been printed in English in *C.S.P. Venetian*, vol. XV, pp. 58–63. This translation, by Allen B. Hinds, silently adds information, alters or omits Busino's impressions at several points, and divides the text into paragraphs.

SEE ALSO

Text: *Works*, 1264

WORKS CITED

Acts of the Privy Council, 1616–1617, vol. 35 (1974)
Analytical Index to the Series of Records Known as the Remembrancia, 1579–1664 (1878)
Beavan, Alfred B., *The Aldermen of the City of London*, 2 vols (1913)
Calendar of State Papers, Venetian, 1617–1619, ed. Allen B. Hinds (1909)
Clode, Charles M., *The Early History of the Guild of Merchant Taylors*, 2 vols (1888)
Coryat, Thomas, *Coryat's Crudities*, 2 vols (1905)
'Diaries and Dispatches of the Venetian Embassy at the Court of King James I', *Quarterly Review* 102 (1857), 398–438
Fairholt, Frederick W., *Lord Mayor's Pageants* (1844)
Foster, Frank Freeman, *The Politics of Stability* (1977)
Hazlitt, W. Carew, *The Livery Companies of the City of London* (1892)
Heal, Felicity, *Hospitality in Early Modern England* (1990)
Heath, John Benjamin, *Some Account of the Worshipful Company of Grocers* (1854)
Holaday, Allan, ed., *The Memorable Masque, The Plays of George Chapman* (1970)
Hope, Valerie, Clive Birch, and Gilbert Torry, *The Freedom: the Past and Present of the Livery, Guilds and City of London* (1982)
Kollock, Margaret R., *The Lord Mayor and Aldermen of London During the Tudor Period* (1906)
Loomie, Albert J., ed. *Ceremonies of Charles I: the Notebooks of John Finet, 1628–1641* (1987)
Malone Society, *Collections III* (1954)
Masters, Betty R., 'The Mayor's Household Before 1600', *Studies in London History* (1969), 95–114
McClure, Norman Egbert, ed., *The Letters of John Chamberlain*, vol. 2 (1939)
Munday, Anthony, *Chrysanaleia* (1616)
—— *Himatia-poleos* (1614)
Purchas, Samuel, *Purchas, His Pilgrimage* (1614)
Reddaway, T. F., 'Elizabethan London—Goldsmith's Row in Cheapside, 1558–1645', *The Guildhall Miscellany* vol. 2, no. 5 (1963), 181–206
Rye, William Brenchley, *England As Seen By Foreigners* (1865), 101–13
Stow, John, *The Survey of London*, 2 vols (1603, reprinted 1971)
—— *The Survey of London*, ed. Anthony Munday (1618)
—— *The Survey of London*, ed. John Strype, 2 vols (1720)
Williams, Sheila, 'The Lord Mayor's Show in Tudor and Stuart Times', *The Guildhall Miscellany* 10 (1959), 3–18

MASQUE OF HEROES; OR, THE INNER TEMPLE MASQUE

Edited by Jerzy Limon

Masque of Heroes; or, The Inner Temple Masque first appears in the quarto edition of 1619 (*BEPD* 358, STC 17887). It was entered in the Stationers' Register on 10 July of that year, although the entry itself is mistakenly dated the previous year:

John Brown — entered for his copy under the hand of Sr Geo[rge] Bucke & Consent of the wardens. The Temple Maske Anno 1618 } vj^d

The quarto edition is collated A–C3^v; it was printed by William Stansby. Editors agree that there are no significant press variants among the nine extant copies, although some minor corrections were made during printing (B4, C1^v). Copies of *Masque of Heroes* are at the British Library (2); the National Library of Scotland (one copy and not three as stated in STC); the Dyce Collection of the National Art Library, Victoria and Albert Museum; the Bodleian Library; the Boston Public Library; the Huntington Library; the Folger Shakespeare Library; and the Pforzheimer Collection, University of Texas at Austin. The original quarto is well printed and contains few errors. The masque has thrice been edited previously: by Alexander Dyce (1840) and A. H. Bullen (1885–6) in their editions of Middleton's works, and by R. C. Bald (1967). The present edition is based on the British Library copies.

SEE ALSO

Text: *Works*, 1324
Music: this volume, 161 (entrance of New Year), 162 (first antemasque), 163 (second antemasque), 164 (entrance of masquers), 164 (their dance), 164 (their exit)
Authorship and date: this volume, 404

WORKS CITED

Previous Editions

Bald, R. C., ed., *The Inner Temple Masque or the Masque of Heroes*, in *A Book of Masques* (1967)
Bullen, A. H., ed., *Works* (1886), vol. 7
Dyce, Alexander, ed., *Works* (1840), vol. 5

Other Works Cited

Anon, *Coleorton Masque* (1618), in *Court Masques*, ed. David Lindley (1995)
Bentley, Gerald Eades, *The Jacobean and Caroline Stage*, 7 vols (1941–68)
Bosanquet, Eustace F., *English Printed Almanacks and Prognostications. A Bibliographical History to the Year 1600* (1917)
—— 'English Seventeenth-Century Almanacs', *The Library*, X, 4 (1930)
Bretnor, Thomas, *A New Almanacke and Progrostication* (1615)
Butler, Martin, 'Ben Jonson's *Pan's Anniversary* and the Politics of Early Stuart Pastoral', *English Literary Renaissance* 22 (1992), 369–404
Durston, Christopher, 'Lords of Misrule: The Puritan War on Christmas, 1642–60', *History Today* 35, 12 (1985), 7–14
Eccles, Mark, 'Ben Jonson, "Citizen and Bricklayer"', *Notes and Queries* 233 (1988), 445–6
Fuller, Thomas, *The History of the Worthies of England* (1662)
Gibson, Abraham, *Christiana-Polemica, or a Preparative to War* (1619)
Hassell, R. Chris, Jr., *Drama & the English Church Year* (1979)
Ingpen, William, *The Secrets of Numbers* (1624)
James VI and I, 'King James on the blazing star: October, 28th 1618', in *The Poems of King James VI of Scotland*, ed. James Craigie (1952), vol. 2
—— *A Declaration of Sports* (1618) in *Minor Prose Works of James VI and I*, ed. James Craigie (1982)
Johansson, Berlin, *Religion and Superstition in the Plays of Ben Jonson and Thomas Middleton* (1950)
Jonson, Ben, *The Complete Masques*, ed. Stephen Orgel (1971)
—— 'An Epistle to a Friend, to Persuade Him to the Wars' in *Ben Jonson*, ed. Ian Donaldson (1985)
Laroque, François, *Shakespeare's Festive World: Elizabethan Seasonal Entertainment and the Professional Stage*, trans. Janet Lloyd (1992)
Leighton, Alexander, *A Short Treatise Against Stage Plays* (1625)
Limon, Jerzy, '"A Silenc'st Bricke-Layer"—An Allusion to Ben Jonson in Thomas Middleton's Masque', *Notes and Queries* 239, December 1994, 512–4
Marcus, Leah, 'The Occasion of *Pleasure Reconciled to Virtue*', *Studies in English Literature, 1500–1900* 19 (1979), 271–93
Orrell, John, 'Amerigo Salvetti and the London Court Theatre, 1616–1640', *Theatre Survey* 20.1 (1979), 1–26
Smuts, Malcolm, 'Cultural Diversity and Cultural Change at the Court of James I' in *The Mental World of the Jacobean Court*, ed. Linda Levy Peck (1991), 99–112
Sugden, Edward H., *A Topographical Dictionary to the Works of Shakespeare and His Fellow Dramatists* (1925)
Tilley, M. P., *A Dictionary of the Proverbs in England in the Sixteenth and Seventeenth Centuries* (1950)

TEXTUAL NOTES

12 DOCTOR ALMANAC] STANSBY (*D. Almanacke.*)
12 Joseph] STANSBY (*Jos.*)
13 William] STANSBY (*W.*)
14 John] STANSBY (*J.*)
15 Hugh] STANSBY (*H.*)
16 William] STANSBY (*W.*)
65 they're] BULLEN; *th'are* STANSBY
89 tail] THIS EDITION; *tale* STANSBY
100–1 DOCTOR ALMANAC (*reading*) The last will and testament of Kersmas, irrevocable.] The laſt WILL and TESTAMENT of | KERSMAS, *Irrevocable.* | *Read;* STANSBY. Although printed as a heading rather than a speech in STANSBY, it is a necessary part of what Doctor Almanac says.

136 Blind Man's Buff] THIS EDITION; *blind man buff* STANSBY, BULLEN
142 ne'er] STANSBY (ne're)
154 DOCTOR ALMANAC] BULLEN; *Fast.* STANSBY
177 ye] THIS EDITION; *you* ALL OTHER EDITIONS. This emendation was made for the sake of rhyme: tell ye—belly.
206 incony] THIS EDITION; *in Cone* STANSBY, BULLEN
213 quean] THIS EDITION; *Queen* ALL OTHER EDITIONS
231 master's] *M*ʳ*s.* STANSBY
239 broke those] THIS EDITION; *these broke* ALL OTHER EDITIONS
319–22 Move on...whiteness.] *repetition of the refrain from 307–10* THIS EDITION; *etc.* ALL OTHER EDITIONS
335.1 *making*] BULLEN; *taking* STANSBY

STAGE DIRECTIONS

3 THE MASQVE.
10–31 The Parts. *The Speakers.* | *D. Almanacke.* Ios. TAYLOR. | *Plumporridge.* W. ROVVLEY. | *A Fasting-day.* I. NEVVTON. | *New-yeere.* H. ATVVELL. | *Time.* W. CARPENTER. | *Harmonie.* A BOY. | *Two* ANTEMASQVES. | In the first, six Dancers. | 1. *Candlemas Day.* | 2. *Shrouetuesday.* | 3. *Lent.* | 4. *Ill-May-day.* | 5. *Midsommer Eue.* | 6. *The first Dog-day.* | The second ANTEMASQVE, presented by | eight BOYES. | *Good dayes*————3. | *Bad dayes*————3. | *Indifferent dayes*————2. | The MASQVE it selfe, receiuing it's Illustration | from nine of the Gentlemen of the House.
31.1 THE | INNER-TEMPLE | MASQVE.
31.2–3 *Enter* DOCTOR ALMANACKE *comming from* | *the funerall of December, or the old yeere.*
64.1 Enter *Plumporridge.* (right, opposite 64)
100–1 The laſt WILL and TESTAMENT of | KERSMAS, *Irreuocable.* | *Read;*
141.1 *Enter New-yeere.* (right, opposite 141, first part)
193.1 *Enter the first Antemasque.* (right, opposite 193, first part)
231.1–3 *The first Dance, and first Ante-Masque,* | *consisting of these six Rude ones.* | Exeunt.
266.1–18 *Here the second Dance, and last Ante-* | *Masque: Eight Boyes, habited accor-* | *ding to their former Cha-* | *racters.* | The three *Good Dayes,* attyred all in white Gar- | ments, sitting close'to their bodies, their Inscriptions | on their Brests. | On the first. | *Cocke a Hoope.* | On the second. | *The Geere Cottens.* | On the third. | *Faint Heart Neuer.* | The three *Bad Dayes* all in blacke Garments, their | Faces blacke, and their Inscriptions. | On the first. | *Rods in Pisse.* | On the second. | *Post for Puddings.* | On the third. | *Put vp thy Pipes.* | *The Indifferent Dayes.* | In Garments halfe white, halfe blacke, their Faces | seamd with that party Colour, and their Inscriptions. | The first. | *Neither full nor Fasting.* | The second. | *In Docke, out Nettle.* | These hauing purchasde a Smile from the Cheekes | of many a Beautie, by their Ridiculous Figures, va- | nish, proud of that Treasure.
278.1–4 *At which loud Musicke heard the first Cloud* | *vanishing, Harmony is discouered* | *with her sacred Quire.* | The first Song.
292.1–5 Then a second Cloud vanishing, the Masquers them- | selues discouered, sitting in Arches of Clouds, | being nine in Number, *Heroes* Dei- | fied for their Ver- | tues. | The Song goes on.
306.1–2 Then the Masquers descending, set to their | first Dance. | The second Song.
322.1–3 Then they order themselues for their se- | cond Dance, after which, | The third Song.
331.1–3 At which, the Masquers make choice | of their Ladyes, and | Dance. | *Time, thus closing all.*
335.1 Then making his honour to the Ladies.
337.2 FINIS.

LINEATION NOTES

39–40 I know...chitterlings] THIS EDITION; *prose* STANSBY
45–6 Nobody...nights] BULLEN; *thought* | STANSBY
80–1 Nay...me not] THIS EDITION; *prose* STANSBY

161–5 The guard...Lancashire] BULLEN; *prose* STANSBY
205–6 Give 'em...admit 'em] BALD; *charge* | STANSBY
211 And tickle...the Cockpit] BULLEN; *Cockpit the* | STANSBY
212 The poor...conscience] BULLEN; *some* | STANSBY

THE PEACEMAKER; OR, GREAT BRITAIN'S BLESSING

Edited by Paul Mulholland

ALTHOUGH it appeared in what might be termed a per-functorily modernized edition in Bullen, *The Peacemaker* has not previously been the subject of textual invest-igation. This five-sheet quarto pamphlet was originally published in 1618 (STC 14387) in accordance with the licence bearing the date, 19 July 1618, granted by James I (*State Papers Domestic*) stipulating sole printing and selling rights for the space of seven years, the executive clause of which reads:

> This Bill conteyneth you^r maies^{ties} licence and priv-iledge vnto William Alley, during seaven yeares, (at ye nomination of Thom^{a}s Midleton) for ye sole print-ing, and selling, of a small booke, lately made by the said Midleton, called the *Peace maker*, or *Great Brittains blessing*, according to ye forme usuall in such cases./
>
> *Signified* to be you^r maies^{ties} pleasure by Maste^r Secretary Naunton/
>
> Thomas Coventrye.

The licence, which bears the king's signature, is further endorsed by Sir Francis Windebank. Secretary of State Sir Robert Naunton had presumably been instructed by James to request his solicitor-general, Thomas Coventry, to draw up the document. No printer named William Alley is known; but W. W. Greg surmised that he may have been related to the Verney Alley who in 1591 was granted a patent in reversion by Elizabeth I. A point of interest in the licence is that William Alley was not the name originally inscribed in the document. The parchment preserves evidence of abrasion on each occasion Alley is cited; and the name is written in a different ink. No record of the pamphlet appears in the Stationers' Register.

Although Thomas Purfoot is named as the printer in the title-page imprint, Purfoot was responsible only for sheets A and B. Six damaged types in sheets C–E of *The Peacemaker* have been identified in single appearances in three other books printed by William Stansby in 1618. The particular 16-point typeface found in sheets C–E occurs only in books printed by Stansby in the 1618–20 period, and not in any books I have examined that issued from the other nineteen shops active in London within this time frame. The fount seems to have been unique to Stansby's shop. In Purfoot's section the 20-line measurement is 112.5 mm, and in Stansby's 113 mm. The former falls within the range of large english, while the latter is an intermediate size between great primer and english perhaps best considered (large) large english.

The different founts that betray the presence of two printers correlate with word forms, spellings, and other matters associated with compositorial idiosyncracy and practice that additionally distinguish sheets A and B from C–E. A preference for terminal '-y' spellings, 'hart' (and cognates), and 'heere' is discernible in the first two sheets in contrast to terminal '-ie', 'heart' (and cognates), and 'here' in the final three. Sheet C marks a fairly clear division between the two sets of forms. A further important difference is also discernible at this point: a liberal use of italics—chiefly for emphasis—decreases sharply from sheet C onward.

Although printing by two establishments constitutes separate and largely independent operations, examination of all extant copies reveals a correspondence between the two sections that compose individual copies in relation to the states of correction/resetting of specific formes. Sheets machined early in the print run at Purfoot's shop, for example, were bound with sheets of an approximately equivalent stage from Stansby's. Matched states are sim-ilarly found in copies containing sheets impressed at later stages. In view of this general correspondence between states of the respective formes in the two sections compos-ing individual copies, the occurrence of states involving rearranged standing type or reset type in one or more cop-ies dated 1618 suggests that such alterations and resetting were effected at an early stage of printing.

The change on A4 from 'Fifteene' to 'Sixteene' (l. 42) in reference to the number of years James I had been king of England carries implications relating to the date of com-position and printing. Since 'Fifteene' would no longer be accurate from 24 March 1618, the anniversary of James's accession to the English throne, the allusion presum-ably preserves reference to the regnal year in which *The Peacemaker* was composed. Alteration to 'Sixteene' would remain correct until the next anniversary date in 1619 and accordingly provides a reasonable indication that the printing was undertaken, and presumably completed, prior to 24 March of this year. The change of imprint date from 1618 to 1619 together with the survival of only four of 27 exemplars bearing the former date, suggests further that printing was initiated near the end of 1618. The alter-ation from 'Fifteene' to 'Sixteene', which occurred at the seventh and final stage of correction, was almost certainly made prior to 24 March 1619. Despite its late position, however, the proportion of seventeen copies containing the variant 'Sixteene' to ten containing 'Fifteene' opposes any suggestion that the change came about towards the latter end of the standing forme's service life. The implied passage of eight or more months separating composition from publication additionally gives a glimpse of the slow progress of such a text from manuscript to print. The dates of the licence granted to William Alley, 19 July 1618, and of the licence's entry into a *Grant Book*, 7 August 1618, mark two stages in this progress.

In the course of printing *The Peacemaker* the imprint date was altered from 1618 to 1619. Four copies are dated 1618 (abbreviations to the left):

BL1 British Library copy 1
LAMBETH Lambeth Palace Library
PETYT Public Library, Skipton, Yorkshire (Petyt Library)
TEXAS University of Texas Library

Nine copies bear the altered date, 1619:

BOD1+2 Bodleian Library copies 1 and 2
CHR.C. Christ Church College, Oxford
COR.C. Corpus Christi College, Oxford
EXETER Exeter College, Oxford
GTS St Mark's Library, General Theological Seminary, New York
PLUME Plume Library, Maldon, Essex
YORK1+2 York Minster Library copies 1 and 2

During the printing of *The Peacemaker*, in addition to conventional press correction, some passages of type were rearranged in Purfoot's section and several pages were reset in Stansby's. The order of impression is often difficult to discern in such instances because press-correction variants are frequently indifferent and betray no sign of direction. In many cases apparent instances of press correction are in fact variant spellings and the like that derive from resetting. Running-title analysis and evidence of type damage preserved in standing-type pages and formes have helped to resolve the stubborn sequence questions, however. Such type rearrangements and reset pages as are encountered in the thirteen extant copies printed by Purfoot and Stansby are, with the exception of resetting that affects only a few lines in outer E, randomly distributed among three of the four copies dated 1618.

A summary of the disposition of type rearrangements and resetting in the 1618 copies will help to clarify the nature and extent of differences separating one or more copies from the others. In inner B in Purfoot's section, the LAMBETH copy contains an arrangement of seven lines of type on B3^v running from l. 198 ('Pride') to l. 203 ('come') different from that found in the BL1, PETYT, and TEXAS copies. And an arrangement of five lines on B4 from l. 221 ('the Father') to l. 224 ('Ifraell') is shared by the LAMBETH and BL1 copies; but an alternate arrangement is found in the PETYT and TEXAS copies. In both instances, except for the replacement of sorts occasioned by press correction and a few changes in spelling (presumably reflecting a different compositor's preferences), the type is the same. Correction further establishes the sequence of impression of each state of inner B: the LAMBETH copy, which uniquely preserves several uncorrected readings on

B3^v ('Euvy' and 'I' in place of the corrected 'Envy' and 'yea', ll. 192 and 199), contains the earliest state of both this page and B4; the BL1 copy contains an intermediate state of the forme in which only one of the rearrangements (B3^v) but various press corrections including those cited above were introduced; and the final state is found in the remaining copies, all of which contain the rearranged passages found on both pages together with the correction of 'fent' to 'fcent' (l. 231) among a range of other changes chiefly involving accidentals.

Similar but more extensive circumstances are encountered in Stansby's section. Three copies, BL1, LAMBETH, and TEXAS, contain the original settings of C2^v and C4^v in outer C and C4 in inner C; damaged type in standing-type pages of both formes in combination with the large proportion of copies containing alternate settings of the three pages (PETYT plus all nine 1619 copies) establish that these pages are in a reset state in the PETYT copy. In outer C an undamaged 's' occurs in 'Friends' on C3 (l. 347) in the BL1, LAMBETH, and TEXAS copies; this sort contains a split in all other copies. Similarly, a 't' in 'the' also on this page (l. 361) is without damage in the same three 1618 copies but has a nick in the lower part of the stem in other copies. In inner C on C3^v these three copies are equipped with a number of clearly printed and unbroken letters: e.g. the initial 'u' in 'ruunt' (l. 373), 'W' in 'Word' (l. 376), 'L' in 'Life' (l. 377); in the remaining copies each of these sorts contains a cut or some other damage.

As in sheet C, determining the original and reset states in sheet D of two different settings of two pages in each forme is frustrated by an absence of press correction clearly signalling sequence on the accompanying standing-type pages. Evidence provided by running-title analysis (described below) and instances of type damage resolves the question, however. In outer D the LAMBETH and TEXAS copies contain the original settings of D1 and D2^v; these pages are reset in the BL1 and PETYT copies (the resetting involves some relineation also). Type damage clearly establishes sequence in this forme. Several undamaged letters in the LAMBETH and TEXAS copies are damaged in some manner in the BL1 copy: e.g. on D3 'h' in 'honourable' (l. 532), the second 'n' in 'permanence' (l. 542), 'o' in 'Eccho' (second instance in l. 547); on D4^v 'F' in 'Fame' (l. 613). Together with these instances of damage the PETYT and other copies contain various additional damaged sorts that point to a further stage in the sequence of impression: e.g. on D4^v 'f' in 'of' (l. 593), 'w' in 'Law' (l. 612), and 'o' in 'Rumors' (l. 613). In inner D, resetting of D3^v that includes relineation of two lines and resetting of D4 separate the BL1, PETYT, and TEXAS copies from the LAMBETH copy. As in the outer forme, type damage affecting the standing-type pages provides evidence that settles the order of impression. On D1^v and D2 a collection of damaged sorts shared by all copies except LAMBETH indicates the precedence of this copy's inner forme through the press: on D1^v 'd' in 'and' (l. 473); on D2 'a' in 'aboue' (l. 489), 'h' in 'which' (l. 491), 'th' in 'their' (l. 496–7). Distortion of an 's' in 'Quarrels' (l. 461) on D1^V found in all other copies but BL1, LAMBETH, and TEXAS establishes a further stage in the printing sequence. In each of the instances concerning sheets C and D set out above the LAMBETH copy stands as an exemplar of the earlier or earliest of two or more states or stages.

Establishment of the original and reset states in the case of sheet E is puzzlingly complicated by an instance of apparent press correction. All four of the 1618 copies contain E2^V in outer E in the same state. In eight of the nine 1619 copies, however, two lines on this page are in a different, and, on the face of it, an earlier state (ll. 683–5). The exceptional Exeter copy has outer E in a later reset state from a subsequent edition. Two of the alterations on this page suggest direction: the 1618 copies read '*vitijs*' (l. 684) and 'the' (l. 685); the 1619 copies have '*vitjs*' and 'thc'. This evidence would seem to indicate that faulty readings in the 1619 copies were corrected and by some unusual circumstance sheets containing the corrections were bound exclusively into the 1618 copies. Such a scenario is problematic in several respects, however. As noted, where press corrections or reset pages are found in the formes of sheets A to D inclusive, whether in Purfoot's or Stansby's section, the LAMBETH copy is always among those containing the original or uncorrected state. An inconsistency in this regard in sheet E would accordingly be most unusual. A related problem concerns the restriction of outer E's apparently corrected state to copies dated 1618 since in other formes a correspondence is discernible between the imprint date and the state of the respective forme. A corrected state found only in 1618 copies runs counter to evidence provided by other sheets. Further, copies containing the apparently uncorrected state of outer E ('*vitjs*' and 'thc') are significantly mated only with the state of inner E bearing the second state '*The Peac-meuker*' running title, a title only latterly transferred to this forme, as established below, and not found in this state in sheet E in any 1618 copies. Assuming that the heap of sheets impressed with one forme was stacked in the order of their impression and that the heap was then turned for perfection, the curious pairing of an early state of an outer forme with a relatively late state of an inner forme would suggest that, regardless of the order of formes, the conventional stacking and turning procedure observed in other sheets printed by Stansby was oddly disrupted or abandoned in the case of sheet E.

Evidence consisting of damaged type in the standing letterpress of outer E, which points uniformly in one direction, however, reveals that '*vitijs*' and 'the' are the original and not corrected readings. On E1 the 1618 copies contain 'other' with a crisp, clear 'o' (l. 615) and 'God' with distinctive rumpling at the upper left curve of the 'G' (l. 633: '*dwelleth in God*'); in the 1619 copies the upper left curve of the 'o' is irregular and sharply defined gaps appear in the lower right curve of the 'G' in all affected copies. In the latter case, the rumpling visible in the 1618 copies establishes unequivocally that the sort is

the same and that the state free of additional damage is the earlier of the two. On E2^V in the 1619 copies the spacing of the initial line and approximately the right half of the subsequent three lines is markedly different from that of the 1618 copies; in addition, much if not all of the roman type in the line containing '*vitjs*' ('Haue Peace with all the') supplemented by at least the final letters of this Latin word, and several sorts in the line immediately below differ from the type found in the 1618 copies. Presumably a disturbance of some kind necessitated partial resetting, which in turn gave rise to the erroneous readings. Also, in the standing type on this page a 'P' in 'Peace' (l. 692) with sharp edges, a clear 'r' in 'our' (l. 693), and an upright 'f' in 'If' (l. 699) appear in the 1618 copies. In the 1619 *vitjs* copies the 'P' is considerably deteriorated, the bracket of the 'r' has been nicked in such a manner as to produce the effect of a hole, and the ascender of the 'f' is bent to the right. The 1618 copies on E3 contain 'Embrace' (l. 713) with an undamaged 'c'; a gap appears in the lower curve of the 'c' in the 1619 copies. Such examples constitute only a representative sampling of damaged type exclusive to the 1619 *vitjs* copies. The direction of alteration or resetting provided by this evidence not only resolves the otherwise problematic circumstances cited above but also agrees with a sequence of running titles that would be impossible to make sense of if a reversed order of impression were postulated. The running title on E2^V (title n in the list below), which appears in the four 1618 copies impressed from the same standing type, seems to have been partially dismantled prior to its appearance in a second state in 1619 copies (n^2): the type of '*e Peace-*' seems to be identical in both titles; but the 'h', the 'k', and the rules are distinctly different. And one or more other letters may well be substitute sorts in the later state of the title.

In light of the rearrangements of type affecting two pages in inner B of Purfoot's section and the resetting of seven pages in Stansby's, recognition of separate editions seems appropriate. Thus the solitary pure exemplar of the first edition, PURFOOT–STANSBY1, is the Lambeth Palace Library copy. The remaining three copies dated 1618 contain various combinations of original and rearranged/ reset states of the respective formes and accordingly span the first and the second editions. With a single exception, all copies of PURFOOT–STANSBY2 bearing the 1619 date contain the rearranged or reset states of pages as described above. The exception, the Exeter College copy, has outer E and E4 of inner E in the later reset states found in the third edition, PURFOOT–THIRD–STANSBY3; this copy is thus made up of four sheets of the second edition and one of the third.

A third edition naming Purfoot as printer on the title--page is also dated 1619: PURFOOT–THIRD–STANSBY3 (STC 14388). As in the first and second editions, Purfoot printed only sheets A and B, both of which were impressed from the standing-type formes used for PURFOOT2. But in contrast to the earlier editions, sheet C was printed by a third, as yet unidentified, printer. Stansby, who was responsible for sheets C–E of PURFOOT-STANSBY1 and 2, printed sheets D and E of PURFOOT-THIRD-STANSBY3. Sheets A and B and three pages of the inner forme of sheet E (E1^v, E2, and E3^v) of PURFOOT-THIRD-STANSBY3 in all thirteen surviving copies were substantially reimpressed from the corrected, rearranged, or reset states of standing type used for PURFOOT-STANSBY2. Sheet D and the remaining pages of sheet E were reset. Two pages in outer E exist in two different reset states in STANSBY3. Presumably in answer to a need for the typeface on another project, at some stage in the printing of this edition Stansby distributed E2^v and E3. This in turn necessitated resetting either to complete the number of an interrupted edition-sheet or to meet a call for additional copies. The 20-line measurement of type in sheet C in this edition is 116.5 mm—slightly larger than that of sheets printed by Purfoot or Stansby and within the range of great primer.

Pertinent in this connection is the survival of E1^v, E2, E3^v in inner E in all copies of PURFOOT-THIRD-STANSBY3: special sorts, different founts, and ornamental pieces—e.g. brackets and small capitals from a larger fount—and more meticulous spacing for the setting of the figure on E3^v (ll. 738–46) representing the twelve tribes of Ebal and Gerizim occur in this forme; these features in combination with the outer forme's three as opposed to the inner's four pages offer a probable explanation for the inner forme being allowed to stand.

The reset states of most of the inner and outer formes of sheet E in the Cambridge University Library copy incorporate a number of wrong-face sorts found neither in other copies of *The Peacemaker* nor in sheet D of this copy. Perhaps most prominent among the wrong-face letters are a collection of 'g's with loops inclined on an angle to the right. The same contamination occurs in another item emanating from Stansby's shop the colophon of which is dated 29 March 1620: the epistle to the reader in Samuel Hieron, *The Workes*, vol. 2 (STC 13377.5). Significantly, the prefatory epistle to a sermon entitled *Penance for Sinne*, also printed by Stansby, bound into the same volume bears an imprint date of 1619 and lacks the wrong-face sorts. Stansby presumably replenished his supply of this typeface at some point probably in the latter part of 1619. The correspondence between the type of sheet E in the Cambridge copy and that of other material printed by Stansby lends further support to the identification of the printer of sheets C–E of PURFOOT-STANSBY1 and 2 and sheets D and E of PURFOOT-STANSBY3 and 4.

The Cambridge University Library copy of *The Peacemaker* is distinguished from all copies of PURFOOT-THIRD-STANSBY3 by further reset states of the three pages of outer E and most of inner E. The only portion of standing type within the latter forme carried over from STANSBY3 is the figure on E3^v in the setting that originally appeared in STANSBY1. Slightly more than six and a half reset pages, although concentrated in a single sheet, may for the sake of convenience be allowed to mark a separate edition, PURFOOT-THIRD-STANSBY4, of which the Cambridge copy stands as the only exemplar. Designation

of a distinct edition prevents confusion when reference to features shared by PURFOOT-THIRD-STANSBY3 copies, but not PURFOOT-THIRD-STANSBY4, is called for.

Preservation of the standing E3^v figure in the Cambridge University Library copy provides additional support for the explanation suggested above for retention of the three standing-type pages of inner E in STANSBY3. A damaged italic '*T*' helps to establish further that the resetting encountered in the Cambridge copy occurred subsequent to that found in copies of STANSBY3. In the reset outer forme of the Cambridge copy a distinctive damaged '*T*' that had previously appeared in a running title (d in the list below) in PURFOOT-STANSBY1 and a large proportion of copies of both PURFOOT-STANSBY2 and PURFOOT-THIRD-STANSBY3 is incorporated into the text of E2^v. Since the title containing the damaged '*T*' had been in service for a lengthy term beginning with an appearance on C2^v in the BL1, LAMBETH, and TEXAS copies and ending on E1^v in eleven STANSBY3 copies, the Cambridge copy's resetting must have followed the distribution of the type composing this running title. On the strength of relationships observed in other sheets between the states of inner and outer formes, presumption of such a correspondence in the case of the Cambridge copy sheet E does not seem inappropriate. Accordingly, the reset state of inner E found in the Cambridge copy is almost certainly contemporary with the resetting of its outer forme.

One of the discrepancies between the STANSBY2 sheet C and the THIRD3 and 4 reset state of this sheet, no doubt attributable in some respects to setting by a different printer, involves the loss by C2 of two lines of type. Contributory factors include the use of a somewhat larger fount and a very likely consequent reduction in the number of lines per page (from 28 to 27). The reduction in turn gave rise to cramping and other spacing economies on C4 in order to match up with the start of sheet D, the content of which, although in a further reset state, remains as in STANSBY1 and 2. Copies bearing this state are readily identified by the C1 catchword, 'canſt', as opposed to the earlier editions' 'Globe'. The reset states of PURFOOT-THIRD-STANSBY3 and 4 are without authority.

Three further editions dated 1619, 1620, and 1621 printed by J. Beale (BEALE5: STC 14388.3; BEALE6: STC 14388.5; BEALE7: STC 14388.7) are essentially page-for--page reprints based on PURFOOT-THIRD-STANSBY3. BEALE6 incorporates approximately seven and a half standing-type pages from BEALE5, almost all of which are found in sheets A and B. About twenty standing-type pages are found in BEALE7 distributed mainly over sheets A, C, and E; B4^v and D4^v are the only standing-type pages in these sheets. Of some significance for the recurrence of the standing--type figure that appears on E3^v in Stansby's section of previous editions is a parallel situation encountered is Beale's editions. The E3^v figure that originated in BEALE5 was retained in standing type and reused for both BEALE6 and 7.

Copies with any claim to authority are accordingly limited to the original 1618 edition by Purfoot and Stansby

(PURFOOT–STANSBY1) extended to include the standing-type sheets A and B, and un-reset pages and standing-type formes of PURFOOT–STANSBY2, and the same standing-type Purfoot sheets and Stansby's standing-type pages of the inner forme of E (E1ᵛ, E2, and E3ᵛ) in PURFOOT–THIRD–STANSBY3 and the standing-type Purfoot sheets of PURFOOT–THIRD–STANSBY4. In practice, however, as discussion of several variants below will demonstrate, authority is for the most part more narrowly restricted to PURFOOT–STANSBY1 and the standing type of PURFOOT–STANSBY2.

Running titles reading 'The Peace-maker' begin on A4ᵛ and end on E4, numbering 31 in total. Since the two sections of the pamphlet constitute two distinct printing operations, the running titles in each section must be treated separately. In Purfoot's sheets A and B nine running titles appear (A4ᵛ to B4ᵛ inclusive). The same nine titles in their respective positions are consistent practically throughout PURFOOT1, 2, 3, and 4. On B2ᵛ in a number of copies of PURFOOT3 a different or a damaged 'k' appears in what is otherwise the same setting of the title, possibly marking a second state. The occurrence of a damaged sort and a damaged rule in some copies preserves evidence of sequence of impression: on B1ᵛ, for example, the BOD1+2, CHR.C., COR.C., EXETER, GTS, and YORK1+2 copies contain an upper rule broken to the right of the running title; the CHR.C. and EXETER copies additionally have a damaged 'T' in the running title and an upper rule bent above the 'T'. As might be expected, all PURFOOT3 and 4 copies contain the same damage in the B1ᵛ running titles as the CHR.C. and EXETER copies. This evidence additionally points to a correspondence between the order of impression and date/edition in Purfoot's sheets.

In Stansby's section 20 different running titles are found in the thirteen copies of STANSBY1 and 2, three of which appear in two states. Since a measure of continuity between the first two editions attends the complement of running titles and their transfers and all evidence points to a relationship between the imprint date and date of impression, in the following arrangement the 1618 copies (BLI, LAMBETH, PETYT, TEXAS) are listed before the 1619 copies. An attempt has been made to present the probable sequence of transfers from forme to forme in the list that follows. The EXETER copy has been eliminated from the list for outer E and E4 of inner E as this forme and page are in reset STANSBY3 states (this copy's excluded sheet E titles conform to the latest STANSBY2 titles except for those on E1, which may be a variant of f, and E2ᵛ, which is a transfer of c).

a. C1: BLI, LAMBETH, TEXAS; D1: BLI, BODI, COR.C., GTS, PLUME, YORK1; E2: LAMBETH, TEXAS, BOD1+2, CHR.C., COR.C., EXETER, GTS, PLUME, YORK1+2

b. C1ᵛ: BLI, LAMBETH, TEXAS; D1ᵛ: LAMBETH; E1ᵛ: BLI, PETYT

c. C2: BLI, LAMBETH, TEXAS; D2: LAMBETH; E2: BLI, PETYT; E1: BOD1+2, CHR.C., COR.C., GTS, PLUME, YORK1+2

d. C2ᵛ: BLI, LAMBETH, TEXAS; D2ᵛ: BLI, BODI, COR.C., GTS, PLUME, YORK1; E1ᵛ: LAMBETH, TEXAS, BODI+2, CHR.C., COR.C., EXETER, GTS, PLUME, YORK1+2

e. C3: BLI, LAMBETH, TEXAS; E4: LAMBETH, TEXAS; C4: PETYT, BODI+2, CHR.C., COR.C., EXETER, GTS, PLUME, YORK1+2

f. C3ᵛ: BLI, LAMBETH, TEXAS; D3ᵛ: LAMBETH; C1ᵛ: PETYT, BODI+2, CHR.C., COR.C., EXETER, GTS, PLUME, YORK1+2

g. C4: BLI, LAMBETH, TEXAS; D4: LAMBETH; E4: BLI, PETYT; D3: BLI, BODI, COR.C., GTS, PLUME, YORK1; E4: BODI+2, CHR.C., COR.C., EXETER, GTS, PLUME, YORK1+2

h. C4ᵛ: BLI, LAMBETH, TEXAS; E3ᵛ: LAMBETH, TEXAS; C2: PETYT, BODI+2, CHR.C., COR.C., EXETER, GTS, PLUME, YORK1+2

i. D1: LAMBETH, PETYT, TEXAS, BOD2, CHR.C., EXETER, YORK2; D2: BLI, PETYT, TEXAS, BODI+2, CHR.C., COR.C., EXETER, GTS, PLUME, YORK1+2

j. D2ᵛ: LAMBETH, PETYT, TEXAS, BOD2, CHR.C., EXETER, YORK2; D1ᵛ: BLI, PETYT, TEXAS, BODI+2, CHR.C., COR.C., EXETER, GTS, PLUME, YORK1+2

k. D3: LAMBETH, PETYT, TEXAS, BOD2, CHR.C., EXETER, YORK2; D4: BLI, PETYT, TEXAS, BODI+2, CHR.C., COR.C., EXETER, GTS, PLUME, YORK1+2

l. D4ᵛ: LAMBETH, PETYT, TEXAS, BOD2, CHR.C., EXETER, YORK2; D3ᵛ: BLI, PETYT, TEXAS, BODI+2, CHR.C., COR.C., EXETER, GTS, PLUME, YORK1+2

l². C4ᵛ (very close to l except for rules, P, and two as): PETYT, BODI+2, CHR.C., COR.C., EXETER, GTS, PLUME, YORK1+2

m. E1: BLI, LAMBETH, PETYT, TEXAS

n. E2ᵛ: BLI, LAMBETH, PETYT, TEXAS

n². E2ᵛ: BODI+2, CHR.C., COR.C., GTS, PLUME, YORK1+2

o. E3: BLI, LAMBETH, PETYT, TEXAS, BODI+2, CHR.C., COR.C., EXETER, GTS, PLUME, YORK1+2

p. E3ᵛ (Peace-muker): BLI, PETYT

p². D4ᵛ (Peac-meuker): BLI, BODI, COR.C., GTS, PLUME, YORK1; E3ᵛ: BODI+2, CHR.C., COR.C., EXETER, GTS, PLUME, YORK1+2

q. C1: PETYT, BODI+2, CHR.C., COR.C., EXETER, GTS, PLUME, YORK1+2

r. C2ᵛ: PETYT, BODI+2, CHR.C., COR.C., EXETER, GTS, PLUME, YORK1+2

s. C3: PETYT, BODI+2, CHR.C., COR.C., EXETER, GTS, PLUME, YORK1+2

t. C3ᵛ: PETYT, BODI+2, CHR.C., COR.C., EXETER, GTS, PLUME, YORK1+2

As the disposition of running titles in the various copies reveals, the titles were transferred from forme to forme, often in accordance with fairly conventional two-skeleton practice. Running title c, for example, appears on C2, D2, and E2; the same title also occurs on E1, however, and latterly on E2ᵛ in the EXETER copy, the text of which is in the reset state of STANSBY3, and in a number of other copies of STANSBY3. In many cases clearly identifiable horizontal rules accompany titles and reveal that the complete headline, including spaces and rules, was normally moved as a unit. These circumstances are presumably responsible for the general adherence to recto and verso positions of running titles (left and right spacing differentiates them), although a few deviations from this practice are found, as in the case of running title c on the occasion of its final appearance in the EXETER copy and other STANSBY3 copies, for example.

In accordance with expectations, such resetting as is encountered in STANSBY2 frequently coordinates with disruption of the arrangement of running titles. Among the 1618 copies, for instance, the same titles appear in outer C in the BL1, LAMBETH, and TEXAS copies. The PETYT copy, which contains two reset pages in this forme, however, introduces different titles that are shared by all of the 1619 copies of STANSBY2. The running titles of inner C in the PETYT copy also differ from those of the other 1618 copies, a circumstance very likely related to the reset state of C4 found only in this 1618 copy but shared by all 1619 copies. A new running title appears on C3^v and the remainder are titles that stood in different positions in the BL1, LAMBETH, and TEXAS copies. In the case of each of the transferred titles, however, the evidence of transfers restricted to 1618 copies and the naturalness of the first transfer positions for the respective titles suggests that the route was circular. The PETYT copy's title on C1^v was apparently initially employed on C3^v in the other three 1618 copies and then on D3^v in the LAMBETH copy before placement in its PETYT position. The two remaining transferred titles similarly appear to have arrived in their respective positions in the PETYT copy after employment in two previous formes: the PETYT copy's C4 and C2 titles seem to have been placed first on C3 and C4^v, then moved to E4 and E3^v respectively prior to occupying the positions reflected by this copy. The PETYT's C2 title additionally involves the relatively unusual movement from a verso to a recto position. Under the circumstances, maintenance of such positions to preserve the left and right spacing seems more likely than switching back and forth and in turn lends further support to the proposed sequence. As with the outer forme, the arrangement in the PETYT copy's inner forme agrees with that encountered in the 1619 STANSBY2 copies. These agreements similarly coordinate with the suggested order of impression.

In outer D no direct relationship is discernible between changes made to the forme and an altered pattern of running titles; but the sequence of title transfers helps to establish the order of impression of the variant states of the forme. The BL1 and PETYT copies contain D1 and D2^v in settings different from those found in LAMBETH and TEXAS. The running titles of the BL1 copy do not match those of the PETYT copy, however: the PETYT copy shares its complement of titles with the LAMBETH, TEXAS, and four 1619 STANSBY2 copies while the BL1 copy contains the same titles as the remaining five 1619 STANSBY2 copies. Although three 1618 copies feature the same set of running titles, the LAMBETH and TEXAS copies are exceptional in sharing the same variant state of outer

D. Resetting of D1 and D2^v must accordingly have been executed at a time when the four running titles remained undisturbed. Since the state of outer D found in the LAMBETH and TEXAS copies is not encountered in any other copies, this must represent the forme's original state. The sequence indicated by the running titles conforms exactly with that established by examination and analysis of stages of type damage. A number of 1619 copies containing the reset STANSBY2 state of outer D (D1 and D2^v) and bearing the same running titles as the three 1618 copies must have been printed, four of which survive. At some point in the course of this impression, the outer D titles were apparently transferred to inner D: D1 to D2, D2^v to D1^v, D3 to D4, and D4^v to D3^v in accordance with conventional single-skeleton practice (the use of two skeleton formes in the present instance notwithstanding). Significantly, only in the LAMBETH copy do the embossed impressions of type in sheet D point to the inner forme preceding the outer on the press. In several other copies in which such evidence can be discerned the embossing indicates a reversal of this order. The transfer of titles presumably marks some unknown interruption of printing—possibly the cessation of a particular print run or impression. A point of particular interest in this transfer is the occurrence of the same set of titles in both formes of sheet D in only two copies: TEXAS and PETYT. If, as evidence derived from other sheets suggests, a correspondence exists between the order of impression of white-paper sheets and the order of their perfection in copies of STANSBY1 and 2, the TEXAS and PETYT copies would seem to stand in closest relation to the transfer of titles from the outer to the inner forme. As a further point of interest, these copies also mark the divide between STANSBY1 and STANSBY2 states.

After the transfer of titles from outer to inner D further impressions of outer D were made employing, along with a pair of other titles, two running titles transferred from inner E, one of which was the distinctive 'The Peace-muker' title that in the process had been partly scrambled to read 'The Peac-meuker'. The titles transferred from inner E additionally coordinate with the sequence of impression since, on the presumption that inner E was set subsequent to the formes of sheet D, impressions would already have been taken of outer D and the latter forme would have been standing when the titles from inner E were transferred to it. In contrast to all other copies, the inner D titles in the LAMBETH copy were transferred from the corresponding pages of inner C. This exceptional situation coupled with LAMBETH's apparently unique precedence of the inner forme may well be related to the special circumstances of an early presentation copy as described below. In all copies of STANSBY2 the relationship between the pattern of running titles and different states of inner D matches that encountered in sheet C: that is, two pages of this forme, D3^v and D4, in these copies are in a reset state variant on the original state represented by the LAMBETH copy, and all such copies are equipped with the alternate set of titles.

As noted above, in outer E, which is composed of only three pages, all four 1618 copies have the same two running titles on E1 and E2ᵛ; all of the 1619 copies of STANSBY2 except EXETER, which has outer E in a later, STANSBY3 reset state, share a different pair of titles on these pages. E2ᵛ and its running title in these copies are in states variant on those encountered in the 1618 copies. As in the case of several of the preceding formes, the running title changes appear to be related to different states of the forme. The running title on E3 originated on this page and was at no point transferred elsewhere; undisturbed in this position, the same title appears in all copies of STANSBY1 and 2, as well as in most copies of STANSBY3 (including EXETER).

In inner E of STANSBY1 and 2 eight running titles appear in puzzling combinations in various copies. BL1 and PETYT are alone in having titles b and c on E1ᵛ and E2 found also on C1ᵛ (BL1, LAMBETH, TEXAS)/D1ᵛ (LAMBETH) and C2 (BL1, LAMBETH, TEXAS)/D2 (LAMBETH) respectively; all other copies have in their place titles d and a found on C2ᵛ (BL1, LAMBETH, TEXAS)/D2ᵛ (BL1 and five 1619 copies) and C1 (BL1, LAMBETH, TEXAS)/D1 (BL1 and the same five 1619 copies) respectively. And on E3ᵛ and E4 the LAMBETH and TEXAS copies differ from all others in containing titles h and e employed on C4ᵛ (BL1, LAMBETH, TEXAS)/C2 (PETYT and nine 1619 copies) and C3 (the same three 1618 copies)/ C4 (PETYT and the same nine copies) respectively. On E4 other copies have title g, found also on C4 (BL1, LAMBETH, TEXAS), D3 (BL1 and five 1619 copies), and D4 (LAMBETH only). The running title on E3ᵛ in all but the LAMBETH and TEXAS copies appears in two states: p, 'The Peace- -muker' and p², 'The Peac-muker'. In the absence of press correction in the standing type of inner E, establishment of the sequence of running-title transfers offers the readiest means of determining the order of impression of this forme. Several pieces of evidence point to 'The Peace- -muker' as the original title used on E3ᵛ. This spelling occurs in only two copies: BL1 and PETYT. Since the sheets in question were printed in a shop different from that responsible for sheets A and B, a cautious approach calls for discounting the value of the 1618 imprint date despite the evidence pointing to a correspondence gathered from other sheets. Pertinent in this connection, however, is the fact that the variant form of this title, 'The Peac-meuker', continues on E3ᵛ in a large proportion of extant copies containing the partially reset state of inner E found in STANSBY2 (i.e. bearing a reset state of E4). In view of the long life of 'The Peac-meuker' title, 'The Peac-muker' almost certainly represents its original rather than its corrected form. If 'The Peac-meuker' were the original spelling, partial correction to 'The Peace-muker' would be difficult to square with reversion to 'The Peac-meuker' at some subsequent point. 'The Peace-muker' additionally indicates that the title originated on E3ᵛ and that the type composing it was probably disturbed on the occasion of the transfer to D4ᵛ. From there it was very likely transferred back to inner E, where it continued in 'The Peac-meuker' form not only in the BL1 and five 1619 copies of STANSBY2 but in ten of

the fifteen copies bearing E4 in a reset STANSBY3 state (i.e. including EXETER). The longevity of the rearranged variant form and the occurrence of 'The Peace-muker' in only two 1618 copies oppose any argument attempting to claim that the latter was the title's final corrected form.

The curious arrangements of running titles that set the LAMBETH and TEXAS copies apart from the BL1 and PETYT copies and both 1618 pairs apart from all other copies are difficult to account for and, since no press correction occurs in inner E, do not coincide with such compositorial intervention in the type. The evidence of the movement of titles from one forme to another, however, suggests that the three dispositions of titles encountered in inner E may be related to successive impressions of the standing type of STANSBY1 and 2. In this regard the variant states of the E3ᵛ title, p and p², provide an important clue to unravelling the sequence. As set out above, the probable original state of the running title occurs only in the BL1 and PETYT copies; from its position on E3ᵛ the title was apparently moved to D4ᵛ and in the process the terminal 'e' from 'Peace-' was displaced to follow the 'm' of 'muker' to produce 'meuker'. After a stint on D4ᵛ, the title in its variant state was returned to E3ᵛ, where it continued in service for an extended term. Accordingly, were it not for the rearranged type, the original state of the running title would appear to be of a piece with its second state and the two distinct impressions of inner E separated by the transfer to outer D would appear to be one. Further, since the same 1619 copies that bear the title from E3ᵛ on D4ᵛ are equipped with the identical title on D3 (g) as occurs on E4, the E4 running title in the BL1 and PETYT copies was most likely transferred to D3 at the same time that the E3ᵛ title was moved to D4ᵛ.

The sequence of impressions of running titles on inner E in the 1618 copies must also, however, take account of the exceptional 'The Peace-muker' setting, which in its first state is exclusive to the BL1 and PETYT copies. The variant 'The Peac-meuker' state helpfully establishes that three of the four running titles in inner E are peculiar to these copies; and the proposed interrupted impression of title g on E4 at least plausibly separates impression of the state found in the BL1 and PETYT copies from impression of what appears to be the same state in the 1619 copies that contain essentially the same two titles, of which p occurs in two states. The set of titles found in the BL1 and PETYT copies is accordingly likely to have been the first through the press. This circumstance is noteworthy and unusual in standing as the solitary instance in which the state of the LAMBETH copy is not the earliest represented by surviving copies. The peculiarity of this situation possibly suggests that very few impressions of the the forme containing the original state of title p were made. Since the LAMBETH and TEXAS copies share two titles (E1ᵛ and E2) with all of the 1619 STANSBY2 copies, inner E in these 1618 copies was probably next in the sequence of impressions. It would appear that the remaining inner E titles, h and e, on E3ᵛ and E4 respectively, which occur only in the LAMBETH and TEXAS copies, were at some subsequent point replaced by titles p² and g from D4ᵛ and D3 formerly transferred from the pages of inner E. Further, the E3ᵛ and E4 titles h and e exclusive to the LAMBETH and TEXAS copies were presumably introduced to enable impression of inner E to continue concurrently, if only for a brief spell, with impression of outer D incorporating the titles transferred from inner E. Return of these titles to their respective positions in inner E produces the arrangement of titles in this forme found in all 1619 copies of STANSBY2. Significantly, the proposed sequence conforms generally to the imprint dates of the respective copies and in sheet E as in other sheets suggests that despite the division of labours between two printing establishments, sheets from the two houses corresponding to at least roughly equivalent stages of correction or change were bound together in individual copies of the pamphlet.

Running titles presumably pied on occasion in the course of transfers from forme to forme or were for some other reason dismantled. Casualties of this nature very likely explain the disappearance of certain titles at various stages and the introduction of new ones. Further, as additional impressions of standing type were taken at various stages more titles were apparently added to extend the total and reduce the need for transfers. The running titles with the briefest service life are those restricted to E1 and E2ᵛ (m and n) in the four 1618 copies. Title b that first appears on C1ᵛ (BL1, LAMBETH, and TEXAS) proceeds in an apparently conventional fashion to D1ᵛ (LAMBETH) and E1ᵛ (BL1, PETYT), but then abruptly vanishes. Since this title appears only in 1618 copies, its life is presumably restricted to an early stage of printing. The fact that it is not common to all four 1618 copies at any of its appearances, however, suggests that procedures of impression and whatever system of transfer may have been in place were more complex than those in operation in a normal book printed with two skeleton formes in which the running titles of one forme would have been transferred to the respective pages of the corresponding forme of the subsequent signature after the set edition--sheet number had been machined. Other running titles restricted to single appearances include those found on the pages of outer C and one page of inner C—C1, C2ᵛ, C3, C3ᵛ, and C4ᵛ—common to the same ten copies (q, r, s, t, l²). Since these titles appear exclusively in 1619 copies they were presumably set to fill gaps left by titles formerly used on these pages but subsequently transferred elsewhere. An attendant implication concerns the number of formes/pages retained in standing type and the quantity of the respective typeface, particularly in Stansby's establishment.

In light of the analysis set out above, the specific running titles as well as their number and disposition in individual copies of Stansby's section of *The Peacemaker* vary considerably. The LAMBETH and TEXAS copies, for example, each contain the same fifteen titles, though not always in identical positions; the BL1 copy has sixteen titles, of which one occurs in two states (p), and the PETYT copy seventeen, of which a different title occurs in two

states (l). Most of these titles are common to the four 1618 copies, but appear on different pages on some occasions. Two running titles are exclusive to 1618 copies (m and n). Except for the anomalous EXETER copy equipped with sheet E in a STANSBY3 state, the 1619 copies contain seventeen titles each, two of which are represented in two states (l and n) and one of which occurs only in its second state (p). All titles found in the 1619 copies are shared among 1618 exemplars of STANSBY2, except for the second state of running title n, which is exclusive to 1619 copies. As in 1618 copies the precise disposition in 1619 copies varies according to the individual copy.

The succession of editions of *The Peacemaker* between 1618 and 1621 gives a fair indication of popularity and steady sales during these years. Although the Stationers' Company rules forbade the use of standing type to exceed the legally allowed edition-sheet size (1250 or 1500), instances of second editions of works incorporating a combination of standing and reset type have come to light. In cases involving resort to standing type, division of a text among several printers would have the natural advantage of reducing the strain on any one establishment's supply of type. Purfoot presumably recognized the potential for sales of the pamphlet over an extended period while at the same time being mindful of duplicate typesetting costs and the implications for his own type-supply. Accordingly, he probably subcontracted the printing to Stansby, who acted in a similar manner in maintaining a substantial proportion of his section in standing type. The licence granted to William Alley for exclusive printing and selling rights for seven years, evidence of royal endorsement, if not authorship, of the work, and the wide readership cited in the title-page's statement, 'Neceſſary for all Magiſtrates, Officers of PEACE, Maſters of *Families, for the conformation of Youth, and for all his* Maieſties moſt true and faithfull Subiects', were very likely perceived as fairly guaranteeing continued sales over a protracted term. Such conditions may reasonably have led in turn to a plan to employ standing type from the start. Although extensive resetting does not concern his section, Purfoot's involvement in a similar arrangement in the printing of a second edition of Marston's *Parasitaster* (1606) may be significant in this regard. In contrast to several other books printed in a second edition from a combination of standing and reset type, however, the second edition of *The Peacemaker* introduces no variant readings in reset type that may derive from authorial revision.

The text of the pamphlet in Purfoot's section occupies slightly more than nine and a half pages, extending from A4 to B4ᵛ. In addition, a little less than a full page of an italic fount of equivalent size is used for the epistle, 'To all Our true-louing, and Peace-embracing SVBIECTS', on A3-A3ᵛ. Two blank pages (A1 and A2ᵛ), a page featuring only the royal coat of arms flanked by 'I' and 'R', for 'Iacobus Rex' (A1ᵛ), as well as the title-page (A2) also figure in Purfoot's four formes. Stansby's section consists of 23 pages of type occupying one page short of six complete formes, a circumstance that would undoubtedly have taxed his type-supply considerably more than the roughly ten and a half pages did Purfoot's. The different quantities of type involved in each establishment offer the likeliest explanation for the relative stability of Purfoot's four formes on the one hand and Stansby's resort initially to resetting and then to a third printer to take over sheet C on the other. Nearly six standing formes of R16 fount constitute an unusually large amount of this typeface. Stansby frequently employed it for preliminary matter in books the main text of which was set in a smaller fount; but he also printed a number of relatively short quarto pamphlets set entirely in it, so he may have been equipped with a larger than 'normal' supply. If the testimony of running-title transfers set out above preserves evidence that may be considered reliable for determining the extent of standing type, Stansby may have had sufficient R16 typeface for nearly all, if not the full complement, of his six formes. Running title h that appears on C4^v in three 1618 copies apparently next occurs on E3^v in two 1618 copies. From here it seems to return to inner C, where it turns up on C2 in one 1618 and a number of 1619 copies. The implication of this movement is that at least parts of sheet C were standing when the final transfer took place. Between the title's appearances in sheet C, two pages of outer and one of inner C were reset. Stansby's type-supply may have reached its limit at some point in the course of setting sheet E. Either his resources were incapable of meeting the needs of almost six quarto formes or, if they were equal to this, could not extend much farther. No positively identified instances of type recurrence have thus far been found in either original or reset states of Stansby's sheets. It is conceivable that while *The Peacemaker* formes were standing, projects such as preliminary matter of one kind or another for other books called for the same R16 typeface. In any case, a dwindling supply, whether deriving from the setting of *The Peacemaker* or from other commitments, very likely necessitated the dismantling of several pages of sheets C, D, and E. After impression of the formes of his section in their original and then partially reset states, Stansby may have distributed both formes of sheets C and D, outer E, and one page of inner E. When called upon to produce yet more copies, he apparently committed himself only to sheet D, which he entirely reset, and sheet E, of which three pages of the inner forme were still standing, and called in a third printer to take over sheet C.

As might be expected of a work blessed with royal favour, *The Peacemaker* was carefully printed. Press corrections are preserved in eight formes out of a possible ten (only outer B in Purfoot's section and inner C in Stansby's contain no evidence of correction, which may mean that they are represented only by the corrected state); and two of Purfoot's formes were subjected to multiple stages of correction (in addition to their original states, seven stages in outer A and three in inner B). With notable exceptions, a single stage of correction beyond the original state is the most common circumstance encountered

in contemporary play quarto texts in instances where evidence of correction survives. But corrected formes in such texts are very rarely found in a proportion equivalent to that encountered in *The Peacemaker*. Further, in one forme of the pamphlet, alterations defy attempts to discern sequence. In inner A the order of the fourth and fifth stages of correction is by no means clear: for example, the accidental inversion of the headpiece on A4 may have occurred on the occasion of the correction on A3^v of 'hauiug' to 'hauing' (l. 22) and change of imprint date on A2 from 1618 to 1619 or at some subsequent point prior to corrections registered in the sixth stage. The headpiece inversion incidentally indicates that this ornament was removed from the skeleton while the type was standing. Unlike the royal headpiece that appears on A2 and A3, which would need to be transferred back and forth between the inner and outer formes, that on A4 occurs only in the inner forme. Although changes encountered on C4 of inner C are indifferent and give no clue as to their direction, establishment that the variants spring from different settings of type assists in determining sequence: 'be'/'bee' (l. 390), 'and'/'&' (l. 395), 'Iniurie'/'iniurie' (l. 396), 'Iniuries'/'iniuries' (l. 397), 'he'/'hee' (l. 398), 'iniurie,'/'iniurie;' (l. 410). A number of variants on D3^v and D4 of inner D, like those found in inner C, very likely signal nothing more than compositorial spelling preferences that arose as a result of partial resetting of the forme: e.g. 'prayfes'/'Prayfes' (l. 549), 'Happie'/'Happy' (l. 554), 'he'/'hee' (l. 555), 'neyther'/'neither' (l. 555), 'and'/'&' (l. 574), 'Blafphemie'/'Blafphemy' (l. 577), the deletion of a comma to the catchword, and a word broken at a different point: 'Repu-|tation'/'Reputa-|tion' (l. 556). In both formes evidence drawn from a combination of running-title analysis and type damage establishes the sequence of impression. Most of these variants, however, involve Jacobean type and spelling idiosyncracies that are of no significance to a modern-spelling edition.

A few corrections not readily attributable to a proof corrector's judgement occur in some formes, however, and are therefore likely to have come about either through reference to the manuscript or by authorial direction; in such instances sequence is generally clear. Among changes introduced in inner A, for example, is that from '*practife*' to '*preferue*' (A3^v; l. 18), which appears designed to register a significantly different meaning—'preserve' conveys an active intention to maintain peace throughout the realm and additionally resonates with sentiments in the pamphlet proper (ll. 217–20), whereas 'practise' appears more narrowly concerned with the establishment of royal example. The alteration's deliberateness in conjunction with the fact that it was made at the sixth stage of correction would appear to coordinate plausibly with authorial intervention. The addition of marginal references in inner B, '*Flamin.* | *Conful.*' (l. 209) and '*Ezech.* | 13.10.' (l. 216), may similarly point to the author's involvement, although the possibility of a proof corrector's intercession cannot be ruled out. The content of these references, however, is of a distinctly different order from other marginalia; placement in the margins presumably reflects the compositor's reluctance to reformat the letterpress to accommodate material either added after setting was complete or inadvertently omitted in setting.

A number of variant readings in pages or formes that have been entirely or partially reset are faulty. On E3 at l. 720 in STANSBY3, for example, the reading of STANSBY1 and 2, 'Promiſe', was altered to 'Paradiſe'. Since 'Paradiſe' coordinates with neither the accompanying Biblical reference nor other allusions to 'the land of promiſe' (ll. 185-6 and 733-4), the reset reading is most likely mistaken. Evidence of compositorial carelessness in the introduction of turned letters in words in the same reset page ('Subnrbes', l. 707, and 'aud', l. 722), and the substitution of the clearly erroneous 'Pacent' for 'Pacem' on E2ᵛ (l. 683) points to the likely source of the incorrect 'Paradiſe'. The unreliability of such variant readings encountered in reset type establishes the importance of distinguishing original from reset states and prompts a cautious response to variants produced by resetting.

Determining the order of substantive variants encountered in outer C involves the resolution of problems of a subtler but related kind. Along with a number of indifferent variants, two that offer the potential for establishing sequence appear: 'diſtraughed'/'diſtraughted' (C2ᵛ; l. 343) and 'ſo little'/'as little' (C4ᵛ; l. 423). At first glance the faulty readings seem to represent the uncorrected state of the forme; but more detailed inspection discloses that the variant readings derive from different settings of the respective pages. The focus of attention thus shifts to determining which state is the original, and hence likely to stand in closer relation to the manuscript, and which reset. Although the apparently incorrect readings suggest that the forme in which they occur preceded the 'corrected' forme, on C4ᵛ in the forme containing 'diſtraughed' and 'ſo little', 'Cōtumely' (l. 427) also appears. In the copies that read 'diſtraughted' and 'as little' tildes are exceedingly rare: a solitary instance in the text of sheets C, D, and E occurs in 'cōmitted' on D4 (l. 575)—a rather tight page offering very little latitude in spacing, and the last page of the forme. They are fairly common, however, in parts of the text that have been reset, where they are generally used to conserve space in compensation for compositorial miscalulation or squandering of space elsewhere in the forme. This appears to be the case on C4ᵛ where the subsequent line—the last in the paragraph—occupies the full printer's measure, in contrast to copies that read 'Contumely' in which a small space equivalent to the width of an 'e' follows the full stop in that line. The likelihood, then, is that 'diſtraughted' and 'as little' occur in the original settings of their pages and that the errors, instead of registering an uncorrected state, were generated when these pages were reset. This conclusion is further supported by the confinement of the original state to three 1618 copies (BL1, LAMBETH, and TEXAS) and confirmed by evidence of type damage, as examined

above; the reset state is shared by the PETYT and all 1619 copies of STANSBY2.

Running-title analysis considerably simplifies discernment of the relative authority of two not very significantly different variants encountered on D1: 'attending' and 'attend' (l. 451). Several minor variants crop up in outer D that at first sight appear to mark the uncorrected state of the forme. Closer examination, however, reveals that the two pages incorporating these variants, D1 and D2ᵛ, are in a different setting. In the variant setting on D1 'drunken' contains a turned 'n' ('druuken', l. 453), 'ſtrokes' is spelled 'ſtroks' (l. 458), and passages of text in several paragraphs on D1 and D2ᵛ are differently lineated. The only substantive variant, however, is 'attend' as against 'attending' in the alternate setting of the forme. As in the foregoing example involving outer C, the question in turn becomes, which state is the original and which reset? Among the implications springing from the proposed sequence of running titles affecting outer D set out above is that the original setting of this forme occurs only in the LAMBETH and TEXAS copies. Accordingly, 'attending', which is exclusive to these copies, represents the original reading, and 'attend' along with several apparently uncorrected readings and lineation rearrangements arose from the partial resetting of this forme. As in other instances, the imprint dates of the respective copies containing the variant states also agree with this sequence.

The single pure exemplar of PURFOOT-STANSBY1, the 1618 Lambeth Palace Library copy, stands as something of a curiosity since it differs in a number of important respects from all copies of PURFOOT-STANSBY2. Most striking, perhaps, is the additional line unique to this copy, 'By the King', set in type below a headpiece ornament of the royal coat of arms on A3 and, separated by a decorative line, above the work's opening address: 'To all Our true-louing, and Peace-embracing SVBIECTS' (see Illustration 1). And on A4 above the head-title set over the beginning of the text proper, in place of an ornament depicting a central vase or fountain flanked by mythological figures found in all other copies (Miller, ornament no. 1), PURFOOT-STANSBY1 contains a headpiece incorporating the Prince of Wales's three ostrich feathers within a crown and 'ICH DIEN' legend (see Illustration 2). The feathers and crown device is also stamped in gold on the handsome contemporary vellum binding. Archbishop Abbot in his will bequeathed his books to the library 'for the use of the Archbishops of Canterbury in succession'. Such books were identified by vellum tabs marked with the letters 'G.C.' (probably standing for 'Georgii Cantuar.'). The LAMBETH copy of The Peacemaker retains the vellum tab so inscribed. A study of Lambeth Palace Library in this period notes, 'It is still possible to distinguish between the collections, for all the books were well bound and the covers of each volume were stamped with the arms of its original owner' (Cox-Johnson). The likelihood is accordingly that the LAMBETH copy was a presentation copy to Archbishop Abbot from Prince Charles.

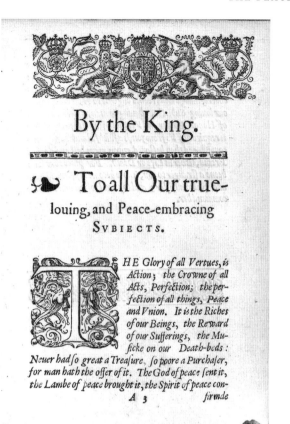

1. Unique ascription to King James in the LAMBETH copy of *The Peacemaker*, A3

2. Headpiece from the LAMBETH copy of *The Peacemaker*, A4

In addition to the authorship attribution unique to this copy, the marginal notations in inner B, '*Flamin.* | *conful.*' and '*Ezech.* | *13.10.*' (B3ᵛ and B4; ll. 209 and 216), present in all other copies, are missing. Successive stages of correction to standing type preserved in copies of PURFOOT–STANSBY2 establish that the respective formes represented by the LAMBETH copy are from a stage of proof correction that in every instance but one antedates all others. And on all occasions involving rearrangements of standing type or resetting of specific pages for PURFOOT–STANSBY2, the LAMBETH copy exceptionally contains the original state. In outer A only this and the TEXAS copies preserve the uncorrected forms of several words, of which those that most clearly indicate direction are 'subftitue' (for 'subftitute', l. 63), 'celebrared' (for 'celebrated', l. 69). Also, in inner A the LAMBETH copy uniquely preserves the distinctive spelling, '*embracft*' (l. 21), subsequently altered first to '*embraft*' and then to '*embraced*', and omits 'Cum Priuilegio' at the foot of the title-page. Among a collection of indifferent variants found in inner B, the uncorrected '*Euvy*' incorporating a turned '*n*' (l. 192), 'I', in place of the corrected 'yea' (l. 199), and the omission

of the two marginal notations, all unique to PURFOOT–STANSBY1, similarly signal that the state of this forme in the LAMBETH copy preceded all others through the press. The Prince of Wales's headpiece ornament coupled with evidence that several formes of sheets A and B are from an incipient stage of printing suggests that a number of the variants peculiar to this copy catered to the special circumstances of a presentation copy and that some of the copy's unique features were very likely set exclusively for the limited number of such copies impressed, probably among the first impressions taken of the respective formes. Although the ornamental and other details connected in some way with a presentation copy are restricted to the sheets printed by Purfoot, sheets C and D in the LAMBETH copy, as resetting in these sheets and running-title transfers have demonstrated, contain evidence that they too were machined early in the initial print run at Stansby's establishment. Only in the case of sheet E does evidence springing from running-title analysis indicate that the state of this sheet in the LAMBETH copy is not from the earliest stage of impression; but even in this instance the introduction of two titles preserved in the LAMBETH and TEXAS copies to replace two titles of the original set found only in the BL1 and PETYT copies is likely to have taken place soon after printing began. In view of the proportion of copies containing each set of titles (an equal split of the four 1618 copies), a disorderly stacking of perhaps only a small number of sheets may reasonably account for this inconsistency.

The line, 'By the King', would appear to be of a piece with the other variants associated with a presentation copy. In an effort to contextualize the apparent pretence of regal authorship of *The Peacemaker*, Rhodes Dunlap cites the instance of a deliberate deception concerning the king's authorship in the matter of *A Pvblication of His Maties Edict and Severe Censure againft Priuate Combats and Combatants* (1614). James I in a proclamation of 26 March 1616 alluded to this work as his own. Although the 'Proclamation against Private Challenges and Combats' of 4 February 1614 makes reference to 'a more large discourse annexed' (i.e. *A Pvblication of His Maties Edict*), neither this proclamation nor the annexed discourse itself provides any indication of the actual author, Henry Howard, Earl of Northampton, preferring instead to give the impression that the work issued from the king. Like *The Peacemaker*, *A Pvblication of His Maties Edict* is characterized by liberal use of royal first-person plurals (*The Peacemaker*, perhaps not insignificantly, lifts several lines from it verbatim). The occurrence of the statement, 'By the King', in only a single surviving copy may signify nothing more than that the printer misconstrued the pamphlet's regal tone, especially as conveyed by the prefatory epistle, in his incorrect assignment of authorship. Whether the provision of the royal headpiece on A2 and A3 and royal coat of arms framed by 'I' and 'R' on A1^v similarly derived from the printer's assumption of authorship or were prescribed in instructions delivered to the printer is beyond recovery; but if the latter, such a direction would serve to reinforce the notion that the work was the king's. In the absence of any supporting evidence there seems no need to suppose some lost political motive pertaining, for example, to James's or Prince Charles's relations with the Archbishop of Canterbury to explain a deliberate deception in specifying the king as the writer of the work. But whatever the line's origin or intent, it was apparently expunged on the occasion of a number of other changes very soon after printing began.

On the basis of the preservation of the distinctive Middletonian form, 'embracſt' (l. 21), in the prefatory epistle together with other spellings associated with the dramatist (e.g. 'confirmde', l. 18, and 'beſtowd', l. 25), there is a reasonable likelihood that the epistle was in his own hand. The relative scarcity of idiosyncratic Middletonian spellings and forms elsewhere suggests that the body of the work was a scribal transcript.

Licence

This is a transcript of the licence for *The Peacemaker*, Public Record Office SP39/9 no. 42; it is printed in facsimile as Illustrations 3 and 4. On the recto:

James R

JAMES by the Grace of God Kinge of England Scotland ffrance and Ireland defendo^r of the faith &c. To all Archbishopps Bishopps deanes Archdeacons Iustices of peace Mayo^{rs} Sheriffes Bayliffes Constables and also other our Magistrates and Officers aswell spirituall as temporall & our Lovinge Subiect*es* whatsoever to whome it shall or maie app*er*teyne Greetinge *Whereas* our welbeloved Subiecte Thomas Middleton hath by his great labo^r & industrie out of his love to the gen*er*all peace and of ou^r lovinge Subiect*es* and others made and compiled a Booke of a small volume nowe called or intituled *The Peacemaker or Brittaines Blessinge*. whereby is manifested the goodnes vertue and benefitt w*hich* springe from love and peace and the vngodliness offence and damage that arise from conten*cions* and quarrells by proofs out of the holie scriptures & manie other thing*es* tendinge to the p*re*serva*cion* and advaunceme*nt* of Christian love & amitie and the avoydinge of conten*cion* and blood sheddinge fitt and necessarie for all men to embrace *Knowe Yee* that we well approvinge and Comendinge the good endevo^r labo^r and study of the said Thomas Middleton in this his pius worke and to the end he maie receaue some recompence out of his owne labo^{rs} and for other Considera*cions* [to] vs herevnto movinge and att the speciall nomina*cion* of

the said Thomas Middleton of our especiall grace certeyne knowledge and meere mo*cion* haue given and graunted and by theis presen*tes* for vs our heires and Successo^{rs} doe giue and graunte full free and sole lib*er*tie licence power priuileges authoritie vnto ou^r welbeloved Subiecte William Alley gent his executo^{rs} Adm*in*istrato^{rs} and Assignes That he the saide William Alley his executo^{rs} Adm*in*istrato^{rs} or Assignes or anie of them or his or their or any of theire deputie or deputies onlie and none other for and duringe the terme and space of seaven yeares next ensueinge the date hereof shall and may imprinte or cause to be imprinted the said Booke intituled *The peacemaker or Brittains blessinge* either in the same forme order or method as it is nowe set downe or in whatsoever other forme order or method the saide William Alley his executo^{rs} Adm*in*istrat*ors* or Assignes duringe the said Terme shall cause the said booke to be digested or set downe & the same see imprinted to publishe vtter sell and putt to sale or Cause to be published uttered sould and putt to sale at anie tyme or times duringe the said Terme to the iust benefitt of the saide William Alley his executo^{rs} Adm*in*istrato^{rs} & Assignes To *have* and to hold the said licence power lib*er*tie priuilege and authoritie vnto the saide William Alley his executo^{rs} Adm*in*istrato^{rs} and Assignes for and duringe the Terme of seaven Yeares from the daye of the date hereof next ensueinge and fullie to be compleate and ended And for the better Confirma*cion* hereof and for the restraint of all others that by anie meanes shall attempt to p*re*vent or p*re*iudice the effecte of theis p*re*sen*tes* or defeate the saide William Alley his executo^{rs} Adm*in*istrato^{rs} and Assignes or anie of them of the benefitt unto him or them herebie intended We doe by theis *presentes* for vs ou^r heires and Successo^{rs} straightlie chardge Com*m*aund prohibite & forbidd aswell the Master and Keep*er*s or Wardens and Com*on*altie of the misterie or arte of Stationers of the Cittie of London for the timebeinge and theire successo^{rs} as all and singuler Printers Booksellers Stationers and other p*er*son & p*er*sons whatsoever beinge either ou^r Subiect*es* or Strangers aswell w^{ith}in lib*er*ties as wthout other then the saide William Alley his executo^{rs} Adm*in*istrato^{rs} and Assignes and his & theire deputies facto^{rs} and s*er*vant*es* y^t neither they nor any of them at anie time or tymes from henceforth for or duringe the said terme of seaven yeares directlie or indirectly by any Cullo^r or meanes shall imprinte or Cause to be imprinted the said Booke before men*cioned* or any abridgm*ent* or epitome thereof or the same imprinted in anie forreigne part*es* to importe into this our Realme or anie other our dominions nor in the same our Realme or dominions or anie p*ar*te of them or anie of them shall sell vtter publishe or put to sale or cause to be soulde vttered published or putt to sale or otherwise dispose of the said booke before men*cioned* or anie abridgm*ent* epitome or abstract of the same contrarie to the true intent and meaninge of theis p^{r}esen*tes* vppon paine of forfeiture of all and eu*er*ie such booke or Book*es* soe to be imprinted sould vttered published

3. Licence to William Alley, as nominee of the author Thomas Middleton, for the
term of seven years of the sole printing and selling of *The Peacemaker*; recto.

imported or putt to sale contrarie to the true meaninge hereof & vppon paine of our high displeasure & of such further paynes penalties forfeitures punishm*entes* & imprisonm*entes* as by anie lawes or statut*es* of this Realme can or maie be inflicted or imposed vppon Offendo*rs* in that behalfe or otherwise for contempt of this our royall Comaundem*ent* And for the better execuc*i*on of our will & pleasure herein we doe by theis p*res*ent*es* for vs our heires and Successo*rs* giue full power and authoritie vnto the saide William Alley his executors Administrato*rs* & Assignes deputie & deputies and eu*er*ie or anie of them takinge w*ith* him or them or anie of them a Constable or other officer of the place where it shall happen during the said terme of seaven yeares to enter into all and eu*er*ie the warehouses workehouses shopps & dwellinge houses or other places of all and eu*er*ie Stationer Printer bookseller Bookebinder or other p*er*son or p*er*sons whatsoever w*ith*in any p*ar*te of ou*r* dominions aswell w*ith*in lib*er*ties as w*ith*out where he the saide William Alley his executo*rs* Administrato*rs* Assignes deputie or deputies or anie of them shall suspect y*t* the said booke or anie p*ar*te or p*ar*cell thereof maie be found and the same to searche And if he or they or

anie of them shall finde that anie such booke or anie epitome or abridgm*ent* thereof or anie p*ar*te or p*ar*cell thereof be or shalbe soe printed imported vttered sould or put to sale contrarie to the true meaninge of this our graunt That then it shall and maie be lawfull to and for the saide William Alley his executo*rs* Administrato*rs* Assignes deputie and deputies or anie of them to seize take and carrie awaie the same to the vse of vs ou*r* heires and Successo*rs*. The one moitie whereof we doe hereby for vs ou*r* heires and Successo*rs* give vnto the saide Willi*am* Alley his executo*rs* Administrato*rs* and Assignes and the other moitie or the benefitt or value thereof we will shalbe distributed amoungst the poore people of the parishe wherein such Book*es* shalbe soe seized or taken *And forasmuch as* the said Booke (whereof the sole printinge is hereby giuen and graunted to the saide William Alley his executo*rs* Administrato*rs* and Assignes as aforesaid) is verie necessarie not onlie for all Magistrates Officers of peace & maysters of families but alsoe for all other our true & lovinge subiect*es* for the informinge & well orderinge of youth p*er*svac*i*on of Christian love & amitie & gen*er*all avoydinge of all contenc*i*on and bloud sheddinge We are well pleased that the same maie be

4. Executive clause of the licence to William Alley; left side at foot of recto

published to the viewe of all the generall good of this our Commonwealth to the encouragement of others in the like lowdable and worthie studies and endevoures Therefore wee will and commaund hereby for vs our heires and Successors aswell the said Master and Wardens of the misterie of Stacioners of our Cittie of London for the time beinge and alsoe all our Officers ministers & subiectes in all and euerie our dominions aforesaid That they and euerie of them at all and euerie tyme or tymes during the said Terme of Seaven yeares vppon request vnto them or any of them made by the saide William Alley his executors Administrators deputies or Assignes or any of them be aidinge and assistinge vnto them and euerie of them in the due excercise and execucion of this our graunte licence and priuiledge and in the publishinge and divulginge of the said booke to all our lovinge Subiectes & in procuring by all due meanes that the same may be the more commonlie and frequentlie vented & vttered amongst all our said Subiectes and in the due execucion of our pleasure herein declared with effecte according to the true meaninge of the same vppon payne of our indignacion & displeasure and as they will avoide the contrarie at theire perills Although expresse mencion &c In Witnes &c. witnes &c./

Exam. Thomas Coventrye

It may please your most excellent Maiestie

This Bill conteyneth your maiesties licence and priviledge vnto William Alley, during seaven yeares, (at ye nomination of Thomas Midleton) for ye sole printing, and selling, of a small booke, lately made by the said Midleton, called the *Peace maker*, or *Great Brittains blessing*, according to ye forme usuall in such cases./

Signified to be your maiesties pleasure by Master Secretary Naunton/

Thomas Coventrye.

On the verso:

Expedit apud Westminster decime nono die Julij Anno Regis Jacobi decimo sexto [i.e., Brought forward at Westminster on the nineteenth day of July in the sixteenth year of the reign of King James]

per Windebank

SEE ALSO

Text: *Works*, 1306
Authorship and date: this volume, 402

WORKS CITED

Previous Edition

Bullen, A. H., ed., *Works* (London, 1886), vol. 8

Other Works Cited

Amussen, Susan Dwyer, *An Ordered Society: Gender and Class in Early Modern England* (1988)
—— 'The Part of a Christian Man', in Susan Dwyer Amussen and Mark Kishlansky, eds., *Political Culture and Cultural Politics in Early Modern England* (1995), 213–33
—— 'Punishment, Discipline and Power: The Social Meanings of Violence in Early Modern England', *Journal of British Studies* 34:1 (1995), 1–34
Bacon, Francis, *The Charge of Sir Francis Bacon Knight, His Majesty's Attorney General, touching duels, upon an information in the Star Chamber against Priest and Wright* (1614)
Clark, Peter, *The English Alehouse: A Social History 1200–1830* (1983)
Cox-Johnson, Ann, 'Lambeth Palace Library, 1610–1664', *Transactions of the Cambridge Bibliographical Society* 2 (1958), 105–26
Dunlap, Rhodes, 'James I, Bacon, Middleton, and the Making of *The Peace-Maker*', *Studies in the English Renaissance Drama*, ed. Josephine W. Bennett, Oscar Cargill, and Vernon Hall, Jr. (1959), 82–94
Foyster, Elizabeth A., *Manhood in Early Modern England: Honour, Sex, and Marriage* (1999)
Greg, W. W., *A Companion to Arber* (1967)
Howard, Henry, Earl of Northampton, *A Pvblication of His Maties Edict, and Severe Censure againſt Priuate Combats and Combatants* (1614)
Ingram, Martin, *Church Courts, Sex and Marriage in England, 1570–1640* (1987)

James VI and I, *Political Writings*, ed. Johann P. Sommerville (1994)

—— *State Papers Domestic*, 39, vol. 9, no. 42

—— *State Papers Domestic*, 14, vol. 141 (*Grant Books*), 241

Kiernan, V. G., *The Duel in European History: Honour and the Reign of Aristocracy* (1988)

Larkin, James F., and Paul L. Hughes, eds., *Stuart Royal Proclamations*, vol. 1 (1973)

Miller, C. William, 'Thomas Newcomb: A Restoration Printer's Ornament Stock', *Studies in Bibliography* 3 (1950–1), 155–70

Sharpe, J. A., 'Defamation and Sexual Slander in early modern England: The Church Courts at York', *Borthwick Papers*, 58 (1980)

Underdown, David, *Fire From Heaven: Life in an English Town in the Seventeenth Century* (1992)

Wrightson, Keith, *English Society, 1580–1680* (1982)

TEXTUAL NOTES

In the following notes distinctions among stages of correction are denoted simply by the addition of '(A)', '(B)', etc. after the printer's name and citation of the edition: e.g. STANSBY2(B). In such instances '(A)' marks the earlier of two or the earliest of more than two states; as some formes of the early edition exist in multiple states, the reader is referred to the list of press variants for a more detailed record of the relationship of one state to another. In instances involving substantive variants in standing and reset type, '(S)' and '(R)' are used to mark the respective settings: e.g. STANSBY1(S), STANSBY2(R). As the formes of Purfoot's sheets A and B remained standing from PURFOOT1 to 4, all citations from this section are to standing type.

6 conformation] PURFOOT2(B) (*conformation*); *confirmation* PUR-FOOT1–2(A). Although '*confirmation*' and '*conformation*' were used interchangeably at this time, the alteration to the latter in PURFOOT2 reflects a sensitivity to more clearly differentiated meanings.

18 preserve] PURFOOT2(B); *practise* PURFOOT1–2(A). Authorial revision or intervention of some kind offers the most likely explanation for the change from '*practife*' to '*preferue*'. The correction extends beyond a proof-corrector's judgement, especially since the original reading makes clear sense and accordingly does not call attention to itself. The authority of the corrected reading is given additional support by reiterations of 'preserve' at ll. 219 and 222, the latter instance bolstered by internal associations of James I with a dove.

21 embraced] PURFOOT1(A) (*embracft*); *embraft* PURFOOT2(B); *embraced* PURFOOT2(C). The original setting, '*embracft*', preserves a spelling highly characteristic of Middleton and suggests that the prefatory remarks at least were in the author's hand.

22 Our] PURFOOT1(B) (*Our*); *our* PURFOOT1(A). Corrections introduced relatively early to the standing type of inner A, since they first appear in a copy dated 1618 (TEXAS), include capitalization of two royal plurals—apparently deliberate alterations.

28 We] PURFOOT1(B) (*We*); *we* PURFOOT1(A). See note above.

32–3 *God ... Apostle ... King*] Although THIS EDITION normally ignores changes of fount when they represent only an obsolete printing convention—for instance, in a text set in roman, the use of italics for proper names—in this text italics and emphasis capitals are used liberally for common and abstract nouns, apparently as a form of emphasis. THIS EDITION therefore preserves this feature for *Peacemaker*, although in other respects its text has been modernized in accordance with general editorial procedures for the *Collected Works* as a whole.

35 practice] PURFOOT1 (*practique*)

42 fifteen] PURFOOT1(A) (Fifteene); Sixteene PURFOOT2(B). The change to 'Sixteene', in coordination with the anniversary of James I's accession to the English throne, 24 March,

presumably stands as a record of the printer's attention to a detail of dating; yet parallel changes in the references to James I's age were not made at ll. 67 and 68.

53 O] PURFOOT1 (ô)

63 substitute] PURFOOT1(B); *subftitue* PURFOOT1(A)

69 O] PURFOOT1 (ô)

97 O] PURFOOT1 (Oh)

105 Suecia, Suecia] THIS EDITION; *Sueuia, Sueuia* PURFOOT1; Suevia, Suecia BULLEN. Copies of all early editions read 'Sueuia', but there can be little doubt that *Suecia* (Sweden) is intended in both references. James I was not involved in diplomatic missions concerning *Sueuia* (Swabia), but did engage in peacemaking efforts between Sweden and Denmark as well as between Sweden and Poland. Although a compositor's simple mistaking of a manuscript 'c' for a 'u' provides a plausible explanation for the error, the mistaken use of *Sueuia* in reference to Sweden was fairly common at this time.

105 Cleves] PURFOOT1 (*Cleue*). The original reading gives the Germanic spelling.

174 O] PURFOOT1 (ô)

185–6 Land of Promise] PURFOOT1 (land of promife). Capitalization, like italicization, for emphasis in PURFOOT–STANSBY1 and 2 is less than consistent. In many instances discrepancies are attributable to the split of the text between two printing establishments, as apparently in the case of 'Land of Promise'. Not capitalized in Purfoot's section, it is given capitals in two occurrences in Stansby's sheet E. In the present, as in other instances, an adjustment has been made in the interests of consistency.

209 Flamin. Consul.] PURFOOT1(B) (*set in margin opposite ll. 208–9*); *not in* PURFOOT1(A). The omission of the marginal commentary in the uncorrected LAMBETH copy in conjunction with a range of other differences unique to this copy indicates that the state of its inner B represents an earlier stage of printing than all others. Placement of the reference in the margin was apparently designed to avoid the need to disturb and reformat type that had already been set.

213 Absalom] PURFOOT1 (*Absolon*)

216 Ezek. 13:10] PURFOOT1(B) (*set in margin opposite ll. 214–15*); *not in* PURFOOT1(A). See note to l. 209 above. The same spacing constraints dictating placement in the margin apply in this instance also.

251 Ham] PURFOOT1 (*Cham*)

260–771 *Alexander ... FINIS*] STANSBY1–3. The section of the pamphlet comprising sheets C–E printed by Stansby begins at l. 260. This section is marked by a dramatic decrease in emphasis italics, probably attributable to some degree to the change of printer. But the tone of the pamphlet also undergoes a transformation at this point (a consequence in part of passages incorporating extensive borrowing from

Seneca and others in Stansby's section) and is less given to the kind of hortatory emphasis common in the first two sheets.

260 *carissimum*] STANSBY1 (*chariſſimum*)
261 wine-bowls] STANSBY1 (Wine-bolles)
262 O...O...O] STANSBY1 (Oh...Oh...Oh)
274 O] STANSBY1 (Oh)
279 O...O] STANSBY1 (Oh...Oh)
286 *chomets ben yayin*] STANSBY1 (*Homets Ben Iin*). STANSBY1's '*Homets Ben Iin*' offers a reasonable phonetic rendering of the Hebrew; the spelling has been regularized in conformity with modern convention.
291 *ægrum*] STANSBY1 (*egrum*). The STANSBY1 spelling, '*egrum*', may have been influenced by the spelling of 'vinegar'; but the initial 'e' has been replaced by the ligature, 'æ', for consonance with '*ægrotum*'.
292 unwholesome] STANSBY1 (unholsome)
296 O] STANSBY1 (Oh)
302 O] STANSBY1 (Oh)
303 Etna] STANSBY1 (*Ætna*)
303 *et*] STANSBY1 (*&*)
310 O] STANSBY1 (Oh)
318 arbiter] STANSBY1 (arbitrer). The form, 'arbitrer', that appears in STANSBY1 and subsequent early editions, if an accurate rendering of the manuscript, derives from the Latin word, '*arbiter*' via Old French. But since the collateral but more widely used form, 'arbiter', occurs at l. 678, and in a similar context of justice serving in the capacity of a judge, preservation of both forms seems inappropriate. 'Arbiter' has accordingly been normalized to agree with the subsequent usage, which became the common literary (as opposed to legal) term from about this time.
323 O] STANSBY1 (Oh)
343 distracted] STANSBY1 (diſtraughted); diſtraughed STANSBY2. The misspelled variant, 'diſtraughed', in STANSBY2 was generated in the process of resetting.
355 *Peace.*] STANSBY1 ((*Peace:*))
413 burdensome] STANSBY1 (burthensome)
423 as] STANSBY1(s); so STANSBY2(R). The compositor may have been influenced by another instance of 'ſo' earlier in the same line on the occasion of resetting C4ᵛ.
451 attending] STANSBY1(s); attend STANSBY2(R). Between impressions of STANSBY1 and STANSBY2 two pages, D1 and D2ᵛ, in outer D were reset. Running-title analysis together with evidence of type damage establishes that the state of the page containing 'attending' (D1) is the original and that the state containing 'attend' (together with a number of relatively inconsequential spelling variants) is reset. The titles found in outer D in the LAMBETH, PETYT, TEXAS, and four 1619 STANSBY2 copies differ from the titles in this forme in the BL1, and the remaining five 1619 STANSBY2 copies. Since the PETYT and four STANSBY2 copies are equipped with the same set of titles found in the LAMBETH and TEXAS copies, resetting must have taken place independent of and prior to replacement of the running titles. Further, the BL1 copy is unique among 1618 copies in carrying on D4ᵛ the running title, 'The Peac-meuker', that appears also on E3ᵛ. Since this title had originated on E3ᵛ, where it was spelled 'The Peace--muker', impressions must already have been taken of outer D prior to the title's transfer to D4ᵛ. Those impressions are represented by the alternate set of titles found in this forme. The set of titles found in the BL1 and five STANSBY2 copies thus reveals that the state of D1 and D2ᵛ in these copies must be the reset state since the same state is shared by the PETYT

and the remaining four STANSBY2 copies, which are equipped with the set of titles found also on copies containing the alternate state of the forme. As the latter state of D1 and D2ᵛ is exclusive to the LAMBETH and TEXAS copies, this state must be the original. Evidence of type damage in standing-type pages of outer D conforms to the findings of running-title analysis. The presumption of the present edition is that the earlier state, in standing in closer relation to the manuscript, has greater authority, a presumption bolstered by numerous errors of various kinds encountered in reset type in this and other formes.

514 latterness] STANSBY1 (laterness)
525 precedents] STANSBY1 (Preſidents)
551 However] STANSBY1 (How euer)
613-14 Rumour's...tongues] BULLEN; Rumors, tenne thouſand tongues, STANSBY1. The conventional emblematic figure of Rumour adorned with many tongues and eyes (cf. Prologue to Shakespeare, *2 Henry IV*) promotes acceptance of the *ten thousand tongues* as attributes of this representation rather than entities grouped collectively with *rumours*. STANSBY1's comma after *Rumors* possibly derives from a misread apostrophe.
617-18 'The voice...earth'] STANSBY1 (*The voice of thy Brothers Bloud cryeth vnto me from the Earth*)
635-6 John 1:29] THIS EDITION; Iohn 11.29 STANSBY1. Probably a simple compositorial error.
651-2 evangelist (John 14:16)] THIS EDITION; Euangeliſt, 16, 17 STANSBY1. The citations for both of the subsequent New Testament references are given together in STANSBY1 and 2; for clarity they have been separated.
656 following (John 14:17)] THIS EDITION; Euangeliſt, 16, 17 (ll. 651-2) STANSBY1. See note to ll. 651-2 above.
657 (John 14:26)] THIS EDITION; *Name, 26.* STANSBY1. As with several other citations, Stansby's arrangement is potentially confusing; the reference has been expanded and repositioned in the interests of clarity.
658-9 He comes...Saviour] THIS EDITION; *26. hee comes all Peace, and in the name of Peace, of Chriſt our Sauior* STANSBY1. The use of italics in conjunction with a preceding verse number suggests a scriptural citation; but no Biblical passage matches the italicized words. The italics in the preceding line presumably influenced the compositor's continued use of italics for the remainder of the paragraph.
683 Pacem] STANSBY1+2(s); *Pacent* STANSBY3(R)(A); *Pacem* STANSBY3(R)(B). The variant reading '*Pacent*', which springs from resetting, is manifestly wrong. Since the copy-text used for resetting was apparently STANSBY2, the error is difficult to account for unless a result of simple compositorial misreading, possibly rendered more plausible if the compositor had no Latin.
684 *vitiis*] STANSBY1 (*vitijs*); *vitjs* STANSBY2(R). The four lines at the top of E2ᵛ display signs of disturbance—different spacing and about a line and a half of resetting that includes at least the final letters of '*vitjs*'. The erroneous spelling arose as a result of resetting.
685 *et*] STANSBY1 (*&*)
693 Judg. 5:8] STANSBY1 (*Iudg. 5. vers. 8.*)
714 letst] STANSBY1 (lett'ſt)
718 Lev.] STANSBY1 (*Leuiticus*)
720 Promise] STANSBY1+2(s) (Promiſe); *Paradiſe* STANSBY3(R)(A); Promiſe STANSBY3(R)(B). As in the case cited above (l. 683), the variant reading in reset type, '*Paradiſe*', is puzzling if, as might be expected, the printed text of STANSBY2 were used as copy. But perhaps the 'm' was

imperfectly printed in the STANSBY2 copy that served as copy-text. Alternatively, the compositor may have been influenced by the memory of a competing biblical reference.

The return to the correct reading, 'Promiſe', was occasioned by a further resetting of E2^v and E3.

PRESS VARIANTS

Included among copies of *The Peacemaker* collated are all those impressed from standing type employed initially for PURFOOT–STANSBY1. The disposition of reset pages, formes, and sheets in individual copies is itemized parenthetically following the imprint date in the list below.

The following copies were collated (abbreviations listed on the left); shelfmarks, where available, distinguish multiple copies in a single location:

BL1 British Library copy 1: C.123.c.12 (3); 1618 (D1, D2^v, D3^v, D4 reset)

BL2 British Library copy 2: C.123.c.12 (4); 1619 (C, D, outer E, E4 reset)

BOD1 Bodleian Library copy 1: 4° Art.L.66 (8); 1619 (C2^v, C4, C4^v, D1, D2^v, D3^v, D4 reset)

BOD2 Bodleian Library copy 2: Ashm. 735 (7); 1619 (C2^v, C4, C4^v, D1, D2^v, D3^v, D4 reset)

BOD3 Bodleian Library copy 3: Pamph. C.16 (4); 1619 (C, D, outer E, E4 reset)

CAMBRIDGE Cambridge University Library; 1619 (C, D, most of E except for part of E3^v in a reset state different from all others)

CHR.C. Christ Church College, Oxford; 1619 (C2^v, C4, C4^v, D1, D2^v, D3^v, D4 reset)

COR.C. Corpus Christi College, Oxford; 1619 (C2^v, C4, C4^v, D1, D2^v, D3^v, D4 reset)

EMMANUEL Emmanuel College, Cambridge; 1619 (C, D, outer E, E4 reset)

EXETER Exeter College, Oxford; 1619 (C2^v, C4, C4^v, D1, D2^v, D3^v, D4, outer E, E4 reset)

GLASGOW Glasgow Public Library; 1619 (C, D, outer E, E4 reset)

KENT University of Kent Library; 1619 (C, D, outer E, E4 reset)

LAMBETH Lambeth Palace Library; 1618

PETYT Public Library, Skipton, Yorkshire (Petyt Library); 1618 (C2^v, C4, C4^v, D1, D2^v, D3^v, D4 reset)

PLUME Plume Library, Maldon, Essex; 1619 (C2^v, C4, C4^v, D1, D2^v, D3^v, D4 reset)

YORK1 York Minster Library copy 1; 1619 (C2^v, C4, C4^v, D1, D2^v, D3^v, D4 reset)

YORK2 York Minster Library copy 2; 1619 (C2^v, C4, C4^v, D1, D2^v, D3^v, D4 reset)

YORK3 York Minster Library copy 3; 1619 (C, D, outer E, E4 reset)

FOLGER Folger Shakespeare Library; 1619 (C, D, outer E, E4 reset)

GTS St. Mark's Library, General Theological Seminary, N.Y.; 1619 (C2^v, C4, C4^v, D1, D2^v, D3^v, D4 reset)

HARVARD Harvard University Library; 1619 (C, D, outer E, E4 reset)

HUNTINGTON Henry E. Huntington Library; 1619 (C, D, outer E, E4 reset)

MCGILL McGill University Library; 1619 (C, D, outer E, E4 reset)

NEWBERRY Newberry Library, Chicago; 1619 (C, D, outer E, E4 reset)

NYPL New York Public Library; 1619 (C, D, outer E, E4 reset)

TEXAS University of Texas Library; 1618 (D3^v, D4 reset)

YALE Yale University Library; 1619 (C, D, outer E, E4 reset)

The sequence of impression of stages marked with an asterisk (*) is unclear; the order may be different from that set out below.

1. **Variants in** PURFOOT–STANSBY1

Sheet A (*outer forme*)

First Stage Corrected: BL1, PETYT
Uncorrected: LAMBETH

A3

on a line below headpiece   *omitted corr*; By the King. *uncorr*
13   peace] *Peace corr*; *Peace uncorr*
16   purchaser] *purchaſer corr*; *Purchaſer uncorr*

A4^v

66   sanctuary] *Sanĉtuarie corr*; *Sanĉtuarie uncorr* (roman/italic variant)

Second Stage Corrected: TEXAS

A4^v

63   substitute] *fubſtitute corr*; *fubſtitue uncorr*
69   celebrated] *celebrated corr*; *celebrared uncorr*

Third Stage Corrected: COR.C., GTS, PLUME, YORK1

A4^v

45   islands] *Ilands corr*; *Iſlands uncorr*
45   glad] *glad*; *corr*; *~, uncorr*
47   thee] *thee*; *corr*; *~, uncorr*
48   confines] *confines*; *corr*; *~, uncorr*
49   climate.] *clymate*: *corr*; *~; uncorr*
52   gates:] *Gates*, *corr*; *~, uncorr*

Fourth Stage Corrected: BL2, BOD1–3, CAMBRIDGE, CHR.C., EM-MANUEL, EXETER, FOLGER, GLASGOW, HARVARD, HUNTINGTON, KENT, MCGILL, NEWBERRY, NYPL, YALE, YORK2+3

A3

8   To] To *with crisp new 'T' corr*; To *with damaged 'T' uncorr*

A4^v

52   there's] *ther's corr*; *ther,s uncorr*

Sheet A (*inner forme*)

First Stage Corrected: PETYT
Uncorrected: LAMBETH

A2

imprint   PVRFOOT: *corr*; *~. uncorr*
10   Cum Privilegio.] Cum Priuilegio. *corr*; *omitted uncorr*

A3^v

21   embraced] *embraſt corr*; *embracſt uncorr*

A4

headpiece   *urn flanked by mythological figures corr*; *Prince of Wales's coat of arms uncorr*

Second Stage Corrected: BL1

A2

imprint   *An. Dom:* corr; *Anno Dom:* uncorr
10   Cum Privilegio.] CVM PRIVILEGIO. corr; Cum Priuilegio. *uncorr*

Third Stage Corrected: TEXAS

A2

10   Cum Privilegio.] CVM PRIVILEGIO. corr; CVM PRIVILEGIO. *uncorr (spacing variant)*

A3^v

21   cheerfulness] *cheerfulnes* corr; *cheerefulneffe uncorr*
21   freeness] *freeneffe* corr; *freenes uncorr*
21   embraced] *embraced* corr; *embraft uncorr*
22   Our] *Our* corr; *our uncorr*
23   power] *Power,* corr; *~_∧ uncorr*
23   it] *it?* corr; *~, uncorr*
25   friend] *Friend* corr; *Freind uncorr*
28   We] *We* corr; *we uncorr*

A4

39   and only] and only *corr;* & ~ *uncorr*
44   handmaid] hand-maid *corr;* handmaid *uncorr*

Fourth Stage Corrected: BOD1, COR.C., YORK1

A2

imprint date   1619 corr; 1618 *uncorr*

A3^v

22   having] *hauing* corr; *hauiug uncorr*

Fifth Stage Corrected: GTS, PLUME

A4

headpiece   *inverted* corr; *right-side up uncorr*

Sixth Stage Corrected: FOLGER

A2

6   conformation] *conformation* corr; *confirmation uncorr*

A3^v

18   preserve] *preferue* corr; *practife uncorr*
24   and] & corr; and *uncorr*

A4

headpiece   *right-side up* corr; *inverted uncorr*

Seventh Stage Corrected: BL2, BOD2+3, CAMBRIDGE, CHR.C., EM-MANUEL, EXETER, GLASGOW, HARVARD, HUNTINGTON, KENT, MCGILL, NEWBERRY, NYPL, YALE, YORK2+3

A4

42   fifteen] Sixteene *corr;* Fifteene *uncorr*

Sheet B (inner forme)

First Stage Corrected: BL1
Uncorrected: LAMBETH

B1^v

96   Solomon] *Salomon* corr; *Salomon uncorr (roman/italic variant)*

B2

117   Peace] *Peace* corr; *Peace uncorr*
119   Peace] *Peace* corr; *Peace uncorr*
122   Peace] *Peace* corr; *Peace uncorr*

125   we] wee *corr;* Wee *uncorr*
125   and] and *corr;* & *uncorr*

B3^v

189   tranquillity] tranquillity *corr;* tranquility *uncorr*
192   Envy] *Envy* corr; *Euvy uncorr*
193   her;] her; *corr;* ~, *uncorr*
197   with her] with her; *corr;* ~ ~, *uncorr*
198   Pride] *Pride* corr; *pride uncorr*
198   overthrow] ouerthrow | corr; o-|uerthrow *uncorr*
199   yea] yea *corr;* I *uncorr*
199   oily] oylie *corr;* oyly *uncorr*
199   dangerous] dan-|gerous *corr;* dangerous | *uncorr*
199   enemy] enemie *corr;* enemy *uncorr*
199   Hypocrisy,] *Hypocrifie,* corr; *~_∧ uncorr*
200   to strangle her;] to | ftrangle her, *corr;* to ftrangle her, | *uncorr*
200   still shall] ftill fhall *corr;* ftil fhal *uncorr*
200–1   stand, and] ftand, and *corr;* ~_∧ & *uncorr*
201   and reign, and conquer. Invidiam] and raigne, | and conquer. *Inuidiam* corr; & raigne_∧ & conquer. Inuidi-|am *uncorr*
201–2   shall mount to *heaven* and] fhall | mount to *Heauen,* and *corr;* fhall mount to *Heauen,* and | *uncorr*
202–3   low as *hell,* where *peace*] low | as *Hell,* where *peace* corr; low as *Hell,* where *peace* | *uncorr*
209   (Flamin. Consul.)] *Flamin.* | *Conful.* corr; *omitted uncorr*
210   mischief] mifchiefe *corr;* mifchief *uncorr*
210   breast] breft *corr;* breaft *uncorr*

B4

211   peace] *peace* corr; peace *uncorr*
211   doubts] doubts, *corr;* ~_∧ *uncorr*
211   horrors;] hor-|rors; *corr;* hor-|rors, *uncorr*
216   (Ezek. 13:10)] *Comm. Ezech.* | 13.10. corr; *omitted uncorr*

Second Stage Corrected: BOD1+3, COR.C., EMMANUEL, GTS, PETYT, PLUME, TEXAS, YORK1

B2

129   go] goe *corr;* go *uncorr*

B4

213   father's] fathers *corr;* Fathers *uncorr*
213   thy] Thy *corr;* thy *uncorr*
221   sung it;] fung it; *corr;* ~ ~, *uncorr*
221   the Father] The Father *corr;* the ~ *uncorr*
221   hath sent it;] hath | fent it; *corr;* hath fent | it, *uncorr*
221   the Son] The Son *corr;* the ~ *uncorr*
221   brought it;] brought it; *corr;* ~ ~, *uncorr*
222   the blessed Dove shall] The bleffed | Doue fhall *corr;* the bleffed Doue fhall | *uncorr*
222–3   with it; our anointed] with it; | our Annointed *corr;* with it, our Annoin-|ted *uncorr*
223   enjoy it, and see it] enioy | it, and fee it *corr;* enioy it, and fee it | *uncorr*
231   scent] fcent *corr;* fent *uncorr*

Third Stage Corrected: BL2, BOD2, CAMBRIDGE, CHR.C., EXETER, FOLGER, GLASGOW, HARVARD, HUNTINGTON, KENT, MCGILL, NEWBERRY, NYPL, YALE, YORK2+3

B2

121.n   Detraction to Peace] *Comm. Detractiõ* | *to Peace.* repositioned lower in margin corr; ~ | ~ ~. positioned higher in margin *uncorr*

129.n Peace answers] *Comm. Peace* | *answers. repositioned lower in margin corr;* ~ | *~. positioned higher in margin uncorr*

Sheet D (outer forme)

Corrected: BL1, BOD1, COR.C., GTS, PLUME, YORK1
Uncorrected: BOD2, CHR.C., EXETER, LAMBETH, PETYT, TEXAS, YORK2

D4^v

running title *Peac-meuker corr; Peace-maker uncorr*

Sheet E (outer forme)

Partially Reset: BOD1+2, CHR.C., COR.C., GTS, PLUME, YORK1+2
Original: BL1, LAMBETH, PETYT, TEXAS

E2^v

684 vitiis] *vitjs corr; vitijs uncorr*
685 the] *thc corr; the uncorr*

Sheet E (inner forme)

First Stage Corrected: LAMBETH, TEXAS
Uncorrected: BL1, PETYT

E3^v

running title *Peace-maker corr; Peace-muker uncorr*

Second Stage Corrected: BOD1+2, CHR.C., COR.C., EXETER, GTS, PLUME, YORK1+2

E3^v

running title *Peac-meuker corr; Peace-maker uncorr*

2. Variants in Reset Pages

This section shows the relationship of the reset pages of STANSBY2 sheets C and D to the original settings of STANSBY1.

Sheet C

Sigs. C2^v and C4^v in outer C and C4 in inner C exist in original (STANSBY1) and reset (STANSBY2) states; the remaining pages of the respective formes in STANSBY2 are standing type held over from STANSBY1.

Sheet C (outer forme)

Reset: BOD1+2, CHR.C., COR.C., EXETER, PETYT, PLUME, YORK1+2, GTS
Original: BL1, LAMBETH, TEXAS

C2^v

326 fearful] *Feareful reset; Fearefull orig*
326-7 spectacle!] *Spectacle! reset;* ~! *orig*
335 neither] *neither reset; neyther orig*
337 he] *hee reset; he orig*
343 distracted] *diftraughed reset; diftraughted orig*

C4^v

412 thereunto] *therunto reset; thereunto orig*
413 Quis] *Quis reset; Quis orig* (roman/italic variant)
417 wise man] *wifeman reset; wife man orig*
423 as] *fo reset; as orig*
425 will] *wil reset; will orig*
426 wise man] *wifeman reset; wife man orig*
427 contumely] *Cõtumely reset; Contumely orig*

Sheet C (inner forme)

Reset: BOD1+2, CHR.C., COR.C., EXETER, PETYT, PLUME, YORK1+2, GTS
Original: BL1, LAMBETH, TEXAS

C4

390 be] *bee reset; be orig*
395 and] *& reset; and orig*
396 injury] *iniurie reset; Iniurie orig*
397 injuries] *iniuries reset; Iniuries orig*
398 he] *hee reset; he orig*
410 injury] *iniurie reset;* ~, *orig*

Sheet D

Sigs. D1 and D2^v in outer D and D3^v and D4 in inner D exist in original (STANSBY1) and reset (STANSBY2) states; the remaining pairs of pages in each forme are preserved in standing type from STANSBY1.

Sheet D (outer forme)

Reset: BL1, BOD1+2, CHR.C., COR.C., EXETER, PETYT, PLUME, YORK1+2, GTS
Original: LAMBETH, TEXAS

D1

436 bull] *Bul reset; Bull orig*
437 another,] *another; reset;* ~, *orig*
439 we. We] *we. We reset; wee. Wee orig*
440 we] *we reset; wee orig*
448 let us] *let | vs reset; let vs | orig*
449 dangerous] *dan-|gerous reset; dange-|rous orig*
450 injuries and] *Iniuries | and reset; Iniuries and | orig*
451 we may] *we | may reset; we may | orig*
451 attending] *attend reset; attending orig*
453 drunken] *druuken reset; drunken orig*
458 strokes] *ftroks reset; ftrokes orig*

D2^v

510 kept for] *kept for | reset; kept | for orig*
510-11 and the] *and the | reset; and | the orig*
511 England] *England | reset; Eng-|land orig*
512 close together] *clofe | together reset; clofe to-|gether orig*
516 Jewish] *Iewifh reset; Jewifh orig*
516-17 Jerusalem] *Ierufalem reset; Ierufalem orig*
523 be] *bee reset; be orig*

Sheet D (inner forme)

Reset: BL1, BOD1+2, CHR.C., COR.C., EXETER, PETYT, PLUME, YORK1+2, GTS, TEXAS
Original: LAMBETH

D3^v

549 praises] *Prayfes reset; prayfes orig*
554 Happy] *Happy reset; Happie orig*
555 he can] *hee can reset; he can orig*
555 neither] *neither reset; neyther orig*
556 reputation] *Reputa-|tion reset; Repu-|tation orig*

D4

574 and] *& reset; and orig*
577 blasphemy] *Blafphemy reset; Blafphemie orig*
catchword flection,] *flection, reset;* ~, *orig*

THE WORLD TOSSED AT TENNIS

Edited by C. E. McGee

THE publication of *A Courtly Masque: The Device called The World Tossed at Tennis* (BEPD 365; STC 17909, 17910) was originally a joint venture of George Purslowe, John Trundle, and Edward Wright. The book was entered in the Stationers' Register on 4 July 1620: 'Ent. G. Purslowe and J. Trundle: lic. G. Bucke: a booke called A Courtly Masque, or The World Tossed at Tennis, acted at the Princes Arms, by the Prince his Highnes servantes.' Although this particular book is not typical of the list of George Purslowe, printer and bookseller whose shop was at the east end of Christ Church (probably in Fowl Lane), it does suit the interests of John Trundle, a London bookseller who regularly invested in 'ballads, news-books, plays and ephemeral literature' (McKerrow, 269). The long list of religious tracts normally published by Purslowe is punctuated from time to time by more topical, secular pamphlets, many printed for John Trundle. The 1620 list of Purslowe books for Trundle, for example, included not only *Tennis* but also the broadside ballad, *A Merry Catch for All Trades* (STC 4793), and *Westward for Smelts* (STC 25292), a collection of traditional fishwives' tales.

Four different states of the first edition of *Tennis*, a quarto of six sheets, can be identified: the first by the lack of an illustrated title-page; the second by a title-page with original woodcut. Copies in this second category can be further divided into those without stop-press corrections, one with most of them, two with all.

Using the term 'issue' somewhat loosely, the STC identifies two issues of *Tennis* on the basis of the variant title-pages. The first 'issue' (STC 17909), of which only one copy is extant (British Library C.34.g.5), is unique in the format, generic block, and imprint of its title-page:

A | COVRTLY | MASQVE: | THE DEVICE | CALLED | The VVorld toſt at Tennis. | *As it hath beene diuers times Preſented* | to the Contentment of many Noble and | *Worthy Spectators,* | [rule] *By the* PRINCE *his Seruants.* | [rule] Inuented, and ſet | downe, By | [bracket] Tho: Middleton | & | William Rowley | [bracket] Gent. | [ornament] LONDON | Printed by *George Purſlowe*, and are to be ſold by *Edward* | *Wright*, at Chriſt Church Gate. 1620.

For the second 'issue' (STC 17910), the title-page was reset to accommodate a woodcut (reproduced above) representing the globe surrounded by characters from the masque. However, the variant title-page and the stop-press corrections evident in three of the ten copies of STC 17910 do not make it, strictly speaking, a separate 'issue'; there is no evidence of distinct setting of any substantial part of

the book. Thus, the extant copies of *Tennis* constitute one issue of a single edition.

The first setting of the title-page of *Tennis* establishes Edward Wright's involvement as a distributor in this publishing venture. The imprint indicates that copies of the masque 'are to be ſold by *Edward Wright*, at Chriſt Church Gate'. When the title-page was reset, Purslowe's compositor deleted 'Edward Wright' from the imprint (thereby introducing an error in all subsequent copies: 'to be ſold by at [*sic*] Chriſt Church Gate'). Given the size of the woodcut evidently commissioned for *Tennis*, the reset title-page was more crowded than the first one, with the result that several copies of the book had parts of the imprint, the title, or the woodcut cropped. Still, since good exemplars of the second title-page have a line with only 'Church Gate. 1620.' on it, Wright's name could have been accommodated. Purslowe probably decided that naming Wright was unnecessary, 'at Christ Church Gate' being in itself sufficient to identify Edward Wright's shop (see STC 3:247, location C.1).

Stop-press corrections characterize the final states of the book. The unique copy of STC 17909 and most copies of STC 17910 (British Library C.34.d.45; Bodleian; Dyce; Folger; Huntington [both copies]; Worcester College) lack these corrections. Of the corrected copies (British Library 162.d.38, Houghton, Library of Congress), those at the British Library and the Houghton Library have several changes not made in the Library of Congress copy. Purslowe's compositor(s) must have worked with a relatively clean copy of the manuscript, for the printed text of *Tennis* is remarkably free of errors in transmission. Considerable care was also taken, perhaps by the authors, in the very first stages of the printing process, for the extant copies provide only a few instances of the gradual incorporation of stop-press corrections. The corrections, all but two found on the inner forme of sig. D, could have been made by alert proofreaders. Some changes eliminate obvious errors ('itch' for 'tich' [481] or 'Simplicity' for 'Simlcity' [452]) while others normalize the style ('Bleſſed Times' for 'bleſſed times' [361]). Some crucial substantive variants may also have resulted from the proofreading. The change of 'Maieſty' to 'Maſtry' (506) for example, a change which confirms the masque's resistance to representations of monarchy as absolute and alters significantly the characterization of the King and the monarchial government he represents, was likely caused by a compositor's error in following copy. It is hard to imagine, however, that a compositor could have misread the manuscript's 'Reapers' as 'ſecond' (484.1) or 'after him' as 'and'

(499.1). Neither the titles of the other songs nor other similar stage directions establish a consistent pattern to justify these substantive changes, which make the heading more descriptive of the song and the stage direction more precise about the blocking. Perhaps Middleton and Rowley, either through revisions registered in the manuscript but not easily deciphered or through more direct, ongoing involvement in the publishing process, required these corrections. If the authors were consulted concerning the details of the woodcut (see Astington, above, p. 226), they may also have been involved throughout the proofreading stage of the publication. Such involvement would help explain the cleanliness of the printed text of the masque and the consistency of the several surviving copies of it.

How many compositors worked on the typesetting of *Tennis* is not clear. Changes in speech prefixes occur within formes: for example, on C1 (66–86) the Soldier and the Scholar are identified as '*Sold*' and '*Sch*'; the same abbreviations are used for the first twelve lines of C1^V (87–98), at which point '*Sould*' (98) and '*Schol*' (100) are introduced. Similarly, the compositor replaces '*King*' on F1 (811) with '*K*' on F1^V and F2 (826–55). If more than one compositor set the book, they collaborated in ways that make it difficult to discern their various shares in the project.

The several states of *Tennis* exhibit various accretions that would distinguish the printed book of the masque from a hypothetical script set down for an intended performance at Denmark House: a prologue and epilogue composed for productions in a public theatre (as opposed to Prince Charles's new London palace); an epistle addressed to readers; a reset title-page with a special woodcut; and a text incorporating stop-press variants. A few other substantive revisions may have been made by the authors when adapting the original script for performance in a public playhouse, but in the absence of an earlier Denmark House script, there is no basis by which to demonstrate such revision, no firm ground for G. E. Bentley's confident conclusion: 'No doubt the piece was altered from its orthodox courtly form for theatre presentation when it was found that the Denmark House performance would not take place.' Arguments for revision take the Jonsonian form of the masque as normative. But the masque as a genre was not narrowly prescriptive—particularly not in this period. From 1617 through 1621, a series of experiments with the masque as a form took place: the girls' school masque, *Cupid's Banishment* (1617); the masque at Coleorton (1618) with its nostalgia for Elizabethan Protestantism; Gray's Inn's 'First Antemasque of Mountebanks' (1618); the 'running masque' repeated at least five times at Christmas 1619–20; the masque for the French ambassadors which was marred, in Chamberlain's opinion, by the entrance of a Puritan who was brought in to be mocked and abused (1621); and *The Gypsies Metamorphosed* adapted for three venues during one summer progress. The oddity of *Tennis*, yet another experiment with the form of the masque, need

not imply that the show was radically reshaped to get it ready for the public theatre.

At one point in the text, a trace of Denmark House staging seems clear. The Stationers' Register specifies 'the Princes Arms' as the venue for performances of *Tennis*. Three years later, in an entry allowing certain 'Italian motions' (*BEPD* 365, note), the Prince's Arms is identified as 'the Swan'. The Swan, however, *if* De Witt's sketch of the playhouse is reasonably accurate, could not have accommodated the entrance of the Worthies as prescribed by the stage direction, which requires that they enter three by three 'at the three seuerall doores' (280.1; see textual note). De Witt's picture of the Swan has, of course, only two doors. This stage direction is problematic in another respect: it is the only one in *Tennis* set in roman; the only one with the verb set in italics and the character's name, Pallas, in small capitals; the only one in which each line is centred. The other stage directions are set as blocks, in italics, with names in roman. This odd stage direction, both in the action it calls for and in its graphic design, seems to be one remnant of the staging projected for Denmark House.

The entire scene with the Muses and the Worthies could have been produced more easily at Denmark House than at the Swan. The stage direction preceding the first song and dance calls for the discovery '*on the vpper Stage*' of the nine Muses '*plac'd by the nine Worthies*' (266.2–3). The array of so many characters seems clearly designed not for the rooms above and behind the Swan stage, but for a large, raised, purpose-built scene such as those employed in the production of masques in great halls. Shakespeare's plays, according to Richard Hosley, never call for more than nine actors 'above'; on average, scenes there require three or four players. The maximum number of characters grouped above in plays barely surpasses the minimum number arrayed on the raised platforms of masque sets. And on a two-tiered scene, such as that for Francis Beaumont's *Masque of the Inner Temple and Gray's Inn* (1613), twenty-seven performers, twelve priests of Jupiter plus fifteen Olympian knights (not to mention an altar, four statues, and two pavilions), could be set forth.

Though more easily and probably more elegantly staged at Denmark House, the Worthies scene could still have been done in accordance with the surviving stage directions at the Swan. The theatre had the rooms above and behind the stage for the discovery of a large, massed group of characters, identified by the speeches as the Muses and the Worthies. If revealed as a stationary tableau rather than as a series of characters processing through the Swan's 'upper stage', the performers would undoubtedly have been crowded, but two rows of nine (the Muses in front of the Worthies) could have occupied the space where De Witt draws eight people on one plane. Such a crowd would not have been unlike Middleton, who was more inclined than Shakespeare to test the limits of the 'upper stage'; hence, the stage direction in *Women Beware* 5.1.37.1–3 implying a gathering of at least ten players above, the four characters named along with other

Cardinals, Lords, and Ladies. Having descended the stairs behind the stage and entered by the Swan's two doors, the characters could easily form the required groups of three as they began to proceed downstage; indeed, it is possible, though unlikely, that the three doors built for the set at Denmark House were transported to the Swan. Once the characters have reached the main platform and re-grouped in threes, Pallas's speech introducing them and setting up their dance would function at the Swan exactly as it would have at Denmark House.

SEE ALSO

Text: *Works*, 1408
Authorship and date: this volume, 408

WORKS CITED

Previous Editions

Bullen, A. H., ed., *Works* (1886), vol. 7
Dyce, Alexander, ed., *Works* (1840), vol. 5

Other Works Cited

Arnold, Janet, 'Three Examples of Late Sixteenth and Early Seventeenth Century Neckware', *Waffen vnd Kostumkunde* (1973), 109–24
Bentley, Gerald Eades, *The Jacobean and Caroline Stage*, 7 vols, vol. 4 (1956)
Butler, Martin, 'Ben Jonson's *Pan's Anniversary* and the Politics of Early Stuart Pastoral', *English Literary Renaissance* 22 (1992), 369–404
Chamberlain, John, *The Letters of John Chamberlain*, ed. Norman Egbert McClure, 2 vols (1939)
Colvin, H. M., *The History of the King's Works*, IV (2) (1982)
Fleay, F. G., *A Biographical Chronicle of the English Drama* (1891)
Furnivall, F. J., 'The Nine Worthies and the Heraldic Arms They Bore', *Notes and Queries*, VII, 8 (1889), 22–3
Gardiner, Samuel Rawson, ed., *Letters and Other Documents Illustrating the Relations between England and Germany at the Commencement of the Thirty Years War. Second Series: From the Election of the Emperor Ferdinand II to the Close of the Conferences at Muhlhausen*, Camden Society, First Series, vol. 98 (1868)
Greg, W. W., *A Bibliography of the English Printed Drama to the Restoration*, 4 vols (1951)
Heal, Felicity, 'The Idea of Hospitality in Early Modern England', *Past and Present* 102 (1984), 66–93
Heinemann, Margot, *Puritanism and Theatre: Thomas Middleton and Opposition Drama under the Early Stuarts* (1980)
Hibbard, G. R., 'The Country-House Poem of the Seventeenth Century', *Journal of the Warburg and Courtauld Institutes* 19 (1956), 159–74
Hosley, Richard, 'Shakespeare's Use of a Gallery over the Stage', *Shakespeare Survey* 10 (1957), 77–89
Hoy, Cyrus, 'The Shares of Fletcher and his Collaborators in the Beaumont and Fletcher Canon (V)', *Studies in Bibliography* 13 (1960), 77–108
McKerrow, R. B., *Dictionary of Printers and Booksellers* (1968)
Nichols, John, *The Progresses, Processions, and Magnificent Festivities of King James the First*, 4 vols (London, 1828)
Notestein, Wallace, *The English People on the Eve of Colonization* (1962)
Rastell, John, *Les Termes de la Ley* (1624)
Raylor, Timothy, *The Essex House Masque of 1621: Viscount Doncaster and the Jacobean Masque* (2000)
Robb, Dewar M., 'The Canon of William Rowley's Plays', *Modern Language Review* 45 (1950), 129–41
Stork, C. W., ed., *'All's Lost by Lust' and 'A Shoemaker a Gentleman'* (1910)
Wiggin, Pauline G., *An Inquiry into the Authorship of the Middleton–Rowley Plays* (1897)

TEXTUAL NOTES

Title-page   sold at Christ] DYCE; sold by at Chrift PURSLOWE; see Textual Introduction
Dedication.0.1   *The Epistle Dedicatory*] located atop sig. A3^V
Dedication.20   Thomas] PURSLOWE (THO:)
Epistle.0.1   *well-reading*] DYCE; -well reading PURSLOWE
Epistle.5   the device] DYCE; *The Deuice* PURSLOWE; the title-page clearly connects this phrase not to 'A Courtly Masque' but to the title that follows
Epistle.11   Brentford] PURSLOWE (*Braine-ford*); see Commentary
Prologue.8   she that] DYCE; *fhe* PURSLOWE
Induction.64   taloner] PURSLOWE (Talenter)
147   SOLDIER] DYCE; *Schol.* PURSLOWE
176   can] THIS EDITION; cap PURSLOWE; 'cup' and 'can' were frequently paired terms. Given the proximity of 'cup', a compositor might easily have erred in setting 'cap'. While it is unlikely that the Soldier could look forward to the high rank symbolized by a cap of maintenance, Pallas could promise that he would find in the city his individual portion ('cup') and an ongoing supply ('can')
280.1   *Enter . . . Worthies*] THIS EDITION; Enter at the three seuerall doores, the nine Worthies PURSLOWE. This part of the stage direction is likely a remnant of the staging planned for Denmark House. Had the set of *Tennis* been built there, the Muses and Worthies would probably have been arrayed on a representation of Mount Helicon, the three doors noted in the stage direction being in front of the base of the mountain. *The Masque of Flowers* (1613) provides a close parallel to the descent and entrance of the Worthies in *Tennis*; in *Flowers*, the masquers 'descend' from an arbour atop the set 'in a gallant march through three several doors of the arbour to the three several alleys of the garden, marching till they all met in the middle alley under the fountain, and from thence to the stage, where they fell into their first measure' (*A Book of Masques in Honour of Allardyce Nicoll* [Cambridge, 1967], p. 169). Although it is not impossible that the three doors were built for the planned performance of *Tennis* at Denmark House and then transported to the Swan, it is unlikely that this one feature of the set would have been moved and reassembled there. Given this improbability, and in the absence of evidence of three doors at the Swan, the entrance through three doors called for in the stage direction in *Tennis* was probably not a part of the first performance of this masque.
379   *frauchen*] Frokin PURSLOWE
407   *Starches*] Straches PURSLOWE
611   victual] vittaile PURSLOWE

633 make] DYCE; makes PURSLOWE
685.1 [an aedituus]] a— PURSLOWE; usage consistent with the arcane, Latin *flamen*
722 swooning] PURSLOWE (sowning); see 'sound', *OED v* 4.

734 'em] DYCE; omitted PURSLOWE
747.1–2 a pettifogger] n ~ PURSLOWE
753 le] *La* PURSLOWE
798 pois'nous] pois'nons PURSLOWE
870 be] THIS EDITION; *omitted* PURSLOWE

PRESS VARIANTS

All but the first two press variants found in the eleven extant copies of *Tennis* (1620) occur on the inner forme of sig. D. The following list registers first the lemma from this edition, then the item (marked PURSLOWEa) as it appears in the uncorrected copies of the book (British Library C34.g.5; British Library C.34.d.45; Bodleian Library, Oxford; Dyce Collection, National Art Library, Victoria and Albert Museum; Folger Shakespeare Library; Huntington Library; Worcester College, Oxford), and finally the item as it appears in corrected copies (British Library 162.d.38; Houghton Library, Harvard University; Library of Congress). Of the corrected copies, British Library 162.d.38 and the Houghton Library copy include four variants (at 266.7, 456, 467, and 499.1) not found in the Library of Congress copy; as a result, the Library of Congress copy (marked PURSLOWEb) appears to be an intermediate one between the uncorrected copies and British Library 162.d.38 and the Houghton Library copy (marked PURSLOWEc).

C (outer)

C4ᵛ

337 snoring] fnorting PURSLOWEa; fnoring PURSLOWEb–c

C (inner)

C4

266.7 *Joshua, etc.*] Iofhua, &c. PURSLOWEa–b; Iofhua. PURSLOWEc

D (inner)

D2

360 world] world PURSLOWEa; *World* PURSLOWEb–c
361 happiness. Blessed times] happineffe; bleffed times PURSLOWEa; happineffe, Bleffed Times PURSLOWEb–c
362 ugly ills] vgly ills PURSLOWEa; ougly Ills PURSLOWEb–c
364 goodness] goodneffe PURSLOWEa; Goodneffe PURSLOWEb–c
365 life—] life; PURSLOWEa; life, PURSLOWEb–c
366 humour, . . . toys] Humour, . . . toyes PURSLOWEa; Humor; . . . Toyes PURSLOWEb–c

368 frenzy . . . mad] phrenzie . . . mad, PURSLOWEa; Phrenzie . . . mad PURSLOWEb–c
369 settle, masculine painting,] fettle Mafculine painting, PURSLOWEa; fettle, Mafculine painting, PURSLOWEb–c
374.8 *Enter the fiue Starches.* PURSLOWEa (following *colours.*); *deleted from corrected version* PURSLOWEb–c
377 gossips] goffip PURSLOWEa; Goffips PURSLOWEb–c
378 primitive] primitiue PURSLOWEa; Primitiue PURSLOWEb–c
380 You, caudle-colour] You Cawdle-colour PURSLOWEa; You, Cawdle-colour PURSLOWEb–c

D3ᵛ

452 Simplicity] Simlcity PURSLOWEa; Simplicity PURSLOWEb–c
456 religions in] Religions together in PURSLOWEa; Religions er in PURSLOWEb; Religions in PURSLOWEc
457 His eyes] his | eyes PURSLOWEa; his eyes PURSLOWEb–c
464 world] world PURSLOWEa; World PURSLOWEb–c
467 pipe, I should] pipe, I | fhould PURSLOWEa–b; pipe, | I fhould PURSLOWEc
470 gone] go PURSLOWEa; gon PURSLOWEb–c
472 learned] learn'd PURSLOWEa; learn't PURSLOWEb–c
478 smack] fmatch PURSLOWEa; fmack PURSLOWEb–c

D4

481 gets but the itch] takes but the tich PURSLOWEa; gets but the itch PURSLOWEb–c
484.1 *Reapers'*] fecond PURSLOWEa; Reapers PURSLOWEb–c
487 age] age PURSLOWEa; Age PURSLOWEb–c
492 health] health PURSLOWEa; Health PURSLOWEb–c
499.1 *Enter King, after him Deceit*] Enter King and Deceit. PURSLOWEa; *Enter King after him Deceit.* PURSLOWEb; *Enter King: after him, Deceit.* PURSLOWEc
500 world] world PURSLOWEa; World PURSLOWEb–c
503 penalties] penalty PURSLOWEa; penaltyes PURSLOWEb–c
504 world] world PURSLOWEa; World PURSLOWEb–c
506 mast'ry] Maiefty PURSLOWEa; Maftry PURSLOWEb–c

STAGE DIRECTIONS

Persons.0.1–Persons.22
   The Figures, and Persons properly raysde for
     Employment through the whole
        MASQVE.

FIrst, Three Ancient and Princely Receptacles:
Richmond, Sᵗ. Iames's, Denmarke-House.

A Scholler. | A Souldier. { Pallas. | Iupiter. } The 9. Worthies. } The first Song, | and first Dance.

        Time, a Plaintiffe.
   But his grieuances deliuered courteously.

The fiue Starches: White, Blue, Yellow, Greene, and Red.
        The second Dance.

Simplicitie, | Deceit, { The Intermedler. | The Disguiser: }

The second Song sung by Reapers.

        A King.
     A Land-Captaine.
     A Sea-Captaine.
        Mariners.
   The third Song, and third Dance.

        The Flamen.
        The Lawyer.
The fourth and last Dance: the Diuell an Intermixer.
Induction.0.3 Enter *Richmond*, and Sᵗ. *Iames's*.
Induction.33.1 Enter *Denmarke-House*.
Induction.95 *Exeunt.*
0.2 Enter *Soldier, and Scholler*.
147.1 *Musique. Pallas descends.*

230.1   *Musique. Iupiter descends.*

266.1–10   *Musique and this Song as an Inuocation to the nine Muses; (who in | the time) are discouer'd on the vpper Stage, plac'd by the nine Wor-|thies, and toward the conclusion descend, each one led by a Muse, the | most proper and pertinent to the person of the Worthy, as* Therpsi-|chore *with* Dauid; Vrania, *with* Ioshua. | *After the Song* Pallas *describes them: Then daunce and Exeunt.* | *The first* SONG.

280.1–3   *Enter at the three seuerall doores, the nine Worthies, | three after three, whom (as they enter)* PALLAS *describes.*

297.1   *The Worthies Daunce; and Exeunt.*

308.1   *Enter Time.*

358   *Exit Time.*

374.1–8   *Musicke striking vp a light fantasticke Ayre, those 5. Starches afore | summon'd come dancing in, and after a ridiculous Straine, White-|Starch challenging precedency, standing vpon her right by An-|tiquity, out of her iust anger presents their pride to vm. | These 5. Starches, White, Blue, Yellow, Greene and Red, all properly ha-|bited to expresse their affected colours.*

407   *The Straches Dance, and Exeunt.*

415.1–6   *Musicke. | Loud Musicke sounding, Iupiter leaues his State; and to shew the | strange Remoues of the World, places the Orbe, whose figure it beares, | in the midst of the Stage: to whom Simplicity, by order of time, | has first accesse. | Enter Simplicity.*

422.1   *Takes vp the Orbe.*

434.1   *Enter Deceit like a Ranger.*

476   *Exit.*

484.1   *The Reapers* SONG.

499.1   *Enter King: after him, Deceit.*

526   *Exit Deceit.*

552.1   *Enter a Land-Captaine and Deceit as a Soldier.*

592   *Exit King.*

608.1   *Exit Deceit.*

624.1–2   *Chambers shot off: Enter a Sea-Captaine and Deceit as a Purser.*

670   *Exit Deceit.*

673.2   *The Mariners Song.*

682.1–3   *A shout within: then, Enter two Mariners with Pipe and Can dan-|cing seuerally by turnes, for ioy the World is come into their hands, | then Exeunt.*

685.1   *Enter a Flamin and Deceit like a—*

735.1   *Exit Deceit.*

747.1–2   *Flourish. Enter King, a Lawyer, and Deceit, as n Pettifog-ger.*

813.1–11   *In this last Dance, (as an ease to memory,) all the former Remooues, | come close together, the Diuell and Deceit ayming at the World, but | the World remaining now in the Lawyers possession, expressing his re-|uerend and noble acknowledgement to the absolute power of Maiesty | resignes it loyally to it's Royall Gouernment: Maiesty, to Valour; Va-|lour, to Law agen; Law to Religion; Religion, to Soueraignty; | where it firmely and fairely settles; The Law confounding Deceit, | and the Church, the Diuell.*

819.1   *They all deliuer the World vp to the King.*

825.1   *Exeunt Deceit | and the Diuell.*

855.1   *Exeunt.*

875.1   *Iupiter ascends.*

888.1   *Exeunt seuerally.*

Epilogue.9.1   FINIS.

LINEATION NOTES

Induction.1   Why ... heavy] PURSLOWE occupies a single type line, but whether it was intended as prose or verse remains ambiguous, as it does in DYCE

Induction.2–4   I ... too] not clearly prose or verse; the compositor, capitalizing 'lead' and using what seem to be line breaks after 'sister' and 'covered with', may have treated prose lines of the manuscript as verse so as to reduce the amount of white space on the page; DYCE first set as prose

Induction.5–7   All ... methinks] whether prose or verse remains ambiguous: now| methinks| PURSLOWE; DYCE first set as prose

Induction.12–13   Thou ... Richmond] THIS EDITION; *1 line* PURSLOWE; *prose* DYCE

Induction.16–17   Nay ... thyself] THIS EDITION; thou| PURSLOWE; *prose* DYCE

Induction.17–19   Thou ... grief] THIS EDITION; *prose* PURSLOWE

70–1   'Tis ... it] THIS EDITION; *1 line* PURSLOWE; DYCE: work| church|

71–2   Prithee ... scholar] DYCE; *1 line* PURSLOWE

73–4   Faith ... best] DYCE; *prose* PURSLOWE, unless the compositor used by mistake a lower-case *t* in 'that' at the start of the second line

141–2   We ... science] DYCE; *1 line* PURSLOWE

150–1   An ... now] THIS EDITION; *1 line* PURSLOWE; DYCE: one|

155–7   A patroness ... soldier] DYCE; *1 line* PURSLOWE

390–1   I ... Sanctity] DYCE; *1 line* PURSLOWE

416–18   Simplicity ... it] DYCE; *prose* PURSLOWE

571–2   How ... captain?] THIS EDITION; *3 lines* PURSLOWE: it is not certain whether 'How cheers our noble captain?' is the completion of l. 569 or the first part of the next line. This edition opts for rests after 'others' both to help the actor playing the King dramatize the process of determining how to negotiate with the challenging rhetorical questions of the Land-Captain and to accelerate the Land-Captain's sharp rejoinder ('Our own captain') to the King's construction of him ('our noble captain'); however, rests before and/or after 'Our own captain' remain playable possibilities that would effectively dramatize the initial conflict between the characters.

591–2   Give't ... treasurer] THIS EDITION; *1 line* PURSLOWE

755–6   All's ... that] THIS EDITION; *1 line* PURSLOWE

771–2   Yes ... again] THIS EDITION; *1 line* PURSLOWE; DYCE: you|

THE TRIUMPHS OF LOVE AND ANTIQUITY

Edited by David M. Bergeron

The Triumphs of Love and Antiquity (STC 17902; *BEPD* 359) has a distinctive rule line about midway down sig. D1. This line demarcates the end of Love's speech and therefore the end of the pageant proper. What follows—a poetic list of fur-bearing animals—exists only for readers in one of the most explicit typographical ways that the Middleton text signals the difference between the dramatic representation and additional material for readers.

The running titles on the inner forme of sheet B are reversed, leading to the verso of *Loue and Antiquity* and the recto of *The Triumphs of*. Press variants are few, scattered in all three sheets. Because no two of the collated copies agree completely, more than one round of press correction likely took place.

SEE ALSO

Text: *Works*, 1399
Authorship and date: this volume, 408

WORKS CITED

Previous Editions

The Progresses of King James the First, ed. John Nichols (1828), vol. 3

Thomas Middleton, *Works*, ed. Alexander Dyce (1840), vol. 5
Thomas Middleton, *Works*, ed. A. H. Bullen (1886), vol. 7

Other Works Cited

Abbot, George, to Sir Robert Naunton, in *Cabala, sive Scrinia sacra: Mysteries of State & Government* (1654), p. 169
Chamberlain, John, *The Letters of John Chamberlain*, ed. N. E. McClure, 2 vols (1939)
Donne, John, *The Sermons of John Donne*, ed. Evelyn M. Simpson and George R. Potter, 10 vols (1954)
Friis, Astrid, *Alderman Cockayne's Project and the Cloth Trade* (1927)
Gerard, G. to Sir Dudley Carlton, Public Record Office, CSPD 87/373, no. 57 (June 14, 1616)
Lodge, Thomas, *A Defence of Poetry, Music, and Stage Plays* (1579), in Smith, p. 1.75
Overall, W. H., ed., *Analytical Index to the 'Remembrancia'* (1876)
Puttenham, George, *The Arte of English Poesie*, ed. Gladys D. Willcock and Alice Walker (1936)
Robertson, Jean, and D. J. Gordon, *A Calendar of Dramatic Records in the Books of the Livery Companies of London 1485-1640*, Malone Society, Collections III (1954)
Sherburn, Edward, to Sir Dudley Carlton, Public Record Office, CSPD 90/422, no. 9 (January 4, 1617)
Smith, G. Gregory, ed., *Elizabethan Critical Essays* (1904; rpt. 1959)
Webbe, William, *A Discourse of English Poetrie* (1586), in Smith, p. 1.231

TEXTUAL NOTES

40   Love] THIS EDITION
237   Allhallowtide] THIS EDITION; Allhollontide DYCE; Alhollontid OKES
304   Philipa] *Philip* OKES
324   Spital] OKES (Spittle). This change reflects the more recent spelling of this word.

325   Bethl'em] OKES (Bethlem). This recognized spelling for 'Bethlehem' reflects probable pronunciation of the word, leading eventually to 'Bedlam'.
373   Philipa] *Philip* OKES
456   *bittern*] Bitter OKES
469   Christmas] OKES (*Crismas*)

PRESS VARIANTS

Copies collated: Harvard, National Library of Scotland, British Library.

Sheet A (outer forme)

Sig. A3

14   the military] the Military HARVARD; his Military NLS, BL

Sheet B (outer forme)

Sig. B3

174   *clemency*] NLS; *Clemency* HARVARD, BL

Sheet C (inner forme)

Sig. C1ᵛ

295   Parliament] NLS, HARVARD; Parliamt BL
295   arrive] arriue BL; ariue NLS, HARVARD

Sig. C2

297   inquisitive] Inquisitiue BL, HARVARD; Inquisit*i*ue NLS

Sig. C3ᵛ

374   Mortimer] *Mortimer* BL, HARVARD; *Mortiner* NLS

HONOURABLE ENTERTAINMENTS

Edited by Anthony Parr

THE TEXT (STC 17886; *BEPD* 3.1093–4) survives in a unique copy of an octavo edition printed by George Eld in 1621. Like a number of other published civic entertainments of the period, it was not entered on the Stationers' Register, and probably appeared in a small edition intended for distribution amongst its dedicatees and other prominent London citizens. The surviving copy was rediscovered just too late (in 1886) to be included in Bullen's edition of Middleton. It was edited by R. C. Bald for the Malone Society in 1953.

Bald lists some obvious misprints and queries a few points of punctuation and layout in an otherwise clean and attractive text. It is a more 'finished' and literary publication than most play texts of the period—Middleton clearly gave the same attention to this as he did to preparing his civic pageants for the press—and at the same time it makes more claim than they do to be a record of particular events. For both reasons it is desirable to keep editorial interference to a minimum: this edition preserves the basic layout of the original and (with one exception, at 8.58) makes no attempt to add directions.

SEE ALSO

Text: *Works*, 1434
Authorship and date: this volume, 410

WORKS CITED

Previous Edition

Bald, R. C., ed., *Honourable Entertainments* (1953)

Other Works Cited

Adams, Thomas, *The Souldiers Honour* (1617)
Analytical Index to . . . the Remembrancia, AD 1579–1664 (1878)
Ascham, Roger, *Toxophilus* (1545)
Brenner, Robert, *Merchants and Revolution* (1993)
Brett-Jones, N., *The Growth of Stuart London* (1935)
Crewdson, H. A. F., *The Worshipful Company of Musicians* (1950)
Dekker, Thomas, *The Shoemakers' Holiday* (1599)
Gerard, John, *The Herball, or Generall Historie of Plantes* (1633)
Girtin, Tom, *The Triple Crown* (1964)
Heinemann, Margot, *Puritanism and Theatre: Thomas Middleton and Opposition Drama under the Early Stuarts* (1980)
Johnson, A. H., *History of the Drapers of London* (1922)
Jonson, Ben, *Pleasure Reconcil'd to Virtue* (1618)
Kenny, R. W., *Elizabeth's Admiral* (1970)
Kingsford, C. L., ed., J. Stow, *A Survey of London* (1908)
Lambert, J. J., *Records of the Skinners of London* (1934)
McClure, N. E., ed., *The Letters of John Chamberlain* (1939)
Onions, C. T., ed., *Shakespeare's England* (1916)
Raikes, G. A., *The History of the Honourable Artillery Company* (1878)
Ripa, Cesare, *Iconologia* (1611)
Whitney, Geffrey, *A Choice of Emblemes* (1586)

TEXTUAL NOTES

1.10.1   *Enter*] THIS EDITION; *not in* ELD
1.84.4   *Second*] THIS EDITION; 2. ELD
3.0.1   *The Third Entertainment*] THIS EDITION; *not in* ELD
3.16, 3.51, 6.15   yon] ELD (yon'd)
4.0.1   *The Fourth Entertainment*] THIS EDITION; *not in* ELD
4.24   council] ELD (Councell)
5.0.1   *The Fifth Entertainment*] THIS EDITION; *not in* ELD
5.15.1   1620] BALD; 162 . ELD (*last numeral erased*)
5.16   1620] BALD; 620 ELD
6.0.1   *The Sixth Entertainment*] THIS EDITION; *not in* ELD
6.41   visor] ELD (Vizard)

6.53   Being] BALD; Bring ELD
7.0.1   *The Seventh Entertainment*] THIS EDITION; *not in* ELD
7.7   ballast] THIS EDITION; Ballace ELD
7.56   be] BALD; me ELD
7.73, 97, 100, 110, 114   SINGER] THIS EDITION; *not in* ELD
7.90–1   [*Echo*] From me to you, | [*Second Echo*] me to you] THIS EDITION; From me to you—Mee—To you, ELD
7.104   *Second Echo*] THIS EDITION; Ecch ELD
8.0.1   *The Eighth Entertainment*] THIS EDITION; *not in* ELD
8.51, 9.61   guests] ELD (*Guesse*)
8.58.1   *Exeunt Hyacinth and Adonis*] THIS EDITION; *not in* ELD
9.3.1   *The Ninth Entertainment*] THIS EDITION; *not in* ELD

THE SUN IN ARIES

Edited by David M. Bergeron

The Sun in Aries (STC 17895; *BEPD* 367) is the only
Middleton pageant text not printed by Nicholas Okes;
Edward Allde's shop printed *Aries*. This quarto text has
two sheets. The compositor who set sheet B clearly
determined to fit everything possible on that sheet so that
an additional one would not be needed. Therefore, the
font changes from sheet A to sheet B as the printer uses a
much smaller Roman type. By contrast, for example, the
text of the 1619 pageant, *Triumphs of Love and Antiquity*,
only some 160 lines longer than *Aries*, nevertheless runs
onto sheet D.

SEE ALSO

Text: *Works*, 1589
Authorship and date: this volume, 421

WORKS CITED

Previous Editions

The Progresses of King James the First, ed. John Nichols (1828),
   vol. 4
Thomas Middleton, *Works*, ed. Alexander Dyce (1840), vol. 5
Thomas Middleton, *Works*, ed. A. H. Bullen (1886), vol. 7
Burridge, Christina Jean, *A Critical Edition of Four Entertainments
   by Thomas Middleton for the Drapers' Company*. Dissertation,
   University of British Columbia, 1978

TEXTUAL NOTES

99   standard-bearers] ALLDE (Standerbearers)
130   *pyramids*] ALLDE *Pyramid's*; the plural seems required by the
         description that precedes the speech (94–8).
175   NEW STANDARD] THIS EDITION; *not in* ALLDE. The speaker is
         inferred from the lines that follow, such as the reference to
         'Fame fixed upon my head' (177), a feature of the actual,
         newly restored, conduit.
195   *o' late*] ALLDE (*alate*)
219   ARIES] THIS EDITION; *not in* ALLDE
228   *gem*] ALLDE (*Iem*)
283   *it; all*] ~ₐ ~, ALLDE. The change in punctuation puts the
         emphasis on all that has been bestowed on the mayor in this
         pageant entertainment.
312   Christmas] ALLDE (*Criſmas*)

PRESS VARIANT

Copies collated: Huntington, British Library, and National Library
of Scotland.

Sheet A (inner forme)

Sig. A2

10-11   Simon and] SIMON and NLS; SIMON BL, HN

AN INVENTION

Edited by Anthony Parr

An Invention survives in a manuscript in the Public Record Office (SP14/129; Conway Papers pp. 81–8). The octavo MS is bound with other papers relating to April 1622 and is written in a mixed italic and secretary hand, demonstrably that of the theatrical scribe Ralph CRANE, also responsible for manuscripts of *Witch* and *Game* (Howard-Hill, 11, 173). Damage to its lower left-hand corner has obliterated words and phrases on most leaves; a nineteenth-century transcript accompanying CRANE attempts to supply the missing words and phrases, with varying success. I have adopted its readings where I am unable to improve on them. The most serious gap occurs near the start, eclipsing the end of line 8 and most of line 8: a makeshift solution is proposed for the former but a gap left for the latter.

As in the case of *Honourable Entertainments*, and for the same reasons, the text of *An Invention* is presented here with as little editorial interference as possible.

SEE ALSO

Text: *Works*, 1446
Authorship and date: this volume, 422

WORKS CITED

Previous Editions

Bullen, A. H., ed., *Works* (1886), vol. 7
Burridge, Christina Jean, ed., *A Critical Edition of Four Entertainments by Thomas Middleton for the Drapers' Company*. Dissertation, University of British Columbia, 1978

Other Works Cited

Howard-Hill, T. H., *Ralph Crane and Some Shakespeare First Folio Comedies* (1972)

TEXTUAL NOTES

6   1622] CRANE; 1623 BULLEN. The title-page of the manuscript in the Conway papers says 'performed for the Service of yᵉ Right honorable Edward Barkham, L. Mayoʳ of the Cittie of London... In the Easter Hollidayes: 162?' The final numeral can be mistaken for a '3', with the bottom curve of the numeral begun just below the line and truncated; but it is almost certainly a '2', as can be seen by comparing it with the numeral '2' in the heading, within the text, '2 Song' (74.1). The tendency to see it as a '3' results from the fact that it is shaped differently than the preceding '2' (where the bottom horizontal stroke of the numeral rises); in the final numeral of the title-page, the bottom horizontal stroke drops. But the latter form also appears in '2 Song'. The different formation in '162?' probably is a result of an upstroke toward the final numeral. In any case, Edward Barkham became Lord Mayor in October, 1621, and therefore the only Easter when he was Lord Mayor would have been the Easter of 1622. Paleographically, it seems likely that the final numeral on the manuscript title-page is a '2' ('1622'); but even if Crane intended a '3', that single numeral is more likely to be wrong than the information about the mayoralty.

8   They appear] THIS EDITION; *not in* CRANE; Come enter TRANSCRIPT
9   [   ]] *opening of Mean's speech missing in* CRANE
17 crest] THIS EDITION; C[   ] CRANE; worth TRANSCRIPT
18 it best] THIS EDITION; [   ]b[   ] CRANE; it both TRANSCRIPT
19 A] TRANSCRIPT; I CRANE; Ay, BULLEN
24 *Fortunae Mater*] TRANSCRIPT; F[   ]n Matre CRANE
24 This honoured] TRANSCRIPT; [   ]rd CRANE
28.1 *Finis the first song*] CRANE (Finis. 1 Song.)
29 appear] TRANSCRIPT; *not in* CRANE
30 thought of fear] TRANSCRIPT; tho[   ] CRANE
39 A station] TRANSCRIPT; [   ]ion CRANE
40 Of our best] THIS EDITION; *not in* CRANE; A christian TRANSCRIPT
50 punishment] TRANSCRIPT; Puni[   ] CRANE
59 Believe we] TRANSCRIPT; CRANE *illegible*
60 Religious] TRANSCRIPT; *not in* CRANE
70 relief] TRANSCRIPT; *not in* CRANE
76 welcome] TRANSCRIPT; [   ]com CRANE
77 That this] TRANSCRIPT; *not in* CRANE
78 Spread as far] TRANSCRIPT; *not in* CRANE
86 wicked deaf] TRANSCRIPT; *not in* CRANE

THE TRIUMPHS OF HONOUR AND VIRTUE

Edited by David M. Bergeron

The Triumphs of Honour and Virtue (STC 17900; *BEPD* 383) is Middleton's most bibliographically complex pageant text. (This quarto text, printed by Nicholas Okes, contains three sheets.) One would not realize the complexity by reading *BEPD* in which Greg notes a single variant in the title-page found in the Folger Library copy. But the Folger copy in fact shows some radical departures from the other three extant copies (British Library, Huntington, and National Library of Scotland).

For some unknown reason, the printing of sheet B occurred in two separate press-runs. During the first, the portion of the edition represented by the original state of the setting, exemplified by both formes of the Folger copy and the outer forme of the National Library of Scotland copy, was printed and perfected. Before the second press-run, two lines of verse following line 131 were deleted from Folger B3^v:5–6, B4:1–2 were pulled back to B3^v:25–26, and B4^v:1–2 were pulled back to B4:26–27, leaving B4^v two lines short. No adjustment to the setting of C1 occurred. Three substantive corrections to the type of B3^v–4 were made at this time, which indicate the priority of the Folger state. By mistake, the previously printed outer forme of the National Library of Scotland copy with B4^v:1–2 in their original location was perfected by the second state of the inner forme with the result that the lines B4^v:1–2 also appear in their new position at the bottom of B4:26–27. The remaining copies exemplify the second state in which the rest of the edition was printed and perfected.

SEE ALSO

Text: *Works*, 1719
Authorship and date: this volume, 427

WORKS CITED

Previous Editions

The Shakespeare Society's Papers, ed. James L. Pearson (1845), vol. 2
Thomas Middleton, *Works*, ed. A. H. Bullen (1886), vol. 7

Other Works Cited

Bergeron, David M., *English Civic Pageantry 1558–1642* (1971)
Coryat, Thomas, 'A Letter of Mr. Thomas Coryat, which travailed by land from Jerusalem to the Court of the Great Mogol…' (1615) in Samuel Purchas, *Hakluytus Posthumus or Purchas his Pilgrimes* (1625), reprinted in vol. 4 (1905)
Dekker, Thomas, *The King's Entertainment*, in *Works*, ed. Ernest Rhys (1949)
Desai, Tripta, *The East India Company, A Brief Survey from 1599 to 1857* (1984)
Hahn, Thomas, 'Indians East and West: primitivism and savagery in English discovery narratives of the sixteenth century', *Journal of Medieval and Renaissance Studies* 8, 1 (1978), 77–114
Hakluyt, Richard, *The Principall Navigations, Voyages and Discoveries of the English Nation* (1598–1600, reprinted 1904)
Heath, Baron, *Some Account of the Worshipful Company of Grocers of the City of London* (1869)
Jonson, Ben, *The characters of two royal masques, the one of blackness, the other of beauty . . . .* (1608)
Jordan, Thomas, *London Triumphant, or the City in Jollity and Splendour* (1672)
—— *London in its Splendour* (1673)
—— *The Triumphs of London* (1676)
Lach, Donald F., *Asia in the Making of Europe* (1965–77)
Munday, Anthony, *The Pageants and Entertainments of Anthony Munday: A critical edition*, ed. David M. Bergeron (1984)
Palmer, Thomas, *The Emblems of Thomas Palmer: Two Hundred Poosees*, ed. John Manning (1988)
Purchas, Samuel, *Hakluytus Posthumus or Purchas his Pilgrimes* (1625, reprinted 1905)
Ramsay, G. D., *English Overseas Trade During the Centuries of Emergence* (1957)
Rees, J. Aubrey, *The Worshipful Company of Grocers, An Historical Retrospect, 1345–1923* (1923)
Ripa, Cesare, *Iconolgie* (1593–1644)
Squire, John, *The Triumphs of Peace* (1620), in Baron Heath, *Some Account of the Worshipful Company of Grocers of the city of London* (1869)
Tatham, John, *London's Triumph* (1659)
Weiss, Adrian, 'A "Fill-In" Job: The Textual Crux and Interrupted Printing in Thomas Middleton's *The Triumphs of Honor and Virtue* (1622)', *Papers of the Bibliographical Society of America* 93 (1999), 53–73
Whitney, Geffrey, *A Choice of Emblemes and Other Devices*, with an introduction by John Manning (1989)

TEXTUAL NOTES

52 THE SPEECH OF THE BLACK QUEEN] THIS EDITION; The Speech. OKES

76 *Enos*] THIS EDITION; *Eoum* OKES; a possible compositor misreading for 'Enos', which at least fits the context of the speech.

80 *such*] OKESb (*fuch*); *whch* OKESa

106 coherence] *cohereuce* OKES; (turned letter *n*)

116 THE SPEECH OF ANTIQUITY] THIS EDITION; The Speech. OKES

131 *recovery.*] In the early state of OKES two lines follow that are cancelled in the later state: '*Thinke and be thankfull euer, there befell* | *More things for this, as much remarkable,*'

140 *Those*] OKESb; *These* OKESa

142 *o'late*] OKES (*alate*)

154 *He's*] OKES (*Ha's*)

202 THE SPEECH OF VIRTUE] THIS EDITION; The Speech. OKES

309 Christmas] OKES (*Crifmas*)

PRESS VARIANTS

Copies collated:

FOLGER Folger Shakespeare Library
HN Henry E. Huntington Library
NLS National Library of Scotland
BL British Library

Sheet A (outer forme)

OKES state a: FOLGER
OKES state b: HN, BL, NLS

Sig. A1

4 Honourable] *Honorable,* OKESa; *Honorable* OKESb
8 return] *Returne* OKESa; *returne* OKESb

Sheet B (inner forme)

OKES state a: FOLGER
OKES state b: HN, BL, NLS

Sig. B1ᵛ

38 approach] ~ OKESa; approch OKESb
39 India,] *India,* OKESa; *India:* OKESb
44 challenging] ~ OKESa; challinging OKESb
54 *black*] *Blacke;* OKESa; *blacke* OKESb
54 *native dye*] *Natiue Dye* OKESa; *natiue dye* OKESb

Sig. B2

57 mind] *Mind* OKESa; *mind* OKESb
58 beauteous] *Beauteous* OKESa; *beauteous* OKESb
58 blackness] *Blackneffe* OKESa; *blackneffe* OKESb
62 examples, blessed] examples; *Bleft* OKESa; examples, *bleft* OKESb
65 abundance] *Abundance* OKESa; *aboundance* OKESb
66 me;] ~; OKESa; ~, OKESb
67 scent] *Sent* OKESa; *fent* OKESb
68 plants . . . youth] *Plants . . . Youth* OKESa; *plants . . . youth* OKESb
69 life,] *Life,* OKESa; *life* OKESb
70 scent] *Sent* OKESa; *fent* OKESb
71 beds] *Beds* OKESa; *beds* OKESb
74 famed] *Fam'd* OKESa; *fam'd* OKESb
75 north,] *North;* OKESa; *North,* OKESb
76 hand] *Hand* OKESa; *hand* OKESb
78 *fruitful,*] *fruitfull;* OKESa; *fruitfull,* OKESb
79 holiness] *Holyneffe* OKESa; *holyneffe* OKESb
80 *such*] *whch* OKESa; *fuch* OKESb
81 enlightenèd] *enlightened:* OKESa; *enlightened,* OKESb

Sig. B3ᵛ

128 *thou*] *Thou* OKESa; *thou* OKESb

128 *unusuring*] *Vnufuring* OKESa; *vnufuring* OKESb
128 *got,*] ~, OKESa; ~, OKESb
129 *wonder-worthy note*] *wonder, worthy Note* OKESa; *wonder worthy note* OKESb
130 *freely*] ~ OKESa; *frely* OKESb
131 *recovery.*] *Recouerie,* | *Thinke and be thankfull euer, there befell* | *More things for this, as much remarkable,* OKESa; *recouerie,* OKESb
134 *degree,*] *Degree,* OKESa; *degree* OKESb
135 *thee;*] ~; OKESa; ~, OKESb
139 those.] *thofe;* OKESa; *those.* OKESb
140 *Those . . . notes;*] *These . . . Notes;* OKESa; *Those . . . notes,* OKESb
141 *friends,*] *Friends* OKESa; *Friends,* OKESb
144 advance] *Aduance* OKESa; *aduance* OKESb
145 *magistrate,*] *Magiftrate;* OKESa; *Magiftrate,* OKESb
146 blest] *Bleft* OKESa; *bleft* OKESb
147 *James . . . breast*] Iames, . . . *Breft.* OKESa; Iames . . . *breft.* OKESb
148 both] *Both* OKESa; *both* OKESb
149 foot.] *Foote;* OKESa; *Foote,* OKESb
151 *citizen:*] *Citizen;* OKESa; *Citizen,* OKESb
152 touches] *Touches* OKESa; *touches* OKESb
152–3 *These . . . endued)*] at head of B4 in OKESa; *moved here in* OKESb

Sig. B4

152–3 *These . . . endued)*] *here in* OKESa; *moved to base of B3ᵛ in* OKESb
153 blessings] *Bleffings* OKESa; *bleffings* OKESb
155 honoured] *Honor'd* OKESa; *honored* OKESb
156 bounds] *Bounds* OKESa; *bounds* OKESb
156 *not . . . place,*] (*not . . . place,*) OKESa; *not . . . place,* OKESb
160 *recòrd . . . joy*] *Record . . . Ioy* OKESa; *record . . . ioy* OKESb
163 *five . . . honour . . . three*] *Fiue . . . Honor . . . Three* OKESa; *fiue . . . honor . . . three* OKESb
164 *triple . . . triple virtue*] *triple, . . . triple Vertue* OKESa; *triple . . . triple vertue* OKESb
171 in the] in OKESa; in the OKESb
176–8 famous worthy . . . said Sir Tho-] *here in* OKESa; *not here in* OKESb

Sheet B (outer forme)

OKES state a: FOLGER, NLS
OKES state b: HN, BL

Sig. B4ᵛ

176–8 famous worthy . . . said Sir Tho-] *here in* OKESa; *not here in* OKESb

677

Sheet C (inner forme)

  OKES state a: FOLGER, NLS

  OKES state b: HN, BL

Sig. C1ᵛ

237 St Paul's] St. *Paules* OKESa; Saint *Paules* OKESb

240 opening] ~, OKESa; ~ₐ OKESb

Sig. C2

250 intentions] Intentions; OKESa; Intentions, OKESb

252 again,] againe; OKESa; againe, OKESb

265 drawn] drawne, OKESa; drawne OKESb

THE TRIUMPHS OF INTEGRITY

Edited by David M. Bergeron

The Triumphs of Integrity (STC 17901; *BEPD* 387), printed by Nicholas Okes, has few problems. It has type font press variants in sheet B. The quarto text has three sheets.

SEE ALSO

Text: *Works*, 1768
Authorship and date: this volume, 438

WORKS CITED

Previous Editions

Thomas Middleton, *Works*, ed. Alexander Dyce (1840), vol. 5
Thomas Middleton, *Works*, ed. A. H. Bullen (1886), vol. 7
Burridge, Christina Jean, *A Critical Edition of Four Entertainments by Thomas Middleton for the Drapers' Company*. Dissertation, University of British Columbia, 1978

Other Works Cited

D'Ewes, Sir Simonds, *The Autobiography and Correspondence*, ed. J. O. Halliwell, 2 vols (1845)
Horace, *The Complete Odes and Epodes*, trans. W. G. Shepherd (1983)
Meres, Francis, *Palladis Tamia* (1598)
Munday, Anthony, *Metropolis Coronata* (1615)

TEXTUAL NOTES

85   *risse*] *rife* OKES; Middleton's past tense form of rise.
94   *risse*] *rife* OKES
121 then] DYCE; the OKES
144 BY MEMORY] THIS EDITION; *not in* OKES
148 *goodness*] *Godneffe* OKES
203 BY INTEGRITY] THIS EDITION; *not in* OKES

225 *evill'st*] THIS EDITION; *euilleft* OKES
232 *translucent*] *Tralucent* OKES; 'tralucent' is a now-obscure word that means 'translucent.'
262 which] DYCE; with OKES
265 an] a OKES
314 Christmas] OKES (*Crismas*)

PRESS VARIANTS

Copies collated:

HUNTINGTON Henry E. Huntington Library
MORGAN Pierpont Morgan Library

Sheet B (inner forme)

Sig. B4

running title   *Integrity* HUNTINGTON; *Integrity* MORGAN (with initial swash italic I)

Sheet B (outer forme)

Sig. B1

running title   *Integrity* HUNTINGTON; *Integrity* MORGAN (with initial swash italic I)

Sig. B3

running title   *Integrity* HUNTINGTON; *Integrity* MORGAN (with initial swash italic I)

THE TRIUMPHS OF THE GOLDEN FLEECE

Edited by David M. Bergeron

The Triumphs of the Golden Fleece (STC 18280; not recorded in *BEPD*) exists in only one copy, that found in the British Library. This brief quarto text fits all on sheet A. The printer is Thomas Snodham.

WORK CITED

Previous Edition

Pageants and Entertainments of Anthony Munday: A Critical Edition, ed. David M. Bergeron (1985)

SEE ALSO

Text: *Works,* 1772
The Triumphs of Integrity: *Works,* 1768

TEXTUAL NOTE

69   device] denise SNODHAM

MEASURE FOR MEASURE: A GENETIC TEXT

Edited by John Jowett

Measure for Measure first appeared occupying quires F and G of the 1623 Shakespeare First Folio, which was printed in William and Isaac Jaggard's shop. The play appears as the fourth text in the opening 'Comedies' section, and is placed between *Merry Wives of Windsor* and *Comedy of Errors*. The text is thought to have been set by the Jaggard compositors identified as B, C, and D. Its position within the 'Comedies' section was probably dictated by considerations of copy, as the first five Comedies were all quite clearly set from 'literary' transcripts. The copyist is believed to have been Ralph Crane, who had strong associations with the King's Men in the early 1620s, and whose transcripts of *A Game at Chess*, *The Witch*, and other works are extant.

The nature of the manuscript of *Measure* that Crane worked from is largely obscured by his own practices of sophistication. Jowett and Taylor ('With New Additions') argue that there is sufficient evidence to indicate that the manuscript in question was not in Shakespeare's hand. The almost complete absence of profanity most likely results from expurgation with performance in mind after the 1606 Act against Abuses of the Players forbade profanity on stage, and the presence of act divisions implies a manuscript used in the theatre after the King's Men began to observe act intervals *c.*1609. Thus Crane's copy appears to have been a promptbook used for a revival of the play after 1609.

Measure is included in this edition of Middleton's works on the basis, initially argued in detail by Jowett and Taylor (1993), that Middleton was partly or wholly responsible for an adaptation of Shakespeare's text that can be dated at 1621. Here, however, the Middleton editor faces a paradox. The Jaggard text is based on the adapted version; it is Shakespeare's pre-adaptation text that is unfamiliar. Even the Oxford Shakespeare text, the editing of which was based on the hypothesis of adaptation, was based on the 1621 text, partly because the hypothesis had not been published and subjected to wider scholarly scrutiny, partly in recognition that the 1603–4 text might lie beyond proper recovery. A Middleton edition that conventionally edited the 1621 text would therefore do little other than reprint *Measure* from the Oxford Shakespeare. Furthermore, such an edition would give no special emphasis to the adapted sections, and so would conspire with the familiarity of the 1623 text as an apparently seamless Shakespeare play to make the play's appearance in a Middleton edition implausible.

This limitation can be turned to advantage. The Middleton *Collected Works* provides an opportunity to affirm the adaptation itself as the prime object in view, and to develop a style of presentation that might be deemed distracting in the context of a Shakespeare edition. The present edition reconstructs a hypothetical Shakespearean version, and imposes upon it the changes made in adaptation. The changes are identified as cancellations and additions (substitution and transposition combine these two processes); cancellations are printed in grey type, and additions are printed in bold type.

Full lines in cancelled passages are identified with an alphabetical suffix to the previous line of the main text. For instance, the third line of the cancel in 1.2 is 1.2.79c. A nominal through scene-numbering has been provided to reflect the continuous action of the pre-adaptation text, the alternative scene-heading 'Sc. 6', for example, indicating that Shakespeare would not have written this scene to follow an act-break. However, the adapted text remains the basis for the standard line numbering, which is therefore on the familiar act–scene–line system. Jaggard's act and scene divisions are followed, though Jaggard's 'Scena Tertia.' in Act 1 indicates a scene break found only (it is argued) in the Shakespearean original; this edition follows the usual editorial continuous action here for the adapted text, and the usual editorial act–scene numbering for the rest of the Act.

Profanity has been restored to the pre-adaptation text where possible. In some passages it is difficult to be certain whether expurgation has or has not affected the text, and in others the reading reconstructed in this edition is conjectural; it is evident, however, that the 1603–4 text would almost certainly have included more rather than less profanity than has been allowed for here.

The arguments and evidence put forward by Jowett and Taylor in 1987 and 1993, identifying changes in 1.2 and around the beginning of Act 4, are presented here in summary form. For the present edition we have conducted substantial new research that confirms and extends the hypothesis. The edition incorporates Taylor's published identifications in ''Swounds Revisited' of expurgated profanity, and a number of suggestions, arguments, and details of evidence put forward privately by Taylor. A fuller and more critically developed account of the 'King of Hungary' allusion, the phenomenon of the news-sheet, and the currency of news, will be found in Jowett, 'Audacity'. The conjectured Italian setting for Shakespeare's original play is fully explored in Taylor, 'Shakespeare's Mediterranean *Measure for Measure*'. This edition publishes for the first time (in the Critical Introduction and commentary unless otherwise noted) the evidence for Middleton's hand in 1.2.99–102 (introducing new roles), 2.1.21–2 (thieves as law-enforcers), 2.1.79–80 and 188–94 (passages naming Mistress Overdone), lines in 2.2 (Lucio's role), 4.2.131 (Barnardine's Viennese upbringing), and 4.3.1–18 (Pompey's catalogue of prisoners; see 'Canon and Chronology' and commentary notes). It proposes for the first time that the adaptation transposed 1.3 and 1.4 (see in particular the scene headnotes), and that Middleton rather than Webster is the author of 4.1.7–25 (the bridge passage between the song and the original text; see 'Canon and Chronology'). It makes a few additions to the examples of expurgation previously suggested by Taylor. It introduces some new evidence for Middleton's authorship of 2.1.262–73 (Escalus and the Justice), and draws attention for the first time to the significance for the origin of 'Take, O take those lips away' in *Rollo* of the song's two stanzas sharing the same source. It also presents new arguments against a 1604 dating for the opening of 1.2 (see 'Canon and Chronology').

The textual notes to the adapted version are based on a summary version of the notes in the Oxford Shakespeare. Matters relating to the original Shakespearean text and the adaptation are documented within a separate section of the textual notes. A specialist commentary provides discursive notes dealing with the adaptation. These aim to define the changes made to the Jaggard text, to clarify the relation between interrelated additions and cancellations, and to set the changes in a Middleton context. It is beyond the scope of this edition to evaluate the entire mass of Middleton parallels and analogues, and to assess it against the occasional (usually unremarkable) case of a word or phrase exampled not in Middleton but in Shakespeare or another dramatist; nor has it usually been found appropriate to record the 'neutral' cases where there are parallels to be found in both Middleton and Shakespeare.

The Critical Introduction, whilst presenting an overview of the textual scholarship, is more concerned to establish a Middletonian and late-Jacobean critical context for the play after adaptation. It draws on the work of Coxe, Dahl, Gardiner, Heinemann, Hirst, Limon, Lockyer, Peck, Sternfeld, and Charles Wilson, as cited below. I am grateful to Anna Kiss for investigating details of early seventeenth century events from a Hungarian perspective. The account of the Hungarian military campaign is also informed by the following details from the *Calendar of State Papers ... [Venetian]* for 1621–3: the majority of English ministers 'abominate the name of Bethlem Gabor owing to suspicion of the Turk, so that any close union between Gabor and the Palatinate would seriously damage and discredit the latter here [in London]' (21 May 1621; p. 52); King James asks Frederick to discontinue his league with Bethlen (16 July 1621; p. 81); Bethlen approaches the Emperor for separate peace (31 July 1621; p. 95); news reaches the Hague of the surrender of Bethlen's troops in Germany (13 December 1621; p. 177); Gondomar declares the affairs of Hungary settled (11 February 1622; p. 233).

SEE ALSO

Text: *Works*, 1547
Music: this volume, 167
Authorship and date: this volume, 417

WORKS CITED

Editions of *Measure for Measure*

A detailed census of editions to 1980 is given by Eccles, xii–xvi. The most important subsequent edition, apart from those recorded below, is that of Brian Gibbons (1991), who introduces no fresh emendations. The following list is confined to editions cited.

Alexander, Peter, ed., William Shakespeare, *Works* (1951)

Bawcutt, Nigel, ed., *Measure for Measure*, by William Shakespeare (1991)

Bullen, A. H., ed., William Shakespeare, *Works*, 10 vols (1904–7), vol. 1

Capell, Edward, ed., William Shakespeare, *Comedies, Histories, and Tragedies*, 10 vols (1767–8), vol. 2

Clark, W. G., and Wright, W. A., eds., William Shakespeare, *Works*, 9 vols (1863–6), vol. 1

Cotes, Thomas, printer, William Shakespeare, *Comedies, Histories, and Tragedies* (1632)

Davenant, William, *The Law against Lovers* (adaptation of *Measure*), in *Works* (1673)

Dyce, Alexander, ed., William Shakespeare, *Works*, 6 vols (1857), vol. 1

Eccles, Mark, ed., *A New Variorum Edition of Shakespeare: 'Measure for Measure'* (1980)

Halliwell, James O., ed., William Shakespeare, *Works*, 16 vols (1853–65), vol. 3

Hanmer, Thomas, ed., William Shakespeare, *Works*, 6 vols (1743–4), vol. 1

Hart, H. C., ed., *Measure for Measure* (1905)

Hayes, John [?], part-printer, William Shakespeare, *Comedies, Histories, and Tragedies* (1663–4)

Hinman, Charlton, ed., *The Norton Facsimile: The First Folio of Shakespeare* (1968)

Hudson, H. N., ed., William Shakespeare, *Works*, 20 vols (1880–81), vol. 6

Jaggard, William and Isaac, printers, William Shakespeare, *Comedies, Histories, and Tragedies* (1623)

Johnson, Samuel, ed., William Shakespeare, *Plays*, 8 vols (1765), vol. 1

Jowett, John, ed., *Measure for Measure*, in William Shakespeare, *Complete Works* (the Oxford Shakespeare), gen. eds. S. W. Wells and Gary Taylor (1986); textual documentation in S. W. Wells and Gary Taylor, with Gary Taylor, *William Shakespeare: A Textual Companion* (1987), 468–75

Keightley, Thomas, ed., William Shakespeare, *Plays*, 6 vols (1864), vol. 2

Knight, Charles, ed., William Shakespeare, *Comedies, Histories, Tragedies, and Poems*, 55 parts [1838–43], Part 29

Lever, J. W., ed., William Shakespeare, *Measure for Measure* (1965)

Malone, Edmond, ed., William Shakespeare, *Plays and Poems*, 10 vols (1790), vol. 2

Nosworthy, J. M., ed., William Shakespeare, *Measure for Measure* (1969)

Pope, Alexander, ed., William Shakespeare, *Works*, 6 vols (1723–5), vol. 1

Rann, Joseph, ed., William Shakespeare, *Dramatic Works*, 6 vols (1786–94), vol. 1

Roberts, Robert, part-printer, William Shakespeare, *Comedies, Histories, and Tragedies* (1685)

Rowe, Nicholas, ed., William Shakespeare, *Works*, 6 vols (1709), vol. 1

—— ed., William Shakespeare, *Works*, 8 vols (1714), vol. 1

Singer, Samuel W., ed., William Shakespeare, *Dramatic Works*, 10 vols (1826), vol. 2

Sisson, Charles J., ed., William Shakespeare, *Complete Works* (1954)

Staunton, Howard, ed., William Shakespeare, *Plays*, 3 vols (1868-60), vol. 2

Steevens, George, with Samuel Johnson, eds., William Shakespeare, *Plays*, 10 vols (1778), vol. 2

Theobald, Lewis, ed., William Shakespeare, *Works*, 7 vols (1733), vol. 1

Warburton, William, ed., William Shakespeare, *Works*, 8 vols (1747), vol. 1

Wilson, John Dover, with Arthur Quiller-Couch, eds., William Shakespeare, *Measure for Measure* (1928)

Other Works Cited

Bawcutt, N. W., 'A Ghost Press-variant in Folio *Measure for Measure*', *Shakespeare Quarterly* 39 (1988), 360

Calendar of State Papers... [*Venetian*], vol. 17, *1621-1623*, ed. Allen B. Hinds (1911)

Chamberlain, John, *Letters*, ed. N. E. McClure, 2 vols (1939)

Cotes, Thomas, and John Benson, eds., William Shakespeare, *Poems* (1640)

Cotgrave, John, *The English Treasury of Wit and Language* (1655)

Coxe, William, *History of the House of Austria*, 3 vols (1847)

Dahl, Folke, *A Bibliography of English Corantos and Periodical Newsbooks, 1620-1642* (1952)

Evans, G. B., ed., *The Riverside Shakespeare* (1974)

Fletcher, John, *Rollo, Duke of Normandy (The Bloody Brother)* (1639 and 1640)

Gardiner, Samuel Rawson, *History of England*, vol. 4, *From the Accession of James I to the Outbreak of the Civil War, 1603-1642* (1883)

Heinemann, Margot, *Puritanism and Theatre: Thomas Middleton and Opposition Drama under the Early Stuarts* (1980)

Hinman, Charlton, *The Printing and Proof-Reading of the First Folio of Shakespeare*, 2 vols (1963)

Hirst, Derek, *England in Conflict, 1603-1660: Kingdom, Community, Commonwealth* (1999)

Holdsworth, R. V., '*Measure for Measure*, Middleton, and "Brakes of Ice"', *Notes and Queries* 236 (1991), 64-7

Jowett, John, 'The Audacity of *Measure for Measure* in 1621', *Ben Jonson Journal* 8 (2001), 1-19

—— and Gary Taylor, '"With New Additions": Theatrical Interpolation in *Measure for Measure*', in Taylor and Jowett, 107-236

Kellner, Leon, *Erläuterungen und Textverbesserungen zu vierzehn Dramen Shakespeares*, ed. Walter Ebisch (1931)

Kerrigan, John, 'Revision, Adaptation, and the Fool in *King Lear*', in Gary Taylor and Michael Warren, eds., *The Division of the Kingdoms: Shakespeare's Two Versions of 'King Lear'* (1983), 195-245

Lambrechts, Guy, 'Proposed New Readings in Shakespeare: The Comedies (I)', in *Hommage à Shakespeare: Bulletin de la Faculté des Lettres de Strasbourg*, 43 (1965), 945-58

Limon, Jerzy, *Dangerous Matter: English Drama and Politics in 1623-24* (1986)

Lockyer, Roger, *The Early Stuarts: A Political History of England 1603-1642* (1989)

Mason, John Monck, *Comments on the Last Edition of Shakespeare's Plays* (1785)

Muir, Kenneth, 'The Duke's Soliloquies in *Measure for Measure*', *Notes and Queries* 211 (1966), 135-6

Nicholson, B., '*Measure for Measure* 1.3.10', *Notes and Queries* VI.12 (1885), 25

O'Connor, Frank [Michael O'Donovan], *The Road to Stratford* (1948)

Orger, J. G., *Critical Notes on Shakespeare's Comedies* (1890)

Peck, Linda Levy, *Court Patronage and Corruption in Early Stuart England* (1990)

Schmidt, Alexander, *Shakespeare-Lexicon*, 2 vols (1874-5)

Sternfeld, F. W., in Lever, ed., 201

Sugden, Edward H., *A Topographical Dictionary to the Works of Shakespeare and His Fellow Dramatists* (1925)

Tannenbaum, Samuel A., *Shaksperian Scraps and Other Elizabethan Fragments* (1933)

Taylor, Gary, '"Swounds Revisited: Theatrical, Editorial, and Literary Expurgation', in Taylor and Jowett, 51-106

—— 'Shakespeare's Mediterranean *Measure for Measure*', in *Shakespeare and the Mediterranean*, ed. Tom Clayton, Susan Brock, and Vicente Forés (2004), 243-69

—— and John Jowett, *Shakespeare Reshaped 1606-1623* (1993)

Tieck, Ludwig, reviser of A. W. von Schlegel, translator, William Shakespeare, *Dramatische Werke*, 9 vols (1825-33), vol. 5

Walker, Alice, 'The Text of *Measure for Measure*', *Review of English Studies* NS 34 (1983), 1-20

Wilson, Charles, *England's Apprenticeship, 1603-1763* (1965)

TEXTUAL NOTES

A. Emendations and Modernizations

1.1.0.2 *Incipit Actus Primus*] *Actus primus, Scena prima.* JAGGARD. Similarly throughout, with '*Scena Secunda.*' etc. for scene-breaks within the act.

1.1.8 But that [   ]] THIS EDITION (Theobald); But that, JAGGARD; Put that, ROWE; But this: JOWETT 1986. See Section B.

1.1.49, 2.4.48 metal] JAGGARD (mettle)

1.1.52 leavened] NOSWORTHY (Dent *MS conj.*, *in* Halliwell); a leauen'd JAGGARD

1.1.76 *Exit*] JAGGARD (*after* l. 75)

1.2.18 wast] JAGGARD (was't)

1.2.33-4 piled...pilled] JAGGARD (pil'd...pil'd)

1.2.79h with maid] JAGGARD; made G.T. *conj.*

1.2.109 bonds] SISSON; words JAGGARD

1.2.121 morality] ROWE 1709 (Davenant); mortality JAGGARD

1.2.139 Unhapp'ly] JAGGARD (Unhappely)

1.2.151 fourteen] RANN (Theobald); ninteene JAGGARD

1.2.170 thy] JOWETT 1986 (Lever); the JAGGARD

1.3(a).10 a witless] WILSON (Nicholson); ˄ ~ JAGGARD; and ~ COTES; with ~ CLARK-WRIGHT (*conj.*)

1.3(a).20 weeds] JAGGARD; Steeds THEOBALD; wills BULLEN (Thirlby, *in* MS note); jades LEVER (Orger)

1.3(a).27 More mocked becomes] JOWETT 1986; More mock'd JAGGARD; become more markt DAVENANT (*conj.*); Becomes more mock'd POPE

1.3(a).43   T'allow] JOWETT 1986; To do JAGGARD; So do THEO-
BALD; To die STAUNTON (*conj.*). Instead, HANMER emends 'in'
to 'it'; HALLIWELL emends 'in' to 'me'.

1.3(a).48   More] JAGGARD (Moe)

1.4.5   sisterhood] COTES; Sifterftood JAGGARD

1.4.6   LUCIO (*within*)] JAGGARD (printing '*Lucio within.*' as stage
direction, then speech-prefix '*Luc.*')

1.4.53   giving] JAGGARD; givings ROWE

1.4.89.3   *Finis Actus Primus*] *not in* JAGGARD. Similarly for Acts
2, 3, and 4.

2.1.12   your] ROWE 1709 (Davenant); our JAGGARD

2.1.21–2   What...on thieves?] JOWETT 1986; *after* 'seizes', l. 23,
JAGGARD

2.1.21   law] ROWE 1709 (Davenant); Lawes JAGGARD

2.1.32.1   *Enter Provost*] JAGGARD (*after* l. 31)

2.1.34   execute] JOWETT 1986; executed JAGGARD

2.1.38   Some...fall] JAGGARD (*in italic, as* sententia)

2.1.39   breaks] JAGGARD (brakes)

2.1.39   ice] JAGGARD; Vice ROWE 1709 (through Brakes of Vice),
STEEVENS. See commentary.

2.1.133.1   *Exit Angelo*] JAGGARD ('Exit.' *after* l. 132)

2.1.218   spay] JAGGARD (fplay)

2.1.248   by the] JAGGARD; by your POPE

2.2.60   it] JAGGARD; it backe COTES; it in WILSON

2.2.75   that were] JAGGARD; that are WARBURTON

2.2.98   raw] JOWETT 1986; now JAGGARD; new POPE; now born
KEIGHTLEY

2.2.101   ere] HANMER (Thirlby, *in MS note*); here JAGGARD

2.2.119   Split'st] JAGGARD (Splits)

2.2.150   with you] JAGGARD; to you THIS EDITION *conj.*

2.2.152   shekels] JAGGARD (Sickles)

2.2.161   prayer is crossed] JOWETT 1986 (Taylor); prayers croffe
JAGGARD

2.3.42   law] HANMER (Thirlby, *in MS note*); Loue JAGGARD

2.4.9   seared] HANMER; feard JAGGARD

2.4.12   in] JOWETT 1986 (Walker); for JAGGARD

2.4.17   now the] JOWETT 1986 (Wilson); not the JAGGARD; yet
the JOHNSON (*conj.*)

2.4.17.1   *Enter Servant*] JAGGARD (*after* 'there')

2.4.30.1   *Enter Isabella*] JAGGARD (*after* 'maid')

2.4.48   moulds] JOWETT 1986 (Malone); meanes JAGGARD; mints
WILSON (Steevens)

2.4.53   or] ROWE 1709 (Davenant); and JAGGARD

2.4.58   for account] JAGGARD (for accompt); accompt ROWE
1714; for compt JOHNSON

2.4.75   craftily] ROWE 1709 (Davenant); crafty JAGGARD

2.4.76   me be] COTES; be JAGGARD

2.4.94   all-binding] JOHNSON (Thirlby, *in MS note*); all-building
JAGGARD

2.4.112   Ignominy] COTES; Ignomie JAGGARD

2.4.143   for't] JAGGARD; for it ROWE 1714 (Davenant)

2.4.185   More] JAGGARD ('More). Jaggard marks the line as a
sententia.

3.1.4   I've] JAGGARD (I'haue)

3.1.20   exist'st] JAGGARD (exifts)

3.1.29   sire] ROBERTS (Cotgrave); fire JAGGARD

3.1.31   serpigo] JAGGARD (Sapego)

3.1.38   in] POPE; yet in JAGGARD

3.1.45.1   *Enter Isabella*] JAGGARD (*after* l. 43)

3.1.51   me...them] MALONE (Steevens); them...me JAGGARD

3.1.67   Though] ROWE 1714; Through JAGGARD

3.1.89   enew] KEIGHTLEY; emmew JAGGARD

3.1.92, 95   precise] KNIGHT (Tieck); prenzie JAGGARD

3.1.94   damnedest] JAGGARD (damneft)

3.1.121   dilated] HANMER; delighted JAGGARD

3.1.130   penury] COTES; periury JAGGARD

3.1.169   falsify] HANMER (THIRLBY, *in MS note*); fatisfie JAGGARD;
fortify LAMBRECHTS (*conj.*)

3.1.253   hear] JAGGARD (heere)

3.1.276   furred with] JAGGARD (furd ~); faced ~ TAYLOR *conj. in*
JOWETT 1986

3.1.276   on] RANN (Thirlby, *in MS note*); and JAGGARD

3.1.292   array] THEOBALD (Hawley Bishop, verbal suggestion);
away JAGGARD

3.1.306   Free from] COTES; From JAGGARD

3.1.306   or] BULLEN (Johnson); as JAGGARD

3.1.313   extracting] JAGGARD; ~ it ROWE 1714

3.1.373   ungenerative] THEOBALD; generatiue JAGGARD

3.1.439   not] HANMER; now JAGGARD

3.1.446.1   *Enter...Bawd*] JAGGARD (*after* l. 447)

3.1.479   it] HAYES; as it JAGGARD

3.1.481   inconstant] HUDSON (Staunton); con-|ftant JAGGARD

3.1.527   Make my] JOWETT 1986 (Walker); Making JAGGARD;
Make a ALEXANDER

4.1.0.2   Mariana...[*discovered*]] JOWETT 1986; *Enter Mariana, and
Boy singing*. JAGGARD

4.1.2   were] JAGGARD; are BODLEIAN MS RAWL. POET. 65, fol. 26ᵛ,
FOLGER MS 452.4, fol. 20. For a full collation and discussion
of the song, see Jowett and Taylor, 'With New Additions',
Appendix 4.

4.1.3   the] JAGGARD; like *Rollo* Q1639, Q1640; that BODLEIAN MS
ENG. POET. f.27, pp. 66–7. The manuscript texts otherwise
agree with Jaggard.

4.1.3   of] JAGGARD; the BODLEIAN MS ENG. POET. f.27, pp. 66–7

4.1.5–6   bring again, bring again...sealed in vain, sealed in
vain] JAGGARD. No other seventeenth-century text of the song
indicates the repeats except COTES and HAYES (both repeats)
and ROBERTS (first repeat only).

4.1.6   though] BODLEIAN MS MUS. b.1, fol. 19ᵛ; but JAGGARD. The
MS is the composer John Wilson's song-book, and its reading
is supported by all other seventeenth-century texts except the
folios and MSS derived from them.

4.1.29   plankèd] JAGGARD (planched)

4.1.49.1   *Enter Mariana*] JAGGARD (*after* l. 48)

4.1.53   and so] LEVER; and JAGGARD; and I POPE; and oft DYCE 2

4.1.60   their] HANMER (*also emending to* 'Quests'), JOWETT 1986;
thefe JAGGARD. See Section B.

4.1.63.1   *Enter...Isabella*] JAGGARD (*after* 'agreed')

4.1.74   tilth's] THEOBALD; Tithes JAGGARD

4.2.55   yare] JAGGARD (y'are)

4.2.57.1   *Exit*] JAGGARD (*after* l. 56)

4.2.64   travailer's] JAGGARD (Trauellers)

4.2.69.1   *Enter Duke*] JAGGARD (*after* 'father')

4.2.89   th'unlisting] WHITE (Mason); th'vnfifting JAGGARD

4.2.101–2   This...DUKE] RANN (Thirlby, *in MS note*); Duke.
This...Pro. JAGGARD

4.2.101   lordship's] JAGGARD (Lordsₐ), ROWE 1714

4.2.121   PROVOST] ROWE 1709; *not in* JAGGARD

4.3.15   Torchlight] THIS EDITION; *Forthlight* JAGGARD; Forthright
WARBURTON. See Section B.

4.3.23   BARNARDINE (*within*)] JAGGARD (printing '*Barnardine
within.*' as stage direction, then speech-prefix '*Bar.*')

4.3.35.1   *Enter Barnardine*] JAGGARD (*after* l. 33)

4.3.62.2   *Enter Provost*] JAGGARD (*after* 'Exit', l. 60)

4.3.86   yonder] ROWE 1714; yond JAGGARD

4.3.96   well-balanced] JAGGARD (weale-ballanc'd)

4.3.103   ISABELLA (*within*)] JAGGARD (printing '*Isabella within.*' as
stage direction, then speech-prefix '*Isa.*')

4.3.108.1 *Enter Isabella*] JAGGARD (*after* 'expected')

4.3.125 convent] JAGGARD (Couent)

4.3.145.1 *Enter Lucio*] JAGGARD (*after* 'here')

4.4.5 redeliver] CAPELL (Thirlby, *in MS note*); re-|liuer JAGGARD

4.4.18 *Exit*] JAGGARD (*after* l. 17)

4.5.6 Flavio's] EVANS (Theobald); *Flauia's* JAGGARD; *Flavius's* ROWE 1709

4.5.8 Valentinus] CAPELL (Thirlby, *in MS note*); *Valencius* JAGGARD

4.5.10 FRIAR PETER] *Peter* JAGGARD. Similarly for the character's speech-prefixes and stage directions for the remainder of the play.

5.1.13 me your] HAYES; we your JAGGARD; we our LEVER

5.1.32 me, hear] CHAMBERS (Keightley); me, heere JAGGARD

5.1.124 and] JAGGARD; in JOWETT 1986 (*conj.*)

5.1.167 her face] COTES; your face JAGGARD

5.1.166.1–2 *Enter . . . Mariana*] JAGGARD (*after* 'witness, friar')

5.1.238 e'en to] THIS EDITION (G.T.); to JAGGARD; unto POPE; even to CAPELL

5.1.242 'gainst] COTES; against JAGGARD. JAGGARD's reading most plausibly originates in Crane's transcript. A similar case might be 'to accuse' at l. 299.

5.1.257.1 *Exit*] JAGGARD (*after* 'slanderers')

5.1.277.1–2 *Enter . . . Provost*] JAGGARD (*after* 'brother')

5.1.277.1–2 *Isabella . . . Duke . . . Provost*] DYCE (*subst.*); *Duke, Prouost, Isabella* JAGGARD

5.1.290 fore] JAGGARD (for)

5.1.372 wast] JAGGARD (was't)

5.1.372 e'er] JAGGARD (ere)

5.1.408 measure still for measure] JAGGARD (*Meafure* still for *Meafure*)

5.1.420 confiscation] COTES; confutation JAGGARD

5.1.422 buy you] JAGGARD; buy G.T. *conj.*

5.1.538 that's] COTES; that JAGGARD

B. Notes on the Adapted and Original Texts

The reconstructed text was first outlined in the Oxford Shakespeare *Complete Works* (JOWETT 1986), which prints the conjectured Shakespearean version of the opening of 1.2 and the passage surrounding the adaptation's Act 4 act-break, and in *Textual Companion*; it was given considerably more substance in Jowett and Taylor (1993). Readings that do not fall in the two passages reconstructed in the Oxford Shakespeare are printed as part of the text for the first time in the present edition. With this caveat in mind, the reconstruction can be attributed editorially to the Oxford Shakespeare and Jowett and Taylor (1993) unless otherwise stated below.

The following notes record subsequent work specifically for the present edition, and the contributions of other editors and textual critics. They include also documentation and discussion that is too technical or indecisive for presentation in the commentary, which supplements many of these notes.

Restored profanities first proposed by Taylor (1993), and first implemented in this edition, are to be found at: 1.1.74; 2.1.66; 2.2.25, 36, 42, 51, 69, 87, 128, 159; 2.4.2, 34; 3.1.107, 142, 338, 363, 376, 387, 412; 4.2.67; 4.4.3; 5.1.82, 118, 146, and 163. These readings are not recorded below.

Persons As printed in JAGGARD, after the play, the list omits the Justice, the Boy, Varrius, the non-speaking parts, and the Clown's name Pompey. The note of the scene (not included in the text of this edition) is printed above 'The names of all the Actors'. It is possible that the scribe Ralph Crane, perhaps with Middleton's help, revised a theatrical list of parts that pre-dated the adaptation, imperfectly bringing it

into line with the adapted text. 'The Scene Vienna' compares with 'The Scene, an vn-inhabited Island' above '*Names of the Actors*' in *The Tempest* (set from a Crane transcript) and '*The Sceane Rauenna*' above the list of '*The Persons*' in Crane's transcript of *The Witch*. Similar headings in other Middleton plays are from texts printed after 1650: *Changeling, Old Law, No Wit, Dissemblers, Women Beware,* and *Quiet Life.*

Persons.1 VINCENTIO] Named in 'The names of all the Actors', but nowhere in the dialogue, stage directions, or speech-prefixes of the play. Shakespeare uses the name for a dramatic role in *Taming of the Shrew*. Middleton refers to a Lord Vincentio in *Dissemblers* and *Women Beware*, both of which have, however, Italian settings. If the Duke's name was supplied by Shakespeare, its survival here could be evidence that a passage or passages naming him were cut during adaptation. See note to 1.1.2.

Persons.5 fantastic] Neither Shakespeare nor Middleton uses this word as a noun.

1.1.2 Vincentio] THIS EDITION (G.T.); *not in* JAGGARD. See Taylor, 'Mediterranean'.

1.1.8 But that [   ]] THIS EDITION (Theobald); But that, JAGGARD; Put that, ROWE; But this: JOWETT 1986. A widely debated crux, combining acute difficulty in sense with metrical irregularity. Those who have inferred an omission include Malone (suggesting eyeskip) and W. W. Greg, in Eccles (suggesting a deliberate cut) as well as Theobald. If Greg is right, the cut is most likely to have been made during adaptation.

1.1.45 Ferrara] THIS EDITION (G.T.); *Vienna* JAGGARD. Similarly throughout.

1.2.0.1–1.2.79 *Enter . . . custom-shrunk*] *identified as unShakespearean addition by* WILSON; *undifferentiated in* JAGGARD

1.2.4 its] To the examples in Middleton listed in Jowett and Taylor, p. 197, we can now add *Banquet* 1.4.172 and 4.2.85, both without apostrophe, and both in scenes attributed to Middleton.

1.2.25 as for example] See Jowett and Taylor, p. 204. Another Middleton parallel is to be found at *Banquet* 2.1.28–9.

1.2.34 speak feelingly] Cited as a 'lesser' Middleton link in Jowett and Taylor, p. 203, but Q2 *Hamlet*'s 'speake sellingly' (sig. N2^v, uncorrected) or 'speake fellingly' (corrected) are almost certainly errors for this phrase. Q3 initiates the usual emendation. The passage is not in the Folio text.

1.2.37 begin thy health] See Jowett and Taylor, p. 201. Further Middleton parallels for the sense 'drink a health to you' are 'begin to me' (*Banquet* 1.4.57) and 'begun to you' (3.3.60).

1.2.60 prithee] JAGGARD (pray'thee). *Prithee* is Middleton's preferred form. Crane evidently expanded, as he did in his transcripts of *Game*, whilst retaining the elision in *prithee* by marking an apostrophe.

1.2.79.2–1.2.79h [BAWD] . . . maid by him.] *Deleted in* JOWETT 1986 (*following Wilson's suggestion of a duplication*); JAGGARD *prints as unbroken dialogue following l. 79, with 'Enter Clowne.' after l. 79a*. The scribe Ralph Crane, when preparing a fresh manuscript, must have copied both the new passage and the lines it was designed to replace. When, prior to typesetting, the page-breaks were marked in the manuscript, it is likely that the replaced seven lines were perceived as a deletion, for the compositor who set them had to squeeze his type to the extent of saving about seven type-lines over the page.

1.2.99 What's to do here] Shakespeare does not elsewhere use the phrase 'What's to do' in the sense required here. 'What's to do?' in *Twelfth Night* 3.3.18 means 'what is there for us to do?', not 'What's going on?', 'What's the fuss?'. Middleton writes *What's here to do?* at least four times, always to mean 'What's going on here?'.

1.2.100.1–1.2.102 *Enter Provost…Juliet.*] JAGGARD places the entry after l. 102, preceding it with a scene-break, '*Scena Tertia.*' (first deleted by ROWE). Hence 1.3 is '*Scena Quarta.*' in Jaggard, and 1.4 is '*Scena Quinta.*'

1.2.102 and there's Madam Juliet] A potential objection to the speech as a whole being by Middleton, raised by Jowett and Taylor (p. 167, n. 109), is that the identification of Juliet is too lamely tacked on to the tacked-on addition for this procedure to be plausible. It can be answered that this reflects the staging: the guarded Juliet enters behind the Provost and Claudio. She will remain strictly in the background of the dialogue between Claudio and the Provost, and remains mentioned at 1.2.130 as though still virtually absent—at least from the leading group of characters.

1.2.102.1 *Exeunt Bawd and Clown*] *Exeunt.* JAGGARD. By one dramatic logic it would make sense for the Clown and Bawd to remain on stage to join Lucio and the Gentlemen as public observers. Considerations of doubling actors' parts might have determined that they left the stage despite the new continuity of action, though whether the doubling issue concerned the Clown and the Friar or the Bawd and the Nun would depend on the sequence of the following scenes, which may itself have been altered during adaptation.

1.3(a).0.2 *Friar Thomas*] JAGGARD. The Folio's list of 'The names of all the Actors' affirms that there are two separate friars called Thomas and Peter. There seems, nevertheless, little dramatic purpose in stipulating that Thomas (in 1.3) and Peter (in 4.5, 4.6, and 5.1) have separate identities. One possibility is that the distinction between Thomas and Peter was enforced to facilitate the doubling of parts. There might have been little room for manœuvre in casting 5.1, in which Friar Peter appears, because this scene contains more parts than any other in the play. A particular difficulty could have arisen after the adaptation, which introduced new speaking parts for the two Gentleman; these characters are on stage until the end of 1.2, and so could not double with the Friar of 1.3. Thus if it were found necessary for Peter to double with one of the Gentlemen, a different actor would need to play the Friar in 1.3. But there is no obvious reason why Friar Peter should have to double in this particular way, and the adaptation does not discernibly add to the overall count of necessary adult actors, which was not in first instance excessive for a King's Men play. Moreover, Middleton never uses his own forename Thomas (or for that matter Peter) as the name for a dramatic role. There may well have been a straightforward inconsistency on Shakespeare's part. Confronted with such ambiguity, Crane might have affirmed two roles by naming Peter in the stage directions and speech-prefixes in the final scenes; 'The names of all the Actors' at the end of the play lists '*Thomas*' and '*Peter*' as '2. Friers'. There is a case, then, for emending 'Thomas' to 'Peter'. The alternative way to approach the issue is to assert that there is no case to answer: the text simply stipulates two friars, it does not have to provide any rationale for doing so, and neither do its editors. Such a line of reasoning leads quickly to the canonization of accident and error, but the doubts are such in the present instance that we have followed the usual editorial practice of leaving the two roles intact, even though as a separate entity Friar Thomas is 'a ghostly father, belike'.

1.4.0.2–1.4.89.2 *Enter Isabella, and Francisca … door*; 1.3(b).0.2–1.3(b).54.1 *Enter Duke … [with Friar]*] THIS EDITION (G.T.); *scenes transposed in* JAGGARD

1.4.2 Holy Francisca] THIS EDITION; *not in* JAGGARD. Like the Friar's name Thomas in 1.3, this name is found here, in the opening direction for the one scene in which the figure appears, and in 'The names of all the Actors' printed after the play, but nowhere else. Francisca is, of course, an Italian name, and as such is consistent with the other names in the play as Shakespeare conceived it. For Shakespeare as he wrote, the significance of 'Francisca' would be that it suggests a follower of St Francis—such as was St Clare, the founder of the order to which the Nun belongs. In *Romeo and Juliet* Shakespeare comparably describes Friar Lawrence as a 'Franciscan Friar' (5.2.1). The textual characteristics are therefore Shakespearean. In contrast, it would not in itself have created any dramatic impact for Middleton as adapter to have inserted the name.

The matter would rest there were it not that the name Francisca appears along with Isabella in Middleton's *The Witch*. In the list of '*The Persons*' in that play, her name is placed immediately after that of the character who happens to share her name with the figure who in *Measure* is named alongside the Nun. The two women in *The Witch* are not only collocated, but also related, as sisters-in-law: a different kind of sisterhood from that invoked in *Measure* at 1.4.4. These coincidences are especially striking because the name 'Francisca' occurs in no other Elizabethan or Jacobean play.

Quite apart from her name, Middleton's Francisca potentially reflects Middleton's awareness of *Measure* in other ways. In *The Witch* Francisca is far from being a nun, and indeed her unchastity has resulted in her becoming pregnant. But in this she resembles Juliet in *Measure*, a figure who is virtually, through her betrothal to Claudio, the other Isabella's sister-in-law. This relationship, together with the role of Isabella in *The Witch* as an unmarried woman facing the consequences of pregnancy, suggest that she is specifically an analogue of *Measure*'s Juliet. Middleton's fascination with the latter role is reflected in his expansion of it when adapting *Measure*, and also in the other similar roles he scripted that are noted in the commentary to 1.2.100.1. His evident awareness of *Measure* when writing the role of Francisca in *The Witch* supports the supposition that he gave his character a name borrowed, in a spirit of irony, from Shakespeare's play.

There is, however, a difficulty with this. As far as is known, *Measure* was not printed before 1623, and, as 'Francisca' is not mentioned in dialogue, no one seeing the play on stage would be aware that this was her name. One explanation would be that, as we argue was the case with Vincentio, Shakespeare originally included the name Francisca in the dialogue. This would have enabled Middleton to associate the name with Isabella when writing *The Witch* from his memory of *Measure* on stage (perhaps there was an earlier revival). Notably, as in the first scene where we postulate that 'Vincentio' was deleted, the opening exchange is metrically defective. As in that instance, a name might have been deleted. If Isabella said 'Holy Francisca' or 'Sister Francisca', the two words would make a verse-line with 'Are not these large enough?' They would also discreetly echo—or anticipate—the Duke's address to the Friar as 'holy father' at the beginning of 1.3.

2.1.21–2 What…on thieves?] *marked as an addition in the adapted text* THIS EDITION (G.T.); *located as in this edition* JOWETT 1986; *after* 'seizes', l. 23, JAGGARD

2.1.79–80 this man's…Master Froth's] THIS EDITION; *the wo-mans…Miſtris Ouer-dons* JAGGARD; *lines missing*, JOHNSON (*conj.*)

2.1.188–94 What...Nine?—] *identified as a later addition in* THIS EDITION; *undifferentiated in* JAGGARD

2.1.262–73 What's...Exeunt] *identified as later addition in* JOWETT 1986 (*following* Wilson); *undifferentiated in* JAGGARD

2.2.25.1 *Isabella*] THIS EDITION (Wilson); *Lucio and Isabella* JAGGARD

2.2.25 God save] CLARK–WRIGHT (Thirlby, *in MS note*); 'Saue JAGGARD

2.2.43, 58, 72, 91, 112, 127, 151 PROVOST] THIS EDITION (G.T.); *Luc.* JAGGARD

2.2.132 LUCIO...that.; 2.2.135 LUCIO...on't.; 2.2.159 LUCIO...away.] *marked as extraneous to the original text in* THIS EDITION (Wilson); *undifferentiated in* JAGGARD

2.2.135 Art advised o' that?] Compare Shakespeare, *Merry Wives*, 1.4.96, 'Are you advised o' that?' and Middleton, *No Wit* 3.170, 'art advised of that?' As *No Wit* and *Measure* share the second person singular, the parallels marginally favour Middleton.

2.2.150 God] THIS EDITION; heauen JAGGARD

2.2.163 God save] HUDSON (Thirlby, *in MS note*); 'Saue JAGGARD

2.4.4 God] NOSWORTHY (Thirlby, *in MS note*); heauen JAGGARD

2.4.45 God's] NOSWORTHY; heauens JAGGARD

3.1.278 God bless] THIS EDITION (Schmidt); 'bleffe JAGGARD

3.1.341 God bless] THIS EDITION (Schmidt); Bleffe JAGGARD

3.1.513a–f O...fancies.] JOWETT 1986, *Additional Passage 2* (Jowett and Taylor); *these lines are printed at* 4.1.58–63 *in* JAGGARD

3.1.513c quests] COTES; Queft JAGGARD. The most plausible alternative emendation of JAGGARD's 'Run with these false, and most contrarious Quest' is to alter 'these' to 'their'. The latter reading is accepted in the present edition where the speech is printed in the same place as in JAGGARD, at 4.1.60. As Warburton first noted, 'These' quests upon the Duke's doings seems to refer to Lucio's slanders; the COTES reading therefore works much more persuasively given the position the speech is thought to have held before the adaptation took place, as here, at the end of Act 3. Warburton considered that this soliloquy should appear *before*, not *instead of*, 'He who the sword of heaven would bear'. His point about the referent of 'these...quests' equally well supports the case for the two soliloquies having been transposed. However, as the line can equally well be emended to 'their...quest' instead of 'these...quests', the reading 'these' carries little weight as evidence for the transposition. It is, in fact, as a consequence of the transposition that 'these' has been retained and 'Quest' emended. 'Quests' produces consistency with plural 'eyes', 'volumes', 'doings', etc.

3.1.513f Enter Isabella] JOWETT 1986, *Additional Passage 2* (Jowett and Taylor); *at* 4.1.20.1 JAGGARD

3.1.513f Very well met.] JOWETT 1986, *Additional Passage 2* (Jowett and Taylor); *as part of* 4.1.25 JAGGARD

4.1.1–6 Take...vain] The song is found, with a second stanza, in John Fletcher's *Rollo, Duke of Normandy* (1617–20; first printed 1639), in Thomas Cotes's and John Benson's corrupt 1640 edition of *Poems* by Shakespeare (and others), in a number of music manuscripts and verse miscellanies, and in four music-books published between 1652 and 1669 by John Playford. One manuscript derives from the Shakespeare Fourth Folio. All other manuscripts, and Cotes–Benson and Playford, follow the *Rollo* version; these include the authoritative text of the composer John Wilson's song-book. In Wilson's and other manuscripts, the music for the last two lines is marked for repetition. The second stanza (not printed in JAGGARD) is quoted in the commentary. There is no

sustainable evidence that *Rollo* was revised to incorporate the song. As F. W. Sternfeld points out, both the first and second stanzas were influenced by the Latin poem '*Ad Lydiam*'; and the song is decidedly better suited to its situation in *Rollo* than to that in *Measure*. Whereas *Rollo* has other songs, 'Take, O take' is unique in *Measure*, where it is sung by a boy who (like the two gentlemen in 1.2) has no other function in the play. Moreover, the composer of the extant music, John Wilson, was himself a mere boy in 1603–4, and cannot be supposed to have written the music at that date. Given that the first stanza must be interpolated in one play or the other, it seems far more probable that the recipient was *Measure*. This would be impossible if *Measure* included the song in 1603–4, but as there are independent reasons for supposing late adaptation of 1.2, the prospect opens up that, as Frank O'Connor and later, more seriously, Alice Walker suggested, the song was transferred from *Rollo* to *Measure* at the same time.

4.1.57a–v He...contracting] JOWETT 1986, *Additional Passage 2* (Jowett and Taylor); *these lines are printed at* 3.1.514–35 *in* JAGGARD. Textual dislocation has been mooted by Theobald (see note to 3.1.513c), Kellner, Muir, and Alice Walker.

4.1.60 their] HANMER (*also emending to* 'Quests'), JOWETT 1986; thefe JAGGARD. COTES retains 'these' and emends 'Quest' to 'Quests'. See note to 3.1.513c, where COTES is followed on account of the changed context. When the speech is located in 4.1 there is no obvious referent for 'these...quests'. The emendation 'their' allows a reference back to the 'false eyes', and so makes the speech self-contained.

4.2.131 but...bred] *identified as unShakespearean addition in* THIS EDITION; *undifferentiated in* JAGGARD

4.3.1–18 CLOWN...sake'.] *identified as unShakespearean addition in* THIS EDITION (G.T.); *undifferentiated in* JAGGARD. The extensive and sometimes distinctive Middleton parallels are recorded in the commentary. These may be set against the following found in Shakespeare but not Middleton: Deepvow (the closest parallel is in Shakespeare: 'deep vow', *Lucrece* l. 1847); Middleton has 'deep oath', *Nice Valour* 2.1.165); tilter (*As You Like It* 4.3.39); Shoe-tie (*Winter's Tale* 4.4.600); doers (seven instances of *doer* in Shakespeare, though without sexual implication).

4.3.15 Torchlight] THIS EDITION; Forthlight JAGGARD; Forthright WARBURTON. The usual reading 'Forthright' is anomalous in a passage attributed to Middleton, as he nowhere else uses the word. But it depends on an emendation made on the assumption of Shakespeare's authorship. The assumed error, 'l' for 'r', is not an easy misreading, whereas 't' can easily be taken as 'f' and 'c' is easily read 'r', and so 'Torchlight' provides graphically the easier misreading. 'Torchlight' indicates the disposition of the tilter (flaming and smoky); moreover the suggestion of the night-time perhaps encourages an association with tilting of a sexual kind. In *Revenger* and elsewhere Middleton associates torchlight with debauchery at court.

4.3.56 Fore God,] THIS EDITION; I fweare JAGGARD; God's will G.T. *conj.* Taylor plausibly identifies removed profanity, but Shakespeare had stopped using 'God's will' by the time he wrote *Measure*.

4.3.68 Ragusine...pirate] The name suggests a seafarer from Ragusa (Dubrovnik), which was a major seafaring city on the fringe of Venetian, Austrian, and Turkish spheres of influence. England had been hostile to it since 1588, when Ragusan ships had joined the Spanish Armada. The occupation recalls the reference to pirates in Middleton's addition to 1.2, but, as a man called Ragusine is very likely to be a pirate rather than any other kind of criminal, as the name occurs three times in the play, and as the Adriatic context is if anything more consistent with an Italian setting for the play, the line probably fits the context of the 1603-4

text better than that of 1621. Ragusa is on the same coast as Illyria, the setting for *Twelfth Night*.

4.3.166 Fore God] THIS EDITION; Yes marrie JAGGARD; By Jesu G.T. *conj.* The same considerations apply here as at 4.3.56.

PRESS VARIANTS

There are no confirmed textual press variants. Hinman (1963, vol. 1, p. 257) lists a single press variant, which merely sets right a typographical imperfection. Hinman, ed. (1968) records a substantive variant at 3.1.528, but it was subsequently discounted by Bawcutt (1988). The following variants were reported by Tannenbaum (3.1.430), and in the editions of Hart and Wilson (5.1.56); they have not subsequently been confirmed by Hinman or any other investigator:

G1ᵛ-6

3.1.430 tundish] Tunner-dish JAGGARD State a; Tunne-dish JAGGARD State b

G3-4ᵛ

5.1.56 characts] characts JAGGARD State a; caracts JAGGARD State b

Catchword Variants

1.2.0.1, 1.4.0.1, 2.2.0.1 *Scena* JAGGARD (*text*); *Scæna* JAGGARD (*c.w.*)
2.3.32 DUKE 'Tis] *Duk.* 'Tis JAGGARD (*text*); *Du.* 'Tis JAGGARD (*c.w.*)
2.4.105 Then] JAGGARD (*text*); That JAGGARD (*c.w.*)
3.1.152 Mercy] JAGGARD (*text*); Mercie JAGGARD (*c.w.*)
4.2.32 Ay,] I, JAGGARD (*text*); I, JAGGARD (*c.w.*)
4.4.2 ANGELO] *An.* JAGGARD (*text*); *Ang.* JAGGARD (*c.w.*)
5.1.274 she] She JAGGARD (*text*); Íhee JAGGARD (*c.w.*)

STAGE DIRECTIONS

1.1.0.1-3 *Actus primus, Scena prima.* | *Enter Duke, Escalus, Lords.*
1.1.25.1 *Enter Angelo.*
1.1.76 *Exit.* (after 1.1.75)
1.1.84.1 *Exeunt.*
1.2.0.1 *Scena Secunda.* | *Enter Lucio, and two other Gentlemen.*
1.2.42.1 *Enter Bawde.*
1.2.76.1 *Exit.*
1.2.79.2 *Enter Clowne.* (after 1.2.79a)
1.2.100.1-2 *Scena Tertia.* | *Enter Prouost; Claudio, Iuliet, Officers, Lucio, & 2. Gent.* (after 'Exeunt.', 1.2.102.1)
1.2.102.1 *Exeunt.*
1.2.175.1-2 *Exeunt.*
1.3(a).0.1-2 *Scena Quarta.* | *Enter Duke and Frier Thomas.*
1.3(a).54.1 *Exit.*
1.4.0.1-2 *Scena Quinta.* | *Enter Isabel and Francisca a Nun.*
1.4.6 *Lucio within.* (on a separate line above 1.4.6)
1.4.89.1-2 *Exeunt.*
2.1.0.1-3 *Actus Secundus. Scæna Prima.* | *Enter Angelo, Escalus, and seruants, Iustice.*
2.1.32.1 *Enter Prouost.* (after 2.1.31)
2.1.40.1 *Enter Elbow, Froth, Clowne, Officers.*
2.1.133.1 *Exit.* (after 2.1.132)
2.1.243 *Exit.*
2.1.273 *Exeunt.*
2.2.0.1-2 *Scena Secunda.* | *Enter Prouost, Seruant.*
2.2.6.1 *Enter Angelo.*
2.2.25.1 *Enter Lucio and Isabella.*
2.2.188.1 *Exit.*
2.3.0.1-3 *Scena Tertia.* | *Enter Duke and Prouost.*
2.3.9.1 *Enter Iuliet.*
2.3.41 *Exit.*
2.3.44 *Exeunt.*
2.4.0.1-2 *Scena Quarta.* | *Enter Angelo.*
2.4.17.1 *Enter Seruant.* (after 'there')
2.4.30.1 *Enter Isabella.* (after 'maid')
2.4.170.1 *Exit*
2.4.187 *Exit.*

3.1.0.1-3 *Actus Tertius. Scena Prima.* | *Enter Duke, Claudio, and Prouost.*
3.1.45.1 *Enter Isabella.* (after 3.1.43)
3.1.180 *Exit.*
3.1.268 *Exit.*
3.1.268.1 *Enter Elbow, Clowne, Officers.*
3.1.307.1 *Enter Lucio.* (after 3.1.306)
3.1.442 *Exit.*
3.1.446.1 *Enter Escalus, Prouost, and Bawd.* (after 3.1.447)
3.1.535 *Exit.*
4.1.0.1-3 *Actus Quartus. Scæna Prima.* | *Enter Mariana, and Boy singing.* | *Song.*
4.1.6.1 *Enter Duke.*
4.1.20.1 *Enter Isabell.*
4.1.24 *Exit.*
4.1.49.1 *Enter Mariana.* (after 4.1.48)
4.1.57.1 *Exit.*
4.1.63.1 *Enter Mariana and Isabella.* (after 'agreed')
4.1.74 *Exeunt.*
4.2.0.1-2 *Scena Secunda.* | *Enter Prouost and Clowne.*
4.2.18.1 *Enter Abhorson.*
4.2.28 *Exit.*
4.2.44.1 *Enter Prouost.*
4.2.57.1 *Exit* (after 4.2.56)
4.2.59.1 *Enter Claudio.*
4.2.69.1 *Enter Duke.* (after 'father')
4.2.100.1 *Enter a Messenger.*
4.2.120.1 *The Letter.*
4.2.208 *Exit.*
4.3.0.1-2 *Scena Tertia.* | *Enter Clowne.*
4.3.18.2 *Enter Abhorson.*
4.3.23 *Barnardine within.* (on a separate line above 4.3.23)
4.3.35.1 *Enter Barnardine* (after 4.3.33)
4.3.44.1 *Enter Duke.*
4.3.60 *Exit*
4.3.62.2 *Enter Prouost.* (after 'Exit', 4.3.60)
4.3.88.1 *Exit.* (after 4.3.87)
4.3.97.1 *Enter Prouost.*

4.3.102   Exit
4.3.103   Isabell within. (on a separate line above 4.3.103)
4.3.108.1   Enter Isabella. (after 'expected')
4.3.145.1   Enter Lucio. (after 'here')
4.3.173   Exeunt
4.4.0.1–2   Scena Quarta. | Enter Angelo & Escalus.
4.4.18   Exit. (after 4.4.17)
4.4.33.1   Exit.
4.5.0.1–2   Scena Quinta. | Enter Duke, and Frier Peter.
4.5.10.2   Enter Varrius.
4.5.13   Exeunt.
4.6.0.1–2   Scena Sexta. | Enter Isabella and Mariana.
4.6.8.1   Enter Peter.
4.6.16   Exeunt.
5.1.0.1–4   Actus Quintus. Scœna Prima. | Enter Duke, Varrius,
    Lords, Angelo, Escalus, Lucio, | Citizens at seuerall doores.
5.1.18.2   Enter Peter and Isabella.
5.1.166.1–2   Enter Mariana. (after 'witness, friar')
5.1.257.1   Exit. (after 'slanderers')
5.1.277.1–3   Enter Duke, Prouost, Isabella. (after 5.1.275)
5.1.376.1–2   Exit.
5.1.396.1   Enter Angelo, Maria, Peter, Prouost. (after 'brother')
5.1.476.1–2   Enter Barnardine and Prouost, Claudio, Iulietta.

[Printed after the play]

The Scene Vienna.
The names of all the Actors.

Vincentio: the Duke.
Angelo, the Deputie.
Escalus, an ancient Lord.
Claudio, a yong Gentleman.
Lucio, a fantastique.
2. Other like Gentlemen.
Prouost.
Thomas. } 2. Friers.
Peter.
Elbow, a simple Constable.
Froth, a foolish Gentleman.
Clowne.
Abhorson, an Executioner.
Barnardine, a dissolute prisoner.
Isabella, sister to Claudio.
Mariana, betrothed to Angelo.
Iuliet, beloued of Claudio.
Francisca, a Nun.
Mistris Ouer-don, a Bawd.

FINIS.

LINEATION NOTES

1.2.44–5   I…to] POPE 1728; verse JAGGARD: roof|
1.2.125   One…you] POPE; 2 lines JAGGARD: friend|
1.2.126–7   A…after] HANMER; hundred| JAGGARD
1.2.169   I pray she may] HANMER (continuing speech as verse),
    WILSON; prose JAGGARD
1.2.174   I'll to her] HANMER (printing rest of speech as verse),
    WILSON; prose JAGGARD
1.4.69–70   To…brother] HANMER; business| JAGGARD
1.4.71   Doth…life] HANMER; 2 lines JAGGARD: so|
2.1.44   How…matter] WILSON; prose JAGGARD
2.1.58   Why…Elbow] POPE; verse line JAGGARD
2.1.133   I…lordship] THEOBALD; prose JAGGARD
2.1.242   Whip…jade] ROWE 1714; prose JAGGARD
2.2.65–6   As…he] CAPELL; 1 line JAGGARD
2.2.85   Tomorrow…him, spare him] POPE; 2 lines JAGGARD:
    sudden|
2.2.116–17   Would…heaven] CAPELL (Thirlby); for thunder|
    JAGGARD
2.4.119   To…mean] ROWE 1714; 2 lines: would have| JAGGARD
3.1.3–4   But…die] CAPELL; prose JAGGARD
3.1.45   Who's…welcome] prose JAGGARD
3.1.49   And…sister] HART; prose JAGGARD
3.1.51   Bring…concealed] HART; prose JAGGARD
3.1.53   Why…indeed] POPE; 2 lines JAGGARD: Why|
3.1.295–6   Indeed…prove] POPE; verse JAGGARD: sir|
3.1.341   Adieu…friar] POPE; verse JAGGARD: Pompey|
3.1.349–50   Go…Duke] CAPELL; verse JAGGARD: go|
3.1.488–9   One…himself] CAPELL; verse JAGGARD: strifes|
3.1.509   If…proceeding] POPE; verse JAGGARD: life|
4.1.33–5   There…him] CLARK-WRIGHT (Walker); 2 lines JAG-
    GARD: upon the|
4.2.3–5   If…woman's head] POPE; verse JAGGARD: can| wife's
    head|

4.2.103–7   My…day] POPE; verse JAGGARD: note| charge| it|
    circumstance|
4.2.116–19   I…before] POPE; verse JAGGARD: you| remiss| me|
    strangely|
4.2.131–2   A…old] POPE; verse (?) JAGGARD: bred| (but PROV-
    OST…bred justified)
4.2.136   His…him] POPE; verse line JAGGARD
4.2.169–72   By…Angelo] POPE; verse JAGGARD: you| guide|
    executed|
4.2.171–3   Angelo…favour] POPE; verse JAGGARD: both|
4.3.20–1   Master…Barnardine] POPE; verse JAGGARD: hanged|
4.3.25–6   Your…death] POPE; verse JAGGARD: hangman|
4.3.28   Tell…too] POPE; verse JAGGARD: awake|
4.3.36–7   How…you] POPE; verse JAGGARD: Abhorson|
4.3.40–1   You…for't] POPE; verse JAGGARD: night|
4.3.49   comfort…with you] HAYES; verse line JAGGARD
4.3.109   Good…daughter] ROWE; prose JAGGARD
4.3.159–60   Nay…Duke] POPE; verse JAGGARD: with thee|
4.4.13–16   Well…him] CAPELL (Thirlby); prose JAGGARD
4.6.13   He…sounded] POPE; 2 lines JAGGARD: you|
4.6.16   The…away] POPE; 2 lines JAGGARD: entering|
5.1.19   Now…him] POPE; 2 lines JAGGARD: time|
5.1.26   Relate…brief] POPE; 2 lines JAGGARD: wrongs|
5.1.32   Or…me, hear] POPE; 2 lines JAGGARD: you|
5.1.68   Have…say] HANMER; 2 lines JAGGARD: reason|
5.1.80–2   I…perfect] CAPELL; then| have| then| JAGGARD
5.1.90–1   Mended…proceed] JOWETT 1986; 1 line JAGGARD
5.1.126   A…Lodowick] HANMER (Thirlby); 2 lines JAGGARD:
    belike|
5.1.278–9   Come…said] COTES; verse JAGGARD: gentlewoman|
5.1.280–1   My…Provost] POPE; verse JAGGARD: of|
5.1.309–10   Be…he] HANMER; dare| JAGGARD
5.1.447–8   For…intent] JOHNSON (Thirlby); 1 line JAGGARD
5.1.521–2   Marrying…hanging] POPE; verse (?) JAGGARD:
    death| (LUCIO…death justified)

THE TRAGEDY OF MACBETH: A GENETIC TEXT

Edited by Gary Taylor

'*Mackbeth*' (BEPD 404) is among the plays listed in the Stationers' Register general entry, on 8 November 1623, for Shakespeare's *Comedies, Histories, and Tragedies*. It was first published in that month in that collection (sigs. ll6–nn4), hereafter identified by its printer, JAGGARD. The most authoritative accounts of the editorial preparation, printing, and publication of JAGGARD as a whole are those by Taylor (1987), Hinman (1963), and Blayney, respectively; an excellent facsimile is available (Hinman 1968, 1996). However, none of the issues raised by these larger studies of the *Comedies, Histories, and Tragedies* is of much relevance to *Macbeth* itself. Aside from some inking quads, only three stop-press variants have been identified, all on a single folio page (sig. nn2): the correction of a page number (from '149' to '147') and of two obvious textual errors (4.3.155, 214).

Macbeth was set by two compositors, A and B; the differing and identifying characteristics of these two workmen were in fact first noticed in this play (Satchell). Compositor A was responsible for all but 96 lines until the end of 3.3; Compositor B then finished the play.

> A: 1.1.0.3–1.6.20 (hermits), 1.7.42–2.4.19 (so), 3.1.22–3.4.0.1
> B: 1.6.20 (where's)–1.7.41, 2.4.19 (to)–3.1.21, 3.4.0.2–end

A survey and assessment of modern studies of all the compositors at work on Jaggard's 1623 collection can be found in Wells and Taylor (1987), 148–54. Most significant for the editor of *Macbeth* have been the studies of compositorial error by Werstine (1978) and Taylor (1981). The evidence collected in Werstine's study of compositorial mislineation (1984) has been applied with particular force by Brooke, who shows that most of the versification problems which have vexed previous editors of *Macbeth* originated in certain recurring bad habits of Compositor A (213–24).

It has been generally thought that JAGGARD was printed directly from the promptbook of the King's Men (Greg 392–5). In part, this conclusion is based upon evidence that the printed text represents a late theatrical adaptation of an earlier original play by Shakespeare; this evidence—which connects Middleton to the play, and which has been widely accepted since 1867—is discussed in 'Canon and Chronology'. However, such evidence only establishes that a promptbook lies behind JAGGARD; it cannot tell us if any, or how many, intermediate manuscripts might lie between the adapted promptbook and JAGGARD. Davenant seems clearly to have had access to a theatrical text

of the play which differed in some important respects from JAGGARD, and which could easily have been the promptbook (Spencer 1961, 58–71); Taylor and Jowett demonstrate that JAGGARD's scene divisions cannot derive from the promptbook, but are instead evidence of a scribal transcript intended for reading (239–42). The scribe has not been identified, but of the 36 plays in Jaggard's collection *Macbeth* most closely resembles *All is True*. Both texts contain scene divisions, make extensive use of round brackets, and prefer the spellings 'ha's' and 'O'; all these features are also shared by the 1622 edition of *Othello*. Another feature shared by all three plays is an apparent attempt to restore, conjecturally, references to the deity which had been forbidden on stage since 1606 (Taylor and Jowett 87–8). None of the texts is supplied with a list of persons (like those appended to transcripts by Ralph Crane). Given these many similarities, it is possible that a single scribe prepared, in the early 1620s, literary transcripts of all three plays.

Editorially, the chief difficulties of this text are related to its adaptation. Since the reason for including Shakespeare's play in an edition of Middleton is that Middleton adapted it, it has seemed desirable—here as in *Measure for Measure*—to highlight the conjectured process of adaptation. The text therefore uses special typography to distinguish passages which we believe were added, altered, or cancelled. However, because the hypothesis that Middleton adapted *Macbeth* has been familiar and indeed orthodox for more than a century, it has not seemed necessary to provide here a detailed commentary substantiating Middleton's presence, like that appended to *Measure for Measure* (where the hypothesis of adaptation is less familiar and more contested).

The songs added in 3.5 and 4.1 exist in several different texts: Ralph Crane's transcript of *The Witch* (CRANE), a manuscript collection of lute songs in the Fitzwilliam Museum (BULL), another such collection in the New York Public Library (Drexel 4257, here cited as GAMBLE), the Yale manuscript of William Davenant's adaptation, *c.*1662, of *Macbeth* (DAVENANT 1), the 1674 edition of Davenant's text, printed by Clark (DAVENANT 2), and an edition of *Macbeth* incorporating some material from Davenant's adaptation, printed in 1673 (by CADEMAN). For Davenant and the Restoration texts, see Spencer (1961, 1965); for a full account of CRANE, see the textual introduction to *The Witch*, p. 995; the fullest account of the relevant texts and their relationships is provided by Brooke (225–33). It is clear that the texts of the songs were, in some respects at least, altered to fit the different dramatic circumstances of *Macbeth*, and as a result none of these variant texts is, in itself, entirely satisfactory or uncomplicated. CRANE is the earliest witness, but gives a text of a different play; the two music manuscripts (BULL, GAMBLE), though they date from c.1630 and provide notes as well as words, remove the song from any dramatic context, and arrange it for a single singer; the three Restoration texts (DAVENANT 1–2, CADEMAN), although they fit the songs into the specific dramatic context of *Macbeth* and in many respects clearly derive from the theatrical practice of the King's Men, may also contain further alterations by Davenant. Moreover, every one of these six texts suffers from some demonstrable error. In these circumstances, one can only construct an eclectic text, based upon individual consideration of every variant; my textual notes are, as a result, exceptionally discursive.

For the rest of the play, JAGGARD is the only text with any substantive authority. It was republished in 1632 (printed by Thomas COTES), 1663 (printed by John HAYES and Robert DANIEL), and 1685 (by an unidentified printer, for a consortium of publishers headed by Henry HERRINGMAN), passing from there into a long tradition of Shakespeare editions from Rowe (1709) to Brooke (1990). Recent editors of this play, as of others in the Shakespeare canon, have become increasingly conservative, often rejecting even the most widely accepted conjectures and emendations of earlier scholars. But programmatic conservatism is hardly warranted by the circumstances of this particular text's transmission: JAGGARD's compositors added their own errors to those accumulated in a literary transcript of an adapted and annotated promptbook which was, itself, almost certainly not in the handwriting of either Shakespeare or Middleton. *Macbeth* was apparently adapted in a period between the first productions of *The Lady's Tragedy* (1611) and of Fletcher and Massinger's *Sir John van Olden Barnavelt* (1619); in neither did the King's Men use an authorial manuscript as their promptbook. In the several known stages of the text's transmission and adaptation, there was plenty of opportunity for human error.

This text differs from all previous editions of *Macbeth*—and from all other texts in the Oxford Middleton—in removing all punctuation and all capitalization at the beginning of sentences or verse lines. The punctuation of JAGGARD bears little, if any, relation to Shakespeare's (or Middleton's) intentions; it reflects the preferences of two different compositors, working from a scribal manuscript which was itself copying, probably, another (annotated) scribal manuscript. On the evidence of the Hand D pages of *Sir Thomas More*, Shakespeare's own manuscripts contained virtually no punctuation, and what punctuation there was would be unlikely to survive into a printed text, or would there be surrounded by so much non--authorial punctuation that the identity and function of any such authorial relics would be irrecoverable. Thus, every comma, colon, semicolon, period, question mark, exclamation mark, or parenthesis in JAGGARD (and every subsequent edition) represents an act of interpretation, not an act of preservation or restoration. Likewise, neither

Shakespeare's manuscripts nor Middleton's capitalized the beginnings of sentences or verse lines. Such capitals are, in effect, punctuation marks.

For the same reason, we have not supplied speech directions ('aside', 'to X', 'aloud'), which almost never occur in contemporary manuscripts, and which some editors replace with different punctuation or a different typeface. We have also not attached a commentary to this text. Every commentary note, like every act of punctuation, makes interpretive choices. So does every dramatis personae list. We have therefore removed the list of persons, and the list of parts, from *The Collected Works*, and placed them instead here in the apparatus.

Spelling produces a more intractable editorial problem. Punctuation and certain kinds of stage direction can be entirely eliminated; but words *have* to be spelled, one way or another. The spelling of JAGGARD, like its punctuation, is primarily compositorial, and to a lesser extent scribal. It would have been possible, using concordances, to impose upon the text Middleton's spelling preferences, but Middleton was not the primary author, and we know little (some would say nothing) about Shakespeare's preferred spellings. In these circumstances, the choice of any early modern spellings would necessarily have been arbitrary, lending an undeserved weight to differences which have no more authority than differences in punctuation. Likewise, any phonetic system would have had to make arbitrary assumptions about early modern pronunciation. Because modern spelling is prescribed, formal, and relatively invariant, not individualized or phonetic, it is the least intrusively interpretive system available. The few cases where modern spelling obscures substantive ambiguity are more than outweighed by the thousands of cases where it removes meaningless arbitrary variation. Of course, the resulting orthography is not authoritative, but that is part of its point: there *is* no authority in these matters.

It would have been possible to go even further in this process. We considered eliminating all apostrophes, but decided in the end that they represented spelling, not punctuation; virtually none involve real ambiguity. We might also have eliminated all stage directions, or refrained from adding editorial directions; but all early dramatic manuscripts contained stage directions, the movement of persons and props was always an essential part of the text, and editorial directions are clearly distinguished by square brackets. Some scholars would prefer us to have avoided any editorial emendation of the text, which—like punctuation and capitalization—cannot be divorced from issues of interpretation. But not to emend would simply have reified and idolized the text of JAGGARD; it would have made a whole series of interpretative choices, while pretending not to make any. We have tried, here, to restore the actual words which we believe Shakespeare and Middleton wrote, and the minimal actions necessary to stage their text, without supplying the apparatus of punctuation, capitalization, indentation, commentary, and arbitrary orthography which usually accompany those words.

The resulting text is, admittedly and deliberately, alien and alienating. It combines modern, familiar, un-Renaissance spellings (including apostrophes) with an unmodern, unfamiliar treatment of punctuation and capitalization, and an entirely editorial use of typography to distinguish between original and adapted material. There are no glossarial notes, many fewer stage directions, and no list of characters, to ease the difficulties of reading. But *Macbeth* is already available in more editions than any other work in this *Collected Works*; readers who want a more comfortable text can find it easily enough elsewhere.

Because there have been so many editions of this play and of Shakespeare's works, the following list of editions only contains texts actually cited in the notes.

SEE ALSO

Text: *Works*, 1170
Music and dance: this volume, 158
Authorship and date: this volume, 383

WORKS CITED

Previous Editions

Braunmuller, A. R., ed., *Macbeth*, New Cambridge Shakespeare (1997)

Brooke, Nicholas, ed., *Macbeth*, Oxford (1990)

Cademan, William [publisher], *Macbeth a tragedy: acted at the Dukes-Theatre* (1673): Wing S2929

Capell, Edward, ed., *Comedies, Histories, and Tragedies*, 10 vols (1767-8)

Clark, W. G., and W. A. Wright, eds., *Macbeth* (1869)

Davenant, William, *Davenant's 'Macbeth' from the Yale Manuscript* (1961)

—— *Macbeth a tragaedy: with all the alterations, amendments, additions, and new songs: as it's now acted at the Dukes Theatre* (1674): Wing S2930

Delius, Nicolaus, ed., *Werke*, 7 vols (1854-61)

Evans, G. Blakemore, ed., *The Riverside Shakespeare* (1974)

Hanmer, Thomas, ed., *Works of Shakespeare*, 6 vols (1743-4)

Hunter, A. (Harry Rowe) ed., *Macbeth*, second edition (1799)

Johnson, Samuel, ed., *Plays*, 8 vols (1765)

Keightley, Thomas, ed., *Plays*, 6 vols (1864)

Malone, Edmond, ed., *Plays and Poems*, 10 vols (1790)

Pope, Alexander, ed., *Works*, 6 vols (1723-5)

—— ed., *Works*, 10 vols (1728)

Rowe, Nicholas, ed., *Works*, 6 vols (1709)

—— ed., *Works*, 6 vols (1709) [second edition]

Schafer, Elizabeth, ed., *The Witch* (1994)

Singer, Samuel W., ed., *Dramatic Works*, 10 vols (1856)

Steevens, George, ed., *Plays*, 10 vols (1773)

—— ed., *Plays*, 10 vols (1778)

—— and Isaac Reed, ed., *Plays*, 15 vols (1793)

Theobald, Lewis, ed., *Works*, 7 vols (1733)

Warburton, William, ed., *Works*, 8 vols (1747)

Wells, Stanley, and Gary Taylor, gen. ed., *William Shakespeare: The Complete Works* (1986)

White, Richard Grant, ed., *Works*, 12 vols (1857-66)

Wilson, John Dover, ed., *Macbeth*, New (1947)

Other Works Cited

Blayney, Peter W. M., *The First Folio of Shakespeare* (1991)

Coghill, Nevill, '*Macbeth* at the Globe, 1606-1616 (?): Three Questions', in *The Triple Bond: Plays, Mainly Shakespearean, in Performance*, ed. Joseph G. Price (1975), 223-239

Cutts, John P., 'Jacobean Masque and Stage Music', *Music and Letters* 35 (1954), 185-200

Ewbank, Inga-Stina, 'The Middle of Middleton', *The Arts of Performance in Elizabethan and Early Stuart Drama*, ed. Murray Biggs et al. (1991), 156-71

Greg, W. W., *The Shakespeare First Folio: Its Bibliographical and Textual History* (1955)

Hinman, Charlton, *The Printing and Proof-Reading of the First Folio of Shakespeare*, 2 vols (1963)

—— ed., *The Norton Facsimile: The First Folio of Shakespeare* (1968, rpt. 1996)

Holdsworth, R. V., 'Middleton and Shakespeare: The Case for Middleton's Hand in *Timon of Athens*', unpublished Ph.D. thesis, University of Manchester (1982)

Holinshed, Raphael, *The Chronicles of England, Scotlande, and Ireland* (1587)

Houston, John Porter, *Shakespearean Sentences: A Study in Style and Syntax* (1988)

Howard-Hill, T. H., '"Lizard's Braine" in Middleton's *The Witch*', *Notes and Queries* 217 (1972), 458-9

Ibsen, Henrik, 'Preface', *The Feast at Solhoug* (rev. edn., 1883), *The Oxford Ibsen*, ed. James Walter McFarlane, I (1970)

Jonson, Ben, *Masque of Queens* (1609), in *The Complete Masques*, ed. Stephen Orgel (1969)

Krabbe, Henning, 'The "Time-Server" in the Porter's Speech in *Macbeth*', *Notes and Queries* 218 (1973), 141-2

Lyle, E. B., 'The Speech-Heading "I" in Act IV, Scene I, of the Folio Text of *Macbeth*', *The Library*, V, 25 (1970), 150-1

Orgel, Stephen, '*Macbeth* and the Antic Round', *Shakespeare Survey* 52 (1999), 143-53

Parsons, Robert, *An ansvvere to the fifth part of Reportes lately set forth by Syr Edward Cooke Knight, the Kinges Attorney generall. Concerning the ancient & moderne municipall lawes of England, Which do apperteyne to spirituall power & iurisdiction* (1606)

Pepys, Samuel, *The Diary of Samuel Pepys*, ed. Robert Latham and William Matthews, 11 vols (1971-95)

Satchell, Thomas, 'The Spelling of the First Folio', *Times Literary Supplement*, 3 June 1920, 352

Scot, Reginald, *The Discovery of Witchcraft* (1584), ed. Brinsley Nicholson (1886)

Seligmann, Raphael, 'The Functions of Song in the Plays of Thomas Middleton', unpublished Ph.D. dissertation, Brandeis University (1997)

Spencer, Christopher, ed., *Davenant's 'Macbeth' from the Yale Manuscript* (1961)

—— ed., *Five Restoration Adaptations of Shakespeare* (1965)

Taylor, Gary, 'The Shrinking Compositor A of the Shakespeare First Folio', *Studies in Bibliography* 34 (1981), 96-117

—— 'General Introduction', in Wells and Taylor (1987), 1-68

—— '"Praestat difficilior lectio": *All's Well that Ends Well* and *Richard III*', *Renaissance Studies* 2 (1988), 27-46

—— and John Jowett, *Shakespeare Reshaped 1606-1623* (1993)

Walker, W. S., *A Critical Examination of the Text of Shakespeare*, ed. W. N. Lettsom, 3 vols (1860)

Wells, Stanley, and Gary Taylor, with John Jowett and William Montgomery, *William Shakespeare: A Textual Companion* (1987)

Werstine, Paul, 'Compositor B of the Shakesperae First Folio', *Analytical and Enumerative Bibliography* 2 (1978), 241-63

—— 'Line Division in Shakespeare's Dramatic Verse: An Editorial Problem', *Analytical and Enumerative Bibliography* 8 (1984), 73-125

TEXTUAL NOTES

1.1.5 set] DAVENANT 1; the ſet JAGGARD

1.1.8 Greymalkin] JAGGARD (*Gray-Malkin*)

1.1.7.1 *a cat mews within*] THIS EDITION; *not in* JAGGARD. WILSON notes the need for such offstage cues, but does not supply them in his text. See 'Canon' and following notes.

1.1.8.1 *a toad croaks within*] THIS EDITION; *not in* JAGGARD.

1.1.8 SECOND] POPE; *All.* JAGGARD. Although editors have agreed on the need to redistribute these words to different speakers, they have not explained the error, which is an unusual kind of speech-prefix confusion. But it could arise from a marginal addition, particularly one which—like the text of 'Come away' in *The Witch*—did not indicate the division of lines among the witches. As emended, this line gives each of the three witches a third speech in this scene: thrice times three.

1.1.8.2 *an owl shrieks within*] DAVENANT (*subst.*); *not in* JAGGARD. Unlike the other two speeches, 'Anon' does not identify the caller by name; like WILSON, I assume it is the 'Harpier' at 4.1.3—presumably a flying creature which, like cats and toads, was associated with witches. One might have guessed 'owl' even without Davenant.

1.1.8 THIRD] SINGER 2 (*conj.* Hunter); *not in* JAGGARD

1.1.9 ALL] POPE; *not in* JAGGARD

1.2.13 galloglasses] COTES (Gallow glaſſes); Gallowgroſſes JAGGARD

1.2.14 quarrel] HANMER; Quarry JAGGARD. WELLS-TAYLOR retains 'Quarry', but in doing so is forced to paraphrase 'his' as 'its' (i.e. Fortune's). But Fortune is always personified as female, making it more likely that 'his' refers to Macdonald, and hence that 'Quarry' was an error for 'Quarrel'; Holinshed supports this reading, too. BROOKE claims that 'quarry' is 'a common form of quarrel', but he cites no evidence, and *OED* provides none.

1.2.26 strike] THIS EDITION; *not in* JAGGARD; breaking COTES; break POPE. Both grammar and metre indicate that a word is missing here. COTES's guess was rationalized by Pope, and from Pope accepted by all editors, but the word has no authority, and conjecture need not be limited to a 1632 guess rationalized a century later. Neither Shakespeare nor Middleton collocated 'break' and 'thunder'. Compare 'thunder, Strike' (*Tragedy of King Lear* 3.2.6–7), 'By thunder struck' (*Quarrel* 3.1.26), and 'May thunder strike me' (*Hengist* 5.2.64). Alternatively, one might insert 'threaten' (a word both Middleton and Shakespeare use in similar contexts). The omission might have been caused by a misunderstood deletion mark; the next line and a half seems to have been written by Middleton, perhaps to replace a longer passage which has been cut. (See Canon and Chronology.)

1.2.31, 49, 1.3.93 Norwegian] JAGGARD (Norweyan)

1.2.32 furbished] JAGGARD (furbuſht)

1.2.44.2 *Ross*] CAPELL (*subst.*); *Roſſe and Angus* JAGGARD. Not only is Angus given nothing to say; both Malcolm and Lennox respond to the entrance with singular pronouns. This looks like a remnant of an earlier version of the scene, in which Angus took part; compare 2.3.87.1. Although DAVENANT substitutes Macduff for Ross here, he anticipates CAPELL by removing the second figure from this entrance. Alternatively, Angus may have entered separately in the original scene, and been added to this stage direction to introduce him

(in preparation for his entrance with Ross in 1.3). But it would have been just as easy to add Angus to the opening stage direction of the scene, if the only purpose were to compensate for an omitted entrance somewhere else. It seems more likely that Angus appears in this stage direction as a relic of his original entrance, an entrance made superfluous in the adaptation by cutting elsewhere in the scene.

1.2.46 haste] COTES, DAVENANT 1; a haſte JAGGARD. EVANS reverts to JAGGARD's reading, but neither Shakespeare nor Middleton offers a parallel for 'a haste', which is extrametrical and could result from the commonest of all interpolations. Compare 'Jesu, what haste' (*Romeo* 2.5.29), 'What haste comes here now?' (*Trick* 4.4.92), 'what haste it makes' (*Changeling* 4.1.110).

1.2.47 seems] JAGGARD; teems JOHNSON *conj.*

1.2.52 numbers terrible] POPE; terrible numbers JAGGARD. Most modern editors revert to JAGGARD, but Shakespeare is unusually fond of postpositioned adjectives (Houston); compare in particular 'sorceries terrible' (*Tempest* 1.2.264) and 'accents terrible' (*Macbeth* 2.3.57)—both, as here, at the end of a verse line. Although there are parallels for the rhythm of 'terrible numbers', transposition not only regularizes the metre but completes the verse line. In general, editors resist emendations involving transposition, but compositorial and scribal studies demonstrate that it is a common form of error.

1.2.62 Colum's] JAGGARD (Colmes)

1.3.21 se'en-nights] JAGGARD (Seu'nights). Modern dictionaries list 'sennight' as an archaic word, but given its obsolescence it seems more helpful to modern readers to use a form which makes its meaning clear (and is in any case closer to JAGGARD).

1.3.30, 1.5.7, 2.1.19, 3.1.2, 3.4.132, 4.1.154 weird] JAGGARD (weyward). JAGGARD uses this spelling throughout.

1.3.37 Forres] POPE; Soris JAGGARD. The emendation presumes the manuscript spelling 'Foris'.

1.3.95 hail] ROWE; Tale JAGGARD

1.3.96 came] ROWE; Can JAGGARD

1.3.117 to me the thane of Cawdor] THIS EDITION; the thane of Cawdor to me JAGGARD. Shakespeare's decisions about where to place the portable prepositional phrase 'to me' (which occurs hundreds of times in his work) are elsewhere based on metre, and he often places it before the verb: compare 'To me you speak not' (l. 55), 'To me came Tarquin' (*Lucrece*), 'to me belongs' (Sonnet 92), 'to me subscribes' (107), 'to me then tendered' (120), 'to me are nothing novel' (123), 'to me she's married' (*Taming*), 'To me she speaks' (*Errors*), 'to me bequeath' (*Midsummer Night's Dream*), 'to me sent' (*Love's Labour's Lost*), 'to me give' (*Henry V*), 'this world to me is' (*Pericles*), 'to me welcome you are' (*Richard II*), 'To me can life be' and 'to me thy secrets tell' (*Winter's Tale*), 'to me you cannot reach' (*All is True*). In this passage the pronoun must be emphasized, in contrast to the subsequent 'to them'; the chiasmus and abnormal position of the prepositional phrase both create emphasis. It would have been very easy for a compositor or scribe to substitute the common word order: see Taylor 1988.

1.4.1 or | are] THIS EDITION; ‸ | Or JAGGARD; Are COTES. Although 'Are' has been preferred by editors, this emendation explains the error equally well, and restores not only sense but metrical regularity in the first line.

1.4.23 doing ₐ] THIS EDITION; ~ it JAGGARD. Metrically preferable, no difference in meaning, and an easy interpolation.

1.5.28 metaphysical] JAGGARD; metaphysic POPE

1.5.46 it] HAYES; hit JAGGARD

1.5.64 the innocent] DAVENANT 1; th'innocent JAGGARD. (An extremely crowded line of type.)

1.6.4 martlet] ROWE; Barlet JAGGARD

1.6.5 loved] loued JAGGARD (= lovèd)

1.6.5 masonry] POPE 2; Manfonry JAGGARD. Compare 'incarnardine' (l. 2.2.60), where there is a similar repetition of a superfluous consonant, emended by everyone.

1.6.9 must] JAGGARD; most ROWE. BROOKE persuasively defends JAGGARD.

1.6.26 count] JAGGARD (compt)

1.7.6 shoal] JAGGARD (Schoole)

1.7.47 do] ROWE; no JAGGARD. DAVENANT 1 agrees with the substance of ROWE's emendation: 'He who dares more is none'.

1.7.68 lie] COTES; lyes JAGGARD. Failure of concord does occur in both Shakespeare and Middleton, but usually for the same reason that it occurs in ordinary speech; here, where nothing intervenes to separate the noun and verb, the clash is glaring, and could easily have resulted—as the first reprint assumed—from simple repetition.

2.1.15 th'] THIS EDITION; the JAGGARD. For the elision 'by th'' compare 2.4.6; it occurs 83 times in Shakespeare.

2.1.52 offerings] DAVENANT 1, HAYES; Offrings JAGGARD

2.1.55 strides] POPE; fides JAGGARD

2.1.56 sure] CAPELL (conj. Pope); fowre JAGGARD

2.1.57 way they] ROWE; they may JAGGARD

2.2.35 sleeve] JAGGARD (Sleeue)

2.2.60 incarnadine] JAGGARD (incarnardine).

2.3.5 time hanger] THIS EDITION; time ₐ JAGGARD; farmer CLARK–WRIGHT; time-server WILSON; time-pleaser KRABBE conj. Although it is true that 'come in time' can mean 'arrived in a timely fashion', this does not fit either the pattern of the rest of his speech ('come in, equivocator...come in, tailor'), and does not seem to have much verbal or dramatic point. Of the conjectures, 'time-server' has the same meaning as 'time-pleaser'; Shakespeare uses the latter twice, the former never. However, a farmer who hoards grain in times of scarcity is not a 'time-pleaser', but one who precisely does *not* provide what would please or serve the times. The logic of these conjectures therefore seems mistaken. The emendation 'farmer' provides obvious sense and the same kind of repetition used elsewhere in the speech, but it is hard to explain why a compositor would have misread 'farmer' as 'time' immediately after he had just correctly set 'farmer' as 'farmer'. The emendation 'time hanger' assumes simple scribal or compositorial eyeskip from 'hanger' to 'haue'. It puns on the notion of hanging, in a way typical of Shakespeare and the Porter. Shakespeare has 'bed-hangers' at 2 Henry IV 2.1.146 and 'hangers' (three times) in Hamlet 5.2.150-60 (where Hamlet jokes about them). The Porter calls the farmer a 'time-hanger' because he hanged himself in expectation of a future time; he was 'hanging' in suspense over future prices; the price of his produce was 'dependent on' (hanging upon) on scarcity or plenty at the time of its sale; the farmer also hanged or killed time, by ending his time on earth. (Compare 'time go hang thee' in Dekker and Ford's The Sun's Darling.) Some of the same meanings would be achieved by 'time-hanger-on' or 'time-hanger-by', but I have not adopted

those alternatives because Shakespeare does not use that compound. Shakespeare does, however, use 'hangman' as a playful term of abuse (Much Ado 3.2.11), which would make sense here, but reduce the range of meanings.

2.3.78 horror] THEOBALD; horror. Ring the Bell. JAGGARD. Probably a marginal promptbook stage direction misread as speech. Lady Macbeth's 'What's the business' seems to complete this verse line.

2.3.87.1 Lennox] DAVENANT 2; Lenox, and Ross JAGGARD. Ross did not exit with Macbeth and Lennox to view the body, and has not hitherto appeared in the scene; moreover, he must enter at the beginning of 2.4. WELLS–TAYLOR defend his presence, on the grounds that a 'ghost' seems 'unlikely in a promptbook'; but an adapted promptbook could easily retain stray signs of altered intentions not systematically imposed. Since Ross and Lennox have until now always appeared as a pair, this direction might well represent the original staging of the scene. (The text of DAVENANT 1 is defective hereabout; DAVENANT 2 presumably represents Restoration staging.)

2.3.109 outran] DAVENANT 1; Out-run JAGGARD. OED does not record 'run' as a past tense; misreading would be easy.

2.4.18 ate] JAGGARD (eate)

3.1.23 talk] MALONE; take JAGGARD. The reverse substitution occurs at Hamlet 1.1.144 and Henry V 2.1.50.

3.1.46 a word] STEEVENS–REED; a word with you JAGGARD. The two phrases—'a word' and 'a word with you'—have the same meaning, which means that they are easy for copyists to substitute for each other, and that there is no subtlety of difference between them which an author might deliberately exploit. In Shakespeare's verse, which of the two is used seems determined solely by metrical regularity ('a word' 16 times, 'a word with you' 9 times, each producing a regular line where the alternative would be irregular). Moreover, in Shakespeare's late verse, from History of Lear to Tempest, 'a word' is used 9 times, 'a word with you' never; this fits his later tendency to avoid pleonasms to fill out verse lines. Here, 'with you' is redundant and extrametrical, almost certainly the result, not of authorial intention, but of the unconscious compositorial substitution of a synonymous phrase, prompted by 'with you' in the preceding line.

3.1.70 seeds] JAGGARD; seed POPE

3.1.75, 115, 139 MURDERERS] JAGGARD (Murth.)

3.2.16 whilst] JAGGARD (whileft)

3.2.35 visors] JAGGARD (Vizards)

3.2.43 shard-born] JAGGARD (fhard-borne). For two recent persuasive defences of this spelling and interpretation of the word, see Timothy Billings, 'Squashing the "shard-borne Beetle" Crux: A Hard Case with a Few Pat Readings', Shakespeare Quarterly 56 (2005), 434–447, and G. Blakemore Evans, '"The shard-borne [-born] beetle," Macbeth, 3.2.42-43', American Notes and Queries 18.4 (2005), 31-4.

3.3.7 and] COTES; end JAGGARD

3.4.1 sit down] JAGGARD. These two (extrametrical and unnecessary) words should perhaps be omitted, on the assumption that they are a stage direction which has been misinterpreted as part of a speech. Confusions apparently arising from marginal stage directions also occur at 2.3.78 and 4.1.128.1-2.

3.4.17 didst it] JAGGARD; ~ that THIS EDITION conj. The emphasis in this clause should surely be on the direct object of the verb: First Murderer has already claimed credit, at l. 15, for Banquo's death—('that I did') and Macbeth replies by encouraging him to claim credit for Fleance's—'if thou didst *that*'. The error is an easy one to make, by simple substitution or misreading; 'that' was often spelled 'y^t'.

3.4.77   time] WHITE; times JAGGARD

3.4.88   of the] ROWE; o'th' JAGGARD. The unelided forms are more metrical.

3.4.143   in deed] THEOBALD; indeed JAGGARD

3.5.33.1–3.5.73.1   *music . . . exeunt singing witches*] WELLS–TAYLOR was the first edition to attempt to sort out the textual problems created here by *Macbeth*'s incorporation of a song from *The Witch*. BROOKE develops and sophisticates their solutions, and provides a much fuller discussion of the variant texts of the song (225–33).

3.5.33.1   *music and a song*] JAGGARD; *Music* BROOKE. Although Jaggard's direction *could*—as Brooke argues—be a duplication deriving from marginal notes in a promptbook, the statement 'I am called' (l. 35) would normally indicate speech, not simply instrumental music. See following notes.

3.5.33.1   *by other witches*] THIS EDITION; *not in* JAGGARD. The additional characters needed to sing this song are not identified here, but at 4.1.38.1 JAGGARD specifies that Hecate should enter with 'the other three witches'. This can only refer to the additional characters in 3.5.

3.5.34   SINGING WITCHES] THIS EDITION; SPIRITS WELLS–TAYLOR; *not in* JAGGARD. See previous note. The attribution of these and subsequent sung lines to 'Spirits' (in WELLS–TAYLOR and BROOKE) has no textual authority, and contradicts their identification in 4.1 as 'witches'. If Hecate is to be called (as her speech indicates) and a song is to be sung (as the stage direction indicates), someone has to call and sing: see following note.

3.5.34   *singing within*] THIS EDITION; *not in* JAGGARD; *singing dispersedly within* WELLS–TAYLOR. BROOKE believes that ll. 33–4 were spoken, because they do 'not fit the music'; this is possible, but the direction at l. 33.1 specifies 'a song'. Likewise, the direction at l. 37 calls for singing 'within', and it seems unlikely that the singers would first appear onstage then retreat off again. Although 'dispersedly' is possible, it is not necessary.

3.5.34   *Hecate . . . away*] DAVENANT; *not in* JAGGARD; *Come away, come away, Hecate, Hecate, come away* WELLS–TAYLOR. The logic of the preceding notes suggests that the offstage spirits must be given something specific to sing—as indeed they are in Davenant's texts, prepared for theatrical performance. The absence of such material from the other texts is not surprising, because as a separate non-theatrical song this summons would be superfluous, and in *The Witch* 3.3 the dramatic situation is different. Here, there are two possibilities: either to adopt Davenant's solution (presuming that it derives from the King's Men's promptbook) or to assume that the offstage summons simply consisted of an extra singing of the first two lines of the song (as WELLS–TAYLOR conjectured). Although either arrangement would work, the one adopted here has the advantage of seventeenth-century authority.

3.5.34.1   *a cloud appears*] WILSON; *Machine descends* DAVENANT (*at l. 36.1*); *not in* JAGGARD. Since a machine is required later (see l. 1–2), it seems sensible to produce it here, where Hecate's speech announces its appearance.

3.5.34.1   *carrying . . . cat*] THIS EDITION; *not in* JAGGARD+. Both Hecate's speech and the direction at l. 1–2 suggest that a single spirit is visible in the cloud.

3.5.36.1   *the song*] CRANE (Song:); *Sing within.* JAGGARD. Practically, this direction makes it unnecessary to repeat 'singing' before each of the following speech prefixes.

3.5.37   FOURTH WITCH] THIS EDITION; I. DAVENANT I, CADEMAN; *not in* DAVENANT 2; SPIRITS WELLS–TAYLOR; FIRST SPIRIT BROOKE; Voices of Witches SCHAFER. See note at 3.5.33.1. Here and throughout the song, the Restoration attribution of parts of the song to numbered singers (1, 2, 3) refers only to the offstage voices, which are in addition to the three (bearded) witches already on stage. In the theatre, there would be no confusion between the offstage actors (with song sheets) and those on stage; but for a modern reader they need to be clearly distinguished. Effectively, 'Fourth Witch' is not an emendation but simply an interpretation of the meaning of the Restoration speech prefix 'I.'

3.5.37   *in the air*] CRANE; *not in* JAGGARD. This direction—which recurs at ll. 42, 43–5—is not quite equivalent to 'within', since it implies that the voices are coming from 'above' and that they are not localized in one part of the building: it suggests 'invisibly dispersed above'.

3.5.37   *within*] JAGGARD, DAVENANT I. Since JAGGARD's direction covers the entire song, it has been added editorially for subsequent lines not sung by Hecate.

3.5.37–73   *come away . . . reach*] DAVENANT, CADEMAN; *Come away, come away, &c.* JAGGARD. The Restoration theatrical texts confirm that the song identified in JAGGARD only by its first line is the song given in full in *The Witch* and in various song manuscripts.

3.5.37   come away come away] come away DAVENANT, CADEMAN

3.5.38   O] *not in* CRANE. From this point until the end of the song, JAGGARD provides no guidance. Except where verbal variants are recorded, all texts agree; for example, all six seventeenth-century texts of the song except Crane's transcript of *The Witch* contain the word 'O' at this point. However, BULL and GAMBLE are arranged for a single voice, and are of no use in distributing speeches; for such variants, only four texts are available for collation.

3.5.39   I come . . . I come] 'I come' is repeated only twice in DAVENANT; only twice here, and then twice again after l. 40, in CADEMAN.

3.5.41   with . . . may] *not in* DAVENANT I

3.5.42   ˄ where's] I. Where's CADEMAN

3.5.42   Stadlin] Stadling BULL, DAVENANT, CADEMAN. BROOKE adopts the variant, but 'Stadlin' is used six times elsewhere in *The Witch*.

3.5.42   FIFTH WITCH] THIS EDITION; 2. DAVENANT; 3. CADEMAN; in ye aire CRANE; SPIRIT WELLS–TAYLOR; SECOND SPIRIT BROOKE; Stadlin SCHAFER. Since the singing spirits are offstage, an audience cannot see who is singing any of these lines divided between the spirits; hence, variants in CADEMAN—apparently based upon witnessing performances of the 1672 revival—are of little value. WELLS–TAYLOR follows CRANE in not specifying which spirit sings which line; however, some division of the lines seems necessary, to convey the experience of different voices singing from different parts of the theatre/tiring-house. For the specific attribution to the Fifth Witch here, see the note on the Fourth Witch at 3.5.37.

3.5.42   HECATE] DAVENANT; *not in* CRANE; I. CADEMAN

3.5.42   SIXTH WITCH] THIS EDITION; 3. DAVENANT; 4. CADEMAN; ANOTHER SPIRIT WELLS–TAYLOR; THIRD SPIRIT BROOKE; Puckle SCHAFER. See note on Fourth Witch at 3.5.37.

3.5.43   ˄ and] OTHER SPIRITS *within* WELLS–TAYLOR. This is an attractive staging. However, the absence of a prefix here from all the Restoration texts makes it clear that this staging was not adopted later in the seventeenth century, and it is hard to see why Davenant should have altered this detail, if it stood in the King's Men's promptbook. Conceivably, the prefix at l. 44 was slightly misplaced, and should have stood here; but even that assumption would only warrant assigning the line to the First Spirit, not to several.

3.5.43 Hoppo] CRANE, GAMBLE; Hopper DAVENANT, CADEMAN, BROOKE; Hope BULL. BULL could be an error for either alternative. All four texts with 'Hopper' derive from the 1672 revival, and hence could result from a single error; CRANE and GAMBLE are evidently independent of one another, and thus reinforce each other as authority for 'Hoppo'. Compare 'Stadlin', where GAMBLE and CRANE are clearly correct.

3.5.43 Hellwain] CRANE; Hellway DAVENANT, CADEMAN, BULL, GAMBLE. CRANE's reading is supported by *Witch* 1.2.5, 105.

3.5.44 FOURTH WITCH] THIS EDITION; 1. DAVENANT, CADEMAN; *not in* CRANE. The absence of a speech prefix in CRANE is not significant, since that text also omits all the preceding prefixes for the spirits.

3.5.44 lack...lack] want...want DAVENANT, CADEMAN. The variant looks like a Davenant improvement.

3.5.46 HECATE] *not in* CADEMAN

3.5.47 I...mount] *not in* CRANE

3.5.47.1 *a spirit...descends*] CRANE (opposite ll. 49–50); *not in* DAVENANT, CADEMAN. Both DAVENANT texts have '*Machine descends*' at l. 36.1; all that is involved here is the further descent of the winch, which need not have been specified. What all three texts agree upon is the use of a flying machine.

3.5.47.1–2 *the other...above*] WELLS–TAYLOR (*subst.*); aboue CRANE (opposite 50–2); *not in* DAVENANT, CADEMAN. The change of stage direction from 'in yᵉ aire' to 'above' seems significant; as BROOKE notes, 'it seems unlikely they remained invisible throughout'.

3.5.47.2 *witches*] THIS EDITION; *Spirits* WELLS–TAYLOR, BROOKE. See note at 3.5.33.1.

3.5.48 FOURTH WITCH] THIS EDITION; 1. DAVENANT, CADEMAN; *not in* CRANE. See note on the attribution at 3.5.37.

3.5.48 here comes] Ther's one CRANE

3.5.48 one down] GAMBLE; comes down CRANE; one BULL; down one DAVENANT; one, it is CADEMAN. Although BROOKE adopts BULL, all five other texts agree on the presence of more, and four agree on 'down'. This is much more likely to be the result of simple omission in one text than contaminated transmission of all. Middleton uses 'come[s] down' 17 times elsewhere.

3.5.49 coll] cull GAMBLE, CADEMAN

3.5.49 a sip] ſip CADEMAN

3.5.50 stay'st] stayest GAMBLE

3.5.50, 52, 54 CAT] THIS EDITION; *not in* CRANE, DAVENANT, CADEMAN. As the associated dialogue variants make clear, the staging of the 1672 revival differed from that imagined in *The Witch*; all the 1672 texts therefore constitute essentially one witness for speech prefixes here. Our only other witness, CRANE, systematically omits speech prefixes for everyone but Hecate in this song. BROOKE's emendation, suppling three prefixes for the Cat, therefore amounts to no more than an interpretation of the ambiguous distribution of speeches in CRANE. As Brooke observes, Firestone's speech after l. 55 (see note) indicates that 'evidently she mews' on the words muse, news, refuse—an effect the 1672 revival removed. The effect might have been removed in earlier productions, but it is the sort of indecorousness to which Restoration adapters particularly objected. BROOKE supplies the prefix between each repetition, so that the Cat echoes the spirits; however, CRANE sets all three repetitions as separate short lines, justified to the right, a format elsewhere used to indicate changes of speaker.

The mewing effect does not require the Cat to echo someone else; the layout of CRANE suggests that, instead, uncannily, it anticipates the completion of the others' sentences.

3.5.50 I muse I muse] I muse DAVENANT, CADEMAN

3.5.51 FOURTH WITCH] THIS EDITION; FIRST SPIRIT BROOKE. This emendation is a consequence of the editorial attribution of the previous words to the Cat; in effect, it continues the attribution already made in seventeenth-century texts at 3.5.48.

3.5.51 sweet] freshe GAMBLE

3.5.52 HECATE] CRANE; *not in* DAVENANT 1, CADEMAN; 2. DAVENANT 2

3.5.52 what news what news] what News? DAVENANT, CADEMAN

3.5.53 FIFTH WITCH] THIS EDITION; 2. DAVENANT 1, CADEMAN; *not in* CRANE, DAVENANT 2; SPIRIT LIKE A CAT WELLS–TAYLOR. BROOKE's interpretation—see note to l. 50—makes better sense of the Cat's role than that adopted in WELLS–TAYLOR, and is supported by the 1672 revival.

3.5.53 still to] CRANE, BULL; well to GAMBLE; for DAVENANT 1; fair for DAVENANT 2, CADEMAN. DAVENANT 1 is a simple error for the reading in the two other texts based on the 1672 revival. However, that shared Restoration reading is contradicted by the indepedent testimony of BULL and CRANE, and GAMBLE is clearly closer to that reading than to the Restoration alternative.

3.5.54 refuse refuse] refuse DAVENANT, CADEMAN

3.5.55 HECATE] CRANE; *not in* DAVENANT, CADEMAN. It is hard to account for these variants, unless there was a deliberate change of staging in the Restoration revival. See note at 55.1.

3.5.55 now] No BULL

3.5.55 I am] I'm DAVENANT 2

3.5.55 flight] *Flight.* | *Fire:* hark, hark, the Catt sings a braue *Treble in* | *her owne language.* | *Hec.* CRANE. Fire-Drake's speech is clearly embedded in the different dramatic context of *The Witch* (although its *content* is relevant to interpretation of what precedes: see note to l. 50).

3.5.55.1 *Hecate...up*] *going up* CRANE; *not in* DAVENANT, CADEMAN. The absence of any direction here, combined with the missing prefix at l. 55, suggests that in the 1672 revival Hecate herself did not fly.

3.5.56 and] *not in* CRANE, CADEMAN; oh GAMBLE. CADEMAN demonstrates how easily this word could drop out; GAMBLE confirms the presence of an extra syllable (and note) here.

3.5.57 Malkin] Malking DAVENANT 2

3.5.58 ʌ O] CRANE; 3: ~ DAVENANT, CADEMAN, BROOKE; HECATE AND SPIRITS ~ WELLS–TAYLOR. The absence of a speech prefix in CRANE here is not in itself significant; but at 69.1 CRANE's direction calls for a repetition of the quatrain '*aboue*', a location it had used earlier for the spirits. If the spirits sing these lines, the direction would be redundant, as none of the other directions in this sparsely-annotated text are. In the 1672 revival, the spirits spoke in turn (1, 2, 3); but in that revival, there is no evidence that Hecate herself ever became airborne. The speech prefixes for the end of the song in the Restoration texts seem to assume a less spectacular staging; in *The Witch*, Hecate, who has been called and then been preparing herself, ends the episode not only with flight but with an extended solo celebrating her flight. This arrangement seems even more desirable in *Macbeth*, since it allows Hecate to dominate the beginning and the ending of the scene. It also makes unnecessary other emendations which editors have felt compelled to make elsewhere in the song (at ll. 61, 65). Finally, at l. 65, it makes more sense for Hecate (speaking for herself and the cat-familiar with which she shares the ascending machine) to say 'We fly by night 'mongst troops of spirits' than for spirits to say they fly among troops of themselves.

3.5.58 pleasure's this] pleafure is this GAMBLE; pleasure 'tis CRANE

3.5.59–60 ride in the air when] saile i'th'aire while DAVENANT, CADEMAN. Clearly a deliberate variant, most likely to have been introduced by Davenant.

3.5.60–1 fair and] ~ To DAVENANT, CADEMAN. Restoration grammatical correction.

3.5.61 feast and dance] BULL, GAMBLE; sing, and daunce CRANE; sing, to Toy DAVENANT, CADEMAN. CRANE agrees with the texts of the 1672 revival on the presence of 'sing' in this verbal catalogue, but 'feast' is a very Middletonian word here: he often associates feasts with 'music' (*Timon* 11.33–4, *Revenger* 3.5.217–8, *Five Gallants* 5.2.6, *Women Beware* 3.2.130), with lust (*Revenger* 1.2.188, *Chaste Maid* 2.1.50, *Tennis* 806, etc.), and with 'dance' (*Dissemblers* 1.3.13); at *Witch* 1.2.25 witches 'feast' a 'hundred leagues in air'. Both readings could be Middletonian, but 'feast' seems preferable. As for 'dance', it is present in every text but CRANE and CADEMAN, but the later is evidently defective anyway. See next note.

3.5.61 and toy and] to Dance, and DAVENANT; to toy and CADEMAN. The repeated 'to' continues the grammatical tidying; CADEMAN is clearly missing a two-word phrase in this line, and although the result is ambiguous it probably was meant to duplicate the other Restoration texts. The issue then is whether 'kiss' is linked to 'toy' or 'dance'; all three early texts link it to 'toy', and the variation in the order of verbs therefore looks like a Restoration attempt at less-predictable coupling.

3.5.62 ‸ over] CRANE, DAVENANT, CADEMAN; CHORUS OF SPIRITS Over BROOKE. BROOKE's emendation contradicts CRANE's direction at l. 69.1 and CADEMAN's prefix at l. 66; and see note at l. 58.

3.5.63 seas our mistress fountains] CRANE; seas [our/and] [cristell/mistris] GAMBLE; seas and misty BULL; Hills and misty DAVENANT; misty Hills and CADEMAN. As BROOKE notes, 'Hills', found in all the texts derived from the 1672 revival, is clearly a copyist's error, suggested by 'rocks and mountains' in the preceding line, and producing mere redundancy. The testimony of these same texts in favour of 'misty' is therefore of dubious value, since 'hills' (unlike seas) could hardly be defined in apposition as 'our mistress fountains'. GAMBLE's 'and' replaces a crossed-out word, probably 'our', and it offers 'cristell' and 'mistris' as bracketed variants. As GAMBLE's text, and the number of variants elsewhere, demonstrate, the line clearly caused problems for copyists, and the problems are likely to be due to difficulty of thought—and there is no difficulty of thought in the simple 'and misty fountains'. In this context, 'mistress' is clearly the more difficult reading, and as BROOKE notes, 'it offends principle to attribute the wittier reading to a copyist'. Previous editors have assumed that the seas are imagined as fountains whose waters are pulled up by the moon (an incarnation of the spirits' 'mistress', Hecate); among other things, this interpretation presumes that the line is not sung by Hecate herself. (See note to l. 58). Alternatively, and I think more plausibly, 'mistress' is here simply a superlative adjective, the appropriately-female equivalent to 'master'. Compare 'master-fountain' (*Hengist* 4.2.69).

3.5.64 steeples] Steepe CRANE

3.5.65 spirits] BROOKE adds after this word '*Hecate and the Cat disappear above*'. The added direction presumes that Hecate is not singing. See note at 58.

3.5.66 no] Cho. No CADEMAN. This direction is probably misplaced; see l. 69.1.

3.5.67 howls] noise BULL. (Probably contamination from the following line.)

3.5.67 nor] GAMBLE, DAVENANT, CADEMAN; no BULL; or CRANE. Both BULL and CRANE contain one half of the reading shared by all other texts.

3.5.67 yelps] elps BULL

3.5.68 nor] not CRANE

3.5.69 or] BULL, CRANE; Nor GAMBLE, DAVENANT, CADEMAN. The texts of the 1672 revival probably agree in a grammatical correction made by Davenant.

3.5.69 throat] BULL, CRANE; throats GAMBLE, DAVENANT, CADEMAN. The texts of the 1672 revival smooth the grammar; in this context, addition of an extra terminal -s would be easy, anyway. There is no such reason to doubt the singular form, which produces a better parallel: waters breach | cannons throat.

3.5.69.1 exeunt . . . heavens] THIS EDITION; *Exeunt into the heavens the Spirit like a Cat and Hecate* WELLS–TAYLOR (*at l. 73.1*); *Hecate and the Cat disappear above* BROOKE (*at l. 65*). None of the early texts provides a direction for the precise moment of the flying exit; this is typical of the vagueness of CRANE, and in the 1672 revival it is unlikely that Hecate herself flew at all.

3.5.70–3 SINGING WITCHES (*above*) no . . . reach] THIS EDITION; SPIRITS *above* no . . . reach WELLS–TAYLOR; *No ring of Bells &c.*} *aboue* CRANE; *not in* BULL, GAMBLE, DAVENANT, CADEMAN. Both the specific 'aboue' and the indentation of the verse suggest that CRANE intends a change of speaker/singer. It is therefore not surprising that this stanza is not repeated in the song manuscripts, designed for a single voice, and therefore unconcerned with the dramatic function of repetition of the same words by a different party. Likewise, in the 1672 revival there is no change of singers, and the repetition would serve no purpose—although, notably, CADEMAN does call for this stanza to be sung by a 'Chorus' [of witches, presumably] (see l. 66). In our edition of *Witch* 3.3.69–72, CRANE is interpreted not as a call for repetition but as a speech prefix and stage direction for the four preceding lines, which are therefore sung once, not twice. Because the scribe's and author's intentions are disputable, we have printed one interpretation in *Macbeth*, and the other in *Witch*.

3.5.73.1 exeunt singing witches] THIS EDITION; *Exeunt Spirits* BROOKE (*at 69.1*); *not in* CRANE, BULL, GAMBLE, DAVENANT, CADEMAN

3.6.23a son] THEOBALD; Sonnes JAGGARD

3.6.23o their] JAGGARD; the DAVENANT 1, HANMER. Most editors have emended, in order to make some sense of the passage; but, as BROOKE notes, 'the only king under discussion has been Edward, and . . . in Act 4, it is Edward, not Macbeth, who is preparing for war.' But this line presents no difficulties, if we assume that the text of this scene—as of the preceding and following scene—has been adapted. See next note.

3.6.24–30 LORD sent . . . provide] JAGGARD. These lines have been the source of insoluble difficulties (well explained by BROOKE, pp. 51–3, and discussed in 'Canon and Chronology'). As the text stands, they must mean that Macbeth sent to Macduff while Macduff was in England (as explained in the immediately preceding lines); this means that Macbeth knows Macduff is in England, which directly contradicts 4.1.157–74 (where Macbeth is first brought word of Macduff's departure). Moreover, they require us to interpret 'their king' (23i) as a reference to Macbeth, the 'he' referred to in the immediately following speech. But if ll. 23–23j were cut, these lines would refer to Macbeth's inviting of Macduff to the feast dramatized in 3.4 (where Lennox was present); 'he' would then refer, without ambiguity, to 'the tyrant' now specified only one line before. The hypothesis that ll. 23–23j were marked for omission removes all the logical and narrative difficulties created by this scene. It is not unusual for printed texts to include material which was marked for omission, or—as seems to have happened here—to omit only a crossed-out line or two at the beginning or end of the intended cut. The (conjectured) cancellation would have required re-ascription of the subsequent speeches between the two lords; either this had not been done in the ancestral adapted manuscript, or the scribe or compositor, confused by an illogical sequence of prefixes, conjecturally emended them, thereby restoring the original attributions (obviously necessary if the intended cut was not made).

4.1.43.1   *music ... vessel*] THIS EDITION; *Musicke and a Song* JAG-GARD; *A Charme Song: about a Vessell* CRANE

4.1.44–58   *black ... wench*] DAVENANT; *Blacke spirits, &c* JAG-GARD; *not in* CADEMAN. The JAGGARD direction calls for the song which DAVENANT's adaptation provides in full, presumably from the King's Men's promptbook. CRANE provides the only early text of the whole song; several of the proper names are taken from Scot.

4.1.44   ∧ black] CRANE; FOURTH SPIRIT BROOKE. It is quite clear that in the seventeenth century Hecate began the song. In *The Witch*, Hecate's previous line ends 'whilst I begin the charm' (5.2.62), making clear that she should sing the first lines of the song; in DAVENANT these lines are preceded by the speech prefix 'Hec:'. The only question is, when did the others join in? See the following notes.

4.1.45   may | ∧] CRANE; I Witch DAVENANT; FOURTH WITCH WELLS–TAYLOR. Unlike the song in 3.5, this song is provided with coherent speech prefixes in CRANE: six different witches are addressed by name by Hecate in ll. 45–7, and there are six witches on stage in *Macbeth*; in *Witch*, she is also accompanied by six helpers (Fire-Drake, and the 'five sisters' she mentions at 5.2.40). DAVENANT took Hecate's lines and divided them up between herself and two witches; but he did the same at 1.3.30–5, where a speech assigned by JAGGARD to 'All' is assigned to the first, second, third, and second witches in succession (an arrangement adopted by no editor of Shakespeare). Thus, although DAVENANT's speech divisions here may derive from the original promptbook, they may also represent DAVENANT's own alteration, whereas CRANE certainly represents Middleton's intention, at some point, for performance of this song. The change in dramatic circumstances from *Witch* to *Macbeth* does not seem to require changing the attribution of lines here: in both plays, Hecate alone has authority over all the witches, and is in the best position to address commands to them.

4.1.46   Titty] CRANE, SCOT; Tiffin DAVENANT. (Bowdlerization or contamination, which turns two separate names into one.)

4.1.47   ∧ Fire-Drake] CRANE, DAVENANT 2; 2: ~ DAVENANT 1

4.1.48   ∧ Liard] CRANE, DAVENANT 2 (*subst.*); HECATE ~ DAVENANT 1

4.1.48   Liard] CRANE, SCOT; Lyer DAVENANT. In DAVENANT this becomes an adjective, so that the line addresses a single witch.

4.1.49   ALL] WELLS–TAYLOR; *not in* CRANE; Chor: DAVENANT; CHORUS OF WITCHES BROOKE. See l. 59. The variant here could result from a simple omission in CRANE; the lines certainly seem more appropriate to the group.

4.1.49   round around around] CRANE; A round a round a round DAVENANT 1; A round, a round DAVENANT 2

4.1.51   FOURTH WITCH] WELLS–TAYLOR; I. witch CRANE; I. DAVEN-ANT; FIFTH WITCH BROOKE. The emendations here and below in WELLS–TAYLOR interpret the 'first', 'second' and 'third' as referring to the three additional witches who enter with Hecate (that is, witches four to six).

4.1.52   HECATE] CRANE, DAVENANT; FOURTH WITCH BROOKE. BROOKE's emendation is based on the assumption that Hecate's participation in the song 'demeans her'; but that is not a view shared by any of our seventeenth-century sources, where Hecate is in charge of the ceremony, giving a series of imperative directions about ingredients suggested by her cohorts.

4.1.52   put in that O] CRANE; O put in that DAVENANT

4.1.53   FIFTH WITCH] WELLS–TAYLOR; 2. CRANE, DAVENANT; SIXTH WITCH BROOKE. See note to l. 51.

4.1.53   leopard's bane] CRANE (*Libbards Bane*); Lizards brain DAVENANT. It is unlikely that Crane would misread words he had written correctly only a few lines before in *The Witch*; as Howard-Hill notes, the manuscript reading is confirmed by Jonson's *Masque of Queens* 189.

4.1.54   HECATE] CRANE, DAVENANT; FOURTH WITCH BROOKE. See l. 52.

4.1.54   a grain] DAVENANT; againe CRANE

4.1.55   FOURTH WITCH] WELLS–TAYLOR; I. witch CRANE; I. DAV-ENANT; FIFTH WITCH BROOKE. BROOKE is forced to make his emendation, for which there is no early authority or plausible explanation, because he has already assigned the preceding speech to Fourth Witch in order to avoid assigning it to Hecate.

4.1.55   the ... the] CRANE; Here's ... here's DAVENANT

4.1.56   ∧ those] DAVENANT, BROOKE; 2. ~ CRANE; FIFTH WITCH ~ WELLS–TAYLOR. The DAVENANT variant is clearly related to that at l. 58 (see note).

4.1.56   charm grow] DAVENANT; yonker CRANE. The variant here has been dismissed as a weak substitution by Davenant, but 'yonker' is specifically appropriate to the dramatic situation in *The Witch*, and inappropriate to *Macbeth*; moreover, Middleton used the phrase 'grow madder' at *Women Beware* 3.2.267. If Davenant had simply wished to avoid the inelegant word 'yonker', he could have substituted some other word referring to Macbeth. The variant changes the charm from one directed at a specific individual (appropriate to the plot of *The Witch*) to something more general (appropriate to the multiplying evil of *Macbeth*).

4.1.57   FIFTH WITCH] THIS EDITION; 2. DAVENANT; Hec: CRANE; FOURTH WITCH BROOKE. See speech-prefix notes at ll. 53, 56, 58.

4.1.57   there's all and rid] CRANE; all these, 'twill raise DAVENANT

4.1.58   HECATE] DAVENANT; Fire⟨stone⟩ CRANE; A WITCH WELLS–TAYLOR; SIXTH WITCH BROOKE. In *The Witch* Fire-Drake is counted as one of Hecate's six assistants here, one who has not yet contributed to the song, who contradicts Hecate's conclusion ('there's all') and adds a final decisive ingredient. In *The Witch* it is appropriate that Fire-Drake, whose insubordination has been dramatized throughout the play, should take these lines. However, in *Macbeth* such an intrusion would serve no purpose, except to diminish the authority of Hecate, which is absolute in this scene. Middleton therefore would have had good dramatic reason to alter the text, and the DAVENANT variant probably reflects the King's Men's promptbook. Re-assigning this line to Hecate would, in turn, have required reassignment of the two preceding lines: see notes above.

4.1.58 a] DAVENANT; *the* CRANE. BROOKE defends the definite article as a reference to Mary Magdalene, the prostitute; but in *The Witch* it clearly refers to 'the red-haired girl I killed last midnight' (5.2.58–9), and in any case the fact that Mary Magdalene was famous for her repentance does not make her good material for an evil charm.

4.1.59 ALL] CRANE; Chor: DAVENANT; CHORUS OF WITCHES BROOKE. It is not at all clear that Davenant's reading differs in substance from Crane's; Brooke's addition is designed, like his other emendations in this scene, to separate Hecate from the song. See l. 49.

4.1.59 round around around] CRANE; A round a round DAVENANT

4.1.59–60 about . . . out] CRANE (&c.), DAVENANT (&c)

4.1.76 germens] POPE; Germaine JAGGARD

4.1.76 all together] JAGGARD (altogether)

4.1.79, 81, 86, 92 HECATE] THIS EDITION; I JAGGARD. The weïrd sisters elsewhere speak in rotation; here the first witch is apparently given five speeches in a row. Since Hecate is identified as 'I' at l. 143, it seems likely that 'I' also refers to her here, where she takes charge. DAVENANT, who dispenses with the apparitions, has Hecate take over until l. 120. Editors have perhaps refrained from this obvious solution because Hecate is not, in these speeches, confined to iambic tetrameter; but she is not so confined in *The Witch* either, and most of these lines would be as metrically uncharacteristic of First Witch as of Hecate. The confusion could have arisen as a consequence of the addition of the apparitions: see Canon and Chronology.

4.1.84, 106, 120, 127 ALL BUT MACBETH] THIS EDITION; All. JAGGARD; ALL THE WITCHES WELLS–TAYLOR. WELLS–TAYLOR's interpretation—adopted also by BROOKE—distances Hecate from the action; there is no reason to rule out her participation.

4.1.110 Dunsinane] ROWE; Dunſmane JAGGARD

4.1.115 our high-placed] JAGGARD; on's high place WELLS–TAYLOR. Although WELLS–TAYLOR's emendation removes the difficulty, felt by many commentators, of Macbeth's reference to himself by the possessive plural, the resulting idiom has not persuaded commentators either. Perhaps 'our' is a simple misreading for 'out': Macbeth shall 'live out' his lease of nature. In support of this conjecture, Davenant has 'thou mayest presume Macbeth | To live out Nature's lease'. But this would produce a very strained word order.

4.1.128.1–2 the last . . . hand and Banquo] HANMER; *and Banquo laſt, with a glaſſe in his hand.* JAGGARD. This error is hard to explain except as a result of confusion created by a marginal afterthought adding 'and Banquo' to the direction.

4.1.137 eighth] JAGGARD (eight)

4.1.141 blood-baltered] JAGGARD (Blood-bolter'd)

4.1.143 HECATE] DAVENANT; I JAGGARD. The emendation is ably defended by Lyle and Brooke; it was first accepted in a Shakespeare edition by WELLS–TAYLOR. Holdsworth compares 145–8 to *Witch* 5.2.87–8: 'Come my sweet Sisters: let the Aire strike our Tune | Whilst we show Reverence to yond peeping Moone. *here they Daunce ye witches Dance & Ext.*'— noting the multiple parallels: 'Come . . . Sisters', 'show', 'our delights/our Tune', 'air', 'while/whilst' [beginning second line of a couplet], and 'the witches dance' vanish/exit. In *Witch* these lines are spoken by Hecate.

4.1.150.1–2 with Hecate] CLARK–WRIGHT; *not in* JAGGARD. JAGGARD may be considering Hecate one of the witches.

4.2.22 none] WILSON (conj. Clark and Wright); moue JAGGARD; wave THEOBALD

4.2.43 with all] withall JAGGARD

4.2.81 shag-haired] SINGER (conj. Steevens); ſhagge-ear'd JAGGARD. The emendation presumes the intended spelling 'hear'd' for 'hair'd'.

4.3.4 downfall] JAGGARD; downfall'n WARBURTON

4.3.29 I pray] JAGGARD; pray W. S. WALKER conj.

4.3.35 affeered] JAGGARD (affear'd)

4.3.60 sullen] THIS EDITION; Sodaine JAGGARD. 'Sodaine' is Compositor B's preferred spelling of 'sudden', which might be a misreading or substitution of 'sullen'. 'Sudden', unlike all the other items in this list, is not a vice; 'sullen'—in the strong contemporary senses 'ill-humoured, obstinant, malignant'—is.

4.3.108 accused] JAGGARD (accuſt); accurſt COTES

4.3.134 thy] COTES; they JAGGARD

4.3.155 with] JAGGARD corr.; my with JAGGARD uncorr.

4.3.161 not] COTES; nor JAGGARD

4.3.169 rend] JAGGARD (rent)

4.3.214 ROSS] JAGGARD corr. (Roſſe.); Roffe. JAGGARD uncorr.

4.3.237 tune] ROWE 2; time JAGGARD

4.3.242a–b come . . . day exeunt] Coghill argued that Edward the Confessor must have appeared in the original play: the audience is led to anticipate his appearance by 3.6.23–31 and by 4.3.139–59. (Coghill might have added that Forman noted, early in his account of the 1611 performance, that 'it was in the days of Edward the Confessor'; the name 'Edward' appears once in the extant text, at 3.6.23, but 'Edward the Confessor' never.) Coghill records a conjecture by E. A. J. Honigmann that Edward appears here in a dumbshow, but it is hard to fit such a stage direction into the extant text, and Coghill notes that a mere procession would do 'nothing to fulfil the notion of a prophecy of victory to Malcolm, which we have been led to expect by the text'. I have therefore conjectured that Edward originally appeared at the end of the scene, after the Scots have themselves united against Macbeth. As Coghill observes, 'Shakespeare had ransacked Holinshed to build up this fabulous national figure, someone on the side of the angels, who would at last appear, to link England and Scotland in amity and order at this very moment, which is the watershed of the play. Imagine how the scene . . . would lift up all hearts, out of all the blood and darkness, when most they need to be lifted'. However, such an effect is most needed not in the middle of the scene (as Coghill assumes), before Macduff receives the news of the slaughter of his family, but after it. Edward's miraculous cure, at the end of Sc. 19 (4.3), would then have stood in direct contrast with the ineffectual secular doctor, at the beginning of Sc. 20 (5.1). Moreover, at the end of the scene Edward could introduce (and bless, as it were) old Siward, and at the same time speak the prophecy of victory which the audience expects—a prophecy in direct contrast to the prophecies of the weïrd sisters, just as his onstage miracle would directly contrast with their satanic rituals. But Shakespeare's reason for wanting to include such a scene would be Middleton's reason for wanting to remove it: 'it may have been deemed wise to cut out the visual presentation of so glamorous a scene, recalling the good old days, when miracles and superstition were still happily allowed' (Coghill, 234). If he reduced it to a mere report, that report would be anticlimactic at the end of the scene, and therefore would have to be moved backward, into a suitable position earlier in the scene. Some of the contents of the cancelled passage can be conjecturally restored, by assuming that Middleton, as much as possible, moved it elsewhere in the scene. (Another speech that might be given him, and that would in fact fit metrically after 'instruments', is the speech currently given to Angus at 5.2.16–22—a powerfully authoritative utterance, often cited by critics, which seems wasted on the colourless Angus.)

5.1.1 two] JAGGARD (too)

5.3.23 disseat] JAGGARD (dif-eate)

5.3.24 May] STEEVENS (*conj.* Johnson); way JAGGARD. Compare 'his May of youth' (*Ado* 5.1.76) and 'He that hath suffered this disordered spring Hath now himself met with the fall of leaf' (*Richard II* 3.4.48–9). Conservative editors have retained 'way', simply because parallels for 'way of life' can be found in the period; but there are no such parallels in the Shakespeare canon. (The parallel cited, at *Pericles* 1.1.54, occurs in a scene apparently written by George Wilkins and preserved in a very corrupt text.) Moreover, the argument for emendation here is that 'way' offers a trite reading, which could easily have been substituted—by the simplest of minim misreadings—for the rarer and more difficult 'May'; the fact that the phrase 'way of life' was common in the period does not disprove but supports the emendation. On the principle of adopting 'the rarer reading', see Taylor (1988).

5.3.37 more] JAGGARD (moe)

5.3.41 cure her] COTES; cure JAGGARD

5.3.46 fraught] WELLS–TAYLOR; ftufft JAGGARD. Many other emendations have been suggested.

5.3.54 pristine] COTES; priftiue JAGGARD

5.3.57 senna] COTES (Cæny), HERRINGMAN; Cyme JAGGARD; sene THIS EDITION *conj.* As BROOKE rightly points out, though 'cyme' has a botanical sense, it is the wrong sense here. The usual emendation, deriving from COTES, is hypermetrical, but *OED* records *sene* as a separate word or form with the same meaning (*sb.*⁴). Paleographically, the conjecture presumes an easier misreading in JAGGARD; it depends upon the assumption that 'purgative' might have been accented on the second syllable, like 'purgation'. (Shakespeare nowhere else uses the word, so its accentuation here is uncertain.)

5.4.0.3 Angus] JAGGARD; ~ and Lennox, Ross MALONE. The absence of these characters is almost certainly due to their doubling the Doctor, Young Siward, or Seyton.

5.4.11 gained] THIS EDITION (*conj.* White); giuen JAGGARD; gone CAPELL (*conj.* Johnson). The repetition is suspicious and undiomatic. For the emendation compare Sonnet 64.5–6 'gain | Advantage'. (As BROOKE notes, CAPELL's 'gone' does not make sense without the additional emendation, also suggested by Johnson, of 'advantage' to 'a vantage'.)

5.5.36 false] COTES; fhlfe JAGGARD

5.5.40 pall] A. HUNTER (*conj.* Johnson); pull JAGGARD

5.8 WELLS–TAYLOR was the first edition to mark a scene division here. JAGGARD, having until now marked a scene division for every clearing of the stage followed by a re-entry, does not provide scene divisions or scene numbers for the final four clearings of the stage. This might be because the battle was considered a single sequence, but if so the marking of 5.7 would seem anomalous, since the alarums which begin in 5.6 are 'continued' into the next scene. Brooke objects that the marking of additional scene divisions 'forgets the reality of the theatre for an impossible series of mini-scenes designated "Another part of the field"' (206); but the issue here is not changes of locale, but the Renaissance convention of marking scenes by the clearing of the stage. Perhaps the scene divisions were present in the manuscript, but omitted in JAGGARD because of space constraints; four additional boxed scene numbers would have made the play run over onto an extra page (nn4ᵛ), where the beginning of *Hamlet* had already been set.

5.8.6 unbattered] vnbattered JAGGARD (= unbatterèd)

5.9 WELLS–TAYLOR was the first edition to mark a scene division here.

5.10 POPE was the first editor to mark a scene division here.

5.11 POPE was the first editor to mark a scene division here.

STAGE DIRECTIONS

1.1.0.3–4 *Actus Primus. Scoena Prima.*

1.1.0.3–4 *Thunder and Lightning. Enter three Witches.*

1.1.10 *Exeunt.*

1.2.0.2–24 *Scena Secunda. | Alarum within. Enter King Malcome, Donal-|baine, Lenox, with attendants, meeting | a bleeding Captaine.*

1.2.44.2 *Enter Rosse and Angus.*

1.2.68.1 *Exeunt.*

1.3.0.2 *Scena Tertia. | Thunder. Enter the three Witches.*

1.3.27.1 *Drum within.* (right margin)

1.3.35.1 *Enter Macbeth and Banquo.*

1.3.76.1 *Witches vanish.* (right margin)

1.3.86.1 *Enter Rosse and Angus.*

1.3.155 *Exeunt.*

1.4.0.1–3 *Scena Quarta. | Flourish. Enter King, Lenox, Malcolme, | Donalbaine, and Attendants.*

1.4.14.1 *Enter Macbeth, Banquo, Rosse, and Angus.*

1.4.53 *Exit.*

1.4.58 *Flourish. Exeunt.*

1.5.0.2 *Scena Quinta. | Enter Macbeths Wife alone with a Letter.*

1.5.29.1 *Enter Messenger.* (right margin)

1.5.37 *Exit Messenger.*

1.5.53.1 *Enter Macbeth.* (right margin)

1.5.72 *Exeunt.*

1.6.0.1–4 *Scena Sexta. | Hoboyes, and Torches. Enter King, Malcolme, | Donalbaine, Banquo, Lenox, Macduff, | Rosse, Angus, and Attendants.*

1.6.10.1 *Enter Lady.* (right margin)

1.6.31 *Exeunt*

1.7.0.1–4 *Scene Septima. | Ho-boyes. Torches. | Enter a Sewer, and diuers Seruants with Dishes and Seruice | ouer the Stage. Then enter Macbeth.*

1.7.28.1 *Enter Lady.* (right margin)

1.7.82.1 *Exeunt.*

2.1.0.1–2 *Actus Secundus. Scena Prima.*

2.1.0.3 *Enter Banquo, and Fleance, with a Torch | before him.*

2.1.9.1 *Enter Macbeth, and a Seruant with a Torch.*

2.1.30.1 *Exit Banquo.*

2.1.32 *Exit.*

2.1.61.1 *A Bell rings.*

2.1.64 *Exit.*

2.2.0.1–2 *Scena Secunda. | Enter Lady.*

2.2.8.1 *Enter Macbeth.*

2.2.55 *Exit.*

2.2.55.1 *Knocke within.* (right margin)

2.2.61.1 *Enter Lady.*

2.2.63.1   *Knocke.* (right margin)
2.2.67.1   *Knocke.* (right margin)
2.2.71.1   *Knocke.* (right margin, after 'deed')
2.2.72.1   *Exeunt.*
2.3.0.1–2   *Scena Tertia.* | *Enter a Porter.*
2.3.0.3   *Knocking within.* (right margin)
2.3.2.1   *Knock.* (not on a separate line, but with blank space before and after)
2.3.6.1   *Knock.* (as preceding)
2.3.11.1   *Knock.* (as preceding)
2.3.14.1   *Knock.* (as preceding)
2.3.18.1   *Knock.* (as preceding)
2.3.20.1   *Enter Macduff, and Lenox.*
2.3.39.1   *Enter Macbeth.* (after 2.3.37–8)
2.3.49   *Exit Macduffe.*
2.3.60.1   *Enter Macduff.*
2.3.71.1   *Exeunt Macbeth and Lenox.* (after 'awake, awake')
2.3.78.1   *Bell rings. Enter Lady.*
2.3.83.1   *Enter Banquo.*
2.3.87.1   *Enter Macbeth, Lenox, and Rosse.*
2.3.93.1   *Enter Malcolme and Donalbaine.*
2.3.131.1   *Exeunt.*
2.3.143   *Exeunt.*
2.4.0.1–2   *Scena Quarta.* | *Enter Rosse, with an Old man.*
2.4.20.1   *Enter Macduffe.*
2.4.42.1   *Exeunt omnes*
3.1.0.1–2   *Actus Tertius. Scena Prima.*
3.1.0.3   *Enter Banquo.*
3.1.10.1–2   *Senit sounded. Enter Macbeth as King, Lady Lenox,* | *Rosse, Lords, and Attendants.*
3.1.41   *Exit Banquo.*
3.1.45.1   *Exeunt Lords.*
3.1.48   *Exit Seruant.*
3.1.72.1   *Enter Seruant, and two Murtherers.*
3.1.72.1–3.1.73   *Exit Seruant.*
3.1.140.1, 142   *Exeunt.* (after 3.1.142)
3.2.0.2   *Scena Secunda.* | *Enter Macbeths Lady, and a Seruant.*
3.2.5   *Exit.*
3.2.9.1   *Enter Macbeth.*
3.2.57   *Exeunt.*
3.3.0.1–2   *Scena Tertia.* | *Enter three Murtherers.*
3.3.9   *within.* (after speech prefix)
3.3.14.1   *Enter Banquo and Fleans, with a Torch.*
3.3.23.1   *Exeunt.*
3.4.0.1–3   *Scaena Quarta.* | *Banquet prepar'd. Enter Macbeth, Lady, Rosse, Lenox,* | *Lords, and Attendants.*
3.4.7.1   *Enter first Murtherer.*
3.4.31   *Exit Murderer.*
3.4.36.1–2   *Enter the Ghost of Banquo, and sits in Macbeths place.*
3.4.87.1   *Enter Ghost.*
3.4.120   *Exit Lords.*
3.4.143   *Exeunt.*
3.5.0.1–2   *Scena Quinta.* | *Thunder.   Enter the three Witches, meeting* | *Hecat.*
3.5.33.1   *Musicke, and a Song.*
3.5.36.1   *Sing within. Come away, come away, &c.*
3.5.74.1   *Exeunt.*
3.6.0.1–2   *Scaena Sexta.* | *Enter Lenox, and another Lord.*
3.6.31.1   *Exeunt*
4.1.0.1–2   *Actus Quartus. Scena Prima.*
4.1.0.3–4   *Thunder.   Enter the three Witches.*
4.1.38.1   *Enter Hecat, and the other three Witches.*
4.1.43.1   *Musicke and a Song. Blacke Spirits, &c.*
4.1.64.1   *Enter Macbeth.*

4.1.85.1   *Thunder.* | *1. Apparition, an Armed Head.* (right margin)
4.1.89.1   *He Descends.* (right margin)
4.1.93.1   *Thunder.* | *2 Apparition, a Bloody Childe.* (right margin)
4.1.98.1   *Descends.* (right margin)
4.1.103.1–2   *Thunder* (right margin) | *3 Apparition, a Childe Crowned, with a Tree in his hand.*
4.1.111.1   *Descend.* (right margin)
4.1.123.1   *Hoboyes* (right margin, opposite 4.1.123)
4.1.128.1–2   *A shew of eight Kings, and Banquo last, with a glasse* | *in his hand.*
4.1.150.1–2   *Musicke.* (right margin) | *The Witches Dance, and vanish.*
4.1.153.1   *Enter Lenox.* (right margin)
4.1.174   *Exeunt*
4.2.0.1–2   *Scena Secunda.* | *Enter Macduffes Wife, her Son, and Rosse.*
4.2.30   *Exit Rosse.*
4.2.62.1   *Enter a Messenger.*
4.2.71   *Exit Messenger*
4.2.77.1   *Enter Murtherers.* (after 'faces')
4.2.83.1   *Exit crying Murther.*
4.3.0.2   *Scaena Tertia.* | *Enter Malcolme and Macduffe.*
4.3.140.1   *Enter a Doctor.*
4.3.146   *Exit.* (after 'amend')
4.3.160.1   *Enter Rosse.*
4.3.242ab   *Exeunt*
5.1.0.1–2   *Actus Quintus. Scena Prima.*
5.1.0.3   *Enter a Doctor of Physicke, and a Wayting* | *Gentlewoman.*
5.1.17.1   *Enter Lady, with a Taper.* (right margin)
5.1.61   *Exit Lady.*
5.1.72.1   *Exeunt.*
5.2.0.1–3   *Scena Secunda.* | *Drum and Colours. Enter Menteth, Cathnes,* | *Angus, Lenox, Soldiers.*
5.2.31.1   *Exeunt marching.*
5.3.0.2   *Scaena Tertia.* | *Enter Macbeth, Doctor, and Attendants.*
5.3.10.1   *Enter Seruant.*
5.3.31.1   *Enter Seyton.*
5.3.64   *Exeunt*
5.4.0.1–4   *Scena Quarta.* | *Drum and Colours. Enter Malcolme, Seyward, Macduffe,* | *Seywards Sonne, Menteth, Cathnes, Angus,* | *and Soldiers Marching.*
5.4.21   *Exeunt marching*
5.5.0.1–3   *Scena Quinta.* | *Enter Macbeth, Seyton, & Souldiers, with* | *Drum and Colours.*
5.5.7.1   *A Cry within of Women.* (after 'noise')
5.5.27.1   *Enter a Messenger.* (right margin)
5.5.50   *Exeunt*
5.6.0.1–3   *Scena Sexta* | *Drumme and Colours.* | *Enter Malcolme, Seyward, Macduffe, and their Army,* | *with Boughes.*
5.6.10.1   *Exeunt* | *Alarums continued.*
5.7.0.1–2   *Scena Septima.* | *Enter Macbeth.*
5.7.4.1   *Enter young Seyward.*
5.7.12.1   *Fight, and young Seyward slaine.*
5.7.14.1   *Exit.*
5.8.0.2   *Alarums. Enter Macduffe.*
5.8.10   *Exit.   Alarums.*
5.9.0.2   *Enter Malcolme and Seyward.*
5.9.6   *Exeunt.   Alarum*
5.10.0.2   *Enter Macbeth.*
5.10.3.1   *Enter Macduffe.*
5.10.8.1   *Fight: Alarum* (right margin)
5.10.34.1   *Exeunt fighting.   Alarums.*
5.10.34.2   *Enter Fighting, and Macbeth slaine.*

5.11.0.2–3   *Retreat, and Flourish. Enter with Drumme and Colours,* | *Malcolm, Seyward, Rosse, Thanes, & Soldiers.*

5.11.19.1   *Enter Macduffe, with Macbeths head.*
5.11.25.1   *Flourish.* (right margin)
5.11.41.1   *Flourish.*   *Exeunt Omnes.* | FINIS.

LINEATION NOTES

1.1.8–9   I…fair] THIS EDITION; Greymalkin| JAGGARD; *three lines* POPE: Greymalkin| anon|. See Textual Notes and Canon. Apparently three short interpolated speeches which make up a single perfect iambic pentameter line.

1.2.19–20   like…slave] STEEVENS; passage| JAGGARD

1.2.34   dismayed…Banquo] JAGGARD; *2 lines* Pope: this|. Editors sometimes treat JAGGARD as though it were prose, since 'Banquo' is printed on the next line, but that is probably an unindented flowover.

1.2.35   yes…lion] WELLS-TAYLOR; *2 lines* JAGGARD: Eagles|

1.2.41–2   I…help] ROWE; faint| JAGGARD. BROOKE preserves JAGGARD, but this produces an eight-syllable line followed by a six-syllable line, a combination of irregularities which almost never occurs in either dramatist; a short four-syllable line followed by a normal pentameter is common (even without the dramatic reason for breaking off after 'tell').

1.2.46–7   what…strange] HANMER; eyes| JAGGARD

1.2.59–60   that…composition] STEEVENS 2; king| JAGGARD

1.3.4   and…I] POPE; *2 lines* JAGGARD: | give

1.3.76   with…you] POPE; *2 lines* JAGGARD: greeting|

1.3.79–80   into…stayed] CAPELL; *3 lines* JAGGARD: corporal| wind|

1.3.100–1   only…thee] SINGER; *2 lines* JAGGARD: sight|

1.3.106–7   the…robes] CAPELL; lives| JAGGARD

1.3.109–12   which…not] MALONE; *5 lines* JAGGARD: lose| Norway| help| laboured|

1.3.129–30   cannot…success] ROWE; good| JAGGARD

1.3.138–40   shakes…not] POPE; man| surmise| JAGGARD

1.3.141   if…crown me] ROWE; *2 lines* JAGGARD: king|

1.3.147–51   give…time] POPE; *7 lines* JAGGARD: favour| forgotten| registered| leaf| them| upon|

1.3.155   till…friends] POPE; *2 lines* JAGGARD: enough|

1.4.1–2   is…returned] CAPELL; Cawdor| JAGGARD

1.4.2–8   my…died] POPE; back| die| he| pardon| repentance| him| JAGGARD

1.4.23–7   in…honour] POPE; *6 lines* JAGGARD: itself| receive our duties| state| should| love

1.5.21–2   and…it] POPE; *3 lines* JAGGARD: win| cries|

1.5.29   to…tidings] *2 lines* JAGGARD: withal|

1.5.37   he…hoarse] ROWE; *2 lines* JAGGARD: news|

1.5.53   to…Cawdor] *2 lines* JAGGARD: hold, hold|

1.6.1–2   this…itself] ROWE; seat| JAGGARD

1.6.17–20   against…hermits] POPE; broad| house| dignities| JAGGARD

1.7.28   and…news] ROWE; *2 lines* JAGGARD: th'other|

2.1.4   hold…heaven] ROWE; *2 lines* JAGGARD: sword|

2.1.7–9   and…repose] ROWE; sleep| thoughts| JAGGARD

2.1.12–13   he…offices] CLARK-WRIGHT; pleasure| JAGGARD

2.1.15–16   by…content] POPE; hostess| JAGGARD

2.1.24–5   if…for you] ROWE; consent| JAGGARD

2.2.2–6   what…possets] ROWE; *6 lines* JAGGARD: fire| shrieked| good-night| open| charge|

2.2.13   my father…husband] ROWE; *2 lines* JAGGARD: done't|

2.2.14   I…noise] ROWE; *2 lines* JAGGARD: deed?

2.2.20–3   there's…sleep] ROWE; in's sleep| other| prayers| JAGGARD

2.2.30–1   I…throat] POPE; *1 line* JAGGARD

2.2.63–4   to…chamber] POPE; *3 lines* JAGGARD: white| entry|

2.2.71–2   to…couldst] POPE; *4 lines* JAGGARD: deed| myself| knocking|

2.3.23–4   faith…things] JOHNSON; *verse (?)* JAGGARD: cock|

2.3.25   what…provoke] JAGGARD. It is unclear whether JAGGARD intends this as prose, or a single verse line, since unindented flowovers are characteristic of Compositor A. Although the speeches of the porter are unmistakeably prose, those of Macduff at ll. 21–2, 25, and 34 are easily scanned as verse.

2.3.48–9   I'll…service] HANMER; *prose* JAGGARD (or unindented flowover of a single line of verse)

2.3.51–3   the…death] ROWE; *4 lines* JAGGARD: unruly| down| air

2.3.56–8   new-hatched…shake] HANMER; *4 lines* JAGGARD: time| night| feverous|

2.3.83–4   O Banquo…murdered] THEOBALD; *1 line* JAGGARD

2.3.117–18   why…ours] BROOKE (conj. Walker); tongues| JAGGARD. Mislineation of speeches consisting of a line and a half of verse is the commonest error in JAGGARD, deriving from a combination of space problems in a two-column format and (probably) ambiguity in the manuscript, where such speeches were often written on a single line.

2.3.119–20   what…hole] THIS EDITION (conj. Walker); here| JAGGARD

2.3.132   what…them] ROWE; *2 lines* JAGGARD: do|

2.3.134   which…England] ROWE; *2 lines* JAGGARD: easy|

2.3.135–8   to Ireland…bloody] ROWE; I| safer| smiles| JAGGARD

2.4.14   and…certain] POPE; *2 lines* JAGGARD: horses|

2.4.19–20   they…Macduff] POPE; *3 lines* JAGGARD: so| upon't|

3.1.36–7   craving…with you] POPE; *3 lines* JAGGARD: horse| night|

3.1.44–5   the…you] ROWE; *3 lines* JAGGARD: welcome| alone|

3.1.46   sirrah…pleasure] CAPELL; *2 lines* JAGGARD: men|

3.1.48–51   bring…dares] ROWE; *5 lines* JAGGARD: us| thus| deep| that|

3.1.72   and…there] POPE; *2 lines* JAGGARD: th'utterance|

3.1.75–80   well…with you] ROWE; *7 lines* JAGGARD: then| speeches| past| fortune| self| conference|

3.1.81–2   how…might] ROWE; *3 lines* JAGGARD: crossed| them|

3.1.85   I…now] ROWE; *2 lines:* so|

3.1.86–91   our point…ever] ROWE; *7 lines:* meeting| predominant| go| man| hand| beggared|

3.1.110–11   hath…world] ROWE; do| JAGGARD

3.1.114–15   both…enemy] ROWE; *1 line* JAGGARD

3.1.128   your…most] POPE; *2 lines* JAGGARD: you|

3.2.18   but…suffer] POPE; *2 lines* JAGGARD: disjoint|

3.2.24   in…grave] ROWE; *2 lines* JAGGARD: ecstasy|

3.2.28–30   come…tonight] CAPELL; on| looks| JAGGARD

3.2.30–4   so…streams] CAPELL; you| Banquo| tongue| lave| JAGGARD

3.2.44–5   hath…note] ROWE; peal| JAGGARD

3.2.51–2   which…wood] ROWE; thickens| JAGGARD

3.3.9–10   then…expectation] POPE; he| JAGGARD

3.3.17   O…fly fly fly] HANMER; *2 lines* JAGGARD: treachery|

3.3.22   we…affair] STEEVENS; *2 lines* JAGGARD: lost|

3.4.1–2   you…welcome] DELIUS; down| JAGGARD; *prose* BROOKE

702

3.4.4–5   and...welcome] WELLS–TAYLOR; *3 lines* JAGGARD: host |
time | ; *prose* BROOKE

3.4.11   the...face] ROWE; *1 line* JAGGARD

3.4.15   my...him] KEIGHTLEY; *1 line* JAGGARD. This emendation
presumes the commonest of lineation errors, and makes it
unnecessary to emend—in a much more irregular fashion,
uncharacteristic of Compositor B—the lineation of the next
speech. This produces in 15 a line with a feminine caesura,
followed in 15–16 with a line-divided foot.

3.4.20   then...perfect] POPE; *2 lines* JAGGARD: again |

3.4.47   here...highness] CAPELL; *2 lines* JAGGARD: lord |

3.4.68   prithee...you] CAPELL; *2 lines* JAGGARD: there |

3.4.108–9   you...disorder] POPE; mirth | JAGGARD

3.4.121   it...blood will have blood] ROWE; *2 lines* JAGGARD: say |

3.5.74   come...again] POPE; *2 lines* JAGGARD: be |

3.6.1   my...thoughts] ROWE; *2 lines* JAGGARD: speeches |

4.1.63–4   open...knocks] THIS EDITION; *1 line* JAGGARD

4.1.88   Macbeth...Macduff] ROWE; *2 lines* JAGGARD: | beware

4.1.96   be...scorn] ROWE; *2 lines* JAGGARD: resolute |

4.1.103–4   what...king] ROWE; *1 line* JAGGARD

4.1.151   where...hour] ROWE; *2 lines* JAGGARD: gone |

4.2.27   fathered...fatherless] ROWE; *2 lines* JAGGARD: is |

4.2.34   poor...lime] THEOBALD; *2 lines* JAGGARD: bird |

4.2.36   why...for] POPE; *2 lines* JAGGARD: mother |

4.2.43–4   thou...thee] BROOKE; *verse* JAGGARD: wit |

4.2.50   everyone...hanged] POPE; *verse* JAGGARD: traitor |

4.2.60–1   if...quickly] THIS EDITION; *prose* JAGGARD. See the
discussion of this scene in 'Canon and Chronology'. The
first twelve syllables are clearly iambic, and make a regular
hexameter, of a kind found in all periods of Shakespeare's
career, and especially often in his Jacobean plays. The
second line lacks a final stressed syllable; Jowett suggests
(private communication) that 'quickely' might be emended
to 'quicklier' (which Shakespeare uses in *All's Well*, a play
which the revised Oxford chronology places in the same year
as the original composition of *Macbeth*). The last four words
of the speech, placed on a separate line in JAGGARD, can be
interpreted as the first half of a verse line completed by Lady
Macduff's next speech; an extra syllable at the caesura is
extremely common in Shakespeare, especially when a verse
line is divided between two speakers.

4.2.77   to...faces] ROWE; *2 lines* JAGGARD: harm |

4.3.26   perchance...doubts] ROWE; *2 lines* JAGGARD: there |

4.3.103–4   fit...miserable] POPE; *1 line* JAGGARD

4.3.141   well...you] ROWE; *2 lines* JAGGARD: forth |

4.3.174–5   O...true] THEOBALD; *1 line* JAGGARD

4.3.212–13   wife...found] CAPELL; *1 line* JAGGARD

4.3.213–14   and...too] CAPELL; *1 line* JAGGARD

5.1.42   go...not] POPE; *verse* JAGGARD: | you have

5.1.46   O O O] *on a separate line* JAGGARD

5.5.27–8   thou...quickly] WELLS–TAYLOR; *1 line* JAGGARD

5.6.1   now...down] ROWE; *2 lines* JAGGARD: enough |

5.11.20   hail...stands] ROWE; *2 lines* JAGGARD: art |

THE LIFE OF TIMON OF ATHENS

Edited by John Jowett

WILLIAM JAGGARD's compositors customarily identified as B and E spent part of the summer of 1623 setting *Timon of Athens* in type so that it would appear later that year in the Folio edition of William Shakespeare's *Comedies, Histories, and Tragedies* (STC 22273). The play was duly entered in the Stationers' Register alongside a number of other previously unpublished titles on 8 November 1623; the first recorded purchase of the Folio was a few weeks later on 5 December (Blayney, 1991). Jaggard's text of *Timon* occupies 21 double-column folio pages identifiable as Gg1^v to hh6^v; the sixth and final leaf of quire hh displays a list of 'THE ACTORS NAMES.' on the recto, with the verso blank. The page signed Gg1 contains the end of *Romeo and Juliet*; the blank page hh5^v faces the opening of *Julius Caesar*.

One could go no further in describing the bibliographical setting of *Timon* without drawing attention to a severe disruption in the setting of the Folio that impinges on the play's very place in the Shakespeare canon. The full quire signed 'Gg' on the first recto (the last page of *Romeo*) is preceded by two leaves of *Romeo* signed 'gg' and 'gg2'. At the end of *Timon* the pagination skips from 98 on the final text-page over the unnumbered leaf hh6 to 109 on the first page of *Caesar* (kk1); quire ii is missing. Furthermore, and most important, a cancel text of pages Gg1–1^v shows the final page of *Romeo* originally signed not 'Gg1' but 'gg3', and backed not with the opening of *Timon* but with the opening of *Troilus and Cressida*.

As Hinman (1963) explained with previously unmatched detail and accuracy (2.231–85), *Troilus* was originally planned to occupy the position in the Folio that *Timon* finally filled. The space for *Troilus*—and so for its replacement—was predetermined in that the tragedies appearing immediately after it in the book, beginning with *Caesar*, had already been printed. Compositor E evidently began work on quire *gg (the asterisk denotes the pre-cancellation quire). He first set, as was usual, the inner pages containing early parts of *Troilus*, and worked outwards, therefore backwards through the first half of the quire towards *Romeo*. After he had composed three pages of *Troilus* and the end of *Romeo* his work was curtailed. *Troilus* was for the time given up as a lost cause, evidently for reasons of copyright. The end of *Romeo* at this stage was partly unprinted (*gg1–1^v) and partly printed on pages forme-mated with *Troilus* (*gg2, 2^v, 3). As a provisional measure ensuring that *Romeo* could be separated from *Troilus*, Compositor E now set what would otherwise have been the opening pages of the abandoned quire as the single, four-page sheet gg1–2 containing most of the

conclusion of *Romeo*. The final lines of *Romeo* were not reset at this stage, and the difficulty was left unresolved for several weeks while work proceeded on other parts of the volume. Yet *Timon* may already have been earmarked, for the printing of the new single-sheet quire gg might assume the eventual provision of two quires (logically hh and ii; in the event Gg and hh), and so anticipate a short text that would occupy 23 pages at most; in contrast 28 pages had originally been alloted to *Troilus*. When it was finally printed, *Timon* may have been brought forward from an anticipated position later in the Folio, but it is strongly to be suspected that there was no original intention to publish it. This has bearings on the question of the play's authorship.

The manuscript made available to Jaggard's compositors was from their point of view conspicuous most of all by its brevity. Though the available space was limited, *Timon* could not be made to fill it. The list of the characters' names was probably assembled specifically to occupy one side of the redundant leaf hh6, and it therefore is unlikely to have authorial or theatrical authority. Notwithstanding the introduction of this space-filler, the text barely stretched to the required length. The text was set by Compositor B, except for one page, Gg3 (2.10–131), which was probably set by Compositor E. Compositor B's prevalence minimizes the extent to which clustered spelling variants can be attributed to the printing house (Hinman 2.285). He used generous spacing, in quire hh especially, to ensure that hh5^v was left with a respectable quantity of type (about half a page). He went further: a passage of stichomythic single lines at 14.360–7, for example, is split into false part-lines, and a widespread confusion between verse and prose that is in any case intrinsic to the text may have been compounded by the compositor's willingness to break to a new type-line.

One technique of space-consumption not available to the compositors was manipulation of the setting of act–scene breaks. After a promissory 'Actus Primus. Scæna Prima.' there are no further indications of act or scene number. This is consistent with the performance practices of the King's Men before 1608–9, and so does not represent a peculiarity of the copy. Various loose ends and inconsistencies do suggest an authorial rough draft, if by this term one does not understand anything radically different in the quality of writing from other texts said to have been printed from collaborative 'foul papers'. The unfinished state combines with the hypothesis of two authors to account for a number of textual discrepancies immediately. The interview between the Steward and Ventidius that Shakespeare arranges at the end of Sc. 4 never materializes, simply because Middleton thereafter takes over. A delay in the episode with the Poet and Painter in Sc. 15 but anticipated at 14.353 may partly be explained by Middleton's interpolation of the Steward episode that intervenes. Sc. 9 is poorly assimilated; certainly if the play were expanded to something nearer full length one might expect the Alcibiades plot to be given fuller exposition. Joint authorship might affect the roles of the lords identified in stage directions and speech-prefixes (though not, while they are on stage, in dialogue) as Lucullus, Lucius, and Sempronius in Scs. 5–7 (Middleton). Consistency would require that they figure amongst the anonymous lords of earlier and later scenes, especially Sc. 11 (mixed authorship; central episode by Shakespeare), but they do not, except for an isolated and ambiguous 'Luc.' at 2.127 (Middleton). Middleton preferred 'Apermantus' and 'Ventidgius' to Shakespeare's 'Apemantus' and 'Ventidius'. The intermixing of prose and verse, unfamiliar and puzzling to readers trained on Shakespeare, is an expected Middleton feature.

The confusion over the value of a talent also lends itself to explanation in terms of authorial stints (Jackson, 1979). One should not too readily infer that Middleton twice wrote 'so many' in Sc. 6 out of hesitance, or that 'fifty fiue hundred' at 6.38 results from a correction inflating 55 to 100; Middleton was far from ignorant on biblically-related matters, and these readings may be admitted as they stand as fragments of comic surreality on his part. Yet different scales of financial value or artistic discretion were surely at work; for instance the explosion from 50 to 1000 talents at 4.188–94 suggests an intervention from Middleton, whereas the sober five talents at 4.221 might indicate Shakespeare in control again.

The present edition has been re-edited from the text I prepared for the Oxford Shakespeare *Complete Works* (JOWETT 1986). In reviewing the readings accepted for that text, I have taken careful note of the preliminary decisions of Roger Holdsworth, whose editorial work for the Middleton *Collected Works* did not reach fruition. Sometimes in response to his readings in the first half of the play, sometimes out of an increased sense of Middletonian idiom (in particular, his relative toleration of metrical irregularity), and sometimes out of an editor's inclination to change his mind over marginal readings, I have made a number of departures from the Oxford text. The textual notes are skeletal in that they avoid repeating discursive comment from the Shakespeare *Textual Companion* and take limited notice of rejected editorial emendations. They give a full record of departures from the 1623 Folio (JAGGARD), and a full record of departures from the Oxford Shakespeare. Scenes are through-numbered, as in the Oxford Shakespeare original-spelling edition.

I would like to thank Kelley Costigan for checking the list of doubling possibilities for this play and *Five Gallants*.

SEE ALSO

Text: *Works*, 471
Authorship and date: this volume, 356

WORKS CITED

Previous Editions Cited

Jaggard, William, printer, and Isaac, printer and co-publisher, William Shakespeare, *Comedies, Histories, and Tragedies* (1623)

Allott, Robert, and others, publishers, William Shakespeare, *Comedies, Histories, and Tragedies* (1632)

Chetwin, Philip, publisher, William Shakespeare, *Comedies, Histories, and Tragedies* (1663-4)

Shadwell, Thomas, *The History of Timon the Man-Hater* (1678)

Herringman, Henry, and others, publishers, William Shakespeare, *Comedies, Histories, and Tragedies* (1685)

Rowe, Nicholas, ed., William Shakespeare, *Works*, 6 vols (1709)

—— ed., William Shakespeare, *Works*, 2nd edn., 6 vols (1709)

—— ed., William Shakespeare, *Works*, 3rd edn., 8 vols (1714)

Pope, Alexander, ed., William Shakespeare, *Works*, 6 vols (1723-5)

—— ed., William Shakespeare, *Works*, 2nd edn., 10 vols (1728)

Theobald, Lewis, ed., William Shakespeare, *Works*, 8 vols (1733)

Hanmer, Thomas, ed., William Shakespeare, *Works*, 6 vols (1743-4)

Warburton, William, ed., William Shakespeare, *Works*, 8 vols (1747)

Johnson, Samuel, ed., William Shakespeare, *Plays*, 8 vols (1765)

Capell, Edward, ed., William Shakespeare, *Comedies, Histories, and Tragedies*, 10 vols (1767-8)

Steevens, George, with Samuel Johnson, eds., William Shakespeare, *Plays*, 10 vols (1773)

—— eds., William Shakespeare, *Plays*, 10 vols (1778)

Rann, Joseph, ed., William Shakespeare, *Dramatic Works*, 6 vols (1786-94)

Malone, Edmond, ed., William Shakespeare, *Plays and Poems*, 10 vols (1790)

Steevens, George, and Isaac Reed, eds., William Shakespeare, *Plays*, 2nd edn., 15 vols (1793)

Knight, Charles, ed., William Shakespeare, *Comedies, Histories, Tragedies, & Poems*, 55 parts [1838-43]

Hudson, H. N., ed., William Shakespeare, *Works*, 11 vols (1851-6)

Collier, John Payne, ed., William Shakespeare, *Plays* (1853)

Delius, Nicolaus, ed., William Shakespeare, *Werke*, 7 vols (1854-61)

Singer, Samuel W., ed., William Shakespeare, *Dramatic Works*, 2nd edn., 10 vols (1856)

Dyce, Alexander, ed., William Shakespeare, *Works*, 6 vols (1857)

White, Richard Grant, ed., William Shakespeare, *Works*, 12 vols (1857-66)

Staunton, Howard, ed., William Shakespeare, *Plays*, 3 vols (1858-60)

Clark, W. G., and W. A. Wright, eds., William Shakespeare, *Works*, 9 vols (1863-6)

Dyce, Alexander, ed., William Shakespeare, *Works*, 2nd edn., 9 vols, (1864-7)

Alexander, Peter, ed., William Shakespeare, *Works* (1951)

Sisson, Charles J., ed., William Shakespeare, *Complete Works* (1954)

Oliver, H. J., ed., William Shakespeare, *Timon of Athens* (1959)

Hibbard, G. R., ed., William Shakespeare, *Timon of Athens* (1970)

Jowett, John, ed., William Shakespeare and Thomas Middleton, *Timon of Athens*, in William Shakespeare, *Complete Works* (the

Oxford Shakespeare), gen. eds. Stanley Wells and Gary Taylor
(1986)

Other Works Cited

Arrowsmith, W. R., 'A Few Supplemental Notes on Some Passages
in Middleton's Plays', *Notes and Queries*, II, 1 (1856), 85–6

Becket, Andrew, *Shakespeare's Himself Again*, 2 vols (1815)

Berry, Ralph, 'Stratford and London, Ontario', *Shakespeare Quarterly*
34 (1983), 462–7

Bevington, David, and David L. Smith, 'James I and *Timon of
Athens*', *Comparative Drama* 33 (1999), 56–87

Blayney, Peter W. M., *The First Folio of Shakespeare* (1991)

Butler, Francelia, *The Strange Critical Fortunes of Shakespeare's
'Timon of Athens'* (1966)

Chambers, E. K., *William Shakespeare: A Study of Facts and
Problems*, 2 vols (1930)

Derrida, Jacques, *Specters of Marx: The State of the Debt, the Work of
Mourning, and the New International*, trans. Peggy Kamuf (1994)

Hayes, Elliot, 'This, Now and Here: Thoughts on Dramaturging
the Classics', *Theatrum* 31 (1992–1993), 22–4

Hinman, Charlton, *The Printing and Proof-Reading of the First Folio
of Shakespeare*, 2 vols (1963)

Holdsworth, R. V. 'Middleton and Shakespeare: The Case for
Middleton's Hand in *Timon of Athens*', unpublished Ph.D. thesis,
University of Manchester (1982)

Holland, Peter, 'Shakespeare Performances in England 1990–1',
Shakespeare Survey 45 (1993), 115–44

Hope, Jonathan, *The Authorship of Shakespeare's Plays: A Sociolinguistic Study* (1994)

Jackson, MacDonald P., *Studies in Attribution: Middleton and Shakespeare* (1979)

Jardine, Lisa, *Still Harping on Daughters: Women and Drama in the
Age of Shakespeare* (1989)

Kinnear, B. G., *Cruces Shakespearianae* (1883)

Konstan, David, 'A Dramatic History of Misanthropes', *Comparative Drama* 16 (1983), 97–123

Lake, David J., *The Canon of Thomas Middleton's Plays* (1975)

Marx, Karl, *Capital: A Critique of Political Economy*, vol. 1, trans.
Ben Fowkes (1977)

—— *Economic and Philosophic Manuscripts of 1844*, trans. Martin
Milligan (1964)

Mauss, Marcel, *The Gift: The Form and Reason for Exchange in
Archaic Societies*, trans. W. D. Halls (1990)

Mellamphy, Ninian, 'Wormwood in the Wood Outside Athens:
Timon and the Problem for the Audience', *'Bad' Shakespeare:
Revaluations of the Shakespeare Canon*, ed. Maurice Charney
(1988), 166–75

Montrose, Louis, *The Purpose of Playing: Shakespeare and the
Cultural Politics of the Elizabethan Theatre* (1996)

Newman, Karen, 'Cultural Capital's Gold Standard: Shakespeare
and the Critical Apostrophe in Renaissance Studies', *Discontinuities: New Essays on Renaissance Literature and Criticism*, ed.
Viviana Comensoli and Paul Stevens (1998), 96–113

O'Dair, Sharon, *Class, Critics, and Shakespeare: Bottom Lines on the
Culture Wars* (2000)

Pettet, E. C., '*Timon of Athens*: The Disruption of Feudal Morality',
Review of English Studies 23 (1947), 21–36

Ruszkiewicz, John J., '*Timon of Athens*': An Annotated Bibliography
(1986)

Sanders, Norman, 'The Popularity of Shakespeare: An Examination of the Royal Shakespeare Theatre's Repertory', *Shakespeare
Survey* 16 (1963), 18–29

Simmonds, Michael, 'Ruskin, Apemantus, and his Father', *Notes
and Queries* NS 26 (1979), 308–10

Tawney, R. H., Introduction, *A Discourse Upon Usury*, 1572, by
Thomas Wilson (1965), 1–172

Taylor, Gary, 'The Canon and Chronology of Shakespeare's
Plays', in Wells *et al.* (1987)

Thomas, Brook, *The New Historicism and Other Old-Fashioned Topics*
(1991)

Thomson, Peter, 'Shakespeare and the Public Purse', *Shakespeare:
An Illustrated Stage History*, ed. Jonathan Bate and Russell
Jackson (1996), 160–75

Veblen, Thorstein, *The Theory of the Leisure Class: An Economic
Study of Institutions* (1934)

Walker, W. S., *A Critical Examination of the Text of Shakespeare*,
ed. W. N. Lettsom, 3 vols (1860)

Wells, Stanley, and Gary Taylor, with John Jowett and William
Montgomery, *William Shakespeare: A Textual Companion* (1987)

Williams, Gary Jay, 'Stage History, 1816–1978', in '*Timon
of Athens*': *Shakespeare's Pessimistic Tragedy*, by Rolf Soellner
(1979), 161–85

Zinman, Toby S., '*Timon of Athens*', *Theatre Journal* 44 (1992),
243–5

TEXTUAL NOTES

Title The Life of Timon of Athens] JAGGARD (*head-title*) (THE LIFE
OF TYMON OF ATHENS); *Timon of Athens* JAGGARD (*Catalogue
and running title*)

Author William Shakespeare and Thomas Middleton] The Oxford Shakespeare was the first edition formally to identify the
play as a Shakespeare–Middleton collaboration.

Persons In JAGGARD a list of 'THE ACTORS NAMES' is printed
after the play; see the list of Stage Directions. Jaggard's list
was probably compiled for the printed text, as it occupies the
recto of an otherwise blank leaf.

1.21 gum] POPE 1723–5; Gowne JAGGARD

1.21 oozes] JOHNSON; issues POPE 1723–5; vſes JAGGARD

1.25 chafes] THEOBALD; chafes JAGGARD

1.56 service] POPE 1723–5; ſeruices JAGGARD

1.88 hands] ALLOTT; hand JAGGARD

1.88 fall] SISSON; fit JAGGARD; slip ROWE; sink DELIUS (*conj.*)

1.108 enfranchised] POPE; enfranchized (= -èd) JAGGARD

1.169 suffered] POPE; suffered (= -èd) JAGGARD

1.179.1 *Enter Apemantus*] POPE 1723–5; *after* 1.177 *in* JAGGARD

1.215 cost] CHETWIN; caſt JAGGARD

1.226 feigned] ALLOTT; fegin'd JAGGARD

1.237 but] HOLDSWORTH (*conj.*); *not in* JAGGARD. Alternatively,
for 'angry wit' read 'augury but', as in JOWETT 1986.

1.249.1 *his horsemen*] JOWETT 1986, *following* CAPELL (*his Company*); *the* reſt JAGGARD

1.253 'mongst] CAPELL; amongeſt JAGGARD

1.258 depart] ALLOTT; depatt JAGGARD

1.261 FIRST LORD] JAGGARD (1.). Similarly formatted as a numeral without a name to the end of the scene for both Lords.
Similarly for the Strangers in Sc. 6, the Friends and Lords
in Sc. 11, the Servants in Sc. 13, the Thieves in Sc. 14, the
Senators in Scs. 16, 17, and 19 (except '1. Sen.', 19.13).

1.276 Come] ALLOTT; Comes JAGGARD

1.277 taste] ALLOTT; raſte JAGGARD

1.286   FIRST LORD] CAPELL; *not in* JAGGARD

2.0.1, 2.143.4   *Oboes*] JAGGARD (*Hoboyes*)

2.1   honoured] POPE; honoured (= -èd) JAGGARD

2.22   Hanged] ALLOTT; Handg'd JAGGARD

2.29   ever] ROWE 1709; verie JAGGARD

2.81   then thou] JAGGARD; thou POPE 1728

2.112.1   *Enter a Servant*] DYCE 1857; *after* 2.113 *in* JAGGARD

2.123   Th' ear,] JAGGARD (There,)

2.124   smell, all] STEEVENS–REED 1793; all JAGGARD; smell THEO-BALD

2.127   welcome] ALLOTT; wecome JAGGARD

2.128   FIRST LORD] CAPELL; *Luc.* JAGGARD

2.128.1–3   *Music…playing*] JAGGARD supplies two directions. The first, continuing after '*Sound Tucket.*' at 2.111.1, reads, '*Enter the Maskers of Amazons, with Lutes in their hands, dauncing and playing.*' The second, at 2.119.1, reads, '*Enter Cupid with the Maske of Ladies.*' Both directions follow information appropriate to the moment ('*Sound Tucket.*', '*Enter Cupid*') with an anticipation of the masque. CAPELL originated the editorial rearrangement.

2.150   LADY] STEEVENS 1778 (Johnson); *Lord* JAGGARD

2.153   attends] JAGGARD; 'tends JOWETT 1986

2.155   *Exeunt Ladies*] JAGGARD (*Exeunt.*)

2.171   Accept it] JAGGARD; Accept ALLOTT

2.177.1   *the Steward*] *not in* JAGGARD. The personal name Flavius is something of an abandoned first thought: it appears in the text a few lines above (2.156) and in the stage direction here, but subsequently vanishes.

2.190   has] JAGGARD (ha's)

3.34   'I go, sir'] JAGGARD (*without quotation marks*); *not in* DYCE 1857

3.35   in. Come] JAGGARD; in compt THEOBALD

4.4   resumes] ROWE 1709; refume JAGGARD

4.9.1   *Servants of*] In JAGGARD these servants are identified by the names of their masters in the stage direction and *speech prefixes*.

4.37   broken] HANMER; debt, broken JAGGARD

4.60   ALL SERVANTS] JAGGARD (*Al.*). Similarly '*All.*' through the rest of the scene, except 4.182, '*Ser.*'.

4.71, 98   master's] JAGGARD; mistress' THEOBALD

4.76   PAGE] *Boy.* JAGGARD

4.124   proposed] ALLOTT; propofe JAGGARD

4.131   summed] JOWETT 1986 (Wells); found JAGGARD; found ALLOTT

4.138   lovèd] CLARK–WRIGHT; lou'd JAGGARD; deare lov'd ALLOTT

4.151   of] HIBBARD (Clark–Wright); or JAGGARD

4.162   Timon's] JAGGARD; Lord Timon's ALEXANDER (Steevens)

4.181   Flaminius] ROWE 1709; *Flauius* JAGGARD

4.200   treasure] ALLOTT; Treature JAGGARD

4.209   cheerly] JAGGARD (cheerely)

5.11   bountiful] ALLOTT; bonntifull JAGGARD

5.46   lived] CHETWIN; liued (= -èd) JAGGARD

5.49   *Exit*] JAGGARD (*Exit L.*)

5.56   this hour] POPE 1723–5; his Honor JAGGARD

6.22–3   he not] JOWETT 1986 (Johnson); hee JAGGARD

6.27, 37, 60   LUCIUS] ALLOTT (*Luci.*); *Lucil.* JAGGARD

6.47   before] HANMER; before for JAGGARD

6.49   I, I] COLLIER 2 (Collier MS); I JAGGARD

6.60   *Exit Servilius*] JOHNSON; *after* 6.59 *in* JAGGARD

6.65   spirit] THEOBALD; fport JAGGARD

7.21   I 'mongst lords] DELIUS; 'mong'ft Lords JAGGARD; 'mongst Lords I ALLOTT

8.1   SERVANT] CAPELL; *man* JAGGARD

8.2   TITUS' SERVANT] As in Sc. 4, the servants are identified by their masters' names from here onwards.

8.57   If] HERRINGMAN; If't JAGGARD

8.76   answer] JAGGARD; an answer ROWE

8.84   VARRO'S…SERVANTS] JAGGARD (2. *Varro.*). Here '2' presumably stands for 'both'.

8.94   *Exit*] JAGGARD (*Exit Timon.*)

9.8   all luxurs] JOWETT 1986 (Fleay); *Vllorxa* JAGGARD; *not in* ALLOTT; Ventidius WHITE

10.4.1   *Enter…attendants*] DYCE 1857. In JAGGARD, instead, the direction opening the scene reads, '*Enter three Senators at one doore, Alcibiades meeting them, with Attendants.*'.

10.4   'im] 'em JAGGARD

10.17   An] JOHNSON; And JAGGARD

10.22   behave] ROWE 1709; behooue JAGGARD

10.49   fellow] JAGGARD; felon JOHNSON

10.61   Why, I] ALLOTT; Why JAGGARD; I POPE 1723–5

10.65   'em] ALLOTT; him JAGGARD

10.100   your] CAPELL; our JAGGARD

11.79   foes] WARBURTON; Fees JAGGARD

11.80   tag] COLLIER 2 (*anon. conj. in* Rann); legge JAGGARD

11.85–6   SOME LORDS…OTHER LORDS] JAGGARD (Some *fpeake*… Some other.)

11.90   with your] WARBURTON; you with JAGGARD

11.90   flattery] DYCE 1864–7 (W. S. Walker); Flatteries JAGGARD

11.106   the] ALLOTT; rhe JAGGARD

11.111–12   THIRD…SECOND] CAPELL; 2…3 JAGGARD

11.114.1   *Exeunt*] JAGGARD (*Exeunt the Senators.*)

12.13   Son] ALLOTT; Some JAGGARD

12.21   yet] JAGGARD; let HANMER (*similarly* Shadwell)

13.33   or to] JAGGARD; or so STAUNTON (White); as to G.T. *conj. in* JOWETT 1986

13.41   does] HERRINGMAN; do JAGGARD

14.9–13   It…lean. | Raise…honour.] JOWETT 1986; Raife… Honor. | It…leaue: JAGGARD. See the Oxford Shakespeare *Textual Companion*, note to 4.3.9–10, 11–13, where it is argued that the two lines 'It…lean' are misleadingly disruptive as printed in JAGGARD and far more meaningful as transposed; the reading could result from a misplaced marginal addition. In further defence of the transposition it should be noted that it allows a referent for It in *great fortune* 14.7: fortune (not, as might otherwise be supposed, nature) is the pasture that fattens one brother and whose lack makes the other lean. Without this referent lines 14.9–10 are relatively banal.

14.10   lean] CHETWIN (leane); leaue JAGGARD

14.11   demit] JOWETT 1986 (Staunton); deny't JAGGARD; denude THEOBALD; deject HUDSON (Arrowsmith)

14.12   senator] ROWE 1709; Senators JAGGARD

14.15   say] ALLOTT; fay JAGGARD

14.39   wappered] SINGER 2 (Malone); wappen'd JAGGARD

14.74–5   promise…not perform] HIBBARD; not promife…per-forme JAGGARD

14.88   tub-fast] THEOBALD (Warburton); Fubfaft JAGGARD

14.105   conquerèd] POPE; Conquer'd JAGGARD

14.117   window-bars] STEEVENS 1778 (Johnson); window Barne JAGGARD

14.122   the] JAGGARD; thy POPE

14.130   giv'st] giueft JAGGARD

14.133   PHRYNIA *and* TIMANDRA] JAGGARD (*Both.*). Similarly at 14.149 and 14.167.

14.135   wholesomeness] JOWETT 1986 (G.T.); Whores JAGGARD; whore POPE 1723–5; whole THEOBALD (Warburton)

14.144   pain-sick] JOWETT 1986 (Becket); paines fix JAGGARD

14.156   scolds] ROWE 1709; fcold'ft JAGGARD

14.186   the] JAGGARD; thy POPE (*similarly* Shadwell)
14.186   doth] CAPELL; do's ROWE 1709; do JAGGARD
14.205   fortune] ROWE 1709 (*similarly* Shadwell), SOUTHERN MS (*in copy of* HERRINGMAN); future JAGGARD
14.224   mossed] HANMER; moyft JAGGARD
14.255   drudges] JAGGARD (drugges)
14.256   command] ROWE 1709; command'ft JAGGARD
14.286   my] ROWE 1709 (*similarly* Shadwell); thy JAGGARD
14.366   I'll] JAGGARD (Ile); I'd HANMER
14.385   son and sire] ROWE 1709; Sunne and fire JAGGARD
14.387   loved] POPE; loued (= -èd) JAGGARD
14.399.1   *Enter . . . Banditti*] JOWETT 1986; *after* 'Exit Apeman.', 14.400.1, *in* JAGGARD
14.400   APEMANTUS] JAGGARD; *not in* HANMER
14.400   them] ROWE 1709; then JAGGARD
14.400.1   *Exit*] JAGGARD (*Exit Apeman.*)
14.411   OTHER THIEVES] JAGGARD (*All.*)
14.414   ALL THIEVES] JAGGARD (*All.*). Similarly at 14.416 and 14.417.
14.436   villains] THIS EDITION; Villaine JAGGARD; villainy (*as object of* 'Do') ROWE 1709. Jaggard's reading is inconsistent with *workmen* and, just as important, *you*. The present emendation is more metrical than Rowe's, and continues the idea that theft is a kind of murder.
14.436   protest] JAGGARD; profess G.T. *conj. in* JOWETT 1986
14.450   less] JAGGARD; not less ROWE; no less COLLIER
14.459.1   *Exeunt*] JAGGARD (*Exit*)
14.476   grant'st] POPE 1723–5; grunt'ft JAGGARD
14.493   mild] HANMER; wilde JAGGARD
14.510   If not a] JAGGARD; A POPE
14.538.1   *Exeunt*] THEOBALD; *Exit* JAGGARD
15.5   *Phrynia*] ROWE 1714; *Phrinica* JAGGARD
15.5–6   *Timandra*] ALLOTT; *Timandylo* JAGGARD
15.22.1   *Enter . . . cave*] JOWETT 1986; *after* 15.29 *in* JAGGARD
15.51   worship] ROWE 1709; worfhipt JAGGARD

15.69   men] ALLOTT; man JAGGARD
15.106   apart] CHETWIN; a part JAGGARD
16.1   is in] CHETWIN; is JAGGARD
16.11   chance] CHETWIN; chanc'd JAGGARD
16.18   cantherizing] JAGGARD; Catherizing (*spelling of* cauterizing) ALLOTT
16.30   Which] JAGGARD; And HANMER; But CAPELL; Where KINNEAR *conj.*
16.32   sense] ROWE 1709; fince JAGGARD
16.33   fall] JAGGARD; fail CAPELL; fault HANMER. *Fall* has suitable spiritual connotations, suitably undermined by the literal fall that threatens Athens.
16.67   reverend'st] JAGGARD (reuerends)
16.105   four] JAGGARD; sour ROWE
16.108.1   *Exit*] JAGGARD (*Exit Timon.*)
17.1, 13   THIRD SENATOR] SISSON; I JAGGARD. JAGGARD numbers anew in this scene, identifying the Senator at 17.5 as '2' and that at 17.14 as '3'. Sisson's emendations create consistency with the previous scene.
18.3–4   Timon . . . man] JAGGARD; *not in* JOWETT 1986. This epitaph is not the one read from the Soldier's wax impression in Sc. 19. As a textual plenitude of epitaphs seems oddly appropriate to the play and the character, I now resist my earlier suggestion that the first epitaph was abandoned as the writing of the play's final scenes progressed. *Interpreter* (18.8), if taken in the sense 'translator', supports Oliver's suggestion that there is a second, unread inscription that is not in the Soldier's native language, or is, for some other reason, illegible to him.
19.6   stepped] HIBBARD (Danchin), flept JAGGARD
19.23   their] ALLOTT; rheir JAGGARD
19.37   revenge] JAGGARD; revenges STEEVENS 1778
19.55   Descend] ALLOTT; Defend JAGGARD
19.65.2–19.66   *Soldier . . . SOLDIER*] THEOBALD: *Meffenger . . . Mef.* JAGGARD

PRESS VARIANTS

Sig. Gg2ᵛ

1.216   APEMANTUS] *Ape* JAGGARD (*some copies*); *pe* JAGGARD (*others*). Mechanical variant.

Sig. hh5

16.78   it] JAGGARD (*some copies*); t JAGGARD (*others*)

STAGE DIRECTIONS

1.0.1–3   *Enter Poet, Painter, Ieweller, Merchant, and Mercer,* | *at seuerall doores.*
1.38.1   *Enter certaine Senators.*
1.95.1–4   *Trumpets sound.* | *Enter Lord Timon, addressing himselfe curteously* | *to euery Sutor.*
1.111   *Exit.*
1.111.1   *Enter an old Athenian.*
1.155   *Exit*
1.179.1   *Enter Apermantus.* (*after* 1.177)
1.242.1   *Trumpet sounds. Enter a Messenger.*
1.249.1   *Enter Alcibiades with the rest.*
1.259.1   *Exeunt.*
1.259.2   *Enter two Lords.*
1.286   *Exeunt.*
2.0.1   *Hoboyes Playing lowd Musicke.*
2.0.1–6   *A great Banquet seru'd in: and then, Enter Lord Timon, the* | *States, the Athenian Lords, Ventigius which Timon re-*|

deem'd from prison. Then comes dropping after all Ape-|*mantus discontentedly like himselfe.*
2.61.1   *Apermantus Grace.*
2.111.1, 2.128.1–2   *Sound Tucket. Enter the Maskers of Amazons, with* | *Lutes in their hands, dauncing and playing.* (*after* 2.111)
2.112.1   *Enter Seruant.* (*after* 2.213)
2.119.1, 2.128.1–3   *Enter Cupid with the Maske of Ladies.* (*after* 2.119)
2.143.1–4   *The Lords rise from Table, with much adoring of Timon, and* | *to shew their loues, each single out an Amazon, and all* | *Dance, men with women, a loftie straine or two to the* | *Hoboyes, and cease.*
2.155   *Exeunt.*
2.164.1   *Exit.*
2.174.2   *Enter a Seruant.*
2.177.1   *Enter Flauius.*
2.182.1   *Enter another Seruant.*

2.187.1   *Enter a third Seruant.*
2.207   *Exit*
2.234.1   *Exeunt Lords*
2.250   *Exit*
2.254   *Exit*
3.0.1   *Enter a Senator.*
3.14.1   *Enter Caphis.*
3.35.1   *Exeunt*
4.0.1   *Enter Steward, with many billes in his hand.*
4.9.1–2   *Enter Caphis, Isidore, and Varro.*
4.13.1–2   *Enter Timon, and his Traine.*
4.44.1   *Exit.*
4.44.2   *Enter Apemantus and Foole.*
4.70.1   *Enter Page.*
4.84   *Exit*
4.115.1   *Enter Timon and Steward.*
4.118.1, 4.119.1   *Exeunt. (at 4.119.1)*
4.181.1–2   *Enter three Seruants.*
4.228.1   *Exeunt*
5.0.1–3   *Flaminius waiting to speake with a Lord from his Master, | enters a seruant to him.*
5.3.1   *Enter Lucullus.*
5.28.1   *Enter Seruant with Wine.*
5.49   *Exit L.*
5.62   *Exit.*
6.0.1   *Enter Lucius, with three strangers.*
6.24.1   *Enter Seruilius.*
6.60   *Exit Seruil. (after 6.59)*
6.62   *Exit.*
6.87   *Exeunt.*
7.0.1–2   *Enter a third seruant with Sempronius, another | of Timons Friends.*
7.26.1   *Exit*
7.41.1   *Exit.*
8.0.1–4   *Enter Varro's man, meeting others. All Timons Creditors to | wait for his comming out. Then enter Lucius | and Hortensius.*
8.5.1   *Enter Philotus.*
8.34.1   *Enter Flaminius.*
8.39.1   *Enter Steward in a Cloake, muffled.*
8.64.1   *Enter Seruilius.*
8.77.1   *Enter Timon in a rage.*
8.94   *Exit Timon.*
8.97.1   *Exeunt.*
9.0.1   *Enter Timon.*
9.14.1   *Exeunt*
10.0.1, 10.4.1   *Enter three Senators at one doore, Alcibiades meeting them, | with Attendants. (at 10.0.1)*
10.101.1   *Exeunt.*
10.115   *Exit.*
11.0.1–3   *Enter diuers Friends at seuerall doores.*
11.25.1   *Enter Timon and Attendants.*
11.40.1   *The Banket brought in.*
11.104   *Exit*
11.104.1   *Enter the Senators, with other Lords.*
11.114.1   *Exeunt the Senators.*
12.0.1   *Enter Timon.*
12.41   *Exit.*
13.0.1   *Enter Steward with two or three Seruants.*
13.15.1   *Enter other Seruants.*
13.29.1   *Embrace and part seuerall wayes.*
13.51   *Exit.*
14.0.1   *Enter Timon in the woods.*

14.45.1   *March afarre off.*
14.48.1–2   *Enter Alcibiades with Drumme and Fife in warlike manner, | and Phrynia and Timandra.*
14.176.1   *Exeunt.*
14.197.1   *Enter Apemantus.*
14.400.1   *Exit Apeman.*
14.399.1   *Enter the Bandetti. (after 'Exit Apeman', 14.400.1)*
14.459.1   *Exit Theeues.*
14.459.2   *Enter the Steward to Timon.*
14.538.1   *Exit*
15.0.1   *Enter Poet, and Painter.*
15.22.1   *Enter Timon from his Caue. (after 15.29)*
15.114.1   *Exeunt*
16.0.1   *Enter Steward, and two Senators.*
16.15.1   *Enter Timon out of his Caue.*
16.108.1   *Exit Timon.*
16.113   *Exeunt.*
17.0.1   *Enter two other Senators, with a Messenger.*
17.13.1   *Enter the other Senators.*
17.17   *Exeunt*
18.0.1   *Enter a Souldier in the Woods, seeking Timon.*
18.10   *Exit.*
19.0.1–2   *Trumpets sound. Enter Alcibiades with his Powers | before Athens.*
19.2.1–2   *Sounds a Parly. | The Senators appeare vpon the wals.*
19.65.2   *Enter a Messenger.*
19.70.1   *Alcibiades reades the Epitaph.*
19.86.1   *Exeunt.*
19.86.2   *FINIS.*

[Printed after the play:]

THE
ACTORS
NAMES.

TYMON *of Athens.*
Lucius, *And*
Lucullus, *two Flattering Lords.*
Appemantus, *a Churlish Philosopher.*
Sempronius *another flattering Lord.*
Alcibiades, *an Athenian Captaine.*
Poet.
Painter.
Jeweller.
Merchant.
Certaine Senatours.
Certaine Maskers.
Certaine Theeues.

[Column break]

Flaminius, *one of Tymons Seruants.*
Seruilius, *another.*
Caphis.
Varro.
Philo.   } *Seuerall Seruants to Vsurers.*
Titus.
Lucius.
Hortensis
Ventigius. *one of Tymons false Friends.*
Cupid.
Sempronius.
With diuers other Seruants,
And Attendants.

LINEATION NOTES

1.7 Hath...merchant] POPE; *2 lines* JAGGARD: attend |
1.19–20 You...lord] POPE; *prose* JAGGARD
1.65 Feigned...mount] ROWE 1709; *2 lines* JAGGARD: throned |
1.146 This...long] ROWE 1709; *2 lines* JAGGARD: mine |
1.152 My...promise] POPE; *2 lines* JAGGARD: thee |
1.156 Vouchsafe...lordship] POPE; *2 lines* JAGGARD: labour |
1.179–80 Look...chid] POPE; *1 line* JAGGARD
1.183 Good...Apemantus] ROWE 1709; *2 lines* JAGGARD: thee |
1.186 Why...not] *prose* JAGGARD
1.210 O...bellies] POPE; *verse* JAGGARD: lords |
1.212 So...labour] POPE; *2 lines* JAGGARD: apprehend'st it |
1.225 Then thou liest] POPE; *verse* JAGGARD
1.237–8 That...merchant] THEOBALD; *verse* JAGGARD: lord |
1.251–5 So...monkey] CAPELL; *prose* JAGGARD
1.259 In...in] ROWE 1709; *2 lines* JAGGARD: pleasures |
1.271–2 No...friend] POPE; *verse* JAGGARD: bidding |
1.273–4 Away...hence] POPE; *verse* JAGGARD: dog |
1.276 He's...in] CAPELL; *2 lines* JAGGARD: humanity |
2.2–3 It...peace] CAPELL; age | JAGGARD
2.23–4 No...welcome] CAPELL; *1 line* JAGGARD
2.51–2 Lest...throats] ROWE 1709 (2nd edn.); *prose* JAGGARD
2.73 Captain...now] POPE; *verse* JAGGARD: Captain |
2.114–15 Please...admittance] POPE; *verse* JAGGARD: ladies |
2.120–3 Hail...bosom] RANN; *prose* JAGGARD; all | taste | freely | POPE; all | senses | come | THEOBALD
2.123–4 Th' ear...rise] RANN; *1 line* JAGGARD
2.126–7 They're...welcome] CHETWIN; *prose* JAGGARD
2.144 You...ladies] POPE; *2 lines* JAGGARD: pleasures |
2.187 Be...news] *2 lines* JAGGARD: entertained |
2.192–3 I'll...reward] HANMER; him | JAGGARD
2.194–5 He...coffer] STEEVENS 1773; *1 line* JAGGARD
2.200–4 That...out] CAPELL (*after* Hanmer); *4 lines* JAGGARD: word | for't | were |
2.207–8 You...merits] MALONE; wrong | JAGGARD
2.210 With...it] POPE; *2 lines* JAGGARD: thanks |
2.216–19 You...to you] JOHNSON; *prose* JAGGARD
2.235–8 What...'em] ROWE 1709; *prose* JAGGARD
2.238 Friendship's...dregs] ROWE 1709; *verse line* JAGGARD
4.29 From...payment] JOWETT 1986; *prose* JAGGARD; *2 lines* CAPELL: Isidore |
4.31 'Twas...past] JOWETT 1986; *prose* JAGGARD
4.43–4 Do...entertained] MALONE; *1 line* JAGGARD
4.66–7 Gramercies...mistress] POPE; *verse* JAGGARD: Fool |
4.73 How...Apemantus] POPE; *verse line* JAGGARD
4.84 Answer...gone] POPE; *verse line* JAGGARD
4.85–6 E'en...Timon's] CAPELL; *verse* JAGGARD: grace |
4.88–9 If...usurers] CAPELL; *verse* JAGGARD: home |
4.91–2 So...thief] POPE; *verse* JAGGARD: I |
4.112–13 Nor...lack'st] POPE; *verse* JAGGARD: man |
4.119 Pray...anon] POPE; *2 lines* JAGGARD: near |
4.179–80 Shall...friends] CAPELL; *3 lines* JAGGARD: perceive | fortunes |
4.227 I...foe] CAPELL; *2 lines* JAGGARD: it |
5.55–6 I...him] POPE; | has JAGGARD
6.64 Why...piece] MALONE; *2 lines* JAGGARD: soul |
6.76–7 For...life] ROWE 1709; *1 line* JAGGARD
7.1 Must...others] STEEVENS 1773; *2 lines* JAGGARD: Hmh |
8.14–15 Is...fear] OLIVER (W. S. Walker *conj.*); *1 line* JAGGARD
8.16–17 'Tis...little] POPE; *prose* JAGGARD

8.28 I'm...witness] ROWE 1709; *2 lines* JAGGARD: charge |
8.31 Yes...yours] POPE; *2 lines* JAGGARD: crowns |
8.35–6 Flaminius...forth] POPE; *prose* JAGGARD
8.38–9 I...diligent] THIS EDITION; *1 line* JAGGARD ('diligent' turned down). Usually taken as prose.
8.45–6 Ay...waiting] CAPELL; *1 line* JAGGARD
8.59–60 VARRO's...worship] *unjustified type line* JAGGARD
8.91 Five...And yours] DYCE 1857; *2 lines* JAGGARD: that |
9.9–12 O...table] POPE; *prose* JAGGARD
10.1 My...bloody] ROWE 1709; *2 lines* JAGGARD: to 't |
10.14–15 He...virtues] JOHNSON; *1 line* JAGGARD
10.32–3 The...carelessly] JOWETT 1986; *3 lines* JAGGARD: breathe | outsides | ; wrongs | POPE
10.49–50 And...judge] ALLOTT; lion | JAGGARD
10.78–9 And...security] JOWETT 1986 (W. S. Walker *conj.*); *1 line* JAGGARD
10.100 Attend...spirit] CAPELL; *2 lines* JAGGARD: judgement |
10.102 Now...live] STEEVENS 1773; *2 lines* JAGGARD: enough |
11.46–7 Let...together] *verse* JAGGARD: remembrance |
11.68–9 The...thanks] *verse line* JAGGARD
14.45 Do...quick] ROWE 1709; *2 lines* JAGGARD: nature |
14.73 Promise...none] *verse line* JAGGARD
14.82–3 TIMON...Yes] *1 type line* JAGGARD
14.84–8 Be...diet] POPE; *prose* JAGGARD
14.130–1 Hast...counsel] CAPELL; *prose* JAGGARD; yet | POPE
14.132 Dost...thee] CAPELL; *prose* JAGGARD
14.145–7 Be...still] CAPELL; *4 lines* (*near foot of page*) JAGGARD: thatch | dead | matter |
14.167 More...Timon] POPE; *prose* JAGGARD
14.168 More...earnest] POPE; *prose* JAGGARD
14.169–70 Strike...again] POPE; *prose* JAGGARD
14.280–1 I...prodigal] CAPELL; *1 line* JAGGARD
14.295–6 Under...Apemantus] CAPELL; *verse* JAGGARD: me |
14.348–50 If...beasts] POPE; *verse* JAGGARD: please me | mightst | here | become |
14.353–6 Yonder...again] POPE; *verse* JAGGARD: painter | thee | way | do |
14.357–9 When...Apemantus] POPE; *verse* JAGGARD: thee | welcome | dog |
14.360 Thou...alive] POPE; *2 lines* JAGGARD: cap |
14.361 Would...upon] POPE; *2 lines* JAGGARD: enough |
14.362 A...curse] POPE; *2 lines* JAGGARD: thee |
14.363 All...pure] POPE; *2 lines* JAGGARD: villains |
14.364 There...speak'st] POPE; *2 lines* JAGGARD: leprosy |
14.365–6 If...hands] CAPELL; beat thee | JAGGARD
14.367 I...off] POPE; *2 lines* JAGGARD: tongue |
14.369–70 Choler...thee] ROWE 1709; me | JAGGARD
14.372–3 Away...thee] *prose?* JAGGARD (Away...shall *set as unjustified type line*)
14.389 That...god] ROWE 1709; *2 lines* JAGGARD: lap |
14.400 More...them] HANMER; *2 lines* JAGGARD: men |
14.405 It...treasure] POPE; *verse* JAGGARD: noised |
14.409 True...hid] POPE; *verse* JAGGARD: him |
14.417 We...want] POPE; *2 lines* JAGGARD: men |
14.456–7 I'll...trade] POPE; *2 lines* JAGGARD: enemy |
14.471–3 He's...life] POPE; *prose* JAGGARD
14.473 My dearest master] POPE; *verse line* JAGGARD
14.476 Then...thee] CAPELL; *2 lines* JAGGARD: man |
14.483 What...thee] ROWE 1709; *2 lines* JAGGARD: weep |

15.3–4   What's…gold] POPE; *verse* JAGGARD: him| true|

15.5–8   Certain…sum] POPE; *verse* JAGGARD: Certain| Timandra| enriched| quantity| steward|

15.9–10   Then…friends] POPE; *verse* JAGGARD: of his|

15.11–16   Nothing…having] POPE; *verse* JAGGARD: else| again| highest| loves| his| us| purposes| for| goes|

15.17   What…him] POPE; *verse* JAGGARD: now|

15.18–19   Nothing…piece] POPE; *verse* JAGGARD: time| him|

15.20–1   I…him] POPE; *verse* JAGGARD: too|

15.22–9   Good…it] POPE; *verse* JAGGARD: best| time| expectation| act| people| use| fashionable| testament| judgement|

15.30–1   Excellent…thyself] POPE; *verse* JAGGARD: workman| bad|

15.32–5   I…opulency] POPE; *verse* JAGGARD: thinking| him| himself| prosperity| flatteries|

15.36–8   Must…thee] POPE; *verse* JAGGARD: needs| work| men|

15.46–8   I'll…feed] CAPELL; turn| worshipped| JAGGARD

15.55   Have…men] ROWE 1709; *2 lines* JAGGARD: lived|

15.56   Sir…tasted] ROWE 1709; *2 lines* JAGGARD: Sir|

15.65   Let…better] POPE; *2 lines* JAGGARD: go|

15.70   We…service] POPE; *2 lines* JAGGARD: come|

15.71   Most…you] POPE; *2 lines* JAGGARD: men|

15.73   What…service] POPE; *2 lines* JAGGARD: can do|

15.74   You're…gold] POPE; *2 lines* JAGGARD: men|

15.94   Ay…dissemble] ROWE 1709; *2 lines* JAGGARD: cog|

15.100   Look…gold] POPE; *2 lines* JAGGARD: Look you|

15.105   You…company] POPE; *2 lines* JAGGARD: this|

16.16   Thou…hanged] HANMER; *2 lines* JAGGARD: burn|

16.20   Of…Timon] POPE; *2 lines* JAGGARD: as you|

16.22   I…plague] POPE; *2 lines* JAGGARD: thank them|

16.80   These…them] POPE; *prose* JAGGARD

16.98   Trouble…find him] POPE; *2 lines* JAGGARD: shall|

16.109–10   His…nature] CAPELL; *1 line* JAGGARD

17.3–4   Besides…approach] POPE; *1 line* JAGGARD

A GAME AT CHESS: GENERAL TEXTUAL INTRODUCTION

Edited by Gary Taylor

Where is the work amid the babble of witnesses?
—T. H. Howard-Hill[1]

SEE ALSO

A Game at Chess (*BEPD* 412) constitutes the most complicated editorial problem in the entire corpus of early modern English drama, and one of the most complicated in English literature. It might be imagined as a kind of Rubik cube, with eight sides instead of six, and each side containing hundreds of squares instead of just nine. Moreover, this editorial problem affects a work which was, by every material historical standard, the most remarkable product of the dramatic industry at that time; it is also a work which, I have argued elsewhere, is one of the great achievements of the Western literary imagination (Taylor, 2000). From a purely editorial point of view, this textual problem crucially affects our understanding of the work of the most famous and important scribe of the period, Ralph Crane, who made at least four copies of *Game*—and who also prepared copies of other dramatic works by Middleton, Shakespeare, Jonson, Webster, Fletcher, and Massinger. Finally, the various early texts of *Game* have often been cited by textual critics of Shakespeare and other early modern English dramatists in support of arguments about the transmission of other plays. The problem is therefore worth solving, not only because of the intrinsic interest of problems of this magnitude, but because of the extrinsic interest of the work that must be editorially constructed out of these materials.

This edition prints two texts of the play, *An Early Form* and *A Later Form*, and the apparatus that follows this introduction is divided accordingly. That apparatus has been organized rather differently than the textual notes for

---

[1] *Pasquin* 152.

other works in this volume, in an effort to make intelligible and accessible the complexity and quantity of textual data about this play. However, the apparatus for both versions must necessarily refer to all the extant witnesses for the text, and to the existing scholarship on the play; moreover, the text of each version will be determined by assumptions about the relationships between the various extant witnesses. All these matters are most conveniently set out in a preliminary overview.

Given the size of the textual domain to be surveyed, the following 'preliminary overview' is dauntingly large. I have accordingly broken it down into numbered sections, and occasionally (within sections) into numbered paragraphs; there is also a sequence of numbered visualizations of the branching data-stream (the 'stemma' of transmission). I begin with a description of the documents (Section I); this is followed, eventually, by my own summary of the relationships between those documents (Section XXIX). Although I'm inclined to believe my own eventual conclusions, others may regard them more sceptically; in any case, it seems desirable to separate premises from conclusions. Some previous discussions of the textual problems of *Game* have failed to clarify whether they are describing 'proof or consequences': the evidence necessary to establish a textual hypothesis, or the editorial consequences of an hypothesis already proven. In order to avoid such invalidating confusions, I have tried to justify each step before I proceed to the next. I have also repeatedly entertained a provisional hypothesis, tested it, identified its weaknesses, and replaced it with an improved hypothesis.

Readers who are prepared to trust anything I say may skip immediately to Section XXIX, and rest in peace. For hardier souls, Sections II through XXVIII contain the data and arguments that support the conclusions I summarize in XXIX; they depend, in part, upon new theoretical models and new analytical techniques, which may be of some interest to readers uninterested in *Game* itself. In particular, my approach to *Game* depends upon a combination of mathematics and literary criticism, a combination I believe is necessary to the solution of all complex editorial problems. It also combines and modifies techniques of textual criticism associated with print production, manuscript production, and dramatic production. Furthermore, it challenges a number of assumptions about Ralph Crane that have governed the editing of Shakespeare.

Having summarized in Section XXIX the history of the textual transmission of *A Game at Chess*, in Section XXX I consider what an editor is to do with such knowledge as has been gleaned by an examination of so many documents. How many forms or versions of *Game* should be edited, and how or why should such forms be chosen, and how once chosen should they be reconstructed? These are matters of editorial principle and literary history, with relevance far beyond *Game*; but *Game* forces us to confront issues that have been elided or obscured in existing discussions of textual variation in early modern drama.

The separate textual introductions to *An Early Form* and *A Later Form*, which follow, deal with issues specific to the editorial reconstruction of each. Throughout, my analysis presupposes the record and discussion of variants contained in the following textual apparatus; unless otherwise noted, line numbers refer to *A Later Form*.[2] However, the textual notes to both *An Early Form* and *A Later Form* provide cross-references to the through-line-numbering of the Malone Society transcription (HOWARD-HILL, 1990), to facilitate cross-reference between the two versions.[3]

I. Description

First, it is necessary to identify the textual 'witnesses'. A text is a material, non-sentient witness to a past human act of witnessing. There are two distinct kinds of witness. Most of this introduction will be devoted to early textual transcriptions, in print and manuscript, of Thomas Middleton's inscription(s) of the play. Those textual transcriptions were produced by human witnesses who looked at an earlier inscription of the words of the text, and then wrote down what they saw, word by word, line by line. Most textual criticism studies that kind of textual transcription. However, for *Game* we also possess an extraordinary number of reports of actual performances of the play. Those reports were produced by human witnesses who looked at and listened to actors in a theatre, and then wrote down a short summary of what they saw and heard. At least one of these witnesses (Holles) wrote an extended eyewitness account of the play, the same day he saw it. Others who did not personally see the play reported what they had been told about it by another person or persons who had seen it; these are secondhand reports of the performed text. In other cases it is unclear whether the report is firsthand or secondhand. But all of our textual transcriptions of the play are secondhand: we do not possess Middleton's first complete draft of the play, or the licensed playbook signed by the Master of the Revels, or any of the 'parts' from which individual actors memorized their roles. Modern scholars all acknowledge that the contemporary reports of the play record details— about the impersonation of specific historical figures, for instance—that are absent from all extant manuscripts, and that are present in the extant printed texts only inferentially (through the correspondence between some of the visual images on the engraved title-pages and other extant visual images of certain historical persons). Thus the direct or secondhand reports of human witnesses to performances have to be considered a fundamentally important category of evidence in reconstructing the

---

[2] *Later* references include three numbers ('act.scene.line'), whereas *Early* references include only two ('act.line'). When I give both numbers they are separated by a slash.

[3] Howard-Hill misnumbers 2179 as 2180, thereby throwing off the numbering for the rest of the play, but for purposes of cross-reference I have let the error stand.

text of the play as performed. Those reports will be cited repeatedly in the textual notes to *A Later Form*. However, even the longest of those reports is a drastically abbreviated account of the play, relevant only to a handful of specific details (particularly stage directions and speech prefixes) of Middleton's creation. Moreover, none of the reports derives, directly or indirectly, from any of the others; there is no genealogical or stemmatic relationship between the reports, which seem to derive independently from a handful of the tens of thousands of spectators who saw the play's first performances. Consequently, these reports will be cited only in relation to specific readings in *A Later Form*.

This General Textual Introduction will focus instead upon the early textual transcriptions of the play. In order not to prejudice the subsequent analysis of their relationships, in this introductory description I have arranged them in alphabetical order of the sigla used in my apparatus. In keeping with the principles of this edition, sigla identify texts by their primary agent of transmission, where known. The sigla for texts which are no longer extant, but which must once have existed, are placed in square brackets. There were presumably other lost manuscripts of the play, because each of the six extant manuscripts seems to be a stemmatic dead-end, and not the direct predecessor or direct copy of any other; however, the number and nature of those other lost manuscripts is a matter for inference, hypothesis, and dispute. Therefore, in this preliminary survey I identify only the specific lost manuscripts which we *know* must have existed, before we even begin a detailed analysis of the relationships of the extant texts.

BRIDGEWATER. The so-called 'Bridgewater–Huntington' manuscript, purchased in 1919 by the Huntington Library from the collection of the Earl of Ellesmere at Bridgewater House (Huntington MS EL 34.B.17). The manuscript entered the Bridgewater collection between 1624 and 1686 as a result of its purchase by the first Earl of Bridgewater (1579–1649) or the second (1622–86). The manuscript is not dated, but the same stock of paper was used for all thirteen and a half sheets (Howard-Hill 1995, 2); therefore it must have been completed before Middleton's burial (4 July 1627). It was initially prepared by three people: BRIDGEWATER^A, an inexperienced and unidentified scribe responsible for *Early* Induction.0.1–2.275.1/*Later* Prologue.0.1–2.2.12; BRIDGEWATER^B, also an inexperienced and unidentified scribe, responsible for *Early* 3.1–5.44.2/*Later* 3.1.0.2–5.2.0.1; and Middleton himself, here identified as MIDDLETON^B, who transcribed the end of the play (from *Early* 5.45/*Later* 5.2.1). Middleton also transcribed and in part composed a bridging passage between the stints of Scribe A and Scribe B, which corresponds to *Later* 2.2.13–17, 2.2.46–57, 2.2.73; this improvised bridge, however, leaves out most of an entire scene. All three copyists occasionally correct themselves as they are writing, but their frequencies of self-correction vary: Middleton does so rarely, Scribe A more frequently

(44 times in 763 lines of text), and Scribe B most of all (111 times in 1013 lines of text). Nascimento (27) attributed three single-word interlineations in Scribe B's portion of the manuscript to a subsequent annotator, whom she identified as 'Corrector 2'.[4] However, Howard-Hill (1995, 19–21) persuasively argues that all three words are corrections made contemporaneously by Scribe B himself.

But this manuscript was also retrospectively annotated by another seventeenth-century hand, identified here as BRIDGEWATER^C. His or her corrections were made in pencil. Ioppolo conjectured that 'some if not all of these penciled corrections appear to be in Middleton's hand' (73), but Howard-Hill's more detailed analysis of the handwriting, spelling, and punctuation concludes that 'the pencil corrector's characteristics overall are not Middleton's' (*Pasquin* 218). Most of the 411 pencil interventions involve punctuation or the formal presentation of speech prefixes. I identify variants *within* BRIDGEWATER as simply *corrected* or *uncorrected*, if they were made in ink; substantive variants introduced in pencil by BRIDGEWATER^C are identified as such.

The first modern editor of *Game*, DYCE, consulted this manuscript, and recorded a few of its variants. Price (1953–4) provided the first physical description of the manuscript, but his account has been superseded by Howard-Hill (1995), which also provides a complete transcription, including a detailed record of variants and corrections. Although I have examined the manuscript myself, and disagree with Howard-Hill about a few small details of interpretation of the handwriting, I refer to his transcription unless otherwise noted. Price (1953) suggested that one of the unidentified scribes was Edward Middleton (85).[5] Howard-Hill (1995) plausibly suggests that BRIDGEWATER^A and BRIDGEWATER^B were amateur scribes, probably members of the same family, indeed perhaps related to Middleton himself. This entire manuscript might therefore be attributed, conjecturally, to the Middleton family. However, those identifications are conjectural, and the main scribes are anonymous. I have therefore retained the traditional modern siglum, identifying the manuscript with its earliest known owner.

CRANE[1]. The so-called 'Archdale' manuscript, once owned by the Irish antiquary Mervyn Archdall (1723–91), now in the Folger Library (MS V.a.231); dated '*August* 13° *Anno Dñi. 1624*.' (when the play was still being performed). Primarily in the hand of Ralph Crane, this text contains subsequent corrections in ink by at least two other hands, one of them Middleton's own, the other(s) unidentified. Crane's scribal work was first

---

[4] The three examples occur at 3.1.99/1164, 3.1.240/1337, 4.4.12/1960.

[5] Howard-Hill calls this 'an attractive notion', but then claims that 'the odds are against Edward being involved in production of transcripts of *Game* before, during, or immediately after its production' because the Privy Council on August 20–21 could not find Thomas but could find Edward (1995, 18–19). But these facts would be relevant only if BRIDGEWATER were transcribed in late August 1624. Howard-Hill provides no evidence for such an early dating of the manuscript; stemmatically, it seems most unlikely.

studied by Wilson; this manuscript was first reported, and briefly described, by Bald (1943). For the study of *Game*, and Middleton, this is obviously the most important of the CRANE manuscripts. But it has never been transcribed or published, despite the fact that less important CRANE transcripts have been published (simply because they were believed relevant to problems in the Shakespeare canon).

CRANE[1] is important because it records—as Bald and all others have recognized—a state of the work earlier than that represented in all other witnesses. That earlier state of the work must, at some time, have existed in a manuscript produced by Middleton himself; that manuscript is now lost, but for the purposes of stemmatic analysis it must often be mentioned. Modernist bibliographers would have called that lost manuscript Middleton's 'foul papers'; but such terminology is now disputed, and carries with it ideological assumptions we would not wish to endorse. We have no way of knowing whether that manuscript was in any important sense 'foul'. But it must have been what I have elsewhere characterized as a 'pre-script': that is, a manuscript which chronologically preceded the 'script' which existed at the time of the first performances of the play (Taylor and Jowett 237–9). We need a way of talking about that 'pre-script' (containing the early form of the play), which Crane, at one or more removes, copied, to create the extant manuscript we here identify as CRANE[1]. I will call that lost autograph manuscript of the earliest known complete form of the play [MIDDLETON[PRE]] (for 'Middleton's pre-script'). The exact relationship between [MIDDLETON[PRE]] and CRANE[1] is disputed; we cannot assume that CRANE[1] was copied directly from [MIDDLETON[PRE]].

Although the attribution of this transcript to Crane is not and cannot be disputed, there is no such agreement on its stemmatic relationship to the other Crane transcripts. The superscript numeral simply indicates that it is the earliest datable Crane witness.

CRANE[2]. The so-called 'Lansdowne' manuscript, now in the British Library (MS Lansdowne 690); in the hand throughout of Ralph Crane, and dated '1624'. Parts of this manuscript have been reproduced in a Malone Society transcription by Bawcutt (1993). In its readings clearly closely related to CRANE[3] (as all investigators have recognized, and as Bawcutt's analysis most lucidly confirms), this is a legible and intelligible text of the play, with few unique variants or obvious errors; it does, however, leave out the entire Jesting Pawn scene in the middle of Act Three ('3.2'), and a few other passages. As Nascimento demonstrated, it imposes more of Crane's habits than CRANE[1]. It is the copy-text for DUTTON's edition.

Although the attribution of this transcript to Crane is not and cannot be disputed, there is no such agreement on its stemmatic relationship to all the other Crane transcripts. It shares with CRANE[1] the date '1624', and could theoretically have been completed earlier than August 13. But unlike CRANE[1] it preserves the revised form of the play, and is (in that sense at least) obviously a 'later' witness. The greater imposition of Crane characteristics

also suggests that it is later than CRANE[1]. Finally, and more conjecturally, it seems likely that the very precise date of CRANE[1] was intended to link the transcript to the period of first performances, and that if CRANE[2] had been prepared at the same time it would have been more precisely dated. For these reasons I have given this Crane manuscript the superscript numeral '2'. This numeral should not prejudice analysis of its underlying stemmatic relationship to other lost and extant witnesses.

CRANE[3]. The so-called 'Malone' manuscript, now in the Bodleian Library (MS Malone 25); never owned by Edmond Malone, it was originally a gift to William Hammond (d. 1635), and was acquired later in the seventeenth century by 'J Pepys', probably John Pepys (1576–1652) of Salisbury Court, London (a long-time associate of Lord Chief Justice Coke). The title-page is dated '1624', but an autograph dedication describes the manuscript as a New Year's gift, presumably referring to 1 January 1625. The rest of the text is in Crane's hand. Although closely related in textual detail to CRANE[2], this manuscript represents a deliberate, systematic, and artistically intelligent abridgement of the play. Its exact stemmatic relationship to CRANE[2] and [CRANE[4]] has been disputed. Nevertheless, I have identified it as the third of the extant Crane manuscripts, because of the date of its dedication, which clearly makes it later than CRANE[1], and almost certainly later than CRANE[2]. Moreover, in at least one passage (1.1.270), a reading in CRANE[3] clearly represents a later stage of textual degeneration than the corresponding reading in CRANE[2] (Bawcutt 8).

The entire manuscript has been transcribed and discussed in a Malone Society edition by Bawcutt (1993). Although variants in this text are systematically recorded in the Textual Notes to *A Later Form*, anyone interested in the abridgement should examine it whole, in Bawcutt's transcription.

CRANE/MATHEWES/ALLDE. The so-called 'third quarto' (Q3) was undated (*BEPD* 412(*c*); STC 17884). The title-page claims that it was printed 'in Lydden by Ian Masse'. No printer of that name is known (Nascimento, 62). As Adrian Weiss has now established from an examination of the type-faces, the text was not printed in Leiden but in London, by two printers: the first five sheets A–E (*Early* Induction.0.1–3.154/*Later* Prologue.0.1–3.1.217) by Augustine Mathewes, and the remaining four sheets F–I (*Early* 3.155–5.375/*Later* 3.1.218–Epilogue.10) by Edward Allde. Such shared printing is, in itself, not unusual, but it might in this instance reflect a desire to get the edition into circulation quickly. The division of the quarto between two printers explains certain features of the text which earlier investigators had attributed to a change in the underlying manuscript: for instance, the abrupt shift in the frequency of -ee endings in pronouns (Nascimento, 71). This quarto contains many fewer unique errors than OKES (see below), and it was the basis of the two nineteenth-century editions of the play (by DYCE and

BULLEN). When referring to the physical printed text alone, I will identify it by the siglum MATHEWES/ALLDE.

Middleton had no known relationship with either Mathewes or Allde.[6] He may not have been responsible for selling the manuscript to either printer, or he may have sold the manuscript to an unknown publisher, who hired Mathewes and Allde to manufacture the book. The printers were working from a manuscript of the play which—as all investigators since Bald (1929) have agreed—displays overwhelming evidence of Crane's influence; accordingly, in the apparatus of this edition readings from this witness are identified as CRANE/MATHEWES for the first five sheets, and as CRANE/ALLDE for the remaining four. The physical integrity of the bound volume is less important than the division of agency between two printers, and its shared origin in a manuscript with Crane characteristics, linked in various ways to the other Crane texts. For the purposes of stemmatic analysis, features of this quarto which appear to originate in the printing houses, rather than in the underlying manuscript, will be identified as MATHEWES or ALLDE (i.e. ligature errors, etc.). It is not immediately apparent whether the underlying Crane manuscript was prepared before or after CRANE[1,2,3], because the manuscript itself does not survive, and the compositors of Mathewes and Allde have obviously interfered with Crane's own spellings and punctuation. For the purposes of stemmatic analysis, the lost manuscript which served as printer's copy-text will be called [CRANE[4]]. The superscript numeral has been chosen because of the date of the quarto printed from it, which cannot have been completed until after the production of the three extant Crane manuscripts. Of course the manuscript used by the printers may have been produced much earlier; theoretically, it could be earlier than all three extant Crane manuscripts. Its exact relationship to the other Crane texts will be considered in detail later in this Introduction.

CRANE. It is sometimes useful to identify as a group all four extant texts associated with the scribe Ralph Crane. Accordingly, when all four share a reading it is attributed to CRANE. Within the Textual Notes, this siglum will also be used when all of the Crane texts which contain a particular passage share the same reading. (This most often occurs when a passage is absent from the abridged CRANE[3] but present in the three other Crane texts.) The fact that these texts were all produced by the same scribe should not be taken to imply that they belong to a separate branch of the stemma of transmission, or that they are directly related genealogically.

[KING'S MEN[1]]. 'A new play called *A Game at Chesse*, written by Middleton' was licensed by Sir Henry Herbert, the Master of the Revels, on 12 June 1624, for the usual fee of £1 (Bawcutt 1996, 152). On August 21, a letter from the Privy Council to Secretary Conway reports that 'some of the principall Actors' of the King's Men, when called to account for performing the play, 'produced a booke being an orriginall and p⟨er⟩fect Coppie thereof (as they affirmed) seene and allowed by Sr Henry

Herbert knight M^r *of the Reuells*, vnder his owne hand, and subscribed in the last Page of the said booke; We demaunding further, whether there were no other parts or passages represented on the Stage, then those expressely contained in the booke, they confidentlie protested they added or varied from the same nothing at all'; the Privy Council decided 'to send herew^th all the booke it self subscribed as aforesaid by the M^r *of the Reuells'* to Conway for perusal by himself or the King (Bawcutt 1996, 154).

The King's Men thus at one time possessed a manuscript of the play signed by Herbert, and presumably also containing other markings by him; no such manuscript survives, and we have no record that it was ever returned to the King's Men by Conway or the Privy Council. That lost 'book'—the usual term for what in later theatrical usage would be called the 'promptbook', and what I will call the 'playbook'—allegedly contained everything that the King's Men performed; whether or not this claim was absolutely accurate, it would surely not even have been made if the manuscript entirely lacked such an extensive, conspicuous and controversial role as the Fat Bishop. Therefore, this lost manuscript must have included the Fat Bishop, who was not in the original version of the play. At some point in the theatrical evolution of the text, Middleton's original papers must have been supplemented by various additions and alterations to produce the lost King's Men's playbook. Although this manuscript does not survive, it can be dated with some precision. It was probably completed by 12 June 1624, when Herbert licensed the play; it was certainly completed by 5 August 1624, when the King's Men began performing the play. It thus antedates the earliest dated extant witness (CRANE[1]).

We do not know whether the playbook was autograph. But other King's Men's playbooks from the second and third decades of the seventeenth century are either scribal—*The Lady's Tragedy* (1611), *Sir John van Olden Barnavelt* (1619), and *The Honest Man's Fortune* (1625)—or a combination of autograph and scribal (*Believe as You List*, 1631); in this last example, the autograph portions of the text are themselves a transcript, or 'fair copy', of Massinger's original version of the play. At the very least, then, we can presume that the King's Men's 'book' was a transcript. For the purposes of stemmatic analysis, I will call it [KING'S MEN[1]]. The playbook of *Honest Man's Fortune*, licensed on 8 February 1624/5, is in the handwriting of a scribe who also marked up the playbook of *Believe as You List* (6 May 1631); this man, Edward Knight, seems to have been a professional scribe employed by the King's Men (Greg 288–300, 321–4). [KING'S MEN[1]] might have been, entirely or partly, in the handwriting of Edward Knight. But that hypothesis remains conjectural;

---

[6] For a summary of stationers who worked on Middleton books during his lifetime see Clegg's essay in this volume. Allde printed but did not publish *Sun in Aries* (1621) and *Phoenix* (1607); Mathewes printed but did not publish the second edition of *Fair Quarrel* (1621), which contains a new scene by Rowley but no evidence of Middleton's renewed involvement.

the existence of such a manuscript, by contrast, is not conjectural.

[KING'S MEN²]. This is not a single complete manuscript but a collection of related smaller manuscripts, produced by the King's Men as necessary textual tools for the rehearsal and performance of the play. From the licensed playbook the King's Men would have had to prepare a 'plot' or 'plat' (a list of stage directions used offstage to control entrances, props, and sound cues) and all the actors' 'parts'.[7] All these would have been separate manuscripts, and the few surviving examples of plats and parts are separates, belonging to different plays. Nevertheless, together the 'plat' and 'parts' would have constituted a complete text of the play. These mini-manuscripts probably had no influence on any other text, but Crane's transcripts of A Game at Chess once provided the basis for theories about texts produced by assembling and collating the actors' parts. Consequently, these lost theatrical documents cannot be ignored. Moreover, they certainly once existed, and they are the graphic intermediaries that led directly to the oral and physical performances of the play reported by various witnesses. They are therefore an invisible stemmatic link between the surviving textual transcriptions and the surviving reports of performance, discussed in the Textual Introduction and notes to A Later Form.

[MIDDLETON/OKES]. The compositor(s) of OKES must have been working from a manuscript, and in particular from a text distinct from any of the surviving manuscripts. Therefore, there must once have existed another manuscript, now lost, which we can provisionally identify as [MIDDLETON/OKES]. The title-page of OKES specifies that the play was acted 'nine days', and hence must postdate the final performance on 14 August 1624; if the printed title-page accurately reproduces the text of the title-page of the underlying manuscript (a big 'if'), then the manuscript itself had a title-page similar to the autograph title-page in ROSENBACH, and must have postdated the last performances of the play. The author is more likely than a printer, nine months later, to have remembered exactly how many performances of the play occurred. Bald, Nascimento, and Howard-Hill all agree that the lost manuscript was in Middleton's handwriting, as a whole or in large part, and that it contained some uniquely authoritative readings. None of these earlier scholars knew that this quarto was printed by Okes—with whom Middleton had a long professional association. Middleton himself thus could have provided OKES with copy-text for the edition. Middleton is also much more likely than OKES to have had the knowledge and incentive to arrange for the title-page engraving—which, whether or not it reflects the play in performance, does accurately represent the play's political referents in a visually creative way.[8] Middleton thus seems to have provided Okes with a manuscript of the play, and with paratext specifically designed for a printed edition.[9]

MIDDLETON[T]. The so-called 'Trinity' manuscript, housed in the library of Trinity College, Cambridge since 1738

(MS O.2.66), and perhaps deriving from the personal library of Patrick Young (1584-1652), Librarian to James I and Charles I. As Bald (1929) was the first editor to realize, this manuscript is in Middleton's hand throughout; it has been most recently transcribed and described in a Malone Society edition by Howard-Hill (1990). The manuscript is not dated, but it must have been completed before Middleton's burial (4 July 1627), and was almost certainly begun before the publication of the first printed edition. Unfortunately for editors, this manuscript 'shows Middleton as a careless and probably hurried scribe. The change in the format of the act-scene divisions; the irregular marking of entrances and exits; the loose and frequently imprecise punctuation and lineation; the mistakes in speech-prefixes; the frequent messiness; and especially Middleton's willingness to omit [Early 4.365.2-428.1/ Later 4.4.48.2-110.1] and to let the errors in act V go uncorrected, argue that he did not give his full attention to this transcription' (Nascimento, 22). Evidence of hurried work becomes increasingly prominent after Early 4.143/ Later 4.1.123 (Nascimento, 21; Howard-Hill, 1990, xi-xii).

NON-CRANE. This category is a corollary of the category CRANE. In attempting to identify features of the texts which represent the habits of Crane rather than Middleton, it is sometimes useful to identify as a group four witnesses: the three extant manuscripts which are not in the handwriting of Ralph Crane (BRIDGEWATER, MIDDLETON[T], ROSENBACH) and the printed quarto which apparently derives from a manuscript not in the handwriting of Crane (OKES). This grouping may or may not have stemmatic significance, and it makes no claims about the chronological priority of the Crane and Non-Crane groupings, or the possible interconnections between the two groups.

OKES. The so-called 'first quarto' ('Q1'), an undated printed edition (STC 17882; BEPD 412(a)). There is some bibliographical confusion about this quarto. It exists in three theoretically distinguishable forms (two editions, one of them in two states), but Bald (1929), Greg (BEPD), and STC do not always agree about which copies belong to which category.[10] The engraved title-page was the expensive, unusual, desirable and detachable feature of the edition, perhaps for the first buyers, and certainly for later collectors; mixed copies might have been produced from the beginning, and West's survey of extant copies of

---

[7] For discussion of both see Greg and Stern 2000. A surviving plot is reproduced in 'The Order of Persons', Illus. 39.

[8] See Astington's essay in this volume.

[9] For Middleton's authorship of the poem opposite the title-page, explaining the engraving, see 'Occasional Poems'. For illustrated title-pages to Middleton plays, see 'Order of Persons'.

[10] Greg distinguishes between states (a) and (b) on the basis of four variants: a has a comma after 'Cheffe-play' at Prologue.1, the incorrect catchword ''Againſt' on E4[v], 'White' (instead of 'Whit') at Epilogue.1, and 'FINJS.' (instead of 'FJNIS.') on K4[v]. STC notes a single variant: STC 17882 has 'me Diſciples' at Induction.4 (sig. B1), where STC 17883 and all other texts have 'my Diſciples'. Combining these criteria, (a) is represented by British Library C.34.l.23, (b) by British Library C.34.d.38. But British Library 161.a.10 is a mixed copy; as Greg notes, it lacks a title-page, and sig. K3-4 belong to (a), although the rest belongs to (b). This

the Shakespeare First Folio demonstrates the prevalence of mixing by later collectors dealing with a particularly desirable book. For stemmatic purposes, the bibliographical problems caused by mixed copies of the quarto are trivial, because the second and third states have no editorial value. (See below.) Therefore, the siglum OKES normally refers only to the first form of the quarto (STC 17882); I identify the first form as OKES[1] only on rare occasions when it is specifically necessary to distinguish it from the later forms.

The play was never entered in the Stationers' Register, and no seventeenth-century edition contained any indication of author, printer, or publisher. Its printing has sometimes been attributed, 'on scanty evidence', to John Haviland (Howard-Hill, 6); but Adrian Weiss has now been able to identify the typeface as that of Nicholas Okes. Though Greg identified it as the earliest of the quartos, whether it was in fact printed before MATHEWES/ALLDE is not self-evident. One British Library copy (C.34.l.23), known to Greg, has 'First Edition' written below the title-page, on the sheet onto which the title-page was pasted in 1798; this bibliographical claim is of dubious authority, but it might have influenced Greg. I will discuss the relative precedence of the quartos in Sections VIII and XX.

Because Middleton declares, in the dedication to CRANE[3], that the text of his play was not then available in any 'Stationers Stall', bibliographers have long assumed that this edition was printed after 1 January 1625. I have now been able to confirm that printing of an edition began soon after the death of James I (27 March 1625): in a letter dated 25 May 1625, Joseph Mead of Cambridge wrote to Sir Martin Stuteville about the publication of a new and enlarged edition of Bacon's *Essays*, and then added 'The play called the game at chesse is also in print but because I haue no skill in the game I vnderstand it not' (British Library, Harleian MS 389, f. 446). Middleton's play had almost certainly not been 'in print' very long at the time this letter was written. Mead regularly kept Stuteville informed of the publication of new books, including corantos and other items that can be dated very precisely. For example, on 24 May 1623 he wrote: '& withall I send a book, which I receiued from London on Thursday, for it came out but on Saturday' (f. 33). Mead's statement that *Game* was 'in print' could have been referring to OKES or MATHEWES/ALLDE. But we do know that the second issue of OKES[2] was printed in 1625 (see below), and OKES[1] therefore must have been printed in that year, too. By contrast, we have no historical evidence whatsoever about the date of CRANE/MATHEWES/ALLDE.

Nascimento collated seven copies of OKES for press variants, and found variants in sheets D (outer forme) and E (outer forme). I record her findings in the Textual Notes to *Later*. I have not systematically collated all the remaining copies, but I have sporadically supplemented her account of variants. She identified two compositors at work, and attempted to reconstruct the sequence of printing, but her

bibliographical analysis is fundamentally unreliable, because based on premises and types of evidence which have since been discredited by McKenzie, Blayney, Weiss, and others; preliminary unpublished investigations by Weiss challenge most of her conclusions. Less conjecturally, Nascimento's collations do demonstrate that OKES contains 'at least three times as many independent corruptions as any other' extant text (14); it has been plausibly described as 'the worst of all the dramatic quartos of the period' (Bald 31)—worse even than Okes's edition of *The History of King Lear* (1608). In this case, Okes's usual sloppiness may have been compounded by the hurried and/or surreptitious nature of the job.

OKES[2]. The so-called 'second quarto' ('Q2'), a reprint of the preceding edition (*BEPD* 412(b)), printed for the most part on the same supply of paper (Nascimento, 63-4). Like its predecessor, this was produced by Okes; unlike its predecessor, it is an entirely derivative edition, of no editorial importance, because it does not seem to reflect consultation of any other source. Sheet K, and most of sheets I and H, were printed from standing type; none of the variants in reset type appears to be anything more interesting than a compositorial error. Variants in OKES[2] are, accordingly, not recorded in my apparatus, and all references to the 'witnesses' to *Game* exclude this document from consideration. It is significant to the textual history of the play only in so far as the printer's decision to leave the type standing suggests at least an expectation of high demand.

That fact in turn tends to confirm Greg's conclusion about the sequence of the quartos (*BEPD* 412(a-c)): if a competing edition were already in print, it seems unlikely that OKES would have invested so much time and money in immediately producing a second edition. By contrast, MATHEWES/ALLDE did not appear in a second edition, despite the fact that it offers a much more legible and intelligible text of the play, with far fewer nonsensical readings. However, Greg's hypothesis about the sequence of the quartos remains conjectural, and raises problems which will be discussed later in this Introduction.

There are two issues of OKES[2]: one issue with the same engraved title-page that is also present in some copies of OKES[1] (*BEPD* 412(b1); STC 17883), and another issue without that engraved title-page, but with an unillustrated printed title-page containing the additional information

third British Library copy is symptomatic of the problems raised by this quarto. STC identifies the Emmanuel College, Cambridge copy and the Bodleian Malone 176(3) copy as STC 17882, but Bald (for both) and Greg (for Bodleian) identify them as STC 17883; Greg is correct about Malone 176(3), at least on the basis of the variants on B1, E4[v], and K4[v], but the absence of A1 and the fact that the engraved title-page might easily have been taken from another copy make it impossible to distinguish between Greg's states '(a)' and '(b)' here. Greg, but not STC, identifies copies at the Library of Congress and Harvard as (b11); but Greg, who never left Britain, would not have examined these American copies personally, and STC is correct. STC correctly claims for Harvard one copy of (b), but Greg does not. STC identifies only three extant copies of Greg's (b11) (STC 17884): Cambridge, Huntington (both identified by Greg) and Yale Elizabethan Club (unknown to Greg).

'Printed. 1625' (*BEPD* 412(*b*II); STC 17885). Greg conjectured that 'Evidently the stock of the engraved title ran out, and a cancel was printed to take its place'. But I am not persuaded by Greg's conjecture—or rather, I am not persuaded by the implication that the cancel was an afterthought. All the printed copies of the play manufactured by Nicholas Okes were financed by a publisher or wholesaler. We can identify the printer Okes because of his typeface, but we have no way of knowing who the publisher was. It might have been Okes himself, or someone else. Whoever he was, that publisher must also have paid for the production of the engraved title-page, which had to be sketched, then etched onto a copper plate, then printed on a rolling press distinct from the machines used by Okes, Mathewes, Allde, and other London printers. How could the publisher who paid for the manufacture of a certain number of title-page engravings, and who also paid for the manufacture of a certain number of copies of sheets B–K, *not* be aware of a discrepancy between the two numbers? The publisher had to supply and pay for the paper for OKES² as well as OKES¹; the use of standing type did not alter the quantity or cost of paper needed for two editions. If the publisher only paid for a certain number of copies of OKES¹, then he would have ordered only a certain number of copies of the engraved title-page; if he later decided to pay for a second edition of the text, he could also have paid for more copies of the engraved title-page. The two issues of the second edition might be more plausibly explained by assuming that two different title-pages were intended from the beginning of printing, with the publisher planning to sell copies with the engraving at a higher price. Certainly, engravings were expensive to produce.[11] The use of standing type for the last three sheets suggests that OKES² might have been ready for sale not long after OKES¹, and at the very least they demonstrate that it was in production before complete copies of OKES¹ went on sale. Commercially, it could have made sense to begin by trying to sell copies of the more expensive version. (Publishers still do this, when they publish a paperback later than the hardback, even when the paperback is simply a different binding of the sheets in the hardback.) This would explain why all the known copies of OKES¹ have the engraving, while copies of OKES² are divided between engraved and unengraved title-pages; moreover, it would also explain why no extant copy of OKES² has a perfect copy of the engraved title-page (the perfect copies being used first). However, some copies of OKES¹ might have acquired their engraved title-pages much later than 1625.[12] Given the obvious value of the engraving, and the fact that such illustrations were printed in separate shops from the rest of the text, it may not be possible to determine the original distribution of engraved and unengraved title-pages.[13]

ROSENBACH. This manuscript, once owned by the collector A. S. W. Rosenbach, is now housed at the Folger (MS V.A. 342). Nothing is known about the earlier provenance of the manuscript, and I therefore retain the traditional label 'Rosenbach'. Discovered in 1928, it was first briefly described by Bald (1930), and more fully by Nascimento. The manuscript is not dated, but the title-page refers in the past tense to the play having been acted 'nine days together', and hence the title-page at least must post-date the last performance on August 14. It must therefore be later than CRANE¹. The title-page is autograph, and must have been written before Middleton's burial (4 July 1627), and probably before the publication of the first printed edition in May 1625 (see above). However, the autograph page was written on a stock of paper that was used only at the beginning and end of the manuscript, and the other pages with that watermark are blank; theoretically, the title-page written by Middleton might have been added to a manuscript produced after his death.[14]

The rest of the text is divided between two unidentified scribes, not present in any other extant witness. ROSENBACHᴬ was responsible for all of the text except for half a page in the expanded version of 3.1 (*Later* 3.1.44–57) and a little over two pages at the beginning of Act Five (*Early* 5.0.1–5.86/*Later* 5.1.0.1–5.2.42); these two brief passages were transcribed by ROSENBACHᴮ. The nature of this manuscript is disputed. Unlike any of the other manuscripts, it provides a virtually complete text of the play (minus only the Prologue). Bald (1930) described it as the 'worst' of the manuscripts, certainly an accurate characterization of its calligraphy, but not necessarily of its textual reliability; Nascimento attempted to rehabilitate

---

[11] For some actual seventeenth-century costings see Tyacke, 70–7.

[12] One of the copies now in the Houghton Library at Harvard (14432.34.8*) lacked the title-page in Malone's lifetime, but had acquired it by the time of the Houghton purchase. Likewise, one of the Folger copies of MATHEWES/ALLDE has the OKES title-page. Interestingly, one of the British Library copies of OKES² (161.a.10) currently lacks a title-page; however, it does include the other leaf of the preliminaries (containing 'The Picture plainly explained' and the 'Prologue'), and on that page reverse inking of a manuscript title ['A Game at | che( )'] is clearly visible; both the positioning and the lettering make it clear that this is not offset from any existing title-page. On that same printed page, above 'Picture plainly explained', the inking of 'Thoˢ' Middleton' also shows through from the other side of the paper. That name (not an autograph signature) is currently visible on the reverse side of the leaf. This copy has been systematically re-mounted; here, a box (7 cm × 3.3 cm) has been cut into the sheet on which the leaf is mounted, presumably because whoever mounted the page thought that the attribution was important, and perhaps autograph. Apparently, in this copy of OKES² a manuscript title-page with the author's name replaced the engraving; the later owner who remounted the leaf pasted over that manuscript title-page, but wanted the attribution to remain visible. As Greg observed, 'It is not certain whether the two preliminary leaves' of OKES¹ 'are conjugate', and for OKES² his only evidence that the two preliminary leaves with the engraving were conjugate was a second-hand report. In some copies (for example British Library c.34.d.38) the page is sewn into the book after the title-page, and facing front, as though it were signature A2 recto; in others (for example, the Huntington copy of STC 17882), the page is sewn into the book as a verso, preceding the title-page and facing it, as though it were signature A1 verso.

[13] Even a detailed bibliographical investigation and comparison of all surviving copies would not necessarily solve the problem. I have not attempted such a survey, because the problem is of more bibliographical than editorial interest. I call attention to it here simply because previous discussions have treated the bibliographical facts as unambiguous, and thereby discouraged further research and analysis.

[14] Nascimento identified two sets of watermarks. The initial half-sheet [A²] and the final half-sheet [X²] 'have a watermark similar to Heawood 2102, found in both gatherings in the centre of the second leaves; since the chain-lines run vertically, the half-sheets at the beginning and end of the manuscript must have come from two different sheets of grapes paper. According to Trinity Librarian Philip Gaskell, a watermark "similar to 2101" is also found in' MIDDLETONᵀ; 'it is probable, then, that Middleton added gatherings [A] and [X] to the manuscript before binding' (Nascimento, 52).

the manuscript's reputation, partly by showing that it alone shared a number of features with the early form of the play represented by CRANE[1], and it was thus (she claimed) earlier in the stemma of transmission than any other witness to the revised version. She also demonstrated that its orthography, punctuation, and treatment of act–scene divisions were all more 'Middletonian' than any other texts but MIDDLETON[T] and BRIDGEWATER; these features characterize the entire manuscript, and suggest that it was copied from a manuscript in Middleton's handwriting—or, at least, that it is not many removes from such an autograph manuscript.

It may be useful here to summarize what is known about the dates of this initial set of documents, which indisputably exist or once existed.

[MIDDLETON[PRE]] Completed no earlier than mid-May and no later than 12 June 1624

[KING'S MEN[1]] Completed after [MIDDLETON[PRE]], probably by 12 June, certainly by 5 August 1624

[KING'S MEN[2]] Completed between 12 June and 5 August 1624

CRANE[1] 13 August 1624

CRANE[2] Certainly completed after 12 June, probably after 15 August; certainly completed before 21 March 1625, probably before 31 December 1624

CRANE[3] Late December 1624

[CRANE[4]] Certainly completed after 12 June 1624, probably after 15 August 1624; completed before the printing of MATHEWES/ALLDE began

[MIDDLETON/OKES] Certainly completed after 12 June 1624, probably after 15 August 1624; completed before the printing of OKES began

BRIDGEWATER, MIDDLETON[T], ROSENBACH Certainly completed after 12 June 1624, probably after 15 August 1624; completed before 4 July 1627, and probably before 25 May 1625

OKES[1] Completed no earlier than mid-May 1625, and no later than 21 March 1626, but earlier than OKES[2]

OKES[2] Completed no earlier than 1 June 1625, and no later than 21 March 1626

MATHEWES/ALLDE Completed no earlier than mid-May 1625, and no later than 21 March 1626

The foregoing summary identifies lost documents only if we are absolutely certain that they once separately existed. It is also useful to identify, at the outset, seven other documents which *might* once have existed.

[PRE-BRIDGEWATER]. The manuscript which the BRIDGEWATER scribes were copying.

[PRE-CRANE[1]]. The manuscript which Crane was copying when he produced CRANE[1].

[PRE-CRANE[2]]. The manuscript which Crane was copying when he produced CRANE[2].

[PRE-CRANE[3]]. The manuscript which Crane was copying when he produced CRANE[3]. This might have been a full-length text of the play, which Crane abridged himself, or it might have been an already-abridged text, by Middleton or Crane or someone else.

[KING'S MEN[3]]. A transcript of [KING'S MEN[1]] or [KING'S MEN[2]], probably made after August 13, to serve as the basis for the production of private transcripts of the performed version of the play. If made from the licensed playbook, it would have been made before August 21; if from the actors' parts, it could have been made at any time before the earliest extant text of the full version.

[PRE-MIDDLETON[T]]. The manuscript which Middleton was copying when he produced MIDDLETON[T].

[PRE-ROSENBACH]. The manuscript which the ROSENBACH scribes were copying.

How many of these documents actually existed is not immediately obvious. Some of them might be identical with lost documents we have already identified: for instance, the lost [PRE-CRANE[1]] might have been the lost [MIDDLETON[PRE]]. Part of the task of the following textual analysis will be to attempt to answer such questions. Nevertheless, in discussing the possible relationships of the extant documents to one another, it can be useful to have names for these hypothetical entities.

From this preliminary description certain facts should be obvious. First, *A Game at Chess* belongs to what is now widely called 'print culture': some of its witnesses are printed texts, produced by post-Gutenberg machines and routines. Such printed texts are best understood through the kinds of bibliographical and editorial analysis developed over the last century for dealing with such objects. Second, *Game* belongs to scribal culture or 'scribal civilization' (Eisenstein, 2005): some of its witnesses are manuscripts, produced for particular individuals or for sale *to* booksellers and/or *by* booksellers. Such manuscripts are best understood through the kinds of paleographical and editorial analysis developed, over many centuries, for dealing with classical and medieval texts. Third, *Game* belongs to the early modern London commercial theatre: most of the extant witnesses advertise or acknowledge its theatrical origins, and some of its lost manuscripts were created within routines of textual reproduction that governed theatre practice 'from Shakespeare to Sheridan' (Stern). Those texts are best understood through the scholarship generated by theatre historians. Finally, as a performed play *Game* belongs to an 'oral' culture: some of its extant witnesses are manuscript reports of oral performances. Those texts are best understood through the scholarship generated by anthropologists and other communication theorists.

The complexity of the problem posed by *A Game at Chess* is not a simple function of the number of witnesses; it is a function of the number of forms and domains of textual reproduction at work here. There are more early editions of *Mucedorus* than early witnesses of *A Game at Chess*, but all the extant texts of *Mucedorus* belong to one domain: hand-press printing culture and its routines. There are many more early witnesses of *The Wife of Bath's Prologue* than of *A Game at Chess*, but the earliest Chaucer witnesses all belong to one domain: scribal culture and its routines. For most of the twentieth century, Anglo-American textual criticism and editorial theory were dominated by the Shakespeare canon, and in particular by the binary created when a single Shakespeare play survived in two substantively different printed editions (Taylor, 1994). That binary also applies to *A Game at Chess*—which, like *King Lear*, survives in two substantively different printed editions, one of them printed by Nicholas Okes. But here that whole binary is itself just one prong of the trinary 'Speech—Manuscript—Print' (McKenzie).

A Game at Chess forces us to attend, not only to the relationship of one text to another text, but to the relationship of one textual domain to another textual domain. As such, the textual problem here has implications far beyond the choice of variants in a particular line of a particular play by a particular author.

II. Textual Proximities

The first scholar to take any serious account of all the extant witnesses was Bald, who has suffered the fate of all pioneers, in having his work both stolen and damned by his successors.[15] His edition (1929) was the basis for those by Brooke and Paradise (1933) and Harper (1966), although its unreliability had been demonstrated by Wagner (1931) and would be more extensively documented by Nascimento (1975). Nascimento's dissertation, containing the first collation of all the known witnesses that comes close to completeness, remains unpublished, although the author summarized many of her conclusions in a later article (Zimmerman, 1982). Work on the play was then taken over by Howard-Hill, who between 1984 and 1995 published thorough transcripts of two important manuscripts, a critical edition, a book of textual and interpretive essays, and half a dozen articles and notes devoted to the play. My own analysis of the text is deeply indebted to the work of these previous scholars, and in particular to Nascimento and Howard-Hill.

It seemed obvious to all editors between Bald (1929) and Howard-Hill (1993) that an edition of *Game* should adopt the authorial manuscript MIDDLETON[T] as control-text. Autograph manuscripts of Renaissance plays are so rare that they inevitably attract the intense attention of editors. Both Nascimento and Howard-Hill edited transcriptions of MIDDLETON[T], and keyed their discussions of variants to MIDDLETON[T]; MIDDLETON[T] was thus positioned, at the very outset of their analysis, as the foundational text. But this policy is based on several dubious assumptions. MIDDLETON[T] is important to Middleton editors because it provides the most extensive surviving database of authorial practices, and as such it is invaluable for the attribution and emendation of other works. But as a witness to *Game*, its value depends in part upon the answers to two questions: (1) what was it copied from? and (2) how reliable a copy is it?

The answer to the second question is both obvious and discouraging. Middleton, unlike Crane, was not a professional scribe, and he was a predictably sloppy copyist. First, as all editors have had to confess, MIDDLETON[T] contains many mistakes found in no other text, mistakes which were almost certainly made by Middleton himself. Second, the inattention which produced such new errors would also certainly have prevented him from noticing many errors present in his 'copy-text' (the manuscript from which he was copying); again, all editors have had to confess that MIDDLETON[T] contains some errors shared with other texts. Finally, Middleton's relative incompetence as a copyist was compounded by his knowledge of and proprietorial attitude toward the work. He might often have decided he could improve upon correct authorial readings present in his copy-text. Such random alterations would obscure the stemmatic relationship between MIDDLETON[T] and other texts—thus making it harder to answer the first question (what was it copied from?).

The editing of Renaissance drama has been dominated by paradigms created for the editing of Shakespeare; because editors of Shakespeare lack authorial manuscripts of his canonical plays, they have been preoccupied with reconstructing such manuscripts editorially. For scholars seeking an unattainable authorial source (and justifying their own activity by the absence of, and need for, such an authority), the existence of an authorial manuscript will seem to nullify the need for further editorial activity. But, as editors working in other periods realize, 'the mere existence of manuscripts in the author's own handwriting does not solve all textual problems, or render editors superfluous' (Taylor 1993, 134). 'Editors seek to establish texts that are proximate to a source of value' (130), and when confronted by eight extant substantive witnesses editors must first establish the proximities of each witness to every other; only then can we identify the relative proximity of each witness to a chosen 'source of value'. If we are seeking an accurate text, a sloppy authorial copy may not be the most valuable witness; if we are seeking a text reflecting the author's first intentions, a late copy will not be the most valuable witness (even if that late copy is in the author's handwriting). More generally, in trying to establish the proximities of a group of objects to one another, it is easier to begin with an object whose location is known, and then situate the others in relation to it.

Therefore, in analysing the relationships of the various textual witnesses of *Game* to one another, it is better to begin, not with the undated and problematic text of MIDDLETON[T], but with a text which can be much more easily and confidently located historically: CRANE[1]. The earliest dated and most precisely dated document, CRANE[1]

---

[15] Bald, for instance, first recognized that both CRANE[2] and CRANE[3] derive from another Crane transcript, which has not survived (what Howard-Hill calls 'Pre-Ln./Ma.' and I call '[PRE-CRANE[2,3]]'). Bald also first proposed that MATHEWES/ALLDE was printed from another lost Crane transcript (what Howard-Hill calls 'Pre-Q3' and I call '[CRANE[4]]').

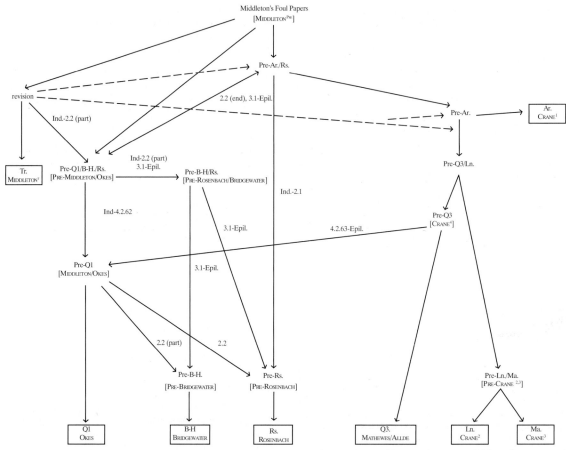

Figure 1. Howard-Hill's stemma, representing the transmission of *A Game at Chess*. Where my labels for manuscripts differ from his, I give my terminology immediately below his. For example, what he labels 'Tr.' I call 'MIDDLETON^T'. The eight extant texts are boxed. Unbroken arrows indicate direct transcription of one text (or part of a text) from another. Dotted lines indicate sporadic contamination of one text by another.

preserves a substantially shorter but coherent version of the work; all modern scholars agree that its version represents the work as originally written, before the composition of various additions and alterations which were incorporated in the play as eventually performed. We might therefore reasonably situate all other witnesses in terms of their relative proximity to CRANE^I.

That is not how the problem was approached by previous investigators. In collating and surveying the mass of variants in the eight substantive texts of *Game*, both Nascimento and Howard-Hill were guided by some dubious assumptions and procedures inherited from the New Bibliography. Howard-Hill presupposes that 'the peculiar characteristics of the individual witnesses' of *A Game at Chess* will help the editor 'to decide whereabouts *the true text*' may be found (*Pasquin* 154; my italics). But what is truth? In a play which so obviously exists in more than one major version, and where different autograph manu-

scripts contain different autograph readings, we need not and indeed cannot look for 'the … text', singular. There is clearly more than one 'true text' of this work; with Middleton as with Shakespeare, the pursuit of a single 'true text' distorts editorial thinking (Taylor, 1987). Although Howard-Hill's analysis sporadically takes account of authorial variation in the analysis of individual variants, his work was organized toward the construction of a single text (the Revels Plays edition). Moreover, the single text toward which he was working would be based, almost inevitably, upon MIDDLETON^T.

This editorial emphasis upon the identity of the copyist affects not only MIDDLETON^T, but also CRANE^I; the fact that Thomas Middleton's hand wrote out MIDDLETON^T lends it an importance it may not possess on stemmatic grounds, while the fact that Ralph Crane's hand wrote out CRANE^I tends to diminish the importance it would otherwise be given on stemmatic grounds. The interest in Crane as a scribe originated in, and has been sustained by, questions about the influence of Crane upon the Shakespeare First Folio; CRANE[I] therefore interests scholars because it belongs to a group of texts which provide evidence of the behaviour of a scribe, not because it provides evidence of Middleton's early intentions. Howard-Hill, not surprisingly, focuses upon relationships between CRANE[I] and other texts which belong to 'The Crane Branch'. But a scribe does not necessarily make a branch. If we ignore Shakespeare, and focus instead upon Middleton's work, it is obvious that the eight *Game* texts belong to two branches: pre-revision (CRANE[I]) and post-revision (everything else). Crane transcribed texts which belong to both branches.

In examining the relationships between the eight substantive texts of *Game*, we must focus upon Middleton (not Shakespeare), upon readings (not scribes), and upon at least two versions (not one). From this perspective, the distribution of variants, which has seemed bewilderingly complex, becomes—if not exactly simple—at least manageable.

III. CRANE[I] and Middleton's First Draft

In his stemmatic analysis (visualized in Figure 1), Howard-Hill concludes that CRANE[I] is at least three removes from Middleton's 'foul papers'.[16] That first draft was first copied in a lost manuscript (which he calls 'Pre-Ar./Rs.', meaning 'pre-Archdale/Rosenbach'), from which was copied another lost manuscript (which he calls 'Pre-Ar.', meaning 'Pre-Archdale'), from which was copied CRANE[I] ('Archdale') itself (*Pasquin* 163–6). By contrast (according to Howard-Hill), MIDDLETON[T] may have been transcribed directly from Middleton's revised foul papers, and hence may be only a single remove from the original draft (*Pasquin* 177). On this reasoning, MIDDLETON[T] (which is a text of the revised version) is a more reliable witness to *the early version* than CRANE[I].

That conclusion is improbable. After all, CRANE[I] is the only text which preserves the early version; all the other texts, including MIDDLETON[T], derive from the revised version. We know, from the very existence of CRANE[I], that the early version must have been preserved in a separate manuscript. If Middleton's original papers had simply been marked up and supplemented to create the revised composite text, then it would have been pointless, and probably impossible, for Crane to reconstruct the original early version. As we know from the date on its title-page, Crane prepared CRANE[I] during the run of the play; by the time he made the existing transcript, the full version already existed, because it was the basis of those performances. Crane could prepare CRANE[I] only because Middleton or the King's Men still possessed an intact, essentially unrevised, manuscript of the original. CRANE[I] must have derived—directly or indirectly, at however many removes—from [MIDDLETON[PRE]]; all other texts must have derived—directly or indirectly, at however many removes—from [KING'S MEN[I]]. We would therefore expect CRANE[I] to be closer than any other text to [MIDDLETON[PRE]].

Of course, it is possible to imagine scenarios in which we do not get what we expect. Howard-Hill indeed imagines such scenarios: that [MIDDLETON[PRE]] was copied twice before CRANE[I]; that, subsequently, [MIDDLETON[PRE]] was modified to incorporate the revisions; that the resulting 'REVISION' became the basis for MIDDLETON[T] and other texts (BRIDGEWATER, ROSENBACH, OKES). The 'REVISION' is not accorded the status of a separate manuscript in Howard-Hill's stemma, although he acknowledges in a footnote that it may have been one.

What could have caused this reversal of our expectations? Why make so many copies of a version of the play that was *not* what potential readers had heard such exciting rumours about? Why, if such copies were made, do we possess only one text of the early version, and seven texts of the revision? It would be more plausible to suppose that CRANE[I] was copied, from [MIDDLETON[PRE]], because during those days in early August [MIDDLETON[PRE]] was the only manuscript Middleton could give to Crane, the only manuscript in his possession, the only manuscript the King's Men were willing to let out of their hands; but while Crane was producing CRANE[I], or at some later date, when the other surviving texts were copied, Middleton or someone else made, or secured from the King's Men, a scribal copy of [KING'S MEN[I]]. That copy of [KING'S MEN[I]]—another lost manuscript, which I have labelled [KING'S MEN[3]]—would then have become the basis for all subsequent copies. Once a private transcript of the full version was available, there was no reason to produce any more copies of [MIDDLETON[PRE]]. Indeed, when someone wanted a shorter text, Middleton (or Crane) did not revert to [MIDDLETON[PRE]], but instead went to considerable trouble to abridge the full version (thus producing CRANE[3]). Potential customers or patrons obviously wanted the full version, including particularly the Fat Bishop and the spectacular ending: they might not notice condensations of the plot and dialogue (hence the economic logic of CRANE[3], an abridgement which could be more cheaply copied, without readers being aware that they had been shortchanged).

The simplified scenario visualized in Figure 2—CRANE[I] copied directly from the first authorial draft, all other extant texts deriving at one or more removes from the playbook—is what the historical and economic circumstances, and the routines of manuscript transmission, would lead us to expect. But will this scenario explain the evidence, the distribution of variants among the eight extant documents?

Yes, it will. Howard-Hill is driven to postulate the existence of a lost manuscript that he calls 'Pre-Archdale' by a handful of 'indisputable errors' in CRANE[I] (*Pasquin* 163). In other words, these 'errors' are the sole basis for the claim (visualized in the upper right side of Figure 1)

---

[16] Howard-Hill gives five partial stemmata: *Pasquin* 166, 176, 179, 184, 187. My Figure 1, which combines his five, does not appear in *Pasquin*. I am grateful to Howard-Hill for checking Figure 1, in January 2007, to make sure that I correctly represented his intentions, particularly in regard to the articulation of his five separate diagrams.

that all the CRANE texts descend from a single lost intermediate manuscript, 'Pre-Ar.', which segregates Crane's work into a distinct branch of the stemma. However, the variants in question are not 'indisputable errors'; they are, in fact, all perfectly sensible variant readings, which are reproduced in the edition of *An Early Form* in *The Collected Works* (*Early* 1.75, 1.307, 1.328, 2.130, 2.171, 2.226, 4.274, 5.57, 5.134, 5.322, 5.371). Some readers may, in each case, prefer the variant reading in MIDDLETON[T]; but that does not prove that the CRANE[I] readings are errors. Indeed, according to the one fact about the stemma of transmission on which all modern scholars are agreed, CRANE[I] readings derive from early authorial papers, and MIDDLETON[T] readings represent an authorial revision.[17] Accordingly, it should hardly surprise us that some readings present in MIDDLETON[T] seem preferable to their CRANE[I] counterparts: Middleton might have made small verbal improvements in transcribing the text.[18] Once we recognize the existence of a revising author, then the aesthetic inferiority of a variant (even if—as seldom happens—it is universally acknowledged) does not prove that the variant is an error. (See Taylor and Warren, *passim*.) Thus, Howard-Hill's personal preference for eleven variants does not demonstrate the existence of an intervening transcript between [MIDDLETON[PRE]] and CRANE[I]; the same evidence could be interpreted to demonstrate that CRANE[I] represents a draft text, later polished and improved by the author when he made a fair copy.

Howard-Hill's stemma depends, not only upon the assertion that these variants in CRANE[I] are errors, but upon the fact that these 'errors…occur also in witnesses of the Crane branch and elsewhere, but not in' MIDDLETON[T] (*Pasquin* 163). However, Howard-Hill's characterization of the distribution of these variants is misleading, because these eleven variants are distributed in six different patterns: those patterns link CRANE[I] to CRANE/MATHEWES (2.130); CRANE[2,3] (4.274); CRANE[2,3,4] (1.328); CRANE[2,3,4], ROSENBACH (1.75, 1.307); CRANE[2,3,4], OKES (5.322); and CRANE[2,3,4], OKES, ROSENBACH—that is, every text but MIDDLETON[T] and BRIDGEWATER (5.57, 5.134, 5.371). The sheer number of patterns undermines Howard-Hill's hypothesis: among the hundreds of variants in these eight witnesses, many different chains of transmission could be justified, if one takes such a haphazard distribution as evidence. Only one of these six patterns, involving only a single variant, connects CRANE[I] to all the other texts in the 'Crane branch', and no others (1.328); the other five patterns, and ten variants, require the 'error' to have been corrected in some CRANE texts, but not others, or to have leaked into some NON-CRANE texts, but not others. Consequently, the preservation of these (inferior?) readings, not only in CRANE[I] but in other texts besides MIDDLETON[T], demonstrates only that the occasional verbal improvements-or-corrections made by Middleton in transcribing his own play were not systematically transferred to all other copies. Again, this should not surprise us. None of the extant texts derives from MIDDLETON[T] (which

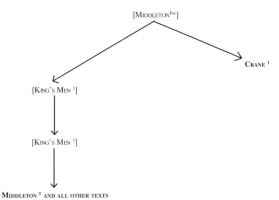

Figure 2. Conjectural relationship of CRANE[I] to other texts. Extant manuscripts are distinguished by bold font.

is a dead-end, stemmatically), and Middleton was demonstrably unsystematic about the verbal details of his text. Authors prone to verbal fidgeting—as Middleton clearly was—may change X to Y in one text, but not another, and may actually revert from Y back to X in yet another text. Howard-Hill's stemma thus presumes processes of authorial improvement-or-correction that, once invoked, make his foundational assumptions superfluous.

Howard-Hill also postulates the existence of a second lost intervening transcript, labelled 'Pre-Ar./Rs.' at the top centre of Figure 1 (for 'prior to Archdale and Rosenbach'). He believes that such a manuscript must have existed because, although the first part of ROSENBACH is close to CRANE[I] (Nascimento, 16), nevertheless ROSENBACH 'sometimes fails to transmit' CRANE[I]'s 'original errors' (*Pasquin* 164). Again, this conclusion depends entirely upon the characterization of those CRANE[I] variants as 'errors'. In fact, the existence of 'Pre-Ar./Rs.' depends on an even smaller sample than the existence of 'Pre-Ar.', because only five of the eleven variants appear in 'the Crane branch' and ROSENBACH. Once we accept that the readings in question may be authorial first versions, then the fact that some readings are shared by CRANE[I] and ROSENBACH reflects nothing more than the manuscripts' joint derivation from [MIDDLETON[PRE]]. ROSENBACH does not

---

[17] See Howard-Hill's own conclusion, in his section on 'Middleton's First Version', confirming CRANE[I]'s 'priority to all other surviving witnesses' (*Pasquin* 29). Note also his acknowledgement of the possibility of 'authorial second thoughts' (28), though not in the context of his discussion of these eleven variants.

[18] How many times Middleton transcribed the text is, at this point, not yet clear. Four of the eleven variants occur in the last two scenes, where two autograph transcripts survive (MIDDLETON[T,8]). The printer's copy-text for OKES is also generally recognized as autograph, at least in large part. The seven other extant texts thus enable us to identify three autograph transcripts; for two of the other four texts he provided autograph front-matter. Given the scale of his involvement in the extant texts, he might also have been responsible for many of the lost transcripts, including [KING'S MEN[I]]. The identification of Middleton's exact role in the production of copies is a central issue in any analysis of the texts of *Game*, but we do not need to have solved all those problems or agreed on all the details of the stemma in order to recognize the weakness of Howard-Hill's claim about these eleven variants. Here, we need only acknowledge that possibility of authorial revision of less than a dozen words.

preserve as many of those original readings as CRANE[1], simply because ROSENBACH is, by all accounts, farther from [MIDDLETON[PRE]].

Howard-Hill's stemma (Figure 1) is complicated and difficult to follow. That is not surprising, given the complexity of the stemmatic problem. Moreover, the fact that my terminology differs from his may make his stemma seem more difficult than it is, by making it even harder for a reader to grasp the essential differences between our two accounts of the history of transmission of the play. Let me try to simplify the issue. For the bottom two-thirds of Figure 1, you can see that I have a name for every extant or lost manuscript in Howard-Hill's stemma. In other words, for most of the stemma we agree on the need to postulate certain lost manuscripts with a similar relationship to the extant manuscripts. We also agree about the very top of the stemma. We agree that there must once have existed an early authorial manuscript (which he calls 'Middleton's Foul Papers', and which I call '[MIDDLETON[PRE]]'). We also agree that Middleton's original version of the play was revised before the play was performed, and we agree that the King's Men must have possessed a 'book' of the play, licensed by Herbert, a manuscript which by the time of the August performances must have incorporated those revisions. This revised version of the play he calls 'revision', without specifying a particular manuscript; I specifically locate the revision in '[KING'S MEN[1]]'. The terminology is different (and the terminology has consequences), so I have not put my own '[KING'S MEN[1]]' anywhere on Howard-Hill's stemma. But up to this point our two alternative hypotheses may be substantively identical, postulating the same relationship between the same lost entities.[19]

At this point, however, our accounts diverge. At the top of Figure 1—that is, at the beginning of the process of transmission—Howard-Hill postulates the existence of three additional manuscripts, which I do not give any names at all: 'Pre-Ar./Rs.', 'Pre-Ar.', and 'Pre-Q3/Ln.'. I see no reason to doubt that the extant CRANE[1] is a direct copy of the lost [MIDDLETON[PRE]]; Howard-Hill, by contrast, believes they are separated by two lost intermediate copies (which he calls 'Pre-Archdale/Rosenbach' and 'Pre-Archdale'). Theoretically, one can never disprove that an apparent 'copy' of X is not instead a 'copy of a copy of a copy' of X. But such multiplication of fictional entities must usually be justified by compelling evidence of their existence. Moreover, CRANE[1] is dated August 13, only eight days after the play's first performance, on August 5 (Howard-Hill 1991). It was presumably the spectacular success of those performances that generated the extraordinary demand for transcripts of the play, and the constraints of time—between the origin of demand and the completion of the extant transcript—only intensify the usual scepticism about multiplying unnecessary entities.[20]

The foregoing criticisms suggest that Howard-Hill's hypothesis is unnecessary and inelegant; they do not prove it is wrong. I have so far offered only an alternative (simpler) explanation of the variants; I have not yet offered

any evidence which actually contradicts Howard-Hill's (more complicated) hypothesis. But several variants do, I believe, decisively invalidate his stemma. At 2.364/ 2.2.177 only CRANE[1] has the expletive 'Lord', where all other texts substitute 'oh'; Howard-Hill quite rightly denies that Crane could have added the oath himself, and instead concludes, 'it is more likely...that "Lord" is a relic of the earliest state of the text, reformed in the sources of the other witnesses' (*Pasquin* 207). Indeed, an exact parallel for this variant (not mentioned by Howard-Hill) occurs at 5.312/5.3.122, where CRANE[1] preserves the Middletonian oath 'faith', absent from all other texts. And both these variants belong, according to Howard-Hill himself, to the same stemmatic category as five other variants unique to CRANE[1], in which the original reading co-exists in CRANE[1] with the alternative which replaces it in all other witnesses (*Early* Induction.26, 1.5, 1.31, 1.167, 2.232). As Howard-Hill observes, those five alterations in the manuscript reflect 'a censorial sensibility', particularly alert to religious issues (*Pasquin* 28).

Howard-Hill does not relate 2.2.177 or 5.3.122 to these five variants, but in all seven cases CRANE[1] uniquely preserves evidence of an uncensored text. It does so again in the exchange at *Early* 5.290-1/*Later* 5.3.103-4, which was 'inexplicably purged' in all other witnesses, probably 'deleted to avoid the imputation that Gondomar was one of the privileged advisors' to the royal family (*Pasquin* 62). In contrast to these eight unique uncensored readings in CRANE[1], there is not a single unique reading in MIDDLETON[T] that can be explained as a consequence of censorship in all the other texts. But how could this have happened? According to Howard-Hill's stemma, MIDDLETON[T] is closer than any other text to Middleton's original foul papers, and therefore should contain more uncensored readings than any other text. Likewise, according to Howard-Hill's stemma CRANE[1] derives from a manuscript ('Pre-Ar.') which is the source of three and a half other extant texts (CRANE[2,3,4] and much of OKES): how could 'Archdale'/ CRANE[1] have preserved censored readings that were not also preserved in some of those other texts? And since the other witnesses (MIDDLETON[T], ROSENBACH, BRIDGEWATER) in any case derive, according to his stemma, from distinct

[19] Although Howard-Hill resists locating the licensed playbook on his stemma, he does argue that 'the impetus' for the major differences between CRANE[1] and the other witnesses 'came from the players' (*Pasquin* 55), and concludes that 'There is no reason to doubt that this significant wrenching of the play from the playwright's fundamental conception was inspired by the theatrical company after Middleton had shown them his early script' (70). I disagree with his evaluation of the literary merit of the changes, but what matters stemmatically is that we both agree that the 'revision' was first incarnated in the playbook.

[20] Even if Crane copied the play by hand several times between August 6 and August 13, one would expect him to keep copying, each time, directly from [MIDDLETON[PRE]]—a manuscript which, whether clean or foul, lacked the refinements supplied by an experienced professional scribe. If demand was so high and so urgent that Crane completed several copies before August 13, then he should have delivered each new and elegant copy to the impatiently waiting customer or patron, as soon as he finished it, and then immediately begun making a new copy from [MIDDLETON[PRE]]. Hence, the known historical constraints of time and circumstance cast considerable doubt upon Howard-Hill's postulate of two intermediary stages of transcription.

sources, how could these readings have been censored in all of them? But if CRANE^I represents the first authorial draft, and all other witnesses derive from the (censored) playbook, there would be no problem explaining 2.2.177 or 5.3.103-4 or 5.3.122, or the five other variants (where the unique and apparently original reading in the first authorial draft was at first transcribed by Crane, and later altered by another hand to the apparently censored reading found in all other texts).

Another anomaly is the presence of a verse line (*Early* 4.135/*Later* 4.1.116) in MIDDLETON^T and CRANE^I, but no other texts (*Pasquin* 202). As Howard-Hill recognizes, this line 'cannot represent an addition during the revision, for then it would not appear [in CRANE^I].... It is difficult to understand why Middleton would have decided to cut the line; it is rhetorically satisfying and eases the transition to line' 4.1.117. Nevertheless, despite his incomprehension of why Middleton or anyone else would have deliber- ately cut this line, his own textual hypothesis 'makes it practically certain that [4.1.116] was not an inadvertent omission.' In other words, according to Howard-Hill him- self, the absence of 4.1.116 from six texts bears every sign of being an accidental omission—except that his stemma cannot explain how the line could have been preserved in both MIDDLETON^T and CRANE^I. In his stemma, MIDDLETON^T and CRANE^I are separated by three intervening documents *that are the ancestors of all the other six texts*; if one of those lost ancestral texts accidentally omitted the line, it should have been omitted from MIDDLETON^T and CRANE^I too (or at least from one of them).

The line preserved at 4.1.116 belongs to a larger class of variants: readings shared only by MIDDLETON^T and CRANE^I. Altogether, there are twenty-three such readings.[21] In the twenty-two other cases, the variant found in other texts makes sense. But all twenty-three cases present the same problem for Howard-Hill's stemma: how can CRANE^I have the reading preserved elsewhere only in MIDDLETON^T?

The insoluble enigma disappears if we eliminate Howard- -Hill's lost intermediate transcripts between [MIDDLETON^{PRE}] and CRANE^I. In the simplified stemma I propose (Figure 2), MIDDLETON^T and CRANE^I preserve 4.1.116 because it was present in Middleton's first completed draft (the immediate ancestor of CRANE^I); but the line was then accidentally omitted in a subsequent transcript—either [KING'S MEN^I] or [KING'S MEN^3]—a transcript that is the ancestor of all the other surviving texts, including MIDDLETON^T. But the author himself, who transcribed MIDDLETON^T, could have corrected the accidental omission in his copy-text. In other words, the presence of this line in MIDDLETON^T is evidence of 'random correction'—in this case, the author remem- bering a reading that has been accidentally omitted in the text he is copying from. This explanation could account for the presence of the correct reading in MIDDLETON^T in either stemma; but Howard-Hill's stemma cannot account for the presence of the correct reading—at 4.1.116, or all the other similar cases—in CRANE^I, which he believes to be a derivative text.

Another, and even more compelling, piece of evidence for this simplified stemma is provided by a variant stage direction: at *Early* 3.103.1/*Later* 3.1.175.1 CRANE^I alone provides an entrance for the White Queen's Pawn. None of the other texts contains this stage direction, but it is clearly necessary; it was editorially supplied by Dyce and Bullen and Bald, who had no knowledge of its existence in CRANE^I. Howard-Hill, too, in his edition of the play recognizes the need for this direction, but obscures its origin: rather than '*Enter White Queen's Pawn*' (the reading of CRANE^I), he interpolates '*Enter White Pawn with White Queen's Pawn*', an emendation he attributes to Dyce. But Dyce contributes only the (dubious) entrance of the anonymous accompanying White Pawn; the central and necessary dramatic fact is the entrance of the White Queen's Pawn, supplied by CRANE^I but by no other text.

A similarly revealing error of lineation occurs at *Early* 4.24-5/*Later* 4.1.21-2. Only CRANE^I has the correct read- ing, adopted by all editors; again, DYCE emended the text, without knowledge of CRANE^I. Howard-Hill also accepts the emendation, but records it (with other errors of lin- eation) in an appendix, without noting the source of the correct reading. The obvious explanation for this lineation variant is that, as with the preceding stage direction, the correct reading is preserved in the earliest text (CRANE^I), that it was accidentally corrupted in some subsequent copy (like KING'S MEN^3), and that all the other extant texts derive from that defective copy.

The same explanation will account for two other vari- ants, not discussed by Howard-Hill or any other invest- igator. These examples are less compelling than the pre- ceding ones, I must admit, because they are not emended by Howard-Hill or other editors; consequently, I have not included them in my tabulation of 'Shared Errors', though I believe they are indeed errors. At *Early* 5.336/*Later* 5.3.144 CRANE^I alone has the reading 'vices'; all other texts read 'others'. The variant 'vices' seems clearly to be correct. In the text of all the other extant witnesses, the word 'others' has no clear antecedent in the preceding lines or speeches; moreover, compellingly, in replying to this speech (*Early* 5.342/*Later* 5.3.148) the Black Knight asks, 'Call you that a vice?'—when in fact the White Knight has *not* called it a vice, except in CRANE^I. The alliteration of 'vices...venom' also supports the CRANE^I reading. It is hard to believe that 'others' is a deliberate

---

[21] 1.1.24 (e'en/even), 1.1.128 (t'/to), 1.1.331 (path/way), 2.2.216-18 (lin- eation), 2.2.217-20 (lineation), 2.2.235 (skonce/brain), 3.1.155.1 (placement of 'and'), 3.1.227-8 (lineation), 3.1.324 (thou'rt/thou art), 3.2.21-4 (lineation), 3.1.350-1 (lineation), 3.1.366 (names/name), 4.1.6 (this/'tis/it's), 4.1.116 (verse line absent from all other texts), 4.2.1 (black/fat), 4.2.27 (e'en/even), 4.2.134 (verse line present in all other texts), 5.2.38 (the/th'), 5.2.87 (voice/Pawne), 5.2.87.1 (stage direction position), 5.3.103 (a/the), 5.3.118 (speech prefixes), 5.3.165 (Queen/Knight/King). The variant at 1.1.331 also occurs as a correction in BRIDGEWATER, but the scribe there originally wrote 'way'; this example might or might not be included, depending on one's attitude to corrections. Howard-Hill does not collate lineation variants or variants in stage direction placement, and his table of shared variants does not include elisions (e'en, t', thou'rt, th'). He creates another example at 3.1.395.2/1576-9 (*Pasquin* 281), but that is a ghost; the phrase is absent from all four CRANE texts. If we eliminated semi-substantives and the ambiguous example at 1.1.331, seventeen examples would remain.

authorial revision which persisted in all other witnesses, and equally hard to believe that 'vices' was an error perpetrated only in CRANE[1] or its antecedents. The same thing happens in the stage direction at *Early* 5.38.1/*Later* 5.1.46.1, where CRANE[1] has the statues move '& dance', where all other texts that contain the direction have them move 'in a Daunce'. Since a dance by definition requires movement, the alternative phrasing is redundant; worse, it conflates two separate theatrical effects, the movement of the statues and then their subsequent dancing.[22] In both cases, the simplest explanation for the variant is that the more precise and apparently correct reading—'vices', '& dance'—stood in Middleton's original papers, from which it was copied into CRANE[1]. Then one of the transcripts which lies behind all the versions of the revised text— either [KING'S MEN[1]] or [KING'S MEN[3]]—accidentally substituted something less precise ('others', 'in a dance'), and those errors were accordingly transmitted to all other witnesses. This could easily happen in the simplified stemma; it could not happen at all in Howard-Hill's stemma.

Thus, CRANE[1] apparently contains four correct readings that are corrupted in every other text, including MIDDLETON[T]: the stage directions at 3.1.175.1 and 5.1.46.1, the lineation at 4.1.21–2, and the substantive variant at 5.3.144. In the first two cases, Howard-Hill himself emends MIDDLETON[T], putting in its place the reading of CRANE[1]. By contrast, MIDDLETON[T] does not contain a single correct reading that has been corrupted in every other text (although it does contain many incorrect readings that are correct in every other text). Either one of these two sets of facts—the presence of uniquely correct readings in CRANE[1], and the complete absence of uniquely correct readings in MIDDLETON[T]—would by itself be enough to invalidate Howard-Hill's stemma. That stemma is also independently invalidated by the presence in CRANE[1], but not MIDDLETON[T], of unique uncensored readings, by the agreement of CRANE[1] and MIDDLETON[T] in at least one demonstrably correct reading corrupted by all other texts, and by their agreement in twenty-two other plausible readings which are variant in all other texts.

The foregoing analysis of substantive textual variants in CRANE[1] seems to me to lead indisputably to the conclusion that CRANE[1] belongs nearer the top of the stemma of textual transmission than MIDDLETON[T]; it provides, I believe, clear positive support for the simplified stemma (Figure 2). Nevertheless, Howard-Hill also spent many years examining the variants in these texts, and he came to a different conclusion. Since the difference between his conclusion and my own will be foundational to any further analysis of the relationship of the extant texts, we need to be confident that the difference is not simply a matter of opinion. To resolve these doubts, it would be useful to consider another category of evidence, one that is independent of these substantive variants, and one that Howard-Hill and other investigators have overlooked.

IV. Middleton's Linguistic Forms, Spelling and Punctuation

Howard-Hill asserts that MIDDLETON[T] 'is undiluted Middleton' (*Pasquin* 177), and he places it alone in the 'Middleton Branch' of his stemma. But its undilutedness is assumed, rather than proven. In Howard-Hill, as in Nascimento and Bald before him, all features of the autograph manuscript are assumed to be Middletonian, and then those features are used to judge the degree to which other witnesses depart from 'pure' Middletonian norms. This may seem unexceptional: MIDDLETON[T] is, after all, autograph throughout. But all scholars agree—because it cannot be denied—that MIDDLETON[T] is a copy of some other manuscript, now lost. Middleton was copying, and all copyists are subject to the influence of what they copy. The study of Crane has had to distinguish Crane's own preferences from those of the manuscripts he was copying—while recognizing that his transformation of his originals was never complete. Crane was a lifetime professional copyist. Middleton was not. We therefore have every reason to suspect that Middleton's own preferences—what he would have done when he was alone with a blank sheet of paper, composing a play from scratch—might have been affected or distorted or weakened in some way by the characteristics of the manuscript he was copying. Since his copy-text is lost, we cannot simply assume that it was in his own handwriting. Indeed, there is a great deal of evidence that what he had in front of him was *not* in his own handwriting.

Linguistic Forms. The most systematic tabulation of Middleton's linguistic preferences is that compiled by Holdsworth. In some cases Holdsworth summarizes and refines features noted by other scholars; in other cases he identifies new features. None of Holdsworth's work was done in order to justify a textual hypothesis about *Game*; instead, *Game* provides only a single set of numbers in tables which record patterns of usage throughout the undisputed uncollaborative Middleton canon. Considering the fact that *Game* is the only text which survives in autograph, and that Holdsworth takes his figures from Bald's edition (based on MIDDLETON[T]), *Game* should provide the largest, or at least the most consistently average, data—or a distribution of data that includes high rankings for some features and balancing low features for others—or a distribution of features clearly related to chronology. Instead, surprisingly, the autograph text of *Game* is repeatedly low in the rankings of Middleton features. Holdsworth's Table 3 (p. 82) provides cumulative figures for the six most characteristic Middleton contractions (I'm, I'd, I've, on't, ne'er, e'en); *Game* has a lower rate per 20,000 words than all but three plays: two written about twenty years before (*Yorkshire* and *Trick*), and one represented by a late scribal transcript (*Hengist*). Table 10 (p. 98) provides raw totals and ratios for -'t contractions; *Game* has a lower ratio than any Middleton play written after 1605–6. It also

---

[22] For fuller discussion, see the text notes at *Later* 5.1.44.2 and 5.1.46.1.

has the highest discrepancy in the ratio between verbal and non-verbal -'t contractions (Table 13, p. 105). For the eleven most characteristic non-verbal -'t contractions (Table 15, p. 110), *Game* has the lowest ratio of any play written after 1606 except *Chaste Maid* (posthumously printed from a scribal manuscript, with many unMiddletonian features). In particular, autograph *Game* is the only Middleton play with no examples whatsoever of the contraction *to't*; nor does it contain any examples of the less common but related contractions *into't* and *unto't*. The average ratio for the Middletonian contraction *they're* is 10 per 20,000 words; the ratio in MIDDLETON[T] is only 6 per 20,000 (Table 20, p. 120). It also has the lowest ratio among Middleton's single-author plays of the contractions *he's* and *she's* (Table 23, p. 123). It has only two examples of the three Middletonian contractions *'bove*, *'mongst* and *yonder's* (Table 26, p. 127); among plays written after 1611, only the exceptionally short *Valour* (with one) has a total as low or lower—and *Valour* survives only in a text printed twenty years after Middleton's death. For various contractions involving the pronoun *thou* (*thou't*, *thou'lt*, *thou'dst*, *th'hadst*, *th'hast*), it is the only play written after 1611 without a single example (Table 33, p. 144). It makes more use of *hath*, proportional to Middleton's preferred *has*, than any play written after 1606 (Table 41, p. 163).

Punctuation. The punctuation of MIDDLETON[T] is also statistically anomalous. Jackson demonstrated that Middleton's uncollaborative works contained very few parentheses (Table II, 185–8), and that in collaborative works the portions attributed to Middleton on other grounds contained many fewer parentheses than the portions attributed on other grounds to Dekker and Rowley (97, 131). By contrast, MIDDLETON[T] contains 54 examples—more than any play but *Witch*, with 162. The only surviving text of *Witch* is, of course, a Crane transcript. If we exclude Crane's *Witch*, the average for the remaining eleven uncollaborative plays is 11 per play. If we further exclude *Women Beware*, printed thirty years after Middleton's death from some sort of transcript, the average of the ten remaining plays is six per play.

Latin spelling and punctuation. These global statistics confirm the suspicion that the contractions, linguistic preferences, and punctuation of MIDDLETON[T] were influenced by some non-Middletonian features of another manuscript. This commonsensical conclusion is confirmed by very specific evidence from one passage. The Latin oration spoken by the Black Bishop's Pawn (*Later* 5.1.10–19, *Early* 5.1–10) was copied, for the most part verbatim, from the printed text of an oration welcoming Prince Charles to Madrid (Price, 1960). Although Middleton had many sources for the political plot of the play, in no other case is the language of the source reproduced so closely at such length. Middleton must have had the original Latin (Pope Gregory XV, sig. H1, H2[v]–H3) in front of him when he was composing the speech in *Game*, since he reproduced its language for the most part word by

word. There are parallels for 56 of the speech's 66 words in the source, and most of those are in sequence; the words original to the speech are confined to two phrases ('a domo Candoris ad domum Nigritudinis' and 'Omnes aduentus tui conflagrantissimi').[23] Fortunately, all nine early texts of *Game* contain this speech in its entirety, and I have collated them against the Latin source. The full collations are given in 'Emendations of Incidentals' to *An Early Form*. The following summary distinguishes between changes of punctuation and changes of spelling (much more significant in Latin than in early modern English). The texts are arranged in order of increasing distance from Middleton's source.

Text	Punctuation	Spelling	Total
CRANE[1]	2	3	5
CRANE[2]	6	4	10
ROSENBACH	5	5	10
MIDDLETON[T]	5	5	10
CRANE[3]	6	5	11
BRIDGEWATER	9	6	15
CRANE/ALLDE	8	8	16
OKES[1]	10	8	18
OKES[2]	10	9	19

Even these raw quantities demonstrate that CRANE[1] is twice as accurate as any other witness, since it has only half the number of variants found in the next closest texts. The qualitative nature of those departures is equally revealing. Two of the five departures found in CRANE[1] are also found in all other texts ('attulisse,' and 'qua'); they might well derive from Middleton's earliest text, transmitted from it to all other witnesses. If we removed these universally shared variants from the table, CRANE[1] would be 2.67 times more accurate than any other text. Another of its departures from the source ('Lætitio') is an error (misreading 'a' as 'o'), which appears in no other text. All other texts correctly have 'a' as the last letter of the word, but omit the accent present in the source; thus, all nine texts depart from the source, but CRANE[1] departs from it differently than all the others. These are patterns that we would expect of a witness which belongs in a separate branch of the stemma. Moreover, CRANE[1] on one occasion preserves a punctuation mark ('possumus,'), altered in all other witnesses, and on another occasion preserves a minuscule ('affectibus') turned into majuscule in every other witness. There is no reason to believe that Crane had access to Middleton's source, or that his 'editing' of his copy-text would have coincidentally reproduced so many details of that source; indeed, the more heavily 'edited' Crane manuscripts are also those farther from Middleton's source. Everything about the spelling and punctuation of this speech indicates that CRANE[1] is closer to Middleton's source than any other transcription. It could easily be

---

[23] The relevant passages are reproduced by Howard-Hill (*Pasquin* 241), but he regularizes certain features of the original, and in particular does not preserve the accents.

only two transcriptions away from the printed source: Middleton's own transcription, in his first draft of the play, and Crane's transcription of that first draft (CRANE[1] itself).

The rest of the table fits well with what we already know, or think we know, about the relationship of the other witnesses. All scholars agree that CRANE[2] and CRANE[3] were copied by Crane later than CRANE[1]. Also as we would expect, the printed quartos—which were, chronologically, almost certainly the last of these texts to be produced—contain the most departures from Middleton's source, and a high proportion of those departures are clearly errors; moreover, this tabulation does not even take account of the fact that all three quartos, alone of all witnesses, set the speech (wrongly) as verse. OKES[2] is less reliable than OKES[1]. The number and nature of their shared departures from the source strongly suggest, as other scholars have suspected, that OKES[1] and CRANE/ALLDE are closely related to one another in some way. (See sections VIII and XX below.) Between these two extremes—the accuracy of CRANE[1] and the cumulative inaccuracy of the printed quartos—stands MIDDLETON[T]. Two of the variant spellings in MIDDLETON[T] are careless errors, present in no other witnesses ('Affectibur' and 'acces- | accessum'); a third such error ('Nigrititudinis') is not counted here, as the word does not appear in the source. Since Middleton was fluent in Latin, and was in a position to correct errors made by intermediaries, we might expect MIDDLETON[T] to contain fewer errors than its copy-text. If so, then the text Middleton was copying might have been as far from the original draft as BRIDGEWATER and [CRANE[4]]. But the exact position of MIDDLETON[T] in the stemma matters less, at this point in our investigation, than the fact that the pattern of its departures from Middleton's source for this speech is incompatible with Howard-Hill's stemma. The autograph transcript is not 'undiluted Middleton'. It is Middleton sometimes actively correcting, and sometimes passively reproducing, features of a non-Middletonian copy-text.

Unique Autograph Preferences. How then are we to distinguish Middleton's active preferences from his passive acceptance of someone else's? We can begin by identifying autograph spellings and punctuation marks that are unique to the autograph text(s). It is of course possible that Middleton's preferences coincided with those of Crane, or one of the other four scribes who worked extensively on surviving manuscripts, or the compositors in three different shops responsible for the printed quartos; it is also possible that his preferences influenced those people. But in order to isolate what is distinctively Middletonian about the autograph manuscript(s) we have to discount, initially, any aspect of the spelling or punctuation which *could* reflect preferences evident in the other surviving texts. The result will be a collection of features unique to autograph. These are not all necessarily correct readings; some of them are unique errors. Moreover, it is always theoretically possible that what seems unique to the manuscript is in fact simply the preference of an oth-

erwise unknown scribe who prepared the lost manuscript which Middleton was copying. However, in so far as they differ from all other known texts, such readings represent a core database of incidentals which are more likely than any others to give us a profile of 'undiluted Middleton'. This database was prepared by checking every spelling and punctuation mark in Middleton's handwriting against the spelling and punctuation of the same word in every other substantive witness.

The database confirms almost all the general conclusions earlier scholars had reached about Middleton's spelling and punctuation. For example, high-frequency autograph features—Middleton's preference for doubling the vowel in the pronouns *hee*, *shee*, *wee*; his preference for 'oh' rather than 'O', for double -tt consonants at the end of words, for redundant apostrophes in monosyllables, etc.—also show up in unique autograph instances. But sometimes Middleton's preference shows up in one of the holograph texts, but not the other. For instance, at 5.3.46/2247 only MIDDLETON[B] has 'neře' (with the typical authorial apostrophe); by contrast, MIDDLETON[T] agrees with all other texts in the unapostrophied 'nere'. In all such cases of disagreement between the two holographs, we may suspect that one form represents the underlying copy-text, rather than the author's own preference; in this example, MIDDLETON[B] actively and uniquely preserves the authorial oddity, and MIDDLETON[T] almost certainly reproduces, passively, the more common form found in all other witnesses to *Game*.[24] The distinction between 'passive' features (also present in other witnesses) and 'active' features (unique to autograph) also immediately explains some of the statistical anomalies described above.

Parentheses. Of the 54 parentheses in MIDDLETON[T], only five are unique to autograph.

418 a great deale harder, (now Sir weere in priuate,
488-90 our most industrious Seruant, famous in all parts of Europe, (our Knight of the black house,
882 (fearefull affrightments, and heart-killing Terrors)
1321 I ioye to iustifie, I was an agent (Sir)
2443 Destroying through (Heauens power) what would destroy

The first two of these open the parenthesis with a bracket but close it with a comma; no other text has this combination of elements around the phrase, but neither element of the combination is itself unique to autograph. At 418 every text but ROSENBACH has the opening bracket

---

[24] See also 5.2.6, where the two holograph manuscripts disagree: MIDDLETON[B] and ROSENBACH have 'o', where MIDDLETON[T] and other texts have 'oh'. Middleton overwhelmingly prefers the 'oh' spelling. The anomalous holograph 'o' confirms much other evidence, discussed later, which establishes the strong stemmatic connection between ROSENBACH and BRIDGEWATER in Act Five; MIDDLETON[B] apparently passively reproduced the spelling of the copy-text, while MIDDLETON[T] reverted to his own preference. Interestingly, at 5.2.129 only CRANE[2,3] have 'oh', where all other texts read 'o'. (The word is missing entirely from MIDDLETON[T].) In Howard-Hill's stemma, CRANE[2,3] are farther from any autograph manuscript than any other extant texts, and yet curiously here they alone preserve Middleton's spelling preference.

where MIDDLETON[T] places it. (ROSENBACH instead brackets 'sir'.) Both MIDDLETON[T] and ROSENBACH close the phrase with a comma. Likewise, in the second example two other texts open a bracket before 'our' (OKES, BRIDGEWATER), and three place a comma after 'house' (CRANE[1,2,4]), so it is only the (incoherent) combination of these different elements that is unique to autograph. Moreover, although the Crane texts do not place the brackets where OKES, BRIDGEWATER, and MIDDLETON[T] do, they do bracket another part of the same sentence ('famous...Europe'). The fifth bracket, like the first two, is only half original. The passage is not present at all in CRANE[1]; CRANE[2,3] bracket, logically, 'through Heauens power'; the alternative autograph text, MIDDLETON[B], places a closing bracket where Crane did, but a comma after 'Destroying' in place of Crane's opening bracket. In three of these cases, an autograph text contains one bracket present in other texts, but at the other end of the bracket uses a comma. But in this instance MIDDLETON[T] places the opening bracket one word later, dividing the phrasing in a grammatically and rhetorically incoherent way that can hardly be called anything other than an error. Of these five unique autograph parentheses, only 882 and 1321 are entirely unique; the other three could easily be explained as Middleton's half-active half-passive response to unMiddletonian brackets in his copy-text.[25]

This hypothesis is further supported by the distribution of parentheses in the CRANE witnesses. The average frequency of brackets rises within the manuscripts from nine every thousand words in CRANE[1] to nineteen in both CRANE[2] and CRANE[3] (Howard-Hill 1965, 335).[26] This internal evidence supports the sequence of Crane texts, based on the external evidence of dates attached to the three manuscripts. This is what we would expect, if indeed CRANE[1] belonged to a distinct branch of the stemma, and was copied directly from the undiluted authorial incidentals of Middleton's original autograph draft. But this pattern also has implications for the origin of the autograph brackets. Of the 54 brackets in MIDDLETON[T], seven involve text not present in CRANE[1]; thus, brackets in MIDDLETON[T] and CRANE[1] could potentially overlap in 47 cases.[27] If all 47 were present in [MIDDLETON[PRE]], we would expect Crane to reproduce them all, while adding many more of his own. 'Crane tended to reproduce the parentheses of his copy, but added to them' (Howard-Hill 1965, 336). Instead, CRANE[1] does not contain brackets in 23 of the 47 places where MIDDLETON[T] does. That is, CRANE[1] fails to 'reproduce' almost half (48.9%) of the brackets in MIDDLETON[T]. This discrepancy cannot be explained by Crane's resistance to bracketing the kind of material Middleton did. By contrast, of the 53 possibilities for brackets in MIDDLETON[T] to overlap with brackets in CRANE[2], the two texts match 49 times (92.5%). Of the 40 possibilities in the abridged CRANE[3], 38 match (95%). Thus, the later and more sophisticated the Crane transcript, the more of the brackets present in MIDDLETON[T] it contains.

Logically, two different processes could account for this pattern. One is that [MIDDLETON[PRE]] contained very few brackets, that Crane added more brackets each time he copied the text, and that MIDDLETON[T] was produced after the later CRANE manuscripts and inherited many of their brackets. The other is that Crane initially removed many of the brackets present in [MIDDLETON[PRE]], but later changed his mind and put almost all of them back in. The second hypothesis is intrinsically less likely, because it requires a radical change in Crane's behaviour. Even then, the unlikely second hypothesis would not prove that MIDDLETON[T] is an early transcript; it permits, but does not require, that assumption. The first hypothesis, by contrast, assumes that [MIDDLETON[PRE]] resembled other authentic Middleton texts in containing very few brackets, and it assumes that Crane's notorious fondness for brackets affected CRANE[1] just as it affected all other known Crane texts.

The statistical anomalies created by the frequency of brackets in MIDDLETON[T] thus seem due to the influence of an underlying manuscript which had inherited brackets from a late Crane transcript. Many of the statistical anomalies in linguistic forms can also be explained by the same assumption.

Hath. Crane often replaced authorial 'has' with his own preferred 'hath': his 1625 transcript of Fletcher's *Demetrius and Enanthe* has 47 *has* and 23 *hath*, compared to a ratio of 65/5 in the 1647 printed text (which better fits Fletcher's high preference for 'has' throughout his career). The proportion of 'hath' rose, as Crane re-copied *Game* (Bald 171). CRANE[2] uses 'hath' 41 times, where MIDDLETON[T] reads 'has'. Thus, if 'hath' were present in

---

[25] Of the two indisputably unique examples, one is a complete verse line; the other—involving a word not present in any other text—is a 'Single Word in Brackets', what Honigmann calls a 'swib'. Honigmann distinguishes between examples like this, which place a vocative within brackets, and other parenthetical single words. He demonstrates that non-vocative swibs are characteristic of Crane, and unusual within the period. He notes that *Michaelmas*, *Phoenix*, and *Chaste Maid* contain no swibs at all; the examples he cites from 'Middleton' texts (p. 163) include five from [Dekker's] *Blurt Master Constable*, three from [Barry's] *Family of Love*, and four from the collaborative *Roaring Girl*. This leaves only a single '(yfaith)' in *Mad World*. Honigmann's data thus tends, without his realizing it, to confirm that Middleton did not write *Blurt* or *Family*.

[26] Howard-Hill's figures are based on Act One. I have taken his raw totals of parentheses and of words in Act One for all the texts, and recalculated them to give number of parentheses per thousand words. The figures might also be expressed as words per parenthesis: one every 111 words in CRANE[1], one every 53 words in CRANE[2,3]. The final column of Howard-Hill's table instead expresses the proportions as 'Px Av. W': I do not understand what that means, but it produces the figures '28' (CRANE[1]), '56' (CRANE[2]), '59' (CRANE[3]). These averages (however they are calculated) clearly demonstrate that CRANE[1] has, proportionally, only about half the number of parenthesis as the other two manuscripts. His figures for CRANE/MATHEWES in Act One are 40 parentheses in 3220 words, or twelve per thousand words, or one every 80.5 words ('38' in Howard-Hill's final column). The figures in CRANE/MATHEWES may, of course, be distorted by compositorial interference, but as they stand they would place [CRANE[4]] later than CRANE[1]. Howard-Hill's subsequent analysis of this data is, as he says, 'made on the necessary assumptions that' MIDDLETON[T] 'corresponds essentially with the holograph from which' CRANE[1] 'was made' (336). But that assumption, which Howard-Hill made in 1965 (long before his detailed work on *Game*), is not 'necessary'.

[27] My figures here and in the remainder of this paragraph are based on the entire play, not just Act One. They therefore differ from Howard-Hill's collation of the distribution of parenthesis in Act One, where he says only that 'most of the parentheses in Middleton's manuscript are repeated in' CRANE[1] (336).

Crane's copy-text, we would expect him to reproduce it. But one of the four examples of 'hath' in MIDDLETON[T] is not present in CRANE[1], which alone of all witnesses uses 'has' at 5.2.63. If we assumed that 'hath' here was a Crane preference, present in all his later transcripts and transmitted from them to MIDDLETON[T] and the other manuscripts, then *Game*'s proportion of *hath* to *has* would be less anomalous, relative to the rest of the canon. Moreover, it is possible that the three other examples in MIDDLETON[T] also originated with Crane, who after all began imposing his preference immediately: CRANE[1] contains eleven examples of 'hath', far too many to attribute to Middleton. Two of those eleven appear in all other texts, including MIDDLETON[T]: 4.1.109 and 5.2.71. In both lines, 'hath' might have originated with Crane, rather than Middleton.

I'd. One or more late Crane texts expands this contraction six times when it is present in MIDDLETON[T], so Crane's preference is clear. On two other occasions, MIDDLETON[T] agrees with all Crane texts in using the expanded form, where OKES (4.2.128) or OKES and ROSENBACH (2.2.35) have the contraction.

I'm. One or more Crane texts expands this contraction 26 times when it is present in MIDDLETON[T], so Crane's preference is clear. But on two occasions (5.2.66, 5.3.145) CRANE[1] agrees with the other autograph text in indicating a contraction, where MIDDLETON[T] has the expanded form also found in later Crane texts. In a passage not present in the early version, MIDDLETON[B] twice has the contraction where MIDDLETON[T] (and all later Crane texts) do not.

i'th'. The autograph text of *Game* has anomalously few examples of this contraction: it occurs only four times in MIDDLETON[T]. According to Lake (Band 1f), the only texts in the Middleton canon with so few are scribal *Lady* (two), scribal *Chaste Maid* (one *i'th'*, but eight examples of *i'the*, almost certainly a scribal expansion of Middleton's preferred form), and *Yorkshire* (five examples of *i'th'* in a text only one-third the length of *Game*). Excluding *Game*, Middleton's non-collaborative full-length plays on average contract 'in the' 17 times per play. The contraction appears nine times in other witnesses to *Game*, where it does not appear in MIDDLETON[T]; adding these nine would bring the total to thirteen, well within Middleton's normal range for a play of this length.

I've. This contraction appears only twice in MIDDLETON[T]; all Crane texts expand both. But on three occasions (1.1.184, 1.1.193, 1.1.258) the Middletonian contraction is present in CRANE[1,2], where later Crane texts and MIDDLETON[T] have the expanded form.

ne'er. MIDDLETON[T] has the lowest relative frequency for this contraction of any full-length Middleton play. Crane expands it twice to 'neuer' where 'nere' is present in MIDDLETON[T]. On another two occasions, the word is spelled out in full by all Crane texts and MIDDLETON[T] where it is elided in ROSENBACH (1.1.173, 3.1.2); the elision regularizes the metre (as it routinely does in *Game* and Middleton). Adoption of these two variants would raise

the frequency per 20,000 words to the range elsewhere attested in the Middleton canon. Moreover, addition of these and of the contracted forms for *I'd*, *I'm*, and *I've* listed above would raise the total for Middleton's six most characteristic contractions by eleven, bringing the total for *Game* within Middleton's post-1606 range.

She's, he's. The anomaly would be reduced by adopting the variant autograph reading *he's*—also present in CRANE[1]—at 5.2.7, where MIDDLETON[T] reads 'hee has'. Another probable example of Crane's characteristic expansion of such contractions, present in all witnesses, occurs at 3.1.406.

't. At 1.1.310 all later Crane texts have 'ere it', where CRANE[1] agrees with MIDDLETON[T] and other NON-CRANE texts in contracting to 'ere't'. Crane was thus obviously capable of expanding this contraction, as he did many others. Twice, CRANE[1] agrees with ROSENBACH in the contracted form, where MIDDLETON[T] agrees with later Crane texts in the expanded form (1.1.311 *though't*, 2.1.209 *see't*). However, these two cases would not be enough to remove the statistical discrepancy, and Crane seems not to have been the only agent of transmission who tended to expand contractions involving Middleton's characteristic terminal *'t*. Altogether, MIDDLETON[T] lacks the contraction an additional 13 times, where it is present in one or more other witnesses; the expanded form also appears three times in ROSENBACH alone, and once in OKES alone.[28] If the contracted form were chosen whenever it appears in other witnesses but not MIDDLETON[T], the total for *Game* as a whole would rise to 68, with a ratio per 20,000 words (77) within Middleton's post-1606 parameters. The same policy would eliminate the discrepancy in the totals for Middleton's eleven most characteristic non-verbal *-'t* contractions: the revised raw total for *Game* would rise to 50, and the frequency per 20,000 words to 57, both within Middleton's post-1606 parameters. The play's totals and ratios for *to't* would also be normalized.

They're. On five occasions a later Crane transcript eliminates the contraction, when it is present in MIDDLETON[T]. Crane's personal preference is therefore clear; so is the fact that CRANE[1], which preserves these examples, better reflects Middleton's preferences. But at 5.1.27 CRANE[1] has the contraction, where all other texts except ROSENBACH eliminate it. Again, MIDDLETON[T] is at this point in the text less Middletonian than CRANE[1]. Restoring the contraction at that point would regularize the metre and raise the ratio for *Game* to the same level as *Women Beware* and *Chaste Maid*.

Yonder's, 'mongst, 'bove. The discrepancy could be eliminated by emending MIDDLETON[T] to adopt variant readings of 'yonder's' at 2.2.41 and 5.2.4 (alternative autograph), and of ''mongst' at 3.1.81.

---

[28] See also *Later* 4.2.142, where I have conjecturally emended ROSENBACH's 'wth it' to 'with't'. Because this contraction is conjectural, I have not included it in the totals.

Summary. 'There is no Jacobean scribe known whose tendency was to introduce colloquialisms; most scribes, presumably, would either transmit them faithfully or replace them with formal literary features' (Lake, 285). In the light of that global historical pattern, and of the evidence specific to the different categories of colloquialism described above, it seems reasonable for an editor of *Game* to adopt many of the elisions not present in MIDDLETON[T] but found in other witnesses.

However, the focus of the preceding analysis is primarily stemmatic, not editorial. Demonstrably, MIDDLETON[T] is, in a variety of features, statistically anomalous. There are only two possible explanations for these discrepancies. The first explanation would postulate (1.a) that all other surviving evidence of Middleton's preferences is incorrect, and that only MIDDLETON[T] preserves the author's 'undiluted' spelling, punctuation, and linguistic forms. But even this radical global assertion would not, in itself, account for the fact that MIDDLETON[T] is farther than CRANE[I] from the incidentals of Middleton's known historical source for the Latin oration. In order to account for the Latin evidence the first hypothesis could only be sustained by several unrelated subsidiary hypotheses: (1.b) that Crane, when copying *Game* in early August 1624, was aware of Middleton's source for the Latin oration, and (1.c) that Crane consulted that source, and (1.d) that Crane preferred the incidentals of that source over Middleton's, or his own, and (1.e) that Crane ignored that source when making his other, apparently later, transcripts of the play.

Alternatively, the statistical anomalies and the Latin oration could both be explained by postulating that (2.a) MIDDLETON[T] has been influenced, in some of its features, by the lost manuscript from which it was copied, a manuscript which contained many characteristics also found in other late transcripts of the play. This second hypothesis is logically, historically, and practically the simpler and more probable of the two available alternatives. It would also—unlike hypothesis 1.a–1.e—explain all the evidence of substantive variants, analysed in the preceding section.

On the basis of the foregoing arguments, it seems reasonable to proceed, tentatively and cautiously, on the assumption that the simplified stemma is correct. If so, then CRANE[I] was copied directly from Middleton's papers, the lost [MIDDLETON[PRE]], and CRANE[I] belongs on a branch of its own at the very beginning of any stemmatic history of *A Game at Chess*. But how can we test that tentative hypothesis? And how can we more precisely determine the position of MIDDLETON[T] in relation to the other witnesses?

My methods up to this point have been local and pragmatic. I began with a consideration of Howard-Hill's stemma, the current prevailing hypothesis. I have presented various specific critiques of one element of that hypothesis (the position of CRANE[I] in Figure 1,

relative to MIDDLETON[T]). Some of those critiques have concerned the logic of Howard-Hill's hypothesis; others have supplied specific counter-evidence. These techniques of argumentation will be familiar to scholars acquainted with the editorial discourse that surrounds Shakespeare and other early modern dramatists. But before we can proceed any further in this analysis, we must clarify certain global theoretical issues, which seldom surface in editorial theories centred on Shakespeare.

V. Shared Errors: Theory

The position of MIDDLETON[T] in relation to the other extant texts can be determined only by applying to *A Game at Chess* the techniques of stemmatology. The importance of stemmatology was recognized by Erasmus and Scaliger in the sixteenth century, but a set of techniques for determining the genealogical relationships between manuscripts first began to be developed in the nineteenth century. Those techniques are often associated with Karl Lachmann; what most people consider 'the Lachmann method' was lucidly and influentially summarized by another German textual critic, Paul Maas, in an extended essay that went through repeated reprintings, revisions, and translations between 1927 and 1958. But the field was revived and revolutionized in the 1990s, as a result of new technical and theoretical resources: technically, the use of computers to correlate massive amounts of data, and theoretically, the use of models drawn from evolutionary biology, including cladistics.[29]

These developments in stemmatology are relatively unfamiliar to textual critics of early modern English, because they are not necessary to the analysis of other early modern plays, which do not survive in many copies; moreover, in that minority of early modern plays preserved in more than one substantive text, the historical sequence of printed editions is either not in doubt, or not significant. Many early modern poems do survive in multiple witnesses of uncertain relationship, but they are so short that individual copies seldom provide enough data for reliable statistical analysis. Indeed, even *Game*, despite its length, does not provide the amount of data required by the 'new stemmatology', which typically deals with works like the New Testament (with thousands of early extant manuscripts) or *The Canterbury Tales* (with scores). Moreover, stemmatology originated in an effort to determine the correct text of works thousands of years old (the Bible, the Greek and Latin classics); for such works, the extant manuscripts may be separated from each other (and from the original) by hundreds of years and an indeterminable number of lost intermediate manuscripts. Even in the case of Chaucer and Langland, the production of new manuscripts continued for more than a century. In the biblical, classical, and medieval traditions, there are, typically, no holograph manuscripts of the texts under

---

[29] For an historical overview see Bordalejo 2003, 39–65.

examination. By contrast, the transmission of *Game* was concentrated in the hands of a few agents over a very short period of time: months, rather than centuries.[30]

Consequently, the methods of the old and the new stemmatology will need to be modified, before they can be applied to *Game*. More generally, both methods have been criticized.[31] I cannot assume that the logic of stemmatology, or its critics, will be familiar to the readers of this book. Therefore, before proceeding to a global analysis of shared errors in the *Game* texts, it is necessary to clarify the principles upon which such an analysis is based. For convenience of subsequent reference, I will divide these into numbered paragraphs.

1. *An attempt to reproduce exactly a pre-existing text is an act of transmission. Every such act of transmission has the potential to corrupt the information content of the original text/message.* The less reliable the method of reproduction/transmission, the greater the probability of corruption of some of that data; human methods of textual reproduction, like those used in manuscript copying and hand-press printing, are intrinsically less reliable than mechanized or automated methods of transmission. Moreover, the larger the quantity of individual particles of information in the original message, the greater the probability of corruption of some of that data. The full text of *A Game at Chess*—including words intended to be spoken, stage directions, speech prefixes, and act and scene directions—contains 19,342 words (Lake, 247, Table I.1). It is extremely unlikely that any human transmission of that text will reproduce every one of those words correctly. Even Howard-Hill's 1990 Malone Society transcript of MIDDLETON[T], subjected to modern routines of repeated and intensive scholarly proofreading, on at least three occasions transmits the wrong word. But the potential for error is much greater than the number of words, because a 'word' is a very imprecise measurement of data. Words are made up of letters, and each letter of a word must, in manual transmission, be separately reproduced. If each word averaged four letters, then the text counted by Lake would contain 77,368 letters. The quantity of data would be even greater than that; since each word in written English will or will not be followed by a punctuation mark, a text with 19,342 words also contains 19,342 bits of punctuation-data (marked or unmarked). Individual letters and punctuation together would constitute 96,710 bits of data to be reproduced. The exact numbers here matter less than the order of magnitude. A message of that size was certain to be corrupted repeatedly, every time it was transmitted, by any method or agent of human transmission in the seventeenth century. Therefore, we can be absolutely certain that every extant seventeenth-century text of *A Game at Chess* contains errors.

2. *Different human agents, attempting to reproduce the same original text/message, will corrupt it in different ways.* To err is human, but different human beings are prone to different sorts of error. Even the same human being, attempting to reproduce the same original text/message

at different times, is likely to corrupt it in different ways on different occasions. This is a corollary of the sheer number of corruptions possible in a text of this magnitude. For instance, for each letter in each word in a text there are, in English, 26 alphabetical possibilities; theoretically, then, each letter might be corrupted in 25 different ways; the postulated 77,368 letters of *Game* therefore offer 1,934,200 different possibilities for corruption. In some ways this is obviously an overestimate, because not every letter-substitution is equally probable. But in another sense it is a gross underestimate. It does not include punctuation, which can sometimes affect our understanding of the information-content of a sequence of words; in MIDDLETON[T] there are at least twelve different possibilities for every punctuation-opportunity in the text. Moreover, errors often involve more than one letter in a text; in a four-letter word, there are fourteen possible letter combinations (first and second letter, first and third, first and fourth, first and second and third, etc.); therefore, each four-letter word in a language with 26 letters could theoretically be corrupted in 350 different ways, and the 19,342 words of *Game* could be corrupted in 6,769,700 ways. Again, this is obviously in one way an overestimate, because many letter combinations do not produce words, and are relatively unlikely to be produced by human transmitters. However, in another way this figure is obviously an underestimate, because letters in an individual word might be added or deleted (rather than simply changed), and indeed whole words might be added or deleted. Besides, some of the variant readings in *Game* are combinations of letters that, to our knowledge, did not constitute words in English at any time. What is true of combinations of letters is also true of combinations of words. Not only might the first word of the text be omitted, or the second word; the first *and* the second might be omitted; the first and the third; the second and the third; the first three words; and so on. The possible combinations of error here are, literally, astronomical ($19,341^2 + 19,340^2 + 19,339^2 \dots$). Again, the exact numbers here matter less than the order of magnitude. We can be absolutely certain that every seventeenth-century text of *A Game at Chess* contains, not only errors involving individual letters, but errors involving combinations of letters; every such text contains, not only errors involving individual words, but also errors involving combinations of words. Likewise, given the orders of magnitude of possibilities-of-error, we can be absolutely certain that, whatever the relationships between them, every seventeenth-century text of *A Game at Chess* contains errors which are not present in any other

---

[30] Completion of Middleton's first draft may have been separated from the publication of the printed editions by twelve or thirteen months, and all eight extant texts were almost certainly produced over a period of less than eleven months, and quite possibly less than ten.

[31] For critiques of the old stemmalogy see Bordalejo. For an influential critique of the new stemmatology see Hanna.

text. All preceding editors of *Game* have agreed on this, if nothing else.

3. *The corruption of a message/text in transmission will be random to the degree that the original message/text is uniformly legible and uniformly reproducible.* Obviously, no seventeenth-century text satisfies these conditions of ideal uniformity. Legibility is not only a matter of the tidiness of handwriting or inking, and the condition of paper, but is also affected by semantic predictability and ease of interpretation. Because all forms of human transmission depend upon interpretation, a message hard to interpret will be hard to reproduce accurately; the more complex and/or unorthodox a message, the more subject it is to misinterpretation, especially in the form of errors which replace 'rare' data with 'commonplace' data (Taylor, 1988). Therefore, since the originals being transmitted were not uniformly legible or uniformly reproducible, the distribution of error in copies is not entirely random. For instance, the speech prefixes in *Game* are very unusual, requiring the repeated copying of unfamiliar combinations of letters (B.K, W.Q.P.), which consist of elements often repeated or recombined in other speech prefixes (W.Q.P, B.Q.P, B.B.P, etc); not surprisingly, the texts of *Game* contain an unusually high number of errors in speech prefixes, by comparison with other plays of the period.

4. *The less uniformly legible and reproducible the original, the less random the production of error; the less random the production of error, the more probable it becomes that different agents, transmitting the same text/message, will independently corrupt it in the same way.*[32] Suppose, for instance, that all eight extant texts of *Game* were copied directly from the same original, each by a different agent, and that a single particular word of that original had been badly inked, or blotted, or rendered less legible by ascending or descending letters from adjacent lines, or by show-through of ink from the other side of the paper, or tearing. Some of the different copyists might, in these circumstances, independently make the same error, because they would all be looking at exactly the same ink-blot; but it is unlikely that all eight copyists would interpret the illegible blot in exactly the same way. Since this kind of material illegibility might happen, accidentally, at any point in any original, it might seem that such coincidences could occur anywhere, and that their probability is therefore entirely incalculable. But the probability of the same error being independently made depends, not only upon unpredictable accidental disuniformities in legibility of the original, but on certain intrinsic features of the original message-medium. Certain letters look more alike than others, and are therefore more easily substituted for one another; certain letters or ligatures are next to one another in a compositor's typecase, and therefore are more likely to be inadvertently substituted for one another in a line of type; only certain letter-combinations produce words in the early modern lexicon. Moreover, the probability of an error, even when the original is not ideally legible, depends upon the magnitude and complexity of the misinterpretation involved. The substitution

of one ascending letter for another ascending letter—'f' and 'l', for instance—is much more probable than the substitution of a majuscule 'H' for a minuscule 'i'; substitution of one letter is more probable than substitution of two, etc. Finally, the probability that an error has been independently made decreases with every increase in the number of independent acts of transmission. We should not be surprised if two independent agents, attempting to transmit the same original text/message, substituted an 'l' for a 'k' in one particular word; but it is much less probable that three different agents would independently make the same mistake; even less probable, that four would independently do so—and so on, in an algorithmically descending scale of probability. Given the original's lack of uniformity and reproducibility, and given that we possess eight different texts, it seems certain that a few simple errors were independently made in two of the eight texts of *Game*; but we should expect few, if any, instances of error independently made in three texts.

5. *The less random the agency of transmission, the less random the generation of corruption.* The same mechanism, trying to reproduce the same original message/text, will tend to produce the same quantity and type of error. Some human transmitters are more error-prone than others. If the same original were being independently copied by eight different scribes, one of the scribes might be less experienced or less capable than any of the others, and the transcript he produced might therefore contain many more errors than the other seven transcripts, even though all eight were copied from the same original.[33] In fact, let us suppose that one copy is being made by Unreliable (who introduces thirty errors in a single transcription), and the other seven are all being made by Reliable (who introduces only four errors in each transcription). Reliable makes copy 2 directly from the original; he makes copy 3 from copy 2, copy 4 from copy 3, etc. Unreliable's single transcript, copied directly from the original, contains thirty errors; Reliable's copy number seven would contain only twenty-eight errors, even though it represents the product of seven different sequential acts of transmission. Therefore, the mere quantity of error contained in a copy does not, in itself, tell us the number of times a text has been transmitted. The first printed edition of *Game* contains more unique undoubted errors than any other text; but that fact is not at all surprising, when we realize that it was printed by Nicholas Okes, one of the least reliable printers of his time.

[32] The kinds of coincidental agreement described in this paragraph are sometimes called 'parallelism'; one of the major problems of stemmatology, old and new, is to distinguish stemmatically significant variants from coincidental 'parallelism'. I prefer 'coincidence', because parallel lines never meet, but coincidences originate in some shared aspect of an original.

[33] This is the logic behind compositor analysis of printed texts; the material apparently set by Compositor E of the 1623 Shakespeare folio, for instance, contains many obvious errors that suggest an inexperienced workman. Compositor analysis, however, is beset by the difficulty of identifying compositorial stints reliably. Scribes, by contrast, are much easier to identify. Serious scholars continue to dispute compositor attributions in the 1623 folio, but no one disputes that Crane transcribed CRANE[1,2,3], or that Middleton transcribed all of MIDDLETON[T] and part of BRIDGEWATER.

6. *The number of new errors generated in a particular act of transmission is a function of the reliability of the transmitter and the legibility and reproducibility of the original being copied.* This conclusion follows from the intersection of paragraphs 3–5.

7. Since every transmission contains the potential for corruption, *the more often a text is transmitted, the more corrupt it will generally become.* If Manuscript 2 is copied from Manuscript 1, and Manuscript 3 is copied from Manuscript 2, then Manuscript 3 will introduce errors of its own; but the text/message it is attempting to reproduce will, itself, already contain errors, and in so far as Manuscript 3 accurately transmits Manuscript 2, it will also accurately transmit readings which are corruptions of the original data in Manuscript 1. That is, Manuscript 3 will 'share' errors which also occur in Manuscript 2. In such circumstances, the sharing of an error between two texts does not depend upon the probabilities of coincidental independent error (discussed above); it depends, instead, upon the routine operation of the normal process of copying and transmission. After all, although manual transmission of large amounts of data inevitably introduces some error, those errors—even in a text as inaccurately printed as OKES—constitute only a very small fraction of the total message. No one will make use of a copyist who corrupts the text more often than he transmits it accurately (i.e., anyone with an error rate higher than 50 per cent). In fact, a copyist who corrupts even one per cent of the text would be exceptionally unreliable, and unlikely to be used more than once.

8. Therefore, *shared errors are intrinsically more likely to occur because a copyist has accurately copied an error in his source, than because two (or more) different copyists— working from different sources—have independently made the same error.* This conclusion follows from paragraph 7.

9. *The more intrinsically improbable the independent, co-incidental production of an error, the more probable that the error is shared between two (or more) texts because those texts are related to each other*—either because one is a copy of the other, or because both are copies of an earlier text which itself already contained the error in question.

10. Since it is intrinsically improbable for two independent acts of transmission to introduce the same errors, *the greater the number of errors two texts share, the greater the probability that they are related.*

11. *The fact that two or more texts share an improbable number of errors clearly indicates that they are related, but it does not in itself indicate the nature or direction of that relationship.* It does not establish which is a copy of the other, or whether both are copies of something else.

12. *The maximum number of shared errors a text can contain depends upon how many errors already exist in its source, and how many new errors of its own it introduces.* Let us suppose that Reliable scribe had copied his own first transcript ('R1') in order to produce another transcript ('R2'), and let us suppose, once again, that R1

contained only four errors. If the scribe's rate of error were consistent, his new transcript ('R2') would add four new errors, and accurately re-transmit the four errors already present in his source. In this logical model, the new transcript ('R2') would contain four errors shared with 'R1', and four new errors not present in 'R1': the *maximum* number of shared errors 'R2' could contain would be eight (if all four of its own new errors were re-transmitted into 'R3' and/or other copies).[34] By contrast, if Reliable scribe copied the transcript produced by Unreliable scribe ('U1') in order to produce another transcript ('U2'), and if Reliable scribe's own rate of error remained consistent, then he would reliably re-transmit the thirty errors already in his source. The text thus produced ('U2') would contain thirty errors shared with 'U1', and—assuming, again, that his accuracy remained consistent— four new errors not present in 'U1'; the *maximum* number of shared errors 'U2' could contain would be thirty-four (if all four of its own new errors were re-transmitted into other copies). But in both of these examples, the copy ('R2' or 'U2') would share errors (whether four or thirty) with the text from which it was copied ('R1' or 'U1'). Since two entirely independent texts are unlikely to share even two errors, the difference between four and thirty, in this instance, does not appreciably affect our statistical confidence that R1 and R2 are stemmatically related, just as U1 and U2 are stemmatically related. What matters more than the difference in quantities is the difference in patterns. Both U2 and R2 contain shared errors, but they share those errors with different texts, and do not share any errors with each other, because they are stemmatically unrelated to each other, except through their shared derivation from the originary message/text.

13. As this logical model demonstrates, if two texts are unrelated—as R2 and U2 are unrelated—then the total number of errors that a given text shares with other texts is not significant as an indication of relative priority of transmission: both R2 and U2 are only two steps away from the original, but R2 might contain only eight shared errors, and U2 might contain thirty-four. However, *if texts are stemmatically related, if they belong to the same branch or sub-sequence of transmission, then the more shared errors a text contains, the later it must have come in that sub-sequence of transmission.* Thus, if Reliable scribe had made a series of seven transcripts, with each new transcript a copy of the one immediately preceding it, and with each new transcript introducing four new errors and accurately reproducing all the errors in its source, then

—R3 would share four errors with R2;
—R4 would add four errors shared with R3, and inherit four more, shared with both R2 and R3;

---

[34] R2 might contain fewer than eight shared errors, if the scribe noticed an error in R1 and corrected it: see the discussion below of correction and transference.

—R5 would add four errors shared with R4, and inherit four shared with R4 and R3, and four with R4, R3, and R2;

—R6 would add four errors shared with R5, and inherit four shared with R5–R4, four with R5–R4–R3, and four with R5–R4–R3–R2;

—R7 would add four errors shared with R6, and inherit four shared with R6–R5, four with R6–R5–R4, four with R6–R5–R4–R3, and four with R6–R5–R4–R3–R2.

As a result of this sequence, R2 would contain four shared errors, all recurring with the pattern R2–R3–R4–R5–R6–R7 (six texts); R3 would contain eight shared errors, four with the preceding pattern, and four with the new pattern R3–R4–R5–R6–R7 (five texts); R4 would contain twelve, four with each of the two preceding patterns, and four with the new pattern R4–R5–R6–R7 (four texts); R5 would contain sixteen, four with each of the three preceding patterns, and four with the new pattern R5–R6–R7 (three texts); R6 would contain twenty, four with each of the four preceding patterns, and four with the new pattern R6–R7 (two texts); R7 would contain the same number and pattern of shared errors as R6, but it would also contain four new errors not shared with any other text.

14. *In such a sequence, the number of shared errors in each text gradually rises, coincident with a rise in the number of patterns in which those shared errors are distributed.* The texts earlier in the sequence of transmission have fewer shared errors and fewer patterns of distribution—but the patterns themselves incorporate more texts, because an error made early in the sequence has the opportunity to be transmitted to more subsequent texts than an error made late in the sequence.

15. This mathematical model is the logical basis of all stemmatic analysis, old or new, and its general outlines can be found in the texts of *A Game at Chess*, and indeed in every other variety of textual transmission.[35] However, *the absolute mathematical regularity of this pyramid of error almost never occurs historically,* for at least four reasons.

16. First, we seldom possess the entire sequence of transmissions: some of the links in the sequence are lost, and have to be inferred. *The more texts that are missing, the greater the number of inferences that need to be made.*

17. Secondly, *even the same scribe is not likely to produce exactly the same number of errors in every act of transcription or transmission.* Some human beings are more erratic than others, but no human being is consistent. Some copies will accumulate more new errors, potentially shareable, than other copies. Thus, in the preceding model, if R4 was produced when Reliable was tired or distracted, and as a result introduced eight new errors, those eight errors would be shared by all subsequent transcriptions; the pattern R4–R5–R6–R7 would therefore contain eight instances, while all the other patterns contained only four. On the basis of this difference, we might be tempted to

infer, incorrectly, the existence of a lost intermediate text ('R3.b'), to explain the increase in shared error in R4. But that mistaken extrapolation would not affect our correct understanding of the relative sequence of transmission of the extant texts.

18. Thirdly, and more significantly, *a new copy is not always made from the immediately preceding copy.* Suppose, for instance, that both R4 and R5 were copied, independently, from R3, and that R6 was made from R4 rather than R5. In that case, R4 and R5 would both share the same errors with R3. But although R4 and R5 would share the same *number* of errors with R3, the *pattern* of their distribution would be quite different. R4 and R5 would each inherit eight errors from R3; but R4 would transmit those eight inherited errors into R6 and R7, and R5 would not. Moreover, the four new errors introduced into R4 itself would also be shared with R6 and R7, creating the new pattern R4–R6–R7; by contrast, the four new errors introduced into R5 would not become shared errors at all, because they would be transmitted to no subsequent text. The patterns of error distribution here do not produce such a tidy pyramid, but they do make clear the relationships between the various texts; they complicate, but do not endanger, stemmatic analysis.

19. The final complication, however, does potentially endanger this entire epistemological enterprise. The foregoing analysis presumes that an error, once made, will be transmitted to all subsequent copies. That seldom happens. Instead, almost all texts are subject to what textual critics usually identify, rather unhelpfully, as 'contamination'. That makes it sound like something unmotivated and undesirable. But it is not unmotivated, and it is not necessarily undesirable, and it would more usefully be described as 'transference'.[36] Copyists are almost always professionally aware that all copying introduces error, and therefore *copyists often do their best to correct errors in what they are copying.* They do so by attempting to 'transfer' correct readings from some other source into the readings of the (apparently corrupt) text at hand.[37] This impulse to correction by transference, routinized among human transmitters of messages, has the goal and the potential of eliminating all shared error, and therefore of eliminating the very data which we use to determine stemmatic relationships. From the perspective of restoring the integrity of transmitted data, correction is usually a good thing; only from the perspective of the textual critic, trying to

---

[35] While the old stemmatologists concentrated on errors, and the new stemmatologists prefer to focus on variants, the logic up to this point regards all variants as errors, because all variants are departures from an original. The distinction between errors and variants will be confronted below.

[36] I adopted the term 'transference' many years ago, but see the recent comparisons made between this textual phenomenon and 'lateral gene transfer' (Howe *et al.*).

[37] The 'source' from which they transfer readings may be an alternative document, or it may be the same document (examined more closely), or it may simply be the corrector's own mind. The distinction between these three sources of transference is important, but for the moment I deliberately ignore it, because from the perspective of a later stemmatologist it can be difficult, often impossible, to prove, in any given case, which 'source' was used.

reconstruct the history of transmission, is it disturbing. This universal tendency to correct texts is the basis of most critiques of the Lachmann–Maas method.

20. But *although routine transference has the potential to eliminate all error (and therefore all shared error), that potential is very seldom realized*—and perhaps never realized in texts of any length. It was certainly never realized within the conditions of transmission governing the reproduction and circulation of commercial plays, or other secular literary texts of comparable length, in early modern Europe.

21. Transference itself requires an act of transmission: the correct readings of the source must be transferred to the to-be-corrected copy. Therefore, *the act of transference is itself subject to error, including most particularly the error of incompleteness.* In order for a variant to be corrected it must first be identified and then altered, and failure of either identification or alteration will leave the error intact. Transference is therefore intrinsically unlikely to remove all errors, or all shared errors, from the to-be--corrected text. Therefore, the process of transference, by removing some errors but not others, produces—like other forms of transmission—not simply correction, but a distinctive new pattern of shared error, which is the corollary of a pattern of successful or bungled transference.

22. *The pattern of transference of shared error will depend upon the source for the corrections being transferred.* If the source for the corrections is the original itself, then that source potentially enables the transference to remove all errors; as already noted, that potential will almost never be realized, but if it were realized it would produce a corrected copy as good as the original in reproducing the substantive intentions of the author.[38] However, it is also possible for the source of the intended act of correction to be itself a copy, which itself contains errors. If the process of transference mechanically transfers variants which are in fact errors from that source into the to--be-corrected copy, then that 'corrected' copy will share errors with that source. For example, at 3.1.48 the pencil corrector in BRIDGEWATER interpolates the speech prefix 'F.B.', where it does not belong; the same error, rejected by all modern editors, also occurs in MIDDLE-TON[T] and OKES. Thus, the source of the pencil corrector's correction was apparently a manuscript that contained an error shared with the source(s) of MIDDLETON[T] and OKES. A text subjected to transference (a 'contaminated' text) may therefore potentially share errors with different texts, which might theoretically belong to entirely different branches of the stemma: the text which was being copied wholesale, and the text from which certain readings were transferred in what was thought to be an act of correction. Because of the transference, there would be fewer errors than we would expect shared with the text being copied wholesale, and more errors than we would expect shared with the source of the retail transference. Thus, transference complicates the pattern of distribution of shared error, but it does not produce a randomness,

or a pattern of distribution which contradicts the actual history of transmission.

23. *Transference does not produce a random or misleading pattern of distribution of shared errors,* precisely because the pattern of correction of shared error will itself be random (in so far as the distribution of shared error is itself random). That is, the process of transference cannot distinguish between different stemmatic sources for the error that is being corrected. Whatever the agent or process of transference, it will not systematically remove shared errors (as opposed to unique errors) or systematically remove errors shared with one text (as opposed to errors shared with another text). Of course, if the source of the transference is an earlier copy from the same branch of the stemma, the transference will systematically discriminate against errors (shared or not) which have originated between the time of the production of that earlier copy (say, X^7) and the production of the copy-to-be-corrected (say, X^{12}); but it will not discriminate between errors introduced at different intermediate stages (errors in X^8 but not errors in X^9, or errors in X^{8-10} but not X^{11}). Transference may therefore diminish the *quantity* of shared error in a text, but—in so far as transference is incomplete—it is not likely to impose a different *pattern* of distribution of shared errors.

24. I have said that the correction of shared error will be random 'in so far as the distribution of shared error is itself random' (para. 23). But as I demonstrated earlier (para. 3–5), the distribution of error itself is not entirely random; therefore, the distribution of shared error cannot be entirely random. Moreover, whether an error, once committed, is reproduced in another text, and therefore becomes a 'shared error', depends upon whether the error is corrected in that subsequent text. But because the impulse to correction is routinized in all human agents of transmission (para. 19), it is entirely possible that an error will be corrected before it ever has the opportunity to become a shared error. Correction, or transference, may therefore preempt the creation of a shared error, and in that way determine the pattern of shared error. *Transference is random in that it does not discriminate between errors on the basis of whether they are shared, or with which other texts they are shared; but this does not mean that transference is random or unpredictable in other senses.*

25. Correction is never random, because it depends upon the identification and rectification of error (para. 21); therefore, *the less easily identifiable or easily rectifiable an error is, the less likely it is to be corrected.*

26. *The smaller an error, the fewer the elements of the original message which it corrupts or disrupts, the greater the similarity between the original reading and the error, the greater the legibility and intelligibility of the error, the less*

---

[38] Editors often use photographic facsimiles as though they were originals, on the assumption that they are equivalent to the originals. I have used photographs myself. But photos are sometimes ambiguous or misleading, and therefore I have personally examined each of the six manuscripts of *Game* and several copies of the original printed editions.

likely it is that the error will be identified—and hence the less likely that it will be corrected, and the more likely that it will become a shared error.

27. On the other hand, *the larger and more disruptive an error, the more likely it is to be identified. But its identifiability may be in inverse proportion to its rectifiability.* An error's rectifiability is a function of the quantity and accessibility of the data required to restore the original reading. For instance, CRANE[3] contains the phrase 'Righ reuerend & holy' (3.1.32; Bawcutt l. 683). This is unintelligible; the first four letters do not constitute a word in English. The error is therefore easily identifiable as such. Moreover, intelligibility can be restored by the addition of a single letter ('Righ[t] reuerend & holy') or by the alteration of a single letter ('[H]igh reuerend & holy'). The only data required to recognize that an error has occurred is a knowledge of English vocabulary and spelling. Any copyist fluent in English would therefore have a 50–50 chance of guessing the correct reading. But in fact the odds are better than that. I have checked the Early English Books Online database for both phrases, including all digitized books up to 1630: 'right reverend' appears 316 times, 'high reverend' does not appear at all. Thus, any copyist in 1624, fluent in English and familiar with early modern formulas of epistolary salutation, could almost certainly have guessed that 'Righ' should be corrected to 'Right' (which is, in fact, the reading of MIDDLETON[T] and all other witnesses). For a native English speaker the missing data is therefore minimal, and easily supplied, without access to other documents. It should therefore not surprise us that this error occurs in no other text of the play. Even if all other extant texts derived from CRANE[3], even if none of the other extant texts had access to any other authoritative source, they could all have independently corrected this particular error. In order to correct such an error, a scribe need only transfer onto the text his own knowledge of the rules of spelling and grammar of the English language. Moreover, in the case of *Game* all the substantive texts were produced within a few months of the first authorial draft, and hence within the same historical state of the language; none of the transmitters of the text need have worried about whether 'Righ' might have been an acceptable form of a recognizable signifier hundreds of years earlier.

28. *Even if an error is both identifiable and rectifiable, the probability of its being rectified depends upon the time and energy required to rectify it, and the reward for doing so.* For instance, Middleton could hardly have failed to notice that the two original scribes of BRIDGEWATER had, between them, left a gap almost three hundred manuscript lines long in the middle of the text, omitting most of 2.2; as the author, he had access—in other manuscripts, or in his own head—to the data that had been omitted. But supplying it would have required a major expenditure of energy, which he was apparently unwilling to make. He therefore patched together, from elements of the missing material, a brief transition, which created a surface of apparent plausibility, not self-evidently corrupt, and

therefore not immediately detectable by a casual reader. Middleton must have calculated that the reward for properly correcting the error (in the prospective satisfaction of a potential purchaser of the manuscript) did not justify the expenditure of time and energy it would have required. If Middleton himself could decide, in some circumstances, that correction was not worth the effort, then we can be sure that other transmitters of his text might also, in some circumstances, make such calculations. Enormous quantities of time and energy, over several centuries, have been expended in editorial attempts to correct the text of Shakespeare; those expenditures testify to the value accorded Shakespeare's work, and the anticipated or actual social, professional, financial, and psychological rewards for successfully correcting it. Until recently, such efforts on Middleton's behalf have not seemed warranted. One could give many other examples of the same principle: transference always requires an expenditure, and transference will occur only to the degree that it satisfies a desire for some sort of reward. Modern scholars, editing early modern texts, are rewarded for certain kinds of accuracy, in a way that seventeenth-century scribes were not. That is why transference occurred less frequently and systematically in the seventeenth-century transmission of secular literature (para. 20).

29. As the foregoing example also reminds us, transference is designed to produce intelligible readings, departures from copy which are not detectable as such by a casual reader. That is, *transference produces readings which do not appear to be errors.* For instance, let us suppose that manuscript X^3 is a copy of manuscript X^2, which is itself a copy of the original text, X^1; let us further suppose that X^2 contains an error, which is unintelligible, and that X^3 at the same point has an intelligible reading, but one which differs from the original reading found in X^1. In these circumstances, with this knowledge, it is clear that the intelligible reading of X^3 is a product of transference, an educated guess, an attempt to correct the obvious error in X^2 by transferring into the new copy X^3 the scribe's own knowledge of the rules of the language. That is, the reading of X^3 is, from the perspective of the original data transmission, an error, just like the reading in X^2. Or, alternatively, let us suppose that the reading of X^2 exactly duplicates the original reading of X^1, but that the copyist of X^3 doesn't understand an unusual word, or disapproves of a smutty joke, or is offended by a blasphemous oath, or considers the original grammar inelegant, or finds the original dialect provincial or the original lexicon old-fashioned (or new-fangled). Such a copyist often 'corrects' the original reading by introducing his own improvement of the text in front of him. In both these scenarios, the copyist does not consult another document, but consults his own mental image of the language, and alters his copy-text in order to make it conform with that neural map. Whether the reading in X^2 is a real error or only a perceived error, the reading introduced in X^3 is a departure from the original text, and from that originary perspective it is an error, even though it makes

sense. Now let us suppose that this intelligible X^3 reading (which is nevertheless an error) is reproduced in X^4, X^5, and X^6; it thus becomes a 'shared error', distributed in the pattern X^{3-6}. But we could not identify it as an error if we did not already know the sequence of transmission. From our perspective, it would certainly be a 'variant', but not necessarily an 'error'. Most obvious 'errors' are produced by human inattention, a lapse of execution, a failure to maintain the artificial order produced by an act of creative resistance against the second law of thermodynamics. Entropy introduces error. By contrast, most 'variants' are deliberately produced by some form of transference, by a secondary effort to repair or improve an already-existing order. Intelligibility, after all, does not just happen. (Shit happens.)

30. *Because transference is designed to produce readings that do not appear to be errors, we can almost never identify such readings as shared errors on any intrinsic basis.* That is, we cannot look at the verbal structure alone, and conclude 'This reading does not make sense; it is obviously an error.' Simple collation will establish whether such a reading is shared by multiple texts; collation can therefore identify some readings as 'shared variants'. But collation cannot determine which members of the large set 'shared variants' belong to the smaller subset 'shared errors'.[39] We can identify intelligible variants as 'errors' only on the basis of extrinsic evidence, in particular a knowledge of the stemma of transmission. Thus, we can identify unique variants in OKES[2] as errors, because we already know that OKES[2] is a wholly derivative text. However, we will only engage in prolonged stemmatic analysis if we do not already know the stemma of transmission; stemmatic analysis is designed to produce exactly such knowledge. Therefore, the kinds of 'error' produced by transference—that is, unauthoritative but nevertheless intelligible readings—do not necessarily provide reliable data for stemmatic analysis, and do not provide the same *kind* of data provided by shared errors. Certainly, one must distinguish between the two kinds of data. Because obvious errors are a small subset of the larger category of variants, two or three indubitable shared errors might establish a genealogical link between texts. But shared variants are always more common, and therefore less valuable, individually. (Errors are diamonds, variants are coal.) Shared variants might establish a stemmatic connection only if there were dozens or scores or hundreds of them belonging to exactly the same set of texts—but only if those large numbers contrasted with no variants, or few variants, suggesting other genealogies. That is, shared variants require a higher threshold of statistical significance, and a greater sensitivity to coincidence.[40]

31. Although it is actually true that 'a text subjected to transference' may share errors with 'the text from which certain errors were transferred in what was thought to be an act of correction' (para. 22), for the purposes of stemmatic analysis those particular shared errors will not be initially identifiable as errors, because they will presumably be intelligible variants. Transference is designed to produce intelligible readings (para. 30). Since, for the purposes of stemmatic analysis, such readings will not have been pre-identified as 'shared errors', transference will not produce 'more errors than we would expect shared with the source of the transference' (para. 22). After the analysis is completed, we may be able to re-evaluate many intelligible variants, and retrospectively identify them as errors; that is, in fact, the editorial usefulness of stemmatic analysis. But *this retrospective editorial use of the stemmatic analysis cannot be allowed to interfere with the initial analysis itself, or prejudice the identification of the indubitable errors which constitute the database to be analysed.*

32. Since 'an error's rectifiability is a function of the quantity and accessibility of the data required to restore the original reading' (para. 27), a copyist's ability to rectify error is in direct proportion to his access to such data. Of all copyists, the original author is the most privileged in this respect: he is more likely to have access to the original documents, he is more likely to be able to identify which documents are most reliable, and even in the absence of original documents he has mental access to the original transmission, in a way most other copyists do not. In other words, *the author is better able than any other copyist to engage in transference.* Therefore, we can expect that the presence of the author, as scribe, will reduce the number of shared errors. To the extent that the author is involved in the preparation of a particular copy, that text should contain fewer shared errors than we would expect. This conclusion is particularly important in *A Game at Chess*, because Middleton was the copyist who produced one entire manuscript, and the copyist who produced a significant part of another (BRIDGEWATER); he has also been identified, by most scholars, in [MIDDLETON/OKES], the lost manuscript used as the printer's copy-text for OKES. We would therefore expect those texts to contain fewer shared errors than their position in the sequence of transmission would have produced. On the other hand, Middleton was demonstrably not the scribe who produced CRANE[1,2,3] or ROSENBACH. We therefore have no reason to suppose that the number of shared errors in those texts has been reduced by the privileged intervention and transference of the author.

33. But although the privileged access of the author makes it possible for him (in this case) or her (in others) to reduce the number of inherited errors, that same privilege makes authors exceptionally prone to increase the number of new 'errors' (whether or not we can identify them as such). An author's pre-existing knowledge of the text may make him bored with it; his familiarity with it will almost certainly incline him to carry more of it in his

---

[39] For a fuller discussion of 'sets' and 'subsets', and the relationship of both to series, see Section X.

[40] Most discussions of the texts of *Game* are logically disabled by a failure to observe this simple rule. See, for instance, my earlier discussion of Howard-Hill's claim about eleven alleged 'indisputable errors' in CRANE[1], which are all perfectly intelligible 'variants' and which are distributed across many different patterns—patterns contradicted by many other variants.

head, without re-consulting the text he is supposed to be copying. *Exact textual transmission is a learned specialist skill, belonging to a subcategory of professional copyists, and seldom possessed by an author.*

34. *An author's sense of privileged access, in respect to the text, readily extends to a sense of privilege in changing it.* Moreover, since authors are in the business of creating new texts, or at least of creating new arrangements of texts out of old ones, they are temperamentally and culturally predisposed to modify existing texts, not to reproduce them with maximum accuracy. Thus, an author is likely to introduce variation into the original transmission. From the perspective of the original, every such variation is an 'error'. But from the perspective of the author, it is 'revision', the creation of a partially new message. However we define it, and however we evaluate its merits, for the purposes of stemmatic analysis such readings cannot be considered errors, or shared errors. Any such authorial intervention will presumably produce a reading which is intelligible; it is thus indistinguishable from other examples of transference, which cannot be included in the initial database of shared errors (para. 30). Indeed, intrinsically there is often no way to distinguish between the two categories of variant: so long as a reading is possible and intelligible, it might represent authorial variation (transference by the author) or an unauthorized scribal 'correction' (transference by a copyist). In the case of *Game*, we know that the author was involved in producing copies, and we also know (by comparing the two autograph copies of the last two scenes) that he varied some of the verbal detail of the text as he copied it. Clearly, such variation could have been introduced into any copy produced by Middleton, and it could appear in any extant text which is itself a copy of a lost text produced by Middleton. Since, theoretically, any of the eight extant texts might be a copy of a lost text produced by Middleton, we must initially allow that any such sensible variant, in any of the eight texts, might be an authorial variant. For the purposes of stemmatic analysis, such variants must therefore not be pre-identified as 'shared errors'.

35. *Any stemmatic analysis of shared error must initially distinguish, rigorously and systematically, between 'shared error' and 'shared variation'* (para. 29–34). Doing so effectively solves the potential problem created by transference (para. 19). Because transferred readings will generally make sense, they will be initially classified as shared variants only, and therefore excluded from the analysis. The analysis will thus be affected by transference only in so far as transference reduces the number of shared errors (para. 22); but that reduction will not discriminate against any particular pattern of error-sharing (para. 23), nor does it operate randomly and unpredictably (para. 24–28).

36. *Within the category of 'shared error', stemmatic analysis must distinguish between two temporal stages which correspond to two material manifestations.* Every 'shared error' is shared both by the text that first introduced the error ('originary shared error') and by any copy of that corrupted text which re-transmits the error ('duplicated shared error'). Materially, the originary shared error and the duplicated shared error are identical; but the first was produced in one text (by an initial failure of transmission) and the other was later copied into another text (by a subsequent faithful transmission). Because the two readings, although temporally distinct, are materially identical, in themselves, intrinsically, they cannot indicate 'which is a copy of the other, or whether both are a copy of something else' (para. 11). Consequently, in order to distinguish between originary and duplicated shared errors, we must be able to identify certain extant texts which were not copied to produce any other extant text.

37. *Whether a text has been copied to produce other texts depends upon the rectifiability of the errors it contains.* Theoretically, any text might be copied to produce any other text; theoretically, the errors in any text A could be rectified in copy B. But certain errors in a text will be much harder to identify and rectify than others (para. 26, 27). In particular, if a copy loses a significant amount of the data contained in the original message, that data can be restored only by access to some other authoritative source, which contains it; moreover, the impulse to restore large chunks of lost data will only be activated if the absence of that data is in some way obvious, and if the effort required to restore the lost data will obviously be commensurably rewarded (para. 28). The less visible the error, and/or the greater the amount of data lost, and/or the less certain a commensurable reward, then the less probable restoration becomes; the less probable such restoration, the less likely that such a transference of data has occurred, the less likely that the damaged text A has been copied to produce any of the whole texts B, C, D, etc. Such calculations make it extremely improbable that certain of the extant texts of *Game* were copied to produce any of the other extant texts. CRANE[1,2,3], ROSENBACH, BRIDGEWATER and MIDDLETON[T] each lack large chunks of the text present in other witnesses; but each lacks different chunks. Taken as a whole, all six extant manuscripts must be dead-ends; that is, none of these manuscripts can have been the copy-text or immediate ancestor of another whole extant text.[41] Likewise, although OKES contains a full text of the play, it contains so many hundreds of unique variants that it is impossible to believe that any extant text is, or descends from, a copy of OKES. In fact, the cost, in paper and labour, of transcribing the play by hand would have been much greater than the cost of purchasing a copy of OKES or MATHEWES/ALLDE; hence, the reward for producing a manuscript copy of either printed text would not have been commensurate with the cost. Hence, taken

---

41 It is not the missing chunk itself which defines a dead-end, but the uniqueness of that missing chunk. For instance, the big chunk missing from BRIDGEWATER might also have been missing from [PRE-BRIDGEWATER] (which, obviously, was not a dead-end). If we discovered another manuscript of the play, also missing that same chunk, then we would know that the new manuscript was either PRE-BRIDGEWATER or POST-BRIDGEWATER, but it would not be immediately clear, from the missing chunk alone, whether BRIDGEWATER itself or the newly discovered manuscript was the dead-end. Nevertheless, we could still say that none of the other extant whole texts was copied from either of them: they would clearly belong together on the same stemmatic cul-de-sac.

as a whole, all eight extant substantive texts must be dead-ends. Any of them *might* have been copied—but, if so, none of those copies (or any derivatives of those copies) survives.

38. *If a text is a dead-end, if it was not copied, then it cannot contain any 'originary shared errors'.* This self-evident observation is worth making only because it is so easy to forget, when deducing genealogical sequences from patterns of shared error. Every dead-end no doubt contains new errors, but because it was not copied, those new errors could never become 'originary shared errors'. Any shared error in a dead-end text is therefore a 'duplicated shared error'. It must have originated in another text, which was produced earlier than the dead-end text.

39. *If an error is shared by two texts which are both dead-ends, then that error must be either a coincidence, or a duplicated shared error in each text; if not a coincidence, the error must have originated in some third text, which was not a dead-end.* If the two dead-ends are the only two texts which share the error—or, more significantly and reliably, if they share several such errors, none shared by any other extant text—then the error(s) the dead--ends share must also have been shared by some other text, no longer extant. For instance, if the two dead-end texts MIDDLETON[T] and BRIDGEWATER share many errors present in no other text, it must be because both MID-DLETON[T] and BRIDGEWATER derive independently, at one or more removes, from a lost manuscript [PRE-MIDDLETON--BRIDGEWATER], which contained the originary error(s). In other words, every well-populated pattern of errors shared by only two dead-end texts implies the existence of a third text. Since all eight substantive texts of *Game* are dead-ends, any well-populated pattern of errors shared by two extant texts demonstrates the existence of a third, now lost.

40. 'The number of shared errors a text can contain depends upon how many errors already exist in its source, and how many new errors of its own it introduces' (para. 12). But 'any shared error in a dead-end text is a "duplicated shared error"' (para. 38); its new errors never become originary shared errors. Therefore, *a dead--end text cannot contain more shared errors than its source.* (This conclusion is important for analysis of *Game*, because all of its extant texts are dead-ends.)

41. But the foregoing analysis, not only of dead-ends but of shared errors generally, presumes that whole texts are the source of other whole texts; it presumes, that is, the unity and integrity of texts. That presumption is self-evidently unwarranted, as the case of *Game* makes clear. ROSENBACH, BRIDGEWATER, and MATHEWES/ALLDE were all produced by more than one transmissional agent; moreover, Nascimento has demonstrated that either ROSENBACH or BRIDGEWATER or both had a different textual source for the second half of the play than for the first. *Stemmatic analysis must therefore examine, not only the pattern of distribution of shared errors between texts, but also the pattern of their distribution within texts.* We cannot assume that texts are stemmatically homogeneous.

VI. Shared Errors: Arithmetical Analysis

With the foregoing principles in mind, we can now proceed to analyse the patterns of shared error in the texts of *Game*. To identify all errors, we must first identify all variants. A complete collation of all eight witnesses is provided, for the first time, in the Textual Notes to *A Later Form*.[42] With a few statistically negligible exceptions, the collation of variants is an empirical process; the results can be duplicated, or corrected, by anyone who examines all the witnesses.

The next step is to produce a database of all errors shared by two or more of the eight texts. Unlike the detection of variation, the detection of error is an interpretive activity, which is inevitably subject to challenge. In constructing this database, 'error' has to be defined as consistently as possible, based upon historical and authorial norms of linguistic usage (dialogue), theatrical practice (stage directions), and literary convention (lineation).[43] In order to avoid logical circularity, error cannot be defined as 'a departure from the text which I have already decided is the most correct', and cannot be defined as 'a reading which I personally prefer'. A reading shared by MIDDLETON[T] and another text is not necessarily evidence that the other text is 'reliable' or 'early in the history of transmission', unless MIDDLETON[T] is itself 'reliable' and 'early in the history of transmission'. To define 'error' in that way—as have all previous investigations—is to presume that we already know what stemmatic analysis is designed to tell us. But we in fact do not know the sequence of transmission of the extant texts of *Game*. If MIDDLETON[T] is late in the history of transmission, then it might inherit, and fail to correct, errors which are also present in other late texts.

In the long process of collating the witnesses and editing (and re-editing, and re-editing) the *Early* and *Later* forms of the play, I identified a small proportion of the variants as clearly mistaken. The resulting database of shared errors is contained in the appendices to this General Textual Introduction, and is divided into three separate categories: Appendix A contains shared errors in dialogue (including speech prefixes), Appendix B in lineation, and Appendix C in stage directions. Within the Textual Notes to *A Later Form*, all readings included in these appendices of shared errors are asterisked and discussed; this allows scholars to examine those readings in context. In many of the Textual Notes I also explain why other readings have *not*

---

[42] Nascimento (1975) is the only scholar to have attempted a complete and reasonably reliable collation, but she did not record lineation variants, substantive punctuation variants, or variants in the positioning of stage directions. Howard--Hill's summary 'List of Divergent Readings' (*Pasquin*, 269–93) derives from Nascimento. Howard-Hill's transcripts of MIDDLETON[T] (1990) and BRIDGEWATER (1995) provided a more thorough record of corrections and overwritings in those manuscripts than had Nascimento; I have been able to add a little to his account, especially of MIDDLETON[T].

[43] I have included speech prefixes as part of 'Dialogue', because they are necessary to readers of the text, uninterested in performance, and because they have been routinely emended even by editors who pay little or no attention to stage directions. But the ten such errors in Appendix A might alternatively be placed in Appendix B, as stage directions.

been counted as shared errors. I do not count as errors any readings which might be authorial variants, or any variants which are sensible and intelligible alternatives; I do not count readings alleged to be the result of censorship, because in each case censorship is only an hypothesis, and both variants make sense. Because I have challenged Howard-Hill's description of various readings in CRANE[1] as 'errors', a reader might suspect that my own tabulation of 'errors' in MIDDLETON[T] is simply the substitution of my biases for his; but HOWARD-HILL himself in his Revels edition emends the overwhelming majority of the readings I describe as 'shared errors' in MIDDLETON[T]. (I have noted HOWARD-HILL's emendations of these readings in the Textual Notes.) Finally, if other editors are aware of a variant, and reject it, I do not include it in the database of shared errors. Thus, although I argued above (Sec. III) that 'others' is an error for 'vices' at 5.3.144, I do not include that variant in the database because, although 'vices' was recorded by Nascimento, it was not adopted in the subsequent editions by Howard-Hill and Dutton.[44]

This system (of appendices, linked to a systematic collation and discursive textual notes) should allow other scholars to check and evaluate the consistency of my procedures. In the subsequent sections of this Introduction, I take for granted the validity of the database, concentrating instead on analysis of the patterns of shared error, and what such patterns can or cannot tell us about the stemmatic relationships of the extant witnesses.

The pattern of shared errors can be analysed in several different ways. First, most simply, the number of shared substantive dialogue errors in each text (Appendix A).

CRANE[1]	4
MIDDLETON[T]	15
CRANE[2]	16
CRANE[3]	20
CRANE/MATHEWES/ALLDE	29
ROSENBACH	44
BRIDGEWATER	50
OKES	53

We expect shared errors to increase as the number of intervening copies multiplies (para. 7, 13, 14); in an ideal stemmatic model, the text with the fewest shared errors is early in transmission, and the text with the largest number of shared errors is late in transmission. That interpretation of this data agrees with what we know about the dates of those texts which are dateable. CRANE[1]—the earliest extant precisely dateable text (13 August 1624), and also a text of an earlier version of the play—has the fewest errors shared with any other text. Both OKES and MATHEWES/ALLDE are much later; one of them was printed in May 1625, and the other some time later that year. The one text which demonstrably belongs, chronologically, between CRANE[1] and the printed quartos, CRANE[3] (completed not long before 1 January 1625), also falls between them in the number of its shared errors.

By such reasoning, CRANE[1] would be the text closest to the originary papers; indeed, Crane transcribed four

of the five most reliable texts. The NON-CRANE text which comes closest to the CRANE texts in accuracy is MIDDLETON[T]: it comes second in the list, with almost the same number of shared errors as CRANE[2]. But MIDDLETON[T] is autograph throughout, and therefore is the text most subject to transference, most likely to have been corrected in ways which would obscure the amount of error in what it copied (para. 32); obviously, the author was uniquely qualified, when producing MIDDLETON[T], to have corrected independently what would otherwise have been inherited and shared errors. Proof of this proposition is provided by the final autograph section of BRIDGEWATER. In the 698 scribal lines from 3.1.319 to 5.2.0.1 BRIDGEWATER contains 20 dialogue errors shared with ROSENBACH, for a rate of one such shared error for every 35 lines; in the 398 autograph lines from 5.2.1 to play's end there are only three dialogue errors shared between BRIDGEWATER and ROSENBACH, for a rate of one such shared error for every 133 lines. If errors in BRIDGEWATER's source had continued in these last 398 lines at the same frequency as in the previous 698 lines, we should have expected eleven or twelve errors shared with ROSENBACH in the last two scenes, instead of only three. Middleton, in other words, in the last four hundred lines of BRIDGEWATER appears to have corrected most of the certain errors he found in the manuscript he was copying, leaving only one error uncorrected out of every four errors he found.

If he was equally efficient in correcting errors over the whole of MIDDLETON[T], then we would expect the manuscript he was copying to have contained 3.8 times as many shared errors as MIDDLETON[T] itself: 57 shared errors, instead of 15. That would make what we might call [PRE-MIDDLETON[T]]—that is, the immediate precursor of MIDDLETON[T], the manuscript he was copying—later in the stemma than all extant texts. That conclusion is, necessarily, speculative: [PRE-MIDDLETON[T]] is not extant, and we cannot be certain that Middleton corrected so many errors. But 'a dead-end cannot contain more shared errors than its source' (para. 40); therefore, we can be absolutely certain that the source from which MIDDLETON[T] was copied itself contained an absolute minimum of 15 errors—that is, almost four times the number in CRANE[1]. It is, moreover, hard to believe that Middleton corrected no errors, so the number of shared errors in [PRE-MIDDLE-TON] must have been at least a little higher than 15, and probably considerably higher. On the evidence of shared substantive errors, MIDDLETON[T] does not belong at the beginning of the sequence of transmission. In itself, the number of shared dialogue errors in MIDDLETON[T] is

---

44 Editors of *Game* have paid most attention to the variants in Appendices A and B; like editors of Shakespeare, they have given much less thought to problems of staging. If editors have discussed the implications of a staging variant, and accepted it, then I have not included it among shared errors; but if they have simply reproduced their copy-text, without any recognition of the staging issues, or when the variant involves issues of timing and positioning never previously collated, I have regarded myself as effectively the first adjudicator of the variant in question, and have therefore been willing to identify a variant as a shared error in stage directions, even when it has been reproduced by some modern editors. See for instance the variant at 5.1.30.1.

sufficient to demonstrate, decisively, that—even on the most optimistic interpretation—it is certainly later than CRANE[1], and almost certainly later than CRANE[2]. With a more realistic estimate of the number of errors it corrected, it would clearly belong to the later half of the sequence of transmission. These are conclusions we have already independently reached, in Sec. IV, on the basis of incidentals.

Another independent test of this conclusion is provided by shared lineation errors (Appendix B). Again, in this category I have not included cases where either arrangement is acceptable. The raw totals are:

CRANE[1]	0
CRANE[2]	4
CRANE[3]	3
CRANE/MATHEWES/ALLDE	8
ROSENBACH	11
MIDDLETON[T]	13
OKES	14
BRIDGEWATER	18

I have put CRANE[2] in the second position, because it has a much longer text than CRANE[3], so its ratio of shared errors per hundred lines of text is lower.

Here, as in the list of dialogue errors, CRANE[1] is clearly the most reliable individual text. Once again, Crane transcripts occupy four of the top five positions; once again, the two least reliable texts are BRIDGEWATER and OKES. The most significant difference between the two lists is the position of MIDDLETON[T]: relative to the other texts, it contains more shared lineation errors than shared dialogue errors. That difference can easily be explained: Middleton was more interested and more thorough in correcting dialogue errors than lineation errors.

That hypothesis is confirmed by comparison with BRIDGEWATER. In the 698 scribal lines tested above there are four lineation errors; in the 398 autograph lines there are three. Although the autograph and scribal sections differ very significantly in their frequencies of shared dialogue errors, when it comes to shared lineation errors the difference is negligible: one every 175 lines (scribal) versus one every 133 lines (autograph). The autograph portion actually has a slightly higher rate, but that in itself is not statistically significant.[45] Again, the significant variable here is the difference between the statistics for shared dialogue and lineation errors within these same two stretches of text: that difference is hard to explain, except on the hypothesis that Middleton was more attentive to correcting the dialogue than to correcting the lineation. If this is true of BRIDGEWATER, then the totals for shared lineation error may give a more reliable picture of the position of MIDDLETON[T] in the stemma.

That specific hypothesis about MIDDLETON[T] must remain conjectural. More securely, this lineation test again independently confirms that CRANE[1] belongs at the beginning of the stemma, and places MIDDLETON[T] somewhere in the later half.

Another independent test of these conclusions is provided by shared errors in stage directions (Appendix C).[46]

CRANE[1]	5
CRANE[2]	26
CRANE/MATHEWES/ALLDE	27
CRANE[3]	26
OKES	37
ROSENBACH	38
MIDDLETON[T]	39
BRIDGEWATER	46

I have placed CRANE/MATHEWES/ALLDE third in this list (although it contains two more errors than CRANE[3]) because it contains a much longer text, and therefore a lower ratio of shared errors per hundred lines.

As in the two earlier tabulations, CRANE[1] is at the top of the list, with BRIDGEWATER at the bottom. In all three lists, Crane transcripts occupy four of the top four or five positions; in all three, CRANE[1] is the most reliable scribal copy, followed by CRANE[2]. In all three lists, ROSENBACH belongs to the bottom half; in the lineation and stage direction lists, so does MIDDLETON[T]. Once again, we can test Middleton's rate of correction by looking at stage direction errors BRIDGEWATER shares with ROSENBACH. In the 698 scribal lines, there are 21 such errors (one every 32 lines); in the 398 authorial lines, there are only four (one every 100 lines). In this case, the comparison is probably misleading, because (unlike dialogue or lineation) stage directions are very unevenly distributed through dramatic texts, and in all witnesses there is less action requiring stage directions in the last two (autograph) scenes than in the preceding six and a half (scribal) scenes. If the rate of authorial correction in the last two scenes of BRIDGEWATER were maintained throughout MIDDLETON[T], then its underlying source would have contained 117 stage direction errors, far more than any extant text. It would be reasonable to assume that Middleton corrected some stage direction errors in his source, but we can only conjecture what his rate of correction might have been. But given that BRIDGEWATER only contains two autograph scenes, while MIDDLETON[T] is entirely autograph, if Middleton corrected any stage direction errors at all, then it would seem that [PRE-MIDDLETON[T]] contained at least as many stage direction errors as [PRE-BRIDGEWATER], and perhaps more.

[45] If MIDDLETON[B] contained one less lineation error, it would have a ratio of one every 199 lines. If the underlying source of the last two scenes had relatively more lineation errors than dialogue errors, Middleton might have corrected one or two of them, and still have retained the existing ratio.

[46] If speech prefixes were classified as stage directions, there would be no change in the totals for CRANE[1] in either list, but for the remaining texts the following quantities of shared error would be subtracted from the 'Dialogue' list and added to the 'Stage Direction' list: CRANE[2] 1, CRANE[3] 4, CRANE/MATHEWES/ALLDE 3, ROSENBACH 1, OKES 6, BRIDGEWATER 3, MIDDLETON[T] 6. In the Stage Direction list, this reclassification would reverse the position of ROSENBACH (40) and OKES (43), but otherwise leave the rank-order intact. In the Dialogue list, the rank-order would remain unchanged, except that OKES (47) and BRIDGEWATER (47) would be tied at the bottom.

I have divided the database of shared errors into three sets because each of these three categories of text is subject to different kinds of error and transference, and presents different editorial problems. None of the shared errors in one category is related to a shared error in the other. Thus, the three databases provide three independent tests of stemmatic relationship. All three lists are also independent of four kinds of evidence surveyed in the previous sections (patterns of censorship, historical norms of theatrical text production, reproduction of a Latin source, authorial linguistic and punctuation preferences). All seven of these independent categories of evidence put CRANE[1] at the top of the stemma.

Although for analytical purposes it was useful to consider shared errors in dialogue, lineation, and stage directions separately, the fact that all three show similar patterns indicates that the three databases can reasonably be combined, providing a statistically more significant single database of 196 shared errors. Adding up the three sets of figures, the totals for shared error for the eight extant substantive texts are:

CRANE[1]	9
CRANE[2]	46
CRANE[3]	49
CRANE/MATHEWES/ALLDE	64
MIDDLETON[T]	67
ROSENBACH	93
OKES	104
BRIDGEWATER	114

These totals demonstrate that CRANE[1] is the text least like any of the others. The text closest to CRANE[1] in its total of shared errors is CRANE[2], which has more than five times as many as CRANE[1]. No extant text has five times as many shared errors as CRANE[2]; the text with the most, BRIDGEWATER, has only 2.5 times as many as CRANE[2]. Thus, CRANE[1] is almost twice as far away from the closest of the other seven texts as any one of those seven is from any other. This result is exactly what we would expect if CRANE[1] belonged to a different branch of the stemma than the other seven texts. Moreover, these statistics make it absolutely clear that we cannot attribute the greater correctness of CRANE[1] to Crane's sophistication as a copyist ('he produced readings which were not obviously nonsensical'), because there are *more* obvious errors in the three other Crane texts.

Despite the fact that MIDDLETON[T] undoubtedly corrects many inherited errors, it ranks fifth in shared errors, with more than seven times as many as CRANE[1]. If MIDDLETON[T] corrected dialogue errors in its copy-text at the same rate as the author apparently did in BRIDGEWATER, but did not correct a single lineation or stage direction error, then that source would have had 109 shared errors—more than any extant text except BRIDGEWATER. If Middleton corrected at least a small proportion of the lineation and stage direction errors in his copy-text, then his immediate source would have been at least as corrupt

as BRIDGEWATER, and maybe more so. These conclusions about [PRE-MIDDLETON[T]] must remain conjectural, but we can be absolutely certain that Middleton corrected some shared errors in his source, and that the total number of shared errors in his source was therefore probably closer to the totals in ROSENBACH, OKES, or BRIDGEWATER than to those in (the longer text of) CRANE/MATHEWES/ALLDE.

VII. Shared Error: Statistical Analysis

The patterns of distribution of shared error are at least as important as the raw numbers (para. 12, 14). Patterns for each of the three separate categories of shared error are listed at the end of each of the three Appendices; the combined set of patterns, with line numbers, is given in Appendix D. For ease of reference I have numbered the patterns there, from 1 to 57.

The distribution of shared errors is clearly not random. For eight texts there are 246 possible patterns combining more than one text but less than eight; of those 246 possibilities, at most only 57 combinations occur in *Game* (23%).[47] Moreover, the distribution of the actual patterns significantly differs from the distribution of possible patterns. In a group of eight, for combinations of two texts there are 28 possibilities, with 18 actual combinations here; for three, 56 possibilities, but only 14 actual; for four, 70 possibilities, only 10 actual; for five, 56 possibilities, only 5 actual; for six, 28 possibilities, 6 actual; for seven, 8 possibilities, 3 actual. In other words, the mathematical possibilities for combination are evenly and symmetrically divided between smaller and larger groupings; but the actual distribution in *Game* is not symmetrical.

Reading Wrong in Only One Text: 8 possible patterns, 8 actual

Reading Right in Only One Text: 8 possible patterns, 3 actual

* * *

Reading Wrong in Only Two Texts: 28 possible, 18 actual

Reading Right in Only Two Texts: 28 possible, 6 actual

* * *

---

[47] Where the existence of an entire pattern would be affected by the absence of a passage or passages exhibiting the pattern from one or more of the eight witnesses, I have indicated that absence, listed such examples at the beginning of the category, and queried each. Thus, the first two examples, under the category 'Shared Errors Linking Two Texts Only', are queried (1–2), and so are the first six examples under 'Three Texts' (19–24), the first two under 'Four' (33–4), and the first under 'Five' (43) and 'Six' (49). There is no doubt that the readings in question are errors, and they have therefore been included in the totals in the previous analysis; the query concerns only the exact definition of the pattern of their distribution. In each case, the pattern may have occurred in at least one other text, and sometimes in more than one. For instance, every one of the patterns that contains only the two texts 'CRANE[2+4]' depends upon shared errors in passages not present at all in the abridged CRANE[3], so it is entirely possible that the unabridged source underlying CRANE[3] also contained the error. This is an important fact, which may be relevant to our analysis of the significance of these patterns. If we eliminate the twelve queried examples, the realized patterns drop to 18% of the possibles.

Reading Wrong in Only Three Texts: 56 possible, 14
actual

Reading Right in Only Three Texts: 56 possible, 5
actual

In each of these three pairings, which should be symmetrical, *Game* heavily favours the top grouping (with the smaller number of texts in error).[48]

The same bias is evident if we examine, not the total number of patterns ('types'), but the total number of errors in each pattern ('tokens'). There are 196 total shared errors. If those errors were randomly distributed among the 246 possible patterns, only 22 errors (11.4% of the total) would occur in patterns involving just two texts; in fact, patterns involving just two texts account for 115 of the actual shared errors in *Game* (58.7%)—more than five times expectation.

Demonstrably, something in the transmission of *Game* significantly disturbed the random distribution of shared error, working against combinations involving larger numbers of texts. That interference can only have come from transference, from regular correction of errors which would otherwise have been inherited and re-transmitted. Such transference, the impulse to correction of error, is routinized in human agents of textual transmission (para. 19); moreover, of all agents of transmission, the original author is the most privileged in his ability to access and restore the original correct reading (para. 32). We know that Middleton was heavily involved in the process of producing copies of *Game*; we could therefore have predicted that the distribution of shared error in the eight texts of *Game* would show statistically significant evidence of correction. Statistically speaking, an error in *Game* was relatively unlikely to be repeated in more than two extant texts, before it was caught and corrected.

But although such routinized correction significantly reduced the reproduction of error, it did not randomize the distribution of the shared errors which do remain (para. 35). There is nothing statistically random about the distribution of *texts* within the actual patterns of error-sharing. Consider, for instance, the distribution of errors in pairs of texts. As already noted, there are twenty-eight potential pairings of the eight texts, but only eighteen actual pairings.[49] The most remarkable fact about those eighteen actual patterns is the predominance of four texts (ROSENBACH, BRIDGEWATER, MIDDLETON[T], and OKES)—the four texts not copied by Crane. There are six possible combinations of any two of those four NON-CRANE texts; all six patterns are indisputably represented in *Game*, by at least two examples, and together those six pairs account for 66 of the actual errors shared by only two texts. In other words, 21% of the possible pairings contain 57% of the actual errors shared by pairs. Or, to put it another way, six combinations out of 246 possibilities (2.4%) contain 66 out of 196 shared errors (34%)—fourteen times the random distribution. Moreover, in nine of the remaining actual pairings (containing another 35 shared errors), one of the two texts is a NON-CRANE text; 101

out of the 115 errors shared by only two texts (88%) are present in one or more of those four NON-CRANE texts (which represent only 50% of the potential pairings).

The same disproportion is evident in the distribution of triplets (errors shared by only three texts). Only three triplet patterns occur, indisputably, more than once: BRIDGEWATER–MIDDLETON[T]–OKES (11), ROSENBACH–BRIDGEWATER–MIDDLETON[T] (11), and ROSENBACH–BRIDGEWATER–OKES (9). Noticeably, these three patterns all involve the same group of four NON-CRANE texts; those three patterns account for 31 of the 44 errors shared by only three texts. Three of the 56 potential patterns of three (5%) thus account for 71% of the actual errors shared by just three texts.

Of the eleven possible combinations which involve those four NON-CRANE texts and no others (six pairs, four triplets, one quadruplet), ten actually occur in *Game*. The exception is therefore interesting: in no case does an error occur in ROSENBACH, MIDDLETON[T], and OKES alone, with the correct reading in BRIDGEWATER. If a reading is correct in BRIDGEWATER, it is also correct in at least one other NON-CRANE text. I will return to the significance of this exception later. For now, the more globally important fact is that 100 shared errors occur in the exclusively NON-CRANE combinations. Those eleven possible combinations, involving only the four NON-CRANE texts, constitute a mere 4.5% of the possible combinations in a group of eight, but they contain 51% of all actual shared errors in *Game*— more than eleven times above random expectation.

The patterns of distribution of shared errors thus not only confirm that the NON-CRANE texts must have been produced relatively late in the sequence of transmission; they also demonstrate that the four NON-CRANE texts form a relatively cohesive grouping. That cohesiveness can be seen more clearly by contrast with the four CRANE texts. Like the NON-CRANE group of four, the CRANE group of four contains six potential pairs, four potential triplets, and one potential quadruplet; but the shared errors in *Game* constitute, from the CRANE quadrant, only three actual pairs, one actual triplet, and one quadruplet. The CRANE texts thus produce only five actual patterns (out of the potential eleven), in contrast to the ten actual patterns in the NON-CRANE texts. The patterns in the CRANE texts contain only 16 shared errors, by contrast with the 100 in NON-CRANE. The total specific to the CRANE texts is higher than the random distribution, which would predict that the eleven patterns possible for that group would contain 11 errors (out of the total of 196). Nevertheless, the difference here between expected and actual distribution is not as significant as the difference in the NON-CRANE texts. In

---

[48] These asymmetries would remain if we eliminated queried patterns. (See previous note.) The pairings would then be 8/3, 16/5, 8/4.

[49] ROSENBACH–BRIDGEWATER (25), CRANE/MATHEWES/ALLDE–OKES (18), BRIDGEWATER–OKES (16), ROSENBACH–OKES (13), CRANE[2,3] (10), BRIDGEWATER–MIDDLETON[T] (8), [CRANE[4]]–ROSENBACH (7), [CRANE[4]]–BRIDGEWATER (3), MIDDLETON[T]–OKES (2), ROSENBACH–MIDDLETON[T] (2), CRANE[3]–MIDDLETON[T] (2), CRANE[3,4] (2), and then six patterns that occur only once (CRANE[1]–OKES, CRANE[2]–[CRANE[4]], CRANE[1]–BRIDGEWATER, CRANE[2]–ROSENBACH, CRANE[3]–BRIDGEWATER, and [CRANE[4]]–MIDDLETON[T]).

a random distribution, the two groups of four texts (CRANE and NON-CRANE) should be approximately symmetrical, in their quantities of possible patterns and errors, types and tokens, but they are massively asymmetrical in both categories.

Demonstrably, the four CRANE texts do not constitute a coherent 'group', in the same way that the four NON-CRANE texts statistically do. What prevents them from constituting such a group is the distinctiveness of CRANE[1], which reproduces a different version of the play, and which—I have argued—belongs to a different branch of the stemma. Its distinctiveness has already been substantiated by the massive difference between its totals of shared error and the totals for all other texts; it is further defined by the patterns of distribution of shared errors.

I have noted that the four CRANE texts contain only one actual instance of the four possible triplets producible by a group of four texts: that one extant triplet pattern involves an error shared by CRANE[2,3,4]. That actual triplet is the only one of the four theoretical possibilities which excludes CRANE[1]; the other three non-existent triplets would all have linked CRANE[1] to two other Crane texts. Moreover, that same extant triplet, CRANE[2,3,4], reappears another eighteen times as a subset of larger groupings of four or more texts linked by shared errors.[50] By contrast, of the other three potential triplets, only one appears (once) embedded in a larger pattern of shared error—and of questionable stemmatic significance.[51] What cannot be disputed is that the nineteen examples of the triplet CRANE[2,3,4] contrast strikingly with only a single example representing any of the three other possible CRANE triplets.

If we focus not upon all four CRANE texts, but only on CRANE[2,3,4]—that is, the three Crane texts of the revised version—we discover an entirely different picture. Patterns produced by this particular group of three exceed statistical expectations. Like any other three texts, CRANE[2,3,4] can be combined in four different groups: a threesome, and three pairs. All four patterns actually occur; they constitute four of the five actualized patterns within the CRANE quartet. That is, within this grouping of three Crane texts (just as within the grouping of four NON-CRANE texts), 100% of the potential patterns are actual; by contrast, in the eight texts as a whole only 24% of the potential patterns are actualized. Moreover, the four patterns possible for this group of three constitute only 1.6% of the patterns possible for the eight texts altogether; but 1.6% of the 196 errors would be only three errors, whereas fourteen actually occur. In terms both of patterns and of quantities, the triplet CRANE[2,3,4] is statistically over-represented. Thus, the three texts CRANE[2,3,4] do constitute a grouping, as the four texts CRANE[1,2,3,4] do not.

The distinction between the cohesiveness of the four NON-CRANE texts and the division within the four CRANE texts is even more apparent if we allow for random variation. We have already established that the more errors two texts share, the greater the probability that they are stemmatically related, and the less likely that

the sharing results from coincidental independent variation (para. 10). Therefore, when two texts (ROSENBACH, BRIDGEWATER) share twenty-five unique errors, there must be some strong and close stemmatic connection between them; when two other texts (OKES, CRANE/MATHEWES/ALLDE) share eighteen unique errors, there must be some strong and close stemmatic connection between them, which is also clearly distinct from the other pair of texts. Even more remarkably, when three different texts (BRIDGEWATER, MIDDLETON[T], OKES) share thirteen unique errors, they must be connected. Such distributions cannot be random.

However, a single error shared by two texts only (out of eight) *could* be the result of coincidence. As already noted, the production of error is not entirely random, and there are circumstances where two different texts might independently make the same mistake (para. 4). An indisputable example of such coincidence occurs at Induction.63, where both OKES[2] and CRANE/MATHEWES have the obviously incorrect 'Nor' for the correct 'Not' found in all other texts. Obviously, a single easily-substituted letter does not provide good evidence for a stemmatic relationship between two witnesses. Likewise, at 4.1.62 an easy misreading of a single letter turned 'uncloses' into 'encloses' (in CRANE[1] and OKES); the error would be facilitated by the universal tendency to substitute common words for rarer ones (Taylor, 1988).[52] At 4.2.82, the Latin word *Poenitentiaria* has been corrupted in CRANE[1] and BRIDGEWATER to *Poenitentia*; the error is produced by simple eyeskip (or mindskip or handskip) from one 'ia' to another 'ia', toward the end of a long and unfamiliar Latin word. This kind of mistake is so common in textual transmission that there is a technical name for it (haplography).

Thus, these two examples, where a single error is shared by a unique pairing of two texts, are both explicable, in context, as easy-to-make errors which *could* have been made independently in different copies. Consequently, the pairing of the two texts could, in these two cases, be coincidental. A single error shared by two texts does not

---

50 It might also be present on another five occasions, where CRANE[2] and [CRANE[4]] share an error in material not present in the abridged CRANE[3]: see queried patterns 2, 19, 20, 33, and 43. In each case, the shared error might have been present in the lost full-length manuscript from which the extant abridged CRANE[3] derives.

51 That single exception, pattern 55, is an exit direction absent from seven texts, and present only in CRANE[3]. Although by the criteria consistently applied in compiling the database, it constitutes an error shared by seven texts, it is possible that the exit was never present in Middleton's first complete draft or in the King's Men's playbook: see the discussion of exit directions in Appendix C. It might have been added by whoever abridged the text, or by the scribe in the course of producing the dead-end text CRANE[3]. That is to say, it may never have been present in the lost full-length manuscript which underlies the abridgement, a lost manuscript which seems to have been closely stemmatically related to the extant CRANE[2] and CRANE/MATHEWES/ALLDE.

52 Texts printed up to 1630 and searchable in Early English Books Online contain no examples of *uncloses* or *vncloses*, but twelve of *encloses* (and twenty-one of *incloses*). Literature Online texts, published by 1625, contain one example of *vncloses* (Day's *Law Tricks*), but eleven of *encloses* and eighteen of *incloses*. If we expand the search to *unclose/vnclose* and *enclose/inclose*, EEBO figures are 56/1013, LION figures 50/250. Both sets of figures confirm that the verb *unclose* is a relatively 'literary' word, and much less common in the period than *enclose*.

in itself provide compelling evidence that they are related to one another stemmatically. There are, altogether, six such errors, involving six different pairings and all eight witnesses. Those six errors are themselves fairly randomly distributed (which increases the suspicion that some or all of them might be coincidence). They might reasonably be subtracted from the total of shared errors for each manuscript, since they *could* be coincidental, and *might* not indicate any kind of shared textual ancestry. They might be simply 'noise'.

If we were to make such an adjustment for coincidence, it would further strengthen the patterns we have already seen. It would reduce the total tokens for CRANE by seven, and for NON-CRANE by five; since the CRANE texts have fewer tokens to begin with, the gap between them and the NON-CRANE texts would widen. Its most significant effect would be upon CRANE[1]. Coincidence might well account for two (22%) of CRANE[1]'s nine shared errors; that fact is itself hard to dismiss as coincidence. Why should the shared errors most likely to be coincidental represent such a disproportionate fraction of the errors shared with only *one* of the eight texts? If we were to dismiss all six of these cases as the result of random independent variation, CRANE[1] would become even more remarkably devoid of errors shared with the seven texts of the revised version. Indeed, only seven shared errors would remain in CRANE[1] (less than one-sixth the total in the next-most-accurate text). Two of the remaining seven shared errors in CRANE[1] are unusual proper names (4.4.37 and 5.3.11)—in both cases, probably Middleton's own error, perpetuated in eight and seven texts, respectively. If we were to discount those two as authorial rather than transmissional errors, we would reduce all the totals, but again such an adjustment would disproportionately affect CRANE[1]. If we made the adjustment for coincidence (pairings of two texts that appear only once) and for authorial verbal error (groupings of seven or eight texts involving a proper name), then the five remaining shared errors in CRANE[1] would all be stage directions: 1.1.328.1, 2.1.150.1, 2.1.194.1, 3.1.155.2–3, 3.1.395.2–3, each of which belongs to a different pattern. All five of these errors link four or more texts; four of them are mid-scene exit directions. As I explain in Appendix C, mid-scene exit directions are the category of stage direction most likely to be absent even in professional playbooks of the period, and it is entirely possible that the four exit directions were never indicated by Middleton himself or the King's Men. The single remaining stage direction error (3.1.155.2–3) consists of a rather loose use of the phrase 'the Black House', when what the context more precisely requires is 'the rest of the Black House'. This might be a scribal error, but the imprecision might also be authorial.[53] In other words, of the nine shared errors present in CRANE[1], two might well be coincidental, and the other seven might all be authorial.

The preceding paragraph could be dismissed as special pleading. But we already have a wealth of independent evidence pointing to the distinctiveness of CRANE[1]. And the preceding analysis does, at the very least, demonstrate that it would be possible to conclude that CRANE[1] does not share *any* non-coincidental, non-authorial errors with any of the other seven witnesses. In other words, it is possible to argue that CRANE[1] belongs to an entirely separate branch of the stemma, earlier than all the others. No such argument can be made for any of the other seven witnesses.

However, in order for this argument to have any validity, the criteria have to be systematically applied. A 'filtered' list of the patterns of shared error is included in Appendix D; it shows the consequences of this filtering out of 'noise' on the whole set of patterns. For ease of comparison I give first the unfiltered cumulative totals (repeated from Sec. VI), then immediately below it I give the filtered summary, which removes the categories of error that might be attributed to random coincidence or to authorial carelessness.

Unfiltered Summary

CRANE[1]	9
CRANE[2]	46
CRANE[3]	49
CRANE/MATHEWES/ALLDE	64
MIDDLETON[T]	67
ROSENBACH	93
OKES	104
BRIDGEWATER	114

Filtered Summary

CRANE[1]	0
CRANE[2]	34
CRANE[3]	32
MIDDLETON[T]	46
CRANE/MATHEWES/ALLDE	52
ROSENBACH	79
OKES	85
BRIDGEWATER	91

The filtered summary reduces the number of shared errors for every text; it actually removes fewer errors from CRANE[1] than from any other text. The filtering does not significantly change the rank order of any of the texts. CRANE[2] has two more errors than CRANE[3], but the relative frequency of error in the abridged CRANE[3] is higher in both lists.[54] In the very middle of both lists,

---

[53] The same kind of error occurs at 2.2.81.1–2 and at 5.1.9.2 (in passages not present in CRANE[1]). The repetition suggests that the imprecision is indeed authorial. All three examples are therefore removed from the filtered database.

[54] CRANE[3] omits, by deliberate abridgement, approximately one-third of the play (Bawcutt 1993, 14). To compare its totals with those for full texts, one should therefore presumably multiply its total by approximately 1.5. The resulting conjectural approximation—[73?]—might better represent the number of shared errors in the lost [PRE-CRANE[3]], if that lost manuscript were unabridged. This conjectural recalculation would push [PRE-CRANE[3]] much closer to CRANE/MATHEWES/ALLDE. The filtered data produces similar results: adjusting for length, [PRE-CRANE[3]] would have [48?] shared errors, slightly fewer than CRANE/MATHEWES/ALLDE. However, we cannot be sure that [PRE-CRANE[3]] was an unabridged text; it might have been an abridgement of [PRE-CRANE[2,3]]. The more reliable conclusion—not dependent on conjectures about its exact antecedents—is that CRANE[3] contains more shared errors per thousand lines than does CRANE[2].

CRANE/MATHEWES/ALLDE and MIDDLETON[T] switch places. Statistically, the difference between those two texts is certainly not significant in the first list, and probably not significant in the second list either. (CRANE/MATHEWES/ALLDE contains about 70 lines more than MIDDLETON[T].)

The significance of this filtering, then, does not lie in the changed arithmetical totals, but in the changed statistical distribution of patterns of error-sharing. Most obviously, the filtering eliminates all patterns linking CRANE[1] to the other Crane texts. That result in turn strengthens the contrast between the NON-CRANE group of four and the CRANE group of four. Filtering the noise out of the data-set makes it even more apparent that CRANE[1] is all alone, and that CRANE[2,3,4] are distinct not only from the early, accurate CRANE[1] but also from the cluster of three especially corrupt NON-CRANE texts (ROSENBACH, OKES, and BRIDGEWATER).

We will eventually need to consider the local relationships of texts within each of these two clusters, but before doing so we need to look at the global problem of the relationship of the two clusters to one another. That is, before micro-mapping the patterns linking the four CRANE texts to each other or the patterns linking the four NON-CRANE texts to each other, we need to examine patterns linking one or more of the CRANE texts to one or more of the NON-CRANE texts. Such patterns should identify how, through what medium and at what point, errors move from the relatively accurate CRANE texts into the increasingly inaccurate NON-CRANE group.

For the sake of symmetry, and to test the preceding conclusions, it will be simpler to set the four texts transcribed by Crane against the four NON-CRANE texts. Obviously, any error that occurs in *both* of the two groups of four will have to occur in *both* of the two groups of four; such patterns are therefore of little value in determining whether the two groups are stemmatically connected. If we exclude errors which occur in five, six, or seven texts there remain 154 potential patterns; eleven of those potential patterns would link the four NON-CRANE texts to each other, and eleven would link the four CRANE texts to each other. Thus, there remain 132 potential patterns, involving errors shared by two, three, or four texts, which would link one-to-three of the Crane texts and one-to-three of the NON-CRANE texts. Of those 132 potential patterns, only 27 actually occur.[55] Indeed, if we limit ourselves to the filtered data, then the total shrinks even further, to only 18.[56]

Obviously, this pattern of distribution cannot be random. If the shared errors had been distributed by chance alone, then shared errors which link the two groups should occur twelve times more often than errors which link only the NON-CRANE texts to each other; in fact, the number of patterns/types represented is less than a quarter of expectation (10 within NON-CRANE, 27 for the cross-groupings), and the quantity of shared errors/tokens is not twelve times higher, but actually *lower* (100 within NON-CRANE, but only 59 for the cross-groupings). If errors shared by the NON-CRANE group occurred only one-twelfth

as often as errors shared by the cross-groupings, the NON-CRANE group would contain only five errors, not 100; if shared errors occurred in the cross-groupings twelve times as often as in the NON-CRANE group, there would be 1200 such errors, not 59. Using the filtered data-set would only worsen these anomalies.[57]

The triplet CRANE[2,3,4] (discussed above) also has a higher proportion of expected links than the cross-groupings. Actual shared errors in CRANE[2,3,4] are distributed in all four (100%) of the potential patterns, whereas the cross-groupings have only 20.5% of potential. On random distribution, the cross-groupings should have 63% of all shared errors, or 123 of the actual 196; instead, they have only 59, less than half the expected number (48%). By contrast, CRANE[2,3,4] should have only five of the 196 shared errors; instead, they have thirteen (260% of the expected number). The cross-over group should have 33 times as many shared errors as CRANE[2,3,4] (not a mere 4.5 times as many). Again, using the filtered data-set only worsens these anomalies.[58] Errors shared by less than five texts are *most* likely to be shared among the NON-CRANE texts alone, and *least* likely to be shared by texts from both groups.

The stemmatic connection *between* the three later Crane texts and the NON-CRANE group is thus statistically much weaker than the connections *within* either grouping. That fact in itself suggests that the two groups are connected through a narrow bottleneck of transmission. The pattern of distribution of the errors shared by texts from both groups should help identify where the bottleneck was. Obviously, when CRANE[2,3,4] share an error, it could have passed from any one of them to the NON-CRANE group; those patterns tell us nothing about this problem. I list the patterns below in descending order of frequency, bracketing the patterns that would be eliminated entirely by filtering the data-set. Where filtering does not eliminate the pattern/type but reduces the quantity of tokens, I give the reduced number in square brackets. I have divided the patterns into three groups: unambiguous patterns (first), queried patterns (second), and filtered patterns (third).

Table of Cross-over Errors

17. CRANE[4]/MATHEWES/ALLDE-OKES: 18 [17]
12. [CRANE[4]]-ROSENBACH: 7
11. [CRANE[4]]-BRIDGEWATER: 3
26. CRANE[2,3]-ROSENBACH: 1
27. CRANE[2,3]-OKES: 1
28. CRANE[3,4]/ALLDE-OKES: 1
37. CRANE[3,4]-ROSENBACH[A]-OKES: 1
45. CRANE[2,3]-MIDDLETON-BRIDGEWATER-OKES: 1

* * *

---

[55] Patterns 1, 3, 4, 5, 6, 8, 11, 12, 17, 19, 20, 21, 22, 23, 24, 26, 27, 28, 29, 33, 34, 36, 37, 38, 39, 41, 42.

[56] The filters eliminate patterns 1, 3, 4, 5, 6, 21, 22, 29, 38.

[57] Filtering reduces the number of cross-overs from 59 to 48, and the number of NON-CRANE errors from 100 to 91.

[58] Filtering eliminates only one shared error from CRANE[2,3,4], but eliminates eleven from the cross-over group.

19. CRANE[2,4]–ROSENBACH: I?
[passage not in CRANE[3]]

20. CRANE[2,4]–OKES: I?
[passage not in CRANE[3]]

33. CRANE[2,4]–MIDDLETON[T]–OKES: I?
[passage not in CRANE[3]]

43. CRANE[2,4]–ROSENBACH–BRIDGEWATER–OKES: I?
[passage not in CRANE[3]]

24. [CRANE[4]]–BRIDGEWATER–OKES: I?
[passage not in CRANE[2,3]]

23. [CRANE[4]]–ROSENBACH–MIDDLETON[T]: I?
[passage not in CRANE[3]]

34. [CRANE[4]]–ROSENBACH–BRIDGEWATER–MIDDLETON[T]:
I? [unspecified in CRANE[3]]

39. CRANE[2]–ROSENBACH–BRIDGEWATER–MIDDLETON[T]:
I? [unspecified in CRANE[3]]

* * *

[4. CRANE[2]–ROSENBACH: I]
[5. CRANE[3]–BRIDGEWATER: I]
[6. [CRANE[4]]–MIDDLETON[T]: I]
[7. CRANE[3]–MIDDLETON[T]: I]
[21. CRANE[3]–ROSENBACH–OKES: I?]
[22. CRANE[3]–BRIDGEWATER–OKES: I?]
[29. CRANE[2,3]–MIDDLETON[T]: I]
[38. CRANE[3]–BRIDGEWATER–MIDDLETON[T]–OKES: I]
[46. CRANE[3,4]–ROSENBACH–BRIDGEWATER–OKES: I]
[47. [CRANE[4]]–NON-CRANE: I]
[49. CRANE[1,2]–NON-CRANE: I]
[51. CRANE[1]–CRANE[3]–NON-CRANE: I]
[52. CRANE[3,4]–NON-CRANE: I]
[55. CRANE[1,2,4]–NON-CRANE: I]

Which of the three Crane texts of the revised version of the play is closest, stemmatically, to the four NON-CRANE texts?[59] Of these three groups of patterns, the second and third both consist entirely of patterns exemplified by a single variant. In the third group, that single variant would be filtered out if we eliminate shared errors probably due to coincidence or authorial carelessness. In the second group, the underlying pattern of affiliation might be larger than it appears, because some of the eight texts lack the relevant passages. Thus, the first four examples in the second group (19, 20, 33, 43) all involve errors shared by CRANE[2,4] in passages not present at all in CRANE[3]; the error might therefore have been present in the lost manuscript of the full text which was subsequently abridged. CRANE[3] is itself a dead-end, and accordingly any link from it to the NON-CRANE group must actually link the NON-CRANE group to its lost full--length antecedent.[60] Effectively then, these four patterns might be additional examples of errors shared by all the full-length CRANE witnesses to the revised version; like other errors shared by the extant CRANE[2,3,4], they tell us nothing about where the two groups intersected. The same logic applies to pattern 24. Thus, five of the eight patterns in the second group are unreliable evidence in resolving this particular stemmatic problem. The three remaining patterns in this group do, however, provide

some potentially useful information. In all three patterns, the material is missing from CRANE[3]. The first two cases (23, 34) are compatible with a link through [CRANE[4]] to NON-CRANE; the third (39) is compatible with a link through CRANE[2].

Obviously, the patterns in the first group are the most important, in both quantity and reliability. Their quantities also enable us to evaluate them statistically. If we combine those eight patterns with the three most reliable patterns in group two, we get the following totals:

[CRANE[4]] *only*: 3 patterns, 28 examples [27]
CRANE[3,4]: 2 patterns, 2 examples
CRANE[2,3]: 3 patterns, 3 examples
CRANE[4,3?]: 2 patterns, 2 examples
CRANE[2,3?]: I pattern, I example
CRANE[2] *only*: 0 patterns, 0 examples
CRANE[3] *only*: 0 patterns, 0 examples

The distribution of the data has clear implications. Statistically, all three texts have an equal number of potential patterns linking them to NON-CRANE. But the actual distribution is not evenly distributed, and not random. Of the three later Crane texts, the one most likely to be linked to NON-CRANE is, on the overwhelming evidence of the foregoing patterns, [CRANE[4]]. It is the only one of the three texts to contain unique filtered and unqueried links to NON-CRANE, and it contains a huge number of examples of such shared errors: at least 27 separate errors, and possibly 28, which link it alone, of the CRANE texts, to NON--CRANE. This is 3.5 times the number of all other cross-over shared errors combined. Moreover, all of these shared errors are 'twins', linking a single CRANE text to a single NON--CRANE text. As we increase the number of texts that share an error, we increase the probability that the error will be shared by texts from different groups.[61] Thus, errors which occur only twice ('twins') but nevertheless cross groups are, far and away, intrinsically the rarest of cross-group patterns. Only [CRANE[4]] contains examples of 'twin' patterns. Thus, the 27 or 28 shared errors linking [CRANE[4]] to NON-CRANE are not only far more numerous than all other cross-over patterns, but each of them is intrinsically rarer and more significant than the other cross-over patterns. Finally, in addition to these 'twins', another four patterns, containing four errors, can also be explained by assuming that CRANE was linked to NON-CRANE through [CRANE[4]].

The foregoing evidence undeniably requires a connection between NON-CRANE and [CRANE[4]]. Nevertheless,

[59] These patterns can also help us determine which of the NON-CRANE texts is closest, stemmatically, to the CRANE group. But for now I wish to postpone that question. (I return to it in Sec. XIV.)

[60] This antecedent might be [PRE-CRANE[3]], or it might be the lost manuscript [PRE-CRANE[2,3]] hypothesized by Bald and Howard-Hill (Figure 1). At this point, we need only recognize that CRANE[3] derives from a full-length text of the play, and that its connection to the NON-CRANE texts must be through that antecedent, or antecedents.

[61] Errors shared by five or more texts *must* include members of both groups (100%); of the 70 possible patterns of error shared by four texts, 68 patterns (97%) will cross groups; of the 56 possible patterns shared by three texts, 48 (86%) will cross groups; but of the 28 patterns shared by two texts, only sixteen (57%) will cross groups.

[CRANE⁴] alone cannot explain everything. Four cross-over patterns, and four examples, do not include [CRANE⁴], but do include CRANE² and CRANE³. Those four patterns require a link to one or the other, and possibly to both.

At one level, these results are contradictory: at least two of the three later Crane texts seem to pass errors forward to NON-CRANE. But this is merely a consequence of the fact that CRANE²,³ are both indisputably dead-ends, and the extant MATHEWES/ALLDE was printed from a lost manuscript we have identified as [CRANE⁴]. The errors shared by CRANE²,³ must also have been present in [PRE-CRANE²,³].[62] In looking for the bridge between the three late Crane texts and NON-CRANE, we are by definition looking for a lost manuscript. The apparent contradictoriness of this data is therefore exactly what we would expect.

The obvious explanation for this distribution would be that the lost manuscript which links the CRANE group to the NON-CRANE group was produced somewhere between CRANE²,³ and MATHEWES/ALLDE. That lost manuscript seems, on the evidence of these cross-over shared errors, to have been much closer to MATHEWES/ALLDE than to CRANE²,³, but it did apparently contain some errors present in [PRE-CRANE²,³] that were not repeated in MATHEWES/ALLDE.

This preliminary hypothesis—that the links between CRANE and NON-CRANE are mediated through a lost manuscript close to MATHEWES/ALLDE—requires further testing. In particular, any further analysis must take account of the fact that MATHEWES/ALLDE itself cannot be the direct intermediary between CRANE and NON-CRANE. Historically, that would be improbable: we would not expect many manuscripts to be produced after the play was available in print, at least nine months after its performances, and we would certainly not expect those manuscripts to be copied from a printed text (para. 37). The links between MATHEWES/ALLDE and the NON-CRANE group must therefore have been mediated not through the printed text (of 1625), but through the printers' manuscript copy-text, [CRANE⁴], a lost manuscript of unknown date. Given its central importance to links between the CRANE and NON-CRANE groups, [CRANE⁴] obviously requires detailed individual analysis.

The fact that [CRANE⁴] is a lost manuscript immediately suggests an explanation for the contradiction in the data. Most of the extant manuscripts were not proofread. The hands that produced CRANE², CRANE³, ROSENBACH, and MIDDLETON^T occasionally caught themselves making an error, and corrected it on the spot, but there is no evidence that they, or anyone else, went through the completed manuscript copy-editing or proofreading what had been copied. A few variants were inserted by others in the early scenes of CRANE¹, but after 2.1 it, too, shows no evidence of subsequent proofreading. Of the extant manuscripts, only BRIDGEWATER was systematically retrospectively proofread. But, like all printed texts of the hand-press era, both OKES and MATHEWES/ALLDE must have been proofread, first in foul proofs and then, at least one more time, while the sheets were being printed

('stop-press' correction).[63] A copyist—whether scribe or compositor—carries in his head small segments of text at a time, and focuses his attention on manually reproducing those small segments. By contrast, a proofreader is, first and foremost, a reader, who reads through the text looking for error. Unlike OKES, MATHEWES/ALLDE is, as all editors have recognized, well printed and well proofread. Consequently, the proofreaders may have deliberately corrected nonsensical or ungrammatical readings that they noticed in the foul proofs. Those errors may have been accurately copied, by the compositor, from the underlying manuscript; but the proofreaders were reading the proof for intelligibility, not just checking it systematically against the manuscript.

This routine process of proofreading in the printing house could, theoretically, explain the few anomalies in the foregoing evidence. The four cases where one or more NON-CRANE texts share an error with an earlier CRANE text might have been errors also present in the lost [CRANE⁴], but corrected by the proofreader in MATHEWES/ALLDE. I will examine the four examples, individually, in later sections, but for now we might begin with the hypothesis that [CRANE⁴] was the single conduit that passed CRANE errors to the NON-CRANE texts.

Nevertheless, before we go any further, I should call attention to an important fact. The *pattern* of cross-group shared error strikingly and independently confirms the evidence of shared error *quantities*. In raw totals of shared errors, CRANE/MATHEWES/ALLDE (65) stands between CRANE¹,²,³ (9–49) and the four NON-CRANE texts (67–114). And that is also precisely where the analysis of patterns places it.

More generally, too, the *patterns* of distribution of shared error reinforce the *quantities* of shared errors for individual texts. The pattern of distribution confirms the absolute priority and distinctiveness of CRANE¹; it also clearly places CRANE² closer to the playbook than any NON-CRANE text. When acting as a scribe, Middleton was copying late, derivative, and corrupt texts; no doubt he corrected and improved his copy-text, but he did not eliminate all the errors those late exemplars had accumulated. If we are attempting to establish an accurate text of *A Game at Chess* as originally written, our most reliable source is undoubtedly CRANE¹, and if we are attempting to establish an accurate text of the play performed in August 1624, our most reliable copy of the whole playbook would seem to be CRANE².

This second hypothesis contradicts the conclusions of earlier scholars. Both Nascimento (12) and Howard-Hill (*Pasquin* 141) regarded [CRANE⁴] as the earliest of the three late Crane transcripts. Certainly, as all investigators have

---

[62] 'If an error is shared by two texts which are both dead-ends, then that error must be either a coincidence, or a duplicated shared error in each text; if not a coincidence, the error must have originated in some third text, which was not a dead-end' (para. 39). Since we are dealing with four separate errors here, shared with several texts, coincidence is not a plausible explanation.
[63] For foul proofing and stop-press proofing, see Blayney 188–218, and Moxon 233–9.

realized, CRANE[2,3,4] are strongly linked to one another in matters of spelling and punctuation. But [CRANE[4]] contains 64 shared errors, 39% more than CRANE[2]'s total of 46; if we use the more reliable filtered totals, [CRANE[4]] contains 53% more shared errors than CRANE[2]. According to Howard-Hill's stemma (Figure I), CRANE[2,3,4] all belong to a single branch; they are the only extant texts that descend from a lost manuscript he calls 'Pre-Q3/Ln.' My own analysis has also concluded that CRANE[2,3,4] form a cohesive group. 'If texts are stemmatically related, if they belong to the same branch or sub-sequence of transmission, then the more shared errors a text contains, the later it must have come in that sub-sequence of transmission' (para. 13). Given this principle, how could [CRANE[4]] possibly, as Nascimento and Howard-Hill claim, be earlier in the sequence of transmission than CRANE[2]? Any attempt to answer that question, or to sort out the relationships between the three Crane texts of the revised version, must systematically take account of the fact that [CRANE[4]] is, in fact, a lost manuscript: we can infer its characteristics only in so far as they are faithfully reflected by the printed quarto, MATHEWES/ALLDE.

But MATHEWES/ALLDE creates a stemmatic problem which we have not yet properly acknowledged or confronted. Because MATHEWES/ALLDE is a printed text, it may, like other printed texts, face in two different directions: on the one hand toward other printed texts, on the other hand towards [CRANE[4]], the manuscript the printers used as copy-text, and the relationships of that manuscript with other manuscripts. For instance, OKES[1] shares more than one hundred errors with OKES[2]; that fact tells us nothing about the manuscript used as printer's copy-text for OKES[1], but simply confirms that OKES[2] is a slavish reprint of OKES[1]. Notably, MATHEWES/ALLDE also shares a large number of errors with OKES. Does that fact tell us something about the relationships between [CRANE[4]] and other manuscripts, or merely something about the relationships between MATHEWES/ALLDE and other printed texts?

VIII. The Relationship between OKES and MATHEWES/ALLDE

Before we can analyse the relationships between [CRANE[4]] and the other Crane manuscripts, we must first analyse the relationship between MATHEWES/ALLDE and the other printed edition, OKES. Those two quartos are linked more strongly to each other than to any other texts: eighteen unique links, a higher total than any combination either text has with any other. But these shared errors are by no means evenly distributed. And any analysis of their distribution must first acknowledge that MATHEWES/ALLDE is itself a composite entity, printed in two different shops.

CRANE/ALLDE–OKES: 16
CRANE/MATHEWES–OKES: 2 [1]

The filtered results (printed above in square brackets) make this contrast even more striking. Moreover, after 5.3.206 there is not a single variant between OKES and ALLDE that would require access to another source.[64] These last 23 lines—all on sig. I4[v] of ALLDE—contain three errors uniquely shared by the printed texts (Epilogue.0.1, Epilogue.5, Epilogue.6); they also contain another error, not unique to the quartos but shared by CRANE/ALLDE and all the NON-CRANE texts (5.3.220.1). Finally, the quartos uniquely share three additional readings which, while not demonstrably errors, occur in no other texts (5.3.207, Epilogue.9, Epilogue.10). I have not attempted a statistical analysis of shared errors in punctuation throughout the play, but there is a clear instance at 5.3.217–18.[65]

For the last 23 lines of the play ALLDE and OKES are substantively—and therefore stemmatically—identical. One possible explanation for that fact would be that the compositors in ALLDE's or OKES's shop possessed, in addition to a manuscript, a copy of the other printed quarto. Which quarto influenced the other depends, of course, on the order of printing of the two quartos. Since 1929, scholars and editors have unanimously regarded OKES as the first quarto ('Q1') and MATHEWES/ALLDE as the third quarto ('Q3').

However, the hypothesis that OKES was printed earlier than MATHEWES/ALLDE is based entirely upon 'comparison of the two engraved title-pages' (Bald 1929, 31). Bald argues that the engraving in MATHEWES/ALLDE 'seems to be copied from that of' OKES. He offers two pieces of evidence for this conclusion. First, in MATHEWES/ALLDE 'the group seated around the chessboard is omitted, and the figures of Spalato and Gondomar are enlarged so as to fill all the available space.' This is inconclusive: one might as easily say that in OKES 'the group seated around the chessboard has been added, and the figures of Spalato and Gondomar are reduced so as to provide the necessary space for the addition.' Secondly, in MATHEWES/ALLDE 'The heading at the top is retained (with slight alterations) with the two inset inscriptions *The White House* and *The Black House*. Though *The Black House* is now on the right side (so as to be above Gondomar) instead of on the left, *The White House* appears over the head of the Archbishop of Spalato. The traitor-bishop is no typical representative of the White House, and the inscription would never have been placed there unless the engraver had had the earlier engraving in front of him, and was imitating it' (Bald 1929, 31–2).[66]

Even if Bald's argument were logically impeccable, it is badly stated, since his language ('retained...alterations') again presupposes what he is trying to prove. In fact, the argument itself is logically flawed. First, the 'slight alterations' demonstrate that the engraver could not have

---

[64] Two variants are unique readings in ALLDE which are clearly printer's errors. At 5.3.208 ALLDE transposes 'me' to 'em', producing a nonsensical reading ('I 'em' instead of 'I'me'). At 5.3.214 it has the unique nonsensical 'Begging' for correct 'Bagging'. At 5.3.213 the extrametrical syllabic spelling of the past participle 'coloured' might be only a spelling variant.

[65] For a list of shared punctuation errors, and discussion of the limited reliability of such evidence, see Appendix E. The most remarkable feature of that Appendix is the dominance of punctuation errors shared by OKES and CRANE/ALLDE.

[66] This argument is repeated by Greg: the title-page of CRANE/ALLDE 'was evidently copied' from that in OKES, 'as shown by the here meaningless headings of the White and Black Houses' (BEPD 412(c)).

been mechanically copying the other title-page.[67] OKES has 'The Black-Houſe' and 'The White-Houſe' (both separately boxed), where MATHEWES/ALLDE has 'the White | Hous' and 'the Black | Hous' (neither boxed, but instead cleverly aligned with the outline of the two respective hats). If one engraver was copying the other, he was doing so very creatively, and that creativity makes it impossible to determine which engraving came first. One might just as easily argue that 'The Black-House' and 'The White-House' in OKES are redundant, because the image immediately below those labels identifies the 'Black' Bishop, Duke, Queen, and King (on the left) and the 'White' Bishop, Duke, Queen, and King (on the right); by contrast, the two figures in MATHEWES/ALLDE are not identified at all, except as representatives of the 'White' and 'Black' houses, respectively; hence, the labels in MATHEWES/ALLDE might be described as providing essential information, while the labels in OKES simply duplicate information in the 'earlier' engraving, which has been rendered superfluous by the other changes in the OKES title-page. Secondly, the Fat Bishop may or may not be 'representative of the White House', depending upon the author/engraver's view of the English episcopate and the hispanophile English court. Associating the Archbishop of Spalato with the White House was, in both the text and the engraving, a political decision.

The fundamental difference between the two engravings may be political rather than aesthetic or commercial. The MATHEWES/ALLDE title-page visualizes only two foreign figures (Spalato and Gondomar, each represented twice), whereas the OKES title-page much more provocatively visualizes the White King, Queen, Duke, Bishop, and Knight; the large image of the White Knight is clearly based on Prince/King Charles, and although the other figures are smaller and less detailed, they do suggest—as Moore demonstrated—King James (King), the Duke of Buckingham (Duke), and Archbishop Abbot (Bishop).[68] We might therefore best characterize the MATHEWES/ALLDE engraving as politically 'safer' or 'more cautious' than the OKES engraving; this caution also explains its false attribution to a Dutch printer (a claim not present in OKES). But it is intrinsically impossible to determine whether the 'safer' image was earlier, or later, than the 'more provocative' image.

An analysis of the content of the two engravings thus cannot determine which preceded the other; there is no 'scientific' or 'bibliographical' argument for priority. Nevertheless, although the reasoning of Bald and Greg was flawed, they *may* have been right in thinking that OKES was printed before MATHEWES/ALLDE. It could be argued that the use of standing type for parts of sheets H and I and all of sheet K of OKES[2] makes it relatively unlikely that, at the time those final sheets were machined, Okes was aware of the existence of a competing edition.[69] The use of standing type suggests that the stationer believed that OKES would be the first available printed text of a scandalously popular play, and that it would therefore be worth his while to exceed the legal limits on the number of

copies produced by a single setting of type. It is harder to explain this confidence if he knew of a competing edition recently published. Of course, it remains possible that MATHEWES/ALLDE and OKES appeared simultaneously—or that MATHEWES/ALLDE appeared just before the outer forme of sheet K of OKES (containing the end of the play) and half-sheet A (containing the title-page) were printed.[70] But the errors shared by OKES and CRANE/ALLDE cluster in the very sheets of OKES where type was left standing for the purposes of printing a second edition. Consequently, if those errors were shared by both quartos because someone in the shop of Nicholas Okes was looking at a copy of MATHEWES/ALLDE, then someone in the shop of Nicholas Okes made a decision to print a second edition, knowing that a rival edition had just appeared. One might argue that the workmen who set the last sheets of OKES into type were unaware of the existence of a rival quarto.

If we accept this reasoning, any direct influence of one quarto upon the other would have been the influence of OKES upon the compositor(s) of ALLDE. I will therefore assume, in the next few sections of this General Textual Introduction, that OKES[1] was printed first, and that pages of that newly printed quarto influenced the compositor(s) of ALLDE, when setting at least some passages in Act Five.

Nonetheless, I want to emphasize that this hypothesis is based upon economic and psychological assumptions, not bibliographical proof or mathematical analysis. I know of no purely textual or bibliographical evidence that would prove whether OKES[1] or MATHEWES/ALLDE was printed first. In this uncertain situation, for the sake of argument I want to entertain the hypothesis that previous investigators have been correct in their assumptions about the order of printing. If OKES[1] was printed first, then the last twenty-three lines of MATHEWES/ALLDE may have used the newly-printed rival quarto as copy-text. That hypothesis has the further implication of reducing the number

---

[67] See the reproductions of both title-pages, and discussion of the many differences between them, in Astington's essay in this volume. Astington's detailed reading of the images (written before I had completed work on the text of *Game*) takes for granted the traditional order of the quartos. If that order were to be overturned, then Middleton's involvement with the engraving for the MATHEWES/ALLDE quarto would be clear, and the OKES title-page would represent a deliberate expansion, also linked to Middleton. The fact that the MATHEWES/ALLDE version more closely resembles the source engraving in *The Second Part of Vox Populi* would support this interpretation. The OKES version would then have been an attempt to compete with the earlier quarto by providing a larger, and more provocative, image—as well as the added paratext of a poem explaining the illustration. Whether or not (as Astington suggests) the same engraver was responsible for both images, certainly the engraver of whichever was second understood that it had to compete with the first.

[68] Moore argues that the White Queen visually represented the dead Queen Anne; for an argument that it represents instead the Queen of Bohemia see the Textual Notes to the dramatis personae in *Later*. In either case, the White Queen would have contributed to the political daring of the image.

[69] This phrasing assumes that Okes was the publisher as well as the printer. Since the book was not entered in the Stationers' Register and the title-page deliberately conceals the identity of the author and stationer(s) involved, Okes is the only stationer we can confidently associate with the quartos of *Game* that he printed.

[70] Then as now, the initial pages of a book, including its title-page, were often the last thing to be composed or printed—especially when, as in OKES, the preliminaries were printed on a separate half-sheet (or rather, two separate leaves, which may or may not be conjugate). The sequence of printing in OKES is unknown.

of shared errors in the underlying manuscript, thereby giving [CRANE⁴] the benefit of any doubt.

Let us assume, then, that an exemplar of OKES¹ was on hand when the final page of ALLDE was set into type. If so, then OKES¹ might also have been consulted at earlier points in the setting of ALLDE. The strongest evidence of such a connection occurs at the beginning of 5.1, where the quartos share seven unique errors in a mere 35 lines (5.1.4, 5.1.9.4, 5.1.10–19, 5.1.15, 5.1.18, 5.1.31, 5.1.39). These errors occur in dialogue (4), lineation (2), and stage directions (1), and none would be removed by filtering. In the same passage the quartos share two unique punctuation errors (a misplaced Latin accent at 5.1.12, a misplaced closing bracket at 5.1.13). In addition, the same lines contain two more stage direction errors, which the quartos share with other texts (both at 5.1.9.2), and one punctuation error shared with another text (5.1.4).

I have insisted on the importance, for stemmatic analysis, of the distinction between shared errors and shared variants. However, it is worth noting that this passage in 5.1 contains, in addition to these shared errors, another four uniquely shared variants, where OKES and ALLDE disagree with all other texts (5.1.28–9, 5.1.30.1, 5.1.33.1, 5.1.33.1–2). The two quartos also share all four parentheses in these lines. Without the shared errors, these shared variants would be ambiguous, but in this context they are certainly suggestive.

Nascimento considered 'the question as to whether the compositors of' MATHEWES/ALLDE 'consulted a copy of' OKES in the printing house, but concluded that the evidence was not 'strong enough ... except in the Epilogue, and possibly in 5.1' (69, 71). But her analysis was seriously weakened by three systematic flaws. First, she treats variants from MIDDLETON^T as errors; she does not rigorously discriminate between shared error and mere shared variation. Secondly, she did not know that MATHEWES/ALLDE was split between two printing houses, and therefore considered this problem across the play as a whole, rather than printer-by-printer. Thirdly, she organized her analysis of variants in all the *Game* texts by scenes, and thus considered the Epilogue separately from the end of 5.3, and considered variants in 5.1 as a whole, rather than in the specific lines where shared errors cluster. However important scene-divisions may be to a formalist analysis, they are clearly irrelevant to the transmission of the text: none of the texts divided between two or more agents (MATHEWES/ALLDE, ROSENBACH, and BRIDGEWATER) is divided at a scene-break. As a result of her division of the material, Nascimento did not realize that the area where OKES matches ALLDE was larger (and therefore even harder to dismiss) than the Epilogue; she also diluted the evidence for contamination in 5.1, by combining material where evidence was strong with material where there was no real evidence at all. If we confine our attention to these two areas, the direct relationship of OKES and CRANE/ALLDE in parts of Act Five cannot seriously be disputed. These two passages at the beginning of 5.1 and at the end of the

play, between them constituting a mere 58 lines, contain eleven unique errors which link OKES to ALLDE.

Nevertheless, Howard-Hill also concluded, even more strongly than Nascimento, that 'there are strong arguments against printing-house consultation of a copy of' OKES 'by the compositor or compositors of' MATHEWES/ALLDE (181). But his chief reason for rejecting this conclusion—the first he mentions, and the one he reiterates at the end of the single paragraph he devotes to this problem—is that a compositor *should not have needed* to consult OKES. 'The hypothesis assumes that the copy for' MATHEWES/ALLDE 'was so difficult that the compositor had to turn elsewhere for clarification, but, since Nascimento and I agree that' MATHEWES/ALLDE 'was almost certainly printed from a Crane transcript, as good contemporary copy for printing as one can conceive, the likelihood that he did is small.... It is unlikely, however, that a compositor would turn from clear scribal copy to a foully printed quarto for elucidation.' This argument is logically flawed at several levels. First, OKES is not 'foully printed', if we take 'printing' as a technical description for the machining of the book; it is perfectly legible in all extant copies (unlike, for instance, the quarto of *Old Law*). A modern editor's dissatisfaction with OKES arises from a recognition that it contains an extraordinary number of errors; but those errors reflect either the carelessness of the *compositorial setting*, or the corruption in the *compositor's copy-text*. Such errors in no way diminish the legibility of the printed quarto, or its usefulness to a compositor in another shop—who would, in any case, have been much less aware than a modern editor of the 'errors' in OKES, since many of them are clearly identifiable *as errors* only by comparison with the readings in all the other texts. For printers, print is *always* more legible than even the cleanest manuscript, and printed texts also include features and options different from those in manuscript. So a compositor's consultation of OKES is intrinsically less surprising than Howard-Hill maintains.

Secondly, Howard-Hill presupposes that the Crane transcript available to the compositors was *uniformly legible throughout*. This is, of course, something that Howard-Hill cannot know. Crane's own transcriptional work may be uniformly legible, but any manuscript can be subsequently damaged, and the *end* of a manuscript is particularly liable to accidental spoilage or loss. The compositor's use of OKES at the end of the play is therefore perfectly compatible with the use of a Crane manuscript for the rest. Likewise, however elegant the penmanship, Latin will be less 'legible' than English for a Latinless compositor; if you doubt this, try transcribing from manuscript a language you do not know. The heavy concentration of shared errors in 5.1 begins with the first speech in the play entirely in Latin (5.1.4). If the compositor were unsure of his own command of Latin, when deciphering his manuscript source it would be natural for him to turn at that point to the available printed text. There follows an even longer speech, in Latin, at 5.1.10–19, where the quartos uniquely share five errors. Our capacity to 'read' any script depends in part upon our knowledge of the available orthographical and semantic possibilities in a particular context. Therefore, the compositor's turn to OKES for assistance with the beginning of Latin in 5.1 is also explicable, whatever the nature of his manuscript copy-text.

Finally, Howard-Hill presupposes that 'if a quarto was consulted at all' it was probably 'consulted throughout'. Certainly, it would be difficult to attribute all the connections between the two texts to consultation of one printed quarto by another. Over the play as a whole there is massive variation between OKES and MATHEWES/ALLDE: 1089 variants, at a conservative estimate (counting stage directions as a single variant, even when many separate words differ, and not counting ambiguous speech prefixes). Likewise with parentheses, which characterize Crane: MATHEWES/ALLDE has 120 not present in OKES, which has 51 not present in MATHEWES/ALLDE; in another eleven cases, the texts agree on only one of the two ends of a parenthesis. If we add these two sets of variants together, over the quartos as a whole there is approximately one variant for every two lines of text. In the context of such massive difference, the compositor(s) of CRANE/ALLDE or CRANE/MATHEWES would have gained nothing by regularly consulting OKES. If they had been doing so, we would expect many more agreements between the two quartos.

Howard-Hill therefore has no difficulty demolishing the hypothesis that the compositors of MATHEWES/ALLDE consulted OKES throughout. But this whole idea is a straw man, and a distraction from the real issue. I suspect that this assumption unconsciously derives (like so much else in the textual criticism of Middleton) from the pattern in Shakespeare. In the Shakespeare folio, quarto copy-text is either used for whole plays, or not used at all. The situation with *Game* is demonstrably different. First (as Howard-Hill did not know), MATHEWES/ALLDE was—unlike the Shakespeare folio—printed in two different shops, and the use of OKES for consultation in one does not require or entail its use in the other. Moreover, the Shakespeare quartos were all clearly published before work on their folio counterparts began. For *Game*, by contrast, we do not know that printing of one quarto was finished before composition of the other quarto began. Indeed, it is not only possible but probable that composition of the two overlapped. Once James I was dead, the text must have seemed publishable, and if this thought occurred to one stationer it may simultaneously have occurred to another. Multiple manuscripts were in circulation, so different stationers might acquire different manuscripts at about the same time. Those who invested time and money in MATHEWES/ALLDE might not have done so if they had known that another surreptitious printing was already underway; if another quarto had been available when they started, we might have expected them to save themselves the trouble of casting off manuscript copy-text, by simply adopting the page-breaks in OKES. At the very least, it is possible (and I think probable) that one of the quartos was published at some point *during* the composition and press-work on the other. Thus, OKES may

only have begun to be consulted at a certain point in the text, because it only became available in Allde's shop at that point.

Howard-Hill's *a priori* rejection of consultation is unjustified. His only other objection to the hypothesis of occasional consultation is that Nascimento does not account for 'the common agreements that are so frequent earlier in the play . . . . not merely in' 5.1 and the Epilogue. This is not an argument against consultation; as phrased, it is an argument in favour of *more* contamination, not less. But it also suffers, as does Nascimento's own analysis, from a failure to distinguish between shared *errors* and mere shared *variants*. The distribution of shared errors (which is concentrated) differs remarkably from the distribution of shared variants (which extends throughout the play). There is, accordingly, no reason to assume that the two categories, and the two patterns of distribution, have a *single* cause. Howard-Hill, looking at the pattern of distribution of the shared *variants*, says that it cannot be due to contamination of MATHEWES/ALLDE by OKES. But that conclusion does not undermine the separate conclusion that the pattern of shared *errors* in Act Five indicates that OKES was used at least once, and perhaps twice, by the compositor(s) of ALLDE.

Of course, if it was used twice, it might have been used more than twice. OKES might be influencing ALLDE in Act Five in ways which cannot be identified simply by tracing the incidence of shared errors. There is, for instance, in Act Five a notable *decrease* in the number of variants where OKES *differs* from ALLDE. In the first four acts of the play, Nascimento records—on a conservative count—924 such substantive differences between the two quartos, or an average of 231 differences per act; in Act Five, by contrast, there are only 148. In 5.1, by Nascimento's count, there are only twelve, the smallest total for any scene in the play (eight less than the nearest low).[71] Equally revealing are features of the text which reflect Crane's strong preferences, and therefore presumably the preferences of the underlying manuscript, [CRANE⁴]. ALLDE shares 33 parentheses with OKES in Act Five; for the rest of the play it shares only 68, or 17 per act, about half as many. By contrast, in the rest of the play MATHEWES/ALLDE adds 105 parentheses not in OKES, or 26 per act; in Act Five it adds only 15, just a little more than half the normal

---

[71] I have used Nascimento's figures here for the sake of consistency throughout the whole play. My counts of variation would be somewhat different, because I include lineation, punctuation, and the placement of stage directions, which she does not. Between 5.1.4 and 5.1.39 (sig. H3–H3ᵛ), where the uniquely shared errors cluster, I identify fourteen variants between OKES and ALLDE. Two of them are unique errors in ALLDE (5.1.25, 5.1.36), one is a unique indifferent variant in ALLDE (5.1.9.4); four are unique errors in OKES (5.1.4, 5.1.23, 5.1.32-3, 5.1.35-6), and one a unique OKES metrical expansion (5.1.23). These eight unique readings might all easily result from compositorial error, or correction, in one quarto or the other. By contrast, variants shared with other texts cannot be explained in that way. Three variants are errors that ALLDE (but not OKES) shares with different texts (5.1.6, 5.1.9.4, 5.1.11-12, each shared with a different single text); three are indifferent variants that ALLDE (but not OKES) shares with other late Crane texts (5.1.9.6-8, 5.1.33.2, 5.1.33.2). This pattern suggests that the compositors of one quarto consulted the other in 5.1, but combined its readings with others from the manuscript; it differs from the pattern at the very end of the play, where no use of manuscript need have occurred.

rate. In Act Five, then, by contrast with the rest of the play, ALLDE's use of parentheses much more significantly resembles their distribution in OKES. Crane adds hyphens as well as parentheses, and from the Prologue to the end of 5.2 MATHEWES/ALLDE omits only one hyphen present in MIDDLETON[T]; in 5.3 it omits ten such hyphens (in each case agreeing with OKES).

Cumulatively, I believe that this evidence—the clustering of uniquely shared errors, the diminution of variants in the vicinity of those error clusters, the associated decline in Crane punctuation—establishes a strong possibility that one quarto directly influenced the composition of Act Five in the other. If we accept my hypothesis about the psychological and economic logic of printing a second edition from standing type, it would have been OKES that influenced ALLDE. Certainly, in analysing the stemmatic relationship of [CRANE[4]] to other manuscripts, making that assumption about the printing of the quartos will give the lost Crane manuscript the benefit of the doubt.

IX. Shared Errors in [CRANE[4]]

Assuming that at least some of the errors uniquely shared between OKES and ALLDE represent the contamination of one printed quarto by another, we are in a better position to examine the nature of the Crane manuscript behind MATHEWES/ALLDE. For the time being, we must leave out of this account any errors shared by CRANE/ALLDE with OKES only, because some of those might be due to contamination of the printed text; the only safe course, at this point, is to consider the profile of [CRANE[4]] without those suspect variants. (I will return to this issue in Sec. XX.) Errors in Act Five shared with OKES and other texts are ambiguous. But when CRANE/MATHEWES/ALLDE shares errors with more than one manuscript, but not OKES, those errors must originate not with the printers, but in the underlying manuscript, [CRANE[4]]. If we set aside the strictly limited problem of printer contamination, then, we can use shared errors to identify the relationship between the lost [CRANE[4]] and the other surviving texts. Once again, I divide the shared errors into three groups: unambiguous patterns (in descending order, from most common to least), then queried patterns, then dubious patterns that would be removed by filtering.[72]

[CRANE[4]] Shared Errors

12. [CRANE[4]]-ROSENBACH: 6–7 (2.2.133–35 [not in BRIDGEWATER or CRANE[3]])
17. CRANE[4]/ALLDE-OKES: 3–6 (3.1.265, 4.4.12.1, 5.3.188: passage not in CRANE[3])
41. CRANE[2,3,4]-MIDDLETON[T]: 3
42. CRANE[2,3]-CRANE/ALLDE-OKES: 3
11. [CRANE[4]]-BRIDGEWATER: 2–3 (2.1.177, passage not in CRANE[3])
7. CRANE[3,4]: 2
53. CRANE[2,3]-ROSENBACH-BRIDGEWATER-CRANE/ALLDE-OKES: 2
56. CRANE[2,3,4]-NON-CRANE: 3–4 [1–2] (2.2.33 [not in BRIDGEWATER], 3.1.175.1 (CRANE/MATHEWES); [3.1.305.1], [5.1.9.2] (CRANE/ALLDE))

17. CRANE/MATHEWES-OKES: 1–2 [1] (1.1.137, [2.2.233.1 not in BRIDGEWATER])
25. CRANE[2,3,4]: 1
28. CRANE[3]-CRANE/ALLDE-OKES: 1
36. CRANE[2,3,4]-ROSENBACH: 1
37. CRANE[3]-CRANE/ALLDE-ROSENBACH[A]-OKES: 1
44. CRANE[2,3]-CRANE/ALLDE-BRIDGEWATER-OKES: 1
51. CRANE[2,3,4]-ROSENBACH-BRIDGEWATER-MIDDLETON[T]: 1

Queried Patterns

19. CRANE[2]-CRANE/MATHEWES-ROSENBACH: 1? [passage not in CRANE[3]]
20. CRANE[2]-CRANE/ALLDE-OKES: 1? [passage not in CRANE[3]]
33. CRANE[2]-CRANE/ALLDE-MIDDLETON[T]-OKES: 1? [passage not in CRANE[3]]
43. CRANE[2]-CRANE/ALLDE-ROSENBACH-BRIDGEWATER-OKES: 1? [passage not in CRANE[2,3]])
24. CRANE/ALLDE-BRIDGEWATER-OKES: 1? (3.2.30–1 [passage not in CRANE[2,3]])
23. CRANE/MATHEWES-ROSENBACH-MIDDLETON[T]: 1? [passage not in CRANE[3]]
34. CRANE/MATHEWES-ROSENBACH-BRIDGEWATER-MIDDLETON[T]: 1? [unspecified in CRANE[3]]

Patterns Filtered Out

[6. [CRANE[4]]-MIDDLETON[T]: 1]
[35. CRANE: 1]
[46. CRANE[3,4]-ROSENBACH-BRIDGEWATER-OKES: 1]
[47. CRANE/ALLDE-NON-CRANE: 1]
[48. CRANE[2,3,4]-ROSENBACH-MIDDLETON[T]-OKES: 1?]
[52. CRANE[3,4]-NON-CRANE: 1]
[54. CRANE-ROSENBACH-MIDDLETON[T]-BRIDGEWATER: 1]
[55. CRANE[1,2,4]-NON-CRANE: 1]

The eight errors/patterns which would be eliminated by filtering are, for the most part, as meaningless as we would expect. They are evenly divided between CRANE/MATHEWES and CRANE/ALLDE. The seven queried patterns are more interesting. Four of them are errors shared by CRANE[2,4] and at least one NON-CRANE text, in a passage missing from CRANE[3]; this again suggests that the error might have been present in all the later full-length Crane manuscripts. However, three of these, and one of the other queried patterns, are CRANE/ALLDE errors shared with OKES, and they might therefore result from contamination by the printed text rather than manuscript transmission. The two remaining queried patterns again involve material not present in the abridged version, and all three occur in CRANE/MATHEWES; they might link the two late lost manuscripts [PRE-CRANE[3]] and [CRANE[4]] to each other, or they might be errors that originated in [CRANE[4]] and were passed from there to some (but not all) manuscripts in the NON-CRANE group.

---

[72] This table omits errors shared uniquely between CRANE/ALLDE and OKES in 5.1.4–39 and 5.3.206-Epilogue.10, and it also omits pattern 58, shared errors linking all surviving witnesses.

There remain between 30 and 38 errors in unambiguous patterns (where the existence of the pattern/type is not in doubt but some of the specific errors/tokens would be queried or filtered). But twelve to sixteen of those specific errors are shared by OKES with CRANE/ALLDE, and might be due to contamination. If we treated all such variants as suspect, on the grounds of possible contamination of CRANE/ALLDE by OKES, then we would have to remove from consideration five patterns (28, 37, 44, 53, 42, 17), and reduce the number of examples in two other patterns (17, 56). This severe reduction is probably excessive, but it is the only way to analyse the underlying pattern of shared error in [CRANE⁴] without using evidence which might theoretically have been contaminated or confused by the relationship between OKES and CRANE/ALLDE.

When we have made all these adjustments, filtering the results to eliminate randomness and contamination, there remain, altogether, twelve patterns/types and at least twenty-four shared errors/tokens which seem certainly to have been present in the lost manuscript [CRANE⁴].[73] This lowest-possible number of shared errors (24), if it were accurate, would make [CRANE⁴] the most accurate of the later CRANE texts; CRANE², by contrast, has a filtered total of 34 shared errors. On the other hand, if we assume instead that OKES directly contaminated CRANE/ALLDE only in the 58 lines we have identified in 5.1 and the end of the play, then [CRANE⁴] might have contained 43 shared errors. This higher end of the range would make it demonstrably less accurate, and later, than CRANE² (though clearly more accurate, and earlier, than MIDDLETON^T). This uncertainty, caused by the relationship between OKES and ALLDE, forces us to take seriously the conjecture, by Nascimento and Howard-Hill, that the lost [CRANE⁴] was an earlier manuscript than the extant CRANE². The total number of shared errors will not, in itself, resolve the problem, because [CRANE⁴] is lost, and depending on our operating assumptions we can deduce a range of shared errors that it might have contained, a range that would be compatible with its being either earlier or later than CRANE².

Nevertheless, although the raw totals do not solve this problem, the patterns of distribution are more helpful. In Sec. VII, I concluded that the patterns linking the three later CRANE texts to the NON-CRANE group could best be explained by the hypothesis that NON-CRANE derives from a lost manuscript somewhere between [PRE-CRANE^{2,3}] and CRANE/MATHEWES, but much closer to the latter. We can now see that the evidence linking the manuscript [CRANE⁴] to the NON-CRANE group may have been distorted by the relationship of printed ALLDE to printed OKES. If we disregard the examples created by possible contamination of one printed text by the other, the links between [CRANE⁴] and the NON-CRANE texts shrink to nine absolutely reliable examples (instead of 27). Nevertheless, these nine shared errors/tokens come from three different patterns, all 'twins'. By contrast, neither CRANE² nor CRANE³ has

any examples of any such pair-patterns of shared error. Thus, even after we have eliminated possible contamination from print, in both tokens/examples and patterns/types [CRANE⁴] remains the dominant cross-over text. We can still say that the stemmatic link between CRANE and NON-CRANE occurred somewhere between CRANE^{2,3} and MATHEWES/ALLDE, perhaps identical with, and certainly close to, [CRANE⁴].

Moreover, it is already possible to say something specific about the pattern of links between [CRANE⁴] and individual texts in the NON-CRANE group. In these filtered totals, discounting possible OKES contamination of ALLDE, there remain eleven to fourteen errors shared with a single text: seven links to ROSENBACH, three to BRIDGEWATER, two to CRANE³ and two to OKES. Notably, the overwhelming majority connects [CRANE⁴] to the NON-CRANE group. This may seem surprising, but it reflects the fact that [CRANE⁴]'s links to the other CRANE transcripts characteristically involve more than one other text. An error made in one of the CRANE texts of the revised version is likely to be passed on to the other texts in the group; an error made in the NON-CRANE group may be corrected in any text, and not corrected in any other.

These patterns can be seen in the total number of errors [CRANE⁴] shares with each of the other texts (again, using the most rigorously filtered database).

OKES: 3 [1 unique]
BRIDGEWATER: 6 [2 unique]
MIDDLETON^T: 8 [0 unique]
CRANE²: 9 [0 unique]
CRANE³: 10 [2 unique]
ROSENBACH : 14 [6 unique]

The low number of links with OKES here is predetermined by exclusion of errors it shares with ALLDE; this eliminates half the text. The *rate* of shared error, per hundred lines of text, is about the same for OKES as for BRIDGEWATER. But the total links to these two texts are still lower than for any other texts of the revised version. This should not be surprising: we have deliberately eliminated many OKES links, and we have already accumulated considerable evidence that BRIDGEWATER is at the very end of the chain of transmission, and therefore, apparently, farther from the whole CRANE group.

MIDDLETON^T has more links with [CRANE⁴] than either OKES or BRIDGEWATER, but unlike them it has no *uniquely* shared errors. Any text in one group of four will have four potential pairings with texts in another group of four; [CRANE⁴] is paired with three of its four potential cross-group mates (OKES, ROSENBACH, BRIDGEWATER). The single

---

[73] Patterns 12, 41, 11, 7, 17, 57, 25, 36, 51, 19?, 23?, 34?. Three of these are queried patterns; if we assumed that, in each queried case, the apparently unique pattern is actually the remnant of a larger pattern, then the number of tokens/errors would remain the same, but the patterns would be reduced from twelve to eleven: 19 would become simply another example of 36, while 23 and 34 would remain as distinctive patterns, but simply add CRANE³ to their list of linked texts.

NON-CRANE text with which it is not uniquely paired is MIDDLETON[T].[74] CRANE/MATHEWES/ALLDE thus seems closely connected to three different texts of the NON-CRANE group, but not to MIDDLETON[T]. This peculiar pattern is almost certainly a consequence of MIDDLETON[T] being autograph throughout. I have already demonstrated that transference, or authorial correction, will not 'systematically remove errors shared with one text, as opposed to errors shared with another text' (para. 23). However, the fewer the errors shared by two texts, the more likely that random correction or transference will eliminate those errors. For instance, if a text (X) uniquely shares 20 errors with one text (Y), but uniquely shares only two errors with another text (Z), then a random process of correction could hardly eliminate the evidence for a connection between X and Y, while leaving the evidence for a connection between X and Z intact; but random correction might entirely eliminate the evidence for a connection between X and Z, while leaving some evidence for a connection between X and Y. That is, transference does not discriminate against particular texts, but a small quantity of evidence is obviously more endangered by random correction than a large quantity. There is massive evidence for a connection between MIDDLETON[T] and BRIDGEWATER (see Sec. XIX); although the process of authorial correction in MIDDLETON[T] must have diminished the total number of errors shared with BRIDGEWATER, it obviously could not eliminate all the evidence for a stemmatic connection. However, BRIDGEWATER uniquely shares with [CRANE[4]] only two errors, and [MIDDLETON/OKES] may have shared only two; if [PRE-MIDDLETON[T]] had a similar number, then random authorial correction might well have eliminated such a small number of shared errors.

Judging from the evidence about the order of texts already accumulated in Sec. VI and Sec. VII, [CRANE[4]]'s strongest links are with two of the later CRANE manuscripts and one of the earliest NON-CRANE manuscripts (CRANE[2,3] and ROSENBACH). Again, these results are easiest to explain if we assume that [CRANE[4]] was produced later, stemmatically, than CRANE[2,3].

Even if we discount all shared OKES/ALLDE errors on the grounds that they might be due to ALLDE consulting OKES, [CRANE[4]] shares at least three errors with OKES. This makes it likely that some of the errors shared by OKES and CRANE/ALLDE actually stood in [CRANE[4]]. The low end of the range of possible totals for [CRANE[4]] is therefore very unlikely to be correct. Moreover, there are very specific reasons for the compositor(s) of CRANE/ALLDE to have consulted OKES in 5.1 and the end of the play; it is less reasonable to suppose that they randomly consulted it everywhere just in order to import extra errors.

The more important and less speculative point is that [MIDDLETON/OKES] must be linked, through the manuscript chain of transmission, to [CRANE[4]]. By discounting contamination of one printed text by another, we have not undermined the essential evidence that [CRANE[4]] is stemmatically connected to the NON-CRANE group; instead, we have more evenly distributed the links between [CRANE[4]] and the NON-CRANE group. Instead of massive linkage with OKES, we can now see that the more important connection of [CRANE[4]] may have been with ROSENBACH. This pattern suggests that—if, for the moment, we ignore OKES—the route of transmission between the CRANE texts and the NON-CRANE texts was from something close to [CRANE[4]] to something close to ROSENBACH. But that evidence in itself does not directly address the crucial question of the stemmatic relationships *within* the CRANE group itself. Are the NON-CRANE texts connected to the CRANE texts at a point early or late in Crane's copying? We have already conclusively proven that CRANE[1] belongs to a distinct and earlier branch, but we have as yet no decisive evidence of the sequence of copying of the three later CRANE texts.

X. Sets and Series

Although the quantity and distribution of shared errors has clarified many aspects of the transmission of *Game*, in determining the sequence of CRANE texts we are hampered by the relative paucity of such errors. CRANE[2] has fewer shared errors than CRANE[3] would have, if CRANE[3] were full-length; CRANE[2] certainly has no more shared errors than did the lost [CRANE[4]], and probably has fewer. But the mere quantities are not decisive here, first of all because the difference in totals is not itself statistically significant, secondly because for both CRANE[3] and [CRANE[4]] the totals are partly conjectural: for CRANE[3] we must extrapolate the probabilities of error for a full-length text, for [CRANE[4]] we must deduce the errors present in the lost printer's copy-text for MATHEWES/ALLDE. Neither conjecture is undisciplined, but neither can give us an exact number, only a range of probabilities. Within the three CRANE texts of the revised version of the play, the difference in quantities of shared error is not statistically significant.

Nevertheless, although quantities of shared error cannot resolve the problem of sequence, another aspect of error distribution should. Up to this point, I have treated patterns of shared errors as mathematical sets: for instance, every error shared by three texts (1,2,3) belongs to a single set containing the elements 1, 2, and 3. But such a description ignores the distinction between sets and series. Every completed set results from a series of actions, and more than one series can produce the same set. For instance, the single set (1,2,3) could be produced by six different series: 1-then-2-then-3, or 2-then-3-then-1, or 3-then-1-then-2, or 1-then-3-then-2, or 2-then-1-then-3,

---

[74] It is also not paired with MIDDLETON[T] in any cross-group triplet except for the filtered pattern 23.

or 3-then-2-then-1. By contrast, the set (1,2) could be produced by only two different series: 1-then-2, or 2-then-1. The more elements in a set, the more possible series could produce that set.[75]

The distinction between sets and series is fundamental to all statistical analysis; for stemmatic analysis, in particular, it cannot be avoided. The textual critic is confronted by a set (of texts, of variants, of errors), and must determine which of the possible series actually produced that set. For *Game* (as for all other works extant in multiple texts), we know that the surviving set of shared errors was produced by one particular historical sequence of transmission of variants and errors from text to text. This applies to the three Crane texts of the revised version, as it does to all other texts. If we re-examine each set of shared errors, and analyse it not as a static set but as the result of a temporal series, we should be able to determine which temporal series produced the extant set.

Why can a set of three items be generated by six different series, while a set of two items can be generated by only two possible series? Because every set consisting of three elements (1,2,3) contains three possible subsets consisting of pairs of those three elements: (1,2), (2,3), (1,3). Since each of those three subsets of pairs could be produced by two different series, the combined triplet set could be produced by six different series (3 subsets times 2 series each).

But a series, unlike a set, adds the dimension of directional time, which restricts the number of possible options. Let us suppose that the three elements of the set (1,2,3) are the result of a series 1→2→3. Unlike the three-element set (1,2,3), the three-element series 1→2→3 could be generated by only two two-element subseries: 1→2 and 2→3. That is, 1 is earlier than 2, and 2 is earlier than 3. Of course, 1 is also earlier than 3, but the subseries 1→3 would leave out the necessary intermediary number in the series 1→2→3: therefore, the subseries 1→3 cannot have helped generate the series 1→2→3.

This fact allows us to use a known pattern of subsets to determine an unknown series. We know that 1, 2, and 3 belong to a single set, but we do not know which series generated that set: 1→2→3, 3→2→1, 2→3→1, 1→3→2, 3→1→2, 2→1→3. However, we do know that any one of these six possible series will eliminate certain subseries, and therefore eliminate certain subsets. Both the series 1→2 and the series 2→1 generate an identical subset (1,2); the existence of the subset (1,2) therefore demonstrates that 1 and 2 are adjacent to one another in a series, but does not indicate the direction of movement between them. Likewise, both the series 2→3 and the series 3→2 generate an identical subset (2,3); the existence of the subset (2,3) therefore demonstrates that 2 and 3 are adjacent to one another in a series, but does not indicate the direction of movement between them. The presence of both the subset (1,2) and the subset (2,3) would therefore demonstrate that the set (1,2,3) was generated by either the series 1→2→3 or

the series 3→2→1. The four other possible series can all be eliminated, because those four other possible series all contain the subset (1,3). In other words, if the set (1,2,3) was the result of a series 1→2→3 or 3→2→1, then it contains the subset (1,2) and the subset (2,3), but it will not contain the subset (1,3).

In stemmatic analysis, these sets and subsets, series and subseries, consist of errors shared by two or more texts. If three texts are copied in sequence—the first copied to produce the second, the second copied to produce the third—then they constitute a series 1→2→3; an error present in the first will also be present in the second and third, thus producing the set (1,2,3); an error introduced in the second will also be present in the third, thus producing the subset (2,3). If there were no transference or correction in the transmission of those texts, then these would be the only possible sets of shared error within the series 1→2→3. However, some degree of transference or correction occurs in almost all acts of transmission (para. 19); consequently, any statistical analysis of shared error must allow for transference. An error present in the first text might be copied in the second text, but corrected in the third, thus generating the subset (1,2). The series 1→2→3 could therefore generate three subsets of shared error: (1,2), (2,3), and (1,2,3). But it could not generate the subset (1,3). An error present in the first text might be corrected in the second text, but if the second text was copied to produce the third then the third text should contain the corrected reading (present in 2), not the error (present in 1). It is intrinsically improbable that the third text (3) would independently re-introduce an error present in an ancestral text in the series (1), but not present in its own intervening immediate source (2).

The three CRANE texts of the revised version of the play share 21 different errors (or at least 14, if we filter the data); one of those errors occurs in CRANE[2,3,4] and in no other texts (Pattern 25).[76] No set of three texts appears in more unfiltered patterns (9).[77] Clearly, then, CRANE[2], CRANE[3], and [CRANE[4]] constitute a set of closely related texts—let's give that set the abbreviated name '(C2, C3, C4)'—which must have been generated by an unknown temporal series. Moreover, CRANE[2] and CRANE[3] share eleven errors present in no other texts (Pattern 14), thus constituting the strong subset '(C2, C3)'; accordingly, we know that CRANE[2] and CRANE[3] are, within the larger set,

[75] This fact does not undermine any of the foregoing statistical conclusions; rather, it makes even more anomalous the anomalies already noted. For example, only two possible series could produce sets/patterns containing an error shared by two texts; but eighteen possible series could produce sets/patterns containing an error shared by six texts. In Section VII I treated sets created by 'Reading Wrong in Only Two Texts' and by 'Reading Right in Only Two Texts' as statistically equivalent, because the number of possible *sets* is the same in both cases—but the number of possible *series* that would produce 'Reading Right in Only Two Texts' is nine times greater. This makes the anomalous predominance of sets containing 'Reading Wrong in Only Two Texts' even more remarkable.
[76] The other patterns of shared error that incorporate CRANE[2,3,4] (but also include various other texts) are [35], 36, 41 (3), 42 (3), 44, 48, 51, 53 (2), [54], 56 (3)[1], and [57 (2)].
[77] The other seven unqueried triplets appear in four (30), five (26, 28, 29, 31, 32), and six (27) unfiltered patterns.

adjacent texts. Although we do not know which came first in the series, we do know that [CRANE⁴] (which does not contain any of those eleven errors) cannot have come between them: we can therefore eliminate from consideration any series which places [CRANE⁴] in the middle of these three texts. The subset (C2, C3) eliminates two of the six possible series that might produce the set (C2, C3, C4). [CRANE⁴] must, accordingly, be either the first or the last of the series: it must be earlier than both CRANE² and CRANE³, or later than both. If [CRANE⁴] is earlier than CRANE², it must also be earlier than CRANE³; alternatively, if [CRANE⁴] is later than CRANE², it must also be later than CRANE³.

But CRANE³ and [CRANE⁴] share two errors present in no other texts (Pattern 8), thus creating the subset (C3, C4). Accordingly, we know that CRANE³ and [CRANE⁴] are, within the larger set, adjacent texts. Although we do not know which came first in the series, we do know that CRANE² (which does not contain either of those errors) cannot have come between them: we can therefore eliminate from consideration any series which places CRANE² in the middle of these three texts. The subset (C3, C4) eliminates two of the six possible series that might produce the set (C2, C3, C4). CRANE² must, accordingly, be either the first or the last of the series: it must be earlier than both CRANE³ and [CRANE⁴], or later than both. If CRANE² is earlier than CRANE³, it must also be earlier than CRANE⁴; alternatively, if CRANE² is later than [CRANE⁴], it must also be later than CRANE³.

The combination of the subset (C2, C3) and the subset (C3, C4) eliminates four of the six possible series that might produce the set (C2, C3, C4). That combination demonstrates conclusively that CRANE³ must have been, temporally, the middle text in the series of three. There is not a single unfiltered, unqueried example of the subset (C2, C4), either as a unique pairing, or as part of a larger set which does not include CRANE³.[78] Thus, we know that the set (C2, C3, C4) must have been produced either by the series (C2→C3→C4) or by the series (C4→C3→C2).

Which one of these two possible series was the actual historical series that produced the extant texts? In theory, there are two ways to identify the historical series. One way would continue to use set theory, analysing other sets in order to try to establish a relationship with the Crane set that would distinguish its beginning from its end. For instance, we have already demonstrated (Sec. VII, VIII, IX) that the bridge to the later NON-CRANE texts was a lost text which stood very near [CRANE⁴]. That conclusion links CRANE⁴ (rather than CRANE²) to a group of later, more corrupt texts, and suggests that [CRANE⁴] belongs at the end of the Crane series. In itself, set analysis cannot go much further.[79]

Alternatively, we might try to establish the priority of CRANE² or [CRANE⁴] by a systematic analysis of progressive error. For example, at 3.1.180 all texts except OKES have the reading 'dares yon'; in OKES¹ the second word is misprinted as 'you', which is nonsensical in its context.

The substitution of 'u' for 'n' is a very common error, in manuscript and print; it might result from misreading, foul case, or a turned type. OKES² changes 'dares you' to 'dare you': that is, OKES² deliberately 'corrects' the form of the verb so that it matches the pronoun. In this case, we know that OKES² is a reprint of OKES¹, and we can therefore identify 'dare you' as an example of progressive error: the error or variant in an earlier text leads to mistaken correction, or further error, in a later text.[80]

Appendix F contains a list of all possible cases of progressive error that I have identified in the textual notes. That evidence is necessarily much more conjectural than the database of shared errors, because it does not depend simply upon identification of an error, but upon a particular conjectural explanation of the *cause* of that error. The plausibility of those explanations cannot be mathematically evaluated, and it varies from case to case; I presume that every reader will be convinced by some explanations, and reject others, and that different readers will disagree about which to accept and which to reject. Nevertheless, for what it is worth, the evidence of progressive error does suggest certain conclusions. In the thirty-one possible examples, fourteen identify OKES as later than one or more other texts. None of the examples identify CRANE¹ or CRANE² as later than any other text. These extremes agree with the independent evidence of shared error totals and patterns, already analysed; the exceptional number in OKES can be explained by the manifestly error-prone compositor(s) of that quarto. Between these extremes fall all the other texts: CRANE³ (2), BRIDGEWATER (4), MIDDLETON (5), ROSENBACH (8). Once

---

[78] Pattern 2 contains the only possible exception, but it is *both filtered and* queried: queried because the material in question does not appear in CRANE³, filtered because it is a pattern created by only a single example yoking only two texts.

[79] Theoretically, one might try to resolve the problem by looking at a group of four texts that contained CRANE²·³·⁴ and another text, which we knew to be earlier or later than that set, in order to try to identify, through analysis of the ten possible subsets, whether CRANE² or [CRANE⁴] was closer to the fourth text. But there are no shared errors linking the three to CRANE¹. The available links are therefore to texts which cannot be dated relative to CRANE, except on the basis of their error totals; the argument thus becomes circular. Moreover, the relationship of CRANE/ALLDE to OKES disqualifies all the relevant patterns involving OKES. The only two unqueried, filtered patterns linking four texts in the required manner are pattern 36 (one example, joining all three to ROSENBACH) and pattern 41 (three examples, joining all three texts to MIDDLETON¹). But the subsets of both these quartets create contradictions. In the case of 36, the pairing [CRANE⁴]-ROSENBACH (6–7 examples) indicates that (C2,C3) cannot come between (C4,RO). That conclusion could be combined with the triplet CRANE²·³-ROSENBACH (1.1.241) to suggest two alternative sequences. On the one hand, [CRANE⁴] might be earlier than ROSENBACH, which might be earlier than CRANE²·³. That possibility seems ruled out by the paucity of Crane spelling and punctuation in ROSENBACH. On the other hand, ROSENBACH might be earlier than [CRANE⁴], but later than CRANE²·³. That runs into the same dilemma: how can ROSENBACH be later than two CRANE texts, when it shows so little evidence of Crane influence? (A solution to that puzzle will be suggested in Sec. XXIII.) As for pattern 41, it runs into the problem that there are no unqueried, filtered subsets (either pairs or triplets) that would determine the sequence. Repeated authorial transference in the NON-CRANE group clearly limits our ability to identify sets and series there, and consequently makes it impossible to use a four-member set to establish the sequence of the three-member set.

[80] For another example, see 3.1.318/1433, where 'flamde' is misprinted in OKES¹ as 'ftand', which is miscorrected to 'ftands' in OKES². The original quarto misreading was made grammatical in the reprint, producing an unauthoritative reading even farther from the shape of the authorial word.

again, we would expect the author to have corrected more errors than he compounded, so the number in MIDDLE-TON[T] probably underestimates the number in its immediate source.

The interpretation of [CRANE[4]] is troubled, again, by the possible relationship of ALLDE to OKES, but there are four cases where the manuscript and/or MATHEWES/ALLDE is identified as later than other texts. Again, these gross totals agree with other evidence that [CRANE[4]] was later than the other CRANE texts. The gross figures are re-inforced by the detail of the CRANE examples. One example (1.1.271) specifically identifies CRANE[3] as later than CRANE[2]. This example was noted by Bawcutt, and is there-fore unlikely to be due to any possible bias on my own part. If accepted, this single variant would clinch the direc-tion of the CRANE subseries (C2→C3), and therefore help clinch the larger series (C2→C3→C4). Likewise, CRANE/ALLDE is later than CRANE[2,3] in two examples (3.1.316, 5.1.13), later than CRANE[1,2] in another (5.2.108). The error at 3.1.316 does not occur in OKES, and hence cannot be attributed to contamination by the other quarto. All these progressive errors might be attributed to the compos-itors of MATHEWES/ALLDE, but that quarto is demonstrably much more accurately printed than OKES, making it likely that at least some and perhaps all of these four progress-ive errors originated in the manuscript, rather than the printing shops.

The security of this conclusion would not be weakened by the existence of lost intermediate manuscripts, because it depends upon sequences of shared error in *relatively* adjacent texts that all belong to a well-defined set. That is, if the subset (C2,C3) contained many lost texts (X[1], C2, X[2], C3, X[3]...X[n]), that expanded subset would still be earlier than [CRANE[4]]. Nor would it matter whether the lost manuscripts in that expanded subset came before, between, or after CRANE[2] and CRANE[3] in a series; for in-stance, the series C2→X[1]→...X[n]→C3 would still precede [CRANE[4]].

This expandability of the subset (C2,C3) is important, because that subset must have contained at least one other manuscript. The evidence for a close relationship between CRANE[2] and CRANE[3], recognized by all editors, is summarized and analysed by Bawcutt (1993). He claims there, as others have, that 'it is unlikely that' CRANE[3] 'is derived directly from' CRANE[2], because CRANE[3] contains two lines (2.2.21–2) and one phrase (3.1.399) not present in CRANE[2] (Bawcutt, 8). Since neither omission leaves an obvious gap in the text, we would not expect the same scribe who actively made or passively transmitted those errors in CRANE[2] to have actively corrected the same errors in CRANE[3]. It is thus virtually certain that Crane did not make CRANE[3] directly from CRANE[2]. Even more obviously, CRANE[2] was not copied directly from CRANE[3] either, because CRANE[3] does not include hundreds of lines present in CRANE[2]. Therefore, either CRANE[3] and CRANE[2] each derives, separately, from a lost manuscript, or CRANE[3] derives from a copy of CRANE[2] corrected by Middleton, a copy in which the two and a half lines missing from

CRANE[2] had been restored. Either the lost manuscript was earlier in the series than CRANE[2] and CRANE[3], or it was later than CRANE[2] and earlier than CRANE[3]. In either case, according to the foregoing analysis that lost manuscript, part of the subset (C3,C3), must have been earlier than [CRANE[4]]. Thus, [CRANE[4]] must have been the last of all extant, or hitherto inferred, CRANE manuscripts of *Game*.

The available evidence thus suggests that the ac-tual chronological series was CRANE[2]→CRANE[3]→[CRANE[4]]. Why then did Nascimento and Howard-Hill place [CRANE[4]] *before* CRANE[2,3]? First, and probably most importantly, because CRANE/MATHEWES/ALLDE contains proportionally less of Crane's characteristic punctuation and spelling; Nascimento and Howard-Hill both presumed that Crane features would progressively increase each time he re-copied the play, particularly if he were producing a new transcript from one of his own previous transcripts. That assumption is almost certainly correct—but there is a fundamental flaw in the way they have *applied* the as-sumption to this particular case. The spelling and punc-tuation of [CRANE[4]] is visible only through the filter of MATHEWES/ALLDE, where Crane's preferences are mixed with those of the unknown compositor(s). For instance, as Howard-Hill (1992) notes, 'in [Mathewes/Allde] there is a general and sporadic diminution of the number of proper nouns and other words distinguished by italic type, probably because the printer's type supply could not cope with Crane's lavish use of the Italian hand' (117).[81] Whatever the sequence of CRANE manuscripts, an actual manuscript in Crane's handwriting (CRANE[2] or CRANE[3]) is certain to preserve more Crane spelling and punctuation than a printed text. Although more than enough Crane features survive in the quarto to prove that the printer's copy-text was indeed a manuscript with many Crane fea-tures, no reliable statistical conclusions can be based on the relative frequencies of such features, when some of the data is taken directly from manuscript and some is merely inferred from a printed text.

Nascimento also characterizes CRANE[2] as the 'least au-thoritative' text (12). Obviously, the 'least authoritative' text cannot be early in the stemma of transmission. But CRANE[2] earns this dubious distinction because it contains the largest number of 'shared substantive variants'. Nas-cimento does not distinguish between shared errors and shared variants; moreover, she defines 'variant' as 'any departure from the reading of' MIDDLETON[T]. Nascimento's 'least authoritative' therefore means 'farthest from MID-DLETON[T]'. But that would only be a reliable measure of the lateness of CRANE[2] if MIDDLETON[T] stood at the beginning of a series. It does not; the quantity of shared error in MIDDLETON[T] demonstrates that it belongs late in the series. Therefore, the text *farthest* from MIDDLETON[T] might well be

---

[81] Howard-Hill was unaware of the division of the text between two printers. The type supply hypothesis will therefore not account for a progressive diminution. It would be better explained by a single copyist, starting out with an effort to preserve Crane's graphic flourishes, and gradually losing interest in doing so. For an hypothesis that the printer's copy-text for MATHEWES/ALLDE was actually a NON-CRANE transcript of [CRANE[4]], see Sec. XIII.

the text *closest* to the beginning of the series of texts of the revised version.

Nascimento and Howard-Hill, in placing [CRANE⁴] before CRANE²,³, relied upon unreliable evidence and arguments. That does not prove they were wrong; it only proves that their claim is unsubstantiated. Their hypothesis is contradicted by the evidence of shared error, and in particular by the logical relationship between interlocking sets and series of shared and progressive error. It is also contradicted by the pattern of accumulating departures from the spelling and punctuation of Middleton's Latin source for 5.1.10–19 (analysed in detail in Sec. IV). However, my own conclusions depend upon methods of analysis unfamiliar to most readers. Fortunately, the same conclusion is supported by other, more familiar kinds of evidence and reasoning.

It is supported, in the first place, by evidence provided by Howard-Hill himself. As noted above, compositors tended to reduce the frequency of many of Crane's characteristics, and consequently a lower incidence of such features in MATHEWES/ALLDE than in CRANE²,³ does not prove that the copy-text for MATHEWES/ALLDE was prepared earlier than the other Crane manuscripts. However, the distribution of one Crane feature—curly brackets for stage directions in the right-hand margin—reverses this expectation: CRANE¹ 0, CRANE² 5, CRANE³ 7, CRANE/MATHEWES/ALLDE 7.[82] These totals confirm all the preceding evidence that CRANE¹ is the earliest in the CRANE sequence, and that CRANE³,⁴ belong at the end of the sequence.

This interpretation of the totals is confirmed by the distribution of actual instances. All three of the later Crane texts share such marginal direction brackets at 3.1.395.1, 5.1.33.1, 5.1.44.1, and 5.3.178.1–2. Apparently, these four brackets originated early in the Crane transcriptions of the revised version of the play, and were then duplicated in Crane's later copies; they were also faithfully reproduced in the printed text. The single example of such a bracket shared by CRANE²,³ but not present in the quarto (at 3.1.262.1–2) occurs in a part of the text set by ALLDE, who also set all four examples of shared curly brackets. This discrepancy is susceptible to two explanations: either the printer reduced the number of such brackets present in [CRANE⁴], or [CRANE⁴] contained fewer curly brackets than the other late Crane texts (and was therefore earlier). But this second explanation is contradicted by the fact that CRANE/ALLDE also contains two additional curly brackets—at 5.1.9.2–5 and 5.3.166.1–3—not present in the other Crane texts (or OKES). It does not seem likely that Allde both added and subtracted examples of this Crane characteristic. Since in general compositors reduce Crane features, and since there are more unique additional brackets than absent ones in CRANE/MATHEWES/ALLDE, it seems likely that the first hypothesis is correct, and that the number of such brackets in the printed quarto was less than the number in lost manuscript [CRANE⁴].

This hypothesis also produces a regular pattern for all four CRANE texts. CRANE² does not contain a single curly bracket not present in one of the other two late Crane texts, but each of them contains two such brackets not present in CRANE². That CRANE² is closest to CRANE¹ is thus indicated not only by the totals of such brackets, but also by their distribution. Because it generally masses entrances at the beginning of a scene, CRANE³ does not contain the mid-scene multi-line entrance directions at 5.1.9.2–5 and 5.3.166.1, which CRANE/ALLDE supplies in the margin with curly brackets; those variants therefore tell us nothing about the relative priority of CRANE³ and [CRANE⁴]. But CRANE³ does uniquely supply curly brackets for mid-scene marginal directions at Induction.52.1–2 and 4.1.97.1–2. These additional brackets indicate that CRANE³ postdates CRANE². But they are more ambiguous evidence of CRANE³'s relationship to [CRANE⁴]. In the second example, CRANE/ALLDE has, presumably accidentally, omitted the entire direction, and there is no way of knowing whether the omission was compositorial or scribal; in any case, where there is no direction there can be no curly bracket, so this example has to be ignored. In the first example, CRANE/MATHEWES moves the direction out of the margin (where it is placed in CRANE¹,²,³), and centres it like a scene-opening entrance direction—an arrangement very unlikely to represent Crane's practice. If that arrangement is compositorial, then it presumably represents further evidence of the quarto reducing the frequency of Crane characteristics—and thus reinforces the conclusion that [CRANE⁴] was the latest of the Crane transcripts. Alternatively, if that arrangement is scribal, then [CRANE⁴] differed from all three extant Crane transcripts; since it cannot be earlier than all three, but could be later, then this explanation, too, would reinforce the conclusion that [CRANE⁴] was the latest of the Crane transcripts.

XI. The Sequence of CRANE Texts: Contractions

As already remarked, English spelling and punctuation provide unreliable evidence of Crane's progressive sophistication of the text, because the practice of [CRANE⁴] was almost certainly sophisticated by the compositors of Mathewes and Allde. The less likely compositorial interference, the more reliable the evidence.

In general, compositors are more likely to re-punctuate or re-spell the text than they are to introduce or remove contractions, in cases where two words might be contracted into one: 'I will' contracted as 'I'll', 'I am' contracted as 'I'm', etc. But Crane's four texts of *Game* demonstrate that he felt free to expand such contractions. Such expansion can take place in two stages: a contraction like 'I'm' can be expanded to 'I'am' (spelling both words in full, but indicating the elision with an apostrophe), or it can be expanded to 'I am' (spelling both words in full, and not indicating the elision in any way). If we take autograph forms in MIDDLETONᵀ and MIDDLETONᴮ as indicative of the author's intention to contract such word pairs (usually

---

[82] Howard-Hill did not give figures for CRANE³ (1992, 117–18); I have supplied that total myself.

for obvious metrical reasons), then we can take expanded forms in CRANE texts as indicative of Crane's unauthorized expansion of authorial contractions. Given Crane's demonstrable tendency to expand such contractions, we might expect that such expansions would increase with each successive re-copying of the text, especially if a new copy was made from one of his own old copies. Therefore, the CRANE text with more expanded contractions should be the later text in the CRANE sequence.

We can test this hypothesis by comparing the treatment of such contractions in CRANE[1] with CRANE[2,3,4], using the table of semi-substantive variants recorded by Nascimento (Appendix 3, pp. 342–51). Nascimento does not record all variants in all texts involving elision, but she does record all cases where an elided form in MIDDLETON[T] is expanded in other texts; these are the cases relevant to this enquiry, since they are cases where the author's intention to provide one of his characteristc elisions has been overridden by Crane's tendency to expand elisions. Since CRANE[1] is clearly the earliest of the CRANE texts, we should expect to find that the three later texts contain many more expanded forms. And that is exactly what we do find. In fifty-five cases, a contracted form in CRANE[1] is expanded in one or more of the three later CRANE texts. By contrast, in only seven cases does one of the three later texts contain a more contracted form than CRANE[1].

This evidence is statistical, and must be interpreted in terms of relative probability. It is not surprising that Crane is sometimes inconsistent, or that there are occasional exceptions to the larger pattern: human beings are not reliable machines. What matters to this kind of argument is not the individual case, but the overall pattern. The fact that there are seven 'exceptions' does not mean that our initial hypothesis has been contradicted; there are almost eight times as many expansions as contractions in the later Crane texts. This is what we would expect: not 'no' contractions in the later texts, but a significantly smaller number of contractions than expansions.

Nevertheless, the seven exceptions are interesting in themselves. (The reading of the lemma is from MIDDLETON[T].)

3.1.117   I'me] I'am CRANE[2]; I am CRANE[1,3,4]
4.1.141   ya'ue] y'aue CRANE[2]; y'haue CRANE[1]; you haue CRANE[3,4]
4.1.144   ya're] y'are CRANE[2]; you'are CRANE[3]; you are CRANE[1,4]
4.2.77   Im'e] I'am CRANE[2]; I am CRANE[1,3,4]
5.2.54   ya're] y'ar CRANE[2,3]; you're CRANE[1]; you are [CRANE[4]]
5.3.158   ya're] y'are CRANE[2]; you're CRANE[1]; you are CRANE[3,4]
5.3.162   Ime lost] I'am ~ CRANE[2]; I am ~ CRANE[1,3,4]

In every one of these seven exceptions, CRANE[2] preserves the contracted form; in one case it is joined by CRANE[3], but never by [CRANE[4]]. This pattern fits the conjectural relationship of the early texts visualized in Figure 2: none

of the later CRANE texts is a direct copy of CRANE[1], because all of them descend from [KING'S MEN[1]]. Thus, CRANE[2] might occasionally have retained contractions present in the playbook, which had been expanded in the dead-end CRANE[1]. Comparison of CRANE[1] with the other Crane texts thus establishes (1) that later Crane texts expand contractions more than early Crane texts, and (2) that CRANE[2] is the only text that has any significant number of such elisions not already present in CRANE[1].

The second observation suggests that CRANE[2] is earlier than CRANE[3], too. If we compare those two texts directly, using Nascimento's table, we find that CRANE[2] has the more contracted form nineteen times, whereas CRANE[3] has the more contracted form only twice (Induction.72, 5.3.115). If CRANE[1] is earlier than the other Crane texts, then CRANE[2] is earlier than CRANE[3]. Likewise, CRANE[3] seems to be earlier than [CRANE[4]]: CRANE[3] has the more contracted form fifteen times, whereas [CRANE[4]] has it only eight times.

Since this test seems to work in discriminating CRANE[1] from the later Crane texts, we should also expect it to identify whether CRANE[2] or [CRANE[4]] is the earlier text; since CRANE[2] seems to be earlier than CRANE[3], which in turn seems to be earlier than [CRANE[4]], then we should expect CRANE[2] to be earlier than [CRANE[4]]. Again, this hypothesis is confirmed, in a further demonstration of the consistency of this kind of evidence. In nine cases, [CRANE[4]] has a more contracted form than CRANE[2].[83] But CRANE[2] has a more contracted form than [CRANE[4]] in thirty-three cases.[84] The difference here cannot be due to the compositors of MATHEWES/ALLDE, because CRANE[2] has fewer expansions in the shares of both printers.[85]

The significant increase in expansions in [CRANE[4]] does not coincide with the change of printers, but occurs between Act Three and Act Four: in the last two acts CRANE[2] has one additional expansion, but [CRANE[4]] has nineteen. A similar pattern is evident by comparison with CRANE[3]: in the first three acts [CRANE[4]] has the more expanded form seven times (to six for CRANE[3]), but in the last two acts it has eight (to only two for CRANE[3]). Perhaps this increase in expansions in the last two acts reflects a change in the copy-text for [CRANE[4]] itself; but even if that were true, [CRANE[4]] would still reflect a later stage than CRANE[2] in Crane's progressive sophistication of the text. The evidence of elisions thus confirms the arguments from set theory, shared errors, progressive errors, and departures from the spelling and punctuation

[83] Induction.65, Induction.72, 1.1.331, 3.1.6, 142, 3.1.207, 3.1.250, 3.1.278, 4.1.132.
[84] Induction.6, 1.1.70, 139, 1.1.224, 1.1.290, 1.1.304, 2.1.164, 2.2.197, 3.1.8, 3.1.62, 3.1.95, 117, 3.1.144, 4.1.66 (two), 4.1.97, 102, 141, 144, 146, 4.2.77, 5.2.20, 5.2.23, 5.2.54, 5.2.58, 5.2.64, 5.3.53, 5.3.82, 116, 158, 162, 199.
[85] CRANE[4]/MATHEWES 14 versus CRANE[2] 6, CRANE[4]/ALLDE 19 versus CRANE[2] 3. Although the disparity is greater in ALLDE's share of the text, even in MATHEWES's share it is more than double.

of Middleton's Latin source for 5.1: CRANE[2] and CRANE[3] are chronologically earlier than [CRANE[4]].

Since the treatment of contractions involving two words seems significant, it might be useful to examine the smaller number of elisions which involve the loss of a prefix: 'gainst (2.2.14, 3.1.88), 'mongst (2.2.17, 3.1.81), 'specially (3.1.66), 'twixt (3.1.146), 'bout (3.1.147, 4.2.61), 'mazed (3.1.186), 'las (3.1.296). None of these ten elided forms is expanded in CRANE[1]; two of the expanded forms occur in CRANE[2], three in CRANE[3], and nine in [CRANE[4]]. These variants show the same pattern as the variants involving two-word contractions, suggesting that the Crane texts were composed in the order in which I have numbered them.

Finally, since these contraction-expansion variants also suggest that CRANE[2] is earlier than CRANE[3], we can further test the reliability of that evidence by comparing it with other evidence of the sequence of those two texts. There are relatively few variants between them; most often, both together agree or disagree with [CRANE[4]], or one of them agrees with both CRANE[1] and [CRANE[4]], and none of those configurations gives any clear indication of sequence. But in a small number of cases either CRANE[2] or CRANE[3] is the only one of the later Crane texts to agree with CRANE[1] in a reading that could be correct. In these few cases, one text seems to be closer than the other to CRANE[1]. Once, CRANE[3] shares a unique reading with CRANE[1]: 2.2.237 ('in' for 'at'). By contrast, CRANE[2] shares such a reading with CRANE[1] four times: Induction.52.2 ('as'), 1.1.242.1 ('Ex[t].'), 5.2.106.1 ('and White Queen'), 5.2.108 ('W.Q.' for 'W.Q.P.').

Crane's expansions of contractions are indifferent variants; by the criteria used to define 'shared error' in the foregoing analysis, they do not constitute errors, and they have not been included in my earlier statistical analysis. However, the expansions do apparently misrepresent the author's metrical intentions, and to that extent they do constitute corruptions of the kind that modern editors would normally wish to correct. To that extent, CRANE[3] is a more corrupt text than CRANE[2], and [CRANE[4]] is even more corrupt than CRANE[3]. In each case, since the same scribe is involved, the more corrupt text is almost certainly a chronologically later text in the sequence of transmission.

XII. The Sequence of CRANE Texts: Censorship and Playhouse Cuts

Just as the foregoing analysis of shared errors has excluded any cases of extrametrical expansion of contractions, so too it has excluded variants that might be attributed to censorship. Almost by definition, and certainly in the case of *Game*, censorship produces variants that cannot be confidently identified as errors. Censored readings generally make sense, even if they do not make the objectionable sense originally intended by the author. We know that *Game* was read and licensed by the Master of the Revels, Sir Henry Herbert. Herbert may or may not have objected to the play's larger political agenda, but he certainly had

strong views about dramatic language, and particularly about oaths and expletives. Editors therefore have good reason to examine variants with the possibility of censorship in mind, and to regard with particular suspicion variants that resemble other known cases of censorship, especially if the variants seem to reflect Herbert's known sensitivities.

1.1.209 by this hand] *not in* CRANE[2,3]
2.1.105 blesse me] he CRANE[3]
2.1.200 by this light] CRANE[1], CRANE[4], ROSENBACH; Anglica CRANE[2,3]; by this hand MIDDLETON[T], BRIDGEWATER, OKES
2.2.177 'Lord] CRANE[1]; oh CRANE[2] +
3.2.31 by this hand] *not in* CRANE[4]/ALLDE, OKES. [Whole scene not in CRANE[2,3].]
4.2.96 masse] *not in* CRANE[2,3,4]
5.2.87 light] MIDDLETON[T], ROSENBACH; slid MIDDLETON[B]; *not in* CRANE, OKES
5.2.116 Death] How CRANE[2,3,4]; How Death ROSENBACH
5.3.122 'faith] CRANE[1]; *not in* CRANE[2] +

These are the only nine variants in *Game* involving oaths or expletives of a kind elsewhere censored by Herbert. We might therefore rank the extant texts in terms of how many of the nine they preserve: CRANE[1] 8; MIDDLETON[T], BRIDGEWATER, ROSENBACH 7; OKES 5; [CRANE[4]] 3; CRANE[2] 1; CRANE[3] 0.

This pattern has clear implications for the transmission of the text. I have already noted (section III, above) that the unique CRANE[1] readings at 2.2.177 and 5.3.122 contradict Howard-Hill's stemma. That evidence can now be seen as part of a larger pattern. CRANE[1] is the least censored of all the extant texts; by contrast, CRANE[2,3,4] are the most censored. The distribution pattern of apparent censorship thus confirms the distribution pattern of shared errors (section VII): CRANE[1] does not belong to the same group as CRANE[2,3,4]. The presence of variants apparently reflecting censorship of oaths and expletives is not a function of the presence of Crane as a scribe.

Howard-Hill ignores this pattern, attributing all the censorship to Crane himself. He notes that Crane felt free to alter the spelling, punctuation, and layout of the text, to provide scene divisions, and to regularize the presentation of speech prefixes and stage directions; these are functions regularly performed by editors of Shakespeare from the seventeenth to the twentieth centuries, and in that sense Crane can be called 'Shakespeare's earliest editor' (Howard-Hill 1992). Middleton might have regarded such formal alterations as embellishments: like the professional elegance of Crane's handwriting, they enhanced the cultural credentials of the text. But a licence to present the text more elegantly did not necessarily or obviously entail a licence to censor or bowdlerize it. Crane exercised his editorial control over punctuation, spelling, and layout in all four texts of *Game* for which he was responsible. By contrast, the treatment of profanity radically differs between one Crane text and the other three. Moreover, we know that *Game* passed through the hands of another agent who, unlike Crane, was specifically entitled and expected to censor it: Henry Herbert. Herbert, unlike Crane, was not employed by the author, instructed by the author, or dismissable by the author. Herbert, unlike Crane, is known to have removed comparable oaths and expletives from other texts.[86]

As I argued elsewhere, there is no reliable evidence of a purely literary or editorial expurgation of dramatic texts before 1623–4.[87] Whether or not that larger claim is accepted, no analysis of apparent expurgation can afford to ignore the possibility that it was demanded by the Master of the Revels—particularly when that Master was Herbert. In attributing the expurgation to Crane, Howard-Hill ignores Herbert's role in the evolution of the text of *Game* in the summer of 1624. By ignoring Herbert, he must also ignore the radical disparity between one Crane text and the other three.

That disparity is easily explained, if we assume that *Game* evolved normally between the author's first draft and the script performed by the actors. As originally written by Middleton, the text almost certainly contained at least some material which was later deleted or altered by the censor. We would therefore expect any copy of the author's first draft to be more profane than copies of the play which derive from the censored playbook; CRANE[1] is a copy of the author's first draft, and it is more profane than any text of the revised version. The obvious explanation for this pattern is that all texts of the revised version derive, at one or more removes, from the censored playbook.

If each text derived from the playbook had simply reproduced the text of its immediate predecessor, without alteration, then profanities removed by the censor would never have been restored. But Middleton himself prepared all or part of at least two, and probably three, of the NON-CRANE texts: MIDDLETON[T], MIDDLETON[B], and [MIDDLETON/OKES]. Since the Master of the Revels had no authority over circulating manuscript texts of *Game*, Middleton could legitimately restore readings that had been expurgated in performance. But 'transference is intrinsically unlikely to remove all errors' (para. 21), and not surprisingly Middleton apparently failed to restore two expurgated profanities at 2.2.177 and 5.3.122. Nevertheless, 'the author is better able than any other copyist to engage in transference' (para. 32), and not surprisingly four profanities that appear to be original are restored by Middleton at 1.1.209, 3.2.31, 4.2.96, and 5.2.116. Elsewhere, Middleton appears to have remembered that the uncensored text had contained some oath, but did not remember exactly what it originally was, or remembered the original reading but chose to revise it: 'an author is likely to introduce variation into the original transmission' (para. 34). Hence, at 2.1.200 what appears to have been the original reading 'by this light' was revised in three later texts to 'by this hand'; at 5.2.87 Middleton in his own hand wrote 'light' in one text and 'slid' in another. Indeed, in this last case

the original text may not have contained any profanity at all: since 'an author is likely to introduce variation into the original transmission' (para. 34), that variation might include adding new profanities, as well as altering original profanities.[88] We can therefore not be certain that Middleton's first draft contained any oath at 5.2.87—which means that there is not a single unambiguous example of expurgation in CRANE[1].

The distribution of variants apparently resulting from expurgation can thus be explained by two normal processes: (1) censorship of the playbook by the Master of the Revels, followed by (2) sporadic authorial restoration of profanity in some late copies. As a consequence of these two opposing processes, the texts with the most profanity would be the first and last in the stemma of transmission: texts deriving from the uncensored authorial first draft (CRANE[1]) and late authorial copies, or copies of late authorial copies (the NON-CRANE group). The pattern of distribution of profanity thus confirms the pattern of distribution of shared error, not only for the CRANE texts, but for all eight texts. The most heavily expurgated texts would be those in the middle of the sequence of transmission, those closest to the censored playbook: CRANE[2] and CRANE[3]. The expurgation of those texts thus apparently has nothing to do with the editorial activities of Ralph Crane, who left profanity intact in CRANE[1]; instead, the expurgation of profanity in CRANE[2] and CRANE[3] reflects Crane's accurate transcription of the playbook version of the play. In so far as both CRANE[2] and CRANE[3] are more heavily expurgated than [CRANE[4]], both appear to be earlier, and closer to the playbook, than [CRANE[4]].

CRANE[2] and CRANE[3] differ in only a single variant which might be due to expurgation: at 2.1.105, CRANE[3] has 'he threatens Me' (Bawcutt 434) where CRANE[2] reads ''blesse me! 'threatens me'. But it is difficult to be sure whether this variant results from expurgation, or is instead related to the systematic abridgement of the text in CRANE[3]. Because CRANE[3] cuts the remainder of the White Queen Pawn's speech (and the next two speeches), it ends this phrase with a full stop, as does no other text of the play.[89] The unique punctuation in CRANE[3] reflects the fact that the following line, cut in CRANE[3], repeats and

---

[86] Crane's transcript of 'vpon my soule' is scribbled over (probably by Crane) at line 2425 of the King's Men's manuscript of Fletcher and Massinger's *Barnavelt*. This manuscript was censored by the Master of the Revels and annotated for playhouse use; the expurgation is therefore, at the very least, anticipatory of censorship and performance. For evidence that Crane was *not* responsible for expurgation of private transcripts, see Taylor and Jowett, 51–106, 115–117. (That analysis did not dwell upon *A Game at Chess*, because when it was written I had not studied the relationships of the extant witnesses; hence, the new evidence here confirms the earlier analysis, and vice versa.) For Herbert's exceptionally strong resistance to a wide range of expletives and profanity see Bawcutt (1996), 73.

[87] Taylor and Jowett 1993, 51–106. This work appeared too late for Howard-Hill to take account of—or challenge—its arguments; it is not listed in the bibliography of *Pasquin*.

[88] For another possible example of a profanity added by Middleton in [MIDDLETON/OKES], see note on 'God bless us' at Add.C.2/1437–8.

[89] MIDDLETON[T] and uncorrected BRIDGEWATER have no punctuation here; a comma suffices for CRANE[1,4], ROSENBACH, and OKES; CRANE[2] has a colon, and the BRIDGEWATER corrector adds an exclamation mark in pencil.

therefore clarifies the grammatical elision ('threatens me, and quite dismays'). In other words, CRANE[3] *cuts* material *after* 'threatens me', and simultaneously *adds* the word 'he' *before* 'threatens me'. That addition, in turn, added an extra syllable to a line already metrically overloaded (twelve syllables in CRANE[2] and all other texts). Since the whole purpose of the abridgement is to shorten the text, 'bless me' might have been sacrificed as part of the same process which cut the rest of the White Queen's Pawn's speech. Given the complexity of interlocking variation here, it is impossible to be sure whether CRANE[3]'s omission of 'blesse me' is a targeted expurgation or a mere side effect of abridgement. If the omission of 'Blesse me' is not an example of expurgation, then CRANE[2] and CRANE[3] contain an equal number of variants due to censorship. In any case, a single ambiguous example cannot provide reliable evidence of the sequence of transmission.

As this variant demonstrates, the problem of expurgation often intersects with the more general problem of cutting. Here, in the deliberately abridged text of CRANE[3], it is impossible to be sure whether, in a specific instance, we are dealing with expurgation or another kind of cutting. The playbook, on which the Master of the Revels would have marked certain objectionable phrases for deletion, could also have indicated any larger cuts made by the acting company, on their own or in response to the censor. Howard-Hill, who attributes every instance of expurgation to Crane, also attributes to Crane all of the cutting of the text in CRANE[2] and CRANE[3].

The problem of censorship thus extends beyond examples of profanity to more general issues of textual abridgement. For instance, although CRANE[1] is generally shorter than the revised version, it contains two lines (*Early* 5.290–1) that are not present at the corresponding point in any of the texts of the expanded version (*Later* 5.3.104–5); as I argue in the textual notes, that omission seems almost certainly due to political censorship. Again, CRANE[1] appears to be the least censored of the extant texts.

Obviously, though, not all cuts can be attributed to censorship. No one supposes that the abridgement evident in CRANE[3] resulted from censorship. Therefore, it must have had some other motive. Moreover, CRANE[3] is the text originally responsible for identifying Crane as the scribe who prepared copy-text for various plays printed in the 1623 Shakespeare folio. Comparison with other texts of *Game*, and with other texts by Middleton, demonstrates conclusively that Crane himself must have been responsible for the so-called 'massed entrances' in CRANE[3], its scene divisions, and most of its spelling and punctuation. But who abridged the play?

Howard-Hill (1992) claims that Crane was responsible. But Middleton, not Crane, was apparently responsible for the abridgements which produced the extant texts of *Penniless Parliament* and *Macbeth*. Describing Middleton's treatment of the Italian play which was the source of *No Wit*, Gordon observed that 'Everything extraneous to the action has been cut out...The quantity of dialogue is cut down. The points are made more quickly, and are not reiterated so much...As usual, Middleton has cut down his original' (404, 408, 411). In his introduction to *Women Beware*, Mulryne concluded that 'in re-organizing his source-material, Middleton compresses a great deal, sharpening up the narrative' (li); likewise, Cawley and Gaines remarked that the playwright 'abbreviates' the source-material for *Yorkshire*, thereby producing a 'telescoping of events' in 'a more concentrated fashion' (12–13). Describing CRANE[3], Bald observed that 'The cuts have been made with considerable skill, and if there were no other texts one would never suspect that so many lines had been omitted' (1929, 29). Middleton, obviously, was a man of 'considerable skill' in constructing intelligible dramatic texts, and in abridging texts; whether Crane had such skills is simply conjecture. Middleton is, intrinsically, the likelier candidate for 'the application of a literary intelligence to familiar material' (Howard-Hill 1992, 124).

What makes Howard-Hill's conjecture possible is the fact that cuts in themselves leave no authorship markers; hence, cuts can always be attributed to someone other than the author. However, if the cuts are accompanied by other changes, then it might be possible to demonstrate that those other changes are authorial. As the autograph texts of *Game* demonstrate, and as Howard-Hill has himself argued elsewhere (1986), Middleton was an unreliable copyist; he could not copy his text without altering its verbal texture, incidentally, not as part of a systematically revised vision of the work, but simply as a kind of verbal restlessness. Consequently, if Middleton himself abridged *Game*, then we should expect to find, within Crane's scribal representation of that abridgement, a scattering of variants which seem to be authorial.

That is, indeed, exactly what we find. Howard-Hill claims that the abridgement 'shows Crane in a more inventive capacity, writing transitional textual adjustments and occasional phrases to compensate for deletions' (124). But he gives no evidence for Crane's authorship of these adjustments and phrases. As I argue in more detail in the Textual Notes, CRANE[3] contains unique verbal variants at 2.1.181, 2.2.17, 3.1.311, and 4.4.63 that are not required by the act of abridgement itself, and which are in each instance demonstrably Middletonian. Equally remarkably, CRANE[3] contains at 3.1.395.1 a unique variant in the form of a stage direction; that form occurs eighteen times elsewhere in Middleton (though in no other text of *Game*), but never appears in any other known Crane text. The number of variants which can be identified as authorial is quite remarkable, given the paucity of variants unique to CRANE[3]; most of the variants—like cutting, or grammatical changes made to smooth transitions—involve changes of a kind which are intrinsically impossible to attribute. Thus, there is strong evidence that Middleton was himself responsible for the abridgement; CRANE[3] apparently derives, at one or more removes, from a lost manuscript of the abridgement made by Middleton himself. Thus, the conclusion which was always intrinsically the most probable is independently supported by strong verbal evidence.

If Middleton himself abridged the play, occasionally making small verbal changes in the process, then there is no reason to attribute to Crane variants like the substitution of 'he' for 'blesse me' at 2.1.105. More significantly, we are left with no reason to believe that Crane felt qualified or entitled to abridge the text on his own initiative. That conclusion, in turn, affects our attitude to certain significant variants shared by both CRANE² and CRANE³.

Although in other respects CRANE² provides a full text of the revised version, it does omit three passages: some lines from the middle of one of the Fat Bishop's speeches (Additional Passage A, after 2.2.22), some lines from the beginning of one of the Black Knight's speeches (*Early* 2.336–8; Additional Passage B, after *Later* 2.2.153), and the whole of '3.2' (Additional Passage D). This third cut must be deliberate: *Early* 3.281—'pray followe mee then and Ile ease you instantlie'—has been altered in CRANE² alone to 'Why then observe: I'll ease you instantly' (*Later* 3.1.345); moreover, the speeches attributed to the Jesting Pawn in the bag in 5.3 are in CRANE² alone attributed instead to an unspecified 'Paw[ne]'. CRANE³ also omits 3.2 (and 3.1.344–5); because it also omits the entire bag sequence in 5.3, like CRANE² it creates no inconsistency by its omission of 3.2. Of CRANE²'s two other cuts, the one after 2.2.153 disappears in the midst of a larger cut in CRANE³; that text also cuts the earlier speech of the Fat Bishop (Add. Passage A). Since CRANE² cannot derive from CRANE³, this overlap between the two texts presumably results from the fact that the process of abridgement began on a text of the play that, like CRANE², had already omitted 3.2, and perhaps also the two passages in 2.2.

As Nascimento remarked, the cuts in CRANE² are deliberate: 'nothing essential has been deleted', and she was 'tempted to think that' CRANE² 'might have derived in some way from the promptbook' (42). The Jesting Pawns are certainly unimportant to the progress of the plot; the comic diversion they provided in the original version of the play is supplied in the revised version, more expansively, by the Fat Bishop. The omitted lines of the Fat Bishop are dispensable; the omitted lines of the Black Knight are not only dispensable, but create a problem in the play's chess allegory. 'There is, then, no omission' in CRANE² 'that might not also have been found in the promptbook' (Nascimento, 43).

Nascimento nevertheless rejects this hypothesis. But her reasons for rejecting it reflect the dubious editorial orthodoxies of the Bowers era. First, she notes that CRANE² contains 'no obvious promptbook features, i.e. anticipatory stage directions, names of actors, props, etc.' (43). But Greg long ago demonstrated that the absence of anticipatory directions is poor evidence for the provenance of a manuscript (1931, 219; 1955, 138). Moreover, there is

no reason to believe that Crane would have reproduced such elements, even if he found them in his copy-text. Crane certainly knew the difference between a promptbook and a literary transcript designed for a private reader. Secondly, Nascimento notes that CRANE² 'contains many descriptive stage directions' (44). Again, Greg demonstrated that playbooks regularly duplicate such gratuitous descriptive details (1931, 208; 1955, 132). Thirdly, Nascimento notes that CRANE² lacks five exits 'which would be necessary in a promptbook' (44). But existing manuscript playbooks often lack exits (Taylor and Jowett 111–2). CRANE² does omit two necessary entrances for the Black Queen's Pawn (3.1.206.1, 5.2.87.1), and playbooks are much less likely to omit entrance directions; but in the first case CRANE² has already called for the entrance of the entire Black House, and in the second case it has already called for the Black Queen's Pawn to speak 'within' in three successive speeches, effectively marking her entrance by the switch from 'within' to an unmarked speech prefix. Even if the playbook supplied a specific entrance direction in both cases, the absence of those two directions from CRANE² would prove only that CRANE² is a copy, not of the playbook itself, but of a copy of that playbook, one which—like all copies—had introduced some errors of its own. This error, in other words, might have been accidentally made in CRANE² or in [PRE-CRANE²]; it may tell us nothing about the King's Men's playbook.

This last point is also relevant to Nascimento's final objection: 'What we know of the circumstances surrounding the play makes it unlikely that Crane had access to a promptbook' (44). But it is not necessary to suppose that CRANE² was copied directly from the playbook; the stemmatic evidence may demonstrate that CRANE² was closer to the playbook than is any other extant text, but it cannot determine how many lost manuscripts stand between that playbook and CRANE². Crane himself, therefore, need never have had access to the playbook. But at some point Middleton or Crane or someone else associated with them must have had such access, in order to copy the revised version of the play from the only texts in which it existed, [KING'S MEN¹], the King's Men's playbook—or, less plausibly, [KING'S MEN²], the collection of parts and plat that regulated performances. That resulting copy of the playbook—a lost manuscript I have been calling [KING'S MEN³]—could have been made at any time before August 21, when the King's Men delivered the playbook itself to the Privy Council. Since CRANE¹ is dated August 13, either Crane or Middleton had at least seven days, after they had begun working to meet the demand for copies of the play, to make a copy of the playbook; because there were no performances after August 14, for six of those days the playbook was not in use by the King's Men. The historical circumstances thus leave plenty of opportunity, and incentive, to produce one or more copies of the playbook. None of Nascimento's arguments, and none of the textual evidence, mitigates against the conclusion that CRANE[2] is a copy—or a copy of a copy—of [KING'S MEN[3]].

Indeed, it is hard to account for the peculiarities of CRANE[2] in any other way. If its cuts do not derive from the playbook, where did they originate? None of the three can be accidental. Howard-Hill attributes them to Crane, but this claim is part of a global misrepresentation of Crane's activities here, which also attributes to him the abridgement of the text (much more plausibly credited to Middleton) and the expurgation of the text (much more plausibly credited to Herbert). Why would Crane cut these three passages, and not others? Howard-Hill imagines that Crane objected to the bawdy of 3.2, but he could have eliminated the bawdy by cutting a few words or phrases, not the whole scene. More obviously, if Crane objected to bawdy he could never have transcribed anything by Middleton (or Fletcher); nor will an aversion to bawdy account for the two other cuts. Why would he cut these passages when producing CRANE[2], but not in CRANE[1] or [CRANE[4]]? Why should the cuts (which look like cuts in a playbook) occur in the very text which is most heavily expurgated (like a playbook)? Why should all these features, which resemble a playbook, be concentrated in a text which, on so many other grounds, seems to be the earliest complete text of the revised version of the play?

XIII. The Sequence of CRANE Texts: Transference

On the evidence of set theory, of shared errors, of progressive errors, of Latin spelling and punctuation, of contractions and elisions, of censorship, and of apparent theatrical cuts, the subset (CRANE[2], CRANE[3]) is closer to the performed play, and chronologically earlier in the sequence of Crane texts, than [CRANE[4]]. On the evidence of variants shared with CRANE[1], of Latin spelling and punctuation, of contractions and elisions, CRANE[2] is chronologically earlier in the sequence of Crane texts than CRANE[3]. On the circumstantial evidence of other works, and the direct evidence of five verbal variants, Middleton himself was responsible for the abridgement of the text, scribally reproduced in CRANE[3]. Middleton might have performed the abridgement by producing, himself, a new, shorter manuscript of the whole play, an autograph manuscript which was later copied by Crane to produce CRANE[3] (and probably other copies); or Middleton might have marked up (in pencil?) a lost full-length manuscript, and then have given that annotated text to Crane, with instructions to produce one or more copies of the play, abridged as he had indicated; or Middleton might have been sitting next to Crane, with both of them looking at a full-length manuscript of the play, and Middleton dictating the abridgement aloud, deciding on the cuts as he went along. Since we cannot be sure of the exact nature of the process, it seems best to refer to this stage of transmission simply as '[MIDDLETON ABRIDGEMENT]'. Given the high frequency of Crane markers in CRANE[3], I suspect there was not an intervening manuscript, with authorial spelling and punctuation throughout. But there might have been, because we have no way of knowing how many lost

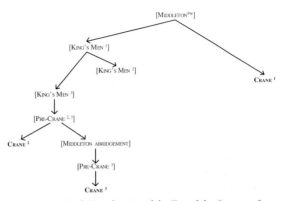

Figure 3. Draft Visualization of the Top of the Stemma of Transmission. The vertical axis is chronological: thus, although CRANE[1] was copied directly from [MIDDLETON[PRE]], it was produced after the play was in performance, and therefore after creation of the licensed playbook, [KING'S MEN[1]], and the parts and plat necessary for performance, [KING'S MEN[2]]. Hence, CRANE[1] is lower on the vertical axis than [KING'S MEN[1,2]].

copies intervened between [MIDDLETON ABRIDGEMENT] and CRANE[3]. Certainly, CRANE[3] itself cannot have been the text produced by dictation. Its massed entrances must have been Crane's work, not Middleton's, and it would not make sense to combine, in one transcription, the process of dictated authorial abridgement and the process of scribal reorganization of entrance directions. In any case, the uniquely-high frequency of Crane spelling and punctuation makes it highly probable that the immediate antecedent of CRANE[3] was another Crane transcript, which we can call [PRE-CRANE[3]].[90]

We are now in a position to expand and clarify my earlier hypothesis (Figure 2) about the initial stages of the transmission of the play; Figure 3 shows the new hypothesis. I have not located [CRANE[4]] on this stemma. Although I believe I have presented strong evidence that it is chronologically later than the extant Crane manuscripts, [CRANE[4]] does present problems that have not been resolved by the preceding analysis. In particular, my argument up to this point has been based on the assumption that each Crane text is an homogeneous entity. None of the three extant Crane manuscripts of *Game* is divided between scribes; Crane typically worked alone. However, a single scribe can work from composite copy-text. We cannot presume 'that *whole texts* are the source of other *whole texts*' (para. 42). Although as a whole [CRANE[4]] is clearly later than CRANE[2,3], it is

---

90 Middleton's involvement makes it theoretically possible that CRANE[3] descends from CRANE[2], since Middleton in the course of abridging the play might have supplied the two and a half lines missing from CRANE[2] but present in CRANE[1]. But it seems relatively unlikely that Middleton would have *added* lines, when engaged in the large-scale task of *abridging* the play. I have therefore agreed with Howard-Hill (Figure 1) in postulating that both CRANE[2] and CRANE[3] derive, separately, from the lost [PRE-CRANE[2,3]]. Whichever scenario we postulate, CRANE[2] is chronologically earlier than CRANE[3], and no extant manuscript can have come between them.

theoretically conceivable that *part* of [CRANE⁴] might be *earlier* than CRANE²,³—or that *part* of it derives from an *earlier* source. At the very least, we need to consider this possibility, which will also force us to examine certain categories of evidence that have led previous scholars to believe that [CRANE⁴] was early rather than late.

CRANE/MATHEWES shares an historical error with CRANE¹ (and uncorrected BRIDGEWATER) at 3.1.188 (ship/ships), which might be coincidental or authorial. The variant has been retained at *Early* 3.120, and has not been counted among shared errors. However, earlier editors did consider it an error of transmission, and my interpretation might be accused of bias.[91] Strikingly, CRANE/MATHEWES shares four unique variants with CRANE¹ in the preceding thirty lines: 3.1.157 (the/that), 159 (Adversaries/Adversary), 168 (Piece/Duke), 173 (t'/to). In isolation, the second and fourth might be dismissed as inadvertent coincidence, but the third cannot; nor can coincidence be plausibly invoked five times in thirty-one lines.

Another clutch of such pairings occurs in a forty-line stretch in the next scene, set by a different printer: CRANE¹ and CRANE/ALLDE are the only texts to supply scene breaks at 3.2.0.1 and 3.3.0.1, to divide 3.2.38–40 after the word 'flies', and to contain the variants 'on' instead of 'upon' at 3.2.25, the expanded form 'I am' at 3.2.28, and '*Enter 2. Bl. Pawne*' at 3.2.29.1. None of these six variants is an error; these are all 'indifferent variants'. Nevertheless, the clustering of unique links between CRANE¹ and [CRANE⁴]—texts that, according to the preceding analysis, are separated by at least five intervening texts—is remarkable, and not easily attributable to random variation.

The anomaly is made clearer by comparison with other possible pairings. Altogether, MATHEWES/ALLDE shares with CRANE¹ sixteen readings not present in any other text (not counting ambiguous spellings, or variant speech prefix forms where the intended speaker is not in doubt): four substantive variants, one lineation variant, two stage directions, two scene divisions, two speech prefixes, and five semi-substantives.[92] Only one other text shares so many unique substantive pairings with CRANE¹: MIDDLETONᵀ shares twenty-three such pairings. But those links between CRANE¹ and MIDDLETONᵀ have already been explained (Sec. III): original readings preserved in CRANE¹, then corrupted or revised in intervening copies, were restored by the author in MIDDLETONᵀ. That is a classic example of what is usually called sophistication or contamination, but what I have proposed to call 'transference' (para. 19). But that mechanism of authorial transference will not explain the number of such 'restorations' in a copy prepared by Crane directly from previous Crane copies.

Of course, for the six shared variants involving 3.2, an alternative explanation is obvious: the scene was not present in CRANE²,³. In conjunction with the restoration of 3.2, CRANE/ALLDE also restores the original last line of 3.1, altered in CRANE² and absent from CRANE³, and the opening stage direction of 3.3, absent in CRANE²,³; these

readings are not unique to CRANE¹ and CRANE/ALLDE, but they cannot have come from CRANE²,³. The presence in CRANE/ALLDE of 3.2, and of the transitional material before and after that scene, must derive from some source other than CRANE²,³. But this explanation of the shared variants implies a larger scenario, with larger implications. If some other source was used to supply a text of 3.2, then CRANE⁴ derives from at least two sources, not one. If that other source was used in 3.2 to supply a deficiency in the earlier Crane manuscripts, then that source could also presumably have been used in the two places in 2.2 where both CRANE² and CRANE³ lack material present in CRANE/MATHEWES (Add. Passages A and B).

If my foregoing arguments about the Crane texts are correct, then [CRANE⁴] was the fullest reading text of the play so far created: it ignored apparently theatrical cuts, while incorporating the additions of the revised playbook. The result is a reading text, not specifically linked to the theatre. In this respect, CRANE⁴ resembles CRANE³, which also offers a literary text specifically designed for readers. But whereas CRANE³ produced a literary text by abridgement, CRANE⁴ produced one by conflation. If my preceding analysis is correct, then [CRANE⁴] offered more text than was ever acted. It thus resembled the 1623 quarto of Webster's *Duchess of Malfi*, for which Middleton had written commendatory verses. The title-page of *Duchess* advertised 'The perfect and exact Coppy, with diuerse things Printed, that the length of the Play would not beare in the Presentment'; that quarto also included a song which the author specifically 'disclaims...to be his' (3.4). Thus, *Duchess* retained material cut in performances, but also included material added for performance by someone other than the author. The manuscript from which Middleton's associate Nicholas Okes printed *Duchess* was apparently in the hand of Ralph Crane (Brown, lxv–lxvii; Gunby *et al.*, 452–6). The expanded text of *Duchess* was thus prepared, obviously with the author's approval and assistance, by the same scribe who prepared the expanded text of *Game* in [CRANE⁴].

In order to create this new 'perfect and exact Coppy, with diuerse things [included], that the length of the Play would not beare in the Presentment', Crane's recent transcripts of the play (CRANE², CRANE³, and probably other lost texts prepared before or after) would have had to be supplemented; another source was needed, an earlier source, containing material that had been cut in the theatre. But it made no sense to abandon all the elegant work Crane had done in making the intervening transcripts; as the preceding analysis has demonstrated, CRANE⁴ was in many respects a chronologically later text than CRANE² or CRANE³. Thus, the preparation of [CRANE⁴],

[91] Previous scholars, however, did not take account of the appearance of this variant in BRIDGEWATER, and considered it a unique agreement between CRANE¹ and the quarto.
[92] 1.1.297, 2.1.120, 2.2.203, 3.1.157, 3.1.159, 3.1.168, 3.1.173, 3.2 (scene numbering), 3.2.25, 3.2.28, 3.2.29.1, 3.2.38–40, 3.3 (scene numbering), 3.1.392.1 (stage direction position), 5.2.7, 5.3.162.

of an expanded reading text, apparently involved some process of macro-transference, combining late Crane features with elements from another, earlier source.

Exactly how was that done? The cluster of variants linking CRANE[4] to CRANE[1] in and around 3.2 could be explained by the interpolation of an extra page into an existing Crane transcript; but that process will not explain the cluster of four such variants at 3.1.157–188. In addition to the four variants uniquely shared by CRANE[1] and CRANE[4], the passage contains their joint historical error (shared with BRIDGEWATER) and a sixth variant where CRANE[4] agrees with CRANE[1] and BRIDGEWATER, against CRANE[2] and all other texts (3.1.187, Admiration/Admirations). Obviously, [CRANE[4]] was influenced by something like CRANE[1] even when that alternative source was not supplying a missing scene or speech.[93]

We might be tempted to explain away these local anomalies by speculating that some unknown damage in the main manuscript compelled Crane to resort to a supplementary manuscript for this passage, just as he did to patch the deliberate cuts in 3.2 and 2.2. But there are problems with that hypothesis even here. We can explain away unique readings in CRANE/MATHEWES by attributing them to compositor error in MATHEWES, rather than supposing that [CRANE[4]] misread a legible text that Crane had copied before; but it is harder to explain readings like those at 3.1.164, where CRANE/MATHEWES agrees with ROSENBACH in reading 'the' (against 'that' of CRANE[1,2], MIDDLETON[T], etc), or 3.1.165, where CRANE/MATHEWES agrees with MIDDLETON[T], BRIDGEWATER and OKES in reading 'Fame' (against 'Fames' in CRANE[1,2]). Such readings cannot be dismissed as compositor errors in MATHEWES; they apparently stood in [CRANE[4]], because they are shared stemmatically with other texts. But they are not shared with any of the three earlier Crane texts. The first might be dismissed as a mere scribal error, originating in [CRANE[4]] and passed from there to ROSENBACH (or vice versa); but the second variant, one line later, is not present in ROSENBACH, but was instead somehow either passed to other NON-CRANE texts, or independently endorsed by them. In these two adjacent lines there is no evidence, substantive or incidental, that [CRANE[4]] derives directly from anything close to CRANE[1].

More fundamentally, the 'patch' hypothesis will not account for the scattering of variants throughout the play in which CRANE[4] uniquely agrees with CRANE[1]. Although these variants do not cluster, like those in 3.1 and 3.2, given the compelling evidence of those conglomerations it is hard to discount the other unique pairings. Since some access to an alternative source must be presumed in order to account for [CRANE[4]]'s added material in 2.2 and 3.2, the simplest explanation for the other uniquely shared readings throughout the play is that they come from the same source. If that is the case, then we are not dealing with a compound *object* (one manuscript with a few patches taken from another manuscript) but with a compound *process* (copying of one manuscript,

complicated by unsystematic transference of readings from another source).

The result is that [CRANE[4]] incorporates, unpredictably, readings from an earlier stage of transmission. Altogether, throughout the play, [CRANE[4]] is closer to CRANE[1] than to CRANE[2,3] at least sixty-two times. (More, if we count details like whether 'the' is placed before the title of a chess piece in stage directions.) On the other hand, CRANE[4] is farther from CRANE[1] between seventy-five and ninety-one times (depending on what kinds of variants we count). The range of numbers here illustrates some of the problems that arise when we move from counting errors to counting indifferent variants. But the looseness does not matter in relation to this particular problem; what matters is that the contrast between the two sets of numbers is not as dramatic as it should be, if [CRANE[4]] derived from a simple act of transmission. Nor do these variants divide neatly into two sets, before and after 3.2. Instead, we find patches of text where [CRANE[4]] seems closer to CRANE[1], and patches where it seems farther. For instance, between the thirty-one line patch of CRANE[1] links at 3.1.157–188 and the forty-line patch of links involving 3.2, there is a thirty-two line stretch of text where CRANE[2] is closer to CRANE[1] thirteen times, while [CRANE[4]] is closer only twice, trivially (3.1.233–347).[94] The only explanation for this kind of pattern is that two different sources are being used, the copyist sometimes tending to favour one, sometimes tending to favour the other, but at all times capable of transferring a reading from one into the texture of the other.

But what was the second source from which such readings were transferred? In the preceding analysis I have described CRANE[4] as being, at certain points, 'closer to CRANE[1]', but that phrasing is deliberately ambiguous, and reflects the ambiguity of the evidence I have been considering. The only conclusion that any of the foregoing evidence warrants is that, at certain points, [CRANE[4]] is 'closer to CRANE[1]' *than* CRANE[2] *is*. In other words, CRANE[4] at such points could be drawing upon a textual source located anywhere along the continuum from Middleton's first completed draft to the lost copy of the playbook that I have designated '[KING's MEN[3]]'. There is no logical justification for assuming, as Howard-Hill does, that these

---

93 Although the spelling and punctuation of CRANE[1,2,3] resemble each other more often than not, where they do differ in this passage CRANE[4] is closer to CRANE[1] twenty-four times, but closer to CRANE[2] only nine times. For instance, at 3.1.175 CRANE[1] and [CRANE[4]] have exactly the same reading ('desert claimes it.'), where CRANE[2] differs in one capital, one spelling, and one punctuation mark ('Desert claymes it:'). In this particular passage of about thirty-one lines, [CRANE[4]] is demonstrably closer to CRANE[1] than is CRANE[2] (or CRANE[3]). However, that resemblance need not entail access to the same manuscript. I return to this problem in Sec. XXVI, below.

94 3.1.233, 3.1.235, 3.1.237, 3.1.238, 3.1.243, 3.1.245, 3.1.246 (twice), 3.1.252 (twice), 3.1.258, 3.1.264, 3.1.265. At 3.1.257 CRANE[2] and all other texts have extrametrical 'the', fully spelled out, where CRANE[1,4] and BRIDGEWATER (corrected) indicate the elision ('th''). The other exception occurs at 3.1.250, where CRANE[2,3] have the fully expanded 'I would', against the characteristic Middletonian elision 'I'd' found in all other witnesses (spelled 'I'll'd' in CRANE[1], 'I'l'd' in CRANE/ALLDE). Neither of these exceptions, notably, is a unique CRANE[1,4] link, and the second is not even identically spelled.

variants link [CRANE⁴] directly to CRANE¹. The variants could just as easily come, not from a CRANE manuscript, but from some early non-Crane source.

Several of the features of 3.2 that link [CRANE⁴] specifically to CRANE¹—the added scene divisions, the expansion of 'I'm' to 'I am'—characterize Crane himself, not his copy-text; those features were presumably not in Middleton's first draft, but added by the scribe in CRANE¹, and the same scribe certainly *would* have added the scene divisions to any version of the play which contained 3.2, and probably would have expanded the contractions, too. The link between CRANE¹ and [CRANE⁴] in these particulars is unique only because Crane did not have the opportunity to impose the same features on CRANE²,³, because CRANE²,³ do not contain the scene. Moreover, the punctuation of 3.2 clearly points to [CRANE⁴]'s derivation from something other than CRANE¹ itself. Nascimento tabulated—for every text, throughout the play, by scene—punctuation variants that might indicate the influence of Crane. CRANE¹, like MIDDLETON^T, contains no parentheses in 3.2; CRANE/ALLDE adds one. That single added parenthesis tells us nothing about the derivation of [CRANE⁴]. But two other statistics are more revealing. Crane added many hyphens to the texts he copied; masses of hyphenated words are a Crane trademark. In 3.2, CRANE¹ presumably added the fourteen hyphens not present in MIDDLETON^T; by contrast, CRANE/ALLDE contains only two hyphens not present in MIDDLETON^T.[95] Crane also used heavier medial punctuation than Middleton, adding commas, turning authorial commas into colons and semi-colons. In 3.2, CRANE¹ apparently strengthened medial punctuation in this way eleven times; by contrast, CRANE⁴ did so only four times. It is impossible to believe that [CRANE⁴] was copied, in 3.2, from CRANE¹, because that would entail believing that Crane drastically reduced two features that he normally drastically increased. Nor is it possible to attribute this reduction of Crane punctuation to the compositor(s) of CRANE/ALLDE: if Allde's shop had so completely disregarded these features of punctuation in other scenes, the printer's copy-text would never have been identified as a Crane transcript. In fact, for the other scenes printed by Allde, Nascimento records 29 added hyphens and 81 instances of strengthened medial punctuation. This evidence accords well with the assumption that most of the time [CRANE⁴] is a copy of another Crane transcript—but 3.2 was apparently *not* so heavily influenced by an earlier Crane transcript.

It is also clear that the supplementary source for CRANE⁴ could not have been CRANE¹ for the rest of the play, outside 3.2. Neither CRANE¹, nor the draft from which it was copied, contained the Fat Bishop; therefore, neither one contained Additional Passage A, one of the three passages cut in CRANE²,³ but restored in CRANE⁴. Since no text of the original version of the play could have supplied these lines, it would be simplest to assume that the supplementary copy-text for these lines was also used as the supplementary copy-text for the rest of the play, including 3.2. Thus, the process of transference that helped produce [CRANE⁴] drew upon elements of the *Early*

version but also upon elements of the later performance version. It included features otherwise unique to the first draft with other features otherwise unique to the licensed playbook. That is to say, not only was [CRANE⁴] produced by some sort of compound process, but one source used intermittently in that process itself seems to have contained compound elements.

Before we proceed any further, it may help to summarize what is already clear. [CRANE⁴] must have been chronologically the last of the known Crane transcripts, because some of its text is demonstrably later than CRANE² and CRANE³; therefore, it must have come into existence, as a physical entity, later than any of the other surviving Crane manuscripts. However, in preparing [CRANE⁴] the copyist also had access to an earlier form or forms of the play, form(s) that belonged stemmatically somewhere between [PRE-CRANE¹] and [PRE-CRANE²]. Consequently, although [CRANE⁴] as a whole is chronologically later than CRANE²,³, some individual readings in [CRANE⁴] come from earlier in the stemma than the corresponding readings in CRANE²,³. But it is hard to pinpoint a particular document within that temporal continuum that could have contained all the readings sporadically transferred into [CRANE⁴].

Some kind of transference is clearly necessary to explain the global pattern of textual variation in [CRANE⁴]. Our difficulty in identifying the source of the transferred readings may arise because we are making an unjustified assumption about the process. I have been assuming, up to this point—and I assumed for many years, as I wrestled with this problem—that Crane was making simultaneous use of two manuscripts, with his eyes literally moving back and forth between them.[96] That is to say, I imagined a particular agent, a particular process, and two particular objects. I thought I had solved the problem by postulating the existence of two objects, instead of just one. But the problem still refused to resolve itself into an intelligible pattern.

Certainly, transference requires an agent, a process, and an alternative source. But that source need not be an alternative material object. Certainly also, the lost manuscript used by the printers Mathewes and Allde contained hundreds of Crane features. But those Crane features do not prove that the agent of transference was Ralph Crane. All the apparent contradictions resolve themselves if we postulate that the agent of transference, and the source of the transferred readings, was Middleton himself. If at some point Middleton took over the work of producing scribal copies, then he could have produced his first such copy by transcribing a Crane transcript, passively reproducing many of its features but importing, from his own memory, passages that had been omitted

---

[95] Nascimento records only one, but there are two: 'Black-beries' (3.2.26) and 'Bird-spit' (3.2.33).

[96] I assumed, in other words, that Crane was like me, or any other modern editor. This unthinking projection of our own professional identity onto textual agents in other times and places is common among editors. See Howard-Hill's description of Crane as 'Shakespeare's Earliest Editor' (1992).

in performance, corrections to accumulated errors, and textual variants from various temporal stages in the play's process of evolution. The resulting manuscript would still have contained many Crane characteristics; but it would also have contained a range of textual variants that Crane was in no position to supply.

Middleton himself would not have needed to keep glancing at another manuscript. He already carried a text of the play in his head. Even if he had wanted to, he could not banish that text-in-his-head from the process of copying the text-on-his-desk. Moreover, that text-in--his-head was not necessarily identical to the playbook, or to any other single physical entity. Middleton actually carried multiple texts-in-his-head, a 'synoptic text' (like the one Gabler produced for Joyce's *Ulysses*), incorporating the whole sequence of texts produced by the evolution of *Game* from his first scribblings to the final performance.

I have already demonstrated that the CRANE manuscripts are all earlier in the process of transmission than the NON-CRANE manuscripts (Sec. V–VIII). At some point, therefore, a CRANE transcript must have been copied by a NON-CRANE agent, and Middleton was the one agent involved in the production of all four NON-CRANE texts. It is therefore reasonable to suppose that at some point Middleton himself produced a new copy of the play, by transcribing a late Crane copy-text. I have also already demonstrated (Sec. IV) that MIDDLETON[T] retains many unMiddletonian features, inherited from previous transcriptions. MIDDLETON[T] seems to have been a very late copy; but despite what seem to have been many intervening transcriptions, MIDDLETON[T] still retains some Crane characteristics. An autograph copy made directly from a late Crane transcript *might* have retained many more Crane features. We simply do not know how many of Crane's spellings, punctuation marks, and formal embellishments Middleton might have duplicated, when working for the first time directly from a late Crane copy--text. After all, Middleton employed Crane, in the first place, because he believed that Crane's scribal expertise made his text more readable, more marketable, and/or more culturally prestigious, and Middleton *might* initially have tried to reproduce many of those features. We do not know. We also do not know whether the printer's copy-text for CRANE/MATHEWES/ALLDE was this postulated authorial transcript, or a copy of that authorial transcript, made by Crane. [CRANE4] *could* have been a Crane copy of a Middleton copy of a late Crane copy.

Of course, in reminding you that certain things *could* have happened, I have not proven that they *did* happen. In the following seven paragraphs I will provide some evidence for this conjecture. The argument takes for granted the conclusions, already reached, that MATHEWES/ALLDE derives in some way from a late Crane transcript, and that it also shows undeniable evidence of transference from another source. That is, the following evidence does

not contradict the conclusions already reached; instead, it supplements those conclusions, in an effort to identify the source of the transferred readings.

1. First, there are aspects of the spelling and punctuation of MATHEWES/ALLDE that are hard to explain on the assumption that [CRANE4] was simply a normal Crane copy of a normal Crane copy. I called attention, above, to the evidence that 3.2 was not printed from a normal Crane transcript, and perhaps not from a Crane transcript at all. Howard-Hill and Nascimento both provided statistical evidence that various Crane characteristics show up less frequently in MATHEWES/ALLDE than in CRANE[2,3]; this reduction might be explained due to interference from the printers, but it might also be due to the intervention of a different copyist. As I noted above (Sec. I), the dramatic shift in the frequency of -ee endings in monosyllables (Nascimento, 71) is clearly related to the change of printers between sheets A–E and sheets F–I (unknown to Nascimento). But the evidence of printer interference is itself ambiguous. It could be explained in either of two ways: (*a*) one printer changed Middleton's preferred *wee, hee, shee, bee* to *we, he, she, be*, or (*b*) one printer changed Crane's preferred *we, he, she, be* to *wee, hee, shee, bee*. The second explanation, required by the hypothesis of an ordinary Crane transcript, has one printer frequently interpolating an obsolete spelling. The first hypothesis, which has one printer more aggressively modernizing the spelling, would indicate that the underlying manuscript had many more Middletonian features than the quarto. If in the case of those common words the division of printers provides ambiguous evidence, in the case of another common word the division of printers strongly suggests continuity in the underlying copy-text. The Middletonian 'Ile' (instead of Crane's preferred 'I'll') is used systematically in both MATHEWES and ALLDE.[97] Of course, the compositors in the shops of both printers might coincidentally have preferred Middleton's spelling. But a simpler explanation for the consistency would be that the manuscript itself contained Middleton's rather than Crane's form.

2. To this statistical evidence of non-Crane spellings in the manuscript can be added many individual, as it were anecdotal, examples. There are, for instance, twenty non-Crane spellings (all apparently Middletonian) in 2.2, the scene with two passages not present in the earlier Crane transcripts: Bodie (52), poynt (139), Hypocrisie (148), dayes (151, 199, 245, 253), combate (157), pang (164), grinde (193), suite (197), been(e) (82, 199, 240), appeare (203), false heart (206), alwayes (218), faults (223), flower (226)—all in addition to a run of eleven

---

[97] CRANE/MATHEWES: 1.1.161, 173, 1.1.210, 1.1.212, 2.1.144, 189, 2.1.211, 2.1.238, 2.2.58, 2.2.61, 2.2.68, 189, 2.2.246, 2.2.251, 3.1.49, 3.1.50, 179, 3.1.204, 3.1.209. At 2.2.252 MATHEWES has 'I'le', which shows up twice in Middleton's autograph. At 3.1.189 MATHEWES has 'Ill', which is probably an error rather than a spelling ('Ill on with't' as an imprecation). The 'Ile' spelling is used without exception in CRANE/ALLDE: 3.1.287, 3.1.293, 3.1.300, 3.1.304, 3.1.345, 3.2.15, 19, 3.2.35, 3.2.36 (twice), 3.1.364, 4.1.148, 4.2.2, 133, 145, 4.4.34, 5.2.29, 5.2.87, 118.

examples of *hee, shee, bee, mee*.[98] Elsewhere in the play, on at least thirty-two occasions MATHEWES/ALLDE is the only other text to share an autograph spelling found in MIDDLETON[T,B].[99] Of course, some or all of these spellings might simply represent compositorial preferences. Then again, they might not.

3. Some of the punctuation of MATHEWES/ALLDE is also eccentrically Middletonian. At 3.1.278 CRANE/ALLDE alone has 'teare 'm', which might reflect the unusual placement of the apostrophe found consistently in MIDDLETON[T] (e'm). The same explanation would account for the unique CRANE/ALLDE reading 'strike 'm' at 4.4.4. Other Middletonian apostrophes occur, in both printers, at 4.1.72 (yon'd), 5.3.146 ('bran'd' for *brand*), and 5.3.214 ('Crow'd' for *Crowd*).[100] Middleton often ends a speech with a comma or semi-colon. Speech-ending commas occur five times in MATHEWES (2.2.176, 3.1.24, 3.1.58, 117, 199), three times in ALLDE (5.2.112, 5.3.130, 143); MATHEWES uses speech-ending semicolons twice (3.1.23, 3.1.216). These anomalies might be attributed to foul case or a local shortage of full stops, but such conjectures will not explain the unusual Middletonian exclamation marks in both printers (3.1.15, 3.1.24, 128, 5.2.114, 115, 5.3.63).

4. Two errors suggest that the printers were dealing with a manuscript containing features that do not occur in the other Crane transcripts.[101] At 2.2.112 CRANE/MATHEWES has the unique error 'fould', probably because the compositor misread the final letter of 'foule' (as the word is spelled in only ROSENBACH and OKES). At 3.1.154–5 CRANE/MATHEWES alone omits eight words, the end of one sentence and the whole of another ('a little. Enough of them in all parts.'). This omission is hard to explain as an accident, unless all eight words were placed on a single manuscript line, which could then accidentally be skipped. Only ROSENBACH and MIDDLETON[T] place the words, apparently incorrectly, on a single manuscript line. This appears to be one of the few examples of a progressive error in CRANE/MATHEWES, and it presupposes NON-CRANE lineation.[102]

5. In addition to the unique agreements in spelling between MATHEWES/ALLDE and autograph, there are also four substantive readings where the two texts agree against all other witnesses.[103] One is certainly correct, and the other three are all plausible readings (adopted in *Later* and defended in the Textual Notes). There are two possible explanations for these variants. It could be conjectured that CRANE[1] and all other texts are in error, and that only MATHEWES/ALLDE and MIDDLETON[T] restore the correct autograph reading. But how then did Crane, or the printer, gain access to that correction? Alternatively, the reading might be one of the many authorial variants found in later transcriptions. (See Sec. XV, below.) In either case, Middleton is the most likely source for the correction/revision.

6. The preceding subset of four variants might be considered part of a larger set of variants which links MATHEWES/ALLDE forward to the later NON-CRANE texts, rather than backwards to CRANE[1]. There are at least twelve such variants.[104] None of these variants is demonstrably incorrect; many are adopted in *Later*, as they were in the editions of DYCE and BULLEN. There are several possible explanations for their presence in MATHEWES/ALLDE. Not all errors are obvious, so all twelve might be errors, shared by [CRANE[4]] with the NON-CRANE group. But one of them is closer to Middleton's source for the passage than the alternative reading (4.2.70), so the hypothesis of error will not by itself easily explain the whole set. This leaves us with the same two explanations described in the previous paragraph: [CRANE[4]] somehow corrected not-obvious errors in the preceding Crane transcripts, or it incorporated some late authorial variants.

7. Finally, both preceding sets of variants might be related to plausible readings that appear in MATHEWES/ALLDE alone. Setting aside obvious errors, there are twenty-two such variants.[105] Again, none of them is obviously mistaken; most were accepted by DYCE and BULLEN, are adopted in *Later*, and defended individually in the textual notes. Again, we might dismiss them all as errors—though they are uncharacteristic of Crane, in both number and kind, and not easily attributed to normal routines of compositorial error (in two different printing shops). If they are not errors, they must be either corrections or authorial variants. In either case, Middleton himself is the likeliest agent and source for the variants.

The foregoing analysis combines evidence about the incidentals of the printers' manuscript (para. 1–4) and evidence about different categories of variant apparently present in that manuscript (para. 5–7). The second type of evidence would not require us to suppose that the printers'

---

[98] Notably, all but one of the other sixteen occurrences of the modern word *been*, in the pages of both printers, are spelled 'bin' (closer to Crane's 'byn' than to Middleton's 'beene'). The one exception is spelled 'ben'.

[99] 1.1.25 (firmnes), 79 (lyes), 2.1.108 (Yon'd), 3.1.91 (flie), 111 (soapes), 132 (their), 180 (yon'd), 311 (knowe), 322 (Youle), 381 (fixe), 3.2.7 (o're), 21 (behinde), 4.2.33 (titelie), 65 (Nauie), 76 (Toade), 81 (Here's), 92 (here's), 4.4.7 (layde), 15 (falshood), 5.2.43 (lips), 77 (voyce), 79 (thankes), 95 (Bawde), 104 (Childe), 108 (lewde), 5.3.6 (burie), 8 (Romane), 19 (Sea-fish), 56 (finde), 91 (Belowe), 99 (sayes), 190 (finde). I say 'at least' because I am not sure I recorded all examples in the play's first three scenes, before I began to pay attention to the unexpected autograph connections with MATHEWES/ALLDE. More generally, manual collation of spellings in eight witnesses is even more prone to errors of omission than manual collation of substantive variants.

[100] This last example occurs in a passage where ALLDE and OKES are substantively identical. The anomalous apostrophe is not in OKES, which might suggest that MATHEWES/ALLDE was, in fact, the earlier of the quartos. See further discussion of that possibility in Section XX.

[101] At 2.1.126 CRANE/MATHEWES shares with MIDDLETON[T] and ROSENBACH the variant 'too,' where all other texts have the required modern 'to'. This is probably only a spelling variant, rather than an error; but it would be unusual for printers to prefer the obsolete form, especially if their copy-text had the modern alternative.

[102] For evidence that a series of errors involving confusion of Black Queen's Pawn and Black Bishop's Pawn—including five in MATHEWES/ALLDE—may all have originated with Middleton, see the textual note at 4.1.38.

[103] 2.2.93, 3.1.89, 132, 3.1.313.

[104] 1.1.183, 1.1.265, 3.1.31, 128, 194, 3.1.211, 3.1.235, 3.1.264, 3.1.276, 3.1.292, 3.1.299.1, 4.2.70, [5.1.9, 5.1.39, Epilogue.10]. The bracketed variants are shared with OKES only, in two passages where the two quartos seem not to be independent witnesses.

[105] Induction.4, 1.1.242, 2.1.104, 138, 175, 2.1.213, 2.2.127, 3.1.62, 3.1.86, 185, 3.1.227, 3.1.246, 3.1.252, 3.1.281, 3.1.293, 3.1.321, 3.2.30, 3.1.395.1, 4.2.144, 5.3.0.3, 5.3.1, 187.

manuscript was itself in Middleton's handwriting; it might have been a faithful Crane transcript of an autograph manuscript that incorporated such readings. The first type of evidence, however, more specifically concerns the features of the manuscript the printers used. Because we can discern those features only through 'the veil of print', it is difficult to assess whether they point to (1) direct use of a Middleton transcript of a late Crane copy, or to (2) a Crane copy of that Middleton transcript.[106] Whichever hypothesis one prefers makes little difference: either will explain all the hitherto-puzzling features of MATHEWES/ALLDE.

XIV. From CRANE to ROSENBACH

I have already established, on the basis of the pattern of shared errors linking the CRANE texts to the NON-CRANE group (Sec. VII, IX), that the link between the two was a text very similar to [CRANE⁴]. We can now see that the last CRANE text may also have been a NON-CRANE text. Nevertheless, I will continue to identify the manuscript used to produce MATHEWES/ALLDE as [CRANE⁴], because it was clearly heavily influenced by Crane's scribal practices; it was either a late Crane transcript, or a direct copy of one, retaining many Crane features. Moreover, as we have already established, it is stemmatically strongly connected to CRANE²·³.

Having established the sequence of CRANE texts, we can now try to establish which of the four extant NON-CRANE texts is most closely linked to the late Crane manuscripts. We can do this, initially, by using the same Table of Cross-over Shared Errors (Sec. VII), which initiated our intervening analysis of the CRANE sequence (Sec. VIII–XIII). Ignoring, at this point, the specific links with specific Crane texts, we can summarize the distribution of cross-over errors for the four NON-CRANE texts.[107]

OKES: 9 patterns, 25 examples
ROSENBACH: 8 patterns, 14 examples
BRIDGEWATER: 6 patterns, 8 examples
MIDDLETONᵀ: 5 patterns, 5 examples

This table immediately suggests that the NON-CRANE texts closest to CRANE are OKES and ROSENBACH. This conclusion also makes sense in terms of the pattern of text-production described above: [CRANE⁴], ROSENBACH, and OKES all provide exceptionally 'full' texts of the play, incorporating theatrical revisions but ignoring theatrical cuts. In this respect all three differ from the earlier CRANE¹·²·³ and the apparently later BRIDGEWATER, MIDDLETONᵀ (which are both seriously defective, in different incoherent ways, which have nothing to do with theatrical cutting).

The raw data identifies OKES as the NON-CRANE text most clearly linked to the CRANE half of the stemma. But the relationship of the printer's manuscript [MIDDLETON/OKES] to the CRANE group is, once again, clouded by the possibility that one quarto contaminated the other (Section VIII). If we eliminate from the above table all errors uniquely shared by OKES with CRANE/ALLDE, the

total number of examples/tokens shrinks to 8 (less than ROSENBACH). If we accept the economic hypothesis that OKES influenced CRANE/ALLDE, the totals would be further reduced to 7 patterns and 7 errors. And if we were to accept the evidence of direct influence of one printed text on the other, without making any assumptions about the direction of influence, the OKES totals would fall even further: 4 patterns, 4 errors. Given these uncertainties, it will be easier to begin by concentrating on ROSENBACH.

Wherever we begin, we are immediately confronted by a conspicuous gap between [CRANE⁴] and the NON-CRANE group. Even if we use the filtered data, the number of shared errors leaps from a maximum of 52 in CRANE/MATHEWES/ALLDE—or, if we rigorously discount any possible contamination from the other printed quarto, a minimum of only 25 in [CRANE⁴]—to the seventy-six of ROSENBACH. How are we to account for this 50–150% increase in magnitude?

The source of that increase is the second half of the play. As Nascimento observed, and as the tabulation of shared errors will demonstrate at a glance, ROSENBACH's remarkably strong links to BRIDGEWATER do not begin until somewhere between 3.1.319 and 3.1.345.1. Before 3.1.345.1, ROSENBACH and BRIDGEWATER do not contain a single uniquely shared uncontestable error; from that point on, they contain as many as 25—the largest category of uniquely shared pairs anywhere in Game. Nor is this discrepancy limited to shared errors. After 3.1.318, ROSENBACH and BRIDGEWATER share 54 variants unattested by other texts. ROSENBACH was not copied directly from BRIDGEWATER, and BRIDGEWATER was not copied directly from ROSENBACH; both are stemmatic dead-ends. Nevertheless, the second half of ROSENBACH is undeniably closely related to the second half of BRIDGEWATER; just as undeniably, the first half of ROSENBACH is *not* directly related to the first half of BRIDGEWATER. I will analyse the second half of ROSENBACH in greater detail below (Sec. XVI), but for now this initial summary establishes that we must distinguish between two parts of ROSENBACH, just as we distinguished CRANE/MATHEWES from CRANE/ALLDE.

If we divide the play in two at 3.1.319, and use the filtered totals, then the second half contains 68 of the shared errors in ROSENBACH. By contrast, before that point ROSENBACH has only 21 shared errors. Thus, 58% of the lines of the text contain only 21 tokens; if that rate had continued, ROSENBACH would have had only 36 shared errors over the play as a whole—almost identical to CRANE², and less than any other text but CRANE¹. On the other hand, in the last 42% of the play ROSENBACH contains 68 shared errors; at that rate, it would have

---

[106] The first alternative seems to me a little more likely, and I have therefore preferred it in my visualizations of the stemma of transmission. But the stemmata would not be substantially affected if, instead, one chose the second alternative.
[107] OKES: patterns 17, 27, 28, 37, 45, 20, 33, 43, 24. ROSENBACH: patterns 12, 39, 26, 37, 19, 43, 23, 34. BRIDGEWATER: patterns 11, 39, 45, 43, 24, 34. MIDDLETONᵀ: patterns 45, 23, 34, 39, 33.

had 162 such errors over the play as a whole—far more than any extant text.[108] In looking at the pattern of shared errors, we must therefore clearly distinguish between the two parts of ROSENBACH: a first part with relatively few shared errors, and a second part with exceptionally many. The first half is the most reliable text not transcribed by Crane. I will therefore begin my analysis of the NON-CRANE texts with it.

The first part of ROSENBACH provides a comprehensible bridge between the relatively low (but rising) rates of shared error in the CRANE texts and the much higher rates of error in the NON-CRANE texts. But the exact nature of that bridge can only be analysed by considering, not simply the quantity of shared errors, but the patterns of their distribution.

Table of Shared Errors in ROSENBACH: Patterns that occur only in Induction–3.1.318

26. CRANE[2,3]: I
36. CRANE[2,3,4]: I

* * *

19. CRANE[2,4]: I? (passage not in CRANE[3])
21. OKES: I? (passage not in BRIDGEWATER, perhaps deliberate variant in CRANE[3])
23. [CRANE[4]]–MIDDLETON[T]: I? (passage not in CRANE[3])
34. [CRANE[4]]–BRIDGEWATER–MIDDLETON[T]: I? (unspecified in CRANE[3])

* * *

[46. CRANE[3,4]–BRIDGEWATER–OKES: I]
[48. CRANE[2,3,4]–MIDDLETON[T]–OKES: I?]
[49. CRANE[1,2]–NON-CRANE: I]
[50. CRANE[1,3]–NON-CRANE: I]
[52. CRANE[3,4]–NON-CRANE: I]
[55. CRANE[1,2,4]–NON-CRANE: I]

Notably, all but one of these errors originates in the CRANE group; there is only one (uncertain) example confined to the three other NON-CRANE texts. Looking in the other direction, these patterns link the first 58% of ROSENBACH once to OKES, once to BRIDGEWATER, and twice to MIDDLE-TON[T]. That is, its links with the other NON-CRANE texts are evenly distributed.

However, the above table does not give a complete picture of the first half of ROSENBACH, because it does not include four patterns that occur in both halves of the play. Those patterns cannot have been caused by whatever change occurred in the vicinity of 3.1.119. In the following table I separate with a vertical rule the subtotals for each of the two sections.

Table of Shared Errors in ROSENBACH: Patterns that occur throughout the play

15. OKES: 4–7 | 5
12. [CRANE[4]]: 3–4 | 3
30. OKES–BRIDGEWATER: I–2 | I–7 [I–4]
56. OKES–BRIDGEWATER–MIDDLETON[T]–CRANE[2,3,4]: I–2 | I [0]

* * *

[57. OKES–BRIDGEWATER–MIDDLETON[T]–CRANE: I | I]

In patterns that persist across the whole play, and in patterns limited to the first section only, ROSENBACH is linked to OKES and to CRANE[2,4]; all its links to other texts could be through those sources. In fact, it might not even be necessary to include CRANE[2] in that list. The only shared error in the first half of ROSENBACH that is not linked to either OKES or [CRANE[4]] is the single example of pattern 26: the indefinite article 'a' is omitted by CRANE[2,3] and ROSENBACH at 1.1.241. This pattern is not queried, because the word's omission by three separate texts means it is unlikely to be coincidental. However, the necessary omitted article could easily have been supplied in MATHEWES by a compositor (consciously or unconsciously) or a proof corrector in foul proofs (consciously).[109] We therefore cannot be certain of the reading in the lost manuscript [CRANE[4]], which might have contained the same error as CRANE[2,3] and ROSENBACH. That is to say, what appears to be Pattern 26 might actually have been another example of Pattern 36. If that were the case, all the links to other texts in the first part of ROSENBACH could be explained by a stemmatic relationship to just two texts, OKES and [CRANE[4]]. This hypothesis would remove the one piece of evidence (dependent on the single letter 'a') that might be thought to contradict the theory that [CRANE[4]] is the only CRANE text to which [PRE-ROSENBACH] was directly connected.

However, we do not have to commit ourselves to that conjecture at this point. Undeniably, for the first part of ROSENBACH the errors shared with CRANE[3], BRIDGEWATER, and MIDDLETON[T] can all be explained through the medium of OKES, [CRANE[4]] and—'less certainly', let us say—CRANE[2].

These patterns invalidate an hypothesis put forward by Nascimento (and subsequently accepted, with modifications, by Howard-Hill). Nascimento recognized the need to separate the end of ROSENBACH (with its strong links to BRIDGEWATER) from the rest of the text; she also recognized that the first half was strongly connected to the CRANE texts. But her unexamined presuppositions about the status of MIDDLETON[T] forced her to assume that ROSEN-BACH's connection with the CRANE texts must be to the early and relatively reliable CRANE[1], rather than CRANE[3,4]. Therefore, Nascimento connected ROSENBACH's first three scenes directly to CRANE[1], and connected the end of ROSEN-BACH (from 3.1.319 on) to BRIDGEWATER.

Even on its own terms, Nascimento's hypothesis has serious weaknesses. It left her with no good explanation for the middle of ROSENBACH (2.2.1–3.1.318). It also left unexplained the fact that the first three scenes of CRANE[1] contain thirteen apparently correct 'early' variants that are not repeated in ROSENBACH. Nevertheless, Nascimento did give several reasons for identifying CRANE[1] as the immediate source of the first three scenes of ROSENBACH, and those reasons also underlie Howard-Hill's belief that

---

[108] Comparing filtered data, it would have had 178% as many shared errors as the second-most corrupt text, BRIDGEWATER.

[109] This is one of the four cross-over links to CRANE[3] identified above in Sec. VII. I there globally conjectured that the four might be attributed to proof-correction; I here offer a specific argument about proof-correction in this one case.

both CRANE¹ and ROSENBACH derive from a lost manuscript he calls 'Archdale-Rosenbach'. Those arguments are therefore worth examining in some detail.

Most significantly, ROSENBACH shares five unique substantive readings with CRANE¹ (1.1.156, 156, 1.1.306, 2.1.197, 2.1.236), and the wording of four stage directions (Induction.0.1–2, 52.2, 2.1.140.1, 152.1). To her examples I can add unique agreements in the wording of a stage direction at Induction.0.1 and in lineation at 2.1.39–41, 137–8, 2.1.207–8. All thirteen examples, in both categories, occur in the play's first three scenes, up to 2.1.236. We have already encountered this category of evidence—unique agreements with CRANE¹—in the preceding analysis of [CRANE⁴] (Section XIII). None of the variants that uniquely link ROSENBACH to CRANE¹ is an error; most are extremely trivial.[110] As I noted then, the only conclusion that these shared variants warrant is that, in the first three scenes, ROSENBACH is 'closer to CRANE¹' than CRANE² is. This fact does not force us to assume a direct documentary link between the two texts.

The first part of ROSENBACH also resembles CRANE¹ in the absence of a Prologue. However, that is not a unique variant: CRANE³ also omits the Prologue. Neither is it a shared error. Middleton's first version of the play apparently contained neither a Prologue nor an Epilogue; the lack of a Prologue in CRANE¹ is therefore not an error in that text. CRANE³ presumably omitted the Prologue deliberately, as part of its more general abridgement; the lack of a Prologue in CRANE³ is therefore not an error in that text, either. The omission is, apparently, an error in ROSENBACH, which represents the revised version of the play. But that error, like any other omission, could have arisen independently of CRANE¹ or CRANE³. Whatever its exact cause, this variant constitutes poor evidence for a link between CRANE¹ and ROSENBACH.

Nascimento also makes much of the fact that only ROSENBACH preserves CRANE¹'s presumably authorial generic speech prefixes (specifying only 'White Pawn' rather than 'White Queen's Pawn', etc.) in 1.1 and 2.1. But that feature of ROSENBACH extends beyond 2.1: ROSENBACH has twenty-three generic prefixes after 2.1. In other words, ROSENBACH contains generic prefixes beyond the first three scenes, and contains generic prefixes when CRANE¹ does not; it also lacks generic prefixes where CRANE¹ has them. Even in 2.1 CRANE¹ has eight such prefixes not present in ROSENBACH; in 3.1, it has another sixteen. We can declare with confidence that both CRANE¹ and ROSENBACH contain more generic prefixes than the other texts, but the patterns of their distribution do not consistently overlap, or support Nascimento's division of ROSENBACH. Again, these features do not require a documentary link between the two texts.

Nascimento believed that ROSENBACH's prefixes came from CRANE¹, because they would not have been permitted to stand in a playbook. Howard-Hill disagrees, and so do I.[111] But even if Nascimento was right about the specificity of speech prefixes in the playbook, this would only prove that CRANE² is closer to the playbook than ROSENBACH. It

would not prove that ROSENBACH was specifically linked to CRANE¹, because generic prefixes are not limited to those two texts; indeed, every text of the play contains some. Since the generic prefixes in CRANE¹ itself must derive, not from Crane, but from Middleton's first draft, we know that Middleton himself thought of the characters in these terms; it is not surprising that a feature preferred by the author shows up, at some point or other, in every text of the play. Therefore, the fact that ROSENBACH contains so many generic prefixes probably indicates that, like CRANE¹, it derives from an autograph manuscript; it certainly does not prove ROSENBACH's dependence on CRANE¹.

These are the shaky foundations on which Nascimento's hypothesis was built. The evidence of shared errors brings it crashing down. As I have already demonstrated (Section VII), the connection between the CRANE texts and the NON-CRANE texts does not come through CRANE¹, but through something close to CRANE⁴. ROSENBACH does not contain a single error shared with CRANE¹ alone, or with CRANE¹ but not the later Crane texts. Conversely, in the 647 lines of the play's first three scenes, ROSENBACH does contain at least four errors that are not present in CRANE¹, but are present in one or more of the later Crane threesome.[112] In the 584 lines from 2.2.1 to 3.1.318, it contains at least eight such shared errors; in the 942 lines of the remainder of the play, the same patterns generate at least another four.[113] There is no statistically significant difference in the relative frequency of such shared errors between the first three scenes and the rest of the play. In addition to shared errors, within the first three scenes ROSENBACH shares another four readings present in the later Crane texts, but not CRANE¹ (1.1.36, 1.1.330, 2.1.131, 2.1.209); three of these involve omission of one or two words, and in all four the reading could easily be an error, since it is endorsed neither by CRANE¹ nor by MIDDLETONᵀ. But whether or not they are errors, the obvious explanation for this pattern would be that those four readings were present in ROSENBACH's copy-text, which was therefore not CRANE¹. Moreover, this evidence of shared error and variation confirms Nascimento's own survey of spelling and punctuation, which found no real distinction between the first three scenes and the rest of the play (77–8). Whatever the origin of ROSENBACH, no part of it seems to derive directly from CRANE¹ (or its immediate source, [PRE-MIDDLETON]). Instead, all of ROSENBACH is somehow connected stemmatically to the later CRANE texts.

---

[110] Nascimento's totals do not count the uniquely shared elisions at 1.1.311, 2.1.209, 5.1.27, perhaps because one of these is in a later area of the text. But it is hard to see how they differ from *they're* (1.1.306) and *he has* (2.1.197).

[111] 'A company bookkeeper would not care what the manuscript read . . . so long as the appropriate lines were written out for each part' (*Pasquin* 34).

[112] 1.1.241, 1.1.279, 2.1.130, 2.1.227.1.

[113] 2.2.33, 2.2.94.1, 2.2.133–5, 3.1.73, 3.1.115, 3.1.154–5, 3.1.175, 3.1.199; 3.1.333, 4.2.44, 5.1.9.2, 5.3.166.3. I do not include in the figures for the last part of the play examples from patterns that do not appear throughout the play, because it is obvious that another manuscript source must have been responsible for those additional patterns.

Nascimento's mistaken hypothesis unnecessarily complicated a simple situation. Why then was ROSENBACH the source of such enormous confusion to Bald, Nascimento, and Howard-Hill? Bald was troubled by the fact that ROSENBACH seemed to mix characteristics which were otherwise separated into two different groups of witnesses, 'the Crane group' (represented for him by CRANE[2,3,4]) and 'the Middleton group' (represented for him by MIDDLETON, BRIDGEWATER, and OKES). Both Nascimento and Howard-Hill accepted Bald's characterization of the problem; indeed, ROSENBACH sits near the middle of the stemma I am constructing, between four texts transcribed by Crane and three texts transcribed in whole or part by Middleton (MIDDLETON, BRIDGEWATER, and OKES).

Of course, that is not the stemma imagined by the play's twentieth-century editors. What so disoriented Bald and his successors was one particular class of variants. In fifty-five cases in the first three scenes alone, ROSENBACH does not contain a reading common to two or more texts in the 'Middleton group'. How are we to account for all these variants? If we assume (as Bald, Nascimento, and Howard-Hill all do) that MIDDLETON[T] is a reliable text early in the stemma, then these variants clearly demonstrate that ROSENBACH cannot also be reliable and early. Any attempt to construct a stemma for *Game* was therefore faced with an insoluble contradiction: ROSENBACH seemed to be both an early text and not an early text, a text simultaneously and throughout its length both very close to the playbook and very far from the playbook.

However, there is another explanation for these readings, which does not produce such an impossible result. These readings not present in ROSENBACH, but present in two or more texts of 'the Middleton group', could derive from two processes: (1) new errors introduced into 'the Middleton group' during the course of repeated transcription, and (2) authorial verbal tinkering in the course of late authorial transcriptions. Nascimento demonstrated that ROSENBACH shows much more evidence of Middletonian orthography and punctuation than any Crane text—even CRANE[I], copied directly from an autograph manuscript. So it takes no great stretch of the imagination to propose that [PRE-ROSENBACH] might have been an autograph manuscript. But that manuscript need not have been an early authorial draft; it could just as easily be an authorial copy, made for readers. Within such a manuscript, the production of new errors and new revisions would both be entirely normal processes. But either of these explanations would place ROSENBACH closer than 'the Middleton group' to the playbook, and therefore earlier in the sequence of transmission.

This simple explanation was not visible to earlier scholars, because their stemmatic analysis was prejudiced by the fact that MIDDLETON[T] and BRIDGEWATER were transcribed, in whole or part, by the author himself. (See Sec. II.) Like Bald's collations, Nascimento's tabulations assumed that departures from MIDDLETON[T] were errors, even though she recognized—in a footnote—that many

variants in CRANE[I] must have had an authorial origin, and even though she acknowledged Middleton's own sloppiness as a copyist. Nevertheless, this illogical definition of 'error' formed the basis of her analysis; once that premise was in place, ROSENBACH—which so often departs from MIDDLETON[T]—seemed to be full of 'errors', and thus could not be close to the playbook. But this reasoning is entirely circular. When the author himself is demonstrably involved in revising and copying a text, the readings of one holograph manuscript clearly do not have a monopoly on textual authority. And because both MIDDLETON[T] and BRIDGEWATER represent a post-revision post-performance version of the work, we have no reason or right to assume that either one is particularly close to the top of the stemma. They *might* be—but equally, they might *not*.

If we abandon the assumption that all variants from MIDDLETON[T] are errors, we can entertain the possibility that the first half of ROSENBACH was copied from an autograph manuscript later than the King's Men's licensed playbook but earlier than MIDDLETON[T]. Indeed, the assumption that Middleton himself was the scribe seems the only possible explanation for the fundamentally dual character of [PRE-ROSENBACH]. On the one hand, that manuscript seems to be related to the late CRANE transcripts. On the other hand, it also contains apparently authoritative readings earlier than CRANE[2,3,4]. The simplest explanation for the pattern of sporadic transference in [PRE-ROSENBACH] is the same explanation already invoked to explain the pattern of sporadic transference in [CRANE[4]]: Middleton, copying a manuscript related to the late CRANE branch, sometimes reverted to older readings that he carried in his head, and sometimes introduced entirely new readings.

Let us therefore entertain the preliminary hypothesis that, for the first part of the play, [PRE-ROSENBACH] was produced by Middleton himself, copying a text related to the late CRANE transcripts. This hypothesis is simpler than the scenarios envisaged by Howard-Hill, and it eliminates an apparently fundamental contradiction. It explains both the quantity and the distribution of shared errors in the first part of ROSENBACH. But it depends on certain claims about authorial transcription; those claims are also crucial to my explanation for the transference that produced [CRANE[4]]. Those claims need to be justified, and Middleton's characteristics as a copyist need to be documented in detail, before we can proceed any further.

XV. Authorial Tinkering, Authorial Error

I have already summarized (Section I) Nascimento's conclusions about Middleton's propensity to error. The entirely autograph text of MIDDLETON[T] contains 124 substantive or semi-substantive readings that occur in none of the seven other texts of the play. At least forty-two of these variants are self-evident errors, emended by Howard-Hill and other editors. In addition, MIDDLETON[T] has forty unique lineation variants; all but one of these seems to be an error, emended by all editors. By itself, the resulting total of unique errors in MIDDLETON[T] is already higher than the number of shared errors of all kinds in any of the four texts of the play prepared by Crane.

Some sceptical readers might object to the arrogant editorial claim that so many readings in MIDDLETON[T], an authorial manuscript, are 'errors'. But for the last two scenes of the play we possess two authorial manuscripts; by definition, unique readings in MIDDLETON[T] are contradicted by the relevant reading in the other authorial manuscript, MIDDLETON[B]. This applies to forty-five of MIDDLETON[T]'s unique substantive variants, eleven lineation variants, and two semi-substantives. Nor is MIDDLETON[B] itself free from mistakes. In a mere nineteen lines in 2.2 MIDDLETON[B] omits an exit present in other texts (2.2.17.1) and gets a speech prefix wrong (2.2.48). At 5.2.115-16 it has a unique lineation error; at 5.3.131 it alone omits the necessary word 'they'; at 5.3.16 it mistakenly substitutes the past tense 'crambd' for the present tense 'cramb'; at 5.3.134 it alone has the nonsensical 'Bond' for 'pond'. Although the 348 lines of 5.2 and 5.3 contain far fewer errors in MIDDLETON[B] than in MIDDLETON[T], that difference is itself predictable: Middleton became less accurate, the more he copied. By comparison, the first 348 lines of MIDDLETON[T]—from the first spoken line of the Prologue to 1.1.260—do not contain a single unique variant: the first unique substantive error in MIDDLETON[T] does not occur until 2.1.68 (446 verse lines, and 547 manuscript lines, into the play); its first unique lineation error does not occur until 2.2.23. At this rate, if MIDDLETON[B] were as long as MIDDLETON[T], it would contain even more errors.

One of the unique MIDDLETON[T] variants is the omission of a necessary entrance direction at 2.1.152.1; another is an omitted 'Exit' at 4.2.134.1.[114] MIDDLETON[T] also is the only text to omit parts of several stage directions: 'he appears black underneath' (3.1.262.2-3), the words 'Dumb show' (4.3.0.1), the light or taper required at 4.3.0.2, the detail that the Black Bishop's Pawn should enter 'above' (5.1.0.5). In particular, MIDDLETON[T] is careless about music directions: it alone omits the specification 'Lowd' (or 'Lowe') for the music at 5.1.0.2, and the indication that oboes/hoboys should be used 'agen' at 5.1.9.

Middleton was not a reliable copyist. The hypothesis that Middleton took over from CRANE would thus account for the increase, between the CRANE texts and the NON-CRANE texts, in the quantity of transmitted error, of all kinds.

Of course, given this demonstrable propensity to inadvertence, many of the other eighty-two unique substantive readings in MIDDLETON[T] might also be errors. However, they might also be corrections of errors: at 3.2.9-10 (Add. Passage D), MIDDLETON[T] alone preserves the correct lineation. I have already noted that on twenty-three occasions MIDDLETON[T] and CRANE[I] uniquely share readings that appear to be correct (Sec. III), and that the last two scenes of BRIDGEWATER share with ROSENBACH far fewer errors than we would expect, presumably because Middleton corrected them (Sec. VI). Therefore, ROSENBACH's

restoration of original readings corrupted or sophisticated in CRANE[2,3,4] might easily be attributed to authorial correction in [PRE-ROSENBACH].

For material present in CRANE[I], we possess a kind of control, a witness earlier than CRANE[2,3,4], but a witness that demonstrably did not itself serve as copy-text for [PRE-ROSENBACH]. Therefore, when ROSENBACH agrees with CRANE[I] against CRANE[2,3,4], we can be reasonably confident that it is restoring an authorial reading (or at least restoring an authorial variant). But for material added in the revision, we have no such control, nothing demonstrably earlier than CRANE[2,3,4]. In the first 95 lines of 2.2, for which CRANE[I] provides no equivalent, ROSENBACH departs twelve times from a reading present in Crane[2,3,4] alone.[115] Those variants might be errors (or revisions) original to ROSENBACH, or they might restore readings that had been present in the playbook but corrupted by CRANE[2,3,4]; without the testimony of CRANE[I] to guide us, we must simply evaluate each reading on its individual merits.

Although MIDDLETON[T] is an autograph text, unique agreements between ROSENBACH and MIDDLETON[T] must also be evaluated on their individual merits. Obviously, given the evidence I have just surveyed, the fact that a reading occurs in MIDDLETON[T] does not prove that it is correct. Just as obviously, a glance at the Table of Shared Errors will demonstrate that the four NON-CRANE texts are stemmatically linked (as ROSENBACH and CRANE[I] are not); therefore, a reading that originated in ROSENBACH might have been transmitted to MIDDLETON[T], even if it was an error—just as errors in ROSENBACH were transmitted to, or received from, the second half of BRIDGEWATER. Unlike CRANE[I], MIDDLETON[T] cannot serve as a completely reliable control for testing the authority of ROSENBACH readings that depart from CRANE[2,3,4].

Nevertheless, the seven variants uniquely shared by ROSENBACH and MIDDLETON[T] do tend to confirm the hypothesis that Middleton transcribed [PRE-ROSENBACH]. The added 'Incipit Quintus' at 5.1.0.1 is demonstrably Middletonian; so is the oath 'light' at 5.2.87. On the other hand, ROSENBACH and MIDDLETON[T] share unique lineation errors at 3.1.154-5 and 4.2.107-8; as his unique mislineations demonstrate, the author was certainly capable of the kind of mislineation that apparently originated in [PRE-ROSENBACH]. Finally, located conceptually between these two clear errors and these two clear restorations are three indifferent variants: 'you' for 'she' at 2.2.179, 'eyes' for 'eye' at 3.1.382, and 'those' for 'these' at 4.2.96.[116] In each of these seven cases, the passage in question is

---

[114] MIDDLETON[B] omits an exit at 2.2.17.1, but the error might have been inherited from other texts.
[115] 2.2 (scene number), 2.2.0.1, 2.2.40.1 (and/wth), 2.2.2, 2.2.14, 2.2.17 (speech prefix), 2.2.27 (mine/my), 2.2.36 (I have/I've), 2.2.56 (doth/does), 2.2.58, 2.2.73, 2.2.82 (hath/has). Most of these seem to be Crane sophistications corrected by ROSENBACH.
[116] Notice that five of the seven variants in this paragraph come from the second half of the play—and possibly all seven, depending on whether we locate the change in the underlying copy-text for ROSENBACH after 2.1 or somewhere in 3.1. I return to that problem in later sections.

present in CRANE¹, which means that ROSENBACH and MIDDLETONᵀ disagree with all the CRANE texts. In the first two cases, we can explain the variant as a reading sophisticated or censored in all CRANE texts; in the second two, we can explain the variant as a reading correct in CRANE, but corrupted by a sloppy copyist (who also happened to be the author). But in the last three, indifferent cases it is harder to claim that all CRANE texts contained an error, because the four CRANE texts are not stemmatically related. If the variant involves a detail of formal presentation that Crane regarded as his own province (as at 5.1.0.1), then the fact that Crane texts in two different branches share an unauthoritative reading can be explained; but it is harder to describe how Crane texts in different branches should agree in accidentally corrupting 'you', 'eye', and 'those'. So these three indifferent variants are most likely to be errors in [PRE-ROSENBACH] (later inherited by MIDDLETONᵀ), or authorial revisions in [PRE-ROSENBACH] (independently confirmed and authorized by MIDDLETONᵀ).

Anyone familiar with the kinds of minor changes authors make in copying their work will be familiar with variants like these. Both MIDDLETONᵀ and MIDDLETONᴮ contain similarly indifferent revisions, as can be seen by comparing them. For the following variants, one or the other authorial manuscript has a unique reading, which is not itself an error; in every case, the reading of the other authorial manuscript, and of the other witnesses, is perfectly sensible, and almost certainly represents the original authoritative reading.

2.2.14   ‸] Sir MIDDLETONᴮ only
2.2.15   Sir] ‸ MIDDLETONᴮ only
2.2.43-4   last | Vouchsafte] did | uouchsafe MIDDLETONᴮ only
2.2.48   sawe] found MIDDLETONᴮ only
*2.2.50   do's worke] ha's wrought MIDDLETONᴮ only
5.2.16   should nere] neuer should MIDDLETONᴮ only
*5.2.20   thinke it most absurd] count it strange MIDDLETONᴮ only
5.2.35   if] when MIDDLETONᴮ only
5.2.42   this] wch MIDDLETONᴮ only
5.2.45   aside] by MIDDLETONᴮ only
5.2.53   name] nam'de MIDDLETONᴮ only
*5.2.60   strickt] hot MIDDLETONᴮ only
5.2.87   light] MIDDLETONᵀ, ROSENBACH; slid MIDDLETONᴮ only
5.2.92   knowne] seene MIDDLETONᴮ only
5.2.96   more‸] ~ Sir MIDDLETONᴮ only
5.2.107.1   and] wth MIDDLETONᴮ only
5.2.116   wert] art MIDDLETONᴮ only
5.3.7   2] 3 MIDDLETONᴮ only
5.3.17   of the] a'th MIDDLETONᴮ only
5.3.179   Baggs Mouth like Hell] Bagg like Hell-Mouth MIDDLETONᴮ only

* * *

5.2.3.1   Enter Iesuite] MIDDLETONᵀ only. (All other texts have him enter with the White Queen's Pawn at 5.2.0.1.)

5.2.7   has] hee has MIDDLETONᵀ only
5.2.50   men] others MIDDLETONᵀ only
5.2.52   sir] ‸ MIDDLETONᵀ only
*5.2.31   they must haue cunning Iudgments] it must bee strange cunning MIDDLETONᵀ only
5.2.80   heeres] this MIDDLETONᵀ only
*5.2.81, 5.2.84, 5.2.86   Bl.Qs.P.] Intus MIDDLETONᵀ only
5.2.102   swell] swells MIDDLETONᵀ only
5.2.113   I'll play] haue MIDDLETONᵀ only
*5.2.114   bloudie Villayne, wouldst thou] Monster-Impudence, wouldst MIDDLETONᵀ only
5.2.115   offence] attempt MIDDLETONᵀ only
5.2.117   that] yon'd MIDDLETONᵀ only
5.3.1   You haue] y'aue both MIDDLETONᵀ only
5.3.71   in] on MIDDLETONᵀ only
5.3.105   haue] ‸ MIDDLETONᵀ only
5.3.120   shutt] lockt MIDDLETONᵀ only
5.3.131   ins] in his MIDDLETONᵀ only
5.3.147   spoke] spake MIDDLETONᵀ only
5.3.165   Bl.K.] Bl.Q. MIDDLETONᵀ only
5.3.166   Bl.Q.] Bl.D. MIDDLETONᵀ only
5.3.169   this] yon'd MIDDLETONᵀ only
*5.3.185   all ‸ hopes] see, alls MIDDLETONᵀ only
5.3.188-9   ouer laid me, | So squelch'd and squeasde mee] squelcht and squeezde mee, so ouerlayde mee MIDDLETONᵀ only
5.3.191   if] and MIDDLETONᵀ only
5.3.209   man that] not in MIDDLETONᵀ only
5.3.211   the] youre MIDDLETONᵀ only
*Epilogue.7   or in priuate] and in Corners MIDDLETONᵀ only

One of these cases of authorial variation (5.2.102) exactly resembles the indifferent difference between 'eye' and 'eyes': in the variant at 5.3.169, 'this' (like 'these') indicates proximity, while the alternative 'yond' (like 'those') indicates distance. Clearly, the three indifferent variants that ROSENBACH uniquely shares with MIDDLETONᵀ could be authorial.

Most or all of these cases of authorial variation between MIDDLETONᵀ and MIDDLETONᴮ would almost certainly be dismissed as scribal or compositorial errors, if we did not possess autograph manuscript verification for both readings; only a few—perhaps the eight I have asterisked— are so unusual or involve such complex variation that an editor might, without access to autograph, recognize them as evidence of authorial tinkering. But even in those cases the variants would be dismissed as errors by the kinds of editorial reasoning that long denied (and in some quarters continues to deny) Shakespeare's revision of *Hamlet*, *King Lear*, *Othello*, *Troilus and Cressida*, and Sonnet 2. Similar variants in non-autograph texts of *Game* continue to be dismissed as errors. Likewise, most of the cases where ROSENBACH departs from the reading of all the preceding CRANE texts could, individually, be dismissed as errors— and no doubt many of them *are* errors, either errors made in [PRE-ROSENBACH] by the sloppy copyist Thomas Middleton, or errors made by the scribes of ROSENBACH itself.

But ROSENBACH also contains variants from CRANE[1,2,3,4] that are more difficult to attribute to simple inadvertence, and more likely to represent authorial variation. In the following list, the ROSENBACH variant departs from all the Crane texts containing the passage, and is supported by at least one authorial manuscript.

Induction.41   Game, what Game] What Game prethee
4.3.0.3   fetching in] conuaies
5.2.1   Dutie] Loue
5.2.4   Yonder's] Hah? tis
5.2.7   much...wrongd] ill...vsd
5.2.87   light] *not in* CRANE, OKES
5.3.0.1   Scaena Vltima] Scea. 3a
5.3.62   if I should] were I to
5.3.98   crambd] full
5.3.113   Sale] weak
5.3.131   How? Ay, how?] ˄ Ay, how?
5.3.145   secretst] smoothest
5.3.153   It is] 'tis like
5.3.157   ˄now y'are a Brother to us, ˄] BRIDGEWATER D. ~ Bl.Kt.
5.3.185   all hopes confounded] 'Tis too apparent
5.3.188   slid] *not in* CRANE[2,4]
5.3.188   Fat] Black OKES, CRANE/ALLDE; Fat Black CRANE[2]
5.3.196–7   art thou showing | thy impudent] I abhor thee | thou show thy ˄
5.3.209   I shall be] to be
5.3.211–12   foh, the politition is not sound ith Vent, I smell him hether] *not in* CRANE[2], CRANE/ALLDE, OKES
5.3.219   malice] Falshood

Some of these may be restoration of censored material (5.2.87, 5.3.188, 5.3.211–12); others might be compound errors (5.3.153, 5.3.157). But it seems difficult to attribute the sequence of interconneted variants at 5.3.196–7, or the transformation of 'weak orisons' to 'Sale orisons' (5.3.113), to anyone but Middleton. Moreover, the variants at Induction.41 and 5.3.131 both create additional instances of the phenomenon Holdsworth christened 'iterative repetition', a technique Middleton used more than any of his contemporaries (236–67). And if Middleton is responsible for any of this variation, then he may well be responsible for all of it.

At this point, nothing prevents us from concluding that [PRE-ROSENBACH] was a Middleton transcript of CRANE[4]—containing many restorations of authoritative readings, many new errors, and a necessarily indeterminable amount of minor verbal revision.

In the preceding few paragraphs, I have treated ROSENBACH as a whole, because in its spelling and punctuation it appears to be both homogeneous and Middletonian. However, it is notable that most of the variants in this final list—ROSENBACH departures from CRANE, which are supported by at least one autograph text—come from 5.2 and 5.3, scenes in which BRIDGEWATER is autograph. That fact is a simple consequence of the fact that, for those two scenes, we possess two autograph manuscripts. That fact does not invalidate the argument I am making

here, because it is clear that ROSENBACH cannot have been copied directly from BRIDGEWATER in those two scenes; the relationship between the two manuscripts must therefore be through some lost underlying manuscript. ROSENBACH, in other words, cannot have picked up those unique authorial readings by copying new variants that had been introduced for the first time by Middleton when he was transcribing the last two scenes of BRIDGEWATER.

Nevertheless, as the preceding paragraph demonstrates, before we can go any further in analysing the stemmatic history of the NON-CRANE texts we must address the relationship, in the second half of the play, between ROSENBACH and BRIDGEWATER.

XVI. ROSENBACH and BRIDGEWATER: Acts Three to Five

So far, my analysis of ROSENBACH has concentrated on its relationship to the CRANE texts. But analysis of the play's second half must begin with ROSENBACH's relationship to BRIDGEWATER.

Table of Shared Errors in ROSENBACH: Patterns that occur only in 3.1.319–Epilogue.10.1

18. BRIDGEWATER: 13–25 [11–22]
31. BRIDGEWATER–MIDDLETON[T]: 9–11
39. BRIDGEWATER–MIDDLETON[T]–CRANE[2]: 2
53. BRIDGEWATER–OKES–CRANE[2,3,4]: 2
40. BRIDGEWATER–MIDDLETON–OKES: 2
9. MIDDLETON[T]: 1–2
51. BRIDGEWATER–MIDDLETON[T]–CRANE[2,3,4]: 1
37. OKES–CRANE[3,4]: 1
* * *
43. BRIDGEWATER–OKES–CRANE[2,4]: 1? [not in CRANE[3]]
* * *
[4. CRANE[2]: 1]
[47. BRIDGEWATER–MIDDLETON[T]–OKES–CRANE/ALLDE: 1]
[54. BRIDGEWATER–MIDDLETON[T]–CRANE: 1]
[56. BRIDGEWATER–MIDDLETON[T]–OKES–CRANE[2,3,4]: 1]

If we limit ourselves to the filtered data-set, the later section of the play contains nine new patterns. In this section of the play, unlike the first, there *are* unique links to both BRIDGEWATER (11–22) and MIDDLETON[T] (1–2), or to the two of them together (9–11) that cannot be explained through the medium of any other text. This section contains no new patterns of links to the CRANE group that cannot be explained through BRIDGEWATER and OKES. However, one of the patterns that occurs throughout the manuscript (listed in the previous Section) includes three errors in this second half, which link ROSENBACH uniquely to [CRANE[4]].[117] There is no reason to suppose that any of these shared errors is authorial, and it is difficult to dismiss three as coincidental. To summarize: the first part of ROSENBACH is linked directly to CRANE[4] and OKES, whereas the second part is linked to two additional NON-CRANE texts (BRIDGEWATER and MIDDLETON[T]).

---

[117] Pattern 12: 3.1.333 (interpolated terminal -s), 4.2.44 (correct 'three', CRANE/ALLDE 'thee', ROSENBACH 'the', probably progressive error), 5.3.166.3 (absence of terminal -s).

The most important and most obvious fact about the second half of ROSENBACH is the new relationship with BRIDGEWATER. Within the filtered data-set, 22 errors are shared with BRIDGEWATER alone, and another 25, belonging to larger patterns, might be linked to other texts *through* BRIDGEWATER (in one direction or the other). Against those 47 shared errors that connect it to BRIDGEWATER, only 11 of the shared errors in the second half of ROSENBACH *require* a link to *any* other text: OKES (6), CRANE[4] (3), or MIDDLETON[T] (1–2).

Neither BRIDGEWATER nor ROSENBACH can be a direct copy of the other; therefore, the links between them must derive from the lost underlying manuscript or manuscripts that connect them. That connection must, in fact, have been even stronger than it appears from the data above. In the 669 scribal lines from 3.1.345.1 to 5.2.0.1, BRIDGEWATER shares from nineteen to twenty-two errors with ROSENBACH alone—one such error every 30 to 35 lines. But in the 398 autograph lines from 5.2.1 to Epilogue.10.1, it shares only three errors with ROSENBACH alone (5.3.5, 12, 5.3.20–1)—one such error every 133 lines. The last two scenes of ROSENBACH contain 37 unique errors; clearly, ROSENBACH does not suddenly become four times more accurate than it had been in earlier scenes. But fewer of its errors are shared with BRIDGEWATER: the frequency of such errors in the last two scenes is only 23–26% of what it was in the preceding 669 lines. This massive discrepancy can be easily explained by a change in BRIDGEWATER: between 3.1.345 and 5.2.0.1 the BRIDGEWATER scribe passively repeated inherited errors, but in the last two scenes Middleton spotted and corrected many such errors, thereby drastically reducing the amount of error shared by BRIDGEWATER and ROSENBACH. We might therefore reasonably extrapolate that, in the lost manuscript that Middleton was copying in the last two scenes of BRIDGEWATER, there were about nine additional errors shared uniquely between ROSENBACH and [PRE-BRIDGEWATER].

As this last paragraph demonstrates, in order to explain this extraordinary connection between ROSENBACH and BRIDGEWATER we need to suspend momentarily the analysis of ROSENBACH itself, and acquire an overview of the stemmatic patterns in its companion. We have already divided ROSENBACH into two sections, to analyse the pattern of its shared errors; we now need to do the same thing for BRIDGEWATER.

Table of Shared Errors in BRIDGEWATER: Patterns that occur only in Prologue.0.1–3.1.319

38. OKES–MIDDLETON[T]–CRANE[3]: 1
45. OKES–MIDDLETON[T]–CRANE[2,3]: 1
56. OKES–MIDDLETON[T]–ROSENBACH–CRANE[2,3,4]: 1

* * *

22. OKES–CRANE[3]: 1? (CRANE[3] may be deliberate)
34. MIDDLETON[T]–ROSENBACH–[CRANE[4]]: 1? (unspecified in CRANE[3])

* * *

[5. CRANE[3]: 1]

[46. OKES–ROSENBACH–CRANE[3,4]: 1]
[49. OKES–MIDDLETON[T]–ROSENBACH–CRANE[1,2]: 1]
[50. OKES–MIDDLETON[T]–ROSENBACH–CRANE[1,3]: 1]
[52. OKES–MIDDLETON[T]–ROSENBACH–CRANE[3,4]: 1]
[55. OKES–MIDDLETON[T]–ROSENBACH–CRANE[1,2,4]: 1]

Only five patterns survive the normal filtering process. Of those, two are queried; in one case, the query might eliminate any connection with the CRANE group, and in the other case it might add another CRANE manuscript to a larger pattern. These queries are, in context, irrelevant. In all five reliable patterns, all the links to other texts can be explained through a stemmatic relationship with just two texts: MIDDLETON[T] and OKES. As in ROSENBACH, however, these patterns unique to the first half of the play cannot be properly understood without taking account of patterns present in both halves.

Table of Shared Errors in BRIDGEWATER: Patterns that occur throughout the play

16. OKES: 5–9 | 5–6 [4–6]
32. OKES–MIDDLETON[T]: 10–12 [7–9] | 1
31. MIDDLETON[T]–ROSENBACH: 1? | 9–10
13. MIDDLETON[T]: 3–4 [2–3] | 3–4
30. OKES–ROSENBACH: 1–2 | 1–7 [1–5]
11. [CRANE[4]]: 1? | 2

These six patterns include unique pairings with OKES, MIDDLETON[T], and [CRANE[4]]. In these and the patterns specific to the first half, all the links to ROSENBACH can be explained through a stemmatic relationship with MIDDLETON[T] or OKES. Thus BRIDGEWATER, unlike ROSENBACH, has a connection to MIDDLETON[T] from the outset. The links to OKES and MIDDLETON[T] (29) are far stronger than the single Crane connection. Actually, the first 58% of the play in BRIDGEWATER is, stemmatically, a distinct entity, because it obviously derives from a different textual source than the second half; consequently, its single error uniquely shared with the CRANE group belongs to the category of fragile patterns created by a single error shared by only two texts. Therefore, according to the criteria we established earlier (sec. VII), the single example of pattern 11 in the first part of BRIDGEWATER constitutes a potentially coincidental agreement, which should be removed from the filtered data-set.[118] By these strict criteria, the first 58% of BRIDGEWATER would become the only extant witness without a single unmediated link to the CRANE group. Since the analysis of shared error totals (Sections VI and VII) consistently puts BRIDGEWATER farthest from the CRANE texts, this pattern in the *distribution* of shared errors strongly confirms the evidence of *quantities* of shared error, placing BRIDGEWATER near the very end of the sequence of extant texts.

---

[118] The error, the transposition of 'barques' and 'vessels' at 2.1.177, could easily have been made independently by two separate copyists: it reverses the order of two synonymous nouns in parallel constructions in a single verse line, the kind of unit which a copyist would normally carry in his head. Elimination of this example as a coincidence would transform Pattern 11 from the category 'errors shared throughout the play' and transfer it to the category 'errors shared in the second half only'.

By contrast, in the same section of the play ROSENBACH contains seven errors shared with the CRANE group but with no member of the NON-CRANE group. Those required connections to the CRANE group constitute one-third of the shared errors in that part of ROSENBACH. In that section of the play, ROSENBACH's total of shared errors is only 72% of the total in the comparable part of BRIDGEWATER; consequently, the complete absence of reliable CRANE connections in BRIDGEWATER indicates that the two texts have radically different origins. The first part of ROSENBACH is as close to CRANE as the first part of BRIDGEWATER is far away from it.

These distinct patterns of shared error demonstrate conclusively that there must once have existed two distinct physical entities, two manuscripts, now lost: on the one hand, [PRE-ROSENBACH] (which was the source for the first part of ROSENBACH, and was linked to [CRANE⁴] and OKES), and on the other hand [PRE-BRIDGEWATER] (which was the source for the first part of BRIDGEWATER, and was linked to MIDDLETON^T and OKES). For the first part of the play, at least, ROSENBACH and BRIDGEWATER cannot have been copied from a single manuscript, but must have been copied from different sources. We must keep these two lost manuscripts in mind, as we analyse the pattern of shared errors in the second part of the play.

Table of Shared Errors in BRIDGEWATER: Patterns that occur only in 3.1.319–Epilogue.10.1

18. ROSENBACH: 13–25 [11–22]
40. ROSENBACH–MIDDLETON^T–OKES: 3 [2]
39. ROSENBACH–CRANE²–MIDDLETON^T: 2
53. ROSENBACH–CRANE^{2,3,4}–OKES: 2
51. ROSENBACH–CRANE^{2,3,4}–MIDDLETON^T: 1
44. OKES–CRANE^{2,3,4}: 1

* * *

24. OKES–[CRANE⁴]/Allde: 1? (not in CRANE^{2,3})
43. ROSENBACH–OKES–CRANE^{2,4}: 1? (not in CRANE³)

* * *

[3. CRANE¹: 1]
[47. ROSENBACH–MIDDLETON^T–OKES–CRANE/Allde: 1]
[54. ROSENBACH–CRANE–MIDDLETON^T: 1]

Here, eight patterns survive the filtering process. The two queries might both add another Crane text to a larger pattern. But the queries are irrelevant, because all the links specific to this portion of the play can be explained through a stemmatic connection with ROSENBACH (27–30) and OKES (2–4). If we add to these eight patterns the seven that stretch across the whole play, another 22 errors connect this part of BRIDGEWATER to ROSENBACH. But there also remain at least thirteen errors that must have come from some other source, including unique links with OKES (6), MIDDLETON^T (4), and [CRANE⁴] (2). These are the same three texts that the second part of ROSENBACH is linked to. In other words, not only are ROSENBACH and BRIDGEWATER uniquely linked to each other in the second half of the play; in that part of the play, both of them are also linked to the same other texts. This global pattern of shared secondary connections provides further,

compelling evidence of the close stemmatic connection between ROSENBACH and BRIDGEWATER in the second half of the play.

Logically, three possible scenarios could account for the pattern of shared errors in the second half of ROSENBACH and BRIDGEWATER.[119]

1. [PRE-ROSENBACH] became the copy-text for BRIDGE-WATER in the second half of the play.
2. [PRE-BRIDGEWATER] became the copy-text for ROSEN-BACH in the second half of the play.
3. A third lost manuscript became the copy-text for both ROSENBACH and BRIDGEWATER in the second half of the play.

The first and second scenarios differ only in the vector of transmission; both require the existence of only two lost manuscripts. We may call this The Two-Manuscript Hypothesis. By contrast, the third scenario requires a third lost manuscript, different from the other two. We may call this The Three-Manuscript Hypothesis. We will eventually have to face the problem of determining which of these scenarios is right (or the problem of determining whether we can determine which of these scenarios is right). For now, the important point is that *one of these three possibilities must be correct.*

Whichever of these scenarios is correct, three stemmatic consequences are already clear. First, within the sequence of transmission, ROSENBACH and BRIDGEWATER are *not* unified entities. In each manuscript, the first two and a half acts contain, demonstrably, a very different set of stemmatic links than the last two and a half acts.

Secondly, after 3.1.318 ROSENBACH and BRIDGEWATER are closer to each other than either is to any other text. They belong, that is, to a clearly defined subset. For clarity's sake, let us call the second part of ROSENBACH 'R2', and the second part of BRIDGEWATER 'B2'; we can then call the subset they form '(R2,B2)'. That subset is the most strongly defined two-member subset among all the possible two-member subsets formed by the extant witnesses to *A Game at Chess*: its integrity is established by more uniquely shared errors (in less than half a play) than any other pairing of two *complete* plays. That is, the subset (R2,B2) is even more strongly defined than the subset (C2,C3). If the Three-Manuscript Hypothesis were to be proven correct, then the subset (R2,B2) would also have contained a third member. But the inclusion in the subset of a third, lost member—let us call it ['RB2']—would not alter the integrity of the subset. (See Sec. X.) In the transmissional series created by the extant texts, the second halves of ROSENBACH and BRIDGEWATER *must be adjacent.*

Thirdly, before 3.1.319 ROSENBACH ('R1') and BRIDGEWA-TER ('B1') do *not* form a subset. Within the first half of the

---

119 All three scenarios could be rephrased, replacing 'BRIDGEWATER' with '[PRE--BRIDGEWATER]' and replacing 'ROSENBACH' with '[PRE-ROSENBACH]'. That distinction will become important later, in our global analysis of divided copy (Section XXVIII), but here what matters is only the distinction between vectors of error and between the Two-Manuscript and Three-Manuscript hypotheses.

play, there are no errors uniquely shared between BRIDGE-WATER and ROSENBACH. Instead, the first half of BRIDGEWA-TER has unique pairings with OKES and with MIDDLETON[T], forming two alternative subsets: (B1,O1) and (B1,M1). The absence of any two-member subset that contains both R1 and B1 means that, within the larger transmissional series created by the extant texts, R1 *and B1 cannot be adjacent.* In particular, the first part of ROSENBACH cannot have come between the series formed between BRIDGEWATER and OKES, or the series formed between BRIDGEWATER and MIDDLETON.

These three facts should help us clarify the relationships to one another of all four extant NON-CRANE texts.

XVII. The Sequence of NON-CRANE Texts

The sequence is most clearly established by examining all errors shared by at least two members of the NON-CRANE group.[120] Since our interest here is in the relationships of the NON-CRANE texts to one another, I have reorganized the display of these patterns to highlight those relationships; when part of a NON-CRANE pattern includes one or more CRANE texts, I have not specified which CRANE text, but simply put 'Crane' in square brackets. Thus, in the third group clustered below, patterns 39, 34, and 51 look identical, because they differ only in regard to which Crane text(s) are linked to ROSENBACH, BRIDGEWATER and MIDDLETON[T].

Table of Errors shared among the Non-Crane Texts

18. ROSENBACH–BRIDGEWATER: 23–25 [20–22] (3.1.345.1–5.3.21)

* * *

30. ROSENBACH–BRIDGEWATER–OKES: 5–9 [5–7] (3.1.7–5.3.191)
53. [Crane]–ROSENBACH–BRIDGEWATER–OKES: 2 (4.1.116, 5.1.1.1)
43. [Crane]–ROSENBACH–BRIDGEWATER–OKES: 1 (4.1.21–2)

* * *

31. ROSENBACH–BRIDGEWATER–MIDDLETON[T]: 11 (3.1.155–5.3.178)
39. [Crane]–ROSENBACH–BRIDGEWATER–MIDDLETON[T]: 2 (5.1.30.1, 5.1.33.1)
34. [Crane]–ROSENBACH–BRIDGEWATER–MIDDLETON[T]: 1 (3.1.115.1)
51. [Crane]–ROSENBACH–BRIDGEWATER–MIDDLETON[T]: 1 (5.3.162.1)

* * *

16. BRIDGEWATER–OKES: 14 (Induction.14–4.4.110.2)
22. [Crane]–BRIDGEWATER–OKES: 1 (2.1.179)
44. [Crane]–BRIDGEWATER–OKES: 1 (3.1.410)
24. [Crane]–BRIDGEWATER–OKES: 1 (3.2.30–1)

* * *

13. BRIDGEWATER–MIDDLETON[T]: 8 (1.1.205–5.2.114)

* * *

32. BRIDGEWATER–OKES–MIDDLETON[T]: 13 (Induction.23–4.1.93)
38. [Crane]–BRIDGEWATER–OKES–MIDDLETON[T]: 1 (3.1.44)

45. [Crane]–BRIDGEWATER–OKES–MIDDLETON[T]: 1 (Induction.52.1)

* * *

15. ROSENBACH–OKES: 11–12 (1.1.201–5.3.116)
37. [Crane]–ROSENBACH–OKES: 1 (5.2.108)
21. [Crane]–ROSENBACH–OKES: 1? (2.2.94.1: passage not in BRIDGEWATER)

* * *

9. ROSENBACH–MIDDLETON[T]: 2 (4.2.81–107)
23. [Crane]–ROSENBACH–MIDDLETON[T]: 1 (3.1.154–5)

* * *

10. MIDDLETON[T]–OKES: 2 (3.1.33, 3.1.75)
33. [Crane]–MIDDLETON[T]–OKES: 1 (5.3.19–20)

* * *

40. NON-CRANE: 3 [2] ([1.1.331.1], 5.1.0.4–5, 5.3.178.1–2)
56. [Crane]–NON-CRANE: 3–4 [1–2]   (2.2.33?, 3.1.175.1, [3.1.305.1], [5.1.9.2])

* * *

[46. [Crane]–BRIDGEWATER–OKES: 1]
[48. [Crane]–MIDDLETON[T]–OKES: 1?]
[54. [Crane]–MIDDLETON[T]–BRIDGEWATER: 1]
[47. [Crane]–NON-CRANE: 1]
[49. [Crane]–NON-CRANE: 1]
[50. [Crane]–NON-CRANE: 1]
[52. [Crane]–NON-CRANE: 1]
[55. [Crane]–NON-CRANE: 1]

Three important facts should be immediately apparent from this table; a fourth is much harder to see, but even more important.

First, BRIDGEWATER is strongly linked to both MIDDLETON[T] and OKES. Even using the lowered filtered figures, it shares, altogether, 44 errors with OKES, and these are distributed throughout the entire play, ranging from Induction.14 to 5.3.191. Likewise, it shares, altogether, at least 29 errors with MIDDLETON[T], and these errors too are distributed throughout the entire play, ranging from Induction.23 to 5.3.178. BRIDGEWATER shares errors with both OKES and MIDDLETON[T] twenty times. This evidence unequivocally establishes that BRIDGEWATER is stemmatically connected to both MIDDLETON[T] and OKES throughout its length—even though, stemmatically, it is not a unified entity. In other words, both [PRE-B1] and [PRE-B2] are linked to OKES and MIDDLETON[T].

Secondly, ROSENBACH is not only linked to BRIDGEWATER from somewhere in 3.1 to the end of the play; it is also linked, from somewhere in 3.1 to the end of the play, to BRIDGEWATER-and-MIDDLETON[T]-together (at least fifteen times from 3.1.155), and to BRIDGEWATER-and--OKES-together (at least eight times from 3.1.7). That is, the triplet BRIDGEWATER–ROSENBACH–MIDDLETON does not appear before 3.1.155, and the triplet BRIDGEWATER–ROSENBACH–OKES does not appear before 3.1.7.

---

[120] That is, this table does not include errors shared by only one NON-CRANE text. I gave totals for such cross-over errors above, in Sec. VII, and I will analyse their patterns in subsequent sections.

Thirdly, although BRIDGEWATER is strongly linked to both MIDDLETON[T] and OKES throughout the play, it shares an error with both those texts, but not ROSENBACH, only if the error occurs *before* 4.1.94.

Finally, there is a fourth important pattern to these shared errors, although unlike the others it may not be immediately apparent. Various combinations of the four NON-CRANE texts share at least 112 errors, in at least 25 different patterns. But there is not a single error shared by the three texts ROSENBACH–MIDDLETON[T]–OKES, unless that error is also shared by BRIDGEWATER. In other words, unless an error is shared by *all* NON-CRANE texts, it is not shared by the three specific texts ROSENBACH–MIDDLETON–OKES.[121]

Like CRANE[2,3,4], the NON-CRANE texts constitute a set, which we need to translate into a series. But the NON-CRANE texts differ from CRANE[2,3,4] in two important respects. First, the NON-CRANE set has four members, not three: pattern 40 contains errors in all four of the NON-CRANE texts, and no others. Secondly, there are in fact *two* NON-CRANE sets: as we have already established, the second halves of ROSENBACH and of BRIDGEWATER (R2 and B2) are stemmatically distinct from the first halves (R1 and B1). For stemmatic purposes, then, we need to distinguish the set containing the first half of all four NON-CRANE texts (B1,M1,O1,R1) from the set containing the second half of all four NON-CRANE texts (B2,M2,O2,R2).

Let us begin with the set formed by the first half of the play, using the mathematical reasoning we applied earlier to CRANE[2,3,4] (Section X). We already have one element of the series created by the set (B1,O1,M1,R1): we know that ROSENBACH and BRIDGEWATER cannot be adjacent in the series. Thus, we know that R1 and B1 *could* be first and third (1,3), first and fourth (1,4), or second and fourth (2,4). But they *cannot* be the first and second items in the series (1,2), the second and third (2,3), or the third and fourth (3,4). In other words, one of them must be either first or last in the series, and the other must be separated from it by at least one intermediate text.

In order to narrow those three possible positions further, we have to look at sets of three. If four texts produce the sequence 1→2→3→4, there are only two possible series of three. In terms of textual transmission, an error present in 1 might easily be passed to 2 and 3, and then corrected in 4 (producing an error shared by the series 1→2→3); or the correct reading in 1 might be corrupted in 2, and passed from it to 3 and 4 (producing an error shared by the series 2→3→4). But from such a series we should not get an error shared by the set (1,2,4); an error corrected in 3 should not re-occur in 4. Likewise, from such a series we should not get an error shared by the set (1,3,4): an error corrected in 2 should not re-occur in 3, and be passed from there to 4.

Every set of four contains four possible subsets of three: (1,2,3), (1,2,4), (1,3,4), and (2,3,4). Only one of these four possible subsets occurs among the NON-CRANE texts in the first part of the play: pattern 32, OKES–BRIDGEWATER–

MIDDLETON (O1,B1,M1). Of the six possible pairs formed by a set of four, only three appear in the first part of the play: (R1,O1), (O1,B1), and (B1,M1). Thus, two elements of the lone triplet subset (O1,B1,M1) also appear as pair subsets, but the third possible pair subset (O1,M1) does not appear. This is exactly the same situation we encountered within the three-member set (C2,C3,C4), and as there it indicates that the excluded two-member set must contain the first and last items in the series. Thus, for the first part of the play the sequence of transmission must have been O1→B1→M1 or M1→B1→O1.

In other words, the distribution of subsets of two and subsets of three demonstrates that B1 must be in the middle. We have already established that R1 cannot be adjacent to B1, and that one of those two texts must be either the first or last text in the series. Therefore, since we now know that B1 is in the middle, we also know that R1 must be either first or last. Finally, the third subset of two that does not appear in the first half of the play is (R1,M1). Therefore, R1 cannot be adjacent to M1, either. These exclusions leave only two possible sequences: R1→O1→B1→M1 *or* M1→B1→O1→R1. In short, for the first part of the play ROSENBACH and MIDDLETON must be the first and last of the NON-CRANE texts. But this set-logic will not, in itself, tell us which was which.

We can now turn to the set formed by the second half of the play, (B2,M2,O2,R2). We already have one element of the series created by that set: we know that ROSENBACH and BRIDGEWATER form the strongest of all subsets (R2,B2), and must be adjacent in the series. The problem is to situate the two other extant texts in relation to that pair. Thus, we know that (R2,B2) *could* be the first and second items in the series (1,2), or the second and third (2,3), or the third and fourth (3,4). But they could *not* be any of the disjunctive pairs: they could not be first and third (1,3), or first and fourth (1,4), or second and fourth (2,4).

The complete absence of the triplet ROSENBACH–MIDDLETON–OKES indicates that those three texts must belong to the excluded series 1→2→4 or the excluded series 1→3→4, for both halves of the play. That is, one of those three texts must be at the very beginning of the sequence of four NON-CRANE texts, and one must be at the very end. Just as the triplet ROSENBACH–MIDDLETON–OKES does not appear anywhere in the play, so the triplet BRIDGEWATER–MIDDLETON–OKES does not appear after 4.1.93. So, in the last 709 lines of the play, two of the four possible sets of triplets—(M2,O2,R2) and (B2,M2,O2)—do not appear. The two triplets that do appear, and appear repeatedly—(R2,B2,M2) and (R2,B2,O2)—must therefore belong to the series 1→2→3 and 2→3→4. Logically, the texts that appear in both sets must be in the middle: only 2 and

[121] The only apparent exception to this rule, the error at 2.2.38, occurs in a passage entirely omitted by BRIDGEWATER. In other words, BRIDGEWATER does not have the correct reading, corrupted in the other three NON-CRANE texts; it has no reading at all. The error thus appears in all extant NON-CRANE texts of the passage. I have therefore listed it as a queried example of Pattern 56, rather than as the sole (queried) example of a separate pattern containing errors shared by the six texts CRANE[2,3,4]–ROSENBACH–MIDDLETON[T]–OKES.

3 belong to both series. Therefore, in the second half of the play, ROSENBACH and BRIDGEWATER must be the middle texts in the series 1→2→3→4.

Since we already know that the subset (R2,B2) must be an adjacent pair, the patterns of triplets is compatible with what we know about the (R2,B2) pair. Indeed, by looking at other pairings we can clarify the series even further. In Act Five, two other pairs never appear: (O2,R2) and (B2,M2). For Act Five we therefore have, as we do for Acts One and Two, three present subsets of two and three absent subsets of two, which gives us the following information:

> B2 is adjacent to M2 and R2 but not O2
> R2 is adjacent to B2 and O2 but not M2
> M2 is adjacent to B2 but not O2 or R2
> O2 is adjacent to R2 but not B2 or M2

Combining this information with what we already know from the excluded and included triplets, we know that in Act Five the series must have been either OKES→ ROSENBACH→ BRIDGEWATER→ MIDDLETON[T] or MIDDLETON[T]→ BRIDGEWATER→ ROSENBACH→ OKES.

The foregoing logical proof leaves us with five questions, which the following analysis will attempt to answer:

1. In the first part of the play, is ROSENBACH or MIDDLETON[T] the first text in the series?
2. In the second part of the play, is OKES or MIDDLE-TON[T] the first text in the series?
3. In the second part of the play, is ROSENBACH or BRIDGEWATER earlier in the series?
4. Why do the breaks between the two parts of the play fall in different places—after 3.1.7, or after 3.1.319, or after 4.1.93, or after 4.4.110.2—in different pairs and triplets among the NON-CRANE texts?
5. Is the connection between ROSENBACH and BRIDGE-WATER best explained by the Two-Manuscript Hypothesis, or the Three-Manuscript Hypothesis?

Not surprisingly, the answer to each of these questions is related to the others.

XVIII. ROSENBACH and BRIDGEWATER: The Vector of Error

We have, as yet, no specific indication of the vector of error in the set (R2,B2). 'The fact that two texts share an improbable number of errors clearly indicates that they are related, but . . . it does not establish which is a copy of the other' (para. 11).

In what follows I will be analysing the later part of the play, where ROSENBACH and BRIDGEWATER are undeniably stemmatically connected, in order to determine the vector of transmission within the subset (R2,B2). My conclusions depend on an argumentative chain, and I have therefore numbered the paragraphs of the chain.

1. If both R2 and B2 derive, independently, from the same lost manuscript that was used as copy-text for B1 ('PRE-B1'), or from the same lost manuscript that was used as copy-text for R1 ('PRE-R1'), then neither extant

text need be earlier than the other: they are both dead-ends, and might be separate branches from the same root. Historically, one would almost certainly have been copied later than the other, but stemmatically that chronological fact would be irrelevant. Stemmatically, both ROSENBACH and BRIDGEWATER would be equally distant from the origin of the textual stream. In that case, for the NON-CRANE texts of the later part of the play we would have only a three-text series: either OKES→[BRIDGEWATER/ROSENBACH]→MID-DLETON[T] or MIDDLETON[T]→[BRIDGEWATER/ROSENBACH]→OKES.

2. Therefore, for the second half of the play the vector question is dependent on whether the Two-Manuscript hypothesis or the Three-Text Hypothesis is correct. If there was a third lost manuscript—'PRE-(R2,B2)'—then we might be able to determine whether 'PRE-(R2,B2)' was earlier, or later, than 'PRE-B1' or 'PRE-R1'. And we could then identify BRIDGEWATER or ROSENBACH as stemmatically later, dependent on whichever extant text was derived from the later of the lost manuscripts.

3. It seems immediately apparent that the lost ancestor of the extant subset (R2,B2) more closely resembled 'PRE-B1' than 'PRE-R1'. The later part of both ROSENBACH and BRIDGEWATER contains undeniable links to MIDDLE-TON[T]—as does the first part of BRIDGEWATER (but not the first part of ROSENBACH). More generally, the first part of ROSENBACH is more distinct from the rest of the manuscript: it contains six unique patterns—as opposed to only four patterns that occur throughout the play. That is, 60% of the patterns in the first half of ROSENBACH are unique to that part. By contrast, the first part of BRIDGEWATER contains only four unique patterns—as opposed to seven that occur throughout the play. That is, only 36% of the patterns in the first half of BRIDGEWATER are unique to that part. In both respects, BRIDGEWATER is, relatively, more homogeneous than ROSENBACH, in its stemmatic relationships to other texts.

4. On the evidence of the preceding paragraph, BRIDGE-WATER could have been copied throughout from a single, stemmatically homogeneous, lost manuscript ('Pre-B1'), and the link between the two extant manuscripts would begin clearly and abruptly when the copy-text for ROSEN-BACH changed from 'PRE-R1' to 'PRE-B1'.

5. The foregoing evidence is compatible with the Two-Text Hypothesis. But it does not prove that hypothesis. It demonstrates only that the lost manuscript copy-text for (R2,B2) resembled 'Pre-B1' more than 'Pre-R1'. It does not prove that the lost manuscript was *identical* to 'Pre-B1'. It proves that the copy-text for ROSENBACH was discontinuous, but it does not prove that the copy-text for BRIDGEWATER was continuous.

6. If the Three-Manuscript hypothesis is correct, then the copy-text for BRIDGEWATER would also have been non-homogeneous. The second half of BRIDGEWATER might, in that case, have derived from 'PRE-(R2,B2)', rather than directly from 'PRE-B1'. But if that were so, then there is no reason to assume that the discontinuity in BRIDGEWATER occurred at exactly the same point in the play as the discontinuity in ROSENBACH. In fact, if the Three-Manuscript

hypothesis were correct, it would be rather remarkable—which is to say, exceedingly improbable—if the stemmatic discontinuities in the two manuscripts began at exactly the same point.

7. Anyone dividing the play into two parts would be likely to do so somewhere in the long first scene of the middle act: the play was divided between the two printers Mathewes and Allde at 3.1.216, between two scribes in ROSENBACH at 3.1.44, between two scribes in BRIDGEWATER at 3.1.0.1, and—as demonstrated by paragraph 3, above—between two sources of copy-text in ROSENBACH somewhere between 3.1.319 and 3.1.345.1. None of these known divisions occurs at the same point, but all of them occur in 3.1 (before the material in '3.2', Additional Passage D). It is therefore not at all implausible to suppose that the lost source for BRIDGEWATER might also have been divided in 3.1, but at a point slightly different from any of the other known divisions.

8. There is, in fact, compelling evidence that the lost manuscript source for BRIDGEWATER was discontinuous, and that the discontinuity occurred in 3.1. In the first place, scribe B begins work on BRIDGEWATER at 3.1.0.1. The division of the play between the two scribes might reflect a division in the underlying copy-text: either a discontinuity in that copy-text, or the use of different manuscripts by the two scribes. The change of scribes also coincides with a change in stemmatic relationships. I have already called attention to the fact (Sec. XVII) that the triplet ROSENBACH-BRIDGEWATER-OKES makes its first appearance at 3.1.7, only seven lines after the appearance of a new scribe in BRIDGEWATER. In fact, three of the seven patterns that seemingly persist throughout BRIDGEWATER actually begin after the change of scribes:

30. ROSENBACH-BRIDGEWATER-OKES: 2–9 [2–7]
3.1.7–5.3.187–91

* * *

31. ROSENBACH-BRIDGEWATER-MIDDLETON[T]: 9–11
3.1.155.1–5.3.178.1

* * *

56. CRANE[2,3,4]–NON-CRANE: 2–3 [0–1]
3.1.175.1–[5.1.9.2]

Subtracting these patterns from the group that belongs to the whole play significantly affects our view of the relative homogeneity of BRIDGEWATER (as analysed in paragraph 3 above). If we break BRIDGEWATER at 3.1.1, rather than 3.1.345.1, then the first part of BRIDGEWATER contains four unique patterns, and four that occur throughout the play: that is, 50% (rather than 36%) of the patterns in the first half of BRIDGEWATER are unique to the first part. Moreover, with this new division ten patterns are unique to the second half of the play. Thus, of the eighteen patterns of shared error found in BRIDGEWATER, fourteen (78%) are unique to one part or the other. Of the nineteen patterns of shared error found in ROSENBACH, fifteen (79%) are unique to one part or the other. The difference here in these two sets of percentages is, of course, not statistically significant. It provides strong evidence that,

stemmatically, neither ROSENBACH nor BRIDGEWATER is homogeneous.

9. The preceding paragraph seems to confirm the Three--Text Hypothesis.[122] Both ROSENBACH and BRIDGEWATER are equally discontinuous texts, but their discontinuities occur at different points in the play. This could not have happened if the second half of one of the extant manuscripts was copied from the same lost homogeneous exemplar that was used, for the other extant manuscript, throughout the play.[123] We must therefore assume the existence of at least one additional lost manuscript, distinct from both 'PRE-R1' and 'PRE-B1'. In other words, the clear stemmatic relationship of the two extant manuscripts BRIDGEWATER and ROSENBACH requires the existence of at least three lost manuscripts: [PRE-BRIDGEWATER], [PRE--ROSENBACH], and a third physical entity, earlier than the other two, that we might provisionally call '[PRE--ROSENBACH/BRIDGEWATER].'

10. If the Three-Manuscript hypothesis is correct (as the preceding paragraphs seem to demonstrate), then we would also expect there to be differences in the quantity and the distribution of shared errors in the second halves of ROSENBACH and BRIDGEWATER. Although the discontinuity in BRIDGEWATER begins earlier, for comparison purposes we must use the later break in ROSENBACH, since it is only after that point that both manuscripts demonstrably derive, at one or more removes, from a common source. The second part of ROSENBACH (undoubtedly beginning by 3.1.345.1) contains nine filtered shared errors not linked to BRIDGEWATER; by contrast, the second part of BRIDGEWATER, defined in the same way, contains fifteen errors not linked to ROSENBACH. If both derive from a shared ancestor, why does BRIDGEWATER contain 67% more shared errors than ROSENBACH? I can envisage two possible explanations for this pattern. The first explanation would locate the source of the discrepancy in the two extant texts: it would postulate that BRIDGEWATER was, in those scenes, less 'corrected' than ROSENBACH. BRIDGEWATER, it could be conjectured, passively reproduced errors in the common ancestor, where ROSENBACH often corrected such errors. This explanation seems relatively unlikely: both extant texts were produced by more than one scribe in this portion of the text, and BRIDGEWATER benefited from the attention of two separate post-inscription correctors, which ROSENBACH did not. If either text shows evidence of more transference/correction, it is BRIDGEWATER, not ROSENBACH. Hence, this first explanation for the disparity seems unlikely. The second explanation would locate

---

[122] This conclusion was also reached by Howard-Hill, though he did not articulate the proof offered here. See Figure 1.

[123] Note that the adjective 'homogeneous' is vital to the logic of this sentence. For example, if the copy-text for [PRE-BRIDGEWATER] changed at 3.1.0, and then the copy-text for ROSENBACH changed to [PRE-BRIDGEWATER] at 3.1.319, the two separate discontinuities identified in the preceding paragraphs would both be explained. However, this scenario simply moves the stemmatic location of the Third Lost Manuscript: instead of being necessary in order to explain the change of copy-text for BRIDGEWATER, it would now be necessary in order to explain the change of copy-text for [PRE-BRIDGEWATER]. These alternatives in the analysis of divided copy are more fully explored in Section XXVIII.

the source of the discrepancy in the two lost copy-texts: it would postulate that [PRE-BRIDGEWATER] is later than [PRE-ROSENBACH]. In the later half of the play ROSENBACH, BRIDGEWATER, and their lost copy-texts clearly belong to a series of stemmatically related texts, and in such a series we would expect the later of two adjacent texts to have accumulated more shared errors than the earlier text.

11. The figures in the preceding paragraph are even more remarkable if we take account of the fact that the last two scenes of BRIDGEWATER are autograph. As I have already demonstrated (Sec. VI), when copying the last two scenes of the play in BRIDGEWATER Middleton apparently corrected about three-fourths of the dialogue errors he found in his copy-text. We already know that transference/correction does not discriminate between errors on the basis of their stemmatic ancestry. Hence, authorial corrections in BRIDGEWATER should have been randomly distributed between errors shared with ROSENBACH and errors shared with other extant texts. If that were the case, then in those two scenes [PRE-BRIDGEWATER] probably contained about eight shared errors not linked to ROSENBACH (instead of two). This calculation would raise the total number of such errors in the second half of BRIDGEWATER from 15 to 21. We might therefore extrapolate that [PRE-BRIDGEWATER] contained, from 3.1.345.1 to the end of the play, at least twice as many such shared errors as ROSENBACH. Because the last two scenes of ROSENBACH are not autograph, and contain no evidence of a dramatic increase in scribal accuracy, it seems reasonable to assume that this is not simply a contrast between [PRE-BRIDGEWATER] and ROSENBACH, but a contrast between [PRE-BRIDGEWATER] and [PRE-ROSENBACH]. Again, this would suggest that [PRE-ROSENBACH] is earlier than [PRE-BRIDGEWATER].

12. Section XVII established that the relationship of the NON-CRANE texts in Act Five could be explained by two different series, with the difference between the two depending on the vector of error between BRIDGEWATER and ROSENBACH. It therefore makes sense to re-examine the statistics in the preceding paragraphs, focusing in particular on Act Five. In those three scenes, ROSENBACH and BRIDGEWATER each contains five filtered shared errors that cannot be explained by its relationship to the other extant text.[124] The extant texts are therefore, statistically, equally 'late', from the perspective of the accumulation of shared errors. However, two of those three scenes are autograph in BRIDGEWATER. As we have already noted, authorial correction of dialogue errors in the last two scenes of BRIDGEWATER probably eliminated about six such errors—even if the author made no corrections to errors in lineation or stage directions (which seems unlikely). Thus, it would be reasonable to extrapolate that [PRE-BRIDGEWATER] contained about eleven such errors—in other words, at least twice as many as ROSENBACH. For the same reason noted in the previous paragraph, this is probably a contrast between [PRE-BRIDGEWATER] and [PRE-ROSENBACH].

13. The foregoing reasoning suggests that, in Act Five, [PRE-ROSENBACH] was earlier than [PRE-BRIDGEWATER]. When this evidence is combined with the conclusions already reached in Section XVII, it establishes that the sequence of lost NON-CRANE texts in Act Five must have been [PRE-OKES] → [PRE-ROSENBACH/BRIDGEWATER] → [PRE-ROSENBACH] → [PRE-BRIDGEWATER] → [PRE-MIDDLETON^T].[125] Notably, this sequence exactly agrees with the earlier evidence of shared errors that cross over between the CRANE and NON-CRANE groups (Sec. XIV), which showed OKES with the most such errors, and the quantities then descending through ROSENBACH to BRIDGEWATER, with the lowest total in MIDDLETON^T.

We have now answered three and a half of the five questions I asked at the end of the previous section. In the second part of the play, OKES is earlier than MIDDLETON^T, and ROSENBACH precedes BRIDGEWATER; the different locations of the discontinuities in two of the shared error patterns (at 3.1.345.1 and 3.1.7) have been explained. The Two-Manuscript hypothesis has been disproven.

One and a half questions remain. The half-question concerns the other discrepancies in the location of stemmatic discontinuities. The big question concerns the relative priority of ROSENBACH and MIDDLETON^T in the first half of the play.

XIX. ROSENBACH and MIDDLETON^T

We now know that, for the first half of the play, either ROSENBACH or MIDDLETON^T was the first text in the NON-CRANE series; whichever of the two was *not* first, we know, had to have been last (Sec. XVII). A direct comparison of the two manuscripts, in that area of the play, should identify which was first.

We also know that there are at least two possible positions for the stemmatic discontinuity between the first and second half of the play (Sec. XVIII). In ROSENBACH we have, on the basis of shared errors alone, provisionally located the discontinuity at 3.1.348.1; in BRIDGEWATER a discontinuity apparently begins at 3.1.0. Consequently, in the following table I divide the shared errors in ROSENBACH into groupings different than those in previous tables: first, undoubted patterns from the beginning of the play to the end of Act Two, and then undoubted patterns from 3.1.0 to 3.1.348.[126] In the first group, if the pattern of shared errors is undoubtedly present before the end of Act Two, I specify it below, but query it in the summary. As before, if there is a difference between unfiltered and filtered totals, I give the filtered totals in square brackets.

---

[124] BRIDGEWATER 5.1.7, 5.2.38, 5.2.77, 5.2.70, 5.2.77, 5.2.114. ROSENBACH 5.2.75, 5.2.108, 5.3.116, 5.3.187–91, 5.3.166.3.
[125] Note that this analysis presupposes that the Third Lost Manuscript, [PRE-ROSENBACH/BRIDGEWATER], was not the same physical entity as [PRE-OKES]. I have not yet proven that assumption. I will return to that issue in later sections. However, for the purposes of establishing the vector of error between ROSENBACH and BRIDGEWATER in Act Five that unanswered question is irrelevant.
[126] Since I have already listed ROSENBACH shared errors in Sec. XIV, here I do not repeat patterns that would be removed by the normal filtering process.

Table of Shared Errors in ROSENBACH, Induction–
3.1.348

15. OKES: 5–7 (1.1.201–2.2.81.1–2 + 3.1.44.1,
3.1.203)

12. [CRANE⁴]: 3–4 (1.1.279–2.2.133–35 + 3.1.199)

26. CRANE²ʼ³: 1 (1.1.241)

56. OKES–MIDDLETON^T–CRANE²ʼ³ʼ⁴: 1? (2.2.33, passage
not in BRIDGEWATER)

19. CRANE²ʼ⁴: 1? (2.1.130, passage not in CRANE³)

21. CRANE³–OKES: 1? (2.2.94.1, passage not in BRIDGE-
WATER)

* * *

30. OKES–BRIDGEWATER: 2 [3.1.7, 3.1.127]

56. OKES–BRIDGEWATER–MIDDLETON^T–CRANE²ʼ³ʼ⁴: 1
[3.1.175.1]

23. [CRANE⁴]–MIDDLETON^T: 1? [3.1.154–5, passage
not in CRANE³]

34. [CRANE⁴]–BRIDGEWATER–MIDDLETON^T: 1?
[3.1.115.1, unspecified in CRANE³]

36. CRANE²ʼ³ʼ⁴: 1 [3.1.73]

The first two acts contain six patterns, and twelve (filtered) shared errors, linking ROSENBACH to CRANE³ʼ⁴ and OKES. There are no unique links to MIDDLETON^T, and the single MIDDLETON^T link that belongs to a larger pattern could be explained through the stemmatic relationship with OKES or with CRANE³ʼ⁴. I have argued above (Sec. XIV) that the single link that appears to connect this part of ROSENBACH to CRANE³ is unreliable, and that all the shared errors in this part of ROSENBACH could be explained by a stemmatic connection to just two texts, [CRANE⁴] and OKES. The [CRANE⁴] and OKES links appear throughout the first two acts, and continue into the third. All five patterns that appear in Act Three are explicable as a consequence of the relationships with [CRANE⁴] and OKES, already evident in the first two acts.

We can now look at a similar table of shared errors in the first part of MIDDLETON^T. We have not looked at this pattern of errors in this manuscript before; consequently, to the two subsets of error in the previous table I add, for MIDDLETON^T, a third subset, containing patterns that would be removed by the normal filtering process.

Table of Shared Errors in MIDDLETON^T, Induction–3.1

13. BRIDGEWATER: 4 [3] (1.1.205.1, 1.1.252–4,
2.1.144)

32. BRIDGEWATER–OKES: 11–12 [8–9] (Induc-
tion.23, 52.1–2, 1.1.288–90, 1.1.324, 2.1.39–
41, 2.1.106–7, 2.1.137–8, 155–6)

45. BRIDGEWATER–OKES–CRANE²ʼ³: 1 (Induction.52.1)

* * *

10. OKES: 2 (3.1.33, 3.1.75)

23. ROSENBACH–[CRANE⁴]: 1? (3.1.154–5)

31. BRIDGEWATER–ROSENBACH: 1? (3.1.155.1) [9 in
4.4–5.3]

34. BRIDGEWATER–ROSENBACH–[CRANE⁴]: 1?
(3.1.115.1)

38. BRIDGEWATER–OKES–CRANE³: 1 (3.1.44)

41. CRANE²ʼ³ʼ⁴: 1 (3.1.262.1)

56. BRIDGEWATER–ROSENBACH–OKES–CRANE²ʼ³ʼ⁴: 3 [1]
([2.2.33], 3.1.175.1, [3.1.305.1])

* * *

[40. NON-CRANE: 1]

[48. CRANE²ʼ³ʼ⁴–ROSENBACH–OKES: 1?]

[49. CRANE¹ʼ²–NON-CRANE: 1]

[50. CRANE¹ʼ³–NON-CRANE: 1]

[52. CRANE³ʼ⁴–NON-CRANE: 1]

[55. CRANE¹ʼ²ʼ⁴–NON-CRANE: 1]

In the first three scenes—that is, before the beginning of the gap in BRIDGEWATER–MIDDLETON^T contains only three patterns, involving twelve unfiltered shared errors. Each of those patterns, and each of those errors, is explicable through a stemmatic relationship with BRIDGEWATER. No other witness to *Game* has such a consistent distribution of shared errors, linking it to only a single text. That sort of distribution can occur only at the beginning or ending of a sequence of transmission. A text shares errors with only one other text either because (*a*) it is the earliest extant text, and passes its errors on to a second text, which then accumulates additional errors and passes them on to other texts, or because (*b*) it is the latest extant text, inheriting errors from the penultimate text, but not passing its own new errors on to any descendants. Of course, we already knew that the first two acts of MIDDLETON^T are a stemmatic dead-end. Although that is also apparently true of all eight extant substantive witnesses, only MIDDLETON^T has this peculiar distribution of shared errors.

We already know that MIDDLETON^T cannot be the earliest of the eight extant witnesses. The first two acts contain nine (filtered) shared errors; by contrast, there is not a single (filtered) shared error in the first two acts of CRANE¹. More obviously, MIDDLETON^T does not contain the original version of the play. However, CRANE¹ is the only representative of a different branch of the stemma, and MIDDLETON^T might therefore, theoretically, be the earliest extant witness of the revised version, at least for these first two acts. But wherever it belongs in the sequence of extant texts of the revised version, as a text of that version it must have been a copy of some other manuscript, now lost, which we can call, for the moment, [PRE-MIDDLETON^T]. Because it is autograph, MIDDLETON^T undoubtedly corrected errors in the manuscript it was copying, which means that [PRE-MIDDLETON^T] must have contained more than nine errors. Indeed, Middleton was clearly more attentive and accurate at the beginning of this transcription than at the end.

Table of Unique and Shared Errors in MIDDLETON^T

	Unique	Shared	Unique Extrametrical
Act One	0	7	0
Act Two	14	5	1
Act Three	14	12	8
Act Four	18	8	6
Act Five	41	16	3

This table establishes, clearly enough, that the quality of Middleton's copying was exceptionally high in Act One, and exceptionally poor in Act Five.[127] The first unique error in MIDDLETON[T] does not occur until 2.1.68, and the first unique extrametrical variant comes even later, at 2.2.213. The pattern of unique errors does not correspond neatly with the distribution of shared errors: Acts One and Four have similar numbers of shared errors, but differ dramatically in the number of shared errors and shared extrametrical variants. Moreover, although the number of unique errors rockets in Act Five—nearly equalling the total for the four preceding acts—the number of shared errors does not rise so sharply. Nevertheless, if we were to count unique extrametrical variants as unique errors, the total for each Act would be higher than the preceding Act: 0, 15, 22, 26, 44. Middleton got increasingly unreliable, as a copyist, as he made his way through the play.

Acts are not very precise units, and we might track the quality of Middleton's copying more precisely if we broke MIDDLETON[T] down into ten equal units, each containing 246 lines.[128]

	Unique
1–246	0
247–492	0
493–738	5
739–984	8
985–1230	5
1231–1476	7
1477–1722	6
1723–1968	13
1969–2214	26
2215–2457	16

Nascimento located the beginning of the serious deterioration of MIDDLETON[T] at about 4.1.123 (1752)—which is indeed in the seventh of these ten consecutive units of text, where the ratio of unique errors per line abruptly doubles. But the change actually begins somewhat earlier: between 1583 and 1752 there are eight unique errors, a ratio of one every 21 lines. Roughly speaking, at about the beginning of Act Four Middleton became significantly less reliable as a copyist.

I began this digression about Middleton's shifting accuracy and attentiveness as a copyist in order to make a point about the play's first three scenes. The first Act contains no unique errors, and 2.1 contains only six (four of them in the last one hundred lines of the scene). Given Middleton's very high level of attention in the first three scenes, the number of errors he corrected may have been quite high. In other words, the manuscript from which he was copying might have had considerably more than twelve errors in those first scenes. If MIDDLETON[T] were the earliest extant witness, then of course [PRE-MIDDLETON[T]] must have been stemmatically earlier than any surviving document. But we know that the first three scenes of [PRE-MIDDLETON[T]] must have contained more than twelve shared errors, and probably many more than twelve.

Moreover, as I have already proven (Sec. XVII), if MIDDLETON[T] were the first of the extant witnesses of the revised version of the first two Acts, then BRIDGEWATER

must have been the second earliest witness. But that is clearly impossible. Howard-Hill identified BRIDGEWATER as 'perhaps the latest manuscript' (Pasquin 218), for good reasons. In particular, in the first three scenes BRIDGEWATER contains twenty-two shared (filtered) errors. By contrast, in the first three scenes CRANE[1] contains no shared errors, CRANE/ALLDE only six, ROSENBACH only eight, CRANE[3] only eleven, CRANE[2] only twelve. The only text that exceeds the BRIDGEWATER total in those lines is OKES, with twenty-four (not a statistically significant difference). The second earliest witness, in a sequence of seven, cannot contain one of the two highest totals of shared errors—unless all later texts benefitted from increasingly accurate authorial correction. But the only entirely autograph text of those scenes is MIDDLETON[T] itself, which—in this hypothetical scenario—would have been earlier, not later, than BRIDGEWATER.

Since BRIDGEWATER cannot be the second earliest witness to those lines, MIDDLETON[T] cannot be the earliest. Instead, it must be the last. The derivation of MIDDLETON[T] from something like BRIDGEWATER makes perfect sense, with the author correcting about 60% of the errors he found in the first three scenes of the manuscript he was copying. In any case, we have now proven that MIDDLETON[T] was the last of the extant manuscripts of everything earlier than 2.2.0 and of everything later than 5.1.0.

There remains the stemmatic problem of Acts Three and Four, which is not yet so clear. In 3.1.0–3.1.348 seven new patterns appear, containing eight new unfiltered shared errors; in addition, one error continues a pattern already found earlier in the play. Four of the new patterns perpetuate a connection to BRIDGEWATER; they confirm that the connections to [PRE-BRIDGEWATER] had changed by 3.1.115, but they need not indicate any change in the stemmatic connections of [PRE-MIDDLETON[T]] itself. However, the other three patterns (and four of the nine errors) link MIDDLETON[T], for the first time, to at least two other texts: OKES (pattern 10) and [CRANE[4]] (patterns 23 and 41). Notably, these are the same two texts that explain all indubitable shared errors in the first half of ROSENBACH.

In the 648 lines up to the end of 2.1, 100% of the shared errors in MIDDLETON[T] can be explained through a

[127] The table does not include all readings unique to MIDDLETON[T], but only those which are grammatically, logically, or formally nonsensical. It also does not include unique errors which are corrected by Middleton himself in the manuscript. The variants tabulated as unique errors occur at 2.1.68, 2.1.74, 2.1.152.1, 2.1.183, 2.1.218, 2.1.2281, 2.2.40.1, 2.2.68, 2.2.69, 2.2.87–88, 2.2.96–97, 2.2.122–3, 2.2.178, 2.2.255, 3.1.106–8, 3.1.121–2, 3.1.135, 3.1.149, 3.1.185, 3.1.209–10, 3.1.262.2–3, 3.1.271–2, 3.1.315–16, Add.C.2 [1437–38], 3.1.345, 3.1.375, 3.1.399, 3.1.415, 4.1.21–22, 4.1.33.2, 4.1.38, 4.1.98, 4.1.107, 4.1.118–19, 4.2.1, 4.2.19, 4.2.84–5, 4.2.109–10, 4.2.134, 4.2.135, 4.3.0.2, 4.4.10, 4.4.11, 4.4.12, 4.4.20–21, 4.4.48.1–4.4.110.1, 5.1.0.2, 5.1.10, 5.1.14, 5.1.14, 5.1.17, 5.1.23, 5.1.30.1, 5.1.33.1, 5.1.33.2, 5.1.36, 5.1.47, 5.1.49, 5.1.49, 5.2.1, 5.2.13, 5.2.67, 5.2.70, 5.2.73, 5.2.75–76, 5.2.84, 5.2.84, 5.2.112, 5.2.113, 5.3.25, 5.3.28, 5.3.52, 5.3.59, 5.3.61–2, 5.3.62, 5.3.81, 5.3.89, 5.3.105, 5.3.131, 5.3.132, 5.3.144, 5.3.154–5, 5.3.163–4, 5.3.187–91, 5.3.199, 5.3.203.
[128] Lines here are numbered according to the Malone Society transcript (Howard-Hill 1990), and therefore include stage directions. The last section contains only 243 lines.

stemmatic relationship with BRIDGEWATER. By contrast, in the 348 lines between the end of 2.2 and the beginning of 3.2, a connection to BRIDGEWATER can explain only 56% of the shared errors in MIDDLETON^T. The same percentage could be explained through a connection to OKES. Clearly, something had changed, and it had changed by 3.1.44 at the latest. Just as clearly, it makes no sense to assume that the change in stemmatic relationships was limited to the first 348 lines of Act Three. In order to understand the change, we need to examine the pattern of shared errors throughout Acts Three and Four.

Before we do so, however, it is important to recognize that we have now answered four and a half of the five questions about the sequence of NON-CRANE texts, posed at the end of Section XVII. The only remaining part-question concerns the discrepancies in the location of two stemmatic discontinuities in Acts Three and Four. That is to say, the problem we have encountered here in the middle acts of MIDDLETON^T is related to the larger, half-resolved issue of stemmatic discontinuities in those very scenes.

We have reached this point through detailed examination of the pattern of shared errors throughout ROSENBACH and BRIDGEWATER, and in the first half of MIDDLETON^T. The only NON-CRANE text that we have not yet examined, in detail, is OKES—which, we now know, was the earliest of the four NON-CRANE texts in Act Five. It is time to confront, directly, the problem of OKES—or rather, the problem not of the printed text, but of the lost manuscript from which it derives, [MIDDLETON/OKES].

XX. [MIDDLETON/OKES] and CRANE/MATHEWES/ALLDE

Earlier, in trying to determine the sequence of CRANE texts, I wanted to give [CRANE^4] the benefit of any possible doubt, and thereby give the benefit of the doubt to previous accounts of the Crane manuscripts. So I discounted errors shared by CRANE/ALLDE and OKES, accepting the tentative hypothesis that those errors represented a direct connection between the two printed quartos, rather than a stemmatic relationship between the two lost manuscripts [CRANE^4] and [MIDDLETON/OKES]. In particular, I argued that there might have been a direct connection between the printed text of ALLDE and the printed text of OKES from 5.3.208 to the end of the play, and possibly also in 5.1.5–40 (Section VIII). The direction of influence was not bibliographically or logically determinable, but an economic and psychological hypothesis suggested that OKES was likelier to have influenced ALLDE. By adopting this hypothesis, I minimized the number of shared errors in [CRANE^4], thereby making the best possible case for the theory that [CRANE^4] was earlier than CRANE^{2,3}. But even with the benefit of this best-possible-scenario, [CRANE^4] demonstrably turned out to be, chronologically, the last of the extant or inferred CRANE manuscripts.

By a completely independent line of reasoning, it has now been proven that [MIDDLETON/OKES] was the earliest of the NON-CRANE texts, possibly from the beginning of Act Three, and certainly for the whole of Act Five. In other words, the lost manuscripts [CRANE^4] and [MIDDLETON/OKES] were, in Act Five, closer to each other, stemmatically, than any other CRANE text to any other NON-CRANE text. Obviously, this new evidence of the stemmatic relationship of the manuscripts forces us to reconsider the problem of the relationship between the two printed quartos.

That relationship cannot be plausibly attributed entirely to a compositor or compositors in Allde's shop consulting an exemplar of the printed text of OKES in two passages. OKES and CRANE/ALLDE also share unique errors at 3.1.265, 3.1.307, 4.4.10, 4.4.12.1, and 5.3.32, far from the two clusters of shared errors and readings. In addition to these five shared errors, OKES and CRANE/MATHEWES share unique variants at 3.1.7, 3.1.31, 3.1.98, 3.1.154.1, and 3.1.201. Outside the two passages of suspected contamination, OKES shares unique variants with CRANE/ALLDE at 3.2.30, 4.2.4, 4.2.70, 4.2.86, 4.2.120, 4.4.10, 5.2.55, 5.3.53, 5.3.118, 5.3.61, 5.3.62, and 5.3.187.[129] In three other cases, although the two quartos are not identical, they are closely related in a reading that differs from all other texts, linking OKES to CRANE/MATHEWES at 3.1.210, and to CRANE/ALLDE at 3.1.264.[130] To sum up: after the beginning of 3.1, OKES uniquely shares five variants with CRANE/MATHEWES; with CRANE/ALLDE, outside the suspect clusters, it shares five unique errors and another thirteen variants. The unique links between the two lost manuscripts overlap the division between the two printers.

But the connection between the two quartos is particularly strong in Act Five, where the other evidence that [MIDDLETON/OKES] directly descends from [CRANE^4] is strongest and clearest. I noted earlier (Sec. VIII) that, compared to the rest of the play, the number of variants where OKES *differs* from ALLDE significantly decreases in Act Five. I also noted earlier that the use of parentheses and hyphens in the two quartos is much more similar in Act Five than elsewhere. Obviously, that decline in differences between the two quartos could reflect the closer proximity of the two manuscripts there, rather than consultation of one quarto by the compositor(s) of the other.

Indeed, it would be much more plausible to suppose that, outside the two suspect passages in Act Five—amounting to a mere 75 lines—all the errors and variants uniquely shared between OKES and MATHEWES/ALLDE actually represent readings shared in the underlying manuscripts, [MIDDLETON/OKES] and [CRANE^4]. After all, we have already established that those two manuscripts must have shared at least thirteen other errors in the last three Acts.[131] Because those errors are shared with other texts,

129 OKES and CRANE/MATHEWES also share unique variants at Induction.0.2 (two variants), 1.1.183, 2.1.52, 2.1.129, and 2.1.187.

130 Another unique OKES link to CRANE/MATHEWES occurs at 1.1.137.

131 Patterns 20 (5.3.210–11), 24 (3.2.30–1), 28 (5.2.106.1), 33 (5.3.19–20), 37 (5.2.108), 42 (5.1.0.2, 5.1.9.2, 5.1.46.1), 43 (4.1.21–2), 44 (3.1.410), 53 (4.1.116, 5.1.1.1), 56 (2.2.33, 3.1.175.1, [3.1.305.1], [5.1.9.2]). Notably, only one of these errors occurs before Act Three, and it—at 2.2.33—is incorrect in all surviving witnesses. It therefore tells us only that both [CRANE^4] and [MIDDLETON/OKES] belonged to the group that included all texts of the revised version.

they must have been transmitted stemmatically, through the manuscripts. Twelve of those thirteen errors occur in at least two CRANE texts; consequently, they cannot have originated in the NON-CRANE group, and then been transmitted through OKES into the CRANE texts.[132] Instead, they must have originated in the CRANE texts, and passed from there into the NON-CRANE texts. In other words, in twelve of the thirteen cases where the error is shared by OKES, MATHEWES/ALLDE, and at least one extant manuscript, [MIDDLETON/OKES] must have inherited the error from [CRANE⁴].

That overlap between the two adjacent manuscripts, for the whole play, contrasts strikingly with the overlap between OKES and ALLDE, which clusters in two brief passages of Act Five. Indeed, that disparity first suggested contamination of one printed quarto by the other in those two passages. That same disparity indicates that contamination will not account for the distribution of variants in the play as a whole, which must instead reflect the proximity of one manuscript to the other. Their proximity is particularly certain in Act Five, which is also the site of the strongest links specifically between OKES and ALLDE. Consequently, in Act Five it may be difficult, at times, to distinguish what was passed from one manuscript to the other from what might have been passed from one printed quarto to the other.

The cluster of shared errors in 5.1 illustrates these problems. At 5.1.8, OKES agrees with all the CRANE texts in reading 'hath' where the other NON-CRANE texts all read 'has'; Middleton himself overwhelmingly preferred 'has', while Crane just as clearly preferred 'hath'. At 5.1.9, OKES agrees with all the CRANE texts in the extrametrical expansion 'They are', where all the other NON-CRANE texts have the metrical contraction 'they're'. Likewise, both quartos share a punctuation error with CRANE³ at 5.1.4, and at 5.1.9.2 both quartos omit a necessary music cue also omitted from CRANE²,³. Both these errors originated in earlier CRANE texts, and therefore probably passed through [CRANE⁴] to [MIDDLETON/OKES]. Finally, the entrance in OKES at 5.1.9.3–8 radically differs from that in CRANE/ALLDE; the two quartos uniquely agree in erroneously calling for a character whose title begins with 'K.', but given the other differences between the two stage directions it is hard to believe that one compositor ignored everything about the other printed quarto except the single false letter it contained. Thus far, the direction of influence at the beginning of 5.1 seems to be what is normal in the second half of the play: the text of OKES derives from the text of [MIDDLETON/OKES], which in turn derives from a late CRANE manuscript.

Two lineation errors occur only in OKES and CRANE/ALLDE at 5.1.10–19 and 5.1.31. However, OKES has unique lineation errors at 5.1.5–6, 5.1.32–3, 5.1.35–6: clearly, ALLDE is not a simple copy of OKES here. Moreover, the misinterpretation of the Latin oration as verse could easily arise from Crane's habits as a scribe. Crane's manuscripts use emphasis capitals in this speech much more

generously than other manuscripts: although there are no such capitals in this oration in ROSENBACH, there are 19 in CRANE¹, 29 in CRANE², and 31 in CRANE³. It is therefore not surprising to find 24 in CRANE/ALLDE. That number includes capitals at the beginning of 'verse' lines, but many of those words are capitalized in one Crane transcription or another: six of the nine words treated as the beginning of verse lines in CRANE/ALLDE are capitalized in both CRANE² and CRANE³. In a seventh case, CRANE³ breaks the line exactly where CRANE/ALLDE does; since Crane sometimes did not capitalize the first letter of a verse line, the compositor might have interpreted that as a case where he should supply the capital himself. Thus, something very like CRANE³ might have led the compositor of CRANE/ALLDE to interpret 5.1.10–19 as verse. The similarity between CRANE/ALLDE and OKES might therefore result from the tendency of both compositors to reproduce their manuscript copy-text much more exactly than usual, when dealing with a foreign language.

The other shared lineation error, at 5.1.32, may also be due to a peculiarity of Crane manuscripts. In all three extant Crane manuscripts of *Game*, the stage direction at 5.1.31.1–3 is written in the right margin; in CRANE² and CRANE³, a curly bracket on the left side of the direction points to the exact location in the dialogue to which the action is keyed. Both those texts also use brackets for the marginal direction at 5.1.45.1. It is thus not surprising that CRANE/ALLDE reproduces the Crane marginal position and the Crane brackets for both directions. OKES, as we would expect of a text descended from the Crane manuscripts, retains the marginal position, but not the brackets. (So do ROSENBACH and BRIDGEWATER.) The brackets point to Crane copy-text for ALLDE here, not contamination by OKES; so do differences in the wording of the stage direction ('divers Images about it' versus 'Images standing on each side'). Equally important, the marginal direction would have created a problem for any compositor trying to reproduce the layout of his manuscript text: with a stage direction beginning in the right margin opposite 5.1.31 and continuing down to a point opposite 5.1.36, there was simply not room in the measure to fit the whole of line 5.1.32, with its speech prefix. The obvious solution would have been to break the line after 'Hark'. The shared mislineation at 5.1.32 may therefore reflect a technological problem, shared only by the two machined texts, in working from a manuscript with actual or inherited Crane characteristics.

Another indication of that pattern is provided by the scene's punctuation. The four pairs of parentheses shared by the two quartos all occur in one or all of the extant Crane manuscripts; by contrast, only one occurs in MIDDLETON^T (which begins the parenthesis at the same point,

---

[132] The single possible exception, at 3.2.30–1, occurs in a scene absent from CRANE²,³, where corroboration of the CRANE origins of the error is therefore impossible. Notably, though, there is no clustering of shared errors between OKES and CRANE/ALLDE in the vicinity, and this error probably has the same origin as the other twelve.

but ends at a different one). Both hyphens ('Seed-Plots' at 5.1.22, 'sweet-sounding' at 5.1.32) occur in all three Crane manuscripts; but OKES reproduces only the second one, and MIDDLETON[T] neither. Most of the emphasis capitals throughout the scene in CRANE/ALLDE are found in other Crane texts, but not MIDDLETON[T]; OKES, as we would expect from its transitional position in the stemma of transmission, has fewer than the Crane manuscripts or CRANE/ALLDE, but more than MIDDLETON[T].

The two quartos share unique substantive errors in the Latin at 5.1.4, 5.1.15, and 5.1.18, and they share unique punctuation errors in the Latin at 5.1.12 and 5.1.13. The mislineation at 5.1.10-19 also involves misreading of Latin prose as Latin verse; nobody with an understanding of Latin scansion would have made that mistake. Without the Latin, 5.1 would contain only three errors uniquely shared between OKES and ALLDE. One of those three errors, the mislineation at 5.1.32, probably originated, as I have suggested above, in a shared technical problem. It is worth remembering, at this point, that 'the distribution of error in copies is not entirely random' (Sec. V, para. 3); here, the presence of two Latin speeches, and the technical problem of translating a particular manuscript practice into print, between them can account for seven of the nine uniquely shared errors in this scene. Clearly, then, what distinguishes 5.1.4-19 from other parts of the play is the concentration of Latin text, and what distinguishes OKES and ALLDE from other texts at this point is the concentration of uniquely shared errors in Latin. As I have already observed (Sec. VIII), that eruption of Latinity could, in itself, explain a compositor's resort, at this point, to consultation of a printed text, but it does not tell us which printed text influenced the other. The one indication of the direction of influence may be the number of departures from the spelling of Middleton's Latin source (Sec. IV): there are eight departures in ALLDE here, but ten in OKES. In themselves, those statistics are compatible with what we know about the manuscripts: [CRANE[4]], which contains fewer departures, is earlier than [MIDDLETON/OKES]. But if one printed quarto influenced the other, this evidence would suggest that ALLDE influenced OKES. Otherwise, how would a Latinless or Latin-poor compositor in ALLDE restore two original spellings, which had been changed in his copy of OKES?

The cluster of uniquely shared errors in 5.1.4-39 could therefore be explained by two different hypotheses: (1) [MIDDLETON/OKES] descends from [CRANE[4]], and (2) the compositor of OKES consulted an exemplar of ALLDE in order to help decipher the Latin. We already know that the first hypothesis is correct, but the second might *also* be correct. There is no way of being sure. I do not know of any rule of probability that would answer the question, 'To what degree does a sudden spike in the number of shared errors indicate direct consultation of another quarto?' The one thing that now seems ruled out is consultation of OKES by the compositor of ALLDE. In other words, the only possibility ruled out, in 5.1, is the very hypothesis that previous

investigators have entertained—and which I accepted, for the sake of argument, in my earlier discussion of [CRANE[4]].

With this new conclusion in mind, we can now return to the other passage that suggests a direct connection between the quartos. To summarize the earlier discussion: in the last twenty-three lines of the play the quartos uniquely share three substantive errors and one punctuation error; they share another three variants that occur nowhere else, and they share two additional errors that also appear in other texts.[133] They are substantively identical.[134] No other passage in the play, outside the Latin of 5.1.4-19, contains such a high concentration of shared error, or such a paucity of variation between the two quartos. Unlike 5.1.4-19, this passage does not contain any substantive evidence of consultation of more than one manuscript. The concentration of errors here cannot be explained by an unfamiliar language; it could be explained by damage at the end of a manuscript (the likeliest place for damage to occur). Damage at the end of a manuscript would be sufficient reason for a compositor to seek an alternative source for the text, if one was available; unless the quartos were printed absolutely simultaneously, then the earlier-printed quarto would have been available by the time the compositor(s) of the other quarto reached the end of the play.

The substantive evidence in the last 23 lines makes a strong case for contamination of one quarto by the other. But the spelling and punctuation suggest that ALLDE, at least, was set from a manuscript. At 5.3.213, ALLDE has the Crane spelling 'Olife', where OKES has the Middleton spelling 'Oliue'.[135] Since the autograph Middleton spelling with 'u' (= 'v') is also the normal modern form, it might have been imposed by a compositor, but it is harder to explain why a compositor would reject the modern spelling for one that happens to coincide with Crane's, unless he were in fact looking at a manuscript influenced by Crane. Likewise, at Epilogue.1 ALLDE has Crane's preferred 'Mistris' where OKES alone has 'Mistresse'. I have argued earlier (Sec. XIII) that the manuscript behind MATHEWES/ALLDE contained a combination of features suggesting a Middleton copy of a late Crane transcript, and the punctuation of the last page of ALLDE fits what we would expect from such a manuscript. Both quartos preserve Crane's parentheses in Epilogue.1; at 5.3.217-18 they both preserve the beginning of one Crane parenthesis and the end of another, producing exactly the kind of incoherent half-inherited use of brackets found

---

[133] At 5.3.210-11 CRANE[2,3,4] and OKES lack two sentences present in the other NON-CRANE texts; at 5.3.220.1 they lack an exeunt direction present only in CRANE[1,2,3]. Thus, one of these errors is shared only with other CRANE texts, one is shared only with other NON-CRANE texts. At 5.3.217 and 5.3.218 CRANE[2,3,4] and OKES agree with each other and differ from the other non-Crane texts in two indifferent variants.
[134] The quartos differ in the abbreviations they use for speech prefixes ('Fat B'/'F.B.', 'Wh.K'/'W.Ki.'), but each quarto simply follows its normal practice, and the difference is almost certainly compositorial.
[135] In the same line CRANE[2] has 'Olliff', and at 2.2.226 CRANE[1,2,3] all have 'oliffe'.

elsewhere in autograph. On six occasions in the last 27 lines of the play, ALLDE is the only text to contain *no* punctuation; five of these absences are at the end of verse lines, one at the end of a speech. Again, this pattern is typical of Middleton himself, and hard to explain if ALLDE were set from a copy of OKES. Finally, at 5.3.214 ALLDE alone has 'Crow'd' for 'Crowd'; the odd superfluous apostrophe resembles those often found elsewhere in Middleton's autograph.[136]

Once again, then, if one quarto influenced the other, it must have been ALLDE that influenced OKES. If that were the case, ALLDE (not OKES) was 'Q1'. As I argued earlier (Sec. VIII), the order of printing of the two quartos cannot be determined bibliographically.[137] But in both passages where contamination is likeliest, the vector of influence seems to have been ALLDE→OKES. In both stemmatic and editorial terms, that vector of influence between the two quartos duplicates the vector in the two lost manuscripts: [CRANE⁴]→[MIDDLETON/OKES].[138]

In either case, it is now clear that *all the errors shared by the quartos originated in* [CRANE⁴] *or* CRANE/ALLDE, and were from there inherited by [MIDDLETON/OKES] or OKES. No more than seven shared errors, in thirty-eight lines of text (5.1.4-19, 5.3.207-end), can be plausibly attributed to the influence of ALLDE rather than [CRANE⁴]. This means that [CRANE⁴] contained at least 46, and quite possibly 52, shared errors.[139] Either figure confirms its status as the latest of the four known CRANE transcripts. Which is to say: the evidence analysed in Sections X–XIII has now been independently confirmed by the evidence of shared error quantities and patterns.

Likewise, depending on whether OKES was contaminated directly by ALLDE in those two passages, [MIDDLETON/OKES] contained between 77 and 84 shared errors—a total just slightly lower or higher than the total for ROSENBACH.

However, as we have already seen (Sec. XIV), the two halves of ROSENBACH differ dramatically in their totals of shared error. In fact, the copy-text for each of the three other NON-CRANE texts seems to have been divided somewhere in 3.1. In both halves, [MIDDLETON/OKES] and [PRE-ROSENBACH] were apparently adjacent. Since ROSENBACH apparently descends from [MIDDLETON/OKES] in the second half of the play, was the copy-text for [MIDDLETON/OKES] also divided? Was it divided at the same place that copy-text for [PRE-BRIDGEWATER] or [PRE-ROSENBACH] was divided?

XXI. [MIDDLETON/OKES] and CRANE³,⁴

The preceding section has established that errors shared between OKES and ALLDE cannot be attributed to contamination of ALLDE by OKES. We therefore need no longer question the stemmatic vector of links between OKES and the CRANE texts: those links are all inherited by OKES. In contrast, for Act Five in particular we know that errors shared by OKES with other NON-CRANE texts must have originated with OKES, which was the earliest of the NON-CRANE texts for that part of the play (and perhaps also

for Acts Three and Four). Consequently, we are finally in a position to determine, more precisely than before, the stemmatic transition from the late CRANE texts to the (even later) NON-CRANE texts.

We can begin by establishing which CRANE text is closest to OKES. You will recall our earlier conclusion (Sec. VII) that the transitional text between the CRANE and NON-CRANE texts was a text somewhere between [CRANE²,³] and MATHEWES/ALLDE, apparently very similar to the lost [CRANE⁴].

Table of CRANE-OKES Errors (filtered data)

CRANE²,³: 2 (Induction.52.1, 1.1.311)
[CRANE⁴]: 1 (1.1.137)
CRANE²,³,⁴: 1 (2.2.33)

         * * *

[CRANE⁴]: 14 + 3? (3.1.265-Epilogue.6)
CRANE³,⁴: 2 (5.2.106.1, 5.2.108)
CRANE²,³,⁴ (after 3.1.410): 6

         * * *

20. CRANE²,⁴: 1? (5.3.210-11)
33. CRANE²,⁴-MIDDLETONᵀ: 1? (5.3.19-20)
43. CRANE²,⁴-ROSENBACH-BRIDGEWATER: 1? (4.1.21-2)

The three patterns clustered at the bottom of this table are queried because the passage in question is not present at all in the abridged CRANE³. But all three examples fall in the second half of the play, where OKES clearly derives from [CRANE⁴]. After 3.1.265 at the latest, not a single error in OKES appears to be directly inherited from anything other

---

[136] In my earlier discussion of the relationship between the quartos (Sec. VIII), I noted that they share all four parentheses in the relevant section of 5.1; this can now be seen as further evidence of ALLDE's possible influence on OKES.

[137] The engraved title-page of MATHEWES/ALLDE fits the same page-frame as the remainder of the text, and the text begins on sig. A2; apparently, the publisher and printer always intended to supply an illustrated title-page. By contrast, the engraved title-page of OKES is oversized, and printed on a separate half-sheet; the text begins on sig. B1. But it is not clear that this contrast favours one scenario over the other. Conceivably, the unengraved '1625' titlepage may have been the original, displaced because the publication of CRANE/ALLDE convinced Nicholas Okes (or the unknown publisher) that his own edition would not be able to compete without its own illustrated title-page. See the discussion of mixed copies in Sec. I.

[138] We can leave to future speculative bibliography the delicate question of whether the sudden rise in errors shared between these two passages in Act Five reflects manuscript or print influence. I can imagine two explanations for the evidence. On the one hand, the 23 lines at the end of the play may simply be too small a patch of text to yield statistically significant results. On the other hand, the economic or psychological motive that I have been using as evidence for the priority of OKES may conflate two different agents, the publisher and the printer. The physical evidence of the type-face demonstrates that Nicholas Okes printed OKES, and physical evidence also demonstrates that the same setting of type was used for the last sheets of both OKES¹ and OKES². However, such physical evidence does not prove that Nicholas Okes was the stationer who paid for the printing. Another stationer, acting as publisher or wholesale or bookseller, might have paid for the paper and the printing. In those circumstances, the printer Okes might have acquired a copy of the freshly-printed ALLDE before the publisher knew of the competitor's existence—or both might have become aware of its existence only as the final forme of OKES was being set. This second hypothesis would explain the influence of one title-page engraving on the other, since the engraved title-page of OKES might have been added at the last minute, shortly after composition and printing of the final forme.

[139] These figures are based on the filtered data-set, and differ only in the seven substantive errors uniquely shared by the two quartos in the two passages.

than [CRANE⁴], which can account for 28 different errors shared with the CRANE group.[140] Since we already know the sequence of NON-CRANE texts in Act Five, at least, this clear connection between OKES and [CRANE⁴] now makes it possible for us to reconstruct the NON-CRANE stemma for that part of the play (Figure 4).

There is, however, one problem with the visualization in Figure 4, a problem that only becomes apparent now that we have established that the links between ALLDE and OKES must be primarily, and perhaps entirely, links between the underlying manuscripts, not links between the printed quartos. The two quartos are at the bottom of this draft stemma, on the assumption that the demand for manuscripts disappeared once hundreds of copies of the play were available in print. OKES is a dead-end, because the two quartos printed by OKES do not seem to have been copied by any other extant text. By even a conservative estimate, OKES contains at least 311 unique errors, and more unique variation than any other text. But this raises a question: is it *only* the printed text which is a dead-end? Are *all* those unique variants printer's errors? Might the manuscript used by the printer also be a dead-end? As already noted (Sec. I), it seems likely that OKES used a manuscript especially prepared for him by Middleton. Howard-Hill lists fifty-seven 'Potentially Authorial Exclusive Q1 Variants' (*Pasquin* 305–6); he dismisses eighteen as errors, but that still leaves thirty-nine, and even his most conservative calculation identifies at least thirteen as certainly authorial. But HOWARD-HILL does not list there one of the more spectacular examples (the correction by OKES of the error present in all other texts at 5.3.11). Howard-Hill's edition adopts fifteen unique OKES variants—including four that occur in the play's last two scenes, when two autograph manuscripts offer an alternative reading that he rejects, preferring OKES. In determining my text of *A Later Form* I have been able to check variants against concordances of Middleton usage that were not available to Howard-Hill, and I adopt ninety-three unique OKES readings, which I identify as authorial variants.[141] Other editors may find my tolerance of OKES excessive, but for stemmatic purposes the difference between my calculation of unique authorial readings in OKES (93) and Howard-Hill's calculation (15) is irrelevant. We both agree that, throughout the play, OKES contains unique readings that can hardly be anything other than authorial variants. Those readings must have been present in the lost printer's copy-text, [MIDDLETON/OKES]. But since those readings do not appear in any other text, that lost printer's manuscript must have been a dead-end.

The evidence of these unique authorial readings (indicating that [MIDDLETON/OKES] must have been a dead-end) conflicts with the evidence of shared errors (indicating that [MIDDLETON/OKES] must have been near the middle of the stemma of transmission). That contradiction establishes that the lost collection-of-variants-entity that we have been calling '[MIDDLETON/OKES]' was, in fact, not one manuscript but two. On the one hand, there must

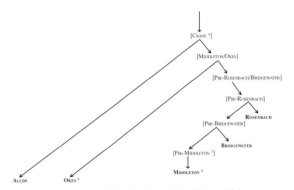

Figure 4. Draft Visualization of the Bottom of the Stemma of Transmission in Act Five. The vertical axis is chronological. The quartos are on the same horizontal line because they seem to have been produced at about the same time; no direct connection between them is assumed, but if one existed it probably went from left to right.

have existed a manuscript in Middleton's handwriting, containing a significant number of unique authorial readings, which was used as printer's copy-text for OKES, and may have been specifically prepared to serve that function: that manuscript was, so far as we can tell, never copied to produce another manuscript. We can continue to call that lost manuscript '[MIDDLETON/OKES]'. On the other hand, there must once have existed another lost manuscript, closer to OKES than any other known manuscript, which did *not* contain those unique authorial readings and was *not* a dead-end, but instead passed its variants and errors on to other extant manuscripts. That second lost manuscript was probably not intended to serve as printer's copy-text for OKES, and it was not necessarily in Middleton's handwriting; indeed, for all we know it might have been another CRANE transcript, perhaps the last of them. In any case, we do not know, and at this stage cannot even guess, the identity of the scribe of that second lost manuscript. But we do know that it was copied, at some

---

[140] Pattern 17 contains seventeen errors uniquely shared by [CRANE⁴] and OKES; the single example of pattern 24 (3.2.30–1) must also come from that source, because the scene in question is absent from CRANE²⁻³ and, presumably, any manuscript linking the two of them. The eight ambiguous examples in the second half of the play come from patterns 28, 37, 42, 44, 53.

[141] 1.1.5, 1.1.97, 1.1.216, 1.1.231, 1.1.254, 2.1.0.1 (twice), 2.1.63, 2.1.68, 2.1.166, 2.1.169, 2.1.174, 2.1.207, *2.1.209, 2.1.210, 2.1.213, 2.1.216, *2.1.225, 2.1.227, 2.2.9, *2.2.25, 2.2.27, *2.2.49, 2.2.72, 2.2.106, 2.2.122, 2.2.147, 2.2.152, 2.2.171, *2.2.180, *2.2.181, 2.2.185, 3.1.17, 3.1.45, 3.1.174, *3.1.186, 3.1.211, 3.1.215, 3.1.222, 3.1.226, 2.1.246, 3.1.248, C.2, 3.1.324, 3.1.328, 3.1.336, 3.1.337, 3.2.10, 3.2.25, 3.2.38–40, 3.1.367, 3.1.401, 3.1.402, 4.1.5, 4.1.33, 4.1.131, 4.1.146, 4.2.2, 4.2.40, 4.2.45, 4.2.128, 4.2.140, *4.2.145, 4.4.3, 4.4.18, 4.4.45, 4.4.71, 4.4.72, 4.4.106, 5.2.3.1, 5.2.26, *5.2.33, 5.2.36, 5.2.61–2, 5.2.79, 5.2.80, 5.2.99, 5.2.110, 5.2.133, *5.3.11, 5.3.56, 5.3.105, 5.3.107, 5.3.108, 5.3.110, 5.3.124, *5.3.162.1, 5.3.164, 5.3.166.2, 5.2.166.3, 5.3.167, 5.3.185, *5.3.198. I have asterisked cases where HOWARD-HILL also adopts the OKES variant. HOWARD-HILL also adopts unique readings which I reject at 2.1.136 (to guide me), 4.1.4 (worn), 4.1.5 (By), and 5.3.39 (th'). According to Howard-Hill (*Pasquin* 194), DYCE adopted twenty-eight OKES variants in Act One alone; I have not checked how many of these are unique OKES readings.

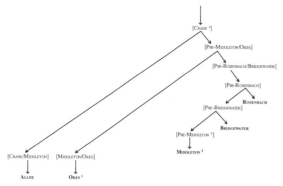

Figure 5. Revised Visualization of the Bottom of the
Stemma of Transmission in Act Five. This differs
from Figure 4 only in recognizing the existence
of [PRE-MIDDLETON/OKES] and [MIDDLETON/CRANE].

point, to produce [MIDDLETON/OKES], and we can therefore
call it '[PRE-MIDDLETON/OKES]'.

The foregoing analysis of the printer's copy for OKES is
also relevant to the printer's copy for MATHEWES/ALLDE.
I have argued (Sec. XIII) that MATHEWES/ALLDE must derive from a Middleton copy of a late Crane transcript.
Although that quarto contains fewer unique errors than
OKES, the printers' copy-text did contain unique errors and
unique readings that seem to be authorial; it also apparently contained independent restorations of authorial
readings. Thus, the printers' copy for MATHEWES/ALLDE
does not seem to have been [CRANE⁴] itself, but a copy
of it, at least partially autograph, that I propose to call
'[MIDDLETON/CRANE]'. Like the lost [MIDDLETON/OKES], the
lost [MIDDLETON/CRANE] seems to have been a manuscript,
wholly or partly autograph, which did *not* have any
manuscript descendants, but *was* used as printer's copy.
An obvious explanation for this situation would be that
both manuscripts were specifically prepared for sale to
printers (Figure 5).

Unfortunately, the clarity of the relationship between
OKES and [CRANE⁴] at the end of the play contrasts with
considerable confusion at the beginning. In the initial
scenes, two errors appear in OKES and in CRANE²˒³, but
not in CRANE/MATHEWES.[142] A third shared error (at 2.2.33)
could link OKES to any of the late Crane texts. However,
this apparently contrasting distribution of shared error
in the two parts of OKES is disturbed by the variant
at 1.1.137, where OKES and MATHEWES share the error
'found' for the correct 'fond', present in all other texts.
This is a double misreading: of 'f' as 'ſ', and of the
minims 'n' as 'un'. By contrast, the error OKES shares
with CRANE²˒³ at Induction.52.1 is a simple omission of
one word ('Music'), and the error they share at 1.1.311
is also a simple omission ('wound' for 'wounded', skipping
from one 'd' to the other). One could describe the situation
here either as (1) OKES shares two errors with CRANE²˒³
and one with [CRANE⁴], or (2) OKES shares one double
error with [CRANE⁴] and two simple errors with CRANE²˒³.

Depending on one's perspective, the first part of OKES
seems to derive either from a lost manuscript equidistant
between CRANE²˒³ and CRANE/MATHEWES, or from a lost
manuscript somewhere between the two but closer to
CRANE²˒³.

In either case, the first part of OKES differs from the
second part in its relationship to the CRANE texts, in three
different ways:

1. In the second part, all the links can be explained
by [CRANE⁴] alone, whereas the CRANE source for the first
part seems to have been somewhere between CRANE²˒³ and
[CRANE⁴].

2. In the second part the number of links to the
CRANE texts, and to [CRANE⁴] in particular, dramatically
increases.

3. Unlike most of the links to [CRANE⁴], none of the early
links to CRANE²˒³ is a unique pair ('twin').

We cannot assume that texts are homogeneous (Sec.
V, para. 41); in the face of repeated evidence of divided copy-text among the NON-CRANE texts, and of these
linked contrasts between the two halves of OKES, we must
consider the two parts of OKES as potentially distinct,
stemmatically. For the second half of OKES, a direct link
between [PRE-MIDDLETON/OKES] and [CRANE⁴] seems indisputable. For the earlier scenes, the connection seems less
clear and less direct.

We may be able to explain these three anomalies in
the first part of OKES by looking at the contrast in the
two parts of ROSENBACH. We can contrast the distribution
of shared errors in the first part of OKES not only with
the distribution in the second half of OKES, but with the
distribution in the first half of ROSENBACH. As we have
already seen (Sec. XIV), the later scenes of ROSENBACH are,
like the later scenes of OKES, linked to [CRANE⁴]; the two
texts uniquely share four errors in the last three Acts,
and in those later scenes no other Crane manuscript is
needed to explain ROSENBACH's link to the CRANE texts.
By contrast, the first scenes of ROSENBACH do contain
an error that is not present in CRANE/MATHEWES: the
indefinite article 'a' is omitted by CRANE²˒³ and ROSENBACH
at 1.1.241. This might be a coincidence, of course;
this single omitted letter is the only example of pattern
26. However, there are only two shared errors, in the
first scenes of the play, that uniquely link ROSENBACH
to CRANE/MATHEWES: 1.1.279 ('this' for correct 'these')
and 2.1.227.1 ('Exit' for correct 'Ex.' or 'Exeunt'). We
have already established that many texts of the period
are sloppy about exit directions, so this second example
may not be very reliable. But even if we include it, the
contrast with the later scenes of ROSENBACH is clear:
the first part contains fewer direct links with CRANE/
MATHEWES/ALLDE, and some evidence of a link with a
different CRANE manuscript. In fact, all three disparities
between the two parts of OKES (noted above) are also
present, to a lesser degree, between the two parts of
ROSENBACH.

[142] Patterns 45 (Induction.52.1), 27 (1.1.311).

In other words: the pattern of links to [PRE-CRANE²,³] is shared by both by the first part of ROSENBACH and the first part of OKES, and by no other NON-CRANE texts. Between them, ROSENBACH and OKES contain, in the first three scenes of the play (Induction, 1.1, 2.1), three errors shared with CRANE²,³ but not present in CRANE/MATHEWES. Those three shared errors are, in fact, the only indisputable evidence of a link between CRANE²,³ and the NON-CRANE texts. In those same three scenes, there are only three shared errors indisputably linking ROSENBACH or OKES to CRANE/MATHEWES. For those three scenes, the cross-over evidence linking CRANE to NON-CRANE is equally divided between CRANE²,³ and CRANE/MATHEWES. By contrast, for the rest of the play the evidence overwhelmingly and univocally identifies [CRANE⁴] alone as the conduit that links CRANE texts to NON-CRANE texts.

We can now localize, and state more precisely, the small anomaly we noticed in the cross-over evidence earlier (Sec. VII). For most of the play, the conduit text was undoubtedly [CRANE⁴], passing errors on to [PRE-MIDDLETON/OKES]. But for the play's first three scenes, at least, the conduit text is not so clear: the evidence is divided between CRANE²,³ and CRANE/MATHEWES.

I have already offered (Sec. VII) a 'global' conjecture to account for the sprinkling of evidence that links the NON-CRANE texts to CRANE²,³: that the shared errors in question were present in the lost [CRANE⁴], but that they were emended by the proofreader(s) in the printing house.[143] But that explanation paid no attention to the fact that more than one printing house was involved. All three of the anomalies noted above occur in CRANE/MATHEWES, which we would expect to have been checked by a proofreader in the shop of Augustine Mathewes. If the proofreader in Mathewes's shop was more accurate than the proofreader in Allde's shop, he would have corrected more errors present in [CRANE⁴]—and thereby he would have created the impression that various NON-CRANE texts were linked to the CRANE texts through the medium of [PRE-CRANE²,³]. This would explain both the scattering of links to CRANE²,³ in those scenes, and the fact that none of those links are 'twins': all of them link multiple texts. The anomaly here, in other words, is not the presence of three links to CRANE²,³, but the absence, in those three places, of the expected link to [CRANE⁴]—an absence attributable to the more scrupulous eye of the proofreader in the shop of Augustine Mathewes. This theory will also explain why the seeming links to CRANE²,³ do not involve a single NON-CRANE text, but two: ROSENBACH and OKES.[144]

However, the hypothesis of a more vigilant proofreader in CRANE/MATHEWES will not explain why the play's early scenes contain so many *fewer* shared errors linking the late Crane texts to OKES and/or to ROSENBACH. And while it may be easy to believe that a proofreader might have supplied the necessary article 'a' and corrected 'wound' to 'wounded', it is less plausible to conjecture that he restored the missing stage direction for 'Music'. That variant at least, and the discrepancy in numbers, suggests

that there may have been a change in the stemma, which might offer an alternative to the proofreader hypothesis, or might be combined with the proofreader hypothesis. In order to arbitrate between these possibilities, we have to do two things. First, we need to identify, if possible, the precise point at which the change occurred. Secondly—and this problem may or may not be related to the first—we need to sort out the relationship between ROSENBACH and OKES in the first three scenes.

To solve these problems, we need to consider some new categories of evidence. As I argued at the beginning of this analysis (Sec. II), shared variants are a less reliable indication of the stemma of transmission than shared errors, because they are much likelier to be coincidental—especially in a case like *A Game at Chess*, where the author is clearly an important agent of re-transmission, and where one scribe (Crane) is responsible for several texts, and might therefore be another agent of transference. There will, accordingly, be more anomalies in the distribution of shared *variants* than in the distribution of shared *errors*. Nevertheless, because we are dealing, in the NON-CRANE texts, with a repeated pattern of divided copy-text, the catchment area for shared errors is repeatedly reduced to half (or less than half) of a play. It may therefore be useful to supplement, cautiously, the evidence of shared errors with the evidence of shared variants.

Ignoring shared errors, the 648 lines in the first three scenes of OKES contain three variants that link it to CRANE²,³ instead of CRANE/MATHEWES.[145] By contrast, the

---

[143] In Sec. VII I identified four shared errors that pointed to a text other than [CRANE⁴] as the conduit for the transition between CRANE and NON-CRANE. Three of the four are discussed in the text, above. The fourth occurs at 5.1.33.1, where four texts (CRANE², ROSENBACH, BRIDGEWATER, and MIDDLETON^T) all misplace a stage direction. The direction is present and correctly placed in CRANE³. Consequently, this is the only example of a link between the NON-CRANE texts and CRANE² alone; it is also the only example of pattern 39. It cannot be explained as the result of simple proof-correction, because the passage was not set by MATHEWES; moreover, both OKES and CRANE/ALLDE agree in the correct reading. Only ROSENBACH and BRIDGEWATER misplace the direction in exactly the same way, and the strictest definition of the shared error would identify it only as another example of the ROSENBACH–BRIDGEWATER pairing common in that part of the play; if we assumed one coincidence instead of two, it would be another example of the common triplet ROSENBACH–BRIDGEWATER–MIDDLETON^T. Pattern 39 has been retained in the filtered data-set, because none of the global filtering rules applies to it; but it seems to me that the approximate agreement of CRANE² with the three other texts is almost certainly a coincidence, of no stemmatic significance.

[144] Both MIDDLETON^T and CRANE²,³ lack the words 'in his reverend habit', describing the Black Bishop's Pawn upon his entrance in 5.2. But MIDDLETON^T (uniquely) places his entrance at 5.2.3.1; CRANE²,³, like all other texts (including the autograph MIDDLETON^B), make it part of the stage direction at the beginning of the scene, 5.2.0.1. Moreover, MIDDLETON^T (uniquely) identifies the character only as 'the Iesuite', whereas CRANE²,³, like all other texts, specify 'Bl.Bps.Pawne'. Thus, there can hardly have been any stemmatic connection between the very differently worded and placed stage directions for the entrance of this character in CRANE²,³ and MIDDLETON^T. The shared omission must result from coincidence. Because MIDDLETON^T separates the two entrances, it was no longer necessary to specify that the two characters enter from different directions; because MIDDLETON^T uniquely identified him as the 'Jesuit', his costume was implied. The omissions of both pieces of information from CRANE²,³ are indeed shared errors, and have been counted as such in the filtered data-set, but the variants in MIDDLETON^T have *not* been counted as an example of the same errors. Thus, pattern 29 has been removed from the filtered data-set (Appendix D), where this shared error has been categorized as another example of pattern 14.

[145] 1.1.1 ('neuer' for authorial 'ne'er'), 2.1.30 'prescription' (singular for plural), 2.1.138 ('me' omitted in CRANE²,³); also perhaps relevant is 2.1.227 (punctuation error in CRANE³).

1523 lines of the rest of the play also contain only three such variants.[146] If we count variants per line, the links in the first three scenes are more than twice as frequent. As we would expect, the pattern of shared variants is not as clean as the pattern of shared errors, but it does point in the same direction.

This evidence of divided copy-text for OKES might explain a crucial fact about the NON-CRANE texts. For most of Act Four and all of Act Five, [PRE-MIDDLETON/OKES] inherits errors from [CRANE⁴], and passes them on to ROSENBACH, BRIDGEWATER, and MIDDLETONᵀ. Therefore, in those later scenes all four NON-CRANE texts clearly belong to a coherent set: (O2,R2,B2,M2). All the NON-CRANE texts, for that part of the play, share a single CRANE ancestor ('[CRANE⁴]'). By contrast, in the first part of the play [PRE-ROSENBACH] inherited errors from [CRANE⁴], but [PRE-MIDDLETON/OKES] instead inherited its errors from something that mixed readings in CRANE²,³ with readings in [CRANE⁴], and OKES passed those errors on to BRIDGEWATER and MIDDLETON. Consequently, in the first part of the play the NON-CRANE texts do not form a coherent set of four; instead, they constitute a set of three (O1,B1,M1), with a fourth text (R1) linked to the CRANE texts rather than the set of three related NON-CRANE texts.

With this hypothesis in mind, we can now look again at the relationship between the CRANE and NON-CRANE texts, this time from the perspective of shared variants rather than shared errors. Once again, I want to stress that shared variants are a less reliable category of data, which will inevitably contain more examples of random association. Nevertheless, certain broad patterns of distribution are discernible. Moreover, the reliability of shared variant patterns will increase as the number of examples increases.

We know that the CRANE texts include two different branches of the stemma: CRANE¹ derives from an early authorial draft of the play, and CRANE²,³,⁴ derive instead from a revised version, probably contained in the licensed playbook. There is not a single reliable example of an error shared by these two branches. Consequently, any variants uniquely shared by all four CRANE texts, and by no NON-CRANE text, are not shared errors, but must instead result from some other cause. There are three possible explanations for these variants.

First, the CRANE variants might be the product of Ralph Crane's own preferences as a scribe, accumulated over decades, and imposed upon all the copies he made. This explanation will account for such obviously deliberate variants as scene divisions and scene numbers, for 'Actus' in places where Middleton was content simply with the Latin numeral ('Quintus'), and for recurring patterns of variants (a preference for older forms such as 'hath', euphonic 'thine' and 'mine', unelided 'I am' and 'it had').

Secondly, the CRANE variants might be correct original readings, corrupted in all the NON-CRANE texts. We have already encountered examples of this pattern in the necessary entrance directions omitted by all NON-CRANE texts at 5.1.0.4–5 and 5.3.178.1–2. But there are also examples

at 3.1.392.1 and 4.4.55.1—which have not been counted as 'NON-CRANE' errors only because the relevant material is missing entirely in one of the NON-CRANE texts (OKES in one case, MIDDLETONᵀ in the other). In both these cases all the CRANE texts contain the correct reading, which is present in none of the extant NON-CRANE texts.

Thirdly, the CRANE variants might be correct original readings, revised by the author in all the NON-CRANE texts. Examples of this category are, necessarily, more conjectural; previous editors have been willing to identify Crane's scribal characteristics, and forced to supply necessary stage directions omitted by MIDDLETONᵀ and other NON-CRANE texts, but whether a variant results from authorial revision (in one group of texts) or scribal error (in another group of texts) is harder to prove, or to judge. Past editors have usually preferred to minimize the problem of authorial revision. But it is hard to dismiss the double variant at Induction.41 ('Game? What game' against 'What game, prithee?'), and there are other plausible examples at 1.1.224 (not/out), 4.1.33 (this/the), 4.4.107 (you/go).

Alternatively, all these examples of the third category might be interpreted as examples of the second category (error in NON-CRANE). More generally, although there are cases where the relevant category is clear enough, there are also ambiguous cases, which different editors will interpret differently. (That is one reason that shared variants are a less reliable category of stemmatic evidence.)

Nevertheless, the patterns of shared variation we have found in all four CRANE texts can be extended in a way that illuminates the stemmatic transition from CRANE to NON-CRANE. We can call this category of evidence 'Crane Plus One'. This category consists of variants shared by all four CRANE texts with only one NON-CRANE text.

We already know that none of these variants can be an error, because CRANE¹ does not share errors with the stemma of the revised version of the play. We also know that none of these variants can be a direct result of the activity of Ralph Crane, because 'Crane Plus One' includes at least one text not transcribed by him. Again, there are three possible explanations for these readings. First, Crane's preferences might have been inherited by another text, because the fifth text was being copied from a Crane text. Second, correct readings in five texts might have been corrupted in three NON-CRANE texts. Third, correct original readings might have been revised by the author in three NON-CRANE texts.

These categories have editorial implications, but for the moment I am interested only in their relevance to the stemma of transmission. Whichever of these three explanations is operating in any given instance, overall the NON-CRANE text closest to the four CRANE texts should have the most 'Crane Plus One' variants.

Unsurprisingly, BRIDGEWATER contains only three 'Crane Plus One' variants: Crane's 'hath' for Middletonian 'has' at 3.1.149, and the correct lineation at 3.1.399 and

---

[146] 3.1.370 (metrical 'th'' for unelided 'the'), 5.2.58 ('one' for 'on'), 5.3.116 ('whom' for 'which').

4.2.107–8. Because these are shared variants, not shared errors, and because there are so few of them, they need not reflect any direct stemmatic link between BRIDGEWATER and the four CRANE texts; indeed, their quantitative and qualitative insignificance suggest the opposite. Since BRIDGEWATER contains more shared errors than any other text, and for a variety of reasons seems to be very late in the stemma of transmission, this paucity of links with the four Crane texts is exactly what we would expect.

Unsurprisingly also, MIDDLETON[T] has more 'Crane Plus One' variants than BRIDGEWATER: sixteen.[147] This may seem a little odd, since for the beginning and end of the play we have already established that MIDDLETON[T] is the last of the NON-CRANE texts. But it is also autograph throughout, which means that it is uniquely positioned to restore correct CRANE readings corrupted by intervening manuscripts. I will return to the distribution of these variants below, but for now the important point is that they are spread throughout the play.

In dramatic contrast with BRIDGEWATER and MIDDLETON[T] both, OKES contains 21 'Crane Plus One' variants. This evidence of shared variants strongly confirms the conclusion, based on the evidence of shared errors, that OKES is much closer than BRIDGEWATER or MIDDLETON[T] to the CRANE texts. But the distribution of those 'Crane Plus One' variants in OKES is as significant as their number: 21 of the 22 occur after 4.1.145.[148] I will return to the one exception below (Sec. XXIV). But the almost complete absence of such variants in the first half of the play provides further confirmation for the hypothesis of divided copy-text: for those earlier scenes, [PRE-MIDDLETON/OKES] derives from something other than [CRANE⁴].

We may be able to locate this discontinuity in the copy-text for [PRE-MIDDLETON/OKES] even more precisely. In my analysis of patterns of shared error, I have already pointed out (Sec. XVII) that the triplet BRIDGEWATER–MIDDLETON–OKES does not appear after 4.1.93. In other words: after 4.1.93, if OKES is linked to BRIDGEWATER and MIDDLETON, it is also linked to ROSENBACH. That is not true in the first part of the play. We might therefore conjecture that the copy-text for [PRE-MIDDLETON/OKES] changed at some point between 4.1.93 and 4.1.146.[149]

An equally dramatic contrast is provided by ROSENBACH: it contains 48 'Crane Plus One' variants. Again, though, these are not evenly distributed: 44 of the 48 occur before 4.1.1. Since we are dealing with shared variation, rather than shared error, the four exceptions are probably insignificant.[150] The contrast between the two texts—ROSENBACH 4, OKES 21—is enough to confirm that, for most of Acts Four and Five, OKES is closer to the CRANE group. Even more remarkable is the contrast between ROSENBACH (44) and OKES (1) up to the beginning of Act Four. Clearly, in the first three Acts ROSENBACH is closer than OKES to the CRANE texts.

One discrepancy remains to be explained. As I noticed in the preceding analysis of shared errors, the links between OKES and CRANE²'³ all occur in the play's first three scenes;

but the sustained cluster of variants linking OKES to all four CRANE texts does not begin until 4.1.146, and the change in its relationship to all the NON-CRANE texts does not occur until 4.1.93 at the earliest. What happens in the middle of the play, from the beginning of 2.2 until 4.1.93?

XXII. Divided Copy-text in the NON-CRANE Texts: 4.1.143–4.4.110.2

My first examination of the stemma of the NON-CRANE texts (Sec. XVII) established that the relationships of those texts were simple and logical at the beginning of the play (Prologue to end of 2.1) and at the end (5.1 to Epilogue). The middle was more confusing. In the extant witnesses, those middle scenes are divided between printing houses (MATHEWES/ALLDE) and between scribes (ROSENBACH, BRIDGEWATER); we have also demonstrated that there is a stemmatic discontinuity, in those scenes, in the underlying lost manuscripts [PRE-MIDDLETON[T]], [PRE-BRIDGEWATER], [PRE-ROSENBACH], and [PRE-MIDDLETON/OKES]. Those discontinuities in all the NON-CRANE texts were almost certainly caused by divided copy-text. Thus, at some point after creation of the last extant CRANE manuscript, the process of producing new copies of the play seems to have routinely involved division of the text between different agents and/or different exemplars to be reproduced. This mode of production makes a global stemmatic analysis of those scenes much more complicated, and in some areas of the text the stemma may remain indeterminable, simply because as the area of text shrinks the number of pieces of reliable evidence also diminishes. Nevertheless, by now we are perhaps as well positioned as it is possible to be, and can attempt to resolve the interrelated problems in the middle scenes.

As I noted at the end of the preceding section, something about the copy-text for OKES seems to have changed at some point between 4.1.93 and 4.1.146. This argument is based partly on the evidence of triplets, which were crucial to determining the sequence of NON-CRANE texts at the beginning and end of the play. So it makes

[147] 1.1.278 (t'), 1.1.311 (tak'st), 2.2.163 (thee), 3.1.108 (questiond), 3.1.127 (and), 3.1.151 (Bishop's White), 3.1.318 (flamed), 3.1.355 (vainer), 3.1.369 (Egyptic), 3.1.395.1 (absence of 'and'), 4.1.91 (our chaste delights), 4.1.97 (confirmd), 4.1.100 (you not), 4.3.0.4 (then), and, 4.4.38 (Mechlin), 5.3.39 ('specially).

[148] 4.1.146, 4.2.66, 4.2.141, *4.4.1, *4.4.11, *4.4.12.1, *4.4.31, *5.1.44.1, 5.2.1, 5.2.3, *5.2.7 (lineation), 5.2.7, 5.2.87 (oath), 5.2.11, 5.3.19, 5.3.62, 5.3.98, 5.3.131 (speech prefix), 5.3.131, 5.3.153, 5.3.158. Asterisked readings are identified as shared errors in the other three texts.

[149] Howard-Hill also concluded that the copy-text for OKES derived from [CRANE⁴] in the play's later scenes: see Figure 1. However, Howard-Hill located the change somewhat later: 'from [4.2.64] 1851' (*Pasquin* 180), 'from around [4.2.66]/1853 onward' (p. 180, n. 27) or at 4.2.63/'1850' (p. 184, Diagram 4). I cannot discern why he locates the change where he does. He claims that, beginning in this vicinity, OKES 'shares variants... with the other witnesses of the Crane branch' (180); however, he gives orthographical evidence for the influence on Crane on OKES beginning at 4.4.57 (p. 182), which leads him to declare that the evidence for a stemmatic relationship 'is conclusive in' Act Five, 'but is less convincing' in 4.4 (p. 183). Still later, he announces that 'the question of how' [CRANE⁴]'s 'influence was exerted on the copy for' OKES 'remains impossible to describe convincingly' (p. 208). My own arguments and conclusions here were developed independently.

[150] All four occur in 5.2, where two NON-CRANE texts are autograph, and in two of those four cases the three other NON-CRANE texts have different readings.

sense to look at the evidence of triplets from 4.1.93 to the end of Act Four, in order to establish how the text after that change might differ from the text before the change. Of the four possible triplets in any set of four, only two appear: (02,R2,B2) and (R2,B2,M2).

> 30. OKES–ROSENBACH–BRIDGEWATER: 1–2 (4.4.38 + 4.4.55.1? *passage not present in* MIDDLETON[T])
> 53. [Crane]–OKES–ROSENBACH–BRIDGEWATER: 2 (4.1.116)
> 31. ROSENBACH–BRIDGEWATER–MIDDLETON[T]: 4 (3.1.155–4.4.1, 4.4.11, 4.4.12.1, 4.4.31)

There are no examples of (02,R2,M2) or of (02,B2,M2). This distribution of triplets is compatible with a set of four that also produces a series of four. Since the doublet (R2,B2) appears in both triplets, it would have to occur in the middle of the series; 02 and M2 must be at the beginning and end. This hypothesis is confirmed by the pattern of two-member subsets. Of the six possible pairs in a set with four members, only four appear: (R2,B2), (02,B2), (R2,M2), and (02,R2).

> 18. ROSENBACH–BRIDGEWATER: 7–8 (4.1.97, 4.2.4, 4.2.16, 4.4.15, 4.4.20, 4.4.33, 4.4.39 + 4.4.74.1? *passage not in* MIDDLETON[T])
> 16. OKES–BRIDGEWATER: 4 (4.2.47, 4.2.74, 4.2.83, 4.4.110.2)
> 9. ROSENBACH–MIDDLETON[T]: 2 (4.2.81, 4.2.107)
> 15. ROSENBACH–OKES: 1–2 (4.2.44 + 4.1.129–30?)

There are no examples of (B2,M2) or of (02,M2). Given the pattern of triplets, the absence of that last pair is not surprising; OKES and MIDDLETON[T] are apparently at opposite ends of the series of four in this stretch of text, and they should not be uniquely paired. Likewise, it is not surprising to find that the strongest subset is (R2,B2), because the pattern of triplets already identified those two texts as adjacent.

However, a series of four should produce only three adjacent pairs, not four. One of these four pairs must therefore be an anomaly, presumably produced by coincidental error. The anomaly cannot be the strong (R2,B2) pair, with seven clear examples, or the strong (02,B2) pair, with four. The weakest of the four pairs is (02,R2). Because the change in the copy-text for OKES could have occurred at any point between 4.1.93 and 4.1.146, I have recorded all shared errors after 4.1.93; but the shared error at 4.1.129–30 might well be *before* the change of copy-text. If so, this would leave only one example of the (02,R2) pair in the relevant stretch of text. Moreover, that (02,R2) pair contradicts two other pairs. According to the evidence of the triplets, OKES must be at the beginning or end of the series of four; it should therefore be paired with only one other NON-CRANE text in this part of the text. Since patterns 16 and 15 both involve OKES, one must be coincidental, and 16 is four times stronger than 15. Likewise, since OKES and MIDDLETON[T] are at opposite ends of the series, no text can be linked to *both* of them. Either

pattern 15 or pattern 9 must therefore be coincidental, and pattern 9 is twice as strong as pattern 15. Altogether, the single clear example of pattern 15 is logically incompatible with six clear examples in patterns 16 and 9. If we dismiss the single pairing at 4.2.44 as a coincidental minim misreading, all the remaining twenty-two shared errors from 4.1.131 to 4.4.110.2 make perfect sense.[151] We might therefore pinpoint the change in the copy-text for OKES even more precisely, to the stretch of text between 4.1.131 and 4.1.145.

The three remaining pairs, when combined with the two triplets, could be explained by two different series. OKES, at one end of either possible series, is linked to BRIDGEWATER, and MIDDLETON[T], at the other end of either possible series, is linked to ROSENBACH. The pattern in this part of the text therefore must differ from the pattern we have seen at the beginning and end of the play. At the beginning, MIDDLETON[T] is strongly and uniquely linked to BRIDGEWATER; here, it has no unique links at all to BRIDGEWATER. Likewise, in Act Five OKES is linked to ROSENBACH, and MIDDLETON is linked to BRIDGEWATER—the exact opposite of the pattern here.

The nature of the difference between this stretch of text and Act Five depends on which series is correct. One possible series, which would explain all the foregoing evidence, is: OKES→BRIDGEWATER→ROSENBACH→MIDDLETON[T]. This series would keep OKES at the beginning of the series, and MIDDLETON at the end—the positions they occupy at the beginning and end of the play. But it would reverse the order of ROSENBACH and BRIDGEWATER. The alternative series, which would also explain all the foregoing evidence, is: MIDDLETON[T]→ROSENBACH→BRIDGEWATER→OKES. This retains the order of ROSENBACH and BRIDGEWATER found elsewhere, but reverses the positions of OKES (from first to last) and MIDDLETON[T] (from last to first).

As we have seen before, the pattern of shared error sets cannot, in itself, arbitrate between these two possible series. But the pattern of shared variants makes one interpretation much more probable than the other. In the preceding section I argued that 'Crane Plus One' variants could reliably identify which NON-CRANE text was closest to the (earlier) CRANE texts. One of the two possible series puts OKES at the beginning of the NON-CRANE sequence, and the alternative puts MIDDLETON[T] in that position. But MIDDLETON[T] does not contain a single 'Crane Plus One' variant in this stretch of text. OKES, by contrast, contains seven.[152] OKES must therefore be at the beginning of the NON-CRANE series, here as in Act Five—and MIDDLETON[T] must be, again, the last of the NON-CRANE texts. What changes, between Act Four and Act Five, is the relative order of the two adjacent texts ROSENBACH and BRIDGEWATER.

---

[151] The misreading of 'mummy' as 'mony' substitutes a very common word for a very rare one: in printed books up to 1630 EEBO-TCP lists 37 examples of *mummy*, but 32,841 of *money*.
[152] 4.1.146, 4.2.66, 4.2.141, *4.4.1, *4.4.11, *4.4.12.1, *4.4.31.

Logically, all the foregoing evidence is explained by the series OKES→BRIDGEWATER→ROSENBACH→MIDDLETON[T] — or, more precisely, by the stemma visualized in Figure 6.[153]

This stemma raises a number of questions. We investigated this section of text, as a discrete unit, because of an apparent change in the stemmatic relationships of OKES. But why should a change in OKES coincide with a change in the relative position of BRIDGEWATER and ROSENBACH? Why should the copy for both BRIDGEWATER and ROSENBACH have changed, simultaneously, at the beginning of Act Five? How can we reconcile this stemma with the evidence that ROSENBACH is stemmatically earlier than BRIDGEWATER in the second half of the play? These questions will eventually have to be addressed, but answering them will require a global picture of the shifting copy for the NON-CRANE texts.

XXIII. Divided Copy-text in the NON-CRANE Texts: 2.1–2.2

Having worked backward from Act Five toward the beginning of Act Four, I now want to work forward from the Prologue to the end of Act Two. I am adopting this rather strange procedure because Act Three creates seemingly insuperable problems, and we will be better positioned to unknot that tangle if we have a provisional picture of the stemma of transmission that governs the text before and after it.

The second scene of Act Two creates several problems for analysis of the relationships of the NON-CRANE texts. For most of 2.2.13–257, BRIDGEWATER is absent, leaving only three NON-CRANE texts. As usual, CRANE[3] abridges the text, and whenever it does so, in that stretch of text, we are reduced to six witnesses. Moreover, CRANE[T] does not contain 2.2.0.1–2.2.95 (a later addition), so for that part of the scene there are (at most) only three CRANE texts. Some lines in that section are also absent from CRANE[2] and/or CRANE[3], leaving in some cases only one CRANE text, and in other cases only two. For 2.2.13–95, there are at most six witnesses, and sometimes as few as four. Of the four witnesses that provide a full text of the scene, one is autograph; MIDDLETON[T] could correct errors at any point, thereby obscuring its stemmatic connections to other witnesses. In the early scenes of the play MIDDLETON[T] is more accurate than it later becomes, and consequently more likely to have covered its stemmatic tracks. Finally, we have already established that the three scenes which precede 2.2 have certain stemmatic peculiarities not present in the last three Acts, and that certain stemmatic anomalies begin in the scene which follows 2.2. Thus, we cannot assume that the patterns present in the preceding scenes, or the following scenes, are also present throughout 2.2, which in one way or another seems to have been transitional: the copy-text for one or more NON-CRANE texts *must* have changed just before 2.2, just after 2.2, or somewhere in the middle of 2.2. Given these obstacles to analysis, the stemmatic relationships of the NON-CRANE texts of 2.2 may be impossible to determine—and any hypothesis will

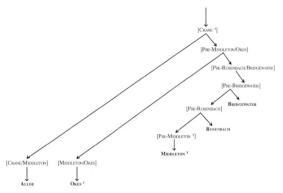

Figure 6. Visualization of the Bottom of the Stemma of Transmission in 4.1.145–4.4.110.2. This is the same as Figure 5, except that the sequence of BRIDGEWATER and ROSENBACH is reversed.

certainly be less secure than our hypotheses about other parts of the play.

Nevertheless, I will describe the available evidence, which at least limits the range of possible solutions.

Table of Shared Errors in 2.2

16. OKES–BRIDGEWATER: 2.2.3, 2.2.68
21. CRANE[3]–ROSENBACH–OKES: 2.2.94.1? [passage not in BRIDGEWATER; CRANE[3] ambiguous]
12. [CRANE[4]]–ROSENBACH: 2.2.133–35 [passage not in BRIDGEWATER or CRANE[3]]
15. ROSENBACH–OKES: 2.2.81.1–2 [passage not in BRIDGEWATER; unspecified in CRANE[3]]
48. CRANE[2,3,4]–ROSENBACH–OKES–MIDDLETON[T]: 2.2.33? [passage not in BRIDGEWATER]

Two things are immediately apparent from this list. First, OKES is closely linked to BRIDGEWATER, as it is in the first three scenes (two unequivocal examples, despite the absence of BRIDGEWATER from most of the scene). Secondly, more weakly, OKES is linked to ROSENBACH, as it is in the first three scenes (two examples). Clearly, certain features of the stemma of transmission in the first scenes of the play remain unchanged in 2.2.

However, the final shared error listed above has some interesting implications which disturb the postulate of continuity. As noted above (Sec. XVII), there are no examples anywhere in the play of the three texts ROSENBACH–OKES–MIDDLETON[T] sharing an error which is not also shared by BRIDGEWATER. That triplet nevertheless appears, as part of a larger pattern, at 2.2.33. There are two possible explanations for that exception. Either (1) this stretch of text is stemmatically unique, in permitting the triplet ROSENBACH–OKES–MIDDLETON[T], or (2) the error at 2.2.33 was shared by the lost [PRE-BRIDGEWATER], and the

---

[153] Although the preceding discussion pays no attention to [PRE-ROSENBACH/BRIDGEWATER], it is included in Figure 6, because we have already demonstrated that it must have existed and must have influenced the transmission of ROSENBACH and BRIDGEWATER. I will return to its possible significance here in Sec. XXVIII.

apparent anomaly results simply from the unavailability of BRIDGEWATER here—in which case, what seems like the lone example of Pattern 48 is actually an example of Pattern 56. But if the second explanation is correct, then 2.2 contains the first clear example of an error shared by all the NON-CRANE texts. Another example of Pattern 56 (combining all four NON-CRANE texts with the three later CRANE texts) occurs at 3.1.175.1. Act Five contains two errors shared by NON-CRANE, which do not occur in any CRANE text (Pattern 40). Consequently, in the second half of the play all four NON-CRANE texts are, in one way or another, stemmatically linked.[154] Either the shared error at 2.2.33 represents a unique pattern, or it represents the first appearance of a new pattern. Either way, something has changed.

The significance of this anomalous shared error is confirmed by patterns of shared variants in 2.2. The parts of the scene missing from BRIDGEWATER contain nine variants uniquely shared by ROSENBACH-OKES-MIDDLETON[T], and two more where the same three share a reading with CRANE[I].[155] Such variants appear nowhere else in the play. We are therefore presented with the same choice: either (1) this scene is stemmatically unique, or (2) these apparent triplets are in fact examples of readings shared throughout the NON-CRANE texts, accidentally disguised by the absence of BRIDGEWATER in this scene.

If we interpret the ROSENBACH-OKES-MIDDLETON[T] triplets as variants that were shared by all the underlying NON--CRANE texts, then the issue of continuity concerns the presence of similar NON-CRANE variants in the earlier scenes of the play, before the break in BRIDGEWATER. There are ten such variants in the play's first three scenes, and three at the beginning of 2.2 (before the break in BRIDGEWATER).[156] If we compare the ratios for the first three scenes (10/648) with the ratio in 2.2 (14/266), the difference is striking: one every 65 lines in the first three scenes, one every 19 lines in the fourth scene.[157] Thus, 2.2 not only contains the first clear error shared by all the extant NON-CRANE texts; it also has, proportionally, at least three times as many variants shared by all the extant NON-CRANE texts.

The anomalous shared error, and the anomalous pattern of shared variants, both require us to investigate the issue of continuity. Whichever explanation we adopt, something seems to have changed between the play's first three scenes and 2.2. Therefore, in order to understand the textual lineage of 2.2 we have to relate its variants to those in the three preceding scenes.

One of the strongest patterns in the first three scenes is the triplet OKES-BRIDGEWATER-MIDDLETON[T]. These three texts, in those three scenes, uniquely share ten errors.[158] They also uniquely share another twenty-one substantive variants.[159] In other words, for the first three scenes of the play (648 lines), these three texts uniquely share thirty--one readings, about a third of them errors. Naturally, for most of 2.2 that pattern is impossible, because the lines are not present in BRIDGEWATER. But that absence should not affect the stemmatic connection between the three texts,

which is indirect: all three texts are dead-ends, and the stemmatic connection really links [PRE-MIDDLETON/OKES], [PRE-BRIDGEWATER], and [PRE-MIDDLETON[T]]. Therefore, if the underlying stemmatic connection remained the same, then it should appear, in 2.2, as a spike in the number of variants uniquely shared by OKES and MIDDLETON[T]. That is, the pervasive underlying triplet OKES-BRIDGEWATER-MIDDLETON[T] should now look like a pair, OKES-MIDDLETON[T]. That pair-pattern is rare in the first three scenes: the two texts do not uniquely share any clear errors, but they do share two variants.[160] So, for the first three scenes as a whole the unique patterns OKES-BRIDGEWATER-MIDDLETON[T] and OKES-MIDDLETON[T] occur thirty-three times, averaging one shared variant every twenty lines. If the stemmatic connection between all three underlying texts remained unchanged in 2.2, then we should, in the 266 lines of 2.2, find about nine unique examples of OKES-MIDDLE-TON[T]. Instead, the scene contains only a single certain example.[161] If that ratio had been present in the play's first three scenes, they would have contained only five of these variants.

In my initial global analysis of the NON-CRANE texts (Sec. XVII), I concluded that, in the first part of the play, the four NON-CRANE texts did not form a unified set. There were two arguments for that proof, one weak, one strong. The weak argument was the absence of any reliable examples of an error uniquely shared by all four NON-CRANE texts. The presence of shared NON-CRANE variants in the first three scenes does not weaken this argument, any more than the presence of CRANE variants weakens the evidence that CRANE[I] belongs to a different branch of the stemma than CRANE[2,3,4]; in each case,

---

[154] At 1.1.242.1 the NON-CRANE texts, and CRANE[3,4], lack an exit direction. That error resembles the one at 2.2.33, in that it is shared by the NON-CRANE texts and more than one late CRANE text; but it differs from the example in 2.2, because like other missing exit directions it has been removed from the filtered data-set.

[155] 2.2.36 (I've), 2.2.50 (does), 2.2.59 (a), 2.2.73 (has), 2.2.81 (wording of stage direction), 2.2.82 (has), 2.2.96-7 (mislineations), 2.2.109 (of), 2.2.197 (they've), 2.2.199 (has), 2.2.246 (You're).

[156] Induction.16 (my), Induction.41 (Game? What game?), 1.1.32 (can), 1.1.59 (the), 1.1.224 (not), 1.1.236 (thy), 1.1.305 (Italica this), 2.1.71 (the), 2.1.235 (the), 2.2 (scene break and number), 2.2.0.2 (wth), 2.2.2 (Bs.). The NON-CRANE texts uniquely lack an exit direction at 1.1.331.1; this was counted as a shared error, but like other errors involving exit directions it has been removed from the filtered data-set. In this tabulation it has been counted simply as a shared variant.

[157] The total number of lines in 2.2 includes the nine lines, present in OKES and MIDDLETON[T], which this edition places in the appendix as Additional Passages A and B. Even if we excluded the two examples in 2.2 where the ROSENBACH-OKES-MIDDLETON[T] triplet coincides with the original CRANE[I] reading, the contrast would still be remarkable (1/22 vs. 1/65).

[158] Induction.23, Induction.52.1-2, Induction.78.1, 1.1.70.1, 1.1.324, 2.1.39-41, 2.1.106-7, 2.1.137-8, 2.1.155-6, 2.1.227.1. Other shared errors linking these three texts occur at *3.1.44, *3.1.48, *4.1.93.1.

[159] Induction.0.1-2, Induction.44, Induction.61, Induction.65 (spelling of contraction), 1.1.0.1, 1.1.249, 1.1.255, 1.1.257, 1.1.288-90, 1.1.306, 2.1.58-9, 2.1.63, 2.1.75-6, 2.1.105 (odd spelling), 2.1.118, 2.1.140, 2.1.141, 2.1.155, 2.1.156, 2.1.200, 2.1.235, 2.1.236. The sum of 'twenty-one' does not include the two spellings. These three texts also share unique variants at 3.1.175, 3.2.29.1, 3.1.395, 4.1, 4.1.0.1, 5.2.56.

[160] 1.1.0.3, 1.1.233. There is one example in 2.2 (2.2.93) and the rest of the play contains ten: 3.1.33, 3.1.75, 4.1.73, 4.1.94, 4.2.85, 4.2.100, 5.3, 5.3.0.1-3, 5.3.0.2, 5.3.188.

[161] At 2.2.141, OKES and MIDDLETON[T] alone have Middleton's preferred 'has'. At 2.2.93, OKES has 'out of', MIDDLETON[T] has 'Plague of'; they agree only in the preposition.

a shared agent (Crane in one case, Middleton in the other) could introduce such variants into texts that were not stemmatically related. Shared errors demonstrate a stemmatic connection; shared variants may or may not. Nevertheless, with or without the shared variants this argument against the stemmatic integrity of the NON--CRANE texts is weak, because one of those texts was autograph throughout the early scenes, and the other three seem to have derived from partially or wholly autograph texts. The author might have caught any new errors before they were perpetrated throughout the whole set of four texts. The argument is weak because the negative evidence on which it is based could be the result of authorial transference.

The second argument against the unity of the NON--CRANE set is much stronger. If the four texts formed a set/series, they should have contained examples of two patterns of triplets: one triplet at the beginning of the set (1,2,3), another at the end (2,3,4), with the two medial texts present in both triplets. But the early scenes in fact contain only one triplet pattern, the one I have just documented: OKES–BRIDGEWATER–MIDDLETON[T], with eight uniquely shared errors and twenty-eight other uniquely shared variants. This triplet includes errors as well as variants; it also includes the autograph text, thereby demonstrating that even authorial correction could not overcome the stemmatic link between the three texts.

How, then, are we to account for the absence of any other triplet patterns in these early scenes? They cannot have been eliminated by authorial correction, because such correction left the other triplet intact. In any case, the number of examples of the extant triplet makes it impossible to attribute the absence of a second triplet to random distribution. If anything, we would expect *more* examples of the other triplet, not fewer. One member of the extant triplet is autograph, and we have already proven (Sec. XIX) that the autograph text is the last of the extant texts for the early part of the play. In these scenes, MIDDLETON[T] is connected to the other extant texts only through BRIDGEWATER. Since we know that the extant triplet results from the series OKES→BRIDGEWATER→MIDDLETON[T], we know that, if the NON-CRANE texts formed a coherent series, then the other triplet *should have been* ROSENBACH→OKES→BRIDGEWATER. But no such triplet materializes, either among shared errors or shared variants.

We already have an explanation for the absence of that triplet, because we know that, in the first three scenes, ROSENBACH is embedded stemmatically among the CRANE texts. In those scenes, the pattern 'Crane Plus One' links ROSENBACH to all four CRANE texts at least 37 times.[162] By contrast, 'Crane Plus One' does not link the other NON-CRANE texts to all four CRANE texts in those scenes: there are no examples of 'Crane Plus OKES' or 'Crane Plus BRIDGEWATER', and only one example of 'Crane Plus MIDDLETON[T]' (almost certainly the result of the author restoring the correct original elision at 1.1.278). This statistical evidence establishes that ROSENBACH is, in those

three scenes, much closer than any other NON-CRANE text to the CRANE texts. Moreover, in those three scenes ROSENBACH contains a remarkably low number of shared errors. I have already observed that for the whole first half of the play, up to 3.1.319, ROSENBACH has a lower ratio of shared error per line than any text except CRANE[1], and about the same number as CRANE[2] (Sec. XIV). If we were to assume, instead, that the copy-text for ROSENBACH changed at the end of 2.1, the ratio would be even more remarkable: only eight shared errors in 648 lines, a ratio of one shared error every 81 lines. If that ratio had been sustained for the whole play (2178 lines), ROSENBACH would have contained only 27 filtered shared errors—making it much less reliable than CRANE[1] (with none), but slightly more reliable than CRANE[2] (with thirty-four).[163]

'Crane Plus One' groups five texts together; it cannot, in itself, tell us where in that grouping any one text belongs. Thus, although 'Crane Plus One' demonstrates that the first three scenes of ROSENBACH belong, stemmatically, among the CRANE texts, it does not identify *where* in the CRANE series we should place it. Nascimento and Howard-Hill linked ROSENBACH directly to CRANE[1]; but that hypothesis, as I have already shown, cannot be correct. 'Whatever the origin of ROSENBACH, no part of it seems to derive directly from CRANE[1] (or its immediate source, [PRE-MIDDLETON]). Instead, all of ROSENBACH is somehow connected to the later CRANE texts' (Sec. XIV). We know that CRANE[1] is the only member of a distinct branch, so ROSENBACH must be related, instead, to the later CRANE texts, either the three extant ones or the unknown number of lost ones. In itself, 'Crane Plus One' does not resolve the stemmatic problem, but it does establish that any solution must put ROSENBACH somewhere *inside* the four CRANE texts, later than CRANE[1] but earlier than the distinct NON-CRANE sequence.

It may help, at this point, to give a complete list of filtered shared errors in the play's first three scenes, in descending order of frequency and significance.

Table of Shared Errors in Prologue, Induction, 1.1, 2.1

32. OKES–BRIDGEWATER–MIDDLETON[T]: 8
16. OKES–BRIDGEWATER: 8
14. CRANE[2,3]: 7
13. BRIDGEWATER–MIDDLETON[T]: 4
15. ROSENBACH–OKES: 4
12. [CRANE[4]]–ROSENBACH: 2
45. CRANE[2,3]–OKES–BRIDGEWATER–MIDDLETON[T]: 1
25. CRANE[2,3,4]: 1
26. CRANE[2,3]–ROSENBACH: 1
27. CRANE[2,3]–OKES: 1
17. [CRANE[4]]–OKES: 1

162 In addition, at 1.1.324 ROSENBACH agrees with CRANE[2,3,4] in a passage absent from CRANE[1], and at 2.1.200 it agrees with CRANE[1,4] in a passage absent from CRANE[2,3]; in both cases, it agrees with all extant CRANE texts against all other extant NON-CRANE texts.
163 If the ratio in the first three scenes (8/648 lines) had been continued in the fourth scene (266 lines), ROSENBACH would have had only three shared errors in 2.2. Instead, it contains four. In itself, the difference is not statistically significant.

* * *

19. CRANE^{2,4}–ROSENBACH: 1? [not in CRANE^3]
11. [CRANE^4]–BRIDGEWATER: 1? [not in CRANE^3]

The most significant triplet is the one we have already discussed, OKES–BRIDGEWATER–MIDDLETON^T, which clearly establishes a set of three related texts. The evidence of errors shared by those three texts is confirmed by the evidence of shared variants: there are, in addition to the shared errors, 28 uniquely shared variants—more than any subset of texts except 'Crane Plus ROSENBACH'. The most significant pair, OKES–BRIDGEWATER, belongs to that triplet; the triplet and the pair together produce sixteen errors in the subset (O1,B1), more than any other set or subset of shared errors in these scenes. Again, the evidence of twenty-one uniquely shared variants confirms the evidence of shared errors: no pair of texts has a greater number of shared variants in these scenes. The same triplet also contains a second significant pair, BRIDGEWATER–MIDDLETON^T: four uniquely shared errors, an additional eleven uniquely shared variants. But the third possible pairing within that triplet (OKES–MIDDLETON^T) produces no shared errors, and only two shared variants, both of which could easily be coincidental.[164] This is the distribution we would expect in a series of three, and it establishes that BRIDGEWATER is the middle text in the series. It does not, in itself, establish which text is earliest, and which latest. But it does clearly establish that these texts must be late in the larger sequence of transmission: OKES contains 23 shared errors, BRIDGEWATER 22, and even MIDDLETON^T, despite the advantage of autograph correction, has thirteen—more than any of the other texts. This is very much what we would expect, from all our preceding analysis. For these three late texts, the evidence from these three scenes is satisfyingly clear, unconflicted, and unambiguous.

The next most important pair, CRANE^{2,3}, does not contain any text in the preceding linked set of three. However, the number of examples of this pairing in these scenes does demonstrate that the two texts are an adjacent pair; they also appear together in four larger sets, producing a subset (C2,C3) with a total of eleven shared errors in the play's first three scenes. An additional twenty-one variants uniquely link the two texts. And the only error in these scenes which occurs in more than three texts—pattern 45, at Induction.52.1—links that strong pair (C2,C3) to the strong triplet discussed in the previous paragraph (O1,B1,M1). The simplest explanation for that linkage is that one of the three NON-CRANE texts inherited the error from the CRANE pair. There are no examples of errors uniquely shared by CRANE^{2,3} and BRIDGEWATER, or by CRANE^{2,3} and MIDDLETON^T. There is, however, one error uniquely shared by CRANE^{2,3} and OKES (1.1.311). Thus, the only separately established link that would explain pattern 45 is the link between OKES and CRANE^{2,3}. The assumption that OKES was the conduit, linking CRANE^{2,3} to BRIDGEWATER–MIDDLETON^T, would also explain why the four NON-CRANE texts are not a coherent set. Two of them are, in these scenes, more closely linked to CRANE^{2,3} than

to ROSENBACH. BRIDGEWATER and MIDDLETON^T do not share a single error with ROSENBACH in these scenes; ROSENBACH and MIDDLETON^T do not uniquely share even a single variant.

There are only two other sets here which are exemplified by more than one shared error: ROSENBACH–OKES (4) and [CRANE^4]–ROSENBACH (2). As I demonstrated earlier (Sec. XIV), all the shared errors in the first part of ROSENBACH can be explained by its relationship to those two texts. These two well-established pairs suggest that the three texts are connected, with ROSENBACH as the middle term: either [CRANE^4]→ROSENBACH→OKES or OKES→ROSENBACH→[CRANE^4]. The first sequence would be ruled out by the evidence (Sec. XXI) that OKES, in this part of the play, is related to CRANE^{2,3}. I have conjectured that those apparent links might be due to proofreading in CRANE/MATHEWES, but if my conjecture were wrong then the first possible sequence here would also be wrong. We might therefore hypothesize that, in these scenes, ROSENBACH represents a separate branch of the stemma, connected to [CRANE^4], and that OKES instead inherits errors from CRANE^{2,3} and passes them on to BRIDGEWATER and MIDDLETON^T.

But this hypothesis raises two questions. First, what about those four errors uniquely shared by ROSENBACH and OKES? Two of these occur in passages not present in CRANE^3, and the errors might therefore have been present in the lost, full-length [PRE-CRANE^3] or in a copy of it, a conjectural lost text between [PRE-CRANE^3] and [CRANE^4], which we might call [CRANE$^{3.5}$]. Two of the four errors might therefore have originated in one of those conjectured lost texts, produced just before or just after CRANE^3, and been passed from there to both ROSENBACH and OKES. We could conjecture that both ROSENBACH and OKES derive, separately, from that lost manuscript, somewhere before or after CRANE^3. Since the text that separates them is lost, any errors they shared with it would appear to be pairs, not triplets. [PRE-ROSENBACH] could have passed its additional errors on to [CRANE^4], while [PRE-MIDDLETON/OKES] passed its additional errors on to the other NON-CRANE texts. This scenario would explain why ROSENBACH, but not OKES, is linked to all four CRANE texts by the 'Crane Plus One' evidence: OKES would only be linked to [CRANE^4] through the medium of ROSENBACH. If we accepted this line of reasoning, then we would get the stemma visualized in Figure 7.

The right side of this diagram is much more securely defined than the middle and the left side, because there are more shared variants and shared errors in the extant right-side texts. But this conjecture might begin to explain the absence of ROSENBACH–OKES–BRIDGEWATER errors. OKES is closely connected to BRIDGEWATER, but more indirectly

---

[164] At 1.1.0.3 both texts lack the word 'and', found in all other texts, and at 1.1.233 they both have 'fellow' instead of the 'fellon' of other texts. Since Middleton apparently transcribed the copy-text for OKES, he might have introduced both readings, or both might represent inadvertent variants independently made in different texts.

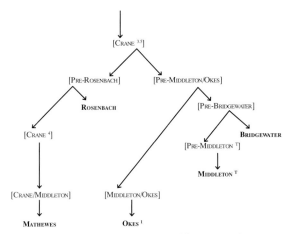

Figure 7. Draft Visualization of the Bottom of
the Stemma of Transmission in Prologue–2.1

connected to ROSENBACH. The stemmatic distance between
texts, and the amount of correction in each, directly affects
the number of errors they share. There are, in these
three scenes, sixteen errors shared by BRIDGEWATER and
OKES, but only eight of them make it through to MID-
DLETON[T]; eight got corrected. By contrast, there are only
four links between ROSENBACH and OKES. If eight OKES–
BRIDGEWATER errors got corrected between BRIDGEWATER
and MIDDLETON[T], then it need not stretch the imagination
to suppose that four ROSENBACH–OKES errors got corrected
in BRIDGEWATER. Part of the analytical problem here is that
the first three scenes of ROSENBACH do not contain many
errors at all; therefore, the maximum potential number of
shared errors was small, much smaller than for the other
NON-CRANE texts. As it is, OKES accounts for *half* of the
errors that ROSENBACH shares with other extant texts. So
ROSENBACH and OKES must be related, but their relationship
need not have produced enough shared errors to make it
through the filtering process into other extant texts.

Nevertheless, although the conjectural stemma visualized in Figure 7 might explain the absence of shared
errors, it cannot plausibly explain the statistically more
improbable absence of shared variants. Moreover, the left
side of the diagram leaves two other features of ROSENBACH
hard to account for: the paucity of shared errors we have
just invoked, and the relatively high number of variants
uniquely shared with CRANE[I]. Those were the very factors
that led Nascimento and Howard-Hill to conclude that
ROSENBACH derived directly from CRANE[I] or its immediate
source. Their conjecture cannot be correct, but it does
point to real anomalies that must be acknowledged in
any reconstruction. Indeed, their chief mistake was to
assume that MIDDLETON[T] was early and authoritative; that
postulate distorted their analysis of the variants. Once we
abandon that mistaken assumption, we can 'place ROSEN-
BACH closer to the playbook, and therefore earlier in the
sequence of transmission' (Sec. XIV) without assuming

that it must be linked to CRANE[I]. Instead, ROSENBACH might
descend from the lost King's Men's licensed playbook, or
from a lost transcript of that playbook. Those manuscripts
would have contained the later version of the script, as
do ROSENBACH and CRANE[2,3,4], and one or both of those
lost early manuscripts might also have contained errors
shared by ROSENBACH and the later CRANE transcripts. But
because those lost manuscripts were produced very early
in the sequence of transmission, they might have contained substantive readings and authorial features also
preserved in CRANE[I] and ROSENBACH.

For instance, ROSENBACH's fondness for generic speech
prefixes clearly reflects an authorial preference, evident
in CRANE[I] and elsewhere. But it might also reflect the
playbook used by the King's Men. The generic prefixes
in the first three scenes create problems for readers, but
not for an acting company, because they chiefly affect
three characters: a boy actor dressed in white (White
Queen's Pawn), a boy actor dressed in black (Black
Queen's Pawn), and an adult actor dressed in black
(Black Bishop's Pawn). The theatrical distinction between
boy and adult, and between black and white costumes,
makes the action perfectly clear. Precision was vital in
the actors' parts and the backstage 'plat' (because those
documents regulated performances), but it was much less
relevant to the playbook, which was first and foremost a
document licensed by the censor. But there was no reason
for Middleton and the actors to make the play easier for
the censor to read. Indeed, Middleton and the actors had
strong reasons to make the play *difficult* for the censor to
understand. In this play, more perhaps than any other of
the period, it is difficult *for a reader* to keep track of the
identity of the characters (see Critical Introduction to *A
Later Form*). Consequently, the generic prefixes may have
been deliberately retained in the playbook, in order to help
disguise the play's outrageous political significance. Thus,
the generic prefixes in ROSENBACH may be an accurate
reflection of the King's Men's playbook. By contrast, the
later CRANE texts and the later NON-CRANE texts were
clearly designed to make the play more comprehensible
for ordinary readers. Once such clarification had been
provided, why would anyone systematically revert to the
earlier speech prefixes? Why should Middleton have done
so in ROSENBACH, when he did not do so in the other
NON-CRANE texts?

Derivation from an early theatrical text might also
account for ROSENBACH's omission of the Prologue. Middleton's first version of the play did not contain a prologue;
neither did his abridged version (CRANE[3]). That abridgement, like ROSENBACH, retained the Epilogue, but not the
Prologue. Why? Perhaps because—as we are told in a
Prologue written for a posthumous revival of *Valour*—
'our Poet . . . scorn'd this crowching veine: We stabb'd him
with keene daggers when we pray'd Him write a Preface
to a Play well made'. Since *Game* is Middleton's last known
play, and since the Prologue for *Game* was not a part of the
author's original conception, the passage in the Prologue
to *Valour* may be specifically remembering Middleton's

reaction to the actors' request that he write a Prologue to *Game*. Certainly, if Middleton objected to prologues in general, he might have felt particularly ambivalent about the Prologue in this case, where the play already contains an Induction. Although the Prologue is the first of the major revisions in the *A Later Form* that readers encounter, it may well have been the last of the revisions that Middleton made. It is not connected, thematically or verbally, to any of the others. Moreover, prologues were often written on a separate loose sheet (Stern 2004). That the Prologue for *Game* was originally written on a loose scrap of paper seems particularly clear. Otherwise, it is hard to explain the Prologue's misplacement in CRANE[2] (which puts it, absurdly, *after* the Induction). Thus, none of the three earliest CRANE texts has a Prologue at the beginning of the play—and neither does ROSENBACH.

Not counting the many generic speech prefixes or the Prologue, in the first three scenes ROSENBACH uniquely shares ten variants with CRANE[1].[165] None is an error— nor should we expect them to be. Because it belongs to a different branch of the stemma, CRANE[1] does not share filtered errors with any other extant text.[166] Even discounting the many uniquely shared generic speech prefixes, the ten uniquely shared verbal variants in these three scenes exceed the total for ROSENBACH's pairings with any other text. They also exceed CRANE[1]'s pairings with any other text. The text which comes closest in these three scenes, CRANE[2] (with eight), is also the CRANE text apparently closest to CRANE[1]. Like the totals for shared error in these scenes, these totals for uniquely shared variants again suggest that ROSENBACH is, if anything, marginally earlier in the sequence of transmission than CRANE[2]. But the differences between CRANE[2] and ROSENBACH in these scenes are not statistically significant. What *is* significant is that, stemmatically, both texts appear to be at about the same distance from CRANE[1], and both are earlier than any other extant text.

Cumulatively, the foregoing evidence suggests that, in the first three scenes, ROSENBACH derives from a manuscript associated with the King's Men, a manuscript earlier than CRANE[2,3,4]. We must therefore revise our earlier visualization of the stemma for these scenes.

The bottom right corner of the stemma in Figure 8, containing OKES–BRIDGEWATER–MIDDLETON[T], remains exactly the same as in Figure 7. Once again, that part of the stemma is linked to [PRE-ROSENBACH] through the medium of a lost late Crane transcript. Once again, CRANE/MATHEWES descends from [PRE-ROSENBACH]. But in this revised stemma [PRE-ROSENBACH] itself derives from a lost transcript of the King's Men's licensed playbook, and it is linked to CRANE[2,3] through that lost transcript. It is, consequently, deeply embedded, stemmatically, among the extant CRANE texts. The other NON-CRANE texts, by contrast, are linked to the CRANE texts only through [PRE-ROSENBACH] and two or more additional lost texts.

This conjectural stemma will account for all the features of variant distribution explained by the earlier visualization, but it also solves the problems caused by that

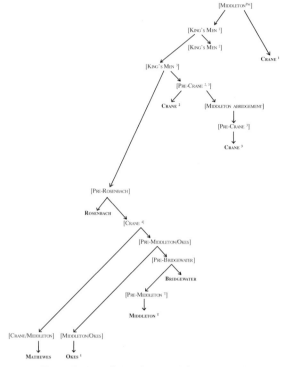

Figure 8. Revised Visualization of the Stemma of Transmission in Prologue-2.1. The vertical axis is chronological. Four manuscripts intervene between [KING'S MEN[3]] and CRANE[3], whereas [CRANE[4]] was only a single manuscript away from [KING'S MEN[3]]; nevertheless, [CRANE[4]] is lower in the stemma, because Crane produced it at some point after he finished CRANE[3].

earlier hypothesis. Moreover, it explains why Nascimento and Howard-Hill considered [CRANE[4]] the earliest CRANE transcript of the revised version of the play. Nascimento and Howard-Hill cannot be right, as I demonstrated in my earlier global analysis of the CRANE witnesses (Sec. X–XII). Chronologically, [CRANE[4]] was apparently the latest of the identifiable CRANE texts; by comparison with CRANE[1,2,3], it contains a higher incidence of Crane expansions, is farther from the performed text of the play, and shares more errors with the late texts OKES, BRIDGEWATER, MIDDLETON[T]. However, [CRANE[4]] also confusingly mixes these late Crane features with other evidence that links it to an autograph text and an earlier stage of the stemma, later

---

[165] Induction.0.1 (discovered), Induction.52.2 (they are sett for the Game), 1.1.156 (A), 1.1.306 (they'ue), 1.1.311 (though't), 2.1.39–41 (lineation relic), 2.1.137–8 (correct lineation), 2.2.207–8 (lineation relic), 2.1.209 (see't), 2.1.236 (come in).

[166] Another non-error is the reading the two texts share with the late manuscript MIDDLETON[T] at 2.1.206 ('three'), a combination which probably results from the author independently restoring the early reading contained in CRANE[1] and ROSENBACH. Stemmatically, the MIDDLETON reading here is therefore probably coincidental, meaning that the ROSENBACH–CRANE[1] link should be considered another unique pairing of those two texts.

than CRANE[1] but earlier than CRANE[2,3] (Sec. XIII). Both sets of features can be explained if we postulate that [CRANE[4]] was *chronologically* late but *stemmatically* early: that is, a late copy that derives from an earlier stage of transmission. [CRANE[4]], like ROSENBACH, seems to derive from a manuscript close to the King's Men, rather than from CRANE[2,3]; but it was apparently produced *after* CRANE[2,3], at a time when Crane's familiarity with the material and his repeated transcriptions led him to impose more of his own preferences on the text.

If this conjectural stemma is correct, then for the first three scenes of the play ROSENBACH and CRANE[2] both derive from something close to the licensed playbook of the King's Men. Those two manuscripts (and their descendants) differ radically from one another, in part because Ralph Crane seems to have had no influence on any of the textual ancestors of ROSENBACH: neither the playbook itself, nor [PRE-ROSENBACH], can have been a CRANE manuscript.[167] But the two branches also differ because they represent two different approaches to the playbook. As *The Lady's Tragedy* demonstrates, a theatrical playbook often contains, within the same physical document, two or more temporal stages. A copyist or editor of the playbook might decide to separate out those temporal layers, producing a text that represents the performed play: that seems to have been the intention that produced CRANE[2], which lacks material probably omitted in performance. Alternatively, a copyist might decide to incorporate everything in the playbook, conflating different temporal layers: that seems to have been the intention that produced ROSENBACH. In both cases, the chosen logic was taken further in subsequent copies: CRANE[3] goes even farther than CRANE[2] in stripping the play down to its essentials, and CRANE/MATHEWES goes even farther than ROSENBACH toward incorporating everything. Neither strategy is exclusively associated with Crane, who adopted the minimalist non-conflationary mode in CRANE[2,3], *The Merry Wives of Windsor*, and *The Tempest*, and the maximalist conflationary mode in [CRANE[4]], *The Duchess of Malfi*, and *Measure for Measure*. Consequently, Crane himself is unlikely to be responsible for the choice of strategies, in either case.

Now that we have a provisional picture of the stemmatic relationships of the extant texts up to 2.1, we should be in a better position to describe what changes, or does not change, in 2.2. As noted above, the filtered shared errors in the scene demonstrate that the strong connection between OKES and BRIDGEWATER persists; given the absence of most of BRIDGEWATER, in frequency of shared errors per lines of text those two texts form the strongest stemmatic pair in the scene. We therefore have no reason to suspect any change in the stemmatic relationship between [PRE-MIDDLETON/OKES] and [PRE-BRIDGEWATER] at any point before the end of Act Two.

But other relationships do change dramatically. The absolute and relative frequency of 'Crane Plus ROSENBACH' variants plummets in 2.2: from 37 in the first three scenes

(one every 18 lines) to only two in 2.2 (one every 118 lines).[168] Simultaneously, the pattern 'Crane Plus OKES' appears for the first time (at 2.2.179), and 'Crane Plus MIDDLETON[T]' appears seven times.[169] In other words, 'Crane Plus ROSENBACH' not only drops absolutely, but also falls precipitously as a proportion of 'Crane Plus One' variants.

Moreover, Figure 8 does not explain our primary evidence of a discontinuity between 2.1 and 2.2 (either a rise of errors and variants shared by all four NON-CRANE texts, or the appearance of the otherwise unparalleled triplet ROSENBACH–OKES–MIDDLETON[T]). Whichever explanation is correct, the change boils down to a strengthening of the relationship between ROSENBACH and MIDDLETON[T]—two texts which, in both Figure 7 and Figure 8, are at opposite ends of the sequence of four extant NON-CRANE texts. In the 648 lines up to the end of 2.1, there is not a single example of a variant uniquely shared by ROSENBACH and MIDDLETON[T]; in the 257 lines of 2.2, there are six. At that ratio, there should have been fifteen in the earlier scenes.

If, as all the foregoing evidence suggests, ROSENBACH in 2.2 is no longer embedded among the CRANE texts, then we might expect it to lose its hitherto exclusive relationship with CRANE[1]. Indeed, the disappearance of that relationship was noted by Nascimento, and formed the basis of her hypothesis (endorsed by Howard-Hill) that the copy-text for ROSENBACH changed at the beginning of 2.2. Not counting generic speech prefixes, ROSENBACH shared ten unique variants with CRANE[1] in the first three scenes; 2.2 contains no such variants. Likewise, the earlier scenes contained seven variants linking ROSENBACH to CRANE[1] and [CRANE[4]]; no such variants appear in 2.2.

In 2.2, we have, for the first time, evidence of ROSENBACH–OKES–MIDDLETON[T] as a triplet. But the triplet OKES–BRIDGEWATER–MIDDLETON[T] and the couplet BRIDGEWATER–MIDDLETON[T], both very frequent in the first three scenes, completely disappear. This might be a coincidence, because BRIDGEWATER is missing for most of the scene. But even in its truncated version of the scene, BRIDGEWATER shares two errors with OKES: why does it share no errors with MIDDLETON[T]? If the disappearance of the common triplet OKES–BRIDGEWATER–MIDDLETON[T] were simply a consequence of the unavailability of BRIDGEWATER for much of the scene, we should have a corresponding boom in the pairing OKES–MIDDLETON[T]; but in fact there are only two examples in 2.2, instead of the fifteen we would expect.

How are we to explain all these anomalies? On the one hand, ROSENBACH is farther from the CRANE texts; on the other hand, MIDDLETON[T] is farther from BRIDGEWATER and closer to ROSENBACH. These two sets of problems could have a single cause. We already know that in 2.2 ROSENBACH must be linked to OKES (two shared errors),

---

[167] See Nascimento's scene-by-scene statistics for spelling and punctuation, which clearly establish the overwhelmingly Middletonian, and un-Crane-like, nature of ROSENBACH.

[168] 2.2.122–3 (correct lineation), 2.2.141 ('hath', versus autograph 'has').

[169] 2.2.117 (correct past participial elision), 2.2.126 (ditto), 2.2.141 (correct 'seized'), 2.2.163 (correct 'the'), 2.2.184–5 (correct lineation), 2.2.225 ('leave' against 'leaves'), 2.2.226 (correctly elided 'th'').

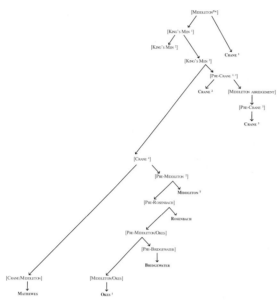

Figure 9. Draft Visualization of the
Stemma of Transmission in 2.2.

and that OKES must be linked to BRIDGEWATER (two shared errors). MIDDLETON[T] would therefore seem to belong after those three texts, or before all three. The disappearance of links between MIDDLETON[T] and BRIDGEWATER rules out the last position in the NON-CRANE group; the appearance of links between MIDDLETON[T] and ROSENBACH strongly points to the first position in the NON-CRANE group. So does the sudden eruption of 'Crane Plus MIDDLETON[T]' variants: the seven examples in 2.2 exceed the raw totals or the relative frequency in any other scene, indeed in any other act. Finally, so does the disappearance of variants exclusively linking ROSENBACH, or ROSENBACH and [CRANE⁴], to CRANE¹; in their place are two variants uniquely linking CRANE¹ to MIDDLETON[T]-ROSENBACH-OKES. Together, these relationships suggest a provisional stemma for 2.2 (Figure 9).

We do not yet have an explanation for the changes from Figure 8 to Figure 9. Nevertheless, we now have provisional models of the stemmatic relationships of all eight extant texts up to the end of Act Two (Figures 8 and 9). Earlier, working backward from the end of the play, we deduced a logical sequence of changes of copy-text that led us to 4.1.145 (Figure 6). We should now be positioned to examine the stemmatic problem in Act Three and the beginning of Act Four, the uncharted territory that lies between.

XXIV. Divided Copy in the NON-CRANE Texts: 3.1

In six of the eight substantive texts of the play, and in all previous modern editions, 3.1.0.1–3.1.345 constitute a single continuous scene. But the division of copy between MATHEWES and ALLDE occurs in the middle of it (3.1.218),

and it is also divided between two scribes in ROSENBACH (with the second responsible for only half a page, 3.1.44–57). We therefore cannot assume that this whole long passage is stemmatically homogeneous. We can begin assessing its homogeneity by examining a list of shared errors throughout the entire passage.

First, there are nine cross-over errors, linking the CRANE and NON-CRANE texts.

Table of Filtered Shared Errors 3.1.1–3.1.345

17. [CRANE⁴]-OKES: 2 (3.1.265, 3.1.307)
12. [CRANE⁴]-ROSENBACH: 2 (3.1.199, 3.1.333)
23. [CRANE⁴]-ROSENBACH-MIDDLETON[T]: 1 (3.1.154-5)
34. [CRANE⁴]-ROSENBACH-BRIDGEWATER-MIDDLETON[T]: 1 (3.1.115.1)
36. CRANE[2,3,4]-ROSENBACH: 1 (3.1.73)
41. CRANE[2,3,4]-MIDDLETON[T]: 1 (3.1.262.1)
56. CRANE[2,3,4]-NON-CRANE: 1 (3.1.175.1)

All nine cross-over errors can be explained by assuming that [CRANE⁴] was the conduit text; six of them require that assumption. This pattern establishes that the top half of the stemma—as visualized in Figure 9—continues into Act Three. Likewise, the appearance of an error shared by all the NON-CRANE texts confirms that, as in 2.2, the NON-CRANE texts form a set, as they do for the rest of the play. Again, this confirms the middling position of [CRANE⁴], between the other three extant CRANE texts and an extant group of four NON-CRANE texts.

However, although the position of [CRANE⁴] remains stable, the NON-CRANE text to which it is linked does not: it shares errors with ROSENBACH (3), OKES (2), MIDDLETON[T] (1), ROSENBACH and MIDDLETON[T] (1), ROSENBACH and BRIDGEWATER and MIDDLETON[T] (1), and with all the NON-CRANE texts (1). The last pattern tells us nothing specific about the conduit text on the NON-CRANE side, but the other six patterns are all potentially relevant—and contradictory.

We cannot explain this distribution by looking at cross-over errors alone. In an attempt to clarify the problem, I list the NON-CRANE shared errors in the order in which they appear in the text.

Table of NON-CRANE Shared Errors between 2.2 and 3.2

30. ROSENBACH-BRIDGEWATER-OKES: 3.1.7

* * *

10. MIDDLETON[T]-OKES: 3.1.33
32. BRIDGEWATER-OKES-MIDDLETON[T]: 3.1.44
15. ROSENBACH-OKES: 3.1.44.1
32. BRIDGEWATER-OKES-MIDDLETON[T]: 3.1.48

* * *

10. MIDDLETON[T]-OKES: 3.1.75
34. [CRANE⁴]-ROSENBACH-BRIDGEWATER-MIDDLETON[T]: 3.1.115.1
30. ROSENBACH-BRIDGEWATER-OKES: 3.1.127
23. [CRANE⁴]-ROSENBACH-MIDDLETON[T]: 3.1.154-5
31. ROSENBACH-BRIDGEWATER-[MIDDLETON[T]]?: 3.1.155.1
56. CRANE[2,3,4]-NON-CRANE: 3.1.175.1
15. ROSENBACH-OKES: 3.1.203

* * *

[change from Mathewes to Allde at 3.1.218]

* * *

17. [CRANE⁴]–OKES: 3.1.265, 3.1.307
16. BRIDGEWATER–OKES: 3.1.322

I have differentiated triplets with bold type, because triplets are so useful in determining the sequence of texts within a set of four. But they are not particularly helpful here. In the first place, the sole example of an error shared by all four NON-CRANE texts is, in fact, shared by all seven texts of the revised version of the play; it does not clearly establish that NON-CRANE is a coherent set in these lines. If it were, there should not be three sets of triplets: (R2,B2,O2), (B2,O2,M2), (R2,B2,M2). Each of these three triplets appears twice in the scene, a parity which makes it difficult to dismiss any one of the three as mere coincidence. Actually, all three are problematic.

The first triplet ROSENBACH–BRIDGEWATER–OKES appears here for the first time. But that triplet could result from an error shared by all NON-CRANE texts, which was corrected in the dead-end autograph text MIDDLETONᵀ. If so, then the triplet tells us nothing about the underlying sequence of NON-CRANE texts. The fact that it did not appear earlier in the play might simply reflect the fact that NON-CRANE was not a coherent set in the first three scenes, and BRIDGEWATER was missing for almost all of the fourth scene. Either, or both, of the examples of this triplet might well be misleading, if taken as evidence of sequencing. Normally, we could assign some weight to the fact that the second example of this triplet occurs only 20 lines after the first. But the first and second examples are separated by examples of both other triplets; moreover, the second example occurs between the two examples of another sequence. Hence, the individual examples of these three overlapping triplet patterns cannot *all* be accurate indicators of sequence.

By contrast, the two examples of the second triplet occur within four lines of each other (3.1.44, 3.1.48), and no examples of any other triplet intervene between them. The uninterrupted concentration of examples of this triplet makes it extremely unlikely to result from coincidence. Moreover, unlike the other triplet, this one (BRIDGEWATER–OKES–MIDDLETONᵀ) cannot be instantly explained as a by-product of authorial correction, because in this pattern the one NON-CRANE text which has the correct reading, ROSENBACH, is not autograph. However, I have argued that [PRE-ROSENBACH] was an autograph manuscript (Sec. XIV, XV). As such, it might have contained authorial corrections; if [PRE-ROSENBACH]'s only extant descendent was ROSENBACH itself, then those corrections might not have been made in any other NON-CRANE manuscript. Moreover, both examples of this pattern fall within a mere thirteen lines that were copied by ROSENBACH Scribe B. The two errors are related, and indeed they might be described as one error, rather than two: at 3.1.44, the absence of a necessary speech prefix, and at 3.1.48, the insertion of that same prefix in the wrong place. Therefore,

it is entirely possible that a fresh, attentive scribe in ROSENBACH might have spotted the mistake and corrected it on his own initiative. Whether the correction was made by Middleton in [PRE-ROSENBACH] or by the newly arrived Scribe B in ROSENBACH itself, this apparent triplet would be another example of an error shared by all NON-CRANE texts except one manuscript that independently corrected it. Finally, the stemmatic significance of this triplet is undermined, here, by another complication: the error at 3.1.48 is not actually present in the original transcription of BRIDGEWATER. The misplaced speech prefix was added, retrospectively, by the pencil corrector, BRIDGEWATERᶜ. In general, stemmatic analysis cannot assume that readings introduced by a later hand come from the same source as the readings in an original transcription.[170] Specifically, in this case, we have no way of knowing whether BRIDGEWATERᶜ had access to a different source than BRIDGEWATERᴮ, who omitted a speech prefix at 3.1.44 but did not insert a new one at 3.1.48. Strictly speaking, the error at 3.1.48 tells us that the copy-text for BRIDGEWATERᴮ did *not* share an error present in OKES and MIDDLETONᵀ. Unfortunately, this is the only substantive variant in the whole play that indicates anything about the stemmatic connections of the manuscript consulted by BRIDGEWATERᶜ.[171] Consequently, we can only acknowledge the ambiguity.

The third triplet, ROSENBACH–BRIDGEWATER–MIDDLETONᵀ, could result from the same process. In that triplet, the correct reading is again found in only a single NON-CRANE text; but we already know that OKES was set from an autograph manuscript, [MIDDLETON/OKES], which had no manuscript descendants. Therefore, the error could well have been present in [PRE-MIDDLETON/OKES], which might have passed it to, or inherited it from, the other NON-CRANE texts. Again, this would tell us that the four NON-CRANE texts are a set, but would not tell us anything about their sequence. Even if the examples of this triplet were not rendered suspect by this general problem, both examples are problematic for particular reasons. As noted above (Sec. XXIII), the misplaced stage direction at 3.1.155.1 is perhaps better interpreted as a paired error, BRIDGEWATER–

---

[170] See for instance Mink 18.

[171] For a complete list of 'Substantial Pencil Alterations' in BRIDGEWATER see Howard-Hill, *Pasquin* 307. He there classifies the variant at MSR 808 (*Later* 2.2.41) as a 'miscorrection', because it disagrees with MIDDLETONᵀ, and classifies the inserted speech prefix at MSR 1112 (*Later* 3.1.48) as a 'correction'. because it agrees with MIDDLETONᵀ; but like me he adopts 'Yonder's' at 2.2.41 and omits the misplaced speech prefix at 3.1.48. The unique reading (restoration?) at 2.1.41 might indicate access to an otherwise unknown manuscript, but if so that otherwise unknown manuscript contained the error at 3.1.48. The only other variant that might provide evidence of shared error occurs att MSR 1065 (*Later* 3.1.7), but damage to the manuscript makes it unclear whether the Corrector inserted the mistaken 'for' (found elsewhere only in CRANE/MATHEWES), or the correct 'for't' (found elsewhere only in MIDDLETONᵀ). In other cases, BRIDGEWATERᶜ either restores a clearly correct reading (MSR 1394, 1433, 1528, 1705, 1997), or supplies a unique reading, which might be interpreted either as a late authorial variant, or as a conjectural miscorrection exemplifying the process that produces progressive errors (MSR 124, 1066, 1168, 1247, 1988). The number of variants is simply too small, and the degree of ambiguity too great, to permit us to differentiate the copy-text for BRIDGEWATERᴮ from the copy-text for BRIDGEWATERᶜ, or to confirm that the same manuscript was used as copy-text for both.

ROSENBACH, because MIDDLETON^T misplaces it differently. Likewise, the stage direction at 3.1.115.1 is placed too late in four texts, but this error might be interpreted as two pairs rather than a quadruplet: it is identically misplaced by [CRANE^4] and ROSENBACH, and (even more badly) identically misplaced by BRIDGEWATER and MIDDLETON^T. What looks at first glance like two examples of a single NON-CRANE triplet might be, instead, one example each of three different pairs.

One or more of these apparent triplets may reflect a real stemmatic sequence. But how can we determine which one or ones? The fact that all six shared errors might be interpreted, instead, as examples of NON-CRANE makes it likely that at least one, and probably more, should be interpreted in that way; as such, the presence of all six does point toward the coherence of the NON-CRANE set in this scene, as in those before and after. Elsewhere, high frequencies of these triplets concentrated in different parts of the play make it impossible to dismiss their distribution as random. Here, by contrast, low frequencies, local uncertainties, and contradictory distribution patterns make them dubious evidence. It would be possible to construct an argument that the copy-text was divided between 3.1.7 and 3.1.44, and/or that it was divided between 3.1.48 and 3.1.115.1 (in either case presuming some relationship with the change of scribes in ROSENBACH), and/or that it was divided between 3.1.127 and 3.1.155, and/or that it was divided in the vicinity of the break between MATHEWES and ALLDE at 3.1.218.

Another category of high-frequency evidence, which has proven useful in identifying stemmatic relationships in earlier and late scenes—'Crane Plus One'—is also confusing in this section of the play. Again, I will try to clarify the evidence by listing it in order of sequence.

Table of 'Crane Plus One' Variants Between 2.2 and 3.2

3.1.0.1 ROSENBACH (twice)

* * *

3.1.21 MIDDLETON^T (CRANE^{2,3,4})
3.1.44 ROSENBACH (CRANE^{2,3,4})
3.1.72 BRIDGEWATER (CRANE^{2,3,4})
3.1.73 ROSENBACH (CRANE^{2,3,4}: shared error?)

* * *

3.1.108 MIDDLETON^T
3.1.117 BRIDGEWATER (uncorrected)
3.1.127 MIDDLETON^T
3.1.149 BRIDGEWATER
3.1.151 MIDDLETON^T
3.1.175 ROSENBACH
3.1.300 ROSENBACH
3.1.318 MIDDLETON^T

If we limit ourselves to examples where all four CRANE texts are available, we have four examples from MIDDLETON^T, three or four from ROSENBACH (depending on whether we count the variants in the opening Act division as one or two), and two from BRIDGEWATER. This differs remarkably

from the pattern up to 2.1 (overwhelmingly ROSENBACH), the pattern in 2.2 (predominantly MIDDLETON^T), and the pattern in Acts Four and Five (overwhelmingly OKES). Only two examples of the same 'Crane Plus One' pattern occur together; all the others are interrupted by one or more examples of another pattern. The same thing happens if we include cases where CRANE^1 is not available, but all three extant CRANE texts agree with one NON-CRANE text. That loosening of the rules would add two more examples from ROSENBACH, and one each from BRIDGEWATER and MIDDLETON^T, but it would not produce any sequence of two consecutive examples of the same pattern. In other words, the contrasting examples cannot be grouped into patterns based on proximity, which would point to a clear division in the copy-text. This contradictory evidence confirms the contradictory evidence we have already seen in the table of cross-over errors, with no single text emerging as the conduit text on the NON-CRANE side.

Nevertheless, the 'Crane Plus One' evidence does limit the range of possibilities. The one thing absolutely clear, from this data, is that OKES cannot be the NON-CRANE text stemmatically closest to all the CRANE texts. Of the fourteen examples of the pattern in this scene, none links CRANE to OKES. That cannot be a coincidence.

This example reminds us that the absence of evidence may be as significant as its presence. Although there are too many shared error triplets in 3.1, one such triplet remains absent: ROSENBACH–OKES–MIDDLETON^T. The absence is remarkable because that triplet was so significant in the immediately preceding scene. In 2.2, its presence was ambiguous: I argued that it might represent either a real subset of three, or a larger group, NON-CRANE (with BRIDGEWATER fortuitously unavailable). In the 257 lines of 2.2 it appeared alone eight times; in the 345 lines here, it appears alone only once, or possibly twice.[172] The substantive absence of this triplet means that its members are not a distinct subset-sequence. Again, that would indicate that the stemma for 2.2 (Figure 9) cannot apply to 3.1.

The hypothesis that something must have changed between 2.2 and 3.1 is confirmed by another telling absence. In 2.2 ROSENBACH and BRIDGEWATER apparently became, for the first time, stemmatically adjacent texts, as they clearly are later in the play. Nascimento located the beginning of the link between the two texts at 3.1.318, where a shared variant is quickly followed by two others at 3.1.326 and 3.1.327. It might have begun a little earlier: Nascimento did not have access to the original manuscript of BRIDGEWATER, and so missed the uncorrected reading at 3.1.215, and she did not collate variations in the position of stage directions, and so missed the shared variant at 3.1.155.1 (which might or might not be shared with MIDDLETON^T). The two texts also uniquely share an unelided 'the' at 3.1.100. But

---

[172] 3.1.72 (unelided 'the'). At 3.1.69 its existence depends on my interpretation of an uncorrected, partially obscured reading in MIDDLETON^T; ROSENBACH and OKES certainly share the unelided 'fearfullest', but whether the subset contains a third member is conjectural. At 3.1.187 the reading is also shared with CRANE^2.

even if we accept all three examples, their character and frequency does not at all resemble the pattern found after 3.1.318. The absence of examples in 2.2 is not surprising, given the absence of BRIDGEWATER itself for almost the whole of that scene. But it is harder to explain the complete absence of such pairs in the first 99 lines of 3.1, and the small number of dubious examples between 3.1.100 and 3.1.318. The complete absence of unique links between BRIDGEWATER and ROSENBACH at the beginning of 3.1, and the ambiguous insignificance of the few examples in the middle of that scene, makes it hard to believe that the stemma for 2.2 could apply at the beginning of 3.1.

That absence also has implications for our interpretation of two of the three extant patterns of triplets in that scene. Both ROSENBACH–BRIDGEWATER–OKES and ROSENBACH–BRIDGEWATER–MIDDLETON[T] contain both texts; if those two triplets really constituted a sequence of four texts, then the two texts which appear in both triplets— ROSENBACH and BRIDGEWATER—would *have* to be in the middle. But if they were in the middle, they would *have* to be a pair throughout the scene, and they clearly are not. Consequently, at least one of the two triplets (and possibly both) *must* be misleading. In other words, at least one of the seeming triplets in fact represents an error shared by all the underlying NON-CRANE texts, which was corrected in a single dead-end autograph manuscript (either MIDDLETON[T] or [MIDDLETON/OKES]). This conclusion confirms that all the extant NON-CRANE texts are more closely related to each other than to any extant CRANE text, but it tells us nothing about the particulars of the sequencing. We suspected this before, but now we have logical proof.

Because at least one triplet is misleading, we have to re-examine both. In the triplet ROSENBACH–BRIDGEWATER–MIDDLETON[T], in order to prevent ROSENBACH and BRIDGEWATER from forming a pair, MIDDLETON[T] would have to stand between them. If MIDDLETON[T] stood between them, it would be adjacent to ROSENBACH. But if those two texts were adjacent, why do they not uniquely share even a single variant in these 345 lines? Remember, they shared six unique variants in the 257 lines of 2.2. The absence of that pair demonstrates, once again, that something changed between 2.2 and 3.1. But it also logically eliminates any possible combination of ROSENBACH, BRIDGEWATER and MIDDLETON[T] as a coherent triplet, rather than a mere remnant of the larger NON-CRANE set.

In the other affected triplet, ROSENBACH–BRIDGEWATER–OKES, the 'Crane Plus One' evidence has already established that OKES cannot be the earliest of the three texts, and in order to prevent a ROSENBACH–BRIDGEWATER pair it would have to be in the middle position. But if it were in the middle position, it would be adjacent to BRIDGEWATER, and we would expect to find many unique BRIDGEWATER–OKES pairs; there are 29 such pairs in the play's first three scenes, and even in 2.2 the two texts uniquely share two errors before BRIDGEWATER disappears. By contrast, there is only a single such pair here, and it does not occur till

3.1.322—that is, after the beginning of the ROSENBACH–BRIDGEWATER link.[173] So BRIDGEWATER and OKES cannot be adjacent in 3.1, which logically eliminates any possible combination of ROSENBACH, BRIDGEWATER, and OKES as a coherent triplet, rather than a mere remnant of the larger NON-CRANE set.

Logically, neither ROSENBACH–BRIDGEWATER–OKES nor ROSENBACH–BRIDGEWATER–MIDDLETON[T] can represent a coherent subset of three; each must be a mere side effect of the larger NON-CRANE set, accidentally created by a dead-end authorial correction in either MIDDLETON[T] or [MIDDLETON/OKES].

It may help to summarize what we think we know at this point about the first 345 lines of 3.1.

(1) The four extant NON-CRANE texts form part of a larger set of NON-CRANE texts, which is separated from, and does not include, any extant CRANE texts.

(2) The CRANE text closest to the NON-CRANE set is [CRANE[4]].

(3) There is no single NON-CRANE text which is closest to the CRANE set.

(4) ROSENBACH and BRIDGEWATER are *not* adjacent texts at the beginning of the scene, and perhaps not before 3.1.318.

(5) BRIDGEWATER and OKES are *not* adjacent texts at the beginning of the scene, and perhaps not before 3.1.322.

(6) The three-text subset MIDDLETON[T]–ROSENBACH–OKES does not appear in the scene, which means that at least one other text must intervene somewhere in the middle of any sequence that contains those three texts.

(7) The stemma that explains 2.2 will not explain 3.1, so there must have been a change in the relationships of the NON-CRANE texts at the beginning of 3.1.

On the basis of these seven observations, we may logically arrive at five further deductions.

(8) The combination of observations 4 and 5 means that OKES cannot stand alone between ROSENBACH and BRIDGEWATER. Therefore, MIDDLETON[T] must stand between ROSENBACH and BRIDGEWATER (with OKES either on the far side of ROSENBACH, or between ROSENBACH and MIDDLETON[T]).

(9) The combination of observations 4 and 5 means that ROSENBACH cannot stand alone between OKES and BRIDGEWATER. Therefore, MIDDLETON[T] must stand between OKES and BRIDGEWATER (with ROSENBACH either on the far side of OKES, or between OKES and MIDDLETON[T]).

(10) The combination of deductions 8 and 9 produces four possible sequences of four extant NON-CRANE texts: ROSENBACH→OKES→MIDDLETON[T]→BRIDGEWATER (or the reverse, BRIDGEWATER→MIDDLETON[T]→OKES→ROSENBACH), or OKES→ROSENBACH→MIDDLETON[T]→BRIDGEWATER (or the reverse, BRIDGEWATER→MIDDLETON[T]→ROSENBACH→OKES).

(11) All four potential four-text sequences identified in deduction 10 place BRIDGEWATER at one end of the

---

[173] There is a shared punctuation error at 3.1.238, and a shared anomalous spelling at 3.1.26, but the shared error at 3.1.322 is the first substantive agreement between the two texts in Act Three.

sequence or the other, and therefore place adjacent to one another the three-text subset (MIDDLETON[T]–ROSENBACH–OKES), a triplet which does not appear in the scene.

(12) The combination of observation 6 and deduction 11 proves that no four-text sequence will explain the distribution of shared NON-CRANE errors and variants in 3.1.

We may seem here to have reached an impasse: deduction 12 seems to contradict observation 1. But there is an important distinction between the terms of the two statements. The extant NON-CRANE texts do form a distinct *set*, stemmatically separated from the extant CRANE texts (observation 1), but they do not form a single *sequence* (deduction 12). In other words, at some point after the NON-CRANE texts separate from the CRANE texts, they must branch off into at least two separate sequences.

We can identify those two branching sequences by looking at the evidence of pairs, and particularly of the pairs that occur with the highest frequency throughout the scene. If we look at the total number of variants shared by only two of the eight extant texts in this scene, we immediately discover five strong pairs.

CRANE[2,3]: 17 variants (3.1.6–3.1.338)[174]
MIDDLETON[T]–BRIDGEWATER: 7 variants, 1 or 2 errors (3.1.0.1–3.1.299.1)[175]

These two sets of pairs are unconnected to each other, and unconnected to the three remaining strong sets of pairs. This suggests that both pair-sets are dead-ends.

[CRANE[4]]–OKES: 10 variants, 2 errors (3.1.7–3.1.307)[176]
[CRANE[4]]–ROSENBACH: 6 variants, 2 or 3 errors (3.1.66–3.1.338)[177]
OKES–ROSENBACH: 7 variants, 2 errors (3.1.44.1–3.1.262.1)[178]

These three strong pair-sets are connected to each other, but not connected to the other pair-sets above. The obvious explanation for this distribution of variants is that MIDDLETON[T] and BRIDGEWATER belong to one branch, while ROSENBACH and OKES belong to another. The pairs themselves will not tell us which of the two NON-CRANE texts in each branch is closer to the CRANE texts, but cross-over errors and 'Crane Plus One' clearly place ROSENBACH closer than OKES. To a much lesser degree, the same evidence would place MIDDLETON[T] closer than BRIDGEWATER; but this apparent difference might result from autograph transference. Nevertheless, for the moment let us assume that sequence. Combining these different kinds of evidence produces the stemma illustrated in Figure 10.

Figure 10 differs from all previous draft stemmata in two ways. First, obviously, it divides the four extant NON-CRANE texts into two distinct branches. Secondly, and more significantly, it requires the existence of a lost manuscript which has, until now, not been necessary: a manuscript earlier than all the extant NON-CRANE texts, but also later than the CRANE texts. I have christened this lost manuscript '[PRE-NON-CRANE]', because we do not know whether it was in the handwriting of Ralph Crane,

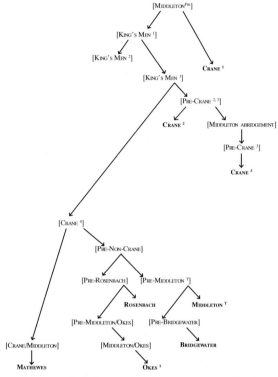

Figure 10. Draft Visualization of 3.1.0.1–3.1.317. This is the same as Figure 9 for the CRANE texts (top half), but identifies a new lost manuscript—[PRE-NON-CRANE]—as the conduit of variants and errors to the NON-CRANE texts.

or someone else. But we do know that it must have existed, because it is otherwise impossible to explain the contradictory features of 3.1. Without [PRE-NON-CRANE], the necessary division of the NON-CRANE texts into two branches cannot be reconciled with the necessary unity of the NON-CRANE set against the CRANE set.

The 'discovery' of [PRE-NON-CRANE] may have implications for interpretation of the evidence for other parts of the play. However, before we can consider those implications we need to finish with 3.1 itself.

XXV. The Copy-text for [PRE-NON-CRANE] in 2.2 and Act Three

The stemma in Figure 10 will explain the distribution of variants and errors for most of the original 3.1. But clearly something must have changed before the end of

---

[174] 3.1.6, 7, 33.1, 34, 44.1, 45, 108, 116 (speech prefixes), 155.1–6, 205, 207, 207.1, 231, 250, 301, 316, 338.
[175] 3.1.0.1, 37, 39, 44.1, 45, 111, 115.1 (shared error, possibly triplet), 194, 281, 299.1 (shared error).
[176] 3.1.7, 31, 99, 133, 155.1–6, 202, 211, 228–9, 264, 265 (error), 292, 307 (error).
[177] 3.1.66, 89, 115.1 (shared error, possibly triplet), 159, 164, 199 (error), 235, 273, 338 (error).
[178] 3.1.44.1 (error), 69, 162, 170, 178, 187, 203 (error), 236, 262.1.

the scene. Variants linking ROSENBACH to BRIDGEWATER begin to appear frequently after 3.1.318. Even before that, something happens to the relationship between the CRANE and NON-CRANE sets. I will begin with the evidence for this second problem, because it is local, concentrated, and specific, and because it turns out to have implications for analysis of the other problem.

I have already discussed (Sec. XIII) the cluster of four variants uniquely shared by CRANE[1] and CRANE/MATHEWES between 3.1.157 and 3.1.188, and the two additional variants in those same lines shared by CRANE[1,4] with BRIDGEWATER. But in my earlier analysis of this problem I asked only one question: why, if CRANE[1] is the earliest Crane text and [CRANE[4]] is the latest, do they share these variants? Now we are positioned to rephrase the question: why do the NON-CRANE texts *not* contain these variants? After all, given the stemma illustrated in Figures 9 and 10, it is not surprising that CRANE[1,4] often share variants; the frequency of variants uniquely shared by CRANE[2,3] throughout the play makes that combination natural enough. But usually those variants shared by CRANE[1,4] are also passed to some or all of the NON-CRANE texts. What is remarkable, in these thirty-one lines, is that CRANE[1,4] seem to be a dead-end, as CRANE[2,3] are elsewhere. In other words, for this small area of the text, it appears that [CRANE[4]] was *not* the conduit between the CRANE texts and the NON-CRANE texts.

What we have been calling a two-member set (CRANE[1,4]) can be reconceptualized as a six-member set (CRANE[2,3], NON-CRANE). Interestingly, in these thirty-one lines the alternative two-member set (CRANE[2,3])—the most heavily populated set, in this scene and indeed throughout the play—disappears entirely. Although there are seventeen specimens of that (CRANE[2,3]) set in 3.1, there are none between 3.1.155 and 3.1.205. Again, though, it may help to reconceptualize that two-member set as the six-member set (CRANE[1,4], NON-CRANE). Between 3.1.156 and 3.1.205 (forty-nine lines), or 3.1.157 and 3.1.188 (thirty-one lines), the overwhelmingly dominant six-member set (CRANE[1,4], NON-CRANE) is temporarily replaced by the six-member set (CRANE[2,3], NON-CRANE). Figure 10 is replaced by Figure 11.[179]

The existence of [PRE-NON-CRANE], already established by the otherwise contradictory distribution of variants and errors in 3.1, also makes it easier to explain the concentration of CRANE[1,4] variants here in 3.1. We need only postulate a single, brief change in the copy-text for [PRE-NON-CRANE], perhaps the intervention of a scribe patching the gap between the beginning and end of the play, already transcribed by one or more other scribes.

However, the existence of [PRE-NON-CRANE], and this tentative hypothesis about divided copy-text in it, inevitably raises questions about its role in the sequence of transmission before and after 3.1. The lost manuscript's existence was not initially established on the basis of CRANE[1,4] variants, but such variants do seem to tell us

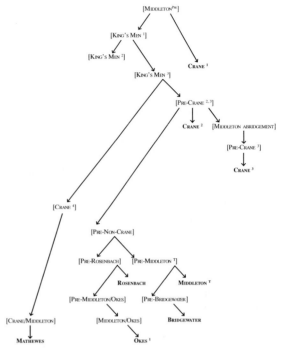

Figure 11. Draft Visualization of 3.1.157–3.1.188 (or 3.1.156–3.1.198). This is identical to Figure 10, except that the link between [CRANE[4]] and [PRE-NON-CRANE] has been replaced by a link between [PRE-CRANE[2,3]] and [PRE-NON-CRANE].

something about it, so we might begin by looking at the larger pattern of such variants throughout the play.

In the first three scenes of the play (Figure 8), there are only two examples of CRANE[1,4] alone, but there are nine examples of those two texts sharing a variant with ROSENBACH. We might describe this pattern as 'CRANE[1,4] Plus One', where the one additional text belongs to the NON-CRANE group. As with the earlier 'Crane Plus One' variants, we already know that CRANE[1] and [CRANE[4]] belong to different branches of the stemma, and consequently this set serves many of the same functions as 'Crane Plus One'. ROSENBACH monopolizes such 'CRANE[1,4] Plus One' variants in the early scenes, but that pattern never appears elsewhere in the play. This binary distribution reinforces the other evidence of the uniqueness

179 Only three variants challenge this hypothesis. Two occur at the end of the passage: an error shared by [CRANE[4]] and ROSENBACH at 3.1.199 ('attempt' for correct 'attempter') and an indifferent variant shared by [CRANE[4]] and OKES at 3.1.202 ('the' for that'). The shared error is particularly difficult to dismiss, and the variant involving a different NON-CRANE text only three lines later (and only three lines before the resumption of CRANE[2,3] pairs) makes it clear that the anomaly ends between 3.1.188 (the last CRANE[1,4] link) and 3.1.199 (the first undoubted link between [CRANE[4]] and a NON-CRANE text). Within those thirty-one to forty-two lines, only a single indifferent variant contradicts the proposed stemma: at 3.1.164 both CRANE/MATHEWES and ROSENBACH have 'the' (where all other texts have 'that'). That variant could easily be due to coincidence—unlike the cluster of CRANE[1,4] links and the absence of unique CRANE[2,3] pairs.

of those early scenes, with ROSENBACH embedded among the CRANE texts. The two examples of CRANE[1,4] do not challenge that pattern, because the two texts would have been linked through [PRE-ROSENBACH] (which might have contained the variant), rather than through ROSENBACH itself (which does not). Thus, [PRE-NON-CRANE] might have come between [PRE-ROSENBACH] and [CRANE4], or between [CRANE4] and the other three NON-CRANE texts.

By contrast with the play's first three scenes, Act Four does not contain a single example of CRANE[1,4] alone, and the single 'CRANE[1,4] Plus One' triplet involves MIDDLETON[T] (4.1.2); it could therefore be an independent authorial restoration, unrelated to the stemmatic sequence of transmission. Likewise, the one triplet in Act Five (5.3.0.2) involves MIDDLETON[B], and is subject to the same explanation. In these two cases we have two different manuscripts, but a single copyist, Middleton himself, who seems the likeliest source of the two unique patterns (and is certainly, at the very least, a *possible* source of those patterns). A single example of CRANE[1,4] appears at 5.3.162. Thus, the final two Acts contain only one example of the pair, and no reliable examples of the triplet. In those two Acts, readings shared by CRANE[1,4] are most likely to be shared by all NON-CRANE texts; on at least one occasion, and probably three, a CRANE[1,4] reading was altered in a manuscript that precedes all the NON-CRANE texts. This evidence is perfectly compatible with our reconstruction of the sequence of transmission in Acts Four and Five (Figures 5 and 6). We need only assume that [PRE-NON-CRANE] followed [CRANE4] and preceded all four extant NON-CRANE texts. Theoretically, in Figures 5, 6, and 8 [PRE-NON-CRANE] could be the same manuscript as [PRE-MIDDLETON/OKES]. But since they cannot have been the same manuscript in 3.1, it would be simpler to suppose that they remained separate entities throughout the play.

But in this respect, as in so many others, the tidy patterns of the beginning and ending of the play do not govern the middle. The pattern in 2.2 radically differs from that in the preceding scenes. There are no examples of 'CRANE[1,4] Plus One'. Instead, there is a single clear example of CRANE[1,4] alone (2.2.203), and two cases where those two texts are closer to each other than to any other text (both in the stage direction at 2.2.81). Obviously, this looks like the pattern in the middle of 3.1 (Figure 11). Indeed, the whole of Act Three looks similar: sixteen examples of CRANE[1,4] alone, against only eight examples of 'CRANE[1,4] Plus One.' Four of those eight triplets involve MIDDLETON[T], and *could* be examples of independent authorial restoration of the original reading (3.1.87, 3.2.20-1, 3.2.32, 3.2.38), unconnected to the stemma of transmission. But it is harder to dismiss the single example involving OKES (3.2.22) and the three involving BRIDGEWATER (3.1.187, 3.1.188, 3.1.257). At the beginning of the play CRANE[1,4] are clearly linked to a single NON-CRANE text; in Acts Four and Five they are just as clearly linked to all NON-CRANE texts. From 2.2 to the end of Act Three they are most often linked to none of the NON-CRANE texts (seventeen to nineteen examples)— but they are also sporadically and uniquely linked to three different NON-CRANE texts.

Between 3.1.157 and 3.1.198 the concentration of unique CRANE[1,4] links coincides with a complete absence of unique CRANE[2,3] links: hence Figure 11. But in the larger sweep of 2.2 to the end of Act Three no such tidy binary appears: the seventeen to nineteen CRANE[1,4] pairs in those scenes cohabit with thirty-five CRANE[2,3] pairs (including the complete absence of 3.2 from those two texts). Thus, the contradictory evidence of CRANE pairs coincides with the equally contradictory evidence linking 'CRANE[1,4] Plus One' to different NON-CRANE texts.

The contradictory pattern of NON-CRANE errors and variants in 3.1 could be resolved by postulating the existence of [PRE-NON-CRANE]. But those contradictions involved texts stemmatically and chronologically *later* than [PRE-NON-CRANE]. By contrast, the contradictions we are here considering involve stemmaticaly *earlier* texts. Beginning in 2.2 and continuing till the end of Act Three, [PRE-NON-CRANE] apparently contained a mix of readings that had elsewhere diverged into two distinct streams: one stream that led to a dead-end of unique CRANE[2,3] variants, another stream that led to a dead-end of unique CRANE[1,4] variants. Those two streams could only have been united relatively early in the play's transmission. Because the scenes in question contain much material present only in the revised performance version, the antecedent for the middle of [PRE-NON-CRANE] cannot have been earlier than the licensed playbook, [KING'S MEN[1]]. It might have been the playbook itself. Alternatively, it might have been another lost early manuscript, already identified as a necessary physical entity: [KING'S MEN[3]] or [PRE-CRANE[2,3]]. However, if it were either of those other texts, then we would have to reconsider their relationships to one another and to the playbook.

Up to this point my visualizations of the upper half of the stemma (Figures 3, 8, 9, 10, 11) have presupposed that only one private transcript of the playbook was made: [KING'S MEN[3]]. This postulate has then forced me to hypothesize that [KING'S MEN[3]] was itself copied twice: one copy led toward CRANE[2,3], and the other led toward CRANE/MATHEWES/ALLDE and the NON-CRANE texts. The new evidence that [PRE-NON-CRANE] derives, in 2.2 and Act Three, from a manuscript that predates the separation of these two data-streams forces us to modify that scenario in one way or another. If [PRE-NON-CRANE] derives from [KING'S MEN[3]], then there were three copies of that manuscript, not two; if [PRE-NON-CRANE] does not derive from [KING'S MEN[3]], then it must derive from the playbook itself, in which case two private transcripts of the playbook were made, not one. Either assumption requires another act of copying, very early in the transmission of the revised theatrical version of the play.

In either scenario, one data-stream leads toward CRANE[2,3], and at least one data-stream leads toward

CRANE/MATHEWES/ALLDE and NON-CRANE. Both data-streams contain material that the playbook apparently contained. As the playbook of *The Lady's Tragedy* demonstrates, playbooks are typically layered documents: they contain a base text which has subsequently been altered by various agents, adding material, altering words, and indicating that certain elements of the original text should be deleted. Typically, the additions are visibly distinct (a pasted-on piece of paper, a different ink or handwriting); typically, deletions and alterations leave the original text still visible and legible. Anyone looking at the playbook itself therefore confronts a visible set of options. Which layer should be copied? Should I copy the original layer, before changes were made by the censor and the acting company? Should I copy the final layer, representing the play as performed? Should I copy everything? Modern editors confront the same choices. However, unlike a modern editor the copyists of *A Game at Chess* did not provide a textual apparatus, documenting the choices they had rejected. Consequently, once the copyist had chosen a particular strategy, the resulting copy would eliminate the visible layering of the playbook itself. If he copied only the final layer, the original layer would simply disappear. If he copied the original layer, the final layer would simply disappear. If he copied everything, the visible layering that had separated the different chronological strata would disappear. Whichever strategy was chosen, any copy of the playbook would be a temporally homogeneous rather than a temporally layered document.

Consequently, if only one private transcript of the playbook had been made—[KING'S MEN[3]]—then all seven extant texts of the revised version would have reproduced a single layer of the licensed playbook: either the original layer, or the final layer, or the undifferentiated totality containing all layers. But that did not happen. As I argued earlier (Sec. XIII), the extant early texts represent two distinct and undoubtedly conscious editorial strategies. CRANE[2,3] derive from the final layer of the playbook, the lightly trimmed and censored text that seems to have been performed. By contrast, CRANE/MATHEWES/ALLDE and NON-CRANE derive from the undifferentiated totality, with a sporadic authorial preference for the original layer. Since these separate choices would only have been visible in the licensed playbook itself, both data-streams must derive directly from [KING'S MEN[1]]. Hence, there must have been two copies of the playbook, not one. We might call these two copies [KING'S MEN[3]] and [KING'S MEN[4]], but we have no way of knowing which was produced first. Rather than arbitrarily chronologically privilege one or the other, I will retain the labels I have been using. For the sake of convenience and consistency, I will continue to call one of those copies [PRE-CRANE[2,3]]; this lost manuscript led to two extant Crane manuscripts, and the lost ancestral transcript was itself almost certainly a Crane manuscript. The other lost copy of the playbook I will continue to call [KING'S MEN[3]], in part because we do not know who made that copy.

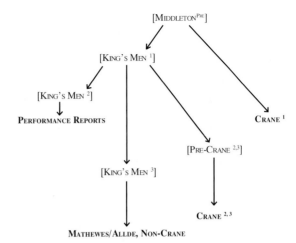

Figure 12. Final Visualization (Source Model) of the Top of the Stemma Throughout *A Game at Chess*. As in all previous figures, the source of all other extant and lost texts is [MIDDLETON[PRE]], the author's first complete draft of the play. In contrast to previous figures, there are here three copies of [KING'S MEN[1]], instead of two.

We know that [PRE-NON-CRANE] cannot derive from [PRE-CRANE[2,3]], because in these middle scenes of the play it includes four passages absent from CRANE[2,3]. (See *Later Form*, Additional Passages A, B, C, and D.) Moreover, errors and variants uniquely shared by CRANE[2,3] occur throughout the play, in a way that demonstrates that those two texts belong to a data-stream that for the play as a whole does not connect to the NON-CRANE texts. For most of the play—leaving aside for a moment the apparently anomalous patch at 3.1.157–98—[PRE-NON-CRANE] must therefore derive either from [KING'S MEN[1]] or from [KING'S MEN[3]].

Since both these manuscripts are lost, since we do not know the identity of the copyist who produced either, and since one was a copy of the other, it is obviously difficult, and probably impossible, to determine which was the immediate ancestor of [PRE-NON-CRANE]. However, we do know that [KING'S MEN[1]] was available for only six days between the end of performances and its delivery to the Privy Council. This was certainly enough time to make two copies of the licensed playbook (as the distribution of variants seems to require). But why should a third copy have been made? We can explain the almost-immediate production of a second copy, because it represents a deliberate editorial alternative to the first: 'someone was dissatisfied with the editorial strategy chosen in producing the first copy, and wanted to make another copy which represented a different temporal layer of the chronologically-layered playbook' or 'someone wanted to satisfy the desires of two different individual readers, or two different kinds of readers'. But why make further copies, using one of the two editorial strategies already available? It is possible [KING'S MEN[1]] was copied three times, but two copies will explain the distribution of all the extant variants and errors, and the time constraints make fewer copies intrinsically likelier than more copies. In what follows, then, I will assume that [PRE-CRANE[2,3]] and [KING'S MEN[3]] were the only copies made directly from [KING'S MEN[1]] after performances began (Figure 12).[180]

Notice that, in the transmission of the play up through the production of [KING'S MEN[3]] and CRANE[2,3], there is no evidence of divided copy-text for any extant or hypothesized text of the play. Each copy was produced by reproduction or alteration of a single existing copy-text. Consequently, this upper part of the stemma, representing the early stages of transmission, applies to the entire play. Only in subsequent stages does the practice of dividing the copy-text—which has caused so many complications in our stemmatic analysis—seem to begin.

Moreover, the clarity of the pattern in Figure 12 allows us to recognize that the same information could be visualized and conceptualized in a different way. Hitherto we have been attempting to identify a chronological sequence, tracing the descent from an original authorial first draft through various lost intermediary texts toward all the extant surviving texts of the whole play. That procedure has dominated textual criticism of early modern English drama, in part because the artisanal routines of the commercial theatre required a movement from authorially produced texts toward theatrical performance and, potentially, subsequent dissemination in private transcripts or printed editions. In this particular case, the attention to authorial intentions makes sense, given the presence of Middleton's hand in five of the six extant manuscripts. The chronological focus also makes sense in this particular case, because we know that at least four of the extant texts—CRANE[1,2,3] and one printed edition—were produced within twelve months of the completion of the first authorial draft of the play; almost certainly, all extant texts were produced within eighteen months of that original manuscript; certainly, three of the four undated texts—ROSENBACH, BRIDGEWATER, MIDDLETON[T]—predate Middleton's own death in July 1627. This precisely defined, compressed time-frame makes chronological analysis more secure. All these factors encourage and enable a form of stemmatic analysis which begins with a single textual source and traces the various data-streams which descend from it in a chronological sequence that moves farther and farther away from that original. In this model, the source resembles a spring, rising from an underground source (the author's mind), creating a river which eventually splays out into a delta (the many extant and lost early texts), and finally opening out into the ocean of the text's later historical reception and reproduction.

Nevertheless, stemmatic analysis does not require this emphasis on authorship, source, or chronology. Philosophically, a source cannot be equated with a centre, and it is possible to measure proximities without establishing vectors. We can know that two texts are closely connected, without knowing which came first. Consequently, we can reconstruct the stemma visualized in Figure 12 in a

way that emphasizes the centre, rather than the source (Figure 13).[181]

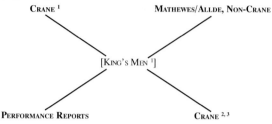

Figure 13. Final Visualization (Centre Model) of the Stemma Throughout *A Game at Chess*. In contrast to previous and subsequent figures, this one lacks arrows of direction, since it records the affiliations of extant witnesses, rather than their derivations. The only lost text identified in this model is the King's Men's licensed playbook, the central text to which all four extant groups are related. The vertical axis in this model has no chronological significance.

This alternative model does not trace the flow of data. Instead, it resembles a tree, seen from above. We know that the tree has a trunk, but all we see are the tops of the branches; the trunk is invisible, somewhere in the centre. In this case, the centre is the lost licensed playbook of the King's Men. For texts associated with the early modern theatre, the centrality of the licensed playbook makes sense: it is the document where the interests of authors, censors, and acting companies intersect. Partly

---

[180] Figure 12 might seem to contradict my earlier analysis of the sequence of CRANE texts, which concluded that [CRANE[4]] must have been chronologically later than CRANE[2,3]. Here, they belong to separate branches of the stemma, both descending from the playbook [KING'S MEN[1]]. But much of the evidence for the relative lateness of [CRANE[4]] concerns Crane's own habits, and the increasing accumulation of Crane markers, each time he copied the text. That is, much of that evidence points to [CRANE[4]] as the chronologically later work of a particular scribe; it does not necessarily prove that [CRANE[4]] is stemmatically later work, or that it belongs on the same sub-branch of the stemma. The key stemmatic arguments are in Section X, the analysis of sets and series. CRANE[2,3,4] do belong to a stemmatic set, because—for the play as a whole—they are the three earliest extant descendants of the playbook [KING'S MEN[1]]. Figure 12 recognizes the existence and stemmatic importance of the subset formed by CRANE[2,3], which was one of the two pair-subsets crucial to my determination of the sequence of the three latest CRANE texts. Figure 12 might seem to be contradicted by the other pair-subset, CRANE[3,4]. Notably, the filtered data-set contains eleven examples of CRANE[2,3] (Pattern 14), and only two examples of CRANE[3,4] (Pattern 8), so the second subset is clearly much weaker than the first. Moreover, although the two examples of Pattern 8 are clearly shared errors, the mechanism of its transmission, in each case, may be scribal rather than stemmatic. At 5.1.11 CRANE[3,4] have 'per amantibus' for the correct Latin 'peramentibus'. This is certainly an error, but I do not normally even record such variants in word-spacing or word-division; I have done so here only because the passage is in Latin. But if Crane in CRANE[3] divided 'per amantibus' into two words, then Crane in a later manuscript might have done exactly the same thing, regardless of the spacing of the manuscript in front of him. Likewise, at 4.2.99–100 CRANE[3,4] fail to provide a line-break between the end of prose and the beginning of verse. But both texts do mark that formal division by a shift from italic to roman—a shift that is certainly scribal, not authorial. Thus, Crane in one manuscript was repeating a formal feature he had imposed in an earlier manuscript, marking a formal division with a change of script rather than a line division. Again, Crane might have repeated himself in this way, regardless of the layout of the manuscript in front of him on the second occasion. Pattern 8 thus confirms that [CRANE[4]] was chronologically closer to CRANE[3] than to CRANE[2]. But it does not prove that CRANE[3] was on the same branch of the stemma as [CRANE[4]].

[181] The best-known example of a centred image is probably the multi-coloured split-tree cladistic model of the textual relationships in Chaucer's *Canterbury Tales* published in Barbrook *et al.*

for that reason it was a composite document, containing different chronological layers and at least two hands (at least one who produced the manuscript itself, the other the official licenser/censor), and often more than two (one or more authors, one or more theatrical functionaries). The playbook will always bear some relationship to performance, and some relationship to an authorial precursor or 'pre-script'; it may or may not be directly related to subsequent printed texts or private transcripts, but it is always at least indirectly related to such documents, either because the success of performances generated market demand for texts of the play, or because authorial dissatisfaction with the performances motivated production of reading texts. Those post-performance texts might be based on different attitudes toward the composite playbook: they might try to reproduce the text as actually performed, or they might try to reproduce some alternative compound text. In this model, the authorial original is simply one of the many forms that can be connected to a central document. In the case of early modern theatre, we might generalize this model in the form visualized in Figure 14.

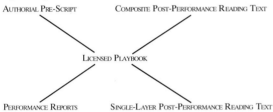

Figure 14. Visualization (Centre Model) of a Generalized Stemma for Early Modern Commercial Plays. Like Figure 13, this stemma lacks arrows of direction, and its vertical axis has no chronological significance.

A Game at Chess is the only early modern play that survives in as many as four of these five forms. An example of the fifth form survives for *The Lady's Tragedy*, making Middleton the only early modern playwright whose work survives in all five forms. But individual examples of all five forms can certainly be found in the work of other playwrights. Most plays of the period do not survive at all, and the overwhelming majority of extant plays have been preserved in only one of these five potential forms. The textual criticism of early modern drama therefore consists, almost entirely, of an attempt to locate the one surviving text of a play in one of these five groups. On rare occasions we possess two substantive early texts, and must determine whether they belong to the same group or to different groups; unfortunately, such circumstances produce a habit of binary thinking, and as we have already seen it is difficult to determine the vector of influence when we possess only two reference points. The playbook-centred, five-group model in Figure 14 provides a more complex picture of the stemmatic problem generated by the particular artisanal routines of the early modern theatre.

Nevertheless, for our ongoing analysis of *A Game at Chess* it makes sense to continue using the source and data-stream chronological model visualized in Figures 2–12. In particular, using the overall pattern visualized in Figure 12, we can now return to the original anomaly identified in 3.1.157–88. In those thirty-one lines, a cluster of CRANE[1,4] variants coexists with an absence of CRANE[2,3] variants. However, if we evaluate those two phenomena statistically, their implications are less local. Random distributions regularly produce some clustering. Even within this scene, there are two longer stretches of text where no CRANE[2,3] variants happen to occur, and even longer gaps occur elsewhere.[182] Thus, the very local pattern—in which the presence of CRANE[1,4] pairs coincides with the complete absence of CRANE[2,3] pairs—is statistically unreliable. Moreover, even within these few lines the apparent tidiness of that binary is interrupted by the triplet which combines CRANE[1,4] with BRIDGEWATER. Much more significant than the local binary is the larger pattern present throughout the middle of the play, from the beginning of 2.2 to the end of Act Three—a pattern in which an exceptional number of CRANE[1,4] pairs coincide with the normal frequency of CRANE[2,3] pairs, and a scattered distribution of 'CRANE[1,4] Plus One' triplets. That larger pattern cannot be attributed to the inevitability of random micro-clustering—and it also cannot be explained by the stemma visualized in Figure 11. We must therefore modify that stemma, so that it applies not just to that small patch but to the larger sequence of 2.2 and Act Three.

Let us suppose that some variants originate in [PRE-CRANE[2,3]], either because they were scribal errors or sophistications or because they preserve a particular chronological layer of [KING'S MEN[1]] which was rejected elsewhere. Those readings were never present in CRANE[1] or [KING'S MEN[3]], and therefore were not passed to CRANE/MATHEWES/ALLDE or to NON-CRANE. In those cases, we would find the binary distribution which regularly shows up in these scenes and indeed throughout the play, with unique CRANE[2,3] pairs set against variants that belong to the larger set (CRANE[1,4], NON-CRANE). But how then are we to account for unique CRANE[1,4] variants? There are two potential sources for the presence of such readings in CRANE/MATHEWES/ALLDE. In one scenario, Middleton himself might have sporadically restored original readings present in CRANE[1] but not present in [KING'S MEN[1]] or any text copied from it. (I discuss the evidence of sporadic authorial intervention in the manuscript antecedents of MATHEWES/ALLDE in Sec. XIII.) Alternatively, if the variant does not result from a unique authorial restoration in [CRANE[4]], then the variant might have been present in at least one layer of [KING'S MEN[1]]; if so, it must have been

---

[182] There are none in the patch after 3.1.45 and before 3.1.108 (53 lines), or after 3.1.250 and before 3.1.301 (51 lines). Similar gaps occur between 1.1.37 and 1.1.98 (sixty-one lines), 1.1.115 and 1.1.209 (ninety-four lines), 1.1.209 and 1.1.270 (sixty-one lines), 2.1.46 and 2.1.135 (eighty-nine lines), 2.1.200 and 2.2.18 (fifty-seven lines), 2.2.113 and 2.2.153 (forty lines). I have not systematically checked Acts Four and Five.

rejected or miscopied in [PRE-CRANE[2,3]]. But in that case, how are we to explain the absence of the CRANE[1,4] variant from NON-CRANE? The original reading, present in at least one layer of [KING'S MEN[1]] and from there copied into [KING'S MEN[3]], must have been independently altered at some point between [KING'S MEN[3]] and all the NON-CRANE texts. The obvious location for such alterations would be [PRE-NON-CRANE]. The existence of [PRE-NON-CRANE], and the sequence of transmission visualized in Figure 15, would explain the repeated coexistence of CRANE[1,4] pairs with CRANE[2,3] pairs in the middle scenes of the play.

At this point we have, I believe, identified the manuscript from which [PRE-NON-CRANE] was copied, for about one third of the play. But it is also clear that the copy-text for [PRE-NON-CRANE], unlike the copy-text for earlier extant or conjectured manuscripts, must have been non-homogeneous.

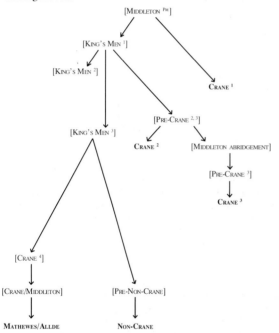

Figure 15. Draft Visualization (Source Model) of the Top of the Stemma in 2.2 and Act Three. This differs from Figure 12 only by specifying the split that separates MATHEWES/ALLDE from the other descendants of [KING'S MEN[3]]. As in Figures 2–12, the vertical axis is chronological.

The nature of the copy-text for [PRE-NON-CRANE] for the beginning and end of the play is suggested by the triplets that belong to the set 'CRANE[1,4] Plus One'. In the first three scenes of the play, the uncontested and unparalleled dominance of the three-member set (CRANE[1,4], ROSENBACH) can hardly be attributed to a random scatter of authorial restorations: nine examples in 648 consecutive lines, zero examples in the remaining 1523 consecutive lines. Likewise, the complete absence of any reliable 'CRANE[1,4] Plus

One' triplets from Acts Four and Five must be stemmatically significant. In isolation, either pattern might be explained by the assumption that [PRE-NON-CRANE] was, in those parts of the play, a copy of [CRANE[4]]. In those 1449 lines of the play (two consecutive sequences of 648 and 801 lines), only three CRANE[1,4] pairs appear. The difference between the two sections, in respect to the distribution of 'CRANE[1,4] Plus One' variants, might reflect nothing more than the different position of [PRE-ROSENBACH]: in the first three scenes it preceded both [CRANE[4]] and [PRE-NON-CRANE], in the last two Acts it followed them both.

But that assumption will not explain a very real contrast, between the first three scenes and the last two Acts, in the relationship of the CRANE texts to the NON-CRANE texts. In examples of the triplet CRANE[1,4]–ROSENBACH, the variant merely passed through [PRE-ROSENBACH] on its way from CRANE[1] to CRANE/MATHEWES; stemmatically, a reading present in CRANE[1] survived through various lost manuscripts into [CRANE[4]], but was then stopped, corrupted or revised, and did not go any further. Because ROSENBACH was there embedded among the NON-CRANE texts, for the first 648 consecutive lines of the play we can combine the pairs and the triplets, and say that nine CRANE[1] readings survived, stemmatically, as far as [CRANE[4]], but no further. By contrast, in the 801 consecutive lines at the end of the play this happened only once, possibly, or only three times at most—*even though*, according to our draft stemmata (Figures 5 and 8), [CRANE[4]] was in both sections the conduit between CRANE[1,2,3] and OKES, BRIDGEWATER, MIDDLETON[T], *and even though* in the final section of the play there were, according to our draft stemmata, fewer intermediaries between CRANE[1] and [CRANE[4]], which would lead us to expect *more* links between them. The transition between the CRANE and NON-CRANE texts cannot have been identical in the first three scenes and the last two Acts. Likewise, in 722 consecutive lines in the middle of the play, what happened only one to three times in 801 lines at the end of the play happened at least seventeen times.[183] Again, this seems proof of a change that took place in the copy-text for [PRE-NON-CRANE] at about the beginning of Act Four.

The question that remains, though, is whether the copy-text for [PRE-NON-CRANE] changed once, or twice: that is, whether we are dealing with one stemmatic discontinuity, or two, in that lost manuscript. In order to answer that question, we will have to re-examine our hypotheses about Acts One and Two, in the light of the existence of [PRE-NON-CRANE].

But one thing is already clear. Nothing discernibly changes in the copy-text for [PRE-NON-CRANE] from the beginning of 2.2 to the end of Act Three. Consequently, the change in stemmatic relationships that we have previously identified at 3.1.0.1 (Sec. XVII), and the apparent but

[183] It might theoretically have happened twenty-four times, depending on the causes of the 'CRANE[1,4] Plus One' triplets. But see my explanation, below, of those 'Plus One' variants.

as yet unanalysed change near 3.1.318, must all result from discontinuities in copy-text within manuscripts that postdate [PRE-NON-CRANE].

XXVI. Divided Copy-text in the NON-CRANE Texts: 3.1.318 to 4.1.144

There remains only one continuous stretch of text that we have not yet examined in detail: from near 3.1.318, where pairs of variants shared uniquely by ROSENBACH and BRIDGEWATER begin to cluster, until near 4.1.145, where 'Crane Plus One' variants begin to be completely dominated by OKES.

Although we have separated off this section of text because something dramatically changes near 3.1.318, most patterns of distribution that appear earlier in Act Three remain the same. I have just noted that the copy-text for [PRE-NON-CRANE] apparently continues unchanged. So does the distribution of filtered NON-CRANE triplets.

Table of Shared Error Triplets in NON-CRANE Texts from 3.1.318 to 4.1.116

30. ROSENBACH–BRIDGEWATER–OKES: 1–2 (3.1.355 + 3.1.369?)
43. [Crane]–ROSENBACH–BRIDGEWATER–OKES: 1 (4.1.21–2)
53. [Crane]–ROSENBACH–BRIDGEWATER–OKES: 1? (4.1.116)

* * *

31. ROSENBACH–BRIDGEWATER–MIDDLETON[T]: 1 (3.1.392.1)

* * *

32. BRIDGEWATER–OKES–MIDDLETON[T]: 1 (4.1.93.1)

These three triplets all appeared earlier in Act Three, and were discussed in Sec. XXIV. Here as earlier, their co-presence contradicts the assumption of a simple sequence of four texts; here as earlier, we might try to argue away the significance of one or more of them, but the very fact that the contradictory pattern continues makes it likelier that it appears here for the same reason it appeared earlier. The four extant NON-CRANE texts form a single coherent set, but not a single sequence. The distribution of filtered paired errors supports the same conclusion.

Table of Paired Shared Errors in NON-CRANE Texts from 3.1.318 to 4.1.129–30

18. ROSENBACH–BRIDGEWATER: 9–11 (3.2.6, 3.2.9–11, 3.2.29.1, 3.2.40, 3.1.352, 3.1.395.1, 3.1.398, 4.1.38–9, 4.1.53 + 3.1.155.1? 3.1.392.1?)

* * *

15. ROSENBACH–OKES: 1–2 (3.1.399 + 4.1.129–30?)

* * *

16. BRIDGEWATER–OKES: 1 (3.1.322)
44. [Crane]–BRIDGEWATER–OKES: 1 (3.1.410)
24. [Crane]–BRIDGEWATER–OKES: 1 (3.2.30–1)

* * *

13. BRIDGEWATER–MIDDLETON[T]: 1 (3.2.39–40)

In a series of four members there should logically only be three pairs; here, there are four. Moreover, in a single sequence of four texts, a text might be paired with one other (if it were at the beginning or end of the sequence) or with two others (if it were in the middle). It cannot be paired with three. But BRIDGEWATER is here paired with three different NON-CRANE texts: ROSENBACH, OKES, and MIDDLETON[T]. The only explanation for this pattern of pairs, combined with this pattern of triplets, is that the four extant NON-CRANE texts all descend from [PRE-NON-CRANE], but they do so in two or more separate data-streams.

Further evidence for this conclusion is provided by 'Crane Plus One' variants. You will recall that in the first three scenes of the play that test is overwhelmingly dominated by ROSENBACH, and that after 4.1.145 it is overwhelmingly dominated by OKES. By contrast, earlier in Act Three such variants are seemingly randomly distributed, with scattered examples linking CRANE to three different NON-CRANE texts: MIDDLETON[T] (4–5), ROSENBACH (5–6), and BRIDGEWATER (2–3). A similarly scattered distribution continues in the remainder of Act Three. 'Crane Plus One' links to MIDDLETON[T] eight times, to ROSENBACH four times, to BRIDGEWATER once (3.1.399).[184]

Because CRANE[2,3] do not contain 3.2, for those forty lines the pattern 'All Four CRANE Texts Plus One NON-CRANE Text' cannot occur. However, the logic of 'Crane Plus One' can still apply. Since CRANE[1] and CRANE/ALLDE belong to different branches of the stemma, they should not share errors. Therefore, even when 'Crane Plus One' includes only those two extant CRANE texts, it should still tell us something about which NON-CRANE text is closest to the earlier CRANE series. In 3.2, 'Crane Plus MIDDLETON[T]' occurs three times: (3.2.6, 3.2.20–1, 3.2.38). But 'Crane Plus OKES' also occurs once (3.2.22). I will return later to the fact that MIDDLETON[T] dominates the list; for now, we need only note that in the 283 lines from 3.1.318 to 4.1.145 there are examples of 'Crane Plus One' for all four NON-CRANE texts. That scatter, like the scatter of triplets and pairs, suggests that the NON-CRANE texts here, once again, descend from [PRE-NON-CRANE] in more than one stream.

These continuities very clearly localize the discontinuity: somewhere near 3.1.318, something changes in the way the extant NON-CRANE texts branch off from [PRE-NON-CRANE]. The nature of that change should be clarified by changes in NON-CRANE triplets and pairs. One error-pair does not appear at all in Act Three: (ROSENBACH, MIDDLETON[T]).[185] Clearly, those two texts cannot be adjacent on the same branch. The absence of that pair is probably related to the complete absence of the triplet OKES–ROSENBACH–MIDDLETON[T]; clearly, those three texts cannot be together on the same NON-CRANE branch, and BRIDGEWATER must come somewhere between them.

---

[184] MIDDLETON[T]: 3.1.355; 3.1.369; 3.1.395.1, 4.1.24, 4.1.33.1, 4.1.91, 4.1.97, 4.1.100. ROSENBACH: 4.1.0.1 (three separate variants), 4.1.101. BRIDGEWATER: 3.1.399.
[185] The two texts uniquely share only a single variant—eye(s)—which could easily be coincidental.

Against these continuities of absence, we can set several changes in patterns of shared-error pairs. The most conspicuous change is the sudden cluster of at least nine errors uniquely shared by ROSENBACH–BRIDGEWATER, beginning at 3.2.6. Before that point the two texts share three variants, beginning thirty lines before (at 3.1.318). The strength of this pairing dwarfs all others, and the two texts must be adjacent on the same branch. This positive evidence complements the negative evidence cited in the preceding paragraph: ROSENBACH and BRIDGEWATER must be adjacent on one of at least two branches descending from [PRE-NON-CRANE]. If MIDDLETON[T] is on the same branch, it must be adjacent to BRIDGEWATER, rather than ROSENBACH.

Since ROSENBACH and BRIDGEWATER are clearly adjacent, there cannot be four separate branches descending from [PRE-NON-CRANE]. There might be three or two; if there are only two, the other branch might contain one text or two. The fact that MIDDLETON[T] and OKES do not share a single error in 1183 consecutive lines (from 3.1.75 to the end of the play) does not encourage the hypothesis that they share a separate branch of the stemma here. Indeed, in the 283 lines from 3.1.318 to 4.1.145 they share only four variants.[186] This leaves only two options: three separate branches, or two uneven branches (one with three members, the other with only one).

If there were really three separate branches descending from [PRE-NON-CRANE], then the ROSENBACH–BRIDGEWATER branch should be equally distant from both OKES and MIDDLETON[T]. The distribution of shared errors does not support that assumption.[187] BRIDGEWATER and ROSENBACH here share a triplet error with OKES four times; by contrast, they share a triplet error with MIDDLETON[T] only once. Likewise, either ROSENBACH or BRIDGEWATER shares an error pair with OKES five times here; by contrast, one or the other shares an error pair with MIDDLETON[T] only once. Altogether, the BRIDGEWATER–ROSENBACH set shares nine errors with OKES, and only two with MIDDLETON[T]. This disparity does not suggest three separate branches. It would be most easily explained if MIDDLETON[T] belonged to a branch of its own, with OKES–BRIDGEWATER–ROSENBACH together on a separate branch. This hypothesis tends to be confirmed by the fact that, altogether, OKES–BRIDGEWATER–ROSENBACH share twenty-two variants, either uniquely or in combination with NON-CRANE texts. By contrast, using the same definitions, MIDDLETON[T]–BRIDGEWATER–ROSENBACH share only five variants. That is, whether we count total shared variants (22/5), shared errors (9/2), or shared variants not classified as errors (13/3), BRIDGEWATER–ROSENBACH share more readings with OKES than with MIDDLETON[T]. ROSENBACH and BRIDGEWATER share twenty-nine paired errors and variants. Since MIDDLETON[T] is autograph, theoretically it might have corrected all those errors and variants, restoring the original reading or inventing a new one; since OKES was apparently set from an autograph manuscript [MIDDLETON/OKES], it too might have corrected all those errors. However,

OKES overall contains a much higher number of shared errors, which makes it less likely to be responsible for such systematic correction: correction does not discriminate against errors inherited from one source, rather than another (Sec. V, para. 23). Consequently, if OKES is indeed on the same branch as ROSENBACH–BRIDGEWATER, it must be higher on that branch, descending from a manuscript which did not contain the errors made later and shared by ROSENBACH–BRIDGEWATER.

On the basis of all the foregoing arguments, we can now attempt a visualization (Figure 16) of the stemma of transmission for the extant NON-CRANE texts in this stretch of text from the beginning of regular ROSENBACH–BRIDGEWATER pairs to the beginning of regular 'Crane Plus OKES' variants.

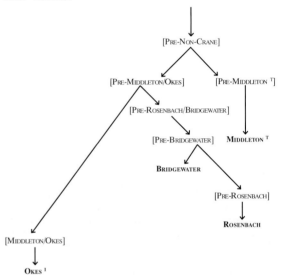

Figure 16. Draft Visualization of the Stemma of Transmission for the extant NON-CRANE texts from 3.1.318 to 4.1.130.

At this point, I have provided a draft stemma for every part of the play (Figures 5–16). But I have not yet attempted to relate all those partial reconstructions to one another. For instance, the area of the text covered by Figure 15 is bisected by the change in the copy-text for [PRE-NON-CRANE], analysed above (Sec. XXV). The two areas of the text, before and after the beginning of Act Four, therefore have to be visualized differently.

Which is to say: Figures 12 and 16 have to be superimposed on each other, and related to each other. Indeed, that process of superimposition and relationship has to

---

[186] 3.2.29.1 (the word 'a' in a stage direction), 3.1.395.1 (position of stage direction), 4.1.73 ('my' for 'mine'), 4.1.94 (omission of 'now'). The last and potentially most significant of these variants is probably related to BRIDGEWATER—see text note—and thus may be a triplet instead of a twin.
[187] Since MIDDLETON[T] is autograph and OKES was apparently set from an autograph manuscript, authorial correction should not be distorting these figures.

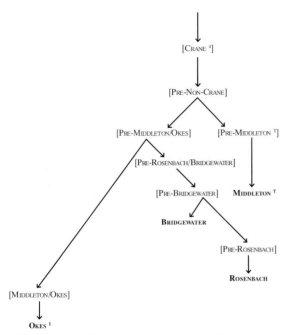

Figure 17. Draft Visualization of the Stemma of Transmission for the extant NON-CRANE texts from *c.*4.1.0 to *c.*4.1.130.

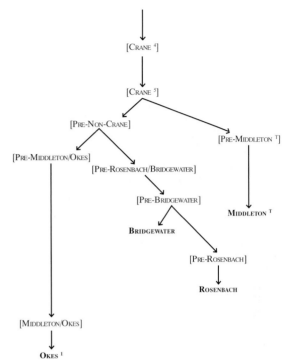

Figure 18. Revised Visualization of the Stemma of Transmission for the extant NON-CRANE texts from *c.*4.1.0 to *c.*4.1.130.

be done for the whole play, if we are to understand the mega-pattern formed by the separate individual patterns.

XXVII. MIDDLETON[T] and [CRANE[5]]

The change in the copy-text for [PRE-NON-CRANE] apparently took place at about the beginning of Act Four.[188] If we superimpose Figure 12 on Figure 16, then for the beginning of Act Four we get something like Figure 17.

The top of Figure 17 recognizes the end of the CRANE[1,4] pairs, and the subsequent derivation of all the NON-CRANE texts from [CRANE[4]]. By doing so, Figure 17 returns us to something resembling Figure 6 (covering 4.1.145–4.4.110.2) and Figure 5 (covering Act Five): in both those preliminary visualizations of the end of the play, I concluded that [CRANE[4]] led to [PRE-MIDDLETON/OKES], the first of the NON-CRANE texts. But Figures 5 and 6 did not take any account of [PRE-NON-CRANE], which was not an entity obviously necessary to explain the distribution of errors and variants in that part of the play. However, since we now have compelling evidence that such an entity existed, we might reasonably assume that it included a text of the whole play, and it must therefore somehow be included in the stemma for those later scenes. Theoretically, it might not have influenced any extant text in Acts Four and Five, but given its importance in Act Three that seems a little unlikely. More importantly, the distribution of variants and errors in Act Three demonstrates that—thanks to [PRE-NON-CRANE]—the four extant NON-CRANE texts can form a single set, without forming a single series. My earlier analysis of Acts Four

and Five, visualized in Figures 5 and 6, presupposed that the existence of a coherent NON-CRANE set indicated that its four members belonged to a single series. That assumption can no longer be taken for granted. Consequently, the fact that Figure 17 resembles Figures 5 and 6 may not be an indication that Figure 17 is correct, but that all three figures are wrong together.

But let us confine our attention, for the moment, to the local issue at the beginning of Act Four. Figure 17 does not presuppose a single NON-CRANE series; instead, it conjectures that (as in Act Three) the NON-CRANE texts form a set because they all derive from [PRE-NON-CRANE]. But by recognizing *both* the branching of the NON-CRANE texts *and* the ancestral influence of [CRANE[4]], Figure 17 raises an obvious question. In order to form a coherent set, all four NON-CRANE texts must share a common ancestor—but how do we know that the common ancestor was [PRE-NON-CRANE] rather than [CRANE[4]]?

The answer is simple: we know that their common ancestor was a text later than [CRANE[4]], because otherwise the four NON-CRANE texts would not form a complete

---

[188] The penultimate CRANE[1,4] pair occurs at 3.1.392.1, where the two texts agree on placement of the stage direction for music. Another such pair—the final one in the play—does not appear until 5.3.162, and is probably coincidental. The only 'CRANE[1,4] Plus One' triplet in Act Four (the obsolescent plural 'yeare' where other texts read 'years' at 4.1.2), may be an autograph restoration of the original reading, or a coincidence.

set; they would instead just be members of a set that included five extant texts (NON-CRANE and MATHEWES/ALLDE), instead of four. In the data-set of filtered shared errors, there is no such five-member set.

But the phrasing of this answer creates an important loophole. To say (correctly) that 'the common ancestor must be later than [CRANE[4]]' is not the same as saying (incorrectly) that 'the common ancestor must be [PRE-NON-CRANE]'. Of course, this may be merely a semantic difference. [PRE-NON-CRANE] *might* have been the only text produced chronologically and stemmatically later than [CRANE[4]] but earlier than the four extant NON-CRANE texts. But, equally, it *might not* have been. Any set of extant texts might be simply the randomly visible members of a larger set that originally included an unknown number of now-lost, and hence now-invisible, members. The principle of economy requires us to conjure into existence the minimum number of lost entities necessary in order to explain the data. But the universe does not always make do with the minimum number of necessary entities, and neither does textual culture.

Let us suppose, for the moment, that another lost manuscript intervened between [CRANE[4]] and [PRE-NON-CRANE]. For reasons that will soon become apparent, I will christen this lost entity '[CRANE[5]]'. If such an entity existed, then it would be possible to replace Figure 17 with Figure 18, and thereby reconceptualize the distribution of variants at the beginning of Act Four.

Figure 18 has the same number of branches as Figure 17, but it distributes them slightly differently. As in Figure 17, in Figure 18 all the extant NON-CRANE texts descend from a single ancestor, which is not the ancestor of any extant CRANE text: the NON-CRANE texts therefore form a set. In Figure 18, the extant NON-CRANE texts first split off into two branches after the lost [CRANE[5]], rather than after the lost [PRE-NON-CRANE]. Although OKES and [PRE-ROSENBACH/BRIDGEWATER] are still closer to each other than any of them is to MIDDLETON[T], those three texts do not form a series or a single branch. They are closer to each other because all three descend from a single lost manuscript; errors and variants shared by those three texts presumably originated in [PRE-NON-CRANE]. All three texts are farther from MIDDLETON[T] because it is separated from them by another lost text, [CRANE[5]]; variants and errors shared by MIDDLETON[T] with the other three presumably originated in [CRANE[5]] and were transmitted from there to [PRE-NON-CRANE].

Figure 18 much more plausibly explains the distribution of pairs in the NON-CRANE texts. The sheer number of errors and variants uniquely shared by ROSENBACH and BRIDGEWATER suggests that they belong together in a textual cul-de-sac. For instance, the two-member cul-de-sac formed by CRANE[2,3] contains a total of thirteen paired errors and variants in the 283 lines between 3.1.318 and 4.1.144; this is fairly typical of its distribution of uniquely shared variants throughout the play. By contrast, in the same number of lines ROSENBACH and BRIDGEWATER share twenty-nine paired errors and variants—more than

double the frequency of CRANE[2,3], the play's clearest consistent cul-de-sac pair.

Figure 18 also more plausibly explains the distribution of triplets in the NON-CRANE texts. As noted above, ROSENBACH and BRIDGEWATER share more variants and errors with OKES (22) than with MIDDLETON[T] (5). But if [PRE-MIDDLETON/OKES] were the immediate ancestor of [PRE-ROSENBACH/BRIDGEWATER] (as in Figure 17), then ROSENBACH and BRIDGEWATER should not have shared any errors with MIDDLETON[T] that were not also present in [PRE-MIDDLETON/OKES]. Of course, the discrepancy can be explained by postulating correction in [MIDDLETON/OKES] or in the printing house. But given the high number of unique errors in OKES and shared errors in [MIDDLETON/OKES], correction of 23% of the shared errors does not seem particularly likely. I have therefore assumed that [PRE-NON-CRANE] is indeed a separate manuscript, and not simply another name for [PRE-MIDDLETON/OKES].

Finally, Figure 18 more economically explains the stemmatic change that takes place near the beginning of Act Four. This becomes clear if we superimpose Figure 12 and Figure 16 for the end of Act Three, to produce Figure 19.

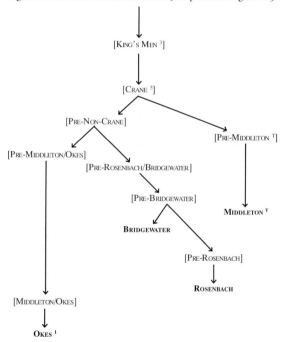

Figure 19. Revised Visualization of the Stemma of Transmission for the extant NON-CRANE texts from *c*.3.1.318 to *c*.3.1.392.1 (including the whole of '3.2').

Figure 19 differs from Figure 18 in only a single detail: at the top of the diagram, [KING'S MEN[3]] has replaced [CRANE[4]]. Or, to put the change in the sequence of *A Game at Chess*, rather than the sequence of this General Textual Introduction: near the beginning of Act Four, [CRANE[4]] replaced [KING'S MEN[3]] as the copy-text for [CRANE[5]].

Like Figure 15, the stemma reflects the change in the ancestral copy-text for all the extant NON-CRANE texts that I identified above (Sec. XXVI). The difference between Figure 16 and Figure 19 arises simply from a different conjecture about *which* lost manuscript divided its copy-text near the beginning of Act Four: in Figure 16, the divided copy-text was conjecturally located in [PRE-NON-CRANE], but in Figure 19 it is conjecturally located in [CRANE5].

Figure 19 is more plausible than Figure 16 for the same reasons that Figure 18 is more plausible than Figure 17. But Figures 18 and 19, together, have a further advantage: they better explain the relationship between MIDDLETON[T] and the CRANE texts. The proposed change of copy-text near the beginning of Act Four explains the disappearance of CRANE[1,4] pairs, which were so anomalously common in 2.2 and Act Three. But something else, also anomalously common in those scenes, does *not* change at the beginning of Act Four: the predominance of MIDDLETON[T] in the 'Crane Plus One' statistics.

The fact that MIDDLETON[T] has more examples of 'Crane Plus One' than the other NON-CRANE texts might not seem surprising, because an autograph text might at any time restore variants from earlier in the stemma. But why does MIDDLETON[T] 'restore' CRANE readings so frequently in the middle of the play, and so rarely at the beginning or end? In the first three scenes of the play, 'Crane Plus MIDDLETON[T]' occurs once; it also occurs once at 5.3.39. By contrast, from the beginning of 2.2 until 4.1.100 it appears thirty times.[189] The ratios make this disparity even more telling: 30 times in 822 lines in the middle of the play (once every 87 lines), twice in 1349 lines at the beginning and end of the play (once every 675 lines). To deny that this difference has any stemmatic significance, we would have to conjecture that Middleton became much, much, much more nostalgic for original readings in the middle of the play—and that at about the beginning of Act Four he again reverted to the indifference he showed in the first three scenes. Figures 18 and 19 provide a much more plausible explanation for the pattern: MIDDLETON[T] contains more 'Crane Plus One' readings because it is closer to the CRANE texts than any other NON-CRANE text.

MIDDLETON[T] does not monopolize the 'Crane Plus One' pattern, in these middle scenes, in the way that ROSENBACH virtually monopolized them for the first three scenes. As noted above, all the NON-CRANE texts contain, in these middle scenes, some examples of 'Crane Plus One'; that scatter itself contributed to the evidence for a divided NON-CRANE set.[190] But dominance rather than a monopoly makes sense here. In the first three scenes, ROSENBACH was embedded in the midst of the CRANE texts, but MIDDLETON[T] here is not embedded: it is, in Figures 18 and 19, simply the closest NON-CRANE text to the last of the CRANE texts. The texts in the other NON-CRANE branch are farther away, but they could still inherit occasional CRANE readings that MIDDLETON[T] had independently corrected or corrupted.

Finally, Figure 19 in particular explains a pattern in the distribution of variants that should never have

occurred, if all the NON-CRANE texts in Act Three derived directly from [PRE-NON-CRANE] which in turn derived from [KING'S MEN3]. We know that [PRE-NON-CRANE] cannot have been in the handwriting of Ralph Crane, because the shared NON-CRANE variants include regular departures from Crane's strong preferences. We also know that [KING'S MEN3] cannot have been, in its entirety, in the handwriting of Ralph Crane, because the first three scenes of ROSENBACH seem to have been directly copied from [KING'S MEN3], and yet they betray few (if any) signs of Crane influence. Theoretically, the first scenes of [KING'S MEN3] might have been produced by one scribe, and the rest by Crane. But all extant CRANE manuscripts are in Crane's handwriting throughout; there is no evidence, in *A Game at Chess* or elsewhere, of him copying only one part of a manuscript, begun or finished by someone else. We can therefore reasonably assume that, if three scenes of [KING'S MEN3] were in someone else's handwriting, then Crane was not responsible for any part of that manuscript. This argument applies equally well to [KING'S MEN1]; if the licensed playbook had been in Crane's handwriting, then Crane characteristics should have made their way from [KING'S MEN1] through [KING'S MEN3] into the first three scenes of ROSENBACH. They do not.

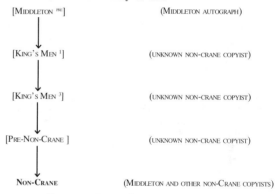

Figure 20. Excerpt from Figure 15, showing its visualization of the antecedents of all four extant NON-CRANE texts in 2.2 and Act Three.

As Figure 20 makes clear, the draft stemma visualized in Figure 16 does not at any point permit Ralph Crane to have influenced any feature of the four extant NON-CRANE texts. That conclusion cannot be correct. Nascimento and Howard-Hill both acknowledge, in their different ways, Crane's influence on more than one NON-CRANE

[189] The statistics in this paragraph are based on the expanded definition of 'Crane Plus One', which includes examples of CRANE[1,4] where CRANE[2,3] are absent entirely.
[190] ROSENBACH 14, BRIDGEWATER 4, OKES 2. Of the 'Crane Plus Rosenbach' examples, five involve the form of act divisions. In each case ROSENBACH shares with CRANE—as it does throughout the play—the formula most common in the entire early modern period. That is to say, Middleton's idiosyncratic form of Act division is not favoured by either CRANE or ROSENBACH. In itself, such variants probably provide poor evidence of a stemmatic connection. If we discounted the act divisions, ROSENBACH would contain only nine 'Crane Plus One' variants here, and MIDDLETON[T] would contain twice as many as the three other NON-CRANE texts combined.

text. I have provided further evidence of such influence in Section IV, and more pervasively in the collation of spelling, punctuation, and capitalization variants in the textual apparatus for *An Early Form*.

The nonsensical result excerpted by Figure 20 proves that Figure 15 cannot be correct, and that for 2.2 and Act Three, at least, a lost CRANE text must have intervened at some point between [KING'S MEN³] and [PRE-NON-CRANE]. Naturally, since that manuscript does not survive, we cannot be certain that it was, chronologically, the last of the known or inferred CRANE transcripts. But the pattern of data visualized in Figure 18 would place it later than [CRANE⁴] for that part of the text. We have no evidence that Crane worked on more than one transcript at a time, so it seems reasonable to assume that [CRANE⁵] was, throughout its length, chronologically later than [CRANE⁴].

This hypothesis is confirmed by the pattern of metrical variants and contractions. I have already established that Crane tended to expand Middletonian contractions, and that later Crane texts expand more contractions than earlier Crane texts (Sec. XI). We would therefore expect that, if [CRANE⁵] ever existed, it would have expanded more contractions than [CRANE⁴]. The NON-CRANE texts restore many of these contractions, but not all. In other words, the NON-CRANE texts—and, in particular, MIDDLETONᵀ itself—occasionally contain unMiddletonian Crane- -like expansions of contractions, in places where those contractions do not appear in any extant CRANE text. This is exactly what we would expect to happen if [CRANE⁵] were placed where Figures 18 and 19 locate it, and if it were indeed the latest of the CRANE texts. As I noted above (Sec. XIX), the unique extrametrical variants in MIDDLETONᵀ are not distributed evenly throughout the play. The first occurs at 2.2.213, but it is followed by twelve examples between the beginning of 3.1 and 4.1.93. The rest of Acts Four and Five—where Middleton was clearly at his least attentive—contain only five examples. In other words, for the play's middle 550 lines, the ratio is one every 46 lines; for the play's first four scenes, the ratio is one every 913 lines; for most of Act Four and Five, Middleton's sloppy rate was one every 118 lines.

The identification of [CRANE⁵] obviously has implications beyond 3.1.318–4.1.144, the portion of the text covered by Figures 18 and 19. The preceding analysis has already indicated that the patterns linking MIDDLETONᵀ to the CRANE texts begin in 2.2. Moving backward from 3.1.318 (Figure 20), we can use what we have learned to reconceptualize our earlier draft stemmata for the earlier part of Act Three (Figure 21).

Figure 21 combines the top of Figure 15 with the bottom of Figure 10. But it also redefines the transition between the top and bottom of the stemma on the basis of Figures 18 and 19, and the arguments that supported them. The four extant NON-CRANE texts form a coherent set, because all four descend from a single lost manuscript—but that manuscript is now identified as [CRANE⁵]. From there, they descend into two separate

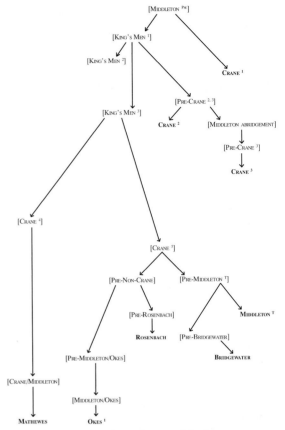

Figure 21. Draft Visualization of the Stemma of Transmission from 3.1.0.1 to *c.*3.1.318.

data-streams, one of them headed by the lost manuscript we have been calling [PRE-NON-CRANE]. I will continue to call it that, even though it is no longer the ancestor of all NON-CRANE texts, but simply of a certain number of NON-CRANE texts. Since the number of NON-CRANE texts that descend from it varies, depending on the particular divisions of copy-text, it is difficult to give it any other name. It remains, throughout, a lost manuscript relatively late in the stemma, later than all extant or inferred CRANE manuscripts, and always earlier than two or more extant NON-CRANE texts.

In Figure 10, [PRE-ROSENBACH] had to be the ancestor of both ROSENBACH and OKES, in order to explain their shared errors and variants. But because the bridging function of [PRE-NON-CRANE] has now been taken over by [CRANE⁵], that assumption is no longer necessary. The unique similarities uniting ROSENBACH and OKES could have originated in [PRE-NON-CRANE]. As a result, the stemma for OKES does not change between Figures 19 and 21: it still descends on a separate branch from [PRE-NON-CRANE].

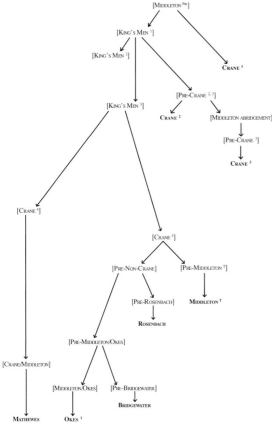

Figure 22. Draft Visualization of the
Stemma of Transmission for 2.2.

Thus, for the middle section of the play, from the beginning of 2.2 until *c.*4.1.93, the distribution of errors and variants can be most economically explained by assuming that all four extant NON-CRANE texts descend from the lost [CRANE⁵], with divisions in the copy-text of one or more extant or lost NON-CRANE texts at or near 3.1.0.1, 3.1.318, and 4.1.0.1. This evidence forces us to reconsider our provisional account of the NON-CRANE texts at the beginning and end of the play, where we have hitherto taken no account of either [CRANE⁵] or [PRE-NON-CRANE].

Given the pattern of divided copy-text, it is of course possible that [CRANE⁵] did not influence any of the extant NON-CRANE texts at the beginning or end of the play. But one important category of variants suggests that, throughout the play, most NON-CRANE texts descend from a late CRANE manuscript. Consider the following list of necessary stage directions, missing in two or more of the extant NON-CRANE texts.

Induction.52.1 *Music*] *not in* CRANE²·³, MIDDLETONᵀ, BRIDGEWATER, OKES
Induction.52.1–2 *Enter...game*] *not in* MIDDLETONᵀ, BRIDGEWATERᴬ, OKES
2.2.94.1 *Enter...Pawn*] *not in* CRANE³, OKES, ROSENBACHᴬ. Passage not present in BRIDGEWATER.
4.4.12.1 *Enter Black Knight*] *not in* CRANE³, ROSENBACH, BRIDGEWATER, MIDDLETONᵀ
4.4.55.1 *Enter Fat Bishop*] *not in* CRANE³, OKES, ROSENBACHᴬ, BRIDGEWATERᴮ. Passage not present in MIDDLETONᵀ. Hence, the direction is not present in any extant NON-CRANE text.
4.4.74.1 *Enter White King*] *not in* CRANE³, BRIDGEWATERᴮ, ROSENBACHᴬ. Passage not present in MIDDLETONᵀ; hence, the only NON-CRANE text which contains the direction is OKES.
5.3.178.1–2/2398.1 *and the Black lost...appear in it*] *not in* NON-CRANE.

To the foregoing list can be added the following examples of stage directions misplaced in two or more of the NON-CRANE texts.

1.1.205.1 *Enter...Pawn*] *not in* CRANE³. This direction is placed too late in BRIDGEWATERᴬ and MIDDLETONᵀ.
1.1.243.2 *Enter Black Knight*] *not in* CRANE³. Both BRIDGEWATER and OKES misplace this direction one line below, after he speaks.
2.1.228.1 *Enter...Pawn*] *not in* BRIDGEWATER; OKES and MIDDLETONᵀ misplace the entrance (in different ways). Passage not present in CRANE³.
2.2.81.1–6 *Enter...black pawns*] *not in* CRANE³. ROSENBACHᴬ and OKES wrongly place this entrance to the right of 2.2.96.
3.1.155.1 *Enter...White House*] *not in* CRANE³. ROSENBACHᴬ, BRIDGEWATERᴮ, and MIDDLETONᵀ place the direction too late.

The continuity between Figures 19 and 21 can also be maintained in Figure 22.

The only difference between Figures 21 and 22 is in the position of BRIDGEWATER. In Figure 21, BRIDGEWATER is the last extant manuscript on one of the branches descending from [CRANE⁵]; in Figure 22, it is the last extant manuscript on the other branch descending from [CRANE⁵]. As a result, in 2.2 MIDDLETONᵀ is alone on a separate branch descending from [KING'S MEN³] through the single intermediary of [CRANE⁵]. This helps explain the paucity of shared errors in MIDDLETONᵀ. In the 648 lines that precede 2.2, MIDDLETONᵀ contains nine shared errors (one every 72 lines); in the 457 lines of Act Three, it contains twelve (one every 32 lines). In-between, in 2.2, it contains only a single shared error (one every 265 lines)—and that single error is the apparently mistaken singular at 2.2.33, shared by all extant texts of the scene, and therefore presumably present in the playbook itself.

4.2.81.1 *Enter Fat Bishop*] not in CRANE[3]. ROSENBACH[A] and MIDDLETON[T] mistakenly place this entrance one manuscript line too late.

Why should six mid-scene entrances be misplaced in multiple NON-CRANE texts? Why should another six mid-scene entrances be omitted entirely in multiple NON-CRANE texts? Entrances are absolutely necessary, both for performance and for reading. Moreover, the distribution of missing and misplaced entrances is not random. In the first three scenes of the play, ROSENBACH does not omit or misplace any mid-scene entrances, or any necessary mid-scene stage direction. Since we already know that ROSENBACH is embedded among the extant CRANE texts for those very scenes, it makes perfect sense that it would not be affected by a pattern that affects the other NON-CRANE texts in those scenes. The first affected mid-scene entrance in ROSENBACH occurs at 2.2.81.1-6, and ROSENBACH examples then occur repeatedly till the end of the play. Again, this fits the stemmatic patterns we have already observed: in 2.2, ROSENBACH becomes an integral part of the NON-CRANE set, and remains so for all the remaining scenes.

What mechanism could account for so many missing and misplaced mid-scene stage directions? Simple sloppiness does not provide a convincing answer. By 1624–5 Middleton had been writing plays professionally for more than twenty years, and the provision of entrances must have become pretty routine. Middleton was obviously deeply involved in the production of the NON-CRANE texts, and must have been responsible for all or part of several of the lost intermediate texts. It is hard to believe that he was personally responsible for omitting or misplacing so many necessary entrances. The quality of MIDDLETON[T] does not begin to deteriorate until the beginning of Act Four, but in the first three Acts eight of the examples on the foregoing lists include MIDDLETON[T]. Finally, if sloppiness were the cause, it should affect entrances at the beginning of scenes, not just in the middle.

If the explanation is not simple carelessness, then it must be stemmatic. As noted above, the distribution of such errors mirrors the stemma, and suggests that their source was a text later than ROSENBACH in the first three scenes of the play, but earlier than ROSENBACH thereafter. In other words, the source of the errors seems to have been either [CRANE[5]] or [PRE-NON-CRANE]. Of these two possibilities, one provides an immediate explanation for the problem. When Crane massed entrances at the beginning of a scene—as he did in CRANE[3]—he produced a text with few if any mid-scene stage directions. Although the only extant example of such a text of *A Game at Chess* is CRANE[3], Crane did not limit that formal device to abridgements: it appears also in the 1623 editions of Webster's *Duchess of Malfi* and Shakespeare's *The Two Gentlemen of Verona*, *The Merry Wives of Windsor* and *The Winter's Tale*, all apparently printed from Crane transcripts. [CRANE[5]] would have been the last of the known or inferred CRANE manuscripts. Or, to put it another way: [CRANE[5]] would have been

the last known Crane transcript descended from [KING'S MEN[3]], just as CRANE[3] is the last known Crane transcript descended from the other branch of the post-performance stemma. It is therefore entirely possible that [CRANE[5]] used the same system of massed entrance directions found in CRANE[3]. If so, then the NON-CRANE texts descended from [CRANE[5]] would have had to re-insert entrance directions in mid-scene. In these circumstances, it would have been particularly easy for them to omit mid-scene directions, or to insert them in the wrong place.

In the preceding lists, I have indicated that nine entrances are 'not in CRANE[3]'. Strictly speaking, those directions are present in CRANE[3], but included at the beginning of the relevant scene; they are not present *at the particular point in the text* that dramatic and narrative logic requires. Since this systematic repositioning of stage directions is clearly intentional, and since Crane does provide the required information about who enters in each scene, in the filtered list of shared errors in Appendix D I have not counted any of those entrance directions as an error shared by CRANE[3] with more than one NON-CRANE text. Clearly, those missing entrance directions do not provide reliable evidence of a close stemmatic connection between CRANE[3] and the NON-CRANE texts. Like Howard-Hill and Nascimento, I place CRANE[3] in a position where it could have had no direct stemmatic connection with any NON-CRANE text. But although these errors do not at all indicate a direct connection with CRANE[3], they do very strongly suggest that the NON-CRANE texts descend from a manuscript which, like CRANE[3], did not place mid-scene entrances at the point in the text where they should occur. In other words, these errors do not establish a link with a particular *manuscript*, but instead establish a link with a particular *form* of manuscript: a manuscript with massed entrances. Since Crane is the only scribe or author known to produce theatrical manuscripts of that kind, and since we have already been forced to postulate the existence of the lost late manuscript [CRANE[5]], it seems reasonable to explain these missing and misplaced entrances as evidence that [CRANE[5]] resembled CRANE[3] in its treatment of entrance directions.

Notice that I am proposing resemblance, not identity. Crane would have been influenced, in a general way, by the fact that he had already prepared one such manuscript of *A Game at Chess*. But he could not have used CRANE[3] as a direct model for [CRANE[5]]—even if it had still been accessible—because CRANE[3] reproduced an abridged text, and [CRANE[5]] must have contained an unabridged text. Thus, the fact that CRANE[3] included, anomalously, the mid-scene entrance at Induction.52.1–2 does not mean that he also included it in [CRANE[5]]. Likewise, the missing music cue at Induction.52.1 is typical of Crane generally; he might well have omitted it in [CRANE[5]], whether or not he included the associated entrance direction.

If this line of reasoning is correct, then for the first three scenes of the play [CRANE[5]] must have stood between

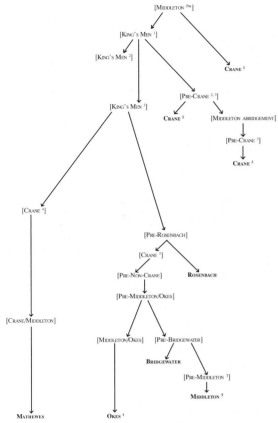

Figure 23. Draft Visualization of the Stemma of
Transmission for Prologue, Induction, 1.1, and 2.1.

[CRANE⁴] as an ancestor of OKES (as Figure 8 assumed). The earlier assumption cannot be correct. ROSENBACH and OKES share four unique errors in the first three scenes of the play; OKES and CRANE/MATHEWES share only one; hence, as in Figure 23, OKES must be closer to ROSENBACH than it is to [CRANE⁴]. Likewise, Figure 8 imagined [CRANE⁴] as an intermediary between ROSENBACH and OKES. But ROSENBACH's four errors shared with OKES contrast with its only two errors shared with CRANE/MATHEWES; again, this indicates that, as Figure 23 proposes, ROSENBACH is closer to OKES than it is to [CRANE⁴].

The first three scenes of ROSENBACH contain only eight shared errors; Figure 23 better accounts for six of those eight (the four unique errors it shares with OKES and the two unique errors it shares with [CRANE⁴]). The two remaining errors are shared with two texts, not one: one linking it to CRANE²,³, the other linking it to CRANE²,⁴. Both those errors can be explained through ROSENBACH's immediate relationship, in Figure 23, with [KING'S MEN³]. Moreover, ROSENBACH's intermediate position, in these scenes, between the CRANE texts and the other three NON-CRANE texts explains why it shares exactly half its errors with CRANE texts and half with NON-CRANE texts.

Let us assume, for the moment, that Figure 23 is correct, and that Figure 22 is also correct. If so, then two things changed in the stemmatic relationships of the extant texts between the end of 2.1 and the beginning of 2.2. First, the copy-text for [PRE-ROSENBACH] changed: for the first three scenes, it was copied from [KING'S MEN³], but in 2.2 it began to be copied from [PRE-NON-CRANE]. Secondly, the copy-text for [PRE-MIDDLETONᵀ] changed: for the first three scenes, it was copied from [PRE-BRIDGEWATER], but in 2.2 it began to be copied from [CRANE⁵]. These changes of copy-text happened, apparently, independently of one another, in the sense that the change in the copy-text for [PRE-ROSENBACH] does not seem to have required the change in the copy-text for [PRE-MIDDLETONᵀ]. But although stemmatically unrelated, the two changes might not have been entirely random, if we assume that one of the people involved in preparing copy-text for one of these manuscripts was also involved in preparing copy-text for the other. In each case, someone apparently decided to divide the copy-text at the beginning of 2.2; historically, it might have been the same someone. Middleton himself, for instance.

Nascimento and Howard-Hill recognized that the copy-text for ROSENBACH changed at the beginning of 2.2, but they did not recognize that the copy-text for MIDDLETONᵀ also changed. Indeed, their procedures took for granted the homogeneity of MIDDLETONᵀ. Because they evaluated all other texts in terms of their distance from MIDDLETONᵀ, almost by definition they could not see changes in the copy-text for that autograph text. But the evidence for a stemmatic change here in the immediate antecedent(s) of MIDDLETONᵀ is varied and overwhelming.[191]

ROSENBACH and the other three extant NON-CRANE texts, and from 2.2 to the end of the play [CRANE⁵] must have stood between all the extant NON-CRANE texts and all the extant CRANE texts. In the light of these arguments, we can modify Figure 8, to produce a more convincing stemma for the first three scenes of the play (Figure 23).

Figure 23 differs from Figure 8 in two important respects. First of all, it reflects the final version of the top of the stemma of transmission for the whole play, visualized in Figure 12. As a result, ROSENBACH in these first scenes still descends directly from [KING'S MEN³], but it no longer shares that origin with CRANE²,³. As a result, [PRE-ROSENBACH] can be closely connected to [CRANE⁴] without being the immediate ancestor of that text; instead, both [PRE-ROSENBACH] and [CRANE⁴] could be separate descendants of [KING'S MEN³]. In this scenario, ROSENBACH is still embedded among the CRANE texts, because the only link between the four extant CRANE texts and the three other extant NON-CRANE texts necessarily passes through [PRE-ROSENBACH].

Secondly, as a consequence of this change at the very top of the stemma, Figure 23 need no longer identify

[191] See the conclusion of Sec. XIX: 'In the 648 lines up to the end of 2.1, 100% of the shared errors in MIDDLETONᵀ can be explained through a stemmatic relationship

I have already discussed, in considerable detail, the distribution of shared errors in Act Three. But we can now examine shared errors in the last three Acts globally. First, let's look at the twelve patterns of error individually, beginning with those that might link MIDDLETON[T] to BRIDGEWATER.

Table of Shared Errors in MIDDLETON[T], 3.1.0-Epilogue
13. BRIDGEWATER: 3.2.38-40, 5.2.38, 5.2.77, 5.2.114

The example at 3.2.38-40 has been included as a shared error, because BRIDGEWATER and MIDDLETON[T] both have a mistaken line division after 'with'. But in fact it is not clear from the physical layout on the page that MIDDLETON[T] intends the lines to be interpreted as verse. That single line division is one of only two shared variants between BRIDGEWATER and MIDDLETON[T] in the second half of Act Three, in the area of text covered by Figure 19 (from 3.1.318 to the end of Act Three). The other shared variant is not an exact match, either (3.1.375). By contrast, the three examples of this pattern in Act Five are clearly errors, as are the three examples in the first three scenes.

31. BRIDGEWATER-ROSENBACH: 11 (3.1.155.1-5.3.178.1)

As noted above (Sec. XXIII), the misplaced stage direction at 3.1.155.1 is perhaps better interpreted as a paired error, BRIDGEWATER-ROSENBACH, because MIDDLETON[T] misplaces it differently. Exactly the same is true of 3.1.392.1. If those examples are interpreted strictly, that would leave no examples in Act Three, four examples in Act Four, and five examples in Act Five.

32. BRIDGEWATER-OKES: 3 (3.1.44, [3.1.48], 4.1.93.1)

These are all earlier than the nine reliable examples of the previous pattern. In the 648 lines of the first three scenes this pattern appears at least eight times. It is completely absent from the last 707 lines of the play (Figures 5 and 6). As I noted above (Sec. XXIV), the misplaced speech prefix at 3.1.48 is not present at all in BRIDGEWATER[B]; the prefix, and the corresponding speech rules, were added by the pencil corrector. The manuscript source consulted by the pencil corrector (BRIDGEWATER[C]) need not have been the same manuscript used for the original transcription produced by Scribe B. Consequently, this error might well not have been shared by MIDDLETON[T] with [PRE-BRIDGEWATER].[192]

40. BRIDGEWATER-ROSENBACH-OKES: 2 (5.1.0.4-5, 5.3.178.1-2)

These two stage direction errors in Act Five are shared by all NON-CRANE texts.

51. BRIDGEWATER-ROSENBACH-CRANE[2,3,4]: 1 (5.3.162.1)

The music cue appears only in CRANE[I] and OKES, but is differently worded and positioned in the two texts, indicating that the restoration in OKES almost certainly results from authorial transference. But that authorial recovery must have been present in the lost [MIDDLETON/OKES], which

did not pass readings to any other manuscript; it apparently was not present in [PRE-MIDDLETON/OKES], which linked OKES to the other NON-CRANE texts. Consequently, this variant tells us nothing about the stemmatic relationships of MIDDLETON[T], beyond the fact that it is a careless transcription which has inherited a CRANE error.

56. BRIDGEWATER-ROSENBACH-OKES-CRANE[2,3,4]: 1 (3.1.175.1)

Like the preceding pattern, this one demonstrates only that MIDDLETON[T] belongs stemmatically among manuscripts later than CRANE[I].

34. BRIDGEWATER-ROSENBACH-[CRANE[4]]: 1 (3.1.115.1)

The 404 lines of Act Five contain eleven of these nineteen potential links with BRIDGEWATER (58%), and all three of the reliable unique links to BRIDGEWATER. By contrast, there are only eight such shared errors in the 579 lines from the beginning of 2.2 till 4.1.94—and four of those eight are, for different reasons, dubious. If we remove those four, Act Five (with only 37% of the lines after 2.1) would contain 73% of the potential BRIDGEWATER links, and 100% of the unique links.

We can now examine, in the same way, the five patterns of shared error from Acts Three, Four, and Five that link MIDDLETON[T] to texts other than BRIDGEWATER. None of these patterns occurs in the first three scenes.

9. ROSENBACH: 2 (4.2.81.1, 4.2.107-8)

Both occur in the section of the text covered by Figure 6, which contains no links with BRIDGEWATER except four errors shared by MIDDLETON[T] with both BRIDGEWATER and ROSENBACH. This pattern strongly suggests that Pattern 31, above, should be interpreted in this area of the text as evidence of MIDDLETON[T]'s proximity to ROSENBACH, not BRIDGEWATER.

10. OKES: 2 (3.1.33, 3.1.75)

Both occur in the section of the text covered by Figure 21.

23. [CRANE[4]]-ROSENBACH: 1 (3.1.154-5)
33. CRANE[2,4]-OKES: 1 (5.3.19-20)
41. CRANE[2,3,4]: 3 (3.1.262.1, 4.3.0.1, 5.1.0.3-4)

Of these nine shared errors, only two (22%) occur in Act Five. Thus, eleven of the thirteen shared errors in Act Five of MIDDLETON[T] (85%) can be explained through its close association with BRIDGEWATER. One of the two exceptions,

with BRIDGEWATER. By contrast, in the 348 lines between the end of 2.2 and the beginning of 3.2, a connection to BRIDGEWATER can explain only 56% of the shared errors in MIDDLETON[T]. The same percentage could be explained through a connection to OKES.'

[192] At 4.1.93.1 only ROSENBACH fully spells out the correct reading 'Exeunt'. The shared error is simply an agreement in misinterpreting the ambiguous 'Ex[t]' of the CRANE tradition. The error therefore probably originated in [PRE-NON-CRANE]—that is, in the first NON-CRANE text confronted with the ambiguous abbreviation. The error might been copied by all the NON-CRANE texts, including [PRE-ROSENBACH], and independently corrected by ROSENBACH[A]. In this case, MIDDLETON[T] presumably did share the error with [PRE-BRIDGEWATER], but might well have shared it with all the NON-CRANE texts except ROSENBACH (and possibly the autograph [PRE-ROSENBACH]).

at 5.3.19-20, might have been present in [PRE-BRIDGE-WATER], but corrected in the autograph text of that scene in BRIDGEWATER itself. If we discount that example, as the result of autograph transference, then eleven of the twelve shared errors in Act Five (92%) could result from MIDDLETON[T]'s close connection to [PRE-BRIDGEWATER]. This approaches the figures for the first three scenes: in the first three scenes and the last three, together accounting for 1052 lines, 24 of the 25 shared errors in MIDDLE-TON[T] can be explained through a direct connection with [PRE-BRIDGEWATER]—and six of those errors *require* such a connection. Moreover, the single exception (at 5.1.0.3-4) might well be due to independent sloppiness or hurry on Middleton's part; Middleton's accuracy as a copyist had begun dropping in Act Four, he had just omitted much of 4.4, and in 5.1 itself would omit several lines of dialogue. He was thus perfectly capable, at that moment, of independently omitting part of a stage direction. Thus, the evidence of shared errors provides strong and consistent support for an exceptionally close stemmatic connection between MIDDLETON[T] and [PRE-BRIDGEWATER] at the beginning and end of the play.

The strength of that evidence at the beginning and end of the play emphasizes, by contrast, its weakness in the middle scenes. Of the fifteen shared errors in the middle, only eight (53%) can *possibly* be attributed to a link with BRIDGEWATER. If we limit ourselves to reliable examples, *none* of the eleven secure shared errors *requires* a connect to BRIDGEWATER, which at best could potentially account for only four out of eleven examples (36%). That proportion contrasts remarkably with the ratio in the first three scenes (100%) or the last three (92%).

Another way to look at this evidence is through unique pairs. All the reliable examples of errors uniquely shared with BRIDGEWATER occur in the first three and last three scenes. All the reliable examples of errors uniquely shared with ROSENBACH occur in Act Four; all the unique pairings with OKES occur in Act Three.

The distribution of shared errors thus overwhelmingly indicates a stemmatic discontinuity in the copy-text for MIDDLETON[T], distinguishing the middle scenes of the play from its first three and last three scenes. The evidence of shared errors cannot tell us anything about the copy-text for 2.2, because BRIDGEWATER is not available for most of that scene, and not available for the only shared error in that scene (shared by all extant texts of the revised version of the play). That shared-error evidence has already been supplemented by 'Crane Plus One' variants (the most significant five-member set of variants) and 'NON--CRANE Plus CRANE[1,4]' (the most significant six-member set of variants). That evidence can now be expanded by examining all variants that MIDDLETON[T] shares with one, two, or three other texts.

Variants Shared by MIDDLETON[T] with One Other Text
BRIDGEWATER 43 (15 before 2.2, 14 in Act Five)
CRANE[1] 23 (evenly distributed)
OKES 19

ROSENBACH 16 (none before 2.2)
[CRANE[4]] 7
CRANE[2] 2
CRANE[3] 1

This table makes it clear that MIDDLETON[T]'s relationship with BRIDGEWATER and ROSENBACH changes at 2.2, and again in Act Five. MIDDLETON[T] is closer to the other three NON-CRANE texts than to any CRANE text except CRANE[1], and the high total of randomly distributed agreements with CRANE[1] exemplifies authorial transference, in this case the autograph return to original readings. This pattern of paired variants supports our current visualizations of the stemma for MIDDLETON[T] throughout the play.

Variants Shared by MIDDLETON[T] with Two Other Texts
BRIDGEWATER-OKES 54 (41 before 2.2; 4 in Act Five)
BRIDGEWATER-ROSENBACH 40 (1 before 2.2; 24 in Act Five)
OKES-ROSENBACH 11 (10 in 2.2)
BRIDGEWATER-[CRANE[4]] 7
CRANE[1,4] 7
CRANE[2,3] 6
CRANE[2,4] 5 (all in 2.2-3.1.411)
CRANE[1], BRIDGEWATER 5 (3 before 2.2)
CRANE[1], ROSENBACH 5
CRANE[2], BRIDGEWATER 4
CRANE[4], ROSENBACH 3
CRANE[4], OKES 3
CRANE[1,2] 2
CRANE[3,4] 1
CRANE[3], BRIDGEWATER 1

* * *

BRIDGEWATER 111 (48 before 2.2, 33 in Act Five)
OKES 68 (none between 4.1.93.1 and 5.2.56)
ROSENBACH 59 (2 before 2.2)
[CRANE[4]] 26
CRANE[1] 19
CRANE[2] 12
CRANE[3] 8

Again, both parts of this table demonstrate that MID-DLETON[T]'s relationship with BRIDGEWATER and ROSENBACH changes at 2.2 and again in Act Five; but it also indicates a change in its relationship to OKES in Act Four. The high final total for BRIDGEWATER actually originates in two contrasting triplets, with the first three scenes of the play in dramatic contrast to the last three scenes. A third triplet completely dominates 2.2. In three-member variant sets, MIDDLETON[T] is even more clearly linked to the other NON-CRANE texts, overall. CRANE[1] has fallen from second to fifth place, since its presence now depends not on a lone autograph retrieval but on its appearance in autograph and one other text. The highest triplet total involving CRANE[1] here (7) almost entirely depends (5 of 7 examples) on passages completely absent from CRANE[2,3]. That pattern artificially inflates the totals for both CRANE[1] and [CRANE[4]]; the highest alternative total for [CRANE[4]] is similarly inflated by passages absent from CRANE³ and/or CRANE¹. In other words, the particular distribution of three-members sets involving two Crane texts is almost entirely due to absent text in one or more of the CRANE witnesses, and hence not reliable as evidence of strong links to particular CRANE texts.

There are 25 separate patterns of four-member variant sets that include MIDDLETON^T.[193] I list below only those patterns that occur more than ten times.

NON-CRANE 57 (17 in Act Five)
* * *

CRANE¹–ROSENBACH–BRIDGEWATER 20 (1 before 3.1, 12 in Act Five)
* * *

CRANE¹–BRIDGEWATER–OKES 13 (7 before 2.2, 5 in Act Five)
* * *

Including BRIDGEWATER–ROSENBACH 26 (25 after 2.1)
Including BRIDGEWATER–OKES 19 (10 before 2.2)
Including ROSENBACH–OKES 15 (14 before 3.1.188)
* * *

Including BRIDGEWATER 113
Including ROSENBACH 107
Including OKES 101
Including CRANE¹ 59
Including [CRANE⁴] 47
Including CRANE² 29
Including CRANE³ 21

Once again, MIDDLETON^T is closest to the other NON-CRANE texts. As we have already noted, many of the NON-CRANE variants reflect Middleton's preferences over those of CRANE, and testify to the frequent involvement of the author in preparation of the extant and lost NON-CRANE texts. The relative frequency of four-member variant sets that include both MIDDLETON^T and CRANE¹ suggests the same pattern, with authorial transference a factor repeatedly in the NON-CRANE texts. Notably— and in accordance with our current visualizations of the stemma—in all three tables CRANE³ is farthest away, and CRANE² occupies the penultimate position. In all three, BRIDGEWATER has the highest total.

Although they did not display it in this form, this is the sort of evidence that persuaded Nascimento and Howard-Hill that BRIDGEWATER was closest to MIDDLETON^T throughout, and that CRANE^{2,3} were farthest away. However, they misinterpreted the distance of CRANE^{2,3} because they assumed that MIDDLETON^T was an early text representing 'undiluted Middleton'. Moreover, the overall proximity of BRIDGEWATER and MIDDLETON^T does not prove that either text is stemmatically homogeneous, in relation to each other or to other texts. The overall numbers are useful in a general sort of way, in establishing groups of texts (like 'Non-Crane'), but for stemmatic purposes the distribution of variants (like the distribution of errors) is more important than gross totals. The distribution of MIDDLETON^T variants and errors is not homogeneous.

Like all the other extant NON-CRANE texts, MIDDLETON^T apparently derives from divided copy-text. The first such division occurs at the beginning of 2.2. Thus, it was not only ROSENBACH that divided its copy-text at that point. Nascimento and Howard-Hill assumed that the division of copy-text in ROSENBACH at that point occurred because CRANE¹, or some other text of Middleton's first draft of the play, did not contain the beginning of 2.2. But clearly that explanation cannot apply to MIDDLETON^T. Nascimento and Howard-Hill could not see the similarity of the problem in ROSENBACH and MIDDLETON^T because their formula for collating the texts presupposed the centrality, authority, and homogeneity of MIDDLETON^T. Once we escape the circularity of such reasoning, we can begin to see a larger pattern in the division of copy-text.

One ambiguity remains. Did the discontinuity in the underlying copy-text, which the evidence clearly requires, occur in the production of MIDDLETON^T itself, or in the production of [PRE-MIDDLETON^T]?

XXVIII. The Sequencing of Divided Copy-text in the NON-CRANE Texts

Up to this point, my stemmata have presupposed the existence of all the various lost NON-CRANE manuscripts identified as potential physical and historical entities in Section I, including [MIDDLETON/OKES], [PRE-ROSENBACH], [PRE-BRIDGEWATER], and [PRE-MIDDLETON^T].[194] To that initial list I have added, in the course of my analysis of the NON-CRANE set, four additional lost manuscripts: [CRANE⁵], [PRE-NON-CRANE], [PRE-MIDDLETON/OKES], and [PRE-ROSENBACH/BRIDGEWATER].[195] It is now time to apply Occam's parsimonious razor to this expanding undergrowth, and try to determine whether all these lost manuscripts are necessary to the stemmata. It may be that, on occasion, we are giving two different names to a single lost manuscript.

This problem of potential duplication is directly related to the problem of divided copy-texts, because all these lost manuscripts have been invoked in order to determine the immediate or intermediate ancestors of the extant texts. The proliferation of lost entities is concentrated among and between the NON-CRANE texts, where the copy-text for one manuscript seems sometimes, and perhaps all the time, to have been a sequential combination of two or more manuscripts. Up to this point, I have looked at the problems of

[193] I do not include cases where only five texts are available for the passage in question: for instance, since CRANE¹ and BRIDGEWATER are both missing for large chunks of 2.2, whenever CRANE³ abridges a passage there are only five possible witnesses, which means that variants apparently linking four witnesses are, in fact, variants shared by all extant texts of the passage except one, which usually contains an obvious error. Such variants—what Salemans calls 'Category 1'—are generally of no stemmatic value.
[194] All four lost entities were also independently identified by Howard-Hill, though he sometimes gives them different names. He does not make it clear whether 'Revision' was a physical entity, but he does acknowledge that MIDDLETON^T must have descended from something now lost. (See Figure 1.)
[195] Howard-Hill also presupposed the existence of the last two of these four. He does not recognize the existence of [CRANE⁵] or [PRE-NON-CRANE], because in his stemma the only common ancestor shared by the four NON-CRANE texts was 'Middleton's Foul Papers' (See Figure 1.)

divided copy-text one discontinuity at a time, without attempting to link the various discontinuities to one another. But we must now reconsider those earlier conjectures by placing each discontinuity within the global historical and material context of the production of all these NON-CRANE texts.

Consider as an initial example the stemmatic discontinuity in MIDDLETON[T] between 2.1 and 2.2, which was documented at the end of the preceding section. That discontinuity can be interpreted in more than one way, stemmatically. In Figures 22 and 23, the change in the antecedent of MIDDLETON[T] is visualized as a change in the source of [PRE-MIDDLETON[T]]. If we excerpt from those larger flow-charts only the local change of copy-text, we can see that we have imagined something like Figure 24.

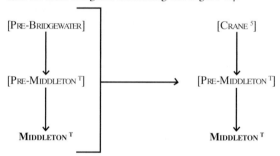

Figure 24. Visualization of the change of copy-text
between 2.1 and 2.2, hitherto assumed.

This is certainly a possible interpretation of the data. It leaves the copy-text for MIDDLETON[T] itself unchanged: behind MIDDLETON[T] lies a single manuscript, which itself derived from two different manuscripts. But the nature of the data does not distinguish, in such cases, between a change in the copy-text for MIDDLETON[T] and a change in the copy-text for [PRE-MIDDLETON[T]]. Hence, the same data could be interpreted as evidence for Figure 25.

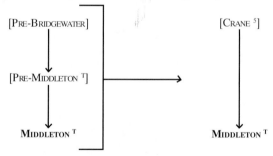

Figure 25. First alternative visualization of the
change of copy-text between 2.1 and 2.2.

In this scenario, the copy-text for the lost manuscript [PRE-MIDDLETON[T]] would have remained the same, but the copy-text for MIDDLETON[T] itself would have changed from [PRE-MIDDLETON[T]] to [CRANE5]. However, the same data could also be interpreted as evidence for Figure 26.

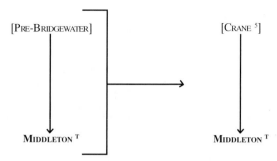

Figure 26. Second alternative visualization of
the change of copy-text between 2.1 and 2.2.

In this scenario, [PRE-MIDDLETON[T]] need never have existed at all; MIDDLETON[T] could have been copied directly from parts of two different manuscripts, using one and then the other. That possibility, in turn, opens up yet another alternative visualization of the genealogical data.

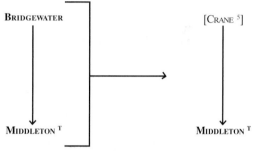

Figure 27. Third alternative visualization of
the change of copy-text between 2.1 and 2.2.

At the outset of this investigation, we defined BRIDGEWATER as a dead-end text, one that could not be the direct ancestor of any other extant text. That is certainly true of BRIDGEWATER *as a whole*; given its omission of most of 2.2, it could not have served as the copy-text for any other extant text. But the strongest evidence for MIDDLETON[T]'s relationship with BRIDGEWATER is concentrated in the play's first three scenes, where there are no major omissions. Moreover, as Nascimento concluded, and as my own analysis has confirmed, Middleton was most attentive as a scribe at the beginning of the manuscript: only one unique MIDDLETON[T] error is present in the first three scenes, and those scenes do not contain any examples of unique extrametrical variants. Consequently, we might reasonably argue that in the first three scenes Middleton was alert enough, as a copyist and author, to have rectified almost all errors in BRIDGEWATER. The difference between the hypothesis visualized in Figure 27 and the alternatives (visualized in Figures 24, 25, and 26) is that MIDDLETON[T] would have needed to correct *all* unique variants in BRIDGEWATER. (Variants that appear in BRIDGEWATER and another text presumably also appeared in [PRE-BRIDGEWATER], and hence would have needed to be corrected in any hypothesis.) Not counting readings corrected in

BRIDGEWATER itself, there are 48 unique variants in the first three scenes, which Middleton would have needed to spot and correct. These 48 corrections would be required by Figure 27 alone; they are in addition to the corrections required by the alternative stemmata. Some of the unique BRIDGEWATER readings, like 'ant' for 'and' at Induction.23, might easily be corrected by almost any scribe; others, like the omitted line at Induction.25–6 and the omitted phrase at 1.1.35, could not have been corrected by any ordinary scribe, but might have been restored by the author. But eleven of the unique BRIDGEWATER readings are perfectly sensible—and, indeed, perfectly Middletonian.[196] Middleton *might* have restored the original readings in those eleven cases, but nothing about the context or the idiom would have disturbed him. Since Middleton reverted to unique CRANE[1] readings only three times in these three scenes, I am not persuaded he would have restored eleven original readings in those same scenes, when the BRIDGEWATER alternative was sensible and Middletonian. Likewise, I have doubts about adding 48 readings to the number that Middleton needed to alter in these first three scenes. Therefore, like previous investigators I will continue to assume that MIDDLETON[T] derives from a lost manuscript here, rather than being copied directly from BRIDGEWATER. But I know of no infallible mathematical or logical proof that would determine for us how many errors or variants an author—or *this* author—might correct in copying his own text from a corrupt manuscript. We must rely, here as elsewhere, on editorial judgement. My own editorial judgement rules out Figure 27.

If we accept the evidence of the preceding paragraph, then [PRE-BRIDGEWATER] must have existed as a physical entity. Certainly, it must have existed in Act Five (Figure 28).

Because 5.2 and 5.3 are autograph in BRIDGEWATER, it has been obvious to all scholars that MIDDLETON[T] cannot derive directly from BRIDGEWATER in those scenes. Hence, the close stemmatic relationship between the two extant texts must be mediated through a text earlier than BRIDGEWATER, which shares readings with MIDDLETON[T] and other NON-CRANE texts. Our proof of the Three-Manuscript hypothesis (Sec. XVIII) has already demonstrated that [PRE-BRIDGEWATER] must have existed for the second half of the play, in order to explain the relationship of BRIDGEWATER to ROSENBACH. We can now say that [PRE-BRIDGEWATER] is also necessary, in Act Five, to explain the relationship of BRIDGEWATER to MIDDLETON[T]. Thus [PRE-BRIDGEWATER] certainly existed for the last three scenes. That physical entity presumably also contained the first three scenes. The most economical hypothesis would be that [PRE-BRIDGEWATER] is a close stemmatic ancestor of MIDDLETON[T] in both sets of scenes. This conclusion rules out the stemmata visualized in Figures 25, 26, and 27.

It also seems reasonable to assume that [PRE-MIDDLE-TON[T]] existed as a physical entity. Otherwise, the stemmatic evidence visualized in Figures 18, 19, 21, and 22 would force us to assume that, in 2.2, the whole of Act

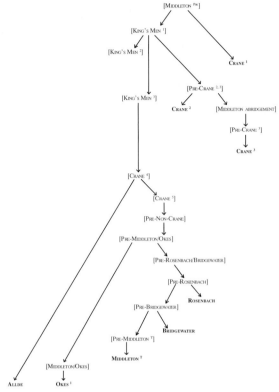

Figure 28. Draft Visualization of the Stemma for Act Five. This replaces Figure 5.

Three, and the first hundred or so lines of 4.1, MIDDLE-TON[T] was a direct copy of a Crane transcript—indeed, the very last Crane transcript, presumably containing more of Crane's own preferences than any extant CRANE text. Although the autograph text preserves some Crane features, it contains only a small fraction of the number preserved in MATHEWES/ALLDE, which was apparently printed from an authorial copy of a Crane transcript. Moreover, although there is stemmatic evidence that those middle scenes derive from different copy-text than the beginning and ending scenes, we would expect much more difference in their spelling and punctuation if the middle scenes were copied directly from a late CRANE transcript, in contrast to the late NON-CRANE manuscript which served as copy-text for the beginning and ending scenes. It makes much more sense to assume that at least one lost NON-CRANE manuscript intervened between [CRANE[5]] and MIDDLETON[T]. Hence, the lost manuscript that we have been conjecturally calling [PRE-MIDDLETON[T]] does seem to have existed, as a physical entity, in the middle scenes.

[196] See text notes at Induction.52 ('will'), 1.1.180, 1.1.238, 1.1.241, 1.1.287, 1.1.313, 2.1.3, 2.1.8.2, 2.1.18, 2.1.26, 2.1.147.

We thus have good evidence for the existence, as physical entities, of [PRE-BRIDGEWATER] for the first and final scenes, and of [PRE-MIDDLETON^T] for the middle scenes. But we do not have any clear evidence that [PRE-MIDDLE-TON^T] served as copy-text for MIDDLETON^T in the first three and last three scenes. For those scenes, the autograph manuscript could have been copied directly from [PRE--BRIDGEWATER]. The clear stemmatic change that occurs between 2.1 and 2.2 could have resulted from a change in the copy-text for MIDDLETON^T itself, rather than a change in the copy-text for [PRE-MIDDLETON^T] (Figure 29).

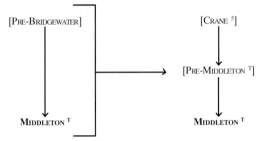

Figure 29. Final visualization of the change of copy-text for MIDDLETON^T between 2.1 and 2.2.

This solution in turn has implications for our understanding of what happens between Act Four and Act Five. Two different lost manuscripts seem to have been accessible while Middleton was producing his late autograph transcript. The lost manuscript that served as his copy-text for the first three scenes of the manuscript also served as his copy-text for the last three scenes. The simplest explanation for the stemmatic change that takes place in Act Five would therefore be to assume that it reverses the change visualized in Figure 29.

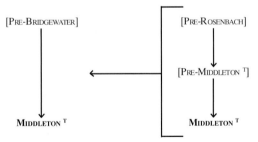

Figure 30. Final visualization of the change of copy-text for MIDDLETON^T between 4.4 and 5.1.

Figure 30 visualizes MIDDLETON^T's return, in the final Act, to the same manuscript that had served as copy-text for the first three scenes. Thus, we need assume only two changes in the copy-text for MIDDLETON^T itself: one that occurred between 2.1 and 2.2, another that occurred between 4.4 and 5.1. Both changes involved the same two late lost manuscripts, [PRE-BRIDGEWATER] and [PRE--MIDDLETON^T]. At 2.2, Middleton switched from one to the other; at 5.1, he switched back to the first. This second

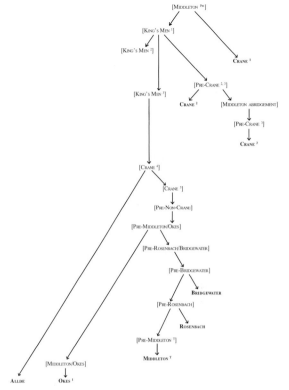

Figure 31. Draft Visualization of the Stemma for c.4.1.145 to 4.4.110.2. This replaces Figure 6.

change coincides—coincidentally or not—with a major disruption in MIDDLETON^T itself: the omission of the end of 4.4.

The only difference between Figure 29 and Figure 30, besides the change in the direction of the arrow, is the identity of the manuscript in the upper right corner. The lost [PRE-MIDDLETON^T] served as copy-text for the extant autograph manuscript from the beginning of 2.2 to the end of Act Four; but the copy-text for [PRE-MIDDLETON^T] itself changed during that interim. The change from [CRANE^5] to [PRE-ROSENBACH] has already been identified, in the difference between Figure 18 and Figure 28. But between the two stretches of text visualized in these two stemmata comes the stretch of text visualized in Figure 31.

Because [PRE-MIDDLETON^T] has not survived, and because it has no known extant descendants in the first three scenes and last three scenes of the play, we cannot tell what manuscripts served as its copy-text at the beginning and end of the play. But we can say that at least two manuscripts served as the copy-text for that lost NON-CRANE manuscript, just as two served as copy-text for MIDDLETON^T. The one known change of copy-text in

[PRE-MIDDLETON^T] occurred at some point between 4.1.130 and 4.1.145.

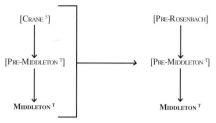

Figure 32. Draft visualization of the stemmatic change in MIDDLETON^T *c.*4.1.145.

There is no break in the dramatic structure at that point, just as there is no break in the dramatic structure between CRANE/MATHEWES and CRANE/ALLDE; hence, the break may have coincided with a page-break or quire--break in one of the lost manuscripts. Just as the divided copy-text for MIDDLETON^T involved two adjacent late manuscripts—[PRE-BRIDGEWATER] and [PRE-MIDDLETON^T]—so likewise the divided copy-text for [PRE-MIDDLETON^T] apparently involved two adjacent late manuscripts: [PRE--BRIDGEWATER] and [PRE-ROSENBACH].

Having identified the changes in the copy-text for MIDDLETON^T and [PRE-MIDDLETON^T], we are now positioned to attempt to do the same for [PRE-BRIDGEWATER], the other lost manuscript from which the autograph manuscript directly descends. Indeed, portions of two autograph manuscripts directly descend from it: the beginning and ending of MIDDLETON^T, and the last two scenes of BRIDGEWATER.

In the play's first three scenes (Figure 23), [PRE-BRIDGE-WATER] must have existed, and must have descended from [PRE-NON-CRANE] or from [PRE-MIDDLETON/OKES]—if there was indeed any difference between those two entities. BRIDGEWATER supplies less stemmatic evidence for 2.2 (Figure 22), because it uniquely omits most of the scene. But the available evidence links it strongly to [PRE-MIDDLETON/OKES], which by now is definitely stemmatically distinct from [PRE-NON-CRANE]. On the other hand, for 2.2 BRIDGE-WATER could, theoretically, have been copied directly from [PRE-MIDDLETON/OKES], without presuming the existence of an intermediary [PRE-BRIDGEWATER]. Nevertheless, it would be more economical to suppose that there was no change in the copy-text for BRIDGEWATER or [PRE-BRIDGEWATER] at this point; given the paucity of evidence, that also seems the safest assumption.

If so, then the copy-text for BRIDGEWATER remained the same for Acts One and Two: it was copied from [PRE-BRIDGEWATER], which was itself copied from [PRE--MIDDLETON/OKES]. But something did change, stemmatic-ally, at the beginning of Act Three, between Figure 22 and Figure 21. As with the change of copy-text in MIDDLETON^T between Act Four and Act Five, the change of copy--text in BRIDGEWATER^T between Act Two and Act Three coincides—coincidentally or not—with a major textual disruption, the omission of the end of 2.2.

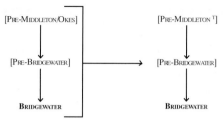

Figure 33. Draft visualization of the change of copy-text for BRIDGEWATER between 2.2 and 3.1.

Figure 33 resembles Figure 24: in both, the two bottom layers of the diagram are identical. In this case, we know that [PRE-BRIDGEWATER] must have existed for the left side of the diagram (in Acts One and Two). But we have no reliable evidence that [PRE-BRIDGEWATER] belongs on the *right* side of Figure 33. In the first three hundred or so lines of 3.1, BRIDGEWATER might be a direct descendant of [PRE-MIDDLETON^T]. Indeed, it would make sense to locate the change of copy-text in BRIDGEWATER itself, because that would best explain the attendant textual disruption.

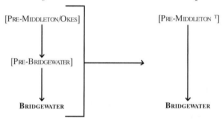

Figure 34. Draft visualization of the change of copy-text for BRIDGEWATER between 2.2 and 3.1.

Figure 34 identifies a change in the copy-text for BRIDGEWATER itself. We have no way of knowing what, if anything, happened in [PRE-BRIDGEWATER] at this point, because that manuscript is lost and has no known descendants for that part of the play. Indeed, if Figure 34 is correct, then from the break at 2.2.13 to 3.1.318 (a space of 570 lines) we do not know anything about [PRE-BRIDGEWATER].

When [PRE-BRIDGEWATER] again becomes stemmatically visible (Figure 19), it has clearly undergone a significant change.

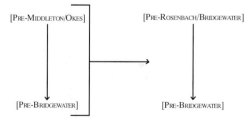

Figure 35. Draft visualization of the change of copy-text for [PRE-BRIDGEWATER] at some point between 2.2.13 and 3.1.318.

Within the area of the play covered by Figure 35, [PRE-MIDDLETON/OKES] and [PRE-NON-CRANE] are clearly separate physical and stemmatic entities. Consequently, the copy-text for [PRE-BRIDGEWATER] must have been divided at some point in those 570 lines. There is no reason to suppose that the change necessarily happened at 3.1.0.1 (the site of the change visualized in Figure 34), or that it happened at 3.1.318 (the site of the change visualized in Figure 36).

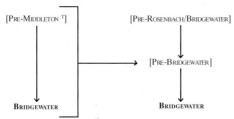

Figure 36. Draft visualization of the change of copy-text for BRIDGEWATER at *c*.3.1.318.

If Figures 34–36 are correct, then in the first four Acts of the play we can identify two different manuscripts that served as copy-text for BRIDGEWATER, and two different manuscripts that served as copy-text for [PRE-BRIDGEWATER]. The one stemmatic discontinuity in the lost manuscript occurred at some indeterminable point between 2.2.13 and 3.1.318. One discontinuity in the extant BRIDGEWATER itself occurred at the beginning of 3.1, and then another occurred at about 3.1.318, when BRIDGEWATER reverted to the same manuscript it had used in Acts One and Two. The apparent pattern of return to the initial manuscript in BRIDGEWATER resembles the one in MIDDLETON^T.

However, another stemmatic discontinuity occurs at the beginning of Act Five. BRIDGEWATER's ancestry for Act Five (Figure 28) differed from its ancestry for the end of Act Four (Figure 31).

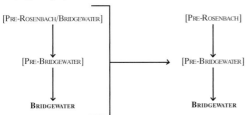

Figure 37. Draft visualization of the change of copy-text for BRIDGEWATER between 4.4 and 5.1.

Like Figures 28 and 31, Figure 37 places the change of copy-text in [PRE-BRIDGEWATER]. Alternatively, the change might have occurred in the preparation of BRIDGEWATER itself, as visualized in Figure 38.

In isolation, Figure 38 is more economical than Figure 36. But it has to be evaluated in the global context of Figure 28, which gives [PRE-BRIDGEWATER] two extant descendants in Act Five. Moreover, we have already revised Figure 28 once, by demonstrating that there is no need to assume the stemmatic influence in Act Five of

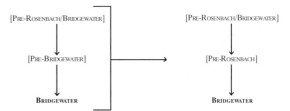

Figure 38. Alternative visualization of the change of copy-text for BRIDGEWATER between 4.4 and 5.1.

[PRE-MIDDLETON^T] (Figure 30). If we were to adopt Figure 38, then in Act Five three different manuscripts would have to be direct copies of [PRE-ROSENBACH]: ROSENBACH itself (Figure 28), BRIDGEWATER (as imagined in Figure 38), and the lost manuscript ancestor of MIDDLETON^T, which we previously identified as [PRE-BRIDGEWATER] (Figure 30). That is to say, the manuscript we are calling [PRE-BRIDGEWATER] on the left side of Figure 38 would, in Act Five, cease to be the direct ancestor of BRIDGEWATER, and instead become the direct ancestor of MIDDLETON^T (Figure 30).

The nomenclature is confusing here, because we initially identified the lost manuscripts in terms of their relationship to extant manuscripts, and we are now discovering that in a situation of shifting and divided copy-text those relationships do not remain stable. But the pattern envisaged would make sense: the same manuscript is divided between Act Four and Act Five, the earlier part is used as copy-text for BRIDGEWATER and the later part is used as copy-text for MIDDLETON^T. Two manuscripts can then be produced, simultaneously, from a single copy.

However, we have as yet no way of arbitrating between Figure 37 and 38. Figure 37 has the advantage that it would leave us with two changes of copy-text in [PRE-BRIDGEWATER] and two changes of copy-text in BRIDGEWATER. Figure 38 is more economical in itself, but it produces an asymmetrical pattern: one change of copy-text in [PRE-BRIDGEWATER], three changes of copy-text in BRIDGEWATER. Moreover, although Figure 38 elegantly interlocks with Figure 30, globally that combination does not eliminate a manuscript, since the two manuscripts we are calling [PRE-BRIDGEWATER] and [PRE-MIDDLETON^T] still apparently must have existed, in order to explain other aspects of the evidence in the play as a whole.

Whichever is correct, Figures 37 and 38 lead us from the problem of divided copy-text in BRIDGEWATER to the problem of divided copy-text in ROSENBACH. Indeed, one feature of the preceding stemmata for BRIDGEWATER that we have not yet properly considered is the role of the manuscript that connects it to ROSENBACH, the lost [PRE-ROSENBACH/BRIDGEWATER]. Section XVIII demonstrated that such a manuscript must have existed, and that it was fundamentally important to the transmission of the extant NON-CRANE manuscripts for the second half of the play. But before we can say more about it, we must first trace the evidence of divided copy in the other extant manuscript it most directly influenced, ROSENBACH.

As we have already seen, the copy-text for ROSENBACH dramatically changed at the beginning of 2.2.

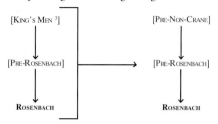

Figure 39. Draft visualization of the change of copy-text for ROSENBACH between 2.1 and 2.2.

Figure 39 identifies a division of copy-text in the lost precursor, but presumes continuity in the copy-text for ROSENBACH itself.

However, the difference between Figures 21–22 and Figure 19 demonstrates that another change of copy-text, in one manuscript or the other, must have occurred in the middle of Act Three.

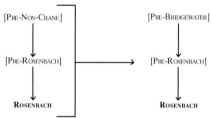

Figure 40. Draft visualization of the change of copy-text for ROSENBACH c.3.1.318.

Together, Figures 39 and 40 produce two divisions in the copy-text for [PRE-ROSENBACH], and none in the copy-text for ROSENBACH. Indeed, Figure 28 visualized yet another change in the copy-text for [PRE-ROSENBACH], and continuing homogeneity in the copy-text for ROSENBACH.

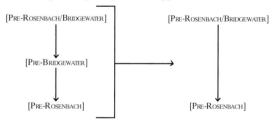

Figure 41. Draft visualization of the change of copy-text for ROSENBACH between Act Four and Act Five.

If all these stemmata (Figures 39, 40, 41) were correct, then parts of four different manuscripts would have served as copy-text for [PRE-ROSENBACH]—and hence all would have had to be available at approximately the same time: from the stemmatically early [KING'S MEN³] to the stemmatically medial [PRE-NON-CRANE] to the later [PRE--ROSENBACH/BRIDGEWATER] and the late [PRE-BRIDGEWATER]. This scenario also juxtaposes an exceptionally complicated

process of copying for [PRE-ROSENBACH] with an anomalously homogeneous process of copying for ROSENBACH itself.

It thus seems extremely likely that Figure 39, and/or Figure 40, and/or Figure 41, is incorrect. But how can we determine which, or how many, of the three is wrong, and whether they are wrong on the left side or the right? In both MIDDLETON^T and BRIDGEWATER the combination of autograph and of major disruptions in the extant texts could help us arbitrate between such alternatives. But ROSENBACH contains no major textual disruptions and no scenes in Middleton's own handwriting.

ROSENBACH does, however, have more than one scribe. One of the changes in the underlying copy-text for BRIDGE-WATER (Figure 34) coincides with a change of scribe (at the beginning of 3.1). Likewise, Figure 41 here coincides with the change, in ROSENBACH, from Scribe A to Scribe B. We might therefore conjecture that the change of scribe in ROSENBACH was associated with a change of copy-text for ROSENBACH itself.

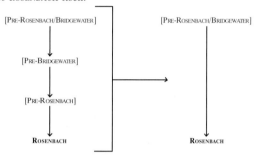

Figure 42. Alternative visualization of the change of copy-text for ROSENBACH between Act Four and Act Five.

But Figure 42 cannot be correct. Stemmatically, we cannot eliminate all the intermediate lost texts within the NON-CRANE group in Act Five. In Figure 38, we considered eliminating [PRE-BRIDGEWATER] from the stemma there; in Figure 30, we eliminated [PRE-MIDDLETON^T]. We cannot also eliminate [PRE-ROSENBACH]. Nevertheless, a change of copy-text at the beginning of Act Five could have occurred in the opposite direction.

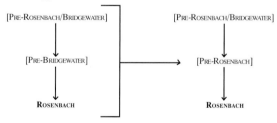

Figure 43. Alternative visualization of the change of copy-text for ROSENBACH between Act Four and Act Five.

Figure 43 proposes a change of copy-text in ROSENBACH that coincides with the change of scribe. It does so without creating a stemmatic tangle in Act Five. However, accepting Figure 43 would entail revising Figure 40.

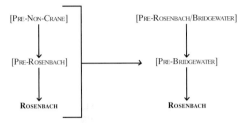

Figure 44. Alternative visualization of the
change of copy-text for ROSENBACH *c*.3.1.318.

The combination of Figures 44, 43, and 39 would explain the distribution of errors and variants in ROSENBACH more economically and logically than the combination of Figures 39, 40, and 41. In the new combination, ROSENBACH itself derives from only two manuscripts, the relatively late and apparently adjacent manuscripts [PRE-ROSENBACH] and [PRE-BRIDGEWATER]. The copy-text for ROSENBACH itself would have changed initially *c*.3.1.318, and then later would have reverted to the initial manuscript. This is the pattern of reversion we have already seen in both BRIDGEWATER and MIDDLETON[T].

Likewise, in the new combination the copy-text for [PRE-ROSENBACH] also changed twice. At the beginning of 2.2 the use of [KING'S MEN[3]] ended, and the use of [PRE-NON-CRANE] began. Between *c*.3.1.318 and 4.4.110.2 [PRE-ROSENBACH] becomes invisible to us, because it is not an ancestor of ROSENBACH, but somewhere during that stretch of the play its copy-text changed from [PRE-NON-CRANE] to [PRE-ROSENBACH/BRIDGEWATER]. In this scenario, the three lost manuscripts that apparently served as copy-texts for [PRE-ROSENBACH] are, as we would expect, all earlier than the two lost manuscripts that apparently served as copy-texts for ROSENBACH itself.

Before we proceed any further, it is worth summarizing the results of the foregoing complex analysis. We have, up to this point, not succeeded in eliminating any of the lost NON-CRANE manuscripts previously conjectured to exist. Instead, we have confirmed the separate material existence of [PRE-MIDDLETON[T]], [PRE-BRIDGEWATER], and [PRE-ROSENBACH]. The separate existence of [PRE-ROSENBACH/BRIDGEWATER] was already proven by the confirmation of the Three-Manuscript hypothesis (Section XVIII). What has emerged from this analysis is not a smaller number of lost manuscripts, but a regular pattern in the division of copy-text within the late NON-CRANE manuscripts [PRE-BRIDGEWATER], [PRE-MIDDLETON[T]], ROSENBACH, BRIDGEWATER, and MIDDLETON[T]. In the production of all these five manuscripts, the copy-text was apparently divided between two adjacent manuscripts. The copy-text for [PRE-ROSENBACH] was also divided, but unlike the others it seems to have been divided between three manuscripts, not two.

However, the use of three different manuscripts as copy-text for [PRE-ROSENBACH] itself depends on the distinction between [PRE-ROSENBACH/BRIDGEWATER] and other lost

NON-CRANE manuscripts. We know that [PRE-ROSENBACH/BRIDGEWATER] must have existed, but we know nothing about its stemmatic relationships before *c*.3.1.318. We do not know, in Act Five, whether [PRE-NON-CRANE] and [PRE-MIDDLETON/OKES] and [PRE-ROSENBACH/BRIDGEWATER] are all physically distinct entities. Stemmatically, the three adjacent ghosts cannot be distinguished in those three scenes (or the first three scenes). It would be most economical to suppose that two of the three are, in these scenes, simply different names for the same entity. This assumption would permit the conclusion that [PRE-ROSENBACH]—like all the other NON-CRANE texts examined so far—was divided between only two manuscripts.

What we have hitherto perceived as a change in the copy-text for [PRE-ROSENBACH] at 3.1.318 might instead be a change in the copy-text for [PRE-ROSENBACH/BRIDGEWATER]. In other words, perhaps the manuscript we have been calling [PRE-NON-CRANE] in Figures 21 and 22 is actually just another name for [PRE-ROSENBACH/BRIDGEWATER]. This assumption would have the advantage of integrating the first half of [PRE-ROSENBACH/BRIDGEWATER] into the sequence of transmission.

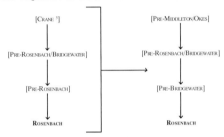

Figure 45. Draft visualization of the change
of copy-text for [PRE-ROSENBACH] in the
middle of Act Three (replacing Figure 40).

Figure 45 differs from all my previous conjectures about the divisions of copy-text in the NON-CRANE texts. Since all the manuscripts in Figure 45 are lost and adjacent, we have no direct physical evidence that Figure 45 correctly visualizes the relationships between them. Consequently, Figure 45 *depends upon the assumption* that the pattern of divided copy-text found in the other five late NON-CRANE manuscripts also operated in [PRE-ROSENBACH] and [PRE-ROSENBACH/BRIDGEWATER]. Figure 45 thus visualizes the extrapolation of a previous pattern. By contrast, the earlier stemmata representing changes of copy-text were all based upon the stemmatic and material evidence of extant texts.

Nevertheless, Figure 45 may be less arbitrary than at first appears. It addresses a problem with my previous analysis of the stemmatic changes that take place *c*.3.1.318. We should distinguish between two categories of location for a change of copy-text. In the first category, some changes of copy-text coincide with major structural divisions within the play itself. To this category belong the apparent stemmatic shifts at the beginning of 2.2, 3.1, 4.1, and 5.1. The number of potential divisions of this kind is strictly limited: four divisions between Acts, an additional eight to ten divisions between scenes (depending on whether, in a given text, Act Three was a single scene, or three). In the second category, some changes of copy-text appear in the middle of scenes, at points apparently unconnected to any formal division within the play. To this category belong the division of MATHEWES/ALLDE at 3.1.218 and two apparent stemmatic divisions, one *c*.3.1.318, the other somewhere between 4.1.130 and 4.1.145. Because the locations in the second category have no formal significance, they presumably represent page-breaks or quire-breaks in a lost manuscript. The number of potential divisions of this kind is immeasurably greater: theoretically, they could occur between almost any two lines of the play. Because the number of structural divisions is intrinsically small, it should not surprise us when the same structural division coincides with a division of copy-text in more than one manuscript. On the other hand, because the number of random material divisions is intrinsically large, we would not expect more than one manuscript to have divided its copy-text at exactly the same random point. For example, the division between MATHEWES and ALLDE does not coincide with any apparent stemmatic division in any extant or inferred manuscript.

This reasoning suggests that there is something wrong with my existing visualization of the change in stemmatic relationships at *c*.3.1.318. Up to this point, my stemmata have assumed that the copy-text for at least two different manuscripts changed at that same random point; indeed, Figure 45 requires us to assume that *three* different manuscripts changed their copy-text at that random point. Whether we call the affected manuscripts [PRE-BRIDGEWATER] and [PRE-ROSENBACH] and [PRE-ROSENBACH/BRIDGEWATER], or something else, hardly matters, because the presupposed coincidence is intrinsically implausible. Indeed, the implausibility of such a coincidence was one of the proofs of the Three-Manuscript hypothesis (Sec. XVIII). That implausibility is compounded with another: my preceding stemmata have assumed that, from *c*.3.1.318 to 4.4.110.2 either [PRE-ROSENBACH] or ROSENBACH was a direct descendant of [PRE-BRIDGEWATER]. That assumption contradicts the evidence, marshalled in Section XVIII, that ROSENBACH was stemmatically earlier than BRIDGEWATER. In that stretch of the play ROSENBACH contains only four shared errors that cannot be explained through its relationship with BRIDGEWATER; in contrast, BRIDGEWATER contains ten shared errors that cannot be explained through its relationship with ROSENBACH.

Figure 45 helps us to re-think this problem, by collapsing into one physical entity the two ghosts we have been calling [PRE-NON-CRANE] and [PRE-ROSENBACH/BRIDGEWATER]. Indeed, some such re-naming is the only way out of the stemmatic dilemma created by the proof of the existence of [PRE-ROSENBACH/BRIDGEWATER]. That physical entity is necessary to explain the unique relationship between two manuscripts; if the entity first appears *c*.3.1.318, then at an arbitrary mid-scene point two different manuscripts acquire a new copy-text. That dilemma

can only be avoided if the same manuscript, by a different name, was already serving as copy-text for one of the two manuscripts. If Figure 45 is correct, then ROSENBACH's stemmatic relationship with that lost manuscript began long *before* 3.1.318. And Figure 35 visualizes a change of copy-text for [PRE-BRIDGEWATER], beginning *c*.3.1.318, which links it to the same manuscript to which ROSENBACH already had a connection. This would be enough to explain the beginnings of a stemmatic connection between ROSENBACH and BRIDGEWATER.

However, I have hitherto ignored a discrepancy between two different categories of evidence for the beginning of that stemmatic relationship. The first variants indicating a unique connection between the two extant manuscripts occurs at 3.1.318, but the first filtered error uniquely shared by the two manuscripts does not occur until 3.2.6. That is, the first indisputable evidence of a direct and unique link emerges after the formal division between 3.1 and 3.2. Since shared variants are a less reliable category of evidence than shared errors, we might postulate that a change of copy-text occurred at the beginning of 3.2. The location of the change would then not be arbitrary, and more than one manuscript might have divided its copy-text at the same point.

This solution is attractive, but I do not think it makes sense to ignore the eruption of links between the two manuscripts beginning at 3.1.318. Like Nascimento and Howard-Hill, I believe that the following sequence of shared readings cannot be plausibly attributed to chance.[197]

3.1.318/1433   Qs] B. ROSENBACH; Ks BRIDGEWATER *uncorrected*

3.1.318/1433   flamde] flame ROSENBACH; framed BRIDGEWATER

3.1.320/1435   saist thou] ROSENBACH; *not in* BRIDGEWATER+

C.1–3/1436–39   Bl.Qs.p. that contaminating…of marriage,] *not in* ROSENBACH, BRIDGEWATER

C.3/1440   yes, yes, you doo marrie,] *not in* BRIDGEWATER

3.1.326/1448   or I or] for ∧ ∧ ROSENBACH; for I, and BRIDGEWATER

3.1.327/1449   ouerrules] ouʳrules ROSENBACH; our rules BRIDGEWATER

3.1.345.1/1470   exeunt] *not in* ROSENBACH, BRIDGEWATER

The omission at 1436–39 has not been counted as a shared error, but I am the first editor to adopt it as an authorial variant; previous scholars have considered it an error. As the Textual Notes argue in more detail, the unique variants on either side of it—one in ROSENBACH, one in BRIDGEWATER—are clearly related to the omission

---

[197] Like other missing exits, the omitted exeunt direction at 3.1.345.1 has been removed from the filtered totals, but its presence in other texts indicates that it was apparently present in the earlier stages of the stemma, so its omission here is certainly a uniquely shared variant and probably a uniquely shared error. However, it occurs at the very end of 3.1. Including it would not affect the argument that the stemmatic link begins, or is solidified, at the formal break between the two scenes. At the very hinge of the difference, it could go either way.

of the intervening material. That is, whether or not we consider the omission an error or an authorial variant, ROSENBACH and BRIDGEWATER respond to it in different ways.[198] This pattern applies, in fact, to all the variants till the end of the scene. Again at 3.1.318 (twice), 3.1.320, 3.1.326, and 3.2.327, ROSENBACH and BRIDGEWATER both depart from the correct reading present in all other texts, but they do so *differently*. This pattern certainly suggests that both derive, separately and equidistantly, from a single shared ancestor. Hence, a stemmatic link between them does seem to have started at an arbitrary mid-scene point.

Nevertheless, that link does seem to have grown stronger at the beginning of 3.2. The forty lines of that scene contain four filtered errors, uniquely shared by the two texts. They share additional unique variants at 3.2.2 (Jesting), 3.2.20 (then), 3.2.22 (push), 3.2.30 (Second), and 3.2.38 (nobody).

We might explain this difference, and resolve the stemmatic dilemma created by [PRE-ROSENBACH/BRIDGEWATER], but postulating that we are dealing, here, with division of copy-texts at two locations, rather than one. The division in the copy-text for PRE-BRIDGEWATER visualized in Figure 35 could indeed have taken place *c.*3.1.318. No division of copy for ROSENBACH or [PRE-ROSENBACH] need be assumed at that point. Instead, the divisions in the copy-text for ROSENBACH and [PRE-ROSENBACH/BRIDGEWATER] imagined in Figure 45 could have occurred at the formal break between 3.1 and 3.2.

Nevertheless, wherever we locate the change visualized in Figure 45, re-locating that break does not solve the other problem. The shared error totals identify ROSENBACH as the earlier text in this stretch of the play, but all my stemmata hitherto have placed it later than [PRE-BRIDGEWATER] from the middle of Act Three to the end of Act Four. The evidence of shared variants from 3.1.318 to the end of that scene suggests that the two extant texts were equidistant, stemmatically, from [PRE-ROSENBACH/BRIDGEWATER]. The stronger relationships between the two extant texts, and the stemmatic priority of ROSENBACH, could both be explained by a single change to Figure 45.

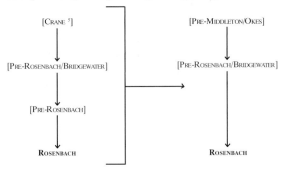

Figure 46. Final visualization of the change of copy-text for [PRE-ROSENBACH] at 3.2 (replacing Figure 45).

In this scenario, two branches would descend from [PRE-ROSENBACH/BRIDGEWATER], beginning *c.*3.1.318, one leading to [PRE-BRIDGEWATER], the other leading to [PRE-ROSENBACH]. Those two branches would remain at the beginning of 3.2. But the ROSENBACH branch would be shorter. If Figure 46 were correct, from the beginning of 3.2 to the end of Act Four ROSENBACH would have been copied directly from [PRE-ROSENBACH/BRIDGEWATER]: stemmatically, it would be only one stage removed from that lost manuscript. By contrast, BRIDGEWATER would be two stages removed: it would be a copy of [PRE-BRIDGE-WATER], which was a copy of [PRE-ROSENBACH/BRIDGE-WATER]. This arrangement would explain the uniquely strong links between the two extant texts, while also explaining ROSENBACH's lower total of shared errors.

The re-conceptualization of Acts Three and Four in Figures 45 and 46 would also compel us to alter Figure 43.

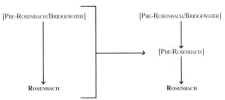

Figure 47. Final visualization of the change of copy-text for ROSENBACH between Act Four and Act Five.

It may help to summarize the preceding analysis. The copy for ROSENBACH was divided between [PRE-ROSENBACH] and [PRE-ROSENBACH/BRIDGEWATER]. The necessary entity Howard-Hill christened [PRE-ROSENBACH/BRIDGEWATER] can now be situated in the stemma of the NON-CRANE texts from the beginning of 2.2 till the end of the play. The copy-text for [PRE-ROSENBACH/BRIDGEWATER] seems to have been divided between [CRANE⁵] and [PRE-MIDDLETON/OKES].

Figures 45 and 46 both include [PRE-MIDDLETON/OKES]. Inevitably, the examination of [PRE-ROSENBACH/BRIDGE-WATER] pushes us toward a global consideration of the copy-text for OKES. It should be recognized at the outset, however, that this will be the most difficult part of the analysis. For the other three extant NON-CRANE texts, we possess a manuscript, which materially aids the analysis. The printed text of OKES conceals and possibly distorts the underlying manuscript. Moreover, as it happens that concealed manuscript was closer than any of the extant NON-CRANE manuscripts to the crucial transition between the CRANE texts and the NON-CRANE texts. Finally, the area of the stemma closest to OKES is also the area that contains the largest concentration of ghost manuscripts. Those manuscripts have each been invoked to explain different features of the stemma. [CRANE⁵] (first identified in Section XXVII) explains certain late Crane features in the extant NON-CRANE texts. [PRE-NON-CRANE] (first identified in

[198] This is true whether one regards the different responses as authorial revision or scribal sophistication.

Section XXIV) explains variants and errors shared by all the NON-CRANE texts, and also explains the otherwise contradictory, split-series distribution of variants and errors in the play's middle scenes. [PRE-MIDDLETON/OKES] (first identified in Section XXI) explains the links between OKES and other NON-CRANE texts, which cannot have transited through a dead-end manuscript or dead-end printed-text. [PRE-ROSENBACH/BRIDGEWATER] (first identified in Section XVIII) explains the uniquely close relationship between ROSENBACH and BRIDGEWATER in the second half of the play, and also explains the relationship of both to OKES. The functions served by these conjecturally-identified manuscripts are all stemmatically necessary, but one physical manuscript might have served more than one of these functions—especially given the routine use of divided copy-text.

However, my previous stemmata do not envisage any division of copy-text for OKES or any of its three immediate predecessors, at any point in the play.

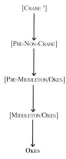

Figure 48. Draft visualization of the copy-text for OKES (based on Figures 18, 19, 21, 22, 23, 38, 31).

The uniformity of this pattern seems unlikely, for at least two reasons. First, copy-text seems to have been divided for the extant manuscripts ROSENBACH, BRIDGEWATER, MIDDLETON^T, and for the lost manuscripts [PRE-ROSENBACH/BRIDGEWATER], [PRE-ROSENBACH], [PRE-BRIDGEWATER], and [PRE-MIDDLETON^T]. Thus, all the other NON-CRANE texts for which we have evidence are discontinuous. There might have been one homogeneous NON-CRANE text, or even several, but it seems odd that all of them would be concentrated in the stemmatic line of a single extant text. Secondly, the number of lost entities here is suspicious, especially because—as we have already noted—they are sometimes stemmatically indistinguishable.

One of the anomalies here makes sense. Thomas Middleton might well have prepared a manuscript specifically for his long-time associate Nicholas Okes. There is, accordingly, a logical reason for OKES itself to differ from the other extant NON-CRANE texts: it was produced from a homogeneous copy-text because [MIDDLETON/OKES] was a single manuscript prepared for a printer, sold to a printer, and used by a printer. That assumption might also explain why [MIDDLETON/OKES] contains so many unique authorial readings: it might have been delivered to the printer as soon as it was completed, and consequently it

might never have been used as whole or partial copy-text for any other manuscript. But both [PRE-NON-CRANE] and [PRE-MIDDLETON-OKES] were apparently used as copy-text for other manuscripts, and neither of them seems to have been intended for sale to a printer; consequently, no known external circumstances would explain the anomalous stemmatic homogeneity I have hitherto attributed to both of them.

I have already noted (Figure 44) that it would be most economical to assume, in Act Five, that [PRE-NON-CRANE] was the same as [PRE-MIDDLETON/OKES]. Likewise, in the play's first three scenes (Figure 23) it is difficult to discern the difference between [PRE-NON-CRANE] and [PRE-MIDDLETON/OKES]. The two lost manuscripts are imagined as adjacent; they have the same ancestors and the same descendants For the first and last three scenes, we need only one physical entity, where my initial stemmata imagined two.

The principle of parsimony therefore urges us to re-imagine the relationship between Figure 23 (covering the play's first three scenes) and Figure 22 (covering 2.2).

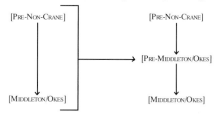

Figure 49. Alternative visualization of the change of copy-text for [MIDDLETON/OKES] between 2.1 and 2.2.

Figure 49 explains all the stemmatic evidence, for OKES and all the other NON-CRANE texts. The same circumstances apply in Act Five, except that there the vector of change is reversed.

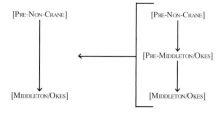

Figure 50. Alternative visualization of the change of copy-text for [MIDDLETON/OKES] between 4.4 and 5.1.

Figure 50 represents the return, in Act Five, of the copy-text used in the first three scenes. It produces a pattern that should now be immediately recognizable. Two different, stemmatically adjacent manuscripts served as copy-text for [MIDDLETON/OKES]; the first manuscript was used at the beginning of the play, a second was used in the middle, and the end of the play returned to the first manuscript.

However, Figures 49 and 50 do nothing to diminish the anomalous homogeneity of [PRE-NON-CRANE] itself.

As Figure 48 makes clear, the stemmata assume that [PRE-NON-CRANE] is a copy, throughout, of a single manuscript, [CRANE⁵]. However, the anomaly is greater than Figure 48 suggests, because the alleged homogeneity of [PRE-NON-CRANE] forces us to assume that the copy-text for [CRANE⁵] was divided between *three* different manuscripts: [PRE-ROSENBACH] (Figure 23), [KING'S MEN³] (Figure 22), and [CRANE⁴] (Figure 18). The contrast between the hyper-divided [CRANE⁵] and the totally homogeneous [PRE-NON-CRANE] would be suspicious in itself; it is especially suspicious because the two contrasting manuscripts are stemmatically adjacent and, often, stemmatically indistinguishable. Finally, and perhaps most suspiciously of all, this contrast reverses the well-established global pattern of undivided copy for all other known CRANE texts and divided copy for all other known NON-CRANE texts (except the two sold to printers).[199]

The first apparent discontinuity, according to the current stemmata, occurs at the beginning of 2.2.

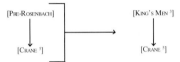

Figure 51. Draft visualization of the change of copy-text for [CRANE⁵] between 2.1 and 2.2.

For the first three scenes, the massive 'Crane Plus One' evidence establishes that [PRE-ROSENBACH] must have stood, stemmatically, between the CRANE texts and OKES, BRIDGEWATER, and MIDDLETON^T. In particular, [PRE-ROSENBACH] must stand between the other NON-CRANE texts and [CRANE⁴].

Figure 51 is based on two assumptions. The first, and most important, is that the lost manuscript identified here as [PRE-ROSENBACH] is the same physical entity identified as [PRE-ROSENBACH] in the stemmata for the later scenes of the play. This might, of course, be true. But it also might not be true. The assumption is, in part, purely nominal: the lost manuscript identified in these early scenes as [PRE-ROSENBACH] is an antecedent of ROSENBACH, and so is the lost manuscript identified in later scenes as [PRE-ROSENBACH], and so I have followed Howard-Hill in calling it or them 'Pre-Rosenbach'. However, we have already seen different lost manuscripts serve as exemplars of different parts of extant manuscripts; indeed, our analysis has already concluded that the copy-text for ROSENBACH was divided. Moreover, we have already encountered one necessary lost manuscript, [PRE-BRIDGE-WATER], which influenced extant texts for one part of the play, but apparently did *not* belong to the lineage of any extant text in another part of the play (Figure 34). Consequently, we could distinguish between two different lost manuscripts: [PRE-ROSENBACH¹], an early copy which strongly influenced all the NON-CRANE texts, and [PRE-ROSENBACH²], a later copy. But this solution multiplies lost entities. We have already identified a lost manuscript

'which strongly influenced all the NON-CRANE texts'. That is, what might be called [PRE-ROSENBACH¹] is just another name for what we have been calling [PRE-NON-CRANE], but a [PRE-NON-CRANE] whose position has now been shifted to *precede* [CRANE⁵], rather than follow it. In that case, we could visualize the stemmatic change in Figure 51 differently.

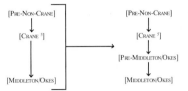

Figure 52. Revised visualization of the change of copy-text for [CRANE⁵] between 2.1 and 2.2.

Figure 52 presumes that the copy for [CRANE⁵] remained the same, but that the Crane transcript itself was subsequently divided, in order to serve as copy-text for different parts of two different NON-CRANE manuscripts. This assumption not only preserves the routine homogeneity of CRANE copy-texts, but also simplifies the stemmata imagined in Figure 22 and 23. Moreover, it locates the first use of divided copy-text in the earliest NON-CRANE texts: [PRE-NON-CRANE], [PRE-MIDDLETON/OKES], and [MIDDLETON/OKES].

The second apparent discontinuity in [CRANE⁵] occurs at the beginning of Act Four.

Figure 53. Draft visualization of the change of copy-text for [CRANE⁵] between Act Three and Act Four.

Figure 53 attempts to account for the increased links between CRANE/ALLDE and the NON-CRANE texts in Acts Four and Five; the stemmatic evidence clearly requires some new conduit between [CRANE⁴] and the extant NON-CRANE texts. But now that we have relabelled the [PRE-ROSENBACH] in the top left corner of Figure 53 as [PRE-NON-CRANE], we can account for that evidence without presupposing divided copy-text for a Crane manuscript.

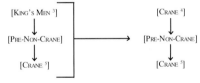

Figure 54. Revised visualization of the change of copy-text for [CRANE⁵] between Act Three and Act Four.

[199] [MIDDLETON/CRANE] is presumed to be an authorial transcript of [CRANE⁴]. In that sense it belongs among the NON-CRANE manuscripts. Chronologically, it might have been produced between [CRANE⁴] and [CRANE⁵], in which case its homogeneity might reflect its position among the CRANE texts.

Figures 52 and 54 solve the problems associated with divided copy-text at the juncture of the CRANE and NON--CRANE texts by denying that [PRE-ROSENBACH] is the same manuscript as [PRE-NON-CRANE]. Instead, they postulate one change in the copy for [PRE-NON-CRANE] (at 4.1.0) and another in the copy for MIDDLETON/OKES (at 2.2).

I began this section with the suspicion that we might be using more than one label for the same lost manuscript. That suspicion seems to have been justified by the foregoing analysis, which suggests that the manuscripts we have identified as 'Pre-X' are also often 'Pre--Y', and that 'Pre-Y' might for parts of the play be the copy-text for X instead of Y. This means that the traditional; names are confusing, and are probably impeding rather than enabling our analysis. But tracing the apparent divisions of copy-text has not actually reduced the number of lost manuscripts required by the stemma. Nor should that surprise us. 'Since all eight substantive texts of *Game* are dead-ends, any well-populated pattern of errors shared by two extant texts demonstrates the existence of a third, now lost' (Sec. V, para. 39). Even after rigorous filtering, there remain nine patterns containing two or more errors shared by two texts, both of them descendants of [KING'S MEN³].[200] What is true of patterns of pairs also applies to patterns of triplets. After rigorous filtering, there remain three patterns containing seven or more errors shared by three NON-CRANE texts.[201] These twelve patterns of shared error would lead us to expect a *minimum* of twelve lost manuscripts among the descendants of [KING'S MEN³]. Even if we raised the bar, and counted only patterns that contained at least three filtered shared errors, ten such pairs and triplets would remain. The preceding analysis presupposes, in fact, exactly ten such manuscripts.[202] The number of postulated lost manuscripts is the bare minimum required.

This means that the principle of economy, in this analysis of divided copy, cannot reduce the number of lost entities required—but it can reduce the number of changes or divisions of copy required. For example, I have already called attention to the improbability of more than one division of copy having occurred at 3.1.318, an arbitrary point in the middle of a scene. Exactly the same logic makes it unlikely that more than one division of copy occurred in the middle of 4.1, between 4.1.130 and 4.1.145. A change of copy for [PRE-MIDDLETON⊤] is stemmatically required there, but no such change needs to be presupposed for [PRE-BRIDGEWATER]. We have already conjectured that the copy-text for [PRE--BRIDGEWATER] from there to the end of the play was [PRE--ROSENBACH]; in fact, [PRE-ROSENBACH] could have occupied exactly the same stemmatic position—between [PRE--ROSENBACH/BRIDGEWATER] and [PRE-BRIDGEWATER]—since the beginning of 3.2. There is, to my knowledge, no way to prove whether this lost manuscript [PRE-ROSENBACH], wedged between two other lost manuscripts, moved into this position at 3.2 or 4.1. But since the manuscript

clearly must have existed and clearly played an important role in the stemma before 3.2 and after 4.1.145, it makes sense to assume that it was also used for some purpose during that intervening stretch of the text. By locating its movement to the beginning of 3.2, we make the division of copy in the middle of 4.1 much more plausible, and the overall sequence of divided copy more economical.

The conjecture in the preceding paragraph does not reduce the number of changes of copy-text in [PRE-BRIDGE-WATER], or the number of difference manuscripts that influenced [PRE-BRIDGEWATER]; it simply moves one of the changes of copy-text to a different location. But it does demonstrate the way in which the conjectural repositioning of 'invisible' lost manuscripts can produce a simpler and more rational sequence of divisions of copy-text. That principle is particularly important in relation to [PRE--BRIDGEWATER]. The preceding analysis has left us with a tidy pattern in which four of the ten lost manuscripts were produced from homogeneous copy-text: [CRANE⁴,⁵] and the two manuscripts sent to printers, [MIDDLETON/CRANE] and [MIDDLETON/OKES]. Five of the six remaining lost manuscripts were produced by dividing the copy-text between two different manuscripts. The lone anomaly is [PRE-BRIDGEWATER], where the copy-text would have to be divided between four different manuscripts: [CRANE⁵], [PRE-MIDDLETON/OKES], [PRE-ROSENBACH/BRIDGEWATER], and [PRE-ROSENBACH]. This implausible scenario is created by my foregoing interpretation of the position of [PRE-BRIDGE-WATER] in Acts One and Two, where my efforts to economize on unnecessary lost manuscripts has eliminated from the stemma several intermediate manuscripts that certainly existed. Thus, if we combined all the conjectures about divided copy-text in this section, my provisional stemma for the play's first three scenes would have no place for [PRE-MIDDLETON/OKES], [PRE-ROSENBACH/BRIDGE-WATER], or [PRE-MIDDLETON⊤]. We could conjecture that those three manuscripts were being used, at the time, to produce additional copies of the first three scenes. But that conjecture would actually *increase* the number of lost NON-CRANE manuscripts that have to be postulated. Thus, by minimizing the number of entities at play in the first three scenes we create two anomalies: (1) the assumption that three manuscripts were either being left atypically idle or were being used to produce yet more lost manuscripts, and (2) the assumption that the copy--text for [PRE-BRIDGEWATER] here was a third manuscript, [CRANE⁵] (Figure 55). These two anomalies are, of course, related.

---

[200] Patterns 9, 10, 11, 12, 13, 15, 16, 17, 18: ROSENBACH–MIDDLETON⊤ (2), OKES–MIDDLETON⊤ (2), MATHEWES/ALLDE–BRIDGEWATER (3), MATHEWES/ALLDE–ROSENBACH (7), BRIDGEWATER–MIDDLETON⊤ (7), ROSENBACH–OKES (14), BRIDGEWATER–OKES (16), MATHEWES/ALLDE–OKES (17), 18 ROSENBACH–BRIDGEWATER (22).
[201] Patterns 30, 31, 32: ROSENBACH–BRIDGEWATER–OKES (7), ROSENBACH–BRIDGE-WATER–MIDDLETON⊤ (11), OKES–BRIDGEWATER MIDDLETON⊤ (11).
[202] The relevance of paragraph 39 to the number of lost manuscripts in the NON-CRANE group was one of the very last things added to this analysis; the matching numbers came as a surprise to me, after I had already completed my analysis of divided copy.

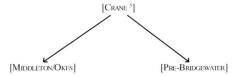

Figure 55. Partial draft visualization of
the stemma for the first three scenes.

But where in the stemma should we interpolate those three lost manuscripts? Once we have freed lost manuscripts from their traditional labels, we can see that they are floating signifiers, which can be moved into blank spaces in order to produce the most economical possible arrangement. In the last three acts of the play, [PRE-BRIDGEWATER] and [PRE-ROSENBACH] served as copy-text for [PRE-BRIDGEWATER], so it would be reasonable to conjecture that one of them also served as its copy-text for these first three scenes. It would certainly be easy enough to interpolate the unused [PRE-ROSENBACH/BRIDGEWATER] into the empty stemmatic space between [CRANE⁵] and [PRE-BRIDGEWATER], thereby eliminating one of the extra copy-texts for [PRE-BRIDGEWATER]. Since [CRANE⁵] apparently served as copy-text for [PRE-ROSENBACH/BRIDGEWATER] in 2.2, this move has the further advantage of creating continuity in the copy-text for [PRE-ROSENBACH/BRIDGEWATER].

As the previous paragraph demonstrates, where in the stemma we place 'floating' lost manuscripts depends on the assumption that continuity of copy-text is desirable, and that we should if at all possible reduce both the number of changes of copy-text that the global stemma for the whole play requires. This principle has implications for exactly where, in the blank space below [CRANE⁵], we place [PRE-ROSENBACH/BRIDGEWATER]. In Figure 55, the stemma branches below [CRANE⁵], with one branch leading to [PRE-BRIDGEWATER] and the other leading to [MIDDLETON/OKES]. So [PRE-ROSENBACH/BRIDGEWATER] could be placed on the branch leading to [PRE-BRIDGEWATER]— or it could be placed at the top of both branches. In other words, the stemma might branch below [PRE-ROSENBACH/ BRIDGEWATER], rather than below [CRANE⁵].

For the moment, let's leave [PRE-ROSENBACH/BRIDGE-WATER] hanging, and consider [PRE-MIDDLETON/OKES] instead. Where does it belong, in our stemma for the first three scenes. It does not seem to have been used as copy for [MIDDLETON/OKES], but we would expect it to have been used somewhere early in the transmission of the NON-CRANE texts. If it was not a descendant of [CRANE⁵], the obvious place to look for it would be on the other branch of the NON-CRANE stemma. This would place it somewhere between [PRE-NON-CRANE] and ROSEN-BACH.

These conjectures can then be combined, to explain more economically the stemmatic changes that took place between 2.1 and 2.2. If, in the first three scenes, [PRE-MIDDLETON/OKES] was the copy for [PRE-ROSENBACH], then it might have continued to do so in 2.2, after its own copy changed from [PRE-NON-CRANE] to [CRANE⁵]. Thus, the movement of [PRE-MIDDLETON/OKES], from the right

to the left branch of the descendants of [PRE-NON-CRANE], would have carried [PRE-ROSENBACH] and ROSENBACH with it. At the same time, the copy for [PRE-ROSENBACH/ BRIDGEWATER] would have changed from [CRANE⁵] to [PRE-MIDDLETON/OKES]. But [PRE-ROSENBACH/BRIDGEWATER] would continue to occupy the same space in relation [MID-DLETON/OKES] and [PRE-BRIDGEWATER]—that is, it would continue to occupy the same space, if we choose the second of the two options for its position in the first three scenes, as copy-text for both those other manuscripts.

These conjectures about the position of [PRE-MIDDLETON/ OKES] and [PRE-ROSENBACH/BRIDGEWATER] in the first three scenes eliminate two of the four manuscripts that otherwise have to be postulated as copy-text for [PRE-BRIDGE-WATER]: for the first two acts. Instead, the copy-text for [PRE-BRIDGEWATER] would have remained [PRE-ROSENBACH/ BRIDGEWATER] until the change at some point between 4.1.130 and 4.1.145, when it changed to [PRE-ROSEN-BACH]. Moreover, these conjectures leave the copy-text for [PRE-MIDDLETON/OKES] and [PRE-ROSENBACH/BRIDGEWATER] divided between only two manuscripts.

This leaves only the invisible [PRE-MIDDLETONᵀ] to account for. Elsewhere in the play, its copy-text was divided between [CRANE⁵] and [PRE-ROSENBACH]; in 2.2. To create the maximum continuity between 2.1 and 2.2, we would need to assume that its copy-text for the first three scenes was [CRANE⁵]. This assumption makes no difference to the stemma there, because it places [PRE-MID-DLETONᵀ] in the position of a dead-end. Taken together, these conjectures about the three invisible manuscripts in the first three scenes would change Figure 55 into Figure 56.

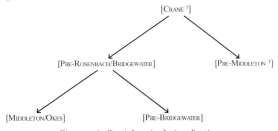

Figure 56. Partial revised visualization
of the stemma for the first three scenes.

The complexity of the foregoing argumentative chain can now be reduced to a fairly simple summary. In order to provide an alternative to the misleading traditional nomenclature for lost manuscripts that served as copy-text for parts of different manuscripts, I have assigned a Greek letter to all seven lost NON-CRANE manuscripts that belong to the same part of the stemma as the four extant NON-CRANE manuscripts. The order of Greek letters, like the order of the following list, is based on the apparent sequence of the completion of each manuscript. For the purposes of this list, I assume that a manuscript cannot be completed until the manuscript(s) that served as its copy-text were completed.

Summary of Divided Copy-Texts for the Extant and Inferred Descendants of [KING'S MEN³]

[CRANE⁴]: [KING'S MEN³] (homogeneous)

[CRANE/MIDDLETON]: [CRANE⁴] (homogeneous)

MATHEWES/ALLDE: [CRANE/MIDDLETON] (homogeneous)

α [PRE-NON-CRANE]: [KING'S MEN³] (Acts I, II, III), [CRANE⁴] (Acts IV, V)

[CRANE⁵]: [PRE-NON-CRANE] (homogeneous)

β [PRE-MIDDLETON/OKES]: [PRE-NON-CRANE] (Prologue–2.1), [CRANE⁵] (2.2–Epilogue)

γ [PRE-ROSENBACH/BRIDGEWATER]: [CRANE⁵] (Prologue–2.1, Act V), [PRE-MIDDLETON/OKES] (2.2–4.4)

δ [MIDDLETON/OKES]: [PRE-ROSENBACH/BRIDGEWATER] (Acts I, II), [PRE-MIDDLETON/OKES] (Acts III, IV, V)

OKES: [MIDDLETON/OKES] (homogeneous)

ε [PRE-ROSENBACH]: [PRE-MIDDLETON/OKES] (Acts I, II), [PRE-ROSENBACH/BRIDGEWATER] (Acts III, IV, V)

ζ [PRE-MIDDLETON^T]: [CRANE⁵] (Prologue–4.1.130), [PRE-ROSENBACH] (4.1.145–4.4)

ROSENBACH: [PRE-ROSENBACH] (Prologue–3.1, Act V), [PRE-ROSENBACH/BRIDGEWATER] (3.2–4.4)

η [PRE-BRIDGEWATER]: [PRE-ROSENBACH/BRIDGEWATER] (Prologue–3.1), [PRE-ROSENBACH] (3.2–Epilogue)

BRIDGEWATER: [PRE-BRIDGEWATER] (Prologue–2.2, 3.1.318–Epilogue), [PRE-MIDDLETON^T] (3.1.0.1–3.1.317)

MIDDLETON^T: [PRE-BRIDGEWATER] (Prologue–2.1, Act V), [PRE-MIDDLETON^T] (2.2–4.4)

This exact sequence of divided copy-text is, necessarily, more conjectural than the earlier conclusions of this investigation, because as the size of the data sample shrinks the security of the hypothesis diminishes. Moreover, there may have been many more lost manuscripts that I have imagined here. My purpose has been to explain the available evidence with the smallest possible number of related texts and the smallest possible number of changes of copy-text. What can hardly be disputed is that the use of divided copy-texts was pervasive among the extant and lost but necessary NON-CRANE manuscripts.

XXIX. The Transmission of *A Game at Chess*: Summary

The following summary re-describes the materials surveyed in Section I; but whereas that survey was organized alphabetically, this one is organized chronologically.

Middleton in the spring of 1624 composed a draft of the play, [MIDDLETON^PRE]. This lost autograph manuscript was probably completed by late May.[203]

From that manuscript was prepared a transcript, incorporating various additions and alterations by Middleton; we do not know who wrote out that copy, but it became the property of the King's Men. That lost transcript, [KING'S MEN¹], was licensed by Herbert on June 12, and returned to the King's Men.

Between June 13 and August 4, that manuscript was copied to produce a collection of lost playhouse documents, [KING'S MEN²]: manuscript 'parts' for the actors, and a backstage 'plat' to regulate performances.

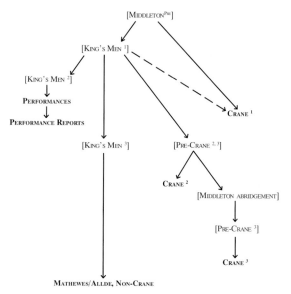

Figure 57. The Transmission of *A Game at Chess*: Global Stemma. The vertical axis is chronological. The dotted line indicates a small number of subsequent alterations by other hands, importing onto CRANE¹ readings from the playbook, made after Ralph Crane completed his initial transcription.

By August 5, when the play was first publicly performed, these playhouse documents—[KING'S MEN^{1,2}]—had incorporated final revisions by the author and the company, and changes demanded by the censor; they had reached their final state as a representation of the play in performance.

The performances of the play between August 5 and August 14, regulated most immediately by [KING'S MEN²], generated a large number of written **Performance Reports**, describing the play, in more or less detail. It is the nature of such responses that they are relatively brief records scattered in letters, archives, and longer texts. A surprising number of such responses survive and have been identified; others have undoubtedly been lost, or remain to be discovered. Although some are retrospective, thirteen of the surviving records were generated during the period when the play was being performed, and another fourteen were written later in August.

The scandalous theatrical success of the play generated an immediate demand for copies of the text; but during the play's uninterrupted run the playbook could not easily be used to make copies. Middleton therefore commissioned his associate Ralph Crane to make a copy or copies from [MIDDLETON^PRE]. On August 13 Crane completed and dated the first such extant transcript of the play, CRANE¹. The first three scenes of this copy were checked sporadically, by Middleton and someone else, importing a few revised

203 See 'Canon and Chronology', p. 439.

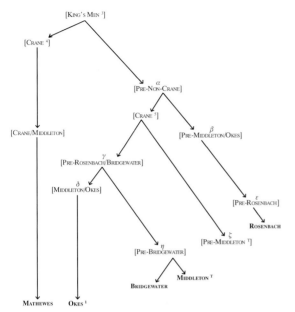

Figure 58. Partial Stemma A: Descendants of [KING'S MEN³] in Prologue, Induction, 1.1, and 2.1.

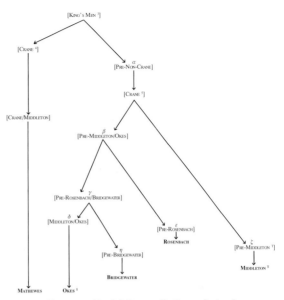

Figure 59. Partial Stemma B: Descendants of [KING'S MEN³] in 2.2. Between 2.1 and 2.2, the copy-text for [PRE-MIDDLETON/OKES] changed from [PRE-NON-CRANE] to [CRANE⁵], the copy-text for [PRE-BRIDGEWATER] changed from [CRANE⁵] to [PRE-MIDDLETON/OKES], and the copy-text for MIDDLETON^T changed from [PRE-BRIDGEWATER] to [PRE-MIDDLETON^T].

readings that probably reflect censorship in [KING'S MEN¹]. At the beginning of 2.2 the playbook contains a major addition, not present in CRANE¹; at that point, any attempt at collation stopped.

The final performance of the play was the next day, August 14; [KING'S MEN¹] was then available to be copied, until August 21 when it was delivered to the Privy Council. During that interim two lost copies of the licensed playbook were apparently made. All subsequent extant texts derive from these two lost manuscripts.

One copy, the lost transcript [PRE-CRANE²,³], was based on the final layer of [KING'S MEN¹]: it reproduced cuts made in rehearsal and alterations demanded by the censor, in an attempt to produce a textual witness that resembled as closely as possible what was actually performed. This editorial strategy might reflect a specific desire, on the part of a patron or purchaser, for a text of the performed play.

Another copy, the lost transcript [KING'S MEN³], did not attempt to sort out different layers of the playbook. Instead, it reproduced the fullest possible text, including material added *and* material deleted in the playbook. This copy might be described as a more 'naïve' transcription (since it did not recognize differences that were important in regulating performance). On the other hand, [KING'S MEN³] might also be described as a more 'authorial' transcription. Rather than subtracting, it adds together all the elements that Middleton had ever written for the play, restoring material that had been removed from the performance script.

On 18 August a warrant was issued, summoning Middleton to appear before the Privy Council; he was still being sought on 20 August; on 30 August his son Edward was brought before the Privy Council, presumably because the father was still in hiding; at some point thereafter Middleton himself was 'committed to prisson'. (See 'Occasional Poems'.) We do not know how long he was incarcerated. There is no evidence, direct or indirect, of Middleton's personal involvement in the only other text dated '1624', CRANE². That transcript derives from the lost [PRE-CRANE²,³].

After CRANE¹,², the production of the extant texts of *Game* ceased to reflect the evolution of the performance text; increasingly, *Game* began to be regarded as a literary text, rather than a play. Middleton himself, at some unknown point in the last four months of 1624, apparently abridged the play, producing a succinct reading version. [MIDDLETON'S ABRIDGEMENT] may have been produced orally (by dictating to a scribe, presumably Crane), by autograph transcription, or by marking a lost transcript in pencil; whatever the exact process, the abridgement was made from something that derived from [CRANE²,³]. Middleton's abridgement removed material that had already been removed in the playbook, but he also removed some material added to the playbook, after completion of [MIDDLETON^PRE]. The abridgement thus drew upon a knowledge of stages of evolution of the performance text, but it combined material from different stages, and further abbreviated the text to create the shortest possible intelligible reading text of the revised version. Middleton's

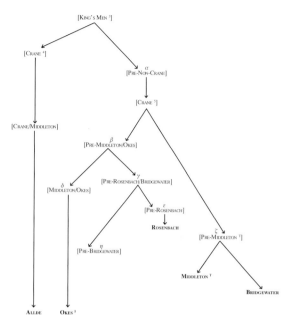

Figure 60. Partial Stemma C: Descendants of [KING'S MEN³] from 3.1.0.1 to 3.1.317. Between 2.2 and 3.1 the copy-text for [MIDDLETON/OKES] changed from [PRE-ROSENBACH/BRIDGEWATER] to [PRE-MIDDLETON/OKES], the copy-text for [PRE-ROSENBACH] changed from [PRE-MIDDLETON/OKES] to [PRE-ROSENBACH/BRIDGEWATER], and the copy-text for BRIDGEWATER changed from [PRE-BRIDGEWATER] to [PRE-MIDDLETON^T].

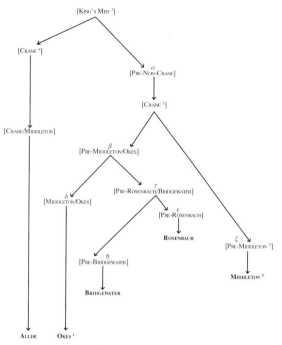

Figure 61. Partial Stemma D: Descendants of [KING'S MEN³] from 3.1.318 to 3.1.345. At or shortly before 3.1.318 the copy-text for BRIDGEWATER changed from [PRE-MIDDLETON^T] back to [PRE-BRIDGEWATER].

abridgement was almost certainly either written down by Crane, or soon copied by Crane, in a lost manuscript, [PRE-CRANE³].

By 1 January 1625 Middleton was probably out of prison, since he wrote a preface to CRANE³, referring to it as a New Year's gift. The rest of that manuscript could have been prepared some time before the dedication was added, and thus probably dates to December 1624. CRANE³ reproduced the text of [MIDDLETON ABRIDGEMENT], but further modified the text by systematically transforming the description of entrances and their relationship to scenes. Crane's explicitly literary massed entrances were not reproduced in any other extant text of the play. Among the extant texts, CRANE³ is the end of the line of texts that derive from [PRE-CRANE²,³].

But Crane was also involved in producing copies of [KING'S MEN³]. Although they are now lost, both [CRANE⁴] and [CRANE⁵] apparently derived, in whole or part, from that alternative transcription of the licensed playbook. Altogether, five extant copies derive from [KING'S MEN³]. The three exceptions are the three extant texts known to have been produced in 1624, CRANE¹,²,³. This may mean that [KING'S MEN³] only became available to Middleton or Crane after 1 January 1625. The timing may or may not be related to Middleton's release from prison. Certainly, Middleton was personally involved in the production of

all five extant texts that derive from [KING'S MEN³]: his handwriting appears in all three of the manuscripts, and he seems to have prepared the manuscript used by the printers of both quartos. Near the point where Crane ceases to be an important agent of transmission for *Game*, Middleton becomes increasingly prominent.

All four extant NON-CRANE texts—OKES, ROSENBACH, BRIDGEWATER, and MIDDLETON^T—derive, ultimately, from [KING'S MEN³]. All four postdate [CRANE⁴,⁵]. Moreover, all four derive from divided copy-text. Each must be separated from the others by at least one lost manuscript. The same agents and processes that produced these four extant texts also probably produced the lost α [PRE-NON-CRANE], the lost β [PRE-MIDDLETON/OKES], the lost γ [PRE-ROSENBACH/BRIDGEWATER], the lost δ [MIDDLETON/OKES], the lost ε [PRE-ROSENBACH], the lost ζ [PRE-MIDDLETON], and the lost η [PRE-BRIDGEWATER]. All four extant NON-CRANE texts—and the seven lost pre-texts associated with them—were probably produced after 1 January 1625, and before June 1625.

This explosion of new copies of *Game* was probably related to the death of James I on 27 March 1625. The play's representation of King James is, at best, ambivalent, and James had acted to punish, at least momentarily, both the author and the acting company. But the play had presented his son and heir, the Prince of Wales, in a

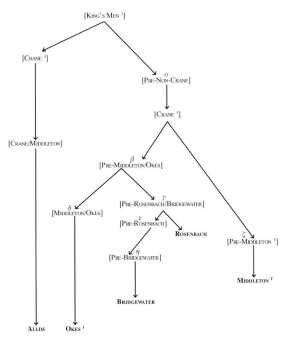

Figure 62. Partial Stemma E: Descendants of [KING'S MEN³] from 3.2 to the end of Act Three. At the beginning of 3.2 the copy-text for [PRE-BRIDGEWATER] changed from [PRE-ROSENBACH/BRIDGEWATER] to [PRE-ROSENBACH], and the copy-text for ROSENBACH changed from [PRE-ROSENBACH] to [PRE-ROSENBACH/BRIDGEWATER.]

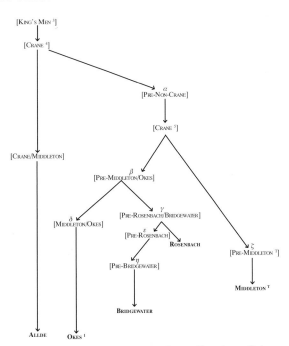

Figure 63. Partial Stemma F: Descendants of [KING'S MEN³] from 4.1.0 to 4.1.130. Between Act Three and Act Four the copy-text for [PRE-NON-CRANE] changed from [KING'S MEN³] to [CRANE⁴].

much more favourable light, and there was every reason to suppose that Charles I would be more sympathetic to Middleton's play—or at least less aggressively hostile—than his father. Middleton probably sold [MIDDLETON/OKES] to his old business associate Nicholas Okes shortly after March 27; in any case, Okes subsequently used that lost autograph manuscript to print OKES¹. At about the same time, someone must have sold [CRANE/MIDDLETON]—Middleton's transcription of [CRANE⁴]—to an unknown stationer, who used it to print MATHEWES/ALLDE. By May 25 the first printed edition of the play had been seen and at least partially read by Joseph Mead in Cambridge. We do not know which edition Mead saw. But the two editions probably came out almost simultaneously. The compositor(s) in Allde's shop, or Okes's shop, may have used the quarto produced in the other shop as copy-text for the last twenty-three lines of the play, and one engraved title-page was clearly influenced by the other. Okes, anticipating high demand, had already begun work on OKES² by the time OKES¹ was published. The almost simultaneous publication of the quartos suggests that the separate stationers may also have acquired their different manuscripts at about the same time, a few weeks before.

This timetable explains several puzzling features of the final texts. All of the extant or inferred Crane manuscripts

were prepared by the same scribe, working from undivided copy-text; the three extant Crane manuscripts were all produced between August 13 and December 31, 1624. During this same period, all of the known lost manuscripts were also apparently prepared by a single scribe working from undivided copy-text: so far as we can tell, this was true of [KING'S MEN¹,³], of [PRE-CRANE²,³], and of [MIDDLETON ABRIDGEMENT]. Although we do not know who produced some of these lost manuscripts, they must all have been careful and professional: although the number of shared errors in the earliest extant texts rises slowly with each transcription, the totals remain relatively low in the earliest known copies.

This process seems to have changed radically at about the time that Ralph Crane ceased to be involved in the production of copies. I have tried to track the divisions of copy-text in various lost and extant manuscripts; some of those divisions are more conjectural than others, and there may well have been more lost intervening manuscripts than I have assumed. But the conjectural nature of any specific proposed stemma for any one section of the play should not obscure the larger pattern, which is uncontestable: all the extant NON-CRANE manuscripts derive, directly or at second hand, from divided copy-text. Moreover, two of the three extant NON-CRANE manuscripts were produced by multiple scribes: ROSENBACH was divided between two scribes, BRIDGEWATER between two unknown scribes and Middleton. Not one of those four scribes has

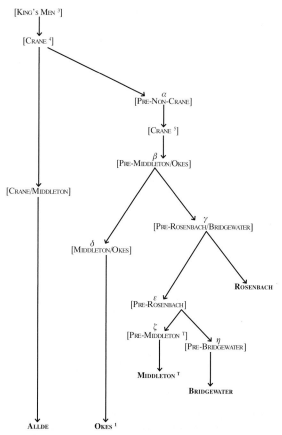

Figure 64. Partial Stemma G: Descendants of [KING'S MEN³]
from 4.1.145 to the end of Act Four. Somewhere
between 4.1.130 and 4.1.145 the copy-text for
[PRE-MIDDLETON^T] changed from [CRANE⁵] to [PRE-ROSENBACH].

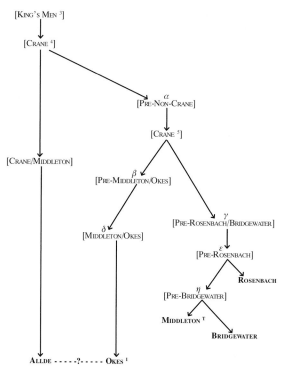

Figure 65. Partial Stemma H: Descendants of [KING'S
MEN³] in Act Five. The dotted line indicates possible
consultation of one printed quarto by the compositor(s) of
the other. Between Act Four and Act Five the copy-text
for [PRE-BRIDGEWATER/ROSENBACH] changed from
[PRE-MIDDLETON/OKES] back to [CRANE⁵], the copy-text for
ROSENBACH changed from [PRE-ROSENBACH/BRIDGEWATER]
back to [PRE-ROSENBACH], and the copy-text for MIDDLETON^T
changed from [PRE-MIDDLETON^T] back to [PRE-BRIDGEWATER].

been identified in other literary manuscripts of the period, and the quality of their work is significantly lower than Crane's.

The process that produced the five extant descendants of [KING'S MEN³] makes it impossible to display their transmission in a single stemma, like Figure 57. In the later stages of transmission, the copy-text for a single new manuscript was often divided between two existing manuscripts. Moreover, these divisions of copy-text did not always occur at the same point in the text. Every time the copy-text for a new manuscript was divided at a certain point, the flow of variants descending from that manuscript was also divided. Hence, the sequence of transmission for the five remaining extant texts can only be visualized in a series of separate stemmata, covering different parts of the play (Figures 58–65).[204]

The advantage of divided copy-text and multiple scribes is that they increase the number of copies that can be produced in a short time. While the second half

of [CRANE⁵] was being copied by Scribe X to produce the second half of [PRE-MIDDLETON/OKES], the first half could be copied by Scribe Y to produce the first half of [PRE-BRIDGEWATER/ROSENBACH]. This cuts in half the time needed for production of the new copy. This is presumably why MATHEWES/ALLDE was divided between two printing houses, but the logic applies equally well to scribal copying. Moreover, the different rates of copying by different scribes can lead to further divisions of copy-text.

This mode of production suggests that, at some time after 1 January 1625, there was a motive for hastening production of manuscript copies, a motive apparently not so pressing in the autumn of 1624, when a number of elaborate dated copies were produced by a single

[204] My figures 57–65 are intended as a replacement for the stemma constructed by Howard-Hill (Figure 1). My partial stemmata differ from those offered by Howard-Hill in *Pasquin*. His stemmata are divided between different groups of textual witnesses, rather than different parts of the play. Thus, his five stemmata can be combined in a single overall map of transmission (Figure 1). Figures 57–65 cannot be combined into a single image.

professional scribe. This evidence of haste in the overall mode of production—multiple scribes, divided copy-text—is confirmed by evidence of haste in the texts themselves. BRIDGEWATER omits most of 2.2, perhaps because of a confusion in the division of copy-text between two scribes; Middleton, rather than properly repairing the gap, instead improvised a short transition, in order to conceal the defect. MIDDLETON[T] likewise omitted sixty-two lines from the second half of 4.4 (again perhaps because of a confusion in the division of copy-text) and dozens of other lines of dialogue, stage directions, and speech prefixes from Act Five.

Obviously, something more important than accuracy was motivating Middleton in the preparation of these two late copies. Equally obviously, Middleton was trying to save money: given the quality of his work, Crane must have been a more expensive scribe than the anonymous copyists who produced ROSENBACH and BRIDGEWATER. Since Middleton was involved in the final form of both those manuscripts, he must have been to some extent responsible for, or at least amenable to, the copying of his text by those persons. Likewise, the fact that two different printed editions of the play were produced at about the same time—OKES and MATHEWES/ALLDE—at least opens the possibility that Middleton may have deliberately sold manuscripts to two different stationers. The fact that the banned play could not be licensed and therefore could not be registered at Stationers' Hall would have made this double sale easier to manage. Middleton had done something similar with *Sir Robert Sherley*, printing separate dedications to different patrons. Personal financial difficulties apparently prompted the 1609 subterfuge, and the same motive may explain the apparent double-sale of 1625.

Moreover, there may well be a relationship between the haste in producing low-quality copies and the apparent double-sale to two stationers. Given his personal relationship with Okes, Middleton must have known that the play was being set into type by at least one stationer; he would therefore also have known that the demand for manuscripts was about to plummet. Once hundreds of printed copies went on sale, manuscripts would immediately cease to be rare and uniquely valuable commodities. A more accurate text would be a less valuable text, if the pursuit of accuracy delayed completion, as both Middleton and the stationers raced to take maximum economic advantage of the demand for texts of the play.

XXX. Editorial Procedures

This edition differs from previous treatments of *A Game at Chess* in several respects. For the first time, it publishes two versions of the play in a single book. What we identify as *An Early Form* is printed here for the first time. What we identify as *A Later Form* is the first systematically eclectic edition of the play ever published. Thus, these two versions of the play not only enable readers to compare Middleton's

original conception with its eventual theatrical realization; they also embody two quite different editorial philosophies.

An Early Form attempts to reconstruct a particular lost manuscript, [MIDDLETON[PRE]], the author's first complete draft of the play. *An Early Form* represents an originary text, determinedly authorial in its substance and presentation: words, spellings, punctuation, capitalization, spatial configuration. Necessarily, it fails in this editorial objective, because it is impossible to recover a lost authorial presence; only 'proximities' are achievable (Taylor, 1993). The text of *An Early Form* has been reconstructed using an editorial model articulated most influentially, in this century and this field, by McKerrow, Greg, Bowers, and Tanselle—which is to say that it is not merely a diplomatic transcript, not a photographic or digital reproduction of a single document. Nevertheless, in its recognition of the artistic integrity of separate versions of the work, this edition departs from that mid-century model, in the direction of the kind of 'versioning' advocated most influentially, in this field, by Taylor, Warren, and Wells. The editorial principles that govern *An Early Form* are similar to those which governed the old-spelling text of *The History of King Lear* (Wells and Taylor, 1987). *An Early Form* reproduces many more features of early modern manuscripts than did *The History of King Lear*, but it does commit itself to recovering the substantive readings of a single originary document of the play.

By contrast, *A Later Form* is not governed by the same editorial principles which governed the corresponding Wells-Taylor companion text, *The Tragedy of King Lear*. For *Lear*, there was only one substantive witness to the revised text; for *Game*, there are seven. In this as in other respects, the debates about 'versioning' and editorial theory in early modern drama have been simplified, and distorted, by the massive canonical dominance of Shakespeare (Taylor, 1993). The paucity of substantive documents in the Shakespeare canon leaves his editors with only one document per version (if that), a mathematical accident which allows them to elide the difference between versions and documents. That elision cannot be entertained in *Game*, where the plurality of documents, each in some way an inadequate representation of the revision, forces us to attend, not 'The Marriage of Good and Bad Quartos', but the marriage of versioning and eclecticism. *A Later Form* does not attempt to reproduce one of the extant documents, or to reconstruct one of the lost documents.

As often, marriage is accompanied by divorce. The defence of editorial versioning, in the Shakespeare canon, relied heavily upon the claim that Shakespeare himself was personally responsible for both versions. Given Shakespeare's relationship to the theatrical company which performed his plays, that claim was and is plausible; but in a critical culture saturated with bardolatry, that claim inevitably had to be articulated with a vehemence which obscured a number of editorial issues. By equating 'versions' with 'authorial revision', the textual radicals of the 1980s—including myself—did not challenge the orthodox editorial pursuit of an originary text; we simply supplied *two* originary texts, each a witness to an independent act of authorial creation. Each 'version' constituted not only a materially distinct document, but an aesthetically distinct object of desire, with its own alleged coherence, integrity, and purpose. But the production of such independent versions does not require the reappearance of an originary author; nor does the reappearance of an originary author inevitably produce independent versions. The freelance Middleton could hardly have controlled performances of his text as routinely or securely as the shareholder Shakespeare did. And although we possess texts of *Game* wholly or partly in Middleton's own handwriting, Middleton doubles in each such document the roles of scribe and author: a not very competent scribe, rather carelessly copying a text, and a sporadic reviser, introducing verbal variants into whatever he copied, but doing so haphazardly and inconsistently, without any sustained or determinable intention to produce a significantly different 'work'.

The insistence on the independence of the two versions of *Lear* was and is made plausible by the evidence that the revision of that play was made several years after the original composition; but all the extant documents of *Game* were probably produced within months of its first performance. Versions do not require authorial revisions, authorial revisions do not always produce independent versions—and new authorial versions are not always improvements. Howard-Hill has argued that the macro-revisions to *Game*, although undoubtedly composed by Middleton, were suggested by the King's Men, and betray the spirit and coherence of Middleton's original conception; I disagree with Howard-Hill's assessment, but my assessment, like his, is critical, not editorial. It may affect whether we think a version is worth reproducing, but it does not affect our conclusions about who wrote the words, or where a text belongs in a genealogical stemma. Such editorial objectivity is unimaginable in the case of Shakespeare: critical distaste for a revision immediately leads to the editorial conclusion that Shakespeare could not have been responsible for it—and evidence that Shakespeare was not responsible for a revision leads (as in *Macbeth* and *Measure for Measure*) to devaluation of the unShakespearian material.

The change in editorial perspective is epitomized by the difference between *Shakespeare's Revision of King Lear* (Urkowitz, 1980) and 'A Game at Chess: A Later Form': the difference between that singular 'Revision'/version, attributed to an originary author, and 'a' form, one of many possible shapes, not labelled authorially but temporally, vaguely, positionally. Our titular *Later* has meaning only in relation to the *Early* which editorially labels a preceding text in the same volume. How much later? In one sense, weeks or months, between completion of the first authorial version (in late May 1624) and public circulation of the revised version (in the last four months of 1624 and the first five months of 1625); in another sense, centuries.

The documents produced in 1624-5 differ significantly from our edition of *A Later Form*, produced early in the twenty-first century, in modern spelling, punctuation, and typography, with a paratext of introduction and commentary designed for postmodern readers. This *Later Form* is an attempt to realize, in practice, McGann's theoretical elevation of the 'socialized text' into an object of editorial desire. It seeks to reconstruct, not only the play as collaboratively produced and performed in August 1624, but a *reading text* which could effectively represent those performances: a reading text cumulatively constructed not only by Middleton, but by Ralph Crane and many other collaborators in 1624 and 1625—and by another set of intermediaries working centuries later: not only myself and my immediate collaborators, but the previous scholars and editors who have made this edition possible.

WORKS CITED

Editions

Bald, R. C., ed., *A Game at Chesse* (1929)

Bawcutt, N. W., ed., *Ralph Crane's Transcript of 'A Game at Chess'*, Bodleian Manuscript Malone 25, in *Collections XV*, Malone Society (1993)

Brooke, C. F. Tucker, and N. B. Paradise, eds., *A Game at Chess*, in *English Drama, 1580-1642* (1933), 943-77

Dutton, Richard, ed., *Thomas Middleton: 'Women Beware Women' and other plays*, Oxford World's Classics (1999)

Harper, J. W., ed., *A Game at Chess*, New Mermaids (1966)

Howard-Hill, T. H., ed., *A Game at Chess by Thomas Middleton 1624*, Malone Society (1990)

—— ed., *A Game at Chess*, Revels Plays (1993)

—— ed., *The Bridgewater Manuscript of Thomas Middleton's 'A Game at Chess'* (1624) (1995)

Lamb, Charles, ed., *Specimens of English Dramatic Poets* (1835)

Secondary Works

Adams, Simon, 'Spain or the Netherlands? The Dilemmas of Early Stuart Foreign Policy', in *Before the English Civil War*, ed. Howard Tomlinson (1983), 79-101

B., G., tr., [Vida], *Ludus Scacchiae: Chesse-play* (1597)

Bacon, Francis, 'On the Fortunate Memory of Elizabeth Queen of England', in *Works*, ed. James Spedding (1857-9)

Bald, R. C., 'A New Manuscript of Middleton's "Game at Chesse"', *Modern Language Review* 15 (1930), 474-8

—— 'An Early Version of Middleton's "Game at Chesse"', *Modern Language Review* 38 (1943), 177-80

Barbrook, Adrian C., Christopher J. Howe, Norman Blake, and Peter Robinson, 'The phylogeny of *The Canterbury Tales*', *Nature* 394 (1998), 839

Bawcutt, N. W., ed., *The Control and Censorship of Caroline Drama: The Records of Sir Henry Herbert, Master of the Revels 1623-73* (1996)

Bergeron, David M., ed., *King James & Letters of Homoerotic Desire* (1999)

Blayney, Peter W. M., *The Texts of 'King Lear' and their Origins*, Volume I: *Nicholas Okes and the First Quarto* (1982)

Bordalejo, Barbara, 'The phylogeny of the tale-order in the *Canterbury Tales*', unpublished doctoral dissertation (New York University, 2003), available online at http://www.bordalejo.net/theses.html

Braunmuller, A. R., '"To the Globe I rowed": John Holles Sees *A Game at Chess*', *English Literary Renaissance* 20 (1990), 340–56

Brecht, Bertolt, *Little Treatise on the Theatre* (1949)

Brown, John Russell, ed., *The Duchess of Malfi*, Revels Plays (1974)

Butler's Lives of the Saints, edited, revised, and supplemented by H. Thurson and D. Attwater, 4 vols (1956)

Capablanca, J. R., *My Chess Career* (1920)

Carlton, Sir Dudley, *Letters* (1778)

Cawley, A. C., and Barry Gaines, ed., *A Yorkshire Tragedy*, Revels Plays (1986)

Chamberlain, John, *The Letters of John Chamberlain*, ed. N. E. McClure, 2 vols (1939)

Cogswell, Thomas, 'Thomas Middleton and the Court, 1624: *A Game at Chess* in Context', *Huntington Library Quarterly* 47 (1984), 273–88

—— *The Blessed Revolution: English Politics and the Coming of War, 1621–1624* (1989)

—— 'Phaeton's chariot: The Parliament-men and the continental crisis in 1621', in *The Political World of Thomas Wentworth, Earl of Strafford, 1621–1641*, ed. J. F. Merritt (1996), 24–46

Cranfield, Nicholas, and Kenneth Fincham, ed., 'John Howson's Answer to Archbishop's Abbot's Accusations', *Camden Miscellany* XXIX, Fourth Series, vol. 34 (1987), 319–42

Cust, Richard, 'News and Politics in Early Seventeenth Century England', *Past and Present* 111 (1986), 60–90

D., J., *The Coronation of Queen Elizabeth, With the Restauration of the Protestant Religion: or, The Downfal of the Pope* (1680)

Dekker, Thomas, *A Critical Old-Spelling Edition of Thomas Dekker's 'Blurt Master Constable'*, ed. Thomas Leland Berger (1979)

Derrida, Jacques, 'The Law of Genre', in *On Narrative*, ed. W. J. T. Mitchell (1981), 51–77

D'Ewes, Sir Simonds. *The Autobiography and Correspondence of Sir Simonds D'Ewes, Bart. during the reins of James I and Charles I*, ed. J. O. Halliwell, 2 vols (1845)

Dibdin, Charles, *Complete History of the Stage* (1795)

Donne, John, *The Sermons of John Donne*, ed. Evelyn M. Simpson and George R. Potter, 10 vols (1953–62)

—— *Ignatius his Conclave*, ed. T. S. Healy (1969)

Drayton, Michael, *The Works of Michael Drayton*, ed. J. William Hebel, 5 vols (1961)

Eisenstein, Elizabeth, 'Afterword', *The Printing Revolution in Early Modern Europe*, rev. edn. (2005), 313–58

Eliot, T. S., 'Thomas Middleton' (1927), in *Selected Essays* (1951), 161–70

—— 'Fifty Years On', *Times Literary Supplement* (25 January 1980), 89; reprint of original review of Bald's edition of *Game*, published anonymously, *Times Literary Supplement* (23 January 1930)

Elliott, J. H., *The Count-Duke of Olivares: The Statesman in an Age of Decline* (1986)

Fincham, Kenneth, 'George Abbot', *Oxford Dictionary of National Biography* (2004)

Fleay, F. G., *A Biographical Chronicle of the English Drama, 1559–1642*, 2 vols (1891)

Fletcher, John, and Philip Massinger, *The Tragedy of Sir John van Olden Barnavelt*, ed. T. H. Howard-Hill, Malone Society (1980)

Foakes, R.A., *Illustrations of the English Stage, 1580–1642* (1984)

Foucault, Michel, *The History of Sexuality*, Volume I: *An Introduction*, trans. Robert Hurley (1980)

Frank, Joseph, *The Beginnings of the English Newspaper, 1620–1660* (1961)

Geertz, Clifford, *Negara: The Theatre State in Nineteenth-Century Bali* (1980)

George, David, 'A Critical Study of Thomas Middleton's Borrowings and of his imitations of other authors in his prose, poetry and dramatic work', unpublished Ph.D. thesis (University of London, 1966)

Goodman, Godfrey, *The Court of King James the First* (1839)

Gordon, D. J., 'Middleton's *No Wit, No Help like a Woman's* and Della Porta's *La Sorella*', *Review of English Studies* 17 (1941), 400–14

Greenblatt, Stephen, *Shakespearean Negotiations: The Circulation of Social Energy in Renaissance England* (1988)

Greg, W. W., *Dramatic Documents from the Elizabethan Playhouses* (1931)

—— *The Shakespeare First Folio: its bibliographical and textual history* (1955)

Gunby, David, David Carnegie, Antony Hammond, Doreen DelVecchio, and MacDonald P. Jackson, eds., *The Works of John Webster: An Old-Spelling Critical Edition* (1995–2007), 3 vols

Pope Gregory XV, *The Popes Letter To the Prince: in Latine, Spanish, and English. Done according to the Latine and Spanish Coppies Printed at Madrid. A Iesuites Oration to the Prince, in Latine and English* (1623)

Habermas, Jürgen, *The Structural Transformation of the Public Sphere: An Inquiry into a Category of Bourgeois Society*, trans. Thomas Burger and Frederick Lawrence (1989)

Hanna, Ralph, 'The Application of Thought to Textual Criticism in All Modes—with Apologies to A. E. Housman', *Studies in Bibliography* 53 (2000), 163–72

Hazlitt, William, *Characters of Shakespeare's Plays* (1815)

Heinemann, Margot, *Puritanism and Theatre: Thomas Middleton and Opposition Drama under the Early Stuarts* (1980)

Honigmann, E. A. J., *The Texts of 'Othello' and Shakespearian Revision* (1996)

Hope, Jonathan, *Shakespeare's Grammar* (2003)

Hotson, Leslie, *Shakespeare's Wooden O* (1959)

Howard-Hill, T. H., 'Ralph Crane's Parentheses', *Notes and Queries* 210 (1965), 334–40

—— *Ralph Crane and Some Shakespeare First Folio Comedies* (1972)

—— 'The Author as Scribe or Reviser? Middleton's Intentions in *A Game at Chess*', *TEXT* 3 (1987), 305–18

—— 'The Unique Eye-Witness Report of Middleton's *A Game at Chess*', *Review of English Studies* 42 (1991), 168–78

—— 'Shakespeare's Earliest Editor, Ralph Crane', *Shakespeare Survey* 44 (1992), 113–29

—— *Middleton's 'Vulgar Pasquin': Essays on 'A Game at Chess'* (1995)

Howe, Christopher, Adrian Barbrook, Linne Mooney, and Peter Robinson, 'Parallels between stemmatology and phylogenetics', in Reneen *et al*, 3–11

Howell, James, *Epistolae Ho Elianae: familiar letters domestic & forren* (1673)

Ioppolo, Grace, *Revising Shakespeare* (1991)

James I, *Political Works*, ed. Charles H. McIlwain (1918)

Jonson, Ben, *Ben Jonson*, ed. C. H. Herford, Percy and Evelyn Simpson, 11 vols (1925–52)

Joyce, James, *Ulysses: A Critical and Synoptic Edition*, ed. Hans Walter Gabler *et al*. (1984)

Lake, Peter, 'Lancelot Andrewes, John Buckeridge, and Avant-Garde Conformity at the Court of James I', in *The Mental World of the Jacobean Court*, ed. Linda Levy Peck (1991), 113–33

Limon, Jerzy, *Dangerous Matter: English Drama and Politics in 1623/4* (1986)

Lockyer, Roger, *Buckingham: The Life and Political Career of George Villiers, First Duke of Buckingham 1592–1628* (1981)

Maas, Paul, *Textual Criticism*, trans. Barbara Flower (1958)

McKenzie, D. F., 'Speech—Manuscript—Print', in *Making Meaning: Printers of the Mind and Other Essays*, ed. P. MacDonald and M. Suarez (2002), 237–58

Milton, John, *Works*, ed. Jonathan Goldberg and Stephen Orgel (1994)

Mink, Gerd, 'Problems of a highly contaminated tradition: the New Testament: Stemmata of variants as a source of a genealogy for witnesses', in Reneen *et al.*, 13–86

Moore, J. R., 'The Contemporary Significance of Middleton's *A Game at Chess*', *PMLA* 50 (1935), 761–8

More, Thomas, *Utopia*, ed. Edward Surtz and J. H. Hexter (1965)

Moretti, Franco, *Signs Taken for Wonders: Essays in the Sociology of Literary Forms*, trans. Susan Fischer (1983)

Morris, E. C., 'The Allegory in Middleton's *A Game at Chess*', *Englische Studien*, 38 (1907), 39–52

Moryson, Fynes, *An Itinerary…containing his ten yeares trauell* (1617)

Moxon, Joseph, *Mechanick Exercises on the Whole Art of Printing (1683–4)*, ed. Herbert Davis and Harry Carter (1962)

Mulryne, J. R., ed., *Women Beware Women*, Revels Plays (1975)

Nascimento, S. Z., 'Thomas Middleton's *A Game at Chesse*: A Textual Study', unpublished Ph.D. diss. (University of Maryland, 1975)

Nashe, Thomas, *Works*, ed. Ronald B. McKerrow, 5 vols (1904–10)

Owen, Lewis, *The Running Register* (1626)

Pastor, Antonio, 'Un Embajador de España en la Escena Inglesa', in *Homenaje ofrecido a Menéndez Pidal* (1925), 3:241–61

Patterson, Annabel M., *Censorship and Interpretation: The Conditions of Writing and Reading in Early Modern England* (1984)

Peck, Linda Levy, *Court Patronage and Corruption in Early Stuart England* (1990)

Pocock, J. G. A., *The Machiavellian Moment: Florentine Political Thought and the Atlantic Republican Tradition* (1975)

Pound, Ezra, *Personae* (1926)

Price, George R., 'The Huntington MS. of *A Game at Chesse*', *Huntington Library Quarterly* 17 (1953–4), 83–8

—— 'The Latin Oration in *A Game at Chess*', *Huntington Library Quarterly* 23 (1960), 389–93

Pursell, Brennan C., *Gondomar: A Spaniard in King James's Court*, North American Society for Court Studies, Occasional Pamphlet 1 (2000)

—— 'The End of the Spanish Match', *Historical Journal* 45 (2002), 699–726

—— *The Winter King: Frederick V of the Palatinate and the Coming of the Thirty Years' War* (2003)

Puttenham, George, *The Arte of English Poesie*, ed. Gladys D. Willcock and Alice Walker (1936)

Rabelais, François, *Oeuvres Complètes* (1973)

Raymond, Thomas, *Autobiography of Thomas Raymond and Memoirs of the Family of Guise of Elmore, Gloucestershire*, ed. G. Davies (1917)

Redworth, Glyn, *The Prince and the Infanta: The Cultural Politics of the Spanish Match* (2003)

Reneen, Peter van, August den Hollander, Margot van Mulken, eds., *Studies in Stemmatology II* (2004)

Rhodes, Elizabeth, *This Tight Embrace: Luisa de Carvajal y Mendoza (1566–1614)* (2000)

Russell, Conrad, *Parliaments and English Politics, 1621–1629* (1979)

Salemans, B. J. P., 'Building Stemmas with the Computer in a Cladistic, Neo-Lachmannian, Way: The Case of Fourteen Text Versions of Lanseloet van Denemerken' (unpublish. Ph.D. dissertation, Nijmegen, 2000)

Shami, Jeanne, '"Twice a day on the banke side"?: A Contemporary Report on Middleton's *A Game at Chesse*', *Notes and Queries* 45 (1998), 367–70

Sharpe, Kevin, *Faction and Parliament* (1978)

Sidney, Philip, *A Defence of Poetry*, in *Miscellaneous Prose*, ed. Katherine Duncan-Jones and Jan van Dorsten (1973)

Spencer, Matthew, Linne R. Mooney, Adrian C. Barbrook, Barbara Bordalejo, Christopher J. Howe, and Peter Robinson, 'The effects of weighting kinds of variants', in Reneen *et al.*, 227–39

Stern, Tiffany, *Rehearsal from Shakespeare to Sheridan* (2000)

—— '"A Small-Beer Health to His Second Day": Playwrights, Prologues, and First Performances in the Early Modern Theater', *Studies in Philology* 101 (2004), 172–99

Strauss, Leo, *Persecution and the Art of Writing* (1952)

Stuart Royal Proclamations, ed. James F. Larkin and Paul L. Hughes, 2 vols (1973–83)

Sugden, Edward H., *A Topographical Dictionary to the Works of Shakespeare and His Fellow Dramatists* (1925)

Tacitus, Cornelius, *Annales*, ed. F. R. D. Goodyear (1972)

Tanselle, G. Thomas, 'External Fact as an Editorial Problem', *Studies in Bibliography* 32 (1979), 1–47

Taylor, Gary, 'Copy-Text and Collation (with special reference to *Richard III*),' *The Library*, VI, 3 (1981), 33–42

—— '*Praestat Difficilior Lectio*: *All's Well that Ends Well* and *Richard III*', *Renaissance Studies* 2 (1988), 27–46

—— 'The Renaissance and the End | of Editing', in *Palimpsest: Editorial Theory in the Humanities*, ed. George Bornstein and Ralph G. Williams (1993), 121–49

—— 'Forms of Opposition: Shakespeare and Middleton', *English Literary Renaissance* 24 (1994), 283–314

—— *Castration: An Abbreviated History of Western Manhood* (2000a)

—— 'c:/wp/file.txt 05:41 10-07-98', in *The Renaissance Text: Theory, History, Editing*, ed. Andrew Murphy (Manchester University Press, 2000b), 44–54

—— 'Divine [ ]sences', *Shakespeare Survey* 54 (2001), 13–30

—— *Buying Whiteness: Race, Culture, and Identity from Columbus to Hip Hop* (2005)

—— and John Jowett, *Shakespeare Reshaped 1606–1623* (1993)

Thorius, Raphael, 'Ignatius Loyolae Apotheosis', in *A Variorum Edition of the Poems of John Donne*, vol. 8, *The Epigrams, Epithalamiums, Epitaphs, Inscriptions, and Miscellaneous Poems* (1995), 253, 467–71

Trollope, Anthony, *Notes on the Old Drama*, ed. Elizabeth R. Epperly (1988)

Tyacke, Nicholas, *Anti-Calvinists: The Rise of English Arminianism c. 1590–1640* (1987)

Tyacke, Sarah, 'Mapsellers and the London map trade c.1650–1710', in Helen Wallis and Sarah Tyacke, ed., *My Head is a Map: Essays and memoirs in honour of R. V. Tooley* (1973), 63–80

Urkowitz, Steven, *Shakespeare's Revision of King Lear* (1980)

Wadsworth, James, *The memoires of Mr. James Wadswort [sic], a Jesuit that recanted* (1679)

Wagner, Bernard M., untitled review of Bald's edition, *Modern Language Notes* 46 (1931), 195–6

Wallace, David, 'Periodizing Women: Mary Ward (1585–1645) and the Premodern Canon', *Journal of Medieval and Early Modern Studies* 36 (2006), 395–451

Ward, A. W., *A History of English Dramatic Literature* (1875), 2:98–102

Watt, Tessa, *Cheap Print and Popular Piety, 1550–1640* (1991)

West, Anthony James *The Shakespeare First Folio: The History of the Book*, Volume II: *A New Worldwide Census of First Folios* (2003)

Williams, Gordon, *A Dictionary of Sexual Language and Imagery in Shakespearean and Stuart Literature*, 3 vols (1994)

Wilson, F. P., 'Ralph Crane, Scrivener to the King's Players', *The Library*, IV, 7 (1926), 194–215

Wright, Louis B., 'A Game at Chess', *Times Literary Supplement* (16 February 1928), 112

Yachnin, Paul, 'A Game at Chess and Chess Allegory', *Studies in English Literature, 1500–1900* 22 (1982), 317–30

——'A Game at Chess: Thomas Middleton's "Praise of Folly"', *Modern Language Quarterly* 48 (1987), 107–23

Zimmerman, Susan [= S. Z. Nascimento], 'The Folger Manuscripts of Thomas Middleton's *A Game at Chess*: A Study in the Genealogy of Texts', *Papers of the Bibliographical Society of America* 76 (1982), 159–95

APPENDIX A: SHARED ERRORS IN DIALOGUE

In this and the following appendices I provide analytical lists of the data used in the analysis of shared error, which is central to my conclusions about the stemmatic relationship of the extant texts of *A Game at Chess*. I begin with a list of the readings identified as shared errors, in the order in which those errors appear in the text of the play. These lists do not attempt an analysis of the readings, or give a full collation of variants; they simply identify which texts share the error. Readers seeking more information should consult the full note in the Textual Notes to *Later*. [I have listed variants in 3.2 in the sequence that they occupy in the texts that contain the scene; in the edited text of *Later* they are placed at the end of the text, as Additional Passage D.]

This preliminary list of shared errors is followed by a summary of their distribution ('Patterns of Shared Error'). I group the patterns in order of complexity, beginning with the simplest (errors linking only two texts), and proceeding to the most complex (errors linking up to eight texts). Within each such grouping, I list the patterns in order of frequency, from rarest to commonest.

This summary of patterns of distribution is followed by a summary of totals of shared error per individual text.

List of shared errors in dialogue (including speech prefixes)

Induction.14/28   and their] ~ ₐ BRIDGEWATER[A], OKES

Induction.23/37   Let] letts MIDDLETON[T], BRIDGEWATER[A], OKES

1.1.7/110   They're] Theis are CRANE[2,3]

1.1.137/249   fond] found OKES, CRANE/MATHEWES

1.1.165/282   then] *not in* BRIDGEWATER[A], OKES

1.1.201/323   comes] come ROSENBACH[A], OKES [passage not in CRANE[3]]

1.1.241/366   a] *not in* CRANE[2], CRANE[3], ROSENBACH[A]

1.1.248/375   kingdoms] kingdome ROSENBACH[A], OKES

1.1.270/396   Priapus...gardens,] *not in* CRANE[2,3]

1.1.271/397   is] are CRANE[2,3]

1.1.272/398   keep] be CRANE[3]; b BRIDGEWATER[A] *uncorrected*

1.1.279/407   these] this ROSENBACH[A], CRANE/MATHEWES

1.1.307/439   work] word OKES, BRIDGEWATER[A] *uncorrected*

1.1.311/444   wounded] wound CRANE[2,3], OKES

1.1.324/459   strength] *not in* MIDDLETON[T], BRIDGEWATER[A], OKES

2.1.16/489   industrious] induftirous BRIDGEWATER[A]; indufterous OKES [passage not in CRANE[3]]

2.1.130/617   by] *not in* CRANE[2,4], ROSENBACH[A] [passage not in CRANE[3]]

2.1.146/639   master swelled] Maſ= ſweld BRIDGEWATER[A]; Maſ--ſwell OKES [passage not in CRANE[3]]

2.1.177/674   barques...vessels] Veſſells...Barkes CRANE/MATHEWES, BRIDGEWATER[A] [passage not in CRANE[3]]

2.1.179/677   BLACK BISHOP'S...none.] *not in* CRANE[3], BRIDGEWATER[A], OKES. [The omission from CRANE[3] may well be deliberate abridgement.]

2.1.212/720   facetious] factious ROSENBACH[A], OKES

2.1.237/753   And...throughly] *not in* BRIDGEWATER[A], OKES [passage not in CRANE[3]]

2.1.239/757   troubled with much] much troubled with BRIDGEWATER[A], OKES [passage not in CRANE[3]]

2.2.3/763   but for] ~ ₐ BRIDGEWATER[A], OKES

2.2.33/800   Venus-baths] DYCE; Venus Bath CRANE[2]+; ~ borth OKES. The passage is not present in CRANE[1] or BRIDGEWATER.

2.2.68/840   BLACK KNIGHT] *not in* OKES, BRIDGEWATER

2.2.141   seized] ceard ROSENBACH; ſcarde OKES. Shared misreading of 'z' as 'r'.

3.1.7/1067   for't] *not in* ROSENBACH[A], OKES, BRIDGEWATER[B] *uncorrected* [phrase not in CRANE[2,3]]

3.1.33/1095   FAT BISHOP] *not in* MIDDLETON[T], OKES

3.1.44/1108   FAT BISHOP] *not in* CRANE[3], BRIDGEWATER[B], MIDDLETON[T], OKES

3.1.48/1112   ₐThis] F B ~ BRIDGEWATER[C], MIDDLETON[T], OKES

3.1.73/1137   And...syrup] *not in* CRANE[2,3,4], ROSENBACH[A]

3.1.75/1139   Ambition's] Ambitious MIDDLETON[T], OKES

3.1.127/1195   and] *not in* ROSENBACH, BRIDGEWATER[B], OKES

3.1.199/1281   attempter] attempt CRANE/MATHEWES, ROSENBACH[A]

3.1.203/1285   waked] walkd ROSENBACH[A], walkt OKES

3.1.265/1368   their] this CRANE/ALLDE; his OKES [passage not in CRANE[3]]

3.1.307/1420   KNIGHT] K. OKES, CRANE/ALLDE

3.1.322/1444   you'll] You'de OKES, yould BRIDGEWATER[B]

3.1.333/1455   person] perſons ROSENBACH[A], CRANE/ALLDE

3.2.6/1476   pranced] praunceſt ROSENBACH, BRIDGEWATER *uncorrected* [scene not in CRANE[2,3]]

3.2.40/1519   buttocks] Buttock BRIDGEWATER[B], ROSENBACH[A]. The scene is not in CRANE[2,3].

3.1.352/1528   boads] bounds ROSENBACH[A], BRIDGEWATER[B] *uncorrected* [passage not in CRANE[3]]

3.1.355/1531   vainer] vaine ROSENBACH[A], BRIDGEWATER[B], OKES [passage not in CRANE[3]]

3.1.369/1547   Egyptic] Egipte ROSENBACH[A]; Aegipted BRIDGEWATER[B], OKES. This is counted as a shared error in three texts, since all three mistakenly have an 'e' after 'pt'; however, it might alternatively be interpreted as an example of an error exactly shared between two texts only.

3.1.410/1595   tetrarch] Tetrach CRANE[2,3,4], OKES, BRIDGEWATER[B]

4.1.44–5   bring...And] *not in* CRANE[2,3]

4.1.53/1669   strait, too] *not in* ROSENBACH[A], BRIDGEWATER[B] [passage not in CRANE[3]]

4.1.62/1680   uncloses] encloſes CRANE[1], OKES [passage not in CRANE[3]]

4.1.97/1721   confirmed] confident ROSENBACH[A], BRIDGEWATER[B]

4.1.107/1735 BLACK] wh. CRANE², ROSENBACH^A *uncorrected*

4.1.116/1744 Their...'em] *not in* CRANE²,³,⁴, ROSENBACH, BRIDGE-WATER, OKES

4.2.4/1788 pounds] OKES, CRANE/ALLDE; pound CRANE¹+; paund ROSENBACH, BRIDGEWATER

4.2.16/1801 yet] it ROSENBACH, BRIDGEWATER [passage not in CRANE³]

4.2.44/1831 three] thee CRANE/ALLDE; the ROSENBACH

4.2.44/1831 mummy] money OKES, mony ROSENBACH

4.2.47/1834 baked] backt OKES; backte BRIDGEWATER

4.2.74/1861 thousand] *not in* OKES, BRIDGEWATER *uncorrected*

4.2.82/1871 *Poenitentiaria*] Poenitentia CRANE¹, BRIDGEWATER

4.2.83/1872 prices] prizes OKES, BRIDGEWATER

4.4.1/1949 Duke] Knight MIDDLETON^T, BRIDGEWATER, ROSENBACH

4.4.10/1958 glitt'ring'st] glittering OKES, CRANE/ALLDE

4.4.11/1959 his] theire MIDDLETON^T; theife ROSENBACH^A; this BRIDGEWATER^B [all three share 'th' in place of the correct 'h']

4.4.15/1963 that] yonder BRIDGEWATER, ROSENBACH

4.4.20/1970 your] the ROSENBACH^A, BRIDGEWATER^B

4.4.31/1980+1 For...thoughts] *not in* MIDDLETON^T, BRIDGEWA-TER, ROSENBACH [passage not in CRANE³]

4.4.33/1982 made] make BRIDGEWATER, ROSENBACH [passage not in CRANE³]

4.4.37/1986 Rombaut's] Rambants CRANE¹; Rumbants MIDDLE-TON^T+. The 'n' in the second syllable, present in all witnesses, is apparently a misreading of 'u'. [The error was probably authorial.]

4.4.38/1987 Mechlin] Methlin ROSENBACH, BRIDGEWATER, OKES

4.4.39/1988 my] *not in* ROSENBACH, BRIDGEWATER *uncorrected*

5.1.1/2004 Hold, hold!] *not in* CRANE²,³

5.1.4/2007 *arce*] Arte OKES, CRANE/ALLDE

5.1.6/2009 snapped] fnap BRIDGEWATER^B, CRANE/ALLDE

5.1.7/2010 *sic*] Sir BRIDGEWATER^B, ROSENBACH^B

5.1.11–2/2018 *peramantibus*] *per amantibus* CRANE³,⁴

5.1.15/2022 *promisisse*] promiffiffe OKES, CRANE/ALLDE

5.1.18/2026 *sospitem*] Sofpitim OKES, CRANE/ALLDE

5.1.39/2043 thee] *thee the* CRANE/ALLDE, OKES

5.2.70/2132 BLACK BISHOP'S PAWN] Bl.Q.P. CRANE/ALLDE, MIDDLETON^B *uncorrected*

5.2.75/2138 suffered'st] fuffereft ROSENBACH^A, OKES

5.2.81/2145 BLACK QUEEN'S PAWN] *not in* CRANE³, MIDDLETON^T

5.2.86/2155 BLACK QUEEN'S PAWN] *not in* CRANE³, MIDDLETON^T

5.2.108/2183 QUEEN] Q.P. CRANE³,⁴, ROSENBACH^A, OKES

5.2.114/2192 O merciless bloodhound] *not in* MIDDLETON^T,B

5.3.5/2206 WHITE KNIGHT I...on't] *not in* MIDDLETON^B, ROSEN-BACH^A

5.3.11/2212 Ebusus] Eleusis CRANE, ROSENBACH, BRIDGEWATER, MIDDLETON^T

5.3.12/2213 Chalcedon] Caldedon MIDDLETON^B, ROSENBACH^A

5.3.32/2235 often] after CRANE/ALLDE, OKES

5.3.116/2328 Plutus] Pluto ROSENBACH^A, OKES

5.3.188/2408 Fat] *not in* CRANE/ALLDE, OKES [passage not in CRANE³]

5.3.210-11/2433-4 Foh...hither.] *not in* CRANE²,⁴, OKES. This entire bag sequence is not present in CRANE¹ (an earlier version of the ending) or CRANE³ (an abridgement).

Epilogue.5/2452 denoted] deuoted CRANE/ALLDE, OKES

Epilogue.6/2453 devoted] denoted CRANE/ALLDE, OKES

Pattern of Shared Dialogue Errors

Shared Dialogue Errors Linking Two Texts

CRANE¹–OKES: 1?

    4.1.62 [passage not in CRANE³]

CRANE¹–BRIDGEWATER: 1

    4.2.82

CRANE²–ROSENBACH: 1

    4.1.107

CRANE³,⁴: 1

    5.1.11–12

CRANE³–BRIDGEWATER: 1

    1.1.272

BRIDGEWATER–MIDDLETON^T: 1

    5.2.114

CRANE³–MIDDLETON^T: 2

    5.2.81

    5.2.86

MIDDLETON^T–OKES: 2

    3.1.33

    3.1.75

[CRANE⁴]–BRIDGEWATER: 2–3

    2.1.177 [passage not in CRANE³]

    [gap in Bridgewater]

    5.1.6

    5.2.70

CRANE²,³: 5

    1.1.7

    1.1.269

    1.1.270

    4.4.44–5

    5.1.1

[CRANE⁴]–ROSENBACH: 4

    1.1.279

    3.1.199

    3.1.333

    4.2.44

ROSENBACH–OKES: 7–9

    1.1.201 [passage not in CRANE³]

    1.1.248

    2.1.146 [passage not in CRANE³]

    2.1.212

    2.2.141

    3.1.203

    4.2.44

    5.2.75

    5.3.116

BRIDGEWATER–OKES: 9–12

    Induction.14

    1.1.165

    1.1.307

    2.1.16 [passage not in CRANE³]

    2.1.237 [passage not in CRANE³]

    2.1.239 [passage not in CRANE³]

    2.2.3

    2.2.68

    [gap in BRIDGEWATER]

    3.1.322

    4.2.47

    4.2.74

    4.2.83

OKES–CRANE⁴/MATHEWES/ALLDE: 10–12

    1.1.137

    [Change from CRANE/MATHEWES to CRANE/ALLDE]

    3.1.265 [passage not in CRANE³]

    3.1.307

4.4.10
5.1.4
5.1.15
5.1.18
5.1.39
5.3.32
5.3.188 [passage not in CRANE[3]]
Epilogue.5
Epilogue.6

ROSENBACH–BRIDGEWATER: **8–14**
3.2.6 [scene not in CRANE[2,3]]
3.2.40 [scene not in CRANE[2,3]]
3.1.352 [passage not in CRANE[3]]
4.1.53 [passage not in CRANE[3]]
4.1.97
4.2.4
4.2.16 [passage not in CRANE[3]]
4.4.15
4.4.20
4.4.33 [passage not in CRANE[3]]
4.4.39
5.1.7
[BRIDGEWATER becomes autograph]
5.3.5
5.3.12

Shared Dialogue Errors Linking Three Texts
CRANE[2]–[CRANE[4]]–ROSENBACH: 1?
2.1.130 [passage not in CRANE[3]]

CRANE[3]–BRIDGEWATER–OKES: 1?
2.1.179 [absence of the line in CRANE[3] may be deliberate abridgement]

CRANE[2]–[CRANE[4]]–OKES: 1?
5.3.210–11 [passage not in CRANE[3]]

CRANE[2,3]–ROSENBACH: 1
1.1.241

CRANE[2,3]–OKES: 1
1.1.311

ROSENBACH–BRIDGEWATER–MIDDLETON[T]: **2–3**
4.4.1
4.4.11
4.4.31 [passage not in CRANE[3]]

BRIDGEWATER–MIDDLETON[T]–OKES: **3**
Induction.23
1.1.324
3.1.48

ROSENBACH–BRIDGEWATER–OKES: **3–5**
[gap in BRIDGEWATER ends at 3.1.1]

3.1.7 [phrase not in CRANE[2,3]]
3.1.127
3.1.355 [passage not in CRANE[3]]
3.1.369 [perhaps belongs under BRIDGEWATER–OKES]
4.4.38

Shared Dialogue Errors Linking Four Texts
CRANE[2,3,4]–ROSENBACH: 1
3.1.73

CRANE[3,4]–ROSENBACH[A]–OKES: 1
5.2.108

CRANE[3]–BRIDGEWATER–MIDDLETON[T]–OKES: 1
3.1.44

Shared Dialogue Errors Linking Five Texts
CRANE[2,3,4]–BRIDGEWATER–OKES: 1
3.1.410

Shared Dialogue Errors Linking Six Texts
CRANE[2,3,4]–ROSENBACH–BRIDGEWATER–OKES: 1
4.1.116

Shared Dialogue Errors Linking Seven Texts
CRANE–ROSENBACH–MIDDLETON[T]–BRIDGEWATER: 1
5.3.11

CRANE[2,3,4]–NON-CRANE: 1
2.2.35

Shared Dialogue Errors Linking Eight Texts: 1
4.4.37 [probably authorial]

Dialogue Shared Error Totals by Text
CRANE[1] (4): with one (2), with six (1), with seven (1)
CRANE[2] (16): with one (6), with two (4), with three (1), with four (1) with five (1), with six (2), with seven (1)
MIDDLETON[T] (15): with one (5), with two (6), with three (1), with six (2), with seven (1)
CRANE[3] (20): with one (9), with two (3), with three (3), with four (1) with five (1), with six (2), with seven (1)
CRANE/MATHEWES/ALLDE (29): with one (20), with two (2), with three (2), with four (1) with five (1), with six (2), with seven (1)
ROSENBACH (44): with one (28), with two (10), with three (2), with five (1), with six (2), with seven (1)
BRIDGEWATER (50): with one (32), with two (13), with three (1), with four (1), with five (1), with six (2), with seven (1)—3.1.319–20 removed from total and from subtotal for 'with one'
OKES (53): with one (35), with two (12), with three (2), with four (1) with five (1), with six (1), with seven (1)
Total Shared Dialogue Errors: 93

APPENDIX B: SHARED ERRORS IN LINEATION

For the purpose and organization of this material, see headnote to Appendix A.

List of shared lineation errors
1.1.36–7/145–6 But…still] meek| CRANE[2,3]
1.1.252–4/379–80 The great…less] nor| hierarchy MIDDLETON[T], BRIDGEWATER[A]
1.1.288–90/416–18 Ay…private] your| ply| MIDDLETON[T], BRIDGEWATER[A]
1.1.302/433 Ay…this] *2 lines* CRANE[2,3]: sir|
2.1.39–41/515–16 Boundless…goodness] all| MIDDLETON[T], BRIDGEWATER[A], OKES [passage not in CRANE[3]]
2.1.106–7/591–2 And…safety] should| MIDDLETON[T], BRIDGE-WATER[A], OKES [passage not in CRANE[3]]
2.1.137–8/626–7 Take…vowed since,| If…me] vowed| since MIDDLETON[T], BRIDGEWATER[A], OKES
2.1.144/636–7 I'll…now] *2 lines* MIDDLETON[T], BRIDGEWATER[A]: dangers|
2.1.155–6/649–50 Time…us] he| MIDDLETON[T], BRIDGEWATER[A], OKES
2.1.187–8/688–9 But…unspied] how| BRIDGEWATER[A], OKES

2.2.133-35/911-13 The...method] fell| master| CRANE/MATHEWES, ROSENBACH^A. Passage not in BRIDGEWATER or [CRANE[3]].

3.1.154-5/1228-9 It's...parts] way| ROSENBACH^A, MIDDLETON^T, [CRANE[4]]. Passage not in CRANE[3].

3.2.9-11/1482-4 A...me] like| ROSENBACH^A, BRIDGEWATER^B. Passage not in CRANE[2,3].

3.2.30-1/1506-7 Soft...you] such| BRIDGEWATER^B, OKES, CRANE/ALLDE. Passage not in CRANE[2,3].

3.2.38-40/1517-19 The worst...buttocks] draw| with| MIDDLETON^T, BRIDGEWATER^B. Passage not in CRANE[2,3].

3.1.398/1582 If...soon] *two lines* ROSENBACH^A, BRIDGEWATER^B: he|

3.1.399/1583-4 why...you] yours| ROSENBACH^A, OKES

4.1.21-2/1629-30 The...sir] his| see| CRANE[2,4], ROSENBACH, BRIDGEWATER, OKES. Passage not in CRANE[3].

4.1.38-9/1652-3 And...by] most| ROSENBACH^A, BRIDGEWATER^B

4.1.129-30/1758-9 We...so] given| ROSENBACH^A, OKES

4.2.99-101/1888-90 Thirty-three...too] CRANE[3,4] do not mark division between prose text and verse comment.

4.2.107-8/1897-8 Sodomy...Bishop] euer| MIDDLETON^T, ROSENBACH^A

5.1.10-19/2017-27 *Si...congratulamur*] *verse* OKES, CRANE/ALLDE: hilarem| peramantibus| peperitue| praelucentissime| Domum| fatemur| qua| Acclamatione| obsequiis|

5.1.31/2031 Hark...parts] *2 lines* OKES, CRANE/ALLDE: Hark|

5.2.7/2063-4 How...not] *2 lines* ROSENBACH^B, MIDDLETON^{T,B}: he|

5.2.38/2095-6 Yes...power] *2 lines* MIDDLETON^{T,B}: of|

5.3.19-20/2220-1 And...throat] his| MIDDLETON^T, CRANE[2,4], OKES. Passage not in CRANE[3].

5.3.20-21/2220-2222 Of...followed] the| ROSENBACH^A, BRIDGEWATER. Passage not in CRANE[3].

5.3.187-91/2407-11 They'd...bag] if you| ROSENBACH, MIDDLETON^T, OKES. The passage is not present in CRANE[1,3].

Pattern of Shared Lineation Errors

Lineation Errors Shared by Two Texts

[CRANE[4]]-ROSENBACH: 1?
  2.2.133-35 [not in BRIDGEWATER or CRANE[3]]

CRANE[3,4]: 1
  4.2.99-100

ROSENBACH-MIDDLETON^T: 1
  4.2.107-8

BRIDGEWATER-OKES: 1
  2.1.187-8

CRANE[2,3]: 2
  1.1.36-7
  1.1.302

CRANE[4]/ALLDE-OKES: 2
  5.1.10-19
  5.1.31

ROSENBACH-OKES: 2
  3.1.399
  4.1.129-30

BRIDGEWATER-MIDDLETON^T: 3-4
  1.1.252-4
  2.1.144
  [gap in BRIDGEWATER]
  3.2.38-40 [not in CRANE[2,3]]
  [BRIDGEWATER becomes autograph]
  5.2.38

ROSENBACH-BRIDGEWATER: 3-4
  3.2.9-11 [not in CRANE[2,3]]
  3.1.398
  4.1.38-9
  [BRIDGEWATER becomes autograph]
  5.3.20-21 [not in CRANE[3]]

Lineation Errors Shared by Three Texts

[CRANE[4]]-ROSENBACH-MIDDLETON^T: 1?
  3.1.154-5 [not in CRANE[3]]

[CRANE[4]]-BRIDGEWATER-OKES: 1?
  3.2.30-1 [not in CRANE[2,3]]

ROSENBACH-BRIDGEWATER-OKES: 1?
  5.3.187-91 [not in CRANE[3]]

ROSENBACH-BRIDGEWATER-MIDDLETON^T: 1
  5.2.7

BRIDGEWATER-MIDDLETON^T-OKES: 3-5
  1.1.288-90
  2.1.39-41 [passage not in CRANE[3]]
  2.1.106-7 [passage not in CRANE[3]]
  2.1.137-8
  2.1.155-6

Lineation Errors Shared by Four Texts

CRANE[2,4]-MIDDLETON^T-OKES: 1?
  5.3.19-20 [not in CRANE[3]]

Lineation Errors Shared by Five Texts

CRANE[2]-CRANE[4]/ALLDE-ROSENBACH-BRIDGEWATER-OKES: 1?
  4.1.21-2 [not in CRANE[3]]

Shared Lineation Errors Text Totals

CRANE[1] (0)
CRANE[3] (3): with one (3)
CRANE[2] (4): with one (2), with three (1), with four (1)
CRANE[4]/MATHEWES/ALLDE (8): with one (4), with two (2), with three (1), with four (1)
ROSENBACH (11): with one (7), with two (3), with four (1)
MIDDLETON^T (13): with one (5), with two (7), with three (1)
OKES (14): with one (5), with two (7), with three (1), with four (1)
BRIDGEWATER (18): with one (9), with two (8), with four (1)
Total Shared Lineation Errors: 29

Relics

I define a lineation 'relic' as the writing or setting of two part-lines (or one and a half verse lines) on one line of paper. This arrangement saves paper (then far more expensive than it is now), and it was therefore, in the early seventeenth century, a very common practice among authors, scribes, and compositors setting quarto texts. It is consequently of little value as evidence of a stemmatic relationship between texts. In each of the following examples, the text is set as one line by the witnesses listed after the lemma.

Induction.49-50/65-6 'Tis...think] ROSENBACH, CRANE[1] *uncorrected* (?). Crane began to write the beginning of the second half-line at the end of the first, perhaps because they were written on one line in his copy.

1.1.28-9/133-4 From...heresies] CRANE, ROSENBACH^A
1.1.133-4/245-6 Of...thoughts] CRANE[1,4], ROSENBACH^A
2.1.39-41/515-16 Boundless...goodness] CRANE[1], ROSENBACH^A
2.1.50-1/527-8 With...duty] ROSENBACH^A, OKES
2.1.150-1/644 Confusion...undoing] MIDDLETON^T, BRIDGEWATER^A
2.1.207-8/713-14 A...there] CRANE[1], ROSENBACH^A
2.1.238-9/755-6 If't...welcome] ROSENBACH^A, OKES

2.2.27–28/790 In…best] MIDDLETON[T] *only* [passage not in CRANE[1,2,3], BRIDGEWATER[A]]. This has not been counted in the totals of shared error.

2.2.81–2/854–5 No…fill] ROSENBACH[A], OKES

2.2.184–5/971–2 O…thee] ROSENBACH[A], OKES

3.1.227–8/1318–19 Then…intended] ROSENBACH[A], BRIDGEWATER[B], OKES, CRANE/ALLDE [passage not in CRANE[3]]

3.1.350–1/1526 Under…turtle] CRANE[1,2], MIDDLETON[T] [passage not in CRANE[3]]

3.1.374–5/1553 Not…another] ROSENBACH[A], OKES

4.2.109–10/1900–1 What's…encouragement] CRANE[1] +

5.1.7–8/2011 All…him] CRANE[2] + [passage not in CRANE[1]]

5.1.28–29 They…giver] OKES, CRANE/ALLDE [passage not in MIDDLETON, CRANE[3]]

5.3.77–8/2286–7 The…ambition] ROSENBACH[A], OKES

Pattern of Shared Relics

Relics Shared by Two Texts

OKES, CRANE/ALLDE: 1?
  5.1.28–29 [passage not in MIDDLETON, CRANE[3]]

MIDDLETON[T], BRIDGEWATER[A]: 1
  2.1.150–1

ROSENBACH, CRANE[1]: 3
  Induction.49–50 (?)
  2.1.39–41
  2.1.207–8

ROSENBACH[A], OKES: 6
  2.1.50–1
  2.1.238–9
  2.2.81–2
  2.2.184–5
  3.1.374–5
  5.3.77–8

Relics Shared by Three Texts

CRANE[1,4], ROSENBACH[A]: 1
  1.1.133–4

CRANE[1,2], MIDDLETON[T]: 1?
  3.1.350–1 [passage not in CRANE[3]]

Relics Shared by Four Texts

ROSENBACH[A], BRIDGEWATER[B], OKES, CRANE/ALLDE: 1?
  3.1.227–8 [not in CRANE[3]]

Relics Shared by Five Texts

CRANE, ROSENBACH[A]: 1
  1.1.28–9

Relics Shared by Seven Texts

CRANE[2,3,4], NON-CRANE: 1
  5.1.7–8 [passage not in CRANE[1]]

Relics Shared by Eight Texts: 1
  4.2.109–10

Shared Relics: Text Totals

CRANE[3] 3: with four (1), with six (1), with seven (1)

BRIDGEWATER 4: with one (1), with three (1), with six (1), with seven (1)

CRANE[2] 4: with two (1), with four (1), with six (1), with seven (1)

MIDDLETON[T] 4: with one (1), with two (1), with six (1), with seven (1)

CRANE[4]/MATHEWES/ALLDE 6: with one (1), with two (1), with three (1), with four (1), with six (1), with seven (1)

CRANE[1] 7: with one (3), with two (2), with four (1), with seven (1)

OKES 10: with one (7), with three (1), with six (1), with seven (1)

ROSENBACH 14: with one (9), with two (1), with three (1), with four (1), with six (1), with seven (1)

Total Shared Relics: 17

As we would expect, the distribution of relics contrasts strikingly with the distribution of other lineation errors. CRANE[1], at the top of the previous list, is near the bottom of this list; its ratio of relics per line of verse is closest to OKES, a text which was produced at least nine months later, and which in all other respects seems late in the chain of transmission. BRIDGEWATER (in all other respects clearly toward the end of the chain of transmission) has fewer relics per verse line than CRANE[2], which contains few of any other category of error. And ROSENBACH is far and away the most relic-prone text, whereas in other categories it is consistently in the middle. Moreover, although ROSENBACH and BRIDGEWATER are strongly and specifically linked to each other in the second half of the play, they do not uniquely share a single relic. Finally, the prominence of paper-saving relics in ROSENBACH is immediately comprehensible to anyone who looks at the very cramped manuscript, whereas the relative paucity of relics in CRANE[3] is just as clearly related to the spacious elegance of the presentation copy.

I might be accused here of special pleading, because the text that I have identified as the earliest in the sequence of transmission (CRANE[1]) does badly on this test. In the interests of full disclosure, in the following chart I have combined the two sets of figures, giving totals that include relics.

Combined Text Totals, Shared Lineation Errors and Shared Relics

CRANE[1] $0+7 = 7$
CRANE[2] $4+4 = 8$
CRANE[3] $3+3 = 6$
CRANE[4]/MATHEWES/ALLDE $8+6 = 14$
MIDDLETON[T] $13+4 = 17$
BRIDGEWATER $18+4 = 22$
OKES $14+10 = 24$
ROSENBACH $11+14 = 25$

I list the texts here by the ratio of errors per line of dialogue. CRANE[1] and CRANE[2] are nearly equal, since CRANE[2] contains more text. Although CRANE[3] has the smallest gross total, it also has a much abbreviated text, and its total error ratio is therefore higher than the other two extant Crane manuscripts. Thus, the combined figures produce the same sequence of the four Crane texts supported by other evidence. Likewise, all four Crane texts contain fewer errors than any of the NON-CRANE texts.

My foundational conclusions about the relationship of CRANE[1] to the other texts, and about the relatively late production of MIDDLETON[T], would not be endangered by inclusion of all relics as lineation errors. Nevertheless, it remains a less reliable category of shared error, and by the conventions of the time may not be an error at all. My analysis of stemmatic relationships in the General Textual Introduction therefore does not include these variants.

APPENDIX C: SHARED ERRORS IN STAGE DIRECTIONS

For the purpose and organization of this appendix, see the headnote to Appendix A.

List of shared errors in stage directions

Induction.0.2/14 *asleep*] *not in* CRANE[2,3]

Induction.52.1 *Music*] CRANE[1,4], ROSENBACH[A]; *not in* CRANE[2,3], MIDDLETON[T], BRIDGEWATER, OKES

Induction.52.1–2 *Enter…game*] *not in* MIDDLETON[T], BRIDGEWATER[A], OKES

Induction.78.1 *Exeunt*] *not in* OKES, BRIDGEWATER[A], MIDDLETON[T]

1.1.0.2–4/99–100 *from the Black House…from the White House*] *not in* CRANE[2,3]; *seuerally* CRANE/MATHEWES

1.1.0.2–4/99–100 *Black…White*] *white…Black* CRANE[2,3,4]

1.1.70.1 *Exit*] *not in* MIDDLETON[T], BRIDGEWATER[A], OKES

1.1.205.1/332–3 *Enter…Pawn*] This direction is placed too late in BRIDGEWATER[A] and MIDDLETON[T]. CRANE[3] is not specific.

1.1.242.1/367.1 *Exeunt…Pawn*] *not in* CRANE[3,4], NON-CRANE

1.1.243.2/369 *Enter Black Knight*] Both BRIDGEWATER and OKES misplace this direction one line below, after he speaks. CRANE[3] is not specific.

1.1.328.1/463 *Exit…Pawn*] *not in* CRANE[1,3], NON-CRANE

1.1.331.1 *Exit*] *not in* NON-CRANE

2.1.150.1/643.1 *Exit*] *not in* CRANE[1,2], NON-CRANE

2.1.194.1/699 *Exit*] *not in* CRANE[1,2,4], NON-CRANE

2.1.227.1/737 *Exeunt*] *not in* MIDDLETON[T], BRIDGEWATER[A], OKES

2.1.227.1/737 *Exeunt*] *Exit* CRANE/MATHEWES, ROSENBACH[A]

2.2.17.1/780 *Exit*] MIDDLETON[T] (exit B[x]p.), CRANE[2]; *not in* CRANE[3,4], ROSENBACH[A], BRIDGEWATER[A], OKES. Passage not present in CRANE[1].

2.2.81.1–6/855 *Enter…black pawns*] ROSENBACH[A] and OKES wrongly place this entrance to the right of 2.2.96. Passage not present in BRIDGEWATER. CRANE[3] is not specific.

2.2.81.1–2/855 *from the White House…and from the Black House*] CRANE[2,3,4] and ROSENBACH, MIDDLETON[T], OKES all call for the entrance of both houses, even though some characters from each are already on stage. (The entire passage is missing in BRIDGEWATER; CRANE[1] has a different start to the scene.)

2.2.94.1/871 *Enter…Pawn*] *not in* CRANE[3], OKES, ROSENBACH[A]. (BRIDGEWATER lacks the entire passage; no separate entrance is needed in CRANE[1], which begins the scene differently.)

2.2.233.1/1033 *Exeunt*] *not in* OKES, CRANE/MATHEWES. Passage not present in BRIDGEWATER.

3.1.44.1/1108 *reads*] OKES (typographically) and ROSENBACH[A] (calligraphically) share the error of distinguishing the first passage read aloud from the letter, but not the second, therefore implying that the first is a quotation but the second not.

3.1.115.1/1182 *Enter…Pawn*] The direction is placed too late, after the Black Knight addresses his pawn, in ROSENBACH, CRANE/MATHEWES, MIDDLETON[T], BRIDGEWATER[B]. CRANE[3] does not indicate exact placement of entrances.

3.1.155.1/1230–31 *Enter…White House*] ROSENBACH[A], BRIDGEWATER[B], and MIDDLETON[T] place the direction too late. CRANE[3] does not indicate exact placement of entrances.

3.1.155.2–3/1231 *Black King…from the Black House*] All texts call for the entrance of the 'Black House', even though at least two of its members are already on stage.

3.1.175.1/1252 *Enter…Pawn*] CRANE[1]; *not in* CRANE[2] +

3.1.262.1 *His…off*] *not in* CRANE[2,3,4], MIDDLETON[T]

3.1.299.1/1410 *Exeunt*] *not in* MIDDLETON[T], BRIDGEWATER[B]

3.1.305.1/1418 *Exeunt…Pawn*] *not in* CRANE[2] +

3.1.348.1/1470 *Exeunt*] *not in* BRIDGEWATER[B], ROSENBACH[A]. The direction is also absent from CRANE[2,3], but is not an error there, because the text has been adapted.

3.2.29.1/1505 *Pawn*] *Pawnes* ROSENBACH[A], *P.s* BRIDGEWATER[B]. Scene not in CRANE[2,3].

3.1.392.1/1572 *Music*] ROSENBACH[A], BRIDGEWATER[B] and MIDDLETON[T] place the direction too late.

3.1.395.1–3/1576–9 *The Jesuit…exit*] CRANE[2,3] place this direction too early.

3.1.395.1–3/1576–9 *The Jesuit…exit*] ROSENBACH[A] and BRIDGEWATER[B] place this direction too late.

3.1.395.2–3/1578–9 *and…exit*] *not in* CRANE

3.1.415.1/1601 *Exit*] *not in* OKES, BRIDGEWATER[B]

4.1.33.1/1644 *Exit*] *not in* ROSENBACH, BRIDGEWATER, OKES. [Passage not present in CRANE[3].]

4.1.93.1/1717 *Exeunt*] *exit* MIDDLETON[T], OKES, BRIDGEWATER

4.1.149.1/1783 *Exeunt*] *not in* BRIDGEWATER[B], ROSENBACH[A]

4.2.81.1/1868 *Enter Fat Bishop*] ROSENBACH[A] and MIDDLETON[T] mistakenly place this entrance after the Pawn's speech (one manuscript line too late). CRANE[3] is not specific.

4.2.134.2/1927 *Enter Black King*] CRANE[2,4] clearly place this direction too late. (The position of the direction is not determinable in CRANE[3], which groups all the entrances for the scene in its opening stage direction.)

4.2.145.1/1940 *Exit*] *not in* BRIDGEWATER[B], ROSENBACH[A]

4.3.0.1/1941 *Recorders.*] *not in* CRANE[2,3,4], MIDDLETON[T]

4.4.12.1 *Enter Black Knight*] *not in* ROSENBACH, BRIDGEWATER, MIDDLETON[T]

4.4.12.1 *Enter Black Knight*] In OKES and CRANE/ALLDE this direction is misplaced. CRANE[3] is not specific.

4.4.55.1 *Enter Fat Bishop*] *not in* OKES, ROSENBACH[A], BRIDGEWATER[B]. Passage not present in MIDDLETON[T].

4.4.74.1 *Enter White King*] *not in* BRIDGEWATER[B], ROSENBACH[A]. Passage not present in MIDDLETON[T].

4.4.110.1 *Exeunt*] *not in* BRIDGEWATER[B], ROSENBACH[A], OKES. Passage not present in MIDDLETON[T].

4.4.110.2 *Quartus*] *Tertus* OKES, BRIDGEWATER *uncorrected*. Phrase not present in CRANE[2,3,4].

5.1.0.2/2002 *Loud music*] *not in* CRANE[2,3,4], OKES

5.1.0.2/2002 *Loud*] *Lowe* BRIDGEWATER[B], ROSENBACH[B]. Phrase not present in CRANE[2,3,4], OKES.

5.1.0.3–4/2003 *as…stage*] *not in* CRANE[2,3,4], MIDDLETON[T]. [CRANE[1] begins the scene differently.]

5.1.0.4–5/2003 *and the…above*] *not in* NON-CRANE

5.1.1.1/2004 *calls*] *not in* CRANE[2,3,4], ROSENBACH, BRIDGEWATER, OKES

5.1.9.2/2013 *Oboes.*] *not in* CRANE[2,3,4], OKES

5.1.9.2/2014 *from*] *not in* CRANE[2,3]

5.1.9.3/2015 *Bishop*] CRANE/ALLDE and OKES are both clearly wrong in calling here for a character whose title begins with 'K'.

5.1.9.4/2015 *with Pawns*] *not in* MIDDLETON[T], CRANE/ALLDE

5.1.30.1/2030 *Music*] MIDDLETON[T], ROSENBACH, BRIDGEWATER mistakenly combine this with the subsequent stage direction.

5.1.30.1/2030 *Music*] CRANE[2], MIDDLETON[T], ROSENBACH, BRIDGEWATER place the music cue too late.

5.1.33.1/2033 *An altar...side*] CRANE², ROSENBACH, BRIDGEWA-
TER, MIDDLETON^T place the direction too late.

5.1.33.1-2/2033 *with tapers on it*] not in CRANE¹, ROSENBACH,
BRIDGEWATER, MIDDLETON^T

5.1.44.1 *The...dance*] not in MIDDLETON^T, BRIDGEWATER^B, ROSEN-
BACH^B

5.1.46.1 *The statues dance*] *in a Daunce* CRANE²,³,⁴, OKES

5.2.3.2/2059 *in...habit*] not in CRANE²,³, MIDDLETON^T

5.2.3.2/2059 *meeting her*] not in CRANE²,³, MIDDLETON^T

5.2.77/2140 *within*] not in MIDDLETON^{T,B}

5.2.106.1/2180 *with White Queen*] not in CRANE³,⁴, OKES

5.3.162.1/2381.1 *flourish*] not in CRANE²,³,⁴, ROSENBACH, MIDDLE-
TON^{T,B}

5.3.166.3/2386 *Pawns*] *Pawne* ROSENBACH^A, CRANE/ALLDE

5.3.178.1 *The bag opens*] not in MIDDLETON^{T,B}, ROSENBACH^A

5.3.178.1-2/2398.1 *and the Black lost...appear in it*] not in
NON-CRANE

5.3.220.1 *Exeunt*] not in CRANE/ALLDE, OKES, ROSENBACH^A, MID-
DLETON^{T,B}

Epilogue.0.1/2447 *the White Queen's Pawn*] not in CRANE/ALLDE,
OKES

Pattern of Shared Stage Direction Errors

Stage Direction Errors shared by two texts

CRANE²,⁴: 1?
  4.2.134.2 [unspecified in CRANE³]

[CRANE⁴]-MIDDLETON^T: 1
  5.1.9.4

ROSENBACH-MIDDLETON^T: 1?
  4.2.81.1 [unspecified in CRANE³]

[CRANE⁴]-ROSENBACH: 2
  2.1.227.1
  5.3.166.3

ROSENBACH-OKES: 1-2
  2.2.81.1-2 [passage not in BRIDGEWATER; unspecified in
    CRANE³]
  3.1.44.1

CRANE²,³: 4
  Induction.0.2
  1.1.0.2-4
  3.1.395.1
  5.1.9.2

BRIDGEWATER-MIDDLETON^T: 2-3
  1.1.205.1 [unspecified in CRANE³]
  3.1.299.1 *Exeunt*
  5.2.77

BRIDGEWATER-OKES: 1-3
  1.1.243.2 [unspecified in CRANE³]
  3.1.415.1 *Exit*
  4.4.110.2 [phrase not present in CRANE²,³,⁴]

[CRANE⁴/MATHEWES/ALLDE-OKES]: 2-4
  2.2.233.1 *Exeunt* [passage not in BRIDGEWATER]
    [change from CRANE/MATHEWES to CRANE/ALLDE]
  4.4.12.1 [unspecified in CRANE³]
  5.1.9.3
  Epilogue.0.1

ROSENBACH-BRIDGEWATER: 3-7
  3.1.348.1 [passage not in CRANE²,³]
  3.2.29.1 [passage not in CRANE²,³]
  3.1.395.1
  4.1.149.1 *Exeunt*
  4.2.145.1 *Exit*

4.4.74.1 [passage not in MIDDLETON^T]
5.1.0.2 [phrase not in CRANE²,³,⁴, OKES]

Stage direction errors shared by three texts

CRANE³-ROSENBACH-OKES: 1?
  2.2.94.1 [not in BRIDGEWATER]

ROSENBACH-BRIDGEWATER-OKES: 3?
  4.1.33.1 *Exit* [passage not present in CRANE³]
  4.4.55.1 [passage not present in MIDDLETON^T]
  4.4.110.1 *Exeunt* [passage not present in MIDDLETON^T]

CRANE²,³,⁴: 1
  1.1.0.2-4

CRANE³-CRANE/ALLDE-OKES: 1
  5.2.106.1

CRANE²,³-MIDDLETON^T: 1-2
  5.2.3.2
  5.2.3.2 [these might be considered a single omission,
    instead of two]

BRIDGEWATER-MIDDLETON^T-OKES: 6
  Induction.52.1-2
  Induction.78.1
  1.1.70.1
  1.1.331.1
  2.1.227.1 *Exeunt*
  4.1.93.1

ROSENBACH-BRIDGEWATER-MIDDLETON^T: 6-7
  3.1.155.1 [not specified in CRANE³]
  3.1.392.1
  4.4.12.1
  5.1.30.1
  5.1.33.1-2
  5.1.44.1
  5.3.178.1

Stage direction errors shared by four texts

[CRANE⁴]-ROSENBACH-BRIDGEWATER-MIDDLETON^T: 1?
  3.1.115.1 [unspecified in CRANE³]

CRANE: 1
  3.1.395.1

CRANE²-ROSENBACH-BRIDGEWATER-MIDDLETON^T: 2
  5.1.30.1
  5.1.33.1

NON-CRANE: 2
  5.1.0.4-5
  5.3.178.1-2

CRANE²,³,⁴-MIDDLETON^T: 3
  3.1.262.1
  4.3.0.1
  5.1.0.3-4

CRANE²,³-CRANE⁴/MATHEWES/ALLDE-OKES: 3
  5.1.0.2
  5.1.9.2
  5.1.46.1

Stage direction errors shared by five texts

CRANE²,³-MIDDLETON-BRIDGEWATER-OKES: 1
  Induction.52.1

CRANE³-CRANE⁴/MATHEWES/ALLDE-ROSENBACH-BRIDGEWATER-
OKES: 1
  2.2.17.1 *Exit*

CRANE⁴/MATHEWES/ALLDE-NON-CRANE: 1
  5.3.220.1 *Exeunt*

Stage direction errors shared by six texts

CRANE[2,3,4]–ROSENBACH–MIDDLETON[T]–OKES: 1?
2.2.81.1-2 [not present in BRIDGEWATER]

CRANE[1,2]–NON-CRANE: 1
2.1.150.1 *Exit*

CRANE[1]–CRANE[3]–NON-CRANE: 1
1.1.328.1 *Exit*

CRANE[2,3,4]–ROSENBACH–BRIDGEWATER–MIDDLETON[T]: 1
5.3.162.1

CRANE[2,3,4]–ROSENBACH–BRIDGEWATER–OKES: 1
5.1.1.1

CRANE[3,4]–NON-CRANE: 1
1.1.242.1 *Exeunt*

Stage direction errors shared by seven texts

CRANE[1,2,4]–NON-CRANE: 1
2.1.194.1 *Exit*

CRANE[2,3,4]–NON-CRANE: 2
3.1.175.1
3.1.305.1 *Exeunt*

Stage direction errors shared by eight texts

3.1.155.2-3

Shared Stage Direction Errors, Text Totals

CRANE[1] (5): with three (1), with five (2), with six (1), with seven (1)

CRANE[2] (26): with one (5), with two (4), with three (8), with four (1), with five (4), with six (3), with seven (1)

CRANE[3] (26): with one (4), with two (6), with three (6), with four (2), with five (5), with six (2), with seven (1)

[CRANE[4]]/MATHEWES/ALLDE (27): with one (8), with two (3), with three (6), with four (2), with five (4), with six (3), with seven (1)

OKES (37): with one (9), with two (11), with three (5), with four (3), with five (5), with six (3), with seven (1)

ROSENBACH (38): with one (10), with two (11), with three (5), with four (1), with five (7), with six (3), with seven (1)

MIDDLETON[T] (39): with one (5), with two (15), with three (8), with four (2), with five (5), with six (3), with seven (1)

BRIDGEWATER (46): with one (13), with two (16), with three (5), with four (3), with five (5), with six (3), with seven (1)

Total Stage Direction Errors: 74

Exit Directions

The preceding summaries do not include the following exit directions, which are missing from all witnesses.

Prologue.10.1   Exit [passage not present in CRANE[1,3], ROSENBACH]
Induction.76.1   Exeunt both houses
1.1.282.1   Exit White Queen's Pawn
1.1.314.1   Exit Black Bishop's Pawn
2.1.192.1   Exit Black Queen's Pawn (and re-enter at 2.1.194.2)
2.1.207.1   Exit Black Queen's Pawn (and re-enter at 2.1.216.1)
2.2.233.1   Exeunt six white pieces
2.2.242.1   Exeunt three white pieces
3.1.159.1   Exit a pawn
5.1.9.1   Exeunt black pawns carrying litter [passage not present in CRANE[1]]
Epilogue.10.1   Exit [passage not present in CRANE[1]]

Even licensed playbooks often omitted exits, and when an exit is absent from all witnesses that almost certainly indicates that it was omitted both by the author and by the King's Men's playbook. These errors are, as it were, errors made by the whole culture, not by individual, distinguishable agents of transmission. Every one of these examples is either a mid-scene exit, or the exit of Prologue or Epilogue (whose entrances and exits are more often absent than present, since the very title indicated an isolated entrance and isolated exit). Adding these eleven examples would only swell the numbers of shared errors, without telling us much; it would in fact further distinguish CRANE[1] from all other texts, since three of the examples occur in passages not present in *An Early Form* (meaning that the error would not be counted in the totals for CRANE[1]).

APPENDIX D: PATTERNS OF SHARED ERROR (CUMULATIVE)

For the purpose and organization of this appendix, see the headnote to Appendix A. This appendix presents, in a single list, the patterns of distribution of shared error in the three previous appendices.

As in the earlier appendices, it is important to emphasize that examples marked with a query are indeed shared errors; the query concerns only the pattern to which they belong. In each case, the query indicates that the error might have been shared with additional texts. For instance, in the second pattern listed below, the error may well have been present in the full-length version of the play from which the abridgement contained in CRANE[3] was made; but we cannot be sure, because the passage is not present in CRANE[3] at all.

I list these patterns twice. In the first 'unfiltered' listing, I include the patterns created by all shared errors.

Shared Errors Linking Two Texts Only: Unfiltered

1. CRANE[1]–OKES: 1?/0/0 = 1?
4.1.62 [passage not in CRANE[3]]

2. CRANE[2,4]: 0/0/1? = 1?
4.2.134.2 [unspecified in CRANE[3]]

3. CRANE[1]–BRIDGEWATER: 1/0/0 = 1
4.2.82

4. CRANE[2]–ROSENBACH: 1/0/0 = 1
4.1.107

5. CRANE[3]–BRIDGEWATER: 1/0/0 = 1
1.1.272

6. [CRANE[4]]–MIDDLETON[T]: 0/0/1 = 1
5.1.9.4

7. CRANE[3]–MIDDLETON[T]: 1+1?/0/0 = 1-2
5.2.81
5.2.86 [these might be considered a single error, rather than two]

8. CRANE[3,4]: 1/1/0 = 2
4.2.99-100
5.1.11

9. ROSENBACH–MIDDLETON[T]: 0/1/1? = 1-2
4.2.81.1 [unspecified in CRANE[3]]
4.2.107-8

10. MIDDLETON[T]–OKES: 2/0/0 = 2
3.1.33

3.1.75

11. [CRANE[4]]–BRIDGEWATER: 2+1?/0/0 = 2–3
2.1.177 [passage not in CRANE[3]]
[gap in BRIDGEWATER]
5.1.6
5.2.70

12. [CRANE[4]]–ROSENBACH: 4/1?/2 = 6–7
1.1.279
2.1.227.1
2.2.133–35 [not in BRIDGEWATER or CRANE[3]]
3.1.199
3.1.333
4.2.44
5.3.166.3

13. BRIDGEWATER–MIDDLETON[T]: 1/3+1?/2+1? = 6–8
1.1.205.1 [unspecified in CRANE[3]]
1.1.252–4
2.1.144
3.1.299.1
3.2.38–40 [not in CRANE[2,3]]
5.2.38
5.2.77
5.2.114

14. CRANE[2,3]: 5/2/4 = 11
Induction.0.2
1.1.0.2–4
1.1.7
1.1.36–7
1.1.269
1.1.270
1.1.302
3.1.395.1
4.1.44–5
5.1.1
5.1.9.2

15. ROSENBACH–OKES: 7+2?/2/1+1? = 10–13
1.1.201 [passage not in CRANE[3]]
1.1.248
2.1.146 [passage not in CRANE[3]]
2.1.212
2.2.81.1–2 [not in BRIDGEWATER; unspecified in CRANE[3]]
2.2.141
3.1.44.1
3.1.203
3.1.399
4.1.129–30
4.2.44
5.2.75
5.3.116

16. BRIDGEWATER–OKES: 9+3?/1/1+2? = 11–16
Induction.14
1.1.165
1.1.243.2 [unspecified in CRANE[3]]
1.1.307
2.1.16 [passage not in CRANE[3]]
2.1.187–8
2.1.237 [passage not in CRANE[3]]
2.1.239 [passage not in CRANE[3]]
2.2.3
2.2.68
[gap in BRIDGEWATER]
3.1.322

3.1.415.1
4.2.47
4.2.74
4.2.83
4.4.110.2 [phrase not present in CRANE[2,3,4]]

17. [CRANE[4]]/MATHEWES/ALLDE–OKES: 10+2?/2/2+2? = 14–18
1.1.137
2.2.233.1 [not in BRIDGEWATER]
[Change from CRANE/MATHEWES to CRANE/ALLDE]
3.1.265 [passage not in CRANE[3]]
3.1.307
4.4.10
4.4.12.1 [unspecified in CRANE[3]]
5.1.4
5.1.10–19
5.1.15
5.1.18
5.1.31
5.1.39
5.3.32
5.3.188 [passage not in CRANE[3]]
Epilogue.5
Epilogue.6
5.1.9.3
Epilogue.0.1

18. ROSENBACH–BRIDGEWATER: 8+6?/2+2?/3+4? = 13–25
3.1.345.1 [passage not in CRANE[2,3]]
3.2.6 [scene not in CRANE[2,3]]
3.2.29.1 [scene not in CRANE[2,3]]
3.2.40 [scene not in CRANE[2,3]]
3.2.9–11 [scene not in CRANE[2,3]]
3.1.352 [passage not in CRANE[3]]
3.1.395.1
3.1.398
4.1.38–9
4.1.53 [passage not in CRANE[3]]
4.1.97
4.1.149.1
4.2.4
4.2.16 [passage not in CRANE[3]]
4.2.145.1
4.4.15
4.4.20
4.4.33 [passage not in CRANE[3]]
4.4.39
4.4.74.1 [passage not in MIDDLETON[T]]
5.1.0.2 [phrase not in CRANE[2,3,4], OKES]
5.1.7
[BRIDGEWATER becomes autograph]
5.3.5
5.3.12
5.3.20–21 [passage not in CRANE[3]]

Shared Errors Linking Three Texts

19. CRANE[2,4]–ROSENBACH: 1?/0/0 = 1?
2.1.130 [passage not in CRANE[3]]

20. CRANE[2]–[CRANE[4]]/ALLDE–OKES: 1?/0/0 = 1?
5.3.210–11 [passage not in CRANE[3]]

21. CRANE[3]–ROSENBACH–OKES: 0/0/1? = 1?
2.2.94.1 [passage not in BRIDGEWATER]

22. CRANE[3]–BRIDGEWATER–OKES: 1?/0/0 = 1?
2.1.179 [absence of the line in CRANE[3] may be deliberate abridgement]

23. [CRANE[4]]-ROSENBACH-MIDDLETON[T]: 0/1?/0 = 1?
  3.1.154-5 [not in CRANE[3]]
24. [CRANE[4]]/ALLDE-BRIDGEWATER-OKES: 0/1?/0 = 1?
  3.2.30-1 [not in CRANE[2,3]]
25. CRANE[2,3,4]: 0/0/1 = 1
  1.1.0.2-4/99-100
26. CRANE[2,3]-ROSENBACH: 1/0/0 = 1
  1.1.241
27. CRANE[2,3]-OKES: 1/0/0 = 1
  1.1.311
28. CRANE[3]-CRANE/ALLDE-OKES: 0/0/1 = 1
  5.2.106.1
29. CRANE[2,3]-MIDDLETON[T]: 0/0/1+1? = 1-2
  5.2.3.2
  5.2.3.2 [perhaps one error, instead of two]
30. ROSENBACH-BRIDGEWATER-OKES: 2+3?/1?/3? = 2-9
  [gap in BRIDGEWATER ends at 3.1.1]
  3.1.7 [phrase not in CRANE[2,3]]
  3.1.127
  3.1.355 [passage not in CRANE[3]]
  3.1.369 [perhaps belongs under BRIDGEWATER-OKES]
  4.1.33.1 [passage not in CRANE[3]]
  4.4.38
  4.4.55.1 [passage not in MIDDLETON[T]]
  4.4.110.1 [passage not in MIDDLETON[T]]
  5.3.187-91 [passage not in CRANE[3]]
31. ROSENBACH-BRIDGEWATER-MIDDLETON[T]: 2+1?/1/6+1? = 9-11
  3.1.155.1 [not specified in CRANE[3]]
  3.1.392.1
  4.4.1
  4.4.11
  4.4.12.1
  4.4.31 [passage not in CRANE[3]]
  [passage at end of 4.4 absent from MIDDLETON[T]]
  5.1.30.1
  5.1.33.1-2
  5.1.44.1
  5.2.7
  5.3.178.1
32. BRIDGEWATER-MIDDLETON[T]-OKES: 3/3+2?/5 = 11-13
  Induction.23
  Induction.52.1-2
  Induction.78.1
  1.1.70.1
  1.1.288-90
  1.1.324
  2.1.39-41 [passage not in CRANE[3]]
  2.1.106-7 [passage not in CRANE[3]]
  2.1.137-8
  2.1.155-6
  2.1.227.1
  [gap in BRIDGEWATER]
  3.1.48
  4.1.93.1

Shared Errors Linking Four Texts
33. CRANE[2,4]-MIDDLETON[T]-OKES: 0/1?/0 = 1?
  5.3.19-20 [not in CRANE[3]]
34. [CRANE[4]]-ROSENBACH-BRIDGEWATER-MIDDLETON[T]: 0/0/1? = 1?
  3.1.115.1 [unspecified in CRANE[3]]

35. CRANE: 0/0/1 = 1
  3.1.395.1
36. CRANE[2,3,4]-ROSENBACH: 1/0/0 = 1
  3.1.73
37. CRANE[3,4]-ROSENBACH-OKES: 1/0/0 = 1
  5.2.108
38. CRANE[3]-BRIDGEWATER-MIDDLETON[T]-OKES: 1/0/0 = 1
  3.1.44
39. CRANE[2]-ROSENBACH-BRIDGEWATER-MIDDLETON[T]: 0/0/2 = 2
  5.1.30.1
  5.1.33.1
40. NON-CRANE: 0/0/3 = 3
  1.1.331.1
  5.1.0.4-5
  5.3.178.1-2
41. CRANE[2,3,4]-MIDDLETON[T]: 0/0/3 = 3
  3.1.262.1
  4.3.0.1
  5.1.0.3-4
42. CRANE[2,3]-[CRANE[4]]/ALLDE-OKES: 0/0/3 = 3
  5.1.0.2
  5.1.9.2
  5.1.46.1

Shared Errors Linking Five Texts
43. CRANE[2]-CRANE[4]/ALLDE-ROSENBACH-BRIDGEWATER-OKES: 0/1?/0 = 1?
  4.1.21-2 [not in CRANE[3]]
44. CRANE[2,3,4]-BRIDGEWATER-OKES: 1/0/0 = 1
  3.1.410
45. CRANE[2,3]-BRIDGEWATER-MIDDLETON[T]-OKES: 0/0/1 = 1
  Induction.52.1
46. CRANE[3,4]-ROSENBACH-BRIDGEWATER-OKES: 0/0/1 = 1
  2.2.17.1
47. CRANE[4]/MATHEWES/ALLDE-NON-CRANE: 0/0/1 = 1
  5.3.220.1

Shared Errors Linking Six Texts
48. CRANE[2,3,4]-ROSENBACH-MIDDLETON[T]-OKES: 1?/0/1? = 2?
  2.2.33 [not present in BRIDGEWATER]
  2.2.81.1-2 [not present in BRIDGEWATER]
49. CRANE[1,2]-NON-CRANE: 0/0/1 = 1
  2.1.150.1
50. CRANE[1,3]-NON-CRANE: 0/0/1 = 1
  1.1.328.1
51. CRANE[2,3,4]-ROSENBACH-BRIDGEWATER-MIDDLETON[T]: 0/0/1 = 1
  5.3.162.1
52. CRANE[3,4]-NON-CRANE: 0/0/1 = 1
  1.1.242.1
53. CRANE[2,3,4]-ROSENBACH-BRIDGEWATER-OKES: 1/0/1 = 2
  4.1.116
  5.1.1.1

Shared Errors Linking Seven Texts
54. CRANE-ROSENBACH-MIDDLETON[T]-BRIDGEWATER: 1/0/0 = 1
  5.3.11

860

55. CRANE[1,2,4]-NON-CRANE: $0/0/1 = 1$
2.1.194.1

56. CRANE[2,3,4]-NON-CRANE: $0/0/2 = 2$
3.1.175.1
3.1.305.1

Shared Errors Linking Eight Texts
57. CRANE-NON-CRANE: $1/0/1 = 2$
3.1.155.2–3 [probably authorial]
4.4.37 [probably authorial]

Shared Errors: Filtered

In this listing, in an effort to eliminate 'noise' I remove four categories of shared error: patterns created by a single example linking two texts only (1–7), shared errors in obscure proper names, which are probably authorial (54, 57), shared stage direction errors which involve imprecise use of the word 'House', which could also be authorial (14, 46, 57), and omitted exits. The fourth category involves the largest number of shared errors, and is discussed and tabulated in Appendix C. For the same reason I have omitted pattern 7, where the 'error' involved the use of a speech direction instead of a speech prefix; in context there is no ambiguity, and the two texts involved (CRANE[3] and MIDDLETON[T]) have radically different forms of the speech direction. It is not unusual in the period for speech directions for offstage speech to substitute for speech prefixes; this example seems therefore to belong to the same category of acceptably loose period usage. The 'filtered' list retains the numbering in the full list, even though seventeen patterns disappear completely, and the totals for other patterns are diminished. Notably, the patterns entirely removed by these three kinds of filtering come at the beginning and end of the list: 1, 2, 3, 4, 5, 6, 7, and then 35, 46, 47, 49, 50, 52, 54, 55, and 57. In addition, when a pattern involving three or more texts is created by only a single shared error, and if one of the texts forming that pattern is ambiguous, I have discounted the ambiguous case, removing the larger pattern and shifting the error undoubtedly shared by the remaining texts to a smaller, well-established pattern: see examples in patterns 21, 22, 29, and 38. This reduces the total number of undoubted patterns, but not the total number of undoubtedly shared errors. For further discussion of the filtered list see Sec. VII.

Shared Errors Linking Two Texts Only
8. CRANE[3,4]: $1/1/0 = 2$
4.2.99–100
5.1.11–12

9. ROSENBACH-MIDDLETON[T]: $0/1/1? = 1–2$
4.2.81.1 [unspecified in CRANE[3]]
4.2.107–8

10. MIDDLETON[T]-OKES: $2/0/0 = 2$
3.1.33
3.1.75

11. [CRANE[4]]-BRIDGEWATER: $2+1?/0/0 = 2–3$
2.1.177 [passage not in CRANE[3]]
[gap in BRIDGEWATER]
5.1.6
5.2.70

12. [CRANE[4]]-ROSENBACH: $4/1?/2 = 6–7$
1.1.279
2.1.227.1
2.2.133–35 [not in BRIDGEWATER or CRANE[3]]
3.1.199
3.1.333
4.2.44
5.3.166.3

13. BRIDGEWATER-MIDDLETON[T]: $1/3+1?/1+1? = 5–7$
1.1.205.1 [unspecified in CRANE[3]]
1.1.252–4
2.1.144
3.2.39–40 [not in CRANE[2,3]]
5.2.38
5.2.77.1
5.2.114

14. CRANE[2,3]: $5/2/4 = 11$
Induction.0.2
1.1.0.2–4
1.1.7
1.1.36–7
1.1.269
1.1.270
1.1.302
3.1.395.1
4.1.44–5
5.1.1
5.2.3.2 [shifted from pattern 29]

15. ROSENBACH-OKES: $7+2?/2/1+2? = 10–14$
1.1.201 [passage not in CRANE[3]]
1.1.248
2.1.146 [passage not in CRANE[3]]
2.1.212
2.2.81.1–2 [not in BRIDGEWATER; unspecified in CRANE[3]]
2.2.94.1 [not in BRIDGEWATER; shifted from pattern 21]
2.2.141
3.1.44.1
3.1.203
3.1.399
4.1.129–30
4.2.44
5.2.75
5.3.116

16. BRIDGEWATER-OKES: $10+3?/1/2? = 11–16$
Induction.14
1.1.165
1.1.243.2 [unspecified in CRANE[3]]
1.1.307
2.1.16 [passage not in CRANE[3]]
2.1.179 [shifted from pattern 22]
2.1.187–8
2.1.237 [passage not in CRANE[3]]
2.1.239 [passage not in CRANE[3]]
2.2.3
2.2.68
[gap in BRIDGEWATER]
3.1.322
4.2.47
4.2.74
4.2.83
4.4.110.2 [phrase not present in CRANE[2,3,4]]

17. CRANE[4]/MATHEWES/ALLDE-OKES: $10+2?/2/2+1? = 14–17$
1.1.137
[Change from CRANE/MATHEWES to CRANE/ALLDE]
3.1.265 [passage not in CRANE[3]]
3.1.307
4.4.10
4.4.12.1 [unspecified in CRANE[3]]
5.1.4
5.1.9.3

5.1.10-19
5.1.15
5.1.18
5.1.31
5.1.39
5.3.32
5.3.188 [passage not in CRANE[3]]
Epilogue.0.1
Epilogue.5
Epilogue.6

18. ROSENBACH-BRIDGEWATER: 8+6?/2+2?/1+3? = 11-22
3.2.6 [scene not in CRANE[2,3]]
3.2.29.1 [scene not in CRANE[2,3]]
3.2.40 [scene not in CRANE[2,3]]
3.2.9-11 [scene not in CRANE[2,3]]
3.1.352 [passage not in CRANE[3]]
3.1.395.1
3.1.398
4.1.38-9
4.1.53 [passage not in CRANE[3]]
4.1.97
4.2.4
4.2.16 [passage not in CRANE[3]]
4.4.15
4.4.20
4.4.33 [passage not in CRANE[3]]
4.4.39
4.4.74.1 [passage not in MIDDLETON[T]]
5.1.0.2 [phrase not in CRANE[2,3,4], OKES]
5.1.7
[BRIDGEWATER becomes autograph]
5.3.5
5.3.12
5.3.20-21 [passage not in CRANE[3]]

Shared Errors Linking Three Texts

19. CRANE[2,4]-ROSENBACH: 1?/0/0 = 1?
2.1.130 [passage not in CRANE[3]]

20. CRANE[2,4]-OKES: 1?/0/0 = 1?
5.3.210-11 [passage not in CRANE[3]]

21. CRANE[3]-ROSENBACH-OKES: 0/0/1? = 1?
2.2.94.1 [passage not in BRIDGEWATER] Because CRANE[3] is ambiguous, and there are no other examples of this pattern, the error clearly shared by ROSENBACH and OKES has been categorized as another example of pattern 15.

22. CRANE[3]-BRIDGEWATER-OKES: 1?/0/0 = 1?
2.1.179 [Because the absence of the line in CRANE[3] may be deliberate abridgement, the error undoubtedly shared by the other two texts has been categorized as another example of pattern 16.]

23. [CRANE[4]]-ROSENBACH-MIDDLETON[T]: 0/1?/0 = 1?
3.1.154-5 [not in CRANE[3]]

24. [CRANE[4]]-BRIDGEWATER-OKES: 0/1?/0 = 1?
3.2.30-1 [not in CRANE[2,3]]

25. CRANE[2,3,4]: 0/0/1 = 1
1.1.0.2-4

26. CRANE[2,3]-ROSENBACH: 1/0/0 = 1
1.1.241

27. CRANE[2,3]-OKES: 1/0/0 = 1
1.1.311

28. CRANE[3]-CRANE/ALLDE-OKES: 0/0/1 = 1
5.2.106.1

29. CRANE[2,3]-MIDDLETON[T]: 0/0/1 = 1
[Because the link with MIDDLETON[T] is ambiguous, the undoubtedly shared CRANE error has been categorized as an example of pattern 14.]

30. ROSENBACH-BRIDGEWATER-OKES: 2+3?/1?/1? = 2-7
[gap in BRIDGEWATER ends at 3.1.1]
3.1.7 [phrase not in CRANE[2,3]]
3.1.127
3.1.355 [passage not in CRANE[3]]
3.1.369 [perhaps belongs under BRIDGEWATER-OKES]
4.4.38
4.4.55.1 [passage not present in MIDDLETON[T]]
5.3.187-91 [not in CRANE[3]]

31. ROSENBACH-BRIDGEWATER-MIDDLETON[T]: 2+1?/1/6+1?
= 9-11
3.1.155.1 [not specified in CRANE[3]]
3.1.392.1
4.4.1
4.4.11
4.4.12.1
4.4.31 [passage not in CRANE[3]]
[passage at end of 4.4 absent from MIDDLETON[T]]
5.1.30.1
5.1.33.1-2
5.1.44.1
5.2.7
5.3.178.1

32. BRIDGEWATER-MIDDLETON[T]-OKES: 4/3+2?/2 = 9-11
Induction.23
Induction.52.1-2
1.1.288-90
1.1.324
2.1.39-41 [passage not in CRANE[3]]
2.1.106-7 [passage not in CRANE[3]]
2.1.137-8
2.1.155-6
[gap in BRIDGEWATER]
3.1.44 [shifted here from pattern 38]
3.1.48
4.1.93.1

Shared Errors Linking Four Texts

33. CRANE[2,4]-MIDDLETON[T]-OKES: 0/1?/0 = 1?
5.3.19-20 [not in CRANE[3]]

34. [CRANE[4]]-ROSENBACH-BRIDGEWATER-MIDDLETON[T]: 0/0/1? = 1?
3.1.115.1 [unspecified in CRANE[3]]

36. CRANE[2,3,4]-ROSENBACH: 1/0/0 = 1
3.1.73

37. CRANE[3,4]-ROSENBACH[A]-OKES: 1/0/0 = 1
5.2.108

38. CRANE[3]-BRIDGEWATER-MIDDLETON[T]-OKES: 1?/0/0 = 1
Because CRANE[3] is ambiguous, and there are no other examples of this pattern, the error undoubtedly shared by BRIDGEWATER, OKES and MIDDLETON[T] has been categorized as another example of pattern 32.

39. CRANE[2]-ROSENBACH-BRIDGEWATER-MIDDLETON[T]: 0/0/1?
= 1?
5.1.33.1 [not in CRANE[3]]

40. NON-CRANE: 0/0/2 = 2
5.1.0.4-5
5.3.178.1-2

41. CRANE[2,3,4]–MIDDLETON[T]: 0/0/3 = 3
   3.1.262.1
   4.3.0.1
   5.1.0.3–4

42. CRANE[2,3]–[CRANE[4]]/ALLDE–OKES: 0/0/3 = 3
   5.1.0.2
   5.1.9.2
   5.1.46.1

Shared Errors Linking Five Texts

43. CRANE[2,4]–ROSENBACH–BRIDGEWATER–OKES: 0/1?/0 = 1?
   4.1.21–2 [not in CRANE[3]]

44. CRANE[2,3,4]–BRIDGEWATER–OKES: 1/0/0 = 1
   3.1.410

45. CRANE[2,3]–MIDDLETON–BRIDGEWATER–OKES: 0/0/1 = 1
   Induction.52.1

Shared Errors Linking Six Texts

48. CRANE[2,3,4]–ROSENBACH–MIDDLETON[T]–OKES: 1?/0/0 = 1?
   2.2.33 [not in BRIDGEWATER]

51. CRANE[2,3,4]–ROSENBACH–BRIDGEWATER–MIDDLETON[T]: 0/0/1 = 1
   5.3.162.1

53. CRANE[2,3,4]–ROSENBACH–BRIDGEWATER–OKES: 1/0/1 = 2
   4.1.116
   5.1.1.1

Shared Errors Linking Seven Texts

56. CRANE[2,3,4]–NON-CRANE: 0/0/1 = 1
   3.1.175.1

Shared Errors, Text Totals: Filtered

CRANE[1] (0)

CRANE[2] (34): with one (12), with two (5), with three (10), with four (3), with five (4), with six (1)

CRANE[3] (32): with one (13), with two (4), with three (8), with four (2), with five (4), with six (1)

MIDDLETON[T] (46): with one (11), with two (22), with three (9), with four (1), with six (1)

[CRANE[4]]/MATHEWES/ALLDE (52): with one (29), with two (6), with three (10), with four (2), with five (4), with six (1)

ROSENBACH (79): with one (44), with two (22), with three (7), with four (1), with five (4), with six (1)

OKES (85): with one (49), with two (22), with three (7), with four (3), with five (3), with six (1)

BRIDGEWATER (90): with one (47), with two (30), with three (6), with four (3), with five (3), with six (1)

APPENDIX E: SHARED ERRORS IN PUNCTUATION

This list differs from those in Appendices A, B, and C because it contains, by definition, no shared errors in autograph texts. Any punctuation found in autograph, which by grammatical or rhetorical standards would appear to be mistaken, is assumed to be evidence of eccentric authorial practice. This list therefore cannot give us any useful information about the relative position, in the stemma, of MIDDLETON[T] and the autograph portion of BRIDGEWATER (5.2, 5.3, and a few lines in 2.2). For similar reasons, if what seems to be anomalous punctuation occurs in too many texts, one begins to suspect that it was acceptable in the period. Given the required deference to autograph, the maximum number of texts that could share a punctuation error would be seven, and for the play's final two scenes would be only six. In practice, I have not identified as an error any punctuation that occurs in more than four texts.

As the foregoing provisos suggest, this list differs from the others, more generally, because it is more difficult to be confident that a punctuation variant is really an error. For that reason, I have not included any of these variants in the arithmetical or statistical analysis of shared error.

The list would be further reduced if we applied the filtering rules for eliminating apparently random combinations. Those rules would remove 2.1.187 (the only example of the pattern CRANE[1,2]), and they would cast doubt on 2.1.179 and 5.3.97 (the only examples of the patterns CRANE[2,4]–ROSENBACH and CRANE[1]–CRANE/ALLDE–ROSENBACH–OKES, respectively). The latter variant is also the only example listed here of a punctuation error apparently shared by four texts. Notably, this filtering would reduce the total number of shared punctuation errors in CRANE[1] to zero, and in CRANE[2] to one; indeed, even the more restrained filtering would reduce the totals for CRANE[1,2] to one shared error each, which given their greater length would place them both higher on the list than CRANE[3]. This would remove the only serious anomaly in the CRANE totals.

The most striking feature of this list is the strong association between OKES and CRANE/ALLDE. By contrast, CRANE/MATHEWES

looks more like a late CRANE text, or an early NON-CRANE text. Two of its five examples would be eliminated by strong filtering; another two, apparently shared only with OKES, are queried because they might belong to larger patterns. The punctuation evidence, although of limited usefulness in relation to the stemma as a whole, does strongly confirm other indications of a close connection between OKES and CRANE/ALLDE.

List of shared punctuation errors

1.1.204/326   confined)...joys∧] ~∧ ~, OKES, CRANE/MATHEWES. Passage not in CRANE[3].

2.1.179/678   Gross!] ~∧ ROSENBACH[A], CRANE/MATHEWES, OKES

2.1.187/688   But, good sir,] ~ ∧ ~ (~) CRANE[2,4], OKES

2.2.43–4/810–11   halter. When...lodgings,] Both autographs and all other texts have stronger punctuation after 'halt' than 'lodgings'—except CRANE/MATHEWES (halt:...lodgings∧) and OKES (halt,...lodgings,). Passage not in CRANE[1].

2.2.195/984   time? Stand firm,] ~~ stand ~: CRANE/MATHEWES; ~∧ ſtands ~, OKES. Only the two quartos separate 'stand firm' from 'now to your scandal'. Passage not in BRIDGEWATER.

3.1.228–9/1320–21   truth,...justify.] The two quartos agree in placing their only punctuation mark in the first position.

3.1.238/1334   I:] ~ ∧ BRIDGEWATER[B], OKES

4.1.77/1697   it,...ghesse,] ~:~∧ CRANE[1,2]. Passage not in CRANE[3].

4.4.61   can,∧] ~ : OKES, CRANE/ALLDE. Passage not in MIDDLETON[T].

4.4.88   ∧thee, Black holiness,] (~∧~~) OKES, CRANE/ALLDE. Passage not in MIDDLETON[T].

5.1.4/2007   *triumphanti*∧] ~, CRANE[3,4], OKES. Passage not in CRANE[1].

5.1.12/2019   *peperitvè*] *peperitùs* CRANE/ALLDE; *perperitùr* OKES. Both quartos agree in misplacing the accent, which disappears entirely in BRIDGEWATER[B] and ROSENBACH[B]. The misplacing of an accent is much more significant than its absence.

5.1.13/2020   Candidissime∧ prælucentissime]] ~)~∧ CRANE/ALLDE, OKES

5.3.97/2308   comes,] Four texts have lighter punctuation at mid-line than at line-end: CRANE[1,4], OKES, ROSENBACH.

5.3.183/2403   perdition-branded] ~,~ ROSENBACH, OKES. A shared punctuation error, perhaps caused by misinterpretation of the lack of a hyphen in [CRANE[4]]. Passage not in CRANE[1].

5.3.217–18/2441–2   (the fitteft...Fallhood) whilft we winner like,] (~,~) CRANE/ALLDE, OKES. Misplaced close of parenthesis in the quartos. Passage not in CRANE[1].

Pattern of Shared Punctuation Errors

Shared Punctuation Errors Linking Two Texts

CRANE[1,2]: 1
  2.1.187

ROSENBACH–BRIDGEWATER: 1
  5.1.12/2019

ROSENBACH–OKES: 1
  5.3.183/2403

BRIDGEWATER–OKES: 1
  3.1.238/1334

CRANE/MATHEWES–OKES: 1–3
  1.1.204/326 [passage not in CRANE[3]]
  2.2.43–4/810–11
  2.2.195/984 [passage not in BRIDGEWATER]

CRANE/ALLDE–OKES: 6
  3.1.228–9/1320–21
  4.4.61

  4.4.88
  5.1.12/2019
  5.1.13/2020
  5.3.217–18

Shared Punctuation Errors Linking Three Texts

CRANE[2,4]–OKES: 1?
  4.1.77/1697 [passage not in CRANE[3]]

CRANE[3,4]–OKES: 1
  5.1.4/2007

ROSENBACH–CRANE/MATHEWES–OKES: 1
  2.1.179/678

Shared Punctuation Errors Linking Four Texts

CRANE[1]–CRANE/ALLDE–ROSENBACH–OKES: 1
  5.3.97/2308

Shared Punctuation Errors: Text Totals

CRANE[3] 1: with two (1)
CRANE[1] 2: with one (1), with three (1)
CRANE[2] 2: with one (1), with two (1)
BRIDGEWATER 2: with one (2)
[CRANE[4]]/MATHEWES 4: with one (3), with two (1)
ROSENBACH 4: with one (2), with two (1), with three (1)
[CRANE[4]]/ALLDE 9: with one (6), with two (2), with three (1)
[CRANE[4]]/MATHEWES/ALLDE 13: with one (9), with two (3), with three (1)
OKES 14: with one (10), with two (3), with three (1)

APPENDIX F: PROGRESSIVE ERRORS

Explanations of one error in terms of another error are, necessarily, conjectural, unless the sequence of transmission is already known. For the argument that the errors in question are progressive, see the relevant textual notes. Here I simply summarize the stemmatic implications of my explanation of the errors. Those summaries do not specify all the possible intervening links between an error in one text and its progressive sophistication in another. For instance, in every instance below where OKES is said to be 'later than' another text or texts, the printed text OKES is certainly later than the lost manuscript used by the printer—[MIDDLETON/OKES]—which might have contained the form found in those other specified extant texts. In other words, what is 'later' may be OKES itself, or it may be [MIDDLETON/OKES], and the variant itself does not distinguish between those two possibilities.

This list does not include examples of progressive error in OKES[2].

1. 1.1.271/397 Bacchus', and Venus' chit, is] CRANE[3] later than CRANE[2].

2. 2.1.75–6/555–6 Good men...one] OKES later than BRIDGEWATER, MIDDLETON[T].

3. 2.1.180/679 a man] OKES later than BRIDGEWATER (and CRANE[3]?).

4. 2.2.195/984 time? Stand firm,] OKES later than ROSENBACH, MIDDLETON[T].

5. 3.1.44/1108 fat bishop] BRIDGEWATER, MIDDLETON[T], OKES later than CRANE[3].

6. 3.1.48/1112 ,This] BRIDGEWATER, MIDDLETON[T], OKES later than CRANE[3].

7. 3.1.154–5/1229 a little...parts] MATHEWES or [CRANE[4]] later than ROSENBACH, MIDDLETON[T].

8. 3.1.313.1/1428 Exeunt] ROSENBACH[A] later than CRANE[1,2,3] and OKES.

9. 3.1.316/1431 my] CRANE/ALLDE later than CRANE[2,3].

10. 3.1.238/1334 I:] OKES later than BRIDGEWATER.

11. 3.1.265/1368 their] OKES later than [CRANE[4]] or ALLDE.

12. 3.1.299.1/1410 Exeunt] ROSENBACH later than CRANE[2,3].

13. 3.2.6/1476 pranced] OKES later than ROSENBACH, BRIDGEWATER.

14. 3.2.8/1480 o'er] OKES later than ROSENBACH.

15. 3.3.24/1547 Egyptic] BRIDGEWATER, OKES later than ROSENBACH.

16. 3.1.375/1554 You...will] MIDDLETON[T] later than BRIDGEWATER.

17. 4.1.4–5/1609–10 to be known, by, | Worn by] OKES later than BRIDGEWATER.

18. 4.1.82/1703 there cause?] OKES later than BRIDGEWATER.

19. 4.2.4/1788 pounds] ROSENBACH, BRIDGEWATER later than CRANE[1,2,3] (and MIDDLETON[T]?)

20. 4.2.7/1791 drum, Pawn] MIDDLETON[T] later than ROSENBACH.

21. 4.2.23/1809 White House] OKES later than MIDDLETON[T], ROSENBACH.

22. 4.2.30–31/1816–17 BLACK KNIGHT'S PAWN Ay...BLACK KNIGHT] OKES later than [CRANE[4]] (or ALLDE), ROSENBACH, BRIDGEWATER, MIDDLETON.

23. 4.2.39/1826 becalmed] ROSENBACH later than BRIDGEWATER, OKES.

24. 4.2.41/1828 six times] ROSENBACH later than BRIDGEWATER, MIDDLETON[T], OKES.

25. 4.2.44/1831 three] ROSENBACH later than [CRANE[4]].

26. 4.2.73/1860 neutrality] OKES later than ROSENBACH, BRIDGEWATER

27. 4.2.76/1863 toad] ROSENBACH later than BRIDGEWATER.

28. 4.2.125/1917 your] OKES later than ROSENBACH.

29. 4.4.11/1959 his] MIDDLETON[T] later than ROSENBACH, which is later than BRIDGEWATER.

30. 5.1.13/2020 Candidissime, prælucentissime]] OKES and [CRANE[4]] (or ALLDE) later than CRANE[2,3], BRIDGEWATER.

31. 5.2.108/2183 QUEEN] CRANE[3], ROSENBACH[A], OKES, and [CRANE[4]] (or ALLDE) later than CRANE[1,2].

APPENDIX G: CONTEMPORARY REFERENCES TO THE PLAY, 1624–63

HOWARD-HILL (1993, 192–213) provides the most recent collection of transcriptions of early documents referring to *A Game at Chess*. This appendix is heavily indebted to his. However, the following list does not include 'The Picture Plainly Explained' or 'To the King', which are both printed (along with Middleton's dedicatory poem in CRANE[3]) in 'Occasional Poems'. It adds two new documents, discovered since 1993 (Ryves and Mead). Howard-Hill gives translations of the documents in French, Spanish, and Italian; for the purposes of scholarly reference, the original languages have been reproduced here.

Sir Henry Herbert, 12 June 1624

'A new play called *A Game at Chesse*, written by Middleton,' was licensed by Sir Henry Herbert, June 12. 1624. So his Office Book ms.

Source: Note by Edmond Malone in his copy of MATHEWES/ ALLDE, Bodleian Malone 247. See Bawcutt (1996), 152.

John Woolley to William Trumbull, Friday 6 August 1624

...All the nues I haue hearde since my comming to toune is of a nue Play acted by his M[t]..seruants, It is called a game at Chess. but it may be a Vox popoly, for by reporte it is 6. tymes worse against the spanyard. In it Gundomars diuilish plotts and deuices are displaid, and many other things to long to resight, the Conclusion expresseth his H: returne and a Mastery ouer the k. of sp: who being ouer come is putt into a great sack with D: Maria, Count of Oliuares, Gundemar, and the B. of Spalato. and there tyed vp together [and by his H. trodde vpon,] such a thing was neuer before invented. and assuredly had so much ben donne the last yeare, they had eueryman ben hanged for it....

Source: British Library, Trumbull Papers, alphabetical series 48/134. The bracketed phrase was added in the margin.

George Lowe to Sir Arthur Ingram, Saturday 7 August 1624

...There is a new play called the *Game at Chestes* acted yesterday and to-day, which describes Gondo-mar and all the Spanish proceedings very boldly and broadly, so that it is thought that it will be called in and the parties punished.

Source: 'The manuscripts of the hon. Frederick Lindley Wood', Historical Manuscripts Commission, *Report on Manuscripts in Various Collections*, vol. VIII (1913), 27.

Note that this is in modern spelling; I have not checked the original.

Don Carlos Coloma, Spanish Ambassador, to King James I, Saturday 7 August 1624

Sire.

Pendent ꝗ ie suis attentant commandem du Roy mon M[re] d'aller donner a sa Ma[te] compte de cette mienne embassade com d'heure a autre ie l'attends, Je ne puis obmettre d'adiouster aux deuoirs de ma function [*sic*], et de representer a VM[te] ce qui conuient pour ma descharge.

Les Comediens ꝗ l'on appele du Roy, ont hier et auiourdhuy exhibe une comedie si sandaleuse, impie, barbare, et si offensiue au Roy mon M[re] (si la grandeur et valeur inestimable de sa persoñe royale fut capable de receuoir offence de personne, et signam d'homes si bas come le sont d'ordinaire les autheurs et repntateurs de semblabes follies: qu'elle m'a obligé de mettre la main a la place et a supplier en peu de paroles, et auec l'humilite ꝗ ce dois a VM[te] pour l'une de deux choses. Qu'elle soit seruie de donner ordre ꝗ les d. Autheurs et Comediens soient publicquem et exemplairem chasties, par ou VM[te] satisfera a son honneur et a la reputation et ciuilite de la nation Angloise; ou ꝗ: comandant ꝗ lon me donne un nauire pour passer en Flandres auec les asseurances requises et qu'elle donne aux Ambassad des autres Roys: le bon plaisir de VMa[te] soit de me donner permission ꝗ je le puisse faire auplustost l'une ou l'autre chose m'obligera indifferemment a rester...

Source: *State Papers* (Spain), PRO SP94/31, fol. 132; printed in P. G. Phialas, 'An Unpublished Letter about *A Game at Chess*', MLN 69 (1954), 398–9. The letter is dated 20 August (continental style), equivalent to 10 August in England. That day Coloma also wrote to Conway, requesting a 'response cathegorique' (fol. 134).

Don Carlos Coloma to the Conde-Duque Olivares, Tuesday 10 August 1624

Poco ha que escriui al Rey, ya ve lo que aca se ofreçia que hauissar hasta los 16 deste, despues aca so a ofreçido una cossa no indigna de que V. Ex[a] y aun S. M. la sepan para que se eche de ver la desberguença desta gente si acasso ay neçessidad de nuevos exemplos y es esta:

Los comediantes que aqui llaman del Rey an repres-sentado estos dias y todavia rrepressentan en esta corte una comedia con tanto concurso de gente que el dia que menos ha havido han passado de tres mill perssonas y con tanto contento algaçara y aplausso que aunque yo me hallara muchas leguas de aqui me fuera inposible dejar de tomar noticia dello y conoçida bajeça no solamente sobrada toleraçia el passarlo en disimulaçion. Es el asumpto de la comedia un juego de ajedrez con cassas de blancos y negros sus reyes y las demas pieças rrepressentados por los personajes donde el rey de los negros por su poca hedad, traje y otras çircunstançias ha sido façil de aplicar al Rey nuestro señor. El primer auto o llamemosle juego le repressentaron sus ministros entendidos por los blancos y los jesuitas por los negros; bieronse aqui notables sacrilejios y entre otras abominaçiones hazer un ministro salir del infierno a San Ignaçio, el qual embiendose otra vez en el mundo lo primero que hiço fue forzar a una hija suya de confession todo con actos tan obçenos y tan torpes como estos maldros y abominables herejes lo son. El segundo auto se libro en el arçobispo de Espalatro, por entonzes blanco aunque despues llevado al bando negro por el Conde de Gondomar el qual traido cassi al bivo, al teatro en su literilla y sentandosse en su silla agujerada dijeron que confessava todas sus trayciones con que habia engañado y adormecido al rey de los blancos y discurriendo con los jesuitas en materia de confession saco el figurado por el Conde un libro en donde estavan tassados todos los preçios porque de alli adelante se habian de perdonar los pecados; y sobre esto cuentan los que vieron la comedia tantas particularidades y tan negandas y suçias palabras que no me ha pareçido ofender los oydos de V. E. con ellas. En estos dos autos y en el terçero que no se particularmente sobre que se fundo, no se trataba apenas de otra cossa que de la crueldad d'España, de la falsedad de los españoles y todo esto tan individuo que ni aun a las perssonas reales excluyeron. El ultimo auto se remato con una larga y porfiada contienda entre todos los blancos y negros y en que el que repressentaba la figure entendida por el Principe de Gales echasse en el infierno que hera una gran sima con figuras horrendas a muy buenas puñadas y coçes al que ymitaba al Conde de Gondomar y el rey de los blancos al rey de los negros y aun e la dama con poco menos bituperio; todo esto con tanto aplauso y regocijo del bulgo que con no repressentarse aqui mas que un dia ninguna comedia se ha repressentado, esta quarto ya y cada dia ay mas concurso.

Si yo hubiera creydo al Marques de la Inojossa que me aconssejava me fuesse con el no llegaran a mis oydos semejantes cossas ni viera por tantos caminos ultrajado de gente tan infame y tan vaja el nombre sagrado de mi Rey, ni interpretadas tan indignamente sus santas y gloriossas acciones que hera solo lo que me faltava para poder llamar infierno justissimamente a las penas que aqui padezco siendo la mayor que en el material se passa el oyr las blasfemias que se diçen contra Dios y añadiendo a esto el no haver

podido averiguar en dos messes si hiçe bien o mal en quedarme si servi o deservi en ello al Rey me tiene con el desconsuelo que V. E. crehera façilmente deste su berdadero servidor; pero dejado esto a cargo de V. E. que como tan gran cavallero y tan prinçipal ministro de S. M. me hara merced de ponerlo en sus reales oydos con la recomendaçion devida al çelo con que e deseado y procurado açertar. Digo señor que en teniendo relaçion de la desverguenza de los comediantes despache al secretario de lenguas a este rey que se halla quarenta leguas de aqui festejando y llevando en palmitas al embajador de Françia con la carta cuyo tenor es el quo se sigue:

Entre tanto que me llega orden del Rey mi señor para hir a dar raçon a S. M. desta mi embajada como por momentos la espero no puedo dejar de acudir a las obligaçiones de mi ofiçio ni de repressentar a V. M. lo que me pareze conviene para mi descargo. Ayer y oy se ha repressentado en esta corte publicamente por los farsantes que llaman de V. M. una comedia tan escandalossa tan impia, tan barvara y tan ofensiva al Rey mi señor, si acasso su conoçida grandeza y el inestimable balor de su real perssona fuera capaz de reçivir ofenssa por nadie quanto mas por gente tan vaja como de ordinario lo son los autores y reçitantes de semejantes locuras, que me a obligado a tomar la pluma y suplicar a V. M. en breves palabras una de dos cossas con la humildad que devo o que V. M. se sirva de mandar castigar publica y exsemplarmente a los autores y reçitantes de la dicha comedia en que satisfara V. M. a su onor mismo y la reputaçion de la naçion inglessa tan ofendida con acziones tan vajas y tan indignas de hombres de honra, o que sirviendose mandarme dar navio en que passar a Flandes y las seguridades neçessarias y conzedidas a embajadores de otros reyes me de lizençia de poderlo hacer luego luego [sic] una destas dos cossas aguardo indiferentemente. Rogando a Dios etc.

La respuesta por estar este Rey lejos y por hir el secretario de lenguas con poca salve no la aguardo hasta los 23 or 24 deste, entretanto haviendo tomado por expediente escrivir a España todos los martes por via del Marques de Miravel con el ordinario a Paris como lo hare lo que aqui me detubiere, no a querido dejar de havissar a V. E. des oy ni de advertir que si el Rey de Inglaterra escoge el darme lizencia y no el castigar tan gran insolençia me hire enfaliblemente a Bruselas y alli aguardare la orden que S. M. fuere servido de mandarme dar, seguro de que se tomara en buena parte esta mi resoluçion como salida de un pecho no acostumbrado a sufrir agravios ni desberguenzas quando menos contra su Rey y contra su patria. Guarde Nuestro Señor a V. E. muchos años como yo desco. Londres 20 de Agosto 1624.

E le dado a escoger a este Rey entre el castigo desta bellaqueria o mi liçenzia pidiendo toda Buena reçon y conjetura que escogeria lo primero y pareçiendome que si escoje le segundo acava de condenar sus acciones no solamente para con Dios sino tanvien para con el mundo y espero que no le parezera a nadie leve la caussa de haver llegado con la Marques de la Inojossa y conmigo los menospreçios que se an hecho y hacen de la grandeza y poder de S. M. per escrito y de palabra y que su embajador a quien por esto se le devo tan conoçido respecto y tan particular estimaçion esta dos meses a sin exerziçio de tan ençerrado en su cassa sin poder tratar con este Rey ni con sus ministros por si ni por terzeras perssonas y considerando finalmente que aunque para con todo genero de gente tiene el sufrimiento, sus limites son mucho mas cortos los de quien tomo a su cargo desde que naçio las obligaçiones de soldado y pudiendose fiar de mi que en calidad de tal sabre con el favor de Dios suplir las faltas en que ubiese caido como envajador y quando al fine merezca culpa per aver puesto a este Rey a peligro de enojarsse quiero mas castigo por haber mostrado valor sinembargo de verme aqui desamparado de tantas maneras que una simple reprehension por haver sufrido demasiado no mis agravios sino del Rey nuestro señor Dios le guarde y no ay decir que son quarto picaros los que lo diçen y los que lo oyen que en cuatro dias hasta oy son mas de doçe mill perssonas las que an oydo la comedia del juego de axedrez que ansi la intitulan y entre ellos toda la nobleza que agora se halla en Londres de la qual salen todos tan yrritados contra España que como me an asigurado algunos catholicos que por disimulaçion la an hido aver no andaria mi perssona segura por essas calles y otros me an aconsejado a estar en mi cassa con buena guarda come so hace. Mire V. E. como pudiera passarlo en disimulazion; basta haver dissimulado tanta diferençia de cossas dichas y hechas y en fin unas cançiones infam es que hace cantar a sus musicos Boquingan alla a donde andar agora, que son tales que el Marques de Hamilton y el Conde de Mongomerli, el de Queri y otros en un gran sarao se salieron por no oyllas que me lo a escripto quien lo vio. Al fin señor no ay que esparar destos otra cossa que guerra y crea V. E., yo se lo suplico, si por algunos respectos nos conviene dilatarlo no es tan buen camino el de su firmamento come el demostrar balor y resolucion . . .

Source: Biblioteca Nacional, Madrid. Ms. 18203, transcribed by Don Ricardo Magdaleno and published by Edward M. Wilson and Olga Turner, 'The Spanish Protest against *A Game at Chess*', *Modern Language Review* 44 (1949), 476–82. The letter is dated continental style.

John Woolley to William Trumbull, Wednesday 11 August 1624

. . . The play of Gundomar is not yett suppressed but it is feared it will be eare longe, for the Spanish Amb^r. hath sent Post after Post, with l^{res} to complayne to the king of it, and takes it very haynously that such a thing should be plaid against his Master. but the Players looseth no tyme, nor forbeareth to make haye while the Sunn shyneth, acting it euery day without any intermition and it is thought they haue already gott neere a thousand pound by it . . . .

Source: British Library, Trumbull Papers, alphabetical series 48/135.

John Holles, Lord Haughton to the Earl of Somerset, Wednesday 11 August 1624

To my Lo. of Summersett at Cheswik y^e ii of August i624. My Lo. though from Mr. Whittakers, or others, this vulgar pasquin may cum to your eares, yet whether he, or y^{ei} saw it, I know not, muche beeing y^e difference between ey=sight, & hear=say: when I returned from your Lo^{ip}? hither upon munday, I was saluted with a report of a facetious comedy, allreddy thryce acted with extraordinary applause: a representation of all our spannishe traffike, where Gundomar his litter, his open chayre for the ease of y^t fistulated part, Spalato &ca. appeared uppon ye stage. I was inuited by ye reporter Sr Edward Gorge (whose ballance giues all things waight to ye aduantage) to be allso an auditor therof, & accordingly yesterday to ye globe I rowed, wch hows I found so thronged, y^t by scores y^{ei} came away for want of place, though as yet little past one; neuertheless lothe to check y^e appetite, wch came so seldome to me (not hauing been in a playhouse y^{es} io. years) & suche a daynty not euery day to be found, I marched on, & heard y^e pasquin, for no other it was wch had been y^e more complete, had y^e poet been a better states=man: y^e descant was built upon y^e popular opinion, y^t y^e Iesuits mark is to bring all y^e christian world vnder Rome for y^e spirituality, & vnder Spayn for y^e temporalty: heeruppon, as a precept, or legacy left those disciples from their first founder Ignatius Loyola, this their father serues for the prologue, who admiring no speedier operation of his drugg, is inraged, & desperate, till cumforted by one of his disciples, ye plott is reuealed him, prosperously aduanced by their designe vppon England: with this he vanisheth, leauing his benediction ouer ye work. The whole play is a chess board, England ye whyt hows, Spayn ye black: one of ye white pawns, wth an vn der black dubblett, signifying a Spanish hart, betrays his party to their aduantage, aduanceth Gundomars propositions, works vnder hand ye Princes cumming into Spayn: wch pawn so discouered, ye whyt King reuyles him, obiects his raising him in wealth, in honor, from meane condition, next classis to a labouring man: this by ye character is supposed Bristow: yet is [*sic*] is hard, players should iudge him in iest, before ye State in ernest. Gundomar makes a large account of all his great feartes heer, descrybes in scorne our vanities in dyet, in apparell, in euery other excess, (ye symptoms of a falling state) how many Ladies brybed him to be groome of ye stoole to ye Infanta, how many to be mother of y^e mayds, with muche suche trashe, l^rs. from y^e nunnry in Drury lane, from those in Bloomsbury &ca. how many Iesuites, & priests he loosed out of prison, & putt agayn into their necessary work of seducing how he sett y^e Kings affayrs as a clock, backward & forward, made him belieue, & vn=belieue as stood best with his busines, be y^e caws neuer so cleere: how he couered y^e roguery of y^e Ie-suits in abusing wemen licentiously: how he befooled Spalato with a counterfett l^re. from Cardinall Paolo his kinsman, promising to leaue his Cardinals hatt to him, himself then beeing elected Pope: with muche suche like stuff, more wittily penned, then wysely staged: but at last ye Prince making a full discouery of all their knaueries, Olliuares, Gundomar, Spalato, Iesuite, spannish bishop, & a spannish euenuke ar by ye Prince [putt] putt into ye bagg, & so ye play ends. Your Lo^p may giue to this a morall; me thinks this is a hardy part, & beyond my vnderstanding: & surely y^es gamsters must haue a good retrayte, else dared y^ei not to charge thus Princes actions, & ministers, nay their intents: a foule iniury to Spayn, & no great honor to Englan d, rebus sic stantibus: euery particular will beare a large paraphrase, wch I submit to your better iudgment &ca: Westminster ii. of Aug.

Source: Holles Letter Book, Nottingham University Library, Ne C 15,405; P. R. Seddon, *Letters of John Holles*, 1587–1637, vol. 2, Thoroton Society Records series, xxxv (Nottingham, 1983), pp. 228–90. See A. R. Braunmuller, '"To the Globe I rowed": John Holles Sees *A Game at Chess*', *English Literary Renaissance* 20 (1990), 340–56, and Howard-Hill, 'The Unique Eye-Witness Report of Middleton's *A Game at Chess*', *Review of English Studies* 42 (1991), 168–78.

Sir Edward Conway, Secretary of State, to the Privy Council, Thursday 12 August 1624

...His Matie hath receaued information from the Spanish Ambassador of a very scandalous Comedie acted publikly by the Kings Players, Wherein they take the boldnes, and presumption in a rude, and dishonorable fashion to represent on the Stage the persons of his Matie, the Kinge of Spaine, the Conde de Gondomar, the Bishop of Spalato, &c. His Matie remembers well there was a commaundment and restraint giuen against the rep^rsentinge of anie moderne Christian kings in those Stage-playes, and wonders much both at the boldnes nowe taken by that Companie, and alsoe that it hath ben permitted to bee soe acted, and that the first notice thereof should bee brought to him, by a forraine Ambassador, while soe manie Ministers of his owne are thereaboutes and cannot but haue heard of it. His Maties pleasure is that your LL^ps p^rsently call before you, aswell the Poett, that made the comedie, as the Comedians that acted it, And vpon examinacion of them to co~mit them,

or such of them, as you shall find most faultie, vnto prison, if you find cause, or otherwise take securitie for their forthcominge; And then certefie his Matie what you find that Comodie to bee, in what points it is most offensiue, by whom it was made, by whom lycenced, and what course you thinke fittest to bee held for the exemplarie, and severe punishment of the present offendors, and to restrayne such insolent and lycencious presumption for the future.

This is the charge I have receaued from his Matie and wth it I make bold to offer to your LL^ps the humble service of...
Rufford
August .12. 1624

Source: *State Papers (Domestic)*, James I, vol. 171, no. 39; SPI4/171.

Sir Edward Conway to Don Carlos Coloma, undated [probably 12 August 1624]

Yo e representado a S. M. la carta de V. E. que esta muy maravillado de la grande insolençia y temeridad que sigun V. E. representa an cometido los comediantes de que S. M. esta con tanto sentimiento que V. E. puede asigurarse de que en este caso se hara la justicia y demostracion que es justo y a este fin me a mandado que escriva muy particularmente a los señores del Consejo para que proceda al exsamen del hecho y a la execuçion de la justiçia con que puede V. E. asigurarle como V. M. [sic] me ha mandado lo haga de su parte que en todo dara entera satisfaçion y contentamiento.

Source: Biblioteca Nacional, Madrid. Ms. 18203. See Wilson and Turner.

Paul Overton to Dr William Bishop, Bishop of Chalcedon, Friday 13 August 1624

...The present time affordeth nothinge newe. wee haue noe stay of persecution, nor any likelyhood yet. one mr. Coale a Preist was lately taken by Gee, and is in newegate. At the globe playhouse is dayly presented an odious play against Spaine, but principally Gondomar, and the Jusuits. This beinge all this barren time doth afford I take my leaue. 23. July. 1624....

Source: Westminster Diocesan Archives B26 (Roman Letters), no. 92. Discovered by Thomas Cogswell, printed in Howard-Hill, who notes that the month is obviously mistaken. The letter is dated continental style.

Amerigo Salvetti, Florentine Ambassador, to Piccena, Friday 13 August 1624

Da otto giorni in qua, si recita in questa città da questi comedianti publici, quasi ogni giorno una comedia, che loro chiamano il giuoco degli scacche; nella quale rappresentano al vivo tutte le azioni del Conte di Gondemare, durante il tempo che fu qui Ambasciatore, non lasciando nulla adietro, che in loro oppinione gli paia di scuoprire, come dicono suoi machinazioni et falsità con tanto applauso et concorso di questo popolo, che si crede, che ogni volta che l'hanno recitata habbino i comedianti guadagnato da 300 scudi di oro. Vi introducono ancora l'Arcivescovo di Spalatro, et in somma e'una cosa molto satirica, et che da'grandissimo gusto. Si crede nondimeno che sarà prohibita subito che il Re n'habbia notiza; perché non possono tanto lacerare il Conte di Gondemar nel scuoprire la sua maniera di trattare, che non dipinghino contro lor voglia per huomo di valore, et consequentemente, che non rifletta fiacchezza sopra di quelli che gli davano credenza, et che giornalmente trattavano seco etc.

Source: British Library Ms. Addit. 27,962, vol. C, fol. 189^r. See Bernard M. Wagner, 'New Allusions to *A Game at Chess*', *Review of English Studies* 6 (1930), 827-34, and John Orrell, 'Amerigo Salvetti and the London Court Theatre', *Theatre Survey* 20 (1979), 1–26. The letter is dated continental style (23 August).

Amerigo Salvetti to Sir John Scudamore, Bart., Saturday 14 August 1624

Gondemar is dailie upon the stage with great applause of the people, but greater of the plaiers, that gett well nigh 200l. a day. In going about to discouer his trickes, me thinkes they make him a man of understanding with a great reflection upon them that he daylie treated wth ... the bishoppe of Spalato is ioyned with him, but the maine runnes all together upon the other and his phistula &c More this uacation doth not affoord....

Source: Public Record Office, Ms C115/N1/8488. Discovered by Thomas Cogswell, published in Howard-Hill.

Sir Francis Nethersole to Sir Dudley Carleton, Saturday 14 August 1624

...Yet we haue now these ten dayes a new play here, the plot whereof is a game of Chesse, vnder wch the whole Spanish business js ripped vp to the quicke, and Gondomar brought on ye Stage in his chayre, wch fitteth skorners so well that the players haue gotten 100^{li} the day euer since, for they play no thing els, knowing there time cannot be long.

Source: *State Papers* (Domestic), James I, vol. 171, no. 49; SPI4/I71. See Wagner.

Dr Thomas Ryves to James Ussher, Bishop of Meath, Saturday 14 August 1624

I have noe newes, to send y^r] Lp: but that Gondomar is plaied twice a day on the banke side; with such infinite concourse of people, as the like was never scene; what the end of this plaie is, or what good will come thereof I knowe not, unless it bee to lett all men know that one fistula in Gondamars bodie had more in it, then all the veines in or bodie ...

Source: Bodleian MS Rawlinson letters 89, fol. 42^r. See Jeanne Shami, '"Twice a day on the banke side"?: a contemporary report on Middleton's *A Game at Chesse*', *Notes and Queries* 45 (1998), 367-4. Not in Howard-Hill.

Privy Council, Wednesday 18 August 1624

A warrant directed to Raphe Robinson one of the Messengers of his ma:^{ts} Chamber to bring [   ] Middleton before theire Llo:^{pps} to answer &c.

Source: *Privy Council Register*, James I, vol. VI, 421; PC 2/32. The space before 'Middleton' is left blank.

Don Carlos Coloma to the Conde-Duque Olivares, Wednesday 18 August 1624

Londres 28 de Agosto 1624.
Como escribi a V. E. la semana passada embie al secretario de lenguas a este Rey que bolvio el savado con la respuesta del secretario Conve, que va aqui traduçida pero se vera si es verdadero el enojo contra el autor y reçitantes de la comedia por el castigo que se les diese. Lo çierto es haverse representado nueve dias arreo con tan general aplausse de los malos como sentimientos de los de sanas intenciones que sin este adminiculo nos juzgavan ya por bastantemente yrritados contra el barvarismo y vajo termino desta gente.

Source: Biblioteca Nacional, Madrid. Ms. 18203. See Wilson and Turner. The letter is dated continental style. It includes the translated letter from Conway, given above and provisionally dated 12 August.

Sir Francis Nethersole to Sir Dudley Carleton, Thursday 19 August 1624

...The players were yesterday called before some of the LL^s. of ye Counsell who met here for that purpose, by whom they are forbidden to play any more at all till they may be licensed agayne by his Ma^{ty}, and must appeare agayne at his returne from his Progresse, for which they haue putt in bondes....

Source: *State Papers* (Domestic), James I, vol. 171, no. 60; SPI4/I71.

John Woolley to William Trumbull, Friday 20 August 1624

...The Spanish Amb^r hath at last though wth much adoe, gott the Players to be silenste, and enter into bond not to Play Gundomar or any other till they know his Ma^{ts}. farther pleasure. Middleton the Poet is sought after, and it is [thought] supposed shall be clapt in prison, if he doe not cleere him selfe by the M^r. of the Reuells, who alowed of it; and it is thought not wthout leaue, from the higher powers I meane the P. and D. if not from the K. for they were all loth to haue it forbidden, and by report laught hartely at it....

Source: British Library, Trumbull Papers, alphabetical series, 48/136. See Bawcutt (1996), 153.

Amerigo Salvetti, Florentine Ambassador, to the Secretary, Friday 20 August 1624

La comedia, che rappresentava il Conte di Gondemar e'state dipoi porhibita da questi Signori consiglieri di stato, per ordine venuto di Corte, dove si crede, che l'Ambasciatore di Spgna si fusse fatto sentire.

Source: British Library, Ms. Addit. 27,962, vol. C, fol. 191ᵛ. See Wagner and Orrell.

Alvise Valaresso, Venetian Ambassador, to the Doge and Senate, Friday 20 August 1624

In uno di questi pubblici mercenarii teatri é stata ultimamente più volte replicata certa rappresentatione sotto nomi finti di molte attioni seguite per occasione dil matrimonio col Infante. L'opera non é di gran succo per quanto dicono ma habbi un infinito concorso per la curiosità della materia. Gli spagnoli vengono tocchi per esser scoperti i loro artifitii, ma é ferita più la riputation del Re per rappresentarsi la facilità con che fu ingannato. L'ambasciatore spagnolo n'ha fatta passare in doglienza, et si crede che il compositor almen resterà castigato.

Source: Archivio di Stato a Venezia, Senato, Dispacci, Inghilterra, f. XXV: 1624, Alvise Valareso e Giovanni Pesaro Ambasciatori; Lettera n. 136, fol. 261ᵛ (modern numbering). The letter is dated continental style ('da Londra, 30 agosto 1624'). The original has been transcribed for this edition by Ilaria Andreoli. Previous scholarship cites the English translation in *State Papers* (*Venetian*), 1623–1625, no. 557, p. 425; SP99/25. The English translation is misleading at several points. It reads the Italian 'nomi finti' (feigned, fictional names) as 'different names', and the Italian 'infinito concorso' (infinite crowd) as 'great crowds'. By a simple slip, Italian 'facilità' (facility, ease) becomes English 'case' (for intended 'ease', presumably).

Privy Council to Sir Edward Conway, Saturday 21 August 1624

...According to his Maᵗⁱᵉˢ pleasure signified to this Board by your lʳᵉ of the]2th of *August* touching the suppressing of a scandalous Comᵈⁱᵉ Acted by the *Kings Players*. Wee haue called before vs some of the principall Actors, and demaunded of them by what lycence and authoritie they have presumed to act the same, in answer wherevnto they produced a booke being an orriginall and perfect Coppie thereof (as they affirmed) seene and allowed by Sʳ *Henry Herbert knight*, Master of the *Reuells*, vnder his owne hand, and subscribed in the last Page of the said booke; We demaunding further, whether there were no other partes or passages represented on the Stage, then those expressely contained in the booke, they confidentlie protested, they added or varied from the

same nothing at all. The *Poett* they tell vs is one Midleton, who shifting out of the way, and not attending the Board with the rest as was expected, Wee haue given warrant to a Messenger for the apprehending of him. To those that were before vs, we gaue a round and sharpe reprooffe making them sensible of his Maᵗⁱᵉˢ high displeasure herein, giving them strict charge and com̃aund, that they presume not to Act the said Com̃edie any more nor that they suffer any Play or *Enterlude* whatsoeuer to be Acted by them, or any of their Company vntill his Maᵗⁱᵉˢ pleasure be further knowne. Wee haue caused them likewise to enter into Bond for their attendance vpon the Board whensoeuer they shalbe called; As for our certifieing to his Maᵗⁱᵉ (as was intimated by your lʳᵉ) what passages in the said Comedie we should finde to be offensiue and scandalous, Wee haue thought it our duties for his Maᵗⁱᵉˢ clearer informacon to send herewᵗʰ all the booke it self subscribed as aforesaid by the Mʳ of the *Reuells*, that so either yʳ self or some other whom his Maᵗⁱᵉ shall appoint to pervse the same, may see the passages themselues out of the orriginall and call Sʳ *Henry Herbert* before you to know a reason of his lycenceing thereof, who (as we are giuen to vnderstand) is now attending at *Court*. So hauing done as much as we conceived agreable with our duties in conformitie to his Maᵗⁱᵉˢ Royall commaundementes and that wᶜʰ we hope shall giue him full satisfaction, we shall continue our humble praiers....

From Whitehall the 21th of August 1624...

Source: *State Papers* (*Domestic*), James I, vol. 171, no. 64; SP14/171. This is the original letter, first transcribed and printed by Howard-Hill.

John Chamberlain to Sir Dudley Carleton, Saturday 21 August 1624

...I doubt not but you haue heard of our famous play of Gondomar, which has ben followed with extraordinarie concourse, and frequented by all sorts of people old and younge, rich and poore, masters and seruants, papists and puritans, wise men et[c] churchmen and statesmen as sir Henry wotton, Sir Albert morton, Sir Beniamin Ruddier, Sir Thomas Lake, and a world besides; the Lady Smith wold haue gon yf she could haue persuaded me to go with her, I am not so sore nor seuere but that I wold willingly haue attended her, but I could not sit so long, for we must haue ben there before one a'clocke at farthest to find any roome. they counterfeited his person to the life, with all his graces and faces, and had gotten (they say) a cast sute of his apparell for the purpose, with his Lytter, wherein the world sayes lackt nothing but a couple of asses to carry yt, and Sir G. Peter, or Sir T. Mathew to beare him companie. but the worst is in playeng him, they played sombody els, for which they are forbidden to play that or any other play till the kings pleasur be further knowne; and they may be glad yf they can so escape scot-free: the wonder lasted but nine dayes, for so long they played yt.

Source: *State Papers* (*Domestic*), James I, vol. 171, no. 66; SP14/171.

Sir Edward Conway to the Privy Council, Friday 27 August 1624

...His Matie havinge receaued satisfacion in y^r Ll^ps indeavours, and in the significacon thereof by yo^rs of the 25. of this present, hath commaunded mee to signifie the same to you. And to add further that his pleasure is, that your LL^ps examine by whose direccon, and applicacon the personnatinge of *Gondemar*, and others was done. And that beinge found out, that partie, or parties to bee severely punished. His Matie beinge vnwillinge for ones sake, and only fault to punish the innocent or vtterly to ruine the Companie. The discovery on what partie his M^ties Iustice is properly, and duly to fall, and your execucon of it, and the accompt to bee retorned thereof, his Matie leaues to y^r LL:ps wisdomes, and care...

    Woodstock
    August, 27. 1624

Source: *State Papers* (*Domestic*), James I, vol. 171, no. 75; SP14/171.

The Earl of Pembroke, Lord Chamberlain, to the President of the Council, Viscount Mandeville, Friday 27 August 1624

...Complaynt being made vnto his M^tie against ye Company of his comedians for Acteing publiquely a Play knowne by the name of a Game at Chesse, Contayning some passages in it reflecting in matter of scorne and ignominy vpon ye King of Spaine some of his Ministers and others of good note and quality. His Ma^ty out of ye tender regard hee has of that Kings honnour, and those his Ministers who weare Conceived to bee wounded thereby, Caused his letters to bee addressed to my LL^s and ye rest of his most hon^rble privy Counsell, thereby requireing them to Convent those his comedians before them, and to take such Course with them for this offence as might give best satisfacion to ye Spanish Ambassadour and to Their owne Honnors. After exarninaccion, that hon^rble Board thought fitt not onely to interdict them ye playing of that play, but of any other also untill his Ma^ty should give way vnto them; And for their obedience herevnto they weare bound in 300^li bondes. Which punishment they had suffered (as his Ma^ty Conceives) a Competent tyme; vpon their peticon delivered heare vnto hym; it pleased his Ma^ty to comaund mee to lett y^ur L^p vnderstand

(which I pray your Lo^p) to impart to ye rest of that ho^rble Board. That his Ma^ty nowe Conceives the punishment if not satisfactory for that their Insolency, yet such, as since it stopps ye Current of their poore livelyhood and maintãuce without much preiudice they Cannot longer vndergoe. In Cõmiseracõn therefore of those his poore servantes, his Ma^ty would have their LL^ps Connive at any Cõmon play lycenced by authority, that they shall act as before; As for this of ye Game at Chesse, that it bee not onely antiquated and sylenced, but ye Players bound as formerly they weare, and in that poynt onely never to Act it agayne: Yet notwithstanding that my LL^s proceed in their disquisicõn to fynd out ye originall roote of this offence, whether it sprang from ye Poet, Players, or both, and to Certefy his Ma^ty accordingly....

    Court at Woodstock the 27th of August 1624.

Source: British Library, Egerton Ms. 2623, fol. 28.

Alvise Valaresso to the Doge and Senate, Friday 27 August 1624

Li comedianti che rappresentarono quanto scrissi con le passate per pena hebbero de non recitar sino ad altro ordine. La sentenza venne dal Consiglio al qual il Re ne rimette il giuditio. Queste son le materie ch'egli volentieri gli devolve, per mantenir a questi Sig.ri con qualche impiego il nome di Consigliero, et per scaricar se stesso dall'impaccio di tali rissolutioni.

Source: Archivio di Stato a Venezia, Senato, Dispacci, Inghilterra, f. XXV: 1624, Alvise Valareso e Giovanni Pesaro Ambasciatori; Lettera n. 137, fol. 267^v (modern numbering). The letter is dated continental style ('da Londra, 6 settembre 1624'). The original has been transcribed for this edition by Ilaria Andreoli. Previous scholarship cites the English translation in *State Papers* (*Venetian*), 1623–1625, no. 568; SP99/25.

John Woolley to William Trumbull, Saturday 28 August 1624

...Some say (how true it is I know not) that the Players are gone to the Courte to Act the game at Chesse before the Kinge. wch doth much truble the spanish Amb^r...

Source: British Library, Trumbull Papers, alphabetical series, 48/137.

Privy Council, Monday 30 August 1624

A warrant directed to Robert Goffe, one of the Messengers of his Maties Chamber to bring one Midleton sonne to Midleton the Poet before theire Ll^ps to answer &c.

Source: *Privy Council Register*, James 1, vol. VI, p. 429; PC2/32.

Privy Council, Monday 30 August 1624

This daie Edw. Middleton of London gent, being formerly sent for by warrant from the Board tendred his Apparaunce, which for his Indempnitie is here entred into the Register of Councell Causes nevertheless he is enioyned to attend the Board, till he be dis'charged by Order from their lo^pps.

Source: *Privy Council Register, James I*, vol. VI, p. 429; PC2/32.

Thomas Salisbury in Sir Thomas Dawes's commonplace book, 1 December 1624

Brother
my muse when yow were past, past too
from her associate Nimphes bid, write to yow
not for my promise only but my vse
Improue yor wordes, so spake my thriving Muse?
She counseld well, I heard, y^is thence require
good Pieties practice, late some holy fire
mildly inflames me, continue yow ye flame

The Induction generall to ye abbreuiate of ye game at Chess acted by^e Princes players at globe. 1624

vpon peruse I shall returne the same,
y^is is my vse yor kindnes: if beside
youle gladly heare some news: from tother side
we heare o^r souldgiers safely are arriud,
in Holland: but how since ye men haue thriud
I haue not heard: somewhat did discouer
their Summer plot?: thence they are forc'd to
    houer;
as for ye Court it is so farr from thence

the speciall manuduction to ye ordering & playing ye men.

we haue no certantie to write from hence:
the rumor buzzes now in euery eare
is: bought a Game at Chess but y^t I fear
to shew my small skill in y^t royall play
I could tell most of that, y^t most men say:
take but y^e [   ] & Gamesters: mongst ye rest
ye seuerall dishes of Ambitions Feast:
and y^en yould wish or y^t ye Scene lay there.

ye description of ye black howse

or yow were, where ye scene is wth vs heere:
For ye black howse, they chose to represent
ye King, Queene, Bishop, Knight, Duke, to each
    lent
their seuerall Paunes as Guards ye first yow
    knowe
ye rest to life y^is present Verse shall shewe
ye Bishop stood for Roomes corrupted chayre
ye Knight for no Knight errant; but a Rare
subtill Embassadour: y^e like o^r shoare
neuer r^d: nor may it euermore!

Lerma

y^e Duke for y^e Duke Fauorite of Spaine;
highly belou'd of y^e black Soueraigne.
3 Paunes were famous: those we shall expresse
y^e Bishop: a Shy Jesuite, adde on S
y^e Queenes Paune was a seculare Jesuitesse;
y^e Knights a State=flye: whome he did addresse

to vndermine o^r Candor: one he tooke
and made an Eunuch: y^is y^e Blackhowse: looke
now to y^e white: (uirtues pure sacred Reste)
o^r ma^ties like heauens: are best exprest
in duteous Silence, opposite agen
to y^e blacke=house, wee had as many men
one Sup^rnumerus Bishop did appeare
to fill upp a vacante sede there
and did it by Reuolt; Apostates Hire,
their turne once seru'd, they damn him to y^e Fire
y^e Queenes Paune was a Lady! hard besett
to become Nunne: but came off cleerely yet:
but two remaine y^e Princely Knight; Lou'd Duke
y^t Royall Payre y^t a close iourney tooke
vnto Iberia: why? to what successe?
I tell not nowe: I onely haue one messe
was sett before o^r Knight: to sett to yow
and I haue s^d when I haue s^d Adieu.

Entranc to ye Feast.

to compasse his owne ends our valiaunt Knight
pretends himself Ambitious: in such height
Y^t one might sooner Bound, ye Boundlesse Fire
y^en quench y^ose thoughts y^t did to rule aspire.
to cure y^is sore ye Black Knight vndertakes
to cure all els y^t fowle disturbance makes
in his greate Harte, y^is first he slights & sayes
we hold y^is but for Pufpaste a light Messe.

ye Feast self

wch eury Cardinals cooke hath skill to dresse.
y^en smild & s^d: yow doe not Couet Moe
y^en ye whole world white Knight, y^t yow may
    knowe
w'are 'bout y^is already; where y^t Land
from whence yow came with vs no more doth
    stand

England ye salle

y^en for a garden whence o^r Cooke may picke
a sallet for o^r Feast.—

y^e seur dishes

Our Food's Leane Fraunce larded with Germany
but first their enters in y^e Graue [Signiory]
of Venice: Seru'd in (though y^e Sirs be Loth)
like to o^r English Capons in white Broth
Italy's o^r Ouen: thence o^r baked meates come
Sauoy o^r Salt: Geneua pure we doome
for o^r chip'd Man=cheate: beneath y^e Salt doth
    lye
y^e Netherlands, lowe pride will sett y^em high
for o^r next Course, there Enters in at dores
for Plouers Portugals for Black=Birds Mores
and last on all handes, least o^r Feast proue Drye
Holland, for Sauce stands ready melted By.
y^e Voyder come, we thus o^r hope suffice
Zealand sayes Grace for fashion then we Rise.
I rise & rest when yow haue cause to send
to proue my self yor Brother &
yor freinde ...

y^e Candide deljnea[of ye white house.

Source: British Library, Add. MS 29,492, fols. 33v–5. See Geoffrey Bullough, "'The Game at Chesse': how it struck a contemporary', *Modern Language Review* 49 (1954), 156–60.

Joseph Mead to Sir Martin Stutevile, 25 May 1625

The play called the game at chesse is also in print but because I haue no skill in the game I vnderstand it not...

Source: British Library, Harleian MS 389, fol. 446. First printed in this edition; discussed in General Textual Introduction above, Sec. I.

Anonymous inscription, no earlier than May 1625

After nyne dayse wherein I have heard some of the acters say they tooke fiveteen hundred Pounde the spanish faction being prevalent gott it supprest the chiefe actors and the Poett Mr. Thomas Middleton that writt it committed to prisson where hee lay some Tyme and at last gott oute upon this petition presented to King James...

Source: manuscript annotation on sig. A1ʳ of the Dyce copy of OKES² in the Victoria and Albert Museum Library, 25.D.42. For the text of the poem which follows, see the textual notes on 'To the King' in 'Occasional Poems', p. 993.

Ben Jonson, 1626

.... THO. O! yes.

Spal-ato's *Legacy to the Players.*
There is a *Legacy* left to the *King's Players,*
Both for their various shifting of their *Scene,*
And dext'rous change o'their persons to all shapes,
And all disguises: by the right reuerend
Archbishop of Spalato. LIC. He is dead,
That plai'd him! THO. Then, h'has lost his share o'
the *Legacy.*

Gundo-mar's *vse of the game at Chesse, or Play so called.*
LIC. What newes of *Gundomar?* THO. A second *Fistula,*
Or an *excoriation* (at the least)
For putting the poore *English-play,* was writ of him,
To such a sordid use, as (is said) he did,
Of cleansing his *posterior's.* LIC. Iustice! Iustice!
THO. Since when, he liues condemn'd to his [chair],
at *Bruxels.*
And there sits filing certaine politique hinges,
To hang the *States* on, h'has heau'd off the hookes.

Source: *The Staple of Newes* in *The Workes of BenJamin Jonson. The second Volume* (1640), sig. F3 (3.2.201–14). The play was entered in the Stationers' Register on 14 April 1626, and completed no earlier than 11 February 1626 (the date of William Rowley's burial).

Richard Brome, 1629

I do see Signior I thanke the light, that you are a goodly man of outward parts, and except it were the black Knight himselfe, or him with the Fistula, the proprest man I haue seene of your Nation. They are a People of very spare dyet, I haue heard, and therefore seldome fat.

Source: *The Northern Lasse* (1632), sig. L4ᵛ. The play was acted by the King's Men on 29 July 1629. On the popularity of this play see G. E. Bentley, *The Jacobean and Caroline Stage*, vol. III (1956), 83–4.

William Heminges, 1631–2

Mʳ Thomas Randall the Poett, his finger being cut of by a Riotous Gentleman, his frinde Mʳ William Hemminges made this Eligie on the same...
...Thay Quakte at Iohnson as by hym thay pase because of Trebulation Holsome and Annanias,
But Middleton thay seemd much to Adore
fors learned Exercise gaynst Gundomore.
To whom thay thus pray, Can you Edifye
our understandings In this misterye?
wᵗʰ Teares the storye hee begane whilest thay
prickt vpp thayr eares and did begin to pray.

Source: Bodleian Library, Ashmolean MS 38, fol. 26. See G. C. Moore Smith, *William Hemminge's 'Elegy on Randolph's Finger'* (1923).

William Prynne, 1633

...our moderne Stageplayes...*curiously survey, and maliciously divulge the faults of others.* Not to particularize those late new scandalous invective Playes, wherein ᵇ*sundry persons* of place and eminence have beene particularly personated, jeared, abused in a grosse and scurrilous manner.

Prynne's marginal note: ᵇ Gundemore, the late Lord Admirall, Lord Treasurer, and others

Source: William Prynne, *Histrio-mastix* (1633), 124. See Martin Butler, 'William Prynne and the Allegory of Middleton's *Game at Chess*', Notes and Queries 228 (1983), 153–4, and T. H. Howard Hill, 'More on "William Prynne and the Allegory of Middleton's *Game at Chess*"', *Notes and Queries* 234 (1989), 349–51. Whether or not all the individuals Prynne names were 'personated' in *Game at Chess*, Gondomar certainly was.

William Davenant, 1663

There's such a crowd at door, as if we had
A New Play of *Gundamar.*

Source: *The Play-House To Be Lett*, in *The Works of Sʳ William Davenant Kᵀ* (1673), 2:73.

A GAME AT CHESSE: AN EARLY FORM

Edited by Gary Taylor

THE TEXT of *An Early Form* contained in *The Collected Works* attempts to represent the first complete authorial text of *A Game at Chess*. In particular, it attempts to reproduce the lost manuscript which I have christened '[MIDDLETON^{PRE}]', a manuscript in Middleton's own handwriting that predated the preparation of the licensed playbook owned by the King's Men. This early version of the play has never heretofore been made available in print—not even by Howard-Hill, who as a literary critic prefers it to the composite version which he has edited and printed in three different publications.

A Game at Chess survives in two subtantially different authorial versions. There has been no agreement on what to call those versions. In Shakespeare, we can refer to 'the Quarto text' or 'the Folio text', but that bibliographical binary is irrelevant here. On the analogy of *Piers Plowman*, we might call the different versions of *A Game at Chess* 'The A-Text' (the first complete draft), 'The B-Text' (the expanded version performed in August 1624), and 'The C-Text' (the abridged reading text which was produced later in 1624). A critical comparison of *A Game at Chess* and *Piers Plowman* might be fruitful, and Skeat's labels might be useful when describing the three underlying archetypes of *Game*. However, we would still need a way to describe the editorial texts reproduced in *The Collected Works*. After all, 'The A-text', or the abridged version, might be editorially reconstructed or displayed in more than one way. It might, for instance, be presented in modern spelling and punctuation, like the other plays in *The Collected Works*, or like *The History of King Lear* in the 1986 *Complete Works* of Shakespeare. I have christened the text in *The Collected Works* 'An Early Form'. I use the indefinite article in recognition of the variety of forms in which that version might be reproduced; I use the word 'Form', rather than 'Version', because 'Form' emphasizes the aesthetic dimension of the text, and because 'version' and 'versioning' have a very particular history in editorial theory, which I wish to avoid.

The only extant document which contains the shorter early form of the play is CRANE^I (which previous scholars called 'Archdale'). CRANE^I is therefore, inevitably, the control text for *An Early Form*. The Textual Notes record substantive departures from its readings, and discuss other CRANE^I readings which have sometimes been regarded as errors. The Lineation Notes record all departures from CRANE^I. The list of Stage Directions contains a transcription of all directions in CRANE^I (and another list of all autograph directions in MIDDLETON^T and MIDDLETON^B). The Historical Collations provide a comprehensive list of

variants unique to CRANE^I, in order to enable readers to distinguish between *An Early Form* and *A Later Form*.

CRANE^I is not an autograph text. It was prepared by the scribe Ralph Crane, and incorporates Crane's distinctive punctuation, spelling, capitalization, and italicization. Old-spelling editions of Shakespeare and Webster have reproduced such Crane features in their texts of, for instance, *The Winter's Tale* and *The Duchess of Malfi*. That editorial practice is understandable in such cases, because we possess no autograph manuscripts of those plays, or indeed of any full-length play by either author. Consequently, in those cases Crane's spelling and punctuation at least represent *an* early form of the play, if not *the* authorial incidentals. However, we do possess autograph manuscripts of *A Game at Chess*. Even in a modern-spelling edition, an editor seeking to recover an authorial text would reject readings in CRANE^I which seem to reflect Crane's practice, rather than Middleton's. Thus, although CRANE^I is necessarily the control-text (for substantive readings) in *An Early Form*, it is not the copy-text (for incidentals). This distinction between control-text and copy-text has been made for other texts (Taylor 1981), but it is especially important here.

The obvious copy-texts for incidentals are MIDDLETON^T, written throughout in Middleton's own hand, and the autograph portions of BRIDGEWATER, which I identify as MIDDLETON^B. Moreover, it seems valuable to incorporate an autograph text into an edition of Middleton's collected works. By combining the authorial structure of CRANE^I with the authorial texture of MIDDLETON^T and MIDDLETON^B, *An Early Form* (re)produces a text that represents Middleton's early version of the play, in both content and form: an authorial inscription of the earliest recoverable coherent version of the work.

In practice, this edition has been constructed by beginning with a complete transcription of MIDDLETON^T, which has then been modified to incorporate the substantive variants of CRANE^I, and then further modified by emending a few of the incidentals, where either CRANE^I or MIDDLETON^T appears to misrepresent Middleton's preferred practice. This procedure creates two practical editorial problems. The first problem concerns the authority and consistency of the incidentals in the edited text. These issues are discussed in detail in the headnote to the list of Emendations of Incidentals.

Included in that list are variants that some editors describe as 'semi-substantives': differences in linguistic forms ('has' versus 'hath'), metrical markers ('i'th'' versus 'in the'), and colloquialisms ('a' versus 'on', 'my' versus 'mine'). Such stylistic variants do not make any difference to the paraphrasable meaning of the text, and Crane clearly considered such matters the province of the scribe rather than the author. That is, Crane treated all such differences as spellings. Consequently, in the textual apparatus to *An Early Form* we have also regarded them as spellings, recording and discussing them among 'Emendations of Incidentals'. But (in recognition of their ambiguous status) we also record them in the Textual Notes to *A Later Form* (which does not normally record mere spelling and punctuation variants).

The editorial problems created by incidentals are fiddly and time-consuming, but they can be 'solved' by the systematic adoption of a set of logical routines. The editorial problems involving substantives are less amenable to such mechanical solutions. Essentially, all these problems boil down to a single question: how faithfully does CRANE[I] represent, substantively, the first authorial draft of the play?

For the most part, CRANE[I] represents that version very well. About the larger structural differences between the two versions, there can be little doubt: the early version did not include the Fat Bishop, the Prologue, the Epilogue, Gondomar's special chair or litter, or the final episode with the black pieces in the bag; it portrayed the White King's Pawn rather differently, and it differed in dozens of verbal details where CRANE[I] preserves a unique—but intelligible, and sometimes demonstrably Middletonian—reading. The editorial uncertainty involves only the reliability of a smaller number of scattered verbal variants.

That uncertainty is created by the simple fact that CRANE[I] is a transcript. It is not Middleton's own 'foul papers', or his own fair copy of his original version of the play. Therefore, CRANE[I] might—indeed, almost certainly does—contain scribal sophistications and errors, which do not represent authorial intentions at any time. Moreover, because all texts of the play derived, by one route or another, from the authorial papers of that earliest version of the work, some readings from 'the A-text' might be preserved, not in CRANE[I], but (theoretically) in any one of the other surviving texts. Any reconstruction of the early version must be based upon an understanding, not only of CRANE[I], but of CRANE[I]'s relationship to all the other witnesses. Thus, CRANE[I] might contain two kinds of error: (1) new scribal errors introduced by Crane, and (2) errors inherited by Crane from previous transcriptions.

Scholarly investigations of Crane's scribal practices (by Wilson, Bald, Nascimento, and Howard-Hill) have demonstrated his substantive accuracy and reliability. An editor can therefore be reasonably confident that Crane committed few *unintended* changes in transcribing the text he was copying. However, simply because CRANE[I] is a transcript, we do not know how many intermediate texts might stand between it and the authorial original we wish to reconstruct: Crane might have accurately transcribed a corrupt copy. In order to assess the reliability of CRANE[I], we must locate CRANE[I] in a textual stemma, which establishes its

relationships with all the surviving texts, and with various other texts now lost which must at one time have existed. The General Textual Introduction concludes that CRANE[I] was copied directly from [MIDDLETON[PRE]], and that all the other extant texts derive from a later manuscript, [KING'S MEN[I]]. The General Textual Introduction also concludes that, although Crane freely altered the styling of the text, he did not 'edit' the text by conjecturally emending, prudishly censoring, or deliberately 'improving' it.

Crane alone is clearly responsible for the scene divisions added in all four CRANE texts—and those only—in Acts Two, Three, Four, and Five. Our text of *Early* therefore numbers lines by acts (reflecting the structure of the play in Middleton's manuscripts, and in performance), rather than by scene.

Finally, CRANE[I] is not entirely homogeneous. All variants *within* CRANE[I] are recorded in the apparatus, and distinguished as 'corrected' or 'uncorrected' states of the text. Sometimes Crane corrects or alters his own text; in each case, we have adopted the reading which appears to represent Middleton's earliest intention. But there are also a handful of early alterations to the text made by other hands; all of these interpolate readings that occur in witnesses to the later, post-performance text of the play. Most of these changes could be explained as the result of censorship by the Master of the Revels: such alterations would probably have been easy to spot in the King's Men's playbook. Someone might therefore have begun going through the playbook, looking for cases of censorial intervention, and transferring those emendations onto CRANE[I]. The last of these censorial alterations in CRANE[I] occurs at 2.236, shortly before the first major alteration in the performance version, the addition of the Fat Bishop. From that point on, it might have been more difficult to locate the passage in CRANE[I] that corresponded to a censored word in the playbook. Either the rest of CRANE[I] is uncensored, or comparable changes had already been made, for the rest of the play, in the manuscript which Crane was copying (perhaps while he was copying the first scenes of the play).

Because *The Collected Works* includes an alternative, modernized text of the play (*A Later Form*), this edition of *An Early Form* gives substantive variants in CRANE[I] the benefit of the doubt, and does not attempt to make the texture of autograph incidentals more intelligible or familiar for modern readers.

Throughout the textual apparatus for *An Early Form* (and *A Later Form*), + indicates that the variant in question occurs in all the other extant substantive texts not specifically mentioned elsewhere in that note. For example, in the following note

Induction.4/18 anie₄] CRANE/MATHEWES (any); ~ of CRANE[I] +

the preposition 'of' occurs not only in CRANE[I], but in all early texts except CRANE/MATHEWES.

The commentary to *An Early Version* differs from those elsewhere in *The Collected Works* in its extensive citation of early modern texts which might have influenced Middleton. When the commentary note gives all the information a reader would need in order to identify the work cited—for instance, the reference to John Buckeridge's *A Sermon Preached before His Maiesty...Touching Prostration, and Kneeling* (1618) in the commentary note at 5.24.1—

the title is not included in the list of Works Cited appended to the General Textual Introduction.

SEE ALSO

Text: *Works*, 1779
General textual introduction: this volume, 712
List of works cited: this volume, 848
Authorship and date: this volume, 439

TEXTUAL NOTES

Substantive Emendations of CRANE[I] ('Archdale')

Title.2   Compoſde...Middleton.] ROSENBACH; by T. Middleton MIDDLETON[T]; by Tho: Middleton. MIDDLETON[B]; August 13⁰ Anno Dm̃ 1624 CRANE[I]. Middleton did not normally date his manuscripts. (If he had, it would be much easier to establish his chronology!) All three title-pages which name the author are autograph. The use of this subheading here is designed to emphasize the authorial character of *Early*.

Induction.0.3/13   *Error*] MIDDLETON[T]; *and* ~ CRANE[I]. Crane routinely adds 'and' to stage directions: see 1.0.2, 4.0.2, 5.0.1–2, 5.178.1, 5.362.1, where CRANE[I] contains copulatives not present in MIDDLETON[T].

Induction.4/18   anie‸] CRANE/MATHEWES (any); ~ of CRANE[I]+. For the construction compare 'any your' (*Valour* 3.2.172). The specific 'any my', in the same construction, is found in Randolph's *Conceited Pedlar*, Wotton's 'Noble, lovely, virtuous creature', the anonymous 1628 translation of 'Hipolito and Isabella,' and other seventeenth-century texts. The unusual grammatical form may have been normalized by Crane—who often supplies grammatically necessary but elided words and syllables—and passively reproduced in most other texts. CRANE/MATHEWES shows other evidence of authorial correction and revision: see General Textual Introduction, Sec. XIII.

Induction.27/41   Vrslie] MIDDLETON[T]+; Vrsula CRANE, ROSENBACH[A]. Probably a scribal sophistication, typical of Crane's expansion of contractions.

Induction.54/69   keepe] MIDDLETON[T]; ~. *Musick—Ent*[| (*seuerally*) *the Wh*[| *& Black-hous*[*as they are sett f*[| *yᵉ Game.* CRANE[I] (direction in right margin, 52–5, cropped). See Historical Collation at 64.1. This direction appears to belong to a later state of the text.

Induction.58–77/73–92   Ig:...Ign—] MIDDLETON[T]. The left margin of this page of CRANE[I] has been cropped, removing all trace of the speech prefixes; there is, however, no disagreement among the extant texts about the assignment of speeches in this scene, and it is difficult to imagine how they could have been distributed differently between the two speakers.

1.0.1/98   *Primi*] MIDDLETON[T] (only); *Prima* OKES; *Primus* CRANE[I]+. For the alternative authorial form here, see notes at 2.0.1 and 3.0.1; it appears in CRANE[I] at the end of acts two, three, four and five. 'Primi' appears at the end of Act One in *Widow* and *Old Law*.

1.18   Bl.] *not in* CRANE[I] (cropped)

1.23   wh.] | h. CRANE[I] (cropped)

1.25   Bl.] *not in* CRANE[I] (cropped)

1.39/144   admiration] CRANE[I] *corrected* (Admiracon); Admonition CRANE[I] *uncorrected*; admiration MIDDLETON[T]+. An easy misreading.

1.47/152   a] A CRANE[I] *corrected*; The CRANE[I] (*original reading, overwritten*). The indefinite article agrees with all other texts, and there seems little point in making the change, unless 'The' were a simple error on Crane's part.

1.261/367   *exit*] CRANE[2] (—*Exᵗ*); *not in* MIDDLETON[T]+; —*Exᵗ* CRANE[I] *at* 1.262.1. This exit in CRANE[I] is certainly misplaced: it cues the exit of the Black Knight's Pawn, not the White Queen's Pawn.

1.330/437   pens] MIDDLETON[T]; P'ees CRANE[I]. The unique variant here makes local sense: the article of clothing called a *pee* was worn from the sixteenth century through the first third of the seventeenth (*OED N.*[1]), and like a shirt or jacket it could theoretically be worn backward. But the variant does not make sense in the larger context, unless there is an innuendo not otherwise recorded. In any case, the requisite innuendo is supplied by 'pens'. See Williams, *Dictionary*, 'pease' and 'pen' (2: 1006–9).

1.353.2/467   *Finit*] MIDDLETON[T]+; *Finis* CRANE[I] (?). The manuscript is cropped, and although the top of the 'F', the dot over the 'i', and 'Act' are clear enough, the last letter of 'Fini⟨.⟩' is not unambiguously determinable. In the Literature Online database, in printed plays up to 1662 'Finis' occurs at the end of an act 258 times in 85 different plays. By contrast, Middleton is one of only two early modern dramatists to use 'Finit' at the end of an act. The sixteenth-century polemicist John Bale used 'finit' eleven times in three plays; it survives three times in *Mad World*, once in *Michaelmas*, and fourteen times in four different NON-CRANE texts of *Game* (four times in OKES and ROSENBACH, three times in MIDDLETON[T] and BRIDGEWATER, which both lack such a direction at the end of Act Two). As Crane's interference with this detail throughout *Game* demonstrates, other occurrences in other Middleton plays were probably regularized by scribes and compositors. See next note and 2.452.2.

2.0.1   *Incipit*‸] OKES; ‸ *Actus* CRANE[I]+. Here in OKES, as in autograph at 4.0.1 and 5.0.1, 'Actus' is elided, having just been used in the preceding line: 'the first act ends, the second begins'. Altogether, 'Incipit' occurs three times in MIDDLETON[T], three times in BRIDGEWATER, and four times in OKES. In the Literature Online database, Middleton is one of only four early modern dramatists who uses 'Incipit' at the beginning of an act: John Bale has eleven examples in two plays, William Hemings has three in *The Jewes Tragedy* (printed 1662), and Thomas May one in *The Old Couple* (printed 1658). Thus, in Middleton's lifetime, this feature appears only in Middleton's plays. In addition to the ten examples in three texts of *Game*, three survive in *Mad World*, three in *Michaelmas* (including 'Incipit quartus' and 'Incipit Quintus', eliding the 'Actus', as here), and three in *Trick*. As Crane's interference here demonstrates, other occurrences were probably regularized by scribes and compositors. (See previous note.) This is one of many OKES variants that points to an autograph manuscript as the printer's copy.

2.0.1 *Secundi*] MIDDLETON[T] *only*; *Secundus* CRANE[1]+. See 1.0.1. Although Crane clearly preferred the -us termination for act numbers, the alternative form 'Secundi' is also preserved in CRANE[1] at 2.452.2, where it presumably derives from the underlying authorial papers. It occurs also in *Old Law* and *Widow*.

2.126/602 Reuerence,] CRANE[1] *uncorrected*; ~ againe CRANE[1] *corrected*+. The line makes sense and is more metrical as originally transcribed by Crane; it is possible that Crane's interlinear addition reproduces an authorial change of mind.

2.152.1 *a noyse wthin*] CRANE[1], ROSENBACH[A]. Every witness contains this stage direction, but only CRANE[1] and ROSENBACH[A] have a single such direction placed here; CRANE/MATHEWES also places one here, and then repeats it again at 165. This position in CRANE[1] seems too early for the action; but it is hard to explain why a scribe would have mistakenly anticipated a direction which belongs several lines later. Perhaps the noise begins here, and gradually becomes louder, intensifying the suspense. Or perhaps ll. 153-6 are an authorial addition in the early draft, making the stage direction's original position misleading after the addition; the abridgement in CRANE[3] omits those lines. This position probably does reflect [MIDDLETON[PRE]].

2.157/633 confound noyse?] CRANE[1]+ (~ Noise?); confound,— DYCE. DYCE gives no explanation for his emendation; BULLEN, who adopts it, justifies it by conjecturing that 'The stage direction has slipped into the text.' But that explanation would only make sense if the text had omitted the stage direction—which is, in fact, present in all eight witnesses (and five lines earlier in CRANE[1]: see Historical Collation and Stage Directions). We know that an error of the kind proposed by Dyce should look like: at the beginning of Act Four, OKES prints part of a scene's initial stage direction, 'The Iefuit in his gallant habit,' in roman type as the first line of the first speech. The line is not duplicated, as both stage direction and dialogue, and the error appears in one text only. The situation here is radically different. If Dyce's emendation were correct, then what must have happened here is not a stage direction being misinterpreted as text, but a stage direction being duplicated in the text, and then one of those duplications being misinterpreted; but that is a much more complicated and implausible chain of error. And where did this dialogue 'error' originate, that it persists through all the branches of a complicated stemma? Why did Middleton let such an egregious error stand? And what is it that Black Bishop's Pawn proposes to confound? What he fears, in the preceding sixteen lines, is the 'discovery' of his secrets, which will be 'disperse[d]' by 'a woman's tongue,' which cannot be counted on to preserve 'secrecy.' In other words, it is precisely the 'noise' she is making that he must forcibly confound. Ironically—and the irony is typically Middletonian—at the very moment when he resolves to stop *her* noise, another woman's noise confounds *him*.

2.185/665 yeare] MIDDLETON[T], CRANE/MATHEWES; years CRANE[1]+. Middleton often uses the obsolescent singular for plural, which scribes were inclined to modernize. The obsolescent form is preserved here, and the modern plural in *Later*.

2.266, 2.273/748, 755 Bl.K[ts.]p.] MIDDLETON[T]+; Bl.B[s].P. CRANE[1]. The alternative attribution cannot be correct; perhaps suggested by 'Bishops' in 2.262/744.

2.269 what's that?] CRANE[1] (What's ~), CRANE[2], CRANE/ MATHEWES, ROSENBACH[A]; *not in* MIDDLETON[T], BRIDGEWATER[A], OKES; *whole passage not in* CRANE[3]. In CRANE[1] this speech is on the same manuscript line as the preceding speech, and could easily be an addition to the text as originally composed or transcribed; this is probably related to the error in attribution in the next line.

2.270/752 Bl.p.] CRANE[1] *corrected*; Bl.B[s].P. CRANE[1] *uncorrected*; Bl.Qs.P. ROSENBACH[A], CRANE[2], CRANE/MATHEWES. CRANE[1]'s original attribution cannot be right, as Crane realized, erasing the medial 'B[s].' This error seems to be connected to the initial omission of the preceding line. All other texts attribute the lines to the Black Queen's Pawn, who is hereabouts in CRANE[1] identified by the generic 'Bl.P.'.

2.273 Bl.K[ts.]p.] ROSENBACH[A], CRANE[2], CRANE/MATHEWES (Bl.Kts.P.); Bl.B[s].P. CRANE[1]; *not in* MIDDLETON[T], BRIDGEWATER[A], OKES. See note at 2.266.

2.275.1/855 Enter] MIDDLETON[T]; *Enter (seu[er]ally)* CRANE[1,2,3]. Howard-Hill shows convincingly that 'severally' is a Crane convention, not a Middleton one. It might replace a Middletonian idiom, in the original manuscript, like 'meeting' or 'from the white house... from the black house'.

2.301/897 mine] my MIDDLETON[T] *only*. LION lists nine examples of 'mine hono*' in six Middleton texts; 'my hono*' occurs thirty-five times in fifteen works. This may therefore be just another example of authorial vacillation.

2.319/915 greiues] MIDDLETON[T]+; glues CRANE[1] (*original reading*); griues CRANE[1] (*corrected reading created by interlining*). The corrected CRANE[1] reading is an alternative spelling of the autograph variant.

2.452.2 Finit] OKES, ROSENBACH[A]; *Finis* CRANE[1]; *not in* MIDDLETON[T]+. Middleton uses this formula at the end of Acts I, III, and IV, always in the form preserved here in OKES and ROSENBACH[A]; Crane prefers the formula found in CRANE[1].

3.0.1/1059 *Incipit,*] OKES; ~ *Actus* MIDDLETON[T], BRIDGEWATER[B]; ₐ *Actus* CRANE[1]+. See 2.0.1. Here, MIDDLETON[T] and BRIDGEWATER[B] had omitted the preceding 'Finit' direction, making the usual elision impossible.

3.0.1/1059 *tercij*] THIS EDITION; *Tercius* CRANE[1,2]; *tertius* MIDDLETON[T]; *Tertius* CRANE[3,4], ROSENBACH[A]; *Tertus* OKES. Since Crane elsewhere prefers the medial 't', the medial 'c' in the two earliest surviving witnesses is probably authorial, and 'Tercij' appears in CRANE[1] at the end of this act. For Crane's preference for terminal -us in place of Middleton's terminal -i, see 1.0.1.

3.53/1200 you... S[r],] MIDDLETON[T]+; *not in* CRANE[1]. This question must have been omitted by accident, since the Black Knight's next line answers it.

3.120/1269 seuerd] MIDDLETON[T]+; fecurd CRANE[1]. An easy misreading. Although what 'severed' the Spanish fleet might be said to have 'secured' the English one, 'scatterd theire Admirations' makes it clear that dispersal is the appropriate action here.

3.158/1309 on] ROSENBACH[A]; of CRANE[1]+. See text note at *Later* 1.1.255. The characteristic Middletonian 'on' is preserved in a single text. The collocation 'think(e)(s) on' occurs more than forty times in the Middleton canon (including 'thinks on me' at *Women Beware* 4.2.198). The obsolete idiom is preserved here; the modern 'of' is retained at *Later* 3.1.220.

3.218/1370 gratious] CRANE[1] (*interlined*), MIDDLETON[T]+; *not in* CRANE[1] (*original*). Metrically necessary.

3.243/1435 wh.Qs.p.] CRANE[1]+ (wh.Q[s]P.); wh.p. BRIDGEWATER[B]. The presence of this relic of the previous generic speech prefixes in BRIDGEWATER[B] suggests that the more specific speech prefixes of CRANE[1] may originate at this point with Crane; but the inconsistency could just as easily be Middleton's, since we have only a single witness to a single prefix, which might result from simple accidental omission. The preceding prefixes for a different 'white pawn' could have precipitated Middleton's shift to a more specific identifier here.

3.319/1512   i Bl.p.] MIDDLETON[T] only; Bl.P. CRANE[1]+. Middleton's unique inconsistency has been preserved, on the grounds that it might have been regularized by copyists. Given his occasional use of 'i' for the numeral 'I', it here might mean 'first' or an abbreviation of 'iesting'.

3.327/1522   Bl.p.] THIS EDITION; Bl.Q[s].P CRANE[1]+. Throughout this scene CRANE[1] employs the more specific prefixes for both pawns, as do all other Crane texts. However, relics of the original generic prefixes occur at lines 329 (ROSENBACH[A], BRIDGEWATER[B]), 333 (ROSENBACH[A], BRIDGEWATER[B]), 343 (OKES, ROSENBACH[A]), 344 (OKES), 348 (ROSENBACH[A]), and 400 (ROSENBACH[A], BRIDGEWATER[B]). Moreover, since only the two women speak in this scene, the authorial draft might naturally have reverted to the generic prefixes (even if they had been abandoned briefly at the end of 3.1, with its more complicated onstage cast). I have therefore used generic prefixes throughout the scene, on the assumption that the specificity of CRANE[1] here is scribal, not authorial.

3.329/1524   wh.p.] THIS EDITION; wh.Q[s].P. CRANE[1]+. Likewise throughout scene. See preceding note.

3.400.1/1602   Finit] MIDDLETON[T]+; Finis CRANE[1]. See 1.353.2.

4.0.1/1603   Incipit_] MIDDLETON[T], BRIDGEWATER[B], OKES; _ Actus CRANE, ROSENBACH[A]. See 2.0.1.

4.0.1/1603   Quarti] THIS EDITION; Quartus CRANE[1]+. See 3.0.1. The 'Quarti' form appears in CRANE[1] at the end of this act.

4.0.2/1604   meeting the] MIDDLETON[T]; & CRANE[1]+. This is an unusual, ambiguous, but characteristic Middleton idiom in stage directions, here apparently regularized by Crane. See Induction.0.3.

4.73/1680   uncloses] MIDDLETON[T]+; enclofes CRANE[1], OKES. An easy misreading, which produces the opposite of the required sense.

4.170.2/1784   wth] MIDDLETON[T], BRIDGEWATER[B]; & CRANE[1]+. Crane texts eliminated a 'wth' present in other texts in stage directions at 5.362.1 (CRANE[1,2,3,4]), 5.162.1 (CRANE[1,2]), 5.0.2 (CRANE[1]), and Later 2.1.0.2, 2.2.40.2, L 5.3.0.3 (CRANE[2,3,4]). This habit naturally coexists with Crane's tendency to insert 'and' in stage directions (for which, see Induction.0.3). Neither is likely to represent Middleton's own papers particularly well.

4.171/1785   _Pawne] MIDDLETON[T]; Bl.Kt. ~ CRANE[1]+. Compare 3.1, and see next note.

4.185/1799   Paw.] THIS EDITION; Bl.K[ts].P. CRANE[1]+. Relics of what were presumably the original generic prefixes survive in the opening stage direction and at lines 185, 201, 248, 244, 260, 297 (CRANE[2,3]). I have therefore reverted throughout the scene to what presumably stood in Middleton's first draft, here editorially regularized by Crane.

4.202/1817   trebled] MIDDLETON[T]+; troubled OKES. Howard-Hill (Pasquin, 283) has the variant shared by OKES with CRANE[1]; but the manuscript seems clearly to read 'trebled' (as Nascimento also concludes), not 'trobled'.

4.205/1820   titelie] MIDDLETON[T]+; lightly ROSENBACH[A], OKES. Howard-Hill (Pasquin, 283) includes CRANE[1] among texts with the variant; but the manuscript seems clearly to read 'titely' (as Nascimento also concludes).

4.225/1840   our] MIDDLETON[T]+; not in CRANE[1]. Defective metre and sense; almost certainly a simple scribal error.

4.242/1857   brest] beft OKES, CRANE/ALLDE. 'Brest' (as Howard-Hill recognizes) is a sensible and imaginative reading (a metaphor for 'native'), more likely to be an authorial variant than an inadvertency preserved in the most reliable witnesses in both branches of the stemma. For the variant see Later 4.2.70.

4.255/1871   poenitentiaria] MIDDLETON[T]+; Poenitentia CRANE[1], BRIDGEWATER[B]. Simple scribal eyeskip with a long foreign word.

4.264/1881   of] MIDDLETON[T]+; on CRANE. See 3.158. The obsolete autograph idiom is preserved here, the modern 'on' in Later.

4.273/1889   pound] MIDDLETON[T], CRANE[2,3]; pounds CRANE[1]+. Clearly not a difference between original and revised versions, this variant—and the next—should probably be listed among incidentals, not substantives, since there is no difference in meaning. It is impossible to tell whether the variants derive from authorial inconsistency or scribal regularization; I have adopted the autograph spelling here, and the 'correct' modern plural in A Later Form. Compare 3.158.

4.273/1889   shilling] MIDDLETON[T], OKES; shillings CRANE[1]+. See preceding note.

4.297/1918   fowler] MIDDLETON[T]+; fowle CRANE[1]. Both metre and sense suggest that Crane has accidentally omitted the last letter of the word in his copy-text.

4.304   him] All texts but CRANE[1] and MIDDLETON[T] have an additional line here, 'And by that act obtaine full abfolution'. It seems virtually certain that MIDDLETON[T] has omitted the line accidentally, as it does several other individual lines (2.1.106, 3.3.33-4, 3.3.77, 4.5.52-3, 5.3.81-2), not to mention more extended passages; moreover, MIDDLETON[T]'s scribal work has demonstrably deteriorated by this point. The omission may also be accidental in CRANE[1], but Crane is a more reliable copyist than Middleton, and the line more probably represents an expansion and clarification of the original version: see the variants at ll. 109, 134, and 147.

4.305/1928   _ why] MIDDLETON[T]; Bl.K. ~ CRANE[1]+. Compare 3.1.

4.314.3   the White] MIDDLETON[T]; wh. Qs Pawne CRANE[1]+. Autograph preserves the more generic form here; CRANE[1]'s more specific reading might well result from scribal normalization.

4.353/1986   Rombauts] THIS EDITION; Rambants CRANE[1]; Rumbants MIDDLETON[T]+; Rumold's HOWARD-HILL (conj. Dyce); Rumbold's DYCE conj. CRANE[1]'s 'n' and the vowel in the first syllable are both evidently incorrect. Howard-Hill reproduces a passage in Gee's New Shreds (p. 40, sig. E4[V]), which refers to 'the Histories of S[t] Columban, S[t] Rumuld, and S[t] Fursius' (Pasquin, 258, modernized to 'Romuld'), but this does not refer to the anecdote of the court lady and the breeches. Middleton's source for the anecdote was Thomas Scott's The second part of Vox populi, where the saint's name is the first word of p. 39; Howard-Hill's transcription of the 'Folger copy' of STC 22103 reads 'Romold's' (Pasquin, 251), but that is his own modernization of the spelling; all Folger and British Library copies of STC 22103 and STC 22103.3 read 'Rombauts' (in both the catchword on p. 38 and the text on p. 39). This alternative form 'Rombaut' is recorded in Butler 3:13. HOWARD-HILL's emendation is paleographically unlikely: neither the interpolation of 'b' nor the omission of 'l' is a normal or common scribal error. In the first syllable of the name, CRANE[1] must be in error: neither Scott nor Gee has an 'a' in the first syllable; the vowel in the other seven texts ('u'), may derive from a misreading of 'o', or from Middleton conflating the first syllable of Gee's form of the name with the second syllable of Scott's. For a misreading of Middleton's autograph 'a' as 'o' (as here in CRANE¹), compare *Later* 4.4.4. By contrast with the errors in the first syllable, the minim error in the second syllable occurs in all witnesses, and was probably authorial: the italic 'u' in *Vox Populi* is hard to distinguish from an italic 'n', and 'ants' is a much more common English sequence of letters than 'auts'.

4.379 weeue] DYCE (we've); wee ROSENBACH^A, BRIDGEWATER *corrected*; I euer BRIDGEWATER^B *uncorrected*; we haue CRANE, OKES. In its 'corrected' state, with 'wee' interlined to replace 'I' and 'euer' underlined for deletion, BRIDGEWATER agrees with ROSENBACH^A in a reading more metrical than the 'we haue' contained in CRANE and OKES. However, Crane is less likely to have interpolated 'haue' than to have expanded an original contraction 'we've'. The conjectured contraction would also explain the otherwise inexplicably interpolated extrametrical 'euer' in BRIDGEWATER^B: 'weeue' could be misread as 'we eue[r]'. For the absence of the apostrophe, compare unique autograph 'weere' for 'wee're'.

4.417 you] BRIDGEWATER^B+; they CRANE¹. A confusing pronoun, which could easily have resulted from contamination by the preceding 'their'.

4.428.1 *Finit...Quarti*] NON-CRANE; *Finis...Quarti* CRANE¹. See 2.0.1 and 2.452.2.

5.0.1 *Incipit*ᴧ] NON-CRANE; ᴧ*Actus* CRANE. See 3.0.1.

5.0.1 *et Vltimus*] BRIDGEWATER^B, OKES; *not in* CRANE¹+. This formula does not appear in any of the Crane witnesses, but does appear here in two other texts which show evidence of authorial involvement. An almost identical formula appears at *Michaelmas Term* 5.1.0.1 (*Incipit Actus Quintus et Vltimus*), set by Edward Allde in 1607 from a manuscript showing many signs of autograph origins. See also 5.178.1.

5.0.2 *wth pawnes*] BRIDGEWATER^B, ROSENBACH^B, OKES; *& Pawnes* CRANE¹; *not in* MIDDLETON^T, CRANE^{2,3,4}. For Crane's interpolated ampersands, see Induction.0.3. The ampersand appears only six times in the whole of MIDDLETON^T, always in long dialogue lines; Crane consistently uses it in stage directions. See 4.170.2.

5.1/2017 ᴧ Si] MIDDLETON^T; Bl.B^s.P. ~ CRANE¹+. Compare 3.1.

5.8/2024 lætitià] MIDDLETON^T+; *Lætitio* CRANE¹

5.16 noble] BRIDGEWATER^B+; Nobe CRANE¹

5.33/2043 Whitehouse Knight] MIDDLETON^T+; White-Knight CRANE¹. Metrically deficient, and an easy error, substituting the more common idiom.

5.124.1 *Bl.Qs.p wthin*] CRANE¹ (~Q^s.Pawne within), ROSENBACH^A, OKES, CRANE/ALLDE; *not in* MIDDLETON^{T,B}, CRANE^{2,3}. The spread of this direction across apparently unrelated texts, and its absence from two of the most heavily sophisticated Crane texts, suggests that it is not Crane's addition, but instead a reflection of his copy. In CRANE^3 (and MIDDLETON^T) the direction is replaced with more specific speech prefixes, and in OKES and CRANE/ALLDE it is duplicated by specific prefixes; if anything, Crane preferred prefixes as a way of handling this problem. MIDDLETON^B, which has neither direction nor specific prefixes, is very confusing, and that confusion is most easily explained by the accidental omission of one direction (like this one), rather than the accidental alteration of four specifying prefixes. For this unusual form of stage direction as a specifically theatrical idiom, see Taylor and Jowett, 113-15; Middleton the playwright is more likely to have used it than Crane the preparer of literary transcripts.

5.129/2144 this] MIDDLETON^T *only*; heere's CRANE¹, MIDDLETON^B+. Both variants have autograph authority, and 'here's' crosses the border between early and revised versions; I have therefore adopted the obsolescent authorial form here in the

old-spelling text, and the modern alternative in *A Later Form*.

5.130, 5.136, 5.140/2145, 2151, 2155 Intus] MIDDLETON; Bl.Qs.P. CRANE¹, MIDDLETON^B, ROSENBACH^A; within CRANE³ (*as speech prefix*); Bl. Q^s.P. within CRANE² (*as speech prefix*); B.Q.P. OKES, CRANE/ALLDE (*with 'within' in the right margin as a stage direction, each time*). MIDDLETON^T preserves what is unmistakably an unusual authorial form, which any scribe was likely to normalize away. At 5.140, in MIDDLETON^T the initial 'I' is written over 'w' (indicating that Middleton started to write 'within', which presumably stood in his copy).

5.137/2152 mischeife] CRANE¹+; a pox MIDDLETON^{T,B}. For the idiom compare 'A mischief on't' (*Michaelmas* 2.1.73, *Old Law* 3.2.50), 'A mischief swell 'em' (*Mad World* 2.6.93), 'Mischief on your officious forwardness' (*Changeling* 1.1.230), and 'Mischief on thee!' (*Valour* 3.4.44)—the closest parallel being, noticeably, the closest in date. There is no need to suppose censorship or scribal interference here; the autograph reading may simply represent a late authorial variation.

5.162.1/2181 *wth*] MIDDLETON^B; *&* CRANE^{1,2}, MIDDLETON^T. See 4.170.2.

5.172/2190 ᴧYond's] MIDDLETON^T; Bl. K^{ts}. P. ~ CRANE¹+. Compare 3.1.

5.178.1 *Scæna Vltima.*] MIDDLETON^B, ROSENBACH^A; *Sce^a. 3^a.* CRANE. Middleton himself is responsible for this scene marker; moreover, the 'Vltima' formula does not appear elsewhere in the Crane witnesses, but does occur elsewhere in Middleton. See 5.0.1.

5.183/2205 a] CRANE¹ (*catchword*), MIDDLETON+; *not in* CRANE¹ (*text*)

5.190/2212 Ebusis] OKES; Eleusis CRANE¹+. The emendation is based upon the reading of Middleton's source, Philemon Holland's translation of Pliny's *History of the world* (bk. 9, chap. 18). Since the error is corrected in OKES (printed from an autograph manuscript), the error may well be scribal (as at 5.229 and 5.248), rather than authorial. Confronted with the same unknown word, Crane may have misinterpreted it in the same way, and passed his misinterpretation on to subsequent texts.

5.196/2218 Crata] Orata DYCE. The emendation is based upon the reading of Middleton's source, Philemon Holland's translation of Pliny's *History of the world* (bk. 9, chap. 54). This error occurs in all witnesses to both the original and revised versions of the play. George has suggested that Middleton 'wrote the extracts in a commonplace book first' (350). Since this error seems to be Middleton's own, it has been preserved here, like the generic speech prefixes, as an accurate reflection of authorial papers. But see *Later* 5.3.17.

5.229/2252 Corduba] MIDDLETON^T+; Curduba CRANE¹. An easy misreading.

5.238/2262 rayst] THIS EDITION; raise CRANE¹+; talke OKES. If Crane had understood this word as a contraction of 'raise it', he would certainly have inserted an apostrophe, as he did elsewhere with 'is't' and 'was't', and probably would have spelled out 'raise't'. However, the similarity of the letter forms for 'fe' and 'ft' in secretary hand (Crane's or Middleton's) demonstrates how easy it would be for Crane to misread 'rayft' as the common verb 'rayse'. HOWARD-HILL, retaining *raise*, glosses it ''to utter or produce (a sound)', *OED*, hence, talk.' However, the difference between the actual *OED* definition and HOWARD-HILL's gloss is precisely the absence of a direct object: the text does not specify 'a sound' that he will 'raise' from anything. This problem is easily solved if we assume that Middleton here elided the direct object *it* to *'t*, attached to the word that precedes it. I have not included this in the computation of shared errors, because other editors do not regard it as an error; but if as I suspect it is indeed a shared error, then it presents the same pattern as 5.195, where OKES corrects an error present in all other texts. Here, however, Middleton apparently substituted a synonym rather than restoring the original reading; accordingly, the OKES variant is adopted in *Later*, and the original reading conjecturally restored here.

5.248/2273 Cabrito] MIDDLETON[T]+; Cabuto CRANE[I]. An easy misreading of an unfamiliar word from a foreign language.

5.298/2322 why...prayers] MIDDLETON[T]+; *not in* CRANE[I] (*text*); why CRANE[I] (*catchword*). CRANE[I]'s catchword indicates that a line at least similar, and probably identical, to that found in MIDDLETON[T] was in Crane's copy-text, but accidentally omitted by Crane. The simplest explanation for the error

would seem to be that he first wrote the catchword ('why') for the first line of the next page, which should have been followed by 'we' ('why we...'); instead, he then skipped to 'we' at the beginning of the next line. This suggests that at least the first two words of the line in [MIDDLETON[PRE]] were identical to the line in all other witnesses.

5.362.1 ‸white] MIDDLETON[T,B], CRANE[3,4]; wth OKES: & CRANE[I,2]. See Induction.0.3 and 4.170.2.

5.375.4/2444+1 T.m.] MIDDLETON[B]; *not in* CRANE[I]+

5.375.5/2445 Finit] THIS EDITION; Finis CRANE[I]+; *not in* OKES, ALLDE. For Crane's preference for 'Finis' over 'Finit' see 2.452.2. Only in CRANE[I] does this line take the form of an act-ending; the two autograph examples of simple 'Finis.' therefore have a different meaning than the 'Finit' that Middleton normally uses before 'Actus'.

HISTORICAL COLLATION

Variants Unique to CRANE[I] (Archdale)

These notes record all substantive and semi-substantive (metrical) variants unique to CRANE[I] (including variants *within* CRANE[I], when one or the other is unique). The list therefore includes cases where THIS EDITION does not adopt the CRANE[I] variant; those readings are also recorded, and discussed, in 'Emendations of CRANE[I] (Archdale)', and in such cases I provide a cross-reference. But whereas 'Emendations' provides readers with a record of editorial intervention, this list provides readers with a comprehensive account of the variants unique to CRANE[I] itself. The variants in CRANE[I] are particularly important, because they provide our only direct evidence of the early form of the play.

This list is not designed to provide a complete historical collation of all the witnesses to *A Game at Chess*. A comprehensive list is provided in the apparatus to *A Later Form*.

The variants are keyed to the line numbering of this edition of *An Early Form*, followed by a slash and the line numbering of Howard-Hill's Malone Society transcription of MIDDLETON[T]. Where there is some difference between the incidentals of CRANE[I] and this edition, CRANE[I]'s exact incidentals are recorded in brackets (as at Induction.26); where the incidentals are identical, the only thing to the right of the bracket will be the reading of all other witnesses (as at 2.79). Where no MSR line number is given (as at Induction.65.1), MIDDLETON[T] does not contain the line or passage, and CRANE[I]'s incidentals have been emended to bring them into conformity with Middleton's practice elsewhere.

This edition includes elsewhere a complete list of Middletonian stage directions (transcribed from MIDDLETON[T] and MIDDLETON[B]), and a separate list of Crane stage directions (transcribed from CRANE[I]). Therefore, when recording CRANE[I] stage directions, below, I have not noted differences in spelling or punctuation between CRANE[I] and the holograph texts. Moreover, stage direction variants are only noted below in order to call attention to the uniqueness of a variant in CRANE[I], which may be evidence of differences between the staging originally imagined by Middleton and the eventual staging of the revised version. (Italics in stage direction lemmas are editorial.)

Title.3 *Anno Dm̃.* 1624] CRANE[I] (*August.* 13°. *Anno Dm̃.* 1624.); 1624 CRANE[3]; *not in* MIDDLETON[T]+. 'August 13' is presumably the date of the manuscript, not the date of completion of the version of the play it represents. 'A new play called *A Game at Chesse*, written by Middleton' was licensed by Sir Henry Herbert on 12 June 1624; but critics continue to debate whether Herbert licensed a text which included the major

additions not present in *Early*. See 'Canon and Chronology'.

Induction.26/40 vicar] CRANE[I] (Vicar), *boxed for deletion, with* Parſon *written in the margin by another hand and ink, to replace it*; parson MIDDLETON[T]+. As Howard-Hill notes, this and the alterations at 1.5, 1.31, 1.166-7, and 2.232 reflect 'a censorial sensibility', particularly sensitive to religious issues (*Pasquin* 28). Parson 'was a term associated with the non-established clergy and pejorative in connotation' by contrast with the 'dignified "vicar"'. The motive for the change can hardly be alliteration alone, since 'icar' is echoed in the last two syllables of 'Polycarpe'.

Induction.64.1/79 Enter...Bps.] CRANE[I] (*uncorrected*); *not in* MIDDLETON[T]+. See 'Emendations' note at Induction.54. The deletion of this stage direction calls attention to the fact that it duplicates or contradicts the marginal direction in CRANE[I] opposite Induction.52-5. But the more modest direction here, found in no other text, probably represents Middleton's first thought, later superseded by the more ambitious stage direction found in CRANE[I,2,3,4] and ROSENBACH[A]. Knowing how many actors would be necessary to bring on an entire chess board, Middleton may initially have imagined Loyola and Error looking offstage at an imagined board, with only the two Jesuit pawns actually entering (because their identification is crucial to establish the opening Queen's Gambit Declined).

1.0.2-3/99-100 *a Weoman-pawne in Black, and*] CRANE[I] (*a Woman-Pawne (in Black) &*); the Bl. Queenes pawne, MIDDLETON[T]+. The pawns seem originally to have been identified generically, by colour and gender.

1.0.3-4/100-101 *a Weoman-pawne in white;*] CRANE[I] (*a Woman-Pawne (in White)*); the white Qs: pawne; MIDDLETON[T]+

1.5/107 Ignorance] CRANE[I] *uncorrected* (*crossed out and replaced, in another hand and ink, with* Herefie); herefie MIDDLETON[T]+. See Induction.26.

1.31/134 Errors] CRANE[I] (*uncorrected reading, later deleted, and replaced by another hand with* herefies); herefies MIDDLETON[T]+. See Induction.26.

1.39/144 admiration] Admonition CRANE[I] *uncorrected*. See 'Emendations'.

1.47/152 a] The CRANE[I] (*uncorrected*). See 'Emendations'.

1.56/161 th'] the MIDDLETON[T]+

1.76-7 weomens...exit] CRANE[I] (sub), *uncorrected reading, later deleted*; *not in* MIDDLETON[T]+

1.167/271 Puritane] CRANE[I] *uncorrected reading, crossed out by another hand*; Heretique CRANE[I] *corrected*+. See Induction.26 and Incidentals note.

1.193/297 princesse] CRANE[1] (Princesse); Princes MIDDLETON[T]+. Crane's reading might be no more than an alternative interpretation of Middleton's ambiguous spelling; but its gendering also suggests a reference to either the Spanish Infanta or Princess Elizabeth, which might have been deliberately removed by the censor.

1.261/367 exit]—Ex[t.] CRANE[1] (at 1.262.1). See 'Emendations'.

1.277/384 ha'] haue MIDDLETON[T]+. It is hard to attribute the contraction here to Crane's sophistication, when all the other Crane texts report 'haue'—which could easily have resulted from assimilation to 'haue' earlier in the line. Middleton's use of this form at 4.1/1606 is unique to autograph; in a passage not present in CRANE[1], at Later 3.1.6/1067, both quartos expand the contraction reported by MIDDLETON[T] and all other witnesses. This evidence suggests that these contractions are more likely to be expanded, than the reverse. 'I ha'' occurs 72 times in 13 uncollaborative Middleton plays.

1.330/437 pens] P'ees CRANE[1]. See 'Emendations'.

1.346/454 and...Frend:] CRANE[1] uncorrected (sub), deleted by another ink; not in MIDDLETON[T]+. See Later 1.1.319–24: the added material is present in all texts but CRANE[1].

1.353.2/467 Finit] Finis CRANE[1] (?). See 'Emendations'.

2.0.2/468 White-weoman] CRANE[1] (uncorrected reading, with 'woman' later boxed for deletion); White-Q[s] CRANE[1] corrected (by later deletion and interlining). The first of the specifying alterations seen later in the manuscript.

2.4/474 I erè] CRANE[1] (ere); erè I MIDDLETON[T]+

2.45/520 m'Intent] my Intent MIDDLETON[T]+. There are no parallels elsewhere in Middleton for such an elision of 'my' to 'm' (though there are three parallels for reduction of 'them' to the single letter 'm'). I have not found any parallels in Crane, either, so it is not clear that the scribe was imposing a preference of his own; the expansion of the elision in his other transcripts would be typical of his tendency to spell out in full words that should be elided metrically. Since Middleton's spelling 'youre' (so frequent and consistent in his autograph pages) never shows up in printed editions, it is conceivable that these two passages preserve an unusual Middleton elision, present in his draft manuscript and preserved in Crane's first copy, but subsequently expanded by Crane and reproduced in its expanded form in all subsequent copies. The very same elisions do occur (rarely) in colloquial texts printed in the 1630s: 'm'obedience' in Davenant's Love and Honour (1639), 'm'intents' in Wither's 'A Satyre' (1633). This unusual elision of 'my' is certainly the 'rarer reading' in terms both of Game witnesses and of period usage (Taylor 1988).

2.68/543 m'obedience] my obedience MIDDLETON[T]+. See preceding note.

2.79/554 mistooke] miftaken

2.126/602 Reuerence,] CRANE[1] uncorrected. See 'Emendations'.

2.182/662 Hugonites] Lutherans

2.212/692 litle] CRANE[1] uncorrected (Litle), deleted and replaced by another hand with interlined bounfeinge CRANE[1] corrected; bouncing MIDDLETON[T]+. It is hard to interpret the original reading as a simple scribal error; it more likely represents an authorial first thought, altered to the revised reading of all other witnesses.

2.232/712 wthout Temple Bar] CRANE[1] (original reading, crossed out); in Drury Lane CRANE[1] (corrected, later insertion by another hand), MIDDLETON[T]+. See Induction.26. Temple Bar was a gate marking the limit of the jurisdiction of the city of London, at the west end of Fleet Street (Sugden, 505); 'outside' it stood not only an increasingly fashionable suburb,

associated with the lawyers of the Inns of Court, but also Westminster. The original location thus could be interpreted as a criticism of Parliament, the courts of law, and the royal court. Drury Lane was also outside Temple Bar, and also associated with women of ill repute, but the more specific street name had no particular associations with lawyers or government, and was if anything associated primarily with the Phoenix or Cockpit theatre (Sugden, 157).

2.233/713 what haue you there] CRANE[1] (later insertion in Middleton's handwriting), MIDDLETON[T]+; not in CRANE[1] (uncorrected). Middleton has here apparently corrected an accidental omission by Crane. Unlike other variants in the manuscript, this is hard to attribute to censorship or revision; it asks a question answered in the following line. As I know from frequent experience, an author glancing over a finished copy of his own text occasionally spots a random error, even when not attempting a complete proofreading of the text.

2.253/734 ont] out MIDDLETON[T]. Although the variant could result from an easy misreading, 'to pick out syllables on't' in fact makes sense, includes the characteristic Middleton contraction on't (which occurs more than four hundred times in the canon), and avoids the pleonasm of 'to pick out...out'.

2.266, 2.273/748, 755 Bl.K[ts.]p.] Bl.B[s].P. CRANE[1]. See 'Emendations'.

2.270/752 Bl.p.] CRANE[1] corrected; Bl.B[s].P. CRANE[1] uncorrected. See 'Emendations'.

2.273 Bl.K[ts.]p.] Bl.B[s].P. CRANE[1]. See 'Emendations'.

2.275.1 Enter] CRANE[1]. See Later 2.2.0.1–2.2.95/759–870 for a major addition in the revised version.

2.280, 2.356/876, 954 wh.p.] CRANE[1] (wh.P.); wh.Q[s].p. MIDDLETON[T]+. Generic prefixes continue.

2.312/908 wthout any] CRANE[1] (without ~); unadmirde MIDDLETON[T]+

2.319/915 greiues] giues CRANE[1] (uncorrected). See 'Emendations'.

2.322/919 Sir] not in MIDDLETON[T]+

2.364/962 Lord,] CRANE[1] ('Lord,); oh, MIDDLETON[T]+. A clear instance of censorship in all later texts; Herbert was particularly sensitive to oaths.

2.373/973 Kinred,,] CRANE[1] (kindred:); ~ too, MIDDLETON[T]+

2.398/998 Iewell] Treafure

2.404-5/1005-9 Bl....endeerde,] CRANE[1]. For an addition to the revised version here, see Later 2.2.212-14.

2.404/1005 Hat] ~ | reserud for you; MIDDLETON[T]+. This variant might have resulted from a simple error of transmission in CRANE[1]. However, the metrical structure of CRANE[1] is regular as it stands, and would be disturbed by the addition of this phrase, which might have been added—at the same time as other additions to this passage, in the revised text—in order to clarify the meaning. 'There's an infallible staff' might be a metaphorical description of the papers Black Knight hands at this moment to White King's Pawn: in taking hold of these papers, he is effectively taking hold of his promised ecclesiastical promotion.

2.410/1014 profession] CRANE[1] (Profession); profeffor MIDDLETON[T]+

2.412/1016 most] not in MIDDLETON[T]+

2.413/1017 th'] the MIDDLETON[T]+. For 'offence' in this sense, stressed on the first syllable, compare Witch 5.3.58 and Widow 1.1.76.

2.418/1022 I am...Flower,] am I...~?

2.425/1029 most] worke

2.436/1041 th'] the MIDDLETON[T]+

2.452.2 Finit] Finis CRANE[1]. See 'Emendations'.

2.452.2 *Actus Secundi*] ~ Secundus ROSENBACH[A], OKES; *not in* MIDDLETON[T]+. Middleton marks the ending of every other act, and the autograph omission of the formula here is almost certainly an accidental failure to correct something in his copy-text. None of the Crane texts, except CRANE[I], marks the ending of any act, so the presence of these markers in CRANE[I] presumably reflects the underlying authorial papers. This hypothesis is further supported by the unusual form 'Secundi' (for which, see the 'Emendations' note at 2.0.1).

3.0.3/1080 *Enter Bl.K[t].*] CRANE[I]. In the revised version the scene begins with extra material involving the Fat Bishop and then also the Black Knight; this entrance therefore occurs earlier in MIDDLETON[T], at a point for which CRANE[I] offers no exact parallels. See *Later* 3.1.0.2–3.1.81/1061–1146.

3.1 ‸ lett] CRANE[I] (Lett); but ~ MIDDLETON[T]+. In other witnesses this speech begins with a speech prefix for the Black Knight, and four additional lines referring to the Fat Bishop; hence 'but' to mark the change of subject. The omission of the speech prefix immediately after an entrance direction (as here in CRANE[I]) is common in dramatic manuscripts of the period, although Crane and other scribes often supply them.

3.16/1162 rayses] Rowzes. The reverse variant occurs at 3.218.

3.24/1170 Suffrers] Sufferers MIDDLETON[T]+

3.28/1174 Venice] *not in* MIDDLETON[T]+. This extrametrical word seems designed to deny the obvious referent for the rest of the line (London). Either Middleton was anticipating censorship (and originally wrote this word to disarm or distract it), or—less plausibly—CRANE[I] here represents a censored text. In either case, the word seems not to have been present in the playbook, which lies behind all other witnesses. Perhaps the censor took the bait and removed it, since it implies that Venice (which had ejected the Inquisition and resisted the Spanish) was more fortunate than England.

3.34.1/1182 *Bl.*] his

3.36/1183 Bl.p.] CRANE[I] (*Bl.P.*); Bl.K[ts].p. MIDDLETON[T]. Another example of the generic speech prefixes apparently common in the author's first draft.

3.53/1200 you . . . S[r],] *not in* CRANE[I]. See 'Emendations'.

3.57, 3.59/1204, 1207 K.] K[t] MIDDLETON[T]+. See 'Incidentals' note at 3.48. The number of cases of this variant abbreviation in CRANE[I] makes it unlikely to be a scribal mistake.

3.80/1228 a'th] CRANE[I] (o'th'); of the MIDDLETON[T]+

3.82/1230 all‸] ~ then

3.103.1/1252.1 *Enter . . . pawne.*] CRANE[I] (~ *wh: Q[s]. Pawne.*); *not in* MIDDLETON[T]+

3.107/1256 makes] makft MIDDLETON[T]+. For the obsolete verb form, see Hope 2.1.8a (p. 161). Crane's subsequent modernization was followed by all other texts.

3.120/1269 seuerd] fecurd CRANE[I]. See 'Emendations'.

3.142/1292 Bl.p.] CRANE[I] (~P.); Bl.Q[s] p. MIDDLETON[T]+. Generic prefixes for this character continue throughout the scene, in CRANE[I] only.

3.143/1294 ‸ in] ftrangelie ~

3.196/1348 that peice] CRANE[I] (~ Piece); the Duke MIDDLETON[T]+

3.213/1365 hir heart,] CRANE[I] (hart); his ~‸ MIDDLETON[T]+. The reading of the other witnesses makes obvious sense, and Nascimento included CRANE[I]'s variant in her table of 'nonsensical' errors. But Crane's 'hir' is graphically quite distinct from the following 'his,' and the punctuation of the line also suggests that Crane quite deliberately differentiated 'hir heart' and 'his intents'—a gendered contrast between female emotion and male intellect and action. The whole point of the Black Knight's speech, and the action which

precedes it, is to make the White House doubt the integrity of their own pieces ('See what sure piece you lock your confidence in'); by demonstrating the treachery of their King's Pawn he could easily suggest the black-heartedness of their Queen's Pawn, standing next to him. He has, throughout the scene, been publicly stubbornly sceptical of the White Queen's Pawn's claim to virtue and truth. Finally, 'hir' is characteristically ironic: while seeming (to the White House) to impugn the whiteness of the White Queen's Pawn, it more accurately (to the Black House, and the audience) declares the blackness of the Black Queen's Pawn, despite her apparent treachery to her own side. While 'his' is merely redundant, 'hir' adds more meaning to the line and the scene.

3.218/1370 gratious] *not in* CRANE[I] (*uncorrected*). See 'Emendations'.

3.218/1370 rousd] rayfde. For the reverse variant see 3.16. Although the variant here could result from misreading, it makes Middletonian sense: compare *Virtue* 274, *No Wit* 2.156. The reading of all other texts may well be related to the added lines: see next note.

3.218/1370 thee] See *Later* 3.1.267–9/1373–5 for one of the additions to the revised version.

3.233/1389 too] See *Later* 3.1.283–305.1/1389–1418 for one of the major additions to the revised version.

3.234/1419 wh.p.] CRANE[I] (wh.P.); wh.K[s] p. MIDDLETON[T]+; wh.Q.P. BRIDGEWATER[B]; *Wh.K[t] p.* OKES. The prefix is ambiguous, but CRANE[I] must reflect Middleton's manuscript; the errors in BRIDGEWATER[B] and OKES suggest that their copy was ambiguous, like CRANE[I]. See 3.239.

3.235/1420 Staff S[ir], the strong Crosier-Staff] CRANE[I] (Staff, Sir); Staff, the ftrong Staff that will hold

3.244/1430 thou'st] CRANE[I] (thou'hast); thou haft MIDDLETON[T]+

3.275/1462 resolud] CRANE[I] (refolu'd); applied

3.278/1465 nor] or

3.291/1482 ‸ pox] a ~

3.297/1489 Drudgerie, and durtie Busines] CRANE[I] (~ ~ durty Busynes); durtie-Drudgerie MIDDLETON[T]+

3.326/1519 in] thorough

3.345/1540 diffrence] difference MIDDLETON[T]+

3.355/1552 you see] CRANE[I] (yo[u] ~); fee you MIDDLETON[T]+

3.396/1597 desire] requeft

3.400.1/1602 Finit] Finis CRANE[I]. See 'Emendations'.

3.400.1/1602 *Tercij*] CRANE[I]; 3[HS] MIDDLETON[T] *only; tertius* ROSENBACH[A], BRIDGEWATER[B]; *Tertus.* OKES. See 'Emendations' at 1.0.1, 2.0.1, 3.0.1. The form with a numeral followed by a superscript suffix appears repeatedly in Crane texts (as does the terminal -us), and may therefore represent MIDDLETON[T] following an intermediary text prepared by Crane or influenced by Crane's practice.

4.3/1608 litterate] CRANE[I] (Litterate); letterd MIDDLETON[T]+

4.17/1622 Vniuersall] CRANE[I] (Vniverfall); Catholicall MIDDLETON[T]+

4.29/1634 pawne] CRANE[I] (Pawne.); ~ (S[ir]) MIDDLETON[T]+

4.67/1674 him] mee

4.170/1780 then,] For the two additional lines added by all other witnesses, see *Later* 4.1.148–9.

4.173/1787 Golden Stoole, my Stoole] Chayre of eafe, my Chayre

4.174/1788 weoman] CRANE[I] (Woman); weomen MIDDLETON[T]+

4.225/1840 our] *not in* CRANE[I]. See 'Emendations'.

4.240/1855 then] CRANE[I] (Then); agen MIDDLETON[T]+. See 2 *Vox Populi*, p. 16: 'I was no less diligent for the discovery of the Inland, then for the Shores . . .'

4.250/1865 t'entrap] to entrap MIDDLETON[T]+

4.252/1867 Black] Fat

4.253.1/1870.1 *Enter Bl. Bishop*] CRANE[1] (~ ~ B[p]); ~ Fat ~ MIDDLETON[T]+

4.255/1871 Bl.B.] F.B. See preceding note. This identification of the Bishop continues in speech prefixes throughout this scene in CRANE[1] only.

4.263/1880 Killing] Only CRANE[1] repeats 'killing' four times; other texts have three (CRANE[2,3]), seven (BRIDGEWATER[B], ROSENBACH[A]), or six (MIDDLETON[T], OKES, CRANE/ALLDE).

4.264/1881 ₐheres] why ~

4.268/1884 at it] in't

4.269/1884-5 2] a Couple of

4.278/1894 pound] See *Later* 4.2.105-7/1895-7 for an addition to the revised version.

4.280/1898 Booke,ₐ] ~, Biſhop

4.284/1903 forₐ] ~ the

4.285/1904-5 5 thousand ducketts] CRANE[1] (fiue...Ducketts); ducketts 5 thouſand MIDDLETON[T]+

4.288/1909 20] CRANE[1] (twenty); ducketts ~ MIDDLETON[T]+

4.297/1918 fowler] fowle CRANE[1]. See 'Emendations'.

4.297/1918 permitted] remitted

4.301/1922 downe,] CRANE[1] (~.); ~, | but none for Gelding; MIDDLETON[T]+

4.314/1937 Side:] See *Later* 4.2.144-5/1938-9 for an addition to the revised version.

4.314.1 *Musique.*] CRANE[1] (*Musick.*); *not in* MIDDLETON[T]+; *Recorders* BRIDGEWATER[B], ROSENBACH[A]; *Recorder* OKES

4.314.2 *Lights*] a light BRIDGEWATER[B], ROSENBACH[A], OKES; *a Taper* CRANE[2,3,4]; *not in* MIDDLETON[T]

4.314.4 *and exit*] puts out the light and ſhee followes MIDDLETON[T]. Although they differ in minor details of wording, all other witnesses have 'put[s] out the light, and...follows...'—thus confirming two important pieces of staging information not present in CRANE[1].

4.322/1956 Sᵢʳ] CRANE[1] (Sir); why MIDDLETON[T]+; *not in* OKES

4.324/1958 glistringſt] CRANE[1] (gliſteringſt); glittrinſt MIDDLETON[T]; glittering OKES, CRANE/ALLDE; glittringſt BRIDGEWATER[B]+. The substantive difference here is between the verbs 'glister' and 'glitter': the first occurs at least twelve times elsewhere in the Middleton canon, the second only four times. Moreover, Middleton also refers elsewhere to the noun *glister*, an enema, which might naturally be associated with the Black Knight and his fistula. Clearly, CRANE[1]'s reading can be defended as Middletonian, perhaps more so than the alternative.

4.327/1961 will] would

4.345/1979 reall] CRANE[1] (Reall); royall MIDDLETON[T]+. The pun in CRANE[1] depends upon a sense of 'real' last recorded by *OED* in 1602 (*a*[1]); perhaps an obsolescent authorial usage, modernized in other texts.

4.353/1986 Rombauts] Rambants CRANE[1]. See 'Emendations'.

4.356/1989 into the] ~ her

4.375 the Bishop of the blackhouse] oh tis the Turnecoate Biſhop BRIDGEWATER[B]+. Clearly related to the change from Black Bishop to Fat Bishop. See next note.

4.376.1 *Enter Bl. Bp.*] *Enter Fat B*[p.] CRANE[2] (at 4.372), CRANE/ALLDE (at 4.371); *not in* ROSENBACH[A], BRIDGEWATER[B], OKES. MIDDLETON[T] lacks this entire passage. CRANE[1] is unique in its adjective and in the position of the entire direction. Although (like licensed playbooks) the original authorial manuscript seems to have been occasionally careless about exits, it also (like playbooks) seems to have been careful about entrances, and the absence of this entrance direction looks like a shared error in the NON-CRANE manuscripts, rather than a scribal interpolation by Crane. The exact

placement of the direction is debatable; the 'massed entrance' in CRANE[3] specifies only that the Fat Bishop enters after the White Queen and before the White Bishop, and the three texts which do specify a position locate the entrance at different moments. Either CRANE[2] or CRANE/ALLDE might be correct, reflecting the common practice of directing an entrance shortly before the character is noticed by others onstage; but CRANE[1]'s later position is certainly possible, presuming that the White Queen is looking offstage, where she has just witnessed the exit of the White Knight and now sees the approach of the Black Bishop; her use of the third person at 4.376 suggests that he is not yet on stage.

4.378 Bl.B.] F. B. BRIDGEWATER[B]+. This identification of the Bishop continues to the end of Act Four, in CRANE[1] only. See 4.255.

4.398 wh K.] See *Later* 4.4.82-5 for an addition in the revised version.

4.417 you] they CRANE[1]. See 'Emendations'.

4.428 agen] See *Later* 4.4.109-10 for an addition in the revised version.

4.428.1 *Finit*] *Finis* CRANE[1]. See 'Emendations'.

4.428.1 *Quarti*] *Quartus* MIDDLETON[T]+. See 1.0.1 and 3.0.1.

5.0.2/2003 Lowde] *not in* MIDDLETON[T]+; Lowe BRIDGEWATER[B], ROSENBACH[A]. For the accuracy of the unique CRANE[1] variant, see the Textual Note at *Later* 5.1.0.2.

5.0.2/2003 *Musique*] CRANE[1] (*original*); ~ *Litter.* CRANE[1] (*by interlining*). The interlineation suggests that the litter was an afterthought, which was later developed in the revision; it plays no part in the original version. See *Later* 5.1.1-5.1.9.2/2004-2013 for a related addition.

5.0.2 wth] & CRANE[1]. See 'Emendations'.

5.8/2024 lætitià] *Lætitio* CRANE[1]. See 'Emendations'.

5.16 noble] Nobe CRANE[1]. See 'Emendations'.

5.25.1/2033 ₐrichlie adorndₐ] CRANE[1] (, richely ~,); *not in* MIDDLETON[T]

5.33/2043 Whitehouse Knight] White-Knight CRANE[1]. See 'Emendations'.

5.38.1 *The...dance.*] *not in* MIDDLETON[T]+; *The Images moue in a Daunce* CRANE[2,3,4], OKES. For an argument that only CRANE[1] accurately represents the action here, see Text Note at *Later* 5.1.46.1.

5.102/2116 by] wth

5.109/2123 ha's] CRANE[1] (has); hath MIDDLETON[T]+. This variant reverses the direction of Crane's normal substitutions (six times in the opposite direction in CRANE[1] alone; another 33 times in one or more other Crane witnesses). It is therefore almost certainly the original authorial reading, preserved in the first Crane transcript, sophisticated in all others, and passively preserved in later copies.

5.124/2139 th'] the MIDDLETON[T]+

5.132/2147 Ile] CRANE[1] (I'll); I will MIDDLETON[T]+

5.138/2153 thou didst præpare thy selfe] CRANE[1] (~ prepare thyſelf); you were præparde for't MIDDLETON[T]+; you did prepare Youre ſelfe MIDDLETON[B]. The pronouns in CRANE[1] are inconsistent: in the remainder of this sequence, 'thou' is addressed to the offstage voice, 'you' to the onstage White Queen's Pawn. The mistaken pronoun reference in CRANE[1] could have arisen from association with the first half of the line (addressed to a different person). However, the pronoun shift would account only for a variant like 'you did prepare yourself,' not a complete rewriting of the phrase, and a corresponding thy/your variant in the next line. The inconsistency thus seems to have originated with Middleton, who later revised it away.

5.139/2154 thy] youre
5.147/2163 there…Engine] that Engine was not
5.149/2165 th'] the MIDDLETON^T+
5.154/2170 can] could
5.178.2/2199 *and pawnes*] *not in* MIDDLETON^T+. For a discussion of the changed staging, see Text Note at *Later* 5.3.0.2.
5.183/2205 a] *not in* CRANE^I (*text*). See 'Emendations'.
5.224/2247 not] nere
5.229/2252 Corduba] Curduba CRANE^I. See 'Emendations'.
5.236/2260 meekelie] CRANE^I (meekely); mildlie MIDDLETON+. *OED* defines *meek* as 'mild, gentle' (*a.*3a), but also as 'indulgent', when used of a superior's relationship to a socially inferior person (*a.*1).
5.248/2273 Cabrito] Cabuto CRANE^I. See 'Emendations'.
5.248/2273-4 Ton's] CRANE^I (Tone's); Ton's | eate, and eate euerie daye, twice if you pleafe, MIDDLETON+. This might be an accidental omission by Crane, but the following 'nay' fits the syntax better without the additional line.
5.270/2296 of] for
5.290-2/2316 I…| wh.Kt. when] CRANE^I (~ Yo^u ~ we'are your Cabbynetts ~); when MIDDLETON+. This exchange establishes Gondomar as the confidant and 'cabinet' of the Prince of Wales. As originally written, this was a highly censorable exchange, and it is not surprising that it is absent from all texts that derive from the playbook.

5.292/2316 my] the
5.298/2322 why…prayers] *not in* CRANE^I (*text*). See 'Emendations'.
5.309/2333 neuer mind] quite forgett
5.312/2336 fayth,] CRANE^I ('faith,); *not in* MIDDLETON+. A Middletonian oath preserved only in CRANE^I.
5.312/2336 thats] that are
5.316/2340 Claye,; ,] ~ Venerie! MIDDLETON+
5.326/2350 laugh] fmile
5.336/2360 Vices] others MIDDLETON+. See General Textual Introduction, Sec. III.
5.340/2364 I er'e] ere I
5.348/2372 unknowen] CRANE^I (vnknowne); not knowen MIDDLETON+
5.357/2380 , the] King, ~
5.360 ,Dissembler] Wh.D. ~
5.360 *Flourish.*] *not in* MIDDLETON+; *A great fhout and flourifh* OKES (*at* 5.357-8)
5.362/2383 Bl.K.] Bl.D. MIDDLETON^T *only*; Bl.q. MIDDLETON^B+
5.364/2387 Meekenes] Sweetnes
5.369/2392 , twas] CRANE^I ('twas); as twas MIDDLETON+
5.375/2398 of] for
5.375/2398 Shame;] CRANE^I (~.). See *Later* 5.3.178.1-Epilogue.10.1/2399-2457 for a major addition in the revised version.
5.375.5/2445 Actus Quinti] *not in* MIDDLETON^T+

EMENDATIONS OF INCIDENTALS

Almost no one reads editorial lists of Emended Incidentals. The lists exist, normally, to legitimate an edition, by demonstrating its attention to even the most insignificant aspects of the text. They are read, normally, only by critics with an interest in de--legitimating the edition in question, by finding tiny holes in its scholarly armature. The following list is as subject to criticism as any other. But it also has a different function, and is more significant, than most such lists.

This edition of *An Early Form* aspires to reproduce Middleton's spelling and punctuation as accurately as type can represent script; in particular, it aspires to reproduce the spelling and punctuation of the lost manuscript [MIDDLETON^PRE], completed in late May or early June of 1624, which contained the first complete draft of *A Game at Chess*. Many old-spelling editions emend incidentals in order to make the text more intelligible for modern readers. Since this edition of the *Collected Works* also provides readers with a modern-spelling version of the play, we have not modified the spelling or punctuation of *An Early Form* for the sake of intelligibility.

Nevertheless, our printed text of *An Early Form* does deliberately and systematically alter certain manuscript features. It ignores turn-overs and turn-unders of long lines; it ignores differences in letter size, and line breaks within stage directions and prose passages. It supplies speech rules of uniform length between speeches (ignoring variations in length, and occasional omissions of such lines). It removes spaces between letters and the following punctuation marks. It does not attempt to reproduce the exact placement of headings and stage directions on the page; it places them at the appropriate point in relation to the text, but not necessarily as far to the right or left, up or down, as they are in the manuscript. Stage directions are in fact systematically displayed using the editorial conventions of this edition (entrance directions on a separate line, and indented; exit directions justified to the right). Also in line with the conventions of this edition, speech prefixes are systematically indented to the left of the text column. These systematic changes of layout do not affect the particularities of punctuation and spelling, which might have expressive significance.

Any attempt to reproduce Middleton's incidentals must begin with the extant manuscripts which, in whole or part, were written out by Middleton himself, in particular MIDDLETON^T and MIDDLETON^B. To begin with, then, we must decipher those manuscripts. My reading of the incidentals of Middleton's autograph manuscripts is fundamentally indebted to Howard-Hill's published transcriptions; I have used his transcription of MIDDLETON^T as the copy-text for this edition. Nevertheless, I have checked his transcriptions against photographs of the originals and against the originals themselves. I have restored the anomalously placed apostrophes in MIDDLETON^T and MIDDLETON^B, which he regularized, and corrected two substantive errors in his transcription: 'or' (an error for 'of' at 2.30/MSR 503), and 'are' (an error for 'art' at 2.421/MSR 1025). My occasional disagreements with his interpretations of spelling, punctuation, and capitalization are all noted below. When I disagree with the transcription of autograph by Howard-Hill (as for example at Induction.31), I give my reasons for doing so, usually by comparing the reading in question with nearby examples of the same orthographic features. I also normally record the interpretation of the feature in Nascimento, and sometimes in Bald. When I cite parallels, I give the line numbering of Howard-Hill's 1990 transcription of MIDDLETON^T, which provides a reference system tied to that manuscript; anyone wishing to check my interpretation of the letter or punctuation mark would want to look at MIDDLETON^T rather than at this edition of *Early*. Most of the disagreements recorded below involve initial 'k' or 'y' or 'w', where minuscule differs from majuscule only or primarily in the relative size of the letter. Howard-Hill acknowledges that Middleton's minuscule and majuscule 'k' are extremely difficult to distinguish (xvi), and that Middleton often uses minuscules even for proper names (xx). For all three letters, Bald, Nascimento, and Howard-Hill sometimes disagree about whether minuscule or majuscule is intended. Previous scholars have, I believe, associated initial majuscules with nouns. But Middleton often undoubtedly used initial majuscules with adjectives and verbs and even prepositions, and initial minuscules with nouns, so I have tried to base my own interpretations on the physical size of the letter, rather than on normative expectations.

The great majority of the following notes record deliberate editorial departures from autograph spelling or punctuation; that is, they record cases where there is no disagreement about the interpretation of the autograph manuscript, and I have chosen, for one reason or another, to reject that autograph reading in favour of something else. In most cases, I have rejected one autograph reading because an alternative autograph reading is available. For the last two scenes of the play, MIDDLETON[T] and MIDDLETON[B] both provide autograph texts, which often differ, and the printed text of *An Early Form* must choose between them. Elsewhere, Middleton corrects or alters the text, so that both the corrected and uncorrected reading are in his own handwriting, and the printed text must choose one form or the other.

These notes record changes usually of a single punctuation mark or a single letter in a word, and differences between the minuscule and majuscule form of the same letter; I have therefore adopted conventions different from those used in the substantive textual notes elsewhere in this edition. The lemma uses bold type to indicate the letter or punctuation mark at issue. Thus, the following note concerns variation only in the first letter of the word; the bold type used in the lemma does not imply that the letter in question is written in a script different from the rest of the word, but simply calls attention to that letter as the object of analysis in the note.

1 7 **N**ostrills] no∫trills MT *uncorr* RO OK

Here, the note records a variant within autograph, involving majuscule and minuscule forms of the same letter. When further variants are noted, each group is set off with a grey bullet (●). As this example also illustrates, because these notes treat tiny features of the text, they adopt a more abbreviated system of reference, including abbreviated sigla.

BAL = Bald, ed., *A Game at Chess*
BR = BRIDGEWATER
C1 = CRANE[1]
C2 = CRANE[2]
C3 = CRANE[3]
C4 = [CRANE[4]]
CMA = CRANE/MATHEWES/ALLDE
GT = THIS EDITION
THH = T. H. Howard-Hill, ed., *Bridgewater Manuscript* (1995)
MB = MIDDLETON[B]
MSR = Malone Society Reprint, ed. Howard-Hill (1990)
MT = MIDDLETON[T]
NAS = NASCIMENTO (transcription of MIDDLETON[T])
OK = OKES
RO = ROSENBACH

I have been deliberately inconsistent about attributing readings in CRANE/MATHEWES/ALLDE. Where the possibility of direct influence of one printed quarto upon the other seems strong, or where the variant for one reason or another seems more likely to be compositorial than scribal, I have preferred 'CMA'. When the variant seems clearly related to Crane preferences, I have preferred 'C4'. Readers may of course disagree with my interpretation; both sigla refer to the same extant document.

MIDDLETON[T] and MIDDLETON[B] are the copy-texts for incidentals; for most of the text, BRIDGEWATER is not autograph, and therefore only one authorial manuscript is available. For all those areas of the text, when MIDDLETON[T] and CRANE[1] agree on the words of the text, I adopt MIDDLETON[T] incidentals without comment. In the play's title, for instance, 'A GAME at CHESSE.' occurs on three autograph title-pages (MIDDLETON[T], ROSENBACH, MIDDLETON[B]), in contrast to 'A Game att Chesse.' in CRANE[1]; this variation, and others like it, is nowhere recorded in this textual apparatus. Likewise, when the substantive variant is a transposition, it does not affect the spelling or punctuation, which is therefore reproduced from autograph. When the substantive variant consists simply of the absence or presence of a terminal 's', I have also reproduced the autograph spelling, with or without the substantively variant final letter. Angle brackets enclose material which other causes (paper damage, blotting) have removed or made difficult or impossible to decipher. In such cases, dots indicate illegible characters (thus ⟨.⟩).

When substantive variants adopted from CRANE[1] are more substantial or more complicated, they have been modified to conform with the pattern of authorial incidentals represented in other manuscripts. Some of those emendations of incidentals are recorded in the Historical Collation; I have not duplicated that information here. Nor have I recorded changes in the incidentals of stage directions, since all autograph stage directions are reproduced elsewhere in this apparatus.

Because of its relevance to the textual stemma—discussed in the General Textual Introduction, Sec. IV—I give below a complete collation of incidentals variants in the Latin oration (5.1-10). The following list also includes: (1) variants *within* either MIDDLETON[T] or CRANE[1], including cases where the text differs from the catchword; (2) cases of indentation, where I depart from the autograph copy-text; (3) emendations of incidentals in three passages (4.365-428, 5.14-23, 5.41-2), and some isolated individual lines and phrases, for which there is no autograph manuscript; (4) incidentals variants between different autograph transcriptions; (5) conjectural emendations of autograph spelling or punctuation.

For editorial procedure the last three categories are the most important. As Howard-Hill has demonstrated, CRANE[1] preserves relatively little of the incidentals in MIDDLETON[T]: about 30%, by contrast with 94% for BRIDGEWATER (*Pasquin*, 205). Because CRANE[1] is *in general* a poor source for Middleton's spelling and punctuation, for the passages where no autograph text is available I have used BRIDGEWATER as copy-text for incidentals, since (even in its scribal portions) its incidentals are elsewhere closest to those of MIDDLETON[T]; the notes to these passages therefore record departures from the spelling and punctuation of BRIDGEWATER[B] (not MIDDLETON[T] or CRANE[1]). However, I have checked all spellings in these passages against autograph spellings elsewhere. Where spellings coincide with CRANE[1], they do so because CRANE[1] preserves Middleton's autograph preference. In BRIDGEWATER[B], speech prefixes are routinely followed by a dash; these dashes, and the occasional use of / as terminal punctuation, I have systematically removed, and they are not recorded below.

As the preceding paragraph makes clear, in passages where no autograph text is available I have not hesitated to emend the incidentals of BRIDGEWATER to bring them into conformity with Middleton's known preferences. This presumes that Middleton's preferences can be determined, and that Middleton's preferences were consistent. These assumptions may seem questionable, because the differences between MIDDLETON[B] and MIDDLETON[T] demonstrate that Middleton was not entirely consistent. However, Middleton's preferences in those two late autograph transcripts seem to have been distorted, occasionally, by the influence of his copy-texts. For evidence of this conclusion, see the General Textual Introduction (for the late and derivative nature of the extant autograph manuscripts), and particularly Section IV (for the distortion of Middleton's spelling and punctuation preferences). Middleton's preferences have therefore been determined on the basis, not simply of numerical totals of individual spellings or punctuation marks in the autograph texts, but by a comprehensive collation of incidentals in all eight extant texts. That collation identifies 'unique' autograph readings, which do not appear elsewhere in the extant documents. Those 'unique' incidentals might also reflect the influence of an unknown scribe in one or more lost manuscripts, but at least we know that they cannot reflect the influence of any *known* agent other than Middleton himself. In fact, the pattern of unique incidentals generally confirms the raw numerical totals, and/or the collateral evidence of incidentals in the Middleton canon as a whole.

When the incidentals of MIDDLETON[T] and MIDDLETON[B] disagree, and one of the two is unique, I have adopted the unique form, on the assumption that it is less likely to reflect the influence of copy-text. When the incidentals of both autographs are unique, in different ways, I have preferred the form best attested by other unique autograph readings. I have also, in evaluating incidentals variants in the autograph texts, paid particular attention to CRANE[1]. The stemma constructed in the General Textual Introduction shows that there was no direct connection between CRANE[1] and the extant autograph manuscripts; indeed, they are at opposite ends of the sequence of transmission. Therefore, if CRANE[1] agrees with one of the autograph texts, against other CRANE texts, then it is likely that CRANE[1] preserves the incidentals of the lost autograph first draft, [MIDDLETON[PRE]]. Although statistically CRANE[1] as a whole may be far from the overall pattern of incidentals in Middleton's autograph, in particular cases it may very well represent the spelling and punctuation of Middleton's first draft better than one of the later manuscripts.

Thus, on numerous occasions CRANE[1] agrees with an autograph spelling or punctuation mark, which does *not* appear in the other autograph text. This pattern strongly suggests that, on other occasions, CRANE[1] might preserve Middletonian incidentals, which have been altered by later copyists, up to and including MIDDLETON[T]. Many of the differences between CRANE[1] and MIDDLETON[T] involve the vocative 'sir'. As is now well known, Crane was exceptionally fond of round brackets; he apparently added many such brackets, not present in the texts he was copying, so it is not surprising to find 'sir' surrounded by round brackets in CRANE[1]. Nevertheless, CRANE[1] has fewer such brackets than the other CRANE texts. More remarkably, CRANE[1] sometimes does not use round brackets, when they are present in MIDDLETON[T]. The absence of brackets in CRANE[1] corresponds to the practice found elsewhere in Middleton's printed texts. The vocative 'sir' appears very often in Middleton's plays: *Hengist* (96), *Changeling* (139), *Dissemblers* (151), *Women Beware* (158), *Chaste Maid* (198), *Quiet Life* (225), *Roaring Girl* (236), *Valour* (236), *Quarrel* (287), *Widow* (331); of these 2057 uses of the vocative 'sir' in ten collaborative and uncollaborative plays written from 1611 to 1623 and printed between 1611 and 1661, only five are bracketed, and three of those are in *Women Beware*, clearly set from scribal copy with an unusual number of brackets: the other two are at *Widow* 4.1.100 ('but (sir) scorn') and *Quiet Life* 2.3.1–2, where the brackets surround the two words 'noble sir'. Thus, when 'sir' is bracketed by MIDDLETON[T] and other texts, but not bracketed in CRANE[1], it seems probable that CRANE[1] better represents Middleton's original draft.

I have already mentioned the occasional paleographical ambiguity of majuscules. Another editorial problem about majuscules

is their use at the beginning of verse lines. In the printed texts, this is an invariable convention, and those texts therefore tell us nothing about Middleton's manuscript practice. This leaves at the most only four witnesses to compare with the two autograph texts at the end of the play (and sometimes less, when CRANE[3] is abridged or *Early* does not contain lines present in the revised version). Consequently, when the two autograph texts disagree about such cases, it can be difficult to choose between them, on the basis of a clear distinction between an undeniable autograph preference and an undeniable instance of the influence of Middleton's copy. In the Induction and 1.1—where the *Early* and *Later* forms are very similar, in all eight texts—there are 439 lines in MIDDLETON[T] which begin a verse line or begin a verse speech. Of those, there are 31 lines that begin with the uncompounded pronoun 'I', which is always majuscule in autograph, and therefore irrelevant. Of the remaining 408 shared lines, only 44 (10.8%) begin with a majuscule; by contrast, 89.2% begin with a minuscule. In any given case, the odds are 9-to-1 against Middleton beginning a verse line with a majuscule. Only one of those majuscules (2.3% of the majuscules, and 0.2% of the eligible verse lines) is unique to autograph: 'Vnperfect' (Induction.12). The exception results from the fact that Middleton never used minuscule 'v' or majuscule 'U': ignoring the modern distinction between the vowel 'u' and the consonant 'v', ignoring also the early modern convention of 'v' at the beginning of a word and 'u' within it, Middleton instead used minuscule 'u' anywhere in a word (including the beginning) and majuscule 'V' at the beginning. This practice is for the most part duplicated in BRIDGEWATER, but in this instance BRIDGEWATER follows the normal convention and uses initial 'v' (like the other witnesses). Middleton had to choose between 'u' and 'V' (either of which would have been a unique autograph reading); in this case he chose 'V'. Clearly, this case does not permit us to generalize about anything other than the specific problem of words beginning with initial u/v. The fact that all the other autograph majuscules at the beginning of verse lines occur in one of the other witnesses does not suggest that Middleton himself favoured this practice: the three scribes who in other respects come closest to his autograph incidentals, BRIDGEWATER[A] and ROSENBACH[A,B], rarely begin verse lines with a majuscule. Of the 42 autograph examples in the Induction and 1.1, many are words that might have been capitalized regardless of their position in the line: proper nouns (Roch, Sislie, Priapus, Bacchus, Germanica, Italica, Hispanica), or titles (Kings, Dukes) and emphatic nouns that are capitalized elsewhere (Obedience, Fate, Sir, Sonne, Trifle). One signals the shift from aside to direct address (the vocative 'Daughter!' at 1.126).

Scholars have always recognized Crane's fondness for emphasis capitals. We can test his practice at the beginning of verse lines by comparing the same passage in his three surviving transcripts of those two scenes, again counting only verse lines that begin with something other than the lone pronoun 'I' (which is always a majuscule in Crane). In CRANE[1], the Induction and 1.1 contain 406 such lines, of which 96 (23.6%) begin with a majuscule. In CRANE[2], there are 408 eligible lines, of which 151 (36.9%) begin with a majuscule. In the abridged CRANE[3], there are 347, of which 134 (38.6%) begin with a majuscule. This evidence confirms the scholarly consensus that Crane was responsible for many of the majuscules in his manuscripts, and that the proportion of majuscules increased with subsequent re-copyings; it agrees with other evidence that CRANE[1] is the first of the extant CRANE manuscripts, and CRANE[3] the latest. Since even the earliest of Crane's copies contained over twice as many such majuscules as Middleton's late autograph transcript, we would expect CRANE[1] to reproduce all the majuscules it found in Middleton's first draft. In fact, all but five of the 44 relevant majuscules in these scenes of MIDDLETON[T] appear in CRANE[I]: 'Vnperfect' (MSR 46), 'The' (79), 'Vntill' (97), 'Blessed' (120), and 'It' (441). Two of these result from Middleton's peculiar treatment of u/v. Thus, in the first two scenes CRANE[I] fails to duplicate a relevant autograph majuscule in only 3 of 42 cases (7.1%). Moreover, in all three cases the majuscule does appear in the two other Crane transcripts. Given all the other evidence that MIDDLETON[T] was influenced by the late lost manuscript from which it was copied, it seems probable that in these three cases CRANE[I] better preserves the first draft than MIDDLETON[T] does. Of course, it is also possible that some, or many, of the 39 relevant majuscules in MIDDLETON[T] in these two scenes also derive from his copy, having been added by Crane and passed on to subsequent manuscripts; but in those other cases we simply cannot discriminate between Middleton's own preferences and his passive repetition of copy forms. However, the presence of some unique autograph majuscules demonstrates that Middleton did occasionally use them, at the beginning of verse lines and elsewhere—but not nearly as frequently as Crane. His first draft almost certainly contained fewer than MIDDLETON[T].

As the preceding paragraphs suggest, the editorial attempt to reproduce the incidentals of the lost [MIDDLETON[PRE]] at many points requires a detailed analysis, not only of the autograph manuscripts themselves, but of a variety of evidence about Middleton's own preferred spelling and punctuation—including his colloquial contractions and metrical elisions. We hope that it may be of use to scholars interested in such issues.

Induction.3/17 Nostrills] noftrills MT *uncorr* RO OK. The change in autograph suggests that his copy had the minuscule, and that he consciously preferred the majuscule.

Induction.9/23 here͵s] BR • here's MT. See unique autograph 'heres' (2311 MB MT, 2316 MT), and the thirteen other unique autograph examples of absent apostrophes for compounds that include elided 'is'.

Induction.15/29 Yeares] GT • yeares CI+. See unique autograph majuscule at 42 47 601 923 2166 (MB).

Induction.18/32 theyde] GT • they'had C2 C3 • they had CI+

Induction.29/43 one] CI+. There are no specific autograph examples of the numeral rather than the word 'one' (although there are plenty of examples of other numerals).

Induction.30/44 twenti͵th] CI C2 C3 RO • twenteth OK • twentieth CMA BR MT

Induction.31/45 Loue] loue NAS MSR. Both in size and shape the initial letter clearly differs from the following 'lame' and 'leape' (both with smaller looped ascenders, which resemble those in mid-word 'Policarpe', 'place', 'fall', 'else', etc.). Although not identical to the initial letter in 'Loyola', it more closely resembles it than any other example of the consonant on the page. That Middleton probably intended the majuscule is also indicated by the unique autograph 'Love' at 2055 (MB).

Induction.33/47 Wraths] BAL NAS • wraths MSR. Both in size and shape the initial letter clearly differs from that in adjacent 'waye', 'were', 'blowe', 'wake', 'what'; it also differs from the initial minuscule in all other textual witnesses.

Induction.33/47 Yeare] yeare MSR CI+. Although the initial autograph letter is somewhat smaller than at 42 (perhaps to avoid the descender of f in 'Confcience'), the letter is still very notably larger than in the adjacent 'my', 'by', and 'daye'; a majuscule was probably intended. See Induction.15.

Induction.38/52 you] You MT *corr* • don MT *uncorr*. The anomalous majuscule 'Y' covers the original 'd', so that the ambiguous final minims can then be interpreted as 'u' rather than 'n'. Middleton's copy may have omitted 'you' entirely.

The need for clarity in the overwriting is presumably the only reason for the majuscule.

Induction.41/55 Eye] CMA (Eie) • eye MT+. The word was originally omitted in MT, then interlined above a caret, both in darker ink; so the initial minuscule in autograph might have resulted from the influence of copy, or from the position of the correction. Middleton began the word with a majuscule in the autograph preface to c3 and fourteen times in MT.

Induction.42/56 pre͵thee] GT • pre'thee CI • *not in* MT

Induction.44/58 ͵twixt] CI ('twixt) • betwixt MT+

Induction.45/59 to't] to it OK BR MT

Induction.50/64 lett] BR • let CI+. Autograph uniquely reads 'lett' at 739, 806, 1261, 1580, 2084 (MB (*only*)), and 2441 (MT (*only*)).

Induction.55/70 Wish] wish NAS MSR. Contrast the preceding 'pawne...power...showe...what...what'. The initial letter here is at least as likely to be majuscule as that in 'Whitehouse' (58).

Induction.56/71 there͵s] BR • there's MT+. See the unique autograph 'theres' (without apostrophe) at 432, 433, 1004, 1010, and 2338 (MT MB). By contrast, none of the examples of the contraction with the apostrophe is unique.

Induction.60/75 Word] word NAS MSR. Contrast the preceding 'pawnes' and following 'whome'.

Induction.63/78 Worth...Well] worth...well NAS MSR. Contrast the preceding 'whome' and following 'Answeres... pawnes'.

Induction.64/79 the] CI BR • The C2 C3 RO NAS MSR. The initial letter in MT does not remotely resemble the majuscule in the preceding 'Titles'; the vertical stroke goes somewhat lower than usual, but the cross-bar is clearly in mid-stroke.

Induction.64.1/80 the bl.] ~ Q MT *uncorr* • ~ Bl. MT *corr* • *black* OK • Black CI+. The MT majuscule was clearly necessary to cover the initial mistake; see the immediately following 'bl: Bishops' and the unique autograph 'black' at 1785.

Induction.65/80 the] C2+ • ye CI • *not in* MT BR OK

Induction.66/81 præfermnts] The Latinate ligature appears only in BR. For unique autograph parallels see 'prævayle' (120), 'prævalde' (875), 'præsident' (921, 1878, 1915), 'præpare' (2153 MT), 'præuented' (2194 MT), 'prætious' (2371 MT). The ligature is preserved only by MT and BR in 'præsentation' (143), 'prævented' (170), 'præuent' (719), 'prætext' (1154), 'præpard' (1410), 'præmeditated' (1411), 'præuent' (1501), 'præsidents' (1901), 'præuent' (1950), 'præsentation' (1979).

Induction.67/82 Worthie] worthie NAS MSR. Contrast the preceding 'pawnes' (twice) and 'would' (twice).

Induction.69/84 I͵de] BR • I'de MT+. Autograph prefers the unapostrophied form of this elision (5 to 2); compare unique autograph 'youde' (2421 MT) and 'Ime' (2278 MB MT • 2381 MT). Crane heavily uses the apostrophe in this and similar forms.

Induction.70/85 Loue] loue NAS MSR. Contrast the initial letter with the letter in 'would', 'place', 'told', 'tale', 'pulse', 'Elixir', and compare it with 'Light' (23) and 'Le Roc' (75).

Induction.75/90 push] MT BR • pifh CI+. A scribal sophistication of Middleton's unusual interjection. The same variant occurs at 1035 and 1779.

1.1/102 p.] GT • *pawne* OK • P. MT+. This is the only autograph example of a majuscule 'p' in speech prefixes, and could easily be due to copy influence. See unique autograph 'p.' at 120, 125, 127, 137, 471, etc. Generally only OK and MT use minuscule 'p' for speech prefix abbreviations.

1.1/103 ne're] CI MT • nere C4 RO • neuer C2+. See unique autograph apostrophe in this word at 1792 and 2247.

1.5/107 **daughter**] BR RO • Daughter MT+. Contrast unique autograph 'daughters' (2169 MB MT), and 17 other autograph examples of the minuscule in this word.

1.6/108 **Eyes**] CMA (Eies) • eyes MT+. See Induction.41.

1.8/110 **theire**] BR (their'e) • they're MT+ • Theis are C2 C3. The unusual 'theire' spelling for the contraction occurs in MT and BR at 73 and 2012, and in *Truth* 756. Such a spelling might also explain the error in C2 C3 ('their' misread as 'theis').

1.17/119 mee] MT BR CMA • me CI+. Although MSR prints 'me', the double vowel is as clear here as in 'mee' (111) and 'shee' (111, 114).

1.18/120 blessed] CI • Bleffed C2+

1.22/124 **Worke**] MT NAS •worke MSR. Contrast 'sweete' and 'were' before, and 'what' after.

1.31/134 all] CI+ • All MT. The majuscule in MT adjoins a large blot, and is almost certainly connected to that accident: this is the only autograph example of a majuscule beginning this word, which appears more than 150 times in the play.

1.35/140 **princes**] CI • Princes CI+. The autograph majuscule is written over something else. Contrast unique autograph 'princes' at 34 and 2373 (MB MT).

1.49/154 that‸s] BR CMA • that's MT+. Autograph uniquely lacks the apostrophe at 923, 2205 (MT), 2266 (MB MT) 2321 (MB MT)—and autograph often elsewhere uniquely lacks apostrophes for compounds with contracted 'is'.

1.74/179 doo] GT • doe CI+ • do'ft MT BR OK

1.76 **weomens**] womens CI (*catchword*) • Womens CI (*text*)

1.77 man‸s] CI (Man's)

1.78/181 lett] BR • let MT • Let CI+. See 64.

1.85/188 youth‸] CI • ~) C2 C3 C4 • ~, MT RO OK

1.87/190 Eye‸lids] CI BR RO • eye-lids C2+. What MSR and NAS record as an autograph hyphen is an unbroken line linking Middleton's characteristically horizontal terminal e to the initial upstroke of the 'l'; the mark clearly differs from the preceding hyphens in 'ague-Curers' (38), 'leape-yeare' (42), 'Love-tale' (85), 'Mr-peice' (104) and 'Ground-worke' (124), which are all disconnected from both the preceding and following letters. The hyphen is typical of Crane; autograph often uniquely treats compounds as a single unhyphenated word, and that seems Middleton's intention here too.

1.90/193 **delightfullie**] GT • delightfully CI+. This, the only autograph example of Crane's preferred '-fully', contradicts Middleton's overall preference for 'lie' and specifically the unique autograph 'cheerefullie' (1029) and 'wrongfullie' (989, 996). See also 'fullie' (368), 'gracefullie' (1534), 'wishfullie' (1592).

1.104/207 rest‸] CI RO • ~, MT OK BR. The autograph comma could easily be a response to the heavier punctuation in C2 C3 C4. The most common feature of punctuation unique to autograph is the absence of punctuation where all other texts contain punctuation.

1.116/219 blab‸d] BR C3 • blabbd RO • blabb'd OK • blab'd CI+. This is the only use of the past participial ending 'd in the first 300 lines of MT (MSR, xviii); there are only three other examples in the whole of MT, and one of those is contradicted by autograph MB (2238). The only other examples of this word in the Middleton canon in the past tense, at *Puritan* 2.1.181 (blabt) and 5.4.27 (blabd), do not contain an apostrophe. It seems highly probable that the apostrophe originated with Crane, and was passed from a late Crane transcript to other texts (including MT).

1.119/222 that‸s] BR • that's MT+. See 1.49.

1.122/225 us‸] CI C2 • ~, C4+

1.123/226 em'‸] CI • ~; MT C4 • ~, C2+

1.124/227 enclines‸] ~, C4 OK MT

1.125/228 **Knowe**] knowe NAS MSR. Contrast with 'make' and 'worke' earlier in the speech; compare with 'Kinds' and 'Kingdomes' (which MSR interprets as majuscule, NAS as minuscule). The position of the first letter here is affected by the frame-line at the bottom of the page and the descender from 'finding' above. See unique autograph 'Knowe' at 1691 (MT), 1694 (MT, Knowing), 2129 (MB), 2120 (MB).

1.126/229 Errors‸] CI • ~, C2+

1.131/234 uncomlie] BR • vncomly OK • uncomelie CI+. See unique autograph 'Comlie' (2389), where 'ie' is unique; this authorial preference is confirmed by 'comlye' (143, MT BR) and 'Comlines' (2266).

1.132/235 til't] CI+ • tilt BR. Contrast unique unapostrophied 'fort' and 'ist'. BR may here be the only text to preserve Middleton's preference.

1.134/237 nòw] MT (*only*). MSR notes the 'left inclined penstroke above n' but does not transcribe the penstroke (actually above the vowel) in the text itself. Possibly for emphasis: see 355. OK places a comma before the word; CMA also has the comma, but moves 'Now' to begin the next line; both quartos thereby emphasize the word.

1.147/251 they‸de] they'de MT. See unique autograph 'theyue' (438).

1.155/259 discharg‸d] discharged MSR. This appears to be a typographical error (substituting the normal modern spelling) rather than a difference of interpretation, since there is clearly nothing in the manuscript between the 'g' and 'd'.

1.158/262 forgett] GT • forget CI+. Contrast unique autograph 'forgett' (MB MT 2333) and 'gett' (2430 MB MT).

1.159/263 sordid‸] CI RO OK • ~) C2 C3 • ~, C4 MT

1.160/264 dutie‸] CI RO OK • ~, C2+

1.163/267 uestall] BR • veftall CI (*catchword*) C3 OK RO • Veftall CI (*text*) C2+. We can actually witness here, within CI, Crane adding one of his many extra initial majuscules, repeated in two other Crane texts and in MT. Middleton would have written the initial minuscule as 'u' (as in BR), not 'v'.

1.166/270 ‸ blest S^ir,] RO • (~~) CI+

1.166/271 Purita‸ne] GT • Puritaine CI. 'Puritaines' occurs in *Witch*, but the spelling there probably reflects Crane's preference rather than Middleton's: it also appears in *Duchess of Malfi* (printed from a Crane transcript), its only occurrence in the Webster canon. It occurs nowhere else in the Middleton canon, and autograph always uses the spelling 'tayn', never 'tain', in other words with such a suffix. By contrast, 'Puritane(s)' occurs often in texts published in Middleton's lifetime (*Honest Whore*, *Heroes*, *Mad World*, *Revenger* (twice), *Five Gallants*, *Tennis*).

1.169/273 præparde] GT • prepard CI+. Contrast unique autograph 'præparde' (2153 MT). See Induction.67.

1.171/275 Reuenges‸] CI BR RO OK • ~) C2 C3 • ~, C4 MT

1.180/284 marriage‸] CI • ~, MT • *heavier* C2+

1.183/287 S^ir] Sir MSR

1.187/291 ne're] RO • neuer CI+. See 1.1.

1.188/292 ‸em] CRANE ('em) RO • them MT BR OK. This is a favourite Middleton colloquialism, which Crane is unlikely to have introduced; this is the only occasion where CI gives the contracted form when it is not in MT.

1.191/295 y‸au'e] C2 (you'haue) • you haue CI+

1.193/297 **princesse**] RO • Princesse CI+. See 1.35. For the substantive variant here see Historical Collations.

1.193/297 Loue‸] CI • ~? C2 • ~, C4+ • ~: OK

1.194/298 exactᵥ] CI OK • ~, C2+

1.196/300 then?] MT (Nascimento), CI OK • ~, C2+. MSR notes 'following vertical penstroke not shaped like ! or ?'—but there is certainly a stroke there, its shape perhaps a little distorted by its intersection with the right frame line. Of Middleton's fourteen unique autograph queries, the only three with an interrogative sense all occur, as here, in mid-question, followed by another query at the end of the phrase.

1.199/210,303,314 Iᵥue] CI C2 (I'haue) • I haue MT+. 'I've' is one of Middleton's most characteristic elisions; it could easily have been expanded in the 'Jonsonian elision' in the two earliest Crane transcriptions, then wholly abandoned in later derivative texts.

1.203/307 shees] BR RO • fhee's MT+. The Crane apostrophe contrasts with Middleton's preference: see unique autograph 'hees' (2186 MT).

1.205/309 muchᵥ] CI • ~. C2 • ~: C4 • ~, MT+

1.207/311 Tract] last letter blotted MT (MSR); perhaps 't' over original 'k'; compare RO 'trackt'.

1.209/313 Sⁱʳ] Sir, MSR

1.212/316 prætious] GT • pretious CI+. See unique autograph 'prætious' (2371 MT), and Induction.67.

1.212/316 bothᵥ] CI • ~, C4 RO • ~(C2 MT+

1.212/316 Sⁱʳ] Sir MSR

1.212/316 Sⁱʳ,] CI RO • ~) C2+ • ~. C4

1.223/328 Ladie] ladie NAS MSR. The initial letter is larger and more distinctive than any other example of the consonant on this page; all other examples of the word in autograph begin with a majuscule.

1.228/334 feather] CI+. Contrast unique autograph 'Fether' (1615).

1.228/334 featherᵥ] CI C2 • ~. C3 • ~: C4 • ~, MT+

1.232/338 bin] byn CI C2 C3 • been CMA. Contrast unique Middleton 'beene' at 856.

1.238/344 ᵥmost] (~ C2 C3 BR MT

1.238/344 Virginᵥ] CI • ~) C2+ • ~. OK CMA • ~! RO

1.246/352 t'] CI MT • to C2+

1.249/355 yòu] MT • You CI C2 C3. MSR notes the 'oblique penstroke above o' but does not include it in his text, presumably regarding it as accidental. But it may well be intended to serve a metrical/rhetorical function, indicating that the pronoun should be stressed in delivery, for the sake of both the sense and the iambic rhythm: 'may better become you, some shirt of hair'. The majuscule in CI C2 C3 may be intended to serve the same function.

1.250/356 Albe] MT corr. The majuscule appears to be written over a minuscule (though MSR claims what lies beneath it is a semicolon). Only RO begins the word with a minuscule.

1.251/357 Fellon] BR C2 C4 • ffellon CI C3 • Fellow MT OK

1.252/358 thatᵥs] CMA BR • that's CI+. See 1.49.

1.253/359 charitie] cheritie MT uncorr

1.256/362 no] BR • No CI+. Compare unique autograph 'no' (1425), also the first word of a speech.

1.261/367 merittsᵥ] CI RO • ~, MT BR • ~. C2+

1.268/375 thorough] MT • through CI+. MT's spelling produces a metrically regular line.

1.269/376 and] not in MT BR OK

1.271/378 putt] GT • put CI+. The unique autograph spelling 'putt' occurs seven times: 261, 833 and 1083 (not in Early), 1715, 1845, 2398 (MB MT). It belongs to Middleton's general preference for doubled terminal consonants. By contrast, when 'put' appears (as here) it is almost always (as here)

the spelling in all other witnesses, making the probability that it stood in Middleton's copy exceptionally high.

1.272/380 Hierarchieᵥ] CI • ~, (C2 BR MT • ~ (C3 OK • ~, C4 RO

1.273/380 principalitye;] CI • ~) C2+ • ~. CMA • ~, RO

1.273/380 I haue] I'ue MT BR • I OK. Metre could go either way

1.274/381 Iᵥue] CI C2 (I'haue) • haue MT+

1.274/381 ᵥem] MT BR. The contraction appears in MT with an apostrophe 35 times; autograph lacks an apostrophe only here, at 2170 (MB MT), 2247 (MB MT), and 2406 (MB).

1.275/382 partsᵥ] CI • ~, C2+ • ~: OK

1.277/384 Iᵥue] C2 (I'haue) • I haue CI+

1.281/388 Iᵥue] C2 (I'haue) • I haue CI+

1.282/389 crackt] CI+. Contrast unique autograph 'Thundercraks' (955); the same unusual spelling, without medial 'c', also appears in Quarrel 1.9 ('crakes') and No Wit Epilogue.9 ('craks'). But I have found no examples of the past participle with this unusual spelling.

1.286/393 Youth] MT CI • youth C2+

1.287/394 hee] BR RO • Hee MT corr • I MT uncorr • He CI C2 C3. Middleton needed the majuscule to cover the mistaken 'I'. Crane routinely began new sentences with a majuscule.

1.291/398 you,] CI C4 RO • ~(C2+

1.291/398 Sⁱʳ] Sir MSR

1.291/398 Sir,] CI • ~,) MT • ~) C2+ • ~). OK • ~. CMA

1.291/399 Bl.] CRANE • Black MT corr • H MT uncorr. Having started the line of dialogue without the speech prefix, Middleton immediately corrected his mistake by writing 'Bl' over 'H', and then for clarity spelled out the word in full instead of using his usual abbreviation.

1.292/399 due, Sⁱʳ,] CI RO • ~(~) C2+ • ~(~). OK • ~,~. CMA

1.291/399 Sⁱʳ] Sir MSR

1.296/403 you] You MT corr, CI C2 C3 • I MT uncorr. The majuscule is needed to cover the original autograph error; in CI C2 C3 the word is preceded by a colon.

1.307/414 sheeᵥs] BR • fhee's MT+. See 1.203.

1.307/414 whitehouse] BR RO (1 word unhyphenated) • white house MT CMA OK • white-house CI C2 C3. See unique autograph 'whitehouse' at 100, 650, 813, 815, 1417, 1809, 2242 (MB MT), 2406 (MT MT), 2450 (MB).

1.309/416 Know] know MSR. The larger initial letter contrasts with all other examples of the consonant on this page. See 228.

1.309/417 ouldᵥ] ~, MT BR OK. Here and below, the comma indicates the correct line-break in a mislined passage.

1.310/418 Gameᵥ] ~ MT BR. See above.

1.311/418 Sⁱʳ] Sir MSR

1.320/427 a'thᵥ] CI C4 (o'th') • of the MT+

1.322/429 hereᵥs] here's MT. See Induction.9.

1.324/431 th'] CI C2 C3 • the MT+

1.326/433 Sⁱʳ] Sir MSR

1.330/437 theyᵥue] GT • they'ue CI RO • they'haue C2 • they haue C3 C4

1.330/437 putt] GT • put CI+. See 378.

1.333/440 ha's] GT • has MT BR • hath CI+. MSR notes that only nine of the thirty-six occurrences of this auxiliary verb in MT lack an apostrophe (xviii); twenty of the twenty-seven apostrophes are unique to autograph (and there is another example unique to MB). By contrast, not one of the exceptions is unique to autograph; in several cases—including 856, not present in Early—the absent idiosyncratic apostrophe is supplied by OK.

1.333/440 writt] CI C2 • writ C3+. See unique autograph 'writt' (865).

1.334/441 it] CI • It C2+. See unique autograph 'it' (also at the beginning of a line and a sentence) at 963.

1.337/444 though't] CI RO • though it C2+

1.337/444 youre] MT BR • your MSR, CI+

1.337/444 name] CI C4 RO • Name C2 C3 • Fame MT BR • fame OK

1.339/447 Kings] MT corr, CRANE+ • Qs MT uncorr • k: BR • kings RO. Elsewhere Middleton consistently begins this word with a majuscule, and does not abbreviate it in dialogue.

1.340/448 hee‸s] BR • hee's MT+. See 1.203.

1.342/450 prætiouslie] GT • pretiously CI+. See 316.

1.344/452 there‸s] BR • there's MT+. See Induction.57.

1.346/454 my selfe youre] GT • myfelf your CI uncorr • not in C2+

1.348/461 Iealious] Iealous MT BR. The extra syllable indicated by six of the eight texts seems metrically required.

1.349/462 Valued] GT • ualued MT+. This is the only example of this word beginning with a minuscule, and it specifically contradicts unique autograph 'Valued' (1043).

1.351/464 poore‸] ~- C3 RO MT. Five texts (CRANE and BR) have a hyphen after 'Iesuite', producing the sense 'poor soul who is ridden by a Jesuit'. The extra hyphen in C3 makes sense ('ridden by a poor Jesuit'), but RO and MT uniquely keep the first hyphen and drop the second. This linking of the first two words as an integral unit leads to the error in OK (which has no hyphens here, but a comma after 'Iesuit'). The error apparently results from retaining one copy hyphen but omitting another.

1.353/466 wch] MSR interprets 'w' as a majuscule, but the letter is no larger than any of the first letters of the preceding lines, no larger than the 'w' in 'Pawne' at the end of the line, almost identical to the speech prefix 'wh' (451) and hardly larger than 'now' and 'drawen' in preceding lines. Contrast 'What' in the first word of the Prologue, at 'What…Waters' at 317, or 'Wch' in autograph at MB 1910 (MSR), in all which the majuscule is clearly intended, and clearly distinct from this 'w'. (NAS interpreted as minuscule.)

1.353/466 pawne] BR • Pawne CI+. There are 15 examples of autograph uniquely beginning this word with a minuscule—100 (twice), 816, 872, 1423, 1471, 1604, 1605, 1876, 1941, 1944, 1385 (MB MT), 2447 (MB MT)—and many more examples where the minuscule is not unique but found elsewhere in the NON-CRANE witnesses.

2.0.3/470 hand;] BR • ~. CI+. The semicolon at the end of a stage direction is a rare Middletonian usage.

2.4/474 tis] RO CMA OK • tìs MT+. Contrast unique autograph 'tis' (without apostrophe) at 2060 (MT). This is the only example of the word in MT with an apostrophe, against 40 examples without it.

2.9/480 shee‸s] BR • fheês MT+. See 1.203.

2.15/487 pawne] BR • Pawne CI+. See 1.353.

2.15/487-8 politick] GT • politique CI+ • politike CMA • politicke OK. The spelling 'politick' occurs twice in autograph only (1170, 1192); the -ique suffix never appears in any word as a unique autograph choice.

2.26/499 ‸Sir‸] CI RO OK • (~) C2 BR MT • ‸~, CMA

2.26/499 Sir] S^{ir} MSR

2.26/499 ha's] MT BR OK • hath CRANE, RO

2.26/499 Iulepp‸] ~, MT CMA

2.34/507 I‸ue] C2 C3 (I'haue) • I haue CI+

2.35/508 ‸worthie Sir‸] GT • (~) CI+ • ;~, C2. That Crane's brackets were not present in his original is suggested by

c2, which interprets the passage differently, probably because a complete absence of punctuation made the grammar ambiguous.

2.40/516 duties‸] CI • ~; MT BR (which share the same mislineation)

2.44/519 She‸es] BR RO • Sheès MT+. See 1.203.

2.53/528 præpare] BR • prepare CI+. See Induction.67.

2.63/538 præsuming] BR • prefuming CI+. See Induction.67.

2.67/542 by't] by it MT BR OK

2.72/547 mine] my OK. The euphonic 'mine arm(s)' appears at least thirteen times elsewhere in the Middleton canon (none in a text transcribed by Crane); 'my arm(s)' only five times elsewhere. The variant probably is a late authorial revision or vacillation (or a compositorial modernization).

2.75/550 th'] the NON-CRANE

2.85/560 some] CI+ • Some MT corr, BR • a MT uncorr. The autograph majuscule was used to cover the original error.

2.85/560 Village‸] CI BR uncorr • ~, c2+ • ~. OK

2.86/561 putt] GT • put CI+. See 378.

2.93/569 uowde] GT • w MT uncorr • Vowde MT corr. The initial autograph error makes it clear that the word in Middleton's copy began with minuscules and minims. On all three other occasions autograph has the verb 'uowde' (contrasting with the three autograph occurrences of the noun as 'Vowe').

2.108/584 neerer?] CI • cleerer MT uncorr • Neerer? C2+

2.118/594 Yon'd] MT BAL • yon'd NAS MSR. The initial letter here contrasts not only in size but in the shape and direction of the descender with the seven other examples of 'y' on this page.

2.120/596 sacred‸] CI • ~, MT BR • ~. C2+

2.121/597 Offrer] CI C2 • Offerer MT+

2.123/599 weoman] BR • woman CI+. The 'weom-' spelling occurs only in autograph at 284, 1788, and 2226 (MT MB); it also occurs in autograph three other times, seconded either by BR (289) or OK (1813), or both (141). The 'wom-' spelling, by contrast, is never unique to autograph, and always originates in Crane.

2.127/603 carrie't] carrie it MT BR OK

2.130/606 to't] to it MT BR

2.130/606 to't‸] CI BR • ~, MT C2 • ~. C4+

2.136/612 there‸s] BR CMA RO • there's CI+. See Induction.57.

2.137/613 to] too RO CMA. The intention of MT is ambiguous: MSR interprets the anomalously thick inking to the right of the normal 'o' as a second 'o', but it might be insignificant, and certainly does not resemble the unambiguous 'too' at MSR 23, 46, etc. NAS and all previous editors interpreted the word as 'to'. Autograph elsewhere consistently spells the preposition 'to'.

2.140/616 can'st] GT • canst CI+. See unique autograph 'can'st' (953).

2.147/623 weomans] BR • womans CI+. See 599.

2.147/623 tong‸] GT • tongue CI+. See unique autograph 'Tong' (2259, MB).

2.150/626 I‸ue] MT BR • I haue CI+. Metre favours the contraction. See 1.274.

2.151/627 Longer] MT corr, C3 • longer MT uncorr, CI+

2.152/628 oh] o MT BR. Middleton overwhelmingly prefers 'oh'.

2.154/630 t'] to MT BR OK

2.155/631 princes] RO • Princes CRANE • nations MT BR OK. See 140. The fact that autograph uses a minuscule for the corresponding noun here supports the autograph preference elsewhere for 'prince(s)'.

2.158/635 thee‸] CI RO • ~, MT BR • ~. C2+

2.160/638 pawns] OK • p: BR • Pawnes CI+. See 1.353.

2.162/640 i‸th‸] CI C4 RO • in the C2+

2.162/640 Conuocation] MT *corr*, CI + • conuocation MT *uncorr*, BR

2.163/641 shr)ueld] BR OK • fhriueled MT RO • fhriuelld CI C2 • fhriuel'd CMA. Autograph elsewhere consistently avoids 'ed' after a consonant, unless the metre requires it to be a separately pronounced syllable.

2.172/650 ath‸] GT • o'th CRANE RO • of the MT BR OK

2.173/651 a] MT BR • on CRANE, RO • of OK

2.178/656 maynelie‸] CI • ~ : C2 • ~. C4 • ~, MT+

2.180/660 white‸house] GT (1 word unhyphenated) white--house CI C2 • white house C3+ • wh house CMA BR. See 1.308.

2.182/662 cheeke‸] CI C2 • ~, C3+

2.186/666 still‸] CI C2 • ~, MT BR • ~. C4+

2.188/668 blackhouse] BR • black houfe MT OK • Black-house CRANE RO. See 4.375.

2.190/670 euer‸] CI BR • ~: C2 C4 • ~, MT+

2.192/672 bottome‸] CI BR OK • ~, C2+

2.196, 198/676, 678 wittnesse] GT • witneffe MT+. The -tt- spelling occurs in *Revenger*, *Trick*, and *Witch*. See unique autograph 'wittnesse' (680) and 'Switterland' (2312).

2.198/678 grosse!] MT • ~? BR • ~: CI C2 C3 • ~‸ RO OK CMA. MSR interprets MT as a comma, but notes the 'vertical stroke at right of comma possibly added for !'. Certainly, there is more than a comma in autograph, and the result most closely resembles some of Middleton's exclamation marks: compare 1437 ('Rape!'), where the raised vertical stroke is just as far to the right of the comma.

2.202 cast] GT • Cast CI + • *not in* MT

2.202 30] RO • thirtie CI+ • thirty OK CMA • *not in* MT. Autograph often uniquely gives numerals instead of words in such cases.

2.202 leagues] Leagues C3 BR • *not in* MT

2.202 earth] C2+ • Earth CI • *not in* MT

2.202 suddenlie] GT • suddainlie BR • fuddenly OK • sodainely CRANE. For this spelling of the adverb see 2251, where both autographs uniquely spell 'suddenlie'. Crane's form (with 'o' in the first syllable, and/or 'ai' in the second) does not appear in autograph.

2.208/688 S^ir] Sir MSR

2.208/688 S^ir‸] CI BR • ~, MT RO • ~) C2+

2.211/691 that!] MT *corr* • ~? MT *uncorr*, BR • ~‸ C2 • ~. CI+

2.222/702 ‸ha's] MT BR OK • he has CRANE RO. Unmetrical expansion by Crane; contrasts with Middleton elision in preceding lines (which CMA alters on both occasions to 'he hath').

2.223/703 ha's] GT • has CI+. See 440.

2.223/703 writt] GT • writ CI+. See 1.334.

2.226/706 bawdie] baudy RO. MSR notes that the 'wd' in MT have been 'altered and retraced'; it is possible that Middleton first wrote 'bau', then altered the 'u' to 'w'.

2.230/710 2] RO • two CI+. See unique autograph '2' at 1701, 1843, 2208 (MT), 2224 (MB MT), 2232 (MB MB).

2.232/712 w‸thout] GT • without CI • *not in* C2+

2.233/714 there‸] CI (autograph) • ~? C2+. There is an ink blot after the word in Rosenbach, but Heather Wolfe and Valerie Wayne agree there is a question mark under it.

2.236/717 see't] CI RO • fee it C2+

2.238/719 that‸s] BR CMA • that's CI+. See 1.49.

2.239/720 Obseruation] CI • obseruation C2+. See unique autograph 'Obseruation' (1466). MT might intend a majus-cule; the initial 'o' is larger than all others in the vicinity.

2.239/720 now‸] CI BR • ~. C3 • ~: RO • ~, C2+

2.244/725 there‸s] BR RO • there's CI+. See Induction.57.

2.245/726 subteller] MT BR • fubtler CI+. Autograph con-sistently spells 'subtel-', not 'subtl-'. Intepreting the word as trisyllabic produces an extra syllable at the caesura (a metrical license Middleton allows elsewhere).

2.246/727 em̄] GT • 'em CI+ • *not in* MT

2.247/728 putt] GT • put CI+. See 378.

2.251/732 there‸] CI BR *uncorr* • ~: C2 • ~, C4+

2.253/734 ath‸] GT • o'th CI • of the C2+. For examples of the extrametrical expansion compare 1.320/427, 2.172/650, 2.290/886, 4.213/1828, 5.196/2218. The context differs in the revised version: see Historical Collations.

2.267/749 for‸t] BR • for't CI+. See unique autograph 'fort' (1045, 2411), and general autograph preference for no apostrophe with contractions that elide 'it' (tis, twas, ist).

2.268/750 toth'] to the NON-CRANE

2.273/755 bee] MT BR • be CI+. MSR has 'be', but the 'ee' is as clear here as at 751 (hee) and 752 (mee). Autograph consistently prefers the 'ee' spelling.

2.284/880 præserude] GT • preferude MT+. See Induction.67.

2.285/881 suff‸rings] CI C2 C3 (Suffrings) • fufferings MT+

2.290/886 a'th‸] GT • o'th CRANE • of th' OK • of the MT RO BR

2.295/891 that‸s] RO • that's CI+. See 1.49.

2.299/895 præserue] GT • preferue CI+. See Induction.67.

2.308/904 Sin‸] CI OK • ~, C2+

2.311/907 Monster] monster MT RO OK. This is the only example of the word beginning with a minuscule in autograph, in contrast with the unique autograph majuscule 'Monster--Impudence' at 2191.

2.317/913 method‸] CI • ~) C2 C4 • ~. RO • ~, MT OK

2.318/914 Deuill‸] CI • ~. C2 • ~, RO • ~; MT, C4

2.319/915 It] GT • It CI+. See unique autograph 'it' beginning line 963.

2.322/919 ha's] GT • has MT+. See 440.

2.322/919 pawne, Sir‸] CI • ~)‸ C2 • ~; ‸ C3 RO MT • ~.‸ OK CMA

2.338/936 the'yde] MT • they'll'd CI • they would C4 RO OK

2.342/940 th'] C2 C4 OK • the CI+

2.342/940 Respected‸] CI C2 • ~. RO • ~, C4+

2.345/943 do'st] CI C2 • doft CMA+. See unique authorial 'do'st' (179).

2.345/943 distraction‸] CI OK • ~? C2 • ~: C4 • ~, MT RO

2.348/946 Waters] MT NAS • waters MSR. Contrast with pre-ceding 'wth' and 'wise' and 'rowling', and with following 'what'.

2.356/954 ostentation‸] CI RO • ~; OK • ~, C2+

2.359/957 Æquiuocation] MT • æquiuocation OK • Equivoca-tion CI+. See Induction.67.

2.363/961 conception‸] CI C3 • ~, C4 MT • ~. C2+

2.366/965 shee] C2+ • She CI • *not in* MT RO BR

2.366/965 shee] CMA • She CI+ • *not in* MT RO BR

2.368/967 urge] GT • ug MT *uncorr* • Vrge MT *corr* • vrge CI+. Middleton originally wrote a minuscule, but when overwriting used a majuscule to cover his initial error.

2.368/967 to‸] CI • ~, C2+

2.371/970 yesterdayes] MT CI (c.w.) • Yefterdaies CI (text) +

2.372/972 can't] OK • cannot CI+. The contraction appears at least six times elsewhere in Middleton; I have not found it anywhere in Crane's transcripts, which suggests that Crane might have expanded it, as he did so many other contractions.

2.374/974 honors sake] MT+ • Honor-fake CI. Elsewhere in the Middleton canon 'sake' is preceded by a terminal possessive plural 's' at least 49 times, while the 's' is elided before 'sake' only five times, three of those being in later Interregnum texts (LION); there are no Middleton examples of the hyphenated compound. Hence CI's unique variant here is unlikely to be an authorial survival. Crane omits the autograph possessive and creates a compound in similar cases at 2.47/521 'Vertues sake' (c2 c3) and 2081 'decorums sake' (c2 c3 c4).

2.375/975 confusion∧] CI C2 • ~: RO • ~, c4+

2.377/977 putt] GT • put CI+. See 378.

2.377/977 king] King MSR. Compare 'meekemans' and 'knowe'.

2.378/978 heauie∧] CI • ~: c4 • ~, c2+

2.387/987 theyůe] CI+ • y MT uncorr • Theyůe MT corr (only). The majuscule was probably used only to clarify the overwrite.

2.387/987 long∧] CI • ~, MT RO • ~. c2+

2.395/995 light] MT (catchword) • Light MT (text), CI+. See 362. Autograph often uniquely begins a speech with a minuscule (818, 857, 927, etc.)

2.397/997 suffer?] CI RO • ~(c2 c3 MT • ~, OK CMA

2.397/997 Sir,] RO • ~) c2 MT • ~)? c3 • ~? CI c4 • ~. OK

2.399/999 step] CI RO • Step c2+

2.400/1000 amazement] CI • Amazement c2+

2.410/1014 accuser] Accufer c2 c4 MT

2.411/1015 youre] Youre MT corr • h(i)s MT uncorr (only). The unique initial majuscule was probably designed to clarify the overwriting.

2.414/1018 let] RO • Let CI+. See unique autograph 'let' (1303, 1378) and 'letts' (1036), all three at line beginnings.

2.418/1022 Flower∧] CI • ~? c2+

2.419/1023 Frendlesse∧] CI c3 • freindles c2+ • Harmlesse MT. The unique MT variant begins the parallel adjective with a majuscule, as does CI.

2.419/1023 Frendlesse] c2 c3 RO • Freindles CI • friendlesse OK CMA • Harmlesse MT. Middleton's preferred spelling occurs, uniquely, just two lines earlier.

2.419/1023 Frendlesse] OK CMA • Freindles CI+ • Harmlesse MT. Middleton's preferred spelling of the suffix is demonstrated in the MT variant.

2.421/1025 no] CI (noe) RO (noe) • No c2+. See 362.

2.422/1026 let] RO • Let CI+. See 2.414.

2.422/1026 putt] GT • put CI+. See 378.

2.439/1044 thou'st] DYCE • thou haft CI+. See 3.245 and Later 2.1.117.

2.441/1046 4] GT • fowre CI+. Contrast the autograph numerals before and after, and '4' at 1053. Autograph often uniquely uses numerals where other texts spell out the word (as with 'i2' at 1049).

2.444/1049 Luxurie∧] CI • ~: c2 c4 • ~. c3 • ~, MT RO • ~) OK

2.448/1053 th'] c2 c3 • the CI+

2.450/1055 Noblie] GT • noblie CI+. See unique autograph 'Noblie' (1995) and Middleton's unusual tendency to capitalize adverbs.

3.3/1149 futuritie] Futuritie c3 BR MT

3.5/1151 cal∧d] calld CI (c.w.) • call'd CI (text), c2 c4 RO

3.6/1152 prætious] GT • pretious CI+. See 316.

3.8/1154 th'] CI c2 OK • the c4+

3.10/1156 who] MT (catchword), RO • Who MT (text), CI+. Middleton often uniquely begins verse lines with a minuscule.

3.14/1160 they∧ue] CI+ (they'ue) • they haue MT c4

3.19/1165 Scent∧] CI c2 OK • ~, c3+

3.21/1167 putt] GT • put CI+. See 378.

3.22/1168 Tong∧men] Tonguemen MT • tong-men OK • Tongue--men CI+. For Middleton's preference for 'Tong' see 623.

3.25/1172 on't∧] CI c4 BR • ~. c3 • ~, c2+. Autograph punctuation may be related to mislineation.

3.26/1173 thought∧] CI RO OK • ~, c2+. See preceding.

3.27/1173 question∧d] CI c2 c3 • questionďd MT CMA • queftion-ed OK BR RO. See 219.

3.30/1176 too∧] ~, c4 MT

3.32/1178 some∧] ~, c2 c4 MT

3.33/1179 i∧th∧] BR RO • I'th' CI • in th' c2 c3 CMA OK • in the MT (only)

3.34/1180 Aerium] MT corr, CI • Erium RO. The autograph majuscule has, as MSR noted, been 'altered', but it is hard to imagine how what lies beneath it could have been any form of 'A'. From its size it was obviously a majuscule, and may well have been 'E'.

3.37/1184 ∧Sir] RO • ,~, BR • (~) CI+

3.37/1184 Im,e] BR (corr) • Iṁe MT c2 RO OK • I am CI+. See the unique autograph absence of punctuation in this contraction at 2278 (MB MT) and 2381 (MT)—and, more generally, Middleton's avoidance of apostrophes in contractions of two words.

3.39/1186 nayle] Nayle MT c2 CMA BR

3.42/1189 mine] Mine CI+

3.42/1190 Driuer∧] CI c2 BR • ~, c4+. Autograph punctuation may be related to mislineation.

3.45/1192 needle] Needle c2 c4 MT

3.45/1192 prickt∧ a Litle∧] BR RO • ~∧~, MT OK • ~,~∧ CI+. Crane's interpretation suggests that his copy did not contain the autograph comma.

3.48/1195 K∧.] CI CMA • Kt. MT+. Since the Black King is not present, no ambiguity is created by the abbreviation, which might represent authorial inconsistency.

3.49/1196 can'st] CI CMA • canft c2+. See 2.142.

3.53/1200 Knowe] knowe MSR NAS. The largest 'k' on this page, clearly distinct from 'keepe' in the preceding line.

3.53/1200 Names,] RO • ~ (c2+

3.53/1200 Sr,] GT • ~) c2+

3.59/1207 e're] GT • ere CI+. See the unique autograph apostrophes in this word at 116, 1490, and 2081 (MB MT), and in the parallel word 'ne're' (278, 1792, 2247 MB).

3.60/1208 braynes] Braynes MT c2 c4 BR

3.61/1209 like] Like c4+

3.61/1209 Cuntryes] BR (Countryes) • Cuntries CI+. See the two unique autograph spellings of the plural with 'y' at 1203 and 1215. (There is no unique autograph evidence of Middleton's preferred spelling of the first syllable.)

3.66/1214 Im,e] BR (ime) • Im'e MT+ • I am CRANE. See 1184.

3.66/1214 Sir] Sir NAS MSR. The two letters are high above the line (and the following comma).

3.67/1215 theyle] BR • they'll CI+. See unique autograph 'theyde' (20) and 'theyue' (438).

3.68/1216 they∧de] BR RO • they'de CI+. See preceding note, and 'youde' (2421 MT).

3.69/1217 plott] GT • plot CI+. See the unique autograph spelling 'plott' (1198), and Middleton's general preference for double-consonant terminations.

3.70/1218 Brat,] CI BR • ~∧ OK • ~ (c2+

3.70/1218 Sir∧] CI • ~, OK CMA BR • ~) c2+

3.75/1223 ha's] GT • has CI+. See 440.

3.80/1229 a litle∧] CI c2 BR • ~, MT RO OK. Autograph punctuation may be related to mislineation.

3.81/1229 parts∧] ~, MT BR • ~. c2+

3.83/1232 Wonders] MT NAS CMA • wonders MSR+. Contrast with preceding 'enow' and following 'wth' and 'pawnes'.

3.83/1232 for,t] BR • for't CI+. See 749.

3.84/1233   wrongs] Wrongs C2 C3 MT

3.84/1233   wrongs‸] CI BR • ~: C3 • ~, C2+

3.93/1242   præseruing] BR • preferuing CI+. See Induction.67.

3.96/1245   peice] GT • Peice CI • Piece C4 • Duke MT+

3.97/1246   respect] Respect C2 C3 BR MT

3.98/1247   Graces‸] CI C2 BR • ~, C4+

3.101/1250   t'] CI C4 • to C2+

3.105/1254   fidelitie] Fidelitie C2 C4 MT

3.115/1264   Im‸e] BR • Im'e MT+ • I am CRANE. See 1184.

3.118/1267   I‸ue] I'ue OK I'haue C2 • I haue CI+

3.119/1268   scatterd] Scattered BR MT

3.120/1269   putt] GT • put CI+. See 378.

3.124/1273   Impartiall] C2 • impartiall CI+. Compare unique autograph 'Impartiall' (995)—and other unusual autograph majuscules in adjectives.

3.127/1276   this] GT • This CI+ • that MT BR

3.129/1278   do's] CI RO • dos MT+. Compare unique autograph 'do's' at 1078 (not in *Early*), 1599.

3.131/1280   do's] GT • dos CI+. See preceding note: Crane seems to have retained the odd apostrophe on his first encounter with it, then normalized it the second time.

3.134/1283   10] GT • ten CI+. Autograph prefers numerals (often unique): see 785 (6 and 30), 990 (10), 1047 and 1049 (12).

2.135/1284   K^t.] MSR notes that the abbreviation is 'followed by two periods like oblique colon', but does not transcribe any punctuation in the text; the usual single point was probably intended.

3.141/1290   ner'e] ne're CMA RO • nere CI+. See unique autograph apostrophe in the preface to C3, and at 277, 1775, 1792, and 2247 (MB).

3.142/1293   p.‸now] ~ | ~ MT RO

3.142/1293   now] CI • Now C2+

3.142/1293   Trech‸rie] CI C2 (Treachrie) • Trecherie MT+

3.142/1293   Wth] MT NAS • wth MSR CI+. Contrast preceding 'how' and 'were' and 'wise' and following 'where'. Graphically, the majuscule seems obvious here, but BAL and MSR probably felt that it *should* not be capitalized here in mid-line. Perhaps the mausucle indicates the iambic stress.

3.142/1293   tong] Tong MT C3 C4

3.143/1294   since] CI (c.w. and text) C2 • Since C3+

3.152/1303   lett] BR • let CI+. See 64.

3.156/1307   Side‸] CI • ~, C4 RO MT • ~. C2+

3.161/1312   Sanctitie‸] CI BR • ~, C2+

3.164/1315   Deuill‸] CI BR • , C4 MT • ~—RO • ~. C2+

3.166/1317   ‸t‸ad] It had CRANE. 'T'ad is a characteristic Middleton elision, metrically preferable here.

3.170/1322   noyse] Noyfe MT C2 C3

3.172/1324   told,] CI BR • ~(C2+

3.180/1332   traytrous] CI BR • Trayterous MT+

3.180/1332   trayt‸rous] OK • Trayterous MT+

3.180/1332   pawne] OK BR • Pawne CI+. 1478 1509 1785 2412 (MSR, emended in my text). See 1.353.

3.181/1333   youre] MT. Although MSR prints 'your', the terminal 'e' is as visible as in all the many other autograph occurrences of the word.

3.190/1342   went‸] CI C2 • ~. RO • ~, C4+

3.191/1343   too'te] BR^C • toote BR *uncorr* • to it MT • to't CI+. Compare the unique autograph 'doo'te' (1770).

3.193/1345   hott‸] BR RO • ~, CI • ~ (C2+

3.193/1345   S^ir‸] BR • ~, CI RO • ~) C2+

3.194/1346   quicklie] BR • quickly CI+. Compare the unique autograph 'quicklie' at 1486. and Middleton's general preference for -lie.

3.194/1346   quicklie‸] CI BR • ~: C2 • ~. C3 • ~, C4+

3.195-8/1347-1350   White...Whitenes] white...whitenes NAS MSR. Contrast the intervening 'will...follow...would... were'.

3.199/1351   immediatlie] GT • immediatly MT+ • immediatelye BR. See the unique autograph spelling 'immediatelie' at 1113 (not in *Early*).

3.200/1352   knowe‸] CI BR • ~: C2 • ~, C4+

3.201/1353   doo'te] GT • Doot BR • do't CI+ • doo it MT • Doe CMA. See 3.191.

3.204/1356   hee‸s] BR • hee's MT+. See 1.203.

3.205/1357   negligence] Negligence C2 C3 MT

3.207/1359   th'] CI C4 BR *corr* • the C2+

3.208/1360   in‸] CI BR • ~, C2+

3.209/1361   ours‸] CI • ~, C2+

3.217/1369   h'as] GT • has CI+. See 1.333.

3.220/1375   th'] GT • the' C2 • the CI+

3.220/1375   do'st] CI • doft C2+. See 2.345.

3.220/1376   rottennes‸] ~, MT (*only*). Related to unique mislineation.

3.223/1378   lett] Lett BR • let MT • Let CI+. See 64.

3.225/1380   crieng] BR • crying CI+. Compare unique autograph 'Lieng' (1887), and 'glorieng' (1959 BR MT).

3.246/1432   it‸] CI • ~. C2 C3 OK • ~; C4 BR • ~, MT RO

3.248/1434   for‸sawe] MT • for sawe MSR. The gap between 'r' and 'f' is no greater than in 'firft' (1422) or 'person' (1455). One word in all other witnesses.

3.251/1438   all‸] CI • ~: C2 MT • ~. OK CMA

3.258/1445   house‸] CI C2 RO • ~. C3+ • ~, MT

3.260/1447   I‸ue] GT • I haue CI+. A unique autograph addition makes the line metrical (in a different way) in *Later*. Here, Crane probably expanded an elision, as usual.

3.260/1447   Affections‸] CI RO • ~, MT BR • ~. C2+

3.261/1448   all on's] CI+ • all's one OK • all of us MT (*only*). OK must be an error of transposition of the terminal 's'; thus all texts except the autograph preserve a contraction that appears at least 20 times in 14 different Middleton plays. See 3.313.

3.266/1453   præsented] BR • prefented CI+

3.280/1467   ist] Ist C2 BR MT

3.284/1474   cheese‸] CI • ~; OK • ~, C4+

3.285-6/1475-6   Whitmeates...White] whitmeates...white NAS MSR. Contrast the initial letters with 'white' in 1472 and 'when' in 1486, and the other minim letters in 1475-6.

3.286/1476   I‸de] BR • I'de MT+. See 84.

3.287.1/1478   pawne] GT • Pawne CI+. See 1.353.

3.288/1479   youde] BR • you'll'd CI+ • you would MT (*only*)

3.291/1483   Im‸e] BR • Im'e MT OK RO • I am CI CMA. See 1184.

3.295/1487   smut thee‸] CI BR • ~. OK CMA • ~, MT+

3.296/1488   putt] GT • put CI+. See 378.

3.296/1488   snapt thee‸] CI C4 • ~, MT+

3.298/1490   putt] GT • put CI+. See 378.

3.300/1492   undonne] GT • vndon CI • undon BR MT • vndone OK CMA RO. Autograph contains no examples of 'undone'. Of the two alternatives, 'don' occurs five times, but none are unique. By contrast, 'donne' occurs twelve times, and six are unique to autograph (53, 1430, 1544, 1780, 2376).

3.300/1492   then‸] CI BR • ~; C4 • ~, MT+

3.301/1493   Im‸e] BR • Im'e MT+ • I am CI CMA. See 1184.

3.305/1497   puh] MT • pish CI CMA OK • push RO BR. The scene is not present in C2 C3. Only the autograph text preserves this characteristic Middletonian form of the interjection; see Induction.76.

3.309/1501   Blackberries‸] CI BR • ~, C4+

3.311/1503 Im‸e] BR • Im'e MT OK RO • I am CI CMA. See 1184.

3.312/1504 Ord‸narie] MT (*only*). This is unlikely to be an autograph minim error because—as Howard-Hill notes (1990, xvi)—Middleton's 'i' is 'invariably formed and dotted with precision'.

3.313/1506 on‸t] BR • out RO • on't CI+ • of it MT (*only*). A Middletonian elision, supported by all other witnesses. See 3.262. See the unique autograph 'ont' (without apostrophe) at 2156.

3.313/1506 ont‸] CI RO • ~, C4+. Comma probably related to mislineation.

3.316/1509 pawne] GT • Pawne CI+. See 1.353.

3.317/1510 3] BR RO • three CI+. For Middleton's preference for numerals see 2.208, See unique autograph '3d' (1359) and '3' (1831, 2208 MB, 2235 MB MT).

3.319/1512 Im‸e] BR • Imě MT RO OK • I am CRANE. See 1184.

3.327/1522 in‸] CI • ~. C2 C4 • ~: C3 • ~; BR • ~, MT+

3.339/1534 præsented] BR • prefented CI+. See Induction.67.

3.345/1540 putt] GT • put CI+. See 378.

3.346/1541 practise‸] ~, C2 C4 MT

*3.350-5/1546-51 Thou...seene:] CI (unindented) • indented C2+. Since Crane indents the lines in his other texts, and begins indenting them in CI with the third incantation, it seems clear that his copy did not indent them.

3.352/1548 th'] CI C2 C3 OK • the C4+

3.353/1549 uniuersall] CI • Vniuersall C2 C3 OK MT • vniuersall C4 RO BR. Initial 'u' is as typical of Middleton as anomalous for Crane.

3.357 ‸praye] 'pray CI C2 C3 • not in MT

3.357 praye] GT • pray CI+ • not in MT

3.357 praye‸] ~, BR • not in MT

3.357 an‸other] an other CI C2 C3 • not in MT

3.357 another,] RO • ~‸ BR • ~: C3 • ~. CI+ • not in MT. Crane's heavy punctuation is unlikely to be authorial; both RO and BR could be Middletonian, but the stemma provides little guidance in choosing between them. Unique autograph commas are five times likelier than unique autograph punctuationlessness at the end of a speech.

3.358 youre] BR • your CI+ • not in MT

3.358 will‸] BR • ~, RO • ~ OK • ~. CI+. Again, the stemma cannot adjudicate between BR and RO. Unique autograph punctuationlessness is twice as likely as unique autograph commas at line-ends.

*3.359-62/1554-7 I...same:] CI (unindented) • indented C2+. See note at 3.350-5.

3.360/1555 hower‸] CI C2 BR • ~. C3 • ~, C4 MT • ~: OK

3.361/1556 inuoke] CI RO • Inuoke C2+

3.361/1556 Name‸] ~, OK CMA MT

3.366-77/1562-73 Thou...place] GT • indented CI+. See note at 3.350-5.

3.366/1562 drawen] MT (*only*). MSR reads 'drawn' deliberately, noting but not accepting Nascimento's interpretation as 'drawen'. But for the handwriting compare 'drawen' at 465 (where the word also rhymes with 'pawne'): in both cases there is the characteristic minimal Middletonian 'e' between the very clear 'w' and the two minims of the 'n' (evident throughout these lines).

3.367/1563 to] CI • To C2+. See unique autograph 'to' at 1073 (not in *Early*) and 1831.

3.368/1562 thou] OK CMA BR RO • Thou MT corr, CI C2 C3 fh MT uncorr. The autograph majuscule covers the autograph false start. Elsewhere in autograph the pronoun begins with a majuscule only twice, both times as the first word of an invocation.

3.368/1564 ‸by...met‸] CMA • (~) CI+

3.383/1583 shadowe] Shadowe MT C2 C3

3.385/1586 certayntie] Certayntie MT C2 C3 Br

3.390/1591 hee‸s] GT • hee is MT+. See 1.203.

3.395/1596 i‸th‸] BR RO+ • i'th CI+ • in the MT (*only*)

3.397/1598 Knowe] knowe NAS MSR. Contrast 'like' and 'make' above and below on the same page.

3.398/1599 do's] MT • doth CI+. This would be the only instance of 'doth' in the entire text. Since 'doth' cannot be exclusive to the original version, and could easily be a Crane sophistication, the autograph—Middleton's strongly preferred form—has been preserved.

3.400 shees] RO • She's CI+ • not in MT

3.400 shees] BR RO OK • She's CI+ • not in MT

3.400 shee‸s] BR • She's CI+ • not in MT

3.400 w‸ch] BR RO • which CI+ • not in MT

4.1/1606 ha'] MT • haue CI+. The elision might easily have been eliminated by Crane.

4.4/1609 Knowen] knowne NAS MSR. Compare to 'Kᵗˢ' in the speech prefix.

4.4/1609 Knowen] GT • knowne CI+. See unique autograph 'knowen' at 578 1856 2372 (MT (*only*)) 2454 (MB MT), and parallel unique autograph 'growen', 'drawen', etc.

4.4/1609 Knowen by‸] CI • ~, c2+

4.6/1611 this] CI RO • This C2+. See unique autograph 'this' at 856 and 1112 (both at line beginning).

4.7/1612 præsident] BR • prefident MT+. See Induction.67.

4.12/1617 weere] GT • weère RO • we're CI • w'are CI • we are OK CMA • wee are BR • wee åre MT. Although MSR prints 'wee'are', Middleton separated 'wee' from 'are' with a blank space, treating them as distinct words, and placing the apostrophe over 'a' rather than in the space between 'e' and 'a'; contrast 'weare' (1622), where 'e' and 'a' are joined. This is, as MSR notes (p. xviii) the only autograph example of 'Jonsonian elision', where two words are written out in full with their intended contraction indicated by an apostrophe; but this anomaly could easily have resulted from Middleton following copy 'wee are' (as in BR), then retrospectively adding the apostrophe as a partial correction. Compare the unique autograph 'weere' at 2293 (MB).

4.12/1617 t'] to C4 RO MT

4.12/1617 to't] to it MT (*only*)

4.15/1620 putt] GT • put CI+. See 378.

4.18/1623 Marke] CI C2 • marke CMA+. See unique autograph 'Marke' (2452 MT). Autograph intentions here are ambiguous; although less unmistakably a majuscule than 'Marke' in the preceding line, the initial letter is much larger and more emphatic than the letter in preceding 'Trim' and 'formost' and following 'ambitious'.

4.24/1630 playe‸] CI OK • ~, c2+. Autograph comma probably related to mislineation.

4.25/1630 ‸Sⁱʳ,] CI • (~) c2+

4.27/1632 Game‸] CI • ~: c2 MT • ~. C4+

4.33/1637 make] MT RO CMA (c.w.) • Make CMA (text), CI+

4.33/1638 youre] NAS • your MSR. At 1.338/444 and 4.33/1638 (in both cases—as at MSR 455, for which there is no equivalent in CI—I read Middleton's normal 'youre' instead of 'your').

4.39/1645 politick] CI BR OK • politique c2+. See 488.

4.44/1651 præsented] BR • prefented CI+. See Induction.66.

4.61/1668 for‸t] BR • for't CI+. See 749.

4.69/1676 neglect] Neglect C2 C3 MT

4.70/1677 hin't] OK • hint CI+. Compare the unique, and similarly anomalous, autograph apostrophe in 'mean't' (2365 MB MT).

4.72/1679   Vnderstanding,] ~, c2 c4 OK MT

4.73/1680   ,till] CI (text), MT+ ● 'till CI (c.w.)

4.78/1685   you,re] you are MT (only)

4.78/1685   intoote] BR ● intot RO ● into it MT ● into't CI+. Compare unique autograph 'see'te' (422) and 'doo'te' (1770).

4.83/1690   it,s] Its CI c2 c3 ● i'ts CMA. See the discussion of Middleton's spelling of this word (with or without apostrophe) in Taylor and Jowett 196-8. To the examples there should be added Banquet 538, 1396, both 'its'.

4.85/1692   my] MT OK ● mine CI+

4.87/1694   Knowing] MT BR ● knowing MSR. Compare the first letter of 'Knowledge' in the preceding line.

4.88/1695   shee,s] BR ● shee̊s MT+. See 1.203.

4.90/1697   Im,e] GT ● Im'e CI+ ● I am c2 c4. See 1184.

4.90/1697   it,...ghesse,] OK BR ● ~:~, CI c2 ● ~,~, CMA MT RO. See text note at Later 4.1.77.

4.91/1698   for,] CI ● ~, c2+

4.101/1708   ,of...one,] (~) c2 c4 MT

4.103/1710   Wife] MT CI c2 c3 ● wife NAS MSR c4+. The initial letter is strikingly larger than the preceding 'will' and 'showe' (in the same line), or any other 'w' on this page except 'Wonder' (1699), which MSR reads as a majuscule.

4.103/1710   Wife] wife NAS MSR. The initial letter is strikingly larger than the preceding 'will' and 'showe' (in the same line), or any other 'w' on this page except 'Wonder' (1699), which MSR reads as a majuscule.

4.103/1710   Wife, Sr,] CI BR ● (~) c2+

4.109/1716   from,t] BR ● from it MT ● from't CI+. For the absent apostrophe compare the unique autograph 'fort' at 1045 and 2411.

4.110/1718   glasse now,] CI ● ~, c2+

4.113/1721   Im,e] BR ● Im'e MT+. See 1184.

4.113.1/1722   agayn,] NAS MSR. The uncharacteristically long horizontal bar to the right of 'n' might be an example of Middleton's minimalist terminal 'e'; contrast the terminal 'n' in the preceding 'proportion' 'in' 'on an' 'then' 'can' 'Creation'.

4.114/1724   wth,] ~, c3 c4 RO MT. Autograph comma probably related to mislineation.

4.117/1726   farder,] CI RO ● ~, BR ● ~(c2+

4.117/1726   S^ir,] BR ● ~. CI RO ● ~) c2+

4.119/1728   ld'e] MT+ ● I'had CI c2

4.120/1729   præsented] prefented CI+. See Induction.67.

4.121/1730   mee,] CI BR ● ~ (c2+

4.121/1730   S^ir,] BR ● ~. CI ● ~.) OK CMA ● ~) c2+

4.126/1735   lett] BR ● let CI+. See 64.

4.129/1738   ,S^ir,] BR ● (~) CI+

4.136/1745   Knowe] knowe NAS MSR. Contrast 'lockt' and 'speake' in the preceding and following line.

4.137/1746   truth] Truth c3 MT

4.137/1747   then,] ~, c4 MT OK. Autograph comma probably related to mislineation.

4.141/1750   Knowe] knowe NAS MSR. See 1745.

4.147/1756   weoman] GT ● woman MT+. See 599.

4.148/1757   weoman] GT ● woman MT+. See 599.

4.148/1757   ,Sir,] CI ● ,~, BR ● (~) c2+

4.152/1761   Im,e] BR ● Im'e CI+ ● I am c2 c3 ● I'am c4. See 1184.

4.154/1763   Knowe] knowe NAS MSR. The initial letter is actually larger and more prominent than in 'Knowledge' (four lines above), and than 'knowe' 'take' 'thinke' below.

4.155/1767   maye] NAS ● may MSR. The terminal 'e' is clearly visible.

4.162/1772   Spring,] CI BR RO ● ●: ● ~: c2 ● ~. c3 ● ~; c4 ● ~, MT OK

4.163/1773   youùe] OK (You'ue) ● y'haue CI ● yhaue BR ● you haue c3 c4 ● y'aue c2 RO MT

4.166/1776   you,re] OK (your) ● you're CI ● yåre c2 RO MT ● you are c2 c3 c4. The apostrophe is almost certainly Crane's addition: see unique autograph 'youre' at 1046 and 2118. Although 'y'are' appears 8 times in autograph, none of those are unique; all of them—like this reading—could result from passive acceptance of the form in Middleton's copy. By contrast, of the 7 examples of autograph 'you're', five are unique: that is, they do not appear in any witnesses except autograph ones. This strongly suggests that Middleton's personal preference was 'you're' (with or without the apostrophe). Every single example of 'y'are' in autograph is contradicted by at least one other authoritative text that contains 'you're': either CI or OK or both (both apparently copied from different autograph manuscripts, at the beginning and end of the chain of transmission). This conclusion is supported by the distribution of forms in Crane's transcripts. In the earliest transcript (CI), 'you'r(e)' appears 7 times, and 'y'ar(e)' only twice. By contrast, in the two manuscripts which in general show a much stronger array of Crane preferences (c2 and c3), 'you'r(e)' does not appear at all, and 'y'ar(e)' occurs 11 times. Whatever our hypotheses about the copy for these three manuscripts, Crane preferred 'y'ar(e)', and only the earliest of his surviving transcripts shows any tolerance for 'you're', a form which presumably appears in CI only because it stood in his copy. Likewise, in Webster's Duchess of Malfi (1623), apparently printed from a Crane transcript, 'you'r(e)' appears only once, by contrast to the six examples in Webster's White Devil, not associated with Crane. Both forms appear in plays of the Shakespeare folio associated with Crane, but since Shakespeare's own preference is unknown those plays provide uncertain evidence of Crane's preferences with this contraction. On the evidence of the eight Game witnesses, Middleton clearly preferred 'you're', but the various agents involved in transmitting his text preferred 'y'are'. This is typical of the period. Although autograph demonstrates that Middleton consistently preferred the spelling 'youre' for the possessive pronoun, that spelling never once occurs in the printed and scribal texts of the rest of his canon (and only 11 times in early modern printed plays). In the period 1580-1640 'y'ar(e)' was strongly preferred by authors, compositors, and scribes: it appears at least 1,946 times in surviving plays, against only 547 examples of 'you'r(e)'—and 98 of those 547 (18%) come from the Middleton canon. Moreover, examples of 'you'r(e)' strongly cluster at the end of the period (Glapthorne, Hausted, Killigrew, Lower, Rutter), and are much rarer before 1626: outside Middleton, only 15 plays contain 5 or more examples, and ten of those are late. By contrast, the Middleton canon alone contains ten plays with five or more examples: Puritan (5), Dissemblers (5), Game (5 in MT, 7 in OK), Phoenix (6), Witch (6), Mad World (7), Roaring Girl (7), Widow (9), Weapons (10), and Five Gallants (14). None of these totals can be due to Middleton's collaborators: outside their collaborations with Middleton, Dekker furnishes only two examples, and Rowley only four (all in the form 'you'r', which never appears in Middleton's autograph). Thus, Middleton alone personally contributed 40% of the plays with five or more examples, and 67% of the plays in his lifetime with five or more examples. Again, this evidence strongly confirms the autograph evidence of Middleton's unusual use of 'you're'. By contrast, at least 50 plays in the period contain five or more examples of 'y'ar(e)'. Of those, 19 do come from the Middleton canon, but seven of those are collaborative plays, and in six of them the form reflects someone else's demonstrable preference: Dekker in *Honest Whore* (28) and *Roaring Girl* (15), Rowley in *Weapons* (6), *Quarrel* (11), *Old Law* (10), and *Changeling* (20). Of the remaining 12, one is a Crane transcript (*Witch*, 5), and several scholars believe that another was printed from a Crane transcript (*Women Beware*, 33). Another survives only in a scribal copy (*Lady*, 14). Nine of the nineteen examples come from late printings (1647 and after). Thus, although it is possible that Middleton used both forms—both do appear in autograph in *Game*, and both do appear elsewhere in his canon—it is more likely that his relatively unusual early use of 'you(')re' was often sophisticated by copyists and compositors. In *Game*, since other texts copied from authorial manuscripts support the authorial preference 'you're', I have adopted it throughout *Early*. Notably, Middleton consistently kept to his preference in the first half of the text; 'y'are' only appears in the last 650 lines of MT, when he was demonstrably becoming tired and increasingly careless.

4.169/1779 **you‚re]** GT • you're OK • you'are C3 • yar'e MT C2 RO • you are C1 C4 BR. See preceding note.

4.177/1791 **i‚th‚]** BR RO • i'th' C1+ • in the MT. See the unique autograph 'ith', without apostrophes, at 2430 (MB MT).

4.180/1794 **e're]** RO (eř) • ere C1+. See 1207.

4.184/1798 **for‚t]** BR • for't C1+. See unique autograph 'fort' at 1045 and 2411.

4.185/1799 **toote]** BR • too't C1: to't C2+ tot RO • to it MT. See Induction.56.

4.185/1799 **S'ir]** Sir NAS MSR. Contrast 'Sin' two lines earlier, where the minims remain on the same horizontal level as the words before and after; here, 'ir' are clearly above that line.

4.188/1802 **I‚th‚]** C2 (i'th'), OK CMA (i'th‚) • in the C1+. For the unapostrophied form see 4.177.

4.192/1807 **soft‚]** ~, C4 MT

4.193/1808 **Im‚e]** BR RO • Im̃e MT C1 OK. See 1184.

4.194/1809 **Whitehouse]** whitehouse NAS MSR. Contrast 'wrought' 3 lines below.

4.202/1817 **io]** GT • IO RO • ten C1+. See 1283.

4.207/1822 **‚daughters]** C4 RO • (~ C1+

4.207/1822 **Seducement‚]** RO • ~, C4 • ~) C1+

4.211/1826 **rather‚]** C1 • ~, BR MT OK • ~. C2+

4.213/1828 **ha']** C1 • ha‚ RO BR OK • haue C2+. See the unique autograph 'ha'' (with apostrophe) at 1067 and 1606. See 1.278. The contraction is unlikely to be a Crane sophistication.

4.213/1828 **a‚th]** BR OK • a'th MT C1 C2 C3 RO • of the CMA

4.216/1831 **Matrons‚]** C1 C2 OK • ~, c3+

4.217/1832 **a‚th]** BR OK • o'th CRANE MT

4.217/1832 **I‚ue]** OK (I'ue) • I'haue C2 • I haue C1+

4.218/1833 **Whitehouse]** white house NAS MSR. Contrast with the medial 'w' in 'Whirlwinde' above and 'hallowed' below.

4.218/1833 **White‚house]** GT • White-house CRANE • white houſe RO+. For Middleton's preference for the unhyphenated single word see 1.308.

4.219/1834 **Pasties]** paſties MT OK BR. The majuscule is supported by 2 *Vox Populi*. In MT, the initial letter is not the unequivocal majuscule in 'Pedlars', but it is certainly more prominent than the same letter in 'Mothership' above or 'Shape' below.

4.220/1835 **Pardons]** pardons MT OK. The majuscule is suppor-

ted by 2 *Vox Populi*; OK uses minuscule for all the nouns in the line.

4.222/1837 **donne]** GT • don C1 C2 C3 BR MT • done OK CMA RO. See 1492.

4.223/1838 **conuayde]** BR • conuaied OK • conuayd C1 MT • conuaid C2 C3 RO • conuay'd CMA. All texts except BR end the word with 'd', so the MT spelling might easily reflect copy influence. The 'ayde' spelling occurs in autograph at 1406 and 1988.

4.223/1838 **roules]** RO OK • Roules MT+. The minuscule is supported by 2 *Vox Populi*.

4.223/1838 **balls]** RO (OK) • Balls C1+

4.224/1839 **politick]** BR • politicke OK • politique C1+. See 488.

4.225/1840 **gentleman]** 2 *Vox Populi* • Gentleman C1+

4.226/1841 **Park]** park OK MT. The majuscule is supported by 2 *Vox Populi*.

4.226/1841 **Keepers]** MT 2 *Vox Populi* • keepers C1+

4.226/1841 **huntsman]** BR OK 2 *Vox Populi* • Huntſman MT+

4.227/1842 **one]** RO BR 2 *Vox Populi* • One C1+

4.231/1846 **t']** to C4 RO MT

4.231/1846 **knowledge]** Knowledge BR MT. The minuscule in C1 reproduces that in Scott (Middleton's source, almost verbatim, for this passage).

4.232/1847 **Fortificatiō]** fortificatio MT RO OK. The majuscule is supported by 2 *Vox Populi*.

4.233/1848 **White]** white NAS MSR. Contrast the 'w' in 'Knowledge' above and below.

4.235/1850 **knowledge]** Knowledge BR MT

4.236/1851 **rocks]** MT • Rocks C1+ 2 *Vox Populi*

4.238/1853 **burden]** Burthen C1 C2 C3 MT. The minuscule is supported by 2 *Vox Populi*.

4.238/1853 **ship]** Ship CRANE MT. The minuscule is supported by 2 *Vox Populi*.

4.241/1856 **state]** C1 CMA 2 *Vox Populi* • State C2+

4.243/1858 **reuennues]** BR OK 2 *Vox Populi* • Reuenues C1+

4.248/1863 **sure]** Sure BR RO MT

4.248/1863 **putt]** GT • put C1+. See 378.

4.248/1863 **phisick,]** C1 • ~‚ BR • ~ (C2+

4.248/1863 **S'‚]** BR • ~: RO • ~. C1 • ~). C4 MT • ~) C2 C3 OK

4.248/1864 **Im‚e]** BR • Im'e MT C2 RO OK • I am C1 C3 C4. See 1184.

4.254/1869 **hee‚s]** BR • heês MT+. See 1.203.

4.255/1871 **here‚s]** BR (Hearcs) • her'es MT+. See Induction.9.

4.255/1871 **pœnitentiaria]** MT CRANE • penitentia BR RO • Penitentiaris OK. Only the Crane texts preserve the latinate autograph digraph.

4.255/1871 **pœnitentiaria]** Pœnitentia C1 • Penitentia BR RO. Eyeskip.

4.258/1874 **uppon‚t]** BR • uppo'nt MT+. See the unique autograph absence of punctuation with a contraction where the second element is 'it' at 1045, 2331 (MB MT), and 2411 (MT).

4.259/1875 **see't]** ſee it MT OK • feete BR. Compare *Trick* 5.1.18 'see'te'. The 'see't' form of the contraction appears more than 30 times in the Middleton canon.

4.260/1876 **ha's]** OK • has MT+. See 440.

4.260/1876 **donne]** GT • don C1+ • done OK CMA. See 1492.

4.262/1878 **13]** OK • thirteene C1+

4.262/1878 **4]** OK • fowre C1+. See 1046.

4.263/1881 **here‚s]** BR RO • here's C1+. See Induction.9.

4.268/1884 **Adult‚rie]** C1 • Adulterie C2+

4.268/1884 **Im‚e]** BR • Im'e MT RO OK. See 1184.

4.269/1885 **2]** GT • two C1. See 710, and the unique autograph '2' in the next line.

4.269/1885 **fiue‚pence]** GT • fiue pence C1+. Compare 1879, where only autograph treats 'sixepence' as a single unhyphenated word (which in both cases throws the stress onto the first syllable, as metre requires, rather than the spondee or iamb of two separate monosyllables).

4.270/1886　these] theis CI C2 C3 ● thofe MT RO

4.271/1887　him selfe] himselfe NAS MSR. As elsewhere, the two words are clearly separated.

4.273/1888-9　33] RO ● thirtie three CI+ ● thirteene C2 C3 ● thirtie 3 BR. See 1510.

4.274/1890　the] CI RO ● The C2+. See unique autograph 'the' at the beginning of lines 1754 and 2237 (MT MB). Autograph uniquely begins a verse line with a minuscule 43 times.

4.275/1891　y'aue] C2 (You'haue) ● You haue CI+

4.275/1891　ₐSir,] CI BR ● (~) C2+

4.278/1894　9] RO ● nine CI+

4.279/1897　putt] GT ● put CI+. See 378.

4.281/1899　there,s] BR RO ● there's CI+. See 71.

4.281/1899　on 's] MT+ ● ons BR ● ones RO. There are no unique autograph parallels either way.

4.281/1899　forward,] CI C4 BR ● ~, RO ● ~ (C2+

4.281/1899　Sir] Sir NAS MSR

4.281/1899　Sir,] CI ● ~,) MT ● ~) C2 C3 OK ● ~. C4 ● ~, RO BR

4.282/1900　here,] CI BR ● ~, RO ● ~ (C2+

4.282/1900　Sir;] RO ● ~, BR ● ~) C2 C3 C4 MT ● ~? CI C2 C3 OK

4.284/1903　gratuitie] Gratuitie C3 C4 BR MT

4.291/1911　io] GT ● ten CI+. See 1283.

4.291/1912　Vse] vse NAS MSR. The reading 'vse' would be the only minuscule 'v' in the entire manuscript, and since it is larger than surrounding minuscules and as large as other examples of the letter that MSR interprets as majuscule, I read 'Vse'.

4.293/1914　Conscience,] CI ● ~? C2 C3 C4 RO ● ~ₐ MT BR OK

4.293/1914　ₐworthie] CMA ● (~ CI+

4.293/1914　Holines,] CMA ● ~) CI+

4.299/1920　there,s] RO BR ● there's CI+. See 71.

4.300/1921　Kill] kill NAS MSR. Contrast 'ducketts' above and 'pickt' below, and see unique autograph 'Kild' (2251).

4.301/1922　there,s] BR (Theres) ● there's CI+. See 71.

4.301/1922　præsident] GT ● prefident CI+. See Induction.67.

4.304/1926　him,] CI ● ~. MT. Only in these two texts does this line end the speech, and MT omits the exit. BR lacks punctuation at the end of both lines. Unique autograph full stops are very rare; the speech ends with a full stop in C3 C4 OK RO MT.

4.305/1928　wheres youre] NAS ● wheres your MSR. The terminal 'e' is not disputable.

4.310/1934　Sir] not in MT. Middleton normally raises the last two letters; the other witnesses do not.

4.310/1934　, Sir,] BR ● (~) CI+. Vocative not present in MT C3 OK.

4.313/1936　Eagle ₐ pride] ~-~ C2 C3 MT

4.313/1936　pride] Pride C3 MSR. Although MT may intend a majuscule, the letter is not much different than in 'puzzle' and 'surprizall'; even if a majuscule was intended in that manuscript, Middleton's first draft almost certainly had a minuscule, or we would expect Crane to have reproduced the majuscule for the noun.

4.316/1950　lett] BR (Lett) ● let CI+. See 64.

4.317/1951　truth] Truth C3 MT

4.317/1951　Plotts] CI C2 C3 RO BR ● Plots OK CMA MT. See 1217. The shorter autograph spelling here may be due to the fact that that word crosses the frame-line of the page.

4.318/1952　grou,ling] OK (grauling) ● groueling CI+

4.320/1954　ha's] OK ● has CI+. See 440.

4.324/1958　e're] OK ● ere CI+. See 1207.

4.326/1960　heauen] Heauen C2 OK MT

4.327/1961　looke] CI ● Looke C2+. See unique autograph 'looke' 818 (also begins line).

4.347　youre] GT ● your CI+ ● not in MT RO BR

4.349/1982　3 score] BR ● three score CI+ ● 60 RO. See 1510.

4.352/1985　promist] GT ● promifd CI+ ● promifde BR. See the unique authorial 'promist' at 1831. The only other autograph example of a word ending '-isd' (or '-is'd') is 'deuisde' (1475), which suggests that BR's spelling might be authorial. But autograph has 'promist' two other times (377, 447), and also 'mist' (508).

4.361/1994　ha's] MT OK BR RO ● has CI (text) ● hath CI (catchword), C2 C3 C4. The disparity between text and catchword provides an excellent example of Crane's normalizing of the text, in progress (and completed in the three other Crane texts).

4.365/1998　ner'e] GT ● nere CI+. See 1290.

4.365.1-4.428　Enter...exeunt] not in MT. In the absence of any autograph text for these lines, the copy-text is BR, and all departures from it are collated. See headnote.

4.365.1　Q.] C4 ● Queene CI+

4.366　my loue] RO ● My ~ CI+

4.367　amongst] a mongst BR

4.367　ones] ons BR

4.368　Extreamitie] CMA ● Extremitie CI+

4.368　ₐlike] OK CMA ● (~ CI+

4.370　like] C2 ● CI+

4.371　interposde,] OK ● ~) CI+

4.373　loue,] OK CMA ● ~, CI+

*4.375　black,house] Black-House CI. See unique autograph 'Blackhouse' (one word, no hyphen) at 774, 1309. The only autograph examples of hyphenated 'Black-house' (99, 427, 1550) are probably inherited from Crane.

4.375　watcht] CMA RO ● wachd BR ● watchd CI C2 C3

4.376　th'] the CI RO BR

4.376　playe] GT ● plaie BR ● Play CI+

4.377　Ime] I am CRANE

4.377　besett] CI RO ● besette BR

4.377　distrest] GT ● Distresd BR ● distreffd CI

4.378　waye] GT ● way CI+

4.380　Queene] queene BR RO

4.380　downe:] C3 ● ~. CI+

4.383　Vertue] CRANE ● vertu BR. Middleton prefers the initial majuscule.

4.384　Inflammation] Inflamation CI+

4.384　instantlie] instantly CI+

4.386　deflower] OK ● deflowre CI+. Autograph never uses the '-owre', preferring 'flower' ('hower,' 'power,' 'tower'), regardless of the required pronunciation.

4.386　not—] RO CMA ● ~. CI+

4.387　streight] ftraight BR RO. See autograph 'streight' (1669). There is no parallel for the 'a' spelling.

4.389　Deuills] CI C2 C3 ● Diuills BR

4.389　Deuill,s] Deuill's CI C2 C3

4.389　Ime] I'am CI

4.390　stood,] stoode BR

4.390　sawe] sowe BR

4.391　lookte] GT ● lookt OK CMA RO BR ● lookd CI+

4.392　aymde] aimde BR ● aim'd RO ● aym'd CI+

4.392　Queene] queene BR

4.393　glorie] ylorie BR

4.393　Game] game RO BR. See 2144.

4.394　waye] GT ● way CI+

4.394　Mr] GT ● Master CI+

4.394　Mr:check] GT ● ~ₐ~ BR RO ● Master- CI+. See 2284.

4.396 Vertue] CRANE • vertu BR

4.397 oh‚] CI C2 CMA RO • ~, c3 OK • ~: BR. Autograph never has any punctuation immediately after 'oh'.

4.399 no longer] nolonger BR

4.400 the] RO • The CI+

4.403 donne] GT • don CI+ • done OK CMA RO. See 1492.

4.404 worthie] CI C2 c3 • worthy BR+

4.404 fayre] GT • faire CI+

4.406 Sonne] CMA OK RO • Son CI+

4.408 destroyde] Deſtroide BR • Deſtroyd c2

4.408 destroyde] Deſtroide BR • deſtroid CI

4.408 i‚th‚] RO BR • i'th CI c4 • i'th' c2 • in the OK

4.409 twere] tware BR

4.410 Verminous] CI C2 c3 • verminous BR+

4.411 putts] CI C2 RO • puts c3+

4.412 Bagg] GT • Bagge BR • Bag CI+

4.413 no] c2 c3 RO • No CI+

4.415 2] GT • Two CI+. See 710.

4.415 princelye] OK RO • Princely CI+. See 140.

4.415 thy‚] ~, BR

4.417 Vertues] CI C2 c3 • vertues BR+

4.418 untruths] GT • Vntruthes CI C2 c3 • vntruths BR+. Autograph occasionally has majuscule for the prefix 'un', but minuscule is more common.

4.418 agaynst] GT • againſt CI+

4.423 stayde] GT • ſtaid CRANE • ſtayd OK • ſtaide BR. There are no parallels in autograph for 'aid', but autograph does contain many examples of past participial layde, sayde, afrayde, unlayde, betrayde, payde, conuayde, playde, and overlayde. The only parallel for OK's spelling (without terminal 'e') is a single 'conuayd' (1838), probably reproduced from copy.

4.424 too much] toomuch BR

4.425 the‚re] theire BR. Compare 714 ('theire' in BR, 'there' in autograph in CI and MT, and all other texts). The BR spelling never occurs with this meaning in autograph.

4.428 putt] GT • put CI+. See 378.

4.428 agen] a gen BR

5.1–10/2017–27 Si…congratulamur] See General Textual Introduction, Sec. IV. Unless otherwise noted, Middleton's Latin source (STC 12357) is the copy-text for incidentals; all departures from it are collated.

5.1/2017 mortalibus‚] ~, OK CMA

5.1/2017 unquam] Vnquam c2 c3 • vnquam OK CMA

5.1/2017 oculis] Oculis CI C2 c3 MT. Although CI in spelling and punctuation more closely resembles the source than any other text of *Game*, as always Crane multiplied the number of initial majuscules he found in his copy—although CI (with eleven) has fewer such additions than any other Crane text (c2 sixteen, c3 seventeen, c4 twelve). It is possible that the majuscule originated with Middleton, but more likely that autograph here simply perpetuates Crane's fondness for them. (Bawcutt mistranscribes c2 as minuscule.)

5.1/2017 hilarem‚] ~, c2 c3

5.2/2018 diem] Diem c2 c3 BR

5.2/2018 diem,] ~: c2 OK CMA

5.2/2018 si] Si CRANE OK

5.2/2018 amicorum] MT RO • Amicorum CI+. Not in the source.

5.3/2019 animis] Animis c2 c3 OK CMA

5.3/2019 animis‚] ~, RO

5.3/2019 gaudium] Gaudium c3

5.3/2019 attulit,] ~‚ OK

5.3/2019 peperituè] peperitue RO BR • peperitùe CMA • peperitùr OK. Both quartos misplace the accent; OK is farther from the source.

5.3/2019 lætitiam] MT RO • Laetitiam CI+

5.3/2019 lætitiam‚] ~, RO. Although the source contains a comma after this word, Middleton here skips over nineteen words to a bracketed vocative phrase, so it is not at all clear that the source comma should be retained. (This variant has not been counted in the totals.)

5.3/2019 (Eques] The source places within brackets the vocative phrase '(clarissime & serenissime Princeps)' just before the word 'fœlicem'. Middleton's parallel vocative—substituting 'Eques' (= Knight) for 'Princeps' (= Prince) and using two adjectives that instead emphasize his whiteness—is placed just before the same word 'fœlicem', and is also in brackets.

5.3/2019 Eques] eques RO. 'Princeps' in the source.

5.4/2020 Candidissime] CI C2 c3 MT • candidissime CMA OK RO BR

5.4/2020 Candidissime‚ prælucentissime)] ~-~) c2 c3 BR • ~)~‚ OK CMA. The hyphen is unnecessary but not misleading, since it joins two adjectives that belong together; the quartos instead erroneously place the closing bracket so that it separates the two adjectives from each other. The presence of a punctuation mark after the first adjective links the quarto error to the earlier Crane texts. Moreover, Middleton's source on eight other occasions places within brackets the word 'Princeps' preceded or followed by an adjective (including '*prælucentissime Princeps*' on p. 30).

5.4/2020 fœlicem] faelicem NAS • fælicem MSR. MSR notes that 'The shapes of the "æ" and "œ" digraphs do not always indicate clearly which of the two forms was intended, but some guidance may be derived from the etymology of the words concerned' (xxii). The ambiguity here attributed to Middleton in particular is characteristic of all the witnesses. However, Middleton's source very clearly distinguishes between 'lætitiam' and 'fœlicem', and I have therefore interpreted the ambiguous digraph here as 'œ'.

5.4/2020 profectò] CI C2 c3 • profecto CMA+

5.4/2020 tuum] Tuum c2 c3

5.4/2020 tuum] tuũ MT (due to crowding of margin)

5.5/2021 domo] MT RO • Domo CI+. The parallel nouns in the source are 'Hesperias' and 'Hispaniam', so the majuscules in CI and other texts may well reflect Middleton's original draft. However, since the source does not contain the same wording, since its proper nouns may not be comparable, and since Crane obviously added majuscules, the autograph minuscule has been given the benefit of the doubt.

5.5/2021 Candoris‚] ~, CI C2 c3. Not in source.

5.5/2021 domum] MT RO BR • Domum CI+. See note above on 'domo'.

5.5/2021 domum] domam BR *uncorr.*

5.5/2021 Nigritudinis] Nigritutidinis MT (*only*). Not in source.

5.5/2021 accessum] MT RO • Accessum CI+

5.5/2021–2 accessum] acceſ= | acceſsum MT (*only*). Not in the source. Dittography across the line-break.

5.5/2022 accessum,] ~‚ OK CMA RO MT • ~₅ BR

5.6/2022 promisisse] promimiſliſſe OK CMA • Pro= | mi ſiſse BR. Another shared quarto error.

5.6/2022 promisisse] ~‚ BR

5.6/2022 peperisse] Peperiſſe BR

5.6/2022 attulisse‚] None of the eight witnesses contains the source's comma, which was probably omitted by Middleton himself.

5.6/2022 fatemur.] ~; CMA • ~: OK • ~, RO BR MT

5.6/2023 Omnes] omnes BR. There is no exact equivalent in the source for this phrase, which begins a new sentence in *Game*, and therefore occupies the same grammatical position as 'Omni' in the source.

5.7/2023 aduentus] Aduentus C1 C2 C3 BR

5.7/2023 tui] Tui C1 C2 C3 OK CMA ('tibi' in source)

5.7/2023 conflagrantissimi,] ~ₐ R. This phrase is not in the source.

5.7/2023 Omni] C2 C3 MT ● omni C1+. See 'Omnes' above. Because of the addition, 'omni' does not begin a new sentence in *Game*; the source, in comparable subsequent positions, has 'omnia' (twice).

5.7/2023 Omni quâ] C1+. The source has 'quâ', but Middleton might have been responsible for the indifferent variant.

5.7/2024 possumus,] C1 ● ~ₐ C2+

5.8/2024 lætitiâ] Laetitia C1 C2 C3 MT

5.8/2024 lætitiâ] Loetitio C1 ● letitiæ BR. The last letter in C1 presumably resulted from simple misreading of Crane's copy. No *Game* text preserves the accent.

5.8/2024 gaudio] Gaudio C2 C3 OK CMA

5.8/2024 congratulatione] Congratulatione C2 C3 OK CMA

5.8/2024 congratulatione,] ~ₐ BR

5.8/2024-5 acclamatione] RO ● Acclamatione C1+

5.8/2024-5 acclamatione,] ~ₐ OK CMA

5.8/2025 animis] RO ● Animis C1+

5.9/2025 obseruantissimis] Obseruantiſsimis MT C2. In both texts the initial letter is smaller than some other majuscules ('Omnes') but larger than normal mid-word 'o'; the intention is ambiguous.

5.9/2025 obseruantissimis,] ~ₐ C3 BR

5.9/2025 affectibus] C1 ● Affectibus C2+

5.9/2025 affectibus] Affectibur MT (*only*)

5.9/2025-6 diuotissimis] Diuotiſsimis BR

5.9/2026 obsequiis] Obsequijs C1 C2 C3

5.9/2026 obsequiis] MT ● obsequijs C1+. Autograph agrees with the source, which has '*obsequiis*' (the terminal *is* ligature being clear under magnification). Crane imposed the more normal 'ij' formula used with doubled 'i'. The intention of BR is not absolutely clear: the penultimate letter is probably an 'i' (as THH transcribes it) but it does extend lower than the preceding letter.

5.10/2026 uenerabundis] GT ● venerabundis C1 RO BR ● Venerabundis C2+. Middleton normally uses 'u' for the minuscule 'v' found here in the source.

5.10/2026 uenerabundis,] RO ● ~ₐ C1+. The different sentence structure in the source may account for this variant, but in the parallel phrase 'affectibus diuotissimis' all *Game* texts reproduce the source's comma.

5.10/2026 te] Te C1 C2 C3 OK CMA ('tuum' in source)

5.10/2026 sospitem] Sospitem C1 C2 C3 OK CMA ● ſcoſpitem BR

5.10/2026 sospitem] Soſpitim OK CMA. Another shared quarto error.

5.10/2026 sospitem,] ~, RO

5.10/2026-7 congratulamur] congratulamor BR

5.10/2026-7 congratulamor.] ~; BR ● ~? OK

5.14-23 wh.Kᵗ· tis ... Donation | Bl.Kᵗ·] *not in* MT. The copy-text for incidentals is therefore BR.

5.14 acknowledgd,ₐ] ~, (C1 CMA BR ● ~ₐ(C2+. The vocative parentheses are probably Crane's addition, repeated in all subsequent texts.

5.14 Royall,] Ryall, BR ● royoll (OK

5.14 Sⁱʳ] GT ● ~) C1+

5.15 rarities, delights] RO ● Rarities, Delights C1+

5.16 thinke] OK CMA ● thinck C1+

5.17 fayre] GT ● faire C1+

5.18 circuit] OK CMA ● Circuit C1 C2 ● circle BR RO

5.19 black,] ~- C1 C2 C3 BR

5.19 Kingdome] kingdome BR

5.19 theyre] RO ● they're C1 ● they are C2+. For the form without apostrophe see unique autograph 'theyde' (20), 'theyue' (438), and 'youde' (2421 MT).

5.26/2034 t'] to MT RO

5.28/2036 there,ₛ] BR ● ther'es MT+. See 71.

5.30/2037 th'] C3 ● the' C1 ● the C2+

5.41-2 Bl.Kᵗ· ... waye;] *not in* MT. The copy-text for incidentals is BR.

5.41 a] GT ● A C1+ ● *not in* MT. Scribe B in BR routinely begins verse lines and speeches with a majuscule.

5.44/2053 Nights,] C1 BR ● ~. C2+

5.45/2056 tryall] MB C1 OK RO ● Triäll MT C2 C3 C4. From here to the end of the play BR is also autograph, and identified as MB. See headnote.

5.45/2056 tryall] MB (*only*)

5.46/2057 and] & RO MB

5.47/2058 mee !] MT ● ~; MB C1 CMA

5.49/2061 agen,] MT ● ~ ? C1+

5.49/2061 Traytor] OK CMA ● Traitoʳ C1+ ● *not in* MB MT RO

5.49/2061 Holines] CMA ● Holineſſe OK ● Holynes C1 C2 C3 ● *not in* MB MT RO. Middleton used majuscule as often as the minuscule, and there are no unique authorial parallels to determine his preference of minuscule or majuscule for this word.

5.49/2061 Holines,] C2 OK ● ~: C1 ●) C3 ● ~? CMA

5.50/2062 oh] o RO MB. Middleton overwhelmingly prefers the longer spelling.

5.50/2062 marble] Marble MT C3

5.50/2062 marble,] ~-Fronted MB C2

5.50/2062 Impudence!] RO MB ● ~, MT+

5.50/2062 Knowes] MB ● knowes MT+. Although THH interprets MB as minuscule, it is actually larger than the letter in 'Kindnes' in MT, four lines below. See 5.54. MT here may also intend a majuscule, in contrast with undisputable cases of the minuscule elsewhere on the same page, but it is more ambiguous. A number of unique autograph uses of initial majuscules are verbs.

5.51/2063 ₐha's] MB C1 ● hee has MT ● has RO ● 'has OK ● 'hath C2 C3 C4

5.51/2063 usde] GT ● vſd C1+ ● wrongd MB MT RO

5.51/2063 Im,e] GT ● Imͤe MT MB C2 C3 RO OK ● I am C1 C4. See 1184.

5.51/2064 not,] MT ● ~; RO MB

5.52/2065 anie] MB ● anye MT ● any C1+. In terms both of raw totals and of unique autograph spellings, Middleton preferred 'anie'. The alternative 'anye' might in part be a response to 'any' in his copy.

5.52/2065 Weomans] MB C1 L, M ● womans CMA RO MT OK

5.52/2065 Weomans] GT ● Womans C1+. See 599.

5.53/2066 You] MB ● you MT+. Although THH interprets MB as minuscule, it contrasts clearly not only with MT, but with 'you', 'yet' 'youre' and 'youre' in the same speech. Even in Howard-Hill's transcriptions, there are at least five cases of autograph 'You' elsewhere (not counting those at the beginning of lines and speeches). There's another unique MB example at 5.60.

5.53/2066 M,ris] MB ● Mistris MT+

5.53/2066 deuotion] MT OK CMA ● devotion MB C1 C2 C3 RO. Among the manuscripts only MT preserves this spelling. The medial 'v' is the only exception to Middleton's otherwise consistent autograph practice (MSR, xv), and is almost certainly evidence of copy influence.

5.54/2067 **Kindnes**] MB MT. Although THH interprets MB as minuscule, it is actually larger and more distinctive than MT's letter; both contrast with the 'k' in 'fake' (2069) and 'speake' (2073).

5.55/2068 **Loue**] loue MB RO. See unique autograph 'Loue' at 2056 (MB MT).

5.55/2068 **Suffrer**] fufferer MT RO OK CMA

5.55/2068 **yet**] Yet RO MB

5.55/2068 **yet_A**] ~? MB C2 C3 RO

5.56/2069 **onelie;**] MT ● ~: CI ● ~? MB+

5.57/2070 **S^ir**] Sir NAS MSR

5.57/2070 **reuerend**] Reverend c3 (adjective) ● Reuerence MT (noun)

5.57/2070 **respect**] Respect C2 C3 MT

5.58/2071 **mee_A**] MB ● ~, MT ● ~) CI+

5.59/2072 **uowde**] MT ● Vowde MB ● vowd CI C2 C3 ● vow'd OK CMA ● vowed R

5.59/2072 **Liuerie**] MB CRANE ● liuerie MT+. Although MB is unmistakably majuscule, MT's intention is ambiguous: the letter clearly is more like the majuscule in 'Language' than like the minuscule in 'onelie' above or 'counsell' and 'should' below.

5.59/2072 **Liuerie_A**] MT ● ~, MB+ ● ~: C2

5.60/2073 **if**] MB CI (yf), RO ● If MT C2 (OK CMA)

5.60/2073 **you _AYou**] MB ● ~, you MT+

5.61/2074 **habit_A**] MB ● ~, MT+

5.62/2075 **you!**] MB ● ~, MT OK ● ~: CI

5.63/2076 **Worlds**] MT MB ● world THH (MB). Contrast MB with 'how' and 'wth' just before, and 'wth' just after; the letter is actually larger than that in MT.

5.63/2076 **World_As**] MB CMA RO ● World's MT+. Unique autograph readings often eliminate the apostrophe when a compound elides the verb 'is' (theres, tis, thats, twas, heres, whats, worths, alls, hopes).

5.64/2077 **youde**] Youde MB C3 OK CMA ● you'de THH (MB). Contrast MB with MT, and with the preceding 'you', 'playde', and the following 'yours'.

5.64/2077 **you_Ade**] RO ● you'de MT+. Compare unique autograph 'youde' (2421 MT), 'theyde' (20) and 'youre' (1046, 2118 MB).

5.65/2078 **deuills**] MB ● Deuills MT+. In the previous line both autograph texts are unique in beginning 'deuill' with a minuscule.

5.65/2078 **shape_A**] MB CMA ● ~, MT+

5.66/2079 **yours_A**] MB RO ● ~, MT+

5.67/2080 **youde**] MB RO (yould) ● Yo'ude MT. Howard-Hill (MSR and THH) interprets both initial letters as minuscule, but contrast the immediately preceding word 'yours' and immediately following 'rayle'.

5.67/2080 **youde**] MB RO (yould) ● Yo'ude MT+. Middleton's preference in unique autograph spellings is to omit the apostrophe in contractions of two words (precisely where modern orthography uses it).

5.67/2080 **Absurditie**] MT CI C2 C3 ● abfurditie MB+. Here and elsewhere, where there is no reliable evidence of Middleton's preferences in relation to a specific form, but when one autograph agrees with CI that autograph's choice is preferred, on the grounds that neither autograph is at all likely to derive directly from CI C2 C3. Hence, the majuscule is likely to represent a deliberate authorial restoration.

5.68/2081 **decorums**] MT CI RO ● Decorums MB+

5.68/2081 **then_A**] MB OK ● ~, MT+

5.69/2082 **Sacred**] MB ● sacred MT+

5.70/2083 **youle**] MB RO ● youle MT+

5.71/2084 **lett**] MB ● let MT+. The doubled consonant appears 13 times elsewhere in autograph in this word; there are many unique autograph examples of doubled terminal consonants.

5.72/2085 **Goodnes**] MB CI C2 C3 ● goodnes MT+. Middleton uses both, but prefers the majuscule.

5.73/2086 **habit_A**] MB ● ~, MT+

5.74/2087 **fitted_A**] MT ● ~, MB+

5.75/2088 **Knowe**] knowe NAS MSR. Contrast 'speake' above and 'make' below, in both autograph texts.

5.75/2088 **Iudgments**] MB+ ● *not in* MT

5.76/2089 **else_A**] MB ● ~, MT OK RO ● ~; CI

5.77/2090 **deceaue**] MB ● deceiue MT+

5.78/2091 **naye_A**] MB CMA OK RO naye, MT CI C2

5.79/2092 **Assemblie**] MT ● Assemblye MB ● Assembly CI+. The MB spelling appears nowhere else in autograph; the MT spelling occurs four times, including the unique autograph 'assemblie' (2451, MB MT).

5.80/2093 **you_A**] MT CI RO ● You_A MB C2 (OK CMA). MT is ambiguous: the initial letter is smaller and less distinctive than in MB, but looks majuscule if compared with the preceding 'naye' and 'they' or following 'playe' and 'you'.

5.80/2093 **mee_A**] MB ● ~, MT+

5.80/2093 **Loue**] MB CI ● loue MT+. See 5.55 (and Middleton's often-unique use of majuscules to begin verbs).

5.80/2093 **you;**] MT ● ~, RO MB ● ~. CMA OK

5.81/2094 **smile_A**] MB CI RO ● ~, MT ● ~ (C2+

5.81/2094 **S^ir;?**] MT ● ~? MB CI C2 C3 RO

5.82/2095 **th'**] MB+ ● the MT CI

5.83/2097 **youth**] Youth MB C2 CMA. In OK and RO all three nouns begin with a minuscule; in C2 and MB all three with a majuscule; in CMA only the first begins with a minuscule.

5.84/2098 **Knowing**] MT C3 ● knowing MB+ ● knowing NAS MSR. Compare with 'make' in the preceding line: MB is almost identical, whereas MT is strikingly different.

5.85/2099 **You**] MB ● you CI+

5.85/2099 **Frends**] MT CI C2 C3 frends MB+. See 5.67.

5.85/2099 **comfort_A**] MB ● ~, MT+

5.86/2100 **Weaknes,**] MT ● ~; RO MB ● ~. CI

5.87/2101 **so**] MB CI C2 C3 ● So MT RO (OK CMA). In terms both of raw totals and of unique autograph variants, Middleton preferred to begin speeches with a minuscule; Crane would probably have used a majuscule if there had been one in his copy.

5.87/2101 **hott**] MB CI C2 ● hot MT+. Autograph often uniquely doubles terminal -t.

5.87/2101 **hott-burning**] MT CI ● ~_A~ MB+

5.89/2103 **hell**] Hell MB C2 C3 OK

5.89/2103 **hell;**] ~; MB ● ~_A MT CMA ● ~. CI+

5.90/2104 **dish**] Dish MT C2 C3. With nouns (where Crane tends to add emphasis majuscules), if one autograph agrees with CI in a minuscule, I have preferred the CI reading.

5.91/2105 **Wch**] MB ● (OK CMA) ● wch MT+

5.91/2105 **Betters**] MT CI C2 C3 ● betters MB+

5.91/2105 **Betters_A**] MB ● ~, MT C3 ● ~) CI+

5.93/2107 **'hope**] MB CI ● _A~ MT RO ● I hope C2 C3 C4 OK

5.93/2107 **you;**] MB ● ~, RO MT ● ~? CI

5.94/2108 **there_As**] GT ● there's CI+. See 71.

5.94/2108 **rellish**] Rellish MB C2 C3 C4

5.94/2108 **office;**] MB ● ~, MT ● ~. RO ● ~_A CI

5.95/2109 **strange!?**] MB RO ● ~_A MT OK CMA ● ~: CI

5.95/2109 **him_A**] MB CI ● ~, MT RO

5.96/2110   t'] CI C2 C3 ● to C4+

5.96/2110   Knott] MT ● Knot MB (RO CRANE ● knote OK. Another uniquely doubled terminal -t.

5.97/2111   busines] OK CMA RO ● Bufynes CI C2 C3 ● office MT MB. The parallel noun in both autograph texts begins with a minuscule, thus tending to confirm that the initial majuscule represents Crane's habit, not Middleton's.

5.97/2111   ‸Sⁱʳ?] CI ● (~) MB+ ● ?‸‸‸ MT

5.97/2111   Sⁱʳ] MB ● not in MT ● Sir CI+

5.98/2112   Token;] MB ● ~‸ MT ● ~. CI ● ● ~: C2 ● ~, RO

5.99/2113   Sⁱʳ;] MT ● sir MB RO OK ● Sir CRANE

5.99/2113   Sⁱʳ;—] MB ● ~‸^ MT ● ~: CI ● ~) C2+

5.100/2114   youre] GT ● you're CI OK ● ya're MT MB ● y'ar C2 C3 ● yare RO ● you are CMA. See 4.166.

5.100/2114   hope‸s] hope's MB CI C2 C3. Compare unique autograph 'hopes' at 2405.

5.100/2114   you‸] MB CI ● ~, MT RO

5.101/2115   You'le] MB (OK CMA) ● you'le MT+. Although probably a minuscule, MT's letter is larger than those in the preceding 'y'are' and 'you', and the following 'you' and 'tye' and 'anye'. The non-authorial manuscripts all use the minuscule; MB is either unique among the manuscripts, or both autographs are unique.

5.101/2115   Knott] MT ● Knot MB+. See 5.96.

5.101/2115   once‸] MB ● ~, MT RO CI

5.102/2116   by] CI ● Wth MB (OK CMA) ● wth MT+. Although for the revised text MB's unique majuscule would be preferred, there are no autograph examples of 'By'.

5.102/2116   sollicitng] Solliciting MT C2 C3

5.103/2117   Craft‸s] Craft's CI C2 C3

5.103/2117   Knitt] MB ● knit MT+. Middleton's unusual use of majuscules to begin verbs.

5.103/2117   Knitt] MB CI C2 ● knit MT+. Another terminal double -t.

5.104/2118   you‸re all] MB ● youre ~ MT ● you'r ~ CI ● you'are ~ C2 ● y'are ~ RO ● You are ~ C3 C4 OK. Of texts with the contracted form, only MB lacks an apostrophe. See 4.166.

5.104/2118   market‸] MB ● ~, MT RO ● ~: CI

5.105/2119   marrier‸] MB RO OK ● ~, MT CRANE

5.105/2119   man‸] MB ● ~, MT RO ● ~; CI

5.105, 106/2119, 2120   Knowe] MB ● knowe MT+. Unusual majuscule to begin a verb.

5.106/2120   Nice] nice MB RO C3 OK

5.106/2120   Iniquitie,] MT CI ● ~?RO MB

5.106/2120   Luxurie‸] MB ● ~, MT CI

5.107/2121   Whoredome‸] MT ● ~, MB CI RO

5.107/2121   Marriage] marriage RO MB

5.108/2122   Wth] MB (OK CMA) ● wth MT+

5.109/2123   see] MT RO ● See MB+

5.110/2124   Mayde,] MB ● ~‸ MT RO ● ~: CI

5.110/2124   youre] GT ● you'r OK ● ya're MB MT ● y'ar CI C3 ● you are CMA RO. OK. See 4.166.

5.112/2126   I‸m‸e] MT ● Im'e MB OK RO ● I'am CI ● I am MT+. Elsewhere in CI Crane expands Middleton's contraction nine times. The contraction (indicated by the Jonsonian elision 'I'am') here reverses Crane's normal practice (demonstrated in C2 C3 C4), and is supported by an autograph text. For removal of the apostrophe, see 1184.

5.112/2126   now‸] MB ● ~, MT RO ● ~: CI

5.112/2126   discouerye] MB ● difcouerie MT C2 C4 ● difcouery CI+

5.113/2128   Brokage²] MT ● ~, MB ● ~‸ CI ● ~., RO

5.114/2129   naye] Naye‸ MB C3 (OK CMA)

5.114/2129   naye‸] ~, MT C2 C3

5.114/2129   staye,] MB CI ● ~‸ MT RO

5.114/2129   thankes] MT OK ● thanks MB+. The word only appears twice in the play, and both times MT and MB disagree; on both occasions, MT's spelling is duplicated in only one other witness, and MB's matches RO, with which it is otherwise closely linked. Moreover, compare 'thinkes' (437), where the penultimate 'e' is unique to autograph. Given Middleton's often minimalist 'e', the graphic difference between the two autographs here is much smaller than print makes it.

5.114/2129   Litle] MT ● litle MB+

5.114/2129   Litle‸] MB CI C2 ● ~, MT+ ● ~ (OK

5.115/2130   Eare] eare MB RO C2 OK

5.116/2131   You...Youre] MB ● you...youre MT+. THH transcribes only the first word in MB with a majuscule, but the initial letters are almost identical, and clearly contrast with the minuscule in 'youre' in the previous line, and with both letters in MT.

5.117/2132   donne] GT ● don CI+ ● done OK CMA RO. See 1492.

5.117/2132   that;] MT ● ~, MB ● ~. CI+

5.120/2135   cheif‸] MT CI C2 C3 ● cheife RO MB ● chiefe OK CMA

5.120/2136   hell‸] MB ● ~, MT CI RO. MT punctuation related to its mislineation.

5.121/2136   Master;] MB ● ~, MT ● ~. CI RO

5.122/2137   merit] MT ● merit MB+

5.123/2138   suffredst] MT ● fufferdft MB CI C2 C3 ● fufferedft CMA ● fuffereft RO OK. The MB reading duplicates the letter forms of 'merit' in the line above. In MT they are instead reversed, but there is no sign of an 'e' after 'f': for the sequence of letter forms compare 'Kindreds' at MSR 643.

5.123/2138   Lust] MB ● lust MT+

5.123/2139   lead] MT ● led MB RO OK CMA ● ledd CI C2 C3. There is no autograph parallel for 'led', which might easily have been repeated from copy; for the past participle spelled 'lead', compare MSR 860.

5.123/2139   lead‸] ~, MT (only). The unique punctuation is associated with MT's unique mislineation: the comma marks the real line-ending.

5.124/2139   night‸] MT CI RO ● ~, MB+

5.124/2139   Actïon] MT ● Action MB+

5.124/2139   Common] common MB OK CMA. Autograph often uniquely capitalizes adjectives. This adjective in particular begins with a majuscule in the autograph C3 preface and at 2303 (MB MT).

5.124/2139   bed;] MB ● ~: MT ● ~‸ RO ● ~. CI+

5.125/2140   ouer‸common] MT ● ouer common MB+ (two words) ● ouercome RO ● ~-~ C3. Middleton often uniquely writes a compound as a single unhyphenated word.

5.125/2140   neyther!] MT ● ~; MB ● ~, RO ● ~. CI+

5.126/2141   hah.] MT ● ~? RO MB CI

5.126/2141   that;] MT ● ~? MB+

5.127/2142   honored:] MT ● ~; MB ● ~, RO ● ~‸ CI

5.128/2143   ‸now]—~ C2

5.128/2143   goe‸] MB ● ~, MT+ ● ~: CI C2 C3

5.128/2143   I‸ue] GT ● I'ue OK ● I haue CRANE+. As Lake and Jackson demonstrated, 'I've' was a relatively rare contraction found in Middleton and few other dramatic authors of the period before 1625. Here, Crane's typical (and extra-metrical) expansion has been passively followed by all subsequent texts except OK.

5.128/2143   thankes] MT CMA ● thanks MB+. See 5.114. Here MT's penultimate 'e' is very clear; MB is badly blotted.

5.128/2143   Sⁱʳ] MT ● Sir MB+

5.128/2143   S^{ir}$_∧$] MB ● ~, MT ● ~. CI ● ~) C2+

5.129/2144   Game] game MT RO. The minuscule occurs only three other times in autograph (54 1092 1782, none unique). By contrast, autograph uses the majuscule on three title-pages and 39 other times in the text.

5.129/2144   Game,] MT ● ~? MB RO ● ~: CI+

5.130/2145   Noh] MB MT ● noe CRANE ● No OK RO. This is the only occurrence in *Game* of this unique autograph spelling, perhaps under the influence of Middleton's preferred 'oh'. It also occurs at *Witch* 1.2.68. The only other occurrences recorded by LION or EEBO in the period are five in 3 speeches by Curvetto in Dekker's (?) *Blurt, Master Constable* (4.1.8, 4.1.13, 4.3.2, 5.3.144, 149), two in 3.2 of *The Wasp* (anonymous manuscript), and one in Breton's *Grimellos Fortunes* (1604). The pattern in *Blurt* suggests that Dekker may have had a collaborator, responsible for part of the Curvetto subplot.

5.132/2147   S^{ir}] MT *only* ● Sir CI+ ● sir MB RO

5.132/2147   S^{ir}$_∧$] MB ● ~, MT ● ~,, CI ● ~) C2+

5.133/2148   thank**s**giuing] MT MB RO ● thankes-giuing OK+. THH mistranscribes MB as 'thankgiuing', but the medial ʃ is clearly present.

5.133/2148   thank**s**giuing;] MT ● ~, MB ● ~$_∧$ CI ● ~. C2+

5.136/2151 $_∧$yes—] MB CI ●—~; MT ● ~: C2 C3 ● ~. RO+

5.137/2152   mis**chiefe**] RO ● miʃcheif CI C2 C3 ● Miʃchiefe OK ● a pox MT MB

5.138/2153   thee,—] MB ● ~$_∧$~ MT ● ~$_∧$: CRANE+

5.138/2153   præpare] prepare CI MB ● præparde MT ● prepard C2 RO ● prepar'd C3 C4 ● prepared OK. The Latinate diphthong often shows up in unique autograph spellings.

5.138/2153   selfe$_∧$] MB CI ● for't, MT RO

5.139/2154   high—] MB ● ~, MT C2 CMA ● ~? CI C3: ~$_∧$ RO ● ~. OK

5.140/2155   — then] MT ● $_∧$~ MB+

5.140/2155   reach$_∧$] MB CMA ● ~, MT RO CI ● ~ (C2 C3 OK

5.140/2155   S^{ir}] MT MB. Howard-Hill (MSR, THH) transcribes MB as 'Sir', but the last two letters are clearly raised in both manuscripts.

5.140/2155   S^{ir};] MT ● ~, MB ● ~. CI ● ~) C2+

5.140/2156   I$_∧$le] I'le MB ● I'll CI C2 C3

5.140/2156   on$_∧$t] MT ● on't MB+

5.143/2159   Kindlie] MB MT ● kindly CI+ ● kindlie NAS MSR. In both manuscripts the initial 'k' here is larger than the medial 'k' of 'workes', just before it.

5.143/2159   Kindlie$_∧$] ~, MB C3 CMA

5.143/2159   Rape] rape MB RO OK

5.147/2163   Was] MB ● was MT+. THH (1995) does not transcribe as majuscule, but it clearly contrasts with the initial minuscules in the preceding lines, and with the equivalent form in MT.

5.147/2163   Knowen] GT ● Knowne MT+ ● ʃeene MB. See 1609.

5.148/2164   Wonder] MT MB ● wonder CI+. THH (1995) does not transcribe the majuscule in MB but the letter is of a similar size and shape in both autographs, and in both contrasts with the initial 'w' of the following word.

5.149/2165   ist] MT CI ● Is't MB+

5.149/2165   is$_∧$t] MT ● Is't MB+. Compare 2321, where both autographs uniquely omit the apostrophe from 'ist'.

5.149/2165   Wilde] MT MB. See preceding notes on 'Was' and 'Wonder'. Howard-Hill (in both THH and MSR) transcribes the initial letter in both autographs as minuscule, but that a majuscule was intended in MT is suggested by the contrast with 'bawde' in the following line; in MB this is the largest 'w'

on the page. Autograph often indisputably begins adjectives with majuscules.

5.150/2166   Can] can MB RO

5.150/2166   Yeares] MB ● yeares MT+

5.150/2166   Bawde?] MB CI ● ~, MT RO

5.150/2166   Looke] MB ● looke MT+

5.150/2166   mee$_∧$] MT CI ● ~, MB

5.150/2166   S^{ir}] MB ● Sir CRANE ● sir RO OK ● *not in* MT C2

5.150/2166 $_∧$S^{ir}$_∧$] MB (*at* 5.151) ● (~.) CI ● (~) C3 C4 OK ● (~$_∧$ RO ● *not in* MT C2

5.151/2167   I$_∧$ue] GT ● I'ue RO ● I'haue CI ● I haue C2 CMA MT MB ● I'me OK. The variant in OK does not make sense, and is presumably a compositor's minim misreading of a manuscript identical to RO here. An unusual Middleton contraction, typically extrametrically expanded by Crane (in two stages), and then passively accepted in other transcriptions. See 1.274.

5.151/2167   Youth] MB ● youth MT+

5.152/2168   Since] MT ● ʃince MB+

5.153/2169   remembred$_∧$] MB ● ~, MT+ ● ~. RO

5.154–5/2170–1   Who...Were...Worldlie] MB MT ● who... were...worldlie MSR THH. Contrast with 'were' and 'twice' and 'twas'.

5.154/2170   em,] MB ● ~$_∧$ MT+

5.155/2171   cares] MT ● Cares RO MB CI C2 C3

5.156/2172   fingers?] MB ● ~; MT ● ~$_∧$ CI ● ~. RO+

5.157/2173   Shall] MT ● (OK CMA) ● ʃhall MB+

5.158/2174   Holie] holly CI C2. Middleton often uniquely uses majuscules for adjectives.

5.158/2174   Holie] MB ● Holye MT ● Holy OK+. See unique autograph 'holie' at 885, 1611, 1618, 2121 (MB MT). MT could have resulted from following copy 'Holy' and then adding his characteristic terminal 'e', but 'Holie' required a more thorough departure from the spelling of all other witnesses. There are 142 examples of 'lie' terminations in MT (not counting monosyllables); this is one of only 8 examples of 'lye' endings (not counting monosyllables).

5.158/2174   Derision!] MB ● ~$_∧$ MT OK ● ~, CRANE RO

5.158/2174   yes!] MB ● ~, MT+ ● ~: C2 C3

5.158/2174   Eare] MB CI C2 C3 ● eare MT+

5.159/2175   wth] With MB (OK CMA). Whether Middleton intended a majuscule in MB is debatable.

5.159/2175   Lifes] MB ● lifes MT+

5.159/2175   Vomit!] MB ● ~; MT ● ~, RO ● ~) C2 ● ~: CI+

5.160/2176   was] MB+ ● Was THH (1995)

5.160–1/2176–7   twice? | and] ~$_∧$ | and CI ● ~? | then MB ● ~, | then MT ~, | and C2+. The change of wording in the two autographs does not seem to alter the pointing of the passage; MT's comma duplicates that of five other texts with 'and'. As usual I have preferred the unique autograph variant.

5.162/2178   Bastard;] MT ● ~, RO MB ● ~? CI+

5.164/2181   myne] MT ● mine MB+

5.166/2183   Shame] MB ● shame MT+

5.166/2183   weomanhood] CI RO ● Womanhood C2+

5.166/2183   weomanhood] GT ● womanhood CI+. See 599.

5.166/2183   weomanhood;] MB ● ~: MT ● ~$_∧$ CI C3 ● ~. RO C2 OK ● ~, CMA

5.167/2184   Im$_∧$e] GT ● Imè MT MB RO OK ● I am CRANE. See 1184.

5.167/2184   hands;] MB ● ~, MT ● ~. CI RO

5.169/2186   hee$_∧$s] MT ● hee's MB+. See 1.203.

5.169/2186   taken$_∧$] MB ● ~, MT+ ● ~. C3

5.170/2187 ˏtàs] MT MB RO • 't'hath CI C2 • It hath C3 C4 OK. A rare, characteristically Middleton contraction, progressively sophisticated.

5.170/2187 burden] Burden MT C2 C3

5.171/2188 Order] MB C2 • order MT+. Although MSR interprets MT as a minuscule, in both autographs this 'o' is larger and more separated from other letters than the other five examples of 'o' in this line.

5.171/2188 Voto;] MB • ~, MT CMA • ~. CI+

5.172/2190 Bishops] Biſhop's MB C3. The possessive appears 15 times in MT, never apostrophied.

5.172/2190 now!] MB • ~, MT • ~. CRANE RO • ~ˏ OK (turnover)

5.173/2191 how now] Hold MT

5.173/2191 how now,] hold, MB • ~ˏ MT+ • ~ (CI C2 C3

5.173/2192 murderˏ] ~, MT OK. The comma in MT may be related to its mislineation.

5.174/2192 oh] C2 C3 • O CI+ • not in MB MT. See 5.50.

5.174/2192 merciles] CI C4 OK • mercyles C2 • Merciles C3 • mercileſſe RO • not in MB MT

5.174/2192 Bloudhound] bloudhound C4 OK RO • not in MT MB

5.174/2192 Bloudˏhound] ~-~ CI C2 C3 • not in MT MB

5.175/2193 wer't] CI • wert C2+ • art MB. For the superfluous apostrophe see 1677.

5.176/2194 Death] MT • (OK CMA) • death MB+

5.176/2194 Death!] MB • ~? MT • ~? C2+ • ~ˏ CI OK • ~, RO

5.176/2194 præuented] MT • preuented MB+

5.176/2194 præuented!] MB RO • ~? MT+ • ~. OK

5.178/2196 farder,] MB • ~ˏ MT+

5.178/2197 exeuntˏ] MT RO • ~. MB+

5.178.2/2198 Dukeˏ] ~, MB OK

5.179/2201 You] yau'e MT you RO

5.179/2201 Knowledge,] MT • ~ (CI+. Although OK also lacks the opening bracket here, it supplies it one word later, thereby changing the meaning of the sentence.

5.180/2202 Content] MT CI C2 C3 • content MT+

5.180/2202 together;] MT • ~, MT RO • ~. CI+

5.181/2203 King;] MT • ~. MB+

5.183/2205 wee] MB RO • we CI • thats MT+

5.183/2205 off] MB • of MT+. See also autograph 'off' at 277.

5.183/2205 parts:] MB • ~; MT • ~, C3 RO • ~. CI+

5.185/2207 doo] MB • do MT OK • doe CI+

5.185/2207 Bellyes] MT • bellies RO MB • Bellies CRANE

5.186/2208 thowsand] MB • thousand MT+

5.186/2208 ducketts] MT OK • Ducketts MB+

5.186/2208 oṅtˏ] MB (on't) • ~, MT RO • ~: CI

5.187/2209 th'] MB C2 C3 C4 • the MT CI RO OK. See 5.81–2.

5.187/2209 Romane] MB CMA • Roman MT RO • Romaine CI+

5.187/2209 paynfull-Idlenes] MB • ~ˏ~ MT+

5.189/2211 Golden] MT C2 CMA • golden MB+

5.190/2212 pelamis] MB (THH) MT (NAS) • Pelamis MT (MSR) CI+. The two autograph readings are very similar here; both might be minuscule. Given the uncertainty, and THH's interpretation of one as minuscule, I have adopted the rarer reading here, especially as Middleton elsewhere begins some proper nouns with a minuscule.

5.190/2212 pelamis, | ˏ] MB • ~,ˏ MT RO OK • ~ˏ(CRANE

5.191/2213 Summer] MT OK • Sommer MB+

5.191/2213 Summer-whiting] ~ˏ~ MB OK CMA • ~,~ RO

5.191/2213 Calcedon,] MT C2 • Caldedonˏ RO MB • ~: CI C3 OK • ~; CMA

5.193/2215 Fatted] MB • fatted MT+

5.194/2216 Sapaˏ flowerˏ] MT • ~,~ˏ MB CI RO • ~,~, C2 • ~;~ˏ CMA • ~ˏ~, OK. Middleton's source in Pliny makes it clear that OK's punctuation is in error; the error could easily

have arisen from misinterpretation of an authorial absence of punctuation, as in MT.

5.195/2217 Birds] birds MB RO OK

5.195/2217 Like] MB • like MT+. See the unique autograph 'Capon-Like' at 2299 (MB).

5.196/2218 Enclose] MT • encloſe MB+

5.196/2218 a'thˏ] MB • o'th CI+ • of the MT (only). The metrical elision is here confirmed by an autograph text (with Middleton's preferred 'a' spelling); RO's error ('at') is more likely to arrive from copy 'ath' than 'of the'.

5.198/2220 Fish] MB CI C2 • fiſh MT+

5.198/2220 beside,] MT MB RO • beſides CRANE, OK. This seems to be in the period only a spelling variant; both autograph texts here prefer the short form.

5.199/2221 Throate] MB C2 • throate MT+. See unique autograph 'Throate' at 788.

5.199/2221 Throate,] MT • ~, MB+ • ~; CMA

5.199/2221 th '] CI C2 MT • the MB+

5.199/2221 Inuention] Inuentiõ MT. The abbreviated form seems to have been caused by the line exceeding the page frame.

5.199/2221 Inuention;] MB RO • ~, MT+ • ~ˏ CMA

5.200/2222 followed;] MT OK CMA • ~, RO MB • ~. CI C2

5.201/2223 nor] MT RO • Nor MB+

5.201/2223 arch] MB RO CI • Arch MT+

5.201/2223 Gurmundizerˏ] MB CI C3 • ~, MT CMA OK RO

5.202/2224 twentye] MT • twenty RO OK • twentie MB+

5.202/2224 dinner] MB • Dinner MT+

5.202/2224 dinner,] MT CMA • ~, MB+ • ~; OK

5.203/2225 courseˏ] MT • Course, MB RO CI

5.204/2226 weomen] Weomen MB CI C2 C3

5.204/2226 weomen,] MT • ~, MB+ • ~ˏ CI • ~,; C3

5.204/2227 strenghtnd] MB • ſtrengthn'd OK • ſtrenghtned MT • ſtrenghthned, RO CMA • ſtrengthend CI C2 C3. For the -ned suffix MT duplicates RO and CMA. MB is unique, and its oddity is confirmed by OK, which retains the spelling but tries to normalize it with an apostrophe.

5.204/2227 strenghtnd;] MT • ~: OK • ~, MB+ • ~ˏ C3 C4

5.205/2228 Dishes] MT CI C2 C3 • dishes MB+

5.205/2228 Dishes;] MB CI CMA • ~, MT RO OK • ~: C2 C3

5.206/2229 Was] MB (OK CMA) • was MT+

5.206/2229 tastedˏ] MT RO • ~, MB+

5.206/2229 Vented:] MB • ~, MT • ~ˏ RO C3 • ~. CI+

5.207/2230 Epicures?] MT • ~! RO MB • ~. CI+

5.209/2232 pertinax] MT • Pertinax MB+

5.210/2233 Halfe] MB • halfe MT+

5.211/2234 Iulianˏ] MT CMA • ~, MB+

5.212/2235 Meales] MT C2 • meales MB+

5.212/2235 hare] MB RO • Hare MT+

5.213/2236 Figgˏ] MB CMA • ~; CI • ~, MT+

5.213–20/2236–43 Wipe … Was … Warhorse … White-house … Wealthie] THH interprets the initial letters of MB in these words as minuscule, but all are notably larger, in both autographs, than the 'w' in 'wee', 'bewaylers', 'now', and 'wch'. Middleton elsewhere uses unambiguous majuscules to begin verbs and adjectives.

5.213/2236 Beard] beard MB RO OK

5.214/2237 Excesse] excesse MB RO OK

5.214/2237 dayes,] MB • ~ˏ MT+

5.215/2238 complaynde] Complayn'd MT C3

5.215/2238 complaynde] MB • Complaynd MT OK CMA • com-plaind CI C2 RO. The medial 'y' is unique to the autograph texts. There are many unique autograph examples of the 'de' spelling of the past participle.

5.215/2238 coyne] MT OK ● Coyne MB+

5.216/2239 purchasde] MB ● purchaſd MT CI C2 ● purchaſed C3 RO OK ● purchas'd CMA. The MT reading crosses the right border of the text-page at 'a', and Middleton probably abbreviated his normal past participial form as a result.

5.217/2240 Rate] MT ● rate MB+

5.217/2240 Triumphs] triumphs MB RO

5.218/2241 Rate] MT ● rate MB+

5.219/2242 ˏspetiallie] MT CRANE ● eſpeciallie MB RO OK

5.219/2242 spetiallie] MB ● ſpetially MT+

5.220/2243 plumpe-] MB CI ● ~ˏ MT+

5.220/2243 plebeians] MT ● Plebeians MB+

5.220/2243 Hoggs] MB RO C2 ● Hogs MT C3 ● Hogge CI ● Hogges OK CMA. Middleton typically doubles terminal consonants.

5.221/2244 Scalliger] MT ● Scaliger MB+

5.221/2244 citesˏ] MB ● ~ˏ MT+

5.222/2245 Prick] MT ● prick MB+

5.222/2245 Goadeˏ] ~, MT RO OK CMA

5.223/2246 Needle] MT ● needle MB+

5.223/2246 Buttocks] buttocks MT RO OK

5.224/2247 eˏm] MT OK ● em̄ MB RO ● 'em CI +

5.224/2247 em;] MT ● ~, RO MB ● ~: CRANE, OK

5.225/2248 choackte] MT OK (choackt) ● choakte MB ● choakd CI C2 RO ● choaked CMA. See the related variant at 5.232, where only MT has the medial 'c'. Its absence from MB is more likely due to the influence of copy.

5.225/2248 choackte] MB (only). See preceding note, and 5.232, where both autograph texts have the unusual Middletonian past participial ending 'te'. The spelling of the ending is apparently not related to the presence or absence of medial 'c'.

5.225/2248 Paunch] MB CI C2 C3 ● paunch MT+

5.225/2248 Paunchˏ] MT ● ~, MB+ ● ~: RO

5.226/2249 Wch] MB (OK CMA) ● wch MT+

5.227/2250 Infinite] MB ● infinite MT+

5.228/2251 Kild] MB MT ● kild OK+. MSR interprets MT as a minuscule, but like the letter in MB it is clearly larger than the 'k' in 'taken' and 'make', one line below; moreover, in the undoubtedly minuscule medial 'k' the upstroke is much lower than the vertical stem of the letter, whereas in both autographs of 'Kild' they are equally high.

5.228/2251 Herbe] MB CI C2 ● herbe MT+

5.229/2252 Leane] MT C2 ● leane MB+

5.230/2253 K.] MT ● King MB+

5.230/2253 counceld] MT RO ● counſeld MB+

5.230/2253 toˏ] MT ● ~, MB+ ● ~) CI

5.232/2255 choackte] MT ● choakte MB ● choakt OK ● choakd CI C2 RO ● choak'd CMA. See 5.225.

5.233/2257 youˏre] MT ● your'e MB ● you'r CI ● yare RO ● y'are C2 ● y'ar C3 ● you are OK CMA. See 5.104.

5.233/2257 Spokesman,] MB ● ~ˏ MT+

5.233/2257 ˏSʳ,] MB ● (~) MT+

5.233/2257 Sʳ] MT ● ~Sⁱʳ~ MB ● Sir CI +

5.233/2257 parsimony,] MT C3 ● ~, MB+

5.234/2258 cleane] CI ● Cleane MT MB+

5.234/2258 Abstinence] MT CI C2 C3 ● abstinence MB+

5.234/2258 dayeˏ] MB CI ● ~, RO MT

5.235/2259 Tongˏ] MB ● tongue MT+

5.235/2259 Tong;] MB ● ~, MT ● ~. CI+

5.236/2260 King] MB CI ● K. MT+

5.236/2260 King—] MB ● K. MT+

5.236/2260 meekelie] CI (meekely) ● mildlie MT MB ● mildly C2 RO OK ● mildely CMA. Middleton's preference for the suffix -lie does not seem affected by the adverb's stem adjective.

5.236/2260 meekelie,] MB CI ● ~ˏ MT+

5.236/2260 Sⁱʳ,] MB MT. MSR does not transcribe 'ir' as superscript in MT but there is no difference between the two autographs.

5.237/2261 discourseˏ] MT ● ~, MB ● ~. CI+

5.238/2262 heele] MT RO ● hee'le MB+. See the unique autograph absence of apostrophe at 2430 (MB MT).

5.239/2263 hereafter,] MT ● ~, RO MB ● ~. CI+

5.240/2264 I,] MB CI ● ~ˏ MT+ ● ~, (C2 ● ~ˏ (CMA

5.240/2264 heartˏ] MB ● ~, RO MT ● ~; CI ● ~) C2 C4 ● ~: OK

5.240/2264 heartˏ] MB ● ~, RO MT ● ~; CI

5.241/2265 Fogg] MB ● Fognes MT ● fog CI+

5.241/2265 Fatnesˏ] MT OK ● ~, RO MB CI ● ~) C2 CMA

5.241/2265 Dragon,] MT ● ~, MB CI ● ~: C2 CMA OK ● ~; RO

5.242/2266 Comlines] comlines MB RO OK

5.242/2266 forˏ] MT ● ~, MB+

5.242/2266 glorious;] MT RO ● ~. MB+ ● ~ˏ OK

5.244/2268 sideˏ] MT ● ~, MB RO C2 ● ~, (CI ● ● (OK CMA

5.244/2268 y'aue] C2 (you'have) ● yoᵘ haue CI+. Typical Crane sophistication, passively reproduced.

5.244/2269 to't] CI C2 ● to it MT MB RO

5.245/2270 misprize;] MB ● ~, RO MT ● ~: CI ● ~? C2 C3 OK ● ~! CMA

5.245/2270 youˏward] MT (one word unhyphenated) ● you- -ward MB+

5.245/2270 youwardˏ] MT ● ~, MB RO C2 ● ~: CI OK CMA ● ~. C3

5.246-8/2271-3 You...You] you...youCI RO ● You...You MB MT C2 C3. MSR interprets MT as a minuscule in both cases, but neither is significantly different from MB's form, and both are clearly distinguished from the 'y' in 'youward' and 'naye', in both autographs. But both may have been minuscule in the first draft.

5.247/2272 Customeˏ] ~, MB C3 C4

5.247/2272 dispencst] MB ● dispenĉst MT ● diſpenc'd CI+ ● diſpencd C2 C3. Both autographs share the unusual Middletonian spelling -cst, but MT preserves the apostrophe present in most other texts.

5.247/2272 wthall;] MT ● ~, MB RO OK ● ~: CI CMA ● ~ˏ C2 C3

5.248/2273 eate] eat MB RO

5.248/2273 Ton's,] MT CI ● ~, MB+ ● ~: C2 OK

5.250/2276 Riot,] MB CI C2 ● ~ˏ MT+

5.250/2276 th'] CI C2 ● the MT+

5.251/2277 Were] MB MT (only). MSR interprets MT as minuscule, but the autographs are very similar, and both notably bigger than the 'w' in 'wch' and 'will'.

5.251/2277 Cockle] MT ● ~: MB C2 ● ~. CI+

5.252/2278 Well] MT MB+ ● well RO. Howard-Hill (1990, 1995) interprets both autographs as minuscule, but they resemble those at 5.251; contrast 'weere' and 'whence'.

5.252/2278 Foodeˏ] MB CMA OK ● ~, MT+

5.252/2278 Ime] MT+ ● I am CRANE

5.252/2278 resolude] MB ● refolud MT ● refolu'd CI+ ● refolued OK. Both autograph texts omit the apostrophe, but only MB preserves the characteristic Middleton termination.

5.253/2279 Diett] MB ● Diet MT+

5.253/2279 Disposition] MB CI C2 C3 ● disposition MT+

5.255/2281 foode] MT RO ● Foode MB+

5.256/2282 it] MB C2 ● It MT+. See unique autograph 'it' (also at the beginning of a speech) at 963.

5.256/2282   nature] Nature MT C2 C3 C4

5.257/2283   policie] MT RO • Policie C3+. Although THH may
be right to interpret MB as a majuscule, it is much less
certainly so than the same manuscript's own 'Pertinax'
(5.209) and 'Paunch' (5.225; so it seems safer to prefer MT's
unambiguous minuscule.

5.258/2284   Mr] MT • m^r RO • Master MB+. For Middleton's
preference for the abbreviation see C2 preface, 1864 Mr:peice
[unique combo, colon], 798 Mr: [RO abbreviation, colon
unique], 823 [colon unique], 103 Mr-peice, 296 Mr-peice
[unique], 905 Mrpeice [unique], 1210 Mr-Polititian [RO m^r],
1301 Mr-prize [ditto].

5.259/2285   Youre] MB MT. Although MSR interprets MT as
minuscule, it is actually larger than MB's form; both contrast
with the minuscule in 'praye', 'youre', and 'certayne'.

5.259/2285   diett] MB C1 C2 C3 • dyet MT RO OK CMA

5.259/2285   diett] C2 • diet C1+. See unique autograph 'Diett'
at 5.253.

5.261/2287   Ambition!] MT • ~: MB • ~ₐ C3 • ~. C1+

5.262/2288   that‚s] MB RO • that's MT+. Autograph uniquely
omits the apostrophe in this compound at 923, 2205 (MT),
2266, and 2321. See 1.49.

5.262/2288   serude] MB • ferud₍ₐ₎ MT • ferued RO • feru'd₍ₐ₎ C1+

5.262/2288   puff paste] MB MT RO • ~~: C1+. Although THH
interprets MB as a single word, there is as much space
between 'f' and 'p' as between other words.

5.262/2288   puffpaste₍ₐ₎] MB • ~, MT RO • ~: C1+

5.264/2290   dinner;] MB C1 • ~, MT RO • ~: C2 C3 C4 OK

5.264/2290   Ambition‚ S^ir₍ₐ₎] MB • ~, ~, MT • ~, ~) RO • ~, ~₍ₐ₎
C1 • ~ (~) C2 C3 C4 OK

5.264/2290   S^ir] MB MT • Sir C1+. Although THH does not
interpret 'ir' as superscript in MB, in both autographs the
two letters are written opposite the top half of 'S' (as opposed
to the lower level in all other manuscripts).

5.265/2291   world;?] MB • ~? MT+ • ~. RO

5.266/2292   Sir;] MT • ~, MB • ~) C2 C3 C4 RO • ~.) OK • ~. C1

5.267/2293   weere] MB • weere̊ MT C1 RO • We'are C2 • We are
C3+

5.268/2294   Large] MB C1 C2 C3 • large MT+

5.268/2294   Ambition₍ₐ₎] MT C1 C2 C3 • ~, MB+

5.269/2295   white] White MT C3 C4

5.269/2295   white₍ₐ₎] ~- MT C2 C3

5.269/2295   came] Came MB. The majuscule was used to cover
an error: Middleton originally wrote 'f', anticipating the
beginning of the next word.

5.269/2295   from₍ₐ₎] MT C1 • ~, RO MB • ~) C2 C3 C4 OK

5.270/2296   Salletts;] MB RO • ~: MT C3 C4 OK • ~. C1 C2

5.272/2298   Chast] MB MT. Although THH interprets MB as an
initial minuscule, it is the same shape and size as the letter
in MT. Both differ clearly from the minuscule 'c' in 'comes'
three words before and 'Venice' three words after.

5.273/2299   Venice₍ₐ₎] MB RO • ~, MT+

5.273/2299   Like] MB • like MT+. Honigmann demonstrates that
Crane is particularly likely to enclose in parentheses this kind
of hyphenated 'X-like' compound: this example is bracketed
in all texts but the two autograph texts and RO. By contrast, I
have found twenty examples of 'X-like' compounds elsewhere
in Middleton's uncollaborative works (*Solomon*, *Michaelmas*,
Five Gallants, *Widow*); none is enclosed in brackets.

5.273/2299   whitebroath₍ₐ₎] MB • ~, MT C1 • ~: C2 CMA OK • ~.
C3 RO

5.274/2300   Cheife] MT C1 C3 • cheife C2 RO MB OK CMA

5.274/2300   Ouen₍ₐ₎] ~, MT C3

5.274/2300   Italie₍ₐ₎] ~, MT C1 C3

5.275/2301   Sauoye₍ₐ₎] ~, MB RO C3

5.275/2301   Geneua₍ₐ₎] ~, MT C2

5.276/2302   plac‚st] MT • plac'ft MB • placd C1 C3. RO • plac'd
C2 OK CMA

5.277/2303   Dish] difh MT RO OK

5.277/2303   Lower] MT C3 • lower MB+

5.277/2303   a‚th] MT • a'th MB OK CMA • o'th C1 C2 C3 RO

5.278/2304   Course] courfe MB RO OK

5.279/2305   portugalls] MT MB • Portugalls C1+. Although THH
interprets MB as a majuscule, it does not significantly differ
in size or shape from MT, or from the forms in 'Spit' and
'plouers', elsewhere in the same line; there seems no effort to
differentiate or emphasize this initial letter. MSR acknowledges
that Middleton often uses miniscules even for proper nouns
(p. xx).

5.281/2307   melted₍ₐ₎] ~, MT C1 C2 C3

5.282/2308   On] MB (OK CMA) • on MT+

5.282/2308   Occasions;] MT • ~, MB+ • ~: C2 C3

5.283/2309   full] C1+ • crambd MB • Crambd MT RO

5.283/2309   Hopes] MT C1 • hopes MB+

5.283/2309   suffize] MT MB • fuffice C2+ • suffise C1 RO.
Although THH interprets the penultimate letter in MB as 'c',
the horizontal upper bar more closely resembles Middleton's
'z' than the 'c' found anywhere else in the vicinity. The
ambiguity is created by the fact that the lower bar of the 'z'
does not extend so far to the left as it does in MT. However,
this is also true of the penultimate letter of the next line
('rize'), which Howard-Hill interprets as 'z'. The majuscule
'Z' which begins the next line is not identical in the two
autographs, either. Here, the letter could easily be 'z', and it
is probably not 'c'.

5.283/2309   suffize₍ₐ₎] MT • ~, MB+ • ~; CMA

5.284/2310   Grace] grace MB RO OK

5.285/2311   meate] Meate MT C3 C4

5.285/2311   conscience] Conscience MB RO C3

5.286/2312   Bl₍ₐ₎] MT • ~. MB+

5.286/2312   anie] MB • anye MT • any C1+. See 5.52.

5.286/2312   want₍ₐ₎] MB C3 OK • ~, MT C2 CMA (only)

5.286/2312   Switzerland] Switterland MT (*only*). The spelling
variant is not recorded elsewhere; given how sloppy MT has
become by this point, it probably results from unintended
dittography.

5.286/2312   Switzerland₍ₐ₎] MB • ~, MT+

5.287/2313   Polonia] polonia MB (probably minuscule, but not
certainly so)

5.288/2314   Table;] MT • ~, RO MB • ~. C1+

5.289/2315   You] MT (OK CMA) • you MB+

5.289/2315   well₍ₐ₎] MB • ~, RO MB C1 • ~ (C2+

5.289/2315   S^ir] MB • fir MT RO OK • Sir CRANE. THH does not
transcribe the last two letters as superscript, but they are
level with the top half of the 'S' and above the horizontal
line created by the preceding words (in very clear contrast
with their lower positioning in MT).

5.289/2315   S^ir:] MT C1 • ~, MB RO • ~) C2 C3 C4 • ~.) OK

5.290/2316   here‚s] MT • here's MB+

5.290/2316   mistrie] MB RO (miferie • miserie, MT CMA OK •
~ : C1 • mifery: C2 • mifery; C3. The substantive variant
does not make any difference to the grammar or metre of the
sentence, and so the variants in punctuation seem relevant
to *Early*.

5.291/2316   weere] GT • we'are C1 • *not in* C2+

5.293/2317   Vice₍ₐ₎] MB C1 • ~, MT+

5.293/2317   there‚s] MT RO • there̊s MB+

5.293/2317   Foode] MT C1 C2 C3 • foode MB+

5.295/2319 what‸s] MT • what's MB+

5.295/2319 rauennous] Rauennous MB RO C3

5.296/2320 ‸Sⁱʳ;] MT • ‸~: CI • ,~) RO • (~) MB+

5.297/2321 housbandrie] MB • huſbandrie CI+. For Middleton's preference, see the unique autograph spelling 'hous-
band' at 723 and 2098 (MB MT).

5.298/2322 fayths‸] MB RO • ~, MT+

5.298/2322 prayers‸] MT • ~, MB+ • ~; CMA • *not in* CI

5.299/2323 death‸bed] MB • death bed MT OK • death Bed RO
• Death-bed CRANE. In MB the tail of the 'h' rises to the
beginning of the 'b'; in MT, by contrast, the tail curves
backward, leaving a clear space between the two words.

5.299/2323 Comforts] comforts MB RO OK

5.299/2323 Comforts‸] MB OK CMA • ~, MT+

5.300/2324 Counsells] counſells MB RO. Given compelling evidence that MB's copy derives from a text resembling RO, the
minuscule in MB could easily be the influence of copy on
autograph.

5.300/2324 Counsells‸] MB • ~, MT+ • ~: CI • ~; CMA

5.301/2325 Reuennewes] MT+ • Reuennues MB CMA RO •
Reuennewes MT+. See unique autograph 'Reuennewes' at
2221 (MB MT).

5.302/2326 or] Or MB *corr* (OK CMA). The quartos automatically
begin every verse line with upper case, and MB does so only
to overwrite the initial error 'and'.

5.302/2326 ‸em] MT OK • em̄ MB • 'em CI+ • them RO CI

5.302/2326 em;] MB C2 • ~, MT OK RO • ~. CI C3 C4

5.303/2327 uiew] MT • View MB C3 • view CI+

5.303/2327 Monasterys] MB • Monasteries MT+

5.303/2327 Monasterys‸] ~, MB C2 CMA OK

5.304/2328 Youde] MT. The initial letter in MB might (as THH
interprets) be minuscule: it is smaller than the letter in MT.
But it is larger than the letter in the preceding 'you' and
'Monaſterys', and in the following 'faye'.

5.304/2328 Yo‸ude] MB RO • Yo'ude MT+ (all other texts
with the contraction, however spelled or placed, have an
apostrophe).

5.304/2328 Plutus‸] MT • ~, MB RO CI • ~ (C2+

5.306/2330 you] You MT C3 (OK CMA)

5.306/2330 Tuns?] MB • ~‸ MT • ~: RO • ~. CI+

5.307/2331 possible;] MT • ~? MB CI C2 C3 • ~! CMA • ~. OK

5.308/2332 bring‸] MT CI • ~, MB (RO)

5.308/2332 bring‸‸] CI • ~‸ (MT+ • ~, ‸ OK • ~, (MB. All
texts but CI and OK (from autograph) have brackets, which
therefore probably originated with Crane; if Middleton's
original draft had brackets, it is hard to believe that Crane
would have removed them in CI. The brackets in both
surviving autograph texts probably reflect copy, rather than
authorial preference.

5.308/2332 Sⁱʳ] MB • Sirs MT+

5.308/2332 Sⁱʳ,] OK • ~) MB MT CMA RO • ~? CI • ?) C2 C3.
See preceding notes. Since autograph reproduces the suspect
brackets, and the grammatical query occurs elsewhere in
three Crane texts, the characteristically minimal comma in OK
(set from a late autograph), is probably closest to Middleton's
original preference.

5.310/2334 Life] MB MT. Although MSR interprets MT as minuscule, and it does differ from MB's indisputable majuscule,
MT's form even more clearly differs in size and shape from
the preceding minuscules in 'shall' and 'lockt', and is virtually identical to the first letter of 'Lord' (5.305) in both
autographs, which THH and MSR interpret as majuscule. Like
NAS, I interpret MT as 'Life'.

5.311/2335 Yours] MB • yours MT+

5.311/2335 ‸Sⁱʳ;] ‸~;? MB • (~) MT • ? ~, RO • , ~? CI •
(~?) C2 C3 C4 • (~.) OK. MB's semicolon in unique (but
its query probably inherited from copy); MT's brackets are
probably inherited from copy, but it uniquely lacks terminal
punctuation within or without brackets. I have retained the
unique aspects of the punctuation of each autograph.

5.312/2336 that‸s] GT • that's CI. See 5.262.

5.312/2336 Wanton] MT MB. Although THH interprets MB as
minuscule, in both autographs it is obviously larger and
differently formed than the 'w' in 'were' and 'wthin' and
'fowle' and 'showe' and 'wee', etc.

5.312/2336 on̄t‸] ~, MT OK RO

5.313/2337 Flesh-Frayltie] MT CI C2 • ~‸~ MB+ • ~,~ RO

5.314/2338 Name] MT CI C2 C3 • name MB+

5.314/2338 for‸t] MB RO • foṙt MT+. See unique autograph 'fort'
at 1045, 2411 (MT).

5.315/2339 Innocent‸] MB CI CMA • ~, MT+ • ~: C3

5.316/2340 Claye;] MT • ~; MB • ~: CRANE+

5.317/2341 hard‸] MT • ~, MB+

5.318/2342 Fruite] MB CI C2 C3 • fruite MT+

5.318/2342 Supper;] MT C2 • ~, MB RO CMA • ~: CI OK • ~. C3

5.319/2343 naye‸] MB • ~, MT+

5.320/2344 Fishpond] fishpond MT+

5.320/2344 Fishpond:] MB • ~, MT CMA • ~. RO OK • ~‸ CI C2
C3

5.323/2347 in‸s] MB • in's CI+ • in his MT (*only*)

5.324/2348 how‸] MB • ~, MT+ • ~: C2 • ~. C3

5.325/2349 Was] MB MT. Although MSR interprets MT as minuscule, it hardly differs from MB, and both are notably larger
(and differently shaped) than the 'w' in the four examples of
'how' in this speech.

5.325/2349 Pond;] MT CMA • ~: RO CI • Bond: MB • ~. C2 C3
•) OK

5.327/2351 Mother] mother MB RO OK

5.328/2352 Knowe] MB MT • knowe NAS MSR CI+. Compare
'thinke' above and 'Wh.Kt.' below.

5.328/2352 head,] MT CMA • ~? RO • ~?. MB • ~. CI C2 • ~:
C3 • ~; OK

5.330/2354 more,] MT CI C2 OK • ~‸ CMA RO MB • ~; C3

5.332/2356 io...io] GT • ten...ten CI+. See 1283.

5.332/2356 Forerunners;] MB • ~, MT • ~. CRANE+

5.333/2357 Bl:] MT RO • ~ MB+

5.333/2357 is it] MB • Is ~ MT+. The majuscule in MT was a
correction, written to cover the original mistaken contraction
'iſt'. Middleton's intention in both autographs was to use a
minuscule (which does not appear in any text except the two
autographs).

5.333/2357 uilde] MT CI • uile MB • vile RO • vilde OK • vild
C2 C3 C4

5.333/2357 ordaynde] MT • ordayn'd MB+ • ordaind CI C2

5.333/2357 for‸t] MB • for't MT+

5.333/2357 fort‸] MT • ~, MB • ~? CI+

5.335/2359 knowen] MB • knowne MT+

5.335/2359 by‸] MT • ~; MB • ~, CMA • ~. CI+

5.336/2360 beares] bear'st MT *uncorr* • bear'es MT *corr* • beare's
MSR. The normalization of apostrophe placement in MSR is
especially misleading here. The apostrophe belongs to the
original MT reading; when Middleton overwrote the mistaken
'st' he did not remove the apostrophe, probably because doing
so would have made the correction even messier.

5.337/2361 poyson,—] MT • ~; • RO MB • ~: CRANE • ~, OK

5.337/2361 Ime] RO • Imė MB • I'am CI C2 • I am MT+. The
contraction here reverses Crane's normal practice (demonstrated in C3 C4, and is supported by the alternative autograph text. See 5.112. For the apostrophe see 1214.

5.337/2361 Arch**d**issembler] MB ● Arch-Diffembler MT CI C2 C3 ● arch-diffembler CMA ● Arch-diffembler OK ● arch diffembler RO. An unhyphenated single word only in MB.

5.337/2361 Archdissembler₄₄] MT ● ~ (, MB ● ~, ₄ CI ● ~₄ (C2+ ● ~. OK. Although the combination of punctuation marks in MB is unique, both elements appear elsewhere.

5.337/2361 Sʳ] MT ● Sir MB+

5.337/2361 Sʳ,] MT ● ~) MB+ ● ●. CI

5.338/2362 Kt.] ~.. MB

5.339/2363 Brand] MT CI C2 ● brand MB+

5.339/2363 Brand,] MB ● ~₄ MT OK ● ~: CRANE

5.339/2363 mee,] MT CI ● ~ (MB C2 OK ● ₄ CMA

5.339/2363 Sⁱʳ,] MT CI ● ~) C2 MB ● ~,) OK ● ~₄ CMA

5.340/2364 er'e] MB ● ere MT+. See 1207.

5.340/2364 spake] MT ● fpoke MB RO ● fpoake CI +. Clearly the distribution of variants does not support a clear distinction between an *Early* and *Later* version; I have adopted the obsolete unique autograph form in the old-spelling text, and the modern autograph form in the modern-spelling text.

5.341/2365 meȧnt!] MB ● ~? MT ● ~. CI +

5.342/2366 Vice!] MB ● ~, MT ● ~? CRANE RO ● ~: OK

5.343/2367 you₄] MT CMA ● ~, RO MB ● ~) CI ● ~: C2 C3 ● ~; OK

5.344/2368 prime-] MB CI OK ● ~₄ MT+

5.345/2369 Empires!] MB ● ~, MT OK ● ~: CI +

5.345/2369 heede₄] MB ● ~, MT CI ● ~ (C2+

5.347/2371 ₄tis] OK ● 'tis CI CMA ● It's It is MB MT RO

5.347/2371 præitious] MT ● pretious MB+

5.348/2372 worth₄s] MB ● worth's MT+

5.348/2372 unknown] CI (vnknowne) ● not Knowen MT ● not Knowne MB+. The -wen terminal spelling shows up repeatedly as a unique autograph preference. See 1609. Although Howard-Hill (MSR and THH) interprets the 'k' in both autographs as minuscule, in size and shape it clearly contrasts with the preceding 'forfake' and following 'fkilfull' and 'picks'.

5.348/2372 skillfull] fkilfull MB RO CMA ● skilful OK

5.350/2374 Motion;] MT ● ~, MB+ ● ~: CI C3 OK

5.351/2375 you] MB MT. Although THH interprets MB as a majuscule, the letter is no different than the MT reading, or than 'yaue' in the line below in both autographs, and it is notably smaller than the initial letter of 'Yet'.

5.351/2375 Yet] MB ● yet MT RO CI

5.351/2375 Soules] soules MT RO OK

5.351/2375 now₄] MB ● ~, RO MT ● ~. CI + ● ~; C2

5.352/2376 you₄re] GT ● you're CI OK ● ya̋re MT MB C2 RO ● you are C3 C4. See 4.166.

5.353/2376 donne₄] ~, MB C2 OK

5.355/2378 Lye] MT ● lye MB+

5.356/2379 ours—] MT ● ~, MB RO OK ● ~: CI C2 C4 ● ~; C3

5.356/2379 Check₄mate] MT RO ● Check-Mate MB CI C2 C3 ● Check-mate CMA ● checke mate OK

5.356/2380 discouerye] MB ● difcouerie MT+ ● Discouery CI OK RO. See 5.112.

5.356/2380 discouerye;] MB ● ~, MT RO OK ● ~ (C2 C3 ● ~, (CMA ● ~. CI

5.357/2380 all;] MB ● ~, Ime MT *uncorr* ● ~,-MT *corr* ● ~. CI +

5.358/2381 Im₄e…Im₄e] MT ● Imè…Im'e MB OK ● Im…Im̋ RO ● I am…I'am CI ● I'am…I am C2 ● I am…I am C3 C4. Only MT omits apostrophes for both words; indeed, it omits

the apostrophe a third time, because Middleton originally wrote 'Ime' at the end of the preceding line, then cancelled it.

5.358/2381 taken;] MB ● ~. MT+

5.360/2381 Falshood—] CI ● ~₄ MB C3 ● ~. C2+. The dash is preferred because related to CI's unique lineation; the autograph alternative uses the line-break as punctuation.

5.361/2382 confounded₄] MB ● ~, MT ● ~. CI +

5.362/2383 Condition!] MT ● ~₄ MB C2 ● ~. CI + ● ~: C3

5.362.1/2384-5 White…white] MT ● White…White MB ● wh…. wh. CI RO ● white C2 C3 ● *White* CMA ● *W*….*W.* OK. MT uniquely (and unambiguously) treats the two words differently.

5.362.1/2386 King] MB CI C3 ● *Ki* OK ● K MT+

5.362.1/2386 King:] MB ● ~. MT+

5.363/2386 treasure₄] MB CMA ● ~, MT+ ● ~/ CI

5.364/2387 Masterpeice] mafterpeice MB RO

5.364/2387 Masterpeice!] MB RO ● ~, MT OK ● ~: CI C2 ● ~; C3 C4

5.365/2388 hee₄s] GT ● heès CI +. See 1.203.

5.366/2389 blest₄] ~- CI. As THH notes, there is a faint stroke to the right of the adjective in MB which 'may indicate hyphen intended', but which could also be described as the right 'footstroke of t'. Since adjective–noun hyphens occur fairly often in Crane, since only the two autographs supply the rarer adjective–adjective hyphen here (true-blest), and since the faint broken mark to the right of 'blest' in MB contrasts with the very clear hyphen in both autographs, it does not seem safe to interpret MB as a hyphen here, or to prefer that uncertain hyphen to MT's blank space.

5.366/2389 Assistant,] MT ● ~: MB ● ~. CI OK CMA ● ~) C2 ● ~.) C3 ● ~! RO

5.368/2391 Sanctuarie;] MB ● ~, MT ● ~. CI +

5.369/2392 Wh] wh MB CI C2 C3 RO. What may be a minuscule in MB (though not much different from the preceding or following speech prefixes, where THH interprets the initial letter as majuscule) may have been affected by an attempt to write the letter under the tail of the 'h' from the first word of the line above.

5.369/2392 (Sⁱʳ)] CI + ● , ~, RO

5.370/2393 Wun] MT (NAS). Although MSR interprets MT as minuscule, it is actually larger than the first letter of the speech prefix in the preceding line (which he interprets as majuscule), and certainly majuscule if compared with the preceding ('twas) and following ('wth').

5.370/2393 Triumph] triumph MT RO OK

5.370/2393 Triumph,] ~₄ MB RO ● ~: CI

5.373/2396 perdition₄] MT CMA ● ~, MB+ ● ~: CI C2

5.374/2397 Lost] MB ● lost MT+. See unique autograph 'Lost' at 116 (verb, as here).

5.374/2397 fame₄] MT C2 ● ~, MB+ ● ~) CI

5.375/2398 Heads] MT CI ● heads MB+

5.375/2398 Shame] MT CI C3 ● fhame MB+

5.375/2398 Shame;] MB RO OK ● ~, MT ● ~. CI C3 ● ~₄ C2 CMA. This is the end of the play only in CI; but the double-autograph epilogue does not end with a full stop, but a colon. Normally the autograph-only comma would have been preferred here, but given the different context I have chosen the stronger pointing, closer to Middleton's play-ending punctuation in autograph; the semicolon is in any case characteristically Middletonian.

STAGE DIRECTIONS

Stage Directions: Middleton

The first list includes stage directions from MIDDLETON[T], and from those portions of the Bridgewater manuscript in Middleton's hand (MIDDLETON[B], here identified with an asterisk (*). The location of the direction in this edition is keyed to the line number of *An Early Form* (when the passage is present in that version), then of *A Later Form*. Where the manuscript position differs from its editorial position in *Early*, the difference is specified in brackets after the text of the direction itself.

Later Prologue.0.1   Prologue | (∴)

Induction.0.1   The Induction! | (∴)

Induction.0.3/Induction.0.1–2   Ignatius Loyola appearing, Error | at his foote as asleepe.

1.0.1/1.1.0.1   *Actus Primi, Scæna prima.*

1.0.2–4/1.1.0.2–5   Enter from the Black-house, the Bl. Queens | pawne, from the whitehouse the white Qs: | pawne;

1.32.1/1.1.30.1–2   Enter the Bl B.s p. | a Iesuite

1.212.1/1.1.195.1–2   Enter wh: Bps. pawne

1.222.1/1.1.205.1–2   Enter Bl Kts | pawne (right margin at 1.226–7/*Later* 1.1.207.1–1.1.208.1)

1.262.1/1.1.243.1   Enter Bl: K[t]

1.337.1/1.1.311.1   Enter wh. K[s] | pawne (right margin at 1.336–7/*Later* 1.1.311.1)

1.353.2/1.1.331.2   *Finit Actus primus.*

2.0.1/2.1.0.1   *Actus Secundi Scæna prima.*

2.0.2–3/2.1.0.2–3   Enter wh: Q[s] pawne wth a booke in her | hand.

2.9/2.1.8.1–2   Enter Bl.B[s] p.

Later 2.1.14.1   the Letter | (∴)

2.152.1/2.1.142.1   a Noyse wthin

2.178.1/2.1.162.1–2   Enter Bl. Bp, and Bl. | K[t] (at 2.176/*Later* 2.1.163.1–2)

2.258.1/2.1.228.1   Enter   Bl.K[ts]   pawn,   (at   2.259/*Later* 2.1.229.1)

2.275/2.1.239.1   exeunt

Later 2.2.0.1–3   Enter Fat Bishop wth a | pawne.

Later 2.2.17.1   exit B[s]p.

*Later 2.2.41.1   *Enter Bl. Kt.*

Later 2.2.48.1–2   Enter his pawne wth | Bookes!

2.275.1/2.2.81.1   Enter both houses, (right margin, opposite *Later* 2.2.82.1, 'fill')

2.275.2/2.2.94.1   Enter wh.Q[s] pawne (at *Later* 2.2.95.1)

2.428.1/2.2.233.1   exeunt

2.452.1/2.2.257.1   exeunt

3.0.1/3.1.0.1   *IncipitActus tertius* | (∴)

Later 3.1.0.2   Enter Fat Bishop.

Later 3.1.0.2   Enter fat Bishop. BRIDGEWATER[B]; *altered, following omission of Later 2.2.58–3.1.0.1, by* MIDDLETON[B] *to* The Fat Bishop.

Later 3.1.19.1   Enter Bl.k[t] (right margin)

Later 3.1.33   the Letter.

Later 3.1.77.1   exit

3.34.1/3.1.115.1   Enter his pawne: (right margin at 3.35/*Later* 3.1.116.1)

3.80.1/3.1.155.1   Enter Bl.Bishop | and both the houses (right margin, opposite 3.82/*Later* 3.1.155, 'then')

3.141.1/3.1.207.1   Enter Bl.Q[s]p.

3.242/3.1.313.1   exeunt

3.281.1/3.1.345.1   exeunt

3.281.2/Add. D 3.2.0.1   Enter a Bl. Iesting pawne

3.287.1/Add. D 3.2.6.1   Enter a Wh: Pawne, (right margin)

3.312.1/Add. D 3.2.28.1   Enter a 2 Black pawne.

3.326/Add. D 3.2.39.1   exeunt

3.326.1/Add. D 3.3.0.1   Enter Bl.Q[s] p. and wh.Qs.p.

3.349/3.367.1   the Inuocation | (∴)

3.376–3.377.1/3.392.1–95.1–3   {Musique, enters the Iesuite in | rich attire like an Apparition | presents himselfe before | the Glasse, then exit (after 3.379/*Later* 3.395)

3.400/3.415.1   exeunt (at 3.399/*Later* 3.414.1)

3.400.1/3.415.2   *Finit Actus 3[us]* (at 3.399/*Later* 3.414.2)

4.0.1/4.1.0.1   *Incipit Quartus.*

4.0.2/4.1.0.2–4   Enter Bl.K[ts] pawne meeting the Black B[s] | pawne richlie accoultred.

4.38/4.1.33.1   exit

4.38.1/4.1.33.2–3   Enter wh.Qs p. and | Bl.Qs.p. (right margin at 4.40.1/*Later* 4.35.1)

4.109.1/4.1.93.1   exit

4.113.1/4.1.97.1   Enter agayn. (right margin)

4.170.1/4.1.149.1   exeunt

4.170.2/4.2.0.1   Enter Bl. K[t] wth his pawne | (∴))

4.253.1/4.2.81.1   Enter Fat Bishop, (right margin, at 4.254.1/*Later* 4.2.81.1, 'sir')

4.304.1/4.2.134.2   Enter Bl. King

4.314/4.2.145.1   exeunt

4.314.2–4/4.3.0.1–8   Enter Bl. Queenes pawne as | Conducting the White to a | Chamber, then fetching in | the Bl. Bishops pawne the | Iesuite conuayes him to | another puts out the Light | and shee followes.

4.314.5/4.4.0.1–2   Enter white Knight, and wh. Duke.

4.365/4.4.48.1   exeunt

4.428.1/4.4.110.2   *Finit Actus Quartus.* (at 4.365.1/*Later* 4.4.48.2)

5.0.1/5.1.0.1   *Incipit Quintus.*

Later 5.1.0.2–5.1.1   Musique, Enter the Black Knight | in his Litter! calls

5.0.2–5/5.1.9.1–7   Hoboyes, Enter Bl.K. | Q. D. meeting the | wh. Knight and Duke. | the Oration. | (∴)

5.24.1, 25.1–5.25.2, 30.1/5.1.30.1, 33.1–2, 36.1   Musique an Altar discouerd | and Statues, wth a Song | Song. (at 5.30.1/*Later* 5.1.36.1)

5.44/5.1.50.1   exeunt

5.44.1/5.2.0.1   Enter wh.Qs.p.

5.44.1/5.2.3.1–2   Enter Iesuite (at 5.47.1)

5.141.1/5.2.87.1   Enter Bl.Qs.p.

*5.141.1/5.2.87.1   Enter Bl qs. p.

5.162.1/5.2.106.1–2   Enter white B[s]p. and | white Queene. (right margin, opposite 5.163–4/*Later* 5.2.106–7)

*5.162.1/5.2.106.1–2   Enter white Bs. | p. wth wh.Q. (at 5.163–4/*Later* 5.2.106–7)

5.171.1/5.2.112.1   Enter Bl.K[ts].p.

*5.171.1/5.2.112.1   Enter Bl: Kts.p.

5.178/5.2.118.1   exeunt

*5.178/5.2.118.1   exeunt.

*5.178.1–3/5.3.0.1–4   Enter Bl. King, Q. | Kt. Duke, wth white | Kt and his Duke | Scæna Vltima.

5.178.2–3/5.3.0.1–4   Enter Bl.K.Q. Duke | Bl.K[t] wth the white | K[t] and his Duke

5.362.1/5.3.166.1–3   Enter White King | Q. white pawnes.

*5.362.1/5.3.166.1 Enter white King | Q. white pawnes.

5.375.4/5.3.220.1 *Finis.* | (∴)

*5.375/5.3.220.1 T.m. | *Finis*

Later Epilogue.0.1 Epilogue. | wh:Queenes pawne!

*Later Epilogue.0.1 Epilogue | *The white Queenes pawne.* (∴)

Stage Directions: Crane

This second list includes all stage directions in CRANE[1]. The location of the direction in the manuscript—not necessarily identical to its location in our edited texts—is keyed to the line numbers of *An Early Form*.

Induction.0.1 *The Induction*

Induction.0.3 *Ignatius discovered; and Error, a-sleepe.*

Induction.53-6 —*Musick—En[| (seuerally) the Wh[| & Black- | -hous[| as they are sett f[| ye Game./* (right margin)

Induction.65-7 —*Enter y^e | Bl. Qu^s | Pawne & | Bl. B^{ps}.* (right margin; crossed out)

Induction.82 —*Exeun[*

1.0.1 *Actus Primus. Sce^a. Pri^a.*

1.0.2-4 *Enter (from ye Black-house) a Woman-Pawne (in | Black) & (from the White-house) a Woman-Pawne | (in White).*

1.32.1 —*Enter Black | B^{ps}. Pawne.* (right margin)

1.77 —*Exit.* (crossed out)

1.212.1 —*Enter | wh. B^{ps}. Paw[* (right margin, opposite 1.211-12)

1.222.1 —*Enter Bl[| Knights Pa[* (right margin, opposite 1.221-2)

1.262.1 —*Ex^t.—Ente[| Bl. Knigh[* (right margin)

1.337.1 —*Enter white | Kings Pawne* (right margin, opposite 1.337)

1.353 —*Ex^t*

1.353.1 *Finis Act[* (right margin, cropped beneath and to the right)

2.0.1 *Actus Secundus.*

2.0.2-3 *Sce^a. pri^a. Enter White-woman Pawne (wth a | Booke in her hand).* ['woman' marked for deletion, and 'Q^s' interlined to replace it]

2.9 —*Ent^r. Bl. B^s. | Pawne.* (right margin)

2.152.1 —*a noise w^{th}.in* (right margin)

2.167.1 —*Enter Black | woman-Pawne* (right margin)

2.178.1 —*Enter | Bl. B^p & | Bl. Knig[* (right margin)

2.256 —*Ex^t.*

2.258.1 —*Enter Bl.K^{ts} | Pawne.* (right margin)

2.275 —*Exeunt.* (below and right of line)

2.275-2.275.1 *Sce^a. 2^a. Enter (seu^rally) wh. King: Q: B^p. | Duke. Knight: Pawnes: & Q^s. Pawne: and Bl. | King. Q B^p. &c.*

2.428.1 —*Ex^t.*

2.452.1 *Exeunt.*

2.452.2 *Finis Actus Secundj.*

3.0.1 *Actus Tercius.*

3.0.1 *Enter Black-Knight.*

3.34.1 —*Enter | Bl. Pawne.* (right margin)

3.80.1 —*Enter | Bl. B^p. & | the wh. House, & | Bl. House.* (right margin, opposite 3.80-1)

3.103.1 —*Enter wh: Q^s. | Pawne.* (right margin)

3.141.1 —*Enter Bl. | Q^s. Pawne.* (right margin, opposite 3.140-1)

3.212.1-2 —*his vpper garment | taken of, he ap- | peeres Black - | vnderneath* (right margin, opposite 3.211-13)

3.230.1 —*Ex^t.*

3.241 —*Ex^t.*

3.280 —*Exeunt.*

3.281.2 *Sce^a. 2^a. Enter Black-Iesting-Pawne.*

3.287.1 —*Enter a wh. Pawne* (right margin)

3.312.1 —*Enter 2. Bl. | Pawne.* (right margin)

3.326 —*Exeunt.*

3.326 *Sce^a. 3^a. Enter Bl. Q^s. Pawne ,& white Q^s. Pawne.*

3.376-3.377.1 —*Musick—Ent[| Bl. B^s. Pawne, in | rich Attire, like | an Apparition.* (right margin, opposite 3.376-8)

3.400 —*Exeunt.*

3.400 *Finis Actus Tercij*

4.0.1 *Actus Quartus:*

4.0.2 *Sce^a. pri^a. Enter Bl. K^{ts}. Pawne, & Bl. B^s. Pawne.*

4.38 —*Exit*

4.38 —*Enter wh. Q^s P. | & Bl. Q^s. Pawne.* (right margin)

4.109.1 —*Ex^t.*

4.113.1 —*Enter agen.* (right margin)

4.170.1 *Exeunt*

4.170.2 *Sce^a. 2^a. Enter Bl. Knight, & his Pawne.*

4.253 —*Enter Bl.B^p.* (right margin)

4.304 —*Ex^t*

4.304 —*Enter | Bl. King* (right margin)

4.314 —*Exeunt.* (right margin)

4.314 —*Musick.* (right margin)

4.314.1-3 *Domb shew}* (left margin)

4.314.1-3 *Enter Bl. Q^s. P. wth Lights, conducting wh. Q^s. Pawne | to a Chamber: and then ye Bl. B^{ps}. Pawne to an other, & Ex[*

4.314.4 *Sce^a. 3^a. Enter White-Knight, & wh. Duke.*

4.326.1 —*Enter Bl. | Knight* (right margin, opposite 4.325-6)

4.365 —*Exeunt.*

4.365 *Sce^a. 4^a. Enter White Queene.*

4.376.1 —*Enter | Bl. B^p.* (right margin)

4.385.1 —*Enter wh.B^p.* (right margin)

4.393.1 —*enter Wh.King* (right margin)

4.428 —*Exeunt.*

4.428 *Finis Actus Quarti.*

5.0.1 *Actus Quintus.*

5.0.2-5 *Sce^a. pri^a. (Lowd Musick) Enter Bl. King: Queene, | Duke & Pawnes, & Bl. Knight: meeting the | white Knight, & Duke: (y^e Bl. B^{ps}. Pawne aboue, | Enterteines them, wth this Lattin Oration)* ['Litter.' inserted by interlining between 5.0.1 and 5.0.2, above and between 'Musick') and 'Enter']

5.24.1 —*Musick* (right margin)

5.25.1-2 —*An Altar disco= | -uerd, richely adorned, | and diuers Statues | standing on each-side.* (right margin, opposite 5.25-8)

5.30.1 *Song.* (left margin before 5.31)

5.38.1 —*The Statues | moue, & Dance.* (right margin)

5.44 —*Exeunt.*

5.44-5.44.1 *Sce^a. 2^a. Enter wh.Q^s. Pawne, & Bl. B^{ps}. Pawne (in | his reuerend habit) meeting hir.*

5.124.1 —*Bl. Q^s. Pawne | within* (right margin)

5.141.1 —*Enter B[| Q^s. Pawn[* (right margin)

5.162.1 —*Enter wh. B^s. | Pawne, & wh. Queene* (right margin)

5.171.1 —*Enter Bl.K^{ts}. | Pawne.* (right margin)

5.178 —*Exeunt.*

5.178-5.178.2 *Sce^a. 3^a. Enter Bl. King: Queene: Knight, Duke | & Pawnes wth white Knight, & Duke.*

5.360 —*Flourish.* (right margin)

5.362.1 —*Enter wh. King | Queene: Bishop & | w^h. Pawnes.* (right margin, opposite 5.362-3)

5.375 —*Exeunt.*

5.375 *Finis Actus Quinti*

LINEATION NOTES

These notes identify every editorial emendation of the lineation of CRANE[1], and every instance of lineation which is unique to CRANE[1] (identified by an asterisk). They do not systematically record variants between the lineation of CRANE[1] and other texts. For lineation variants more generally, see the Textual Notes to *Later*. As elsewhere in THIS EDITION, the lemma cites the spelling but not punctuation of our text.

Induction.51 tis...thinke] *1 line* ROSENBACH[A]; dream| MIDDLE-TON[T]+. In CRANE[1] the scribe began to write 'a ⟨.⟩' on the same line, then partially erased it and began 'a Vision' on the next manuscript line. In Middleton's original draft the two part-lines were probably written on a single manuscript line, as in ROSENBACH.

1.31 from...Errors] CRANE[1,2,3,4], ROSENBACH; *2 lines* eye| MIDDLETON, BRIDGEWATER[A], OKES. It seems apparent that Middleton often wrote on a single manuscript line what the metre would identify as a line and a half. As the following notes demonstrate, virtually the only 'errors' in the lineation of CRANE[1] result from this practice, which occurs fourteen times in CRANE[1], more than in any other witness. Moreover, the practice is in every other instance contradicted by other Crane texts, and it is often supported by autograph texts; it never occurs in more than two Crane texts without being supported (as it is here) by at least one non-Crane text. Because it seems to be a relic of the authorial draft, this formal arrangement has been preserved here; every instance is, however, noted below.

1.142 of...thoughts] CRANE[1], ROSENBACH[A], CRANE/MATHEWES; *2 lines* MIDDLETON+: food|. Another relic.

1.272-3 the...lesse] CRANE[1,2,4], ROSENBACH[A]; nor| hierarchy MIDDLETON[T], BRIDGEWATER[A]; monarchy| OKES; *3 lines* CRANE[3]: stands| hierarchy|. Another relic. The shared error in MIDDLETON[T] and BRIDGEWATER[A] probably testifies to the fact that their copy derives from a lineation like CRANE[1], which produces a line so long that a copyist is forced to break it somewhere; if the formal structure had been indicated as it is in CRANE[3], the error in MIDDLETON[T] and BRIDGEWATER[A] (and the variant in OKES) would be hard to explain.

*1.339 take...pawne] MIDDLETON[T]+; *2 lines* CRANE[1]: the—|. The dash here presumably indicates that these two manuscript lines are only a single verse line; if Crane had continued on the same line, he would have run into the marginal stage direction. The dash here functions in the same way as a parenthesis, used to mark a turnover.

2.40-1 Boundlesse...Goodnes] CRANE[1], ROSENBACH[A]; all| MIDDLETON[T], BRIDGEWATER[A], OKES; *3 lines*: obedience| duties| CRANE[2], CRANE/MATHEWES; *not in* CRANE[3]. Another relic. As at 1.272-3, the shared error in MIDDLETON[T], BRIDGEWATER[A], and OKES suggests that something like CRANE[1]'s lineation stood in the manuscript(s) from which they were copied.

2.62-3 I...meaning] CRANE[1]+; plaintiffe| MIDDLETON[T], BRIDGEWATER[A], OKES; *not in* CRANE[3]. Either arrangement is metrically defensible.

2.79-80 Goodmen...one] CRANE[1] (mistook sure,| if), ROSENBACH[A]+; mistaken| sure, if MIDDLETON, BRIDGEWATER[A], OKES. Either arrangement is defensible. In this and the preceding variant, in most texts the metrical break coincides with a grammatical one.

2.90 haue...seruitude] ROSENBACH[A]; *2 lines*: myself| CRANE[1]+. Since Crane's other transcripts almost always eliminate the practice of writing a line and a half of verse on a single manuscript line, it seems reasonable to assume that some examples of that practice in Middleton's papers would have been caught and 'corrected' in CRANE[1] also. In cases where CRANE[1] preserves the authorial practice, it is most often seconded by ROSENBACH[A] (five times); ROSENBACH also has the second-highest total of this feature (nine). Here, ROSENBACH probably reflects the lineation in [MIDDLETON[PRE]] better than does CRANE[1].

2.166 Confusion...undoing] MIDDLETON[T], BRIDGEWATER[A]; *2 lines*: voice| OKES; Confusion| CRANE[1]+. See preceding note. Here an autograph text preserves the practice, which all the Crane manuscripts correct away; MIDDLETON[T] confirms the practice on at least five other occasions, twice seconding CRANE[1] (3.331, 4.278-9), and three times similarly aligning passages not present in the *Early* version (*Later* 2.2.27-8, 3.1.6, 4.2.105-6). The mislineation in OKES suggests that something like MIDDLETON[T] stood in its copy, and that OKES broke the line randomly, in order to fit its measure.

2.198 grosse...Societie] OKES; *2 lines*: witness| CRANE[1]+. See the two preceding notes. One of many authorial features which OKES shares sporadically with other witnesses outside the 'Crane' group.

2.233 a fire, a...there] CRANE[1], ROSENBACH[A]; *2 lines*:| what MIDDLETON[T]+. Another relic. In CRANE[1], the authorially added half-line is placed in the right margin, without any indication that it should be placed on a separate line; CRANE[1]'s placement thus tends to confirm ROSENBACH[A]'s.

*2.269 cause...what's that] CRANE[1]; *second speech not in* MIDDLETON[T], BRIDGEWATER[A], OKES; *whole passage not in* CRANE[3]; *2 lines* ROSENBACH[A], CRANE[2], CRANE/MATHEWES: way|. As the text notes explain, this unusual manuscript lineation probably reflects a marginal insertion in the foul papers; there is no other example in CRANE[1] of two short speeches on a single line.

*2.320 wth his...out] CRANE[1]; *2 lines*: name| MIDDLETON[T]+; *passage not in* BRIDGEWATER[A]. Another relic.

*2.336 a...to] CRANE[1]; *2 lines* retort| MIDDLETON[T]+; *passage not in* CRANE[3], BRIDGEWATER[A]. Another relic.

2.372 oh...thee] ROSENBACH[A], OKES; *2 lines* CRANE[1]+. See 2.90.

2.407-8 behold...good] CRANE[1], MIDDLETON[T]; *not in* BRIDGEWATER[A], CRANE[3]; *3 lines*: all| one| OKES, ROSENBACH[A]; *2 lines*: one| CRANE/MATHEWES. Another relic. Here autograph confirms the pattern seen repeatedly in CRANE[1]; the variants in OKES and CRANE/MATHEWES could both derive from something like the autograph lineation.

3.169 tis...agent] OKES; *2 lines*: truth| CRANE[1]+. See 2.198-9.

*3.291 pox...Black-bird] CRANE[1]; *2 lines*: on you| MIDDLETON; *not in* CRANE[2], CRANE[3]; *altered in* CRANE/ALLDE; *prose* BRIDGEWATER[B], ROSENBACH[A]; taken| OKES. Another relic. The metrical structure is correctly indicated by MIDDLETON, only; the confusion in the other texts could easily have arisen from an arrangement like that in CRANE[1].

3.331 under...Turtle] CRANE[1], MIDDLETON[T], CRANE[2]; *not in* CRANE[3]; *2 lines*: omen| BRIDGEWATER[B], ROSENBACH[A], OKES, CRANE/ALLDE. Another relic. See 2.407-8.

*3.355 I...yet] CRANE[1]; *2 lines*: seen| MIDDLETON[T]+. Another relic.

*3.362 wth...yet] CRANE[1]; *2 lines*: same| MIDDLETON[T]+. Relic.

4.268 Adultrie?...Adulterie] CRANE[1], CRANE[3], OKES; *prose* MIDDLETON[T]; *2 lines* ROSENBACH[A], CRANE/ALLDE: Adultery| shillings|; *2 lines* CRANE[2]: Adultery| for adultery|. Another relic: ROSENBACH[A], CRANE[2], and CRANE/ALLDE indicate the metrically implied break after the first word.

4.269 2...fiuepence] OKES; *prose* CRANE[1], MIDDLETON[T]; fornication| CRANE[2], CRANE[3]; couple| BRIDGEWATER[B]; shillings| ROSENBACH[A], CRANE/ALLDE. The verbal variants in CRANE[1] help to constitute a normal pentameter.

4.282 whats...Encouragement] CRANE[1]+; *prose?* MIDDLETON[T] *only*: encou| ragement. Another relic, this one preserved by all witnesses.

5.21 they...giuer] OKES, CRANE/ALLDE; *2 lines* CRANE[1], CRANE[2], ROSENBACH[B], BRIDGEWATER[B]: fauours|; *not in* MIDDLETON[T], CRANE[3]. See 2.198–9.

*5.356-7 and...all] CRANE[1]; by| MIDDLETON[T]+; checkmate| OKES. Another relic.

*5.359-60 Ambitious...all] CRANE[1]; falsehood| MIDDLETON[B]+; *3 lines*: ambitious| falsehood| CRANE[3]; covetous| falsehood| CRANE[2]; *not in* MIDDLETON[T]

A GAME AT CHESS: A LATER FORM

Edited by Gary Taylor

ALL modern editions of *A Game at Chess*—those by DYCE, BULLEN, BALD, BROOKE AND PARADISE, HARPER, HOWARD--HILL, and DUTTON—have been editions of the revised version. Thus, whereas *The Collected Works* prints *An Early Form* for the first time, *A Later Form* belongs to a well--established editorial tradition, surveyed by Howard-Hill in 1995 (*Pasquin* 193–9). Moreover, like all these previous editions, *A Later Form* is an eclectic text, drawing upon more than one early witness. Even Lamb—who in 1835 anthologized a sixteen-line excerpt from the play, and thereby put it into print for the first time in more than two centuries—combined readings from two early witnesses (419–20). Bald's edition, which many scholars treated as a reliable transcript of the autograph manuscript, was criticized for its eclecticism by Nascimento, who comprehensively documented its editorial departures from MIDDLETON[T]. Howard-Hill's rigorously scholarly transcript of MIDDLETON[T] (1990) included also a transcript of MIDDLETON[B], and Bawcutt's rigorously scholarly transcript of CRANE[3] (1993) included also a transcript of extended excerpts from CRANE[2]. For editors of the version of the play performed and published in Middleton's lifetime, the question is not *whether* to be eclectic, but *how* eclectic to be (or how to be eclectic).

Reconstructing the verbal texture of a work like *A Game at Chess*, which survives in multiple witnesses, entails two distinct operations. First and foremost, the editor must eliminate errors. Errors are readings that were never consciously intended by the author, at any time. The adverb 'consciously' is important, because Middleton, like any other copyist, sometimes inattentively executed his own intentions. Baseball players seldom intend to strike out, quarterbacks seldom intend to throw an interception, but occasionally all such players empirically fail to execute real intentions. Sometimes Middleton caught himself in the process of making an error, and immediately corrected it; all such self-corrections are recorded in the Textual Notes, because they tell us a great deal about Middleton as a copyist, and may also tell us something about his copy-text. However, on other occasions (as all editors agree) Middleton as copyist made a mistake that he did not correct. Thus, even the autograph manuscripts contain errors, and so of course do all the other witnesses.

Usually, the errors made in one text are corrected in one or more other texts. Therefore, the first step in identifying and correcting error is to collate all the early witnesses. The following Textual Notes publish, for the first time, a comprehensive list of readings in all eight substantive witnesses. (Variants unique to the unauthoritative reprint

OKES[2] are recorded by Nascimento.) Unlike the textual apparatus to *An Early Form*, and unlike Nascimento's analytic apparatus, the Textual Notes to *A Later Form* combine all categories of substantive variant in a single list. The Textual Notes also include all known press variants in OKES[1] and MATHEWES/ALLDE, even when they are not substantive. They also include so-called 'semi-substantive' variants, primarily colloquial contractions that may affect our understanding of Middleton's metrical intentions. In *An Early Form* such semi-substantive variants are recorded among 'Emendations of Incidentals'; in *A Later Form* they are recorded among substantive variants. This difference between the *Early* and *Later* apparatus reflects the ambiguous status of such variants, as orthographical forms which may substantively alter verse form but which do not alter meaning. Otherwise, the Textual Notes do not include spelling and punctuation variants, unless in a particular instance the spelling or punctuation of some witnesses seems to be so misleading that it might be considered a substantive error.

Whenever I believe that a variant in one or more texts is an error, I attempt to explain how or why the error was made. This explanatory imperative, combined with the number of extant substantive witnesses, accounts for the unprecedented length of the apparatus to *A Later Form*. But the identification and explanation of error is especially important in *A Game at Chess*, because it may have implications for the stemma of transmission of the extant witnesses. I therefore distinguish, in the Textual Notes, between two categories of rejected readings: (1) variants that are certainly errors, and (2) variants that are probably errors, or which I personally consider errors, but which have been or might be defended by another scholar. In the editing of *A Later Form*, the two categories have the same result: the reading is not printed in *The Collected Works*. But in the analysis of the stemma of transmission in the General Textual Introduction, I have limited myself to variants in the first category. Particularly important, within that category, are errors that occur in more than one witness. All such substantive 'shared errors' are identified, in the Textual Notes, with an asterisk preceding the line number. Those asterisked errors are tabulated in Appendices A–D. (Appendix D further refines and filters those totals; but the Textual Notes do not distinguish between the filtered and unfiltered items.)

The identification and elimination of error is an editorial activity relevant to every text in *The Collected Works*. But *A Game at Chess* also imposes on editors a second imperative, which is much less common. In addition to identifying errors, the editor must identify authorial variants: that is, identify places where the author had more than one intention. Having located such variants, the editor must normally choose which authorial intention to prioritize. In a printed edition like *The Collected Works*, only one authorial variant will be placed in the reading text. But even in an electronic edition, one reading will normally be prioritized as the default reading (Taylor 2000b).

The identification of authorial variation is easier when we possess—as we do for 5.2, 5.3, the Epilogue, and parts of 2.2—two autograph manuscripts of the work. In other cases, the identification of authorial variation is sometimes related to the identification of error. Any reading that cannot be plausibly explained as an error may be an authorial variant. In this case, the identification is negative: what cannot be an error must be an authorial variant. But authorial variants can also be identified positively, either by demonstrating their relationship to Middleton's known sources for the play, or by demonstrating that they reflect verbal habits found in Middleton's other work ('verbal parallels'). In searching for collateral evidence of Middleton's vocabulary and style, previous editors have been hampered by the unavailability of basic research tools (a standard edition, printed and electronic concordances). This is the first edition based on the systematic use of a printed modern-spelling concordance (a draft concordance to *The Collected Works*, generated by John Lavagnino in 1993) and of electronic databases which include old-spelling texts of much of Middleton's canon (LION, EEBO-TCP). Although such resources are valuable in editing all of Middleton's work, they have been especially important in establishing the Middletonian character of many verbal variants in *Game*.

The identification of authorial variants can also be aided by an understanding of the relationship of the extant witnesses to one another and to important lost manuscripts like [MIDDLETON^{PRE}] and [KING'S MEN^1]. The General Textual Introduction attempts to construct a stemma of transmission for all extant, known, or inferred early texts of *Game*. All modern editors agree that four of the eight extant substantive texts are sources of unique authorial readings: CRANE^1 (a transcript of the earliest autograph text, which contains original readings subsequently censored or corrupted in all surviving witnesses of the revised version), MIDDLETON^T (autograph in its entirety), BRIDGEWATER (partially autograph), and OKES (printed from an autograph manuscript). To these four may now be added CRANE^2, chosen by DUTTON as his copy-text, and (according to my analysis of the textual stemma) only one intervening text away from the licensed playbook of the King's Men. In addition, in the following Textual Notes I am able to identify several unique authorial readings in CRANE^3, readings that apparently originated in Middleton's own work on the abridgement of the text. Where both CRANE^2 and CRANE^3 agree on a sensible variant that does not appear in other witnesses, they may well be reflecting the reading in [PRE-CRANE^{2,3}], which was apparently copied directly from the playbook. For the approximately one-third of the play omitted from the abridged CRANE^3, the only extant witness of that branch of the stemma is CRANE^2. Thus, on occasion either CRANE^2 or CRANE^3 might contain unique authorial variants; more often, the two together might contain an authorial variant unique to that branch of the stemma.

Other, later texts descend from another copy of the playbook, [KING'S MEN^3]. Nascimento demonstrated that ROSENBACH, while containing a text of the revised version, also preserves many early authorial features; I conclude that it derives from an autograph transcript of the revised version. According to my stemmatic analysis, ROSENBACH is the earliest surviving witness to dozens of variants also present in MIDDLETON^T and BRIDGEWATER; thus, like every surviving autograph manuscript, the source of ROSENBACH apparently contained new authorial variants (alongside new errors). Thus, ROSENBACH, too, may contain unique authorial variants.

So far, stemmatic analysis has identified authorial variants in three of the extant CRANE texts and three of the extant NON-CRANE texts. The fourth NON-CRANE text, BRIDGEWATER, contains unique readings in its autograph sections. But most of the text is scribal, and authorial readings in those sections could only have come from its copy-text. Unique readings in the scribal portions of BRIDGEWATER, which seem to be authorial, occur at 1.1.287, 2.1.8.1, 2.1.218, 2.2.41, 3.1.279, 3.1.320, and 3.2.29, and are discussed in the Textual Notes. These variants suggest that the copy-text for BRIDGEWATER was autograph, at least for the first half of the play. So do variants shared only by MIDDLETON^T and BRIDGEWATER. Since MIDDLETON^T was a dead-end, it could not have transmitted any new authorial variants directly to BRIDGEWATER; hence, any such readings must have come to both MIDDLETON^T and BRIDGEWATER from some antecedent, lost authorial manuscript that was a copy-text or ancestor for both. Such readings are discussed in the Textual Notes at Induction.71, 1.1.0.1, 1.1.30.1, 1.1.253, 1.1.307, 1.1.308, 2.1.137, 2.1.157, 3.1.0.1, 3.1.193, 4.2.0.1, 4.2.3, and 4.2.66.

The single remaining substantive text, MATHEWES/ALLDE, is a descendant of [KING'S MEN^3] for its entire length, and for Acts Four and Five it is closer to the playbook than any of the four NON-CRANE texts. I have argued in the General Textual Introduction that it was printed from Middleton's transcription of [CRANE^4]. Thus, MATHEWES/ALLDE might also contain unique authorial variants.

To summarize: stemmatically, every one of the eight extant witnesses might be expected to contain some unique authorial variants, and in practice every one of them apparently does. The stemma informs editorial choice, but it does not do so by eliminating whole classes of variants; indeed, the only document discredited by stemmatic analysis is OKES^2. Instead, the stemma indicates that the author was deeply involved in the early reproduction and dissemination of the text. Stemmatic analysis actually increases the field of potential authorial variation.

Having identified, by such means, a large pool of certain or probable authorial variants, an editor still must decide which authorial intention to prioritize, in any given case. Most editorial theorizing about what to do in such circumstances presupposes a linear model of intention, which moves smoothly from an 'original' intention to a 'final' intention, or from 'authorial' to 'social' intentions. Theorists and practitioners disagree about which end of the spectrum to prefer, but all tend to reinforce the authority of a linear model. The witnesses of *A Game at Chess* disturb that model, and therefore disturb our sense of editorial options and responsibilities. 'Final' intentions sometimes circle back to 'original' intentions, revoking 'middle intentions', perhaps deliberately, perhaps unconsciously or half-consciously, perhaps simply because of the influence of different copy-texts. Authorial revisions made in one document seem to have been ignored or forgotten in the next. The messiness of the evidence should not surprise anyone familiar with the oceanic instability of human intentions. How are editors to make up our minds, if authors refuse to do so? Howard-Hill concludes one of his many important studies of *A Game at Chess* with a despairing declaration of independence: 'an editor may receive some comfort from the reflection that, *whatever* may be the character of his representation of Middleton's "final intentions", the author himself would have accepted it' (1987, 316). Nevertheless, Howard-Hill spent a decade of scholarly activity trying to distinguish error from revision, and to produce an edition of *Game* more reliable and responsible, editorially, than the texts produced or overseen by Middleton himself.

At the very least, an editor can tell readers what they are getting. This edition of *A Later Form* attempts to represent the structure of the play performed by the King's Men in August 1624. Thus, the main body of *A Later Form* does not include four passages apparently omitted from performances; those are printed in an appendix of Additional Passages, instead. More pervasively, the stage directions and speech prefixes of *A Later Form* indicate the historical and theatrical identity of the chess characters, because those identities were a fundamental and well--documented aspect of the 1624 performances. In both respects, this edition of *A Later Form* differs from all previous editions. Moreover, the added information in speech prefixes and stage directions affects every scene of the reading text—just as it affected every scene in early performances. Each of these historical identifications is discussed in the Textual Notes to the preliminary list of characters; most of them are explicitly supported by early comments on the play (collected in Appendix G). Those for which there is no explicit historical witness are bracketed, as conjectural, whenever they occur in *A Later Form*. Whenever such information is provided in the text, it will also be provided in the lemma for a textual note to the relevant passage ('Black Knight Gondomar', 'White King James'). But the additional information ('Gondomar', 'James', etc) will be ignored in the collation to the right of the bracket, because it does not occur in any of the eight substantive transcriptions of the play. Thus,

the textual notes pay attention to speech prefixes or stage directions only where variants occur among the eight substantive witnesses, or where emendation is at issue; after the preliminary list of characters, the textual apparatus ignores the historical identifications.

Nevertheless, despite its fidelity to these structural aspects of the performed play, *A Later Form* does not attempt to represent the verbal texture of the 1624 performances, of the licensed playbook, or of the actors' parts. *A Later Form* is, first and foremost, a text for readers. It supplies the historical and theatrical identifications of the characters not simply, or even primarily, because those identities were visible in early performances; it supplies that information in order to make the play as intelligible for twenty-first century readers as it was for Jacobean spectators. Likewise, the four passages deleted from performances seem to have been cut in order to eliminate unnecessary elaborations that might detract from the clarity of the play's very complicated action. Again, what once served the interests of early modern spectators also serves the interests of postmodern readers.

The correspondences that recommend the structure of early performance do not necessarily apply once we descend to the level of verbal detail. Moreover, we have outstanding historical evidence for the historical identifications of characters. By contrast, the playbook and the actors' parts are lost, and the early responses to the play provide almost no information about its verbal detail. (Consequently, those reports are seldom cited after the preliminary list of characters.) An editor could attempt to reconstruct the verbal detail of [KING'S MEN[1]], and in fact I have prepared such a reconstruction, which I hope to publish as part of the electronic edition. If it had been possible to print more than two texts of *A Game at Chess* in *The Collected Works*, then a reconstructed text of 'The Playbook Form' would have been a prime candidate for inclusion. (So would an edited, modern-spelling text of 'The Abridged Form'). However, my decision about how many 'Later Forms' to print in *The Collected Works* was limited by the constraints of space in a large volume that was already pushing the limits of contemporary paper thickness and binding technology. Likewise, the decision about *which* of the many 'Later Forms' to print was affected by the fact that it would sit alongside *An Early Form*. Because *An Early Form* gives readers Middleton's earliest complete version of the play, it seems valuable to give readers an alternative from the other end of the chronological spectrum. The eclectic text of *A Later Form* printed here therefore attempts to recover Middleton's 'final' revisions of the verbal texture of the play. But I do not assume that those 'final' revisions are all contained in a single document or that such fossils of authorial intention can all be found deposited in a single chronological layer. Rather, I interpret 'Middleton's final intentions' to mean 'Middleton's intention at any point in the chronological evolution of the play *later* than his first complete draft,

[MIDDLETON[PRE]], whenever that later intention consciously differed from his earlier intention'.

What does this mean in practice? If Middleton at any time between spring 1624 and summer 1625 wrote two alternative versions of a particular phrase or line, then in almost all cases *The Collected Works* prints one version of that phrase in *An Early Form* and the other version in *A Later Form*. The logic of editorial choice is thus governed by the desire to give readers as many Middletonian intentions as possible.

If Middleton changed his mind about a word or a phrase at any point between the preparation of the playbook and his last transcription of part or all of the play, sometime in 1625, then that revised verbal intention will be printed in *A Later Form*. Thus, if Middleton changed word X in Text A, and changed phrase Y in Text B, *A Later Form* will contain the revised word X and the revised phrase Y, even if those two variants did not appear together in any extant early witness of the play. *A Later Form* is, consequently, a systematically 'conflated' text. This will dissatisfy some readers, and it may surprise or distress (or delight) readers who are familiar with my programmatic rejection of conflated texts of *King Lear* or *Hamlet*. But the circumstances that produced the extant texts of *A Game at Chess* fundamentally differ from the circumstances that governed the routine artisanal production of texts in the London commercial theatres. The movement from the original authorial complete draft represented by *An Early Form* and the script performed at the Globe produced two distinct versions of *A Game at Chess*. So far, so normal. If that had been the end of the story, we would be left with something like the two versions of *The Lady's Tragedy* printed in *The Collected Works*. But later—in response to the combination of censorship, unparalleled public demand, and authorial indigence—many different texts of *Game* were produced, texts specifically designed for reading, and probably designed for different markets (whether individual readers or classes of readers). The authorial verbal variants contained in these many different reading texts do not seem to reflect the transition from textual to performance, or a changed view of any of the characters, or a refocusing of the play's overall structure or meaning. Instead, the authorial revisions in later reading texts are, apparently, purely localized attempts to improve a particular phrase or word or image. Even the wholesale abridgement of the play, in CRANE[3], does not evince any discernible intention to change the meaning of the play; it is remarkably and cunningly faithful in delivering a condensed version of the same aesthetic, intellectual, and political experience.

The object of editorial desire is proximity to a 'source of value' (Taylor 1994); here, forced by the economics of print to limit myself to two texts instead of five or six, I have chosen the value of local authorial verbal revision, rather than the value of editorial fidelity to the unity of a single lost document. That lost document, in any case, was certainly a composite, containing layers of text added, altered, and deleted; hence, any attempt to produce a reading edition of the playbook would have to make decisions about which layer(s) of the composite document to reproduce. Moreover, the stemma of transmission reconstructed in the General Textual Introduction establishes that no single extant witness reliably reproduces all features of the playbook; hence, any reconstruction of the lost [KING'S MEN[1]] would be an eclectic text based on a reconstruction of the lost [PRE-CRANE[2,3]] and the lost [KING'S MEN[3]]. Finally, any such reconstruction of the lost document would not include historical identifications of the chess characters, which were demonstrably not present in the playbook, but were—equally demonstrably—present in performances. Finally, Middleton himself clearly did not regard the playbook as the only source of editorial value. None of the eight substantive witnesses produced after performances began is consistently faithful to the playbook.

Moreover, fidelity to the playbook would entail acceptance of Sir Henry Herbert's censorship of the text. Since the play itself satirizes the silencing of opposition writing, in this case more than most it would seem bizarre to perpetuate editorially the censor's interventions. This particular editorial policy reduces the amount of variation between *An Early Form* and *A Later Form*, but it does not reduce the amount of *authorial* verbal variation.

Finally, the policy of maximizing authorial variation leaves open, in a few cases, the question of which text should contain which variant. Since *A Later Text* is printed in modern spelling and punctuation, I have preserved obsolete or archaic forms ('I', 'a purpose') in *Early*, and preferred their modern counterparts ('yes', 'on purpose') in *Later*. Usually, Middleton himself used both forms—or, at least, both forms occur in the earliest extant texts of his work—and the distribution of forms is not consistently segregated between the two versions of *Game*. Those who appreciate Middleton's embedded embodiment of early modern experience can find the exotic authenticity of the archaic in *An Early Form*, while those who prefer the clarity of Middleton's modernity can find that in *A Later Form*.

SEE ALSO

Text: *Works*, 1830
General textual introduction: this volume, 712
List of works cited: this volume, 848
Authorship and date: this volume, 439

TEXTUAL NOTES

Title *as . . . together*] OKES, MIDDLETON[R]; *as it hath bine sundrey times acted* CRANE/MATHEWES; *not in* CRANE[1]+. This information is clearly not necessary, and could not have been supplied when CRANE[1] was dated (before the play's run was abruptly ended). Of the verbal variants, 'nine days' provides more precise information (independently confirmed by Coloma 18 August, Chamberlain, and the manuscript annotator of the Dyce copy of OKES[2]), and OKES agrees with autograph; by contrast, 'hath' departs from Middleton's normal preference (for 'has').

Title *by the King's Men*] THIS EDITION; *not in* MIDDLETON+. This information is implied by the reference to the Globe, and independently specified in several contemporary documents: Woolley ('by his Ma[ts.] seruants'), Colona 7 August ('The Actors who are called "the King's"'), Colona 10 August ('The actors whom they call here "the King's men"'), Conway ('the Kings Players'), Privy Council ('by the *Kings Players*'), Pembroke ('his Ma[tie] . . . y[e] Company of his comedians'). The omission of the name of the company may have been tactful.

Title *at . . . bankside*] OKES (banks fide), CRANE/MATHEWES (Banck fide); *not in* CRANE[1]+. See preceding notes. The Globe is independently specified by Holles, Overton, and Salisbury. Either form of 'bankside' was acceptable.

Persons.0.2–**Persons.**76 PERSONS . . . Statues] THIS EDITION; *not in* CRANE[1]+. It would have been politically extremely dangerous for Middleton or anyone else to provide a list of characters, like those that appeared in other Middleton works from 1611 on, for any of the early texts of *Game*. (See Taylor, 'Persons.') Modern editions, if they provide a list of Dramatis Personae at all, simply list the generic names found in early texts (Black Knight, etc.), without describing them as persons or specific chess pieces, or identifying the historical persons that some of them demonstrably represented. THIS EDITION lists the characters in descending order of dramatic importance, based on the number of words each speaks.

Persons.4 GONDOMAR] THIS EDITION (*conj.* DYCE); *not in* CRANE[1]+. This identification is confirmed by the title-page engravings, the play's sources, and contemporary accounts of the play by Woolley, Coloma, Holles, Conway, Overton, Salvetti, Nethersole, Chamberlain, Salisbury, Ryves, Jonson, and Heminges. This first identification is crucial to all the others. 'Once [Gondomar] was identified,' Howard-Hill notes (*Pasquin* 119), 'the analogical relationship of the other pieces to the Black Knight established their historical identity, so far as the contemporary political situation provided appropriate counterparts for the chessman.' All insertions in entrance directions and speech prefixes of this and other historical identifications are likewise editorial, and not recorded.

Persons.4 (Black Queen's Knight)] THIS EDITION; *not in* CRANE[1]+. Since he is repeatedly paired with the Black [Queen's] Bishop, this piece presumably begins on an adjoining square. From the perspective of hostile Protestant critics, Gondomar was the chief diplomatic advocate of the Spanish Match, designed to give England a future Black Queen.

Persons.10 JESUIT] THIS EDITION; *not in* CRANE[1]+; Father Henry Floyd BULLEN *conj*. Bullen's conjecture was based upon the details given at 5.2.91–101. That identification is at least more appropriate than Maximilian, Duke of Bavaria (suggested by Morris) or the Dominican Fray Diego de Lafuente

(suggested by Sherman). But it is highly unlikely that Middleton expected an actor to impersonate Floyd, or expected spectators to recognize him, even in 5.2 (let alone earlier), and it would make no difference to the play if they did so. Although never so identified in the speech prefixes of the early texts, Black Bishop's Pawn is repeatedly called a 'Jesuit' in stage directions and dialogue; if he represents 'all that Anglicans feared and detested in the Jesuits' (HOWARD-HILL, 74), then he cannot represent a particular individual, since one of the paranoid beliefs about Jesuits was that England was filled with thousands of them.

Persons.10–11 (Black Queen's Bishop's Pawn)] THIS EDITION (*conj.* HARPER); *not in* CRANE[1]+. From beginning to end of the play the Black Bishop's Pawn is closely associated with the Black Queen's Pawn, so we would expect him to be on an adjoining file. When the two Jesuit pawns are first seen, Loyola's comment at Induction.64–6 indicates that, if the Black Bishop's Pawn took the place of his Bishop, he would be immediately adjacent to the Black Queen. The Induction's introductory positioning of the two Jesuit pawns makes it possible for the audience to recognize the opening moves of the game, in 1.1, as a classic chess opening, Queen's Gambit Declined (with Black beginning the game, as was common in the seventeenth century): Black Queen's Pawn to d4, White Queen's Pawn to d5, Black Queen's Bishop's Pawn to c4, which enables and invites White Queen's Pawn to capture Black Queen's Bishop's Pawn; but she does not do so (though he says 'I never was so taken', and in a sense his infatuation with her does lead to his eventual capture in 5.2).

Persons.15 VIRGIN] THIS EDITION; *not in* CRANE[1]+. She calls herself 'A virgin' at 4.1.127; the vocative 'virgin' is used of her at 1.1.32, 1.1.220; her 'virginity' is explicitly acknowledged at 2.1.122, implicitly at 3.1.164, 5.2.78. Her virginity is symbolically related to her whiteness, and throughout the plot she is implicitly compared to the 'Maiden Queen of the White Kingdom' (4.2.117–18), who like her was tempted by various Catholic suitors, but in the end resolved to 'never know man farther than by name' (5.2.118). DYCE conjectured that she 'seems intended to stand for the Church of England', but that function is much more obviously performed by the White Bishop. Fleay conjectured that she 'may be Katherine, daughter of the Earl of Rutland, who was converted before her marriage to the Marquis Buckingham, 1620 May' (2:105), and Morris identified her with Elizabeth Stuart, Princess Palatine and Queen of Bohemia. But neither conjecture has been accepted by subsequent critics. Her virginity throughout the play and rejection of future marriage at the end makes it impossible to believe that she represents a married woman (let alone one so remarkably fertile as Elizabeth); it seems ridiculously inappropriate for a Queen to be called a pawn. Middleton's sources for her role (for which, see the commentary to *Early*) identify her with various English laywomen, tempted by Catholics to convert.

Persons.18 JESUITESS] THIS EDITION (*conj.* Ward); *not in* CRANE[1]+. Fleay conjectured she was '?Mrs. Ward, the Jesuitess' (2:106). Mary Ward (1585–1645) was the founder of an order of female Jesuits in England, and although such an order is implied, nothing in the play identifies Black Queen's Pawn as its founder. Morris identified her as the Archduchess

Isabella of Brussels, but this was inferred from a larger political allegory which has been universally discredited; there
is nothing in the part itself to suggest the (aged) dowager
Isabella. Pastor identified her as Donna Luisa de Carvajal, 'a
Spanish woman from Valladolid', resident in London, whom
Owen called 'a holy Jesuitess, or a she Jesuit' (64). But
nothing in the texts requires so specific an identification.
Howard-Hill is right to emphasize her generic identity within
the larger pawn-plot allegory of the Catholic effort to convert
individual Protestants. She calls herself a Jesuitess at 1.1.41,
and the word is used of her at 2.1.189 and 2.1.207. Coloma
says that in 'The first act...the Jesuits [were impersonated]
by the black' pieces; Overton describes *Game* as 'an odious
play against Spaine, but principally Gondomar, and the Jesuits'; describing the 'black howse', Salisbury records that
the 'Queenes Paune was a seculare Jesuitesse'.

Persons.21 OF SPALATO] THIS EDITION (*conj.* DYCE); *not in*
CRANE² +. The identification is confirmed by the title-page
engravings, Middleton's sources, and contemporary accounts
of the play by Woolley, Holles, Conway, Salvetti, and Jonson.

Persons.21 WHITE KING'S BISHOP] THIS EDITION; *not in* CRANE² +.
Spalato was closely associated with his chief patron, King
James, whose ecumenical project he supported. The position
of White Queen's Bishop is already occupied. (See below.)
Moreover, since no Black King's Bishop is represented in the
play, the Fat Bishop can easily switch into that position while
remaining in the same file.

Persons.26 JAMES] THIS EDITION (*conj.* DYCE); *not in* CRANE¹ +.
This identification is made explicitly by Valaresso and Hollis,
implicitly by Salvetti and Chamberlain, ambiguously by Conway. Whether or not the actors dared to impersonate King
James physically, the role of the White King is based—as
the sources make clear—on the historical James I, as would
have been apparent to all early spectators and readers; once
Gondomar was identified as the Black Knight, James had to
be understood as White King.

Persons.30 GELDER] THIS EDITION; *not in* CRANE¹ +. He is identified as 'the gelder' on his first entrance at 1.1.207. Morris
conjectured that 'the Black Knight's Pawn is the Emperor
Ferdinand', on the grounds that 'Ferdinand drove Frederick
from the throne of Bohemia and so prevented the union of
the Electorate of the Palatine and the Kingdom of Bohemia'
and that Ferdinand's action is comparable to 'the gelding
of the White Bishop's Pawn'. Like his other interpretations
of the seduction, rape, and marriage plot, this identification
has found no supporters. For a detailed analysis of early modern gelding metaphors and allegories—which, among other
things, shows what is wrong with Moore's allegory—see
Taylor, *Castration*. 74-83. It seems obviously inappropriate
to the chess allegory for an Emperor to be identified with
a pawn. Howard-Hill notes that, in performance, he could
have been 'distinguished from the Jesuit Black Pawns by his
secular apparel' (*Pasquin* 135).

Persons.30-1 (Black Queen's Knight's Pawn)] THIS EDITION; *not
in* CRANE¹ +. He is explicitly identified by the Black [Queen's]
Knight as 'My pawn' (3.1.116). In order to have attacked
the White [Queen's] Pawn he needs to be in an
adjoining file; his attraction to the White Queen's Pawn also
indicates that he belongs on the Queen's side of the board.

Persons.35 CHARLES] THIS EDITION (*conj.* WARD); *not in* CRANE¹ +;
Buckingham BULLEN *conj.* Bullen's unexplained conjecture—
rejected by all subsequent commentators—was presumably
based on a belief that the Prince of Wales should have a
higher rank, in the play, than Knight, and that Charles
Stuart should outrank his companion George Villiers. But

the identification of the White Knight with Prince Charles is
confirmed by the title-page engravings, and by the comments
of Woolley, Colona, Holles, and Salisbury. Charles is a knight
in order to oppose him to Gondomar, and because he had
been made a Knight of the Order of the Garter in 1616, in
a ceremony for which Middleton composed *Civitatis Amor*.
Commenting on their trip to Madrid, King James called the
Prince of Wales and Duke of Buckingham 'venturous knights,
worthy to be put into a new romance' (letter of 27 February
1623, in Bergeron, 151).

Persons.35 (White Queen's Knight)] THIS EDITION; *not in*
CRANE¹ +. Portrayed as the chief opponent of the Black
[Queen's] Knight, in order to face him in the array the
White Knight would have to be on the Queen's side. That
position also suits his protection of the White Queen's Pawn,
his verbal defence of the White [Queen's] Bishop at 2.2.149-
52, his alliance with the White [Queen's] Bishop's Pawn at
2.2.232-3, and his familial connection to the White Queen;
it separates him from the White King's mistaken support
of the Fat Bishop and White King's Pawn (and James's
unpopular commitment to the Spanish Match).

Persons.49 OF BOHEMIA] THIS EDITION; *not in* CRANE¹ +. No contemporary equated the White Queen with any specific historical person; Ward identified her as Queen Anne, Fleay as the
'English Church' (2:106). Neither identification is plausible.
Queen Anne had died early in 1619, making it ridiculous to
have her celebrate the triumphant 1623 return of Charles
and Buckingham from Spain (allegorized in the final scene).
The Church of England is undoubtedly best represented by
a Bishop; Queen Anne had no obvious connection, constitu-
tionally or personally, to the Anglican church; she was (and
is) widely suspected of Catholic sympathies. Moreover, she
had first suggested the Spanish Match (Adams 88), whereas
the White Queen's most important scene dramatizes her distress when Charles and Buckingham go to Madrid to finalize
that very alliance. From 1619 to the play's performance in
1624 and printing in early 1625, the only Queen in the
Stuart royal family was Elizabeth Stuart, Queen of Bohemia,
also called 'the Winter Queen', having been evicted from her
kingdom after the Protestants were defeated at the battle of
White Mountain: she was thus a Queen, a leading member
of the House of Stuart, and personally associated with winter
and whiteness. Chamberlain refers to her as 'Queen Elizabeth'
(2:331). She was repeatedly championed and celebrated by
Middleton's sources, appearing with Prince Charles in engraved title-pages for Thomas Scott's *Vox Dei* (1624) and *Vox
Regis* (1624). The daughter of King James and sister of Prince
Charles, her presence between them, on stage, would make
obvious sense. Her anxiety in 4.4, when the White Knight
and White Duke enter the Black House, makes sense, not only
because of her familial connection to Charles ('My love, my
hope, my dearest'), but because the marriage of Charles to
the Infanta was opposed by hard-line Protestant supporters of
the Queen, who wanted a war against the Habsburgs, not an
alliance with them. The White King's first words addressed
to her—'Let heaven's blessing | Be mine no longer than I
am thy sure one. | The Dove's house is not safer in the
rock | Than thou in my firm sanctuary' (4.4.78-81)—make
no sense as an address to Queen Anne, but directly respond
to criticism that King James did not care about the fate of
his daughter (Redworth, 19-25, 31, 136-7). For more on
the historical context, see commentary notes to *Early* 4.366-
421. Finally, the Black King's lust for the White Queen makes
sense, as an expression of the Catholic desire for Bohemia and
the Palatinate.

Persons.38–9 OF BUCKINGHAM] THIS EDITION (*conj.* WARD); *not in* CRANE[I]+; Prince Charles BULLEN *conj.* Among contemporary commentators, Salisbury specifically identifies the White Duke with George Villiers, Duke of Buckingham (1592–1628), who accompanied Charles to Madrid in 1623 to negotiate the Spanish Match, to which many commentators refer (thus implicitly making the identification with Buckingham). On Bullen's conjecture, see the note on Charles, above. No commentator since Bullen has doubted the identifications of the White Duke or White Knight proposed by Ward. Howard-Hill suggests that the easiest way for the actors to have distinguished Buckingham from Charles would be 'to deck the White Duke's person with jewels (or at least baubles, for which Buckingham was renowned)' (*Pasquin* 132).

Persons.46 (White Queen's Duke)] THIS EDITION; *not in* CRANE[I]+. By 1624, Buckingham was more closely aligned with Prince Charles—the White [Queen's] Knight—than with King James; in the play they are repeatedly associated with each other.

Persons.43 JESUIT] THIS EDITION (*conj.* Ward); *not in* CRANE[I]+; the Archbishop of Toledo BULLEN *conj.* See 'Your Father General, Bishop o'th' Black House' (1.1.297). Unlike other Spanish clerics, the Jesuits supported the Spanish Match, designed to give England a future Black Queen. In describing the bagging of the Black characters in the final scene, Holles refers to 'Iesuite, spannish bishop'; that may be one character or two, but in any case links the bishop to the Jesuit; 'the Jesuit' is called 'his' pawn (2.1.161), and the Jesuit's master would presumably be another Jesuit.

Persons.43 (Black Queen's Bishop)] THIS EDITION; *not in* CRANE[I]+. Since this character is the master of the Black [Queen's] Bishop's Pawn—see 2.1.161 and 2.2.142—he must be Black Queen's Bishop.

Persons.53 MARIA] THIS EDITION (*conj.* Hotson); *not in* CRANE[I]+. Ward identified the Black Queen with Queen Isabella of Spain; Fleay, with the 'Church of Rome' (2:106). Hotson's conjecture (p. 40) is implicit in the earliest recorded response to the play: Woolley, describing 'the Conclusion', writes of 'the k. of sp: who being ouer come is putt into a great sack with D: Maria, Count of Oliuares, Gundemar.' Doña Maria is named immediately after her brother, the Black King of Spain. The only female on stage in 5.3 is the Black Queen; the only other Black female in the play, the Black Queen's Pawn, can hardly be the Infanta Doña Maria. Although Woolley did not personally see the play, he did hear what others were saying about it, which means that some witnesses of the first performance interpreted the Black Queen as the Infanta. Braunmuller recognizes that the eyewitness account also supports this identification: Holles, in his first phrase describing the play, calls it 'a representation of all our spannishe traffike', which it could hardly be without representing the Infanta; later, quoting the Black Knight's phrase about 'groom of the stool' he adds 'to the Infanta.' Lowe also says it 'describes Gondomar and all the Spanish proceedings very boldly and broadly', Nethersole says that in it 'the whole Spanish business is ripped vp to the quicke', and Valaresso describes it as 'several representations under different names of many of the circumstances about the marriage with the Infanta.' All these references to the Spanish Match make it likely that the play contains some representation of the Infanta herself. The actual Queen of Spain, Isabella, was of no real interest in England; Howard-Hill acknowledges that 'Isabella's appearance . . . would not be familiar to London audiences' (*Pasquin* 118). But the

English public was, instead, obsessed with the Infanta—who would, if Charles married her, soon become *Queen* of England. When White Knight Charles arrives in Spain, in 5.1, the Black Queen's first words to him are to tell him that whatever 'Your fair eye [can] fix on' is his servant; he replies, 'How amply you endear us' (5.1.25–8). In Madrid, Charles would 'have his eyes immovably fixed upon the Infanta half an hour together in a thoughtful speculative posture, which sure would needs be tedious, unless affection did sweeten it' (Redworth, 89). The exchange between White Knight and Black Queen may have included some stage business, because White Duke immediately follows it with a reference to 'favours That equally enrich the royal giver As the receiver in the free donation' (28–30): 'giver' is singular, and although it could refer to the Black King the most immediate referent would be the Black Queen; if so, she has just given some unspecified 'favours' to the White Knight. The two Queens represent the two royal women Charles had to choose between: his own (Protestant) sister or the (Catholic) sister of King Felipe. For more on the identification of Black Queen with Maria, see the notes and commentary, particularly 5.1. (Notably, the end of 4.4 is the White Queen's major scene, immediately followed by 5.1, the Black Queen's major scene; the juxtaposition dramatizes the political choice between the Winter Queen and the Infanta.)

Persons.56 FELIPE] THIS EDITION (*conj.* DYCE); *not in* CRANE[I]+. This identification was made explicitly by Woolley ('the k. of sp:'), Colona ('the king of the blacks has easily been taken for our lord the King, because of his youth, dress, and other details'), Conway ('the King of Spaine'), and Pembroke ('y[e] King of Spaine'); in calling 'England y[e] whyt hows, Spayn y[e] black', Holles implicitly identified the Black King as Felipe IV. Since the Black King 'was the Black Knight's (Gomdomar's) master, he *was* Philip of Spain, regardless of his appearance' (Howard-Hill, *Pasquin* 119).

Persons.59 GELDED] THIS EDITION; *not in* CRANE[I]+. He is called 'the gelded' on his first appearance at 1.1.207; there are many other references to his castrated condition. Morris identified him as Frederick of Bohemia; for criticism of this and other political allegories, and discussion of the early modern symbolism of castration, see Taylor 2000. Like his other identifications, Morris's conjecture ignores the class structure of chess.

Persons.59–60 (White Queen's Bishop's Pawn)] THIS EDITION; *not in* CRANE[I]+. Since this piece was once betrothed to the White Queen's Pawn (d-file), one would expect him to be on an adjoining file (c-file). This also explains his rivalry with the Black [Queen's] Knight's Pawn (b-file), since each could diagonally capture the other; moreover, Black Queen's Knight's Pawn could only reach the c-file, adjoining the White Queen's Pawn, if he could diagonally capture the White Queen's Bishop's Pawn. Comparing the White Bishop's Pawn with the Black Bishop's Pawn, Howard-Hill argues it is likely he 'would be identified by clerical dress also' (*Pasquin* 134).

Persons.63 COUNSELLOR] THIS EDITION; *not in* CRANE[I]+. The only contemporary witness to identify this character was Holles, who wrote that he 'is supposed Bristow', i.e. Sir John Digby, 1st Earl of Bristol (1580–1635). Modern scholars have conjectured that he represents Robert Carr, the disgraced Earl of Somerset (Ward), or Sir Toby Matthew (Bullen and Pastor), or Lionel Cranfield, Earl of Middlesex (Bald); before the discovery of Holles, most twentieth-century scholars favoured

Bald's interpretation. However, even Holles says only that the identification is 'supposed', which means that it was conjectural even for early spectators. What is not in doubt is the Pawn's relationship as a minister and trusted confidant of King James.

Persons.66 OF CANTERBURY] THIS EDITION (*conj.* Bullen); *not in* CRANE[1] +. BULLEN first conjectured that this character represented George Abbot, Archbishop of Canterbury (1562–1633). Abbot strongly opposed the Spanish Match, the Roman Catholic church, and the Arminian faction that increasingly dominated the late Jacobean episcopate; he urged support for the Queen of Bohemia; he had also attended the same Oxford college as Middleton. No contemporary made this identification, and there is no evidence that the King's Men attempted to represent Abbot physically. But the Archbishop of Canterbury was in any case the head of the English church, which is the role of the White Bishop. Howard-Hill accepts this identification (*Pasquin* 34).

Persons.66 (White Queen's Bishop)] THIS EDITION; *not in* CRANE[1] +. Although the connection is never explicitly verbalized, it is natural to take this piece as the master of the White [Queen's] Bishop's Pawn. The Fat Bishop of Spalato already has a pawn of his own, and no other White Bishop is demanded by any text of the play. This piece captures the Fat [Black King's] Bishop; he could do so only if he were on the same diagonals, which means that he must be the White Queen's Bishop.

Persons.69 PROLOGUE] THIS EDITION; *not in* CRANE[1] +

Persons.70 OLIVARES] THIS EDITION (*conj.* BULLEN); *not in* CRANE[1] +. This identification was made explicitly by Woolley and Holles; Salisbury correctly saw that the character represented 'the Duke Fauorite of Spaine', but in the margin revealed his own out-of-date grasp of Spanish affairs by naming the old favourite 'Lerma' instead of his successor under the new king, Olivares (whose name is clearly behind the joke at 5.3.212–13).

Persons.70 (Black Queen's Duke)] THIS EDITION; *not in* CRANE[1] +. Historically, Olivares was linked to King Felipe, but in chess neither Duke begins the game adjoining a King. Notoriously, Buckingham had clashed with Olivares, and it would make sense to represent them as opposing pieces on the same file.

Persons.76 Dancing Statues] THIS EDITION; *not in* CRANE[1] +. These are required in 5.1, and given the technology of the time must have been actors (like the statue of Hermione in *Winter's Tale*, and the statues in Beaumont's 1613 masque).

Prologue.0.1–Prologue.10/1–10 Enter...check.] *not in* CRANE[1,3], ROSENBACH[A]; *placed after Induction* CRANE[2]; *placed opposite title-page* OKES. The first addition in the revised version; it is unusual to combine a Prologue with an Induction. The odd placement in CRANE[2] might relate to the fact that Prologues were, in the theatre, usually written on separate loose sheets of paper, which might therefore be misplaced. The misplacement suggests that Crane did not see performances of the play.

Prologue.0.1 Enter] THIS EDITION; *not in* CRANE[2] +. The absence of this direction has not been taken as a shared error, because such an entry was implicit in the word 'Prologue'. This is effectively a modernization rather than an emendation.

Prologue.0.1/1 the Prologue] CRANE[2]; ˬ ~ CRANE/MATHEWES, OKES, MIDDLETON[T], BRIDGEWATER[A]

Prologue.0.1/1 in a black cloak] THIS EDITION; *not in* CRANE[2] +. This was the conventional dress of a prologue. See Thomas Heywood, *Four Prentices of London* (1615), sig. A4: 'Do you not see this long black velvet cloak upon my back?...Nay,

have I not all the signs of a Prologue about me?' This conventional costuming will, of course, soon take on an unconventional meaning within the play's emergent and unique black–white colour scheme: *Game* begins with figures in black, and ends with figures in white, controlling the stage.

Prologue.1/2 PROLOGUE] THIS EDITION; *not in* CRANE[2] +. The entrance/heading clearly doubled as a speech prefix in the early witnesses: this is effectively a modernization rather than an emendation.

Prologue.2/3 shall] This word is accidentally omitted in Howard-Hill's transcription of BRIDGEWATER (1995).

Prologue.9/10 fair'st] faireſt BRIDGEWATER[A]

Prologue.9/10 can] cou BRIDGEWATER[A] *uncorrected* (beginning to write 'could')

Prologue.10/11 t'] to MIDDLETON[T], BRIDGEWATER[A]

Prologue.10/11 avoid] awoid MATHEWES. Compositorial error (foul case?).

Prologue.10 Exit] THIS EDITION; *not in* CRANE[2] +. See Prologue.0.1. The absence of this direction has not been taken as a shared error, because such an exit was implicit in the word 'Prologue'. This is effectively a modernization rather than an emendation.

Induction.0.1–2/13–14 Ignatius...asleep] OKES, BRIDGEWATER[A], MIDDLETON[T]. Late authorial variant. See following notes. ROSENBACH[A] and CRANE/MATHEWES most closely resemble CRANE[1].

Induction.0.1/13 ˬIgnatius] Enter ~ CRANE/MATHEWES

Induction.0.1/13 Loyola] *not in* CRANE[1,4], ROSENBACH[A]

Induction.0.1–2/13 in his black Jesuit habit] THIS EDITION; *not in* CRANE[1] +

Induction.0.2/13 appearing] *not in* CRANE[2,3]; *discovered* CRANE[1], ROSENBACH[A]; *discouring* CRANE/MATHEWES

Induction.0.2/13 ˬ Error] *and* ~ CRANE[1,2,3], ROSENBACH[A]

Induction.0.2/14 at his foot] *not in* CRANE, ROSENBACH[A]. Not strictly necessary, additional information for the benefit of a reader, presumably reflecting performance.

Induction.0.2/14 foot] feete OKES. To be at his 'foot' Error could be on one side, but 'feet' would require him to lie in front of Loyola. Probably the first of many misreadings in OKES.

Induction.0.2/14 as] *not in* CRANE, ROSENBACH[A]. The addition calls attention to the theatricality of the opening.

*Induction.0.2/14 asleep] *not in* CRANE[2,3]; *ſleeping* CRANE/MATHEWES. The omission removes a detail necessary for understanding the action; without it, almost the whole of the first speech appears to be addressed to Error.

Induction.3/17 refined] refinèd OKES

Induction.3/17 taste] caſt CRANE/MATHEWES. Misreading.

Induction.4/18 any ˬ] CRANE/MATHEWES; ~ of CRANE[1] +. See *Early Induction.4.*

Induction.4/18 my] me OKES

Induction.5/19 institution] inſtitutions OKES. Possibly authorial, but an easy error of assimilation, and Loyola's institutional legacy was singular.

Induction.6/20 they'd] they'had CRANE[2,3]; they had CRANE/MATHEWES

Induction.7/21 Covered] Couerèd CRANE/MATHEWES, OKES, ROSENBACH[A]

*Induction.14/28 and their] ~ ˬ BRIDGEWATER[A], OKES. Apparently a shared error, since nothing seems gained by the omission but metrical irregularity.

Induction.15/29 It's] CRANE[2,3]; 'tis CRANE[1] +. Both forms occur in Crane texts, so Crane might have changed the contraction in either direction; but Crane was older than Middleton, and his linguistic preferences are in general more old-fashioned (doth, hath, etc). The modern contraction appears often in Middleton's canon: *Patient Man* (10), *Widow* (6), *No Wit* (4), *Roaring Girl* (3), *Chaste Maid* (2), *Dissemblers* (2), *Women Beware* (2), *Valour* (2), *Mad World* (1), *Michaelmas* (1), *Quarrel* (1), *Changeling* (1), *Tennis* (1). In transcribing Middleton's *Witch*, Crane transcribed ''tis 86 times, and 'Jt's' only once; in Fletcher and Massinger's *Barnavelt*, Crane transcribed ''tis 71 times, and the alternative 'it's' only once; most of the Shakespeare plays for which Crane is believed to have supplied printer's copy contain no examples of the modern form. Moreover, the modern form appears three times in OKES, apparently set from Middleton's autograph. Although like others of his generation Middleton preferred the older form, he seems occasionally to have vacillated toward the modern alternative, and it would not be surprising if his last full-length play contained more examples than usual. Where early witnesses vary, I have printed the older form in *Early*, and the modern form in *Later*. This still leaves 'tis as the dominant form (24 times).

Induction.15/29 five] 7 BRIDGEWATER[A]

Induction.15/29 sainted] faluted OKES. Misreading.

Induction.16/30 my] mine CRANE. Crane seems to have imposed the more old-fashioned form.

Induction.17/31 canònise] Cannonze MATHEWES. Omitted type.

Induction.18/32 they'd] CRANE[2,3] (they'had); they had CRANE[1]+

Induction.18/32 sainted me] faluted ˄ OKES. The same misreading occurs at Induction.15.

Induction.19/33 no] not BRIDGEWATER[A]

Induction.20/34 removed] remoouèd OKES

*Induction.23/37 Let] letts MIDDLETON[T], BRIDGEWATER[A], OKES. A shared error, emended by HOWARD-HILL.

Induction.23/37 and] ant BRIDGEWATER[A]

Induction.24/38 Maine, and] ~ ˄ ROSENBACH[A]

Induction.24/38 Petronill] Pecronel OKES. Misreading t/c.

Induction.25-6/39-40 Abbess...The] *not in* BRIDGEWATER[A]. Eyeskip.

Induction.25/39 Cunigund] Cunigung CRANE[3]

Induction.26/40 Marcell] Alarcell CRANE/MATHEWES. Misreading, probably compositorial.

Induction.26/40 parson] Vicar CRANE[1] *uncorrected*. Although there can be little doubt that Middleton first wrote 'Vicar' (which is accordingly preserved in *Early* Induction.26), the change to 'parson' may or may not have been due to censorship.

Induction.26/40 Polycarp] *Policary* OKES. Misreading.

Induction.27/41 Urs'ly] Vrfula CRANE, ROSENBACH[A]. Possibly a late authorial revision.

Induction.29/43 but] CRANE/MATHEWES (Worcester, Huntington, Bodleian Malone 247, British Library C.34.d.37); but but CRANE/MATHEWES (Folger copy). Unrecorded press variant (sig. A3[v], which includes Induction.25-52). See Induction.38.

Induction.30/44 twenti'th] CRANE[1,2,3], ROSENBACH[A] (twentith), OKES (twenteth); twentieth MIDDLETON[T], CRANE/MATHEWES, BRIDGEWATER[A]

Induction.31/45 See] fee BRIDGEWATER[A] *uncorrected* (misreading of 'fee')

Induction.32/46 Their...too] *not in* ROSENBACH[A]

Induction.32/46 to thrust] ˄ truft OKES. Eyeskip.

Induction.33/47 methinks] For the first of these two words (mee thinkes), BRIDGEWATER[A] *uncorrected* has 'wch', which is then deleted and replaced by 'may', which is then altered to the correct 'mee'.

Induction.35/49 wake] awake OKES. Extrametrical synonym substitution.

Induction.36/50 supererogation] Superogation OKES. Haplography.

Induction.37/51 Ignatius] Ingnatius ROSENBACH[A]

Induction.38/52 What...ignorance] *2 lines* CRANE/MATHEWES: done |

Induction.38/52 you] In MIDDLETON[T] the initial 'Y' is written over 'd' (by eyeskip or mindskip, anticipating 'donne'), thus immediately correcting the error.

Induction.38/52 sleep] fleepe MATHEWES (Worcester, Huntington, Bodleian Malone 247; British Library C.34.d.37); flleepe MATHEWES (Folger). Ligature error (and therefore almost certainly originating in the printing shop, not in the underlying manuscript). Press variant (sig. A3v). See Induction.29.

Induction.41/55 my] mine CRANE[2,3,4]

Induction.41/55 eye] *not in* MIDDLETON[T] *uncorrected*

Induction.41/56 'Game'? What game?] what *Game* pre'thee CRANE. Late authorial variant.

Induction.43/58 'Twixt] CRANE[1]; betwixt CRANE[2]+. For a similar Crane expansion see 3.1.146.

Induction.44/59 to't] to it MIDDLETON[T], BRIDGEWATER[A], OKES

Induction.47/62 That...Bishop's] *2 lines* CRANE/MATHEWES: Pawn |

Induction.48/63 pow'r] power CRANE[1], MIDDLETON[T], ROSENBACH[A], OKES

Induction.48/63 mast'ry] CRANE[2], BRIDGEWATER[A], MIDDLETON[T]; Maftery CRANE[1,3,4], ROSENBACH[A], OKES

Induction.49-50/65-6 It's...think] *1 line* ROSENBACH[A]. See lineation note at *Early* Induction.51-2.

Induction.49/65 It's] CRANE[2]; 'tis CRANE[1]+. See Induction.15.

Induction.51/68 ˄ behold] could ~ CRANE/MATHEWES

*Induction.52.1 *Music*] CRANE[1,4], ROSENBACH[A]; *not in* CRANE[2]+. A shared error in MIDDLETON[T], emended by Howard-Hill. Crane often omitted directions for music: see Taylor and Jowett, 71-2. MATHEWES separates this direction from the following entrance, placing it in the right margin opposite Induction.51 (near the bottom of sig. A3[v]), with the entrance in the middle of Induction.52, between the two speeches (at the top of sig. A4). There seems little point in the separation, which is probably simply a printer's solution to the fact that the manuscript's marginal direction extended across a printed page-break.

*Induction.52.1-2 *Enter...game*] *not in* MIDDLETON[T], BRIDGEWATER[A], OKES. A shared error in autograph, emended by Howard-Hill. For variants in the remaining five texts, see following notes. Again, ROSENBACH[A] and CRANE/MATHEWES most closely resemble CRANE[1]. For the placing of the direction in CRANE/MATHEWES see preceding note. All four manuscripts which contain the direction place it in the right margin, opposite ll. 50-2 ('what...wish' in CRANE[1,3], 'whaf' to 'keepe' in CRANE[2]), opposite ll. 51-4 ('cunning...Byfhops') in ROSENBACH[A]. The later placing seems in error, and determined partly by the page-break in ROSENBACH[A] (after 'what' in l. 50). The curly bracket in CRANE[3] points to the position preferred here.

Induction.52.1 *severally*] *not in* CRANE[2]

Induction.52.1 *White House*] CRANE[2,3]; ~ ˄ CRANE[1,4], ROSENBACH[A]

Induction.52.1 and˄] ~ y[e] CRANE[2]

Induction.52.1-2 *Black House*] CRANE[3]; hous | CRANE[1]; ~ ˄ CRANE[2]; ~ Houfes ROSENBACH[A], [CRANE[4]]

Induction.52.2 as] *not in* CRANE[3,4]. Again, as at Induction.0.2, a reminder of the theatricality of the action, which might have been accidentally omitted.

Induction.52.2 in…game] CRANE[2,3]; ~ ~ ~ ˌ ~ CRANE/MATH-
EWES; *they are sett* fl | *y[e] Game.* CRANE[1], ROSENBACH[A] (for).
CRANE/MATHEWES places the phrase before rather than after
'the White…Houses'.

Induction.52/70 wish] will BRIDGEWATER[A]. Compare *Mad World*
5.2.293, 'You have your wish'. This might be a scribal
synonym substitution, but Middleton uses 'you…have your
will' at least three times elsewhere (in *Michaelmas*, *Mad
World*, and *Game*), and uses 'your will' much more often
than 'your wish'.

Induction.53/71 of ˌ] ~ all BRIDGEWATER[A]. Error: metre.

Induction.54/72 Kings…dukes] *2 lines* ROSENBACH[A]: bishops |

Induction.54/72 pawns] Pawne ROSENBACH[A]

Induction.55/73 They're] they are CRANE[2,3,4], ROSENBACH[A]

Induction.55/74 Corruptively] Corruptedly CRANE/MATHEWES

Induction.56/75 Le] *La* CRANE[3]

Induction.56/75 Custode] cuſtodie OKES

Induction.58/77 trust'] MIDDLETON[T] + (trust); truſt's ROSENBACH[A].
Throughout his career Middleton overwhelmingly preferred
not to elide the possessive 's' before 'sake': see *Early* 2.156.
Only ROSENBACH preserves the authorial preference. However, in this case the unpronounceable consonantal cluster
of 'tru*stss*ake' may have encouraged the autograph elision.

Induction.60/79 Thy] OKES, BRIDGEWATER[A]; the CRANE[1] +. Both
readings make sense: 'thy answer' occurs also at *Puritan*
1.4.120.

Induction.60/79 I] *not in* OKES. Haplography: the line, carried in
the copyist's head, repeats the same vowel sound ('high I'),
tempting the copyist to write it once instead of twice.

Induction.60/79 daughter] Daughters CRANE/MATHEWES. In the
right margin, connected to the end of this line by a horizontal
line, CRANE[1] (*uncorrected*) has a stage direction, preserved in
Early Induction.64.1: Enter *y[e]* | *Bl.Qu[s]* | *Pawne & | Bl. B[ps]*.

Induction.61/80 Those…Bishop's] *2 lines* CRANE/MATHEWES:
Pawns |

Induction.61/80 pawns] ~ of ROSENBACH[A]

Induction.61/80 Black] In MIDDLETON[T] the initial correct 'B' is
written over 'Q' (anticipating the next word), thus immediately correcting the error before the next letter was written.

Induction.61/80 Queen's] Queene OKES

Induction.61/80 and Black] OKES, BRIDGEWATER[A], MIDDLETON[T]; ~
the CRANE, ROSENBACH[A]. Late authorial variant.

Induction.62/81 slight preferments] light performents OKES. DYCE
reprinted the OKES variant, glossing the noun as 'performance'; HOWARD-HILL calls it a misspelling, but *OED* records
the spelling in 1527 and 1641. However, if Middleton had
intended 'performance' we would expect him to have used
that form (which appears at least 21 times in 13 different
Middleton works); the graphic resemblance suggests that this
is yet another misreading in OKES.

Induction.63/82 Not] Nor OKES[2], CRANE/MATHEWES. Apparently
independent misreadings (or an unrecorded press variant in
OKES[1]).

Induction.64/83 nigh] ~ that BRIDGEWATER[A] *uncorrected*

Induction.65/84 but] and BRIDGEWATER[A] *uncorrected*

Induction.65/84 I'd] Ill'd CRANE[1,4], ROSENBACH[A]; I'would
CRANE[2,3]. Only MIDDLETON[T], BRIDGEWATER[A], and OKES entirely
drop (Crane's) 'l' from the contraction. Hereafter, forms of
the contraction with 'ld' or 'lld' will be regarded as spelling
variants only, and not recorded unless otherwise relevant.
See Induction.72.

Induction.67/86 make] haue made OKES. The grammatical
change could be a late authorial variant.

Induction.67/86 no] ˌ OKES. Clearly mistaken omission of a
single short word.

Induction.68/87 or] and OKES. Possibly authorial, but an easy
misreading.

Induction.69/88 'em] them CRANE[3,4]. A favourite Middleton
contraction, repeatedly expanded by Crane.

Induction.69/88 themselves] themſeues MATHEWES. Omitted
type. Compare Induction.17.

Induction.70/89 That's] y[t] ROSENBACH[A]

Induction.70/89 rule of] *not in* OKES

Induction.71/90 Push] BRIDGEWATER[A], MIDDLETON[T]; piſh
CRANE[1] +

Induction.71/90 observe rule] ~ game ROSENBACH[A]

Induction.72/91 then] *not in* OKES. See next note.

Induction.72/91 you'd] MIDDLETON[T] *only*; you'll'd CRANE[1,3,4],
ROSENBACH[A]; you'ld BRIDGEWATER[A]; you'would CRANE[2];
you yould OKES. See Induction.65. Only MIDDLETON[T] drops
(Crane's) 'l' entirely from the contraction. The printer's error
might arise from a manuscript reading 'you would', which
would compensate metrically for the absence of 'then' in the
same line. Both variants might thus be related, and the result
of late authorial revision. However, because this conjecture
about origins further depends upon conjectural emendation
of 'you yould', adoption of the OKES readings here would be
more than usually speculative.

Induction.74/93 It's] CRANE[2], ROSENBACH[A]; 'tis CRANE[1] +. See
Induction.15.

Induction.74/93 rare] hard ROSENBACH[A]

Induction.74/93 world reined] word rulde OKES. The alternative
verb must be an inadvertent synonym substitution, since 'in'
is retained.

Induction.74 reined] MIDDLETON[T] (reignd)

Induction.74/93 one] me CRANE/MATHEWES

Induction.75/94 'em…'em] Them…them CRANE[3]

Induction.75/94 anon] *not in* ROSENBACH[A]

Induction.75/94 mark] view OKES. The synonym repeats the
meaning of 'see', without the added emphasis of 'mark' [pay
attention].

Induction.76.1/95 *Exeunt both houses*] DYCE (~ *the two* ~); *not
in* CRANE[1] +

Induction.77/96 longings] longing OKES. The concrete plural is
the 'rarer reading', of a kind that copyists often replace with
the more commonplace singular: see Taylor 1988.

*Induction.78 *Exeunt*] *not in* OKES, BRIDGEWATER[A], MIDDLETON[T]. A
shared error in autograph, emended by HOWARD-HILL, who
notes that the eyewitness Holles explicitly stated that Ignatius
'vanisheth' at this point, and Coloma had heard that Ignatius
appeared 'from hell.'

1.1.0.1/98 *Incipit*] THIS EDITION; *not in* MIDDLETON[T] +. Compare
the beginnings of Acts 2, 3, 4, and 5.

1.1.0.1/98 *Primus*ˌ] *Primi, Scæna prima.* MIDDLETON[T], BRIDGE-
WATER[A]; *Prima, Scæna Prima.* OKES; ~. *Sce[a]. Pri[a].* CRANE,
ROSENBACH[A]. For the Latin forms here see note at 2.1.0.1.

1.1.0.2-5/99-100 *Enter…in white*] *The white-queenes, & y[e]
Black-queenes Pawnes. Then ye Black Bishop's Pawne: then
ye whi: Bishop's Pawne, & ye Bl. Knights Pawne, Then y[e]
black-knight, Then y[e] wh. Kings Pawne.* CRANE[3]. This is the
first example in CRANE[3] of the so-called 'massed entries':
see Bawcutt's discussion (12-14). These list in sequence
all the characters who appear in the scene; as a result,
the characters who appear after the opening direction of a
scene are not given separate directions at the point where
they actually enter, or (in later scenes) re-enter. In this
apparatus, I will record each of these directions in CRANE[3]

at the beginning of the relevant scene; if they call for the entrance of a character given an entrance later in the scene, I will not record the absence of that direction at the later point (where the other texts have it), but take the direction at the beginning of the scene as evidence that CRANE³ also contains the direction. If there are peculiarities in the massed entry relevant to the text, or to variants in other witnesses, I will generally discuss those at the point where the other witnesses have a mid-scene stage direction.

*1.1.0.2–4/99–100 *from the Black House...from the White House*] *not in* CRANE²,³; *feuerally* CRANE/MATHEWES. (The prepositional phrases are present in ROSENBACHᴬ, but placed after the character names, rather than before.) The lack of this important information about staging can be considered a shared error; CRANE/MATHEWES supplies the information about separate entrances, but in a form characteristic of Crane rather than Middleton, which leaves out the association of each stage door with a particular 'House'.

1.1.0.2–4/99–100 *the Black...the White*] ₐ~...ₐ~ CRANE/MATHEWES

*1.1.0.2–4/99–100 *Black...White*] *white...Black* CRANE²,³,⁴. As HARPER noted, 'either side could move first in seventeenth-century chess', and the order of the first four entries—Black Queen's Pawn, White Queen's Pawn, Black Bishop's Pawn, White Bishop's Pawn—reproduces that of a famous chess opening, Queen's Gambit Declined. HARPER took for granted the autograph form of this direction, and did not remark on the variants. But Crane's transposition of the order of entry destroys this effect. Crane's reordering, if deliberate, was presumably based upon the fact that the Black Queen's Pawn's first speech presumes that the White Queen's Pawn is already on stage. But both characters might have entered, sequentially, before either spoke.

1.1.0.3–5/99–100 *a woman-pawn in black...a woman-pawn in white*] CRANE¹ *only*; *not in* CRANE² +. The first two speeches establish that the characters are female; placing the information in the stage direction is not necessary, but it is helpful for a modern reader.

1.1.0.3/100 *then*] THIS EDITION; *&* CRANE, ROSENBACHᴬ, BRIDGEWATERᴬ; *not in* MIDDLETONᵀ, OKES. On the unreliability of the Crane form of this opening direction see preceding notes. 'And' is ambiguous, suggesting simultaneity; the autograph form, without a conjunction, is more likely to indicate sequential entries—especially in OKES, where the two clauses are separated by a full stop and a line-break.

1.1.1/102 QUEEN'S] *not in* CRANE¹, ROSENBACHᴬ. The two texts use this generic prefix for all her speeches in this scene (1.1.16, 22, 36, 49, 70). See 1.1.6.

1.1.1/103 ne'er] *neuer* CRANE²,³, OKES, BRIDGEWATERᴬ. A favourite Middleton contraction. For other examples of Crane expanding the elision, see 1.1.172, 3.1.2, 5.2.16.

1.1.3/105 heaven's] *heau's* MATHEWES. Omitted type. See Induction.17, 69.

1.1.4/106 And...eternally] *not in* OKES

1.1.5/107 that] OKES; *that fhe is* BRIDGEWATERᴬ; *being* CRANE¹ +. 'Being not' occurs four times elsewhere in Middleton; 'that not' three times elsewhere (in each case preceded by a monosyllable, at the beginning of a verse line). Late authorial variant.

1.1.5/107 heresy] *Ignorance* CRANE¹ *uncorrected*. There is no doubt that Middleton originally wrote 'Ignorance' (which is accordingly preserved in *Early* 1.5), and the variant may well result from censorship. That would explain why the original reading in CRANE¹ was altered. But the variant might be

a deliberate theatrical revision: although a Catholic might well attribute a Protestant's beliefs to 'Ignorance', for an audience 'heresy' establishes the sectarian difference without suggesting that White Queen's Pawn is an uneducated character.

1.1.6/109 QUEEN'S] *not in* CRANE¹, ROSENBACHᴬ. See 1.1.1. The two texts use this generic prefix for all her speeches in this scene and the next, and for all but two of her speeches in 2.2. The abbreviated form of the prefix occurs in CRANE¹ alone at 2.2.99, 179.

1.1.6–7/109–10 Where...plainly] *sorrow* | ROSENBACHᴬ. Suggesting that in some antecedent manuscript this line and a half of verse was written as a single line.

*1.1.7/110 They're] *Theis are* CRANE²,³; *they are* CRANE/MATHEWES. See Induction.55. The variant 'Theis' must be a shared error, since her distance on stage from the Black Queen's Pawn would require 'those'. Probably 'they'are' (Crane's Jonsonian elision) was misread as 'thefare' (with the tale of the 'y' misread as the tale of an 's'). Compare 'they'are' in CRANE² at 1.1.224.

1.1.8/111 Beshrew...heartily.] *not in* CRANE³
1.1.8/111 weep] *wept* CRANE/MATHEWES
1.1.8/111 heartily] *hartity* OKES. Foul case error.
1.1.10–14/113–17 If...eye?] *not in* CRANE³
1.1.13/116 best] *not in* OKES
1.1.14/117 of] *ot* MATHEWES. Foul case error.
1.1.14/117 eye] *Eies* CRANE/MATHEWES
1.1.15/118 It's] CRANE²,³; *'tis* CRANE¹ +. See Induction.15.
1.1.20/124 ground-work] ~ *workes* BRIDGEWATERᶜ (correction in pencil). Howard-Hill identifies this as a miscorrection (*Pasquin* 307).
1.1.20/124 firmer] *firme* CRANE/MATHEWES
1.1.21/125 has] *hath* CRANE²,³,⁴
1.1.22/127 the enemy |] *your* ~: CRANE³. Replacement for the two following lines.
1.1.23–4/128–9 That...battle.] *not in* CRANE³
1.1.23/128 ₐ your strength away] *away* ~ ~ ₐ ROSENBACHᴬ
1.1.24/129 Disarms] *This-Armes* CRANE/MATHEWES
1.1.24/129 e'en] MIDDLETONᵀ (*een*'), CRANE¹ (*ev'n*); *euen* CRANE² +. Autograph restores the contraction present otherwise only in the first transcription. Although Crane's initial 'ev'n' moves in the direction of his fully expanded 'euen', in subsequent notes 'ev'n' will be regarded only as a spelling variant of the elided form, and not recorded unless relevant to a particular set of variants.
1.1.24/129 the] *that* OKES
1.1.27/132 flew] *flied* BRIDGEWATERᴬ. The variant form appears nowhere else in Middleton. Contamination from 'spied'.
1.1.28–9/133–4 From...heresies] *1 line* CRANE, ROSENBACHᴬ. Relic.
1.1.28/133 eye] *eyes* OKES
1.1.29/134 heresies] *Errors* CRANE¹ *uncorrected*. The original reading is probably authorial—and is retained in *Early* 1.31—but the variant produces a regular iambic pentameter.
1.1.30.1/136 *from the Black House*] THIS EDITION (*conj.* Hotson); *not in* CRANE¹ +. See 1.1.0.2–4. The call for entrances from the Black and White House in the first stage direction of the chess game may be understood as a global direction to govern entrances and exits for the whole play. Hotson's interpretation of the use of contrasting stage doors is supported by Foakes.
1.1.30.1/136 the] *not in* CRANE¹,⁴, ROSENBACHᴬ, BRIDGEWATERᴬ
1.1.30.2/137 *a Jesuit*] MIDDLETONᵀ, BRIDGEWATERᴬ; *not in* CRANE¹ +

1.1.32/139   Can] will CRANE

1.1.35/143   and the habit] *not in* BRIDGEWATER[A]

*1.1.36-7/145-6   But...still] meek | CRANE[2,3]

1.1.36/145   the heart, the heart] ~ ~ ᴀ ᴀ CRANE[2,3,4], ROSENBACH[A]. Although either reading makes sense, the shorter variant could easily result from eyeskip or haplography; the longer form appears in the earliest and latest texts, and the shorter in a succession of closely related texts, suggesting that it is a shared error. It has not been counted as such, however, because the shorter variant does make sense.

1.1.40/149   E'en] even CRANE[2,3,4], ROSENBACH[A]

1.1.40/149   his bosom] ~ armes OKES; ~ A BRIDGEWATER[A] *uncorrected*. The scribe apparently began to write the same word present in OKES, then corrected the error before writing the second letter. The variant probably originated from contamination from two lines above; it is probably, but not certainly, an error.

1.1.40/149   dear] *not in* OKES

1.1.41/150   Jesuitess] OKES, BRIDGEWATER[A]; Iesuite CRANE[1]+. Middleton so calls her later in the play, specifically referring to the Jesuit order founded by Mrs. Ward and suppressed by the Pope in 1631. 'Praestat insolitior lectio' (Taylor 1988): a late authorial revision.

1.1.42/151   worth] OKES, BRIDGEWATER[A]; wealth CRANE[1]+. Late authorial revision. See preceding note.

1.1.44/153   the] their CRANE/MATHEWES. Assimilation.

1.1.46-7/155-6   This...pleasure] receive | CRANE/MATHEWES

1.1.46/155   now stands, for] to] ~ ~, now, to OKES. Nascimento incorrectly records the OKES reading (omitting 'to').

1.1.47/156   college] reuerend ROSENBACH[A]. The variant seems to result from memory of 1.1.35-6 ('habit...reverend').

1.1.48-62/157-72   WHITE QUEEN'S PAWN...sound.] *not in* CRANE[3]

1.1.48/156   those] thefe OKES

1.1.49/159   They're] They are CRANE[2,4]

1.1.50/160   'em] them CRANE/MATHEWES

1.1.50/160   vineyard] ROSENBACH[A]; Work CRANE[1]+. The telling biblical echo is likelier to be Middleton's than a copyist's. For an argument that [PRE-ROSENBACH] was at least in part autograph, see General Textual Introduction, Sec. XIV-XV. For other variants unique to ROSENBACH that appear to be authorial see 1.1.173, 2.2.125, 2.2.39, 2.2.40, 3.1.2, 3.1.274, 3.1.197, D.22, 4.2.61, 5.2.95-6. Stemmatically, many authorial variants that appear in both ROSENBACH and BRIDGEWATER must have originated in [PRE-ROSENBACH] or [PRE-ROSENBACH/BRIDGEWATER].

1.1.51/161   th'] CRANE[1]; the CRANE[2]+; *not in* OKES

1.1.53/163   maintained] maintaynèd OKES, ROSENBACH[A]

1.1.54/164   by] ~ th' CRANE/MATHEWES

1.1.59/169   th'] the NON-CRANE

1.1.59/169   are] o[r] ROSENBACH[A]

1.1.60/170   Oft] Often OKES

1.1.60/170   important] importune CRANE/MATHEWES; importinant OKES. The quartos' variants are perhaps related.

1.1.61/171   state] States CRANE/MATHEWES. Probably assimilation to the preceding plurals (designs...times...secrets).

1.1.62/172   those] they CRANE/MATHEWES

1.1.65/175   Checked] Ceeck'd MATHEWES. Foul case.

1.1.66/176   Your] our ROSENBACH[A]

1.1.69/179   Dost] doe you CRANE, ROSENBACH[A]. Late authorial variant.

1.1.70/180   There's] There is CRANE/MATHEWES. A typical Crane expansion of a Middletonian elision.

1.1.70/180   made] *not in* CRANE, ROSENBACH[A]. Late authorial variant.

*1.1.70/180.1   Exit] CRANE, ROSENBACH[A]; *not in* OKES, BRIDGEWATER[A], MIDDLETON[T]. A shared error in autograph, emended by Howard-Hill. For the additional lines present in CRANE[1] only, see *Early* 1.76-7.

1.1.72-4/182-4   With...goodness] *not in* CRANE[3]

1.1.75/185   not] no CRANE[2]

1.1.76/186   catholical] Cathalccall OKES (Huntington); Cathalecall OKES (Worcester, Bod.Vet.A2, British Library). Nascimento noted this variant on sig. B3[v], but no others on this page or forme. The second 'l' is broken in British Library copies C.34.d.38 and 161.a.10, in a way that makes it look, to a casual observer, like an 'i'.

1.1.77/187   Does] Doth CRANE[2,3,4]. 'Does' is Middleton's overwhelming preference, occasionally sophisticated by Crane.

1.1.79/189   pearl] a ~ CRANE[2,3], ROSENBACH[A]

1.1.80/190   from the] ~ ᴀ OKES

1.1.80/190   op'ning] THIS EDITION; opening CRANE[1]+. See l. 287.

1.1.83/193   delightfully] delightfull OKES, BRIDGEWATER[A]

1.1.88/198   which] MIDDLETON[T]+ (wch); well OKES. Misreading.

1.1.91/201   that] the OKES

1.1.92/202   since] feythence OKES. Middleton uses 'sithence' (in *Sherley*, *Gates*, *Owl*, and *Industry*), but it does not appear elsewhere in dialogue.

1.1.93/203   Th'] the ROSENBACH[A], OKES

1.1.94/204   labour] labours BRIDGEWATER[A] *uncorrected*

1.1.95/205   it's] CRANE[2]; 'tis CRANE[1]+. See Induction.15.

1.1.96/206   desire] deafires BRIDGEWATER[A] *uncorrected*

1.1.96/206   transgressed] tranfgreffe BRIDGEWATER[A]

1.1.97/207   It's] OKES; that's CRANE[1]+. See Induction.15.

1.1.98/208   that] *not in* CRANE[2,3]

1.1.104/214   locks] lookes OKES. Misreading.

1.1.105/217   Who is] MIDDLETON[T] *only*; ~ ᴀ BRIDGEWATER[A], OKES; Who's CRANE, ROSENBACH[A]. Late autograph variant. The variant shared by BRIDGEWATER and OKES might be an accidental omission by haplography ('who's so'), but the ellipsis produces a perfectly comprehensible sentence, so it might also be a late authorial variant. MIDDLETON[T] might be a correction of the shared error, or an expansion of the original contraction. Since the line is extrametrical in any case, and 'Who's' is retained in *Early* 1.114, the autograph variant has been preferred here.

1.1.108/220   unblessed] imbleft OKES. Misreading.

1.1.112-16/224-8   For...designs] *not in* CRANE[3]

1.1.112/224   by] my OKES

1.1.112/224   disclosing] discouering BRIDGEWATER[A]

1.1.114/226   in the] i'th' THIS EDITION *conj*.

1.1.115/227   point] paynt BRIDGEWATER[A] *uncorrected*

1.1.116/228   best] how BRIDGEWATER[A] *uncorrected*

1.1.117/229   errors] Error[ors] CRANE[2]

1.1.118/230   recovery] recouery OKES

1.1.119-30/231-5   To be...cure.] *not in* CRANE[3]

1.1.120/232   Toward] towards CRANE/MATHEWES, ROSENBACH[A], OKES. Middleton uses both forms, though he somewhat prefers 'toward'.

1.1.121/233   ulcer] vlter OKES. Foul case error.

1.1.122/234   the tumor] that ~ BRIDGEWATER[A], OKES. Possibly a late authorial variant.

1.1.123/235   far] faire OKES. Misreading.

1.1.125/237   In] into BRIDGEWATER[A] *uncorrected*

1.1.127/239   your] yours OKES. Terminal 's' error.

1.1.127/239   night-counsel] Night Counfels CRANE/MATHEWES. The compound (adjective + singular noun) is likelier to be authorial, because it is a rarer verbal formula than the overwhelmingly common uncompounded adjective + plural noun (Taylor 1988).

1.1.128/240 action] account OKES. Misreading.

1.1.133–4/245–6 Of...thoughts] *1 line* CRANE[1,4], ROSENBACH[A]. Relic.

1.1.135/247 more] ʋore MATHEWES

1.1.136/248 with...safety] for...fafely OKES. Misreading and assimilation.

1.1.137/249 fond, some sinful] finful, some found OKES

*1.1.137/249 fond] found OKES, CRANE/MATHEWES. She cannot mean to say that she gave 'sound' thoughts 'small encouragement to come again.'

1.1.138/250 But] *not in* OKES

1.1.139/251 They'd] they'had CRANE[1,2]; they had CRANE[3,4], ROSENBACH[A]

1.1.139/251 small] *not in* OKES

1.1.140/252 profess] profeffd BRIDGEWATER[A] *uncorrected*

1.1.143/256 passage] paaffge OKES

1.1.145/259 discharged] difchargèd OKES

1.1.149/263 Clad] Cal'd CRANE/MATHEWES

1.1.149/263 sordid] forbid ROSENBACH[A]

1.1.150/264 by] be BRIDGEWATER[A] *uncorrected*

1.1.151/265 lock] fhut CRANE[2]

1.1.153/267 prayer] grace CRANE/MATHEWES. A misreading of 'praire' (the spelling in CRANE[1,2,3]); the NON-CRANE texts spell 'prayer', which makes the misreading much less plausible.

1.1.154/268 modestlier] modeftier OKES

1.1.156/271 A] CRANE[1], ROSENBACH[A]; An CRANE[2]+. See next note.

1.1.156/271 Puritan] CRANE[1] *uncorrected*; Heretique CRANE[1] *corrected*, CRANE[2]+. This variant almost certainly results from censorship—applied, or anticipated—of the specifically English original reading; it is hard to dismiss 'Puritaine' as a scribal error. It presumably represents Middleton's original intention—and as such a reliable guide to the play's allegory. 'Puritan' identifies the White Bishop's Pawn as a particular kind of 'heretic' (i.e. Protestant): a dedicated Calvinist (like Archbishop Abbot), at odds with the increasingly Arminian court clergy. The play's sympathetic representation of a Puritan, as a victimized but constant opponent of Spanish/Jesuit plotting, helps explain why Puritans 'seemed much t' adore' Middleton for *A Game at Chess*.

1.1.157/273 prepared] preparèd OKES

1.1.157/273 his] the OKES. Assimilation.

1.1.157/273 competitor] Competitors CRANE/MATHEWES

1.1.162–4/278–81 WHITE QUEEN'S PAWN...nature.] *not in* CRANE[3]

1.1.162/279 BISHOP'S] Q. CRANE/MATHEWES. Assimilation to preceding prefix?

1.1.164/281 unmanning] vnmarring OKES. Misreading.

*1.1.165/282 then] *not in* BRIDGEWATER[A], OKES. Shared error: the absence of the word disturbs the metre and removes the logical connective, to no discernible advantage.

1.1.165/282 refused] refufe OKES. Probably a misreading, though possibly a revision.

1.1.166/283 Therein...desire] *not in* OKES. Eyeskip.

1.1.167/284 That] which CRANE[2]

1.1.167/284 ˄ ends] the ~ BRIDGEWATER[A], OKES. Possibly a late authorial variant; metrically acceptable, if elided.

1.1.170/288 acknowledge] confeffe BRIDGEWATER, OKES. Unmetrical synonym substitution. This may be a shared error, but since both words make sense it has not been tabulated as such.

1.1.173/291 ne'er] ROSENBACH[A]; neuer CRANE[1]+. See 1.1.1.

1.1.175–85/293–304 BLACK BISHOP'S PAWN...glory.] *not in* CRANE[3]

1.1.175/293 BLACK BISHOP'S PAWN] *not in* MIDDLETON[T] *uncorrected*; BlB[s.]p. MIDDLETON[T] *corrected* (interlined)

1.1.177/295 you've] CRANE[2] (you'haue); you haue CRANE[1]+

1.1.178/296 composed] compofèd OKES

1.1.179/297 princess' favour] *not in* BRIDGEWATER[A] *uncorrected*. See next note.

1.1.179/297 princess'] CRANE[1]; Princes CRANE[2]+. Censorship. See *Early* 1.193.

1.1.180/298 exact] ~ in all things BRIDGEWATER[A]. The extrametrical prepositional phrase anticipates 2.1.2, something likelier to be done by an author than a scribe. The phrase also occurs at least ten times elsewhere in the Middleton canon (all after 1611). Compare the extrametrical addition at 4.4.71. This variant suggests that [PRE-]BRIDGEWATER was autograph, at least in this vicinity. However, the addition is metrically disruptive, and may not have been a conscious decision to revise.

1.1.182/300 wish] wifhes BRIDGEWATER[A], OKES. The plural ruins the parallel with 'desire' in the following phrase (and turns a feminine ending into a hexameter).

1.1.183/301 stir] CRANE/MATHEWES (ftirre), OKES (ftirre); fteere CRANE[1]+. Compare *No Wit* 4.8 ('stir up her Blood') and *Women Beware* 4.1.132 ('a blood soon stir'd'). This is either a late autograph variant, or an error in all six extant manuscripts, or a spelling variant (since *OED* records 'steere' as an early modern spelling of *stir*, and 'stirre' as an early modern spelling of *steer*). Middleton uses the verb *steer* twice in *Truth*, but *stir* occurs more than 70 times in 28 works in his canon.

1.1.184/303 I've] CRANE[1,2] (I'haue); I haue [CRANE[4]]+. For this characteristic Middletonian elision see General Textual Introduction, Sec. IV.

1.1.185/304 Maker's] workes OKES. Misreading.

1.1.186–9/306–9 A second...much.] *not in* CRANE[3]

1.1.186/306 fall] bee BRIDGEWATER[A] *uncorrected*

1.1.188/308 some] ~ to knowe BRIDGEWATER[A] *uncorrected*

1.1.192/312 forward] forwards ROSENBACH[A]. Middleton strongly prefers 'forward'.

1.1.192/313 that's] that is OKES

1.1.193/314 I've] CRANE[1,2] (I'haue); I haue CRANE[3]+

1.1.193/314 especial] a fpeciall CRANE/MATHEWES

1.1.194/315 You...duty] *2 lines:* that | OKES

1.1.194 pow'r] CRANE (powre); power NON-CRANE

1.1.195/316 WHITE...sir.] *not in* OKES. Eyeskip.

1.1.195/316 both] all BRIDGEWATER[A] *uncorrected*

1.1.195.1–2/317 *Enter...Pawn*] CRANE/MATHEWES places this direction in the right margin opposite 'well' at 1.1.192.

1.1.195.1/317 *from the White House*] THIS EDITION (*conj.* Hotson); *not in* CRANE[1]+. See 1.1.30.1.

1.1.195.1/317 ˄ White] y[e] ~ CRANE[2,3]. One of thirteen directions where CRANE[2,3] are the only texts to use the definite article; in another eight directions only CRANE[2] does so. Theoretically, these might derive from the playbook, but in seven cases the article appears only in CRANE[3], usually in massed entrance directions, a trademark of Crane rather than Middleton or the King's Men. Moreover, MIDDLETON[T] does not contain any unique definite articles in directions.

1.1.196/318 waters] water OKES

1.1.197/319 that] yond OKES. Probably contamination from preceding line.

1.1.197/319 But that] ~ ˄ OKES

1.1.200/322 suff'rings] fufferings CRANE/MATHEWES, ROSENBACH[A], OKES

1.1.200–5/322–7 which...possess her.] *not in* CRANE[3]

*1.1.201/323 comes] come ROSENBACH^A, OKES. Shared error.
1.1.204/326 confined)…joys_∧] CRANE^{1,2}, MIDDLETON^T; ~_∧ ~_∧ ROSENBACH^A, BRIDGEWATER^A; ~_∧ ~, OKES, CRANE/MATHEWES. Shared punctuation error in the quartos.
1.1.204/326 confined] confinèd OKES
1.1.205/327 I] I'would CRANE^2; Il'd CRANE/MATHEWES; not in ROSENBACH^A
*1.1.205.1–2/332–3 Enter…Pawn] CRANE^2, OKES, CRANE/MATHEWES; at 204.1 CRANE^1; at 203.1 ROSENBACH^A; at 208.1 BRIDGEWATER^A, MIDDLETON^T. The slightly earlier positions of CRANE^1 and ROSENBACH^A are possible, but the later position of BRIDGEWATER^A and MIDDLETON^T must be mistaken, since it follows the Black Bishop's Pawn's speech, which refers to both characters as already on stage. If the direction had been accidentally omitted in an intervening text, then it might have been reinserted at this later point, just before the character's speech reminded the copyist that he needed an entrance. Shared error in autograph, emended by HOWARD-HILL.
1.1.205.1/332 from the Black House] THIS EDITION (conj. Hotson); not in CRANE^1+. See 1.1.30.1.
1.1.205.1/332 _∧ Black] y^e ~ CRANE^2, OKES. See 1.1.195.1.
1.1.205/328 Behold, lady,] not in ROSENBACH^A
1.1.207/330 Bishop's] ~ pawne BRIDGEWATER^A uncorrected
1.1.207/330 the gelder…gelded] not in CRANE^1 uncorrected
1.1.209/333 Knight's] B. OKES^2 uncorrected. The error is corrected by hand (to 'K') in British Library copy 161.a.10 (which is OKES^2 for this sheet). Bodleian Malone 176(3)—which is also OKES^2—prints 'B.', as does the New York Public Library copy, so this is apparently a press variant in OKES^2. I record it here only because of the handwritten annotation.
1.1.209/333 By this hand] not in CRANE^{2,3}. Censorship of playbook (with the original reading restored in later copies).
1.1.213/337 return] veturne BRIDGEWATER^A. (Assimilation: vsurers veturne.)
1.1.214/338 Have I] I'haue CRANE^2; I haue CRANE^{3,4}
1.1.216/340 of it] OKES; oft' BRIDGEWATER^A (misplaced apostrophe added in pencil); of CRANE^1+. One would expect Middleton to have written 'on't' rather than 'of't', if he had intended the contraction. But Middleton used the full form 'of it' more than 80 times elsewhere. Although the text makes sense without the pronoun (and so has been retained in Early 1.234), the variant clarifies the meaning, and could be a late authorial revision.
1.1.220/344 virgin] Lady CRANE^3
1.1.221–8/345–52 WHITE QUEEN'S PAWN…building?] not in CRANE^3
1.1.223/347 virgin] virgins ROSENBACH^A
1.1.224/348 They're] they'are CRANE^2; They are CRANE/MATHEWES
1.1.224/348 not] out CRANE. Late authorial variant.
1.1.227/351 a] the OKES. Assimilation.
1.1.228/352 t'] CRANE^1, MIDDLETON^T; to CRANE^2+. Autograph restoration of original reading.
1.1.228/352 building] bulding BRIDGEWATER^A
1.1.229/353 evil] diuell OKES
1.1.230/354 eyes] eye BRIDGEWATER^A
1.1.231/355 Would] will CRANE^3
1.1.231/355 ye] OKES (yee); you CRANE^1+. Although not a favourite Middleton form, 'yee' or 'ye' occurs altogether 65 times in 20 of his uncollaborative works (No Wit 10, Chaste Maid 7, Phoenix 6, Five Gallants 6, Mad World 5, Michaelmas 5, Lady 4, Solomon 3, Trick 3, Widow 3, Yorkshire 2, Women Beware 2, Valour 2, Truth 1, Integrity 1, Antiquity 1, Puritan 1,

Revenger 1, Witch 1, Hengist 1). Even if we invoke interference by Shirley and a scribe to account for the two highest totals, 48 examples in 18 works remain. (If we include collaborative works, the total rises to more than 100.) The variant here can hardly be attributed to a compositorial preference, since this is its only appearance in the quarto. But it could well be a late authorial variant.
1.1.232/356 BLACK KNIGHT'S PAWN] not in BRIDGEWATER^A uncorrected (no speech rule)
1.1.232/356 a] fo BRIDGEWATER^A uncorrected (beginning to write 'some'; contamination from previous line)
1.1.232/356 alb] Abbey OKES. Misreading of 'Albe'.
1.1.233/357 An] And CRANE/MATHEWES
1.1.233/357 felon] fellow MIDDLETON^T, OKES. The variant could easily result from minim misreading of 'Fellon' (CRANE^1+), which produces a typical Middletonian oxymoron. Contrast the unique autograph spelling 'bedfellowe' (2158 and 2160 in MIDDLETON^{T,B}). The variant has not been counted as a shared error, because 'fellow' does make minimal sense, and might result from authorial memory and anticipation of 'this fellow' at l. 248.
1.1.234/358 Robs] robd MIDDLETON^T uncorrected
1.1.234/358 safe] faf't OKES. Possibly a late authorial revision, but there are no Middleton parallels.
1.1.235/359 White_∧] ~ Bs BRIDGEWATER^A corrected
1.1.235/359 to accept] CRANE+; t'accept THIS EDITION conj. An exact parallel for the elision occurs at Timon 14.489 (attributed to Middleton). However, charity seems to be treated as disyllabic at 1.1.15, 37.
1.1.236/360 thy] thine CRANE
1.1.236/360 own conditions] one Condition BRIDGEWATER^A
1.1.237/361 extremely] extteamely MATHEWES (Folger, Worcester, Huntington, Bodleian Malone 247, British Library C.34.d.37). Nascimento records 'extrreamely' (perhaps a press variant).
1.1.237/361 burdened] burthenèd CRANE/MATHEWES, ROSENBACH^A
1.1.238/362 or] nor BRIDGEWATER^A; no OKES. Middleton uses the idiom 'no [noun] nor' at least nine times elsewhere, including Game 5.3.16.
1.1.238/362 protested] proteſt OKES
1.1.239/363 quittance] acquittance OKES
1.1.240/364 diffidence] difference OKES. 'Insolitior lectio'.
1.1.241/365 conference] confrence BRIDGEWATER^A only. LION contains seven examples of the elision in the period. Here, it produces an extra unstressed syllable at the caesura, rather than a speaker-divided hexameter. There is not much to choose between the variants, metrically, and Middleton's verse elsewhere occasionally requires both the elided and the unelided pronunciation.
1.1.241/366 KNIGHT'S] Bs BRIDGEWATER^A uncorrected
*1.1.241/366 a] not in CRANE^{2,3}, ROSENBACH^A
*1.1.242.1–2/367.1 Exeunt…Pawn]—Ex^t CRANE^1 (after 'fully' one line below);—Ex^t CRANE^2; not in CRANE^{3,4}, NON-CRANE. A shared error in autograph, emended by Howard-Hill.
1.1.243/368 fully] throughly CRANE/MATHEWES. Possibly a late authorial variant.
*1.1.243.1/369 Enter Black Knight] Both BRIDGEWATER^A and OKES misplace this direction one line below, after he speaks, in the right margin opposite 'So, so.' By contrast, CRANE/MATHEWES places it three lines earlier, in the right margin after 'conference' (1.1.241), a possible position, but relatively unlikely.

1.1.243.1–2/369 *from the Black House*] THIS EDITION (*conj.* Hotson); *not in* CRANE[1]+. See 1.1.30.1.

1.1.245/372 great] *not in* OKES

1.1.247/374 intelligences] intelligencers OKES

1.1.248/375 Thorough] MIDDLETON[T] *only*; through CRANE+. HOWARD-HILL claims that the disyllabic pronunciation 'is not necessary for the meter', but the line is a syllable short without it.

*1.1.248/375 kingdoms] kingdome ROSENBACH[A], OKES. A shared error: in the play and the world it represents, there is more than one Christian kingdom (as the following dialogue with its letters from various kingdoms make explicit).

1.1.249/376 ‿one] MIDDLETON[T], OKES, BRIDGEWATER[A]; and ~ CRANE, ROSENBACH[A]. Possibly a late authorial variant.

1.1.250/377 sev'n] 7 MIDDLETON[T], BRIDGEWATER[A], ROSENBACH[A]; feauen CRANE[1]+. Middleton's preference for the numeral—which appears often in his printed texts, as well as autograph—makes it impossible to tell whether he intended one or two syllables. But LION records the elided spelling 'sev'n' fifty times in English poetry printed in Middleton's lifetime, so the monosyllabic pronunciation was clearly available, and widely used. Perhaps pronounced 'se'n' (as in the contraction *sennight* for 'seven-night').

1.1.250/377 years] yeare CRANE[1,3], ROSENBACH[A]

*1.1.252–4/379–80 The great...less] CRANE[3]; *2 lines* hierarchy | CRANE[1,2,4], ROSENBACH[A]; nor | hierarchy MIDDLETON[T], BRIDGEWATER[A]; monarchy | OKES

1.1.252/379 great] *not in* CRANE/MATHEWES

1.1.252/379 work stands] worke-ſtaues OKES. Misreading.

1.1.253/380 hierarchy] Hererazie OKES

1.1.254/380 Diviner] Diuine CRANE/MATHEWES

1.1.254/380 principality] principallities OKES

1.1.254/380 I brag] OKES; I haue bragd CRANE, ROSENBACH; Iu'e bragd MIDDLETON[T], BRIDGEWATER[A]. Late authorial variant.

1.1.255/381 have] MIDDLETON[T], BRIDGEWATER[A], OKES; I'haue CRANE[1,2]; I haue CRANE[3,4], ROSENBACH[A]. Late authorial variant.

1.1.255/381 of] CRANE[2]; on CRANE[1]+. Middleton's now-obsolete 'on' is preserved in *Early* 1.274; the normal modern 'of' is preferred in the modernized text where (here and elsewhere) it is present in one or more early witnesses. This is comparable to the treatment of pound(s), year(s), etc.

1.1.256–7/382–3 Take...boot] *not in* CRANE[3]

1.1.256/382 assistant] *not in* BRIDGEWATER[A] *uncorrected*

1.1.256/382 fathers] father BRIDGEWATER[A]

1.1.257/383 Yea] CRANE[2,4]; I CRANE[1]+. Middleton uses the stronger form twelve times in nine uncollaborative works, from *Solomon* to *Valour*; if we add collaborative works the total rises to at least nineteen examples. The variant is unlikely to be Crane's work: it does not occur at all in *Witch* or in Webster's *Duchess of Malfi*, and occurs less often in Crane's Shakespeare transcripts than elsewhere in the Shakespeare canon. Authorial variation.

1.1.257/383 and] or MIDDLETON[T], BRIDGEWATER[A], OKES. Error: 'to boot' (in addition) makes it clear that the phrase is additive, not alternative. This is not tabulated as a shared error because HOWARD-HILL accepts the autograph reading.

1.1.258/384 I've...I've] CRANE[2] (I'haue...I'haue); I haue... I ha' CRANE[1]+; I haue...I haue CRANE[3]+. The elisions in the two earliest texts produce a regular iambic pentameter. Without them, the line is hypermetrical, and the iambic stress—'and *what* I *have* done'—seems to emphasize what he *has* done (as opposed to what he has *not* done), when the

emphasis instead should be on the repeated 'done' (which the elisions preserve, stressing the contrast between his *action* and their *inaction*).

1.1.258/384 facetiously] faƈtiouſly OKES. Misreading.

1.1.260/386 Abused] Abuſe OKES. Misreading.

1.1.261/387 a] *not in* OKES

1.1.262/388 I've] CRANE[2] (I'haue); I haue CRANE[1]+

1.1.265/391 mischief] CRANE/MATHEWES, OKES, BRIDGEWATER[A]; Miſcheifes CRANE[1]+. *Women Beware* contains two examples of 'all the mischief' (singular) (2.2.415, 3.1.225); Middleton uses the singular more often than the plural. Authorial vacillation?

1.1.266/392 way of] *not in* ROSENBACH[A]

1.1.268/394 He] I MIDDLETON[T] *uncorrected* (skipping ahead to next phrase)

1.1.268/394 me] one ROSENBACH[A]

1.1.269/395 public] priuat CRANE[3]

*1.1.270/396 Priapus...gardens,] *not in* CRANE[2,3]. This is not an accidental error originating in CRANE[2]: after 268, there is a page break, and the catchword is 'Bacchus' (270). The omission therefore seems to have originated in an earlier text. See next notes. (The cluster of variants is noted and discussed by Bawcutt, 8).

1.1.270/396 of the] ~ the' CRANE[1]. At *Women Beware* 3.2.8 'guardian' is treated as two syllables.

1.1.270/396 gardens] Garden BRIDGEWATER[A]. Assimilation.

*1.1.271/397 Bacchus‿, and Venus' chit, is] ~, ~ ~ ~, are CRANE[2]; ~, ~ ~ ~ ~ ‿ are CRANE[3]. As Bawcutt notes, the punctuation in CRANE[2] suggests it is closer to the correct original (8). Progressive error?

1.1.272/398 accumulation] accumiliation OKES

*1.1.272/398 keep] be CRANE[3]; b BRIDGEWATER[A] *uncorrected*. Scribe A began to write 'bee', but changed the 'b' to 'k'. This variant is clearly an error, anticipating the verb in the same position in the next line. Black Knight already has an accumulation of material blessings, and the question in the play is whether he will be able to *keep* them.

1.1.272/399 BLACK] In MIDDLETON[T] *corrected* the initial 'Bl' was created by altering 'H', indicating that Middleton at first skipped over the speech prefix, beginning with the first word of the spoken text, but then immediately corrected his error before writing the second letter of the word 'Honors'. We see here the beginning of an autograph sloppiness about speech prefixes, here being committed and quickly corrected, with the inattention later increasing so that the error goes uncaught.

1.1.274/400 his...plunges] in...plunge OKES

1.1.277/404 Sh'as] Sh'ath CRANE[2,3,4]

1.1.277/405 KNIGHT] K. OKES. The same misleading abbreviation occurs in OKES alone at 1.1.304, 2.1.216, 2.1.220. Since the play contains a Black King, it is essential to distinguish between him and the Black Knight, and all eight witnesses do so with remarkable consistency. In these early scenes, however, no Black King is on stage—indeed, the Black King has not yet appeared as a speaking character—so the OKES abbreviation, although technically incorrect, is not seriously misleading. But see 4.4.16.

1.1.278/406 T'amaze] CRANE, MIDDLETON[T]; to ~ ROSENBACH[A]; t'maze BRIDGEWATER[A]; To maze OKES. Middleton does not elsewhere use *maze* as a verb.

*1.1.279/407 these] this ROSENBACH[A], CRANE/MATHEWES

1.1.279/407 *guitonens*] great ones OKES. Misreading of a rare word: see Taylor 1988.

1.1.283 pucelles] MIDDLETON[T]+ (Pufills). Howard-Hill modernizes as 'pucills' (OED n.1), deriving from Latin pusillus 'very
small', and glosses as 'weak-minded, easily-led persons'; but
OED gives no examples of his figurative meaning, instead
recording this passage as a variant spelling of 'pucelles'.
Howard-Hill claims 'the context bears no sexual connotation', but Black Knight repeatedly complains about Black
Bishop's Pawn's lechery, and the audience also knows his
sexual intentions toward the White Queen's Pawn.

1.1.283.1/411 *Exit...Pawn*] HARPER; *not in* CRANE[1]+. The character could exit at any point between the Black Bishop's
Pawn's final words to her ('sons and daughters') at 1.1.277
and the Black Knight's statement at 1.1.284 that she has
'vanished'; DYCE placed the exit after 1.1.281. An extended
mimed farewell would cover the Black Knight's aside. An
error shared by all texts, and probably authorial in origin;
the exit is clearly implied.

1.1.284/412 vanished] gone OKES

1.1.285/413 It's] CRANE[2], OKES; 'tis CRANE[1]+. See Induction.15.

1.1.285/413 pawn] game OKES

1.1.286/414 of] in CRANE, ROSENBACH[A]. Late authorial revision.

1.1.287/415 op'ning] BRIDGEWATER[A]; opening CRANE[1]+. The
elision seems metrically required, and is graphically marked
in other verse texts of the period.

*1.1.288–90/416–18 Ay...private] your | ply | MIDDLETON[T],
BRIDGEWATER[A]; play | ply | OKES. Shared errors. The line-
-break after 'your' is clearly mistaken; although OKES's arrangement is defensible, in that it produces two pentameters,
Middleton consistently prefers end-stopped lines, and in any
case OKES simply moves the hexameter from the first to the
third line of the speech.

1.1.289/417 ply] playe BRIDGEWATER[A]. Assimilation.

1.1.289/418 the] your CRANE[2,3]

1.1.290/418 we're] we'are CRANE[2]; we are CRANE[3,4], ROSEN-
BACH[A]

1.1.291/419 main...great] great...maine BRIDGEWATER[A]

1.1.293/423 You may deny so] So you may deny OKES

1.1.295/425 cedar] Cedars OKES

1.1.297/427 o'th'] CRANE[1,4]; of the' CRANE[2]; of the CRANE[3],
NON-CRANE

1.1.300/431 th'] CRANE[1,3]; the CRANE[4]+

1.1.301/432 you] *not in* CRANE[2,3,4]

1.1.301/432 Anglica] Angelica ROSENBACH[A]

*1.1.302/433 Ay...this] *2 lines* CRANE[2,3]: sir |. Shared error.

1.1.304/435 ˌ'Think] I ~ CRANE[2,3,4]. Extrametrical expansion of
a colloquial elision found often in Middleton. (The apostrophe
is present in CRANE[1].)

1.1.304/435 they've] they'haue CRANE[2]; they haue CRANE[3,4];
they'n OKES (foul case or turned letter)

1.1.305/436 *Italica*, this] this *Italica* CRANE

1.1.306/437 They] MIDDLETON[T], BRIDGEWATER[A], OKES; they'ue
CRANE[1], ROSENBACH[A]; they'haue CRANE[2]; they haue CRANE[3,4].
Late autograph variant.

1.1.307/438 here] there OKES. Possible revision.

*1.1.307/439 work] word OKES, BRIDGEWATER[A] *uncorrected*

*1.1.307/439 this] OKES, BRIDGEWATER[A]; tis CRANE[1]+. Late au-
thorial revision.

1.1.308/440 has] BRIDGEWATER[A], MIDDLETON[T]; hath CRANE+

1.1.310/442 Ere't] ere it CRANE[2,3,4]

1.1.310/443 will] would CRANE/MATHEWES

1.1.311/444 Though't] CRANE[1], ROSENBACH[A]; though it CRANE[2]+

*1.1.311/444 wounded] wound CRANE[2,3], OKES. A shared error
(haplography), which produces a metrically and grammatically inferior reading.

1.1.311/444 fame] name CRANE, ROSENBACH[A]. Late authorial
revision.

1.1.311.1–2/444–6 *Enter...Pawn*] CRANE[1] and OKES place this
direction in the right margin opposite 'Pecunia'.

1.1.311.1/444 *from the White House*] THIS EDITION (*conj.* Hotson); *not in* CRANE[1]+. See 1.1.30.1.

1.1.311.1/444–6 ˌ White] y[e] ~ CRANE[2], OKES. See 1.1.195.1.

1.1.311.1–1.1.312/445–7 *King's...King's*] K[s]...Kings MIDDLE-
TON[T] *corrected*; Q...Qs MIDDLETON[T] *uncorrected*. In both cases
the correct reading has been written over the uncorrected
one. The repetition of the unique error suggests that it stood
in Middleton's copy (one of many indications that the copy
was not any extant manuscript).

1.1.312/447 bishop's] Kts BRIDGEWATER[A] *uncorrected*.

1.1.312/447 The...Pawn!] *not in* OKES. The position of the
stage direction in the right margin created an apparent
duplication, which might account for the omission.

1.1.312/447 we're] we'are CRANE[2]; we are CRANE[3,4]

1.1.313/448 man] (Sir) BRIDGEWATER[A]. Possible revision: Middleton is extraordinarily fond of 'sir', and here it would
eliminate the potential ambiguity of 'our own man'.

1.1.314/449 heart's] hart is CRANE[3]

1.1.314.1/449 *Exit...Pawn*] DYCE; *not in* CRANE[1]+. See ll. 283.1
and 331.1.

1.1.315/450 all] all's BRIDGEWATER[A]. Assimilation ('alls friends').

1.1.315/450 endeared] indeed OKES. Misreading, producing a
common instead of a rare idiom (Taylor, 1988).

1.1.315/450 special] eſpetiall ROSENBACH[A]

1.1.316/451 you know] *not* OKES

1.1.316/451 knight] (Sir) BRIDGEWATER[A]. Possible revision: see
3.1.313.

1.1.318/453 ripens] ripeneſſe OKES. Misreading.

1.1.319–24/454–9 There...part] and my selfe your Frend:
CRANE[1]

1.1.321/456 her] his ROSENBACH[A]

1.1.322/457 and] or CRANE[3]

1.1.323/458 supplies] ſupply ROSENBACH[A]

1.1.323/458 back] *not in* OKES

*1.1.324/459 strength] CRANE[2,3,4], ROSENBACH[A]; *not in* OKES,
BRIDGEWATER[A], MIDDLETON[T]. A shared error in autograph,
emended by Howard-Hill: metrically deficient, with no object
for the transitive verb. Since this passage is not present in
CRANE[1], this is effectively another correct reading shared by
CRANE, ROSENBACH.

1.1.325/460 discuss] diſcuſſe OKES

1.1.326/461 jealous] CRANE+ (iealous); iealous MIDDLETON[T],
BRIDGEWATER[A]. Although this is not counted in the tabulation
of shared errors, the extra syllable indicated by six of the eight
texts seems metrically required.

1.1.328/463 fleet] Fleece OKES. Misreading of 'Fleete'.

*1.1.328.1/463 *Exit...Pawn*] DYCE; *Exit* CRANE[2,4] (*after l.* 326);
not in CRANE[1]+. The actor clearly begins his exit at the end
of his speech, but must remain within earshot and therefore
presumably on stage during the first two lines of the Black
Knight's speech. This is a matter of convention (whether
to mark exits when they begin or when they end), not
a substantive error. Omission of the direction entirely is,
however, a shared error.

1.1.330/465 of thy] ~ the ROSENBACH[A]

1.1.331/466 way] path CRANE[1], MIDDLETON[T], BRIDGEWATER *corrected*. This autograph return to the original reading may be
a correction of intervening error, or simply authorial vacillation. The collocation 'which way' occurs at least nineteen
times in nine uncollaborative Middleton works, connected to

the verb *take* at least three times. By contrast, 'which path' is unique; but *path* occurs four times elsewhere in *Game*, and is connected to *take* at least twice. Both readings are thus Middletonian, and the non-autograph variant arguably more Middletonian.

1.1.331/466 thou] tho BRIDGEWATER[A]

1.1.331/466 tak'st] takeſt ROSENBACH[A], BRIDGEWATER[A], OKES

1.1.331/466 thou'rt] Thou'art CRANE[2,3]

1.1.331/446 a] the OKES

*1.1.331.1/466 Exit] CRANE[1,2,3]; *Exeunt.* CRANE/MATHEWES; *not in* NON-CRANE. A shared error in autograph, emended by HOWARD-HILL. Apparently also an independent error in CRANE/MATHEWES, which correctly calls for an exit but incorrectly makes it plural; however, the Black Bishop's Pawn, though silent, might still be on stage. See 1.1.314.1.

1.1.331.2/467 *Finit Actus Primus*] *not in* CRANE[2,3,4]

1.1.331.2/467 *Finit*] *Finis* CRANE[1]

2.1.0.1/468 *Incipit*] OKES; *not in* CRANE+. For this authorial form see text note at *Early* 2.1.0.1.

2.1.0.1/468 *Actus*] *not in* OKES. For OKES see *Early* 2.0.1.

2.1.0.1/468 *Secundus*] OKES; *Secundi Scæna prima.* MIDDLETON[T] *only*; ~ *Sceᵃ. priᵃ.* CRANE+. Although we have preserved Middleton's alternative Latin forms for act numbers in *Early* 2.0.1, it is clear that Middleton himself was inconsistent, and for *Later* we adopt throughout the more recognizable forms used in modern (and most early modern) editions of Renaissance plays.

2.1.0.2-3/469-70 *Enter...hand*] *The white-Queenes Pawne* (reading) *The Black Bſ. Pawne. Then yᵉ Black-Queenes-Pawne. Then yᵉ Black-Bishop, & Black-Knight.* CRANE[3]. For the massed entry, see note at 1.1.0.2-5.

2.1.0.2/469 *Enter* ∧] ~ yᵉ CRANE[2]; ∧ The CRANE[3]

2.1.0.2/469 *White Queen's*] White-woman CRANE[1] *uncorrected*

2.1.0.2-3 *from the White House*] THIS EDITION (*conj.* Hotson); *not in* CRANE[1]+. See 1.1.30.1.

2.1.0.3/469-70 *with...hand*] *reading* CRANE[2,3,4]

2.1.1 *reading*] DYCE ('reads'), CRANE[2,3,4] (in entrance direction). See previous note.

2.1.1/471 it] is BRIDGEWATER[A] *uncorrected*

2.1.1/471 daughter's] daughter ROSENBACH[A]

2.1.2/472 confessor's] feſſors OKES

2.1.3/473 exception or expostulation] expoſtulatior ~ exception BRIDGEWATER[A]; ~ ~ expoſtulations OKES

2.1.4/474 It's] CRANE[2,3]; 'tis CRANE[1]+. See Induction.15.

2.1.4/474 e'er I] I ere CRANE[1]

2.1.4/474 read] heard OKES. Possible revision.

2.1.6/476 it's] CRANE[2]; lies OKES; 'tis CRANE[1]+. See Induction.15.

2.1.6/476 gently] lately CRANE/MATHEWES

2.1.6/476 reconciled] reconcilèd OKES

2.1.8/478 dispenser] diſperſer MIDDLETON[T] *uncorrected*. The incorrect 'r' may have been changed to 'n' before the last three letters were written.

2.1.8/478 as] are's OKES

2.1.8.1 *She reads silently.*] THIS EDITION; *not in* CRANE[1]+. The action is specified by the Black Bishop's Pawn's first line, and explains her failure to notice him for 24 lines.

2.1.8.1-2/479 *Enter...Pawn*] *& to her, the Black Bishop's Pawne* CRANE[2] (after 'reading' in that manuscript's entrance direction 2.1.0.2). For 'to her' in an entrance direction like this, see *Mad World* 3.2.0.3. In the massed entrance direction for the whole scene, in CRANE[3], the absence of the word 'Then', or a colon or full stop, between the two names here, suggests that CRANE[3] derives from a text which, like CRANE[2], includes

both characters in the scene's opening stage direction. This has not been counted as a shared error, because in performance he could enter and be watching her, seen by the audience but unseen by her, before he speaks.

2.1.8.1/479 *from the Black House*] THIS EDITION (*conj.* Hotson); *not in* CRANE[1]+. See 1.1.30.1.

2.1.8.2/479 *Jesuit*] BRIDGEWATER[A] (after 'Bl:Bs:P:'); *not in* CRANE[1]+. Late authorial variant. See 1.1.30.1.

2.1.9-28/480-501 She's...yours.] *not in* CRANE[3]

2.1.9/480 most] mode MIDDLETON[T] *uncorrected* (anticipating 'modest')

2.1.12/483 What have we here?] CRANE[2]; *not in* CRANE[1]+. Compare 'What have we here?' (*Quarrel* 3.2.141, probably by Rowley), and 'What have we there, sirs?' (*Widow* 4.2.270). CRANE[3] omits this entire passage. The addition makes it clear that the verse continues until he actually begins reading the letter; it also clarifies the action. It could have been added in the playbook, and lost in later copies.

2.1.14/485 Strange...he] *not in* CRANE/MATHEWES. Eyeskip ('*mee*' to '*hee*').

2.1.14/485 subscribes] ſubſcribed BRIDGEWATER[A]; ſubſ MIDDLETON[T] *uncorrected*

2.1.14.1/486 *the letter*] *not in* CRANE, ROSENBACH[A]

*2.1.16/489 industrious] induſtirous BRIDGEWATER[A]; induſterous OKES. This inverted form, with the unstressed syllable before rather than after 'r', is not recorded by *OED*, and contradicts both the Latin and French etymology of the word.

2.1.16/489 servant] ſerpent ROSENBACH[A]

2.1.18/490 instant] time BRIDGEWATER[A]. Possible revision: Middleton uses 'at this time' at least 23 times elsewhere; in contrast, 'at this instant' appears in his canon only eleven other times. I have preserved 'instant' only because it is a much rarer word, attested here by many more textual witnesses.

2.1.19/492 your] the ROSENBACH[A]. Misreading?

2.1.26/499 has] hath CRANE, ROSENBACH[A]

2.1.26/499 took] taken BRIDGEWATER[A]. Compare *Early* 2.79, where the original obsolescent 'mistook' is changed to modern 'mistaken' in all witnesses but CRANE[1].

2.1.29/502 She's] Sh'ath CRANE[2,3,4]

2.1.29/502 ∧ the large] of ~ ~ OKES

2.1.30/503 prescriptions] Prescription CRANE[2,3]; preſciption OKES. The plural/singular distinction might be authorial instability; Middleton does not use either elsewhere.

2.1.31/504 what] that CRANE/MATHEWES

2.1.32/505 eye moves] eyes moue CRANE/MATHEWES

2.1.32/505 letters] Letter OKES. Terminal-s error.

2.1.33/507 I've] CRANE[2,3] (I'haue); ∧ haue ROSENBACH[A]; I haue CRANE[1]+

2.1.33/507 O] *not in* ROSENBACH[A]

2.1.35-46/509-21 Lay...WHITE QUEEN'S PAWN] *not in* CRANE[3]

2.1.38/514 Which...for] *not in* BRIDGEWATER[A] *uncorrected*

2.1.38/514 too narrow] to morrow OKES. Misreading.

*2.1.39-41/515-16 Boundless...goodness] CRANE[2], CRANE/MATHEWES; all | MIDDLETON[T], BRIDGEWATER[A], OKES; *1 line* CRANE[1], ROSENBACH[A]; *not in* CRANE[3]. Shared false line-break in three NON-CRANE texts.

2.1.41/516 here set] ~ ſett BRIDGEWATER[A] *uncorrected*; ſet her OKES

2.1.43/518 Has] hath CRANE, ROSENBACH[A]

2.1.44/519 farther] farre OKES

2.1.45/520 my] m' CRANE[1]. See *Early* 2.45.

2.1.46/521 For...something] *2 lines* OKES: sir |

2.1.46/521 virtue's] Vertue CRANE[2,3]. See incidentals note at *Early* 2.46.

2.1.46/521 good sir] Goodnes BRIDGEWATER[A] *uncorrected*

2.1.49/525 sweetly] wel BRIDGEWATER[A] *uncorrected*

2.1.50-1/527-8 With...duty] *1 line* ROSENBACH[A], OKES. Relic.

2.1.50/526 then] *not in* BRIDGEWATER[A]

2.1.52/530 lip] lips OKES, CRANE/MATHEWES. Middleton uses both 'my lip' and 'my lips', and neither variant can be securely identified as a shared error. Nevertheless, the singular provides the only conjunction with 'kiss' (*Revenger* 1.2.119), the only conjunction with 'seale' (*Five Gallants* 2.1.316), and the only prepositional phrase 'upon my lip' (*Mad World* 3.2.258, *Women Beware* 3.1.104, *Quiet Life* 4.1.230). The parallels all strongly support the stemmatic authority of the singular, which would also be endorsed here by the principle that the abstract singular is rarer than the concrete plural (Taylor 1988).

2.1.54/532 in] and CRANE/MATHEWES

2.1.55/533 greater] great ROSENBACH[A]

2.1.57/536 My] mine CRANE[2,3,4]

2.1.57-64/536-43 Be...best] *not in* CRANE[3]

2.1.58-9/537-8 I...meaning] MIDDLETON[T], BRIDGEWATER[A], OKES; who | CRANE[1]+; *not in* CRANE[3]. Either arrangement is defensible.

2.1.58/537 much] moft CRANE/MATHEWES

2.1.62/541 own] CRANE[2], ROSENBACH[A]; good CRANE[1]+. These variants may result from authorial instability. Middleton used 'own cause', preceded by a possessive pronoun, twice in *Phoenix* 12.55; 'good cause' appears in *Widow* 2.2.80, *Five Gallants* 2.4.375, *Entertainments* 61, *No Wit* 7.68, *Old Law* 1.1.92, and *Patient Man* 14.44, but in Middleton is not elsewhere preceded by a possessive pronoun. The variant is therefore demonstrably Middletonian; it cannot be dismissed as a misreading, or a common error; it appears in two witnesses prepared by different scribes and not directly stemmatically connected.

2.1.63/542 the] OKES; his CRANE[1]+. There is no obvious mechanical explanation for OKES's variant, and 'the Adversary' allows a secondary meaning ('the devil') not available for 'his aduersary'; the OKES idiom occurs four times later in the play, making it more likely to be a late authorial variant than a compositorial inadvertence.

2.1.63/542 by't] CRANE, ROSENBACH[A]; by it MIDDLETON[T], BRIDGEWATER[A], OKES

2.1.64/543 my] m' CRANE[1]. See 2.1.45.

2.1.67-75/546-54 BLACK BISHOP'S PAWN...sure,] *not in* CRANE[3]

2.1.68/547 Is it] is ∧ MIDDLETON[T] *only*; ift BRIDGEWATER[A]

2.1.68/547 in] *not in* ROSENBACH[A]

2.1.68/547 my] OKES; mine CRANE+. The euphonic 'mine arm(s)' appears at least thirteen times elsewhere in the Middleton canon (none in a text transcribed by Crane); 'my arm(s)' only five times elsewhere. The variant probably is a late authorial revision or vacillation, and the autograph (and CRANE[1]) reading 'mine' has been retained at *Early* 2.72.

2.1.69/548 ∧ from...dealt abroad] abroad ∼...dealt ∧ OKES

2.1.69/548 these] thofe ROSENBACH[A], BRIDGEWATER[A]

2.1.69/548 abroad] out BRIDGEWATER[A] *uncorrected*

2.1.71/550 th'] the NON-CRANE

2.1.73/552 which] wth BRIDGEWATER[A] *uncorrected*; wch BRIDGEWATER *corrected*

2.1.74/553 of] on MIDDLETON[T] *only*. HOWARD-HILL glosses 'on' as 'of', but it is difficult to see how it could take that meaning here, especially where the idiom 'look on' intervenes (and probably accounts for the error). This is probably another unique autograph error. In any case, see 1.1.255.

2.1.74/553 hear] ∼ of ROSENBACH[A]

2.1.75-6/555-6 Good men...one] CRANE, ROSENBACH[A]; mistaken | MIDDLETON[T], BRIDGEWATER[A], OKES. In the abridged CRANE[3], the first line is absent, but the second begins 'If', indicating that its copy agreed with the lineation in the other CRANE texts. Either arrangement is defensible metrically and contextually; consequently this has not been treated as a shared lineation error. However, only OKES places a punctuation mark after 'mistaken', and this kind of mislineation (with one or more words at the end of a line flowing over into the next, probably prompted by shortage of space) is elsewhere shared by the same three texts. The related punctuation error in OKES might be compositorial.

2.1.75/554 Good men] ROSENBACH[A], BRIDGEWATER[A], OKES; Goodmen MIDDLETON[T], CRANE[1]; Good-men CRANE[2]. The spacing in CRANE/MATHEWES is ambiguous. In a modern-spelling context, two words seem required.

2.1.75/554 You are] you're OKES. Possibly due to justification.

2.1.75/554 mistaken] miftooke CRANE[1]

2.1.78-81/558-61 And...one] *not in* CRANE[3]

2.1.78/558 idiot] edict OKES. Misreading.

2.1.80-1/560-1 If...village, | 'Tis...one.] Tis...one, | If...Village. OKES

2.1.80/560 some] one ROSENBACH[A]. In MIDDLETON[T] *uncorrected* the initial 'S' is written over 'a', which may have stood in Middleton's copy. The two variants may well be stemmatically related, but since each makes sense they cannot be clearly labelled errors, and neither text shares the exact reading of the other.

2.1.81/561 that] If BRIDGEWATER[A], OKES. This variant almost certainly preceded OKES's transposition of the two lines; it seems to have originated in contamination from the 'if' which precedes it in the correct arrangement.

2.1.84-5/565-6 Have...servitude] *1 line* ROSENBACH[A]. Relic.

2.1.86-90/567-71 Is...forgot?] *not in* CRANE[3]

2.1.86/567 top] tye OKES. Possible revision.

2.1.90/571 the most forgot] they ∼ forget OKES

2.1.90/571 virgin's] virgine is ROSENBACH[A]

2.1.90/571 ruined] raine OKES. Misreading.

2.1.92-101/574-84 BLACK BISHOP'S PAWN...Nearer?] *not in* CRANE[3]

2.1.92/574 BLACK] Wh BRIDGEWATER[A] *uncorrected*

2.1.94/576 forward] forwards OKES. See 1.1.192.

2.1.98/580 care] carage BRIDGEWATER[A] *uncorrected*

2.1.101/583 be] *not in* BRIDGEWATER[A]

2.1.101/584 Nearer] cleerer MIDDLETON[T] *uncorrected*

2.1.101-2/585-6 Was...hopes] I | BRIDGEWATER[A] *only*

2.1.101/585 that] ∼ in OKES

2.1.102/586 prove] prooud BRIDGEWATER[A], proued OKES. Probably a simple e/d misreading, later expanded in OKES: 'turn out to be' seems more relevant than 'be demonstrated juridically'. However, because both readings are possible, neither has been counted as a shared error.

2.1.103/587 great] OKES, BRIDGEWATER[A]; grand CRANE[1]+. Late authorial variant: compare 'great monarchal business' (167), 'so great a business' (*His Lordship's Entertainment* 31-2), and 'great business' (*Five Gallants* 4.5.78, *Nice Valour* 5.3.131, *Women Beware* 2.2.180).

2.1.104/588 stir] flye OKES; fpread CRANE/MATHEWES. The minimal 'stir' makes the threat stronger. But both variants might be late authorial vacillations: 'spread abroad' occurs in *Chaste Maid* 3.2.54.

2.1.105/589 ill] I OKES

2.1.105/589 with't] with it ROSENBACH[A]; wcht BRIDGEWATER[A] *uncorrected*

2.1.105/590   Bless me!] He[,] CRANE[3]. This variant may be related to the cutting of the following lines: it clarifies the statement, which now becomes the totality of her reaction. See General Textual Introduction, Sec. XII.

2.1.105/590   Threatens] MIDDLETON[T], BRIDGEWATER[A] (threatnens), OKES (threatnes), CRANE, ROSENBACH[A]. *OED* records the variant spelling from the 16th to 18th c.

2.1.106-12/591-7   And…wicked] *not in* CRANE[3]

*2.1.106-7/591-2   And…safety] CRANE, ROSENBACH[A]; should | MIDDLETON[T], BRIDGEWATER[A], OKES. Shared error.

2.1.107/592   safety] fayth BRIDGEWATER[A]. Probably a misreading.

2.1.108/593   ’Twas…sweetness] *2 lines* CRANE/MATHEWES: jealousy |

2.1.109/594   Yon] Yours OKES. Misreading.

2.1.109/594   venom] veonome OKES. Probably a miscorrection of a transposition error in foul proofs (‘veonme’).

2.1.112/597   to] *not in* BRIDGEWATER[A], OKES. Haplography, producing a metrically deficient line.

2.1.112/597   off’rer] CRANE[1,2]; Offerer MIDDLETON[T], ROSENBACH[A], BRIDGEWATER[A]; offerors OKES; Offices CRANE/MATHEWES

2.1.115/600   freely] fleely ROSENBACH[A]

2.1.115/600   off’ring] offering [CRANE[4]], ROSENBACH[A], OKES

2.1.116-21/601-8   My…BLACK BISHOP’S PAWN] *not in* CRANE[3]

2.1.117/602   thou’st] THIS EDITION; thou haſt CRANE[2]+. For the original reading, where ‘thou hast’ is metrical, see *Early* 2.126. For the elision see 3.1.315. Middleton used the contraction at least 29 times elsewhere, and it is metrically preferable here. This seems to be another example of an expanded form passively reproduced in later transcripts. MIDDLETON[T] is anomalously low in *thou* contractions, in relation to the rest of the canon: see General Textual Introduction, Sec. IV.

2.1.118/603   thy] the CRANE/MATHEWES

2.1.118/603   carry’t] CRANE, ROSENBACH[A]; carrie it MIDDLETON[T], BRIDGEWATER[A], OKES

2.1.119/605   Thou’rt] thou art CRANE[2,4], ROSENBACH[A]

2.1.119/605   so] MIDDLETON[T]; *not in* CRANE[1]+. Late authorial revision.

2.1.120/606   deep] great CRANE[1,4]. This variant could theoretically be an error, in one or both texts, by contamination from the ‘too great’ of the preceding line. But the parallelism could just as easily be deliberate, and ‘great…loser’ deliberately oxymoronic. If the variant is authorial, its distribution might result from authorial vacillation; if it is an error, the same association which led Crane to make the mistake in one transcription might have led him to make it again in another transcription. I have therefore kept the CRANE[1] reading at *Early* 2.130, and kept the autograph reading here.

2.1.120/606   to’t] to it MIDDLETON[T], BRIDGEWATER[A]

2.1.122/609   stir’st] ſtirreſt ROSENBACH[A]

2.1.123/610   my] thy CRANE[2]. Assimilation.

2.1.123/610   love] loss DYCE *conj*

2.1.125-33/612-21   Thy…thee.] *not in* CRANE[3]

2.1.125/612   thy] ROSENBACH[A]; thine CRANE+. The euphonic ‘thine own(e)’ occurs at least 43 times in the Middleton canon, in 21 different works; ‘thy own(e)’ appears 14 times in 10 works. This variant may therefore be late authorial revision or vacillation: modern ‘thy’ is preferred here, and ‘thine’ has been retained at *Early* 2.136.

2.1.126/613   to] ROSENBACH[A], [CRANE[4]] (too), CRANE[1]+ (to)

2.1.129/616   make] ~ me OKES, CRANE/MATHEWES. Syntactical normalization at expense of metre.

*2.1.130/617   by] *not in* CRANE[2,4], ROSENBACH[A]. This error, shared by ROSENBACH and the post-playbook CRANE texts, presumably originated in [KING’S MEN[1]], and was corrected by Middleton in later transcripts.

2.1.130/617   thy] thine CRANE/MATHEWES

2.1.130/617   awe] arme CRANE/MATHEWES. Misreading.

2.1.131/619   thou] CRANE[1], MIDDLETON[T], BRIDGEWATER[A]; *not in* CRANE[2,4], ROSENBACH[A], OKES. Autograph restores the original (metrical) reading.

2.1.135/624   sir] *not in* CRANE[2,3]

2.1.136/625   my honour] mine ~ CRANE[2,3,4]

2.1.136/625   for my guide] to guide me OKES. This variant is adopted by HOWARD-HILL, and it may indeed be authorial, but it produces a less regular line, metrically.

*2.1.137-8/626-7   Take…vowed since | If…me] CRANE[1], ROSENBACH[A]; vowed CRANE[2,3,4]; vowed | since MIDDLETON[T], BRIDGEWATER[A], OKES. Shared lineation error. CRANE[2,3,4] omit ‘since’; MIDDLETON[T], BRIDGEWATER, and OKES misplace it. See following notes.

2.1.137/626   I’ve] MIDDLETON[T], BRIDGEWATER[A]; I haue CRANE, ROSENBACH[A], OKES. Late authorial restoration of a favourite Middleton contraction. See next note.

2.1.137/626-7   since] *not in* CRANE[2,3,4]. Possibly a shared error, but not counted as such because the line is metrical and sensible.

2.1.138/627   resist] reiect CRANE/MATHEWES. The variant could be an authorial variant; Middleton uses both verbs, and there is no exact parallel for either. But the variant could also result from scribal or compositorial synonym substitution, and *resist* is more often and more naturally modified by adverbs (‘longer’ here, ‘valiantly’ in *Parliament* 171, ‘hardly’ in *Phoenix* 3.1, ‘well’ in *Five Gallants* 3.6.143). Rejection is absolute; resistance comes in degrees.

2.1.138/627   me] *not in* CRANE[3], OKES

2.1.138/628   Help, O] ~ help: ~ CRANE[3]. Perhaps related to preceding omission in CRANE[3], since this added ‘help’ restores metrical regularity.

2.1.139-42/629-32   BLACK BISHOP’S PAWN…sake—] *not in* CRANE[3]

2.1.139/629   bubble] bable OKES. Misreading.

2.1.140/630   T’] CRANE, ROSENBACH[A]; to MIDDLETON[T], BRIDGEWATER[A], OKES

2.1.141/631   nations] MIDDLETON[T], BRIDGEWATER[A], OKES; Princes CRANE, ROSENBACH[A]. Late authorial revision.

2.1.142/633   confound noise?] confound[,]—DYCE. See note to *Early* 2.157.

2.1.142.1/634   *A noise within*] CRANE[2,3], MIDDLETON[T]. All witnesses contain this direction, but they vary in its positioning: after 138 CRANE[1,4], ROSENBACH[A]; after ‘sake’ at 142 OKES; after 143 BRIDGEWATER[A] (clearly mistaken); after ‘earth. *Exit*’ at 150 CRANE/MATHEWES (the direction’s second occurrence in that text, and in this position obviously mistaken, unless it indicates that the noise gradually increases between the two directions). The CRANE/MATHEWES duplication perhaps reflects the strategy of transcription apparently adopted in [KING’S MEN[3]], which seems to have reproduced everything in the playbook, including both material added and material deleted; such a policy of comprehensive reproduction might incorporate the original position of the direction (seen in CRANE[1] and ROSENBACH) and a revised position. For the CRANE[1] position, see *Early* 2.152.1 (where it is retained): alternatively, it may be anticipatory, and given the presence of anticipatory directions in various theatrical texts it cannot be confidently categorized as an error.

2.1.142.1/634   A] *not in* CRANE[2,3,4]

2.1.142.1/634   *within*] *not in* BRIDGEWATER[A]

2.1.143/635   Ha...thee.] *not in* CRANE[3]

*2.1.144/636-7   I'll...now] *2 lines* MIDDLETON[T], BRIDGEWATER[A]: dangers|. Shared error.

2.1.144/636   upon] on OKES. HOWARD-HILL is confused by the passage, citing definitions of *upon* at *OED prep* 5.c and 5.d; but the idiom is explained in *OED venture n.* 9b.

2.1.144/636   dangers] danger BRIDGEWATER[A]

2.1.145-9/638-42   BLACK BISHOP'S PAWN ... WHITE QUEEN'S PAWN I] ∧ And CRANE[3]. The verbal variant is a consequence of the deliberate cut.

2.1.145/638   Who...face] *2 lines* CRANE/MATHEWES: me |

2.1.145/638   me] him BRIDGEWATER[A] *uncorrected*

2.1.145/638   that] the CRANE/MATHEWE

*2.1.146/639   master swelled] MIDDLETON[T]+ (M[r] fweld); Maf=fweld BRIDGEWATER[A]; Maf-fwell OKES. Misreading.

2.1.147/640   Which] who BRIDGEWATER[A]. Possible revision.

2.1.147/640   i'th'] CRANE[1,4], ROSENBACH[A]; in the CRANE[2]+. See General Textual Introduction, Sec. IV. CRANE[1] here preserves a Middletonian elision which was expanded in later Crane transcriptions, and passively repeated in most subsequent texts.

2.1.148/641   air] are BRIDGEWATER[A] *uncorrected*

2.1.148/641   puffs] puff ROSENBACH[A]

2.1.149/642   thee] the OKES. Ambiguous.

*2.1.150/643.1   Exit] CRANE[3,4]; *not in* CRANE[1]+

2.1.150-2/644-5   BLACK BISHOP'S PAWN...me?] *not in* CRANE[3]

2.1.150-1/644   Confusion...undoing] CRANE, ROSENBACH[A]; *1 line* MIDDLETON[T], BRIDGEWATER[A]; *2 lines* OKES: voice|. The mislineation in OKES suggests that something like the relic in MIDDLETON[T] stood in its copy, and that the compositor broke the line randomly; the full line would not fit his measure.

2.1.152.1/645   Enter...Pawn] *not in* MIDDLETON[T]. In CRANE[3] her entrance is listed in the opening 'massed entry' direction, which means it is not present at this point in the text. CRANE/MATHEWES and OKES place it in the right margin opposite ll. 151-2 ('undoing...me?'); BRIDGEWATER[A] places it to the right of, and slightly below, 'are you mad?' (2.1.152). This confusion about placement in three later texts, and absence from MIDDLETON[T], might be due to the omission of a specifically placed direction in a text which resembled CRANE[3], but these variants cannot be considered an unambiguously 'shared' error.

2.1.152.1/645   ∧Black] y[e] ~ CRANE[2]

2.1.152.1/645   Queen's] woman CRANE[1], ROSENBACH[A]. For this generic form of the character's name, see 1.1.0.2.

2.1.152.1/645   *from the Black House*] THIS EDITION (*conj.* Hotson); *not in* CRANE[+]. See 1.1.30.1.

2.1.154/648   No...sure] *not in* CRANE[3], ROSENBACH[A]. The dog-star did indeed reign during the August of the original performances, but thereafter this allusion would have made little sense, and may have been deliberately cut by Middleton not only in the abridgement but in other copies. This has not been counted as a shared error because it could be due to abridgement in CRANE[3].

*2.1.155-6/649-50   Time...us] CRANE, ROSENBACH[A]; he | MIDDLETON[T], BRIDGEWATER[A], OKES. Shared error.

2.1.155/649   fair] fire OKES

2.1.155/650   pliant] MIDDLETON[T], BRIDGEWATER *corrected*, OKES; playnlie BRIDGEWATER[A] *uncorrected*; pleafant CRANE, ROSENBACH[A]. Late authorial revision.

2.1.156/650   of the] MIDDLETON[T], BRIDGEWATER[A], OKES; o'th' CRANE, ROSENBACH[A]. Either reading is rhythmically possible.

2.1.157/651   on] CRANE, ROSENBACH[A]; a MIDDLETON[T], BRIDGEWATER[A]; of OKES. Middleton's elision is preserved in *Early* 2.173, and Crane's modernization in the modern-spelling text.

2.1.157/651   warning] warrant BRIDGEWATER[A], OKES. The variant might be a late authorial revision, but is probably a misreading. *Warrant* has several relevant senses—'defence, security' (*OED n.*[1] 1–3, Sternhold and Hopkins *Psalms* 121), 'witness' (5a)—and takes secondary meanings that fit the following aside: 'justification, authorization, sanction' (7a, 8a) and 'license to travel' (9b). But 'giue' is followed by 'warning' six times elsewhere in Middleton; the only example of 'giue' followed by 'warrant' (*Phoenix* 6.11–12) refers to a physical document, and is not comparable.

2.1.158   Aside] CRANE[2,3,4] place the line within parentheses.

2.1.158/652   end] ends BRIDGEWATER[A], OKES. Possible revision.

2.1.159-63/653-7   BLACK BISHOP'S PAWN...too.] *not in* CRANE[3]

2.1.161/655   BLACK...pawn.] *not in* OKES

2.1.162/656   It's] CRANE[2]; 'tis CRANE[+]. See Induction.15.

2.1.162.1/658-9   Enter...Knight] CRANE[1,2], ROSENBACH[A]. The direction is placed after 2.1.163 in CRANE/MATHEWES, MIDDLETON[T], OKES, and after 2.1.164 in BRIDGEWATER[A]; this later entry is usually reproduced by editors, but the characters must already be entering when she says 'here he comes'.

2.1.162.1/658   Enter ∧...and ∧] ~ y[e] ~ y[e] CRANE[2]

2.1.162.2/659   *from the Black House*] THIS EDITION (*conj.* Hotson); *not in* CRANE[1]+. See 1.1.30.1.

2.1.163/657   And...too.] *not in* ROSENBACH[A]

2.1.163/657   haply] CRANE/MATHEWES (happely), CRANE[+] (happily)

2.1.164/660   O...House] *2 lines* ROSENBACH[A]: work |

2.1.164/660   you've] MIDDLETON[T], BRIDGEWATER[A] (yau'e); y'haue CRANE[1]; you'haue CRANE[2,3]; you haue [CRANE[4]], ROSENBACH[A]; you OKES. Depending on its copy, OKES might have misread 'yaue' or omitted 'haue'.

2.1.164/660   House∧] OKES, BRIDGEWATER[A]; ~ yonder CRANE[1]+. The variant may be a late authorial revision; it makes the line metrically regular without eliding 'the' (which may originally have been intended, but is indicated by no extant text).

2.1.165/661   fill] *not in* OKES

2.1.166/662   Luth'ran's] OKES (Luthrens); Lutherans CRANE[2]+; Hugonites CRANE[1]. The variant might result from censorship, or self-censorship; 'Hugonites' (i.e. modern 'Huguenots') is preserved in *Early* 2.182. But 'Lutheran' may simply be an authorial revision, and is more immediately intelligible to a modern reader.

2.1.166/662   cheek till't] CRANE[1], MIDDLETON[T], BRIDGEWATER; ~ till it ROSENBACH[A]; cheeks till they CRANE[2,3,4]; cheeks ~ OKES. Howard-Hill cites the plural here as an example of Crane's intrusive editing, but the variant could easily be another example of authorial vacillation between singular and plural. See 'cheeks have cracked' at 1.1.263. Middleton is likelier than any scribe to have been influenced by an image 234 lines earlier, in a speech about 'the business of the universal monarchy'—also the subject of the next line here ('the great monarchal business'). The likeliest explanation for the variant is contamination by another context in the author's mind. The original reading has been retained because it produces a more regular line metrically, and because it continues the singular nouns of the preceding line ('act... the advesary...mouth').

2.1.167-70/663-6   BLACK KNIGHT...still.] *not in* CRANE[3]

2.1.169/665   What] Which OKES. Misreading.

2.1.169/665   have] OKES; in CRANE[1]+. This is easier to explain as a late authorial variant than as a misreading or compositorial error.

2.1.169/665   sev'n] 7 MIDDLETON[T], BRIDGEWATER[A], ROSENBACH[A]; feauen CRANE[1]+. See 1.1.250.

2.1.169/665   years] year MIDDLETON[T], CRANE/MATHEWES

2.1.169/665   laboured] labourèd ROSENBACH[A], OKES

2.1.172-8/669-75   BLACK BISHOP...door).] not in CRANE[3]

2.1.173/670   ever] ftill BRIDGEWATER[A], OKES. Variant probably from contamination from l. 170 (where it occupies the same position in the verse line).

2.1.174/671   I've] OKES; I have CRANE[1]+. Possibly a late authorial revision, since the original reading is metrically defensible as a line-divided foot.

2.1.174/671   travelled] trauillèd ROSENBACH[A], OKES. Howard-Hill (1990) notes that the 'd' in MIDDLETON[T] has been 'retraced'. It is possible that Middleton started with his characteristically minimalist 'e' (duplicating the extrametrical syllabic ending found in his copy?) and then changed his mind and made the lone 'd' as clear as possible.

2.1.175/672   all] CRANE/MATHEWES; moft CRANE[1]+. There is no obvious explanation for the variant other than authorial vacillation. Middleton refers to a woman who sexually welcomes 'all nations' at Mad World 1.2.102, and writes all shortly after most at least 26 times. The line alludes to the mixing of populations ('nations') in Spain, historically, and in the new global Spanish empire.

2.1.175/672   Of] on OKES. See 1.1.255.

2.1.176/673   I have] I've DYCE. The emendation may be correct: see 2.1.174. However, 'bottom | I' is defensible as an iambic foot divided between two lines.

2.1.176/673   Venus'] Vennes OKES

2.1.177/674   trimmer] ~ and OKES

2.1.177/674   sounder] founder BRIDGEWATER[A]

*2.1.177/674   barques...vessels] Veffells...Barkes CRANE/MATHEWES, BRIDGEWATER[A]. Easy transposition of synonymous nouns in parallel construction. Metre supports the order in MIDDLETON[T]+.

2.1.177/674   barques] MIDDLETON[T]+ (Barkes)

2.1.178/675   that is] that's ROSENBACH[A]

2.1.179/676   has] hath CRANE[2,3,4]

*2.1.179/677   BLACK BISHOP'S...none.] not in CRANE[3], OKES, BRIDGEWATER[A]. Eyeskip. The omission from CRANE[3] may well be deliberate abridgement, but in the other two witnesses this looks like shared error.

2.1.179-80/678-9   Gross...Society] 1 line OKES only

2.1.179/678   Gross!] ~ᴧ ROSENBACH[A], CRANE/MATHEWES, OKES. Shared punctuation error: 'gross' does not modify 'witness', so the absence of punctuation gives a demonstrably false meaning to the passage.

2.1.179/678   witness] wirneffe OKES. Foul case.

2.1.180/679   a man] one OKES. This may be an example of progressive error: the omission of the Black Bishop Pawn's two-syllable speech left the original regular iambic pentameter 2.1.179 a foot short; OKES sets 'Gross...society' as one line, thereby leaving 'She...then' as an unassimilated part-line. The newly created verse line could be made rhythmically regular, after adding 'Gross witness' to it, only by removing a syllable. Although this conjectural reconstruction explains the variant as authorial in origin, it also makes it the consequence of an inadvertent omission earlier in the chain of transmission.

2.1.181/681   Be it thus] CRANE[3]; I haue don't CRANE[1]+. Despite Bawcutt (1993, 10), this variant cannot be due to 'the pro-cess of abbreviation', since CRANE[3] preserves the immediately preceding and following lines of the full text, and the variant here does not save words or lines. Middleton uses the imperative 'be it' (or 'be't') more than a dozen times, and the collocation 'thus then' three times elsewhere: No Wit 1.123, Lady 4.1.116, Old Law 4.2.83. This looks like authorial revision. For other evidence of authorial involvement in CRANE[3] see 2.2.17, 3.1.311, 4.4.63.

2.1.183   Cast...suddenly,] not in MIDDLETON[T]

2.1.183   suddenly] prefently ROSENBACH[A]

2.1.184/683   with] at OKES

2.1.185/684   least] ~ paft BRIDGEWATER[A]

2.1.185-7/685-7   BLACK KNIGHT...journey.] not in CRANE[3]

2.1.187/687   the] thy OKES, CRANE/MATHEWES. Although it makes sense, and therefore has not been tabulated among shared errors, this variant could easily result from misreading of Crane's or Middleton's 'the', and there is no Middleton parallel for 'thy iourney'.

*2.1.187-8/688-9   But...unspied] how | BRIDGEWATER[A], OKES. Shared error.

2.1.187/688   But, good sir,] ~ ᴧ ~ (~) CRANE[2,4], OKES. Shared punctuation error.

2.1.188/689   forth] for the OKES. Misreading.

2.1.188/690   bishop] OKES (B.), BRIDGEWATER[A] (Bs:); K[L] CRANE[1]+; Kin. CRANE/MATHEWES. Although 'Kin.' is clearly just an error for 'Kni⟨ght⟩', the speech could be spoken by the Black Bishop: since the Bishop, his master, had come up with this plan, the Pawn's previous speech might naturally have been addressed to him, and he might naturally respond. Late authorial revision.

2.1.189-90/692-3   BLACK KNIGHT...BLACK QUEEN'S PAWN] not in CRANE[3]

2.1.189/692   bouncing] little CRANE[1] uncorrected

2.1.190.1/693   She...trapdoor] THIS EDITION; not in CRANE[1]+. See the use of a trapdoor leading to a 'secret vault' in Banquet 4.3.123. There, as here, it is used by a lecherous woman character, and makes it possible for a male to enter or exit an indoor space without being perceived; in both plays, it associates the character who uses it with hell.

2.1.190/694   BLACK KNIGHT...then!] not in CRANE[3]

2.1.191/695   intelligences] Intelligencies CRANE[2,3,4]. No substantive or metrical difference; perhaps only an alternative (obsolete) spelling.

2.1.192/696   For...rather] 2 lines CRANE/MATHEWES: house |

2.1.192.1/696   Exit...Pawn] DYCE; not in CRANE[1]+. Even playbooks from the period usually omit mid-scene exits followed by a quick re-entrance. See 194.2.

2.1.192/696   rather] not in OKES. With this final word the line would not fit OKES's measure.

2.1.193-4/698-9   BLACK BISHOP...you.] not in CRANE[3]

2.1.193-4/698-9   Be gone...you] 1 line OKES. Relic.

*2.1.194.1/699   Exit] CRANE[3]; not in CRANE[1]+. CRANE[3] places his exit immediately after his last speech, following l. 193; but it omits the intervening speech. The exit here could have been added, editorially, by Crane—although, if so, it is surprising he did not do so in his three other copies. Alternatively, it might derive from the lost playbook, or be further evidence of authorial involvement in preparing the abridgement. See 2.1.181.

2.1.194.1/699   by the trapdoor] THIS EDITION; not in CRANE+. See 2.1.190.1.

2.1.194.2-3/699   Enter...cabinet] DYCE; not in CRANE+. See 2.1.192.1.

2.1.195/701   formally] formerly OKES. Misreading.

932

2.1.195/701 he's] 'hath CRANE^{2,3}; he hath [CRANE^4]

2.1.195/701 packed] pack CRANE^3

2.1.195/701 intelligences] Intelligencies CRANE^{2,3}. See the same variant at 2.1.191.

2.1.196-8/702-4 He's…Anglica!] not in CRANE^3

2.1.196/702 He's] CRANE^1+ (Has); 'hath CRANE^2; He hath [CRANE^4]

2.1.196/702 'em] them CRANE/MATHEWES, OKES

2.1.197/703 he's] MIDDLETON^T, BRIDGEWATER^A, OKES (has); he has CRANE^1, ROSENBACH^A; he hath CRANE^{2,4}. Two words in CRANE, ROSENBACH.

2.1.198/704 their] the OKES

2.1.198/704 Anglica] Angellica ROSENBACH^A. The same error occurs in the same manuscript at 1.1.301.

2.1.200/706 Ha…hand] Anglica CRANE^{2,3}. This variant might be due to censorship of profanity in the playbook. Alternatively, it might be related to the cutting of ll. 196–8, including the earlier use of the word 'Anglica'. If those lines were cut, then 'Anglica' would need to be substituted here, to compensate; the lines marked for omission were duly omitted in the abridged CRANE^3, but restored in CRANE^2.

2.1.200/706 hand] MIDDLETON^T, BRIDGEWATER^A, OKES; light CRANE^{1,4}, ROSENBACH^A. Late authorial variant.

2.1.201/707 Time…'em.] not in CRANE^3

2.1.201/707 bundles] boundles BRIDGEWATER^A. This is probably only a spelling variant: it combines a known sixteenth-century spelling of the first syllable ('boundell') with a seventeenth-century spelling of the second ('bundle'). However, OED does not record this spelling, which might have been avoided because it duplicated a contemporary form of boundless.

2.1.201/707 of] CRANE^{2,4}, OKES; on CRANE^1+. See 1.1.255.

2.1.201/707 'em] them CRANE/MATHEWES

2.1.202/708 from] for ROSENBACH^A

2.1.203/709 their] the OKES. Assimilation.

2.1.204/710 These] Thofe OKES. Misreading.

2.1.204/710 Sisters of Compassion] MIDDLETON^T capitalizes both nouns, as do all three Crane manuscripts; CRANE^3 italicizes both nouns. Such incidentals suggest that both Middleton and Crane were thinking of an order of nuns.

2.1.206/712 These] CRANE^{2,3,4}; 3 MIDDLETON^T, CRANE^1, ROSENBACH^A; thefe 3 BRIDGEWATER^A, OKES. All three readings could be authorial, but the variant in BRIDGEWATER^A and OKES is extrametrical, and given the close stemmatic relationship of those two texts might result from a single error (substitution misinterpreted as addition). Since '3' is preserved in Early 2.232, 'These' has been adopted here.

2.1.206/712 without Temple Bar] CRANE^1 uncorrected; in Drury Lane CRANE^1 (corrected)+. Censorship. See Early 2.232.

2.1.207-8/713-14 A…there] 1 line CRANE^1, ROSENBACH^A. Relic.

2.1.207/713 go] OKES; good CRANE^1+. Late authorial variant. See next note.

2.1.207.1/713.1 Exit…Pawn] THIS EDITION; not in CRANE+. Unless the Black Knight is calling for some action on her part, the line hardly makes sense. All texts also omit her exit and re-entry earlier in the scene (2.1.192.1, 194.2).

2.1.208/714 What…there] not in CRANE^1 uncorrected

2.1.208/715 sir] not in BRIDGEWATER^A

2.1.209/716 an] OKES; one CRANE^1+. OKES's variant is adopted by most editors.

2.1.209/717 Pray] not in ROSENBACH^A

2.1.209/717 see't] CRANE^1, ROSENBACH^A; fee it CRANE^2+

2.1.209/717 sir] not in CRANE^{2,3}, ROSENBACH^A

2.1.210/718 in the] OKES; ~ a CRANE^1+. Previous editors have overlooked this variant; the definite article makes it clear that England is intended.

*2.1.212/720 facetious] factious ROSENBACH^A, OKES. Misreading. Clearly an error, both because of metre and because the political meaning is less appropriate than the sexual one.

2.1.213/721 That] OKES; and CRANE^1+. Late authorial revision.

2.1.213/721 suits] fits CRANE/MATHEWES. Both verbs are used in the period to modify humour; 'suits' is the rarer idiom, and has been preserved in Early 2.241. Atlhough 'fits' might be an authorial variant, it could easily result from misreading, encouraged by the more common idiom (Taylor 1988). This and the preceding word are variant in one text only; it would be misleading to conflate the two variants, and of the two, this is likelier to be a misreading.

2.1.214/722 adult'ry] ROSENBACH^A, BRIDGEWATER^A; Adulterie CRANE^1+

2.1.215/723 send] fent ROSENBACH^A

2.1.215/723 Rome] Roome BRIDGEWATER^A uncorrected

2.1.216.1-2/724.1 Enter…fire] THIS EDITION; not in CRANE^1+. See note at 207.1. Her entrance before or after the Black Knight's 'O…subtler' lends a point to his observation, which it otherwise lacks; it does not directly answer the Black Bishop's question, shifting as it does from plural ('Some wives' and 'they') to singular ('female').

2.1.216/725 KNIGHT] K. OKES. For king/knight abbreviations generally see 1.1.277. The same misleading abbreviation occurs again at 2.1.220. See also the discussion of 'Knight's' in speech prefixes at 2.1.229.

2.1.216/725 no familiar] OKES; there's ~ Female MIDDLETON^T+. Late authorial revision. OKES's noun might be dismissed as a misreading, but it coexists with another otherwise-unexplained variant (the absence of 'there's') which complements it metrically; coincidental metrical omission and misreading seem less likely than deliberate authorial tinkering—especially given the range of relevant meanings of the noun 'familiar' (used at Parliament 219, Timon 13.10, Roaring Girl 5.125). For the elision of 'there's' after 'oh' and before 'no' at the beginning of a speech, compare Trick 3.1.247.

2.1.217/726 and subtler] not in OKES. Eyeskip: 'sweeter and subtler'.

2.1.217/726 these] thofe OKES. Misreading.

2.1.218/727 me 'em] BRIDGEWATER corrected (me'em), BRIDGE-WATER^A uncorrected (meem); 'em-me CRANE, ROSENBACH; mee MIDDLETON^T; em OKES. The alternative unmetrical omissions in MIDDLETON^T and OKES make it impossible to determine the order of the pronouns in their copy.

2.1.218-27/727-37 burn…pawn] not in CRANE^3

2.1.220/730 strangely] not in BRIDGEWATER^A

2.1.221/731 in] at ROSENBACH^A

2.1.221/731 Venice] Venis OKES corrected; Vennis OKES uncorrected

2.1.223/733 When] Where OKES. Misreading.

2.1.223/733 all] not in CRANE/MATHEWES

2.1.223/733 spectacled] fpecktacl'd OKES corrected; fpecturald OKES uncorrected

2.1.224/734 pick out] ~ our MIDDLETON^T uncorrected

2.1.224/734 out of the] ont o'th' CRANE^1

2.1.225/735 their] OKES; out CRANE^1+. Late authorial revision (avoiding using 'out' three times in a line and a half).

*2.1.227.1/737 Exeunt] CRANE^3 (after 2.1.228);—Ex^t. CRANE^{1,2}; Exit CRANE/MATHEWES, ROSENBACH^A; not in MIDDLETON^T, BRIDGE-WATER^A, OKES. A shared error of omission in autograph, emended by Howard-Hill. A different error is shared by ROSEN-BACH^A and CRANE/MATHEWES, expanding the ambiguous form

in CRANE[1,2] to the clearly mistaken singular. The unambiguous plural form, found only in CRANE[3], is ambiguous because of its placement: because the abridgement removes the last ten lines of the scene, its 'Exeunt' might be interpreted as the equivalent of 2.1.239.1. Nevertheless, it is notable that the three earliest texts, stemmatically, all have an ambiguously or unambiguously plural exit in this vicinity, where one is clearly required.

2.1.227/738 Faith] OKES; feare CRANE[1]+. Although the variant is not an impossible misreading, the oath is Middletonian, and produces a characteristically ambivalent aside: she does not obey the Black Knight, or the Black House, in everything. Probably a late authorial variant.

2.1.227/738 not₍ in all.] ~₍~, CRANE[3], OKES, BRIDGEWATER[C]; ~,~, MIDDLETON[T]; ~:~, CRANE[1,2,4], ROSENBACH[A]. The OKES punctuation makes sense with its preceding verbal variant, but is probably an error in CRANE[3] and BRIDGEWATER[A].

2.1.228-9/739-40 roguery...How now,] rogarie...~~~ OKES corrected; roguria...~~₍ OKES uncorrected

2.1.228.1-2.1.239/741-57 Enter...sir.] not in CRANE[3]

2.1.228.1/741 Enter...Pawn] CRANE, ROSENBACH[A]; not in BRIDGEWATER[A]. MIDDLETON[T] and OKES contain the direction, but both misplace it, OKES at 227.1 (after 'pawn') and MIDDLETON[T] to the right of, and slightly below, 'you' in 2.1.229. The misplacements may be related to the omission, the absence of a direction leading to conjectural editorial restorations. However, because each of the three texts differs, these variants have not been treated as shared errors.

2.1.228.1/741 Enter ₍] ~ yᵉ CRANE[3]

2.1.228.1-2/741 from the Black House] THIS EDITION (conj. Hotson); not in CRANE[1]+. See 1.1.30.1.

2.1.229/740 How now,] ~ ~ ₍ OKES uncorrected

2.1.229/740 what] whats BRIDGEWATER[A] uncorrected

2.1.229/742 KNIGHT'S] K. OKES. The same abbreviation occurs in OKES at ll. 233 and 238. But since the play contains no Black King's Pawn, the abbreviation is not ambiguous and cannot be considered an error. See 2.1.216.

2.1.230/743 Afflicts] Afflicts MATHEWES. Foul case.

2.1.231/744 On] one BRIDGEWATER[A]

2.1.232/745 joy,] ~ ₍ OKES uncorrected

2.1.232/746 QUEEN'S] B. CRANE/MATHEWES

2.1.232/746 an] and CRANE/MATHEWES

2.1.234 absolved] obfolu'd OKES. Misreading.

2.1.234/749 Where's] where is OKES

2.1.235/750 Why...ground?] not in BRIDGEWATER[A] uncorrected

2.1.235/750 th'] the NON-CRANE

2.1.235/751 way.] MIDDLETON[T], BRIDGEWATER[A], OKES; Bl.K[ts].P. what's that? | Bl.Q[s]P. CRANE[2,4], ROSENBACH[A]. See Early 2.269. In ROSENBACH[A] the third letter of the first speech prefix was originally written 'B', then immediately corrected by overwriting 'K'. The larger variant might be a shared error of omission in three texts; but if so it must be a two-stage error, since simple eyeskip would have left at least one speech prefix. Moreover, the following line has been revised to make it metrical in this new context. The resulting variant resembles the deliberate excision, in CRANE[3], of very short speeches by minor characters. The revision might have been stimulated in the first place by an accidental omission, but the complex result seems to be a late authorial revision.

2.1.236/752 come help me in] MIDDLETON[T], BRIDGEWATER[A], OKES; ₍ ~ ₍ ~ CRANE[1], ROSENBACH[A]; ₍ ~ ~ ₍ CRANE[2,4]

*2.1.237/753 And...throughly] not in BRIDGEWATER[A], OKES. Shared error.

2.1.237/753 throughly] CRANE[1]+; thoroughly HOWARD-HILL

2.1.238/755 KNIGHT'S] Bs. CRANE[1]; K. OKES, CRANE/MATHEWES. See l. 229. This is the first occurrence of the misleading abbreviation in CRANE/MATHEWES.

2.1.238-9/755-6 If't...welcome] 1 line ROSENBACH[A], OKES. Relic.

2.1.238/755 If't] If it ROSENBACH[A]

2.1.238/755 sad,] ~ ₍ OKES uncorrected

2.1.239/756 It's] CRANE[2]; 'tis CRANE[1]+. See Induction.15

2.1.239/757 QUEEN'S] K. CRANE/MATHEWES. Assimilation to the preceding line.

*2.1.239/757 troubled with much] much troubled with BRIDGEWATER[A], OKES. Unmetrical transposition.

2.1.239.1 with cabinet and fire] THIS EDITION; not in CRANE[1]+. Even when early modern theatrical texts call for characters to enter with a property, they seldom direct them to exit with it (assuming that the actor will have the wits to do so). However, for a modern reader such information is useful.

2.2 CRANE (Sce.ᵃ. 2ᵃ); not in NON-CRANE

2.2.0.1-2.2.95/759-870 Enter...storm] not in CRANE[1]. A major addition in the revised version, introducing the Fat Bishop.

2.2.0.1-3/759-60 Enter...Pawn] The Fat-Bishop: & his Pawne: Then yᵉ Bˡ. Bᵖ. & Bˡ. Knight. Then yᵉ wh. & Bl. Houses (feuerally) CRANE[3]. For the massed entry see 1.1.0.2-5.

2.2.0.1/759 Enter] The CRANE[3]

2.2.0.1-2/759 from the White House] THIS EDITION (conj. Hotson); not in CRANE[2]+. See 1.1.30.1.

2.2.0.2-3/759 dressed in white...white] THIS EDITION; not in CRANE[2]+. It must be immediately apparent, on this entry, that the Bishop and his Pawn belong to the White party. The Bishop is identified corporeally ('Fat') rather than sartorially ('white'), because he will eventually change sides; but the visual effect here, taken for granted in all the early texts and confirmed in the engraved title-pages to all the early printed editions, must clearly be white.

2.2.0.2/759 followed by] THIS EDITION; & CRANE; wth NON-CRANE. Early theatrical texts seldom provide the level of detail required to distinguish simultaneous entry from entry of the servant a few steps or seconds after the master. But the Fat Bishop's first word, and his later question, indicate that the two characters have been separated until the scene begins.

2.2.0.2-3/759 his servant, a] THIS EDITION; his CRANE, OKES; a MIDDLETON[T], BRIDGEWATER[A], ROSENBACH[A]. The information provided by the stage direction in CRANE is supplied by the speech prefix in MIDDLETON[T]. 'His' implies 'his servant', which in turn implies a costume and demeanour immediately recognizable on stage.

2.2.2/762 FAT BISHOP'S] DYCE (F.B.); Bs. MIDDLETON[T], ROSENBACH[A], OKES; not in CRANE; Bl.Bs. BRIDGEWATER[A]. Apparently the King's Men's playbook identified this minor role only as 'Pawn', since that formula is used consistently in the earliest texts of the scene; in context that would not have been ambiguous. See 2.2.14.

2.2.2/762 great] not in OKES uncorrected

2.2.2/762 holiness's] holines MIDDLETON[T]+; holiness' DYCE. The grammar is not in doubt; the pronunciation is ambiguous. The metre would be more regular if the possessive produced an extra syllable.

2.2.3/763 great₍] ~, OKES corrected

*2.2.3/763 but for] ~ ₍ BRIDGEWATER[A], OKES. The variant is unmetrical and ungrammatical, and eliminates the parallelism with the first half of the line.

2.2.4/764 soil] foyld OKES. Misreading of 'soyle' (the spelling of MIDDLETON[T]+).

2.2.5/765 but] not in OKES. Accidental omission: metre.

2.2.7/767 great] gread ROSENBACH[A]. Assimilation.

2.2.8/768   pure] purer BRIDGEWATER[A] *uncorrected*

2.2.9/769   That's] OKES; is MIDDLETON[T]+. The emphatic variant is hard to explain as a misreading or common substitution.

2.2.10/770   this] a OKES; his CRANE/MATHEWES. The OKES variant probably arose through assimilation to the other 'a' in the line in all witnesses (since compositors and scribes alike often carried a line at a time in their heads); 'this' is dramatically specific and deictic. 'His' is possible, but it could be a misreading, which sacrifices dramatic effect to logic.

2.2.11-12/771-2   Like...mouse-flesh] *not in* CRANE[3]

2.2.12/772   to bed] OKES, CRANE/MATHEWES; abed MIDDLETON[T]+. Both variants are Middletonian: he uses 'a-bed' 23 times elsewhere, and 'brought a-bed' at *Phoenix* 13.24, *No Wit* 4.243, 7.76, *Chaste Maid* 3.3.136; but 'brought to bed' occurs at *Microcynicon* 4.82. Middleton's preferred contraction is preserved in *Early*, and the alternative here in the modern-spelling text.

2.2.12/772   mouse-flesh] MIDDLETON[T]+ (Mouffleſh); mans fleſh OKES. An easy misreading (ou/an); 'mouse' is supported by the source in Horace.

2.2.13-3.1.0.1/773-1060   My last...*Tertius*] *not in* BRIDGEWATER. This gap has been partially filled by Middleton, as noted below.

2.2.13-17/773-9   My last...sir.] Middleton autograph in BRIDGEWATER. See previous note.

2.2.13/773   books] booke OKES

2.2.13/773   invectives] *Inuectiue* CRANE/MATHEWES

2.2.14/774   'Gainst] CRANE[2]; againſt CRANE[3]+

2.2.14/775   FAT BISHOP'S] MIDDLETON[B], OKES; Bs. MIDDLETON[T], ROSENBACH[A]; *not in* CRANE[2,4]; B[l]. CRANE[3]. Only CRANE[3] is clearly erroneous (perhaps a misreading of 'Bſ' or 'Bi'); its error may be related to the error in BRIDGEWATER[A] at 2.2.2.

2.2.14-15/775-6   publication [Λ]...morning, sir] ~, S[ir]...~ [Λ] MIDDLETON[B]. Metre supports the reading of all other witnesses.

2.2.15/776   books] booke ROSENBACH[A]

2.2.17/778   'mongst] amongſt [CRANE[4]], ROSENBACH[A], OKES

2.2.17-18/779-81   FAT BISHOP'S PAWN...sir. *Exit*...| FAT BISHOP] Goe, be gon: CRANE[3]. See 2.1.181. The replacement phrase seems authorial: it occurs also at *Patient Man* 5.195 (Middleton and/or Dekker), also at the end of a verse line; Middleton also has 'begone' at the end of a verse line at 2.1.193, *Heroes* 136 and *Valour* 1.1.143 ('Groom, begone').

2.2.17/779   FAT BISHOP'S] MIDDLETON[B], OKES; Bs. MIDDLETON[T], ROSENBACH[A]; *not in* CRANE[2,4]

*2.2.17.1/780   *Exit*] MIDDLETON[T] (exit B[s]p.), CRANE[2]; *not in* CRANE[3,4], ROSENBACH[A], MIDDLETON[B], OKES. One of the two autograph texts (but not the other) restores the original reading, present in the earliest text of the revised script but accidentally omitted thereafter.

2.2.18/781   It's] CRANE[2,3]; 'tis CRANE[4]+. See Induction.15.

2.2.19/782   Sit] Set OKES. Probably only a spelling variant: *OED* shows that confusion of 'sit' and 'set' began as early as the 14th c. Compare *Revenger* 1.2.142 ('set you a-horseback').

2.2.19/782   feed] drinke OKES. Although DYCE and BULLEN follow OKES, one does not normally drink fat, or drink *upon* fat; Middleton uses 'feed upon' at least four times, and here 'feed' alliterates with 'fat' and echoes 'ease' and 'eat' assonantally. The variant is probably an inadvertent substitution, caused by the familiarity of the idiom 'eat and drink'.

2.2.21-2/784-5   I have...meal.] *not in* CRANE[2]. See notes below. These two lines have been retained because they are present in CRANE[3].

2.2.22/785   six-and-thirty] 36 ROSENBACH[A]. The variant does not alter the meaning, but disrupts the metre. Compare OKES error

at 5.3.23.

2.2.22/785   meal.] Five verse lines, present in most texts of the revised version after this word, are absent from CRANE[2,3]. It is hard to explain the variant, except as a reflection of a deliberate cut in the performance text. For the lines, see Additional Passage A. Textual variants in the passage are keyed to its appearance there.

2.2.23-7/790-94   Of...truth] *not in* CRANE[3]. See notes above. These lines have been retained because they are present in CRANE[2].

2.2.25/792   House] OKES; Side MIDDLETON[T]+. Late authorial variant, removing the only occurrence in the play of 'Black side' (or 'White side').

2.2.26/793   turn] reuolt OKES. Anticipation.

2.2.27/794   my] mine CRANE[2,4]

2.2.27/794   truth] OKES; true CRANE[2]+. Probably a late authorial variant. In parallels for 'to say tru—' in the Middleton canon, 'true' appears only once elsewhere (*Revenger* 3.1.22), but 'truth' five times (*Phoenix* 2.48, 15.23, *Michaelmas* 2.3.176, 3.1.222, *Weapons* 2.2.221).

2.2.28/795   I've] DYCE; I have CRANE[2]+. For Crane's expansion of Middleton's characteristic elision, see General Textual Introduction. Since the preceding line does not end with an extra unstressed syllable, the elision seems metrically required.

2.2.29/796   th'] THIS EDITION; the CRANE[2]+. A characteristic Crane expansion of a Middletonian elision.

2.2.32/799   marigolds] Marie-gold OKES. Perhaps deliberately altered to provide numerical concord with 'shuts and opens'.

*2.2.33/800   Venus-baths] DYCE; Venus Bath CRANE[2]+; ~ borth OKES. All the other six items in this two-line floral catalogue are plurals, so the emendation appears justified. OKES must be a misreading; the whole passage is not present in CRANE[1]. An error apparently shared by all texts of the revised version, which must therefore have originated in the playbook.

2.2.34/801   Pinks...daffadowndillies] *not in* CRANE[3]

2.2.34/801   hyacinths] Hyanths OKES

2.2.35/802   There] Therh MATHEWES. Foul case.

2.2.35/802   I'd] OKES, ROSENBACH[A]; I had CRANE[2]+. Metre; a favourite Middleton elision.

2.2.35/802   more such drabs] much more drab OKES

2.2.36/803   I've] I haue CRANE[2,3,4]

2.2.37-40/804-7   Yet...again.] *not in* CRANE[3]

2.2.37/804   hole-sale] CRANE[2] (hole-Sale), MIDDLETON[T] (Holefale), ROSENBACH[A] (holefale); whole fale CRANE/MATHEWES; whole-fayle OKES. The dominant meaning is sexual; the printed texts are more modest than the manuscripts.

2.2.38/805   clapped a bargain] clap ~ barging OKES

2.2.39/806   I've] CRANE[2]; I haue CRANE[2]+

2.2.40/807   that] *not in* CRANE[2]. Eyeskip.

2.2.40/807   they've] ROSENBACH[A]; then'ue OKES; they haue CRANE[2]+

2.2.40.1-2.2.52/808-22   Enter...party.] Middleton autograph in BRIDGEWATER. See at 2.2.13-17.

2.2.40.1/807.1   Enter...Knight] *not in* MIDDLETON[T]; Enter Bl. Kt. | F.B. MIDDLETON[B]. The two quartos place the direction differently: OKES in the right margin opposite 41-2, CRANE/MATHEWES opposite 38-9. Both these variants may reflect the fact that 2.2.40 is too long to permit the stage direction even to begin on the same type line. The direction is completely missing from MIDDLETON[T], and half of it is missing from MIDDLETON[B] (since the Bishop should enter here, as well as the Knight). However, the omission of the Black Bishop from the BRIDGEWATER stage direction may be deliberate, since it is

directly related to the added speech prefix which immediately
follows, and to the fact that this passage is part of an
autograph transition bridging a scribal gap between 2.2 and
3.1. (See previous note.) The Black Bishop's role is thereby
eliminated, and he has nothing to do until his (correctly
marked) entrance in 3.1. Consequently, this variant has not
been tabulated as a shared error.

2.2.40.1/807   *from the Black House*] THIS EDITION (*conj.* Hotson);
not in CRANE² +. See 1.1.30.1.

2.2.40.1–2/807.1   *Knight...Bishop*]   CRANE²;   Bᵖ...*Knight*
CRANE³˒⁴, ROSENBACHᴬ, OKES. See preceding note. The CRANE²
order indicates the character first noted by the Fat Bishop,
which we would expect to be the first of the two characters
to become visible on stage; the Knight is also the first of the
two characters to speak, again suggesting that he is closer
to the Fat Bishop than is his Black companion. The variant
instead prioritizes social rank, which puts bishops before
knights.

2.2.40.1/807   *Knight*] K. OKES

2.2.40.2/807   *with*] ROSENBACHᴬ, OKES; & CRANE. On Crane's
preference for 'and' in stage directions, see text note at *Early*
4.170.2.

2.2.41/808   *Yonder's*] BRIDGEWATERᶜ, HOWARD-HILL; Yonder
CRANE² +. 'Yonder's' appears at least 24 times elsewhere in
the Middleton canon. Without the emendation, the sentence
lacks a verb.

2.2.43–4/810–11   halter. When...lodgings,] Both autographs
and all other texts have stronger punctuation after 'halter'
than 'lodgings'—except CRANE/MATHEWES (halter:...lodg-
ings₍ₐ₎) and OKES (halter,...lodgings,). Shared punctuation
error.

2.2.43–4/810–11   did | Vouchsafe] MIDDLETONᴮ; laft | Vouch-
fafe MIDDLETONᵀ +. Late authorial variant.

2.2.44/811   privileged] priuiledgèd CRANE/MATHEWES, OKES

2.2.45/812   found] MIDDLETONᴮ; faw MIDDLETONᵀ +. Late authorial variant.

2.2.45/812   there] *not in* OKES

2.2.47/814   not]₍ₐ₎ ROSENBACHᴬ

2.2.48/815   turned] turnèd OKES

2.2.48.1–2/816–17   *Enter...books*] *not in* MIDDLETONᴮ, CRANE³˒⁴.
The omission of this stage direction in MIDDLETONᴮ might be
deliberate, part of the major disturbance hereabouts. (See
note at 2.2.40.1–2.2.52.) However, 'more books' have to
appear on stage, in order to provoke the response 'Look, more
books yet.' Nevertheless, it is not clear whether the direction
was absent in the manuscript from which Middleton copied
this section of BRIDGEWATER—if indeed he consulted copy at
all—or whether it was simply omitted as part of the general
carelessness of the patching operation. CRANE³ does not have
the direction because it groups entrances at the beginning of
the scene (and does not indicate re-entrances). As a result
of these uncertainties, this omission has not been tabulated
as a shared error; if it were, it would link BRIDGEWATER to
[CRANE⁴]. This might also be another case where 'massed
entrances' in a text like CRANE³ led to omission of situated
directions in later texts.

2.2.48.1/816   *Fat Bishop's*] DYCE; his MIDDLETONᵀ *only*; *not in*
CRANE² +

2.2.48.1–2/816   *from the White House*] THIS EDITION (*conj.* Hotson); *not in* CRANE² +. See 1.1.30.1.

2.2.48/818   KNIGHT] B. MIDDLETONᴮ. This late autograph variant
may simply be an error (by contamination from the last
word of the previous line, 'Bishop'), but even if intentional it
cannot be reproduced in a full text of the scene.

2.2.49/819   Yonder greasy ₍ₐ₎] OKES, HOWARD-HILL; yon ~ turncoat CRANE² +. The omission of 'turncoat' makes the image
relevant to a lot of bishops, not just this one. By itself it might
be accidental, but the compensatory change to 'Yonder'
makes it more likely to be deliberate.

2.2.50/820   Has wrought] MIDDLETONᴮ; dos worke MIDDLETONᵀ,
OKES, ROSENBACHᴬ; doth work CRANE²˒³˒⁴. Late authorial variant.

2.2.51–2/821–2   His...party] whole | CRANE/MATHEWES

2.2.53/823   O...subtlety] *2 lines* CRANE/MATHEWES: 'twere |

2.2.54/824   on] CRANE²˒³; a NON-CRANE; 'o CRANE/MATHEWES. See
2.1.157.

2.2.54/824   this] *not in* MIDDLETONᵀ *uncorrected only*

2.2.54–8/825–9   And...already.] *not in* CRANE³

2.2.56/827   part] party OKES

2.2.56/827   now he] hee now ROSENBACHᴬ

2.2.56/827   upon] on OKES

2.2.58/829   Has] hath CRANE²˒⁴

2.2.59/830   On] CRANE²˒³˒⁴; a MIDDLETONᵀ, ROSENBACHᴬ, OKES. See
2.2.54.

2.2.59–60/830–1   prescribed...provided] CRANE²˒³; prouided...
inuented [CRANE⁴], OKES, ROSENBACHᴬ, MIDDLETONᵀ; *not in*
CRANE¹, BRIDGEWATER. These variants seem related: 'prescribed' is appropriate to 'physic' (and paralleled elsewhere
in Middleton), and the Fat Bishop 'provided' rather than
'invented' the surgeon. CRANE²˒³ are apparently the earliest extant texts of the revision; the variants might be late
authorial revision, but they could also have arisen as a miscorrection of an intermediate error ('provided...provided') in
a manuscript no longer extant.

2.2.61/832   you] thee ROSENBACHᴬ, CRANE/MATHEWES

2.2.61/832   uncatholic] vncatholicall OKES. Metre.

2.2.64/835   of] ROSENBACHᴬ; on CRANE² +. See 1.1.255.

2.2.66/837   at₍ₐ₎] ~ a ROSENBACHᴬ

*2.2.67–8/839–40   O insufferable! | BLACK KNIGHT] *not in* OKES.
Eyeskip, with the effect of attributing the following speech
to Black Bishop instead of Black Knight—and thus giving
him two speeches in a row. That speech is also given to the
Black Bishop in MIDDLETONᴮ, as part of the improvised patch
covering the omission of most of this scene. (See note at
2.2.40.1–2.2.52.) In both texts, the line needs to be spoken
by the Black Knight, and both texts are therefore mistaken.

2.2.67/839   O] *not in* CRANE²˒³

2.2.68/840–1   I'll...churches] Middleton autograph in BRIDGE-
WATER, inserted between ll. 53–4 (and therefore attributed to
the Black Bishop). See note at 2.2.40.1–2.2.52.

2.2.68/840–1   I'll...churches] of the | MIDDLETONᵀ; ball | OKES;
not in CRANE¹

2.2.69–72/841–4   And...absent] he | drink | side to | MIDDLE-
TONᵀ; *not in* CRANE¹˒³, BRIDGEWATER

2.2.69–72/841–4   He...write] *not in* CRANE³

2.2.70/843   urine] wine OKES. Minim misreading.

2.2.71/843   will] well MIDDLETONᵀ *uncorr* (anticipating 'well')

2.2.72/844   write:] CRANE; ~ , MIDDLETONᵀ, ROSENBACHᴬ; ~ ₍ₐ₎
OKES. See next note.

2.2.72/844   Bishop absent] bifhops dead OKES *corrected*; bifhops
deedes OKES *uncorrected*. See previous note. The variant can
hardly be a misreading or inadvertent substitution; it was
the death of Pope Paul V that prompted Spalato to return
to Rome. This is almost certainly a late authorial revision.
However, this local variant conflicts with the text at 3.1.33–
41, so it has not been integrated into the larger context, and
may be inadvertent.

2.2.73/845   has] h'as OKES *uncorrected*; hath CRANE[2,3,4]. A redundant Middletonian apostrophe in the original typesetting of OKES, 'corrected' by the proofreader.

2.2.74–5/846–7   Perhaps…ours] *not in* CRANE[3]

2.2.75/847   most] *not in* OKES. Possible metrically if three-syllable 'motion'; but that is unusual in mid-line for Middleton.

2.2.76/848   flattered] flatterèd ROSENBACH[A], OKES

2.2.76/848   *vacante*] *vacant* OKES

2.2.79–81/851–3   For…lecherous] *not in* CRANE[3]

2.2.80–1/852–3   When…lecherous] mind | ROSENBACH[A]; *not in* CRANE[1,3], BRIDGEWATER

2.2.80/852   meets] meet OKES

2.2.81/853   As] *not in* ROSENBACH[A]

2.2.81–2/854–5   No…fill] *1 line* ROSENBACH[A], OKES; *not in* CRANE[1,3], BRIDGEWATER. Relic.

*2.2.81.1–6/855   *Enter…black pawns*] CRANE[2] (position); *Enter Kin.Qu.Kni.Duke, Bishops of both | fides, and Pawnes.* CRANE/MATHEWES (below 'fill' at 82); *Enter both houfes,* MIDDLETON[T] (opposite 'Both…fill' at 82), ROSENBACH[A], OKES (both to the right of 96). In CRANE[1] this stage direction begins the scene, which lacks the Fat Bishop sequence and accordingly begins with the White Queen's speech at 96. It is surely no coincidence that the shared error of ROSENBACH[A] and OKES misplaces the stage direction at exactly that point (which is clearly wrong in the revised version of the play). However, the *form* of the direction in those two texts does not at all resemble the direction's form in CRANE[1]. (See *Early* 2.275.1.) Rather than a direct manuscript link, the coincidence suggests 'memorial contamination' by someone familiar with the earlier version (Crane or Middleton). Again, this error might have occurred as a result of the absence of the direction, *in situ*, in a text with massed entrances resembling those in CRANE[3].

2.2.81.1–4/855   *from…from*] THIS EDITION; *seu[r]ally* CRANE[1,2,3]; *on one side…on the other* DYCE. See 1.1.30.1, and next note. The emendation retains the original wording, supplementing it to remove the logical contradiction. This should perhaps be considered a shared error in [CRANE[4]] and all the extant NON-CRANE texts (ROSENBACH[A], OKES, and MIDDLETON[T]), since those texts lack useful information about staging; but it has not been counted as such because Howard-Hill does not adopt (or even record) the variant.

*2.2.81.1–5/855   *from the White House…and from the Black House*] ∧ ~ ~ ~ & ∧ ~ ~ ~ CRANE[2]; *Then* ~ ~ & ∧ ~ ~ *Houfes* CRANE[3] (as part of massed entrance direction at 2.2.0.1); *both houfes,* ROSENBACH[A], OKES, MIDDLETON[T]. (The entire passage is missing in BRIDGEWATER.) See preceding notes. One Knight and two Bishops are already on stage, so neither House enters in its entirety. The error might have resulted from a confusion of the meaning of 'House', which can refer either to the persons or to the place. The confusion was repeated in all texts of the revised version except CRANE/MATHEWES, which specifies 'Kin. Qu. Kni. Duke, Bishops of both | fides, and Pawnes.' This repeats the formula 'both [plural noun]', substituting 'Sides' for 'Houses'; it thus more closely resembles the ROSENBACH–MIDDLETON–OKES group than CRANE[2,3]. But where the shared direction for the entrance of both houses is guilty of an excessively inclusive vagueness, CRANE/MATHEWES is uniquely and explicitly wrong (in specifically calling for the entrance of three characters already on stage). That unique error presumably originated when a desire to provide more specificity than the common direction was mechanically fulfilled by listing all the major characters in both houses, describing the scenic effect produced after

the two entrances are completed, rather than the entrances themselves.

2.2.81.1–6/855   *White King…black pawns*] THIS EDITION; *Wh. King: Q: B[p]. | Duke. Knight: Pawnes: & Q[s] Pawne: and Bl. | King. Q. B[p]. &c.* CRANE[1]; *Kin. Qu. Kni. Duke, Bishops of both | fides, and Pawnes.* CRANE/MATHEWES. The CRANE[1] specifics make sense in the Early Form, where the direction begins the scene, no one is already on stage, and the White Queen's Pawn enters after the rest of the White House. For the errors in the CRANE/MATHEWES direction, see preceding note.

2.2.81.4–6/855   *white pawns…black pawns*] THIS EDITION; *not in* CRANE[2]+; *Pawnes…&c.* CRANE[1]; *of both | fides, and Pawnes.* CRANE/MATHEWES; *White King's Pawn, and White Bishop's Pawn…Black Knight's Pawn* DYCE. Full ranks of pawns are implied by the call for the entrance of both houses. DYCE presumes that the only pawns to appear on stage are those that speak. The absence of the Black Bishop's Pawn would be more conspicuous if all the other Black (and White) aristocrats had a pawn in place.

2.2.81.3–6/855   *White Duke…Black Duke*] Duke CRANE/MATHEWES. Although the singular 'Duke' also appears in CRANE[1], there it belongs to a list of specifically White pieces, and is therefore correct; in CRANE/MATHEWES it occurs in a completely different context, and is incorrect. This is not a shared error, because it is in an error only in one text. (See preceding notes.)

2.2.82/855   Both…fill.] *not in* CRANE[3]

2.2.82.1–2   *Fat…King James*] THIS EDITION; *not in* CRANE[2]+

2.2.82/856   has] hath CRANE[2,3,4]

2.2.84/858   I'm] ROSENBACH[A], OKES; I am CRANE[2]+

2.2.84/858   ashamed] afhamèd CRANE/MATHEWES

2.2.86/860   blindness] boldneffe CRANE/MATHEWES. Misreading.

2.2.87–8/861–2   I must…now] DYCE; played | CRANE[2,3], OKES; fool | MIDDLETON[T]; *1 line* ROSENBACH[A]; *not in* CRANE[1], BRIDGEWATER. 'I must confess' is not present in CRANE/MATHEWES, which sets 'I have…now' as a single verse and type line; even if the variant is an error, accidental omission would be likelier to occur if 'I must confess' were a separate line (encouraging eyeskip from one line beginning 'I' to the line below it, also beginning 'I'). Thus the copy for MATHEWES or for [CRANE[4]] probably had DYCE's lineation. ROSENBACH[A] presumably represents the ambiguous authorial original, but Middleton's verse-breaks more often coincide with sense-breaks (rather than enjambing between a verb and its object).

2.2.87/861   I must confess] *not in* CRANE/MATHEWES. See preceding note.

2.2.87/861   I've] OKES, ROSENBACH[A]; I haue CRANE[2]+. A favourite Middleton elision, here producing a more metrical line.

2.2.88/862   till] iill OKES *uncorrected*

2.2.89/863   And…knave] *2 lines* CRANE[2,3]: parts |. A possible arrangement, depending on how the preceding speech is aligned.

2.2.90–4/864–8   FAT BISHOP…heart.] *not in* CRANE[3]

2.2.90/864   There's] ROSENBACH[A], OKES; There is CRANE[2]+. A typical Crane expansion of a characteristic Middleton contraction. Alternatively, Crane's 'in the' might be emended to the elided form 'i'th''; but I have adopted the elision for which there are early witnesses.

2.2.91/865   Writ] Wer't OKES. Misreading or miscorrection.

2.2.92/866   BISHOP] P. CRANE/MATHEWES. There are white pawns present, but it seems unlikely that one of them intervenes here.

2.2.92/866 plainer] better OKES. It seems unlikely that Middleton would have had the idealized White Bishop claim that Latin serves 'better' than English for 'pure honesty'.

2.2.93/867 Plague] MIDDLETON[T], CRANE/MATHEWES; Out CRANE[2], ROSENBACH[A], OKES. See next note. Middleton uses 'Plague of' at *Puritan* 3.5.180, *Women Beware* 5.1.178, and 'Plague o'' at *No Wit* 4.369; there are no exact parallels for 'Plague on' (the CRANE/MATHEWES reading), although 'a plague on' occurs at *Patient Man* 15.132 (Dekker?), and 'A plague upon' at *Microcynicon* 5.88. For the interjection 'Out on', see *Dissemblers* 5.2.47. The variant probably arises from late authorial revision.

2.2.93/867 of] MIDDLETON[T], OKES; on CRANE[2,4], ROSENBACH[A]. See previous note.

2.2.94/868 th'] CRANE/MATHEWES; the CRANE[2]+

*2.2.94.1/871 Enter...Pawn] CRANE[2]; *not in* CRANE[3], OKES, ROSENBACH[A]. The direction is placed later by CRANE/MATHEWES (in the right margin after 'anger') and MIDDLETON[T] (below 2.2.95), but it seems most likely that the character begins to enter before the Black Bishop sees her. BRIDGEWATER lacks the entire passage; no separate entrance is needed in CRANE[1], which lacks the preceding lines, and therefore has a mass entrance of both houses begin the scene here. The massed initial direction for the scene in CRANE[3] does not indicate a separate entrance for the White Queen's Pawn, and a text with similar massed entrances—[CRANE[5]]?—might be responsible for the omission in OKES and ROSENBACH[A] and the late placement in MIDDLETON[T].

2.2.94.1/871 ‸White] y[e] ~ CRANE[2]

2.2.94.1–2/871 *from the White House*] THIS EDITION (*conj.* Hotson); *not in* CRANE[2]+. See 1.1.30.1.

2.2.94/869 Here‸] ~, OKES *uncorrected*. Something is certainly missing in OKES *uncorrected*; it might have been missing in the underlying manuscript, too. Perhaps (instead of 'Heere,') the correction should have been 'Heeres'. See next note.

2.2.94/869 comes more anger ‸] ‸ ~ ~ yet OKES. Possibly authorial. See previous note.

2.2.95/870 BLACK KNIGHT...storm.] *not in* CRANE[3]

2.2.96–7/872–3 Is...dejection] CRANE; our | MIDDLETON[T]; *3 lines* pawn | person | ROSENBACH[A]; *3 lines* should | person | OKES

2.2.98–9/874–5 Sorrow...her.] *not in* CRANE[3]

2.2.99/875 Has] Hath CRANE[2,4]

2.2.99/875 prevailed] preuailèd OKES

2.2.103/880 wondrously] wonderoufly CRANE/MATHEWES

2.2.103/880 preserved] preferuèd OKES

2.2.104/881 suff'rings] CRANE[1,2,3]; fufferings [CRANE[4]]+

2.2.105/882 terrors] terrour CRANE/MATHEWES

2.2.106/883 all] OKES; *not in* CRANE[2]+

2.2.107/884 absolut'st] abfolute OKES; absoluteft ROSENBACH[A]. Middleton elsewhere uses 'absolute' 24 times. But the superlative is the 'rarer reading' (Taylor 1988). *OED* cites examples in 1602, 1615, and 1642.

2.2.108/885 Fair] Fayrer OKES. The comparative is less metrical; it seems unlikely that 'peace' would be considered 'fairer' than 'true sanctity'.

2.2.109/886 o'th'] CRANE; of th' OKES; of the MIDDLETON[T], ROSENBACH[A]. Middleton elsewhere elides *th'* ten times before words beginning 'un'. For the OKES form of the elision compare 'of th'other' (*Women Beware* 2.2.132) and 'of th'unwise' (*Truth* 425).

2.2.112/889 foul] fould CRANE/MATHEWES. Misreading of 'foule' (as the word is spelled in ROSENBACH[A] and OKES).

2.2.113/890 WHITE QUEEN [OF BOHEMIA] Ha?] *not in* CRANE[2,3].

This may be deliberate abridgement in CRANE[3], and hence cannot be certainly tabulated as a shared error, but that is probably what it is. It is hard to imagine the playbook bothering to cut such an exclamation.

2.2.115/892 ear] eares CRANE[3]. The plural produces a more commonplace expression: see Taylor 1988.

2.2.116–36/894–914 WHITE QUEEN'S PAWN...devil.] *not in* CRANE[3]

2.2.117/895 offered] offerèd ROSENBACH[A], OKES

2.2.119/897 my] MIDDLETON[T] *only*; mine CRANE+

2.2.120 pleased] pleafèd OKES

2.2.121/899 give] gaue ROSENBACH[A]

2.2.122–3/900–1 When...there] com- | MIDDLETON[T]; *3 lines* OKES: sins | companies |

2.2.122/900 desp'rate] CRANE[2]; defperate CRANE[1]+

2.2.122/900–901 company] OKES; companies CRANE[1]+. Both readings make sense; though the plural might have been added by assimilation, the singular is less easy to explain as an error.

2.2.125/903 wonder] wounds CRANE/MATHEWES

2.2.126/904 answered] anfwerèd ROSENBACH[A], OKES

2.2.127/905 Yea...sheltered] *not in* OKES

2.2.127/905 Yea] CRANE/MATHEWES; I CRANE[1]+. See 1.1.257.

2.2.128/906 robe] rape OKES *uncorrected*. Nascimento did not collate Bodleian Vet.A2; it has 'robe' here, and the corrected state through this forme.

2.2.129/907 wonder] number OKES. Minim misreading.

2.2.130/908 unadmired] without any CRANE[1]; vnadmirèd OKES

*2.2.133–5/911–13 The...method] fell | master | CRANE/MATHEWES; fell | master | order | ROSENBACH[A]. Shared error.

2.2.136/914 Takes...devil.] *not in* OKES

2.2.137–8/915–6 It...name] that | CRANE[3]

2.2.138/916 infested] infected CRANE/MATHEWES. Possibly only a ligature error (ċt instead of ft).

2.2.140/918 which] that OKES

2.2.141/919 has] hath CRANE, ROSENBACH[A]

*2.2.141/919 seized] ceard ROSENBACH[A]; fcarde OKES. ROSENBACH seems to be a misreading of 'ceazde' (MIDDLETON[T]) or 'ceizd' (CRANE[1,2,3]), but OKES looks like a misreading of 'feiz'd' (CRANE/MATHEWES). Both texts misread 'z' as 'r'.

2.2.141/919 Pawn‸] ~ Sir CRANE[1]

2.2.142–56/920–40 BISHOP...respected,] *not in* CRANE[3] (which preserves only the speech prefix 'K[t].', to govern the words that follow the cut)

2.2.142/920 his] this CRANE/MATHEWES

2.2.143/921 prime] prince ROSENBACH[A]. Minim misreading.

2.2.143/921 of] on OKES. There are authorial parallels for both variants. For 'on the earth', see *Magnificent Entertainment* 3.927 (specifically attributed to Middleton).

2.2.147/926 thou] OKES; you CRANE+. Late authorial variant.

2.2.148/927 BISHOP] Bi.P. CRANE/MATHEWES. The Black Bishop's Pawn is not on stage.

2.2.148/927 you] ~ with DYCE. The emendation clarifies the grammar, and would be metrical if *sincerity* were elided to three syllables.

2.2.149/928 Spiced] Spake OKES. Misreading of 'Spicft' (MIDDLETON[T]).

2.2.149/929 there] their OKES

2.2.152/932 after] OKES; following CRANE[1]+. Late authorial variant. For 'all the year following' compare *Industry* 143–4; for 'year after', *Dissemblers* 1.4.83.

2.2.153/937 White] Before this word most of the texts contain three and a half verse lines, which are however not present in CRANE[2]. The passage is also missing from CRANE[3] (as part of a larger cut). (BRIDGEWATER lacks the entire passage, so it is impossible to know whether it would have seconded the cut.) These lines might well have been cut in the playbook. They are printed as Additional Passage B; textual variants in the lines are recorded there.

2.2.153/937 there is] ther's OKES. Metre.

2.2.155/939 loved] Lord OKES. Minim misreading of 'lou'de' (MIDDLETON[T]).

2.2.156/940 th'] CRANE[2,4], OKES; the CRANE[1] +

2.2.156/940 aforenamed] aforenamèd CRANE/MATHEWES, ROSEN-BACH[A], OKES

2.2.157-74/941-59 If . . . BLACK KNIGHT GONDOMAR I] And CRANE[3]. The substitution of 'And' for 'I' is clearly deliberate, smoothing the transition after the cut.

2.2.157/941 with all] withall OKES

2.2.159/943 distraction] deſtruction OKES. Misreading.

2.2.163-4/947-8 Or . . . discover] enough | ROSENBACH[A]

2.2.163/947 thee] the ROSENBACH[A], OKES. Possibly only a spelling variant.

2.2.165/949 vexing] vexed ROSENBACH[A]

2.2.165/949 strong] ſtrongly OKES

2.2.167/951 remove] roome CRANE/MATHEWES

2.2.169/953 thou canst] you can OKES

2.2.171/955 blood-threats] OKES; lowd Threates CRANE[1] +. Late authorial variant. Compare *Weapons* 4.1.242, 'so much blood is threatened', and other Middleton compounds beginning with 'blood' (-guiltiness, -hasty, -letting, -pot, -quaffing, -raw, -shedder, -sucker, -thirsty). See next note.

2.2.171/955 that thunder cracks] OKES; those thunder-cracks CRANE[1] +. This variant might also be authorial: for the verb, see *Tennis* 638, 'I'll thunder thee a-pieces'.

2.2.172/956 Ush'ring] Vſhering [CRANE[4]], ROSENBACH[A], OKES. Shared extrametrical expansion.

2.2.173/957 Craft] Truſt OKES; Crafts CRANE/MATHEWES. Misreading (craf/truſ).

2.2.177-83/962-9 WHITE QUEEN'S PAWN . . . Pawn?] *not in* CRANE[3]

2.2.177/962 Lord] CRANE[1]; oh CRANE[2] +. Censorship.

2.2.178/963-4 It . . . it] *2 lines* MIDDLETON[T]: to |

2.2.179/965 you] MIDDLETON[T], ROSENBACH[A]; She CRANE, OKES. Late authorial variant.

2.2.180/966 you] your OKES. Possible authorial variant.

2.2.180/966 more unclean] OKES; uncleaner CRANE[1] +. Late authorial variant.

2.2.181/967 ‸ impious] OKES; more ~ CRANE[1] +; moſt ~ CRANE/MATHEWES. Related to the variant in the preceding line.

2.2.182/968 show] now OKES. Foul case ('n' for 'ſh').

2.2.182/968 i'th'] in th' CRANE[2]

2.2.183/969 wronged] wronges OKES

2.2.184/970 Yesterday's] Yeſterday CRANE/MATHEWES

2.2.184/970 cursèd] haples CRANE[2,3]. Possibly censorship.

2.2.184-94/971-82 BLACK KNIGHT . . . now?] *not in* CRANE[3]

2.2.184-5/971-2 O . . . thee] *1 line* ROSENBACH[A], OKES. Relic.

2.2.185/972 can't] OKES; cannot CRANE[1] +. The contraction appears at least six times elsewhere in Middleton.

2.2.187/974 honour's] Honor CRANE[1]

2.2.191/978 hand's] CRANE[1,2]; hands CRANE/MATHEWES, NON-CRANE. This is not an error, since Middleton often omits the apostrophe with such compounds. But the correct meaning is 'our hand is too heavy' (*not* 'the cause is too heavy for our hands').

2.2.192/980 her] het OKES. Foul case.

2.2.194/982 Has] hath CRANE[1,2]

2.2.194/982 raised] rayſèd OKES

2.2.195/984 time? Stand firm‸] CRANE[1,2,3]; ~~ stand ~: CRANE/MATHEWES; ~‸ ſtands ~, OKES; ~,~~~ MIDDLETON[T], ROSEN-BACH[A]. Shared punctuation error: only the two quartos separate 'stand firm' from 'now to your scandal'. The substantive variant in OKES ('stands') seems to be a progressive error, related to the lighter autograph punctuation in the first half of the line (which led to 'time' being understood as the subject of the verb).

2.2.196/986 treacheries] treachery OKES. The next word ('They') confirms the plural.

2.2.197/987 They've] they'haue CRANE[2,3]; they haue CRANE/MATHEWES. In MIDDLETON[T] *corrected* the initial 'T' is written over 'y', suggesting that Middleton started to write 'y'aue' (you have).

2.2.198/989 accused] accuſèd OKES

2.2.199/990 Has] hath CRANE[2,3,4]

2.2.200-1/991-2 WHITE KNIGHT . . . BLACK KNIGHT] *not in* CRANE[3]

2.2.202/993 WHITE QUEEN'S PAWN . . . unblasted?] *not in* CRANE[3]

2.2.202/993 QUEEN'S] *not in* CRANE[1], ROSENBACH[A], OKES. In CRANE[1] and ROSENBACH[A] this variant is part of the more general pattern of generic speech prefixes; in OKES it is not, but might result from simple compositorial omission (or vacillating authorial reversion to the original generic form).

2.2.203/994 KING] Kt. CRANE[1], Kni. CRANE/MATHEWES. The variant is adopted at *Early* 2.394.

2.2.205/997 KING'S] Kt. OKES; Q. CRANE/MATHEWES. Each quarto repeats its separate error at 2.2.212 (Qu. CRANE/MATHEWES).

2.2.206/998 treasure] Iewell CRANE[1]. The variant, like several other changes in the revised version, associates the White King's Pawn with the Lord Treasurer.

2.2.207-11/999-1004 WHITE KING . . . BLACK KNIGHT] *not in* CRANE[3]

2.2.207/999 KING] Kni. CRANE/MATHEWES. The quarto makes the same error at 2.2.216, 231.

2.2.207.1-2/999.2 *White . . . Gondomar*] THIS EDITION; *not in* MIDDLETON[T] +; *Exit B. Kt.'s Pawn, who presently returns with papers* DYCE, BULLEN; *Exit a* BLACK PAWN *who returns with papers* HARPER, HOWARD-HILL, DUTTON. There seems no reason to have a character exit and re-enter; nor does it make sense for the White King to give orders to a black pawn. This staging makes possible the private exchange between Black Knight and White King's Pawn.

2.2.208/1001 so] *not in* OKES. Eyeskip ('ſo ſo . . .').

2.2.209/1002 strong] wrong MATHEWES. Type error ('w' for 'ſt').

2.2.211 *aside . . . Pawn*] HARPER; *not in* MIDDLETON[T] +. See note to 212.1.

2.2.212/1005 Reserved] Referuèd OKES

2.2.212.1-2 *Black . . . Pawn*] THIS EDITION; *not in* MIDDLETON[T] +. See 207.1-2.2.207.2.

2.2.212.1-2.2.212/1006 WHITE KING'S COUNSELLOR PAWN . . . en-deared!] *not in* CRANE[3]

2.2.212.2/1006 KING'S] See note on variants at 2.2.209.

2.2.212/1006 endeared] indeede OKES. Misreading.

2.2.212-14/1007-9 A . . . of] *not in* CRANE[1]. One of several additions to the revised version that characterize the White King's Pawn.

2.2.213/1008 eas'ly break, you may trust to't] ‸ breake ‸‸‸‸ CRANE[3] (abridgement to produce an iambic pentameter verse line within the structure created by the preceding cut)

2.2.213/1008 eas'ly] ROSENBACH[A] (eaſely); eaſily CRANE[2] +

2.2.213/1008 to't] to it MIDDLETON[T] *only*

2.2.216-18/1011-12 Behold . . . good] OKES, ROSENBACH[A]; all | held | CRANE[2]; *2 lines* all | CRANE[1], MIDDLETON[T]; *2 lines* one | CRANE/MATHEWES; all | CRANE[3] (which continues with a half line from 2.2.222 after 'one'); *not in* BRIDGEWATER[A]. 'Behold all' is an amphibious section, which can complete either the preceding half-line (an interpretation made explicit in CRANE[2]) or the following half-line (an interpretation made explicit in CRANE/MATHEWES).

2.2.217–20/1012–15 How...vicious] OKES, ROSENBACH[A]; *3 lines* good | rather | CRANE[1], MIDDLETON[T]; *3 lines* one | good | rather | CRANE/MATHEWES; *4 lines* held | holiness | rather | CRANE[2]; *not in* BRIDGEWATER[A], CRANE[3]; *4 lines* held | professed | false | HOWARD-HILL. The emendation adopts CRANE[2]'s unique line-break after 'held', then abandons the reading of all witnesses, to no discernible benefit to the metre, since the witnesses produce one hexameter ('To...rather') and the emendation produces two hexameters ('A...professed' and 'I...false', the second requiring a stress on 'the') and an incomplete line ('Than...vicious').

2.2.217/1012 cohere] were OKES. Misreading.

2.2.218–22/1012–17 I...WHITE KING] *not in* CRANE[3]

2.2.219/1013 ᴧ I] that ~ CRANE[2]. Extrametrical interpolation of implied connective (typical of Crane's tendency to expand contractions and elisions, without regard to metre).

2.2.219/1013 ever] er'e ROSENBACH[A]

2.2.219/1013 believed] beleeuèd OKES

2.2.220/1014 false[ᴧ] ~, OKES *corrected*

2.2.220/1014 than] you OKES. Misreading.

2.2.220/1014 profession] CRANE[1]; Profeſſo[r] CRANE[2]+. Censorship: the original reading (through the irony of the White King's misperception of what the audience knows to be the truth) indicts clerics generally. By contrast, the alternative indicts only a single individual.

2.2.221/1015 your] Youre MIDDLETON[T] *corrected*; his MIDDLETON[T] *uncorrected only*. 'You' is written over 'his'.

2.2.222/1016 ᴧGracious] most ~ CRANE[1]

2.2.222/1017 settles] ſits OKES[1] *corrected*; ſets OKES[1] *uncorrected*, OKES[2]. Nascimento does not record this press variant, but 'ſets' is clear in the Worcester copy (which has the uncorrected state of eight other press variants in this forme, including another on this page). The uncorrected state is obviously the source of the OKES[2] reading; it is also closer to the reading in all other witnesses, and suggests that 'sets' is simply an error for 'settles', conjecturally corrected in proof.

2.2.222/1017 the] th' CRANE[1]

2.2.223/1018 derived] deriuèd OKES

2.2.225/1021 Queen] frend MIDDLETON[T] *only*; Queenes OKES *uncorrected*. The autograph variant anticipates 'frendless', two lines below, and is confusing for a reader or spectator: since several White characters are leaving, 'frend' could apply to any.

2.2.225/1021 leave] leaues ROSENBACH[A], OKES. Though this might be an authorial variant, error could easily substitute the more common indicative present tense (Taylor 1988).

2.2.226/1022 Am I] I am CRANE[1]

2.2.226/1022 th'] the ROSENBACH[A], OKES

2.2.226/1022 flower] leafe ROSENBACH[A]

2.2.227/1023 friendless] Harmleſſe MIDDLETON[T] *only*. The autograph variant is almost certainly related to the unique variant at 2.2.225 ('frend'): having just used 'frend', he wanted to avoid the original 'frendless', and so substituted 'harmless', which produces the tautological 'harmless innocuousness'.

2.2.228/1025 KNIGHT] K. CRANE/MATHEWES. Since CRANE/MATHEWES uses 'Kni.' as the abbreviation for 'Knight' and 'K.' for 'King', this variant seems erroneous, not simply ambiguous. See 2.2.207 (for the opposite CRANE/MATHEWES error) and

2.2.232 (for the same error in a different text). All texts later attribute this plan to the White Knight.

2.2.228/1025 No] Nor OKES

2.2.228/1025 art] HOWARD-HILL (1990) mistakenly transcribes MIDDLETON[T] as 'are'.

2.2.231/1029 work] moſt CRANE[1]

2.2.231/1029 cheerfully] chiefely OKES. Misreading.

2.2.232/1030 KNIGHT] K. ROSENBACH[A]. See 2.2.228.

2.2.232/1031 my] mine CRANE[2,3]

2.2.233/1032 her] *not in* OKES

*2.2.233.1/1033 *Exeunt*] *not in* OKES, CRANE/MATHEWES

2.2.234–5/1034–5 BLACK KNIGHT...wonders.] *not in* CRANE[3]

2.2.234/1034 BLACK] In MIDDLETON[T] the initial 'B' is written over 'K', indicating that Middleton originally omitted the first part of the speech prefix and then immediately corrected his error before writing the second letter.

2.2.235/1035 Push!] MIDDLETON[T] *only*; Piſh CRANE[1]+. Unusual Middleton interjection replaced with a more common one, probably by misreading: *praestat insolitior lectio* (Taylor 1988).

2.2.235/1035 That] the OKES. Misreading

2.2.235/1035 brain] Skonce MIDDLETON[T], CRANE[1]. Because '*Galitian* braine' occurs in Middleton's source (quoted in the commentary to *Early* 2.430), it is unlikely to be a scribal error. This seems to be another example of authorial vacillation.

2.2.236/1036 the] *not in* OKES

2.2.237/1037 used] vſèd OKES

2.2.237/1037 at] in CRANE[1,3]

2.2.238/1038 Begin] being OKES. Perhaps a foul proof miscorrection (original error 'bein' with a 'g' marked in the margin, then reinserted in the wrong place).

2.2.239–44/1039–44 Vessel...tainted.] *not in* CRANE[3]

2.2.239/1039 freight] fright OKES. Misreading or omitted single type.

2.2.240/1040 there] *not in* OKES

2.2.241/1041 of] *not in* OKES

2.2.241/1041 th'] CRANE[1]; the CRANE[2]+

2.2.243/1043 't'ad] t'had CRANE[1], ROSENBACH[A]; it had CRANE[2,4]

2.2.244/1044 that] the ROSENBACH[A]

2.2.244/1044 thou'st] DYCE; thou haſt CRANE[1]+. The passage is not in CRANE[3] or BRIDGEWATER. For the contraction see 2.1.117.

2.2.245/1045 KING] Biſh. CRANE/MATHEWES

2.2.246/1046 You're] you are CRANE[2,3,4]

2.2.246/1046 I'll] ill OKES

2.2.247/1047 I, to[ᴧ]] I[ᴧ] too: ROSENBACH[A]

2.2.249/1049 twice twelve] ᴧ ~ OKES. The variant could easily result from eyeskip.

2.2.250/1050 see so...pommel ᴧ] ſo...pummell ſee OKES. The variant is less metrical; it could have arisen from initial omission (by eyeskip from 'see' to 'so'), followed by a foul proof correction in the right margin, misplaced by the compositor at the end of the line (where it was written) rather than within the line (where it belonged).

2.2.251/1051 Lucrece'] Lucreſes ROSENBACH[A]

2.2.253/1053 fast] laſt OKES. Misreading.

2.2.253/1053 to] into OKES. Contamination from following 'Inquisition', producing a fourteen-syllable line.

2.2.253/1053 th'] CRANE[2,3]; the CRANE[1]+

2.2.255–6/1055–6 Why...aggravated] *prose*? MIDDLETON[T]: ag-gra= | uated

2.2.255/1055 Why] *not in* CRANE[2,3]. Eyeskip.

2.2.257.1/1059 *Exeunt*] *not in* OKES

2.2.257.1/1059 *into the Black House*] THIS EDITION (*conj.* Hotson); *not in* CRANE[1]+. See 1.1.30.1. Pieces have until now always exited into the same house from which they had entered; part of the theatrical tension at the end of Act Two is that the White Queen's Pawn enters Black territory.

2.2.257.2/1059 *Finit Actus Secundus*] ROSENBACH[A], OKES; *Finis ~ Secundj* CRANE[1]

3.1.0.1/1060 *Incipit*] MIDDLETON[T], BRIDGEWATER[B], OKES; *not in* CRANE, ROSENBACH[A]. See 2.1.0.1.

3.1.0.1/1060 *Actus Tertius*] MIDDLETON[T], BRIDGEWATER[B]; ^ *Tertus* OKES; ~ *Tercius* CRANE[1]; ~ *Tercius.* | *Sce[a]. Pri[a].* CRANE[2]; ~ ~ | *Sce[a]. prima.* CRANE[3,4], ROSENBACH[A]

3.1.0.2–3.1.82/1061–1147 *Enter...shame 'em.* | *But*] *not in* CRANE[1]. Part of the addition of the Fat Bishop to the revised version.

3.1.0.2–3/1061 *Enter... in white*] *The Fat-Bishop: Then the B[l]. K[t]. Then his Pawne. Then y[e] white, & Black-Houses (feverally.)* CRANE[3]. For the massed entry, see 1.1.0.2–5.

3.1.0.2/1061 *Enter*] *The* MIDDLETON[B] (written over 'Enter' as part of the improvised transition filling a gap in the manuscript). See 2.2.13.

3.1.0.2/1061 ^ *Fat*] *y[e] ~* CRANE[2,3], MIDDLETON[B]

3.1.0.2–3/1061 *from the White House*] THIS EDITION (*conj.* Hotson); *not in* CRANE[2]+. See 1.1.30.1.

3.1.0.3/1061 *dressed in white*] THIS EDITION; *not in* CRANE[2]+. See 2.2.0.1.

3.1.2/1063 ne'er] ROSENBACH[A]; neuer CRANE[2]+. See 1.1.1.

3.1.3–5/1064–6 It...come.] *not in* CRANE[3]

3.1.3/1064 has] NON-CRANE; hath CRANE[2,4]

3.1.4/1065 strike] fticke OKES. Perhaps authorial, but easily explicable as misreading.

3.1.5/1066 orifex] Orifice BRIDGEWATER[C]. Howard-Hill calls this an 'orthographical variation' (*Pasquin* 307).

3.1.6–7/1067 But...for't] THIS EDITION; *1 line* MIDDLETON[T], ROSENBACH[A], OKES, CRANE/MATHEWES; *not in* CRANE[1], BRIDGEWATER[B]. The extrametrical syllables 'I...for't' are not present in CRANE[2,3].

3.1.6/1067 where is] CRANE[2,3]; where's CRANE[4]+

3.1.7–12/1067–72 I ha'...trial] *not in* CRANE[3]. See next note.

3.1.7/1067 I ha' gaped for't] *not in* CRANE[2,3]. See previous note. This may well be part of the deliberate abridgement in CRANE[3], not an error, and hence not a shared error. Perhaps the line marking the beginning of a cut in the promptbook was misunderstood in CRANE[2], and interpreted as cutting only this phrase.

3.1.7/1067 ha'] haue OKES, CRANE/MATHEWES

3.1.7/1067 gaped] got OKES

*3.1.7/1067 for't] MIDDLETON[T]; for CRANE/MATHEWES; *not in* ROSENBACH[A], OKES, BRIDGEWATER[B] *uncorrected*; for[| BRIDGEWATER[C]. In BRIDGEWATER[B], Howard-Hill (1995) notes that 'for' was 'added in pencil and rewritten in black ink; possibly not contemporary ink' (71). The original transcription thus shared with ROSENBACH[A] and OKES the error of omission. Moreover, although only 'for' is visible, another letter may once have been present at the margin of the page; even the added reading is therefore ambiguous. BRIDGEWATER[C] may share the error 'for' with CRANE/MATHEWES, but given the ambiguity that has not been tabulated among shared errors. Only MIDDLETON[T] unquestionably has the favourite Middleton elision 'fort'.

3.1.8/1068 I'd] NON-CRANE; I'would CRANE[2]; I would CRANE/MATHEWES

3.1.8/1068 preferment] peeferment OKES. Foul case.

3.1.9/1069 breadth] breath OKES. Misreading or omitted type.

3.1.10/1070 fill] fit OKES. Possibly authorial, but more probably a simple misreading.

3.1.12–13/1072–3 If...hospital] *1 line* OKES *only*. Relic.

3.1.13/1073 a] CRANE[2]+ (an). Like HOWARD-HILL, I have modernized the spelling of the article, since the euphonic 'n' presumes an obsolete pronunciation.

3.1.14/1074 diseased bedrid] difeafe bred OKES. Misreading.

3.1.15/1075 dean] dreame OKES. Misreading.

3.1.16/1076 lazy] large ROSENBACH[A]. Misreading of 'lazye' (MIDDLETON[T]).

3.1.17/1077 I've] OKES; I haue CRANE[2]+

3.1.18/1078 does] NON-CRANE; doth CRANE[2,3,4]

3.1.19.1/1078 *from the Black House*] THIS EDITION (*conj.* Hotson); *not in* CRANE[2]+. See 1.1.30.1.

3.1.19–20/1081–2 O...master-trick] holiness | OKES. The error suggests that the printer's copy treated this as a single long line (an authorial relic), which the compositor broke randomly to fit the measure.

3.1.19/1081 O] *not in* BRIDGEWATER[B] *uncorrected*

3.1.19/1081 ^ walks] he ~ ROSENBACH[A]; walke OKES

3.1.20/1082 master-trick] Maifter-peece OKES. The rare word 'master-trick', not recorded in *OED* and possibly a Middleton coinage, has been replaced in OKES by the commonplace 'masterpiece'. See Taylor 1988.

3.1.21/1083 T'undo] To vndo ROSENBACH[A], OKES. BRIDGEWATER[B] began to write 'To', then wrote 'u' over the 'o', so that the corrected text reads 'Tundoo'.

3.1.21/1083 everlastingly] euerlafting OKES

3.1.23/1085 a] an OKES. See 3.1.13.

3.1.25/1087 KNIGHT] K. OKES

3.1.25/1087 ^ reverend] most ~ BRIDGEWATER[B]. Unmetrical anticipation of following line.

3.1.27–32/1089–94 FAT BISHOP...not.] *not in* CRANE[3]

3.1.27/1089 FAT BISHOP] Bl. BRIDGEWATER[B] *uncorrected*

3.1.27/1089 sayst thou] fayth ~ OKES. Assimilation.

3.1.31/1093 skip] flip OKES, CRANE/MATHEWES. The variants here might result from a shared ligature error in the two quartos ('fl' for 'fk'), or from misreading in any of the texts, or from authorial revision. The knight does 'skip', but it does a chess piece no harm if a knight 'skips over' it onto another square. See *OED* slip v.[1], 'to move quickly and softly, without attracting notice; to glide or steal.' Although skip makes sense if *over* means 'onto', that meaning also would render slip intelligible. I have retained autograph skip because of its clearer allusion to chessplay, but without confidence that the alternative is an error.

3.1.32/1094 thou shalt be] you shalbe ROSENBACH[A]

*3.1.33/1095 FAT BISHOP] *not in* MIDDLETON[T], OKES. See next note.

3.1.33/1095 *reads the letter*] *reades* CRANE[2,3] (immediately to the right of the speech prefix, with the text of the letter immediately following on the same line); *Hee ~ ~ ~.* CRANE/MATHEWES (below 3.1.31); ^ ~ ~. MIDDLETON[T], OKES (centred before text of letter begins on following line); ^ ~ ~. BRIDGEWATER[B] (in right margin opposite speech prefix, before text of letter begins on following line), ROSENBACH[A] (centred opposite speech prefix, before text of letter begins on following line). Only the Crane texts contain the verb, but it is implicit in the stage directions of the other witnesses. MIDDLETON[T] and OKES agree not only in accidentally omitting the speech prefix (see previous note), but also in their placement of the direction (which most closely resembles the layout of ROSENBACH). See 3.1.44.

3.1.33–41/1096–1104 Right...supremacy] *verse* CRANE/MATH-
EWES: our | your | proves | fortune | the | you | remove | ;
verse? BRIDGEWATER[B]: our | affection | proves | fortune |
the | you | which | have | . BRIDGEWATER[B] and CRANE/MATH-
EWES share line-breaks at five of the first six lines of this
passage; but it is not clear that BRIDGEWATER[B] intends verse,
and therefore not clear that this is a shared error.

3.1.33/1096 Right] Righ CRANE[3]

3.1.34/1096 noble] holy CRANE[2,3]. Either reading is defensible,
and either could be an error for the other. Although 'reverend
and holy' might seem redundant, 'holy and reverend' occurs
at 4.1.13; a scribe is less likely than an author to be
responsible for the same phrasing, so far apart in the play.
Because this passage is not present in CRANE[1], I cannot
reproduce one reading in *Early* and the other in *Later*. I have
chosen 'noble' as a late authorial variant, but regard both
readings as Middletonian.

3.1.34/1096 ourself] MIDDLETON[T] *only*; Me CRANE[2]+. Late authorial variant.

3.1.34–5/1097–8 our...affection,] *not in* CRANE[3]

3.1.34/1097 true] *not in* CRANE/MATHEWES

3.1.34–5/1097–8 blood...affection] affection...blood OKES

3.1.36–7/1099–1100 at this time the...fortune,] ∧ the...for-
tune at this time OKES. Unlike the immediately preceding
transposition, this one does not produce nonsense, but the
preceding error does not inspire confidence in an authorial
origin of this variant.

3.1.37/1101 general election] ∧ ~ MIDDLETON[T], BRIDGEWATER[B].
Although retained by HOWARD-HILL and therefore not tabulated among shared errors, the variant is hard to explain
except as an error: neither Crane nor any other copyist is
likely to have gratuitously inserted the information provided
by 'general', but it could easily have dropped out by accident.

3.1.39/1102 ha] MIDDLETON[T] *only*; how CRANE[2]+. Late authorial variant.

3.1.39–43/1103–6 which...letter.] *not in* CRANE[3]

3.1.39/1103 at] by MIDDLETON[T], BRIDGEWATER[B]. Anticipation of
'by' four lines later.

3.1.40/1103 have] *not in* OKES. Obviously accidental omission
that produces nonsense.

3.1.42/1105 How] MIDDLETON[T] *only*; hah CRANE[2]+. Late authorial variant. See 3.1.39.

3.1.42/1105 ∧ to my] up ~ ∧ BRIDGEWATER[B]

*3.1.44/1108 FAT BISHOP] CRANE[2,4], ROSENBACH[A]; *reades.* CRANE[3];
not in BRIDGEWATER[B], MIDDLETON[T], OKES. It is clear from the
earlier part of the scene that the Fat Bishop, and not the
Black Knight, should read this second excerpt from the letter,
as he had read the first. At 3.1.32 CRANE[3] has '*fat B. reades*',
so its '*reades*' here may be unambiguous; but like the other
texts it lacks the speech prefix here, and so has been initially
counted among the texts that share the error. The complete
absence of any stage direction or speech prefix in MIDDLETON[T],
OKES, and BRIDGEWATER[B] is clearly a shared error, emended
by HOWARD-HILL. See 3.1.48. This looks like an example of
progressive error, from the ancestral source of CRANE[3] to all
the NON-CRANE texts except ROSENBACH.

*3.1.44/1108 reades] CRANE[2,3]; *not in* [CRANE[4]], NON-CRANE. In
CRANE/MATHEWES the following text of the letter (ll. 43–6)
is typographically distinguished from the dialogue, as had
been the preceding quotation from the letter (ll. 32–40); the
same distinction is made calligraphically for both quotations
in CRANE[2,3]. No calligraphic distinction, for either passage,
is made in MIDDLETON[T] or BRIDGEWATER[B], which therefore are
not necessarily in error (though certainly unhelpful). But OKES

(typographically) and ROSENBACH[A] (calligraphically) share the
error of distinguishing the first passage but not the second,
therefore implying that the first is a quotation but the second
not.

3.1.44–7/1108–11 Think...conclave] *verse* OKES: then | ac-
knowledgement | obedience | loving | ; *verse* ROSENBACH[A]:
through | disobedience | conclave |

3.1.44–5/1108 Think...seriously] *not in* CRANE[3]

3.1.45/1108 then] OKES; *not in* CRANE[2]+. It is hard to explain
the interpolation as accidental; probably a late authorial
variant.

3.1.45/1109 through] tho- | rough BRIDGEWATER[B], thorough
MIDDLETON[T]. In prose the difference between these two
spellings is probably not substantive.

3.1.45–6/1109–10 the...acknowledgement of your disobedi-
ence] your...acknowledgement ∧∧∧ CRANE[3]. Abridgement.

3.1.45/1109 submiss] submissiue CRANE[2,3], DUTTON. BRIDGE-
WATER[B] began to write 'submissi', then altered the final 'i'
to 'e'. Probably 'submissive' results from substitution of a
common for a rare word (Taylor 1988); but 'submiss' could
be a late authorial revision.

3.1.46–7/1110–11 lovingly...brotherly] brotherly...louing
OKES. See transpositions in 3.1.34–7.

3.1.47/1110 received] MIDDLETON[T]; receiuèd CRANE[2]+. Because
this is prose the non-autograph texts apparently paid no
attention to the syllabic distinction in the past participle.

*3.1.48/1112 ∧This] CRANE[2,3,4], ROSENBACH[B], BRIDGEWATER[B] *un-
corrected*; F B ~ BRIDGEWATER[C] (interlined in pencil, with
horizontal and vertical framing lines); F.B. ~ MIDDLETON[T],
OKES. A shared error in autograph, emended by HOWARD-HILL.
See 3.1.44. Apparently, the pencil corrector of BRIDGEWATER
recognized that there must be a speech prefix for the Fat
Bishop between the speech prefixes for the Black Knight
correctly placed at 3.1.42 and 3.1.58; but he misplaced
the necessary speech prefix, inserting it here rather than at
3.1.44. That error also occurs in MIDDLETON[T] and OKES. This
seems to be a clear example of progressive error, following
upon the error at 3.1.44.

3.1.49/1113 bonfire] bondfire BRIDGEWATER[B]. A rare spelling:
OED cites a single 1582 example.

3.1.52–6/1116–20 By...flourishing] *not in* CRANE[3]

3.1.53/1117 Another recantation and inventing] And inuent-
ing another Recantation CRANE/MATHEWES (transposed to follow rather than precede 3.1.53). This looks like a two-stage
or even three-stage error: first the accidental omission of
3.1.52, then its re-insertion one line too late, then transposition of its two phrases to make sense of the result. The
entire sequence of error and miscorrection probably occurred
in Mathewes's shop.

3.1.55/1119 I'm in o' t'] I am ~ on th' CRANE[2,4]; I'me ∧ at OKES

3.1.57/1121 be long] belong OKES

3.1.58/1122 You shall] MIDDLETON[T] *only*; thou ſhalt CRANE[2]+.
Late authorial variant (which substitutes the normal modern
idiom).

3.1.58/1122 shortly] *not in* OKES

3.1.61–7/1125–31 If...th'adversary's] *not in* CRANE[3]

3.1.62/1126 you've] you haue CRANE/MATHEWES

3.1.62/1126 life blood] liue bood OKES

3.1.62/1126 yea] CRANE/MATHEWES; the CRANE[2]+. See 1.1.257.

3.1.63/1127 your primitive] ∧ ~ OKES. Although OKES might
appear to be the more metrical reading, Middleton elsewhere
treats 'primitive' as though it were a two-syllable word. The
repetition of the possessive pronoun after an adjective but

before the noun is definitely a 'rarer' idiom than pronoun–adjective–adjective (Taylor 1988).

3.1.64/1128 of] & BRIDGEWATER[B]

3.1.65/1129 sweet] ſecret ROSENBACH[A]. Misreading.

3.1.66/1130 Which a] ~ the OKES

3.1.66/1130 'specially] eſpecially CRANE[4], ROSENBACH[A]

3.1.67/1131 than] (then); you OKES uncorrected

3.1.67/1131 th'] CRANE/MATHEWES; the CRANE[2]+

3.1.69/1133 fearful'ſt] fearefullſt MIDDLETON[T] (corrected), CRANE[2]+; fearefule MIDDLETON[T] (uncorrected); fearfulleſt ROSENBACH[A], OKES. Though Howard-Hill (1990) noted that the second 'l' in MIDDLETON[T] had been 'altered', the thick clumsy letter seems instead to be overwriting an 'e' like the third letter in 'Sleepers' two lines below; the downstroke of the 'e' is still visible, and the shape of the 'l' is distorted in a way that seems designed to cover that vowel. This suggests that the manuscript Middleton was copying had the same extrametrical expansion present in ROSENBACH and OKES.

3.1.71/1135 urns] veines OKES. Misreading of 'vrnes'.

3.1.72-3/1136-7 Forbear...syrup.] not in CRANE[3]

3.1.72/1136 melt] met OKES uncorrected

3.1.72/1136 i'th'] CRANE[2,4], BRIDGEWATER[B]; i'the ROSENBACH[A], OKES; in the MIDDLETON[T] only. The contraction i'th'—usually spelled without apostrophes—occurs at least 239 times in Middleton's uncollaborative plays; by contrast, the contraction i' the occurs only three times in three uncollaborative plays, and eight times in Chaste Maid (where it almost certainly reflects scribal copy). The metre seems to require one syllable only. See 2.1.147.

*3.1.73/1137 And...syrup] not in CRANE[2,3,4], ROSENBACH[A]. CRANE[3] also omits the preceding line, so the absence of this line might be part of a larger, apparently deliberate abridgement. This line could be a late authorial addition, and therefore should perhaps not be counted among shared errors, since the text makes perfect sense without it. It might also have been censored, since 'a fat bishop' could apply irreverently to other members of the English episcopate. However, in order not to prejudice the tabulation of shared errors by incorporating assumptions about the sequence of texts or their sources, for the purposes of stemmatic analysis it has been treated as a shared error.

3.1.74/1138 Suffices] Suffice OKES

*3.1.75/1139 Ambition's] CRANE[2]+ (Ambitions); Ambitious MIDDLETON[T], OKES. Absence of the possessive apostrophe is normal in Middleton. Nascimento reads MIDDLETON[T] as 'Ambitions'; Howard-Hill reports that 'the u is distinct but incorrect' (1990), and my own examination of the manuscript confirms his observation. Neither Howard-Hill nor Nascimento records the (unambiguous) OKES variant, or its agreement in error with MIDDLETON[T].

3.1.75/1139 fodder] fooder OKES uncorrected

3.1.75/1139 pow'r] CRANE[2,3] (powre); power CRANE/MATHEWES+

3.1.75/1139 draws] draw ROSENBACH[A]

3.1.77/1141 leads me through] ~ ~ throgh OKES corrected; lead ~ ~ OKES uncorrected

3.1.77/1141 field] feilds ROSENBACH[A]

3.1.77.1/1142 Exit] not in BRIDGEWATER[B]

3.1.78/1143 Here's...on] 2 lines BRIDGEWATER[B]: propagate |

3.1.78/1143 paunch] paune OKES corrected; pange OKES uncorrected

3.1.79-80/1144-5 Like...quagmire] not in CRANE[3]

3.1.81/1146 'Mongst] CRANE[3]; amongſt CRANE[2]+; Amongſt MIDDLETON[T] (corrected); up MIDDLETON[T] (uncorrected). Though Howard-Hill (1990) noted that 'Am' had been altered, the

initial originally-written 'u' is still visible above the cross-bar of the 'A'. Middleton mistakenly began to repeat the first word of the line immediately above, then tried to cover the mistake with an uncharacteristic majuscule 'A'. (Elsewhere in autograph 'amongst' always begins with a minuscule.)

3.1.81/1146 and not shame 'em] not in CRANE[3] (regularizing the metre after the previous cut)

3.1.83/1148 With] In CRANE/MATHEWES

3.1.85-90/1150-55 Whose...expedition] not in CRANE[3]

3.1.86/1151 world] Earth CRANE/MATHEWES. Substitution of synonyms. The variant could be authorial: Middleton has 'of the earth' and 'of the world' elsewhere (and earlier in Game).

3.1.87/1152 I] not in OKES. Nonsense-producing omission of single word.

3.1.87/1152 procured] procurèd OKES

3.1.87/1152 gallant fleet] CRANE[2], ROSENBACH[A], BRIDGEWATER[B], OKES; pretious safeguard CRANE[1,4], MIDDLETON[T]. Both readings make sense, and have a claim to authorial origins. The variant adopted in Later is confirmed by Middleton's source for this passage, John Reynolds's Vox coeli (1624), p. 57; it is hard to attribute to anyone other than the author. It is equally hard to explain 'precious safeguard' (preserved in autograph, and adopted in Early 3.6) as a scribal substitution. It might theoretically be due to censorship, but it is hard to see why either phrase would have been censored. Howard-Hill identifies 'gallant fleet' as a late authorial revision (Pasquin 211), reverting to a reading in the book Middleton had in front of him when he originally composed this passage; in principle this is no different than an authorial revision to an original phrase corrupted by intermediaries (or revised by himself at an earlier stage); in both cases the author returns to an earlier reading, which only he is likely to have remembered.

3.1.88/1153 coasts] coaſt BRIDGEWATER[B]

3.1.89/1154 'Gainst] 'Gainſt OKES (text), CRANE[1]+; Againſt OKES (c.w.), CRANE/MATHEWES, ROSENBACH[A]. Shared extrametrical expansion.

3.1.89/1154 th'] CRANE[1,2], OKES; the MIDDLETON[T]+

3.1.89/1154 piràte] CRANE/MATHEWES (Pyrat), MIDDLETON[T] (Pyrate); Pirats CRANE[1]+. Middleton's source used the plural, which has been preserved in Early 3.8: see Reynolds, Vox Coeli, 'to secure the coast of Spain, against the Turkish Pirates' (p. 57). However, the autograph singular-for-plural is possible, and elsewhere Middleton vacillates between singular and plural.

3.1.90/1155 necessitous] neceſſities OKES. Misreading.

3.1.93/1158 property is] property's OKES

3.1.93/1158 with] without OKES. Antonym substitution.

3.1.94/1159 heretic] Heretiques CRANE/MATHEWES. Substitution of common possessive construction for rarer adjectival metaphor.

3.1.94/1159 minute] houre CRANE/MATHEWES. It is typical of Middleton's imagery to seize on the 'minute'.

3.1.95/1160 they've] they'haue CRANE[3]; they haue [CRANE[4]], MIDDLETON[T]

3.1.97/1162 rouses] rayſes CRANE[1]

3.1.99/1164 couches] coaches OKES; chambers BRIDGEWATER[B] uncorrected; couches BRIDGEWATER corrected (interlined). Nascimento attributed the correction to a different hand, but Howard-Hill notes that 'the ink is obviously current and the graphs are those of scribe B' (1995, 19).

3.1.99/1164 there's] their CRANE/MATHEWES, OKES, BRIDGEWATER[C] (altered in pencil from 'theres' to 'their', with a comma inserted after the preceding word).

3.1.100/1165   th'] th'e CRANE[3]; the ROSENBACH[A], BRIDGEWATER[B]

3.1.102/1167   silenced] silent ROSENBACH[A]

3.1.103/1168   barking tongue-men] barking=tongued-~ BRIDGEWATER[C]

3.1.103/1168   of the] ~ that ROSENBACH[A]. The scribe was thinking of the historical past of the real Gondomar, not the dramatic present of the speech.

3.1.104/1169   Made] Mad OKES

3.1.105/1170   suff'rers] CRANE[1]; Sufferers CRANE[2] +

3.1.106–8/1171–3   My light…questioned] to | but | MIDDLETON[T]

3.1.107/1172   drifts] drift OKES

3.1.107/1172   walked] walke CRANE/MATHEWES

3.1.107/1172   uncensured] vncensurèd OKES

3.1.108/1173   whistle…whisper] whisper…whistle CRANE[2,3]

3.1.108/1173   would] might ROSENBACH[A]

3.1.108/1173   questioned] queſtionèd ROSENBACH[A], BRIDGEWATER[B], OKES

3.1.109/1174   of] in OKES. Contamination from earlier in the line.

3.1.109/1174   world,] ~, Venice CRANE[1]

3.1.110/1175   has] hath CRANE[2,3,4]

3.1.111/1176   I have] ˄ haue ROSENBACH[A]. Nascimento records the variant as '& I haue'; 'aue' is clear, and the mark before it might be 'h' or '&', but is certainly not three distinct letters.

3.1.111/1176   got] had BRIDGEWATER, MIDDLETON[T]. Middleton uses both idioms, but the emphatic alliteration of 'got good' seems preferable here, and the variant could easily have arisen from scribal substitution of the much more common word (had).

3.1.111/1176   good] not in BRIDGEWATER[B]

3.1.111/1176   sops] sopes CRANE[1,2,3], BRIDGEWATER[B]; soapes MIDDLETON[T], CRANE/MATHEWES, soaps ROSENBACH[A]; soups OKES. OED records 'sope' but not 'soap(e)' or 'soup' as variant spellings of sop n.[1]; the latter are certainly ambiguous, and perhaps erroneous.

3.1.111/1176   too] not in CRANE/MATHEWES

3.1.112/1177   country ladies] Countries OKES. Unconscious compression of two words into one ('country ladies').

3.1.113/1178   hoped ˄] ~ for OKES. Extrametrical repetition of 'for' from earlier in the line.

3.1.114/1179   i'th'] CRANE[1], ROSENBACH[A], BRIDGEWATER[B]; in th' CRANE[2,3,4], OKES; in the MIDDLETON[T] only. See 2.1.147.

3.1.115/1180   aerium] acrim OKES. Misreading.

3.1.115/1180   mirth] milch ROSENBACH[A]

*3.1.115.1/1182   Enter…Pawn] OKES ('Enter blacke' right margin opposite 'manna'), CRANE[1,2] ('—Enter' right margin between 3.1.115 and 3.1.116). Because CRANE[3] masses entries for the scene, its exact positioning of the direction cannot be determined. But in all other texts the direction is placed too late, after the Black Knight addresses his pawn: in the right margin opposite the first half of 3.1.116 (after 'news') ROSENBACH, CRANE/MATHEWES, and—even more explicitly wrong—below the first half of 3.1.117 MIDDLETON[T], BRIDGEWATER[B].

3.1.115.1/1182   ˄Black Knight's] CRANE/MATHEWES, OKES, ROSENBACH[A]; Bl.˄ CRANE[1]; yᵉ Bl.K[ts] CRANE[2]; Bl.Kts. BRIDGEWATER[B]; Then his CRANE[3] (after 'Bl.K[t]' in massed direction at 3.1.0.1); his MIDDLETON[T]. Given the difference in position and wording, the shared variant 'his' probably reflects authorial preference rather than a direct stemmatic relationship here between CRANE[3] (which shares with earlier Crane texts and BRIDGEWATER[B] the abbreviated 'Bl.Kt') and MIDDLETON[T]. See 2.1.181.

3.1.115.1–2/1182   from the Black House] THIS EDITION (conj. Hotson); not in CRANE[1] +. See 1.1.30.1.

3.1.116/1181   the] what ROSENBACH[A]

3.1.116/1183   BLACK KNIGHT'S] not in CRANE[2,3]; Bl. ˄ CRANE[1]. Given the stage direction and the Black Knight's 'My pawn', identification of the speaker is clear even with the more generic speech prefix, and these variants have not been counted as errors. They probably represent a form used by the author and playbook. CRANE[1,2,3] consistently use, for all his speeches in this scene, the form each uses here. See also 3.1.119.

3.1.117/1184   I'm] I'am CRANE[2]; I am CRANE[1,3,4], BRIDGEWATER[B] uncorrected

3.1.117/1184   for sad things] ſo ~ ˄ OKES. This might be a late authorial revision: Middleton has 'so sad' at Dissemblers 2.1.26.

3.1.118–26/1185–94   BLACK KNIGHT…BLACK KNIGHT'S PAWN] not in CRANE[3]

3.1.118/1185   of late] CRANE[2,4]; alate NON-CRANE; o' late CRANE[1]. See 2.1.157.

3.1.119/1187   BLACK KNIGHT'S] not in CRANE[2]; Bl.˄ CRANE[1], BRIDGEWATER[B]. See 3.1.116. In this scene, the so-called generic speech prefixes link CRANE[1] to CRANE[2,3], ROSENBACH[A], and (here) BRIDGEWATER[B].

3.1.119/1187   yours] yoᵣ BRIDGEWATER[B]

3.1.121–2/1189–90   Mine…driver] CRANE[2]; 1 line CRANE[1] +; and | MIDDLETON[T]. The single syllable is an amphibious section, which fits equally well (or extrametrically) at the end of the preceding or the beginning of the following verse line.

3.1.123/1190   machiavel] Matchauile OKES

3.1.125/1192   Compunction] compunctions ROSENBACH[A]

3.1.125/1192   pricked] pricke OKES. Misreading of 'prickt' (MIDDLETON[T] +).

3.1.126/1193   Unbind] vnkind ROSENBACH[A]. Misreading.

3.1.126/1193   wound] wounded ROSENBACH[A]

3.1.126/1194   discovered] diſcouerèd CRANE[3,4], ROSENBACH[A], OKES

3.1.127, 135/1194, 1207   KNIGHT] K. CRANE[1], CRANE/MATHEWES. From the first line of sig. E3[v] to the bottom of sig. E4 (3.1.126–85, both belonging to the inner forme of the sheet), CRANE/MATHEWES contains a series of errors and changes of speech prefix practice, almost certainly caused by shortage of some italic types. 'Knight' or Knight's has heretofore been abbreviated 'Kni.', but on these two type pages, in speeches that belong to the Black Knight or Black Knight's Pawn, MATHEWES uses the following abbreviations: K. Kni. K. Kts. Kt. K. Kt. Kts. K. K. K. K. K. K. K. K. K. K. K. Kt. K. The catchword at the bottom of E4 reads B.K. (referring to 3.1.186), but the usual form Kni. appears at the top of E4[v], and is used consistently (seven times altogether) on that page. The ambiguous or misleading abbreviations in this stretch of CRANE/MATHEWES thus seem clearly to have originated in the printing house (MATHEWES), and not in the underlying manuscript (CRANE[4]). The variants thus seem entirely independent of the three occurrences in CRANE[1] of K. instead of Kt. in this scene—especially because one of the CRANE[1] examples of K. (at 3.1.134) is Kt. in CRANE/MATHEWES. See 3.1.246.

3.1.127/1195   KNIGHT] Kt[s] BRIDGEWATER[B] uncorrected

*3.1.127/1195   and] not in ROSENBACH[A], BRIDGEWATER[B], OKES. The omission does not change the sense but does disrupt the metre, to no purpose.

3.1.127/1195 hundred] OKES (hundreth), CRANE[2] + (hundred). Spelling variant only.

3.1.128/1196 Fourscore] CRANE/MATHEWES, BRIDGEWATER[B], MIDDLETON[T]; three-score CRANE[1,2,3], ROSENBACH[A], OKES. Late authorial variation. Middleton uses both numbers frequently.

3.1.128/1196 canst tell] not in BRIDGEWATER[B]

3.1.128-45/1197-1217 BLACK KNIGHT'S PAWN...discovered?] not in CRANE[3]

3.1.129/1198 do] CRANE[2,4], MIDDLETON[T]; do's CRANE[1], BRIDGEWATER[B], ROSENBACH[A], OKES. For the variant see note at Early 3.51.

3.1.130/1199 yet] & ROSENBACH[A]

3.1.131/1200 You...sir.] not in CRANE[1]

3.1.131/1200 know] not in OKES. Nonsense-producing omission.

3.1.131/1200 their] theis CRANE[2]

3.1.132/1201 their] MIDDLETON[T], CRANE/MATHEWES; the CRANE[1]+. This could be an error, repeating 'their' from the end of the previous line: 'the number' appears at least ten times elsewhere in the canon. But I have given autograph the benefit of the doubt, and assumed this is a late variant.

3.1.132/1201 number] uumbers CRANE/MATHEWES. The initial turned letter clearly originated in the printing house, but the plural might have been in the manuscript.

3.1.132/1201 trebled] treble BRIDGEWATER[B]

3.1.133/1202 stands] ſtand OKES, CRANE/MATHEWES. Nascimento did not record the CRANE/MATHEWES variant.

3.1.134/1203 sir] not in BRIDGEWATER[B] uncorrected

3.1.134/1203 full of] drawne with OKES. Probably an authorial anticipation of the following line.

3.1.135/1204 KNIGHT] K. CRANE[1]

3.1.135/1204-5 True...oblique] 2 lines: drawn | OKES; some | oblique MIDDLETON[T]

3.1.135/1204 drawn] BRIDGEWATER[B] uncorrected first wrote 'ſ' (skipping ahead to next word), then immediately corrected it to 'd' and continued with 'rawen'.

3.1.136/1206 can scarce] MIDDLETON[T] only; ſcarce can CRANE[1]+. Late authorial variant.

3.1.137/1207 opened] openèd ROSENBACH[A]

3.1.139/1210 Yes] CRANE[2]; I CRANE[1]+. Middleton's early preference for ay (spelled 'I') shifted, during the second decade of the seventeenth century, to a preference for the more modern yes. The older form is preserved in Early 3.62, the modern alternative here.

3.1.140-1/1211-12 That...fastened] pick | ROSENBACH[A]

3.1.140/1211 has] hath CRANE[2]

3.1.140/1211 state] not in CRANE/MATHEWES

3.1.140/1211 pick] pricke CRANE/MATHEWES. Misreading.

3.1.141/1212 every] the CRANE/MATHEWES. Unmetrical repetition from earlier in line.

3.1.142/1213 'Twill] it will CRANE[2]; And will OKES (probably resulting from a misreading of 't' as '&').

3.1.142/1214 I'm] I am CRANE[1,2,4]

3.1.143/1215 to fall thick] too full ∧ OKES. Misreading compounded (or caused) by single word omission.

3.1.144/1216 They'd] They'had CRANE[2]; They had CRANE/MATHEWES; The'd OKES

3.1.144/1216 need] ~ to BRIDGEWATER[B] uncorrected

3.1.144/1216 use] of CRANE[2]. (Not recorded by Nascimento, but the variant is clear by comparison with other examples of 'vse' and 'of' in the same manuscript.)

3.1.145/1217 discovered] diſcouerèd ROSENBACH[A], CRANE/MATHEWES, OKES

3.1.145/1218 brat] bruite OKES. Misreading.

3.1.146/1219 'twixt] betwixt CRANE[2,3,4]; between ROSENBACH[A]

3.1.147/1220 'bout] about CRANE/MATHEWES

3.1.148-9/1221-2 BLACK KNIGHT...BLACK KNIGHT'S PAWN] not in CRANE[3]

3.1.148/1221 KNIGHT] P BRIDGEWATER[B] uncorrected

3.1.148/1221 Discovered] diſcouerèd ROSENBACH[A], CRANE/MATHEWES, OKES

3.1.149/1222-3 The...seems] 2 lines MIDDLETON[T]: policy |

3.1.149/1223 has] hath CRANE, BRIDGEWATER[B]

3.1.149/1223 it seems] not in CRANE[3]

3.1.150/1224 Joined] Ioynèd OKES

3.1.150/1224 th'] the BRIDGEWATER[B]

3.1.150/1224 his] this OKES. Misreading.

3.1.151/1225 Bishop's White] white bishops BRIDGEWATER[B], ROSENBACH[A], OKES. Unmetrical transposition, substituting a common for a rare word-order. See Taylor 1988. Because the variant was preferred in HOWARD-HILL, it has not been tabulated among shared errors.

3.1.152/1226 discharged] diſchargèd OKES

3.1.152/1226 like] as BRIDGEWATER[B]

3.1.153/1227 I] CRANE[1]+; And HOWARD-HILL. 'The Black Knight's Pawn is not likely to have fitted his adversary to frustrate the Black Knight's plot' (Howard-Hill). The emendation misunderstands a sexual joke. Black Knight's Pawn, by castrating White Bishop's Pawn, has removed his testicles, which in early modern slang were called 'stones'; by removing stones, you make something light (particularly because a 'stone' is also a measurement of weight, equivalent to fourteen pounds). Domestic animals were routinely castrated precisely in order to improve their usefulness. This is a typical Middletonian irony: thinking to disable White Bishop's Pawn, the Black House has actually improved his ability to defeat them. See Taylor 2000, 43–6, 257.

3.1.153/1227 the] his BRIDGEWATER[B]

3.1.154-6/1228-32 BLACK KNIGHT...for't.] not in CRANE[3]

*3.1.154-5/1228-9 It's...parts] CRANE[1,2], BRIDGEWATER[B], OKES; way | ROSENBACH[A], MIDDLETON[T]; not in CRANE[3]. For CRANE/MATHEWES see note after next. The mislineation must have been shared by [CRANE[4]], ROSENBACH[A], and MIDDLETON[T].

3.1.154/1228 It's] CRANE[2]; 'tis CRANE[1]+. See Induction.15.

3.1.154-5/1229 a little...parts] not in CRANE/MATHEWES. This omission indicates that in the copy for MATHEWES, or the copy for [CRANE[4]], these words were a single line of manuscript, as they are (incorrectly) in ROSENBACH[A] and MIDDLETON[T]. See preceding lineation note. This is therefore an example of progressive error: the mislineation precedes the related substantive error. But since the substantive error does not appear in any other witness, it is likely that the printer was responsible for it.

3.1.155/1229 ∧ Enough] There's ~ OKES

*3.1.155.1-6/1230-31 Enter...White House] CRANE[2,4], OKES (position). Uniquely, CRANE[1] places the direction earlier (beginning in the right margin, opposite 3.1.154). By contrast, ROSENBACH[A] places it below 3.1.156; this is clearly mistaken, since the Black Bishop must either be given a separate entrance before he speaks, or he must be included with the entrance for the rest of the Black House (which then must enter before he speaks). BRIDGEWATER[B] places an identically worded direction in the same late position, but it also adds 'Enter' to the right of the speech prefix for the Black Bishop in 3.1.155, pushing the half-line of his speech down onto the next line of text. This bears every appearance of an afterthought: the scribe copied the speech prefix for the speech, then realized that the character was not on stage, and added

'Enter' after the name (rather than before it). MIDDLETON[T] puts 'Enter Bl.Bishop' in the right margin after the character's half-line completing 3.1.155: that is, after the character has entered, and after the speech prefix (as in BRIDGEWATER[B]), but also after the character's actual short speech; then on the following line, MIDDLETON[T] adds 'and both the houses.' The three texts which erroneously place the direction too late are clearly linked to one another, with BRIDGEWATER[B] seemingly representing an intermediate stage between the other two.

3.1.155.1/1230 *Black Bishop*] CRANE[1], MIDDLETON[T], BRIDGE-WATER[B]; *not in* CRANE[2]+. For BRIDGEWATER see preceding note. The omission of a separately-indicated entry for the Black Bishop cannot be considered an error, since he is implied in the direction for entry of the Black House; but the autograph specification, seconded (independently) by the earliest extant manuscript, suggests that Middleton imagined the Black Bishop as the first character on stage.

3.1.155.1/1231 *followed by*] THIS EDITION; *&* CRANE[1] (after 3.1.154), and MIDDLETON[T] (after 'then' in 3.1.155). See previous notes. I regard 'followed by' not as an emendation but as an interpretation of the separately specified initial entrance of the Black Bishop, and of three texts' placement of the entrance of both houses later than his first words.

3.1.155.1-6/1231 *Black King ... White House*] THIS EDITION; *the wh. House, & Bl. House.* CRANE[1]; *y[e] white & Black-houses* (seuerally) CRANE[2,3]; *both Houfes feuerally.* CRANE/MATHEWES; both the houfes ROSENBACH[A], BRIDGEWATER[B], MIDDLETON[T]; *both Houfes.* OKES. See 2.2.81.1-4 and 5.1.9.2 for comparable emendations; see 3.1.175.1 and 207.1 for the separate entrances of White Queen's Pawn and Black Queen's Pawn. As the Black Knight and Black Knight's Pawn are already present, and as some witnesses also give a separate entrance to the Black Bishop, 'both houses' must describe the general visual effect produced by this direction, rather than indicate precisely who enters. The entrance is clearly meant to echo the similar moment in 2.2. The editorial emendation changes the early witnesses in three ways. First, it specifies which characters enter. Second, it interprets 'severally' to refer to separate doors, and equates those doors with the White and Black Houses, as in 1.1.0.2-4. Third, as a consequence of the first two changes, it reverses the order in which the 'white' and 'black' houses are mentioned, on the assumptions that the entries are simultaneous, not sequential, and that the Black Bishop enters from the same door as other Black characters.

3.1.155.3/1231 *and pawns*] THIS EDITION; *not in* CRANE[1]+. It is possible that the Black Bishop's Pawn remains absent, since he was absent in the preceding scene, and does not speak; however, his superior (the Black Bishop) is there to speak for him. The scene could be played intelligibly with or without him.

3.1.155/1230 *then*] *not in* CRANE[1]

3.1.157/1233 WHITE KING] BRIDGEWATER[B] *uncorrected* placed this prefix (in the form 'wh. k[g].') at the end of the stage direction for the entrance of both houses (at 3.1.155.6), then deleted it there and placed it on a separate line above the beginning of this speech.

3.1.157/1233 *that*] the CRANE[1,4]

3.1.159/1235 *adversary*] Aduersaries CRANE[1,4]

3.1.159-60/1236 *WHITE ... WHITE KING*] *not in* CRANE[3]

3.1.159/1236 KNIGHT] k. ROSENBACH[A], CRANE/MATHEWES. For the quarto's ambiguous abbreviations throughout this section of text, see 3.1.127. Consequently, ROSENBACH[A] is in effect the only witness for this variant. It would certainly be appropriate

for the Black King to respond to the White King's speech, and to be the first black character to speak in the 'public' part of the scene. But given the ease with which a 't' could be omitted from one speech prefix, and the tendency of the Black Knight to dominate and stage manage the action, the variant is probably a simple error.

3.1.159/1236 *Exit a pawn*] THIS EDITION; *not in* CRANE[1]+; *Exit W. Kg's Pawn* DYCE; *Exit a* WHITE PAWN HARPER. The White King's speech calls for someone to go fetch the White Queen's Pawn, and even promptbooks of the period often omit such exit directions for attendants. However, since she is imprisoned in the Black House, it is not clear whether a white or a black pawn goes to fetch her, and neither could do so unless authorized by someone in the Black House; hence, the direction should (as in THIS EDITION) follow rather than precede (as in DYCE and other modern editions) 'Good'. Otherwise, 'Good' serves no discernible purpose.

3.1.160-2/1237-9 *a title ... comprised in*] *not in* CRANE[3]

3.1.162/1239 *comprised*] comprizèd ROSENBACH[A], OKES

3.1.164/1241 *that*] her CRANE[3]; the CRANE[4], ROSENBACH[A]. 'Her' could be an authorial variant, corrupted in CRANE/MATHEWES and ROSENBACH[A].

3.1.165-6/1242-3 *Where ... consecrated*] *not in* CRANE[3]

3.1.165/1242 *fame*] Fames CRANE[1,2], ROSENBACH[A]. In order to explain 'fame ... are', HOWARD-HILL glosses the singular as 'a collective noun'; it would be easier to explain the failure of concord as a result of the intervening 'knights'. Although the plural is the rarer idiom (Taylor 1988), it could be explained as a scribal correction of Middleton's grammar; alternatively, the singular could be a late shared error. In the absence of certainty the plural has been retained in *Early* 3.93 and the singular in *Later*.

3.1.165/1242 *of*] *not in* OKES

3.1.168/1245 *Duke*] piece CRANE[1,4]. The reading in CRANE/MATHEWES cannot be compositorial, but must represent a conscious or unconscious reversion to the original reading.

3.1.170-6/1247-54 *WHITE DUKE ... fidelity.*] *not in* CRANE[3]

3.1.170/1247 *blest*] bleffèd OKES, ROSENBACH[A]

3.1.170/1247 *throned*] throand BRIDGEWATER[B]; throughand BRIDGEWATER[C]. The interlinear pencil correction is ambiguous: it might intend 'through and in all royal graces' (*Pasquin* 215) or simply 'through' (neglecting to delete 'and', when the replacement was inserted).

3.1.171/1248 *reward*] rewards OKES

3.1.172/1249 *enterpriser*] enterprize ROSENBACH[A]. Common substituted for rare word (Taylor 1988).

3.1.173/1250 *t'*] CRANE[1,4]; to CRANE[2]+

3.1.174/1251 *munificency*] OKES; Munificence MIDDLETON[T]+; Magnificence CRANE/MATHEWES. The terminal -y produces the much rarer form, which could be a late authorial revision.

*3.1.175.1/1252 *Enter ... Pawn*] CRANE[1]; *not in* CRANE[2]+. The need for an entrance was recognized by DYCE and other editors, even before the discovery of CRANE[1]. DYCE supplied the entrance after 3.1.178, which was a reasonable guess in the absence of CRANE[1]; but HARPER and HOWARD-HILL retain that position, without explaining their departure from the sole authority for the direction. It is unlikely that CRANE[1] placed the direction four manuscript lines too early, without reason. Conceivably, the intervening lines are an authorial afterthought; Middleton's original draft might have placed the direction at that point, before he decided to add the White King's speech. But it is also possible that she appears in the doorway before she is noticed, and that the White King's 'appear' calls her forward to receive his personal attention; her presence might then render 'desert(s)...zeal and fidelity' ironically more applicable to her than to White Duke Buckingham. It does not make sense for her to enter as the result of a speech by the White King, when someone has already been sent to fetch her.

3.1.175.1/1252 *Enter*] CRANE[1]; *Re-enter White King's Pawn with* DYCE; ~ WHITE PAWN *with* HARPER. See 3.1.159. Although logically the pawn that went to fetch her should accompany her return, such symmetries are not always observed in the theatre, even now, because they may clutter and distract from the entrance of an important character. The exit in response to a command is a necessary theatrical sign of the authority of the commander, and a suspense-producing promise of an imminent entrance; but when that promised entrance comes it is theatrically self-sufficient. A re-entrance of the unidentified messenger pawn is possible but not necessary.

3.1.175.1-2/1252 *from the Black House*] THIS EDITION (conj. Hotson); *not in* CRANE[1] +. See 1.1.30.1. This entrance *from* the 'wrong' house echoes and reverses the effect of her entrance *into* the 'wrong' house at the end of 2.2.

3.1.175/1253 deserts claim] MIDDLETON[T], BRIDGEWATER[B], OKES; defert claimes CRANE, ROSENBACH. Late autograph variant.

3.1.176-8/1254-6 Appear...glorious] innocence | mak'st | CRANE[3] (omitting 3.1.170-6, 'Most...fidelity', and 3.1.179, 'I'll...on't')

3.1.177/1255 innocence] Innocency CRANE/MATHEWES. Extrametrical misreading. The form 'innocency' was not at all rare: in the period 1580–1640 LION records 359 examples.

3.1.178/1256 Of patience...glorious] *2 lines* ROSENBACH[A]: suff'rings |

3.1.178/1256 mak'st] mad'ft OKES; makeft ROSENBACH[A]; makes CRANE[1]

3.1.178/1256 suff'rings] sufferings ROSENBACH[A], OKES. Shared extrametrical expansion.

3.1.179/1257 I'll...on't.] *not in* CRANE[3]

3.1.179/1257 knowledge] notice ROSENBACH[A]

3.1.180/1258 dares yon] ~ you OKES[1]; dare OKES[2]. A good example of progressive error: the accidental u/n leads to deliberate 'correction' of 'dares' to 'dare'.

3.1.182/1260 Has] hath CRANE

3.1.183-94/1261-75 Let...shroud in.] *not in* CRANE[3]

3.1.184/1262 that's] 'tis CRANE/MATHEWES. Anticipation.

3.1.184/1262 born] bound OKES. Misreading.

3.1.185/1263-4 KNIGHT...KING] *K....Kt.* CRANE/MATHEWES. See 3.1.127. The variant here cannot be directly due to type shortage, since MATHEWES does distinguish between the two prefixes. This might be a late authorial variant: for an exact parallel, with a unique autograph variant reversing the order of attribution of two consecutive short speeches, see 3.1.264-5. However, the variant might have occurred as a consequence of a miscorrection in foul proof of two consecutive 'W.K.' speech prefixes—or the compositor may have set 'W.K.' for the first prefix (in line with his practice elsewhere in these two pages), and only when setting the second prefix realized that it would be identical, and consequently, in order to save time and labour, changed the second prefix rather than going back to the first.

3.1.185-6/1265-6 Assist...again] *1 line* ROSENBACH[A]. Relic.

3.1.185/1263 this] 'tis MIDDLETON[T] *only*

3.1.185/1264 I'm] I am CRANE

3.1.185/1265 QUEEN's] *not in* CRANE[1], ROSENBACH[A], BRIDGEWATER[B]. For the generic prefix for this character in earlier scenes, in both CRANE[1] and ROSENBACH[A], see 1.1.6. This is her

first speech in this scene, and the only example of this generic prefix in BRIDGEWATER[B] (perhaps by a simple inadvertent omission). See 3.1.216, 232.

3.1.186/1267 I've] OKES; I'haue CRANE[2]; I haue CRANE[1] +

3.1.186/1267 'mazed] amazed CRANE/MATHEWES; mard ROSENBACH[A]

3.1.187/1268 Scattered] fcattered ROSENBACH[A], OKES

3.1.187/1268 their] by OKES

3.1.187/1268 admiration] CRANE[2], MIDDLETON[T], ROSENBACH[A], OKES; Admirations CRANE[1,4], BRIDGEWATER[B]. Either reading could be an error for the other; the singular could be an authorial variant present in the playbook, later corrupted or deliberately replaced with the original reading. Given the impossibility of determining the sequence of intentions or inadvertencies here—and the fact that the singular appears both in autograph and in an early text stemmatically distant from it (CRANE[2])—I have printed the plural in *Early* 3.119 and the singular in *Later*.

3.1.187/1268 innocence] inncence ROSENBACH[A]. Perhaps intended to signal an elision, but the form is unrecorded elsewhere (and ambiguously suggests 'incense'), and is probably just a slip of the pen.

3.1.188/1269 ships] Ship CRANE[1,4], BRIDGEWATER[B] *uncorrected*. Although the plural is historically correct, the error may be authorial: see *Early* 3.120, where the singular is defended and retained. The presence of the singular in two later texts might be a simple error of omission of terminal -s, by scribe or compositor, or an inconsistent return to the author's original reading. The uncorrected BRIDGEWATER[B] reading is recorded in Howard-Hill's transcript, but not in his 1995 list of shared variants (*Pasquin*, p. 278), or in Nascimento.

3.1.188/1269 severed] fecurd CRANE[1]

3.1.189-90/1270-71 In...justice] is | CRANE/MATHEWES

3.1.190/1271 this] his OKES

3.1.190/1272 Is] *not in* OKES (eyeskip: 'Is Iniured')

3.1.191/1272 injured] Iniurèd OKES

3.1.193/1274 most equal] iuft BRIDGEWATER[B]; vnequall OKES. BRIDGEWATER[B] substitutes a cliché: in literary works published between 1580 and 1640 LION records 46 examples of 'iust heauen(s)'. By contrast it has only eleven examples of 'most equal(l)', none of them modifying 'heauen(s)'. OKES, by contrast, has the opposite of the sense apparently required.

3.1.194/1276 KNIGHT] CRANE/MATHEWES (*Kni.*), BRIDGEWATER[B] *uncorrected* (K[t]); K[g] BRIDGEWATER[B] *corrected*; K. CRANE[2], ROSENBACH[B]; Ki. OKES; King. CRANE[1,3], MIDDLETON[T]. Unlike the variants at 3.1.185, 'Kni.' here occurs on a page without evidence of systematic disruption of speech prefixes due to type shortage; it therefore probably derives from [CRANE[4]], rather than the printing shop. Its presence in uncorrected BRIDGEWATER[B] also suggests that it originated in the manuscript stages of the stemma. The variant makes sense, as White Knight was responsible for the plan to expose the antedated letters—and had also become, by the time MATHEWES/ALLDE was printed, King of England. Although either abbreviation could be an error for the other, the coexistence of three such variants, all contributing to the same shift of attention from King/James to Knight/Charles, looks less like error and more like authorial intervention: see 3.1.227, 235.

3.1.194/1276 That] MIDDLETON[T], BRIDGEWATER[B]; This CRANE[1] +. Late authorial variant.

3.1.195/1277 an] any OKES

3.1.195-8/1277-80 'Tis...else.] *not in* CRANE[3]

3.1.196/1278 does] doth CRANE[2,4]

3.1.197-8/1279-80 When…testimony] 3 lines ROSENBACH^A: clear | else |

3.1.197/1279 conscïence] ROSENBACH^A; vnderſtanding CRANE¹+. This could well be a late authorial variant, deliberately removing the repetition 'understand…understanding', which seems redundant rather than functional. There is nothing in the immediate context to prompt the substituted word. Middleton has 'clear conscience' at *Virtue* 244-5 and *Aries* 132, and 'the clearness of her conscience' at *Truth* 357. For trisyllabic *conscïence* see *Timon* 6.87, *Widow* 5.1.126, etc.

3.1.198/1280 does] doth CRANE^{2,4}

3.1.199/1281 Confirmed] Confirmèd OKES

3.1.199/1281 men] mens BRIDGEWATER^B uncorrected

3.1.199/1281 foul] falce CRANE³

*3.1.199/1281 attempter] attempt CRANE/MATHEWES, ROSENBACH^A

3.1.201/1283 forged] forgèd OKES

3.1.201/1283 for ten] ₍ fix OKES. The printer's error would be easier to explain if the manuscript read 'for fix', permitting easy eyeskip; in which case 'six' might be a late authorial variant.

3.1.202/1284 that] the OKES, CRANE/MATHEWES

3.1.203/1285 you have] CRANE¹+. On four occasions—1.1.177, 4.2.102, 5.3.1, 5.3.62—the contraction is indicated in only a single manuscript, so it is entirely possible that an intended contraction *you've* might occasionally have been marked in none of the surviving witnesses. But here the extra unstressed syllable at the caesura is common enough, and the context seems to demand a stress on *you* that the contraction would discourage.

*3.1.203/1285 waked] walkd ROSENBACH^A, walkt OKES. Misreading.

3.1.204/1286 rash] much BRIDGEWATER^B uncorrected; much rafs BRIDGEWATER corrected

3.1.205/1288 That] this CRANE^{2,3}

3.1.206/1289 as wise] CRANE¹, MIDDLETON^T, ROSENBACH^A; ſo ~ CRANE²+. There are no exact parallels in Middleton for 'so [adjective] as [adjective]', or for 'half so…as', but Middleton uses 'as…as' often in this situation, and compare 'half as ill as' at *Solomon* 2.15. Late autograph agrees with the earliest witness in a Middletonian construction, which was probably sophisticated in intermediate texts.

3.1.206/1289 impudent] impudence CRANE/MATHEWES

3.1.207/1290 She'd] She'would CRANE²; She would CRANE³

3.1.207/1290 farther] MIDDLETON^T (Farder), CRANE¹+; further CRANE/MATHEWES. Middleton's autograph consistently prefers 'fa-'.

3.1.207.1/1291 Enter…Pawn] not in CRANE^{2,3}. Both CRANE¹ and CRANE/MATHEWES begin the direction in the right margin opposite 3.1.206, but this is probably because there is not enough space for the whole direction in the margin opposite 3.1.207, or space to continue the direction opposite 3.1.208.

3.1.207.1-2/1292 from the Black House] THIS EDITION (conj. Hotson); not in CRANE¹+. See 1.1.30.1.

3.1.208/1292 QUEEN'S] not in CRANE¹. This variant, unique to the *Early* version, is recorded only because ROSENBACH^A, beginning here, does *not* use the generic prefix for the Black Queen's Pawn, a variant that continues in CRANE¹ for the rest of her speeches in this scene. But see the ROSENBACH^A speech prefix variants at 3.1.237, 238, 239.

3.1.208/1291 aside] CRANE² places the first two lines of the speech within round brackets, presumably to indicate that they are spoken aside.

3.1.208/1293 treach'ry] CRANE^{1,2} (Treachrie); Treacherie CRANE³+

3.1.209-10/1294-5 Since…goodness] in | MIDDLETON^T

3.1.209/1294 all's] all ours OKES

3.1.209/1294 strangely] not in CRANE¹

3.1.209/1294 strangely in] in ſtrongly OKES. Misreading and transposition.

3.1.210/1295 is this] ~ his OKES

3.1.211/1296 prize] OKES; price CRANE/MATHEWES; peice MIDDLETON^T+. The quarto readings are essentially identical, since *prize* was not consistently orthographically distinguished from *price*. Both 'peice' and 'prize' make sense, and could be authorial; the same variant recurs, in different witnesses, four lines below. See next note.

3.1.211/1296 equal] OKES; value CRANE¹+. Late authorial variant, difficult to attribute to misreading or any other obvious source of error. For 'can equal' compare *Revenger* 2.1.152.

3.1.212-13/1297-8 This…fury?] not in CRANE³

3.1.212/1297 rock] worke ROSENBACH^A. Misreading.

3.1.213/1298 made] makes ROSENBACH^A

3.1.214/1299 distracted] detracted OKES

3.1.214/1300 think] thinik BRIDGEWATER^B (intending 'thinck')

3.1.215/1301 There's] OKES; there is CRANE¹+. Late authorial metrical revision; *Early* 3.150 presupposes a line-divided foot.

3.1.215/1301 masterpiece] ROSENBACH^A, BRIDGEWATER^B uncorrected; Master-Prize CRANE¹+. The meaning is the same; the obsolete form is preserved in *Early* 3.150, the modern form here in *Later*.

3.1.216/1302 This] The CRANE/MATHEWES

3.1.216/1303 QUEEN'S] not in BRIDGEWATER^B uncorrected. See 3.1.185.

3.1.216-23/1303-13 Let…other.] not in CRANE³

3.1.217.1 She…Pawn] THIS EDITION; not in CRANE¹+

3.1.218/1306 BLACK KNIGHT…still.] This is the first line on sig. F1 of MATHEWES/ALLDE, the beginning of the text printed by Allde.

3.1.218/1306 Well] not in OKES

3.1.220/1309 of] on ROSENBACH^A. The collocation 'think(e)s of' occurs about forty times in the Middleton canon, including 'thinks of me' at *Old Law* 3.2.311. See 1.1.255.

3.1.221/1311 unlaid] vnlayèd OKES

3.1.222/1312 However] OKES (How euer); how any CRANE¹+. In literature printed in Middleton's lifetime LION lists 'how any' only five times, 'however' 330 times: the autograph variant is undoubtedly the 'rarer reading' (Taylor 1988), and has been retained in *Early* 3.161. But Middleton uses 'however' at least thirteen times, and there are no Middleton parallels for 'how any'. The OKES variant could therefore easily by an authorial revision, and has been preferred in *Later*.

3.1.226-7/1316-17 BLACK…duel.] not in CRANE³

3.1.226/1316 QUEEN] OKES (Q.); K^t CRANE¹+. The three preceding speeches by the Black Queen's Pawn have been immediately followed by a speech by her mistress, the Black Queen. The OKES variant extends this formal pattern, and expands the Black Queen's role. The variant could easily be authorial, and is not particularly likely to be a scribal or compositorial error.

3.1.226/1316 there] here BRIDGEWATER^B

3.1.227/1317 'T'ad] It had CRANE. In BRIDGEWATER^B uncorrected something was originally written between 'T' and 'ad' (perhaps 'h') before being deleted.

3.1.227/1317 duel] Diuell OKES. Misreading of 'Duell'.

3.1.227/1318 KNIGHT] CRANE/ALLDE (Kni.); D. BRIDGEWATER^B uncorrected; Kg BRIDGEWATER^B corrected; K. MIDDLETON^T, CRANE², ROSENBACH^A; Ki. OKES; King. CRANE^{1,3}. See 3.1.193, where CRANE/MATHEWES has the same unique, and apparently deliberate, variant 'Kni.'. The presence of the variants in work by two different printers suggests that they originated in [CRANE[4]]. Here, as there, the variant gives the White Knight a stronger role in justifying and defending the White Queen's Pawn. The same effect would be achieved by giving the line to the White Knight's partner in her vindication, the White Duke. Given the normal abbreviations, either 'Knight' or 'King' could be a misreading of the alternative; the presence of 'Duke' as a further alternative—harder to explain as a simple misreading—suggests that Middleton vacillated over attribution of these speeches. See 3.1.234.

3.1.227-8/1318-19   Then ... intended] CRANE[1,2], MIDDLETON[T]; *I line* CRANE/ALLDE, OKES, ROSENBACH[A], BRIDGEWATER[B]; *passage not in* CRANE[3]. Relic. BRIDGEWATER has a unique comma after 'heardst'; as elsewhere, punctuation is used to compensate for mislineation.

3.1.228-9/1320-1   'Tis ... agent] *I line* OKES. Relic.

3.1.228-9/1320-21   truth, ... justify.] CRANE[3]; ~,~: CRANE[1,2]; ~,~, MIDDLETON[T], ROSENBACH[A]; ~,~,~, BRIDGEWATER[B]; ~.~, CRANE/ALLDE; ~,~, OKES. All the texts except BRIDGEWATER[B], OKES, and CRANE/ALLDE have punctuation only in the second position; BRIDGEWATER[B] has no punctuation at all, and the two quartos agree in placing their only punctuation mark in the first position. The punctuation of both quartos seems clearly and substantively wrong.

3.1.229/1321   sir] MIDDLETON[T] *only; not in* CRANE[1]+. Late authorial variant, providing a respectful vocative in her address to the King.

3.1.230/1322   confused] confuſèd OKES

3.1.231/1323   startled] ſtarted OKES. The variant is synonymous, and appears elsewhere with this meaning in *Phoenix* 9.236 and *No Wit* 9.254.

3.1.231/1323   him] CRANE[2,3]; his Attempt CRANE[1]+. The variant is not only metrically more regular, but Middletonian: compare 'startled you' (5.2.65) and 'startles him' (opening stage direction of *Changeling* 4.1).

3.1.232-6/1324-8   WHITE QUEEN'S PAWN ... done.] *not in* CRANE[3]

3.1.232/1324   QUEEN'S] *not in* CRANE[1], ROSENBACH[A]. See 3.1.185. Notice that, in the character's second speech in this scene, BRIDGEWATER[B] does not share the generic variant.

3.1.232/1324   has] hath CRANE[2,4]

3.1.233/1325   stand] ſtood CRANE/ALLDE; ſtands OKES

3.1.233/1325   engaged] engage OKES[1]. An obvious error, probably from misreading, corrected even in OKES[2] (and therefore perhaps in some copies of OKES[1]).

3.1.235/1327   KNIGHT] ROSENBACH[A] (K.[t]), CRANE/ALLDE (*Kni.*); *King.* CRANE[1,3]; *K.* CRANE[2], MIDDLETON[T]; *Ki.* OKES; *D.* BRIDGEWATER[B] *uncorrected*; *Kg* BRIDGEWATER *corrected*. The attribution of this speech to White Knight in ROSENBACH[A] confirms that the variant (differently spelled) in CRANE/ALLDE did not originate in the printing house but almost certainly stood in [CRANE[4]]. Since both CRANE/MATHEWES and CRANE/ALLDE normally use 'K.' for King and 'Kni.' for Knight, those forms probably stood in [CRANE[4]] (unless the printers had agreed beforehand on certain features of the book). Attribution of the speech to White Knight might be a shared error, but it might also be a late authorial variant: see the related variants at 3.1.194, 227. Moreover, the uncorrected BRIDGEWATER[B] reading suggests that another potentially authorial variant, White Duke, might have been present in a lost manuscript. The speech could be attributed to any White character.

3.1.235/1327   Does] Doth CRANE[2,4]

3.1.236/1328   believed] beleeuèd ROSENBACH[A], OKES

3.1.236.1   *The Black House speaks apart*] THIS EDITION; *not in* CRANE[1]+

3.1.237/1329   BLACK KING] *W.Kni.* CRANE/ALLDE. This error presumably arose from contamination from the speech prefix at 3.1.235 (the copyist lapsing into the assumption of an alternating pattern). Alternatively, eyeskip might have led to the accidental omission of 3.1.235-6 ('Does ... Bl.K.'), subsequently corrected but with the speech prefix inadvertently repeated.

3.1.237/1331   BISHOP] P. ROSENBACH[A]

3.1.237/1332   DUKE] P. ROSENBACH[A] *uncorrected* (inadvertent repetition from preceding line)

3.1.237/1332   Trait'rous] OKES; Trayterous MIDDLETON[T]+

3.1.238, 239/1333, 1336   BLACK QUEEN'S PAWN] Bl.P. CRANE[1]; Bl: P. ROSENBACH[A]. See 3.1.208. Nascimento recorded the gap in ROSENBACH[A] as a variant, presumably because it might mean that the ROSENBACH[A] scribe could not read the intermediate letter form, or perhaps was unsure how to expand and clarify a generic speech prefix like that in CRANE[1]. However, on other occasions there is a similar gap where no intermediate letter could be inserted, and which Nascimento does not record as a variant: compare 3.1.299 ('wh. D.').

3.1.238/1333   beside yourselves] mad BRIDGEWATER[B] *uncorrected*

3.1.238/1333   beside] beſides ROSENBACH[A], CRANE/ALLDE, OKES. In early modern usage, only a spelling variant.

3.1.238-9/1334-5   But ... Pawn] *I line* OKES. See next note.

3.1.238/1334   I:] ~, BRIDGEWATER[B], OKES. See preceding note. Progressive error: the lack of punctuation here, combined with the mislineation in OKES, produces in the quarto the false sense 'But I remember that pawn' (instead of 'except me: remember that fact, pawn').

3.1.239/1335   Pawn] Knight ROSENBACH[A] *uncorrected*

3.1.240/1337   pleasures] comeforts BRIDGEWATER[B] *uncorrected*. Nascimento attributed the interlined correction to a different hand, but Howard-Hill notes that 'the ink is obviously current and the graphs are those of scribe B' (1995, 19).

3.1.241/1338   in my] in my in my BRIDGEWATER[B] *uncorrected*

3.1.242/1340   ‸ won] not ~ OKES. Possibly authorial, but anticipating the beginning of the next line.

3.1.243/1341   not I] I not CRANE/ALLDE

3.1.243/1341   machination] machiuation OKES. Foul case.

3.1.244-5/1342-3   I ... to't.] *not in* CRANE[3]

3.1.244/1342   smelt] ſmell OKES. Misreading.

3.1.245/1343   covered] couerèd OKES

3.1.245/1343   I'm] I'am CRANE[2]; I am CRANE/ALLDE

3.1.245/1343   to't] to it MIDDLETON[T] *only*

3.1.246/1344   DUKE] CRANE/ALLDE (*D.*); Kt BRIDGEWATER[B] *uncorrected*; *King.* CRANE[1], *Ki.* OKES, Kg BRIDGEWATER[B] *corrected*, K. MIDDLETON[T]+. The CRANE/ALLDE variant occurs in both the text and catchword, and is not easily explained by contamination from anything in the immediate vicinity. In chess, a king can take a queen only if the opponent makes an elementary mistake; a duke can much more easily capture a queen—and in fact the Duke of Bavaria wanted, and by 1624 had taken, possession of the Palatinate. Moreover, it may have seemed inappropriate to have a knight correct a king so brusquely. This is more likely to be a late authorial variant than a scribal or compositorial error.

3.1.246/1345   KNIGHT] K. CRANE/ALLDE. The seduction of the White Knight is elsewhere consistently conducted by the Black Knight, not the Black King.

3.1.246/1345   You're] You are CRANE[2,3,4], OKES

3.1.246/1345   hasty] OKES; hott CRANE[1]+. Late authorial variant: 'too hasty' appears at least seven times elsewhere in the Middleton canon. It is also the reading of what may be Middleton's source (quoted in *Early* commentary at 3.193).

3.1.248/1347 t'] OKES; *not in* CRANE[1]+. Late authorial variant.

3.1.249/1348 The Duke] that Pei ce CRANE[1]

3.1.249/1349 I] *not in* OKES. Possibly deliberate revision; but less metrical than the original reading.

3.1.250/1350 I'd] I would CRANE[2,3]

3.1.251/1351 Sir] *not in* BRIDGEWATER[B]

3.1.252/1353 BISHOP] CRANE/ALLDE (B.); *King.* CRANE[1], Ki. OKES, K. MIDDLETON[T]+. Elsewhere the Black Knight and Black Bishop work as a team, so they could easily do so here. The Black Knight's 'Sir' could be directed to the Black Bishop, rather than the Black King; the reassignment of this speech to the Bishop might well be related to the reassignment of 3.1.246 to the King. This is the first example of roman 'B' in speech prefixes in ALLDE, and the only one on sig. F1[v] (inner forme); this might result from foul case. But there are eight (beginning at 3.1.278) on sig. F2 (inner forme), seven on F2[v] (outer forme), then none on F3 (outer forme) and F3[v] (inner forme), with the single example on F4 (inner forme) occurring in the last speech prefix on the page; finally, nine substitutions occur on F4[v] (outer forme). The substitutions undoubtedly occur because the recurrent speech prefix abbreviation 'B' for 'Black' (and Bishop) resulted in a shortage of italic 'B'. If this sheet had been set seriatim, once the shortage appeared it should have continued till the end of F4[v], unless the stock of italic B was being periodically replenished by distribution of type from some other text being composed at the same time, which was also using lots of italic 'B'. The pattern here suggests setting by formes. But a systematic examination of recurrent types would be necessary to determine the issue, and I have not attempted one.

3.1.252/1353 Do't] doo it MIDDLETON[T] *only*; Doe ₄ CRANE/ALLDE

3.1.253.1–2 *Black ... Pawn*] THIS EDITION; *Seizes W. Kg.'s Pawn.* DYCE. This is the first piece actually taken in the game; some repeated stage action must be used to indicate the taking of opposing chess pieces (which also occurs in 3.2, 4.5, 5.2, and 5.3).

3.1.254/1356 He's ... default] HOWARD-HILL and DUTTON assign this phrase (without a textual note) to Black Knight as part of preceding speech; all extant witnesses give it to the White Knight, as the beginning of his speech. This shared error in two modern editions demonstrates DUTTON's derivation from HOWARD-HILL.

3.1.257/1359 th'] CRANE[1,4], BRIDGEWATER *corrected*; the CRANE[2]+

3.1.258/1360 KNIGHT] K. CRANE/ALLDE. The variant is at best ambiguous, but probably an error: the Black Knight is elsewhere associated with the treason of the White King's Pawn, and historically the ambassador to England is likelier than the King of Spain to have personally corrupted an English minister.

3.1.258/1360 lock] took CRANE/ALLDE. Misreading.

3.1.259–60/1361–2 I ... yours.] *not in* CRANE[3]

3.1.259/1361 this] this this BRIDGEWATER[B] *uncorrected*

3.1.261/1363 This] The OKES. Perhaps anticipation (in compositorial memory) of 'the' later in the line.

3.1.261/1363 leprosy] leaprofly OKES. Foul case.

3.1.262/1364 dissimulation] diffemulation BRIDGEWATER[B], OKES. The variant spelling is etymologically wrong, and should perhaps be considered a shared error.

*3.1.262.1 *His ... off*] CRANE[1], OKES, ROSENBACH[A], BRIDGEWATER[B]; *not in* CRANE[2,3,4], MIDDLETON[T]. Late authorial restoration. CRANE[1], apparently correctly, begins the whole direction opposite 'View him now'; BRIDGEWATER[B] and ROSENBACH[A] begin it two manuscript lines later (opposite 'hypocrite',

3.1.264), and OKES a line early (opposite 3.1.261), suggesting that the presence of the directions in these manuscripts does not derive directly from CRANE[1], but results from authorial restoration.

3.1.262.1 *being*] ROSENBACH[A], OKES; *not in* CRANE[1]+. The added word could easily be a late authorial variant.

3.1.262.1–2 *the White King's Counsellor Pawn*] THIS EDITION; *not in* CRANE[1]+

3.1.262.2–3 *he ... underneath*] *not in* MIDDLETON[T]

3.1.263/1365 His heart] hir ~ CRANE[1]

3.1.263/1365 our] one ROSENBACH[A]

3.1.264/1366 KING] OKES (Ki.), CRANE/ALLDE (K.); K[t]. CRANE[1]+. Late authorial variant. The unambiguous OKES reading (not recorded by Nascimento) makes it clear that the CRANE/ALLDE variant is not an ambiguous abbreviation due to type shortage—which, in any case, we have no reason to suspect at this point in the text. See next note.

3.1.264–5/1367–8 QUEEN ... DUKE] MIDDLETON[T] *only*; D. ... Q. CRANE[1]+. Late autograph variant: in the Duke/Buckingham's mouth the phrase 'against us' makes a general claim about Catholic/Protestant rivalry, but in the Queen's mouth 'against us' can also refer to the struggle for Bohemia and the Palatinate, and to the Stuart royal family. For a parallel paired variant, see 3.1.185.

3.1.264–78/1367–83 WHITE QUEEN ... substitute.] *not in* CRANE[3]

3.1.265/1368 His] This OKES. Misreading.

3.1.265/1368 of] o BRIDGEWATER[B]

*3.1.265/1368 their] this CRANE/ALLDE; his OKES. Misreading. 'This' is closer than 'his' to the correct reading, so the misreading (or miscorrection) in OKES looks like a progressive error, deriving at one or more removes from a manuscript that already contained the misreading printed in ALLDE. In any case, the quartos agree on the mistaken 'is' instead of correct 'eir'.

3.1.265/1369 Has] Hath CRANE[2,4]

3.1.266/1370 raised] roufd CRANE[1]

3.1.267–9/1371–3 From ... adventures] *not in* CRANE[1]. Another of the additions to the revised version's representation of the White King's Pawn.

3.1.271–2/1375–6 And dost ... fruit] by the | MIDDLETON[T]

3.1.271/1375 th'] CRANE[2] (the'); the CRANE[1]+

3.1.273/1377 ripened] ripenèd CRANE/ALLDE, ROSENBACH[A]

3.1.274/1378 thy] thine CRANE

3.1.274/1378 ha'] ROSENBACH[A]; haue CRANE[1]+. Late authorial metrical variant: the extra syllable at the caesura, preserved in *Early* 3.217, is an acceptable alternative.

3.1.276/1380 trespass] fin [CRANE[4]], BRIDGEWATER[B] *uncorrected*. This variant might be a late authorial variant; but *trespass* is a much rarer word than 'sin'. This has not been tabulated as a shared error, because 'sin' makes sense; but BRIDGEWATER obviously regarded it as an error, and restored the reading found in all other texts.

3.1.278/1382 I'd] I would CRANE[2]

3.1.278/1382 tear 'em] ~ him CRANE[2]; teare 'm CRANE/ALLDE. CRANE/ALLDE could easily be due to simple transposition, or to the unusual form found routinely in MIDDLETON[T] (e'm). But its ambiguity also permits it to be understood as 'him'.

3.1.278/1383 Spoke] Speke BRIDGEWATER[B] *uncorrected*. Easy misreading.

3.1.279/1384 QUEEN] BRIDGEWATER[B] (Q.); *King.* CRANE[1], K. CRANE[2]+. The BRIDGEWATER variant, clearly present in the manuscript, was noted by Nascimento; Howard-Hill's 1995 transcription incorrectly reads 'K.' (presumably because of his years of familiarity with the standard reading, which led him to substitute a common for a rare reading). This is probably a late authorial variant; it expands the White Queen's role, it is hard to explain as a misreading, there is no other obvious explanation for the substitution.

3.1.281–2/1386–8   BLACK KNIGHT…too.] *not in* CRANE[3]

3.1.281/1386   KNIGHT] MIDDLETON[T], BRIDGEWATER[B] (K[t]); *King* CRANE[I], *Ki.* OKES, *K.* CRANE[2,4], ROSENBACH[A]. Late authorial variant. There is no reason to doubt the original (CRANE[I]) reading, which has the White King respond to the Black King (and has the White King cue the White House's departure). The variant cannot be explained by simple omission, and it makes sense to associate the Black Knight with 'cunning'. See next note.

3.1.281/1387   WHITE KNIGHT] CRANE/ALLDE (*W.Kni.*); Bl.K. MIDDLETON[T] *only*; *Bl.K[t]* CRANE[I]+; *not in* BRIDGEWATER[B] (thus continuing the speech of the Black Knight). Certainly one, probably two, late authorial variants. MIDDLETON[T] transposes the original speech prefixes, as it does also at 3.1.264–5 (and as CRANE/MATHEWES does at 3.1.185). CRANE/ALLDE, by contrast, retains the second element (attributing the speech to a Knight), and alters the first (attributing it to the White side, rather than the Black). This variant produces a demonstration of White House strength; instead of two consecutive Black speeches, the Black Knight's speech is answered by the White Knight's speech. Although it makes sense, in the original version, to have two consecutive Black speeches here, the variant here better prepares for the immediately following added speech of the Fat Bishop, which refers to the response of the White House, not the Black. Also see 3.1.264, where a variant in CRANE/ALLDE eliminates the White Knight's only response to the White King's Pawn's treason; the variant here compensates for that one, giving the White Knight the last response to that development, rather than the first.

3.1.282/1388   Play…can—perhaps…too] phapps…too, play…can ROSENBACH[A]. Phrasal transposition. Almost by definition it is difficult to distinguish authorial transpositions from unauthorized transpositions, and this could be a late revision. But it seems more effective to end with the threat of 'mate'—especially given the punning reference to the Spanish Match.

3.1.282/1388   mate] make OKES

3.1.283–3.1.299.1/1389–1418   FAT…*Exeunt*] *not in* CRANE[I]. One of the major additions to the revised version, related to the Fat Bishop.

3.1.288/1394   WHITE KING] *not in* BRIDGEWATER[B] *uncorrected*

3.1.288/1394   thy] they BRIDGEWATER[B] *uncorrected*

3.1.289/1396   farther] further CRANE/ALLDE. See 3.1.207.

3.1.289/1396   then] CRANE/ALLDE (than), CRANE[2]+

3.1.292/1400   KING] OKES (*Ki.*), CRANE/ALLDE (*K.*); K[t] CRANE[2]+. Late authorial variant. See 3.1.264.

3.1.292/1400   matched] match OKES

3.1.293/1401–2   FAT BISHOP…him.] *not in* CRANE[3]

3.1.293/1401   FAT BISHOP] CRANE/ALLDE (*Fat B.*); *not in* BRIDGEWATER[B] *uncorrected*; *Bl.B.* CRANE[2]+. The variant makes dramatic sense, and is hard to explain as an inadvertent error. Probably a late authorial variant.

3.1.293/1401   Knight] *not in* BRIDGEWATER[B]

3.1.293/1402   K. CRANE/ALLDE. This variant (about halfway down sig. F2) is the first example in ALLDE of the abbreviation *K.* in a speech that should be spoken by the Black Knight (because 'halter' alludes to the earlier anecdote about a halter curing his fistula). For another clear example,

later on the same page, see 3.1.301. These variants cannot be due to a shortage of italic 't' (which continues to be used in prefixes for 'Fat B.'). Moreover, since ALLDE uses roman 'B' and 'P' in speech prefixes, when the italic forms are unavailable, it is not clear why a shortage of italic 'ni' should have produced these speech prefix variants. There is thus no mechanical explanation in the printing house for the variant, which presumably results from simple omission of a single letter by scribe or compositor (or author).

3.1.293/1402   him] THIS EDITION (italic); him CRANE[2]+ (roman); *not in* BRIDGEWATER[B] *uncorrected*

3.1.294/1403   Next] Now BRIDGEWATER[B] *uncorrected*

3.1.295/1404   Spalato] MIDDLETON[T]+ (Spoletta, Spolletta, *Spoleta*)

3.1.296/1405   seized] feafe BRIDGEWATER[B] *uncorrected*

3.1.296/1406   BISHOP] *not in* CRANE[2]. A simple error of omitting the letter 'B'; since no other character has the speech prefix 'Fat', there is no ambiguity.

3.1.296/1406   'Las] alas CRANE[3]

3.1.297/1407   water] water-gate OKES. The unmetrical variant ('Last night by watergate') seems to have arisen by contamination from 3.1.52 ('Last night at watergate'). Since the earlier line was set by a compositor in a different printer's shop, the variant was almost certainly introduced by Middleton in [PRE-OKES], and it could be adopted as a late authorial variant. However, since it is unmetrical and repetitive, the variant was probably an inadvertent authorial substitution rather than a conscious revision.

3.1.298/1408   of] to CRANE/ALLDE. Contamination from preceding prepositional phrase.

3.1.298/1408   cause] houfe OKES. Contamination from end of preceding line.

3.1.298/1409   KNIGHT] K[t] CRANE[3], MIDDLETON[T], BRIDGEWATER[B]; *K.* CRANE[2,4], ROSENBACH[A]; *Ki.* OKES. Late autograph variant. Both attributions appear in Crane texts: 'King' in the earliest and latest, supported by two non-Crane texts (one set from an autograph manuscript); 'Knight' in the abridgement CRANE[3], supported by two non-Crane texts (one autograph). This variant might be taken as further evidence of Middleton's involvement in preparing the abridgement. In any case, it seems to represent yet another example of authorial wavering about speech prefixes in this scene. The variant adopted here pairs the White Knight and Duke in righteous indignation, just before the exeunt of the White House.

*3.1.299.1/1410   *Exeunt*] OKES, CRANE/ALLDE; *not in* MIDDLETON[T], BRIDGEWATER[B]; *Ex[t].* CRANE[2,3]; *Exit* ROSENBACH[A]. The unique ROSENBACH[A] error here and at 3.1.313.1 probably derives from the ambiguity of the Crane abbreviation; it might be considered an example of progressive error.

3.1.299.1–2/1410   all…*Pawn*] THIS EDITION; *not in* CRANE[2]+; W. King, W. Queen, W. Knight, W. Duke, *and* W. Bishop. DYCE. Although Dyce's emendation is commonly followed, it presumes that the White House entrance earlier in the scene does not include pawns. The phrasing adopted here leaves the pawn option open. It is common, even in playbooks, for exeunt directions not to specify the group that goes off; consequently, the absence of this supplementary information from all early texts has not been treated as a shared error.

3.1.300/1412   writings] books ROSENBACH[A]. This variant is metrical within ROSENBACH's context. (See next note.) The variant could be authorial, but we have adopted the rarer word ('writings') which is paired with the Middletonian contraction ('I'm').

3.1.300/1412   I'm] I am CRANE, ROSENBACH[A]

3.1.301/1413   BLACK] In MIDDLETON[T] *only* the initial 'B' is written over 'wh', indicating that Middleton initially misattributed the speech to a White character (perhaps as a consequence of routinely alternating black and white speeches), then corrected his error before writing the second part of the prefix. This error was made easier by the absence two lines earlier of the necessary exeunt direction; Middleton as copyist could therefore have forgotten, momentarily, that there was no White House response to this taunt. For comparable autograph errors, not corrected, see 5.1.49, 5.2.13, 5.3.55.

3.1.301/1413   KNIGHT] K. CRANE/ALLDE. See 3.1.293. CRANE/ALLDE here, near the bottom of sig. F2, has two 'Bl.K.' prefixes in a row; one must belong to the Knight, to which all other texts attribute this speech.

3.1.301/1413   honours] honor CRANE[2,3]

3.1.303/1415–16   BLACK KING...you!] *not in* CRANE[3]

3.1.305/1418   raise] prayfe OKES

*3.1.305.1–3/1418   *Exeunt...Pawn*] THIS EDITION; *Exeunt B. King, B. Queen, B. Duke, B. Bishop, and Fat Bishop.* DYCE; *not in* CRANE[2]+. Only two Black characters play any subsequent part in the scene, and the Black Knight would not want his treatment of one turncoat to be witnessed by the other. There is no need for a separate exit in CRANE[1], because the final exchange can be overheard by the entire Black House.

3.1.306/1419   KING'S] CRANE[2,3]; ROSENBACH[A], MIDDLETON[T] (K[S].); K. CRANE/ALLDE; *not in* CRANE[1]; Q. BRIDGEWATER[B]; Kt. OKES. The absence of the specific indicator in the earliest text is probably authorial, since Middleton seems to have used many generic pawn prefixes in his first draft; but the other variants in OKES and BRIDGEWATER are clearly errors. OKES's error cannot be due to type shortage, but perhaps resulted from miscorrection. (See 3.1.307.) BRIDGEWATER[B]'s error might be the result of mistaken expansion of an ambiguous 'Wh.P.': rather than identify a character hitherto silent in this scene, someone assumed the white pawn was a character who has spoken earlier in the scene and has been identified in at least some manuscripts as 'wh.p.' (See 3.1.311, 320.)

3.1.306/1419   Knight] now BRIDGEWATER[B] *uncorrected*

3.1.306/1419   my] me BRIDGEWATER[B] *uncorrected*

3.1.306/1419   advancement,] MIDDLETON[T]; ~ now CRANE[1]+. NASCIMENTO records this as a substantive agreement of MIDDLETON[T] with CRANE/ALLDE, and HOWARD-HILL duplicates her claim (*Pasquin*, 279). But 'now.' is present in the quarto: it has simply been turned up onto the preceding type line (justified to the right, with an opening but no closing bracket, in the normal convention for dealing with lines too long for the measure). The absence of 'now' is therefore a reading unique to MIDDLETON[T], and may be one of many unique errors of simple carelessness in autograph; but because it makes sense and could be a late authorial variant, it has been retained here.

*3.1.307/1420   KNIGHT] K. OKES, CRANE/ALLDE. A shared error in the two quartos. The error in OKES cannot be due to type shortage, since it has 'Kt' in the type line before and five lines after (in the Black Knight's next speech). However, it might be related to the opposite error in the immediately preceding type line, where 'W.Kt.p.' is nonsensical: if the compositor or his copy had initially accidentally omitted the 't' in this speech prefix, and the error were noticed in foul proofs (because of the vocative 'Knight' in the preceding speech), then the 't' might accidentally have been inserted in the identical position immediately above. As for the variant in ALLDE, in seriatim setting this 'K.' (at the top of F2[v])

would have been set immediately after the erroneous 'K.' for 'Knight' at ll. 293, 301 (at the bottom of F2). But since the variants seem not to be due to type shortage, and since seriatim setting produces the same sequence as manuscript transcription, the run of ambiguous/erroneous speech prefixes may have originated in the manuscript rather than the printing house.

3.1.307/1420   the staff, the strong staff, that will hold] ~ ~, Sir, the ftrong Crofier-ftaff CRANE[1]

3.1.308/1421   And] BRIDGEWATER[B] *uncorrected* began by writing 'I' (apparently skipping to the following line) but then immediately corrected the error by altering 'I' into 'A'.

3.1.308/1421   mazard] mazure OKES. Either a misreading, or a spelling of the older form (recorded in *OED* under *mazere n.*, with the same meanings as *mazard*).

3.1.309/1422   thy] the OKES. Contamination from four words before.

3.1.311/1424–5   WHITE KING'S COUNSELLOR PAWN...BLACK KNIGHT] *not in* CRANE[3]

3.1.311/1424   KING'S] *not in* CRANE[1], ROSENBACH[A], BRIDGEWATER[B]. For a related generic speech prefix in the same three texts see 3.1.185. Not an error, because unambiguous in context, and apparently an authorial form.

3.1.311/1425   replications] replication OKES. This could be an indifferent authorial variant, but there are no grounds for distinguishing it from the many minor compositorial errors in OKES. 'No replication' appears elsewhere, in the singular, in seventeenth-century legal texts, but its very currency as a legal idiom might explain an unauthorized substitution.

3.1.311/1425   me] ~ well enough CRANE[3]. See 2.1.181. This unique addition is further evidence of Middleton's involvement in the abridgement. Middleton uses 'well enough' at least seventeen times elsewhere (not counting examples attributed to collaborators, or uncertainly attributed); after the verb 'know', it occurs at *Phoenix* 9.143–4, *Black Book* 381, 513, 636, *Timon* 5.39–40; the whole phrase 'You know me well enough' very closely resembles 'You read me well enough' (*Changeling* 5.3.16, attributed to Middleton). Here the phrase is added to complete the verse line, made defective by the omission of the White King's Pawn's speech. (See note above.) The addition seems specific to the abridgement, and also eliminates the rhyme. Bawcutt (1993, 11) notes two other occasions where, in the abridgement, a character loses a brief speech, even though he is clearly required in the scene (2.2.17, 4.4.63); in each case, as here, eliminating the speech saves a line of manuscript. In fact, there are many more examples of the same pattern of abridgement: 2.1.179, 2.1.189, 2.1.190, 2.2.113, 2.2.200, 2.2.212, 3.1.148, 3.1.159, 3.1.320, 3.1.397, 4.1.36, 4.1.136.

3.1.313/1427   'twill] to ROSENBACH[A]

3.1.313.1/1428   *Exeunt*] MIDDLETON[T], CRANE/ALLDE; *Ex[t].* CRANE[1,2,3]; *Ex.* OKES; *Exit* ROSENBACH[A]; exu- BRIDGEWATER. The mistaken singular in ROSENBACH[A] results from misinterpretation of the ambiguous abbreviated form. At least two characters on the stage must leave it.

3.1.313.1–2/1428   *Black Knight Gondomar, taking off White King's Counsellor Pawn*] THIS EDITION; *not in* CRANE[1]+; *Puts* WHITE KING'S PAWN *into the bag* HARPER. 'Here, perhaps,' DYCE had conjectured, 'the Black Knight thrust the White King's Pawn into the bag *on the stage*: compare the concluding scene of the play.' Despite the reference here to the bag, it seems likely that Middleton and the King's Men would want to save that dramatic special effect for the climax of the play. However, the Black Knight's physical treatment of the White

King's Pawn, for this exit, could and probably should indicate the pawn's fate and changed status. The rough treatment might begin earlier, and prompt the pawn's 'How's this?'

3.1.313.1/1428 *Black Knight*] THIS EDITION; *not in* CRANE[1]+. Editors from DYCE to HOWARD-HILL add the Black Knight's Pawn to this exit direction; this is possible, but his presence is not necessary in 3.1.306-13. In chess terms a knight alone can take a pawn, without being threatened by it.

3.1.315-16/1430-1 Let…service] this | MIDDLETON[T]

3.1.315/1430 Thou'st] CRANE[1] (thou'hast); thou haſt CRANE[2]+

3.1.316/1431 my] mine CRANE[2,3]; many ALLDE. Compositorial misreading of 'mine' in [CRANE[4]].

3.1.317/1432 of] in CRANE[3]

3.1.317/1432 not transcend it ᴧ] ᴧ traſend ~ not OKES. Perhaps a miscorrection: if 'not' were accidentally omitted, a correction in the right margin of the foul proofs to reinsert it might have been misunderstood, leading to its insertion at the end of the line (near the correction in the right margin) rather than in mid-line. The variant is less regular metrically than the original, and also uncharacteristically old-fashioned in its post-position of the adverb.

3.1.318/1433 QUEEN's] *not in* CRANE[1]; B. ROSENBACH[A]; Ks. BRIDGEWATER[B] *uncorrected*. The correction was made by BRIDGEWATER[C] (in pencil). The error could have resulted from a misreading of 'Bs' as 'Ks'; although this might be evidence of a shared error in ROSENBACH and [PRE-BRIDGEWATER], the link remains conjectural, and has not been counted. For the first clear evidence of the beginning of a close stemmatic connection between the two texts, see D.0.1/1470; but there are several suspicious shared readings from this point to that shared error.

3.1.318/1433 flamed] framde BRIDGEWATER[B]; flame ROSENBACH[A]; ſtand OKES[1]; ſtands OKES[2]. A good example of miscorrection: the original quarto misreading was made grammatical in the reprint, producing an unauthoritative reading even farther from the shape of the authorial word.

3.1.319/1434 it mounted] I amounted OKES. Misreading.

3.1.319/1434-9 mounted.ᴧ] CRANE[3], ROSENBACH[A]; *Bl.P.* that Contaminating Act | would haue spoild all your fortunes: a Rape? bleſſe vs all | *wh.Qˢ.P.* thou talkſt of Marriage? | *Bl.P.* yes CRANE[1]+. BRIDGEWATER[B] also omits these two speeches (see below). Although this looks like many other deliberate abridgements in CRANE[3], the fact that it skips from 'marriage' at the end of one short speech (*Early* 3.249; C.1) to the same word at the end of another short speech (*Early* 3.252; C.3) means that it could be due to eyeskip. Theoretically, the omission might not be deliberate in any of the three texts; or it might be deliberate abridgement in CRANE[3] but accidental in BRIDGEWATER[B] and ROSENBACH[A]. However, none of the three texts is identical. CRANE[3] makes two further abridgements in 3.1.320-1 ('The man?' and 'a complete one'), which are hard to dismiss as accidental, and that therefore suggest that this other omission is also deliberate. BRIDGEWATER[B] also omits 'Yes, yes, you do marry' (the second half of *Early* 3.253); the speech prefix is present, but placed before *Early* 3.254. This repositioning means that we are not dealing with simple omission, and the omission is in any case larger than the one in CRANE[3], and harder to attribute to simple eyeskip; it regularizes the metre of the whole passage. ROSENBACH[A] modifies *Early* 3.249 (the first part of 3.1.320) by adding 'saist thou' (thus producing an iambic pentameter line, split between *Early* 3.249/1435 and *Early* 3.254/1440)—which looks like an authorial attempt to correct the metrical deficiency created by the CRANE[3] omission. Although this is one of several

indications of the beginnings of a close stemmatic relationship between BRIDGEWATER and ROSENBACH[A] hereabouts, it cannot be confidently characterized as a shared error (as other investigators have claimed), because the boundaries of the omission are not the same in any two texts, and there is evidence of authorial intervention in at least one of the three cases, and of deliberation rather than simple inadvertence in all three texts. The omitted material is in fact dramatically superfluous (as Middleton might have realized when abridging the text); it looks backward instead of forward; moreover, the emphasis on rape reduces the parallel between the promised but never intended marriage of the White Queen's Pawn and the promised but never intended marriage of the White Knight/Charles. Since the passage is preserved in *Early* 3.249-52, this intelligent cut, apparently authorially endorsed, has been accepted here in *Later*. The fuller version is printed as Additional Passage C, and textual variants are keyed to its appearance there.

3.1.320/1435 QUEEN's] *not in* BRIDGEWATER[B]. See 3.1.305, 310.

3.1.320/1435 sayst thou] ſaiſt thou ROSENBACH[A]; *not in* CRANE[1]+. The added phrase appears at least a dozen times in the Middleton canon, including a remarkable parallel at *Trick* 4.4.100 ('How? a precontract, sayst thou?')—which is identical except for the variant 'marriage'/'a precontract'. The two added words in ROSENBACH are thus almost certainly a late authorial variant, designed to regularize the metre after the following lines had been cut. See preceding notes. Notably, this apparently-authorial variant in ROSENBACH does not appear in BRIDGEWATER.

3.1.320/1440 BLACK QUEEN's PAWN ᴧ I] BRIDGEWATER[B]; *Bl.P.* yes: yes: you doe Marry. | I CRANE[1]+. See two previous notes. This variant cannot be a simple extension of the earlier omission, since the speech prefix had to be moved; it has the effect of regularizing the metre of the entire passage.

3.1.320-1/1442-3 WHITE QUEEN's PAWN…BLACK QUEEN's PAWN] *not in* CRANE[3]. Another example of the abridgement saving a line of manuscript by omitting a very short speech.

3.1.321/1443 honest] CRANE/ALLDE; handſome CRANE[1]+. Late authorial variant: the exact phrase 'honest gentleman' appears nine times elsewhere in undisputed Middleton plays. How could she know, from seeing him in the mirror, that he was honest? On the other hand, her knowledge of his inheritance prospects also indicates more than visual knowledge. The Black Queen's Pawn knows that her victim is likelier to be interested by claims of honesty than good looks.

3.1.321/1443 a complete one] *not in* CRANE[3] (thus regularizing the metre after the previous cut)

*3.1.322/1444 You'll] MIDDLETON[T]+ (you'le); You'de OKES, yould BRIDGEWATER[B]

3.1.324-7/1446-9 WHITE QUEEN's PAWN…methinks.] *not in* CRANE[3]

3.1.324/1446 ᴧ Sure] OKES; why ~ CRANE[1]+. It is curious that OKES does not contain a single one of the three examples of initial 'Why' in the three lines of verse spoken by the White Queen's Pawn in ll. 324-8, and that two of the three omissions are unique to OKES. It also uniquely omits 'why' at 4.4.8 and 5.2.83. By contrast, among all seven other witnesses the interjection is omitted only twice: 2.2.255 (not in CRANE[2,3]) and 4.2.91 (not in CRANE[1]). This pattern is hard to attribute to compositorial error: there is no such selective omission of the remaining instances of 'Why' in OKES[2], nor in Shakespeare's *History of King Lear* (printed by Okes in 1608, and available in a variant Folio text). However, the variants might be due to Middleton's own declining use of the interjection. According to Lake (Band 1(a)), *Game* (1624) has only 16 examples (based on Bald's edition of MIDDLETON[T]), and *Changeling* (1623) only 18; these figures are strikingly lower than earlier Middleton/Rowley collaborations (*Weapons* 47, *Quarrel* 42) and Middleton's own high numbers in earlier single-author plays of similar length (*Mad World* 60, *Trick* 57). Late Middleton thus seems to have been reducing his use of the interjection, and is the agent of transmission most likely to have cut the number in OKES.

3.1.324/1446 thou art] CRANE[2]+; thou'rt CRANE[1], MIDDLETON[T]. The autograph text restores the original elision. However, the alternative solution to making the line metrical again, found in OKES (see preceding note), presumes the unelided text. The elision is preserved in *Early* 3.259, the alternative here.

3.1.324/1446 much] *not in* OKES. Eyeskip: 'much mistaken'.

3.1.324/1446 mistaken_] ~, ~ ~ ~_ OKES

3.1.325/1446 for] in CRANE[2]

3.1.325/1447 Why] MIDDLETON[T] *corrected*; who MIDDLETON[T] *uncorrected* (?); *not in* CRANE[1]+. Howard-Hill (1990) notes that the 'y' is retraced, but rather than retracing it was probably written over a round letter. The false start 'who' or 'whose' might occur naturally after 'Man' (especially for a copyist who knew the following speeches). For the handwriting and the sense compare 'whofe' at 3.1.330. The unique and extrametrical 'why' here might be no more than an effort at minimalist correction. Only MIDDLETON[T] has the interjection at the beginning of two consecutive verse lines by the same speaker.

3.1.326/1448 or I, or] CRANE, OKES, MIDDLETON[T]; for _ ROSENBACH[A]; for ~, and BRIDGEWATER[B]. The original 'or' puts the White Queen's Pawn in the same category as the Black Queen's Pawn, and 'us'; by contrast, 'for' (incorrectly) makes a distinction between 'you' and 'I', and/or 'you' and 'all of us'. Although 'for' is probably a shared error, it has not been tabulated as such, because ROSENBACH[A]'s variant line makes sense, and its metrical deficiency is not due to the word 'for'. With 'for' the sentence is less elegant—'there's a fate rules for all of us, and overrules all of us'—but not demonstrably wrong. Another of the indications of the beginning of a close stemmatic relationship between BRIDGEWATER and ROSENBACH, but not an indisputable shared error.

3.1.326/1448 all on's] all's one OKES; ~ of us MIDDLETON[T] *corrected*; ~ of ⟨??⟩ MIDDLETON[T] *uncorrected*. Though Howard-Hill (1990) describes the autograph 'us' as 'retraced', it is difficult to be sure it is not overwriting, perhaps of 'ne' or 'ns'; the blotting of the second letter is particularly indecipherable.

3.1.327/1449 rules _] ~ vs OKES. Probably contamination from later in the line.

3.1.327/1449 overrules] ou[r]rules ROSENBACH[A]; our rules BRIDGEWATER[B]. Howard-Hill's transcription explains 'our' as 'i.e. ouer', but (like ROSENBACH[A]) it may suggest an elided pronunciation (one syllable rather than two). However, the metre seems to require two syllables here.

3.1.328/1450 _ How] OKES; why ~ CRANE[1]+. See 3.1.324.

3.1.328/1450 see or know] know or fee ROSENBACH[A]

*3.1.333/1455 person] perfons ROSENBACH[A], CRANE/ALLDE. The plural is clearly wrong: she is describing 'the man' and 'him', not anyone else.

3.1.336/1459 cannot feel] OKES; can feele no CRANE[1]+. Late authorial variant.

3.1.337/1460 feel] feeke OKES. Misreading.

3.1.337/1460 the] OKES; our CRANE[1]+. This is probably a late authorial variant: it is hard to explain as a misreading or

common substitution. Middleton uses 'our faith' at 5.3.110, but 'the faith' occurs at least six times in his canon.

3.1.338/1461 upward] vpwards CRANE[2,3]. Probably only a spelling variant.

3.1.339/1462 WHITE] BRIDGEWATER[B] *uncorrected* began to write 'B', then immediately corrected to 'wh'.

3.1.339/1462 'Twas] It was OKES

3.1.339/1462 applied] refolu'd CRANE[1]

3.1.342/1465 or] nor CRANE[1]

3.1.342/1465 spectre] fpeaker CRANE/ALLDE. Misreading.

3.1.343-4/1466-7 That's...man] it | OKES

3.1.344-5/1467-69 Is't...instantly.] *not in* CRANE[3]

3.1.345/1468-9 Why...instantly] 2 *lines* you | MIDDLETON[T]; 2 *lines* then | OKES

3.1.345/1468 Why then, observe] CRANE[2]; 'pray follow me then, and CRANE[1]+. CRANE[2] rewrites the final line of the scene, in order to accommodate the omission of 3.2—which means the omission must have been deliberate. (CRANE[3] also omits the scene, but it abridges more of the text, and has no equivalent to this line.) The phrase 'why then' occurs at least sixty times in the Middleton canon, including 'why then behold' (*Valour* 4.1.335) and the rhythmically identical 'Why then farewell' (*Roaring Girl* 4.102) and 'why then content' (*Mad World* 3.1.127); Middleton uses 'observe' as an imperative without an object in *Heroes* 186 and *Michaelmas* 1.2.122. It is therefore conceivable that Middleton wrote the bridging phrase, but an exact parallel occurs in *The Bloody Brother*, by Fletcher and others, another late Jacobean King's Men play; it's therefore also possible the bridge was written by someone in the playhouse, after 3.2 was censored (or cut during rehearsals). Despite the number of contemporary responses to the play's early performances, none mentions this scene, which means we have no evidence it was ever performed. As originally written, the 'Jesting Pawn' scene provided a comic interlude and a brief part for the company's clown; but those functions were rendered obsolete by the late addition of the Fat Bishop. There may also have been other factors, though the clown issue was probably primary. The scene's references to anal penetration—'in the breach of me' and 'one straw thorough their buttocks'—makes it clear that the pawns are captured by being taken from behind; this is a typically Middletonian sodomy joke, but a pawn can never be taken by another pawn from behind; pawns face each other across the board, and take other pieces by moving forward toward the opposing side. Moreover, the scene's position forces another departure from chess allegory: after the three anonymous pawns exit, White Queen's Pawn and Black Queen's Pawn must enter together, rather than from separate doors. These practical visual problems could all have become more obvious in rehearsal. The most obvious explanation for the scene's omission from two manuscripts is thus theatrical. It is hard to see why the censor should have objected so strenuously to this scene that he demanded its omission, when the more obviously objectionable political material elsewhere in the play was permitted. Howard-Hill argues that Crane removed the scene on his own initiative, but he gives no plausible motive for Crane to do so. Since the scene is printed in *Early*, since it was clearly deliberately omitted, and since comprehensible artistic motives for the omission can be found, it has been omitted from *Later*. The scene is reproduced as Additional Passage D at the end of the text, and textual variants within the scene are therefore listed below, at the end of the Textual Notes, keyed to the text there.

3.1.346.1/1523 *She reveals a large mirror*] THIS EDITION; *not in* CRANE[1]+. DYCE began the scene with the direction 'A *chamber, with a large mirror*', but in the original performances (apparently without 3.2) the action was continuous, and Black Queen's Pawn would have had to reveal the mirror herself. That was probably always Middleton's intention, as the phrase 'look you' suggests.

3.1.348-61/1524-37 WHITE QUEEN'S PAWN...loves).] *not in* CRANE[3]

3.1.348-50/1524-6 I...omen] should I | me | OKES. This error resembles the mislineations elsewhere in MIDDLETON[T].

3.1.348, 352/1524, 1528 QUEEN'S] *not in* ROSENBACH[A], BRIDGE-WATER[B]. The generic prefixes continue in ROSENBACH even after they cease in CRANE[1]. See 3.1.362.

3.1.350-1/1526 Under...turtle] *1 line* CRANE[1,2], MIDDLETON[T]; *passage not in* CRANE[3]. Relic.

3.1.351/1526 As is] is ROSENBACH[A]; As OKES. Eyeskip.

3.1.351/1526 felt] fet ROSENBACH[A]

*3.1.352/1528 bodes] bounds ROSENBACH[A], BRIDGEWATER[B] *uncorrected*. The correction 'boades' was made by BRIDGEWATER[C] (in pencil).

*3.1.355/1531 vainer] vaine ROSENBACH[A], BRIDGEWATER[B], OKES. The variant is both unmetrical and pointless. In MIDDLETON[T] the initial 'V' is written over the start of 'f', indicating that Middleton started to write the next word (omitting 'vaine(r)' entirely) and then immediately corrected his error before writing the second letter.

3.1.359/1535 creates] treats OKES. Misreading.

3.1.360/1536 sounds] sinne OKES. Misreading.

3.1.360/1536 entered] enters OKES. Assimilation to the present tenses elsewhere in the context (conspires, creates, argues).

3.1.361/1537 your] *not in* CRANE/ALLDE

3.1.362/1538 QUEEN'S] *not in* OKES, ROSENBACH[A]. See 3.1.3 and next note.

3.1.363/1539 QUEEN'S] *not in* OKES. Since no one believes that OKES is directly connected to CRANE[1], this and the preceding variant are probably evidence that Middleton himself occasionally reverted to the generic prefixes widely used in *Early*.

3.1.364/1540 that] all BRIDGEWATER[B] *uncorrected*

3.1.364/1540 diff'rence] CRANE[1]; difference CRANE[2]+

3.1.366/1542 name] names CRANE[1], MIDDLETON[T]. This variant could well result from authorial vacillation. The independent agreement of the two most authoritative texts on the plural is not likely to be an error. But the singular could also be authorial: the Middleton canon elsewhere has nine examples of 'in the name of'—including 'in the name of the black angels' (*Michaelmas* 1.2.147) and 'in the name of all the brethren' (*Hengist* 5.1.169), where singular 'name' is followed by a plural.

3.1.367/1543-4 WHITE QUEEN'S PAWN...done.] *not in* CRANE[3]

3.1.367/1543 QUEEN'S] *not in* ROSENBACH[A]. See 348, 362.

3.1.367/1543 That will...much ₐ] OKES; twill ... ~ that CRANE[1]+. Late authorial variant. Compare 'that satisfies me' (*Witch* 5.1.7). If only transposition were involved, the variant might be attributed to substitution of a common for an unusual word-order; but transposition is here combined with the alteration of 'twill' to 'will'. The extra initial stressed syllable produces a line-divided foot, and a rhythm much more frequent in Middleton than the original reading (with an extra stressed syllable after the caesura).

3.1.367.1/1545 *the invocation*] MIDDLETON[T]; *not in* CRANE[1]+. This stage direction is not at all necessary, and its absence has not been counted as a shared error.

3.1.368/1546 whose] with OKES. The variant makes sense locally but not for the speech as a whole.

*3.1.369/1547 Egyptic] MIDDLETON[T] (Ægiptick), CRANE; Egipte ROSENBACH[A]; Aegipted BRIDGEWATER[B], OKES. Middleton's adjective 'Egyptic' is not recorded in *OED*, and antedates the earliest examples of 'Egyptiac'. Although Middleton could have turned a noun into a past participial (Egyped), we have already been told that she bought the glass 'of an Egyptian' (3.1.329), so the mirror seems to be of Egyptian origin, rather than a glass transformed into something Egyptian. In all three texts the correct 'Egipt' is incorrectly followed by 'e'.

3.1.370/1548 th'] CRANE[1,2,3], OKES; the CRANE/ALLDE, ROSEN-BACH[A], BRIDGEWATER[B], MIDDLETON[T]

3.1.370/1548 imperious] Emperours ROSENBACH[A]. The other invocations give a single name only. Probably a misreading, but perhaps Middleton was responsible, momentarily thinking of the Holy Roman Emperor.

3.1.370/1548 pow'rful] CRANE[1,2,3] (powrefull); powerfull MID-DLETON[T]+

3.1.374-5/1553 Not...another] *1 line* OKES, ROSENBACH[A]. Relic.

3.1.374/1552 see you] yo[u] fee CRANE[1]

3.1.374/1552 you nothing] ~ ₐ ROSENBACH[A]; youn,othing ALLDE

3.1.375 ₐPray] Bl.Q.P. ~ BRIDGEWATER[B]. All other texts except MIDDLETON[T] place the speech prefix one manuscript or type line below, before the half-line beginning 'you'. BRIDGE-WATER[B], too, divides the iambic pentameter line in two, which would not be necessary unless it were split between two different speakers.

3.1.375 Pray...another] *not in* MIDDLETON[T] *only*

3.1.375 You...will] *not in* MIDDLETON[T]. See preceding notes. If these two omissions of spoken text resulted from simple eyeskip, the speech prefix between the two half lines in six of the other witnesses would have been omitted too. However, if the underlying manuscript being copied had misplaced the speech prefix (as in BRIDGEWATER[B]), then simple eyeskip would have produced the text as it stands in MIDDLETON[T]. This looks like progressive error. It has not been counted as a shared error, because the two texts are not identical; but MIDDLETON[T] and BRIDGEWATER[B] both misplace the speech prefix, in ways that seem related.

3.1.381-2/1560-61 My...forever] *3 lines* OKES: clearer | eye |

3.1.381/1560 clearer. Then₄] MIDDLETON[T]+ (subs); ~_ₐ~: DYCE. Middleton uses the seemingly oxymoronic 'then now' in the sense 'therefore now' at *Women Beware* 2.2.177 and *Dissemblers* 5.1.186; it also appears in *Changeling* 1.1.136.

3.1.382/1561 eyes] MIDDLETON[T], ROSENBACH[A]; Eie CRANE[1]+. Authorial vacillation: either reading makes sense.

3.1.383/1562 fate's] Fats BRIDGEWATER[B]

3.1.385/1564 thou] In MIDDLETON[T] the initial 'T' is written over 'sh', indicating that Middleton started to write the next word (omitting 'thou' entirely) but corrected his error before writing the third letter.

3.1.385/1564 met] meete OKES

3.1.386/1565 graceful issues] issues gracefull ROSENBACH[A]. The variant might be authorial: it has the rarer word order, and creates a semantic double-meaning ('graceful issues' and 'gracefully get').

*3.1.392.1/1572 *Music*] *not in* OKES. The music cue is placed here by CRANE[1] and CRANE/ALLDE: this lets the offstage instrumental music overlay the climactic line of the incantation. CRANE[2,3], by contrast, cue it after 3.1.389, which seems pointlessly early; their positioning of the direction might have been driven by space considerations, since there is more open space in the right margin opposite the short incantation lines (3.1.383–92) than opposite the longer iambic penta-meter (393–5). However, since the music could begin at any point during the incantation, the earlier placement cannot be clearly identified as an error (and might be an early play-house warning). However, directions which place the music cue after Black Queen's Pawn says 'Hark' (the first word of l. 394) are clearly wrong: ROSENBACH[A] and BRIDGEWATER[B] place it in the right margin opposite 396, MIDDLETON[T] after and below 395.

3.1.393/1573   thou art] thou'rt OKES. The variant changes the rhythm of the line, but it could be authorial.

3.1.393/1575   these] this OKES (perhaps in error for 'theis').

*3.1.395.1–3/1576–9   The Jesuit...exit] MIDDLETON[T], OKES (posi-tion of direction). For verbal variants within this direction, see subsequent notes. CRANE[1] begins the entrance at 3.1.392.1; in CRANE[2,3], the three-line marginal entrance direction is bracketed and pointed after 3.1.391. All three entrances are clearly too early, since they precede the summons in 393. The error in CRANE[1] may have originated in nothing more than the scribe moving the single word 'Enter' backward onto the same line as 'Music', but the earlier and specifically pointed placement of the entrance direction in CRANE[2,3] is a more serious, and shared, error, probably due to manuscript spacing considerations. (See 3.1.392.1.) A different error is shared by ROSENBACH[A] and BRIDGEWATER[B], which both place the entrance after 3.1.396, after he has already begun to exit. The remaining texts give two different placements, both pos-sible. CRANE/ALLDE places 'Enter' after 3.1.393, immediately after he is summoned; MIDDLETON[T] (centred below) and OKES (marginally) place it two lines below, after 395, which refers to 'his approach'. I have adopted the later placement because it is supported by two texts, one autograph; theatrically, this position gives two lines to respond to the music, then lets the entrance itself take centre stage, as both women watch without speaking, a verbal pause broken only when he begins to leave. Note that MIDDLETON[T] and OKES minimally correct the ROSENBACH/BRIDGEWATER error—or, to put it another way, that the autograph placement would require only a minimal error to be corrupted into ROSENBACH–BRIDGEWATER.

3.1.395.1/1576   The Jesuit] MIDDLETON[T]; not in CRANE[1]+. Late authorial variant. See next note.

3.1.395.1/1576   Black Bishop's Pawn] not in MIDDLETON[T]; y[e] ~~~ CRANE[2,3]

3.1.395.1/1576   comes] CRANE[3] (verb after noun clause); Ente[CRANE[1]; Enters CRANE[2] (verb after noun clause); enters MID-DLETON[T]; Enter CRANE/ALLDE, ROSENBACH[A], BRIDGEWATER[B]; En. OKES. Bawcutt calls CRANE[3]'s unique variant an 'odd form' (1993, 13), and it is certainly odd—indeed, apparently unparalleled—in a Crane text. But Middleton uses the verb 'come' in stage directions at least eighteen times: Phoenix 15.19.1, Patient Man 6.143.3, Michaelmas 3.1.0.3, Trick 1.3.0.3, Timon 2.0.5, 8.0.3, Puritan 3.5.0.2, 4.2.299.1, 4.3.23.1, Revenger 5.3.48.3, Banquet 1.1.0.4, No Wit 9.62.7, 9.170.12, Roaring Girl 5.155.1, Hengist 2.2.0.12 (Quarto), 4.3.0.3 (Quarto), Tennis 374.2, Valour 3.4.0.2. In most of these cases, the verb occurs in a descriptive stage direction, as here. This looks like an authorial variant in the abridgement.

3.1.395.1–2/1577   like ∧ an apparition] as in ~ ~ CRANE[2,3]; as in ∧ ~ CRANE/ALLDE. Thus, CRANE[2,3,4] all share 'as in' in place of 'like'.

3.1.395.2/1577   in rich attire] richlie habited CRANE[2,3] (after 'Apparition') ; richly attired CRANE[4] (after 'apparition'). Thus, CRANE[2,3,4] all share the adverb 'richly'.

*3.1.395.2–3/1578–9   and...exit] not in CRANE. As noted else-where, even playbooks often omit exits, particularly for characters who enter and immediately leave; the informa-tion provided by this phrase is helpful for a literary reader, and was probably an addition intended for that purpose. However, for the sake of consistency, its absence—like the absence of other strictly necessary directions—is counted as a shared error, for the purposes of statistical analysis. Howard--Hill (1995, p. 281) notes the absence of this direction from CRANE[2,3,4], but does not record its absence from CRANE[1]. This is important, because Crane is usually supposed (as part of his 'editing' of texts) to have added exit directions.

3.1.395.2/1578   and] OKES, ROSENBACH[A], BRIDGEWATER[B]; not in CRANE, MIDDLETON[T]

3.1.395.2/1578   presents himself] MIDDLETON[T]; stands OKES, ROSEN-BACH[A], BRIDGEWATER[B]. Late autograph variant.

3.1.397–8/1581–2   BLACK QUEEN'S PAWN...WHITE QUEEN'S PAWN] not in CRANE[3]

*3.1.398/1582   If...soon] two lines ROSENBACH[A], BRIDGEWATER[B] : he |. Shared error.

*3.1.399/1583–4   Why...you] 2 lines: how | MIDDLETON[T]; yours | ROSENBACH[A], BRIDGEWATER[B]. Shared error.

3.1.399/1583–4   How do you?] not in CRANE[2]

3.1.400/1585   O] not in BRIDGEWATER[B] uncorrected

3.1.401/1586   bloods, our states] OKES; bloud or state CRANE[1]+. Late authorial revision. The triple variant, and the related rhyme-change in the following line, make it very unlikely that the plurals are accidental. Middleton uses 'our bloods' at Phoenix 9.80 and Revenger 3.6.79, 'our states' at Trick 1.1.68, and the two phrases are juxtaposed in Chaste Maid 2.1.14 ('our bloods') and 2.1.20 ('our states'); indeed, the earlier line ('And till our state rise, make our bloods lie still') should perhaps be emended to 'states', and in any case uses 'our' twice before the same two nouns.

3.1.402/1587   still] doe ROSENBACH[A]

3.1.402/1587   fates] OKES; fate CRANE[1]+. Late authorial variant: see above. Middleton uses plural 'fates' at least fifteen times elsewhere.

3.1.403/1588   that is] thats ithe ROSENBACH[A]; that are BRIDGE-WATER[B] uncorrected. The ROSENBACH[A] variant might be au-thorial; but it replaces a rare compound (law-tossed) with a commoner explanatory prepositional phrase (in the law tossed). The double contraction (that's i'th') seems typical of Middleton's elided style, but I have not found that particular combination elsewhere in his canon (though he uses both 'that's' and 'i'th'' often). See 2.1.147.

3.1.406/1591   It's] CRANE[3]; 'tis CRANE[1]+. See Induction.15.

3.1.406/1591   He's] THIS EDITION; hee is CRANE[1]+. A typical Crane expansion, reproduced in all subsequent witnesses. The phrase 'He's a gentleman', with the contraction (vari-ously spelled), occurs twice in Widow 1.1.61–2, 2.1.131–2, and once each in Michaelmas 1.2.263, Witch 3.2.197, Quarrel 2.1.43, and Changeling 1.1.134. The contraction makes the line more regular metrically. Moreover, MIDDLE-TON[T] has an anomalously low rate of the contractions he's and she's, relative to other Middleton plays. (See General Textual Introduction, sec. IV.)

3.1.407/1592   composed] compoſèd OKES

3.1.408/1593   has] 'hath CRANE[2,3]

*3.1.410/1595   tetrarch] Tetrach CRANE[2,3,4], OKES, BRIDGEWATER[B]. Shared error: the second 'r' is present in the Greek and Latin forms, and in OED's list of English spellings. The unfamiliar-ity of the word no doubt accounts for the repeated passive transmission of the error.

3.1.410–11/1595–6   which…pleasure] not in CRANE³

3.1.411/1596   I'th'] In th' CRANE²⁺⁴; in the MIDDLETONᵀ only. See 2.1.147.

3.1.412/1597   request] defire CRANE¹

3.1.413/1599   What] ~ to BRIDGEWATERᴮ uncorrected

3.1.413/1599   does] MIDDLETONᵀ (do's); doth CRANE¹+. See Incidentals note at Early 3.398.

3.1.414/1600   Exit] CRANE²; not in CRANE¹+. See note at 3.1.415.1.

3.1.415   BLACK…wronger.] not in MIDDLETONᵀ

3.1.415   QUEEN'S] not in ROSENBACHᴬ, BRIDGEWATERᴮ; B. CRANE/ALLDE. For the generic prefix see 3.1.348. For the CRANE/ALLDE error see 4.1.38.

*3.1.415.1/1601   Exit] CRANE²; Exeunt CRANE¹+; not in OKES, BRIDGEWATERᴮ. It is common for an exeunt direction to cover two separate exits when one follows the other almost immediately; only the complete absence of an exit direction is actually an error. CRANE² more likely represents the playbook, and hence performance.

3.1.415.2/1602   Finit Actus Tertius] MIDDLETONᵀ, ROSENBACHᴬ, BRIDGEWATERᴮ corrected; Finis ~ ~ BRIDGEWATERᴮ uncorrected; Finis ~ Tercij CRANE¹; ~~ Tertus OKES; not in CRANE²,³,⁴

4.1   CRANE, ROSENBACHᴬ (Sceᵃ. priᵃ.). The scene number is not in OKES, BRIDGEWATERᴮ, MIDDLETONᵀ.

4.1.0.1/1603   Incipit] OKES, BRIDGEWATERᴮ, MIDDLETONᵀ; not in CRANE, ROSENBACHᴬ. See 2.1.0.1.

4.1.0.1/1603   Actus] not in OKES, BRIDGEWATERᴮ, MIDDLETONᵀ

4.1.0.2–4/1604–5   Enter…accoutred] The Black Bᵖˢ. Pawne: & yᵉ white, & Bl: Queenes Pawnes. CRANE³. For the massed entry, see 1.1.0.2–5. An entry for the Black Knight's Pawn is omitted, because as part of its abridgement CRANE³ omits 4.1.1–33.

4.1.0.2/1604   from the Black House] THIS EDITION (conj. Hotson); not in CRANE¹+. See 1.1.30.1.

4.1.0.2–3/1604   ₐBlack Knight's….ₐBlack Bishop's] yᵉ ~~ … yᵉ ~~ CRANE²

4.1.0.2–3/1604–5   Knight's…Bishop's] Bᵖˢ…. Knights CRANE²,⁴. The alternative order probably represents traditional hierarchy of bishop over knight, rather than stage practice.

4.1.0.3–4.1.33.1/1603–44   meeting…deeper. Exit] not in CRANE³ (which also leaves Black Knight's Pawn out of the massed entrance directions for this scene, because it has cut the first part of the scene)

4.1.0.3/1604   meeting] MIDDLETONᵀ; & CRANE¹+

4.1.0.3–4/1604   the Jesuit…in his gallant habit] THIS EDITION; The Iefuit in his gallant habit, OKES; not in CRANE¹+. OKES prints these words in roman type after the speech prefix, as though they were the first line of spoken text. I have inserted the two phrases at separate points in the stage direction, so that they supplement the information given to readers.

4.1.0.3/1604   the] CRANE²,³, MIDDLETONᵀ; not in CRANE¹+

4.1.0.4/1605   richly accoutred] MIDDLETONᵀ; not in CRANE¹+

4.1.1/1606   KNIGHT'S] K. CRANE/ALLDE. This variant can hardly be due to type shortage. It occurs at the top of G1, immediately after the stage direction spelling out 'Knights' in full, and followed by three occurrence of 'Kni.' in speech prefixes on the same page; italic 'n' and 'i' were clearly available to the compositor here. The omission of ni may have been an accidental or deliberate result of following the spelled-out stage direction, which made it less necessary to give a full form of the speech prefix. For other examples of this unambiguous form for this character, see 2.1.229 (in OKES) and 4.2.14 (in CRANE/ALLDE).

4.1.1/1606   It's] CRANE²⁺⁴; 'tis CRANE¹+. See Induction.15.

4.1.1/1606   ha'] MIDDLETONᵀ only; haue CRANE¹+

4.1.1/1606   passed] paffed BRIDGEWATERᴮ

4.1.2/1607   Sev'n] 7 MIDDLETONᵀ, ROSENBACHᴬ; feauen CRANE¹+. See 1.1.250.

4.1.2/1607   years] yeare CRANE¹,⁴, MIDDLETONᵀ. The obsolete form is preserved in Early 4.2.

4.1.3/1608   lettered] letterèd OKES

4.1.3/1608   hatband] OKES (Hat bond), MIDDLETONᵀ+

4.1.4–5/1609–10   The…consent] worne, | OKES. See next note.

4.1.4–5/1609–10   to be known, by, | Worn by] ~ ~ ~,~, | ~ ~ BRIDGEWATERᴮ; ~ ~ worne, | By OKES. OKES makes sense, and is adopted by HOWARD-HILL; it would work metrically if 'Jesuitical' were pronounced as five syllables. But the variant produces an uncharacteristically strong enjambment, and probably results from simple inadvertent omission (skipping from 'knowne by' to 'worne by'). Both BRIDGEWATER and OKES place an anomalous comma after the third word of the phrase; these punctuation errors seem related to one another, and OKES may be another example of progressive error. The mislineation does not encourage confidence in OKES here.

4.1.5/1610   with consent] OKES; by ~ CRANE¹+. Late authorial variant. There is nothing in the context to explain 'with' as an error; Middleton might have wished to avoid three uses of 'by' within a line and a half. For 'with consent' see OED n.2.

4.1.6/1611   It's] CRANE²; 'Tis CRANE⁴, OKES, ROSENBACHᴬ, BRIDGEWATERᴮ; This CRANE¹, MIDDLETONᵀ. The obsolete autograph contraction is preserved in Early 4.6. For it's, see Induction.15.

4.1.6/1611   strange] ftrong ROSENBACHᴬ. Misreading.

4.1.6/1611   Father] Feather CRANE/ALLDE. Perhaps a miscorrection, in foul proofs, of the error four lines below (also at the end of a verse line).

4.1.10/1615   humbly] MIDDLETONᵀ+ (humblie); humble BRIDGEWATERᴮ, OKES. Although adjective and adverb are often interchangeable, here the adjective seems inept ('confess ourselves [to be] as humble'), and is probably a shared error.

4.1.10/1615   feather] Father CRANE/ALLDE. See 4.1.6.

4.1.11/1616   spur] fpeare OKES. Misreading.

4.1.11/1616   alb] MIDDLETONᵀ+ (Albe); Abbey OKES. Misreading.

4.1.12/1617   we're] CRANE¹ (we're), CRANE² (w'are), ROSENBACHᴬ (weére); weeáre MIDDLETONᵀ; we are [CRANE⁴], BRIDGEWATERᴮ, OKES

4.1.12/1617   highly] mighty CRANE/ALLDE. This might be a late authorial variant, but alliteration favours 'highly'; I have found no parallels for Middleton using mighty as an adverb before a verb or past participle. The variant could result from scribal or compositorial misreading, or miscorrection of a foul case error.

4.1.12/1617   t'] to [CRANE⁴], ROSENBACHᴬ, MIDDLETONᵀ

4.1.12/1617   attain] taine BRIDGEWATERᴮ. See previous note.

4.1.12/1617   to't] to it MIDDLETONᵀ only

4.1.13/1619   hast] has OKES

4.1.14/1620   trim] trane CRANE/ALLDE. Misreading.

4.1.15/1621   knew] know OKES. Possibly authorial, but an easy misreading. The question used the past tense.

4.1.16/1622   Catholical] Catholicke CRANE/ALLDE; Vniverfall CRANE¹. Middleton never elsewhere uses CRANE/ALLDE's form of the adjective.

4.1.17/1624   bishop's] Kts. BRIDGEWATERᴮ uncorrected

4.1.17–18/1624–5   Are…bus̑iness] CRANE/ALLDE; grown | CRANE¹+. CRANE/ALLDE produces an hexameter with an extra unstressed syllable at the caesura and the line-end, followed by a regular iambic pentameter; the alternative produces a regular iambic pentameter here, but in the next line produces two initial trochees, followed by a four or five stress iambic line. Neither arrangement is perfectly regular, and Middleton may well have vacillated.

4.1.19/1627 And] ROSENBACH[A], BRIDGEWATER[B]; *not in* CRANE[1]+. Late authorial vacillation. The Middleton canon has at least 27 examples of the phrase 'and I have', at least once immediately after a speech prefix (*Changeling* 1.1.68).

*4.1.21-2/1629-30 The...sir] CRANE[1]; his | MIDDLETON[T]; see | CRANE[2]+; *not in* CRANE[3]. Shared lineation error.

4.1.22-4/1630-32 Might...game] pleasure | conscience | courage | OKES. This error resembles mislineations elsewhere in MIDDLETON[T].

4.1.24/1632 ply] play OKES, ROSENBACH[A], BRIDGEWATER[B]. Possibly authorial, but it substitutes a common idiom (and a verb already used three lines earlier) for an unusual one, and could easily be a shared error.

4.1.25/1634 schismatic] Schifamticke OKES. Compositorial transposition.

4.1.25/1634 sir] *not in* CRANE[1]

4.1.26/1635 nobility] ability OKES. Misreading.

4.1.27/1636 Suffices] 'Suffice CRANE/ALLDE. Probably an omitted type.

4.1.30/1639 in't] not BRIDGEWATER[B] *uncorrected*

4.1.31/1640 Black] Fat HOWARD-HILL. This may be, as Howard-Hill believes, a relic of the original version, inadvertently transmitted to all later texts. But at this point the word makes perfect sense: we do not yet know that the Fat Bishop will appear later, to serve this function, and when he does appear, 197 lines later, we have no reason to remember this word—or, if we do, we would immediately understand it, because the Fat Bishop has by that point fully transformed himself into (again) a black bishop.

4.1.31/1640 clemency] fauor BRIDGEWATER[B] *uncorrected*

4.1.31/1640 have wrought] hau'wroght OKES; ha' wrought THIS EDITION *conj.*

4.1.32/1641 singular] fingle OKES. *OED*'s first instance of *single* with the meaning 'unique, singular' (a. 7) is from Ford's *Perkin Warbeck*, printed in 1634 but possibly written as much as a decade earlier. But that usage may be anticipated by *Roaring Girl* Epilogue.7-11: 'our plays follow the niceness of our garments: single plots, quaint conceits, lecherous jests, dressed up in hanging sleeves...Such a kind of light-colour summer stuff, mingled with diverse colours, you shall find this published comedy'. Editors have been confused by 'single' there, because the phrase 'mingled with diverse colours' (and the play itself) shows that it does not mean 'undivided' or 'one only'; but the sense 'unique, singular' would fit with 'niceness' and 'quaint'. The OKES variant therefore might make sense, but 'single' is a much more common word than 'singular', especially after the indefinite article and followed by a noun; it is almost impossible to understand 'a single piece' as anything other than 'one piece'. The variant probably results from the substitution of a common for an unusual word (Taylor 1988).

4.1.33/1642 It's] OKES; that's CRANE[1]+. See Induction.15.

4.1.33/1643 KNIGHT'S] K. CRANE/ALLDE. See 4.1.1. Here on G1[v] the compositor may have reduced the form of the prefix because of the crowding produced by the presence on the same type line of one stage direction and part of another (*Exit. (Bl.Q.Pawne.*).

4.1.33/1643 This] the CRANE. Late authorial variant.

4.1.33/1643 deeper] deepe BRIDGEWATER[B], ROSENBACH[A]. Possibly authorial, but Black Knight's Pawn has mentioned the 'sting'

before, and the comparative emphasizes the deepening of his despair since that earlier reference.

*4.1.33.1/1644 *Exit*] *not in* OKES, ROSENBACH[A], BRIDGEWATER[B]. It may be relevant that the direction was also omitted from CRANE[3], because the abridgement omitted the first part of the scene; but the absence of the direction is not an error in that text, as it is in the others.

4.1.33.2/1644 *Enter...Pawn*] CRANE[1,2], ROSENBACH[A]. For verbal variants see following notes. BRIDGEWATER[B], OKES, CRANE/ALLDE place the entrance a half-line earlier, after 'refuge now' (which is certainly possible); MIDDLETON[T] places it after 'see' (4.1.35), which is almost certainly an error.

4.1.33.2/1644 *aloof off*] THIS EDITION; *not in* CRANE[1]+. The scene requires them to occupy at first a different part of the stage than the Black Bishop's Pawn. This idiom occurs in stage directions in *No Wit* 8.0.4 and *Patient Man* 6.143.4.

4.1.33.2-3/1644 *White Queen's Pawn...Pawn*] ~ ∧ ∧...*Pawnes* CRANE[2,3]; *w.Q....pawne* OKES

4.1.33.2-3/1644 *White...Black*] B: ...Wh: ROSENBACH[A]

4.1.33.2/1644 ∧ *White*] *y*[e] ~ CRANE[2,3]

4.1.33.2/1644 *and*] *not in* BRIDGEWATER[B]

4.1.33.3/1644 ∧ *Black*] *y*[e] ~ CRANE[2]

4.1.34/1645 chessmaster] Cheffner OKES. Misreading of 'mr' as 'ner'.

4.1.35/1647 'Tis he] CRANE[2,3]; *not in* CRANE[1]+. Bawcutt (1993) defends the possible authority of this variant, noting that 'It would certainly seem that "that tis" is a better reply to "'tis he" than to "oh my heart"' (p. 9). Middleton uses *'tis he* at least fourteen times elsewhere. This could be a change in the playbook, which was overlooked in [KING'S MEN[3]] or [CRANE[4]], and thereby dropped out of all later copies.

4.1.36-7/1649-50 BLACK QUEEN'S PAWN...WHITE QUEEN'S PAWN] *not in* CRANE[3]

4.1.37/1650 self-same] CRANE[1]+ (felfe fame); ∧ fame OKES. Eyeskip.

4.1.37/1650 mirror] *not in* OKES

4.1.38/1651 to] vnto OKES. Possibly authorial, but the only two Middletonian examples of 'unto me' I have found are both early (*Solomon* 7.72 and *Five Gallants* 1.2.42).

4.1.38/1652 QUEEN'S] Bs. MIDDLETON[T] *only*. The same error—again, as here, unique to an autograph text—occurs at 4.1.107. At 2.1.232 CRANE/MATHEWES makes the same substitution of 'B' [= Bishop's] for 'Q' [= Queen's]; it occurs also in CRANE/ALLDE at 3.1.412. This suggests that the errors may have originated in [CRANE[4]], not the two printing shops. The same error occurs in ROSENBACH[A] at 3.1.318, and in OKES at 4.1.81 (set in a third printshop from an autograph manuscript). For another example, with both the error and its correction in a single manuscript, see *Early* 2.270. The reverse error occurs in OKES at 4.1.101, in CRANE/MATHEWES at 1.1.162, then in CRANE/ALLDE at 4.1.118 and 5.2.70. Since 'Q' and 'B' are not adjacent in the standard lay of the case, and do not resemble one another in Middleton's or Crane's handwriting, the error—which occurs in autograph, in at least one scribal text, and in texts set by three different printshops—probably originated with Middleton himself, as it does here. Apparently, Middleton strongly associated these two black Jesuit pawns, and occasionally absent-mindedly wrote the initials of one in place of the other. (If the copy for MATHEWES/ALLDE were Middleton's transcript of a Crane transcript, then all these examples might have originated in autograph.)

*4.1.38-9/1652-3 And...by] most | ROSENBACH[A], BRIDGEWATER[B]. Shared error.

4.1.39/1653 most] ſtrange CRANE/ALLDE. Anticipation.

4.1.40/1654 his] this OKES. Misreading.

4.1.40/1654 minded] indeede OKES. Misreading.

4.1.41/1655 principal'ſt] principalleſt ROSENBACH[A]

4.1.43/1659 pow'r] CRANE[1,2,3], BRIDGEWATER[B] (powre); power [CRANE[4]]+

4.1.43/1659 now] *not in* CRANE/ALLDE

*4.1.44-5/1660-61 bring...And] *not in* CRANE[2,3]. Probably eyeskip, rather than deliberate revision. If the cut had been intended to clarify the meaning, 'it' should have been changed to 'time'. For consistency, this omission has been counted as a shared error.

4.1.44/1660 mast'ry] MIDDLETON[T], BRIDGEWATER[B], [CRANE[4]]; Mastery CRANE[1], OKES; mistery ROSENBACH[A]

4.1.46/1662 I...virtue] *2 lines* OKES: nothing |

4.1.46/1662 its] MIDDLETON[T], CRANE[1], BRIDGEWATER[B]; it's CRANE[2,3,4], OKES; it ROSENBACH[A]. *It is* the obsolescent form of the neuter possessive pronoun. See Taylor and Jowett (p. 197) for its/it's in Middleton.

4.1.47/1663 I'd] I had CRANE[2,3,4]

4.1.48/1664 undiscovered] vndiſcouerèd OKES, ROSENBACH[A]

4.1.49/1665 Than] You OKES

4.1.49/1665 suffer] offer ROSENBACH[A]

4.1.51-3/1667-9 How...sudden?] *not in* CRANE[3]

4.1.51/1667 altered] alterèd ROSENBACH[A], BRIDGEWATER[B] *uncorrected*

4.1.52/1668 for't] fot't OKES. Foul case error.

*4.1.53/1669 strait, too] *not in* ROSENBACH[A], BRIDGEWATER[B]. Eyeskip producing metrical deficiency; no reason for change.

4.1.53 strait] MIDDLETON[T]+ (ſtreight)

4.1.57/1674 me] him CRANE[1]

4.1.58/1676 drowned] downe OKES. Misreading.

4.1.59-62/1677-80 Without...it] *not in* CRANE[3]

4.1.59/1677 hint] *not in* ROSENBACH[A]. The scribe left a blank space for a word he presumably could not decipher; this suggests that the word was present in [PRE-ROSENBACH].

4.1.60/1678 fortunes] MIDDLETON[T]; Fortune CRANE[1]+. Late autograph variant.

4.1.61/1680 the] *not in* ROSENBACH[A]

4.1.62/1680 sun's] Sons BRIDGEWATER[B] *uncorrected*

4.1.62/1680 flow'r] Flower NON-CRANE

*4.1.62/1680 uncloses] encloſes CRANE[1], OKES. Probably coincidental independent error. An easy misreading of one letter (u/e), facilitated in this case by the tendency to substitute a common word for a rare one (Taylor 1988).

4.1.63/1681 'Twere] 'Tis OKES. Possibly authorial, but it substitutes the common present tense for the more unusual subjunctive.

4.1.64-6/1682-5 WHITE QUEEN'S PAWN...into't.] *not in* CRANE[3]

4.1.65/1684 still] skill OKES. Probably a misreading, because if the compositor had intended to set the correct word one would expect a ligature.

4.1.66/1685 You're] you'ar CRANE[2]; You'are [CRANE[4]]; you are MIDDLETON[T] *only*. The unique autograph reading almost certainly derives from Crane's 'Jonsonian elision', with the apostrophe at some stage overlooked and omitted.

4.1.66/1685 changed] chain'd OKES. Probably misreading, possibly miscorrection in foul proofs.

4.1.66/1685 if] CRANE[2,4]; and CRANE[1]+; *not in* OKES. Both Crane and Middleton vacillated between these two forms: see 5.3.191. The obsolete variant is preserved in *Early* 4.78. See next note.

4.1.66/1685 you'd] you would CRANE/ALLDE; you'll ROSENBACH[A]; *not in* OKES. The omission of 'and you'd' turns the conditional subordinate clause into a separate imperative sentence. It could be an authorial variant, but it could also easily result from careless omission in (the often careless) OKES, and I cannot find a Middleton parallel for 'look into't' as an imperative.

4.1.66/1685 into't] into it MIDDLETON[T] *only*. Middleton uses 'look into't' three times elsewhere.

4.1.66.1 *Black...Pawn*] THIS EDITION; *not in* CRANE[1]+

4.1.70/1689 it would] would it OKES. Transposition (error).

4.1.70/1689 arrive] appeare BRIDGEWATER[B] *uncorrected*

4.1.72/1691 yon] CRANE[1]+ (yond); your ROSENBACH[A]. Misreading.

4.1.73/1692 my] MIDDLETON[T], OKES; mine CRANE[1]+

4.1.75/1695 liked] like'd CRANE/ALLDE. A unique combination of the elided form ('lik'd') and the extrametrical expansion ('lik⟨e⟩d'), both in contrast to the metrical autograph form 'likte'.

4.1.75/1695 then?] CRANE[1,2,3], BRIDGEWATER[B]; ~, MIDDLETON[T]+. The autograph punctuation is preserved in *Early* 4.88. Middleton's all-purpose comma could cover a variety of interpretations.

4.1.76-86/1696-1708 Pray...found.] *not in* CRANE[3]

4.1.76/1696 There is] there's OKES

4.1.77/1697 I'm] I am CRANE[2,4]

4.1.77/1697 it] *not in* BRIDGEWATER[B] *uncorrected*

4.1.77/1697 it, you must guess;] ~, ~ ∧ OKES, BRIDGEWATER[B]; ~:~ CRANE[1,2]; ~,~, CRANE[4], ROSENBACH[A], MIDDLETON[T]. The meaning of 'guess' closely resembles the meaning of 'think for' (*v.*[2] 12.d., 'expect, suppose'). The free-floating phrase 'you must guess' would therefore be less redundant if it modified the preceding clause rather than the following one. However, Middleton often omitted necessary punctuation at the end of a verse line, and if his draft had contained a comma after 'ghesse' one would have expected Crane to reproduce it. Middleton also sometimes has commas in mid-line and none at line-end; the only explanation for much of his punctuation practice is that he treated the line-end as always a break of some sort. It is therefore entirely possible that his original draft had no punctuation at all in this line, or even contained a mid-line punctuation mark of some sort, and none at the end. However, for the sake of consistency the reading in CRANE[1,2] and OKES, BRIDGEWATER, where the mid-line punctuation is stronger than the end-line punctuation, should be considered a shared punctuation error.

4.1.77/1697 guess] thinck BRIDGEWATER[B], ROSENBACH[A]. Anticipation of the verb in the following line. The word makes sense, and has not been counted as a shared error, but that is almost certainly what it is: it reduces information content without any increase in stylistic effect.

4.1.79/1699 the] *not in* BRIDGEWATER[B]

4.1.80/1700 reciprocal] recipicall OKES. Compositorial error.

4.1.81/1701 QUEEN'S] B. OKES. For this error see 4.1.38.

4.1.81-2/1701-2 And...acquainted] better | ROSENBACH[A]; worth | OKES

4.1.82/1703 there cause?] theire ~ ? BRIDGEWATER[B]; their ~ ∧ OKES. The odd spelling in itself is not ambiguous, but combined with the absence of punctuation it produces a different (and erroneous) meaning in OKES: 'Is their cause affinity'? Perhaps an example of progressive deterioration, the anomalous spelling in BRIDGEWATER leading to the error in OKES.

4.1.83/1704   courteous] couetous OKES. Misreading.

4.1.84/1705   To bring] tloringe ROSENBACH[A]; T bring BRIDGE-WATER[B] *uncorrected*. The two errors seem related. BRIDGE-WATER[C] corrects the error by adding the 'o' in pencil.

4.1.84/1705   forward] forwards ROSENBACH[A]; worke forward OKES. See 1.1.192. OKES's variant recollects l. 78.

4.1.87/1709   then] you OKES

4.1.89/1711   BISHOP'S] K. BRIDGEWATER[B] *uncorrected*

4.1.89/1711   extends] exceds OKES. Misreading.

4.1.90/1712   Has] hath CRANE[2,3,4]

4.1.91/1713   out chaste delight] OKES, ROSENBACH[A], BRIDGE-WATER[B]; our ~ delights CRANE[1]+. The linked variants look authorial. For 'choose out' compare *Old Law* 2.2.120, *Truth* 727. For 'chaste delight' compare *Entertainments* 7.95–6; although Middleton uses the plural noun, he does not else-where collocate it with 'chaste.'

4.1.92/1715   art] heart OKES. Aural error (in the compositor's memory).

4.1.92/1715   me on an] in on one OKES. Misreading.

4.1.93/1716   from't] from it MIDDLETON[T] *only*.

*4.1.93.1/1717   *Exeunt*] CRANE[1,2,3] (*Ex^t.*), ROSENBACH[A]; *not in* CRANE/ALLDE; exit OKES, BRIDGEWATER[B], MIDDLETON[T]. As the dialogue indicates and as all editors since DYCE recognize, two characters must leave the stage here. The abbreviation in the earliest texts can mean 'exeunt', but the singular 'exit' is incorrect.

4.1.94/1718   prove] bee BRIDGEWATER[B] *uncorrected*

4.1.94/1718   check] chcek OKES. Compositorial transposition.

4.1.94/1718   magical] Magick OKES. Possibly authorial.

4.1.94/1718   glass] MIDDLETON[T], OKES; glasse now CRANE[1]+. The omission of the extrametrical word could well be authorial. However, in BRIDGEWATER[B] there is a comma after and below 'glasse', with '(now' interlined above as a turn-up; the punctuation suggests that 'now' was initially overlooked by the scribe, as it easily could be in that position. The BRIDGE-WATER mispunctuation and turn-up seem suspiciously related to the omission in OKES and MIDDLETON[T].

4.1.95/1719   my] by OKES. Aural contamination from preceding word (*but by*).

4.1.96/1720   eye] eyes OKES

4.1.96/1720   his] *not in* ROSENBACH[A]

4.1.97/1721   Then] You OKES

4.1.97/1721   I'm] I'am CRANE[2]; I am CRANE[3,4]

*4.1.97/1721   confirmed] confident ROSENBACH[A], BRIDGEWATER[B]; confirmèd OKES. The alternative adjective is unmetrical.

4.1.97/1721   he is] hee's ROSENBACH[A]

4.1.97/1721   own] *not in* OKES

4.1.97.1/1722   *Enter again*] *not in* CRANE/ALLDE. The error might be related to the format in BRIDGEWATER[B], which places the direction to the right of the following speech prefix.

4.1.97.1/1722   *Black Bishop's Pawn*] OKES (*B.B.p.*). By specifying one of the two characters who must re-enter, OKES produces a less correct text than all the other witnesses, since in other texts 'Enter again' could easily refer to the two who had just left. Perhaps the compositor anticipated the speech prefix on the following line, or accidentally omitted a second abbreviation ('B.Q.P.'). However, at 4.1.93.1 OKES is one of the three texts that has incorrect singular 'Exit', so it is possible that the error here derives from that earlier error.

4.1.97.1–2/1722   *with Jesuitess Black Queen's Pawn*] THIS EDI-TION; *not in* CRANE[1]+. See preceding note. The need for her re-entrance was recognized by DYCE, but he put the two

names in the reverse order ('Re-enter Black Queen's Pawn and Black Bishop's Pawn.'), and has been followed by other editors.

4.1.98–9/1723–4   The...habit] mirror | MIDDLETON[T]

4.1.98/1723   The...with] 2 lines ROSENBACH[A]: same |

4.1.98/1723   the mirror] my ~ OKES; the Mag BRIDGEWATER[B] *uncorrected*

4.1.100/1725   you not] not you OKES, ROSENBACH[A], BRIDGE-WATER[B]. Possibly authorial.

4.1.101/1726   farther] MIDDLETON[T], BRIDGEWATER[B] (farder), CRANE[1,2,3], ROSENBACH[A] (farther); further CRANE/ALLDE; *not in* OKES. See 3.1.207.

4.1.101/1727   BISHOP'S] Q. OKES. See 4.1.38.

4.1.102–3/1728–9   I...presented] substance | ROSENBACH[A]. Same kind of mislineation that appears elsewhere in MIDDLETON[T].

4.1.102/1728   I'd] NON-CRANE; I'had CRANE[1,2]; I had CRANE[3,4]

4.1.103/1729   'Twas] was ROSENBACH[A]

4.1.104/1730   E'en] MIDDLETON[T], BRIDGEWATER *corrected*; Ev'n CRANE[1]; Euen CRANE[2]+

4.1.104/1731   Saw] Pawne, saw OKES. Perhaps unconscious duplication/expansion of the final element of the speech prefix.

4.1.105–6/1732–3   Perfectly...appeared] no | OKES. This error may indicate that in the printer's manuscript copy this was a single long line, a relic of authorial practice that was arbitrarily divided by the compositor in order to fit the measure.

4.1.105/1733   used] vśèd OKES

4.1.106/1733   appeared] appeares ROSENBACH[A]; appearèd OKES

4.1.106/1734   Just] *not in* ROSENBACH[A], BRIDGEWATER[B]. Unmet-rical; probably a shared error.

4.1.106/1734   now] too ROSENBACH[A]. Possibly a late authorial variant.

*4.1.107/1735   BLACK] wh. CRANE[2], ROSENBACH[A] *uncorrected*. The error was probably caused by the pattern of alternating 'Black' and 'White' speeches in the preceding lines (92–106).

4.1.107/1735   QUEEN'S] B[s.] MIDDLETON[T] *only*. This error results from the substitution of one letter ('B[s]' in place of 'Q[s]'). See 4.1.38.

4.1.107–10/1735–38   Why...bashfull'st] 5 *lines* OKES: time | those | you | blushing |. The mislineation here might be due to deliberate space wasting by a compositor, stretching cast-off copy.

4.1.108–11/1736–9   Protracting...any] *not in* CRANE[3]

4.1.108/1736   Protracting] Protacting ROSENBACH[A]

4.1.108/1736   benefits] Beuties CRANE[2]. Misreading.

4.1.109/1737   fate has] faith OKES (combining the beginning of the first word with the end of the second)

4.1.109/1737   has] THIS EDITION; hath CRANE+. This is the first occurrence in autograph of the obsolescent form, preferred by Crane over Middleton's overwhelmingly preferred 'has'. Middleton was demonstrably becoming less attentive as a transcriber, and in correcting his copy, by the beginning of Act Four.

4.1.109/1737   marked] work'd CRANE/ALLDE. Misreading (prob-ably compositorial) of 'mark'd'.

4.1.109/1737   marked] markèd OKES

4.1.109/1737   you?] You] you, ᴧ BRIDGEWATER[B]. Haplography.

4.1.110/1738   bashfull'st] bafhfull OKES; shamefulst ROSENBACH[A]

4.1.112/1740   assigned] assigne OKES; affignèd ROSENBACH[A]. OKES might result from misreading or (if the compositor's copy resembled ROSENBACH) from an omitted final letter.

4.1.113/1741 irrevocable] irrecouerable CRANE/ALLDE. Misreading, probably compositorial.

4.1.114-17/1742-5 Others...coupled.] *not in* CRANE³

4.1.115/1743 shame] chance CRANE/ALLDE. Misreading.

*4.1.116/1744 Their...'em] MIDDLETON^T, CRANE^I; *not in* CRANE²+. There seems no explanation for omission of this line, beyond simple error, perpetuated in all subsequent texts except MIDDLETON^T, where it was restored because the author remembered it.

4.1.116/1744 fortune's...event's] MIDDLETON^T, CRANE^I (fortunes...events). Although editors interpret 'fortunes' and 'events' as plural, that would make the whole line modify 'Others', two lines earlier; it seems likelier that, as often elsewhere, the intended contraction was not indicated by an apostrophe.

4.1.118/1746 BISHOP'S] Q. CRANE/ALLDE. See 4.1.38.

4.1.118-19/1746-7 She...night] reason | MIDDLETON^T

4.1.118/1746 She...then] *2 lines* OKES: this |. Space wasting?

4.1.120/1748 that] *not in* OKES. Possibly a late authorial variant, but if so indistinguishable from the carelessness of this printer.

4.1.121/1750 therein] thetein ALLDE. Foul case.

4.1.122-4/1751-3 Your...miserable] *4 lines* ROSENBACH^A: loose | my | mind |

4.1.123/1752 my] by OKES

4.1.125/1754 wingèd] wing'd [CRANE⁴], ROSENBACH^A. Metre requires the obsolescent disyllabic form.

4.1.126-7/1755-6 Have...virgin] justly | OKES

4.1.126/1755 desires] defites ALLDE. Foul case.

4.1.127/1756 unfortunate] infortunate OKES, ROSENBACH^A. Probably a simple misreading, since Middleton used the obsolete form of the adjective only at *Solomon* 16.183, twenty-seven years before.

4.1.127/1756 A] *not in* OKES

4.1.128/1757 woman] women ROSENBACH^A

4.1.128/1757 that] *not in* OKES

4.1.128/1757 has] hath CRANE²,³,⁴

4.1.128/1757 ordained] ordaynèd OKES, ROSENBACH^A

*4.1.129-30/1758-9 We...so] given | OKES, ROSENBACH^A. Shared lineation error.

4.1.129/1758 should be] shalbe ROSENBACH^A

4.1.129/1758 man] both ~ CRANE/ALLDE

4.1.129/1758 has] hath CRANE²,³,⁴

4.1.130/1759 For...so] till | OKES

4.1.130/1759 any] ayme OKES. Misreading.

4.1.130.1/1759 *She weeps*] THIS EDITION; *not in* CRANE^I+

4.1.131/1760 How] the BRIDGEWATER^B *uncorrected*

4.1.131/1760 grieves] OKES; giues CRANE^I+. The variant makes excellent Middletonian sense: compare 'grieve at' (*Solomon* 14.111) and 'grieve a modest eye' (*Witch* 5.3.40). The majority reading could be a shared error: for 'giues' in place of correct 'griues' or 'grieues', see *Early* 2.319. However, here *gives* can be defended in the sense 'yield, give way' (*OED* give v. 40a). This could be another case of late authorial revision.

4.1.131.1-2/1760 *Black...apart*] THIS EDITION; *not in* CRANE^I+

4.1.132/1761 I'm] I'am CRANE/ALLDE; I am CRANE²,³

4.1.133/1762 As] at MIDDLETON^T *uncorrected only*

4.1.134/1763 marry] be married CRANE/ALLDE. The variant would be metrical if 'cannot' were contracted to 'can't' (as at 2.2.185).

4.1.134/1763 my] mine CRANE²,³,⁴

4.1.135-6/1764-5 I...contract] yet you | OKES

4.1.136/1765 Upon] on OKES. Possibly a late authorial variant: 'venture on' would produce a line-divided foot.

4.1.136/1765 contract] conctract ALLDE. Compositorial error.

4.1.136/1766-7 BLACK BISHOP'S PAWN...BLACK QUEEN'S PAWN] *not in* CRANE³

4.1.136/1767 Surely] Sure OKES

4.1.138/1769 may take] make take OKES. Assimilation.

4.1.139/1770-1 Nay...too] *2 lines:* the | MIDDLETON^T, you | OKES

4.1.139/1770 you] thou BRIDGEWATER^B *uncorrected*

4.1.141/1773 You've] You haue CRANE³,⁴

4.1.142/1774 love] loues ROSENBACH^A. Possibly authorial, but it substitutes a common possessive for an unusual compound.

4.1.143/1775 ne'er] neuer ROSENBACH^A, BRIDGEWATER^B. See 1.1.1.

4.1.144/1776 we're] we are CRANE²,³,⁴

4.1.144/1776 contracted] marri BRIDGEWATER^B *uncorrected*

4.1.144/1776 you're] you'are CRANE³; you are [CRANE⁴]; you BRIDGEWATER^B *uncorrected*

4.1.146-9/1779-82 Push...for] *7 lines* OKES: wife | ceremony | first | then | both | have |. Space wasting?

4.1.146/1779 Push] pish CRANE, OKES

4.1.146/1779 you're] you'are CRANE³; you are CRANE^I,⁴, ROSENBACH^A

4.1.146/1779 ceremonies] OKES; Ceremonie MIDDLETON^T+. Middleton has 'holy ceremonies' at *Women Beware* 4.3.3; 'reverend ceremonies' and 'holy service and ceremonies' both occur in *Antiquity* 402, 403-4 and *Industry* 249-50, 252. There is nothing in the immediate context to encourage a compositor to substitute plural for singular here, and since Middleton used both forms in similar contexts the vacillation is probably authorial.

4.1.147/1780 that] it OKES. Misreading of 'yᵗ'.

4.1.148-9/1781-2 Now...for] *not in* CRANE^I

4.1.148/1781 'em] CRANE²,³; you CRANE⁴, NON-CRANE; *not in* CRANE^I. One of Middleton's favourite contractions; here it clarifies that the line is spoken aside. The variant may be authorial, but it could have arisen from a memory of 'cozen you' at D.16 and 4.1.107, or simply from the assumption that dialogue was continuing.

4.1.149/1782 worked] wrought CRANE³

*4.1.149.1/1783 *Exeunt*] *not in* ROSENBACH^A, BRIDGEWATER^B

4.2 CRANE (*Sce.ᵃ. 2ᵃ.*); *not in* NON-CRANE

4.2.0.1/1784 *Enter...Pawn*] Enter B. K.ᵗ P his BRIDGEWATER^B (justified right like an exit direction); *The Bl. Knight, & his Pawne: Then yᵉ Fat-Bishop: Then the Black-king.* CRANE³. For the massed entry, see 1.1.0.2-5.

4.2.0.1/1784 *Enter* ₐ] ~ yᵉ CRANE²,³

4.2.0.1/1784 with] MIDDLETON^T, BRIDGEWATER^B; & CRANE^I+

4.2.0.2/1784 *from the Black House*] THIS EDITION (*conj.* Hotson); *not in* CRANE^I+. See 1.1.30.1.

4.2.1/1785 BLACK KNIGHT] *not in* MIDDLETON^T *only*

4.2.1/1785 Pawn...thee] *2 lines* ROSENBACH^A: to |. (Stage direction in margin cramps line.)

4.2.1/1785 spoke] spoken HARPER, HOWARD-HILL, DUTTON. The past tense form 'have spoke' is recorded by *OED* from 1387 to 1840; 'spoken' is extrametrical. The form here in all eight witnesses to *Game* appears at least seven times elsewhere in the Middleton canon; the only occurrence of 'have spoken' appears in the Crane transcript of *Witch* 5.3.121.

4.2.1/1785 the] thee CRANE/ALLDE

4.2.1/1785 Fat] black CRANE^I, MIDDLETON^T. A relic of the original version, correct in CRANE^I but also present in MIDDLETON^T alone of the revised texts. This is not a 'shared error', since it is *not* an error in CRANE^I, and not really an error in

MIDDLETON[T] either, since it makes sense, though that sense is not pursued in the subsequent narrative. Even if regarded as an error, it belongs to the (large) category of unique errors in MIDDLETON[T]. If MIDDLETON[T] were a scribal text, this variant might suggest a close connection between MIDDLETON[T] and CRANE[I]; but since MIDDLETON[T] is authorial, and the author knew the original version preserved in CRANE[I], he could at any point have reverted to an original reading, even if the manuscript he was copying contained the revised form.

4.2.2/1786   thy] OKES; thee CRANE[I]+. Either reading makes sense, and 'thy' is less repetitive ('thee' having appeared only three lines before).

4.2.3/1787   chair of ease, my chair] Golden stoole, my stoole CRANE[I]. The phrase 'chair of ease' is glossed by HOWARD-HILL and DUTTON as 'privy, commode', presumably on the basis of *OED ease n.*8.b. But the first recorded example of that sense, from *c.*1645, is the predicate 'doing his Ease', and the noun 'seats of ease' is not recorded until *c.*1850. The referent is clearly, as HARPER noted, to Gondomar's special chair, with a hole cut in the middle of the seat (shown on the title-page of *2 Vox Populi*), which allowed him to sit without irritating his fistula; in performances, the King's Men had Gondomar 'seated in his chair with a hole in it' (according to Coloma), he was 'brought on the Stage in his chayre' (Nethersole), and 'his open chayre for the ease of that fistulated part...appeared uppon the stage' (Holles).

4.2.3/1787   coz'nage] MIDDLETON[T], BRIDGEWATER[B] (coofnage); Cozonage CRANE, OKES, ROSENBACH[A]

4.2.4   Sev'n] 7 MIDDLETON[T], BRIDGEWATER[B], ROSENBACH[A]; feauen CRANE[I]+. See 1.1.250.

*4.2.4/1788   pounds] OKES, CRANE/ALLDE; pound CRANE[I,2,3], MIDDLETON[T]; paund ROSENBACH[A], BRIDGEWATER[B]. In the modern-spelling text we have preferred the normal modern form: see *Early* 4.2.104. The variant 'paund', i.e. 'pawned', is clearly a shared error; it presumably originated from misreading a text which used the archaic singular, and is therefore a 'progressive' error (although there is nothing wrong with the singular form from which it derives).

4.2.4/1788   women] woman CRANE[I]

4.2.4/1788   reach] read ROSENBACH[A]

4.2.5/1789   love] live CRANE[3]

4.2.5/1789   o'] of CRANE[3,4]; to BRIDGEWATER[B] *uncorrected*

4.2.6/1790   gently] gentle OKES, HOWARD-HILL (unrecorded)

4.2.7-9/1791-93   There's...qualm] *4 lines* ROSENBACH[A]: drum | soldier | Europe|.

4.2.7/1791   i'th'] in the MIDDLETON[T] *only*. See 2.1.147.

4.2.7/1791   drum] bum OKES. A possible authorial variant; certainly, the literal meaning of the line, where the other texts supply a metaphor. But 'bottom of my bottom' seems redundant. Probably an unconscious substitution/paraphrase.

4.2.7/1791   drum, Pawn] Drum; P. MIDDLETON[T]. No other text abbreviates the final word of the line, or has such strong punctuation after the penultimate 'drum'; the abbreviation, squeezed into the end of the line, might be an afterthought correction, if Middleton's copy were a manuscript mislined like ROSENBACH, with 'Pawne' at the beginning of the following line. On that assumption, one might identify the punctuation here as evidence of progressive error.

4.2.8/1792   treacher] CRANE[I]+; trencher HOWARD-HILL (*conj.* Mulryne). The emendation is justified on the grounds that the reading of all the witnesses 'is rather meaningless' while the emendation 'maintains the image of Black House voracity,

developed prominently in 5.3.82-9'. But in the immediate context of this speech, there is no reason for the Black Knight to describe himself as a voracious eater; in fact, in 5.3 he is the spokesman for anorexia, and elsewhere criticizes the Fat Bishop for his very fatness. The unemended passage depends upon a simple but widespread and ideologically powerful early modern contrast between soldiers (still considered honourable, according to a feudal aristocratic code) and politicians like Gondomar (dishonourable courtiers, who achieve their power by talking and have no loyalty to anyone but themselves).

4.2.9/1793   qualm] quality OKES. Probably a misreading (of 'qualme' as 'qualitie'); in ROSENBACH[A] the upturn at the bottom of the tail of the 'h' in 'treacher' looks like an ascender in the middle of the three minims of 'm'.

4.2.10/1794   puking'st soul] paultreſt foole OKES. Misreading, substituting a much commoner adjective.

4.2.10/1794   puking'st] puklingſt BRIDGEWATER[B]; pukelingſt ROSENBACH[A]. The variant is not recorded in *OED*, and might be an authorial portmanteau, yoking 'puking' with the contemptuous diminutive suffix 'ling' (as in 'groundling'). But the combination of the 'ling' suffix (indicating a noun) with the superlative suffix (indicating an adjective) is awkward.

4.2.10/1794   with] wth MIDDLETON[T] *corrected*. Howard-Hill (1990) notes that this word is 'altered'; the original reading is indecipherable.

4.2.11/1795   one] a ROSENBACH[A], BRIDGEWATER[B]

4.2.12/1796   crudity] credit OKES. Misreading, producing a much commoner noun.

4.2.14/1799   BLACK KNIGHT'S] *Bl. K.* CRANE/ALLDE; *not in* CRANE[2,3]; *Bl:* . ROSENBACH[A]. For 'B.K.P.' as a mere spelling variant, particularly preferred by printed texts, see 2.1.229, 238 and 3.1.127. Alone of the eight witnesses, CRANE/ALLDE also uses 'K.' for 'Knight's' at 4.2.40, 122, 131. CRANE[2,3] use abbreviations of 'Pawne' for the speech prefixes of this character consistently in this scene, probably a relic of authorial practice in contexts where the generic form would be unambiguous: see note at 3.1.116, and further examples at 4.2.30, 33, 40, 76, 81, 86, 122, 126, 131. Thus, in this scene, the generic speech prefixes occur in two late Crane transcripts, and nowhere else.

4.2.14/1799   ˄ You] CRANE[3]; I, ~ CRANE[I]+. This variant can hardly be part of the abridgement, since it does not save a line of paper, and is the only word missing from the verse line. The variant produces a regular hexameter, which may have been Middleton's intention all along: 'you have' might be Crane's expansion of 'you've', passively repeated in all subsequent texts. See 3.1.203. Rather than emend a reading present in all eight witnesses, it seems preferable to adopt an existing variant that has the same effect—especially given the other evidence of Middleton's involvement in the abridgement. (See 2.1.181.)

4.2.14/1799   to't] to it MIDDLETON[T] *only*

4.2.15-17/1800-1802   That's...down.] *not in* CRANE[3]

4.2.16/1801   Has] Hath CRANE[2,4]

*4.2.16/1801   yet] it ROSENBACH, BRIDGEWATER

4.2.17/1802   i'th'] CRANE[2,4], OKES; in the CRANE[I], ROSENBACH[A], MIDDLETON[T], BRIDGEWATER[B]. See 2.1.147.

4.2.18   sev'n] 7 MIDDLETON[T], BRIDGEWATER[B], ROSENBACH[A]; feauen CRANE[I]+. See 1.1.250.

4.2.18/1803   pounds] ROSENBACH[A], OKES, CRANE/ALLDE: pound CRANE[I]+. See note to 4.2.4.

4.2.19/1804–5 And...bigger] *2 lines* MIDDLETON[T]: been |

4.2.19/1804 that] you OKES. Misreading.

4.2.19/1805 bigger] MIDDLETON[T] *corrected*+. As Howard-Hill (1990) notes, the first letter has been 'altered', but the original is undecipherable; perhaps 'm'?

4.2.20/1806 KNIGHT] K[S] BRIDGEWATER[B] *uncorrected*

4.2.20–2/1806–8 Nay...thee] *not in* CRANE[3]

4.2.20/1806 Nay] Naie BRIDGEWATER[B]; Nai ROSENBACH[A] *uncorrected*; Naÿ ROSENBACH[A] *corrected*. The odd original ROSENBACH spelling, obviously considered an error by the scribe, suggests that its copy had the same spelling as BRIDGEWATER's unique 'Naie'. (Further evidence, if any were needed, of the close stemmatic connection between the two manuscripts.)

4.2.20/1806 if] an OKES. See 5.3.191.

4.2.20/1806 prov'st] proueft ROSENBACH[A]

4.2.20/1806 facetious] faċtious OKES. Misreading.

4.2.21/1807 soft, rare, poor-poached] poore-pocht-foft, reare, OKES. Transposition. Conceivably authorial, but there is no way of testing.

4.2.21/1807 rare] MIDDLETON[T]+ (reare)

4.2.22/1808 ride] rude OKES. Misreading.

4.2.22/1808 I'm] I am CRANE[2,4]

4.2.22/1808 ashamed] afhamèd ROSENBACH[A]

4.2.23/1809 Hadst] Haft ROSENBACH[A]

4.2.23/1809 betrayed] betrayèd OKES

4.2.23/1809 White House] witneffe OKES. In MIDDLETON[T] 'white-house' is a single word; in ROSENBACH[A] the compound is abbreviated ('wh:howse'); either form would make the OKES misreading more plausible. Elsewhere it is two distinct words (CRANE/ALLDE) or two full words joined by a hyphen. This might be considered an example of progressive error (with the error in OKES deriving from the specific spellings in two late manuscripts).

4.2.25/1811 Unjointed...traffic,] *not in* CRANE/ALLDE

4.2.26/1812 Poisoned] poyfonèd ROSENBACH[A]

4.2.27/1813 e'en] MIDDLETON[T] (eeṅ), CRANE[1] (eu'n); euen CRANE[2]+

4.2.27/1813 masculine] the ~ OKES. Extrametrical interpolation.

4.2.29/1815 are] as OKES. Misreading.

4.2.29/1815 thee] them ROSENBACH[A]

4.2.30–1/1816–17 BLACK KNIGHT'S PAWN Gelder Ay...BLACK KNIGHT GONDOMAR] *not in* OKES. This is not a simple error of omission of one line, since two sequential speech prefixes are missing. An original error of eyeskip from one speech prefix to the next (causing the omission of 4.2.30 in its entirety) could have been followed by a mistaken correction of what was then a duplicated speech prefix for the Black Knight (in 4.2.31). The original eyeskip would have been less likely to occur if the underlying text had used the simple prefix 'Paw.'. Thus, the OKES reading might be considered a progressive error, deriving from a manuscript other than CRANE[2,3].

4.2.31–40/1817–27 All...sir.] *not in* CRANE[3]

4.2.31/1817 All] I BRIDGEWATER[B] *uncorrected*

4.2.31/1817 trebled] CRANE[1,2,4], MIDDLETON[T]; troubled OKES; treble ROSENBACH[A], BRIDGEWATER[B]. Divergent misreadings.

4.2.31/1817 has] CRANE[1], NON-CRANE; hath CRANE[2,4]

4.2.33/1820 lightly] OKES, ROSENBACH[A]; titely CRANE[1]+. For *tightly* see OED *adv.*1 (the only sense available in the seventeenth century); he might jest 'properly, effectively, vigorously.' For *lightly* several senses are relevant: OED *adv.*3 ('without depression or heaviness...merrily'), 4 ('easily, readily'), 5 ('facilely...immediately'), 6.b ('often'), 7 ('carelessly'), 9 ('not chastely'). Either meaning is possible, and either could be a misreading of the other; *lightly* has a wider

range of relevant meanings, and could be a late authorial variant, or an original reading restored.

4.2.34/1821 stirring] strange OKES. Probably a misreading, substituting a common adjective for an unusual participle.

4.2.35/1822 seducement] feducements OKES. This could be an authorial variant; there are no Middleton parallels for the plural or singular. But it could also result from inadvertent assimilation to three preceding plural nouns. In the absence of parallels OKES alone does not seem reliable enough to warrant preferring its indifferent variant.

4.2.36/1823 hearty] heartily OKES. Extrametrical and ungrammatical.

4.2.36/1823 innocence] Innocency ROSENBACH[A]. See 3.1.177.

4.2.38/1825 ˌfeel no tempest, not a] never feele a Tempest, ˌa CRANE[2]. This phrase, involving three words out of five, might be a playbook variant, with Middleton later reverting to his original reading. But the repetition of 'never' from the preceding line is weaker than the emphatic 'no...not'.

4.2.39/1826 becalmed] becalmd MIDDLETON[T] only; be-calmd CRANE[1,2]; becalm'd CRANE[4]; be calm'd OKES; bee calmde BRIDGEWATER[B] (two words); to be Calmd ROSENBACH[A]. The interpolation seems to be the result of progressive error, following from the division of the word in BRIDGEWATER and OKES (and, presumably, their copy). Although Middleton consistently prefers 'bee' for the spelling of the verb, autograph never uses 'bee' for the prefix (as in BRIDGEWATER here).

4.2.40/1827 I'm] I am CRANE[2,4]

4.2.40/1827 there's] OKES; there is CRANE[1]+. For other examples of Crane texts with the expanded form see 1.1.70, 2.2.89, 3.1.215. Here the line is metrical with a line-divided foot.

4.2.40/1827 huffs] *not in* BRIDGEWATER[B], ROSENBACH[A]. This has not been included among shared errors, because the line makes sense and is metrical without this vivid verb; but the omission is almost certainly accidental.

4.2.40/1827 sir] *not in* OKES. Possibly authorial, but the word is often enough omitted accidentally, and Middleton used it ubiquitously at the end of verse lines.

4.2.41/1828 KNIGHT] K. CRANE/ALLDE. After a string of five examples of *Kni.* in speech prefixes on sig. G3[V], on the last two prefixes of the page CRANE/ALLDE switches to *B.K.P.* (4.2.40) and *B.K.* (4.2.41). The first is not technically incorrect, and may have stood in the printer's manuscript: see 2.1.229. However, this speech cannot be spoken by the Black King, which the CRANE/ALLDE prefix suggests. The shortening of both prefixes might be due to compositorial concerns about justifying too very long lines. But with these two prefixes at the bottom of G3[V] CRANE/ALLDE begins a run of *B.K.* prefixes which continues until *Kni.* reappears at 4.2.142 (in a speech all other texts attribute to the Black King) near the bottom of sig. H1 and again in 4.4.1 at the top of H1[V].

4.2.41/1828 ha'] haue CRANE[2,3,4], MIDDLETON[T]

4.2.41/1828 o'th'] MIDDLETON[T] (a'th), CRANE[1]+ (o'th); o'the ROSENBACH[A]; of the CRANE/ALLDE

4.2.41/1828 six times] 6 times MIDDLETON[T], BRIDGEWATER[B]; be-times ROSENBACH[A]. ROSENBACH's error is almost certainly related to the numeral in MIDDLETON[T] and BRIDGEWATER[B] (much more likely to be misread as 'be' than the spelled-out word 'six'). It thus seems to be a progressive error, deriving from a NON-CRANE manuscript (since Crane consistently spells out numerals).

4.2.42/1829 received] receiuèd BRIDGEWATER[B], OKES

4.2.42/1829 of] for ROSENBACH[A]

*4.2.44/1831   three] CRANE[1,2,3], OKES, BRIDGEWATER[B]; thee CRANE/ ALLDE; the ROSENBACH[A]; 3 MIDDLETON[T]. Shared error (omitted 'r'), which also seems to be progressive (from 'thee' to 'the').

*4.2.44/1831   mummy] money OKES, mony ROSENBACH[A]

4.2.44/1831   promised] promiſèd ROSENBACH[A]

4.2.45/1832   o'th'] MIDDLETON[T] (a'th), CRANE+ (o'th'); or' ROSEN- BACH[A] (perhaps intending 'o'er')

4.2.45/1832   I've] OKES; I'haue CRANE[2]; I haue CRANE[1] +

*4.2.47/1834   baked] MIDDLETON[T] + (bakte); backt OKES; backte BRIDGEWATER[B]. OED does not record the 'ck' variant as an historical spelling of bake, so this has been treated as a shared substantive error.

4.2.47/1834   and] not in OKES. Unmetrical.

4.2.47/1834   ₍cozen₎] to ~ the ROSENBACH[A]. Extrametrical inter- polations.

4.2.47/1834   searchers] Searchrrs OKES (foul case)

4.2.48/1835   hallowed] halbow'd OKES (foul case)

4.2.48/1835   medals] needles OKES (misreading)

4.2.50/1837   i'th'] in th' CRANE[2,3,4]; i' the ROSENBACH[A]. See 2.1.147.

4.2.51/1838   tobacco balls] Tobaco-roles OKES. This repeats the preceding 'roles'. However, the mistake might be authorial, because his source for the passage uses both nouns: 'I haue knowne some vnder the cullour of selling Tobacco, have carried Letters handsomly, privily in the balls or roules' (Scott, 2 Vox Populi, 57).

4.2.53/1840   our] not in CRANE[1]

4.2.53/1840   turn] turned CRANE/ALLDE. An easy mistake, sub- stituting the historical past tense (since the passage is re- ferring to recent events) for the present tense of the play. The present tense is confirmed also by Middleton's source: 'some [Jesuits] will turn schoolmasters in private men's houses' (Scott, 2 Vox Populi, 29). For a similar autograph error, turning dramatic present into historical past tense, see 5.3.16.

4.2.54/1841   falc'ners] Faulconers CRANE[2,3]. Shared unmetrical expansion.

4.2.54/1841   park-keepers] park-keeper OKES

4.2.56/1843   chores] MIDDLETON[T] + (chares)

4.2.56/1843   in] on CRANE[2,3,4]

4.2.57/1844   Pray] I'pray CRANE[3]. Typical Crane expansion.

4.2.58/1845   summer] Sommers ROSENBACH[A]. The singular is confirmed by 2 Vox Populi, 15.

4.2.59/1846   t'] to [CRANE[4]], ROSENBACH[A], MIDDLETON[T]

4.2.60/1847   fortification] fortifications OKES. The singular is confirmed by 2 Vox Populi, 15.

4.2.61/1848   or] ROSENBACH[A]; not in CRANE[1] +. Late authorial variant, apparently prompted by a memory of Middleton's source: 'no Fortification, Hauen, Creeke, or Landing-place about the Coast of England' (2 Vox Populi, 15). Metrically, this works if one assumes a line-divided foot.

4.2.61/1848   'bout] about [CRANE[4]], ROSENBACH[A]. The prose source has 'about' (see preceding note). This variant might therefore be authorial. However, both texts that contain it also contain many other extrametrical expansions of au- thorial forms, substituting statistically common words (like 'about') for statistically rare alternatives (like 'bout').

4.2.61/1848   coast] Coasts ROSENBACH[A]. The singular is con- firmed by 2 Vox Populi.

4.2.62/1849   ₍learned] and learn'd CRANE/ALLDE. The conjunc- tion is not in 2 Vox Populi, 15.

4.2.63/1850   their] the OKES. The possessive pronoun is con- firmed by 2 Vox Populi, 15.

4.2.64/1851   invasion] Nauigacon ROSENBACH[A]; [e]vasion BRIDGE- WATER[B] uncorrected. The BRIDGEWATER correction to 'Invasion' (confirmed by 2 Vox Populi, 15) was apparently made by Middleton himself, and covered one letter; that the letter originally written was an 'e' is my conjecture.

4.2.64/1851   prop'rest] propereſt ROSENBACH[A]; not in OKES

4.2.66/1853   burden] Burrhen OKES (foul case)

4.2.66/1853   the ships] MIDDLETON[T], BRIDGEWATER[B]; their shipps ROSENBACH[A]; each Ship CRANE, OKES. Late authorial variant. Both the singular and the plural are supported by Middleton's source (2 Vox Populi, 15): 'the names of all the Ships of King James his Navy Royal, I knew to a hair of what burden every ship was' (my italics). The singular is closest to the immediate phrase in the source, and is preserved in Early 4.238, composed when Middleton obviously had 2 Vox Populi in front of him; the plural is in the preceding phrase, suggesting a later looser recollection of the source. The ROSENBACH variant is clearly related to the autograph plural.

4.2.66/1853   brassy] braſſe OKES. Misreading as the more com- mon word (Taylor 1988).

4.2.68/1855   Again] then CRANE[1]

4.2.68/1855   inlands] Ilands ROSENBACH[A]. The autograph read- ing is confirmed by 2 Vox Populi, 16.

4.2.70/1857   best] CRANE/ALLDE, OKES; brest CRANE[1] +. The quarto reading is supported by Scot, 2 Vox Populi, 16: 'I better know the estate, power, and quality thereof than the Inhabitants, even the best of them themselves did'. For a comparable late authorial reversion to a source phrase, see 3.1.87.

4.2.71/1858   pow'r] CRANE[2], BRIDGEWATER[B] (powre); Powres CRANE[3]; power CRANE[1] +. The singular is confirmed by 2 Vox Populi, 16.

4.2.71/1858   gentry's₍] CRANE[1] + (gentries); gentries, CRANE/ ALLDE, OKES; Gentry₍ ROSENBACH[A]. Probably a shared punc- tuation error, but not counted as such because the source is ambiguous.

4.2.72/1859   our side, who] your ~ how OKES

4.2.72/1859   side] State CRANE[3]. This could be an authorial variant, but is more likely an inadvertent substitution, by contamination from its use twice in the previous twelve lines. Neither noun is present in the phrase in 2 Vox Populi.

4.2.73/1860   well] will OKES

4.2.73/1860   the] that ROSENBACH[A]

4.2.73/1860   neutrality] Newtralitie BRIDGEWATER[B]; newtrality ROSENBACH[A]; new trality OKES. Progressive error: the changed spelling of the first syllable ('new') precipitated the OKES misunderstanding as two words.

*4.2.74/1861   thousand] not in OKES, BRIDGEWATER uncorrected

4.2.74/1861   seduced] ſeducèd OKES

4.2.74/1861   Pawn] Pawnd ROSENBACH[A]; P. MIDDLETON[T] (heavily inked and lower than the rest of the line, after a unique comma; perhaps an afterthought or correction)

4.2.75/1862   with] CRANE[1] +; wi'th' THIS EDITION conj.

4.2.76/1863   KNIGHT'S] B. ROSENBACH[A]; K. OKES, CRANE/ALLDE. See note to 4.2.41. The abbreviation 'K.' for 'Knight's' is consistent throughout this stretch of text in CRANE/ALLDE (ll. 76–137, with a single exceptional 'Kni.' at 4.2.82), but it is anomalous in OKES. The two texts agree again in the shortened form at 4.2.86 and 4.2.126. The few cases in OKES cannot have caused the more consistent pattern in CRANE/ALLDE, so if there is contamination here it must be from ALLDE to OKES, or from [CRANE[4]] to [PRE-OKES]. But since the normal speech prefix form in OKES is 'Kt.', the scattered agreements involve a single occasionally omitted letter in

OKES. In any case, unlike ROSENBACH's 'B.', the quartos' 'K.' is not an error in this context: see 2.1.229.

4.2.76/1863   toad] Cod ROSENBACH[A]; tode BRIDGEWATER[B]. Progressive error? The absence of 'a' in BRIDGEWATER—and, presumably, [PRE-BRIDGEWATER]—would make the ROSENBACH misreading much likelier. Another indication of the similarity of [PRE-ROSENBACH] and [PRE-BRIDGEWATER] in this section of the text.

4.2.76/1863   into] in CRANE/ALLDE

4.2.76/1863   sir] *not in* ROSENBACH[A]. In MIDDLETON[T] the word is written into the margin, and not separated from the preceding word—'phifick(S[r]).'—with the small majuscule 'S' written on the line framing the margin, and over a full stop, which is then duplicated after the closing bracket. The 'S' is much smaller than the majuscule 'S' in the first word of the line, and slightly raised above the rest of the line. (Howard-Hill inserts a space between the two words, and does not transcribe the first full stop.) It is possible that Middleton originally wrote 'phifick.' and then corrected the error by squeezing in the additional '(S[r]).' This suggests that Middleton's copy might have been a text which, like ROSENBACH, did not contain the vocative. It has not, however, been counted as a shared error, because my explanation of the physical circumstances in MIDDLETON[T] is conjectural.

4.2.77/1864   I'm] NON-CRANE; I'am CRANE[2]; I am CRANE[1,3,4]

4.2.78/1865   T'entrap...allurements] *2 lines* BRIDGEWATER[B]: allure- | ments

4.2.78/1865   T'] CRANE[1]; To CRANE[2]+

4.2.79/1866   the] our OKES. Possibly an authorial variant; *Early* 4.251 had 'our Black' in the following line.

4.2.80/1867   Fat] Black CRANE[1]. Through the remainder of the scene, in stage directions and speech prefixes, CRANE[1] has the Black Bishop where all texts of the revised version have the Fat Bishop.

*4.2.81.1/1868   *Enter Fat Bishop*] ROSENBACH[A] and MIDDLETON[T] mistakenly place this entrance after the Pawn's speech (one manuscript line too low).

4.2.81.1-2/1868   *from the Black House*] THIS EDITION (*conj.* Hotson); *not in* CRANE[1]+. See 1.1.30.1.

4.2.81.2/1868   *in his black habit*] THIS EDITION; *not in* CRANE[2]+. This is his first appearance since 3.1.305; his change of allegiance would surely be signalled visually. Originally this was an entrance for the Black Bishop, so Middleton took the character's black costume for granted.

4.2.81.2/1868   *with a book*] DYCE; *not in* CRANE[1]+. Stage directions in the period often fail to mention necessary props, so this has not been counted as a shared error.

*4.2.82/1871   *Pœnitentiaria*] Poenitentia CRANE[1], BRIDGEWATER[B]; *Penitentiaris* OKES. An easy error: in a foreign language, writing 'ia' once, instead of twice, thereby skipping inadvertently from the middle to the end of the word. This error might have been made separately in the two manuscripts: CRANE[1] and BRIDGEWATER[B] do not share any other features suggesting a direct transcriptional link between them.

*4.2.83/1872   prices] prizes OKES, BRIDGEWATER[B]

4.2.84-5/1873-4   I...upon't] half | MIDDLETON[T]

4.2.85/1874   upon't] vpon it OKES

4.2.85-7/1875-78   BLACK KNIGHT GONDOMAR That's...for?] *not in* ROSENBACH[A]. Eyeskip from one speech of the Black Knight to the next.

4.2.85/1875   That's] That is OKES

4.2.85/1875   see't] fee it MIDDLETON[T], OKES

4.2.86/1876   Pawn] *not in* CRANE/ALLDE, OKES. An easy error, since the first spoken word repeats the last element of the

speech prefix. Not included among shared errors (as the word is not necessary for sense or metre), but almost certainly inadvertent.

4.2.86/1876   that] as OKES, BRIDGEWATER *uncorrected*. Although both 'that I am' and 'as I am' appear in Middleton, and 'wretched' is followed by either idiom in the period, the closest Middleton parallel is 'Wretch that I am' (*Hengist* 3.3.180); the fact that the variant is corrected in BRIDGEWATER also casts doubt on its authority.

4.2.86/1876   has] hath CRANE[2,3,4]

4.2.88-90/1878-80   For wilful...killing] *verse?*: shillings | For killing | CRANE/ALLDE, OKES, ROSENBACH[A], BRIDGEWATER[B]. Although it breaks the lines where CRANE/ALLDE does, OKES does not capitalize the first letter; since the first two lines fill the measure, they are apparently interpreted as prose. Likewise, BRIDGEWATER[B] normally begins verse lines with an initial majuscule, and does not begin any of these lines so, suggesting that it understood them as prose; the first two fill the measure.

4.2.89/1879   sixpence] MIDDLETON[T] (one word); fixe-pence OKES, CRANE[3]; six pence CRANE[1]+ (two words)

4.2.90-1/1880   killing...killing] MIDDLETON[T], OKES, CRANE/ALLDE (six times). The word is repeated four times in CRANE[1], three times in CRANE[2,3], seven times in ROSENBACH[A], BRIDGEWATER[B]. This is probably an authorial variant, expanding the number of repetitions from the original 3 or 4 to the later 6 or 7.

4.2.91-2/1880-81   killing'— | Why] ~ Sr | ~ CRANE[2]; ~ ∧ CRANE[1]

4.2.92/1881   Why...side] This is a single distinct line in all witnesses except CRANE[1], where it continues the preceding prose. An intended shift to verse is explicitly indicated by the fact that the preceding line does not fill the measure in the quartos, or in ROSENBACH. In the other manuscripts the length of the preceding line leaves the intention ambiguous.

4.2.92/1881   Bishop] *not in* OKES

4.2.92/1881   on] CRANE; of NON-CRANE. See 1.1.255. The obsolescent 'of' is preserved in *Early* 4.265.

4.2.93/1882   the sheet over] 'ore the fheete OKES

4.2.93/1882   you] and ~ CRANE/ALLDE

4.2.94-100/1884-9   Adultery...threepence] *prose* MIDDLETON[T], BRIDGEWATER[B]; *verse*: For adultery | are | himself | sir | CRANE[1]; Adultery? | For adultery | fornication | see | mother | pound, three | CRANE[2]; For adultery | fornication | see | mother | pound, three | CRANE[3]; Adultery? | shillings | good | mend | daughter | shillings three | CRANE/ALLDE; For adultery | fivepence | penniworths | lying | sir | OKES; shillings | mass | how | mother | pounds | ROSENBACH[A]. This has not been counted as a shared lineation error, because the quartos do not agree on any of the actual line breaks. The intention of MIDDLETON[T] and BRIDGEWATER[B] is clear, because all lines fill the measure. With the other manuscripts it can be more difficult to know whether prose or verse is intended, because the layout is less consistent. In CRANE[1] only 'two... himselfe' fills the measure; but the textual variants there create a different rhythm. (See *Early* 4.268-73.) Verse seems to be intended in CRANE[2,3] through 'fornication', then clearly prose thereafter. In ROSENBACH[A] only the two lines 'those... mother' are arguably full measure. See following lineation notes for further discussion.

4.2.94-5/1884   Adultery? | O] CRANE[2,4]. All other texts continue the first line of the speech, as verse or prose, breaking it later. (See preceding and following.) Because of the textual variants in *Early*, CRANE[2] is probably the earliest witness of this version of the speech, and its first word would complete a regular verse line begun by the last words of the preceding speech. The first four words of 4.2.95 also have a regular iambic rhythm (before he begins reading from the book again).

4.2.94/1884   Adultery?] *not in* ROSENBACH[A]. This omission would be easier to explain if the word were on a separate manuscript line in the scribe's copy (as in CRANE[2,4]).

4.2.95/1884   I'm] I am CRANE

4.2.95/1884   in't] at it CRANE[1]; met OKES. Compositorial misreading.

4.2.96/1885   fivepence] ROSENBACH[A] (one word); fiue pence CRANE[1] + (two words)

4.2.96/1886   Mass,] *not in* CRANE[2,3,4]. Censorship.

4.2.96/1886   those] MIDDLETON[T], ROSENBACH[A]; thefe CRANE[1] +. Late autograph variant.

4.2.97/1886   two] the OKES; too CRANE/ALLDE

4.2.98/1888   and] or OKES. Possibly a late authorial variant, producing a more logical text; but the ambiguity of 'and' produces a sense of fantastic specificity and depravity (there is a payment specified for someone who commits all three sins).

*4.2.99–101/1888–90   thirty-three…too] pound, three | CRANE[3]; shillings, three | CRANE/ALLDE. Shared lineation error. All other witnesses clearly mark a spatial division between the last line of the speech and the preceding lines perhaps the clearest evidence that the middle of the speech was considered prose. In both texts the division between the text Black Knight is reading and his own comment on it is marked by Crane's shift from italic to roman (*pence. The*), but without a line-break. The comment is a metrically regular iambic pentameter sentence with a feminine ending; it seems clearly to be verse (like his comment at the end of his preceding speech), as is indicated by all other witnesses.

4.2.99/1888–89   thirty-three] thirteene CRANE[2,3]. Probably contamination from his preceding speech.

4.2.99/1889   pounds] pound MIDDLETON[T], CRANE[2,3]. See note to 4.2.4.

4.2.100/1889   shillings] fhilling MIDDLETON[T], OKES. See note to 4.2.4.

4.2.100/1889   ₐthreepence] and ~ ~ OKES

4.2.100/1889   threepence] 3 pence MIDDLETON[T] + (two words)

4.2.101/1890   sins'] THIS EDITION; Sins MIDDLETON[T]+; sin's DYCE+. Typically, Middleton does not indicate the possessive apostrophe; nor does any other early witness, and in performance there would be no difference. The modern editorial possessive singular insists that only a single sin is involved; the possessive plural emphasizes the plurality of incests and the plural logic of the payments. A man's mother cannot be his daughter, and consequently more than one form of incest is involved (whether or not committed by one man).

4.2.101/1890   too] [CRANE[4]], NON-CRANE; *not in* CRANE[1,2,3]. Late authorial variant.

4.2.102/1891   You've] CRANE[2] (You'haue); You haue CRANE[1] +

4.2.102/1891   the story of that] that ~ ~ the ROSENBACH[A]

4.2.103/1891   his wife] ₐ ~ OKES

4.2.104/1894   KNIGHT] B BRIDGEWATER[B] *uncorrected*. Misreading.

4.2.104/1894   pounds] OKES, ROSENBACH[A]; pound CRANE[1] +. See note at 4.2.4.

4.2.105–7/1895–7   FAT BISHOP…BLACK KNIGHT] *not in* CRANE[1]. Another 'Fat Bishop' addition to the revised version.

4.2.106/1896   Before…sums] *2 lines* DYCE: came |

4.2.106/1896   I've] DYCE; I haue CRANE[2] +. See 2.2.28. In both cases, the passage is not present in *Early*; the elision is often preserved in only a single witness. Here, a fourteener is

likelier than a fifteen-syllable line.

4.2.106/1896   sums] Sinnes CRANE/ALLDE (easy misreading)

*4.2.107–8/1897–8   Sodomy…Bishop] euer | MIDDLETON[T], ROSENBACH[A]; *3 lines* OKES: should haue | book |. Shared lineation error.

4.2.107/1897   sixpence] MIDDLETON[T], BRIDGEWATER[B] (one word); six pence CRANE[1] + (two words)

4.2.107/1897   ₐ put] haue ~ OKES

4.2.108/1898   on] in DUTTON (not justified as a deliberate emendation, probably an error)

4.2.108/1898   Bishop] *not in* CRANE[1]

4.2.109–10/1900–1   What's…encouragement] HARPER; *1 line* CRANE[1] +; *prose?* MIDDLETON[T] *only*: encou- | ragement. Another relic, preserved by all witnesses.

4.2.109/1899   on's] ones ROSENBACH[A]. Misreading.

4.2.109/1899   forward] forwards ROSENBACH[A]. See 1.1.192.

4.2.109/1900   here, sir] ~ ₐ OKES

4.2.111/1902   are ₐ] ~ too ROSENBACH[A]

4.2.112–14/1903–5   Given…thousand] *verse* CRANE/ALLDE: heretical |

4.2.112/1903   gratuity] gratitud OKES

4.2.113/1903   the] *not in* CRANE[1]

4.2.113/1904   poisoned] poyfonèd ROSENBACH[A]. (Prose).

4.2.114/1905   thousand] thoufands CRANE/ALLDE

4.2.115/1906   sir] *not in* CRANE[2]

4.2.115/1906   paid] payèd OKES

4.2.116–21/1907–13   Promised…Antwerp] *verse* CRANE/ALLDE: maiden | thousand | alms | thousand |

4.2.116/1907   also] *not in* OKES

4.2.117/1907   Lopez] Lopus OKES. Misreading.

4.2.117–18/1908   Maiden…Kingdom] white howfe Queene ROSENBACH[A]. The paraphrase might well be authorial: Middleton wrote 'White House Bishop' (2.2.48) and 'White House Knight' (5.1.39). But the paraphrase confusingly implies that the play's White Queen is Elizabeth I. Again, the confusion might be authorial, since the White Queen probably represented another Elizabeth.

4.2.118/1909   ducats] *not in* CRANE[1]

4.2.118/1909   twenty] 20 20 BRIDGEWATER[B]

4.2.120/1912   pounds] CRANE/ALLDE, OKES; pound CRANE[1] +. See note to 4.2.4.

4.2.121/1913   of] at CRANE[2], ROSENBACH[A]. Possibly authorial vacillation; probably contamination from earlier in the line.

4.2.125/1917   your] yo[r] ROSENBACH[A]; that OKES. Progressive error? Misreading 'y[r]' as 'y[t]'.

4.2.126/1918   remitted] permitted CRANE[1]; forgiuen ROSENBACH[A]. The second variant is an example of synonym substitution of a common for a very rare word (Taylor 1988).

4.2.127/1919   Nay] BRIDGEWATER[B]+; may HOWARD-HILL (1995)

4.2.127/1920   there's] there is OKES

4.2.128/1921   you] yon OKES. Foul case.

4.2.128/1921   I'd] OKES; I would CRANE[1] +. Late authorial variant. As Holdsworth, Lake, and Jackson demonstrate, *I'd* is a typical Middleton contraction, relatively rare elsewhere; its presence here in OKES is much more likely to be authorial than compositorial. See General Textual Introduction, Sec. IV.

4.2.132/1925   that] the OKES, ROSENBACH[A]

4.2.132/1925   cabalistic] Carbuliftique OKES. Misreading.

4.2.133/1926   estate] State CRANE/ALLDE

4.2.134   And…absolution] *not in* CRANE[1], MIDDLETON[T]. This is probably an error of omission in MIDDLETON[T], because all other texts of the later version include the line. But in the original version (preserved in CRANE[1]), the speech makes sense without the line, which could have been added in rehearsals in order to clarify the moral point. MIDDLETON[T]'s omission might therefore have been a conscious or half--conscious return to the original reading. But the omission of the exit—see next note—suggests that it may have been simple eyeskip.

4.2.134/1926   Exit] *not in* MIDDLETON[T]

*4.2.134.1/1927   Enter ˏ *Black King*] ~ *the* ~ ~ OKES. CRANE[2,4] clearly place this direction in the right margin after 4.2.133, before the exit direction for Black King's Pawn at 4.2.134.1; the direction is not present at all in CRANE[3], which groups all the entrances for the scene in its opening stage direction. (See note to 4.2.0.1.) Although sometimes a character might enter a line before they speak, in this case the urgency of his speech makes that implausible. This shared error is not recorded by Nascimento or Howard-Hill.

4.2.134.1/1927   *from the Black House*] THIS EDITION (*conj.* Hotson); *not in* CRANE[1]+. See 1.1.30.1.

4.2.135/1928   BLACK KING] *not in* MIDDLETON[T] *only*

4.2.135-6/1928-9   Why…game] removes | OKES

4.2.135/1928   Why…traps] *2 lines* ROSENBACH[A]: knight | . (Marginal stage direction cramps line.)

4.2.135/1928   traps] troopes OKES. Misreading.

4.2.136/1929   now] *not in* ROSENBACH[A]

4.2.136/1929   heat] heart OKES. Misreading.

4.2.137/1930   game's] game is OKES

4.2.139/1932   his] this OKES. Misreading.

4.2.139/1932   'em] them OKES

4.2.139/1932   coming both] very cunning OKES. Although 'cunning' could be an easy misreading of 'com(m)ing', it is harder to account for 'very' as a misreading, especially when combined with transposition. Perhaps Middleton was thinking of Prince Charles and Buckingham, rather than his characters. See variant at 4.4.3.

4.2.140/1933   And] OKES; then CRANE[1]+. Middleton often begins verse lines with 'And for', and begins speeches with the two words at least four times elsewhere (in *Phoenix* 10.152, *Mad World* 5.1.131, *Trick* 3.1.172, and *Five Gallants* 1.1.276).

4.2.140/1933   surprisal] ~ (Sir) CRANE[1,4], ROSENBACH[A], BRIDGEWATER[B]

4.2.141/1934   that] this ROSENBACH[A], BRIDGEWATER[B], MIDDLETON[T]. Although the variant could be a late authorial revision, 'that' identifies the 'state-puzzle and distracted hurry' with the 'coming' [to Spain] of Charles and Buckingham; by contrast, 'this' must refer to the present moment, when the Black Knight and Fat Bishop have been in anything but a hurry, and concerned with private rather than 'state' matters. The variant has not been counted among shared errors, but it probably belongs among the group of such errors linking these three texts.

4.2.142/1935   with't] THIS EDITION; wth it ROSENBACH[A]; with ˏ CRANE[1]+. Late authorial variant. For the elision, see 2.1.105, where ROSENBACH[A] alone expands 'with't' to 'with it'.

4.2.142-4/1936-38   KING…KNIGHT] CRANE[2,3] (K….K[t]), OKES (Ki.…Kt.), MIDDLETON[T] (K…K[t].); K.…ˏ BRIDGEWATER[B], ROSENBACH[A]; Kni.…K. CRANE/ALLDE. Although CRANE[1] does not contain the second speech, it confirms attribution of the first speech to Black King. The CRANE/ALLDE variant might have arisen as a mistaken correction of the problem created by its use of 'Bl.K.' as a speech prefix for the Black Knight; in this exchange, one 'Bl.K.' answers another. See 4.2.41. The reversed attribution of the two speeches might be a late authorial revision, but here printing house confusion seems more probable. It seems more appropriate for the King to refer

to the Habsburg eagle, and for the Black Knight to anticipate in an aside, once again, his revenge against the Fat Bishop.

4.2.143.1/1937   Exeunt] CRANE[2] (*Ex.[t]*); *not in* CRANE[3]+. At this point in the original version, where CRANE[1] has 'Exeunt', the scene ended; in the added speech, Black Knight stays behind for a sardonic address to the audience. The variant requires Black King and Fat Bishop to remain on stage for Black Knight's aside; this is possible, but a bit awkward, and an exit direction is more likely to accidentally drop out than to be unauthoritatively added. See note at 4.2.145.

4.2.144-5/1938-9   BLACK KNIGHT…more.] *not in* CRANE[1]. Another 'Fat Bishop' addition to the revised version.

4.2.144/1938   BLACK KNIGHT] *not in* BRIDGEWATER[B], ROSENBACH[A]. Probably an inadvertent omission, but not counted as a shared error because it is a performable option.

4.2.144/1938   Bishop] Bifhops CRANE/ALLDE

4.2.144/1938   snapped] fnatch'd CRANE/ALLDE. Possibly an authorial variant, but the verb *snap* is used four times elsewhere in this play for the taking of a chess piece.

4.2.144/1938   ˏnext] MIDDLETON[T], BRIDGEWATER[B], ROSENBACH[A]; at ~ CRANE[2,3,4], OKES. Possibly a late authorial variant; but 'at' is also the kind of extrametrical grammatical clarification of an elliptical form that Crane sometimes supplies.

4.2.145/1939   the] their ROSENBACH[A]

4.2.145/1939   game stands] OKES, HOWARD-HILL; Men stand CRANE[2]+. Late authorial revision.

4.2.145/1939   never] nere BRIDGEWATER[B], ROSENBACH[A]. The variant is metrically possible (producing a line with a missing unstressed syllable at the caesura), and a typical Middleton contraction.

*4.2.145/1940   Exit] CRANE[2]; Exeunt CRANE[3,4], OKES, MIDDLETON[T]; *not in* ROSENBACH[A], NON-CRANE. In his first transcription of the play Crane did not treat the dumb show as a separate scene but as a stage direction, perhaps because it is cramped at the bottom of a page. In his subsequent transcripts he did identify it as a scene. According to the law of re-entry, it is one, because it begins after a cleared stage with the entrance of new characters and ends with a cleared stage before the entrance of new characters.

*4.3.0.1/1941   Recorders] ROSENBACH[A], BRIDGEWATER[B]; *Recorder* OKES; *Musick* CRANE[1]; *not in* CRANE[2,3,4], MIDDLETON[T]. The call for one or more recorders apparently specifies the kind of 'music' originally generically called for in the first draft. Elsewhere in the period, 'directions almost invariably use the plural *recorders*, probably indicating that typically more than one was played' (Dessen and Thomson, 177). Howard--Hill does not emend, or even record this variant, but it is impossible to believe that anyone would invent the specific 'recorder(s)', especially when it is independently supported by 'music' in a text in another part of the textual stemma. For Crane removing music cues, see Induction.52.1.

4.3.0.1/1941   *within, playing soft music*] THIS EDITION; *Musick.* CRANE[1]; *not in* CRANE[2]+. The recorders, like other musical instruments, were usually played 'within' (Dessen and Thomson, 177, 253); recorders are associated with 'soft music', in turn associated with quiet or supernatural actions, and sleeping (Dessen and Thomson, 177, 205-6).

4.3.0.1/1941   ˏEnter] MIDDLETON[T] *only*; *Domb shew. Enter* CRANE[1], OKES, ROSENBACH[A], BRIDGEWATER[B]; A ~ ~ˏ CRANE[2,3]; *Enter as in a* ~ ~ [CRANE[4]]. Authorial vacillation. The phrase 'dumb show' is superfluous, since the stage directions themselves describe a series of mimed actions without dialogue.

4.3.0.1/1941   the] CRANE[2,3]; *not in* CRANE[1]+

4.3.0.2/1941   *with a taper*] CRANE[2,3,4]; ~ ~ *light* OKES, ROSEN-
BACH[A], BRIDGEWATER[B]; ~ ∧ *Lights* CRANE[1]; *not in* MIDDLETON[T]
only. The more specific item is confirmed by OKES, which has
her put out 'the Candell' later in the direction.

4.3.0.2–3/1941   *in her hand*] CRANE[2]; *not in* CRANE[1]+. This
specification, which may seem redundant, makes it clear that
the taper is an object, not a person carrying an object. The
preceding CRANE[1] variant is incompatible with this phrase,
so it does not seem to have been omitted from that text, in
the way we can say it was omitted from others.

4.3.0.3/1941–2   *as conducting*] MIDDLETON[T] *only*; ∧ *conducting*
CRANE[1], OKES, ROSENBACH[A], BRIDGEWATER[B]; *and Conducts*
CRANE[2]; *Conducts* CRANE[3,4]. Late autograph variant.

4.3.0.3–4/1942   *the Virgin White Queen's Pawn*] CRANE[2,3,4], OKES;
the White∧∧ MIDDLETON[T] *only*; ∧ ~ ~ ~ CRANE[1], ROSENBACH[A],
BRIDGEWATER[B]

4.3.0.4/1942   *in her night attire*] CRANE[2,3]; *not in* CRANE[1]+. Crane
is unlikely to have invented this detail of the staging, which
might have been copied straight from the King's Men's
playbook.

4.3.0.4/1943   *one*] CRANE[2,3,4]; *a* CRANE[1]+. Middleton uses the
'one...another' formula elsewhere in stage directions as well
as dialogue. Authorial vacillation.

4.3.0.4/1943   *chamber,*∧] CRANE[3,4], MIDDLETON[T]; ~ *and* CRANE[1]+

4.3.0.4/1943   *then*] *not in* OKES, ROSENBACH[A], BRIDGEWATER[B]. This
might be authorial vacillation, but unlike the preceding
omitted word it is attested in autograph, and it provides useful
information/clarification (about sequence).

4.3.0.5–6/1943–5   *fetching in...conveys him*] NON-CRANE; ∧ *Conuaies the Black B.ˢ Pawne* CRANE[2,3,4]; ∧∧ *yᵉ Bl. Bᵖˢ. Pawne*
CRANE[1]. This is not the sort of information required in a
playbook, and it has therefore not been counted as a shared
error. There is no reason for Crane deliberately to have
omitted this clarification of the action (that before conveying
him to another chamber she must first go to a door and
bring him onto the stage with her), both in the early version
and the later version. What the actor needed to do would
have been apparent in any case. It seems more likely that
the 'fetching' clause was added later to clarify the action for
readers.

4.3.0.5/1944–5   *the Jesuit*] MIDDLETON[T]; *not in* CRANE[1]+. BROOKE
and HOWARD-HILL interpret this as a reference to the Black
Queen's Pawn, making it the subject of the verb *conveys*; but
'the Jesuit' is used seven times elsewhere, always of the Black
Bishop's Pawn.

4.3.0.6/1945   *in his night habit*] CRANE[2]; *not in* MIDDLETON[T]+. See
note to the parallel variant at 4.3.0.4.

4.3.0.6–7/1945–6   *into another chamber*] CRANE[2,3,4]; *to an other*
CRANE[1]+. This could be authorial vacillation, or scribal
clarification, but the intended action is clearer for a reader
in the more expansive version.

4.3.0.7/1946   *then shuts the door, pauses,*] THIS EDITION; *not in*
CRANE[1]+. In order for the substitution to work, she must
seem to leave, and then allow a minimal pause for the arrival
of what he imagines to be another woman. The separate
chambers presumably were indicated by different stage doors.
For 'shut' and 'pause' directions, see Dessen and Thomson,
198, 160.

4.3.0.7–8/1946   ∧ *puts out the candle, and*] OKES; *So* ~ ~ ~ *light* ~
CRANE[2,3]; ∧ ~ ~ ~ *light* ~ ROSENBACH[A], BRIDGEWATER[B], MIDDLE-
TON[T]; *and putting* ~ ~ *light* ∧ CRANE[4]; *not in* CRANE[1]. Another
unique OKES variant that looks authorial.

4.3.0.8/1947   *follows him*] ~ ~ OKES; *fhee* ~ ∧ MIDDLETON[T]. This
variant might be authorial, but it could also result from

simple omission of the pronoun, and for clarity's sake I have
retained the pronoun.

4.3.0.8–9/1947   *into the second chamber*] THIS EDITION; *not in*
CRANE[1]+. This phrase is not strictly necessary, but I have
added it for clarification of the action.

4.4   CRANE[2,3,4] (Sce.ᵃ 4ᵃ.); Sce.ᵃ 3ᵃ. CRANE[1]; *not in* NON-CRANE.
See note to 4.3.

4.4.0.1–2/1948   *Enter...House*] *The white-Knight, & wh. duke,
yᵉⁿ yᵉ Bl. Knight: Then yᵉ white-Queene: yᵉ Fat Bishop: yᵉ white
Bishop; & yᵉ wh. King.* CRANE[3]

4.4.0.1/1948   *Enter*] ~ yᵉ CRANE[2]

4.4.0.2   *from the White House*] THIS EDITION (*conj.* Hotson); *not in*
CRANE[1]+. See 1.1.30.1.

4.4.1/1949   Duke] *Knight* ROSENBACH[A], BRIDGEWATER[B], MIDDLE-
TON[T]. A shared error in autograph, emended by HOWARD-HILL.

4.4.1/1949   *virtue's*] *Vertue* CRANE/ALLDE

4.4.1/1949   *one*] *on* CRANE/ALLDE. Although 'on' might be a
legitimate alternative spelling of 'one', in context CRANE/
ALLDE has clearly misunderstood the line.

4.4.3/1951   *of cause and*] & ~ *of* ROSENBACH[A]. Transposition.

4.4.3/1951   *cunning*] OKES; *courage* CRANE[1]+. See variant at
4.2.139. Retrospectively Middleton may have wanted to
strengthen the emphasis on Charles and Buckingham as
Machiavellian politicians. Moreover, the variant here avoids
repetition of the word *courage*, which occurs in all texts at
4.4.9.

4.4.4/1952   *strike 'em*] *strike 'm* CRANE/ALLDE; ~ *them* OKES.
Compare the variant at 3.1.278 ('m).

4.4.4/1952   *grov'ling*] THIS EDITION; *grauling* OKES; *groueling*
CRANE[1]+. The emendation retains the syncopation indicated
by OKES; after the simple a/o substitution in the third letter
there is no indication of a letter or syllable between *u* and
l.

4.4.6/1954   *has*] *hath* CRANE[2,3,4]

4.4.6/1954   *on*] *not in* OKES

4.4.8/1956   KNIGHT] *K.* CRANE/ALLDE, which repeats this technically ambiguous abbreviation throughout the remainder of
the scene.

4.4.8/1956   *Why*] *Sir* CRANE[1]; *not in* OKES. Possibly authorial
omission, creating a line-divided foot.

4.4.8/1956   *triumphs*] OKES, BRIDGEWATER *uncorrected*; *Triumph*
CRANE[1]+. The author of *The Triumphs of Truth* is more likely
than anyone else to have changed the original singular to a
plural.

4.4.9/1957   *constant*] *conftantie, &* ROSENBACH[A]. Although the
variant might be authorial, I have found no Middleton parallels for it; by contrast the autograph reading is confirmed
by 'constant courage' (*Aries* 76).

4.4.10/1958   glitt'ring'st] *glittrinft* MIDDLETON[T]; *glitteringft* RO-
SENBACH[A]; *glittering* CRANE/ALLDE, OKES; *gliftringft* CRANE[1];
glitteringest HOWARD-HILL. Shared quarto error: the superlative is grammatically required.

4.4.10/1958   *fashioned*] *fafhonèd* OKES

4.4.11/1959   his] *theire* MIDDLETON[T]; *theife* ROSENBACH[A]; *this*
BRIDGEWATER[B]. A shared error; although each has a slightly
different reading, all three late manuscripts share 'th' in
place of the correct 'h'. This looks like progressive error:
simple 'his' first mistakenly expanded to 'this', then further expanded/corrected to 'theise' (to agree with plural
'poisons' later in the line), then mistakenly corrected to
'theire'. As originally written, the passage goes from singular 'serpent' to singular 'his' to singular 'his'; autograph's unique variant introduces a confusing plural in
the middle of the sequence. HOWARD-HILL emends, restor-

ing 'his', but does not comment on the autograph error.

4.4.12/1960 can] will BRIDGEWATER[B] *uncorrected*. Nascimento attributes the interlined correction to a 'much finer pen' and a different hand (27), but Howard-Hill (1995, 20) cites a similar style of correction in other *currente* corrections by scribe B.

4.4.12/1960 bolt] blott ROSENBACH[A]

4.4.12/1960 bruise] buize MIDDLETON[T] *only*; braize ROSENBACH[A]

*4.4.12.1/1960 *Enter . . . Black Knight] not in* ROSENBACH[A], BRIDGEWATER[B], MIDDLETON[T]. In OKES and CRANE/ALLDE this direction is misplaced in the right margin opposite 4.4.14–15; the direction needs two lines of type in the margin, so it would not fit opposite 4.4.13, which is fully justified in both quartos. CRANE[1,2] place it here; CRANE[3] includes it in the scene's opening massed entrance direction.

4.4.12.1/1960 *from the Black House*] THIS EDITION (*conj.* Hotson); *not in* CRANE[1]+. See 1.1.30.1.

4.4.13/1961 would] MIDDLETON[T] *corrected*; y MIDDLETON[T] *uncorrected* (anticipating 'you')

4.4.13/1961 you] *not in* OKES

4.4.13/1961 sunning] finning ROSENBACH[A]. Misreading.

*4.4.15/1963 that] yonder BRIDGEWATER[B], ROSENBACH[A]. Contamination from preceding line, unmetrical.

4.4.15/1963 face] falce CRANE/ALLDE. Anticipation.

4.4.16/1965 KNIGHT] *K.* CRANE/ALLDE, OKES. The two quartos share the incorrect abbreviation again at 4.4.47. This abbreviation is part of a consistent pattern in CRANE/ALLDE: see notes at 4.2.41 and 4.4.8. For four earlier examples of the same variant in OKES alone, see note at 1.1.277. For the unreliability of this variant as evidence of contamination of one quarto by the other, see 4.2.76 and 5.1.1.

4.4.16–17/1965–6 What . . . little] *I line* CRANE[2]. Relic.

4.4.16/1965 a] *not in* CRANE[2]

4.4.18/1968 the] OKES; that CRANE[1]+. Late authorial variant. See 2.2.100–1: 'the House professors *Of* noble *candor*'. The author is more likely than a compositor to have produced such a parallel.

4.4.20–1/1970–71 Lost . . . soul] con- | fidence MIDDLETON[T]

*4.4.20/1970 your] the ROSENBACH[A], BRIDGEWATER[B]. Misreading of 'y[r]' as 'y[e]'.

4.4.21/1971 vowed] vowèd OKES

4.4.21/1971 my] ROSENBACH[A], BRIDGEWATER[B]; the CRANE[1]+. The possessive pronoun could be a shared error, but there is nothing in the context to prompt an inadvertent substitution, and the variant could well be authorial. It creates a useful contrast with 'youre' in the following line (a contrast that requires the person responsible for the variant to know the line not yet transcribed). Compare 'my filial faculties' (*Old Law* 1.1.335).

4.4.23–7/1973–7 *Your . . . admirer?] not in* CRANE[3]

4.4.25/1975 observer] obseruers OKES (contamination from other terminal sibilants in line)

4.4.26/1976 tainted] taunted OKES. Misreading.

4.4.27/1977 your] you CRANE/ALLDE

4.4.29/1979 royal] Reall CRANE[1]

4.4.30–3/1980–82 *and . . . tomboy] not in* CRANE[3]

4.4.30/1980 mimic . . . and,] minicke . . . and and ROSENBACH[A]

4.4.30/1980 jester] CRANE/ALLDE (Iesture), Iester CRANE[1]+. It is not clear whether these are substantive variants or only alternative spellings. Although *OED* does not list 'iester' as a possible spelling of modern *gesture*, it does record *iesticulation*, *iesticular* and many other examples of initial i/j where modern texts have initial g. Moreover, the relationship between modern *jester* and *gesture* is indicated by its citation, under

jester.2, of the Elizabethan definition 'A Gester, or dizard faining and counterfeiting all men's gestures' (1573–80). Middleton probably intended both 'mimicking jester' and 'mimic's gesture', with *gesture* taking not only its modern sense but also the older senses 'deportment' (1.a) and 'posture' (2.a).

*4.4.31 *For . . . thoughts] not in* ROSENBACH[A], BRIDGEWATER[B], MIDDLETON[T]. A shared error in autograph, emended by Howard-Hill. By definition a parenthetical phrase is disposable, and it is always possible that Middleton deliberately cut a phrase he had originally written; but for the sake of consistency this is counted—like other dialogue omissions of uncertain origin—as an error. The absence of this line from CRANE[3] is part of a larger, clearly deliberate abridgement.

4.4.31 th'] OKES

4.4.32/1981 grave] great OKES (misreading)

4.4.32/1981 sire] Sir CRANE/ALLDE (substition of common for rare word); fice OKES (foul case error for 'fire')

*4.4.33/1982 Made] make ROSENBACH[A], BRIDGEWATER[B]

4.4.33/1982 threescore] 60 ROSENBACH[A]. I have found no Middleton parallels for 'sixty', but more than 35 for 'threescore'.

4.4.33/1982 years] yeare OKES

4.4.37/1986 could] would OKES

*4.4.37/1986 Rombaut's] THIS EDITION; Rambants CRANE[1]; Rumbants CRANE[2]+. See text note to *Early* 4.353. The 'n' in the second syllable, present in all witnesses, is probably a misreading of 'u', since the 'n' form of the name apparently appears nowhere else, and it has accordingly been listed as a shared error. However, the error was probably authorial: compare 'Orata' at 5.3.17. In both cases one letter in the proper name of a relatively obscure person has been mistranscribed; in neither case would the dramatic effect of the proper name have been affected. Few poets maintain the standards of historical accuracy expected of scholars. (Notably, CRANE[1] has a different form of the name than all other texts.) Although the vow 'u' in the first syllable is probably an error, present in all the post-playbook texts (CRANE[2]+), it has not been counted as one, because the 'Rum-' spelling does occur elsewhere in the period, in texts Middleton may have read.

*4.4.38/1987 Mechlin] Methlin OKES, ROSENBACH[A], BRIDGEWATER[B]. Shared error. The autograph spelling is confirmed by Middleton's source (*2 Vox Populi*, 39). 'Mechlin' appears more than 40 times in printed books of 1475–1700 (EEBO-TCP, October 2005); the same source records only two examples of 'Methlin' (neither referring to the continental town). A simple c/t misreading of an unfamiliar proper name.

*4.4.39/1988 my] *not in* ROSENBACH[A], BRIDGEWATER[B] *uncorrected*; o[r] BRIDGEWATER[C] (in pencil)

4.4.39/1988 conveyed] counayde ALLDE (type transposition); conueyèd OKES

4.4.40/1989 her] the CRANE[1]

4.4.40/1989 tried] trièd ROSENBACH[A]

4.4.43/1993 To any shape to please you] To please you, to any shape OKES (unmetrical transposition)

4.4.44/1994 Has] Hath CRANE[2,3,4]

4.4.45/1995 nobly] noble BRIDGEWATER[B] *uncorrected*

4.4.45/1995 I] OKES; wee CRANE[1]+. Late authorial variant.

4.4.47/1997 BLACK KNIGHT] *not in* BRIDGEWATER[B] *uncorrected* ('Bl.Knt' inserted by BRIDGEWATER[C])

4.4.48/1999 *Exeunt] Exit* CRANE/ALLDE

4.4.48.1–4.4.110.1 *Enter . . . Exeunt] not in* MIDDLETON[T] *only*. An apparently deliberate decision to save time in transcription. The omitted material is necessary to make sense of the next scene (which refers to the Fat Bishop's bagging) and the final scene (when the Fat Bishop appears in the bag).

4.4.48.1 ‸*Enter*] (Sce.[a] 4.[a]) ~ CRANE[1]. For the scene numbering here see note to 4.3. Perhaps as a result of having seen the play after transcription of the Early Form, Crane in subsequent copies did not recognize a scene-break here. The action is continuous, and the stage is probably not cleared. See next note.

4.4.48.1–2 *from the White House, as they go into the Black House*] THIS EDITION; *not in* CRANE[1]+. See preceding note. This addition clarifies the implicit staging. See 1.1.30.1.

4.4.49 love] luoe OKES *uncorrected* (Worcester, Bodleian Vet.A2, Huntington); loue OKES *corrected* (British Library C.34.l.23), CRANE[1]+. A simple transposition of type. Nascimento records the OKES reading as 'lure', which might be a conjectural press correction of the original 'luoe' error; but I have not found the reading reported by Nascimento in the copies I have examined.

4.4.50 Ensnared, entrapped] Entrapt, enſnard OKES. There is no way of distinguishing authorial from compositorial or scribal transposition in a case like this, so it is safer to stick to autograph.

4.4.50 surprised amongst] ſurpriſèd amongſt OKES; ſurpriz̀èd mongſt ROSENBACH[A]

4.4.52–6 Thick...horror.] *not in* CRANE[3]

4.4.54 interposed] interpoſe OKES. Misreading or omitted single type.

*4.4.55.1 *Enter...Fat Bishop*] CRANE[2] (at this point in the text), [CRANE[4]] (after 4.4.54); ~ Bl. ~ CRANE[1] (after 4.4.59); *not in* OKES, ROSENBACH[A], BRIDGEWATER[B]. CRANE[3] includes an entrance for the Fat Bishop in its opening massed entry between the entrances of the White Queen and the White Bishop.

4.4.55.1 *from the Black House*] THIS EDITION (*conj.* Hotson); *not in* CRANE[1]+. See 1.1.30.1.

4.4.56 of love] in ~ ROSENBACH[A]. This might be an authorial variant.

4.4.57 I'm] I'am CRANE[2]; I am CRANE[3]

4.4.58 turncoat] Turne‸ BRIDGEWATER[B] *uncorrected*

4.4.58 watched] watchèd OKES

4.4.59 Th'] the CRANE[1], ROSENBACH[A], BRIDGEWATER[B]

4.4.59 play] place BRIDGEWATER[B] *uncorrected* (corrected to 'plaie')

4.4.59 comes] is BRIDGEWATER[B] *uncorrected*

4.4.60 I'm] I am CRANE

4.4.60 distressed] BRIDGEWATER[B] *uncorrected* has been overwritten in a way that makes the original hard to discern: '..ſh.pf.' Perhaps 'worship' or 'worshipful' or 'miſhapt'.

4.4.60 miserably] miſerable OKES (misreading). BRIDGEWATER *corrected* reads 'miſerablye', but the terminal 'e' was added when 'y' was written over some other letter; HOWARD-HILL'S transcription does not identify the reading in BRIDGEWATER[B] *uncorrected*, but it appears to me to have been 'miſerable'. This has not been counted as a shared error because the original reading is not certain, and in any case the variant could be defended.

4.4.61 ‸vain] in ~ OKES

4.4.61 can‸] ~, ROSENBACH[A]; ~ : CRANE/ALLDE, OKES. The substantive punctuation error in the quartos seems related to the ambiguous punctuation of ROSENBACH[A].

4.4.62 we've] DYCE; wee ROSENBACH[A], BRIDGEWATER *corrected*; I euer BRIDGEWATER[B] *uncorrected*; we haue CRANE, OKES. See *Early* 4.379.

4.4.63–4 WHITE QUEEN OF BOHEMIA No...deliverer? | FAT BISHOP] ‸ there is no remedie | ‸ CRANE[3]. For other evidence of Middleton's involvement in the abridgment, see 2.1.181. The added phrase, which metrically replaces the removed speech, is clearly Middletonian: 'there's no remedy' occurs six times

elsewhere in his work, and 'there is no remedy' at *Plato* 269.

4.4.63 deliverer] CRANE[1,2], OKES; Deliuer CRANE/ALLDE; deliuerance ROSENBACH[A]; Deliuererance BRIDGEWATER[B]. Although 'deliuerance' makes sense and could be an authorial variant, I have not found an example of the word elsewhere in Middleton, and the final syllable could have been supplied conjecturally by someone confronted with the error in CRANE/ALLDE.

4.4.68.1 *Enter...White Bishop*] CRANE/ALLDE, OKES, ROSENBACH[A], BRIDGEWATER[B]. The entrance is placed one line earlier in CRANE[1,2]; that is also possible, and is reproduced in *Early* 4.385.1.

4.4.68.1 *from the White House*] THIS EDITION (*conj.* Hotson); *not in* CRANE[1]+. See 1.1.30.1.

4.4.68.1 *White...Bishop*] THIS EDITION; *not in* CRANE[1]+

4.4.70 I'm] NON-CRANE; I'am CRANE[1]; I am CRANE[2,3,4]

4.4.71 all this while] OKES; *not in* CRANE[1]+. Who but the author is likely to have added this phrase? The thirteen-syllable line is well within Middleton's metrical range, and the added colloquialism would be typical of the Fat Bishop (more than the Black Bishop, for whom the speech was originally written). Compare the Fat Bishop's 'And where is my advancement all this while I ha' gaped for't'? (3.1.6–7).

4.4.71 saw] ſowe BRIDGEWATER[B]. Misreading.

4.4.72 O] OKES; *not in* CRANE[1]+. There is no obvious reason for a compositor or scribe to add this interjection.

4.4.74 of the] ~ ‸ BRIDGEWATER[B]

*4.4.74.1 *Enter White King*] CRANE[1,2]; *not in* ROSENBACH[A], BRIDGEWATER[B]. The King must presumably enter before the pronoun reference to him at 4.4.76, and therefore OKES is mistaken in placing it after l. 77. CRANE/ALLDE puts it in the margin opposite ll. 76–7, which is possible if we interpret it to mean that he enters in the middle of l. 76. The OKES error might derive from the ambiguous placement in [CRANE[4]].

4.4.74.1 *from the White House*] THIS EDITION (*conj.* Hotson); *not in* CRANE[1]+. See 1.1.30.1.

4.4.76–7 Which...station] honour | ROSENBACH[A]

4.4.76 Which] why ROSENBACH[A]

4.4.76 and] or CRANE[1], ROSENBACH[A], BRIDGEWATER[B]. Either reading makes sense, dramatically and politically; *and* makes better sense in terms of chess, but *or* makes a specific political point, distinguishing James I from his son Charles and favourite Buckingham. Middleton might well have wavered back and forth between these alternatives. Since *or* is preserved in *Early* 4.395, I have adopted *and* here.

4.4.76 live] CRANE[3]; liues CRANE[1]+. A logical grammatical development from the variant *and*. See preceding note.

4.4.79 mine no longer] no longer mine OKES; no longer BRIDGEWATER[B] *uncorrected*. OKES's unmetrical variant could have resulted from an omission like that in BRIDGEWATER[B] *uncorrected*, with the needed word reinserted in the wrong place. But there are other examples of transposition in OKES with no such explanation.

4.4.79 I am] I'm̂ ROSENBACH[A]. The elision is Middletonian, and would produce a metrically regular line if combined with OKES's variant. However, each variant is confined to a single, separate text, and the probability of deliberate authorial revision does not seem high enough to warrant conflation here.

4.4.81 QUEEN] Q[s]. CRANE[3]

4.4.82–5 Is...kingdom?] *not in* CRANE[1] (original version), CRANE[3] (abridgement). Another 'Fat Bishop' addition to the revised version.

4.4.84 forgetful] ROSENBACH[A]; malitious CRANE[2,4], OKES, BRIDGE-
WATER[B]. Although 'malitious' seems clearly to have been
what was spoken on stage, 'forgetful' is almost certainly a
late authorial revision; it is hard to explain as a scribal error,
and it echoes Induction.17 ('Could they be so forgetful...').
It also produces two relevant senses: 'Could he (who has
partaken etc.) be so forgetful' (the original grammar of the
sentence) and 'Could he be so forgetful *that* he has partaken
etc.'

4.4.84 has] hath CRANE[2,4]

4.4.85-6 Of...service] Bishop | OKES

4.4.86 White] not in BRIDGEWATER[B] uncorrected

4.4.88 ‸thee, Black holiness,] (~‸~~) CRANE/ALLDE, OKES. Shared
punctuation error.

4.4.88 work'st] workeſt ROSENBACH[A]; workes OKES

4.4.89-92 the proper'st...work] not in CRANE[3]

4.4.89 proper'st] prop'rest CRANE/ALLDE, OKES; propereſt ROSEN-
BACH[A]

4.4.90 the] not in OKES

4.4.91 destroyed] deſtroyèd OKES

4.4.91 i'th'] in the OKES. See 2.1.147.

4.4.92 advancèd] aduanc'd CRANE/ALLDE, OKES

4.4.92 well,] ~ indeed CRANE[3]. The word was added to complete
an iambic pentameter line from the combination of 'As the
blind mole' (89) and ''twere well with thee' (92). Although
Howard-Hill attributes the change to Crane, it could easily
have been made by Middleton, who wrote 'well indeed' at
Revenger 1.3.167, and possibly elsewhere in his collaborative
work.

4.4.93 imitat'st] imitateſt OKES, ROSENBACH[A]

4.4.95 thy] the OKES. Misreading and/or assimilation to 'the'
earlier in the line.

4.4.100 you] they CRANE[I]

4.4.103-6 WHITE KING...set, sir.] not in CRANE[3]

4.4.103 were never] neuer were CRANE/ALLDE. Unmetrical transposition.

4.4.104 stayed] stands ROSENBACH[A] (misreading of 'staide')

4.4.106 Place] play ROSENBACH[A]; plaie BRIDGEWATER[B]. The fourth
letter in BRIDGEWATER[B] is not dotted, and although Howard-
-Hill transcribes it as 'i' he notes that it may be 'c'. Because
the manuscript reading is not certain I have not included it
in the tabulation of shared errors, but it probably is one.

4.4.106 strong] OKES; good CRANE[I]+. Late authorial variant.
The phrase 'a strong guard' also occurs at *Dissemblers*
3.2.116.

4.4.107 you] OKES, ROSENBACH[A], BRIDGEWATER[B]; Goe CRANE. Late
authorial variant.

4.4.109-10 FAT BISHOP...crack.] not in CRANE[I]. Another 'Fat
Bishop' addition to the revised version.

4.4.109 sound] ſtrong CRANE[3] (anticipatng the adjective in the
next line of the couplet).

*4.4.110.1 Exeunt] CRANE; not in OKES, ROSENBACH[A], BRIDGE-
WATER[B]

*4.4.110.2 Finit Actus Quartus] MIDDLETON[T], ROSENBACH[B]; ~ ~
Quarurtus BRIDGEWATER corrected; ~ ~ t BRIDGEWATER[B] uncorrected; ~ ~ Tertus OKES; Finis ~ Quarti CRANE[I]; not in
CRANE[2,3,4]. It is clear that BRIDGEWATER[B] started to commit the
OKES error, but immediately corrected it, before the second letter was written. This suggests that the copy for BRIDGEWATER[B]
shared the error.

4.4.110.2 Finit] Finis CRANE[I]

5.1.0.1/2001 Incipit] not in CRANE

5.1.0.1/2001 Actus] not in NON-CRANE

5.1.0.1/2001 Quintus et Ultimus] OKES, BRIDGEWATER[B]; ~ ‸‸ MID-
DLETON[T], ROSENBACH[B]; Quintus. | Sce.[a]. pri[a]. CRANE. See *Early*
5.0.1.

*5.1.0.2/2002 Loud music] not in CRANE[2,3,4], OKES. For Crane
removing music cues, see Induction.52.1.

*5.1.0.2/2002 Loud] CRANE[I]; Lowe ROSENBACH[B], BRIDGEWATER[B];
not in MIDDLETON[T]. (See preceding note: the whole phrase
is absent from CRANE[2,3,4], OKES.) Of the four texts that call
for music, only MIDDLETON[T] lacks an adjective modifying the
noun, and that omission is probably inadvertent, given other
evidence of carelessness in this section of that manuscript.
'Low' is never elsewhere used in stage directions for music,
which is often elsewhere specifically 'loud' (Dessen and
Thomson, 137); nor does 'low' fit the historical welcome of
Charles and Buckingham to Madrid. The shared error 'Lowe'
could easily result from misreading.

5.1.0.2-5/2002-3 Enter...habit] Enter Bl. King: Queene, Duke,
& Pawnes, & Bl. Knight: meeting the white Knight, & Duke: (y[e]
Bl. B[ps]. Pawne aboue, Entertaines them wth this Lattin Oration)
CRANE[I]; The Black-Knight (in his Litt[r]) & ye Bl: B[ps]. Pawne
aboue: Then y[e] Black-house, (meeting the white Knight, and white
Duke. CRANE[3]. The original staging of the scene combined
what became, after the *Later* version added new dialogue at
the beginning of the scene, two separate entrances. For the
massed entry in CRANE[3], see 1.1.0.2-5. As in the Induction
(both houses) and 3.1 (Black Bishop's Pawn), the massed
entry does not list characters/actors (here, the statues) who
appear later in the scene but do not speak.

5.1.0.2-3/2003 in his litter] not in CRANE/ALLDE. Although
'Litter' was added to the stage direction in CRANE[I], its absence
from the initial transcription of that text apparently reflects
Middleton's original intention. Thus its absence is not an
error in CRANE[I] (*uncorrected*), but it is certainly an error—
probably a simple omission of a prepositional phrase—in a
copy of the revised version. Since CRANE[I] interpolated the
word in a different position than all other texts, CRANE/
ALLDE's error certainly represents an omission from a different
point in the text.

5.1.0.3/2003 carried by Black Pawns] THIS EDITION; not in
CRANE[I]+. The litter does not carry itself, and the Black
Knight's 'hold, hold!' must be addressed to someone. The
title-page of Scott's *Second Part of Vox Populi* (1624) shows
it carried by two horses, but (as we would expect), John
Chamberlain specifies that horses were not used: 'his Lytter,
wherein the world sayes lackt nothing but a couple of asses
to carry yt' (21 August 1624). For theatrical purposes, 'litter'
implied an entrance for litter-carriers, so the absence of the
specific information added here, for the benefit of modern
readers, has not been considered a shared error in all the
early texts.

*5.1.0.3-4/2003 as...stage] OKES, ROSENBACH[B], BRIDGEWATER[B];
not in CRANE[2,3,4], MIDDLETON[T]. Because CRANE[I] begins the
scene differently—see below—the absence of this material
from its opening stage direction is not an error. Dessen and
Thomson (158-9) list numerous examples of such directions
(including *Puritan*, *Revenger* and *Five Gallants*); they do not
cite this example, because it does not occur in MIDDLE-
TON[T].

*5.1.0.4-5/2003 and the...above] CRANE[2,3,4]; ~~~~~ CRANE[I];
not in NON-CRANE. Although the NON-CRANE texts later specify—see note at ll. 9.6-5.1.9.7—that the Black Bishop's
Pawn speaks his long oration from 'above', they do not
provide him with an entrance; he must enter at the very

beginning of the scene, not later with the rest of the Black House.

5.1.1–5.1.9.2/2004–13 BLACK KNIGHT...*Oboes.*] *not in* CRANE[1]. An addition in the revised version, expanding the characterization of the Black Knight and Black Bishop's Pawn, and connecting the scene more clearly to Madrid.

5.1.1/2004 KNIGHT] *K.* CRANE/ALLDE. The quarto repeats the misleading abbreviation at 5, 7 (also on sig. H3) and 28 (on H3[v]). But it uses the correct '*Kni.*' at 5.1.21, 22, 31, 35, 47 (bottom of H3 to bottom of H3[v]). Notably, although there is exceptionally strong evidence of a direct link between OKES and CRANE/ALLDE here (5.1.4–39), OKES does not share any of these erroneous abbreviations. This tends to confirm that the scattered agreements in abbreviations earlier are not good evidence of a stemmatic link between the two quartos: see 4.4.16.

*5.1.1/2003 *calls*] MIDDLETON[T] *only* (before speech prefix, as part of entrance direction for Black Knight); *not in* CRANE[2]+. This helpful direction might theoretically have been a late addition for the benefit of literary readers; but such directions occur often in theatrical texts (Dessen and Thomson, 40–41, which includes examples from *Five Gallants* and *Revenger*). For consistency, this omission has therefore been counted as a shared error in all texts of the revised version except Middleton's autograph.

5.1.1–2/2004–5 Hold...Jesuit] *1 line* CRANE/ALLDE. This is the only example of a 'relic' line-and-a-half preserved in CRANE/ALLDE but no other text; however, according to the stemma of transmission [CRANE[4]] was also the earliest extant text to contain the longer version of this line. (See next note.) The autograph line-division in all four NON-CRANE texts makes dramatic sense, since the litter must stop after the command and before the question.

*5.1.1/2004 Hold, hold!] *not in* CRANE[2,3]. This extrametrical interjection is clearly linked to the stage action of 'passing in haste over the stage', a particular also absent from the earliest texts. That haste might well have developed in rehearsal, in turn prompting an ad-libbed interjection: Black Knight needs to call out to stop his carriers only if they are hurrying. Thus the direction for haste and the interjection to stop the haste might never have been present in the playbook, but added to later texts as a description of a detail of the actual performances. However, if the two words were on a distinct line the line might have been skipped over accidentally. In order not to bias the stemmatic analysis, this omission from the dialogue has, like others, been tabulated as a shared error.

5.1.1.1 *The litter stops*] THIS EDITION; *not in* CRANE[2]+. Though not specified, implied in the early witnesses.

5.1.3/2006 Planted] Placed ROSENBACH[B], BRIDGEWATER[B]. An easy misreading, which eliminates the image. The obsolescent syllabic -ed is relatively rare in Middleton's late work. Not counted as a shared error—though it probably is one—because it makes sense.

5.1.3/2006 above] *not in* OKES

5.1.3/2006 concise oration] courfe Oration CRANE/ALLDE; confecration OKES. Unrelated misreadings.

5.1.4/2007 BISHOP'S] K[ts] BRIDGEWATER[B] *uncorrected*

5.1.4/2007 *triumphanti,*] CRANE[2], MIDDLETON[T], BRIDGEWATER[B] *corrected*; ~, CRANE[3,4], OKES; *triumphantis,* ROSENBACH[B], BRIDGEWATER[B] *uncorrected*; *triumphante,* BROOKE. The comma is undoubtedly a shared punctuation error. Brooke's reading—followed by HARPER, HOWARD-HILL, and DUTTON—was presumably considered a mere modernization of spelling; in classical

Latin, either -e or -i could be used to indicate the ablative. However, 'Latin verse chose which termination to use based on metrical convenience. Here, *triumphanti* produces a regular Latin hexameter verse, as *triumphante* does not. Whether the speech is prose or verse matters, because the separation of adjective and noun ("triumphanti...arce") is normal in verse, and abnormal in prose' (Francis Cairns, private communication, 6 January 2006). Although Brooke's translation of the line—'Behold me fixed on Caesar's triumphal arch'— is repeated by HARPER, HOWARD-HILL, and DUTTON, it cannot be correct; *arcu triumphalis* would be the correct noun and adjective to indicate 'triumphal arch'. See Glare, 164 (arcus), 179 (arx), 1979 (triumphalis, triumpho). The ablative adjective can only mean 'triumphing', and the noun must mean citadel, city, or summit—all intelligibly related to the Black Bishop Pawn's onstage position, and to the historical circumstances in Madrid. DYCE, without being aware of the supporting manuscript readings, emended to 'triumphantis' (producing the sense 'the citadel of triumphing Caesar'). This is a plausible reading, and has not been counted as a shared error. I have preferred 'triumphanti' because it is supported by autograph and by the earliest witness to the revised version. It also better fits the historical circumstances of 1623: the city did triumphantly celebrate the arrival of Charles, but King Felipe did not have any personal military victories to celebrate.

5.1.4/2007 *me*] m ROSENBACH[B]; mi BRIDGEWATER[B]

5.1.4/2007 *Caesaris*] Cafaris OKES. This is not simply a spelling variant but, in Latin, an error.

*5.1.4/2007 *arce*] Arte CRANE/ALLDE, OKES; Axe ROSENBACH[B]

5.1.5–6/2008–9 Art...time] MIDDLETON[T]; Bishop | OKES; Tumbrel | CRANE[2] + . MIDDLETON[T] splits the line in mid-word (Tum: | brel), suggesting that the author thought of the line as prose (at least at that moment), and the ambiguous line division in OKES may reflect the same view. Aligned as verse, the first line has twelve syllables (three iambs followed by three trochees), and the second line has seven syllables (two iambs followed by an ambiguous three-syllable foot). Given the intervention of the preceding fourteen syllables of the Black Bishop Pawn's Latin, the very irregular rhythm of this speech makes it hard to discern a clear verse structure.

*5.1.6/2009 snapped] MIDDLETON[T]+ (fnapt); fnap CRANE/ALLDE, BRIDGEWATER[B]

5.1.6/2009 i'th'] in the MIDDLETON[T] *only*. See 2.1.147.

5.1.7/2010 BISHOP'S] K BRIDGEWATER[B] *uncorrected*

5.1.7/2010 Haeretici] Heretici CRANE/ALLDE, OKES, ROSENBACH[B]. For Middleton's attention to 'ae' see *Early*, 'Emendations of Incidentals', Induction.67.

*5.1.7/2010 *sic*] Sir ROSENBACH[B], BRIDGEWATER[B]

5.1.7–8/2011 All...him] THIS EDITION; *1 line* MIDDLETON[T]+. A relic, preserved in all texts of the revision.

5.1.8/2011 has] hath CRANE[2,3,4], OKES. 'Hath' appears nine times in OKES (as opposed to only four in MIDDLETON[T]); eight of those nine occur in Act Five.

5.1.9/2012 Away] Away, away CRANE/ALLDE, OKES. This may be an authorial variant, alternative to 'Oboes again!' (see below), as a way of filling out the verse line.

5.1.9/2012 they're] they are CRANE[2,3,4], OKES

5.1.9.1 *Exeunt...litter*] THIS EDITION; *not in* CRANE[2]+. The litter has served its purpose, and would only clutter the rest of the scene, which has other spectacles to display. The imperative 'away' must be addressed to his porters, who presumably obey it. Such exit directions for mute characters are routinely omitted in almost every kind of text (including playbooks).

5.1.9/2013 Oboes again!] BRIDGEWATER[B] (hoboyes ayen!), ROSEN-BACH[B] (hoboyes agen.); Hoboyes,_∧_ MIDDLETON[T] *only*; *not in* CRANE[2,3,4], OKES. In MIDDLETON[T] the music cue is unam-biguously a stage direction; in ROSENBACH[B] it is spoken by the Black Knight, indented like dialogue and completing an iambic pentameter line; in BRIDGEWATER[B] it is clearly sep-arated from the rest of the following stage direction, but also indented in a way that differentiates it from normal dialogue. If the only issue were the single word *Hoboys*, we might dismiss this variant as a misunderstanding, but the added word *again* seems unlikely to be mere inadvertence: it completes the verse line, it supplies unnecessary information, and it also explains that the music of the scene's opening stage direction was provided by hoboys. It also—especially with the exclamation mark present in BRIDGEWATER—puts the Black Knight in the (characteristic) position of stage manager and director of the action, a position which the added beginning of the scene seems to have been created in order to emphasize. The author is much more likely than a scribe to have produced such a variant; alternatively, it might record a detail added by the actor in performance. In either case it seems to represent a late, deliberate variant, probably never present in the playbook. Because other editors do not print the phrase as dialogue, the omission of 'Hoboyes again' has not been considered a shared error.

5.1.9 Oboes] MIDDLETON[T] + (Hoboyes). Although Wells argues that there are physical differences between the Renaissance instrument and its modern equivalent (*Modernizing*, 15), that is true of almost all musical instruments. Modern 'oboes' is actually closer to the autograph 'hoboyes' than is the French spelling 'hautboyes', adopted by some modern editors.

*5.1.9.2/2013 Oboes.] MIDDLETON[T] *only*; *not in* CRANE[2,3,4], OKES. See preceding note. Probably another example of Crane's tendency to omit music directions. Although the dialogue call for music is optional and disputed, omitted music cues are counted consistently as shared errors.

*5.1.9.2/2014 *from*] THIS EDITION (*conj.* Hotson); *not in* CRANE[2,3]. See next note. As at 2.2.81.1–2 and 3.1.155.2–3, 'the Black House' cannot enter here, because some of its members are already on stage.

5.1.9.2/2014 *the Black House*] CRANE[2,3]; *not in* CRANE[1] +. See preceding note.

5.1.9.2–3/2013–14 *Black King Felipe, Black Queen Maria, Black Duke Olivares*] *not in* CRANE[2,3]

*5.1.9.4/2015 *Bishop*] THIS EDITION; *K.* CRANE/ALLDE; *and B. Kt* OKES; *not in* MIDDLETON[T] +. OKES is clearly incorrect, as the Black Knight is already on stage. For the same reason, CRANE/ALLDE also is clearly incorrect, and the problem is not solved by the ambiguity of 'K.', because the Black King has already been specified in the same stage direction (*Enter* | *Bl.K.Q.* | *D.K.and* | *Wh.Kni.* | *and D.*). Both texts agree in erroneously calling for the entrance of a character whose title begins with 'K.' Given the other evidence linking the two quartos in this scene, it is possible that the error in one quarto derives directly from the error in the other, without intermediaries. However, the fact that the quartos are not necessarily independent witnesses here still leaves the original error (in whichever text) unexplained. It is conceivable that this error derives from a mistaken recollection of *Early*, since the mass entrance direction at the beginning of the scene in CRANE[1] includes '& Bl. Knight'; in *Early* that is correct, but in the changed staging of *Later* it is wrong. But since the beginning of the scene is not present in *Early*, it is hard to explain how any text of *Early* could have directly

influenced this scene, and also hard to explain how anyone transcribing the first part of the scene could have deliberately called for the Black Knight (who spoke the preceding speech) to enter here. The reading therefore seems more likely to result from inadvertence, the fact that the copyist had just been dealing with the Black Knight leading to an associative contamination of the text here. The CRANE/ALLDE 'K.' might be a misreading of or substitution for manuscript 'B.' Likewise, the OKES 'B.' might stand for 'Bishop', rather than a (redundant) 'Black' before 'Knight' (not used before the preceding initials 'Q.' and 'D.'); alternatively, 'B.Kt.' could be an error for 'B.Bi.', easily explicable as the Knight appears on the same page, and the Black Bishop has not been seen or heard of since the end of 3.1. In any case, though, inclusion in the entrance direction of an abbreviation for 'Bishop' would account for the error in both quartos. The Black Bishop was not originally included in the scene (in *Early*), because—before the introduction of the Fat Bishop—he had been captured in the preceding scene; but in all texts after CRANE[1], the Black Bishop would be a natural participant in this scene, and may be implied by the general direction in CRANE[2,3] calling for the 'Black House' here. (See preceding notes.) On that interpretation, his omission from the list of entering characters in ROSENBACH, BRIDGEWATER, MIDDLETON[T] would represent a shared error in those texts; however, because this new emendation is conjectural, I have not counted this as an instance of shared error in those three linked texts. (I have, however, counted it as an error shared by the two quartos, since they are both clearly wrong in calling here for a character whose title begins with 'K'.)

*5.1.9.4/2015 *with Pawns*] OKES, ROSENBACH[B], BRIDGEWATER[B]; *not in* CRANE/ALLDE, MIDDLETON[T]. The pawns are specified in CRANE[1], and implied in 'the Black House' of CRANE[2,3]. Hence, although they have no speaking part in the scene, they seem to have been part of Middleton's intention from the beginning of his work on the play, to the late transcription of the other NON-CRANE texts; moreover, the sheer number of Black figures on stage, surrounding the White Knight and Duke, provides a theatrical corollary for the perilous situation of Prince Charles and Buckingham in Madrid, surrounded by Spanish Catholics. Omission of the pawns therefore seems to me—as to HOWARD-HILL and other editors—to be an error shared by MIDDLETON[T] and CRANE/ALLDE, rather than a revision. Contrast the absence of black pawns from 5.3.0.1–3.

5.1.9.4/2014 *meeting*] *and* CRANE/ALLDE

5.1.9.5/2015 *White Duke*] CRANE[3]; _∧_ ~ CRANE[1] +

5.1.9.6/2015 *who enter from the White House*] THIS EDITION (*conj.* Hotson); *not in* CRANE[1] +. See 1.1.30.1. We have seen them exit toward the Black House in 4.4; now we see them from, as it were, the opposite side of the facade, entering the space they had exited into.

5.1.9.6–8/2016 *The Jesuit Black . . . oration*] CRANE[1], OKES, ROSENBACH[B], BRIDGEWATER[B]; *the Oration.* MIDDLETON[T]; *not in* CRANE[2,3,4]. Although CRANE[1] contains substantively the same phrase, it has a different beginning to the scene, and hence is not likely to be the direct transcriptional source of OKES, ROSENBACH, BRIDGEWATER. This is probably another instance of authorial recovery. CRANE[2,3,4] provide an entrance for the Black Bishop's Pawn at the beginning of the scene, and (however useful for a reader) this phrase is not strictly necessary in a playbook; hence its absence cannot be categorized as a shared error.

5.1.9.7/2015 *above*] *from above* OKES

5.1.9.7/2015 *entertains*] OKES, CRANE[1]; *entertaining* ROSENBACH[B], BRIDGEWATER[B]

5.1.9.7/2015 *them*] *him* OKES. This might be an authorial variant, since Middleton's source emphasized that the oration was made in honour of Charles, specifically.

5.1.10/2017 BLACK BISHOP'S PAWN] *not in* MIDDLETON[T] *only*

*5.1.10–19/2017-27 *Si…congratulamur*] *verse* OKES, CRANE/ ALLDE: hilarem | peramantibus | peperitue | praelucentissime | Domum | fatemur | qua | Acclamatione | obsequiis |

*5.1.11–12/2018 *peramantibus*] *per amantibus* CRANE[3,4]; *permantibus* OKES; peramantibur BRIDGEWATER[B]. Nascimento and Howard-Hill do not record these variants. According to Francis Cairns (private communication) '*peramantibus* should be one word' (as it is in Middleton's source); 'it is a form of *peramans*, a rare intensive of *amans*.' The rarity of the form might account for Crane's mis-spacing in two late manuscripts. Normally word-spacing is not treated as a substantive error, but I have included it among shared errors in this case because the passage is in Latin.

5.1.12/2019 *peperitvè*] peperituè MIDDLETON[T], CRANE[1,2,3]; peperitue BRIDGEWATER[B]; *perpetue* ROSENBACH[B]; *peperitùs* CRANE/ ALLDE; *perperitùr* OKES. The penultimate 'u' would have been ambiguous in old typography, meaning either modern 'u' or modern 'v'. The final letter of CRANE/ALLDE is difficult to read, and could be either an 'e' or an 's', but it most closely resembles the final letter of the 'us' ligature in 'peramantibus' at the end of the previous line (and seems to be a ligature). Both quartos agree in misplacing the accent (shared punctuation error), which disappears entirely in BRIDGEWATER[B] and ROSENBACH[B].

5.1.13/2020 *candidissime*ᴀ *prælucentissime*)] ~-~ CRANE[2,3], BRIDGEWATER[B]; ~)~ᴀ CRANE/ALLDE, OKES[1]. Shared punctuation error. Middleton's source places within brackets the vocative phrase '(clarissime & serenissime Princeps)' just before the word 'fœlicem', and Middleton's parallel vocative, substituting Knight for Prince and using adjectives that instead emphasize his whiteness, placed just before the same word 'fœlicem', is also in brackets: '(Eques candidissime prælucentissime)'. Moreover, Middleton's source on eight other occasions places within brackets the word 'Princeps' preceded or followed by an adjective (including '*prælucentissime Princeps*' on p. 30). Though not in the source, the hyphen is unnecessary but not substantively misleading, since it joins two adjectives that belong together; the quartos instead erroneously place the closing bracket so that it separates the two adjectives from each other. The error is progressive: the presence of a punctuation mark after the first adjective links the quarto error to the earlier Crane texts.

5.1.13/2020 *candidissime*] candiffime BRIDGEWATER[B]; Candififfime MIDDLETON[T] *uncorrected*. The variants might be connected, as the error in the uncorrected state of MIDDLETON[T] could easily produce eyeskip, resulting in the BRIDGEWATER[B] error.

5.1.14/2021 *Domum*] domam BRIDGEWATER[B] *uncorrected*

5.1.14/2021 *Nigritudinis*] Nigritutidinis MIDDLETON[T] *only*

5.1.14/2021 *accessum*] accef = | acceffum MIDDLETON[T] *only*

5.1.15–16/2023-4 *adventus…lætitia*] Adven= | tiæ BRIDGE-WATER[B] *uncorrected* (thereby omitting 'tui…possumus')

*5.1.15/2023 *promisisse*] promiffiffe CRANE/ALLDE, OKES; Pro= | mi fiſse BRIDGEWATER[B]

5.1.16/2024 *lætitia*] Lætitio CRANE[1]

5.1.17–18/2025 *affectibus*] Affectibur MIDDLETON[T] *only*

5.1.18/2025 *devotissimis*] MIDDLETON[T]+ (diuotifsimis). In Renaissance Latin the 'di-' spelling (under the influence of Italian) was common, and used in Middleton's source.

*5.1.18/2026 *sospitem*] Sofpitim CRANE/ALLDE, OKES; fcofpitem BRIDGEWATER[B]

5.1.20/2028 KING] K: BRIDGEWATER[B] *uncorrected*; K[g] BRIDGE-WATER[B] *corrected* (recognizing and correcting the potential ambiguity of 'K.', the reading of all other texts except OKES, which has 'Ki.').

5.1.20/2028 *congratulatory*] congratulary ROSENBACH[B]. The variant is not recorded in *OED* or Literature Online, but it does produce a more regular line, metrically, and might be an authorial coinage, influenced perhaps by the phrase 'adventum tuum tibi congratulari' in Middleton's source for 'this… speech' (p. 32).

5.1.21/2029 *affects*] affecty BRIDGEWATER[B]

5.1.23–31 WHITE KNIGHT…'Tis…donation….BLACK KNIGHT] *not in* MIDDLETON[T] *only*. The CRANE[3] abridgement made almost the same cut, but began it one line later (and therefore did not need to omit the speech prefix at the beginning of 5.1.31). Middleton, trying to finish the autograph copy quickly, may have remembered the abridgement.

5.1.23 KNIGHT] Ki. OKES. This impossible variant might be simply an omitted type; CRANE/ALLDE has 'Kni.' here. Or it might be a simple i/t error.

5.1.23 *acknowledged*] acknowledgèd OKES

5.1.24–30 BLACK KING FELIPE What…donation.] *not in* CRANE[3]

5.1.24 KING] K. CRANE/ALLDE; K[t] ROSENBACH[B]; K[ts] BRIDGEWATER[B] *corrected*; K[g] BRIDGEWATER[B] *uncorrected*. The CRANE/ALLDE reading is ambiguous, but part of a larger pattern of abbreviations: see 5.1.1. The deliberate alteration in BRIDGEWATER makes it share with ROSENBACH a reading found unambiguously in no other witnesses. Either reading could be defended: 'Knight' might reflect performance (the leading actor stealing two lines from an actor with a very small part, who was certainly less accomplished). But it seems more appropriate for the King and Queen to share the sentence, and ROSENBACH–BRIDGEWATER share many unique errors in this part of the play.

5.1.25 *noble*] Nobe CRANE[1]

5.1.25 *thought*] thoughts ROSENBACH[B]

5.1.25 *fix*] fixed CRANE/ALLDE

5.1.26 *circuit*] circle ROSENBACH[B], BRIDGEWATER[B]. Though the synonym substitution might be authorial, 'circuit' is the rarer word (Taylor 1988), and I can find no significant parallels for the variant.

5.1.27 *they're*] CRANE[1], ROSENBACH[B]; they are CRANE[2]+

5.1.28–9 They…giver] *1 line* CRANE/ALLDE, OKES. Relic.

5.1.30 *in*] of BRIDGEWATER[B] *uncorrected*

*5.1.30.1/2030 *Music*] CRANE/ALLDE, OKES; as a separate line in right margin, opposite l. 32 CRANE[1], opposite 'you', l. 35 CRANE[2]; *not in* CRANE[3]. In ROSENBACH[B] and BRIDGEWATER[B] the word is immediately followed, without punctuation or a line break, by 'an altar', in the right margin opposite 'you', l. 35; in MIDDLETON[T] it is immediately followed, without punctuation or a line break, by 'an Altar discouerd', on a new line below l. 36. For the altar see note at l. 33 below. The word 'Hark' (l. 31) clearly indicates that the music must begin just before the Black Knight's speech—or, at the very latest, at the end of that sentence, cued by 'airs' (the position of CRANE[1]'s direction). Three texts (ROSENBACH, BRIDGEWATER, MIDDLETON[T]) thus agree in mistakenly combining the two stage directions, and all three also place the music cue too late; MIDDLETON[T] uniquely places it farthest from its correct position, and the other two share their late position with CRANE[2].

*5.1.31/2031 Hark … parts] 2 lines CRANE/ALLDE, OKES: Hark |
5.1.32-3/2032-3 Is … altar] things | OKES
5.1.32/2032 sounding] founds BRIDGEWATER[B] uncorrected
*5.1.33.1-2/2033 An altar … side] CRANE[1] (four lines in the margin, beginning opposite 5.1.33, and with a dash linking the direction to that line); four lines in the margin opposite ll. 33-5, with a bracket pointing to the space between l. 34 and 35 CRANE[3]; seven lines in the margin, opposite the text lines from 'Hark' to 'taste', ll. 31-5, with ambiguous brackets CRANE/ALLDE; six lines in the margin, opposite the text lines from 'hark' to 'you', ll. 31-5, without brackets OKES; three lines in the margin opposite ll. 35-6, with a bracket pointing to 'still' CRANE[2]; four lines in the margin, opposite the text lines from 'The virtues' to 'still', ll. 35-6, without brackets ROSENBACH[B], with ambiguous brackets BRIDGEWATER[B]; centred below l. 36 MIDDLETON[T]. The word 'yon(d)' either demonstrates that the altar is already visible, or cues its discovery. This position is indicated most clearly by CRANE[1,3], which both have the words 'An altar' opposite l. 33; the correct action may also be indicated by OKES and CRANE/ALLDE, which because of space limitations in the printed margin spread the direction across the Black Knight's entire speech. But CRANE[2], ROSENBACH[B] and BRIDGEWATER[B] mistakenly place the direction opposite the end of his speech and the White Knight's reply, and MIDDLETON[T] uniquely misplaces the whole thing after his reply. See note at 5.1.30.1.

5.1.33.1/2033 discovered] is ~ CRANE/ALLDE, OKES
5.1.33.1/2033 richly adorned] CRANE[1]; not in CRANE[2]+. Although this descriptive phrase does not appear in any of the later texts, there is no reason to believe that the revision (which strengthened the play's political allegory) would have used a plain altar to represent Catholic Spanish ritual. See next note.
*5.1.33.1-2/2033 with tapers on it] CRANE[2,3]; ~ ~ ʌʌ CRANE/ALLDE, OKES; not in CRANE[1], ROSENBACH[B], BRIDGEWATER[B], MIDDLETON[T]. Not adopted or recorded by HOWARD-HILL. But four texts of the revision specify a detail clearly related to the original generic direction in Early 4.25.1; for the political and religious significance of these props, see Taylor 2001. It is difficult to imagine why Crane or any other scribe should add such a detail, if it did not reflect authorial intention and/or performance practice.
5.1.33.2/2033 divers] CRANE[1,2,4]; not in CRANE[3], NON-CRANE. Probably a shared error, but the word is not absolutely necessary, and might be attributed to Crane.
5.1.33.2/2033 statues] CRANE[1], ROSENBACH[B], BRIDGEWATER[B], MIDDLETON[T]; Images CRANE[2,3,4], OKES. In MIDDLETON[T] the initial 'S' is written over 'I', suggesting that the manuscript he was copying had 'Images' but that he preferred 'Statues' (also the reading of CRANE[1]). The two words were synonymous, and this might be an example of authorial vacillation.
5.1.33.2/2033 standing on each side] CRANE[1], OKES, ROSENBACH[B], BRIDGEWATER[B]; about it CRANE[2,3,4]; not in MIDDLETON[T] only
5.1.34/2034 t'] to ROSENBACH[B], MIDDLETON[T]
5.1.35-6/2036-7 There's … still] 1 line OKES. Relic.
5.1.35/2035 with you] ~ ʌ BRIDGEWATER[B]
5.1.36/2037 WHITE DUKE … relish.] not in CRANE/ALLDE; ʌ ~ MIDDLETON[T] only. CRANE/ALLDE omits the whole speech, MIDDLETON[T] omits only the speech prefix, thereby re-attributing the three words to the White Knight. Given his carelessness and space-saving throughout this part of the manuscript, this

does not seem to be a considered artistic revision of the text, and may be only a partial correction of an error in his copy.
5.1.36/2037 Th'] CRANE[3]; the' CRANE[1]; the CRANE[2]+
*5.1.37 BLACK QUEEN MARIA (sings a] THIS EDITION; not in CRANE[1]+. All texts insist that the following rhymed lines are a song, but no extant witness specifies who sings it. The omission is not an error, because dramatic texts often leave the singer unspecified. Although music is often played from offstage, songs are almost always sung by onstage actors, and overwhelmingly they are sung by boy actors. The only specified onstage boy actor is the one playing the Black Queen. Given the theatrical norm of the singing boy, and the presence here of only one boy, the absence of a speech prefix makes sense: it would have been obvious to any theatrical professional who should have sing the song. There may also have been a political reason for the absence of a speech prefix. Since this scene clearly represents the arrival of Charles and Buckingham in Madrid, everyone in the audience would expect the scene's key figure to be a woman of the Black House; but the Black Queen speaks only nineteen words. Giving her the climactic song makes the political meaning of the scene, and the song, much clearer: 'our hopes' and especially 'our love' (the last words of the song) acquire a much more particular relevance when sung by a woman to a man, in a context where 'our' can be interpreted as a royal plural. It is indecorous for a Queen to sing, but no more indecorous than her interruption of the King, or the spectacle of religious statues dancing.
5.1.37/2039-40 song] wth a Song | Song. MIDDLETON[T] only
*5.1.39/2043 thee,] THIS EDITION; thee the CRANE/ALLDE, OKES; the MIDDLETON[T]+. The reading of the quartos, adopted by no modern editor, seems to be clearly mistaken: metrically it produces not only an extra syllable but a very uncertain rhythm, unparalleled in the other lines of the song. However, the erroneous duplication 'thee the' might have arisen from a misunderstood attempt to correct or revise 'the' to 'thee'. The spelling 'the', although normally used for the definite article, occasionally represented the second person singular pronoun 'thee.' Metrically, the pronoun produces the strong iambic (or trochaic) rhythm found consistently in the rest of the song. The article not only produces an irregular rhythm, but oddly shifts to the third person, departing from the otherwise consistent direct address to the White Knight in the rest of the scene. Elsewhere he is addressed with the more formal 'you', but the use of 'thee' make sense as a deliberate, climactic shift to the more intimate register; if indecorous, it would be no more so than everything else in the scene. Because 'the' makes sense, as a spelling variant or substantive variant, and because it is used by all modern editors, it is preserved in Early 5.33, and not counted as a shared substantive error; but I have interpreted 'thee' as a deliberate variant (and perhaps correction), botched in the quartos, in this scene where they share so many errors that apparently originate in a shared source.
5.1.39/2043 White House] white CRANE[1]
5.1.42/2046 on fire] CRANE, OKES, ROSENBACH[B]; a fire BRIDGEWATER[B], afire MIDDLETON[T]. Middleton's obsolete elision is preserved in Early 5.36. See 2.1.157.
*5.1.44.1 The … move] CRANE, OKES; not in ROSENBACH[B], BRIDGEWATER[B], MIDDLETON[T]. A shared error in autograph, emended by Howard-Hill. See next two notes. All five texts that contain the direction for the statues to do something place it in the right margin, spreading it across two lines (CRANE[1,2]) or three (CRANE[3]+). All CRANE texts have a line or bracket pointing to a specific position in the dialogue: CRANE[1,3,4] point to 'Move'

(44), CRANE[2] to 'above' (45). The three OKES lines are centred opposite 'move' (44).

5.1.44.1 *statues*] CRANE[1]; *Images* CRANE[2,3,4], OKES. On the variant see 5.1.33.2. Middleton apparently preferred 'Statues', which is also more intelligible to modern readers.

*5.1.46.1 *The statues dance*] THIS EDITION; *, & dance* CRANE[1]; *in a Daunce* CRANE[2,3,4], OKES; *not in* ROSENBACH[B], BRIDGEWATER[B], MIDDLETON[T]. The omission has already been counted as a shared error; but there seems also to be a second error, shared by all texts that contain the stage direction, except CRANE[1]. The second half of the scene calls for five spectacular effects, each separated from the other, so that each can wow the audience and make its intellectual point before the next occurs: offstage music coming from all directions (30.1), discovery of the altar (33.1–5.1.33.2), self-ignition of the candles (42), the movement of the statues (44), and then, in the final line of the song, something even 'more strange' than their movement (46–5.1.46.1). It is unclear what that climactic strangeness could be, if not the 'dance' called for by five texts, and commented on in the following speech. The earliest witness separates the movement of the statues from the dancing by a comma and the word 'and', providing a sequence of two verbs and two actions. In the four later texts that contain a direction, the duality and the sequence have been destroyed by removing the punctuation and transforming 'dance' into a noun in a prepositional phrase; this also has the effect of making 'move' redundant, since every 'dance' requires and presupposes movement. Dessen and Thomson do not record 'move' in their dictionary of stage directions, and LION does not record it elsewhere in stage directions of the period; its uniqueness and significance here derives from the fact that statues should, by definition, not move at all. Hence the first magical effect of the statues should be a simple movement of some kind—of an arm, or a head, or even stepping down from a pedestal—only later followed by a 'quickened' movement and then complex group dancing. This edition therefore follows CRANE[1] in calling for two distinct actions. The wording and position of CRANE[1] are preserved in *Early* 5.38.1, because it is not technically wrong, in an early modern stage direction, to call in a single direction for actions that may take place over several subsequent lines of text. However, for the convenience of modern readers it is helpful to move the second part of the direction to its appropriate place in the text (which in turn makes it necessary to repeat the initial noun).

5.1.47–8 BLACK KNIGHT GONDOMAR A . . . way.] *not in* MIDDLETON[T]. Further evidence of the author cutting corners toward the end of this transcript.

5.1.48 *right-hand*] HARPER suggests that 'the dance goes clock-wise and thus toward the White House' (p. 78), referring to his earlier note on Induction.52.1–2, where he speculates that 'The White House would presumably be on stage-right and the Black House, appropriately, on the "sinister side" (cf. *Ecclesiastes*, x, 2)' (p. 8). The symbolism of this seems convincing, but 'stage-right' is first recorded in 1947, and for the symbolism to make sense to an audience the White House would need to be located on stage-left (i.e., on the right side of the stage, as seen from the point of view of the spectators, or of the Black Knight, standing downstage, looking upstage at the dancing statues).

5.1.49/2051 BLACK] Wh: MIDDLETON[T] *only*. 'White Knight' would be possible, but 'White King' is not.

5.1.49/2051 KING] K. P. CRANE/ALLDE; Kt: ROSENBACH[B]. Since the Black Knight has just spoken, ROSENBACH[B]'s variant is impossible—unless we were to conflate it with MIDDLETON[T]'s 'Wh:', and assign the speech to the White Knight. But that seems dramatically as well as textually improbable. Nor does it seem credible to give this closing rhyming speech, commanding the rest of the company, to the Black King's Pawn, who has not spoken, or been addressed, anywhere else in the play. Perhaps CRANE/ALLDE, which elsewhere uses 'K.' for 'Knight', here intended the Black Knight's Pawn, but that too seems improbable, since he has not spoken in this scene, and the speech would be entirely uncharacteristic of his role.

5.1.49/2051–2 Come . . . delights] *choice* | MIDDLETON[T] *only*

5.1.49/2051 the] *not in* OKES *only*

5.1.49/2052 delights] *delight* BRIDGEWATER[B]

5.1.50.1/2054 *into the Black House*] THIS EDITION (*conj.* Hotson); *not in* CRANE[1]+. See 1.1.30.1.

5.2 CRANE (*Sce.*[a]. 2[a].); *not in* NON-CRANE

5.2.0.1–2/2055 *Enter . . . House*] *The white Queenes Pawne, & Black-Bishop's Pawne. Then y*[e] *Black Queenes-Pawne: Then y*[e] *white Bishop's Pawne, & ye Bl Knights Pawne* CRANE[3]. For the massed entry, see 1.1.0.2–5. For the absence, here, of an entrance for the White Queen, see 5.2.106.1.

5.2.0.1/2055 *Enter*,] ~ y[e] CRANE[2,3]

5.2.0.1/2055 *Pawn*] MIDDLETON[T] *only*; ~ *and* CRANE+. All texts but MIDDLETON[T] give a double entrance here, including the Black Bishop's Pawn: see notes at 5.2.3.1–2. The staging echoes that at the beginning of 2.1.

5.2.0.1–2/2055 *from the White House*] THIS EDITION (*conj.* Hotson); *not in* CRANE[1]+. See 1.1.30.1.

5.2.1/2056 QUEEN'S PAWN] Q., MIDDLETON[T] *only*

5.2.1/2056 love] *duty* CRANE, OKES. Beginning with this line, BRIDGEWATER is autograph, and cited as MIDDLETON[B]. Thus, both autograph texts and ROSENBACH[B] have the late authorial variant 'loue' in this line. There is strong evidence that ROSENBACH is the earliest of these three texts; hence, the variant probably originated in [PRE-ROSENBACH].

5.2.2/2057 H'as] *'h'ath* CRANE[2,3,4]

5.2.2/2057 more] *moft* CRANE/ALLDE

5.2.3/2058 has] *hath* CRANE, OKES

5.2.3.1/2059 *Enter*] MIDDLETON[T] *only*, which has a separate entrance here for the Black Bishop's Pawn; details cited in the following notes appear, in the other texts, at 5.2.0.1–2.

5.2.3.1/2059 *from the Black House*] THIS EDITION (*conj.* Hotson); *not in* CRANE[1]+. See 1.1.30.1.

5.2.3.1/2059 *the Jesuit*] OKES (after '*Blacke B.p.*'); ∧ *Iefuite* MIDDLETON[T]; *not in* CRANE+. Late authorial variant.

5.2.3.1–2/2059 *Black Bishop's Pawn*] MIDDLETON[B], ROSENBACH[B], CRANE[1,3]; y[e] ~ ~ ~ CRANE[2,4], OKES; *not in* MIDDLETON[T] *only*

*5.2.3.2/2059 *in . . . habit*] *not in* CRANE[2,3], MIDDLETON[T]. It is necessary to mark the change of costume, to explain her immediate recognition of him as the Jesuit (as opposed to her earlier failure to recognize him in 3.3 and 4.1). Emended by Howard-Hill.

*5.2.3.2/2059 *meeting her*] CRANE[1], ROSENBACH[B], MIDDLETON[B]; ~ *them* OKES; *seuerally* CRANE/ALLDE (after 'Enter'); *not in* CRANE[2,3], MIDDLETON[T]. A characteristically Middletonian direction; the two characters do not come on together, but from separate directions, presumably entering from the separate doors associated with the White and Black Houses. CRANE/ALLDE's direction has the same meaning, but in a form favoured by Crane.

5.2.4/2060 Yonder's] MIDDLETON[B], ROSENBACH[B]; hah? tis MIDDLE-
TON[T]+. Late authorial variant.

5.2.5/2061 traitor to holiness] *not in* ROSENBACH[B], MIDDLETON[T,B].
HOWARD-HILL supposes that 'the words were either deleted in
revision or (more probably) composed by Crane to complete
the verse'. Compare 'traitor to' at *Hengist* 5.1.2 and 'to
holiness' at *Hengist* 3.3.293. It would be relatively unusual
for Middleton to leave a half-line in mid-speech, and it is
hard to see why he or anyone else would have deliberately
omitted the line. The simplest explanation is that this is an
inadvertent omission in the archetype which lies behind
the three latest NON-CRANE manuscripts. However, this has not
been tabulated as a shared error, because HOWARD-HILL does
not regard it as such. (See next note.)

*5.2.7/2063-4 How...not] *2 lines* ROSENBACH[B], MIDDLETON[T,B]:
he |

5.2.7/2063 much...wronged] MIDDLETON[T,B], ROSENBACH[B]; ill...
vsd CRANE, OKES. Late authorial variant.

5.2.7/2063 he's] ha's MIDDLETON[B], ROSENBACH[B], CRANE[1], OKES;
'hath CRANE[2,3,4]; hee has MIDDLETON[T] *only*. 'He's' is the
modern spelling of the contraction 'H'as' (when *have* is an
auxiliary verb, as here).

5.2.7/2063 I'm] NON-CRANE; I'am CRANE[2,3]; I am CRANE[1,4]

5.2.10/2067 or] MIDDLETON[B], ROSENBACH[B]; and MIDDLETON[T]+.
Late authorial variant.

5.2.11/2068 suff'rer] CRANE[1,2,3]; fufferer CRANE/ALLDE+.

5.2.12/2069 For...only] *not in* CRANE[3]

5.2.13/2070 WHITE QUEEN'S] Bl.Bs. MIDDLETON[T] *uncorrected only*;
Bl.Qs. MIDDLETON[T] *corrected only*. Half-correction of an error
of assimilation to preceding and following speech prefixes.

5.2.13/2070 reverence and respect] MIDDLETON[T,B]; reuerend respect CRANE+. Late authorial variant.

5.2.16/2073 you, you should ne'er] ᴧ, ~ ~ neuer CRANE/ALLDE,
OKES; you You neuer fhould MIDDLETON[B]. Possibly a late
authorial variant, or two: in the quartos the omitted repeated
pronoun is complemented by expansion of the elision to
produce a regular iambic pentameter.

5.2.17/2074 unchasteness] Vnchaftity OKES. Compositorial synonym substitution of common 'unchastity' for the much rarer
'chasteness'. See EEBO (for relative frequencies) and Taylor
1988 (for the editorial principle).

5.2.18/2075 would] will OKES

5.2.18/2075 does] doth CRANE[2,3,4]

5.2.19/2076 stage] Stage MIDDLETON[T] *corrected*. The uncorrected
reading is disputable: Howard-Hill records 'ag blotted and
altered', but the original third letter seems to have been
dotted, and the fourth letter had an ascender: it looks
as though Middleton started to write 'Stät[ue]' (under the
influence of the preceding scene), but corrected the error in
mid-transcription.

5.2.20/2077 You'd] You would CRANE/ALLDE

5.2.20/2077 count it strange] MIDDLETON[B] *only*; thinke it moft
abfurd MIDDLETON[T]+. Late authorial variant, preventing the
repetition within three lines of 'absurd...absurdity'.

5.2.20/2077 have] MIDDLETON[T,B] *only*; fee CRANE+

5.2.23/2080 You'd] You would CRANE/ALLDE

5.2.23/2080 rail] In MIDDLETON[T] *only*, the 'l' of 'rayle' is altered
from the start of 'f', indicating that Middleton started to write
'rayfe' but corrected his error before finishing the fourth
letter.

5.2.24/2081 decorum's] decorum CRANE[2,3,4], OKES. See note on
'sake' at Induction.58.

5.2.26/2083 dev'lish] OKES (diulifh); Deuills MIDDLETON[T]+. Late
authorial variant: Middleton uses the adjective at least four

times elsewhere, and the elision 'dev'lishly' occurs at *Women
Beware* 4.2.77.

5.2.27/2084 do] *not in* OKES. Possible authorial variant, but it
produces a less regular line, and compositorial carelessness
seems a likelier explanation.

5.2.30-6/2087-93 Then...love you] *not in* CRANE[3]

5.2.31-2/2088-9 Know...you] judg- | ments MIDDLETON[B] *only*

5.2.31/2088 they must have cunning judgements] ~ ~ ~ ~
Iudgm[t] CRANE/ALLDE, ROSENBACH[B]; it ~ bee ftrange cunning
MIDDLETON[T] *only*. The unique autograph variant probably
resulted from unconscious anticipation of 'it must be a
strange nature' (5.3.74).

5.2.33/2090 auditory] OKES; Audience CRANE+. 'Auditory' occurs only 80 times in other plays printed by 1662; by
contrast, the more common 'audience' occurs 699 times.
A compositor or scribe is unlikely to have substituted the
'rarer reading': see Taylor 1988.

5.2.35/2092 when] MIDDLETON[B] *only*; if MIDDLETON[T]+. Late authorial variant (removing repetition of 'if').

5.2.36/2093 the] OKES; youre MIDDLETON+. Late authorial variant: compare 'play' [or 'ply'] 'the game' at 1.1.289.

*5.2.38/2095-6 Yes...power] *2 lines* MIDDLETON[T,B] *only*: of |

5.2.38/2095 th'] the MIDDLETON[T], CRANE[1]

5.2.39/2097 time, youth, fortune.] ~ᴧ (youths, fortune) OKES.
Possibly a late authorial variant, but I can find no Middleton
parallels.

5.2.39/2097 fortune] Fortunes MIDDLETON[T] *uncorrected*

5.2.42/2100 Which] MIDDLETON[B] *only*; this MIDDLETON[T]+. Late
autograph variant.

5.2.44/2103 cast] laft CRANE/ALLDE

5.2.45/2104 BLACK BISHOP'S PAWN] Bl. . CRANE/ALLDE (failure to
ink?)

5.2.45/2104 by] MIDDLETON[B] *only*; afide MIDDLETON[T]+. Late
autograph variant.

5.2.45/2104 loathe] loue OKES *only*. The variant might be
authorial: compare 'so much desir'd and lov'd' (*Revenger*
2.1.93). But although it makes local sense, it does not work
in the larger context, and probably resulted from antonym
substitution, prompted by the graphic similarity of the two
words. The mistake could be a compositor's, or the author's
scribal error.

5.2.46/2105 has] hath CRANE[2,3,4], OKES

5.2.47/2106 th'] CRANE[2] (th'e); the CRANE[1]+

5.2.48/2107 ᴧHope] I hope CRANE[2,3,4], OKES. Typical Crane expansion.

5.2.48/2107 pleases] pleafeth OKES. Middleton makes little use of
the obsolescent form, especially in his later work. For another
unique example of the -th form in OKES, see 3.1.27.

5.2.50/2109 others he should ᴧ] MIDDLETON[T] *only*; men ~ ~
ᴧ OKES; men ~ ~ first MIDDLETON[B]+. The unique authorial
variant 'others' might be an attempt to repair the metre
after the accidental omission of 'first' (as in OKES) in the lost
manuscript from which Middleton was copying the Trinity
transcript. However, this cannot be considered a shared
error, since MIDDLETON[T] makes sense—arguably better sense,
because she has no way of knowing that this was his 'first'
choice.

5.2.51/2110 t'] CRANE[1,2,3]; to CRANE[4]+

5.2.52/2111 office,] MIDDLETON[T] *only*; ~ (S[ir]) MIDDLETON[B] *only*;
Bufynes Sir CRANE[1]+. 'Office' is probably a deliberate late
authorial variant, since it makes sense and appears in both
autograph texts. However, it exactly repeats the phrase 'that
office', also at the end of the line, just three lines above; the
variant could therefore easily result from inadvertent con-

tamination by a copyist (whoever that copyist was). White Queen's Pawn might repeat 'that office', sarcastically; alternatively, the verbatim repetition might be designed to minimize the significance of the direct object (containing no new information), thereby clearly throwing the sentence's stress onto the verb 'were you requested'. The absence of 'Sir' from MIDDLETON[T] might also result from carelessness, but it has the effect of making more exact the repetition of the ending of l. 49, for purposes either of sarcasm or of de-emphasis—while also preventing, by anticipation, the pointless repetition of 'sir' at the end of two successive verse lines (52–3). These (related?) variants illustrate the occasional difficulty of distinguishing deliberate authorial revision from inadvertency. In this case, because the manuscripts are autograph, and because the alternative is readily available in *Early* 5.97, the hypothesis of revision has been preferred.

5.2.53/2112   named] MIDDLETON[B] *only*; name MIDDLETON[T]+. Late authorial variant, which clarifies that the 'token' (evidence) was given in his previous speech. HOWARD-HILL, printing 'name', suggests that he 'may display' at this point some token of affection exchanged during 4.3, but 'name' would be an odd way to say 'display'. The variant 'name' might be a simple misreading of 'namd', repeated in all witnesses until authorially corrected in MIDDLETON[B]; but use of the extended present tense to cover a statement spoken seconds before is well within the range of acceptable usage.

5.2.54/2114   you're] you are CRANE/ALLDE

5.2.55/2115   You'll] You'ld CRANE/ALLDE, OKES

5.2.55/2115   the] that CRANE[3]

5.2.55/2115   tie] tyde OKES. Misreading.

5.2.56/2116   With] by CRANE[1]

5.2.56/2116   solicitings] MIDDLETON[T,B], OKES; solliciting CRANE[1]+. Late authorial variant.

5.2.58/2118   You're] You'are CRANE[2]; You are CRANE[3,4], OKES

5.2.58/2118   on fire] CRANE[2,4]; one fire CRANE[3], OKES; afire MIDDLETON+. Since the earliest manuscript and the two late authorial manuscripts agree, it seems probable that 'one fire' is an error; however, it does make sense—the phrase 'all one fire' occurs at least six times before 1660 (LION and EEBO)—and it cannot be certainly categorized as a shared error. Here, as elsewhere, the elided form is preserved in *Early* (5.104): see 5.1.42.

5.2.58/2118   coz'ning] cozening CRANE, ROSENBACH[A]

5.2.59/2119   I am] I'm all ROSENBACH[A]. This might be deliberate parallelism introduced in a late authorial revision, but it might also result from contamination from the preceding line. The 'all' is not recorded by Nascimento or HOWARD-HILL.

5.2.60/2120   strict] hot MIDDLETON[B] *only*. This may well be a late authorial variant, but it loses the paradox of 'nice iniquity' and 'holy whoredom'; it also anticipates 'hot speed', two lines below, producing a pointless repetition of the adjective instead of the meaningful contrast between 'strict' and 'luxury'. An author, who knows the text better than most scribes, is particularly prone to such inadvertent or unconscious substitutions by anticipation.

5.2.61–2/2121–2   Ay...the game] OKES (I); that...youre ~ MIDDLETON+. There is no obvious error that would account for these variants in OKES. The letter 'I' could stand for the singular first person pronoun ('I') or the affirmative interjection ('Ay'), and both would be relevant here: 'Yes' [that's what kind of woman you are, described in the preceding phrases; or yes, you know me], and [Do you remember that I said, or did you think] 'I would marry you

right away in order to make legitimate the sexual game I wanted to play?' or 'would [you] get married right away in order to make legitimate the sexual game you play?' The change of 'you' to 'the' makes possible the ambiguity of 'game' (his or hers).

5.2.61/2121   marriage] Marriage MIDDLETON[T] *corrected*; L MIDDLETON[T] *uncorrected* (probably starting to write 'Luxurie', the word immediately above)

5.2.63/2123   See] So OKES. Simple e/o misreading.

5.2.63/2123   scourge] ſtrong OKES. Misreading.

5.2.63/2123   has] CRANE[1]; hath CRANE[2]+. This variant in CRANE[1] reverses the direction of Crane's normal substitutions (six times in the opposite direction, in CRANE[1] alone; another 33 times in one or more other Crane witnesses). It is therefore almost certainly the original authorial reading, preserved in the first Crane transcript, sophisticated in all others, and passively preserved in later copies.

5.2.64/2124   you're] yo[u] are ROSENBACH[A], [CRANE[4]]

5.2.66/2126   I'm] I'am CRANE[1]; I am CRANE[2,3,4], MIDDLETON[T]

5.2.67/2127–8   your...brokage] *2 lines* MIDDLETON[T]: farewell |

5.2.67/2127   cunnings] Cunning OKES. For concrete plurals as the 'rarer reading', see Taylor 1988.

5.2.67/2128   brokage] Brokage MIDDLETON[T] *corrected*; Brokere ROSENBACH[A]. The initial letter in MIDDLETON[T] has been 'altered, possibly from L' (Howard-Hill 1990). *OED* treats broker and brokage as exact synonyms, and HOWARD-HILL glosses as 'trafficking in matchmaking, pimping'; but here *brokage* also surely alludes to the broken hymen which is the subject of the last four lines of this speech.

5.2.68–9/2129–30   Nay...gracious] *a* | OKES

*5.2.70/2132   BLACK BISHOP'S PAWN] Bl.Q.P. CRANE[4], MIDDLETON[B] *uncorrected*; *not in* MIDDLETON[T] *uncorrected*; Bl.[ᴧᴧ] MIDDLETON[T] *corrected*. The 'Bl.Q.P.' error results from assimilation to the preceding and following speech prefixes. But for the recurrent confusion of these two speech prefixes see 4.1.38.

5.2.71/2133   *kneels, praying*] THIS EDITION; *not in* CRANE+

5.2.71/2133   pow'r] CRANE[2,3,4] (Powre); power MIDDLETON+

5.2.71/2133   preserved] preſerueд OKES

5.2.71/2133   this] that ROSENBACH[A]. Possibly authorial, but impossible to tell.

5.2.73, 75, 78   *praying*] THIS EDITION; *not in* CRANE+

5.2.73–4/2135–6   This...master] chair | MIDDLETON[T] *only*

5.2.75–6/2138–9   That...bed] lust to | MIDDLETON[T] *only*; last | OKES *only*

*5.2.75/2138   suffered'st] MIDDLETON[T,B], CRANE[1,2,3] (fufferdft); fufferedeft CRANE/ALLDE; fuffereft ROSENBACH[A], OKES. The metre requires two syllables here, eliminating a vowel in the second half of the word: Howard-Hill's transcript of MIDDLETON[T] (1990) reads 'sufferedst', but he acknowledges in a note that the reading might be 'possibly *suffredst*', and my own examination of the manuscript supports this alternative. More significant, the sense and the action of the play require the past tense; the present tense—a variant not recorded by Nascimento or Howard-Hill 1995—is a shared error resulting from e/d misreading (or from eyeskip from 'ed' to 'est', if the form in CRANE/ALLDE was also present in [PRE-OKES]).

5.2.76/2139   th'] CRANE[1]; the CRANE[2]+

*5.2.77/2140   *within*] *not in* MIDDLETON[T,B]

5.2.77/2140   over-common] ouercome ROSENBACH[A]

5.2.78.1   *She...Pawn*] THIS EDITION; *not in* CRANE+

5.2.79/2143   Now you may] you may now CRANE[2,3]

5.2.79/2143   I've] OKES; I haue CRANE+. See *Early* 5.128.

5.2.80/2144   Here's] this MIDDLETON[T] *only*; Here is OKES. See text note at *Early* 5.129.

5.2.80/2144 indeed] OKES; *not in* MIDDLETON+. Late authorial revision. The variant is hard to attribute to inadvertent scribal or compositorial intervention; it produces a twelve-syllable iambic line, but those are common in *Game*, especially with such a strong caesura. The interjections of the Black Bishop's Pawn, beginning with this mild one, become more blasphemous as his confusion increases.

*5.2.81, 86/2145, 2155 BLACK QUEEN'S PAWN] *not in* CRANE³, MIDDLETON^T

5.2.81/2145 within] CRANE^{2,3,4}, OKES; Intus MIDDLETON^T; *not in* MIDDLETON^B. Although CRANE¹ and ROSENBACH^A also lack specific directions here, their stage direction at 5.2.77 might be taken to apply to the entire sequence of her speeches until her entry; consequently, only MIDDLETON^B is clearly in error, in omitting any indication of speech within. See text note at *Early* 5.124.1.

5.2.82/2146 a] the CRANE/ALLDE

5.2.82/2147 WHITE] *B.* OKES. Assimilation. Compare autograph error at 5.2.13.

5.2.82/2147 I'll] CRANE¹; I will CRANE²+. A typical extrametrical Crane expansion, passively followed in all subsequent texts.

5.2.83/2149 Why] *not in* CRANE¹, OKES. Of witnesses to the revised version, only OKES lacks the interjection, a variant that could result from simple inadvertence or from Middleton's own temporary reversion to the original reading.

5.2.83/2149 a] MIDDLETON^{T,B}; *not in* CRANE¹+. Late authorial variant: the indefinite article completes the metrical transformation begun with addition of the interjection 'Why' (the original eleven-syllable iambic line with a feminine ending having finally become a thirteen-syllable iambic line with a feminine ending).

5.2.84/2150 the contract] thanksgiuing MIDDLETON^T *only*. Contamination from the preceding line.

5.2.84–5/2151–3 BLACK QUEEN'S PAWN...thee.] *not in* CRANE³. Abridgement (saving two manuscript lines).

5.2.84/2151 BLACK QUEEN'S PAWN] *not in* MIDDLETON^T; Bl.B^s.p. MIDDLETON^B *uncorrected*. See 5.2.81, 86. This differs from the other two examples only because the line is not present in CRANE³, and hence there can be no shared error; however, the error could have been present in CRANE³'s full-length source. Here as elsewhere in dealing with shared error, the connections between existing documents are not direct, because no existing manuscript was the direct source for another existing document.

5.2.84/2151 within] CRANE^{2,4}, OKES; Intus MIDDLETON^T; *not in* MIDDLETON^B. See 5.2.81.

5.2.84/2152 A pox] MIDDLETON^{T,B}; Mischief CRANE¹+. Late autograph variant. See text note at *Early* 5.137.

5.2.84/2152 thee] yee MIDDLETON^B *uncorrected*

5.2.85/2153 were prepared for't] did prepare youre felfe MIDDLETON^B *only*; thou didſt prepare thyſelf CRANE¹. Late authorial variant, which returns to the active construction of the original version. However, all other texts of the revision contain Middleton's characteristic contraction 'for't', and since the active construction is already available at *Early* 5.137, I have here retained the alternative autograph reading.

5.2.86/2154 your] thy CRANE¹

5.2.86/2155 within] CRANE^{2,3,4}, OKES; Intus MIDDLETON^T *corrected*; *not in* MIDDLETON^B. See 5.2.81. In MIDDLETON^T the initial 'I' is written over 'w', indicating that Middleton started to write 'within', which presumably stood in his copy. This suggests that MIDDLETON^T derives from something like CRANE^{2,3}

(where *within* is a speech prefix, rather than a stage direction in the right margin).

5.2.87/2156 'Slid, 'tis] MIDDLETON^B; light, tis MIDDLETON^T, ROSENBACH^A; ₍ tis CRANE¹; ₍ This is CRANE^{2,3,4}, OKES. There is nothing intrinsically suspicious about CRANE¹ here; its extra initial stressed syllable is at least as common and regular, metrically, as the alternative twelve-syllable line. However, Crane does not elsewhere expand 'tis to This is—which suggests that the revised playbook may have contained an oath here, crossed out by the censor, and later restored by the author in subsequent transcriptions. Alternatively, the oath, in its variant forms, may simply be a late authorial revision. Among the autograph alternatives, 'slid is the more objectionable oath.

5.2.87/2156 a] ſome OKES. This might well be a late authorial revision. Because 'some' indicates uncertainty, it makes better sense of the noun 'pawn' later in the line (see next note): what he hears is undoubtedly a bawdy *voice*, but he might guess that it is the voice of *some* bawdy *pawn*. Hence, acting on the conjecture that this variant is authorial (rather than a compositorial or scribal substitution) would require an editor to ignore the certainly autograph oath and the certainly autograph noun 'voice.'

5.2.87/2156 voice] MIDDLETON^T, CRANE¹; Pawne CRANE²+. Despite its adoption by some editors (including HOWARD-HILL), 'Pawn' cannot be correct, because the Black Bishop's Pawn knows nothing about the identity of the offstage voice—except the probability that it is a woman's or a boy's. Moreover, 'Pawn' loses the wit and logic of the movement from 'voice' to 'throat'. Given the immediately following entry for the Black Queen's Pawn, any copyist might have made the substitution, and it could easily have been passively repeated, until the author restored the original reading. (Not counted among shared errors because some editors adopt it.)

5.2.87.1/2157 *Enter Jesuitess Black Queen's Pawn*] MIDDLETON^{T,B}, CRANE¹; *in the right margin opposite ll.* 88–9 CRANE/ALLDE, OKES, ROSENBACH^A; *not in* CRANE²; *in massed entrance direction at* 5.2.0.1–2 CRANE³. The placement of the entrance is actually not ambiguous in CRANE^{2,3}, because the speech prefixes switch from *within* to the simple *Bl.Q^s.P.*, indicating that she is visible when she speaks 5.2.88. By contrast, in ROSENBACH^A and the printed texts it is not clear whether she enters before or after that line. A shared ambiguity, rather than a shared error.

5.2.87.1–2/2157 *from the Black House*] THIS EDITION (*conj.* Hotson); *not in* CRANE¹+. See 1.1.30.1.

5.2.88/2157 offer violence to me] THIS EDITION; ₍ ₍ ₍ ~ OKES; ~ ~ ~ ₍ CRANE¹+. The first person personal pronoun usefully clarifies the meaning of a crucial dramatic moment (which in my experience students, reading other editions, sometimes find confusing); moreover, its addition produces a more regular line, metrically (since *violence* elsewhere in the play seems to be trisyllabic). However, in itself OKES does not make sense, because the 'To' which begins the next line depends on the phrase omitted in this line. The emendation is based on the assumption that 'me' results from late authorial revision, and that the omission results from compositorial error.

5.2.89/2158 To] do MIDDLETON^B *uncorrected*

5.2.92/2163 That...not] there was no such engine CRANE¹

5.2.92/2163 seen] MIDDLETON^B *only*; knowne MIDDLETON^T+. Late authorial variant.

5.2.93/2164 up] *not in* OKES

5.2.94/2165 Is't] It ROSENBACH^A. Although this variant makes sense at the level of the individual sentence—turning a question into a statement—it does not work at the level of the speech as a whole.

5.2.94/2165   th'] CRANE¹; the CRANE²+. Typical Crane extrametrical expansion, passively followed by all other texts.

5.2.95-6/2166-7   Pray...'Tis] It is CRANE³. This abridgement (with the related expansion of 'tis to it is, for metrical reasons) might be authorial. It has the advantage of clarifying, for readers, a complicated theatrical moment: 'no longer' or 'no more' immediately follows the 'five years' to which it refers.

5.2.95/2166   upon] on ROSENBACHᴬ

5.2.95/2166   sir] not in MIDDLETONᵀ,ᴮ, CRANE²

5.2.96/2167   I've] ROSENBACHᴬ (I'ue); I'haue CRANE¹; I haue CRANE²,⁴, MIDDLETONᵀ,ᴮ; I'me OKES. See Incidentals note at Early 5.151. OKES could result from an easy minim misreading of the form in ROSENBACH.

5.2.96/2167   more] MIDDLETONᵀ,ᴮ only; longer CRANE+. Late authorial variant. Metrically, the line can work with either reading.

5.2.96/2167   more,] ~ Sⁱʳ MIDDLETONᴮ, CRANE³; not in CRANE¹+. The late authorial variant is anticipated by CRANE³, in a way clearly related to its deliberate omission of the two preceding half-lines: the same 'Sir' occurs, after 'me' (and therefore at the end of a verse line), in CRANE¹, CRANE/ALLDE, OKES, and ROSENBACHᴬ. Thus, only CRANE² and MIDDLETONᵀ lack her first use of the coldly impersonal 'Sir' at this point in the text. That omission is probably a shared error (although not counted as one, since the presence or absence of 'sir' can never certainly be identified as an error). Perhaps significantly, CRANE³'s 'sir' may represent not only a deliberate transfer of the word from one line to the next, but a restoration of a word omitted in intervening manuscripts. But no text has the vocative more than once here, so its presence at the end of this line is an alternative to its presence at the end of the preceding line. It seems more effective in its original position, following closely on 'bawd'.

5.2.99/2170   could] can CRANE¹

5.2.99/2170   you] OKES; who CRANE¹+. Late authorial variant, hard to explain as an error. See note at 5.2.88. Another clarification of this crucial exchange.

5.2.99/2170   pursed] MIDDLETON+; pursued DUTTON. The emendation is not recorded, but is deliberate, since 'pursued' occurs not only in the text (p. 301) but twice in the commentary (p. 452). The reading of all early witnesses is unambiguously the monosyllable 'purst' (variously spelled, but never with a second 'u').

5.2.100/2171   dispossessed] diſpatchd ROSENBACHᴬ

5.2.101/2173   Shall] not in ROSENBACHᴬ

5.2.102/2174   thy] thine CRANE³

5.2.102/2174   ear swells] MIDDLETONᵀ only; ~ ſwell MIDDLETONᴮ+; eares ſwell OKES. Since the variant in one autograph text appears in Early 5.158, the variant in the other autograph text has been preferred in Later. The OKES variant may also be authorial.

5.2.103/2175   With...vomit] not in CRANE³

5.2.103/2175   With thy] NON-CRANE; ~ thine CRANE¹,²,⁴

5.2.104/2176   niece] Child CRANE³ uncorrected

5.2.105/2177   Then] MIDDLETONᵀ,ᴮ only; and CRANE+. Another late autograph clarification of this speech.

5.2.106.1/2180   Enter White Bishop's Gelded Pawn] The stage direction is placed here by CRANE¹,² and ROSENBACHᴬ; MIDDLETONᵀ, CRANE/ALLDE and OKES place it in the right margin, opposite the two half-lines of the Black Bishop Pawn's speech; in MIDDLETONᴮ it follows that speech. None of the positions can be clearly identified as an error, but the physical

drift in later witnesses may not be deliberate. See next notes.

5.2.106.1-2/2180   White Bishop's Gelded Pawn...White Queen] White Q.... yˢ Wh. Bˢ Pawne CRANE²

*5.2.106.1-2/2180   with White Queen] not in CRANE³,⁴, OKES. This character is missing from the sequential list in CRANE³'s massed entry at 5.2.0.1–2 (Bawcutt 1340–42), so the stage direction may have been missing from [PRE-CRANE²,³]. Although White Queen's Pawn (who is already on stage) could take Black Queen's Pawn, this variant would leave no one onstage to take Black Knight's Pawn; it would be theatrically awkward, to say the least, for White Queen's Pawn to stop an attempted assassination while still holding on to her female prisoner. Moreover, it is hard to imagine the variant as a deliberate revision, since the character enters both in Middleton's first version of the play, and also in two late autograph texts. By contrast, it is easy to explain the error: facing the form of the direction in CRANE² (White Q.... Wh. Bˢ), a copyist could easily skip, by eye or hand, from one 'White' (or 'Wh') to the next, thereby omitting the Queen. The changed order in CRANE² reflects his usual preference for hierarchical sequence in stage directions, and may have been present in other transcripts.

5.2.106.1/2180   with] MIDDLETONᴮ; and MIDDLETONᵀ, CRANE¹, ROSENBACHᴬ; ₍ CRANE³

5.2.106.2/2180   from the White House] THIS EDITION (conj. Hotson); not in CRANE¹+. See 1.1.30.1.

5.2.107.1   White Bishop's...takes...Pawn] THIS EDITION; not in CRANE¹+. Which piece takes which is probably indicated by who speaks to the taken pawn. If what we are seeing is snapshots of the endgame, the chess moves are sensible enough, on that assumption. But if speeches do not indicate which pieces take others, then it would be possible to arrange the moves differently. In chess, the White Bishop's Pawn cannot take the Black Bishop's Pawn unless one of them has already taken some other piece; we have not seen either of them do so in the play. If the White Queen's Pawn took the Black Bishop's Pawn here, then the White Bishop's Pawn could take the Black Knight's Pawn.

*5.2.108/2183   QUEEN] MIDDLETONᵀ,ᴮ, CRANE¹,²; Q.P. CRANE³,⁴, OKES, ROSENBACHᴬ. See 5.2.106.1. Although intrinsically either character could speak the line, without it the White Queen is given nothing to say, and no reason to enter. Omission of the stage direction for the White Queen's entrance could have led to a false 'correction' of this speech prefix; this may be an example of progressive error. In chess terms, too, White Queen makes more sense than White Queen's Pawn. (Both autograph texts, and the earliest text, agree on 'White Queen'.) This looks like late authorial restoration of an original reading, corrupted in intervening copies.

5.2.108.1   White Queen...takes...Pawn] THIS EDITION; not in CRANE¹+

5.2.109/2184   I'm] I am CRANE

5.2.109/2185   And] not in OKES. Perhaps authorial, but it leaves the line a syllable short.

5.2.109/2185   cannot] connot OKES

5.2.110/2186   affection] OKES only; perdition CRANE¹+. Late authorial revision. Psychologically, OKES is a plausible, indeed fascinating, variant, which cannot be explained as a misreading or an obvious substitution. For the rare collocation of weight and affection, compare 'I weigh my friends' affection with mine own' (Timon 2.218); for 'my affection' see Phoenix 1.161, Michaelmas 4.3.75, Trick 4.1.61.

5.2.111/2187 'T'as] MIDDLETON[T,B], ROSENBACH[A]; 't'hath CRANE[1,2]; It hath CRANE[3,4], OKES. A rare, characteristic Middleton contraction, progressively sophisticated.

5.2.111/2187 not the] ∧ ~ ROSENBACH[A]

5.2.112/2188 BLACK BISHOP'S PAWN] not in MIDDLETON[T] uncorrected only; Bl. MIDDLETON[T] corrected only. Another example of a speech prefix omitted by Middleton, and another example of autograph half-correction.

5.2.112.1/2189 Enter Black Knight's Pawn] not in CRANE/ALLDE. In OKES placed opposite 5.2.111–12.

5.2.112.1/2189 Black] y[e] ~ CRANE[2,3]

5.2.112.1–2 from the Black House] THIS EDITION (conj. Hotson); not in CRANE[1]+. See 1.1.30.1.

5.2.112.2 with a weapon] THIS EDITION; not in CRANE+. He must have a knife, sword, or pistol, if he intends to attack the White Bishop's Pawn's 'heart'; an edge tool seems likelier, given his earlier assault by gelding.

5.2.113/2190 BLACK KNIGHT'S PAWN] not in MIDDLETON[T]; B.K.P. CRANE/ALLDE. For the variant abbreviated spelling see 2.1.229.

5.2.113/2190 Yonder's...now] 2 lines: Pawn | ROSENBACH[A]; heart | MIDDLETON[B] only

5.2.113/2190 Yonder's] OKES; Yond's CRANE+. Of these synonyms, yonder is more immediately comprehensible to a modern audience, and Middleton was quite capable of beginning a line with an extra stressed syllable (especially when it creates a line-divided foot, as it does here: 'in voto. Yonder's...').

5.2.113/2190 Have at his] MIDDLETON[T] only; Ile play at his MIDDLETON[B]; I'll play at's CRANE+. Late authorial variant.

5.2.114/2191 WHITE] Bl: ROSENBACH[A]. See the identical autograph error at 5.2.13.

5.2.114–16/2191–3 Hold...taken] prose MIDDLETON[T] only: a | that |

5.2.114/2191 Hold] MIDDLETON[T,B] only; Oh OKES; how now CRANE, ROSENBACH. Late authorial revision. See next note.

5.2.114/2191 monster-impudence! Wouldst∧] MIDDLETON[T] only; bloudie Villayne ~ thou MIDDLETON[B], OKES; (Black Villaine) ~ thou CRANE, ROSENBACH. Late authorial revisions. MIDDLETON[T] is not only the most original compound, but the farthest from the original reading.

5.2.115/2192 attempt] MIDDLETON[T] only; offence CRANE+; offences OKES. Late autograph variant.

5.2.115–16/2192–3 On...taken] 1 line MIDDLETON[B] only

*5.2.115/2192 O merciless bloodhound] not in MIDDLETON[T,B]. A shared autograph error, emended by HOWARD-HILL. Compare 5.2.5; here, HOWARD-HILL cannot dismiss the omitted phrase as a Crane interpolation, because it is also present in ROSENBACH[A] and OKES. Unlike other omitted phrases or lines, this variant is hard to explain as a conscious cut, designed to serve an explicable dramatic purpose. The error was presumably accidentally made in the lost manuscript from which both autograph texts of this part of the play derive.

5.2.116/2193 that thou] ∧ ~ ROSENBACH[A]. Eyeskip.

5.2.116/2193 art] MIDDLETON[B] only; wert CRANE+. Late autograph variant.

5.2.116.1 White...takes...Pawn] THIS EDITION; not in CRANE+

5.2.116.1/2194 BLACK KNIGHT'S PAWN] B.K.P. CRANE/ALLDE, OKES. For the acceptability of this variant and its unreliability as evidence of a stemmatic connection see 2.1.229 and 4.2.76.

5.2.116/2194 Death!] How CRANE[2,3,4]; how, Death ROSENBACH[A]. Censorship of the playbook, later restored by the author. ROSENBACH[A] treats the restored original reading as an addition to (rather than replacement for) the censor's variant.

5.2.117/2195 yon] MIDDLETON[T] (yon'd); that CRANE+. Late autograph variant.

5.2.118/2196 never] ner ROSENBACH[A]

5.2.118/2196 farther] further CRANE/ALLDE, OKES

5.3 CRANE (See[a]. 3[a].); Scaena Vltima ROSENBACH[A], MIDDLETON[B]; not in OKES, MIDDLETON[T]

5.3.0.1–4/2198–2200 Enter...White Duke] not in ROSENBACH[A]; The Black-House, & y[e] white-knight, & Duke: Then the white King, Queene, Bishop. CRANE[3]. For the massed entry, see 1.1.0.2–5.

5.3.0.1/2198 from] THIS EDITION; not in CRANE[1]+. See 1.1.0.2–4.

5.3.0.1/2198 the Black House] CRANE[2,3] (without listing individuals); not in CRANE[1]+

5.3.0.1/2198 Black] All early texts use this adjective at least once here; MIDDLETON[T] and OKES use it twice (before the King and Knight); I have added it, for consistency, before all the Black pieces.

5.3.0.2/2198 Duke] MIDDLETON[T], OKES. In CRANE[1,4] and MIDDLETON[B] the Black Duke enters, anti-hierarchically, after the Black Knight, not before. Notably, in contrast with 5.1.9.4, not a single witness to the revised text specifically calls for black pawns in this scene. Three have just been captured, and the movement from the public welcome of 5.1—with many Black pieces commanding not only the stage but the balcony—to private negotiations in 5.3 might well be conveyed by the contrasting number of black pieces on stage in this final scene. Moreover, once the climactic action of putting black pieces in the bag had been added, there would have been a strong reason to omit any black pawns from this entrance, since putting them into the bag would be anti-climatic and would prolong the final action at a point when the audience is ready for closure. Moreover, within the terms of the allegory the return of Charles and Buckingham was a defeat for Spanish aristocrats, particularly.

5.3.0.3/2198 Bishop] CRANE/ALLDE; not in CRANE[1]+. The Black Bishop has already been captured in Early, so his absence from the direction there is not an error. However, in the revised version he is available, and would be implied by 'the Black House' (CRANE[2,3]); hence, the three earliest witnesses of the revised version all explicitly or implicitly include him here. Although he plays no part in the dialogue, he does apparently make a spectacular visual contribution: see note to 178.2 (which records a fourth text of the revised version which presupposes his presence in this scene). His absence from this entrance direction in the three NON-CRANE texts that include the direction (OKES, MIDDLETON[T,B]) is probably just another error shared by those texts, but it has not been counted as such, because some modern editors endorse his absence.

5.3.0.3/2199 with] MIDDLETON[T,B], CRANE[1]; & CRANE[2,3,4]; not in OKES

5.3.0.3–4/2199 ∧White Knight] the ~ ~ CRANE[2,3], MIDDLETON[T]

5.3.0.4/2199 his] MIDDLETON[T,B]; not in CRANE[1]+. The possessive pronoun is significant, indicating the degree to which the favourite of King James had shifted allegiances, becoming the chief ally and favourite of Prince Charles (perhaps King by the time these manuscripts were copied).

5.3.0.4/2199 White Duke] CRANE/ALLDE, OKES; ∧ ~ CRANE[1]+

5.3.1/2201 knight] K. ALLDE. The misleading abbreviation is used repeatedly by ALLDE in this scene: ll. 5, 28, 53, 57, 61, 71, 77, 82, 100, 117, 143, 158, 171, 198, 205. The only exceptions in speeches of the White Knight are ll. 103, 137,

145, 162, which all have *Kni.* (presumably the reading of the underlying manuscript). This ALLDE abbreviation also affects speeches of the Black Knight: see 5.3.28. For both characters, the correct 'Kni.' prefixes cluster in two stretches of text: 5.3.74–107 (I2ᵛ–I3, five examples out of nine possible) and 5.3.137–62 (I3ᵛ–4, eight out of ten).

5.3.1/2201 You've both] MIDDLETONᵀ *only*; You haue CRANEᴵ+. Late autograph variant.

5.3.1/2201 royal] Noble CRANE/ALLDE. Possibly an authorial variant.

5.3.2/2203 KING] Kt. OKES, CRANEᴵ; K. CRANE/ALLDE (ambiguous). The variant here might result from authorial wavering. 'Knight' is preserved in *Early* 5.179.

5.3.4/2205 that's seldom heard] wee seldome heare MIDDLETONᴮ, ROSENBACHᴬ, CRANEᴵ. Of the two autograph readings here, we have printed in *Later* the one not present in *Early* 5.183.

*5.3.5/2206 WHITE KNIGHT CHARLES I...on't] *not in* ROSENBACHᴬ, MIDDLETONᴮ. A shared error in autograph, emended by Howard-Hill.

5.3.6/2207 do] In MIDDLETONᵀ *only* the initial 'd' is written over 'n', indicating that Middleton started to write 'not' (omitting 'do' altogether), but corrected his error before finishing the word.

5.3.7/2208 Three] MIDDLETONᴮ *only* (3); 2 MIDDLETONᵀ+; a ROSENBACHᴬ. Late authorial variant.

5.3.8/2209 th'] CRANE²,³,⁴, MIDDLETONᴮ; the CRANEᴵ, OKES, ROSENBACHᴬ, MIDDLETONᵀ

5.3.8/2209 painful] vainfull ROSENBACHᴬ. Although *OED* records three examples of *vainful* in the sixteenth century, here it repeats rather than complicates 'idleness', and is probably an inadvertent synonym substitution under the influence of context.

5.3.8/2209 idleness] exercife ROSENBACHᴬ. Contamination from earlier in the line.

5.3.9/2210 fishes] fisher ROSENBACHᴬ

*5.3.11/2212 Ebusus] OKES (Ebufis); Eleusis CRANE+. Late authorial correction of what was probably an authorial error. See note to *Early* 5.190. I have modernized the spelling. Eleusis is in eastern Greece—which would place all three sites in the eastern Mediterranean, thus defeating the impression of fish imported from all directions.

5.3.12/2213 whiting] writing ROSENBACHᴬ

*5.3.12/2213 Chalcedon] CRANEᴵ+ (Calcedon); Caldedon ROSENBACHᴬ, MIDDLETONᴮ. A shared c/d misreading in autograph, emended by Howard-Hill. The correct reading is confirmed by Middleton's source (Pliny).

5.3.13–15/2214–16 Salmons...wine] *not in* CRANE³

5.3.13/2214 ellops] CRANEᴵ+ (Helops). All early witnesses include the initial 'h', which is not present in modern editions of Pliny's Latin or in Holland's 1601 translation; I have adopted the lemma in *OED*, which notes that modern zoological 'elops' has a different sense (which Howard-Hill reproduces in his commentary).

5.3.14/2215 fatted] flatted ROSENBACHᴬ; falted OKES. Misreading.

5.3.16/2217 cram] crambd MIDDLETONᴮ *only*. Probably another example of Middleton momentarily thinking in the historical past tense (of Prince Charles's visit to Madrid) rather than the present tense (of performance).

5.3.16/2217 Epicurean] *Epicidean* CRANE/ALLDE

5.3.17/2218 o'th'] CRANE, OKES; of the MIDDLETONᵀ *only*; a'th MIDDLETONᴮ *only* (alternative spelling); at ROSENBACHᴬ (an error, apparently based on the alternative spelling *a'th* instead of *o'th*)

5.3.17/2218 Orata] DYCE; Crata CRANEᴵ+. This is almost certainly an authorial error. (See note to *Early* 5.196.) However, Middleton's intention was to refer to the historical person identified in his source, Pliny (perhaps supplemented by Macrobius's *Saturnalia*, which also gives the name as 'Orata', and explains that he was 'surnamed Orata on account of his passion for the fish called *aurata*' (tr. Davies, 235)). In such circumstances, an editor may emend to restore the intended reading, concealed by an autograph mistranscription. For the editorial principle see Tanselle.

5.3.18–21/2219–22 He...followed] *not in* CRANE³

*5.3.19–20/2220–1 And...throat] CRANEᴵ, ROSENBACHᴬ, MIDDLETONᴮ; his | CRANE²,⁴, OKES, MIDDLETONᵀ. Shared error.

5.3.19/2220 besides] CRANE, OKES; befide ROSENBACHᴬ, MIDDLETONᵀ,ᴮ. Though treated as substantive by modern editors, this was only a spelling variant at the time. Compare 3.1.238. In each case I have chosen the spelling idiomatic in modern English.

5.3.19/2220 besides] befide MIDDLETONᵀ *corrected*; bef MIDDLETONᵀ *uncorrected* (presumably starting to write 'before', under the influence of 'for' immediately above)

*5.3.20–1/2220–2222 Of...followed] the | ROSENBACHᴬ, MIDDLETONᴮ. Shared error in autograph, emended by Howard-Hill.

5.3.20/2221 th'] MIDDLETONᵀ, CRANEᴵ,²; the CRANE/ALLDE, OKES, ROSENBACHᴬ, MIDDLETONᴮ

5.3.23/2224 two-and-twenty] twenty two OKES. See similar error in ROSENBACHᴬ at 2.2.22.

5.3.23/2224 one] a OKES. Possibly authorial.

5.3.25/2226–7 Washed...strengthened] *2 lines* MIDDLETONᵀ *only*: down and |

5.3.28/2230 WHITE KNIGHT] *not in* MIDDLETONᵀ *only* (which nevertheless has speech rules to indicate a change of speaker)

5.3.28/2231 KNIGHT] K. ALLDE. See also 5.3.1. Use of this abbreviation for the Black Knight is more sparing than for the White Knight, presumably because the Black King is on stage from the beginning of the scene, and had been given the first speech by a Black character. Nevertheless, *K.* reappears at ll. 63, 82, 120, 124, 130/2270, 2293, 2335, 2339, 2346. In the Black Knight's ten other speeches in this scene ALLDE has the prefix *Kni.*. In novelistic or realistic terms, it would make good sense to attribute all those speeches (amounting in all to 74 lines) to the Black King, leader of the Black House; however, in theatrical terms, the Black Knight was played by the company's leading actor, and Gondomar was much more familiar to London audiences (and the object of more visceral loathing) than Felipe, a distant figure they had never seen. Hence, ALLDE's *K.* must be interpreted as *Knight* unless other witnesses support *King*.

5.3.29/2232 extremes] extreame ROSENBACHᴬ

*5.3.32/2235 often] after CRANE/ALLDE, OKES. An easy misreading. Middleton's source confirms 'often'.

5.3.33/2236 I] MIDDLETONᴮ, ROSENBACHᴬ; we CRANE+. Late authorial variant. Gondomar had a beard; not all the Black pieces on stage did. Apart from the Black Queen, the Black King was young, and the Black Duke is referred to as a 'Ganymede' (hence young and presumably beardless).

5.3.35–9/2238–42 Complained...'specially] bid for a | are | some | needs | OKES. Similar to mislineations in MIDDLETONᵀ.

5.3.35/2238 was] were OKES. Possible, since 'coin' could be interpreted as plural.

5.3.37/2240 triumphs] Tryumphant OKES (probably resulting from dittography in an earlier stage of transmission: 'and and' interpreted as 'ant and').

5.3.39/2242 your] th' OKES, HOWARD-HILL. Probably a misreading, since Middleton does not elsewhere elide 'the' when the preceding word ends with a consonant and the following word begins with one. Perhaps 'o'th'' was the intended reading, which would reduce the hexameter to an iambic pentameter line with an extra initial stressed syllable.

5.3.39/2242 'specially] CRANE, MIDDLETON[T]; eſpeciallie OKES, ROSENBACH[A], MIDDLETON[B]. The contracted form is metrically preferable; the expanded form is probably another shared error, but—because HOWARD-HILL adopts it—has not been counted as such in the stemmatic analysis.

5.3.40/2243 plump] fat CRANE[2,3]. Probably an unconscious synonym substitution (perhaps anticipating 5.3.46); the alliteration seems too good to give up.

5.3.42-52/2245-56 So...him] not in CRANE[3]

5.3.44/2247 ne'er] not CRANE[1]

5.3.45/2248 Cyrene's] Cyrenus OKES. Misreading. (Does the unique autograph apostrophe here—the only autograph example of an apostrophe to indicate a possessive—instead indicate that the 'e' should be pronounced as a distinct syllable?)

5.3.46/2249 fat] not in ROSENBACH[A]

5.3.46/2249 Sanctius] Sauetius CRANE/ALLDE. This error seems to result from misreading rather than two foul case errors; the correct reading should have been set with a ligature ('Sanɔtius'), as it is in OKES.

5.3.49/2252 Cordoba] MIDDLETON+ (Corduba); Cordeba OKES. An easy misreading in the quarto (u/e); 'Cordoba' is the modern spelling.

5.3.50/2253 Morocco] MIDDLETON[T] corrected; Mora MIDDLETON[T] uncorrected

5.3.50/2253 counselled] counſellèd OKES, ROSENBACH[A]

5.3.51/2254 stunk] ſtrucke CRANE/ALLDE; ſtung OKES

5.3.52/2255-6 As...him] 2 lines MIDDLETON[T] only: choked |

5.3.53/2257 you're] you are CRANE/ALLDE, OKES. Typical Crane hypermetrical expansion, inherited by OKES.

5.3.53/2257 sir] not in OKES. This might be an authorial variant, since Middleton vacillated elsewhere over the presence or absence of 'sir'. Here, though, in mid-line, its presence seems metrically preferable.

5.3.54/2258 ₐClean] And cleare OKES. The added conjunction could be authorial, creating a line-divided foot. But 'cleare' looks like a simple misreading.

5.3.55/2259 spoke] MIDDLETON+ (spake)

5.3.55/2260 BLACK] W. MIDDLETON[T] uncorrected only

5.3.55-6/2260-61 Censure...discourse. | BLACK QUEEN] not in CRANE[3]. Probably abridgement, possibly eyeskip. In either case the effect is to re-attribute 'He'll...anything' to the Black King instead of the Black Queen.

5.3.55-6/2260-1 Censure...discourse] 1 line OKES. Relic.

5.3.55/2260 mildly] meekeley CRANE[1]

5.3.56/2262 talk] OKES; raiſe CRANE[1]+. Late authorial variant. See note at Early 5.238. Perhaps 'raise' was originally a mistake for 'rail': see 5.2.23.

5.3.58-62/2264-9 White Duke...to't).] not in CRANE[3]

5.3.59/2265 fog] Fognes MIDDLETON[T] only (assimilation to and anticipation of 'fatness')

5.3.61-2/2267-9 Your...to't] 3 lines MIDDLETON[T] only: trans- | much |

5.3.61/2267 shall] ROSENBACH[A], MIDDLETON[B]; ſhould CRANE+. Late authorial variant (as indicated by the related change in the following line).

5.3.61/2268 sure] (Sir) CRANE/ALLDE, (ſir) OKES. This could be a late authorial variant, but it could also easily result

from simple misreading. Whereas 'sure' is emphatic, 'sir' misleadingly singles out one person, rather than addressing this remark to the whole Black House; there is no obvious single antecedent for 'sir'. Probably a shared error.

5.3.62/2268 If I should] ROSENBACH[A], MIDDLETON[B]; Were I to CRANE+. Late authorial variant (as indicated by the related change in the preceding line).

5.3.62/2268 as...to't] me | ROSENBACH[A]; wrought | MIDDLETON[B] only; much | MIDDLETON[T] only; not in CRANE[3]

5.3.62/2268 you've] CRANE[2] (you'have); you haue CRANE[1]+

5.3.62/2269 to't] CRANE[1,2]; to it ROSENBACH[A], MIDDLETON[T,B]; not in CRANE/ALLDE, OKES

5.3.63/2270 This is] 'tis OKES. Possibly authorial, but also easily compositorial eyeskip, and producing a less regular line metrically.

5.3.64/2271 height] heights ROSENBACH[A]

5.3.66/2273 cabrito] Cabuto CRANE[1]. THIS EDITION italicizes this as a Spanish word, recorded in English only here and in Middleton's source, Scott's 2 Vox Populi ('leane Kid, or Cabrito'); in both cases it is spoken by a Spanish speaker and preceded by the English word. See OED cabrie, cabrit.

5.3.66/2273 tunas] MIDDLETON+ (Ton's). The meaning is not in doubt (OED ton[4]). Modern tuna was listed in the first edition of OED as an obsolete form of 'tunny', revived in American usage c.1900; but it has now become universal, and has been preferred in the modernized text.

5.3.67/2274 Eat...please] not in CRANE[3]

5.3.67/2274 twice] & ROSENBACH[A]

5.3.69-70/2276-7 A riot...cockle] not in CRANE[3]

5.3.69/2276 th'] CRANE[1,2]; the CRANE[4]+

5.3.71/2278 WHITE KNIGHT] not in MIDDLETON[T] only

5.3.71/2278 I'm] I am CRANE

5.3.71/2278 on] MIDDLETON[T] only; in CRANE[1]+. Late authorial variant.

5.3.75/2283 for] for't OKES. This could be an authorial variant, if the compositor accidentally omitted 'and' or 'if' at the beginning of the line.

5.3.75/2283 policy] plo MIDDLETON[T] uncorrected

5.3.77-8/2286-7 The...ambition] 1 line OKES, ROSENBACH[A]. Relic.

5.3.78/2288 BLACK KNIGHT] not in MIDDLETON[B] only (but with speech rules added, clearly indicating a change of speaker)

5.3.79/2290 cardinals'] Cardinall ROSENBACH[A]

5.3.81/2291 farther] MIDDLETON+ (farder); further CRANE/ALLDE, OKES

5.3.82/2293 We're] We'are CRANE[2]; We are CRANE[3,4], OKES

5.3.84-5/2295-6 but...ₐ The] ₐbut ~ ROSENBACH[A] (substituting the more common word order, at the expense of metre)

5.3.84/2295 came] come CRANE/ALLDE, ROSENBACH[A]. Probably a misreading, but both variants make sense and could be authorial.

5.3.85/2296 salads] Sallasd ALLDE uncorrected (Folger); Sallads ALLDE corrected (Huntington; Bodleian Malone 247; British Library C.34d.37). An unrecorded press variant (sig. I2[v]).

5.3.89/2300 our] her MIDDLETON[T] only

5.3.93/2304 fall to] ~ too ROSENBACH[A], OKES

5.3.97/2308 occasions;] MIDDLETON[T] only; ~, MIDDLETON[B]+; ~: CRANE[2,3]. See next note.

5.3.97/2308 comes,] MIDDLETON[T,B]; ~, CRANE[2]; ~: CRANE[1,3,4], ROSENBACH[A]; ~; OKES. See preceding note. Four texts have lighter punctuation at mid-line than at line-end: CRANE[1,4], OKES, ROSENBACH[A]. Given Crane's fondness for, and tendency to add, colons, this shared punctuation error presumably originated with Crane (working from authorial papers that may have had no punctuation in the line at all). That it is indeed an error is demonstrated not only by the agreement of the two autographs with the earliest text of the revised version (and with Salisbury's paraphrase), but by the sense: 'on all occasions' (anytime) directly contradicts 'when the voider comes' (a very specific time, at the end of the meal); there is no reason to restrict the making of sauces to the arrival of the voider, which instead seems clearly related to the end of the meal (when everyone has had enough, grace is said, and the guests 'rise'). The second half of the line clearly relates, grammatically and semantically, to what follows, and the first half to what precedes. The two most heavily punctuated texts here are CRANE[3] (which places colons at both points in the line, and two commas in the following line) and CRANE/ALLDE (which places a semicolon here and at the end of the following line, and commas in the middle of both lines); this over-punctuation is consistent with the assumption that Crane's punctuation grew heavier with each copying, and that CRANE[3,4] were the last of the known Crane transcripts.

5.3.98/2309   crammed] full CRANE, OKES. Late authorial revision.

5.3.100/2311   in] OKES, ROSENBACH[A]; a MIDDLETON[T,B] *only*; on' CRANE. The elided form found in both autograph texts is preserved in *Early* 5.285. The Middleton canon uses 'in conscience' at least eight times elsewhere, and 'in' is probably a late authorial variant.

5.3.103/2314   the] a CRANE[1], MIDDLETON[T]. Given the indifference of the variants, I have chosen to consider this authorial vacillation (preserving the indefinite article in *Early*, and the definite article here), but it might also be a transcriptional error in the playbook passed to all subsequent copies and corrected by Middleton.

5.3.104/2316   myst'ry] CRANE[1] (miftrie); mifery CRANE[2]+. The 'mystery' anticipates and explains the request for privacy, and the variant is almost certainly related to the censorship of the following words: see next note.

5.3.104–5/2316   I...cabinets. | WHITE KNIGHT] CRANE[1]; *not in* CRANE[2]+. Censorship: see note at *Early* 5.290–1.

5.3.105   we're] CRANE[1] (we'are)

5.3.105/2316   ha'] OKES; *not in* MIDDLETON[T] *only*; haue CRANE[1]+. See comparable variants at 1.1.258, 3.1.7, 3.1.274, D.22, 4.1.1, 4.2.41.

5.3.106/2317   gapes] ftands gaping OKES

5.3.107/2318   I'm] OKES; I am CRANE[1]+. Possible authorial variant, or late authorial restoration of Middleton's characteristic contraction.

5.3.108/2320   We're] OKES; we are CRANE[1]+. Late authorial metrical variant. Middleton treats 'ravenous' as disyllabic at *Revenger* 1.4.44 and *Chaste Maid* 2.2.63; hence, the speaker-divided verse line is either an iambic hexameter (as in CRANE[1] and other texts) or iambic pentameter with an extra stressed syllable at the caesura (as in OKES alone).

5.3.109/2321   heinous] hanoufneffe OKES. Although this might be a late authorial variant, all *OED*'s examples of the word are followed by 'of'. The autograph adjective better fits the grammar and metre.

5.3.110/2322   Why,ᴀ] ~ when OKES. Perhaps a miscorrection in foul proofs.

5.3.110/2322   we...prayers.] *not in* CRANE[1] (eyeskip)

5.3.110/2322   faith] OKES; faiths CRANE[2]+. I can find no parallels for 'our faiths' or 'our faith', but this could easily be an authorial variant, since 'our faith' would mean 'Catholicism', whereas 'faiths' individualizes the meaning of the phrase,

so that 'our faiths, our prayers' becomes almost redundant.

5.3.110/2322   our] or CRANE[2]. Misreading.

5.3.112/2324   her] their CRANE/ALLDE. Misreading.

5.3.113/2325   sale] ROSENBACH[A], MIDDLETON[T,B]; weake CRANE, OKES. Late authorial revision.

5.3.114/2326   Or] and MIDDLETON[B] *uncorrected only*

5.3.116/2328   You'd] You'would CRANE[2]; You would CRANE/ALLDE

5.3.116/2328   swear] fay ROSENBACH[A], MIDDLETON[B]. This might be late authorial revision, but the substitution of a weaker and commoner verb seems pointless, and might easily be inadvertent synonym-substitution by a scribe passively repeated by the author.

*5.3.116/2328   Plutus] Pluto OKES, ROSENBACH[A]

5.3.116/2328   whom] CRANE[3], OKES; which CRANE[1]+. This looks like authorial vacillation; Middleton used both 'which' and 'whom' as a relative pronoun referring to god(s) in *Solomon* 13.24, 16.163. The autograph is preserved in *Early* 5.304, and the more modern form here.

5.3.117/2329   is] ROSENBACH[A], MIDDLETON[B]; were CRANE+. Late autograph variant, substituting the more modern indicative for the older subjunctive.

5.3.117/2329   within 'em] there OKES. Perhaps a late authorial variant, but it weakens the metre and removes the wit of 'without 'em...within 'em'. Perhaps OKES should have read 'therein'.

5.3.118/2330–1   WHITE KNIGHT CHARLES Is't possible? | BLACK DUKE OLIVARES You...tuns.] CRANE[2,3,4], OKES; ᴀ You...Tuns | wh.K[t.] ist possible; MIDDLETON[T], CRANE[1]; Bl.D. You...Tuns | wh.Kt. ist possible? MIDDLETON[B] *corrected*; Bl:D. yo[u]... Tuns. ROSENBACH[A] *corrected*. The original reading, represented by CRANE[1], has been restored by MIDDLETON[T]. However, the dominant variant must be deliberate, because it not only transposes the two half-lines, but adds a new speech prefix, attributing to the Black Duke the half-line originally intended for the Black Knight as the conclusion of his speech; this provides an answer to the White Knight's question, gives the Black Duke something to say, and provides a transition for the next speech (as an intervention by the Black Duke leads to an intervention by the White Duke). This change (which appears in the earliest texts of the revised version) presumably originated in the playbook. Both ROSENBACH[A] and MIDDLETON[B] (*corrected*) attribute 'You...tuns' to the Black Duke, rather than regarding it as a continuation of the Black Knight's speech; hence, both clearly derive, at one or more removes, from the playbook version. As the speech prefix for the first half line, MIDDLETON[B] originally wrote 'W', then replaced it with 'B' and wrote out 'Bl.D. You... Tuns'. This suggests that his copy might have contained the two half-lines in their playbook order, and he might have consciously decided to restore the original order (without abandoning the new speech ascription). Alternatively, his copy might have contained only the White Knight's half-line, and he spotted the error just as he began to write the prefix, and supplied the missing half-line before rather than after the White Knight's speech. ROSENBACH[A], by contrast, omits the White Knight's half-line, presumably accidentally; we therefore cannot tell whether [PRE-ROSENBACH] put the two half-lines in the playbook order, or in the original order, restored by both autograph texts. However, the 'D' in the speech prefix has been heavily written over something else, probably 'K[t]'. If so, as originally written ROSENBACH[A] re-attributed the half-line to the Black Knight. However, such a speech prefix would have been unnecessary, since the Black Knight spoke the preceding speech. Perhaps in an earlier text the playbook order was retained, but the second half line was reattributed to the Black Knight, instead of the White Knight. That would have made it easier to accidentally skip over and omit the White Knight's short speech, perhaps explaining both ROSENBACH[A]'s omission and ROSENBACH[A]'s original error in the speech prefix. These explanations are conjectural. Only ROSENBACH[A]'s omission seems to be a simple error; ROSEN-BACH[A] and MIDDLETON[B] uniquely agree in placing the Black Duke's speech immediately after the Black Knight's. The reversion of the autograph texts to one feature (order) or both features (order and attribution) of the original reading might or might not have been precipitated by an intervening omission. Since the original version is printed in *Early* 5.306, the playbook version is printed in *Later*.

5.3.118/2330 pass] ROSENBACH[A], MIDDLETON[B]; walke CRANE[1]+. Late authorial variant.

5.3.119/2332 WHITE] *not in* MIDDLETON[B] *uncorrected only*

5.3.119/2332 sirs] MIDDLETON[T], CRANE[2,3,4]; (Sir MIDDLETON[B], CRANE[1], ROSENBACH[A], OKES. Either reading is defensible, and each occurs in autograph. Since the singular is printed in *Early* 5.308, the plural is printed in *Later*.

5.3.120/2333 quite forget me] neuer mind me CRANE[1]

5.3.120/2333 locked] MIDDLETON[T]; ſhut CRANE[1]+. Late authorial variant.

5.3.121/2335 foul] vild CRANE[2,3,4], OKES. This might be authorial vacillation, and the distribution of witnesses in different branches of the stemma makes it clear that 'vild' must have been present in the playbook. But it appears in neither autograph text, and it could result from scribal synonym substitution, or even censorship (*foul* being the stronger word, and more often associated with specifically sexual impropriety). Even if the variant is authorial, it anticipates (and was probably prompted by a memory) of 'Is it so vile' twenty lines below.

5.3.122/2336 Faith, some that's] CRANE[1]; Some that are CRANE[2]+. Censorship.

5.3.124/2338 book] OKES; bookes CRANE[1]+. For an audience the singular would recall the onstage 'Book' discussed by members of the Black House in 4.2; for Middleton, it suggests the 'black book' of which he had elsewhere written.

5.3.126/2340 Venery] *not in* CRANE[1]; verily OKES (misreading)

5.3.128/2342 It's] CRANE[2]; 'tis CRANE[1]+. See Induction.15.

5.3.129/2343 a] the CRANE/ALLDE. Assimilation to 'the' earlier in the line.

5.3.130/2344 heads] hee's ROSENBACH[A]

5.3.131/2345 WHITE KNIGHT] ROSENBACH[A], MIDDLETON[B]; wh.D. CRANE, OKES; *not in* MIDDLETON[T] *only* (which nevertheless has speech rules to indicate a change of speaker). It is possible that the revised speech ascription occurred after the accidental omission of the speech prefix (as in MIDDLE-TON[T]), and subsequent (mis)correction. But both readings are possible, and 'Knight' may be a later authorial variant.

5.3.131/2346 How? Ay] ₐ ~ CRANE, OKES. Late authorial variant.

5.3.131/2346 they] *not in* MIDDLETON[B] *only*. Eyeskip.

5.3.132/2347 in's] in his MIDDLETON[T] *only*

5.3.132 Ulric] CRANE, MIDDLETON[T,B] (Huldrick), OKES, ROSENBACH[A] (Huldricke)

5.3.132/2347 Augsburg] Auſburge ROSENBACH[A], MIDDLETON[T,B]; Asburge CRANE[1]; Awsberge CRANE[2]; Ausberge CRANE[3,4], OKES. None of these variants in the proper name seems to be definable as an error, and Middleton's exact source for this detail cannot be determined, but several details are notable:

CRANE[1] is the closest of all Crane texts to the autograph form, ROSENBACH and BRIDGEWATER are again identical (even in 'ſ' instead of 's'), and the 'berge' suffix is shared by late Crane and OKES.

5.3.134/2349 pond] Bond MIDDLETON[B] *only*

5.3.135/2350 smile] laugh CRANE[1]

5.3.136/2351 those parts] that place ROSENBACH[A], MIDDLETON[B], CRANE[1]. Some of the late texts apparently revert to the author's memory of the original reading. Since 'that place' is printed in *Early* 5.327, 'those parts' is printed in *Later*.

5.3.140/2356 'Tis ten times] *not in* ROSENBACH[A]. Eyeskip.

5.3.141/2357 Is it] ist MIDDLETON[T] *uncorrected only*

5.3.144/2360 vices] CRANE[1]; others CRANE[2]+. See note to *Early* 5.315. Although this seems to me clearly a shared error, it has not been included in the statistical analysis of the stemma, because other editors have not recognized it as an error (or even commented on it).

5.3.144/2360 bears] bearst MIDDLETON[T] *uncorrected only*

5.3.144/2360 hidden'st] hiddeſt MIDDLETON[T]; hiddeneſt ROSEN-BACH[A] (suggesting three syllables)

5.3.144-5/2360-1 venom...poison] poyson...venome OKES. Although the transposition might be authorial, 'venom' alliterates with 'vices': see note above.

5.3.145/2361 secret'st] ROSENBACH[A], MIDDLETON[B]; ſmootheſt CRANE[1]+. Late authorial variant.

5.3.145/2361 I'm] ROSENBACH[A], MIDDLETON[B]; I'am CRANE[1,2]; I am CRANE[3,4], OKES, MIDDLETON[T]. Progressive Crane sophistication.

5.3.145/2361 sir] *not in* OKES. Possibly authorial, eliminating the repetition at the end of two successive verse lines.

5.3.146/2362-3 BLACK KNIGHT GONDOMAR How!...sir.] *not in* CRANE[3], ROSENBACH[A] (eyeskip from 'Sir' at the end of one line to 'Sir' at the end of the next line). This has not been tabulated among shared errors, because its absence from CRANE[3] might well be due to deliberate abridgement.

5.3.146/2363 It's] CRANE[2]; 'tis CRANE[1]+. See Induction.15.

5.3.146/2363 brand] brain OKES. Misreading.

5.3.147/2364 e'er I] I ere CRANE[1]

5.3.153/2371 It is] MIDDLETON[T,B], ROSENBACH[A]; 'tis like CRANE[1,4]; Tis ₐ OKES; It's like CRANE[2,3]. Late authorial variant.

5.3.154-5/2372-3 Whose...hearts] skillfull | MIDDLETON[T] *only*

5.3.154/2372 not known] vnknowne CRANE[1]. Nascimento mis--records the autograph reading as 'now knowne' (p. 330).

5.3.157/2375 came so] CRANE[2,3,4]; yet came CRANE[1], ROSENBACH[A], MIDDLETON[T,B]. This variant might result from scribal error, but the double change (of adverb and position) seems more likely the result of authorial wavering: an initial revision followed by a subsequent return to the original reading.

5.3.157/2375 souls] foule ROSENBACH[A]

5.3.157/2375 till] as CRANE[2,3,4]. Possible authorial variation, but also possible scribal error under the influence of 'so'. Since OKES preserves 'till', the two variants seem not to be necessarily related.

5.3.158/2376 BLACK DUKE...BLACK KNIGHT] CRANE, OKES; ₐ....ₐ ROSENBACH[A], MIDDLETON[T,B]. Even CRANE[3], systematically reducing the text, retained the original speech prefixes, though removing them could have saved a manuscript line. There seems no artistic reason to have taken 'now...us' away from the Black Duke, thereby reducing the complexity of dramatic interaction and the amount of information conveyed by the text. Although it is possible that these two linked variants are a late authorial revision, they might also have arisen from simple laziness (like a number of omissions in MIDDLETON[T], especially toward the end of the play) or as a reaction to the accidental omission of a line or a speech prefix in a lost intermediate text.

5.3.158-9/2376-7 What...ever] *1 line* OKES *only*. Relic.

5.3.158/2376 you're] you are CRANE[3,4]

5.3.159/2377 Has] hath CRANE[2,3,4]

5.3.160-1/2379-80 And...all] discovery | CRANE[1]; checkmate | OKES

5.3.161/2380 King] *not in* CRANE[1]

5.3.161.1-3/2380.1 *White Knight...Black King*] THIS EDITION; *not in* CRANE[1]+

5.3.162/2381 KING] *Kni.* CRANE/ALLDE, *K.*[t] CRANE[1]. 'Knight' is perfectly possible (and retained in *Early* 5.358): the taking of the Black Knight, the architect and expositor of Black House policy and their key player against the White House, leads to checkmate; the White Knight's following line refers specifically to the vices confessed by the Black Knight, and the subsequent responses of the other Black characters indicate their recognition of the consequences of loss of the Black Knight. Moreover, the ALLDE reading must be deliberate, given the quarto's systematic reduction of 'Kni.' to 'K.'. (See 5.3.1.) Finally, CRANE/ALLDE's variant reverts to the original reading. Nevertheless, 'King' (spelled out in MIDDLETON[B], thereby removing any ambiguity) is probably a deliberate change, representing the revised version performed at the Globe: it seems related to the addition, in all seven witnesses to the revised version, of the word 'King' at 5.3.161, not present in CRANE[1]. For audiences unfamiliar with chess, the word 'king', combined with ascription to the opposing king of the first spoken response to 'checkmate', would clarify the action.

5.3.162/2381 I'm] NON-CRANE; I'am CRANE[2]; I am CRANE[1,3,4]

5.3.162/2381 I'm] NON-CRANE; I'am CRANE[1]; I am CRANE[2,3,4]

*5.3.162.1 *A...flourish*] OKES (right margin, opposite 5.3.161-2); *Flourish* CRANE[1] (after 5.3.163); *not in* CRANE[2]+. HOWARD-HILL adopts OKES, but silently moves the direction one line backward (to follow 5.3.160). The absence of this important direction from all but one witness to the revised text may have resulted from Crane's general removal of sound cues: see Induction.52.1.

5.3.163-4 WHITE KNIGHT...all.] *not in* MIDDLETON[T]. Another example of authorial skimping on time and paper in the last two Acts.

5.3.163-4 Ambitious...all] MIDDLETON[B]+; luxurious | CRANE[1]; *3 lines* ambitious | falsehood | CRANE[3]; covetous | falsehood | CRANE[2]

5.3.164 WHITE DUKE] *not in* CRANE[1]

5.3.164 that] OKES; *not in* CRANE[1]+. Late authorial variant.

5.3.165/2382 KNIGHT] CRANE[2,3], OKES; *K.* CRANE/ALLDE, ROSENBACH[A], MIDDLETON[B]; *Q.* MIDDLETON[T], CRANE[1]. The abbreviation in CRANE/ALLDE is ambiguous, and could refer to King or Knight: see 5.3.1. MIDDLETON[T] reverts to the original reading, which must have been deliberately altered in the playbook, since 'Q' could hardly have been misread as 'K' or 'Kt'. The playbook must therefore have attributed the speech to Black Knight or Black King. The playbook had reattributed the previous Black House speech from the Knight to the King (see 5.3.162); it seems very unlikely that anyone with any theatrical competence (author or actors) would deliberately alter the speech prefix here in order to give two successive speeches to the Black King (a minor character), and leave only two words for the reaction by three other onstage Black characters—leaving nothing at all for the Black Knight (the play's most important character) to say

in response to his capture and the defeat of his entire side. Thus, 'K.' appears to be another error shared by BRIDGEWATER/ROSENBACH. However, I have not counted it as such, in the stemmatic analysis, because HOWARD-HILL adopts it.

5.3.166/2383 QUEEN] D. MIDDLETON[T] *only*; *K..* CRANE[1]. Authorial revision. CRANE[1]'s assignment to the Black King made sense, given its attribution of 5.3.162 to the Black Knight: there should be *some* response to checkmate from the Black King. However, since the revised version gave 5.3.162 to the Black King, this speech could be reassigned to any one of the other Black characters on stage: in performance (apparently) the Black Queen, in late authorial revision the Black Duke. Given the sloppiness of MIDDLETON[T] hereabouts, I have preferred the well-attested autography alternative.

5.3.166.1-3/2384-5 *Enter...Pawns*] CRANE/ALLDE places this direction in the right margin opposite 5.3.164-6, but that is probably because those three short lines afford the only available marginal space for the long direction, between the long measure-filling lines 163 and 167.

5.3.166.1/2385 *from the White House*] THIS EDITION (*conj.* Hotson); *not in* CRANE[1]+. See 1.1.30.1.

5.3.166.2/2386 *White Queen*] OKES (*W. ~*); ʌ ~ CRANE[1]+

5.3.166.2/2386 *White*] THIS EDITION; *not in* CRANE[1]+

5.3.166.2/2386 *Bishop*] CRANE; *not in* NON-CRANE. HOWARD-HILL's commentary at this point asserts that 'The Bishop is not present', and cites his commentary note for 5.3.0.1; but that note in turn insists upon the absence of the *Black* Bishop; he claims that 'Presumably the White Bishop was omitted because there was no Black Bishop for him to bag', but the pawns also have no one to bag, and are present simply to swell the size and impressiveness of the White House entrance. Although this variant is not included in my tabulations of 'shared error' (because Howard-Hill adopts it), I regard the shared omission as accidental.

5.3.166.3/2386 *with their*] OKES; *&* CRANE[1], ROSENBACH[A]; *not in* CRANE[2]+. Another sign of authorial revision in OKES: this formula indicates that the pawns present are specifically those belonging to the White aristocrats mentioned in the stage direction. See next notes.

5.3.166.3/2386 *White*] *not in* CRANE[2,3,4], OKES. This is necessary to clarify that the characters do not enter with the black pawns captured earlier.

*5.3.166.3/2386 *Pawns*] MIDDLETON[T,B], OKES, CRANE[1]; *&cc* CRANE[2]; *not in* CRANE[3]; *Pawne* CRANE/ALLDE, ROSENBACH[A]; WHITE QUEEN'S PAWN, *and other White Pawns* HOWARD-HILL. Surely, more than one pawn enters here, and the singular is a shared error. HOWARD-HILL's note states, confusingly, that 'Reputable witnesses do not specify the pawns'; the presence of white pawns is confirmed by two autograph texts, and two others which apparently derive directly from autograph. Perhaps he means only that the direction should specify the presence of some white pawns but not others; but precisely that specificity is provided by OKES, a text which he elsewhere treats as reputable. (See preceding notes.) The distinction between 'reputable' and (implicitly) 'disreputable' may refer to the fact that ROSENBACH[A] and CRANE/ALLDE call for only a single pawn; but they do not specify which one. In CRANE/ALLDE there is no comma after *Bishop*, but there is a space and then a line break, so it seems unlikely that 'White Bishop's Pawn' is intended. There seems no reason to single out the White Queen's Pawn as present (although she is, according to OKES, but only in the context of a direction which simultaneously specifies others).

986

5.3.167/2386 KING] See 5.3.1. CRANE/ALLDE from here to the end of the play has two characters on stage, the White King and White Knight, which it represents with the speech prefix 'Wh.K.' (seven times in sequence, including adjacent speeches).

5.3.167 *embracing White Knight*] THIS EDITION; *not in* CRANE[1] +

5.3.167/2386 O...treasure] *2 lines* OKES *only:* arms |

5.3.167/2386 my arms be blessed] OKES *only;* me bleſſe mine Armes CRANE[1] +. Late authorial variant.

5.3.167/2386 my] OKES, ROSENBACH[A]; mine CRANE+

5.3.168/2387 sweetness] ſweenes CRANE/ALLDE; meekenes CRANE[1]

5.3.169/2388 this] yon'd MIDDLETON[T] *only*. This late authorial variant may be as accidental as most of this manuscript's other variants in the last pages of the text; it has the effect of physically distancing the White King (James) from the White Duke (Buckingham), thereby removing any hint of the physical relationship between them; this sanitizing, if conscious, may have been made in deference to the sensibilities of a particular patron for whom the manuscript was intended. It seems to contradict the claim that the White Duke is 'in my bosom safe', and the White Queen's reference to both the White Duke and the White Knight possessing 'that' sanctuary.

5.3.172/2391 pow'rful] powrefull CRANE[2,3,4], OKES; peaceful CRANE[1] +. Authorial vacillation.

5.3.172/2392 KNIGHT] K. CRANE/ALLDE. See 5.3.162. The double 'sir' in this speech makes it clear that it is addressed to a social superior, which in turn means that it cannot be spoken by the White King.

5.3.172/2392 As] *not in* CRANE[1]

5.3.173/2393 Won...triumph] *2 lines* CRANE/ALLDE: hazard |

5.3.174/2394 We] MIDDLETON[T,B] *only;* I CRANE+. Late autograph variant: the royal plural is also appropriate to the chess strategy of checkmate by discovery, which requires the cooperation of at least two pieces.

5.3.177/2397 It's] CRANE[3]; 'tis CRANE[1] +. See Induction.15.

5.3.177/2397 have] hath OKES

5.3.178/2398 for] of CRANE[1]

5.3.178.1-Epilogue.10/2399-2457 *The bag...again.*] *not in* CRANE[1]. A major addition in the revised version, transforming the play's ending.

*5.3.178.1/2398.1 *The bag opens*] CRANE[2,3,4], OKES; *not in* ROSENBACH[A], MIDDLETON[T,B]. A shared error in both autographs, emended by Howard-Hill. In CRANE/ALLDE the three-line direction begins in the right margin opposite 179, with a curly bracket pointing to 180; in OKES, the four-line direction, without a bracket, also begins opposite 179. The quarto placement could be interpreted to mean that the bag opens during 179, after 'Behold' or 'opens'. Either positioning is possible; I have chosen that in the earliest witnesses.

*5.3.178.1-2/2398.1 *and the Black lost...appear in it*] CRANE[2]; *& the Black-Side put into it* CRANE[3]; *the Bl. Side it it* CRANE/ALLDE; *not in* NON-CRANE. The CRANE[3] direction compresses two different actions in the unabridged texts: the appearance of already-lost black pieces in the bag when it opens, and the putting into the bag of the Black aristocrats just captured. CRANE/ALLDE uses similar language ('the Bl. Side'), as though the entire Black House were already in the bag when it opens; this suggests that the wording in CRANE/ALLDE derives from a version of the direction later than CRANE[2] and close to CRANE[3].

5.3.178.1/2398.1 *pieces*] THIS EDITION; *Pawnes* CRANE[2]. Perhaps a simple misreading. The Fat Bishop is the most prominent character already in the bag.

5.3.178.2/2398.2 in] CRANE[2]; *into* CRANE[3]; *it* CRANE/ALLDE. The nonsense in CRANE/ALLDE—*it it*—might be a compositorial error for either 'in it' or (less probably) 'into it'.

5.3.178.2/2398.2 *The Jesuit Black Bishop slides in it*] OKES *only* (right margin, opposite ll. 180-2, but as a continuation of 'The bag opens'). Although HOWARD-HILL does not adopt or record it, this is another unique OKES addition, supplying information about performance not present in any other witness. It seems impossible to attribute the direction to scribal or compositorial error. OKES's 'B.B.' is the only black piece not otherwise explicitly bagged by the end of the play in the revised version; the direction presumably indicates that he slides into the bag when it opens, perhaps because it opens under his feet. See 5.3.0.3. This is not counted as a shared error, even though OKES supplies theatrical information not present in any other witness, because other editors have ignored or rejected it.

5.3.179/2399 bag, like hell-mouth,] MIDDLETON[B] *only;* bag like hells mouth ROSENBACH[A]; Baggs Mouth like Hell CRANE[2]+. Late authorial variant.

5.3.181/2401 fellowship] followſhip CRANE/ALLDE. Nascimento (p. 341) mistakenly identifies this as a variant in 'Q2' (OKES[2]) rather than 'Q3' (MATHEWES/ALLDE).

5.3.183/2403 perdition-branded] MIDDLETON[T,B], CRANE[2,3]; ∼∧∼ CRANE/ALLDE; ∼,∼ OKES, ROSENBACH[A]. A shared punctuation error, perhaps caused by misinterpretation of the lack of a hyphen in [CRANE[4]].

5.3.183/2403 foreheads] heads CRANE[2]

5.3.184/2404 issues] ROSENBACH[A], MIDDLETON[B]; iſſue CRANE[2]+. Late authorial variant.

5.3.185-217/2405-41 BLACK BISHOP'S PAWN...WHITE KING] *not in* CRANE[3]

5.3.185, 186, 187, 192, 194, 196, 197, 201, 204, 207, 214 *in the bag*] DYCE; *not in* CRANE[2]+

5.3.185/2405 'Tis too apparent] CRANE[2,4], OKES; see, alls confounded MIDDLETON[T] *only;* all hopes confounded ROSENBACH[A], MIDDLETON[B]. The late autograph variants repeat the sentence at 5.3.165 ('all hope's confounded'), which is probably inadvertent, whether or not authorial: it reduces the information content of the scene, and has been regarded as an unintentional or inattentive scribal variant (even if the scribe responsible was Middleton). MIDDLETON[T] reduces the exact correspondence, which suggests that the ROSENBACH[A]/MIDDLETON[B] variant originated earlier. Progressive revision?

5.3.185/2405 King] OKES; King's CRANE[2]+. Either reading makes sense, and OKES is if anything less likely to be an error (since it does not repeat the elided 'is').

5.3.186/2406 has] NON-CRANE; hath CRANE[2,4]

5.3.187, 196/2407, 2415 ∧ PAWN] CRANE[2]; Ieſting ∼ [CRANE[4]], NON-CRANE. This variant is clearly related to the omission of the original Jesting Pawn scene, 3.2 (providing further evidence that the omission was a deliberate cut).

*5.3.187-91/2407-11 *They'd...bag*] CRANE[2,4]; your- | overlaid me | verjuice | if you | ROSENBACH[A]; bag | squelched | ver- | goodness | MIDDLETON[T]; by | overlaid me | verjuice | if you | MIDDLETON[B]; bag | yourself | overlaid me | verjuice | if you | OKES; *not in* CRANE[1,3]. Shared error (break after 'if you').

5.3.187/2407 They'd] OKES, ROSENBACH[A]; They'had CRANE[2]; They had [CRANE[4]], MIDDLETON[T,B]

5.3.187/2407 have given] giue CRANE/ALLDE. Possibly authorial.

5.3.188/2408 'Sfoot] MIDDLETON[T], OKES; slid ROSENBACH[A], MIDDLETON[B]; *not in* CRANE[2,4]. Omission of the oath, in the two texts closest to the playbook, was probably due to censorship. Late authorial variation in the choice of oaths.

*5.3.188/2408 Fat Black] CRANE²; ~ ‸ ROSENBACH^A, MIDDLE-
TON^{T,B}; ‸ ~ CRANE/ALLDE, OKES. Perhaps late authorial variation, rather than simple omission of 'Black'; the autograph
reading produces a more metrical line. However, the omission
of 'Fat' seems an error, since he is never called 'Black Bishop'
elsewhere.

5.3.188/2408 has] NON-CRANE; hath CRANE^{2,4}

5.3.188-9/2408-9 so squelched...me, So overlaid me] MID-
DLETON^T only; so ouerlayde mee, so squelcht...mee MIDDLE-
TON^B+. Late authorial variation.

5.3.191/2411 If] and MIDDLETON^T only. Late autograph variation. The obsolete synonym is printed in Early, the modern
variant here. For another example see 4.1.66.

5.3.191/2411 for't] for it ROSENBACH^A

5.3.195/2416 scant] little OKES. Substition of a common for a
rare synonym (Taylor 1988)—in this case, extrametrical.

5.3.195/2416 your] his ROSENBACH^A. Possibly authorial.

5.3.195/2416 Spalato] MIDDLETON^{T,B}, CRANE², ROSENBACH^A (Spoletta); CRANE/ALLDE, OKES (Spalletto). HOWARD-HILL notes that
'different contemporary forms were common'; the shared
quarto spelling has not been counted as an error.

5.3.196-7/2417-18 Art thou showing | Thy impudent whor-
ish] ROSENBACH^A, MIDDLETON^{T,B}; I abho^r thee. | Thou ſhow
thy Whoriſh CRANE^{2,4}; I abhorre thee, | Thou't ſhew thy
whoriſh OKES. Late authorial revision. (Nascimento does not
record the OKES variant 'Thou't.)

5.3.198/2420 bag] OKES; pit CRANE²+. Late authorial variant.

5.3.199/2421 WHITE KING] not in MIDDLETON^T only (which also
lacks speech rules to indicate a change of speaker)

5.3.199/2421 You'd] NON-CRANE; you'had CRANE²; You had
CRANE/ALLDE

5.3.200.1-2/2422.1 White King...bag] DYCE (sub); not in
CRANE²+

5.3.201/2423 I'm not so] ROSENBACH^A, MIDDLETON^B; I am not
CRANE^{2,4}, OKES, MIDDLETON^T. Late authorial variant.

5.3.201/2423 moved] mouèd OKES, ROSENBACH^A

5.3.201/2423 I'm] NON-CRANE; I am CRANE^{2,4}

5.3.203-4/2425-7 WHITE QUEEN...FAT BISHOP] Fat. B....Wh.Q.
CRANE/ALLDE

5.3.203.1-2/2425-6 Here...her] 2 lines MIDDLETON^T only: then |

5.3.203.1-2/2427.1 White Queen...bag] DYCE (sub); not in
CRANE²+

5.3.205/2428 mightiest] greateſt OKES. Possibly a late authorial
variant, but it sacrifices the alliteration to no apparent
purpose, and may be a compositorial substitution.

5.3.206/2429 e'er the] the ere OKES. A clearly mistaken transposition.

5.3.206/2429 e'er] euer CRANE/ALLDE. Typical Crane expansion.

5.3.206.1-2/2429.1 White...bag] THIS EDITION; not in CRANE²;
Puts B. Knight in the bag DYCE. See the letter of the Spanish
Ambassador to the Duke of Olivares: 'The Prince of Wales...
beat and kicked...Gondamar into Hell, which consisted of
a great hole with hideous figures': Edward M. Wilson and
Olga Turner, 'The Spanish Protest Against A Game at Chess',
Modern Language Review 44 (1949), 477.

5.3.207/2430 peck] pick OKES, ROSENBACH^A. Probably only a
spelling variant.

5.3.207/2430 i'th'] CRANE², MIDDLETON^{T,B}; i'the ROSENBACH^A; in
the CRANE/ALLDE, OKES. See 2.1.147.

5.3.208/2431 But I shall] MIDDLETON^T, ROSENBACH^A; I am ſure
to CRANE²; I 'em ſure to CRANE/ALLDE; I'me ſure to OKES; But
Ime ſure I ſhall MIDDLETON^B only. Late authorial revision. See
next note.

5.3.208/2431 last man that] ~ ‸‸ MIDDLETON^T only

*5.3.210-11/2433-4 Foh...hither.] ROSENBACH^A, MIDDLETON^{T,B};
not in CRANE^{2,4}, OKES. This variant could be due to accidental
omission, censorship, or late authorial addition. Censorship
seems probable, and I have therefore retained the passage.
However, for consistency, and so as not to prejudice construction of the stemma, the variant has, like other omissions of
dialogue, been counted as a shared error.

5.3.210/2433 the] ROSENBACH^A, MIDDLETON^B; your MIDDLETON^T+.
Late authorial variant.

5.3.213/2436 coloured] colourèd CRANE/ALLDE, OKES, ROSEN-
BACH^A

5.3.213.1-2/2436.1 White Duke...bag] DYCE (sub); not in
CRANE²+

5.3.214/2437 bagging] Begging CRANE/ALLDE

5.3.217/2441 ‸ let...close now] CRANE^{2,3,4}, OKES; now lett...
close ‸ ROSENBACH^A, MIDDLETON^{T,B}. This might be a late authorial variant, but metrically the original reading seems
superior, and the variant could be an inadvertent transposition.

5.3.218/2442 malice] falcehood CRANE^{2,3,4}, OKES. Late authorial
revision.

5.3.218/2442 malice)...winner-like,] ~,...~) CRANE/ALLDE,
OKES. The parenthesis should close in the middle of the line,
not the end. Shared punctuation error in the quartos.

5.3.220/2444 our] of ROSENBACH^A

*5.3.220.1 Exeunt] CRANE^{1,2,3}; not in CRANE/ALLDE, NON-CRANE.
A shared error in autograph, emended by Howard-Hill.

5.3.220.1/2445 Exeunt ‸] ~ Finis. CRANE³, ROSENBACH^A, MIDDLE-
TON^{T,B}; ~ Finis Actus Quinti CRANE¹ (after 5.3.178); not in
CRANE/ALLDE. CRANE² and OKES place 'Finis' after the Epilogue,
rather than here.

Epilogue.0.1/2446 Enter] HOWARD-HILL; not in CRANE²+. The
entrance was probably considered implicit in the word
'Epilogue', which occurs in all witnesses to the revised version; its omission has therefore not been counted as a shared
error. (Compare Prologue.)

*Epilogue.0.1/2447 the Virgin White Queen's Pawn] not in CRANE/
ALLDE, OKES

Epilogue.0.1/2447 the] not in MIDDLETON^T

Epilogue.1/2448 WHITE QUEEN'S PAWN] by the white Queenes
Pawne CRANE²; spoken by the white-Queenes Pawne CRANE³;
not in CRANE/ALLDE, OKES. In the manuscript witnesses to
the revised version the character's name occurs only once,
serving both as entrance direction and speech prefix; the
absence of the name from the quartos is therefore treated as
a single shared error, rather than two.

Epilogue.1/2448 bowing] THIS EDITION; not in CRANE²+

Epilogue.1/2448 Queen] queenes ROSENBACH^A

Epilogue.1/2448 hath] The same phrase—'hath sent me forth'—
appears in Honourable Entertainments, so hath is likely to be
authorial.

*Epilogue.5/2452 denoted] deuoted CRANE/ALLDE, OKES

*Epilogue.6/2453 devoted] denoted CRANE/ALLDE, OKES

Epilogue.7/2454 and in corners] MIDDLETON^T only; or in priuate
MIDDLETON^B+. Late authorial variant.

Epilogue.9/2456 assured] aſſured ROSENBACH^A

Epilogue.9/2456 what they'd] that they ROSENBACH^A; ~ they'll
CRANE/ALLDE, OKES. Though the double variant 'that they'
might be a late authorial revision, 'they'll' is almost certainly
just a misreading of the Crane contraction 'they'lld', with one
quarto repeating the other. However, because 'they'll' makes
sense it has not been counted among shared errors.

Epilogue.9 they'd] MIDDLETON^{T,B}, They'would CRANE^{2,3}. See previous note.

Epilogue.10/2457 hands] CRANE/ALLDE, OKES; loues CRANE[2]+. Late authorial revision. 'Hands' does double work, alluding to the applause of the audience, which becomes thereby a demonstration of the power of the White cause.

Epilogue.10.1 Exit] HOWARD-HILL; not in CRANE[2]+. As with her entrance, her exit may have been considered implicit in the word 'Epilogue', and its omission from all texts of the revised version has therefore not been taken as a shared error. Compare the absence of entrance and exit directions for the Prologue.

A.1/786 of,] ~ the ROSENBACH[A]

A.3/788 throat] roote OKES. Misreading.

A.4/789 ate] MIDDLETON[T]+ (eate)

A.5/790 In the conception.] not in CRANE[1,2,3], BRIDGEWATER[A]. MIDDLETON[T] alone prints these three words on the same manuscript line as 'of all things I commend the Wh. house best' (2.2.23). This mislineation—a typical 'relic'—crosses the barrier between the deleted passage (Add. A) and the surrounding text (2.2.22–3).

B.4/936 or] & CRANE/MATHEWES

B.4/936 they'd] MIDDLETON[T] only; they'll'd CRANE[1]; they would [CRANE[4]], ROSENBACH[A], OKES

C.1/1436 That] Thus CRANE/ALLDE. Misreading, probably compositorial.

C.1/1436 act] Art OKES. Misreading.

C.2/1437-8 Would...us] prose? MIDDLETON[T]: blesse|; not in ROSENBACH[A], BRIDGEWATER[B], CRANE[3]

C.2/1437 rape] Rope ALLDE. Compositorial misreading or foul case error. Compare the variant robe/rape in OKES at 2.2.128.

C.2/1437-8 God bless us ,] OKES; , bleffe vs all CRANE[1]; , 'bleffe ~ , CRANE[2]; , bleffe ~ all MIDDLETON[T], CRANE/ALLDE; passage not in CRANE[3], ROSENBACH[A], BRIDGEWATER[B]. This entire passage is not present in CRANE[3], ROSENBACH[A], or BRIDGEWATER[B]. All texts that contain the line have the two words 'bless us'; they differ on the presence or absence of the preceding 'God' and following 'all'. Because of the Act to Restrain Abuses, Middleton generally avoided use of 'God' in dramatic texts written after 1606. 'God bless us' could well be an authorial variant: Middleton used 'God' regularly in non-theatrical texts, and he might have supplied it here, knowing that the printed text would not be censored by the Master of the Revels.

C.3/1439 talk'st] talkeft OKES

C.3/1440-41 Yes...man?] 1 line ROSENBACH[A]

3.1.345-6/1470-1521 instantly. | This] Between these two words six texts include an exeunt, a new scene, and a re-entrance for the two Queen's Pawns. The omission of this scene from the abridged CRANE[3] is not surprising; but its absence from the otherwise unabridged CRANE[2] presumably originated in the playbook. The scene is not necessary to the plot.

*D.0.1/1470 Exeunt] ROSENBACH[A] and BRIDGEWATER[B] retain the Jesting Pawn scene, but omit this exit direction. The direction is also absent from CRANE[2,3], but is not an error here. (See preceding note.) Its absence in BRIDGEWATER[B] and ROSENBACH[A], by contrast, is undoubtedly a shared error. The error might have originated in a text into which 3.2 had been reinserted, without this necessary adjustment being made; but it might also have resulted from simple carelessness by one scribe. Given the number of omitted exits in various texts of this play, there seems no reason to seek a special explanation here.

D.0 3.2] CRANE[1,4] (Sce[a]. 2[a].); not in NON-CRANE

D.0.1/1471 a] not in CRANE[1], ROSENBACH[A], OKES

D.0.1-2/1471 from the Black House] THIS EDITION (conj. Hotson); not in CRANE[1]+. See 1.1.30.1.

D.1/1472 BLACK JESTING PAWN] not in MIDDLETON[T] uncorrected only (?). Howard-Hill (1990) describes this speech prefix as 'interlined', and prints it on the same line as 'I would... now', but it is clearly an afterthought, and given much less space than the separate-line speech-prefix immediately after the entrance of the Black Queen's Pawn at 3.1.208 in MIDDLETON[T]. The conjectured initial omission might be related to the fact that in BRIDGEWATER[B] the speech prefix is on a separate line from the beginning of the speech, separated from it by a stage direction and a page break.

D.1/1472 JESTING] ROSENBACH[A], BRIDGEWATER[B]; Iest. CRANE[1], MIDDLETON[T] corrected; I. OKES; not in CRANE/ALLDE. The generic CRANE/ALLDE form anticipates the generic prefix that will become standard in all texts at D.8.

D.1/1472 I...now] 2 lines ROSENBACH[A]: take |

D.1/1472 take] meete BRIDGEWATER[B] uncorrected

D.2/1473 I'd] I would CRANE/ALLDE. Unmetrical Crane expansion of characteristic Middleton elision.

D.2/1473 under] durty ROSENBACH[A]. Anticipation and hence duplication of D.15/1489, suggesting that the copyist knew the material; probably a late authorial variant, but if so likely to be unconscious rather than deliberate.

D.3/1474 asses' milk] afhes, milke OKES. This might be a foul-case ligature error (fh for ff), but the punctuation suggests it is a two-stage error.

D.4/1475 could] can OKES. Although the variant might be authorial, it substitutes a simpler (and less appropriate) grammatical construction, and could easily result from a copyist's substitution.

D.4/1475 devised] deuifed OKES

D.5/1476 I'd] So OKES. Misreading of 'Ide' as 'foe'.

*D.5/1476 pranced] praun'cft MIDDLETON[T], CRANE[1,4]; praunceft ROSENBACH[A], BRIDGEWATER[B] uncorrected; prance it OKES. Although 'prance it' is an early modern idiom and could be a late authorial variant, it does not appear elsewhere in Middleton, and could easily result from misreading of Middleton's unusual -cst spelling of the past participle. It might also be an example of progressive error, resulting from a conjectural correction of the shared error 'prauncest'.

D.6/1477 Black] Blacks CRANE/ALLDE. Contamination from following word.

D.6.1/1478 Enter...Pawn] not in OKES

D.6.1/1478 from the White House] THIS EDITION (conj. Hotson); not in CRANE[1]+. See 1.1.30.1.

D.6/1479 And] not in OKES. This variant may, like others before and after in OKES, be authorial.

D.6/1479 you'd] you would MIDDLETON[T] only

D.7/1480 o'er] MIDDLETON[T] (oře), CRANE[1], BRIDGEWATER[B] (ore), CRANE/ALLDE (o're); ou[r] ROSENBACH[A]; ouer OKES. This looks like progressive error from ROSENBACH to OKES.

D.7/1480 night-mare] night mare ROSENBACH[A], OKES

D.8.1/1481 White...Jesting Pawn] THIS EDITION; not in CRANE[1]+. See 3.1.253.1-2.

D.8.1/1482 JESTING] DYCE (J.); not in CRANE[1]+. The character is generically identified, in all texts, for the remainder of the scene; in context, there is no ambiguity, and hence this generic prefix (retained in Early 3.291) has not been considered an error.

D.8.1/1482 PAWN] p. MIDDLETON[T] corrected; a MIDDLETON[T] uncorrected. Though HOWARD-HILL (1990) describes the abbreviation as simply 'altered', under magnification one can clearly see the original overwritten 'a': as happens elsewhere, Middleton originally omitted the second part of a speech prefix and began the verse line, but in this case he caught the error and immediately corrected it.

*D.8–10/1482–4 A...me] MIDDLETON[T]; 2 *lines* blackbird | CRANE[1]; like | pawn | ROSENBACH[A]; like | grinning | BRIDGEWATER[B]; taken | white | OKES; Were...near | snow | CRANE/ALLDE; *not in* CRANE[2,3]. The mistaken line-break after 'like' is shared by ROSENBACH[A] and BRIDGEWATER[B].

D.8/1482 A pox on you] *not in* CRANE/ALLDE. It's impossible to tell whether the omission resulted from censorship or carelessness; it would be hard to defend as an authorial revision.

D.9/1483 nigh] OKES; neere CRANE+. Middleton uses the synonym at least 26 times elsewhere; it is also the rarer idiom (Taylor 1988).

D.9/1483 I'm] NON-CRANE; I'am CRANE[1]; I am CRANE/ALLDE. Crane expansion of a characteristic Middleton elision.

D.11/1485 WHITE PAWN] *not in* MIDDLETON[T] *only*

D.13/1487 Ay...thee] 2 *lines* OKES: then |

D.13 Ay,] MIDDLETON[T]+ (I,). A modernization of ambiguous 'I', not an emendation. 'Ay' confirms the White Pawn's previous statement ('yes, white does quickly soil'), and is parallel to the 'Nay' at the beginning of the White Pawn's next line.

D.14/1488 WHITE PAWN] W.Q.P. OKES. The error can only be due to the author or compositor thinking of the preceding scene.

D.14–15/1488–9 Nay...drudgery] have | OKES

D.14/1488 Nay] MIDDLETON[T] *only*; no CRANE[1]+; *not in* OKES. The autograph synonym occurs eleven times elsewhere in *Game* alone.

D.14/1488 venture:] OKES, ROSENBACH[A] (~,); ~ , CRANE[1]+. See next note.

D.14/1488 thee,] ~, MIDDLETON[T], BRIDGEWATER[B], ROSENBACH[A]. See preceding note. The issue here is the relative weight of punctuation at the middle and end of the line. The two texts with no punctuation at all in the line (CRANE[1,4]) or with a comma in both places (ROSENBACH, OKES) are ambiguous in a way common enough elsewhere in Middleton's unique autograph practice. But OKES punctuates mid-line more heavily than end-line, whereas MIDDLETON[T] and BRIDGEWATER punctuate end-line but not mid-line. Since the autograph punctuation is not unique, it might be a shared error. 'Now' seems to pick up the thread of the White Pawn's preceding speech ('And now because...'), interrupted by the Black Pawn's speech. If so, it should be separated from 'Nay... venture', which is a direct response to the interruption. The White Pawn could not have 'put...to venture' whether the Black Pawn would smut him *until* he had captured him; subordinating 'now...thee' to the preceding clause makes it logically redundant. But there could be a real difference between the Black Pawn's situation before and after his capture: *now* that he has been snapped, he will have to work like a slave (in contrast to his previous laziness). It seems to make better sense to put the heavier punctuation in mid-line. (That also has the effect of marking the mid-line caesura.)

D.14/1488 snapped] MIDDLETON[T]+ (snapt); fcap'd CRANE/ALLDE. Minim misreading.

D.16/1490 e'er] euer CRANE[1], ROSENBACH[A], OKES

D.17/1492 then] *not in* OKES. Although the variant might be a late authorial revision, it is impossible to distinguish from another example of careless omission of short words.

D.18/1493 I'm] NON-CRANE; I am CRANE[1,4]; Iam BRIDGEWATER[B] *uncorrected*. The uncorrected BRIDGEWATER reading is not certain; the 'a' is 'perhaps a blot only' (Howard-Hill 1995, 1215).

D.19–20/1495–6 And...behindhand] CRANE[1,4], MIDDLETON[T]; not | ROSENBACH[A]; shall | BRIDGEWATER[B]; black | OKES. The three separate mislineations suggest that the copy behind ROSENBACH[A], BRIDGEWATER[B], and OKES had a single long line, randomly broken in two by different copyists.

D.19/1495 And I'll] CRANE/ALLDE; I will CRANE[1]+. It is not characteristic of Crane to add such elisions, or copulatives; Middleton often begins speeches with a copulative, and 'I'll fit' echoes 'I'll starve'. Late authorial variant.

D.19/1495 then] *not in* ROSENBACH[A], BRIDGEWATER[B]. Perhaps another authorial variant; but 'then' usefully clarifies the causal and temporal relationship between the two threats.

D.20/1496 whip—] ROSENBACH[A], CRANE/ALLDE, OKES (~,); ~ , MIDDLETON[T]+. Middleton usually omits mid-line punctuation, even when some sort of pause is required by grammar or rhythm. Punctuating in mid-line allows 'that' to be understood either as a relative or a demonstrative pronoun. As a phrasal unit '*that* shall not be behindhand' exactly echoes 'I tell you that beforehand'.

D.21–4/1497–1500 Push...hands] *verse* CRANE/ALLDE, BRIDGEWATER[B], ROSENBACH[A] (whipped | morning, and | meat |), OKES (whipping | town | fortnight and |). Both CRANE[1] (myself | a |) and MIDDLETON[T] (whipping I have | morning and | meat |) independently and clearly set this speech as prose, driving the lines out to the margin and breaking them at points uncharacteristic of Middleton's verse practice. Both attempts to align as verse produce a succession of four irregular lines. In the most popular arrangement (adopted by HARPER, HOWARD-HILL, and DUTTON), the first line and third lines both have an extra initial stressed syllable; the second begins with an iambic but then follows with a spondee, two anapaests, and two unstressed final syllables; the fourth line is an unassimilated part-line with six syllables, beginning with two trochees. This is not at all characteristic of Middleton's late verse, and not supported by autograph or by the manuscript closest to Middleton's original papers.

D.21/1497 Push] ROSENBACH[A], BRIDGEWATER[B]; puh MIDDLETON[T] *only*; Pißh CRANE[1,4], OKES. Both 'puh' and 'push' are rare Middleton oaths: see Jackson, 190–91. Since 'puh' is preserved in *Early* 3.305, the equally rare Middletonian 'push' is preferred in *Later*.

D.21/1497 ha' been] ROSENBACH[A]; haue ~ CRANE[1]+

D.23/1498 morning, and] ~ , ROSENBACH[A]

D.23/1499 all] *not in* BRIDGEWATER[B] *uncorrected*

D.24/1500 upon] OKES; a MIDDLETON[T], ROSENBACH[A], BRIDGEWATER[B]; on CRANE[1,4]. The phrase 'upon your hand' appears at *Gypsy* 3.2.157 (one of the two passages most strongly linked to Middleton).

D.24/1500 hands] hand CRANE/ALLDE. Idiomatically (in the sense 'uselessly') the plural seems required.

D.25–8/1501–4 To...frisk] be | pickled | to | OKES; that | days | anchovies | ordinary | CRANE/ALLDE

D.26/1502 And] A BRIDGEWATER[B]

D.27/1503 an] *not in* BRIDGEWATER[B], OKES. Probably eyeskip. At *Valour* 5.1.57 (Middleton's only other use of the word), 'anchovies' is clearly accented on the second syllable.

D.27/1503 anchovy] MIDDLETON[T]+ (Anchouis), CRANE/ALLDE (Anchouas). Like other editors I modernize the spelling.

D.27/1503 I'm] NON-CRANE; I am CRANE[1,4]

D.28/1504 monkey's] MIDDLETON[T]+ (Monckeys); monthes OKES. Misreading.

D.28 ordinary] MIDDLETON[T] (Ordnarie); Ordinary CRANE[I]+. This is unlikely to be an autograph minim error because—as Howard-Hill notes (1990, xvi)—Middleton's 'i' is 'invariably formed and dotted with precision'. The elided form is preserved in *Early* 3.312. See next note.

D.28/1504 ∧frisk] BRIDGEWATER[B]; will you ~ CRANE[I]+. Although this variant could be an inadvertent omission, there is no obvious explanation for omission here, and 'come, sir' is followed by an imperative at least four times in the Middleton canon, including *Widow* 3.2.130 ('come, sir, follow me') and *Witch* 5.1.31 ('come, sir, along with me'), which are situationally exactly parallel. Although the *Early* 3.312 form of the sentence is acceptable and well-attested, this variant produces a more metrical line, and a master's command rather than the polite 'will you'.

D.28/1504 frisk] firke OKES. Misreading and/or anticipation.

D.28.1/1505 *Enter...Pawn*] CRANE/ALLDE begins this direction in the right margin opposite 'ordinary'.

D.28.1/1505 *a*] MIDDLETON[T], OKES; *not in* CRANE[I]+. A late authorial addition, clarifying the sense, probably in response to the error in BRIDGEWATER and ROSENBACH[A]. (See below.)

D.28.1/1505 *second*] OKES; 2 CRANE+. The word clarifies the meaning of the ambiguous numeral.

*D.28.1/1505 *Pawn*] Pawnes ROSENBACH[A], P.s BRIDGEWATER[B]

D.28.1–2/1505 *from the Black House*] THIS EDITION (*conj.* Hotson); *not in* CRANE[I]+. See 1.1.30.1.

D.29/1506 SECOND] *not in* ROSENBACH[A], BRIDGEWATER[B]. Almost certainly a shared error, but not counted as such, because the lines could be intelligibly spoken by the Black Jesting Pawn (for whom the prefix 'Bl.P.' is used).

*D.29–30/1506–7 *Soft...you*] such | BRIDGEWATER[B], CRANE/ALLDE, OKES. Shared error.

D.29/1506 soft you] ~ ∧ BRIDGEWATER[B]. Haplography.

D.29/1506 on't] of it MIDDLETON[T] *only*

D.30.1/1506 *Black...White Pawn*] THIS EDITION; *not in* CRANE[I]+. See 3.1.253.1–2.

D.30/1508 By this hand] *not in* CRANE/ALLDE, OKES. This completes the preceding half-line. It might have been omitted because it creates a distracting ambiguity (either an oath or a prepositional phrase modifying 'snapped'). The scene was perhaps marked by the censor before it was cut wholesale; see the omission of exactly the same oath at 1.1.209. This

has not been counted as a shared error for the sake of consistency, because the omission may be due to censorship.

D.31/1509 I'm...me] *2 lines*: pawn | ROSENBACH[A]; the | BRIDGEWATER[B]; breech | OKES

D.31/1509 I'm] ROSENBACH[A], OKES; I am CRANE+. Probably late authorial metrical revision, since the expansive version in early witnesses produces an iambic hexameter. See below.

D.33/1512 BLACK JESTING] i Bl. MIDDLETON[T] *only*; Bl. CRANE[I]+. See D.8.

D.33/1512 I'm] I am CRANE

D.33/1512 so] *not in* OKES. Metrically possible as an authorial revision.

D.34/1513 But] *not in* ROSENBACH[A]

D.35/1514 Then] And OKES. Anticipation.

D.35/1514 Then I'll] ~ wee'll ROSENBACH[A]

D.35/1515 him] you OKES. The effect of this and the preceding variant in OKES is to make the two speeches identical; perhaps authorial, but probably an unconscious duplication, which reduces the complexity of the dialogue.

D.36–7/1516–17 Mass...nobody] shall | OKES; the | CRANE/ALLDE

D.36/1516 Mass] *not in* CRANE/ALLDE. This may be further evidence that the copy for ALLDE derived from a text censored before this scene was cut: see D.30.

*D.37–9/1517–19 The worst...buttocks] OKES; draw | with | MIDDLETON[T] (*prose?*), BRIDGEWATER[B] (*verse*); draw | flies | CRANE[1,4]; we | three | ROSENBACH[A]. The line-break after 'with' seems to be a shared error.

D.37/1517 for] OKES, ROSENBACH[A], BRIDGEWATER[B]; *not in* CRANE[1,4], MIDDLETON[T]. Late authorial variant. The phrase 'for I can' appears also at *Valour* 2.1.81.

D.37/1517 nobody] ROSENBACH[A], BRIDGEWATER[B] (nobodie), MIDDLETON[T]+ (no bodie). See *OED*: the spacing as two words was normal in the period.

D.38/1518 now] non BRIDGEWATER[B] *uncorrected*

D.39/1519 thorough] MIDDLETON[T] *only*; in CRANE[I]; through [CRANE[4]]+

*D.39/1519 buttocks] Buttock BRIDGEWATER[B], ROSENBACH[A]

D.39.1/1520 *Exeunt*] *not in* OKES

D.39.2 3.3] CRANE[1,4] (*Sce.*[d]. 3[a].); *not in* NON-CRANE. There is no scene division marked in CRANE[2,3], either, because both omit 3.2, thereby turning Act 3 into a single long uninterrupted scene (like Act 1). Consequently, the absence of a scene division in CRANE[2,3] is not comparable to its absence in the NON-CRANE texts.

OCCASIONAL POEMS

Edited by Gary Taylor

THE POEMS collected here are dispersed in various seventeenth-century documents, and their editorial circumstances therefore differ. I will consider them here in the sequence in which they are printed in *Works*. The edited texts of the poems are printed opposite a photographic reproduction of the only authoritative early witness in all cases except 'To the King', where more than one witness survives. There are no textual notes to any of the poems except 'To the King'.

The Burbage epitaph is known from only a single copy: Rosenbach Museum and Library, MS 1083/16, p. 271; it was first printed by Collier (p. 26). The miscellany as a whole was edited by Redding. It was apparently compiled by Robert BISHOP, *c.*1630. The only edition to include the poem is Bullen's (7:413), but it is also (mis)quoted by Edmond, who prints the third line as 'Death interposing Burbage and there staying'. As often with poems in miscellanies, the exact wording of the title may or may not be authorial.

The Bolles epitaph and the St James verses were both printed in John Stow, *The Survey of London*, revised by Anthony Munday, Humfrey Dyson, *et al.* (1633), printed by PURSLOWE (STC 23345), p. 870, sig. 4E1^v (Bolles), pp. 147-9, sig. O2-O3 (St James). The most authoritative text of both sets of verses would have been those inscribed in the two churches, but both were destroyed by fire in 1666. I have not collated the many surviving copies of PURSLOWE for press variants. This is the first edition of Middleton to include either poem.

The Webster poem appeared in the first edition of *The Duchess of Malfi* (1623), printed by OKES (STC 25176), sig. A4. Subsequent seventeenth-century editions save paper by omitting Webster's dedication and all three commendatory poems. It has been included in modern editions of the play and of Webster's works; the 1995 edition, which collated 29 exemplars of OKES, found no press variants on this page.

'To the King' has been preserved in five known manuscript texts, listed in Beal (MiT 1-4.5). I list them here, in alphabetical order, by the name used to identify them in this edition.

DAWES: British Library Add. MS 29492, f. 43 (reproduced in *Works*, p. 1895). A miscellany compiled by Sir Thomas Dawes, *c.*1624-8.

FLOYD: Bodleian MS Douce f.5, fol. 22v. A verse miscellany, *c.*1614-1630s, owned in 1630 by Hugh Floyd.

DYCE: Victoria and Albert Museum, Dyce Collection, Cat. No 6561 (No. 1) (Pressmark 25.D.42). An anonymous manuscript note on the title-page of an exemplum of

the edition of the play printed by Nicholas Okes in May 1625. Tannenbaum (who reproduced a photograph of this document) considered this manuscript note a forgery; it could have been written at any time after the edition was printed.

HULSE: Bodleian MS Rawlinson poet.152, f. 3. A quarto verse miscellany apparently compiled by Sir Thomas Hulse, *c.*1624-40s, later incorporated in a composite volume of verse collected by Peter Le Neve (1661-1729).

INNS: Meisei University, 'Crewe MS', p. 62. A small quarto verse miscellany associated with the Inns of Court, *c.*1624. I have examined the set of photographs of this manuscript at the British Library (RP 2031). On the basis of its other contents this appears to be the earliest manuscript witness.

Since only a single version would have been sent to King James, the textual variants between these manuscripts are not likely to result from authorial revision; they illustrate, instead, the normal vagaries of transmission in early modern miscellanies. The text constructed here is therefore an eclectic one, evaluating individual variants in relation to Middleton's practice elsewhere and/or their contribution to the poem.

The Hammond poem exists only in the autograph page reproduced in *Works*: Bodleian MS Malone 25, p. vii (modern numeration in pencil). The entire manuscript is transcribed and discussed by Bawcutt.

'The Picture Plainly Explained' is printed opposite the title-page of the first edition of *A Game at Chess* printed by Nicholas OKES in 1625 (STC 17882; *BEPD* 412(*a*)). Nasciamento recorded no press variants on this page.

SEE ALSO

Text: *Works*, 1889
Authorship and date: 'Burbage', this volume, 404; 'Bolles', 416; 'St James', 427; 'Malfi', 438; 'To the King', 441; 'Hammond', 441; 'Picture', 442

WORKS CITED

Bawcutt, N. W., ed., *Ralph Crane's Transcript of 'A Game at Chess', Bodleian Manuscript Malone 25*, in *Collections XV*, Malone Society (1993)

Beal, Peter, *Index of English Literary Manuscripts: Volume I: 1450-1625* (1980); *Volume II: 1626-1700* (1987-93)

Bretnor, Thomas, *A new almanacke and prognostication for the yeare of our redemption 1619...for the latitude and meridian of the honorable city of London* (1619: STC 420.12)

Chandler, Wayne A., *Commendatory Verse and Authorship in the English Renaissance* (2003)

Collier, John Payne, *New Facts regarding the Life of Shakespeare* (1853), p. 26

Edmond, Mary, 'Richard Burbage', *Oxford Dictionary of National Biography* (2004)

Hannay, Patrick, *Two Elegies, On the late death of our Soueraigne Queene Anne. With Epitaphs* (1619), sig. A4ᵛ

Jonson, Ben, 'LXXXIX. To Edward Allen', in 'Epigrammes' (1616), in *Ben Jonson*, ed. C. H. Herford and Percy and Evelyn Simpson, vol. 8 (1947), 56–7

Nascimento, S. Z., 'Thomas Middleton's *A Game at Chesse*: A Textual Study', unpublished Ph.D. diss. (University of Maryland, 1975)

North, Marcy L., *The Anonymous Renaissance: Cultures of Discretion in Tudor–Stuart England* (2003)

Pembroke, William, British Library Egerton MS 2592, fol. 81 (letter of 20 May 1619)

Redding, David Coleman, *Robert Bishop's Commonplace-Book: An Edition of a Seventeenth Century Miscellany*, unpub. Ph.D. thesis, University of Pennsylvania (1960)

Taylor, Gary, '*Praestat Difficilior Lectio*: *All's Well that Ends Well* and *Richard III*', *Renaissance Studies* 2 (1988), 27–46

Webster, John, *The Works of John Webster*, Volume One, ed. David Gunby, David Carnegie, Antony Hammond, and Doreen DelVecchio (1995)

Williams, Franklin B., Jr., 'Commendatory Verses: The Rise of the Art of Puffing', *Studies in Bibliography* 19 (1966), 1–14

TEXTUAL NOTES

St James

4   bring] THIS EDITION; brings PURSLOWE. Although grammatically possible, 'brings' suggests that the verb is governed by 'mirror' instead of 'times'. An easy error of assimilation.

To the King

Title   To the King] THIS EDITION; to yᵉ Kinge   Middletons Verſes who was committed to yᵉ Fleet for yᵉ play calld the 'Game at Chefs:' INNS; Verses sent to King James DAWES; after nyne dayſe wher in J haue heard ſome | of the acters ſey they tooke: ſiueteene hundred | pounde the ſpain'ſh factōn being preualent | gott it ſuppreſt the Cheife actors and | the Poett Mt [*sic*] Thomas Middleton | that writt it Comitted to priſſon | where hee ley ſome Tyme and at | laſt gott oute vpon this petition | preſented to King James DYCE; The petition of poet Midleton | to king Iames HULSE; On the author of the | play called yᵉ game | at chefse FLOYD. Another (contemporary) hand has added to the HULSE title the words 'Authoʳ of yᵉ Game | at Chefs,' after 'Midleton'. In the original transcription, the first line of the title identified the author, and the second line (centred) was the prepositional phrase 'to king Iames'. That same phrase occurs just before the first line in DYCE, and the comparable 'to yᵉ Kinge' is physically separated in INNS. The specification 'James' was only necessary after the accession of another 'king'; this suggests that INNS may represent the earliest extant transcription of the poem, or at least that it represents the earliest form of the title. The plain name 'James' would be unnecessary and inappropriate in a petition; the unspecific 'King' also better fits the chess allusion.

1   raised] raiſèd FLOYD

1   merely] only DYCE, FLOYD. Compare 'a mere delight, a game' (*Entertainments* 2.25) and 'What I do is merely recreation' (*Chaste Maid* 2.2.5). 'Only' is the commoner word, and more likely to be substituted for the rarer 'merely'.

2   lately] *not in* DYCE, FLOYD. The choice of variants here affects the choice of variants and hence the rhythm of the rest of the line. The adjective here makes more sense closer to the time of composition; later copies might easily omit it. The variants which make the line metrical, in other copies, are mere metrical fillers, without substantive significance.

2   played] playèd HULSE; acted FLOYD

2   by] INNS, DAWES; twixt HULSE, FLOYD; betwixt DYCE. Compare *Game* Induction.72 ('you'd *play a game* all *by* yourself'), *Mad World* 2.1.157.1 ('A strain *plaid by* the consort'), *Michaelmas*

1.1.67 ('play by'). I have found no comparable collocations of *play* and [*be*]*twixt*.

2   and] & the DYCE, FLOYD. This is a metrical variant, related to preceding variants in the line.

3   White side] DAWES, INNS; ~ houſe HULSE, FLOYD, DYCE. Middleton uses both idioms in *Game*; 'house' could easily have resulted from duplication of the preceding line.

3   won] wann DAWES, DYCE. A spelling variant only, interesting only because it might suggest some connection between the two manuscripts. However, they share no other unique readings.

3   but now] DAWES, INNS; but yet HULSE; & yet FLOYD; yet ſtill DYCE. The 'now' contrasts with 'lately', and suggests the immediacy of an original reading.

3   House] ſide DAWES; doth DYCE. Middleton uses the auxiliary 'doth' no more than eleven times in the 1620s; here it would be purely a metrical filler. Although 'side' is possible here, as earlier in the line, the unique DAWES reading could easily result from assimilation to the preceding phrase: in our edited text, as in INNS, the assonance of 'White side' in the first half of the line contrasts with the assonance of 'now...House' in the second half.

4   changed the game and] had the power to DYCE. The majority variant permits a variety of word-play on *game*: the rules of the game, the outcome of the game, and the quarry being pursued (and 'put...in the bag', bagged, like a dead animal). The idiom 'have power to' is very common, and has no special pertinence here: the exact phrase 'had the power to' occurs at least nine times in texts printed between 1597 and 1630 (including once in *Mad World* 3.2.51). By contrast, there are no parallels in those years for 'changed the game' (with any spelling of the verb), which makes it the 'rarer reading' (Taylor 1988), less likely to be a scribal substitution.

4   ‚changed] DAWES; ha' chaun'gd INNS; have Changed HULSE; have chang'd FLOYD. The elided 'ha' could be Middleton's; the full 'have' looks like a scribal expansion. Perhaps Middleton's original was 'They've' (a relatively rare contraction, which first appears in print in a Middleton text in 1619 in *Antiquity* 430, then several times in *Game* texts, and in posthumous printings of *Valour*, *No Wit*, and *Women Beware*). In undoubted Middleton 'they ha' appears only in *Widow* 4.2.228 (printed in 1652 from a scribal text).

4   game] name FLOYD

5–6   And...Fleet] *not in* DYCE. For the phrasing, compare 'make joy more glad' (*Virtue* 160) and 'make my joys proud' (*Roaring Girl* 11.186); 'She lay with one o' the navy, Her husband lying in the Fleet' (*Roaring Girl* 8.116–17), where there is the same pun on the prison and the navy.

5 that which makes] for to make HULSE. Middleton has 'for to make' three times in *Solomon*, and once at *Chaste Maid* 5.1.93. But 'that which makes' occurs in later plays: *Dissemblers* 4.3.25 and *Women Beware* 3.2.334.

5 joy] ioyes FLOYD

6 lie now] now lie FLOYD

7 Use but] HULSE, DYCE; Yet vſe DAWES, INNS; But vſe FLOYD. 'But' adds the sense 'only', which emphasizes how little James needs do. The exact phrase 'use but' occurs at *Witch* 4.2.48 and *Changeling* 1.2.100; I have found no Middleton parallels for 'yet use' or for 'but use' (as a verb).

7 hand] hands FLOYD. The plural destroys the reference to handwriting.

7 my hopes are] DAWES, INNS, HULSE; my thoughts are FLOYD; Twill set mee DYCE. DYCE simplifies the grammar and the content. Compare 'my hopes are' at *Five Gallants* 1.1.273, *Dissemblers* 2.1.145, 3.1.73, *Witch* 4.1.91; Middleton has

'my hopes' 19 times. The only Middleton parallel for the Dyce variant is ''Twill set off' at *No Wit* 7.324. The collocation 'set(t)…free' is very common in the period: it occurs 15 times in Middleton, 281 times in other texts published between 1600 and 1630 (LION).

8 removing] remounceing FLOYD

8 one] a DYCE. The emphatic 'one man' (six times in Middleton's uncollaborative works, 300 times in LION texts printed between 1597 and 1630) is a much rarer idiom than 'a man' (at least 330 times in Middleton, 5767 times in the comparable LION corpus); scribes are likelier to substitute the commoner phrase.

8 Tho. Middleton] THIS EDITION; T.M DAWES; *not in* INNS, HULSE, FLOYD, DYCE. Other texts move the attribution to the heading of the poem, but Middleton would not have described himself in the third person, as those headings do. Instead, we would expect him to 'sign' his petition to the King, as he often signed dedicatory poems and prefaces. In this case, the signature is part of the syntax of the poem, identifying the 'me' of its final rhyme.

THE WITCH

Edited by Marion O'Connor

Not printed until 1778, the text of *The Witch* was transmitted in a manuscript, now Malone MS 12 in the Bodleian Library, Oxford. The tidy and legible handwriting of this presentation copy is that of Ralph Crane, a scrivener from whose pen eight dramatic manuscripts are known to have survived. Crane put no date on his transcript of *The Witch*, but his title-page quite clearly identifies the theatrical provenance of the play: 'A Tragi--|Coomedie, Called | the | Witch, | long since Acted by his Majesties Servants | at the Black-Friars'. By his own account elsewhere, Crane took particular pride in his professional association with the King's Men:

> And some employment hath my useful Pen
> Had 'mongst those civil, well-deserving *men*,
> That grace the *Stage* with *honour* and *delight*,
> Of whose true honesties I much could write,
> But will comprise't (as in a Cask of Gold)
> Vnder the *Kingly Service* they do hold. (*The Works of Mercy*, 1621)

This boast is of limited use in determining the date of Crane's transcript of *The Witch*. By 1621 Crane's pen had been employed upon at least one other King's Men play, John Fletcher's and Philip Massinger's *Sir John van Olden Barnavelt*: consequently, Crane's transcript of *The Witch* is not necessarily to be included among the professional achievements of which he boasted that year. Indeed, there is reason to doubt that he had prepared the transcript even by two years later. From the first of two parenthetical protests which Middleton lodges within the epistle dedicatory of Malone MS 12, it seems clear that at least one earlier manuscript—authorial or playhouse—went missing for an appreciable time: 'I have...recovered into my hands (though not without much difficulty) this (ignorantly-ill-fated) labour of mine' (Epistle.4–5). It would not seem to have been discovered, recovered, or replaced by 1623. In preparing the text of *Macbeth* for publication in *Mr William Shakespeare's Comedies, Histories & Tragedies*, the editors of the First Folio appear to have been unable to lay hands on a copy of *The Witch*: their abbreviation of the two Middletonian songs, down to the mere titles 'Come away, come away &c.' and 'Blacke Spirits, &c', suggests that no copy—neither authorial nor playhouse nor presentation—of Middleton's play was available to Shakespeare's editors in 1623. 1623 is thus a reasonable *terminus a quo* for Crane's preparation of the presentation copy. The dedicatory epistle also supplies a rather stronger *terminus ante quem*: giving no indication

that the author is not alive, the dedication almost certainly antedates Middleton's death in 1627.

This probable range of dates, 1623–7, for Crane's transcript of *The Witch* is narrowed by some of the bibliographical evidence which Malone MS 12 presents. One striking feature of the manuscript is the fact that Crane used two different papers for it. The dedicatory epistle and the title-page are respectively verso and recto of a sheet which is distinct from the bulk of the manuscript: it has a different watermark; the box rule which frames the page is out of alignment; and while the italic script is recognizably by the same hand as that of the manuscript, it is also perceptibly different—as if it had been made at another time and/or with another pen. In preparing at least two other transcripts (that of *A Game at Chess*, now Bodleian Library MS Malone 25, in December–January 1624–5 and that of Beaumont and Fletcher's *Demetrius and Enanthe*, now MS Brogyntyn II.42 in the National Library of Wales, Aberystwyth, in November 1625) Crane is known to have used paper from one stock for the bulk of the manuscript and from another or others for the preliminaries. Moreover, the three transcripts share paper stocks: the sheet which Crane used for the preliminaries to *The Witch* bears the upper half of the post/pillar watermark found on the title-leaf of *Demetrius and Enanthe* (Greg and Wilson, viii); and the paper which Crane used for the bulk of his transcript of *The Witch* bears the same pot watermark as that of the paper he used for the bulk of his transcript of *A Game at Chess*. (The slight differences which a recent editor of *The Witch* has observed between the watermarks of Malone MS 12 and MS 25 [Esche, 9–10] can also be discerned between the watermarks on different sheets of MS 12 and should probably be attributed to the use of two moulds in the making of that paper stock.) Two of the three transcripts can be firmly dated within a period of eleven months, from December 1624 to November 1625. Scribal practice and paper stock, then, together suggest that the third transcript, Malone MS 12, the undated presentation copy of *The Witch*, is contemporaneous with the other two transcripts and can therefore be dated, with them, to 1625.

Another material oddity of Malone MS 12 deserves special remark here. The ruled stub of a cancelled sheet survives between pages 84 and 85, the break falling in the middle of line 9 of the penultimate scene of the play. It seems clear that the sheet was excised by the scribe: the tag-word which Crane has put at the bottom of 84 matches the first word of dialogue on 85. The fact that on page 84 Crane misheaded the scene ('Scena 3a' for

'Scena 2a') invites the hypothesis that he proceeded to make further mistakes on his next page before giving that one up as a bad job and starting page 85 afresh in the morning. (Whatever occasioned the excision of the sheet, Crane's misnumbering of scenes continued through the final act.) Page 85, however, contains a long passage of quotation from Ovid's *Metamorphoses*. For this quotation, as elsewhere for some stage directions, Crane changed his script. He also omitted an entire line mid-way through the quotation, let his letter formation get crude in the penultimate line, and imperfectly aligned the final italic half-line of Latin with the secretary half-line of English that continues it. The fact that the quotation thus appears to have been crammed into insufficient space suggests that Crane may have left a blank until he could change pens and/or check quotations.

In addition to Malone MS 12, there are early manuscript texts for two of the three songs in *The Witch*. Firstly, 'Come away, Hecate' survives in New York as No. 52 (misnumbered LIV) in Drexel MS 4175 at the New York Public Library and in Cambridge on folios 107^v–108^r of Fitzwilliam Museum MS 52.D / MU.MS 782 (the John Bull MS). The New York manuscript, inscribed 'Ann Twice, Her Booke', is currently dated to the 1620s (Jorgens, vii). The Fitzwilliam manuscript contains several layers in different hands: the relevant layer, the second, is thought to have been added by around 1650 (Fenlon, 149). The musical setting which these manuscripts give for 'Come away, Hecate' is accepted to have been the work of Richard Johnson. Although they disagree about the bass accompaniment to the song, the two manuscripts give it virtually identical melodic lines for a single voice. The textual variants in 'Come away, Hecate' are, however, more pronounced—both between the two song manuscripts and also between each of them and the song as it appears in 3.3, the second coven scene, of Crane's transcript of *The Witch*. Secondly, 'In a maiden-time professed' survives in New York as No. 32 in Drexel MS 4257 (a songbook inscribed 'John Gamble, His Booke Amen 1659') and in Oxford on folio 21^r of Bodleian MS MUS.b.1, where its musical setting is credited to John Wilson (who presented this manuscript volume of his work to the University before 1656). Again, the melodic line, for a single voice, is the same in both settings, but there are differences between the bass lines. Both of these manuscripts give two further verses for 'In a maiden-time professed' but otherwise they vary only slightly from the text of the song as assigned to Isabella in 2.1 of Crane's transcript of *The Witch*. Both Johnson ([c.1582]-1633) and Wilson ([c.1595]-1674) were associated with the King's Men, Johnson for six or seven years from about 1610 and the younger man (who got off to an early start with a masque for the wedding festivities of Frances Howard and Robert Carr) from about 1615.

The provenance of Malone MS 12 is uncertain until the eighteenth century. Its first owner is named on the verso of the title-page, where an epistle dedicatory above the name of 'Tho. Middleton' presents the copy 'To

the | truely-worthie and gene-|rously-affected | Thomas Holmes, Esquire.' Holmes has not been firmly identified among a handful of possible candidates: the field is led by, on the one hand, a Gray's Inn lawyer (Phelps) and, on the other (and stronger) hand, a musician, composer and gentleman of the Chapel Royal (Schafer, 1996) who died in 1638. Later in the century Malone 12 may possibly have come into the possession of William Davenant (1606-68). Davenant's early writings include a play (*Albovine*, published in 1629) which overlaps with the third plot of *The Witch* and is dedicated to Robert Carr. His post-Restoration revivals included *Macbeth*, of which his adaptation survives in three different versions—one manuscript and two printed after Davenant's death. Of the printed versions, the earlier (1673) varies from the Folio *Macbeth* only in its songs, while the later (1674, promptly running through five editions in quarto) claims to give 'all the alterations, amendments, additions, and new songs. As it is now Acted at the Dukes Theatre'. These improvements also appear in the manuscript version. All three Restoration versions give a text of the song 'Come away Hecate' from 3.3 of *The Witch*; and both the manuscript and the 1674 printed versions give a text for the song 'Black spirits' from 5.2 of *The Witch*. (The 1673 printed version gives only the title of this song.) That Davenant was working from a copy of Middleton's play rather than, or perhaps as well as, from a manuscript of stage and masque music is suggested by an emendation which he made to the text of 'Black Spirits' and which looks to have been cued by a Middletonian line of dialogue some lines before this song begins in *The Witch*. (See Textual Notes.) The continuous history of the ownership of Malone MS 12 begins with Benjamin Griffin: Griffin (1680-1740) was an actor whose London career began with employment by Christopher Rich (c.1658-1714), the manager who bought out the Davenant family's theatrical interests. None of these connections with Davenant amounts to incontrovertible proof that he ever held Crane's transcript of *The Witch* in his hands, for each admits of alternative explanation; but the ensemble does point in his direction.

Griffin's ownership of the manuscript was recorded in the entry for it in the printed catalogue of Major Thomas Pearson's library, sold at auction over three weeks in the spring of 1788. The catalogue entry for No. 3872, the manuscript of *The Witch*, notes: 'N.B. The above MS of the Witch, was purchased from the Collection of Benj. Griffin, the actor.' This entry is pasted onto a preliminary leaf of Malone MS 12: below it a note handwritten and initialled by George Steevens amplifies the Georgian history of the manuscript. Steevens records that the manuscript had 'passed from the hands of [Benjamin] Griffin...into those of Lockyer Davis Bookseller in Holborn, who sold it to Major Pearson'. (Lockyer Davis's sale catalogues survive from as early as December 1747 [Munby and Lenore, 53].) Steevens also records the price which he himself paid for the manuscript at the auction of Pearson's books: £2 14s. 0d. (The auctioneer's copy of the sale catalogue gives this sum as the price paid by Steevens on 1 May 1788 and records other figures against which to measure it: on the same day, for example, Malone paid £7 for a 1592 imprint of John Lyly's *Midas*.) Yet another fly-leaf note, this one in the handwriting of Edmond Malone, shows that, by the time he bought Crane's transcript of *The Witch* a dozen years later, its sale value had almost trebled: 'Bought at the sale of Mr. Steevens's books, May 20th 1800, at the enormous price of £7.10.0.' After Malone's death, the manuscript went to the Bodleian Library.

Before becoming an owner of the manuscript, Steevens had copied it out. His transcription, which survives in the Folger Shakespeare Library, has been shown to have been the copy for the text of *The Witch* printed in 1778 by John Nichols at the expense of Isaac Reed (Mulholland, 78). This first printed edition of Middleton's play was thus at least one and a half centuries, and two transcriptions, away from any authorial draft. Evidently transcribed afresh (Mulholland, 79), passages from *The Witch* (parts of 1.2, and the entireties of 3.3 and 5.2) were then included in the 1793 edition of *The Plays of William Shakespeare*, revised by Reed from Steevens's and Samuel Johnson's edition fifteen years earlier. These passages appeared again both in subsequent editions of *The Plays of William Shakespeare* and also, with a few alterations, in Charles Lamb's 1808 *Specimens of English Dramatic Poets*. A complete text of *The Witch* was included in the three-volume collection of *Ancient British Drama* published in 1810 and attributed to Walter Scott: an introductory note acknowledges that 'the present edition is printed from the one... printed in 1778. The orthography is reduced to the present standard, and directions are added to the several scenes.' Scott's text also makes some independent emendations of manuscript readings. The play was re--edited by Alexander Dyce for his edition of *The Works of Thomas Middleton*, published in 1840. Both Dyce's text of *The Witch* and his annotations were recycled— the former wholly and without acknowledgement, the latter but partially and with acknowledgement—by A. H. Bullen in his 1885 *Works of Thomas Middleton*. In 1890 Dyce's edition of the play soon got a further recycling, by Havelock Ellis in the second of his two--volume selection of Middleton's plays. Of the five editions of *The Witch* published in the twentieth century, the three latest (those of Peter Corbin and Douglas Sedge in 1986, of Edward Esche in 1993, and of Elizabeth Schafer in 1994) modernize spelling and punctuation. (Spelling and musical notation were also modernized by Ian Spink when he edited 'Come away, Hecate' for a volume of Robert Johnson's songs published in 1961 and 'In a maiden-time professed' for a collection of seventeenth-century English songs published in 1971.) Editions of *The Witch* published mid-century, however, present more or less diplomatic texts: the edition of L. Drees and Henry de Vocht (1945) is faulted by its indifference to the manuscript lineation of passages which the editors reckoned to be prose; but the edition of W. W. Greg and F. P. Wilson (1950 for 1948) is highly trustworthy in this and other respects. T.

H. Howard-Hill's transcription of Malone MS 12, deposited with the Oxford Text Archive, also gives a diplomatic text: it lacks a line here and there, but is otherwise extremely accurate.

Thanks in largest measure to Howard-Hill (1965, 1972, 1973, and 1992), Crane's transcripts have received scholarly attention. Studies of Crane's work, and in particular comparative analyses of his transcript of Middleton's *Game of Chess* and the authorial manuscript of the play, have revealed a high level of scribal intervention, with Crane introducing: hyphens; italics to emphasize quotations and sententiae as well as scene and speech headings; parentheses to mark off asides and changes of address; and elisions to modify metre. Save where Crane's deployment of them happens to coincide with modern conventions, neither his hyphens nor his italics nor his parentheses have been retained in this edition; and their removal has not been signalled. They have, in other words, been put on a par with the punctuation marks of subsequent editors. The elisions in Crane's transcript of *The Witch* have been more problematic. It is likely that some of them are Middleton's elisions, while others are Crane's elisions of words which Middleton (being less scrupulous in matters metrical) spelled out in full, and still others are Crane's alterations of elisions which Middleton (having different orthographical habits) actually wrote. It has seemed regrettably impossible, however, to determine which is which and thence to reconstruct, letter for letter, what Middleton actually wrote. Where Crane gives an elision, in general this edition also elides, but does so in accordance with twentieth-century orthographical convention. Where this convention dictates a form different from that given by Crane, the change is recorded in the Textual Notes.

SEE ALSO

Text: *Works*, 1129
Music and dance: this volume, 151 ('In a maiden time professed'), 153 ('Come away'), 158, 160 (dances)
Authorship and date: this volume, 382

WORKS CITED

Previous Editions: Complete Texts

CRANE: Malone MS 12, Bodleian Library
STEEVENS: [Steevens, George, ed.,] *A Tragi-Coomedie Called The Witch* (1778)
SCOTT: [Scott, Walter, ed.,] *The Ancient British Drama*, vol. 3 (1810)
DYCE: Dyce, Alexander, ed., *Works*, vol. 3 (1840)
BULLEN: Bullen, A. H., ed., *Works*, vol. 5 (1885)
ELLIS: Ellis, Havelock, ed., *Selected Plays*, vol. 2 ([1890])
DREES–DE VOCHT: Drees, L., and Henry de Vocht, eds., *The Witch* (1945)
GREG–WILSON: Greg, W. W., and F. P. Wilson, eds., *The Witch* (1950 for 1948)
Howard-Hill, T. H., ed., *The Witch* (digital transcript deposited with the Oxford Text Archive)
CORBIN–SEDGE: Corbin, Peter, and Douglas Sedge, eds., *Three Jacobean Witch Plays* (1987)
ESCHE: Esche, Edward J., ed., *The Witch* (1993)
SCHAFER: Schafer, Elizabeth, ed., *The Witch* (1994)

Previous Editions: Songs/Passages Only

JAGGARD: Shakespeare, William, *Comedies, Histories & Tragedies* (1623), facsimile edn. Helge Kökeritz and Charles Tyler Prouty (1955)

TWICE: *English Song 1600–1675*, vol. 11. Miscellaneous Manuscripts...Drexel MS 4175, 'Ann Twice, Her Booke', introd. Elise Bickford Jorgens (1987)

BULL: Fitzwilliam Museum MS 52.D / MU.MS 782

BODLEIAN: Bodleian MS MUS.b.1

GAMBLE: *English Song 1600–1675*, vol. 10. New York Public Library Manuscripts, Part II: Drexel MS 4257, 'John Gamble, His booke, Amen, 1659', introd. Elise Bickford Jorgens (1987)

CADEMAN: [Davenant, William,] *Macbeth: A Tragedy acted at the Dukes-Theatre* (1673)

CHETWIN: [Davenant, William,] *Macbeth, A Tragedy: with all the Alterations, Amendments, Additions, and New Songs. As it is now acted at the Dukes Theatre* (1674)

CLARK: [Davenant, William,] *Macbeth, A Tragædy: with all the Alterations, Amendments, Additions, and New Songs. As it is now acted at the Dukes Theatre* (1674)

YALE: Davenant, William, *Macbeth from the Yale Manuscript*, ed. Christopher Spencer (1961)

REED: Johnson, Samuel, and George Steevens, eds., *The Plays of William Shakespeare* (1778), revised by Isaac Reed, vol. 7 (1793)

LAMB: Lamb, Charles, ed., *Specimens of English Dramatic Poets Who Lived about the Time of Shakspeare* [sic] (1808)

Spink, Ian, ed., *Robert Johnson: Ayres, Songs and Dialogues*, The English Lute Songs, 2nd Series, No. 17 (1961)

Spink, Ian, ed., *English Songs 1625–1660*, Musica Britannica 33 (1971)

WELLS–TAYLOR: Wells, Stanley, and Gary Taylor, *William Shakespeare: The Complete Works* (Oxford: Clarendon, 1986)

BROOKE: Brooke, Nicholas, ed., *Macbeth* (Oxford: Oxford University Press, 1990)

Other Works Cited

Bibliotheca Pearsoniana: A Catalogue of the Library of Thomas Pearson...sold by auction (London, 1788)

Bodin, Jean, *La Demonomanie des Sorciers* (1580)

—— *De Magorum Daemonomania* (1581)

Chamberlain, John, *Letters*, ed. Norman Egbert McClure, 2 vols (1939)

Clowes, William, *A Short and Profitable Treatise touching the cure of the disease called (Morbus Gallicus)* (1579)

Crane, Ralph, *The Workes of Mercy* (1621), rpt. as *The Pilgrimes New-yeares-gift: or fourteene steps to the throne of glory* ([1625])

Cutts, John P., 'Jacobean Masque and Stage Music', *Music and Letters* 35 (1954), 185–200

Della Porta (Neapolitanus), Iohannes, *Magia naturalis* (1561)

Fenlon, Iain, ed., *Cambridge Music Manuscripts 900–1700* (1982)

Fraunce, Abraham, *The Third Part of...Ivychurch* (1592)

Greg, W. W., 'Some Notes on Crane's Manuscript of *The Witch*', *The Library*, IV, 22 (1942), 208–22

Howard-Hill, T. H., '"Lizard's Braine" in Middleton's *The Witch*', *Notes and Queries* 218 (1973), 458–9

—— 'Ralph Crane's Parentheses', *Notes and Queries* 210 (1965), 334–40

—— *Ralph Crane and Some Shakespeare First Folio Comedies* (1972)

—— 'Shakespeare's Earliest Editor, Ralph Crane', *Shakespeare Survey* 44 (1992), 113–29

James I, *Daemonologie, in Form of a Dialogue* (1597)

Jonson, Ben, *The Complete Masques*, ed. Stephen Orgel (1969)

Jorgens, Elise Bickford, 'Introduction' to *English Song 1600–1675*, Vol. 11, *Miscellaneous Manuscripts* (1987), v–viii

Le Loyer, Pierre, trans. Zacharie Jones, *A Treatise of Specters or Straunge Sights, Visions and Apparitions appearing sensibly unto men* (1605)

Lynche, Richard, *The Fountain of Ancient Fiction* (1599)

Machiavelli, Niccolò, *Istorie fiorentine*, trans. Thomas Bedingfield (1595)

Mulholland, Paul, 'Notes on Several Derivatives of Crane's Manuscript of Middleton's *The Witch*', *Papers of the Bibliographical Society of America* 78 (1984), 75–81

Munby, A. L., and Lenore Coral, *British Book Sale Catalogues 1676–1800: A Union List* (1977)

Pharmacopoeia Londinensis (1618)

Phelps, Wayne H., 'Thomas Holmes, Esquire: The Dedicatee of Middleton's *The Witch*', *Notes and Queries* 225 (1980), 152–4

Ripa, Cesare, *Iconologia* (1593)

Schafer, Elizabeth, 'Thomas Holmes of Salisbury and Winchester and the Dedicatory Letter of Thomas Middleton's *The Witch*', *Notes and Queries* 241 (1996), 188–90

Scot, Reginald, *The Discoverie of Witchcraft* (1584)

Smith, Irwin, *Shakespeare's Blackfriars Playhouse: Its History and Its Design* (1964)

A true and just Record of the Information, Examination and Confession of all the witches, taken at S. Oses in the county of Essex (1582)

Tuke, Thomas, *A Treatise Against Painting and Tincturing of Men and Women* (1616)

Vicary, Thomas, *The English mans treasure* (6th edn., 1613)

A warning for faire women. Containing, the most tragicall murther of master G. Sanders (1599)

Wilson, F. P., 'Ralph Crane, Scrivener to the King's Players', *The Library*, IV, 7 (1926), 194–215

TEXTUAL NOTES

Title A Tragi-|Coomodie, Called | the | Witch; | long since Acted, by his Maties. Seruants | at the Black-Friers. | Written by. Tho. Middleton. CRANE

Persons CRANE writes *The Sceane Rauenna.* before the *dramatis personae* list; following the procedures of this edition Crane's editorial indication of place is omitted from the text.

Persons.20 [&]] THIS EDITION; *not in* CRANE. In CRANE the *dramatis personae* list contains three pairs of names, each pair being governed by a single curly bracket. As the other two pairs are internally linked by ampersands, it seems appropriate to insert an ampersand here as well.

Persons.29 mutes] Not all of the roles which are comprehended by this label are completely silent: the Servant who comes on near the beginning of 1.1, the Old Woman who enters with Aberzanes at the beginning of 3.2, and the Stableboy who comes on at the end of the latter scene all have to speak a few words.

1.1.8 fast'ning] CRANE (fastning)

1.1.18 lose] CRANE (loose). Also at 2.1.70, 3.1.45, 4.2.43 and 4.3.102.

1.1.23.1 *Exit*] STEEVENS; Ex^t CRANE. All subsequent usages of this abbreviation signify the plural verb. There is, however, no one available to accompany Sebastian in his departure. At this point near the beginning of his transcript, either the scrivener may not have determined the rule governing his marking of exits, or proximity to the right-hand rule may have caused him to forget it.

1.1.38 Duke's] DYCE; King's CRANE

1.1.40 he's] CRANE (h'as); has DYCE. Crane's elisions tend to pare the pronoun where modern usage reduces the verb instead. See also 2.1.210 (CRANE ha's), 2.2.111, 4.2.51 (CRANE ha's), and 4.3.43.

1.1.41 has the least, he's] CRANE (has the least, ha's); ESCHE (has the least, he's); STEEVENS (has the least has). Being consistent with scribal practice throughout the manuscript, the modernization given by ESCHE appears to me to be correct. However, modern ears, accustomed to hearing 'he's' as a contracted form of 'to have' only in its use as an auxiliary verb (as in the immediately preceding line 40), might be better served in performance by the reading given by STEEVENS: grammatically possible here (as it was not in the immediately preceding line), 'has' has been adopted in all other modernizing editions.

1.1.44 malaga] CRANE (Malego)

1.1.65 yon] CRANE (yond). Also at 5.2.32, 5.2.88, and 5.3.38.

1.1.66 ven'son] CRANE (venson)

1.1.66 parsnip] STEEVENS; pasnip CRANE

1.1.69 She's] CRANE (Sh'as). Also at 2.2.52, 3.2.40 (CRANE sha's), 3.2.52 (CRANE sha's), 3.2.56, 3.2.87, and 4.1.84.

1.1.77 blessed] CRANE (blessd). The word 'bless[e]d' appears 11 times in CRANE. Five occurrences, all spelled 'blessd' and monosyllabic, are past participles: 1.1.77, 2.1.78, 2.2.113, 4.2.58, and 5.3.85. The six occurrences as an adjective are variously spelled 'blessd' (2.2.37, 3.2.130, 4.2.118, and 5.3.117) and 'blessed' (3.2.210 and 5.3.82). None of them is definitely disyllabic.

1.1.87 holy] CRANE (holly); silly STEEVENS. As CORBIN-SEDGE point out, 'holy' is both appropriate to the dramatic situation and consistent with scribal orthography elsewhere (2.1.228, 5.1.13, and 5.3.61) in the manuscript.

1.1.98 power] CRANE (powre). Also at 1.2.125, 1.2.175, 3.2.34, and 4.1.83.

1.1.99 you've] CRANE (y'have). Also at 1.2.218, 2.1.22, 3.2.76, 3.2.95, 3.2.112, 4.2.71, 4.2.122, 5.1.35, 5.1.131,

1.1.112 LORD GOVERNOR Fie, how you fright the women!] THIS EDITION. In CRANE this half-line is part of the Duke's speech. This scribal assignment has been preserved by all previous editors: CORBIN-SEDGE rescue it from nonsense by means of a direction which requires the Duke to address the half-line to the skull. It makes even better dramatic and theatrical sense to reassign the half-line. The exclamation is not the Duke's style: nowhere else in this scene does he personify the skull as living, and nowhere else in the play does he re-address his speech twice within a line and a half. An explicit expression of concern for his female guests and an implicit rebuke of the Duke for dreadful manners is, however, appropriate to the high style of the speech of the Lord Governor.

1.1.115 Marry] CRANE (mary')

1.1.119 e'er] CRANE (ere). Also at 1.2.74, 2.2.43, 3.2.47, 4.1.59, 4.3.40, and 5.1.132.

1.1.123 We're] CRANE (We'are). Also at 1.2.127, 1.2.181, 3.2.78, 4.1.25 (We'ar), and 4.2.8.

1.1.123 than] CRANE (then). Also in all subsequent occurrences of this conjunction.

1.1.129 rose's] CRANE (rose')

1.1.133 This's] CRANE (This'). See also 2.1.233 and 3.1.1.

1.1.143 it's] ESCHE; it'has CRANE; it has STEEVENS

1.1.149 ne'er] CRANE (nere). Also at 1.2.50, 1.2.122, 2.1.5, 2.1.21, 2.1.83, 4.3.109, and 5.1.42.

1.2.0.1 *Enter Hecate*] DYCE; Enter Hecate and other witches CRANE; Hecate, and the other witches, at their charms LAMB. The direction in CRANE proposes a theatrical impossibility on which a great deal of editorial energy has been expended. One solution (of which a variant is considered but rejected in DYCE) is to make Hecate enter to the front of the stage and the other witches be discovered around a cauldron on an inner stage. Another is to bring on the entire coven but make all the witches except Hecate pass over the stage and leave it to her. However, the first solution is rendered impossible by Firestone's account (at ll. 182–93) of Almachildes's arrival: such bumbling and tumbling must remain matters of report only rather than being mimed on an inner stage. The second solution avoids the problems of tone, timing, and traffic control raised by the first but does seem to be precluded by 1.2.5. On balance it seems preferable to regard the direction in CRANE as one of the massed entries which betray distance from the theatre (Howard-Hill, 1992, 110). So construed, its mass may be reduced.

1.2.0.2 [*including a baby, serpents and snakes*]] THIS EDITION; *not in* CRANE. It was recognized by SCHAFER that 'Hecate must have the "dead baby" with her at the beginning of the scene': this can be achieved by her bringing it on. (Her entrance is thus visually linked to the appearance of the Old Woman with Aberzanes's and Francisca's child in arms at 3.2.0.1.) If Hecate is carrying a doll or dummy (rather than just a bundle) and it is exposed to audience view (rather than under wraps), then its mouth should be begrimed in accordance with l. 39. That she must also be carrying serpents and snakes (presumably in a basket) is required by l. 12, the first in the series of references which determine the deployment of these personal properties across the entire scene.

1.2.2 Pidgin] THIS EDITION (following Reginald Scot's *Discoverie of Witchcraft* [1584]); pidgen CRANE; Pigeon ESCHE

1.2.5 Hellwain ... Puckle] LAMB, DYCE (the latter following Scot's *Discoverie of Witchcraft*); Hellwin ... Prickle CRANE; Hellwyn ... Prickle STEEVENS; Hellwayn ... Prickle SCOTT.

1.2.8 seeton] CRANE; seeten STEEVENS; seething (?) LAMB

1.2.19 o'er] CRANE (or); on STEEVENS. The emendation is possible, but is rejected on grounds of both orthography and—in context of a speech celebrating transvection—topography.

1.2.21 towers] CRANE (towres). Also at 3.3.67.

1.2.23 e'en] CRANE (ev'n). Also at 1.2.65 and 2.2.79.

1.2.23 leek] CRANE (leeke); like LAMB. The archaic form has been retained in order to preserve eye-rhyme—to which, as Howard-Hill (1992, 119) points out, Crane was attentive.

1.2.30–3 Last night ... mounting] These three and a half lines are omitted in LAMB, whose preface gives warning: 'Where a line or more was obscure, as having reference to something that had gone before, which would have asked more time to explain than its consequence in the scene seemed to deserve, I have had no hesitation in leaving the line or passage out.' If this sentence can be taken as the explanation of the omission, then the omission suggests that, as Mulholland (1984, 80) puts it, 'Lamb did not know the play in its complete form'.

1.2.30 Whelpley's] STEEVENS (*subst.*); Wlelplies CRANE

1.2.32 thou'st] CRANE (thou'hast). Also at 4.2.112.

1.2.37–42 *eleoselinum ... oleum*] The list of magical ingredients being a *verbatim* conflation of two recipes in Scot's *Discoverie of Witchcraft* (x, 8), this edition generally adopts the spelling of Latin herbal names as given in that source. (But see note below to 1.2.40.) CORBIN-SEDGE note that 'Hecate's grasp of

Latin terminology seems less secure in this passage' than in her quotation from Ovid at 5.2.20–8. (See note below to 5.2.25.) Any incorrect spellings in CRANE could therefore be defended as dramatically significant. However, it seems likelier that Hecate's access of linguistic competence should be ascribed to the qualitative difference in the Latinity of the sources.

1.2.37   *eleoselinum*] CRANE; Eleaselinum LAMB

1.2.38   *populeas*] LAMB; *Populeus* CRANE

1.2.39   black] STEEVENS; backe CRANE

1.2.40   *acorum vulgare*] DYCE; *Acharum, vulgaro* CRANE; Acharum, Volgaro STEEVENS; *Acharum, Vulgaro* LAMB; *acarum vulgaro* CORBIN–SEDGE; *acharum vulgaro* SCHAFER. The reading given by DYCE slightly varies the spelling (*acarum vulgare*) given by Scot's *Discoverie of Witchcraft* (x, 8), but it is confirmed by Scot's own source for his recipes, the *Magia Naturalis* (1561) of Giovanni Baptista della Porta. DYCE's emendation, moreover, produces a botanical name which befits the speech.

1.2.41   *Pentaphyllon*] DYCE; Dentaphillon CRANE

1.2.42   *Solanum somniferum*] ESCHE; *Solanum Somnificum* CRANE

1.2.45   wife's] CRANE (wives)

1.2.46   They're] CRANE (They'are). Also at 3.3.15.

1.2.52.1–2   [*Squeezing...skins*]] The skins which are the residue of Hecate's work must remain onstage. Her retention of them can be motivated by 1.2.57–8, where Hecate seems to indicate that the serpents' skins are to be used as a charm affecting dairy production. They probably see onstage service in connection with Hecate's incantation at 1.2.102–1.2.106.1. They are certainly onstage when, at 1.2.153–4, Hecate draws them to the attention of Sebastian, who, upon his exit after 1.2.178, takes them away to use as a charm rendering Antonio impotent.

1.2.53   I've] CRANE (I'have). Also at 2.1.67, 2.1.102, 2.1.141, 3.1.19, 3.2.125, 4.1.48, 4.2.26, 5.1.91, and 5.3.77.

1.2.55   And a hog fell lame] & a hog: | And | Fell lame CRANE. GREG–WILSON excepted, editors have silently removed the redundant conjunction, which in the manuscript stands as a tag-word between pages 10 and 11, in favour of its abbreviated incarnation in the last line of verse on page 10.

1.2.56   sope] GREG–WILSON; soape CRANE; soupe STEEVENS; sup DYCE; sop CORBIN–SEDGE; soap ESCHE. The word in CRANE is a variant spelling of a word which survives in modern English as a Northern dialect form.

1.2.58   dew'd-skirted] STEEVENS; dew-d-skirted CRANE; dew-skirted DYCE. Following Greg (1942, 214), CORBIN–SEDGE point out that the substitution of a hyphen for an apostrophe is among the characteristic scribal practices of CRANE.

1.2.60   frothy] CRANE (froathie); swathie STEEVENS; swathy DYCE, who glosses *swathie feastings* in the following note: 'i.e., (I suppose) feastings among the *swaths*—the mown rows of grass'. As an indication of what the milk-maids and parish youths consume under the cows' bellies, the word in CRANE is preferable to an emendation which has them feasting on (or tumbling in) mown hay there.

1.2.65   o'clock] CRANE (a clock). Also at 1.2.66 (a-clock) and 1.2.116.

1.2.79   portion] CRANE; potion CORBIN–SEDGE *conj.*

1.2.103   Silens,] CORBIN–SEDGE; Silence. CRANE; Silence! SCOTT; Sylvans, DYCE. The speech is taken *verbatim* from Scot's *Discoverie of Witchcraft*, wherein the corresponding word is 'sylens'. The transformation of Scot's plural noun into an imperative verb may have been Middleton's doing, but the

initial majuscule on the word in CRANE makes it look likelier that the change was wrought by his pen.

1.2.104   dwarves] SCHAFER; dwarffes CRANE

1.2.109   religious] CRANE; religion's STEEVENS

1.2.119   Whate'er] CRANE (What ere). Also at 2.3.15.

1.2.125   as] REED; and CRANE

1.2.145   ricks] CRANE (reekes). All nineteenth-century editions preserve the obsolete form but, LAMB and SCOTT excepted, gloss it with the modern one.

1.2.149   powers] CRANE (powres). Also at 1.2.177, 2.2.37, 4.2.118, and 5.3.83.

1.2.160   *Chirocineta*] DYCE, following Scot's *Discoverie of Witchcraft* (VI, 3); *Chiroconita* CRANE. This list, like those at 1.2.36–7 and 1.2.39–41, is taken from Scot.

1.2.161   *Archimedon*] DYCE, following Scot's *Discoverie of Witchcraft* (VI, 3); *Archimadon* CRANE

1.2.166   gristle] CRANE (grizzell)

1.2.173   o'er] CRANE (ore). Also at 4.3.110 'o'erflows' CRANE (ore-flowes).

1.2.175   disjoint] CRANE; disjoin LAMB

1.2.184   fall'n] CRANE (falne)

1.2.189   Hey-day] CRANE (Hoy-day)

1.2.207   sea-lamprey] DYCE; stalamprey CRANE

1.2.208   must't] CRANE (must')

1.2.210   pismires] CRANE (Pize mires)

1.2.217   marzipan] CRANE (March-pane)

1.2.220   handkerchief] CRANE (handkercher)

1.2.227   i'th'] STEEVENS; i'th CRANE. Also at 3.2.135 and 3.2.161.

1.2.230   Fiddle?] CRANE; Fidle's STEEVENS. The punctuation mark in CRANE is defective: GREG–WILSON think it probably an alteration of a semicolon.

2.1.11   Give order...to jelly] CRANE has cancelled a redundant speech heading assigning this line to Antonio, who is already speaking. The situation of the line, third down after a page has been turned over, may partly explain the error.

2.1.19   You'd] CRANE (You'had). Also at 2.1.92.

2.1.22   panada] CRANE (ponado)

2.1.47   once] The reading in CRANE could be either 'oure' (preferred by STEEVENS, SCOTT and DYCE) or 'once' (adopted by DREES–DE VOCHT, GREG–WILSON, CORBIN–SEDGE, ESCHE and SCHAFER). This edition joins the scholarly majority because Francisca's speeches tend to deploy first-person pronouns in the singular.

2.1.48   they] CRANE; they'll SCOTT

2.1.52   chewets] CRANE (chewitts)

2.1.53   currant-custards] CRANE (curran-custards)

2.1.68   I'm] CRANE (I'am). Also at 2.1.71, 2.1.109, 2.1.113, 2.1.157, 2.1.189, 2.2.47, 2.2.75, 3.2.28, 3.2.123, 3.2.179, 4.1.47, 4.2.5, 4.3.41, 5.1.1, 5.1.63, 5.1.130 and 5.3.19.

2.1.78   happily] CRANE (happely). Also at 4.3.20 and 5.1.116.

2.1.83   He'd] CRANE (Hee'll'd)

2.1.117   bit] SCOTT; bitt CRANE. The word is quite clear in CRANE and has been accepted by all modernizing editors. However, 'bite' ([*a*] morsel, and [*b*] female pudendum) is a tempting emendation. A substitution of terminal 'e' for 't' is a very possible scribal error.

2.1.124   he'd] CRANE (he'had)

2.1.127   everything] CRANE (every thing)

2.1.131   professed] CRANE, BODLEIAN; possessed GAMBLE

2.1.132   life] CRANE, BODLEIAN. In GAMBLE, the word is 'tyme' has been cancelled and 'life' written above it, by the same hand.

2.1.133   married] CRANE; marrid'g BODLEIAN; marriage GAMBLE

2.1.136   women] CRANE, GAMBLE (woemen); woman BODLEIAN

2.1.138 The middle's...give me] In BODLEIAN and GAMBLE two further verses are inscribed below the musical setting of the song. In BODLEIAN they read:

> Cupid is an Idle toy
> never was there such a boy
> yf there were, let any show
> or his quiver or his Bow
> or a wound by him they gott
> or a broaken Arrow shott
> Mony Mony makes vs bough
> there is no other Cupid now
>
> Whilst yᵉ wold [sic] continued good,
> People loud for flesh, and bloud
> Men about them bore the dart
> that would catch a womans hart
> wemen likewise great, and small
> with a pretty thinge they call
> Cunny Cunny wun the Men
> And this was all the Cupid then

In GAMBLE they read:

> Cupid is an idle toy
> Neuer was there such a boy
> If there were let any show
> Or his quiuer or his bow
> Or a wownd by him begott
> Or a broken Arrow shott
> Mony Mony makes vs bow
> There is noe other Cupid now
>
> While the world continued good
> People lou'd for flesh & bloud
> Men about them bore the darte
> That will winn a woeman's heart
> Woemen likewise greate & smale
> With a pretty thing they call
> Cony cony wonn the men
> Loe was the only Cupid then

These verses appear impossibly inappropriate for their singer and incongruous with the dramatic situation at this point in *The Witch*. While they may not be proper to that play as dramatic fiction, they are quite possibly germane to it as topical satire on Frances Howard and Robert Carr. The entertainment which Middleton wrote for their wedding festivities was, after all, a *Masque of Cupids*, performed at Merchant Taylors' Hall on 4 January 1614 (see *Works*, p. 1027). Two days later, the Banqueting Hall at Whitehall gave place to the performance of a *Masque of Flowers*, for which the music was composed by John Wilson, then still in his teens. Wilson's responsibility for the musical setting of 'In a Maiden Time Professed' is proclaimed in BODLEIAN. This attribution seems secure: Wilson, who spent part of the interregnum as Professor of Music in the University of Oxford, himself presented the manuscript volume (Bodleian MS Mus.b.1) to the Bodleian Library—on condition that its contents were to remain unexamined during his lifetime! The provenance of the volume is also some assurance both of the authenticity of the second and third verses of the song and of the occasion for which they were first written.

2.1.142 the] CRANE (yᵉ)

2.1.143.1-2 [*with watermen carrying provisions*]] THIS EDITION; *not in* CRANE. It would be possible for Aberzanes to enter alone and unencumbered and then address his commands offstage. It is preferable, however, that he make his entrance with at least two well-laden supernumeraries: at 2.1.143-5 Francisca comments on Aberzanes's entourage and on his baggage, on which Antonio also remarks at 2.1.150 and 156.

2.1.146 into th'] CRANE (into'th')

2.1.150 you're] CRANE (y'ar). Also at 2.2.123, 3.2.93, 3.2.149, and 4.2.79.

2.1.176 You're] CRANE (You'are). Also at 2.1.184

2.1.177 healt' varray well] THIS EDITION; heale-varray-well CRANE; heale varray well SCOTT; heal varray well DYCE; heal verray well CORBIN-SEDGE. Any phonetic approximation of pseudo-Scottish would do, and the phonier the better.

2.1.178 ANTONIO] The margin of CRANE gives the letter an eponymous heading as 'Letter.' but does not assign it to any speaker. Editors since SCOTT have required it to be read out by its addressee, Antonio.

2.1.193 to th'] CRANE (to'th). The even more than usually high density of contractions in this speech may perhaps be taken to indicate affectation in its utterance.

2.1.194 ne'er] CRANE (ne'ur)

2.1.203 at] CRANE (at')

2.1.210 he's no] CRANE (ha's no); he's not SCOTT; has no DYCE. The reading given by SCOTT makes an unnecessary emendation, while that given by DYCE is ungrammatical.

2.1.224 red sighs] CRANE (redd-sighes); sighs bred SCOTT, *conj.*

2.1.233 I've done't...this's a less] CRANE (I'ha' don't...this' a lesse)

2.2.6 Eat] CRANE (eate); ate SCOTT. While it might assist a reader unfamiliar with obsolete verb forms, the emendation would be inaudible in performance, at least by a British actor.

2.2.14 bouts] CRANE; boughts DYCE. Both readings being semantically possible, both would be audible in onstage utterance.

2.2.31 nethermost] CORBIN-SEDGE; hethermost CRANE; hithermost DYCE. The reading in CRANE is quite clear, but the emendation proposed by CORBIN-SEDGE is confirmed by the passage in Scot's *Discoverie of Witchcraft* (VI, 7) which is the source for this speech.

2.2.32 pest'lence] CRANE (pestlence)

2.2.77 was] CRANE; were SCOTT

2.2.98 retain'st] CRANE (retainst)

2.2.107 It's] CRANE ('Thas)

2.2.108 has't not] CRANE (ha'st-not)

2.2.110 flutt'ring] CRANE (fluttring)

2.2.116 competent] CRANE (computent)

2.2.118 soe'er] CRANE (so ere)

2.2.124 you'd] CRANE (you'll'd). Also at 2.2.125, 2.3.36 and 5.1.34.

2.2.125 ruled] SCOTT; rude CRANE

2.2.134 Wilt hear] CRANE (wil't heare); wilt have STEEVENS

2.2.136 snarer] CRANE; suarer STEEVENS

2.3.3 OLD WOMAN] SCOTT; Wom. CRANE

2.3.7 ne'er] CRANE (nev'r). Also at 2.3.8, 3.2.4, 3.2.137, 4.1.68, 5.1.73, and 5.1.77.

2.3.21 Give] CRANE ('Give); SCOTT (Give)

2.3.31 probably] CRANE; properly SCOTT

2.3.46 wi' th' least] CRANE (with'least); with 'least STEEVENS; with least DYCE; with' least ESCHE. Although most modernized editions have followed DYCE in excising the apostrophe after the preposition in CRANE, its enunciation would be both audible and, within an idiomatic phrase requiring the definite article, significant. The contraction is clarified for the reader by the insertion of another apostrophe.

2.3.50 STABLEBOY] THIS EDITION; Boy. CRANE. Also at 2.3.52 and 2.3.53.

3.1.0.1 Tertius] CRANE (Tercius)

3.1.2 I'd] CRANE (I'had). Also at 4.3.85.

3.1.39 For...methinks] An entrance for Gaspero has been cancelled after this line in CRANE.

3.1.39 Thou'st] CRANE. Also at 3.2.195 and 5.1.24.

3.2.23 city-tuck] CRANE; city-truck BULLEN conj. BULLEN's tentative emendation increases the insult—'truck' = 'trash'—but mitigates the metaphor.

3.2.32 at] CRANE (at'); at the STEEVENS

3.2.59 her] STEEVENS; here CRANE

3.2.75 you're] CRANE (you'ar). Also at 4.2.38 and 4.2.68.

3.2.89 travailed, travailld] CRANE (travaild, travaild); travail'd, travail'd STEEVENS; travelled, travelled DYCE. The interpretation proposed by DYCE has been adopted by all modernizing editors. However, as both participles make sense, each is a possible usage, and each audibly implies a quibble on the other, it seems preferable to retain the reading of CRANE.

3.2.106 you've] CRANE (yoᵂ ha')

3.2.115 fine] STEEVENS; five CRANE

3.2.117 hast'ning] CRANE (hastning)

3.2.176 Till] CRANE ('till). All other occurrences of the word in CRANE lack the initial apostrophe.

3.2.218 I'd] CRANE (I'll'd). Also at 4.2.86 and 4.3.59.

3.3.0.1 Hoppo and Stadlin] THIS EDITION; witches CRANE; Stadlin, Hoppo, with the other Witches, preparing for their midnight journey through the Air LAMB; Stadlin, Hoppo and other Witches SCOTT; [two] Witches ESCHE; [Stadlin, Hoppo, three other] Witches CORBIN-SEDGE; Witches [Stadlin, Hoppo, Puckle, Hellwain] SCHAFER. In CORBIN-SEDGE this direction is amplified by notes identifying the three as 'Hellwain, Puckle and one unnamed witch' and pointing to 5.2.40 as proof 'that [Hecate] is habitually accompanied by "five sisters"'. Whatever Hecate's line implies about her social habits, the dialogue subsequent to her entrance in this scene (as before in 1.2) requires only that she be accompanied by Hoppo and Stadlin, both of whom must speak before she sends them off at 3.3.14. Other witches may enter and exit with them, but Hoppo and Stadlin alone are needed.

3.3.0.1–3 [through one door...unnoticed]] That Firestone does not come onstage with the others is implied by the last sentence of his first speech within the scene. That he is equipped with a basket or similar conveyance is required by his tally of necromantic fauna and flora at 3.3.23–32.

3.3.10 screech-owl] CRANE (schreich-owle). In YALE, CHETWIN, and CLARK, a stage direction 'A shriek like an owl' is placed after the line 'There to meet with Macbeth' in the first of the witches' scenes. In so far as Davenant's stage direction can be taken as his re-presentation of Middleton's line here, then the sound effect affords some further evidence that the Restoration adapter of Macbeth had access to more of The Witch than just the songs. However, owls being fairly standard equipment for witches in visual representations of them, Davenant's stage direction may be without textual significance for The Witch. Its theatrical significance for his adaptation of Macbeth is obvious: the owl's shriek punctuates the first naming of Macbeth.

3.3.14.1 [Exeunt Stadlin and Hoppo]] ESCHE; not in CRANE; The other witches mount LAMB; They ascend SCOTT; Exeunt all the Witches except Hecate DYCE

3.3.18 after it] CRANE; affer'd STEEVENS; offer'd LAMB, who notes 'Probably the true reading is "after 't".'

3.3.23 hast] CRANE (ha'st)

3.3.28 Here's...thee] In CRANE, this line is somewhat squeezed in between its immediate predecessor and successor, with the result that it is at first unclear which speech heading governs it. The fact that in CRANE it stands as a complete line on its own does establish that its seven syllables are to be uttered by the speaker (Hecate) of the regular decasyllabic line before it rather than the speaker (Firestone) of the six syllables which comprise the line following it. It is, however, assigned to Firestone in STEEVENS, REED, LAMB, SCOTT, and DYCE; but editors since DREES-DE VOCHT have recognized it as a continuation of Hecate's speech.

3.3.38 there] CORBIN-SEDGE; they CRANE; (omitted) LAMB

3.3.38.1 Song] CRANE; Sing Within. Come away, come away, &c. JAGGARD; Musick & song | Heccat, Heccat, Heccat, oh come away YALE; Musick, and a Song. CADEMAN; Musick and song. Heccate, Heccate, Heccate! Oh come away CHETWIN, CLARK; Song in the Air LAMB; SONG [in the air above] SCOTT; Song above DYCE; The Song WELLS-TAYLOR

3.3.39 VOICES [from off-stage or above]] THIS EDITION; in the aire CRANE; Machine descends | 1 Sing wᵗʰin YALE; Sing within.1 CADEMAN; Sing Within. [Machine descends CHETWIN, CLARK; Voice. [Above.] ELLIS; [Voices.] (in the air.) CORBIN-SEDGE; Spirits [within] WELLS-TAYLOR; First Spirit BROOKE; [Voices of witches] (in the air)] SCHAFER. The attempt to assign a local habitation and name to each line of this song is above all an exercise in editorial ingenuity and theatrical imagination. Some guidance is given by the way the lines of the song are placed on the page in CRANE, and some musical hints are given by (it is thought) Robert Johnson in BULL and TWICE. As song manuscripts, neither BULL nor TWICE distributes the song, and neither localizes its utterance. However, the melody given in them is at points suggestive in pitch, tempo, or phrasing of text.

3.3.40 O] BULL, TWICE, YALE, CADEMAN, CHETWIN, CLARK; not in CRANE. The 'O' is obviously an embellishment for musical effect: the note on which it falls in the song manuscripts is marked out by its pitch and duration.

3.3.41 HECATE] CRANE, YALE, CHETWIN, CLARK; 2. CADEMAN

3.3.41–3 I come...I may] CRANE, BULL; I come I come I come wᵗʰ all the speede I may TWICE; I come I come with all the speed I may YALE; I come, I come, with all the speed I may | I come, I come, with all the speed I may CADEMAN; I come, I come, with all the speed I may | With all the speed I may CHETWIN, CLARK

3.3.44 Stadlin] CRANE, TWICE; Stadling BULL, YALE, CADEMAN, CHETWIN, CLARK. In CADEMAN this question is assigned to '1.'

3.3.44 VOICE [from off-stage or above]] THIS EDITION; in the aire CRANE; 3. CADEMAN; 2. YALE, CHETWIN, CLARK; [Above.] LAMB; [Voice above.] DYCE; Voice. [Above.] ELLIS; [Voice.] (in the air.) CORBIN-SEDGE; In the air ESCHE; Spirit [within] WELLS-TAYLOR; Second Spirit BROOKE; [Stadlin] in the air SCHAFER

3.3.44 HECATE] CRANE, YALE, CHETWIN, CLARK; 1. CADEMAN

3.3.44 VOICE [from off-stage or above]] THIS EDITION; in the aire CRANE; 3. YALE, CHETWIN, CLARK; 4. CADEMAN; [Above.] LAMB; [Voice above.] DYCE; Voice. [Above.] ELLIS; [Voices.] (in the air.) CORBIN-SEDGE; In the air ESCHE; Another spirit [within] WELLS-TAYLOR; Third Spirit BROOKE; [Puckle] in the air SCHAFER

3.3.45 Hoppo] CRANE, TWICE; Hope BULL; Hopper YALE, CADEMAN, CHETWIN, CLARK

3.3.45 Hellwain] CRANE; Hellway BULL, TWICE, YALE, CADEMAN, CHETWIN, CLARK

3.3.46–7 We...count] In YALE, CHETWIN, and CLARK these lines are assigned to '1.'

3.3.46–53 We...news] In CADEMAN these lines are assigned to '1.': as the heading is unnecessarily repeated at l. 49, the intervening omission of a heading for Hecate at l. 48 looks to have been a typographical rather than editorial error.

3.3.46 lack...lack] CRANE, BULL, TWICE; want...want YALE, CADEMAN, CHETWIN, CLARK

3.3.48 then] CRANE, BULL, TWICE, YALE, CADEMAN, CLARK; the CHETWIN

3.3.48 I will...I mount] A single line in CRANE, this is repeated in BULL, TWICE, YALE, CADEMAN, CHETWIN, CLARK, BROOKE. In the Restoration texts the repetition of the line is abbreviated: 'I will but 'Noint &c' YALE; 'I will &c' CADEMAN; and 'I will but, &c' CHETWIN, CLARK.

3.3.48.1 *A spirit like a cat descends*] CRANE; not in BULL, TWICE, YALE, CADEMAN, CHETWIN, nor CLARK; *A spirit descends in the shape of a cat* SCOTT; MALKIN *a spirit like a cat descends* CORBIN-SEDGE. In WELLS-TAYLOR, the reading from CRANE is amplified with the further direction '[*Spirits appear above*]', this amplification being refined to '*The other three Spirits appear above*' in BROOKE.

3.3.49 VOICE [*from off-stage or above*]] THIS EDITION; above CRANE; 1. YALE, CADEMAN, CHETWIN, CLARK; [Above.] LAMB; [Voice above.] DYCE; Voice. [Above.] ELLIS; [Malkin.] (above) CORBIN-SEDGE; First Spirit BROOKE; [Voices of Witches] *above* SCHAFER

3.3.49 There's one comes down] CRANE; here comes one BULL, BROOKE; heare comes one downe TWICE; here comes down one YALE, CHETWIN, CLARK; Here comes one, it is CADEMAN

3.3.49 dues] CRANE, BULL, TWICE; due YALE, CADEMAN, CHETWIN, CLARK. Evidently a Restoration regularization.

3.3.51 CAT] THIS EDITION. Placed in the left margin of CRANE, the stage direction for the descent of the cat appears to be doing double duty as a speech heading for l. 51. (Such is clearly the case at l. 59, headed *Hec. going up* in left margin of CRANE.) In CORBIN-SEDGE ll. 49–52 are assigned to the cat. In BROOKE the cat is assigned only the last two syllables of ll. 51, 53 and 55, as echoes.

3.3.52 VOICE [*from off-stage or above*]] THIS EDITION; First Spirit BROOKE

3.3.52 the air's] CRANE, BULL, CADEMAN, STEEVENS; ye aire TWICE; th'aire YALE; th'air's CHETWIN, CLARK, SCOTT

3.3.53–6 O, art...the flight] In CHETWIN and CLARK these lines, with ll. 3.3.59–60 appended to them, are assigned to '2.'

3.3.53 [CAT] THIS EDITION; not in CRANE

3.3.53 What news, what news?] CRANE, TWICE; wth nues, wth nues BULL; what news? YALE, CADEMAN, CHETWIN, CLARK

3.3.54 [HECATE] THIS EDITION; not in CRANE; Spirit LAMB

3.3.54–6 All goes still...the flight] In YALE and CADEMAN these lines, with 3.3.59–60 appended to them, are assigned to '2.'

3.3.54 still to] CRANE, BULL; well to TWICE; for YALE; fair for CADEMAN, CHETWIN, CLARK

3.3.55 VOICE [*from off-stage or above*]] THIS EDITION; not in CRANE

3.3.55 [CAT] THIS EDITION; not in CRANE

3.3.55 Refuse, refuse] CRANE, BULL, TWICE; refuse YALE, CADEMAN, CHETWIN, CLARK

3.3.56 Now] CRANE, TWICE, YALE, CADEMAN, CHETWIN, CLARK; no BULL

3.3.56 I am] CRANE, TWICE, BULL, YALE, CADEMAN; I'm CHETWIN, CLARK

3.3.57–8 Hark...language] CRANE. Firestone, whose line this is, does not appear in any version of *Macbeth*.

3.3.59 HECATE (*going up* [*with Cat*)] SCOTT, *subst.* (Hecate [Ascending with the Spirit.]); Hecate going up CRANE; 3. CADEMAN; Hecate. (Going up [with Malkin.]) CORBIN-SEDGE. In WELLS-TAYLOR the bare assignment to Hecate is amplified by the direction, *She ascends with the spirits and sings*, immediately after the line.

3.3.59 Now I go, now I fly] CRANE, CADEMAN; Now I go, o now I fly TWICE; Now I go and now I fly BULL, YALE, CHETWIN, CLARK

3.3.60 Malkin] CRANE, BULL, TWICE, YALE, CADEMAN; Malking CHETWIN, CLARK

3.3.61 what a dainty pleasure 'tis] CRANE; what a dainty pleasure's this BULL, YALE, CHETWIN, CLARK; what a dainty pleasure is this TWICE; what dainty pleasure 'tis SCOTT. In WELLS-TAYLOR the speech heading requires [*Spirits and Hecate*] for this line (in the reading from CRANE). In BROOKE (where the reading given by BULL is, as usual, preferred), this line and the next two are assigned to *Third Spirit*.

3.3.62 To ride in the air] CRANE, BULL, TWICE; To saile i'th'aire YALE, CADEMAN, CHETWIN, CLARK

3.3.63 When] CRANE, BULL, TWICE; While YALE, CADEMAN, CHETWIN, CLARK

3.3.64 And sing and dance and toy and kiss] CRANE; And feast and sing and toy and kiss BULL, TWICE; To sing, to toy and kiss CADEMAN; To sing, to toy, to dance and kiss YALE, CHETWIN, CLARK

3.3.66 seas, our mistress'] CRANE; seas, our cristall/mistris TWICE; seas and misty BULL; hills and misty YALE, CHETWIN, CLARK; misty hills and CADEMAN. From STEEVENS on, all modernizing editors of *The Witch* have accepted the reading of CRANE: an image of seas as the fountains of the moon presents no difficulty within a scene that has begun with a personification of the moon as a gallant and within a play that is preoccupied with the three faces of Diana. See Introduction and Commentary.

3.3.67 steeple] THIS EDITION; steep CRANE; steeples, BULL, TWICE, YALE, CADEMAN, CHETWIN, CLARK. In DYCE, copied *verbatim* by BULLEN, the reading from CRANE is given but then, in a footnote, taken away in favour of 'steeples'. Both the metre of the verse line and the melody of its musical setting demand the second syllable. The emendation suggested here is the minimal correction of an easily imagined slip.

3.3.69–72 [ALL] [*from off-stage or above*] No ring...can reach] THIS EDITION; *No Ring of Bells &c.* above CRANE, where it falls immediately after l. 72. All previous modernized editions of *The Witch* have resolved that Hecate sing everything from 3.3.59 ('Now I go, now I fly') through 3.3.68 ('Or cannon's throat, our height can. reach'), and then that the last four lines of her solo be repeated by the massed spirits or witches 'above'. The direction in CRANE can, however, be construed as governing those lines in their first and only utterance rather than as requiring their repetition. The other stage directions localizing lines of the song 'above' or 'in the air' are all inscribed to the right of those lines (which are marked by brackets) but within the box-rule which surrounds every page. Here, however, Crane appears not to have left himself enough room for this layout. Neither BULL nor TWICE repeats these four lines, for which Johnson's setting changes tempo and then builds to a firm musical conclusion. Nor are they repeated in YALE, CADEMAN (which heads them '*Cho.*'), CHETWIN, or CLARK.

3.3.70 howls] CRANE, TWICE, YALE, CADEMAN, CHETWIN, CLARK; noise BULL

3.3.70 no yelps] CRANE; or elps BULL; nor yelps TWICE, YALE,
CADEMAN, CHETWIN, CLARK

3.3.71 not] CRANE; nor TWICE, BULL, YALE, CADEMAN, CHETWIN,
CLARK

3.3.72 Or cannon's throat] CRANE (Or cannons throat), BULL;
nor cannons throat TWICE; Nor cannons throats YALE, CADE-
MAN, CHETWIN, CLARK. Another Restoration regularization.

4.1.9 aqua vitae] CRANE (aqua-vite)

4.1.45 I have] CRANE (I have'); I 'have GREG–WILSON (conj). The
conjecture of GREG–WILSON would produce the form which
CRANE most often adopts for 'I've': see notes to 1.2.53,
2.1.233, and 4.2.116. However, as there is no metrical need
for a contraction in this pentameter line, the apostrophe is
probably superfluous rather than stray, and the conjecture
can be rejected.

4.1.59 grievèd'st] CRANE (grievedst)

4.1.68 pray'rs] CRANE (praires)

4.1.90 of honour] In CRANE 'horror' has been cancelled between
these words.

4.2.27 he] CRANE. Attempting to 'make sense of an otherwise
incomprehensible narrative,' SCHAFER emends this pronoun
to the feminine nominative singular and construes it as
referring to Isabella. However, with the mere introduction of
an aside, the masculine pronoun in CRANE can be construed
as referring to Fernando, and the rest of the scene confirms
this construction: Florida is sent off to waylay Isabella with
tales of Antonio's intimacy with the house and therefore
with her (Florida's) own liaison with Antonio; Isabella enters
and indicates that Florida has just told her of Antonio's
familiarity with the house and with Florida herself; and
Fernando, presenting himself, in his own house, as landlord
of a somewhat dubious establishment, at first denies, then
confirms, Florida's story before leading Isabella off to Florida's
chamber and a bed in which the lady expects to find her
husband, Antonio.

4.2.59 feed] GREG–WILSON (conj.); feele CRANE

4.2.74 ent'ring] CRANE (entring). Also at 5.3.27.

4.2.79 on's] STEEVENS; o'n's CRANE

4.2.116 I've] CRANE (I ha'). Also at 4.3.98.

4.2.118 blessed] CRANE (blessd)

4.2.124 e'er] CRANE (ev'r)

4.2.125 does] CRANE (do's). Also at 4.3.11.

4.3.0.1 [above,] in her chamber] The location of Francisca's
chamber is implied by 4.3.22–4.3.22.1 and required by both
4.3.56–7 and also 4.3.99. The stage directions of more than
fifty plays known to have been performed at the Blackfriars
Theatre require action to be set on an upper stage; and such
action above was usually—as here in The Witch—related to
action on the platform below. (See Smith, 1964, 363.)

4.3.2 fortnight's] SCOTT; forthrights CRANE

4.3.17 maidservants] SCOTT (maid-servants); Maides-servants
CRANE

4.3.20.1 [She produces key]] Francisca's production of a key,
probably from her own pocket, is clearly required by her
announcement of its discovery.

4.3.21.1 [undressed, below]] Gaspero's appearance, probably
wearing only his shirt, is indicated by 4.3.30.

4.3.22.1 [She drops key onto stage behind him]] Those previous
editors who have commented on Francisca's half-line here
have construed it figuratively. The extended sense is unnecessary because the literal one obtains: the speaker is on the
upper level of the stage, whence she throws down an object,
the key which 4.3.20 has just put into her hand.

4.3.34.1 [armed, above]] That Antonio is armed—at least to
the extent of wearing sword and scabbard—is implied by
4.3.40 and required by 4.3.100. That he here enters above
is inferred from 4.3.35, the line immediately following this
his first entrance, which apparently requires Francisca to
hand a torch to him. This transfer, which quickly proves to
be of considerable iconographic consequence, demands that
Francisca and Antonio be on the same level when it is made.

4.3.36 his] In CRANE, the word appears to have been 'his',
overwritten to 'her'. All editors have preferred to take the
pronoun as referring to Gaspero rather than to Isabella.

4.3.40 FRANCISCA] CRANE; FLORIDA DYCE, CORBIN–SEDGE, SCHAFER.
In consequence of these editors' reassignment of this half-
-line, the utterance of both it and also Antonio's lines from
4.3.36.1–37 through at least 4.3.41 (or 4.3.46 in DYCE) has
to be moved offstage: this would be both acoustically difficult
and visually deleterious. (See Introduction and Commentary.)
Taking the exclamation to be an earnest attempt to hold
Antonio back from violence, the editorial emendation is
also unnecessary. Such an exclamation, prompted by her
brother's brandishing of his sword, would be quite suitable
for the pose of solicitude which Francisca has adopted.

4.3.47 She'd] CRANE (sh'ad). Also at 4.3.49.

4.3.51 burden's] CRANE (burthens)

4.3.54 it'd] CRANE (it'had)

4.3.68 ruinous] DYCE; ruynes CRANE; ruines STEEVENS; ruins
ESCHE

4.3.74 Ha'] THIS EDITION; The CRANE; Have SCHAFER. The manuscript reading is quite clear, the letter formation being
identical with the first three letters of 'then' [= 'than'] in
the immediately preceding line. Justifying an emendation
which deftly rescues the grammar, and with it the sense,
of the lines, SCHAFER suggests that 'The' in CRANE could be a
misreading of 'Ha''. That contracted form of the verb being
both orthographically plausible and metrically preferable, it
has been adopted here.

4.3.85 troth] CRANE (troth')

4.3.110 o'erflows] CRANE (ore-flowes)

5.1.0.2 Antonio] SCOTT; Sebastian CRANE. In STEEVENS the reading
of CRANE is retained here, and again for the speech headings
at 5.1.1 and 5.1.3, but a footnote makes the correction:
'Instead of sebastian, we should read antonio'. Subsequent
modernizing editors have all emended accordingly.

5.1.1 ANTONIO] STEEVENS; Seb. CRANE

5.1.3 ANTONIO] STEEVENS; Seb. CRANE

5.1.71 for't] STEEVENS; fo't CRANE

5.1.88 off] CRANE (of)

5.1.90.1 Enter Lord Governor] CRANE. In the editions of CORBIN–
SEDGE and of SCHAFER the Lord Governor enters with an
unspecified number of gentleman attendants. This amplification of his entrance—and then of both his exit and that
of Florida—is unnecessary. The only role for attendants in
this scene is to respond to the Lord Governor's command
(at ll. 108–9) that Florida be put under arrest. If Gaspero
escorts Florida offstage, however, that command is picked
up, and Gaspero himself is given an exit (something which
both CRANE and SCHAFER omit). Not required in this scene,
supernumeraries can come on for the witches' dance in the
next.

5.1.110 wear'st] CRANE (wearst)

5.1.113 LORD GOVERNOR] STEEVENS; Flo. CRANE All editors since
STEEVENS have given 5.1.113–14 to the Lord Governor. As
both claimants are making exits at this point, the fact
that the lines form a rhyming couplet strengthens neither

claim. The manuscript assignment is tempting: Florida has elsewhere (4.2.48–53) been given a speech informed by rigorously traditional standards of female sexual morality; and the utterance of this metaphor by a courtesan would neatly anticipate the final scene's disclosure of the identity of Almachildes's veiled partner. Moreover, Crane's errors of speech assignment are so few that it may be prudent to accept what he gives unless it is impossible. But on balance, the assignment of these lines to Florida, who has just announced that Isabella and 'Celio' are in bed together, is, even within *The Witch*, an impossible inconsistency. And as the Lord Governor has just been asserting his faith in his niece's sexual propriety, the lines can appropriately be spoken by him.

5.1.132   wicked'st] CRANE (wickedst)

5.2.0.1–2   [*with … cauldron*]] THIS EDITION; *not in* CRANE; [a cauldron in the centre] DYCE. By 5.2.54, a cauldron must be set for Hecate's necromantic cuisine. It could be discovered on an inner stage; but since it is to be circled during the charm song, it is better placed downstage. If it be so situated, then probably Firestone carries it on at the beginning of the scene. Its removal by Firestone at 5.2.84–6 would both clear the stage floor for the witches' dance and also occasion a visual/verbal quibble on the word 'burden' in 5.2.85.

5.2.11   may possibly] CRANE; may possible STEEVENS; be possible LAMB

5.2.12   Here's] CRANE (Her's); REED (Here's)

5.2.25   *Vivaque … terra*] THIS EDITION, not in CRANE. The absence of this line from Hecate's quotation of Ovid's *Metamorphoses* (Book VII) occasioned some editorial comment from DYCE, amplified by ESCHE. The line is also missing from the passage as quoted in Jean Bodin's demonological treatise for French jurists, initially published in French as *La Demonomanie des Sorciers* (1580) and then in Latin as *De magorum demonomania* (1581). Since the line appears in the passage as quoted, and translated, in Scot's *Discoverie of Witchcraft* (XII, 6), DYCE and ESCHE inferred that Middleton had transcribed the passage from Bodin rather than from Scot. However, the fact that in *The Witch* the missing line of Latin gets glossed (as 'Whole earth's foundation bellow' at l. 30) within Hecate's self-translation suggests that the omission of the Ovidian line was not Middleton's, nor his source's, but Crane's. The absence of the same line from both Bodin's and Crane's texts is an entirely possible coincidence of errors in transmission: grammatically otiose bits of text are especially liable to copyist's oversights, and the Ovidian passage can be construed without the stray line. Moreover, the evidence of the manuscript suggests that in copying out *The Witch*, Crane encountered difficulties around this point. The page bearing the quotation appears to be a second attempt, the stub of a cancelled first attempt surviving in the binding. (See Textual Introduction.) And Crane's italic transcription of Hecate's Ovidian quotation looks as if it has been made later than, and been uncomfortably cramped by, his secretary-hand transcription of her Middletonian lines around it.

5.2.28   *Teque*] CRANE (*Teque*); *Te quoque* STEEVENS. Transforming an enclitic particle meaning 'and' into a word meaning 'also', the emendation of '-que' to 'quoque' matters more for metrics than it does for meaning. It is, however, most important for the question of the text from which Middleton transcribed the quotation: in both Ovid's *Metamorphoses* and Bodin's *Demonomania*, the line begins 'Te quoque'. In Scot's *Discoverie of Witchcraft* (XII, 7), however, it reads, as in the manuscript of *The Witch*, 'teque'.

5.2.37   power's] CRANE (powre's)

5.2.48   [*Exit Duchess*]] SCOTT, *not in* CRANE. The addition of an exit for the Duchess at this point has been accepted in all modernized editions since SCOTT. A case can be made for her to remain onstage: her exit can be comprehended within the final stage direction of this scene, and her next re-entry will be fully 60 lines into the next scene. Her presence through the Witches' Dance would swell numbers for this last exhibition of the coven, and it would also give visual reinforcement to the verbal association made by the informal, even intimate, terms of address between her and Hecate during the first part of the scene. On balance, however, it seems preferable that Duchess depart at this point: Hecate's conciliatory speech to the Duchess at ll. 40–8 appears to signal a dismissal, while her next, to Firestone at ll. 52–3, marks a sharp change of tone and pace.

5.2.50   t'other] CRANE (thother)

5.2.54   All … forsooth] After this line, LAMB adds a stage direction: 'The other Witches appear.'

5.2.62.1   *A Charm Song: about a vessel*] CRANE; *Musick and a Song. Black spirits, &C.* JAGGARD, CADEMAN (neither of whom gives any text for the song other than this title); *Musick and Song* YALE, CHETWIN, CLARK; A CHARM SONG. The Witches going about the Cauldron SCOTT

5.2.63–9   Black spirits … keep out] CRANE assigns all of this part of the song to Hecate. In YALE it is distributed among: *Hec[ate]* (5.2.63–4); *1 Witch* (5.2.65); *2 [Witch]* (5.2.66); *Hec[ate]* (5.2.67); *Chor[us]* (5.2.68–9). In CHETWIN and in CLARK it is distributed among: *Hec[ate]* (5.2.63–4); *I[st] Witch* (5.2.65–7); and *Chor[us]* (5.2.68–9). With *4th Witch* replacing *Ist Witch*, this distribution is also adopted in WELLS–TAYLOR.

5.2.65   Titty, Tiffin] CRANE; Tiffin, tiffin YALE, CHETWIN, CLARK

5.2.66   Fire-drake, Pucky] CRANE; Fire drake ˏ Puckey YALE; Fire-drake ˏ Puckey CHETWIN, CLARK. The Restoration punctuation has the same grammatical effect here as is noted below for the first half of 5.3.67 and is rejected for the same reason.

5.2.67   Liard, Robin] STEEVENS; Liand, Robin CRANE; Lyer Robin YALE, CHETWIN; Liar Robin CLARK. The Restoration emendation and punctuation put the first word in this line into an adjectival relationship with the second. Knowledge of Middleton's source, however, both confirms the emendation given by STEEVENS and also leaves no doubt but that the words are to be construed as names in series. See Commentary on 1.2.1–4.

5.2.68   Round … about] CRANE; A round a round a round about about YALE; A round, a round, about, about CHETWIN, CLARK

5.2.69.1   *Enter Witches*] THIS EDITION; not in CRANE, which gives no entrance for the witches in this scene, nor does the manuscript anywhere clearly indicate their number. Modernizing editors since LAMB have put an entrance for witches at 5.2.53–4, cued by Hecate's question and Firestone's reply there. However, Firestone's assertion that Stadlin and all the other witches are 'at hand' need not mean that they are already onstage, or stepping onto it, but only that they are near. Rather than upstage Firestone's collection of ingredients, this edition prefers to delay the witches' entrance until the middle of the charm, cued by 5.2.68–9. As for the number of witches to enter the scene, the editions of CORBIN-SEDGE, ESCHE and SCHAFER, taking up Hecate's reference to her 'five sisters' at 5.2.40, bring on five of them. Hecate and Firestone excepted, only two witches are required to open their mouths in this scene, as is the case in the other witch scenes. (In both of those other scenes, however, CRANE identifies the speaking witches as Hoppo and Stadlin, while in this last scene CRANE reduces them to anonymity as Witch

1 and Witch 2.) Middleton and/or Crane being presumed to have let the number of mute witches be determined by the availability of supernumeraries, this edition has also left them untallied.

5.2.70 [STADLIN]] 1. Witch CRANE; I. YALE, CHETWIN, CLARK. Also at 5.2.74.

5.2.71 Put in that, O] CRANE; O put in that YALE, CHETWIN, CLARK

5.2.72 [HOPPO]] 2. CRANE, YALE, CHETWIN, CLARK

5.2.72 libbard's bane] CRANE; lizards brain YALE, CHETWIN, CLARK. The Restoration emendation may have been prompted by Hecate's demand at 5.2.52 and Firestone's response at 5.2.56. If so, the emendation suggests that Davenant had access to more of the text of *The Witch* than the songs alone: see Textual Introduction.

5.2.73 again] CRANE; a grain YALE, CHETWIN, CLARK. The Restoration emendation has been adopted in CORBIN–SEDGE, WELLS–TAYLOR, and SCHAFER. Either reading being grammatically, dramatically and poetically possible, the reading of CRANE is preferable on grounds not just of priority but also of plausibility. The basic unit of all European systems for the measurement of weight, a grain represents a mere 1/7000th of a pound avoirdupois or 1/5760th of an apothecary's pound. The recipes in the *Pharmacopoeia Londinensis* (1618) rarely call for any measure less than a dram (60 grains): even imaginary witches should not be pressed to greater pharmaceutical precision than the professionals. To put the objection differently, if the emendation is adopted, the proportion of human flesh to libbard's bane in the cauldron would be 1420:1 apothecaries' weight or 2625:2 avoirdupois weight.

5.2.74 The...the] CRANE; Here's...here's YALE, CHETWIN, CLARK

5.2.75 [HOPPO]] 2. CRANE. In YALE, CHETWIN, and CLARK, I[st Witch] speaks this line as well as the one immediately preceding it; 2[nd Witch] takes over 5.2.76; and Hec[ate] gets 5.2.77.

5.2.75 Those] CRANE; That YALE, CHETWIN, CLARK. The Restoration emendation, substituting a relative pronoun for a plural demonstrative one, has been required by the redistribution of the couplet: 5.2.75 becomes a continuation of 5.2.74 instead of a rejoinder to it.

5.2.75 younker] CRANE (yonker); charm grow YALE, CHETWIN, CLARK

5.2.76 Put in. There's all, and rid] CRANE; Put in all these, 'twill raise YALE, CHETWIN, CLARK (in all of which this line is assigned to 2[nd Witch])

5.2.77 ounces of the] CRANE; ounces of a YALE, CHETWIN, CLARK. In CRANE, the definite article governs an ingredient mentioned at 5.3.58–60: the absence of that earlier reference from the dramatic context of this song in the Restoration necessitated the emendation to an indefinite article.

5.2.78 ALL] CRANE (where the word is placed not as a speech heading but as the beginning of the line of the song); Chor.[us] YALE, CHETWIN, CLARK

5.2.78-9 Round...keep out] SCHAFER; Round: around: around &c CRANE; A round, around, &c YALE, CHETWIN, CLARK

5.2.81 't hath] CRANE ('thath)

5.2.88.1 Witches' Dance] A pair of Witches' Dances survive in several different manuscript versions, most notably British Library Additional MS 10444. Although John Cutts (1954, 191–3) argued that the second of these dances should be associated with *The Witch* rather than with *Masque of Queens*, both are now thought to have been composed (by Robert Johnson) for Ben Jonson's masque (Sabol, 1978, 568 [Notes 76-7], 599 [Notes 76-9]). Current opinion about the genesis of the witches' dances leaves open the hypothesis that one of them might have been recycled for Thomas Middleton's play. However, the manuscript dances, like Jonson's evocation of the *mise en scène* for *Masque of Queens* in 1609, cannot be taken as more than an ensemble of possibilities for the performance of *The Witch* in 1616.

5.3.0.1-2 Florida...Francisca, Aberzanes] Florida, Aberzanes CRANE; omitted by DYCE. After Antonio sends Francisca and Aberzanes packing at 5.1.51–3, neither of them speaks again, nor is either spoken to. Their banishment from the final scene in DYCE is, however, theatrically pointless: it would not secure any further possibilities for doubling. Francisca has been alarmingly silent throughout her most recent appearance onstage (5.1.29–5.1.53.1): any explanation of her silence there, and of the silence of both herself and Aberzanes here, has to be left to directorial discretion.

5.3.5 Where'er] CRANE (where ere)

5.3.63 HERMIO] In CRANE this speech heading is an overwriting of 'Duch', whose entrance is being announced.

5.3.65 Ends] CORBIN–SEDGE; Ever CRANE. In the manuscript this word begins a seventeen-syllable line which editorial ingenuity has been unable to construe in a way that befits English syntax and dramatic situation. As this hypermetrical nonsense occurs just two lines after the self-corrected error in the speech heading at 5.3.65, it does appear that CRANE was making—or meeting—mistakes in this passage. DYCE suspected a lacuna after 'now'. The emendation proposed by CORBIN–SEDGE assumes an at least equally plausible error: moreover, it makes the line make sense.

5.3.67 prince's] THIS EDITION; princesse CRANE; princess' SCOTT. The manuscript reading can be taken as the possessive form of either 'princess' or 'prince'. The latter (unlike 'princess') could refer to either male or female, and this androgyny sustains the semantic ambiguity of 'to match'—(i) 'to equal' (ii) 'to marry'.

5.3.68 lives] CRANE (lifes)

5.3.83 thee] CRANE; there SCOTT

5.3.85 be'st] CRANE (beesst)

5.3.93 Perform] STEEVENS (performe); performes CRANE

5.3.122 scarves] CRANE (scarffes)

STAGE DIRECTIONS

[Preceding the play:]

The Sceane Rauenna.

The Persons:

Duke
L. Gouerno^r.
Sebastian} Contracted to Isabella.
Fernando} his Frend.
Antonio} Husband to | Isabella.
Abberzanes} a Gent. neither honest, wise, nor | valiant.
Almachildes} a fantasticall | Gentleman.
Gaspero, & Hermio} Seruants to | Antonio
Fire-Stone} ye Clowne & | Heccats Son.

[Column break]

The Persons.

Duchesse.
Isabella} Neice to ye Gouerno^r.
Francisca} Antonio's Sister
Amoretta.} ye Duchess-woman.
Florida} a Curtezan.
Heccat} ye cheif Witch
Stadlin | Hoppo} witches
other Witches & Seruants} Mutes.

1.1.0.1–2 *Actus Primus: | Sce^a. Prima. Enter Sebastian, & Fernando.*
1.1.23.1 Ex^t
1.1.36.1 *Enter | Gaspero, & Seru^t.* (right, opposite 1.1.35–6)
1.1.41 Exit
1.1.45.1 *Enter | Florida.* (right, opposite 1.1.44–5)
1.1.68 Exit
1.1.75.1 *Enter | Almachildes | & Amoretta* (right, opposite 1.1.75–6)
1.1.95.1–3 *Enter | Duke, Duchess, | L. Gouerno^r, Antonio, & | Isabella | Francisca.* (right, opposite 1.1.91–5)
1.1.148.1 Ex^t
1.1.149.1 Exit
1.2.0.1–2 *Sce^a. 2^a. Enter Heccat: & other witches: (with | Properties, and Habitts fitting.)*
1.2.62.1 *Enter | Fire-Stone* (right, opposite 1.2.62[a])
1.2.101.1 Exit
1.2.101.2 *Enter Sebastian* (right, opposite 1.2.101[b])
1.2.178.1 Exit
1.2.193.1 *Enter Almachildes* (top right, above 1.2.191–3)
1.2.229.1–2 *She Coniures: And | Enter a Catt (playing | on a Fidle) and | Spiritts (wth Meate)* (right, opposite 1.2.229–31)
1.2.232.1 Ex^t
1.2.236 Exit
1.2.236.1 *Finis Actus pri^i*
2.1.0.1–2 *Actus Secundus. | Sce^a. pri^a. Enter Antonio, & Gaspero.*
2.1.13 Exit
2.1.24.1 *Enter | Francisca* (right, opposite 2.1.24)
2.1.33.1 Exit
2.1.64.1 *Enter | Isabella* (right, oppoisite 2.1.64[a])
2.1.109.1 *Enter | Antonio* (right, opposite 2.1.109)
2.1.130.1 *Song* (centred)
2.1.143.1–2 *Enter | Aberzanes* (right, opposite 2.1.143)
2.1.167.1 *Enter | Sebastian & | Gentleman* (right, opposite 2.1.167[b]–168)
2.1.204.1 Ex^t.
2.1.209.1 Ex^t

2.1.228.1 *Enter | Gaspero, & L. | Gouerno^r.* (right, opposite 2.1.228–9)
2.2.0.1 *Sce^a. 2^a. Enter Almachildes.*
2.2.36.1 *Enter | Amoretta.* (right, opposite 2.2.35–6)
2.2.46.1 Exit
2.2.56.1 *Enter | Duchesse* (right, opposite 2.2.56)
2.2.114 Exit
2.2.118 *Enter | Almachildes* (right, opposite 2.2.114)
2.2.142.1 Ex^t.
2.3.0.1 *Sce^a. 3^a. Enter Abberzanes: & an old woman.*
2.3.22 *Enter | Francisca.* (right, opposite 2.3.22)
2.3.55 Ex^t.
2.3.55.1 *Finis Acte. 2^i.* (right, below 2.3.55)
3.1.0.1–3 *Actus Tercius | Sce^a. pri^a. Enter Duchesse, leading Almachildes | (blindfold)*
3.1.39 *Enter | Gaspero* (cancelled; right, opposite 3.1.39[a])
3.1.58 Ex^t
3.2.0.1 *Sce^a. 2^a. Enter Gaspero, & Florida*
3.2.13.2 *Enter | Sebastian* (right, opposite 3.2.13)
3.2.29.1 *Enter | Gaspero* (right, opposite 3.2.29)
3.2.47.1 *Enter | Isabella* (right, opposite 3.2.47[b])
3.2.50.1 Ex^t
3.2.62.1 *Enter | Gaspero* (bottom right, after 3.2.60)
3.2.74.1 *Enter | Abberzanes | & Francisca* (right, opposite 3.2.73–4)
3.2.90.1 Exit
3.2.113 Exit
3.2.141.1 *Enter | Antonio* (right, opposite 3.2.141[a])
3.2.168.1 *Enter | Isabella* (right, opposite 3.2.166[b])
3.2.179 Exit
3.2.180.1 *Enter | Sebastian* (right, opposite 3.2.179–80)
3.2.231 Ex^t
3.3.1–3 *Sce^a. 3^a. Enter Heccat: Witches, & Fire-stone*
3.3.38.1 *Song:* (placed to left, at 3.3.39, as speech heading within song)
3.3.39–40 *in ye aire* (right, pointed by bracket governing 3.3.39–40)
3.3.44 *in ye aire* (right, pointed by bracket governing 3.3.44)
3.3.44 *in ye aire* (right, pointed by bracket governing 3.3.45–7)
3.3.48.1 *aboue* (right, pointed by bracket governing 3.3.49–51)
3.3.48.1 *A spirit like | a Cat descends* (left, governed by bracket pointing to 3.3.51)
3.3.59 *Hec. going up* (left, governed by bracket pointing to 3.3.59)
3.3.68 *aboue* (after 3.3.72, at end of centred line 'No Ring of Bells &c.', to which it is referred by a bracket)
3.3.75 Exit
3.3.75.1 *Finis Actus Tercii* (right, below 3.3.75)
4.1.0.1–2 *Actus Quartus | Sce^a. pri^a. Enter Almachildes* (Crane appears to have started to misnumber the scene but has contrived to transform *sec* into *pri*.)
4.1.23.1 *Enter Duchess* (top right, above 4.1.24)
4.1.45.1 Exit
4.1.55.1 *Enter | L. Gouerno^r* (right, opposite 4.1.54–5)
4.1.87 Exit
4.1.96 Exit
4.2.0.1 *Sce^a. 2^a. Enter Sebastian, & Fernando*
4.2.22.1 *Enter | Florida.* (right, opposite 4.2.19–20)
4.2.67.2 *Enter Isab.* (right, below 4.2.67)
4.2.94.1 Ex^t

4.2.94.2 *Enter | Sebastian* (right, opposite 4.2.94)
4.2.111.1 *Enter | Isabella* (right, opposite 4.2.111)
4.2.125.1 Ex^t
4.3.0.1 *Sce^a. 3^a. Enter Francisca, in her Chamber.*)
4.3.21.1 *Enter | Gaspero.* (right, opposite 4.3.21–4.3.22.1[a])
4.3.34.1 *Enter | Antonio* (right, opposite 4.3.33–4)
4.3.104.1 *Enter | Hermio* (right, opposite 4.3.103–4)
4.3.111.1 Ex^t
4.3.111.2 *Finis Actus Quarti* (right, below 4.3.111)
5.1.0.1–3 *Actus Quintus. | Sce^a. pri^a. Enter Sebastian, & Aberzanes.*
5.1.69 *Enter Gaspero* (right, opposite 5.1.69[b])
5.1.90.1 *Enter | L. Gouerno^r.* (right, opposite 5.1.89)
5.1.95.1 *Enter | Florida* (right, opposite 5.1.95)
5.1.105 Exit
5.1.114 Exit

5.1.121.1 *Enter Isabella | & Sebastian* (right, opposite 5.1.121)
5.1.131.1 Ex^t
5.1.135 Exit
5.2.0.1–2 *Sce^a. 3^a. Enter Duchesse: Heccat. Firestone*
5.2.62.1 *A Charme Song: about a Vessell.* (centred)
5.2.88.1 *here they | Daunce ye witches | Dance & Ex^t.* (right, opposite and below 5.2.88)
5.3.0.1–3 *Sce^a. 4^a. Enter L. Gouerno^r. Isabella, [Antonio. (cancelled)] | , Florida, Francicsa: Abberzanes, Gaspero, | Hermio:*
5.3.62.1 *Enter | Duchess* (right, opposite 5.3.62)
5.3.80.1 *Duke is | discouerd* (right, opposite 5.3.80)
5.3.104.1 *Enter | Almachildes* (right, opposite 5.3.104[a])
5.3.114.1 *Enter | Amoretta* (right, opposite 5.3.115)
5.3.137 Exeunt
5.3.137.1 *Finis Actus Quinti* (below 5.3.137 and with a flourish under *Quinti*)

LINEATION NOTES

1.1.52–3 Why…reputation] CRANE; not| CORBIN-SEDGE
1.1.81–2 'Tis…little] SCOTT; *1 line* CRANE
1.1.84–6 Amsterdam…Queenhithe] CRANE; *prose* SCOTT
1.1.88–93 Sweet…town] CRANE; *prose* SCOTT
1.1.94–5 Like…conclusions] DYCE; *3 lines* CRANE: kind| try|; *prose* SCOTT
1.2.1–5 Titty…Puckle] CRANE; *prose* DYCE; *verse* CORBIN-SEDGE: Tiffin| Pidgen| Robin| black spirits| red spirits| devil-ram| devil-dam|
1.2.46 Laid down…Good] CRANE; *2 lines* ESCHE: too
1.2.54–5 Of…too] CORBIN-SEDGE; hog| and| CRANE; hog| STEEVENS; litter| hog| DYCE. For CRANE's superfluous 'and', see Textual Notes.
1.2.57–9 Each…cursing] CRANE; send| beforehand| stroke| CORBIN-SEDGE; snakes| beforehand| dairy-wenches ESCHE
1.2.66–77 And may you…before him] CRANE; *verse* STEEVENS, preserving manuscript lineation: Mother| No| bakers| hundred| give| from the| through| be the| tailor| him|; REED divided the passage between *verse* (mother| No| bakers|) and *prose* (Your spirits…before him); *prose* DYCE, DREES-DE VOCHT
1.2.83–5 Dear…shorter] CRANE; *prose* REED,
1.2.85–6 Thou'rt…villainy] DYCE; *1 line* CRANE
1.2.87–9 Truly…daughter] REED (*prose* from 'Not I'); *verse* CRANE: think| straight| and| pray| the| overlay|; *prose* from 'there's' DREES-DE VOCHT
1.2.93–5 And who…kind son] CORBIN-SEDGE; *prose* DYCE; *verse* CRANE: then| night| son; REED divided into *prose* (And… once) and *verse* (son|)
1.2.102–6 Urchins…A-Ab-Hur-Hus] CRANE; *verse* STEEVENS, preserving manuscript lineation: fawns| centaurs| Man| fire-Drake, the|
1.2.183–92 There's…covered] CRANE; *verse* STEEVENS, preserving manuscript lineation: and the| fall'n| child's| and in| heels| hey-day| save her| be|
1.2.193–4 See…flat tumblers] THIS EDITION. In CRANE, followed by DREES-DE VOCHT, Firestone's exclamation is *prose* and Almachildes's entrance lines are *verse*: witches|; SCOTT and DYCE preserve the same division into *prose* and *verse* but differ on the lineation of the *verse*—*1 line* SCOTT, and *2 lines* (methinks|) DYCE; ESCHE divides the exchange as *verse*: Mother| witches|.
1.2.202–3 Thou…dry] CORBIN-SEDGE; *1 line* CRANE
1.2.207–8 Some…buttered] CRANE; *1 line* CORBIN-SEDGE

1.2.210–11 The flesh…chamber-pot] CRANE; *1 line* CORBIN-SEDGE
1.2.212–13 You…anon] CRANE; *prose* REED
1.2.220–1 I…sir] CRANE; *prose* REED
1.2.230–1 The Cat…fox-skin] CRANE; *prose* SCOTT
1.2.233–6 How…him] CRANE; *verse* STEEVENS, preserving manuscript lineation: to the| and| twain|
2.1.34–6 I have…year] THIS EDITION; *2 lines* CRANE: hundred; *1 line prose, 1 line verse* SCOTT gentlewomen|.
2.1.36 Some] At this point DYCE appended an apology: 'In this speech I have printed several lines as prose, which might, perhaps, be tortured into verse.' The editorial problem is double: Middleton switches so easily between prose and verse that it is hard to determine whether a given line is a change of mode or an irregularity, and Crane's scribal practice does not always make clear whether he is presenting a passage as verse or prose. In STEEVENS the whole of Francisca's speech (2.1.34–64) is presented as *verse*, preserving manuscript lineation. Subsequent editors retained the manuscript lineation for most of Francisca's speech but cast a portion of it as *prose*: If I had been married…promised me *prose* SCOTT; These bastards…too fast *prose* DYCE; If I had been married…here i'th'house *prose* DREES-DE VOCHT. Dyce's solution has been accepted by all modernizing editors to date, and it may still be the most satisfactory.
2.1.43–4 These…children] CRANE: *prose* DYCE
2.1.45–7 If…whipped] THIS EDITION; *2 lines* CRANE: child|
2.1.48–54 Ere…fast] THIS EDITION; ambiguous in CRANE: come| stay| of| wine| curse|
2.1.55 This…night] CRANE; *prose* SCOTT
2.1.56–61 Honesty…house] THIS EDITION; ambiguous in CRANE: been| fared| think| me| devise|; *verse* DYCE, preserving manuscript lineation
2.1.143–5 That…and I] CRANE; comes| lead| SCOTT; here| born| DYCE
2.1.164 Nor…sir] CRANE, where this single line got near enough to the righthand rule to induce ELLIS to set an acceptable alexandrine as *prose*
2.2.3–6 I could beat…spoiled the rest] THIS EDITION; rascals| then| CRANE
2.2.26–32 Here…pest'lence] DYCE; *verse* CRANE: on't| gentlewoman| the| bade| And a| tail|; STEEVENS divides among *verse* (on't| gentleman [*sic*]|), *prose* (The whoreson…And a), and again *verse* (tail| pestilence|); SCOTT divides between

verse (on't | gentleman [*sic*] |) and *prose* (The whoreson...
pestilence)

2.2.33–6 Nay...luckily] CRANE; *prose* DYCE

2.2.111–12 About...faithfully] THIS EDITION; perform | CRANE;
me | perform | DYCE

2.2.118 Whose...already] CRANE; be | SCOTT

3.1.57–8 Be...thee] CORBIN-SEDGE; *3 part-lines* CRANE; ourself |
thee | ESCHE

3.2.2–5 I warrant...handsomely] CRANE; *verse* STEEVENS, pre-
serving manuscript lineation: of | every | wife |

3.2.186 What's...toward] *1 line* CRANE; *2 lines* DYCE: sir |

3.3.4–5 O...yet] LAMB; *1 line* CRANE

3.3.15–19 They're...me now] REED; *verse* CRANE: tonight |
day | sluts | after it | infect | now |; CORBIN-SEDGE divides
between *prose* (They're all...whole region) and *verse* (son |)

3.3.21–2 A little...me] *prose* CRANE; *verse* STEEVENS, preserving
manuscript lineation: were |

3.3.23–4 Nineteen...eggs] *verse* CRANE; *prose* REED

3.3.31–2 Every...mother] CRANE; *prose* (*1 line*) REED

3.3.34–7 Aloft...musicians] CRANE; *prose* REED

3.3.39–40 Come away...come away] CRANE; *1 line* YALE, CA-
DEMAN, CHETWIN, CLARK

3.3.44–5 Where's...too] THIS EDITION; *5 lines* CRANE: (Stadlin |
Here | Puckle | Here |); *4 lines* YALE, CADEMAN, CHETWIN,
CLARK: Stadling | here | Puckle |; *3 lines* CORBIN-SEDGE: Here |
Here |

3.3.49–50 There's one...of blood] CRANE; kiss | blood | YALE,
CHETWIN, CLARK; Here comes one, it is | kiss | blood | CADE-
MAN

3.3.57–8 Hark...language] CRANE; *verse* STEEVENS, preserving
manuscript lineation: in |; *verse* (*1 line*) LAMB

3.3.73–5 Well...mortal] CRANE; *verse* STEEVENS, preserving
manuscript lineation: be | here |

4.1.1–16 Though...*Hair-Bracelets*] CRANE; *verse* STEEVENS,
preserving manuscript lineation: a | at | make | a | young |
there | condition | quite | aqua- | a | the | reckning | be | a |
about | a | be |

4.3.56–7 Come...too] DYCE; *1 line* CRANE

5.1.5–7 Nay...me] CRANE; *verse* STEEVENS, preserving manu-
script lineation: acquainted | good |

5.1.9–10 I love...Commendable] THIS EDITION; ambiguous in
CRANE: thing |; *verse* (*1 line*) STEEVENS; *prose* DYCE

5.1.123–4 Here...Madam] THIS EDITION; madam | CRANE

5.1.128–9 Then...business] THIS EDITION; madam | CRANE

5.2.28 *Teque*...daughter] CRANE; *2 lines* STEEVENS, where the
Ovidian quotation is set out from the rest of Hecate's speech

5.2.33–5 I know...Latin] REED (*prose*); ambiguous CRANE;
verse STEEVENS, preserving manuscript lineation: mad |
then |; *verse* LAMB: our |

5.2.49–51 They...pudding] CRANE; *verse* STEEVENS, preserving
manuscript lineation: eat | good |

5.2.65–7 Titty...bob in] CRANE; *6 lines* DYCE: Tiffin | stiff in |
Pucky | lucky | Robin |

5.2.70–3 Here's...again] CRANE; *2 lines* CORBIN-SEDGE: that |

5.2.84–6 A...burden] CRANE; *verse* STEEVENS, preserving manu-
script lineation: warrant |

5.3.64–6 One...than ours] SCOTT; *2 lines* CRANE: night |. See
Textual Notes.

5.3.82 Blessed...happy] CRANE; *2 lines* DYCE: powers |

THE TRIUMPHS OF HEALTH AND PROSPERITY

Edited by David M. Bergeron

The Triumphs of Health and Prosperity (STC 17898; *BEPD* 413) has no significant textual problems. This quarto text has two sheets. All the press correction occurred on a single page of the inner forme of sheet A, corrections of obvious errors. Unlike the case in some other texts, in this one the printer wants to use sig. B4 and therefore cuts short the material on sig. B3^v. On B4 the printer uses a larger italic type and includes an ornament, thereby filling the page.

SEE ALSO

Text: *Works*, 1903
Authorship and date: this volume, 443

WORKS CITED

Previous Editions

Thomas Middleton, *Works*, ed. Alexander Dyce (1840), vol. 5
Thomas Middleton, *Works*, ed. A. H. Bullen (1886), vol. 7
Burridge, Christina Jean, *A Critical Edition of Four Entertainments by Thomas Middleton for the Drapers' Company*. Dissertation, University of British Columbia, 1978

Other Works Cited

Brückner, Martin, and Kristen Poole, 'The Plot Thickens: Surveying Manuals, Drama, and the Materiality of Narrative Form in Early Modern England', *ELH* 69 (2002), 617–48
Casey, Edward S., *The Fate of Place: A Philosophical History* (1998)
Certeau, Michel de, *The Practice of Everyday Life* (1984)
Fitzpatrick, Joseph, and Bryan Reynolds, 'The Transversality of Michel de Certeau: Foucault's Panoptic Discourse and the Cartographic Impulse', *Diacritics* 29:3 (1999), 63–80
Hedrick, Donald, and Bryan Reynolds, 'I Might Like You Better If We Slept Together: The Historical Drift of Place in *The Changeling*', in Reynolds, *Transversal Enterprises in the Drama of Shakespeare and his Contemporaries: Fugitive Explorations* (2006), 112–23
Reynolds, Bryan, *Becoming Criminal: Transversal Performance and Cultural Dissidence in Early Modern England* (2002)
Robertson, Jean, and D. J. Gordon, *A Calendar of Dramatic Records in the Books of the Livery Companies of London 1485–1640*, Malone Society, Collections III (1954)
Turner, Henry S., *The English Renaissance Stage: Geometry, Poetics, and the Practical Spatial Arts 1580–1630* (2006)
Weimann, Robert, *Author's Pen and Actor's Voice: Playing and Writing in Shakespeare's Theatre* (2000)

TEXTUAL NOTES

64   *showers*] DYCE; *flowers* OKES
221 Christmas] OKES Chrismas

PRESS VARIANTS

Copies collated: Huntington, Guildhall.

Sheet A (inner forme)

Sig. A4

52   graze] GUILDHALL; grace HUNTINGTON
52   platform,] platforme, GUILDHALL; platforme. HUNTINGTON
52   come] GUILDHALL; Come HUNTINGTON
67   *unvalued*] *vnvalued* GUILDHALL; *vnvaleed* HUNTINGTON
68   *handmaid*] *Hand-mayde* GUILDHALL; *Hnnd-mayde* HUNTINGTON
69   *wait*] *waite* GUILDHALL; *waire* HUNTINGTON

A CHASTE MAID IN CHEAPSIDE

Edited by Linda Woodbridge

A Chaste Maid in Cheapside was first printed three years after Middleton's death. The earliest surviving text (STC 17877, *BEPD* 433) is dated 1630 on its title-page, which also records the claim 'neuer before printed'. The full title-page reads: 'A | CHAST MAYD | *IN* | CHEAPESIDE. | *A* | Pleafant conceited Comedy | neuer before printed. | As it hath beene often acted at the | Swan on the Banke-fide, by the | Lady ELIZABETH her | *Seruants*. | [rule] By THOMAS MIDELTON Gent. | [rule] *LONDON*, | Printed for *Francis Conftable* dwelling at the | figne of the *Crane* in *Pauls* | Church-yard. | 1630.' On the verso of the title-page are 'The Names of the principall *Persons*'. The pages are numbered from 2 (B1ᵛ) to 71 (K4). The title had been entered in the Stationers' Register on 8 April 1630 by Francis Constable; the entry reads: 'Master Constable   Entred for his Copie vnder the hand*es* of Sʳ Hen: Herbert and Mʳ Bill warden A play called *The Chast Mayd of Chepeside*.' The Register also records two copyright transfers: to Richard Thrale by Alice Constable (Francis Constable's widow) in 1648, and to Benjamin Thrale by Dorothy Thrale (Richard Thrale's widow) in 1681; but the copyright holders apparently did not see fit to reissue the play after 1630.

The printer of the 1630 edition was identified by George as Thomas Cotes, on the basis of type ornaments, capitals, and a bent italic 'd'; Adrian Weiss has confirmed this identification through typographical evidence consisting of 17 identified types which exhibit a total of 59 recurrences in *A Chaste Maid in Cheapside* and another book with a signed imprint that specifies Thomas Cotes as the printer (*Pathomachia*, STC 19462). This pica roman font also appears in other books printed by Cotes. Except for a number of passages set as prose which appear to be verse, the printing of the 1630 edition is a clean job with a fairly small complement of printing errors. The printing is, however, plain and unornamented compared to other works of the same printer, giving an impression, as Parker says, of 'skilled but casual execution'.

George's edition (lxiv–lxxx) provides the most detailed evidence on presswork, based on extensive comparison of the crispest copies, with the aid of a Martin lamp. Parker, who also undertook an extensive presswork collation, summarizes the sequence of formes and skeletons: 'B (outer), skeleton I; B (inner), skeleton II; C (outer), an aberrant, composite skeleton; C (inner), skeleton I; D (inner), skeleton I; D (outer), skeleton I; E (outer), skeleton I; E (inner), skeleton I; F (outer), skeleton II; F (inner), skeleton I; G (outer), skeleton I; G (inner), skeleton I; H (inner), skeleton II; H (outer), skeleton II; I (inner),

skeleton I; I (outer), skeleton II; K (inner), skeleton II; K (outer), skeleton I. When skeleton II was reintroduced in H (inner), it still had the page numbers of F (outer) in it; so, in uncorrected copies of Q, Hᵛ is numbered 36 instead of 50; H2, 33 instead of 51; H3ᵛ, 40 instead of 54; and [H4], 37 instead of 55' (xxiv).

Variant spellings of Allwit/All-wit, Dahumma/Dahanna, and Yellowhammer/Yellow-hammer/Yellow-hammar, and different ways of punctuating abbreviations and contracted speech headings, suggest two compositors. The most detailed analysis of the compositors' roles is in George's edition, pp. lii–lxiv, though Barber believes that George often goes beyond what the evidence warrants. The compositors' stints suggested by George are:

Compositor A: 1.2.85–2.1.30; 2.1.97–154; 2.1.183–2.2.13; 2.2.71–100; 3.1.13–41; 3.2.38–70; 3.2.125–51; 3.2.184–215; 3.3.31–60; 3.3.114–48; 4.1.21–86; 4.1.213–43; 4.4.14–70; 5.1.19–51; 5.1.110–34; 5.1.166–5.2.79; 5.4.0.8–5.4.34; 5.4.67–96.

Compositor B: 1.2.23–84; 2.1.31–96; 2.1.155–82; 2.2.14–70; 2.2.100–3.1.12; 3.1.42–3.2.37; 3.2.71–124; 3.2.152–83; 3.2.216–3.3.30; 3.3.60–113; 4.1.87–212; 4.1.244–4.4.13; 4.4.70–5.1.18; 5.1.52–110; 5.1.134–65; 5.2.79–5.4.0.8; 5.4.35–66; 5.4.97–5.4.122.1.

George, however, marks the attribution of a number of pages to each compositor as uncertain, and Parker believes that 'the different compositorial habits of spelling, abbreviation, and spacing do not fall into any pattern of regular alternation, and without such a pattern the statistics for individual pages are too meagre and contradictory to identify particular compositors' characteristics or stints' (xxv). The two putative compositors seem to have been of nearly equal competence.

There is general agreement among editors that, as Parker says, 'the copy text for the edition was either a Middleton holograph or a copy closely derived from his manuscript' (xxv). Traces of Middleton's known habits of punctuation, capitalization, act but not scene division, and speech headings abound. The text contains some of Middleton's preferred spellings, such as medial 'oy' for 'oi', but other characteristic spellings such as '-nes' for '-ness' or '-nesse' and '-ie' for final 'y' are missing, opening the possibility of a transcribed copy between the holograph and print (Parker xxvi, George xxxvi–xxxix). But, according to Barber, 'there is even more decisive evidence for an intermediate transcription: there are numerous distinctively non-Middletonian spellings which occur consistently throughout the play, and it would be a strange coincidence if both compositors happened to favour these same forms (a necessary hypothesis if they set up from a Middleton holograph)' (11). Lake writes, 'The style of the play is clearly Middletonian throughout, though somewhat diluted as to certain features; for instance, there are only 17 *'em* beside 27 *them*. Middleton's more distinctive spellings, such as *e'm* and words ending in *-cst*, are absent, so that we may suppose that a scribal copy underlies the printed text. Nevertheless, several distinctive contractions occur, namely *I've*, *you're* and *they're*' (27).

Some details, such as the reference to the music room (5.4.0.12–13) suggest a copy marked for stage use; against such evidence, however, are the fact that prompt books did not usually contain Dramatis Personae, the literariness of some stage directions, and a number of omissions which would have been rectified if the text were being used for a production—for example, about 28 missing exits and exeunts and three missing entrances (the nurse at 3.2.100.1 and 3.2.113.1, and the Puritans, Maudline, Lady Kix, and nurse with child at 3.2.0.1–2—though the nurse's appearances are both re-entries within the scene, and the opening entry for 3.2, '*Enter all the Gossips*', may well include the other figures). Staging symbols penned into margins might easily be omitted by a printer, but this is a large number of omissions: 28 is an abnormal number of missing exits for a promptbook, and missing entrances are rare in theatrical manuscripts. One possible explanation for the text's rather inconsistent internal signals is that a manuscript copy was made for private, readerly use from a promptbook (see George xlv–xlvii). If the promptbook was indeed transcribed in this way, it might be inferred that the promptbook manuscript itself is likely to have been mainly in Middleton's own hand.

COTES divides the play into acts but not scenes. Dyce first added the scene divisions, and the present edition follows his division, except that (following Parker and Barber) it adds a scene division to Act 4; Dyce does not change scenes after the exit of Moll and Touchwood Junior at 4.3.28.

The list of 'The Names of the principall *Persons*' in COTES is grouped according to family affiliations. Not evident in COTES's list is the extent of the play's cast of anonymous characters—34 or 35 of them—who help create the sense of a densely-populated urban neighbourhood.

It is often difficult in the play to distinguish between verse and prose, since little division between them is made on class lines and because the prose is often rhythmic while the verse is unmetrical with irregular syllable counts. A factor that contributes further to the difficulty is that COTES, following the usual arrangement in a theatrical manuscript but not the usual typesetting conventions, frequently fails to capitalize the first letter of verse lines. Furthermore, the text does not indent flow-over lines. In distinguishing verse from prose, then, a number of judgement calls have had to be made.

Given the dubious erudition of Tim and his Tutor, it seems fair to allow them to make grammatical errors in Latin rather than to correct them, except where they seemed obvious misprints. To reduce Middleton's phonetic Welsh to the intelligible Welsh of a native speaker (the Welsh gentlewoman), I have accepted the translations and conjectures of Parker and of Wall, who acknowledges the expert assistance of Margery M. Morgan.

The song sung by the Welsh Gentlewoman (4.1.167–93) is of textual interest because it exists in three variant versions: one in *Dissemblers* and the others in two manuscript songbooks, British Library, Additional MS. 29481, fol. 6ᵛ, and New York Public Library, Drexel MS. 4175, Item 24. For the light that is thrown on the text of this song by the other versions, see Jowett and Cutts. Cutts argues that an English song was substituted for what was originally a song in Welsh: the song is headed 'Welch Song', Maudline has said that the Welsh Gentlewoman sings 'the sweetest British songs' (4.1.162), and there is enough Welsh spoken in the play to suggest that Middleton would not have hesitated to incorporate a song in Welsh. Jowett argues that the two manuscript versions preserve a fragment of a lost work, Middleton's *Masque of Cupids*, and that the song was introduced into *Chaste Maid* for a revival, perhaps in 1614. The replacement of the Welsh song with an English song is certainly suggestive of a revival, and this strengthens the case for the printed text deriving directly or indirectly from a theatre playbook.

As R. B. Parker points out in his edition, '*A Chaste Maid* has the distinction of being the only play that we know for certain was acted at the Swan, and the Swan in turn happens to be the only theatre of which we possess an eyewitness drawing and description [by Johannes de Witt, 1596]. Since all discussions of Elizabethan theatre structure—and hence of production methods—centre on this drawing, the evidence afforded by the original stage-directions of *A Chaste Maid* is of the utmost historical and theatrical importance' (lx–lxi). Though the evidence of early modern staging is no longer so sparse as when Parker wrote of *Chaste Maid*'s staging, the play's stage directions remain of considerable importance. Stage directions bear out De Witt's drawing in suggesting no inner or upper stages, except for a small upper area called 'the music room', probably adapted from part of the upper gallery in which spectators sat. The rapid movement from private to public scenes as indicated by the stage directions suggests fluid staging on various parts of the main stage rather than rigid locales associated with different sets of characters.

COTES's stage directions are clear but fairly sparse. There are several early 'enter' directions (people enter before they are summoned, or enter so as to interrupt dialogue proceeding onstage although they do not yet speak), which some regard as evidence that COTES was set from a copy marked for theatrical use. The phenomenon could also be an effect of that 'fluid staging' of which Parker speaks, with characters continually impinging on others, and it could reflect the sheer lack of privacy that is so conspicuous a feature of Cheapside life in the play: even the lovers are never allowed an intimate scene with each other, and eavesdropping, surveillance, spying, informing, and gossip are important to the plot. A number are nevertheless relocated to a more plausible position in this and other editions.

It is interesting that Eton College, the school of Sir Walter Whorehound's putative son (see 4.1.249), owns a copy of the 1630 edition, and Oxford University, where Middleton himself was a student, owns three. Cambridge University, home of the ignominious Tim and his Tutor, does not own a copy. And the most copies—four— are where they should be considering the play's own allegiances: in London.

SEE ALSO

Text: *Works*, 912
Music: this volume, 145 ('Weep eyes, break heart'), 149 ('Cupid is Venus' only joy')
Authorship and date: this volume, 373

WORKS CITED

Previous Editions

A Chaste Maid in Cheapside (1630), STC 17877; facsimile reprint (1969) from the British Library Ashley copy
Barber, Charles, ed., *A Chaste Maid in Cheapside* (1969)
Brissenden, Alan, ed., *A Chaste Maid in Cheapside* (1968)
Bullen, A. H., ed., *Works* (1885), vol. 5
Dyce, Alexander, ed., *Works* (1840), vol. 4
Ellis, Havelock, ed., intro. Algernon Charles Swinburne, *A Chaste Maid in Cheapside*, in *Thomas Middleton*, vol. 1 (1887)
Fisher, Margery, ed., *A Chaste Maid in Cheapside* (unpublished B.Litt. thesis, University of Oxford, 1937)
Fraser, Russell A., and Norman Rabkin, eds., *A Chaste Maid in Cheapside*, in *Drama of the English Renaissance*, vol. 2, *The Stuart Period* (1976)
Frost, David L., ed., *A Chaste Maid in Cheapside*, in *The Selected Plays of Thomas Middleton* (1978)
George, David F., ed., 'A Critical Edition of *A Chaste Maid in Cheapside*, by Thomas Middleton, with Introduction' (unpublished MA thesis, University of Manchester, 1962)
Loughrey, Bryan, and Neil Taylor, eds., Thomas Middleton, *Five Plays* (1988)
Muir, Kenneth, ed., *A Chaste Maid in Cheapside*, in *Thomas Middleton: Three Plays* (1975)
Parker, R. B., ed., *A Chaste Maid in Cheapside* (1969)
Wall, John Richard, ed., 'A Critical Edition of Thomas Middleton's *A Chast Mayd in Cheape-side*' (unpublished Ph.D. dissertation, University of Michigan, 1958)
Walley, Harold Reinoehl, and John Harold Wilson, eds., *A Chaste Maid in Cheapside*, in *Early Seventeenth-Century Plays 1600–1642* (1930)

Other Works Cited

Aleman, Mateo, *Guzman de Alfarache*, trans. James Mabbe (1622)
Altieri, Joanne, 'Against Moralizing Jacobean Comedy: Middleton's *Chaste Maid*', *Criticism* 30 (1988), 171–87
The Bachelor's Banquet (1603) (anonymous trans. of *Le Quinze Joyes de Mariage*)
Bakhtin, Mikhail, *Rabelais and His World*, trans. Helene Iswolsky (1965)
Bald, R. C., 'The Sources of Middleton's City Comedies', *Journal of English and Germanic Philology* 33 (1934), 373–87
Bruster, Douglas, *Drama and the Market in the Age of Shakespeare* (1992)
Calmo, Andrea, *La Potione* (1552)
Campion, Thomas, *Observations in the Art of English Poesie* (1602)
Chatterji, Ruby, 'Theme, Imagery, and Unity in *A Chaste Maid in Cheapside*', *Renaissance Drama* NS 8 (1965), 105–26
Cutts, John P., 'The Music for *A Chaste Maid in Cheapside*', appended to R. B. Parker's edition of the play (1969)
—— *La Musique de scène de la troupe de Shakespeare: The King's Men sous le règne de Jacques Ier*, second edn. rev. (1971)
—— 'Two Jacobean Theatre Songs', *Music and Letters* 33 (1952), 333–4
Forsythe, Robert Stanley, *The Relations of Shirley's Plays to the Elizabethan Drama* (1914, 1965)
Goux, Jean-Joseph, 'Banking on Signs', *Diacritics* 18 (1988), 15–25
—— *Symbolic Economies: After Marx and Freud*, trans. Jennifer Curtiss Gage (1990)
Harbage, Alfred, *Shakespeare and the Rival Traditions* (1952)
Heywood, Thomas, *If You Know Not Me, You Know Nobody, Part Two* (1605)
Hibbard, G. R., 'Love, Marriage, and Money in Shakespeare's Theatre and Shakespeare's England', *The Elizabethan Theatre VI: Papers Given at the Sixth International Conference on Elizabethan Theatre Held at the University of Waterloo, Ontario, in July 1975*, ed. G. R. Hibbard (1977), 134–55
Hoey, Allen, 'The Name on the Coin: Metaphor, Metonymy, and Money', *Diacritics* 18 (1988), 26–37
Honigmann, E. A. J., 'Re-Enter the Stage Direction: Shakespeare and Some Contemporaries', *Shakespeare Survey* 29 (1976), 117–25
Hotz-Davies, Ingrid, '*A Chaste Maid in Cheapside* and *Women Beware Women*: Feminism, Anti-feminism and the Limitations of Satire', *Cahiers Elisabethains* 39 (1991), 29–39
Jowett, John, 'Middleton's Song of Cupid', *Notes and Queries* NS 41 (1994), 66–70
Leggatt, Alexander M., *Citizen Comedy in the Age of Shakespeare* (1973)
Leinwand, Theodore, *The City Staged: Jacobean Comedy, 1603–1613* (1986)
Levin, Richard, 'The Four Plots of *A Chaste Maid in Cheapside*', *Review of English Studies* NS 16 (1965), 14–24
—— *The Multiple Plot in English Renaissance Drama* (1971)
Machiavelli, Niccolò, *Mandragola* (1524)
Paster, Gail Kern, *The Idea of the City in the Age of Shakespeare* (1985)
—— 'Leaky Vessels: The Incontinent Women of City Comedy', *Renaissance Drama* NS 18 (1987), 43–65
Reeves, John D., 'Thomas Middleton and Lily's Grammar: Some Parallels', *Notes and Queries* 197 (1952), 75–6
Richman, David, 'Directing Middleton's Comedy', in *Accompaninge the Players: Essays Celebrating Thomas Middleton*, ed. Kenneth Friedenreich (1983), 79–88
Roberts, Marilyn, compiler, 'A Preliminary Check-List of Productions of Thomas Middleton's Plays', *Research Opportunities in Renaissance Drama* 28 (1985), 37–61
Rubin, Gayle, 'The Traffic in Women: Notes on the "Political Economy" of Sex', in *Toward an Anthropology of Women*, ed. Rayna R. Reiter (1975), 157–210
Schoenbaum, Samuel, '*A Chaste Maid in Cheapside* and Middleton's City Comedy', in *Studies in the English Renaissance Drama: In*

Memory of Karl Julius Holzknecht, ed. Josephine W. Bennett, Oscar Cargill, and Vernon Hall, Jr. (1959), 287–309

Shakespeare, William, *The Complete Works*, gen. ed. Stanley Wells and Gary Taylor (1986)

Shell, Marc, *Money, Language, and Thought: Literary and Philosophical Economies from the Medieval to the Modern Era* (1982)

Slights, William, 'The Incarnations of Comedy', *University of Toronto Quarterly* 51 (1981-2), 13–27

Spenser, Edmund, *The Faerie Queene*, ed. A. C. Hamilton (1977)

Stow, John, *A Survey of London*, ed. Charles Lethbridge Kingsford (1908)

Taylor, John, 'The True Cause of the Watermen's Suit concerning Players', in *All The Works of John Taylor, the Water Poet* (1630)

Van Gennep, Arnold, *The Rites of Passage*, trans. Monika B. Vizedom and Gabrielle L. Caffee (1960; first published in French, 1908)

Vernon, John, *Money and Fiction: Literary Realism in the Nineteenth and Early Twentieth Centuries* (1984)

Wakefield Master, *The Second Shepherd's Play* (c.1425)

Wells, Susan, 'Jacobean City Comedy and the Ideology of the City', *English Literary History* 48 (1981), 37–60

Wigler, Stephen, 'Thomas Middleton's *A Chaste Maid in Cheapside*: The Delicious and the Disgusting', *American Imago* 33 (1976), 197–215

Woodbridge, Linda, 'The Gossips' Meeting', in *Women and the English Renaissance: Literature and the Nature of Womankind, 1540-1620* (1984), 224–43

TEXTUAL NOTES

Title A Chaste Maid in Cheapside] A CHAST MAYD *IN* CHEAPESIDE COTES (*title-page*); A Chaſt Mayd in Cheape-side. COTES (*half-title and running titles*)

Persons This list is based on COTES (see 'Stage Directions' below). Of the minor roles (from Susan onwards), COTES lists only two Promoters, Servants, and Watermen.

1.1.35 e'en] PARKER; eeue COTES; even DYCE

1.1.70 *Amantissimis carissimis*] DYCE; *Amantiſſimus chariſſimus* COTES

1.1.89 *Exit*] Exit Porter. COTES

1.1.93 *Maximus*] COTES; *Maxime* GEORGE

1.1.100.3 *Dahumma*] PARKER; *Dahanna* COTES. Similarly at 1.1.110 and 1.2.2.

1.1.102 *Duw cato chwi*] THIS EDITION (*conj.* Wall); *Dugat a whee* COTES

1.1.119 *Exit*] Exit Moll. COTES

1.1.123.1 *Moll*] DYCE; *Mary* COTES. Moll was a nickname for Mary; Moll is called Mary at 1.1.25. Changing it to Moll avoids confusion for readers, since otherwise 'Mary' enters four lines after 'Moll' exits, and a reader might take her for a different character.

1.1.130 sound] WALL (*conj.* Dyce); wound COTES

1.1.146 peak] PARKER (*conj.* Dyce); picke COTES

1.1.147 spoil] DYCE; ſpoy COTES

1.1.156 Tim, sir, Tim!] GEORGE (*conj.* Dyce); turne Sir, turne COTES. No textual hiatus need be inferred here: Yellowhammer's seemingly abrupt introduction of the topic of Tim, when he has been speaking of the Welsh gentlewoman, suggests that he has continued conversing with Sir Walter in quiet tones in the background while Touchwood Junior's remarks have been foregrounded.

1.1.168 kind] PARKER; *not in* COTES

1.1.210 served] DYCE; ſerued (=èd) COTES

1.1.211 wear] COTES (were)

1.1.214.1 *Exit*] Printed in COTES before Moll's half-line addressed to Touchwood Junior.

1.1.218 *Exeunt*] Exit. COTES

1.2.4 In to] COTES (Into)

1.2.6 My wife's] Speech prefixes in the play refer to both Allwit's and Touchwood's spouses simply as 'Wife'; since these two characters are never onstage together, no confusion is likely. Of all the female characters in the play, only Moll, Maudline, and (at one point) Susan are identified in speech prefixes and stage directions by their names, a depersonalization that vitiates the feminism some critics find in the play. This edition retains the 'Wife' speech prefixes, as well as 'Lady' for 'Lady Kix'.

1.2.64.1 *Enter Sir Walter and Davy*] Printed after 1.1.63 in COTES, interrupting the exchange between the First Servant and Allwit.

1.2.26 chaldron] Not modernized to 'cauldron' to avoid confusion with the cooking utensil.

1.2.71 i'faith] COTES (a faith)

1.2.75 put] DYCE; but COTES

1.2.107 poisoned] DYCE; poyſoned (=èd) COTES

1.2.110 Wat] DYCE; *1 Boy.* COTES

1.2.110, 111 Good e'en] COTES (god-den)

1.2.111 Nick] DYCE; *2 Boy.* COTES

1.2.141.1 [*Exeunt*]] *not in* COTES

1.2.141.2 *Finis Actus Primus*] *not in* COTES

2.1.13 prudent'st] DYCE; prudents COTES

2.1.45 desires] DYCE; deſire COTES

2.1.52 Merely] COTES (Meerely); Merrily DYCE

2.1.52 sin] BARBER; ſing COTES

2.1.68 called] DYCE; called (=èd) COTES

2.1.80 An] COTES (and)

2.1.140 withal] COTES (with all)

2.1.144.1 *Exit Touchwood Senior*] Touchwood, after remaining onstage long enough to overhear the Kixes' plight, exits for long enough to enlist the maid in his scheme; otherwise, the maid would be acting on her own initiative, unlikely since the miraculous 'water' she reports is actually Touchwood Senior's fabrication, tailored to this situation.

2.1.165 Master] COTES (M^r); Mistress PARKER

2.1.177 proved] PARKER; proued (=èd) COTES

2.1.192 SIR OLIVER] GEORGE; *not in* COTES. Such confident disposal power over the family income ('stands me | In some five hundred pound'; 'I'll about it') sounds more husbandly than wifely in this age when married women had no property rights. The passage is in character for Sir Oliver, who has just said 'I spare for nothing, wife, no, if the price | Were forty marks a spoonful; | I'd give a thousand pound to purchase fruitfulness' (2.1.142-4). Nowhere else in the play does Lady Kix mention a specific sum of money.

2.1.195.1 *Exeunt*] Exit. COTES

2.2.16.1 *Enter Dry Nurse*] Printed between 2.2.13 and 2.2.14 in COTES, causing Dry Nurse to enter before summoned.

2.2.16.1 DRY NURSE] Nurſe COTES

2.2.17.1 *Exit [Dry Nurse]*] Printed at 2.2.16 in COTES, causing the Dry Nurse to exit before Allwit tells her she is not needed.

2.2.18.1   *Enter Wet Nurse*] Printed before 2.2.18 in COTES, causing the Wet Nurse to enter before summoned.

2.2.21, 24, 32   WET NURSE] *Nurſe* COTES

2.2.62   corpses] COTES (corps). The original 'corps' was a plural
form.

2.2.89   nature] DYCE; Natnre COTES

2.2.100   foutre] COTES (footra)

2.2.124, 127   SECOND MAN] *Man* COTES

2.2.128   mistress'] COTES (*Miſtriſſes*)

2.2.162   Now] WALL; Not COTES; No, ELLIS

2.2.166   I'll] DYCE; *not in* COTES

2.2.186   Queenhithe] COTES (Queene-hiue)

2.2.188   Brentford] COTES (Branford)

2.3.2   kers'ning] COTES (Kurſning). 'Kursen', 'kursning', and
'kersten' have been given a standard spelling throughout
the text. Because they are dialect words, they have not been
modernized to 'christen' and its derivatives.

2.3.3   an] COTES (and)

2.3.9.1   *Enter a Servant with a box*] Printed before 'So well ſaid' in
COTES, creating ambiguity about the status of that utterance.

2.3.19   Mistress] DYCE; Mr COTES

2.3.22   *Exeunt*] Exit COTES

2.3.34   beholden] COTES (beholding)

2.3.44   *Exeunt*] Exit COTES

2.4.19   *Exeunt*] Exit COTES

2.4.19.1   *Finis Actus Secundus*] *not in* COTES

3.1.18   ne'er] COTES (ne're); near GEORGE *conj.*

3.1.21   you] DYCE; *not in* COTES

3.1.29   received] DYCE; receiued (=èd) COTES

3.1.36   posy] COTES (Poeſie). The word has been given in its two-
-syllable form to agree with the metre and the form appearing
at 1.1.200 and 201.

3.2.3   FIRST PURITAN] COTES (*Pur.*). Similarly throughout the scene
except at l. 45, where '1 Pur.' is pragmatically distinguished
from '2 Pur.' in the following line.

3.2.6   NURSE] The character may be identical with the earlier
Wet Nurse or Dry Nurse, but COTES stage directions seem to
distinguish among them; this nurse performs a number of
maid-like food catering services not easily accomplished by
one simultaneously attending to a baby. It makes most sense
to assume that she briefly displays the child, exits at 3.2.24.1
with the child (whom she perhaps deposits with the Dry or
Wet Nurse), and returns to hand round wine and comfits.
There *is* a superfluity of nurses, but extravagant attendance
is part of the point of such satire; Allwit complains of 'nurse
upon nurse' (2.2.7).

3.2.11   Eyed] COTES *corr* (ey'd); ey's COTES *uncorr*

3.2.36   lady] THIS EDITION; Goſſip COTES. 'Gossip' seems a very
unlikely term for a god-father to employ in addressing the
mother. He calls her 'lady' at 3.2.39. ('Gossip' would be
appropriate if he were addressing the Puritan who speaks
just before him, but the remark to her would sit oddly in
context, both with the Puritan's remark and with Allwit's
wife which follow's Sir Walter's.)

3.2.51   handkerchiefs] COTES (Handkerchers)

3.2.63   an] COTES (and)

3.2.83   an] COTES (and)

3.2.96.1   *Exit Nurse*] The Nurse must exit before she can return
with tidings that a gentleman has arrived.

3.2.100.1   *Enter Nurse*] The Nurse must re-enter in order to
report the arrival of the gentleman.

3.2.104.1   *Exit Nurse*] The Nurse goes out to call Tim.

3.2.100.1   *Enter Nurse*] The Nurse must re-enter before she can
be sent in pursuit of Tim at 3.2.114.

3.2.123   answered] DYCE; answered (=èd) COTES

3.2.148   beholden] COTES (beholding)

3.2.159.1   *She kisses Tim*] Kiſſe COTES

3.2.161   handkerchief] COTES (Handkercher)

3.2.163.1   *She kisses Tim*] Kiſſe COTES

3.2.173   Mistress] DYCE; Mr COTES

3.2.179   Heyday] COTES (Hyda)

3.2.185.1   *Exeunt*] Exit COTES

3.2.187.1   *Exeunt*] Exit COTES

3.2.202   shuttle-cork heels] COTES *corr* (ſhittle-corke-heels);
ſhittle-cokre-heels COTES *uncorr*

3.2.210   gave the spoon] On the question of whether this
reference implies the need for a textual emendation to
introduce Moll into the scene where the spoons are presented
(say at 3.2.23.1-2), see Commentary, note to 3.2.202.

3.3.5   I] DYCE; *not in* COTES

3.3.16   eryngoes] COTES (Oringoes)

3.3.19   an] COTES (and)

3.3.21   Common Pleas] COTES (Common place)

3.3.40   (*to his lady, within*)] COTES prints 'Kix *to his Lady within.*'
to the right of the speech.

3.3.89   *aside*] Printed right of 'Almond-milke' in COTES.

3.3.102   An] COTES (and)

3.3.112.1   [*He*] *drinks*] 'Drinkes' printed right of ''tis gone' in
COTES.

3.3.113   Ay,] COTES (I_)

3.3.116-17   the [   ]] COTES prints a long dash after 'the'.

3.3.124   *Aside*] Printed right of 'necke Sir' in COTES.

3.3.135   wife is] DYCE; Wifes is COTES

3.3.152.1   *Exeunt*] Exit COTES

3.3.152.2   *Finis Actus Tertius*] *not in* COTES

4.1.16, 23   disputas] DYCE; diſputus COTES

4.1.19, 23   sumus] DYCE; ſum COTES

4.1.82.1   *Exeunt*] Exit COTES

4.1.87   kith] COTES (kiſſ)

4.1.99   Romford] COTES (Rumford)

4.1.112   Fertur] DYCE; Ferter COTES

4.1.120   homunculus] DYCE; homauculus COTES

4.1.120-1   simul et arte] DYCE; ſimule arte COTES; simule et artis
GEORGE

4.1.121   baccalaureus] COTES (bachalarius)

4.1.121   paratus] GEORGE; parata COTES; parato DYCE

4.1.123   *A ſedrwch ... Cymraeg*] THIS EDITION (*conj.* Wall); Auedera
whee comrage COTES

4.1.123   *Er ... gennyſf?*] THIS EDITION (*conj.* Wall); der due cog
foginis COTES

4.1.127-8   *Rhyw ... dro*] THIS EDITION (*conj.* Parker); Rhegoſin a
whiggin harle ron corid ambre COTES

4.1.150   an] COTES (and)

4.1.153   He] ho COTES

4.1.166.1   *Music and Song*] THIS EDITION; Muſicke and Welch Song
| [rule] THE SONG. COTES. 'Welsh' has been removed from
the stage direction, since the song is in English; the vestigial
'Welsh' probably indicates that the song originally planned
was in Welsh. 'Music and song' presumably means that some
instrumental prelude precedes the vocal rendition of the song.

4.1.174   thought] DYCE; taught COTES. 'Thought', more idiomatic
than 'taught' when joined to 'upon', is also the reading in
Dissemblers and in the two music manuscripts.

4.1.177   pranks] The music manuscripts read 'tricks'. The possibility that Middleton wrote 'tricks' rather than 'pranks' here
is enhanced by the fact that he uses 'tricks' in a similar sense
four times in the play (2.1.96, 3.2.133, 4.4.26, 5.4.112),

and nowhere else in the play does he use 'prank' in this sense.

4.1.180 hurt] The music manuscripts read 'wound', but 'wound...with cruel wounding' is graceless. 'Hurt' occurs four times and 'wound' or its derivatives seven times in the play.

4.1.181 Ay me] MUSIC MSS; *ah me* COTES. 'Ay me' forms a parallel with 'I mean' in the same line in stanza 1 (4.1.172).

4.1.185-93 The third stanza's omission of Cupid and Venus and failure to return to the notion of keeping ladies' lips in play, with which the first two stanzas close, may suggest that it was composed independently of the song as recorded in *Dissemblers* and the music manuscripts. The third stanza also fails to develop the parallelisms of the first two: 'Venus' as fourth and fifth syllables of line 1 of both, 'wanton' appearing in line 3 of both, and 'he shoots' beginning line 4 of both.

4.1.187 quickly, quickly] BARBER; *quickly* COTES. The emendation restores the metre, giving a sense of quickness rather than an otherwise drawn-out line, and echoes the 'very, very' of the third line of stanza 1.

4.1.190 [   ]] A line seems to be missing here, to judge from the fact that stanza 3 has only 8 lines compared with the 9 lines each of stanzas 1 and 2, from the lack of a rhyme for line 5, and from the lack of a subject for the clause introduced by 'And' in line 6. The missing line cannot be supplied from other versions of the song, since of the four extant versions, only the one in *Chaste Maid* contains the third stanza.

4.1.195.1 *in disguise*] COTES does not specify disguise, but it makes most sense to stage the scene this way. Maudline knows Allwit (she was at the christening), and if he were not disguised, it would be odd that she, onstage when he enters, does not demur when he is called 'strange' (4.1.198), or that (on seeing Maudline) Allwit betrays no anxiety about his identity's being disclosed.

4.1.198.1 *Exeunt*] *Exit* COTES

4.1.212 confirmed] COTES *corr* (confirm'd); confir'd COTES *uncorr*

4.1.228 [   ]] THIS EDITION; COTES prints a long, heavy dash at beginning of 4.1.229. As the line is already long, a full verse-line is probably missing.

4.1.232 but [   ]] COTES prints a long dash after 'but'.
4.1.247 Corderius] DYCE; Cordelius COTES
4.1.263 *anno* [   ]] COTES has a blank after '*Anno*'.
4.1.275 *Exeunt*] *Exit* COTES
4.2.4 coral] COTES (Curral)
4.2.8.1 *Exeunt*] *Exit* COTES
4.3.11 bandied] COTES (banded)
4.3.24 *Exeunt*] *Exit* COTES
4.4.23.1 *Exeunt*] *Exit* COTES
4.4.72.1 *Finis Actus Quartus*] *not in* COTES
5.1.44 parts] DYCE; part COTES
5.1.71 her too] PARKER; ho to COTES; O too DYCE; go too GEORGE
5.1.110.1 *Enter a Servant [of Sir Walter's]*] COTES distinguishes between the servants only by the fact that they enter separately, but gives each the speech prefix '*Seru*.'; THIS EDITION follows the editorial tradition in designating servants 'First', 'Second', and so forth.
5.1.171.1 *Exeunt*] *Exit* COTES
5.2.15 his] BULLEN; *not in* COTES
5.2.26 ingredients] COTES (ingredience)
5.2.37.1-5.2.38 *The Song* | MOLL] THE SONG. COTES
5.2.69 Ay] COTES (I)
5.2.105.1 *Exeunt*] *Exit* COTES
5.3.0.1 *[four] Servants*] COTES does not distinguish among the servants in this scene; THIS EDITION follows the editorial tradition in designating servants 'First', 'Second', and so forth.
5.3.3 all together] COTES (altogether)
5.3.11 joy] DYCE; ioyes COTES
5.3.24, 5.3.25 handkerchiefs] COTES (Handkerchers)
5.3.31 *Exeunt*] *Exit* COTES
5.4.32 lose] THIS EDITION; haue COTES
5.4.34 TOUCHWOOD JUNIOR] DYCE; *T.S.* COTES
5.4.92 Brentford] COTES (Brainford)
5.4.99 *nequeo*] DYCE; *neguro* COTES
5.4.99 *movebo*] DYCE; *mourbo* COTES
5.4.109 *falleris*] DYCE; *falacis* COTES
5.4.117 upon [   ]] COTES prints a long dash after 'upon'.
5.4.122 *[Exeunt]*] *not in* COTES

PRESS VARIANTS

Press variants recorded in this edition are as reported by David F. George, Charles Barber, and R. B. Parker. Variants in the following copies are mentioned below:

Bodleian Library, Oxford, Malone 245(8)
British Library: (1) 162. d. 30; (2) C. 34. f. 9; (3) Ashley 5353
Chapin Library, Williamstown, Massachusetts
Eton College, Windsor
Folger Shakespeare Library, Washington, D.C.
Harvard University Library
Library of Congress, Washington, D.C.
National Art Library, Victoria and Albert Museum, London, Dyce Collection 6562
Worcester College, Oxford

Other copies are located as follows:

Bodleian Library, Oxford, Douce MM 465
Boston Public Library, Massachusetts
Henry E. Huntington Library, San Marino, California
National Library of Scotland: H. 28. 1. 6(5); Bute 371; Bute 372
Pierpont Morgan Library, New York
Pforzheimer Collection, University of Texas at Austin

Sheet B (outer forme)

State a: Folger. State b: others.

Sig. B1

1.1.13 dancing] Dauning COTES State a; Dauncing COTES State b

Sig. B2^v

1.1.90 merry] mirry COTES State a; merry COTES State b

Sheet E (outer forme)

State a: British Library 1–3, Eton, Worcester, Victoria and Albert. State b: others.

Sig. E4^v

3.2.11 Eyed] ey's COTES State a; ey'd COTES State b

Sheet F (inner forme)

State a: reading reported by Parker, with no identification of copies.

Sig. F3ᵛ

3.2.202 shuttle-cork heels] ſhittle-cokre-heels COTES State a; ſhittle-corke-heels COTES State b

Sheet H (inner forme)

State a: Library of Congress, Folger, Chapin, Harvard. State b: others.

Sig. H1ᵛ

page number   36 COTES State a; 50 COTES State b
4.1.199 You're] Your COTES State a; You'r COTES State b

4.1.212 confirmed] confir'd COTES State a; confirm'd COTES
State b

Sig. H2

page number   33 COTES State a; 51 COTES State b

Sig. H3ᵛ

page number   40 COTES State a; 54 COTES State b

Sig. H4

page number   37 COTES State a; 55 COTES State b

Sheet I (outer forme)

State a: British Library 1–3, Victoria and Albert, Bodleian (Malone), Eton, Worcester. State b: others.

Sig. I2ᵛ

5.1.98 curses] Curſrs COTES State a; Curſes COTES State b

STAGE DIRECTIONS

Unless otherwise indicated, COTES stage directions are centred on the page.

[Printed before the play:]

The Names of the principall
Persons.

Mʳ YELLOWHAMMER, *A Gold-Smith.*
MAVDLINE, *His Wife.*
TIM, *Their Sonne.*
MOLL, *Their Daughter.*
TVTOR *to* TIM.
Sʳ WALTER WHOREHOVND, *A Suter to* MOLL.
Sʳ OLIVER KIXE, *and his Wife, Kin to* Sʳ WALT.
Mʳ ALLWIT, *and his Wife, Whom* Sʳ WALT. *keepes.*
WELCH GENTLEWOMAN, Sʳ WALT. *Whore.*
WAT *and* NICKE, *His Bastards.*
DAVY DAHVMMA, *His Man.*
TVCHWOOD SENIOR, *and his Wife, A decayed Gentleman.*
TVCHWOOD IVNIOR, *Another Suter to* MOLL.
2 PROMOTERS.
SERVANTS.
WATERMEN.

1.1.0.1 *Actus Primus.*
1.1.0.2 *Enter Maudline and Moll, a Shop being discouered.*
1.1.22.1 *Enter Yellow-hammar.*
1.1.59.1 *Enter Porter.*
1.1.89 *Exit Porter.*
1.1.98.1 *Enter a Gentleman with a Chayne.*
1.1.100.2–3 *Enter Sir Walter Whorehound, Welch Gentlewoman, | and Dauy Dahanna.*
1.1.119 *Exit Moll. (after 'O Death')*
1.1.123.1 *Enter Mary.*
1.1.142.1 *Enter Tuchwood Iunior.*
1.1.215 *Exit.*
1.1.218 *Exit.*
1.2.0.1 *Enter Dauy and All-wit seuerally.*
1.2.11.1 *Exit.*
1.2.57.1 *Enter two Seruants.*
1.2.64.1–2 *Enter Sir Walter, and Dauy; (after 1.1.63)*
1.2.108.1 *Enter two Children.*
1.2.128.1 *Enter Allwits Wife.*
2.1.0.1 *Actus Secundus.*
2.1.0.2 *Enter Tuchwood Senior, and his Wife.*

2.1.42.1 *Exit.*
2.1.61.1 *Enter a Wench with a Child.*
2.1.106.1 *(Exit. (right, turned up)*
2.1.115.1 *Enter Sir Oliuer Kix, and his Lady.*
2.1.124.1 *Enter Tuchwood Iunior.*
2.1.132 *Exit.*
2.1.172.1 *Enter a Mayd.*
2.1.195.1 *Exit.*
2.2.0.1 *Enter All-wit.*
2.2.10.1 *Enter Sir Walter Whorehound.*
2.2.16.1 *Enter Dry Nurse. (after 2.2.13)*
2.2.17.1 *Exit.*
2.2.18.1 *Enter Wet Nurse. (before 2.2.18)*
2.2.32 *Exit (after 'Sir.')*
2.2.45.1 *Enter Dauy.*
2.2.52.1 *Exit*
2.2.56.1 *Enter two Promoters.*
2.2.100 *Exit*
2.2.102.1 *Enter a Man with Meat in a Basket.*
2.2.116 *Exit (after 'Milke-potage')*
2.2.122.1 *Enter another with a Basket.*
2.2.136.1–2 *Enter a Wench with a Basket, and a Child in it | vnder a Loyne of Mutton.*
2.2.156.1 *Exit*
2.3.0.1 *Enter Allwit in one of Sir Walters Sutes, and Dauy | trussing him.*
2.3.9.1 *Enter a Seruant with a Box. (after 2.3.8)*
2.3.12.2 *Enter two Puritans.*
2.3.22 *Exit*
2.3.23.1 *Enter two Gossips.*
2.3.32.2 *Enter Tuchwood Iunior, and Moll.*
2.3.36.1 *Enter Sir Walter Whorehound.*
2.3.44 *Exit*
2.4.0.1–2 *Enter Midwife with the Child, and the Gossips to the | Kursning.*
2.4.19 *Exit*
3.1.0.1 *Actus Tertius.*
3.1.0.2 *Enter Tuchwood Iunior, and a Parson.*
3.1.9.1 *Enter Moll, and Tuchwood Senior.*
3.1.17.1 *Enter Yellow-hammer, and Sir Walter.*
3.1.49 *Exit*
3.1.56 *Exit*
3.1.59 *Exit*

3.1.60   *Exit*
3.2.0.1   *A Bed thrust out vpon the Stage, Allwits Wife in it,* | *Enter all the Gossips.*
3.2.23.1   *Enter Sir Walter with two Spoones and Plate* | *and Allwit.*
3.2.49.1   *Enter Nurse with Comfits and Wine.*
3.2.88.1   *Exit*
3.2.113.1   *Enter Tim.*
3.2.113   *Exit*
3.2.118.1   *Enter Nurse and Tim.*
3.2.142.1   *Enter Tutor.*
3.2.159   *Kisse*
3.2.163   *Kisse*
3.2.171   *Reels & fals*
3.2.177.1   *Enter Allwit, and Dauy.*
3.2.184   *Exit*
3.2.185.1   *Exit*
3.2.187.1   *Exit*
3.2.212.1   *Exit*
3.2.218   *Exit*
3.3.0.1   *Enter both the Tuchwoods.*
3.3.35.1   *Exit*
3.3.40   *Kix to his Lady within.*
3.3.48.1   *Enter Sir Oliuer Kix, and his Lady.*
3.3.83   *Weepes*
3.3.89   *Aside*
3.3.109.1   *Enter a Seruant.*
3.3.112   *Drinkes*
3.3.120   *Capers*
3.3.124   *Aside*
3.3.141.1   *Enter a Seruant.*
3.3.144   *Exit*
3.3.152.1   *Exit*
4.1.0.1   *Actus Quartus.*
4.1.0.2   *Enter Tim and Tutor.*
4.1.20.1   *Enter Maudline.*
4.1.82.1   *Exit*
4.1.99.1   *Enter Welch Gentlewoman.*
4.1.133.1   *Enter Maudline.*
4.1.166   *Musicke and Welch Song* | [rule] THE SONG.
4.1.195.1   *Enter Yellow-hammer, and All-wit.*
4.1.259.1   *Exit*
4.1.270.1   *Enter Maudline.*
4.1.275   *Exit*
4.2.0.1   *Enter Tim and Tutor.*

4.2.8.1   *Exit*
4.3.0.1   *Enter both the Tuchwoods.*
4.3.13.1   *Enter three or foure Watermen.*
4.3.24   *Exit*
4.3.24.1   *Enter Moll.*
4.4.0.1   *Enter S* Walter, Yellowhammer, Tim and Tutor.*
4.4.21.1-2   *Enter Maudline drawing Moll by the Hayre,* | *and Watermen.*
4.4.23.1   *Exit*
4.4.43   *Exit*
4.4.51   *Exit*
4.4.55.1   *Enter Tuchwood Iunior with a Waterman.*
4.4.59.1   *Exit Wat.*
4.4.61   *Both draw* | *and fight* (opposite 'thou' and 'I')
4.4.72   *Exit*
5.1.0.1   [rule] *Actus Quintus.* [rule]
5.1.0.2   *Enter Allwit, his Wife, and Dauy Dahumma.*
5.1.6.1-2   *Enter Sir Walter led in hurt.*
5.1.64.1   *Enter Dauy with the Children.*
5.1.110.1   *Enter a Seruant.*
5.1.129.1   *Enter a Seruant.*
5.1.151.1   *Exit*
5.1.153.1   *Exit*
5.1.171.1   *Exit*
5.2.0.1   *Enter Yellowhammer, and his Wife.*
5.2.7.1   *Enter Tim.*
5.2.18.1   *Enter Moll.*
5.2.37.1   THE SONG.
5.2.45.1   *Enter Tuchwood Senior with a Letter.*
5.2.90.1   *Enter Susan.*
5.2.105.1   *Exit*
5.3.0.1   *Enter Sir Oliuer and Seruants.*
5.3.31   *Exit*
5.4.0.1-13   *Recorders dolefully playing: Enter at one Dore the Cof-* | *fin of the Gentleman, solemnly deck't, his Sword vpon it,* | *attended by many in Blacke, his Brother being the chiefe* | *Mourner: At the other Doore, the Coffin of the Virgin,* | *with a Garland of Flowres, with Epitaphes pin'd on't,* | *attended by Mayds and Women: Then set them downe* | *one right-ouer- -against the other, while all the Company* | *seeme to weepe and mourne, there is a sad Song in the* | *Musicke-Roome.*
5.4.58.1   *Enter Yellow-hammer, and his Wife.*
5.4.83.1   *Enter Tim and Welch Gentlewoman.*
5.4.122.1   *FINIS.*

LINEATION NOTES

Dyce in his 1840 edition did yeoman's labour in detecting verse misprinted as prose in COTES; but he was sometimes overzealous, and editors who followed him have sometimes gone to extremes in re-setting in new patterns of verse what was set in lines of intelligible verse in COTES. In some cases the present edition restores the COTES lineation. The present edition's departures from COTES are listed below.

1.1.15-22   Last...ware] DYCE; *prose* COTES
1.1.27-37   Errors...bracks] DYCE; *prose* COTES
1.1.47-8   We...enters] DYCE; *prose* COTES
1.1.62-3   O...Tim] DYCE; *prose* COTES
1.1.98-100   Nay...gentleman?] DYCE; *prose* COTES
1.1.104-9   'Twill...maid] DYCE; *prose* COTES
1.1.112-13   Pure...Brecknockshire] DYCE; *prose* COTES
1.1.114-15   I have...years] DYCE; *prose* COTES
1.1.126-8   Why...servant] DYCE; *prose* COTES

1.1.129-34   Pish...niece] DYCE; *prose* COTES
1.1.135-6   You...mountains] DYCE; *prose* COTES
1.1.136   Bless...all] DYCE; *prose* COTES
1.1.176-7   We...lack] DYCE; *1 line* COTES
1.1.202-3   Love...eyes] DYCE; *1 line* COTES
1.1.208-9   Do...carried] DYCE; I | COTES
1.2.4-5   In...instantly] DYCE; *prose* COTES
1.2.6-8   My...boy] FROST; *prose* COTES
1.2.65   *Negatur...Walter*] DYCE; *prose* COTES
1.2.105   That...awe] THIS EDITION; *prose* COTES; slave | DYCE
1.2.106-8   I'll...virgins] THIS EDITION; gap | poisoned | already | COTES
1.2.115-16   O...ha] DYCE; school | COTES
1.2.125-8   I'll...i'faith] THIS EDITION; Yellowhammer | gold-smith | COTES; goldsmith | be | vintner | DYCE
1.2.138-40   No...fear] DYCE; *prose* COTES

2.1.17–18 Sir...house] DYCE; *1 line* COTES
2.1.72 I'll...to't] THIS EDITION; *prose* COTES; have| DYCE; parson's| PARKER
2.1.103 And...myself] THIS EDITION; *prose* COTES; wench| DYCE
2.1.128 With...me] THIS EDITION; *prose* COTES; canst| DYCE
2.1.136–7 To...child] DYCE; *1 line* COTES
2.1.149 Give...children] DYCE; find| COTES
2.2.30–1 Here...spoon-meat] WALL; her| COTES
2.2.78 How...bird] DYCE; Dick| COTES
2.2.95–6 This...apron] DYCE; the| COTES
2.2.101–2 That...us] DYCE; *prose* COTES
2.2.106–7 No...sir] DYCE; *prose* COTES
2.2.139 Look...too] DYCE; fool| COTES
2.2.178–9 Nothing...us] DYCE; *prose* COTES
2.2.187–8 And...Brentford] DYCE; *prose* COTES
2.3.13–15 Here...i'faith] DYCE; *prose* COTES
2.3.21 There...home] DYCE; *prose* COTES
2.3.26 Faith...thou] DYCE; *prose* COTES
2.3.30 Ay...master] DYCE; get| COTES
2.3.31–2 They...wenches] DYCE; things| minutes| 'em| COTES
2.3.34–5 Here's...hour] DYCE; *prose* COTES
2.3.37–8 Mistress...cup.] DYCE; *prose* COTES
3.1.1–2 O...me] DYCE; *prose* COTES
3.1.21–2 Thou...end] DYCE; strumpet| COTES
3.1.24–5 An...more] DYCE; *prose* COTES
3.1.37–8 Love...eyes] DYCE; *1 line* COTES
3.1.42–4 As...on't] DYCE; sun| COTES
3.1.44–5 O...me] | DYCE; *one line* COTES
3.1.45 Away] DYCE; *prose* COTES
3.1.45–6 Farewell...comfort] DYCE; sir| COTES
3.1.49–50 Your...soon] DYCE; lately| COTES
3.2.18–19 She...neighbour] DYCE; *prose* COTES
3.2.20–1 We...i'faith] DYCE; COTES: once| again| faith|
3.2.29 Methinks...him] DYCE; *prose* COTES
3.2.43–4 Now...gilt] DYCE; *prose* COTES
3.2.45 Sure...beard] DYCE; *prose* COTES
3.2.47–9 For...colour] PARKER; *prose* COTES
3.2.55–6 Now...end] DYCE; COTES: pocketing|
3.2.61–71 Had...Bucklersbury] DYCE; *prose* COTES
3.2.89–90 Bring...grief] DYCE; *prose* COTES
3.2.101–2 A...forsooth] DYCE; Cambridge| COTES
3.2.103–4 'Tis...well] DYCE; faith| women| COTES
3.2.126 What...up] DYCE; *prose* COTES
3.2.135–7 You'll...church-yard] DYCE; *prose* COTES
3.2.143–4 Yes...him] GEORGE; *prose* COTES
3.2.147 That...him] GEORGE; *prose* COTES
3.2.160–1 O...kisses] THIS EDITION; *verse line* COTES
3.2.196 Nothing...belike] THIS EDITION; *prose* COTES; sir| DYCE
3.3.3–7 For...brother] DYCE; me| vow| none| gameful| COTES
3.3.13–14 Prithee...blood] DYCE; *one line* COTES

3.3.25–6 Why...brother] DYCE; right| COTES
3.3.33–4 I...yours] DYCE; *one line* COTES
3.3.55–6 That...destiny] DYCE; thee| COTES
3.3.68 Singleness...smock] PARKER; her| COTES
3.3.135–7 Another...still-born] DYCE; *prose* COTES
3.3.142–3 I...farewell] DYCE; *one line* COTES
4.1.32 Why...now] THIS EDITION; mother| COTES
4.1.36–7 to...here] THIS EDITION; *prose* COTES; myself| PARKER
4.1.44–6 Some...so] DYCE; *prose* COTES
4.1.46–9 Faith...hither] DYCE; *prose* COTES
4.1.49 Why...him] DYCE; *prose* COTES
4.1.83–4 I mar'l...me] THIS EDITION; be| COTES; gentlewoman| marriage| PARKER
4.1.88–91 Life...together] THIS EDITION; body| knew| stranger| neither| COTES
4.1.97–101 I have...graduate] THIS EDITION; letter R| neither| hogs| not| comes| now| graduate| COTES
4.1.104–7 She shall not...cursy] THIS EDITION; her| it| her| COTES; speak| it| PARKER; her| it| DYCE
4.1.107–9 *Salve...heart*] DYCE; *pulcherrima* | *curo* | COTES
4.1.110 I...quoth a] DYCE; means| COTES
4.1.141–2 No...London] DYCE; boy| COTES
4.1.145 Why...gentlewoman] DYCE; *prose* COTES
4.1.146 As...Latin] PARKER; *prose* COTES
4.1.156–7 Tim...you, forsooth] THIS EDITION; pardoned, forsooth| her| COTES; quickly| her| PARKER
4.1.203 The...Abingdon] DYCE; Oxfordshire| COTES
4.1.204–5 And...citizen] DYCE; *prose* COTES
4.1.238–9 Tush...do] DYCE; that| COTES
4.1.253–4 Ay...mark] DYCE; *prose* COTES
4.2.1 Thieves...her] DYCE; stolen| COTES
4.3.25 I found...for] DYCE; *prose* COTES
4.4.1–2 Life...devil] DYCE; COTES: keeping| lock| devil|
4.4.7 Heart...out] DYCE; *prose* COTES
4.4.25 I'll...daughters] THIS EDITION; *prose* COTES; example| DYCE
4.4.35–9 You...joined] DYCE; *prose* COTES
4.4.55 And...forty] DYCE; maidenhead| COTES
4.4.67–8 There...pounds] DYCE; *prose* COTES
4.4.68 O...sir] DYCE; *prose* COTES
5.1.84 Tell...moan] DYCE; *prose* COTES
5.1.94 My...now] DYCE; *prose* COTES
5.1.103 There's...with't] DYCE; legacy| COTES
5.1.122 Am...forsooth] DYCE; chamber| COTES
5.2.12 And...mother] DYCE; 'tis done| COTES
5.2.69–70 Ay...quickly] | DYCE; *one line* COTES
5.2.71–5.2.72.1 He...servants] DYCE; *one line* COTES
5.2.82 O...this] DYCE; me| COTES
5.2.85–6 Moll...heart] DYCE; speak| COTES
5.3.5–7 Upon...night] DYCE; *prose* COTES
5.4.70–3 What...greedy] DYCE; sir| now| him| COTES

THE BLOODY BANQUET: A TRAGEDY

Edited by Julia Gasper and Gary Taylor

THE only early edition of *The Bloody Banquet*, a quarto dated 1639, was printed by Thomas COTES (STC 6181, *BEPD* 567), but not entered in the Stationers' Register. In some copies, the title-page was cropped, leading to the date being misread as 1620 or 1630; but Cole showed that this was an error, and that only one edition exists.

Lake conjectured, and Taylor (2000) has confirmed, that COTES was set from a scribal transcript, prepared by the scribe also responsible for the manuscript behind the printed text of Robert Davenport's *A New Trick to Cheat the Devil* (*BEPD* 561). The scribe divided each act into numbered scenes (using the formula 'Scene. [arabic numeral]'), and also imposed an unusual form of speech prefix for numbered characters in 1.3, 2.1, and 3.2 (with the number after the noun, rather than before); he also imposed his own linguistic preferences (*of't* rather than *on't*, *them* rather than *'em*, *hath* rather than *has*, etc.). We have generally restored the original authorial forms, when there is a consistent authorial preference, or when metre offers auxiliary evidence: see notes to 1.4.9, 1.4.32, 1.4.65, 1.4.163, 2.3.13, 3.1.22, 3.1.117–18.

COTES also apparently preserves a version of the play adapted for the theatre, probably after 1625. Although apparently written *c.*1609, the play belonged to the repertory of Beeston's boys, at the Cockpit, in 1639 (see Canon and Chronology). Schoenbaum's Malone Society transcript—the first and only reprinting of the text between COTES and our edition—conjectured that the play was abridged, and Taylor (2000) provides more evidence of both abridgement and adaptation. The Induction and 2.5 were probably written by an adapter to replace omitted material; the adapter may also be responsible for 3.2. If COTES represents an adaptation, then it presumably derives, at one or more removes, from a theatrical manuscript. For some evidence of this, see note to Induction.0.2. More generally, the stage directions in COTES are thorough and clear. Although COTES might owe these characteristics to its scribal source, its apparently complete and precise account of music cues is unusual, and tends to confirm derivation from the theatre.

The history of the manuscript behind COTES may explain two characteristics of the text, relevant to an editor. First, we have identified (in a short play) five probable lacunae: see notes to Induction.11, 1.1.154, 1.4.29, 4.3.106–7, 4.3.166–7. As the rest of the *Collected Works* makes clear, it is unusual to find so many lacunae. It did not occur to us until after we had finished editing the play that some or all of these gaps might result from ambiguities in the marking of theatrical cuts: on the evidence of manuscripts which do mark cuts, a scribe or compositor might easily have been misled into omitting a line or phrase which should have been retained, just before or just after a passage marked for omission. Secondly, some errors in the text are most plausibly explained by a two-stage process, of error then attempted conjectural correction: see notes to 3.3.36.2, 4.3.166–7, 5.1.165.

There is a good deal of mislineation in COTES, but this seems in large part to reflect the copy, which reflects authorial practices. In the 570 lines of the play attributed to Dekker or the adapter (Induction, 1.1, 1.2, 1.3, 2.2, 2.4, 2.5, 3.2, 5.1.110.2–5.1.248.1), we have identified only fourteen lineation errors, or one per every forty-seven lines; in the 1153 lines in the seven scenes clearly attributable to Middleton (1.4, 2.3, 3.1, 3.3, 4.1, 4.2, 4.3, 5.1.1–5.1.110.1), we record seventy-six such errors, or one per every fifteen lines. Moreover, the nature of the errors differs between the two authorial shares. In the non-Middleton scenes, the errors are those commonly found throughout plays of the period: short verse speeches of a line and a half, or of two half-lines, were often written and printed on a single line, and the same practice also often applied to a line and a half which begins or ends a longer speech. In the Middleton scenes, such errors are themselves more frequent, because Middleton more frequently divides verse lines between speakers; but the Middleton scenes also mix verse and prose, often within a single speech, in ways which copyists found confusing. Holdsworth (1982) demonstrated that the pattern of mislineation found in the Middleton scenes in COTES is characteristic of Middleton's work, particularly in his first decade as a playwright, and can differentiate him from his collaborators.

The conventions of Malone Society editions did not permit Schoenbaum to emend the text, but he did append a list of 'Irregular and Doubtful Readings' (pp. ix–xi) in which he identified errors he would have corrected; we have attributed all such corrections to SCHOENBAUM. When he queried a passage, we have regarded his query as a conjecture, which we have sometimes adopted, and sometimes not. Most of his corrections involve obvious typographical errors and added stage directions. He made no attempt to emend lineation, and all lineation emendations recorded below originate with this edition. Our edition is the first to annotate the text, and in doing so we have identified a number of passages, not noted by Schoenbaum, which seem not to make sense without emendation.

SEE ALSO

Text: *Works*, 641
Authorship and date: this volume, 364

WORKS CITED

Previous Editions

SCHOENBAUM, Samuel, ed., *The Bloody Banquet* (1961)

Other Works Cited

Alabaster, William, *Roxana* (1632)

Cole, G. W., 'Bibliographical Ghosts', *Papers of the Bibliographical Society of America* 12 (1919), 103-12

Cotgrave, John, ed., *The English Treasury of Wit and Language, Collected Out of the most, and best of our English Drammatick Poems* (1655)

Eliot, T. S., *Selected Essays* (1951), 65-105, 126-40

Freud, Sigmund, *The Standard Edition of the Complete Psychological Works*, tr. James Strachey *et al.*, 24 vols (1955-74), 21:10-11

Holdsworth, R. V., 'Middleton and Shakespeare: The Case for Middleton's Hand in *Timon of Athens*', unpublished Ph.D. diss. (University of Manchester, 1982)

Hunter, G. K., 'Seneca and the Elizabethans: A Case-Study in "Influence"', *Shakespeare Survey* 20 (1967), 17-26

—— 'Seneca and English Tragedy', in *Seneca*, ed. C. D. N. Costa (1974)

Kristeva, Julia, *Powers of Horror: an essay on abjection*, tr. Leon S. Roudiez (1982)

Oliphant, E. H. C., '*The Bloodie Banquet*: A Dekker-Middleton Play', *Times Literary Supplement* (17 December 1925), 882

Taylor, Gary, 'Gender, Hunger, Horror: The History and Significance of *The Bloody Banquet*', *Journal for Early Modern Cultural Studies* 1 (2001), 1-45

—— *Moment by Moment by Shakespeare* (1985)

—— 'Thomas Middleton, Thomas Dekker, and *The Bloody Banquet*', *Papers of the Bibliographical Society of America* 94 (2000), 197-233

Tricomi, Albert H., *Anticourt Drama in England 1603-1642* (1989)

Warner, Marina, *Managing Monsters: Six Myths of Our Time* (1994)

Warner, William, *Pan his Syrinx*, ed. Wallace A. Bacon (1950)

TEXTUAL NOTES

Persons.0.2 *Dramatis Personae*] A heading favoured by Dekker, not Middleton. Because the list is accurate and seems to be authorial, we have preserved its wording and layout; editorial additions are signalled by square brackets.

Persons.4-6 The…daughter] These characters only appear in the Induction dumbshow; however, they might have appeared as speaking characters in scenes originally belonging to the Lapyrus plot which were omitted from the extant text. If so, they would have appeared in the part of the play which seems to have been written by Dekker. (This is not an error in the list.)

Persons.7 and TYRANT of Lydia] THIS EDITION; *not in* COTES. After 1.1 he is identified, in stage directions and speech prefixes, as 'Tyrant'. The form in the list agrees with the form in a scene apparently written by Dekker.

Persons.11 a LADY in waiting] THIS EDITION (G.T.); *not in* COTES. A 'Lady' sent by the Young Queen on a domestic errand (carrying wine) speaks once, at 3.3.60-1, then exits. The Young Queen's 'maid' is then mentioned in an entrance direction at 3.3.77.2-3 (carrying a shirt) and 4.3.0.1 (carrying a lantern), but does not speak. Since the 'maid' attendant upon a queen would almost certainly be a lady, the two forms could easily refer to a single character; given the similar social and dramatic function performed by a 'maid' who enters only a few lines after a 'lady' exits, the existence of only a single character (identified by synonyms) seems especially likely.

Persons.13 ROXANO] SCHOENBAUM; Roxona COTES. An easy compositorial or scribal transposition.

Persons.16 SERTORIO] THIS EDITION; Sextorio COTES. The form in the dramatis personae list agrees with the form of the name found in 1.1 (apparently written by Dekker), but not elsewhere.

Persons.17 LODOVICO] THIS EDITION; Lodovicus COTES. See preceding note.

Induction.0.2 *Flourish. Enter*] THIS EDITION (G.T.); Enter [*broad space*] Floriſh. COTES. The music cue is separated from 'Enter' by more than three inches of white space, and justified flush to the right margin; moreover, it interrupts the syntax of the sentence begun by 'Enter' and continued by 'at one door'. Clearly, the flourish is meant to precede the entrance, and its position in COTES presumably reflects its position in the right margin of a manuscript page; it might easily be a theatrical addition to the original text. See next note.

Induction.0.2 *Chorus, then*] THIS EDITION (G.T.); *not in* COTES. Here as in other plays, the long stage direction describing a dumbshow is, in the printed or manuscript text, placed before the speech which explains the mimed action. This is a convention of textual display, which almost certainly does not reflect performance; performance can and regularly does present simultaneously material which has to be presented sequentially in the very different medium of a written text (Taylor 1985, p. 39). The complex action of this opening dumbshow would be unintelligible to any audience without the Choric commentary which seems meant to accompany and explain it. See note to Induction.1.

Induction.0.16 with] SCHOENBAUM; *vith* COTES

Induction.1 CHORUS] THIS EDITION (G.T.); *Enter Chorus*. COTES. We are given a stage direction in COTES, but no speech prefix; clearly, the direction is meant to double as a prefix, and may well have originated as a prefix. In *Hengist*, the 1662 quarto twice adds an 'Enter' (not present in the manuscripts) before a speech of Ranulph; in both cases, as here, the choric speech follows a long and complicated stage direction, which it is clearly meant to accompany and explain. See note to Induction.0.2.

Induction.4 constrainèd] THIS EDITION (J.G.); confeigned COTES. *O.E.D.* does not recognize 'confeigned', but it could mean 'mutually feigned'. However, we see nothing in the context to suggest that the Old King is insincere; feigning would undermine his credentials as a good king, which he is throughout the play. Some emendation therefore seems required. Dekker uses 'constrain'd' at *Satiromastix* 3.2.59, 60. Moreover, since COTES seems to have been set from a scribal manuscript, the spelling of the word in the printer's copy need not have been Dekker's. In secretary hand, 'conſtreigned' could easily have been misread as 'confeigned'. Other possibilities include 'consigned' (i.e. signed by both), 'confirmed', 'confessed' (i.e. public) and 'conferred'.

Induction.11 By [   ],] THIS EDITION (G.T.); *not in* COTES. SCHOENBAUM conjectured that a line was missing here; the confusion of sense could have resulted from eyeskip, if the missing line began (like the next line) with a short word beginning with the letter 'b' (or 'B'). Moreover, one would expect a 'by' somewhere in the missing line, to provide the seemingly necessary contrast with the following line's 'but chiefly by'. The sense must be that Lapyrus [was] 'entertained and welcomed' [by the king and his court], 'but chiefly by' Eurymone.

1.1.1 TYRANT] THIS EDITION; *Arm.* COTES. This form of the speech prefixes—an abbreviation of 'Armatrites'—is used consistently in 1.1, and not thereafter. The character does not appear again in a scene which seems to be written by Dekker alone; he is identified as 'Tyrant' in the final scene, apparently of mixed authorship. Its persistence in the final scene might also be scribal; by the time he reached the final scene, the scribe knew the play well enough to retain 'Tyrant', even if his copy reverted to 'Armatrites'. Schoenbaum says that the character 'becomes a tyrant in this scene', so that 'there is no real confusion'; but he usurps the throne in the opening stage direction, where he is called 'the Tyrant', so the speech prefix variation cannot be attributed to a change in political status; it is more likely due to collaborative authorship.

1.1.21 your] THIS EDITION (G.T.); *our* COTES. There is nothing extraordinarily deserving about putting their lives at risk in fighting their own foes; the Tyrant's point is that they have risked their lives in fighting someone who is not their own natural foe, but Lydia's. The emendation also produces a powerful succession of pronouns (our, their, your), in place of a pointless repetition (our, their, our). The error could easily have arisen from contamination by the pronoun earlier in the line. Compare 65–8, where the Tyrant addresses the old King repeatedly with 'you' and 'your'.

1.1.31 are] SCHOENBAUM; *are are* COTES

1.1.40 rightfully] THIS EDITION (G.T.); *rightly* COTES. A metrical emendation. But also compare 143–4, where 'wrongfully' and 'unforcedly' contrast with 'rightfully' and 'force' here.

1.1.45 MAZERES] SCHOENBAUM; *Max.* COTES

1.1.73 sadness] THIS EDITION (*conj.* Schoenbaum); *fadneffe* COTES. A metrical emendation; the superfluous plural could easily have resulted from contamination from the other terminal sibilants in the line.

1.1.76 I have] SCHOENBAUM; *Ihave* COTES. Elision does not seem to be required by the metre.

1.1.76 AMORPHO] THIS EDITION (*conj.* Schoenbaum); *Arma.* COTES. Elsewhere in this scene the speech prefix for Armatrites/Tyrant is always '*Arm.*'; he nowhere else addresses the old king as 'my lord' (appropriate for a servant, not a rival king), but instead as 'old king' or 'doting Lydia'. Since this would be the first speech of Amorpho, the compositor or scribe could easily have misread the abbreviation.

1.1.121 gloss] THIS EDITION (G.T.); *glaffe* COTES. An easy misreading. A glass which is dim does lose its value (for seeing through, or reflecting); but the surface gloss may be restored to many objects, whose worth is therefore unaffected.

1.1.130 weep] THIS EDITION (G.T.); *weepe for* COTES. A metrical emendation: 'weep' can take the obsolete sense 'shed tears over, lament with tears' (*OED v.* 6), thus being synonymous with the more common expression 'weep for', which a compositor or scribe might easily substitute, thereby disrupting the metre of this otherwise formal utterance.

1.1.154–5 bounties [   ] I] THIS EDITION (G.T.). We have marked a lacuna because something seems necessary after the 'or if' clause: either they are acting out of charity, or if [they intend to supply him with] larger bounties, then I was mad etc.

1.3.4 country] SCHOENBAUM; *Counttey* COTES

1.3.8 FIRST THIEF] COTES (*The.* 1.) Throughout, COTES postpositions the numerals for the two thieves; this seems to be a scribal eccentricity, and we have used the normal form.

1.3.21 within] COTES; *without conj.* G.T.

1.3.45 your name] SCHOENBAUM; *you name* COTES

1.3.50 Lurks in this forest that] THIS EDITION (G.T.); *In this Forreft lurkes that* COTES. Both the metre and the rhetorical pattern suggest that a scribe or compositor has transposed the verb.

1.3.78 honour] SCHOENBAUM; *honours* COTES

1.4.9 O'] THIS EDITION (G.T.); *On* COTES. Middleton almost invariably uses the contracted form 'a purpose' (modern-spelling 'o' purpose'): compare *Phoenix* 9.35, *Michaelmas* 3.4.87, *Mad World* 4.5.34, *Trick* 1.1.93, 3.1.135, *Puritan* 3.5.72, *Roaring Girl* 4.19, *No Wit* 7.148, 9.124, *Lady* 4.1.153, 5.1.56, *Old Law* 4.2.130, *Hengist* 4.2.18, *Quiet Life* 2.2.203, *Changeling* 5.2.24, *Game* 2.1.157. Scribes or compositors alter Middleton's preferred form to 'on' in other texts of *Hengist* and *Game*, and the scribe who prepared printer's copy for COTES elsewhere avoids a = o'.

1.4.11 unworth] THIS EDITION (G.T.); *unworthy* COTES. Substitution of common for rare word; 'unworth' (*OED a.*^{2}) seems required by both the metre and the rhetorical parallelism.

1.4.29 padlocks, [   ].] THIS EDITION (*conj.* Schoenbaum); *padlockes,* COTES. The metre, grammar, and the lack of an expected rhyme all suggest that half of a verse line is missing. Perhaps evidence of a larger cut?

1.4.32 'em] THIS EDITION (G.T.); *them* COTES. The scribe who prepared the manuscript used by COTES seems to have systematically expanded Middleton's favourite contraction, leaving only three instances. We have restored it, in scenes which seem clearly to be Middleton's, when metre or syntax does not require a stress on the pronoun: 1.4.64, 1.4.210, 2.3.12, 2.3.41–2, 4.1.32, 4.1.34, 4.3.10, 4.3.191, 4.3.273 (end of line), 5.1.27, 5.1.51. This leaves a total of 15 'em, 6 them, in Middleton scenes.

1.4.65 on't] THIS EDITION (G.T.); *of't* COTES. The unusual contraction 'of't' appears to be a scribal sophistication of Middleton's favoured 'on't'; it appears seven times, always in scenes apparently written by Middleton. We have restored Middleton's form: 1.4.211, 2.1.40, 4.1.19, 4.1.21, 4.2.45, 5.1.72.

1.4.66 I...fantasy] Schoenbaum suggested this line was a sign of cuts since 'she has done no such thing' (p. vii). However, the Queen may be referring to the business of the pledges.

1.4.84 he] THIS EDITION (G.T.); *thee* COTES. She uses the second person pronoun elsewhere in this speech only when apostrophizing herself, but here the word must contrast with 'myself' and rhyme with 'me'. An easy error.

1.4.108.1 *Enter...guard*] THIS EDITION (G.T.). COTES places this direction after 106, where it is unmotivated and seems out of place; but it would naturally follow the Tyrant's call 'Why, villains!', which would also alert the Queen to his presence. If the direction were placed in the margin, a scribe or compositor might easily have been unsure about the exact position where it should be interpolated into the dialogue.

1.4.111 Thetis] THIS EDITION (G.T.); *Tethis* COTES. This is the only occasion in the text where the Young Queen is named. The corresponding character in the play's source is consistently and repeatedly called Thetis. The single occurrence of 'Tethis' here could easily result from a simple scribal or compositorial transposition.

1.4.127 that's] COTES (that's)

1.4.132 rèceived] For the accent, compare *Mad World* 1.1.102, *Truth* 510, *Game* 4.2.42, *Prosperity* 164, 170.

1.4.147 on't] THIS EDITION; of it COTES. See Taylor (2000), 222-6.

1.4.159 enough] SCHOENBAUM; enongh COTES

1.4.163 i'th'] THIS EDITION (G.T.); in the COTES. In the texts of Middleton's full-length plays apparently unaffected by scribal interference, numbers of this contraction almost invariably reach to double figures. In COTES there are only two—just as there are only two in Davenport's *New Trick*, though Davenport's other plays have 14 and 20 examples each. COTES's 'in the' thus often seems to be a scribal expansion. We have contracted 'in the' when it appears in prose (1.4.220, 3.1.17, 3.1.81, 3.1.82) or in verse when the metre seems to require elision: see notes below at 3.1.22, 3.1.117-18. As emended, our text therefore contains nine examples, which is within Middleton's range for a collaborative play.

1.4.169 safety] SCHOENBAUM; fafety COTES

1.4.182 Then] THIS EDITION (J.G.); than COTES

1.4.207 an he] COTES (and ~)

2.1.0.2-3 In...opened.] THIS EDITION (G.T.); not in COTES. These stage properties remain in place throughout Act Two: the tree, indicating the forest in 2.1, 2.2, and 2.4, suggests a garden in 2.3 (where the trapdoor is ignored). Compare Shakespeare and Fletcher's *Two Noble Kinsmen*, where a bush is present throughout the six scenes of Act Three.

2.1.1 FIRST SHEPHERD] COTES (*Shep.* 1.). Throughout, COTES postpositions the numerals for the two shepherds; this seems to be a scribal eccentricity, and we have used the normal form.

2.1.40 work] THIS EDITION (*conj.* Schoenbaum); weeke COTES. There was no 'cleansing week' in the calendar.

2.1.49 Long Lane] COTES (long lane)

2.1.52 guts] THIS EDITION (G.T.); ftomackes COTES. There is no particular reason to associate fiddlers with stomachs, but a compositor or scribe could have unconsciously substituted 'stomachs' for its synonym 'guts'—which in addition to the sense 'appetite' has the specific musical sense 'strings for a musical instrument': compare *Roaring Girl* 8.78.

2.1.53 bites] COTES (bits)

2.2 *new scene* (*Scene.* 2.). Although the place has not changed, the stage has been cleared of actors. However, the marking of a new scene here—which is probably scribal—may reflect a change of authors, rather than theatrical convention: compare Act Five.

2.2.38.1 *Cover the pit, and*] THIS EDITION (G.T.); *not in* COTES. Another wolf will only fall into the pit if it is covered with boughs, as before; moreover, covering the pit makes more plausible the change of locale for the next scene.

2.3 *new scene* COTES (*Scene.* 3.). The stage has been cleared of actors because Lapyrus, in the pit, is technically off the stage once he stops speaking—until he reappears by speaking again in 2.4.

2.3.7 o'] THIS EDITION (G.T.); on COTES. See 1.4.9.

2.3.9 upon] THIS EDITION (G.T.); on COTES. Metrical emendation.

2.3.13 I've] THIS EDITION (G.T.); I have COTES. The scribe seems to have systematically eliminated Middleton's favoured contraction 'I've'; we have restored it in Middleton scenes where the metre would require it.

2.3.13 gall; instead of ∧ blood,] THIS EDITION (G.T.); Gall ∧ in stead of th' blood, COTES. The scribe or compositor has mis-

understood the speech, contrasting 'the gall' which Tymethes has hit with 'th' blood' he has not hit; in fact, 'the blood' is not a part of the body one aims for, or a part one can avoid hitting if one has also hit any interior organ (like the gall bladder). Instead, 'blood' which Mazeres does not shed (and which he might be expected to shed, if he were physically hit) must be contrasted with 'distractions' which he does shed. Thus, the article ('th'') is intrusive not only metrically but grammatically, interpolated by contamination from the foregoing phrase.

2.3.61 shut your] SCHOENBAUM; fhuty our COTES

2.3.93 but] THIS EDITION (G.T.); and COTES. Tymethes must mean that 'the Tyrant's gem' is the exception to Roxano's claim that the unknown woman is 'the sweetest', and there are no parallels (in Middleton or *OED*) for the construction 'excepting and'. For 'excepting but', compare *Trick* 5.2.159; 'excepting only' (with the same sense) is common.

2.5 *new scene* THIS EDITION (G.T.); *not in* COTES. The stage has been cleared of actors, and the following action and speech therefore constitute a separate scene, as clearly as the Induction, or the other scenes of Act Two.

2.5.0.2 *Chorus, then*] THIS EDITION (G.T.); *not in* COTES. See Induction.0.2.

2.5.0.14 *nurse*] SCHOENBAUM; nu fe COTES

2.5.1 CHORUS] THIS EDITION (G.T.); *Enter Chorus*, COTES. See Induction.1.

3.1.5 throat] SCHOENBAUM; rhroate COTES

3.1.22 i'th'] THIS EDITION (G.T.); in the COTES. Metrical emendation. See 1.4.163.

3.1.63 Play] COTES; Ply *conj.* J.G.

3.1.64 resolved ∧ an...lord?] THIS EDITION; resolv'd? and... Lord. COTES

3.1.117-18 i'th' night...i'th' dark] THIS EDITION (G.T.); in th' night...in the darke COTES. Within the same couplet, the prepositional phrase is spelled *in th'*, *in the*, and *i'th'*, in COTES, though the rhythm and parallelism clearly require the same pronunciation; this seems to be scribal interference with authorial contractions. See 1.4.163.

3.2.2 FIRST SERVANT] COTES (*Ser.* 1.). Throughout, COTES postpositions the numerals for the four servants; this seems to be a scribal eccentricity, and we have used the normal form.

3.2.25.1 *The...exeunt*] THIS EDITION (G.T.); *not in* COTES. She has given them an order to 'Go', which they presumably follow; moreover, since these are the servants who presumably set out the properties at the beginning of 3.3 (the 'charge', presumably, which the paper gives them), they need to exit now, in order not to violate the law of re-entry. The rest of the Queen's speech is not addressed to them, and closely resembles her asides and soliloquies elsewhere in the play. See next note.

3.2.34 *Exit*] THIS EDITION (G.T.); *Exeunt.* COTES. See previous note. Perhaps a mistaken expansion of an original abbreviation 'Ex' (as in *Dick of Devonshire*, which may have been copied by the same scribe).

3.3.7.1 *Pulls...hood*] THIS EDITION (G.T.). COTES places this direction after 'sir' (7); but it treats the entire speech as a single verse line, which means that in the manuscript the direction was placed opposite the speech; by convention, a direction so placed might belong at any point within the line to which it is appended.

3.3.21 visor, and] THIS EDITION (J.G.); vizarded COTES. Roxano is taking the disguise from Valesta so that he can give it to Mazeres (22-4) who enters wearing it a few lines below

(36.1–3). Therefore Valesta cannot also be wearing the visor from this point on.

3.3.22   disguise] SCHOENBAUM; di guiſe COTES

3.3.31   wrong] SCHOENBAUM; wong COTES

3.3.35   o'er] COTES (or). COTES's spelling is ambiguous, but for *over* in this sense compare *Romeo* 1.2.7 ('But saying o'er what I have said before').

3.3.36.2   three] THIS EDITION (J.G.); 4. COTES. Mazeres, in disguise, has now replaced one of the four original servants. Valesta is waiting outside and it is essential that Tymethes does not notice that anything has changed. This error might have been caused by a scribe or prompter who noticed that Mazeres was not included in the original direction, and so added him, without altering the number.

3.3.36.5   Tymethes] SCHOENBAUM adds '*Exeunt servants*', but Mazeres has to stay, and since he is pretending to be one of the servants, it would be odd and unnecessary for them to leave and him to stay.

3.3.76   horrid] THIS EDITION (G.T.); horrible COTES. The line as printed is too long: no amount of elision will make it scan, within even the generous metrical conventions of the play, or Middleton; but 'horrid' appears at 5.1.127, and elsewhere in Middleton; a scribe or compositor could easily substitute the more common synonym, especially under the influence of the following word ('horribul fearful'). As emended, the line is a (common) hexameter, with an extra unstressed syllable before the caesura (also common).

3.3.80   sweetly] SCHOENBAUM; ſwee ely COTES

3.3.86   and] THIS EDITION (G.T.); and a COTES. The article is superfluous and extrametrical; it is easily interpolated almost anywhere, but especially here, by contamination from the preceding phrase; and it has the surely undesired effect of implying that the nightcap is *not* 'fair-wrought'.

3.3.100   a eunuch] COTES (an Eunuch)

3.3.108   are, seek] SCHOENBAUM; areſe,eke COTES. In Schoenbaum's list of corrections, the original reading is reproduced inaccurately (with a space after the comma).

3.3.123   thorough] THIS EDITION (G.T.); through COTES. Metrical emendation. The meaning is identical, and 'thorough' appears (solely for metrical reasons) in Middleton's autograph *Game* 1.1.248.

3.3.130   office'] office, COTES

4.1.18   sights] THIS EDITION (G.T.); lights COTES. In 3.3 'lights' are specifically set out, and Tymethes remarks upon their 'lustre', which is so great that he at first mistakes it for daybreak; by contrast, the servants are 'visored' and the Queen 'masked'; moreover, Tymethes is contrasting himself with them, not himself with their lamps. For the variety of senses in which 'sights' would be relevant, see *OED n.*[1], 3 'appearance, aspect' (*Timon* 1.249, 'I am joyful of your sights'), 7a 'look or glance', 13a 'pupil of the eye'. An easy misreading.

4.1.19   Fore] COTES (For)

4.1.39   I've] THIS EDITION (G.T.); I have COTES. See 2.3.13.

4.1.41.2   exeunt] THIS EDITION (J.G.); exit COTES. Further evidence that the original manuscript probably used the abbreviation 'ex' (as in *Dick of Devonshire*; see note to 3.2.34).

4.1.44.1   cum] THIS EDITION; come COTES. A misreading for the unfamiliar Latin word: compare 1.1.85.1 '*exit cum suis*'.

4.2.18   so vigorously thy affection] THIS EDITION (G.T.); thy affeċtion ſo vigoroufly COTES. Metrical transposition: there is no reason for the author to place the words in an unmetrical sequence, and every possibility of accidental transposition by scribe or compositor.

4.2.51   TYRANT] SCHOENBAUM; Try. COTES

4.2.65   I've] THIS EDITION (G.T.); I have COTES. See 2.3.13.

4.2.79   I've] THIS EDITION (G.T.); I have COTES. See 2.3.13.

4.3.6   darkness] SCHOENBAUM; darkedeſſe COTES

4.3.95   sleights] THIS EDITION (G.T.); fights COTES. Tymethes is not responsible for, and need not repent, things he has seen, but must repent not only his 'dishonest thoughts' but also his dishonest actions, the execution of those thoughts. An easy error.

4.3.106–7   senses, [   ].] THIS EDITION (G.T.); fences: COTES. The text has a conditional clause without the corresponding consequent clause; presumably she is justifying her treachery, in shooting him in the back, by claiming that, if he had had any warning, he would have been able to prevent her. Eyeskip from one verse line to another? or consequent upon a larger deliberate cut?

4.3.116   now] SCHOENBAUM; no w COTES

4.3.117   Who's] COTES (Who's)

4.3.118   deeds] THIS EDITION (G.T.); deed's COTES. The required sense seems to be 'we must be safe, the deeds [must be] unknown'. The apostrophe turns it into a declarative statement of fact, which is not in fact true, and which bears an unclear relationship to the surrounding text. Compare Middleton's superfluous autograph apostrophe in 'Good's' and 'mean't' (*Game* 3.1.51 and 5.3.148).

4.3.166–7   all. | QUEEN . . . TYRANT Nothing] THIS EDITION (G.T.); all; | Nothing COTES. The Tyrant's final sentence (167) seems to be an answer to an unspoken question, which would complete the preceding incomplete verse line (166–7). Part-lines in the middle of a speech are not unexampled in the play, but they are relatively rare, and most of the Queen's speeches hereabouts are short. Such an omission probably would have required two stages: first the accidental omission of the half-line, then a subsequent 'correction' of the apparently duplicated speech prefix for the Tyrant.

4.3.167   but] SCHOENBAUM; bnt COTES

4.3.195   believed] COTES (beleev'd)

4.3.206   whispering] SCHOENBAUM; whiſperlng COTES

4.3.270   I] THIS EDITION (J.G.); he COTES

4.3.279   corpse] COTES (corpes). As the preceding 'those' makes clear, a plural sense seems required. The spelling 'corpes' is listed in *OED* under 'corpse' (*sb.*2.d). The plural form seems less odd when we compare it to the word 'remains'. Since Tymethes has now been cut up into quarters, it is a moot point whether he is singular or plural, and aurally 'corpse' and 'corpes' are identical.

4.3.281.1   Sertorio . . . limbs] THIS EDITION (G.T.); not in COTES. The limbs must be in view for Zenarchus's speech, beginning 5.1, and they are specifically mentioned at 5.1.127–9; it would be dramatically effective to hang them at the end of the act, thus leaving them on display during the interval.

5.1.51   took'st] THIS EDITION (G.T.); tookeſt COTES

5.1.100   threats] SCHOENBAUM; thereats COTES

5.1.110.2   Thunder] THIS EDITION (G.T.); Scene. 2. | Thunder COTES (which also separates the two 'scenes' with a horizontal bar). The two bodies are visible still on stage; the stage has not been cleared, and no change of scene is required. A change of authors (and hence, of paper) might have been misinterpreted as the beginning of a new scene.

5.1.117   both in haste] THIS EDITION (G.T.); for ſome haſt COTES. This line is clearly corrupt, and we are not at all sure that our emendation restores the authorial reading, but it is the best solution we can find. The subject required by 'died' must be a noun or pronoun which refers to 'my children': therefore the auxiliary verb 'hast' does not agree grammatically with the noun. It would be possible to emend 'Their' (the first word of the preceding line) to 'Thy', thereby making the entire couplet an apostrophe to the dead children, and making it possible to retain 'hast'; but it would still be necessary to emend the second and third words of the line, so that this solution complicates rather than simplifies any solution. It would be much simpler to interpret 'hast' as a seventeenth-century spelling of *haste*; this is not an emendation, but a mere modernization/interpretation. It also seems relevant, since his children have died quickly, unexpectedly, and prematurely. The problem then becomes to interpret or emend 'for some' in a way that relates to 'haste', and provides a subject for the verb 'died'. The proposed solution assumes a compound misreading of two words not clearly separated (bothin = forfom). Paleographically, this emendation is much less likely than others proposed in this edition; but it does create a pattern of ascenders and minims which resembles the general shape of the COTES text, and it does produce an intelligible metrical sentence.

5.1.127   inhuman] COTES (inhumaine)

5.1.140   and] SCHOENBAUM; aad COTES

5.1.143.2   *Loud*] SCHOENBAUM; *Lond* COTES

5.1.149   Let't] COTES (Let)

5.1.155.4–5   *She . . . skull.*] THIS EDITION (G.T.); *not in* COTES. These are the climactic actions of the play, and the reason for its title; they must have been performed at some point between her entrance and her death.

5.1.155.6   *wonder*] Schoenbaum adds 'Exit Sertorio', but there is no reason why he should not remain.

5.1.165   spoke] THIS EDITION (G.T.); ſpeakes COTES. The rest of the passage is in the past tense; 'spake' might easily have been corrupted to 'speake', then 'speakes'.

5.1.167.1   *Fidelio*] THIS EDITION (*conj.* Schoenbaum); *Amorpho* COTES. Fidelio returns at 5.1.194.1 and then has two speeches reporting on the situation outside. Possibly an authorial error, or in some way caused by adaptation.

5.1.181   airs] THIS EDITION (G.T.); dares COTES. The printed text does not make any discernible sense. The emendation preserves the rhyme, and has many relevant senses: 'atmospheric conditions', 'scents', 'breaths'. The young Queen is not only forced to eat the body; she is confined in the castle, and allowed no fresh air, just the air in rooms contaminated by the smell of a rotting body. The image depends upon the early modern idioms 'taste the air' and 'eat the air'.

5.1.237   behold] SCHOENBAUM; b hold COTES

STAGE DIRECTIONS

[Printed before the play:]

Drammatis Personae.

The King of Lydia.
Tymethes *his Sonne.*
Lapirus *his Nephew.*

The King of Lycia.
Zantippus *his Sonne.*
Eurimone *his Daughter.*

Armatrites *King of* Cilicia.
Zenarchus *his Sonne.*
Amphridote *his Daughter.*
His Young Queene.
Her Mayd.
Mazeres *his Favorite.*
Roxona *the young Queenes Keeper*

Fidelio. ⎱ *Two faithfull Servants to the*
Amorpho ⎰ *Lydian King.*

Sextorio. ⎱ *Two unfaithfull Servants*
Lodovicus. ⎰ *of his.*

The Old Queene of Lydia.
Her two little Children.

Chorus.   4. Servants.
The Clowne.   Souldiers.
Two Shepheards.

Induction.0.1   *INDVCTIO.*

Induction.0.1   Enter [*broad space*] Florish.

Induction.0.2–20   *At one doore the old King of* Lydia, Tymethes *his | Sonne,* Lapyrus *his Nephew, and Souldiers. At | the other the old King of* Lycia, Zantippus *his Son, |* Eurmone *his Daughter, and Souldiers. The two | Kings parley, and change hostages for peace. La-|pyrus is given to the* Lycian, *and* Zantippus *to the* Lydian. *The |* Lycian *seemes to offer his daughter* Eurymone *to* Lapyrus *to fall | from his Uncle, and joyne with him; he accepts her, drawing his | sword against his Country and Uncle. The* Lydian *sends his sonne |* Tymethes *for ayd; he enters againe with Armatrites King of |* Cilicia, Zenarchus *his sonne, and* Mazeres *a young Prince, the | Cilician Kings follower. All they draw against the Lycians par-|ty, whereat they all with Lapyrus flye; the two other Kings pur-|suing them. Then enter the old Queene of* Lydia *flying from her | Nephew* Lapyrus, *with two Babes in her armes; he pursuing her | with his drawne sword.*

Induction.0.1   *Enter Chorus.* (at Induction.0.20–Induction.1)

Induction.31–1.1.0.1   *Exit.*

1.1.0.1–8   *Act.* 1. *Scene* 1. | *Enter, The two Kings of* Lydia *and* Cilicia, Zenarchus *sonne | to the* Cilician, Tymethes, *sonne to the* Lydian, Mazeres, | Fidelio, Amorpho, Sextorio, Lodovicus, *when they come | unto the Throne, the Tyrant of* Cilicia *puts by the old King, | and ascends alone: all snatch out their swords,* Mazeres *crownes | him, the old King and* Tymethes *stand amazed. | Florish.* (justified right)

1.1.85.1   *Exit cum suis.* (right margin)

1.1.102.1   *Exit. all but Zenarchus and Tymethes.*

1.1.124.1   *Enter Amphrodite.*

1.1.146.1   *Enter Mazeres observing.*

1.1.150.1   *Exeunt.*

1.1.164   *Exit.* (followed by a horizontal line across the page)

1.2.0.1–2   *Scene.* 2. | *Enter the old Queen with two Babes, as being hard pursued.*

1.2.10.1   *Cry within follow, follow.*

1.2.11   *Exit.* (followed by a horizontal line across the page)

1.3.0.1   *Scen.* 3. | *Enter Lapirus disguised.*

1.3.6.1–2   *Enter the Queene and two souldiers pursuing her.*

1.3.16.1   *Exeunt.*

1.3.35   *aside.* (right margin)

1.3.63.1   *Puls off his false beard | and kneeles.* (right margin, opposite 1.3.63–4, 'first . . . do't')

1.3.94.1   *Exeunt.* (followed by a horizontal line across the page)

1.4.0.1   *Scene.* 4. | *Enter Tymethes and Zenarchus.*

1.4.10.1   *Enter Roxano.*

1.4.12.1 *they whisper.* (right margin)

1.4.17 *Exit.*

1.4.34.1 *Enter young Queene with a booke in her hand.*

1.4.55.1 *Enter Roxano with wine.*

1.4.60.1 *Drinkes and gives Roxano the Cup.*

1.4.65.1 *Rox. offers it him.* (right margin)

1.4.73.1 *Gives Roxano the Cup.* (right margin)

1.4.78 *Exit.*

1.4.81 *Exit.*

1.4.100.1 *Enter Tyrant.*

1.4.108–1.4.108.2 *Enter Roxano and guard.* (at 1.4.106)

1.4.111.1–2 *Walkes off with her, and the guard followes.* (justified right)

1.4.128.1 *Enter Queene sad.*

1.4.188.1 *(She swounds and Roxano holds her in his armes.* (justified right)

1.4.223 *Exit.* (followed by a horizontal line across the page)

2.1.0.1–3 *Act 2. Scene. 1.*

2.1.0.3–4 *Enter Clowne, and two Sheapheards.*

2.1.77.1 *Exeunt.* (followed by a horizontal line aross the page)

2.2.0.1 *Scene. 2. | Enter Lapirus, solus.*

2.2.13.1 *He falls in the Pit.* (justified right)

2.2.17.1 *Enter Clowne.* (right margin)

2.2.38.1 *Exit.*

2.3.0.1 *[horizontal line across the page] | Scene. 3. | Enter Zenarchus, Tymethes, Amphridote, and Mazeres.*

2.3.24 *Exit.*

2.3.27.1 *Enter Roxano disguised.*

2.3.92 *Exit.*

2.3.99 *Exeunt.* (followed by a horizontal line across the page)

2.4.0.1 *Scene. 4. | Enter the old King, Fidelio, and Amorpho.*

2.4.4 *[in the pit.]* (between speech prefix and speech)

2.4.19.1 *(Lapi. fals downe.* (right margin)

2.4.30 *Exeunt.*

2.5.0.1–2.5.1 *Dumbe shew. | Enter the old Queene weeping, with both her Infants, the one | dead; she layes downe the other on a banke, and goes to bury the | dead, expressing much griefe. Enter the former shepheards, | walking by carelesly, at last they espie the child and strive for | it, at last the Clowne gets it, and dandles it, expressing all signes | of joy to them. Enter againe the Queene, she lookes for her | Babe and finding it gone, wrings her hands; the Shepheards see | her, then wisper together, then beckon to her; she joyfully runs | to them, they returne her child, she points to her breasts, as mea-|ning she should nu se it, they all give her money, the Clowne kisses | the Babe and her, and so Exeunt severall wayes. Then enter La-|pirus, the old King, Amorpho, and Fidelio, they misse the | Queene and so expressing great sorrow. Exeunt. | Enter Chorus.*

2.5.15.1 *Exit.* (followed by a horizontal line across the page)

3.1.0.1 *Act. 3. Scene. 1. | Enter Roxano with his disguise in his hand.*

3.1.10.1 *Enter Mazeres musing.*

3.1.42 *Exit.*

3.1.60.1 *Enter Mazeres.*

3.1.74.1 *Enter Tymethes.*

3.1.86.1–2 *Exit.*

3.1.116.1 *He puts on the hood.* (right margin)

3.1.124.1 *Exeu.* (followed by a horizontal line across the page)

3.2.0.1–2 *Scen. 2. | Enter the Queene and foure servants, she with a booke | in her hand.*

3.2.34 *Exeunt.* (followed by a horizontal line across the page)

3.3.0.1–4 *Scene. 3. | Soft musicke, a Table with lights set out. Arras spread. | Enter Roxano leading Tymethes. Mazeres meetes them.*

3.3.5 *Exit.*

3.3.7.1–3.3.8 *Puls off the hood.* (right margin)

3.3.19.1–4 *Loud musicke. Enter 2. with a Banquet; other 2. with lights; | they set 'em downe and depart, making obeysance. Rox-|ano takes one of them aside.*

3.3.26.1 *Exit.*

3.3.36.1–5 *Loud Musicke, Enter Roxano, Mazeres and the 4. Servants, | with dishes of sweete meates, Roxano places them: each | having delivered his dish makes low obeysance to Tyme-|thes.*

3.3.59.1 *Enter a Lady with wine.*

3.3.62.1–2 *Spils the wine.* (on separate line, beginning just below semicolon of 'thankefully;')

3.3.77.1–3 *Soft Musicke. Enter the Queene masked in her night-| gowne; her mayd with a shirt and a Night cap.*

3.3.104.1 *He reads.* (left margin, opposite 'Our')

3.3.118 *Exit.*

3.3.119 *Exit.*

3.3.132 *Exit.* (followed by a horizontal line across the page)

4.1.0.1–2 *Act. 4. Scene. 1. | Enter Tymethes and Zenarchus.*

4.1.18.1 *Enter Tyrant and Mazeres observing.*

4.1.22.1 *Enter Amphridote.*

4.1.29.1 *Tymethes kisses her.* (right margin)

4.1.41.1–2 *They kisse, and Exit. Zenarchus and Amphridote.*

4.1.44.1 *Exit. come Mazeres.*

4.1.59.1 *Enter Mazeres and Roxano.*

4.1.62–4.1.62.1 *Exit.* (at 4.1.61)

4.1.74 *Exit.*

4.1.76 *Exit.* (followed by a horizontal line across the bottom of the page; 4.2 begins on next page)

4.2.0.1 *Scene. 2. | Enter Amphridote and Mazeres.*

4.2.2.1 *Enter Tyrant.* (right margin)

4.2.50.1 *Enter Lodovico.*

4.2.54.1 *Enter Sertorio.* (right margin)

4.2.65.1 *Exeunt all but Amphridote.* (centred)

4.2.70.1 *Enter Mazeres.*

4.2.95 *(a side.* (right margin)

4.2.98 *Exit.*

4.2.101.1 *Exit.* (followed by a horizontal line across the page)

4.3.0.1 *Scene. 3. | Enter Queen and her maide with a light.*

4.3.13.1 *She sleepes.* (right margin)

4.3.13.1–2 *Enter Roxano as she sleepes with Tymethes hudwinckt.*

4.3.31.1 *Exit.*

4.3.34.1 *Opens a darke Lanthorne.*

4.3.42.1 *He spies the Queene.*

4.3.45.1 *She awakes.*

4.3.79.1 *Exit.*

4.3.88.1 *Enter the Queene with two Pistols.*

4.3.96.1 *She shootes him dead.*

4.3.125.1 *Enter Tyrant with a Torch.*

4.3.128.1 *She runnes to him.* (right margin)

4.3.170 *aside* (right margin)

4.3.182.1 *Enter from below, Mazeres habited like Roxano.*

4.3.192.1 *Exit.*

4.3.218.1 *They Enter.*

4.3.228 *Exit.*

4.3.231.1 *Enter Mazeres.*

4.3.249.1 *Enter Roxano from below.*

4.3.254 *Runnes at Roxano.* (at 4.3.253, on separate line, beginning just above first letter of 'there's')

4.3.270 *Exit.*

4.3.272.1–2 *Enter Tyrant Sertorio, Lodovico, bringing in | Tymethes limbes.*

4.3.282.1   *Exeunt omn.* (followed by a horizontal line across the bottom of the page; 5.1 begins on next page)
5.1.0.1-2   *Act. 5. Scene. 1. | Enter Zenarchus solus.*
5.1.6.1   *Enter Tyrant.*
5.1.37.1   *Enter Sertorio.* (right margin)
5.1.42.1   *Enter Mazeres and Sertorio.*
5.1.63.1   *Exit.*
5.1.66.1   *Enter Amphridote and Lodovico.*
5.1.81.1   *Enter Lod. with wine and Exit.*
5.1.82-5.1.82.1   *She poysons the wine.*
5.1.108.1   *She dyes.* (right margin)
5.1.110.1   *Dyes.* (right margin, followed by a horizontal line across the page)
5.1.110.2-3   *Scene. 2. | Thunder and lightning. A Blazing starre appeares. | Enter Tyrant.*
5.1.118.1   *Enter Sertorio and Lodovico.*
5.1.124.1-2   *Enter the Old King, Lapirus, Fidelio, Amorpho, all | disguised like Pilgrims.*

5.1.142.1   *Enter Sertorio.*
5.1.143.2-3   *Loud Musicke. A banquet brought in, and by it a small | Table for the Queene.*
5.1.150.1   *Enter Sertorio.*
5.1.151.1   *Exit.*
5.1.155.1-6   *Soft Musicke. Enter the Tyrant with the Queene, her | haire loose, she makes a Curtsie to the Table. Ser-|torio brings in the flesh with a skull all bloody, they | all wonder.*
5.1.167.1   *The Old King sends forth Amorpho.*
5.1.194.1   *Enter Fidelio.*
5.1.205.1   *They discover themselves.*
5.1.210   *He kils his Queene.*
5.1.217.1   *They all discharge at him.*
5.1.218.1   *Dyes.* (right margin)
5.1.226.1   *Enter the Old Queene disguised, a Boy with her.*
5.1.230.1   *She discovers.*
5.1.248.1   *Exeunt omnes. | FINIS.*

LINEATION NOTES

1.1.61-2   A...recompense] *1 line* COTES
1.1.86-7   Farewell...tide] *1 verse line* COTES
1.1.131-2   Alas...beggar] *1 verse line* COTES
1.3.14-15   Whoe'er...villains] *1 verse line* COTES
1.3.59-60   Are...do't] *1 line* COTES
1.4.38-9   'Tis...King] *1 line* COTES
1.4.45-7   A...mother] *1 verse line* COTES
1.4.47-8   He...understand] *1 verse line* COTES
1.4.71-2   Thanks...dangerous] *1 line* COTES
1.4.114-28   I...comes] *verse* COTES: deceitful| face| Christian| lady| 'em| fortunately| ounce| can| none| joint| much|
1.4.147-8   Troth...wouldst] *1 line* COTES
1.4.160-3   Nay...vantage] *verse?* COTES: lady| put| hundred|
1.4.168-70   Do...madam] *verse* COTES: it|
1.4.179-80   And...her] *1 verse line* COTES
1.4.180-1   And...still] *1 verse line* COTES
1.4.189-92   Lady...Why, Madam] *verse* COTES: hear| business|
1.4.194-7   Why...more] *verse* COTES: him| bring you together|
1.4.199-204   And...it is] *verse* COTES: will I| purpose| in him| brain|
1.4.206-13   Why...morning] *verse* COTES: lady| know you| preposterous| of't| said| night|
1.4.219-21   There's...lady] *verse* COTES: many|
2.1.4-6   Mass...it] *verse* COTES: orphans|
2.1.12   I...wolves] *verse* sheep|
2.1.17-18   For...up] *1 line* COTES
2.1.26-7   A...lambs] *1 verse line* COTES
2.1.36-7   First...drinkers] *verse* COTES: be|
2.1.55-6   A...gudgeon] *verse* COTES: them|
2.2.27-8   'Snails...sir] *verse* COTES: surgeon|
2.2.32-3   Yes...country] *1 verse line* COTES
2.2.34-5   Torture...now] *1 verse line* COTES
2.2.36-8   The...rascal] *verse?* COTES: your| one|
2.3.31-2   for...noted] *verse* COTES: gentleman|
2.3.35-7   Good...gentleman] *verse* COTES: relief|
2.3.52-4   kept...honours] *verse* COTES: wives|
2.3.56-7   Perhaps...honour] *verse* COTES: it|
2.3.61-2   But...sir] *1 verse line* COTES
2.3.65-6   I...desired] *verse* COTES: appear|
2.3.68-9   of...creature] *verse* COTES: most|
2.3.73-4   Exceeds...beauteous] *1 verse line* COTES

2.3.74-5   This...pardon] *1 verse line* COTES
2.3.97-9   How...i'faith] *prose* COTES
2.4.2-3   Than...monster] *1 line* COTES
2.4.17-18   One...the poor] *1 verse line* COTES
3.1.15-16   if...me] *verse* COTES: therefore|
3.1.24-6   Tell...blood] *2 lines* COTES: there|
3.1.28-9   As...further] *1 line* COTES
3.1.29-30   Touch...mettle] *1 line* COTES
3.1.62-3   I'll...hand] *1 verse line* COTES
3.1.65-6   It...it] *1 verse line* COTES
3.1.71-2   I...lord] *1 verse line* COTES
3.1.78-84   It...him] *verse* COTES: bastinadoed| blanketting| chambermaids| blankets| th'other| swore enough|
3.1.106-7   Why...knowledge] *1 verse line* COTES
3.1.108-9   I...well] *1 verse line* COTES
3.3.3-4   You...disguise] *verse* COTES: help|
3.3.7-8   And...sir] *1 verse line* COTES
3.3.11-12   Though...hither] *1 verse line* COTES
3.3.52-3   The...prince] *1 verse line* COTES
3.3.70-3   I...munches] *verse* COTES: it| lecher|
3.3.84-6   The...nightcap] upon| streamer|
3.3.87-8   I...this] *1 line* COTES
3.3.95-6   You...crowns] *1 verse line* COTES
3.3.96-7   Ay...mind] *1 line* COTES
3.3.99-100   But...knows] *verse* COTES: hand|
3.3.101-2   O...game] *1 verse line* COTES
3.3.113-14   I'd...heaven] *1 verse line* COTES
3.3.115-16   Nay...cheap] *1 verse line* COTES
3.3.120-1   I'll...upheaped] *1 verse line* COTES
3.3.128   And...breast] COTES (and ~)
4.1.11-12   Canst...place] *1 line*
4.1.12-16   At...nearer] man| cunning| darkness|
4.1.25-6   Worse...lord] *1 verse line* COTES
4.1.28-9   Pardon...lord] forth|
4.1.65-6   Why...words] *1 verse line* COTES
4.2.3-4   I...daughter] lord|
4.2.11-12   So...thee] *1 verse line* COTES
4.2.26-8   When...him] *2 lines* COTES: honours|
4.2.54-5   We...hear] *1 line* COTES
4.2.55-6   From...favour] *1 verse line* COTES
4.2.57-9   Thou...cunningly] *2 verse lines* COTES: off|

4.2.77–8   My...love] *1 verse line* COTES
4.2.93–4   If...deserve] *1 verse line* COTES
4.3.22–3   You...room] *1 verse line* COTES
4.3.25–6   No...enough] *verse* COTES: have |
4.3.62–4   May...ever] *2 lines* COTES: nothing |
4.3.125   That...enjoy] COTES (that ~)
4.3.169–4.3.170.1   And...jewel] *1 verse line* COTES
4.3.177–8   Or...loose] *1 verse line* COTES
4.3.217–18   A...Lodovico] *1 line* COTES

4.3.250–1   Madam...light] *1 line* COTES
5.1.43–5   I...desert] *2 lines* COTES: service |
5.1.51–2   I...lord] *1 line* COTES
5.1.61–2   So...die] *1 line* COTES
5.1.74–5   My...merry] *1 verse line* COTES
5.1.101–2   But...O] *1 line* COTES
5.1.130–1   What...on] *1 verse line* COTES
5.1.136–7   Most...you] *1 verse line* COTES
5.1.200–1   Alas...eats] *1 verse line* COTES

HENGIST, KING OF KENT;
or, THE MAYOR OF QUEENBOROUGH

Edited by Grace Ioppolo

THE textual transmission of *Hengist, King of Kent, or The Mayor of Queenborough* presents clear evidence of authorial, theatrical, and compositorial revision. Two scribal manuscripts survive. Although R. C. Bald dated these manuscripts, which he considered to be in the same hand, from the second quarter of the seventeenth century, Peter Beal noted instead that the manuscripts were in two different hands and should be dated 1650–70. After comparison of these manuscripts with many others extant from the 1610s to the 1670s and after consultation with Dr Beal, I agree that the manuscripts are in two different hands, which cannot be identified, but date the hands in the manuscripts from the 1640s, most likely following the 1641 request by the King's Men to the Lord Chamberlain to prevent the play from being printed. In fact, the watermarks in both manuscripts appear in other manuscripts of this and the following decade, supporting the conclusion that the manuscripts are not later than 1661, after which time the printed quarto was available and a scribal transcription would have possessed less urgency or value.

The two manuscripts, although scribal, should be considered authoritative texts because of their overwhelming agreement in spelling, diction, directions, character names, and speech prefixes, their evident dependence on Middleton's unique spelling and scribal practices, and their clear provenance from a playhouse manuscript. In addition, they strikingly demonstrate the ways in which a scribe can and cannot alter and influence the transmission of a play text. The manuscripts are each written in a mix of secretary and Italian hand with Italian hand used for stage directions and act-scene divisions. The Lambarde–Folger manuscript (J.b.6; Beal MiT 22) and the Portland–Nottingham manuscript (Pw.v.20; Beal MiT 23; Malone Society edition, 2003) both show evidence of having been transcribed as presentation or commissioned copies. Unfortunately the Lambarde manuscript was cropped sometime after its transcription, probably as a result of being bound into the Lambarde volume, resulting in the loss of its title-page and the obscuring of its gilt edge, both of which features exist in the Portland manuscript (the gilt edge was most certainly applied to the paper of this manuscript before transcription rather than after binding because several of the scribe's ink-blots have the gilt mixed into them).

Both manuscripts present compelling evidence that they were transcribed in every detail from the same source, most likely a playhouse manuscript descending from the author's foul papers; both manuscripts preserve ample evidence of Middleton's spellings and scribal practices as well as playhouse notations, including cuts and minor actors' names, slavishly copied out by the scribes exactly as they saw them. The inclusion at 2.1.31–2 (cropped in LAMBARDE), 2.4.2, and 4.2.233–5 of the names of the three minor, unknown actors (Robb. Briggs, Blackson, Robrt Str), not easily recognizable as members of the King's Men, is solely cited by Bentley, who follows Bald, to argue that the play did not originally belong to the King's Men but to another company employing these actors, one of whom, Robert Stratford, had died by the early 1620s. However a 1631 cast list for another play (performed by Prince Charles's Men) contains the name of another Robert Stratford, a boy actor who could not possibly have been the same adult Robert Stratford who Bald and Bentley claim belonged to the original 1619–20 cast. If this boy actor is the same one who appears in the *Hengist* manuscripts, there is no evidence to suggest that the play was not originally a King's Men's play (the company certainly owned the play by 1641 at which time they prevented it from being printed). Any argument that the play was not first performed by the King's Men based on the inclusion of actors' names is purely speculative simply because we have no evidence linking them with any particular acting company other than the King's Men, or 'His Majesties Servants' as noted on the quarto's title-page.

In addition to actors' names, the Lambarde manuscript also preserves four occurrences (at 2.4.2, 3.3.0.1, 4.1.0.1, and 5.1.0.3–4) of what appears to be an orb and cross symbol (or the astrological symbol for a woman drawn upside down) in the left margin, and this symbol most probably served as a promptbook-holder's notation to ready properties or actors (particularly the one playing Simon who appears in all four scenes) to appear on stage (such hand-drawn symbols are very common in theatrical manuscripts of this period). Occasional divergence from LAMBARDE and agreement with HERRINGMAN (as at 1.3.201) suggests that the Portland scribe probably did not transcribe his manuscript from the Lambarde manuscript but from the playhouse manuscript which served as LAMBARDE's source; indeed, he neglected to add the marginal symbols. Rather than being 'not very elegant' (as Bald terms them) or amateurish, the hands of both scribes demonstrate professional practice and concern for the integrity of the text. Strikeouts are neatly and cleanly

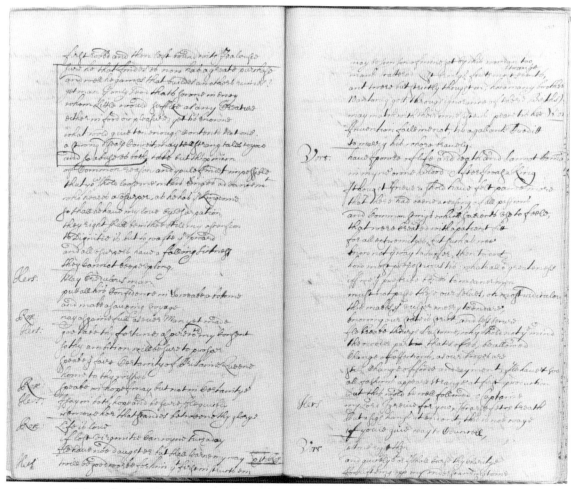

Folio 221^v–222^r of the Lambarde manuscript showing the deletions in Roxena's speech at 3.1.53–60.

made and the occurrence of obvious errors or suspected readings is very rare (most errors are the result of eyeskip).

Each scribe does have unique characteristics. The Lambarde scribe frequently and consistently economizes space in the lines by using abbreviations with superscripts for such common words as 'the' ('y^e'), 'you' ('yo^u'), and 'your' ('yor'), suggesting both that he was a professional scribe accustomed to common scribal practice and that he was used to copying dramatic manuscripts with blank verse which required accurate lineation in the given space. He, in fact, is extremely precise about estimating the amount of space needed to transcribe each line accurately and only rarely runs a line over to the next line. The Portland scribe seems less experienced in both scribal practice and in copying dramatic manuscripts, as he inconsistently uses abbreviations and frequently underestimates the amount of space needed to transcribe, requiring him to carry over the last words of a line to the next line, eventually catching up with the correct lineation some lines later. However, this scribe can be faulted only for creating lineation problems. All in all, it is clear that both scribes took great care to produce transcriptions that were commissioned or could be presented to patrons and members of the nobility who were eager for a copy of a popular play not available in print. Rather than exemplifying the stereotypically incompetent, ignorant, hasty, or careless scribe so frequently proposed by modern textual critics, these two scribes demonstrate that their role was not to interfere in, or to botch, the transcription of the text but to transmit it precisely and accurately.

The play was first entered in the Stationers' Register as the 'Maior of Quinborough' on 4 September 1646 for 'Master [Humphrey] Robinson and Master [Humphrey] Mozeley' along with forty-seven other plays; Middleton's play was the only one in the list not entered with the author's name. However, the play was not printed at that time. The Lord Chamberlain had recorded the play in a list (dated 7 August 1641) of King's Men's plays which they did not want printed; he had also noted in 1637 that printing plays which were still being performed in repertory would financially harm the acting companies and 'would directly tend to their apparent Detriment & great pʳiudice & to the disenabling of them to doe their Maᵗᵉˢ service'. Thus we know that at least until 1641 *Hengist* had remained active in the King's Men's repertoire. The play was entered again on 13 February 1661:

Master Henry Herringman	Entred...under the hand of Master Crooke warden A Comedie called the Maior of Quinborough, By Tho: Middleton	xij𝆩

Herringman published the play once, in quarto form, in 1661 as *The Mayor of Quinborough* (the printer has not yet been identified); the printing of this quarto was interrupted early in the run in order to correct the title--page's original description of the play from a 'tragedy' to a 'comedy'. Some copies of HERRINGMAN suffered 'frisket bite' on E4ᵛ (page 40) during printing: pieces of paper wedged into the frisket to keep it stable came loose and covered portions of the paper during printing, resulting in failure to print some letters and words in the page's right margin. No other press variants have been observed.

This printed text varies significantly from the text represented by the two manuscripts. The title of the play suggests that the play's main character had become Simon the Mayor rather than Hengist the Saxon. In HERRINGMAN only appears the following preface: 'Gentlemen, you have the first flight of him I assure you; this Mayor of Queenborough whom you have all heard of, and some of you beheld upon the stage, now begins to walk abroad in print; he has been known sufficiently by the reputation of his wit, which is enough (by the way) to distinguish him from ordinary mayors; but wit, you know, has skulked in corners for many years past, and he was thought to have most of it that could best hide himself. Now whether this magistrate feared the decimating times, or kept up the state of other mayors, that are bound not to go out of their liberties during the time of their mayoralty, I know not; 'tis enough for me to put him into your hands, under the title of an honest man, which will appear plainly to you, because you shall find him all along to have a great picque to the rebel Oliver; I am told his drollery yields to none the English drama did ever produce; and though I would not put his modesty to the blush by speaking too much in his commendation, yet I know you will agree with me, upon your better acquaintance with him, that there is some difference in point of wit, betwixt the Mayor of Queenborough and the Mayor of Huntingdon'.

As Bald has noted, the quarto (Wing M1984, M1984A) omits 175 lines found in the manuscripts while adding 25 lines not found in the manuscripts. Some of these omissions clearly derive from the playhouse. The two songs at 1.1.29–40 and 4.2.43–6 have been cut as well as the numerous 'Music' stage directions and those requiring musical instruments such as 'Flourish', 'Cornetts', and 'Drum', suggesting either that music was no longer required or fashionable in the play's later venue or that it was now uneconomical. The quarto also reduces the number of characters in particular scenes, for example cutting Aurelius, who speaks only one line, and Uther, who does not speak, from 1.1, as well as reducing the number of generic characters in an attempt to economize by making use of a smaller cast. Other variants offer evidence of compositorial interference, especially in relineating lines so that a half-line which concludes a speech is automatically followed by another half-line in the next speaker's speech. The quarto also shows that some attention has been paid to modernizing what by then was forty-year-old diction and topical expressions, and to presenting the play to a literary rather than a theatrical audience. Similarly, stage directions, especially those involving Simon, the play's later focus, have become more explicit, archaic words and verb forms have been modernized, contractions have almost entirely been eliminated, and the preface alluding to Oliver Cromwell has been added. The King's Men appear to have been willing some time after the rise of Cromwell in the 1630s to capitalize on the coincidence in the two rebel Olivers, Oliver the fustian-weaver, a stock comic character, and Oliver Cromwell.

However, the majority of these omissions derive not from playhouse or printing-house personnel but from Middleton himself. As in the case of *A Game at Chess*, Middleton paid very close attention to the explicit and implicit meanings of the major and minor aspects of his text (Ioppolo); here likewise, rather than reacting to censorship (as Bald and his followers have claimed), Middleton appears to have redrawn certain characters, including Castiza and Roxena, in order to alter the play's focus and direction. Significant cuts appear at 1.1.9–15, 1.3.21–3, 1.3.62–5, 2.3.4–6, 3.1.53–60, 3.1.84–7, 3.1.98–102, 3.2.59–62, 3.3.212–25, 3.3.266–71, 4.2.225–32, 4.4.14–19, 4.4.25–30, 4.4.118–20, 5.1.288–91, 5.2.120–31, and 5.2.139–41. The quarto occasionally adds a few lines within a speech, often to develop particular imagery, as at 4.2.144 and 5.1.270. The quarto frequently and expertly cuts lines within speeches, which may have appeared extraneous to the flow of the action, without disturbing the surrounding lines. These lines are not hastily cut in large chunks from long speeches in only a few scenes, as presumably an amateur, disinterested reviser unfamiliar with the play would do, but instead are carefully and usually slightly cut throughout the text, showing great concern for the dramatic integrity and intention of the play as a whole. Such practice is typical of an experienced, revising dramatist very familiar with the dramatic impact of even his most minor lines of dialogue (Ioppolo).

The quarto's most substantive variant appears at the end of the final scene, which cuts the dialogue from 5.2.206–34 and the epilogue and substitutes two short speeches of six and five lines each, seemingly to present a briefer conclusion to the play's final scene. However, as discussed in the Critical Introduction, this cut prevents Castiza from returning to the stage to be exonerated of adultery and to receive Aurelius's marriage proposal. This quarto exclusion of Castiza, and the major cuts in two of Roxena's speeches on the impact of misogyny at 3.1.53–60 and 5.2.120–31 (marked for deletion but not deleted in the manuscripts), suggest that Middleton had rethought these presentations of the two women, and he evidently made other minor but telling alterations in order to support this later vision of his play as more strictly male-centred. In regard to these features, Middleton's revisions in this play match those in *A Game at Chess*. Middleton may have revised the play as a result of the change of personnel in the acting company over time, to suit the changing taste of his theatrical audience, or to satisfy his own artistic designs for the play. Neither the quarto's nor the manuscripts' text offers any evidence that the text was cut or altered as a result of externally or self-imposed censorship for political reasons, and in fact none of the passages which contain the most overt political criticism of kingship, religious persecution, and civil war has been tampered with between or within the early and later texts of the play. Arguments which insist that an Elizabethan or Jacobean dramatist revised his play solely because he was forced to revise it often also insist that a dramatist would not revise his play only because he wanted to revise it. Middleton evidently revised this play because he wanted to, not because he was forced to. The quarto, then, apparently descends from another manuscript, which postdates the one for the manuscripts' transcription, and its literary characteristics suggest that this later manuscript was especially prepared to serve as printers' copy. This manuscript was at some remove from a revised manuscript made by Middleton; it incorporated the company's later revisions as well as Middleton's own revisions.

Because of the unique nature and the existence of two scribal manuscripts descended from the same playhouse source as well as a later quarto showing signs of authorial revision, the textual notes are necessarily detailed and specific. Thus, unlike the textual notes of the other plays in this volume, these notes record even minor variants which may seem accidental but which clearly distinguish between the manuscripts' scribes, only recently recognized as being different hands; these notes then also include stage direction variants. Incidental variants in spelling and punctuation which do not alter the meaning of words or passages or do not represent unique scribal practice are not recorded. Neither scribe clearly distinguishes between verse and prose passages in his manuscript and neither

capitalizes at the beginning of new lines, even at the beginning of each character's speech; thus I have determined from the length of the lines as well as the syntax, rhythm, and metre which lines appear to be rendered as prose by the scribes. The quarto similarly does not distinguish between verse and prose and in fact prints all lines in the play as verse.

This play exists in two versions, one represented by the manuscripts and one by the quarto; each version is a Middletonian text with its own integrity. LAMBARDE has been used as control-text for this edition of *Hengist, King of Kent* because it represents the manuscript closest to Middleton's most complete draft of the play as first presented in the theatre and because it does not possess the quarto's later, non-authorial alterations. Although cropped after its transcription, and thus occasionally defective in its readings in the extreme right margin of recto pages, LAMBARDE is more reliable in its lineation than the Portland manuscript and displays fewer errors in transcription. All cropped words and directions missing from the Lambarde manuscript have been supplied by the Portland manuscript. Very few emendations from HERRINGMAN have been incorporated into the *Hengist* text; the act and scene divisions in the manuscripts and HERRINGMAN have been altered, making separate scenes of the dumbshows (1.2, 2.2, 4.3) rather than presenting them as part of the following scene. The two passages of Roxena's dialogue marked for deletion but not actually deleted in the manuscripts (3.1.53–60 and 5.2.119–33) have been retained because they are clearly part of the complete draft of the play as first performed. As stated in the Critical Introduction, I consider the deletion of these and other passages as part of a late revision of the play some years after the play's first performance when these passages' topicality in alluding to the Frances Howard case was no longer theatrically effective. In addition, extant manuscripts of this period often have passages ruled-off in order to mark deletions for occasional performances only; this may be the case for this manuscript.

Doubling

Doubling in this play is extremely difficult to determine due to the fact that almost all of the play's characters, with the exception of Hengist and Hersus, appear on stage together in 4.1. Thus none of the actors appearing in 4.1 would have doubled any other role unless in minor parts such as Monks, Fortune, Lords, Gentlemen, or Soldiers. Actors in the main plot would not have doubled other roles in the mainplot as they appear together on stage in various dumbshows. The actor playing Hengist would not double any roles after his appearance in 2.3, as he appears on stage in scenes involving the characters of the main plot (such as Vortiger) as well as scenes involving the characters of the minor plot (such as Simon), most of whom appear in 4.1. The actor playing Hengist could only have doubled roles in 1.1, 1.3, 2.1, and 2.2, including Constantius, Lupus, and Germanus.

The actor playing Hersus could also have doubled roles such as Constantius, Lupus, and Germanus, as well as roles in the Mayor of Queenborough plot, such as Oliver; the actors playing Constantius, Lupus, and Germanus could also have doubled roles in the Mayor of Queenborough plot. The actor playing Raynulph could have doubled any role except those of Vortiger, Hengist, and certain minor characters who appear immediately before or after his appearances.

SEE ALSO

Text: *Works*, 1451
Authorship and date: this volume, 410

WORKS CITED

Previous Editions

A Select Collection of Old Plays, Vol. 11 (1744)
The Ancient British Drama in Three Volumes, ed. Walter Scott, Vol. 3 (1810)
The Works of Thomas Middleton, ed. Alexander Dyce, Vol. 1 (1840)
The Works of Thomas Middleton, ed. A. H. Bullen, Vol. 1 (1885)
The Best Plays of the Old Dramatists: Thomas Middleton, ed. Havelock Ellis, Vol. 2 (1890)

Middleton, Thomas, *Hengist, King of Kent*, ed. R. C. Bald (1938)
Middleton, Thomas, *Hengist, King of Kent, or The Mayor of Queenborough*, ed. Grace Ioppolo (2003) [Malone Society edition of the Portland manuscript]

Other Works Cited

Bentley, G. E., *The Jacobean and Caroline Stage*, 7 vols (1941-68)
Desens, Marliss, *The Bed-Trick in English Renaissance Drama: Explorations in Gender, Sexuality, and Power* (1994)
Foakes, R. A., and R. T. Rickert, eds., *Henslowe's Diary* (1961)
Friis, Astrid, *Alderman Cockayne's Project and the Cloth Trade* (1927)
Green, Mary Anne Everett, *Calendar of State Papers (Domestic Series, James I, 1619-1623)*, vol. 10, (1858)
Greg, W. W., and E. K. Chambers, *Collections*, Vol II, Part III (1931)
Heinemann, Margot, *Puritanism and Theatre: Thomas Middleton and Opposition Drama under the Early Stuarts* (1980)
Henslowe's Diary, ed. R. A. Foakes and R. T. Rickert (1961)
Holdsworth, R. V., 'The Date of *Hengist, King of Kent*', *Notes and Queries* 236 (1991), 516-19
Ioppolo, Grace, *Revising Shakespeare* (1991)
James I, *Basilikon Doron* (1603)
Lambarde, William, *A Perambulation of Kent, Conteining the Description, Hystorie, and Customes of that Shyre* (1596)
McAlindon, Thomas, *English Renaissance Tragedy* (1986)
Munday, Anthony, *The Triumphs of re-vnited Britania* (1605)

TEXTUAL NOTES

LAMBARDE = Lambarde (Folger) Manuscript (Beal MiT 22)
PORTLAND = Portland (Nottingham) Manuscript (Beal MiT 23)
HERRINGMAN = Quarto 1 (Wing M 1984)

Title *Hengist king of | Kent or the^e | Maior of Quinborough | decoration* PORTLAND; THE | MAYOR | OF | Quinborough: | A | COMEDY. HERRINGMAN (*alternate title-page substitutes* 'TRAGEDY' *for* 'COMEDY'); LAMBARDE *lacks the title-page, possibly because it was omitted when this manuscript was bound into the* LAMBARDE *volume, however the play concludes with the note* 'Finis | Hengist King off Kent'

Persons *No title appears in* LAMBARDE *or* PORTLAND; *this list varies only slightly in* LAMBARDE *and* PORTLAND *in accidentals such as spelling and scribal practice; however* LAMBARDE *has been cropped, thus* PORTLAND *remains the authority; it appears as follows:* Raynulph, Munck of Chester | Constantius, King of th^e Brittains | Vortiger | Hengist King of Kent | Aurelius and Vther Brothers to Cons: | Hersus | Deuon: and Staff: two Lordes | Lupus and Germanus two Muncks | | Castiza Daughter to Deuon: | Roxena Daughter to Hengist | two Ladyes | | Symon a tanner Maior of Quinborough | Oliver a fustian Weaver | three Graziers | Glouer | Barbor | Taylor | fellmonger | Buttonmonger | Brazier | Petitioners | Gentleman | Clarke | footeman | Saxons Soldiers | Captain gaurd | and officers; HERRINGMAN *is titled* 'Drammatis Personae' *and appears as follows:* Conſtantius. | Aurelius Ambroſius. | Uther Pendragon. | Vortiger. | Hengiſt. | Horfus. | Devonſhire, | Stafford. [*bracket*] Britiſh Lords. | Gentlemen. | Symon. | Oliver. | Taylour. | Barber. | Aminadab. | Footmen. | Souldiers. | Cheaters. | Caſtiza. | Roxena. | Ladies. | Raynulph Monck of Cheſter. | Germanus. | Lupus. [*bracket*] Moncks. | Graſiers .

Persons.24 Collier] THIS EDITION; *not in* LAMBARDE, PORTLAND, *and* HERRINGMAN *although he is mentioned in all three texts as being on stage in 3.3.174-6.*
Persons.27 Clown] THIS EDITION; *not in* LAMBARDE, PORTLAND, HERRINGMAN
1.0.0.1 *Incipit Actus Primus*] Actus Primus Scena Prima LAMBARDE, PORTLAND; ACT I. SCENA I. HERRINGMAN
1.0.0.2 *Enter... presenter*] LAMBARDE, PORTLAND; Enter Raynulph HERRINGMAN
1.0.3 raises] LAMBARDE, PORTLAND; raiseth HERRINGMAN
1.0.3 do] LAMBARDE, HERRINGMAN; does PORTLAND
1.0.4 (To...again)] LAMBARDE, PORTLAND; To fee long parted light again HERRINGMAN
1.0.6 judgements] LAMBARDE, PORTLAND; Diamonds HERRINGMAN
1.0.7 I shall] HERRINGMAN; Shall LAMBARDE, PORTLAND;
1.0.7 power] LAMBARDE, PORTLAND; powers HERRINGMAN
1.0.8 two] HERRINGMAN; *altered in* PORTLAND *to* 'two' *from* 'twe'; too LAMBARDE
1.0.13 used] LAMBARDE, HERRINGMAN; worne PORTLAND, *probably as a result of eyeskip from* 'worn' *in the line above*
1.0.15 what's] LAMBARDE, PORTLAND; what HERRINGMAN
1.0.17 prove] LAMBARDE, PORTLAND; approve HERRINGMAN
1.0.18 story] *altered in* PORTLAND *from another word*
1.1.0.1 *Shout...Vortiger*] LAMBARDE, PORTLAND; Shouts within. Then enter Vortiger HERRINGMAN
1.1.1 wide-throated] PORTLAND, HERRINGMAN; wided throated LAMBARDE
1.1.2 lin] LAMBARDE (lyn); luy PORTLAND; leave HERRINGMAN
1.1.4 What...by't?] LAMBARDE, PORTLAND (*the corner of the manuscript page is torn, obscuring the final* 'es' *in* 'themselues'); *not in* HERRINGMAN

1.1.6 ever upon] LAMBARDE (*another, later, hand has crossed out the scribe's 'ever' and written 'een' above it*), PORTLAND; even upon HERRINGMAN

1.1.7 tasting] LAMBARDE, PORTLAND; casting HERRINGMAN

1.1.9–10 Poisoned…long] PORTLAND; *the second half of this line appears at the bottom of a damaged page in* LAMBARDE *and survives as* 'poysoned my fortune, they will haue he | as long'; 'Poyſon'd my Fortunes for *Conſtantines* ſons' HERRINGMAN

1.1.9–15 They…Bondage] LAMBARDE, PORTLAND; *not in* HERRINGMAN

1.1.11 vassals] *altered in* LAMBARDE *to* 'vassailes' *from* 'vassal'

1.1.16 close] LAMBARDE; *altered in* PORTLAND *from another word*; neer HERRINGMAN

1.1.17.1 *Enter Devonshire and Stafford*] HERRINGMAN (*Enter* Devon. *and* Stafford:); *Enter Deuon St | afford* LAMBARDE; *Enter Deuon Staff:* PORTLAND

1.1.17 kind] LAMBARDE, PORTLAND; good HERRINGMAN

1.1.18 loves] LAMBARDE, PORTLAND; kind loves HERRINGMAN

1.1.22 DEVONSHIRE] LAMBARDE, HERRINGMAN. This speech prefix as well as those following for Vortiger at 1.1.25 and Stafford at 1.1.28 do not appear in PORTLAND, although all three speeches have been ruled off

1.1.23 will appease 'em] LAMBARDE, PORTLAND; can appeaſe them HERRINGMAN

1.1.24 'em] LAMBARDE, PORTLAND; them HERRINGMAN

1.1.26 stranger] LAMBARDE; straighter PORTLAND; ſtraighter HERRINGMAN

1.1.27 aids] LAMBARDE, PORTLAND; aid HERRINGMAN

1.1.28 They're] their LAMBARDE, PORTLAND; They are HERRINGMAN

1.1.28 They're…service] Both LAMBARDE and PORTLAND have an 'Exit' direction following Stafford's speech; because the entrance directions in the next line for Constantius and the monks are set off as if introducing a new scene, each scribe may have thought he was ending the previous scene with his 'Exit' marker after Stafford's speech. However, there is no marker to begin a new scene with Constantius's entrance, and it is clear that Vortiger and at least Devonshire, who speaks later in the scene at 1.1.159, have remained on stage throughout.

1.1.28.1 Music] LAMBARDE, PORTLAND; *not in* HERRINGMAN

1.1.28.1–3 *Enter…procession*] PORTLAND; *Enter Certaine Muncks, Germanicus; Constantius being one singing as Precession* LAMBARDE; *Enter* Constantius (*as a Monck, attended by other Moncks*) Vortiger *stays him* HERRINGMAN

1.1.28.1 Germanus] LAMBARDE, PORTLAND (Germanicus); *not in* HERRINGMAN

1.1.28.3 *Enter…Uther*] Neither LAMBARDE nor PORTLAND has an entrance marker for Aurelius, who speaks at 1.1.107, or for Uther, who with Aurelius is referred to by Constantius at 1.1.102; HERRINGMAN similarly does not have an entrance marker for Uther or Aurelius, yet his line does not appear in this scene in HERRINGMAN; both he and Uther may have been cut from the scene in HERRINGMAN.

1.1.28.4–1.1.40 *Song* MONKS Boast…folly] LAMBARDE, PORTLAND; *not in* HERRINGMAN

1.1.39 hymn] THIS EDITION; him LAMBARDE, PORTLAND

1.1.40 folly] PORTLAND; ffollyes LAMBARDE

1.1.42 public] LAMBARDE, PORTLAND; general HERRINGMAN

1.1.43 purely] LAMBARDE, HERRINGMAN; holy PORTLAND

1.1.45 on…general] PORTLAND, HERRINGMAN; on the for thee for the generall LAMBARDE

1.1.48 groaning] LAMBARDE, PORTLAND; growing HERRINGMAN

1.1.48 earth] altered in PORTLAND from another word

1.1.48 again] PORTLAND, HERRINGMAN; *cropped in* LAMBARDE *to* 'aga'

1.1.49 forward] LAMBARDE, PORTLAND; forwards HERRINGMAN

1.1.54 be i'th'] LAMBARDE, PORTLAND; there be in the HERRINGMAN

1.1.55 about] LAMBARDE, PORTLAND; about now HERRINGMAN

1.1.55 off] LAMBARDE, HERRINGMAN; oft PORTLAND

1.1.55.1 [*A*] *shout within*] PORTLAND; *cropped in* LAMBARDE *to* 'show' (*at* 1.1.54); *not in* HERRINGMAN.

1.1.56 lose hazard] LAMBARDE, PORTLAND (loose hazard); loſe and hazard HERRINGMAN

1.1.56 Germanus] HERRINGMAN; Germanicus LAMBARDE, PORTLAND

1.1.67 unwillingness] *in* LAMBARDE 'un' *has been altered from* 'an'

1.1.68 departed] LAMBARDE; part PORTLAND; parted HERRINGMAN

1.1.73 as earth] LAMBARDE, HERRINGMAN; a serch PORTLAND

1.1.74 consent] *preceded in* LAMBARDE *by erased* 'des'

1.1.77 sin] LAMBARDE, PORTLAND; fins HERRINGMAN

1.1.79 kneel] LAMBARDE, HERRINGMAN; beg PORTLAND

1.1.81 too] PORTLAND, HERRINGMAN; two LAMBARDE

1.1.81 helps] LAMBARDE, PORTLAND; help HERRINGMAN

1.1.84 was once] LAMBARDE, PORTLAND; once was HERRINGMAN

1.1.85 ended] LAMBARDE, HERRINGMAN; was ended PORTLAND

1.1.89 charge] LAMBARDE, HERRINGMAN; rule PORTLAND

1.1.91 Who's] LAMBARDE, PORTLAND; who is HERRINGMAN

1.1.91 peace] *preceded in* LAMBARDE *by deleted* 'good'

1.1.92 own] PORTLAND, HERRINGMAN; one LAMBARDE

1.1.92 will look] LAMBARDE, HERRINGMAN; lookes PORTLAND

1.1.93 business] LAMBARDE, PORTLAND; actions HERRINGMAN

1.1.100 in] LAMBARDE, PORTLAND; of HERRINGMAN

1.1.101 has] LAMBARDE, PORTLAND; hath HERRINGMAN

1.1.102 of my] *preceded in* LAMBARDE *by deleted* 'yoʳ t'

1.1.104 You…cruelty!] LAMBARDE, PORTLAND; *not in* HERRINGMAN

1.1.106 the Britons] LAMBARDE, PORTLAND; Great *Britain* HERRINGMAN

1.1.106.1 *Flourish*] PORTLAND; *cropped in* LAMBARDE *to* 'Flouri'; *not in* HERRINGMAN

1.1.107 AURELIUS They…already] LAMBARDE, PORTLAND; *not in* HERRINGMAN

1.1.107 tune] THIS EDITION; time LAMBARDE; tim PORTLAND

1.1.107 want] LAMBARDE (*followed by deleted* 'already'), PORTLAND; a want HERRINGMAN

1.1.108 within me] LAMBARDE, PORTLAND; within HERRINGMAN

1.1.112 blest] LAMBARDE, PORTLAND; beſt HERRINGMAN

1.1.113 with…man] LAMBARDE, PORTLAND; by the ruine of another HERRINGMAN

1.1.114 peace] *preceded in* PORTLAND *by* 'filcht'

1.1.114 'em] LAMBARDE, PORTLAND; them HERRINGMAN

1.1.115 if't] LAMBARDE, HERRINGMAN; if it PORTLAND

1.1.117 a] LAMBARDE, PORTLAND; the HERRINGMAN

1.1.121 year] LAMBARDE, PORTLAND; years HERRINGMAN

1.1.121 to him] PORTLAND, HERRINGMAN; *cropped in* LAMBARDE *to* 'to'

1.1.123 from't] LAMBARDE, PORTLAND; from it HERRINGMAN

1.1.126 the least] LAMBARDE, PORTLAND; *not in* HERRINGMAN

1.1.128 subject] LAMBARDE, PORTLAND; ſervant HERRINGMAN

1.1.129 pains] *preceded in* LAMBARDE *by altered and then deleted* 'perish'

1.1.131 Millions of rising actions] LAMBARDE, PORTLAND; Millions of Actions, riſing HERRINGMAN

1.1.132 never] *altered in* PORTLAND *to* 'neuer' *from* 'neere'

1.1.132 done] *altered in* PORTLAND *to* 'dun' *from* 'begun'

1.1.134 insensible] LAMBARDE, PORTLAND; marble HERRINGMAN

1.1.134 o'er-watching] LAMBARDE, PORTLAND; over-watching HERRINGMAN

1.1.137 take] *traced over another word in* PORTLAND

1.1.138 burdensome] LAMBARDE (burthensome); burthenous PORTLAND, HERRINGMAN

1.1.139 to lay't] LAMBARDE, PORTLAND; lay it HERRINGMAN

1.1.142 ourselves] LAMBARDE, PORTLAND; our felf HERRINGMAN

1.1.143 charity] LAMBARDE, PORTLAND; love HERRINGMAN

1.1.150 I'm] LAMBARDE, PORTLAND; I am HERRINGMAN

1.1.155 abst'nence, fastings and vigils] LAMBARDE, PORTLAND; abstinence HERRINGMAN

1.1.156 has] LAMBARDE, PORTLAND; hath HERRINGMAN

1.1.160 must] PORTLAND; *in* LAMBARDE *the scribe has written* 'must' *and a later hand has crossed out the* 'st' *and written above it* 'ch'; fhall HERRINGMAN

1.1.161.1 *Flourish*] LAMBARDE, PORTLAND; *not in* HERRINGMAN

1.1.161.1 *Exeunt...Vortiger*] HERRINGMAN; *Exevnt* PORTLAND; *cropped in* LAMBARDE *to* 'E'

1.1.162 this] LAMBARDE, PORTLAND; the HERRINGMAN

1.1.165 forward] LAMBARDE, PORTLAND; forwards HERRINGMAN

1.1.166 this] LAMBARDE, PORTLAND; the HERRINGMAN

1.1.167 counterfeit] *in* PORTLAND *the* 'u' *in this word has been inserted above the line with a caret*

1.1.169 rise] *in* PORTLAND *the scribe has first written* 'thriue' *and then altered it to this word by erasing the* 'th' *and tracing an* 's' *over the* 'u'

1.1.170 several] PORTLAND, HERRINGMAN; *in* LAMBARDE *the scribe has written* 'seudall' *and a later hand has inserted an* 'r' *above the* 'u'

1.1.174 sing] LAMBARDE, PORTLAND; fink HERRINGMAN

1.1.175 seek all ways] LAMBARDE; speake always PORTLAND; ufe all means HERRINGMAN

1.1.176–8 I...over] LAMBARDE, PORTLAND; *not in* HERRINGMAN *and instead the last part of* 1.1.178 'and in all' *appears as the second part of the line* 'To vex authority from him'

1.1.180 to th'] LAMBARDE, PORTLAND; to the HERRINGMAN

1.1.182.1 *Enter three Graziers*] PORTLAND; *cropped in* LAMBARDE *to* 'Ent | Gra'; *Enter two | Grafiers* HERRINGMAN

1.1.184 an't] LAMBARDE, PORTLAND (and); if't HERRINGMAN

1.1.186 affairs] LAMBARDE, PORTLAND; affair HERRINGMAN

1.1.187 What] LAMBARDE, PORTLAND; For what? HERRINGMAN

1.1.189 friendship] LAMBARDE, PORTLAND; favour HERRINGMAN

1.1.190 Hie to] high to LAMBARDE, PORTLAND; hye you to HERRINGMAN

1.1.192 speed] HERRINGMAN *prints an* 'Exit' *direction after this word; this direction is not in* LAMBARDE *or* PORTLAND

1.1.192 And] LAMBARDE, PORTLAND; If HERRINGMAN

1.1.193 'em] LAMBARDE, PORTLAND; them HERRINGMAN

1.1.193.1 *Exeunt*] LAMBARDE (Ex^t), HERRINGMAN; Exit PORTLAND

1.2.0.1–12 *Dumb Show...forth*] *for variants between the* LAMBARDE–PORTLAND *texts and* HERRINGMAN, *see* Stage Directions

1.2.0.4 hang] *inserted in* LAMBARDE *above the line with a caret*

1.2.0.4 all] *Before this word in* LAMBARDE *the scribe has written* 'imbrace each o' (*evidently through eyeskip to the next line*) *and then deleted it.*

1.2.0.7 of] LAMBARDE; of of PORTLAND

1.2.0.8 and] PORTLAND; & LAMBARDE

1.2.0.13 *Enter Raynulph*] HERRINGMAN; *not in* LAMBARDE *or* PORTLAND

1.2.6 fates] LAMBARDE, HERRINGMAN; fate PORTLAND

1.2.6 in other] *written in* PORTLAND *over another word, possibly* 'there'

1.2.7 two] LAMBARDE; too PORTLAND, HERRINGMAN

1.2.7 that] LAMBARDE, PORTLAND; the HERRINGMAN

1.2.10 the] PORTLAND; ye LAMBARDE; her HERRINGMAN

1.2.12 lover] *altered in* PORTLAND *from* 'Louers'

1.2.14 that maids will] LAMBARDE, PORTLAND; Maids HERRINGMAN

1.2.15 scorn] LAMBARDE, HERRINGMAN; scornd PORTLAND

1.2.15 called] *altered in* PORTLAND *to* 'Call'd' *from* 'Labld'

1.2.16 on't] LAMBARDE, PORTLAND; of't HERRINGMAN

1.2.16 judged] HERRINGMAN; judge LAMBARDE, PORTLAND

1.3.0.1 *Fellmonger*] LAMBARDE, PORTLAND; *Feltmonger* HERRINGMAN

1.3.0.1 *Buttonmonger*] LAMBARDE, PORTLAND; *Button-maker* HERRINGMAN

1.3.0.2 *Petitioners*] PORTLAND, HERRINGMAN; *cropped in* LAMBARDE *to* 'Petit'

1.3.3 yon] LAMBARDE, PORTLAND; yond HERRINGMAN

1.3.4 FELLMONGER] LAMBARDE, PORTLAND; ALL HERRINGMAN

1.3.5 several] HERRINGMAN; scedall LAMBARDE; sceduall PORTLAND

1.3.5 suits] *altered in* LAMBARDE *from another word*

1.3.6 GRAZIER] *Graf.* HERRINGMAN; *1 Graz* LAMBARDE, PORTLAND

1.3.7 That's] LAMBARDE, PORTLAND; That is HERRINGMAN

1.3.7 if he] LAMBARDE, PORTLAND; and doth HERRINGMAN

1.3.9 FELLMONGER] LAMBARDE, PORTLAND; ALL HERRINGMAN

1.3.10 if...suits] LAMBARDE, HERRINGMAN; if you meane to speede PORTLAND

1.3.10 suits] *altered in* LAMBARDE *from another word*

1.3.13 repulse] LAMBARDE, HERRINGMAN; denyall PORTLAND

1.3.15 BUTTONMONGER] LAMBARDE, PORTLAND; ALL HERRINGMAN

1.3.16 an] LAMBARDE, PORTLAND ('and' *in both texts*); if HERRINGMAN

1.3.16 list] PORTLAND, HERRINGMAN; *cropped in* LAMBARDE

1.3.16 know't] LAMBARDE; know it PORTLAND, HERRINGMAN

1.3.17 general] PORTLAND, HERRINGMAN; gendall LAMBARDE

1.3.18 I'll] LAMBARDE, PORTLAND; I HERRINGMAN

1.3.18 for] PORTLAND, HERRINGMAN; *cropped in* LAMBARDE *to* 'f'

1.3.20 To raise] LAMBARDE, PORTLAND; for HERRINGMAN

1.3.21–3 I'll...law] LAMBARDE, PORTLAND; *not in* HERRINGMAN, *and instead* 'it fhall be glad' *is the second part of* 1.3.21

1.3.21 back] LAMBARDE, PORTLAND; vex HERRINGMAN

1.3.22 night's] LAMBARDE; a nights PORTLAND

1.3.23 he] LAMBARDE, PORTLAND; it HERRINGMAN

1.3.25 profess] LAMBARDE, PORTLAND; proteft HERRINGMAN

1.3.26 upward] LAMBARDE, PORTLAND; upwards HERRINGMAN

1.3.30, 36 BRAZIER] LAMBARDE, PORTLAND; *Graf.* HERRINGMAN

1.3.33 i'th] LAMBARDE, PORTLAND; in the HERRINGMAN

1.3.35 afinding on her] LAMBARDE, PORTLAND; in finding her HERRINGMAN

1.3.36 you'd] LAMBARDE, HERRINGMAN; you had PORTLAND

1.3.36 on't] LAMBARDE, PORTLAND; of it HERRINGMAN

1.3.38 find] LAMBARDE, PORTLAND; feel HERRINGMAN

1.3.39 sunk] LAMBARDE, HERRINGMAN; sunk't PORTLAND

1.3.40 a meeting] LAMBARDE, PORTLAND; meeting while I live HERRINGMAN

1.3.42–3 a naked candle] LAMBARDE, PORTLAND; candle naked HERRINGMAN

1.3.43 tak't on my word] LAMBARDE, PORTLAND; *not in* HERRINGMAN

1.3.44 Hark there] LAMBARDE, PORTLAND; Hark, hark HERRINGMAN

1.3.44.1 *Enter...Gentlemen*] HERRINGMAN; *Enter Const 2 Gent* LAMBARDE; *Enter Constan & 2 Gentlemen* PORTLAND

1.3.46 petition now] LAMBARDE; petition for me PORTLAND; petition HERRINGMAN

1.3.46 'Tis] LAMBARDE, PORTLAND; I is HERRINGMAN

1.3.48 do't] LAMBARDE, PORTLAND; do it HERRINGMAN

1.3.51 for me] LAMBARDE, PORTLAND; not in HERRINGMAN

1.3.57 know] LAMBARDE, PORTLAND; know that HERRINGMAN

1.3.58 duty] LAMBARDE; duties PORTLAND, HERRINGMAN

1.3.59 thing's] LAMBARDE; thing is PORTLAND, HERRINGMAN

1.3.60 We] LAMBARDE, PORTLAND; No HERRINGMAN

1.3.60 tremble] altered in PORTLAND to 'tremblell' from 'tremblest'

1.3.61 cowards] BALD; Carrerdes LAMBARDE; Carrerders PORTLAND; fools HERRINGMAN

1.3.62-5 All…fearfully] LAMBARDE, PORTLAND; not in HERRINGMAN

1.3.65 For charity's sake] LAMBARDE, PORTLAND; For Charities fake defilt here I pray you HERRINGMAN

1.3.66 your] LAMBARDE, HERRINGMAN; altered in PORTLAND from 'uery'

1.3.71 faces] In PORTLAND the scribe has first written 'fortunes' and deleted it and then added this word above it.

1.3.71.1 Exeunt Gentlemen] LAMBARDE (cropped to 'Exe Ge'), PORTLAND (Exvnt Gent); not in HERRINGMAN

1.3.73 higher] PORTLAND, HERRINGMAN; altered in LAMBARDE from 'les'

1.3.74 To the] HERRINGMAN; to th' LAMBARDE, PORTLAND

1.3.74 to] LAMBARDE, HERRINGMAN; for PORTLAND

1.3.76 GRAZIER] LAMBARDE, PORTLAND ('1 Graz' in both texts); But. HERRINGMAN

1.3.76 'twill] HERRINGMAN; will LAMBARDE, PORTLAND;

1.3.77 been at begging] PORTLAND; cropped in LAMBARDE to 'ben | begging'; been at the begging HERRINGMAN

1.3.77 a hundred] PORTLAND; a hundreth LAMBARDE; of a hundred HERRINGMAN

1.3.79 no] LAMBARDE, PORTLAND; not HERRINGMAN

1.3.80 kneel to] LAMBARDE, PORTLAND; point at HERRINGMAN

1.3.81 so] LAMBARDE, PORTLAND; too HERRINGMAN

1.3.82 amongst] LAMBARDE, PORTLAND; among HERRINGMAN

1.3.83 If…out] HERRINGMAN; not in LAMBARDE and PORTLAND, probably due to scribal error

1.3.84 served] LAMBARDE, PORTLAND; fpent HERRINGMAN

1.3.84 souls] PORTLAND, HERRINGMAN; cropped in LAMBARDE to 'soul'

1.3.86 fellmonger] LAMBARDE, PORTLAND; Felt-maker HERRINGMAN

1.3.87-8 BRAZIER Here's…grace] LAMBARDE, PORTLAND; But. Here's his Petition and mine, if it like your Grace HERRINGMAN

1.3.88 like] LAMBARDE, HERRINGMAN; please PORTLAND

1.3.90 my lord] LAMBARDE, PORTLAND; not in HERRINGMAN

1.3.91 I] LAMBARDE, PORTLAND; You HERRINGMAN

1.3.92 amongst 'em] LAMBARDE, PORTLAND; among them HERRINGMAN

1.3.93 i'th'] LAMBARDE, PORTLAND; in the HERRINGMAN

1.3.93 bottom] PORTLAND, HERRINGMAN; botton LAMBARDE (altered from 'button')

1.3.93 some] PORTLAND; not in LAMBARDE or HERRINGMAN

1.3.94 Prays] prays LAMBARDE, HERRINGMAN; prayers PORTLAND

1.3.95 request] LAMBARDE, PORTLAND; requests HERRINGMAN

1.3.95 not] added in PORTLAND with a caret above 'heaven'

1.3.99 consider't] LAMBARDE; consider it PORTLAND, HERRINGMAN

1.3.100 to twopence] LAMBARDE, PORTLAND; 2^d HERRINGMAN

1.3.104 this is one] PORTLAND, HERRINGMAN; this one LAMBARDE

1.3.104 afflictions] In PORTLAND the first 'i' has been altered from 'e'.

1.3.107 BRAZIER] LAMBARDE, PORTLAND; But. HERRINGMAN

1.3.107 To mine] LAMBARDE, PORTLAND; Mine HERRINGMAN

1.3.107 CONSTANTIUS] LAMBARDE, HERRINGMAN; not in PORTLAND, although the speech has been ruled off

1.3.108 That's all the] PORTLAND; thats all ye LAMBARDE; that's the HERRINGMAN

1.3.109 half] LAMBARDE; all PORTLAND, HERRINGMAN

1.3.111 BRAZIER] LAMBARDE, PORTLAND; But. HERRINGMAN

1.3.111 to] LAMBARDE, PORTLAND; at HERRINGMAN

1.3.113 There's] LAMBARDE, HERRINGMAN; there is PORTLAND

1.3.113 that] LAMBARDE, PORTLAND; that already HERRINGMAN

1.3.114-15 in the chase] LAMBARDE, PORTLAND; in chafe HERRINGMAN

1.3.115 and go] LAMBARDE, PORTLAND; and then go HERRINGMAN

1.3.117 BUTTONMONGER] LAMBARDE, PORTLAND; Gra. HERRINGMAN

1.3.117 destiny] LAMBARDE, PORTLAND; currifh deftiny HERRINGMAN

1.3.119 tempest] LAMBARDE, PORTLAND; ftorm HERRINGMAN

1.3.120 wished] HERRINGMAN (wifh'd); wis'd LAMBARDE, PORTLAND

1.3.121 All] all LAMBARDE, PORTLAND; all's HERRINGMAN

1.3.121 this] LAMBARDE, PORTLAND; here HERRINGMAN

1.3.121.1 Enter Vortiger] PORTLAND, HERRINGMAN; cropped in LAMBARDE to 'Enter V'

1.3.124 my lord] LAMBARDE, PORTLAND; not in HERRINGMAN

1.3.126 To marry] LAMBARDE, PORTLAND; How, to marry HERRINGMAN

1.3.126 Suddenly] LAMBARDE, PORTLAND; And fuddenly HERRINGMAN

1.3.126 given] LAMBARDE, PORTLAND; to be given HERRINGMAN

1.3.128 of] LAMBARDE; for PORTLAND; of a HERRINGMAN

1.3.129 abstinence] PORTLAND, HERRINGMAN; cropped in LAMBARDE to 'abstinen'

1.3.130 virgin] LAMBARDE, HERRINGMAN; virgins PORTLAND

1.3.131 The heat] added in PORTLAND with a caret above 'course'

1.3.135 'em] LAMBARDE, PORTLAND; them HERRINGMAN

1.3.136 VORTIGER This…lord] LAMBARDE, PORTLAND; not in HERRINGMAN

1.3.136 no] LAMBARDE; not PORTLAND

1.3.138 Their…clouds] LAMBARDE, PORTLAND; not in HERRINGMAN

1.3.139 virgin] altered in LAMBARDE from 'virgins'

1.3.140 sends] LAMBARDE, PORTLAND; fend HERRINGMAN

1.3.140 her] PORTLAND, HERRINGMAN; cropped in LAMBARDE to 'he'

1.3.142 See] LAMBARDE, PORTLAND; Lo HERRINGMAN

1.3.142.1 Enter Castiza] PORTLAND, HERRINGMAN; cropped in LAMBARDE to 'E'

1.3.143 Unhappy] LAMBARDE, PORTLAND; Th'unhappy HERRINGMAN

1.3.146 dangerously] PORTLAND, HERRINGMAN; in LAMBARDE the scribe has written 'strangely', deleted it and then written this word (cropped to 'danger') above it

1.3.148 politicly] LAMBARDE, PORTLAND; politique HERRINGMAN

1.3.151 say] altered in PORTLAND from 'saw'

1.3.152 lord] PORTLAND, HERRINGMAN; cropped in LAMBARDE

1.3.153 already] LAMBARDE, HERRINGMAN; already s^r PORTLAND

1.3.153 contract's] LAMBARDE, PORTLAND; contract is HERRINGMAN

1.3.154 VORTIGER…Leave…still] LAMBARDE, PORTLAND; not in HERRINGMAN

1.3.155 without] LAMBARDE, PORTLAND; void of HERRINGMAN

1.3.156 my projects] LAMBARDE, PORTLAND; projects that HERRINGMAN

1.3.156 I] HERRINGMAN; ne LAMBARDE, PORTLAND

1.3.156 you] *after this word in* LAMBARDE *a later hand has added* 'hee'

1.3.156 *Exit*] HERRINGMAN; *Exit Vort:* LAMBARDE (*at* 1.3.155); *Exit Vorti:* PORTLAND

1.3.157 This' an] LAMBARDE, PORTLAND; This is an HERRINGMAN

1.3.158 like't] LAMBARDE, PORTLAND; like it HERRINGMAN

1.3.159 they're] LAMBARDE, HERRINGMAN ('th'are' *in both texts*); they are PORTLAND

1.3.165 stand] LAMBARDE, PORTLAND; ftand in HERRINGMAN

1.3.168 to th'] LAMBARDE; to the PORTLAND, HERRINGMAN

1.3.168 door] *in* LAMBARDE *the second 'o' has been added*

1.3.169 has] LAMBARDE, PORTLAND; hath HERRINGMAN

1.3.169 this] LAMBARDE, HERRINGMAN; your PORTLAND

1.3.170 immaculate] *in* LAMBARDE *the second 'm' has been added above the line*

1.3.171 lamp] LAMBARDE, PORTLAND; lump HERRINGMAN

1.3.177 corruption] LAMBARDE, PORTLAND; corruptions HERRING-MAN

1.3.179 troth] LAMBARDE; *altered in* PORTLAND *from* 'faith'; truth HERRINGMAN

1.3.182 virtuous] LAMBARDE, HERRINGMAN; *altered in* PORTLAND *from another word*

1.3.182 lord] LAMBARDE, PORTLAND; Sir HERRINGMAN

1.3.183 I'm] LAMBARDE, PORTLAND; I am HERRINGMAN

1.3.184 I carry thoughts away] LAMBARDE, PORTLAND; My thoughts henceforth fhall be HERRINGMAN

1.3.185 immortal] In PORTLAND *the scribe has first written* 'eternall' *and deleted it and then added this word above the line with a caret.*

1.3.185.1 *Enter Vortiger and Gentleman*] PORTLAND (*Enter Vort & Gentle*); *cropped in* LAMBARDE *to* 'Enter Vo | & Gentl'; *As he kisses her | Enter* Vortiger *and | Gentlemen* HERRINGMAN (*at* 1.3.186)

1.3.187 *exit Castiza*] LAMBARDE, PORTLAND; *not in* HERRINGMAN

1.3.188 I'm] LAMBARDE, PORTLAND; I am HERRINGMAN

1.3.189 They're] LAMBARDE (their), HERRINGMAN (Th'are); they are PORTLAND

1.3.189 methinks] PORTLAND, HERRINGMAN; *cropped in* LAMBARDE *to* 'methin'

1.3.190 course] LAMBARDE, PORTLAND; way HERRINGMAN

1.3.192 woman] LAMBARDE, PORTLAND; a woman HERRINGMAN

1.3.193 *Exit*] HERRINGMAN; Exit Vortiger LAMBARDE, PORTLAND

1.3.195 'em] LAMBARDE, PORTLAND; them HERRINGMAN

1.3.196 better] LAMBARDE, HERRINGMAN; *not in* PORTLAND

1.3.196 an] LAMBARDE, PORTLAND (and); if HERRINGMAN

1.3.196 they'd] LAMBARDE, HERRINGMAN (they'ld); they would PORTLAND

1.3.197 And leave the court to me] LAMBARDE, PORTLAND; And leave me to my felf HERRINGMAN

1.3.198 to themselves] *altered in* LAMBARDE *to* 'to them selues' *from* 'to there selues', HERRINGMAN; there selues PORTLAND

1.3.199 upon the] LAMBARDE, PORTLAND; on the HERRINGMAN

1.3.200 memory's] LAMBARDE, PORTLAND; memory is HERRING-MAN

1.3.200 diseased] LAMBARDE (*altered to* 'diseasd' *from* 'deseased'), PORTLAND; difeas'd HERRINGMAN

1.3.201 Agatha, as I take it] PORTLAND; *Agatha's I take it* HERRINGMAN; Agatha I take LAMBARDE. The agreement of PORTLAND and HERRINGMAN suggests here and elsewhere that PORTLAND was not transcribed from LAMBARDE but from the same source as LAMBARDE, a source whose reading survived in the copy used to print HERRINGMAN.

1.3.202 O] LAMBARDE, PORTLAND; *not in* HERRINGMAN

1.3.204 an] PORTLAND (and); & LAMBARDE; if HERRINGMAN

1.3.205 court] PORTLAND, HERRINGMAN; *cropped in* LAMBARDE

1.3.206 pate] PORTLAND, HERRINGMAN; *cropped in* LAMBARDE

1.3.206 scarce] LAMBARDE, PORTLAND; *not in* HERRINGMAN

1.3.207 twelvemonth] PORTLAND; *cropped in* LAMBARDE *to* 'twelve'; twelve months HERRINGMAN

1.3.207 *Exit*] HERRINGMAN; *not in* LAMBARDE *or* PORTLAND

1.3.208 Sure, 'tis] LAMBARDE, PORTLAND; 'Tis sure HERRINGMAN

1.3.209.1 *Enter . . . Stafford*] PORTLAND (Enter Vort Deuon & Staff); *cropped in* LAMBARDE *to* 'Ente | Deuon'; *Enter* Vortiger HERRING-MAN (*at* l. 212)

1.3.211 'em] LAMBARDE, PORTLAND; them HERRINGMAN

1.3.214 duties] LAMBARDE, PORTLAND; duty HERRINGMAN

1.3.215 please] LAMBARDE, HERRINGMAN; *in* PORTLAND *the scribe has altered his original* 'Confesse' *to* 'plesse' *by deleting the* 'Co' *and changing the* 'n' *to a* 'p' *and the* 'f' *to an* 'l'

1.3.224 you'll] LAMBARDE, PORTLAND; you HERRINGMAN

1.3.227 VORTIGER] LAMBARDE, HERRINGMAN; *not in* PORTLAND, *although the speech has been ruled off*

1.3.227 What, will] LAMBARDE, PORTLAND; Will HERRINGMAN

1.3.230 knees] LAMBARDE, PORTLAND (*altered from another word, possibly* 'eues'); Eeves HERRINGMAN

1.3.232 You've] LAMBARDE, PORTLAND (y'haue); I have HERRING-MAN

1.3.232 may well] LAMBARDE, PORTLAND; well may HERRINGMAN

1.3.233.1 *Exeunt*] HERRINGMAN; Exeunt Omnes LAMBARDE, PORT-LAND

2.1.0.1–2 *Incipit . . . Castiza*] LAMBARDE (*Musique Actus Secundus, Sce: Prima Enter Entiger* [*altered from* 'Enter'] *& Castiza*); *Musique Actus Secundus, Sce^a Pr^a Enter Vort: Cast:* PORTLAND; ACT. 2. SCENA 1. | *Enter* Vortiger *and* Castiza HERRINGMAN (*preceded by catchword* 'Actus')

2.1.1 further] LAMBARDE, PORTLAND; farther HERRINGMAN

2.1.3 truth of health] LAMBARDE, HERRINGMAN; way of truth PORTLAND

2.1.6 you'd] LAMBARDE; you would PORTLAND; Youl'd HERRING-MAN

2.1.9 I'm] LAMBARDE, PORTLAND; I am HERRINGMAN

2.1.10 In] PORTLAND, HERRINGMAN; for LAMBARDE

2.1.11 I'm] LAMBARDE, PORTLAND; I am HERRINGMAN

2.1.12 you] HERRINGMAN; youle LAMBARDE, PORTLAND

2.1.13 into me] LAMBARDE, PORTLAND; me into HERRINGMAN

2.1.15 my] *preceded in* LAMBARDE *by deleted* 'ye'

2.1.17 on't] LAMBARDE, PORTLAND; of it HERRINGMAN

2.1.18 somewhat] LAMBARDE, PORTLAND; something HERRING-MAN

2.1.20 was] LAMBARDE; wer PORTLAND; were HERRINGMAN

2.1.22 intent] *preceded in* LAMBARDE *by deleted* 're'

2.1.25 perfections] LAMBARDE, PORTLAND; profperity HERRING-MAN

2.1.26 mine] LAMBARDE, PORTLAND; my HERRINGMAN

2.1.26 am I] LAMBARDE, HERRINGMAN; I am PORTLAND

2.1.29 wrought] LAMBARDE, PORTLAND; brought HERRINGMAN

2.1.29 him] PORTLAND, HERRINGMAN; *cropped in* LAMBARDE *to* 'hi' (*altered from* 'he')

2.1.30 neglect] LAMBARDE, PORTLAND; neglects HERRINGMAN

2.1.31–2 A . . . benefit] In PORTLAND *in the right margin of these lines the scribe has written* 'Brigs | Robrt St | Blackson'; *these actors's names appeared in this place in* LAMBARDE *but have been cropped.*

2.1.33 catches] LAMBARDE, PORTLAND; catcheth HERRINGMAN

2.1.33 beliefs] LAMBARDE, HERRINGMAN; belief PORTLAND

2.1.33 stronger too] PORTLAND, HERRINGMAN; *cropped in* LAM-BARDE *to* 'stron'

2.1.34 to me] PORTLAND; *cropped in* LAMBARDE *to* 'to m'; at me HERRINGMAN

2.1.37 never] LAMBARDE, PORTLAND; ne're HERRINGMAN

2.1.37.1 Exit] LAMBARDE, HERRINGMAN; not in PORTLAND

2.2.0.1–24 Dumb Show...safety] for variants between the LAMBARDE–PORTLAND texts and HERRINGMAN, see Stage Directions

2.2.0.1 Oboes] LAMBARDE, PORTLAND (Hoboys)

2.2.0.7 furies] LAMBARDE; fury PORTLAND

2.2.0.9 on] LAMBARDE; upon PORTLAND

2.2.0.10 and] PORTLAND; not in LAMBARDE

2.2.0.17 all] LAMBARDE; not in PORTLAND

2.2.0.20 and Stafford] PORTLAND (& Stafford); not in LAMBARDE

2.2.0.24 their] LAMBARDE; not in PORTLAND

2.2.0.25 Enter Raynulph] HERRINGMAN; not in LAMBARDE or PORTLAND

2.2.2 death] LAMBARDE, PORTLAND; they HERRINGMAN

2.2.3 In wicked strengths] LAMBARDE, PORTLAND; Two wicked rogues HERRINGMAN

2.2.5 Pity] LAMBARDE, PORTLAND; Of pity HERRINGMAN

2.2.10 slaughterous] LAMBARDE, PORTLAND; flaughterers HERRINGMAN

2.2.11 they him] preceded in LAMBARDE by deleted 'yᵉ King'

2.2.11 maid] PORTLAND, HERRINGMAN; cropped in LAMBARDE to 'may'

2.2.14 kin] LAMBARDE (altered from 'hin'), PORTLAND; Kindred HERRINGMAN

2.2.14 and] LAMBARDE, PORTLAND; not in HERRINGMAN

2.2.14 friends] altered in LAMBARDE to 'friendes' from 'friends'

2.3.0.1 Enter...Gentleman] LAMBARDE, PORTLAND ('Enter Vortiger a Gentleman' in both texts); (Enter Vortiger (Crowned) a Gentleman meeting him) HERRINGMAN

2.3.4–6 I...now] LAMBARDE, PORTLAND; not in HERRINGMAN

2.3.7 power] LAMBARDE, PORTLAND; time HERRINGMAN

2.3.7 thee] PORTLAND, HERRINGMAN; cropped in LAMBARDE to 't'

2.3.8 What's] LAMBARDE, HERRINGMAN; what PORTLAND

2.3.9 'em] LAMBARDE, PORTLAND; them HERRINGMAN

2.3.9.1 Exit] LAMBARDE, PORTLAND (Exit Gentleman); not in HERRINGMAN

2.3.12–13 Compared...wishes] LAMBARDE, PORTLAND; not in HERRINGMAN

2.3.16 their] HERRINGMAN; this LAMBARDE, PORTLAND

2.3.16 hearts] PORTLAND, HERRINGMAN; cropped in LAMBARDE to 'hea'

2.3.17 safety] PORTLAND, HERRINGMAN; cropped in LAMBARDE to 'saf'

2.3.17.1 Shout] LAMBARDE, PORTLAND (at 2.3.16); not in HERRINGMAN

2.3.18 hear] altered in LAMBARDE from 'feare' (the 'f' was changed to an 'h')

2.3.19.1 Enter Gentleman] PORTLAND (Enter Gent); cropped in LAMBARDE to 'Enter Ge'; Enter a second Gentleman HERRINGMAN

2.3.24 hearts] LAMBARDE, PORTLAND; hats HERRINGMAN

2.3.25.1 Enter...soldiers] LAMBARDE ('Enter Her | sus Drum | and Soldiers', with 'Hengist' added above the first line, before 2.3.23); Enter Hengist | Hersus Drum & | Soldiers PORTLAND (before 2.3.23); Enter Hengift, Horfus, Souldiers HERRINGMAN

2.3.27 wished...pleasures] LAMBARDE; wish to a kins pleasure PORTLAND; pleafure to a King HERRINGMAN

2.3.28 speaks] LAMBARDE, PORTLAND; fpake HERRINGMAN

2.3.32 hope-faithful] LAMBARDE, PORTLAND; hope, fruitful HERRINGMAN

2.3.33 Calls] altered in PORTLAND from another word

2.3.33 Hersus] LAMBARDE, PORTLAND; Horsus HERRINGMAN (here and throughout the text). Holinshed uses the name Horsus; however, the name is spelled in varying ways in the sources earlier than Holinshed.

2.3.34 but, sir] LAMBARDE; but PORTLAND; but yet HERRINGMAN

2.3.34 acts of valour] LAMBARDE, PORTLAND; deeds of Arms HERRINGMAN

2.3.39 fate] LAMBARDE (altered to 'fatte' from 'faith'), PORTLAND; Fates HERRINGMAN

2.3.39 bounds] altered in PORTLAND from 'lands'

2.3.40 wounds] altered in LAMBARDE and PORTLAND from 'owne'

2.3.41 dearly] LAMBARDE, PORTLAND; ever HERRINGMAN

2.3.43 HENGIST] LAMBARDE, HERRINGMAN; not in PORTLAND, although the speech has been ruled off

2.3.43 in] added in PORTLAND with a caret above 'vigour'

2.3.43 then] LAMBARDE, HERRINGMAN; now PORTLAND

2.3.44 them that thrive] LAMBARDE; them that liue PORTLAND; such as thrive HERRINGMAN

2.3.44 by th'] LAMBARDE, HERRINGMAN; by the PORTLAND

2.3.44.1 Exeunt] HERRINGMAN; Exevnt | omnes LAMBARDE (at 2.3.43); Exeunt Omnes PORTLAND

2.4.0.1–2.4.1 Alarums...Gentleman] LAMBARDE, PORTLAND; Enter Vortiger and Gentlemen. Alarm and | Skirmishes HERRINGMAN

2.4.1, 4 GENTLEMAN] LAMBARDE, PORTLAND; I Gent. HERRINGMAN

2.4.1 'em] LAMBARDE, PORTLAND; them HERRINGMAN

2.4.2 Stains] LAMBARDE, PORTLAND; Stay HERRINGMAN

2.4.2 Stains...success] In LAMBARDE the scribe has drawn a symbol (either an orb with a cross above it or an astrological symbol, upside down, for a woman) in the left margin, probably representing a reminder for properties or actors to be made ready or to cross reference an interleaved addition or for some other purpose. The symbol suggests that the scribe was copying his text from a playhouse promptbook. The symbol also appears at 3.3.0.1, 4.1.0.1 and 5.1.0.3–4. The name 'Rob: Briggs' is also written in the right margin; in PORTLAND the name appears as 'Robb Briggs' in the same place.

2.4.2 forward] LAMBARDE, PORTLAND; forwards HERRINGMAN

2.4.3 a moment] LAMBARDE, PORTLAND; one minute HERRINGMAN

2.4.4 insurrection] in LAMBARDE the first 'r' has been added

2.4.5 prisoners] in LAMBARDE the 'o' has been added

2.4.6 mercy] PORTLAND, HERRINGMAN; cropped in LAMBARDE to 'm'

2.4.7 with] LAMBARDE, PORTLAND; by HERRINGMAN

2.4.8 are] LAMBARDE, PORTLAND; th'are HERRINGMAN

2.4.9 'Tis] LAMBARDE, PORTLAND; which HERRINGMAN

2.4.9 wondrous] LAMBARDE, PORTLAND; is wonderous HERRINGMAN

2.4.9.1–2 Enter...Prisoners] PORTLAND (Enter Heng: Hers: with | Drum Collours Soldiers | leading prisoners; cropped in LAMBARDE to 'Enter H | Horsus, | Soldiers le | prisoner'; Enter Hengist and Horsus with Prisoners HERRINGMAN

2.4.11 life's] LAMBARDE, PORTLAND; life is HERRINGMAN

2.4.13 immortality] preceded in PORTLAND by deleted 'my soul still'

2.4.13 with't] LAMBARDE, PORTLAND; with it HERRINGMAN

2.4.14 And] LAMBARDE, PORTLAND; But HERRINGMAN

2.4.16 sum] LAMBARDE, PORTLAND; fame HERRINGMAN

2.4.16 praises] LAMBARDE, PORTLAND; merits HERRINGMAN

2.4.16 give] LAMBARDE, HERRINGMAN; giues PORTLAND

2.4.17 all's] LAMBARDE, HERRINGMAN; all is PORTLAND

2.4.19 man] PORTLAND, HERRINGMAN; Mans LAMBARDE

2.4.21 do] PORTLAND, HERRINGMAN; cropped in LAMBARDE

2.4.22 as soon] LAMBARDE, PORTLAND; are as foon HERRINGMAN

2.4.22 taken] LAMBARDE, PORTLAND; ta'ne HERRINGMAN

2.4.22 as in] LAMBARDE, PORTLAND; in the HERRINGMAN

2.4.24 deeds] PORTLAND, HERRINGMAN; cropped in LAMBARDE to 'd'

2.4.25 fortune speaks] LAMBARDE, HERRINGMAN; fortunes speak PORTLAND

2.4.29 we'll] *in* PORTLAND *the scribe has first written* 'will' *and then inserted* 'we' *with a caret above it*

2.4.30 Sir, for our] LAMBARDE, HERRINGMAN; for our PORTLAND

2.4.30.1 *Enter Simon with a hide*] LAMBARDE, PORTLAND; *at* 2.4.33 *in* HERRINGMAN

2.4.33 greatest] PORTLAND, HERRINGMAN; greatess LAMBARDE

2.4.34 men] LAMBARDE, HERRINGMAN; people PORTLAND

2.4.35 grant you that] LAMBARDE, PORTLAND; yield to that HERRINGMAN

2.4.40 blushing] LAMBARDE, PORTLAND; bubbling HERRINGMAN

2.4.47 for I] LAMBARDE, PORTLAND; I HERRINGMAN

2.4.51 the] LAMBARDE, HERRINGMAN; *not in* PORTLAND

2.4.51 buy] *in* LAMBARDE *the* 'u' *has been added above the line with a caret*

2.4.51 house] *altered in* LAMBARDE *and* PORTLAND *from* 'horse'

2.4.52 o'er] LAMBARDE, PORTLAND; over HERRINGMAN

2.4.54 There's] LAMBARDE, PORTLAND; There is HERRINGMAN

2.4.55-6 be the better] PORTLAND; by'th better LAMBARDE; be the blacker HERRINGMAN

2.4.56 o'th' twain] LAMBARDE; of the twaine PORTLAND; of the two HERRINGMAN

2.4.58 gulled] LAMBARDE, PORTLAND; deceiv'd HERRINGMAN

2.4.58 a good calf's] LAMBARDE, PORTLAND; a Calves HERRINGMAN

2.4.59 gather] *altered in* PORTLAND *from* 'Leather'

2.4.59 'em] LAMBARDE, PORTLAND; them HERRINGMAN

2.4.59-60 for shoemakers] LAMBARDE, PORTLAND; for honeſt Shoomakers HERRINGMAN

2.4.63 servant] *preceded in* LAMBARDE *by deleted* 'Master'

2.4.63 man, sir] PORTLAND, HERRINGMAN; *cropped in* LAMBARDE *to* 'm'

2.4.64 How? Prithee, how that now] LAMBARDE, PORTLAND; Prithee how can that be HERRINGMAN

2.4.65 master's] LAMBARDE; master is PORTLAND, HERRINGMAN

2.4.65 and I serve] *altered in* LAMBARDE *to* 'serue' *from* 'haue'; and I haue PORTLAND; and now I ſerve HERRINGMAN

2.4.66 mistress] PORTLAND, HERRINGMAN; *cropped in* LAMBARDE

2.4.66 I] LAMBARDE, PORTLAND; Ergo I HERRINGMAN

2.4.66 she's] LAMBARDE, PORTLAND; she is HERRINGMAN

2.4.70 and] *added in* LAMBARDE *above the line with a caret*

2.4.71 greatly with wit neither] LAMBARDE, PORTLAND; with wit neither greatly HERRINGMAN

2.4.71 are] PORTLAND, HERRINGMAN; *cropped in* LAMBARDE

2.4.72 Now] PORTLAND, HERRINGMAN; *cropped in* LAMBARDE

2.4.73 will] PORTLAND, HERRINGMAN; *cropped in* LAMBARDE

2.4.74 hanging] PORTLAND, HERRINGMAN; *cropped in* LAMBARDE *to* 'ha'

2.4.74 of myself] LAMBARDE, PORTLAND; myself HERRINGMAN

2.4.75 neighbours] PORTLAND, HERRINGMAN; *cropped in* LAMBARDE *to* ' | ghbours'

2.4.76 too, willingly, sir] LAMBARDE, PORTLAND; *not in* HERRINGMAN

2.4.77 labour] PORTLAND, HERRINGMAN; *cropped in* LAMBARDE *to* 'la'

2.4.77 fleaing] LAMBARDE, PORTLAND; fleaing me HERRINGMAN

2.4.78 shall] PORTLAND, HERRINGMAN; *cropped in* LAMBARDE *to* 'sh'

2.4.78 of] *altered in* LAMBARDE *from* 'in'

2.4.78 rate] LAMBARDE, PORTLAND; price HERRINGMAN

2.4.78 man] LAMBARDE, PORTLAND; men's HERRINGMAN

2.4.79 and] PORTLAND, HERRINGMAN; *cropped in* LAMBARDE *to* 'a'

2.4.80 ear] LAMBARDE, PORTLAND; good ear HERRINGMAN

2.4.80 your] LAMBARDE, PORTLAND; the HERRINGMAN

2.4.83 indeed] LAMBARDE, PORTLAND; y'faith HERRINGMAN

2.4.83 go and spoil] LAMBARDE, PORTLAND; Spoil HERRINGMAN

2.4.83 leather] PORTLAND, HERRINGMAN; *cropped in* LAMBARDE *to* 'L'

2.4.85 Do't] LAMBARDE, PORTLAND; Do it HERRINGMAN

2.4.86 Hunch] LAMBARDE, PORTLAND; hum HERRINGMAN

2.4.86 this] PORTLAND, HERRINGMAN; the LAMBARDE

2.4.87 vanity of] PORTLAND, HERRINGMAN; *cropped in* LAMBARDE *to* 'vani'

2.4.87 Roman] *altered in* LAMBARDE *to* 'Romane' *from* 'Romans'

2.4.87 gallants] LAMBARDE, PORTLAND. *In some copies of* HERRINGMAN *the first* 'l' *in this word was not well inked and was not printed.*

2.4.88 suits] PORTLAND, HERRINGMAN; *cropped in* LAMBARDE *to* 'sh'

2.4.88 'em] LAMBARDE, PORTLAND; them HERRINGMAN

2.4.88 gigots] PORTLAND, HERRINGMAN; *cropped in* LAMBARDE *to* 'li'

2.4.89 taffeta sits] LAMBARDE, PORTLAND ('taffety sits' *in both texts*); Taffaties fit HERRINGMAN

2.4.89 their] PORTLAND, HERRINGMAN; *cropped in* LAMBARDE *to* 'the'

2.4.90 sir] sʳ LAMBARDE, PORTLAND; *not in* HERRINGMAN

2.4.90 the] PORTLAND; *cropped in* LAMBARDE; this HERRINGMAN

2.4.91 swaggering] LAMBARDE, HERRINGMAN; swagger in PORTLAND

2.4.91 condition] PORTLAND, HERRINGMAN; *cropped in* LAMBARDE *to* 'c'

2.4.92 an't] LAMBARDE (ant); and it PORTLAND; if it HERRINGMAN

2.4.92 well] PORTLAND, HERRINGMAN; *cropped in* LAMBARDE

2.4.94 gross] LAMBARDE, PORTLAND; croſs HERRINGMAN

2.4.94-5 lighted on] PORTLAND, HERRINGMAN; *cropped in* LAMBARDE *to* 'ligh'

2.4.100 with] *altered in* LAMBARDE *from* 'is'

2.4.100 parcels] LAMBARDE (*altered to* 'parcells' *from* 'peices'), PORTLAND; pieces HERRINGMAN

2.4.101 stretch] LAMBARDE, PORTLAND; ſtretch far HERRINGMAN

2.4.101 circuit] *in* LAMBARDE *the first* 'i' *has been altered from* 'u'

2.4.104 shake] LAMBARDE, PORTLAND; claw HERRINGMAN

2.4.104 lands] LAMBARDE, PORTLAND; land HERRINGMAN

2.4.107 doubled] LAMBARDE, PORTLAND; *not in* HERRINGMAN

2.4.110 devil's in] LAMBARDE, PORTLAND; Devil is HERRINGMAN

2.4.112 away] LAMBARDE, PORTLAND; *not in* HERRINGMAN

2.4.117 sessions, that] LAMBARDE, PORTLAND; Seſsions at *Maidſtone* HERRINGMAN

2.4.118 you are] PORTLAND; yoᵘ are LAMBARDE; y'are HERRINGMAN

2.4.120 I'm] LAMBARDE, PORTLAND; I am HERRINGMAN

2.4.120 make you] LAMBARDE, PORTLAND; make HERRINGMAN

2.4.124 fellows] LAMBARDE, PORTLAND; Followers HERRINGMAN

2.4.124 *Exit*] LAMBARDE, PORTLAND ('*Exit Simon*' *in both texts*); *not in* HERRINGMAN

2.4.125 You, sirs] LAMBARDE, PORTLAND; *not in* HERRINGMAN

2.4.126 foundations] LAMBARDE, PORTLAND; foundation HERRINGMAN

2.4.127 earth] *altered in* LAMBARDE *from* 'errth'

2.4.130 honours] *preceded in* PORTLAND *by deleted* 'promissess'

2.4.130 does't] dost LAMBARDE, PORTLAND; does it HERRINGMAN

2.4.132 departed] LAMBARDE, PORTLAND; had HERRINGMAN

2.4.132 bodies] PORTLAND; bodies sprung HERRINGMAN; *cropped in* LAMBARDE *to* 'body'

2.4.133 carcasses] *In* LAMBARDE *the scribe has first written* 'Carsses' *and then inserted* 'ca' *with a caret above the* 'rs'.

2.4.134-5 college. | HENGIST There's the fruits | Of] HERRINGMAN; Colledge, theirs the fruites. | *Heng:* of LAMBARDE, PORTLAND

2.4.135 shows] PORTLAND (shews); shews shewes LAMBARDE; fhew HERRINGMAN

2.4.137–8 When...charity] LAMBARDE, PORTLAND; *not in* HERRINGMAN

2.4.137 shelter] PORTLAND; *cropped in* LAMBARDE *to* 'shelt'

2.4.138 nor house nor] LAMBARDE; noe house or PORTLAND

2.4.139 our] LAMBARDE, HERRINGMAN; *not in* PORTLAND

2.4.139 Captain] PORTLAND, HERRINGMAN; *cropped in* LAMBARDE *to* 'Cap'

2.4.142 he's] LAMBARDE, PORTLAND (h'as); he has HERRINGMAN

2.4.142 I know] LAMBARDE, PORTLAND; he knows HERRINGMAN

2.4.150 She's] LAMBARDE, PORTLAND; She is HERRINGMAN

2.4.151 is she] LAMBARDE, PORTLAND; she is HERRINGMAN

2.4.156 learns one] LAMBARDE, PORTLAND; learn them HERRINGMAN

2.4.157 Some] LAMBARDE, PORTLAND; Come HERRINGMAN

2.4.157 you forget not] LAMBARDE, PORTLAND; forget none HERRINGMAN

2.4.158 my memory if I should] LAMBARDE; me if I should PORTLAND; my memory HERRINGMAN

2.4.160 you need no help] LAMBARDE, PORTLAND; *not in* HERRINGMAN

2.4.160 memory's] LAMBARDE, HERRINGMAN; memory is PORTLAND

2.4.160.1 *Shouts; flourish*] LAMBARDE (at 2.4.157); showte flourish PORTLAND (at 2.4.157); *not in* HERRINGMAN

2.4.161 sounds] LAMBARDE, PORTLAND; shouts HERRINGMAN

2.4.162.1 *Enter Saxon Gentleman*] LAMBARDE ('Enter Gent: saxon' at 2.4.161); *Enter Gent* PORTLAND (at 2.4.161); *Enter a Gentleman.* HERRINGMAN

2.4.164, 165 SAXON GENTLEMAN] LAMBARDE *cropped to* 't: | Sax'; Gent PORTLAND, HERRINGMAN *Gen*

2.4.165 SAXON GENTLEMAN] *cropped in* LAMBARDE *to* 't: | Sax' *with the* 'S' *altered from* 'G'

2.4.165 here] LAMBARDE, PORTLAND; here, Sir HERRINGMAN

2.4.166 youth] LAMBARDE, HERRINGMAN; age PORTLAND

2.4.171 charitably] LAMBARDE, HERRINGMAN; Charitable PORTLAND

2.4.173 downhill] *altered in* LAMBARDE *to* 'down hill' *from* 'down his'

2.4.174 i'th'] LAMBARDE, PORTLAND; in the HERRINGMAN

2.4.175 'em] LAMBARDE, PORTLAND; them HERRINGMAN

2.4.177 take you] LAMBARDE, PORTLAND; take HERRINGMAN

2.4.178 HENGIST I...for't.] LAMBARDE, PORTLAND; *not in* HERRINGMAN

2.4.179 at] LAMBARDE, PORTLAND; with HERRINGMAN

2.4.181 now] LAMBARDE; *not in* PORTLAND; new HERRINGMAN

2.4.183 current] LAMBARDE, PORTLAND; reverend HERRINGMAN

2.4.187 I know not which, but one, or both] LAMBARDE, PORTLAND; but one or both, I know not which HERRINGMAN

2.4.194 times o'th'] LAMBARDE; time oth PORTLAND; times of the HERRINGMAN

2.4.196 fits it] PORTLAND, HERRINGMAN; *cropped in* LAMBARDE *to* 'fitt'

2.4.196.1–2 *Flourish...attendants*] PORTLAND; *cropped in* LAMBARDE *to* 'Flourish | Enter V | Rox'; *Florish. | Enter* Vortiger, | Roxena, &c. HERRINGMAN

2.4.197 for't] LAMBARDE, PORTLAND; for it HERRINGMAN

2.4.199 Our...grow] LAMBARDE, PORTLAND; *not in* HERRINGMAN

2.4.201 here] LAMBARDE, PORTLAND; to her HERRINGMAN

2.4.202 my lord] LAMBARDE, PORTLAND; *not in* HERRINGMAN

2.4.203 Take't] LAMBARDE; take it PORTLAND, HERRINGMAN

2.4.204 You'll keep] LAMBARDE, HERRINGMAN; You will take PORTLAND

2.4.204 will you] LAMBARDE, PORTLAND; *not in* HERRINGMAN

2.4.205 yet] LAMBARDE, PORTLAND; *not in* HERRINGMAN

2.4.206 I] *preceded in* LAMBARDE *by deleted* 'yet'

2.4.206 a] LAMBARDE, PORTLAND; the HERRINGMAN

2.4.206 husband's] *before this word in* LAMBARDE *the scribe has first written* 'hi' *then changed it to* 'hue' *and then deleted it*

2.4.206 interest] LAMBARDE, HERRINGMAN; part PORTLAND

2.4.207 of majesty] LAMBARDE, PORTLAND; to Majefty HERRINGMAN

2.4.209–10 Come again? | I...thee] LAMBARDE, PORTLAND; Come again, I never thought to hear fo ill of thee HERRINGMAN

2.4.211 So beyond detestable] LAMBARDE ('beyond' *preceded by deleted* 'ill'), HERRINGMAN; soe ill beyond detestable PORTLAND. The agreement of LAMBARDE and PORTLAND in regards to the appearance of 'ill' suggests that the word, possibly deleted, appeared in the manuscript from which both scribes were copying.

2.4.214 only] *preceded in* LAMBARDE *by deleted* 'worst'

2.4.215 hours] PORTLAND, HERRINGMAN; ours LAMBARDE

2.4.215 with it] PORTLAND, HERRINGMAN; wth LAMBARDE

2.4.216 'em] LAMBARDE, PORTLAND; them HERRINGMAN

2.4.218 nobler] LAMBARDE, HERRINGMAN; noble PORTLAND

2.4.221 'twill do't] LAMBARDE, PORTLAND; *not in* HERRINGMAN

2.4.223 helped] HERRINGMAN (helpt); hope LAMBARDE, PORTLAND

2.4.223 Comes't] LAMBARDE; comes it PORTLAND, HERRINGMAN

2.4.225 but't] LAMBARDE; but it PORTLAND, HERRINGMAN

2.4.227 for] LAMBARDE, PORTLAND; *not in* HERRINGMAN

2.4.228 bring] LAMBARDE, HERRINGMAN; brings PORTLAND

2.4.228 upon] LAMBARDE, PORTLAND; into HERRINGMAN

2.4.229 plague] LAMBARDE, PORTLAND; proof HERRINGMAN

2.4.233 undertook] LAMBARDE, PORTLAND; undertaken HERRINGMAN

2.4.239 thou'rt] LAMBARDE (*altered to* 'thou't' *from another word beginning with* 'th'), HERRINGMAN; thou art PORTLAND

2.4.241 what's] PORTLAND; w^{ts} LAMBARDE; what is most HERRINGMAN

2.4.241 precious] LAMBARDE, HERRINGMAN; spretious PORTLAND

2.4.241 yet once more] LAMBARDE, PORTLAND; *not in* HERRINGMAN

2.4.243 find] LAMBARDE, PORTLAND; feel HERRINGMAN

2.4.244 wilt thou] LAMBARDE; wilt thee PORTLAND; do not HERRINGMAN

2.4.244 wilfully] *altered in* PORTLAND *to* 'will fully' *from* 'wish fully'

2.4.244 me] *preceded in* LAMBARDE *by deleted* 'the'

2.4.245 I'm] LAMBARDE, PORTLAND; I am HERRINGMAN

2.4.251 Amongst] LAMBARDE, PORTLAND; Among HERRINGMAN

2.4.251 whose are nicest] PORTLAND; whose are incest LAMBARDE; thofe are nicefl HERRINGMAN

2.4.252 bring] LAMBARDE, PORTLAND; brought HERRINGMAN

2.4.253 ever] LAMBARDE, PORTLAND; e're HERRINGMAN

2.4.253 restored] HERRINGMAN; stored LAMBARDE, PORTLAND

2.4.253 'em] LAMBARDE, PORTLAND; them HERRINGMAN

2.4.255 I am] LAMBARDE, PORTLAND; I'm HERRINGMAN

2.4.257 I am] LAMBARDE, PORTLAND; I'm HERRINGMAN

2.4.259 chain] HERRINGMAN; Chaire LAMBARDE, PORTLAND

2.4.259 means] PORTLAND, HERRINGMAN; *cropped in* LAMBARDE *to* 'meane'

2.4.261 that] PORTLAND; y^t LAMBARDE; my HERRINGMAN

2.4.261 that] LAMBARDE, PORTLAND; my HERRINGMAN

2.4.263 I...on't!] LAMBARDE, PORTLAND; I fay think on it! HERRINGMAN

2.4.263 An] LAMBARDE, PORTLAND ('and' *in both texts*); If HERRINGMAN

2.4.264 shall even] LAMBARDE, PORTLAND; *not in* HERRINGMAN

2.4.264 again] LAMBARDE, PORTLAND; *not in* HERRINGMAN

2.4.266 else is] *added in* PORTLAND *above the line with a caret*

2.4.266 chide] HERRINGMAN; chid LAMBARDE, PORTLAND

2.4.266.1 Flourish...Exeunt] LAMBARDE (*flourish Cornets Exen*) (*at* 2.4.264-5); *flourish | Cornetts* (*at* 2.4.266) PORTLAND; *Exeunt.* HERRINGMAN

3.1.0.1 *Incipit...Tertius*] LAMBARDE (*Actius Tertius Sce Pr:ᵃ*); *tus Tertius Sceᵃ Prᵈ* PORTLAND; ACT. 3. SCENA 1. HERRINGMAN

3.1.0.2 *Enter...Roxena*] PORTLAND; *Enter Horfus and* Roxena HERRINGMAN; *Enter Hersus: Roxena* LAMBARDE

3.1.2 So, so] LAMBARDE, PORTLAND ('soe, soe' *in both texts*); See, see HERRINGMAN

3.1.6 honours] LAMBARDE, HERRINGMAN; honour PORTLAND

3.1.6 and] LAMBARDE, PORTLAND; of HERRINGMAN

3.1.11 call] *altered in* LAMBARDE *from* 'tell'

3.1.13 They are] LAMBARDE, PORTLAND; Th'are HERRINGMAN

3.1.15 desire] LAMBARDE, HERRINGMAN; desires PORTLAND

3.1.16 To examine] LAMBARDE, PORTLAND; T'examine HERRINGMAN

3.1.16 condition] LAMBARDE, HERRINGMAN; Conditions PORTLAND

3.1.19 ours can't] LAMBARDE; yours cant PORTLAND; ours cannot HERRINGMAN

3.1.20 Or never] LAMBARDE, PORTLAND; Nor ever HERRINGMAN

3.1.20 any] *altered in* LAMBARDE *from* 'eny'

3.1.21 greater] *cropped in* LAMBARDE *to* 'greate'

3.1.22 he's] LAMBARDE, PORTLAND; he is HERRINGMAN

3.1.24 'Gainst] LAMBARDE, PORTLAND; Againſt HERRINGMAN

3.1.24 blood's] HERRINGMAN (blouds); blood LAMBARDE, PORTLAND

3.1.24 wronging] *preceded in* LAMBARDE *by deleted* 'riseing'

3.1.24 for this] PORTLAND, HERRINGMAN; *cropped in* LAMBARDE *to* 'fo'

3.1.25 love] HERRINGMAN; haue LAMBARDE, PORTLAND

3.1.26 unknown] *in* LAMBARDE *the first 'n' in this word has been altered from* 'r'

3.1.27 were] *in* PORTLAND *the 'w' in this word has been altered from* 'h'

3.1.29 arising] LAMBARDE, PORTLAND; in riſing HERRINGMAN

3.1.31 now] LAMBARDE, PORTLAND; not HERRINGMAN

3.1.33 admit] LAMBARDE, PORTLAND; in HERRINGMAN

3.1.35 perhaps] PORTLAND, HERRINGMAN; *cropped in* LAMBARDE *to* 'perhapp'

3.1.36 i'th'] LAMBARDE, PORTLAND; in the HERRINGMAN

3.1.37 gentlewoman] PORTLAND; *cropped in* LAMBARDE *to* 'Gentlew'; woman HERRINGMAN

3.1.38 nay, nor never] LAMBARDE, PORTLAND; no nor ever HERRINGMAN

3.1.40 'Tis] LAMBARDE, PORTLAND; Is HERRINGMAN

3.1.40 pleasing'st] LAMBARDE, PORTLAND; moſt pleaſing HERRINGMAN

3.1.40 anyone] LAMBARDE, PORTLAND; they HERRINGMAN

3.1.41 rises] LAMBARDE, PORTLAND; do ſpring HERRINGMAN

3.1.42 from whence] LAMBARDE, PORTLAND; whence HERRINGMAN

3.1.43 for] LAMBARDE, PORTLAND; of HERRINGMAN

3.1.44 fortunes] *altered in* PORTLAND *from another word*

3.1.44 gentlewomen] LAMBARDE, PORTLAND; women HERRINGMAN

3.1.45 Now] LAMBARDE, PORTLAND; *not in* HERRINGMAN

3.1.45 mine] LAMBARDE, PORTLAND; my HERRINGMAN

3.1.45 given] PORTLAND, HERRINGMAN; *cropped in* LAMBARDE *to* 'giu'

3.1.46 their] LAMBARDE, PORTLAND; our HERRINGMAN

3.1.47 which] LAMBARDE, PORTLAND; that HERRINGMAN

3.1.49 stripped] PORTLAND (stript); ſtripp'd HERRINGMAN; *cropped in* LAMBARDE *to* 'strip'

3.1.52 with] LAMBARDE, PORTLAND; by HERRINGMAN

3.1.53-60 Sure...both] In LAMBARDE *and* PORTLAND the scribes have marked these lines for deletion by ruling them off; these lines are not in HERRINGMAN.

3.1.54 gains] PORTLAND; games LAMBARDE

3.1.56 suffice] LAMBARDE (*altered to* 'ſuffize' *from* 'ſuffire'); sustize PORTLAND

3.1.60-1 but th'opinion | Of common reason] LAMBARDE; but the | opinion of Common reason PORTLAND; reaſons advice HERRINGMAN

3.1.61 find it] PORTLAND, HERRINGMAN; *altered in* LAMBARDE *to* 'findet' *from* 'findes'

3.1.62 That you should] LAMBARDE; that you PORTLAND; For you to HERRINGMAN

3.1.63 Who...kingdom] LAMBARDE (who heares a vsurper, as he has yᵉ Kingdome); who heares a usurper, as he has the kingdome PORTLAND; Who's an Uſurper here, and as the Kingdom HERRINGMAN

3.1.65 The] PORTLAND, HERRINGMAN; They LAMBARDE

3.1.66 upward] LAMBARDE, PORTLAND (*altered from another word*); higher HERRINGMAN

3.1.67 a] LAMBARDE, PORTLAND; the HERRINGMAN

3.1.71 yet] *preceded in* PORTLAND *by deleted* 'did'

3.1.72 fortune] LAMBARDE, PORTLAND; fortunes HERRINGMAN

3.1.74 certainty] LAMBARDE, PORTLAND; certainties HERRINGMAN

3.1.74 Britain's] LAMBARDE, HERRINGMAN; a PORTLAND

3.1.77 quickly] LAMBARDE, PORTLAND; ſoon HERRINGMAN;

3.1.78 her] LAMBARDE, PORTLAND; the Lett HERRINGMAN

3.1.78 thy glory] LAMBARDE, PORTLAND; thee and thy Glory HERRINGMAN

3.1.79 is] LAMBARDE, PORTLAND; of HERRINGMAN

3.1.81 *Exit*] HERRINGMAN; *Exit Rox* LAMBARDE, PORTLAND

3.1.82 'em] LAMBARDE, PORTLAND; them HERRINGMAN

3.1.83-9 Maybe...bravely] LAMBARDE; maybe...woman | too...strange | euents...many | brothers...theire | births...sisters | pish...a | gallant...bravely PORTLAND; 3.1.84-7 *not in* HERRINGMAN

3.1.84 strange] *added in* LAMBARDE *with a caret above* 'events'

3.1.85 brothers] PORTLAND; *cropped in* LAMBARDE *to* 'brother'

3.1.86 through] *in* LAMBARDE *the first 'h' has been altered from* 'r'

3.1.87 Peace] LAMBARDE, HERRINGMAN; pish PORTLAND

3.1.87.1 *Enter Vortiger*] PORTLAND (*altered to* 'Enter Vort:' *from* 'Exit Vort:'), HERRINGMAN; *cropped in* LAMBARDE *to* 'Vor'

3.1.88 gallant's] LAMBARDE (gallants); gallant PORTLAND, HERRINGMAN

3.1.89 his] LAMBARDE, PORTLAND; ones HERRINGMAN

3.1.90 command ease] PORTLAND, HERRINGMAN; *cropped in* LAMBARDE *to* 'Comᵐa'

3.1.91 mine] LAMBARDE, PORTLAND; my HERRINGMAN

3.1.95 patience] PORTLAND, HERRINGMAN; patient LAMBARDE

3.1.97 do't] LAMBARDE, PORTLAND; do it HERRINGMAN

3.1.98-102 What's...secure] LAMBARDE, PORTLAND; *not in* HERRINGMAN, *and instead the second half of* 3.1.98 *appears as* 'tuſh, riddles, riddles'.

3.1.99 bounds] *in* LAMBARDE *the 'v' has been added*

3.1.100 ridiculous] PORTLAND; *cropped in* LAMBARDE *to* 'ridiculou'

3.1.104 nobler] LAMBARDE, HERRINGMAN; noble PORTLAND

3.1.106 Still change] LAMBARDE, PORTLAND; change HERRINGMAN

3.1.106 have't] LAMBARDE; have it PORTLAND, HERRINGMAN

3.1.110 on't] LAMBARDE, PORTLAND; of it HERRINGMAN

3.1.110 This] LAMBARDE, PORTLAND but this HERRINGMAN

3.1.110 no] LAMBARDE, PORTLAND; not the HERRINGMAN

3.1.111 you'll] LAMBARDE, PORTLAND; youl'd HERRINGMAN

3.1.111-12 Set...charity] LAMBARDE, PORTLAND; Set me right then, or I ſhall heauily curſe thee HERRINGMAN

3.1.115 slept] LAMBARDE, PORTLAND; then ſlept HERRINGMAN

3.1.117 make] LAMBARDE, PORTLAND; wake HERRINGMAN

3.1.118 so] LAMBARDE, PORTLAND; not in HERRINGMAN

3.1.118 rudely] LAMBARDE, PORTLAND; rudely done HERRINGMAN

3.1.119 you've] LAMBARDE, PORTLAND; you haue PORTLAND

3.1.119 violent] altered in LAMBARDE to 'violente' from 'violate'

3.1.121 none can] LAMBARDE, PORTLAND; nought elfe can HERRINGMAN

3.1.123 our] LAMBARDE, PORTLAND; your HERRINGMAN

3.1.125 whiles] LAMBARDE; while PORTLAND, HERRINGMAN

3.1.126 ignorance] LAMBARDE; Inorance PORTLAND; Innocence HERRINGMAN

3.1.129 that] LAMBARDE, PORTLAND; him HERRINGMAN

3.1.131 friendly league] LAMBARDE, PORTLAND; League HERRINGMAN

3.1.133 would] LAMBARDE, PORTLAND; will HERRINGMAN

3.1.134 act] LAMBARDE, PORTLAND; action HERRINGMAN

3.1.135 VORTIGER] LAMBARDE, PORTLAND; not in HERRINGMAN, and instead the rest of the speech appears as a continuation of Horsus's speech beginning at 3.1.133; some copies of HERRINGMAN have the speech-prefixes added in the owner's hand

3.1.135 to the] altered in PORTLAND to 'to yᵉ' from 'tog'

3.1.135 that's] LAMBARDE, PORTLAND; 'tis HERRINGMAN

3.1.136 further] LAMBARDE, PORTLAND; farther HERRINGMAN

3.1.136 with't] LAMBARDE, PORTLAND; with it HERRINGMAN

3.1.137 Fie] HERRINGMAN (Fye); fly LAMBARDE, PORTLAND

3.1.138 I] LAMBARDE, PORTLAND; I'le HERRINGMAN

3.1.138 thee] LAMBARDE (yᵉ); you PORTLAND, HERRINGMAN

3.1.143 words] LAMBARDE, HERRINGMAN; woundes PORTLAND

3.1.143 should] LAMBARDE, HERRINGMAN; ſhall PORTLAND

3.1.144 i'th'] LAMBARDE, PORTLAND; in the HERRINGMAN

3.1.147 on't] LAMBARDE, PORTLAND; on it HERRINGMAN

3.1.149 light] LAMBARDE, PORTLAND; life HERRINGMAN

3.1.151 sir] LAMBARDE, PORTLAND; not in HERRINGMAN

3.1.152 women] PORTLAND, HERRINGMAN; cropped in LAMBARDE to 'woe'

3.1.153 When 'tis at strongest] LAMBARDE (when tis at stronest); when they are at strongest (the 'est' in 'strongest' has been added above the line with a caret) PORTLAND; at ſtrongeſt HERRINGMAN

3.1.153 well] LAMBARDE; not in PORTLAND or HERRINGMAN

3.1.154 your grace] PORTLAND ('your' has been altered from 'yoʳ'); yᵒʳ grace LAMBARDE; Sir HERRINGMAN

3.1.157 are] LAMBARDE, PORTLAND; be HERRINGMAN

3.1.158 concerns] LAMBARDE, PORTLAND; concern HERRINGMAN

3.1.160-3 Where...purpose] LAMBARDE, PORTLAND; Where Ring-doves ſhould be caught, that's married wives, | Or chaſt Maids, what the appetite has a mind to HERRINGMAN

3.1.160 wives] PORTLAND, HERRINGMAN; cropped in LAMBARDE

3.1.162 therefore] LAMBARDE; theire forth PORTLAND; not in HERRINGMAN

3.1.164 where e'er she be] LAMBARDE, PORTLAND; not in HERRINGMAN

3.1.169 eyes] LAMBARDE, PORTLAND; eye-lids HERRINGMAN

3.1.173 ebb] PORTLAND, HERRINGMAN; ebbs LAMBARDE

3.1.174 coached] PORTLAND, HERRINGMAN; Coach LAMBARDE

3.1.176 spoiled] LAMBARDE, PORTLAND; robb'd HERRINGMAN

3.1.177 Wise] LAMBARDE, PORTLAND; There's the HERRINGMAN

3.1.181 be never] LAMBARDE, PORTLAND; ne're be HERRINGMAN

3.1.184 praised] LAMBARDE; practis'd PORTLAND; praiſe HERRINGMAN

3.1.184.1 Exeunt] LAMBARDE, PORTLAND; not in HERRINGMAN, and instead there are two separate 'Exit' directions after 3.1.183 and 3.1.184, making it clear that in HERRINGMAN Horsus gives his final line while alone on stage

3.2 LAMBARDE (Scena 2ᵃ); Sceᵃ 2ᵃ PORTLAND; ACT. 3. SCENA 2. HERRINGMAN

3.2.0.1 Enter Castiza...Ladies] HERRINGMAN; Enter Castiza A Booke: two Ladyes: LAMBARDE, PORTLAND

3.2.2 The less it grieves me] LAMBARDE, PORTLAND; It grieves me leſs HERRINGMAN

3.2.4 would] in PORTLAND the scribe has altered this word from 'will', adding the 'o' above the line with a caret

3.2.4 bestow't] LAMBARDE, PORTLAND; beſtow it HERRINGMAN

3.2.5 no] PORTLAND, HERRINGMAN; not in LAMBARDE

3.2.5 more] added in PORTLAND above the line with a caret

3.2.6 Than 'tis for] then 'tis for LAMBARDE, PORTLAND; then for HERRINGMAN

3.2.7 For] LAMBARDE, PORTLAND; without HERRINGMAN

3.2.7 so] LAMBARDE, PORTLAND; And so HERRINGMAN

3.2.10 see men] added in PORTLAND above the line with a caret

3.2.10 work] LAMBARDE, PORTLAND; wear HERRINGMAN

3.2.10 and] LAMBARDE, PORTLAND; or HERRINGMAN

3.2.12 to th'] LAMBARDE; to the PORTLAND, HERRINGMAN

3.2.13 as long] LAMBARDE, PORTLAND; ſo long HERRINGMAN

3.2.14 She's] LAMBARDE; she is PORTLAND, HERRINGMAN

3.2.14 will not know] LAMBARDE, PORTLAND; knows not what HERRINGMAN

3.2.14 he's] LAMBARDE, PORTLAND; he is HERRINGMAN

3.2.14.1 Exeunt Ladies] HERRINGMAN; Ex: Ladyes LAMBARDE; Exit Ladyes PORTLAND

3.2.15 amongst] LAMBARDE, PORTLAND; among HERRINGMAN

3.2.15 life's] THIS EDITION; lives LAMBARDE, PORTLAND, HERRINGMAN

3.2.16 speak noblest] LAMBARDE, PORTLAND; did ſpeak nobleſt of HERRINGMAN

3.2.16 yet't] LAMBARDE, PORTLAND; yet it HERRINGMAN

3.2.16 just heaven] LAMBARDE, PORTLAND; the King HERRINGMAN

3.2.18 this] LAMBARDE, PORTLAND; that HERRINGMAN

3.2.20 That's] PORTLAND, HERRINGMAN; that LAMBARDE

3.2.22 on't] LAMBARDE, PORTLAND; on it HERRINGMAN

3.2.22.1 Enter...disguised] HERRINGMAN (at 3.2.18-20); Enter Vort: & Hersus PORTLAND; cropped in LAMBARDE to 'E | Vort | Hers'

3.2.23 then] LAMBARDE, PORTLAND; on HERRINGMAN

3.2.25 HERSUS...I'll...it] LAMBARDE, PORTLAND; not in HERRINGMAN

3.2.26 VORTIGER] LAMBARDE, PORTLAND; Hor. HERRINGMAN

3.2.26 O help] LAMBARDE, PORTLAND; not in HERRINGMAN

3.2.29 rescue] LAMBARDE, PORTLAND; reſcue, reſcue HERRINGMAN

3.2.29.1 [Hersus and Castiza]...again] LAMBARDE (cropped to 'Ext & enter aga'), PORTLAND (Ext & enter again); not in HERRINGMAN

3.2.31 Extend] HERRINGMAN; entend LAMBARDE, PORTLAND

3.2.32 pity] PORTLAND, HERRINGMAN; cropped in LAMBARDE

3.2.43 But if't] LAMBARDE, PORTLAND; If it HERRINGMAN

3.2.44 no immodest] LAMBARDE, HERRINGMAN; more modest PORTLAND

3.2.46 cruelly] LAMBARDE, PORTLAND; Cruelty HERRINGMAN

3.2.48 The] LAMBARDE, PORTLAND; 'Tis the HERRINGMAN

3.2.52 Thus, thus] LAMBARDE, PORTLAND; Thus HERRINGMAN

3.2.54 you] LAMBARDE, PORTLAND; thee HERRINGMAN

3.2.57 spark] preceded in LAMBARDE by deleted 'soule'

3.2.59–62 It...lord] LAMBARDE, PORTLAND; *not in* HERRINGMAN (*the speech continues from* 3.2.59 *with* 'Pifh, let her go')

3.2.60 like] *altered in* PORTLAND *from* 'fitt'

3.2.66 cruelty] LAMBARDE, PORTLAND; cruelties HERRINGMAN

3.2.66 ways] PORTLAND, HERRINGMAN; *cropped in* LAMBARDE *to* 'way'

3.2.67 invention] LAMBARDE, HERRINGMAN; inventions PORTLAND

3.2.69 Of] LAMBARDE, PORTLAND; By HERRINGMAN

3.2.74 cannot] PORTLAND, HERRINGMAN; *cropped in* LAMBARDE *to* 'Canno'

3.2.75 resolved] LAMBARDE, HERRINGMAN; resolue PORTLAND

3.2.76 never] LAMBARDE, PORTLAND; ever HERRINGMAN

3.2.81 secrecy] *altered in* PORTLAND *to* 'secresye' *from* 'secresee'

3.2.82–3 Not...less | King's...torture] LAMBARDE, PORTLAND; Not death fhall pluck it from me, much lefs the King's | Authority or torture HERRINGMAN

3.2.84 whate'er] *altered in* PORTLAND *to* 'what ere' *from* 'what are'

3.2.87 mine] LAMBARDE, PORTLAND; my HERRINGMAN

3.2.88 'em out quite] LAMBARDE, PORTLAND; them quite out HERRINGMAN

3.2.88 light] LAMBARDE, PORTLAND; lights HERRINGMAN

3.2.88 body] PORTLAND, HERRINGMAN; *cropped in* LAMBARDE

3.2.89 but] LAMBARDE, PORTLAND; hut HERRINGMAN

3.2.92 would] LAMBARDE, PORTLAND; will HERRINGMAN

3.2.95 Will] LAMBARDE, PORTLAND; what, will HERRINGMAN

3.2.97 thee] LAMBARDE, PORTLAND; you HERRINGMAN

3.2.98 CASTIZA] LAMBARDE, HERRINGMAN; *not in* PORTLAND, *although the speech has been ruled off*

3.2.98 reverend] LAMBARDE, PORTLAND; reverenc'd HERRINGMAN

3.2.100 HERSUS] LAMBARDE, HERRINGMAN; *not in* PORTLAND, *although the speech has been ruled off*

3.2.100.1 *Exeunt...Castiza*] LAMBARDE, PORTLAND; *Vort. snatches her away* HERRINGMAN

3.2.100 Here's] LAMBARDE, PORTLAND; Ah, ha, here's HERRINGMAN

3.2.104 by't] LAMBARDE, PORTLAND; by it HERRINGMAN

3.2.108 it comes] LAMBARDE, PORTLAND; comes it HERRINGMAN

3.2.109.1 *Exit*] LAMBARDE, PORTLAND; *Exeunt* HERRINGMAN

3.3 *Scena* 3^a LAMBARDE, PORTLAND; ACT. 3. SCENA 3. HERRINGMAN

3.3.0.1 *Enter Hengist*] As at 2.4.2, 4.1.0.1 *and* 5.1.0.3–4, *in* LAMBARDE *the scribe has drawn a symbol (either an orb with a cross above it or an astrological symbol, upside down, for a woman) in the left margin.*

3.3.2 footing] LAMBARDE, PORTLAND; foot HERRINGMAN

3.3.7 the observance] LAMBARDE, PORTLAND; th'obfervance HERRINGMAN

3.3.7 subject] *in* LAMBARDE *the* 'e' *has been added above the line with a caret*

3.3.9 invite] *altered in* LAMBARDE *from* 'limite' *and in* PORTLAND *from* 'limit'

3.3.10 'em] LAMBARDE, PORTLAND; them HERRINGMAN

3.3.10.1 *A noise*] LAMBARDE, PORTLAND (*at* 3.3.4); *not in* HERRINGMAN; LAMBARDE *also has* 'Barber & Taylor wthn' *at* 3.3.7; *these characters do not enter until* 3.3.44.1 *and* 3.3.65.1

3.3.14 ne'er] LAMBARDE, PORTLAND; never HERRINGMAN

3.3.15.1 *Enter Gentleman*] LAMBARDE (*cropped to* 'Enter Gentl'), PORTLAND (Enter Gent); *Enter a Gentleman* HERRINGMAN

3.3.16 Now, what's] LAMBARDE, PORTLAND; Now, Sir HERRINGMAN

3.3.16 clamours, sir] LAMBARDE (Clamo^{rs} sir); Clamor Sir PORTLAND; clamours HERRINGMAN

3.3.21 HENGIST] LAMBARDE, HERRINGMAN; *not in* PORTLAND, *although the speech has been ruled off*

3.3.22 never] LAMBARDE, PORTLAND; ne're HERRINGMAN

3.3.22 in] *preceded in* PORTLAND *by deleted* 'em'

3.3.23 comes] LAMBARDE, PORTLAND; come HERRINGMAN

3.3.24 'Twere] LAMBARDE, PORTLAND; 'Tis HERRINGMAN

3.3.25 slight off] HERRINGMAN; slight of LAMBARDE; slight PORTLAND

3.3.26 foundation] LAMBARDE, PORTLAND; foundations HERRINGMAN

3.3.27 them] LAMBARDE, HERRINGMAN; 'em PORTLAND

3.3.28 first] *altered in* PORTLAND *from* 'as'

3.3.28 ascends up] LAMBARDE, PORTLAND; afcends HERRINGMAN

3.3.29 at] LAMBARDE, PORTLAND; at the HERRINGMAN

3.3.29 comes] *altered in* LAMBARDE *from* 'loues'

3.3.29.1 *Enter Gentleman*] PORTLAND (*at* 3.3.26), HERRINGMAN; *cropped in* LAMBARDE *to* 'Enter' (*at* 3.3.28)

3.3.31–2 HENGIST How? | GENTLEMAN] LAMBARDE, PORTLAND; *not in* HERRINGMAN

3.3.32 for 'em than ever 'twas] LAMBARDE, PORTLAND; then it was before HERRINGMAN

3.3.32 before] PORTLAND, HERRINGMAN; *cropped in* LAMBARDE *to* 'befor'

3.3.33 stood] LAMBARDE, PORTLAND; was HERRINGMAN

3.3.34 they're] LAMBARDE; they are PORTLAND; th'are all HERRINGMAN

3.3.35 says, sir] PORTLAND; says HERRINGMAN; *cropped in* LAMBARDE *to* 'sayes'

3.3.36 he'll] LAMBARDE, PORTLAND; will HERRINGMAN

3.3.37 come all at first] LAMBARDE; come both at first PORTLAND; all come firft HERRINGMAN

3.3.40 town] HERRINGMAN; *not in* LAMBARDE *or* PORTLAND

3.3.41 one] LAMBARDE, PORTLAND; he HERRINGMAN

3.3.42 toil] LAMBARDE, PORTLAND; quoyl HERRINGMAN

3.3.42 I'm] LAMBARDE, PORTLAND; I am HERRINGMAN

3.3.42 they're grown so] LAMBARDE; they are growne so PORTLAND; they are so HERRINGMAN

3.3.44 hope on't] LAMBARDE; hopes ont PORTLAND; hope HERRINGMAN

3.3.49 vouchsafe] LAMBARDE, PORTLAND; think fit HERRINGMAN

3.3.49 it] LAMBARDE, PORTLAND; me HERRINGMAN

3.3.50 this you have] LAMBARDE, PORTLAND; you have this HERRINGMAN

3.3.51 business now] LAMBARDE, PORTLAND; bufinefs HERRINGMAN

3.3.52 lordship] Before this word in PORTLAND, the scribe has written 'Hie' and altered it to 'Him' and then tried to erase it.

3.3.52 high] LAMBARDE, PORTLAND; very high HERRINGMAN

3.3.53 all about] LAMBARDE; about the PORTLAND ('about' *altered from another word*), HERRINGMAN

3.3.54 That's work] HERRINGMAN; That works PORTLAND; that worke LAMBARDE

3.3.55–6 kind of body, a body] LAMBARDE, PORTLAND; Body, a kind of Body HERRINGMAN

3.3.57 Barber's] LAMBARDE; barbour is PORTLAND; Barber is HERRINGMAN

3.3.57 o'th] THIS EDITION; at LAMBARDE, PORTLAND; at the HERRINGMAN

3.3.61 had] *added in* PORTLAND *above the line with a caret*

3.3.62 with't] LAMBARDE; with it PORTLAND, HERRINGMAN

3.3.62–3 I was] *altered in* PORTLAND *from* 'I'll'

3.3.63 o'th] LAMBARDE, PORTLAND; of the HERRINGMAN

3.3.63 here] LAMBARDE, PORTLAND; *not in* HERRINGMAN

3.3.64   go] LAMBARDE, PORTLAND; *not in* HERRINGMAN

3.3.65.1   *Enter Tailor*] LAMBARDE, PORTLAND (*Enter Tay*); *not in* HERRINGMAN

3.3.67   That...business] LAMBARDE, PORTLAND; *not in* HERRING- MAN

3.3.68   rip] LAMBARDE, PORTLAND; rip up HERRINGMAN

3.3.69   on] LAMBARDE, PORTLAND; of HERRINGMAN

3.3.71   factions] LAMBARDE; faſhions PORTLAND, HERRINGMAN

3.3.73   go] LAMBARDE, PORTLAND; we go HERRINGMAN

3.3.74   the] LAMBARDE, HERRINGMAN; this PORTLAND

3.3.75   wove] LAMBARDE, HERRINGMAN; Link't PORTLAND

3.3.77   makes] LAMBARDE, PORTLAND; make HERRINGMAN

3.3.79   Call...yet] LAMBARDE, PORTLAND; I am ne're the wiſer yet, call in the reſt HERRINGMAN

3.3.80–1   I...to] LAMBARDE, PORTLAND; *not in* HERRINGMAN

3.3.81.1   *Enter...Brazier*] LAMBARDE (*Enter Glouer But* | *Brazier*, at 3.3.78); *not in* PORTLAND *or* HERRINGMAN

3.3.82   of] LAMBARDE, PORTLAND; on HERRINGMAN

3.3.84   with] LAMBARDE, PORTLAND; *not in* HERRINGMAN

3.3.85   all that] LAMBARDE, PORTLAND; the HERRINGMAN

3.3.87   pleaſure] LAMBARDE, PORTLAND; preſence HERRINGMAN

3.3.88   We have] PORTLAND, HERRINGMAN; *cropped in* LAMBARDE

3.3.88   town] *in* LAMBARDE *the 'T' has been altered from 'Tw'*

3.3.89   juſtice] PORTLAND, HERRINGMAN; *cropped in* LAMBARDE *to* 'Juſt'

3.3.90   handed] LAMBARDE; handled PORTLAND, HERRINGMAN

3.3.90   take] *altered in* PORTLAND *from* 'like'

3.3.91   hold] LAMBARDE, PORTLAND; hold | On it HERRINGMAN

3.3.93   ſir] LAMBARDE, PORTLAND; *not in* HERRINGMAN

3.3.95   the] LAMBARDE, PORTLAND; our HERRINGMAN

3.3.96   chooſe and part] LAMBARDE; Chooſe and end PORTLAND; part and end HERRINGMAN

3.3.96   the] LAMBARDE, PORTLAND (*altered from* 'thi'), HERRING- MAN

3.3.97   they] PORTLAND, HERRINGMAN; *cropped in* LAMBARDE *to* 'the'

3.3.100   my] LAMBARDE, HERRINGMAN; his PORTLAND

3.3.101   ſir] LAMBARDE, PORTLAND; *not in* HERRINGMAN

3.3.101   too] *altered in* PORTLAND *from* 'Sir'

3.3.103   the] LAMBARDE, PORTLAND; a HERRINGMAN

3.3.105   by't] LAMBARDE, PORTLAND; by it HERRINGMAN

3.3.105   after] LAMBARDE, PORTLAND; *not in* HERRINGMAN

3.3.106   her foreman] LAMBARDE, HERRINGMAN; a foreman PORT- LAND

3.3.110   Does] LAMBARDE, PORTLAND; Do HERRINGMAN

3.3.113   what's...contends] LAMBARDE; whats the other con- tends PORTLAND; what are thoſe that do contend HERRINGMAN

3.3.114   noble] LAMBARDE, HERRINGMAN; *not in* PORTLAND

3.3.115   will] LAMBARDE, PORTLAND; *not in* HERRINGMAN

3.3.115   compare] *in* LAMBARDE *the scribe has altered the 'p' in this word from 't'*

3.3.116   match] *altered in* LAMBARDE *from* 'matcht'

3.3.118   houſe] LAMBARDE, PORTLAND; Hall PORTLAND

3.3.118.1–2   *Enter...[Collier and others]*] In LAMBARDE '*Enter Symon* | *& Oliuer*' appears at 114 and '*fellmonger Brazier* | *Buttonmunger*' at 116–17; in PORTLAND '*Enter Symon* | *& Oliuer*' and '*fellmongers Braziers* | *Buttonmongers*' appear at the same place as in LAMBARDE; HERRINGMAN lacks these entrance directions; it is clear from LAMBARDE and PORTLAND that a small group of townspeople enter at 3.3.81.1 (see note above) and others enter following Oliver, who rushes in ahead of Simon at this line.

3.3.119   Before] LAMBARDE, PORTLAND; How, before HERRINGMAN

3.3.119   wattle-faced] HERRINGMAN (wattle-fac'd); watle faide LAMBARDE, PORTLAND

3.3.122   the] LAMBARDE, HERRINGMAN; that PORTLAND

3.3.123   brook] *in* LAMBARDE *the 'r' has been altered from 'a'*

3.3.125   flax-wench] PORTLAND, HERRINGMAN; *in* LAMBARDE *the scribe has first written* 'flax whench', *deleted* 'whench', *and written* 'wench'

3.3.126   moſt need] LAMBARDE, PORTLAND; need HERRINGMAN

3.3.130   whos'] HERRINGMAN; whoſe LAMBARDE, PORTLAND

3.3.131   ſpirits] LAMBARDE, PORTLAND; ſpirit HERRINGMAN

3.3.132   ſee his] PORTLAND, HERRINGMAN; *cropped in* LAMBARDE

3.3.133   Maſter] LAMBARDE (M^r), HERRINGMAN; my PORTLAND

3.3.134   fine] LAMBARDE, PORTLAND; fair HERRINGMAN

3.3.134   he has] LAMBARDE, PORTLAND; hath he HERRINGMAN

3.3.135   There] PORTLAND; *cropped in* LAMBARDE; then HERRING- MAN

3.3.136   I'm] LAMBARDE, PORTLAND; I am HERRINGMAN

3.3.136   out of love] PORTLAND, HERRINGMAN; *cropped in* LAM- BARDE *to* 'ou'

3.3.136   with't] LAMBARDE, PORTLAND; with it HERRINGMAN

3.3.137   thee and] LAMBARDE, PORTLAND; *not in* HERRINGMAN

3.3.137   I] LAMBARDE, PORTLAND; and HERRINGMAN

3.3.138   man that thrives] PORTLAND, HERRINGMAN; *cropped in* LAMBARDE *to* 'm'

3.3.139   be] *altered in* PORTLAND *from* 'beſt'

3.3.140   to thrive] PORTLAND, HERRINGMAN; *cropped in* LAMBARDE

3.3.140   faith] LAMBARDE, PORTLAND; faith, my Lord HERRINGMAN

3.3.141   a green] PORTLAND, HERRINGMAN; *cropped in* LAMBARDE

3.3.142   Th'aſt] LAMBARDE, HERRINGMAN; thou haſt PORTLAND

3.3.145   ſo] *altered in* PORTLAND *to* 'ſoe' *from* 'are'

3.3.145   hoarſe] *in* LAMBARDE *the 'a' has been altered from 'r'*

3.3.146   drinking] PORTLAND, HERRINGMAN; *cropped in* LAMBARDE

3.3.146   ne'er] LAMBARDE, PORTLAND; *not in* HERRINGMAN

3.3.146   amongſt 'em] LAMBARDE, PORTLAND; among them HER- RINGMAN

3.3.147   that...company] LAMBARDE, PORTLAND; *not in* HERRING- MAN

3.3.147   in this] PORTLAND; *cropped in* LAMBARDE *to* 'i'

3.3.148   both to put all to] LAMBARDE, PORTLAND; to put it to all HERRINGMAN

3.3.150   cenſure] LAMBARDE, PORTLAND; cenſures HERRINGMAN

3.3.152   laſt] LAMBARDE, PORTLAND; laſt, my Lord HERRINGMAN

3.3.152   he] LAMBARDE, PORTLAND; they HERRINGMAN

3.3.153   caſt] PORTLAND, HERRINGMAN; *cropped in* LAMBARDE

3.3.153   town-born] LAMBARDE, HERRINGMAN; Townes borne PORTLAND

3.3.153   'tis] LAMBARDE, PORTLAND; It is HERRINGMAN

3.3.154   forty] LAMBARDE, PORTLAND; ſome forty HERRINGMAN

3.3.155   I'll] LAMBARDE, PORTLAND; I HERRINGMAN

3.3.155.1   *Exit Hengist*] LAMBARDE, PORTLAND; *Exit* HERRINGMAN

3.3.156   view us both well e'er] LAMBARDE, PORTLAND; before HERRINGMAN

3.3.157   let] PORTLAND, HERRINGMAN; *cropped in* LAMBARDE

3.3.158   the] PORTLAND, HERRINGMAN; *cropped in* LAMBARDE *to* 'th'

3.3.158   give] LAMBARDE, PORTLAND; do HERRINGMAN

3.3.159   callimoother] LAMBARDE, PORTLAND; Callymoocher HER- RINGMAN

3.3.160   known to] PORTLAND, HERRINGMAN; *cropped in* LAMBARDE *to* 'know'

3.3.160   thee] LAMBARDE, PORTLAND; the Pariſh HERRINGMAN

3.3.161   muſhrump] LAMBARDE, PORTLAND; muſhroom HERRING- MAN

3.3.161   that] PORTLAND, HERRINGMAN; *cropped in* LAMBARDE

3.3.161 shot] LAMBARDE, PORTLAND; ſhot'ſt HERRINGMAN

3.3.161 one] LAMBARDE, PORTLAND; a HERRINGMAN

3.3.161 with] LAMBARDE, PORTLAND; By HERRINGMAN

3.3.164 would] LAMBARDE, PORTLAND; will HERRINGMAN

3.3.165 rise] *preceded in* LAMBARDE *by deleted* 'lye'

3.3.166 me] *preceded in* LAMBARDE *by deleted* 'thee'

3.3.167-8 SIMON The...asleep] LAMBARDE, PORTLAND; *not in* HERRINGMAN

3.3.169 cease of] LAMBARDE, PORTLAND; leave HERRINGMAN

3.3.171 Barber] *altered in* LAMBARDE *to* 'Barbor' *from* 'Barbur'

3.3.174 Buttonmonger] LAMBARDE, PORTLAND; Button-maker HERRINGMAN

3.3.175 eye] LAMBARDE, HERRINGMAN; *not in* PORTLAND

3.3.176 a-brewing] LAMBARDE, PORTLAND; in brewing HERRINGMAN

3.3.176 this] LAMBARDE, PORTLAND; the HERRINGMAN

3.3.178 A...Simon!] LAMBARDE, PORTLAND; A *Symon,* a *Symon.* HERRINGMAN

3.3.179 My] LAMBARDE, PORTLAND; *not in* HERRINGMAN

3.3.183 all] LAMBARDE, HERRINGMAN; in PORTLAND

3.3.185 thee] LAMBARDE, HERRINGMAN; you PORTLAND

3.3.185 with thee] LAMBARDE; with you PORTLAND; by thee HERRINGMAN

3.3.185 an] LAMBARDE, PORTLAND ('and' *in both texts*); If HERRINGMAN

3.3.187 'em] LAMBARDE, PORTLAND; them HERRINGMAN

3.3.188 scabs] LAMBARDE, PORTLAND; the ſcab HERRINGMAN

3.3.188 lo] PORTLAND; no LAMBARDE; now HERRINGMAN

3.3.190 so fit] LAMBARDE ('fitt' *has been altered from* 'fitting'), PORTLAND; not fit HERRINGMAN

3.3.190 what man] LAMBARDE, PORTLAND; what a man HERRINGMAN

3.3.191 that] LAMBARDE, PORTLAND; *not in* HERRINGMAN

3.3.192 unlearned man] *altered in* PORTLAND *from two other words*

3.3.194 could] LAMBARDE, PORTLAND; can HERRINGMAN

3.3.195 an excellent] PORTLAND, HERRINGMAN; *cropped in* LAMBARDE

3.3.196 have] PORTLAND, HERRINGMAN; *cropped in* LAMBARDE

3.3.197 you] LAMBARDE, PORTLAND; There you HERRINGMAN

3.3.198 all cough] PORTLAND, HERRINGMAN; *cropped in* LAMBARDE *to* 'a'

3.3.198 now] LAMBARDE, PORTLAND; *not in* HERRINGMAN

3.3.199 ALL Hem,...cough] LAMBARDE, PORTLAND ('hum, hum, hum, Cough' *in both texts*); *in* HERRINGMAN *this line of dialogue appears as the stage direction* 'Here they all cough and hem' (*see note on* 3.3.210)

3.3.200 SIMON] LAMBARDE, PORTLAND; *not in* HERRINGMAN

3.3.201 weaver, who] PORTLAND, HERRINGMAN; *cropped in* LAMBARDE *to* 'weau'

3.3.201 threateneth] LAMBARDE, PORTLAND; threatens HERRINGMAN

3.3.202 amongst] LAMBARDE, PORTLAND; among HERRINGMAN

3.3.202 which...number] LAMBARDE, PORTLAND; *not in* HERRINGMAN

3.3.202 which as] PORTLAND, HERRINGMAN; *cropped in* LAMBARDE

3.3.202 seven in number] LAMBARDE; in number seven PORTLAND

3.3.203 let] PORTLAND, HERRINGMAN; *in* LAMBARDE *the* 't' *has been altered from* 'ſ'

3.3.203 'em] LAMBARDE, PORTLAND; them HERRINGMAN

3.3.203 town's] LAMBARDE, PORTLAND; town is HERRINGMAN

3.3.203 big] PORTLAND, HERRINGMAN; *cropped in* LAMBARDE *to* 'bi'

3.3.203 'em] LAMBARDE, PORTLAND; them HERRINGMAN

3.3.204 much] LAMBARDE, PORTLAND; so much HERRINGMAN

3.3.204 a] LAMBARDE; your PORTLAND; you know a HERRINGMAN

3.3.204 Besides] PORTLAND; *cropped in* LAMBARDE *to* 'Beside'; beſides you know HERRINGMAN

3.3.204 sin] LAMBARDE, HERRINGMAN; sins PORTLAND

3.3.205 think] PORTLAND, HERRINGMAN; *cropped in* LAMBARDE

3.3.206 woven, with] PORTLAND; *cropped in* LAMBARDE *to* 'nouen'; beſt woven, with HERRINGMAN

3.3.207 I'll] LAMBARDE, PORTLAND; I will HERRINGMAN

3.3.207 the] LAMBARDE, PORTLAND; through the HERRINGMAN

3.3.207 looms] LAMBARDE, PORTLAND; Loom HERRINGMAN

3.3.207 of their] PORTLAND, HERRINGMAN; *cropped in* LAMBARDE

3.3.208 let] LAMBARDE, PORTLAND; make HERRINGMAN

3.3.208-9 shuttle. Here] PORTLAND, HERRINGMAN; *cropped in* LAMBARDE *to* 'shut'

3.3.209 hem] LAMBARDE, PORTLAND; cough and hem HERRINGMAN

3.3.210 ALL Cough and hem] LAMBARDE, PORTLAND; *They cough and hem again (as stage direction)* HERRINGMAN

3.3.211 SIMON] LAMBARDE, PORTLAND; *not in* HERRINGMAN

3.3.211 you] LAMBARDE, PORTLAND; you all HERRINGMAN

3.3.212 Now for seven] PORTLAND; *cropped in* LAMBARDE *to* 'n | 7'; now for the HERRINGMAN

3.3.212-25 first...by't] LAMBARDE, PORTLAND; Pride, Sloth, Envy, Wrath

3.3.213 uppermost] PORTLAND; *cropped in* LAMBARDE *to* 'upper'

3.3.213 will be] *altered in* LAMBARDE *to* 'wilbe' *from* 'wibbe'

3.3.214 that is] PORTLAND; *cropped in* LAMBARDE *to* 'th'

3.3.214 to] LAMBARDE; for PORTLAND

3.3.215 and] PORTLAND; cropped in LAMBARDE

3.3.216 know] PORTLAND; *cropped in* LAMBARDE *to* 'kn'

3.3.217 requires] PORTLAND; *cropped in* LAMBARDE *to* 'req'

3.3.218 that which] PORTLAND *cropped in* LAMBARDE *to* 'tha'

3.3.219 eats raw] PORTLAND; *cropped in* LAMBARDE *to* 'eat'

3.3.220 pines] LAMBARDE; pins PORTLAND

3.3.220 makes] PORTLAND; *cropped in* LAMBARDE

3.3.221 punish] PORTLAND; *cropped in* LAMBARDE

3.3.222 Wrath] PORTLAND; *cropped in* LAMBARDE

3.3.223 less we] LAMBARDE; lessen PORTLAND

3.3.224 is that] PORTLAND; *cropped in* LAMBARDE

3.3.224-5 many a] PORTLAND; *cropped in* LAMBARDE *to* 'man'

3.3.225 Now] LAMBARDE, PORTLAND; as HERRINGMAN

3.3.225 Covetousness and Gluttony] LAMBARDE, PORTLAND; Gluttony and Covetouſneſs HERRINGMAN

3.3.226 tell] PORTLAND, HERRINGMAN; *cropped in* LAMBARDE

3.3.226 mine] LAMBARDE, PORTLAND; my HERRINGMAN

3.3.227 have] PORTLAND, HERRINGMAN; *cropped in* LAMBARDE *to* 'hau'

3.3.227 I'll] LAMBARDE, PORTLAND; I will HERRINGMAN

3.3.227 'em] LAMBARDE, PORTLAND; them HERRINGMAN

3.3.227 soundly] PORTLAND, HERRINGMAN; *cropped in* LAMBARDE

3.3.228 Covetousness and Gluttony] LAMBARDE, PORTLAND; Gluttony and Covetousness HERRINGMAN

3.3.229 one] LAMBARDE, PORTLAND ('on' *in both texts*); the one HERRINGMAN

3.3.229 i'th'] LAMBARDE, PORTLAND; in the HERRINGMAN

3.3.229 th'other] LAMBARDE, PORTLAND; the other HERRINGMAN

3.3.229 i'th'] LAMBARDE, PORTLAND; in the HERRINGMAN

3.3.230 sirs] PORTLAND, HERRINGMAN; sir LAMBARDE

3.3.230-1 I mean to] LAMBARDE, PORTLAND; I'le HERRINGMAN

3.3.231 nay] LAMBARDE, PORTLAND; my ſelf HERRINGMAN

3.3.231 I will] LAMBARDE, PORTLAND; I'le HERRINGMAN

3.3.232 one] LAMBARDE, PORTLAND; a HERRINGMAN

3.3.232 in all] LAMBARDE, PORTLAND; in the HERRINGMAN

3.3.233 Some] LAMBARDE, HERRINGMAN; sin PORTLAND

3.3.233 may go] LAMBARDE, PORTLAND; muſt HERRINGMAN

3.3.234 i'th'] LAMBARDE, PORTLAND; in the HERRINGMAN

3.3.236 villainies] LAMBARDE, PORTLAND; villany HERRINGMAN

3.3.236 mine] LAMBARDE, PORTLAND; my HERRINGMAN

3.3.239 in] LAMBARDE, PORTLAND; at HERRINGMAN

3.3.239 then] LAMBARDE, PORTLAND; *not in* HERRINGMAN

3.3.240 sink-hole] LAMBARDE, PORTLAND; ſuck-hole HERRINGMAN

3.3.240 out] LAMBARDE, PORTLAND; down HERRINGMAN

3.3.241 bullock] LAMBARDE, PORTLAND; Butcher HERRINGMAN

3.3.243 Here's] LAMBARDE, PORTLAND; This is HERRINGMAN

3.3.244 You may] LAMBARDE, PORTLAND; To HERRINGMAN

3.3.245 a little] LAMBARDE, PORTLAND; *not in* HERRINGMAN

3.3.246 mine] LAMBARDE, PORTLAND; my HERRINGMAN

3.3.249 your lordship] LAMBARDE, PORTLAND; you, Sir HERRING-MAN

3.3.252 my] LAMBARDE, HERRINGMAN; our PORTLAND

3.3.252.1 *Exeunt [all but Hengist and Roxena]]* LAMBARDE, PORTLAND (*'Exeunt' in both texts*); *Exit cum fuis.* HERRINGMAN

3.3.253 Continues] LAMBARDE, PORTLAND; Continue HERRING-MAN

3.3.253 fervour] LAMBARDE; favour PORTLAND, HERRINGMAN

3.3.255 he] PORTLAND, HERRINGMAN; *not in* LAMBARDE

3.3.256 To...it] HERRINGMAN; *not in* LAMBARDE *or* PORTLAND, *probably due to scribal error*

3.3.256 Canst speak low] PORTLAND; Can speak low LAMBARDE; Speak lower HERRINGMAN

3.3.260 first] LAMBARDE, PORTLAND; just HERRINGMAN

3.3.261 me] PORTLAND, HERRINGMAN; *cropped in* LAMBARDE *to* 'm'

3.3.263 half] LAMBARDE, PORTLAND; *not in* HERRINGMAN

3.3.266-71 She...again] LAMBARDE, PORTLAND; *not in* HERRING-MAN

3.3.266 ne'er] LAMBARDE; neuer PORTLAND

3.3.273 O] LAMBARDE, PORTLAND; *not in* HERRINGMAN

3.3.273 sight] LAMBARDE, PORTLAND; firſt fight HERRINGMAN

3.3.281 remembered] PORTLAND, HERRINGMAN; *cropped in* LAM-BARDE *to* 'remem'

3.3.283 low now] LAMBARDE, PORTLAND; lower HERRINGMAN

3.3.285 invitation] PORTLAND; *altered in* LAMBARDE *to* 'invetation' *from* 'invenation'; Inventions HERRINGMAN

3.3.290 Go] LAMBARDE, PORTLAND; Go now HERRINGMAN

3.3.294 taken up] LAMBARDE, PORTLAND; ta'ne HERRINGMAN

3.3.295 has] HERRINGMAN; hus LAMBARDE, PORTLAND

3.3.298 An...so] LAMBARDE, PORTLAND (and...so); To yield ſo much HERRINGMAN

3.3.299 there] PORTLAND; yoʳ LAMBARDE; ſome HERRINGMAN

3.3.303 pray] LAMBARDE, PORTLAND; prithee HERRINGMAN

3.3.303 wake] HERRINGMAN; work LAMBARDE, PORTLAND

3.3.304-5 HENGIST Your...here] LAMBARDE, PORTLAND; *in* HER-RINGMAN *the order of these two lines is reversed so that Vor-gtiger's line appears first then Hengist's, and 3.3.306 has a speech-prefix for Vortiger.*

3.3.306 you that] HERRINGMAN; that yoᵘ that LAMBARDE, PORT-LAND

3.3.308 raised] LAMBARDE, PORTLAND; made HERRINGMAN

3.3.308 make] LAMBARDE, PORTLAND; do HERRINGMAN

3.3.308 favour] LAMBARDE, PORTLAND; favours HERRINGMAN

3.3.309 Which] HERRINGMAN; wᵗʰ LAMBARDE; with PORTLAND

3.3.309 they] HERRINGMAN; yᵉ LAMBARDE; the PORTLAND

3.3.309 now, my] PORTLAND, HERRINGMAN; cropped in LAM-BARDE

3.3.311 such] LAMBARDE, PORTLAND; ſo HERRINGMAN

3.3.312 never] LAMBARDE, PORTLAND; nere HERRINGMAN

3.3.313 for your] LAMBARDE; for you PORTLAND; that your HERRINGMAN

3.3.313 building's name shall] LAMBARDE, PORTLAND; Building may HERRINGMAN

3.3.316 highness] LAMBARDE, PORTLAND; Grace HERRINGMAN

3.3.317 her] LAMBARDE, PORTLAND; its HERRINGMAN

3.3.319 sir] LAMBARDE, PORTLAND; *not in* HERRINGMAN

3.3.320 thy] LAMBARDE, PORTLAND; your HERRINGMAN

3.3.321 forward] LAMBARDE, PORTLAND; forwards HERRINGMAN

3.3.321 love honours] LAMBARDE; loues honours PORTLAND; Honour loves HERRINGMAN

3.3.321.1 *Music. Exeunt]* LAMBARDE, PORTLAND (*musique Exeunt Omnes.*); *Exit* HERRINGMAN

4.1.0.1 *Incipit Actus Quartus]* LAMBARDE (*Actus Quartus Scena Prima*); *Actus Quartus Scᵃ Priᵃ* PORTLAND; ACT 4. SCENA 1. HERRINGMAN (*preceded by catchword Áctus*)

4.1.0.1 *Incipit...Quartus]* In LAMBARDE, as at 2.4.2, 3.0.0.1, and 5.1.0.3-4, the scribe has drawn a properties or cross--referencing symbol in the left margin.

4.1.0.2-5 *Enter...other]* LAMBARDE, PORTLAND; *Enter Symon and all his Brethren, a Mace and Sword before him, meeting* Vortiger, Caſtiza, Hengiſt, Roxena, Horfus, *two Ladies.* HERRINGMAN

4.1.1-14 Lo, I...unto thee.] As noted by BALD (pp. xv, xxxvii), this speech was printed in variant form in *Wit Restor'd* (London, 1658; Wing M1719), pp. 162-3, under the title 'A *Prologue to the Mayor of Quinborough*.':

> Loe I the Maior of *Quinborough Town* by name,
> With all my brethren saving one that's lame;
> Are come as fast as fyery mil-horse gallops,
> To meet thy grace, thy Queene, & her fair Trollops,
> For reason of our comming do no look,
> It must be don, I finde it i'th Town-book:
> And yet not I myself, I scorne to read,
> I keep a Clarck to do these jobbs at need.
> And now respect a rare conceipt before Thong castle see thee,
> Reach me the thing, to give the King, that other too, I prethee,
> Now here they be, for Queene and hee, the guift's all steele, and leather,
> But the conceit of mickle weight, and here they're com together,
> To shew two loves must joyne in one, our Towne presents to thee,
> This gilded scabberd to the Queene, this dagger unto Thee.

4.1.1 Queenborough town] LAMBARDE (*'towne' has been added above the line with a caret*), PORTLAND (*'Quinborough' in both texts*); *Quinborough* WIT, HERRINGMAN

4.1.4 meet] LAMBARDE, PORTLAND, WIT; greete HERRINGMAN

4.1.4 thy fair] LAMBARDE, PORTLAND; her ~ HERRINGMAN, WIT

4.1.4 trollops] PORTLAND, WIT, HERRINGMAN; *cropped in* LAMBARDE *to* 'trollop'

4.1.5 not] LAMBARDE, PORTLAND; no WIT

4.1.6 found] LAMBARDE, PORTLAND; finde WIT; find HERRINGMAN

4.1.7 scorn to] LAMBARDE, PORTLAND, WIT; cannot HERRINGMAN

4.1.8 for] LAMBARDE, PORTLAND, HERRINGMAN; at WIT

4.1.9 expect] LAMBARDE, PORTLAND, HERRINGMAN; respect WIT

4.1.9 so thee] PORTLAND; *cropped in* LAMBARDE *to* 'so'; ſee thee WIT, HERRINGMAN

4.1.10 the other] LAMBARDE, PORTLAND, HERRINGMAN; that ~ WIT

4.1.10 prithee] PORTLAND, WIT, HERRINGMAN; *cropped in* LAM-BARDE *to* 'pr'

4.1.11 thee] LAMBARDE, PORTLAND, HERRINGMAN; hee WIT

4.1.11 gifts] LAMBARDE, PORTLAND; guift's WIT; gift HERRINGMAN

4.1.11 leather] PORTLAND, WIT, HERRINGMAN; *cropped in* LAMBARDE *to* 'le'

4.1.12 they're] LAMBARDE, PORTLAND, WIT; they HERRINGMAN

4.1.13 to thee] PORTLAND, WIT; *cropped in* LAMBARDE *to* 'to'; by me HERRINGMAN

4.1.16 'em] LAMBARDE, PORTLAND; them HERRINGMAN

4.1.16 rotten] LAMBARDE, PORTLAND; *not in* HERRINGMAN

4.1.16–17 you. | You inconstant] LAMBARDE; your | inconstant PORTLAND; your | Inconſtant HERRINGMAN

4.1.17 fits] *preceded in* LAMBARDE *by deleted* 'rable'

4.1.18 bounty] LAMBARDE, PORTLAND; Bounties HERRINGMAN

4.1.18 iron] PORTLAND, HERRINGMAN; Iror LAMBARDE

4.1.19 And get you gone] LAMBARDE, PORTLAND; *not in* HERRINGMAN

4.1.19.1 *Music*] LAMBARDE, PORTLAND; *not in* HERRINGMAN

4.1.19.1 *Exeunt...Lords*] HERRINGMAN (*Exit cum fociis.*); *Exevnt King Lordes* LAMBARDE; *Exeunt king and Lordes* PORTLAND

4.1.20 sir] LAMBARDE, PORTLAND; Sirs HERRINGMAN

4.1.20 'Tis, 'tis] LAMBARDE, PORTLAND; It is, it is HERRINGMAN

4.1.24 that pie is new] LAMBARDE, PORTLAND; this pye shall be HERRINGMAN

4.1.25 all] LAMBARDE, PORTLAND; full HERRINGMAN

4.2 HERRINGMAN (ACT 4. SCENA 2.); *not in* LAMBARDE *or* PORTLAND

4.2.0.1–5 *Oboes...[and attendants]*] LAMBARDE, PORTLAND; *Enter Hengift, Horfus, Vortiger, Devonſhire, Stafford, Caſtiza, Roxena, Ladies.* HERRINGMAN

4.2.0.1 *Oboes*] LAMBARDE, PORTLAND (Hoboys)

4.2.2 talk and toil] LAMBARDE, HERRINGMAN; toil and talk PORTLAND

4.2.3 thankful love and] *in* PORTLAND 'ful loue' *is inserted with a caret above* 'thank and'

4.2.5 that's...implies] LAMBARDE, PORTLAND; there's a Fabrick that implies eternity HERRINGMAN

4.2.6 but] *preceded in* PORTLAND *by deleted* 'full'

4.2.8 Save that great] LAMBARDE, PORTLAND; Saving that HERRINGMAN

4.2.11 last] LAMBARDE, PORTLAND; pass HERRINGMAN

4.2.12 metal] PORTLAND, HERRINGMAN; *cropped in* LAMBARDE *to* 'mettl'

4.2.13 VORTIGER] *altered in* LAMBARDE *from the original* 'Hersus'

4.2.14 a full] HERRINGMAN; of all LAMBARDE, PORTLAND

4.2.16 sir] LAMBARDE, PORTLAND; *not in* HERRINGMAN

4.2.17 And, ay] LAMBARDE, PORTLAND (and I); I and HERRINGMAN

4.2.17 on't] LAMBARDE, PORTLAND; of it HERRINGMAN

4.2.18 o' purpose] LAMBARDE, PORTLAND ('apurpose' *in both texts*); on purpose HERRINGMAN

4.2.20 sticks] *altered in* PORTLAND *from another word*

4.2.25 such] LAMBARDE, PORTLAND; these HERRINGMAN

4.2.26 observance] *altered in* LAMBARDE *from* 'observations'

4.2.27 t'abuse] LAMBARDE, PORTLAND; to abuſe HERRINGMAN

4.2.27 themselves] PORTLAND, HERRINGMAN; *cropped in* LAMBARDE *to* 'themselu'

4.2.29 storm] LAMBARDE, PORTLAND; ſtorms HERRINGMAN

4.2.29 pirates] *altered in* LAMBARDE *to* 'pyratt' *from another word*

4.2.29 venturers] LAMBARDE (ventuers); ventures PORTLAND; Adventurers HERRINGMAN

4.2.29 courage] PORTLAND, HERRINGMAN; *cropped in* LAMBARDE *to* 'C'

4.2.31 venturer] PORTLAND, HERRINGMAN; vetuerer LAMBARDE

4.2.32 they] PORTLAND, HERRINGMAN; the LAMBARDE

4.2.32 their] *altered in* LAMBARDE *to* 'theire' *from* 'theere'

4.2.35 are oft] LAMBARDE, PORTLAND; oft are HERRINGMAN

4.2.35.1 *Music*] PORTLAND; *cropped in* LAMBARDE *to* 'Mu'; *not in* HERRINGMAN

4.2.38 HERSUS My lord. | VORTIGER] LAMBARDE, PORTLAND; *not in* HERRINGMAN

4.2.39 They're] th'are LAMBARDE; they are PORTLAND, HERRINGMAN

4.2.40 They had] LAMBARDE, PORTLAND; th'had HERRINGMAN

4.2.40 cup] LAMBARDE, PORTLAND; Carp HERRINGMAN

4.2.40–1 my lord. | I sit wrong] LAMBARDE, PORTLAND; *not in* HERRINGMAN

4.2.42.1–4.2.46 SONG...If...forth] *in* LAMBARDE *and* PORTLAND *this song appears as part of Hersus's speech; not in* HERRINGMAN

4.2.47–8 HERSUS Welcome...one] LAMBARDE, PORTLAND; *not in* HERRINGMAN

4.2.50 sweetest] *altered in* LAMBARDE *from* 'secretest'

4.2.52 from] LAMBARDE, PORTLAND; for HERRINGMAN

4.2.53 power's] LAMBARDE, HERRINGMAN; powre is PORTLAND

4.2.55 I'm] LAMBARDE, PORTLAND; I am HERRINGMAN

4.2.60 When she] HERRINGMAN; whe she LAMBARDE; who's there PORTLAND

4.2.60 maid] *preceded in* LAMBARDE *by deleted* 'f'

4.2.61 otherwise] LAMBARDE, HERRINGMAN; otherways PORTLAND

4.2.66 desert] LAMBARDE, PORTLAND; deferts HERRINGMAN

4.2.67 intimates] HERRINGMAN; imtinates LAMBARDE; imitates PORTLAND

4.2.71 o'th'] LAMBARDE, PORTLAND; of the HERRINGMAN

4.2.74 'em] LAMBARDE, PORTLAND; them HERRINGMAN

4.2.76 May't] LAMBARDE, PORTLAND; May it HERRINGMAN

4.2.77 with 'em] LAMBARDE, PORTLAND; with them HERRINGMAN

4.2.79 'em] LAMBARDE, PORTLAND; them HERRINGMAN

4.2.80 you have] LAMBARDE, PORTLAND; y'have HERRINGMAN

4.2.80 constancy] PORTLAND; *cropped in* LAMBARDE *to* 'Cons'; conſtancies HERRINGMAN

4.2.82 for't] LAMBARDE, PORTLAND; for it HERRINGMAN

4.2.85 'Troth] LAMBARDE, PORTLAND; Truth HERRINGMAN

4.2.87 motion] PORTLAND; *cropped in* LAMBARDE *to* 'moti'; queſtion HERRINGMAN

4.2.90 May't] LAMBARDE; May it PORTLAND, HERRINGMAN

4.2.90 'Twill] LAMBARDE, PORTLAND; 'Twould HERRINGMAN

4.2.90 wondrous] LAMBARDE, PORTLAND; very HERRINGMAN

4.2.93 shall] *preceded in* LAMBARDE *by deleted* 'all'

4.2.93 never] LAMBARDE, PORTLAND; ne're HERRINGMAN

4.2.94 any] PORTLAND, HERRINGMAN; aniy LAMBARDE

4.2.95 remembrance] LAMBARDE, HERRINGMAN; re remembrance PORTLAND

4.2.97 excuses] LAMBARDE, PORTLAND; excuſe HERRINGMAN

4.2.98 ne'er] LAMBARDE (nere), HERRINGMAN (ne're); neare PORTLAND

4.2.99 I'm] LAMBARDE, PORTLAND; I am HERRINGMAN

4.2.101 were] LAMBARDE, PORTLAND; be HERRINGMAN

4.2.102 mine] LAMBARDE, PORTLAND; my HERRINGMAN

4.2.102 may] LAMBARDE, HERRINGMAN; *not in* PORTLAND

4.2.103 can] *added in* LAMBARDE *above the line with a caret*

4.2.105 I'm] LAMBARDE, PORTLAND; I am HERRINGMAN

4.2.107 has] LAMBARDE, PORTLAND; have HERRINGMAN

4.2.108 VORTIGER] LAMBARDE, HERRINGMAN; *not in* PORTLAND, *although the speech has been ruled off*

4.2.109 ne'er] LAMBARDE, PORTLAND; never HERRINGMAN

4.2.112 'em] LAMBARDE, PORTLAND; them HERRINGMAN

4.2.115 A...many] LAMBARDE, PORTLAND; A thouſand! Nay a million, or as many HERRINGMAN

4.2.117 there, over-holy fearful] LAMBARDE, PORTLAND; thee, over-fearful HERRINGMAN

4.2.118 That...niceness] LAMBARDE; that syns in nothing but into much inocense PORTLAND; That finn'ft in nothing but in too much nicenefs HERRINGMAN

4.2.121 on't] LAMBARDE, PORTLAND; on it HERRINGMAN

4.2.122 these] LAMBARDE, PORTLAND; thofe HERRINGMAN

4.2.126 mine] PORTLAND, HERRINGMAN; *cropped in* LAMBARDE *to* 'min'

4.2.127 he's] LAMBARDE, PORTLAND (has); he has HERRINGMAN

4.2.130 now] LAMBARDE, PORTLAND; *not in* HERRINGMAN

4.2.136 'em] LAMBARDE, PORTLAND; them HERRINGMAN

4.2.141 We...lord] LAMBARDE, PORTLAND; *not in* HERRINGMAN, *and instead the line finishes with the beginning of* 4.2.142 'her Uncle and my felf'

4.2.142 wild] HERRINGMAN; would LAMBARDE, PORTLAND

4.2.144 deprivation] LAMBARDE, PORTLAND; *after this word in* HERRINGMAN *appear the following lines not in* LAMBARDE *and* PORTLAND: 'She fhall accept this oath | VORTIGER You do but call me then | Into a world of more defpair and horrour; | Yet fince fo wilfully you ftand engag'd | In high fcorn to be touch'd, with expedition | Perfect your undertakings with your fames, | Or by the Iffues of abus'd belief | I'le take the forfeit of Lives'

4.2.144 honour] LAMBARDE, PORTLAND; Honours HERRINGMAN

4.2.146 misery] LAMBARDE, PORTLAND; miferies HERRINGMAN

4.2.148 goodness] PORTLAND, HERRINGMAN; *cropped in* LAMBARDE *to* 'goodn'

4.2.150 religious] LAMBARDE, HERRINGMAN; so religious PORTLAND

4.2.150 so vile] HERRINGMAN; so vild LAMBARDE; vild too PORTLAND

4.2.151 true, my lord] LAMBARDE, PORTLAND; truth great sir HERRINGMAN

4.2.152-3 I...sir] LAMBARDE, PORTLAND; *not in* HERRINGMAN

4.2.154 has] LAMBARDE, PORTLAND; hath HERRINGMAN

4.2.155 Give] LAMBARDE, PORTLAND; But give HERRINGMAN

4.2.156 But] LAMBARDE, PORTLAND; 'Twas HERRINGMAN

4.2.157 ravished] LAMBARDE ('rauifhd' *altered from* 'rauisd'), PORTLAND; raught HERRINGMAN

4.2.159 sin] PORTLAND, HERRINGMAN; fim LAMBARDE

4.2.163 lords] HERRINGMAN; words LAMBARDE, PORTLAND

4.2.165 To swift] HERRINGMAN; swifter LAMBARDE, PORTLAND

4.2.166.1 Exeunt] LAMBARDE (*Ex^t*); Exit PORTLAND; *not in* HERRINGMAN

4.2.167 Ha, ha] LAMBARDE, PORTLAND; *not in* HERRINGMAN

4.2.168 saddest] HERRINGMAN; suddest LAMBARDE, PORTLAND

4.2.171 sir] LAMBARDE, PORTLAND; *not in* HERRINGMAN

4.2.171 I'm] LAMBARDE, PORTLAND; I am HERRINGMAN

4.2.172 best] LAMBARDE, PORTLAND; worft HERRINGMAN

4.2.175 I'd] LAMBARDE; I had PORTLAND, HERRINGMAN

4.2.175 myself] LAMBARDE, PORTLAND; my felf elfe HERRINGMAN

4.2.177 this, this shames] LAMBARDE, PORTLAND; this does fhame HERRINGMAN

4.2.178 shall] LAMBARDE, HERRINGMAN; should PORTLAND

4.2.179 and] *preceded in* PORTLAND *by deleted* 'Issue'

4.2.180 Vortiner] LAMBARDE, PORTLAND; Vortimer HERRINGMAN (*also at* 4.2.187)

4.2.181 O that] LAMBARDE, PORTLAND; I would HERRINGMAN

4.2.182 injury] *in* LAMBARDE *an* 'i' *has been added before the* 'u' *to the original* 'inurye'

4.2.182 truth] *altered in* LAMBARDE *from another word*

4.2.186 never] LAMBARDE, PORTLAND; ne're HERRINGMAN

4.2.187 legitimate] *in* LAMBARDE *the* 'g' *has been written over another letter*

4.2.188 Pish] LAMBARDE, PORTLAND; *not in* HERRINGMAN

4.2.188-9 though...ceases] LAMBARDE, PORTLAND; *not in* HERRINGMAN

4.2.190 can ne'er] LAMBARDE, PORTLAND; ne're can HERRINGMAN

4.2.192 this...oath] LAMBARDE, PORTLAND; thy heart for urging this excufe

4.2.193 'T has] LAMBARDE, PORTLAND; Th'haft HERRINGMAN

4.2.193 sir] LAMBARDE, PORTLAND; *not in* HERRINGMAN

4.2.194 Amongst] LAMBARDE, PORTLAND; Among HERRINGMAN

4.2.194 women] *altered in* LAMBARDE *to* 'woeman' *from* 'waeman'

4.2.196 began't] LAMBARDE, PORTLAND; begun HERRINGMAN

4.2.199 I'm] LAMBARDE, PORTLAND; I am HERRINGMAN

4.2.200 less] LAMBARDE, HERRINGMAN; least PORTLAND

4.2.201 life] LAMBARDE, PORTLAND; cafe HERRINGMAN

4.2.201 will] LAMBARDE, PORTLAND; may HERRINGMAN

4.2.202 here] LAMBARDE, PORTLAND; *not in* HERRINGMAN

4.2.204 up] LAMBARDE, PORTLAND; *not in* HERRINGMAN

4.2.210 professes] LAMBARDE, PORTLAND; profeffeth HERRINGMAN

4.2.211 also] LAMBARDE, PORTLAND; likewife HERRINGMAN

4.2.213 death] LAMBARDE, PORTLAND; falfhood HERRINGMAN

4.2.215 know] PORTLAND, HERRINGMAN; knew LAMBARDE

4.2.217 seed] LAMBARDE, PORTLAND; feeds HERRINGMAN

4.2.218 great] LAMBARDE, PORTLAND; black HERRINGMAN

4.2.219-20 by...forever] LAMBARDE, PORTLAND; *not in* HERRINGMAN

4.2.221 restore] LAMBARDE, PORTLAND; we ftore HERRINGMAN

4.2.222.1 Music] LAMBARDE, PORTLAND; *not in* HERRINGMAN

4.2.222.1 Exeunt] LAMBARDE, PORTLAND; Exeunt all but Horfus HERRINGMAN

4.2.223 fortune] LAMBARDE, PORTLAND; fortunes HERRINGMAN

4.2.225 the advantage] LAMBARDE, PORTLAND; th'advantage HERRINGMAN

4.2.225-32 The...train] LAMBARDE, PORTLAND, *not in* HERRINGMAN

4.2.226 a lost] LAMBARDE; lost PORTLAND

4.2.227 as at] LAMBARDE; at PORTLAND

4.2.231 troops] PORTLAND; tropes LAMBARDE

4.2.233 Methinks] LAMBARDE, PORTLAND; Precious Whore. | Methinks HERRINGMAN

4.2.233-5 Methinks...lord] This page is cropped in LAMBARDE and the scribe's marginal transcription of 'Lords | Blackson | Briggs' survives as 'Lor | Black | Brig'; this transcription is not in PORTLAND, probably because the scribe has not left enough room in the margin to accommodate it.

4.2.236 Earl] LAMBARDE, PORTLAND; Earl of

4.2.240 Somewhat] LAMBARDE, PORTLAND; Something HERRINGMAN

4.2.241 Exit] HERRINGMAN; *not in* LAMBARDE *or* PORTLAND

4.3.0.1-21 Dumb Show...severally] *for variants between the* LAMBARDE-PORTLAND *texts and* HERRINGMAN, *see Stage Directions*

4.2.0.1 Oboes] LAMBARDE, PORTLAND (Hoboyes)

4.3.0.2 and Stafford] PORTLAND (& Stafford); Staffo LAMBARDE

4.3.0.2 leading] PORTLAND; *cropped in* LAMBARDE *to* 'Lead' (*altered from* 'Lad')

4.3.0.3 the] LAMBARDE (y^e); *not in* PORTLAND

4.3.0.3 Enter] PORTLAND; *cropped in* LAMBARDE *to* 'E'

4.3.0.5 then] PORTLAND; *cropped in* LAMBARDE

4.3.0.6 out] PORTLAND *cropped in* LAMBARDE *to* 'ou'

4.3.0.7 subborns] PORTLAND; suborne LAMBARDE

4.3.0.7 two] PORTLAND (tow); *cropped in* LAMBARDE *to* 'tw'

4.3.0.8 and] PORTLAND; *cropped in* LAMBARDE

4.3.0.9 exeunt] LAMBARDE (*Ex^t*); Exit PORTLAND

4.3.0.10 draws] PORTLAND; *cropped in* LAMBARDE *to* 'dra'

4.3.0.11 thereon] LAMBARDE; through PORTLAND

4.3.0.11 Hersus and] PORTLAND; *cropped in* LAMBARDE *to* 'Hers'

4.3.0.12 *Hersus. Then*] PORTLAND; *cropped in* LAMBARDE *to* 'Hersu'

4.3.0.14 *they all*] PORTLAND; *cropped in* LAMBARDE *to* 'the'

4.3.0.15 *submission*] PORTLAND; *cropped in* LAMBARDE *to* 'su | ion'

4.3.0.16 *Then*] PORTLAND; *cropped in* LAMBARDE

4.3.0.16 *Hengist*] LAMBARDE (Hen:), PORTLAND

4.3.0.17 *rest*] PORTLAND; *cropped in* LAMBARDE *to* 'res'

4.3.0.19 *amazed*] Before this word in LAMBARDE the scribe has first written 'with diuers Saxons' and then deleted it.

4.3.0.21 *down*] LAMBARDE; by PORTLAND

4.3.0.22 *Raynulph*] LAMBARDE, PORTLAND; Raynulphus HERRINGMAN

4.3.3 Vortiner] LAMBARDE, PORTLAND; Vortimer HERRINGMAN

4.3.3 they crownèd] BALD; the crowned LAMBARDE, PORTLAND; and crown'd him HERRINGMAN

4.3.5 to] LAMBARDE, PORTLAND; unto HERRINGMAN

4.3.10 near] LAMBARDE, HERRINGMAN; of PORTLAND

4.3.15 too] *in* LAMBARDE *the 't' has been altered from* 'v'

4.4.0.1 *Gentleman, and Saxons*] LAMBARDE, PORTLAND; *with* Saxons HERRINGMAN

4.4.7 assure] LAMBARDE, PORTLAND; endure HERRINGMAN

4.4.7, 33, 36, 38 *gentleman*] LAMBARDE, PORTLAND; Sax. HERRINGMAN

4.4.7 resolved] *added in* PORTLAND *above the line with a caret*

4.4.10 Is't] LAMBARDE, PORTLAND; Is it HERRINGMAN

4.4.11 preventions] LAMBARDE, PORTLAND; prevention HERRINGMAN

4.4.12 He's] LAMBARDE, PORTLAND (has); He has HERRINGMAN

4.4.13 made] *altered in* PORTLAND *from another word*

4.4.13 can] LAMBARDE, HERRINGMAN; has PORTLAND

4.4.14–19 Nor...commended] LAMBARDE, PORTLAND; *not in* HERRINGMAN

4.4.21 the] *altered in* LAMBARDE *to* 'thee' *from* 'this'

4.4.22 steel] *altered in* LAMBARDE *to* 'stele' *from* 'seeke'

4.4.23 the] LAMBARDE, PORTLAND; a HERRINGMAN

4.4.23 snake] *preceded in* PORTLAND *by deleted* 'shade'

4.4.24 leaf] HERRINGMAN; lease LAMBARDE, PORTLAND

4.4.24 and as great substance] LAMBARDE; and of greate substance PORTLAND; there fly you on HERRINGMAN

4.4.25–30 Blocks...those] LAMBARDE, PORTLAND; *not in* HERRINGMAN

4.4.27 So in] LAMBARDE; some PORTLAND

4.4.31 loves] LAMBARDE, PORTLAND; love HERRINGMAN

4.4.32 his] LAMBARDE, PORTLAND; the HERRINGMAN

4.4.37 not him] LAMBARDE, PORTLAND; him not HERRINGMAN

4.4.38 fear't] LAMBARDE, PORTLAND; fear it HERRINGMAN

4.4.39 our] *preceded in* LAMBARDE *by deleted* 'her'

4.4.39 lord] PORTLAND, HERRINGMAN; *cropped in* LAMBARDE *to* 'Lor'

4.4.40 They come; calm] LAMBARDE, PORTLAND; Calm HERRINGMAN

4.4.40 you] LAMBARDE, PORTLAND; you all HERRINGMAN

4.4.40.1 *Enter...unarmed*] HERRINGMAN (*Enter* Vortiger *and British Lords*); *not in* LAMBARDE *or* PORTLAND

4.4.41 word] LAMBARDE, PORTLAND; words HERRINGMAN

4.4.42 breath] *altered in both* LAMBARDE *and* PORTLAND *from* 'birth'

4.4.43 word] LAMBARDE, PORTLAND; words HERRINGMAN

4.4.46 we're...met] LAMBARDE; w'are both sides met together PORTLAND; both fides are met HERRINGMAN

4.4.47 other arms] HERRINGMAN; other armyes LAMBARDE; others armyes PORTLAND

4.4.48 Th'are, th'are] LAMBARDE, PORTLAND ('their their' in both texts); They are HERRINGMAN

4.4.49 these only] LAMBARDE, HERRINGMAN; these PORTLAND

4.4.50.1–2 BRITISH LORDS] PORTLAND, HERRINGMAN; *Vortiger* PORTLAND

4.4.50 to th'] LAMBARDE; to the PORTLAND; it to the HERRINGMAN

4.4.51 'tis] LAMBARDE, PORTLAND; It is HERRINGMAN

4.4.52 you're] LAMBARDE, PORTLAND; you are HERRINGMAN

4.4.54 bound] *preceded in* PORTLAND *by deleted* 'vp'

4.4.56 suffice] *followed in* LAMBARDE *by deleted* '& w'

4.4.59 the hard] LAMBARDE, HERRINGMAN; the hard the hard PORTLAND

4.4.60 we] *altered in* LAMBARDE *from* 'he'

4.4.63 you] LAMBARDE, PORTLAND; the HERRINGMAN

4.4.65 the] LAMBARDE, PORTLAND; thy HERRINGMAN

4.4.66 your] LAMBARDE, PORTLAND; thy HERRINGMAN

4.4.66 take your] LAMBARDE, PORTLAND; takeft thou HERRINGMAN

4.4.68 the sudden'st] LAMBARDE (the sodanist); the sodainst PORTLAND; a fudden HERRINGMAN

4.4.70 never] LAMBARDE, PORTLAND; ne're HERRINGMAN

4.4.70 man] LAMBARDE, PORTLAND; a man HERRINGMAN

4.4.72 me] *preceded in* LAMBARDE *by deleted* 'you'

4.4.73 full] LAMBARDE, PORTLAND; sore HERRINGMAN

4.4.74 heaven] LAMBARDE, HERRINGMAN; *not in* PORTLAND, *which has instead the deleted* 'euer'

4.4.76 obtain't] LAMBARDE, PORTLAND; obtain it HERRINGMAN

4.4.77 headstrong] LAMBARDE, PORTLAND; headlong HERRINGMAN

4.4.79 'em] LAMBARDE, PORTLAND; them HERRINGMAN

4.4.80 Have...height] LAMBARDE, PORTLAND; *assigned to* HENGIST *in* HERRINGMAN

4.4.80 height] LAMBARDE, PORTLAND; height of pride HERRINGMAN (*the second 'h' in 'height' has been turned and printed upside down*)

4.4.80 HENGIST] LAMBARDE (*altered from* 'Vort'), PORTLAND; *not in* HERRINGMAN

4.4.80 My lord] LAMBARDE, PORTLAND; *not in* HERRINGMAN

4.4.81 mine] LAMBARDE, PORTLAND; mine HERRINGMAN

4.4.81 enforce it] PORTLAND, HERRINGMAN; *cropped in* LAMBARDE *to* 'enfo'

4.4.83 all...kingdoms] PORTLAND; all yᵉ honorˢ Kingdomes LAMBARDE; all a Kingdom HERRINGMAN (*in some copies the first 'l' in 'all' has not been well inked and the letter has not been printed*)

4.4.83 impart] PORTLAND, HERRINGMAN; *cropped in* LAMBARDE *to* 'impar'

4.4.84 above] LAMBARDE, HERRINGMAN; about PORTLAND

4.4.86 Queen] LAMBARDE, PORTLAND; a Queen HERRINGMAN

4.4.87 Why, y'have] LAMBARDE, PORTLAND; You have HERRINGMAN

4.4.87 for't] LAMBARDE (*preceded by deleted* 'byᵗ'), PORTLAND; for it HERRINGMAN

4.4.88 Y'have crowned] LAMBARDE, PORTLAND; You Crown HERRINGMAN

4.4.89 sirs] LAMBARDE, PORTLAND; Sir HERRINGMAN

4.4.89 reason] LAMBARDE, HERRINGMAN; reason, Sʳ PORTLAND

4.4.90 on't] LAMBARDE, PORTLAND; of it HERRINGMAN

4.4.91 on't] LAMBARDE, PORTLAND; of't HERRINGMAN

4.4.92 The] LAMBARDE, PORTLAND; In HERRINGMAN

4.4.92 possession] PORTLAND; poffeffion HERRINGMAN; *cropped in* LAMBARDE *to* 'pos'

4.4.93 yet] LAMBARDE, PORTLAND; *not in* HERRINGMAN

4.4.94 yet] LAMBARDE, PORTLAND; *not in* HERRINGMAN

4.4.99 be] LAMBARDE, PORTLAND; not be HERRINGMAN

4.4.99 by] LAMBARDE, PORTLAND; with HERRINGMAN

4.4.100 Well] LAMBARDE, PORTLAND (*altered from* 'weele'); Very well HERRINGMAN

4.4.100 take't] LAMBARDE, PORTLAND (tak't); take it HERRINGMAN

4.4.100 resign't] LAMBARDE, PORTLAND; refign it HERRINGMAN

4.4.101 sufficed yet] LAMBARDE; satisfied yet PORTLAND; yet fatisfied HERRINGMAN

4.4.102 There's] LAMBARDE, HERRINGMAN; there is PORTLAND

4.4.104 fearful…late] LAMBARDE, PORTLAND; dangerous thirft of late, my Lord HERRINGMAN

4.4.105 by't] LAMBARDE, PORTLAND; by it HERRINGMAN

4.4.106 seek] preceded in PORTLAND by deleted 'all'

4.4.107 VORTIGER] LAMBARDE, HERRINGMAN; not in PORTLAND, and other speech-prefixes are also missing at 4.4.107, 4.4.108, 4.4.110, and 4.4.113, although the speeches have been ruled off

4.4.107-8 There's…in't] LAMBARDE, PORTLAND; There will nothing be abated, I affure you HERRINGMAN

4.4.108 the advantage] LAMBARDE, PORTLAND; me at advantage HERRINGMAN

4.4.109 captivates] LAMBARDE, PORTLAND; Does captivate HERRINGMAN

4.4.109 'em] LAMBARDE, PORTLAND; them HERRINGMAN

4.4.112.1 Exeunt…Vortiger] HERRINGMAN (Exit cum fuis.); Exit LAMBARDE, PORTLAND

4.4.116 on't] LAMBARDE, PORTLAND; of it HERRINGMAN

4.4.118-20 Here…demolished] LAMBARDE, PORTLAND; not in HERRINGMAN

4.4.118 Here is] LAMBARDE; heers PORTLAND

4.4.119 rank] in LAMBARDE the first letter has been altered from another letter

4.4.120.1 Enter Hersus] PORTLAND; cropped in LAMBARDE to 'Enter'; Enter Horfus (at 4.4.117)

4.4.121 mine] LAMBARDE, PORTLAND; my HERRINGMAN

4.4.122 me] LAMBARDE, PORTLAND; me | I have not a friend left me HERRINGMAN

4.4.131 life's] LAMBARDE, PORTLAND (liues); my lives HERRINGMAN

4.4.131 to your fortunes] LAMBARDE, PORTLAND; not in HERRINGMAN

4.4.132 ruined] LAMBARDE, PORTLAND; fick HERRINGMAN

4.4.133 not] LAMBARDE, PORTLAND; no HERRINGMAN

4.4.133 in] LAMBARDE, PORTLAND; of HERRINGMAN

4.4.133 sea] altered in LAMBARDE from 'see'

4.4.135 made up in thee] PORTLAND, HERRINGMAN; cropped in LAMBARDE to 'mad'

4.4.135 Exit] PORTLAND, HERRINGMAN; cropped in LAMBARDE to 'E'

4.4.140 toiling] LAMBARDE, HERRINGMAN; toyle PORTLAND

5.1.0.1 Incipit Actus Quintus] LAMBARDE, PORTLAND ('Actus Quintus Scena p^{ra}' in both texts); ACT. 5. SCENA 1. HERRINGMAN (preceded by catchword 'Actus')

5.1.0.2-4 Enter…Music] PORTLAND (Enter Symon: Clark Glouer fellmonger etc graz & Musique); Enter Symon: Clark Glouer fell etc: gras Musique LAMBARDE; Enter Symon and his Brethren, Aminadab his Clerk. HERRINGMAN

5.1.0.3-4 Fellmonger…Music] In LAMBARDE As at 2.4.2, 3.3.0.1 and 4.1.0.1, the scribe has drawn the properties or cross-referencing symbol in the left margin.

5.1.1 the fustian-weaver] LAMBARDE, PORTLAND; not in HERRINGMAN

5.1.3 CLERK] LAMBARDE, PORTLAND; Ami. HERRINGMAN (throughout the scene)

5.1.5 that's] LAMBARDE, PORTLAND; that art HERRINGMAN

5.1.6 on] LAMBARDE, PORTLAND; upon HERRINGMAN

5.1.7 an] LAMBARDE, PORTLAND (and); if HERRINGMAN

5.1.14 worn] LAMBARDE, PORTLAND; wore HERRINGMAN

5.1.16.1 Enter Footman] LAMBARDE, PORTLAND; Enter a Footman HERRINGMAN

5.1.17 pumps] PORTLAND, HERRINGMAN. After this word in LAMBARDE a later hand has added '& greasie hair'; no part of this later addition is in the original scribe's hand or ink and thus the addition has no authority.

5.1.19 Shake] altered in PORTLAND from 'shaken'

5.1.20 Footman, thou art welcome] LAMBARDE, PORTLAND; Th'art welcome, Footman HERRINGMAN

5.1.21 year's] LAMBARDE, PORTLAND; year is HERRINGMAN

5.1.22 An't] LAMBARDE, PORTLAND; If HERRINGMAN

5.1.22 come] LAMBARDE, PORTLAND; that came HERRINGMAN

5.1.24 thee] LAMBARDE, PORTLAND; thee, thou HERRINGMAN

5.1.26 Intend] LAMBARDE, PORTLAND; Intends HERRINGMAN

5.1.26 merry] altered in LAMBARDE from 'mere'

5.1.28 evil] LAMBARDE, PORTLAND; ill HERRINGMAN

5.1.29 mayor] LAMBARDE, PORTLAND; not in HERRINGMAN

5.1.30 There's] LAMBARDE, PORTLAND; there is HERRINGMAN

5.1.32 Simon] LAMBARDE, PORTLAND; Sym HERRINGMAN

5.1.34 That] LAMBARDE, PORTLAND; Do I prithee; That HERRINGMAN

5.1.35 enough] PORTLAND, HERRINGMAN; cropped in LAMBARDE to 'e'

5.1.36 King of] PORTLAND HERRINGMAN; cropped in LAMBARDE to 'K'

5.1.36-7 to me] LAMBARDE, PORTLAND; not in HERRINGMAN

5.1.37 you must] PORTLAND, HERRINGMAN; cropped in LAMBARDE to 'y'

5.1.38 that] LAMBARDE, PORTLAND; when HERRINGMAN

5.1.38 Kent stands] PORTLAND, HERRINGMAN; cropped in LAMBARDE to 'Ken'

5.1.39 there] LAMBARDE, PORTLAND; here HERRINGMAN

5.1.39 never] PORTLAND, HERRINGMAN; cropped in LAMBARDE

5.1.41 you're] LAMBARDE, PORTLAND (y'are); you are HERRINGMAN

5.1.41 wit] HERRINGMAN; cropped in LAMBARDE; not in PORTLAND

5.1.43 into] LAMBARDE, PORTLAND; to HERRINGMAN

5.1.44 tonight] PORTLAND, HERRINGMAN; cropped in LAMBARDE to 'ton'

5.1.45 geese] PORTLAND, HERRINGMAN; cropped in LAMBARDE

5.1.45 but] LAMBARDE, PORTLAND; And HERRINGMAN

5.1.46 woodcocks] PORTLAND, HERRINGMAN; cropped in LAMBARDE to 'w | cocks'

5.1.47 mutton] PORTLAND, HERRINGMAN; cropped in LAMBARDE to 'mu'

5.1.47 that's] LAMBARDE, PORTLAND; that is HERRINGMAN

5.1.47 infidel] LAMBARDE, PORTLAND; Infidels HERRINGMAN

5.1.48 of] PORTLAND, HERRINGMAN; cropped in LAMBARDE

5.1.48 Kent's] PORTLAND, HERRINGMAN; cropped in LAMBARDE; Kent is HERRINGMAN

5.1.49 officers] PORTLAND, HERRINGMAN; cropped in LAMBARDE

5.1.50 bring't] LAMBARDE, PORTLAND; Bring it HERRINGMAN

5.1.50 'twill be] PORTLAND, HERRINGMAN; cropped in LAMBARDE to 'twi'

5.1.50 well] LAMBARDE, PORTLAND; the better HERRINGMAN

5.1.50-1 Run….Come hither you] LAMBARDE, PORTLAND; Run, run, come you hither HERRINGMAN

5.1.51 the cushions] PORTLAND; cropped in LAMBARDE to 'y'; my Cushions HERRINGMAN

5.1.52 'em] LAMBARDE, PORTLAND; them HERRINGMAN

5.1.52 feast] PORTLAND, HERRINGMAN; cropped in LAMBARDE to 'f'

5.1.53 has] LAMBARDE, PORTLAND; have HERRINGMAN

5.1.53 flour in] PORTLAND; flower in HERRINGMAN; cropped in LAMBARDE to 'fflow'

5.1.53 'em] LAMBARDE, PORTLAND; them HERRINGMAN

5.1.53 'em] LAMBARDE, PORTLAND; them HERRINGMAN

5.1.54 o'er] LAMBARDE, PORTLAND; over HERRINGMAN

5.1.54 there'll be] PORTLAND; *cropped in* LAMBARDE *to* 'their'; there will be HERRINGMAN

5.1.55 handle] LAMBARDE, HERRINGMAN; order PORTLAND

5.1.55 it] PORTLAND, HERRINGMAN; *cropped in* LAMBARDE

5.1.56 burn a] PORTLAND, HERRINGMAN; *cropped in* LAMBARDE *to* 'bu'

5.1.57 i'th'] LAMBARDE, PORTLAND; in the HERRINGMAN

5.1.57 was] PORTLAND, HERRINGMAN; *cropped in* LAMBARDE

5.1.58 fire] PORTLAND, HERRINGMAN; *added in* LAMBARDE *in a later hand above the line with a caret*

5.1.58 thought] LAMBARDE, PORTLAND; dreamt HERRINGMAN

5.1.59 coming] PORTLAND, HERRINGMAN; *cropped in* LAMBARDE *to* ' | ing'

5.1.61 there's] LAMBARDE, PORTLAND; here are HERRINGMAN

5.1.62 players] PORTLAND, HERRINGMAN; *cropped in* LAMBARDE *to* 'pla'

5.1.64 desires] LAMBARDE, PORTLAND; Desire HERRINGMAN

5.1.65 leave and favour] LAMBARDE, PORTLAND; favour and leave HERRINGMAN

5.1.66 I'th'] LAMBARDE, PORTLAND; In the HERRINGMAN

5.1.66 it] LAMBARDE, PORTLAND; them that HERRINGMAN

5.1.67 'em] LAMBARDE, PORTLAND; them HERRINGMAN

5.1.68–9 a barn to 'em] LAMBARDE, PORTLAND; them a barn HERRINGMAN

5.1.69.1 *Enter [two] Cheaters* LAMBARDE, PORTLAND; *at* 5.1.66–7 *in* HERRINGMAN

5.1.71 anything] LAMBARDE, PORTLAND; *not in* HERRINGMAN

5.1.72 pastoralists] LAMBARDE, PORTLAND; Paſtoriſts HERRINGMAN

5.1.73 and] LAMBARDE, PORTLAND; *not in* HERRINGMAN

5.1.73 'em] LAMBARDE, PORTLAND; them HERRINGMAN

5.1.74 the smile] LAMBARDE, PORTLAND; the hug to the ſmile, from the ſmile HERRINGMAN

5.1.75 handkerchief] PORTLAND, HERRINGMAN; handkercher LAMBARDE

5.1.76 You are] LAMBARDE, PORTLAND; Y'are HERRINGMAN

5.1.76 strong i'th' wrists] BALD; strongists wrists LAMBARDE, PORTLAND; ſtrong in the wriſt methinks HERRINGMAN

5.1.76 shall] LAMBARDE, PORTLAND; muſt all HERRINGMAN

5.1.77 you're endowed withal] LAMBARDE, PORTLAND; *not in* HERRINGMAN

5.1.77 among] LAMBARDE, PORTLAND; upon HERRINGMAN

5.1.78 malt-men] LAMBARDE, PORTLAND; Malt-men, ha? HERRINGMAN

5.1.79 an't] LAMBARDE, PORTLAND (and't); if it HERRINGMAN

5.1.81 Have] LAMBARDE, PORTLAND; Hum; have HERRINGMAN

5.1.82 person] LAMBARDE, PORTLAND; perſon as my ſelf HERRINGMAN

5.1.86 I'm] LAMBARDE, PORTLAND; I am HERRINGMAN

5.1.86–7 My humour 'tis] LAMBARDE, PORTLAND; It is my humour HERRINGMAN

5.1.92 FIRST CHEATER] LAMBARDE, PORTLAND (*1 Chea*); *2 Cheat.* HERRINGMAN

5.1.94 rubbed] *altered in* LAMBARDE *to* 'rubd' *from* 'rubb'

5.1.95 We will] LAMBARDE, PORTLAND; We'le HERRINGMAN

5.1.95 offer't] LAMBARDE, PORTLAND; offer it HERRINGMAN

5.1.95 worship, sir] PORTLAND; woᵖᵖ sirs LAMBARDE; Worſhip HERRINGMAN

5.1.99 i'th'] LAMBARDE, PORTLAND; in a HERRINGMAN

5.1.100 kept] PORTLAND, HERRINGMAN; *cropped in* LAMBARDE

5.1.101 play now] LAMBARDE, PORTLAND; play HERRINGMAN

5.1.101 would I] LAMBARDE, PORTLAND; I would HERRINGMAN

5.1.101 after] PORTLAND, HERRINGMAN; *cropped in* LAMBARDE

5.1.102 Why] LAMBARDE, PORTLAND *not in* HERRINGMAN

5.1.103 all o'er] LAMBARDE, PORTLAND; *not in* HERRINGMAN

5.1.103 choice] PORTLAND, HERRINGMAN; *cropped in* LAMBARDE *to* 'Chois'

5.1.104 trust me] LAMBARDE, PORTLAND; *not in* HERRINGMAN

5.1.106 *Carwidgeon*] LAMBARDE, PORTLAND; the Carwidgen HERRINGMAN

5.1.111 plain yet] LAMBARDE; plain now PORTLAND; *not in* HERRINGMAN

5.1.112 SECOND CHEATER] LAMBARDE, PORTLAND ('*2 Chea*' in both texts); *1 Cheat.* HERRINGMAN

5.1.114 FIRST CHEATER] LAMBARDE, PORTLAND ('*1 Chea*' in both texts); *2 Cheat.* HERRINGMAN

5.1.118 since, sir] LAMBARDE, PORTLAND; of late HERRINGMAN

5.1.119 Clown] LAMBARDE, PORTLAND; your Clown HERRINGMAN

5.1.120 CLOWN I . . . sir] LAMBARDE, PORTLAND; This is our Clown, Sir | *Symon* Fye, fye, your Company HERRINGMAN

5.1.121 SIMON He's . . . laugh] LAMBARDE, PORTLAND; Muſt fall upon him and beat him, he's too fair y'faith | To make the people laugh HERRINGMAN

5.1.124 he'll] PORTLAND; *cropped in* LAMBARDE; He will HERRINGMAN

5.1.125 I have] PORTLAND, HERRINGMAN; *cropped in* LAMBARDE

5.1.125 'em] LAMBARDE, PORTLAND; one of them HERRINGMAN

5.1.126 have] PORTLAND, HERRINGMAN; *cropped in* LAMBARDE

5.1.126 if] LAMBARDE, PORTLAND; though HERRINGMAN

5.1.126–7 had lain] LAMBARDE, PORTLAND; lay HERRINGMAN

5.1.127 a-dying] PORTLAND, HERRINGMAN; *cropped in* LAMBARDE *to* 'ady'

5.1.128 that can] PORTLAND, HERRINGMAN; *cropped in* LAMBARDE

5.1.128 twopence] LAMBARDE, PORTLAND; 2ᵈ HERRINGMAN

5.1.129 with] PORTLAND, HERRINGMAN; *cropped in* LAMBARDE *to* 'w'

5.1.130 world] PORTLAND, HERRINGMAN; *cropped in* LAMBARDE *to* 'w'

5.1.131 puling] PORTLAND, HERRINGMAN; *cropped in* LAMBARDE *to* 'pulen'

5.1.131 stuff] LAMBARDE, HERRINGMAN; stuft PORTLAND

5.1.132 clown's part] LAMBARDE, PORTLAND; Clown HERRINGMAN

5.1.132 on't] LAMBARDE, PORTLAND; on it HERRINGMAN

5.1.136 I mean is one] LAMBARDE, PORTLAND; is one, I mean HERRINGMAN

5.1.138 hope is] LAMBARDE, PORTLAND; hopes are HERRINGMAN

5.1.141.1 *Exeunt Cheaters*] BALD; *Exeunt Cheater* LAMBARDE, PORTLAND; *Ex. Players.* HERRINGMAN (all at 5.1.139)

5.1.141 'em] LAMBARDE, PORTLAND; them HERRINGMAN

5.1.144 an't] LAMBARDE, PORTLAND; if it HERRINGMAN

5.1.150 FELLMONGER] LAMBARDE, PORTLAND; *Felt.* HERRINGMAN (*throughout the scene*)

5.1.151 No, no] LAMBARDE, PORTLAND; Oh no, no HERRINGMAN

5.1.151–2 to it] LAMBARDE, HERRINGMAN; too't PORTLAND

5.1.152 amongst 'em] LAMBARDE, PORTLAND; among them HERRINGMAN

5.1.152.1 *A shout within*] HERRINGMAN; *showte* LAMBARDE, PORTLAND (*at* 5.1.154)

5.1.154 meaning] *altered in* LAMBARDE *to* 'meaneing' *from* 'meaning'

5.1.155 Rebel's ta'en] LAMBARDE, PORTLAND; Rebel is taken HERRINGMAN

5.1.155.1 *Oliver is brought in*] HERRINGMAN (*at* 5.1.160); *Enter Oliuer* LAMBARDE, PORTLAND

5.1.159 amending] LAMBARDE, PORTLAND; in mending HERRINGMAN

5.1.160 forth] LAMBARDE, PORTLAND; out HERRINGMAN

5.1.161 I'm] LAMBARDE, PORTLAND; I am HERRINGMAN

5.1.162 welcome] LAMBARDE, PORTLAND; welcome, I HERRING-MAN

5.1.166 plain] PORTLAND, HERRINGMAN; *cropped in* LAMBARDE *to* 'plai'

5.1.167 away] PORTLAND, HERRINGMAN; *cropped in* LAMBARDE *to* 'aw'

5.1.167 not] LAMBARDE, PORTLAND; no HERRINGMAN

5.1.168 there's] LAMBARDE, PORTLAND; there are HERRINGMAN

5.1.168 charge] *added in* LAMBARDE *above the line with a caret and preceded by deleted* 'pray'

5.1.169 the] PORTLAND, HERRINGMAN; *cropped in* LAMBARDE *to* 'th'

5.1.171 the] LAMBARDE, PORTLAND; a HERRINGMAN

5.1.175 O, O] LAMBARDE, PORTLAND; Oh HERRINGMAN

5.1.175 trumpet] LAMBARDE, PORTLAND; trumpet! oh, oh HER-RINGMAN

5.1.177 mine] LAMBARDE; my PORTLAND, HERRINGMAN

5.1.177 eyes] *preceded in* LAMBARDE *by deleted* 'eares'

5.1.179 tyranny] LAMBARDE, PORTLAND; tyranny, tyranny HER-RINGMAN

5.1.180 SIMON] LAMBARDE, PORTLAND; *not in* HERRINGMAN

5.1.180 deaths] PORTLAND, HERRINGMAN; Death LAMBARDE

5.1.182 OLIVER] LAMBARDE, PORTLAND; *not in* HERRINGMAN

5.1.182 swoon] THIS EDITION; swound LAMBARDE, PORTLAND, HERRINGMAN

5.1.182 SIMON] *in* LAMBARDE *the 'S' has been altered from another letter*

5.1.182 But] LAMBARDE, PORTLAND; Which HERRINGMAN

5.1.182 fright] LAMBARDE, PORTLAND; ſpite HERRINGMAN

5.1.183.1 *Enter . . . Cheater*] PORTLAND, HERRINGMAN; *cropped in* LAMBARDE *to* '*Enter 1 C*'

5.1.184 swoon] HERRINGMAN (ſwound); sound LAMBARDE, PORT-LAND

5.1.186 cannot] *in* LAMBARDE *the 'o' has been added*

5.1.187 wits] PORTLAND, HERRINGMAN; *cropped in* LAMBARDE *to* 'wi'

5.1.189 first] PORTLAND, HERRINGMAN; *cropped in* LAMBARDE *to* 'ſ'

5.1.189 Sure] PORTLAND, HERRINGMAN; *altered in* LAMBARDE *from* 'suee'

5.1.189 lives] LAMBARDE, PORTLAND; live HERRINGMAN

5.1.189 wits, neighbours] PORTLAND; neighbo^rs LAMBARDE

5.1.191 as much] LAMBARDE, HERRINGMAN; *not in* PORTLAND

5.1.191 to] PORTLAND, HERRINGMAN; *cropped in* LAMBARDE

5.1.192 on] LAMBARDE, PORTLAND; of HERRINGMAN

5.1.192 all] *followed in the next line in* LAMBARDE *by deleted* 'all'

5.1.193 you are] LAMBARDE; y'are PORTLAND; then y'are HER-RINGMAN

5.1.193 company, Oliver] LAMBARDE, PORTLAND; company HER-RINGMAN

5.1.193–4 and so] LAMBARDE, PORTLAND; ſo HERRINGMAN

5.1.194.1 *Enter [Second] Cheater*] HERRINGMAN; *Enter Cheater* LAMBARDE; *not in* PORTLAND

5.1.195 Fellows] LAMBARDE, PORTLAND; Fellow HERRINGMAN

5.1.195 welcome] *preceded in* LAMBARDE *by deleted* 'quotha'

5.1.197 Fellows] LAMBARDE, PORTLAND; Fellow HERRINGMAN

5.1.197 a] LAMBARDE, PORTLAND; he HERRINGMAN

5.1.197 'em] LAMBARDE, PORTLAND; him HERRINGMAN

5.1.198 fellows] LAMBARDE, PORTLAND; fellow HERRINGMAN

5.1.198 for they are] LAMBARDE, PORTLAND; I am sure th'are HERRINGMAN

5.1.198 o'th'] LAMBARDE, PORTLAND; at the HERRINGMAN

5.1.199 booty's] LAMBARDE, PORTLAND; Booty is HERRINGMAN

5.1.200 eldest] LAMBARDE, HERRINGMAN; *not in* PORTLAND

5.1.200–1 he comes] LAMBARDE, PORTLAND; He's HERRINGMAN

5.1.201–3 pay . . . th'other] LAMBARDE, PORTLAND; buy houſehold-ſtuff | With one pocket, and to pay rent with the other HERRINGMAN

5.1.205 th'one] LAMBARDE, PORTLAND; the one HERRINGMAN

5.1.206 i'th' old] LAMBARDE, PORTLAND; in HERRINGMAN

5.1.206 th'other] LAMBARDE, PORTLAND; the other HERRINGMAN

5.1.207–8 if he] LAMBARDE, PORTLAND; to HERRINGMAN

5.1.208 on] LAMBARDE, PORTLAND; of HERRINGMAN

5.1.209 He comes, he comes] LAMBARDE, PORTLAND; He comes HERRINGMAN

5.1.210 do . . . small] LAMBARDE, PORTLAND; finally HERRINGMAN

5.1.211 comfort] LAMBARDE, HERRINGMAN; comforts PORTLAND

5.1.212 is't] LAMBARDE, PORTLAND; is it HERRINGMAN

5.1.212 key's o'th] LAMBARDE, PORTLAND; Key is on HERRINGMAN

5.1.214 Ay . . . neighbours] LAMBARDE, PORTLAND; Oh neigh-bours here's the part now HERRINGMAN

5.1.216 play's] LAMBARDE, HERRINGMAN; pay is PORTLAND

5.1.217 cheaters] LAMBARDE, PORTLAND; a Cheater HERRINGMAN

5.1.218 son] *in* LAMBARDE *the scribe has first written* 'sons' *and then erased the final 's'*

5.1.219 in's] LAMBARDE; in his PORTLAND, HERRINGMAN

5.1.220 one of those cheaters] LAMBARDE, PORTLAND; ſome of theſe Creatures HERRINGMAN

5.1.220 I'm] LAMBARDE, PORTLAND; I am HERRINGMAN

5.1.222 I'd] LAMBARDE, PORTLAND; I would HERRINGMAN

5.1.223 'em] LAMBARDE, PORTLAND; them HERRINGMAN

5.1.226 way's] LAMBARDE, HERRINGMAN; was PORTLAND

5.1.226 I'm] LAMBARDE, PORTLAND; I am HERRINGMAN

5.1.227 Come, come] LAMBARDE, PORTLAND; Come HERRINGMAN

5.1.227 familiar] LAMBARDE, PORTLAND; moſt familiar HERRING-MAN

5.1.227 takes] LAMBARDE, PORTLAND; take HERRINGMAN

5.1.230 'Twill but fetch] LAMBARDE, PORTLAND; It will fetch HERRINGMAN

5.1.231 so] LAMBARDE, PORTLAND; too HERRINGMAN

5.1.231 at] LAMBARDE, PORTLAND; out HERRINGMAN

5.1.232 th'other] LAMBARDE, HERRINGMAN; the other PORTLAND

5.1.233 money, current money] LAMBARDE, PORTLAND; currant money HERRINGMAN

5.1.233.1 *They draw*] HERRINGMAN; *not in* LAMBARDE *or* PORT-LAND

5.1.234 Ay, so is] LAMBARDE, PORTLAND (I so is); I say 'tis HERRINGMAN

5.1.234 country, country sir] LAMBARDE; Contry Sir PORTLAND; Countries HERRINGMAN

5.1.235 Here's] LAMBARDE, PORTLAND; Here is HERRINGMAN

5.1.235 I'll] LAMBARDE, PORTLAND; I will HERRINGMAN

5.1.236 whos'] LAMBARDE, PORTLAND (whose); who HERRINGMAN

5.1.236 'em] LAMBARDE, PORTLAND; them HERRINGMAN

5.1.237 sir] LAMBARDE, PORTLAND; *not in* HERRINGMAN

5.1.238 Here comes] LAMBARDE, PORTLAND; here's HERRINGMAN

5.1.238 o'th'] LAMBARDE, PORTLAND; of the HERRINGMAN

5.1.240 Pray] LAMBARDE, PORTLAND; Pray you HERRINGMAN

5.1.241 cannot put it off] PORTLAND, HERRINGMAN; *cropped in* LAMBARDE *to* 'Cann'

5.1.242 FIRST CHEATER] LAMBARDE, PORTLAND ('1 Chea' in both texts); 2 Cheat. HERRINGMAN

5.1.242 SECOND CHEATER] LAMBARDE, PORTLAND (2 Chea in both texts); 1 Cheat. HERRINGMAN

5.1.246 an't] LAMBARDE, PORTLAND; if it HERRINGMAN

5.1.246 let's see't] LAMBARDE; lets see it PORTLAND; Let me ſee it HERRINGMAN

5.1.247   to handle money] PORTLAND; *cropped in* LAMBARDE *to* 'to handl'; money HERRINGMAN

5.1.248   on't] LAMBARDE, PORTLAND; on it HERRINGMAN

5.1.248.1   *They…pocket*] HERRINGMAN (*They pick his pocket.*); *not in* LAMBARDE *or* PORTLAND

5.1.249   need to] LAMBARDE, PORTLAND; both need HERRINGMAN

5.1.249   gentlemen] LAMBARDE (gent), PORTLAND (Gentle); *not in* HERRINGMAN

5.1.250   both so] LAMBARDE, PORTLAND; ſo HERRINGMAN

5.1.250   choleric] PORTLAND, HERRINGMAN; *cropped in* LAMBARDE *to* 'choll'

5.1.251   rub] HERRINGMAN; rubbd LAMBARDE, PORTLAND

5.1.251   spare't] LAMBARDE; spare it PORTLAND; spare HERRINGMAN

5.1.252   'tis] LAMBARDE, PORTLAND; It is HERRINGMAN

5.1.253   you'd] LAMBARDE, PORTLAND (y'had); I had HERRINGMAN

5.1.253   'em] LAMBARDE, PORTLAND; them HERRINGMAN

5.1.255   Th'other] LAMBARDE, HERRINGMAN; the other PORTLAND

5.1.255   men] PORTLAND, HERRINGMAN; *cropped in* LAMBARDE

5.1.255.1   *Exeunt…Cheaters*] HERRINGMAN (*Exeunt.*); *not in* LAMBARDE *or* PORTLAND

5.1.256   to see] LAMBARDE, PORTLAND; of HERRINGMAN

5.1.256-7   this fool so cozened] LAMBARDE, PORTLAND; him thus couzen'd HERRINGMAN

5.1.257   the] LAMBARDE, PORTLAND; his HERRINGMAN

5.1.257   mine] LAMBARDE, PORTLAND; my HERRINGMAN

5.1.258   fain] LAMBARDE, PORTLAND; *not in* HERRINGMAN

5.1.258   this thing] LAMBARDE, PORTLAND; these things HERRINGMAN

5.1.261   endure him no longer] LAMBARDE, PORTLAND; no longer endure him HERRINGMAN

5.1.264   without] LAMBARDE, PORTLAND; LAMBARDE; for HERRINGMAN

5.1.265   cheaters] HERRINGMAN; Cheater LAMBARDE, PORTLAND

5.1.268   commit] *in* PORTLAND *the second* 'm' *has been added*

5.1.269   on't] LAMBARDE, PORTLAND; it HERRINGMAN

5.1.269   Officer] LAMBARDE, PORTLAND; Officers HERRINGMAN

5.1.270   CLOWN With me] *Before this line in* HERRINGMAN *only appear the following lines:* '*Glo*. What means your Worſhip? why you'l ſpoil the Play, Sir. | *Sym*. Before the King of *Kent* ſhall be thus ſerv'd, | I'le play the Clown my ſelf, away with him'.

5.1.270   An't] LAMBARDE, PORTLAND; if it HERRINGMAN

5.1.271   as foolish a part] LAMBARDE, PORTLAND; a fooliſh part HERRINGMAN

5.1.272   for't] LAMBARDE, PORTLAND; for it HERRINGMAN

5.1.273   clown] LAMBARDE, HERRINGMAN; Clown's part PORTLAND

5.1.274   to't] LAMBARDE, PORTLAND; to it HERRINGMAN

5.1.275   pocket] LAMBARDE, PORTLAND; Pocket pickt elſe HERRINGMAN

5.1.275   hear him say't] LAMBARDE, PORTLAND; heard them ſay it HERRINGMAN

5.1.275   mine] LAMBARDE, PORTLAND; my HERRINGMAN

5.1.276   he comes] LAMBARDE, PORTLAND; he's come HERRINGMAN

5.1.276   disguise] *in* PORTLAND *the* 's' *has been added above the line with a caret*

5.1.277.1   *Enter…Cheater*] HERRINGMAN; *not in* LAMBARDE *or* PORTLAND

5.1.277.2   *Exit…Clown*] LAMBARDE, PORTLAND; Exit Clown HERRINGMAN (*at* 5.1.274)

5.1.278-9   He spoils all my part] LAMBARDE, PORTLAND; *not in* HERRINGMAN

5.1.280   let's] LAMBARDE, PORTLAND; let us ſee HERRINGMAN

5.1.281.1-2   *He…back*] HERRINGMAN (*at* 5.1.281-7); *not in* LAMBARDE *or* PORTLAND

5.1.282   think now, rascal] LAMBARDE, PORTLAND; not think HERRINGMAN

5.1.282   no fool] LAMBARDE, PORTLAND; a Clown HERRINGMAN

5.1.283   for] LAMBARDE, PORTLAND; too, for HERRINGMAN

5.1.283-4   so like an ass] LAMBARDE, PORTLAND; *not in* HERRINGMAN

5.1.288-91   SIMON Away…thee] LAMBARDE, PORTLAND; *not in* HERRINGMAN

5.1.289   Everyone] PORTLAND; every ones LAMBARDE

5.1.290   his ending but not his] LAMBARDE; there ending but not there PORTLAND

5.1.291   do] PORTLAND; *cropped in* LAMBARDE

5.1.292   let's] LAMBARDE, PORTLAND; let us HERRINGMAN

5.1.293   not] LAMBARDE, PORTLAND, HERRINGMAN; *cropped in* LAMBARDE

5.1.293   forward] LAMBARDE, PORTLAND; forwards HERRINGMAN

5.1.295   fool all the] PORTLAND; *cropped in* LAMBARDE *to* 'foo'; heels all the HERRINGMAN

5.1.296   who's] LAMBARDE, PORTLAND; who is HERRINGMAN

5.1.296   that] *added in* LAMBARDE *above the line with a caret*

5.1.296   laughed now] PORTLAND; *cropped in* LAMBARDE *to* 'laugh'; laugh'd at me HERRINGMAN

5.1.297   the] LAMBARDE, HERRINGMAN; a PORTLAND

5.1.297   pleasure] PORTLAND, HERRINGMAN; *cropped in* LAMBARDE *to* 'p'

5.1.299   King's] PORTLAND, HERRINGMAN; *cropped in* LAMBARDE *to* 'Ki'

5.1.299   better] LAMBARDE, HERRINGMAN; other PORTLAND

5.1.299   amongst] LAMBARDE, PORTLAND; among HERRINGMAN

5.1.300   chosen to] PORTLAND; choſen HERRINGMAN; *cropped in* LAMBARDE *to* 'Choſe'

5.1.301   an't] LAMBARDE, PORTLAND; if it HERRINGMAN

5.1.303   done] PORTLAND, HERRINGMAN; *cropped in* LAMBARDE

5.1.303   'em] LAMBARDE, PORTLAND; them HERRINGMAN

5.1.303   dares] LAMBARDE, PORTLAND; dare HERRINGMAN

5.1.304   now] HERRINGMAN; note PORTLAND, HERRINGMAN; *cropped in* LAMBARDE

5.1.305   here's] LAMBARDE, PORTLAND; here are HERRINGMAN

5.1.305   purse-strings] purse PORTLAND; purſe HERRINGMAN; *cropped in* LAMBARDE *to* 'pu'

5.1.305   defy you] LAMBARDE, PORTLAND; do defie thee HERRINGMAN

5.1.307   an] LAMBARDE, PORTLAND ('and' *in both texts*); if HERRINGMAN

5.1.312   knavery] PORTLAND; Knavery in it HERRINGMAN; *cropped in* LAMBARDE *to* ' | ry'

5.1.313   deceived] PORTLAND, HERRINGMAN; *cropped in* LAMBARDE

5.1.313   in't] LAMBARDE, PORTLAND; in it HERRINGMAN

5.1.314   or] PORTLAND, HERRINGMAN; *cropped in* LAMBARDE

5.1.316   An] LAMBARDE, PORTLAND ('and' *in both texts*); If HERRINGMAN

5.1.316   mine now] LAMBARDE, PORTLAND; my purse HERRINGMAN

5.1.316   give't] LAMBARDE, PORTLAND; give it HERRINGMAN

5.1.317   you] LAMBARDE, PORTLAND; thee HERRINGMAN

5.1.317   thou'lt] LAMBARDE, HERRINGMAN; thou wilt PORTLAND

5.1.317   answer't] LAMBARDE; answer it PORTLAND anſwer it HERRINGMAN

5.1.318   do't] LAMBARDE, PORTLAND; do it HERRINGMAN

5.1.320   here's] LAMBARDE, PORTLAND; here is HERRINGMAN

5.1.320   me then] LAMBARDE, PORTLAND; me HERRINGMAN

5.1.320.1-2   *He…exits*] HERRINGMAN (*Throws meal in his face, takes his purſe, & Exit*); *Exit* LAMBARDE, PORTLAND

5.1.324 for he'll] LAMBARDE, PORTLAND; He will HERRINGMAN

5.1.324 and] LAMBARDE, PORTLAND; if HERRINGMAN

5.1.325 A] altered from 'ba' in LAMBARDE

5.1.325 of] LAMBARDE, PORTLAND; on HERRINGMAN

5.1.327 in't, remember] LAMBARDE, PORTLAND; in't HERRINGMAN

5.1.327 Call] LAMBARDE, PORTLAND; Calls HERRINGMAN

5.1.328 as] LAMBARDE, PORTLAND; not in HERRINGMAN

5.1.328 out] LAMBARDE, PORTLAND; out in't HERRINGMAN

5.1.328 Brother] LAMBARDE, PORTLAND; Brothet HERRINGMAN

5.1.330 GRAZIER] LAMBARDE, PORTLAND ('Graz.' in both texts); Felt. HERRINGMAN

5.1.331 my] LAMBARDE, PORTLAND; not in HERRINGMAN

5.1.332 I hope] LAMBARDE, PORTLAND; not in HERRINGMAN

5.1.332 within] LAMBARDE, PORTLAND; within these HERRINGMAN

5.1.333 me] LAMBARDE (added above the line with a caret), PORTLAND; me, now HERRINGMAN

5.1.334 of] PORTLAND, LAMBARDE; on HERRINGMAN

5.1.335 ever hereafter] LAMBARDE, PORTLAND; as long as you live HERRINGMAN

5.1.336 you] LAMBARDE, HERRINGMAN; the PORTLAND

5.1.336 'em] LAMBARDE, PORTLAND; them HERRINGMAN

5.1.337 pleased and edified] THIS EDITION; pleasd edifyde LAMBARDE, PORTLAND; pleas'd HERRINGMAN

5.1.338 exercise] LAMBARDE, PORTLAND; exercife. Ha, ha, ha HERRINGMAN

5.1.339 that] altered in LAMBARDE from 'this'

5.1.339 is that rascal's dust he] LAMBARDE, PORTLAND; was the duft | The Rascal HERRINGMAN

5.1.341 'Tis] LAMBARDE, PORTLAND; 'Twas HERRINGMAN

5.1.341 an't] LAMBARDE, PORTLAND; if it HERRINGMAN

5.1.342 I'm] LAMBARDE, PORTLAND; I am HERRINGMAN

5.1.342 on't] LAMBARDE, PORTLAND; of it HERRINGMAN

5.1.343 on't] LAMBARDE, PORTLAND; it HERRINGMAN

5.1.346 on't] LAMBARDE, PORTLAND; it HERRINGMAN

5.1.350 he has] LAMBARDE, PORTLAND; the Rafcal hath HERRINGMAN

5.1.351 the rascal] LAMBARDE, PORTLAND; not in HERRINGMAN

5.1.352 em in's] LAMBARDE (the 'e' has been altered from 's'), PORTLAND; them in his HERRINGMAN

5.1.352 than] LAMBARDE, PORTLAND (then); As HERRINGMAN

5.1.353 done] LAMBARDE, PORTLAND; done mine HERRINGMAN

5.1.353.1 Enter Clerk] LAMBARDE, PORTLAND; not in HERRINGMAN

5.1.354 Where's] LAMBARDE, PORTLAND; Where is HERRINGMAN

5.1.357 You're] LAMBARDE, PORTLAND (y'are); You are HERRINGMAN

5.1.357 CLERK] LAMBARDE, HERRINGMAN; not in PORTLAND, although the speech has been ruled off

5.1.357-8 cheaters professed] LAMBARDE (Cheaters pʳofest); Cheaters and profest PORTLAND; profeffed Cheaters HERRINGMAN

5.1.358 three spoons too] LAMBARDE, PORTLAND; two filver fpoons HERRINGMAN

5.1.361 or two] PORTLAND, HERRINGMAN; cropped in LAMBARDE

5.1.361 they] LAMBARDE, PORTLAND; which they HERRINGMAN

5.1.362 worst] LAMBARDE, PORTLAND; worfe HERRINGMAN

5.1.363 on't] LAMBARDE, PORTLAND; of it HERRINGMAN

5.1.365 could…into't] LAMBARDE; Could looke intot PORTLAND; could fee to look into it HERRINGMAN

5.1.366 slaves] altered in LAMBARDE from 'knaves'

5.1.367.1 Enter Hengist] LAMBARDE (at 5.1.364), PORTLAND (at 365), HERRINGMAN (at 5.1.365)

5.1.368-9 GLOVER 'Ods…lighted] before this line in HERRINGMAN only appears the line 'Heng. Where's Mr. Mayor?'

5.1.368 Kent's] LAMBARDE, PORTLAND; Kent is HERRINGMAN

5.1.368 new] LAMBARDE, PORTLAND; newly HERRINGMAN

5.1.370 Where…he] LAMBARDE; where is he, wheers he PORTLAND; where is he HERRINGMAN

5.1.371 O] LAMBARDE, PORTLAND; not in HERRINGMAN

5.1.372 welcome] PORTLAND, HERRINGMAN; cropped in LAMBARDE to 'we'

5.1.373 Now where's] LAMBARDE, PORTLAND; Where is HERRINGMAN

5.1.373 our] preceded in PORTLAND by deleted 'of'

5.1.374 As] LAMBARDE, PORTLAND; Ah HERRINGMAN

5.1.374 se'night] LAMBARDE; night PORTLAND; fevenight HERRINGMAN

5.1.377 mine] LAMBARDE; my PORTLAND, HERRINGMAN

5.1.379 man's] LAMBARDE, PORTLAND; man is HERRINGMAN

5.1.380 all the villainy] LAMBARDE, PORTLAND; the jeft of it HERRINGMAN

5.1.380 'tis] LAMBARDE, PORTLAND; is HERRINGMAN

5.1.381 been] altered in PORTLAND from another word

5.1.381 'tis] LAMBARDE, PORTLAND; it is HERRINGMAN

5.1.382 to] PORTLAND, HERRINGMAN; cropped in LAMBARDE

5.1.382 but] LAMBARDE, PORTLAND; not in HERRINGMAN

5.1.383 suppertime] PORTLAND; cropped in LAMBARDE to 'sup | time'; Supper HERRINGMAN

5.1.383 on't] LAMBARDE, PORTLAND; of it HERRINGMAN

5.1.383.1 Enter Gentleman] LAMBARDE, PORTLAND; Enter a Gentleman. HERRINGMAN

5.1.387 They're] LAMBARDE, PORTLAND; They are HERRINGMAN

5.1.389 in Britain's] PORTLAND; in Brittaine LAMBARDE; of Britifh HERRINGMAN

5.1.393 afore] LAMBARDE, PORTLAND; e're HERRINGMAN

5.1.394 Set forward] After these words in LAMBARDE and PORTLAND appears the direction 'Exeunt'; it is clear from the text that Hengist does not exit until 5.1.397; not in HERRINGMAN.

5.1.395 I'll] LAMBARDE, PORTLAND; I will HERRINGMAN

5.1.397 Unreasonable] LAMBARDE, PORTLAND; Unfeafonable HERRINGMAN

5.1.397 Exit…Gentleman] HERRINGMAN (Exit cum fuis.); Exit LAMBARDE, PORTLAND

5.1.398 war] LAMBARDE, HERRINGMAN; Warrs PORTLAND

5.1.398 ones] LAMBARDE, PORTLAND; men HERRINGMAN

5.1.400 sight's] LAMBARDE, PORTLAND; fight is HERRINGMAN

5.1.400-1 eyes pulled out] HERRINGMAN (eyes pull'd out); eyes LAMBARDE (a later hand has added 'plvckt out' above this word and then altered it to 'putt out'), PORTLAND

5.1.402 Hang thee! Mine eyes?] LAMBARDE, PORTLAND; My eyes? hang thee HERRINGMAN

5.1.403 'em] LAMBARDE, PORTLAND; them HERRINGMAN

5.1.403 that's] LAMBARDE, PORTLAND; That is HERRINGMAN

5.1.403 resolution] LAMBARDE, PORTLAND; refolution. Ha, ha, ha HERRINGMAN

5.1.403.1 Exeunt] PORTLAND, HERRINGMAN; Exeunt omnes LAMBARDE

5.2 LAMBARDE (Scena 2ᵃ), PORTLAND (Scᵃ 2ᵃ); ACT. 5. SCENA 2. HERRINGMAN (preceded by catchword 'Aĉtus')

5.2.0.1 Enter…Soldiers] LAMBARDE, PORTLAND; Enter Aurelius and Uther with Soldiers, (Vortiger and Horfus above.) HERRINGMAN

5.2.2 So fortified] LAMBARDE, PORTLAND; not in HERRINGMAN

5.2.4 I'th'] LAMBARDE, PORTLAND; In the HERRINGMAN

5.2.4 wrath] Before this word in PORTLAND the scribe has left a large gap, perhaps indicating that he had trouble initially reading his copy and left enough room to fill in later what he could not yet decipher.

5.2.5 haste] LAMBARDE, PORTLAND (hast); Hence HERRINGMAN

5.2.6   till't] LAMBARDE, PORTLAND; till it HERRINGMAN

5.2.6.2   *Enter . . . walls*] LAMBARDE, PORTLAND; *not in* HERRINGMAN (*see note on 5.2.0.1*)

5.2.10   sighting now] LAMBARDE (*altered from* 'sighing not'); sighing PORTLAND; lightning now HERRINGMAN

5.2.13   it] LAMBARDE, PORTLAND; itſelf HERRINGMAN

5.2.14   VORTIGER] *preceded in* LAMBARDE *by deleted* 'Aure:'

5.2.15   on't] LAMBARDE, PORTLAND; of it HERRINGMAN

5.2.16   agone] LAMBARDE, PORTLAND (agen); ago HERRINGMAN

5.2.18   'em] LAMBARDE (*preceded by deleted* 'him'), PORTLAND; them HERRINGMAN

5.2.19   'em over] LAMBARDE, PORTLAND; them HERRINGMAN

5.2.20   'em] LAMBARDE, PORTLAND; them HERRINGMAN

5.2.24   it] LAMBARDE, HERRINGMAN; it now PORTLAND

5.2.24   now] PORTLAND, HERRINGMAN; *cropped in* LAMBARDE *to* 'n'

5.2.25   lord] PORTLAND, HERRINGMAN; *cropped in* LAMBARDE *to* 'Lor'

5.2.28   And] LAMBARDE, PORTLAND; *not in* HERRINGMAN

5.2.30   desert] LAMBARDE, PORTLAND; juſt defert HERRINGMAN

5.2.30   it fell to't] LAMBARDE, PORTLAND; *not in* HERRINGMAN

5.2.31   lesser] LAMBARDE; less PORTLAND; pettier HERRINGMAN

5.2.32   begin] LAMBARDE, PORTLAND; began HERRINGMAN

5.2.33   before I'd] LAMBARDE, PORTLAND; ere I had HERRINGMAN

5.2.34   I'm . . . condition] LAMBARDE, PORTLAND; *not in* HERRINGMAN

5.2.34   i'th' same] LAMBARDE (ith som); it some PORTLAND

5.2.37   could not but] LAMBARDE, PORTLAND; were bound to HERRINGMAN

5.2.37   afterward] LAMBARDE, PORTLAND; after HERRINGMAN

5.2.38   to do't] LAMBARDE ('doot' *altered from* 'Loot'), PORTLAND; to't HERRINGMAN

5.2.39   'em] LAMBARDE, PORTLAND; them HERRINGMAN

5.2.40   faithful] LAMBARDE, PORTLAND; a faithful HERRINGMAN

5.2.41-9   *Vortiger 'Tis . . . do't*] LAMBARDE, PORTLAND; *not in* HERRINGMAN

5.2.44   dangerous] *in* LAMBARDE *the* 'n' *has been added above the line with a caret*

5.2.46   Extremity] LAMBARDE; extremities PORTLAND

5.2.49   those] LAMBARDE, PORTLAND; thefe HERRINGMAN

5.2.50   death in] HERRINGMAN; in teach LAMBARDE, PORTLAND

5.2.50   think] LAMBARDE, PORTLAND; hold HERRINGMAN

5.2.51   acception] HERRINGMAN; exception LAMBARDE, PORTLAND

5.2.52   those] LAMBARDE, PORTLAND; whose HERRINGMAN

5.2.53   lord] LAMBARDE, PORTLAND; Lords HERRINGMAN

5.2.54   those] LAMBARDE, PORTLAND; them HERRINGMAN

5.2.55   none] LAMBARDE, HERRINGMAN; nowe PORTLAND

5.2.56   my lords] LAMBARDE, PORTLAND; *not in* HERRINGMAN

5.2.58   your] HERRINGMAN; their LAMBARDE, PORTLAND

5.2.58   love] LAMBARDE, PORTLAND; loves HERRINGMAN

5.2.59   Was] LAMBARDE, PORTLAND; Were HERRINGMAN

5.2.60   pagan] PORTLAND, HERRINGMAN; paga LAMBARDE

5.2.60   woman] LAMBARDE, PORTLAND; wound HERRINGMAN

5.2.60   thou'dst] LAMBARDE; thou hadst PORTLAND; th'hadſt HERRINGMAN

5.2.60   slept free] LAMBARDE, PORTLAND; kept thee free HERRINGMAN

5.2.62   Was this] LAMBARDE, PORTLAND; This was HERRINGMAN

5.2.64   lord] PORTLAND; *cropped in* LAMBARDE; Lords HERRINGMAN

5.2.68   these] LAMBARDE, PORTLAND; those HERRINGMAN

5.2.72   thinks] PORTLAND, HERRINGMAN; *cropped in* LAMBARDE *to* 'think'

5.2.76   Mine] LAMBARDE, PORTLAND; *not in* HERRINGMAN

5.2.77   VORTIGER Will't do't? | HERSUS What if it would?] LAMBARDE, PORTLAND; *not in* HERRINGMAN

5.2.77   Will't] LAMBARDE; will it PORTLAND

5.2.77   will it] LAMBARDE; will't PORTLAND

5.2.78   it would] LAMBARDE, PORTLAND; 'twould doe't HERRINGMAN

5.2.79   words] LAMBARDE, PORTLAND; word HERRINGMAN

5.2.80   He] LAMBARDE, PORTLAND; it HERRINGMAN

5.2.80   yielded up] PORTLAND, HERRINGMAN; *cropped in* LAMBARDE *to* 'yeilde'

5.2.80-1   I . . . lords] LAMBARDE, PORTLAND; *not in* HERRINGMAN

5.2.81   do't] LAMBARDE, PORTLAND; do it HERRINGMAN

5.2.86.1   *He . . . Hersus*] HERRINGMAN (*Stabs him*); *not in* LAMBARDE *or* PORTLAND

5.2.87   more] LAMBARDE, PORTLAND; other HERRINGMAN

5.2.88   its] HERRINGMAN; it LAMBARDE, PORTLAND

5.2.89   has thy] LAMBARDE, HERRINGMAN; hasty PORTLAND

5.2.93   Ha, ha] LAMBARDE, PORTLAND; Ha, ha, ha HERRINGMAN

5.2.94   on't] LAMBARDE, PORTLAND; of it HERRINGMAN

5.2.96   thou art] LAMBARDE, PORTLAND; th'art HERRINGMAN

5.2.96-7   You . . . sir. | Roxena] HERRINGMAN; Roxena you Change to soone sir LAMBARDE, PORTLAND

5.2.97   thou'st] LAMBARDE; thou has PORTLAND; th'hast HERRINGMAN

5.2.97   thine] LAMBARDE, PORTLAND; thy HERRINGMAN

5.2.99   Your] THIS EDITION; you LAMBARDE, PORTLAND; the HERRINGMAN

5.2.99   violence is] LAMBARDE; violent PORTLAND; violence of whirl-winds HERRINGMAN

5.2.100   sits] LAMBARDE, HERRINGMAN; is PORTLAND

5.2.106   change] *in* LAMBARDE *the scribe has altered the first two letters in this word from* 'st'

5.2.110   trump] LAMBARDE, HERRINGMAN; trumpet PORTLAND

5.2.112   I . . . hope] LAMBARDE, PORTLAND; *not in* HERRINGMAN

5.2.112-13   HERSUS Hold . . . quickly] LAMBARDE, PORTLAND; *this appears after* 'poison' (5.2.116) *in* HERRINGMAN

5.2.113.1-2   *Vortiger . . . fear*] HERRINGMAN (*They ſtab each other. Rox. enters in fear*); *not in* LAMBARDE *or* PORTLAND

5.2.114   save me] HERRINGMAN; saue LAMBARDE, PORTLAND

5.2.114   flame] PORTLAND; *cropped in* LAMBARDE *to* 'flam'; flame HERRINGMAN

5.2.115   It's] LAMBARDE, PORTLAND; 'Tis HERRINGMAN

5.2.115   poor Vortiner] LAMBARDE, PORTLAND; young *Vortimer* HERRINGMAN

5.2.116   out thy soul] LAMBARDE, PORTLAND; thy ſoul out HERRINGMAN

5.2.118   VORTIGER Slave . . . lord] LAMBARDE, PORTLAND; *not in* HERRINGMAN

5.2.119   Hear me, help me] LAMBARDE, PORTLAND; Oh hear me HERRINGMAN

5.2.119-33   Hear . . . consumed] As at 3.1.53-60, *in* LAMBARDE and PORTLAND *the scribes have marked these lines for deletion, from* 'Hear me, help me' *to* 'To see me yet consumed', *by ruling them off*; 5.2.120-31 *are not in* HERRINGMAN.

5.2.123   torment] PORTLAND; *cropped in* LAMBARDE *to* 'Tormen'

5.2.126   sufferings] PORTLAND; *cropped in* LAMBARDE *to* 'suffering'

5.2.132   succour] *added in* LAMBARDE *above deleted* 'suffer'

5.2.135   left] LAMBARDE, HERRINGMAN; left yet PORTLAND

5.2.136.1   *Both . . . [and dies]*] HERRINGMAN (*Both ſtab, Hor. falls.*); *not in* LAMBARDE *or* PORTLAND

5.2.139-41   See . . . actions] LAMBARDE, PORTLAND; *not in* HERRINGMAN

5.2.142   waxes nearer now] THIS EDITION (J.J.); was nearer now LAMBARDE; was neerest now PORTLAND; comes nearer HERRINGMAN

5.2.142 fountains] LAMBARDE (*followed by deleted* 'weare'), PORT-
LAND; fountains fall HERRINGMAN

5.2.143 Guile...blessing] LAMBARDE, PORTLAND, *not in* HERRING-
MAN

5.2.146 O help, help, help] LAMBARDE, PORTLAND; Help, help
HERRINGMAN

5.2.146.1 *She...dies*] HERRINGMAN (*She falls.*); *not in* LAMBARDE
or PORTLAND

5.2.147 torments] LAMBARDE, PORTLAND; torment HERRINGMAN

5.2.152–4 Give...me] LAMBARDE, PORTLAND; *not in* HERRINGMAN

5.2.154 mystical] LAMBARDE, HERRINGMAN; my mystical PORT-
LAND

5.2.156 for a] LAMBARDE, PORTLAND; a most HERRINGMAN

5.2.157 end] LAMBARDE (*the scribe has first written* 'ends' *and
then deleted the final* 's'), HERRINGMAN; ends PORTLAND

5.2.157 'em] LAMBARDE, PORTLAND; them HERRINGMAN

5.2.157.1 *He falls [and dies]*] HERRINGMAN (*He falls*); *falls* LAM-
BARDE, PORTLAND

5.2.157 now] LAMBARDE, PORTLAND; *not in* HERRINGMAN

5.2.158 yon] LAMBARDE, HERRINGMAN (yond); that PORTLAND

5.2.161 injured] LAMBARDE ('iniurd' *altered from* 'inurd'); ruind
PORTLAND; murthered HERRINGMAN

5.2.163–5 Too...few] LAMBARDE, PORTLAND; *not in* HERRINGMAN

5.2.163 clear-eyed] LAMBARDE; cleared PORTLAND

5.2.165.1–2 Enter...prisoner] LAMBARDE (*cropped to* 'Devon
Staff: | Hengist priso'), PORTLAND; Enter Hengift, Devon. Staf.
& Soldiers. HERRINGMAN

5.2.166 How now, my lords] LAMBARDE, PORTLAND; How now!
HERRINGMAN

5.2.168 lies] LAMBARDE, PORTLAND; now lye HERRINGMAN

5.2.170 fierce] LAMBARDE, PORTLAND; deep HERRINGMAN

5.2.172, 175 gentleman] LAMBARDE, PORTLAND; *1 Lor.* HERRING-
MAN

5.2.175 sticks] LAMBARDE, HERRINGMAN; strikes PORTLAND

5.2.182 tasted liberty that lay] LAMBARDE, PORTLAND; tafte our
liberty, who liv'd HERRINGMAN

5.2.189 insolence and treason] LAMBARDE, HERRINGMAN; Insolent treason PORTLAND

5.2.190 bid you] PORTLAND, HERRINGMAN; bid yoᵘ bid yoᵘ LAM-
BARDE

5.2.191 redemption] *in* LAMBARDE *the* 'd' *has been altered from*
'n'

5.2.191 on] *in* LAMBARDE *the* 'o' *has been altered from a* 'u'

5.2.193–5 You...lords] LAMBARDE, PORTLAND; You richly came
provided, I underftood | Not your deferts till now; my
honoured Lords HERRINGMAN

5.2.194 Hengist, King of Kent] LAMBARDE; King of Kent PORT-
LAND

5.2.195 desert] LAMBARDE; desarts PORTLAND; deferts HERRING-
MAN

5.2.195 lords] LAMBARDE, PORTLAND; honoured lords HERRING-
MAN

5.2.202 land must] LAMBARDE, PORTLAND; must doe't HERRING-
MAN

5.2.206 When I'm content, it must be when I'm clay] LAM-
BARDE, PORTLAND; To limit my Ambition, a full cure | For
all my fading hopes and fickly fears; | Nor fhall it be lefs
we come to me now | Then a frefh acquifition would have
been | Unto my new built Kingdoms; Life to me, | ('Lefs it
be glorious) is a mifery. HERRINGMAN

5.2.207–13 My...clear] LAMBARDE, PORTLAND; That pleafure
we will do you; Lead him out, | And when we have inflicted
our juft doom | On his ufurping head, it will become | Our
pious care to see this Realm fecur'd | From the Convulfions
it hath long endur'd. HERRINGMAN

5.2.209 Glories] LAMBARDE; glory PORTLAND

5.2.214–34 DEVONSHIRE Had...virtues] LAMBARDE, PORTLAND;
not in HERRINGMAN

5.2.217 kneel] *in* PORTLAND *the scribe has altered the* 'k' *in this
word from* 'l'

5.2.220 It] PORTLAND; at LAMBARDE

5.2.220 ruin] LAMBARDE; ruins PORTLAND

5.2.221 it is] LAMBARDE; 'tis PORTLAND

5.2.225 kingdom] PORTLAND; *cropped in* LAMBARDE *to* 'Kingd'

5.2.232 With] *preceded in* PORTLAND *by deleted* 'whi'

5.2.232 adulterate] LAMBARDE; adulterous PORTLAND

5.2.234 *Flourish. Exeunt*] LAMBARDE, PORTLAND; *Exeunt omnes.*
HERRINGMAN

5.2.234.1 *Finis Actus Quintus*] *Finis | Hengist King off Kent*
LAMBARDE; *Finis | Hengist King of Kent* PORTLAND; FINIS
HERRINGMAN

Epilogue.0.1–Epilogue.10.1 *Enter...Music*] LAMBARDE, PORT-
LAND; *not in* HERRINGMAN

Epilogue.4 this] LAMBARDE; they PORTLAND

STAGE DIRECTIONS

Although LAMBARDE has been used as control-text for this edition,
its stage directions are frequently cropped, and thus PORTLAND
has been used to supply stage directions when they are cropped
in LAMBARDE. PORTLAND varies only slightly (in accidentals) from
LAMBARDE in the stage directions; both manuscripts vary significantly from HERRINGMAN. Some missing or incomplete stage
directions have been supplied by HERRINGMAN. Below appear separate lists of stage directions as supplied in LAMBARDE, PORTLAND,
and HERRINGMAN. Although the LAMBARDE and PORTLAND scribes
have been inconsistent in rendering stage directions in italic hand,
the directions transcribed below from both manuscripts have been
regularized to italic.

LAMBARDE **Stage Directions**

1.0.0.2 *Enter Raynulph a Munck, yᵉ pʳsenter*

1.0.18 *Exit*

1.1.0.1 *Showte Enter Vortiger*

1.1.16 *Enter | Deuon St | afford:*

1.1.28 *Exit*

1.1.28.1–3 *Musick Enter Certaine Muncks, Germanicus; Constan-
tius being | one singing as Precession.*

1.1.55.1 *show (at 1.1.54)*

1.1.106.1 *flouri*

1.1.161.1 *flourish*

1.1.161.1 *E*

1.1.182.1 *Ent | Gra (at 1.1.178–9)*

1.1.193.1 *Exᵗ*

1.2.0.1–12 *Musique Dumb show: ffortune is discouered vppon an
alter, in | her hand a golden round full of Lotts: Enter Hengist
| and Hersus with others they Draw Lotts and hang them vp |
with Joy, soe* imbracee each o *all departs saueing | Hengist: and
Hersus who kneeles and imbrace | each other as partners in one
fortune, to them | Enter Roxena seeminge to take her leaue of |
Hengist her father; But especeally priuately & | warily of Hersus*

her lover she departs weepeing: | and Hengist: and Hersus goe to
the doore and Bring | in their souldiers with Drum | and Collors
and soe | march forth

1.2.16.1 *Exit*

1.3.0.1–2 *Enter Vortiger felmonger, Buttonmunger Grazier Petit*

1.3.24 *Exit*

1.3.44.1 *Enter Constant | 2 Gent (at 1.3.43)*

1.3.71.1 *Ex | Ge*

1.3.117.1 *Exevnt*

1.3.121.1 *Enter | V*

1.3.142.1 *E*

1.3.156 *Exit Vort: (at 1.3.155)*

1.3.185.1 *Enter Vo | & Gentl (at 1.3.184)*

1.3.187 *Exit Castiza*

1.3.193 *Exit Vortig:*

1.3.209.1 *Ente | Deuon*

1.3.233.1 *Exeunt Omnes*

2.1.0.2 *Musique.*

2.1.0.2 *Entiger & Castiza:*

2.1.26 *Exit*

2.1.37 *Ex^t*

2.2.0.1–24 *Hoboys Dumb show. Enter 2 Villaines to them Vortiger
| seemeing to solissitt him giues them gold, then sweares |
them—Exit Vortiger Enter to them Constantius in | priuate
meditation, they rudely Come to him strike | downe his Booke
and Draw their swordes vpon him | he fairely spredds his armes,
and yeildes to thire furys, | at wch they seeme to be ouer Come w^{th}
pittye, But lookeing | on ye gold kills him as hee turns his Back,
and hurry away | his bodye. Enter Vortiger Deuon: Stafford in
| priuate Conference: to them Enter y^e murderers | p^{re}senting
y^e head to Vortiger, he seems to express much | sorrow, and
before y^e astonished Lordes, makes | officers lay hold on em; who
offering to Com to= | wardes Vortiger are Commanded to be
hurryed | away as to execution: then y^e Lordes all seeming |
respect Crowne Vortiger, then brings in Castiza, who seems to be
brought in | unwillingly Deuon: | & Stafford who Crowne her
and then giue her | to Vortiger, she going forth wth him with a
Kinde of | Constraind Consent; then enter Aurelius & Vther | y^e
two | Brothers who much astonished seeme to fly | for safety.*

2.2.20 *Exit:*

2.3.0.1–2 *Enter Vortiger a Gentleman*

2.3.9.1 *Exit Gentleman*

2.3.17.1 *Showte (at 2.3.19)*

2.3.19.1 *Enter Gen*

2.3.25.1 *Hengist | Enter Her | sus Drum | and Soldier (at 2.3.20–
2)*

2.3.44.1 *Exeunt omnes (at 2.3.42–3)*

2.4.0.1–2.4.1 *Alarums and skirmish. Enter Vortiger & Gentleman*

2.4.9.1–2 *Enter H | Horsus, | Co | soldiers le | prisoner (at 2.4.7)*

2.4.30.1 *Enter Symon | with a hide*

2.4.124 *Exit Symo:*

2.4.160.1 *showtes flourish (at 2.4.159)*

2.4.162.1 *Enter Gent (at 2.4.161)*

2.4.196.1–2 *flourish | Enter | Rox*

2.4.266.1 *flourish | Cornetts Exe: (at 2.4.264)*

3.1.0.2 *Enter Hersus: Roxena:*

3.1.81 *Exit Rox*

3.1.87.1 *E | Vor:*

3.1.184.1 *Exevnt*

3.2.0.1 *Enter Castiza A Booke: two Ladyes:*

3.2.14.1 *Ex Ladyes*

3.2.22.1 *E | Vort: | Hers (at 3.2.20)*

3.2.29.1 *Ex^t & enter aga*

3.2.100.1 *Ex^t Vort: Castiza*

3.2.109.1 *Exit*

3.3.0.1 *Enter Hengist:*

3.3.7 *Barbor & | Taylor w^{th}*

3.3.10.1 *A noyse (at 3.3.4)*

3.3.15.1 *Enter Gente*

3.3.23.1 *Exit Gent (at 3.3.22)*

3.3.29.1 *Enter (at 3.3.28)*

3.3.44.1 *Enter Barbor (at 3.3.42)*

3.3.65.1 *Enter Taylor*

3.3.78 *Enter Glouer But | Brazier*

3.3.118.1–2 *Enter Symo | &Oliuer (at 3.3.114)*

3.3.118.1–2 *fellmonger Brazier | Buttonmunger (at 3.3.116)*

3.3.155.1 *Exit Hengist*

3.3.184 *Ex^t*

3.3.242.1 *Enter Hengist | & Roxena*

3.3.252.1 *Exevnt*

3.3.256.3 *Enter Vort: & | Hersus*

3.3.284.1 *Enter Castiza*

3.3.321.2 *Musique Exevnt Omnes*

4.1.0.2–5 *Enter Vortiger Castiz | two Ladyes | Roxena Devon:
Staff: at one Doore Sy | And his | Brethren at the other*

4.1.19.1 *musique Exevnt King Lordes*

4.1.25.1 *Exevnt:*

4.2.0.1–5 *Hoboys the King and his traine mett by Hengist and
Hersus | they salute & Exevnt; while the Banquet is Brought
forth | Musique plays; Enter Vortig: Hors, Dev: Staff: Castiza
Roxena | and two Ladies.*

4.2.35.1 *Mu (at 4.2.34)*

4.2.166.1 *Ex^t*

4.2.222.1 *Musique | Exvnt*

4.3.0.1–21 *Hoboyes Dumb show Enter Lupus Germanus Devon
Staffo: Lea | Vortiner: they seate him in ye throne & Crowne him
King, E | Vortiger in greate passion and submission they neglect
him, | Roxena expressing greate fury & discontent, they leade
ou | Vortiner, and leaue Vortiger and Roxena she suborne tw |
saxons to murder Vortiner they sweare performance | secresie and
Ex^t wth Roxena, then Vortiger left alone draw | his sword and
offers to run himselfe thereon Enter Hersu | prevents him, then
ye Lordes Enter againe and Ex^t Hersus | is brought in ye Bodye
of Vortiner in a Chaire dead, the | in amazem^t and sorrow take
Vortiger and vpon his su | ion restore him, sweareing him against
ye saxons, t | Enter Hengist with diuers saxons: Vortiger and y^e
re | wth their swordes drawn threaten their expulsion: whereat
| Hengist ~~with diuers saxons~~ amazd sendes one to entreate | a
peaceable parly, wch seeming to be granted by layeng down |
there weapons Exevnt seuerally*

4.3.0.22 *Enter Raynulph (at 4.3.0.21)*

4.3.16 *Exit*

4.4.0.1 *Enter Hengist Gentleman & Saxons*

4.4.120.1 *Enter | Hersus (at 4.4.119)*

4.4.135 *E*

4.4.141 *Exit*

5.1.0.2–4 *Enter Symon: Clark Glouer fell | etci: graz Musique*

5.1.16.1 *Enter | foot: (at 5.1.14)*

5.1.69.1 *Enter | Cheaters*

5.1.141.1 *Exevnt Cheater (at 5.1.139)*

5.1.152.1 *Showte (at 5.1.154)*

5.1.155.1 *Enter Oliuer*

5.1.183.1 *Enter 1 C*

5.1.208.1 *Enter Clowne*

5.1.277.2 *Ex^t with Clowne*

5.1.320.2 *Exi*

5.1.353.1 *Enter | Clark*

5.1.367.1 *Enter Hengis: (at 5.1.364)*

5.1.383.1   *Enter Gentleman*

5.1.397   *Exevnt:*

5.1.403.1   *Exevnt:*

5.2.0.1   *Enter Aurelius and Vther wth Souldiers*

5.2.6.2   *Vortiger | Horsus on | ye walls (at 5.2.7)*

5.2.165.1–2   *Deuon Staff: l | Hengist priso (at 5.2.164–5)*

5.2.215.1   *Enter Castiza a | Gent (at 5.2.210)*

5.2.234   *fflorish: Exevnt:*

Epilogue.0.1   *Enter Raynulph*

Epilogue.10.1   *Musique*

PORTLAND **Stage Directions**

1.0.0.2   *Enter Raynulph a Munck, ye p^r senter*

1.0.18   *Exit*

1.1.0.1   *Showte   Enter Vortiger*

1.1.17.1   *Enter Deuon. | Staff:*

1.1.28   *Exit*

1.1.28.1–3   *Musique Enter certaine Muncks, Germanicus; | Constantius being | one singing as at Precession.*

1.1.55.1   *showte | within (at 1.1.53–4)*

1.1.106.1   *flourish*

1.1.161.1   *flourish*

1.1.161.1   *Exevnt*

1.1.182.1   *Enter | 3 Graz | iers (at 1.1.178–9)*

1.1.193.1   *Exit*

1.2.0.1–12   *Musique Dumb show: ffortune is discouered vvpon an Alter | in her hand a golden round full of Lotts: Enter Hengist | and Hersus with others they draw Lotts and hang them vp with | Joy, soe all departs saueing Hengist: and Hersus who kneeles | and imbrace each other as partners in one fortune, to them | Enter Roxena: seeming to take her leaue of of Hengist | her ffather; but especially priuately and warily of Hersus | her lover she departs weepeing: and Hengist: and Hersus | goe to the doore and bring | in their souldiers with Drum | and Coullers and soe march forth*

1.2.16.1   *Exit*

1.3.0.1–2   *Enter Vortiger felmonger, Buttonmunger | Grazier Petitioners*

1.3.24   *Exit*

1.3.44.1   *Enter Constan | & 2 Gentlemen*

1.3.71.1   *Exvnt | Gent*

1.3.117.1   *Exevnt*

1.3.121.1   *Enter | Vortig*

1.3.142.1   *Enter Castiza*

1.3.156   *Exit | Vorti:*

1.3.185.1   *Enter Vort: | & Gentle*

1.3.187   *Exit Castiza*

1.3.193   *Exit Vort:*

1.3.209.1   *Enter | Vort | Devon | Staff (at 1.3.210–12)*

1.3.233.1   *Exeunt Omnes*

2.1.0.2   *Musique.*

2.1.0.2   *Enter Vort: Cast:*

2.1.26   *Exit*

2.2.0.1–24   *Hoboys Dumb show: Enter 2 Villaines to them Vortiger | seemeing to solisit them gives them gold, then swears them | Exit Vortiger Enter to them Constantius in priuate meditation, | they rudely Come to him strike downe his booke and draw there | swordes vpon him he fairely spredds his armes, and yeildes to | there furye, at which they seeme to be ouer come with pittye | Butt looking vpon the gold kills him as hee turns his back | and hurry away his bodye. Enter Vortiger, Deuon: & Stafford | in priuate Conference to them Enter the Murderers pres | ting the*

head to Vortiger, he seems to express much sorrow, and | before the astonished Lordes, makes officers lay hold on ’em, who | offering to Com towardes Vortiger are Commanded to be hurryed | away as to execution: then the Lordes seemeing respect Crowne | Vortiger, then brings in Castiza, who seemes to be brought in | unwillingly Deuon & Stafford who Crowne her and then giue | her to Vortiger, she goeing forth with him, with a Kinde of a | Constraind Consent; then Enter Aurelius & Vther the two | Brothers, who much astonished seeme to fly for safety.

2.2.20   *Exit:*

2.3.0.1–2   *Enter Vortiger a Gentleman*

2.3.9.1   *Exit Gentleman*

2.3.17.1   *Showte (at 2.3.19)*

2.3.19.1   *Enter Gent*

2.3.25.1   *Enter Hengist | Hersus Drum & | Soldiers (at 2.3.21–2)*

2.3.44.1   *Exeunt omnes*

2.4.0.1–2.4.1   *Alarums and skirmish. Enter Vortiger & Gentleman*

2.4.9.1–2   *Enter Heng: Hers: with | Drum Collours, Soldiers | leading prisoners*

2.4.30.1   *Enter Symon | with a hide*

2.4.124   *Exit Symo*

2.4.160.1   *showte flourish (at 2.4.157)*

2.4.162.1   *Enter Gent*

2.4.196.1–2   *flourish Cornet Enter Vort: | Rox: and attendance*

2.4.266.1   *flourish | Cornetts (at 2.4.264) Exeunt*

2.4.266.1   *Exevnt:*

3.1.0.2   *Enter Hersus & Roxena*

3.1.81   *Exit Rox*

3.1.87.1   *Enter | Vort:*

3.1.184.1   *Exeunt*

3.2.0.1   *Enter Castiza A booke: two Ladyes*

3.2.14.1   *Exit Ladyes*

3.2.22.1   *Enter Vort: & | Hersus*

3.2.29.1   *Ex^t & enter againe*

3.2.100.1   *Ext: Vort: Castiz*

3.2.109.1   *Exit*

3.3.0.1   *Enter Hengist:*

3.3.10.1   *A noyse (at 3.3.4)*

3.3.15.1   *Enter Gent*

3.3.23.1   *Exit Gent*

3.3.29.1   *Enter Gent (at 3.3.26)*

3.3.44.1   *Enter Barbor*

3.3.65.1   *Enter Tay*

3.3.118.1–2   *Enter Symon | &Oliuer (at 3.3.114)*

3.3.118.1–2   *fellmongers Braziers | Buttonmongers (at 3.3.116)*

3.3.155.1   *Exit Heng:*

3.3.184   *Exit*

3.3.242.1   *Enter Hengist | & Rox:*

3.3.252.1   *Exeunt*

3.3.256.3   *Enter Vort: & | Hersus*

3.3.284.1   *Enter Castiza*

3.3.321.2   *Musique Exevnt | Omnes*

4.1.0.2–5   *Enter Vort: Castiza two Ladyes, | Roxena Devon: Staff: at one Doore Symon and his | bretheren at the other:*

4.1.19.1   *Musique Exevnt king | and Lordes*

4.1.25.1   *Exevnt:*

4.2.0.1–5   *Hoboys the King and his traine mett by Hengist and | Hersus they salute and Exevnt, while the Banquet | is brought forth Musique plays, Enter Vort: Hers, Devo, | Stafford Castiza Roxe: and two Ladyes.*

4.2.35.1   *Musique (at 4.2.33)*

4.2.166.1   *Exit*

4.2.222.1 *Musique | Exvnt*

4.3.0.1–21 *Hoboyes Dumb show Enter Lupus Germanus Deuon & | Stafford leading Vortimer: they seate him in throne | and Crowne him king, Enter Vortiger in greate passion and | submission they neglect him, then Roxena expressing greate fury | and discontent, they leade out Vortimer, and | leaue Vortiger | and Roxena she subborns tow Saxons to | murder Vortimer | they sweare performance and secresie | and Exit with Roxena, | then Vortiger left alone dwraws | his sword and offers to run | himselfe through Enter | Hersus and preuents him, then the | Lordes enter againe | and Exit Hersus, then is brought in the | bodye of Vortimer | in a Chaire dead, they all in amazement and | sorrow | take Vortiger and vpon his submission restore him | swearing him against the Saxons, then Enter Hen: | with diuers | Saxons Vortiger and the rest with there | swordes drawn threaten | there expulsion: whereat | Hengist amazed sendes one to entreate | a peaceable parly, | which seeming to be granted by laying by | their | weapons Exevnt seuerally*

4.3.0.22 *Enter Raynulph (at 4.3.0.21)*

4.3.16 *Exit*

4.4.0.1 *Enter Hengist Gentlemen & Saxons*

4.4.120.1 *Enter | Hersus*

4.4.135 *Exit*

4.4.141 *Exit*

5.1.0.2–4 *Enter Symon: Clark | Glouer fellmonger etc: graz & | Musique*

5.1.16.1 *Enter | footm: (at 5.1.14)*

5.1.69.1 *Enter Cheaters*

5.1.141.1 *Exevnt Cheater (at 5.1.140)*

5.1.152.1 *showte (at 5.1.154)*

5.1.155.1 *Enter Oliuer*

5.1.183.1 *Enter 1 Che*

5.1.208.1 *Enter Clowne*

5.1.277.2 *Exit wth Clown*

5.1.320.2 *Exit*

5.1.353.1 *Enter Clark:*

5.1.367.1 *Enter Heng: (at 5.1.365)*

5.1.383.1 *Enter Gentleman*

5.1.397 *Exevnt:*

5.1.403.1 *Exvnt:*

5.2.0.1 *Enter Aurelius and Vther wth souldiers*

5.2.6.2 *Vort: Hers: | on ye walls*

5.2.165.1–2 *Enter Deuon | Stafford | leading Heng: | prisoner (at 5.2.164–5)*

5.2.215.1 *Enter Castiza | Gent (at 5.2.210)*

5.2.234 *florish: Exevnt:*

Epilogue.0.1 *Enter Raynuph*

Epilogue.10.1 *Musique*

HERRINGMAN **Stage Directions**

1.0.0.2 *Enter Raynulph*

1.0.18 *Exit*

1.1.0.1 *Shouts within; Then Enter Vortiger.*

1.1.17.1 *Enter De-|von. and | Stafford: (at 1.1.17–19)*

1.1.28.1–3 *Enter Constantius (as a Monck, attended by other | Moncks) | Vortiger ftays him.*

1.1.161.1 *Ex. all | but Vor. (at 1.1.160–1)*

1.1.182.1 *Enter two | Grafiers. (at 1.1.182–3)*

1.1.192 *Exit.*

1.1.193.1 *Exeunt.*

1.2.0.1 *Dumb fhow. Fortune difcovered, in her hand a round Ball full | of Lots; then enters Hengift and Horfus, with | others; they | draw Lots, and having opened them, | all depart, fave Hengift and | Horfus, who kneel | and embrace; then enter Roxena, feeming*

to take | leave of Hengift in great paffion, but more efpeci-|ally | and warily of Horfus, her Lover; fhe departs | one way, Hengift | and Horfus another.

1.2.0.13 *Enter Raynulph.*

1.2.16.1 *Exit.*

1.3.0.1–2 *Enter Vortiger, Feltmonger, Button-maker, Grafier, Pe-|titioners.*

1.3.24 *Exit.*

1.3.44.1 *Enter | Conftan-|tius and | two Gentle-|men. (at 1.3.44–8)*

1.3.117.1 *Exeunt.*

1.3.121.1 *Enter Vortiger.*

1.3.142.1 *Enter | Caftiza. (at 1.3.141–2)*

1.3.156 *Exit.*

1.3.185.1 *As he kiffes her, | Enter Vortiger and | Gentlemen. (at 1.3.186–7)*

1.3.193 *Exit.*

1.3.207 *Exit.*

1.3.209.1 *Enter Vortiger. (at 1.3.212)*

1.3.233.1 *Exeunt:*

2.1.0.2 *Enter Vortiger and Caftiza.*

2.1.26 *Exit.*

2.1.37.1 *Exit.*

2.2.0.1 *Dumb fhow Enter two Villains, to them Vortiger, who | feems to | follicite them with gold, then fwears them, and Ex-|it. Enter Conftantius meditating, they rudely | ftrike down his | Book, draw their Swords, he kneels | and fpreads his arms, | they kill him, hurry him off. | Enter Vortiger, Devonfhire and | Stafford in Con-|ference, to them the Villains prefenting the head, | he feems forrowful, and in rage ftabbs them both. | Then they | crown Vortiger, and fetch in Caftiza, | who comes unwillingly, | he hales her, and they | crown her. Aurelius and Uther Brothers | of Con-|ftantius, feeing him crowned, draw and fly.*

2.2.0.25 *Enter Raynulph.*

2.2.20 *Exit.*

2.3.0.1–2 *Enter Vortiger (Crowned) a Gentleman meeting him.*

2.3.19.1 *Enter a fecond | Gentleman. (at 2.3.18–19)*

2.3.25.1 *Enter Hengift, Horfus, | Souldiers. (at 2.3.25–6)*

2.3.44.1 *Exeunt.*

2.4.0.1–2 *Enter Vortiger and Gentlemen.*

2.4.0.1–2.4.1 *Alarm and | Skirmifhes.*

2.4.9.1–2 *Enter Hengift and Horfus | with Prifoners.*

2.4.30.1 *Enter Symon with a Hide. (at 2.4.33–4)*

2.4.162.1 *Enter a Gentleman.*

2.4.196.1–2 *Florifh.; | Enter Vortiger, | Roxena, & c. (at 2.4.196–8)*

2.4.266.1 *Exeunt.*

3.1.0.2 *Enter Horfus and Roxena.*

3.1.81 *Exit.*

3.1.87 *Enter | Vortiger.*

3.1.183 *Exit.*

3.1.184.1 *Exit.*

3.2.0.1 *Enter Caftiza (with a Book) and two Ladies.*

3.2.14.1 *Exeunt Ladies.*

3.2.22.1 *Enter Vortiger | and Horfus | difguifed.] (at 3.2.18–20)*

3.2.100.1 *Vort. fnatches | her away. (at 3.2.99–100)*

3.2.109.1 *Exeunt.*

3.3.0.1 *Enter Hengift.*

3.3.15.1 *Enter a Gentleman.*

3.3.23.1 *Exit Gentleman. (at 3.3.22)*

3.3.29.1 *Enter Gent.*

3.3.44.1 *Enter Barber.*

3.3.155.1 *Exit.*

3.3.184 *Exit.*

3.3.198   *Here they all cough and hem.*
3.3.209   *They cough and hem again.*
3.3.242.1   *Enter Hengist | and Roxena. (at 3.3.242–3)*
3.3.252.1   *Exit cum suis.*
3.3.256.3   *Enter Vortiger | and Horsus.*
3.3.284.1   *Enter Castiza.*
3.3.321   *Exit.*
4.1.0.2–5   *Enter Symon and all his Brethren, a Mace and Sword before | him, meeting Vortiger, Castiza, Hengist, Roxena, | Horsus, two Ladies.*
4.1.19.1   *Exit cum sociis.*
4.1.25.1   *Ex.*
4.2.0.1–5   *Enter Hengist, Horsus, Vortiger, Devonshire, Stafford, | Castiza, Roxena, Ladies.*
4.2.222.1   *Exeunt all | but Horsus. (at 4.2.221–2)*
4.2.241   *Exit.*
4.3.0.1   *Dumb show. Enter Lupus, Germanus, Devonshire, and Staf-|ford, leading Vortimer, and Crown him: Vorti-|ger comes to them in passion, they neglect him. Enter | Roxena in fury expressing discontent, then they | lead out Vortimer; Roxena gives two Villains | gold to murther him, they swear performance and | go with her: Vortiger offers to run on his sword, | Horsus prevents him, and perswades him; the | Lords bring in Vortimer dead; Vortiger mourns | and submits to them, they swear him, and Crown him, | Then Enters Hengist with Saxons, Vortiger | draws, threatens expulsion, and then sends a Parley, | which Hengist seems to grant by laying down his | weapons, so all depart severally.*
4.3.0.22   *Enter Raynulphus.*
4.3.16   *Exit.*
4.4.0.1   *Enter Hengist with Saxons.*
4.4.40.1   *[Enter Vortiger | and British | Lords. (at 4.4.39–41)*
4.4.112.1   *Exit cum suis.*
4.4.120.1   *Enter Horsus (at 4.4.117)*
4.4.135   *Exit.*

4.4.141   *Exit.*
5.1.0.2–4   *Enter Symon, and his Brethren, Aminadab his Clerk.*
5.1.16.1   *Enter a | Footman. (at 5.1.16–17)*
5.1.33   *Exit.*
5.1.69.1   *Enter Cheaters. (at 5.1.66–7)*
5.1.141.1   *Ex. Players. (at 5.1.139)*
5.1.152.1   *A shout within. (at 5.1.154–5)*
5.1.155.1   *Oliver is | brought in. (at 5.1.160–1)*
5.1.183.1   *Enter 1 Cheater.*
5.1.194.1   *Enter second | Cheater. (at 5.1.195–6)*
5.1.208.1   *Ent. Clown.*
5.1.233.1   *They draw.*
5.1.248.1   *[They pick | his pocket. (at 5.1.17–19)*
5.1.255.1   *Exeunt.*
5.1.277.2   *Exit Clown. (at 5.1.274)*
5.1.277.2   *Enter second Cheater.*
5.1.281.1–2   *He throws off | his Gown, dif-|covering his doublet with | a fatten fore-|part and a | Canvas back. (at 5.1.280–7)*
5.1.320.1–2   *Throws meal | in his face, | takes his purse, | & Exit. (at 5.1.321–4)*
5.1.367.1   *Enter Hengist. (at 5.1.365)*
5.1.383.1   *Enter a Gentleman.*
5.1.397   *Exit cum suis.*
5.1.403.1   *Exeunt.*
5.2.0.1   *Enter Aurelius and Uther with Soldiers, (Vortiger and | Horsus above.)*
5.2.86.1   *Stabs him. (at 5.2.85)*
5.2.113.1–2   *They stab each other. | Rox. enters in fear. (at 5.2.111)*
5.2.136.1   *Both stab, Hor. falls. (at 5.2.135–6)*
5.2.146.1   *She falls.*
5.2.157.1   *He falls.*
5.2.165.1–2   *Enter Hengist, | Devon.Staf. | & Soldiers. (at 5.2.166–8)*
5.2.234   *Exeunt omnes:*

LINEATION NOTES

1.1.15–16   Bondage…can] PORTLAND; Bondage…the| Means…can; Bondage…means| To…can HERRINGMAN

1.1.105–6   Long…King] HERRINGMAN; long…live| King LAMBARDE; long…King PORTLAND

1.1.187–9   What…ruler] THIS EDITION; What…deserved| my…Ruler LAMBARDE; What…well| deserved…a| Ruler PORTLAND; For what? depart…me| You…Ruler HERRINGMAN

1.3.15–16   Say…list] HERRINGMAN; say…list LAMBARDE, PORTLAND

1.3.16–17   I…sum] HERRINGMAN; I…sum LAMBARDE, PORTLAND

1.3.107–8   No…on't] HERRINGMAN; no…on't LAMBARDE; no…com| fort…on't PORTLAND

1.3.160–1   Never…man] HERRINGMAN; never…Man LAMBARDE, PORTLAND

1.3.174–6   To…pureness] BALD; to…pavements,| y'have…pure| ness LAMBARDE; to…pavements| y'have…your| pureness PORTLAND; To…substance| As…pureness| HERRINGMAN

1.3.216–17   But…me] HERRINGMAN; But…me LAMBARDE, PORTLAND

2.4.108–9   Thus…first] PORTLAND; Thus…Captain| set…first LAMBARDE; Thus…learn| set…first HERRINGMAN

2.4.150–3   She's…name] BALD; she's…self| fair…be| but… the| Close…name LAMBARDE; she's…my| self…she| be…has| been…name PORTLAND; She…Maid,| Fair… be| But…desire| Has…name HERRINGMAN

2.4.260–1   O…hope] HERRINGMAN; Oh…hope,| Besides LAMBARDE; oh…that| hope, besides PORTLAND

2.4.263–4   An…again] THIS EDITION; and…I| shall…again LAMBARDE, PORTLAND; If…disease HERRINGMAN

3.1.3–4   O…this] HERRINGMAN; o…is| this LAMBARDE; o… love| is this PORTLAND

3.2.13–14   Not…for] HERRINGMAN; not…she's| a…for LAMBARDE; like…is| made…he's| good for PORTLAND

3.2.87–91   And…without] HERRINGMAN; and…with| darkness…body| I'll…me| that…world| and…without LAMBARDE; and…with| darkness…light| of…not| from… another| world…without PORTLAND

3.3.34–5   Upon…by't] HERRINGMAN; upon…sir| he…by't LAMBARDE; upon…says| Sir…by't PORTLAND

3.3.42–3   Here's…Call] HERRINGMAN; here's…so| reasonable LAMBARDE; here's…are| grown PORTLAND

3.3.307–10   And…me] HERRINGMAN; and…reading| for… of| favour…my| Lord…me LAMBARDE; and…reading| for…make| of…and| now…conceitedly| Gone…me PORTLAND

4.2.147–9 You…And] HERRINGMAN; you…goodness| And LAMBARDE; you…with| your good PORTLAND

4.4.89–90 Faith…Kent] HERRINGMAN; 'Faith…Kent LAMBARDE, PORTLAND

4.4.91–2 The…possession] PORTLAND, HERRINGMAN; the…possession LAMBARDE

4.4.134–5 O…thee] HERRINGMAN; oh…thee LAMBARDE; oh…made| vp…thee PORTLAND

5.2.59–60 And…free] HERRINGMAN; and…thou'dst| slept free LAMBARDE; and…pagan| woman…free PORTLAND

5.2.79–80 It…up] BALD; It…up LAMBARDE, HERRINGMAN; it…he| shall…up PORTLAND

5.2.80–1 I…do't] THIS EDITION; I…do't LAMBARDE; I…Can| not do't PORTLAND; Believe…it HERRINGMAN

5.2.86–7 See…breeds] HERRINGMAN; see…breeds LAMBARDE, PORTLAND

5.2.98–9 Burst…whirlwinds] BALD; Burst…whirlwinds LAMBARDE, PORTLAND, HERRINGMAN

5.2.101–2 Deafen…world] HERRINGMAN; deafen…ye| world LAMBARDE; deafen…that| starts…world PORTLAND

5.2.113–16 O…poison] HERRINGMAN; oh…flame| follows… Prince| whose…poison LAMBARDE; oh…save| the…poor| Vortiner…by| poison PORTLAND

WIT AT SEVERAL WEAPONS

Edited by Michael Dobson

Wit at Several Weapons (*BEPD* 666) was first published in the Beaumont and Fletcher folio of 1647 (Wing B1581), where it appears as the last of the four plays in section 6, occupying signatures 6I3-6L6ᵛ: exhaustive work by Iain Sharp has identified this section as the work of the printer Moses Bell. In common with five other works in the 1647 folio (including another Middleton play, *Valour*), it had not appeared in the Stationers' Register when the rest of its contents were entered in September 1646, and would not do so until 29 June 1660, when a second edition of the collection was probably already under consideration:

> *Ent H.Robinson and H.Moseley: severall plays, vizt.*
> *The False One The Nice Valour, or the Passionate Mad-*
>   *man*
> *Witt at Severall Weapons. The Faire Maid of the Inne.*
> *A Maske of the Gentlemen of Graies Inne and the Inner*
>   *Temple at the Marriage of the Prince and*
> *Princesse Palatine of the Rhene*
> *Four Plays or Morall Representations in One.*
> *All six copies by Fra. Beamont and John Fletcher.*

It is probable that in September 1646 the folio's chief publisher, Humphrey Moseley, did not have copies of these six titles in his possession (perhaps, it has been suggested in the case of the Fletcherian works, because they were works for which the King's Men, with whom Fletcher had been closely associated, were unable to supply copies—although one of these plays, *The False One*, had certainly been in their repertoire). Sadly there is no specific evidence as to how Moseley *did* belatedly obtain the manuscript of *Weapons* which Moses Bell used as printer's copy.

Whatever the source of the copy, his workshop did its job competently, and the Bell text (on which all subsequent editions are based) poses few notable textual problems: there are, for example, no significant press-variants between different copies. Its inconsistencies and errors are minor and in certain instances positively helpful, providing evidence as to how and in what sequence it was typeset along with various indications as to the nature of the manuscript from which Bell's employees worked.

The typesetting, as Sharp has demonstrated, was carried out by the same two compositors who set the previous play in section 6, *A Wife for a Month*, recognizable by their habits with incidentals. Compositor A set question marks and semicolons immediately after the word they followed, with no space in between, set 'ifaith', 'does' and 'ha' (short for 'have') without apostrophes but 'hunder'd' with an apostrophe, placed no full stop after 'Exit' or 'Exeunt', used a lower-case 'i' when 'ile', 'i'me' or 'i'de' appeared in mid-sentence, and favoured the spellings 'you'le', 'hee'le', 'we'le', 'wee'le', 'beleeve' and 'beleefe'. His colleague Compositor B, by contrast, set a space before question marks and semicolons, preferred 'i'faith' or 'y'faith', 'doe's', 'ha' and 'hundred', placed full stops after 'Exit' and 'Exeunt', used upper-case 'I' for mid-sentence 'Ile' and its analogues, and was more sparing with final 'e' and double 'e', favouring the spellings 'you'l', 'hee'l', 'we'l', 'wee'l', 'believe' and 'belief'. The play was divided between them thus:

Compositor A: 1.1.1-1.2.176; 2.2.177-297; 2.2.49-176; 2.1.1-2.2.48; 1.2.178-319; 3.1.202-61; 5.1.47-5.2.361

Compositor B: 2.2.298-3.1.202; 4.2.62-5.1.46; 4.1.312-4.2.61; 4.1.215-311; 4.1.6-105; 3.1.262-4.1.5

Other incidental variations, however, cannot be attributed to the compositors, and must instead derive from the manuscript from which they were working. Lady Ruinous Gentry, for example, is called '*Lady Gentry*' in 2.1 and 4.1 and '*Lady Ruinous*' in 2.4, 5.1, and 5.2, irrespective of compositor, and since on other evidence the two former scenes are attributed to Middleton and the three latter to Rowley this is likely to reflect authorial preferences preserved by the manuscript. (The same probably applies to variations in the Old Knight's surname, given in hyphenated form as '*Old-craft*' and '*Old-Craft*' in Middleton's 1.1 and 3.1 but simply as '*Oldcraft*' in Rowley's 2.4.) That the manuscript was itself the work of a single hand, however, is suggested by the comma-dominated consistency of the punctuation throughout the Bell text, irrespective of author or compositor, and that this hand belonged to a scribe rather than either Middleton or Rowley is suggested by the clearly non-authorial attempts that have been made in Rowley's scenes (again irrespective of compositor) to 'correct' prose speeches by high-ranking characters such as Lady Ruinous and the Old Knight into verse. Further evidence of the work of a non-authorial scribe is provided by two other misconceived 'corrections' at 2.4.10 and 4.1.52, in both of which the word 'Gentleman', referring to the cross-dressed Lady Ruinous, has been mistakenly altered to 'Gentlewoman' on the strength of her female speech-prefix: one of these is in a section set by Compositor A and the other in a section set by Compositor B, and while it is possible that both compositors made the same well-intentioned error independently it seems more likely that the tampering had already been carried out on the manuscript. One other feature of the Bell text which suggests the work of a scribe is the seven apparently unexceptional words mysteriously set in italic type ('*Daynty*', 2.4.37; '*Chymist*', 2.4.62; '*Mandrake*', 4.1.298; '*humble-bee*', 4.2.61; '*Minion*', 4.3.24, and '*Tortusses*', 5.1.93), which Turner conjectures must have been supplied by a second, italic hand to supply gaps left in the manuscript at points where the scribe was unable to read the authorial draft he was transcribing. Partly illegible, varying in incidentals between Middleton and Rowley scenes, and still showing signs of hasty revision (notably in 4.1, which at one point had clearly been two wholly independent scenes, subsequently fastened rather arbitrarily together by eleven lines of dialogue between Wittypate and Cunningame, 151–61), the manuscript the scribe was working from was almost certainly Middleton and Rowley's own papers.

The question remains as to whether this scribal transcript of authorial papers had previously been employed in the theatre—whether, indeed, it had been made specifically for use as a promptbook. Turner rejects the possibility out of hand, but in fact the evidence provided by the text is distinctly ambiguous. Bell's text, for example, is remarkably conscientious in its provision of stage directions (particularly entrances and exits), and although they are often laconic there are some which are highly suggestive of a manuscript marked for theatrical use: most strikingly, Cunningame's entrance at 4.1.151 is given as '*Enter Cunningame (with a Letter)*', although Cunningame does not produce his letter until a hundred and twenty lines of dialogue later. At the opening of 5.1 appears the distinctly playhouse-oriented direction '*Enter Cunningame (at one doore) Witty Pate, Ruinous, L. Ruinous, and Priscian (at the other)*'; and the ample direction which opens 2.4 is full of information highly pertinent to stage production but not all of it strictly necessary for an understanding of the dialogue which follows: '*Enter Lady Ruinous (as a man) Witty Pate, Sir Ruinous, Priscian, and Master Credulous, (binding and robing her, and in Scarfes) Credulous findes the bagge.*' These latter examples are less conclusive, since similar directions appear in texts which we know do not derive from theatrical copy, but one more detail might support the view that Bell's text does ultimately derive from the playhouse, namely its occasional placing of entrance directions earlier than the dialogue requires them, characteristic of a theatrical text careful to mark cues in good time (a feature for which Bell's compositors may have overcompensated at two points where entrances are instead marked slightly late, 2.2.18.1 and 2.2.98.1). Bell's text is not wholly consistent in these respects (and very few Renaissance dramatic texts, if any, are), but the absence of more extensive traces of playhouse provenance might simply result from Bell's otherwise successful processing of disreputably theatrical copy for an extremely up-market, library-oriented folio publication (a processing visible, perhaps, in the opening stage direction, 1.1.0.1, '*Enter Sir Perfidious Old-craft an old Knight, and Witty-pate his Sonne*', the literary nature of which complements the whole page's elegant design as well as carefully supplying readerly information otherwise unavailable due to the absence of a list of persons). It certainly seems more likely, thirty years after the play's composition but only five since the closure of the theatres made the sale of scripts an acting company's sole source of income, that the folio's publishers would have obtained their copy of *Weapons* via a theatrical source rather than by purchasing a purely literary manuscript of the play.

Bell's text concludes with an undistinguished poem, in six couplets, headed 'The Epilogue at the reviving of this Play'. In fact the poem is clearly a prologue, and despite a cursory reference to 'Wits' in its second line there is nothing to link it specifically with *Weapons*. It borrows its final line from the prologue to Fletcher's *The Elder Brother* (a prologue dating, with the rest of that play, from around 1625), and with its casual crediting of at least 'An Act, or two' of the play it introduces to Fletcher it could have been hastily composed for a revival of any Fletcherian play from 1625 onwards. (It is interesting to note in this respect that the next play in the Folio, *Valentinian*, is also supplied with an epilogue likely to belong to another play: see Maxwell, 225–6.) The evident misrecognition of a prologue as an epilogue recommends the hypothesis that what has been printed as the 'Epilogue' to *Weapons* is actually the prologue to another play entirely: the erroneous assignation might easily have occurred, as Turner suggests, if the prologue had been written on a loose sheet preceding the manuscript of a play stacked directly beneath that of *Weapons*, and was mistakenly picked up as the final sheet of *Weapons* instead of the first of the next play. Accepting that the poem does not really belong to *Weapons* at all, this edition relegates the 'Epilogue' to its textual notes.

Two other distinctive features of Bell's text should perhaps be noted here. One is the lineation of (especially) Rowley's scenes, which seems to have baffled everyone involved with the reproduction of the play from the scribe onwards: as the lineation notes record, there are passages where verse has clearly been mistakenly rendered as prose and others (more frequent) where the opposite has occurred, but these seem to be the responsibility of the scribe rather than of the compositors, who show little evidence of having based choices as to verse or prose on the grounds of space. (Rowley's verse is sufficiently irregular, however, and his prose sufficiently rhythmic, for no two editors to agree on precisely how such passages should be corrected.) The other feature is the text's handling of the exclamation 'Pox': it occurs six times in gatherings I and K and twice in gathering L (at 4.1.317 and 5.1.210), but at six other points in gathering L a dash appears where the context would otherwise lead one to expect another use of 'pox', from which Turner deduces that orders to avoid this mild scurrility were issued during the printing of the play, after the typesetting of the second forme of gathering L, L3:4$^\mathrm{v}$. In this edition as in others, 'pox' has been carefully restored throughout.

Weapons appeared in the Stationers' Register again on 30 January 1673, when the rights to the entire Beaumont and Fletcher collection were reassigned, and the play duly reappeared in the second, expanded Beaumont and Fletcher folio of 1679, *Fifty Comedies and Tragedies. Written by Francis Beaumont and John Fletcher* (Wing B1582), in the half of the volume printed by Thomas Newcomb. (The song from 3.1, 'Fain would I wake you, sweet', had been reprinted in 1653 in *Poems by Francis Beaumont, Gent.*, Wing B1602, but in a version which does not vary significantly from that in the folio and almost certainly derives directly from it.) This second edition of the play is for the most part simply a reprint of the first, but it does carry out a number of emendations, some of them so perspicuous that one subsequent editor, Turner, has plausibly theorized that whoever edited the text for Newcomb must have had access to an authoritative manuscript of the play. As MacDonald Jackson has observed, if an authoritative manuscript was *not* used in 1679, then whoever prepared copy for Newcomb gave this text more rigorous and intelligent scutiny than is displayed elsewhere by any seventeenth-century editor known to modern scholarship, and the present edition is thus happy to prefer Newcomb's readings to Bell's at a number of points.

SEE ALSO

Text: *Works*, 983
Music and dance: this volume, 148
Authorship and date: this volume, 375

WORKS CITED

Previous Editions Consulted

Colman, George, the elder, ed., *Dramatic Works of Beaumont and Fletcher* (1778), vol. 9
Dyce, Alexander, ed., *Works of Beaumont & Fletcher* (1843–6), vol. 4
Glover, Arnold, and A. R. Waller, eds., *Works of Francis Beaumont and John Fletcher* (1905–12), vol. 9
Langbaine, Gerard, ed., *Works of Francis Beaumont and John Fletcher* (1711), vol. 6
—— ed., *Wit at Several Weapons* (1718)
Seward, Thomas, John Sympson, and Lewis Theobald, eds., *Works of Mr Francis Beaumont and Mr John Fletcher* (1750), vol. 9 (ed. Sympson)
Sharp, Iain, ed., *Wit at Several Weapons*, unpublished dissertation, University of Auckland (1982)
Turner, Robert Kean, ed., *Wit at Several Weapons*, in Bowers, Fredson, general ed., *Dramatic Works in the Beaumont and Fletcher Canon* (1966–1996), vol. 7 (1989)
Weber, Henry, ed., *Works of Beaumont and Fletcher* (1812), vol. 9

Other Works Cited

Beaumont, Francis, *Poems by Francis Beaumont, Gent.* (1653)
Cibber, Colley, *The Rival Fools: or, Wit, at several Weapons* (1709)
Guilford, Horace, *Beauties of Beaumont and Fletcher* (1834)
Maxwell, Baldwin, *Studies in Beaumont, Fletcher, and Massinger* (1939)

TEXTUAL NOTES

Persons.0.2–Persons.20   The Persons...niece] NEWCOMB; *not in* BELL. Newcomb's cast list omits the Servants and the Boy.

1.1.0.1   *Oldcraft*] LANGBAINE; *Old-craft* BELL. This hyphenated form (also at 3.1.196) may be Middleton's (see Textual Introduction), although this edition follows Newcomb's List of Persons in favouring the unhyphenated form.

1.1.14   to] NEWCOMB; *too* BELL

1.1.81   wit, thou after my name] BELL; Wit, than after my name NEWCOMB. Newcomb's emendation is plausible, though not necessary.

1.1.105.1   *Cunningame*] THIS EDITION Some editions follow Newcomb's cast list in adopting the usual modern form of this surname, 'Cunningham'; Bell calls him '*Cuningham*' here, but elsewhere usually spells his name '*Cuningame*' (the spelling favoured by Turner). The variant adopted here compromises between the two in such a way as to make both the ordinariness of the name and its evident intended pun(s) as clear as possible.

1.1.106   An] BELL (And). The conditional seems more appropriate than the simple conjunction here, given the Old Knight's subsequent insistence that the Niece should indeed 'seem pleased' with Sir Gregory; the plot suggests that the Niece could conceivably refuse the match, rather than that she has already appeared to consent to it.

1.1.117   I hope] NEWCOMB; Hope BELL

1.1.160.1   *Enter Niece and Guardianess*] Bell places this direction earlier, after l. 158, but since the Old Knight does not see the two women until nearly the end of l. 160 (prompting his exclamation 'Cuds, my niece!') and still has four lines of dialogue apart with Cunningame before they arrive in the conversation, this may be a case of an entrance direction marked early in the manuscript to provide actors with advance warning: see Textual Introduction.

1.1.173   true] NEWCOMB; *truth* BELL

1.1.216   gentleman] LANGBAINE; *Gent.* BELL

1.2.1   Pox] NEWCOMB; *Pax* BELL. Dyce follows Bell here on the grounds that 'Pax' might reflect an affected pronunciation, but since Wittypate is elsewhere firmly committed to 'Pox' it seems more likely that this is merely an arbitrary spelling variant.

1.2.5   still] NEWCOMB; *Sill* BELL

1.2.14   *per fidem*] NEWCOMB; *perfidem* BELL

1.2.19   from] NEWCOMB; *for* BELL

1.2.28–9   brains. [*Giving money to Sir Ruinous*] *Pol, aedepol*, here's toward a *castor, ecastor* for you] THIS EDITION; brains *Pol, aedipol*, here's toward, a Caster ecastor for you BELL. Many editors have been confused by Bell's lack of a full stop after 'brains', for which no room was left here against the right-hand margin, and, missing the fact that *Pol, aedepol* is one of a series of impromptu nicknames for Priscian, have failed to recognize the nature of the action in progress at this point. The passage was unravelled by Dyce (who replaced the missing full stop, however, with a semicolon) and explicated by Turner.

1.2.74   OLD KNIGHT] SYMPSON; *not in* BELL

1.2.83   *propitii*] NEWCOMB; *poopitii* BELL

1.2.83   *juvenem*] SYMPSON; *junenem* BELL

1.2.108   *pernoctet*] SYMPSON; *pernoctat* BELL

1.2.109   *paupertas*] NEWCOMB; *Paupertat* BELL

1.2.109   *habitet*] SYMPSON; *habitat* BELL

1.2.125   'em] BELL (um). The spelling 'um' for this contraction is common throughout Rowley's scenes.

1.2.170   hopped] BELL (hop't). Simpson, Colman and Weber prefer to read Bell's 'hop't' as 'hoped', but 'hopped' (Dyce) is more in keeping with Sir Ruinous's brisk soldierly idiom at this point.

1.2.225   PRISCIAN] LANGBAINE; *not in* BELL

1.2.280   WITTYPATE] LANGBAINE; *not in* BELL

1.2.287   off] BELL (of)

1.2.299   counters] WEBER; contents BELL

2.1.0.1   *Servant*] SYMPSON; *Servants* BELL. As Sharp points out, the dialogue here only calls for a single servant, and Lady Ruinous's complaints about her fallen fortunes look absurd if she is surrounded by superfluous attendants. This stage direction in Bell refers to her as '*Lady Gentry*' and the speech prefixes throughout the scene as '*Lady.*', as is the case in 4.1 (the other wholly Middletonian scene in which she appears); in Rowley's 2.4, 5.1 and 5.2, however, stage directions usually call her '*Lady Ruinous*' and speech prefixes '*L.Ruin*'.

2.1.5   mocks] NEWCOMB; workes BELL

2.1.13   [*Exit Servant*]] WEBER. It is clear that the Servant must exit before Priscian arrives unabashedly to recruit Lady Ruinous to the conspiracy against Master Credulous, and both the anguished tone and compromising content of the second half of Lady Ruinous's speech make it evident that the shift into soliloquy should occur here.

2.1.22   footmen's] SYMPSON; Foot-mans BELL

2.1.41   We've] NEWCOMB (we'ave); Wee'ne BELL

2.1.56   *Exit Priscian*] Bell places this exit earlier, in l. 55 (directly after the end of Priscian's speech), but although this admirably suits Bell's page layout it prevents Priscian from hearing Lady Ruinous's response: the change of mood as she returns to musing on her fallen fortunes at the end of l. 56 makes more sense if it corresponds with a change back into soliloquy.

2.2.18.1   *Enter Guardianess*] In Bell this entrance is postponed until immediately before the Guardianess's first speech, l. 20, but she must be already visible for the audience to understand Cunningame's 'I'm haunted again' at l. 19. This may be an example of Bell 'tidying up' theatrical copy, overcompensating for a tendency to set entrances too early: see Textual Introduction.

2.2.45   wish the knight the better] THIS EDITION; wish the knight better BELL; a metrical emendation.

2.2.54   say] SYMPSON; *not in* BELL

2.2.58   I'll tell you all] BELL; Sympson, Weber, Dyce and Sharp all add 'not', but the sense does not require it if the Guardianess is exclaiming at her own indiscretion, joking that she is already blabbing all her secrets to Cunningame (or will do, if she continues at this rate), rather than stating that it is actually her policy not to do so.

2.2.76   there is] THIS EDITION; there's BELL. A metrical emendation.

2.2.98.1   *Enter Niece and Clown*] In Bell this entrance is placed immediately before the Niece's first line at l. 100, despite Cunningame's earlier exclamation on seeing the Niece at l. 98: cf. 2.2.18.1, above.

2.2.113   (*Toward Cunningame*)] Set in Bell to the right opposite ll. 114–15, the length of l. 113 forbidding its placement precisely where the dialogue requires it.

2.2.127   (*toward Cunningame*)] Set in Bell to the right after l. 128, again the first available space against the right-hand margin.

2.2.127   shoot] LANGBAINE; fhoots BELL

2.2.167   pat] SYMPSON; put BELL

2.2.209   CLOWN] NEWCOMB; *not in* BELL

2.2.210   NIECE] NEWCOMB; *Gard.* BELL

2.2.211   CLOWN] NEWCOMB; *not in* BELL. Newcomb's disentangling of Bell's confusion over speech prefixes here is highly satisfactory.

2.2.248.1   *Exit, humming 'Loath to depart'*] WEBER; Hum's loath to depart. *Exit Clown.* BELL; He humhs loath to depart. *Exit Clown.* NEWCOMB; *Niece.* He hums loath to depart SYMPSON. Bell mistakenly sets the stage direction as dialogue.

2.2.252   gulled] NEWCOMB; gub'd BELL

2.2.255   early] NEWCOMB; erring BELL. Bell's reading, though it makes sense of a kind, could be the result of eyeskip from the next word, 'spring'; Newcomb's emendation is more convincing in context.

2.2.268   stalking] NEWCOMB; stalking BELL

2.2.271   But] SYMPSON; Not BELL. An obscure passage at best; Sympson's emendation seems to offer its only hope of intelligibility.

2.2.281   ail you, aunt?] NEWCOMB; ayld you Ant? BELL

2.2.284   waking] NEWCOMB; walking BELL

2.2.326   task] SYMPSON; taste BELL

2.4.10   gentleman] NEWCOMB; Gentlewoman BELL. See Textual Introduction.

2.4.11   WITTYPATE] LANGBAINE; *not in* BELL

2.4.19   *probos*] SYMPSON; *probas* BELL

2.4.24   You] NEWCOMB; *Wit.* You BELL

2.4.28   I had] NEWCOMB; *Cred.* I had BELL

2.4.35   belly] BELL (bellow)

2.4.44   WITTYPATE He] DYCE (conj. Sympson); He BELL

2.4.46   SIR RUINOUS Secure] NEWCOMB; Secure? BELL

2.4.74   in, in] SYMPSON; in BELL

3.1.34.1   *Enter Boy*] TURNER; *Enter Page* BELL; *Enter Page and Fidlers boy* NEWCOMB. Bell's stage direction and the speech prefix at 3.1.36 call this character 'Page', but subsequent speech prefixes and his exit refer to him as 'Boy', an arbitrary change of synonym probably going back to Middleton's foul papers. Newcomb misreads this to produce a spurious and superfluous extra character, who remains a ghostly and pointless presence in the background of this scene in all subsequent editions until Turner's. Sharp justifies his faith in the existence of the Page by suggesting that 'a servant ushers in a group of players, among them the boy-singer', but although the song clearly is accompanied (3.1.62, 'Pay you the instruments') there seems no need to complicate the scene by bringing the instrumentalists onto the stage. Sir Gregory's instruction as he hands over the fee for the song at 3.1.62–3 (that the Boy should pay his accompanists out of the sum but save what he can of it for himself), so far from suggesting that these musicians (and a by-now wholly ignored Page) are present, surely demonstrates that they are not (as does his question as to whether they have arrived at 3.1.36).

3.1.42   E-la] NEWCOMB; Ely BELL

3.1.98   I've] THIS EDITION; I have BELL. A metrical emendation.

3.1.241   bobbed] NEWCOMB; bold BELL

3.1.284   housewifery] BELL (huswifery)

3.1.300   frampold] BELL (frampell)

3.1.351 pox] COLMAN; — BELL. See Textual Introduction.

4.1.28 and't] LANGBAINE; an't BELL

4.1.52 gentleman] NEWCOMB; Gentlewoman BELL. See Textual Introduction.

4.1.108 debauched] BELL (deboyft)

4.1.111 tobacco whiffers] NEWCOMB; Tobacco ſwivers BELL. Turner prefers Bell's 'swivers', speculating that '[a] "great Tobacco swiver" might be a great copulator with tobacco, one who thoroughly enjoys it and is hardly parted from it', but has to admit that he has found no analogous usage elsewhere. It is true that 'swivers' is a surprising error for 'whiffers', but both the context and the speaker (the naïve cleric Credulous is nowhere else given to obscenities, let alone such inventive ones as this) make 'whiffers' a far more likely reading.

4.1.150-1 Smithfield Pens...Master Cunningame!] THIS EDITION; Smithfield Pens. | Enter Cunningame (with a Letter.) | Wit. Zo,zo,zufficient. Master Cunningame? BELL. Bell uncharacteristically fails to provide an exit for Sir and Lady Ruinous here after Lady Ruinous's parting confirmation of their rendezvous with Wittypate in Smithfield: it must come after Wittypate's 'Zo, zo, zufficient', since Wittypate's zeds are a joke with the Gentries, imitating Sir Ruinous's fake Scots accent at ll. 48-9. The encounter between Wittypate and Cunningame which follows, ll. 151-61, has clearly been added at a late stage of composition; it contributes nothing to the plot (apart from providing the only indication to date that Wittypate and Cunningame know one another) and seems designed purely to join two otherwise unconnected scenes, the first, up to l. 151, set in the Old Knight's house, and the second, from l. 151 onwards, set in a public street. This being the case, Cunningame's entrance should follow the departure of the Gentries, probably using a different door. Bell's '(with a Letter)' is clearly the survival of a reminder to a prompter or actor, since neither an audience nor a reader need know anything of this document until Cunningame produces it at l. 277.

4.1.161.1 Enter Mirabell [behind]] THIS EDITION. The direction is set on a separate line two lines earlier in Bell, during Cunningame's farewell lines to Wittypate, between ll. 159 and 160, although Mirabell's presence is not required at the rear of the stage until l. 162 (after Wittypate's exit), when Cunningame begins to soliloquize about the way in which she has been dogging him. Such a mistake is not surprising in such an evidently half-finished section of the play.

4.1.217 CUNNINGAME] NEWCOMB; not in BELL

4.1.221 CUNNINGAME] NEWCOMB; not in BELL

4.1.221 MIRABELL] NEWCOMB; not in BELL.

4.1.226-8 Do, sweet Confidence...'Tis he] THIS EDITION; Do, ſweet confidence, | Enter Sir Gregory. | If I can match my two broad brim'd hats; 'Tis he BELL. Cunningame's line at 277 seems designed to bridge Mirabell's departure (which Bell fails to record) and Sir Gregory's remarkably apposite arrival, which clearly ought to cue Cunningame's ''Tis he' at l. 228.

4.1.234 pox] WEBER; — BELL. See Textual Introduction.

4.1.240 collet] SYMPSON; Coller BELL

4.1.256 pox!] COLMAN; — BELL. See Textual Introduction.

4.1.289 paned] SYMPSON; pawnde BELL

4.1.292 He never grew where rem in re e'er came] SYMPSON; He never came where Rem in Re e're grew BELL. Cunningame is remarking on Sir Gregory's origin rather than his sexual

inexperience, as Sympson recognized. The switching of 'grew' and 'came' in Bell might reflect an error by either the scribe or Compositor B.

4.1.298.1 Enter Clown, as a gallant] SYMPSON. Bell gives this entrance as 'Enter Clowne (as a Gallant.)', and places it two lines earlier, on a separate line after 'Bridewell in't.', between ll. 296 and 297, although it is clearly the cue for Cunningame's 'How now?' at l. 299, and would distract the audience's attention from the close of Cunningame's soliloquy.

4.1.305-10 I...women] Most editors prefer to recast Bell's wayward verse as prose here, but it seems perfectly fitting to the oddly formal quality of the Clown's garbled mixture of legal phraseology and poetic diction.

4.1.330 An ear] NEWCOMB; And dare BELL

4.1.362-3 whistling. | CUNNINGAME A very good note. | Exit Clown] SYMPSON; whistling. Exit Clow. | Cun. A very good note BELL

4.2.24 I've] THIS EDITION; I have BELL. A metrical emendation.

4.2.26 in] NEWCOMB; not in BELL

4.2.44 You run in] NEWCOMB; Your running BELL

4.2.61 same] SYMPSON; some BELL

4.3.0.2 scarfed,] BELL. Newcomb meant to add the explanatory phrase 'Which is only a Puppet so drest' at this point, but for some reason it appears instead at 4.2.64, just before Sir Gregory's exit.

4.3.5 crone's] NEWCOMB; groane's BELL

4.3.23 [Cunningame falls]] not in BELL. Newcomb adds the direction '(Cun. falls on purpose' to clarify the Niece's 'Your cause trips you': there is no reason to infer, however, that this stumble is deliberate.

4.3.38 I've] NEWCOMB (I have); I'me BELL

4.3.41 one] SYMPSON (conj.); not in BELL

5.1.24 Exit Wittypate] SYMPSON. Bell marks Wittypate's exit at the end of his last speech, at l. 22, but he needs to stay on stage long enough to hear Cunningame's reply.

5.1.34-6 Bell is a little careless with entrances and exits here, marking the Second Servant's entrance with the gown slightly earlier than Cunningame's thanks require it (after 'too', in l. 34, where it suits Bell's page layout), neglecting to mark his exit, and placing the Clown's entrance early (after 'You know him', l. 36, again where it suits Bell's layout and lineation).

5.1.51 CUNNINGAME] NEWCOMB; not in BELL

5.1.70 I lived] NEWCOMB; Iived BELL

5.1.71 thou shalt] NEWCOMB; that shall BELL

5.1.104-5 Silence!— | Enter Mirabell | Lady, your] TURNER; Enter Mirabell | Cun. Silence, Lady, your BELL. Editors prior to Turner have generally left 'Silence' as the first word of a verse line (however clumsily), although from Dyce forwards they have agreed that Mirabell's entrance needs to be postponed (it is important to make it clear that there is no risk of Sir Gregory seeing who she is at this point in the scene).

5.1.119 She kisses [Sir Gregory's] hand] THIS EDITION; She kiſſes his hand. BELL. The comic business of this scene, and the Clown's response to it, makes far more sense if at this point (as at l. 116) it is already Sir Gregory's hand rather than Cunningame's that is in play.

5.1.290 CUNNINGAME] TURNER; Witty. BELL. As Turner points out, only Cunningame, as Sir Gregory's companion, is in a position to make this assurance, just as it is he rather than Wittypate who has been witness to the Niece's flirtation with the Clown, ll. 304-6.

5.1.304   CUNNINGAME] NEWCOMB; *Witty.* BELL

5.1.307   wantonness] SYMPSON; wantons BELL

5.2.21   pair-o'-dice] SHARP; paire of Dice BELL. Without Sharp's emendation the hackneyed pun on 'paradise' is liable to remain obscure.

5.2.26   did] NEWCOMB; did not BELL

5.2.26   LADY] TURNER (conj. Sharp); *Ruin.* BELL

5.2.61   he] NEWCOMB; be BELL

5.2.68   [*To Guardianess, imitating Sir Gregory's voice*]] THIS EDITION; *not in* BELL. It is hard to imagine that the Guardianess would fail to recognize Cunningame's voice if he did not adopt this traditional comic expedient: see also ll. 59–62.

5.2.75–6   prepared for...I'll follow. | *Exit*] SYMPSON; prepar'd for. *Exeunt they two.* | *Gard.* 'Tis the Knight fure, ile follow. | *Exit Cun.Nee.Gardianeffe* BELL; prepar'd for. | *Guard.* 'Tis the Knight fure, I'll follow. | *Exit.Cun.Nee.Guard.* NEWCOMB.

5.2.79   your] THIS EDITION; my BELL. Turner attempts to explain Wittypate's 'Oh, that's my charge, father' as either meaning 'that's the responsibility I charged you with, father' or as a burlesque quotation (or, in fact, misquotation) of the Old Knight's line at 5.1.347, 'That shall be my charges'; but construed either way the line as it stands in Bell seems unlikely, and liable to be actively misleading. Sharp's suggestion that 'charge' here refers to the Niece seems even less plausible, since such a reading would have Wittypate drawing attention to her departure instead of deliberately hindering his father from pursuing her. The whole dramatic situation seems urgently to require the emendation adopted here; cf. 5.2.141.

5.2.92.1   [*Sir Ruinous and Priscian produce pistols*]] THIS EDITION (conj. Turner); *not in* BELL. The 'loud instruments' of l. 93 can only be firearms, without which it is not clear under what compulsion the musicians' exorbitant fee is extorted from the Old Knight.

5.2.105   pox] COLMAN; — BELL. See Textual Introduction.

5.2.155–7   Ha, ha...GUARDIANESS O] NEWCOMB (Oh), (but with the Guardianess's entrance marked after 'you', l. 154–5);

Gard. Ha, ha ... | Oh BELL

5.2.210   Pox, this] COLMAN; — This BELL. See Textual Introduction.

5.2.214   you] NEWCOMB; they BELL

5.2.233   eye] NEWCOMB; dye BELL

5.2.282   Pox] DYCE; — BELL. See Textual Introduction.

5.2.313   of] NEWCOMB; *not in* BELL

5.2.333   decayèd] WEBER; decay'd BELL

5.2.355   not] TURNER; *not in* BELL. As Turner points out, this emendation is needed to make sense of the subsequent exchange with Mirabell (and the opening of the Old Knight's final speech); Sir Gregory's line is otherwise inconsistent with his professed policy towards the Niece. The 'not' might easily have been left out by a compositor or scribe eye-slipping to l. 357.

5.2.361   In Bell and Newcomb, the following poem is placed after the final stage direction:

The Epilogue at the Reviving of this Play

WE need not tell you Gallants, that this night
The VVits have jumpt, or that the scenes hit right,
'Twould but be labour lost for to excufe
VVhat Fletcher had to do in; his brisk Muse
VVas fo Mercuriall, that if he but writ
An Act, or two, the whole Play rife up wit.
Wee'le not appeale unto thofe Gentlemen
Judge by their Clothes, if they fit right, nor when
The Ladies fmile, and with their Fannes delight
To whiske a clinch afide, then all goes right:
'Twas well receiv'd before, and we dare fay,
You now are welcome to no vulgar Play.

Here endeth Wit at feverallWeapons.

Sharp and Turner emend 'Epilogue' to 'Prologue' and print the poem at the beginning of the play (after the List of Persons in the case of Sharp, before it in the case of Turner): all editions prior to Sharp reprint it as an epilogue. See Textual Introduction.

STAGE DIRECTIONS

1.1.0.1   Actus primus, Scæna prima | *Enter Sir Perfidious Old--craft an old Knight, and* | *Witty-pate his Sonne.*

1.1.90.1   *Exit* (Set to the right at the end of 1.1.90)

1.1.105.1   *Enter Sir Gregory Fop, and Cuningham.*

1.1.149.1   *Exit Sir Greg.* (Set to the right at the end of 1.1.149)

1.1.160.1   *Enter Neece and Guardioneffe.* (Set by the folio on a separate line earlier in the Old Knight's speech, between 'twice now,' and 'All with a breath', 158–9: see Textual Notes).

1.1.188.1   *Enter Sir Gregory.*

1.1.268   *Exeunt.* (Set to the right at the end of 1.1.268)

1.2.0.1   *Enter Sir Ruinous Gentry, Witty-pate, and Prifcian.*

1.2.41.1   *Enter Old Knight and Sir Gregory.*

1.2.272   *Exit* (Set to the right, at the end of 1.2.272)

1.2.279.1   *Enter Witty-pate.*

1.2.286.1   *Exeunt the two Knights.*

1.2.319   *Exeunt.* (Set to the right at the end of 1.2.319)

2.1.0.1   Actus Secundus. | *Scæna Prima.* | *Enter Lady, Gentry, and Servants.*

2.1.28   *Enter Prifcian.*

2.1.29   *Pulls off's* | *beard* (right, opposite 2.1.29–30)

2.1.56   *Exit Prif.* (to the right, after 'dispatch', 2.1.55).

2.1.58   *Exit.* (To the right, at the end of 2.1.58).

2.2.0.1   *Enter Cuningame.*

2.2.18.1   *Enter Gardianeffe.* (In the folio, set on a separate line slightly later, immediately before the Guardianess's first speech at 2.2.20).

2.2.98.1   *Enter Neece and Clowne.* (Placed immediately before the Niece's first line at 2.2.100).

2.2.113   *Toward* | *Cuning.* (Set in the Folio to the right opposite 2.2.114–15).

2.2.124–5   *Toward Cun.* (Set to the right after 2.2.128).

2.2.215   *Exit.* (To the right, at the end of 2.2.215).

2.2.228   *Exit.* (To the right, at the end of 2.2.228).

2.2.248.1   *Hum's loath to depart. Exit Clown.*

2.2.273   *Exit..* (To the right, at the end of 2.2.273).

2.2.275.1   *Enter Mirabell.*

2.2.331.1   *Exeunt.* (To the right, at the end of 2.2.331).

2.3.0.1   *Enter Sir Gregory, and Clowne.*

2.3.53   *Exit.* (To the right, at the end of 2.3.53).

2.3.63   *Exit.* (To the right, at the end of 2.3.62).

2.4.0.1–2   *Enter Lady Ruinous (as a man) Witty Pate, Sir Rui-*| *nous, Prifcian, and Mafter Credulous, (binding* | *and robing her, and in Scarfes) Credulous* | *findes the bagge.*

2.4.17.1   *Exit Ruin.Prif.* | *(and Lady.* (to the right, at the end of 2.4.17).

2.4.45.1   *Enter Ruinous, and Prifcian.*

2.4.59.1   *Exit Cred. and Ruin.*

2.4.60.1   *Enter Lady Ruinous.*

2.4.89   *Exeunt.*

3.1.0.1   Actus Tertius. | Scæna Prima. | *Enter Old Knight and Sir Gregory.*

3.1.33   *Exit.* (To the right, at the end of 3.1.33).

3.1.34.1   *Enter Page.*

3.1.62.1   *Enter Neece above.*

3.1.63   *Exit Boy.* (To the right, at the end of 3.1.63).

3.1.99   *Exit.*

3.1.103.1   *Enter Cuningame.*

3.1.131   *Exit Cun.*

3.1.131.1   *Enter Old Knight, and Sir Gregory.*

3.1.165.1   *Neece lets* | *(fall her Scarfe.* (Right, opposite 3.1.164–5).

3.1.172   *Exit.* (To the right, at the end of 3.1.172).

3.1.231.1   *Enter Cuningame.*

3.1.299   *Exit.* (To the right, at the end of 3.1.299).

3.1.301.1   *Enter Old Knight.*

3.1.308.1   *Enter Neece.*

3.1.350.1   *Exeunt Old Knight, and Neece.*

3.1.360   *Exit.*

4.1.0.1   Actus Quartus. | Scena Prima. | *Enter Old Knight and Witty-Pate.*

4.1.29.1   *Enter Servant.*

4.1.37   *Enter Credulous, Sir Ruinous (as a Conftable,) and* | *Lady Gentry (as a man.)*

4.1.105.1   *Exeunt Knight,* | *(Ruin. and Lady.* (Set to the right, at the end of 4.1.105).

4.1.137.1   *Enter Servant.*

4.1.144.1   *Exit Cred. and Servant.*

4.1.149.1   *Enter Ruinous, and Lady Gentry.*

4.1.151.2   *Enter Cunningame (with a Letter.)* (Set on a separate line between the end of Lady Ruinous's last remark, 4.1.150, and Wittypate's 'Zo, zo').

4.1.160.1   *Exit Wit.* (Set to the right, at the end of 4.1.160).

4.1.161.1   *Enter Mirabell* (Set on a separate line two lines earlier, during Cunningame's farewell lines to Wittypate, between 4.1.159 and 4.1.160).

4.1.227.1   *Enter Sir Gregory.* (Placed a line earlier, between 'Confidence' and 'If', 4.1.226.1).

4.1.247   *Drawes.*

4.1.283   *Exit.* (Set to the right, at the end of 4.1.283).

4.1.298.1   *Enter Clowne (as a Gallant.)* (Placed two lines earlier, on a separate line after 'Bridewell in't.', between 4.1.296 and 4.1.297).

4.1.363   *Exit Clow.* (Placed immediately after his last speech, at the end of 4.1.361–2).

4.1.366   *Exit.* (Set to the right, at the end of 4.1.366).

4.2.0.1   *Enter Neece, and Sir Gregory.*

4.2.37   Old Knight's speech prefix given as *Within O.K.*

4.2.51.1   *Enter Gardianeffe.*

4.2.59.1   *(Exeunt Neece and Gard.*

4.2.64   *Exit.* (Set to the right, at the end of 4.2.64).

4.3.0.1   *Enter Cunningame (in difcourfe with a Mask't Gen-*| *tlewoman in a broad hat and fcarf'd,) Neece* | *at another doore.*

4.3.46   *Exeunt.* (Set to the right, at the end of 4.2.46).

5.1.0.1   Actus Quintus. | Scæna Prima. | *Enter Cunningame (at one doore) Witty Pate, Ruinous,* | *L.Ruinous, and Prifcian (at the other.)*

5.1.20.1   *Exeunt Ruin. & Prif.* (right, opposite 'backwards').

5.1.20.2   *Exit.* (right, opposite 'Ladies').

5.1.22.1   *Enter two Servants with a Banquet.*

5.1.24   *Exit* (Set earlier, directly after the end of Wittypate's last speech at 5.1.22)

5.1.34.1   *Enter second Servant with a Gowne.* (placed earlier, on a separate line during 5.1.31, after 'too,').

5.1.36.2   *Enter Clowne.* (Placed on a separate line, between 'know him,' and 'Entertain him').

5.1.78.1   *Enter Servant.*

5.1.83.1   *Enter Sir Gregory.*

5.1.96   *Soft Musick.* (Placed on the right, opposite 'dream' at 5.1.94).

5.1.98   *Both go into the Gowne* (Set to the right, on a separate line).

5.1.104.1   *Enter Mirabell.* (On a separate line after 5.1.102, just before Cunningame's 'Silence!').

5.1.118   *Kiffe her hand.*

5.1.119   *She kiffes his hand.*

5.1.248.1   *Exit Sir Greg. and Mirab.*

5.1.262   *Exit.* (To the right, at the end of 5.1.262).

5.1.262.1   *Enter Witty-pate.*

5.1.280.1   *Enter Old Knight.*

5.1.349.1   *Exit O.K. and Witty.*

5.1.352   *Exit.* (To the right, at the end of 5.1.352).

5.2.0.1–2   *Enter Neece, Lady Ruinous, Gardianeffe, Ruinous,* | *Prifcian, (with inftrumenes mafqu't.*

5.2.46.1   *The Dance, a Cornet is winded.*

5.2.48.1   *Enter Old Knight, Witty-pate, Cuningame,* | *Mafqu'd, and take them to dance.*

5.2.75   *Exeunt they two.* (right, opposite 'His stay's prepared for.')

5.2.76   *Exit Cun.Nee.Gardianeffe.* (right).

5.2.156.1   *Enter Gardianeffe.* (Set on a separate line during the close of the Old Knight's speech, between 'you' and 'Ha, ha' at 5.2.154–5).

5.2.177.1   *Enter Credulous, Cuningame, Neece, Sir Gregory,* | *and Mirabell.*

5.2.215.1   *Enter Clowne.*

5.2.293   *Exit.* (To the right, at the end of 5.2.292–3).

5.2.361   *Exeunt.* (To the right, at the end of 5.2.361).

LINEATION NOTES

1.1.74–81   I hold...nature] THIS EDITION; *verse* BELL: by | cour-age | not, | 'em: | children | rather | foolish | after my |

1.2.1–12   Pox...always.] WEBER; *verse* BELL: fourth | in't | be | year's | vacations and | is a | lay share | have had | as much |

1.2.66–7   'Blows'...that way.] WEBER; *verse* BELL: I'm in |

1.2.74–111   Tush...*argumentum.*] WEBER; *verse* BELL: in a | question | *munificentissimi!* | *salvere* | too. | now | too | him | *abundantia* | *juvenem* | *exulem.* | again | sir | ne'er | wiser | sir | *in ore* | *impudentia* | *indigentia* | *intelligo* | fetch | this | much | *nomen est* | *nunc* | sir | think so | speech | farther | *respondes* | *miseria* | again | *quotidie* | *habitat* | *Responde* |

1.2.129–32   Stay...then?] WEBER; *verse* BELL: first | they | love |

1.2.197–209   Nay...coxcomboy?] WEBER; *verse* BELL: too | learned | easily | enough | is | tried | chief | *et caetera* | *domine* | in | grounded | rest |

1.2.280–1   Look...concealed.] WEBER; *verse* BELL: round |

2.2.50–1   Ne'er . . . two),] SEWARD; you | BELL

2.2.75–6   Whoop! . . . bird,] WEBER; now. | BELL

2.2.166–7   A cheek . . . dalliance!] WEBER; *1 line* BELL

2.2.170–1   When . . . blush.] WEBER; such a | BELL

2.2.186–7   The goodlier . . . over.] THIS EDITION; now | BELL

2.2.194–8   They . . . that?] SEWARD; *prose* BELL

2.2.203–5   I took . . . filthily.] WEBER; to | stomach | BELL

2.2.283–8   No, . . . Baggage!] SEWARD; *prose* BELL

2.2.306–8   If . . . much] SEWARD; *prose* BELL

2.2.326–8   This . . . undertake't?] THIS EDITION; an | injunction | BELL. Bell's placement of a line-break between 'an' and 'unwilling' seems extremely unlikely.

2.4.28–9   Than . . . questions] DYCE; robber | BELL

2.4.46–7   But . . . loss,] WEBER; bullies? | BELL

2.4.68–70   Good . . . under-watchman).] WEBER; sure | from the | BELL

3.1.4–5   Have . . . suitor;] WEBER; music? | wish. | BELL

3.1.121–2   But . . . love!] WEBER; change! | BELL

3.1.159–60   How . . . sir,] WEBER; sides | niece | BELL

3.1.238–9   'Sniggs . . . too?] SEWARD; *prose* BELL

3.1.257–8   And . . . man] THIS EDITION; token | BELL

3.1.282–3   Did . . . sir.] SEWARD; sir | BELL

3.1.337–8   Or . . . now!] WEBER; speak | BELL

4.1.10–12   Lemme . . . sir.] SEWARD; Brute | Holinshed | BELL

4.1.266–9   Troth . . . wear 'em.] WEBER; hers | tokens | BELL

4.1.297–8   A . . . mandrake.] SEWARD; *1 line* BELL

4.1.303–4   How . . . thee!] WEBER; party | parties | BELL

4.2.1–2   Is't . . . you] SEWARD; possible? | in't, | BELL

4.2.13–14   To . . . hers.] SEWARD; mine | BELL

4.2.20–1   What's . . . heart,] THIS EDITION; *1 line* BELL

4.2.23–4   Yes . . . stone-cutter] SEWARD; *1 line* BELL

4.2.32–5   'Tis . . . conceive,] DYCE; bedtime | yet | spider | thee | BELL

4.2.49–51   I trow . . . swear.] WEBER; manners | together | BELL

5.1.12–14   Away . . . dancers.] THIS EDITION; you | BELL

5.1.33–7   Alas . . . man?] DYCE; too | Gramercy | him | BELL

5.1.38–42   'Snails! . . . you] WEBER; *verse* BELL: other | yet | messenger |

5.1.68–70   I warrant . . . else.] WEBER; *verse* BELL: mouth | Queen--Hithe |

5.1.74–103   Choke . . . out] WEBER; *verse* BELL: see | only | modesty | hope | Gregory | seen | private | opportunity | table | serve | you | have | that | dream | extremely | woman | lady | off | me | on | dream | predictions | watchword | now | *nobis* | to | business | chair | out |

5.1.104–5   Silence! . . . illustrates] TURNER; *1 line* BELL

5.1.136–9   I . . . be.] DYCE; him | least | health | BELL

5.1.140   I'll . . . O, o!] THIS EDITION; health | BELL

5.1.144   Yes . . . forsooth] THIS EDITION; *prose* BELL

5.1.171–3   Nay . . . lady.] DYCE; *verse* BELL: much |

5.1.205–6   Good . . . better] SEWARD; *1 line* BELL

5.1.220–2   Content? . . . boldly.] SEWARD; *verse* BELL: life | Old |

5.1.250–2   The . . . 'tis.] SEWARD; *verse* BELL: of |

5.1.273–4   This . . . go] SEWARD; for ever | BELL

5.1.278–9   Help . . . it,] DYCE; only | belief | assurance | BELL

5.1.294–5   Ay . . . again?] WEBER; deeds | BELL

5.1.300–2   But . . . sir.] SEWARD; *prose* BELL

5.1.317–19   Could . . . sir.] DYCE; him | BELL

5.2.5–6   Else . . . was] DYCE; me | BELL

5.2.14–17   Yes . . . him.] DYCE; *verse* BELL: along | device | great |

5.2.49–50   Ha? . . . counsel-keeping.] THIS EDITION; *verse* BELL: then |

5.2.85–6   You . . . now?] SEWARD; sir | BELL

5.2.130–2   Fiddle . . . received] WEBER; robbery | BELL

5.2.137–9   And . . . it] DYCE; force | and | BELL

5.2.180–3   Faith . . . father] SHARP; *verse* BELL: act | him | answer | desire |

5.2.243–4   O, fie! . . . hand—] WEBER; *prose* BELL

5.2.251–2   Pray you . . . much] WEBER; *prose* BELL

5.2.294–5   So . . . sir] SHARP; *prose* BELL

5.2.296–7   And . . . hope.] SHARP; us | BELL

5.2.323–4   Thou . . . sir.] WEBER; full | BELL

5.2.341–2   Something . . . me] DYCE; *verse* BELL: more |

5.2.347–9   She . . . another.] SEWARD; *verse* BELL: matter | been |

5.2.357–8   Why . . . time] SEWARD; sake | BELL

THE NICE VALOUR; OR, THE PASSIONATE MADMAN

Edited by Gary Taylor

The Nice Valour; or, the Passionate Madman (BEPD 652, Wing B1581) was first printed in the Beaumont and Fletcher folio, 'Comedies and Tragedies | Written by Francis Beaumont and John Fletcher Gentlemen. | Never printed before, | And now published by the Authors Original Copies' (1647). It does not appear in the entry for the folio in the Stationers' Register (4 September 1646), nor in the list of plays belonging to the King's Men in 1641 (Public Record Office: L.C. 5/135, printed in Chambers, 398-9). It first appears in the Stationers' Register on 29 June 1660, in a supplementary list (*BEPD*, p. 68); each of the six items in that entry (except *The Nice Valour*) ends its section of the 1647 folio—which, Williams notes, shows that 'the manuscripts of these sections did not reach Moseley till after the sections had been allocated' to the different printers who were working on the volume. Moreover, *Valour*—the one apparent exception to this rule—is itself misplaced, and belongs at the end of its section (see below).

The 1647 folio, published by Humphrey Moseley, was farmed out to different printers, and *Valour* is the seventh item in the third section (after *The Chances*, *The Loyal Subject*, *The Laws of Candy*, *The Lovers' Progress*, *The Island Princess*, and *The Humorous Lieutenant*). Gerritsen, correcting Bald, confirmed Susan ISLIP as the printer of that section of the folio; her shop was also responsible for section seven (*Valentinian* and *The Fair Maid of the Inn*). *Valour* was evidently an addition to ISLIP's original quota for section 3. It follows *The Humorous Lieutenant*, and precedes 'Mr Francis Beaumonts Letter to Ben Johnson, written before he and Master Fletcher came to London, with two of the precedent Comedies then not finisht, which deferred their merry meetings at the Mermaid'. *Valour* apparently reached the printer late and has been inappropriately inserted before the letter to Jonson, which should have come after the two earlier comedies.

It was set by the two main compositors working for ISLIP. Dr Barbara Fitzpatrick and George Walton Williams have analysed compositorial stints; they attribute to compositor A 1.1.85-192, 2.1.32-84, and 3.2.176-end, and to compositor B 1.1.0.1-1.1.84, 1.1.193-2.1.31, 2.1.85-143, and 2.1.249-3.2.175; 2.1.144-248 may have been set by compositor A, or by compositor D, who occasionally appears elsewhere in ISLIP's section. Turner, evaluating the work of these two compositors in *Valentinian*, notes in particular that all but one or two of twenty-five errors 'involving the terminations of words' occur in the stints of Compositor B (272); it may be significant that the only two occurrences of unmetrical -est in *Valour* both occur in B's (shorter) stint (1.1.249, 2.1.117), and that his

stint also contains five of the six apparent errors involving terminal -s or terminal -ed (1.1.3, 1.1.12, 1.1.18, 3.2.27, 3.2.76; 5.3.101). (We had edited the play, and made these emendations, before being aware of Turner's assessment.) But more important than any differences between the two compositors is the relative unreliability of either. Turner concludes that 'Their best was not very good' (273). In the case of *The Humorous Lieutenant*, set in the same shop, chiefly by the same two workmen, we can compare their work with a related manuscript; as Hoy (1982) concludes, the ISLIP 'text of *The Humorous Lieutenant* is in fact a wretchedly printed affair...The quality of the press-work itself, with the many obvious errors on display, does not encourage confidence in the degree of faithfulness with which the [ISLIP] print has reproduced Fletcher's text' (294, 296).

Bald argued that the printer's copy for ISLIP was a private transcript; unlike most of the plays included in the 1647 collection, it seems not to have belonged to the King's Men, or to have been printed from their stock of promptbooks (8-10, 109-110). The Prologue, specifically attributed to a revival, may have come from a separate source; but if, as seems more probable, both prologue and text come from the same source, then that source was not an early authorial draft, and apparently had some connection with the theatre. But many private transcripts are copies of theatrical documents. The stage directions, as we would expect in either a promptbook or a private transcript but not from an authorial draft, are full and relatively unambiguous; no entrances are omitted. Many directions—including entrances—are printed in the right margin, probably reflecting their manuscript location. Nevertheless, nothing specifically points to a promptbook; one detail which a promptbook might specify, which is not noted here, is the need for chairs to be placed on stage during the act interval before the entrance at 2.1.0.1. Several apparent errors in ISLIP seem to result from two stages of error, suggesting that there was an error in the printer's manuscript copy: see notes to 1.1.31-2, 2.1.45, 5.3.183. Unusual Middleton spellings are not much in evidence, which again suggests some sort of transcript. Finally, Middleton did not mark or number scenes, and prompters did not add such divisions; the presence of scene divisions thus points to a literary scribe. More than one scribe may have been involved; Act 5 marks and numbers scene divisions, but Act 3 does not. (Acts 1, 2, and 4 have only one scene apiece.) Bald's hypothesis, that ISLIP was set from a literary transcript, thus seems more probable than any of the alternatives; certainly, the manuscript seems not to have been a rough authorial draft.

The play was next printed, by John MACOCK, in 'Fifty Comedies and Tragedies Written by Francis Beaumont and John Fletcher, Gentleman', the so-called second folio (1679; Wing B1582). MACOCK is a reprint of ISLIP; in our collations, MACOCK is assumed to reproduce the reading of ISLIP, unless otherwise noted. MACOCK adds an editorial dramatis personae list (as it does to other plays); it replaces the subtitle with the generic label 'A Comedy' (followed by all subsequent editions until WILLIAMS). Clearly, some editorial attention was paid to the text, and we adopt eighteen readings from MACOCK; but with the exception of the emendation at 1.1.237, these are all obvious corrections of obvious typographical errors, which require no recourse to any manuscript authority, and little ingenuity. Serious editorial engagement with the text did not begin until the eighteenth century.

Like these first two editions, all subsequent texts of the play have been in collections of Beaumont and Fletcher; *Valour* has never been edited separately. The most reliable of the existing editions is undoubtedly that of WILLIAMS, who identified a surviving manuscript version of the song at 2.1.114-24 (Folger v.A.308, f. 5^r-v; not listed in Beal, probably because it was compiled in the early eighteenth century); the list of press variants in ISLIP, below, derives directly from WILLIAMS. Our own edition is the first to analyse the play's textual and interpretative problems from the perspective of the Middleton rather than the Fletcher canon, and the first to essay a full commentary.

We have also, for the first time, collated all extant texts of the song at 3.3.36-54. 'Hence, all you vain delights' is not only the most popular song from any early modern English play, but also the Middleton text which survives in the most early witnesses. Most of those documents are earlier than ISLIP, and all seem to be independent of it.

We list below the known separate texts of the song; sigla used in the collations are printed in small capitals. In choosing sigla we have, as elsewhere, preferred to identify texts in terms of agents: hence, we adopt as sigla (in descending order) the name of the (a) compiler, or (b) owner, or (c) site of compilation, of manuscripts. When no such information is available, we use (d) some abbreviation of the document's current location. Our information about these manuscripts as a whole, including identification of their dates, owners and compilers, derives from Beal. His 1980 descriptions, in the context of the Beaumont and Fletcher canon (I.1.93-5), have in some cases been expanded or updated by his subsequent work on other authors whose texts appear in the same miscellanies; our listing incorporates his latest conclusions, scattered throughout *Part II* of his *Index*. Beal sometimes provides more information about each manuscript as a whole, and the persons involved; owners may or may not have been compilers. Beal—in accordance with the principles adopted for a reference work intended to enable scholars to find texts—listed the texts in alphabetical order

by archive and shelfmark, beginning with Aberdeen and ending with Yale; our interest in these texts is editorial, and we list them in approximate chronological order, in so far as this can be determined. Unless specified below, these texts have not been collated by previous editors.

Meisei: not listed in Beal; formerly in private hands, now at Meisei University; British Library photos, R.P. 2031 (prob. comp. at the INNS OF COURT[1]), p. 10 (1615-25).

B&F 145: Huntington HM 46323 (prob. comp. CAL-VERLEY family), p. 35 (c.1623-30s).

B&F 144: Harvard, MS Eng 703 (comp. by or for Sir Henry CHOLMLEY), f. 34 (c.1624-41). Collated by Seng.

B&F 124: British Library, Add. MS 15226, f. 28^v (c.1630).

B&F 134: Folger, MS V.a.103, Part I, f. 52 (c.1630). In the same hand as the Nottingham manuscript (below); hence identified as SCRIBE[1]. Collated by Williams.

B&F 147: University of Nottingham, Portland MS Pw V 37 (perhaps once owned by family of William and Margaret Cavendish), p. 107 (prob. Christ Church, c.1620s-30s). In the same hand as Folger V.a.103 (above); hence identified as SCRIBE[2]. Manuscript also contains an autograph text of Strode's 'An Opposite to Melancholy' f. [lv] (Beal StW 642).

B&F 143: Folger, MS V.b.43, f. 21 (OXFORD[1], c.1630). Collated by Williams. Also contains Strode's 'An Opposite', f. 21 (Beal StW 661).

B&F 151: Yale, OSBORN Collection, b 200, p. 46 (c.1630s). This manuscript's text of the song is clearly linked to HIGHMORE: in addition to eight shared variants which are fairly common, they uniquely share three errors, and in a fourth variant are linked with only one other manuscript. Moreover, HIGHMORE appears to be the later text: it contains four errors not present in OSBORN 200 (Moon-like, soules, as, midnights). By contrast, OS-BORN 200 does not contain any errors not present in HIGHMORE. Also contains Strode's 'An Opposite', p. 48 (Beal StW 654).

B&F 130: British Library, Sloane MS 1792 (probably comp. J.A., Christ Church, Oxford), f. 123 (early 1630s). Also contains Strode's 'An Opposite', f. 120^v-121 (Beal StW 648). Linked to LANE and BOYLE?

B&F 137: Folger, MS V.a.160 (comp. Matthew DAY, Mayor of Windsor, 1574-1661), 2nd series, p. 2 (c.1633-4).

B&F 148: Rosenbach Museum & Library, MS 239/27 (owned T.C.), p. 161 (c.1634). Also contains Strode's 'An answer to Melancholly', p. 421 (Beal StW 652).

A Description of the King and Queene of Fayries (London, 1634; entered in the Stationers' Register 29 April), printed by T. HARPER (STC 21512.5, 21513). Collated by Williams.

B&F 118: Bodleian, MS Malone 21, f. 80 (St. John's College (?), OXFORD², *c*.1634–43). Also contains Strode's 'Against Melancholly', f. 80^r–v.

B&F 150: miscellany owned by the late Edwin WOLF 2nd (d. 1991), p. 73. This manuscript is currently owned by The Family Album, and its text of the song has not been collated here; Beal reports that it is 'probably associated with Oxford and possibly related to' OXFORD² and dates it '*c*.1635' (II.2.358). Also contains Strode's 'An Opposite', p. 74 (Beal StW 653).

B&F 112: Aberdeen University Library, MS 29 (owned by Elizabeth LANE and John Finch), pp. 187–8 (*c*.1630s); 'evidently associated with Oxford, probably Christ Church' (Beal II, 2:354). Also contains Strode's 'An Opposite', pp. 188–9 (Beal StW 643). Linked to J.A., BOYLE, HARFLETE?

B&F 125: British Library, Add. MS 15227, f. 75^v (CAMBRIDGE, *c*.1630s).

B&F 129: British Library, Sloane MS 542 (owned by Nathaniel HIGHMORE), f. 42^v (*c*.1630s). Clearly linked to OSBORN 200; see above.

B&F 136: Folger, MS V.a.125, Part I (comp. Richard BOYLE), f. 7 (*c*.1630s). Collated by Cutts and Williams.

B&F 138: Folger, MS V.a.170, p. 29 (OXFORD³, *c*.1630s). Collated by Williams. Also contains Strode's 'An Opposite', p. 184 (Beal StW 651).

B&F 139: Folger, MS V.a.245, f. 58^v (OXFORD⁴, *c*.1630s). Collated by Williams.

B&F 152: Yale, OSBORN Collection, b 205, f. 76 (*c*.1630s). Also contains Strode's 'An Opposite', f. 70^v (Beal StW 655).

B&F 146: Huntington, HM 116, p. 125 (Brasenose College (?), OXFORD⁵, *c*.late 1630s).

B&F 140: Folger, MS V.a.262, p. 131 (INNS OF COURT², *c*.late 1630s).

B&F 114: Bodleian, MS Eng. poet. c. 50 (owned by Peter DANIELL of Oxford), f. 130^r–v (*c*.1630s–40s). Also contains Strode's 'An Opposite', f. 128^v.

B&F 115: Bodleian, MS Eng. poet. e. 14 (owned by Henry Lawson), f. 84 (prob. Christ Church, OXFORD⁶, *c*.1630s–40s).

B&F 142: Folger, MS V.A.322, pp. 33, 37 (*c*.1630s–40s). Collated by Williams.

B&F 149: St. John's College, Cambridge, MS S.32 (owned and poss. comp. John PIKE of Cambridge), f. 9 (*c*.1636–40s).

B&F 116: Bodleian, MS Firth e. 4 (dedicated to Lady Afra HARFLETE), p. 72 (*c*.1640).

B&F 120: Bodleian, MS Rawl. D. 1092, f. 273 (OXFORD⁷, *c*.1640). Also contains Strode's 'An Opposite', f. 273^v (Beal StW 657).

B&F 123: Bodleian, MS RAWLINSON poet. 153, f. 13 (*c*.1640).

B&F 141: Folger, MS V.A.319, f. 35 (*c*.1640). Collated by Williams.

B&F 127: British Library, Add. MS 47111 (comp. Sir John PERCEVAL, Magdalen College, Cambridge), f. 11^r–v (*c*.1646–9).

ISLIP, Susan, printer, *The Nice Valour*, in Francis Beaumont and John Fletcher, *Comedies and Tragedies* (1647), sig. 3U3^r.

B&F 119: Bodleian, MS Mus. Sch. F. 575 (owned by William ILES), f. 7^v (music, mid-century). Collated by Williams.

B&F 121–2: Bodleian, MS Rawl. poet. 84 (comp. PAULET family), ff. 40 rev., 66 rev. (mid-century).

B&F 128: British Library, Egerton MS 2013 (music, arranged by John HILTON), f. 3^v (mid-century). Collated by Williams.

B&F 135: Folger, MS V.a.124 (comp. Richard ARCHARD), f. 20^r–v (*c*.1650–57). Collated by Williams. Also contains Strode's 'An Answere', f. 20^v (Beal StW 660).

[Sir John MENNES], *Wit Restor'd in several select poems not formerly publish't* (1658), sig. F1–F1^v (Wing M1719).

B&F 132: Cambridge University Library, MS Gg.1.4 (prob. comp. J. HINSON), f. 24 (*c*.1658).

B&F 113: Bodleian, MS Ashmole 36/37 (comp. Elias ASHMOLE), f. 26 (*c*.1660).

B&F 131: Cambridge University Library, MS Dd.6.43 (owned by William GODOLPHIN and Henry Savile), f. 23 (late 17th c.).

B&F 133: CHRIST CHURCH, Oxford, MS Mus. 350 (music), pp. 64–5 (late 17th c.).

B&F 153: Yale, OSBORN Collection, b 213, p. 49 (late 17th c.).

B&F 126: British Library, Add. MS 28644 (comp. Charles MONTAGU), f. 74^v (end 17th c.).

B&F 117: Bodleian, MS LYELL 37, p. 144 (17th c.).

SEE ALSO

Text: *Works*, 1683
Music and dance: this volume, 169
Authorship and date: this volume, 423

WORKS CITED

Previous Editions

ISLIP, Susan, printer, *The Nice Valour*, in *Comedies and Tragedies | Written by Francis Beaumont and John Fletcher* (1647)

MACOCK, John, printer, *Fifty Comedies and Tragedies Written by Francis Beaumont and John Fletcher* (1679)

LANGBAINE, Gerard, ed., *The Works of Mr Francis Beaumont and Mr John Fletcher*, volume 7 (1711)

Theobald, Lewis, Thomas Seward, and John SYMPSON, eds., *The Works of Mr Francis Beaumont and Mr John Fletcher*, volume 10 (1750)

COLMAN, George, ed., *The Dramatick Works of Beaumont and Fletcher Collated with all the Former Editions, and Corrected…by various commentators*, volume 10 (1778)

WEBER, Henry, ed., *The Works of Beaumont and Fletcher*, volume 4 (1812)

DYCE, Alexander, ed., *The Works of Beaumont and Fletcher*, volume 10 (1843–6)

WILLIAMS, George Walton, ed., *The Nice Valour*, in Fredson Bowers, gen. ed., *The Dramatic Works in the Beaumont and Fletcher Canon*, volume 7 (1989)

Other Works Cited

Bald, R. C., *Bibliographical Studies in the Beaumont and Fletcher Folio of 1647* (1937)

Beal, Peter, *Index of English Literary Manuscripts: Volume I: 1450–1625* (1980); *Volume II: 1626–1700* (1987–93)

Butler, Martin, *Theatre and Crisis 1632–1642* (1984)

Chambers, E. K., ed., 'Dramatic Records: The Lord Chamberlain's Office', in *Collections: Vol. II. Part III*, gen. ed. W. W. Greg, Malone Society (1913), 321–416

Cutts, John P., *La Musique de scène de la troupe de Shakespeare: The King's Men sous le règne de Jacques Ier*, second edn. rev. (1971)

DiGangi, Mario, *The Homoerotics of Early Modern Drama* (1997), 140–5

Dyce, Alexander, ed., *The Works of Beaumont and Fletcher* (1846)

Gerritsen, Johan, 'The Printing of the Beaumont and Fletcher Folio of 1647', *The Library*, V, 3 (1949), 233–64

Gilman, Sander L., *Seeing the Insane* (1982)

Halliwell, James Orchard, *Letters of the Kings of England*, 2 vol. (1848), 2:16–133 ('James I. to the Earl of Somerset')

Hammersmith, James P., 'The Proof-Reading of the Beaumont and Fletcher folio of 1647: Section 2 and πA, πe, πf; Section 3 and πc', *Papers of the Bibliographical Society of America* 82 (1988), 287–332

Heinemann, Margot, *Puritanism and Theatre: Thomas Middleton and Opposition Drama under the Early Stuarts* (1980)

Hoy, Cyrus, ed., *The Humorous Lieutenant*, in Fredson Bowers, gen. ed., *The Dramatic Works in the Beaumont and Fletcher Canon*, volume 5 (1982)

Hurley, C. Harold, 'The Discovery of Beaumont and Fletcher's *Nice Valour* as a source for Milton's "Il Penseroso"', *Notes and Queries* 218 (1973), 166–7

Mason, J. Monck, *Comments on the Plays of Beaumont and Fletcher* (1798)

Seng, Peter J., 'Early version of a song in Fletcher's *Nice Valour*', *Notes and Queries* 228 (1983), 151–2

Smith, Bruce R., 'Making a difference: male/male "desire" in tragedy, comedy, and tragicomedy', in Susan Zimmerman, ed., *Erotic Politics: Desire on the Renaissance Stage* (1992), 127–50

Taylor, Gary, 'Bardicide', in *Shakespeare and Cultural Traditions: Proceedings of the Fifth World Shakespeare Congress*, ed. Roger Pringle *et al.* (1994), 333–49

—— 'Praestat Difficilior Lectio: *All's Well that Ends Well* and *Richard III*', *Renaissance Studies* 2 (1988), 27–46

—— 'Thomas Middleton, *The Nice Valour*, and the Court of James I', *The Court Historian* 6 (2001), 1–36

Turner, Robert K., Jr., ed., *Valentinian*, in Fredson Bowers, gen. ed., *The Dramatic Works in the Beaumont and Fletcher Canon*, volume 4 (1979)

Wright, Thomas, *The Passions of the Mind in General* (1604)

TEXTUAL NOTES

Persons *The Persons . . . Servants*] THIS EDITION; *not in* ISLIP. The arrangement of parts is editorial, based upon conventions in such lists in early Middleton texts (see Taylor, 'Persons'). Some descriptive phrases are taken from MACOCK, which prints lists for all the plays; although its list has no Middletonian authority, and is anachronistically and conventionally divided by gender and arranged by hierarchy, it does interestingly reflect the views of an early reader.

Persons.1 Duke] WILLIAMS; Duke *of Genoua* MACOCK. As Williams notes, the play 'does not require such localization'; Taylor argues that the Dukedom of Savoy would have been more plausible.

Persons.2 the Duke's favourite] *his Favourite, a superstitious lover of reputation* MACOCK

Persons.4 the Duke's . . . beloved] MACOCK

Persons.5 the Duke's . . . kinsman] MACOCK

Persons.6 Cupid . . . Lord] MACOCK (*subst.*). This combines material from two entries in MACOCK: 'A Lady, *personating* Cupid, *Mistriss to the mad Lord*' and 'Two Brothers *to the Lady, affecting the passionate Lord*'.

Persons.11 Lepet . . . court] THIS EDITION; Lepet, *the cowardly Monsieur of* Nice Valour MACOCK

Persons.12–13 another . . . flesh] MACOCK

Persons.16 two . . . courtiers] MACOCK

Persons.17 A . . . temper] MACOCK

1.1.0.1 Actus] THIS EDITION (Taylor). ISLIP prints, after 5.3.197, a Prologue, which this edition omits from the text, since it seems clearly to belong to a revival, with which the original author was not associated. The text of the Prologue is as follows:

> The Prologue at the reviving
> of this Play.
>
> It's growne in fafh'on of late in thefe dayes,
> To come and beg a fufferance to our Playes;
> Faith Gentlemen our Poet ever writ
> Language fo good, mixt with fuch fprightly wit,
> He made the Theatre fo foveraigne
> With his rare Scænes, he fcorn'd this crowching veine:
> We ftabb'd him with keene daggers when we pray'd
> Him write a Preface to a Play well made.
> He could not write thefe toyes; 'twas eafier farre,
> To bring a Felon to appeare at th' Barre,
> So much he hated bafeneffe; which this day,
> His Scænes will beft convince you of in's Play,

The heading makes it clear that the prologue was not written for the original production, or for the original author, who is spoken of in a past tense which suggests that he is dead, or at the very least no longer writing for the theatres.

1.1.0.2 Chamont] ISLIP (*Shamont*). This name has been modernized throughout to its proper French spelling.

1.1.0.2 Four] ISLIP (4). Like WILLIAMS this edition follows the folio in keeping the gentlemen as numbers rather than using names derived from later in the text.

1.1.0.2–3 of the Chamber] THIS EDITION (Taylor); *not in* ISLIP. Their particular status is defined at 4.1.143, 1.1.181–2, 2.1.256.

1.1.3 Answered] MASON; answer ISLIP. Mason's correction produces agreement with Chamont's reply.

1.1.9 taffeta] ISLIP (Taffitie)

1.1.12 one man's] MACOCK; ones mans ISLIP. MACOCK makes the most obvious correction; but since 'character' could be accented on the first or second syllable, one of ISLIP's two possessives might have been intended as a substitution for the other: Middleton might have written 'on's' (= on his; misinterpreted as 'one's') or 'man's', and the ISLIP reading might result from misinterpretation of a substitution as an addition (Taylor).

1.1.18 disgraces] WILLIAMS; difgrace ISLIP

1.1.31–2 which is indeed | No virtue, and not] DYCE; no vertue, | Which is indeed, not ISLIP. The proposed error could have arisen from omission of the phrase 'which is indeed' at some stage of manuscript transmission, and its subsequent ambiguous or misplaced reinsertion. Certainly, the phrase seems misplaced in ISLIP. Alternatively, one might emend to 'which indeed No virtue is, nor', but this would require more complicated scenarios of error.

1.1.61 in the] SYMPSON; not in ISLIP

1.1.72 disrelish] COLMAN; his rellish ISLIP. The ISLIP reading produces the reverse of the required sense: 'The taste . . . will come into his taste', when the object of the exercise is to make what he now relishes become, by overuse, distasteful.

1.1.77.1 Lepet] ISLIP (Lapet). As the text makes clear, ISLIP's spelling is meant to represent the French for 'the fart'; in modern spelling this would be 'Lepet' not 'Lapet'. The distinction is seldom observed in early modern theatrical transliterations of French.

1.1.82 FIRST GENTLEMAN] COLMAN; Gen. ISLIP; 2 Gent. MACOCK

1.1.105 He's] ISLIP (Has)

1.1.105 switched] ISLIP (fwitz'd)

1.1.126 honour's sake] ISLIP (honour ~). In such phrases, early modern English orthography often did not mark the terminal -s (of the preceding noun) before the initial s- (of 'sake'), since effectively the letter is only sounded once; the modernization of spelling indicates the grammatical relationship more clearly.

1.1.128 assure] THIS EDITION (Taylor); I ~ ISLIP. Middleton uses 'assure you' (as a colloquial metrical variant for 'I assure you') at Phoenix 4.41, Puritan 1.3.53, 4.2.90, Weapons 5.2.11, Changeling 1.2.115. The idiom could easily have been expanded to the more common form by compositor or scribe, even without the possibility of contamination from the preceding 'I'll'.

1.1.128 'less they] MACOCK; lesse then ISLIP—which would imply that Chamont did not take fewer blows than were given to him. Alternatively, one might emend to 'more then' (more than); but 'less' for 'unless' is a Middletonian idiom, and could easily produce ISLIP's error.

1.1.134 as] MACOCK; as a ISLIP

1.1.137 wrongfully] MACOCK; wrong fully ISLIP

1.1.142 nowhere] ISLIP (no where)

1.1.153 lovely worth] ISLIP; lowly ~ MASON. Dyce thinks that it refers to the lady; it could also refer, ironically, to the monster.

1.1.154 LADY] SYMPSON; not in ISLIP. (MACOCK supplies the word at the end of the preceding line; probably a compositorial misunderstanding of the same correction successfully made by Sympson.)

1.1.157 possible] THIS EDITION (Taylor); ~ that ISLIP. Middleton elsewhere idiomatically elides 'that' after 'possible'; alternatively, less frequently, he uses 'that' as a metrical filler; nowhere else is it supplied, superfluously and extrametrically, as here. An easy compositorial or scribal interpolation, which lessens the dramatic force of the question, as well as disrupting the metre.

1.1.161 he was] ISLIP; he's THIS EDITION (conj. Taylor). For compositorial tense errors compare l. 158 where ISLIP 'twas became MACOCK 'tis.

1.1.161 was it] ISLIP; was't MACOCK

1.1.188 too] ISLIP; through MASON

1.1.211 work] ISLIP; worth COLMAN, on the grounds that Chamont 'calls the lady lovely worth'; but, suggesting part of God's creation, 'work' makes good sense.

1.1.219 It's] ISLIP ('Tas)

1.1.237 CHAMONT] MACOCK; 2 Gent. ISLIP

1.1.243 curse] THIS EDITION (Taylor); course ISLIP. There are no clear Middleton parallels for the idiom 'course of [noun indicating social class]'. By contrast, compare Michaelmas 1.2.248 'curse of poverty', Women Beware 5.1.223 'curse of wretchedness', Witch 5.3.84 'shame of greatness', Game 5.3.209 'that's the misery of greatness'. An easy misreading.

1.1.245 I will] THIS EDITION (Taylor); I'le ISLIP. The emendation produces not only a more metrical but also a more emphatic reading; ISLIP's contraction could easily result from contamination from the preceding 'I'le', and certainly the repetition weakens the sentence. Middleton's choice of 'I'll stay' or 'I will stay' is elsewhere governed by metre: compare Microcynicon 6.14 'No, I will stay, the fool to gaze upon' and Women Beware 2.2.171 'I swear you shall stay supper.'

1.1.247 away a passion] THIS EDITION; a paffion away ISLIP. Middleton prefers 'take + away + noun (direct object)' (15 times) to 'take + noun (direct object) + away' (twice); his preferred form produces a more regular line, metrically.

1.1.249 poor'st] THIS EDITION (Taylor); pooreft ISLIP. Middleton's choice of 'poorest' or 'poor'st' is elsewhere based purely on metrical considerations: compare Chaste Maid 2.1.24, Phoenix 4.223.

1.1.263 Though] COLMAN (conj. Sympson); thou ISLIP

2.1.6 employs] ISLIP; implies SYMPSON. Within gender stereotypes, fear (or weariness) is as likely to be an employment as a sign of femininity. The emendation thus does not improve the sense, and ISLIP offers the witty conjunction of 'employment' with a complete idleness which can never feel real exhaustion.

2.1.28 his] ISLIP; its SYMPSON. Although 'its' clarifies the sense for a modern reader, 'his' was the obsolescent neuter possessive.

2.1.29 then] ISLIP; than MACOCK. This edition keeps the ISLIP spelling, which can be glossed roughly as 'in that case', whereas 'than' unwarrantedly complicates the syntax and negatives.

2.1.44 me] COLMAN (conj. Heath); one ISLIP. The emendation, as Williams admits, presupposes an easy error; attempts to justify the meaning of ISLIP require extraordinarily contorted interpretations, impossible to communicate onstage. See next note.

2.1.45 promise] SYMPSON; I ~ ISLIP. Williams objects that 'There is no justification for this second change'; but that is only true if the text only passed through one stage of transmission. If the error in the preceding line were made in one transcript, then 'I' could have been interpolated here—in a second transcript, or in the printing house—to restore the clearly required first person pronoun (removed by the error in the preceding line). This sequence is characteristic of correction by printers or scribes: they often leave the original (hard-to-spot) error intact, instead doing something simpler elsewhere. For other evidence of more than one stage of transmission, see 1.1.31–2.

2.1.62 But as black, sir] ISLIP; Thou'rt as black as sin MASON conj. See next note.

THE NICE VALOUR

2.1.67 Or] SYMPSON; O ISLIP. Whether or not emended, the passage balances 'brother' symmetrically against 'sister'. But ISLIP's reading requires 'sister' to be a vocative in an exclamation, addressed to the Lady, who is *not* the Soldier's sister; 'O' thus produces nonsense. SYMPSON's simple emendation instead makes the whole phrase a subjunctive continuation of the preceding speech, meaning '[I would that] my sister [heard me]'; 'sister' can then mean 'sister-in-law', turning the Soldier's remark into a wish that the Lady should be married to his brother, Chamont.

2.1.69 For] MACOCK; Por ISLIP
2.1.70 on] ISLIP; of COLMAN. See next note.
2.1.75 on] THIS EDITION (Taylor); of ISLIP. Since the whole point of this exchange is that Passionate Lord exactly mimics the Soldier's words, the wording should be the same in ll. 70 and 75. But the autograph Trinity manuscript of *A Game at Chess* has 'on 'em' once (TLN 707), 'of 'em' never. This suggests that ISLIP's 'of' is an unconscious modernization (as it was a conscious modernization in COLMAN).
2.1.84 our] ISLIP; your COLMAN
2.1.87 woo] ISLIP *corr.* (wooe); ISLIP *uncorr.* (woe). Either spelling could represent the modern meaning, but the uncorrected spelling is ambiguous.
2.1.88 Divulge] THIS EDITION (Taylor); Divine ISLIP; discharge SYMPSON. 'Discharge' never elsewhere in Middleton has the required sense (= reveal), and in any case proposes a much more difficult misreading than 'divulge/divine'.
2.1.117 mak'st] THIS EDITION (Taylor); makeſt ISLIP; make'st V.A.308. The forward kern of the italic 'k' and the backward kern of the italic 's' made it necessary for ISLIP's compositor to insert an 'e' to prevent type-damage; metrically, a monosyllable is required here, and the otherwise superfluous apostrophe in V.A.308 may be a 'Jonsonian elision', intended to indicate monosyllabic pronunciation.
2.1.117 a heart thy] ISLIP; thy heart a V.A.308
2.1.119 strik'st the fond] ISLIP; strikest fooll's V.A.308
2.1.122 would] ISLIP; will V.A.308
2.1.155 felicity] ISLIP; multiplicity SYMPSON. A 'felicity' is used ironically as a collective term.
2.1.162 This] DYCE; His ISLIP; your SYMPSON; thy WEBER. DYCE's is the easist emendation of ISLIP; the shame of the pregnancy would have been focused upon the unwed mother, not her social superior, the father, whose 'shame' seems not to exist at all, and is certainly not—as hers is—growing.
2.1.181 have] WEBER; heare ISLIP
2.1.193 them] THIS EDITION (Taylor); her ISLIP. The only 'her' who might be so identified here is the Lady (which seems wholly inappropriate in the context) or the Cupid (which the Soldier does not know to be female); by contrast, 'them' would refer to the six Amazons, which the Passionate Lord has 'engross[ed] all to himself', and with whom he has just left the stage. A common enough misreading or substitution.
2.1.212 hear] ISLIP (here)
2.1.231 Speak] THIS EDITION (Taylor); *not in* ISLIP. Not only the metre but the sense suggests that a word is missing here: otherwise, the consequence ('That...again') is considerably removed from its cause ('excuse him not'), which is further complicated by its negative formulation.
2.1.243–54 FIRST GENTLEMAN...SECOND GENTLEMAN] ISLIP (I Gen...2 Gent); Weber claims that the folios have the speech attributions transposed.
2.1.251 Make] SYMPSON; Made ISLIP

2.1.252.1 *Exit...Gentleman*] LANGBAINE; *Exit. I Gent.* ISLIP (after 'murmur'd' 2.1.254). There is not enough space in ISLIP for this marginal direction at its appropriate point in the text; it is inserted after the first available part-line of dialogue.
2.1.260 His] ISLIP (*corr.*); This ISLIP (*uncorr.*)
2.1.262.1 *two Gentlemen*] MACOCK; *2 Gen.* ISLIP. It appears from the plural pronoun at 265 that more than one gentleman leaves the stage here; although ISLIP's abbreviation would most naturally be interpreted to mean 'Exit Second Gentleman', it is ambiguous, and can be interpreted as a call for the exit of two gentleman (probably the First and Second). Compare 5.1.98.1.
2.1.264.1 *two Gentlemen*] MACOCK; *2 Gent.* ISLIP. See preceding note.
2.1.265 sir] THIS EDITION (Taylor); *not in* ISLIP. Virtually every speech by the gentlemen to the Duke contains an honorific 'sir' or 'my lord', almost always used to fill out the metre, and typically inserted at the end of a clause. Both decorum and metre suggest that 'sir' has been accidentally omitted here by a compositor or scribe.
2.1.277 wrestled] ISLIP *corr.* (wreſled); wreſted ISLIP *uncorr.*
2.1.294 pour] ISLIP (powre), MACOCK. Contrast with the spelling 'power' in the following line.
3.1.1 I] MACOCK; I I ISLIP
3.1.10 shape] ISLIP; ~ on THIS EDITION (*conj.* Taylor). Compare 'Whiles that shape's on' (*Roaring Girl* 11.105).
3.1.36 beat me] ISLIP *corr.*; beaten ‸ ISLIP *uncorr.*; beaten me WILLIAMS. Middleton never elsewhere uses 'beaten' after the auxiliary; the obsolete past tense 'beat' occurs in that position at least seven times elsewhere. (It also produces a more regular line, metrically.) So there seems no reason to doubt the accuracy of ISLIP's correction.
3.1.39 burstness] DYCE; business ISLIP; bruise SYMPSON; bruises COLMAN *conj.*; brewis COLMAN *conj.* See also 3.2.166, 171.
3.1.45 AMBO] THIS EDITION (Taylor); Omnes. ISLIP; Brothers LANGBAINE. 'Omnes' may be technically correct, since 'all' as a speech direction usually does not include the other speaker in a dialogue (here, the Clown); but there are in fact only two other speakers on stage. The confusion may be authorial (although Middleton strongly prefers the form 'All', rather than 'Omnes'); alternatively, a scribe or compositor might have misunderstood/misread 'amb' as 'all', or substituted one conventional Latin speech-prefix for another.
3.1.67 No] WEBER; Now ISLIP. This may well be an anticipation of 'now' two lines down as suggested by COLMAN—'it stands in its right place two lines lower'.
3.2.20 From P. to E.] WILLIAMS; From C.P. to E. ISLIP; From P.A. to C.E. SYMPSON. The 'C.' in ISLIP seems to be a mistake and editors have dealt with this by adding or subtracting letters from 'patience'. It is possible that 'C' was intended as a correction for 'E' (since the word could be spelled 'patienc').
3.2.24 jostle] ISLIP (juſtle)
3.2.27 If I] MACOCK; ~ ‸ ISLIP
3.2.27 hanged;] MACOCK; hang'‸; ISLIP
3.2.67 douse] ISLIP (dowſt). The terminal 'st' may be a variant spelling (though it is not recorded as such by *OED*); however, it would also be the kind of termination error typical of Compositor B.
3.2.68 whelk] THIS EDITION (Taylor); whelpe ISLIP. The only relevant meaning of *whelp* recorded in *OED* is a dialect sense, only recorded in the twentieth century, 'welt' (*welt n²*). By contrast, *whelk* was often used of a variety of pustules on the face (*OED whelk* 2); any such sore on the lips would make them particularly sensitive to a blow. The proposed

error could have arisen from misreading or assimilation to the preceding 'lips'.

3.2.76 table says] LANGBAINE; tables ~ ISLIP. Elsewhere always singular; the plural here creates an unusually awkward failure of concord, which could easily arise from compositorial contamination.

3.2.95 know, it] ISLIP; know it, 'tis LANGBAINE

3.2.117 become] MACOCK; hecome ISLIP

3.2.153 passest] THIS EDITION (Taylor); posest ISLIP. ISLIP could be defended as a spelling of 'possessed', meaning 'persuaded', as at *Michaelmas* 1.2.51. However, the past tense seems inappropriate, because Lepet had not been persuaded in the previous speech; the accentation, on the second syllable, does not fit the metre. The emendation (which presumes a simple a/o misreading) through the use of the present tense indicates a change in Lepet's opinion, effected by the Clown's intervening speech. It is accented on the first syllable, as the metre seems to require, and has two relevant meanings: 'surpass' (outdo me in suffering) and 'pass' (overtake me on the way down the stairs).

3.2.155 filled] ISLIP (fil'd)

3.2.165 men] ISLIP; me WILLIAMS. Lepet does not want *other* people to think of it (lest they use it against him).

3.3.2 not] MACOCK; no ISLIP

3.3.8 mistresses] THIS EDITION (Taylor); Ladies ISLIP. 'Mistresses' seems necessary to prompt 'mischiefs' in the following line; the synonym-substitution of 'ladies' could easily have been encouraged by contamination from Cupid's previous speech.

3.3.12 screech] THIS EDITION (Taylor); *not in* ISLIP. Metrically, there seems to be a syllable missing between 'bird' and 'sometimes', and as the text stands it is not clear which 'bird' is intended, or why a person who hears it should be considered 'happy'. SYMPSON solved this problem by emending 'bird sometimes' to 'night-bird's summons'—not an attractive solution, but a recognition of the problem. The verb 'screech' identifies the bird as a screech-owl (as at *Solomon* 17.58, *Witch* 3.3.10, 5.2.43), which is 'heard' at night (as at *Witch* 3.3.5); this identification picks up the reference to a nest of owls, three lines before, and paradoxically—as elsewhere in this scene—declares that something usually associated with melancholy is a source of pleasure and happiness. The word could have been omitted by simple eyeskip from the first letter of 'screech' to the first letter of 'sometimes'.

3.3.24 knew't] THIS EDITION (Taylor); know't ISLIP. The present tense 'know't' does not agree with the past tense 'when I loved'; 'knew't' assumes an easy o/e misreading, and 'experienced it' seems more relevant than 'am intellectually certain of it'.

3.3.26 neat-sitting] ISLIP; neat-fitting WILLIAMS *conj.* ISLIP's reading is confirmed by 'sit close and neat' (*Quiet Life* 3.1.171).

3.3.32 but] DYCE; out ISLIP

3.3.36 Hence] In the play (ISLIP) the song is not given a title, but HARPER (the earliest printed version, 1634) entitles it 'The melancholly Lovers Song' (suggesting an awareness of its context in the play), and most of the manuscripts also give it a title: Sonnett: INNS[1]; A Sonnett. HARFLETE; Of Melancholy OXFORD[1], OXFORD[4]; The Praise of Melancholy SCRIBE, OXFORD[5]; In laudem Melancholie 15226; On y[e] prayse of Melancholly OSBORN 200; Song in y[e] praise of Melancholly OXFORD[2]; Verses made of Meloncholy J.A., BOYLE; Melancholly OXFORD[3], RAWLINSON, V.A.319, HINSON, GODOLPHIN, MONTAGU;

Melancholicus CAMBRIDGE; A Melancholy OSBORN 205; On Melancholy T.C., HIGHMORE, V.A.322, DANIELL, PIKE, PERCEVAL, ARCHARD; Vpon Melancholy LANE; A Melancholy Meditation DAY, INNS[2]; The Image of Melancolly OXFORD[6]; The Lovers Melancholy OXFORD[7], MENNES; A Song PAULET. Only nine manuscripts have no title: CALVERLEY, CHOLMLEY, WOLF, ILES, HILTON, ASHMOLE, CHRIST CHURCH, OSBORN 213, LYELL.

3.3.36-42 Hence...sweetest melancholy] *not in* DAY, INNS[2], PERCEVAL, HINSON

3.3.36 Hence...delights] *bis* LYELL

3.3.36 Hence] Hence, hence OXFORD[3-4], OSBORN 205, DANIELL, V.A.322, OXFORD[7], V.A.319, HILTON, MENNES, CHRIST CHURCH

3.3.36 all you] *not in* INNS[1]

3.3.36 you] yee CALVERLEY, CHOLMLEY, SCRIBE[2], OXFORD[1], OSBORN 200, HIGHMORE, CAMBRIDGE, V.A.322, PIKE, HARFLETE, HILTON, GODOLPHIN, CHRIST CHURCH, MONTAGU, LYELL. Middleton preferred 'you'.

3.3.36 vain] fond 15226, J.A., LANE, CAMBRIDGE, BOYLE, OXFORD[6], PIKE, HARFLETE, ARCHARD

3.3.36 delights] delight OXFORD[6]

3.3.37 As short] As short, as short ILES

3.3.37 As short as] More ~ then CHOLMLEY, RAWLINSON, ARCHARD; More ~ & fweet then T.C.; so ~ ~ MONTAGU, LYELL

3.3.37 are the] ~ ~ shortest OSBORN 205, DANIELL; all ~ ARCHARD; bee ∧ MONTAGU

3.3.38 Wherein...your] which men consume in LYELL

3.3.38 Wherein] where mad CAMBRIDGE; Where HARFLETE

3.3.38 you spend your] Youths ~ their ASHMOLE; men ~ their 15226, CHOLMLEY, CAMBRIDGE, RAWLINSON; wee ~ our OXFORD[1], PIKE; love spends its J.A., BOYLE, LANE, HARFLETE; yee ~ ~ SCRIBE[2]; ~ ~ all ~ OSBORN 205

3.3.38-9 A stanza break is marked here in 15226, CAMBRIDGE, MONTAGU.

3.3.39 There's...life] This world hath nothing LYELL

3.3.39 There's] Ther OSBORN 213

3.3.39 naught] nothing 15226, OXFORD[1-2], V.A.322, OXFORD[6], PIKE, V.A.319, PAULET, T.C.

3.3.39 in this life] truly 15226, OXFORD[1-2], OXFORD[6], PIKE, PAULET, T.C.; ~ ~ world LANE, CAMBRIDGE, BOYLE, HARFLETE, GODOLPHIN; ~ ~ life's CHRIST CHURCH. Clearly, 'nothing truly' is a compound variant, linking five manuscripts, and probably originating in Oxford. Although no manuscript contains *truly* without *naught*, two manuscripts (V.A.322, V.A.319) have *nothing* with *in this life*, and this pattern suggests that *truly* might be a deliberate attempt to correct the metre, disrupted when *nothing* had been inadvertently substituted for *naught*. The prepositional phrase 'in this life' implies the existence of another life (as in *Hengist* 4.2.201, *Virtue* 290, 297).

3.3.40 If...see't] *not in* GODOLPHIN

3.3.40 men] INNS[1]+; man ISLIP, MACOCK, HARFLETE. All of the other texts agree in the plural; MACOCK is a reprint of ISLIP, and HARFLETE—a relatively late and error-prone text, which clearly is not related to ISLIP stemmatically—demonstrates the ease of the substitution.

3.3.40 were wise to] have eyes ~ CHOLMLEY; had Eyes ~ OXFORD[5], OXFORD[7], RAWLINSON *uncorrected*; could truly OXFORD[6]. The variant substitutes a commoner idiom; for ISLIP, compare 'were you so *wise* to' (*Chaste Maid* 3.1.22), 'if his cares *were wise*' (*Women Beware* 2.2.73), 'view me with an intellectual eye, As *wise* men shoot their beams forth' (*Virtue* 55-6), 'If *sin were* half so *wise*' (*Game at Chess* 3.1.206).

3.3.40   see't] see it 15226, T.C.. Middleton uses the contraction 'see't' at least 31 times, 'to see't' 5 times.

3.3.41   But] Save CALVERLEY, OXFORD¹, J.A., CAMBRIDGE, BOYLE, LANE, OXFORD⁵⁻⁶, HARFLETE, ASHMOLE. Middleton uses both idioms. But ISLIP and most other texts use one here and the other at l. 50, thus producing more lexical variety than the alternative reading here, which may result from assimilation.

3.3.41   only] *not in* CHOLMLEY, PIKE

3.3.42   O sweetest melancholy] OXFORD³, ISLIP, OSBORN 213; ~ sweet ~ HILTON, MONTAGU; *not in* INNS¹, CALVERLEY, CHOLMLEY, 15226, SCRIBE, OXFORD¹, OSBORN 200, J.A., HARPER, OXFORD², LANE, CAMBRIDGE, HIGHMORE, BOYLE, OXFORD⁴⁻⁵, OSBORN 205, DANIELL, V.A.322, OXFORD⁶⁻⁷, PIKE, HARFLETE, RAWLINSON, V.A.319, PERCEVAL, ILES, PAULET, T.C., ARCHARD, MENNES, HINSON, ASHMOLE, GODOLPHIN, LYELL. For the reading in MONTAGU, see its variant at l. 54, where it has the superlative found in other witnesses here. The line is repeated in HILTON and CHRIST CHURCH, a variant which seems due to the composer (as at ll. 53, 54); but the repetition does testify to the presence of the line (at least once) in his source. The absence of the line from the earliest music manuscript (ILES) may be due to the (other) composer, and the currency of that earlier setting of the first stanza may account for the predominance of this variant. The line in ISLIP can hardly result from compositorial interpolation; it might represent an authorial draft, altered by the composer, and therefore preserved only in texts which derive from Middleton himself (at whatever remove). All of the manuscript texts which preserve this line, with the exception of OXFORD³, postdate ISLIP.

3.3.42   O] ISLIP, HILTON, CHRIST CHURCH, OSBORN 213, MONTAGU; a OXFORD³. WILLIAMS records 'a' in HILTON, but Ioppolo reports that the word is clearly 'o'. Middleton uses both interjections.

3.3.42–3   *stanza break* CALVERLEY, 15226, J.A., LANE, CAMBRIDGE, HIGHMORE, BOYLE, OXFORD³⁻⁵, V.A.322, HARFLETE, OXFORD⁷, PAULET², ASHMOLE, MONTAGU (and perhaps INNS¹). In V.A.322, V.A.319 the song is split in two, and treated as two separate poems, with the break between 'Melancholy' and 'Welcome'; in DAY, INNS², PERCEVAL, HINSON the first seven lines are omitted; in GODOLPHIN ll. 42–8 are omitted. The lines before 'Welcome,' with a different metre and rhyme scheme than the rest of the song, clearly belong to one stanza; ISLIP is ambiguous, because the stanza break here coincides with a column break, and WILLIAMS accordingly does not mark a break here. Most manuscripts have no stanza breaks at all.

3.3.43–8   Welcome...loves] *not in* GODOLPHIN

3.3.43   Welcome] Come OXFORD⁶, HINSON; O ~ HILTON; Then ~ RAWLINSON; The ~ LYELL

3.3.43   folded arms] armes folded OSBORN 200, HIGHMORE

3.3.43   arms] hands HARPER

3.3.43   and] *not in* OSBORN 200, HIGHMORE, ARCHARD; with HINSON

3.3.43   fixèd] fix'd LANE

3.3.43   eyes] eye PERCEVAL

3.3.44   sigh] sight INNS¹, CHOLMLEY, SCRIBE, OSBORN 200, CAMBRIDGE, HIGHMORE, OSBORN 205, INNS², PIKE, HARFLETE, OXFORD⁶⁻⁷, V.A.319, PERCEVAL, PAULET, T.C., ARCHARD, MENNES, OSBORN 213; look J.A., LANE, BOYLE, CHRIST CHURCH. 'Look' obviously derives from 'sight'; either 'sigh' or 'sight' could be a misreading/mishearing of the other (especially since the next word begins with 't'). There are parallels in Middleton for either idiom with 'piercing'.

3.3.44   that] that's CHOLMLEY, HARPER, OXFORD⁴, CHRIST CHURCH; which OXFORD⁵, HINSON

3.3.44   that piercing mortifies] shal ~ mortifie PERCEVAL. Obviously related to the same text's error (also unique) in the rhyme word of the previous line. The only other appearance of the verb 'mortify' in Middleton's canon is in this scene; the noun 'mortification' appears only in *Quiet Life* (2.4.18, 5.2.185).

3.3.45–6   A look...ground, | A tongue...sound] A tongue... sound | A looke...ground T.C.

3.3.45   A look] An eye J.A., LANE, BOYLE; A loock HARFLETE

3.3.45   that's] that J.A., PERCEVAL; *not in* MONTAGU

3.3.45   fastened] fixed J.A., LANE, BOYLE, V.A.319

3.3.45   to] on CALVERLEY, 15226, OXFORD¹, J.A., DAY, HARPER, LANE, CAMBRIDGE, BOYLE, PIKE, HINSON, CHRIST CHURCH, MONTAGU; upon V.A.319. Middleton used both idioms.

3.3.45   the] then DANIELL

3.3.46   chained] ty'd OSBORN 200, HIGHMORE, V.A.319; chand OXFORD⁶; strained ARCHARD. Compare *Women Beware* 4.2.155: 'chained up her tongue'.

3.3.46   up] *not in* OXFORD⁶

3.3.46   without a] ~ ∧ MONTAGU

3.3.46   sound,] OSBORN 200, J.A., DAY, LANE, OXFORD⁵, V.A.319, ASHMOLE; ~ ∧ CALVERLEY, 15226, OXFORD¹⁻², CAMBRIDGE, OSBORN 205, INNS², DANIELL, OXFORD⁶, PIKE, HARFLETE, PERCEVAL, PAULET, T.C., HILTON, HINSON, CHRIST CHURCH, OSBORN 213, MONTAGU, LYELL; ~., CAMBRIDGE; ~; SCRIBE; ~. CHOLMLEY?, HIGHMORE?, OXFORD³⁻⁴, V.A.322, OXFORD⁷, RAWLINSON, ISLIP, ILES. Of the texts with a full stop here, ILES ends with this line; RAWLINSON originally omitted the four following lines (later added marginally).

3.3.46–7   ISLIP clearly calls for a stanza break here (as does PERCEVAL); in CHRIST CHURCH the music ends here, although the scribe continues with two and a half additional lines of text under blank staves, so that it is difficult to know what to make of the incompleteness; but in ILES both music and text end here. In any case, there is no break in terms of metre, rhyme scheme, or sense, and the great majority of texts do not mark a stanza-break here (even when they mark them elsewhere). The error might result from the compositor's misinterpretation of a page-break in the manuscript, or from the same process that produced mistaken stanza-breaks elsewhere, in other manuscripts: see 38–9, 48–9.

3.3.47–54   Fountain-heads...melancholy] *not in* ILES

3.3.47–50   Fountain-heads...owls] *not in* RAWLINSON *uncorrected*

3.3.47–8   Fountain-heads...loves] *not in* CAMBRIDGE

3.3.47   Fountain-heads] Fountaines ~ CALVERLEY, 15226, DAY, OXFORD⁵, INNS², DANIELL, OXFORD⁷, ARCHARD; And fountaines ~ OSBORN 200, HIGHMORE; Fountaines woods V.A.319; shady bowers INNS¹; Treadlesse paths OXFORD². Middleton has 'fountain-head' at *Solomon* 15.8; he never uses the noun possessively.

3.3.47   and] *not in* MONTAGU

3.3.47   pathless] walks & OSBORN 200, HIGHMORE; shady OXFORD²; Palelesse HARFLETE

3.3.47   groves] groue PERCEVAL

3.3.48   Places] are ~ HARPER, PERCEVAL

3.3.48   which] yᵗ INNS¹, CALVERLEY, V.A.319, HINSON; where HARPER, OXFORD⁶⁻⁷

3.3.48   loves] shews PERCEVAL (deleted, and replaced with correct 'loues'); moves HINSON; moves | And thoughts of greived weights ASHMOLE. ASHMOLE also adds another line after l. 50, perhaps in order to enable symmetry with its reply-poem 'Come all my deare delights'.

3.3.48–9   Stanza-break marked by J.A., BOYLE, HARFLETE (which divide into three six-line stanzas, numbered in the left margin 1, 2, 3) and by LANE (same stanzas, without marginal numbers).

3.3.49–50   Moonlight...owls] *not in* PERCEVAL; *transposed to follow next couplet* OXFORD[2]

3.3.49   Moonlight walks] Moon-shine ~ CHOLMLEY; A ~ walke 15226, CAMBRIDGE, PIKE, T.C.; Moon like ~ HIGHMORE; Moon--like wakes OXFORD[3]; midnight ~ RAWLINSON *corrected*; ~ faire GODOLPHIN

3.3.49   when] whiles ASHMOLE; where MONTAGU

3.3.49–54   all...melancholy] *not in* CHRIST CHURCH

3.3.49   the fowls] ~ fowle J.A.; ‸ ~ OXFORD[2]; ~ souls CAMBRIDGE, HIGHMORE.

3.3.50   Are] as HIGHMORE

3.3.50   warmly housed] warme ith howse OSBORN 205

3.3.50   warmly] safely 15226, OXFORD[5], PIKE, V.A.319, T.C.; falsly CAMBRIDGE; *not in* ASHMOLE. The CAMBRIDGE variant is more probably a misreading of 'safely' than an independent substitution for 'warmly'.

3.3.50   housed] coucht HINSON

3.3.50   save] but CHOLMLEY, CAMBRIDGE, PIKE, HARFLETE, T.C., HINSON, MONTAGU; save only ASHMOLE. ASHMOLE's interpolation is clearly metrical compensation for the accidental omission of 'warmly', earlier in the line. T.C. spells 'butt batts', which suggests that the variant may have arisen through contamination; on the other hand, it calls attention to the euphonic appeal of 'but bats'.

3.3.50   bats] bat PIKE, OXFORD[7]; backes LYELL

3.3.50   owls] ~; | These are o.r cheife Delights ASHMOLE. See ASHMOLE's related variant at l. 48.

3.3.51   A midnight...groan] *not in* J.A.

3.3.51   A midnight] ~ passing INNS[1], OXFORD[2], LANE, BOYLE, HINSON; ~ passinge ~ DANIELL, ASHMOLE; ~ Parting HARFLETE, T.C.; ‸ Midnight SCRIBE[1], OSBORN 200, OXFORD[7], GODOLPHIN, LYELL; ‸ Midnights SCRIBE[2], HIGHMORE, PERCEVAL; midnight's OXFORD[6], PAULET. The symmetry of the line makes it easy to transpose the two adjectives, especially as the conjunction of the two phrases implies that the midnight bell rings for the departing soul; but 'passing bell' perhaps substitutes a commoner collocation.

3.3.51   bell] bels PERCEVAL, LYELL; Knell OXFORD[7]; psales GODOLPHIN (?prales). Perhaps 'psalms' was intended; although 'pralle' is a recorded fifteenth-century spelling of the verb *prowl*, the noun *prowl* is not recorded until the nineteenth century.

3.3.51   a] or CALVERLEY, HIGHMORE, PIKE; and SCRIBE, OSBORN 200, PAULET[1], GODOLPHIN, LYELL

3.3.51   parting] midnight INNS[1], BOYLE, HINSON, DANIELL, T.C.; midnights LANE, HARFLETE; passing CHOLMLEY. For 'midnight groan' compare *Women Beware* 4.1.262: 'The powers of darkness' groan'.

3.3.51   groan] groanes GODOLPHIN, LYELL

3.3.52   These] *not in* PERCEVAL

3.3.52   are] be CHOLMLEY

3.3.52   the] *not in* CHOLMLEY, OXFORD[1], OSBORN 200, J.A., LANE, HIGHMORE, BOYLE

3.3.52   sounds] delights CHOLMLEY; thoughts 15226; sweetes OXFORD[1], PIKE; sighes HARPER; things LANE, OXFORD[2], BOYLE, RAWLINSON *uncorrected*; Sounde HINSON; sights OSBORN 213. The profusion of alternative nouns here probably results from misunderstanding of the grammar: 'These' refers only to the

two nouns in the preceding line (bell, groan), and therefore 'sounds' is appropriate. However, any reader who did not recognize that ll. 47–50 are governed by the verb 'Welcome' (43) would consider 'sounds' an inept noun, and search for a replacement.

3.3.52   we feed] I ~ INNS[1], HARPER, PERCEVAL; love feeds GODOLPHIN; ~ live LYELL

3.3.53–4   Then...melancholy] *not in* GODOLPHIN

3.3.53   Then] Other ⟨???⟩ mee CAMBRIDGE. The middle word is illegible.

3.3.53   Then...bones] The phrase is repeated in HILTON: See l. 42.

3.3.53   stretch] stretcht HARPER

3.3.53   our bones] OXFORD[5] has an illegible symbol in place of these two words.

3.3.53   our] my INNS[1], CAMBRIDGE, PERCEVAL; your CALVERLEY, CHOLMLEY, 15226, OXFORD[1–4], OSBORN 205, INNS[2], OXFORD[6], RAWLINSON, ARCHARD, ASHMOLE, MONTAGU; the DAY; out HARPER; thy V.A.319, LYELL. For 'out' see next note. None of the four earliest manuscripts has 'our'.

3.3.53   bones] self INNS[1]; Limmes out CHOLMLEY; limbs 15226, OXFORD[2], RAWLINSON, HINSON, T.C.; loue CAMBRIDGE

3.3.53   in] on OXFORD[2]; into DAY

3.3.53   a] some INNS[1], 15226, J.A., LANE, CAMBRIDGE, BOYLE, PIKE, HARFLETE; the V.A.319

3.3.53   still gloomy] glome shady LYELL

3.3.53   still] sadd INNS[1], 15226, OSBORN 200, CAMBRIDGE, HIGH-MORE, PIKE, RAWLINSON, T.C.; *not in* DAY. ISLIP is clearly correct, combining the more complex and less predictable senses 'quiet', 'motionless' and 'perpetually'.

3.3.53   gloomy valley] ~ ally DAY; gloominge alley INNS[2], V.A.319. This looks like a case of progressive error.

3.3.54   Nothing's so dainty sweet] There's nothing ‸ ~~ HILTON (twice)

3.3.54   Nothing's so] OXFORD[1], SCRIBE[1], ISLIP; Nothing ~ OS-BORN 213; for nothing is ~ LYELL; There's nothing ‸ INNS[1], CALVERLEY, CHOLMLEY, 15226, SCRIBE[2], OSBORN 200, DAY, HARPER, ARCHARD[2] CAMBRIDGE, HIGHMORE, OXFORD[4–5], OSBORN 205, INNS[2], DANIELL, PIKE, HARFLETE, OXFORD[7], V.A.319, PER-CEVAL, PAULET, T.C., HILTON, ARCHARD, MENNES, ASHMOLE, MONTAGU; Where's nothing ‸ J.A., LANE, BOYLE, OXFORD[3]; Thers naught ‸ OXFORD[6], RAWLINSON; There nought ‸ HINSON. Only four texts agree with Islip, and two of those—OSBORN 213, LYELL—are among the three latest witnesses, and probably derivative from the printed text of ISLIP. The frequency of the 'there's/where's nothing' variant can hardly be attributed to a scribal error shared by so many different texts; it must represent an authoritative early variant, probably present in the original musical setting; see also the other variant in this line, below.

3.3.54   so dainty] in y.s life OXFORD[6], RAWLINSON (producing, in these two manuscripts, an exact repetition of l. 39)

3.3.54   dainty sweet] pleasant HINSON

3.3.54   dainty] truly CALVERLEY, 15226, SCRIBE, OXFORD[1], OSBORN 200, OXFORD[2], CAMBRIDGE, HIGHMORE, OXFORD[5], PIKE, OXFORD[7], PERCEVAL, PAULET[2], MENNES; *not in* HARFLETE, PAULET[1], LYELL. 'Dainty' is a favourite word of Middleton's, appearing as an adjective or adverb at least 51 times in his works.

3.3.54   sweet] ~ | If men were wise to see't PIKE; ~ ____ If men— RAWLINSON

3.3.54   as...melancholy] *contraction mark* PAULET[2]

3.3.54   as] ISLIP, HINSON, OSBORN 213; faue INNS[1], CALVERLEY, SCRIBE, OXFORD[1], J.A., OXFORD[2], LANE, CAMBRIDGE, HIGHMORE, BOYLE, OXFORD[3], OXFORD[5–6], HARFLETE, PERCEVAL, ASHMOLE;

but CHOLMLEY, 15226, OSBORN 200, DAY, OXFORD[4], OSBORN 205, INNS[2], DANIELL, PIKE, RAWLINSON, V.A.319, PAULET[1], T.C., HILTON, ARCHARD, MENNES, MONTAGU; to ˄ HARPER. Almost all texts collated agree against ISLIP in placing an adversative conjunction here; ISLIP is supported only by two late texts. ISLIP's 'as' could easily result from compositorial or scribal substitution of the commoner reading ('as' almost automatically following 'so'). This variant is probably related to the variant at the beginning of this line, since there is a real difference in sense between 'There's nothing sweet, except melancholy' and 'There's nothing *so* sweet *as* melancholy.' All three variants—as, but, save—can be paralleled in Middleton, but the closest Middleton parallel to the whole image is 'there's nothing tastes so sweet as your Welsh mutton' (*Chaste Maid* 4.1.159-60). It seems likely that ISLIP preserves a Middletonian reading. It is certainly possible, but less certain, that Middleton was responsible for the linked variants in the song texts. In terms of overall frequency in the period, *save*—which also occurs in the earliest extant text—would be the 'rarer' reading, and hence more likely to be authorial than the much more common adversative 'but'.

3.3.54   lovely] ISLIP, OSBORN 213; *not in* INNS[1]+; Deepe HINSON; *only* CAMBRIDGE, HARFLETE, RAWLINSON. The 'only' is clearly designed to create an exact repetition of line 41. None of the other texts contains a modifier here, but ISLIP seems unlikely to be an interpolation, since the word could not have been picked up from anywhere in the immediate context.

3.3.54   melancholy] ~ | O sweetest Melancholy MONTAGU. For this variant see l. 42, which it clearly echoes. In PERCEVAL, PAULET the song is followed, without a stanza break, by six additional lines attributed to Henry King; in OSBORN 200 there are reciprocal cross-references linking the song to the same six lines (p. 109): My woeful monument shall be a cell, | The murmur of the purling brook my knell, | And for my epitaph the rock shall groan | Eternally; if any ask the stone | What wretched thing doth in that compass lie, | The hollow echo answer shall, 'tis I. In ASHMOLE, a sexual parody is written line by line alongside it, on the right ('Come all my dear delights | As pleasing as the nights'). More often, the song is followed by William Strode's 'An Opposite to Melancholy' (LANE, WOLF, ARCHARD, OXFORD[1], OXFORD[2], OXFORD[7], MENNES).

3.3.54.1   *at one door*] THIS EDITION (Taylor); *not in* ISLIP. This is implied by the contrasting 'another door' at 3.4.0.1.

3.4   *scene division* WILLIAMS; *not in* ISLIP, which does not contain any scene-divisions within Act 3. WEBER continues scene 3 for 67 lines more. DYCE follows him—assuming that 'woodcock' (l. 1) refers to the Passionate Lord, having no brains. But according to Williams the empty woodcock is Lepet. This interpretation better fits the dramatic action: Lepet can be 'ginned' [= trapped] by 'keep[ing] this door fast', not allowing him to escape, but the whole point of the trap is that the Passionate Lord is not trapped, but will be loosed upon Lepet. Assuming two doors, the door from which Lepet has entered is kept closed, so he cannot escape the way he came, and the other door will be the one from which the Passionate Lord will emerge.

3.4.5   melancholy] MACOCK; melancho ISLIP

3.4.7.1   *at separate doors*] THIS EDITION (Taylor); *not in* ISLIP. First Brother follows the Passionate Lord, in order to incense him; Second Brother guards 'another door' from which Lepet has entered. See notes above at ll. 54.1, 3.4.

4.1.4   dry-beat] THIS EDITION (Taylor); dry beaten ISLIP. For the form compare *Patient Man* 11.22, *Roaring Girl* 7.216. Middleton only seems to use the form 'beaten' as metrical padding;

here it disrupts the metre. There was a natural tendency for compositors (especially by mid-century) to modernize the form.

4.1.6   'mongst] THIS EDITION (Taylor); amongft ISLIP. The distinction between the two forms, in Middleton, seems to serve no purpose but metre, and the aphetic form would be metrical here.

4.1.54   that] ISLIP; thy WEBER

4.1.68   truth] ISLIP (troth)

4.1.70   am I] ISLIP; I am WEBER

4.1.76   sets] DYCE (*conj.* Heath); lets ISLIP. Although the sense 'allows it to be seen' is not impossible, it seems less relevant than 'displays it prominently'; moreover, there is no Middleton parallel for 'lets out'; for 'sets out' compare *Michaelmas* 3.1.18, *Trick* 1.1.9, *Chaste Maid* 1.1.109, 4.1.214, etc.

4.1.77   sir] ISLIP; sirs THIS EDITION (*conj.* Taylor). See next note. Since the text does not provide an exit direction here, the compositor or scribe could easily have assumed that this speech was spoken to the Duke, and consciously or unconsciously have altered the plural to singular accordingly.

4.1.77.1   *Exeunt Gentlemen*] WILLIAMS (*subst.*); *not in* ISLIP. As Dyce and Williams note, as the First Gentleman enters, with others, at l. 57.1 and again at l. 137.1, he needs to leave the stage at some point between these two entrances. Dyce thinks the gentlemen withdraw before the dialogue between the Duke and Chamont, and Williams positions the exit here. It would be most economical, and least distracting dramatically, for the gentlemen to exit together; they cannot do so before the Duke's entrance, and the Second Gentleman speaks at l. 71; thereafter the dialogue does not mention them again, before the re-entrance at l. 137.1. And this is the only occasion when someone is specifically invited to depart.

4.1.112   curiosity] ISLIP; courtesy SYMPSON *conj.*

4.1.138   GENTLEMEN] ISLIP (*Gent.*), DYCE; *1. Gentleman* COLMAN; *Other Gentlemen* WILLIAMS

4.1.151   my] ISLIP *corr.*; any ISLIP *uncorr.*

4.1.164   he] THIS EDITION (Taylor); the ISLIP. Although the article makes a kind of sense, it is not clear why lechery should be preliminary to the first fault, when we would expect it to be the first fault itself. Middleton often uses *first* as an adverb modifying the verb *begins with* (*Revenger* 2.1.237, 4.4.79) or *begin* (*Black Book* 116, *Meeting* 315-16, *Dissemblers* 5.2.243, *Widow* 2.1.160, 2.2.12, *Old Law* 1.1.159, *Hengist* 3.3.29, 4.2.119, *Entertainments* 2.29, *Women Beware* 3.2.180, *Virtue* 122, *Changeling* 5.3.88); he never uses *the first* to govern the verb, but does use *he begins* (*Puritan* 1.4.206, *Roaring Girl* 5.154, *Women Beware* 5.1.55). The he/the misreading is found often in the period; here, it introduces a characteristic ambiguity ('he first accuses me of lechery; he himself begins with lechery').

4.1.179   mettle] ISLIP (mettall)

4.1.198   redounded] ISLIP; rebounded MASON *conj.*

4.1.203   grinned] ISLIP (grind), MACOCK (grin'd)

4.1.205   jostle] ISLIP (juftle)

4.1.256   truth] ISLIP (troth)

4.1.272   I'fax] ISLIP (I'fex). The apostrophe is not visible in all copies.

4.1.277   Le] ISLIP (La)

4.1.288   not you] ISLIP; you not WEBER

4.1.290   on] THIS EDITION (Taylor); upon ISLIP. Throughout his career, from *Solomon* to *Game at Chess*, Middleton consistently treats 'on earth' and 'upon earth' as metrical variants. Whatever the lineation here, 'upon' would be extrametrical. An easy compositorial or scribal substitution.

4.1.311 'im] WILLIAMS; 'em ISLIP; him LANGBAINE. Elsewhere the printer is consistently singular. This change may, in fact, be only a modernization of spelling, not an emendation.

4.1.315 pikèd] ISLIP (Picked)

4.1.322 one kicked] ISLIP; one kick MACOCK; a kick DYCE

4.1.344 douse] ISLIP (Dowſt). See 3.2.67.

5.1.9 long] DYCE (conj. Mason); longer ISLIP. Although Williams claims that 'A rhyming couplet seems singularly out of place at this point of the text', such mid-scene couplets are characteristic of Middleton. It is not clear why a mid-scene speech-ending couplet would be any less appropriate here than those at 1.1.24–5, 1.1.182–3, 2.1.29–30, 2.1.298–9, 3.1.25–6, 3.2.124–5, 3.4.51–2, 3.4.63–4, 4.1.153–4, 5.1.21–2, 5.1.105–6, 5.2.46–7, 5.3.18–19, 5.3.61–2, 5.3.63–4, 5.3.96–7. Williams himself notes the frequency of scene-ending couplets as evidence of Middleton's authorship; but in dismissing a mid-scene rhyme he seems to have been thinking of Fletcher's practice, not Middleton's. Moreover, the emendation, in addition to providing a characteristic rhyme, improves the sense: in ISLIP this line simply repeats the sense of l. 6, in reference to the Cupid disguise, whereas as emended the line generalizes about 'Cupid' (sexual love). As Williams notes, ISLIP's reading could easily have resulted from contamination by the same word at the end of l. 6.

5.1.45 ho, ho, ho] WILLIAMS; oh, oh, ho, ho. ISLIP; Ho, ho, ho, ho DYCE. Williams, developing Dyce, makes a convincing case for normalizing the form of the song.

5.1.53 ha] ISLIP; ho DYCE

5.1.56 caviary] ISLIP (Caveare). The alternative four-syllable form is necessary for the rhyme.

5.1.67 How] MACOCK; Now ISLIP. Of course the word 'Now' makes local sense almost anywhere, but the exclamation better fits the rest of the song, and ISLIP's emphasis on the present ('I especially miss you now') conflicts with the rest of the line ('I have always missed you').

5.1.67 ha' since] ISLIP; ha-Sense SYMPSON; ha' sense MASON. SYMPSON's reading will 'signify the laughing sense'. Mason's reading is a contraction of 'half-sense' or half-witted. But ISLIP makes sense; the speaker has missed Democritus in intervening ages.

5.1.73 deeper] ISLIP; steeper THIS EDITION (conj. Taylor). The sense must be 'more expensive', which is usually indicated by images of height rather than depth.

5.1.74 BASE] LANGBAINE; Pas. ISLIP

5.1.85 Kicksy] ISLIP (Kicksee). This word seems to have been formed here on the basis of compounds like kickshaw (used five times by Middleton), and kicksey-winsy, first used by Nashe, indicating something fantastic, and leading to other compounds like Shakespeare's 'kickywicky'; but here also including the literal sense of 'kick', given a fake 'French' terminal syllable ('zee' as a French pronunciation for 'the').

5.1.91.1 Exeunt...dancers] WILLIAMS (subst.); not in ISLIP. Although the dancers entered with Lepet and Cupid, they have nothing to do for the remainder of the scene, and theatrically it makes sense to get them off stage as unobtrusively as possible; moreover, it is dramatically effective for Cupid to be left alone on stage with the wounded Passionate Lord, the two of them abandoned by everyone else. The dancers' exit here could be motivated either by terror, or in response to Base's command to pursue the murderer.

5.1.95.1 Exeunt...at another door] THIS EDITION (Taylor); not in ISLIP; Exeunt ambo WILLIAMS. Lepet and Clown have no reason to remain on stage, and naturally exit together; but they clearly do not want to run into their assailant again.

5.1.98.1 two] ISLIP (2.)

5.1.101 lackey] SYMPSON; luckie ISLIP

5.1.104 surgeon] ISLIP (Chirurgeon)

5.1.106 ere] THIS EDITION (Taylor); before ISLIP. The distribution of these synonyms seems to be entirely a matter of metrical convenience, and here there would have been no reason not to use the metrical alternative, especially in the formally more regular context of a couplet. Scribes and compositors are often guilty of synonym-substitution; 'before' is the more modern form, likelier to be unconsciously chosen in such circumstances.

5.2.14 elegance] THIS EDITION (Taylor); elegancy ISLIP. Although 'elegancy' is the commoner form in the period, 'elegance' was used (by Nashe, for instance), and ISLIP's form—which is metrically irregular here—could result from misreading, substitution of the commoner form, contamination from the preceding 'honesty' and 'beauty', or some combination of all three. In contrast to modern usage, 'elegance' is actually 'the rarer reading' here: see Taylor 1988.

5.2.53 noblesse] THIS EDITION (Taylor); nobleneſſe ISLIP. The synonym remained in use through the seventeenth century (OED); again, the compositor or scribe seems to have substituted the commoner, but unmetrical, reading. See preceding note.

5.3.0.1–2, 5.3.1, 5.3.4, 5.3.20, 5.3.113, 5.3.116 Moulebaiser] THIS EDITION (Taylor); Moulbazon ISLIP. Like 'Poltrot' and 'Lepet' and other Middletonian names, this one is almost certain to mean something; as emended, it could be translated 'pussy-kisser', derogatory French slang which is appropriate to his comic status. (Compare modern 'ass-kisser'.) Literally, 'moule' is 'mussel', which anatomically and in other ways suggested the female genitalia. The er/on misreading would be especially easy for a compositor setting a foreign language name; the word would probably have been spelled 'Moulbazer'.

5.3.24 at] ISLIP corr.; it ISLIP uncorr.

5.3.55–6 suitor...sister] ISLIP; sister...suitor WILLIAMS conj. This proposed transposition is much more attractive than WEBER's emendation. (See next note.)

5.3.56 sister] ISLIP (ſiſter); suitor WEBER. 'Suitor' apparently makes a clearer sense: she is a sister already, and she has not been 'made' one by her respect for Chamont. However, the compositor must have set 'sister' (with its two ligatures) deliberately; he could have misread the manuscript, but errors of this kind are more likely to repeat the preceding parallel noun (suitor), rather than vary it. Her respect has not made her a sister, but it has made her—what she has never been before—'a most importunate' one (importunity being considered inappropriate to her gender).

5.3.82 made] THIS EDITION (Taylor); not in ISLIP. ISLIP's line seems incorrect for two reasons: it is metrically irregular, and Middleton does not elsewhere use the idiom 'ha[ve] me a gentleman' in this sense. By contrast, he does use gentleman as the object of the verb 'make' or 'made', as at 2.1.296, Phoenix 8.83–4, etc. It is easy for a compositor or scribe, setting two consecutive words which begin and end with the same letter, to skip from the beginning of the first to the end of the second: 'm[e mad]e'.

5.3.88 I'm] ISLIP uncorrected (I'am); I am ISLIP corrected

5.3.101 affection] MACOCK; affections ISLIP. The plural not only creates a failure of concord with 'Is', but a failure of parallelism with 'will', and could easily have resulted from assimilation to the immediately following 'stronger'.

5.3.159 were] SYMPSON; was ISLIP

5.3.166 wife] MACOCK; wife ISLIP
5.3.183 and admiration are her] ISLIP *corr*.; her and admiration are ISLIP *uncorr*. The uncorrected reading looks like another example of two-stage error: first 'her' was omitted accident-

ally, then re-inserted in the wrong place. It is impossible to tell whether the misplaced reinsertion took place as a result of foul-proof correction (as Hammersmith suggests, p. 316) or in the printer's manuscript copy.

PRESS VARIANTS

Copies collated:

CSMH Henry E. Huntington Library, 112111
HOY Cyrus Hoy
IU¹ University of Illinois, copy 1
MB Boston Public Library, G.3960.27
MNU University of Minnesota, Z823B38/foCa
NCD Duke University, 429544
NIC Cornell University, A951587
NJP Princeton University, Ex.3623.1/1647q., copy 2
PST Pennsylvania State University
VIU¹ University of Virginia, 570973
VIU² University of Virginia, 217972
WAU University of Washington, 29424
WMU¹, WMU², WMU³ University of Wisconsin–Milwaukee, copies 1, 2, 3
WU University of Wisconsin, Madison, 1543420

Partially collated:

ICN Newberry Library, Silver copy
IU² University of Illinois, copy 2
NCU University of North Carolina, Chapel Hill

Quire 3T (outer sheet, outer forme)

Uncorrected: VIU¹

Sig. 3T4ᵛ

2.1.43 good.] ~, *corr*; ~; *unc*
2.1.87 woo] wooe *corr*; woe *unc*

Quire 3U (outer sheet, inner forme)

Uncorrected: WMU¹

Sig. 3U1ᵛ

2.1.260 His] *corr*; This *unc*

2.1.277 wrestled] wreſled *corr*; wreſted *unc*
2.1.292 own.] owne, *corr*; owneₐ *unc*
3.1.36 pain, gentlemen; he's beat me] pain gentlemen; 'has beate me *corr*; paine Gentlemen; 'has beaten ₐ *unc*

Sig. 3U4

page number 159 *corr*; 145 *unc*
4.1.151 my] *corr*; any *unc*
4.1.172 tried,...dross;] try'd,...droſſe; *corr*; try'd;...droſſe, *unc*

Quire 3X (outer sheet, inner forme)

Uncorrected: HOY, ICN, MB, MNU, PST, VIU², WMU²⁻³, WU

Sig. 3X1ᵛ

5.2.36 murderer] *corr*; ɯurderer *unc*

Quire 3X (inner sheet, outer forme)

Uncorrected: CSMH, ICN, IU², MB, NCD, NIC, NJP, VIU¹, WAU, WMU¹

Sig. 3X2

5.3.24 at] *corr*; it *unc*

Quire 3X (inner sheet, inner forme)

Uncorrected: ICN, MB

Sig. 3X2ᵛ

5.3.88 I'm] I am *corr*; I'am *unc*
5.3.162 him] *corr*; hi m *unc*

Sig. 3X3

5.3.183 Honour ₐ and admiration are her] *corr*; ~ her ~ ~ are ₐ *unc*
Prologue.11 baseness;] baſeneſſe; *corr*; baſeneſſeₐ *unc*
Epilogue.6 nicer] Nicer *corr*; nicer *unc*

STAGE DIRECTIONS

1.1.0.1–3 *Actus primus. Scæna prima*
1.1.0.1–3 *Duke, Shamont, and 4 Gentlemmen*
1.1.72 *Exit*
1.1.77.1 *Enter Lapet*
1.1.143 *Exit*
1.1.144.1 *Enter Lady, the Dukes sister, Lapets wife*
1.1.156 *Exit*
1.1.183 *Exit*
1.1.183.1 *Enter the Passionate Lord, the Dukes Kinsman, makes a congy or two to nothing*
1.1.245.1 *Ex.Pas.Lord*
1.1.251 *Ent. a Servant*
1.1.253.1 *Ent. Shamounts brother a Souldier*
1.1.264–2.1.0.1 *Exeunt.*
2.1.0.1–2 *Actus Secundus. Scæna prima*
2.1.0.2–3 *Enter Shamonts brother, a Souldier, and a Lady the Dukes sister*
2.1.48.1 *Enter Shamont & a servant listening*

2.1.66 *Ex. Shamont, Servant*
2.1.69.1 *Enter Passionate Lord*
2.1.90.1 *Enter 1 Gen*
2.1.124.1 *Enter one like a Cupid offering to shoot at him*
2.1.135 *aside*
2.1.139 *exit*
2.1.147.1 *Enter againe the same Cupid, two brothers, 6 women Maskers, Cupids bow bent all the way towards them, the first woman singing and playing, A Priest*
2.1.164.1 *A dance, Cupid leading*
2.1.179.1–2 *Ex. with the Lady, & the Maskers.*
2.1.198.1 *Enter Duke, and Lords*
2.1.198.1 *Exit*
2.1.207.1 *Enter Shamont*
2.1.222–2.1.222.1 *Gives him a touch with his switch*
2.1.224–2.1.224.1 *Drawes*
2.1.254 *Exit. 1 Gent*
2.1.259.1 *Enter 1 Gentleman*

2.1.262.1   *Ex. 2 Gen*
2.1.264.1–2   *Enter 2 Gent. and Shamont*
2.1.299.1   *Exit*
2.1.307.1   {*Enter a Huntsman*
2.1.312–3.1.0.1   *Exit*
3.1.0.2–3   *Actus Tertius. Scæna prima*
3.1.0.3   *Enter the twobrothers, 1 Gentleman, with those that were*
   the Maskers, and the Cupid.
3.1.32   *Exit*
3.1.32.1   *Enter the Clowne*
3.1.95   *Exit*
3.2.0.1   *Enter Lapet*
3.2.32.1   *Enter Shamont*
3.2.100.1   *Enter the Lady, and Servants.*
3.2.125.1   *Ex. Lad and Ser.*
3.2.125.2–3   *Enter the Clowne. He kicks Lapet*
3.2.185   *Exit*
3.2.187   *Exit*
3.3.0.1   *Musick. Enter the paſſionate Couſen, rudely, and careleſly*
   Apparell'd, unbrac'd, and untruſt: The Cupid following
3.3.35   *Exit*
3.3.54.1   *Exit*
3.3.54.1–3.4.0.2   *Enter at another doore Lapet, The Cupids Brothers*
   watching his comming.
3.4.18   *within*
3.4.23–3.4.23.2   *The paſſionate man enters in furie, with a*
   Truncheon
3.4.24   *He Sings*
3.4.39.1–3.4.40.1   *Falls down for dead*
3.4.42   *Sings again.*
3.4.47   *Exit*
3.4.52.1   *Enter the two Brothers*
3.4.53   *Falls againe*
3.4.67–4.1.0.3   *Exeunt*
4.1.1   *Actus Quartus. Scæna prima*
4.1.1   *Enter Shamons Brother, the Souldier, and 1 Gent.*
4.1.21.1   *Enter Shamont*
4.1.57.2   *Enter 1.Gentleman, and others*
4.1.60   *Ex. Sold.*
4.1.68.1   *Enter Duke.*
4.1.134   *Within*
4.1.137.1–2   *Enter 1.Gent. and divers other.*
4.1.154   *Exit*
4.1.167   *Exit*
4.1.175.1   {*Enter a Gallant*

4.1.200.1   *Ex.*
4.1.203.1   *Enter a plain fellow*
4.1.208.1   *Exit*
4.1.216.1–2   *Enter Lapet, and Clowne his servant, and so habited*
4.1.244.1   *Exit*
4.1.304.1   *Enter Clowne*
4.1.365.1–5.1.0.1   *Exeunt*
5.1.0.2   *Actus Quintus. Scæna prima*
5.1.0.2   *Enter the 2.Brothers.*
5.1.1   *Within.*
5.1.12.1   *Ex.Broth.*
5.1.12.2–3   *Enter Passion. and Base his Jester.*
5.1.36   *Enter Servant*
5.1.43.1   *Song*
5.1.79.1–4   *Enter Lapet and Clowne, and foure other like fooles,*
   dancing, the Cupid leading, and bearing his Table, and holding it
   up to Lapet at every ſtrain, and acting the postures
5.1.80.1   *2 Straine*
5.1.81.1   *3 Straine*
5.1.82.1   *4 Straine*
5.1.83.1   *5 Straine*
5.1.84.1   *6 Straine*
5.1.85.1   *7 Straine*
5.1.86   *Enter Soldier, Shamonts Brother, his sword drawne.*
5.1.98.1   *Enter 2. Brothers.*
5.1.109   *Exeunt*
5.2.0.1   *Scæne 2. Enter Shamont*
5.2.22.1   *Enter 1 Gent.*
5.2.47   *Exit*
5.2.67   *Exit*
5.3.0.1–2   *Scæne 3. Enter Lapet, Clown, Poultrot, Moulbazon, and*
   others, the new Court Officers.
5.3.44.1   *Enter Duke, the Lady his sister, 1 Gent.*
5.3.47.1   *Ex.*
5.3.64.1   *Ex.*
5.3.88   *Exit*
5.3.97.1   *Enter Shamont*
5.3.111   *Exit*
5.3.117.1   *Enter Shamont*
5.3.150.1   *Enter 1. Gent.*
5.3.162.1–2   *Enter Passion. the Cupid, and two brothers.*
5.3.180.1   *Enter the Dukes sister.*
5.3.180.2   {*He joyns Shamonts hand and his Siſters.*
5.3.189.1   *Enter Shamonts brother the Souldier.*
5.3.197–Epilogue.12.1   *Exeunt*

LINEATION NOTES

1.1.155–6   That…sir] WEBER; *1 line*
1.1.178–80   He's…court] SYMPSON; *2 lines* ISLIP: me |
1.1.251   In…now] SYMPSON: *2 lines* ISLIP: essence |. The complete verse line, with the accompanying stage direction 'Ent. a Servant', would not fit in a single type line, and could not be turned up or down.
2.1.66–7   You're…you] SYMPSON; *1 line*
2.1.86   I…me] THIS EDITION (Taylor); *2 lines* ISLIP: long |. The full hexameter (common in Middleton) would not fit the printer's measure here.
2.1.265–6   Thanks…he] SYMPSON; *1 line*
3.1.36–40   Then…world] SYMPSON; *4 lines* ISLIP: a | pap | [burstness] |. The apparent mislineation here and below (through 3.2.65–6) may result from a compositorial need to save space on this page (sig. 3U2): the page contains five

instances of lines turned up or down, not blank lines, and one entrance direction placed in the margin (3.2.32.1).
3.1.41–4   Why…dog] THIS EDITION; dead | gallipots | throw | ISLIP; me | mummy | glasses | SYMPSON
3.1.56–8   There's…indignation] SYMPSON; *2 lines* ISLIP: would |
3.1.74–5   Ay…master] COLMAN; *1 line*; ease | SYMPSON
3.1.75–6   No…master] SYMPSON; *1 line*
3.1.77–9   O…wed] THIS EDITION; *2 lines*: wear | ISLIP; *2 lines*: gentlemen | WILLIAMS
3.1.80–1   But…red] THIS EDITION; *1 line*
3.2.44–7   Ay…now] COLMAN; *3 lines* ISLIP: pleasure | no |.
3.2.64–5   You're…too] COLMAN; *2 lines* ISLIP: sir |
3.2.64–6   You're…carried] DYCE; *2 lines* ISLIP: too |
3.2.129–30   Or…to't] COLMAN; one |
3.2.168–9   Or…for't] SYMPSON; *1 line* ISLIP

3.4.1   So...brother] COLMAN; *2 lines* ISLIP: ginned|. Lines like this are common in Middleton's versification (an iambic pentameter, with an extrametrical final vocative); the full line would not at all fit ISLIP's measure.

3.4.3–4   Will't...one] COLMAN; you|

3.4.6–7   Is...powder] COLMAN; close|

3.4.19–20   I...villain] WEBER; on|

3.4.21–2   My...exhibition] WEBER; *1 line*

3.4.43   Mischief...upon thee] THIS EDITION (Taylor); *2 lines* ISLIP: on thee|

3.4.44   All...confound thee] WILLIAMS; *2 lines* ISLIP: plagues|

4.1.31–2   The very...sister] SYMPSON; *1 line* ISLIP. Taylor conjectures that the extrametrical 'the Dukes sister' was written at the end of the line as a clarifying substitution for 'that blest Lady'; the two phrases have exactly the same scansion.

4.1.58–9   Forbear...reputation] THIS EDITION (Taylor); hand| Here. The full first line, as constructed here, would not fit ISLIP's measure; the closing part-line, here, forms an amphibious section with l. 60.

4.1.203–4   And...craven] COLMAN; *3 lines* ISLIP: still| hand|

4.1.206   How...not] COLMAN; *2 lines* ISLIP: sir|

4.1.208   I...by't] COLMAN; *2 lines* ISLIP: need not|

4.1.244   The...mumbling] COLMAN; *2 lines* ISLIP: up|

4.1.248–9   A...name] COLMAN; *1 line*

4.1.268–9   Pray...arms] COLMAN; *1 line*

4.1.285   How...things] COLMAN; *2 lines* ISLIP: colics|

4.1.289–91   No...me] COLMAN; earth| think|

4.1.299   You...now] COLMAN; *2 lines* ISLIP: heed|

4.1.314–15   So...bills] COLMAN; Romans|

4.1.323–4   The...questions] WILLIAMS; *1 line*

4.1.326–7   Marry...*Kick*] COLMAN; *1 line*

4.1.339–41   The...them] WEBER; *2 lines* ISLIP: givers|

5.1.35–6   Ten...sir] WILLIAMS; *1 line*

5.1.54   Laugh...vary] COLMAN; *2 lines* ISLIP | wide

5.2.24   I...sir] COLMAN; *2 lines* ISLIP: death|

5.3.162–3   Let...cousin] COLMAN; *1 line*

THE WIDOW

Edited by Gary Taylor

The Widow was printed in quarto format, by an unidentified stationer, for Humphrey Moseley in 1652 (*BEPD* 705, Wing J1015). Moseley probably acquired his manuscript from the actor Alexander Gough, who supplied an epistle 'To the Reader.' We might therefore suspect a theatrical provenance for the manuscript, and indeed nothing in MOSELEY contradicts this hypothesis. The text systematically supplies all necessary entrances (except for some probable re-entries in 1.1 and 4.2, and such re-entries within a scene were often not marked in promptbooks). Speech prefixes and character designations are uniform, and create no confusions of identity or action. Such features do not point unequivocally to the theatre; they might feature in any literary transcript. However, the separate direction for '*Table and Standish*', which MOSELEY places in the right margin within square brackets opposite 1.1.1, does—in its syntax, content, and position—look like theatrical annotation to a manuscript. Likewise, the names in the marginal stage directions at 3.1.99 and 4.2.33.2 look like additions to an original direction. Indeed, an exceptional proportion of the stage directions in MOSELEY are printed in the right margin, with brackets and/or a distinct type-face. (See list of Stage Directions, below.) None of this evidence is incontrovertible, but it does reinforce the implications of the text's known connection with Gough; it also sits comfortably with other evidence that the play was revived in the 1630s (for which, see 'Canon and Chronology'). This edition assumes that the manuscript used by the printer of MOSELEY came from the theatre. Moreover, the title-page claims that the play was 'Printed by the Originall Copy'—which is likely to mean 'authorized theatrical manuscript', and certainly tells against any kind of private literary transcript.

Twenty-eight copies of MOSELEY are extant; of these, Levine fully collated six, identifying only four press variants, all of them trivial, and none affecting a modern-spelling text: 1.2.178 (turned 'r' in the word 'reading'), 1.2.207 (missing catchword 'I' on sig. C2^v), 2.1.191 ('now fobd me,' corrected to 'now fobd me,'), 3.2.43, 3.2.49 (not indented in the uncorrected state).

The only other authority for the text is provided by four manuscript miscellanies which contain Latrocinio's song at 3.1.22–37 (Beal MiT 24–27). A complete facsimile of one of these—the song manuscript British Library Add. MS 29396—has been published by Jorgens (vol. V; see also XII, 435). Day and Murrie identified another version of the song (no. 1536) under the name 'The Banditte—A Song in the Play of Henry the Fourth'; this was published in John Playford's *The Second Book of the Pleasant Musical*

Companion (1686), Part II, no. 26. It also reappears, as Seligmann notes, in the anonymous comedy *The Factious Citizen, or the Melancholy Visioner* (Wing F78; printed for Thomas Maddocke, 1685), sig. F3 (p. 45). The variants in these texts (recorded in the textual notes) have been ignored by all previous editors of the play, including Levine.

Editorially, the play presents few difficulties. The scene divisions at 3.2 and 3.3 were first recognized by Weber; MOSELEY does not mark the new scenes. The 3.2 break occurs across a page break; the catchword on sig. E3 confirms the absence of a scene number between 'Exeunt.' and *Enter*, but the entrance direction itself is, like other scene beginnings, centred and in large type. By contrast, the entrance direction for what we mark as the beginning of 3.3 is printed in small type, marginally, and bracketed. The omission of a scene break for 3.3 may accurately reflect the underlying manuscript: in all the scene divisions which are marked in MOSELEY, a clearing of the stage coincides with a clear change of locale, whereas 3.2 and 3.3 both take place at Brandino's house. In any case, the scene divisions are not likely to be authorial; Middleton seems characteristically to have marked act divisions, but not scenes.

The British Library catalogue attributes the 1810 edition of the play, included in *Ancient British Drama*, to 'A. Gough', but this seems to be a mistake, based upon misinterpretation of its reprint of the original preface by Alexander Gough. We have instead attributed it to WALTER SCOTT; Todd and Bowden provide documentary evidence for this traditional attribution. The best previous edition of the play is Levine's, to whose commentary Michael Warren and I are in many places indebted.

SEE ALSO

Text: *Works*, 1078
Music: this volume, 152
Authorship and date: this volume, 379

WORKS CITED

Previous Editions

Bullen, A. H., ed., *Works* (1885), V
Chetwood, William R., *Memoirs of the Life and Writings of Ben. Jonson, Esq.... To which are added, Two Comedies* (1756)
Collier, John Payne, ed., *A Select Collection of Old Plays*, 12 vols (1825–7)
Dodsley, Robert, ed., *A Select Collection of Old Plays*, 12 vols (1744), VI
Dyce, Alexander, ed., *Works* (1840), III
—— ed., *The Works of Beaumont & Fletcher*, 11 vols (1843–6), IV

Ellis, Havelock, ed., *Thomas Middleton*, The Mermaid Series, 2 vols (1890)

Levine, R. T., ed., *A Critical Edition of Thomas Middleton's 'The Widow'* (1975)

Miller, William, 'An Edition of Thomas Middleton's *The Widow*', unpublished MA thesis, Rutgers University (1939)

Moseley, Humphrey, publisher, *The Widow* (1652)

Reed, Isaac, ed., *A Select Collection of Old Plays*, 12 vols (1780), XII

Scott, Walter, ed., *The Ancient British Drama*, 3 vols (1810), III

Weber, Henry, ed., *The Works of Beaumont and Fletcher*, 14 vols (1812), XIV

Other Works Cited

Abbott, E. A., *A Shakespearian Grammar*, rev. edn. (1870)

Andrewes, Lancelot, 'Sermon 5 of the Nativitie: Christmas 1610', *Sermons*, ed. G. M. Story (1967)

Bakhtin, Mikhail, *Rabelais and his World*, trans. Hélène Iswolsky (1968)

Barber, C. L., *Shakespeare's Festive Comedy* (1959)

Beard, Thomas, *The Theatre of God's Judgements* (1612)

Berggren, Paula S., '"A Prodigious Thing": The Jacobean Heroine in Male Disguise', *Philological Quarterly* 62 (1983), 383–402

Boccaccio, Giovanni, trans. anonymous, *The Decameron* (1620)

Brodsky, Vivien, 'Widows in Late Elizabethan London: Remarriage, Economic Opportunity and Family Orientations', *The World We Have Gained: Histories of Population and Social Structure*, ed. Lloyd Bonfield, Richard M. Smith and Keith Wrightson (1986), 122–54

Budge, E. A. Wallis, *Amulets and Talismans* (1961)

Carlton, Charles, 'The Widow's Tale: Male Myths and Female Reality in 16th and 17th Century England', *Albion* 10 (1978), 118–29

Crooke, Helkiah, *Microcosmographica: A Description of the Body of Man* (1615)

Day, Cyrus Lawrence, and Eleanore Boswell Murrie, *English Song-Books, 1651–1702: A Bibliography with a First-Line Index of Songs* (1940)

Dent, R. W., *Proverbial Language in English Drama exclusive of Shakespeare, 1495–1616: An Index* (1984)

Dessen, Alan C., and Leslie Thomson, *A Dictionary of Stage Directions in English Drama, 1580–1642* (1999)

Dickenson, John, *Greene in conceit: new raised from his grave to write the tragic history of Fair Valeria of London* (1598)

The Sermons of John Donne, ed. Evelyn M. Simpson and George R. Potter, 10 vols (1953–62)

The Diary of John Evelyn, ed. E. S. de Beer (1955)

Ewbank, Inga-Stina, 'The Middle of Middleton', *The Arts of Performance in Elizabethan and Early Stuart Drama*, ed. Murray Biggs et al. (1991), 156–71

Florio, John, *Queen Anna's New World of Words* (1611)

Freud, Sigmund, *Jokes and their Relation to the Unconscious* (1912), trans. and ed. James Strachey, rev. Angela Richards, Pelican Freud Library 6 (1976)

Gleason, J. H., *The Justices of the Peace in England 1558 to 1640* (1969)

Hanson, Elizabeth, 'There's Meat and Money Too: Rich Widows and Allegories of Wealth in Jacobean City Comedy', *ELH* 72 (2005), 209–38

Heller, Herbert Jack, *Penitent Brothellers: Grace, Sexuality, and Genre in Thomas Middleton's City Comedies* (2000)

Ben Jonson, ed. C. H. Herford, Percy and Evelyn Simpson, 11 vols (1925–52)

Jorgens, Elise Bickford, ed., *English Song 1600–1675: Facsimiles of Twenty-six Manuscripts and an Edition of the Texts*, 12 vols (1986)

Laroque, François, *Shakespeare's Festive World: Elizabethan Seasonal Entertainment and the Professional Stage*, trans. Janet Lloyd (1992)

Miles, Josephine, *Major Adjectives in English Poetry from Wyatt to Auden* (1946)

Panek, Jennifer, *Widows and Suitors in Early Modern English Comedy* (2004)

Perkins, William, *A Commentary on Galatians* (1617)

Seligmann, Raphael, 'The Functions of Song in the Plays of Thomas Middleton', Ph.D. diss. (Brandeis University, 1997)

Sommerville, C. John, 'Puritan Humor, or Entertainment, for Children', *Albion* 21 (1989), 227–47

Sousa, Geraldo de, 'Romance in the Satiric Comedies of Ben Jonson and Thomas Middleton, 1603–1614', Ph.D. diss. (University of Kansas, 1983)

Swinburne, Algernon, 'Thomas Middleton', *The Nineteenth Century* 19 (1886), 138–53

Taylor, Gary, 'Inventing Shakespeare', *Shakespeare Jahrbuch* 122 (1986), 26–44

—— 'Praestat Difficilior Lectio: *All's Well that Ends Well* and *Richard III*', *Renaissance Studies* 2 (1988), 27–46

—— 'Forms of Opposition: Shakespeare and Middleton', *English Literary Renaissance* 24 (1994), 283–314

Todd, William B., and Ann Bowden, *Sir Walter Scott, A Bibliographical History, 1796–1832* (1998)

Trevelyan, G. M., *English Social History* (1941)

Wilson, Thomas, *A Christian Dictionary* (1612)

TEXTUAL NOTES

Title The Widow] MOSELEY (running titles); THE WIDDOW A COMEDIE As it was Acted at the private House in *Black-Fryers*, with great Applause, by His late MAJESTIES Servants. MOSELEY (title-page); The Widdow. A Comedie MOSELEY (head-title)

Persons THIS EDITION. In MOSELEY this is preceded by the following epistle:

To the Reader.

Considering how the curious pay some part of their esteem to excellent persons in the carefull preservation but of their defaced statues, instead of decayed medals of the Romans *greatness, I believed it of more value to present you this lively piece, drawn by*

the art of Johnson, Fletcher, *and* Middleton, *which is thought to have a neer resemblance to the portracture we have in* Terence *of those worthy minds, where the great* Scipio *and* Lælius *strove to twist the Poets* Ivy *with the victors* Bayes. *As the one was deserv'd by their work in subduing their Countries enemies, so the other, by their recreation and delight which was to banish that folly and sadness, that were worse than* Haniball, *or all the monsters and venome of* Africa. *Since our own Countrymen are not in any thing inferior, It were to be wished, they had but so much incouragement, that the past licence and abuses charged on the Stage, might not ever be thought too unpardonable to pass in oblivion, and so good Laws and instructions for manners uncapable of being regulated, which if but according to this pattern, certainly none need think himself the less a good Christian for owning the same desire as*

Your humble Servant.
Alexander Gough.

Persons.1–20 BRANDINO...Servants] THIS EDITION. For MOSELEY's list see Stage Directions. Such paratexts were characteristic of MOSELEY publications; nothing in the language of this one points specifically to Middleton. The arrangement and categorization of persons—particularly, the gendered division of characters, the hierarchical sequence, and the distinction between real and 'supposed' identities—is clearly not Middletonian; see Taylor, 'Persons', above.

Prologue.0.1–Prologue.6 *Enter...laugh*] REED. MOSELEY prints the Prologue on a separate page (sig. K1ᵛ) with the Epilogue, after the play; this suggests that both were a supplement to the original text of the play. However, they are both apparently by Middleton: see Canon and Chronology.

Prologue.0.1 *Enter Prologue*] MOSELEY (Prologue.)

Prologue.2 gay] WEBER; *merry* MOSELEY. Although Middleton was quite capable of writing lines that did not rhyme in passages which did, the word used here in MOSELEY is a synonym of one which would produce a perfect rhyme; moreover, Middleton only used 'gay' three times elsewhere, and in two of those passages it was used for a rhyme (*No Wit* 4.67, *Women Beware* 3.2.216). LEVINE argues that 'it seems unlikely that "gay" could have been misread for "merry"', but the error, if one, is clearly one of synonym-substitution, not misreading. A compositor or scribe could easily have substituted the commonplace idiom 'make...merry' for the much more unusual 'make...gay'. Finally, the fact that one line of the Epilogue does not rhyme does not support the lack of rhyme here: there, the unrhymed line (5.1.463) is an odd line surrounded by couplets (a pattern common enough in Middleton); here, the failure to rhyme produces *two* consecutive unrhymed lines in an otherwise rhyming prologue (a pattern not common in Middleton, or in prologues of the period).

1.1.0.1, 2.1.0.1, 3.1.0.1, 4.1.0.1, 5.1.0.1 *Incipit Actus*] MOSELEY (*Actus*)

1.1.45 It's] MOSELEY ('Tas)

1.1.62 beholden] MOSELEY (beholding)

1.1.69 according] MOSELEY; 'cording THIS EDITION *conj.* For the rare colloquial form, see *Revenger* 4.2.36. The emendation would make this line, like the rest of the speech, regular verse. I have retained 'according' because Martino so often speaks prose.

1.1.71 impudency] THIS EDITION (*conj.* Dyce 1844); impudence MOSELEY. A metrical emendation. The two words (or forms) were, in the seventeenth century, interchangeable in meaning, and manuscript 'impudencie' could easily have been misread as the more common 'impudence'.

1.1.74 Astilio] MOSELEY; Attilio DODSLEY. The emendation is supported by the error at 3.2.76. But it is difficult to judge whether it makes better sense to have Francisco use the name of one of his friends here, or to differentiate the two.

1.1.80.1 *Enter Philippa*] MOSELEY (Philippa)

1.1.101 of his] REED; of MOSELEY

1.1.104 He's] MOSELEY (Has)

1.1.138 it's] MOSELEY ('tas)

1.1.146 Mrs] MOSELEY; Mistress WEBER. There is no doubt that MOSELEY's abbreviation stands for 'mistress', but for a modern audience 'Mrs' conveys the right meaning.

1.1.156 wiseman] MOSELEY; wise man DODSLEY. 'Wiseman' is often treated as a single word—like 'goodman', 'gentleman', etc.—by Middleton.

1.1.178 He's] MOSELEY (H'as)

1.1.193, 200 he's] MOSELEY (h'as, has)

1.1.194 bodily] THIS EDITION; bodly MOSELEY; boldly DODSLEY. MOSELEY's 'bodly', silently corrected to 'boldly' by all editors, could as easily be an error for 'bodily', in the senses 'unspiritually' (*OED* adv 1) and 'in person' (adv 2), both current in the seventeenth century. Middleton uses the adjective at *Solomon* 7.113 and *Michaelmas* 3.1.66.

1.1.228.1 *Exeunt Brandino and Martino*] THIS EDITION; *not in* MOSELEY. Alternatively, Dyce marks Philippa's following speech as an aside; but there is no reason for Brandino to hang around after his exit line. See next note.

1.1.230 *Exit*] THIS EDITION; *Exeunt.* MOSELEY. MOSELEY's direction covers all three exits, indicating the clearing of the stage—even though the men begin their exit just before Philippa.

1.2.32 no thing] MOSELEY (nothing). The modernization makes the primary (obscene) sense clearer.

1.2.65 Ha!—hm] MOSELEY (Ha, humh)

1.2.126 does't] MOSELEY (do'st)

1.2.138.1 *Ricardo throws Francisco down*] THIS EDITION; *not in* MOSELEY. Panek notes that 'the dialogue suggests a violent embrace, bringing the two actors to the ground' (188). For the form of the direction, see Dessen and Thomson, 229.

1.2.140.1 *Attilio...Francisco*] THIS EDITION; *not in* MOSELEY. See preceding note. For the form, see Dessen and Thomson, 173.

1.2.154 two] CHETWOOD; too MOSELEY

1.2.166.1 *Exeunt*] MOSELEY (*Exit.*)

1.2.166.1 *Attilio*] MOSELEY (Attalio). It is hard to be sure whether MOSELEY's reading is a variant spelling or simply a misreading of a foreign word; but Middleton apparently took the name from Giambattista della Porta's *La Sorella* (a major source for *No Wit*), where it is spelled 'Attilio'.

1.2.185 not best] MOSELEY; best not THIS EDITION *conj.*

1.2.252 *punto bello*] THIS EDITION; —— MOSELEY (*indicating lacuna*). Something is clearly missing here, and it seems likely that the missing material produced a doggerel rhyme with 'duello'. *OED* records English uses of *punto* as 'a stroke or thrust' in fencing, with various Italian modifiers, usually postpositioned (*sb* 3, 1595-1624); Middleton uses it at *Fair Quarrel* 3.1.155, 157, written at about the same time as *The Widow*. The use of Italian would be appropriate here, and would itself help to explain the bewilderment of the 1652 compositor; the missing material almost certainly referred to violence of some sort. (Neither Martino or his master would be likely to appreciate a reference to the law, the only other way in which 'a great strife' might have been ended.)

2.1.1, 3 SERVANT] MOSELEY (*Ser.*). The abbreviation could mean either 'Servant' (as in the entrance direction) or 'Servellio' (as in Valeria's speech).

2.1.6 painted] DODSLEY; painted, painted MOSELEY

2.1.12 th'ambition] DYCE; the ambition MOSELEY. For the same contraction, suggested by the metre, see Prologue.3.

2.1.28 widow] DODSLEY; Window MOSELEY

2.1.57 beholden] MOSELEY (beholding)

2.1.68 have't] THIS EDITION; have | it MOSELEY. See 'have't' in the preceding and following lines; MOSELEY's form may result from its setting of the speech as prose.

2.1.80 You're] MOSELEY (You'r)

2.1.113 *Exit Ricardo*] MOSELEY (*Exit.*)

2.1.124 you. Mine] DODSLEY; you | you, mine MOSELEY. This duplication occurs across a page-break (D1–D1ᵛ); the catchword, following a single 'you', is 'mine', thus supporting DODSLEY's emendation.

2.1.124 years] DODSLEY; ears MOSELEY

2.1.125 cause] MOSELEY. Perhaps this should be emended to 'case', which conveys the same literal sense but makes the sexual sense clearer.

2.1.159 and] DODSLEY; and and MOSELEY

2.1.164 shaker] THIS EDITION (*conj.* Jowett); ſhake MOSELEY. *OED* first records the dialect noun 'shake' in the sense 'disreputable person' (*sb.*²) in 1846. By contrast, 'shaker' has that sense in the sixteenth and seventeenth centuries (*sb.* 3), and the sense 'boaster' in the same period (*sb.* 2); it is also used in 1613 for 'ague' (quoted under *sb.* 1). All these senses are relevant, and attested in the period. For comparable omissions of one or two letters see 1.1.194, 2.1.124, 3.1.122, 4.2.158, 4.2.161, 5.1.187, 5.1.204, 5.1.386.

2.1.164–5 marry...wed] THIS EDITION; wed...married MOSELEY. A compositor setting these two lines from memory could easily have transposed their two synonymous verbs, to the detriment of the metre of the second line. Moreover, in the sequence adopted here, the name 'Marcia' leads to 'marry' (like the frequent pun on *mar* and *marry*), while 'wed' alliterates with 'would' and 'wealthy'.

2.1.178 you else] DODSLEY; your else MOSELEY

2.1.180 lemme see, lemme] MOSELEY (le'me see, le' me). See 3.1.17, 4.2.11. The contraction also occurs at *Weapons* 4.1.10.

2.1.202.1 Exit Valeria] MOSELEY (*Exit.*), after Valeria's speech

2.2.28 could] DODSLEY; would MOSELEY

2.2.77–8 OFFICER You...you? | It] DODSLEY (subs); you...you? | *Officer.* It MOSELEY

2.2.95 you] DODSLEY; your MOSELEY

2.2.118 o'] DYCE; O MOSELEY; on DODSLEY

2.2.134 own wife] THIS EDITION; ˄ ~ MOSELEY. However this passage is aligned, a syllable seems missing in this phrase, not only for the metre but for the emphasis. Compare 'to his own wife' (*Quiet Life* 3.1.157) and 'sale of thine own wife' (*Phoenix* 8.272).

2.2.161 ingrateful] MOSELEY; ingrate THIS EDITION *conj.* 'Ingrate' was available in the same sense (as adjective or substantive), and occurs at *Weapons* 2.2.69; compositorial or scribal substitution would be easy; 'ingrate' is metrically preferable. Middleton's other uses of 'ingrateful' are metrical.

2.2.163 wife's] MOSELEY (wives)

3.1.5.2 Ansaldo] MOSELEY (Anfoldo). MOSELEY uses this name—everywhere else spelled 'Ansaldo'—in stage directions and speech prefixes; WEBER (followed by DYCE and BULLEN) changed the direction to 'Martia, *disguised as* Ansaldo'; DYCE (followed by BULLEN) then changed the speech prefixes to 'MARTIA'. These nineteenth-century editorial changes ensured that readers—unlike audiences—responded to the character as a woman, not a man, throughout the play.

3.1.17 Lemme] MOSELEY (Le'me). See 2.1.180.

3.1.22–37 I keep...sir] The song is transcribed in British Library Additional MS 10309 (Margaret BELLASYS, *c.*1630), f. 96; British Library Add. MS 29396 (Edward LOWE, 1654–70s), ff. 77ᵛ–8 (with music); British Library Harley MS 3991, f.92ʳ⁻ᵛ (ANONYMOUS, later seventeenth century). In this last manuscript, the text follows songs from *Evening's Love* (1668), *The Tempest* (1667), *She Would if She Could* (1668), and *Love in a Tub* (1664), as part of a larger anthology of theatrical lyrics from plays performed after the Restoration. ANONYMOUS is the manuscript closest in its readings to MOSELEY, and might have been copied from it, with one or two minor transcriptional

errors. The text farthest from MOSELEY is BELLASYS, which has many unique variants, which either represent an authorially variant version of the song or a very corrupt transcription; clearly, neither BURGHE nor LOWE derives from it, and because of their dates neither BELLASYS nor BURGHE can derive from MOSELEY. In these circumstances, variants attested by only a single witness are suspicious, and we have rejected all such variants; the next most suspicious variants are those attested only by MOSELEY and ANONYMOUS, which are not only both late, but possibly directly related.

3.1.21.1 song] MOSELEY (Song.); On A purse-Taker BELLASYS; Thee Highe Lawyers Song in the playe called the Widdowe BURGHE; In the Widow ANONYMOUS; *Sings an Old Song.* MADDOCKE; [The Banditte.] *A Song in the Play of* Henry *the Fourth.* PLAYFORD

3.1.23 take] MOSELEY+; haue BELLASYS. See next notes.

3.1.23 rents] MOSELEY, BURGHE, ANONYMOUS, MADDOCKE; rent LOWE, PLAYFORD; wealth BELLASYS. Compare 'takes all her rents' (*Ghost* 245)—closer to this passage, than any of Middleton's uses of the singular noun 'rent'. The independent agreement of BURGHE and MOSELEY also supports the plural.

3.1.23 am] MOSELEY+; I'me BELLASYS

3.1.24 travel] BELLASYS+; traverse MOSELEY. An easy misreading could produce MOSELEY's variant, a word which Middleton apparently never used elsewhere—and which produces an awkward clump of consonants, harder to sing than the alliterative 'travel'. Moreover, travelling was particularly associated with the Jacobean nobility, who after the Anglo-Spanish peace of 1604 were freed to travel the continent extensively.

3.1.24 land] MOSELEY+; world BELLASYS. Compare *Puritan* 3.2.77–8: 'travelled all the world o'er'. But 'land' seems required by the next line's 'foot' [of land].

3.1.25 yet] MOSELEY+; it BURGHE. A nonsensical, easily explained error.

3.1.25 ne'er] BELLASYS, BURGHE, LOWE, PLAYFORD; never MOSELEY, ANONYMOUS, MADDOCKE. The metre favours the contracted form, which is common in Middleton, and here supported by three independent manuscripts. (In *Game* Middleton never used the uncontracted form at all.)

3.1.26 with] MOSELEY, BURGHE; & BELLASYS, LOWE, ANONYMOUS, MADDOCKE, PLAYFORD. Either reading could be authorial.

3.1.27 I...often] MOSELEY, BURGHE, ANONYMOUS, MADDOCKE; I often doe at midnight LOWE, PLAYFORD; At midnight oft I vse to BELLASYS. 'Often' (which Middleton generally prefers to 'oft') is juxtaposed with 'dine' at *Michaelmas* 4.1.62, *Timon* 5.23.

3.1.28 if] MOSELEY+; when BELLASYS. See next note.

3.1.28 be not in] MOSELEY+; is out of BELLASYS. Middleton uses 'in' before 'case' 24 times, including the negative constructions 'He's not in case' (*Revenger* 4.2.181) and 'Not in such a case' (*Weapons* 4.1.88); there are no parallels for 'out of case'.

3.1.29 hostess'] MOSELEY+; Hostice's PLAYFORD

3.1.29 takes] BELLASYS, BURGHE, LOWE, MADDOCKE, PLAYFORD; h'as MOSELEY, has ANONYMOUS. There are Middleton parallels for either reading; but the agreement of the three independent manuscripts favours 'takes'. Moreover, the apparently erroneous reading 'take' in the next line is best explained as contamination from this phrase. It would be harder to explain the independent substitution of 'take' twice in two lines.

3.1.30 maids sit] MOSELEY+; mayd sittes BURGHE. The variant is obviously an unintended transpositional error, since BURGHE continues the line as though its subject were plural: see next note.

3.1.30 watch] MOSELEY, ANONYMOUS, MADDOCKE; take BELLASYS, BURGHE, LOWE, PLAYFORD. The context seems to require the meaning 'wait up, stay awake watching for'. Compare *Old Law* 3.2.32: 'They observe turns and hours'. The variant 'take' could easily have arisen from contamination by 29.

3.1.31 long] MOSELEY+; late BELLASYS

3.1.32-3 The...chamberl'in.] MOSELEY+: *not in* BURGHE

3.1.32 has no mind] MOSELEY+; will not yeild BELLASYS

3.1.34 But] MOSELEY+; And BELLASYS

3.1.34 when] MOSELEY+; if LOWE, PLAYFORD

3.1.34 bustle] MOSELEY+; hustle BELLASYS; bruſtle PLAYFORD

3.1.35 ostler yawns] MOSELEY+; Oſtlers yawn PLAYFORD. An easy error, assimilating the first clause to the plural of the second.

3.1.35 ostler] MOSELEY+; tapster BURGHE

3.1.35 geldings] MOSELEY+; Gelding ANONYMOUS. Clearly an unintended variant, since it does not agree with the following verb.

3.1.35 justle] MOSELEY+; gussell LOWE. 'Jostle' is now the more normal spelling, but most dictionaries still record 'justle', which is preferable for the rhyme here. LOWE's unique variant (= modern 'guzzle') seems less attractive, for rhyme or sense.

3.1.36 If...her] MOSELEY+; And then I call bring forth my horse, Sʳ BELLASYS

3.1.36 If] MOSELEY+; and if PLAYFORD. See next note.

3.1.36 maid] MOSELEY, ANONYMOUS, MADDOCKE; a ~ BURGHE; yᵉ ~ LOWE, PLAYFORD. The absence of an article is both the grammatically rarer and the more metrical reading, easily corrupted independently to a more commonplace phrasing.

3.1.36 they] MOSELEY+; I LOWE

3.1.37 all this comes of] MOSELEY+; after comes BELLASYS

3.1.42 your] DODSLEY; yout MOSELEY

3.1.45 th'undoing] DYCE; the undoing MOSELEY

3.1.56 LATROCINIO] DODSLEY (subs); *Anf.* MOSELEY

3.1.65 That's] MOSELEY (That 'as)

3.1.91 he'd] MOSELEY (h'ad)

3.1.111 ALL THIEVES] DYCE (subs); *not in* MOSELEY

3.1.116 There] MOSELEY (*there*); there's DYCE

3.1.122 so] THIS EDITION; ſo it MOSELEY. The 'it' is unnecessary, and could easily have been interpolated in transmission; without it, the rhythm of this line matches that of the other lines.

3.1.122 use] THIS EDITION; us MOSELEY. The point of the song is that everything goes round in a circle; it should therefore end where it begins, in usury. Each person in the rest of the song's sequence is logically and economically linked to those before and after (see commentary), but there is no reason that the court should be specifically linked to thieves—who have, in any case, already been mentioned in 3.1.121-2. The thieves do not see themselves as the culmination of the sequence, and they have not just robbed a courtier; instead, they describe themselves simply as a part of the great round, which begins with moneylenders and ends with an indebted court.

3.2.12 mistress] MOSELEY (Mrs.). Here the abbreviation is misleading for a modern audience: contrast 1.1.150.

3.2.22 he'd] MOSELEY (h'ad)

3.2.24 perceiverance] MOSELEY (perſeverance). See *OED*.

3.2.34, 38, 44, 48 PHILIPPA] WEBER; 1 MOSELEY

3.2.37, 42, 46 VIOLETTA] WEBER; 2 MOSELEY

3.2.49.1 *They...unseen*] THIS EDITION; *not in* MOSELEY; *Exeunt above* REED (subs). It has already been established, in 1.1, that when above the women may not be seen by men below; here the convention is assisted by the pretence of darkness. Interpolating an editorial exit here requires the later interpolation of an editorial re-entrance, and while that

is not impossible, there is nothing in the dialogue here to suggest that the women are about to depart. Moreover, their exit would result in a cleared stage and a change of scene, which MOSELEY does not mark either.

3.2.49.2 *his*] MOSELEY; *a* WEBER. See note to 3.1.5.2.

3.2.59.1 *aloof*] THIS EDITION; *not in* MOSELEY. The remainder of the scene presumes that Ansaldo and Francisco are at some distance from one another.

3.2.62 't'ad] MOSELEY ('thad)

3.2.76 whittles] DYCE; whiſtles MOSELEY

3.2.90 an] THIS EDITION; on MOSELEY. The redundancy of 'on... upon', so juxtaposed, is especially awkward; 'an armour'—in the sense 'a suit of armour'—is common in the period (as for instance at *Antony* 4.8.27, *Pericles* 2.1.128). The proposed error could easily result from misreading or anticipation.

3.2.104-5 obtained,...is] THIS EDITION. Though previous editors have not marked or perceived a lacuna, it seems apparent that something is missing from MOSELEY, probably as a result of eyeskip from the middle of l. 104 to the middle of l. 105. Line 104 begins a sentence concerning the object which 'fond man' ventures for and obtains; l. 105 continues a sentence concerning 'fond man' himself. It is clearly not 'that which [is] obtained' which 'is as he was to his own sense, but removed nearer still to death eternal', but the person who obtained it. The idea which linked these two statements must have been something to the effect that the good obtained is in some way disappointing or transitory, and that he who obtains it has, afterwards, nothing to show for it, no lasting pleasure or good; instead, even from the viewpoint of his senses he seems to be just as he was beforehand—which would be bad enough; in fact, he is spiritually *worse* off than he was before obtaining it. The pleasure is thus not simply transitory or disappointing, but actually harmful. It is impossible to establish exactly how Middleton would have expressed this thought; for the conjectural filling of lacuna of this size, see Taylor (1988). My own conjecture—'For that which, being obtained, [favours the beggar | With a minute's dream; who, waked,] is as he was'—assumes that the scribe or compositor skipped from one mid-line past participle to another. What is 'once obtained' at *Valour* 5.3.192 and *Solomon* Epistles.14 is 'favour'; at *Trick* 4.4.149-50 *ventures* are collocated with riches as a dream, which prove false 'If I be waked'; at *Michaelmas* 2.2.24-5 a man, after a youth spent in swinish riots, 'being sober', does 'awake' and find himself 'a beggar', and in *Mad World* 2.6.14 one rises from sleep 'like a beggar'. Middleton contrasts *minute* with *eternal* at *Mad World* 4.1.5 and *Women Beware* 4.1.233, and gives satiric durations for dreams at *No Wit* 8.139 and *Dissemblers* 2.1.51.

3.3.3 witless] THIS EDITION; worthleſs MOSELEY. MOSELEY's generalized commonplace adjective adds nothing to the context; of course anyone who is 'worthless' would not be fit for women's company. Philippa particularly objects to Francisco's apparent lack of intelligence in deciphering her letter, and Middleton uses 'witless' as *Solomon* 15.49; if spelled 'witteless', it might be misread as 'worthless'. Moreover, 'wit' is a sexual innuendo, like 'short', 'dullest', and 'fit' in the surrounding lines. Alternatively, 'worthless' might be an error for the rarer adjective 'workless', in the now-obsolete senses 'doing no work, idle' (*OED a.* 1) and 'Of faith, without works' (*a.* 2). Francisco seemed to be—in addition to witless—all talk and no action, all faith and no works (another possible sexual innuendo). But Middleton does not elsewhere use 'workless', and he does not elsewhere accept the Catholic emphasis upon 'works' rather than faith.

3.3.40 't'ad] MOSELEY ('t 'had)

3.3.144 ne'er] MOSELEY (nev'r). The form of the contraction here in MOSELEY (which recurs at 5.1.140, 355) does not appear in Middleton's autograph texts, which consistently favour 'nere' or 'ne're'.

4.1.31 you] DODSLEY; your MOSELEY

4.1.65 it's] MOSELEY ('t'as)

4.1.74 quite] MOSELEY (quit)

4.1.81 BRANDINO] DODSLEY (Bra.); Fra. MOSELEY

4.1.121 't'ad] MOSELEY ('t had)

4.1.121 ne'er] MOSELEY (u'er)

4.1.147-8 gaskins...galligaskins] MOSELEY (gafcoyns ...gally-gafcoyns). See OED.

4.2.1.1 A...out] THIS EDITION. In MOSELEY this is placed in parenthesis after the entrance direction; DYCE has Occulto 'Hanging up a banner of cures and diseases' during l. 2. Latrocinio's command makes it likely that the banner is hung out after they enter; but Occulto need not be responsible; or if he is, he might enter after Latrocinio, with the banner.

4.2.11 Lemme] MOSELEY (Le' me). See 2.1.180.

4.2.54.2 disguised] THIS EDITION; not in MOSELEY. Occulto must be disguised before Ansaldo enters at 65.1. See note to 4.2.117.1.

4.2.82 a bout] THIS EDITION (conj. Jowett); about MOSELEY. The idiom 'have a bout with' occurs eight times elsewhere in Middleton. An easy misreading; indeed, even in the printed quarto there is some uncertainty about the spacing here.

4.2.84 New] THIS EDITION (conj. Jowett); now MOSELEY. An easy misreading; the thief wants Ansaldo's 'store of coin' replenished, renewed (so that he can be robbed again); 'new' corresponds to 'better'.

4.2.92 stinks] DODSLEY; ſticks MOSELEY

4.2.94 beleag'r'] MOSELEY (beleaguer). The elision here orthographically indicated is necessary for the rhyme with 'Megrum'.

4.2.100.1 Exit Occulto] THIS EDITION; not in MOSELEY. It seems most unlikely that Occulto is onstage during the following dialogue; not only does he take no part, but there would be no reason for Brandino to 'call for aid' (111) if Occulto were present; moreover, Occulto's presence would spoil the effect of Latrocinio's entrance. Ansaldo's 'sir' in this line could be naturally addressed to Occulto, who could take it as a dismissal. See note to 4.2.140.1.

4.2.112 master, master] MOSELEY (Mr, Mr)

4.2.114 He's] MOSELEY (Has)

4.2.117.1 disguised as an empiric] THIS EDITION; not in MOSELEY. Latrocinio might be disguised on his first entrance, but it would be better if the audience were first allowed to recognize him as the thief of Act Three, and l. 63 suggests that he withdraws in order to transform himself into 'the great man of art'.

4.2.119 professer] MOSELEY (profeſſor). We have adopted this spelling in order to differentiate from the modern 'professor'.

4.2.129 he's] MOSELEY (has)

4.2.140.1 Occulto and] THIS EDITION; not in MOSELEY. If Occulto is to exit at 1 (see note), then he must re-enter before he speaks at 205; he is probably addressed at 187. Alternatively, he could enter behind Latrocinio at 117.1.

4.2.152.1 Stratio leaps] THIS EDITION; not in MOSELEY; Leaps WEBER (after preceding speech). It seems more appropriate for Stratio to leap after the challenging incredulity of Latrocinio's question.

4.2.156.1 Exit] THIS EDITION; not in MOSELEY. The three patients play no further part in the scene, after each is interviewed

by Latrocinio; if they were present throughout the scene, then it would surely seem odd that Brandino and Martino do not even consider that they might be responsible for the pickpocketing. Latrocinio's 'Away' (153) is naturally taken as a dismissal; Stratio leaps one more time, then goes. See notes at 165, 180.

4.2.158 space] MOSELEY; pace DODSLEY

4.2.161 you're] THIS EDITION; ye MOSELEY. Editors have not commented upon or emended MOSELEY, perhaps because of uncertainty about the meaning of the following 'F.U.'. But as the second person pronoun, 'ye' here has no verb; it might be an error for 'yᵉ' (abbreviation for 'the'), but that makes little better sense. The emendation adopted here presumes that Middleton wrote 'yare' (his usual spelling of 'you're'), and that a scribe or compositor accidentally omitted the two medial letters.

4.2.165 jostle] MOSELEY (juſtle)

4.2.165.1 Exit] THIS EDITION; not in MOSELEY. See note to 156.1. The blessing is a natural exit line.

4.2.180 Exit Fiducio] THIS EDITION; not in MOSELEY. See note to 156.1. Latrocinio's speech is surely a dismissal.

4.2.184 't'ad] MOSELEY ('t had)

4.2.185 Cancer] MOSELEY (Canker)

4.2.203.1 Occulto...Martino] THIS EDITION; not in MOSELEY; While Occulto gives a pull at one of his teeth DYCE (after l. 202). It would be difficult for Martino to talk while Occulto had the pliers (or whatever) in his mouth; witness his subsequent speeches. It would also be funnier if Occulto actually pulled out the wrong tooth.

4.2.220 Over] MOSELEY; As e'er WEBER. CHETWOOD rewrites the whole phrase: 'Oh, I'm as light, methinks, as ever I was in my life'. DYCE's interpretation and defence of MOSELEY, as 'above, beyond what', is supported by OED: over, prep. 9b.

4.2.223 I've] MOSELEY (I 'ave)

4.2.248 wife's] MOSELEY (wives)

4.2.261 gentleman] DODSLEY; gedtleman MOSELEY

4.2.262.1 Exit Brandino] MOSELEY (Exit.), after Brandino's speech

4.2.264.1 Enter...Fiducio] THIS EDITION; not in MOSELEY. The song at scene's end, and Latrocinio's 'sirs' at 270, both suggest that the three other thieves must re-enter at some point after Brandino's exit, now presumably having removed their disguises. (See note to 156.1.) Latrocinio's 'none but you' would perhaps make better sense if someone else were onstage; it could be taken as a compliment on the performances of the other thieves.

4.2.279 we] WEBER; he MOSELEY

5.1.46 master] MOSELEY (Mr.)

5.1.57 he's] MOSELEY (h'as)

5.1.75 sir] MOSELEY. MOSELEY can be retained, assuming a shift of address in mid-sentence; but perhaps 'sir' is an error for 'sirra', addressed to Violetta, as elsewhere. Ansaldo is not otherwise addressed in this passage (72–84).

5.1.124 beholden] MOSELEY (beholding)

5.1.139 cruses] MOSELEY (crewzes)

5.1.166.1 Francisco kisses Ansaldo] THIS EDITION; not in MOSELEY. DYCE added a direction—'(after kissing Martia)'—at the beginning of Francisco's aside; but it seems more sensible for him to kiss her after announcing to the audience his feelings; the kiss then provokes, and covers, the following exchange between Philippa and Violetta.

5.1.187 gentleman] DODSLEY; Getleman MOSELEY

5.1.203-4 prettiliest...prettiliest] THIS EDITION; prettieſt... prettieſt MOSELEY; prettiest...prettiest DODSLEY. Presumably Brandino should repeat Martino's word, but the error is more likely to be in Martino's speech than Brandino's: Martino has the shorter and more common form. 'Prettiliest' is the rarer reading: see Taylor (1988). For the obsolete form of the superlative, compare Shakespeare's *maidenliest, busiliest, rudeliest* (also altered by later editions and eighteenth-century editors). Probably pronounced 'prett'liest'.

5.1.268   o'] DODSLEY; O MOSELEY

5.1.270.1   *Enter Brandino*] THIS EDITION; *Enter Bradino and Martino.* MOSELEY; *Enter Brandino and Martino, severally* WEBER (after 'it', l. 271.1); *Re-enter Brandino* DYCE (after 'it', l. 271.1). See next notes.

5.1.271.2   *Exeunt...Violetta*] THIS EDITION; *not in* MOSELEY. Three of these four characters must exit at some point hereabouts: Valeria, Ansaldo, and Francisco are all given specific directions to re-enter at the end of the scene, and it seems likely that Philippa exits and re-enters too, since she has nothing to say in the interim, and since she is trying to shepherd Francisco into what she thinks will be a mock-marriage with Ansaldo. DYCE inserted this exit direction immediately after the kiss (which he was also the first editor to specify in a stage direction); he followed WEBER in moving Martino's entrance direction to follow the general exeunt (see previous note). DYCE's rearrangement creates a break in continuity; it seems better to take Brandino's first words as a comment upon, and endorsement, of the kiss he has witnessed. His entrance—and comment—would help motivate the exit of the others.

5.1.272.1   *Enter Martino*] DYCE (subs); *not in* MOSELEY. See preceding notes. Given Martino's function as messenger here, it does not seem sensible for him to enter with Brandino. If the manuscript direction were written in the margin, with 'Martino' a line or two below 'Brandino', a compositor might easily have misinterpreted it as one direction, not two.

5.1.281   you] MOSELEY (yo')

5.1.303   served] DODSLEY (ferv'd); fer've MOSELEY

5.1.312   without, 'lying] DODSLEY (subs); with out-lying MOSELEY. *OED* first records the adjective 'outlying' in 1663. MOSELEY's hyphen may or may not be followed by a space; in either case, it might result from misinterpretation of a manuscript dash.

5.1.314   Master] DODSLEY (Mr.); me MOSELEY

5.1.352   cure] MOSELEY; ease THIS EDITION *conj.*

5.1.357   reap] THIS EDITION; receive MOSELEY. Both the metre and the image (after 'sow') encourage the emendation; a scribe or compositor could easily have made such a substitution of the commoner word, beginning with the same letters.

5.1.362   Allhallowtide] MOSELEY (Alhallontide). See *OED.*

5.1.381   BOTH SUITORS] MOSELEY (1. 2.)

5.1.384   'T'ad] MOSELEY (T'had)

5.1.386   It] WEBER; I MOSELEY

5.1.453   RICARDO] WEBER; Epilogue. MOSELEY (as centred heading). See next note.

5.1.453–63   Stay...you] WEBER. MOSELEY prints this speech after the Prologue on a separate page (sig. K1ᵛ), at the end of the volume. The epilogue seems to be an afterthought, probably written with the Prologue on a separate sheet of paper. Brandino is the highest-ranking character on stage; his final speech ends with a rhyme (451–2); the concluding phrase 'and that we wish all here' could refer to the characters onstage and to the audience, an ambiguity characteristic of final speeches in plays; moreover, Brandino's speech is followed by a general 'Exeunt' (see next note), whereas the Epilogue clearly seems to be spoken before anyone leaves the stage. See Prologue.0.1–Prologue.6.

5.1.463.1   *Exeunt*] WEBER. MOSELEY places this direction after Brandino's preceding speech, at 5.1.452.

STAGE DIRECTIONS

Persons.1–20

The Persons of the Play.

BRANDINO, *an old Justice.*
MARTINO, *his Clerk.*

FRANCISCO } *2 Gentlemen.*
ATTILIO. }

2 Old men Suters to the Widdow.
RICARDO, *A decayed young Gent. and Suter to the Widdow.*

ANSALDO, MARTIA *disguis'd.*

LATROCINIO }
OCCULTO, }
SILVIO, } *Thieves.*
STRATIO, }
FIDUCIO. }

    VALERIA, *The Widow.*
    MARTIA, *Daughter to one of the old Suters and supposed a man.*
    PHILIPPA, *Justice Brandino's Wife.*
    VIOLETTA, *her waiting Maid.*
  Officers.
  Servants.

Prologue.0.1   Prologue. (at top of new page after 5.1.463.1, and c.w. 'Prologue')

1.1.0.1   *Actus* 1. *Scæna* 1. | *Enter Signior* MARTINO (*an old Justices | Clerk*) *and* FRANCISCO.

1.1.0.1   [*Table and Standish.*] (right, opposite 1.1.1)

1.1.80.1   [*Philippa and* Vio-|letta *at a Window*]. (right, opposite 1.1.80)

1.1.121   *Exit.*

1.1.169   *Exit.*

1.1.172.1   [*Enter* Bran-|dino (*the* Ju-|stice) *and* | [Philippa. (right, opposite 1.1.176–8)

1.1.228.1, 1.1.230   *Exeunt.*

1.2.0.1   *Scæna.* 2. *Enter* FRANCISCO *and* RI-|CARDO *and* ATTILIO.

1.2.166.1   [*Exit. Ricardo & Attalio.*]

1.2.168.1   [*Enter Brandino and Martino.*] (right margin)

1.2.248   *Exit.*

1.2.254   *Exeunt.* | *Finis Actus Primi.*

2.1.0.1   *Actus* 2. *Scæna* 1. | *Enter* VALERIA *the Widow* | *and a Servant.*

2.1.25.1   *Enter* RICARDO.

2.1.58.1   [*Francisco and* | *Attilio: stand* | *unseen.*] (right, opposite 2.1.58–60)

2.1.76.1   [*Enter* Fran-|cisco *and* At-|tilio.] (right, opposite 2.1.66–7)

2.1.113   *Exit.*

2.1.118.2   *Enter two old Suiters.*

2.1.172.1   *Exit.* 1. *Suiter.*

2.1.202   *Exit.* (after Valeria's speech)

2.1.209   *Exit.*
2.2.0.1   *Scæna* 2. *Enter* FRANCISCO.
2.2.11.1   [*Enter* 1 *Suiter* | *with Officers.*] (right, opposite 2.2.10–11)
2.2.27.1   [*Enter* Ricardo *and* Attillio.] (right margin)
2.2.61.1   [*Enter* 2 *Suiter.*] (right, opposite 2.2.57)
2.2.118.1   [*Enter* Brandino *and* Martino.] (right margin)
2.2.173.1   *Exit.*
2.2.176.1   *Exit*
2.2.177   *Exit.*
2.2.182   *Exit.* | *Finis Actus Secundi.*
3.1.0.1–3   *Actus* 3. *Scæna* 1. | *Enter* OCCULTO, SILVIO, *and two or three* | *other Thieves.*
3.1.5.1   *Exit.*
3.1.5.2   *Enter* Latrocinio *the chief Thief, and* Ansoldo.
3.1.6   *sings.*
3.1.21.1   Song.
3.1.78.1–2   —— *A Song:* [*Enter* Stratio.] (right margin)
3.1.83   ——*Exit.*
3.1.98.1   ——[*Enter* Latrocinio *and* | *the rest,* Occulto, Sil–|vio, Fiducio.] (right, opposite 3.1.98–100)
3.1.111   Song.
3.1.126   Exeunt.
3.2.0.1   *Enter* PHILIPPA *and* VIOLETTA *above* | *at the Window.*
3.2.33.1   Song. (c.w. *Song.*)
3.2.49.2   [*Enter* Ansaldo | *in his Shirt.*] (right margin)
3.2.59.1   [*Enter* Francisco. (right margin)
3.2.119   —*Exit.*
3.2.128.1   [*Enter* Vi–|oletta.] (right, opposite 3.2.128–9)
3.2.131.1   *Exeunt.*
3.3.0.1   [*Ent.* Phi–|lippa *be*–|*low.*] (right, opposite 3.2.131–3.3.2)
3.3.9.1   [*Enter* Vio–|letta.] (right, opposite 3.3.9–'mistress, mistress', 3.3.10)
3.3.42.1   *Exit* | Viol. (right, opposite 3.3.42–3)
3.3.59.1   [*Enter* ANSALDO *and* VIOLETTA.]
3.3.124.1   *Exit Ans.*
3.3.144   *Exeunt.* | *Finis Actus Tertii.*
4.1.0.1   *Actus* 4. *Scæna* 1. | *Enter* RICARDO *and* 2 *Suter at one dore, and* | VALERIA, *and* 1 *Suter at an other dore.*
4.1.59.1   [*Enter* Brandino | *and* Martino.] (right, opposite 4.1.59–60)
4.1.90.1   [*Enter* Violetta.] (right margin)
4.1.151.1   *Exeunt.*
4.2.0.1–4.2.1.1   *Scæna* 2. *Enter* Latrocinio *and* Occulto, (*a Banner* | *of Cures and Diseases hung out.*) (at 4.2.0.1)

4.2.33.1–2   *Enter* | *all the rest* | Silvio, | Stratio, | Fiducio. (right, opposite 4.2.32–5)
4.2.54.1   *Exeunt.*
4.2.54.2   [*Enter* Occulto.] (right, opposite 'sir', 4.2.55)
4.2.65–4.2.65.1   *Exit.* [*Enter* Ansaldo.] (right margin)
4.2.87   *Reads.* (right, opposite 4.2.87)
4.2.100.2   [*Enter* | Brandino | *and* Mar–|tino. (right, opposite 4.2.99–102)
4.2.117.1   [*Enter* Latrocinio.] (right margin)
4.2.140.1   [*Ent.* 2 *or* 3 *Servants.*] (right, opposite 'aid', 4.2.140)
4.2.144.1   [*Ex. with* | Ansaldo. (right, opposite 4.2.144–5)
4.2.146.1–2   [*Enter* Stratio, | Silvio *and* Fi–|ducio.] (right, opposite 4.2.146–'sir', 4.2.147)
4.2.256.1   *Exit.*
4.2.262.1   *Exit.* (after 'withal')
4.2.283.1, 283.1–4.2.284   (speech prefix) Song, in parts by the Thieves.
4.2.293   *Exeunt.* | *Finis Actus Quarti.*
5.1.0.1–2   *Actus* 5. *Scæna* 1. | *Enter* PHILIPPA *and* VIOLATTA.
5.1.18.1   [*Ent.* Martino.] (right, opposite 5.1.16)
5.1.54   *Exit.*
5.1.65.1   [*Enter* Ansaldo.] (right, opposite 5.1.63)
5.1.84.1   [*Ex.* Viol. | *and* Ansaldo. (right, opposite 5.1.84–5)
5.1.93.1   [*Enter* Brandino | *with a writing.*] (right, opposite 5.1.92–3)
5.1.121.1   [*Enter* Francisco.] (right margin)
5.1.132.1   [*Enter* Marti–|no.] (right, opposite 5.1.130–1)
5.1.140.1–2   [*Enter* An–|saldo (*as* | Martia) & | Violetta. (right, opposite 5.1.139–41)
5.1.198.1   *Exit.* Fra. & Ansaldo. (after 'sir')
5.1.206.1–2   *Exeunt.*
5.1.226.1   [*Enter* Ansaldo.] (right margin)
5.1.250.1   [*Enter* Francisco.] (right, opposite 5.1.249)
5.1.270.1, 272.1   *Enter* Bradino *and* Martino. (right, opposite 5.1.271.1)
5.1.278.1   *Enter* Valeria, Ricardo, | *and two Suters.* (right, opposite 5.1.276)
5.1.396.1   [*Enter* | Violetta. (right, opposite 5.1.395–6)
5.1.406.1–2   [*Enter* | Francis–|co *and* | Ansaldo (right, opposite 5.1.405–8)
5.1.436.1   *Enter* Martino. (right margin)
5.1.456.1   Epilogue. (after Prologue.6; both Prologue and Epilogue on a separate page after 5.1.453)
5.1.463.1   ——*Exeunt.* (right, opposite 5.1.453)
5.1.463.1   *FINIS.*

LINEATION NOTES

1.1.2–4   Signor…hour] DYCE; *verse* MOSELEY: meet | yet |
1.1.6–7   What…warrant] DYCE; *verse* MOSELEY: do not |
1.1.22   Why…Francisco] DYCE; sir | MOSELEY
1.1.40–3   A goose…turn] THIS EDITION; *2 lines* MOSELEY: lantern |. I have split MOSELEY's fourteeners into ballad form, because they will not fit our column measure.
1.1.67   Here…dispositions] THIS EDITION; *prose* MOSELEY. In MOSELEY 'Here' is capitalized at the beginning of a type line, which then runs on as the first of three prose lines.
1.1.144   You…mistress] THIS EDITION; *prose* MOSELEY
1.1.161   The velvet's…milder] DYCE. In MOSELEY 'The' is capitalized at the beginning of a type line, which then runs on as the first of four prose lines.
1.1.171–2   A man…it] WEBER; *prose* MOSELEY
1.1.198–9   Why…him] WEBER; wife | MOSELEY

1.1.214–15   Exactly…Martino] WEBER; *1 line* MOSELEY
1.2.10–11   Ay…widow] THIS EDITION; *1 type line* MOSELEY (at the bottom of a page, sig. B4)
1.2.30–2   Why…no thing] THIS EDITION; *prose* MOSELEY
1.2.36–8   Nay…suitors] COLLIER; *prose* MOSELEY
1.2.58–9   Right…since] THIS EDITION; *1 line* MOSELEY (fourteener); begun | WEBER; Right | DYCE
1.2.74–6   Ha…you] MOSELEY (two consecutive fourteeners); *prose* DODSLEY
1.2.93   So…sir] DYCE; *prose* MOSELEY
1.2.94–5   Now…else] THIS EDITION; *prose* MOSELEY; So… mildly | COLLIER
1.2.101–2   'Tis…hanged] THIS EDITION; *1 type line* MOSELEY
1.2.116   A…too] WEBER. In MOSELEY, divided after 'gom' (as though completing an iambic pentameter line which begins

with Francisco's 'I...so'); 'And' is then capitalized as the beginning of a new line, which is the first of two prose lines.

1.2.117-18 My...sir] WEBER; *prose* MOSELEY (an-|swer)

1.2.135-6 Tell...mouths] THIS EDITION; *prose* MOSELEY

1.2.171-2 Let's...stay, master] THIS EDITION; *prose* MOSELEY; him| COLLIER. Probably one line in manuscript.

1.2.177 Marry...sir] MOSELEY; *prose* REED+

1.2.210-11 Did...house] MOSELEY; first| COLLIER

1.2.217 Pray...peace] MOSELEY; *prose* WEBER

1.2.251-2 Here...bello] MOSELEY; *prose* WEBER. See text note to 1.2.251.

2.1.45-8 Suffices...again] MOSELEY; *verse* DYCE: valour| pride| comes| (emending to 'gainst and ne'er)

2.1.55-6 All...yours] THIS EDITION; *prose* MOSELEY

2.1.60-1 What...good] WEBER; *verse* MOSELEY: do't|. MOSELEY could not set this speech as prose because of the marginal stage direction on the right.

2.1.65-6 Troth...has] WEBER; *verse* MOSELEY: you|

2.1.67-8 But...anything] WEBER (ambiguous), DYCE; *prose* MOSELEY

2.1.93-5 Life...money] WEBER; *prose* MOSELEY

2.1.133 Why...hope] THIS EDITION; *prose* MOSELEY

2.1.163-4 Your...Marcia] THIS EDITION; *1 line* MOSELEY

2.1.166-7 No...widow] THIS EDITION; *1 line* MOSELEY

2.1.179-81 That...Ricardo] THIS EDITION; *prose* MOSELEY; *2 lines* WEBER: see|. DYCE emended MOSELEY 'between' to ''tween' in order to smooth the meter of the second line created by WEBER; but the last four words of MOSELEY make a perfect pentameter when joined to the beginning of Valeria's following speech.

2.1.188 He...widow] CHETWOOD; *prose* MOSELEY (wi-|dow). The turned-down final syllable is actually placed in the far left of the same type-line with the signature (D2) and the catchword ('I', far right).

2.1.208-9 I...humour] WEBER; *prose* MOSELEY (or one overrun verse line)

2.2.26-7 I'm...sir] WEBER; severity| MOSELEY (the first line run over, as though prose)

2.2.33-4 A...thee] THIS EDITION; old| MOSELEY; leave| WEBER. MOSELEY is almost certainly in error, with its line-break between an adjective and its noun. The compositor probably had created an indented margin, affecting ll. 28-34 (ten type lines on sig. D3).

2.2.43 I...wit] THIS EDITION; *prose* MOSELEY

2.2.58-64 Here...debts] THIS EDITION; *prose* MOSELEY

2.2.64 I'm...now] THIS EDITION; *separate type line* MOSELEY; *prose* REED+

2.2.69-70 I...him] MOSELEY occupies a single type line, and its intention is ambiguous. DYCE first set as prose.

2.2.74-5 There's...me] MOSELEY occupies a single type line, and its intention is ambiguous. DYCE first set as prose; WEBER divided after 'think'.

2.2.122-3 Seest...Martino] THIS EDITION; *1 line* MOSELEY

2.2.129-30 La...honesty] THIS EDITION; *1 line* MOSELEY. The phrase 'La you, sir, now' amphibiously completes the pentameter begun by 'Why...then' and begins the hexameter completed by 'My...honesty'.

2.2.133-5 Luck...expression] THIS EDITION; thee| go to| MOSELEY. The line-break in the middle of a prepositional phrase would be very uncharacteristic of Middleton.

3.1.107 Best...man] WEBER; *verse* MOSELEY: law|

3.1.111-26 How...minute] WEBER; it| minute| runs| thief| husbandmen| again| it| minute MOSELEY. MOSELEY places a comma in the middle of each line (where Weber placed a line-break).

3.2.32-3 Better...lute] REED; *prose* MOSELEY

3.3.16-17 How...indeed] WEBER; *1 line* MOSELEY

3.3.36-41 You'd...on you] MOSELEY; *prose* WEBER. Three successive hexameters are well within Middleton's range; alternatively, one might divide after 'mistress' and 'youth'. Only l. 38 is awkwardly irregular.

3.3.67-8 I...mistress] DYCE; not| MOSELEY

3.3.100 Please...sir] sir| were| MOSELEY; sir| banquet| unluckily WEBER; next| were| DYCE. MOSELEY's lineation produces a regular (split) iambic pentameter, followed by a fourteener (with a feminine caesura), followed by a hexameter. Dyce's rearrangement simply makes l. 99 (instead of l. 100) a fourteener; typographically, Dyce breaks up MOSELEY's long middle line, but there is nothing to choose metrically between the two arrangements, and it is hard to explain why the purported error should have occurred.

4.1.62-3 'Twere...see't] MOSELEY; enough| I am| DYCE

4.1.66-7 It...O! O!] *1 type line* MOSELEY

4.1.137-8 Twirling...well] DYCE; *prose* MOSELEY (you| so)

4.1.139-40 'Twas...matrimony] THIS EDITION; *prose* MOSELEY

4.2.11-12 Lemme...gunpowder] WEBER; *1 line* MOSELEY; *prose* DODSLEY

4.2.31-3 And...Fiducio] THIS EDITION; *2 lines* MOSELEY: shavers|. MOSELEY's first line contains seventeen syllables, which seems excessive even by Middleton's standards.

4.2.129 O...here] DODSLEY; *prose* MOSELEY; *2 lines* REED: e'er|; *2 lines* DYCE: spoiled|

4.2.140-1 Seize...thief] DYCE; *1 line* MOSELEY

4.2.145 You've...sir] WEBER; *prose* MOSELEY. MOSELEY's lineation was probably forced by the stage direction in the right margin.

4.2.146 I...sir] DODSLEY; *prose* MOSELEY. See preceding note.

4.2.229-33 How...thyself] WEBER; *prose* MOSELEY. No printing-house explanation.

4.2.237-8 Then...comfort] DYCE; *1 line* MOSELEY

5.1.10-11 Faith...think] MOSELEY; seemed| WEBER. Weber's line-break seems unlikely for Middleton.

5.1.17-18 Weep...laughing] WEBER; *prose* MOSELEY. Probably one line in manuscript; but Weber's arrangement clarifies the rhythmical structure.

5.1.20-2 Mistress...mistress?] *prose* MOSELEY; *verse* WEBER: for you|. Of these four sentences, the first and third are metrical, the second and fourth irregular. Martino is presumably breathless.

5.1.23 You...you] WEBER; *prose* MOSELEY

5.1.51-4 That...bands] WEBER; *prose* MOSELEY.

5.1.79 Into...again] MOSELEY; *2 lines* DYCE: never|. Fourteeners are not uncommon in Middleton.

5.1.80 A...mistress] MOSELEY; *prose* DYCE. Extrametrical vocative in the final foot.

5.1.81-2 For...nail] THIS EDITION; *1 line* MOSELEY; *prose* DYCE

5.1.82-3 the...hid] DYCE; *verse* MOSELEY: murder|

5.1.109-10 Nay...sir] THIS EDITION; *1 line* MOSELEY

5.1.141 Look...especially] DODSLEY; *prose* MOSELEY. The full line would not fit MOSELEY's measure, here shortened by the long marginal stage direction (140.1-2).

5.1.154-6 In...ourselves] WEBER. MOSELEY probably intends to convey verse: 'mutton' is set as a new (and separate) type line, at the bottom of sig. H4ᵛ; 'We' begins the first line on sig. I1.

5.1.159-60 I...close] DYCE; *1 line* MOSELEY

5.1.160-1 You...sir] DYCE; *1 line* MOSELEY

5.1.174–6 By...mistress] WEBER; *prose* MOSELEY

5.1.199–200 O...again] THIS EDITION; *verse* MOSELEY: tonight|; *verse* WEBER: bedfellow| must|. MOSELEY's first line fills the measure, and might be prose, but the second type-line begins 'For', an emphasis capital unusual for this word, especially after a comma, unless it was intended as the beginning of another verse line.

5.1.205–6 Their...master] WEBER; *1 line* MOSELEY

5.1.206 Never...never] MOSELEY; *2 lines* DYCE: Never|

5.1.215–16 Are...that] THIS EDITION; *1 line* MOSELEY; *prose* WEBER

5.1.216–20 I...finger] WEBER; *verse* MOSELEY: that| thing| speechless| injuries|

5.1.222–3 But...man] WEBER; *prose?* MOSELEY: gentlewoman| be

5.1.236–7 Would...will] WEBER; *1 line* MOSELEY

5.1.237–8 For...gentleman] WEBER; *1 line* MOSELEY

5.1.268–9 Blame...fearful] WEBER; *1 line* MOSELEY

5.1.269–70 Never...man] WEBER; *1 line* MOSELEY

5.1.271–2 Yea...Martino] WEBER; 'em| MOSELEY

5.1.313–14 In...indeed] THIS EDITION; ha| MOSELEY. MOSELEY gives a rhythmically rough sixteen-syllable line, followed by a six-syllable unassimilated part-line. This arrangement—one regular pentameter, followed by a hexameter with a feminine caesura—seems preferable.

5.1.330–2 Ay...still] DYCE; *prose* MOSELEY; too| horses| WEBER

5.1.351–2 I'll...me] DYCE; *prose* MOSELEY

5.1.353–4 And...'em] THIS EDITION; *prose* MOSELEY; they are now| DYCE

5.1.388–9 O...lips] WEBER; *1 line* MOSELEY

5.1.407–8 Here...another] BULLEN; *prose* MOSELEY; *1 line* WEBER. MOSELEY's measure is shortened here by the long marginal stage direction (406.1–2).

5.1.435–6 Ay...fortune] WEBER; forbear| MOSELEY. MOSELEY's mislineation may be deliberate, in order to provide room in the right margin of l. 436 for the stage direction.

5.1.438–9 To...service] THIS EDITION; *1 line* MOSELEY; do| WEBER

5.1.440–1 Art...thus] WEBER; openly| MOSELEY

THE CHANGELING

Edited by Douglas Bruster

FIRST printed for London stationer Humphrey Moseley in 1653 by Thomas Newcomb, *The Changeling* (Wing M1980; *BEPD* 712) is a quarto made up of eight sheets. Newcomb printed three additional plays by Middleton for Moseley in 1657: *No Wit*, in addition to an octavo of *More Dissemblers* and *Women Beware*. Evidence for Newcomb's role in printing *Changeling* comes with the printer's ornament (a male and female centaur) on page B1r. C. William Miller has identified this ornament in twenty-six other publications of the shop Newcomb married into and later passed on to his son. Lawrence (1961) has found certain damaged letters (including 'H', '*ll*', and '*ſt*') in other books of the period which bear Newcomb's name or initials. Newcomb printed two title-pages for the 1653 issue, one reading: 'THE | CHANGELING: | As it was Acted (with great Applause) | at the Privat house in DRURY-LANE, | and *Salisbury Court*. | [rule] Written by [*THOMAS MIDLETON*, and *WILLIAM ROWLEY*.] Gent'. | [rule] *Never Printed before*. | [rule] LONDON, | Printed for HUMPHREY MOSELEY, and are to | be sold at his shop at the sign of the *Princes-Arms* | in St *Pauls* Church-yard, 1653.' The thirteen surviving copies of this version are joined by four with an anonymous imprint (Wing M1981; *BEPD* 828), which repeat the above with the exception of: '[. . .] | [rule] *Never Printed before*. | [rule] LONDON, | Printed in the Year, 1653.' Because both title-pages are conjugate with I4, priority is difficult to determine.

We can only guess why this change occurred. Greg suggested that the anonymous imprint may have been meant for private circulation. But a more compelling explanation involves its potential (wholesale) distribution to other booksellers. Citation of Moseley's address would be seen as an impediment to retail sales of the book from other addresses; these booksellers would thus require an anonymous imprint. This change, then, may represent a marketing strategy.

Although in large type, Alsemero's eight-line Epilogue on I3v allowed room for advertising four books (either 'newly printed' or 'in the Press'): 'The *Wild-goose-Chase* . . . written by *Francis Beamont* and *John Fletcher*, Gent'.'; 'The *Widdow* . . . written by *Ben: Johnson*, *John Fletcher*, and *Thomas Midleton*, Gent'.'; 'Five *Playes* . . . written by Mr *James Shirley*'; and 'Also, The *Spanish Gypsies*.' Robert Lawrence (1961) points out that the play was certainly published by 8 February 1653, when Thomason recorded having received Shirley's *Six New Playes* (Wing S3486), in which Moseley advertised *Changeling* as 'newly printed'. It seems likely, then, that *Changeling* was printed in January, 1653.

The Spanish Gypsy was printed in 1653 by John Grismond, Jr., and connected to *Changeling* not only through title-page attribution to the same authors and the latter play's end-page advertisement, but also by a curious mistake in the former. Both plays indicate, in identical phrasing, a location of Alicante ('The Scene *Allegant*.': *Changeling* A1v; 'The Scene, *Allegant*.': *Gypsy* A2), but only *Changeling* is there laid.

The reason for this duplication might lie close to the play's date of composition. *Gypsy* was licensed 9 July 1623, slightly more than a year after *Changeling* (Bawcutt, 1996, 141). Both plays were in the repertory of Lady Elizabeth's company at the Phoenix, and both plays were acted at court within two months of each other: *Gypsy* on 5 November 1623, followed by *Changeling* on 4 January 1624 (Bawcutt, 1996, 147-8). *Gypsy* also stresses the word 'changeling': as though alluding to the earlier play, Pretiosa vows to 'play the changeling':

> How! Not a changeling?
> Yes, father, I will play the changeling:
> I'll change myself into a thousand shapes
> To court our brave spectators; I'll change my postures
> Into a thousand different variations
> To draw even ladies' eyes to follow mine;
> I'll change my voice into a thousand tones
> To chain attention. Not a changeling, father?
> None but myself shall play the changeling. [2.1.105-13]

Pretiosa's allusion might indicate that the actor who played Pretiosa also played Beatrice-Joanna (rather than Antonio, as is sometimes suggested), a gender 'changeling' in that play as well. Along with other parallels, this reference suggests that its authors still had *Changeling* in mind when writing another Spanish play—part of a genre of such plays concerned with the possible Spanish Match. The similarities between *Changeling* and *Gypsy* may have led those involved with copying, printing, and publishing *Gypsy*—three decades after its composition—to believe that it shared the dramatic location of *Changeling*.

Moseley was a royalist publisher of belles-lettres: among his authors were Donne, Shakespeare, Milton, Webster, Beaumont, Fletcher, Carew, Crashaw, Waller, Cartwright, and Suckling. Plays were one of his specialties; publication of *Changeling* in 1653 was followed by a block entry in the Stationers' Register (9 September 1653) for fourteen plays by various authors, including Middleton's *No Wit*, *Dissemblers*, and *Women Beware*. Although we do not know how Moseley obtained these plays for printing, both

Changeling and *Gypsy* were likely owned by William Beeston, a theatrical manager in great financial difficulty in the early 1650s. Both of these plays appear in a list which Beeston submitted to the King in 1639 for protection. On 10 August of that year the Lord Chamberlain issued an edict recognizing forty-five plays—including *Changeling* and *Gypsy*—as Beeston's: 'all & euery of them properly & of right belong to the sayd House, and consequently... they are all in his propriety' (Bentley I, 331). Beeston had lost possession of the Cockpit theatre by 1651 and was imprisoned in March of that year for debt; 'having sold and pawned his most necessary goods and having took up money upon ill conditions', he eventually regained some control over the Cockpit's lease (Hotson, 103). His 'most necessary goods' may have included such valuable unpublished plays as *Changeling* and *Gypsy*.

Changeling was popular on stage before the closing of the theatres in 1642. N. W. Bawcutt gathers a number of references to the play and to actors associated with the play—particularly with the role of Antonio (identified as 'The Changeling.' in the dramatis personae). That the play enjoyed a continued vitality, and that it struck people as particularly theatrical, is suggested by the subtitle to a broadside by Robert Wild entitled: 'THE | RECANTATION | Of a Penitent | PROTEUS | Or the | CHANGLING, | AS It was Acted with good Applause in St. Maries in *Cambridge*, and St. *Pauls* in *London*, 1663.' This broadside (Wing W2148) has no other connection to Middleton and Rowley's play. As G. Blakemore Evans notes, three 'drolls' from *Changeling* appear in *The Marrow of Complements*, published in 1655 (though the British Museum copy has been dated by Thomason as 'July. 15. 1654'). The first droll (p. 124), drawn from 1.1.137–54, is entitled 'Jasperino, *a merry fellow, at first sight thus boards the Joviall* Diaphanta.'; the second droll (pp. 124–5), drawn from 1.2.1–33, is entitled '*A Dialogue betweixt an old jealous Doctor, and his man.*'; the third (pp. 126–7), from 3.3.130–52, is entitled '*A Gentleman to obtain the love of his Lady, faignes himselfe Mad, and thus courts in his keepers absence.*' Evans notes that these drolls contain 'slight omissions, the addition of a few words, occasional verbal substitutions, and a change of names in the second "droll" to "Doctor" and "Jacomo."' It is almost certain that they are derived from NEWCOMB. Evans goes on to suggest that these drolls are 'possible evidence of the play's popularity during the later Commonwealth period', and may explain the figure labelled 'Changeling.' on the engraved title-page of Francis Kirkman's collection of drolls entitled *The Wits* (1662).

Fifteen years after its original publication a new cancel title-page (with a new setting of the dramatis personae on its reverse) was appended to the quarto. Nine copies (Wing M1982) have survived: 'THE | CHANGELING: | As it was Acted (with great | Applause) by the Servants of His | Royal Highness the Duke of *York*, at | the Theatre in *Lincolns-Inn* Fields. | [rule] | [ornament] | [rule] | *LONDON*, | Printed for *A.M.* and sold by | *Thomas Dring*, at the *White Lyon*, over against | the *Inner Temple-Gate* in *Fleet-street*. 1668. | [rule] Where you may be Furnish'd

with | most sorts of *Plays*.' Moseley had died in 1661, and 'A.M.' here is probably his daughter, Anne, who appears to have continued the business after the death of her mother (also named Anne) in 1673 (Reed). We do not know how or where the original sheets survived decay and the Great Fire of 1666—perhaps in the crypt of St. Paul's—but many did. The issue of 1668 accounts for a third of all surviving quartos recorded.

The nature of printer's copy is difficult to determine. Bawcutt suggests that the play was probably printed from a transcript of theatrical prompt-copy. Certainly at places one finds instructions likely to be helpful to playhouse practice: '*In the Act time Deflores hides a naked Rapier*' (3.1.0.3); '*Exit with Body*' (3.2.27). And in the last Act some of these directions are clearly imperative ('*Strike two*', 5.1.11; '*Enter Deflores*[,] *servants: passe over, ring a Bell*', 5.1.72.1), suggesting instructions from author(s) or bookkeeper. Yet as Lawrence (1961) remarks, elsewhere the stage directions are less ample. Much of the quarto, in fact, seems unsuited for use in the theatre. For example, at many places a character is acknowledged in dialogue before a stage direction indicates the entrance of that character—the reverse of what one would expect from playhouse copy (compare '*Enter Jasperino.*' 4.2.130.1; '*Enter Deflores, passes over the Stage.*' 5.2.8.1; '*Enter Deflores.*' 5.2.23.1; '*Enter Deflores.*' 5.3.88.1). Yet the play lacks spellings we might expect to see in copy derived directly from authorial foul papers. However slight the evidence supporting it, then, Bawcutt's suggestion that the play was printed from a transcript of theatrical prompt-copy remains the most persuasive theory.

At least since E. H. C. Oliphant it has been argued that as printed the play lacks a scene or scenes. Roger Holdsworth (1990) gives the best case for this view in advancing the following claims: (*a*) the counterfeit lunatics are too abruptly introduced to the play and the madhouse—i.e. they are neither identified nor motivated; and (*b*) although plans are prepared as early as 3.3.253 ff. for a wedding-masque with which to draw together the various plots—as well as Antonio and Franciscus, in a (parodic) duel for Isabella (hinted at in the end of 4.3)—such a masque is never seen, and may have been abridged from the quarto version. Yet Holdsworth himself has provided the best evidence against missing scenes. For example, in regard to the need for a scene that would introduce, name, and motivate both Antonio and Franciscus, Holdsworth points out that *Women Beware* is characterized by precisely such structural 'namelessness'; that is, that not only do four characters 'never acquire personal names' (in the dialogue of that play), but many of the other characters are so 'named' only late and then sparingly. (With this one could compare Vermandero in *Changeling*, who is 'named' only late, only in the hospital scenes, and then only by Alibius: 3.3.273, 4.3.58, 4.3.78.) But such a view may confuse 'name' with 'identity', and a better answer to Holdsworth's claim is the fact that Alibius early on expresses fears about 'Gallants' who come to the madhouse (1.2.51 ff.); and, also quite early on, Lollio seems to be

harbouring suspicions about the newly-introduced mad-
men. As regards a scene in Act 5 which would provide us
with a formal version of the wedding-masque rehearsed
earlier, we can take Holdsworth's observation (1989) concerning the absence of Lollio and Jasperino from the play's
final scene (5.3). He argues that their absence may indicate that they are doubled with characters present during
this scene. If such is the case, it would seem of necessity to
preclude a similar group gathering earlier in Act 5. Sarah
Sutherland, in fact, argues that all such theories of a lost
masque miss the point, for the rehearsal 'Dance' indicated
by a stage direction at 4.3.224.1 ('*The Madmen and Fools
Dance [to music]*') 'brings together for the first and last time
all the sub-plot's characters . . . In this dramatic event the
Jacobean audience is given an almost emblematic vision
of all the plotting and counter-plotting that has gone on
in the sub-plot as well as, by several ratios, the main plot'.
It seems safe to conclude that the text of *Changeling* that
has come down to us accurately represents what Middleton and Rowley made available to seventeenth century
theatres.

Lawrence (1961) has provided the best account of the
quarto's printing, detailing various errors and in-press
corrections. One skeleton was used, and was rotated before the printing of the outer forme of the F gathering;
in all other formes the four versions of the running title
follow a regular order. The text appears to have been set
seriatim. Twenty-three incidental and three substantive
proof-corrections were made in the outer formes of the B,
D, and G gatherings. Some of these corrections encompass
no more than turned letters or foul case: e.g. 'bis' (uncorrected) is replaced by 'his' (corrected) at 2.1.139. Others
involve alteration to aid metre, as in the change from
'we are' (uncorrected) to 'w'are' (corrected) at 2.1.151.
At 2.2.132, 'myselfe that' (uncorrected) was altered to
'myself of that' (corrected)—a substantive correction all
editors have accepted as supplying sense to the line;
but an alteration at 4.2.89—'tho' (uncorrected) to 'thou'
(corrected)—while apparently made for 'sense', actually
spoils the sense ('tho' = 'though' in the line in question).
Although many scholars have felt that *Changeling* is a relatively 'clean' text, T. W. Craik seems right in suggesting
that 'a characteristic error of Q is omission': some words
and phrases appear to have been omitted during the setting of type. Two lines of a song at 3.3.98–9, and several
instances of what appear to be lyrics elsewhere in the text
(see 3.3.101–6, 3.3.163–5, 4.1.63–6) are set as prose,
as are numerous lines throughout NEWCOMB which later
editors concur in setting as verse; however, rather than
indicating compositors economizing on space (as Bawcutt
suggests), such is likely to derive from Middleton's manuscript practice. (See Lawrence, 1961, 1956, for further
discussion of printing matters.)

An initial division of compositors is suggested in the
punctuation used with speech prefixes. Of the sixty-one
pages with speech prefixes, thirty-three employ only periods to close the name abbreviation, and can be assigned to
Compositor A on this basis: B1–C3^v, C4^v–D2, D3^v, D4^v,
E1^v, F2–F4, G2, G3^v, H3, I1, I2, I3. Twenty-eight pages
use some combination of periods and colons; the ratio of
periods to colons here varying from a high of 95:5% to
a low of 8:81% (the use of a semicolon here accounts
for the numbers not adding up to 100). In addition to
those given to A above, pages on which more than 85%
of the speech headings are followed by periods include the
following, perhaps set by A: E1^r, E2^r, E2^v, E4^v, F1^r, F1^v,
F4^v, G1^r, G1^v, G2^v, G4^v, H1^r, H2^v, I1^v.

As Holdsworth points out (*Notes and Queries* 234
(1989), 346), that Lollio and Jasperino are absent from
the play's close may indicate they are doubled with characters present during this scene (5.3.12 ff.). If this is true
and if (*a*) the play as we have it accurately represents a
theatrical script and (*b*) acts were separated by an interval
(see 3.1.0.3: 'In the Act time, De Flores hides a naked
rapier'), through elimination we can see that:

  1) Lollio probably doubled Tomazo. (He could not be
doubled with any other character present during 5.3,
so if—as seems likely—his absence is attributable to
doubling, he likely doubled Tomazo.)

  2) Jasperino may have doubled Antonio or Franciscus

  3) Alibius—absent from the Dumb show at 4.1—may
have doubled Alonzo, who appears there

  4) Pedro may have been doubled by either Alsemero
or De Flores. (If the preceding hypotheses (i.e. #1–3) are
correct, Alsemero and De Flores are able to double only
the part of Pedro.)

There are 38 dashes in the quarto. It may be significant that they occur most frequently in parts of the play
now ascribed to Middleton: 2.1.52–3, 2.1.57, 2.1.78,
2.2.41, 2.2.69 (two), 2.2.98, 2.2.102 (two), 2.2.108,
2.2.114, 2.2.127, 2.2.155, 3.2.21, 3.2.22, 4.1.108,
4.2.50, 4.2.81, 4.2.105, 4.2.130, 5.1.1, 5.1.10, 5.1.6,
5.1.12, 5.1.60, 5.1.76, 5.3.13, 5.3.88, 5.3.89, 5.3.174.
These dashes are unlikely to have been compositorial in
nature, as they occur both in pages I have ascribed to
Compositor A, and in those which—because of a high
ratio of colons to periods following speech headings—are
unlikely to have been set by him (e.g. C4^r, D2^v, D4^r, H1^v,
H2^r, H4^v).

SEE ALSO

Text: *Works*, 1637
Authorship and date: this volume, 422

WORKS CITED

Previous Editions

Dilke, C. W., ed., *Old English Plays* (1815), vol. 4
Dyce, Alexander, ed., *Works* (1840), vol. 4
Bullen, A. H., ed., *Works* (1885), vol. 6
Ellis, Havelock, ed., *Thomas Middleton* (1887), vol. 1
Neilson, William A., ed., *The Chief Elizabethan Dramatists* (1911)
Sampson, Martin W., ed., *Thomas Middleton* (1915)
Tatlock, John S. and Robert G. Martin, eds., *Representative English
    Plays* (1916)
The Changeling (1922)

Schelling, Felix E., ed., *Typical Elizabethan Plays* (1926)

Oliphant, E. H. C., ed., *Shakespeare and His Fellow Dramatists* (1929), vol. 2

Oliphant, E. H. C., ed., *Elizabethan Dramatists Other than Shakespeare* (1931)

Schelling, Felix E., ed., *Typical Elizabethan Plays*, rev. and enl. (1931)

Brooke, C. F. Tucker and Nathaniel B. Paradise, eds., *English Drama 1580–1642* (1933)

Spencer, Hazelton, ed., *Elizabethan Plays* (1933)

Baskervill, Charles R., Virgil B. Heltzel, and Arthur H. Nethercot, eds., *Elizabethan and Stuart Plays* (1934)

Tatlock, John S., and Robert G. Martin, eds., *Representative English Plays*, second edition rev. and alt. (1938)

Lawrence, Robert G., ed., *A Critical Edition of The Changeling* (1956)

Bawcutt, N. W., ed., *The Changeling* (1958)

Sazayama, Takashi, ed., *The Changeling* (1961)

Harrier, Richard C., ed., *The Anchor Anthology of Jacobean Drama* (1963), vol. 2

Lawrence, Robert G., ed., *Early Seventeenth Century Drama* (1963)

Ornstein, Robert, and Hazelton Spencer, eds., *Elizabethan and Jacobean Tragedy: An Anthology* (1964)

Thomson, Patricia, ed., *The Changeling* (1964)

Salgādo, Gāmini, ed., *Three Jacobean Tragedies* (1965)

Black, Matthew W., ed., *The Changeling* (1966)

Corrigan, Robert W., ed., *The Changeling* (1966)

Williams, George W., ed., *The Changeling* (1966)

Gomme, A. H., ed., *Jacobean Tragedies* (1969)

Huston, J. D. and Alvin B. Kernan, eds., *Classics of the Renaissance Theater: Seven English Plays* (1969)

Wine, M. L., ed., *Drama of the English Renaissance* (1969)

The Changeling: 1653 (1973)

Muir, Kenneth, ed., *Three Plays* (1975)

Fraser, Russell A., and Norman C. Rabkin, eds., *Drama of the English Renaissance* (1976), vol. 2

Frost, David L., ed., *The Selected Plays of Thomas Middleton* (1978)

Loughrey, Bryan, and Neil Taylor, eds., *Thomas Middleton: Five Plays* (1988)

Daalder, Joost, ed., *The Changeling* (1990)

Other Works Cited

Bawcutt, N. W., ed., *The Control and Censorship of Caroline Drama: The Records of Sir Henry Herbert, Master of the Revels 1623–73* (1996)

Bentley, Gerald Eades, *The Jacobean and Caroline Stage*, 7 vols (1941–68)

Bromham, A. A., and Zara Bruzzi, *The Changeling and the Years of Crisis, 1619–1624: A Hieroglyph of Britain* (1990)

Cogswell, Thomas, *The Blessed Revolution: English Politics and the Coming of War, 1621–1624* (1989)

Craik, T. W., 'Notes on the Text of Three Passages in *The Changeling*', *Notes and Queries* 222 (1977), 120–2

—— 'Further Proposed Emendations in *The Changeling*', *Notes and Queries* 225 (1980), 324–7

Dollimore, Jonathan, *Radical Tragedy: Religion, Ideology, and Power in the Drama of Shakespeare and his Contemporaries* (1984)

Eliot, T. S., 'Thomas Middleton', *Selected Essays* (1958), 161–70

Evans, G. Blakemore, review in *Journal of English and Germanic Philology* (1959), 693–4

Greg, W. W., *A Bibliography of the English Printed Drama to the Restoration*, 4 vols (1939–59)

Heinemann, Margot, *Puritanism and Theatre: Thomas Middleton and Opposition Drama under the Early Stuarts* (1980)

Holdsworth, R. V., 'Notes on *The Changeling*', *Notes and Queries* 234 (1989), 344–46

—— '*Women Beware Women* and *The Changeling* on the Stage', in Holdsworth, ed., *Three Jacobean Revenge Tragedies* (1990)

Hotson, Leslie, *The Commonwealth and Restoration Stage* (1928)

Kirkman, Francis, *The wits; or, sport upon sport. In select pieces of drollery* (1662) (Wing W3218)

Lawrence, Robert G., 'A Bibliographical Study of Middleton and Rowley's *The Changeling*', *The Library*, V, 16 (1961), 37–43

Limon, Jerzy, *Dangerous Matter: English Drama and Politics in 1623/4* (1986)

Malcolmson, Cristina, '"As Tame as the Ladies": Politics and Gender in *The Changeling*', *English Literary Renaissance* 20 (1990), 320–39

The Marrow of Complements (1654/5) (Wing M719)

Miller, C. William, 'Thomas Newcomb: A Restoration Printer's Ornament Stock', *Studies in Bibliography* 3 (1950–1), 155–70

Oliphant, E. H., ed., *Shakespeare and His Fellow Dramatists: A Selection of Plays Illustrating the Glories of the Golden Age of English Drama* (1929)

Reed, John Curtis, 'Humphrey Moseley, Publisher', *Oxford Bibliographical Society Proceedings and Papers* 2 (1928), 61–142

Ricks, Christopher, 'The Moral and Poetic Structure of *The Changeling*', *Essays in Criticism* 10 (1960), 290–306

Roberts, Marilyn, 'A Preliminary Check-List of Productions of Thomas Middleton's Plays', *Research Opportunities in Renaissance Drama* 28 (1985), 37–61

Schoenbaum, Samuel, *Middleton's Tragedies* (1955)

Sutherland, Sarah P., *Masques in Jacobean Tragedy* (1983)

Transcript of the Registers of the Worshipful Company of Stationers from 1640–1708 A.D., A, ed. George Edward Briscoe Eyre, Charles Robert Rivington, and H. R. Plomer, 3 vols (1913–14)

Wiggin, Pauline G., *An Inquiry into the Authorship of the Middleton-Rowley Plays* (1897)

[Wild, Robert], *The Recantation of a Penitent Proteus* (1663) (Wing W2148)

TEXTUAL NOTES

1.1.4 of] DAALDER (conj. Bawcutt); or NEWCOMB. Bawcutt retains Newcomb but as supporting emendation refers to what is more obviously a mistake of 'of' for 'or' at 1.1.111— 'than his of hers' (Newcomb). Although Middleton often uses 'hopes' as a resonant substantive, nowhere else does he follow it with 'or'. For instances supportive of emendation, see *Chaste Maid* 5.1.37–8 and 1.2.116–17, and *Quarrel* 4.2.97. Compare especially *Dissemblers* 1.2.68, 3.1.237, 5.2.104, and 5.2.199. Holdsworth suggests (privately) a parallel in *Revenger* 3.5.170.

1.1.27 inclinations] NEWCOMB; inclination DILKE.

1.1.56 him] NEWCOMB (bim)

1.1.57.1 *Joanna*] NEWCOMB (*Joannna*)

1.1.97 stall] NEWCOMB (ſtall); stale DILKE. Newcomb's reading seems correct, as 'stall' was current as a verb in several senses (see Commentary). It should be pointed out that Middleton nowhere else uses the word, and does use 'stale' as a verb in *Weapons* 1.1.140: 'we'll stale your friend first'. While Rowley does not use 'stall', or 'stale' as a verb, he does use 'forestall' in *All's Lost by Lust* 3.2.25: 'Now I forestall thee, heaven, ere I begin'; and *New Wonder* 4: 'I hold my life this spruce | Citizen will forestall the market'.

1.1.100 Will't] NEWCOMB (Wilt)

1.1.111 or] DYCE; of NEWCOMB. See note to 1.1.4 above.

1.1.117 found] DILKE; found NEWCOMB. Newcomb's long 's' here may have been a misreading of 'f', or perhaps resulted from a sorting error in the compositor's type-case. The emphasis here, on discrepancy of quantity, would be continued in 'found' but less so in 'sound'—which, as Williams argues, may call for a further paradox of logic: 'Almost every man in a thousand healthy people is unhealthy'. Compare *Dissemblers* 1.3.44–5: 'I would have nothing want to your *perfection*...Is there a doubt *found* yet?' (emphasis added: compare 'imperfection' in *Changeling*, l. 118). And see also Laurentius, quoted in Burton's *Anatomy of Melancholy* (1621), 1.3.2: 'for scarce is there one of a thousand that dotes alike'.

1.1.128 What might be] DILKE; And what might be NEWCOMB. Yet arguing against emendation here is Rowley's habit of 'cue-catching' (i.e. repeating words and phrases as a kind of chain through his texts—see Robb).

1.1.160 beholden] NEWCOMB (beholding)

1.1.192 this] NEWCOMB; his (conj. Dyce). Rowley seems to prefer the phrase 'this day' (compare *Old Law* 5.1.539–40; *Birth of Merlin* 3.1.156; *Fortune by Land and Sea* 2.1; *Travels of the Three English Brothers*: 'This day my royal master'; 'My thanks to heaven that overlooked this day'; *Wonder* 2.1: 'But after this day, I protest cuz, you shall never | See me handle those bones again; this day I | Break up school: if ever you call me unthrift after | This day, you do me wrong'). Middleton seems divided in his practice of associating 'triumph' with 'this' (*Civitatis* 230 and 244–5), and sometimes with possessive pronouns (*Dissemblers* 1.2.64 and 1.3.52). *Entertainments*, for example, offers support for either reading; compare 6.23 and 6.58.

1.2.21 this] NEWCOMB; these DILKE. Perhaps best understood as referring to 'this difference (of our ages)', or even 'this—the fact that I am old', with 'concord and sympathise' taking as object the (unstated) plural subject of 'this'. It seems clear that Alibius does not hear or chooses not to acknowledge Lollio's joke in the previous line.

1.2.87 the] DYCE; his NEWCOMB

1.2.103 hee] he NEWCOMB. So modernized throughout this text.

1.2.128 you I'll make] DYCE; you make NEWCOMB. For the attraction of 'warrant' to forms of the future, compare Rowley in three roles he probably acted himself; Sim in *A Match at Midnight* 4.2.52–3: 'Ay, but I'll have more care of the Gentleman I warrant you'; the Clown in *Old Law* 4.1.133–4: 'As long as I have thee by me, she shall not be with child, I warrant thee'; and Chough in *Quarrel* 5.1.296–7: 'I warrant you, sir, he shall do nothing but what I do before him'. It should be noted that all three statements, like Lollio's to Pedro, are custodial in nature. Compare also *Lust* 1.1.157: 'She'll hold out I warrant, hark you my Liege'; *Birth of Merlin* 4.1.34: 'for now will I warrant thee'; *Fortune by Land and Sea* 2.1: 'I'll warrant him fright the birds, here's that will make him look like a scarecrow'; *Maid in the Mill* 2.2: 'I'll warrant you | He dies in't'; *A Shoemaker, a Gentleman* 1.2.10: 'I'll warrant ye'; 2.1.119–20: 'he shall mend it I warrant you, Madam'.

1.2.164 fools goes] NEWCOMB. Common use of plural subject with verb in the singular; compare Abbott 333.

1.2.198 there's] DILKE; there NEWCOMB

1.2.210 goes] NEWCOMB; go DYCE.

2.1.40 pig-haired] THIS EDITION; pick-haired NEWCOMB (pick-haird). Compare Witgood in *Trick* 4.4.299–300: 'you short pig-haired, ram-headed rascals!' (That this is not itself a mistake for 'pickhaired' may be taken from the 'pig'/'ram' contrast.) This reading has the support of the 'trough' and 'swine' references a few lines later in De Flores's speech. Compare also *Roaring Girl* 3.256: 'You, goodman swine's face!' and *Patient Man* 6.173: 'a little pig's wash!' Compare also *Richard III* 5.2.7–10: 'The...boar, | That...Swills your warm blood like wash, and makes his trough | In your in-bowelled bosoms'. But Middleton elsewhere uses 'pick-hatcht' as an adjective ('Pickt-hatch commanders', *Black* 103)— referring to the London resort of prostitutes and thieves. And it is possible that a compositor or scribe of 1653— not recognizing a reference current earlier in the century— took this as 'pickhaird' from the attraction of 'hairs'. *OED* lists three uses of 'picked-hatch' (spelled variously) as an attributive during the period 1598–1634; it seems to have been especially popular in the drama. For yet another use of the adjective, see Samuel Rowlands, *More Knaves Yet? The Knaves of Spades and Diamonds*, 'The Picture of a Swaggerer' (E2ᵛ): 'A Bedlam looke, shag haire, and staring eyes, | Horse coursers tongue, for oths & damned lyes, | A Pickt-hatch paire of pockey lymping legs, | And goes like one that fees in shackels begs'. The force of a phrase like 'pickt-hatched faces' would be to imply damage from venereal disease, got at and common to Pickt-hatch. Spelled, variously, 'Picked', 'Pict', and 'Pick'd' (see Sugden, *Topographical Dictionary*, who collects many references from plays of the period). It is not unimaginable that Middleton would introduce a colourful if local adjective of this sort in a 'Spanish' play that refers to Bedlam and Paris Garden (compare 2.1.81 below).

2.1.46 plucked] NEWCOMB (pluckt); plucks DILKE. For the past in a similar thought, compare 3.4.149: 'by all sweets that ever darkness tasted'. Yet support for the iterative might be found in *Hengist* 2.4.216 and *Women Beware* 2.2.370–4.

2.1.68 wilt] NEWCOMB (wil't)

THE CHANGELING

2.1.86   his] NEWCOMB; their DILKE. See 1.1.27 above, note.

2.1.139   in his absence] THIS EDITION (conj. Sampson); in his paſſions NEWCOMB. This emendation makes sense of an otherwise confusing line; many editors omit 'in his passions'. That thirteen words were packed into this line suggests a reason for compositorial error. Middleton rarely uses 'passions', and almost always connects the word 'absence' with the possibility of adultery and other sexual transgressions; compare especially *Women Beware* 1.1.173–4, where 'absence' is followed by 'restraint' (as in *Changeling*, l. 141). See also *Chaste Maid* 1.2.86–7, Sir Walter: 'No strangers in my absence?' (to which Allwit responds in an aside, 'His jealousy begins'); *Dissemblers* 3.1.125–6; *Widow* 1.1.211–3; and *Lady* 1.2.148. Compare also *Yorkshire* 1.2 ff..

2.2.6   their] THIS EDITION (conj. Holdsworth); the NEWCOMB. Holdsworth (1989) points out that the compositor makes an error in the next line ('lock' for 'lock'd'), and compares *Quarrel* 2.2.65, where a confidante is called 'your closet'. The popular work called *The Ladies Cabinet* (1639) does not internally use its title phrase; yet rather than arguing for retaining Newcomb, this title—postdating the composition of the play—may have contributed to the imposition of the Newcomb form by making 'the ladies['] cabinet' a natural-sounding phrase. Compare *Game* 2.1.191 and *Women Beware* 1.1.56.

2.2.7   locked] DILKE (lock'd); lock NEWCOMB. See previous note, and compare *Game* 2.1.141, 2.2.250.

2.2.10   brings] NEWCOMB; bring BULLEN; see note above to 1.1.27.

2.2.27   'bout] NEWCOMB; about DILKE.

2.2.33   your dangers and not mine, then] NEWCOMB; your danger's and not mine then DILKE; you're danger's and not mine then DYCE. Traditional interpretations of Newcomb are wrong here for at least seven reasons: (*a*) the line makes sense as it stands; (*b*) *Changeling* 4.1.83: 'my fears are not hers else'—also delivered by Beatrice—speaks similarly (if in bad faith) of a desire to share hardships; (*c*) Middleton never follows 'you are'/'you're'/'y'are' with an abstract substantive in the possessive case; (*d*) Middleton is markedly fond of the pronominal deixis one finds in the passage in Newcomb (compare *Dissemblers* 3.1.1, 4.3.7; *Five Gallants* 4.6.000; *Game* 2.2.109, 4.1.106; *Hengist* 1.1.27, 4.2.179; *Patient Man* 15.393; *Roaring Girl* 6.262); (*e*) Middleton never uses the possessive form of 'danger'; (*f*) Middleton often uses 'dangers' to describe similar situations (compare *Women Beware* 1.2.227; *Game* 2.1.144); and (*g*) Middleton often employs 'dangers' in quasi-heroic description, a register that might fit Beatrice's relation to Alsemero here (compare *Sherley* 67 and 160, and *Tennis* 631). If emendation is desired, a more likely reading would be 'your dangers are not mine, then', but as *Quarrel* 2.1.122–3 shows, the reading adopted here finds parallels in Middleton's practice: 'I do but think how wretched I had been | Were this another's quarrel and not mine'.

2.2.41   to blame] NEWCOMB too blame.

2.2.57   I have] NEWCOMB; I've DYCE

2.2.59   Happily] NEWCOMB; haply DILKE. Elsewhere Middleton uses 'haply' only once (*Chaste Maid* 2.1.179), and often employs 'happily' in this sense; see *Game* 2.1.163 and 5.3.71. 'Happily' is used in at least twenty-two of Middleton's works.

2.2.80   Faugh] NEWCOMB (Vauh)

2.2.88   'tis] NEWCOMB; it is DILKE

2.2.109   that's] NEWCOMB; that is DYCE (for reasons of metre)

2.2.118   It's] NEWCOMB; It is DILKE

2.2.125   receive] NEWCOMB; receiv'd DILKE

2.2.132   I have] NEWCOMB; I've DYCE

2.2.159   I am] NEWCOMB; I'm DYCE

2.2.163   I will] NEWCOMB; I'll DYCE

3.1.3   sconce] NEWCOMB. Stage directions that follow here take their logic from Holdsworth, 'Notes on *The Changeling*', who points out that 'A sconce was a small fort but it was also a jocular term for the head, so if one admits the pun (and De Flores's subsequent speeches are full of similar sadistic ironies) this must mean that he intends to club Alonzo with one of the large, heavy keys he is carrying, the very one he is now showing his victim. That he does this is borne out by 3.2.13–17'.

3.3.36   have had a taste] DYCE; have a taſt NEWCOMB. Compare *A Shoemaker, a Gentleman* 4.1.72–3; *Weapons* 5.1.221.

3.3.37   o'th' other side] DYCE; o'th' side NEWCOMB. Dyce's emendation seems in keeping with Rowley's practice elsewhere; the question is whether to insert 'other' or 'tother' (a popular form in other Rowley plays and passages). As Lollio consistently employs 'other' here (there are no occurrences of 'tother'), this seems the correct reading. For 'other' see *Maid in the Mill* 2.1: 'But then o'th'other side'; 'For a Funeral Elegy on the Death of Hugh Atwell', l. 1; *Search For Money*: 'on the other side', 'on the other side', 'in at the one side and out at the other'; *Quarrel* 4.1.223. For 'tother' see *Match at Midnight* 2.1.195 and *A Shoemaker, a Gentleman* 4.1.161.

3.3.57   primroses] DILKE; primrose NEWCOMB. I have found no instance of 'primrose' signalling the plural in relation to actual flowers (i.e. as opposed to uses like 'primrose path'). Compare *Cymbeline* 1.5.83–4: 'The violets, cowslips, and the primroses | Bear to my closet'; and *The Shepherds' Calendar*, April: 62–3: 'Bay leaves between, | And primroses green'.

3.3.71   never] NEWCOMB; ne'er DYCE

3.3.78   say] THIS EDITION (suggested BAWCUTT); not in NEWCOMB.

3.3.92   walks] NEWCOMB; walk DILKE. See above, note to 1.1.27.

3.3.101   (sings)] THIS EDITION; not in NEWCOMB

3.3.101–6   THIS EDITION. Set as a song here because of rhymes otherwise buried within the lines when set as blank verse. Franciscus has just been singing at ll. 98–9, and it seems likely that he continues to sing after Lollio's choric commentary (100); perhaps the copy-text did not bother to signal the continuation. It should be noted that the compositor set the preceeding snatch of a song (98–9) as one line—always expanded by editors. And compare what seems to be similar compression at 3.3.163–5, 4.1.63–6. For songs with similarly alternating short and long lines, see, for a few examples, *Heroes* 279 ff., and *Dissemblers* 1.3.68–89. Compare also 'sweet lady, smile on me', the song of Budget and Ditty in *The London Chanticleers* (in Hazlitt's *Dodsley*, 12:342).

3.3.122   singing] THIS EDITION; not in NEWCOMB

3.3.114   nidget] NEWCOMB (nigget)

3.3.148   she] NEWCOMB; he DYCE. Compare 4.3.107 and note, below.

3.3.149   and the nearest] DILKE; and nearest NEWCOMB. Compare Rowley, *Search for Money*: 'which way first to begin as the likeliest to find the nearest way (being the very nominative case first to find the construction)'; 'we now (sans fear) would go the nearest way'; and Middleton, *Game* 4.1.85.

3.3.168   he is] NEWCOMB; he's DYCE

3.3.199   you but smile] ELLIS; you smile NEWCOMB. Compare the otherwise verbatim repetition of this speech at ll. 245–52.

3.3.273   castle captain] NEWCOMB; castle's captain DILKE

3.3.287   'Tis this] THIS EDITION; This this NEWCOMB

3.4.9 largely] NEWCOMB; largely commended DYCE. Middleton often uses 'largely' by itself at the end of phrases, clauses, and sentences. Compare *Dissemblers* 4.1.12, 5.2.241. Rowley uses 'largely' only once elsewhere, in *New Wonder*, Act 3: 'Let him be largely texted in your love, | That all the City may read it fairly'.

3.4.36 I made] NEWCOMB; I have made DYCE (for metre). But compare *Widow* 3.1.94: 'I made him field it straight again'.

3.4.67–8 gold | For the] DILKE; gold? | The NEWCOMB. Compare *Game* 3.1.62: 'O you've drawn blood, life blood—yea, blood of honour'.

3.4.72–3 have lain at ease, | And] THIS EDITION; have slept at ease DILKE; have, | And NEWCOMB. Compare *Five Gallants* 1.1.86–7; *No Wit* 2.57.

3.4.115 it not] DILKE; it NEWCOMB

3.4.154–5 lovers' plagues...that shooting eye] NEWCOMB (fhooting). Dyce and other editors have emended 'lovers' (Newcomb) to 'love's' or read it as 'lover's'; since Ellis several editors have seen that word as misplaced, and emended to 'love-shooting eye', partly for metre. But Middleton frequently used the possessive plural 'lovers'' (compare *Patient Man* 1.49: 'lovers' rage'; *Quarrel* 1.1.180: 'lovers' arms'; *Roaring Girl* 4.205: 'lovers' hearts'; and *Solomon* 6.124: 'lovers' toys'). And with 'shooting eye' compare also *Patient Man* 1.138: 'wafting eye'. In Middleton, eyes may 'shoot' without further definition; compare *Weapons* 2.2.127; *Yorkshire* 8.36–9; and *Virtue* 56. In *Old Law* 4.2.153, Middleton connects 'plagues' with 'shoot'.

3.4.166 may you weep me] DYCE; may weep me NEWCOMB. Compare *Dissemblers* 1.3.110–11: 'Is not this flesh? Can you drive heat from fire? | So may you love from this'.

4.1.5 One that's ennobled both] BAWCUTT; One both ennobled both NEWCOMB

4.1.45 sleight] NEWCOMB (slight). Compare *Roaring Girl* 6.139: 'no odd sleight, no prevention'.

4.1.63 (Sings)] THIS EDITION; *not in* NEWCOMB. Henke (*Courtesans*, p. 159) quotes lines from 'A Song made on the Power of Women': 'Alexander the Great, who conquered all, | And wept because the World was so small; | In the Queen of Amazon's pit did fall'.

4.1.65 the end] NEWCOMB; th'end DYCE

4.2.55 chins and noses] ELLIS (conj. Dyce); sins and vices NEWCOMB. See Bawcutt's note to 4.2.54. And compare also Drayton in the 1619 *Idea*, no. 8: 'Thy Pearly Teeth out of thy Head so cleane, | That when thou feed'st, thy Nose shall touch thy Chinne' (ll. 11–12).

4.2.61 'Twill] DYCE; I will NEWCOMB

4.2.71 have a] NEWCOMB; have had a DILKE

4.2.102 passed] DYCE; past NEWCOMB

4.2.113–14 I've spent | My study] THIS EDITION; I've | My study NEWCOMB. Apparently a word has been omitted; Bawcutt inserted 'made'.

4.2.149 Keeps] DYCE; Keep NEWCOMB. Compare *Five Gallants* 2.1.120.2. For 'Keeps' in the initial position of a blank verse line with subject understood, see *Five Gallants* Interim.2.89; *Revenger* 2.1.82, 4.1.47.

4.3.1 waning] DYCE (conj. Dilke); waiting NEWCOMB; waxing WILLIAMS. Rowley does not elsewhere use 'waiting'; for 'wane' compare *The Witch of Edmonton* 2.1.55–6. Compare also Middleton in *Mad World* 3.2.176; and *Yorkshire* 4.72. In Wither's *Collection of Emblems*, XL, we learn of Fortune: 'that her *changing* may be showne; | She beareth in her Hand a *Wayned-moone*'.

4.3.2 all at once] DILKE; all once NEWCOMB. Compare *Travels*: 'I do beseech ye take it all at once'; 'They all at once shall take their leaves of you'; *Quarrel* 1.1.219–20.

4.3.3 akin] DYCE; a-kin NEWCOMB

4.3.35 you, mistress] DILKE; your mistress NEWCOMB

4.3.45 Why,] DILKE; We NEWCOMB

4.3.99 yeomanry] DYCE; yeomandry NEWCOMB

4.3.102 rises] DILKE; rife NEWCOMB

4.3.107 she] NEWCOMB (fhe); he DILKE. See 3.3.148 above, and note. It seems likely that Isabella's 'how she treads the air' is the kind of illeism that Franciscus uses later in this scene at l. 216: 'He handles him like a feather. Hey!' (Note also the use of 'Hey' in each instance.) It should be noticed that some editors are confused by Franciscus's illeism as well, and give his line to Lollio.

4.3.111–13 Isabella perhaps creates a song on the lines of the madmen she has heard earlier at 3.3.122–3: 'Bounce! Bounce! He falls! He falls!' And compare the following lines from John Dowland's song, 'Sorrow, stay!': 'But down, down, down I fall, | And arise I never shall'. On the compression of lyrics in this text, see note to 3.3.101–6 above.

4.3.122 straits] DYCE; ftreets NEWCOMB

4.3.144 Why] NEWCOMB (Wy)

4.3.163 desire] NEWCOMB. DYCE queried 'desert' (from the preceding line), a tempting suggestion.

4.3.170 cast off] DYCE; caft off NEWCOMB (caft)

4.3.175 which have made] DYCE; which made NEWCOMB

5.1.105 ruin] DAALDER (conj. Craik); mine NEWCOMB.

5.1.21 a pothecary's] DYCE; a Apothecaries NEWCOMB; elsewhere Middleton does not use what we consider the full form of the word.

5.1.22 thanked] DILKE; thank NEWCOMB

5.1.25 Phosphorus] DILKE; Bosphorus NEWCOMB

5.1.105 ruin] DAALDER (suggested Craik); Mine NEWCOMB

5.2.81 Briamata] NEWCOMB (Bramata). See 4.2.8 above, and commentary note.

5.2.10 bestead] NEWCOMB (befted). Compare *Women Beware* 3.2.118.

5.2.16 touch him with] DILKE; touch with NEWCOMB

5.2.18 near] DYCE; ne're NEWCOMB

5.3.107 that is she's] THIS EDITION; that fhe's NEWCOMB; that she is DYCE; that that *conj.* Jane Sherman in MUIR. Metre as well as sense here suggests a word has dropped out.

5.3.108 It] DILKE; I NEWCOMB. Possibly accurate as stands in Newcomb; compare the verbatim line at 5.1.84, Beatrice to Alsemero: 'I could not choose but follow'. One reading might see Alsemero as repeating her (false) words back to himself, anticipating what he says next: 'O cunning devils! | How should blind men know you from fair-faced saints?' Yet Beatrice's earlier use of this line may equally be cited as a contributing factor in error of transmission here. The use of 'it' as a potentially vague substantive seems in keeping with Middleton's practice: De Flores has just used a similarly vague 'it' (l. 106), and Alsemero will employ another in the Epilogue, l. 4.

5.3.118 adulteress] NEWCOMB (adultreff)

5.3.135 urgent in my blood] DILKE; urgent in blood NEWCOMB. Middleton often uses personal pronouns—'their', 'our', 'your', 'my'—before 'blood'; for the present reading, compare *Phoenix* 15.58: 'Soul-quicking news...pale vengeance to my blood'.

5.3.136 alive or dead] NEWCOMB; or alive or dead DILKE. Middleton uses 'Dead or alive' in *Quarrel* 2.1.120.

5.3.153   sewer] NEWCOMB (fhewer). Perhaps an alternate form:
     See *OED* 'shewer', 'sewer'. And compare *Patient Man* 6.376.
5.3.155   hung] DYCE; hang NEWCOMB. Compare *Black Book* 45–6.

In neither Middleton nor Rowley does 'fate' seem something
humans might manipulate (i.e. as in 'hang my fate').

5.3.164   circumscribes us here] DILKE; circumfcribes here NEW-
     COMB

STAGE DIRECTIONS

[Printed before the play:]

    Drammatis Perfonæ.

Vermandero,   *Father to Beatrice.*
Tomazo de Piracquo,   *A Noble Lord.*
Alonzo de Piracquo,   *His brother, Suitor to* Beatrice:
Alfemero,   *A Nobleman, afterwards married to*

         (Beatrice.

Jafperino,   *His Friend.*
Alibius,   *A jealous Doctor.*
Lollio,   *His man.*
Pedro,   *Friend to Antonio.*
Antonio,   *The Changeling.*
Francifcus,   *The Counterfeit Madman.*
Deflores,   *Servant to Vermandero.*
  Madmen,
  Servants.

Beatrice,   *Daughter to Vermandero*
Diaphanta,   *Her Wayting-woman.*
Ifabella,   *Wife to Alibius.*
    The Scene *Allegant.*

1.1.0.1   ACTUS PRIMUS.
1.1.0.2   *Enter Alsemero.*
1.1.12.1   *Enter Jasperino.*
1.1.44.1   *Enter Servants.* (right, opposite 1.1.44)
1.1.57   *Serv.* | *Exeunt* (right, opposite 1.1.55–7)
1.1.57.1   *Enter Beatrice, Diaphanta, and Servants, Joannna.*
1.1.92.2   *Enter Deflores.*
1.1.154.1   *Enter Vermandero and Servants.* (right, opposite 1.1.155)
1.1.234.1   *Exeunt* (right, opposite 1.1.234)
1.1.241   *Exit.*
1.2.0.1   *Enter Alibius and Lollio.*
1.2.81.1   *Enter Pedro and Antonio like an Idiot.*
1.2.148.1   *Ex. Ped.* (right, opposite 1.2.146–7)
1.2.203.1   *Mad-men within.* (right, opposite 1.2.203)
1.2.223   *Exit.* (right, opposite 1.2.223)
1.2.236   *Exeunt.*
2.1.0.1   ACTUS SECUNDUS.
2.1.0.2   *Enter Beatrice and Jasperino severally.*
2.1.5   *Exit.* (right, opposite 2.1.5)
2.1.26.1   *Enter Deflores.*
2.1.89.1   *Exit Def:* (right, opposite 2.1.89)
2.1.97.1   *Enter Vermandero, Alonzo, Tomazo:*
2.1.124.1   *Exeunt Ver. and Bea.* (right, opposite 2.1.124)
2.1.155.1   *Exit.* (right, opposite 2.1.155)
2.1.157   *Exit.* (right, opposite 2.1.157)
2.2.0.1   *Enter Diaphanta and Alsemero*
2.2.5   *Exit:* (right, opposite 2.2.5)
2.2.7.1   *Enter Beatrice.*
2.2.53.1   *Enter Diaphanta.* (right, opposite 2.2.53)
2.2.56.1   *Ex. Dia. and Als.* (right, opposite 2.2.56)
2.2.56.2   *Enter Deflores.*
2.2.148   *Exit.* (right, opposite 2.2.148)
2.2.157.1   *Enter Alonzo.*
2.2.167   *Exeunt:*
3.1.0.1   ACTUS TERTIUS.

3.1.0.2   *Enter Alonzo and Deflores.*
3.1.0.3   (*In the Act time Deflores hides a naked Rapier.*)
3.1.10.2   *Ex. at one door & enter at the other.* (right, opposite 3.1.10)
3.2.27   *Exit with Body,* (right, opposite 3.2.27)
3.3.0.1   *Enter Isabella and Lollio.*
3.3.39.1   *Ex. Enter presently.* (right, opposite 3.3.39)
3.3.40   *Enter Loll: Franciscus.*
3.3.97   *Sing.* (right, opposite 3.3.97)
3.3.106   *Exit Fra.* (right, opposite 3.3.107)
3.3.109.1   *Enter Antonio.*
3.3.128   *Exit.* (right, opposite 3.3.128)
3.3.160.1   *Enter Lollio.*
3.3.185   *Exit.* (right, opposite 3.3.185)
3.3.193.1   *Enter Lol. above.* (right, opposite 3.3.193)
3.3.207.1   *Exit.* (right, opposite 3.3.207)
3.3.207.1   *Mad-men above, some as birds, others as beasts.*
3.3.215.2   *Enter Lollio.*
3.3.229.1   *Exeunt Lol. and Ant.* (right, opposite 3.3.229)
3.3.235.1   *Enter Lollio.*
3.3.267.1   *Enter Alibius.*
3.3.300   *Exeunt.* (right, opposite 3.3.300)
3.4.0.1   *Enter Vermandero, Alsemero, Jasperino, and Beatrice.*
3.4.10   *Exeunt. Manet Beatrice.* (right, opposite 3.4.10)
3.4.17.1   *Enter Deflores.*
3.4.174.1   *Exeunt:* (right, opposite 3.4.174)
4.1.0.1   ACTUS QUARTUS.
4.1.0.3–15   *Enter Gentlemen,* Vermandero *meeting them with ac-|tion of wonder-|ment at the flight of* Piraquo. *Enter* Alsemero, *with* Jasperino, *and* | *Gallants,* Vermandero *poynts to him, the Gentlemen seeming to ap-|plaud the choyce,* Alsemero, Jasperino, *and Gentlemen;* Beatrice | *the Bride following in great state, accompanied with* Diaphanta, Isa-|bella, *and other Gen-|tlewomen:* Deflores *after all, smiling at the* | *accident;* Alonzo's *Ghost appears to* Deflores *in the midst of his* | *smile, startles him, showing him the hand whose finger he had cut off.* | *They passe over in great solemnity.*
4.1.0.16   *Enter Beatrice:*
4.1.53.1   *Enter Diaphanta*
4.1.130.1   *Exeunt.* (right, opposite 4.1.130)
4.2.0.1   *Enter Vermandero and Servant.*
4.2.17   *Exit Servant.* (right, opposite 4.2.17)
4.2.17   *Enter Tomazo.*
4.2.36.1   *Exit.* (right, opposite 4.2.36)
4.2.36.1   *Enter Deflores.*
4.2.57.1   *Exit.* (right, opposite 4.2.57)
4.2.61.1   *Enter Alsemero.*
4.2.78   *Exit:* (right, opposite 4.2.78)
4.2.80.1   *Enter Jasperino.*
4.2.116.1   *Exit.* (right, opposite 4.2.116)
4.2.122.1   *Enter Beatrice.*
4.2.130.1   *Enter Jasperino.*
4.2.151.1   *Exeunt.*
4.3.0.1   *Enter Isabella and Lollio.*
4.3.54   *Exit.* (right, opposite 4.3.54)
4.3.55.1   *Enter Alibius.*

4.3.84 *Ex. Ali:* (right, opposite 4.3.84)
4.3.86.1 *Enter Antonio.*
4.3.104 *Exit.* (right, opposite 4.3.103)
4.3.106.1 *Enter Isabella.*
4.3.141 *Exit.* (right, opposite 4.3.141)
4.3.141.1 *Enter Lollio.*
4.3.163.1 *Enter Franciscus.*
4.3.215.1 *Enter Alibius.* (after 4.3.216)
4.3.224.1 *The Madmen and Fools dance.* (right, opposite 4.3.224)
4.3.226 *Exeunt.*
5.1.0.1 *ACTUS QUINTUS.*
5.1.0.2 *Enter Beatrice. A Clock strikes one.*
5.1.11 *Strike two.* (right, opposite 5.1.11)
5.1.11.1 *Enter Deflores.*
5.1.57.1 *Enter Alonzos Ghost:*
5.1.60.1 *Exit.* (right, opposite 5.1.60)
5.1.66.1 *Struck 3 a clock:* (right, opposite 5.1.66)
5.1.72.1 *Enter Deflores servants: pass over, ring a Bell.*
5.1.75.1 *Exit:* (right, opposite 5.1.75)
5.1.76 *Enter Diaphanta.*
5.1.81 *Exit* (right, opposite 5.1.81)
5.1.81.1 *Enter Alsemero.*
5.1.87.1 *Enter Vermandero, Jasperino.*
5.1.88.1 *Enter Deflores with a Piece.*
5.1.89.1 *Exit.* (right, opposite 5.1.89)
5.1.94.1 *The piece goes off.* (right, opposite 5.1.94—after 'Ha, there he goes.')

5.1.107.1 *Enter Deflores.*
5.1.115.1 *Enter Servant.* (right, opposite 5.1.116)
5.1.127.1 *Exeunt.* (right, opposite 5.1.127)
5.1.130 *Exit.* (right, opposite 5.1.130)
5.2.0.1 *Enter Thomazo:*
5.2.8.1 *Enter Deflores, passes over the Stage.*
5.2.23.1 *Enter Deflores.* (after 'What, again?')
5.2.42 *Exit.* (right, opposite 5.2.42)
5.2.48.1 *Enter Verman: Ali: and Isabella.*
5.2.87 *Exeunt.* (right, opposite 5.2.87)
5.3.0.1 *Enter Alsemero and Jasperino*
5.3.11.1 *Ex Jas.* (right, opposite 5.3.11)
5.3.13.1 *Enter Beatrice.* (right, opposite 5.3.13—after 'she'd here')
5.3.86.1 *Exit Beatrice:* (right, opposite 5.3.86)
5.3.88.1 *Enter Deflores.*
5.3.113.1 *Exit Def.* (right, opposite 5.3.113)
5.3.120.1–2 *Enter Vermandero, Alibius, Isabella, Thomazo, | Franciscus, and Antonio.*
5.3.142.1 *Enter Deflores bringing in Beatrice.*
5.3.177 *Dyes.* (right, opposite 5.3.177)
5.3.179 *Dyes.* (right, opposite 5.3.179)
Epilogue.0.1 EPILOGUE.
Epilogue.8.1 Exeunt omnes.
Epilogue.8.2 FINIS:

LINEATION NOTES

1.1.42–3 Is…yesterday] THIS EDITION; NEWCOMB: idleness |
1.1.44–5 Backwards…servants] THIS EDITION; *1 line* NEWCOMB. Arranged thus to accentuate Rowley's habit of having one character complete the sentence of another—usually in a different sense than the first speaker intended. Compare 4.3.40–1.
1.1.83–6 O…miss it!] THIS EDITION; NEWCOMB: past | mistaken | come |
1.1.156–7 O…ended?] DILKE; *1 line* NEWCOMB
1.1.174–6 He…truth] DYCE; *2 lines* NEWCOMB: speaks |
1.1.221–2 He's…sir] DYCE; *1 line* NEWCOMB
1.1.223–4 As…else] DYCE; *1 line* NEWCOMB
1.1.235–9 Here's…her] THIS EDITION; NEWCOMB: Now | tanned | fingers | me |
1.2.30–1 You…into't] DYCE; *verse* NEWCOMB: by |
1.2.42–3 Thy…question] THIS EDITION; *1 line* NEWCOMB
1.2.84–5 Ay…patient] BAWCUTT; *1 line* NEWCOMB
1.2.94–5 Sir…hands] DYCE; *verse* NEWCOMB: something |
1.2.99–100 His…Tony] THIS EDITION; NEWCOMB: half |
1.2.107–8 Well…height] DYCE; *1 line* NEWCOMB
1.2.126–7 O…enough] DYCE; NEWCOMB: shorter |
1.2.146–7 I…you] THIS EDITION; *1 line* NEWCOMB. Pedro perhaps breaks his speech here into clauses; first for Lollio ('I…leave you'); then Alibius ('Your…beseech you')—hence Alibius responds to the second half.
1.2.217–19 There's…for't] DILKE; *verse* NEWCOMB: madman | parmesant |
2.1.9–10 Than…choose] THIS EDITION; *1 line* NEWCOMB
2.1.52–4 Again…passions] DILKE; NEWCOMB: disturbs |
2.1.56–7 Soft…now] DYCE; *1 line* NEWCOMB
2.1.57–8 The…toad-pool!] DYCE; *1 line* NEWCOMB
2.1.60–1 My…you] DILKE; *1 line* NEWCOMB

2.1.61–2 What…thee] DILKE; *1 line* NEWCOMB
2.1.64–5 Let…all] DYCE; *1 line* NEWCOMB
2.1.66–7 Signor…Piracquo—] DILKE; *1 line* NEWCOMB
2.1.69–70 The…Tomazo—] DYCE; *1 line* NEWCOMB
2.1.139–40 She…dangerous] THIS EDITION (emending 'passions' to 'absence'); *1 line* NEWCOMB
2.1.144–5 Nay…enough] DILKE; *1 line* NEWCOMB
2.2.5–6 This…cabinets] DILKE; *1 line* NEWCOMB
2.2.12–13 We're…borrow] DILKE; *1 line* NEWCOMB
2.2.25–6 Pray…happy?] DILKE; *prose* NEWCOMB
2.2.48–9 I…side] DILKE; *1 line* NEWCOMB
2.2.51–2 As…opens] DYCE; *1 line* NEWCOMB
2.2.63–4 One…royal] DILKE; *1 line* NEWCOMB (with numbers written: '1, 10, 100, 1000, 10000').
2.2.69–70 And…De Flores!] DYCE; *1 line* NEWCOMB
2.2.72–3 What…physician] DILKE; *1 line* NEWCOMB
2.2.74–5 You've…amorously] THIS EDITION; NEWCOMB: wont |
2.2.75–6 Not…pimple] DILKE; *1 line* NEWCOMB
2.2.77–8 Which…this?] DYCE; *1 line* NEWCOMB
2.2.79–80 Turn…perceive't] DYCE; NEWCOMB: perceiv't |
2.2.83–4 I'll…fortnight] DILKE; *1 line* NEWCOMB
2.2.85–6 Yes…other] DILKE; *1 line* NEWCOMB
2.2.86–7 'Tis…me] DILKE; *1 line* NEWCOMB
2.2.87–90 When…experience] DILKE; *2 lines* NEWCOMB: unpleasing |
2.2.91–2 I…on't] DILKE; *1 line* NEWCOMB
2.2.94–5 It…employment] DILKE; *1 line* NEWCOMB
2.2.95–8 'Twould…to] DILKE; *2 lines* NEWCOMB: it |
2.2.98–9 We…De Flores!] DILKE; *1 line* NEWCOMB
2.2.99–100 How's…'my De Flores'!] *conj.* DYCE; *1 line* NEWCOMB
2.2.102–3 There…on't] *conj.* DYCE; *1 line* NEWCOMB

2.2.107–8 For…bosom] DYCE; *1 line* NEWCOMB

2.2.110–11 O…one] DILKE; NEWCOMB sets 'marry one' on a type line of its own, beneath the preceding

2.2.113–14 Then…sight] DILKE; *1 line* NEWCOMB

2.2.114–15 O…wishes] DILKE; NEWCOMB: you |

2.2.116–17 In…that] DILKE; *1 line* NEWCOMB

2.2.117–18 Put…you] DILKE; *1 line* NEWCOMB

2.2.125–6 This…such] DILKE; *1 line* NEWCOMB

2.2.128–9 Possible…thee] DILKE; *1 line* NEWCOMB

2.2.131–3 That…ravishes] DILKE; *prose* NEWCOMB. Newcomb splits 'before-hand' between two lines without capitalizing 'hand', giving the speech the appearance of prose; the compositor here apparently tried to set thirteen words ('That… beforehand') in one line, but was obliged to move 'hand' to the line following.

2.2.143–5 When…country] DILKE; *prose* NEWCOMB

2.2.146–8 I shall…dog-face] DILKE; *2 lines* NEWCOMB. It is impossible to say whether Newcomb's break after 'time' is meant to signal a verse division.

2.2.148–9 O…already] DILKE; *1 line* NEWCOMB

2.2.159–60 Thou…castle?] DILKE; *1 line* NEWCOMB

2.2.161–3 And if…lord] DILKE; *prose* NEWCOMB

2.2.164–6 I'm…me] DILKE; *prose* NEWCOMB

3.1.9–10 Here…purpose] DYCE; *1 line* NEWCOMB

3.1.10 Lead…thee] THIS EDITION; *1 line* NEWCOMB

3.2.1–2 All…on] DILKE; *1 line* NEWCOMB

3.2.2–3 I am…house] DILKE; *1 line* NEWCOMB

3.2.10–14 Ay…awhile] DYCE; *prose* NEWCOMB

3.2.15–16 De Flores…put on?] DILKE; *1 line* NEWCOMB

3.2.17–18 Do…you] DILKE; *1 line* NEWCOMB

3.3.9–11 NEWCOMB. What may appear to be verse in Newcomb from a capital 'C' ('Corn') is probably prose; there are many capitalized proper nouns in the lines preceding this, and, as MacDonald Jackson points out (privately), 'man's' is justified against the right-hand margin.

3.3.32–4 If I…fool] DILKE; *verse* NEWCOMB: shew | may |

3.3.50–3 For…neither] DILKE; *verse* NEWCOMB: Mistress | first | Chambermaid |

3.3.54–8 Hail…poesy] DILKE; *prose* NEWCOMB

3.3.87–93 Luna…sheep] DILKE; *prose* NEWCOMB

3.3.98–9 *Sweet…thee*] DILKE; *1 line* NEWCOMB (where it is italicized as a song)

3.3.101–6 *No…mouse-hole*] THIS EDITION; *3 lines* NEWCOMB: round | soul | mouse-hole

3.3.124–5 Hark…order] DYCE; *1 line* NEWCOMB

3.3.136–7 O…all] DILKE; *1 line* NEWCOMB

3.3.153–4 Take…you] THIS EDITION; within | NEWCOMB

3.3.163–4 *I'll…morning*] THIS EDITION; *prose* NEWCOMB

3.3.168–9 If…something] DYCE; *1 line* NEWCOMB

3.3.170–2 Ay…six?] DILKE; *verse* NEWCOMB: begins | is |

3.3.174–5 What…seven?] DILKE; *verse* NEWCOMB: is |

3.3.183–5 Again?…together] DILKE; *verse* NEWCOMB home! |

3.3.189–90 How…alone] DILKE; *1 line* NEWCOMB

3.3.195–7 How…that] DILKE; *verse* NEWCOMB Lipsius? | harder |

3.3.198–9 What…smile] DILKE; *1 line* NEWCOMB

3.3.208–9 Of…lunatics] DILKE; *1 line* NEWCOMB. 'Lunatiques' in Newcomb is placed on a line of its own—rather than placed above the line it presumably ends.

3.3.245–6 'What…smile] DYCE; *1 line* NEWCOMB

3.3.253–7 And…on't] DILKE; *verse* NEWCOMB: more | Lacedemonian | thing |. Presumably the scribe or compositor failed to notice that Lollio has finished quoting Antonio's love poetry.

3.3.296–7 You've…commodity] DYCE; *1 line of prose* NEWCOMB

3.4.22–3 All…service] THIS EDITION; circumstance |

3.4.31–2 Why…strings:] DYCE; effectively *1 line* NEWCOMB, who sets 'heart strings', uncapitalized, on a separate line, presumably signalling that it was held to complete the preceding line unit.

3.4.50–2 It…recompense] DILKE; *prose* NEWCOMB

3.4.52–3 No…then] DILKE; *prose* NEWCOMB

3.4.62–3 'Tis…florins] DILKE; *1 line* NEWCOMB

3.4.70–1 I could…rate] DILKE; *1 line* NEWCOMB

3.4.75–6 You…do] DILKE; *1 line* NEWCOMB

3.4.92–3 How…well] DILKE; *1 line* NEWCOMB

3.4.93–4 What…us] DILKE; *1 line* NEWCOMB

3.4.97–8 Take…us] DILKE; *1 line* NEWCOMB

3.4.100–1 I have…pain] DILKE; *1 line* NEWCOMB

3.4.104–5 O…lose] DILKE; *1 line* NEWCOMB

3.4.107–8 I…deed] DILKE; *1 line* NEWCOMB

3.4.108–9 Soft…act] DILKE; *1 line* NEWCOMB

3.4.127–8 I cannot…modesty] DILKE; *1 line* NEWCOMB

3.4.128–9 Push…modesty?] DILKE; *prose* NEWCOMB

3.4.163–4 The…me] DYCE; *1 line* NEWCOMB

4.1.30–2 'If…C—'] DILKE; *verse* NEWCOMB: not |

4.1.33–4 Where's…child] DILKE; *1 line* NEWCOMB

4.1.34–5 she sleeps…not.] DILKE; *verse* NEWCOMB

4.1.45–6 'A merry…Mizaldus':] THIS EDITION; *1 line* NEWCOMB

4.1.47–51 'Give…lumpish.'] Newcomb capitalizes 'In' in the phrase 'water, In the glass M.,' but then evidently decides the passage is prose and sets the speech accordingly.

4.1.52–3 Where…bed-time] DYCE; *1 line* NEWCOMB

4.1.63–5 Earth-conquering…pit-hole] THIS EDITION; *2 lines* NEWCOMB: world |

4.1.84–5 Nay…maid] DILKE; *prose* NEWCOMB

4.1.85–6 You…me] DILKE; *1 line* NEWCOMB

4.1.105–6 And…take it] DILKE; *1 line* NEWCOMB

4.1.107–13 Now…concerns it] NEWCOMB: itself | already | makes | time | contrary

4.1.115–16 As if…another] DILKE; *1 line* NEWCOMB

4.1.118–19 Ay…by't] DILKE; *1 line* NEWCOMB

4.1.120–1 It…Diaphanta] DYCE; *1 line* NEWCOMB

4.1.123–4 I'll tell…business] DILKE; *prose* NEWCOMB

4.2.3–4 Nor…absent?] THIS EDITION; *1 line* NEWCOMB

4.2.7–8 Some…Briamata] THIS EDITION; *1 line* NEWCOMB

4.2.18–19 You're…here] DYCE; *1 line* NEWCOMB

4.2.34–5 'Tis…you] DYCE; *1 line* NEWCOMB

4.2.36–7 The best…on.—] DILKE; *1 line* NEWCOMB

4.2.44–5 O…him] DILKE; *1 line* NEWCOMB

4.2.48–9 'Las…none] DYCE; *1 line* NEWCOMB

4.2.61–2 'Twill…Sir!] DILKE; *1 line* NEWCOMB

4.2.68–9 Your…strangers] DILKE; *1 line* NEWCOMB

4.2.69–70 Time…business] DILKE; NEWCOMB: acquainted |

4.2.74–5 You…sir] DILKE; *1 line* NEWCOMB

4.2.75–6 Fear…meeting] DILKE; *1 line* NEWCOMB

4.2.86–7 This…slowness] DILKE; *1 line* NEWCOMB

4.2.98–9 Still…her] DILKE; *1 line* NEWCOMB

4.2.105–6 Such…earth] DILKE; *1 line* NEWCOMB

4.2.111–12 Done…secret] DILKE; *1 line* NEWCOMB

4.2.134–5 Sir…composition] DILKE; *1 line* NEWCOMB

4.3.8–11 'To the…post.'] DILKE; *verse* NEWCOMB: Chambermaid to the | middle | Pay the |

4.3.90–2 Ay…la, la] DYCE; *verse* NEWCOMB: out |

4.3.98–100 Marry…caper] DILKE; *verse* NEWCOMB: yeomandry | stiffened |

4.3.102–4 Very…Tony?] DILKE; *verse* NEWCOMB: high | again |

4.3.107–10 Hey…moons] DYCE; *verse* NEWCOMB: way | Icarus | moons |

4.3.111–12 He's…had] THIS EDITION; Newcomb prints in one line, ending with 'stand up'

4.3.113–15   *2 lines* NEWCOMB: lower |

4.3.164–7   *Down...bowstring*] THIS EDITION; *2 lines* NEWCOMB: trick |

5.1.14–15   Sure...somebody] THIS EDITION; NEWCOMB: devil | waiting-woman |

5.1.29–30   Tush...all] DILKE; *1 line* NEWCOMB

5.1.31–2   This...chamber] BAWCUTT; *1 line* NEWCOMB

5.1.32–3   How?...house!] BAWCUTT; *1 line* NEWCOMB

5.1.35–6   Push...sure] DYCE; *1 line* NEWCOMB

5.1.50–1   One...servants?] DILKE; *1 line* NEWCOMB

5.1.51–2   I'll...hurry] DILKE; *1 line* NEWCOMB

5.1.79–80   Hie...you] DYCE; *1 line* NEWCOMB

5.1.80–1   I never...bargain] DYCE; *1 line* NEWCOMB

5.1.86–7   I...not] THIS EDITION; *1 line* NEWCOMB

5.1.94–6   Dog...done] THIS EDITION; NEWCOMB: now | goes |

5.1.107–8   O...for't] DYCE; *1 line* NEWCOMB

5.1.110–11   Now...sir!] DILKE; NEWCOMB: are |

5.1.112–14   Not...us] DILKE; *2 lines* NEWCOMB: embrace |

5.1.117–19   All...stifled!] THIS EDITION; NEWCOMB: lords | gentlewoman |

5.1.126–7   He...me] DILKE; *1 line* NEWCOMB

5.3.14–15   How do I?...well] DILKE; *1 line* NEWCOMB

5.3.39–40   You...please] DILKE; *1 line* NEWCOMB

5.3.52–3   He's...saint!] DILKE; *1 line* NEWCOMB

5.3.53–4   Worse...adultery] DYCE; *1 line* NEWCOMB

5.3.55–6   'Twas...Diaphanta] DILKE; *1 line* NEWCOMB

5.3.90–1   I can...to you] DYCE; *1 line* NEWCOMB

5.3.209–10   Your...transformation] DILKE; *1 line* NEWCOMB

5.3.214–15   Into...myself] DILKE; NEWCOMB: Scholars |

THE SPANISH GYPSY

Edited by Gary Taylor

The Spanish Gypsy was first published, by Richard Marriot, in 1653 (*BEPD* 717, Wing M1986); the title-page declares it was 'Never before printed'. The Stationers' Register contains no entry for Marriot's edition. John Wright had entered 'the Spanish Jepsye' on 28 June 1624; this might have been the play or a ballad, but if it was the play it did not result in publication. In any case, Marriot's title was uncontested, and on 11 June 1659 he transferred his claim to 'The Spanish Gipsies' (and 25 other plays) to Humphrey Moseley.

Moseley died before he published an edition of the play. A second quarto (Q2), dated 1661, was probably published before 16 June (when Pepys records having just read it). This second edition, printed by 'T.C. and L.P.', was initially published by Robert Crofts; a cancel title-page identifies the publisher as Francis Kirkman. However, Moseley's heirs continued to claim title to the play. Whatever the relationships between Moseley, Crofts, and Kirkman, and whatever the legal authority of this edition, it has no textual authority, obviously having been printed from a copy of the first edition, which it only sporadically and conjecturally corrects.

Marriot's 1653 edition was printed by John GRISMOND II. Shanti PADHI collated thirteen copies of GRISMOND, and found only three press corrections (pp. 334–5); none is substantive. They are recorded in the textual notes at 1.4.17, 2.1.15, and 2.2.112. As a play quarto, GRISMOND is chiefly remarkable for employing the modern conventions for u/v and i/j (used by none of the four authors to whom the text is here attributed). If the quarto was set from authorial papers, this modernization must have originated in GRISMOND's printing house.

However, the printer's copy was—as both George Price and David Lake concluded—almost certainly scribal. As Lake remarks, 'the general tidiness of the text and the full marking of entrances and exits would seem to rule out foul papers' (215). He rules out a promptbook because 'there are no convincing examples of entrances brought forward to allow time for walking on'; but such early 'warning directions' are not found in all promptbooks. Certainly, at some point in the transmission of the text someone went through the play and provided additional directions in the margins, as may be seen by the marginal placement of directions at 3.2.218.1 (Dance), 4.1.0.5 (A showte within), 4.1.136 (Diego within), 4.2.108 (Florish), 4.3.4.1 (Florish within), 4.3.117.1 (A Picture), 4.3.147.1–2 (A noyse within), 5.1.38.1 (from behinde the Arras), 5.1.81 (Within Servants), 5.2.3.1 (Two Swords), 5.3.35.1 (A Casket), 5.3.110.1 (Dance). In any of the proposed divi-

sions of authorship, these directions appear in the shares of at least two authors; in our division, they appear in the work of four. They are therefore unlikely to be an authorial feature, and more likely the work of a theatrical annotator, concerned with properties, music cues, and speech from 'within'. Lake, citing three of these examples (picture, swords, casket), attributes them to a 'fair draft lightly annotated for theatrical use'; but the degree of apparent annotation is greater than he acknowledged, and the amount of annotation to be expected in a promptbook less (and more variable) than he imagined. Lake postulates the existence of a kind of 'intermediate transcript' (often invoked at that time by Fredson Bowers); I have elsewhere argued that such entities are editorial fictions, which were never a regular part of manuscript production associated with the theatres (Taylor 1987, 12–14; Taylor and Jowett, 242–3). Moreover, in *Gypsy* there are particular reasons for doubting that the printed text derives from a manuscript which antedates performances (and the promptbook). The play was licensed for performance on 9 July 1623 (Bawcutt, 141); the scene-ending couplet at 2.2.178–9 apparently alludes to the 'elephant and camels' given by King Philip of Spain to King James, which entered London about midnight on July 5 (Chamberlain, II, 507). It seems relatively unlikely that a manuscript containing that couplet could have been copied in full (from the putative 'intermediate transcript'), submitted to the Revels office, and approved, between the morning of July 6 and July 9. It is much more likely that the couplet represents an addition. The play was performed at court on 5 November 1623 (Bawcutt, 146), and that occasion provided an obvious opportunity for tinkering with the text. The play's final line—which requires kneeling to 'all these noble guests'—certainly permits and invites the assumption of the kind of aristocratic audience that could be expected at court, and that line might also represent a late alteration.

Moreover, GRISMOND appears to represent a censored text. 'Faith', for instance, does not appear at all—an absence unparalleled in the Dekker or Rowley canon, found in Middleton only in the censored texts of *Game at Chess*, and in only three plays of Ford (which may themselves be censored); the canons of the four dramatists, tabulated by Lake, average 25 per play. The oath 'Marry' also does not appear in *Gypsy*, though it is found in every other tabulated play of the four canons except Middleton's very short *Yorkshire Tragedy* and Ford's *Perkin Warbeck*; the four canons together average almost six per play. Moreover, the three Ford plays which lack an example of the oath 'faith' (*The Fancies Chaste and Noble*, *The Lady's Trial*, *The Laws of Candy*) do contain examples of 'marry'. There is thus no play wholly or even partly by Ford (including the collaborative *Sun's Darling*, *Witch of Edmonton*, and *Welsh Ambassador*) which lacks both asseverations. Likewise, one or both show up in the other collaborative plays of Dekker, not tabulated by Lake (*Sir Thomas More*, *Patient Grissil*, *Sir Thomas Wyatt*, *Westward Ho*, *Northward Ho*, *The Noble Spanish Soldier*). Indeed, no play except *Gypsy*, in the entirety of the four canons, lacks examples of *both* these expletives. Likewise, all Dekker's plays contain at least one example of a group of related oaths ('sblood, 'sdeath, 'sfoot, 'sheart, heart, 'slid, 'snails, 'swounds, 'uds); in the eight uncollaborative plays (including *Blurt*) tabulated by Lake, these oaths occur 88 times (almost nine per play); in his other three collaborations with Middleton they appear 65 times; but not one of these oaths appears in *Gypsy*. As Lake and Jackson demonstrated, the characteristic oaths of Middleton and Rowley are also completely absent from *Gypsy*. Either the external and internal evidence for the authorship of *Gypsy* is all wrong, and the play was written by some unidentified author(s) who avoided all oaths, or the extant text has been systematically expurgated. This edition is based upon the conclusion that *Gypsy* was written by Dekker, Ford, Middleton, and Rowley; but without making assumptions about *which* of these four authors was involved, or *which* of these four authors wrote which scenes, we can nevertheless conclude, on the basis of such statistics, that the extant text has certainly been expurgated.

The statistics may be supplemented by a critical examination of the text itself. Expurgation is intrinsically difficult to detect and correct (especially in prose), but likely verse examples occur at 3.1.30 and 5.1.68, where other editors have already presumed omissions. More generally, we would expect some oaths in Ricardo's performance as a 'rake-hell' in 4.3; swearing is, elsewhere, a regular part of the convention for representing such prodigals. But no oaths appear in those speeches, although there are several obvious opportunities for them (4.3.72, 94, 142); in particular, it seems likely that an oath should have punctuated his first speech (4.3.52) and his first reaction to the picture (4.3.124). Similar dramatic considerations would lead us to expect more profanity in Sancho; indeed, he speaks most of the few serious oaths that GRISMOND contains. The lack of an oath is especially suspicious in his very first speech (2.1.118); later in the same scene, 'foot' (2.1.134) might represent a censorial softening of an original, stronger ''sfoot' (preferred by Dekker and Rowley). Elsewhere, it would have been natural for Sancho to strengthen his exaggerated or defensive assertions with some sort of oath (2.1.155, 2.1.197, 2.2.161, 4.3.16, 4.3.184-5, 5.3.97, 5.3.109). Outside of these two characters, dramatic considerations combine with metrical irregularity to suggest censorship at 1.5.34, 3.2.172, 3.2.183, 4.1.203, 4.1.207, 4.1.210, and 4.3.204. Finally, given this statistical and particular evidence that the text has been censored, there is reason to suspect that in other

cases bland words like 'oh' are expurgated substitutes for more dramatic language (4.3.156). These passages of suspected expurgation occur in the work of all four putative authors, so the emendations are not being used to bolster the evidence for attribution to any single author.

As I have argued elsewhere, such expurgation is itself good evidence for a theatrical origin for the text (Taylor and Jowett, 51-106); it suggests that GRISMOND derives from a manuscript which had been censored by the Master of the Revels. It is necessarily impossible, without the manuscript itself, to know whether it was licensed and used as a company promptbook, but nothing in GRISMOND rules that conclusion out, and much seems to support it. Scene divisions are one of the clearest indications of a scribal literary transcript (Taylor and Jowett, 239-42); but GRISMOND contains only act divisions, which accurately reflect theatrical practice. (The scene divisions marked and numbered in this edition were first supplied by DILKE.) The dramatis personae list printed in GRISMOND is clearly literary, but it might have been added to the manuscript by the publisher; its erroneous attribution of the play's 'Scene' to 'Allegant'— the setting for *The Changeling*—certainly arouses suspicion. Price noted several bibliographical links between *Gypsy* and *The Changeling* (also published for the first time in 1653); *The Changeling* (published by Moseley) contains an advertisement for 'PLAYES in the Press' which includes '*The Spanish Gypsies*' (sig. I3ᵛ). Both quartos contain a list of characters, headed 'Drammatis Personae', dividing the characters by gender and arranging them in descending hierarchical order, and ending 'The Scene, Allegant'. An editor, preparing a list for *Gypsy* right after preparing one for *Changeling*, might have made such an error in *Gypsy*; a scribe, transcribing the entire play and then preparing a list of its characters, would be much less likely to do so. There is, accordingly, no clear evidence that would suggest a literary rather than theatrical manuscript as the copy for GRISMOND.

Further evidence of scribal copy is the play's treatment of exit directions. 'Exeunt' occurs only three times (twice at the end of an Act); the manuscript seems to have been written by someone who either ignored the distinction between 'exit' and 'exeunt', or who used an ambiguous abbreviation (like 'ex.', found at 1.4.22.1, 3.3.108.1, 5.1.208.1). Either usage would be uncharacteristic of Ford (who seems to have written at least two of the scenes with the abbreviation), and the consistency of the pattern defies the clear external and internal evidence that the play was composed collaboratively. It therefore seems likely that this pattern reflects the habits of a scribe.

Neither Price (looking for Middleton and Rowley features) nor Lake (looking for Ford and Dekker features) could find much if any evidence of authorial spelling or punctuation in GRISMOND. Indeed, further evidence of scribal copy is provided by certain anomalous linguistic features. If (as we believe) the play was written by Dekker, Ford, Middleton and Rowley—or, indeed, by any combination of those four playwrights—then its linguistic texture has been pervasively disturbed by some intervening agent(s). There are far too few parentheses for Dekker and Ford or Rowley, and far too few instances of 'I'm' (only two) for any of the four authors, alone or in collaboration (Taylor 2004). In the case of parentheses and 'I'm', the gap between expectations (based on authorial practice elsewhere) and actual instances in GRISMOND is large enough to establish a statistical case for scribal interference. With other possible contractions, the numbers involved are smaller, and not individually compelling; but the pattern of apparent scribal expansion established by 'I am' can also be seen in 'I have' for metrical 'I've' (1.4.2, 1.5.77), 'I ha'' for 'I've' (4.1.154, 159), 'to' for metrical ''t'' (1.5.11, 1.5.54, 2.2.29), the spelling 'thas' or 'thad' for authorial 'tas' or 'tad' (1.5.78, 85, 121), 'on' or 'of' for 'o'' (1.5.92, 96, 3.2.138–9), 'the' for 'th'' (5.1.70), 'them' for ''em' (3.1.120, 122), 'thee' for ''ee' (3.1.136), 'it' for ''t' (3.2.158, 160), 'you are' for 'y'are' or 'you're' (4.1.161, 4.3.208, 5.1.105), 'you have' for 'y'have' (3.2.180), 'we have' for 'we've' (3.2.207), 'spoken' for 'spoke' (3.3.77), 'with you' for 'with ye' or 'with'ee' (3.3.93), 'with the' for 'wi'th'' (4.1.20). Noticeably, in all these cases what should be an elision has apparently been expanded; the reverse situation does not occur. They occur in passages attributed, here, to all four authors.

Because this modern-spelling edition makes no attempt to preserve patterns of punctuation, the paucity of parentheses does not pose an editorial problem. But the apparent scribal expansion of contractions does. Of the seventy instances of 'I am', forty-six are clearly correct, because the metre requires two syllables; thirty-five of those forty-six cases (76%) occur in scenes or passages attributed, on other grounds, to Ford (1.3, 1.5.1–73, 2.2, 3.2.242–300, 3.3, 5.1, 5.2, 5.3.1–71). In contrast, GRISMOND contains eleven instances of 'I am' where the metre requires a single syllable; only three of these (27%) are in passages attributed to Ford. If we were to emend 'I am' to 'I'm' when metre seems to require it, the resulting figure for the Ford scenes (3 I'm/35 I am) would fit well the pattern found in Ford's other work. This leaves, for the remainder of the play, eleven clear cases of correct 'I am', two cases of 'I'm', eight cases where metre would require a monosyllable, and sixteen examples of 'I am' in prose or ambiguous verse. If we adopted the same principles for the rest of the play that have been adopted for Ford's scenes—eliding only when metre requires it—we would have ten cases of 'I'm' to twenty-seven of 'I am'—a figure much more appropriate for a collaboration by Dekker, Middleton, and Rowley. The difference between the Ford scenes and the rest of the play, on this accounting, is itself statistically significant. Although it is likely enough that some instances of prose 'I am' were originally 'I'm', it is impossible to tell which, and therefore none have been emended. But since the evidence of unmetrical expansion of authorial 'I'm' to scribal 'I am' extends across scenes attributed to all four authors—and yet follows a pattern which distinguishes between Ford's intolerance of 'I'm', and the much more frequent use of the contraction by the

other three authors—it has seemed reasonable to emend where the metre seems to require it. The same principle has been applied in the case of other contractions which have apparently been scribally expanded.

Expurgation presents similar problems. Some editors would accept (for the purposes of bibliographical analysis of the printer's copy) the statistical evidence that GRISMOND has been censored, without wishing to restore the expurgated oaths conjecturally. Even when expurgation of the text as a whole is certain, it is necessarily impossible to prove that expurgation has occurred in a particular line, or to prove that one oath rather than another should be inserted to repair the damage; in such circumstances, conservative editors will always refuse to emend. But, as I have argued elsewhere, the conservative editor, 'who is locally judicious in rejecting' such conjectures, 'will also be globally injudicious, in offering readers a text which certainly contains too little profanity' (Taylor and Jowett, 94). An editor is better placed to point to probable expurgation, and probable solutions, than any unassisted reader. I have, accordingly, conjecturally restored a number of oaths, and suggested others; even if the exact details are not right, the overall balance of profanity and asseveration is closer to what the original must have contained—although even this emended text of *Gypsy* is still, no doubt, less profane than it should be.

As the problems of scribal expansion and expurgation demonstrate, editorial decisions about whether (or how) to emend must be based on an analysis of authorial practice elsewhere; just as my analysis of expurgation in the Shakespeare canon was based upon evidence of Shakespeare's practice in unexpurgated works (Taylor and Jowett), so the analysis of individual cases of suspected expurgation in *Gypsy* is based upon a survey of the other work of the author of the passage in question. However, although the principle is the same, the problem of attribution is especially complicated in *Gypsy*, where four authors seem to be involved. The textual notes, in arguing for or against certain readings, therefore sometimes take account of conclusions about the authorship of individual scenes, discussed in 'Canon and Chronology'. There may seem to be some circularity here: the hypothesis of expurgation, and of scribal interference, justifies editorial interventions which make the play 'sound more like' the work of these authors. But the circularity is more apparent than real. These four authors are the only plausible candidates for authorship of this play; scribal copy has been postulated by all investigators, whatever their opinions about authorship, and the conclusion that all four authors are involved was reached before the evidence for expurgation was noticed (late in the editing of the text). Although the textual and authorial hypotheses are necessarily related in the actual editing of the play, line by line, nevertheless each hypothesis can be justified independently of the other.

Although GRISMOND is our only surviving authority for the play's text, one copy of that edition—formerly owned by Alexander Dyce, and now in the Dyce collection at the National Art Library, Victoria and Albert Museum—contains manuscript annotations which occasionally correct and supplement the text in ways which would seem to have required access to another authoritative source. PADHI gives the fullest description and analysis of the annotations (pp. 310–29). Some of the variants—for example, that at 2.1.263—are simple corrections which might have been made conjecturally by an intelligent reader (and in some cases were made, independently, by Q2 or DILKE). But some are difficult or impossible to attribute to mere guesswork: see particularly the added lines at 2.1.146, 153, 177, 3.2.110–13, 4.1.147–8, or the correction confirmed by Cervantes at 3.3.13. The identity of the ANNOTATOR cannot be determined, but access to another authoritative source seems clear enough. It is possible that this source was the printer's manuscript, and that differences between the printed text and the annotations arise from compositorial error in GRISMOND. However, it is equally possible that the ANNOTATOR had access to a different manuscript, and sporadically transferred readings from it; given the play's immediate and enduring popularity in the seventeenth century, the existence of another manuscript is not improbable. In either case, the ANNOTATOR—like all other annotators of printed texts in the period—left many errors in GRISMOND uncorrected.

It is sometimes possible to correct the text, or to clarify the staging, by reference to the play's source, the *Novelas Ejemplares* of Cervantes, first published in Spanish in 1613. Proper names are emended to conform to the Spanish; for details of action the notes quote, for the convenience of readers, the first English translation of 'The Force of Blood' (1640, by James Mabbe) and—because Mabbe's selection did not include 'La Gitanilla'—from the most recent English translation of 'The Little Gypsy' (1998, Lipson).

The most recent and thorough edition of the play is the dissertation by PADHI, who unfortunately died between its completion and our decision to include *Gypsy* in the *Collected Works*. I have drawn extensively on her edition (which I had supervised); I have prepared the text directly from GRISMOND, but I am especially indebted to her account of the ANNOTATOR (pp. 310–329) and her collation of all subsequent editions. Although she would no doubt disagree with many of my decisions, I am sure she would be delighted to see the play restored to the Middleton canon.

SEE ALSO

Text: *Works*, 1727
Music and dance: this volume, 172 ('The Gypsies' Round'), 174 ('The Spanish Gypsy')
Authorship and date: this volume, 433

WORKS CITED

Previous Editions

DILKE, C. W., ed., *A Continuation of Dodsley's Old English Plays* (1814), vol. IV
DYCE, Alexander, ed., *Works* (1840), vol. IV
BULLEN, A. H., ed., *Works* (1885), vol. VI
ELLIS, Havelock, ed., *The Best Plays of the Old Dramatists: Thomas Middleton* (1887), vol. I
MORRIS, Edgar C., ed., *'The Spanish Gipsie' and 'All's Lost by Lust'* (1908)
BUTLER-CLARKE, H., ed., in *Representative English Comedies*, gen. ed. Charles M. Gayley (1914), vol. III
PARKER-SMITH, Kate, ed., *A Critical Edition of Middleton and Rowley's 'The Spanish Gipsie'*, unpub. Ph.D. thesis (Northwestern University, 1944)
PADHI, Shanti, 'A Critical Old-spelling Edition of *The Spanish Gipsie* by Middleton, Rowley (and possibly Ford)', unpub. D.Phil. thesis (Oxford University, 1984)

Other Works Cited

Austern, Linda Phyllis, *Music in English Children's Drama of the Later Renaissance* (1992)
Bawcutt, N. W., ed., *The Control and Censorship of Caroline Drama: The Records of Sir Henry Herbert, Master of the Revels 1623–73* (1996)
Bentley, Gerald Eades, *The Jacobean and Caroline Stage*, 7 vols (1941–68)
Bromham, A. A., and Zara Bruzzi, *The Changeling and the Years of Crisis, 1619–1624: A Hieroglyph of Britain* (1990)
Burelbach, Frederick M., Jr., 'Theme and Structure in *The Spanish Gipsy*', *Bulletin de l'Association canadienne des Humanités* 19 (1968), 37–41
Carlton, Charles, *Charles I the Personal Monarch*, 2nd edn. (1995)
Cervantes, Miguel de, *Exemplary Stories*, tr. Lesley Lipson (1998)
Chamberlain, John, *Letters*, ed. N. E. McClure, 2 vols (1939)
Chappell, W., *Popular Music of the Olden Time* (1859)
—— *The Roxburghe Ballads* (1875, rpt. 1966)
Cogswell, Thomas, *The Blessed Revolution: English Politics and the Coming of War, 1621–24* (1989)
Dawson, Anthony B., '*Women Beware Women* and the Economy of Rape', *Studies in English Literature, 1500–1900* 27 (1987), 303–19
Dessen, Alan C., and Leslie Thomson, *A Dictionary of Stage Directions in English Drama, 1580–1642* (1999)
Foakes, R. A., *Illustrations of the English Stage 1580–1642* (1985)
Gasper, Julia, *The Dragon and the Dove: The Plays of Thomas Dekker* (1990)
Gossett, Suzanne, '"Best Men are Molded out of Faults": Marrying the Rapist in Jacobean Drama', *English Literary Renaissance* 14 (1984), 305–27
—— 'Resistant Mothers and Hidden Children', in *Pilgrimage for Love: Essays on Early Modern Literature in Honor of Josephine A. Roberts*, ed. Sigrid King and Rebecca Crump (1999), 191–207
Gurr, Andrew, *The Shakespearian Playing Companies* (1996)
Hogg, James, '*The Spanish Gypsy* and Francis Manning's *All for the Better, or The Infallible Cure*', in *Elizabethan and Renaissance Studies*, ed. James Hogg (1978)
Kistner, A. L. and M. K., '*The Spanish Gipsy*', *Humanities Association Review* 25 (1974), 211–24
Lake, David J., *The Canon of Thomas Middleton's Plays* (1975)
Levin, Richard, *The Multiple Plot in English Renaissance Drama* (1971)
Levine, Robert T., 'Rare use of *since* in Middleton', *Notes and Queries* 216 (1971), 457–8
Mabbe, James, tr., 'The Force of Blood', in Cervantes, *Delight in Severall Shapes* (1640), 179–208
—— trans., *The Rogue or the Life of Guzman de Alfarache* by Matheo Aleman, ed. James Fitmaurice-Kelly (1967)
Mead, Joseph, British Library MS Harleian 389 (letters to Sir M. Stuteville)

Price, George R., 'The Quartos of *The Spanish Gypsy* and Their Relation to *The Changeling*', *Papers of the Bibliographical Society of America* 52 (1958), 111–25

Southworth, John, *Fools and Jesters at the English Court* (1998)

Steen, Sara Jayne, *Ambrosia in an Earthern Vessel: Three Centuries of Audience and Reader Response to the Works of Thomas Middleton* (1993)

Sykes, H. Dugdale, *Sidelights on Elizabethan Drama* (1924)

Taylor, Gary, 'General Introduction', in Stanley Wells, Gary Taylor *et al.*, *William Shakespeare: A Textual Companion* (1987), 1–68

—— 'Middleton, Habsburg, and Stuart: *The Spanish Gypsy* and *A Game at Chess*', *SEDERI* 18 (2008), forthcoming

—— 'Praestat Difficilior Lectio: *All's Well that Ends Well* and *Richard III*', *Renaissance Studies* 2 (1988), 27–46

—— 'Thomas Middleton, *The Nice Valour*, and the Court of James I', *The Court Historian* 6 (2001), 1–36

—— 'Thomas Middleton, *The Spanish Gypsy*, and Collaborative Authorship', in *Words That Count*, ed. Brian Boyd (2004), 241–73

—— and John Jowett, *Shakespeare Reshaped 1606–1623* (1993)

T. E., *The Lawes Resolutions of Womens Rights* (London, 1632)

TEXTUAL NOTES

Persons.0.2–Persons.19 *Dramatis...Servants*] THIS EDITION. The list in GRISMOND differs substantially in its arrangement and identification of characters: see Stage Directions list.

Persons.15 Carlo] DILKE; *Claro* GRISMOND

Persons.17 Christiana,] ~ A Gentleman GRISMOND; ~ A gentlewoman Q2

Persons.19 Servants,] DILKE; ~. | The Scene, *Allegant*. GRISMOND (bracketing 'Servants' among 'Women'). The scene—as DYCE recognized—is actually 'Madrid'; 'Allegant' is the setting of *The Changeling*.

1.1.0.1, 2.1.0.1, 3.1.0.1, 4.1.0.1, 5.1.0.1 *Incipit*] THIS EDITION; *not in* GRISMOND

1.1.0.2 Luis] GRISMOND (*Lewys*). The 'Lu' form occasionally occurs in speech prefix abbreviations and the text.

1.1.0.2, 1.2.0.1, 1.3.0.1, 1.4.0.1, 1.5.0.1 *as at night*] THIS EDITION; *not in* GRISMOND. Since the play was designed for an indoor theatre, the stage could have been artificially darkened; much of the atmospheric effect of Act One depends upon its darkness, and the contrasting daylight of the remaining scenes.

1.1.5 Englishman] GRISMOND (Englifh man)

1.1.6 *boraccio*] GRISMOND (Borachia)

1.1.6 *malaga*] GRISMOND (Maligo). Named for the southern Spanish seaport.

1.1.6 *calentura*] GRISMOND (Calenture). Both spellings were used, and as with other words in this scene the word would have immediately established a Spanish atmosphere.

1.1.13 scarce] THIS EDITION; *not in* GRISMOND; only DYCE. DYCE seems right to believe that a word has dropped out, but wrong about what it was. For the sense 'only', a better conjecture would be 'but': 'but a glimpse' appears in Dekker's *Brittania's Honour* (1628) and in Lodowick Carlell's *Deserving Favorite*. But 'only' does not seem the right sense: it confirms that Roderigo did indeed glimpse her face—which is not at all evident or necessary: in the rest of the sentence he is conjecturing that it must be beautiful, and the rest of the play depends upon ambiguities about his ability to recognize her face. (In Cervantes he does not.) For the collocation preferred here compare *Michaelmas* 5.3.54 ('a glimpse, scarce something').

1.1.33 he be] Q2; ~ ‸ GRISMOND

1.1.37.1–2 *They...swords*] THIS EDITION; *not in* GRISMOND. From Cervantes: 'They covered their faces with their handkerchers, and drawing their swords...' (tr. Mabbe, p. 181).

1.1.37.2 *veiled*] THIS EDITION; *not in* GRISMOND. The plot requires that her face be concealed (so that Luis does not recognize her immediately); Roderigo veils her at the end of 1.3, presumably using her own veil (not an article of clothing

he would be likely to have in his bedroom, otherwise). Stage directions often neglect to mention female veils or masks required by the dialogue.

1.1.38 Madrid] GRISMOND (*Madrill*). Modernized by Dilke, and in modern translations of Cervantes, and throughout this edition.

1.1.45 know] GRISMOND; not ~ DYCE

1.1.46.1 *Exeunt Luis and Diego*] *Exit*. GRISMOND. The plural form appears only three times in GRISMOND (1.5.125, 2.2.179, 4.3.188.1). Either the original used an ambiguous form like 'ex' (as at 1.4.22.1, 3.3.108.1, 5.1.208.1), or the scribe imposed a personal preference for the singular. I have therefore treated the difference between plural and singular as a clarification of an ambiguous manuscript original.

1.2.1 I am lost, I am] GRISMOND; I'm ~ I'm THIS EDITION *conj*. Although GRISMOND's line has ten syllables, it is not iambic: two trochees (O Diego) are followed by two anapests (I am lost, I am mad). Of the four likely candidates for authorship, only Rowley writes 'blank verse' which consists of ten syllables so irregularly accented. The proportion of feminine endings in this scene also would fit Rowley. (See Canon and Chronology.) If the scene is not by Rowley, this line may be an instance of scribal expansion of contracted forms: see Textual Introduction. With the elisions, two trochees are followed by two iambs, and the first two speeches of the scene would constitute a single hexameter.

1.3.0.1 *A bed.*] THIS EDITION; *not in* GRISMOND; A Bedchamber in Fernando's house. Roderigo and Clara discovered. DYCE. An onstage bed seems clearly implied by l. 38; beds are called for—either 'discovered' or 'thrust out'—in some 150 stage directions in the period (Dessen and Thomson, 24).

1.3.0.1 Clara] DILKE; *Claria* GRISMOND

1.3.14 wanton] GRISMOND (want on)

1.3.17 Too] GRISMOND (To)

1.3.40.1 *She...curtain*] THIS EDITION; *not in* GRISMOND. An actual curtain of some kind is likely. In Cervantes, the opening of the curtain throws light into the room she is in, until then so pitch-dark that she has to grope along the walls to see. Here, it is possible that by drawing the curtains she discovers another room; for 'a chamber behind' curtains, see Dessen and Thomson, 63.

1.3.46, 3.3.8 alabaster] GRISMOND (Alablafter)

1.3.49.1 *She...it*] THIS EDITION; *not in* GRISMOND. DYCE places a similar direction after 'I have enough', but that phrase surely comments upon an action which it follows rather than precedes.

1.3.49.1–2 *in her sleeve*] PADHI; *not in* GRISMOND; *in her bosom* DYCE. Detail supplied by Cervantes (tr. Mabbe, p. 187).

1.3.49.3 *She . . . curtain*] THIS EDITION; *not in* GRISMOND. See note at l. 40.1. Once she has 'enough', she needs to conceal from Roderigo her awareness of her surroundings; otherwise, he might notice the loss of the crucifix.

1.3.94 last] GRISMOND; lost PARKER-SMITH *conj.*

1.3.95 Live] ANNOTATOR; Lay GRISMOND. The error was probably caused by contamination from the 'Say' immediately above.

1.4.2 I've] DILKE; I have GRISMOND. For this and other editorial contractions, see Textual Introduction.

1.4.12 Prado] DILKE; Perado GRISMOND

1.4.16.1–2 *at . . . another door*] THIS EDITION; *not in* GRISMOND; *As Diego is going out* DYCE

1.4.16.2 *Juan*] THIS EDITION; *Iohn* GRISMOND. 'John' or 'Iohn' is the normal Elizabethan and Jacobean transliteration of Spanish 'Juan'; compare 'Don John, Prince of Spain' in Dekker's *Match me in London*. The 1640 edition of Fletcher's *Rule a Wife* is the first English play to transliterate as 'Juan'. Therefore, to the original audiences 'Don John' would have been a recognizable rendering of a recognizably Spanish name, like the names of all the play's other characters. But the modern spelling of the Spanish name, even in English, is 'Juan'; the difference in pronunciation is minimal, and I have modernized the spelling, to preserve the intended Spanish inflection, throughout the play.

1.4.17 true;] GRISMOND(b); ~, GRISMOND(a). The corrected reading is found only in the Bodleian copy (sig. B4).

1.4.18 ennoble] DILKE; enable GRISMOND. Easy misreading.

1.4.22.1 *Exit*] Q2; *Ex.* GRISMOND.

1.5.1 I, ay,] THIS EDITION; if GRISMOND; I ANNOTATOR; if I, DYCE; I, I, BULLEN. My reading is an interpretation of BULLEN's, modernizing the spelling of the second 'I' as the affirmation (used by the same character six lines above) rather than the pronoun. BULLEN's conjecture supplements and corrects the ANNOTATOR's emendation of GRISMOND, presupposing that 'if' is likelier to have been a misreading of a doubled 'I' than a single one; it also regularizes the metre.

1.5.4 travailed] GRISMOND (travell'd)

1.5.6.1 *Enter Roderigo*] DYCE; *at* 1.5.7 GRISMOND (below 'speedily')

1.5.11 t'inherit] DILKE; to inherit GRISMOND

1.5.34 Marry] THIS EDITION; Yes GRISMOND. The line is a syllable short; 'Yes' is substituted for oaths elsewhere in the period; something stronger seems required of Luis in response. 'Marry' is a mild oath, used elsewhere by Ford (and all the other dramatists), but completely absent from GRISMOND.

1.5.51 temptation] DILKE; temption GRISMOND. Although DYCE reverts to 'temption', GRISMOND's form is not recognized by *OED*, and could easily result from a compositor skipping inadvertently from one internal 't' to another. Metrically, an iambic hexameter (as emended) is, in Ford's work, more common than a pentameter with an extra stressed syllable after the caesura (as in GRISMOND).

1.5.54 t'avoid] DILKE; to avoyd GRISMOND

1.5.55 and] GRISMOND; of DYCE *conj.* Perhaps evidence of scribal misexpansion of 'o'?

1.5.66 untold] GRISMOND (untol'd)

1.5.77 I've] THIS EDITION; I have GRISMOND. Neither 'fegary' nor 'vagary' is elsewhere accented on the second syllable, which a regular iambic pattern would require. For the scribal expansion, see 1.4.2, and Textual introduction. 'I've' is characteristic of Middleton, though Ford's works contains a few examples—and without the contraction, the line contains an extra unstressed syllable in mid-line, a metrical licence very rare in Ford. Either way the line would be more characteristic of Middleton than Ford.

1.5.77 vagary] GRISMOND (fegary)

1.5.78 'T'as] THIS EDITION; 'Thad GRISMOND. Neither the conditional nor the past perfect makes sense here; GRISMOND's form could easily arise from contamination by the following 'made'. Taylor (2001) contends that Burton's *Anatomy of Melancholy* (1621)—describing all sorts of erratic behaviour, including mania and uncontrollable laughter—was a source for *Valour* (1622?); here, Diego's fits of laughter are taken as evidence that he has become melancholy.

1.5.85 't'ad] GRISMOND (thad)

1.5.89 i' the] GRISMOND. Metre requires two syllables here; the part-line is linked to the preceding 'not I' to form a perfect pentameter. The form is therefore not scribal, and constitutes strong evidence for Middleton. (See Canon and Chronology.)

1.5.91 Carcámo] THIS EDITION; Carcomo GRISMOND. I adopt the spelling of the name in Cervantes, which also appears at 4.3.118 (Rowley). As often elsewhere, GRISMOND misspells Spanish words, especially proper names, probably as a result of error in transmission. The incorrect spelling appears repeatedly in GRISMOND: 2.1.243 (Dekker), 2.2.66 (Ford), 3.2.0.1 (Ford or Dekker), 3.2.233 (Ford?), 5.3.1 (Ford), 5.3.88 (Ford); since the misspelling occurs in passages apparently written by three different authors, and (according to Padhi) set by different compositors, the error is probably scribal. But only in this line does the metre require an accent on the penultimate (rather than antepenultimate) syllable, although the surname appears in verse on five other occasions, in passages written by Rowley, Ford, and perhaps Dekker. This is the only occurrence of the surname in a passage attributable, on other grounds, to Middleton.

1.5.92 o'] THIS EDITION; on GRISMOND. Middleton uses the oath 'o' my life' elsewhere at *Phoenix* 15.159, *Trick* 5.2.30, and *Weapons* 3.2.77; the oath with 'on' does not appear in his work (although it does appear with 'upon'). Since it seems almost certain from other linguistic, lexical, and metrical evidence that Middleton wrote the ending of this scene, the expanded 'on' is probably scribal, not authorial. (Unlike other emendations involving elisions in *Gypsy*, this one is specifically based upon an hypothesis about authorship.) See 1.5.96.

1.5.93 limed] THIS EDITION; lind GRISMOND. None of the available senses of the verb 'line' recorded in *OED* seems relevant; $v.^3$ ('cover, copulate with') in all examples has a male subject and a female object, and would therefore be inappropriate here. But 'lind' would be an easy minim misreading, by scribe or compositor, of 'limd', in several relevant senses: 'caught with birdlime', used figuratively more often than literally ($v.^1$ 3), 'copulate with, be coupled to' ($v.^3$, of animals, male and female). For the image, compare *Dissemblers* 4.2.157, 'A pox of your lime-twigs' (which juxtaposes, as does this passage, venereal disease, money, and a metaphorical use of 'lime' as a sticky substance).

1.5.96 o' late] THIS EDITION; of late GRISMOND. Middleton contracts 'of' before 'late' on at least twenty-one other occasions; in Middleton passages of texts printed during Middleton's lifetime, 'of late' appears only at *Puritan* 1.2.101 and *Tennis* Induction.29. But this authorial preference was clearly subject to scribal interference. At *Game* 3.1.118, autograph 'a late' was expanded to 'of late' by Ralph Crane in the Lansdowne manuscript, and in the manuscript which served as copy for Q3; thus, at *Witch* 3.2.85 Crane's 'of late' almost certainly is an expansion of authorial 'a late'. The expanded form 'of late' occurs eight times in mid-century manuscripts or printings (*Valour*, *Women Beware*, *Dissemblers*, *Hengist*, and *Quiet Life*). Its appearance here, in a passage where there is considerable evidence of Middleton's presence, thus fits an historical pattern, as well as the pattern of scribal expansion specific to this text (for which see Textual Introduction). See also 3.2.138–9.

1.5.97   often to] DILKE; oft to GRISMOND; oft ˄ MacDonald P. Jackson *conj.* (private communication). As a verb 'frequent' seems to have been accented on the second syllable—see below, l. 113, and *Timon* 1.119. As the line stands in GRISMOND, it is metrically irregular in a manner impossible to attribute to Ford; metrical emendation does not improve the *metrical* evidence for Middleton, since emendation produces a regular iambic pentameter (which could have been written by Ford as easily as by Middleton, metrically). Compare 'I have observed 'em often' (*Five Gallants* 1.2.85), 'I have observed it often' (*Women Beware* 1.1.9).

1.5.98   Gypsies] GRISMOND (*Gipfies*). Capitalized and italicized in GRISMOND, the word is treated as a proper noun indicating a national or ethnic identity; it began in English as an aphetic form of 'Egyptian'—which would of course be capitalized, as would 'Romany', their name for themselves. Since the modern convention of not capitalizing the word constitutes a form of linguistic prejudice, we have abandoned our usual adherence to forms preferred by *COD*, and treated 'Gypsy'/ 'Gypsies' as a proper noun throughout this edition.

1.5.102   reports of] THIS EDITION; ~ ˄ GRISMOND. Compare 'There is report of a fair Gypsy' (3.2.78). For the primary meaning—'describes'—with the preposition, used of a person, see *OED v.*2b, and *Trick* 3.2.16, *Valour* 2.1.75. The addition of the preposition here gives the verb an intensive secondary meaning, 're-echoes, resounds' (*v.* 9b, 9c) with talk 'of, about' her; it seems a nonsequitur to say (as GRISMOND does) that 'she has such amazing qualities that Spain describes her, not unadmiringly'. Metrically, the emendation produces an hexameter with a feminine ending (for which Middleton provides many parallels); unemended, the line has an extra unstressed syllable ('her') before the (unmarked) caesura.

1.5.112   They have] GRISMOND; They've DYCE. The emendation is unnecessary; Middleton often has an extra unstressed syllable before the caesura. (That metrical licence is rare in Ford.)

1.5.115   sackful] GRISMOND (*fack-full*).

1.5.120   fairy] DILKE; Faire GRISMOND

1.5.121   'T'as] GRISMOND (Thas)

1.5.126   evils] GRISMOND; devils THIS EDITION *conj.*

2.1.0.2   the old Father of the Gypsies] THIS EDITION; *Alvarez* GRISMOND. To identify this character as 'Alvarez' from the outset makes the experience of readers radically different from the experience of spectators (who are not informed of his 'real' identity until 5.2). GRISMOND's dramatis personae list identifies 'Alvarez' as 'An old Lord disguised like the Father of the Gypsies'; whatever the source of this list, its description of this character combines 'old' (used of him seven times in the dialogue) with 'Father' (as he is called by both Preciosa and Sancho, the latter clearly using it as a term of respect, not a literal assertion of paternity; for this meaning see *father n.* 4.a, 8.a, 10.a). THIS EDITION systematically alters the stage directions and speech prefixes to identify the character with his theatrical identity.

2.1.0.3   all properly habited as Gypsies] THIS EDITION; *not in* GRISMOND; *disguised as gipsies* DYCE. The usual editorial emendation reveals what a performance does not.

2.1.1   FATHER] THIS EDITION; *Al.* GRISMOND. See note to 2.1.0.2. Altered throughout.

2.1.2   trade] THIS EDITION; Trades GRISMOND. All three characters belong to the single trade ('Gypsy'), which is specified as singular in the two following speeches. The plural here could easily have arisen from contamination by the five preceding plurals ending in -s (boyes, Taylors, sheers, us, shapes).

2.1.8   *emboscado*] GRISMOND (ambuscado). See *OED*: an English import, and recognized at the time as 'a Spanish word'.

2.1.10   style] GRISMOND (ftile). A pun, but the primary meaning is clearly 'style'.

2.1.13   FATHER] Q2 (*Al.*); *Alo.* GRISMOND. See note at 2.1.0.2.

2.1.14   *picaros*] GRISMOND (Pickeroes). First example cited by *OED*.

2.1.15   lifting] THIS EDITION (*conj.* Padhi); Iilting GRISMOND(a); Jilting GRISMOND(b). The uncorrected reading is found only in the Harvard copy (sig. C2). No relevant sense of GRISMOND's word is recorded; but 'lifting' was a favourite cant word for describing theft: see *OED v.*8, Robert Greene's *Black Book's Messenger* (1592), Dekker's *Belman of London* (1608), etc.

2.1.22   *mayordomo*] GRISMOND (Major domo). Originally a Spanish word, and still felt as such until the eighteenth century (as indicated by GRISMOND's italics); I therefore use the Spanish spelling. GRISMOND's 'j' was probably an 'i' in manuscript; GRISMOND systematically adopts the modern convention.

2.1.22   *teniente*] GRISMOND (Teniente). Clearly a Spanish word, as indicated by italics: first example in *OED* not until 1798.

2.1.28   *grandes*] GRISMOND (Grandos). GRISMOND was an acceptable Spanish form, and the word was clearly regarded as Spanish; but *grandes* is the recognizable modern Spanish equivalent. See also 3.1.102 (*Grandoes*).

2.1.29   *condes*] GRISMOND (Condes). First *OED* example 1633.

2.1.29   *titulados*] GRISMOND (Titulados)

2.1.35   do so] DILKE; do GRISMOND; do't DYCE. Haplography seems the likeliest explanation for the error; although 'do't' works well in the following line, here 'so' seems more appropriate, for clarification.

2.1.36   BOTH] GRISMOND; *Carlo* DYCE; *Ant.* PARKER-SMITH

2.1.36   Our] GRISMOND; *Ant.* ~ DYCE; *Carlo* PARKER-SMITH

2.1.48   handkerchiefs] GRISMOND (Handkerchers)

2.1.48   tweezers] GRISMOND (Tweezes)

2.1.49   *maravedi*] GRISMOND (Maruade)

2.1.55   Seville] DILKE; *Sivell* GRISMOND

2.1.55   Valladolid] DILKE; *Vallidoly* GRISMOND

2.1.56   Cordova] DILKE; *Cordica* GRISMOND

2.1.59   Rochelle] DILKE; *Rochill* GRISMOND

2.1.62   sack-butts] GRISMOND (Sackbuts). *OED* distinguishes the meaning 'wine cask' (which seems the primary meaning here) by this hyphenated form.

2.1.63   FATHER] Q2 (*Al.*); *Ala.* GRISMOND

2.1.69.1   *Eugenia, Preciosa*] GRISMOND. All editors since Dyce identify these characters throughout by their 'real' names, Guiamara and Constanza; but the audience does not discover their identities until the final scene, and GRISMOND consistently identifies them by their Gypsy names in both stage directions and speech prefixes.

2.1.69.1   *Preciosa*] GRISMOND (Pretiofa). Both 'precious' and 'preciosity' were often spelled with a medial 't' (in place of modern 'c') from the sixteenth to eighteenth centuries; it is quite clear that the name means 'precious', and it is rendered as 'Preciosa' in modern translations of Cervantes.

2.1.69.1–2   *in new Gypsy clothes*] THIS EDITION; *not in* GRISMOND; *disguised as gipsies* DYCE. Preciosa's first line establishes that the clothes are 'new', but leaves ambiguous whether that means that the Gypsy identity is new, or simply that this particular outfit is new.

2.1.70 I'm] DYCE; I am GRISMOND. Scribal interference: metrically the elision is clearly required.

2.1.75 thee] DILKE; the GRISMOND. Probably only a difference in spelling.

2.1.92 bibbers] THIS EDITION; bubbers GRISMOND. First recorded appearance of 'bubbers' is 1673, half a century after *Gypsy* was written; the root word 'bub', in this sense, is not recorded before 1671–2. By contrast, 'bibbers' is well attested from early in the sixteenth century, and used elsewhere by Dekker (for instance, *Gull's Hornbook*, 1609, sig. B2ᵛ). An easy misreading, assisted by assimilation to preceding 'butt'.

2.1.96 Galicia] GRISMOND (Galifia)

2.1.98 A-many] GRISMOND (amany)

2.1.100 woman's] Q2; Womens GRISMOND

2.1.101 alchemy] GRISMOND (Alcumy)

2.1.103 gyrfalcons] GRISMOND (Jer-falcons)

2.1.104–5 to thyself | Thyself] ANNOTATOR; ~ ~ ‸ GRISMOND; thou ~ ‸ MORRIS

2.1.118 'Swounds] THIS EDITION; not in GRISMOND. We have already heard 'beating' of a drum or on the door, and been told that Sancho and Soto 'swear all the oaths in Spain' in demanding entrance; the unemphatic question offered by GRISMOND is incongruously mild-mannered as the beginning of a role which, even in the censored text, contains more asseverations than any others. This oath is used by both Dekker and Rowley, the two likeliest candidates for authorship of this material.

2.1.119 taffeta] GRISMOND (Taffaty)

2.1.121 diminutive] GRISMOND (deminitive)

2.1.129 PRECIOSA] Q2 (Pre.); Ped. GRISMOND

2.1.134 'Sfoot] THIS EDITION; Foot GRISMOND. See Textual Introduction. The stronger oath is characteristic of Dekker and Rowley.

2.1.144 yon] DILKE; you GRISMOND

2.1.146 SANCHO Hum, hum.] ANNOTATOR (Sanch.); not in GRISMOND

2.1.148 Portocarrero] THIS EDITION; Portacareco GRISMOND. Padhi identified the source for this passage in James Mabbe's translation of *Guzman*, which has (in a short space) 'Portocarrero', 'Don Hortado de Mendonça', 'Condee de Tendilla', 'Francisco de Bouadilla', and 'Commentadors of Alcantara'. The probability of scribal or compositorial error with these foreign words is high (on the evidence of errors elsewhere in the scene), and nothing would seem to be gained, for the original author or audience, by insignificant variations from the Spanish; so I have accordingly emended to make the Spanish titles conform to the source.

2.1.149 Mendonça] THIS EDITION; Mendonza GRISMOND

2.1.150 Tendilla] THIS EDITION; Tindilla GRISMOND

2.1.151 Bovadilla] THIS EDITION; Bavadilla GRISMOND

2.1.151 comendadors] GRISMOND (Commendadors)

2.1.151 Alcantara] DYCE; Aleantaro GRISMOND

2.1.153 FATHER And...style.] ANNOTATOR (Alv.); not in GRISMOND

2.1.155 Good ones?] GRISMOND. An oath would be appropriate after this question.

2.1.160 be] DILKE; been GRISMOND

2.1.162 stocking] GRISMOND (ftocken)

2.1.170 rhymes] ANNOTATOR ('rimes', crossing out the initial 'c'); crime GRISMOND

2.1.171 then] ANNOTATOR; not in GRISMOND

2.1.177 SOTO Do...back.] ANNOTATOR; not in GRISMOND

2.1.192 despairs] DILKE; dfpaires GRISMOND (with fp ligature)

2.1.197 Mine own?] GRISMOND. An oath would be appropriate after this question.

2.1.205 thy] DILKE; thee GRISMOND

2.1.210–12 chewed...chew] GRISMOND (chaw'd...chaw)

2.1.220 senor] GRISMOND (Signior)

2.1.225 burden] GRISMOND (burthen)

2.1.228 morrow] GRISMOND; tomorrow BULLEN

2.1.241 Tarifa] DILKE; Tarisa GRISMOND

2.1.242 trowed] ELLIS (conj. Dyce); told GRISMOND

2.1.263 task] ANNOTATOR, DILKE; taste GRISMOND; test PARKER-SMITH

2.2.8 tears' weary complaints] GRISMOND (teares? | Weary complaints); tears, | Weary heav'n with complaints DILKE; tears | And weary complaints, Maria MORRIS. The emendations do not much improve the sense or the metre. GRISMOND makes sense if we interpret 'teares' as possessive.

2.2.14 MARIA] DILKE; Ped. GRISMOND

2.2.16 thou] DILKE; not in GRISMOND

2.2.27 ‸Here] ANNOTATOR; Die. ~ GRISMOND. The error probably originated from the fact that the preceding entrance direction was written in the left margin, where its final word could easily be misinterpreted as a speech prefix.

2.2.28 you] GRISMOND; your DYCE

2.2.29 T'exchange] DYCE; To exchange GRISMOND

2.2.47 when] GRISMOND; then Q2. For the idiom 'till when' compare Ford's *Love's Trial*, sig. C2.

2.2.49 Exit] PADHI; not in GRISMOND. Editors normally have Clara exit with Maria, but since GRISMOND omits the exit for Diego it might just as easily have omitted a separate exit for Clara.

2.2.87 threatened to] DILKE; threaten'd ‸ GRISMOND. Perhaps 'threatenèd'?

2.2.94 sent] DILKE; fet GRISMOND

2.2.112 sacrificed] facrific'd GRISMOND(b); facrifie'd GRISMOND(b). The uncorrected reading is found only in the Trinity College, Cambridge copy (sig. D3).

2.2.119 ‸How] DILKE; Soto. ~ GRISMOND. See similar error at 2.2.26.

2.2.120 flaying] GRISMOND (fleaing)

2.2.139 spoke] GRISMOND (fpake)

2.2.139 haught] GRISMOND (haute)

2.2.155 Italy, I'll] DILKE; ~ I GRISMOND

2.2.156 Rome, I'll] DILKE; ~ I GRISMOND

2.2.161 If] GRISMOND. An oath would be appropriate here.

2.2.161 woods] DILKE; wookes GRISMOND

2.2.163 maravedi] GRISMOND (Maruedi)

2.2.164 larks] DILKE; markes GRISMOND

2.2.166 to the] GRISMOND; to th' THIS EDITION conj. Pedro elsewhere speaks verse; the elision would make this final speech metrical.

3.1.1 vile] GRISMOND (vild)

3.1.5 caroche] GRISMOND (Caroach)

3.1.24 her] THIS EDITION; the GRISMOND. There is no reason for us to suppose that Roderigo is standing in real 'ruins here'; the 'ruins' must be those of Clara's reputation. Easy misreading.

3.1.30 Faith, what are] THIS EDITION; not in GRISMOND; But who are DILKE; Who are DYCE. All editors have recognized the need for emendation here, but none has explained the error. The deletion of an oath at the beginning of the line (expressing surprise, a change of subject, and a comment upon the appearance of Sancho and Soto) might easily lead to the mistaken omission of one or more other words. (For evidence that the text has been expurgated, see Textual Introduction.)

'What' seems more appropriate than 'who': compare 3.1.45, where he says 'what you are'.

3.1.46   shows] DYCE; ſhew GRISMOND

3.1.61   Wou't] GRISMOND (wut)

3.1.65   calf's head] GRISMOND (Calves-head)

3.1.76.1   *Enter . . . Gypsies*] PADHI; *after* 'march' (*l. 81*) GRISMOND; *after* 'round' (*l. 79*) DILKE

3.1.102   *grandes*] GRISMOND (Grandoes). See 2.1.28.

3.1.120, 122   'em] THIS EDITION; *them* GRISMOND. The metrical pattern throughout the song requires that this final syllable be elided.

3.1.134   Mulled sack] THIS EDITION; *Mull-ſack* GRISMOND. No one has cited any parallels for GRISMOND's form, and I cannot find any. Under various headings *OED* gives three examples of 'mulled' in this sense: Dekker and Webster, *Northward Ho*, sig. B1; Wilkins, *Miseries of Enforced Marriage*, sig. F1ᵛ; Fletcher, *Loyal Subject*, 4.6.

3.1.135   noll] GRISMOND (*nowle*)

3.1.136   malaga] GRISMOND (*Maligo*)

3.1.136   'ee] THIS EDITION; *thee* GRISMOND. See 3.1.120; here, necessary for the rhyme with 'doxy'.

3.1.138   *dancing*] THIS EDITION; *not in* GRISMOND

3.2.14   Castilla's] DYCE; *Castilla* GRISMOND

3.2.15   quarrels] DILKE; *Families* GRISMOND

3.2.19   he mends] THIS EDITION; *hee mindes* GRISMOND; *his mind's* DILKE. DILKE's emendation, accepted by most editors, does not change the sense of GRISMOND; in either reading, 'bravery' is something unequivocally positive (as in modern usage). But 'bravery' in early modern English was more often negative (bragging, or extravagant apparel), or at least ambivalent; moreover, in this specific context the actions for which Luis is praised in the rest of the speech explicitly contradict the code of valour and revenge. By simple alteration of one letter Fernando instead praises Luis because he 'mends' (improves upon, corrects, reforms) the 'bravery' which leads to 'quarrels . . . too large' in the first place. (A secondary sense plays on the patching/mending of clothes.)

3.2.39   Repeat] DILKE; *Repeale* GRISMOND

3.2.42   MARIA] DILKE; *Al.* GRISMOND. A bizarre error, since Alvarez is not present in this scene. Padhi suggests that this speech prefix was caught 'from the next heading for a group speech' (3.2.44); this hypothesis presumes, and may provide some evidence that, the group speech prefixes were originally written '*All*', and later systematically altered by a scribe to his preferred 'Omnes'.

3.2.78   There is‸] GRISMOND; ~ ~ a Q2; There's‸ DYCE

3.2.81   JUAN] ANNOTATOR (John); *not in* GRISMOND. Notably, there are speech prefix errors connected to both of the brief interventions by Juan, before and after the song; perhaps they were insertions (by one author) into the original manuscript (written by a different author).

3.2.82   FATHER] *conj.* Padhi); I. GRISMOND; *not in* DYCE. Since Alvarez is the Gypsy leader, he is the obvious person to sing the first line. The specification 'Omn.' for the two final lines of each stanza makes it clear that the first four lines are sung by an individual voice.

3.2.85   ANSWER] GRISMOND; *not in* DYCE

3.2.86   OMNES] GRISMOND; *Chorus* DILKE

3.2.88   SECOND GYPSY] GRISMOND (2.); *not in* Dyce. GRISMOND numbers each stanza; this may be nothing more than a literary convention, found in some manuscript transcriptions of songs; but it may also indicate that the first lines of each stanza are sung by a succession of different voices.

3.2.110   OMNES] DILKE; *not in* GRISMOND. There seems no reason to abandon the pattern of choruses in the four preceding stanzas, and every reason to close the song with a rousing collective assertion; scribe or compositor could simply have omitted the prefix.

3.2.110–13   Whose . . . own] ANNOTATOR. Each of these two final lines is given once in GRISMOND; ANNOTATOR brackets the two lines and writes in the margin, 'twice sung' (underlined). DYCE did not mention this annotation; it was first transcribed by Padhi.

3.2.115   PEDRO] DILKE; *Ro.* GRISMOND

3.2.117   father?—Disguise] DILKE (sub); *Fathers‸ diſguiſe* GRISMOND

3.2.126–7, 147   I ha'] GRISMOND. Both examples should possibly be emended to 'I've'. See note at 4.1.154.

3.2.130   picked] GRISMOND. This might be modernized to 'peck' (like 'peckd' at 2.1.50), but *pick* overlapped with *peck* in meaning: see *Michaelmas* 1.1.61 ('birds pick'). Moreover, the joke seems to depend on a second meaning ('stolen'), which is recorded by *OED* for *pick v.*[1] but not for *peck*. Compare *Five Gallants* 3.1.133 ('Does my boy pick').

3.2.138–9   o' late] THIS EDITION; *of* ~ GRISMOND. See note at 1.5.96.

3.2.142   have] DILKE; *hath* GRISMOND. The error could have resulted from scribal misexpansion of original *ha'*, to which the text should perhaps be alternatively emended.

3.2.143   foal] GRISMOND (*Fole*)

3.2.157   Sat] GRISMOND (*Sate*)

3.2.158   buy't] THIS EDITION; *buy it* GRISMOND. The elision continues the rhyme with 'white' and 'bright'.

3.2.160   nigh't] THIS EDITION; *nie it* GRISMOND. See preceding note.

3.2.161   Yet] THIS EDITION; *yes* GRISMOND. The point of this closing couplet is that it contradicts the preceding; 'yet' is not only appropriately adversative, but in the sense 'yet to come, at some future time' also appropriately predictive. An easy misreading.

3.2.172   Forsooth] THIS EDITION; *not in* GRISMOND. A two-syllable oath completes the verse line, and emphasizes Fernando's shock at the discovery. Given other evidence that Middleton wrote this passage, I have chosen one of his oaths; *i'faith* or *cuds me* would also fit the metre.

3.2.175   This is] GRISMOND; *This'* THIS EDITION *conj.*

3.2.180   You've] THIS EDITION; *You have* GRISMOND. Metre: the other three lines are regular tetrameters, and 'You have' fits a pattern of scribal expansion.

3.2.183   Vengeance!] THIS EDITION; *not in* GRISMOND. The line is a foot short, and does not provide a very emphatic cue for Alvarez's 'an you threaten'. An oath used elsewhere by Middleton.

3.2.184   an] GRISMOND (*and*)

3.2.195   we'd] DILKE; *hee'd* GRISMOND

3.2.205   you] BULLEN (*conj.* Dyce); *your* GRISMOND

3.2.207   bon voyage] GRISMOND (*boone voyage*)

3.2.207   we've] THIS EDITION; *we have* GRISMOND

3.2.210   I'm] THIS EDITION; *I am* GRISMOND

3.2.213, 217   OMNES] DYCE; *not in* GRISMOND. Perhaps the repetition of lines 212 and 216 was an afterthought, written in the margin; this would explain the absence of a speech prefix for both lines, and the peculiar lineation error at 3.2.213–14: see lineation notes.

3.2.215   sway] THIS EDITION; *ſtay* GRISMOND. Why should their passing lead to the stopping of their bell-ropes? How can the bells chime if the bell-ropes do not move? Surely the bell-ropes must *move* in order to 'chime…holiday', and to indicate that they are 'pleased'. For 'sway' in the sense 'swing', see *OED*. For the plausibility of the proposed error, compare the sway/stay variant in the B-text of *Faustus 1616* (4.2): 'Let us sway/stay thy thoughts from this attempt'.

3.2.216, 217 holiday] GRISMOND (*Holy-day*). See *OED* for *holiday*.

3.2.246 jester] The contemporary source for this incident—described by Joseph Mead in a letter of 16 May 1623 to Sir M. Stuteville—has not been noticed by previous editors of *Gypsy*, or previous accounts of Armstrong. See Harleian MS 389, f. 328ᵛ: 'And Archie the King's foole, fell there also from an horse & is killed.' For other accounts of Armstrong's activities in Spain, as part of Prince Charles's entourage, see Southworth, 144–6.

3.2.253 headstrong] GRISMOND (head ſtrong)

3.2.254 back] THIS EDITION; *not in* GRISMOND; on DYCE. 'Bear' at the beginning of the line seems to mean 'to move (a thing) onward by force of pressure, to push, force, drive' (*OED v.*¹, 26a); this general sense takes a number of different adverbs, including 'bear back', meaning 'to press, force one's way against resistance; to move with effort, with pressure' (*v.*¹, 36); *OED* cites examples from Shakespeare's *Lucrece* 1417 and *Caesar* 3.2.172, both involving crowds. If the (apparently) missing word began with a 'b', the scribe or compositor could easily have skipped to the following 'before'. Alternatively, one might conjecture 'hard': see *bear, v.*¹, 29b ('to press hard(ly) or heav(il)y upon') and *hard, adv.* 1 ('violently, vigorously'), 2a ('severely, cruelly'), 2b ('with an uneasy pace', used of horses). Either of these adverbs would be more appropriate to the violent and jostling context, so important to the narrative, than Dyce's colourless 'on'.

3.2.265 at once] THIS EDITION; *not in* GRISMOND; straightway DILKE. The emendation restores the metre, but also—like Dilke's emendation—emphasizes the immediacy and urgency which the command seems to require; eyeskip would explain the omission of 'at once' just before 'about'.

3.2.275 Callèd] DYCE; Call'd GRISMOND; She's called DILKE

3.2.287 Sir] ANNOTATOR; For GRISMOND. Padhi read the manuscript annotation as 'sᵒ', but there would be no reason to write 'o' as a superscript, and Dyce was almost certainly right to interpret it as superscript 'r', thus producing a common abbreviation for 'sir'.

3.3.6.1 He…curtain] THIS EDITION; *not in* GRISMOND. See note at l. 1.3.40.1.

3.3.9 Thy] DILKE; The GRISMOND

3.3.9 wild] DILKE; wide GRISMOND

3.3.13 Azevedo] THIS EDITION; *Azeutda* GRISMOND; *Azevida* ANNOTATOR. The correct reading is confirmed by *La Gitanilla*, which has '*Azeuedo*'; the *corregidor*'s full name is mentioned nowhere else in the play. ANNOTATOR struck through GRISMOND's 't' and replaced it with 'i'; this gives approximately the correct sense, substantively, and has been followed by subsequent editors, but the minimal correction probably does not restore the authorial form, which is likely to have followed *La Gitanilla*. GRISMOND seems to have originated from a simple e/t misreading, by compositor or scribe (corrected by ANNOTATOR), and a terminal a/o misreading (as often with Spanish words in GRISMOND).

3.3.14 Madrid] DILKE; *Mardrill* GRISMOND. Same error at 4.3.103.

3.3.21 *rising*] THIS EDITION; *not in* GRISMOND. Clara, who is discovered sitting, must rise before l. 25, when Fernando sits, presumably in the same chair.

3.3.24 May] ANNOTATOR; Muſt GRISMOND

3.3.25.1 *Fernando sits*] THIS EDITION; *not in* GRISMOND

3.3.51 Aught] GRISMOND (Ought)

3.3.66 holler] GRISMOND (hollow)

3.3.70 marvel] GRISMOND (marvaile)

3.3.71 Sit] BULLEN (*conj.* Dyce); Sir GRISMOND. The only chair specified in the opening stage direction is that in which Clara is discovered sitting, and which she later urges Fernando to sit in (25); there is no reason for Fernando to tell Pedro to sit, but considerable dramatic and symbolic logic in Fernando telling Clara to reoccupy the chair she earlier yielded to him. The (easy) misreading would have been facilitated by the fact that Pedro spoke the previous line.

3.3.77 spoke] THIS EDITION; ſpoken GRISMOND. Metre. Compare 'hath spoke', as here for metrical reasons, in Ford's *Broken Heart* 3.4.1 and *'Tis Pity* 2.1.63.

3.3.93 with ye] THIS EDITION; ~ you GRISMOND. The stress in this phrase, as in the following one, falls on the preposition, not the pronoun, and 'ye' seems as appropriate here as in the following phrase; the shift in mid-line is awkward, and probably another sign of scribal normalization. (There is much evidence of Ford's authorship of this scene.)

3.3.100 An] GRISMOND (And)

3.3.106 Night] DILKE; Might GRISMOND

4.1.0.2 *A shout within*] THIS EDITION. GRISMOND separates this sentence from the rest of the entrance direction, to the right of '*and Don John*'; this presumably reflects the placement of the direction in the right margin of a manuscript. The shout surely takes place before the entrances; there is no reason (and nobody) to shout 'within', once the characters are on stage.

4.1.0.2–5 *at one door…at another door*] THIS EDITION; *not in* GRISMOND. The repeated 'welcome' presupposes a meeting; the scene begins with the dramatic moment of Juan's coming to join the Gypsies. DYCE reorganizes the list of Gypsy names, adds 'disguised as before', and adds Roderigo, who plays no part in this scene.

4.1.20 Wi'th'] THIS EDITION; With the GRISMOND. Probably another scribal expansion, disrupting the metre.

4.1.21 Mullah] GRISMOND (*Muly*)

4.1.21–2 Crag-a-whee] GRISMOND (*Crag* a whee)

4.1.29 bury] Q2; buy GRISMOND

4.1.34 Thy] DYCE specifies that this entire ceremony should be sung; although GRISMOND does not contain any stage directions to sing, it does set ll. 34–57 and 64–77 in italic, a printing convention used to indicate song elsewhere. However, GRISMOND does not italicize ll. 59–60, 78–9, or 81–2, which DYCE also specifies as song; it does italicize 58, a repetitive exclamation of a kind elsewhere clearly shouted, not sung—and not marked by DYCE to be sung, either. (DILKE set it in roman type.) Such inconsistencies do not encourage great faith in the italic/roman distinction in GRISMOND, as a marker of musical performance; moreover, GRISMOND specifies 'Song' at 85.1 and 138, in contrast to the absence of music directions here. Probably the use of italic is a scribal or printing convention, (inconsistently) interpreting a different metre as evidence of song, when it may only represent the kind of incantatory utterance elsewhere signalled by tetrameter couplets (for instance, in *Game at Chess* 3.3).

4.1.42, 54 sing] THIS EDITION; *not in* GRISMOND. See preceding note. GRISMOND sets these two speeches in italic, and DYCE further implies that they are sung by attributing them to a 'chorus' which follows the singing of Alvarez. These are the lines of the scene most likely to be sung, not only because their repeated content specifies singing and dancing, but because it would be difficult for a group to speak these lines in unison if they were *not* sung.

4.1.65 Teach him how.] GRISMOND. DILKE identified this as a misunderstood marginal stage direction—which is possible, but unnecessary. Moreover, the hypothesis of interpolation seems to require (for metrical purposes) the subsidiary hypothesis of a missing word in what remains of the line: see next note.

4.1.65 what] GRISMOND; well ~ DILKE

4.1.78 CARLO] DYCE; *Cla.* GRISMOND

4.1.81 sing] THIS EDITION; *not in* GRISMOND. See notes at ll. 34 and 42.

4.1.81 Holidays] GRISMOND (Holy dayes). See 3.2.216.

4.1.88 hay-de-guys] GRISMOND (hey de guize). Although the first element of this compound is clearly the dance called the 'hay' in modern spelling (*OED n.*[4]), this particular variant, popular in the sixteenth and seventeenth centuries, is of uncertain etymology, form, and spelling; I have chosen the form most likely to assure modern readers of the rhyme.

4.1.95 wrench] THIS EDITION (*conj.* Dyce); *wench* GRISMOND. Although 'such another wench' makes good sense in isolation, in the context of this particular praise of *dancing* it is less evidently relevant. Do the Gypsies go beyond all nations in their dancing simply because they have one beautiful female dancer? However inelegant it sounds now, in the context of dancing 'wrench' is clearly the more relevant *early modern* word; it also is a more exact rhyme. An easy minim misreading, substituting a very common word for a rarer technical one. For the principle of preferring 'the rarer reading', see Taylor 1988.

4.1.97 grout] GRISMOND (*growte*)

4.1.109 gilt] GRISMOND (*guilt*)

4.1.111 No such,] THIS EDITION; *not ~ a* GRISMOND. Why should any author use the more expansive phrase when the more economical one also preserves the metre evident in the preceding line, and in every comparable line (or phrase) of the three stanzas? GRISMOND's reading could easily be a scribal or compositorial expansion/substitution.

4.1.112 Nineveh] GRISMOND (*Ninivie*)

4.1.127 work-a-day] GRISMOND (*workie-day*)

4.1.129 mauled] GRISMOND (*mall'd*)

4.1.136 DIEGO (*within*)] DILKE; *Diego Within.* GRISMOND (as stage direction, in right margin after the speech). Probably a remnant of theatrical practice: see Taylor and Jowett, 113–15.

4.1.138 fine] GRISMOND; *fare* MORRIS *conj.*; *flie* PADHI *conj.* Probably 'fine' is here adverbial, combining 'Hence...finely' and 'finely to get money'.

4.1.141 Hence bravely, boys!] THIS EDITION; *not in* GRISMOND; *Hence merrily!* PADHI. GRISMOND is indented, as though to indicate a lacuna in its manuscript; certainly, the metrical pattern of the preceding and following stanzas suggests that four syllables are missing here. On the evidence of stanzas one and three, the first word of stanza two should be 'hence'. Moreover, since the third stanza is addressed to the Gypsy 'bonny girls', and since the 'we' of line 142 are Gypsy males, it would make sense for the missing half line to include a vocative addressed to Gypsy males. Gypsy 'girls' are contrasted with Gypsy 'boys' in another song at 3.2.206; Alvarez calls his fellow males 'my brave boys' at 2.1.1.

4.1.143 dell] THIS EDITION; *dill* GRISMOND. *OED* cites this passage as the only occurrence of *dill n.*[2], describing it as 'a variant of, or error for, *Dell*'—a word with the obviously appropriate primary meaning, and appropriate linguistic register, with examples cited from 1567–1688 (and other examples not

cited, like *Dissemblers* 4.2.57). There seems no reason to retain the anomaly, which is either (probably) an error or (at best) a variant spelling which should be modernized.

4.1.147–8 Smug...seemly] ANNOTATOR (who writes 'twice' opposite 145–6); *not in* GRISMOND

4.1.154, 159 I've] THIS EDITION; *I ha* GRISMOND. GRISMOND contains twelve examples of *ha'*, none of *I've*. The consistency of this pattern—in a play by at least two, and probably four, authors—is itself suggestive of the imposition of a scribal preference. In two cases, 'ha' seems to be correct, since they occur in what appears to be verse, where the metre would require the extra syllable (4.3.120), or where elision to a monosyllable is impossible (4.3.121). So the play does contain at least two examples of *ha'*—as we would expect, since it is used elsewhere by all of the four suspected authors but Ford (and Ford cannot have written 4.3). Of the twelve examples of *ha'*, seven occur in the phrase *I ha*. Five are in prose (1.1.11, 18, 2.1.210, 3.2.126–7, 147); but the two here in 4.1 are in verse, and in both cases monosyllabic *I've* would be metrically regular, where disyllabic *I ha* would be irregular. Moreover, one verse occurrence of the parallel form *you ha'* (at 5.3.105, a passage involving Sancho and Soto which could be by any of the four authors) would be metrically regular with 'you've'. (See note.) We therefore have three passages which independently suggest that an original metrical *'ve* has been replaced by an unmetrical scribal *ha'*. Both these examples of suspect *I ha'* occur in a passage which we have other reasons for assigning to Middleton, who used *I've* more frequently than other playwrights; so do two of the prose examples (3.2).

4.1.156 drove of] GRISMOND; ~ *on* THIS EDITION *conj.* Caroline texts sometimes substitute 'of' for Middleton's idiomatic 'on'. See *Bloody Banquet*.

4.1.159 I'm] DYCE; *I am* GRISMOND. See note at 4.1.154.

4.1.161 you're] DYCE; *you are* GRISMOND. Compare 5.1.105.

4.1.161 I'm] DYCE; *I am* GRISMOND

4.1.192 ne'er] THIS EDITION; *never* GRISMOND. In 1.3, 2.1, 2.2, 3.1, and 5.3, metre requires that 'never' be pronounced as two syllables; only here, in a passage which is unequivocally verse, does metre require a monosyllable. The elision is characteristic of Middleton.

4.1.202 young] ANNOTATOR (?), DILKE; *younger* GRISMOND. Padhi doubts whether the ANNOTATOR is responsible for inking out 'er'. It is not obvious why a compositor or scribe should substitute 'younger' for 'young'—but also not obvious why Cardochia should say 'younger' (than Diego, presumably, who seems himself to be young, since he is a friend of the very young Luis). However, omission of the ft ligature would transform 'youngster' into 'younger'; Middleton uses *youngster* in *Meeting* and *Widow*.

4.1.203 Marry] THIS EDITION; *not in* GRISMOND. The line is a foot short, and we would expect Diego—who is in love with Cardochia—to respond with at least a little emphasis. For 'marry' particularly, and expurgation generally, see Textual Introduction.

4.1.205 *reals*] GRISMOND (*Rialls*)

4.1.207 By my troth] THIS EDITION; *not in* GRISMOND. The line is very irregular metrically as it stands; a serious oath seems dramatically appropriate, and 'troth' would specifically relate to his romantic commitment to Cardochia.

4.1.210 on, since:] THIS EDITION; ~, *finne*, GRISMOND; ~, since, ANNOTATOR; ~, since, DILKE. Our reading essentially follows that of the ANNOTATOR, who corrected one letter but left the punctuation intact, thus understanding the word as a rare survival of the contracted form of 'sithence', found elsewhere in Middleton's *Chaste Maid* 3.3.145 and *Widow* 5.1.253. See Levine.

4.1.210 by'r Lady] THIS EDITION; *not in* GRISMOND. The line is metrically a foot short; 'cuds me' would fit the metre perfectly, but an extra syllable after the caesura is common enough, and this oath (also often used by Middleton) seems particularly appropriate to the context.

4.2.1–2 arm … arm] ANNOTATOR; Army … Army GRISMOND. Presumably the Grismond compositor or the scribe of Grismond's manuscript misread terminal 'e' as 'y'.

4.2.9 I will] GRISMOND; I'll DYCE. Although I have elsewhere emended to supply contractions, it is not clear that an extra stressed syllable after the caesura is any more 'regular' than six iambics. The formality of this dialogue does not encourage such elisions.

4.2.18 seek] DILKE; fee GRISMOND

4.2.21 of] DILKE; *not in* GRISMOND

4.2.28.1 *Exit Pedro with Francisco*] DILKE (*subst.*); *Exit.* GRISMOND; *Exeunt Pedro and Francisco* DYCE (after 'here', l. 29). Morris notes that Francisco has no reason to leave, but in the rest of the scene he does not speak and is not acknowledged in any way as present, so it seems likely that he must exit. As Gossett notes in the Critical Introduction, the play departs from theatrical convention in allowing a father (Fernando) to see through his son's disguise; if Francisco were present, we might expect him to see through *his* son's disguise, too; such confusions about what convention is operating would be avoided easily by removing Francisco from the stage. DYCE moved the exit direction so that there would still be someone on stage to whom 'See, they are here' could be addressed. However, because exits and entrances took some time, Pedro and Francisco could still be onstage as the Gypsies appeared, at another door. I have left the stage direction where GRISMOND puts it (where the exit begins, rather than where it is completed) because (1) it clearly marks the division between one scene-section in verse and another which begins with prose, a shift possibly reflecting a change of authorship, and (2) unlike other examples of slightly misplaced exit directions in GRISMOND, this one cannot be due to ambiguity in the manuscript's placement of marginal directions, because lines 28 and 29 are separated by a large entrance direction.

4.2.29 ᴧSee] Q2 (*Fer.* ~); *Al.* GRISMOND. No speech prefix at all is required, since the words that follow are simply a continuation of Fernando's speech. Perhaps a change of authors here, with the entry of the Gypsies, led to the duplicated speech prefix: Fernando switches from verse to prose in mid-speech. But even that hypothesis still leaves the error partially unexplained: 'Al' is not a likely misreading of 'Fer'.

4.2.29 here] GRISMOND. If verse had been desired, iambic pentameter could easily have been achieved by inserting 'already' here. But none of the following seven speeches is clearly verse (including the next three by Fernando).

4.2.49 lay't] THIS EDITION; lay GRISMOND. The sentence obviously lacks a direct object: what did he lay in Spain? DILKE and others solve the grammatical problem by repunctuating the end of Fernando's preceding speech with a dash, apparently understanding an implicit 'which' before 'I lay'. But that produces very awkward sense, difficult to communicate in the theatre across an interruption. One might alternatively add 'it' (rather than 't), but that would disrupt the metre.

4.2.62 Yet,] THIS EDITION; Yes, GRISMOND. There must be a contrast between 'poor' and 'full' (*OED adj* 5, 'abounding in wealth', or 6, 'abundant, satisfactory'). An easy misreading.

4.2.69, 104 debauched] GRISMOND (deboſh'd)

4.2.98 we] Q2; me GRISMOND

4.3.0.2 *Flourish*] THIS EDITION; *Floriſh.* GRISMOND (in right margin opposite preceding '*Exit.*' at 4.2.108); '*Flourish within*' DYCE (after 'places' in first line of Fernando's following speech). Clearly, Roderigo's exit should not be accompanied by a flourish; the misplaced direction indicates ambiguous placement in the right margin of a manuscript. In the right margin it would therefore naturally follow (rather than precede) the entrance; the flourish could continue long enough to cue Fernando's remark.

4.3.1 This'] GRISMOND (this)

4.3.3 fretted,] THIS EDITION; frighted, GRISMOND; freighted, DYCE. GRISMOND's reading is a recorded period spelling for neither 'freighted' nor 'fretted', and fright is clearly inappropriate, so we are dealing here with emendation, not mere modernization of spelling. 'Fretted' seems preferable because it picks up the musical imagery of the preceding lines (and of the context, preceded and followed by flourishes), but also because 'fretted' was often used of various forms of architectural decoration; rooms were often said to be 'fretted', but 'freighted' does not seem elsewhere to have been used of a room. Moreover, as often elsewhere 'fretted' here would pun on the sense 'irritated'; hence, the contrastive and specific 'but' (= only), which would be superfluous with 'freighted'.

4.3.3 gold works,] THIS EDITION; *not in* GRISMOND; pleasures, DYCE. Clearly, something is missing from GRISMOND, and may have been missing in its manuscript copy, since the punctuation of the line suggests an attempt to make sense of it without this word (comma before 'but', no punctuation after 'friends'). DYCE's emendation supplies a positive noun, but has nothing specific to recommend it; he admits 'I am by no means confident that I have supplied the right word.' 'Gold works' would be, literally, architectural fretting done (as it often was) with gold: see *work n.* 15b ('an ornamental pattern or decoration, ornamentation, decoration', with examples from 1477 to 1700, all in the plural). But 'works' are also actions, a sense conveyed by the buried pun on 'good works' (*work n.* 32). In addition 'gold' is, of course, often used adjectivally as an expression of supreme value, as in Fernando's earlier description of 'a golden ring of worthy friends' (3.2.2). 'Welcomes' are elsewhere described as 'golden', and one early modern technical meaning of the term was 'a special award in a lottery', all the cited examples involving gold or sterling (*welcome n.²*, 1.c). The following word ('noble') was also the name of a gold coin, and could have been suggested by association.

4.3.4.1 *Flourish*] THIS EDITION; *Floriſh within.* GRISMOND (in right margin, after 'masters.'); *not in* DYCE. Stage directions for actions which occur in the middle of a line of speech are normally placed in the margin of dramatic manuscripts, where they can be more easily seen. See next note.

4.3.5 SANCHO (*within*)] DYCE; San. ᴧ GRISMOND. The direction 'Floriſh within'—placed by GRISMOND in the right margin opposite the preceding verse line—is probably two separate directions, which stood in the left margin of a manuscript: a 'florish' followed by a 'within' immediately opposite the speech direction for Sancho. Compare '*Diego Within.*' (4.1.136). Flourishes (which would presumably be performed by the theatre musicians in the music room) are not normally specified as 'within': see the example at 4.3.0.2, above.

4.3.7.1 *Flourish*] PADHI; *not in* GRISMOND. Something must cue Fernando's confidence that the actors are beginning; the long dash in GRISMOND at this point perhaps, as elsewhere, signals an action—which is not likely to be Sancho's entrance, since some gap between his speech 'within' and his entrance seems desirable. The reiterated flourishes could themselves become comic; but a prologue also conventionally appeared after the third sounding of a trumpet, to signal the beginning of performances. See Heywood, *Four Prentices of London*: 'Do you not see this long black velvet cloak upon my back? Have you not sounded thrice? . . . Nay, have I not all the signs of a Prologue about me?' (sig. A4).

4.3.28 wife's] GRISMOND (Wives)

4.3.40 He's] GRISMOND (has)

4.3.52 'Swounds] THIS EDITION; *not in* GRISMOND. A 'rake-hell' should employ lots of offensive oaths; the extant text gives him none. This is a particularly strong oath, which immediately establishes his character, and is relevant to the rest of the sentence; it is used elsewhere by Rowley (who probably wrote this scene). Oaths might also have been censored at ll. 72, 94, and 142.

4.3.61 grindstone] GRISMOND (Grinſtone)

4.3.74 taffeta] GRISMOND (Taffaty)

4.3.81 FATHER] Q2 (*Al.*); *A.* GRISMOND

4.3.87 *Exeunt . . . Sancho*] THIS EDITION; *not in* GRISMOND; *Exit Soto* DYCE. Since both characters enter again at 4.3.106.2, they must both exit before then; since both are servants, and both return with the guests which Avero here asks someone to fetch, it makes dramatic sense that both should exit here together. Although logically Sancho is Roderigo's servant in the play-within-the-play, the audience is used to seeing the two clowns enter and exit together, and will not be disturbed by a joint exit here.

4.3.88 ANTONIO] GRISMOND (*Ant.*); *Alv.* DILKE. See next note.

4.3.91 FATHER] PADHI (*Al.*); *not in* GRISMOND. Antonio cannot speak the whole of the lines assigned to him by GRISMOND, since the last sentence clearly belongs to Alvarez. But unless there was a change of speaker at l. 88, there would be no reason for any speech prefix at all, and it would be difficult to explain GRISMOND's interpolation of one. On the other hand, omission of a speech prefix does occasionally occur. PADHI's arrangement also gives Antonio something to say between his entrance at l. 84.1 and l. 99 (the first line assigned to him by all editors since DILKE).

4.3.103 Madrid] Q2 (*Madrill*); *Mardrill* GRISMOND

4.3.106.1 Carlo] DYCE; *Claro* GRISMOND; *Clara* Q2

4.3.106.2 *Sancho and Soto*] GRISMOND; *not in* DILKE. See note at 4.3.87. Every entrance and exit of these characters gives them an opportunity for comic business; modern editors, by removing this double entrance and the corresponding double exits at ll. 87 and 109, have privileged their own sense of realism over the theatricality of GRISMOND.

4.3.108 marquis] GRISMOND (Marqueſſe)

4.3.109 *Exeunt . . . Soto*] PADHI; *not in* GRISMOND; *Exit Sancho* DILKE. See note at 4.3.106.2. Soto enters again at l. 119.1, so he must exit before then.

4.3.117.1 *He draws . . . shows*] THIS EDITION; *not in* GRISMOND. The portrait seems not to be a miniature but a hanging picture: see 'hang' at l. 230. It is visible to Preciosa, Eugenia, and Christiana, who all comment on it. Such pictures were often protected by curtains—as is implied by ll. 235-6, where the curtain protecting a picture is compared to the mask protecting a woman's face. See William Heminges, *The Fatal Contract*, sig. B3ᵛ: 'Draw the curtain and show the picture'.

4.3.118 Cárcamo] GRISMOND (*Carcamo*); *Carcomo* Q2. 'Cárcamo' is the form of the name in Cervantes; editors here, for the sake of consistency, have emended GRISMOND when it agrees with the source! See note at 1.5.91.

4.3.123 Marry] THIS EDITION; *Yes* GRISMOND. The line is a syllable short, and 'yes' is elsewhere substituted for oaths.

4.3.124 'Snails] THIS EDITION; *not in* GRISMOND. We would expect the 'rake-hell' to respond strongly to the picture's ugliness; this is a strong oath used elsewhere by Rowley and Dekker (and relevant to the 'devil').

4.3.131 I'm] DYCE; *I am* GRISMOND

4.3.140 blubber] GRISMOND (blabber). The original spelling no longer conveys the required sense; *OED* cross-refers 'blabber' to 'blubber' and 'blobber', as forms clearly related etymologically.

4.3.146 foh] THIS EDITION; *for* GRISMOND. An interjection expressing disgust or nausea would be more appropriate here than a logical connective: 'foh' appears in, for instance, Rowley's *All Lust by Lust* 2.2.

4.3.155 *Exeunt some with Diego*] THIS EDITION; *not in* GRISMOND; *Servants remove Diego* DYCE. There is no evidence for onstage servants elsewhere in this scene; the resources of the company would be taxed enough by the full complement of onstage spectators and actors in the play within the play (at least seventeen, including six women characters). Neither Clara nor Maria speaks in the remainder of the scene.

4.3.156 Faith] THIS EDITION; *Oh* GRISMOND. We would expect Carduchia to authenticate her testimony against Juan with some sort of asseveration; the neutral 'Oh' is elsewhere in the period substituted for censored oaths.

4.3.157 I'd] THIS EDITION; *I had* GRISMOND. The contraction, though most frequent in Middleton and Rowley, is also used by Dekker and Ford, so the metrical emendation here does not depend upon assumptions about authorship.

4.3.159 gave it] GRISMOND; *gave't* THIS EDITION *conj.*

4.3.176 I am] GRISMOND; *I'm* THIS EDITION *conj.*

4.3.176 weary on't] THIS EDITION; ~ *of it* GRISMOND. All four authors use the contraction (although it is most frequent in Middleton and Rowley). The specific collocation 'weary on't' appears at *Mad World* 2.1.21, 4.3.51 and *Lady* 5.2.159 (and in the quarto of *Five Gallants* 2.4.159, emended to 'wary on't' in this edition).

4.3.179 gentleman] Q2; *Genleman* GRISMOND

4.3.197 I'd] THIS EDITION; *I had* GRISMOND. See 4.3.157.

4.3.199 spoke] GRISMOND (ſpake)

4.3.204 Marry] THIS EDITION; *not in* GRISMOND. The line is a foot short; Fernando needs an asseveration to defend his choice (but not one as strong as the oaths used by a 'rake-hell'). All four dramatists used 'marry', which is completely absent from GRISMOND.

4.3.206 sell] ANNOTATOR; *fee* GRISMOND

4.3.208 You're] DYCE; *you are* GRISMOND

4.3.218 How? She] ANNOTATOR; *How! how* GRISMOND

4.3.219, 221 I'm] DYCE; *I am* GRISMOND

4.3.220.1 *He kneels*] DILKE; *not in* GRISMOND. 'Kneels' is 'written in faded pencil in Jacobean hand' in the Trinity College, Cambridge copy of GRISMOND (Padhi).

4.3.236.1 *He . . . picture.*] THIS EDITION; *not in* GRISMOND. See note at l. 117.1.

5.1.14 sin] DILKE; *fins* GRISMOND

5.1.33 precedent] GRISMOND (preſident)

5.1.36 fall] DILKE; *full* GRISMOND

5.1.45 flow] DILKE; *flew* GRISMOND

5.1.48 am I] THIS EDITION; ~ ‸ GRISMOND

5.1.56.1 *They embrace*] THIS EDITION; —— GRISMOND; *He kisses her* PADHI. PADHI seems right to suspect that the long dash in GRISMOND is, as often, a signal of stage action; perhaps a marginal manuscript direction was omitted by the compositor. In any case, some physical action, embodying the reconciliation, seems theatrically necessary here: it might be initiated by Roderigo or Clara, and might or might not include a kiss.

5.1.68 faith] THIS EDITION; *not in* GRISMOND. Metrically the line is awkward, as editors have recognized (see next note); such irregularity is particularly suspicious in a passage apparently written by Ford. A word like 'here' might have been omitted by simple eyeskip, but given other evidence that the text has been expurgated the problem may be censorship; *faith* would be especially relevant here, where Luis is upbraiding Roderigo's failure to keep faith with his friend. Ford uses *faith* as an expletive at least fifteen times elsewhere.

5.1.68 friend] GRISMOND; ~ to me DYCE. See preceding note. DYCE's emendation produces the needed extra metrical foot, but adds two words instead of one, does not explain the error, and leaves an extra syllable in the first half of the line.

5.1.70 th'university] THIS EDITION; the Univerſity GRISMOND

5.1.72 poor-spirited] THIS EDITION; poore ‸ GRISMOND; poor as BULLEN; poor in spirit DYCE *conj.* Although DYCE's conjecture restores what seems to be the necessary sense, no one has accepted it, presumably because it further confuses the line's shaky metre. By contrast, the emendation adopted here produces a regular hexameter: compare ll. 62, 75, 101, 105, 140, 147, etc.

5.1.74 calm] Q2; calcalme GRISMOND. PADHI points out that GRISMOND's error may conceal an omission from the text, which is metrically short.

5.1.81 SERVANTS (*within*)] DILKE. GRISMOND has no speech prefix, but instead has the stage direction '*Within Servants.*' in the right margin opposite 'My Lord?'. See notes at 4.1.136 and 4.3.5.

5.1.82 SERVANTS (*within*)] DILKE; *Ser.* GRISMOND. See preceding note. There is no entrance direction for servants, so presumably 'within' applies to both speeches.

5.1.83 hussy] GRISMOND (Huſ-wife)

5.1.85 lovely] ANNOTATOR; lively GRISMOND

5.1.97 you are] GRISMOND; y'are THIS EDITION *conj.*

5.1.99 sweet] ANNOTATOR; ſir GRISMOND

5.1.105 You're] DYCE; You are GRISMOND. An extra stressed initial syllable would be anomalous for Ford. Compare 4.1.161, 4.3.208.

5.1.106 poise] THIS EDITION; price GRISMOND. An easy misreading: compare the press variant priſe/poyſe in *History of King Lear* 6.120. The image of balancing weights, as in the traditional scales of justice, seems much more relevant (with 'life *or* death') than 'price'. Ford uses the word 'poise' at 2.2.12.

5.1.108 Here sit they] ANNOTATOR; he ~ ~ GRISMOND; they ſit ‸ Q2

5.1.109 heads] DYCE; head GRISMOND

5.1.121 white] GRISMOND; whiter DYCE *conj.* For the conjectured idiom see for instance William Lower, *The Phoenix in Her Flames* (1639), 'this more whiter skin' (2.1.408).

5.1.122 in] DYCE; is in GRISMOND

5.1.125 sometimes] ANNOTATOR; ſomething GRISMOND

5.1.125 heard] GRISMOND (hard). For the spelling see *OED hear v.*

5.1.127 friend] THIS EDITION (*conj* DYCE); friends GRISMOND. The plural can only be defended by claiming (implausibly) that the class-conscious Luis counts the hostess Cardochia among his 'friends'.

5.1.127.1 in irons] THIS EDITION; *not in* GRISMOND. In Cervantes he is 'bound in chains and wearing handcuffs and an iron collar' and later 'his hands in cuffs, and the iron collar still round his neck'; at 4.3.170 Fernando had ordered 'Iron him'.

5.1.132 mads] GRISMOND; maddens DYCE

5.1.149 the] DILKE; *not in* GRISMOND

5.1.156 determinèd] DYCE; determin'd GRISMOND

5.1.174.1 *Exeunt...Cardochia*] THIS EDITION; *Exit.* GRISMOND. Since these three characters entered together, it makes sense that they exit together; no separate exit directions are provided for either of the men.

5.1.186 you'll] DYCE; you will GRISMOND; that you will DILKE

5.1.208 alike] GRISMOND; like THIS EDITION *conj.*

5.2.2 scurvily] ANNOTATOR; ſecurely GRISMOND

5.2.5 armory] DYCE; Army GRISMOND

5.2.9 This is] GRISMOND; This' THIS EDITION *conj.*

5.2.15 Castro] DYCE; Caſtor GRISMOND. Dyce's emendation restores the form of the name in *Guzman*, used four times in 3.2. Probably a simple compositorial or scribal transposition; possibly, evidence that 5.2 and 3.2.1–182 were written by different authors. See 5.2.28.

5.2.20 Thou] GRISMOND; Beshrew thee! ~ THIS EDITION *conj.* An oath here would be appropriate, and would regularize the verse. Ford uses 'beshrew' as an imprecation often, followed by a variety of nouns or pronouns; 'Beshrew thee' occurs at *Broken Heart* 5.2.14.

5.2.26 I'm] DYCE; I am GRISMOND

5.2.28 Castro's] DYCE; Caſtors GRISMOND

5.2.34 I'm] DYCE; I am GRISMOND

5.2.36 age] ANNOTATOR; rage GRISMOND; rags DILKE

5.2.54 son] THIS EDITION; *not in* GRISMOND; so DILKE. The play is full of emotional verbal repetitions; since something is obviously missing, repeating the charged word 'son' would be more dramatic than the colourless 'so'.

5.3.19 Guiomare] THIS EDITION; *Guyamara* GRISMOND. The name in Cervantes is 'Guiomar', and the variation here is presumably another of the errors caused by foreign words and names. The word occurs three times in this scene, spelled three different ways: see notes at ll. 44, 69.

5.3.39 be yours,] DYCE; be‸ GRISMOND

5.3.40 Because born yours] THIS EDITION; Be yours GRISMOND; Be yours at last DYCE. Clearly, something has been omitted from this line: the phrase that should have stood at the end of the preceding line seems to have ousted what belonged at the beginning of this one. As emended by DYCE, the passage simply repeats the same idea: 'she should be yours, [she should] be yours at last'. But two senses of 'yours' are possible here, in a way that might plausibly be related to the repetition of the word: 'your [comfort]' (as she has been mine) and 'your child' (which she has always been).

5.3.44 Guiomare] THIS EDITION; *Guyamare* GRISMOND; *Guiamara* Q2. See note at 5.3.19.

5.3.45 darkened] GRISMOND (darkenèd)

5.3.56 An] GRISMOND (And)

5.3.58 without] Q2; wichout GRISMOND

5.3.61 digest] GRISMOND (diſgeſt)

5.3.65 lords] DILKE; Lord GRISMOND

5.3.66 ‸Count] GRISMOND; The ~ DYCE

5.3.69 Guiomare] THIS EDITION; *Guyamere* GRISMOND. See note at 5.3.19.

5.3.70 this is] DYCE; ~‸ GRISMOND

5.3.71 I'm] THIS EDITION; I am GRISMOND

5.3.72.2 Cardochia] Q2; Cardocha GRISMOND

5.3.97 As] GRISMOND. An oath for Sancho would be appropriate here.

5.3.101 you are] ANNOTATOR; ~ be GRISMOND; be you DYCE *conj.*
5.3.105 You've] THIS EDITION; You ha GRISMOND. See note at
  4.1.154.

5.3.109 We'll] GRISMOND. A mild oath would be appropriate
  here.

STAGE DIRECTIONS

Persons.0.2–Persons.19

        Drammatis Perfonæ.

FErnando, Corigidor of Madrill.
Pedro de Cortes. ⎫
Francifco de Carcomo. ⎭   Two old Dons.
Roderigo, Son to *Fernando.*
Lewys, Son to *De Caftro,* flaine by *Alvarez.*
Diego, Friend to *Don Lewys.*
Don John, Son to *Francifco De Carcomo,* and a Lover of *Conftanza.*
Sancho, A foolifh Gentleman, and Ward to *Don Pedro.*
Soto, A merry fellow his Man.
Alvarez, An old Lord difguifed like the Father of the Gipfies.
Claro. ⎫
Antonio. ⎭   Two Gentlemen, difguifed like Gipfies.

Women ⎧ *Maria,* Wife to *Don Pedro.*
⎪ *Clara,* Their Daughter.
⎪ *Guiamara,* Wife to Count *Alvarez,* and Sifter
⎪   to *Fernando,* | difgus'd like the Mother
⎪   of the Gipfies, and call'd by | the Name
⎨   of *Eugenia.*
⎪ *Conftanza,* Daughter to *Fernando,* difguis'd like
⎪   a young | Spanifh Gipfie, and call'd by the
⎪   Name of *Pretiofa.*
⎪ *Chriftiana,* A Gentleman, difguis'd like a Gipfie.
⎪ *Cardochia,* A young Hoftes to the Gipfies.
⎩ Servants.

       The Scene, *Allegant.*

1.1.0.1 ACTUS PRIMUS.
1.1.0.2 *Enter Roderigo, Lewys, and Diego.*
1.1.37.2 *Enter Pedro, Maria, and Clara.*
1.1.40.1 *They feize them.* (right margin)
1.1.42.1 *Exit with Clara.*
1.1.46.1 *Exit.*
1.1.55 *Exit.*
1.2.0.1 *Enter Lewys and Diego.*
1.2.15 *Exit.*
1.3.0.1 *Enter Roderigo and Claria.*
1.3.30.1 *Exit.*
1.3.50.1 *Enter Roderigo.*
1.3.105 *Exit.*
1.4.0.1 *Enter Lewys, Diego, and a fervant.*
1.4.11 *Exit.*
1.4.16.1 *Exit.Lewys.*
1.4.16.2 *Enter Don Iohn Reading.*
1.4.21 *Exit.*
1.4.22.1 *Ex.*
1.5.0.1 *Enter Lewys.*
1.5.6.1 *Enter Roderigo.* (at 1.5.7)
1.5.73.1 *Enter Diego.*
1.5.127 *Exeunt.*
2.1.0.1 ACTUS SECUNDUS.
2.1.0.2–3 *Enter Alvarez, Carlo, and Antonio.*
2.1.69.1–2 *Enter Eugenia, Pretiofa, Chrifftiana, Cardochia.*
2.1.83 *Exit.*
2.1.114.1–2 *A beating within. Enter Cardochia.* (at 2.1.114.2)

2.1.117.1–2 *Enter Sancho and Soto.*
2.1.213 *Exit.*
2.1.229 *Exit.*
2.1.229.1 *Enter Don John Muffled.*
2.1.232.1 *Exit. Don John pulls Pretiofa back.*
2.1.266.1 *Exit.*
2.1.270 *Exit.*
2.2.0.1 *Enter Clara.*
2.2.5.1 *Enter Pedro, and Maria.*
2.2.26.1 *Enter Lewys, and Diego.*
2.2.52.1 *Exit.*
2.2.118.1 *Exit.*
2.2.118.2–3 *Enter Sancho, and Soto.*
2.2.166.1 *Exit.*
2.2.179 *Exeunt.*
3.1.0.1 ACTUS TERTIUS.
3.1.0.2 *Enter Roderigo Difguiz'd like an Italian.*
3.1.30.1 *Enter Sancho, and Soto as Gipfies.*
3.1.76.1–2 *Enter Alvarez, Eugenia, Pretiofa, and the Gipfies.* (at
  3.1.81 after 'march')
3.1.106.1 *Song.*
3.1.138 *Exit.*
3.2.0.1–2 *Enter Fernando, Francifco de Carcomo, Don Iohn Pedro,*
  | *Maria, Lewys, and Diego.*
3.2.52.1 *Florifh.*
3.2.53.1 *Enter Soto, with a Cornet in his hand.* (at 3.2.52.1)
3.2.77 *Exit.*
3.2.81.1–4 *Enter Alvarez, Eugenia, Pretiofa, Roderigo, Sancho,* |
  Soto, and all the Gipfies. | *Song.*
3.2.170 *Exit Diego.*
3.2.196.1 *Song.*
3.2.218.1 *Dance.* (right margin)
3.2.232.1 *Exit Gipfies Dancing.*
3.2.240 *Exit Ped. Ma.*
3.2.242.1 *Enter Diego.*
3.2.264 *Exit.*
3.2.267 *Exit.*
3.2.274.1 *Enter Lewys.* (at 3.2.275, after 'lady')
3.2.288.1 *Enter Pedro and Maria.*
3.2.292 *Exit Ped. Ma.* (at 3.2.298)
3.2.300 *Exit.*
3.3.0.1–2 *Clara in a Chaire, Pedro and Maria by her.*
3.3.17.1 *Enter Fernando.* (at 3.3.18, after 'servants')
3.3.69 *Exit.*
3.3.70.1 *Enter Fernando.*
3.3.108.1 *Ex.*
4.1.0.1 ACTUS QUARTUS.
4.1.0.2–5 *Enter Alvarez, Sancho, Soto, Antonio, Carlo, Eugenia,* |
  Pretiofa, Chriftiana, and Don John. A fhowte within.
4.1.6.1 *He offers to kiffe her.* (right margin)
4.1.60.1 *Offers to kiffe.* (right margin)
4.1.85.1 *Song.*
4.1.136 *Diego within.* (right margin, after 'you')
4.1.138 *Song.*
4.1.148.1 *Exit.*
4.1.148.2 *Enter Cardochia, ftayes Soto.*

4.1.153   *Exit.*
4.1.156.1   *Enter Don John.*
4.1.195   *Exit.*
4.1.198.1   *Enter Diego.*
4.1.210.1   *Exit.*
4.2.0.1   *Enter Fernando, Francifco, Pedro, and Lewys.*
4.2.10.1   *Exit.* (after 'done')
4.2.23.1   *Enter Diego.*
4.2.25   *Exit Die.*
4.2.28.1   *Exit.*
4.2.28.2–4   *Enter Alvarez, Don John, Roderigo, Antonio, Carlo, Eugenia, | Pretiofa, Chriftiana, Sancho and Soto.*
4.2.79   *Exit.*
4.2.99.1   *Exit.* (after 'life')
4.2.108–4.3.0.2   *Exit. Florifh.*
4.3.0.1–2   *Enter Francifco, Pedro, Fernando, Diego, | Maria, and Clara.*
4.3.4.1   *Florifh within.* (right margin)
4.3.7.2   *Enter Sancho, the Prologue.*
4.3.13   *Exit.*
4.3.14.1–2   *Enter Alvarez and Soto.*
4.3.37.1   *Enter Sancho.*
4.3.50.1   *Enter Roderigo.* (after 4.3.48)
4.3.84.1   *Enter Antonio.*
4.3.106.1–3   *Enter Claro, Don John, Eugenia, Pretiofa, Chriftiana, Sancho and Soto.*
4.3.117.1   *A Pićture.* (right margin)
4.3.119.1   *Enter Soto.*
4.3.121   *Exit.*

4.3.121   *Exit.*
4.3.121   *Exit.*
4.3.147.1–2   *A noyfe within. Enter Don John, Diego, Cardochia, Sancho, | and Soto in a hurry.*
4.3.185.1   *Exit.*
4.3.188.1   *Exeunt.*
4.3.236.1   *Exit.*
5.1.0.1   Actus Quintus.
5.1.0.2–5   *Enter Fernando, Francifco, Pedro, Roderigo, Clara, Maria, as from | Church over the Stage. Fer. ftayes Roderigo.*
5.1.38.1–2   *Enter Clara, Maria, and Pedro: from behind the Arras.*
5.1.57.1   *Enter Lewys and Francifco.*
5.1.59   *Exit.*
5.1.81   *Within Servants.* (right margin, opposite 'My Lord?')
5.1.82.1–2   *Enter Pretiofa, Eugenia, and Alvarez.*
5.1.127.1   *Enter Don John, Diego, and Cardochia.* (at 5.1.128, after 'ease')
5.1.174.1   *Exit.*
5.1.182   *Exit. Manet Lewys, Alvarez.*
5.1.208.1–5.2.0.2   *Ex. at one dore, | Enter prefently | at the other.* (right margin, opposite 5.1.207–5.2.1)
5.2.3.1   *Two Swords.* (right margin)
5.2.56   *Exit.*
5.3.0.1   *Enter Eugenia, Fernando, and Pretiofa.*
5.3.35.1   (right margin) *A Casket.*
5.3.62.1   *Enter Francifco, Pedro, Maria, Roderigo, Clara.*
5.3.72.1–2   *Enter Alvarez, Lewys, Don John, Diego, Sancho, | Soto, and Cardochia.*
5.3.110.1   *Dance.* (right, opposite 'leave')
5.3.112–Parts.22   *FINIS.*

LINEATION NOTES

1.3.85–7   Whom…me] DYCE; *2 lines* GRISMOND; satisfaction |. Error across page-break between B3 and B3ᵛ.
1.3.88–9   First…passion] DILKE; neither | GRISMOND
1.4.2–3   No…observes] DYCE; known | GRISMOND
1.4.7   The…hear] MORRIS; *2 lines* GRISMOND: strange |
1.5.7–8   The…Speak] DYCE; *1 line* GRISMOND
1.5.22–3   Of…brief] DYCE; *1 line* GRISMOND
1.5.76–7   Yes…vagary] DYCE; *1 line* GRISMOND
1.5.97–9   I…Present] MORRIS; *2 lines* GRISMOND: frequent |; *2 lines* DYCE: sports |. A line and a half at the end of a speech (as in MORRIS) often appears as one manuscript or type line; misdivision of lines in mid-speech (as in DYCE) is much less common. Moreover, MORRIS's arrangement completes the first verse line of Louis's speech (otherwise one foot short), while also eliminating the metrical awkwardness of 'to th' city present'.
2.1.71–2   My…safe] DILKE; *1 line* GRISMOND
2.1.200–1   Past…better] DILKE; out | GRISMOND
2.2.7–8   Why…childish] THIS EDITION; tears | GRISMOND
2.2.29–30   Leave…too] DYCE; *1 line* GRISMOND
2.2.45–6   'Deed…well] DILKE; *1 line* GRISMOND
3.1.77–8   See…'em?] DYCE; *verse* GRISMOND: company |
3.1.105–6   Trip…father] THIS EDITION; arrive | GRISMOND
3.2.56–7   Art…sure] THIS EDITION; *1 line* GRISMOND
3.2.142   Through…stole] DYCE; *2 lines* GRISMOND: ground |
3.2.167–8   Stay…fortune] DYCE; *1 line* GRISMOND
3.2.168–9   'Twill…company] THIS EDITION; *1 line* GRISMOND; her | DYCE
3.2.169–70   Good…her] THIS EDITION; *1 line* GRISMOND

3.2.213–14   Such…away] DILKE; *1 line* GRISMOND. Unlike most other lineation errors in the play, this one is not likely to represent authorial manuscript practice; it could be attributed either to deliberate compositorial space saving on sig. E4ᵛ, or to the writing of 'such clappers please a king' in the margin, so that it looked like the beginning of another line.
3.2.221–2   You…stage] DILKE; *1 line* GRISMOND
3.2.224–5   My…sports] DILKE; *prose* GRISMOND: see | your
3.2.228–9   Denies…Gypsy-ballads] DYCE; *1 line* GRISMOND
3.2.236–7   The…Pedro] THIS EDITION; *1 line* GRISMOND
3.2.242–3   Where's…sir] BULLEN; *1 line* GRISMOND
3.2.268–70   A…wonder] DYCE; what! | noted | GRISMOND; what! | noted | you | DILKE
3.2.274–5   Most…lady] DILKE; *1 line* GRISMOND
3.2.275–6   Callèd…sadness] DILKE; *1 line* GRISMOND
3.2.276–7   Nothing…her] DILKE; *1 line* GRISMOND
3.2.293–5   'Tis…Luis] BULLEN; *2 lines* GRISMOND: time |
4.1.59–60   Now…yours] DILKE; *1 line* GRISMOND
4.1.86–95   Brave…wrench] DYCE; *4 lines* GRISMOND: fashions | nations | French |
4.1.96–105   We…skipping] DYCE; *4 lines* GRISMOND: head | corn-fed | whipping |
4.1.106–15   Jack-in-boxes…see] DYCE; *4 lines* GRISMOND: things | rings | Nineveh |
4.1.126–7   But…hand] DILKE; *prose* GRISMOND
4.1.128–9   When…mauled] DILKE; *prose* GRISMOND
4.1.130–1   When…pease-porridge] DILKE; *prose* GRISMOND
4.1.160–1   I cannot…quick] THIS EDITION; then | GRISMOND
4.1.198–9   Gone…me] DYCE; *1 line* GRISMOND

4.2.28–9   To...number] GRISMOND; See| BULLEN
4.2.39–41   So...plot] DILKE; *prose* GRISMOND
4.2.43–4   We...subject] DILKE; *1 line* GRISMOND
4.2.85–6   One...Hialdo] THIS EDITION; *1 line* GRISMOND
4.3.28   At your...mother's] THIS EDITION; *prose* GRISMOND
4.3.46   And...money] THIS EDITION; *prose* GRISMOND
4.3.49–50   Here...dares] THIS EDITION; *prose* GRISMOND
4.3.51–2   I...tavern] DILKE; *1 verse line* GRISMOND
4.3.55–6   Old...silver] PADHI; *prose* GRISMOND
4.3.57–8   Had...for] THIS EDITION; *prose* GRISMOND
4.3.76   Give...sea] THIS EDITION; *prose* GRISMOND. The rhyme
    suggests that this is verse; it lacks only an unstressed syllable
    at the caesura.
4.3.101–2   When...off] DYCE; *1 type line* GRISMOND
4.3.109–10   Away...Lorenzo] DILKE; *1 line* GRISMOND
4.3.114–16   Fly...me] THIS EDITION; *prose* GRISMOND
4.3.120–1   If...you] THIS EDITION; *prose* GRISMOND
4.3.124–5   'Snails...cuckold] THIS EDITION; *prose* GRISMOND. Like
    other words with a medial 'v,' *devil* is often treated as a
    monosyllable.

4.3.212–13   I cannot...do't] DILKE; *1 line* GRISMOND
5.1.26–7   Hence...reward] DYCE; *1 line* GRISMOND
5.1.47–8   Ha!...wronged] DYCE; *1 line* GRISMOND
5.1.54–5   My care...love] DILKE; *1 line* GRISMOND
5.1.76–7   So...it] THIS EDITION; t'ye| GRISMOND. The metre is
    amphibious here: 'and you shall grant it' both completes the
    pentameter begun by 'I come for justice t'ye' and begins the
    pentameter completed by 'Shall and will.—With speed, too.'
5.1.82–4   What...ballads] DYCE; *2 lines* GRISMOND: tricks|
5.1.100–1   Upon...not] DYCE; *1 line* GRISMOND
5.1.169–70   I would...manifest] DYCE; *2 lines* GRISMOND: not|
5.1.205–7   Apace...fortunate] DYCE; *2 lines* GRISMOND: thee|
5.3.6–7   Why...thee] DYCE; *1 line* GRISMOND
5.3.67–8   Your...theft] DYCE; Juan| GRISMOND
5.3.71–2   And...prisoner] DILKE; man| GRISMOND
5.3.79–80   For ever...Religiously] DYCE; *1 line* GRISMOND
5.3.94–5   Live...ever one] DYCE; *1 line* GRISMOND

LOST PLAYS

Doris Feldmann and Kurt Tetzeli von Rosador

SEE ALSO

Essay: *Works*, 328

WORKS CITED

Adams, Joseph Quincy, 'Hill's List of Early Plays in Manuscript', *The Library*, IV, 20 (1939), 71–99

Anon., *The Raigne of King Edward the Third*, ed. Fred Lapides (1980)

Arber, Edward, *A Transcript of the Stationers' Registers, 1554–1640*, 5 vols (1875–94)

Bullen, A. H., ed., *The Works of Thomas Middleton*, 8 vols (1885–6)

Ellis, Sir Henry, ed., *Holinshed's Chronicles of England, Scotland, and Ireland*, 6 vols (1807–8)

Eyre, G. E. B., and C. R. Rivington, *A Transcript of the Stationers' Registers, 1640–1708*, 3 vols (1913–4)

Foakes, R. A., and R. T. Rickert, eds., *Henslowe's Diary* (1961)

Freehafer, John, 'John Warburton's Lost Plays', *Studies in Bibliography* 23 (1970), 154–164

Greene, Robert, *Friar Bacon and Friar Bungay*, ed. Daniel Seltzer (1963)

Grosart, Alexander B., ed., *The Non-Dramatic Works of Thomas Dekker*, 5 vols (1884–6)

Hebel, J. William, ed., *The Works of Michael Drayton*, 5 vols (1931–41)

Herford, C. H., Percy Simpson, and Evelyn Simpson, eds., *Ben Jonson*, 11 vols (1925–52)

Heywood, Thomas, *An Apology for Actors* (1612) [STC 13309]

Hillebrand, H. N., 'Thomas Middleton's *The Viper's Brood*', *Modern Language Notes* 42 (1927), 35–8

Krueger, Robert, ed., *The Poems of Sir John Davies* (1975)

Langland, William, *Piers Plowman*, ed. George Kane and E. Talbot Donaldson (1975)

[Languet, Hubert] *Vindiciae contra Tyrannos* (1648) [Wing L414]

Lyly, John, *Campaspe*, ed. G. K. Hunter (1991)

Munday, Anthony, *John a Kent and John a Cumber*, ed. Arthur E. Pennell (1980)

—— *The Death of Robert, Earl of Huntingdon*, ed. John C. Meagher, Malone Society Reprints (1967 for 1965)

Perkins, William, *Christian Economy* (1609) [STC 19677]

Rouse, W. H. D., ed., *Plutarch's Lives, Englished by Sir Thomas North*, 10 vols (1898–9)

Rowlands, Samuel, *The Complete Works*, 3 vols (1880)

Topsell, Edward, *The History of Serpents* (1608) [STC 24124]

Webster, John, *The White Devil*, ed. John Russell Brown (1966)

Woodbridge, Linda, *Women and the English Renaissance* (1984)

AN/THE OLD LAW

Edited by Jeffrey Masten

THE 1656 quarto of *Old Law* (Wing M1048, *BEPD* 766), the only text of the play printed in the seventeenth century, announces itself as the product of a culture in which plays were increasingly read as well as watched, consumed as collectible artifacts as well as witnessed on stage. (At the time the quarto was printed, of course, reading was the only *legal* mode of dramatic consumption.) The title-page of the quarto (BELL) suggests its liminal status between 'event' and 'text'; it stresses that the play has been 'Acted before the King and Queene at *Salisbury House*, and at severall other places, with great Applause', and, at the same time, it advertises 'an exact and perfect Catalogue of all the Playes...more exactly Printed then ever before' (Figure 1). (As will be discussed below, at least one copy of BELL includes a variant catalogue, and some copies include no catalogue.)

The idea of BELL as a book and a proto-bibliography may have distracted readers of the play text from its qualities as an essentially theatrical script. Though it is impossible to know for certain, whatever interpretive difficulties face a reader of BELL seem to have arisen in the movement of a play-house book-holder's copy or 'promptbook', a document with its own conventions of reading within a company of theatrical professionals, toward the printed quarto, with its less specialized audience. BELL has many characteristics in common with documents annotated for use in the theatre: frequent anticipatory stage directions and other marginal notations marking entrances of complexity or crucial timing (see Stage Directions list); precisely noted music cues (e.g. 2.1.146 ff., 4.2.55 ff.); and highly detailed stage directions at moments requiring processions, a sequence of actions, and/or significant props (e.g. 4.1.88, 5.1.347.1–4). (See Long, 'Stage Directions' and 'Bookkeepers'.) Many of the unclear passages in BELL seem to involve an inability on the part of whoever typeset the play (or perhaps whoever copied a copy from which it was then set) to interpret and reproduce the reading conventions of centre and margin in a theatrical book-holder's copy—to interpret, that is, the difference between annotations and stage directions in the margin of this *hypothetical* copy for BELL and the speeches, speech headings, and stage directions that constitute the main body of the text (5.1.104.1, 4.1.88).

Nevertheless, though it provides a wealth of information when considered from the perspective of seventeenth--century professional theatrical practice, BELL has been universally vilified by modern, professional readers. In the words of BELL's most recent editor, it is 'a deplorably bad quarto', a 'hodge-podge bad quarto', with 'numererous

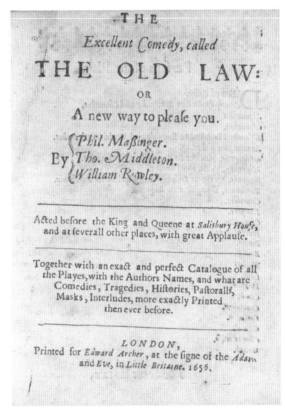

Figure 1. Title-page of BELL.

textual absurdities resulting from misreadings' (Shaw l, *sic*). Though it seems to me more productive to interpret the text than to arraign it, I think it may be said that BELL is 'bad' in one very limited sense: as a material artifact, it has been poorly manufactured in the most literal way. That is, the letters of the type have been inadequately (or sometimes *excessively*) inked, and the result is a text in which some letters (or, more accurately: ostensible letters) do not register on the page. (I thus mean to dissociate my use of the term 'bad' from its traditional usage in New Bibliographic descriptions of so--called 'bad quartos'; 'bad' here applies to the material inking of the text and is meant to imply nothing about: piracy ('unauthorized' printing), irregular entry in the Stationers' Company register, memorial reconstruction, the authority/authorship of the play's readings, etc.) Since some letters—and occasionally, whole words—present in any given copy of BELL are illegible or do not appear at all in other copies, it is often impossible to distinguish a variant (introduced deliberately in the process of printing) from a letter or word that simply does not appear in some copies (4.1.148). Thus, even a full collation of all extant copies (a mode of reading that would have struck an early modern reader as odd) could not produce a 'complete' text of BELL, if by 'complete' we mean the pieces of type lying in a forme in (probably) Jane Bell's print shop in 1656—a text, that is, prior to paper. Early modern readers would have had to make sense of the text as it appeared in the particular copy they read—a process that could have resulted in substantially disparate readings at a number of points in the text (see commentary to 2.1.61). Some readers' readings at other important points in the play have been recorded in surviving copies of BELL and are described in the notes. (For corrections in the Newberry copy, see notes to 5.1.267-74 and Masten, 'Family Values'. A reader of the Folger copy [at an unknown but probably early date] made occasional 'corrections' in the text [5.1.341] and filled in some of the copy's 'missing' letters [4.2.256].)

Though the play and the play-catalogue most frequently bound with it may have been printed and assembled separately, the available evidence suggests that both were printed in the shop of Jane Bell. Probably the widow of the printer Moses Bell, Jane Bell was active 1649-1660, printing a variety of materials, including a number of plays, and several annual 'survey[s] of the yeer' for the Stationers' Company (Morrison 26-27); she published a catalogue of her own 'Bookes Printed' on the title-page verso of her 1655 *True Chronicle History of the life and death of King Lear*. As Price has noted (118), the same ornament appears on the title-page of Bell's 1655 *Lear* and at the end of BELL's catalogue (inverted). While this associates Bell only with the printing of the catalogue, which has signatures (a1-b4^v) separate from the rest of BELL (Shaw li), watermarks occurring within the play text of both Houghton Library copies and within the catalogue bound in the second Houghton copy may suggest a single printer for the entire volume. Further, though the ornamental borders used in the play text and the catalogue are different, some elements of borders from *both* parts of BELL appear on a single page of *The Sun's Darling*, a Dekker-Ford collaboration also printed by Bell in 1656.

Even if the catalogue and the play were both printed by Bell, it is not necessarily the case that they were always bound together. BELL's title-page announces that it was printed 'for Edward Archer', a bookseller apparently active only from 1654-1658 (see ESTC and *BEPD* 1:1491), but the first page of the catalogue advertises the listed plays as available at both 'the *Ben Johnson*'s Head in Thredneedle-street, over against the Exchange', a shop associated with Robert Pollard (Plomer 148), and at Archer's shop 'at the Signe of the *Adam and Eve*, in Little Britain' (a1). This so-called 'Archer catalogue' (*BEPD* 3:1328-38) occurs in only some copies of BELL (of the copies consulted for this edition, FOLGER, HUNTINGTON, HOUGHTON2; also (according to Shaw) the two British Library copies). A different catalogue appears at the end of at least one copy of BELL, at Williams College. It is not clear whether this, the so-called 'Rogers and Ley catalogue' (rpt. *BEPD* 3:1320-1327) was originally bound with the WILLIAMS copy of BELL, or was appended later to supply the perceived lack of a catalogue. BELL's title-page advertisement of a catalogue 'more exactly Printed then ever before' suggests that the 'Archer catalogue' post-dates and responds to the 'Rogers and Ley' list, which is usually found in another volume (*The Careles Shepherdess*, also printed in 1656 [*BEPD* 2:867]) and is the only prior play-catalogue of this kind. (A 1655 Stationers' Company registration also suggests that 'Rogers and Ley' preceded 'Archer' [*BEPD* 3:1320].)

Whatever the location and agency of their production and circulation, the catalogues are themselves significant documents of an emergent bibliophilic and proto-authorial culture. Their publication serves to emphasize the emergence of printed plays as collectible commodities, as well as the emerging (though still highly tentative) notion of singular dramatic authorship in the mid-seventeenth century. (On the emergence of authorship in printed drama, see Masten, *Textual Intercourse*, chapter 4, Masten, 'Ben Jonson's Head', and Taylor, 'Persons', elsewhere in this volume.) The 'Archer catalogue' advertises itself as 'An Exact and perfect CATALOGUE of all the PLAIES that were ever printed ; together, with all the Authors names ; and what are Comedies, Histories, Interludes, Masks, Paftorels, Tragedies...' (a1). Running to 16 pages and 622 titles, this catalogue groups plays alphabetically by title and includes a column of letters noting genre and a column that sometimes attributes authorship (Figure 2). The less elaborate 'Rogers and Ley' catalogue is simply a title list with less frequent notation of authorship in the same column (Figure 3). Many of the authorial identifications in these lists now seem to us to be incorrect ('Hieronimo, both parts... Will.Shakespeare'); some plays whose authorial attributions now seem completely non-controversial are not identified ('Doctor Faustus', 'Troilus and Cressida'); and collaborations are often simplified (the only collaborators identified are Beaumont and Fletcher).

But to take the objective of these catalogues as the factual identification of authorship or authorial shares (Greg, 'Authorship Attributions') is to mistake their function. Unlike the modern *Short Title Catalogue*, of which these lists are only the most distant of analogues, these catalogues are organized to facilitate locating plays by title (rather than by author); to the extent that they treat authorship, the catalogues seem not as interested in consistency with even the available printed attributions as they are in producing an interest (in the literary *and* the economic sense) in printed plays associated with recognizable names—desirable volumes, available for purchase in several London bookshops around 1656. (The 'Kirkman' list of 1661 [rpt. *BEPD* 3:1338f] places an author column first but continues to group the plays alphabetically by title; authorship

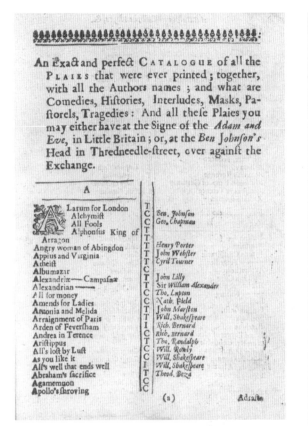

Figure 2. First page of the so-called 'Archer catalogue', bound with some copies of BELL.

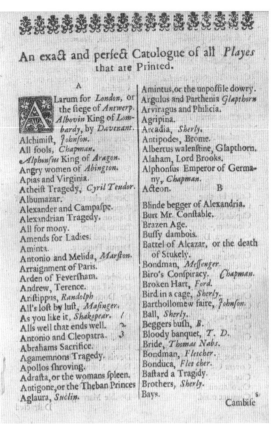

Figure 3. First page of the so-called 'Rogers and Ley catalogue', bound with the WILLIAMS copy of BELL (usually found in *The Careless Shepherdes*, 1656).

is thus marked as more prominent than it had been in the earlier catalogues, but title is still the primary category of organization.) A final indication of this ambivalence toward authorship may be the cataloguing of *Old Law* itself; absent entirely from the 'Rogers and Ley catalogue' in the Williams copy, it appears as the first 'O' entry in the 'Archer catalogue'. There it is listed—in a simplification of the title-page of the very volume in which it is (sometimes) bound—as a comedy by 'Philip Massinger'.

The text of this edition is based on the two copies of BELL in the Houghton Library and one at the Library Company of Philadelphia; copies at the Chapin Library (Williams College), and at the Folger, Huntington, and Newberry Libraries have also been consulted. This edition is an interpretation of BELL that attempts to highlight its own manifold interventions in the 1656 text, and the textual notes for this edition are included with the commentary to the play. Nevertheless, a number of BELL's conventions have been erased in the preparation of a modernized reading text. Unless otherwise mentioned in the notes, stage directions appearing in the right margin of a line in BELL are here printed immediately following that line;

anticipatory stage directions and other apparent notations printed in BELL's right margins can be found in the Stage Directions list. Because of inadequate or excessive inking in the printing of BELL, it is difficult to identify printed ligatures or to distinguish ligatures from letters that have run together; identification of ligatures in the notes should thus be regarded as tentative. As discussed above, the unusual quality of BELL's printing eliminates the possibility of a 'complete' list of press variants; see notes to 1.1.201.1, 2.1.96, and 4.1.148. In some cases of marked divergence from the editorial tradition, a + has been added, following a siglum, to denote the agreement of all subsequent editions after and including the edition cited.

SEE ALSO

Text: *Works*, 1335
Music and dance: this volume, 166
Authorship and date: this volume, 405

WORKS CITED

Massinger, Philip, Thomas Middleton, and William Rowley, *The Excellent Comedy, called The Old Law: or A new way to please you* (1656) (BELL)

Sigla for Copies of BELL consulted

FOLGER, Folger Shakespeare Library
HOUGHTON1, Houghton Library, Harvard University (14432.18)
HOUGHTON2, Houghton Library, Harvard University (14432.18.2)
HUNTINGTON, Huntington Library
LCP, Library Company of Philadelphia
NEWBERRY, Newberry Library
WILLIAMS, Chapin Library, Williams College

Previous Editions Cited

BULLEN, A. H., ed., *Works* (1885), vol. 2
COLERIDGE, Hartley, intr., *The Dramatic Works of Massinger and Ford* (1839/40)
COXETER, Thomas, ed., *The Dramatic Works of Philip Massinger, Compleat* (1761), vol. 4
DYCE, Alexander, ed., *Works* (1840), vol. 1
GIFFORD, William, ed., *The Plays of Philip Massinger* (1805), vol. 4
MASON, John Monck, ed., *The Dramatick Works of Philip Massinger Complete* (1779), vol. 4
SHAW, Catherine M., ed., *The Old Law* (1982)

Additional Sigla in Notes

D, notes attributed to 'D.' (Thomas Davies?), in notes to MASON
PRICE, George R., 'The Authorship and the Manuscript of *The Old Law*', *Huntington Library Quarterly*, 16.2 (1953), 117–39
REVELS, Revels Office manuscript, British Library, Cotton MS Tib.E.X
TAYLOR, Gary, private correspondence

Other Works Cited

'An Act to Restrain Abuses of Players', 3 Jac. I c. 21 (1606)
Arden of Feversham (1592)
The Arte of English Poesie (1589)
Barker, R. H., *Thomas Middleton* (1958)
Barksted, William, *Hiren: or The faire Greeke* (1611)
Barthes, Roland, *S/Z*, trans. Richard Miller (1974)
Bentley, G. E., *The Jacobean and Caroline Stage*, 7 vols (1941–68)
—— *The Profession of Dramatist in Shakespeare's Time, 1590–1642* (1971)
The Bible and Holy Scriptvres, Geneva version (1560)
Brome, Richard, *The New Academy, Or The New Exchange* (1659)
Bromham, A. A., 'The Contemporary Significance of *The Old Law*', *Studies in English Literature, 1500–1900* 24 (1984), 326–39
Bullokar, John, *An English Expositor: Teaching the Interpretation of the hardest words vsed in our Language* (1616, 1621)
Bullokar, William, *Bullokars Booke at large, for the Amendment of Orthographie for English speech* (1580)
Chambers, E. K., Review of Marcham, *Review of English Studies* 1 (1925) 481–4
Coke, Edward, *The First Part of The Institvtes of the Lawes of England* (1628)
Cowell, John, *The Interpreter, or Booke Containing the Signification of Words* (1637)
Dekker, Thomas, and John Ford, *The Sun's Darling* (1656)
The Dictionary of National Biography, vol. 3 (1968)
English Short Title Catalog, online edition (1995–)
Giraldi, Giambattista Cinzio, *Gli Ecatommiti* (1565)
God and the King (1615)

Greg, W. W., 'Authorship Attributions in the Early Play-lists, 1656–1671', *Edinburgh Bibliographical Society Transactions* 2 (1946), 305–29
Hauteseille, Jean de, trans. *Historia septum sapientum* (c.1200)
The Holy Bible, Authorized Version (1611)
Homer, *Odyssey*
James I, *Basilikon Doron. Or His Maiesties Instrvctions to His Dearest Sonne, Henry the Prince* (1603)
—— *His Maiesties Speach in this last Session of Parliament* (1605)
—— *The Trve Lawe of free Monarchies* (1598)
—— *The Workes of the Most High and Mightie Prince, Iames* (1616)
Jonson, Ben, *The Case Is Altered* (1609)
Kyd, Thomas, *The Spanish Tragedie* (1592)
Lant, Thomas, *Sequitur celebritas et pompa funeris [of Philip Sidney]* (1587)
Long, William B., 'Bookkeepers and Playhouse Manuscripts: A Peek at the Evidence', *Shakespeare Newsletter* 44 (1994), 3
—— 'Stage Directions: A Misinterpreted Factor in Determining Textual Provenance', *TEXT* 2 (1985), 121–37
Marcham, Frank, *The King's Office of the Revels 1610–1622* (1925)
Massinger, Philip, *The Picture* (1630)
Masten, Jeffrey A., 'Beaumont and/or Fletcher: Collaboration and the Interpretation of Renaissance Drama', *ELH* 59 (1992), 337–56
—— 'Ben Jonson's Head', *Shakespeare Studies* 28 (2000), 160–8
—— 'Family values: euthanasia, editing, and *The Old Law*', *Textual Practice* 9.3 (1995), 445–58
—— *Textual Intercourse: Collaboration, Authorship, and Sexualities in Renaissance Drama* (1997)
Maxwell, Baldwin, *Studies in Beaumont, Fletcher, and Massinger* (1939)
The Mirrovr of Policie (1599)
Montaigne, Michel de, 'A custome of the Ile of Cea', *Essayes*, trans. John Florio, (1603)
More, Thomas, *Utopia* (1516, rpt. 1597)
Morrison, Paul G., *Index of Printers, Publishers and Booksellers in Donald Wing's Short-title Catalogue* (1955)
Morris, Edgar Coit, 'On the Date and Composition of *The Old Law*', *PMLA* 17.1, NS 10.1 (1902), 1–70
Oxford Classical Dictionary, 2nd edition (1970)
Peck, Linda Levy, *Court Patronage and Corruption in Early Stuart England* (1990)
Pelling, Margaret, and Richard M. Smith, Introduction, *Life, Death, and the Elderly: Historical Perspectives* (1991)
Plato, *Cratylus* (c.369 BCE), trans. B. Jowett, *The Dialogues of Plato*, 4th edition, vol. 3 (1953), 41–106
Plomer, Henry R., *A Dictionary of the Booksellers and Printers Who Were at Work in England, Scotland, and Ireland from 1641 to 1667* (1907)
Plutarch, *Lives of the Noble Grecians and Romans*, trans. Thomas North (1579, rpt. Tudor Translations 1895)
Price, George R., 'The Authorship and the Manuscript of *The Old Law*', *Huntington Library Quarterly* 16.2 (1953), 117–39
Purchas, Samuel, *Purchas His Pilgrimage* (1614)
Rastell, John, *The exposicions of the termes of the lawes* (1618)
Rich, Barnaby, *Farewell to Military Profession* (1581)
Rider, John, *Bibliotheca scholastica: A double dictionarie* (1617)
Shakespeare, William, *True Chronicle History of the life and death of King Lear* (1655)
Sophocles, *Antigonê* (Latin trans. 1581)
'Statute of Artificers', 5 Eliz. c. 4 (1562), sect. 5, 17
Swinburn, Henrie, *A Briefe Treatise of Testaments and Last Willes* (1590)

Taylor, Gary, 'Middleton and Rowley—and Heywood: *The Old Law* and New Attribution Technologies', *Papers of the Bibliographical Society of America* 96 (2002), 165–217

—— '"The Old Law" or "An Old Law"?', *Notes and Queries* 49 (2002), 256–8

Trollope, Anthony, *The Fixed Period* (1882)

Terence, *Eunuchus*, trans. Nicholas Udall, *Floures for Latin Spekynge* (1533)

Vesalius, Andreas, *De humani corporis fabrica libri* (1543)

Virgil, *The Bvcoliks of Pvblivs Virgilivs Maro*, trans. Abraham Fleming (1589)

—— *The First Foure Bookes of Virgils Aeneis*, trans. Richard Stanyhurst (1583)

Waith, Eugene, *The Pattern of Tragicomedy in Beaumont and Fletcher* (1952)

Webster, John, *The Deuils Law-case* (1623)

Whitney, Geffrey, *A Choice of Emblemes* (1586)

Wilson, Thomas, *The Art of Rhetorique* (1585, rpt. *Tudor and Stuart Library* 1909)

STAGE DIRECTIONS

Persons of the Play

BELL's *dramatis personae* list, reproduced in an unedited transcript below, seems to have been prepared by someone not entirely familiar with the play, since it contains a number of mistakes (making Creon and Antigona, for example, parents to both Simonides and Cleanthes). The list originally appeared on the verso of BELL's title-page, facing the first page of the play's text.

Perſons of the Play.

DUke of *Epire.*
Creon, Father to *Simonides* and *Cleanthes.*
Simonides ⎫
⎬ 2 Courtiers
Cleanthes. ⎭
Liſander Husband to *Eugenia* and Uncle to *Cleanthes.*
Leonides an old man.
Antigona, Mother to *Simonides* and *Cleanthes.*
Hippolita, Wife to *Cleanthes.*
Eugenia, Wife to *Liſander* and Mother to *Parthenia.*
Parthenia, Daughter to *Eugenia.*
Courtiers.
Lawyers.
Clowne.
Executioner.
Butler.
Bayliff.
Taylor.
Cook.
Drawer.
Clerk.
Couchmen.
Footmen.
Guard.
Clowns Wife.
Wench.

The Scene EPIRE.

Quarto Stage Directions

If the location of a direction is not noted, it occurs within the column of text at BELL's equivalent of the specified line number. Square brackets enclose the word in the control-text after which a specified stage direction follows, in cases where a line number in this edition continues over onto another of BELL's lines. As discussed in the Textual Introduction, the distinction between stage directions and other text in BELL is not always clear; on specific instances, see Commentary.

1.1.0.1   Act. I. Scen. I. (centred, between rules)
1.1.0.2   *Enter* Simonides, *and two Lawyers.*
1.1.70.1   *Enter* Cleanthes.
1.1.201.1   *Enter* Cre on | & Antigona. (right margin of 1.1.201–2)

1.1.254   —— weeping. (not clearly a stage direction, but interpreted as such, THIS EDITION)
1.1.313.1   *Exeunt.* (right margin of 1.1.313)
1.1.315.1   *Exeunt.* (right margin of 1.1.314–15)
1.1.334.1   *Enter* Leonides | *and* Hippolita. (right margin of 1.1.333–4)
1.1.492   *Exeunt.* (right margin of 1.1.492)
1.1.492.1   *Finis Actus Primi.* (followed by an ornamental border)
2.1.0.1   Act. II. Scen. I. (centred, between rules)
2.1.0.2   *Enter* Duke, 3. Courtiers *and* Executioner.
2.1.70.1   *Enter* Creon, Anti-|gona & Simonides. (right margin of 2.1.70)
2.1.146.1   *Recorders.* (right margin of 2.1.146, possibly an anticipatory stage direction)
2.1.150–2.1.150.2   *Recorders. Enter* | Cleanthes & Hi-|polita *with a hearf* (right margin of 2.1.150 [funerall] through 2.1.152 [Cleanthes.])
2.1.202.1   *Floriſh* (right margin of 2.1.202)
2.1.216.1–2   *Enter* Butler, Tailor,Bayly,Cook,Coachman,*and* Footman.
2.1.275   *Exeunt.* (right margin of 2.1.275)
2.2.0.1   *Enter* Eugenia, *and* Parthenia.
2.2.28.1   *Enter* Courtiers. (right margin of 2.2.28)
2.2.46.1–2.2.47   *Enter* Simonides, Coachman. (right margin of 2.2.46)
2.2.63.1   *Ent.er* Liſander. (right margin of 2.2.63)
2.2.99   *Exit.* (right margin of 2.2.99)
2.2.121.1   *Enter* Parthenia.
2.2.123.1   *Exeunt.* (right margin of 2.2.123 [already ?])
2.2.138.1   *Enter* Hippolita. (between two parts of 2.2.139)
2.2.199   *Exit.* (right margin of 2.2.199)
2.2.208   *Exit.* (right margin of 2.2.208)
2.2.208.1   *Finis Actus Secnndi.*
3.1.0.1   Act. III. Scen. I. (centred, between rules, preceded by an ornamental border)
3.1.0.2   *Enter the Clown and Clark.*
3.1.108.1   *Enter the* Cook, *the* Taylor, Bayliffe, *and* Butler.
3.1.227.1   *Enter* Wife. (right margin of 3.1.227)
3.1.229.1   *Exit.* (right margin of 3.1.229)
3.1.241.1   *Exeunt.* (right margin of 3.1.241)
3.1.321.1   *Swouns.* (right margin of 3.1.321)
3.1.330.1   *Swouns.* (right margin of 3.1.330)
3.1.343   *Exit.* (right margin of 3.1.343)
3.1.354   *Exit.* (right margin of 3.1.353–4)
3.2.0.1–2   *Enter* Eugenia *at one Dore*, Simonides, Courtiers *at the other.*
3.2.41.1   *Enter* Liſander. (right margin of 3.2.41)
3.2.67.1   *Ent.* Dan. (right margin of in the margin of 3.2.67–9, following [there.]) Of the copies consulted, only LCP and WILLIAMS have the period at the end of this direction.

3.2.114   *Entɔr with* | Glasses. (right margin of 3.2.114) (with possible ff ligature)

3.2.131–3.2.131.1   *A Galliard La-|mi niard* (right margin of 3.2.130–1). A space appears in the third word in some copies of BELL.

3.2.194   *Exit.* (right margin of 3.2.194 [ftay.])

3.2.204.1   *Enter* Cleanthes (right margin of 3.2.204 [out fides.])

3.2.216.1   *Exeunt* Courtiers& Eu-|genia. (right margin of 3.2.216–17, contiguous with the text)

3.2.253   *Exit* Lifander. (right margin of 3.2.253)

3.2.255   *Enter* Eugenia. (right margin of 3.2.254)

3.2.300   *Exit.* (right margin of 3.2.300)

3.2.305.1   *Enter* Simonides (right margin of 3.2.305)

3.2.315   *Exeunt.* (right margin of 3.2.315)

3.2.315.1   *Finis Actus Tertii.* (followed by an ornamental border)

4.1.0.1   Act. IV. Scen. I. (centred, between rules)

4.1.0.2–3   *Enter* Clowne, Butler, Bayliff, Taylor, Cooke, Drawer, Wench.

4.1.17.1   *Enter* Drawer. (right margin of 4.1.17)

4.1.77.1   *Enter* Drawer. (right margin of 4.1.76–7)

4.1.88.1   *Old women.* | *Gnothoes:* | *Dance.* (right margin of 4.1.85–8. *Gnothoes* is contiguous with the text [let em come]; THIS EDITION interprets the word as a misplaced speech heading for 4.1.89)

4.1.88.2–4.1.89.1   *The Dance of old women maskt, then offer to take the men, they a-|gree all but* Gnothoes; *he fits with his Wench after they whi^{er}.* (on two lines following 4.1.89)

4.1.91.1–2   *Exeunt each with* | *his wife manet* | Gnothoes *wife unmaskt.* (right margin of 4.1.91–3)

4.1.165   *Ex.* (right margin of 4.1.163–5)

4.1.169   *Exit.* (right margin of 4.1.168–9)

4.2.0.1   *Enter* Cleanthes.

4.2.7   *Hip.* (left of 4.2.7, as if the speech heading, probably a misplaced anticipatory stage direction for Hippolita's entrance at 4.2.22)

4.2.22   *Enter* | Hippolita. (right margin of 4.2.21–2)

4.2.31.1   *Ent.* Leonides. (to the right of 4.2.32, contiguous with the text)

4.2.55.1   *A Horne.* (right margin of 4.2.55)

4.2.59.1   *A Horne.* (right margin of 4.2.59)

4.2.63.1   *A Horne.* (right margin of 4.2.63 [twice.])

4.2.68   *Enter* Duke, Simonides, Courtiers, *and* Executioner. (following 4.2.66–4.2.67.1)

4.2.148.1   *Exeunt* Courtiers & Sim. (right margin of 4.2.148 [ftill.])

4.2.160.1   *Enter* Courtiers Simonides Leonides.

4.2.181.1–2   *Exeunt* | *with* Leonides. (right margin of 4.2.181–2)

4.2.209   *Enter* | Eugenia. (right margin of 4.2.208–9)

4.2.243.1   *Enter* Simonides, *and* Courtiers.

4.2.256.1   *Enter* Officers (right margin of 4.2.256)

4.2.275   *Exeunt.* (right margin of 4.2.274–5)

4.2.275.1   *Finis Actus Quarti.*

5.1.0.1   Act. V. Scen. I. (centred, between rules)

5.1.0.2–4   *Sword and Mace carried before them.* | *Enter* Simonides, *and the* Courtiers.

5.1.10   *Eugenia.* (right margin, an anticipatory stage direction)

5.1.22.1   *Enter* Eugenia (right margin of 5.1.22)

5.1.37   Lifander *and* Guardian. (right margin, following [Aprill.], an anticipatory stage direction)

5.1.46.2   *Enter* Hippolita. (right margin of 5.1.46, [bufinefs])

5.1.80   *without fee.* (right margin of 5.1.81; THIS EDITION interprets these words as part of the spoken text)

5.1.83   *Exit.* (right margin of 5.1.83)

5.1.83.1–2   *Enter* Eugenia, *with* Lifander Prifoner, *a* Guard.

5.1.104   *Florifh.* (right margin)

5.1.104.1   *Duk.* A flemifh (as if a speech, at the top of a new page I3^v, p. 62)

5.1.104.1   *Enter the* Duke. (right margin of previous)

5.1.127–30   *Hip.* (left of first half of 5.1.128–9, as if a speech prefix; probably a misplaced part of the following anticipatory stage direction)

5.1.127–30   Cleanthes Guard. (right margin of 5.1.130 [ftrength], an anticipatory stage direction)

5.1.135.2–3   *Enter a* Guard *with* Cleanthes, Hippollita *weeping after him.* (following the completion of 5.1.135)

5.1.146   *Exit.* (right margin of 5.1.146 [freedome.])

5.1.147   *Exit.* (right margin of 5.1.147)

5.1.249–50   *Recorders.* | *Old men.* (right margin, an anticipatory stage direction)

5.1.251.1–2   *Mufick,* Sons *and the old men appeare.*

5.1.283   *Kneeles.* (margin, to the far right of [Father.])

5.1.311–12   *Eugenia.* (right margin, probably a bookkeeper's mark to emphasize the following entrance)

5.1.312.1   *Enter* Eugenia.

5.1.314.1   *She founds.* (right margin of 5.1.314)

5.1.330–1   *Hippolita.* (right margin, probably a bookkeeper's mark to emphasize the following entrance)

5.1.332.1   *Enter* Hip. (right margin of 5.1.332)

5.1.336.1   *Shee faints.* (right margin of first half of 5.1.336 [Leonides.])

5.1.344.1   *Mufick.* (right margin of 5.1.344)

5.1.346.1   *Mufick* (right margin of 5.1.346)

5.1.347   *Clo. &c.* (at left margin, on the line following 5.1.347; probably a bookkeeper's mark emphasizing this large and important entrance)

5.1.347.1–4   *Enter* Mufick *one carrying a Bridecake,* | *the* Clowne, *the reft with them old* Women. (centred, beginning on the same line as the previous)

5.1.347.1–4   *Enter* Clowne, *and* Wench, *the reft with the old women,* | *the* Clownes *wife,* Mufick, *and a* Bride *Cake to* | *the wedding.* (centred, on the lines following the previous, from which this duplicate direction is separated by a blank line)

5.1.618   *Difcover the* | *Executioner.* (right margin of 5.1.618–19)

5.1.624.2   *F I N I S.* (centred between rules, in large type)

LINEATION NOTES

1.1.127–8 Listen...you.] THIS EDITION; *verse* BELL (*1 line*)

1.1.131 A...not] DYCE; BELL (*ambiguously prose or verse*)

1.1.138 There...certain] GIFFORD; BELL (*ambiguously prose or verse*)

1.1.184–5 'That...death.'] GIFFORD; *verse* BELL: threescore |

1.1.192–4 O...sir:] COXETER; BELL (*ambiguously prose or verse*)

1.1.201 There's...sir] THIS EDITION; BELL (*ambiguously prose or verse*); *verse* GIFFORD

1.1.238–9 And...heat,] COXETER; the | BELL

1.1.255 'Cause...end.] GIFFORD; BELL (*1 line, ambiguously prose or verse*)

1.1.277–8 I...sir.] THIS EDITION follows BELL in setting this speech as two lines of verse, but the scansion may suggest that all or parts of the speech may function as prose.

1.1.314–15 Cleanthes...dead.] BELL. If Cleanthes's 'Why...villain' is not a part-line picking up from the end of Simonides's speech, 'Why...corrupt' may form a full iambic line, followed by a part line ('a...example'), a configuration that smooths the rhythm of the line but abandons BELL's lineation.

1.1.324–7 Weak...it,] BELL; teeming | making | darling | GIFFORD. The disrupted iambic rhythm of these lines makes lineation here uncertain.

1.1.390–1 And...course] COXETER; BELL (*1 line*)

2.1.8–9 He...lord] COXETER; these | BELL

2.1.24–7 An...vamped!] COXETER; *verse* BELL: talks? | endure |

2.1.28–30 Now...us.] THIS EDITION; *verse* BELL: thankfull, |

2.1.31 Ay...know't.] BELL (*1 type line*). See commentary.

2.1.37–40 'Tis...cheeks.] BELL; *prose* COXETER; *verse* GIFFORD: be: | merit; | act, | tongues, |. Depending on syllabic contraction, the lines might be edited as verse, ending as follows: lord, | proves | not | .

2.1.41–2 But...it.] THIS EDITION; *verse* BELL: long, |

2.1.116–17 Worth...read.] THIS EDITION follows BELL in printing two consecutive trimeter lines; alternatively, Antigona's speech may be one hexameter line.

2.1.137–42 'Tis...seven-and-fifty,] BELL; *verse* COXETER: Mother; | yourself, | wise, | Time.

2.1.158–9 One...joy.] GIFFORD; participate | BELL

2.1.163–7 I...yet.] GIFFORD; *verse* BELL: Lord | wept | apparently | ; *verse* COXETER: Lord, | Part of | Sunshine; |

2.1.203–4 I...like.] BELL; *verse* COXETER: e'en |

2.1.214–16 That...covetous.] COXETER; *verse* MASON: else | Way. | ; *verse and prose* BELL: follow | One...be-|gin...covetous. The speech moves from verse to prose at this point, ambiguously: there are initial capitals, but the lines are justified.

2.1.220–3 My...munching] GIFFORD; *prose* BELL. 'Livery' is probably disyllabic.

2.1.227–8 Unless...used to] GIFFORD; *prose* BELL. See next note; in 2.1.226–30, BELL mixes prose and verse.

2.1.228–30 Thou'st...sight.] BELL; *verse* GIFFORD: when | doublet |

2.1.238–9 Butler...without.] COXETER; *verse* BELL: Cooke, |

2.1.240–3 The...me.] COXETER *prose*; BELL (*justified as prose, but capitalizing initial words as if verse*): doe | the | to |

2.1.252–3 But...business?] GIFFORD; *verse* BELL (*1 line*)

2.2.4–28 Yes...lost] BELL; *prose* COXETER, which sets many subsequent speeches in the scene as prose (e.g., 2.2.37–8, 2.2.40–2).

2.2.53 Who's...i'faith.] THIS EDITION *verse*; BELL (*2 lines, ambiguously prose or verse*)

2.2.70–1 I...dead] GIFFORD; *prose* (*1 line*) BELL

2.2.71–3 man...tackling.] COXETER; *verse* BELL: thee, |

2.2.118–19 Gentlemen...house,] GIFFORD; *1 line* BELL

2.2.152–3 Your...blow.] COXETER; fixt | BELL

2.2.198–9 I have...gone.] COXETER; *prose* BELL

3.1.339 Or...conscience] BELL (*1 line, uncapitalized*); *prose* COXETER+

3.1.351 'Tis...gone,] GIFFORD; *prose* BELL

3.1.353–4 'Tis...conscience.] COXETER (*prose*); *ambiguously prose or verse* BELL (*1 line*). The line may be function as a concluding (irregular) verse couplet, rhyming 'o' conscience' and 'a conscience.'

3.2 This scene's verse is rarely regular, and the signs in BELL for the division of prose from verse are ambiguous, especially in the case of the scene's many short, interjections occupying less than a single line of type. Though some editors thus render much of the scene in prose (cf. MASON), THIS EDITION largely follows the lineation of BELL, even where metrically irregular, and (tentatively) constructs metrical lines out of part-line speeches where these seem audible.

3.2.69–71 Come...gentlemen.] THIS EDITION; day, | agen. | Gentlemen BELL;

3.2.74–5 Nay...'tis—] GIFFORD; *1 line* BELL

3.2.104–5 O...longer.] GIFFORD; *1 line* BELL

3.2.140–1 What...time?] COXETER; *1 line* BELL

3.2.155 There...again.] COXETER; *2 lines* BELL: third | and...agen.

3.2.164–6 Ay...no.] THIS EDITION; *verse* BELL: not | ; nothing | not | GIFFORD; voluntarily | out | SHAW. BELL's line-break is also a page-break (G–Gv).

3.2.177–9 O...glass.] BELL; *2 undivided lines* SHAW: rope |

3.2.189–90 No...again.] THIS EDITION; *1 line* BELL

3.2.193–4 Farewell...stay.] COXETER; *1 line* BELL

3.2.246–7 The...equal] COXETER; heart, | BELL

3.2.257–8 'Tis...way] THIS EDITION; *1 line* BELL

3.2.266–7 Bless...woman!] COXETER; *1 line* BELL

3.2.301–2 I'll...pleasure,] COXETER; *1 line* BELL

3.2.309–10 You...minds you] GIFFORD; *1 line* BELL

4.1.38–40 Some...house?] COXETER; *verse* BELL: conscience. |

4.1.65 whether...no.] BELL (c. w.); *verse* BELL (*on a separate type line, capitalized*). The uncapitalized catchword ('whether' G4–G4ᵛ) makes clear that the line continues as prose.

4.1.100 husband...doing?] COXETER; *verse* BELL. In BELL, 4.1.99 breaks off in mid-line of prose (you, |); the next line is set as verse.

4.1.135 The...child.] COXETER; *1 line* BELL (*ambiguously prose or verse*). Possibly a hexameter line.

4.1.138 No...proof] COXETER; *1 line* BELL (*ambiguously prose or verse*). A possible pentameter, with the elision of 'in the.'

4.2.58 What...you] *1 type line* BELL

4.2.66–7 A...before] BELL; knew | GIFFORD

4.2.151–2 O...minute?] COXETER; *1 line* BELL

4.2.159–60 Panting...me.] COXETER; BELL vengeance. |

4.2.196 This...nature] BELL; overturns | COXETER

4.2.218 Less...way] *1 type line* BELL

4.2.245 Yes...one] BELL; Sir, | COXETER

4.2.274–5 I'll...me.] MASON; such | *verse* BELL

5.1.1–2 Be...please] COXETER; an | BELL

5.1.21–2   Hereafter…highness.] DYCE; one,| BELL

5.1.23–8   Widow…seventeenth,] BELL. Possibly prose.

5.1.45–6   Do…sessions.] COXETER; short| BELL

5.1.78–9   You…friends.] COXETER; *prose* BELL: ends| (*2 lines apparently justified, second line beginning lower case, but divided as here*)

5.1.84   Eugenia…guard] GIFFORD; *2 lines* BELL: come.|

5.1.128–9   Your…him.] BELL (*1 type line*)

5.1.139   To…he—] COXETER; *2 lines* BELL: *Cleanthes,*|

5.1.188–9   Hewed…Troy,] THIS EDITION; fire, through| BELL. See textual note.

5.1.242–3   And…madmen.] COXETER; of| BELL

5.1.245–6   'Tis…ends.] BELL suggests two lines of trimeter; alternatively, the Duke speaks a single hexameter line, but BELL's arrangement may stress the Duke's line as a substitute for Simonides's which precedes it.

5.1.249–50   I…effects.] THIS EDITION; doubt| BELL

5.1.252–3   Pray…changed] GIFFORD; *prose* BELL: comforta-|bly (*second line not justified*); *verse* COXETER: Heaven,| comfortably,|

5.1.258–9   I…me.] COXETER; *prose* BELL

5.1.267–9   O…mother.] THIS EDITION; *verse* on| father| BELL

5.1.278–9   That…cruel.] BELL suggests two trimeter lines (but the apparent couplet in THIS EDITION is the result of modernization [BELL: vild]).

5.1.284   That…forgot.] DYCE; *2 lines* BELL: know|

5.1.285–6   I…now.] GIFFORD *prose*; *1 type line* BELL (*ambiguously prose or verse*)

5.1.292–6   'It…goodness.'] COXETER; *verse* BELL: learned| heire| inheritance| time|

5.1.298–9   Though…allowed.] COXETER; *verse* BELL (*2 lines, both beginning lower case but unjustified*): twenty,|

5.1.306   From…sir.] GIFFORD *verse*; BELL (*ambiguously prose or verse*)

5.1.307–8   Whom…such] COXETER; *verse* BELL: such|. The line is unjustified, but after the page-break (K2–K2^v), the speech continues in justified prose.

5.1.321   You…louder,] COXETER; *verse* BELL: lowder,|

5.1.329–31   'And…Cleanthes.'] COXETER; *verse* BELL: offending| *Hippolita,*|

5.1.333–5   Ah…else] COXETER; *prose* BELL

5.1.348   From this point on, the scene shifts frequently between prose and verse. These transitions are not always clearly marked in BELL.

5.1.350–1   Stay…jollity.] GIFFORD; *verse* BELL: reason|

5.1.361–2   Good…forced?] THIS EDITION; *verse* BELL: em|

5.1.364–5   I…forced.] THIS EDITION; *verse* BELL: not|

5.1.376–8   This…*amoris.*] GIFFORD; *verse* BELL: *uxoris ,*|

5.1.391   neck. 'I] COXETER; neck| I BELL (*beginning a new prose paragraph*)

5.1.476   I…pleasant.] GIFFORD *prose*; *1 type line* BELL

5.1.479–81   I'll…women.] MASON; *verse* BELL: come| doe|

5.1.517   The…wipes.] COXETER; *2 lines* BELL: Bridegroome|

5.1.520–2   This…have.] GIFFORD; *verse* BELL: yet,| now,| honestly|

5.1.530–7   Such…terms.] THIS EDITION; *verse* BELL: salt| water,| subjects,| do| not| Law|

5.1.545–52   I…me.] GIFFORD; *verse* BELL: did,| been| you,| Beefe| like.| run| help| keepe|

MORE DISSEMBLERS BESIDES WOMEN

Edited by John Jowett

Two New Plays

More Dissemblers appeared before *Women, Beware Women* in a volume published in 1657 by Humphrey Moseley (see Reed, 1929) titled *Two New Playes* (Wing M1989). On 9 September 1653 Moseley had made a large block entry in the Stationers' Register which included the following:

More Dissemblers besides Women.
A right Woman, or Women
beware of Women.
No Witt, no helpe like a Woman } Mr Tho:
The Puritan Maid, modest Wife Midleton.
& Wanton Widdow. by.

A Right Woman was evidently a different play from *Women Beware*; the title was re-entered in the Stationers' Register for Humphrey Robinson and Moseley in 1660, and reattributed to Beaumont and Fletcher. That Middleton was indeed the author of this lost play is suggested by the similar phrase 'a right man' in *Revenger* 1.1.94.

Three years after the entry the three extant Middleton plays named in it remained unprinted but were announced as amongst '*Books I do purpose to Print very speedtly* [sic.].' in an advertising list of '*Books Printed for Humphrey Moseley*' (BEPD, Separate List VI^A, 1656):

244. More Dissemblers then
Women.
245. Women beware Women. } By *Tho. Midleton*,
Gent.
246. No { Witt }
     { Help } like a Womans.

All three plays were published by Moseley in 1657, the first two as a single octavo volume, 'TWO NEW PLAYES... WRITTEN By *Tho. Middleton*, Gent.'.

Mulryne (1975) used Miller's reproductions of Thomas Newcomb's ornamental stock (1950–1) to identify Newcomb as the printer of *Two New Playes*; Johnson (1976) made the same identification for *No Wit*. Newcomb's business was prosperous and expanding; he provided well-printed texts. The engraving of Middleton and Moseley's advertising list, one or both of which were bound with some copies, were printed separately and are not intrinsic to the collation of the book, which runs: A^4, B–N^8, O^4. Preliminaries are arranged somewhat confusingly:

[A1] Collection title: 'TWO NEW | PLAYES...'
[A1^v] Blank
[A2] Play title: 'MORE | DISSEMBLERS | BESIDES | WOMEN. | [rule] | A | COMEDY, | BY | *Tho. Middleton*, Gent.'
[A2^v] Blank
A3 Epistle: 'TO THE | READER.'
[A3^v] '*To the Reader*:' continued
[A4] Commendatory poem 'UPON | The Tragedy of | My Familiar Acquaintance, | *THO. MIDDLETON*.', signed '*Nath. Richards*.'
[A4^v] 'The Actors Names.'

The epistle is printed as follows:

When these amongst others of Mr. *Thomas Middleton*'s Excellent Poems, came to my hands, I was not a little confident but that his name would prove as great an Inducement for thee to Read, as me to Print them: Since those Issues of his Brain that have already seen the Sun, have by their worth gained themselves a free entertainment amongst all that are ingenious: And I am most certain, that these will no way lessen his Reputation, nor hinder his Admission to any Noble and Recreative Spirits. All that I require at thy hands, is to continue the Author in his deserved Esteem, and to accept of my Endeavors which have ever been to please thee.

Farewel.

The actor and occasional dramatist Nathaniel Richards's commendatory poem reads:

Women beware Women; 'tis a true Text
Never to be forgot: Drabs of State vext,
Have Plots, Poysons, Mischeifs that seldom miss,
To murther Vertue with a venom kiss.
Witness this worthy *Tragedy*, exprest
By him that well deserv'd among the best
Of *Poets* in his time: He knew the rage,
Madness of Women crost; and for the Stage
Fitted their humors, Hell-bred Malice, Strife
Acted in State, presented to the life.
I that have seen't, can say, having just cause,
Never came *Tragedy* off with more applause.

One might have expected the individual play title (A2) to follow the epistle to the reader (A3), which refers to plural 'Poems', and the commendatory poem (A4), which refers to *Women Beware*. Yet another feature of the text that causes confusion over the relationship between *More Dissemblers* and the volume as a whole is that after the half-title to *Dissemblers* on B1 NEWCOMB misleadingly adds 'The First Part.'.

The text of *More Dissemblers* occupies B1–G2, numbered 1–83; p.6 is mispaginated 4. A press correction to the running title on C7^v alters 'Dissembers' to 'Dissemblers'.

G2ᵛ is blank; the title-page 'WOMEN | BEWARE WOMEN. | [rule] | A | TRAGEDY, | BY | *Tho. Middleton*, Gent.' follows on G3. After an untitled list of dramatic parts on G3ᵛ, the text of *Women Beware* begins on G4 and continues to O3; G4ᵛ–O3 are numbered 88–197, with pp. 142–3 mispaginated 140–1. The blank leaf O4 is absent in some copies.

Moseley's book-list VIᴬ is appended to many copies of both *No Wit* and *Two New Playes*; the section titled '*Incomparable Comedies and Tragedies written by several Ingenious Authors*', and headed by the Beaumont and Fletcher folio, suggests a planned drama series. Moseley adopted the octavo format for other dramatists who were not seen to merit publication in folio. Along with *No Wit*, which was published in the same year, *Two New Playes* contributed to an unprecedented project amounting to 'a single publisher's bibliographically standard series' of pre-Interregnum drama (Kewes, 1995). 'Two [or more] New Plays' was a formula favoured for general titles, and the typography and layout of the title-pages take a standardized form. An optional extra leaf prefixed to some copies of *Two New Playes* and some of *No Wit* presents a handsome engraved portrait of Middleton inscribed '*Vera Effigies* | *Tho: Middletoni Gent:*'; the engraving follows the example of Moseley's octavo editions of Shirley, Brome, and others, and is in accordance with Moseley's claim to have been 'very ambitious to have got Mr. *Beaumonts* picture' for the 1647 Beaumont and Fletcher Folio.

As with other Moseley play collections, the separate title-pages enabled the individual plays to be bound and sold separately. However, the preliminaries anticipate the Middleton volume as a collection, and so does the continuous page numbering—in contrast with the separate pagination of, for example, the texts in Philip Massinger's *Three New Playes* published by Moseley in 1655. Indeed only one identified copy (in the British Library) is of one play alone (*More Dissemblers*). Moseley had other options available to him. Gerald Langbaine in 1691 described *More Dissemblers*, *Women Beware*, and *No Wit* as 'all in one Volume'. One such book in Worcester College may have originally been owned by Langbaine himself. Another can be found in the Library of Congress. On the collective title-page, 'TWO' has been inked out by hand and '3' written to the left of it; the bracket left of the two printed titles has been extended downwards, and '3 [extended bracket] No Wit like a Woman's' has been very carefully handwritten in black ink. Moseley's similar bracketing of the three plays in his advertising list shows that he conceived of them as a group. It seems likely that some copies of the two books were bound together for purchasers from Moseley's shop. One might wonder why they were not brought out as three new plays in the first place, but the procedure was not unique: in another instance Moseley printed two of the three advertised plays by Lodowick Carlell as 'TWO NEW PLAYES'.

One might also wonder as to whether the full titles could have been modified to suit Moseley's purposes, for

they are surprisingly close in theme and wording for three plays that casually happened into a stationer's hands from at least two different theatre companies. But a variation on the *No Wit* title is found heading the new prologue (published in 1646) that Shirley wrote for the 1638 Dublin revival; *Dissemblers* is recorded as a King's Men play in 1641 (see below); and in his commendatory verse Richards was happy to recognize *Women Beware* by the name on Moseley's title-page. *Dissemblers* finds further witness by way of a strong echo in the play's final line, 'There's more dissemblers than of womenkind'; and the closing lines of *Women Beware* include the paraphrase 'O, the deadly snares | That women set for women'. Though *No Wit* could conceivably have been renamed by Shirley almost twenty years before the three plays were published, even this seems relatively unlikely (Jowett, 1991).

As might be expected in a book printed so long after the plays were first written, the spellings, punctuation, and most details of page layout are heavily regularized as compared with Middleton's autograph manuscripts of *A Game at Chess*. It is very difficult to tell whether the printing process is responsible for this regularization in its entirety or merely a part of it, hence there is some difficulty in determining the nature of the manuscript used as the printer's copy. The text of both plays is characterized by a sprinkling of colons in place of full stops at the end of speeches. As many of these are italic with a faint upper point, they probably result from a peculiarity of the type-case, and so offer no evidence as to the copy.

More Dissemblers

In NEWCOMB, stage directions are relatively detailed and full, and most of them probably derive from Middleton's hand. Mason (ed., 1974) cited the direction after 1.3.87 as designed for the reader rather than for theatrical use, but narrational phrasing is here necessary to provide a clear statement of complex dramatic action. If Moseley obtained the manuscript from someone who had been involved with the King's Men, that manuscript is likely to have derived from a playbook. Indeed, a comparison with *No Wit* suggests that the papers must have been too well ordered to have constituted an authorial draft. The marking of scenes is further testimony against a Middleton autograph.

The play's songs were recycled. 'Cupid is Venus' only Joy' probably originated in Middleton's lost *Masque of Cupids* (1614) as the two-stanza song preserved in extant manuscripts. The text for *Dissemblers* was evidently reduced and the stanzaic form modified (see Jowett, 1994, and Textual Note to 1.4.89–99). A third stanza appears in the song as printed in *Chaste Maid*, where the song was evidently added for a revival. Similarly, the Gypsy song 'Come, my dainty doxies' is quoted, in part, in *The Widow*.

In 1623 *More Dissemblers* was relicensed as an old play. It was subsequently performed at Court in 1624. Herbert described the play as 'free from alterations' in 1623, but the play could hypothetically have been revised for Whitehall the following year. Such a revision might in principle have sought to strengthen the links with *The Duchess of Malfi*, which was itself revived between 1619 and 1623 and published in quarto in 1623. But a better candidate for revision would have been the Gypsy scenes, which would have become topical after Jonson's masque *The Gypsies Metamorphosed* (1621; see Critical Introduction). The palm-reading episode could have been highlighted in a revision so as to remind an audience of Buckingham playing the role of the masque's First Gypsy. However, it is necessary to the plot for Dondolo to be robbed and so disillusioned from his infatuation with the Gypsy life, and there is no specific evidence of revision.

An initial attempt to publish the play may have been made in 1641, when 'More dissemblers beside women' was listed amongst plays belonging to the King's Men which the new Lord Chamberlain, the Earl of Essex, forbade in a letter to the Stationers' Company to be printed without the Company's consent.

Notwithstanding the compositorial stints suggested by Mulryne for *Women Beware*, compositors have not been effectively distinguished in *Dissemblers*. In addition to the variant running title (see above), there were, as Mason noted, press corrections in the outer forme of sheet B and the inner forme of D. These are mostly minor alterations, but include a substantive change of punctuation (1.2.72) and an emended word (3.1.94). The former seems unauthoritative (see Textual Note), but in the latter case at least the manuscript was probably consulted.

NEWCOMB is carefully divided into acts and scenes, in the form 'Act 1. Scæn. 1.', 'Scæn. 2.', etc., but our 2.2 and 2.3 are numbered 'Scæn. 3.' and 'Scæn. 4.' There is specific evidence against a scene being missing, as, unusually, the last line of 2.1 and the first of 2.2 are complementary part-lines that make up a single verse-line. NEWCOMB's numbering must accordingly be an error. We follow NEWCOMB's divisions with C. W. Dilke's correction of the misnumbering in Act 2.

The Gypsy scenes were adapted by John Leanerd in his Restoration play *The Rambling Justice* (Hogg, 1978). His emendations have occasionally been recorded as conjectures where they anticipate readings followed in this edition.

SEE ALSO

Text: *Works*, 1037
Music: this volume, 149
Authorship and date: this volume, 378

WORKS CITED

Previous Editions

[Dilke, C. W.], ed., *Old English Plays* (1815), vol. 4

Dyce, Alexander, ed., *Works* (1840), vol. 3

Bullen, A. H., ed., *Works* (1885), vol. 6

Mason, Frank Tolle, 'A Critical Edition of Thomas Middleton's *More Dissemblers Besides Women*', Ph.D. diss. (Michigan State University, 1974)

Tytle, Thomas Allen, '*More Dissemblers Besides Women* by Thomas Middleton', Ph.D. diss. (University of Toronto, 1976)

Other Works Cited

Bawcutt, N. W., ed., *The Control and Censorship of Caroline Drama: The Records of Sir Henry Herbert, Master of the Revels 1623–73* (1996)

Beaumont, Francis, and John Fletcher, *Comedies and Tragedies* (1647)

Cutts, John P., *La Musique de scène de la troupe de Shakespeare: The King's Men sous le règne de Jacques Ier*, second edn. rev. (1971)

Dekker, Thomas, *English Villainies Discovered by Lantern and Candle-light* (1608), in *Thomas Dekker*, ed. E. D. Pendry (1969), 169–308

—— *O per se O* (1610)

Geller, Lisa, 'Widows' Vows and *More Dissemblers Besides Women*', *Medieval and Renaissance Drama in England* 5 (1991), 287–308

Hogg, James, 'John Leanerd's *The Rambling Justice*', in *Salzburg Studies, Elizabethan Studies*, vol. 70 (1978), 111–24

Holmes, David M., *The Art of Thomas Middleton* (1970)

—— and H. D. Janzen, 'A Note on Editing Jacobean Drama', in *Editing Seventeenth Century Prose*, ed. D. I. B. Smith (1972), 25–30

Johnson, Lowell Edward, ed., *No Wit, No Help Like a Woman's* (1976)

Jonson, Ben, *The Gypsies Metamorphosed*, in *Works*, ed. C. H. Herford and Percy and Evelyn Simpson, 11 vols (1925–52), vol. 7, pp. 539–622

Jowett, John, 'Middleton's Song of Cupid', *Notes and Queries* 239 (1994), 66–70

—— 'Middleton's *No Wit/Help like a Woman's* at the Fortune', *Renaissance Drama* NS 22 (1991), 191–208

Kewes, Paulina, '"Give me the Sociable Pocket-books..."': Humphrey Moseley's Serial Publication of Octavo Play Collections', *Publishing History* 38 (1995), 5–21

Langbaine, Gerard, *An Account of the English Dramatic Poets* (1691)

Leanerd, John, *The Rambling Justice, or, The Jealous Husband* (1678)

Miller, C. William, 'Thomas Newcomb: A Restoration Printer's Ornament Stock', *Studies in Bibliography* 3 (1950–51), 155–70

Montaigne, Michel Eyquem de, 'Of the Force of Imagination', in *The Essays*, trans. John Florio (1603), vol. 1, Chapter 20

Mulryne, J. R., 'Half-Sheet Imposition and Running-Title Transfer in *Two New Plays* by Thomas Middleton, 1657', *The Library*, V, 30 (1975), 222–8

—— ed., *Women Beware Women* (1975)

Randall, Dale B. J., *Jonson's Gypsies Unmasked* (1975)

Reed, John Curtis, 'Humphrey Moseley, Publisher', *Oxford Bibliographical Society Proceedings and Papers* II.2 (1929), 60–142

TEXTUAL NOTES

Title More...Women] NEWCOMB, SR, *Moseley's advertising list VI^B*, Herbert; *More dissemblers beside women Earl of Essex's list of plays not to be published without the King's Men's permission, 1641*; *More Dissemblers then Women Moseley's advertising list VI^A*, *list of King's Men plays assigned to Thomas Killigrew, 1669*. The testimony for *than* comes from two independent sources, and the variant gains some further credibility as the word used in the echo of the title in the play's final line. However, *beside(s)* has testimony from four sources, three of them independent, and NEWCOMB itself is decisive. Both versions of the title may have been current.

After the title, NEWCOMB adds, between rules, 'The First Part.'—a misunderstanding probably in the printing house, where this play and *Women Beware* were brought together to be printed as one book.

Persons The present list rearranges the order of names and modifies the descriptions in NEWCOMB, which probably originates in the print culture of the mid-seventeenth century rather than earlier theatrical culture. It also omits 'Scæn Milan.' NEWCOMB omits the Cupid, Captain of Gypsies, other Gypsies, and Officers of the Guard.

1.1.0.2 *Lactantio*] THIS EDITION; *Lactantio, and Aurelia, and Servant* NEWCOMB. See note to l. 6.1.

1.1.0.3 *Song, music*] NEWCOMB (SONG. | Muſick.). The two separate directions are usual for a song in NEWCOMB, and might result from annotation. This edition follows NEWCOMB's positioning after the first entry, though the entry, or separated entries, might plausibly occur during the song.

1.1.6.1 *Enter...servant*] THIS EDITION. NEWCOMB includes these characters in the opening entry, but Lactantio indicates that he has been listening to the song alone.

1.1.17 for't] NEWCOMB; for it DILKE (*conj.*)

1.1.20 were thy] NEWCOMB (wear thy). *OED* records 'weare' as a 16th-century form. Similar is *Women Beware* 5.1.3, and 'near' for *ne'er* at l. 165.

1.2.0.1–2 *two...closet*] THIS EDITION; *L. Cardinal in his Cloſet, and two or three Lords* NEWCOMB. 'In his Closet' signals a discovery and strongly hints that the Lord Cardinal is initially alone. The speech-prefixes for '3. Lord.' arbitrate on the stage direction's permissive 'two or three', but the speeches could easily be redistributed.

1.2.18 We're] NEWCOMB (We'are)

1.2.19 spheres'] NEWCOMB (~,)

1.2.29 deceased] deceaſed (= èd) NEWCOMB

1.2.52 her‸ face] NEWCOMB; ~‸ faith DILKE; ~. Face BULLEN. The Duchess 'wears | A constancy will not deceive my praises', and 'art' etc. cannot make *her* a dissembler. Her outward face can be trusted.

1.2.56 sins] THIS EDITION (Taylor); ſin NEWCOMB. The emendation is urged not only by *beat*, but also *owners* and the image of repeated waves beating against a rock.

1.2.59 wish] DILKE; with NEWCOMB

1.2.71 hopes] NEWCOMB; hope TAYLOR (*conj.*). Taylor's reading would change the referent of *it* from *Opinion* to *hope*.

1.2.72 as] NEWCOMB; are TAYLOR (*conj.*). But compare 1.3.29, 'Welcome, as peace to temples'.

1.2.88 I've] NEWCOMB (I'have)

1.2.95.1 *Enter...book*] THIS EDITION; after 'comes' in NEWCOMB

1.2.118 *Hei*] DILKE; *Heu* NEWCOMB

1.2.142 o'late] NEWCOMB (alate)

1.2.148, 160 Lord] NEWCOMB (L.)

1.2.158.1 *Enter...gentleman*] DYCE; after 'gentleman' in NEWCOMB

1.2.165 ne'er] NEWCOMB (near). See note to 1.1.20. In context a confusion remains possible.

1.2.170 *Exit*] NEWCOMB (*Exit Cardinal.*)

1.2.188 laughter'] NEWCOMB (laughter)

1.2.200 fool-urchin, old] *in italic in* NEWCOMB

1.2.215 of] NEWCOMB (off)

1.2.232 villainy] DILKE; Villain NEWCOMB. Both sense and metre suggest error. Probably a simple '-ainie'/'-aine' misreading. There seems to be the reverse error at 5.2.227.

1.2.241 reck'nings] rock'nings NEWCOMB

1.3.51 hope] DILKE; bope NEWCOMB

1.3.68 ALL THE NOBILITY] THIS EDITION; *not in* NEWCOMB. Suggested by *hymns*, l. 63. Similarly l. 88.

1.3.87.1 *He ascends*] NEWCOMB (Aſcend.)

1.3.128 *Exeunt*] DYCE; *Exit.* NEWCOMB

1.4.2 I'd] NEWCOMB (I'had)

1.4.24 off] NEWCOMB (of)

1.4.27 marrowbones] NEWCOMB (Maribones)

1.4.38 cut] *OED* quotes this line under *keep cut* (Cut, sb.², 34), glossing 'to keep one's distance, be coy or reserved'; this cannot apply here. *Cut* is instead primarily 'style of clothing' (sb.², 16).

1.4.51 puling] THIS EDITION; paling NEWCOMB. The line is *OED*'s only illustration of *paling* (ppl.a.2) before the 19th c. *Puling* is both 'whining' and 'sickly'; it occurs at 3.1.98 and elsewhere in Middleton.

1.4.51 some] DILKE; ſo me NEWCOMB

1.4.62 Wilt] NEWCOMB (Wil't)

1.4.64 well] NEWCOMB; well as TAYLOR (*conj.*). NEWCOMB sets 'Give...too' as a verse line, in which case metrical emendation is desirable, especially in view of the Page's 'As well as' in the previous line. 'Well' ends the type line, which would make omission easy. But the prose/verse distinction is insecure in a passage of transition from prose to verse.

1.4.89–99 Cupid...play] Found also, without the 8th and 9th lines, as the first stanza of the three-stanza song in *Chaste Maid* beginning 4.1.167. A similar two-stanza song, 'Cupid is an Idle Toy', is also found as an expansion of 'In a Maiden Time Professed' in two music manuscripts; for a transcript and further details, see Textual Note to *The Witch* 2.1.138. The more closely related texts in *More Dissemblers* and *Chaste Maid* probably derive from a two-stanza version preserved in other extant music manuscripts (BM Add. MS. 29481, fol. 6^v, and New York Public Library, Drexel MS. 4175, Items 24 and 56; Item 56 omits the second stanza). The version in the music MSS has the shorter stanza form of *Chaste Maid*, probably indicating that the eighth and ninth lines were added specifically for the song's inclusion in *More Dissemblers*. A conjectural sequence of events is: (*a*) the two-stanza version preserved in the music MSS was written for Middleton's *Masque of Cupids*, which was performed 6 January 1614; (*b*) the song was then adapted for *More Dissemblers*, in order to strengthen allusions to the earlier masque already present in the play's own masque of Cupid in 1.3, and to make further use of a song perhaps notorious for its sexual content as well as its association with the masque; (c) it was later expanded from the music MSS version to replace the anticipated Welsh song in a revival of *Chaste Maid*, perhaps in part because a Welsh-speaking singer was no longer available. See Cutts for details of the MSS and transcription of the music; Jowett, 'Middleton's Song of Cupid', for further textual analysis; and the present volume, p. 149, for the musical text.

1.4.90   he's] NEWCOMB; *he is Chaste Maid and* MUSIC MSS

1.4.96-7   Of... wiser.] NEWCOMB; *not in Chaste Maid or* MUSIC MSS

1.4.97   husbands] NEWCOMB (husband's)

1.4.98   thought] NEWCOMB, MUSIC MSS; *taught Chaste Maid*

1.4.104   *Exit [Page]]* DYCE; *Exit.* NEWCOMB (*after* 'straight, Dondolo')

2.1.16.1   *Exit [Celia]]* DYCE; *Exit.* NEWCOMB (*after* 'madam')

2.1.57   gain] NEWCOMB; guile DYCE (*conj.*); stain TAYLOR (*conj.*). See following note.

2.1.57   of] THIS EDITION; or NEWCOMB. It is difficult to make sense of NEWCOMB's 'gain or art'. Compare *Fair Quarrel* 4.3.89, 'With honest gain of fortune'.

2.1.60   fellows] NEWCOMB; *fellow* DILKE. A typical Middleton dislocation: for 'we, fellows of life, must part'.

2.1.63   calmer] THIS EDITION; calm NEWCOMB. The line is metrically defective and probably corrupt. DILKE added '[then]' after 'calm'; BULLEN awkwardly emended Q's 'T'would' to 'It would'. 'Calmer' would easily be misread 'calme', especially as the error normalizes a double comparative.

2.1.70   your] DILKE; you NEWCOMB

2.1.75   thy promise] DILKE; the promise NEWCOMB

2.1.128   without] withont NEWCOMB

2.1.135   He's] NEWCOMB (Has)

2.1.144   off] NEWCOMB (of)

2.2.29   bear] NEWCOMB. For the distinctive intransitive use, compare *Lady* 4.2.36.

2.3.3   good fellow] NEWCOMB (~-|~). The modernization distinguishes between the Governor's familiar form of address and Andrugio's interpretation, *good-fellow*, 'thief'.

2.3.60   Does't] NEWCOMB (Do'st)

2.3.66-7   ANDRUGIO... love] NEWCOMB. This exchange is rather awkward. Andrugio's 'Thou art in raptures' might be a misinserted annotation, in which case one could conjecture:

AURELIA

   Most virtuously delivered! My love, my love!

ANDRUGIO

   Thou art in raptures. (*Aside*) 'Most virtuously delivered'!

This gives a more fluent text, but NEWCOMB is playable; if NEWCOMB lends greater dislocation to the dialogue as a love-exchange, this could be seen as a virtue.

2.3.92.1   *Exit]* NEWCOMB (*Exit Andrugio.*)

3.1.5   Well fare] NEWCOMB (Welfare)

3.1.87   O'] DILKE; Oh NEWCOMB

3.1.94   me] NEWCOMBb; no NEWCOMBa

3.1.108   daintiest] NEWCOMB (dantieft). The spelling is not usual; perhaps an error.

3.1.116   those] NEWCOMB; 'em LEANERD; them THIS EDITION (*conj.*)

3.1.116   trifling] triffling NEWCOMB

3.1.126   Will... affection] NEWCOMB is metrically deficient. Two possible remedies are: (a) 'him' for 'himself' (assuming sophistication, and taking *affection* as four syllables); (b) a monosyllable presumably beginning 'a-' before *affection* (for instance *apt*).

3.1.147   *Exit]* NEWCOMB (*Exit Page.*)

3.1.189-90   vow's. | LACTANTIO The... [*Aside*] My] DILKE; vows, the... | *Lact.* My NEWCOMB. A defence of NEWCOMB is attempted by Holmes and Janzen. Dilke's reattribution remains difficult to resist. The Lord Cardinal is happy to urge Lactantio forward to the Duchess throughout this scene, and indeed after 2.2 shows no further sign of a troubled conscience. The contrast between the reattributed comment and the aside 'My blood dances' is wholly consistent with Lactantio. Coming from him, the reattributed phrase anticipates his speech beginning l. 201. Presumably the words were annotated marginally in a manuscript, and subsequently misincorporated.

3.1.208.1   *Enter Lords]* THIS EDITION; *after l. 207 in* NEWCOMB

3.1.209   advised] advifed (= èd) NEWCOMB

3.1.221   honoured] honored (= èd) NEWCOMB

3.1.282   missed] DILKE; wafte NEWCOMB. NEWCOMB establishes no contrast between the act and the perception.

3.1.313   *Exeunt]* DILKE; *Exit.* NEWCOMB

3.2.7   fortunately] NEWCOMB; fortunate TAYLOR (*conj.*)

3.2.10.1   *Knocks within]* DYCE (Knocking within.); *after* 'knocks', l. 11, *in* NEWCOMB

3.2.16-3.2.16.1   *Exit... Lactantio]* Exit | Enter Lactantio. NEWCOMB (*after l. 15*)

3.2.33   be] NEWCOMB; be [well] DILKE

3.2.46   Of] NEWCOMB; Oft THIS EDITION (*conj.*). NEWCOMB's 'Of', though awkward, may be defended as equivalent to 'for'.

3.2.95   rèport] Compare rècord, rèdeem, rèmain, rèspect, rèturn, rèveal, rèvenge, etc., all cited by Cercignani, pp. 37-8.

3.2.109   service] NEWCOMB; services THIS EDITION (*conj.*). NEWCOMB sets ll. 109-10 as one line. The emendation would establish 'One... affections' as a regular pentameter and would highlight the bawdy innuendo. But the metrical consideration carries little weight as the line can be split after 'service'.

4.1.9   she not] DILKE; fhe NEWCOMB. By a strained reading, 'Yet comes she' might mean 'she is still on her way', but this places an exceptional burden on *comes* in a dramatic situation where the whole point is that Aurelia has *not* come.

4.1.25   possess] THIS EDITION; poffeffes NEWCOMB

4.2.26   woman] DILKE; one woman NEWCOMB. NEWCOMB might be defended as stressing the thematic duplicity of disguises: Aurelia is in effect two women; she explicitly sheds the double identity in the final scene, where 'This is she peace dwells in' affirms the loss of both the Gypsy woman and the deceiver. But this justification is somewhat contrived; the reading should logically refer to womankind and offer an allusion to the play's title.

4.2.41   pullen] DILKE (Leanerd); Pully NEWCOMB. NEWCOMB is remotely possible as an old spelling, but *OED* does not record it. The form could result from misreading of 'Pullin' (compare 'pullin' in *Revenger* 4.2.55) as 'Pullie'.

4.2.60, 80   ALL GYPSIES] NEWCOMB (*All.*)

4.2.87-8   camcheateroon... house-drows] NEWCOMB (camcheteroon, puscatelion, howf-drows). Middleton was probably familiar with the canting lore and word-lists compiled by Thomas Harman (*A Caveat or Warning for Common Cursitors, Vulgarly called Vagabonds*, 1567) and adapted by, amongst other later writers, Thomas Dekker (*Lantern and Candlelight*, 1608; *O per se O*, 1610). Although the flavour of Middleton's Gypsy cant is plausible enough, he did not base it other than incidentally on the available word-lists. Instead, he wrote nonsense interspersed with half-disguised English words, which are sometimes meaningful and sometimes merely add to the comic nonsense. In this edition, recognizable English elements have been modernized as such: here, for instance, *cheater, puss, cat, lion, house.*

4.2.90 *piss-kitch*] NEWCOMB (*Piskitch*)

4.2.92 *Piss-kitch*] NEWCOMB (*Piskitch*)

4.2.92 *house-clout*] NEWCOMB (*howſe-clout*)

4.2.106, 132 ALL GYPSIES] NEWCOMB (*All.*)

4.2.144 line] DILKE; live NEWCOMB. 'Live' is possible as a form of *life*, but arouses suspicion. *Line* is clearly both 'line of life', 'pedigree, family', and 'hangman's line'.

4.2.158 cache] NEWCOMB (caſh). The point is that the money has been placed in hiding, though there is no doubt wordplay or confusion between words.

4.2.198 whither] NEWCOMB (whether)

4.2.199 can] DILKE (Leanerd); cau NEWCOMB

4.2.217 *Signoros*] NEWCOMB (*Seignoroes*)

4.2.217 *cavallario*] THIS EDITION; *Calavario* NEWCOMB

4.2.217 *folkadelio*] NEWCOMB (*Fulkadelio*)

4.2.218 *Lagnambrol*] NEWCOMB (*La gnambrol*). The 'g' is presumably pronounced, making a syllable with 'La'.

4.2.256 She's] NEWCOMB (She'is)

4.2.261 dreamed] dreamed (= èd) NEWCOMB

4.2.262.1 *Exeunt*] DILKE; *Exit* NEWCOMB

4.2.266, 277 ALL GYPSIES] NEWCOMB (*All.*)

4.2.277.1 *Exeunt*] DYCE; *Exit* NEWCOMB

4.3.0.1 *and other Lords*] THIS EDITION. NEWCOMB adds 'Celia'. The phrasing 'and other Lords, Celia' probably betrays an unauthoritative annotation. Celia has no part in the scene until l. 76 (presuming that the Lord Cardinal does not indicate her at l. 19, 'your own women'), and the Duchess's speech beginning l. 52, apparently a soliloquy, is more effective with Celia's absence. She probably enters, as indicated in this edition, when she is summoned at l. 76. NEWCOMB's long dash after the Duchess calls 'Celia' is probably shorthand for the stage action.

4.3.51.1 *Exeunt...Lords*] DYCE; *Exit Lords.* NEWCOMB

4.3.76.1 *Enter Celia*] See note to 4.3.0.1.

4.3.79 sprawling] NEWCOMB; squalling DILKE (*conj.*). *OED* does not record the verb *squall* until '*a.*1631'; it is there applied to animals and means 'screaming loudly or discordantly'—not the sense required here.

4.3.90.1 *Exeunt*] *Exit* NEWCOMB

4.3.93.1 *Enter...guard*] THIS EDITION; *after* 'near', l. 95, *in* NEWCOMB

4.3.115 up] DILKE; up to NEWCOMB

4.3.115 puckfist] NEWCOMB (puckfoiſt)

4.3.130.1 *Exeunt...guard*] THIS EDITION; *Exit* Lactantio *and Guard:* NEWCOMB (*after* 'indeed')

4.3.147 walk and breathe] THIS EDITION; walks and breath NEWCOMB; walks and breathes DILKE. Whether indicative or subjunctive, the pair of verbs seems to require consistency. The subjunctive, as the more marked form, would be more liable to be corrupted.

4.3.206-9 *Exit with the guard...Exit*] THIS EDITION; *Exeunt.* NEWCOMB (*after* l. 209)

4.2.277.2 oboes] NEWCOMB (Hoboys)

5.1.7 whos'] NEWCOMB (whoſe). DILKE emends 'who as', and MASON emends 'whoso'; but NEWCOMB gives an acceptable monosyllabic form of *whoso* found elsewhere in Middleton (*Lady* 1.2.182, *Women Beware* 3.3.180, *Microcynicon*, 2.68). In her note on the first of these parallels in her edition of *Lady*, Lancashire notes that the idiom occurs in bawdy contexts.

5.1.18 Gam ut, A re, B mi,] NEWCOMB (Gamot, *a re, b me,*)

5.1.18 C...sol—] THIS EDITION; *&c:* NEWCOMB. The situation is the same as when 'etc.' stands for missing but known

words such as the refrain of a song. An alternative expansion would include 'E-la', on the assumption that the Page sings it off-pitch.

5.1.23 clefs] NEWCOMB (Cliffs). Similarly throughout.

5.1.26 one] THIS EDITION; I NEWCOMB. Probably the Roman or Arabic numeral misread as pronoun 'I'.

5.1.38 re, mi,] THIS EDITION; me re NEWCOMB. The song is clearly a learners' piece based on the scale, which is given simply before the song proper. NEWCOMB must therefore give a misreading, an error of transposition or, just possibly, an authorial slip (though Middleton's knowledge of the hexachord system otherwise seems competent). The form 'me' cannot be taken as more than a spelling variant, but would encourage confusion.

5.1.38.1-5.1.39.1 *Here...again*] NEWCOMB prints: 'Crotch. Keep time you foolish Boy——(Here they sing Pricksong)'. This does not clearly establish how the stage direction relates to Crotchet's admonition. Presumably Crotchet must begin singing before the Page gets out of time, and the singing must be continued before Crotchet can ask Celia's opinion of it.

5.1.40 madonna] DILKE; *Madova* NEWCOMB

5.1.50.1 *Enter...dancer*] THIS EDITION; *after* l. 51 *in* NEWCOMB

5.1.56 B fa, B mi] NEWCOMB (*Be fa beme*)

5.1.61 la-sol] THIS EDITION; *fa fol* NEWCOMB. Hexachords could be based on C, F, or G, none of which renders D as 'fa'. Probably again an error of transmission, as is confirmed in that 'D la-sol' substitutes for 'dilate'; compare the correct formula at l. 76.

5.1.84 cithern] NEWCOMB (Cittron)

5.1.85 E la-mi] NEWCOMB (*Ela me*)

5.1.88 lavoltas] (Lavolto's)

5.1.89.1 *Exit* [Crotchet with his books]] THIS EDITION; *Exit.* NEWCOMB (*after* ll. 86-7); *after* 'you, sir', l. 88, *in* DYCE

5.1.95 His] DYCE; 'Tis NEWCOMB; At his DILKE

5.1.165.1-2 *The...dance*] NEWCOMB prints '(Dance.)', without locating as a stage direction or italicizing.

5.1.166 boys...springals] NEWCOMB; boy...springal DYCE. *Springal* does not imply a springing movement. The Usher is a boy (ll. 193-4), and is described as a 'dainty stripling' (l. 215).

5.1.173 *fortune*] NEWCOMB (Fortune)

5.1.173 *guerre*] DILKE; *guardo* NEWCOMB; guerra DYCE

5.1.174 We're] NEWCOMB (W're)

5.1.190 O...(etc.)] NEWCOMB (...ᴀ*&c.*ᴀ). Here accepted as Cinquepace's disparagements (compare l. 57), but possibly a marginal note for the Page to groan that has become assimilated into the speech.

5.1.207, 208 Lactantio] THIS EDITION; *Laurentio* NEWCOMB. An easy initial misreading, and the compositor would be influenced by his first error when setting the name the second time. Laurentio is nowhere else named; Lactantio was the Page's earlier master and as such responsible for her courtly education. The 'dance' the Page learnt can be seen, in the light of the emendation, as the cause of her present difficulties.

5.2.17 her] DILKE; his NEWCOMB. It is *her* lips which provoke greed and are like (red or black) berries. Probably a *his/hir* misreading (or eyeskip from the line above).

5.2.31.1 *Enter Celia, and Aurelia*] DYCE; *after* 'there' *in* NEWCOMB

5.2.50 *Exit Aurelia*] DYCE; *after* l. 48 *in* NEWCOMB

5.2.55 but] bnt NEWCOMB

5.2.70 He'd] NEWCOMB ('had)

5.2.111.1 *Enter Celia, and Aurelia*] DYCE; *after* l. 112 *in* NEWCOMB

5.2.118.1–2 *Celia...clothes*] It seems insufficient to follow Bullen's 'CELIA *points to* AURELIA.', especially in view of Aurelia's
double demonstrative, surely indicating the disguise itself, at
l. 123.

5.2.153.1 *She...Celia*] We follow previous editors in marking
the Page's entry after l. 213. Lactantio could hardly fail
to respond to her presence earlier in the scene, especially
if, as seems necessary to conclude the story of the Page's
pregnancy, she is carrying her new-born baby. Her entry is
not only unspecified in NEWCOMB but also unprepared for. We
envisage that Celia brings her on, as she did Aurelia twice
earlier in the scene, and Andrugio once. The present line
provides a cue for Celia's exit in a context where Lactantio's
arrogance provides a sufficient hint as to what the Duchess
is about. This reading of the action affects the interpretation
of *mark* (see commentary).

5.2.153 I've] NEWCOMB (I'have)
5.2.205 'tis] DILKE; is NEWCOMB
5.2.227 villain] DILKE; villainy NEWCOMB. An error would be
influenced by 'Penitency' at the end of the next line. 'Villainy'
as a personification is not impossible, but the article 'th''
tells against such a reading, and other personifications in the
passage have capital initials.
5.2.234 weight] NEWCOMB (wait)
5.2.239 He's] NEWCOMB (h'as)
5.2.267 womenkind] NEWCOMB (Women kinde); womankind
DILKE. The plural *Women-kind* is not recognized in *OED*
but databases such as *Literature Online* reveal numerous
examples. The form echoes the play's title.

PRESS VARIANTS

Sheet B (outer forme)

Sig. B2^v

1.2.11 pity] pitty NEWCOMBa; pity NEWCOMBb
1.2.17 woman,] ~_∧ NEWCOMBa; ~, NEWCOMBb
1.2.38 her,] ~_∧ NEWCOMBa; ~, NEWCOMBb

Sig. B3

1.2.58 owners,] ~_∧ NEWCOMBa; ~, NEWCOMBb
1.2.67 err.] ~, NEWCOMBa; ~; NEWCOMBb
1.2.72 joys,] ~_∧ NEWCOMBa; ~. NEWCOMBb

Sig. B4^v

1.2.147 lord,] ~; NEWCOMBa; ~, NEWCOMBb
1.2.147 credit,] ~_∧ NEWCOMBa; ~, NEWCOMBb

Sig. B6^v

1.3.10 pity.] ~. NEWCOMBa; ~? NEWCOMBb

Sig. B8^v

1.3.121 me,] ~_∧ NEWCOMBa; ~, NEWCOMBb

Sheet D (inner forme)

Sig. D1^v

3.1.94 me] no NEWCOMBa; me NEWCOMBb

Sig. D7^v

4.1.6 shape,] ~, NEWCOMBa; ~_∧ NEWCOMBb
4.1.7 freedom,] ~, NEWCOMBa; ~_∧ NEWCOMBb

Sig. D8

4.1.31 crosses!—] ~; NEWCOMBa; ~! NEWCOMBb

Catchword Variant

F3-3^v

5.1.126 understanding.] un-|derstanding; NEWCOMB (*c.w.*); un-
-|derstanding, NEWCOMB (*text*)

STAGE DIRECTIONS

[Printed before the play:]

The Actors Names.

Lord Cardinal of *Milan*.
Lactantio, his Nephew.
Andrugio, General of *Milan*.
Father to *Aurelia*.
Lords of *Milan*.
Governor of the Fort, Servant to *Aurelia*.
Crotchet, a Singing Master.
Sinquapace, a Dancing Master.
Usher to Sinquapace.
Dondolo, Servant to *Lactantio*.

Dutchess of *Milan*.
Celia, her Waiting-Gentlewoman.
Aurelia, Mistress to *Andrugio* and *Lactantio*.

Page, *Lactantio*'s old Sweet-heart disguised.
Servants.

Scæn *Milan*.

1.1.0.1 Act 1. Scæn. 1.

1.1.0.2, 1.1.6.1 Enter *Lactantio, and *Aurelia, *and *Servant*. (at
1.1.0.1)
1.1.0.3 SONG. | Musick.
1.1.68.1–2 *Exeunt.*
1.2.0.1 Scæn. 2.
1.2.0.1 *Enter L. Cardinal in his Closet, and | two or three Lords.*
1.2.76 *Enter a Servant.*
1.2.95 *Enter Lactantio with a Book.* (after 'comes')
1.2.135 *Enter Page with a Letter.*
1.2.158 *Enter Aurelia like a Gentleman.* (after 'gentleman')
1.2.170 *Exit Cardinal.*
1.2.190.1 *Enter Father and Governor.*
1.2.222 *Exeunt:*
1.2.241 *Exit.*
1.3.0.1 Scæn. 3.
1.3.0.1 *Enter Dutchess, above, | and Celia.*
1.3.25.1 *Enter Lord Cardinal.*
1.3.58.1 *Cornets: | And a shout | within* (opposite 'Hold...
sudden', 1.3.58–9)
1.3.67.1–2 *Enter Andrugio, attended with the Nobility | and State,
like a Victor.*
1.3.67.5 SONG. | *Musick.*

1.3.76.1-2   *A* Cupid *discending, sings this.*
1.3.87.1   *Ascend.*
1.3.87.2-4   *During these Songs,* Andrugio *peruses a Letter* | *delivered him by a Lord, and then closes with this* | *Song* below.
1.3.89.1   *Exeunt in State.*
1.3.103   *Exit.*
1.3.128   *Exit.*
1.4.0.1   *Scæn. 4.*
1.4.0.1   *Enter Dondolo, and the Page* | *with a Shirt.*
1.4.88.1   *SONG.* | *Musick.*
1.4.104   *Exit.* (after 'straight, Dondolo')
1.4.109   *Exit.*
2.1.0.1   *Act 2. Scæn. 1.*
2.1.0.2   *Enter Dutchess and Celia.*
2.1.16.1   *Exit.* (after 'madam')
2.1.24.1   *Enter Lord Cardinal.*
2.1.133   *Exit.*
2.1.145   *Exit.*
2.2.0.1   *Scæn. 3.*
2.2.0.1   *Enter L. Cardinal.*
2.2.30   *Exit:*
2.3.0.1   *Scæn. 4.*
2.3.0.1   *Enter Father, Governor, Aurelia,* | *and* Andrugio *disguised.*
2.3.18.1   *Exeunt Father and Governor.*
2.3.92.1   *Exit Andrugio.*
2.3.108   *Exit.*
3.1.0.1   *Act 3. Scæn. 1.*
3.1.0.2   *Enter Lactantio, and Page.*
3.1.28.1   *Enter Dondolo.*
3.1.123.1   *Exit:*
3.1.131.1   *Enter Lord Cardinal.*
3.1.147   *Exit Page.*
3.1.208.1   *Enter Lords.* (after 3.1.207)
3.1.220   *Exit:*
3.1.313   *Exeunt.*
3.2.0.1   *Scæn. 2.*
3.2.0.1   *Enter Dutchess and Celia.*
3.2.10.1   *Knocks within.* (after 'knocks', 3.2.11)
3.2.16   *Exit.* (after 3.2.15)
3.2.16.1   *Enter Lactantio.* (after 'Exit'; see previous direction)
3.2.119   *Exit.*
3.2.124   *Exit.*
4.1.0.1   *Act 4. Scæn. 1.*
4.1.0.2   *Enter Andrugio.*

4.1.16.1   *Enter Lactantio with a Guard.*
4.1.33   *Exeunt:*
4.2.0.1   *Scæn. 2.*
4.2.0.1   *Enter Aurelia like a Gipsey.*
4.2.28.1   *Enter Dondolo.*
4.2.55.1-2   *Enter a company of Gipseys, Men and Women,* | *with Booties of Hens, and Ducks, &c.* | *singing.*
4.2.55.3   *Musick.* | SONG.
4.2.215.1   *Enter Father and Governor.*
4.2.262.1   *Exit Father and Governor.*
4.2.277.1-2   *Exit with a* | *strange wilde fashion'd dance to the Hoboys or* | *Cornets.*
4.3.0.1   *Scæn. 3.*
4.3.0.1   *Enter Dutchess, Lord Cardinal,* | *and other Lords, Celia.*
4.3.51.1   *Exit Lords.*
4.3.60.1   *Enter Page.*
4.3.90.1   *Exit Celia and Page.*
4.3.93.1   *Enter General, Lactantio and the Guard.* (after 'near', 4.3.95)
4.3.130.1   *Exit Lactantio and Guard:* (after 'indeed')
4.3.197.1   *Enter Lactantio, and the Guard.*
4.3.200.1   *Exit.*
4.3.209   *Exeunt.*
5.1.0.1   *Act 5. Scæn. 1.*
5.1.0.2   *Enter Page, Celia, and Crotchet.*
5.1.38.1   *(Here* | *they sing Pricksong)* (after long dash at end of 5.1.39)
5.1.49.1   *Musick. Song.*
5.1.50.1   *Enter Sinquapace the Dancer.* (after 5.1.51)
5.1.89.1   *Exit.* (after 5.1.86-7)
5.1.142   *Exit.*
5.1.145.1   *Enter Usher.*
5.1.165.1-2   *(Dance.)*
5.1.228.1   *Exeunt Sinquapace and Page.*
5.1.239   *Exit.*
5.2.0.1   *Scæn. 2.*
5.2.0.1   *Enter the Dutchess and Celia.*
5.2.25.1   *Exit Celia.*
5.2.31   *Enter Celia and Aurelia.* (after 'there')
5.2.50   *Exit Aurelia.* (after 5.2.48)
5.2.58.1   *Exit.*
5.2.73.1   *Enter Andrugio.*
5.2.111.1   *Enter Celia and Aurelia.* (after 5.2.112)
5.2.135.1   *Enter Lactantio.*
5.2.171.1   *Enter Lord Cardinal and the Lords.*
5.2.267.1   *Exeunt.*

LINEATION NOTES

1.2.10-12   To...follies] DYCE; *2 lines* NEWCOMB: 'em | (with 'but pity 'em' as flow-over); love | momentary | DILKE
1.2.57-8   That...weeping] DYCE; *1 line* NEWCOMB
1.2.197-9   He...shaw] DYCE; *2 verse lines* NEWCOMB: tufftee |
1.2.200   Quisquimken...astrata] DYCE; *1 verse line* NEWCOMB
1.2.201-2   Nay...whoremongeria] *2 verse lines* NEWCOMB: strumpetikin |; Nay...too *1 verse line, then prose* DYCE
1.3.124-5   My faith...Cardinal] DILKE; *1 line* NEWCOMB
1.4.84-5   That's...so] DILKE; *verse* NEWCOMB: after |
2.1.8-9   Lactantio...General] DILKE; Cardinal | NEWCOMB
2.1.88-9   What...vow] DYCE; *1 line* NEWCOMB
3.1.30-1   Soft...there] DYCE; castle | NEWCOMB
3.1.31-2   As...anywhere] DYCE; *1 line* NEWCOMB
3.1.36   Nay...certain] DYCE; *1 verse line* NEWCOMB

3.1.45-6   If...belly] THIS EDITION; mind | NEWCOMB; know | DYCE
3.1.66-8   Come...away] BULLEN; *2 lines* NEWCOMB: went |; *3 lines* DYCE: went | say |
3.1.76-97   You...breeches] DYCE; *prose* NEWCOMB
3.1.102-3   I...gibbet] THIS EDITION; *2 verse lines* NEWCOMB: trick |. 'Fool...unreasonable' (3.1.101) and 'It...leap' (3.1.104) are valid verse lines, and are set as such in NEWCOMB, but the passages between and immediately after them resist versification. The beginning of the speech seems to vacillate between verse and prose. 'I will turn Gypsy presently' initiates a consistent verse pattern, but the compositor's difficulties with the opening lines seem to have persuaded him to abandon verse layout.

3.1.107-17 I...'em] DYCE; *prose* NEWCOMB

3.1.201-2 O...virtue] DILKE; *1 line* NEWCOMB

3.2.70-1 Stay...ink] DILKE; *1 line* NEWCOMB

3.2.97-8 But...at 'woman'] THIS EDITION; *1 line* NEWCOMB

3.2.103-4 Sharp...oftentimes] THIS EDITION; *1 line* NEWCOMB; *prose* DYCE. Here, and again when the letter is read at 4.3.171-4, NEWCOMB sets 'But...more sharp set' and 'And...weapon' as verse lines. Their irregularity is explained by the interruptions after 'sharp-set'; otherwise 'And I know' would complement 'But...set'.

3.2.105-6 And...weapon] THIS EDITION; *1 line* NEWCOMB; *prose* DYCE

3.2.109-10 One...such-a-one] THIS EDITION; *1 line* NEWCOMB

4.1.2-4 Make...own] DYCE; *2 lines* NEWCOMB: eyes|; safe| castle| DILKE

4.2.9-11 And...money] THIS EDITION; *verse* NEWCOMB: quickly| some|

4.2.82-3 O...me] THIS EDITION; *1 line* NEWCOMB; *prose* DYCE

4.2.87-8 *Ousabel...house-drows*] THIS EDITION; *1 verse line* NEWCOMB; *puscatelion*| DYCE. The speech rhymes once, perhaps twice, with the following one, and requires the same metre.

4.2.92 *Piss-kitch in house-clout*] DYCE; *1 verse line* NEWCOMB

4.2.150-1 O...indeed] DILKE; *1 verse line* NEWCOMB

4.2.155-7 Nay...already] DYCE; *prose* NEWCOMB. Following the usual convention, 'Nay...love' would probably be written as a single long line in the compositor's copy manuscript, giving a semblence of prose.

4.2.212 *Nosario...then*] DILKE; *1 verse line* NEWCOMB

4.2.214-15 *Arsinio...for't*] DILKE; *1 verse line* NEWCOMB

4.2.216-17 Stop...*folkadelio*] THIS EDITION; *Signoros*| NEWCOMB

4.2.219-20 How...too] DILKE; *1 verse line* NEWCOMB

4.2.232-3 I...company] DILKE; *1 line* NEWCOMB

4.2.264-5 *Filcheroon...too*] THIS EDITION; *1 line* NEWCOMB; *prose* DYCE

4.2.267-8 I...bell-wethers] DILKE; *1 verse line* NEWCOMB

4.3.173-4 And...weapon] THIS EDITION; *1 line* NEWCOMB; *prose* DYCE

4.3.175-6 Weapon...fencer] THIS EDITION; *1 verse line* NEWCOMB; *2 verse lines* DYCE: Weapon|

5.1.10-14 But...back] THIS EDITION; *4 lines* NEWCOMB: man's| I| of|; *5 lines* DILKE: spoil| singing| methinks| spare|; *5 lines* DYCE: rather| singing| methinks| spare|. In NEWCOMB, 'man's' and 'if I' flow over onto second indented type-lines. This suggests that the printer's copy was already faulty, written as prose that could be mistaken for verse. The original error is probably connected with the short lines of the rhyming couplet, which Middleton may have written on a single line.

5.1.30-1 Will...sir] THIS EDITION; *1 line* NEWCOMB; prose DILKE

5.1.32-3 A...semiquaver] DYCE; crotchet| NEWCOMB. NEWCOMB probably reflects copy manuscript layout, which would indicate a misinterpretation of a prose speech on account of the verse context. We therefore reject the possible verse division after 'semibreve', which gives one regular and one irregular line.

5.1.52-3 A...name] DYCE; *1 verse line* NEWCOMB

5.1.55-6 The horriblest...dancer] THIS EDITION; *1 line* NEWCOMB; *prose* DILKE

5.1.56-7 B fa...man] THIS EDITION; *1 line* NEWCOMB

5.1.85-7 E...sir] THIS EDITION; *3 verse lines* NEWCOMB: other| your|; *3 verse lines* DILKE: sir| away|. NEWCOMB presumably follows manuscript layout, mistaking prose lines for long verse lines. Similarly 5.1.117-19.

5.1.92-4 Signor...yet] THIS EDITION; *2 verse lines* NEWCOMB: of|; *3 verse lines* DILKE: Cinquapace| dancer|. Alternatively the verse begins at '*Metereza*' (5.1.91) and is divided after 'Cinquapace' (DYCE). NEWCOMB's line-ending probably stood in the compositor's copy, as 'man alive of' is indented on a second type-line.

5.1.117-19 Nay...Florence] DILKE; *2 verse lines* NEWCOMB: on't|

5.1.124-5 Gentlewomen...can] THIS EDITION; *2 verse lines* NEWCOMB: scholars|. Rather irregular verse, but note the rhyme.

5.1.125-30 I have...linen] DYCE; *prose* NEWCOMB. NEWCOMB sets 'I have...better un-' as the last type line of a page; 'derstanding' could not be turned up or turned down, and became the catchword. This may have committed the compositor to setting the speech as prose.

5.1.141-2 It...you] DILKE; him| NEWCOMB

5.1.142 How, love him] DYCE; *prose* NEWCOMB. The speech seems freely to mix verse and prose. The compositor, or a scribe, settled for prose throughout.

5.1.145 One...tolerable] DYCE; *prose* NEWCOMB. See previous note.

5.1.147-8 How...conscience] DYCE; *prose* NEWCOMB. See note to 5.1.142.

5.1.149-50 Now...yet] DYCE; *1 line* NEWCOMB; *prose* DILKE

5.1.154-6 Troth...now] DYCE; *prose* NEWCOMB. The compositor, or a scribe, was probably confused because (*a*) the previous lines are prose, and (*b*) 'I'll...now' was probably written as a single line in the manuscript.

5.2.153-4 I've...time] DILKE; *1 line* NEWCOMB

WOMEN, BEWARE WOMEN: A TRAGEDY

Edited by John Jowett

Women, Beware Women was first printed by Thomas Newcomb after *Dissemblers* in Humphrey Moseley's 1657 octavo 'TWO NEW | PLAYES...WRITTEN By *Tho. Middleton*, Gent.' (*BEPD* Middleton 1657; Wing M1989; see Textual Introduction to *Dissemblers*, page 1131, for fuller details). Nathaniel Richards's verse in commendation of *Women Beware* appears on sig. A4, before *Dissemblers*. Before *Women Beware* itself, on sig. G3, comes a title-page specific to the play reading: 'WOMEN | BEWARE | WOMEN. | [rule] A | TRAGEDY, | BY | *Tho. Middleton*, Gent. | [rule] [device] [rule] *LONDON*: | Printed for *Humphrey Moseley*, 1657.' A list of characters appears on sig. G3ᵛ.

The text of the play is on the whole well printed. Mulryne (ed., 1975) tentatively identifies four compositors who respectively set the following portions: sheets G and H (up to 'will not', 2.1.177); sheets I and K (from Livia's speech, 2.1.177, to 3.1.277); sheets L (3.1.278 to 3.3.18), N, and O (from '*Enter Leantio*', 4.2.19, to the end); and sheet M (3.3.19 to 'preferment', 4.2.19). These attributions should be regarded as speculative and unconfirmed. For instance, the alleged lighter punctuation in sheet M is hard to verify statistically, and the parentheses supposedly characterizing sheets I and K probably derive from copy (see below). During the print-run, press corrections were made in at least three formes, the inner formes of sheets H, I, and M. The list of press corrections in this edition is based on Mulryne's collation.

Mulryne conjectures that Richards provided Moseley with the manuscript that served as printer's copy. This is plausible, though speculation as to that manuscript's immediate origin is of limited help in determining its nature. The speech prefix 'Neece.' consistently used for Isabella in 1.2 alone might be a survival from Middleton's hand. Although some crucial directions are missing for the masque in Act 5, stage directions are usually very ample, and sometimes elaborate. The more detailed and descriptive wording, and the occasionally permissive directions ('*two or three Boys*'), can be taken to be authorial.

Yet the immediate copy must have been too well ordered for a rough draft. And there are signs of non--authorial transcription. The consistent error 'Brancha' for Bianca, though it can scarcely have been Middleton's form (see the textual note on her name, Persons.1), presumably stood in the printer's copy. In localized parts of the text there is a modest upsurge in the frequency of parentheses, especially in I5–K3 (2.2.151–472), which accounts for over half the parentheses in the text. There is no particular correspondence between these sections and sheets or formes such as might have been set by a single

compositor. It would seem that the parentheses were localized in the copy. But, once allowance is made for the influence of Crane on the Trinity MS of *Game at Chess*, the parentheses cannot be reconciled with Middleton's habits. Moreover, NEWCOMB's division of the text into scenes is not characteristic of a manuscript in Middleton's hand. The catchword 'Scæn.' in the middle of 1.2 (after 1.2.87; see textual note) seems to reflect an annotator's abandoned first thought, and so suggests that scene divisions were imposed retrospectively on the manuscript. More precisely, it looks like an abandoned initial attempt to introduce scene divisions on literary Jonsonian lines.

As Mulryne notes, certain curt marginal notes suggest annotation for the theatre, such as 'Brancha and Mother above', 'Table and Chess', 'Duke above', and 'Cupids shoot:'; the first three of these are set off from the text by a dash or dashes. Directions for music also look theatrical, especially those that are set off from the accompanying main stage direction. The inadequacies of the stage directions for the masque and elsewhere are not necessarily incompatible with a theatrical manuscript (Long, 1985). The printer's copy may therefore have been a careful transcript of a playbook that had been itself based on an authorial fair copy.

NEWCOMB's act divisions would have been required for act-intervals in performance; they structure the play coherently and are presumptively authorial. The act and scene divisions are followed in this edition. NEWCOMB is almost certainly correct in observing continuous action after 3.1.81. Here, Oliphant (1931) and subsequent editors have supplied an exit for Leantio's Mother, giving a cleared stage and so a scene break. An entry is certainly missing for Bianca towards the end of Leantio's soliloquy, but it does not follow that both an exit and an entry are missing for the Mother. It is perfectly consistent with Middleton's stagecraft for the Mother to remain on stage for the duration of Leantio's speech without seeing him or being seen by him (see Shand, 1985; Jowett and Taylor, 1993).

SEE ALSO

Text: *Works*, 1493
Authorship and date: this volume, 414

WORKS CITED

Previous Editions

[Dilke, C. W., ed.,] *Old English Plays*, 6 vols (1815), vol. 5
[White, T., ed.,] *Old English Drama* 3 vols (1830), vol. 3
Dyce, Alexander, ed., *Works*, 5 vols (1840), vol. 4

Bullen, A. H., ed., *Works*, 8 vols (1885), vol. 6

Ellis, Havelock, ed., *Thomas Middleton*, Mermaid, 2 vols (1887), vol. 1

Oliphant, E. H. C., ed., *Shakespeare and His Fellow Dramatists*, 2 vols (1929), vol. 2

—— ed., *Elizabethan Dramatists Other than Shakespeare* (1931)

Jacobs, Elizabeth R., ed., 'A Critical Edition of Thomas Middleton's *Women Beware Women*', unpublished Ph.D. dissertation (Wisconsin, 1941)

Parker, R. Brian, ed., Thomas Middleton, *Women Beware Women*, unpublished Ph.D. diss. (University of Liverpool, 1957)

Mulryne, J. R., 'A Critical Edition of Thomas Middleton's *Women Beware Women*', Ph.D. diss., 2 vols (Cambridge University, 1962)

Gill, Roma, ed., Thomas Middleton, *Women Beware Women*, New Mermaid (1968)

Gomme, A. H., ed., *Jacobean Tragedies* (1969)

Barber, Charles, ed., Thomas Middleton, *Women Beware Women*, Fountainwell (1969)

Lawrence, Robert G., ed., *Jacobean and Caroline Tragedies* (1974)

Muir, Kenneth, ed., Thomas Middleton, *Three Plays* (1975)

Mulryne, J. R., ed., Thomas Middleton, *Women Beware Women*, Revels (1975)

Kriegel, Harriet, ed., *Women in Drama: An Anthology* (1975)

Frost, David L., ed., Thomas Middleton, *Selected Plays* (1978)

Loughrey, Bryan, and Neil Taylor, eds., Thomas Middleton, *Five Plays* (1988)

Other Works Cited

Daileader, Celia R., *Eroticism on the Renaissance Stage: Transcendence, Desire, and the Limits of the Visible* (1998)

Gossett, Suzanne, '"Best Men are Molded out of Faults": Marrying the Rapist in Jacobean Drama', *English Literary Renaissance* 14 (1984), 305–27

Holdsworth, R. V., 'Notes on *Women Beware Women*', *Notes and Queries* 238 (1993), 215–22

—— Review of J. R. Mulryne's edition (1975), *Review of English Studies* NS, 29 (1978), 83–93

—— '*Women Beware Women*: An Octavo Reading Vindicated', *Notes and Queries* 223 (1978), 15

Jowett, John, and Gary Taylor, 'With New Additions', in Taylor and Jowett, *Shakespeare Reshaped, 1606–1623* (1993), 107–236

Lamb, Charles, *Specimens of English Dramatic Poets, Who Lived About the Time of Shakespeare* (1808)

Long, William B., 'Stage Directions: A Misinterpreted Factor in Determining Textual Provenance', *TEXT* 2 (1985), 121–37

McLuskie, Kathleen, *Renaissance Dramatists* (1989)

Middleton, Thomas, *A Game at Chess, 1624*, ed. T. H. Howard-Hill, Malone Society Reprints (1990)

—— and Howard Barker, *Women Beware Women* (1986)

Mulryne, J. R., 'Annotations in Some Copies of *Two New Plays by Thomas Middleton*, 1657', *The Library*, V, 30 (1975), 217–28

Shand, G. B., 'The Stagecraft of *Women Beware Women*', *Research Opportunities in Renaissance Drama* 28 (1985), 29–36

Simpson, Percy, 'Thomas Middleton's *Women Beware Women*', *Modern Language Review* 33 (1938), 45–6

Stachniewski, John, 'Calvinist Psychology in Middleton's Tragedies', in R. V. Holdsworth, ed., *Three Jacobean Revenge Tragedies* (1990), 226–47

Thomson, Leslie, '"Enter Above": The Staging of *Women Beware Women*', *Studies in English Literature, 1500–1900* 26 (1986), 331–43

Tricomi, Albert H., *Anticourt Drama in England 1603–1642* (1989)

TEXTUAL NOTES

Title   *Women, Beware Women: A Tragedy*] NEWCOMB (title-page: WOMEN | BEWARE | WOMEN. | [rule] A | TRAGEDY, | BY | *Tho*. Middleton, Gent.); A right Woman, or Women beware of Women *SR*; Women beware Women *Moseley's advertising list*, NEWCOMB (*half title and running title*). *A right Woman* is believed to be a different play; see Textual Introduction to *Dissemblers*. The comma in the present modernized text identifies the first 'Women' as a vocative, though the same punctuation would be neccesary if it anticipated the second 'Women' as object of 'beware'.

Persons   The present list is editorial in organization. NEWCOMB prints an unheaded list and note of the scene. NEWCOMB's list is hierarchically organized, and omits the two Ladies and all persons listed after the Servants, including those in the masque. It appears to be post-Jacobean and was probably prepared for the printed edition (see Taylor, 'the Order of Persons', p. 65).

Persons.1   BIANCA] DYCE; Brancha NEWCOMB. Similarly throughout. Middleton's sources (or at least the closest extant analogues) and the repeated metrical requirement for a trisyllable establish 'Brancha' as a consistent error in NEWCOMB. Mulryne posits an inital misreading of Middleton's 'Beancha'. The persistence of the error suggests that an annotator or, more likely, a scribe made an initial misreading then arbit-

rarily imposed the reading throughout the text. See Textual Introduction.

1.1.24   aught] NEWCOMB (ought). Similarly elsewhere in NEWCOMB.

1.1.40   died] NEWCOMB (di'd)

1.1.61   done] DILKE; doue NEWCOMB

1.1.92   swinge] NEWCOMB (fwindg). DYCE modernized 'swing'.

1.1.104   perfect] NEWCOMB (per-|fit)

1.1.122   spake] NEWCOMB; spoke DILKE

1.1.127   send] NEWCOMB; sent FROST (*conj*.)

1.1.149   Will't] NEWCOMB (Wilt)

1.1.150.1   *Mother and Bianca*] *not in* NEWCOMB

1.2.22   seemed] NEWCOMB (feem'd); seemes MULRYNE (*conj*.)

1.2.24   An] NEWCOMB (And). Similarly elsewhere.

1.2.34   Counting] DILKE; Connting NEWCOMB

1.2.48   blown, man] NEWCOMB (~ʌ ~); ~ʌ woman SIMPSON (*conj*.)

1.2.56   Light] NEWCOMB; Plight SIMPSON (*conj*.); Flight FROST (*conj*.). Another emendation of this much-suspected utterance is 'Like ennow' for 'Light her now' (ELLIS), either deleting 'Brother' (ELLIS) or transferring the word to the beginning of Livia's next speech (OLIPHANT). This solution is not convincing in either of its variants. The emended sense is weak; it seems highly dubious that 'ennow' would be construed 'her now'; and *OED* records no '-nn-' spellings of *enow*. 'Brother' is not a real difficulty, as Guardiano may be speaking as anticipated brother-in-law. There has been no satisfactory emendation of the single word 'Light'. An initial 'p' or 'f' would be resistent to oversight, and neither 'Plight' nor 'Flight' nor even 'Flite' gives a convincing reading. 'Light' is defensible. The sense might be either 'provide intellectual enlightenment to' (ironic: Fabritio has proved himself stupid), or 'comfort, gladden, cheer'. The latter would pick up on Livia's anxiety that Fabritio will make Isabella marry irrespective of her feelings. Compare 'to lighten her of one grief' (*No Wit* 3.69), where the grief is a mother's for the plight of her daughter.

1.2.80 ISABELLA] NEWCOMB (*Neece:*). Similarly in speech-prefixes throughout scene. By 2.1 the personal name is established in speech-prefixes, following a mention of it in dialogue (2.1.58). A feature of Middleton's original draft has evidently survived subsequent regularization.

1.2.87.1 *Enter*] NEWCOMB (*text*); Scæn. NEWCOMB (*c.w.*). The variant is between G8ᵛ and H1. Though erroneous by the criteria adopted elsewhere in the text, the catchword must have been prompted by the copy.

1.2.104 guardianer] NEWCOMB (Guardianer). The usual forms in NEWCOMB are 'guardiner' and 'gardiner'. These are primarily to be taken as variants on *guardianer*, though puns on *gardner* occasionally demand a modified form in the edited text (see note to 2.2.89, 100).

1.2.123 ne'er] NEWCOMB (nev'r). A common form in NEWCOMB for the monosyllable; not subsequently recorded.

1.2.153 that] NEWCOMB; thy DILKE. Editors often follow Dilke. The idiom is equivalent to 'that niece of yours'.

1.2.223 Then] NEWCOMB. GILL modernizes 'Than', positing a contrast between hearing too soon and understanding too soon. But this depends on a distinction that is hard to uphold (the understanding cannot be without hearing, and hearing too soon is meaningless without understanding). More plausibly, the news is intuitively understood before it is heard, in which case the understander hears too quickly, in that an intuitive 'hearing' pre-empts the literal hearing that *then* follows.

1.2.223 prevent] In so far as the intuited and actual news of Hippolito's desire are the same, what can be *prevented*, in any sense of the word? The *news* becomes, in Isabella's mind, an *over-quick* anticipation that she and Hippolito will have an incestuous affair. This she attempts to forestall.

1.2.224 Welcome it?] NEWCOMB (~ it,); well fare it: MULRYNE. The difficulties lie in explaining the apparent syntactic parallel between 'prevent it' and 'welcome it', and in understanding the sense in which Isabella can offer to welcome bad news. A purely neutral or ironic welcome seems untenable because (*a*) the parenthesis raises the possibility of, and so creates the conditions for, a more usual, positive, welcoming, and (*b*) there is no logic that can equate a welcome with a refusal of either first or further entry. In emending 'welcome', Mulryne creates a new difficulty of interpretation (*well fare* as 'farewell', which is not specifically supported in *OED*), destroys a Middletonian collocation, 'welcome...come' (see Jowett and Taylor, p. 226) and posits a relatively unlikely compositorial error. The troublesome *prevent it...welcome it* parallel can simply be broken by taking 'Welcome it?' as a self-contained rhetorical question. It poses the alternative to prevention; it is prompted by Isabella's thought of her 'joys', and is immediately answered in the negative.

1.3.12.1 *Enter*] not in NEWCOMB

1.3.17 quay] NEWCOMB (Key)

1.3.22 The] NEWCOMB; then MULRYNE

1.3.57.1 *Exit Leantio*] Exit. NEWCOMB (*after* 'thee')

1.3.68 good] NEWCOMB; glad MULRYNE (*conj.*)

1.3.72.1 *two or three*] NEWCOMB. NEWCOMB's sequence of speech-prefixes indicates at least three boys. The permissive '*two or three*' shows that the disposition of speech-prefixes is not rigid.

1.3.73 BOYS] NEWCOMB. The First Boy presumably takes the lead.

1.3.101.5 *exeunt*] Exit. NEWCOMB

2.1.17 summed] DYCE; fow'd NEWCOMB. 'Sow'd' is possible as a form of *sewed*, which Gill accepts, but *sewed up* still does not seem right: it surely suggests 'made silent'. Error would be easy if, for instance, 'som'd' was misread 'sow'd'. *Summed* anticipates *Counting*. Holdsworth ('Notes') adduces parallels in Middleton for the play on the senses 'summarized' and 'reckoned up'.

2.1.36 lift] NEWCOMB; list MULRYNE (*conj.*)

2.1.49 I'll] NEWCOMB; I'd MULRYNE. The sense is 'I'd', but Middleton often implies the conditional where others would state it.

2.1.57.1 *Enter Servant*] *after* 'news' *in* NEWCOMB

2.1.60 bless you simply.—Lead] BULLEN; bless; you ſimple, lead NEWCOMB; bless you: Simple! lead DILKE. Editors following NEWCOMB or DILKE take 'simple' as an address to the servant. Middleton probably wrote something like 'bless you simplie, lead'. Compare *simply* at 4.1.43, where it means 'absolutely, greatly', and the corresponding adjective *simple* at 3.3.136. See also *Phoenix* 12.161.

2.1.62.1 *Exit*] NEWCOMB (*Exit Hippolito*). It is possible that Hippolito remains on stage to be berated into leaving at 2.1.67: NEWCOMB frequently regularizes exits by bringing them back to the character's last speech, and Hippolito's name might have been added to the direction precisely because it was not originally attached to his speech. But Livia's speech works well, perhaps better, as a confessional soliloquy.

2.1.73.1 *Enter...niece*] DILKE; *after* 'towards', 2.1.75, *in* NEWCOMB

2.1.109 fruitfulness] DILKE; fruit-|nefs NEWCOMB

2.1.179.1 *Enter Hippolito*] *after* 'Exit' *in* NEWCOMB

2.1.204 does't] NEWCOMB (do'ft). Middleton was careless in placing apostrophes, and commonly wrote 'st' as a ligature. Compare *Game*, Trinity MS, 1167, 'wa'st', for *was it*.

2.2.21 strangely] NEWCOMB (ftrangely); strongly FROST (*conj.*). Compare *No Wit* 1.234.

2.2.42 three] DILKE; theee NEWCOMB

2.2.42.1 *Enter Fabritio*] *after* 2.2.43 *in* NEWCOMB

2.2.70 *Exit*] Exit Fabritio. NEWCOMB

2.2.79 world's] NEWCOMB; word's GILL (*conj.*)

2.2.79.1–2 shuttlecock] NEWCOMB (Shittle-|cock). There is nothing exceptional in NEWCOMB's spelling, which in this edition is modernized to the usual form except where the context indicates a pun on *shit* (3.3.89).

2.2.87 asked] DILKE; ask NEWCOMB. The space after the word would accommodate an uninked or worn 't'.

2.2.89, 100 guard'ner] NEWCOMB (Guardiner). The form has been adopted to give a disyllable and signal the potential pun on *gardener*. The pun is certain at 4.2.95.

2.2.96 her cony-way] THIS EDITION; her——way NEWCOMB. Mulryne and others unconvincingly print 'her—'way', explaining 'way as 'away, leave it to me'. Instead, it seems that an obscenity has been omitted. *Arse-way* (compare *arseward*) would give a plausible compound with the added figurative sense 'perversely'. A genital term would more effectively indicate that the *fault* might be sexual misdemeanours or venereal diseases, and would also lead to a more effective quibble on *hair* as pubic hair. The specific possibility adopted here, *cony-way*, 'rabbit-hole', puns on *cun*, 'cunt'. The wordplay would continue with *hair* as not only pubic hair but also 'hare', which gives a particular reason for considering this conjecture the right one. For *cony*, with a comparable innuendo, compare *Chaste Maid* 4.1.236; for *to a hair* ('exactly') quibbling on pubic hair see 1.1.199 in the same play; for a proverbial phrase involving hair (*against the hair*) which gives rise to a pun on *hare* see *No Wit* 1.1.273–77. The voyeurism of *cony-way* would be entirely appropriate to Sordido. The repression of obscenity compares with *Romeo and Juliet* 2.1.38: 'open *Et cætera*' in Q1, 'open, or' in Q2, 'open arse' in most modern editions. As in *Romeo*, the playwright is extremely unlikely to have euphemized the text himself. In some situations, as for example with a missing rhyme-word in the second line of a couplet, a silence or physical gesture can be more effective than the word itself, but this justification can scarcely be applied here.

2.2.102 Her] DILKE; Heir NEWCOMB

2.2.108 plumped] DYCE; plump NEWCOMB. Probably copy 'plumpt' misread 'plumpe'.

2.2.135.1 *Enter Mother*] after 'returned', 2.2.136, *in* NEWCOMB

2.2.153 merrily] DILKE; meerly NEWCOMB. Perhaps from copy 'merely'.

2.2.158 account] NEWCOMB (ac-|compt)

2.2.241.1 *Enter . . . Servant*] after 'madam' *in* NEWCOMB

2.2.249 our] THIS EDITION; your NEWCOMB. NEWCOMB gives a very forced reading. The context would encourage a simple error.

2.2.292 chokes] NEWCOMB; chok'd DILKE

2.2.308 simplicity] NEWCOMBb (Simplicitie); Simplicities NEWCOMBa

2.2.314.1 *Enter*] not in NEWCOMB

2.2.328 here] DILKE; here's NEWCOMB

2.2.342 makes] NEWCOMB; make DILKE. Strictly speaking the verb should agree with *bless*. The singular, however, helps to establish that the subject is not *figures*. There is ambiguity as to whether the clause beginning *such as* qualifies *meekness* and *gentleness* or just *meekness*. *Bless* might possibly be a metrical compression of *blesses*.

2.2.381 wife] NEWCOMB; wise DILKE. Editors usually follow Dilke, but they are probably underestimating Middleton's capacity for irony. The Duke means (*a*) play the housewife, don't squander beauty but *provide for ever* (*b*) put yourself in the role of my wife (a strained hyperbole for becoming a mistress if it were the only sense of the words, though Bianca does of course eventually become the Duke's actual wife) (*c*) don't take being a wife too seriously, play the game.

2.2.386.1 *Exeunt . . . above*] Exit above. NEWCOMB

2.2.403 stay] NEWCOMB. This seems to be the right word, as is evidenced by parallel phrasing at 3.2.47–8 ('a fine bit | To stay a cuckold's stomach') and *No Wit* 6.236–7 ('that stay their wedding stomachs with a hot bit of a common mistress'). For discussion of the sense, see Mulryne.

2.2.423 why] DILKE; who NEWCOMB

2.2.442 He . . . traitor] NEWCOMB sets in italic, marking a sententia.

2.2.460 may't] DYCE; may NEWCOMB

2.2.464 *Aside to her*] Indicated in NEWCOMB by parentheses round 'Y'are a damn'd Baud'.

2.2.467.1 *Guardiano and Bianca*] not in NEWCOMB

3.1.8 I'll] NEWCOMB; I'd MULRYNE

3.1.12 of] NEWCOMB; or BULLEN (Dyce). Though 'grumbling', the more usual sense of *grudging*, is relevant, the idea of a slight symptom 'of' an approaching illness gets taken up in the following line.

3.1.15.1 *Enter Bianca*] after 'comes', 3.1.16, *in* NEWCOMB

3.1.31 Yes] NEWCOMB; Yet MULRYNE (*conj.*)

3.1.39 good] DILKE; gook NEWCOMB

3.1.68 where'er] NEWCOMB (where ere); whate'er THIS EDITION *conj*.

3.1.77 pewterer] NEWCOMB (Pew-|terer); pewter MULRYNE (Oliphant). See Holdsworth, 'Octavo Reading'.

3.1.81 so.] NEWCOMB. Editors usually provide an exit and a scene-break here, and introduce an entrance for the Mother with Bianca at 3.1.108. See Textual Introduction.

3.1.111 this?—as] NEWCOMB (~? as); ~∧ is DILKE; ~∧ as MULRYNE (Hoeniger). Mulryne takes *this* as 'this is'. NEWCOMB is, however, satisfactory.

3.1.146 'Tis] DILKE; 'till NEWCOMB

3.1.176 thou] NEWCOMB; thou['rt] DYCE; thou art MULRYNE. See following note.

3.1.176 please] FROST (Mulryne); pleas'd NEWCOMB

3.1.176.1 *Exit Bianca*] Exit. NEWCOMB

3.1.195, 197 Capella] NEWCOMB; Capello DYCE

3.1.270 marzipan] NEWCOMB (March-pain)

3.1.275 to] NEWCOMB; with THIS EDITION *conj*. With could be understood as either 'to' or 'by'. The emendation would therefore lend coherence to the secondary sense of *knit* as the forming or setting of fruit.

3.2.12 little] DILKE; lettle NEWCOMB

3.2.23.2 *Isabella*] Listed in NEWCOMB after '*Mother*'. In grouping the women together NEWCOMB probably misrepresents the staging.

3.2.40, 44 Ruinse] NEWCOMB (Rouans). Mulryne plausibly identifies NEWCOMB's name with a place Moryson calls 'le Ruinate', near a fort on the walls of Florence. If so, Middleton is likely to have picked up on the name for its meaning, 'ruinous'. He may have written 'Ruinse' as a disyllabic Anglification. 'Rouans' is perhaps by way of confusion with the familiar Normandy city Rouen.

3.2.41 Supplied] DILKE; Suppli' NEWCOMB

3.2.41 GENTLEMAN] NEWCOMB (Gentlem.). Some editors expand to the plural.

3.2.71 tenpence] NEWCOMB; twopence WHITE. OED does not record *twopence* as 'a type of a very small amount' before 1691. But beginning with Marlowe's use in *Jew of Malta* 4.4.43–4, *tenpence* could be 'used contemptuously because the amount wants something of a shilling' (*OED*). Compare *Fair Quarrel* 3.1.73, and see Mulryne's longer defence of NEWCOMB.

3.2.103 rite] NEWCOMB (right). The forms were often used interchangeably, especially in relation to marriage. *Rite* seems the primary idea.

3.2.130 of] DYCE; of a NEWCOMB

3.2.134 They're] NEWCOMB (They'are)

3.2.145 ISABELLA (*sings*)] SONG. NEWCOMB

3.2.145–57 What . . . kitlings] NEWCOMB prints the Ward's speech right, opposite the song. Mulryne suggests that the song was pasted into the manuscript. There are two other alternatives: that the Ward's speech was added as an afterthought (it is entirely extraneous to the action), or that the layout indicates simultaneous delivery. The latter is the most likely explanation. The Ward's speech evidently is spoken during the song, and the layout is probably deliberate. NEWCOMB therefore probably reflects, directly or indirectly, a characteristic of Middleton's manuscript.

3.2.153 *speaking . . . song*] THIS EDITION; *not in* NEWCOMB. Probably implied by NEWCOMB's layout: see previous note.

3.2.180 whos'] NEWCOMB (who's); whoso DYCE; who WHITE. See note to *Dissemblers* 5.1.7.

3.2.187 Ay,] NEWCOMB (I,). GOMME prints 'I?'.

3.2.201.1–3 *Hippolito...after*] *right, opposite* 3.2.202–4, *in* NEWCOMB

3.2.201.1 [*Hippolito and Isabella*] *dance*] *A dance* NEWCOMB

3.2.214 Well,] DILKE; We'll, NEWCOMB. *OED*'s first example of the playful use of *we* to mean the person addressed is dated 1702.

3.2.219 Your...your] DILKE; You...you NEWCOMB

3.2.228.1 *Music*] *right, opposite* 3.2.227, *in* NEWCOMB

3.2.241.1 *Cornetts...Livia*] NEWCOMB places the flourish after the exeunt.

3.2.272 to] DILKE; too, NEWCOMB

3.2.316 as] NEWCOMB; as for DILKE. Editors usually accept the emendation without comment, but it merely smooths the metre. 'As tempt' would give a stronger reading, but assumes a more substantial error.

3.3.30 an] NEWCOMB (and)

3.3.44 what] MULRYNE; *not in* NEWCOMB; which DILKE. Holdsworth (1993) finds a slightly better Middleton parallel for *which* than for *what*, but *what* produces the easier misreading.

3.3.54 once] NEWCOMB; ones WHITE

3.3.89 shittlecock] NEWCOMB. See note to 2.2.79.1–2. The pun is taken up in *stool*.

3.3.115 and the] DILKE; and he NEWCOMB

3.3.141 In to] NEWCOMB (Into)

4.1.1 o'clock] NEWCOMB (a clock)

4.1.22.1 *Exeunt*] NEWCOMB (*Exit*)

4.1.88 An] NEWCOMB (And). Editors usually read 'And', accepting Dilke's 'know'.

4.1.88 knew] NEWCOMB; know DILKE. See previous note. Mulryne finds difficulty with the sense in NEWCOMB, but sarcasm, implying 'if only I could believe you were in reality such a great woman', is appropriate.

4.1.111 he's] NEWCOMB (has)

4.1.128 *Exit Bianca*] DYCE; *Exit.* NEWCOMB (*after* 4.1.126)

4.1.131.1 *Exit Messenger*] *Exit.* NEWCOMB (*after* 'lord')

4.1.135 honour's] NEWCOMBb (honors_); honor: NEWCOMBa

4.1.140–1 poise | Of] NEWCOMBb; ~, | If NEWCOMBa

4.1.141.1 *Enter Hippolito*] *after* 'welcome', 4.1.142, *in* NEWCOMB

4.1.177 cure's] NEWCOMB; care's DYCE (*conj.*)

4.1.180.1 *Enter...attended*] *after* 'welcome', 4.1.181 *in* NEWCOMB

4.1.203 love-private] NEWCOMB; low private DILKE. Editors usually follow Dilke, but 'love-private' is entirely appropriate as a reference to men like Leantio who, in contrast to the Duke, secretly hide their sexual affairs. It effectively anticipates the equation of the 'offences' of love (punning on *fences?*) and 'enclosèd grounds'.

4.1.228 sets] NEWCOMB; set DILKE

4.1.236 if] NEWCOMB; if [that] DYCE

4.1.248 their] NEWCOMB; her THIS EDITION *conj.* NEWCOMB may be defended as a slide from the particular to the general. Middleton may have been writing carelessly: compare 'Or death resist' (4.1.250) which, though clear enough as to the required sense, actually means the opposite.

4.1.267.1 *Exit...Servants*] *Exit Cardinal, &c.* NEWCOMB (*after* 'brother')

4.2.19.1 *Enter Leantio and a Page*] NEWCOMB. Some editors print the Page's entry at 4.2.22, but there is no tendency to 'massed' stage directions in NEWCOMB, and an entry with Leantio allows the Page to make stronger impact as an absurd

courtly accoutrement for the former factor. The 'court sun' is on Leantio too, and his access to a coach underlines the point.

4.2.22–3 LEANTIO...I'll go...I'll hurry] DILKE; I'll go...*Lean.* I'll hurry NEWCOMB

4.2.38 metal] NEWCOMB (mettle)

4.2.40 own] DYCE; *not in* NEWCOMB

4.2.42 prayed] NEWCOMB (praid); paid GILL

4.2.46.1 *Livia...Guardiano*] THIS EDITION; *Guardiano, Livia* NEWCOMB. Livia logically enters from the same door as Leantio, representing her house.

4.2.82 reprobate] DILKE; rebrobate NEWCOMB

4.2.95 guard'ner's] NEWCOMB (Gardiners)

4.2.117 or] NEWCOMB; and MULRYNE. Holdsworth ('Notes') provides a good defence of NEWCOMB, explaining 'to' as redundant.

4.2.123 wife's] NEWCOMB (wives)

4.2.166 all 's] NEWCOMB (all's); all DILKE

4.2.187 this'] THIS EDITION (Holdsworth, 1993, *following* Mulryne); thus NEWCOMB; that's DILKE; this is MULRYNE.

4.2.195 He's] NEWCOMB (Has)

4.2.229.1 *Exeunt all but Livia*] *Exit.* NEWCOMB

4.2.235 *Exit*] *Exeunt.* NEWCOMB

4.3.0.1 *Oboes*] NEWCOMB (Hoboys), before the scene heading

4.3.67 Than] NEWCOMB; Or THIS EDITION *conj.* Mulryne dubiously glosses *Than* as 'or'. NEWCOMB could be corrupt, but it seems more likely that the lines were written carelessly.

4.3.72 have] NEWCOMB; hear THIS EDITION *conj.*

5.1.0.2 *An...masque*] THIS EDITION; *not in* NEWCOMB. An altar is clearly required, and here is the obvious opportunity to bring it on stage. This scene-setting activity provides a fitting context for Guardiano's plot machinations. The scenic structure repeats 3.2, where NEWCOMB specifies preparation for the banquet before Guardiano and the Ward enter. The set establishes continuity of action throughout the act, notwithstanding the cleared stage after 5.1.37 and NEWCOMB's 'Scæn 2.' before the following entry.

5.1.2 were] NEWCOMB (wear). See textual note to *Dissemblers* 1.1.20.

5.1.27.1 *Exit*] *Exit Ward.* NEWCOMB

5.1.37.1 *Flourish. Enter*] THIS EDITION; *Flourish:* | *Scæn 2. Enter* NEWCOMB. See Textual Introduction and note to 5.1.0.2.

5.1.66 souls] OLIPHANT; foul NEWCOMB

5.1.95.1–2 *He...cup*] *not in* NEWCOMB; *To the Duke the wrong cup by mistake* MS note in Yale copy of NEWCOMB. The Yale note (see Mulryne, 'Annotations') states what happens from a narrative viewpoint, but does not sufficiently specify the stage action.

5.1.100 forbear. For...heart] THIS EDITION; ~, for...fake NEWCOMB. BULLEN conjectured restoring rhyme by emending 'part' (5.1.101) to 'leave take'; MULRYNE improved metrically by reading 'parting take', but still left a four-foot line rhyming with a five-footer. The present emendation, though radical, is less so than these, and gives a balanced couplet. *Heart*, as often in Middleton, means 'inclination, wishes, purposes' (see for instance *Lady* 3.1.101); it also anticipates *love*. The error may be classified as substitution of a weaker near-synonym.

5.1.101 *masquers*] *not in* NEWCOMB

5.1.107 peace] NEWCOMB. The form can be a mere spelling variant of *piece*. There is almost certainly wordplay.

5.1.109.1–4 *Enter...it*] *after* 'indeed' *and continuous with* 5.1.109.5–7 *in* NEWCOMB

5.1.110 ISABELLA...NYMPHS] Ditty. NEWCOMB

5.1.110   Juno] NEWCOMB (Iuno); [Io] Juno DILKE; Juno, Juno THIS
EDITION conj.
5.1.126   one] BARBER; me NEWCOMB
5.1.134   HIPPOLITO and GUARDIANO] NEWCOMB (Both.)
5.1.134.1   Livia...Juno] right, opposite 5.1.135, in NEWCOMB
5.1.134.1-2   with...arrows] THIS EDITION. NEWCOMB provides no
entry or part in the masque for the Cupids who shoot
Hippolito. Swift-winged (5.1.30) seems to imply a flight; Juno
promises 'Love's arrows' (5.1.147), which must refer to the
Cupids and so strongly suggests that they have already
appeared with Juno. If there is an impropriety in Cupids
appearing with Venus's rival Juno, it is a fitting impropriety
for Livia.
5.1.139   be long] DILKE; belong NEWCOMB
5.1.151   savour] DILKE; favor NEWCOMB
5.1.154.1-5.1.156.1   She...lap...Isabella...dies] Based on the
MS note at 5.1.154 in the Yale copy of NEWCOMB: 'Throws
flaming gold upon Isabella, who falls dead'.
5.1.173.1   Cupids shoot] NEWCOMB. Some editors move the direction to after 5.1.176, but the shooting represents Livia's
revenge for Hippolito's approval of Isabella's poisoning, and

as an ironized emblem of love it effectively coincides with
Hippolito's embrace of Isabella. Fabritio's temporary refo-
cussing of the audience's attention is typical of the scene's
disjunctions.
5.1.196   plagues] DILKE; plague NEWCOMB
5.1.197   all together] NEWCOMB (altogether)
5.1.206.1   He...dies] Based on the MS note in the Yale copy
of NEWCOMB: 'Runs on a guard's halbert; dies'. The detail
of the halberd suggests to Mulryne recollection of stage
performance. Unless it was distantly recalled after 1657 by
a member of a pre-1640 audience, we must assume such
a performance would belong to an unrecorded Restoration
revival. In either case the detail is questionably authoritative.
However, the halberd was probably a standard stage property
to denote a guard.
5.1.209   play] NEWCOMB; plays WHITE. NEWCOMB is an acceptable
subjunctive.
5.1.210   Masque] NEWCOMB (Mask)
5.1.256   enemy, no enemy] NEWCOMB; enemy WHITE. Compare
Oswald's death in King Lear (Q 1608, K1): 'The Brittiſh partie,
ô vntimely death! death.'—and similarly F 1623 (4.5.249).

PRESS VARIANTS

Copies collated by Mulryne are:

British Library, 643.b.37 (= BM 1)
British Library, 162.d.28 (= BM 2)
Bodleian Library, Art. 8° C.19.BS (= Bod 1)
Bodleian Library, Malone 247 (= Bod 2)
Boston Public Library, Boston, Massachusetts
Brown: copy owned by Professor Arthur Brown (lacks
everything after N6ᵛ)
Chaplin Library, Williams College, Williamstown, Massachu-
setts
Dyce Collection (National Art Library, Victoria and Albert
Museum), D.17.P.28 (= D 1)
Dyce Collection (National Art Library, Victoria and Albert
Museum), D.17.P.29 (= D 2)
Fletcher: privately owned copy sold at Sotheby's on 28
March 1961 to H. M. Fletcher
Folger Shakespeare Library, Washington, D.C.
Harvard University Library
Huntington Library, San Marino, California
Library of Congress, Washington, D.C.
Newberry University Library
Princeton University Library
Harry Ransom Humanities Research Center, University of
Texas, Austin, Texas
Trinity College, Cambridge (lacks sheet O)
Worcester College, Oxford
Yale University Library

The rarer uncorrected formes are found in the following copies:

H (inner): Library of Congress
I (inner): Bodleian Art.; Fletcher; Newberry; Princeton
M (inner): Chaplin; Fletcher; Huntington; Newberry; Texas;
Trinity

Sheet H (inner forme)

Sig. H1ᵛ

1.2.119   exercise_∧] NEWCOMBb; ~, NEWCOMBa
1.2.126   sir?] Sir? NEWCOMBb; ~, NEWCOMBa

Sig. H2

1.2.164   it.] NEWCOMBb; ~, NEWCOMBa

Sig. H5ᵛ

headline   106 NEWCOMBb; 306 NEWCOMBa

Sig. H8

2.1.119   father's_∧] Fathers_∧ NEWCOMBb; ~, NEWCOMBa

Sheet I (inner forme)

Sig. I1ᵛ

2.1.211   now.] ~; NEWCOMBb; ~, NEWCOMBa
2.1.213   either,] NEWCOMBa; ~; NEWCOMBb
2.1.226   love] NEWCOMBa; Love NEWCOMBb
2.1.226   sir;] Sir, NEWCOMBa; ~; NEWCOMBb
2.1.231   her?] ~, NEWCOMBa; ~_∧ NEWCOMBb
2.1.233   art] NEWCOMBa; Art NEWCOMBb

Sig. I2

2.2.8   window;] NEWCOMBb; ~, NEWCOMBa
2.2.16   folly:] ~; NEWCOMBb; ~, NEWCOMBa
2.2.21   heart.] ~; NEWCOMBa; ~! NEWCOMBb

Sig. I3ᵛ

2.2.74   vein] NEWCOMBb; vain NEWCOMBa
2.2.79   heir!] NEWCOMBb; ~. NEWCOMBa
2.2.85   ward,] Ward, NEWCOMBb; ~_∧ NEWCOMBa
2.2.87   anywhere] NEWCOMBb; any where NEWCOMBa
2.2.90   herb-woman,] Herb-woman_∧ NEWCOMBb; ~, NEWCOMBa

Sig. I5ᵛ

2.2.178   evening,] NEWCOMBa; ~! NEWCOMBb
2.2.186   heartsease?] hearts-eaſe? NEWCOMBb; ~. NEWCOMBa
2.2.200   request?] NEWCOMBb; ~_∧ NEWCOMBa

Sig. I6

2.2.204   now_∧] NEWCOMBb; ~, NEWCOMBa
2.2.210   truth.] ~; NEWCOMBb; ~, NEWCOMBa

Sig. I8

2.2.308   simplicity] Simplicitie NEWCOMBb; Simplicities NEW-
COMBa

Sheet M (inner forme)

Sig. M1ᵛ

3.3.63   by∧] ~, NEWCOMBb; ~; NEWCOMBa
3.3.72   well?] NEWCOMBb; ~. NEWCOMBa
3.3.80   bottom?] NEWCOMBb; ~: NEWCOMBa

Sig. M2

3.3.84   th'] NEWCOMBa; ~∧ NEWCOMBb
3.3.88   dancing?] NEWCOMBa; ~, NEWCOMBa
3.3.102   handkerchief!] Handkercheif; NEWCOMBb; ~, NEWCOMBa

Sig. M3ᵛ

4.1.22.1 *Exeunt Ladies*] *Exeunt* NEWCOMBb; *Exit* NEWCOMBa
4.1.27-8 enough…me. Yet] ~,…~; yet NEWCOMBb; ~;…~, yet NEWCOMBa
4.1.30   kindred!] kinred; NEWCOMBb; ~, NEWCOMBa
4.1.31   days.] ~; NEWCOMBb; ~, NEWCOMBa
4.1.36   me.] ~; NEWCOMBb; ~, NEWCOMBa

Sig. M4

4.1.53   sir?] Sir? NEWCOMBb; ~. NEWCOMBa
4.1.55   slippers.] Slippers; NEWCOMBb; ~? NEWCOMBa
4.1.56   shoemaker?] Shoomaker? NEWCOMBb; ~, NEWCOMBa
4.1.57   pair?] NEWCOMBb; ~, NEWCOMBa

Sig. M5ᵛ

4.1.125   go.] ~, NEWCOMBb; ~∧ NEWCOMBa
4.1.129   there?] NEWCOMBb; ~. NEWCOMBa

Sig. M6

4.1.135   honour's∧] honor's∧ NEWCOMBb; honor: NEWCOMBa
4.1.140-1 poise∧ | Of] poyfe∧ | Of NEWCOMBb; ~, | If NEWCOMBa
4.1.143   sister?] Sifter? NEWCOMBb; ~; NEWCOMBa
4.1.146   lord?] Lord! NEWCOMBb; ~: NEWCOMBa
4.1.149   fast∧] faft; NEWCOMBb; ~, NEWCOMBa

Sig. M7ᵛ

4.1.229   done,] NEWCOMBa; ~∧ NEWCOMBb
4.1.233   minute's] minutes NEWCOMBb; minuts NEWCOMBa
4.1.236   now?] ~! NEWCOMBb; ~, NEWCOMBa
4.1.237   on't.] ~; NEWCOMBb; ~, NEWCOMBa

Sig. M8

4.1.244   brother.] Brother; NEWCOMBb; ~, NEWCOMBa
4.1.247   beauty∧] NEWCOMBb; ~; NEWCOMBa
4.1.248   neither?] NEWCOMBb; ~: NEWCOMBa
4.1.250   resist?] NEWCOMBb; ~, NEWCOMBa
4.1.258   place∧] NEWCOMBb; ~, NEWCOMBa
4.1.260   conversion∧] NEWCOMBb; ~, NEWCOMBa
4.1.261   hymn] Hymn NEWCOMBb; Himn NEWCOMBa
4.1.264   lord.] Lord: NEWCOMBa; ~! NEWCOMBb

STAGE DIRECTIONS

[Printed before the play]

Duke of *Florence.*
Lord Cardinal, Brother to the
    Duke.
Two Cardinals more.
A Lord.
Fabritio, Father to *Isabella.*
Hippolito, Brother to *Fabritio.*
Guardiano, Uncle to the *Foolish Ward.*
The Ward, a rich young Heir.
Leantio, a Factor, Husband to *Brancha.*
Sordido, the Wards Man.

Livia, Sister to *Fabritio.*
Isabella, Neece to *Livia.*
Brancha, Leantio's Wife.
Widow, his Mother.

States of *Florence.*
Citizens.
A Prentice.
Boys.
Messenger.
Servants.

The Scæn.
F L O R E N C E.

1.1.0.2   Act. I. Scæn. I. | *Enter* Leantio *with* Brancha, | *and Mother.*
1.1.150.1 *Exeunt.*
1.1.176.1 *Exit.*
1.2.0.1   Scæn. 2. *Enter* Guardiano, Fabritio, | *and* Livia.
1.2.69.1-2 *Enter* Hippolito, *and* Isabella *the Neece.*
1.2.87.1-2 *Enter the Ward with a Trap-stick, and* | Sordido *his man.*
1.2.129.1 *Exit.*

1.2.141   *Exit.*
1.2.230.1 *Exit.*
1.2.232   *Exit.*
1.3.0.1   Scæn. 3. *Enter* Leantio *alone.*
1.3.12.1 —*Brancha* | *and* Mother | *above.* (right, opposite 1.3.12-13)
1.3.57.1 *Exit.* (after 'thee')
1.3.72.1-2 *Enter two or three Boys, and a Citizen or two,* | *with an Apprentice.*
1.3.98.1 *Musick.*
1.3.101.1-5 *Enter in great solemnity six Knights bare-headed, then* | *two Cardinals, and then the Lord Cardinal, then the* | *Duke; after him the States of* Florence *by two and* | *two, with varity of Musick and Song. Exit.*
1.3.112   *Exeunt.*
2.1.0.1-2 Act.2. Scæn. I. | *Enter* Hippolito, *and Lady* Livia | *the Widow.*
2.1.57.1 *Enter Servant.* (after 'news')
2.1.60.1 *Exit Servant.*
2.1.62.1 *Exit Hippolito.*
2.1.73.1 *Enter* Isabella *the Neece.* (after 'towards', 2.1.75)
2.1.179.1 *Enter* Hippolito. (after '*Exit*')
2.1.179.1 *Exit.* (after 'go')
2.1.228   *Exit.*
2.1.238   *Exit.*
2.2.0.1   Scæn. 2. *Enter* Guardiano *and* Livia.
2.2.34.1 *Enter Servant.*
2.2.38   *Exit.*
2.2.42.1 *Enter* Fabritio. (after 2.2.43)
2.2.70   *Exit* Fabritio.
2.2.79.1-2 *Enter* Ward *and* Sordido, *one with a Shittle-|cock, the other a Battledoor:*
2.2.126   *Exit.*
2.2.134   *Exit.*
2.2.135.1 *Enter Mother.* (after 'returned', 2.2.136)

2.2.176.1   *Table and | —Chess.* (right, opposite the 2 part-lines)
2.2.225.1   *Enter Servant.*
2.2.241.1   *Enter Brancha, and Servant.* (after 'madam')
2.2.292.1   *Exit Guardiano & Brancha.*
2.2.309.1   *Enter above Guardiano and Brancha.*
2.2.314.1   *—Duke above*
2.2.316   *Exit.*
2.2.386.1   *Exit above.*
2.2.392.1   *Enter Guardiano:*
2.2.418.1   *Enter Brancha.*
2.2.460.1   *Enter Servant.*
2.2.467.1   *Exeunt.*
2.2.476   *Exit.*
3.1.0.1–2   *Act.3. Scæn. I. | Enter Mother.*
3.1.15.1   *Enter Brancha:* (after 'comes', 3.1.16)
3.1.60   *Exit.*
3.1.81.1   *Enter Leantio.*
3.1.173.1   *Knock | within.*
3.1.176.1   *Exit.*
3.1.176.2   *Enter Messenger.*
3.1.204.1   *Exit Messenger.*
3.1.206.1   *Enter Brancha.*
3.1.268.1   *Exit.*
3.1.270   *Exit.*
3.1.295.1   *Enter Messenger.*
3.1.302.1   *Exeunt.*
3.2.0.1   *Scæn 2. A Banquet prepared: Enter | Guardiano and Ward:*
3.2.20.1   *Cornets:*
3.2.23.1–2   *Enter Duke, Brancha, Fabritio, Hippolito, Livia, | Mother, Isabella, and Attendants.*
3.2.29.1   *Enter Leantio.*
3.2.135.1   *Musick.*
3.2.144   SONG.
3.2.201.1   *Musick.*
3.2.201.1–3   *A dance, making | Honors to the D. | and cursie to them- | selves, both before | and after.* (right, opposite 3.2.202–4)
3.2.228.1   *Musick.* (right, opposite 3.2.227)
3.2.228.1–2   *Ward and Isabella | dance, he ridicu- | lously imitates | Hippolito.* (right, opposite 3.2.228–9)
3.2.241.1   *Exe. all but Leantio and | Livia; Cornets flourish.*
3.2.320.1   *Exit.*
3.2.349.1   *Enter Livia.*
3.2.377   *Exeunt.*
3.3.0.1–2   *Scæn 3. Enter Guardiano and Isabella at one door, | and the Ward and Sordido at another.*
3.3.100.1   *He yawns.*
3.3.139.1   *Enter Guardiano:*
3.3.144   *Exeunt.*
4.1.0.1–2   *Act.4. Scæn. I. | Enter Brancha attended by two Ladies.*
4.1.22.1   *Exit Ladies.*
4.1.40.1   *Enter Leantio.*

4.1.105   *Exit:*
4.1.112.1   *Enter the Duke:*
4.1.128   *Exit.* (after 4.1.126)
4.1.129.1   *Enter Messenger.*
4.1.131.1   *Exit:* (after 'lord')
4.1.141.1   *Enter Hippolito.* (after 'welcome', 4.1.142)
4.1.177   *Exit.*
4.1.180.1   *Enter Lord Cardinal attended.* (after 'welcome', 4.1.181)
4.1.264   *Enter Servants.*
4.1.267.1   *Exit Cardinal, &c.* (after 'brother')
4.1.279.1   *Exit.*
4.2.0.1   *Scæn 2. Enter Hippolito:*
4.2.19.1   *Enter Leantio, and a Page:*
4.2.46.1–2   *Enter Guardiano, Livia, Isabella, Ward, | and Sordido:*
4.2.94.1   *Exeunt Livia and Guardiano.*
4.2.129   *Exeunt Ward and Sordido.*
4.2.156.1   *Enter Guardiano and Livia.*
4.2.229.1   *Exit.*
4.2.235   *Exeunt.*
4.3.0.1   *Hoboys.* (before scene heading)
4.3.0.1–5   *Scæn 3. Enter in great state the Duke and Brancha, | richly attir'd, with Lords, Cardinals, Ladies, and | other Attendants, they pass solemnly over: Enter | L Cardinal in a rage, seeming to break off the Cere- | mony.*
4.3.71   *Hoboys.*
4.3.71, 1   *Exeunt.* (at 'Exit', 4.3.72.1)
5.1.0.1–3   *Act. 5. Scæn. I. | Enter Guardiano and Ward.*
5.1.27.1   *Exit Ward.*
5.1.37   *Exit.*
5.1.37.1–2   *Florish:*
5.1.37.1–2   *Scæn 2. Enter above, Duke, Brancha, L. Cardinal, | Fabritio, and other Cardinals, Lords | and Ladies in State.*
5.1.69.1   *Reads.*
5.1.85.1   *Musick.*
5.1.87.1–4   *Enter Hymen in Yellow, Ganymed in a Blue robe | powdered with Stars, and Hebe in a White robe | with golden Stars, with covered Cups in their | hands: They dance a short dance, then bowing | to the Duke, &c. Hymen speaks.*
5.1.101   *Exeunt.*
5.1.108   *Musick.*
5.1.109.1–4   *Enter two drest like Nymphs, bearing two Tapers | lighted; then Isabella drest with flowers and | Garlands, bearing a Censor with fire in it; they | set the Censor and Tapers on Juno's Altar with | much reverence; this Ditty being sung in parts.* (after 'indeed')
5.1.110   *Ditty.* (in place of speech-prefix)
5.1.126.1–2   *Enter Hippolito and Guardiano, | like Shepherds.*
5.1.134.1   *Livia descends | like Juno.* (right, opposite 5.1.135)
5.1.173.1   *Cupids | shoot:* (right, opposite 5.1.173–4)
5.1.205.1   *Enter a Lord with a Guard.*
5.1.266.1   *Exeunt.*

LINEATION NOTES

Mislineation in NEWCOMB can be attributed to the conventions of lineation adopted in the manuscript, except where otherwise noted.

1.3.78–9   CITIZEN...sir] DYCE; 1 *type line* NEWCOMB

2.2.33–4   After...there] DILKE; 1 *verse line* NEWCOMB

2.2.42–3   At...Fabritio] DILKE; 1 *line (with* 'Signor Fabritio' *as wrap-over)* NEWCOMB

2.2.257–8   'Tis...acquaintance] DYCE; 1 *line* NEWCOMB

2.2.258–9   All...mistresses] DYCE; 1 *line* NEWCOMB

2.2.414–15   Yes...game] DYCE; 1 *line* NEWCOMB

3.1.2–3   Or...since] DILKE; 1 *line* NEWCOMB

3.1.125–6   Unless...pride] DYCE; 1 *line* NEWCOMB

3.1.260–1   But...hope] DYCE; 1 *type line* NEWCOMB

3.2.60–1   Yes...now] DYCE; 1 *line* NEWCOMB

3.2.150–1   But...be] DILKE; fresh | NEWCOMB. The rhyme establishes the line-end. The song may have been written in a MS with two verse lines on a single line.

3.2.220–1   Here's...minstrels] DILKE; *verse* NEWCOMB: him |; *verse* DYCE: finds |. NEWCOMB sets a prose line-end as verse, influenced by the previous verse passage.

3.2.251–2   Whose...oil] DILKE; 1 *line (at foot of page)* NEWCOMB

3.3.45–6   O...question] DILKE; 1 *verse line* NEWCOMB. Single prose line in MS

3.3.47–8   Methinks...with] DILKE; 1 *verse line* NEWCOMB. Single prose line in MS

3.3.133–4   Faith...sweetheart] DILKE; 1 *line* NEWCOMB

3.3.137–9   Nay...bagpipes] DYCE; *prose* NEWCOMB. MS run-on part line interpreted by the compositor as prose

4.1.3–4   St Antony's...truer] DYCE; 1 *line* NEWCOMB

4.1.128–9   It...there] DYCE; 1 *line* NEWCOMB

4.1.164–5   He...talk] DYCE; 1 *line* NEWCOMB

4.2.79   O...damned] DILKE; 1 *verse line* NEWCOMB. Single prose line in MS

4.2.81–2   One...cuckold] DILKE; 1 *verse line* NEWCOMB. Single prose line in MS

4.2.83–6   Nay...myself] DYCE; 3 *verse lines* NEWCOMB: sir | wife |. A logical continuation of the attempt to set the passage as verse (see previous notes).

5.1.10–12   Prithee...then] DYCE; *prose* NEWCOMB. The speech is clearly metrical, like Guardiano's previous speeches in the scene. Verse is confirmed by the Ward's completion of Guardiano's final part-line in a speech otherwise prose (though NEWCOMB sets the part-line as prose also).

5.1.12   If...me] THIS EDITION; *prose* NEWCOMB. The part verse-line, probably unmarked in the MS, gives a transition from verse to prose.

5.1.59–60   In...on] DILKE; 1 *line* NEWCOMB. The emendation restores a rhyming couplet.

5.1.110–17   Juno...equally] DILKE; 4 *lines* NEWCOMB: bodies | maker | me |

5.1.160–1   This...lords] DILKE; 1 *line* NEWCOMB

5.1.164–5   Stark...that] DYCE; 1 *line* NEWCOMB

5.1.206–7   Behold...point] DYCE; 1 *line* NEWCOMB

NO WIT/HELP LIKE A WOMAN'S

Edited by John Jowett

HUMPHREY MOSELEY entered *No Wit* (*BEPD* 778) in the Stationers' Register on 9 September 1653, in a block entry including several Middleton plays (see Textual Introduction to *Dissemblers*). He published the play in an octavo volume some four years later in 1657 (Wing M1985), in the same format and year as *Two New Plays*. There is a strong association between the two books: the title-page of *No Wit* and the individual play title-pages in *Two New Plays* are printed from the same setting from the author's name to the publisher's name, and some copies of the books were probably stitched and bound together for sale as a single volume. Like *Two New Plays*, the play was printed by Thomas Newcomb. His edition runs to seven and a half sheets collated A–G8, H4, with the pages taken up as follows: A1, title-page; A1ᵛ, blank; A2, Prologue; A2ᵛ, 'The Actors Names'; A3–H3, the play; H3ᵛ, Epilogue; H4 and H4ᵛ blank. The book is paginated from 5 (A3) to 117 (H3), with p. 30 misnumbered '32' and 83 misnumbered '77'. A number of the extant copies of *No Wit* are prefixed with the engraved portrait of Middleton found also in some copies of *Two New Plays*; others have the Moseley advertising list cited in *BEPD* as 'Separate List' VIᴬ appended.

Johnson (ed., 1976) detects two compositors, the second taking over from the first between the end of Sc. 4 (on C8) and the beginning of Sc. 7 (on E2). These limits are specified because Sir Gilbert is given the speech-prefix '*Lambst.*' until C8 but on E2 and after '*Sir Gilb.*'. Taken alone, this is insecure evidence in that the change in form could easily be a feature of the manuscript. However, it coincides with at least suggestive evidence that the second part of the book was set by a more space-conscious workman. Although we have been unable to confirm that the second compositor set more contractions than the first, Johnson's identification of two compositors has some plausibility. He suggests that the text was set seriatim and that a single press was used to print it. After collating six copies of NEWCOMB, he was able to identify no true press corrections.

The manuscript from which NEWCOMB was printed must have differed in kind from Newcomb's copy for *Dissemblers* and *Women Beware*. Although the forms used for speech-prefixes and the name-forms in stage directions are on the whole stable (those for Sir Gilbert being an exception), the text has a number of irregularities that point to a less 'finished' and sophisticated manuscript. The following traits suggest a writer at work on a draft:

(*a*) at 1.36–7 there appears to be a misincorporated marginal addition, more likely in an authorial draft than a promptbook;

(*b*) in Sc. 4 Middleton seems to have changed his first intention to bring on Mistress Low-water at 4.154.1, but left the entry direction standing (the wording of the first direction is authorial in character, and cannot be a prompt anticipation);

(*c*) a double speech-prefix at 9.24 is most likely to indicate an authorial alteration (the change seems too trivial to indicate an adaptator);

(*d*) there are a marked number of errors and two probable omissions in NEWCOMB, all of which suggest difficult copy.

Even allowing for such inadequacies as might remain in a promptbook, the stage directions look pre-theatrical. Exits are omitted frequently, as are entries for speaking servants; Master Low-water is given no entry in Sc. 9; Jane is omitted from the catalogue of '*all the Guests*' at 9.349. The printer perhaps made use of an authorial rough draft that would have required further modification in a transcript before becoming fit for stage realization, but in which the speech-prefixes and names in stage directions might have been reasonably uniform.

However, as Bullen first recognized, this manuscript was in at least one place altered in the course of bringing the play to the Dublin stage. In NEWCOMB, at 7.293, Weatherwise stipulates that the current year as 'One thousand six hundred thirty and eight'. In his 1646 *Poems &c.* James Shirley published 'A Prologue to a Play there [in Dublin] Call'd, *No Wit to a Womans*'. Shirley was in Ireland for about four years from 1636, so there can be little doubt that the alteration to the manuscript was made in anticipation of the Dublin revival at the Werburgh Street theatre.

The theoretical possibility arises that the text was altered in other respects in 1638. As suggested below, NEWCOMB's act divisions were most probably introduced at this time. No evidence has been found for other revisions, but two passages require special consideration before this conclusion can be admitted:

First, George (1966) notes that the reference to 'the Bear at Bridge foot in Heaven' (9.477) is a rare allusion to the tavern called the Bear at the Southwark end of London Bridge. There is another such allusion in Shirley's *The Lady of Pleasure*, which was written in 1637, a year before Shirley's revival of *No Wit*. But a better parallel is found in *Puritan* 1.4.256–7: 'yon Bear at Bridgefoot in Heaven'. In contrast to Middleton in *Puritan*, Shirley does not pun on the constellation. One might conjecture that

Shirley had obtained the manuscript of *No Wit* by the time he wrote *The Lady of Pleasure*; but in any case Middleton's authorship of the passage is favoured.

Secondly, Mistress Low-water's repeated entries in Sc. 4 could hypothetically result from the insertion of an additional passage in Shirley's hand. Apart from the recognized alteration in Sc. 7, this passage is the one part of the play where a textual anomaly might be explained as a non-authorial revision. In fact the passage in question (4.155–76) is emphatically Middletonian in tone, motifs, and language. It is extremely doubtful that a case could be made for Shirley's hand here.

One cannot exclude the possibility that Shirley or someone else involved in the Dublin theatre nonetheless made minor alterations to the dialogue that are preserved in NEWCOMB, but apart from the reference to the year 1638, the text can be regarded as essentially Middleton's.

The printer's copy manuscript would have been no more functional as a promptbook in Dublin than in London, and is unlikely to have served as such. Shirley's new Prologue establishes an important textual difference between NEWCOMB, with its older Prologue by Middleton, and the play as performed in the revival. It would therefore seem that the manuscript was annotated in anticipation that a new promptbook would be transcribed from it. Shirley presumably took the manuscript back to London with him. As Moseley printed a number of works by Shirley, including the 1646 *Poems &c* and a 1653 collection of *Six New Plays*, Moseley may have obtained the manuscript directly from Shirley.

NEWCOMB is marked with act divisions but, unlike *No Wit* and *Women Beware*, with no scene divisions. This is consistent with Middleton's usual practice, but a question arises as to the authenticity of the act divisions (Jowett, 1991). The short final Act begins in NEWCOMB (at the equivalent to 9.208):

> The Dial of my sleep goes by your eyes.   *Exit.*
>   *Manent Widow and Mrs.* Low-water.
> [G2]   Act 5. Scaen 1.
>   *Widow and Mrs* Low-water.

In other words, it is emphatically stipulated that the Widow and Mistress Low-water stay on stage during the act interval. The situation is similar to that in texts such as *Midsummer Night's Dream* and *King John* in the Shakespeare Folio, where it seems that theatrical act divisions have been belatedly imposed on a text originally written for continuous performance (Taylor, 1993). The difference is that in both Shakespeare plays the interval is introduced at a point where a definite pause in the action is dramatically plausible; the reverse is true here. The Widow is 'greedy' to embrace Mistress Low-water; the act interval can represent no time-lapse and indeed undermines the immediacy of the action. In 1611 some of the adult acting companies, including Prince Henry's Men, had yet to make the transition from continuous action to act intervals. Thus there are no act divisions in *Roaring Girl*.

The conclusion must be that NEWCOMB's act divisions are unauthoritative. They could have been introduced for the Dublin revival, or, less plausibly, could have been marked in the printing-house. In either case, the same hand would have introduced the stage directions immediately either side of the Act 5 act-break. The consequence for an edition seeking to establish the text as Middleton wrote it for the original performances is that the act divisions should be removed. This is the first edition to do so.

Editorial intervention is required also for the passages in Dutch spoken by the Dutch Merchant and his Boy. In dealing with these speeches I have benefitted from informal assistance from Yvonne Steimitz and, in the later stages of editing, expert advice from Johan Koppenol. It seems that Middleton wrote roughly intelligible transliterations of Dutch that by the time they reach print have sometimes degenerated towards incoherence. A relatively straightforward example of NEWCOMB's Dutch is the first sentence in the language, which is printed '*War es you neightgen an you thonkes you*'. This can be regularized and modernized to '*Waar is je nijgen en je dank-je?*', which gives a meaningful sequence of recognizable words without actual emendation. There is no completely unintelligible phrase in the Dutch passages, but radical intervention is sometimes needed if a semblance of sense is to be established. Easily the most troublesome example is NEWCOMB's '*Ick an sawth no int hein clappon de heeke*', which is the boy's response to Savourwit's nonsense. I emend and modernize to '*Ik antwoord niet zijn klap van de hik*', on the basis that here too there must, presumably, be something communicable underlying the printed words. In such an extreme case there will inevitably be other ways of reconstructing the passage and the editorial task becomes arbitrary; but to leave an utterly meaningless formulation would be more seriously against the tenor of the text, which is to have a simple and roughly correct Dutch.

SEE ALSO

Text: *Works*, 783
Authorship and date: this volume, 371

WORKS CITED

Previous Editions

Dyce, Alexander, ed., *Works* (1840), vol. 5

Bullen, A. H., ed., *Works* (1885), vol. 4

Johnson, Lowell E., 'A Critical Edition of Thomas Middleton's *No Wit, No Help like a Woman's*', unpublished Ph.D. diss. (University of Wisconsin, 1963)

—— ed., *No Wit, No Help like a Woman's* (1976)

Other Works Cited

Balch, Marston Stevens, *Thomas Middleton's 'No Wit, No Help like a Woman's' and 'The Counterfeit Bridegroom' (1677) and Further Adaptations* (1980)

Behn, Aphra [?], *The Counterfeit Bridegroom, or, The Defeated Widow* (1677)

Bergeron, David M., 'Middleton's *No Wit, No Help* and Civic Pageantry', *Pageantry in the Shakespearean Theater*, ed. Bergeron (1985), 65–80

Bretnor, Thomas, *A Prognostication for This Present Year of Our Lord God, 1611* (1611)

Dade, John, *A New Almanac* (1611)

Eccles, Mark, 'Middleton's Comedy *The Almanac, Or No Wit, No Help like a Woman's*', *Notes and Queries* 232 (1987), 296–7

George, David, 'Weather-wise's Almanac and the Date of Middleton's *No Wit No Help like a Woman's*', *Notes and Queries* 211 (1966), 297–301

—— 'Some Later Uses of Middleton's *No Wit*', *Notes and Queries* 219 (1974), 290–2

Guazzo, Stefano, *Civil Conversation*, 4 vols, vols 1–3 trans. George Pettie (1583), vol. 4 trans. Bartholomew Young (1586), ed. Sir E. Sullivan, Tudor Translations, II, vols 7–8 (1925)

Jowett, John, 'Middleton's *No Wit/Help like a Woman's* at the Fortune', *Renaissance Drama* NS 22 (1991), 191–208

Neve, Jeffrey, *A New Almanac and Prognostication, with the Foreign Computation, Serving for the Year…1611* (1611)

Petronius, *The Satyticon*, with Seneca, *The Apocolocyntosis*, trans. J. P. Sulivan, revised edn. (1986)

Porta, Giambattista della, *La Sorella* (1584)

Potter, Lois, 'Arbitrary Adulteries', *Times Literary Supplement* 22 November 1985

Rowe, George E., *Thomas Middleton and the New Comedy Tradition* (1979)

Shirley, James, *Poems Etc.* (1646)

Swinburne, Algernon Charles, 'Thomas Middleton', *The Nineteenth Century* 19 (1886), 138–53

Taylor, Gary, 'The Structure of Performance', in Taylor and John Jowett, *Shakespeare Reshaped 1606–1623* (1993), 3–50

Traub, Valerie, 'The (In)Significance of "Lesbian" Desire in Early Modern England', *Erotic Politics: Desire on the Renaissance Stage*, ed. Susan Zimmerman (1992), 150–69

Trollope, Anthony, marginal note in his copy of Dyce's edition of Middleton (1840), dated 10 March 1877

Ward, Adolphus William, *History of English Dramatic Literature to the Death of Queen Anne* (1875)

TEXTUAL NOTES

Title *No…Almanac*] THIS EDITION; NO WIT/HELP LIKE A WO-MANS NEWCOMB (*title-page, with 'WIT' bracketed above 'HELP'*; *similarly half-title*), *Moseley's advertising list VI^A, with similar bracketing; No wit like a Womans* NEWCOMB (*running title*); No Witt, no helpe like a Woman SR, *Moseley's advertising list VI^B*; the Almanak *Accounts of the Revels at Court*; *The Almanac; or, No Wit, No Help Like a Woman's* ECCLES (*conj.*). Most editors follow the Stationers' Register's 'No Wit, No Help', but the slash adopted in this edition more accurately reflects the bracketing of 'Wit' and 'Help' consistently adopted by Moseley. The identification of 'A play called the Almanak' acted at Whitehall by Prince Henry's Players on 29 December 1611 with Middleton's play was first made by Eccles. This suggestion is highly plausible; but 'the Almanak' was probably a subtitle to 'No Wit…', not, as Eccles argues, Middleton's original and only name for the plays (see Jowett). For its running titles, this edition uses the original running title and versions of the half-title reading, the Stationers' Register reading, and the Revels reading (the last in its original spelling and in the spellings found in Middleton's texts, 'Alamanck' and 'Alamancke'; they never use 'Almanak').

Persons In NEWCOMB this list is printed after the Prologue. NEWCOMB omits the Prologue, Servants, Tenants, and Winds. THIS EDITION omits 'The Scene LONDON.'

Persons.16 Peccadill] NEWCOMB (*Pickadille*). Similarly throughout. Johnson over-ingeniously suggests that 'the name of the clown, Pickadille, suggests the analogy between a pickadille (an intricate, delicate edging on a collar) and the intricate schemes in the plot for which the clown is responsible' (Johnson, 1976 edition, p. 3). Rather, '*Pickadille*' is simply a spelling of *peccadill*, itself an anglicization of *peccadillo*, and so immediately fitting as a name for a clown.

Persons.16 CLOWN] Fool NEWCOMB

Prologue.0.1 *Enter Prologue*] *not in* NEWCOMB. NEWCOMB and previous editors treat the Prologue as if it were not part of the performance text; there is no entry or exit. In NEWCOMB the speech precedes 'The Actors' Names', and is printed in italic.

Prologue.7 errand] NEWCOMB (*arrant*). As neither form rhymes properly with *warrant* there is no reason not to modernize.

1.15 woos] NEWCOMB (*woes*). Also 1.112.

1.17 'Twixt] DYCE; 'Bwixt NEWCOMB

1.19 hath] NEWCOMB; have DYCE

1.20.1 *Enter Sandfield*] THIS EDITION; *after* 'comes', 1.20, NEWCOMB

1.36–7 O…silent!] THIS EDITION; How…filent! | Phil. O… Friendfhip NEWCOMB. NEWCOMB duplicates the speech-prefix, assigning both lines to Philip. DYCE follows NEWCOMB's line-order but assigns *O…friendship* to Sandfield. But 'O defend me, friendship' is a protestation of innocence, and is more appropriate to the speaker indicated in NEWCOMB. It responds effectively to Sandfield's accusation that Philip is wooing through his father, and happens to complement the part-line. Similarly, if symptomatic rather than an overwhelming objection in its own right, Savourwit's 'True…' responds to 'How…silent' (DYCE, recognizing the awkward sequence in NEWCOMB, conjecturally emends 'True' to 'Tush'). The duplicated prefix probably arises because '*Phil…. Friendship*' was added in the manuscript as an afterthought; it appears to have been inserted at the wrong point when it was transcribed or set in print.

1.39 now] NEWCOMB; ne'er DYCE

1.41 'Tis] DYCE; 'Ts NEWCOMB

1.43 you'd] NEWCOMB (y'would)

1.51 mad] DYCE; made NEWCOMB. *OED* records 'made' as a 15th c. spelling of *mad*, but NEWCOMB probably gives an imperfect modernization of 'madde'.

1.62 Jersey] NEWCOMB (*Jernfey*). The 'n' gives an acceptable spelling variant of *Jersey* (though *OED* records it only as 16th c.). The usual emendation to *Guernsey* (DYCE) is unnecessary.

1.73 crowns] The final letter is a type resembling a small turned '3'. Here it might stand for 's' or 'e', but the ambiguity is resolved by 'time[s]', 9.44, where it must stand for 's'.

1.110 soldered] NEWCOMB (foader'd)

1.113 arrant] NEWCOMB. Johnson reads the variant *errant*. In modern use *arrant* is primarily 'downright' and *errant* is (a) 'wandering', (b) 'erring'. All these senses are present, as too is 'rascally', which is better communicated by *arrant*. The choice between forms is somewhat arbitrary; but *errant* is perhaps too Quixotic, whereas *arrant* is consistent with *mere sot*, *rank fox*, etc.

1.115 dow'r] DYCE (dower); Down NEWCOMB. *Down* cannot here be of the feathery kind. It might be understood as referring to the smock being taken off, but *OED* gives no support for *down* as a substantive from the verb before 1710 except as the refrain of a song. NEWCOMB could result from the easiest minim error. The collocation 'portion...dowry' occurs in 2.9–10.

1.116 covetous] DYCE; courteous NEWCOMB

1.118 masty] THIS EDITION; waste NEWCOMB; waste her on DYCE. *Waste*, if taken as a verb, requires an emendation such as Dyce made. But the error Dyce posited is relatively unlikely. Two of *OED*'s obsolete senses of *Waste* as an adjective fit the portrayal of Weatherwise. Sense 4 is 'Of speech, thought, action: Profitless, serving no purpose, idle, vain'; sense 8 is 'Of a person: ?Worthless', citing an example from Ben Jonson in which the person is again a potential partner in marriage. And the usual modern meaning might apply to the imagined almanac fragments. Yet bearing in mind that the phrasing (especially *To save* in the previous line) prompts *waste* to be read as a verb and that the metre is awkwardly irregular, it remains probable that *waste* is an error. Disyllabic *masty* (fed with mast, fatted, swinish) would seem to be the best emendation. Compare Pilia-Borza's description of Barabas as 'a masty slave' (Marlowe, *Jew of Malta*, 5.1.75).

1.149.1 *Enter Grace Twilight*] DYCE; *after* 'come', 1.150, NEWCOMB

1.153 sport'st with] THIS EDITION; fport'ft NEWCOMB; sportest DYCE. Dyce identified metrical corruption, but the sense is also problematic: no recorded sense of *sport* current in the period fits the context. *In* or *with* is required. Compare *Old Law* 1.1.216, 'play and sport with sorrow'.

1.153.1 *A noise within*] THIS EDITION; *not in* NEWCOMB. Savourwit's *Hark* responds to the offstage noise of the gathering.

1.161.1–5 *Enter...Sunset*] THIS EDITION; *after* 'Peace', 1.162, NEWCOMB

1.168 widow weight] NEWCOMB. *OED* records no such expression as *widow weight*. It is probably a nonce variation, for the sake of irony and rhyme, on *widow right*. The rhyme with *estate* confirms the reading.

1.170 Master Overdone] NEWCOMB; [and] Master Overdone DYCE

1.173 SIR GILBERT] NEWCOMB (*Lambft.*). NEWCOMB continues to designate the character by his surname until after Sc. 4 (C8), but the speech-prefix form is 'Sir Gilb.' from Sc. 7 (E2) onwards.

1.182, 190 GRACE *and* JANE] NEWCOMB (*Both.*)

1.183–4 WIDOW There's...I now] JOHNSON; There's...*Wid.* I now NEWCOMB

1.186 does't] NEWCOMB (do'ft)

1.196 WIDOW] DYCE; *No speech prefix in* NEWCOMB

1.224 which] THIS EDITION; with NEWCOMB.

1.243 doting] THIS EDITION; do-|ing NEWCOMB. The literal would be easily dropped at the line-break.

1.250 To, marry,] NEWCOMB (to, ~,); Marry, to, THIS EDITION conj. NEWCOMB prints as prose. *Marry* must be the interjection, which is strained after *to*. The compositor might have misunderstood the sense and taken *marry* as the verb.

1.269 eighth] NEWCOMB (eight)

1.272 eleventh] THIS EDITION; tenth NEWCOMB. In NEWCOMB Weatherwise breaks off to wish himself luck before reading the tenth day, but when he resumes he skips to the eleventh

day; it is accordingly the eleventh day which brings the bad luck which he tried to avert before reading the tenth, which he never reads. DYCE emends 'eleventh' at l. 273 to make both readings 'tenth'. This is plausible, but that eleven was regarded as an unlucky number, associated with sin and death, both in Middleton's writings (see, for example, *Black Book*, 206) and in a tradition going back at least to St Augustine. It is unlikely that there is an omission due to eyeskip, because any such break would have to be after 'tenth' by the logic of number but before 'but now' by the logic of rhetoric. Equally, 'but now' strongly suggests that the day in question, today, has been reached. This can be established by emending 'tenth' to 'eleventh', on the basis of a simple misreading of an Arabic numeral or a deliberate 'correction' to maintain numerical continuity in NEWCOMB. Weatherwise presumably loses patience with the recitation as he approaches the eleventh day, and passes over the tenth silently.

2.4 devil's] NEWCOMB (Devils); Devil DYCE

2.19 husband] THIS EDITION; Uncle NEWCOMB. 'Middleton failed to change the relationship from the source play's "uncle"' (Johnson). There is no need to perpetuate the slip.

2.49 prize] NEWCOMB (price); piece BULLEN (Dyce). NEWCOMB has not previously been interpreted as a form of *prize* ('Property seized as in war', *OED*, *Prize*, *sb.*3.2.c). This reading involves no emendation and fits the situation well.

2.60 you] DYCE; your NEWCOMB

2.62.1 *Jane begins to leave*] *not in* NEWCOMB. Jane is close to the door when the Footman enters, and perhaps admits him in.

2.71.1 *She...away*] *not in* NEWCOMB. See 2.81 and 110.

2.84–97 If...another's] NEWCOMB (*in italics*)

2.89 a long] THIS EDITION; *a longer* NEWCOMB; an DYCE

2.107 nearest] DYCE; near'ft NEWCOMB

2.116 loose] NEWCOMB (lofe); taste DYCE (conj.). JOHNSON first read *loose*. This gives the sense required, though *lose* could be defended as ironic. NEWCOMB's 'lose' is probably no more than a spelling variant.

2.117 suits] DYCE; Suiters NEWCOMB

2.122 you] DYCE; yon NEWCOMB

2.124 MISTRESS LOW-WATER] DYCE; *Mrs Lambft.* NEWCOMB

2.140 east port] BULLEN; vaft part NEWCOMB. A compelling emendation that seems necessary to sustain the image of sunrise (compare 1.141, 'here it sets'). NEWCOMB's reading obliterates anything but the sexual reading, as *part* can in context mean only 'organ'. But the emendation far from disallows this genital reference. *Port* can be specifically and even technically 'entrance to the vagina' (see *OED*, *sb.*3, 1b, 1545 quotation) and is used in such a sense, or at least with reference to it, by Middleton (*Revenger's*, 2.2.104–4, 'I'll guard her honour, | And keep the ports sure'). In this respect *port* makes the genital image more precise, even as *port* as 'gateway of the sun' heightens the poeticism.

2.145.1 *Exit*] NEWCOMB (*Exit Sir Gilbert Lambston.*)

2.147 Wherein] BULLEN (Dyce); Herein NEWCOMB

2.148 shuts] NEWCOMB; shut DYCE

3.0.2 and Savourwit] THIS EDITION; Philip, *and* Savorwit NEWCOMB. See following note.

3.24.1 *Enter Philip*] THIS EDITION; *placed after* 'Philip', 3.25 NEWCOMB; *not in* DYCE. More noteworthy than the misplacement is that NEWCOMB's direction duplicates the opening entry. It also coincides with another apparent duplication, 'boys, *Philip*', in 3.25. Philip's presence in the opening direction is consistent with 'boys', whereas his entry mid-scene makes '*Philip*' more natural. Here is an evident change of intention. As Philip is not the last-named character in the opening direction, as his name follows 'boys' in 3.25, and as a mid-scene entry is both more sophisticated and more contextually effective, his entry at the beginning of the scene would have been the original arrangement. We emend to establish the revised staging.

3.25 Philip] THIS EDITION; boys, *Philip* NEWCOMB. See previous note.

3.29 PHILIP *and* SANDFIELD] NEWCOMB (*Both.*)

3.29 *Exeunt...Sandfield*] NEWCOMB (*Exeunt.*)

3.32 ye] DYCE; you NEWCOMB. The emendation attractively establishes a rhyme with *belly*. Compare the oddly similar 5.148 and *Heroes* 177-8. *Ye* is not a particularly characteristic Middleton form, occurring, for instance, only an average of five times per play in five early comedies (Jackson, *Studies in Attribution*, pp. 189-90). But in these three cases it must be more than suspected that Middleton broke his normal preference for *you* for the sake of the rhyme, and that (*a*) the compositor regularized 'ye' to *you*; or (*b*) Middleton wrote a confusible form such as 'yᵉ', misread 'yᵘ'; or (*c*) Middleton indifferently wrote 'you' whilst anticipating that 'ye' would be spoken.

3.33 *Exit*] NEWCOMB (*Exit Savourwit.*)

3.40 owed] NEWCOMB (ought)

3.40 shows] NEWCOMB; sh'owes DYCE. NEWCOMB acceptably shifts the 'love and care' from affection given to affection demonstrably received. Dyce's emendation requires a similar shift in the sense of the repeated verb *owe* from 'owe as a debt' to 'own, have'. *Sh'owes* (as distinct from *she owes* or *owes*) can only with difficulty be distinguished in sound from *shows*. Its relevance is probably as a secondary sense, through wordplay.

3.42 How] NEWCOMB (*Sir Oliv.* How)

3.43 now] NEWCOMB. NEWCOMB's idiom recurs at 3.137, making emendation to *new* implausible.

3.45 in to...trow] NEWCOMB (into...tro)

3.73 boggling] NEWCOMB (budgelling)

3.80 son] NEWCOMB (Son); sum BULLEN (Dyce). Sir Oliver is not (otherwise) talking about the ransom, and the emendation creates a difficulty in establishing an antecedent for *this*, and even *his*, in the following line. NEWCOMB is a little tangled, but intelligible; the sense is that the act of sending Philip led to the return home of his sister in addition to him, the son. *With* means 'as well as', and *this* refers back to the news.

3.81.1 *Enter Grace*] THIS EDITION; *after* 'she', 3.82, NEWCOMB

3.93 Yea?] DYCE; Ye! NEWCOMB. The space before the exclamation mark might fit an 'a', but it is the compositor's usual spacing. NEWCOMB gives a late example of an old spelling, or, more likely, a compositorial omission.

3.104-5 *Waar...*DUTCH BOY...*Ik*] JOHNSON; *Dutch Boy. War... Ick* NEWCOMB

3.104 *Waar...je*] NEWCOMB (*War es you neighen an you thonkes you*). For general comments on editorial treatment of NEWCOMB's Dutch, see Textual Introduction.

3.105 *Ik...vriendelijkheid*] NEWCOMB (*Ick donck you, ver ew Edermon vrendly Kite*). NEWCOMB's *Edermon* is the substantive where the qualifier *edele*, 'noble', is required. *Edermon*, modernized to *edelman*, is retained as intrinsic to Middleton's Dutch.

3.113.1 *Exit Dutch Merchant*] DYCE; '*Exit.*' after 3.112 NEWCOMB

3.115 and] DYCE; aud NEWCOMB

3.140 I'll] NEWCOMB; I'd DYCE

3.145 *Ik...niet*] NEWCOMB (*Ick wet neat watt hey zacht; Ick un-|verſton ewe neat*). *En...niet* is an obsolete double negative. *Verstaan* should properly be *versta*.

3.154 Tells] DYCE (*following 'Counterfeit Bridegroom'*); Tell NEWCOMB

3.159 Ik] NEWCOMB (*Ick*)

3.159 antwoord...hik] THIS EDITION; *an ſawth no int hein clappon de heeke* NEWCOMB. NEWCOMB is seriously confused or corrupt here. Koppenol suggests that the second half of the sentence might be '*een klap van de giek*', a blow from the boom (of a sailing ship), meaning that Savourwit is mad, but the expression does not seem to be idiomatic and it leaves the beginning of the sentence unresolved.

3.159-60 *Ik...zinnen*] NEWCOMB (*I dinke ute zein zennon*)

3.161 Aha] NEWCOMB (Ah ha)

3.175 artichokes, and cabbages] NEWCOMB (Hartichalks, and Cabiſhes)

3.180 *Neem...kakk'*] NEWCOMB (*Nimd aweigh de cack*). *Eige'* should properly be *eigen*, and *kak* is short for *kakken*.

3.199 tail] DYCE; tale NEWCOMB. 'Tail' was an acceptable spelling of *tale*, but *OED* records 'tale' for *tail* only in Scotland.

3.207 *Exit*] NEWCOMB (*Exit Savourwit.*)

3.220.1 *Dutch Merchant*] NEWCOMB (*Dutchman*)

3.234-5 *Zeg...maan, en*] NEWCOMB (*Zeicke yongon, ick ben ick quelt medien dullek heght, ee vntoit van the mon, an*)

3.235 *koeterwalend*] THIS EDITION (Koppenol); *koot uram'd* NEWCOMB

3.236 *Wee...zegt*] NEWCOMB (*Wee ek, heigh lieght in ze Bokkas, dee't ſite*)

3.242-3 *Zei...we*] NEWCOMB (*Zeicke hee ewe ek kneeght, yongon, dat wee*)

3.243 *niet kijf*] THIS EDITION; *neeky* NEWCOMB. The emendation is not entirely satisfactory; as Koppenol points out the only use of 'kijf' is in the set expression 'buiten kijf'.

3.243 *bij Antwerpen*] NEWCOMB (*by Antwarpon*)

3.243 *vandaan*] THIS EDITION; *ne don* NEWCOMB

3.243-4 *komen...daar*] NEWCOMB (*cammen no ſeene de doughter Dor*)

3.245-6 *Ik...rabauw*] NEWCOMB (*Ick hub ham hean ſulka dongon he zaut, hei es an ſkallom an rubbout*). In *hean* and *he zaut* the 'h' seems to stand for an initial 'g'. This may be a feature of Middleton's transliteration rather than a repeated error.

4.0.1-2 *the Clown...servants*] NEWCOMB (*two or three*). Though NEWCOMB does not specify the Clown, he is plausibly included amongst the 'two or three'. After 4.9 he has no part in the scene until 4.141, and can accordingly leave the stage with the other servants at 4.9.1. NEWCOMB provides no re-entry, but omits a re-entry for the servants generally. Weatherwise addresses his servants as amongst those present before the banquet enters; they can be presumed to enter setting forth the banquet when Weatherwise returns at 4.87.1, and the Clown would be amongst them.

4.5 CLOWN] NEWCOMB. The character later acquires the personal name Peccadill. The generic name is found in all the Clown's speech-prefixes and most stage directions; the personal name occurs three times in the text and in one stage direction.

4.22.1 *The...apart*] *not in* NEWCOMB. At 4.28 the explicit dialogue is resumed midstream.

4.27 in th'] NEWCOMB (in 'th')

4.39 to th'] NEWCOMB (t'th')

4.42 o'] NEWCOMB (a'). The form is common in NEWCOMB and is not subsequently recorded.

4.66-7 Now...gay] *in italics (except 'May')* NEWCOMB

4.66 'Now'] NEWCOMB; PEP. *Now* DYCE

4.71 much] The type for 'u' resembles a small turned 'B' and might be taken as an 'a'. In the previous line, the first letter of 'away' is again an unusual type, in this instance resembling a small ampersand.

4.74–7 Now...dry] *in italics* NEWCOMB

4.74 physics] NEWCOMB; physic GEORGE (*conj.*). The motto is taken word for word from Jeffery Neve's 1611 almanac, which reads 'physicke'. However, there is a comparable alteration from the almanac's '*fieldes*' to NEWCOMB's '*field*' at 4.67.

4.95.1–2 the...the] *not in* NEWCOMB. See note to 4.0.1–2.

4.95.2 *Weatherwise's*] NEWCOMB (*his*)

4.95.4 in order] *not in* NEWCOMB. NEWCOMB's list must prescribe the order in which the signs enter.

4.117 back] DYCE; hack NEWCOMB

4.120 Since] NEWCOMB (fence). Similarly at 5.18.

4.144 Push] The first of five instances in NEWCOMB of this characteristically Middletonian expletive. The form is not found in Moseley's 1657 edition of *Dissemblers* and *Women Beware*, where it may have been regularized to *pish* in the copy.

4.154.1 *Enter a Servant*] DYCE. NEWCOMB instead gives here the stage direction printed at 4.177.1–2. For discussion, see note to 4.177.1–2.

4.157 Has] NEWCOMB (H'as)

4.177.1–2 *Enter...her*] NEWCOMB gives the full version of this direction, as printed here, after 4.154 (see note). It duplicates this version with the brief '*Enter Mistress Low-water.*' here. The wording of the longer direction looks distinctly authorial, so it is not likely to be a bookkeeper's anticipatory note in a promptbook. Its position is puzzling unless Middleton added the intervening passage after he first drafted the scene. For implications as to the compositor's copy, see Textual Introduction.

4.206 low water] NEWCOMB (Low-water). Middleton often failed to mark proper names with capital letters, hence the confusion. Or a deliberate ambiguity.

4.246 ALL THE REST] NEWCOMB (*All.*)

4.254 who's] NEWCOMB (whofe)

4.257 taking...Clown] *not in* NEWCOMB. Necessary so that the cup can remain on stage.

4.268 yon] DYCE; you NEWCOMB

4.281–2 fill t'...Fill t'] NEWCOMB (filt...fil't)

4.288 knight] THIS EDITION (Eccles); Knave NEWCOMB. Sir Gilbert is consistently distinguished from the other suitors by his rank, and there is no contextual justification in calling him a knave. Error might have been facilitated by an abbreviation such as 'Kt', which is regularly used in speech-prefixes in the Trinity MS of *Game*.

4.313 these] NEWCOMB (this)

4.331 ALL THE SUITORS] NEWCOMB (*All.*)

4.347 Frames] THIS EDITION; From NEWCOMB; To free JOHNSON. Johnson identifies a real difficulty in NEWCOMB, but his emendation is not convincing. *Frames* is more conducive to the error, and varies the idea of the letter as 'a glass | Will show him...' (4.342–3).

4.395 Heart] DYCE; Hear't NEWCOMB. The expletive occurs also at 9.95 (NEWCOMB 'Heat') and 9.125. Here the compositor seems to have been confused by *hear* in the previous line, unless Middleton, perhaps influenced by the same word, introduced an irregular apostrophe.

4.409 knight's] DYCE; nights NEWCOMB

4.410 flutter] THIS EDITION; flatter NEWCOMB. The point about the end of the scene is that the suitors are ruffled; one of them has been exposed and the others depart, presumably separately, to pursue their separate courses. *Flatter* has no

application here; *flutter* anticipates the image of cocks and hens, and is entirely apposite.

5.33.1–2 *Master...scholar*)] THIS EDITION; a Gentleman | a Scholler NEWCOMB. Johnson identifies the gentleman as Beveril and the scholar as another character, but NEWCOMB is probably based on copy 'Gentleman Scholler'. Compare 7.180.

5.33.2 and servants] NEWCOMB (&c.). These figures probably exist to bear the travellers' luggage and so to indicate that they are 'new landed'.

5.48 worn] DYCE; worm NEWCOMB

5.56 I] DYCE; It NEWCOMB

5.102.1 *Philip...Mother*] NEWCOMB ('*Shogs his* | *Mother.*' opposite the two part-lines of 5.103)

5.148 ye] DYCE; you NEWCOMB. The emendation completes the rhyme. See note to 3.32.

5.176 hufty-tufty] NEWCOMB (Hoffte Toftee). NEWCOMB's form resembles the pseudo-Dutch nonsense '*Hoff Tofte*' at 3.158. The modern equivalent is *hoity-toity*, but the expressions probably have separate derivations.

5.185.1–5.193.1 *Exeunt; manet Savourwit...Exit*] DYCE; *Exeunt:* NEWCOMB (after 5.193)

6.0.1 *Kate Low-water*] NEWCOMB (Kate)

6.15 is] DYCE; his NEWCOMB

6.22 these] DYCE; thofe NEWCOMB. Mistress Low-water is referring to her own disguise, not her husband's.

6.23 lies] NEWCOMB; lies now G.T. conj.

6.25.1–3 *Enter...suitors*] THIS EDITION;. after 6.31 NEWCOMB; after 'fellows', 6.26, DYCE

6.39 ALL THE SUITORS] NEWCOMB (*All.*). Similarly 6.191.

6.45 gentlemen's] DYCE; Gentlemans NEWCOMB

6.52 PEPPERTON...Peg] NEWCOMB (*Peppert. Overd. How Befs, Peg?*); PE. How! Bess? | OVER. Peg? DYCE. Dyce indicates one of several ways of interpreting NEWCOMB.

6.80 *Exeunt suitors*] NEWCOMB (*Exeunt.*)

6.89 make a] DYCE; make NEWCOMB

6.155 kneeling] *not in* NEWCOMB. A strongly emotive gesture is needed; and see 6.157.

6.161 *Rising*] THIS EDITION; *not in* NEWCOMB. This is the first opportunity to rise, and almost the last: Mistress Low-water is certainly standing for her next speech.

6.182 Within there!] DYCE. NEWCOMB prints in italic, set to the right margin as a stage direction, with a full stop instead of an exclamation mark. Middleton would use a dash either to mark a change of addressee or to set off a stage direction, and did not usually write stage directions in italic.

6.204 California] NEWCOMB (Californic) The form derives from Neve's 1611 almanac, B3^v (George), and is probably a current spelling rather than an error.

6.209 *Exeunt suitors*] DYCE; *Exit.* NEWCOMB (after 6.206–7)

6.211.1–2 the...Servant] *not in* NEWCOMB

6.212, 214 SERVANT] NEWCOMB (*1 Serv.*)

6.214 What] NEWCOMB; What['s] DYCE

6.214 worship'] NEWCOMB (worfhip); worship's DYCE. Compare the irregular idiom of the Servant's 'privilege place', 9.7.

6.250 parbreaking] NEWCOMB; Barbreaking NEWCOMB

6.260 feed] NEWCOMB; fleet DYCE (*conj.*). *Feed* alarmingly collapses the metaphor, but is taken up in *past hand-to-mouth* and is probably right.

6.269.1 *Enter Beveril*] DYCE (*subst.*); '*Enter Beveril.*' after 'How now', 6.270, NEWCOMB

6.273 affection] DYCE; affliction NEWCOMB

6.279 suffice] DYCE; suffer NEWCOMB

6.280 kneeling] *not in* NEWCOMB. Not absolutely required, but highly plausible in view of 6.282.

6.300.1   *Enter Widow*] THIS EDITION; *after* 'comes', 6.301, NEW-COMB

7.15   Tail] DYCE; tails NEWCOMB

7.50   slander] DYCE; ſlaue NEWCOMB

7.95   they're] NEWCOMB (their)

7.126   beer] NEWCOMB (Bear)

7.137   believed] DYCE; bely'd NEWCOMB. NEWCOMB, as *belied*, just might mean that almanac posies only come true according to their bad (knavish) interpretation because they are calumniated through misinterpretation. But this is very strained, and the point of view contradicts Sir Gilbert's belief that the posies themselves are *mere delusions*.

7.137.1   *Sir...apart*] *not in* NEWCOMB. Weatherwise appears to address Sir Gilbert amongst the *gentlemen* in his following speech, but it is clear from 7.143 that Sir Gilbert has ceased taking any notice of him.

7.150   candles] NEWCOMB; caudles DYCE (*conj.*). A plausible emendation, in so far as Middleton refers elsewhere to *caudles* (e.g. *Dissemblers* 5.1.6). But *candles* makes perfect sense as a requirement for Beveril to study late into the night.

7.157   shrewdly] NEWCOMB (ſhroudly)

7.173-4   persons...Parsons] NEWCOMB (Parſons...Parſons). Modernized texts cannot fully preserve the wordplay. We give the primary sense in each case.

7.178.1   *with a pasteboard*] *not in* NEWCOMB. At 7.234.1 Beveril evidently shows the suitors an abstract of the device they will perform. This could be on a piece of paper, but is more likely to be the same pasteboard that NEWCOMB stipulates at 9.52.1. Beveril certainly enters looking studious and thoughtful; the pasteboard could assist here, and would provide a way for him to demonstrate before he speaks at 7.189 that he is attempting to concentrate on his work but cannot. The pasteboard would have the same relation to the device that Weatherwise's almanac has to the conceited banquet.

7.199   smothered] NEWCOMB (ſmothered) (=èd)

7.210-11   her—...Whether] THIS EDITION; ~. | *Sir Gilb.* Whether NEWCOMB. The combination of uncomplemented part-line and double speech-prefix in NEWCOMB suggests strongly that a part-line is missing. The situation that would most readily account for such an error would be an echoic part-line that induced eyeskip. In support of the present emendation, compare 'Both lovers of her honour...And think our service well' below (7.220-2).

7.233   disposed] diſpoſed NEWCOMB (= disposèd)

7.250   men] DYCE; me NEWCOMB

7.293   now] THIS EDITION; now in One thouſand ſix hundred thirty and eight NEWCOMB; now in one thousand six hundred and eleven ECCLES *conj.* The date mentioned in NEWCOMB but omitted in this edition was clearly introduced for the revival in Dublin. The dominical letter for 1611, the year of first performance, was, as Eccles notes, F, not G. This is really only a problem if one assumes that 1611 was stipulated in the original text. Shirley was later able to make the G-for-goose joke topical because G happened to be the dominical letter for 1638, but the joke is Middletonian (see *Dissemblers* 3.2.110-13), and Eccles's suggestion that Middleton originally wrote the weaker 'F' and 'fool' therefore seems unlikely. See Jowett, pp. 202-4.

7.295   though't] THIS EDITION; though that NEWCOMB. The sequence *this...that...that's* is confusing, and the demonstrative seems wrong in an anticipatory position. Compositorial expansion of 'though't' to 'though that' would be prompted by 'that's' in the following line.

7.304   Air] DYCE; fair NEWCOMB. Perhaps a *currente calamo* alteration from 'f[ire]' to 'air'.

7.321.1   *Exeunt suitors*] NEWCOMB (*Exeunt.*)

7.323.1   *Enter...man-husband*] DYCE; *after* 'it', 7.326 NEWCOMB

8.0.2   *Sir Oliver's redeemed...Mother*] NEWCOMB (*his redeemed Lady*)

8.13   these] THIS EDITION; that NEWCOMB. NEWCOMB makes strained sense as 'For that [because] my joy's [joy is] unlooked for', but it is hard not to think that heaven should wishedly requite Beveril *for* the joys. Dyce's emendation (see following note) highlights the awkwardness of *that* from a new angle. NEWCOMB could result from a substitution of demonstrative pronouns, or from a rationalization of the old form 'this' for *these*, as at 4.313. And the compositor may have been confused as to the sense; NEWCOMB's punctuation is 'requite him!...unlook'd for;—'.

8.13   joys] NEWCOMB; joy DYCE. See previous note.

8.62   she] DYCE; he NEWCOMB

8.91   risse] NEWCOMB (rife); risen DYCE. *Risen* gives a plausible metrical emendation, but NEWCOMB otherwise gives a satisfactory and distinctively Middletonian form (*Lady* A1.1.113, *Michaelmas Term* 3.1.126, etc.). Here it is possibly used to echo the previous line more closely.

8.115   and I] NEWCOMB; ay and THIS EDITION *conj.*

8.159.1   *Exeunt*] DYCE; *Exit.* NEWCOMB

8.159.1-2   *Sister (Grace)*] NEWCOMB (*Siſter*)

8.178.1   *Philip...apart*] THIS EDITION; *not in* NEWCOMB. At 8.196 and after, Philip remains unaware of the exchange between Grace and the Mother. See also following note.

8.193   *showing...Grace*] THIS EDITION; *not in* NEWCOMB. Like Philip, Savourwit is here unaware of the exchange that has just taken place (see 8.203), and his comment is without irony: he takes the embrace as an encouraging sign.

8.240   approve] THIS EDITION; approv'd NEWCOMB. Dyce and subsequent editors retain NEWCOMB, glossing 'have proved'; but if that is the sense, the text requires emending to 'a' proved'. Terminal '-e'/'-d' error is more likely.

8.257.1   *Exit...(Grace)*] DYCE (*subst.*); *after* 8.256 NEWCOMB (reading '*Exit cum Filia.*')

9.7   privilege] NEWCOMB; privileged DYCE. NEWCOMB's reading is retained because the Servant may be given a characterizing idiom.

9.20.1   *Loud music [within]*] THIS EDITION; *Loud Musick.* (*before* 'Enter', 9.22.1-2) NEWCOMB. The Clown's *Hark* is clearly a response to the approaching music.

9.22.1-2   *Low-water*] *not in* NEWCOMB

9.24   ALL THE REST] THIS EDITION; *All. Sir Ol* NEWCOMB. DYCE prints 'SIR O. TWI., &c.', but NEWCOMB probably gives a duplicated prefix. Either of NEWCOMB's alternatives is possible; the assignation to '*All*' is an arrangement which is highly characteristic of Middleton, and which corresponds to the addressee of the previous speech, *This fair assembly*. If there were a change of intention, the outer prefix is likely to be the revised one, confirming the choice of '*All.*'. But alternatively, the double prefix could result from confusion between 'al' and 'ol'. In that case the direction of the error would be less certain, were it not for the contextual consideration.

9.28   No,] THIS EDITION; Nay, NEWCOMB

9.32   knows] DYCE; that knows NEWCOMB. The line rhymes with 9.30, making metrical emendation attractive. NEWCOMB might give a conscious or unconscious sophistication.

9.52.1   *Enter...pasteboard*] THIS EDITION; *after* 9.53 NEWCOMB

9.62.4   streaks] DYCE; ſtroaks NEWCOMB

9.62.20 Beveril] *not in* NEWCOMB

9.63   *as* FIRE] NEWCOMB instead prints 'FIRE' centred on a separate type-line after the first part-line of 9.63. Similarly 'AIR' after 9.98, 'WATER' after 9.131, and 'EARTH' after 9.153.

9.83   son] DYCE; Sun NEWCOMB

9.95   Heart] DYCE; Heat NEWCOMB. The context may have reinforced a misreading.

9.109 sun's] THIS EDITION; Signs NEWCOMB. The idiom in NEWCOMB is wrong: a sign can scarcely be *in* a sign. For the emendation, compare 'when the Sun enters into the Crabs room' (7.106) and the table George adduces as Middleton's source of information at that point, John Dade's 1611 almanac, table for June: 'Sol in cancer'.

9.118 gown-skirts sweeps] NEWCOMB; gown-skirt sweeps *Counterfeit Bridegroom; gown-skirts sweep* DYCE

9.125 *Exit*] NEWCOMB (*Exit Beveril.*)

9.130 Rosa Solis] NEWCOMB (*Roſa Solace*). The expression is: (*a*) the alcoholic cordial (which, as is clear in Dekker's (?) *Blurt, Master Constable* 3.3.14–15, is appropriately smelly to be something for which the nose is a pledge: 'He so smells of ale and onions, and rosa-solis'), and (*b*) the name of the woman whose *solace* is the syphilitic undoing of the nose. I take the cordial to be the primary sense, but retain capitals to indicate the pun.

9.130 bleaching-house] NEWCOMB (Bleaking-houſe)

9.138 'lay] NEWCOMB (lay). The verb is more likely to be *allay* than *lay*.

9.144 prey] THIS EDITION; play NEWCOMB. NEWCOMB surely makes no sense in terms of the Sirens' behaviour. *Prey* was commonly spelled with 'a', which would have facilitated misunderstanding as *pray* and miscorrection, or error of transmission. A double emendation *their prey* would avoid the absolute and aurally ambiguous use of *prey*. In defence of that ambiguity, there may be some wordplay involving (*a*) the alternation of singing and prayer in a church service, and (*b*) prayer as metonymic for the wedding ceremony. *Their prey* would give a closer verbal parallel with the previous line but a less close parallel in sense. But the double error would be much less likely to have occurred, and it is unnecessary to suppose that it did.

9.146 least] NEWCOMB (left)

9.170 warring] DYCE (*following* 'Counterfeit Bridegroom'); waiting NEWCOMB

9.170.14 Beveril] *not in* NEWCOMB

9.192.1 *Exeunt...Low-water*] *not in* NEWCOMB. Low-water is available to fulfil the role of servant here without any need to bring on additional servants.

9.207.1 *Exeunt*] DYCE; Exit NEWCOMB

9.207.1 *manent...Low-water*] THIS EDITION; *Manent Widow and* Mrs *Low-water.* [page-break] Act 5. Scæn I. | *Widow and Mrs Low-water.* NEWCOMB. NEWCOMB's combination of the call for the Widow and Mistress Low-water to remain at the end of its Act 4 and the omission of the word 'Enter' before '*Widow and Mrs Low-water*' at the beginning of its Act 5 gives a peculiarly emphatic insistance that the stage is not cleared for the act-break. DYCE ends 4.2 with '*Scene closes*', implying perhaps that the Widow and Mistress Low-water retire into the discovery space, and begins 5.1 with a discovery, but there is no reason to compromise NEWCOMB's unambiguous '*Manent*'. The act-break is evidently superimposed on a previously uninterrupted scene, which is restored in this edition. See Introduction, and Jowett.

9.284 missed] DYCE; muſt NEWCOMB

9.292 pores] JOHNSON (Dyce); powers NEWCOMB. A minimal error, as both words could be spelled 'powres'.

9.293.1 *Enter Master Low-water*] DYCE; *after* 'work', 9.294, NEWCOMB

9.297.1 *Master...back*] *not in* NEWCOMB. Prompted by *to your office*, which requires some sort of response. It would be at least unnaturalistic for Low-water to relinquish his disguise while still in the Widow's house. But in the Jacobean theatre naturalism would not be mandatory, so Low-water may indeed appear with part of his disguise off (say a beard) and resume it here. More probably, he simply assumes the demeanour of a servant, as he does at 6.25.1.

9.304–15 Kind...for't] NEWCOMB (*in italics*)

9.311 bargain] DYCE; bagain NEWCOMB

9.314 he's] NEWCOMB (*has*)

9.317–23 Being...wife] NEWCOMB (*in italics*)

9.324–6 I have...coming] NEWCOMB uses no quotation marks for the letter but prints the rest of it in italics. These lines are in Roman type, so are undistinguished from Beveril's own words.

9.336 he's] NEWCOMB (has)

9.338 best bow.] THIS EDITION (Dyce); beſt— NEWCOMB. Dyce's conjecture gives a rhyming couplet and a sexual innuendo.

9.338.1 *Exit Mistress Low-water*] DYCE; '*Exit.*' *after* 9.337 NEWCOMB

9.349.1 Low-water] *not in* NEWCOMB

9.349.3 Twilight] *not in* NEWCOMB

9.349.4–5 Twilight's...(Grace)] Wife, Daughter NEWCOMB

9.349.5 *after them,*] THIS EDITION; *not in* NEWCOMB. By interposing 'Mr Sunset' between 'Sir Oliver' and 'Wife, Daughter', NEWCOMB follows the decorum whereby the men are listed before the women irrespective of their family. Philip, Sandfield, and Savourwit are named after the women; this arrangement can only reflect the staging, which therefore repeats the staggered entry in the previous scene.

9.357 ALL THE GUESTS] NEWCOMB (*All.*)

9.364 within] NEWCOMB (*opposite* 'him')

9.364.1–4 Enter...scholar] DYCE; *after* 9.363 NEWCOMB

9.364.3–4 Mistress...Beveril] NEWCOMB (*her Brother*)

9.429 pound] THIS EDITION; *not in* NEWCOMB; pounds DYCE. The ametrical line is especially likely to be corrupt as the absent stressed syllable coincides with the absent currency denomination. *Pound* accords with 'Ten thousand pound' at 1.220, 'ten pound' at 4.33 and 'a hundred pound' at 9.1–12. The repeated '-nd' termination would encourage eyeskip. Alternatively the compositor might have faced '£5000', in which case it would be easy to miss transposing and expanding the pound sign.

9.441 rule] NEWCOMB; yet rule DYCE (*conj.*). 'Yet let us rule' would be more conducive to error.

9.463.2–3 Sir...Overdone] *not in* NEWCOMB

9.476 near] NEWCOMB (nere)

9.514 Now] NEWCOMB; No, THIS EDITION *conj.*

9.549 Jacobi] NEWCOMB (Iac)

9.559.1 She...herself] DYCE; *not in* NEWCOMB. Dyce adds '*embracing Beveril*', suggesting that the *neck-verse* is her arms around his neck. This is possible. Johnson is probably closer to the mark in printing '*revealing her bosom*', but he is over-literal in explaining the *neck-verse...here and here* as specifically Mistress Low-water's breasts. *Here and here* probably accompanies the removal of two garments, or a false beard and a garment, baring her lower neck. A boy actor could not, of course, expose a cleavage.

9.561 ALL THE OTHERS] NEWCOMB (*All.*)

9.562.1   *Exit*] NEWCOMB (*Exit Sir Gilbert*)

9.565   coil's] NEWCOMB (quoils)

9.568   you've] NEWCOMB (Y'have)

9.575   exercised] DYCE; examin'd NEWCOMB. The various meanings of *examine* do not fit the context. *Exercised* happens to restore metre as well as sense. One must posit an error of substitution influenced by a general graphic similarity of the words which would be more marked in early seventeenth--century handwriting.

9.596   wife's] NEWCOMB (Wives)

9.616   gentlemen's] DYCE; Gen-|mens NEWCOMB

9.630   banns] NEWCOMB (Banes)

9.635   Zounds] NEWCOMB (Zunes)

9.659   Whoop] NEWCOMB (Hoop)

9.670   here] DYCE; *not in* NEWCOMB. Primarily a metrical emendation, but the sense is also improved. *Here* would easily be omitted after *her.*

9.674.1–2   *Philip*...'*Jane*'] *not in* NEWCOMB. *Well said* (i.e. well done) is testimony that the boys do as Sir Oliver suggests.

9.681   neatness] THIS EDITION (G.T.); weaknefs NEWCOMB; keanness JOHN MITFORD *conj. in Gentleman's Magazine*, NS, 14

(1840), p. 586; workings BULLEN *conj.*; wittiness JOHNSON (Dyce); quickness THIS EDITION *conj.* Dyce's conjecture introduces a redundant syllable and a reading not readily corrupted to *weakness. Keanness* is not Middletonian, and *workings* is paleographically implausible. *Quickness* may be idiomatically more attractive than *neatness*, but less so paleographically (northern and Scottish forms with 'w' or 'wh' for 'qu' seem unlikely from Middleton). Middleton refers elsewhere to neatness of spirit, art, invention, etc.

Epilogue.1   WEATHERWISE] DYCE; *not in* NEWCOMB

Epilogue.20   [   ] Cancer,] THIS EDITION (Dyce); *not in* NEWCOMB. Dyce noted that a line has dropped out ending in 'Cancer', to rhyme with 'answer'. The line probably made reference to a crab's claws, with jocular reference to the hands as claws. This would be especially appropriate as the association of *clap* and *claw* suggests *clapperclaw*, 'to thrash'. The line may have read something like, 'Though claws hold hardest when the sign is Cancer'.

Epilogue.23.1   *Exit*] THIS EDITION; *not in* NEWCOMB. Like the Prologue, the Epilogue has not been fully treated as a part of the performance text, and is printed in italics.

STAGE DIRECTIONS

Prologue   PROLOGUE.

Persons   [*Printed between the Prologue and Sc. 1*]

The Actors Names.

Sir *Oliver Twilight*, a rich old Knight.

Philip his Son, servant to Mistress *Grace.*

Sandfield, friend to *Philip*, servant to Mistress *Jane.*

Mr. *Sunset*, true Father of Mistress *Grace.*

Mr. *Low-water*, a decayed Gentleman.

Sir *Gilbert Lambston*
Mr. *Weatherwise*   } Suitors to the Lady *Golden-* | *fleece.*
Mr. *Pepperton*
Mr. *Overdon.*

Mr. *Beveril*, Brother to Mistress *Low-water:*

Dutch Merchant.

Dutch Boy.

Savor-wit, Sir *Oliver's* man.

Footman.

Pickadille, Lady *Golden-fleeces* Fool.

Lady *Twilight.*

Lady *Golden fleece*, a rich Widow.

Mistress *Low-water.*

Mistress *Grace*, Sunsets Daughter, but supposed *Twi-* lights.

Mistress *Jane*, Twilights Daughter, but supposed *Sunsets:*

The Scene

LONDON.

1.0.1–2   Act 1. Scæn 1. | *Enter* Philip, Sir Oliver Twilights Son, with Savor-|wit his Fathers man.

1.20.1   *Enter* Sandfield: (after 'comes', 1.21)

1.147   *Exit.*

1.149.1   *Enter* Grace Twilight. (after 'come', 1.150)

1.161.1–5   *Enter the Lady Widow* Golden-fleece *with* Sir Gil-|bert Lambston, Mr. Pepperton, Mr. Overdon, | *suiters; after them the two old men*, Sir Oliver | Twilight, *and* Mr. Sunset, *with their Daughters,* | Grace Twilight, Jane Sunset. (after 'Peace', 1.162)

1.197.1   *Exeunt.* | *Manet* Sir *Oliver with* Savorwit.

1.260.1   *Exit.*

1.262.1   *Enter* Weather-wise.

1.306   *Exit.*

2.0.1   *Enter* Mistress Low-water.

2.26.1   *Enter* Mistress Jane, Sunsets *Daughter.*

2.64   *Enter* Footman.

2.74   *Exit.*

2.111.2   *Enter* Sir *Gilbert* Lambston.

2.145.1   *Exit* Sir *Gilbert* Lambston.

2.152.1   *Enter* Master Low-water.

2.171   *Exeunt.*

3.0.1–2   *Enter* Sir Oliver Twilight, *with* Mr Sandfield, | Philip, *and* Savorwit.

3.24.1   *Enter* Philip. (after 'Philip', 3.25)

3.29   *Exeunt.*

3.33   *Exit* Savorwit.

3.41.1   *Enter* Servant.

3.45.1–2   *Enter* Dutch Merchant, *with a little Dutch* | Boy *in Great slops:*

3.81.1   *Enter* Grace. (after 'she', 3.82)

3.113.1   *Exit.* (after 3.112)

3.116   *Enter* Savorwit.

3.207   *Exit* Savorwit.

3.220.1   *Enter* Dutchman.

3.260.1   *Exeunt.*

4.0.1–2   Act 2. Scæn 1. | *Enter* Weatherwise *the Gull, meeting two or three* | *bringing out a Table.*

4.9.1   *Exeunt.*

4.9.2–3   *Enter* Weatherwise *with the Widow,* Sir Gilbert | Lambston, Mr. Pepperton, | Mr. Overdon.

4.27.1   *Exit.*

4.87.1   *Enter* Weatherwise.

4.95.1–5   *Strike Musick.* | *Enter* Banquet, *and six of his Tenants with the* | Twelve Signs, *made like Banquetting-stuff.* | *Aries, Taurus, Gemini, Cancer, Leo, Virgo, Libra,* | *Scorpio, Sagittarius, Capricorn, Aquarius, and* | *Pisces.*

4.154.1   *Enter* Mistress Low-water *as a gallant Gentleman,* | *her Husband like a Serving-man after her.*

4.177.1–2 *Enter Mistress* Low-water.

4.249.1 *Enter Clown.*

4.260 *Exit:*

4.279.1 *Enter Clown.*

4.411.1 *Exeunt.*

5.0.1–2 *Enter Mr Sandfield, Philip, Sir Oliver Twilights | Son with* Savorwit.

5.33.1–2 *Enter his Mother new landed, with a Gentleman | a Scholler, &c.*

5.102 *Shogs his | Mother.* (opposite the two part-lines of 5.103)

5.185.1, 193.1 *Exeunt:* (after 5.193)

6.0.1 *Enter Kate with her Man-husband.*

6.4.1 *Exit.*

6.25.1–3 *Enter Master* Weatherwise, *Mr* Pepperton, | *and Mr* Overdon, *Suiters.* (after 6.31)

6.80 *Exeunt.*

6.107 *Exit.*

6.107.1 *Enter Widow:*

6.170.1 *Enter Mr* Low-water.

6.171.1 *Throws | somewhat | at him.* (opposite 6.171–2)

6.182 *Within there.* (see textual note)

6.185.1 *Enter Servant, with the Suiters.*

6.195 *Exit.*

6.209 *Exit.* (after 'you well', 6.206–7)

6.211.1 *Enter Servants.*

6.269.1 *Enter Beveril.* (after 'How now', 6.270)

6.300.1 *Enter Widow.* (after 'comes', 6.301)

7.0.1–3 *Act 3. Scæn 1. | Enter the three late Suiters,* Weather-wise, | Pepperton, *and* Overdon, *joyn'd with | Sir* Gilbert Lambston.

7.80.1 *Enter Clown.*

7.178.1 *Enter Mr* Beveril: (after 7.179)

7.187 *Exit.*

7.319 *Exit.*

7.321.1 *Exeunt.*

7.323.1 *Enter Mrs* Lowwater *and her Man-husband.* (after 'it', 7.326)

7.330.1 *Exit.*

7.332 *Exit.*

8.0.1–4 *Act 4. Scæn 1. | Enter at Sir* Oliver's *house, himself, old* Sunset, | *his redeemed Lady, Master* Sandfield, *the | Dutch Merchant,* Philip *Sir* Oliver's | *Son, and* Savorwit *alooff off, | and Servants.*

8.78.1 *Enter Grace.*

8.159.1–2 *Exit. | Manent Mother, Sister,* Philip, *and* Savorwit.

8.257.1 *Exit cum Filia.* (after 8.256)

8.291 *Exeunt.*

9.0.1–3 *Enter two or three Servants placing things in order, | with* Pickadille *the Clown like an Overseer.*

9.22 *Exeunt.*

9.20.1 *Loud Musick.* (after 'Exeunt', 9.22; before the entry)

9.22.1–7 *Enter the new married Widow, and* Kate *her Husband, | both changed in Apparel, Arm in arm together; | after them Sir*

Oliver Twilight, *Mr* Sunset, *and | the Dutch Merchant; after them the Mother, |* Grace *the daughter sad, with* Jane Sunset; *after | these, melancholy* Philip, Savorwit, *and Mr* Sand-|field.

9.52.1 *Enter Mr* Beveril *with a Pastboord.* (after 9.54)

9.62.1–22 *Loud Musick a while. | A Thing like a Globe opens of one side o'th' Stage, | and flashes out Fire, then Sir Gilbert that pre-|sents the part, issues forth with Yellow-hair and Beard, | intermingled with stroaks like wilde flames, a three | forked Fire in's hand; and at the same time Air comes | down, hanging by a cloud, with a Coat made like an | Almanack, all the Twelve Moons set in it, and the | Four Quarters, Winter, Spring, Summer, and Au-|tumn, with change of Weathers, Rain, Lightning, | and Tempest, &c: | And from under the Stage at both ends, arises Wa-|ter and Earth, two persons; Water with green flags | upon his head, standing up in stead of hair; and a | Beard of the same, with a Chain of Pearl. Earth with | a number of little things like Trees, like a thick Grove | upon his head, and a wedg of Gold in his hand, his Gar-|ment of a Clay colour. | The Fire speaking first, the Schollar stands | behinde, give's him the first word, which he now fol-|lows.*

9.63 *FIRE.* (after 'zeal')

9.99 *AIR.* (after 9.98)

9.125 *Exit* Beveril.

9.132 *WATER.* (after 9.131)

9.154 *EARTH.* (after 9.153)

9.170.2–14 *Enter four at several corners, addrest like the four | Winds, with Wings, &c. and dance all to the Drum | and Fiff; the four Elements seem to give back, and | stand in amaze; the South Wind has a great red | face, the North wind a pale bleak one, the Western | wind one cheek red, and another white, and so the | Eastern wind; at the end of the dance, the Winds | shove off the disguises of the other four, which | seem to yeeld and almost fall off of themselves | at the coming of the Winds; so all the four old | Suiters are discovered. Exeunt all the Winds but | one, which is the Schollar in that disguise, so shows | all.*

9.203.1 *Exeunt.*

9.207.1 *Exit. | Manent Widow and Mrs* Low-water. [page-break] *Act 5. Scæn 1. | Widow and Mrs* Low-water.

9.290.1 *Exit Widow.*

9.293 *Enter Mr* Low-water. (after 'work', 9.294)

9.296.1 *Above.* (opposite 'often', 9.297)

9.338.1 *Exit.* (after 9.337)

9.338.2 *Enter Mr* Beveril.

9.349.1–6 *Enter* Kate *with all the Guests, Sir* Oliver, | *Mr* Sunset, *Wife, Daughter,* Philip, | Sandfield, *and* Savorwit.

9.360.1 *Break open door, | rush in.*

9.364.1–4 *Enter confusedly with the Widow, and her Brother | the Schollar.* (after 9.363)

9.364 *Within.* (opposite 'him')

9.463.1 *Enter Servants with two Caskets, | and the Suiters.*

9.562.1 *Exit Sir* Gilbert:

Epilogue.23.2 FINIS.

LINEATION NOTES

1.85–6   Till…it] DYCE; *1 line* NEWCOMB
1.123–4   Thus…you] DYCE; *1 line*
1.161–2   The…Peace] DYCE; *1 line* NEWCOMB
1.169–70   Those…Overdone] DYCE; *1 line* NEWCOMB
1.174–5   It…both] DYCE; *1 line* NEWCOMB
1.178–9   Ah…madam] DYCE; *1 verse line* NEWCOMB
1.196–7   Thanks…welcome] JOHNSON; *3 verse lines* NEWCOMB: Twilight | Pepperton | ; *2 verse lines* DYCE: Welcome |
1.215–18   Play…lad] DYCE; *2 lines* NEWCOMB: long |
1.241–2   He…list] DYCE; *prose* NEWCOMB
1.249–50   That…buttock] DYCE; *1 line* NEWCOMB
2.11–12   O…mean] DYCE; *1 line* NEWCOMB
2.117–18   Sir…lately] DYCE; oft | NEWCOMB
2.165–6   Hope…thee] DYCE; ill | NEWCOMB
3.71–2   That…there] DYCE; *1 line* NEWCOMB
3.93–4   Yea…then] DYCE; *1 line* NEWCOMB
3.119–20   Pox…after-reckonings] JOHNSON; *1 line* NEWCOMB; *3 lines* DYCE: on't | abide |
3.233   How, how's this] DYCE; *prose* NEWCOMB
4.57–8   And…Madam] DYCE; *1 line* NEWCOMB
4.117–18   I…belly] THIS EDITION; *prose* NEWCOMB; Leo | JOHNSON
4.119–22   I…enough] BULLEN; *prose* NEWCOMB
4.139   How…widow] BULLEN; *prose* NEWCOMB
4.188–9   Take…gentlemen] DYCE; *1 verse line* NEWCOMB
4.194   How…banquet] JOHNSON; *2 lines* NEWCOMB: mine | ; *prose* DYCE
4.206   It…then] BULLEN; *2 lines* NEWCOMB: water |
4.221–2   Fair…him] DYCE; *1 line* NEWCOMB
4.230–2   And…Lane] THIS EDITION; *1 line* NEWCOMB; *2 lines* DYCE: old | ; *2 lines* JOHNSON: crabbed |
4.241–3   An…water-bearer] THIS EDITION; *1 line* NEWCOMB; *2 lines* DYCE: married her |
4.270–1   Here…signs] THIS EDITION; *1 verse line* NEWCOMB; *2 verse lines* DYCE: all |
4.289–90   I…Lambstone] DYCE; *1 line* NEWCOMB
4.296–8   Yet…Garden] DYCE; *2 verse lines* NEWCOMB: here |
4.299–300   Why…signs] DYCE; *1 verse line* NEWCOMB
4.301–2   But…ears] DYCE; *1 verse line* NEWCOMB
4.328–9   Why…you] DYCE; *1 verse line* NEWCOMB
4.332–3   Look…villain] DYCE; *1 verse line* NEWCOMB; *2 verse lines* BULLEN: white |
4.334–5   Aqua…here] DYCE; *1 verse line* NEWCOMB
4.374–5   Does…oaths] DYCE; *1 line* NEWCOMB
4.397   Life…here] THIS EDITION; *prose* NEWCOMB
4.400–1   'Twas…for't] DYCE; *1 verse line* NEWCOMB

5.10–11   A…'em] DYCE; *1 line* NEWCOMB
5.22   Why, master] THIS EDITION; *prose* NEWCOMB
5.38–9   I…since] DYCE; *1 line* NEWCOMB
5.92–3   The…time] DYCE; *1 line* NEWCOMB
5.95–6   And…man] DYCE; *1 line* NEWCOMB
5.106–8   Was…time] THIS EDITION; *2 lines* NEWCOMB: tide | ; been | DYCE
5.174–5   We're…own] THIS EDITION; *verse line* NEWCOMB
6.7–8   Desires…Kent] DYCE; *1 line* NEWCOMB
6.19–21   I…beforehand] JOHNSON; *prose* NEWCOMB
6.22–3   You…gown] JOHNSON; *prose* NEWCOMB
6.25   I…sir] JOHNSON; *prose* NEWCOMB
6.90–1   And't…enough] DYCE; *1 line* NEWCOMB
6.103–4   Marry…all] DYCE; *1 verse line* NEWCOMB
6.122–3   Some…interest] DYCE; *1 verse line* NEWCOMB
6.127–8   I…more] DYCE; *1 verse line* NEWCOMB
6.183–4   I've…beds] DYCE; *1 line* NEWCOMB
6.230–1   No…tavern] DYCE; *1 verse line* NEWCOMB
6.249–51   And…you] THIS EDITION; *2 verse lines* NEWCOMB: over | ; *prose* DYCE; *3 verse lines* JOHNSON: over | chops |
6.306–7   Methinks…is] DYCE; *1 line* NEWCOMB
6.316–17   'Gainst…weather] DYCE; *1 line* NEWCOMB
7.105–7   You…aside] DYCE; *prose* NEWCOMB
7.122   By…then] THIS EDITION; *1 verse line* NEWCOMB
7.135–6   How…sir] DYCE; *1 line* NEWCOMB
7.143–4   How…thou] DYCE; *1 verse line* NEWCOMB
7.145   Why…yet] DYCE; *1 verse line* NEWCOMB
7.161–2   Why…together] DYCE; *1 verse line* NEWCOMB
8.33–4   No…yet] DYCE; *prose* NEWCOMB
8.90–1   All…son's] DYCE; *1 line* NEWCOMB
8.132–3   'Twas…too] DYCE; lady | NEWCOMB
9.28–9   'Las…money] DYCE; *1 line* NEWCOMB
9.33–6   That's…bride-house] DYCE; *prose* NEWCOMB
9.40   Take…then] JOHNSON; *prose* NEWCOMB
9.195–6   The…elements] DYCE; *1 verse line* NEWCOMB
9.226–7   No…on't] DYCE; *1 line* NEWCOMB
9.324–6   I…coming] DYCE; *3 verse lines* NEWCOMB: admittance | have | . Misinterpreted prose/verse break.
9.343–6   It…her] THIS EDITION; *3 lines* NEWCOMB: man | will | ; so | warily | come | DYCE; now, sir | any | come | JOHNSON
9.375–6   She…gross, too gross] DYCE; *1 line* NEWCOMB
9.398–9   That…Christendom] DYCE; substance | NEWCOMB
9.415–16   Let…was] DYCE; *1 line* NEWCOMB
9.513–14   I…suitors] DYCE; *1 line* NEWCOMB
Epilogue.6–7   That's…whistle] DYCE; pockets | NEWCOMB

ANYTHING FOR A QUIET LIFE

Edited by Leslie Thomson

ALTHOUGH written c.1621, *Anything for a Quiet Life* (BEPD 821; Wing M1979) was not printed until 1662; there is no Stationers' Register entry for the play. According to the imprint, Thomas Johnson printed the play for Francis Kirkman and Henry Marsh to be sold at the Prince's Arms in Chancery Lane, which was Marsh's shop, although he and Kirkman were close collaborators. *Anything for a Quiet Life* is advertised among 'Plays newly Printed' in a list of books sold by Henry Marsh which appears in *The Wits*, Part I, 1662 (Wing C3218).

The quarto consists of only seven sheets or 28 leaves (it collates A2, B–G4, H2), a paper saving made possible by printing almost the whole play as prose and by making the speeches continuous rather than starting a new line for each. Other space-saving measures not so readily apparent, such as spelling changes (and perhaps the omission of some stage directions), were also used. Eleven of the surviving copies of the quarto have been examined for variants, but a complete collation has not been done. Only one variant page has been found (G2^r, not previously noted), uncorrected in the Folger copy and the Malone copy at the Bodleian Library and corrected in the other nine copies examined. For the most part, the quarto is free of obvious printing errors, although a phrase is duplicated on the last leaf.

While the imprint and advertisement imply that Henry Marsh had a greater share in the publication, Francis Kirkman was probably responsible for getting *Anything for a Quiet Life* into print. In 1661–2 he openly published four other plays also printed by Thomas Johnson: *The Birth of Merlin* (BEPD 822) with Marsh, *The Two Merry Milkmaids* and *A Cure for a Cuckold* (BEPD 364(b) and 817) with Nathaniel Brooke, *The Thracian Wonder* (BEPD 819) by himself. Some copies of the 1661 quarto of *The Beggar's Bush* (BEPD 643(b)) have an advertisement on the title-page in which the publishers, Henry Robinson and Anne Moseley, accuse Kirkman of the piracy of several unidentified plays. That question has been examined by W. W. Greg, Fredson Bowers, and Johan Gerritsen, and it has been shown (in particular by Gerritsen's analyses of damaged types etc.) that falsely dated quartos of at least three other plays were also printed by Thomas Johnson at about this date: *The Scornful Lady*, *Philaster*, and *Love's Mistress* (BEPD 334(h), 363(g), and 504(c)). The involvement of Kirkman's 'regular' printer suggests that these are the Kirkman piracies complained of by Robinson and Moseley.

Kirkman boasts in several prefaces of his large collection of plays, which he was willing to sell or, he implies, rent, to customers. In his 1661 preface to *The Thracian Wonder* he informs his readers: 'I have several manuscripts of this nature [i.e. old plays], written by worthy authors, and I account it much pity they should now lie dormant, and buried in oblivion, since ingenuity is so likely to be encouraged, by reason of the happy restoration of our liberties'. He concludes: 'if you please to repair to my shop, I shall furnish you with all the plays that were ever yet printed. I have 700 several plays, and most of them several times over, and I intend to increase my store as I sell . . .'. While this was no doubt an exaggerated claim, the writer is the same Francis Kirkman who produced two detailed catalogues of plays, in 1661 and 1672, which with their numerous misattributions have both helped and hindered later critics.

Kirkman's claim to have manuscripts of plays, and the title-page assertion that *Anything for a Quiet Life* was '*Never before Printed*', together with the absence of any previous reference to the play all support the inference that Johnson's compositor(s) worked from a manuscript. As to whether the manuscript was authorial or scribal, it is impossible to say for certain. Although attribution studies of the quarto have found characteristics typical of Middleton and Webster, this does not mean the manuscript was in the hand of either. The title-page gives the only extant indication that the play was performed when written, 'at *Black-Fryers*, by His late Majesties Servants'. As to whether the source manuscript was theatrical in origin, there are three cryptic prop cues of the sort that can occur in a playbook marked by a bookkeeper—*table* (2.1.0.2), *map* (4.1.179.1), *indenture* (5.1.66.1)—but they could equally be a playwright's shorthand reminders. At several points additional stage directions must be added to make the action clear to readers, although the dialogue tells the actor what he must do. Given the crammed state of the quarto, possibly some of these stage directions were omitted by Johnson's compositor(s) as a space-saving measure.

The main problem confronting an editor of *Anything for a Quiet Life* is that while the quarto was printed almost completely in prose, the underlying manuscript was probably an intricate and idiosyncratic combination of prose and verse. Evidence supporting this conclusion can be adduced from the practices of Middleton and Webster in other plays of about the same date, and from several plays printed by Johnson for Kirkman which, unlike *Anything for a Quiet Life*, exist in an earlier form as well. While Middleton's early plays for the boys' companies are largely in prose, his later work contains an ever greater proportion of verse. Both *Women, Beware Women* (1621) and the sections of *The Changeling* (1622) attributed to Middleton make effective use of an intricate, sophisticated verse grounded in iambic pentameter but also including longer and shorter verse lines. All of Webster's plays are predominantly verse; *The Devil's Law-Case* (BEPD 388) (c.1617-20), perhaps closest in time to *Anything for a Quiet Life*, provides numerous examples of a verse style not unlike Middleton's in its variety and range. This complexity in each playwright's versification makes it virtually impossible to restore the play to more than an approximation of its manuscript form. Nevertheless, everything indicates that the play was not written completely in prose, and in printing it as such Johnson's compositor(s) distorted and flattened what Middleton and Webster gave their characters to say. Something near the original verse must be offered to do the play and its authors justice.

The best example of a play printed by Johnson for Kirkman and Marsh which also exists in an earlier version is *The Two Merry Milkmaids* by 'J. C.' The first quarto, dated 1620, was printed by Bernard Alsop for Lawrence Chapman (STC 4281; BEPD 364(a)), and the Johnson quarto was printed from it in 1661 (BEPD 364(b)). Alsop's version of *Milkmaids* fills 58 leaves, Johnson's version only 38. Even a casual comparison of the two quartos reveals immediately how this considerable saving of costly paper was achieved. Verse became prose, speeches once begun on separate lines were run continuously, spelling changes were made which not only modernized but shortened the words ('Drinke, and Countrey Libertie' becomes 'Drink, and Country Liberty', for example). Similarly, one of the extant versions of *Love's Mistress* (Wing H1786A; BEPD 504(c)) has been shown by Gerritsen to be a product of Johnson's printing house, probably for Kirkman. This pirated quarto, falsely dated 1640 on the title-page, was probably printed by Johnson in 1661 and it fills only 28 leaves. This play was first printed in 1636 on 46 leaves in a small quarto format and reprinted in 1640 on 36 leaves in regular quarto size (STC 13352, and 13353; BEPD 504(a) and 504(b)). Because *Love's Mistress* contains more rhymed verse than either *The Two Merry Milkmaids* or *Anything for a Quiet Life*, the condensing principles of Johnson's compositor(s) are more apparent. Almost without exception, rhymed verse remains as such; unrhymed verse becomes prose. The main reason why *Anything for a Quiet Life* was printed almost completely in prose is probably that the manuscript contained very little rhymed verse. As the Lineation Notes indicate, rhyme is restricted to sententious and/or scene-ending couplets scattered through the play.

Such evidence that much, but by no means all, of *Anything for a Quiet Life* was originally in verse helps to corroborate what one senses in reading the quarto, but the specific problems of lineation still remain. As noted, Middleton and Webster each had developed extremely variable verse forms which stretched the limits of blank verse. The iambic pentameter line is there, but often more

apparent by its absence—acting as a base for numerous short lines and hexameter or longer lines, as well as for passages which are probably, but not certainly, rhythmic prose. The effect is colloquial, and well-suited to the city setting and topical concerns of the play, but not to an editor's irrational desire for a fixed text. The verse of this edition of *Anything for a Quiet Life* is presented in a layout more regular and consistent than either playwright ever used. Nevertheless, the lineation of this version is certainly closer to that of the source manuscript than is the quarto produced by Johnson.

Alexander Dyce, A. H. Bullen, and F. L. Lucas each returned some of the prose to verse. Bullen followed Dyce for the most part, but not always; Lucas often differed from both. Nancy Ruth Katz left the text in prose. Overall, the lineation of Dyce, Bullen, Lucas, and this editor is the same. While it would be satisfying to believe that this agreement indicates that the text has been returned to its original form, more realistic is that non-authorial prose has been returned to blank verse.

The 1662 edition is divided into acts but not scenes (as is generally the case with other Middleton plays both printed and in manuscript). Editorial division into scenes is generally straightforward, but poses problems at several points. Lucas and Katz have only three scenes in Act 2, since neither begins a new scene when the stage is cleared at Franklin's exit before the entrance of the Barber, his boy, and Ralph. Dyce and Bullen have four scenes in Act 2, as does this edition. In Act 4 at the stage direction 'manet Knavesbe' (4.1.210.1), all four previous editors begin a new scene because the fictional location obviously changes. Yet the text at this point specifically indicates that Knavesbe was to remain on stage (possibly Webster stopped here and Middleton picked up the plot he had begun). Changes of place on the unlocalized stage for which the authors were writing were usually indicated by dialogue; scene changes meant nothing on a stage where the action was continuous through an act; and the usual signal for scene breaks, when they were included, was a cleared stage; consequently, there is no justification for creating a new scene here and this edition does not do so. Whereas Lucas has only one scene in Act 5, Dyce, Bullen, and Katz have three. Again, there is a change of fictional location at 5.1.128, but George Cressingham remains on stage when the other characters leave; there is no new scene. Conversely, where this edition begins Scene 2, and all the previous editors except Lucas begin Scene 3, the stage has been cleared before the entrance of Beaufort and Knavesbe, justifying the new scene.

The other textual problem is posed by the French in 3.2. This scene is attributed to Middleton, and is the only time French occurs in a play by him—or by Webster, for that matter. Like the play's English, the French is colloquial and suggestive, creating translation problems. Lucas left it pretty much as printed; Dyce, Bullen, and Katz each modernized, and formalized it in the process. In this edition the obsolete spellings are modernized, as is done with the

English in the rest of the play, but some attempt has been made to convey the colloquial quality of the original, and to indicate and explicate the bawdy-house French.

SEE ALSO

Text: *Works*, 1596
Authorship and date: this volume, 422

WORKS CITED

Previous Editions

Bullen, A. H., ed., *Thomas Middleton, Works*, vol. 5 (1885)
Dyce, Alexander, ed., *Thomas Middleton, Works*, vol. 4 (1840)

Katz, Nancy Ruth, ed., *Anything for a Quiet Life*, unpublished dissertation, University of California, Berkeley (1975)
Lucas, F. L., ed., *The Complete Works of John Webster* (1927), vol. 4

Other Works Cited

Bowers, Fredson, 'The First Series of Plays Published by Francis Kirkman in 1661', *The Library*, V, 2 (1948), 289–91
Gerritsen, Johan, 'The Dramatic Piracies of 1661: A Comparative Analysis', *Studies in Bibliography* 11 (1958), 117–31
Marlowe, Christopher, *Doctor Faustus*, ed. John D. Jump (1962)
Shakespeare, William, *King Edward III*, ed. Giorgio Melchiori (1998)
Supple, B. E., *Commercial Crisis and Change in England, 1600–1642* (1964)

TEXTUAL NOTES

Persons.7   Master Walter CAMLET] THIS EDITION; Mr. *Water Chamlet* JOHNSON. 'Mr.' was the abbreviation of 'master' and indicates social status; 'Water' was a variant of 'Walter', indicating pronunciation; 'Chamlet' is the obsolete form of 'camlet', a kind of fabric.
Persons.7   mercer] THIS EDITION; *not in* JOHNSON
Persons.14   BARBER-SURGEON] THIS EDITION; a Barber JOHNSON
Persons.23   3 or 4 Citizens (CREDITORS)] THIS EDITION; *not in* JOHNSON. At 5.2.35.2–3 in JOHNSON: '*three or four citizens, creditors*' enter; they are likely the same thing
1.1.28   Than] JOHNSON (then). This change is made silently hereafter.
1.1.64   Whither] JOHNSON (Whether)
1.1.85   parcels] LUCAS; farcels JOHNSON
1.1.101   do] DYCE; does JOHNSON
1.1.116   George] DYCE; *Frank* JOHNSON, clearly an error.
1.1.196   bevers] DYCE; Beavers JOHNSON
1.1.234   an] JOHNSON (and). This change is made silently hereafter.
1.1.244   counsel] JOHNSON (council)
1.1.365   even then] LUCAS (*conj.* DYCE); ever there JOHNSON
2.1.0.2   and chair] THIS EDITION; *not in* JOHNSON. Knavesbe tells Sib to sit at 2.1.5. In JOHNSON the word 'Table' follows the entrance direction.
2.1.0.3   *Sib Knavesbe*] KATZ; *and his Wife* JOHNSON
2.1.5.1   *She sits*] THIS EDITION; *not in* JOHNSON. Since there is no discussion about it, she probably complies.
2.1.101   it] DYCE; *not in* JOHNSON
2.1.159   *He hands her a mirror*] LUCAS; *not in* JOHNSON
2.1.170   holiday] JOHNSON (Holy-Day)
2.1.175   *aside to Beaufort*] KATZ; *not in* JOHNSON. It seems likely that this is an aside, but it need not be.
2.2.0.1   Camlet] JOHNSON adds *his wife Rachel*, but she does not enter until 2.2.9.1.
2.2.50   vend] JOHNSON (vent)
2.2.57–8   FIRST CHILD...SECOND CHILD] THIS EDITION; *Mar.....Ed.* JOHNSON (throughout the scene). The children are named only in the speech prefixes in this scene; in 4.1 JOHNSON has *1 Childe* and *2 Childe*.
2.2.73   [*Exit children*]] THIS EDITION; *not in* JOHNSON. Camlet's words of dismissal probably signal the children's exit.
2.2.98   through] JOHNSON (thorow)
2.2.203   o'] JOHNSON (o)
2.2.221   Protests] LUCAS; Protest JOHNSON

2.2.240   holiday] JOHNSON (Holy-day)
2.2.267   live] LUCAS; love JOHNSON
2.2.279   she] DYCE; *not in* JOHNSON
2.2.281   wor'st] JOHNSON (wore'ſt)
2.4.3   cauterizer] DYCE; *Cauterize* JOHNSON, which prints *Cauterizer* at 2.4.67.
2.4.5   *lixivium*] LUCAS (*conj.* DYCE); luxinium JOHNSON
2.4.6   rollers] JOHNSON (rowlers)
2.4.6   pledgets] JOHNSON (pleggets)
2.4.10   *preputium*] JOHNSON (prepuſium)
2.4.11   lose] JOHNSON (loofe)
2.4.15   *os pubis*] JOHNSON (Os pubes)
3.1.44.1   [*She*]] THIS EDITION; *not in* JOHNSON
3.1.64   you] DYCE; yuo JOHNSON
3.1.156   To corrupt a] DYCE; to a corrupt JOHNSON
3.2.31   *os coxendix*] JOHNSON (ofcox-index)
3.2.32   *humour*] JOHNSON (humore)
3.2.33   *thorax*] JOHNSON (thoric)
3.2.37   *conquassation*] JOHNSON (conquaſſition)
3.2.39   migraine] THIS EDITION; *megrum* JOHNSON
3.2.55   *ceux-ci*] THIS EDITION; ceftui ci JOHNSON
3.2.56   *ses*] JOHNSON (ces)
3.2.63   *trois*] DYCE; erois JOHNSON
3.2.64   canailles] JOHNSON (Quenailles)
3.2.65   *donné*] JOHNSON (donner)
3.2.68   *s'ils ne*] DYCE; fi ne JOHNSON
3.2.86   *retardé*] DYCE; retarge JOHNSON
3.2.89   *vrai*] DYCE; vay JOHNSON
3.2.90   *d'échapper*] JOHNSON (de chaper)
3.2.90   *changeant*] DYCE; chanfant JOHNSON
3.2.92   *bordel*] THIS EDITION; bordeau JOHNSON
3.2.103   *quassative*] JOHNSON (quaſſitive)
3.2.136   *canailles*] JOHNSON (Quenailles)
3.2.161   precedent] JOHNSON (preſident)
3.2.196   candied] DYCE; candid JOHNSON
3.2.203   principle] JOHNSON (principal)
3.2.212   vend] JOHNSON (vent)
3.2.225   venture] JOHNSON (venter)
3.2.229   by th'ears] DYCE; bi'th' years JOHNSON
4.1.12   controller] JOHNSON (Comptroller)
4.1.69   beneplacito] JOHNSON (*bene placita*)
4.1.92   precedent] JOHNSON (preſident)
4.1.97   charged] JOHNSON (charge)
4.1.129   grudged] JOHNSON (grutcht)

4.1.142 waistcoat] LUCAS (conj. DYCE); wainscot JOHNSON
4.1.161.1 [Exit George with children]] THIS EDITION; not in JOHN-
    SON. Lady Cressingham signals this exit in the previous line.
4.1.184 Blackwater] JOHNSON (black water)
4.1.185 Cusacks'] THIS EDITION; Coffacks JOHNSON. Lucas, emend-
    ing to C[u]ssacks, reasons that cossacks would be unlikely in
    Ireland, and that 'Cusack or Cussack is a well-known Irish
    name'.
4.1.201 not] DYCE; no JOHNSON
4.1.210.1 Exeunt, manet Knavesbe] All previous editors begin a
    new scene here, but the stage is specifically not cleared.
4.1.223 a] DYCE; not in JOHNSON
4.1.244 beholden] JOHNSON (beholding)
4.1.262 f-u-x-o-r] JOHNSON (f u x o r)
4.1.333 byrlakins] JOHNSON (birlakins)
4.1.336 cursed] JOHNSON (curst)
4.1.339 sought] DYCE; fonght JOHNSON
4.1.341 'm] JOHNSON ('em)
4.1.356 through] KATZ; thorough JOHNSON
4.1.361 enough] JOHNSON (enow)
4.2.0.1 at Camlet's shop] THIS EDITION; not in JOHNSON. At the
    end of this scene Rachel Camlet asks about and seems to be
    shown a piece of cloth (4.2.85), requiring a prop; the shop
    is likely visible again, and was probably 'discovered'.
4.2.10 beholden] JOHNSON (beholding)
4.2.19 'eartily] JOHNSON (artely)
4.2.28 through] KATZ; thorough JOHNSON
4.2.48 be] DYCE; by JOHNSON
4.2.79 woo thee] JOHNSON (wooe the)
4.2.93 ride] JOHNSON (rid)
5.1.17 deceit] THIS EDITION (conj. DYCE); defeat JOHNSON
5.1.52 owed] JOHNSON (ought)
5.1.99 owed] JOHNSON (ought)
5.1.106 o'th'] JOHNSON ('ath')

5.1.121 George] DYCE; in JOHNSON the name appears erroneously
    as a speech heading for 'Sir, rest assured...you.'
5.1.127.1 Enter Saunder] DYCE, BULLEN, and KATZ begin a new
    scene here, but the stage is not cleared.
5.1.134 o'th'] JOHNSON ('ath')
5.1.208-9 great ones may] JOHNSON corr, DYCE; greatories | my
    JOHNSON uncorr. This is a press variant of which previous
    editors might not have been aware.
5.1.242 sore] JOHNSON corr (fore); foar JOHNSON uncorr. A second
    press variant on the same page, the only one which seems
    to have been corrected.
5.1.262 e'er] JOHNSON (ere)
5.1.262 your] DYCE; you JOHNSON
5.2.3 is] KATZ; his JOHNSON
5.2.3 fiddling] DYCE; fidling JOHNSON
5.2.16 hot-reined] JOHNSON (hot-rain'd)
5.2.21 passed] JOHNSON (paft)
5.2.33 Queenhithe] JOHNSON (Queen-hive)
5.2.103 lose] JOHNSON (loofe)
5.2.113 cunning man] JOHNSON (cunning-man). See Comment-
    ary.
5.2.158 Be wi' ye] JOHNSON (Bewy ye)
5.2.158 bye] JOHNSON (buoy)
5.2.234 came] DYCE; can JOHNSON
5.2.242-3 anchor, | Bulked] JOHNSON (Anchor-bulkt)
5.2.267 dues] JOHNSON (dews)
5.2.282 bankrupt] JOHNSON (banquer-out)
5.2.288 which] JOHNSON (with)
5.2.316 parsons'] JOHNSON (persons)
5.2.327 shalt] JOHNSON (fha't)
5.2.353 hire] DYCE; her JOHNSON
5.2.364 spermaceti] JOHNSON (Sperma Cate)
5.2.378 But...return] In JOHNSON this phrase is printed twice,
    at the bottom of one page and at the top of the next, clearly
    a printing error which occurs in every copy examined.
5.2.387 passed] JOHNSON (paft)

PRESS VARIANTS

Sheet G (inner forme)

Uncorrected: Folger, Bodleian 2 (Malone)
Corrected: BL (644. f. 11; 162. d. 31), Bodleian 1, Dyce,
    Chapin, Huntington, LC, Worcester, Yale

Sig. G2

5.1.208-9 great ones may] corr; greatories my uncorr
5.1.242 sore] fore corr; foar uncorr

STAGE DIRECTIONS

[Printed before the play:]

Drammatis Personae.

The Scene LONDON.

Lord *Beaufort.*
Sir *Francis Cressingham,* an Alchymist.
Old *Franklin,* a Countrey Gentleman.
George Cressingham, son to Sir *Francis.*
Franklin a Sea-Captain, son to old *Franklin,* and Compa-|nion to
    George Cressingham.
Mr. *Water Chamlet* a Citizen.
Knaves-bee a Lawyer, and Pandor to his Wife.
Selenger, Page to the Lord *Beaufort.*
Saunder, Steward to Sir *Francis.*

George and *Ralph,* two Prentices to *Water Chamlet.*
A Surveyor.
Sweetball, a Barber.
Barbers boy.
Flesh-hook and *Counter-buff,* a Sergeant and a Yeoman.
Two Children of Sir *Francis Cressinghams,* nurs'd by *Wa-|ter*
    Chamlet.
Lady *Cressingham,* wife to Sir *Francis.*
Rachel, wife to *Water Chamlet.*
Sib, Knaves-bee's wife,
Margarita, a French Bawd.
1.1.0.1 ACTUS I.
1.1.0.2-3 Enter the Lord Beaufort, and Sir Francis Cressingham.
1.1.48.1 Enter Mr. Water Chamlet (right, opposite end of 1.1.48)

1.1.112.1 *Enter George Cressingham & Franklin.* (right, opposite end of 1.1.112)
1.1.202.1 *Enter Knaves-bee.*
1.1.255.1 *Exeunt George Cressingham and Franklin.*
1.1.281.1 *Enter Lady Cressingham and Saunder.* (right, opposite end of 1.1.281)
1.1.313.1 *Exit Chamlet.* (right, opposite 1.1.313)
1.1.328 *Exit Saunder.* (right, opposite 1.1.328)
1.1.360.1 *Ent. Saunder.* (right, opposite 1.1.359–60)
1.1.371.1 *Exeunt.* (right, opposite 1.1.371)
2.1.0.1 Actus. II.
2.1.0.2 *Enter Knaves-bee and his Wife. Table.*
2.1.118.1 *knock within.* (right, opposite 2.1.118)
2.1.124.1 *Enter Beaufort.* (right, opposite end of 2.1.124)
2.1.129 *Exit Knaves-bee.* (right, opposite 2.1.129)
2.1.170.1 *Ent. Knaves-bee.* (right, opposite start of 2.1.169)
2.1.178 *Ex. Beaufort & Knaves-bee* (right, opposite start of 2.1.178)
2.1.193 *Exit Lady.* (right, opposite 2.1.193)
2.2.0.1–2 *Enter (a Shop being discover'd) Walter Chamlet, his Wife* Rachel, | *two Prentices, George and* Ralph.
2.2.9.1 *Enter Rachel.* (right, opposite 2.2.9)
2.2.53.1 *Enter two children* (right, opposite 2.2.53)
2.2.56.1 *Exit Rachel.* (right, opposite 2.2.56)
2.2.69.1 *Ent. Frank. & yong Cress. disguis'd* (right, opposite 2.2.69)
2.2.180 *Exit Cress.* (right, opposite 2.2.180)
2.2.217.1 *Enter yong Cressingham.* (right, opposite end of 2.2.217)
2.2.252.1 *Exeunt Frank. Cress. Ralph.* (right, opposite 2.2.252)
2.2.282 *Exeunt.* (right, opposite 2.2.282)
2.3.0.1 *Enter Franklin, yong Cress. as before, Ralph, Barber, Boy.*
2.3.16 *Exeunt Barber & Ralph.* (right, opposite 2.3.15–16)
2.3.23 *Exit yong Cressingham.* (right, opposite end of 2.3.23)
2.3.29 *Exit boy.* (right, opposite 2.3.29)
2.3.31 *Exit Franklin.* (right, opposite 2.3.31)
2.4.0.1 *Enter Barber, Ralph, Boy.*
2.4.47.1 *Exit boy.* (left, at end of 2.4.47)
2.4.66 *Exit Ralph.* (right, opposite 2.4.66)
2.4.70.1 *Exeunt.* (right, opposite 2.4.70)
3.1.0.1 Actus III.
3.1.0.2 *Enter Selenger, Mris. Knaves-bee.*
3.1.3 *Exiturus.* (right, opposite 3.1.3)
3.1.44.1 *grasps the skain be-|tween his hands.* (right, opposite 3.1.43–5)
3.1.77.1 *Enter Beaufort.*
3.1.82.1 *Beaufort puts off his Hat.* (right, opposite start of 3.1.83)
3.1.98 *Exit Selenger.* (right, opposite 3.1.98)
3.1.163.1 *Exit Beaufort.* (right, opposite 3.1.163)
3.1.171 *Exit.* (right, opposite 3.1.171)
3.2.0.1 *Enter Flesh-hook, Counter-buff, and Sweetball the Barber.*
3.2.33.1 *Enter Ralph.* (right, opposite end of 3.2.33)
3.2.43.1 *Enter Franklin.*
3.2.57.1 *Enter Chamlet and Ralph hastily.* (right, opposite end of 3.2.57)
3.2.80.1 *Enter Margarita a French Bawd.*
3.2.97.1 *Embrace and complement.* (right, opposite 3.2.97)
3.2.138 *Ex. Frank.* (right, opposite 3.2.137–8)
3.2.152 *Ex. Marg.* (right, opposite 3.2.151–2)
3.2.174.1 *Exeunt.* (right, opposite 3.2.173–4)
3.2.175.1 *Enter George.* (right, opposite 3.2.175)
3.2.181 *Exit Ralph.* (right, opposite 3.2.181)

3.2.237.1 *Exeunt.* (right, opposite 3.2.237)
4.1.0.1 Actus IV.
4.1.0.2 *Enter Sir Francis Cressingham, and a Surveyor.*
4.1.7 *Exit Surveyor.* (right, opposite 4.1.6)
4.1.12.1 *Enter Saunder.* (right, opposite 4.1.12)
4.1.36.1 *Exit Saunder.* (right, opposite 4.1.35–6)
4.1.36.2 *Enter young Cressingham.*
4.1.109.1 *Enter George with the two Children.* (right, opposite 4.1.109)
4.1.135.1 *Enter Saunder, Knaves-bee, and Surveyor.*
4.1.152.1 *Enter Lady Cressingham.*
4.1.179.1 *(Map.* (right, opposite 4.1.184)
4.1.210.1 *Exeunt. manet | (Knaves-bee.* (right, opposite 4.1.210–210.2)
4.1.210.2 *Enter Knaves bee's Wife.*
4.1.255.1 *Enter George with Rolls of Paper.*
4.1.322.1 *Exit George.* (right, opposite 4.1.322)
4.1.327.1 *Enter Mris Chamlet.* (towards right, opposite 4.1.327)
4.1.361 *Exeunt.* (right, opposite 4.1.360–1)
4.1.364 *Exit.* (right, opposite 4.1.364)
4.2.0.1 *Enter George, Margarita.*
4.2.4.1 *Enter Chamlet.*
4.2.8 *Exit George.* (right, opposite 4.2.7–8)
4.2.13.1 *Enter Mris. Chamlet, and Knavesbee.*
4.2.52 *Exit Margarita.* (right, opposite 4.2.52)
4.2.62.1 *Enter George.*
4.2.87.1 *Exeunt.* (right, opposite 4.2.87)
4.2.94 *Exit Knaves-bee.* (right, opposite 4.2.94)
5.1.0.1 Actus. V.
5.1.0.2–4 *Enter old Francklin in mourning: young Cressingham with young | Francklin disguis'd like an old Serving-man.*
5.1.49.1 *Enter George.* (right, opposite 5.1.49)
5.1.66.1 *Indenture.* (left, opposite 5.1.65)
5.1.125 *Exeunt. Old Franklin, George, and Young Francklin.* (right, opposite 5.1.125)
5.1.127.1 *Enter Saunder.* (right, opposite 5.1.126–7)
5.1.147.1 *Enter Sir Fran. Cressingham.* (right, opposite 5.1.147)
5.1.183.1 *Enter the Lady Cressingham.* (right, opposite 5.1.182)
5.1.212 *Exeunt old Cress. and Saund.* (right, opposite 5.1.211)
5.1.281 *Exeunt.* (right, opposite 5.1.281)
5.2.0.1 *Enter Lord Beaufort, and Knaves-bee.*
5.2.35 *Exit* (right, opposite 5.2.34–5)
5.2.35.1 *Enter Old Franklin; his son as before, George, three or four | Citizens, Creditors.*
5.2.65.1 *Enter Chamlet.* (right, opposite 5.2.65)
5.2.114.1 *Enter Mris Chamlet.*
5.2.119–20 *Slips behinde the Arras.*
5.2.136 *within.* (added to speech heading)
5.2.141 *within.* (added to speech heading)
5.2.158 *Exit* (right, opposite 5.2.157–8)
5.2.168.1 *Enter Barb. & Knavesbee.* (right, opposite 5.2.168)
5.2.215.1 *Enter Selenger as a woman, and Mris Knavesbee.* (right, opposite end of 5.2.215)
5.2.225.1 *Enter Young Cressingham.* (right, opposite 5.2.224–5)
5.2.227.1 *Enter Old Cressingham.*
5.2.260.1 *Enter Lady Cress. in civil habit, Saund. and children very gallant.* (right, opposite end of 5.2.260)
5.2.294.1 *Enter George, and Mris Chamlet.* (right, opposite 5.2.293–4)
5.2.350.1 *Knaves-bee kneels.* (right, opposite 5.2.350)
5.2.389 *Exeunt.* (right, opposite 5.2.389)
5.2.389.1 FINIS.

LINEATION NOTES

When this edition agrees with DYCE no note is given. When this edition departs from DYCE a note indicates the difference, citing the originating editor or indicating that the lineation is original with this edition.

The only segments of the control text printed as verse are rhymed passages (with the exception of two lines). These are: the Prologue; 1.1.254-5, 312-13; 2.1.192-3; 2.2.1-9, 280-1; 2.3.30-1; 2.4.67-70; 3.1.170-1; 3.2.232-7; 4.1.209-10, 363-4; 4.2.83-4, 93-4; 5.2.388-9; Epilogue. All changes to JOHNSON are from prose to verse, none from verse to prose.

1.1.4   Can...see] LUCAS; error | DYCE

1.1.52-60   Nothing...book] THIS EDITION; *prose* DYCE

1.1.146-7   Her...as] THIS EDITION; it | misdemeanours | DYCE

1.1.309-11   I...leave] THIS EDITION; *verse* DYCE: done | dotage | leave |

2.1.1-7   Have...be] BULLEN; *prose* DYCE

2.1.178-9   You...think] LUCAS; husband | think | DYCE

2.2.25-6   Peace...I'll] THIS EDITION; *verse* DYCE: speak | I'll |

2.2.59-61   No...worse] THIS EDITION; *verse* DYCE: no | Ralph | worse |

2.2.70-1   Why...so] LUCAS; *prose* DYCE

2.2.263-4   But...bullets] LUCAS; *verse* DYCE: George | bullets |

3.1.76-7   This...too] LUCAS; prison | too | DYCE

3.1.83-5   Nay...you] LUCAS; *verse* DYCE: both | perceive | you |

3.1.144-5   Yet...prostitute] LUCAS; that | prostitute | DYCE

3.2.178-80   And...together] THIS EDITION; *verse* DYCE: still | countenance | together |

3.2.218-19   She...falsehood] THIS EDITION; *verse* DYCE: truth | falsehood

3.2.221-2   'Tis...pardon] THIS EDITION; *verse* DYCE: redressed | pardon

4.1.57-110   I...compassion] LUCAS; *prose* DYCE

4.1.177-9   Show...year] THIS EDITION; *verse* DYCE: mean | yours | year |

4.1.222-3   I...burst] THIS EDITION; *prose* DYCE

4.1.232-5   You...thee] LUCAS; DYCE: way | kiss'd | memory | thee |

4.2.62-6   Your...so] THIS EDITION; *prose* DYCE

5.1.4-7   He...lighter] THIS EDITION; DYCE: nearest | perpetual | continuèd | weigh | lighter |

5.1.161-6   Ha...destruction] THIS EDITION; *prose* DYCE

5.1.167-9   Surely...condition] BULLEN; *prose* DYCE

5.1.230-44   I...use] BULLEN; *prose* DYCE

5.1.245-9   When...vices] LUCAS; *prose* DYCE

5.1.250-6   So...person] LUCAS; DYCE: sir | oath | woman | expected | not | wife | then | answer | person |

5.1.256-72   A...presently] LUCAS; *prose* DYCE

5.2.17-21   This...lord] LUCAS; DYCE: house | return | lost |

5.2.230   Sir...you] THIS EDITION; DYCE: met | at |

5.2.271-84   O...extinct] LUCAS; *prose* DYCE

LOST POLITICAL PROSE, 1620–7: A BRIEF ACCOUNT

Thomas Cogswell

WORKS CITED

Manuscript Sources

Beaulieu to Trumbull, 7 January 1625, BL Trumbull MSS, VII/172; Dorchester to Master and Company of Stationers, 5 February 1629, BL Trumbull MSS, Misc. 18/104; Wimbledon's report to the Council, [early 1626], the earl of Clare's commonplace book, Nottingham University Library, Newcastle MSS, NeC 15,406, fol. 417–8; 'To the right honorable the Lord Maior and Court of Alderman', 1 February 1626, Corporation of London Record Office, Rep. 41, fols. 216–9; Locke to Carleton, 23 March 1621, PRO SP 14/120/36; and Brown to Bennett, 19 December 1621, Westminster Diocesan Archives, A17/253.

Contemporary Works

John Stow, *Annales, or a General Chronicle of England* (London, 1631), pp. 1042–3; Thomas Scott, *Vox Dei* ([Utrecht], 1624), and esp. pp. 59-2 and 68–70; *The Protestant's Plea for Priests and Papists* (London, 1621); George Musket, *The Bishop of London his Legacy* ([St. Omer], 1624); Henry King, *Upon Occasion of that false and scandalous Report touching the supposed Apostacie of . . . J. King* (London, 1621); and Thomas Fuller, *The Church History of Britain* (London, 1837), III, pp. 293–4.

Printed Primary Sources

William Oldys's note on the auction, quoted in *The Works of Thomas Middleton*, ed. by Alexander Dyce (London, 1840), I, xxiii–iv; *Proceedings in Parliament 1625*, edited by Maija Jansson and William Bidwell (New Haven, 1987), p. 460; *Proceedings in Parliament 1628*, edited by Robert C. Johnson *et al.* (New Haven, 1977), II, p. 109; T. H. B. M. Harmsen, *John Gee's 'Foot Out of the Snare'* (Nijmegen, 1992); Conrad Russell, 'The Examination of Mr Mallory after the Parliament of 1621', *Bulletin of the Institute of Historical Research* (1977), pp. 125–32; and Chamberlain to Carleton, 30 October 1620, 22 December 1620, and 19 May 1621, *The Letters of John Chamberlain* (Philadelphia, 1939), II, pp. 268, 331 and 376.

Secondary Sources

On the general background, see S. L. Adams, 'Spain or the Netherlands? the Dilemmas of Early Stuart Foreign Policy', in *Before the Civil War*, ed. by H. Tomlinson (London, 1983), pp. 79–101; David Bergeron, 'Charles I's Royal Entries into London', *The Guildhall Miscellany* 3 (1970), pp. 91–3; D. R. Woolf, *The Idea of History in Early Stuart England* (Toronto, 1990), pp. 3–76; W. W. Greg, *Licensers for the Press, &c. to 1640: A Biographical Index, Based Mainly on Arber's 'Transcript of the Registers of the Company of Stationers'* (Oxford, 1962); Linda Levy Peck, *Court Patronage and Corruption in Early Stuart England* (London, 1990); and W. J. Jones, *Politics and the Bench* (London, 1971).

On the politics in the decade, see Richard Cust, *The Forced Loan and English Politics, 1626-1628* (Oxford, 1987); and Cust, 'News and Politics in Early Seventeenth Century England', *Past and Present*, no. 112 (1986), pp. 60–90; Conrad Russell, *Parliaments and English Politics, 1621-1629* (Oxford, 1979); Russell, 'The Foreign Policy Debate in the House of Commons in 1621', *Historical Journal* XX (1976), pp. 289–309; Robert Zaller, *The Parliament of 1621* (Berkeley, 1971), pp. 72–90; Jonathan L. Marvil, *The Trials of Counsel: Francis Bacon in 1621* (Detroit, 1976); Christopher Thompson, *The Debate on Freedom of Speech in the House of Commons in February 1621* (Orsett, Essex, 1987); Robert Ruigh, *The Parliament of 1624: Politics and Foreign Policy* (Cambridge, Mass., 1971); Roger Lockyer, *Buckingham; the Life and Political Career of George Villiers, the First Duke of Buckingham* (London, 1981); Gordon Albion, *Charles I and the Court of Rome* (London, 1935); Charles Dalton, *The Life and Times of General Edward Cecil* (London, 1878); Vernon L. Snow, *Essex the Rebel* (Lincoln, 1970); Thomas Cogswell, *The Blessed Revolution: English Politics and the Coming of War, 1621-1624* (Cambridge, 1989); Cogswell, 'England and the Spanish Match', in *Conflict in Early Stuart England*, ed. by R. Cust and Ann Hughes (London, 1989), pp. 107–33; Cogswell, 'Foreign Policy and Parliament: the Case of La Rochelle, 1625-1626', *English Historical Review* (1984), pp. 241–67; and Cogswell, 'The Politics of Propaganda: Charles I and the People in the 1620s', *Journal of British Studies* XXIX (1990), pp. 187–215.

INDEX TO NOTES ON MODERNIZATION

Trish Thomas Henley

This index identifies Textual Notes, in Part III, which record or discuss modernizations of spelling. (Modernization notes to *Old Law* in the *Works* volume are also included.) Items are alphabetized by the spelling adopted in this edition (the lemma of the relevant textual note). An asterisk indicates that the note in question contains a discussion of whether and/or how to modernize the original spelling.

This index records proper names, references to all Middleton's works, and a selection of important topics. It covers the Preface, all of Part I and Part II, and the Textual Introductions of Part III.